Country Music Records A Discogra

By Tony Russell

With editorial research by

Bob Pinson

Assisted by the staff

of the Country Music Hall of Fame® and Museum

Country Music Records
A Discography, 1921–1942

OXFORD
UNIVERSITY PRESS

Oxford University Press, Inc., publishes works that further
Oxford University's objective of excellence
in research, scholarship, and education.

Oxford   New York
Auckland   Bangkok   Buenos Aires   Cape Town   Chennai
Dar es Salaam   Delhi   Hong Kong   Istanbul   Karachi   Kolkata
Kuala Lumpur   Madrid   Melbourne   Mexico City   Mumbai   Nairobi
São Paulo   Shanghai   Taipei   Tokyo   Toronto

With offices in
Argentina   Austria   Brazil   Chile   Czech Republic   France   Greece
Guatemala   Hungary   Italy   Japan   Poland   Portugal   Singapore
South Korea   Switzerland   Thailand   Turkey   Ukraine   Vietnam

Copyright © 2004, 2008 by The Country Music Foundation, Inc.

First published by Oxford University Press, Inc., 2004
198 Madison Avenue, New York, New York 10016

www.oup.com

First issued as an Oxford University Press paperback, 2008

Oxford is a registered trademark of Oxford University Press

All rights reserved. No part of this publication may be reproduced,
stored in a retrieval system, or transmitted, in any form or by any means,
electronic, mechanical, photocopying, recording, or otherwise,
without the prior permission of Oxford University Press.

Library of Congress Cataloging-in-Publication Data
Russell, Tony.
Country Music Records: A Discography, 1921–1942 / by Tony Russell; with editorial research by
Bob Pinson assisted by the staff of the Country Music Hall of Fame and Museum.
   p. cm.
Includes bibliographical references and indexes.
ISBN 978-0-19-513989-1; 978-0-19-536621-1 (pbk.)
1. Old-time music—Discography. 2. Country music—To 1951—Discography.
I. Pinson, Bob. II. Country Music Hall of Fame & Museum (Nashville, Tenn.). III. Title.
ML156.4.C7 R87 2002
016.781642'0266—dc21   200202264

9 8 7 6 5 4 3 2 1

Printed in the United States of America
on acid-free paper

This publication was made possible in part by support from the National Endowment for the Arts and by the National Academy of Recording Arts and Sciences.

Acknowledgments

A large number of people have contributed to this work, with no other motive than wishing to see things done right and no other reward than my gratitude and a promise of acknowledgment. That promise I am happy now to keep.

In the early 1970s, curious about the recording history of this music that had begun to fascinate me, I started gathering the few discographies of country artists that had been published in collectors' magazines and tentatively began to compile some of my own. I came to realize that much of the root-and-trunk information grew in the gardens of jazz and blues discographers, who had long before obtained for their own purposes copies of crucial record company files or, where such files no longer existed, had gone far in reconstructing them. I made contact with one of the keenest members of this fraternity, Bert Whyatt, who over the years has lent me, sometimes *for* years, such basic source material as Columbia, OKeh, and ARC matrix listings and label numericals (originally furnished to the discographical community by Helene Chmura of Columbia Records), Gennett matrix files (painstakingly transcribed many years earlier by Dan Mahony), and much else. Though publishing relatively little himself, Bert has contributed immeasurably and with unstinting generosity to the work of others. For my part, I can say with perfect accuracy that without his assistance this project could hardly have begun.

I was encouraged from the start and later given much practical help by several of the leading collectors of country records, in particular, David Crisp, Gene Earle, David Freeman, and Frank Mare, who have responded promptly and attentively to innumerable requests for information. David Crisp has not only been an authoritative source of data on Australian issues of country material, but he has checked many of the entries, including some of the longest and most complicated, against his enviable collection. I much appreciate his unflagging encouragement. Gene Earle furnished copies of important label numericals and gave Bob Pinson, my colleague from the Country Music Foundation, and me many hours' access to his richly stocked shelves. Frank Mare offered me similar hospitality and let me inspect his copy of a vital Gennett ledger.

Many entries herein are based on data gathered by David Freeman, Richard Nevins, and the late Guthrie T. Meade, including their invaluable primary research into music featured in reissue albums on Freeman's County and Nevins's Morning Star labels. They preceded me by some years in documenting the recording history of early country fiddlers and string bands, yet they unselfishly shared their work and gave me numerous leads that enabled me to augment it. I am also grateful to Rich Nevins for organizing the circulation of parts of the manuscript to a panel of collectors, for timely financial assistance at a late stage of the project, and for his constant encouragement.

Anyone engaged in the discography of American vernacular music must soon come upon the legacy of its pioneers. Though I never dealt with them in person, I have gratefully derived much essential data from the files and writings of George Blacker, Floy Case, John Edwards, Will Roy Hearne, John K. MacKenzie, and Joe Nicholas.

Robert M. W. Dixon, co-author of *Blues & Gospel Records 1890–1943*, lent me a mass of Brunswick/Vocalion data, while Howard Rye, co-author of the fourth edition of that exemplary work, drew on his experience as a blues and jazz discographer to clarify many areas of mystery.

Richard K. Spottswood, in compiling his enormous discography of the music of America's ethnic communities, followed a similar path to my own in the territory of Cajun recordings and discovered much information that I have gratefully borrowed. But his contribution goes further for, in examining company files for his own work, he was able to amplify or illuminate parts of mine.

Robert Olson has been the most assiduous discographer of "citybilly" artists, and I am indebted to his extensive work on the entries for such figures as Vernon Dalhart, Carson Robison, Frank Luther, Frank Marvin, Bob Miller, and the McCravy Brothers. I am glad to acknowledge, at Bob's request, some of his own sources, in particular the Victor discographer Ted Fagan, the Canadian Dalhart collector Jerry Ormond, and the Australian discographer Mike Sutcliffe. Bob also provided copies of label numericals that he and various colleagues have assembled individually and/or collaboratively.

In Texas, Kevin Coffey has conducted a remarkable amount of skillful firsthand research into the history of western swing, and most of the entries in that category have profited from his work. Kevin's informants are too numerous to list, but I thank them all.

I owe Richard Weize of Bear Family Records special thanks for the wealth of data he elicited from MCA files and for his constant interest in the entire project.

John Stoten lent his expertise as the major collector of country records released in Britain. I am also grateful for his research, first published in *Old Time Music*, into Indian pressings of country material. I also thank Rob Allingham, who has been a prime source of information on country recordings issued in South Africa, and acknowledge my debt to the voluminous work of the Canadian discographer Alex Robertson. I have also drawn, indirectly, on the Canadian discographical work of Eric Wadin.

Richard Johnson's close knowledge of the Gennett ledgers enabled me to refine the dating of this company's complex activities.

Among the other collectors and researchers who have contributed to this book, I should especially mention Joe Bussard, Norm Cohen, Harlan Daniel, Steve Davis, Bob Healy, John Larsen, Kip Lornell, Donald L. Nelson, Robert Nobley, Robert K. Oermann and Mary Bufwack, Kinney Rorrer, Chris Strachwitz, E. S. (Stan) Turner, Gayle Dean Wardlow, and Charles K. Wolfe. But some of these need to be singled out. Norm Cohen made it possible for Bob Pinson and me to examine the holdings of the John Edwards Memorial Foundation, at the time when it was held at the University of California at Los Angeles; in addition, he has shared his thoughts on the structure and methodology of country discographies. Bob Oermann and Mary Bufwack gave me much data from their extensive research into the women of country music and also a delightful pied-à-terre on several of my visits to Nashville.

Charles and Mary Dean Wolfe too have been frequent and liberal hosts to this visiting discographer. No one who has given much time to the study of early country music needs to be alerted to Charles Wolfe's prolific and varied writings on the subject, many of which are digested or excerpted in these pages. Charles has also acted as a clearinghouse of information from all directions and given me the chance to join him on many rewarding investigations in the field.

I have been happy to find friends and helpers not only among collectors and students of country music but also among the musicians who made it. To list all of them would be impossible, but these are some whose aid and, in many cases, hospitality I remember with special gratitude: Chester Allen, Hubert (Hugh) Ashley, Claude Boone, Cliff Bruner, Cecil Campbell, Bill Carlisle, Claude Casey, J. R. Chatwell, Stan Clements, Jimmie Davis, John Foster, S. Carlton Freeny, Ausie B. Grigg, Lucille Collier Lutts, Lewis McDaniels, Asa Martin, Hoyt Ming, Rozelle Ming, Patsy Montana, John W. "Knocky" Parker, Leo Raley, Randall Raley, Melvin Robinette, Leo Soileau, Carl Swanson, David "Pee Wee" Wamble, John I. White, Scott Wiseman, and Preston Young.

The following have given more selective but no less valuable assistance to the project, either to me or to Bob Pinson:

Shelly Lee Alley, Jr.	Wayne W. Daniel	Ben Hollis
Billy Altman	Luderin Darbone	Frank Johnson
Hobart Ashley	John R. T. Davies	Clifton "Sleepy" Johnson
Jesse Ashlock	Bill Dean-Myatt	Willard Johnson
Bob Atcher	George C. Edens, Jr.	Thomas Jordan
David Barnes	David Evans	Homer Kellogg
Robert Barres	Buster Ferguson	Don Kent
Bruce Bastin	Joe Ferguson	Rich Kienzle
Jerry Bethel	Carl Fleischhauer	Walker Kirkes
Malcolm V. Blackard	Ray Funk	Darrell Kirkpatrick
Kerry Blech	Paul Garon	Klaus Kuhnke
Vernon Bogle	Aubrey Gass	Ross Laird
Johnny Bond	Cary Ginell	Bert Layne
Jim Boyd	Artie Glenn	Bill Legere
Cecil Brower	Wayne Glenn	Columbus Lewis
Ron Brown	John Godrich	Guy Logsdon
Hoyt "Slim" Bryant	Archie Green	Pete Lowry
Floyd Bucy	Douglas B. Green	Leon McAuliffe
Fred Calhoun	Clarence Greene	Larry McBride
Homer Callahan	Ken Griffis	Mack McCormick
Luther Carden	Sydney Guidry	Brad McCuen
Joyce Cauthen	Jim Hadfield	Clayton McMichen
Keith Chandler	Piers Harker	W. K. McNeil
Robin Clayton	Danny Hatcher	Wade Mainer
John Coffey	Benno Haupl	Bill C. Malone
John Cohen	Jim Hayes	Doug Meade
Lawrence Cohn	Dick Heil	Jerry Mills
Chris Comber	Bill Helms	Marvin Montgomery
Pat Conte	Michael Helwig	Joe Moore
John H. Cowley	Jim Hibbits	Bill Morris
Jack Crysel	Ralph Hodges	John Morris
Lou Curtiss	Fred Hoeptner	Bill Mounce

Kurt Nauck
Jack Palmer
Wilson "Lefty" Perkins
Nolan Porterfield
Bronson "Brownie" Reynolds
Brian Rust
Dave Samuelson
Ann Savoy
Elizabeth Schlappi
Mike Seeger
Charlie Seemann
Doug Seroff
Arthur "Guitar Boogie" Smith
Hank Snow
Mike Stewart
M. L. "Rocky" Stone
Al Stricklin
Charlie Stripling
Ira Stripling
Keith Summers
Allen Sutton
Paul Swinton
Bill Thompson
Harold Timmons
Keith Titterington
Ivan M. Tribe
George Tye
Gerald F. Vaughn
Crawford Vincent
Max Vreede
Thurman "Tex" Walker
Frank Weston
Pete Whelan
Glenn P. White
Gene Wiggins
D. H. Williams
Mark Wilson
Marshall Wyatt
Mike Yates
Henry Young
Larry Zwisohn

In addition to all of that private help and support, I have been fortunate in having the assistance of several commercial and institutional bodies. RCA Records in New York allowed me unlimited access to its archives; I must record my thanks to Herb Helman and to Mary Ann Leavitt and Bernadette Moore of the Listings Department. I was also able to visit MCA Records in Universal City, California, thanks to Arnold Stone. Leah Burt, archivist of the Edison National Historical Site in East Orange, New Jersey, kindly supplied material from its remarkably preserved files. Bob Pinson was further assisted by Kenn Scott of MCA Records; Martine McCarthy, Nick Shaffran, Nathaniel Brewster, and Michael Brooks of Columbia Records; and Chick Crumpacker and Frank Driggs of RCA Records.

And, since I have mentioned him again, this must be the place to thank Bob Pinson. But "thank" is scarcely an adequate word. From his desk at the Country Music Foundation, he oversaw the entire project. He read and checked every entry and corrected or added to many of them. Some, like that on Bob Wills, he authored himself. He spent countless hours amid the Foundation's collection, now dropping in to verify a take number or a title variant, now giving long stretches of his time to listening to records and reporting in detail on their contents. Most of that, I should add, was an extra task beyond his day-to-day duties. I am grateful for his patience, his enthusiasm, his accuracy, his enormous knowledge and experience as a collector and discographer, and above all for his friendship. But "grateful," too, is a puny sort of word, so let me put it this way: if there had been no Bob Pinson, there would have been no book. I am very sorry indeed that he did not live to see it published.

I also thank the other officers of the Country Music Foundation who have been involved in the project, particularly Director Kyle Young and former deputy directors Paul Kingsbury, John Knowles, and Peggy Sherrill. Kyle and Paul have been responsible for steering the book to publication, and I am grateful for their patience. I extend my thanks, too, to Karen Raizor, Karen Willard, and Elek Horvath for carefully entering the discographical data into a manageable computer database and to CMF intern Summer Yates for keying in the introductory matter. I am indebted to Ronnie Pugh for the many hours he spent revising the database and for his ever-vigilant eye for errors and inconsistencies and to Alan Stoker for his help in identifying instrumentation and vocal parts in many of these recordings.

I am also grateful to Dick and Anne Bower of AnDix Indexing Associates for their meticulous work in compiling the indexes.

Finally, I thank the people who made a formal investment of faith, time, and resources in me and in this project. Bill Ivey, then director of the CMF, drew up the grant proposal, and the board of the National Endowment for the Arts issued the generous grant that enabled me to spend three months at the CMF working uninterruptedly on the project and creating a large part of the manuscript. Later, the National Academy of Recording Arts and Sciences (NARAS) also gave grant support to the development of this discography. I am further grateful to Bill Ivey for facilitating my several subsequent spells of work at the CMF. It would be dutiful to say that its library is the most pleasant and well-resourced place I know to do this kind of work; it would also be true.

Tony Russell
London, 2004

Contents

Introduction   3

Record Label Histories   9

User's Guide   35

Abbreviations   43

Discography   47

Bibliography   981

Index to Performers   985

Index to Titles   1013

Country Music Records A Discography, 1921–1942

Introduction

Over the years, many terms have been used for the music documented in this book. Some of them were, consciously or not, partisan and therefore too narrow in their application, such as "mountain" or "hill and range" music. Others carried overtones that some have considered undesirable, such as "hillbilly." Yet others, attempting comprehensiveness by piling up phrases like "white Anglo-American folk-based music," were simply too unwieldy.

"Country and western" (or "country-western"), for a long time the most widely accepted term, has fallen out of favor, partly because the country music establishment has not consistently acknowledged the western element in the music's history. Some factions have employed the term "old-time," which was indeed what it was called by several of the music's first publicists, the record companies. No doubt some of the musicians called it that too, but others vigorously rejected it, as they rejected "hillbilly," because it seemed to imply musical or social backwardness. ("That 'hillbilly,' we fought it tooth and nail," remarked fiddler Clayton McMichen.) Certainly there is material in this book, for instance at the progressive end of western swing, that it would seem eccentric to call old-time—and, for that matter, inappropriate to call hillbilly.

So the world has largely settled on "country music" as the name of the idiom that began, so far as records are concerned, with Eck Robertson and Fiddlin' John Carson and that lives on, eighty years later, as a distinct strain of American—and indeed international—popular music.

Clearly a term so routinely applied to so many diverse performers and styles is likely to be questioned by the academically rigorous, and I should go no further without explaining that when I use the expressions "country" and "country music" in this book, I am under no illusion that they are precise or comprehensive terms. To the best of my knowledge, no precise or comprehensive definition of country music has ever been agreed upon. Naturally, I hope this book may contribute to the framing of such a definition. But for the present, the reader has a right to know upon what principles the book was assembled.

Its primary purpose is to document recordings that were designed to be sold principally to a market identified by the sellers as largely white, initially southern, and substantially composed of rural or small-town dwellers.

The point of qualifying words like "principally," "initially," and "substantially" is that the market for those recordings was not homogeneous in the first place, and within a few years had become significantly less so, encompassing other areas, such as the Midwest, and other demographic elements, such as southern enclaves in northern cities. But it is clear from the record companies' policies and the publicity with which they advanced them that, at the start, they perceived a sectional audience that they believed would buy records of certain types of music already familiar to it, recognized that those musics were as yet unexploited, and made it their business to exploit them.

The American record industry had discovered the value of sectional marketing early in the twentieth century, when it began to meet the cultural needs of immigrant and first-generation-American communities by recording the music they regarded as their own. To enable distributors and dealers to identify these records, so that they could order them if they had a market for them and avoid them if they did not, some record companies eventually adopted a policy of placing their releases in discrete numerical catalogs, each of which contained recordings exclusively or predominantly of interest to a single ethnic group or to several groups with close cultural connections.

The companies' response to the discovery of a market for country music (though they did not yet call it that) was to treat that market no differently, and, throughout the first decade of the period covered by this book, recordings of that music were generally placed in idiomatically specific numerical listings, such as the Brunswick 100, Columbia 15000-D, OKeh 45000, Paramount 3000, Victor V-40000, and Vocalion 5000 series.

The records issued in those and similar series are the core of this book, a substantial core, but by no means the whole of it. Some companies did not divide their output among such sectional lists or did so inconsistently. From the mid-1930s onward, most companies separated their "specialty" records—country, blues, jazz—from their mainstream, "popular" output but not from each other. Nevertheless, from company catalogs and other publicity material, we can discern a continuity of marketing practices or attitudes; we can therefore identify what was considered to be country material even after it ceased to be segregated.

What was that material? From the evidence gathered in this book, we can perceive such genres as tunes played on the fiddle, banjo, and other instruments, sometimes with incidental singing; "traditional" ballads, event songs, love songs, comic songs, and new compositions more or less similarly conceived; material from the minstrel and vaudeville stages, the ragtime library, and writers of popular songs; cowboy songs; blues; the music of the Louisiana Cajuns; the fusion of various elements, including blues and jazz, in western swing and honky-tonk music; and a mass of material that mingled in different proportions several of these strains.

Such a catalog—and it is far from complete—clearly poses enormous problems of definition and discrimination. It would be a relief if we could securely identify a country music aesthetic and thereby distinguish, say, a "country" performance of a song from one in a "popular" style, so as to include the former in this book and in good conscience exclude the latter. Indeed, there are many instances when I have silently made just such a decision. But no hard-and-fast rule can be applied. To raise one massive objection: by far the largest entry in this book is claimed by Vernon Dalhart, a journeyman singer of the early record business whose output included many records in the popular and light classical idioms but many too that were expressly made for the country catalogs of the numerous companies that employed him. While there are differences of style among his several approaches, it would probably be agreed by most experienced listeners today that Dalhart's recordings even of country songs evince an aesthetic somehow different from, say, Charlie Poole's, even when (as happened at least once) Dalhart deliberately imitated Poole's manner. But there is little evidence that such a view would have been shared by either the producers or the purchasers of those records.

Although it has been impossible to compile this discography—indeed, it may be impossible to compile any discography—without sometimes yielding to aesthetic judgments that may reflect the compiler's world rather than his subject's, I have tried to follow one article of faith, namely, that the persistence and the frequent success with which the record companies marketed this music allow us to assume that they were broadly in tune with the tastes of the market and that what was recorded and sold as music for a particular audience was largely accepted as such by that audience. The diversity of the recordings listed here may at first seem bewildering. What unites them is that they were units of a common cultural currency, recognized and used in specific cultural contexts.

But even that statement must be qualified, for it would be a mistake to assume that the recordings in this book were made by, any more than they were offered to, a single, homogeneous community. The stereotypes of early country music, many of them created and promulgated by the music's promoters in the offices of record companies and radio stations and some of them still influential today, have obscured a great deal of social and regional diversity. The country catalogs gave a voice not only to the blind street singer and the fiddling farmer but to the urban stringed-instrument club and the amateur folksong collector; to the quartet from the local church as much as to the entertainer on a powerful radio station; to a band from a Texas Bohemian community no less than one from the backwoods of Appalachia.

That said, this book is predominantly a record of white southern music. It has been argued by some scholars that country music was not, even in this early period, a purely southern phenomenon. There is a good deal of evidence to support that view—but little of it on records, since for most of the period covered by this book the record companies rarely visited or solicited material from the areas where non-southern country music was to be found. By the late 1930s, however, much of the country music that was being recorded in New York and Chicago, in particular, was neither made by southern artists nor exclusively marketed to southern audiences. Records and radio were rapidly creating a nationwide country music industry, thereby encouraging the development of a national country music.

It has also been suggested, in my view rightly, that some forms of African-American music in the period covered by this book had much in common with contemporary white idioms, and some scholars have suggested that there might be a case for including them in a discography of this kind. The practical reply to that is that African-American music already has exhaustive discographies of its own, notably Dixon, Godrich, and Rye's *Blues & Gospel Records 1890–1943*, which I heartily recommend to any reader interested in investigating those connections. A small number of recordings by African-American musicians, however, were issued in country catalogs rather than, or as well as, in their own sectional lists, and although those recordings are generally not included here, the instances are noted. (An exception has been made for harmonica player DeFord Bailey, who was so long associated with the Grand Ole Opry.) An even smaller, indeed a tiny, group of recordings that were collaborations by white and African-American musicians has been judged to be country music, and these records are duly included.

Virtually all of the recordings listed in this book were made in the United States; the very few exceptions are the early Canadian recordings of Hank Snow and Wilf Carter and the records made while visiting Britain by Vernon Dalhart and Carson Robison. I have not attempted to investigate the work of American artists who recorded in a country idiom only outside the United States or that of non-American artists who pursued a country music career in other countries, such as the British band the Hill Billies or the many admirable figures of the early Australian country music scene.

Some further definitions and exclusions need to be mentioned. This book deals almost entirely with 78-rpm records made by commercial companies for sale through normal retail outlets. I have also included "personal" recordings that were sold by or for the artists themselves and a few items recorded for, and presumably sold through, radio stations. Transcriptions made solely for broadcast use, however, such as those manufactured by Sellers, Standard, and World, have not been included. I have also ruled out all recordings made in a spirit of folkloric or documentary inquiry either by institutions, such as the Archive of American Folk-Song at the Library of Congress, or by individual folklorists. Though many such recordings have been made available, particularly since the 1950s, to a general or sectional public, they were not originally made for that purpose, and the principles on which they were collected were not always akin to—indeed, were sometimes deliberately different from—those adopted by commercial concerns.

At the same time, some recordings made for what might now be called folkloric reasons were issued by commercial companies, and these too have been omitted from this book. Among these are the work of folksong interpreters like Bentley Ball, Carl Sandburg, John Jacob Niles, John A. Lomax, and the American Ballad Singers under the direction of Elie Siegmeister, as well as the recordings of Henry Ford's Old Time Dance Orchestra.

Also excluded are recordings of folk or minstrel songs by professional recording artists, such as Billy Golden, Arthur Collins, Byron G. Harlan, Harry C. Browne, Wendell Hall, and Frank Kamplain; comic sketches in a rural vein by monologists like Charles Ross Taggart and Cal Stewart; and, by and large, fiddle tunes played by studio or stage musicians, such as Don Richardson, Joseph Samuels, and Charles D'Almaine. (A small number of Samuels's recordings have been included.) Such material, much of which predates the earliest recordings listed in this book, undeniably forms part of the history of recorded American vernacular music but, in my judgment, a subsidiary part.

The inclusion of Vernon Dalhart, however, provides grounds for arguing the case for other professional recording artists, who sometimes made recordings evidently conceived for a similar market (even, in some cases, deliberately imitating Dalhart's manner), such as Arthur Fields, Al Bernard, and Ernest Hare. These, and some other comparable figures, have been awarded selective entries, which contain material that I and the collectors whom I have consulted judge to be too close to the heart of the matter to be excluded. Here is one of those aesthetic judgments mentioned earlier, and no doubt some readers will think me to have been too generous and others will think me not generous enough. In our defense, I should say that those entries have been subjected to scrutiny and discussion by several authorities, and decisions about what to include and what to exclude have been based on careful balancing of the claims of repertoire, accompaniment, and performance style. But it is in the nature of such decision making that the ground upon which it stands shifts and reforms as time passes and perceptions become more finely tuned, and the judgments enshrined in this edition should not be regarded as irrevocable.

Another category of recordings that has entailed decisions about relevance is Hawaiian-style music. Some groups that recorded exclusively in this idiom had their records issued in country catalogs, for example, the Honolulu Strollers, Hauulea Entertainers, and North Carolina Hawaiians; these have been included, as have other groups that, though not sectionally cataloged, seem similar enough to be treated likewise, for example, the Hawaiian Song Birds, Kelly Brothers (Masters' Hawaiians), Jim & Bob, and Price-Prosser-Teasley. Also included are groups that played in this idiom only occasionally, such as the later Tennessee Ramblers. Artists who recorded exclusively Hawaiian-style material that was generally not issued in country catalogs—who proved in most cases to be genuine Hawaiian musicians, if not always playing authentically Hawaiian material, such as Charles Kama & M. T. Salazar, Walter Kolomoku, Sol Hoopii, and Benny Nawahi—are excluded, except when accompanying country artists. (But their appearance, if any, in country catalogs is noted.) Also excluded are all authentically Hawaiian groups, such as Kalama's Quartette.

Many of the recordings in this book are of gospel music. Some are arguably country, as I have used the term, for they were made by artists who also recorded secular material and were issued in the same sectional catalogs. Being listed in country catalogs also determined the inclusion in this book of many exclusively gospel artists, such as gospel quartets and similar singing groups, among them those affiliated with the Stamps-Baxter, Vaughan, Hartford, and other gospel publishing houses; soloists and duets in the tradition of the traveling musical evangelists; singing ministers, with or without their congregations; Sacred Harp groups; and a few choirs. I have ruled out the recordings of the Chicago hymnographer, publisher, and singer Homer Rodeheaver and most of his associates and those of certain quartets, such as the Criterion Quartet, which are significantly different in approach from the groups that have been included. However, further research into the gospel music herein—at present a scantily studied genre—may produce good arguments for revising my criteria, and, if so, that will be reflected in subsequent editions.

Finally, I should answer the other question implied in this book's title: why does it start and finish when it does? Until now, the recording history of this music has been supposed to begin in June 1922, with the first Victor recordings of A. C. (Eck) Robertson and Henry Gilliland; that date is now preempted by the first recordings of the Vaughan Quartet in 1921. As for the end-date, by concluding at the close of 1942 the book falls into line with most other discographies of American vernacular music. The reason for that cut-off point has been well put by the blues and gospel discographers Dixon, Godrich, and Rye (p. viii): after that date, "styles of performance changed rather radically, and so did methods of recording and issuance. Far more obscurity surrounds the operations of the many small companies issuing records for black audiences in the late forties than of those of the twenties and thirties." The same is true in country music. Documenting the pre-1943 record business is complicated enough, but it has the advantage that record making was conducted almost entirely by a small number of major firms whose catalogs and methods have been studied for decades. The landscape of later recording is both much larger and much less well mapped. I wish the discographical explorers of postwar country music the very best of luck: having spent so long on my own journey of discovery, I have some idea of the extent and challenges of theirs.

Additions and corrections will be welcomed and included in subsequent editions. They should be sent to Tony Russell, 22 Cranbourne Road, London N10 2BT, England, or e-mailed to tonyrussell@bluetone.demon.co.uk.

Record Label Histories

American

ARC The American Record Corporation (ARC) came into being in August 1929 as an amalgamation of three New York companies, each controlling several labels relevant to this book.

The **Cameo** Record Corporation had its offices (until 1927) at 249 West 34th Street and studios at 200 West 57th Street; its records were pressed at plants in Framingham, Massachusetts, and Jersey City, New Jersey. The company's chief labels were Cameo, Lincoln, and Romeo; others were Muse, Tremont, and Variety. Cameo operated a single matrix series for all of its labels, beginning in the early 1920s at 100 and continuing to somewhere beyond 4100.

The **Pathé** Phonograph & Radio Corporation had its offices (until 1927) and pressing plant at 10-34 Grand Avenue, Brooklyn, New York, and studios at 150 East 53d Street in New York. Its labels included Actuelle, Pathé, and Perfect. Some Pathé issues also appeared, with the same catalog number, on a Supertone label operated by the Chicago-based store chain of Straus & Schram (unconnected with the Sears label of that name). Early recordings used a five-digit matrix series, followed, from around 1924, by a series beginning at 105000 and rising to beyond 109000.

In 1927, both Cameo (then in receivership) and Pathé were acquired by James McPherson, who had previously operated a pressing plant, the American Record Manufacturing Company, at Framingham, Massachusetts, which was used by Cameo. McPherson ran Cameo and Pathé from a common office at 114 East 32d Street in New York, preserving their distinct identities but from late 1927 frequently operating a split numbering policy, whereby a recording would be assigned a Cameo matrix for use on Cameo-group labels and a Pathé matrix for Pathé-group labels; this process is evident in the contemporaneous matrix ranges 2800–3800 (Cameo) and 108000–108800 (Pathé). In most instances, the Cameo-matrix and Pathé-matrix versions of a recording are identical—some issues even bear both matrices—but there is evidence to suggest that this practice was not hard and fast and that the Cameo and Pathé versions may sometimes be distinct takes.

The third component of what would be ARC was the **Plaza** Music Company, based at 10-20 West 20th Street, with studios at 55 West 16th Street in New York; its records were pressed by the Scranton Button Company of Scranton, Pennsylviania, which was also subsumed in the 1929 merger. Its labels were Banner, founded in 1921; the previously independent Domino, acquired in 1924; Jewel, founded in 1926; Oriole, founded in 1923, which joined Plaza in 1923–1924; and Regal, acquired from Emerson in 1923. A single matrix series for this group began in February 1923 at 5000; it was this series that ARC continued to use for its New York recordings.

Throughout the 1920s, Cameo, Pathé, and Plaza often exchanged or licensed material, both internally and with companies like Emerson and Grey Gull and the labels of the New York Recording Laboratories (Broadway, Paramount, and Puritan). Not all of the possible channels were used: for example, before the 1929 union, Cameo seldom swapped material with Plaza. But the interrelationships of Plaza and Pathé and of Plaza and NYRL are extremely complex, with original matrices sometimes surviving the exchange, sometimes being suppressed, and sometimes being replaced by new matrices or control numbers.

Before their amalgamation, Cameo, Pathé, and Plaza were chiefly concerned with popular and standard recordings. Each of them had ventured into the "race" (African-American) recording field; Pathé's Perfect had begun what was intended to be an exclusively race 100 series as early as 1926. In country music, they had done little more than commission work regularly from Vernon Dalhart and occasionally from Frank Luther and Carson Robison. Plaza was the most committed of the three groups, recording, though sporadically, such artists as John Baltzell and Ernest Stoneman.

After the creation of ARC, country and race material generally appeared simultaneously, or approximately so, on all or most of the Banner, Oriole, Perfect, and Romeo labels. Oriole and Romeo are the most closely linked of these; the Oriole 8000 and Romeo 5000 series worked in tandem—and, for a short period, in tandem too with a Jewel 20000 series. Thus Oriole 8050 = Romeo 5050 = Jewel 20050. (The highest known Jewel in this series is 20053.) The Oriole, Romeo, and Jewel series were devoted to country and race recordings, while Banner and Perfect issued this music within their regular series, which included popular material. Recordings were also released on the other ARC labels, chiefly Cameo, Domino, and Regal, but infrequently, and within a year or so those labels were phased out. ARC recordings of around 1929–1930 were also occasionally issued on Challenge, Homestead, and ARC-Broadway.

ARC was bought in October 1930 by Consolidated Film Industries. In December 1931, CFI purchased from Warner Brothers Pictures the Brunswick, Vocalion, and Melotone labels, administering them through a subsidiary company, the Brunswick Record Corporation, which in August 1934 also acquired Columbia and OKeh. ARC-BRC was bought in February 1938 by the Columbia Broadcasting System and became the Columbia Recording Corporation. (Pre-1932 Brunswick/Vocalion holdings were excepted from this deal and were acquired by Decca.)

Neither "American Record Corporation" nor "ARC" was ever used as a label name, but the latter is used in this book, as in other discographies, as a shorthand reference to the issuing method employed by ARC-BRC between September 1935 and April 1938. During that period, country and race material was released on Banner, Melotone, Oriole, Perfect, and Romeo with a common numbering system usually taking the form x-xx-xx, in which the first element denotes (by its lone digit) the year of issue, the second the month, and the third the record's place in that month's sequence of issues (starting after 50). Thus 5-11-51 is the first country/race issue for November 1935. (There was a similar system for popular releases, except that the third element started not from 50 but from 0; thus the first popular issue for November 1935 is 5-11-01.)

At the start, in September and October 1935, the system was slightly different. The year was denoted in the first *two* digits and the month's sequence began at 01 for all types of material. Thus, the first issue for September 1935 was 35-09-01. In most cases, the hyphens were omitted, so the numbers are generally in the form 350901.

The use of a collective issue description like ARC 5-11-51 therefore implies that the coupling with that number appeared on all five of the main ARC-BRC labels. This assumption, generally made by discographers, does not, however, receive unqualified support from the evidence of the records that have been recovered. ARC-BRC issues of that period are commonly found on Melotone, fairly often on Perfect, but relatively seldom on Banner, Oriole, and Romeo. There is a strong possibility either that fewer copies were pressed on the latter labels than on the former or that each label had a different marketing and therefore selection policy: Melotone issuing all or nearly all of the material and Perfect a good deal of it, but Banner, Oriole, and Romeo operating much more selectively, perhaps choosing only material of proven or predicted popularity. It should be noted that each of these three labels, unlike Melotone and Perfect, was handled exclusively by one store chain: Banner by W. T. Grant, Oriole by McCrory's, and Romeo by S. H. Kress.

Many ARC-BRC sides also appeared on Vocalion, initially (about 1931–1933) in the latter part of the 5000 series, then from 1933 in an 02500 series (though its earliest issues were numbered from 25001 to 25021). After the demise of the x-xx-xx list in April 1938, Columbia, the new owner, issued new country and race recordings exclusively on Vocalion. That label name was preserved until the sequence had reached 05621, in the summer of 1940; thereafter, all new releases were on OKeh, as were reissues of earlier Vocalion couplings, which retained their original issue numbers. Further reissues of ARC-BRC and Vocalion material appeared after World War II on Columbia's red-label 37000 and later 20000 series. ARC-BRC, Vocalion, and OKeh recordings were often licensed to, and occasionally appeared only on, the Sears label Conqueror.

During 1938, Vocalion issued more than a hundred country and race couplings that were assigned four-digit numbers used earlier for popular recordings, those numbers now being prefixed with 0 to fit them into the 02500 series. Thus, Vocalion 02957 by the Westerners, containing recordings made in 1937, has no connection with the earlier issue Vocalion 2957 by the Mound City Blues Blowers, recorded in 1935.

Most of the material in the ARC x-xx-xx and Vocalion/OKeh catalogs was recorded in New York, in the 10000 matrix sequence that continued Plaza's, or in Chicago, in a matrix sequence beginning at C-500; there was also a CP-1000 Chicago matrix series, operative around March to September 1934. Recordings were also obtained at various field sessions held between 1934 and 1941; those relevant to this book were in San Antonio, Fort Worth, Dallas, and Saginaw, Texas; Jackson and Hattiesburg, Mississippi; Augusta, Georgia; Hot Springs, Arkansas; Birmingham, Alabama; Columbia, South Carolina; and Memphis, Tennessee. All of these field sessions were assigned their own matrix series and identifying prefixes (DAL-, HAT-, and so on). Sessions were also held in San Francisco, California (prefixed SF-), Los Angeles, California (prefixed LA-), and later, for OKeh, in Hollywood, California (prefixed H- or HCO-).

Bluebird

Victor launched its Bluebird B-5000 series, for popular, race, and "Old Familiar Tunes" (country) material, in January 1933. (There was also a short-lived Bluebird series numbered from 1820 to 1853, duplicating the first 34 issues in the B-5000 series, and a handful [1800–1809] of eight-inch Bluebirds identical in numbering and contents to an Electradisk sequence.)

Many early Bluebirds were reissues of material originally released several years earlier on Victor, but gradually new recordings came to predominate. Initially 25 cents,

Bluebird's price rose in February 1934 to 35 cents. From October 1938, popular material was issued in a B-10000 series, leaving the original series for country and race material. (A few items that appeared in the B-10000 list have been judged relevant to this work.) Much Bluebird material was also issued under license by Montgomery Ward.

The B-5000 series ended at B-9042 in October 1942, and country material was thereafter issued in a 33-0500 series. A small number of the recordings listed in this book was issued there, but the catalog was predominantly stocked by post-1942 recordings. It ended with 33-0541, released in December 1945.

Other Bluebird series relevant to this book are the B-2000, in which Cajun material was issued (or reissued from Victor), and the B-2500 and B-3000 Mexican series, in which a small number of country items was issued, usually with the artists listed under pseudonyms and the titles translated into Spanish.

While some of Bluebird's original country recordings (as distinct from reissues from Victor) were made at Victor studios in New York and Chicago, many were made at field sessions in Charlotte, North Carolina; Atlanta, Georgia; New Orleans, Louisiana; and San Antonio and Dallas, Texas. For a time in the later 1930s, to circumvent restrictions imposed by the Charlotte, North Carolina, local union chapter of the American Federation of Musicians, sessions that would normally have been held in that city were moved to Rock Hill, South Carolina.

On the evidence of the session sheets, as soon as a satisfactory take of a Bluebird recording had been made, it would be suffixed -1 and, much more often than not, no further take would be attempted. Sometimes, however, a take -2 is also logged, but since these second takes almost invariably have the note "Hold," perhaps implying that they were made as safeties, I have worked on the principle that only first takes were issued and have noted the existence of second takes only for a few unissued recordings. But there are a few instances in which it appears that second takes *were* issued—usually instead of, rarely as well as, the first—and in those cases that fact is noted.

Toward the end of the period covered by this book, Bluebird session sheets begin to report the recording of both -1 and -1A (and sometimes also -2 and -2A) takes. It seems likely that the -A takes are not second attempts but simultaneously recorded duplicates, probably safeties.

Bluebird country recordings were licensed in considerable numbers to Regal-Zonophone in Britain, Australia, India, and Ireland, and to HMV and Twin in India.

Brunswick/ Vocalion

The Brunswick-Balke-Collender Company was founded in the mid–nineteenth century to manufacture pianos. It later became a manufacturer of bowling equipment. The company started to make records in 1919, issuing material of all types on the Brunswick label. In December 1924, it acquired Vocalion (founded in 1917) from the Aeolian Company. In 1926, BBC launched a Vocalion 1000 race series, followed in 1927 by a 5000 country series. These were joined in 1927 by the Brunswick 100 country series and in 1928 by its 7000 race series. All of these were full-price (75-cent) labels.

At first, the Brunswick 100 series reissued items from the Vocalion 5000s, often in new couplings, but by 1928 most Brunswick releases were original, though material continued to be transferred between the two labels from time to time, as well as being licensed to Sears's Supertone S2000 series and selectively to Canadian and British companies.

Brunswick/Vocalion recordings were chiefly made in New York in a five-digit matrix series prefixed E-. The Chicago studio, used more for race than for country material, used a four-digit matrix series prefixed C-. Recordings made at the Los Angeles studio were prefixed LA-. From early 1928, field sessions were held in a number of other cities. In 1928 and 1929, fresh matrix blocks, beginning at 100, were assigned for this work, while in 1930, the August–September 1929 sequence was carried on until it reached 999 and then was succeeded by an 8000 series. For the last round of field sessions, in November and December 1930, a block was taken from the Chicago sequence. All of these field recordings carry prefixes that identify their locations.

The field trips relevant to this book are as follows. The matrix spans given are complete or as nearly so as our knowledge permits, and they include race, popular, and country recordings. Popular material was issued in the Vocalion 15000 and Brunswick 4000 series, to which country and race items were occasionally assigned, and from and to which they were sometimes transferred.

Location	Matrix	Date
Ashland, KY	AL-100?–327	February 1928
Atlanta, GA	AT-326 ½–394?	early March 1928
Indianapolis, IN	IND-622?–666	late June 1928
Dallas, TX	DAL-675?–745?	October 1928
New Orleans, LA	NOR-747–768	early November 1928
Birmingham, AL	BIRM-769–815	mid-November 1928
Memphis, TN	M-816–853	late November 1928
New Orleans, LA	NO-100–131	February–March 1929
Knoxville, TN	K-100–172?	August–September 1929
Memphis, TN	M-175?–217	late September 1929
New Orleans, LA	NO-218–264?	September–October 1929
San Antonio, TX	SA-269?–442	October 1929
Dallas, TX	DAL-443–576?	October–November 1929
Kansas City, MO	KC-579?–611?	early November 1929
Memphis, TN	MEM-730?–807?	February 1930
Atlanta, GA	ATL-900?–999, 8000–8021	March 1930
Knoxville, TN	K-8022–8113?	March–April 1930
Atlanta, GA	ATL-6295–6299, 6600–6699	November 1930
New Orleans, LA	NO-6700–6742	November 1930
Dallas, TX	DAL-6743–7003	November–December 1930

Though company files often identify the catalog for which unissued recordings would have been destined, they do not always do so. Hence, some items are described in this book as "Br/Vo unissued."

Brunswick's Australian branch issued some country material from the 100 series, using the original catalog numbers. A few country items appeared in Britain in the general Brunswick series or on Decca and in Ireland on Rex or in the Decca W4000 series. The later South African Brunswick SA series drew exclusively from U.S. Decca.

In April 1930, BBC was taken over by Warner Brothers Pictures, which in November created Melotone, a chiefly popular catalog in which a considerable number of country and a few race items appeared. Many of the country issues were also issued on the custom-made Polk label (see entry for Polk). The Brunswick/Vocalion/Melotone complex soon was constituted as the Brunswick Record Company. In December 1931, BRC was acquired by Consolidated Film Industries, which already owned ARC. The Brunswick 100 series ended at 601 in about February 1933, and the Vocalion 5000 series ended at 5504 about six months later. The last thirty-one issues in the latter series, 5474–5504, also appeared on various ARC-BRC labels. For the subsequent history of Brunswick and Vocalion holdings, see the entry on ARC.

Clarion This label issued recordings made by Columbia for its Harmony, Velvet Tone, and Diva subsidiaries and some material made for Columbia itself, in a green-label series spanning 5001–5477, all catalog numbers being suffixed -C. The first releases were on August 30, 1930, and the last some time in 1932. The bulk of the catalog is popular material, but more than 100 issues employed material listed in this book.

As a rule, original artist credits and matrices were preserved, but some batches of Clarion releases, drawn from Columbia rather than from Harmony/Velvet Tone/Diva—including much of the country material—substituted control numbers in the 100000 series for the original matrices, generally replacing the original artist credits with pseudonyms.

From early in 1931, Clarion and Velvet Tone were closely linked, issuing the same couplings in almost the same order:

Clarion 5248-C to 5330-C = Velvet Tone 2314-V to 2396-V
Clarion 5333-C to 5400-C = Velvet Tone 2397-V to 2464-V
Clarion 5405-C to 5477-C = Velvet Tone 2465-V to 2537-V

Columbia The earliest issues of country material on Columbia were in the predominantly popular, full-price series that began in 1923 with 1-D. The -D stood for "domestic"; Columbia also had many series of foreign recordings, suffixed -F, which were either licensed from overseas companies or made within the United States by members of non-Anglophone minorities.

In 1924, the company initiated a 15000-D country series to match its 13000-D/14000-D race series, and thereafter virtually all of its country material appeared in that catalog. (So did a scattering of popular and race items that evidently were deemed marketable to the country audience.) This catalog closed in 1932 at 15782-D.

Early country recordings by Columbia, all made in New York, carry matrices from a five-digit series, which ended in September 1924 at 81999. Thereafter, all species of domestic recordings were in the 140000/150000 matrix series, while foreign material was generally logged in the 105000/110000 matrix series, a fact relevant here because two batches of Cajun masters were so numbered.

Other Columbia matrix series occasionally appear in this book. The 130000s are believed to have been used for dubbed or transferred items. The 190000 series may have been used for simultaneously recorded duplicates, possibly safety copies, of items in the 150000 series, since recordings bearing 190000 numbers are also logged in company files with 150000 numbers. A few records are believed to exist in both versions, some copies with 190000 numbers and others with 150000 numbers.

A good deal of the material issued in the 15000-D series was recorded at the company's studios in New York, but much was derived from field sessions in the South, chiefly in Atlanta, Georgia, which the company visited more than a dozen times between 1925 and 1931. There were also spells of recording in Dallas, Texas; New Orleans, Louisiana; and Memphis and Johnson City, Tennessee. Blocks of the domestic matrix series were assigned to these trips (as were blocks of the foreign matrix series, occasionally for Cajun recordings as mentioned above, but chiefly for Mexican and other foreign material outside our scope).

Some Cajun items were issued in the 15000-D series, but others appeared in an exclusively Cajun 40500-F list, which were later reissued in an OKeh 90000 series in the same numerical sequence (that is, Columbia 40510-F became OKeh 90010).

In November 1926, Columbia was amalgamated with OKeh. Around 1931–1932, there was some sharing of artists between the Columbia 15000-D and OKeh 45000 catalogs and some collaborative organization of field sessions. The two companies subsequently passed into the ownership of Grigsby-Grunow (1931), ARC-BRC (1934), and the Columbia Broadcasting System (1938). From 1948, country, race, and popular material from the extensive CBS holdings—chiefly from ARC-BRC but in some cases from the earlier Columbia and OKeh catalogs—was reissued on the red-label 37000 series. Later, many of these reissues were themselves reissued on the red-label 20000 series.

During the 1920s and early 1930s, Columbia maintained several subsidiary labels, the most important of which were Harmony, Velvet Tone, and Diva. For the most part, material was not derived from the Columbia label itself but recorded specifically for this label group; the odd feature of these recordings was that they continued to be made acoustically even after 1925, when Columbia adopted, for its primary label, the Western Electric system. However, some electric recordings appeared on the subsidiary labels before mid-1930, and thereafter all new recordings were electric.

These recordings customarily appeared, along with much noncountry material, in the Harmony 100-H and Velvet Tone 1000-V series; many were also issued in a 2000-G series on Diva, which Columbia manufactured expressly for the W. T. Grant store chain. During the period covered by this book, such issues were numerically linked so that, for example, Harmony 800-H = Velvet Tone 1800-V = Diva 2800-G. When Harmony passed 1000-H, the linking took this form: Harmony 1100-H = Velvet Tone 2100-V = Diva 3100-G. The three labels also had shorter series—Harmony 5000-H, Diva 6000-G, and Velvet Tone 7000-V—used primarily for country and race material; the Diva and Velvet Tone lists are numerically linked. Recordings from the Harmony/Velvet Tone/Diva stock and from the primary Columbia label were also selectively released on another subsidiary, Clarion (see entry on Clarion).

Around 1932–1933, Columbia departed from the previous policy, issuing on Velvet Tone and Clarion some recordings that were also appearing on Columbia or OKeh and initiating recordings for those labels in a 365000 matrix series.

Some Harmony/Velvet Tone/Diva recordings also appeared in a 1000-S series on Puritone, made for the Chicago-based Straus & Schram store chain. The Harmony label was revived in 1949, and some reissued recordings by the Sons of the Pioneers appeared thereon.

Overseas, Columbia masters appeared in Great Britain, Australia, South Africa, and Japan in local Columbia series and, in the first two of those nations, on Regal and Regal-Zonophone. (French and Swiss Columbia, however, had access to Victor masters, hence the appearance on those labels of a few country items derived from Victor and Bluebird.)

Crown

The Crown Record Company, operating from 10 West 20th Street, New York, New York, was founded by Eli Oberstein. Issues were in a 3000 series, which began about September 1930. The company dealt primarily in popular material but issued small quantities of Irish, race, and country items; all recordings were made in New York, in a matrix series beginning at 1000. From December 1931 or January 1932, Crown records (including, probably, repressings of items that had already been issued) were manufactured by Victor, for whom Oberstein had worked. The series ended, at 3532, in the summer of 1933, possibly because Oberstein was committed to A&R work for Victor's new Bluebird line.

Also part of the Crown enterprise was Gem, similarly custom-made by Victor. Few issues are known on Gem; those that appear in this book are numerically identical reissues or co-issues of Crown couplings. Crown material was also reissued shortly afterward in the Homestead 22000/23000 series, from 1939 on Oberstein's Varsity label, and in the 1940s on Continental and Joe Davis-owned labels, such as Beacon, Davis, Joe Davis, and the briefly revived Gennett.

Decca Founded in the summer of 1934 as a U.S. partner of the English nameholder, Decca directly competed with Victor's Bluebird label at the 35-cent price level. The company initially generated recordings from two locations, each with its own matrix series: the 38000/39000s (later 60000s/70000s) in New York and the C-9000s (later 90000s) in Chicago. Popular material was issued in the 100 and 1000/2000/3000/4000 series, country in the 5000/6000 series, and race in the 7000 series. An 8000 "sepia" series, intended for race material with wider appeal, ran alongside the 7000 series in 1940–1942 and continued in 1944–1945 after the 7000 series' demise.

Unlike the popular and race catalogs, the 5000/6000 list was substantially stocked with field-recorded material made on visits to New Orleans, Louisiana; Charlotte, North Carolina; and, in particular, Dallas, Houston, and San Antonio, Texas. For these trips, blocks were assigned from either the New York 60000 or, less often, the Chicago 90000 matrix series. Except for some New Orleans recordings, whose matrices are prefixed NO-, these field matrices carry no clue to their recording location.

Recordings for the popular and country catalogs were also made in Los Angeles, initially as location recordings, later probably at permanent studios; these had their own matrix series with a DLA- prefix.

The 5000/6000 list included some releases by artists outside the scope of this book, such as polka bands; conversely, some country material was issued only in the aforementioned popular series. A few country items were also issued, with appropriate pseudonyms, in the Mexican 10000 and Irish 12000 series. Cajun material was occasionally placed in the 5000 series (if the vocals were in English) but chiefly in its own 17000 catalog.

Decca country recordings were occasionally issued by the company's branches in other territories, particularly in Australia (the X series), Great Britain (the F series), Ireland (the W4000 series), and South Africa (the FM5000 and Brunswick SA series). (See the entries on Australian and British labels for other licensing agreements.) Many Decca recordings were issued in Canada on Melotone and some on Minerva.

The blue-label country list ended in 1945 at 6112. It was succeeded by a short-lived 9000 series and a year later by a black-label 46000 series, in which some material from the 5000/6000 series was reissued and some held-over items first issued.

In 1935, Decca acquired the Champion trademark from Gennett and created (among others) a Champion 45000 country series, chiefly to reissue Gennett material but occasionally using it for new recordings of its own. A small number of Gennett-derived sides was also reissued in the Decca 5000 series. An association with Montgomery Ward led to the issue on that label, in an 8000 series, of both Gennett and original Decca items.

Edison This pioneering recording company issued material within the scope of this book on four-minute Blue Amberol cylinders (containing one musical item) and ten-inch, double-sided, vertical-cut Diamond Discs, which were playable only on Edison phonographs. By the time Edison came to be involved in recording country music, its cylinders were probably always dubbed from disc recordings. Country recordings generally appeared in both formats, which may be distinguished thus: discs, which are listed first, are numbered in the 50000 series, whereas cylinders carry numbers in the 4000s and 5000s.

During the period covered by this book, all of Edison's country recordings were probably made in its studios at 16 Sixth Avenue and 216 Sixth Avenue, New York,

New York. Like most other companies, Edison recorded several takes of each item, but it was unique in also issuing most or all of those takes. Therefore, while all reported takes have been listed here, it may be assumed that other, unlisted takes were also issued.

From 1928, recordings were cut simultaneously for Diamond Discs and for the new, lateral-cut electrical discs, issued in 11000 and 20000 series. The matrices designated for the latter were in an N-1 series. (It should be noted that although the Diamond Disc and electrical N- masters of an item are shown in this book on consecutive lines as if they were discrete, they represent a single recording.) Although numerous Edison recordings were assigned numbers in the 11000 and 20000 series, it is doubtful whether they were all actually issued. Edison ceased all recording activities in October 1929.

Electradisk   Manufactured by Victor for sale by the F. W. Woolworth Company, Electradisk recordings made their first appearance in June 1932 as eight-inch records in an 1800 series. From October they were on ten-inch discs in a series that ran from 1900 to 2177. (There was also a short run from 2500 to 2509.) Material was shared with Bluebird and Sunrise. Electradisk was discontinued in January 1934; its issues are relatively scarce and were probably pressed in small quantities.

Gennett   Gennett was the flagship label of the Starr Piano Company of Richmond, Indiana (founded in 1893 by proprietor Harry Gennett). The company began manufacturing phonographs and records in 1916; country material began to appear on the Gennett label in 1922, issued alongside race, popular, and other material in a 4000/5000 and later a 3000 series. Once the company was using exclusively electrical recordings, it instituted, probably in December 1926, the 6000 Electrobeam series, which ran until 7323, issued about the beginning of 1931; this series too was used for a variety of genres.

Much of the material recorded by Gennett (properly speaking, by Starr, but collectors' usage has established Gennett as the company's umbrella name) appeared also, or instead, on a cheaper label, Champion, which started its 15000 series (at 15001) in September 1925 and ran to 16832 in December 1934. Champions were at first manufactured for sale through the Kresge store chain but were later sold through other outlets. Company files also log issues in a Champion 33000 series, about which almost nothing is known.

A later Gennett low-price label, Superior, ran from 2501 to 2839 in 1930–1932; releases in all genres were generally reissues from Gennett or Champion, with pseudonyms replacing the original artist credits, but some were unique to Superior. Pressing runs were customarily small, and the records are consequently rare.

Gennett recordings also appear profusely, generally pseudonymously, and sometimes uniquely on the Sears labels Challenge, Conqueror, Silvertone, and Supertone (see entry for Sears) and on independent labels such as Bell, Black Patti, Buddy, Herschel Gold Seal (made for the Northwestern Supply Company of St. Paul, Minnesota), and Herwin.

Gennett had its main recording studios in Richmond, Indiana, and New York. The Richmond studio used a matrix sequence starting (for the purposes of this book) in the 11000s and running into the early 20000s. The New York studio, at 9–11 East 37th Street, initially used a 7000 vertical-cut matrix series (irrelevant to this book), then a 9000 lateral-cut matrix series, which when it reached 9999, in March 1926, continued from X-1. The prefix was soon afterward altered to GEX-, while the numbering ran on to 2953. Latterly the New York recordings were made at a studio in

Woodside, Long Island, New York. There were occasional sessions in Chicago, Illinois (some at the Starr Piano Store); Cincinnati, Ohio; and St. Paul, Minnesota, all using Richmond matrices, and one field session in Birmingham, Alabama (at the Starr Piano Store on Third Avenue, in July–August 1927), using New York matrices.

Gennett recordings were commonly made in two, three, or occasionally four takes, the first denoted by the unsuffixed matrix number (customarily described as the "plain take"), the others by the addition of -A, -B, and -C, thus: 12000, 12000-A, 12000-B, 12000-C. Most Gennett-group issues do not carry matrix or take information either in the wax or on the label, but company files usually note which take was judged to be the most suitable for issue, and that information has been incorporated in this book.

The dating of Gennett recordings presents some complexities. The dates provided in Gennett files for recordings made at the Richmond studios appear to be genuine recording dates. Those given for recordings made in New York, Chicago, and other locations, however, do not denote the recording date but, probably, the date the masters were received in Richmond, which consequently must be later than the recording date, though how much later is uncertain: probably days rather than weeks. Hence, all Gennett sessions outside Richmond have, in this book, been assigned an approximate (c.) date, which should be interpreted as implying a recording date probably no more, and possibly less, than a week earlier. Where Richmond sessions have been assigned approximate dates, it is because the files report processing rather than recording dates.

Gennett also did a good deal of custom recording, both for other companies and for individuals. Some of the earliest Gennett-recorded material in this book was in the latter category, produced with personalized labels for such artists as the Vaughan Quartet, E. Arthur Lewis, and the Garner Brothers, who were on the Jubilee Gospel Singers label. A later example is the 1931 session by the Vagabonds for their own Old Cabin label. Among the record companies that did business with Gennett, the most significant for users of this book is Paramount, which commissioned recording sessions by several Cajun artists, such as John H. Bertrand, Roy Gonzales, Leo Soileau, and Moise Robin. Another is Chapel, whose products were designed for use in funeral parlors.

An obscure group of recordings in Gennett's files is the block of Paramount-commissioned matrices extending from GEX-2397 to GEX-2478. The use of this matrix prefix implies that the material was recorded in New York, but the date of October 23, 1929, which is assigned in the files to the entire sequence, cannot be a recording date—the workload would have been much too great—and it seems certain that the recordings were made earlier and bought or processed by Gennett *en bloc* on or about the quoted date. There is some evidence to suggest that the sessions were organized by the independent producer Harry Charles of Birmingham, Alabama.

Like other companies, Gennett also made some recordings for sale or distribution by radio stations, for example, the John McGhee item for KWKH/KLEA.

By the mid-1930s, much of the company's work was in recording sound effects. It remained in business, in a desultory way, at least until the end of the decade, when some of its masters were used in a custom job for the Fireside Melodies label by Warren Caplinger and Andy Patterson.

The Champion trademark was acquired by Decca in June 1935, and a selection of material from the 15000/16000 catalog was reissued in 40000 (popular), 45000 (country), and 50000 (race) series. Gennett-derived material was also reissued, usually pseudonymously, in 1939–1940 on Eli Oberstein's Varsity label, though more in the 6000 race series than in the 5000 country list.

Some Gennett rights were acquired in the mid-1940s by the New York music publisher and label owner Joe Davis, who revived the Gennett name for a handful of newly recorded blues issues, chiefly by Gabriel Brown, and older, previously issued country items by, for example, the McCravy Brothers.

The location of its head office in Richmond, Indiana, made Gennett uniquely accessible to artists and artists' representatives in the upper South, and the company's holdings are richer than any of its contemporaries' in country music from West Virginia, Kentucky, Ohio, Indiana, and Illinois. It may be, however, that among the more knowledgeable artists, its reputation was inferior to that of Victor or Columbia, chiefly because of its lower standards of recording and pressing and, in some cases, because of its poorer distribution.

Grey Gull

This New York company began operations in 1920 as a full-price label, but within a few years its products were being sold at lower prices through five-and-ten-cent stores and mail-order outlets, not only on Grey Gull but on the associated labels Radiex, Van Dyke, Supreme, Globe, and others. Except for Radiex and Van Dyke, these sister labels were short-lived, and little of the material contained in this book was issued on them.

Issues were in 1000 (dance), 2000 (popular vocal), and 4000 (standard vocal) series, the last of these containing the majority of the country recordings that Grey Gull produced, as well as sacred, Hawaiian, comedy, and other items. The 2000-series issues included in this book are mostly by Al Bernard, Vernon Dalhart, and Arthur Fields. The highest reported number in the 2000 series is 2548 and in the 4000 series, 4321. It appears that the company ceased business sometime in 1930.

The majority of Grey Gull's material originated with the company and bore matrix numbers in a four-digit series beginning somewhere before 2000 and ending soon after 4000. Recordings were also acquired from Emerson, Paramount, and Plaza.

During the period covered by this book, it seems to have been standard practice for a coupling to be issued on Grey Gull and Radiex (and, for a time, Supreme and Globe) with the same catalog number, and on Van Dyke with that number prefixed by 7 (later 8). Thus, Grey Gull 4131 = Radiex 4131 = Supreme 4131 = Globe 4131 = Van Dyke 74131. Pseudonymous rather than genuine artist credits were frequently employed, and Van Dyke issues sometimes used different artist credits from those on the Grey Gull and Radiex issues.

Numerous Grey Gull and associated-label issues exist in two or more forms, where the titles were rerecorded—sometimes, but not always, by the same artist(s)—and assigned either new matrices or the same matrices with higher take letters. Such instances are further complicated by the use of pseudonyms rather than the original, "true" credits, or, more often, new pseudonyms rather than the original pseudonyms.

To take a particularly complex example, Grey Gull/Radiex 4131 existed in at least four forms, always coupling the titles "Wreck Of The Old 97"/"Wreck Of The Titanic" but using various combinations of recordings by Vernon Dalhart, Arthur Fields, and Frank Luther. All of them usually used the pseudonym Jeff Calhoun, but sometimes, as in the case of Fields's version of "Wreck Of The Old 97," the pseudonym is Mr. X or Vel Veteran, pseudonyms also used on other discs, occasionally by artists other than Fields. Yet a further complication is that there are sometimes discrepancies between the matrix pressed or embossed in the wax and that printed on the label. In an attempt at clarification, quite detailed notes are usually attached to sessions—mostly by Dalhart, Fields, and Luther—which involve such multiple issues.

There was also a Van Dyke 5000 series of predominantly standard vocal material, which ran to at least 5122 and contained a number of country items, very often with pseudonymous artist credits. The same issues also appeared on Madison in the numerically matching 5000 series (until 5099) and 50000 series (until 50051). Thus, Van Dyke 5018 = Madison 5018 = Madison 50018. Some items additionally appeared in Madison's 1000 popular series.

The matrices found on issues in these series are partly from Grey Gull's four-digit matrix series and partly from an obscure, possibly Madison-originated, three-digit matrix or, more probably, control series, but some items may carry numbers from both series. Some titles in these linked Van Dyke/Madison series duplicate titles by the same artists in the Grey Gull/Radiex 4000 and Van Dyke 74000/84000 series, and while the recordings often prove to be identical, in some instances they certainly are not.

Herwin

This St. Louis label, active probably from late 1925 to 1929, took its name from brothers Herbert and Edwin Schiele, owners of the parent company, the Artophone Corporation. Artophone entered the record arena in 1918 as a manufacturer of phonographs and within a few years had become a major distributor of other companies' records. Herwins appeared in a 55000 popular series, 92000 and 93000 race series, and the 75500 country series, which ran from 75501 at least as far as 75571. Material was chiefly drawn from Gennett and Paramount and a smaller amount from Plaza; pseudonymous artist credits were frequently employed.

Some Herwin 75500-series releases exist in two forms: one version employs Gennett or Paramount matrices for the titles, while the other uses Plaza matrices, sometimes by the same artist(s), sometimes not. A few issues couple matrices from both sources, and some pressings of Herwin 75532 couple a Paramount matrix by Harkreader & Moore with a Grey Gull matrix by Vernon Dalhart.

Herwins were sold mainly, perhaps entirely, by mail order, through Artophone's subsidiary the St. Louis Music Company, which advertised regularly in newspapers and magazines that reached the rural white and black markets. Initially offered at 75 cents, by the spring of 1927, they were being advertised at a special price of eight for $2.98. With some exceptions, mostly Vernon Dalhart items, they are relatively scarce.

Homestead

Owned by the Chicago Mail Order Company, this label was active from about the mid-1920s, issuing in a black-label 15000/16000 series a large number of popular and some country and race items derived from Plaza and subsequently ARC.

In January 1932, Victor took over the manufacture of Homestead labels (but probably not pressings) from the Simeon Company. A 22000/23000 series, of which the earliest reported number is 22984, drew on Crown, which was then manufactured by Victor, and consisted entirely of reissues of Crown couplings. However, a few of the Homestead catalog numbers so employed were also used for different, ARC-derived recordings previously issued in the 15000/16000 series.

The 22000/23000 series was sold through the catalogs of the CMOC at a price of five for $1.19. Issues therein are considerably scarcer than those in the earlier series.

Montgomery Ward

The famous mail-order house issued a large number of records in several numerical series. Its most lasting association was with Victor, which from June 1933 provided Ward with recordings from all of its categories of music. These recordings, which Victor also pressed, appeared first on buff labels with red type, then from October 1933 on black labels with gold type. The main Montgomery Ward series, of country (including Cajun), race, foreign, and popular material, appears to have begun with M-4200 and to have run with only occasional numerical gaps until approximately M-5041. An M-6000 series was devoted to classical material. The country/race/foreign/

popular issues recommenced at M-7001 and ran, again with some gaps, until M-7999. The sequence resumed at M-8306 and ran through M-8961. While the majority of Montgomery Ward records are reissues of Victor and, later, Bluebird items, a good deal of material recorded for Bluebird never appeared on that label but solely on Montgomery Ward. Montgomery Ward records were primarily advertised in and sold through the company's retail outlets and through its mail-order catalogs, which were distributed to innumerable rural households.

There were, however, some intrusions into these Victor-derived series. The majority of releases within the numerical block of 4926–5022 (those without the M- prefix) uses Gennett matrices through an arrangement with Decca, which had obtained certain Gennett rights in January 1935. The unprefixed release numbers in the 8000–8072 block also stem from Decca and employ both Decca and Gennett-derived recordings. There was also a blue-label M3000 series, evidently brief (the highest reported number is M3026), drawn from Crown.

Through an autumn 1933 arrangement whose details are still obscure, some Montgomery Ward issues in the range (approximately) M-8050 to M-8305 replicated both the catalog numbers and the titles of couplings previously issued on the Paramount subsidiary Broadway but substituted recordings of those titles made by Victor artists. Thus, Montgomery Ward M-8109 contains the titles "Daddy And Home"/"Waiting For A Train," which had appeared on Broadway 8109 by Ed (Jake) West, but the Ward version uses the recordings of those titles made for Victor by Jimmie Rodgers, whom it duly credits. There are many gaps in this part of the Montgomery Ward listing, and it seems likely that only selected numbers were used, presumably on those relatively few occasions when Victor had appropriate recordings of the titles that had been used on the original Broadways. (Though on at least one occasion Victor material was retitled to fit the Broadway mold; compare Bill Helms & His Upson County Band on Montgomery Ward M-8234 with Chumbler, Coker & Rice on Broadway 8234.)

Similarly, a small number of Montgomery Wards with numbers between 4000 and 4199 replicated the numbers and titles of couplings previously issued on the ARC-Broadway 4000 series. A few others replicated the numbers and titles of couplings on Paramount; for example, M-3272, "Blue Yodel"/"Away Out On The Mountain" by Jimmie Rodgers, "covered" the similar titles on Paramount 3272 by Frank Marvin.

Certain Montgomery Wards, mostly in the M-7900s, though known from Victor files to have been planned and to have had labels printed (they were even listed in Montgomery Ward catalogs), were almost certainly never shipped out to the retail trade; this, at least, is my supposition, based on evidence in Victor's archives that these items registered zero sales totals. In this book, these questionable issues are enclosed in square brackets: [MW M-7913].

Montgomery Ward's association with Victor probably ended in December 1941.

OKeh   This label of the Otto Heineman Phonograph Supply Company issued miscellaneous popular material in 1919 in a purple-label 1000 series of vertical-cut discs. In October of that year, Heineman formed the General Phonograph Company and soon began issuing lateral-cut records in a 4000 series, which was succeeded in 1923, when it had reached 4999, by a 40000 series. Race issues were awarded their own catalog, the 8000 series, in 1921. Country music, which OKeh began to record in 1923, was at first issued in the 4000/40000 popular catalog, but from 1925 was generally placed in its own 45000 list. A small number of longer performances was issued during 1924–1926 on twelve-inch discs in the 7000 series, priced at $1.25 (the ten-inch price was 75 cents).

OKeh was merged with Columbia in November 1926, when the German parent firm was acquired by Columbia's owners, the British Columbia Graphophone Company. The joint concern was sold in 1931 to Grigsby-Grunow and in 1934 to ARC-BRC. The country catalog operated throughout most of these transactions, reaching 45579 in 1934.

Field recording sessions were organized frequently between 1923 and 1931, chiefly in Atlanta, Georgia; Dallas, Texas; New Orleans, Louisiana; and St. Louis, Missouri; and occasionally in Memphis, Tennessee; San Antonio, Texas; Richmond, Virginia; Winston-Salem, North Carolina; Shreveport, Louisiana; and Jackson, Mississippi. From October 1929 onward, these field trips were conducted in some liaison with Columbia's, and later sessions would be held in some locations with both labels in mind. Sometimes material recorded on those occasions was assigned OKeh matrices but then diverted to be issued on Columbia and, rarely, vice versa.

Early country recordings on OKeh employ matrices drawn from the 70000 (New York) and 8000 (Chicago) sequences; field trips were assigned blocks of matrices from the Chicago sequence. The 80000 matrix series, begun in the summer of 1926, was used for electrical recordings; it was succeeded in January 1928 by a 400000 matrix series, which was used for all recordings, wherever made. Matrices in the 480000 series are transfers or dubbings from the normal series. The W- prefix that appears on discs, added to 80000-series matrices from December 1926 onward and to all 400000 matrices, denotes the Western Electric process.

Some recordings from the OKeh 45000 catalog were also issued in the company's 16000 Mexican series, usually with their titles translated into Spanish and artist credits appropriately altered. The OKeh 90000 series was a short-lived catalog of Cajun material, reissued from the Columbia 40500-F series. Overseas, OKeh country items appeared in small numbers on both British and Australian Parlophone and more seldom on the British Ariel and Australian Kismet labels.

ARC-BRC passed in January 1938 into the ownership of the Columbia Broadcasting System, which in 1940 revived the OKeh trademark to replace Vocalion. (See ARC entry.) It has been employed at irregular intervals ever since by CBS and the present proprietors, Columbia/Sony.

Paramount   Paramount was owned by the Wisconsin Chair Company of Port Washington, Wisconsin (1888–1954), and operated through its subsidiary company, the New York Recording Laboratories, which incorporated in July 1917. It achieved its greatest impact as a race label, with the institution in July 1922 of its 12000 series. Earlier (popular) releases had been in 2000, 30000, 50000, and (from June 1920) 20000 series, the last of which continued to be used for popular and some race items. Recordings were also issued on the company's Broadway, Famous, and Puritan labels.

Paramount's first ventures into country music appeared during 1924–1926 in a 33000 series (begun in September 1919), which until then had been, and continued to be, used chiefly for standard and sacred material. Many of these issues also appeared in the Puritan 9000 series, numerically linked so that, for example, Paramount 33176 = Puritan 9176. There was also a connection with the Sears label Silvertone's 3500 series.

In the early months of 1927, Paramount decided to create an exclusively country catalog, and the first issues in the black-label 3000 series of "Olde Time Tunes" appeared in April or May. The catalog closed in the latter part of 1932 at 3323. Closely linked with this was the black-label Broadway 8000 series, in which Paramount material usually appeared in the same couplings but with pseudonymous artist credits; this series ran until 8337. (See the entry on Montgomery Ward for a curiously associated series.)

Many Paramount recordings included in this book were made in Chicago, Illinois, the majority probably at the Marsh Laboratories studio, located first on the sixth floor of the Lyon & Healy Building on South Wabash Street and later on the seventh floor of the Lyon & Healy Building at 64 East Jackson Avenue, though other independent studios in the Loop area were also used by the company from time to time. These Chicago recordings were logged first in a 4000 and then in a 20000 matrix series. Some early items, however, fall in a 2000 series, which appears to have been used in both Chicago and New York, where Paramount had studios at 1140 Broadway until about the end of 1926.

In late 1929, the company opened studios in Grafton, Wisconsin, across the street from its pressing plant, and commenced a matrix series with L-1 (the L probably stood for recording manager Arthur C. Laibly). The latest known recordings in this block are from around July 1932. By that time, what little country material Paramount was recording was being issued in the last stretches of the Paramount 3000 and Broadway 8000 series or in the brief, mixed-idiom Paramount 500 series. (Judging from the artists involved, the company was associating itself closely with the Chicago radio station WLS.)

As well as producing its own masters, Paramount commissioned recordings from Gennett, which were made in either New York or Richmond, Indiana, and licensed material from and to Plaza, QRS, and Crown.

Broadway had at least two other relevant manifestations. In the mid-1930s, it reappeared as an ARC subsidiary. A 4000 series drew on ARC-owned material, using pseudonymous artist credits, while occasional issues in what is here termed the ARC-Broadway 8000 series duplicate the earlier Broadway titles and catalog numbers but substitute ARC recordings of the titles by different artists. (In some instances, however, these issues couple a new ARC item and an original Paramount/Broadway one.)

Much earlier, about 1924–1925, a few country items appeared in a Broadway 5000 series, a list later reserved for race material. These items, by, for example, Osey Helton, derive their catalog numbers (which are distinct for each side of the record) from their matrices. In the absence of further information, their recording locations and dates must remain speculative.

Polk   This label, custom-made by Brunswick-Balke-Collender for an Atlanta-based store chain, drew its material exclusively from Melotone and probably came into being soon after the creation of that label in November 1930. (Some of the recordings were made as much as three years earlier and had already been issued, prior to their Melotone release, on Brunswick and/or Vocalion.) The latest Melotone recordings to appear on Polk were made in late 1931, and it is likely that the association with BBC ended with, or soon after, that company's purchase from Warner Brothers Pictures by Consolidated Film Industries in December 1931.

The label design was based on that of the Vocalion 5000 series. Issues were in a P9000 series, of which the highest known number is P9094. A few issues were of blues or jazz, but the bulk of the catalog, particularly from P9047 onward, was country material. Artist credits, whether genuine or pseudonymous, were as on the Melotone issues. Initial pressings were of 500 copies, and from the scarcity of most Polks, it seems likely that few were awarded a second pressing.

QRS   Based in Long Island City, New York, this company was chiefly involved in the manufacture of piano rolls, but during 1928–1929 produced discs in R.7000 (race) and R.9000 (country) series. Early releases in the latter (up to R.9009 inclusive) are reissues from Plaza, but thereafter they are original recordings, employing matrices in a 100 series within the span 391–481, which implies a recording date in the spring of 1929. The circumstances of that recording activity are still obscure, but the artists concerned, like many of those in the race series, were all from Georgia, and the sessions were almost certainly organized by the Birmingham, Alabama, recording agent Harry Charles. They may have been held in Gennett's studios, then located on Long Island. Most of these R.9000 issues were also released in the Paramount 3000 and Broadway 8000 catalogs. The highest number identified in the series is R.9037.

It was probably after the demise of these black-label QRS series that a Q1000 catalog came into being, using pale red labels and bearing as a manufacturer's name the Cova Recording Corporation of New York. Issues in that series included some by Carson Robison & Frank Luther, Arthur Fields, and Gene Autry.

Sears

The Sears, Roebuck mail-order company in Chicago created a number of labels to issue popular, country, and race recordings licensed from other companies.

Challenge (1927–1931) issued country and popular material in several three-digit series, spanning 101–999 but not issued consecutively and with numerous gaps where numbers were not assigned. Material was derived chiefly from Gennett (101–271, 301–431, 501–506) but also from Plaza (532–698, 811–859, 900–999), Bell (700–760), ARC (763–793, 860–899), and Paramount (801–810). The label was Sears's cheapest line, offered at various prices between 19 and 24 cents, or even more cheaply if bought in tens. Pseudonyms were used for much of the country material.

Conqueror (1928–1942) drew almost exclusively on material controlled by ARC (or later, Columbia), in all genres. The series began at 7000 and ran into the high 9000s. Some ARC-recorded items never appeared on the original owner's labels but only on Conqueror. There was also a batch of Gennett-derived country and race items (7254–7277); these employed pseudonymous artist credits, but ARC-derived issues seldom did. Conquerors were offered for sale at 29 cents, or three for 85 cents.

Silvertone may have been Sears's oldest label; it was in existence as early as 1916. The series relevant to this book, all operating in the mid-to-late 1920s and issuing material in all genres, are the 3000, chiefly drawn from Brunswick/Vocalion but including a few items from Columbia; the 3500, drawn from Paramount; and the 4000, 5000, 8000, and 25000 drawn from (and manufactured by) Gennett. The 25000s are, except for the prefix 2-, identical to the 5000s. Silvertones were regarded as higher-grade pressings than Challenges and (at that period) Conquerors and were priced around 39 cents. The label was discontinued in 1930 but had a brief revival in the 1940s.

Supertone drew from Gennett for its mixed-genre 9000 series, active in 1929–1931. The identity of the original artist was generally hidden by a pseudonym. (Exceptions are artists associated with the radio station WLS, such as Bradley Kincaid and the Arkansas Woodchopper.) The highest known number in this series is 9778.

The mixed-genre S2000 series drew exclusively from Brunswick/Vocalion, often using the original artist credit. It was launched in March 1931 and may not have survived long into the following year; certainly many items listed in the fall 1931 Sears catalog did not reappear in the spring 1932 volume.

Sunrise

A Victor subsidiary, active from August 1933 to May 1934, Sunrise differed from its predecessor Timely Tunes in amounting to an extensive catalog: it ran from S-3100 to S-3467. Such is the scarcity of the records, however, that there must be some doubt whether all of the issues that Victor archives report as scheduled were actually put on the market. Sunrises are without exception reissues (or co-issues) of Bluebird couplings in popular, race, and country genres.

Timely Tunes This 25-cent label was in operation, according to Brian Rust in the *Victor Master Book*, from April 6, 1931, to July of that year. A Victor brand, it dealt in popular, race, and country music recorded specifically for it by the parent label. These items often duplicated material recorded for Victor, frequently at the same sessions. Artist credits were almost always pseudonyms. The series spanned C-1550 to C-1590. Its issues are scarce.

Varsity Varsity was founded by Eli Oberstein in 1939 as a 35-cent label, issuing country material in a blue-label 5000 series, as well as race (6000), foreign (7000), and popular (8000) series. Much of the material in the first hundred issues of the 5000 series was dubbed from Oberstein's earlier Crown catalog, including a few items never issued on that label, but there were also some (also dubbed) reissues of Gennett and Paramount masters to which Varsity had obtained rights. Some Crown-derived Varsity recordings were licensed to Montgomery Ward and appeared in a blue-label M3000 series.

Subsequent Varsity releases (and reissues or co-issues on Elite) were of newly recorded material, represented in this book by, for example, Bill Bender. Varsity had a full-price sister label, Royale, which during the period covered by this book confined itself to popular and classical material; its dealings with country music were after World War II.

Victor One of the most venerable companies in the history of American recorded music, Victor was incorporated as the Victor Talking Machine Company on October 3, 1901. The company was merged in January 1929 with the Radio Corporation of America.

Country recordings on Victor first appeared in the early 1920s in the general domestic black-label series, priced at 75 cents; items show up in the 18000s and 19000s and then more frequently in the 20000s. The company's term for country material was initially "Hillbilly," later "Southern." In May 1929, Victor created a country catalog, the V-40000 series, first called "Native American Melodies," then, from May 1930, "Old Familiar Tunes & Novelties." A few dozen releases in this series were by popular vocalists and dance bands; they are not listed in this book, but the relevant artist credits appear with explanatory entries.

In January 1931, the V-40000 series, like the V-38000 race list, was discontinued; the last release was V-40335. Race issues thereafter were in the 23000 (jazz) series (which had begun in September 1930) and the 23250 (blues and gospel) series; country music was in the 23500 series. It was arranged that the main domestic series, when it had reached 22999, would skip the apportioned race and country blocks and recommence at 24000. The 23500 series was terminated at 23859 in early 1934, and thereafter virtually all of the company's country recording was for its cheaper label, Bluebird (see entry).

Much Victor recording was conducted at studios in New York, New York; Camden, New Jersey; and Chicago, Illinois, but the company also made many southern field recording trips, generally under the supervision of Ralph S. Peer. Between 1925 and 1932, Victor visited Atlanta, Georgia; Dallas, Texas; Memphis, Tennessee; and New Orleans, Louisiana, while also making important stops in Bristol, Tennessee; Charlotte, North Carolina; Nashville, Tennessee; San Antonio and El Paso, Texas; and other locations.

Apart from certain recordings in Central and South America, Cuba, and Puerto Rico, a single matrix series was employed for virtually all of Victor's recordings, in all genres (including foreign material) and at all recording locations. (The three-digit Pacific Coast matrix series, used between June 1924 and June 1927, did not include any recordings relevant to this book.) The main series began at 1 in May 1903; the first electrically recorded ("Orthophonic") matrix was 32160, made in March 1925. This matrix series was employed more or less chronologically, but some blocks were used out of sequence, and remakes of individual titles generally used the original matrix with higher take numbers. By August 1936, this series had reached well into six figures. At that point, a fresh series was begun at 01; it terminated at 075904 at the end of 1942. The sequence also supplied matrices for recordings designed for Bluebird.

The matrix prefixes BVE-, BSHQ-, and BS-, used in Victor files, do not appear on discs or labels and are therefore ignored in this book. The matrix itself does not appear on disc or label either, except for a six-month period in 1928 when it was shown on both.

In addition to Bluebird, Victor created the shorter-lived subsidiaries Sunrise and Timely Tunes and provided material exclusively for Electradisk (see entries). The company also manufactured pressings for Montgomery Ward (of Victor-owned material under license) and, for a period, Crown and associated labels.

Victor's country recordings were licensed in Australia and Britain to HMV, Zonophone, and Regal-Zonophone and in India to HMV and Twin. Some sixty-odd issues of Victor-derived material were pressed in Britain in the Zonophone 4000 series for export to South Africa. Victor recordings also appeared in Japan, generally in the local JA and Jr series but in a few cases with the original U.S. catalog numbers.

The Victor name reappeared on country material in 1945 on the 20-1500 series, which was chiefly concerned with recordings made after 1942 but also reissued some items first released on Bluebird. A few Bluebird-derived sides also appeared on Victor with numbers drawn from the domestic series, usually when they were selected for reissue, in the early 1940s, in album sets.

Canadian

A substantial number of recordings listed in this book was issued in Canada, either by regional offices of U.S. companies, such as Brunswick, Columbia, and Victor, or by Canadian companies, in particular the Compo group. (I am indebted to material assembled by Alex Robertson for much of the information below.)

Aurora Two Aurora catalogs are relevant to this book. A series drawn from U.S. Victor ran from 36-101 to 36-140, from 36-201 to 36-240, and from 400 to 431. Many of the issues in the first of those blocks, including all of the country ones, were drawn from Timely Tunes and replicated that label's pseudonymous artist credits. The second and third blocks were drawn from Victor itself or, in a few cases in the third block, Electradisk; the majority of the issues in those blocks are of country material.

An A22000 series was drawn from and manufactured by U.S. Brunswick. The sequence ran to A22039; twenty-four of the forty issues are of country material, and pseudonyms peculiar to the series are employed for all artists except Vernon Dalhart. Brunswick's file cards for the series, prepared on June 12, 1931, are headed "Aurora–Syndicate" and bear the note "Canada May 1931" or "Toronto May 1931."

Bluebird Bluebird's B-4000 series included blocks dedicated to French-Canadian, Irish, and West Indian recordings and a sequence reserved for Canadian recordings, represented in this book largely by the early work of Wilf Carter (Montana Slim) and Hank Snow.

A few items from U.S. Victor/Bluebird also appeared in that series. Numerous U.S. Bluebird issues were pressed by Victor's office in Montreal and used the same catalog numbers. Except where there is some anomaly peculiar to the Canadian pressing, these issues are not identified here with a C suffix.

Brunswick A few items in the U.S. Brunswick 100 series were made for sale only in Canada and are therefore shown as Canadian issues. The 52000 series, which reissued a good deal of material from the country holdings of U.S. Brunswick and Vocalion, with the titles translated into French and with French artist credits, presumably for the French-Canadian market, was manufactured in the United States and so is not given a C suffix here.

Columbia In the late 1930s and early 1940s (and subsequently), a number of recordings made for the U.S. Columbia labels OKeh and Vocalion were issued in Canada in a Columbia C series.

Compo The Compo company of Lachine, Quebec, probably Canada's largest recording group in the 1920s and 1930s, controlled the following labels relevant to this book: Apex, Crown, Domino, Royale, Sterling, and, from 1932, Melotone (see entry).

The Apex 8000 series ran from 1923 to 1929. Other catalogs dependent on it for material were the Starr 10000, Domino 21000, Microphone 22000, and Lucky Strike 24000 series. The Apex 41000 series was begun in October 1929 and may have lasted no later than March 1930. Very little country material appeared in any of these series, and that small amount was predominantly by Vernon Dalhart.

The linked series Crown 81000, Domino 181000, and Sterling 281000 were launched in the spring of 1929 and drew material from the Apex 8000 and, later, 41000 series. Early Crown and Domino issues were on brown wax, but by the time the series ended, at 81533, in the spring of 1931, all issues were on black wax. Material was licensed from Plaza and ARC and was predominantly in the popular idiom but included some recordings by Vernon Dalhart, Frank Luther, and the like. A few items were re-pressed, with the Crown number, on Melotone.

A shorter and more obscure series, linking Crown 83000, Domino 183000, and Sterling 283000, seems to have existed in 1929–1930. Some of these issues, too, were repressed with Crown numbers on Melotone. A few sides by Vernon Dalhart, Carson Robison, and Frank Luther are the only known country items.

Another linked series, Crown 91000, Sterling 291000, and Royale 391000, began in early 1931. When it reached 91227, Sterling and Royale dropped their 2 and 3 prefixes, so that all three labels used an identical number. In January 1932, Melotone was added to this group and also used numbers in the 91000 series; the first was around 91300. The series, which ran to 92156, was drawn exclusively from ARC and included a higher proportion of country material than the earlier series.

A fourth linked series, Crown/Melotone 93000, Sterling 293000, and Royale 393000, may have begun about the same time as the third or not long afterward. It ended, at 93165, in 1941 or 1942. Like the Minerva M-14000 series, which shared many of the same issues, it drew material, both country and popular, from U.S. Brunswick and Vocalion, U.S. Crown, Gennett, Plaza, and ARC, as well as Canadian material from Compo.

A couple of Vernon Dalhart's recordings included in this book appeared on Ajax, a Compo label chiefly concerned with African-American music (see Dixon, Godrich, and Rye).

Leonora   A few of Vernon Dalhart's recordings appeared on this uncommon label in a 10000 series, which was apparently identical to the Starr 10000 series.

Lucky Strike   This label was manufactured by Compo for an as-yet-unidentified store chain, probably in Ontario, in the middle to late 1920s. The few country items known in its 24000 series are mostly by Vernon Dalhart.

Melotone   Melotone, a label of the U.S. Brunswick group, was distributed in Canada in 1931 (its first year of operation) by T. Eaton, a mail-order company. Acquired by Compo in January 1932, though it continued to be sold through Eaton's, the label was used in tandem with the Compo labels Crown, Domino, Royale, and Sterling (see entry on Compo).

Later in the 1930s, a Melotone 45000 series drew from Gennett's Champion catalog and to a greater extent from Decca; it probably came into being after Decca acquired the Champion trademark in 1935. The series, which ran to more than 550 issues and consisted almost entirely of country material, chiefly from the Decca 5000/6000 series (a few issues were by Canadian artists), was withdrawn from the retail trade in 1942 but continued to be sold through Eaton's until at least 1948.

An M18000 series was evenly divided between French-Canadian material and recordings from the country holdings of U.S. Brunswick and Vocalion. As with the Brunswick 52000 series, which shares many of the same issues, the titles were translated into French and the artists were given French pseudonyms, though different ones from those used in the Brunswick series. Also like the Brunswick 52000s, this series, which ran to M18052, was manufactured in the United States and is not given a C suffix.

Microphone   Like Lucky Strike, this label was manufactured by Compo for an unidentified store chain. It first appeared in March or April 1925; its issues, in a 22000 series, were exclusively drawn from the Apex 8000 catalog. The country items that appeared on Microphone are by Vernon Dalhart, Frank Luther, and the Pickard Family, all from Plaza. The label probably disappeared in 1929–1930.

Minerva   This label was made for the Eaton mail-order company. The brand was registered in 1926 and amended to include records in September 1935. The label was introduced to customers in the company's fall–winter 1935–1936 catalog and made its last appearance in the spring–summer 1942 catalog. Two series were used simultaneously, both including a considerable amount of country material. The M-900 series, which ran to M-938, drew from Plaza and ARC, while the M-14000 series, which ran to M-14168, was derived from U.S. Brunswick, U.S. Crown, Gennett, Plaza, ARC, and, after M-14061, entirely from Decca. (Both series also included some Canadian recordings derived from Compo.) A small number of Minerva M-900-series items were also issued with the same catalog number on Melotone.

Victor   Numerous U.S. Victor issues were also pressed by the company's office in Montreal, using the same catalog number. Except where there is some anomaly peculiar to the Canadian pressing, these issues are not identified here with a C suffix.

Australian   (by David L. Crisp)

Considering the small population of Australia during the period covered by this book (between five and six million) and the huge quantity of records manufactured there, it is hardly surprising that many of them had extremely small sales. Some items, though they make tantalizing appearances in catalogs and advertisements, have yet to turn up in collectors' hands.

Before 1927, when a tariff was imposed which added significantly to their price and virtually drove them out of the market, many U.S. labels were imported into Australia, and recordings on such labels as Banner, Edison, Jewel, Lincoln, Oriole, and Victor, including a few country items, were not infrequently found there.

Between 1927 and 1932, an occasional country item appeared on the twenty or so labels produced by Clifford Industries (later the Klippel Record Company) and Vocalion (later Moulded Products), such as Angelus, Bellbird, Clifford, Electron, Gaiety, Gracelon, Lyric, Melotone, Paramount, Starr, Sterling, Summit, and Worth. Melotone and Paramount were not connected with the U.S. labels of those names, nor Sterling with the Canadian label. The material was drawn from such U.S. sources as Cameo, Gennett, and Grey Gull. Grand Pree, which issued (under pseudonyms) a few Vernon Dalhart items from Pathé, was initially (c. 1926–1927) manufactured in Britain and exported to Australia, but from 1928 formed part of the Clifford Industries family. Most of the country items issued in Australia, however, appeared on the major labels listed below.

From 1931 onward, most Australian major labels used the pressing services of Columbia Graphophone, which employed the CPS (coated paper surface), or laminated, process. This had the curious result of producing pressings that were often of higher quality than the original U.S. issues on labels such as Decca, Gennett, and Victor.

Brunswick — D. Davis & Company, Brunswick's Australian distributor, began pressing records in 1923, drawing upon U.S. Brunswick's various numerical catalogs and generally employing the same issue numbers. Nearly a hundred country items were issued, many from the U.S. Brunswick 100 series.

Columbia — Columbia Graphophone issued a handful of country items, drawn from the U.S. company, between 1926 and 1930, in a five-digit series beginning with 0.

Decca — The Decca X series, pressed by Columbia Graphophone, included nearly a hundred country items drawn from U.S. Decca (including some Gennett recordings acquired by that company), issued between 1936 and 1946.

HMV — The Gramophone Company's Australian branch began pressing material derived from U.S. Victor in 1926, issuing it in its EA series. This catalog was continued until the 1950s, but no country items appeared after 1936. From 1931 onward, the recordings were pressed by Columbia Graphophone. The most significant country material in this series was twenty-seven couplings by Jimmie Rodgers.

Panachord — Brunswick (Australia), which took over from Davis & Company in 1930, introduced the cheap Panachord label in March 1931 in an effort to boost sales. The catalog began at 12000 and ran both backward to 11980 (or lower) and forward to 12299 before ceasing, with the rest of the Brunswick operation, in June 1933. Some fifty country items were issued, drawn from U.S. Brunswick and Melotone. The blue-and-silver or blue-and-gold label design, like that of British Panachord, was based on Melotone's.

Parlophone — The Australian branch of British Parlophone introduced its A series in 1926. Apart from a few of the earliest issues, which were imported, records were pressed in

Australia by Columbia Graphophone, which eventually absorbed the label in the early 1930s. Between 1927 and 1935, a small number of mostly obscure country items from OKeh was issued, probably more by mistake than by design, since the label was primarily devoted to what were considered better types of music.

Regal/Regal-Zonophone Beginning in 1926 with recordings drawn from the British Regal catalog, Columbia Graphophone soon introduced the Regal G20000 series, which lasted until the 1950s. It was combined with Zonophone in May 1933 to form Regal-Zonophone, but the numbering was unaffected. Some items first issued on Regal were repressed with Regal-Zonophone labels but retained their catalog numbers.

This series was by far the most prolific in country material, including about four hundred issues listed in this book. The recordings were originally drawn from U.S. Columbia and, in a few cases, OKeh; later, they were taken from ARC, including some records originally issued in the United States on Brunswick and Vocalion. The bulk of the country material, however, was derived from Bluebird.

Zonophone The Gramophone Company began pressing this label in Australia in 1926. About seventy-five country couplings were issued; a few were drawn from the British Zonophone 5000/6000 series, including several of Carson Robison's English recordings, but most were derived from U.S. Victor and were issued in Australia in the EE series. As with HMV, pressings after 1931 were made by Columbia Graphophone. After the amalgamation with Regal in May 1933, many of these items were also issued on Regal-Zonophone.

British and Irish

Recordings listed in this book were often issued on British, and sometimes on Irish, labels, some the subsidiaries or partners of the original U.S. companies, others independent concerns that had licensing agreements with U.S. producers. The following list is not comprehensive but includes the labels that had the most significant dealings with country material. Relevant material also appeared, less frequently, on Ariel, Broadcast International, Broadcast Twelve, Brunswick, Eclipse, Empire, Filmophone, Goodson, HMV, Mayfair, Perfect, Phonycord, Piccadilly, Plaza, and Solex.

Many recordings on British labels by Carson Robison were actually recorded in England, during his visits in 1932, 1936, and 1939. Vernon Dalhart also recorded a single session there, for Regal in 1931.

Columbia Scarcely any country material appeared on the British Columbia label's primary four-digit series or in the DB series instituted in March 1930 for standard and popular vocal items. However, about twenty couplings from the U.S. Columbia 15000-D series were issued in a British-pressed 19000 series, and about a half dozen couplings from the same source were issued on a DE500 series, probably pressed in Britain, which was sold in South Africa.

Decca The British Decca company was launched in the spring of 1929. Of its several numerical series, the blue-label popular list beginning with F1501 is of interest to users of this book, since it issued approximately seventy-five couplings of country material drawn from Brunswick, Vocalion, U.S. Decca, and (seldom) ARC. Some of these couplings were also issued in Ireland in the Rex U100 and R5000 and Decca W4000 series. The South African Decca FM series drew its country issues from U.S. Decca.

Durium	Durium discs were pressed on thin celluloid on a flexible brown linoleum-like base; only one side carried recorded material, generally two full-length performances, with an intervening scroll. The model was the U.S. Durium label (1931–1932), a subsidiary of the Hit-of-the-Week label, from which some noncountry material was leased. Vernon Dalhart had four U.S. Durium releases in 1931. The British Durium label was launched in March 1932; the weekly releases, priced at a shilling, were sold only on newsstands. The company is believed to have lasted for less than a year. The only British Durium material relevant to this book is a handful of Carson Robison items recorded in England in 1932. (Robison also recorded for Durium Junior, produced by U.S. Durium.)
Edison Bell Winner	Founded in 1910, this label licensed material at different stages in its existence from Gennett, Plaza, Paramount, Crown, and other U.S. sources. Originally independent, it was sold to Decca in 1933; by the summer of 1935, it had been discontinued. The main four-digit series contained few country items; the most significant of them was a Gene Autry coupling from ARC under the pseudonym Hank Bennett. The W series, which began at 1 in October 1933, released a handful of ARC items by Cliff Carlisle and Tex Ritter. The cheaper eight-inch Edison Bell Radio discs never featured any country material.
Imperial	This label of the Crystalate group, extant from 1920 to 1934, drew some material from Paramount, Plaza, and Crown, including a few items listed in this book.
Panachord	Owned by the Warner Brothers–Brunswick concern and active from April or May 1931 to November 1939 in a numerical series beginning at 25001 and reaching 26041, Panachord modeled its label, initially blue and silver, later blue and gold, closely on Melotone's. It issued country items first from the ARC-BRC group, later from Decca, and constitutes by far the largest British catalog of such material in that period, amounting to several hundred items, some of which are now exceedingly rare.
Parlophone	Founded in October 1923, Parlophone was a British subsidiary of Carl Lindström's German Odeon-Parlophon concern but later joined British HMV and Columbia in what would become the EMI group, of which it is still a part. Material was drawn from various European labels, original British recordings, and U.S. OKeh masters, the last providing a number of country items, issued in the red-label E and purple- (later black-) label R series. A sequence of 20 couplings, R3859–R3878, derived from the OKeh 45000 series, appeared in the Parlophone catalog amid West Indian material; these records are believed to have been manufactured in England for export to that territory.
Regal/Regal-Zonophone	Regal, founded in April 1914 as a subsidiary of the British label Columbia, issued during the 1920s a few country items from the U.S. Columbia catalog. The G6000 numerical series ceased at G9473 in February 1930, and in the following month a new series began with MR1. The amalgamation in January 1933 of HMV and Columbia led to a merging of Regal and Zonophone as Regal-Zonophone, and country items appeared in some profusion on that label, drawn initially from the U.S. Columbia 15000-D series, later and more numerously from Victor/Bluebird, including many by Jimmie Rodgers, and later still from OKeh, including some by Gene Autry (some of which are post-1942 recordings). This series closed at MR3824 in 1949. Other Regal-Zonophone series included country issues, but always of material that had already appeared in the MR catalog. The IZ series was sold exclusively in Ireland.

The ME series, spanning 1–83 (at least), consisted largely of country material—again, mostly from Victor/Bluebird but occasionally from Columbia. It was produced in Britain around 1947–1948 and, from its title of "Special International Records," was probably destined primarily for overseas markets, including New Zealand. Some issues in this series were of material recorded after 1942. (For the Regal/Regal-Zonophone G20000 series, see the entry on Australian labels.)

Rex This label of the Crystalate group was launched in September 1933 at 8001. Though primarily concerned with local product, it drew U.S. recordings of all types, including a little country material, from ARC. In March 1937, the label was taken over by Decca and continued in operation until 1948. Apart from some English recordings by Carson Robison, several by the Hoosier Hot Shots from ARC, and a batch of Gene Autry masters from Gennett (via U.S. Decca), the label is chiefly of interest to users of this book for material in its green-label Irish U100 series drawn from U.S. Brunswick. A later Irish R5000 series drew some items from U.S. Decca.

Zonophone Originally independent, Zonophone was acquired by the Gramophone Company in 1903. Numerous country items from Victor, including many by Jimmie Rodgers, were issued in the 5000/6000 series and a more diverse selection in the 4000 export series, destined for the South African market. (Some Zonophones in the 5000/6000 series were also issued in Australia with the same catalog numbers.) The label was merged with Regal in January 1933 to become Regal-Zonophone. (See entry on Regal.)

Indian *(by John Stoten and Tony Russell)*

A remarkable quantity of country material—between 300 and 400 couplings—was issued in the Indian subcontinent in the 1930s and early 1940s, chiefly on HMV and Twin, labels of the Gramophone Company, a subsidiary of the British firm of that name. The records were made at the company's factory in Dum Dum. Some country issues appeared on Regal-Zonophone, made by the Columbia Graphophone Company of Calcutta.

HMV The first issue in the HMV N series was N3637 in August 1931, but systematic and continuous numbering seems to have begun with N4199 in May 1932. The U.S. material was drawn from Victor and, later, Bluebird. The label was primarily green until December 1933, when it adopted the plum color familiar on British HMVs. In that month's new-release supplement, it was announced that a section would henceforth be devoted to U.S. recordings that would not customarily be issued in Britain but had proved popular in India, including material by Cuban and South American dance bands, Hawaiian groups, and hillbilly artists.

Between July 1932 and November 1938, almost a hundred couplings of country material appeared by such artists as Jimmie Rodgers, Carson Robison & Frank Luther, Jimmie Davis, and the Girls of the Golden West. Items were often cross-coupled with recordings by different artists.

The N series continued until the end of 1944. It had been partnered since May 1935 with a magenta-label NE series, which began at NE200; no country material appeared herein until 1943, when a half dozen items from Bluebird were issued. (Post-1942 country recordings may have been issued later in this series, which survived until at least 1949.)

Regal-Zonophone   Some two or three dozen country issues appeared in the Regal-Zonophone MR20000 series; the material originated on Victor/Bluebird (e.g., Jimmie Rodgers) or ARC/Vocalion/OKeh (e.g., Gene Autry), but the couplings were derived from the British Regal-Zonophone MR1 series.

Twin   Various series of Twin records issued material in the languages of the subcontinent; the first to carry English-language material originating in Britain and the United States was the FT1000 series, which began in July 1928 (at T1001; the FT-prefix was substituted in November of that year). It ran until FT2000 in May 1936, then jumped to FT8000 and continued to FT9119 in September 1941. (The block FT9000–FT9100 was not used.) The label color was primarily yellow except for a period in 1929–1932, when it was red.

More than 220 couplings of country material were issued, drawn from Victor and Bluebird. As on HMV, the most popular artists appear to have included Jimmie Rodgers, Robison & Luther, and Jimmie Davis, but there were also numerous issues by Bill Boyd, Milton Brown, Cliff Carlisle, the Delmore Brothers, Fred Kirby, Montana Slim, Riley Puckett, and others. Also as on HMV, items were sometimes cross-coupled with recordings by other artists. As well as U.S. country material, the series also included several dozen issues by the British group the Hill Billies and the yodeler Harry Torrani; these were derived from Regal-Zonophone, as were some of Carson Robison's British recordings.

User's Guide

The layout of the entries in this book is based upon the model of R. M. W. Dixon, John Godrich, and Howard Rye's *Blues and Gospel Records 1890–1943*, 4th edition (1997). I have occasionally departed from that model, chiefly in order to deal with problems peculiar to a country music discography. The user accustomed to that work should find the organization of this book familiar, but for the sake of others I have composed this user's guide.

Entries

Entries (i.e., sections headed with an artist or group credit) are of two basic kinds:

1. discographies proper;
2. explanatory entries, which serve one of three functions:
    a. to reveal the artist or group concealed by a pseudonym;
    b. to cross-refer the reader to another entry; or
    c. to state that an artist or group has been judged to be outside the scope of the work, and sometimes to explain why. (For more on this, see the introduction.)

Artist Credits

At the head of each entry is the artist credit: the name of the artist or group, usually in the form most commonly used on record labels (or, in the cases of artists who had no issued recordings, the form used in company files). These are listed in alphabetical order of surname, then first name; if the first name is in the form of an initial or initials, it precedes full first names beginning with that letter. Descriptive titles such as Blind, Little, or Rev(erend) are, for this purpose, ignored, unless they take the place of a first name, in which case they are treated as such. Duet credits are listed by the name of the first artist. If a first name is lacking, as in duet credits using only surnames, the entry appears after all full-name entries for that surname. Multiple-surname or group credits appear after any of the above, in alphabetical order of the next word. Thus:

B. Smith
B. J. Smith
Rev. Bill Smith
Bob Smith & Bill Brown
Bob Smith's Band
Rev. Smith
Richard Smith
Smith & Brown
Smith & Wilson
Smith Brothers
Smith, Brown & Wilson
Smith County String Band
Smith Family
Smith String Band
Smith, Wilson & Brown
Smith's Entertainers
Smithers Brothers
Smithville String Band

The artist credit that appears at the head of the entry applies throughout, unless a different artist credit is given at the head of a session. This new credit then applies until another artist credit replaces it.

Personnel and Instrumentation

At the head of each session are listed the personnel and instrumentation involved. Musicians' full names, if known, are given only on their first appearance in an entry; thereafter, they are referred to by the name by which they were usually known. Thus,

Shelby "Tex" Atchison

—as he is listed at the beginning of the Prairie Ramblers entry—becomes on subsequent occasions

Tex Atchison

The order in which the instruments are listed is approximately based upon the conventions created by jazz discographers, whereby brass instruments come first, followed by reeds, keyboards, stringed instruments, and drums/percussion, but the nature of the subject matter has dictated some variations from this principle. In this book, the fiddle has been granted first place, followed by brass and reeds (where present), harmonica, accordion, kazoo, stringed instruments playing lead roles (such as electric steel guitar), keyboards, other stringed instruments, drums/percussion, and miscellaneous instruments, such as washboard, ocarina, and jug. The abbreviations used for instruments and other musical components are listed in the abbreviations section.

If personnel and instrumentation data are not provided, it may be assumed that the details given for the previous session still apply.

Any uncertainty about the personnel or instrumentation is signaled by the use of "prob." (probably) or "poss." (possibly), the latter denoting a greater degree of uncertainty. In addition to these standard terms, I have introduced the use of "unidentified," where it is virtually certain that the role concerned is taken by one of the named personnel but it is impossible at present to identify which one.

Title-to-title variations in the personnel or instrumentation of a session are described by the use of numerical suffixes (-1, -2, and so on). Thus,

John Doe, v-1/g; James Doe, v-2/g

describes a session on which both Does play guitar throughout; John is the vocalist on items suffixed -1, James is the vocalist on titles suffixed -2, and titles suffixed -1, 2 are vocal duets.

Not infrequently, musicians play several instruments in turn during a session; this is similarly denoted, thus,

Jane Doe, md-1/g-2; Julia Doe, bj-3/g-4.

A title suffixed -1, 4 therefore has Jane Doe playing mandolin and Julia Doe guitar, while a title suffixed -3 has Julia Doe playing banjo and Jane Doe taking no instrumental part.

Occasionally, such instrumental doubling takes place within a single performance. Thus, taking the previous example, a title suffixed -1, 2, 4 has Jane Doe playing both mandolin and guitar and Julia Doe playing guitar. Note that

John Doe, f/t-1

signifies that John Doe plays fiddle on all of the titles in the session but also trumpet on titles suffixed -1.

Suffix numbers are assigned in the order in which the roles they denote first appear in the personnel and instrumentation details, not in the order in which they occur during the session. Thus, a session may be headed

John Doe, v-1/g; James Doe, v-2/g

even though suffix -2 may be attached to the first title in the session, and suffix -1 may not be used until later in the session.

Where two or more suffixes denoting vocal roles are attached to a title, and it is known which singer took the lead vocal part, this state of affairs may be signified as follows:

Julian Doe, f/v-1; Jeremiah Doe, bj/v-2; Junior Doe, g/v-3.

The title listing will look like this:

Way Out There -1, 2 (lead), 3.

When vocal roles are frequently repeated, they will be defined by the use, in the personnel and instrumentation details, of lv (lead vocal) and hv (harmony vocal); when they are fixed, they will customarily be noted after the session:

Jeremiah Doe sings lead and Junior Doe tenor.

When two (or more) suffixed numbers are separated by a slash, -2/3, *either* suffix -2 *or* suffix -3 applies, but it is not known which. For example, an instrument is known to have been used on a title; either of two (or any of several) musicians known to have been present might have played it, but it has been impossible to ascertain which. Alternatively, a single musician is known to have played two instruments during a session, but on a title suffixed in this way it has not been determined which of those instruments was used.

When a title is followed by a hyphen but no suffixed number, it means that one or more of the suffixes in the personnel/instrumentation are likely to apply, but it has not been determined which.

If neither the personnel nor the instrumentation is known, the heading is customarily in the form

John Doe, v; acc. unknown, or

No details.

If personnel or instrumentation data are given for sessions from which nothing was issued, it may be assumed that these have been obtained from company files or related sources, from information supplied by the artist(s) or associates, or in some instances from extant test-pressings.

Location and Date

Following the personnel and instrumentation data, on a new line, are the location and date of the recording session.

Only the city in which the session was held is cited. In a few cases, matrix prefixes (see below) imply a different location from the one cited, as in the case of OKeh recordings prefixed DAL- but actually made in Fort Worth or Saginaw, Texas. In such instances, the cited location is known to be correct.

Precise dates, in the form

Sunday, January 1, 1928

are in almost all cases derived from company files or related sources. If there is a sound reason to suspect the accuracy of this information, it is duly noted.

In the absence of company files, I have given approximate dates based on the best research available. These are of varying degrees of probable accuracy, so sessions are ordered on the page according to the firmness of their chronology, thus:

Sunday, January 1, 1928
c. January 1, 1928
January 1928
c. January 1928
January/February 1928
c. January/February 1928

Gennett recordings pose a special dating problem (see the entry in Record Label Histories). In the case of Gennett recordings made elsewhere than at Richmond, Indiana, a date preceded by a "c." can only imply an earlier, never a later, recording date. Therefore, if such a session dated, for example, c. January 1, 1928, appears in an entry that also includes a session firmly dated to January 1, 1928, the "c."-dated session will precede, not follow, the firmly dated one.

Matrix Numbers

The number given to the left of the recording's title is the matrix. Most companies assigned a matrix number to each recording at the time it was made, and from this practice it has been assumed reasonably enough that matrix numerical order represents recording order. In most instances, this assumption is probably justified, but the discographer should always be prepared to consider other possibilities: for example, matrices may sometimes have been assigned after the session, not necessarily in the exact order of recording. It was the practice, too, of some companies, such as Victor, to reuse a matrix number—obviously, out of sequence—when a rerecording of the item was made; this is often signaled by an unusually high take number or letter.

The matrix number is often engraved or embossed in the area between the run-out groove and the label or under the label; this is standard practice on Columbia, OKeh, Paramount, and other records. In other cases, such as most Gennett-group and Victor-group records, the matrices do not appear on the records but have been derived from company files.

Several companies prefixed matrix numbers with a letter or letters (which do not always appear on the records); these have been included when they convey geographically useful information, like ARC's prefixes C-, LA-, and so on, which denote recording locations, but not when they are merely elements of a company's filing system, like the BVE-, BSHQ-, and BS- prefixes to Victor and Bluebird matrices.

Some companies also employed control numbers. These are pseudomatrices, which generally do not refer to recording order, though when they are connected, as they often are, with the catalog (issue) number, they bear some relation to release order. Control numbers are customarily excluded from discographies, but in this book they have been included on certain occasions:

1. Brunswick and Vocalion. E—W numbers, though hitherto taken to be controls, are in fact transfer matrices, used when an item was transferred from Brunswick to Vocalion, or vice versa. It is this transfer matrix, or part thereof, that then appears on the record, so it seems helpful to cite both matrices.

2. Plaza, Pathé, Cameo. These companies engaged in complex exchanges of recordings, in which one company's original matrix might be replaced by another's. This new and necessarily "false" matrix is thus a kind of control. Further sale or license of an item might introduce further false matrices or even actual controls. Since all of these numbers provide useful information, which can aid in the identification of an obscure recording, they are all listed: the original matrix in the usual place, the false matrices or controls in a note following the session. Few attempts have been made to tie these false matrices and controls to the specific issues on which they appear.

3. Diva, Velvet Tone, Clarion. These Columbia subsidiary labels, when using items originally recorded for Columbia, frequently replaced that company's matrix with a transfer matrix, which is all that appears on the record. Such transfer matrices are specified in a note following the session.

Take Numbers and Letters

During a large part of the period covered by this book, virtually every relevant record company had a policy of making at least two, and sometimes three or more, attempts at a complete recording of each selection. These multiple versions are known as takes. Most companies assigned each selection a matrix number and distinguished the takes by suffixed numbers or letters, thus: 140000-1 (the first take of matrix 140000), 80000-B (usually, the second take of matrix 80000). Note that while some companies employing letter takes called the first take -A, others, such as Gennett, began with the unsuffixed matrix (known as the "plain take"); in those instances, the second take would be -A, the third -B, and so on.

Since, in the absence of some company files, it is not always known how many takes were made of a selection, I have followed the common practice of listing only the number or letter of the issued take (or takes, in cases where more than one was issued). Thus 140000–1 indicates that the first take was the one issued, but should not be taken to imply that second or subsequent takes were not recorded.

The possibility should also be noted that takes may in some company files be numbered not according to their chronology but according to their quality, that is, the take numbered -1 may not have been the first take to be recorded but the first acceptable take.

With unissued recordings, all the takes are listed that are known to have been recorded. These data naturally vary in detail according to the availability and quality of company files.

Some companies followed a different system, whereby a new matrix number was assigned to each take; this is true, for example, of early Brunswick and Vocalion recordings. The issued take in these instances is denoted by an asterisk. Thus 13000/01*/02 denotes that matrices 13000, 13001, and 13002 were assigned to three attempts at the selection concerned and that the second of these was the issued take.

Where a take number or letter is presently unknown, this is indicated by a single hyphen, thus, 60000-; C-2276-. Where a take number or letter is never likely to be known, this is indicated by a second hyphen, thus: 60000--; C-2276--.

Recording Title

The title of the recording is given as it appears on the record label(s) on which it was issued. Variant wordings and spellings and other differences are given in a note following the session. The titles of unissued recordings are given as they are listed in company files or, occasionally, as written on the labels of test-pressings.

Sometimes a recording would be logged (entered in a company file) under one title and issued under another; these instances are reported in a note following the session.

Variations from standard spelling or usage are reproduced generally without comment, but sometimes, where the reader might suspect an error on the discographer's part, [sic] has been inserted. Titles in Cajun French, however, are more often than not misspelled—sometimes grossly—on record labels and in company files alike. It would be futile to call attention to all of these errors with a litter of [sic]s, and I have not done so.

Issue Number

The label(s) or label abbreviation(s) and number(s) to the right of the recording's title are the issues of that recording. Label abbreviations are interpreted in the Abbreviations section.

Many recordings appeared on several issues, sometimes simultaneously, sometimes months or years apart. In the latter case, these multiple issues would ideally be listed in chronological order of release, and sometimes, where I have enough information to be clear about that chronology, I have listed the issues in that way. But in many cases, that information is not available, and the order in which issues have been listed should not be taken as firm evidence of release order.

As for recordings released on several labels at once, the issues are usually listed according to established discographical conventions. For example, a Columbia recording issued on the company's subsidiary labels Diva, Harmony, and Velvet Tone and the associated Clarion will have its issues in numerical order, thus:

Ha 1000-H, Ve 2000-V, Di 3000-G, Cl 5000-C

Many recordings were issued not only in the United States but also in other countries. In such cases, the U.S. issues are listed first, followed by Canadian, English, Australian, South African, Indian, Irish, and other issues (in that order). However, non-U.S. issues on the same label as the U.S. issue are listed immediately after it, thus:

Br 300, BrAu 300, BrSA SA250, Spt S2000, and so on,

where the second and third items are issues on Australian and South African Brunswick, or

Ba 33000, Me M13000, MeC 93000, Or 8300, and so on,

where the MeC 93000 is an issue on Canadian Melotone.

Company files occasionally report the making of test recordings, sometimes with matrices from an exclusive "test series," such as ARC's TO- sequence, sometimes with matrices from the same series as recordings intended for issue. Any such item is described as a "trial recording." (To avoid ambiguity, the term "test" is used only in the phrase "test-pressing.")

There are several reasons why a recording may not have been issued, and some attempt has been made, relying on the admittedly partial evidence of company files, to distinguish differing fates. An item described as "rejected" or "canceled" is so termed in the relevant company file, and it may be assumed that it did not survive long after its recording but was destroyed. In a few cases, company files actually report that action, and those items are described as "destroyed." The more common description "unissued" means just that, and in many cases it may be assumed that the recording in question could have survived, for example, in company archives or on a test-pressing given to the artist. In numerous instances, such unissued recordings *have* survived, but this fact is noted only when the item has been issued in a more modern format such as on an LP, CD, or cassette.

An issue printed in italics is a dubbing, that is, a copy made from another issue, rather than a pressing from the original master. This usage is employed both for dubbed 78-rpm reissues and for LP/CD/cassette issues, which are necessarily copies of records rather than of master pressings. The latter are distinguished from each other by the use of (LP), (CD), or (Cass) after the catalog number(s). LP/CD/cassette issues are cited only for recordings that were not issued as 78-rpm discs.

Notes

Beneath the data of a recording session will often be found a note containing matter relevant to the recording or issue information. Such data include:

- pseudonyms or variant artist credits used on certain issues
- variant forms of an item's title on certain issues
- changes between logged and issued versions of an item's title
- miscellaneous information, often drawn from company files
- information on intervening or surrounding matrices recorded by other artists, sometimes with parenthetical descriptions such as (popular), or, for artists listed in other discographies, (see *JR*) or (see *B&GR*).

- identifications of reverse sides of certain issues, where these were by other artists. For example, Cameo 9192 coupled a recording by Frank Marvin with one by Carson Robison. In the note to the relevant session in Marvin's entry, this will be denoted by "Rev. Cameo 9192 by Carson Robison." Likewise, in the relevant session in Robison's entry, the note will report "Rev. Cameo 9192 by Frank Marvin."

Abbreviations

Instruments and Frequently Used Terms

ac	accordion	emd	electric mandolin
acc.	accompanied/accompaniment	EMOR	*Ethnic Music On Records*
		eo	electric organ
ah	autoharp	esg	electric steel guitar
as	alto saxophone	etg	electric tenor guitar
av	alto vocal	exc.	except
B&GR	*Blues & Gospel Records 1890–1943*	f	fiddle
		fl	flute
bb	brass bass	g	guitar
bj	banjo	h	harmonica
bj-g	banjo-guitar	Ho	Hammond organ
bj-md	banjo-mandolin	hv	harmony vocal
bj-u	banjo-ukulele	j	jug
bs	baritone saxophone	jh	jew's harp
bscl	bass clarinet	JR	*Jazz Records*
bss	bass saxophone	k	kazoo
bsv	bass vocal	ldr	leader
bv	baritone vocal	lg	lead guitar
c	cornet	LP	long-playing record
c.	circa	lv	lead vocal
Cass	(audio) cassette	md	mandolin
CD	compact disc	o	organ
cel	celeste	oc	ocarina
cl	clarinet	orch.	orchestra
conc	concertina	p	piano
d	drums	pac	piano accordion
dir.	director/directed	perc	percussion
du	dulcimer (Appalachian)	p-o	pipe organ
ef	electric fiddle	poss.	possibly
eff	effects	prob.	probably
eg	electric guitar	rev.	reverse

43

Abbreviations

s	saxophone	tu	tuba
sb	string bass	tv	tenor vocal
sg	steel guitar	u	ukulele
sp	speech	unacc.	unaccompanied
ss	soprano saxophone	v	vocal
sv	soprano vocal	vb	vibraphone
sw	slide whistle	vc	violoncello
t	trumpet	vla	viola
tb	trombone	VMB	Victor Master Book
tbj	tenor banjo	vn	violin
tg	tenor guitar	wb	washboard
ti	tiple	wh	whistling
tri	triangle	x	xylophone
ts	tenor saxophone	y	yodeling

Record Labels

Aj	Ajax	CoJ	Columbia (Japanese)
Ang	Angelus	CoSA	Columbia (South African)
ARC	American Record Corporation	CoSs	Columbia (Swiss)
		Co-Lucky	Columbia-Lucky
ARC-Bwy	ARC-Broadway	Cont	Continental
Au	Aurora	Cq	Conqueror
Ba	Banner	Cr	Crown
BB	Bluebird	CrC	Crown (Canadian)
BF	Bear Family (LP, CD)	CSP	Columbia Special Products (LP)
BP	Black Patti		
Br	Brunswick	Cx	Claxtonola
BrAu	Brunswick (Australian)	Cy	County (LP, CD)
BrC	Brunswick (Canadian)	De	Decca
BrE	Brunswick (British)	DeAu	Decca (Australian)
BrSA	Brunswick (South African)	DeE	Decca (British)
Bu	Buddy	DeIr	Decca (Irish)
Bwy	Broadway	DeSA	Decca (South African)
Ca	Cameo	Di	Diva
Cam	Camden (CD)	Do	Domino
Cap	Capitol	DoC	Domino (Canadian)
Cd	Cardinal	Doc	Document (LP, CD)
Ch	Champion	EBW	Edison Bell Winner
Chg	Challenge	Ed	Edison
Cl	Clarion	Eld	Electradisk
CMF	Country Music Foundation (LP, CD)	Em	Emerson
		Ep	Epic (LP, CD)
Co	Columbia	Fa	Famous
CoAu	Columbia (Australian)	FM	Franklin Mint (LP)
CoC	Columbia (Canadian)	Fo	Fossey's
CoE	Columbia (British)	FV	Folk Variety (LP)
CoF	Columbia (French)	Fwy	Folkways (LP)
CoIr	Columbia (Irish)	Ge	Gennett

GG	Grey Gull	Pe	Perfect
Gn	Goodson	PeE	Perfect (British)
GP	Grand Pree	Pic	Piccadilly
Ha	Harmony	Pl	Plaza
Her	Herwin	Pm	Paramount
Hg	Harmograph	PmAu	Paramount (Australian)
HGS	Herschel Gold Seal	Po	Polk
Hi	Historical (LP)	Pu	Puritan
HMV	His Master's Voice	Rad	Radiex
HMVAu	His Master's Voice (Australian)	Rdr	Rounder (LP, CD)
		Re	Regal
HMVE	His Master's Voice (British)	ReAu	Regal (Australian)
HMVIn	His Master's Voice (Indian)	ReE	Regal (British)
HMVPg	His Master's Voice (Portuguese)	Ro	Romeo
		Roy	Royale
HMVSA	His Master's Voice (South African)	RZ	Regal-Zonophone
		RZAu	Regal-Zonophone (Australian)
Htd	Homestead		
Imp	Imperial	RZIn	Regal-Zonophone (Indian)
ImpE	Imperial (British)	RZIr	Regal-Zonophone (Irish)
ImpIr	Imperial (Irish)	Sil	Silvertone
ImpSd	Imperial (Swedish)	Spr	Superior
JDs	Joe Davis	Spt	Supertone
Je	Jewel	Sr	Sunrise
JGS	Jubilee Gospel Singers	St	Starr
LC	Library of Congress (LP, CD)	StAu	Starr (Australian)
Leo	Leonora	Stg	Sterling
Lin	Lincoln	StgAu	Sterling (Australian)
LS	Lucky Strike	TR	Texas Rose (LP)
Mad	Madison	TT	Timely Tunes
Mc	Microphone	VD	Van Dyke
Me	Melotone	V-D	V-Disc
MeAu	Melotone (Australian)	Ve	Velvet Tone
MeC	Melotone (Canadian)	Vi	Victor
Min	Minerva	ViC	Victor (Canadian)
MS	Morning Star (LP)	ViJ	Victor (Japanese)
MW	Montgomery Ward	Vo	Vocalion
NW	New World (LP)	Vri	Variety
OH	Old Homestead (LP, CD)	Vs	Varsity
OK	OKeh	WHAA	West Hill Audio Archives (CD)
Or	Oriole		
PaAu	Parlophone (Australian)	WS	Wax Shop
PaE	Parlophone (British)	Yz	Yazoo (LP, CD)
PAE	Pathé Actuelle (British)	Zo	Zonophone
Pan	Panachord	ZoAu	Zonophone (Australian)
PanAu	Panachord (Australian)	ZoSA	Zonophone (South African)
Pat	Pathé		

Discography

A

JERRY ABBOTT & "THE MAIN STREETERS"

Jerry Abbott, v; acc. The Main Streeters: unknown, f; unknown, cl; unknown, ac; unknown, g; unknown, sb; band v-1; unknown, wh-1.
    prob. New York, NY   c. January/February 1942

	Get A Move On, Cowboy -1	Standard T-2058
	Tend To Your Knitting	Standard T-2058
	Young McDonald Had A Horse	Standard T-2071
	You Never Cared For Me	Standard T-2071

ABERNATHY QUARTET

Arthur Williams, tv; Roy Holbrook, tv; J.B. Hadaway, bv; D. Abernathy, bsv; acc. Leroy Abernathy, p.
    Atlanta, GA   Tuesday, February 23, 1932

71607-1	Don't Forget To Pray	Vi 23663
71608-1	Redeemed	Vi 23663

LOREN H. ABRAM

Domino George: Loren H. Abram, v; acc. own g.
    Richmond, IN   Wednesday, December 23, 1931

18271-A	I'll Remember You Love In My Prayers	Ch S-16394, Spr 2792
18272-A	All Aboard For Blanket Bay	Ch S-16394, Spr 2792
18273-A	We'll Have Weather	Spr 2774
18274	Eleven Cent Cotton – Forty Cent Meat	Spr 2774

Superior 2774, 2792 as by **The Texas Ranger**.

L.H. Abram & Arnold Frazier, dialogue.
    Richmond, IN   Wednesday, December 23, 1931

18275	Ham And Bone Part No. 1	Ge rejected
18276	Ham And Bone Part No. 2	Ge rejected

Loren Abram was certainly, and Arnold Frazier possibly, associated with the Corn Cob Crushers.

NASON ABSHER & THE RAYNE-BO RAMBLERS

See Nathan Abshire.

NATHAN ABSHIRE

Nason Absher & The Rayne–Bo Ramblers: Norris Savoy, f; Nathan Abshire, ac/v-1; Leroy (Happy Fats) LeBlanc, g; Warnest Schexnyder, g.
    New Orleans, LA   Saturday, August 10, 1935

94408-1	Gueydan Breakdown	BB B-2177
94409-1	La Valse De Riceville -1	BB B-2174
94410-1	One Step De Morse	BB B-2174
94411-1	French Blues -1	BB B-2177
94412-1	One Step De Laccissine	BB B-2178
94413-1	La Valse De Boutte Dechuminen -1	BB B-2178

Bluebird B-2174 as by **Rayne-Bo Ramblers**. Matrices 94402 to 94407 are by the Rayne-Bo Ramblers without Abshire. Nathan Abshire recorded after 1942.

LOUIS ACKER

Pseudonym on Aurora for Goebel Reeves.

E.F. "POSS" ACREE

E.F. "Poss" Acree, h solo.
Atlanta, GA   late March 1924

| 8611-A | Missouri Waltz | OK 40197 |
| 8612-A | Chicken Reel | OK 40197 |

ROY ACUFF

Roy Acuff & His Crazy Tennesseeans: Roy Acuff, f/v-1; Sam "Dynamite" Hatcher, h-2/v-3; Clell Summey, sg/v-4; Jess Easterday, g/v-5; Red Jones, sb/v-6.
Chicago, IL   Tuesday, October 20, 1936

C-1579-4	Singing My Way To Glory -2, 3, 4, 5, 6	Vo/OK 04730, Cq 9256
C-1580-2	Charmin' Betsy -1, 4, 6	ARC 7-02-53
C-1581-1	Great Speckle Bird -1	ARC 7-01-59, Vo/OK 04252, Cq 8740, Co 37005, 20031, 54003, CoC C1139
C-1582-1	My Mountain Home Sweet Home -1, 4, 6	ARC 7-01-59, Vo/OK 04252, Cq 8740, Co 37005, 20031, CoC C1139
C-1583-1	Gonna Raise A Rukus Tonight -1, 2, 3, 4, 5, 6	ARC 7-01-60

Columbia 20031, 54003 as by **Roy Acuff & His Smoky Mountain Boys**.
Take 4 of matrix C-1579 is a technical remastering, made on October 21, 1938, of take 1 or 2.

Roy Acuff, f-1/v-2/train-wh eff-3; Sam "Dynamite" Hatcher, h-4/v-5; poss. unknown, h-6; Clell Summey, sg/v-7; Jess Easterday, g/v-8; Red Jones, sb/v-9.
Chicago, IL   Wednesday, October 21, 1936

C-1588-1,-2	Coney Island Baby	ARC unissued
C-1589-1	Wabash Cannon Ball -3, 5	Vo/OK 04466, Cq 9121, Co 37008
C-1590-2	Freight Train Blues -3, 5	Vo/OK 04466, Cq 9121, Co 37008
C-1591-1	You've Got To See Mama Every Night (Or You Can't See Mama At All) -1, 2, 4	ARC 7-02-53
C-1592-1	Gonna Have A Big Time Tonight-1, 2, 4, 7, 8, 9	ARC 7-04-75, Cq 8842
C-1593-1	Yes Sir, That's My Baby -4, 5, 6	ARC 7-04-75, Cq 8842
C-1594-2	You're The Only Star (In My Blue Heaven) -1, 2, 4	ARC 7-04-51, Vo/OK 04505, Cq 8791
C-1595-1,-2	You're A Heavenly Thing	ARC unissued
C-1596-4	Please Don't Talk About Me When I'm Gone -4, 9	ARC unissued: *Time-Life TLCW-09 (LP)*

Vocalion/OKeh 04730 as by **Roy Acuff & His Smoky Mountain Boys** (as are those issues of Columbia 37008 which use 1947 masters of the songs rather than C-1589 and C-1590).
Take 4 of matrix C-1596 is a technical remastering, made on October 21, 1938, of take 1 or 2.

Roy Acuff, f-1/v-2; Clell Summey, sg/v-3; Jess Easterday, g/v-4; Red Jones, g-5/sb-6/v-7; Sam "Dynamite" Hatcher, v-8.
Chicago, IL   Thursday, October 22, 1936

C-1597-2	All Night Long -1, 2, 6	ARC 7-01-60
C-1598-1	New Greenback Dollar -1, 2, 3, 6, 7	ARC 8-03-59, Vo/OK 03255, Cq 9122, 9781, Co 37614, 20213
C-1599-1	Steamboat Whistle Blues -5, 8	ARC 8-03-59, Vo/OK 03255, Cq 9122, Co 37614, 20213
C-1600-1	She No Longer Belongs To Me -1, 3, 4?, 6, 7?	ARC 7-04-51, Vo/OK 04505, Cq 8791

Columbia 20213 as by **Roy Acuff & His Smoky Mountain Boys**.

Bang Boys: Roy Acuff, f/v; Sam "Dynamite" Hatcher, k-1; Clell Summey, sg; Jess Easterday, g; Red Jones, sb.
Chicago, IL   Friday, October 23, 1936

| C-1604-1 | When Lulu's Gone | Vo/OK 03372, Cq 9123 |
| C-1605-1 | Doin' It The Old Fashioned Way -1 | Vo/OK 03372, Cq 9123 |

Matrices C-1601 to C-1603 are by Patsy Montana and/or Prairie Ramblers.

Roy Acuff & His Crazy Tennesseeans: Roy Acuff, f-1/v-2/bj eff-3; Clell Summey, sg/v-4; Jess Easterday, g/v-5; Red Jones, sb/v-6.

Birmingham, AL   Monday, March 22, 1937

B-1-4	An Old Three Room Shack -1, 2, 5, 6	Vo/OK 04795, Cq 9255, 9782
B-2-2	Red Lips - Kiss My Blues Away -1, 6	ARC 7-08-64
B-3-1	Trouble Trouble -1, 2, 4, 6	ARC 7-11-62
B-4-1	Sailing Along -1, 3, 6	ARC 7-11-62
B-5-1	Steel Guitar Chimes	ARC 7-07-52, Vo/OK 04376, Cq 9086, Co 37007, 20033
B-6-4	Lonesome Valley -1, 2, 4, 6	Vo/OK 04730, Cq 9256, 9781
B-7-	Hi Hattin' Blues	ARC unissued
B-8-	Bonnie Blue Eyes	ARC unissued
B-9-1	Sad Memories -2	Vo/OK 04975, Cq 9791
B-10-2	Steel Guitar Blues -2	ARC 7-07-52, Vo/OK 04376, Cq 9086, Co 37007, 20033
B-11-4	Old Fashioned Love -1, 6	Vo/OK 05359, Cq 9528, 9783
B-12-2	My Gal Sal -1, 6	ARC 7-08-64
B-13-1	Great Speckle Bird No. 2 -2	ARC 7-06-54, Vo/OK 04374, Cq 8877, Co 37006, 20032, 54003
B-14-2	Tell Mother I'll Be There -2, 5, 6	ARC 7-06-54, Vo/OK 04374, Cq 8877, Co 37006, 20032

Vocalion/OKeh 04730, 04795, 04975, 05359, Conqueror 9528, 9781, 9782, 9783, 9791, Columbia 20032, 20033, 54003 as by **Roy Acuff & His Smoky Mountain Boys**.
Most issues of matrices B-13 and B-14 show -3 takes, which are technical remasterings of B-13-1 and B-14-2 respectively.

Roy Acuff & His Smoky Mountain Boys: Roy Acuff, f-1/v-2; Clell Summey, sg/v-3; Jess Easterday, g/sb/v-4; Red Jones, g/sb/v-5; Bob Wright, g/y-6.

Columbia, SC   Thursday, November 3, 1938

SC-58-1	Down In Union County -1, 3, 5	Vo unissued: *Time-Life TLCW-09 (LP)*
SC-59-1	The Rising Sun -2	Vo/OK 04909
SC-60-1	What Would You Do With Gabriel's Trumpet -2, 5	Vo/OK 04531, Cq 9170, 9670, Co 20480
SC-61-1	Shout, Oh Lulu -1, 2, 3, 5, 6	Vo/OK 04867
SC-62-1	Good-bye Brownie -5	Vo/OK 04909, Cq 9782
SC-63-1	Blue Ridge Sweetheart -4?, 5	Vo/OK 04531, Cq 9170, 9739, Co 20479
SC-64-1	One Old Shirt -2, 4, 5	Vo/OK 04657, Cq 9257
SC-65-	An Old Three Room Shack -2, 5	Vo unissued
SC-66-1	Bonnie Blue Eyes -2	Vo/OK 04795, Cq 9255
SC-67-1	The Automobile Of Life -2, 5	Vo/OK 04975, Cq 9783
SC-68-1	Smoky Mountain Rag	Vo/OK 05450, Co 37743, 20320
SC-69-1	Wabash Blues -1	Vo/OK 04867
SC-70-	The Longest Train -1, 2	ARC unissued
SC-71-1	That Beautiful Picture -2, 5	Vo/OK 04590, Cq 9740, Co 20478
SC-72-1	The Great Shining Light -2	Vo/OK 04590, Co 20478
SC-73-1	Honky Tonk Mammas -2	Vo/Ok 04657, Cq 9257

Matrix SC-62 is titled *Goodbye Brownie* on Conqueror 9782.

Roy Acuff, v; acc. own f-1; Pete "Oswald" Kirby, sg-2/bj-3/v-4; Lonnie Wilson, g; Jess Easterday, sb.

Memphis, TN   Wednesday, July 5, 1939

MEM-38-1	Haven Of Dreams -1, 2	Vo/OK 05244, Cq 9432
MEM-39-1	Answer To Sparkling Blue Eyes -1, 2, 4	Vo/OK 05041, Cq 9324
MEM-40-1	Smoky Mountain Moon -2	Vo/OK 05450, Co 37743, 20320
MEM-41-1	Fly, Birdie, Fly -2, 4	Vo/OK 05093, Cq 9740
MEM-42-1	Ida Red -1, 3, 4	Vo/OK 05359, Cq 9404
MEM-43-2	Beautiful Brown Eyes -1, 2, 4	Vo/OK 05163, Cq 9579
MEM-44-1	Mother's Prayers Guide Me -1, 2, 4	Vo/OK 05403, Cq 9324
MEM-45-1	Living On The Mountain, Baby Mine -1, 3, 4	Vo/OK 05163
MEM-46-1	A Vagabond's Dream -2	Vo/OK 05041
MEM-47-1	Old Age Pension Check -2	Vo/OK 05244, Cq 9432
MEM-48-1	Eyes Are Watching You -2, 4	Vo/OK 05297
MEM-49-1	I'm Building A Home -1, 2, 4	Vo/OK 05403, Cq 9579, 9671

Acc. own f-1/train-wh eff-2; Pete "Oswald" Kirby, sg/v-3; Lonnie Wilson, g; Jess Easterday, sb/v-4.

Memphis, TN   Thursday, July 6, 1939

MEM-50-1	Railroad Boomer -2	Vo unissued: *Time-Life TLCW-09 (LP)*
MEM-50-2	Railroad Boomer -2	Vo unissued: *NW NW287 (LP)*
MEM-51-1	Walkin' In My Sleep -1, 3	Vo/OK 05093, Cq 9739
MEM-52-1	Wonder Is All I Do	Vo unissued: *Co FC39998 (LP); CK39998 (CD)*
MEM-53-2	Drifting Too Far From The Shore -4	Vo/OK 05297, Cq 9670

Acc. own f-1/train-wh eff-2; Pete "Oswald" Kirby, sg-3/bj-4/g-5/v-6; Jess Easterday, md-7/sb-8; Lonnie Wilson, g-9/sb-10.

Saginaw, TX   Thursday, April 11, 1940

DAL-944-1	Come Back Little Pal -1, 3, 8, 9	OK 05956, Cq 9791, Co 37017, 20043
DAL-945-1	Will The Circle Be Unbroken -1, 3, 6, 8, 9	Vo/OK 05587, Cq 9671, Pe 16-101
DAL-946-1	Coming From The Ball -1, 6, 8, 9	Vo unissued: *Time-Life TLCW-09* (LP)
DAL-947-1	When I Lay My Burden Down -1, 4, 6, 8, 9	Vo/OK 05587, Cq 9433, 9667
DAL-948-1	Beneath That Lonely Mound Of Clay -3, 8, 9	OK 05695, Cq 9435, Co 37015, 20041
DAL-949-1	The Streamlined Cannon Ball -2, 5, 7, 10	OK 05638, Cq 9434, Co 37012, 20038
DAL-950-1	Weary River -3, 8, 9	OK 05766, Cq 9434
DAL-967-1	Just To Ease My Worried Mind -1, 5, 6, 7, 10	OK 05820, Cq 9404, Co 20479

Acc. own f-1; Pete "Oswald" Kirby, sg-2/g-3/v-4; Jess Easterday, md-5/sb-6; Lonnie Wilson, g-7/sb-8.

Saginaw, TX   Friday, April 12, 1940

DAL-951-1	Farther Along -1, 2, 4, 6, 7	OK 05766, Cq 9433, 9667, Co 20480
DAL-951-2	Farther Along -1, 2, 4, 6, 7	Vo unissued: *Ha HL7342* (LP)
DAL-952-1	Blue Eyed Darling -2, 6, 7	OK 05695, Cq 9435, Co 37015, 20041
DAL-952-2	Blue Eyed Darling -2, 6, 7	Vo unissued: *Ha HL7342* (LP)
DAL-953-1	The Precious Jewel -1, 2, 4, 6, 7	OK 05956, Cq 9741, Co 37017, 37597, 20043(?), 20196
DAL-953-1c, d	The Precious Jewel -1, 2, 4, 6, 7	Co 37597, 20043(?), 20196, 52014, C6343
DAL-954-1	The Broken Heart -2, 6, 7	OK 05820, Cq 9741
DAL-955-1	Would You Care -3, 5, 8	Vo/OK 05512, Cq 9436
DAL-956-1	Lonesome Old River Blues -1, 2, 4, 6, 7	Vo unissued: *Co FC39998* (LP); *CK39998* (CD)
DAL-956-2	Lonesome Old River Blues -1, 2, 4, 6, 7	Co 20626
DAL-957-1	What Good Will It Do -1, 2, 6, 7	Vo/OK 05512, Cq 9436
DAL-958-1	Mule Skinner Blues (Blue Yodel #8) -2, 6, 7	OK 05638, Cq 9528, Co 37012, 20038
DAL-958-2	Mule Skinner Blues (Blue Yodel #8) -2, 6, 7	Vo unissued: *Ha HL7342, Co CS1034* (LPs); *CK1034* (CD)

Matrices DAL-953-1, DAL-953-1c, and DAL-953-1d variously appear on Columbia 37597, 20196, and possibly 20043. Matrices DAL-953-1c and -1d are probably technical remasterings of DAL-953-2.

Acc. own f-1; Pete "Oswald" Kirby, sg-2/v-3; Jess Easterday, md; Lonnie Wilson, g; Oral Rhodes, sb.

Chicago, IL   Tuesday, April 29, 1941

C-3700-1	Be Honest With Me -2	OK 06229, Cq 9889, Co 37020, 20046
C-3701-1	Worried Mind -2	OK 06229, Cq 9889, Co 37020, 20046
C-3702-1	Things That Might Have Been -1, 2	OK 06585, Cq 9812, Co 37421, 20148
C-3703-1	You're My Darling -2	OK 06463, Cq 9810, Co 37436, 20163, CoC C569
C-3704-1	It Won't Be Long (Till I'll Be Leaving) -3	OK 06623, Cq 9811, Co 37413, 20140
C-3705-1	Just Inside The Pearly Gates -3	OK 06623, Cq 9811, Co 37413, 20140
C-3706-1	I Know We're Saying Goodbye -2, 3	OK 06550, Cq 9813, Co 37424, 20151
C-3707-1	Brother Take Warning -2, 3	OK 06512, Cq 9888, Co 37429, 20156
C-3708-1	The Great Judgment Morning -2	OK 06512, Cq 9888, Co 37429, 20156

Acc. Oral Rhodes, f; Pete "Oswald" Kirby, sg/v; Lonnie Wilson, g; Jess Easterday, sb.

Chicago, IL   Tuesday, April 29, 1941

| C-3709-1 | Stuck Up Blues | OK 06300, Cq 9808 |

Acc. own f-1; Pete "Oswald" Kirby, sg/v-2; Jess Easterday, md; Lonnie Wilson, g; Oral Rhodes, sb.

Chicago, IL   Tuesday, April 29, 1941

C-3710-1	Lying Woman Blues -1	OK 06300, Cq 9808
C-3711-1	You Are My Love	OK 06550, Cq 9812, Co 37424, 20150
C-3712-1	Branded Wherever I Go -1, 2	OK 06463, Cq 9813, Co 37436, 20163, CoC C569
C-3713-1	No Letter In The Mail -2	OK 06585, Cq 9810, Co 37421, 20148
C-3714-1	Are You Thinking Of Me Darling?	OK 06384, Cq 9809, Co 37442, 20169
C-3715-1	I Called And Nobody Answered -1, 2	OK 06384, Cq 9809, Co 37442, 20169

Acc. own f-1; Pete "Oswald" Kirby, sg/v-2; Lonnie Wilson, g; Velma Williams, sb.

Hollywood, CA   Thursday, May 28, 1942

HCO-807-1	Wreck On The Highway -1, 2	OK 6685, Co 37028, 37596, 20195, 52023
HCO-808-1	Fire Ball Mail	OK 6685, Co 37028, 37596, 20195
HCO-809-1	I'll Reap My Harvest In Heaven -2	OK 6704, Co 37031, 20056
HCO-810-1	Night Train To Memphis	OK 6693, Co 37029, 20054

Roy Acuff, f-1/v-2; Pete "Oswald" Kirby, sg-3/bj-4/g-5/v-6; Rachel Veach, bj-7/v-8; Lonnie Wilson, g; Velma Williams, sb.

Hollywood, CA   Monday, June 1, 1942

| H-811-1 | The Prodigal Son -2, 3 | OK 6716, Co 37032, 20057 |

HCO-812-1	Low And Lonely -2, 3	OK 6693, Co 37029, 37599, 20054, 20198
H-813-1	Write Me Sweetheart -1, 2, 3, 6	OK 6723, Co 37035, 20060
HCO-814-	I Didn't Want You To Know -2, 3	OK unissued
HCO-815-	Roll On Buddy -1, 2, 4, 6, 8	OK unissued
HCO-816-1	Weary Lonesome Blues -1, 5, 6, 7, 8	OK unissued: *Co FC39998* (LP); *CK39998* (CD)
HCO-817-	Come Back Little Darling -2, 3	OK unissued
H-818-1	They Can Only Fill One Grave -1, 2, 3, 6	Co 37943, 20378

Roy Acuff, v; acc. Pete "Oswald" Kirby, sg/v-1; Lonnie Wilson, g; Velma Williams, sb.
Hollywood, CA   Thursday, June 4, 1942

H-819-	Live And Let Live -1	OK unissued
H-820-1	Don't Make Me Go To Bed And I'll Be Good	OK 6704, Co 37031, 20056
H-821-1	The Heart That Was Broken For Me	OK unissued: *Co FC39998* (LP); *CK39998* (CD)
H-822-1	Not A Word From Home -1	OK 6716, Co 37032, 20057
H-823-1	Do You Wonder Why	Co 37943, 20378
H-824-1	I'll Forgive You But I Can't Forget	OK 6723, Co 37035, 20060

Roy Acuff recorded after 1942.

GREEN B. ADAIR

Green B. Adair, sp.
Atlanta, GA   Saturday, March 26, 1927

143777-2	Talkin' About My Gal	Co 15166-D
143778-1	A Trip To The City	Co 15166-D

Green B. Adair, sp; unknown second man, sp; poss. unknown third man, sp-1.
Atlanta, GA   Wednesday, November 9, 1927

145190-2	Lucy Wants Insurance	Co 15316-D
145191-3	Malinda Gets Married -1	Co 15316-D

BILLY ADAMS

Pseudonym on Clarion and Velvet Tone for Frank Hutchison.

CLARENCE ADAMS

Pseudonym on Challenge for Welby Toomey.

DAVID ADAMS

Pseudonym on Australian Grand Pree for Vernon Dalhart.

JOE ADAMS [& JAMES CLARK]

Pseudonym on Madison, Radiex, and Van Dyke for Bob Miller [& Barney Burnett].

PAUL ADAMS

Pseudonym on Australian Grand Pree for Vernon Dalhart.

RAYMOND ADAMS

Pseudonym on Superior for the Long Family Trio (see Jimmy Long).

ADAMS & MORRIS

Pseudonym on Australian Grand Pree for Vernon Dalhart & Carson Robison.

LOUIS ADLER

Louis Adler & His Swiss Yodelers: Louis Adler, zither; unknown, v/y; or **Louis Adler**-1: Louis Adler, zither solo.
Richmond, IN   Thursday, April 18, 1929

15066,-A	And Now You Farmers	Ge 20351
15067	Mountaineers Song	Ge 20351
15068	Lullaby Song; Cuckoo Song -1	Ge rejected

JAMES AHERN

Pseudonym on Madison 1918 for Vernon Dalhart.

AIKEN COUNTY STRING BAND

Unknown, h-1; unknown, md; two unknowns, g; unknown, calls; unknown, wh-2; unknown, perc-3.
Winston-Salem, NC   Monday, September 19, 1927

81339-A	Carolina Stompdown -1, 3	OK 45153
81340-A	Hard Times Breakdown -2, 3	OK 45153
81341-A	Harrisburg Itch -3	OK 45294
81342-B	High Sheriff -1, 2	OK 45219, PaE E6144

| 81343-B | Charleston Rag -1 | OK 45219, PaE E6144 |
| 81344-B | Savannah River Stride -3 | OK 45294 |

THE AIRPORT BOYS

Buck Nation, v/g; Ed West, v/g; Lloyd West, v/sb.
    New York, NY   Monday, September 30, 1940

056413-1	Don't Leave Me Now	BB B-11074
056414-1	South	BB B-11074
056415-1	You Are My Sunshine	BB B-10939
056416-1	Bad Girl	BB B-10939

Bluebird B-11074 as by **Two Guitars And A Bass**.

    New York, NY   Wednesday, August 13, 1941

067563-1	Worried Mind	BB unissued
067564-1	It Ain't Gonna Rain No Mo'	BB B-11290
067565-1	You Can Depend On Me	BB unissued
067566-1	Pay Me No Mind	BB unissued
067567-1	You're My Inspiration	BB unissued
067568-1	You Belong To Me	BB B-11290

This group was originally logged as **The Quaker Town Boys**. Buck Nation also recorded in his own name.

GEORGE AKE

George Ake, v; acc. the Jolly Four Orch. (sic): unknown, f; unknown, bj; unknown, g.
    Richmond, IN   Thursday, April 30, 1925

| 12229 | Sand Cave | Ge 3062, Ch 15048, Sil 4019 |

Champion 15048 as by **Edward Johnson**. On most pressings of Champion 15048, however, matrix 12229 is replaced by one or the other of two Vernon Dalhart recordings of *The Death Of Floyd Collins*, correctly credited. Silvertone 4019 as by **John Ferguson**. Revs: Gennett 3062, Silvertone 4019 by David Miller; Champion 15048 by Vernon Dalhart.

LUNDY AKERS

See Fred Pendleton.

AKINS BIRMINGHAM BOYS

E.E. Akins, f; prob. Johnny Motlow, bj/v; T.H. "Red" Phillips, g/v.
    Atlanta, GA   Wednesday, October 31, 1928

| 147356-2 | I Walked And Walked | Co 15348-D |
| 147357-1 | There Ain't No Flies On Auntie | Co 15348-D |

THE ALABAMA BARN STORMERS

This pseudonym was used on English and Australian Regal and Regal-Zonophone for various artists, as follows:

(English)

G9458   McCartt Brothers & Patterson (147242)/Leake County Revelers (148324)
ME30   Elzie Floyd & Leo Boswell (143767)/Tom Darby & Jimmie Tarlton (149309)
MR20   Roy Harper & Earl Shirkey (148136)/Gid Tanner & His Skillet-Lickers (148203)
MR56   Hugh Cross & Riley Puckett (146027)/Ira & Eugene Yates (149262)
MR70   as ME30
MR209   Eddie Younger & His Mountaineers (see Arthur Fields & Fred Hall)
MR2458   Dixie Reelers/(rev. Cliff Carlisle & Junior under their own names)
MR3021   The Blue Sky Boys

(Australian)

G20753   as G9458
G21139   Leake County Revelers
G21475   McMichen's Melody Men (145101)/Leake County Revelers (151120)
G21659   as MR70
G22150   as MR209

This artist credit sometimes appears as **The Alabama Barnstormers**.

ALABAMA FOUR

Pseudonym on Broadway for the Charles Brothers (see Phil Reeve & Ernest Moody) or North Georgia Quartette.

ALABAMA SACRED HARP SINGERS

Vocal group; unacc.
    Atlanta, GA   Monday, April 16, 1928

146091-2	Rocky Road	Co 15274-D
146092-2	Present Joys	Co 15274-D
146093-	The Christians Hope	Co unissued
146094-	Victoria	Co unissued

Alabama Sacred Harp Singers Under direction of J.C. Brown and Whit Denson: vocal group; unacc.
Atlanta, GA   Monday, October 29, 1928

| 147329-2 | Religion Is A Fortune | Co 15349-D |
| 147330-2 | Cuba | Co 15349-D |

ALBEE SISTERS

Vocal trio; acc. unknown, f; unknown, p.
New York, NY   Saturday, May 14, 1932

| TO-1155 | Rocky Mountain Lullaby | ARC unissued trial recording |

ALBERTVILLE QUARTET

Vocal quartet; acc. unknown, p.
Atlanta, GA   Tuesday, November 5, 1929

| 149387-2 | Workers For Jesus | Co 15666-D |
| 149388-2 | I Hold His Hand | Co 15666-D |

JOHN ALBIN

Pseudonym on Marathon for Carson Robison & Frank Luther.

ALCOA QUARTET

J.E. Thomas, tv; J.H. Thomas, tv; J.L. Wells, bv; W.B. Hitch, bsv; unacc.
Atlanta, GA   Thursday, January 29, 1925

| 140294-2 | Throw Out The Life Line | Co 15022-D |
| 140295-2 | Shall We Gather At The River | Co 15022-D |

Bristol, TN   Tuesday, August 2, 1927

| 39756-2 | Remember Me, O Mighty One | Vi 20879 |
| 39757-2 | I'm Redeemed | Vi 20879 |

ALEC'S STRING BAND

This credit is used on Victor 21587 for Kiriloff's Balalaika Orchestra, a group outside the scope of this work.

E.F. "PAT" ALEXANDER

E.F. "Pat" Alexander, v-1; acc. prob. own h-2/g-3; unknown, g-4.
Richmond, IN   Wednesday, January 15, 1930

16101,-A	Summer's County Rag -3, 4	Ge rejected
16102,-A	Mame -3, 4	Ge rejected
16103	Devil's Dream -2, 3/4	Ge rejected
16104,-A	There Is Joy -2, 3/4	Ge rejected
16105,-A	Moonshine In The Kentucky Hills -1, 2, 3/4	Ge rejected

Martices 16101 to 16104 are uncredited in Gennett files but seem likely to be by this artist.

ALEXANDER & APPLE

One of them, f; one of them, g.
Richmond, IN   Wednesday, March 26, 1930

| 16398,-A | The Little Red Shawl That Mother Wore | Ge unissued |
| 16399,-A | Give Us Another Lincoln | Ge rejected |

ALEXANDER & MILLER

Bj duet.
Richmond, IN   Saturday, February 23, 1929

14827	Darling Nellie Gray; Girl I Left Behind Me; Buffalo Girl	Spt 9398
14829,-A	Silver Threads Among The Gold; Massa's In The Cold Cold Ground; My Old Kentucky Home	Ge rejected
14830,-A	Medley Of Old Songs	Ge rejected
14831	Old Polka; Stony Point; Stonewall Jackson	Spt 9398

This session was logged as by **Miller & Alexander** but Supertone 9398 was issued as shown. Matrix 14828 is unrelated.

BIG SLIM ALIFF

Harry C. McAuliffe, v; acc. own h/g.
  New York, NY   Thursday, December 17, 1936
    61488-A   Little Rag Doll   De 5329
    61489-A   Footprints In The Snow   De 5316
    61490-A   New Birmingham Jail   De 5316
    61491-A   Put My Little Shoes Away   De 5329
This artist recorded after 1942.

ALL STAR ENTERTAINERS
This group had two releases in the Brunswick old-time series (226, 245) but is outside the scope of this work.

ALLEGHENY HIGHLANDERS
This was essentially a Charlie Poole band, and its Brunswick recordings are listed under his name.

ALLEMAN & WALKER

Prob.: Lawrence Walker, f; Toney Alleman, g/v; unknown, g.
  New Orleans, LA   Friday, January 18, 1935
    87616-1   La Femme Qui Jovait Les Cartes   BB B-2193
    87617-1   Mon Dernier Bon Soir   BB B-2193

AUSTIN & LEE ALLEN
See the Allen Brothers.

CHARLIE ALLEN

Charlie Allen, v; acc. poss. own h/g.
  Richmond, IN   Wednesday, July 17, 1929
    15362   I Have No Mother In This World   Ge rejected
  Richmond, IN   Thursday, July 18, 1929
    15367,-A,-B Sadie Ray   Ge rejected
    15368,-A   I Truly Love But One   Ge rejected

CHESTER ALLEN & CAMPBELL

Chester Allen, Grady "Red" Campbell, v duet; acc. own g duet.
  Atlanta, GA   Monday, August 5, 1935
    94324-1   The Huntsville Jail   BB B-6195
    94325-1   Drinkin' Blues   BB B-6195
    94326-1   Railroad Blues   BB B-6224, MW M-4825
    94327-1   Booze Drinkin' Daddy   BB B-6224, MW M-4825

MISS JIMMIE ALLEN

Jimmie Allen, v/y-1; acc. "string ork" (thus Vocalion files).
  Columbia, SC   Friday, November 11, 1938
    SC-143-   Freight Train Blues -1   Vo unissued
    SC-144-   Renfro Valley   Vo unissued

JULES ALLEN

Jules Allen "The Singing Cowboy", v; acc. own g.
  El Paso, TX   Saturday, April 21, 1928
    42193-2   Little Joe, The Wrangler   Vi 21470, MW M-4344, M-4780, Au 420
    42194-2   Jack O' Diamonds   Vi 21470, MW M-4464, M-4779, Au 420
    42195-1   Po' Mourner   Vi unissued
  El Paso, TX   Tuesday, April 24, 1928
    42195-2   Po' Mourner   Vi 23834
    42211-2   Somebody But You Don't Mean Me   Vi 23598
    42212-2   The Days Of Forty-Nine   Vi 21627, BB B-4959, MW M-4463, Au 421
    42213-2   Home On The Range   Vi 21627, BB B-4959, MW M-4343, Au 421
Rev. Montgomery Ward M-4343 by Carl T. Sprague.

Acc. unknown, f-1; D.A. Champaigne, h-2; own g.
  El Paso, TX   Monday, April 30, 1928
    42254-1   The Texas Cowboy -2   Vi V-40068, MW M-4781
    42255-1   A Prisoner For Life -1   Vi V-40068

| 42256-1 | The Gal I Left Behind Me -1, 2 | Vi V-40022 |
| 42257-1 | Zebra Dun | Vi V-40022, MW M-4464 |

Acc. own g.
  Hollywood, CA   Thursday, March 28, 1929

50567-2	The Cow Trail To Mexico	Vi 23757
50568-2	Chisholm Trail	Vi V-40167, MW M-4463
50569-2	Cowboy's Love Song	Vi V-40167, MW M-4101, M-4779
50570-2	Sweetie Dear	Vi 23598

Rev. Montgomery Ward M-4101 by Bud Billings Trio (see Frank Luther).

Jules Allen (The Singing Cowboy), v; acc. Charles Coffey, f-1/v-2; own g.
  Los Angeles, CA   Monday, April 8, 1929

50594-1	'Long Side The Santa Fé Trail -1	Vi V-40118, MW M-4344, M-4780, Au 231
50595-3	Two Fragments	Vi V-40118, MW M-4781, Au 231
50596-1	The Cowboy's Dream -1	Vi V-40178
50597-1	Cowboy's Lament	Vi V-40178, MW M-4099
50598-2	Little Old Sod Shanty -1	Vi 23757
50599-1,-2	The Dying Cowboy -1, 2	Vi unissued

Montgomery Ward M-4099 as by **Jules Allen The Singing Cowboy**. Rev. Montgomery Ward M-4099 by Carl T. Sprague.

Jules Allen, The Singing Cowboy, v; acc. own g.
  Culver City, CA   Saturday, April 27, 1929

50865-2	When The Work's All Done This Fall	Vi V-40263
50866-2	Punchin' The Dough	Vi V-40263
50867-	The Dying Cowboy	Vi 23834

MACK ALLEN

Pseudonym on Diva, Harmony, Velvet Tone, and English Regal for Vernon Dalhart.

ALLEN BROTHERS

Austin Allen, v/tbj; Lee Allen, k/g.
  Atlanta, GA   Thursday, April 7, 1927

143927-	Free A Little Bird	Co unissued
143928-	Wedding Bells	Co unissued
143929-2	Salty Dog Blues	Co 15175-D
143930-2	Bow Wow Blues	Co 15175-D

Austin Allen, v-1/sp-2/tbj; Lee Allen, v-3/k/g.
  Atlanta, GA   Thursday, November 4, 1927

145112-1	Chattanooga Blues-1, 2	Co 14266-D
145113-	Coal Mine Blues	Co unissued
145114-	Beaver Cap	Co unissued
145115-1	Laughin' And Cryin' Blues -3	Co 14266-D

Columbia 14266-D as by **Austin & Lee Allen**.

  Atlanta, GA   Friday, April 20, 1928

146150-2	Ain't That Skippin' And Flyin' -1	Co 15270-D
146151-1	Cheat 'Em	Co 15270-D
146152-	Monkey Blues	Co unissued
146153-	Ain't That A Shame	Co unissued

Austin Allen, v/tbj; Lee Allen, v-1/k-2/g; acc. Robert Douglas, f-3; Jimmie Medley, g-4.
  Atlanta, GA   Monday, October 15, 1928

47167-3	Frisco Blues -2, 4	Vi V-40003, BB B-5224, Eld 2110, Sr S-3307
47168-3	Tiple Blues -2, 4	Vi V-40003, BB B-5104, Eld 2020, Sr S-3187, MW M-4438, M-4798
47169-3	Free A Little Bird -1, 3, 4	Vi V-40266, BB B-5668
47170-3	Skipping And Flying -3, 4	Vi V-40266, BB B-5772
47171-1,-2,-3	I'm A Diamond From The Rough -1	Vi unissued
47172-1,-2,-3	Meet Your Mother In The Skies -1	Vi unissued
47173-3	Prisoner's Dream -1, 2	Vi V-40210
47174-3	I'll Be All Smiles Tonight -1, 2, 4	Vi V-40210

Austin Allen, v-1/sp-2/tbj; Lee Allen, v-3/k/g.
  Memphis, TN   Friday, June 5, 1930

62589-2	I've Got The Chain Store Blues -1	Vi V-40276
62590-2	Jake Walk Blues -1, 2	Vi V-40303, BB B-5001, Eld 1959, 1831, Sr S-3105, MW M-4281
62591-1	The Enforcement Blues -1	Vi V-40276

62592-2	Reckless Night Blues -1, 2	Vi V-40303, BB B-5224, Eld 2110, Sr S-3307
62593-2	New Chattanooga Blues -1	Vi V-40326, BB B-5380, Sr S-3461
62594-1	Shanghai Rooster Blues -3	Vi V-40326, BB B-5668

Austin Allen, v-1/sp-2/wh-3/tbj-4; Lee Allen, v-5/k/g.
Memphis, TN   Saturday, November 22, 1930

62991-2	Price Of Cotton Blues -1, 4	Vi 23507
62992-2	I'm Always Whistling The Blues -1, 3, 4	Vi 23507, BB B-5104, Eld 2020, Sr S-3187, MW M-4438, M-4798
62993-2	Roll Down The Line -1, 4, 5	Vi 23551, BB B-5700, B-6148, MW M-4799, Twin FT1828
62994-2	Old Black Crow In The Hickory-Nut Tree -1, 4, 5	Vi 23551, BB B-5448, HMVIn N4305
62995-2	No Low Down Hanging Around -1	Vi 23536, BB B-5448, MW M-4797, HMVIn N4305
62996-2	Maybe Next Week Sometime -2	Vi 23536, BB B-5165, Eld 2062, Sr S-3246, MW M-4439
62997-2	A New Salty Dog -1, 4	Vi 23514, 20-2132, BB B-5403, MW M-4750, HMVIn N4324
62998-2	Preacher Blues -1, 4	Vi 23514, BB B-5820

Revs: Bluebird B-5403, Montgomery Ward M-4750, HMV N4324 by Delmore Brothers; Victor 20-2132 by Modern Mountaineers.

Austin Allen, v/h-1/tbj; Lee Allen, k/g.
Charlotte, NC   Wednesday, May 20, 1931

69319-1	When You Leave, You'll Leave Me Sad -1	Vi 23567, BB B-5702, Twin FT1828
69320-1	Chattanooga Mama	Vi 23567, BB B-5470, Twin FT1736
69321-2	It's Too Bad For You	Vi 23631, BB B-5872
69322-2	Slide Daddy, Slide	Vi 23590, BB B-5317, Sr S-3398
69325-2	Moonshine Bill	Vi 23631
69326-2	Pile Drivin' Papa	Vi 23578, BB B-5772

Matrices 69323/24 are by Selma & Dewey Hayes. Revs: Bluebird B-5470, Twin FT1736 by Fleming & Townsend.

Austin Allen, v-1/sp-2/h-3/tbj-4; Lee Allen, v-5/k-6/g.
Charlotte, NC   Thursday, May 21, 1931

69327-2	Shake It, Ida, Shake It -1, 4, 5, 6	Vi 23607, BB B-5165, Eld 2062, Sr S-3246, MW M-4439
69328-1	Roll It Down -1, 2, 5	Vi 23590, BB B-5317, Sr S-3398, MW M-4797
69329-2	Mother-In-Law Blues -1, 4, 6	Vi 23607, BB B-5380, Sr S-3461
69330-2	Unlucky Man -1, 3, 4, 5	Vi 23623
69331-1	Laughin' And Cryin' -2, 4, 5, 6	Vi 23623, BB B-5533
69332-2	Monkey Blues -1, 4, 6	Vi 23578, BB B-5820

Austin Allen, v/tbj-1/g-2; Lee Allen, k/g-3.
Atlanta, GA   Wednesday, February 17, 1932

70700-1	Glorious Night Blues -1, 3	Vi 23707, BB B-5701, B-6149
61387-1,-2	Misbehavin' Mama -1, 3	Vi unissued
61388-2	Inspiration -2	Vi 23678

Austin Allen, v/sp-1/tbj-2/g-3; Lee Allen, v-4/k-5/g-6.
Atlanta, GA   Thursday, February 18, 1932

61389-2	Crossfiring Blues -2, 4, 6	Vi 23692, BB B-5872
61390-2	I'll Be Here A Long, Long Time -3, 4, 5	Vi 23662, BB B-5702
61395-2	It Can't Be Done -1, 3, 5	Vi 23662, BB B-5533

Matrices 61391 to 61394 are by Fleming & Townsend.

Austin Allen, v-1/sp-2/h-3/tbj-4/g-5; Lee Allen, v-6/k/g.
Atlanta, GA   Friday, February 19, 1932

61396-2	Windowshade Blues -1, 3, 4	Vi 23692, BB B-5701, B-6149
61397-2	Maybe Next Week Sometime – No. 2 -1, 2, 5	Vi 23678, BB B-5700, B-6148, MW M-4799
61398-1,- 2	Free-Wheeling Blues -1, 3, 4, 6	Vi unissued

Austin Allen, v/tbj; Lee Allen, k/g.
Camden, NJ   Monday, December 5, 1932

74805-1	Fruit Jar Blues	Vi 23756, BB B-5001, Eld 1959, 1831, Sr S-3105, MW M-4281
74806-1	Lightning Bug Blues	Vi 23805
74807-1	Warm Knees Blues	Vi 23805
74808-1	My Midnight Man	Vi unissued
74809-1	Red Hot Rambling Dan	Vi 23786
74810-1	Won't You Come Home?	Vi unissued

Austin Allen, v/h-1/tbj-2/g-3; Lee Allen, k/g-4.
    Camden, NJ   Tuesday, December 6, 1932

74811-1	When A Man's Got A Woman -1, 2, 4	Vi 23773
74812-1	Rough Neck Blues -2, 4	Vi 23756
74813-1	Slipping Clutch Blues -3	Vi 23773
74814-1	Here I Am -3	Vi unissued
74815-1	Please Pay In Advance -3	Vi 23786
74816-1	Allen's Lying Blues -3	Vi 23817
74817-1	So Straight, My Lad -2, 4	Vi unissued
74818-1	Midnight Mama -2, 4	Vi 23817

Austin Allen, v/tbj; Lee Allen, v-1/k/g.
    New York, NY   Wednesday, October 3, 1934

16095-2	Baby When You Coming Back Home	Vo 02853
16096-1	Long Gone From Bowling Green -1	Vo 02817
16097-3	Red Pajama Sal	Vo 02817
16098-2	New Deal Blues	Vo 02890

Austin Allen, v-1/tbj-2; Lee Allen, v-3/k/g.
    New York, NY   Friday, October 5, 1934

16107-1	Mercy Mercy Blues -1	Vo 02874
16108-1	Padlock Key Blues -1	Vo unissued: Doc DOCD-8035 (CD)
16109-2	Daddy Park Your Car -1, 2	Vo 02853
16110-2	Salty Dog, Hey Hey Hey -1, 2	Vo/OK 02818
16111-1	Hey Buddy, Won't You Roll Down The Line -1, 2, 3	Vo/OK 02818
16112-1	Allen Brothers' Rag -2	Vo 02939, ARC 6-12-57

    New York, NY   Saturday, October 6, 1934

| 16046-2 | Skippin' And Flyin'-1, 2 | Vo 02939, ARC 6-12-57 |
| 16047-2 | Tipple Blues -1, 2 | Vo 02891 |

Austin Allen, v-1/sp-2/tbj-3; Lee Allen, v-4/k-5/g.
    New York, NY   Monday, October 8, 1934

16048-2	Mary's Breakdown -1?, 3, 5	Vo 02891
16049-2	Can I Get You Now -1, 3, 5	Vo 02890
16050-1	The Prisoner's Dream -1, 3, 4	Vo 02874
16121-1	Drunk And Nutty Blues -2, 3, 4	Vo unissued: Co C2K47466, Co(E) 472886, Doc DOCD-8035, Indigo IGODCD2520 (CDs)
16122-1	Misbehavin' Mama -1, 3, 5	Vo 02841
16123-2	Midnight Mama -2, 5	Vo 02841
16124-1,-2	I'm In Here A Long Long Time -1, 4	Vo unissued
16125-2	Chattanooga Mama -1, 3, 5	Vo unissued: Co C2K47466, Co(E) 472886, Doc DOCD-8035 (CDs)

ALLEN QUARTETTE

Vocal quartet; unacc.-1; or acc. unknown, o-2.
    Atlanta, GA   Tuesday, March 22, 1927

80611-B	Redeemed -2	OK 40797
80612-B	When The Sweet Bye And Bye Is Ended -1	OK 45109
80613-A	Try To Win Some Soul To Him -1	OK 45109
80614-A	My Old Cottage Home -2	OK 45130
80615-B	My Precious Saviour -2	OK 45130
80616-B	We Are Going Down The Valley -2	OK 40797

    Atlanta, GA   Saturday, October 8, 1927

81713-	Death Is Only A Dream	OK unissued
81714-	My Far Away Home	OK unissued
81715-A	Beautiful River	OK 45196, PaE R3866
81716-A	God's Children Are Gathering Home -2	OK 45168
81717-A	Life's Railway To Heaven	OK 45196, PaE R3866
81718-	A Child At Mother's Knee	OK unissued
81719-B	My Mother's Bible -2	OK 45168

ALLEN'S CREEK PLAYERS

Pseudonym on Champion for Taylor's Kentucky Boys.

SHELLY LEE ALLEY & HIS ALLEY CATS

Shelly Lee Alley, f/v-1; Cliff Bruner, f; Anthony Scanlin, cl/ts/p; Ted Daffan, esg; unknown, 2nd p (on some items); Chuck Keeshan, g/v-2; Jack Moran, sb; Don Law, wb.

San Antonio, TX			Thursday, November 4, 1937
SA-2887-1	Let Me Bring It To Your Door -1	Vo 03975	
SA-2888-1	I'm Still In Love With You -2	Vo 03975	
SA-2889-	She's So Different -1	ARC unissued	
SA-2890-	Alone -1	ARC unissued	
SA-2891-	Why Are You Blue -1	ARC unissued	
SA-2892-	Houston Blues -1	ARC unissued	
SA-2893-1	You've Got Me Worried Now -1	Vo 03939	
SA-2894-	Nonie -1	ARC unissued	
SA-2895-	Don't You Care -1	ARC unissued	
SA-2896-	Deep Congress Avenue -1	ARC unissued	
SA-2897-1	My Precious Darling -1	Vo 03891	

San Antonio, TX			Friday, November 5, 1937
SA-2898-1	Train Whistle Blues -1	Vo 04451	
SA-2899-1	Women, Women, Women -1	Vo 03939	
SA-2900-	You Can Make Me Happy -1	ARC unissued	
SA-2901-1	You've Made A Dream Come True -1	Vo 03891	
SA-2902-	She's My Red Hot Gal (From New Orleans) -1	ARC unissued	

Shelly Lee Alley, v; acc. own f; Cliff Bruner, f; Anthony Scanlin, cl/ts; Ted Daffan, esg; Douglas Blaikie, p-1; unknown, p-2; Chuck Keeshan, g; Lester J. Voss, sb-1; Pinkie Dawson, sb-2.

Dallas, TX			Tuesday, May 10, 1938
DAL-478-1	I'll Get It -1	Vo 04371	
DAL-479-1	Nine Or Ten Times -1	Vo 04371	
DAL-480-1	Try It Once Again -1	Vo 04145	
DAL-481-	My Steppin' Gal -1	Vo unissued	
DAL-482-1	Deep Congress Avenue -2	Vo 04276	
DAL-483-	She's My Red Hot Gal -2	Vo unissued	
DAL-484-1	She's So Different -2	Vo 04276	
DAL-485-1	Houston Blues -2	Vo 04201	

Dallas, TX			Wednesday, May 11, 1938
DAL-486-	You Can Make Me Happy -2	Vo unissued	
DAL-487-	Why Are You Blue -2	Vo unissued	
DAL-488-1	You've Got It -2	Vo 04145	
DAL-489-1	You Know What I Mean -2	Vo 04451	
DAL-490-	Alone -2	Vo unissued	
DAL-491-1	Bring It On Home To Grandma -2	Vo 04201	
DAL-492-	Blonde Headed Mama Blues -2	Vo unissued	

Acc. own f; Leon Selph, f; Smoky Miller, cl/as; Ernest "Deacon" Evans, esg; Ralph Smith, p; Gus Plant, g; Chet Miller, sb.

Dallas, TX			Monday, December 5, 1938
DAL-715-1	She Just Wiggled Around	Vo 04600	
DAL-716-1,2	I Got The Blues	Vo unissued	
DAL-717-1,2	I See That Certain Something (In Your Eyes)	Vo unissued	
DAL-718-1	She Wouldn't	Vo 04793	
DAL-719-1	What's The Matter Now	Vo 04879	
DAL-720-2	Don't You Care	Vo 04670	
DAL-721-1	Why Should I Worry Now	Vo 05391	

Shelly Lee Alley, f/v-1; Leon Selph, f; Smoky Miller, cl/as; Ernest "Deacon" Evans, esg; Ralph Smith, p; Gus Plant, g; Chet Miller, sb.

Dallas, TX			Tuesday, December 6, 1938
DAL-729-1	What Size Do You Need -1	Vo 04879	
DAL-730-	Those Loving Lies -1	Vo unissued	
DAL-731-1	She Loves It So -1	Vo 04728	
DAL-732-1	New Mean Mama Blues -1	Vo 05256	
DAL-733-1	I'll Take You Back Again -1	Vo 04728	
DAL-734-1	I'm So Used To You Now -1	Vo 04670	
DAL-735-1	Can't Nobody Truck Like Me	Vo 04793	
DAL-736-1	Alley Cat Stomp	Vo 04600	

Shelly Lee Alley, f/v-1; Leon Selph, f; George Ogg, cl/ts; Ted Daffan, esg/v-2; Ralph Smith, p; Gus Plant, g; Chuck Keeshan, g/v-3; Chet Miller, sb; unidentified, 3rd v-4.

Dallas, TX			Monday, June 12, 1939
DAL-772-1	I've Got The Blues #2 -1	Vo 05053	
DAL-773-1,-2,-3	Big House Blues -1	Vo unissued	
DAL-774-1	I'm Wondering Now -1	Vo/OK 05106	

DAL-775-1	It Makes A Lot Of Difference Now -1	Vo/OK 05106, Cq 9306
DAL-776-1	I Wish I'd Never Learned To Love You -1, 3	Vo 04986
DAL-777-1	Tired Of You -2	Vo 05391
DAL-778-1	Let's Do It Honey -1	Vo 05053
DAL-779-1	My Texas Sweetheart -1, 3	Vo 05322
DAL-780-3	Two More Years (And I'll Be Free) -3	Vo 04986
DAL-781-1	Hang Your Pretty Things By My Bed -1	Vo/OK 05202
DAL-782-1	My Little Dream Girl -1	Vo 05322
DAL-783-1	Goodbye Forever -3	Vo 05256
DAL-784-1	I'll Keep Thinking Of You -1, 3, 4	Vo/OK 05202

Rev. Conqeror 9306 by Light Crust Doughboys.

Shelly Lee Alley, v; acc. Leon Selph, f; Ernest "Deacon" Evans, esg; Ralph Smith, p; Howard Oliver, tbj; Gus Plant, g; Chet Miller, sb.

Saginaw, TX   Monday, April 29, 1940

DAL-1088-1	I'm Smiling (Just To Hide A Broken Heart)	OK 05667
DAL-1089-1	How Can You Treat Me This Way	OK 05738
DAL-1090-1	Don't Leave Me (With A Broken Heart)	OK 05667
DAL-1091-2	Oh What A Fool I've Been	OK 05930
DAL-1092-1	I Just Can't Forget The Past	OK 05930
DAL-1093-1	It Won't Be Long	OK 05738
DAL-1094-2	It Doesn't Matter Now	Vo/OK 05585
DAL-1095-2	It Took My Breath Away	Vo/OK 05585

Acc. own f; unknown, f; prob. Harry Choates, esg; unknown, g; unknown, sb; band v-1.

Dallas, TX   Thursday, October 9, 1941

071142-1	Answer To "My Precious Darling"	BB B-8888
071143-1	Beer Joint Blues	BB B-8934
071144-1	The Big House Blues -1	BB B-8934
071145-1	Why Are You Blue	BB unissued
071146-1	My Love	BB B-8888
071147-1	Sweetheart Of Mine	BB unissued

Shelly Lee Alley recorded after 1942.

THE ALLEY BOYS OF ABBEVILLE

Frank Mailhes, f/v-1; Lourse Leger, sg; Murphy Guidry, g/v-2; Sidney Guidry, g/v-3; Maxie Touchet, d.

Memphis, TN   Friday, June 30, 1939

MEM-1-1	Pourquois Te En Pen -2	Vo 05423
MEM-2-1	Moi Et Ma Belle -3	Vo unissued: *Co CK46220 (CD)*
MEM-3-1	Apres Jengler A Toi -1	Vo 05057
MEM-4-1	Es Ce Que Tu Pense Jamais A Moi? (Do You Ever Think Of Me?) -3	Vo 05424
MEM-5-1	Tu Peu Depend Si Moi (You Can Depend On Me) -2	Vo 05167
MEM-6-1	Se Toute Sain Comme Moi Ma Saine -2	Vo 05058
MEM-7-1	Jolie Petite Fille -1	Vo unissued: *Co CK46220 (CD)*
MEM-8-1	Tu Ma Quite Seul (The Prisoner's Song) -2	Vo 05423
MEM-9-1	Tu Peus Pas Me Faire Ca (You Can't Put That Monkey On My Back) -3	Vo 05058
MEM-10-1	Jolie Petite Blonde -2	Vo 05167
MEM-11-2	Quel Espoire (What's The Use) -1	Vo 05424
MEM-12-1	Abbeville Breakdown	Vo 05168
MEM-13-1	Pourquoi Tu M'Aime Pas -1	Vo unissued: *Co C4K47911 (CD)*
MEM-14-1	Te Bonne Pour Moir Estere -3	Vo 05057
MEM-15-1	Je Vas Jamais Lessair Pleurer (I'll Never Let You Cry) -1	Vo 05168
MEM-16-1	Te A Pas Raison -1	Vo unissued: *Co CK46220 (CD)*

Frank Mailhes reportedly performed and possibly recorded after 1942 as Frank Miles.

[J.T.] ALLISON'S SACRED HARP SINGERS
ALLISON'S SACRED HARP QUARTETTE

J.T. Allison's Sacred Harp Singers, vocal group; acc. unknown, o.

Birmingham, AL   c. August 10, 1927

GEX-786-A	I Belong To This Band	Ge 6255
GEX-787-A	I'm A Long Time Traveling Away From Home	Ge 6255

Allison's Sacred Harp Singers-1/Allison's Sacred Harp Quartette-2, vocal group; acc. unknown o-3/p-4.
Richmond, IN   Tuesday, May 1, 1928

13755	The Heavenly Port -2, 3	Ge 6514
13756	Long Sought Home -2, 3	Ge 6550
13757	Exhilaration -2, 3	Ge 6550
13758-A	The Loved Ones -1, 3	Ge 6584
13759	The Old Ship Of Zion -1, 3	Ge 6583
13760-A	Primrose Hill -1, 3	Ge 6584
13761	Sweet Morning -1, 3	Ge 6606
13762	Sweet Canaan -1, 3	Ge 6499
13763	The Golden Harp -1, 3	Ge 6499
13764	Weeping Pilgrim -1, 3	Ge 6583
13765	Traveling Pilgrim -1, 3	Ge 6622
13766-A	Hallelujah -1, 3	Ge 6514
13767	Esther -2, 3	Ge 6606
13768-A	The Morning Trumpet -2, 3	Ge 6622
13769-B	Journey Home -2, 3	Ge 6639
13770-A	Sweet Rivers -2, 3	Ge 6639
13771,-A,-B	I Would See Jesus -2, 3	Ge unissued
13772-A	Bound For Canaan -2, 3	Ge 6482
13773	Jewett -2, 3	Ge 6675
13774	Heaven's My Home -2, 3	Ge 6482
13775	Sweet Prospect -2, 4	Ge 6658
13776,-A	Soft Music -2, 4	Ge unissued
13777	Murillo's Lesson -2, 4	Ge 6564
13778	Pisgah -2, 4	Ge 6675
13779	Antioch -2, 4	Ge 6658
13780-A	Weeping Mary -2, 4	Ge 6794
13781	Penick -2, 4	Ge 6794
13782	Sharpsburg -2, 4	Ge 6564
13783	Happy Land -2, 4	Ge 6691
13784-A	Not Made With Hands -2, 4	Ge 6691

AMORY MALE QUARTETTE

Vocal quartet; unacc.
Memphis, TN   Monday, February 27, 1928

400364-B	We're Drifting On	OK 45288
400365-B	Keep Your Eyes On Jesus	OK 45288
400366-	Do Not Wait 'Till I'm Laid 'Neath The Clay	OK unissued
400367-B	Oh! Beautiful City	OK 45210
400368-B	Hold To God's Unchanging Hand	OK 45210

ANDY ANDERSON

Pseudonym on Clarion and Velvet Tone for Frank Marvin.

ELROY ANDERSON

Pseudonym on Broadway for Emry Arthur.

LE ROY ANDERSON (THE RED HEADED BRIER HOPPER)

See The Red Headed Brier Hopper.

ANDREWS BROTHERS

James Andrews, Joshua Floyd Bucy, v/y-1 duet; acc. Slim Smith, f-2; own g duet.
Memphis, TN   Friday, July 7, 1939

MEM-54-1	Prisoner's Farewell	Vo/OK 05272
MEM-55-1	Filling Station Blues	Vo 05029
MEM-62-	Trouble Worries Me -2	Vo unissued
MEM-63-	A Hobo's Life Is Lonely -1	Vo unissued
MEM-64-1	Far Away From My Old Virginia Home	Vo 05109
MEM-65-1	When I'm Travelling Little Darling	Vo 05381
MEM-66-1	Mother's Gone From The Cabin	Vo 05109
MEM-67-1	Weak And Sinful Soul	Vo 05381
MEM-68-1	West Virginia Railroad Blues -1	Vo 05029
MEM-69-1	Mother Watch O'er And Guide Me	Vo/OK 05272

Intervening matrices are by Slim Smith.

The Andrews Brothers who recorded after 1942 are different artists.

ANGLIN BROTHERS
THE ANGLIN TWINS & RED

The Anglin Twins (Jack & Jim)-1, v duet; or **The Anglin Twins & Red**-2: Jack Anglin, Jim Anglin, Red Anglin, v trio; or **Jack & Red Anglin**-3: Jack Anglin, Red Anglin, v duet; acc. Jack Anglin, g.

San Antonio, TX   Friday, November 5, 1937

SA-2903-1	When It's Time For The Whippoorwill To Sing -2	ARC unissued
SA-2904-1	See Them Pine Trees Waving -2	ARC unissued
SA-2905-1	Just Inside The Pearly Gates -1	Vo/OK 04078
SA-2906-1	Take Me Back To Alabama -2	ARC unissued
SA-2907-1	Columbus Stockade Blues -3	ARC unissued
SA-2908-1	Don't Say Good-Bye When You Go -1	Vo 02963, ARC 8-04-52, Cq 8985
SA-2909-1	Lost On The Ocean -2	ARC unissued
SA-2910-1	Short Life Of Trouble -1	ARC unissued
SA-2911-1	No Drunkards Can Enter There -1	Vo/OK 04078
SA-2912-1	Uncle Eph's Got The Coon -2	Vo 03904, ARC 8-02-52
SA-2913-1	Bye And Bye You'll Soon Forget Me -2	Vo 03904, ARC 8-02-52

San Antonio, TX   Saturday, November 6, 1937

SA-2914-1	The Broken Hearted Family -2	ARC unissued
SA-2915-1	In The Land Where's She's At Rest	ARC unissued
SA-2916-1	They Are All Going Home But One -1	Vo 02963, ARC 8-04-52, Cq 8985
SA-2917-1	A Mother's Answer (To All Going Home But One) -1	ARC unissued
SA-2918-1	Nobody Knows The Trouble I've Seen -2	ARC unissued
SA-2919-1	Blow That Lonesome Whistle -2	ARC unissued
SA-2920-1	You Give Me Your Love (And I'll Give You Mine) -2	ARC unissued
SA-2921-1	No Place To Pillow My Head -1	ARC unissued
SA-2922-1	I've Got To Be Gittin' Away -2	ARC unissued

Anglin Brothers: Jack Anglin, Jim Anglin, v duet; or Jack Anglin, Jim Anglin, Red Anglin, v trio-1; acc. one of them, g; poss. another, g on at least some items.

Columbia, SC   Saturday, November 12, 1938

SC-155-	Leaving On That Train	Vo unissued
SC-156-1	When You Don't, Others Do	Vo 04774
SC-157-1	Money Cannot Buy Your Soul	Vo 04579
SC-158-1	Southern Whoopee Song	Vo 04774
SC-159-1	I Loved You Better Than You Knew -1	Vo 04896
SC-160-1	Where The Soul Of Man Never Dies	Vo 04692, Cq 9243
SC-161-	Blow That Lonesome Whistle -1	Vo unissued
SC-162-	Take Me Back -1	Vo unissued
SC-165-1	It's An Unfriendly World	Vo 04579
SC-166-	But Now It's Only A Dream -1	Vo unissued
SC-167-1	You Give Me Your Love (And I'll Give You Mine) -1	Vo 04896
SC-168-	What Does The Deep Sea Say -1	Vo unissued
SC-169-1	It Won't Be Long Till I'll Be Leaving	Vo 04692, Cq 9243
SC-170-	When It's Time For The Whippoorwill To Sing -1	Vo unissued

Matrices SC-163/64 are by Fisher Hendley.

Jack Anglin recorded after 1942 (with Johnnie Wright as Johnnie & Jack).

ANN(I)E, JUDY, & ZEKE (WITH PETE)

See the Canova Family.

GEORGE ANTHONY

Pseudonym on Madison 5006, and probably Madison 50006 and Van Dyke 5006, for Jack Weston.

THE APPALACHIA VAGABOND

Pseudonym on Vocalion for Hayes Shepherd.

AMEDIE ARDOIN

Amédé Ardoin, v; acc. Denus McGee, f; own ac.

New Orleans, LA   Monday, December 9, 1929

111384-2	Taunt Aline (Aunt Aline)	Co 40514-F, OK 90014
111385-2	Two Step De Mama (My Mother's Two Step)	Co 40514-F, OK 90014
111386-2	Madam Atchen (Mrs. Atchen)	Co 40515-F, OK 90015
111387-1	Two Step De La Prairie Soileau (Prairie Soileau Two Step)	Co 40515-F, OK 90015
111388-2	La Valse Ah Abe (Abe's Waltz)	Co 40511-F, OK 90011
111389-2	Two Step De Eunice	Co 40511-F, OK 90011

McGee & Ardoin: Denus McGee, f; Amédé Ardoin, ac/v.
   New Orleans, LA   Thursday, November 20, 1930

Matrix	Title	Issue
NO-6717-A	Amadie Two Step	Br 576, Me M18050
NO-6718-A	La Valse A Austin Ardoin	Br 576, Me M18050
NO-6719-	Blues De Basille	Br 531
NO-6720-	La Valse A Thomas Ardoin	Br 531
NO-6721-	Two Step D'Elton	Br 513
NO-6722-	La Valse De Gueydan	Br 513
NO-6737-	Valse Des Opelousas	Br 559, 80083
NO-6738-	One Step Des Chameaux	Br 559, 80083

Matrix NO-6721 may have been recorded on November 21. Intervening matrices (except NO-6735/36, for which see below) are by other artists.

   New Orleans, LA   Friday, November 21, 1930

Matrix	Title	Issue
NO-6735-	Valse A Alcee Poulard	Br 495
NO-6736-	One Step D'Oberlin	Br 495

Amede Ardoin–Denus McGee: Denus McGee, f; Amédé Ardoin, ac/v.
   San Antonio, TX   Wednesday, August 8, 1934

Matrix	Title	Issue
83854-1	Les Blues De Voyage (Travel Blues)	BB B-2189
83855-1	La Valse De Amities (Love Waltz)	BB B-2189
83856-1	Les Blues De Crowley (Crowley Blues)	BB B-2190
83857-1	Oberlin	BB B-2190
83858-1	Sunset (Sunset)	BB B-2192
83859-1	Tout Que Reste C'Est Mon Linge	BB B-2192

Amedie Ardoin, v; acc. own ac.
   New Orleans, LA   Saturday, December 22, 1934

Matrix	Title	Issue
39195-B	Tostape De Jennings (Tostape Of Jennings)	De 17002
39196-B	Le Midland Two-Step	De 17003
39197-A	La Valse Des Chantiers Petroliferes (Waltz Of The Oil Field)	De 17002
39198-A	Valse Brunette	De 17007
39199-A	Tortope D'Osrun	De 17007
39200-A	La Valse Du Ballard	De 17014
39201-A	La Turtape De Saroied (The Turtape Of Saroied)	De 17023
39202-A	Valse De La Pointe D'Eglise (Church Point Waltz)	De 17023
39203-A	Les Blues De La Prison (The Jail House Blues)	De 17014
39204-A	Valse De Mon Vieux Village (My Old Home Town Waltz)	De 17003
39205-A	Si Dur D'Etre Seul (So Hard To Be Alone)	De 17033
39206-A	Aimez-Moi Ce Soir (Love Me Tonight)	De 17033

THE ARIZONA WRANGLERS

Poss.: Len "Dynamite" Dossey, f; Cal "Sleepy" Short, h; Joe "Hungry" Ivans, md/v-1; Chas. "Irontail" Hunter, bj-md/v-2; Laverne "Slicker" Costello, bj; J.E. "Nubbins" Patterson, g; Loyal "Sheriff" Underwood, sp. (This is the lineup shown in a photograph in an approximately contemporary folio and may not be wholly accurate for this session, but the vocalists' identities are confirmed by the session-sheets.)
   Los Angeles, CA   Monday, March 16, 1931

Matrix	Title	Issue
LAT-971-A,-B	Little Joe The Wrangler -2	Br unissued trial recording
LAT-972-A,-B	Tying Knot's [sic] In The Devil's Tail -1	Br unissued trial recording

Same as or similar to above. Loyal Underwood, sp introductions; band v-2.
   prob. Hollywood, CA   unknown date

Matrix	Title	Issue
L-930-A	Red River Valley -1	Merry Xmas unnumbered
L-931- -	Twelfth Street Rag	Merry Xmas unnumbered
L-932-A	Going Back To Arizona -2	Merry Xmas unnumbered
L-933- -	West Coast Special	Merry Xmas unnumbered

The mandolinist featured on L-931 is identified as "Shorty." Matrix L-933 consists of a band instrumental of *Casey Jones* and a harmonica solo of the title tune. These items were recorded by Freeman-Lang, Hollywood, and coupled L-930/L-931, L-932/L-933.

   prob. Hollywood, CA   unknown date

Matrix	Title	Issue
L-948- -	Wreck Of The 97 -1	Merry Xmas unnumbered

J.E. "Nubbins" Patterson, v; acc. unidentified, md; unidentified, bj; poss. own g.
   prob. Hollywood, CA   unknown date

Matrix	Title	Issue
L-949- -	Strawberry Roan	Merry Xmas unnumbered

Matrices L-948/L-949 are coupled on a 12-inch disc.

ARKANSAS BAREFOOT BOYS

Cyrus Futrell, f/v eff-1; James Leroy "Roy" Sims, h; William Campbell, h; Hubert Haines, g.
 Memphis, TN   Tuesday, February 14, 1928
   400227-   Benton County Hog Thief -1   OK unissued
   400228-B   I Love Somebody   OK 45217
   400229-B   Eighth Of January   OK 45217
   400230-   The Prisoner At The Bar   OK unissued

ARKANSAS CHARLIE

See Charlie Craver.

ARKANSAS RAMBLER

Pseudonym on ARC-Broadway for Arkansas Woodchopper.

[THE] ARKANSAS WOODCHOPPER

This artist's real name is Luther W. Ossenbrink.

The Arkansas Woodchopper, v; acc. own g.
 Dallas, TX   Thursday, December 6, 1928
   147585-1   The Cowboy's Dream   Co 15463-D
   147586-1   The Dying Cowboy   Co 15463-D

Arkansas Woodchopper, v/y-1; acc. own g.
 Richmond, IN   Thursday, October 17, 1929
   15777-A   Barney McCoy   Ge 7095, Ch 15897, Spt 9569
   15778-A   The Prisoner At The Bar -1   Ge 7154, Spt 9639
   15779   Home On The Range   Ge 7065, Spt 9571
   15780-A   The Cowboy's Dream   Ge 7065, Ch 15897, Spt 9571
   15781-A   Zeb Turney's Gal   Ge 7095, Ch 16053, Spt 9570, Spr 2590
   15782-A   Frankie And Johnnie   Ge 7036, Ch 15852, 45058, 33064, Spt 9569, Spr 2590
   15783-A   In The Jailhouse Now -1   Ge 7036, Ch 15852, 45058, Spt 9570
   15784   The Gypsy's Warning   Ge rejected

Champion 15852, 15897, 16053 as by **The West Virginia Rail Splitter**. Champion 45058, Supertone 9569, 9570, 9571, 9639 as by **The Arkansas Woodchopper**. Superior 2590 as by **James Burke**. Rev. Champion 33064 by Merritt Smith.

 Richmond, IN   Monday, February 10, 1930
   16236-B   Write Me A Song About Father   Spt 9665
   16237   If Brother Jack Were Here   Ge 7126, Spt 9628
   16238-B   Old And Only In The Way   Ge 7154, Ch 15943, 45192, Spt 9639
   16239   Take Me Back To Colorado   Ge 7126, Ch 15943, Spt 9628
   16240   An Old Man's Story   Ge rejected
   16241   A Hard Luck Guy   Ge 7184, Ch 15990, Spt 9664
   16242   The Habit -1   Ge 7184, Ch 15990, Spt 9664
   16243   The Gypsy's Warning   Ge rejected
   16244   The Little Green Valley   Ge 7264, Ch 16095, 45192, Spt 9643
   16245   Sweet Evelina   Ch 16053
   16245-A   Sweet Evelina   Ge 7264, Spt 9643
   16246   The Dying Ranger   Ch 16095, Spt 9665

Champion 15943, 15990, 16053, 16095 as by **The West Virginia Rail-Splitter**. Champion 45192, Supertone 9639 as by **The Arkansas Woodchopper**.

 New York, NY   Wednesday, November 11, 1931
   10980-3   Little Green Valley   Cq 7884, Bwy 4053
   10981-2   When It's Harvest Time My Sweet Angeline Cq 7884
   10982-1   I'm A Texas Cowboy -1   Cq 7883

Rev. Broadway 4053 by Vernon Dalhart & Carson Robison.

 New York, NY   Thursday, November 12, 1931
   10991-2   Little-Ah-Sid -1   Cq 7887
   10992-1   Sweet Sunny South -1   Cq 7880
   10993-2   If I Could Only Blot Out The Past   Cq 7880
   10994-2   Old Pal -1   Cq 7885
   10995-2   Daddy And Home -1   Cq 7885, ARC-Bwy 8109
   10996-2   Little Blossom   Cq 7886
   10997-2   Mrs. Murphy's Chowder   Cq 7879
   10998-2   Just Plain Folks -1   Cq 7881
   10999-3   Cowboy Jack   Cq 7882, MeC 91539

ARC-Broadway 8109 as by **Arkansas Rambler**.
Revs: ARC-Broadway 8109 by Ed (Jake) West; Melotone 91539 by Cliff Carlisle & Wilbur Ball.

    New York, NY   Friday, November 13, 1931

10983-1	The Last Great Roundup	Cq 7882
11006-2	Mary Dow	Cq 7886
11007-2	Frankie And Albert	Cq 7879
11008-2	The Bronc That Wouldn't Bust -1	Cq 7883, MeC 91541
11009-1	What Is A Home Without Love -1	Cq 7881
11010-2,-3	Dollar Down And A Dollar A Week With Chicken Pie	Cq 7887

Rev. Melotone 91541 by Asa Martin.

Arkansas (Arkie) Woodchopper & His Square Dance Band: unknown, f; unknown, bj; unknown, sb; Arkansas Woodchopper, calls.

    Chicago, IL   Tuesday, June 10, 1941

C-3875-1	Arkansas Traveler	OK 06296, Co 20444
C-3876-1	Mississippi Sawyer	OK 06296, Co 20444
C-3877-1	Soldiers Joy	OK 06297, Co 20445
C-3878-1	Sallie Goodwin	OK 06297, Co 20445
C-3879-1	Walkin' Up Town	OK 06298, Co 20446
C-3880-1	Wagoner	OK 06298, Co 20446
C-3881-1	My Love Is But A Lassie 'O	OK 06299, Co 20447
C-3882-1	Light Foot Bill	OK 06299, Co 20447

ARMSTRONG & HIGHLEY

Vocal duet; acc. prob. one of them, g.

    Grafton, WI   c. January/February 1932

L-1392-1	Climbing Jacob's Ladder	Pm 3291
L-1393-2	No More Dying	Pm 3291

ARMSTRONG & JACOBS

Pseudonym on Supertone for Nicholson's Players.

ARMSTRONG'S PLAYERS

Pseudonym on Supertone for Nicholson's Players.

GENE ARNOLD

This artist's work is beyond the scope of this book. The name was also used as a pseudonym on Lyric for Frank Marvin.

BROTHER JAMES ARNOLD & CONGREGATION

Sermons with singing; acc. prob.: William Rexroat, g/v; Emry Arthur, g/v; Jossie Ellers, v.

    Chicago, IL   Wednesday, January 9, 1929

C-2775-	Husks With The Swine	Vo 5304
C-2776-	Get Understanding	Vo 5304

ARNOLD BROTHERS

Pseudonym on Aurora A22038 and A22039 for the Kessinger Brothers and on Aurora A22023 for The Pickard Family.

ART, ANDY, BERT & DAVE

Pseudonym on Clarion and Velvet Tone for the Buck Mt. Band.

EMRY ARTHUR

Emry & Henry Arthur, v duet; acc. Emry Arthur, h-1; unknown, sg; Henry Arthur, bj-2; unknown, g-3.

    Chicago, IL   Tuesday, January 17, 1928

C-1531*/32	Love Lifted Me -1, 2	Vo 5205
C-1533*/34	Shining For The Master -1, 2	Vo 5205
C-1543*/44	Heave Ho – The Anchor -1	Vo 5209
C-1545*/46	I Can Never Forget -1, 2	Vo 5206
C-1551/52*	The Little Black Train Is Coming -2, 3	Vo 5229
C-1553/54*	She's A Flower From The Fields Of Alabama -2, 3	Vo 5234

Matrices C-1547 to C-1550 are by Rochford & Peggs (with Emry Arthur).

Emry Arthur, v; acc. unknown, sg; Henry Arthur, bj.

    Chicago, IL   Wednesday, January 18, 1928

C-1539/40*	I Am A Man Of Constant Sorrow	Vo 5208
C-1541*/42	Down In Tennessee Valley	Vo 5208

Emry & Henry Arthur, v duet; acc. Emry Arthur, h; unknown, sg; Henry Arthur, sg.
 Chicago, IL   Thursday, January 19, 1928
  C-1535/36*   Goodbye, My Lover, Goodbye   Vo 5209
  C-1537*/38   I'll Remember You Love In My Prayers   Vo 5206

Emry Arthur, v; acc. own h-1/g.
 Indianapolis, IN   Wednesday, June 20, 1928
  IND-639-   Wandering Gypsy Girl   Vo 5234
  IND-640-   Let That Liar Alone -1   Vo 5229
  IND-641-   Going Around The World -1   Vo 5230
  IND-642-   Nobody's Business -1   Vo 5230

Emry Arthur & Frank Owens, v duet; acc. prob. Emry Arthur, h-1/g.
 Indianapolis, IN   Monday, June 25, 1928
  IND-637-   Bring Back To Me My Wandering Boy   Vo 5244
  IND-638-   Your Mother's Going To Leave You Bye And Bye -1   Vo 5244

Emry Arthur & The Cumberland Singers: Emry Arthur, prob. Frank Owens, v duet; or Emry Arthur, prob. Frank Owens, unknown, v trio-1; acc. unknown, o-2; poss. Emry Arthur, g-3.
 Indianapolis, IN   Monday, June 25, 1928
  IND-654-   Where The Gates Swing Outward Never -2   Vo 5228
  IND-655-   I Shall Know By The Print Of The Nails On His Hand -2   Vo 5228
  IND-656-   Where The Silvery Colorado Wends Its Way -1, 3   Vo 5225
  IND-659-   In The Heart Of The City That Has No Heart -3   Vo 5225
Matrices IND-657/58 are by Floyd Thompson & His Home Towners.

Arthur's Sacred Singers, vocal group; acc. unknown, o.
 Chicago, IL   Thursday, July 19, 1928
  C-2077-A,-B   Meet Mother In The Skies   Vo unissued
  C-2078-A,-B   There's A Joy In Righteous Living   Vo unissued
  C-2079-A,-B   No, Not One   Vo unissued
  C-2080-A,-B   Why Not Tonight   Vo unissued
  C-2081-A,-B   Victory Ahead   Vo unissued
  C-2082-B   If Jesus Goes With Me   Vo unissued

Emry Arthur, v; acc. unknown, f-1; poss. own h-2/g.
 Chicago, IL   Thursday, July 19, 1928
  C-2083-A,-B   The Rich Man And Joe Smith -1   Vo unissued
  C-2084-A,-B   Ethan Lang -1, 2   Vo unissued
  C-2087-A,-B   Train Whistle Blues   Vo unissued
  C-2088-A,-B   Empty Pocket Blues   Vo unissued
Matrices C-2085/86, C-2089 to 2092 are by Floyd Thompson & His Home Towners (latter block with Emry Arthur).

Acc. own h-1/g.
 Chicago, IL   Thursday, August 30, 1928
  C-2276-   Ethan Lang -1   Vo 5249
  C-2277-   Empty Pocket Blues   Vo 5264
  C-2278-   The Rich Man And Joe Smith   Vo 5249
  C-2279-   Train Whistle Blues   Vo 5264

Arthur's Sacred Singers: Emry Arthur, poss. Frank Owens, v duet; acc. unknown, o.
 Chicago, IL   Thursday, August 30, 1928
  C-2880-   Meet Mother In The Skies   Vo 5326
  C-2881-   There's A Joy In Righteous Living   Vo 5326
  C-2882-   No, Not One   Vo 5245
  C-2883-   Why Not Tonight   Vo 5245
  C-2884-A,-B   If Jesus Goes With Me   Vo unissued
  C-2285-A,-B   Victory Ahead   Vo unissued
Matrices C-2286 to C-2289 are by Floyd Thompson & His Home Towners with Emry Arthur.

Emry Arthur & William Rexroat, v duet; acc. Emry Arthur, h-1/g; unknown, bj-2; prob. William Rexroat, g-3.
 Chicago, IL   Tuesday, January 8, 1929
  C-2766   The Wanderer -1   Vo 5335
  C-2769   The White Rose -2, 3   Vo 5335
Matrices C-2767/68 are by Jossie Ellers.

 Chicago, IL   Wednesday, January 9, 1929
  C-2772-   I Tickled Her Under The Chin   Vo 5323
Matrices C-2770/71 are by William Rexroat's Cedar Crest Singers.
Rev. Vocalion 5323 by William Rexroat's Cedar Crest Singers.

Emry Arthur, v; acc. own g.
    Chicago, IL   Wednesday, January 9, 1929

| C-2773- | My Girl – She's A Lulu | Vo 5288 |
| C-2774- | Mary Don't Go | Vo 5288 |

The Jack Harmonica Player: Emry Arthur, h solo.
    Chicago, IL   Wednesday, June 17, 1929

| C-3622- | Mouth Harp Blues | Vo 5353 |
| C-3623- | Five Miles/Intro: Turkey In The Straw – Arkansas Traveller | Vo 5353 |

Emry Arthur, v; acc. own g.
    Chicago, IL   Wednesday, June 17, 1929

| C-3624- | The Blind Boy | Vo 5358 |

    Chicago, IL   Thursday, June 18, 1929

C-3629-	Frankie Baker – Part I	Vo 5340
C-3630-	Frankie Baker – Part II	Vo 5340
C-3631-	My Mother-In-Law	Vo 5354
C-3632-	Mother's In Heaven Tonight	Vo 5358
C-3633-	The Bootlegger's Song	Vo 5385
C-3634-	Remember The Old Folks Back Home	Vo 5396
C-3635-	Prison Bound Blues	Vo 5351
C-3636-	Mountain Daddy Blues	Vo 5351
C-3637-	I Got Drunk And I Got Married	Vo 5354

Matrices C-3625 to C-3628 are by Leroy Carr (see *B&GR*). Rev. Vocalion 5385, 5396 by Clarence Ganus.

    Grafton, WI   c. September 1929

| L-30-3 | The Broken Wedding | Pm 3221, Bwy 8261 |
| L-31-3 | I'm Always Thinking Of You | Pm 3221, Bwy 8261 |

Broadway 8261 as by **Elroy Anderson**.

Emry Arthur, v; or **Emry Arthur & Della Hatfield**-1, v duet; acc. Emry Arthur, g.
    Grafton, WI.   c. October/November 1929

L-105-1	The Bluefield Murder -1	Pm 3222
L-106-2	George Collins -1	Pm 3222
L-107-1	Reuben Oh Reuben	Pm 3237, 3295, Bwy 8216
L-108-1	She Lied To Me	Pm 3237, 3295, Bwy 8216
	The Bloodstained Dress -1	Pm 3243
	The Day I Left Home -1	Pm 3243

Paramount 3295, Broadway 8216 as by **Elroy Anderson**. Matrices L-109/10 are untraced and may apply to Paramount 3243.

Emry Arthur, v; or **Emry Arthur & Della Hatfield**-1, v duet; acc. Emry Arthur, g.
    Grafton, WI   c. October/November 1929

L-130-1,-2	Gone But Not Forgotten	Pm unissued
L-131-2	Jennie My Own True Love -1	Pm 3249, Bwy 8266
L-132-2	A Railroad Lover For Me -1	Pm 3249, Bwy 8266
L-133-1	Sunshine And Shadows -1	Pm 3251, Bwy 8267, LA 3
L-134-1	True Love Divine -1	Pm 3251, Bwy 8267, LA 3

Emry Arthur, v; or **Emry Arthur & Della Hatfield**-1, v duet; acc. unknown, bj-2; Emry Arthur, g.
    Grafton, WI   c. April/May 1931

L-956-2	The Married Man	Pm 3289
L-957-2	I'm A Man Of Constant Sorrow -2	Pm 3289
L-958-1	Got Drunk And Got Married	Pm 3301
L-959-1	I Tickled Her Under The Chin	Pm 3301
L-962-1	I'm Going Back To The Girl I Love	Pm 3298
L-967-3	Careless Love	Pm 3298
L-969-2	There's A Treasure Up In Heaven -1	Pm 3290
L-970-1	Short Life Of Trouble -2	Pm 3290

Paramount 3301 as by **Emery Arthur**. Despite the label credit, matrix L-970 is a vocal solo by Arthur. Intervening matrices are untraced, but some at least are likely to be by Emry Arthur.

Emry Arthur & Delle [sic] **Hatfield**, v duet; acc. prob. Emry Arthur, g.
    Richmond, IN   Tuesday, September 29, 1931

| 18063 | Wait Till The Clouds Roll By | Ge rejected |

Emry Arthur, v; acc. own g; unknown, train-wh eff-1.
    Chicago, IL   Thursday, January 17, 1935

| C-9662-A | The Broken Wedding | De 5067 |
| C-9663-A | Six Months In Jail Ain't Long | De 5127, Min M-14151 |

C-9664-A	Look Out For The Window	De 5085
C-9665-A	Ramblin' Hobo Blues -1	De 5068, Min M-14152
C-9666-A	I'm Always Thinking Of You	De 5085
C-9667-A	Don't Get Married	De 5068, Min M-14152
C-9668-A	The Bootlegger's Lullaby	De 5127, Min M-14151
C-9669-A	My Own True Lover	De 5067

ARTHURS CAMP BOYS

Pseudonym on Elite for Arthur Fields & Fred Hall.

ARTHUR'S SACRED SINGERS

See Emry Arthur.

ASHABRANER & SPURGEON

See Nicholson's Players.

ASHFORD QUARTETTE

Vocal quartet; acc. unknown, g.
    Chicago, IL   Tuesday, December 3, 1929

C-4781-A	Grand Old Chariot	Br 393
C-4782-A	Lost	Br 393
C-4783-A	You Can't Make A Monkey Out Of Me	Br 456
C-4784-A,-B	Work – Watch – Pray	Br rejected
C-4785-A,-B	Waiting The Boatman	Br rejected
C-4786-A	Out On The Ocean	Br 456

Brunswick 456 as by **Ashford Quartet**.

    Chicago, IL   Wednesday, December 4, 1929

C-4789-A	Ready To Go, I'll Be	Br 402
C-4790-A,-B	Beautiful Home Somewhere	Br rejected
C-4791-A	Where Is Your Boy Tonight?	Br 402
C-4792-A,-B	In The Golden Bye And Bye	Br rejected

Matrices C-4787/88 are untraced.

CLARENCE ASHLEY

See Thomas C. Ashley.

CLYDE ASHLEY

Pseudonym on Superior for Bill Cox.

THOMAS C. ASHLEY

Thomas C. Ashley, v; acc. Dwight Bell, bj-1; own g.
    Richmond, IN   Thursday, February 2, 1928

13419	Ohio Lovers -1	Ge unissued
13420,-A	Drunkard's Dream -1	Ge rejected
13421	You're A Little Too Small -1	Ge 6404, Ch 15525, Chg 391
13422	Four Night's Experience	Ge 6404, Chg 405

Champion 15525 as by **Oscar Brown**. Challenge 391, 405 as by **Tom Hutchinson**.
Revs: Champion 15525 by H.K. Hutchison; Challenge 391 by John McGhee, 405 by Vernon Dalhart.

Clarence Ashley, v; acc. own bj.
    Johnson City, TN   Wednesday, October 23, 1929

149250-2	Dark Holler Blues	Co 15489-D
149251-2	The Coo-Coo Bird	Co 15489-D
149252-2	Little Sadie	Co 15522-D
149253-2	Naomi Wise	Co 15522-D

    Atlanta, GA   Monday, April 14, 1930

150210-; 194982-1	The House Carpenter	Co 15654-D
150211-; 194983-1	Old John Hardy	Co 15654-D
150212-	Ain't Got No Money Babe	Co unissued
150213-	Bitter Pill Blues	Co unissued
150214-	Dear, I Love You	Co unissued
150215-	I Once Knew A Little Girl	Co unissued

Ashley & Foster: Gwen Foster, h/g/v-1; Thomas C. Ashley, g/v.
   New York, NY   Wednesday, September 6, 1933

13959-2	Sideline Blues	Vo 02611
13960-1	Rising Sun Blues	Vo 02576
13961-1	Sadie Ray -1	Vo 02900
13962-1	Greenback Dollar	Vo/OK 02554, Cq 9112
13963-2	East Virginia Blues	Vo 02576
13964-1,-2	You're Going To Leave The Old Home, Jim -1	Vo unissued

Ashley & Foster-1/**Gwyn Foster**-2: Gwen Foster, h/g-3/v-4; Thomas C. Ashley, g/v-5.
   New York, NY   Thursday, September 7, 1933

13967-1	One Dark And Stormy Night -1, 3, 4, 5	Vo 02750
13968-1	Faded Roses -1, 4, 5	Vo 02666
13969-1	The Old Arm Chair -1, 3, 4, 5	Vo 02647
13970-2	Let Him Go God Bless Him -1, 3, 5?	Vo 02666
13971-2	Bay Rum Blues -1, 5	Vo 02611
13972-2	My North Carolina Home -2, 3, 4	Vo 02900

Ashley & Foster-1/**Gwyn Foster**-2: Gwen Foster, h-3/g-4/v-5; unknown, md-6; Thomas C. Ashley, g/v-7.
   New York, NY   Friday, September 8, 1933

13975-1	Ain't No Use To High Hat Me -1, 3, 7	Vo 02789
13976-1,-2	When I Had But Fifty Cents -1, 3, 7	Vo unissued
13977-1	Times Ain't Like They Used To Be -1, 3, 7	Vo/OK 02554, Cq 9112, Pan 25616
13978-	We Courted In The Rain -1, 6, 7	Vo unissued
13979-1	Down At The Old Man's House -2, 3, 5	Vo 02750, Pan 25642
13980-1	Go 'Way And Let Me Sleep -1, 3, 4, 7	Vo 02789
13981-	I Love My Baby -2, 3, 4, 5	Vo unissued
13982-	Bull Dog Sal -1, 3, 4, 7	Vo unissued
13983-2	Frankie Silvers -1, 3, 4, 7	Vo 02647
13984-	My Mother Scolds Me For Flirting -1, 3, 4, 7	Vo unissued

Revs: Panachord 25616 by Frank Welling & John McGhee, 25642 by Frank Marvin.

Thomas Clarence Ashley also recorded with the Blue Ridge Entertainers (some items being issued as by Tom Ashley) and the Carolina Tar Heels, and after 1942.

ASHLEY & ABERNATHY
ASHLEY & FOSTER
ASHLEY & GREEN[E]

See Thomas C. Ashley and Blue Ridge Mountain Entertainers entries.

ASHLEY'S MELODY MAKERS
ASHLEY'S MELODY MEN

Ashley's Melody Men: Anson Fuller, f-1; Vern Baker, f-2; Hobart N. Ashley, sg/v-3; Homer Treat, bj; Arle Baker, g; unidentified, calls-4; band sp-4.
   Memphis, TN   Wednesday, October 2, 1929

56331-2	There'll Be No Kisses To-night -3	Vi V-40199
56332- -	Sweetest Flower Waltz -1	Vi V-40199
56333-1	Bath House Blues -1	Vi V-40158
56334-1	Searcy County Rag -1, 2, 4	Vi V-40158

Ashley's Melody Makers: Hobart N. Ashley, sg-1/v-2; Homer Treat, bj; Hubert M. Ashley, v/y-3.
   Memphis, TN   Wednesday, June 4, 1930

62569-1	Somewhere In Arkansas -1, 2, 3	Vi V-40300
62570-2	I'm Lonely Too -1, 2	Vi 23767
62571-1,-2	If Father And Mother Would Forgive	Vi unissued
62572-1,-2	The Lonely Child	Vi unissued
62573-2	The Rambling Woman -1, 3	Vi V-40300
62574-2	Come Back, Lottie -3	Vi 23767

Ashley's Melody Men: Gerald Ashley, h-1; Hobart N. Ashley, sg-2/v-3; Hubert M. Ashley, g/v/y-4.
   Dallas, TX   Wednesday, February 10, 1932

70672-1	Methodist Pie -3, 4	Vi 23661
70681-1	I Settled It All -2, 3	Vi unissued
70682-1	I Never Felt So Blue -2, 4	Vi 23661
70683-1	Dandy Dan -1	Vi unissued

Matrices 70673 to 70678 are by Walter Davis; 70679/80 by James "Stump" Johnson (see *B&GR* for both).

P.H. ASHWORTH

P.H. Ashworth, v; acc. unknown.
    Atlanta, GA   Saturday, November 5, 1927

145118-	Walking Home With Jesus	Co unissued
145119-	Come On Board The Ship Of Glory	Co unissued

ASPARAGUS JOE

Pseudonym on Champion for Pie Plant Pete.

BOB ATCHER
BOB & RANDALL ATCHER
BOB ATCHER & BONNIE BLUE EYES

Bob Atcher, v; or **Bob Atcher & Bonnie Blue Eyes**-1, v duet; or **Bonnie Blue Eyes**-2, v; acc. Reggie Cross, h; Rusty Gill, g; Bob Atcher, g; Howard Black, sb.
    Chicago, IL   Monday, May 15, 1939

WC-2562-1	Those Eyes Of Grey -1	Vo 04882
WC-2563-1	My Buddy, My Daddy, My Pal -1	Vo/OK 04948
WC-2564-1	I Found My Cowgirl Sweetheart	Vo 05001, Cq 9338
WC-2565-1	The Lonesome Mountain -2	Vo/OK 04948
WC-2566-1	Family Prayers -1	Vo/OK 05069
WC-2567-2	Blow, Whistle, Blow -1	Vo 04882
WC-2568-1	The Letter That Went To God	Vo/OK 05069
WC-2569-1	When The Locust Is In Bloom -1	Vo 05001, Cq 9338

    Chicago, IL   Friday, September 15, 1939

WC-2738-A	You Love Me Or You Don't (Make Up Your Mind) -1	Vo/OK 05134, Cq 9379, Co 37443, 20170
WC-2739-A	Whisper Goodbye	Vo/OK 05323, Cq 9677
WC-2740-A	Oh Darling -1	Vo/OK 05245
WC-2741-A	The War Baby's Prayer -2	Vo/OK 05177
WC-2742-A	I'm Always Dreaming Of You	Vo unissued
WC-2743-A	Going Home To Mother -1	Vo/OK 05177
WC-2744-A	Broken Vows -1	Vo/OK 05323, Cq 9676
WC-2745-A	I'm Thinking Tonight Of My Blue Eyes	Vo/OK 05134, Cq 9379, Co 37443, 20170, M-412, OK 6925
WC-2746-A	The Picture On The Mantle -2	Vo/OK 05245

Matrix WC-2745 is titled *The Crying Song (I'm Thinking Tonight Of My Blue Eyes)* on Columbia 20170.
Rev. OKeh 6925 (a 1952 issue) *The Laughing Record No. 1* (anonymous early-'20s recording).

Acc. Shorty Michaels, f; Eddie Powers, ac; Randall Atcher, g; Bob Atcher, g; Bill Vance, sb.
    Chicago, IL   Wednesday, January 17, 1940

WC-2862-A	You Are My Sunshine -1	Vo/OK 05370, Cq 9381, Co 37741, 20318, L3
WC-2863-A	Crying Myself To Sleep	Vo/OK 05370, Cq 9381, Co 37741, 20318
WC-2864-A	You're My Darling -1	Vo/OK 05402, Cq 9380, Co 37742, 20319
WC-2865-A	The Last Letter -1	Vo/OK 05402, Cq 9380, Co 37742, 20319

Bob Atcher, v; or **Bob Atcher & Bonnie Blue Eyes**-1, v duet; or **Bonnie Blue Eyes**-2, v; or **Bob & Randall Atcher**-3, v duet; or **Bob & Randall Atcher & Bonnie Blue Eyes**-4, v trio; acc. Randall Atcher, md; Bob Atcher, g; Bill Vance, sb.
    Chicago, IL   Thursday, June 13, 1940

WC-3116-A	I'm Not Coming Home Tonight -1	OK 05652
WC-3117-A	Sal's Got A Meatskin Laid Away -1	OK unissued
WC-3118-A	Papa's Going Crazy – Mama's Going Mad -3	OK unissued: Co C4K47911 (CD)
WC-3119-A	Cool Water -4	OK 05808, Cq 9674, Co 37815, 20354, CoC C1008
WC-3120-A	Seven Beers With The Wrong Man -2	OK 05652
WC-3121-A	Are You Sure -1	OK 05993, Cq 9673

    Chicago, IL   Tuesday, June 18, 1940

WC-3132-A	I Won't Care (A Hundred Years From Now) -1	OK 05755, Cq 9595, Co 37751, 20328
WC-3133-A	I Dream Of Your Bonnie Blue Eyes -3	OK 05697, Cq 9597, Co 37649, 20248
WC-3134-A	I Wish It Wasn't So -1	OK 05993, Cq 9674
WC-3135-A	Pennsylvania Pal -4	OK 05808, Co 37815, 20354, CoC C1008
WC-3136-A	She's Not My Curly Headed Baby -1	OK 05697, Cq 9597, Co 37649, 20248
WC-3137-A	Now I Know Somebody Doesn't Care -1	OK 05755, Cq 9595, Co 37751, 20328

Bob Atcher & Bonnie Blue Eyes, v duet; or Bonnie Blue Eyes, v-1; acc. poss. Shorty Michaels, f; Eddie Powers, ac; Randall Atcher, g; Bob Atcher, g; Bill Vance, sb.
    Chicago, IL   Wednesday, October 9, 1940

C-3399-1	A Face I See At Evening	OK 05866, Cq 9578, Co 37753, 20330
C-3400-1	No One To Kiss Me Goodnight -1	OK 05928, Cq 9578, Co 37755, 20332
C-3401-1	You Waited Too Long -1	OK 05866, Cq 9677, Co 37753, 20330
C-3402-1	We Never Dream The Same Dream Twice -1	OK 05928, Cq 9676, Co 37755, 20332

Although issued as by **Bob Atcher & Bonnie Blue Eyes**, matrices C-3400 and C-3402 are vocal solos by Bonnie Blue Eyes.

Bob Atcher, v; or **Bob Atcher & Bonnie Blue Eyes**-1, v duet; or Bonnie Blue Eyes, v-2; or **Randall Atcher**-3, v; acc. poss. Shorty Michaels, f; Eddie Powers, ac; Randall Atcher, g; Bob Atcher, g; Bill Vance, sb.

Chicago, IL   Tuesday, January 21, 1941

C-3532-1	Don't Say Goodbye Little Darling	OK 06041, Cq 9816
C-3533-1	I'm Lending You To Uncle Sammy -2	OK 06041, Cq 9673
C-3534-1	Blues In Jail -3	OK 06138, Cq 9672
C-3535-1	Now That You're Gone (Oh My Darling!) -1	Cq 9816, Co 20527
C-3536-1	Answer To You Are My Sunshine -1	OK 06090, Cq 9672, CoC C330
C-3537-1	You'll Always Have My Heart	OK 06090, Cq 9675, CoC C330
C-3538-1	Goin' South -3	OK 06138, Cq 9675

Although issued as by **Bob Atcher & Bonnie Blue Eyes**, matrix C-3533 is a vocal solo by Bonnie Blue Eyes.

Acc. unknown, f; unknown, ac; two unknowns, g; unknown, sb; Lou Singer, vb.

Chicago, IL   Sunday, April 27, 1941

C-3799-1	Always Alone -1	OK 06326
C-3800-1	Weary, Worried And Blue -1	OK 06326
C-3801-1	Poor Little Rose -1	OK 06395
C-3802-1	Will You Be True -1	OK 06453, Cq 9817
C-3803-1	There'll Be A Day -1	OK 06453, Cq 9817
C-3804-1	Doesn't Matter Anymore	OK 06395
C-3805-1	Take Me Back Again -1	OK 06263, Cq 9815
C-3806-1	I Wonder Where You Are Tonight -1	OK 06263, Cq 9815

At least some of the accompanists may be Columbia house musicians.

Acc. Koby Sirinski, f; prob. Marshall Sosson, f; Eddie Fritz, ac; unknown, g; unknown, sb.

Chicago, IL   Tuesday, November 11, 1941

C-4036-1	Walking The Floor Over You	OK 06496, Co 37432, 20159
C-4037-1	Sweethearts Or Strangers -1	OK 06496, Co 37432, 20159
C-4038-1	I'm Reading Your Letter Again, Dear -1	OK 06495
C-4039-1	Let's Start Life All Over -1	OK 06495

Acc. Koby Sirinski or Marshall Sosson, f; Eddie Fritz, ac; unknown, g; unknown, sb.

Chicago, IL   Tuesday, January 20, 1942

C-4129-1	Let's Tell Our Dream To The Moon -1	OK 06602, Co 37418, 20145
C-4130-1	In The Echo Of My Heart -1	OK 06602, Co 37418, 20145
C-4131-1	Nobody Knows But Me And You	Co 20527
C-4132-1	Time Will Tell -1	Co 20468, CoC C1158
C-4133-1	Don't Let Your Sweet Love Die	OK 06639, Co 37411, 20138
C-4134-1	Honest I Do	OK 06639, Co 37411, 20138

Matrices C-4131 and C-4132 were scheduled for OKeh 06677 but never issued.

Bob Atcher & Bonnie Blue Eyes: Bob Atcher, v; acc. Koby Sirinski or Marshall Sosson, f; Eddie Fritz, ac; unknown, p-1; unknown, g; unknown, sb; Ken Carson, wh-2.

Chicago, IL   Tuesday, May 5, 1942

CCO-4240-1	Sorrow On My Mind	OK 6686, Co 37409, 20136
CCO-4241-1	Why Should I Cry Over You -1	OK 6686, Co 37409, 20136
CCO-4242-1	Time Alone	OK 6689, Co 37407, 20134
CCO-4243-1	Pins And Needles (In My Heart) -2	OK 6689, Co 37407, 20134

Bob and Randall Atcher recorded after 1942.

THE ATCO QUARTET

Will Hartsey, Grady Looney, Bill Cagle, Dee Abernathy, vocal quartet; acc. Velma Abernathy, p.

Atlanta, GA   Monday, November 7, 1927

| 145140-1 | The Rich Young Ruler | Co 15312-D, Ve 7110-V |
| 145141-2 | Don't Be Knocking | Co 15312-D, Ve 7102-V |

Leroy Abernathy is thought to have attended the session as a non-participant.
Revs: Velvet Tone 7102-V by Grant Brothers & Their Music, 7110-V by Stroup Quartet.

THE AUGUSTA TRIO

Pseudonym on Champion for Shores' Southern Trio (see Bill Shores).

AUSTIN BROTHERS
Pseudonym on ARC-Broadway 4061 and 8194 for Frank & James McCravy.

GENE AUTRY

Gene Autry–Jimmie Long, v duet; acc. unknown, f-1; Frank Marvin, sg/y; Johnny Marvin, sg.
New York, NY   Wednesday, October 9, 1929

| 56761-2 | My Dreaming Of You | Vi V-40200 |
| 56762-2 | My Alabama Home -1 | Vi V-40200 |

Gene Autry, v/y; acc. Frank Marvin, sg-1; own g.
Long Island City, NY   mid-October 1929

3684	Stay Away From My Chicken House	GG 4314, Rad 4314, VD 84314, 5114, 5120
3685-A	My Oklahoma Home-1	GG 4281, Rad 4281, VD 74281, 5115
3965	I'll Be Thinking Of You Little Gal -1	QRS 1044, Sr 33070
3966	Cowboy Yodel	GG 4304, Rad 4304, VD 84304
3967	Why Don't You Come Back To Me	VD 5119, Sr 33070
3968-A	No One To Call Me Darling	GG 3007, 4310, Rad 3007, 3070, 4310, VD 84310
	Living In The Mountains	QRS 1044
	Blue Yodel No. 6	QRS 1047
	Oh For The Wild And Wooley West	QRS 1047
	That's Why I Left The Mountain	QRS 1048
	Yodelin' Gene	QRS 1048

All Grey Gull/Radiex/Van Dyke issues probably as by **Sam Hill**, except Grey Gull 4310, Radiex 4310 as by **John Hardy**. Sunrise 33070 as by **Tom Long**.
These items were recorded under the supervision of Art Satherley at the Gennett studio, reportedly between October 9 and 24, on behalf of the Cova Recording Company. Six items were released on Cova's QRS label, with no visible matrices. Subsequently all the masters were sold to Grey Gull, which assigned the matrices shown.
Revs: Grey Gull 4281, Radiex 4281, Van Dyke 74281 by Chezz Chase; Grey Gull 4304, Radiex 4304, Van Dyke 84304 by Al Bernard (popular); Grey Gull 4310, Radiex 4310, Van Dyke 84310 by Bobby Gregory; Grey Gull 4314, Radiex 4314, Van Dyke 84314 by Bob Miller; Van Dyke 5114, 5115 untraced, 5119 by Smith & James, 5120 untraced.

Gene Autry (Yodelin' Cowboy), v/y; acc. own g.
New York, NY   Thursday, October 24, 1929

| 149179-3 | Blue Yodel No. 5 | Ha 1046-H, Ve 2046-V, Di 3046-G, ReE/RZ MR74, RZAu G22149 |
| 149180-3 | Left My Gal In The Mountains | Ha 1046-H, Ve 2046-V, Di 3046-G, Cl 5239-C |

Regal-Zonophone G22149 as by **Gene Autry (The Yodelling Cowboy)**; Regal/Regal-Zonophone MR74 as by **Gene Autry – The Yodelling Cowboy**. Rev. Clarion 5239-C by Jim Andrews (popular).

Gene Autry, v/y; acc. own g.
New York, NY   Tuesday, December 3, 1929

149661-2; 404398-A	Why Don't You Come Back To Me	Cl 5058-C, OK 45472
149662-2	Hobo Yodel	Ve 7056-V, Di 6030-G, Cl 5025-C
149663-2	Dust Pan Blues	Ve 7056-V, Di 6030-G, Cl 5154-C
149664-2; 404249-	No One To Call Me Darling	Ve 7061-V, Di 6035-G, Cl 5026-C, OK 45462, ReE/RZ MR74, RZAu G22149
149667-1,-2	Yodeling Them Blues Away	Co unissued
149668-3; 403729-A	Frankie And Johnny	Ve 7063-V, Di 6037-G, Cl 5026-C, OK 45417, PaAu A3061

OKeh 45417, 45462, 45472, Parlophone A3061 as by **Johnny Dodds**. Regal/Regal-Zonophone MR74 as by **Gene Autry – The Yodelling Cowboy**. Regal-Zonophone G22149 as by **Gene Autry (The Yodelling Cowboy)**.
Matrix 149668 is titled *Frankie And Johnnie* on Parlophone A3061. Matrices 149665/66 are by Clarence Williams (see JR).
Revs: Diva 6037-G, Velvet Tone 7063-V by Chick Bullock (popular); Parlophone A3061 by Greene Brothers (see Arthur Fields & Fred Hall).

Acc. own g; Frank Marvin, v eff-1; unknown, sp/train-wh eff-2.
New York, NY   Thursday, December 5, 1929

149678-1,-2	My Dreaming Of You	Co unissued
149679- ; 403730-A	Railroad Boomer	OK 45417
149680-2	My Alabama Home	Ve 7059-V, Di 6033-G, Cl 5075-C
149686-1; 404399-A	Slue-Foot Lue	Ve 7057-V, Di 6031-G, Cl 5154-C, OK 45472
149687-2; 404250-1	Stay Away From My Chicken House -1	Ve 7058-V, Di 6032-G, Cl 5155-C, OK 45462

| 149688-3 | Waiting For A Train -2 | Ve 7057-V, Di 6031-G, Cl 5155-C |
| 149689-2 | Lullaby Yodel | Ve 7059-V, Di 6033-G, Cl 5243-C |

Matrix 149686/404399 is titled *Slue Foot Sue* on some issues. Matrix 149681 is untraced; 149682/83 are by Will Osborne (popular); 149684/85 are by Lee Morse (popular). Rev. Clarion 5243-C by Carson Robison.

New York, NY   Friday, December 6, 1929

149692-1,-2	California Blues (Blue Yodel No. 4)	Ve 7058-V, Di 6032-G
149693-	I'm Sorry We Met	Co unissued
149694-2	Daddy And Home	Ve 7061-V, Di 6035-G, Cl 5240-C

Rev. Clarion 5240-C by Jim Andrews (popular).

Acc. Frank Marvin, sg-1/g; own g.

New York, NY   Monday, March 3, 1930

| 150048-2 | That's Why I Left The Mountains -1 | Ve 7075-V, Di 6049-G, Cl 5025-C |
| 150049-2; 403839-B | Cowboy Yodel | Ve 7083-V, Di 6057-G, Cl 5075-C, OK 45560 |

OKeh 45560 as by **Johnny Dodds**. Matrix 150048 is titled *The Day I Left The Mountains* on some issues.

New York, NY   Wednesday, March 5, 1930

| 150064-2; 403838-B | I'll Be Thinking Of You Little Girl | Ve 7083-V, Di 6057-G, Cl 5058-C, OK 45560 |
| 150065-2 | My Rough And Rowdy Ways | Ve 7075-V, Di 6049-G |

OKeh 45560 as by **Johnny Dodds**. Matrix 403838 is titled *I'll Be Thinking Of You Little Gal* on OKeh 45560.

New York, NY   Wednesday, March 5, 1930

| GEX-2623 | I'll Be Thinking Of You Little Gal | Ge rejected |
| GEX-2624 | Cowboy Yodel | Ge rejected |

Richmond, IN   Thursday, June 5, 1930

16712	Whisper Your Mother's Name	Ge 7243, Ch 16030, Spt 9705, MW 4978, De 5501, MeC 45007, 45172, Rex 9457
16714-A	The Girl I Left Behind	Spr 2561
16715-A	I'll Be Thinking Of You Little Gal	Ch 16030, Spt 9705
16717-A	Cowboy Yodel	Ge 7243, Ch 16096, 45172, Spt 9706, MW 4932, 8017, MeC 45172
16719,-A	Why Don't You Come Back To Me	Ge rejected
16720,-A	Dust Pan Blues	Ge rejected

Intervening matrices (and 16721) are popular. Rev. Melotone 45007 by Jimmy Long.

Richmond, IN   Friday, June 6, 1930

16722-A	In The Shadow Of The Pine	Ge 7265, Ch 16050, 45071, Spt 9704, MW 4933, De 5464, DeAu X1090, MeC 45071, Rex 9462
16723-A	Hobo Yodel	Ge 7290, Ch 16096, Spt 9702, MW 4932
16724	They Cut Down The Old Pine Tree	Ge 7265, Ch 16050, 45071, Spt 9704, MW 4933, De 5464, DeAu X1090, MeC 45071, Rex 9462, Ang 3329, Lyric 3329, Clifford 5329, Embassy 9329
16727,-A	The Tie That Binds	Ge rejected

Decca X1090 and possibly Rex 9462 use what appears to be the plain take of matrix 16722 but is indistinguishable from take A. Matrices 16725/26 are by Ivy Smith (see *B&GR*).
Revs: Angelus 3329 by Jack Turner or Karl & Kenny; Lyric 3329 by Karl & Kenny; Clifford 5329 by Jack Turner; Embassy 9329 probably by Jack Turner or Karl & Kenny (all popular).

Gene Autry, v/y-1; acc. own g.

Richmond, IN   Monday, August 4, 1930

16878	Texas Blues -1	Ch 16119, 33054, Spt 9703, MW 8034
16879-A	Hobo Bill's Last Ride -1	Ge 7290, Ch 16073, Spt 9702, Spr 2769
16880-A	Dust Pan Blues -1	Ge 7310, Ch 16119, Spt 9703, Spr 2769, MeC 45013
16881,-A	I'm Sorry We Met -1	Ge rejected
16882-A	My Carolina Sunshine Girl -1	Ge 7153, Spt 9651, Spr 2561, MW 4978, De 5501, Rex 9461
16883-A	Train Whistle Blues -1	Ge 7310, Ch 16073, Spt 9706, MW 8034, MeC 45013
16884,-A	I'm Lonely And Blue	Ge rejected
16885,-A	That's Why I'm Blue -1	Ge rejected

Matrix 16882-A appears on later pressings only of Gennett 7153 and Supertone 9651; earlier pressings use matrix 16321-A, *My Carolina Sunshine Girl* by Wilbur Ball. Decca 5501 and possibly Rex 9461 use what appears to be the plain take of matrix 16882 but is indistinguishable from take A. Rev. Gennett 7153, Supertone 9651 by Cliff Carlisle.

Gene Autry, v/y; acc. own g.
   Richmond, IN   Thursday, November 6, 1930

17231	Anniversary Blue Yodel No. 7	Ch 16141
17232-A	In The Jailhouse Now No. 2	Ch 16141, MW 4975
17233,-A	Any Old Time	Ge rejected
17234,-A	I'm Sorry We Met	Ge rejected
17235,-A,-B	That's Why I'm Blue	Ge rejected

   New York, NY   Tuesday, November 18, 1930

10257-1,-2	The Yodeling Hobo	Ba 32082, Je 20035, Or 8035, Pe 12667, Re 10259, Ro 5035, Cq 7708, CrC/MeC/Roy/Stg 91540, Pic 872
10258-2	Pictures Of My Mother	Cq 7843, Bwy 4068, CrC/MeC/Roy/Stg 91540
10259-2	Blue Days	Ba 32123, Je 20045, Or 8045, Pe 12686, Re 10295, Ro 5045, Cq 7831

Broadway 4068 as by **Bob Clayton**. Piccadilly 872 as by **Gene Autry, The Yodelling Hobo**.
Matrix 10257 is titled *Yodelling Hobo* on Piccadilly 872.

   New York, NY   Thursday, November 20, 1930

10263-1,-2	He's In The Jail House No. 2	Ba 32082, Je 20035, Or 8035, Pe 12667, Re 10259, Ro 5035, Cq 7708, Bwy 4062, Pic 872
10264-1	Cowboy's Yodel	Ba 32123, Je 20045, Or 8045, Pe 12686, Re 10295, Ro 5045, Cq 7831, Bwy 4100, Min M-14007, Pan 25603
10265-1	Dad In The Hills	Ba 32133, Je 20053, Or 8053, Pe 12696, Re 10311, Ro 5053, Cq 7702, Bwy 4068

Broadways as by **Bob Clayton**. Piccadilly 872 as by **Gene Autry, The Yodelling Hobo**.
Matrix 10263 is titled *I'm In The Jail House* on Piccadilly 872. Matrix 10264 is titled *Cowboy Yodel* on Panachord 25603. Rev. Broadway 4062 by David Miller.

Gene Autry, v/y-1; acc. own g.
   New York, NY   c. November 24, 1930

GEX-2829-A	High Powered Mama -1	Ch 16166, De 5527, MW 8033, MeC 45254
GEX-2830,-A	Whisper Your Mother's Name	Ge rejected
GEX-2831,-A	I'll Be Thinking Of You Little Gal	Ge rejected
GEX-2832-A	Yodeling Hobo -1	Ch 16166, 45172, MW 4932, 8017, De 5527, MeC 45172, 45254

Gene Autry, v/y; acc. unknown, md-1; own g.
   Richmond, IN   Thursday, January 29, 1931

17496	Mean Mama Blues -1	Ch 16210, 45183, Spr 2660, MW 8033, MeC 45183
17497	Blue Yodel No. 8 -1	Ch 16210, Spr 2637, MW 4976
17498-B	Pistol Packin' Papa -1	Ch 16230, 45025, Spr 2637, MW 4977, De 5544, MeC 45025, 45261, Rex 9458
17499	Dad In The Hills	Ch 16372, 45060, Spr 2596, MeC 45060, Rex 9460, DeAu X1232
17500-B	Pictures Of My Mother -1	Ch 16372, 45060, Spr 2596, MW 4931, MeC 45060, Rex 9461
17501,-A	Texas Blues -1	Ge rejected

Gene Autry, v/y-1; acc, own g.
   Richmond, IN   Monday, February 9, 1931

17515-B	Any Old Time -1	Ch 16230, 45025, Spr 2660, De 5544, DeAu X1232, MeC 45025, 45261, Rex 9460
17516-C	Money Ain't No Use Anyway -1	Ch 16245, 45156, Spr 2732, MW 8016, De 5426, DeAu X1236, MeC 45156, Rex 9459
17517	Blue Days -1	Ch 16245, 45156, Spr 2710, MW 8016, De 5426, DeAu X1236, MeC 45156, Rex 9459
17518,-A,-C	Call Me Back Pal Of Mine	Ge rejected

Decca X1232 and X1236 use what appear to be the plain takes of matrices 17515 and 17516 respectively but are indistinguishable from the issued takes.

Gene Autry, v/y; acc. own g.
   New York, NY   Tuesday, February 17, 1931

151321-1	A Gangster's Warning	Co 15687-D, Ve 2374-V, Cl 5308-C
151322-1	Pictures Of My Mother	Ve 2338-V, Cl 5272-C, ?Diamond 2338
151323-1	That's How I Got My Start	Ve 2374-V, Cl 5308-C
151324-1	True Blue Bill	Ve 2338-V, Cl 5272-C, ?Diamond 2338

Columbia 15687-D as by **Overton Hatfield**. Rev. Columbia 15687-D by Roy Evans (popular).

Acc. Frank Marvin, h-1/sg-2; own g.
New York, NY						Wednesday, February 18, 1931

67455-1	Do Right Daddy Blues -2	Vi 23548, MW M-4244
67456-2	Money Ain't No Use Anyway	Vi 23530, MW M-4243
67457-1	That's How I Got My Start -1	Vi unissued: BF BDP15204 (LP)
67457-2	That's How I Got My Start -1	Vi 23548, ZoSA 4374, HMVIn N4233
67458-1	Bear Cat Papa Blues -2	Vi unissued: BF BDP15204 (LP)
67458-2	Bear Cat Papa Blues -2	Vi 23530

Bear Family BDP15204 claims, erroneously, to use matrix 67456-1. Rev. Zonophone 4374, HMV N4233 by Jimmie Rodgers.

Gene Autry, v/y-1; acc. Frank Marvin, h-2/sg-3/g-4; own g.
New York, NY						Wednesday, February 25, 1931

10444-A	True Blue Bill -2, 4	Ba 32132, Je 20052, Or 8052, Pe 12695, Re 10310, Ro 5052, Cq 7843, Apex 41346, CrC/MeC 91113, Stg 291113, Roy 391113, Min M-14003, EBW 5558, Pan 25625
10445-1,-2,-3	A Gangster's Warning -3	Ba 32132, Je 20052, Or 8052, Pe 12695, Re 10310, Ro 5052, Cq 7704, Apex 41346, CrC/MeC 91113, Stg 291113, Roy 391113, EBW 5558, Pan 25625
10446-3	I'll Always Be A Rambler -1, 3	Ba 32244, Or 8090, Pe 12742, Ro 5090, Cq 7842, Bwy 4100
10447-1	The Death Of Mother Jones -3	Ba 32133, Je 20053, Or 8053, Pe 12696, Re 10311, Ro 5053
10448-2,-3	Bear Cat Papa Blues -1, 4	Ba 32200, Me M12383, Or 8069, Pe 12721, Re 10378, Ro 5069, Cq 7838, RZ MR3513, RZIn MR20237, RZIr IZ1142
10449-	The Old Woman And The Cow	ARC unissued

Broadway 4100 as by **Bob Clayton**. Regal-Zonophone MR3513, MR20237 as by **Gene Autry (The Yodling Cowboy)**. Edison Bell Winner 5558 as by **Hank Bennett**.
Matrix 10448 is titled *Bear Cat Papa* on Oriole 8069, Perfect 12721, and Conqueror 7838, and subtitled *(Once I Had A Sweetheart)* on Regal-Zonophone issues.
Revs: Conqueror 7704 by Frank Marvin; Minerva M-14003 by Goebel Reeves.

Gene Autry, v/y; acc. own g.
New York, NY						Tuesday, March 31, 1931

68839-1	High Steppin' Mama	TT unissued: BF BDP15204 (LP)
68839-2	High Steppin' Mama Blues	Vi 23589, MW M-4244, ZoSA 4346
68840-2	She Wouldn't Do It	Vi 23589, ZoSA 4346
68841-2	Don't Do Me That Way	Vi 23617, MW M-4243, Au 36-103, ZoSA 4361
68842-1	High Steppin' Mama Blues	TT C-1550, Au 36-101
68843-1	She Wouldn't Do It	TT C-1551, MW M-4768, Au 36-102
68844-1	Do Right Daddy Blues	TT C-1552
68845-1	T. B. Blues	TT C-1550, Au 36-101
68846-1	Jimmie The Kid	TT C-1551, Au 36-102
68847-1	Travellin' Blues	TT C-1552, Au 36-103

Timely Tunes and Aurora issues as by **Gene Johnson**. Matrix 68839-2 is titled *High Steppin' Mama* on Montgomery Ward M-4244. Bear Family BDP15204 claims, erroneously, to use matrix 68841-1.

Gene Autry, v/y-1; acc. Frank Marvin, h-2/sg-3/jh-4; own g.
New York, NY						Wednesday, April 1, 1931

68848-1	There's A Good Gal In The Mountains -1	Vi 23561, MW M-4767
68849-1	There's A Good Gal In The Mountains -1	TT C-1557, Au 36-106
68850-2	She's A Low Down Mamma -1	Vi 23617, MW M-4768, ZoSA 4361
68851-1	She's A Low Down Mama -1	TT C-1556, Au 36-105
68852-1,-2	The Old Woman And The Cow -2, 4	Vi unissued
68853-1	The Old Woman And The Cow -2, 4	MW M-4767
68854-1	Bear Cat Mama From Horner's Corners -3	TT C-1556, Au 36-105
68855-1	She's A Hum Dum Dinger -3	TT C-1557, Au 36-106

Timely Tunes and Aurora issues as by **Jimmie Smith**. Rev. Victor 23561 by Frank Marvin.

Frank Marvin & Jimmie Smith: Frank Marvin, v-1/y-2/sg-3; Gene Autry, v/y-4/g.
New York, NY						Wednesday, April 1, 1931

68860-1	Valley In The Hills -1, 3	TT C-1555, Au 36-104
68860-2	Valley In The Hills	Vi unissued
68861-1	Valley In The Hills -1, 3	Vi unissued

| 68863-1 | She's Always On My Mind -1, 2, 3, 4 | TT C-1554, Eld 1932 |
| 68864-1 | I'm Blue And Lonesome -2, 3, 4 | TT C-1555, Eld 1932, Au 36-104 |

Matrix 68862 is by Frank Marvin.

Gene Autry, v/y-1; acc. own g.
New York, NY   Friday, April 10, 1931

10555-1	Pistol Packin' Papa -1	Ba 32200, Me M12383, Or 8069, Pe 12721, Re 10378, Ro 5069, Cq 7765, Bwy 4064, Pan 25475, RZ MR3537, RZIn MR20260, RZIr IZ1163
10556-3	Jail House Blues -1	Ba 32350, Me M12384, Or 8110, Pe 12776, Ro 5110, Cq 7838, Bwy 4067, CrC/MeC/Stg/Roy 91307, Pan 25475, RZ MR3537, RZIn MR20260, RZIr IZ1163
10557-3	That's How I Got My Start -1	Ba 32242, Or 8093, Pe 12745, Ro 5093, Cq 7845, Bwy 4070, Mel-O-Dee 302, Apex 41413, *DoC/MeC 51023, Sun 251023, Ace 351023*, CrC/MeC 91181, Stg 291181, Roy 391181
10558-2	Methodist Pie	Ba 32308, Or 8103, Pe 12764, Ro 5103

Broadways as by **Bob Clayton**. Regal-Zonophone MR3537, IZ1163 (and probably other Regal-Zonophone issues) as by **Gene Autry (The Cowboy Film Star)**.
Domino/Melotone 51023, Sunrise[?] 251023, Ace 351023 are double-play issues; the other item on the same side and both items on the rev. are by Carson Robison.
Revs: Perfect 12764 by Frank & James McCravy; Broadway 4070 by Asa Martin & James Roberts; Conqueror 7765 by Miller Wikel; Romeo 5093, Conqueror 7845, Apex 41413, Crown/Melotone 91181, Sterling 291181, Royale 391181 by Carson Robison.

Gene Autry, v/y; acc. Frank Marvin, h-1/sg-2/g-3; own g.
New York, NY   Monday, April 13, 1931

10563-3	Do Right Daddy Blues -3	Ba 32201, Or 8070, Pe 12722, Re 10379, Ro 5070, Cq 7832
10565-2	Money Ain't No Use Anyhow -1	Ba 32263, Or 8094, Pe 12750, Ro 5094, Cq 7840
10566-2	I'll Be Thinking Of You Little Girl-2	Ba 32245, Or 8091, Pe 12743, Ro 5091, Cq 7835

Matrix 10564 is by The O'Connor Trio (popular). Rev. all issues of matrix 10566 by The O'Connor Trio.

Acc. Frank Marvin, sg; own g.
New York, NY   Tuesday, April 14, 1931

10567-3	Dallas County Jail Blues	Ba 32201, Or 8070, Pe 12722, Re 10379, Ro 5070, Cq 7832, Bwy 4064
10568-3	She Wouldn't Do It	Ba 32263, Or 8094, Pe 12750, Ro 5094, Cq 7840
10569-3	T.B. Blues	Ba 32244, Or 8090, Pe 12742, Ro 5090, Cq 7842, Bwy 4067

Broadway 4064, 4067 as by **Bob Clayton**.

Gene Autry, v/y-1; acc. own g.
Richmond, IN   Thursday, April 16, 1931

17683	T.B. Blues -1	Ch 16275, 45073, Spr 2710, MW 4975, De 5517, DeAu X1234, MeC 45256
17684	True Blue Bill	Ch 16328, Spr 2681, MW 4976
17685	That's How I Got My Start -1	Ch 16485, 45027, Spr 2681, De 5488, DeAu X1234, MeC 45027
17686	I'll Always Be A Rambler -1	Ch 16328, 45183, MW 4931, MeC 45183, Rex 9458
17687-A	Bear Cat Papa Blues -1	Ch 16485, 45027, De 5488, MeC 45027
17688-A	I've Got The Jail House Blues -1	Ch 16275, 45073, Spr 2732, MW 4977, De 5517, MeC 45256, Rex 9457

Matrix 17688 is titled *I've Got The Jailhouse Blues* on Rex 9457.

Gene Autry, v/y-1; or **Gene Autry & Jimmy Long**, v-2/y-3 duet; acc. Frank Marvin, sg-4; Roy Smeck, sg-5/bj-6; Gene Autry, g; unknown, train-wh eff-7.
New York, NY   Thursday, October 29, 1931

10940-2	Rheumatism Blues -1, 4?	Ba 32350, Me M13098, Or 8365, Pe 13026, Ro 5365, Cq 7913
10941-1	I'm Atlanta Bound -1, 6	Ba 32350, Me M12384, Or 8110, Pe 12776, Ro 5110, Cq 7907, Bwy 4071, CrC/MeC/Stg/Roy 91307, Pan 25357
10942-1,-2	High Steppin' Mama Blues -1, 6	Ba 32473, Me M12429, Or 8147, Pe 12817, Ro 5147, Cq 7909, Pan 25357

10943-1	Silver Haired Daddy Of Mine -2, 5?	Ba 32349, Or 8109, Pe 12775, Ro 5109, Vo 5489, 02991, OK 02991, Cq 7908, Bwy 4073, CrC/MeC/Stg/Roy 91282
10944-2	Missouri I'm Calling -2, 5?, 7	Ba 32472, Me M12430, Or 8146, Pe 12811, Ro 5146, Cq 7914, Bwy 4071, Pan 25603
10945-1	My Alabama Home -2, 3, 4, 6	Ba 32472, Me M12430, Or 8146, Pe 12811, Ro 5146, Cq 7907

Matrix 10941 on Broadway 4071 as by **Bob Clayton**; matrix 10944 on Broadway 4071 as by **Clayton & Greene**; Broadway 4073 as by **Clayton & Green**.
Matrix 10941 is titled *Atlanta Bound* on Perfect 12776, Conqueror 7907, Panachord 25357. Matrix 10943 is titled *That Silver Haired Daddy Of Mine* on Vocalion 5489, Broadway 4073. Rev. Broadway 4073 by Cliff Carlisle.

Gene Autry & Jimmy Long, v/y-1 duet; acc. Frank Marvin, h-2/sg-3/g-2/y-2; Roy Smeck, sg-4; Gene Autry, g.
New York, NY   Friday, October 30, 1931

10946-2	Mississippi Valley Blues -3/4	Ba 32349, Or 8109, Pe 12775, Ro 5109, Vo/OK 02991, Cq 7908, CrC/MeC/Stg/Roy 91282, Pan 25375
10947-1	My Old Pal Of Yesterday -3/4	Ba 32431, Me M12392, Or 8133, Pe 12804, Ro 5133, Vo 5489, Vo/OK 04274, Cq 7910, CrC/MeC/Stg/Roy 91323, RZAu G22575
10948-2	My Cross-Eyed Girl -1, 2	Ba 33485, Me M13452, Or 8489, Pe 13159, Ro 5489, Cq 7911, CrC/MeC/Stg/Roy 92039

Regal-Zonophone G22575 as by **Gene Autry & Jimmie Long**. Matrix 10948 is titled *My Cross Eyed Girl* on Conqueror 7911. Rev. Regal-Zonophone G22575 by Bradley Kincaid.

Long Brothers: Jimmy Long, Gene Autry, v/y duet; acc. unidentified, k-1; Jimmy Long, sg; Gene Autry, g.
New York, NY   Friday, October 30, 1931

70924-1	Mississippi Valley	Vi 23622
70925-1	My Old Pal Of Yesterday	Vi 23637, ZoSA 4381
70926-1	Missouri Is Calling	Vi 23637
70927-1	Cross-Eyed Gal That Lived Upon The Hill -1	Vi 23622
70928-1	I'm Always Dreaming Of You	Vi 23673, MW M-4333, RZ ME54, RZIr IZ1331
70929-1	Why Don't You Come Back To Me	Vi 23673, MW M-4333, RZ ME54, RZIr IZ1331

Rev. Zonophone 4381 by Luther – Stokes Trio (see Frank Luther).

Gene Autry, v/y; acc. own g.
New York, NY   Friday, October 30, 1931

70930-1	Jailhouse Blues	Vi 23642, MW M-4067, Zo 6117, RZ T6117, Twin FT1785
70931-1	Rheumatism Blues	Vi 23630, MW M-4245
70932-1	I'm Atlanta Bound	Vi 23630
79033-1	Wildcat Mama	Vi 23642, MW M-4245, Zo 6117, RZ T6117, Twin FT 1785

Matrix 70933 is titled *Wild Cat Mamma* on Montgomery Ward M-4245, Zonophone 6117.

Gene Autry, v/y-1; acc. Frank Marvin, sg-2/g-3; Roy Smeck, sg-4/bj-5; own g.
New York, NY   Wednesday, November 11, 1931

10984-2	Birmingham Daddy -1, 5	Ba 33131, Me M13098, Or 8365, Pe 13026, Ro 5365, Cq 7909
10985-2	Why Don't You Come Back To Me? -2/4	Ba 32431, Me M12392, Or 8133, Pe 12804, Ro 5133, Vo/OK 04272, Cq 7914, 9450, CrC/MeC/Stg/Roy 91323
10986-2	She's A Low Down Mama -1, 3	Cq 7911

Matrix 10985 is titled *Why Don't You Come Back To Me* on Conqueror 7914.

Gene Autry, v/y-1; acc. Roy Smeck, sg-2/bj-3; own g.
New York, NY   Monday, November 16, 1931

11011-1	I'm A Railroad Man (Waiting On A Weary Train) -1, 2	Cq 7912
11012-2	Under The Old Apple Tree -2	Cq 7910
11013-3	Wild Cat Mama Blues -3	Ba 32473, Me M12429, Or 8147, Pe 12817, Ro 5147, Cq 7913, RZ MR3513, RZIn MR20237
11014-2	There's A Good Girl In The Mountains -1, 3	Ba 32552, Or 8161, Pe 12837, Ro 5161, Cq 7912

Regal-Zonophone MR3513 (and probably MR20237) as by **Gene Autry (The Yodling Cowboy)**.
Matrix 11013 is titled *Wild Cat Mamma Blues* on Regal-Zonophone MR3513.

Gene Autry, v; acc. unknown, g; own g; unknown, v-1.
    New York, NY   Friday, June 24, 1932
    11970-2   That Ramshackle Shack   Ba 32610, Me M12523, Or 8177, Pe 12858,
                                                             Ro 5177, Cq 7999, Bwy 4093
    11971-2   Back To Old Smoky Mountain -1   Ba 32610, Me M12523, Or 8177, Pe 12858,
                                                             Ro 5177, Cq 7999, Bwy 4094

Broadway 4093, 4094 as by **Bob Clayton**.

Gene Autry, v/y; acc. Roy Smeck, sg; own g.
    New York, NY   Monday, June 27, 1932
    11986-2   Back Home In The Blue Ridge Mountains   Cq 8002, Bwy 4097

Broadway 4097 as by **Bob Clayton**.

Gene Autry, v/y; or **Gene Autry & Jimmy Long**, v duet-1; acc. Roy Smeck, sg; Gene Autry, g.
    New York, NY   Tuesday, June 28, 1932
    11987-1   The Crime I Didn't Do -1   Ba 32521, Me M12472, Or 8153, Pe 12830,
                                                             Ro 5153, Cq 8000, Bwy 4093,
                                                             CrC/MeC/Stg/Roy 91401
    11988-3   Kentucky Lullaby   Cq 8059
    11989-2   Alone With My Sorrows -1   Ba 32652, Me M12572, Or 8189, Pe 12873,
                                                             Ro 5189, Cq 7998, Bwy 4095,
                                                             CrC/MeC/Stg/Roy 91478

Broadway 4093, 4095 as by **Clayton & Green**.

Acc. Roy Smeck, sg-2/bj-3; Gene Autry, g.
    New York, NY   Wednesday, June 29, 1932
    11997-2   I'm Always Dreaming Of You -1, 2   Ba 32521, Me M12472, Or 8153, Pe 12830,
                                                             Ro 5153, Cq 8000, CrC/MeC/Stg/Roy 91401,
                                                             Pan 25375
    11998-2   Moonlight And Skies -2   Ba 32552, Or 8161, Pe 12837, Ro 5161,
                                                             Vo 5500, Cq 8002, CrC/MeC/Stg/Roy 91394
    11999-2   Returning To My Cabin Home -3   Cq 8095, CrC/MeC/Stg/Roy 91394
    12001-2   In The Cradle Of My Dreams -1, 2   Cq 8001

Matrix 12000 is by Boswell Sisters (popular).

    New York, NY   Thursday, June 30, 1932
    12002-1   My Carolina Mountain Rose -1, 3   Ba 32928, Me M12871, Or 8290, Pe 12964,
                                                             Ro 5290, Cq 8001, Bwy 4095
    12003-1   Have You Found Someone Else -1, 2   Ba 32652, Me M12572, Or 8189, Pe 12873,
                                                             Ro 5189, Cq 7998, Bwy 4097,
                                                             CrC/MeC/Stg/Roy 91478
    12004-1   In The Hills Of Carolina -2   Cq 8059, Bwy 4094

Broadway 4094 as by **Bob Clayton**, 4097 as by **Clayton & Greene**. Matrix 12003 is titled *Have You Found Some One Else?* on Conqueror 7998.

Gene Autry, v/y-1; acc. own g.
    New York, NY   Thursday, June 30, 1932
    73046-1   Gangster's Warning   Vi 23725, MW M-4326
    73047-1   Back To Old Smokey Mountain   Vi 23726
    73048-1   Back Home In The Blue Ridge Mountains -1 Vi 23726
    73049-1   That Ramshackle Shack -1   Vi 23720, MW M-4326
    73054-1   Black Bottom Blues -1   Vi 23707
    73055-1   Kentucky Lullaby -1   Vi 23720

Intervening matrices are by Jimmy Long. Revs: Victor 23707 by Allen Brothers, 23725 by Bud Billings (Frank Luther).

Gene Autry, v/y-1; acc. unknown, f-2; unknown, g-3; own g.
    Chicago, IL   Friday, January 27, 1933
    74897-1   Cowboy's Heaven -1, 3   Vi 23783
    74898-1   The Little Ranch House On The Old Circle B -1, 3   Vi 23783
    74899-1   The Yellow Rose Of Texas -1, 3   Vi 23792
    74900-1   Your Voice Is Ringing -1, 3   Vi 23810
    75101-1   Louisiana Moon -2   Vi 23792

Intervening matrices are by other artists on other dates. Rev. Victor 23810 by Dwight Butcher.

Gene Autry & Jimmy Long, v duet; acc. unknown, f; poss. Bob Miller, p-1/cel-2; unknown, g.
    New York, NY   Wednesday, March 1, 1933

13102-1	Louisiana Moon -2	Ba 32843, Me M12772, Or 8261, Pe 12936, Ro 5261, Vo/OK 04375, Cq 8092, 9512, CrC/MeC/Stg/Roy 91627, RZ ME3, RZIn MR20081, Twin FT8913
13103-1	Cowboy's Heaven -2	Ba 32723, Me M12652, Or 8217, Pe 12899, Ro 5217, Vo 5498, Cq 8093, CrC/MeC/Stg/Roy 91520, RZAu G22166
13104-2	The Little Ranch House On The Old Circle B	Ba 32771, Me M12700, Or 8233, Pe 12912, Ro 5233, Vo 5500, 04998, OK 04998, Cq 8093, CrC/MeC/Stg/Roy 91577
13107-2	If I Could Bring Back My Buddy -2	Ba 32723, Me M12652, Or 8217, Pe 12899, Ro 5217, Vo 5497, Cq 8138, CrC/MeC/Stg/Roy 91520, RZAu G22175
13108-1	The Old Folks Back Home -2	Ba 32761, Me M12690, Or 8230, Pe 12910, Ro 5230, Cq 8094, CrC/MeC/Stg/Roy 91576
13109-2	The Yellow Rose Of Texas -1	ARC unissued: *Co CK48957 (CD)*
13109-3	The Yellow Rose Of Texas -1	Ba 32771, Me M12700, Or 8233, Pe 12912, Ro 5233, Vo 5498, 04998, OK 04998, Cq 8096, CrC/MeC/Stg/Roy 91577, RZAu G22166

Regal-Zonophone G22166, G22175 as by **Gene Autry & Jimmie Long**. Matrices 13105/06 are by Ruth Etting (popular).

New York, NY   Thursday, March 2, 1933

13110-2	Gosh! I Miss You All The Time	Ba 32981, Me M12931, Or 8308, Pe 12980, Ro 5308, Cq 8096, CrC/MeC/Stg/Roy 91726
13111-2	The Answer To 21 Years -2	Ba 32761, Me M12690, Or 8230, Pe 12910, Ro 5230, Vo 5497, Cq 8092, CrC/MeC/Stg/Roy 91576, RZAu G22174
13114-1	When It's Lamp Lightin' Time In The Valley -1	Cq 8094
13115-2	Watching The Clouds Roll By	Ba 32928, Me M12871, Or 8290, Pe 12964, Ro 5290, Cq 8138

Regal-Zonophone G22174 as by **Gene Autry & Jimmie Long**. Matrices 13112/13 are by Anson Weeks Orchestra (popular). Rev. Regal-Zonophone G22174 by Fisher Hendley.

Gene Autry, v; acc. unknown, f; unknown, g.
New York, NY   Thursday, March 2, 1933

13116-1	Don't Take Me Back To The Chain Gang	Ba 33444, Me M13411, Or 8470, Pe 13144, Ro 5470, Cq 8095, CrC/MeC/Stg/Roy 92025

Gene Autry & His Trio: Gene Autry, Jimmy Long, Smilie Burnette, v trio; acc. unknown, f; Bob Miller, cel; unknown, g.
Chicago, IL   Monday, April 17, 1933

C-558-4	In The Valley Of The Moon	Cq 8152, CoC C558
C-559	When The Mailman Says No Mail Today	ARC unissued

Gene Autry, v/y; acc. unknown, sg; own g.
Chicago, IL   Monday, April 17, 1933

C-560-3	When The Humming Birds Are Humming	Cq 8152, CoC C560

See note on matrix 13495 (below).

Gene Autry, v/y-1; acc. unknown, sg; prob. own g.
New York, NY   Tuesday, June 20, 1933

13480-1	Roll Along Kentucky Moon -1	Cq 8224
13481-1	That Mother And Daddy Of Mine	Cq 8223

Acc. two unknowns, g.
New York, NY   Thursday, June 22, 1933

13491-2	'Way Out West In Texas	Ba 32887, Me M12832, Or 8279, Pe 12952, Ro 5279, Vo/OK 04485, Cq 8193, 9513
13492-1	The Dying Cowgirl	Cq 8193

Matrix 13491 is titled *Way Out West In Texas* on Vocalion/OKeh 04485.

Acc. unknown, f; unknown, g.
New York, NY   Thursday, June 22, 1933

13493-1	When The Humming Birds Are Humming	Cq 8152
13494-2	The Death Of Jimmie Rodgers	Ba 32800, Me M12733, Or 8246, Pe 12922, Ro 5246, Vo 5504, Cq 8168, CrC/MeC/Stg/Roy 91575, RZAu G22176

Rev. Regal-Zonophone G22176 by Asa Martin & James Roberts.

Acc. Jimmie Dale's Oklahoma Cowboys: no details.
New York, NY   Thursday, June 22, 1933
    13495-1   In The Valley Of The Moon   Cq 8152

It has been reported that Conqueror 8152 was issued in two forms, using matrices 13493/13495 and using the earlier matrices C-558/C-560; only the latter version has been verified.

Acc. unknown, f; unknown, g.
New York, NY   Thursday, June 22, 1933
    13496-2   The Life Of Jimmie Rodgers   Ba 32800, Me M12733, Or 8246, Pe 12922,
                                                                 Ro 5246, Vo 5504, Cq 8168,
                                                                  CrC/MeC/Stg/Roy 91575, RZAu G22175
    13497-1   If You'll Let Me Be Your Little Sweetheart   Ba 32886, Me M12822, Or 8277, Pe 12950,
                                                                  Ro 5277, Cq 8192, CrC/MeC/Stg/Roy 91642

Acc. Frank Marvin, sg-1; Bob Miller, p; unknown, g.
New York, NY   Friday, June 23, 1933
    13502-1,-2   That Old Feather Bed On The Farm   Ba 32886, Me M12822, Or 8277, Pe 12950,
                                                                   Ro 5277, Cq 8244, CrC/MeC/Stg/Roy 91642
    13503-2   There's An Empty Cot In The Bunkhouse Tonight -1   Ba 32843, Me M12772, Or 8261, Pe 12936,
                                                                   Ro 5261, Vo/OK 04375, Cq 8191,
                                                                  CrC/MeC/Stg/Roy 91627

Acc. unknown, f; unknown, bj; two unknowns, g.
Chicago, IL   Wednesday, October 4, 1933
    C-618-1   A Hill-Billy Wedding In June   Ba 32981, Me M12931, Or 8308, Pe 12980,
                                                           Ro 5308, Cq 8192, CrC/MeC/Stg/Roy 91726

Acc. unknown, f; two unknowns, g.
Chicago, IL   Monday, October 9, 1933
    C-619-1   Moonlight Down In Lovers' Lane   Cq 8223
    C-620-1   The Last Round-Up   Ba 32887, Me M12832, Or 8279, Pe 12952,
                                              Ro 5279, Vo/OK 04485, Cq 8191

Acc. unknown, f-1; unknown, g.
Chicago, IL   Wednesday, November 1, 1933
    C-656-1   When Jimmie Rodgers Said Good-bye -1   Ba 32902, Me M12843, Or 8283, Pe 12957,
                                                              Ro 5283, Cq 8246
    C-657-1   Good Luck Old Pal ('Till We Meet Bye And Bye)   Ba 32902, Me M12843, Or 8283, Pe 12957,
                                                               Ro 5283, Cq 8246

Gene Autry, v/y; acc. unknown, f; unknown, g.
Chicago, IL   Monday, March 26, 1934
    CP-1071-2   The Round-Up In Cheyenne   Ba 33294, Me M13261, Or 8411, Pe 13094,
                                            Ro 5411, Cq 8295, CrC/MeC/Stg/Roy 91992

Matrix CP-1071 is titled *The Roundup At Cheyenne* on Conqueror 8295.

Gene Autry & Jimmy (or **Jimmie**) **Long**, v duet; acc. unknown, f; unknown, g; unknown, sb-1.
Chicago, IL   Monday, March 26, 1934
    CP-1072-2   Memories Of That Silver Haired Daddy Of Mine   Ba 33225, Me M13192, Or 8384, Pe 13065,
                                                               Ro 5384, Cq 8296, CrC/MeC/Stg/Roy 91928,
                                                               Min M-917
    CP-1073-3   After Twenty-One Years   Ba 33055, Me M13017, Or 8334, Pe 13003,
                                                               Ro 5334, Cq 8297, CrC/MeC/Stg/Roy 91771
    CP-1076-2   Eleven Months In Leavenworth-1   Ba 33444, Me M13411, Or 8470, Pe 13144,
                                                               Ro 5470, Cq 8297, CrC/MeC/Stg/Roy 92025

Matrices CP-1074/75 are by the Maple City Four.

Gene Autry, Jimmy Long, v duet; or **Gene Autry**, v-1; acc. unknown, f; unknown, md; unknown, g; unknown, sb.
Chicago, IL   Tuesday, March 27, 1934
    CP-1086-3   Little Farm Home   Ba 33055, Me M13017, Or 8334, Pe 13003,
                                            Ro 5334, CrC/MeC/Stg/Roy 91771, Min M-907
    CP-1087-2   There's A Little Old Lady Waiting   Me M13034
    CP-1088-1   Dear Old Western Skies -1   Cq 8295, CrC/MeC/Stg/Roy 92095

Rev. Minerva M-907 by Dick Robertson.

Acc. unknown, f; unknown, md; unknown, g.
Chicago, IL   Saturday, March 31, 1934
    C-703-3   Beautiful Texas   Ba 33070, Me M13034, Or 8340, Pe 13009,
                                          Ro 5340, Vo/OK 04267,
                                          CrC/MeC/Stg/Roy 91814

    Chicago, IL   Saturday, April 28, 1934

| CP-1087-3 | There's A Little Old Lady Waiting | Ba 33070, Or 8340, Pe 13009, Ro 5340, Vo/OK 04267, Cq 8296, 9613, CrC/MeC/Stg/Roy 91814, Min M-905 |

Rev. Minerva M-905 by Asa Martin & James Roberts.

Acc. unknown.
    Chicago, IL   Thursday, May 24, 1934

| C-703-4 | Beautiful Texas | ARC unissued |

Acc. Roy Smeck, bj; unknown, g.
    New York, NY   Monday, May 28, 1934

| 15258-1,-2 | Memories Of My Silver Haired Daddy | ARC unissued |
| 15259-2 | When The Moon Shines On The Mississippi Valley | Ba 33225, Me M13192, Or 8384, Pe 13065, Ro 5384, Cq 8296, CrC/MeC/Stg/Roy 91928, Min M-917 |

Acc. unknown, md; unknown, g.
    New York, NY   Tuesday, May 29, 1934

15260-1,-2	Shine On, Pale Moon	ARC unissued
15262-1,-2	The Stump Of The Old Pine Tree	ARC unissued
15264-1	Seven More Days	Me M13070, Cq 8386

Matrices 15261, 15263, and 15265 are by Smilie Burnette.

Acc. unknown.
    New York, NY   Thursday, May 31, 1934

| 15266-1,-2 | My Shy Little Bluebonnet Girl | ARC unissued |

Acc. unknown, sg-1; Bob Miller, cel-2; unknown, md-3; unknown, g.
    New York, NY   Monday, June 11, 1934

15258-3	Memories Of My Silver Haired Daddy	ARC unissued
15262-3	The Stump Of The Old Pine Tree -1, 2	Ba 33102, Me M13070, Or 8352, Pe 13016, Ro 5352, Cq 8386, CrC/MeC/Stg/Roy 91840
15264-3	Seven More Days -3	Ba 33102, Me M13070, Or 8352, Pe 13016, Ro 5352, ?Cq 8386, CrC/MeC/Stg/Roy 91840
15266-3	My Shy Little Bluebonnet Girl -1, 3	Ba 33294, Me M13261, Or 8411, Pe 13094, Ro 5411, Cq 8467, XL Radio Productions 80, CrC/MeC/Stg/Roy 91992

Matrix 15266 is titled *My Shy Little Blue Bonnet Girl* on Crown/Melotone/Sterling/Royale 91992.

Acc. unknown.
    New York, NY   Monday, June 25, 1934

| 15260-3 | Shine On, Pale Moon | ARC unissued |

Gene Autry Trio: Gene Autry, Jimmy Long, Smilie Burnette, v trio; acc. Tex Atchison, f; Chick Hurt, md; Salty Holmes, g; Jack Taylor, sb.
    New York, NY   Friday, January 11, 1935

| 16629-1 | Tumbling Tumbleweeds | Ba 33348, Me M13315, Or 8434, Pe 13113, Ro 5434, Vo/OK 03007, Cq 8465, Co 37000, 20027, CrC/MeC/Stg/Roy 91960 |

Gene Autry, v/y; acc. Tex Atchison, f; Chick Hurt, md; Salty Holmes, g; Jack Taylor, sb.
    New York, NY   Friday, January 11, 1935

| 16630-1 | Texas Plains | Ba 33349, Me M13316, Or 8435, Pe 13114, Ro 5435, Cq 8466, CrC/MeC/Stg/Roy 91970, Lucky 1046 |

Gene Autry & Smilie Burnette, v duet; acc. Tex Atchison, f; Chick Hurt, md; Salty Holmes, g; Jack Taylor, sb; poss. Smilie Burnette and others, animal imitations.
    New York, NY   Friday, January 11, 1935

| 16631-1 | Uncle Noah's Ark | Ba 33485, Me M13452, Or 8489, Pe 13159, Ro 5489, Cq 8467, CrC/MeC/Stg/Roy 92039 |

Gene Autry & Jimmie Long, v duet/y duet-1; acc. Tex Atchison, f; Salty Holmes, h-2/g; Chick Hurt, md; Jack Taylor, sb.
    New York, NY   Monday, January 14, 1935

16566-2	Angel Boy	ARC 35-10-10, Cq 8484, CrC/MeC/Stg/Roy 92095
16567-2	Red River Lullaby	ARC 7-01-51, Cq 8485, CrC/MeC/Stg/Roy 92154
16568-1	Some Day In Wyomin' -1, 2	Ba 33386, Me M13354, Or 8448, Pe 13127, Ro 5448, Vo/OK 04415, Cq 8468, 9613, CrC/MeC/Stg/Roy 91989

Gene Autry, v; or **Gene Autry & Smilie Burnette**, v duet-1; acc. unknown, sg; unknown, g; unknown, sb.
    New York, NY   Tuesday, January 15, 1935

16569-2	Dear Old Western Skies	ARC 35-10-10
16570-1	The Old Covered Wagon -1	ARC 5-12-53, Cq 8484, CrC/MeC/Stg/Roy 93085

Matrix 16570 is titled *The Covered Wagon* on Conqueror 8484.

Gene Autry Trio: Gene Autry, Jimmy Long, Smilie Burnette, v trio; acc. Tex Atchison, f; Salty Holmes, h/g; Chick Hurt, md; Jack Taylor, sb.
    New York, NY   Wednesday, January 16, 1935

16575-1	Hold On, Little Dogies, Hold On	Ba 33349, Me M13316, Or 8435, Pe 13114, Or 5435, Cq 8466, CrC/MeC/Stg/Roy 91970, Lucky 1046

Gene Autry & Jimmie (or **Jimmy**) **Long**, v duet; acc. Tex Atchison, f; Salty Holmes, h-1/g; Chick Hurt, md; Jack Taylor, sb.
    New York, NY   Wednesday, January 16, 1935

16576-1	Answer To Red River Valley-1	ARC 6-08-51, Vo/OK 03101, Cq 8485, 9512, CrC/MeC/Stg/Roy 92154, MeC/Min M-935
16577-2	Silver Haired Mother Of Mine	ARC 5-12-53, Cq 8581, CrC/MeC/Stg/Roy 93085

Rev. Melotone/Minerva M-935 by McFarland & Gardner.

Gene Autry & Smilie Burnette, v duet; acc. Tex Atchison, f; Chick Hurt, md; Salty Holmes, g; Jack Taylor, sb.
    New York, NY   Wednesday, January 16, 1935

16578-2	Ridin' Down The Canyon	ARC 35-10-18, Cq 8483, CrC/MeC/Stg/Roy 92084

Matrix 16578 is titled *When The Desert Sun Goes Down* on Conqueror 8483.

    New York, NY   Thursday, January 17, 1935

16581-1	Wagon Train	ARC 35-10-18, Cq 8483, CrC/MeC/Stg/Roy 92084

Gene Autry & Jimmie (or **Jimmy**) **Long**, v duet; acc. Tex Atchison, f; Chick Hurt, md; Salty Holmes, g; Jack Taylor, sb.
    New York, NY   Thursday, January 17, 1935

16582-1	Old Missouri Moon	Ba 33348, Me M13315, Or 8434, Pe 13113, Ro 5434, Vo/OK 03007, Cq 8465, Co 37000, 20027, CrC/MeC/Stg/Roy 91960, RZAu G25125

Gene Autry Trio: Gene Autry, Jimmy Long, Smilie Burnette, v trio; acc. Tex Atchison, f; Chick Hurt, md; Salty Holmes, g; Jack Taylor, sb.
    New York, NY   Thursday, January 17, 1935

16583-1	Ole Faithful	Ba 33387, Me M13354, Or 8448, Pe 13127, Ro 5448, Vo/OK 04415, Cq 8468, CrC/MeC/Stg/Roy 91989, Lucky 60286

Rev. Lucky 60286 by Patsy Montana.

Gene Autry & Jimmie (or **Jimmy**) **Long**, v duet; acc. Art Davis, f; Jim Boyd, g.
    Dallas, TX   Sunday, September 22, 1935

DAL-121-1	Vine Covered Cabin In The Valley	Cq 8582
DAL-122-1	Rainbow Valley	Cq 8581
DAL-124-1	I'd Love A Home In The Mountains	Cq 8582

Gene Autry, v; acc. prob. Frank Marvin, sg; unknown, g.
    Dallas, TX   Sunday, September 22, 1935

DAL-125-1	Nobody's Darling But Mine	ARC 6-04-52, Vo/OK 03070, Cq 8629, Co 37001, 20453, CoC C1136, C20435, RZAu G25141, Lucky 60268

Gene Autry & Jimmie (or **Jimmy**) **Long**, v duet; acc. Art Davis, f; Jim Boyd, g.
    Dallas, TX   Monday, September 23, 1935

DAL-123-1,-2,-3	Just Come On In	ARC unissued

Gene Autry, v/y-1; acc. Art Davis, f-2; Frank Marvin, ac-3/sg-4/v-5; unknown, md-6; unknown, g.
    Chicago, IL   Thursday, December 5, 1935

C-1173-1	My Old Saddle Pal -1, 2, 4, 6	ARC 7-05-54, Vo/OK 03138, Cq 8828, 9442
C-1174-2	Ridin' The Range -2, 3	ARC 6-02-58, Cq 8634, CrC/MeC/Stg/Roy 93088, Min M-14028
C-1175-2	The End Of The Trail -2, 5	ARC 6-02-58, Cq 8634, CrC/MeC/Stg/Roy 93088, Min M-14028

C-1176-1	Don't Waste Your Tears On Me -1	ARC 6-04-52, Vo/OK 03070, Cq 8632, Co 37001, 20453, CoC C1136, C20435, RZAu G25125
C-1177-1	You're The Only Star (In My Blue Heaven) -2, 4	ARC 6-05-59, Vo 03097, Cq 8652, 9098, CoC C255

Later pressings of Vocalion 03097 and Conqueror 9098, and all pressings of OKeh 03097, use matrix LA-1849 rather than C-1177.

Gene Autry, v; acc. Art Davis, f; unknown, g; unknown, sb.
Chicago, IL   Tuesday, December 24, 1935

C-1194-1	Mexicali Rose	ARC 6-05-59, Vo/OK 03097, Cq 8629, Co 37002, 20028, CoC C255

Acc. Art Davis, f; unknown, cel-1; unknown, md-2; unknown, g.
Los Angeles, CA   Tuesday, May 12, 1936

LA-1108-A	The Answer To Nobody's Darling -2	ARC 6-08-51, Vo/OK 03101, Cq 8685
LA-1109-A,-B	Mother Here's A Bouquet For You -1	ARC unissued; *ASV Living Era CD AJA5264 (CD)*
LA-1110-A,-B	Riding All Day -2	Cq 8828

Gene Autry, v/y-1; acc. Art Davis, f; Frank Marvin, sg-2/wb-3/v-4/y-5; unknown, g.
Los Angeles, CA   Tuesday, August 25, 1936

LA-1162-A	The Old Gray Mare -1, 3, 4, 5	Cq 8686
LA-1163-B	Guns And Guitars -2	ARC 7-01-51, Cq 8685
LA-1164-A	I'll Go Riding Down That Texas Trail -1, 2	ARC 7-05-54, Vo/OK 03138, Cq 8686

Conqueror 8686 as by **Gene Autry With Frankie Marvin**.

Gene Autry, v; acc. Art Davis, f-1; poss. Frank Marvin, sg; unknown, g.
Los Angeles, CA   Monday, March 22, 1937

LA-1312-A	The Convict's Dream	ARC 7-05-73, Vo/OK 03229, Cq 8808
LA-1313-A	That's Why I'm Nobody's Darling -1	ARC 7-05-73, Vo/OK 03229, Cq 8808

Gene Autry, v; or **Gene Autry & Jimmie Long**, v-1/y-2 duet; acc. Art Davis, f-3; poss. Frank Marvin, esg; unknown, g.
Chicago, IL   Saturday, May 29, 1937

C-1908-1	The One Rose (That's Left In My Heart) -3	ARC 7-10-58
C-1909-3	End Of My Roundup Days	ARC unissued: *Murray Hill M61072 (LP)*
C-1910-2	Sing Me A Song Of The Saddle	Cq 8880
C-1911-1	With A Song In My Heart -1	ARC 7-08-53, Cq 8878
C-1912-2	My Star Of The Sky	ARC unissued: *Murray Hill M61072 (LP)*
C-1913-1,-2	I Hate To Say Goodbye To The Prairie -1, 2	ARC 7-10-58, Vo/OK 03262, Cq 8879, Co 37702, 20281, CoC C973
C-1914-2	My Rose Of The Prairie -1	ARC unissued: *Murray Hill M61072 (LP)*
C-1915-1,-2	When The Tumbleweeds Come Tumbling Down Again	ARC unissued

Matrix C-1908-1 has been reported on Melotone 7-10-58; at least some pressings of Perfect 7-10-58 use instead matrix LA-1451-A (see below). Some pressings of Melotone 7-08-53 and Conqueror 8878 use C-1911-3, a remastering of take 1 (made on July 6, 1937). Similar "take 3" remasterings of matrices C-1909, C-1914 and C-1915 were made on August 27, 1937.

Gene Autry & Jimmie Long, v duet; acc. poss. Frank Marvin, esg; unknown, g.
Chicago, IL   Wednesday, June 2, 1937

C-1918-	Down A Mountain Trail	ARC unissued: *Murray Hill M61072 (LP)*
C-1919-1	When The Golden Leaves Are Falling	ARC 7-08-53, Cq 8878

Some pressings of Melotone 7-08-53 and Conqueror 8878 use C-1919-3, evidently a remastering of take 1 (though made the same day). A 'take 3' remastering of matrix C-1918 was made on August 27, 1937; the take issued on Murray Hill M61072 is unascertained.

Gene Autry, v; or Gene Autry, poss. Jimmy Long, poss. Smilie Burnette, v trio-1; acc. Carl Cotner, f; Frank Marvin, esg; unknown, g; unknown, sb.
Los Angeles, CA   Monday, October 11, 1937

LA-1451-A	The One Rose (That's Left In My Heart)	ARC 7-10-58, Vo/OK 03262, Cq 8879
LA-1452-B	Blue Hawaii	OK 05693, RZ MR3754, RZIr IZ1264
LA-1453-D	Dust -1	ARC 8-04-58, Vo/OK 04172, Cq 9427, Co 20681, CoC C1506, RZ MR2862

Matrix LA-1451-A has been reported on Perfect 7-10-58; at least some pressings of Melotone 7-10-58 use instead matrix C-1908-1 (see above). (For issues from LA-1451-D see session of November 24, 1937.)

Gene Autry & His String Band: Gene Autry, v; acc. Carl Cotner, f; Frank Marvin, esg; unknown, g; unknown, sb.
Los Angeles, CA   Monday, October 11, 1937

LA-1454-A	Rhythm Of The Range	ARC 7-12-60, Vo/OK 03291, Cq 8882, 9513
LA-1455-B	Eyes To The Sky	Vo/OK 04091, Cq 8983, 9428

Vocalion/OKeh 04091, Conqueror 8882, 8983, 9428, 9513 as by **Gene Autry**.

Gene Autry, v; acc. Carl Cotner, f; Hymie Gunkler, cl-1; Frank Marvin, esg; unknown, g; unknown, sb.
   Los Angeles, CA   Friday, October 15, 1937

LA-1456-B	Old Buckaroo Goodbye	ARC 7-12-60, Vo/OK 03291, Cq 8882, 9444
LA-1457-A	In The Land Of Zulu -1	ARC 7-12-61, Vo/OK 03317, Cq 8960, 9441
LA-1462-A	It's Roundup Time In Reno -1	ARC 7-12-61
LA-1462-C	It's Roundup Time In Reno -1	ARC 7-12-61, Vo/OK 03317, Cq 8946, 9441
LA-1463-A	Were You Sincere -1	OK 05693, Cq 8960, RZ ME11, RZIn MR20147

Gene Autry, v; acc. Carl Cotner, f; Frank Marvin, esg; unknown, g; unknown, sb.
   Los Angeles, CA   Friday, October 15, 1937

| LA-1464-A | End Of My Round-Up Days | Vo/OK 04146, Cq 8946, 9550, Co 37004, 20030, CoC C309, RZAu G25201 |

Matrices LA-1458 to 1461 are by Johnny Mercer (popular). Rev. Regal-Zonophone G25201 postwar.

Gene Autry, v; or Gene Autry, poss. Jimmy Long, poss. Smilie Burnette, v trio-1; acc. Carl Cotner, f; Frank Marvin, sg; unknown, g; unknown, sb.
   Los Angeles, CA   Monday, October 18, 1937

LA-1469-A	My Star Of The Sky	Vo/OK 04340, Cq 8880, 9442, RZAu G23608
LA-1470-A	When The Tumbleweeds Come Tumbling Down Again	ARC 8-04-58, Cq 8982, Vo/OK 04091
LA-1471-A	When It's Springtime In The Rockies -1	Vo 03448
LA-1471-B	When It's Springtime In The Rockies -1	ARC 8-03-51, Cq 8982, Vo/OK 03448, Co 20865
LA-1472-A	I Want A Pardon For Daddy	Vo/OK 04146, Cq 8933, Co 37004, 20030, CoC C309
LA-1473-A	Take Me Back To My Boots And Saddle -1	ARC unissued: *Co CK48957 (CD)*
LA-1473-B	Take Me Back To My Boots And Saddle -1	Vo/OK 04172, Cq 8933, Co 20861, CoC C1506

Conqueror 8880, Columbia 20865 as by **Gene Autry & His String Band**.

   Los Angeles, CA   Wednesday, November 24, 1937

LA-1451-D	The One Rose (That's Left In My Heart)	Co 37702, 20281, CoC C973
LA-1530-B	There's A Gold Mine In The Sky	ARC 8-02-51, Cq 8968, Vo/OK 03358, Co 37003, 20029, CoC C1019
LA-1531-B	Sail Along, Silv'ry Moon	ARC 8-02-51, Cq 8968, Vo/OK 03358, Co 37003, 20029, CoC C1019
LA-1532-A	At The Old Barn Dance	ARC 8-03-51, Cq 8983, Vo/OK 03448, CoC C256

Gene Autry, v/y-1; acc. unknown, f; poss. Frank Marvin, esg; unknown, g; unknown, sb.
   Los Angeles, CA   Wednesday, June 22, 1938

LA-1667-A	I Don't Belong In Your World (And You Don't Belong In Mine)	Vo unissued: *Murray Hill M61072 (LP)*
LA-1668-A	Ride Tenderfoot Ride	Vo/OK 04262 Cq 9058, CoC C310, RZAu G23593
LA-1669-A	Good-Bye Pinto	Vo/OK 04340, Cq 9098, RZAu G23608
LA-1670-A	As Long As I've Got My Horse	Vo/OK 04246, Cq 9057

Gene Autry, v; acc. unknown, f; poss. Frank Marvin, esg; two unknowns, g; unknown, sb.
   Los Angeles, CA   Thursday, June 23, 1938

LA-1671	I'm Beginning To Care	Vo unissued
LA-1672-A	If Today Were The End Of The World	Co 20495, CoC C1185
LA-1673-A	The Dude Ranch Cowhands	Vo/OK 04246, Cq 9057, 9427
LA-1674-A	Panhandle Pete	Vo unissued: *Murray Hill M61072 (LP)*
LA-1675-A	The Old Trail	Vo/OK 04262, Cq 9058, CoC C310, RZ MR2862, RZAu G23593

Acc. Sam Koki, esg; unknown, g; unknown, 2nd g-1; unknown, sb; unknown, vb-2.
   Los Angeles, CA   Thursday, April 13, 1939

LA-1847-A	Paradise In The Moonlight -2	Vo/OK 04810, Cq 9259, 9449, RZ ME6, MR3754, RZAu G23938, RZIn MR20094, RZIr IZ1264
LA-1848-A	Old November Moon -2	Vo/OK 04908, Cq 9260, 9444, CoE FB2279, CoSs MZ170
LA-1849-A	You're The Only Star (In My Blue Heaven) -2	Vo/OK 03097, Cq 9098, Co 37002, 20028
LA-1850-A	I Just Want You -1	Vo/OK 04809, Cq 9194, RZAu G24894
LA-1851-A	I Don't Belong In Your World (And You Don't Belong In Mine) -1	Vo/OK 05015, Cq 9426
LA-1852-A	Blue Montana Skies -1	Vo/OK 04947, Cq 9261, RZ ME3, RZIn MR20081, Twin FT8913

Columbia MZ170 possibly as by **Gene Autry, The Singing Cowboy-Filmstar**.
Earlier pressings of Vocalion 03097 and Conqueror 9098 use matrix C-1177 rather than LA-1849.

Acc. Carl Cotner, f; unknown, f; prob. Sam Koki, esg; unknown, g; unknown, sb.
  Los Angeles, CA   Friday, April 14, 1939
    LA-1853-A   When I First Laid Eyes On You   Vo/OK 04810, Cq 9259, 9449, RZAu G23938
    LA-1854-A   If It Wasn't For The Rain   Vo/OK 04908, Cq 9260, 9428
    LA-1855-A   Little Old Band Of Gold   Vo/OK 05080, Cq 9614, Co 37010, 20036,
                                                         CoC C287, RZ ME14, MR3497, RZAu G24289,
                                                         RZIn MR20186, RZIr IZ1135
    LA-1856-A   Rhythm Of The Hoof Beats   Vo/OK 04947, Cq 9261, 9450, CoE FB2270,
                                                         CoSs MZ170
    LA-1857-A   Little Sir Echo   Vo/OK 04809, Cq 9194

Columbia MZ170 possibly as by **Gene Autry, The Singing Cowboy-Filmstar**.

Acc. Carl Cotner, f; unknown, f-1; unknown, ac; prob. Frank Marvin, esg; unknown, g; unknown, sb.
  Los Angeles, CA   Tuesday, April 18, 1939
    LA-1864-A   I Wonder If You Feel The Way I Do -1   Vo/OK 04854, Cq 9258
    LA-1865-A   Back In The Saddle Again -1   Vo 05080, OK 05080, Cq 9341, 9544, Co 37010,
                                                         20036, CoC C287, Min M-14138, RZ ME9,
                                                         RZAu G25141, RZIn MR20161
    LA-1866-A   I'm Gonna Round Up My Blues   Vo/OK 05015, Cq 9426
    LA-1867-A   We've Come A Long Way Together -1   Vo/OK 04854, Cq 9258, RZ ME6,
                                                         RZIn MR20094

Matrix LA-1865 is titled *Back To The Saddle* on Vocalion 05080, Conqueror 9341.

Acc. unknown, f-1; unknown, ac; poss. Frank Marvin, esg; unknown, eg; unknown, g; unknown, sb.
  Chicago, IL   Monday, September 11, 1939
    WC-2696-A   South Of The Border (Down Mexico Way) Vo/OK 05122, Cq 9305, Co 37195, 20242,
                                                         CoC C293, M-595, Co-Philco 3, RZ ME1,
                                                         MR6, RZIn MR20059
    WC-2697-A   Little Pardner -1   Vo/OK 05190, Cq 9341, RZ ME12,
                                                         RZIn MR20163
    WC-2698-A   The Merry-Go-Roundup -1   Vo/OK 05257

Rev. Columbia-Philco 3 by Blind Boy Fuller (see *B&GR*).

Acc. unknown, f; unknown, ac; unknown, eg; unknown, g; unknown, sb.
  Chicago, IL   Tuesday, September 12, 1939
    WC-2699-A   A Gold Mine In Your Heart   Vo/OK 05122, Cq 9305, Co 37643, 20242,
                                                         C293, RZ ME1, RZIn MR20059
    WC-2700-A   I'm Beginning To Care   Vo/OK 05257, Cq 9390
    WC-2701-A   Darling How Can You Forget So Soon   Vo/OK 05190, Cq 9390, RZ ME9, MR3738,
                                                         RZAu G24501, RZIn MR20161, RZIr IZ1252

Regal-Zonophone MR3738 as by **Gene Autry (The Yodling Cowboy)**. Rev. Regal-Zonophone MR3738 postwar.

Acc. Carl Cotner, f; Spade Cooley, f; Paul Sells, pac; Frank Marvin, esg; Oliver E. (Eddie) Tudor, g; Walter Jecker, sb; band, v eff-1.
  Los Angeles, CA   Tuesday, March 12, 1940
    LA-2174-A   The Singing Hills   Vo/OK 05513, Cq 9388
    LA-2175-A   Good-Bye Little Darlin' Good-Bye   Vo/OK 05463, Cq 9389, Co 37011, 20037,
                                                         CoC C83, *V-D 20*, RZ ME11, RZAu G24101,
                                                         RZIn MR20147
    LA-2176-A   El Rancho Grande (My Ranch) -1   Vo/OK 05513, Cq 9388, RZ ME12, MR3497,
                                                         RZIn MR20163, RZIr IZ1135
    LA-2177-A   Mary Dear   Vo/OK 05599, Cq 9387, CoC C21, RZ ME10,
                                                         MR3588, RZIn MR20162, RZIr IZ1192
    LA-2178-B   There's Only One Love In A Lifetime   Vo/OK 05599, Cq 9387, CoC C21, RZ ME10,
                                                         RZIn MR20162
    LA-2179-B   When I'm Gone You'll Soon Forget   Vo/OK 05463, Cq 9389, Co 37011, 20037,
                                                         CoC C83, RZ ME14, RZAu G24101,
                                                         RZIn MR20186

  Los Angeles, CA   Tuesday, August 20, 1940
    LA-2311-A   Blueberry Hill   OK 05779, Cq 9545, Co 20485, CoC C1165, L3,
                                                         RZ MR3404, RZAu G24289, RZIn MR20138,
                                                         RZIr IZ1108
    LA-2312-A   A Face I See At Evening   OK 06089, Cq 9614, Co 37655, 20254,
                                                         CoC C277, CoSs MZ243, RZAu G25053
    LA-2313-A   Be Honest With Me   OK 05980, Cq 9549, Co 37018, 20044,
                                                         CoC C207, C729, RZ MR3477, RZAu G24501,
                                                         RZIn MR20207, RZIr IZ1126

LA-2314-A	The Call Of The Canyon	OK 05890, Cq 9544, Co 37652, 20251, CoC C162, C977, RZAu G24230, G24950
LA-2314-B	The Call Of The Canyon	OK unissued: *Co CK48957 (CD)*

Columbia MZ243 possibly as by **Gene Autry, The Singing Cowboy-Filmstar**.

Los Angeles, CA   Wednesday, August 21, 1940

LA-2315-A	There'll Never Be Another Pal Like You	OK 06239, Cq 9800, Co 37660, 20259, CoC C367, C913
LA-2316-A	Broomstick Buckaroo	OK 05890, Cq 9550, Co 37652, 20251, CoC C162, C977, RZAu G24230
LA-2317-A	Sycamore Lane	OK 05779, Cq 9545, Co 20485, CoC C1165, RZAu G25053
LA-2318-A	There Ain't No Use In Crying Now	OK 06089, Cq 9415, Co 37655, 20254, CoC C277, CoSs MZ243, RZAu G24950

Columbia MZ243 possibly as by **Gene Autry, The Singing Cowboy-Filmstar**.

Los Angeles, CA   Thursday, August 22, 1940

LA-2319-A	You Waited Too Long	OK 05781, Cq 9547, Co 37016, 20042, CoC C93, RZ MR3455, RZAu G25010, RZIn MR20191, RZIr IZ1123
LA-2320-A	That Little Kid Sister Of Mine	OK 05781, Cq 9547, Co 37016, 20042, CoC C93, RZ MR3455, RZAu G24988, RZIn MR20191, RZIr IZ1123
LA-2321-B	What's Gonna Happen To Me	OK 05980, Cq 9549, Co 37018, 20044, CoC C207, C729, RZ MR3477, RZIn MR20207, RZIr IZ1126
LA-2322-A	Tears On My Pillow	OK 06239, Cq 9415, Co 37660, 20259, CoC C367, C913, RZAu G24827
LA-2323-A	Sierra Sue	OK 05780, Cq 9548, RZ MR3404, RZAu G24219, RZIn MR20138, RZIr IZ1108

Los Angeles, CA   Tuesday, August 27, 1940

LA-2336-A	Good Old Fashioned Hoedown	Cq 9425, Co 36904, 20012, CoC C782, RZ ME56, RZIr IZ1334
LA-2337-A	When The Swallows Come Back To Capistrano	OK 05780, Cq 9546, RZ MR3738, RZAu G24219, RZIr IZ1252
LA-2338-B	We Never Dream The Same Dream Twice	OK 05793, Cq 9546
LA-2339-A	The Cowboy's Trademarks	Cq 9425, Co 20635
LA-2340-A	The Last Letter	Cq 9800, Co 20495, CoC C1185
LA-2341-A	I'll Never Smile Again	OK 05795, Cq 9548

Rev. Columbias and Regal-Zonophone ME56, IZ1334 postwar.

Acc. Carl Cotner, f; Mischa Russell, f; Paul Sells, pac; Frank Marvin, esg; Johnny Bond, g; Dick Reinhart, sb.

Hollywood, CA   Wednesday, June 18, 1941

H-315-1,-2	You Are My Sunshine	OK 06274, Cq 9799, Co 37021, 20047, RZ MR3588, RZAu G25105, RZIr IZ1192
H-316-1,-2	It Makes No Difference Now	OK 06274, Cq 9799, Co 37021, 20047, *V-D 240, V-D Navy 20*, RZAu G25105
H-317-1	After Tomorrow	OK unissued
H-318-1	A Year Ago Tonight	OK 06360, CoC C438, RZ MR3632, RZIr IZ1200

There may be only one fiddle on matrix H-315.

Acc. Carl Cotner, f; Don Linder, t; Paul Sells, pac; Frank Marvin, esg; Eddie Tudor, g; W. Fred Whiting, sb.

Hollywood, CA   Monday, July 28, 1941

H-384-2	I'll Never Let You Go (Little Darlin')	OK 06360, CoC C438, RZ MR3633, RZAu G24988, RZIr IZ1200
H-385-1,-2	I'll Be True While You're Gone	OK 6648, Cq 9801, Co 37023, 20029, CoC C649, CoIr IFB395, RZ MR3728, RZAu G24858, RZIr IZ1236
H-386-1	Under Fiesta Stars	OK 6694, Cq 9802, CoC C685, RZAu G24806
H-387-2	Spend A Night In Argentina	OK 6694, Cq 9802, CoC C685, RZAu G24816

Hollywood, CA   Wednesday, July 30, 1941

H-392-1,-2	I'll Wait For You	OK 06511, Cq 9801, Co 37430, 20157, CoC C548, RZ ME25, MR3758, RZAu G24858, RZIr IZ1298
H-393-1	Too Late	OK 06549, Cq 9803, Co 37425, 20152, CoC C575, RZAu G24827
H-394-1	Don't Bite The Hand That's Feeding You	OK 06359, Co 37663, 20262

| H-395-1 | After Tomorrow | OK 06434, Cq 9797, V-D 240, V-D Navy 20, CoC C490, RZ MR3699, RZAu G24950, RZIr IZ1203 |

Hollywood, CA   Friday, August 1, 1941

H-399-1	God Must Have Loved America	OK 06359, Co 37663, 20262
H-400-1	You Are The Light Of My Life	OK 06567, Cq 9803, Co 37423, 20150, CoC C576, RZAu G24858
H-401-1,-2	Lonely River	OK 06511, Cq 9804, Co 37430, 20157, CoC C548, RZ ME25, RZ MR3758, RZAu G24958, RZIr IZ1298
H-402-1	Dear Little Dream Girl Of Mine	Cq 9804

Acc. Carl Cotner, f; Mischa Russell, f; Ted Bacon, vla; Andy Iona Long, esg; Eddie Tudor, g; Fred Whiting, sb.
    Hollywood, CA   Monday, August 11, 1941

H-423-1	Purple Sage In The Twilight	OK 6725, Cq 9805, Co 37036, 20061
H-424-1	I Wish All My Children Were Babies Again	OK unissued
H-425-1	Dear Old Dad Of Mine	Cq 9805
H-426-1	I'm Comin' Home Darlin'	OK 06461, Cq 9806, Co 37437, 20164, CoC C511

Acc. Carl Cotner, f; Spade Cooley, f; Frank Marvin, esg; Eddie Tudor, g; Fred Whiting, sb.
    Hollywood, CA   Wednesday, August 27, 1941

H-486-1	If You Only Believed In Me	OK 6725, Cq 9807, Co 37036, 20061
H-487-1	Keep Rollin' Lazy Longhorns	OK 06643, Co 37410, 20137
H-488-1	Blue-Eyed Elaine	OK 06549, Cq 9807, Co 37425, 20152, CoC C575

Matrix H-486 is titled *If You Believed In Me* on Conqueror 9807.

Acc. Carl Cotner, f; unknown, f-1; Don Linder, t-2; Thurman Ratraff, cl; Paul Sells, pac; Karl Farr, g; Fred Whiting, sb; unknown, v trio-3.
    Hollywood, CA   Friday, September 26, 1941

H-424-2	I Wish All My Children Were Babies Again -2	OK 06461, Cq 9806, Co 37437, 20164, CoC C511, RZ MR3649, RZAu G25010, RZIr IZ1203
H-520-1	Amapola (Pretty Little Poppy) -2, 3	OK 06435, Cq 9798
H-521-1	Maria Elena -1, 3	OK 06435, Cq 9798
H-522-1	I Don't Want To Set The World On Fire -3	OK 06434, Cq 9797, Co 20865, CoC C490

Acc. Carl Cotner, f; Mischa Russell, f; Jack Mayhew, cl-1; Paul Sells, pac; Frank Marvin, esg; Johnny Bond, g; Fred Whiting, sb.
    Hollywood, CA   Saturday, December 13, 1941

H-598-1	Take Me Back Into Your Heart	OK 6680, Co 36587, 37024, 20050, CoC C656, RZAu G24844
H-599-1	Sweethearts Or Strangers -1	OK 06567, Co 37423, 20150, CoC C576, RZAu G24674
H-600-1	I Hang My Head And Cry -1	OK 06627, Co 37412, 20139, CoC C635, RZAu G24971
H-601-1	You'll Be Sorry	OK 06627, Co 37412, 20139, CoC C635, V-D 20, RZAu G24971

Acc. Carl Cotner, f; Don Linder, t; Joe Krechter, cl; Paul Sells, pac; Frank Marvin, esg; Johnny Bond, g; Fred Whiting, sb; band v-1/clapping-1.
    Hollywood, CA   Tuesday, February 24, 1942

H-676-1	Tweedle-O-Twill	OK 6680, Co 36587, 37024, 20050, CoC C656, RZAu G24707
H-677-1	Deep In The Heart Of Texas -1	OK 06643, Co 37410, 20137, RZAu G24674
H-678-1,-2	I'm Thinking Tonight Of My Blue Eyes	OK 6648, Co 37023, 20049, CoC C649, CoIr IFB395, RZ MR3728, RZAu G24806, RZIr IZ1236
H-679-1	Rainbow On The Rio Colorado	OK 6682, Co 36598, 37026, 20052, CoC C659, RZAu G24844

There may be no trumpet on matrix H-679.

Acc. Carl Cotner, f; Mischa Russell, f; Paul Sells, pac; Frank Marvin, esg; Johnny Bond, g; Fred Whiting, sb.
    Hollywood, CA   Thursday, March 26, 1942

H-759-1	Private Buckaroo	OK 6682, Co 36598, 37026, 20049, CoC C659
H-760-1	Call For Me And I'll Be There	OK 6684, Co 37027, 20053, RZAu G24881
H-761-1	Yesterday's Roses	OK 6684, Co 37027, 20053, RZAu G24881

Acc. Carl Cotner, f; Don Linder, t; Jack Mayhew, cl; Paul Sells, pac; Frank Marvin, esg; Johnny Bond, g; Fred Whiting, sb; unknown, male v group; unknown woman, v-1.

Hollywood, CA   Wednesday, June 10, 1942

| H-831-1 | Jingle Jangle Jingle -1 | OK 6690, Co 37406, 20133, CoC C662, RZ MR3666, RZAu G24707, RZIr IZ1229 |
| H-832-1 | I'm A Cow Poke Pokin' Along | OK 6690, Co 37406, 20133, CoC C662, RZ MR3666, RZIr IZ1229 |

There may be no trumpet on matrix H-831.
Gene Autry recorded after 1942.

AVOCA QUARTETTE

O.M. Hunt, K.T. Hunt, W.R. Stidman, W.H. Bowers, vocal quartet; acc. two unknowns, f; unknown, g.

Winston-Salem, NC   Tuesday, September 20, 1927

81355-B	He Lives On High	OK 45182
81356-	Walking With Jesus	OK unissued
81357-	Gates Of Gold	OK unissued

Winston-Salem, NC   Wednesday, September 21, 1927

81358-B	My Precious Mother	OK 45182
81359-	Swinging 'Neath The Old Oak Trees	OK unissued
81360-	Down Where The Watermelons Grow	OK unissued

AVONDALE MILLS QUARTET

F.M. Tanton, tv; F.G. Tapley, tv; unknown, bv; T.T. Pitts, bsv; unacc.

Atlanta, GA   Sunday, October 21, 1928

| 47221-2 | Rejoicing On The Way | Vi V-40211 |
| 47222-2 | Stilling The Tempest | Vi V-40211 |

B

PERCY BABINEAUX–BIXY GUIDRY

Percy Babineaux, f/v-1; Bixy Guidry, ac/v-2.

New Orleans, LA   Wednesday, November 6, 1929

56494-2	Vien A La Maison Avec Moi (You'll Come Home With Me) -2	Vi 22210
56495-2	J'Vai Jouer Celea Pour Toi (I'll Play This For You)	Vi 22210
56496-2	Qu'Est Que J'Ai Fait Pour Etre Peuni Si Longtemps? (What Did I Do To Be Punished So Long?) -2	Vi 22365
56497-2	La Valse Du Bayou (The Waltz Of The Bayou) -2	Vi 22563
56498-1	Je Tai Toujors Dis Dene Pas Fair Sa (I Always Told You Not To Do That) -2	Vi 22563
56499-2	Elle A Plurer Pour Revenir (She Cried To Come Back But She Couldn't) -1	Vi 22365
56500-2	Waltz Of The Long Wood -1	BB B-2084
56501-2	I Am Happy Now	BB B-2084

Victor 22210 as by **Bixy Guidry–Percy Babineaux**.

BACHELOR BUDDIES

Richmond, IN   Thursday, February 8, 1934

| 19489,-A,-B | Tennessee Coon | Ge unissued trial recording |

BACK HOME BOYS

Pseudonym on Varsity for Bob Miller.

LES BACKER

Recordings by this artist on Gennett and Vocalion are outside the scope of this work.

DEFORD BAILEY

DeFord Bailey, h solo.

Atlanta, GA   Friday, April 1, 1927

| 143846-1,-2 | Pan American Express | Co unissued |
| 143847-1,-2 | Hesitation Mama | Co unissued |

New York, NY			Monday, April 18, 1927
E-22475*/76	Pan American Blues	Br 146, Vo 5180	

New York, NY			Tuesday, April 19, 1927
E-22501*/02	Dixie Flyer Blues	Br 146, Vo 5180	
E-22503/04*	Up Country Blues	Br 147, BrC 434	
E-22505/06*	Evening Prayer Blues	Br 148, BrC 435, Vo 5147	
E-22507/08*	Muscle Shoal Blues	Br 147, BrC 434	
E-22509/10*	Old Hen Cackle	Vo 5190	
E-22511	Alcoholic Blues	Br 148, BrC 435, Vo 5147	
E-22512	Fox Chase	Vo 5190	

At least some copies of Brunswick 147 have the labels reversed.

Nashville, TN			Tuesday, October 2, 1928
47110-1,-2	Lost John	Vi unissued	
47111-2	John Henry	Vi 23336, 23831	
47112-1	Ice Water Blues	Vi V-38014, BB B-5147, Sr S-3228, MW M-4910	
47113-1,-2	Kansas City Blues	Vi unissued	
47114-1,-2	Casey Jones	Vi unissued	
47115-1,-2	Wood Street Blues	Vi unissued	
47116-1	Davidson County Blues	Vi V-38014, BB B-5147, Sr S-3228, MW M-4910	
47117-1,-2	Nashville Blues	Vi unissued	

Revs: Victor 23336 by Noah Lewis (see *B&GR*), 23831 by D.H. Bilbro.

DeFord Bailey recorded after 1942.

GREEN BAILEY

Green Bailey, v; acc. Doc Roberts, f-1; Asa Martin, h-2/g-3; own g-4.

Richmond, IN			Friday, November 30, 1928
14487	The Santa Barbara Earthquake -1, 3	Ge 6702, Ch 15652, Spt 9320	
14489	I Wish I Were A Mole In The Ground -2, 3, 4	Ge 6732, Cq 7255	
14490-A	The Fate Of Ellen Smith -1, 4	Ge 6702, Spt 9372	

Champion 15652 as by **Aaron Boyd**. Supertone 9320 as by **Harry Farr**, 9372 as by **Harvey Farr**. Conqueror 7255 as by **Amos Baker**. Matrix 14488 is by Dick Parman. Rev. Supertone 9372 by John D. Foster.

Acc. Doc Roberts, f-1; own g.

Richmond, IN			Saturday, December 1, 1928
14495,-A	Fate Of Talt Hall -1	Ge rejected	
14496-A	If I Die A Railroad Man -1	Ge 6732, Ch 15652, Spt 9320	
14497	Twenty Years In Prison	Cq 7255	

Champion 15652 as by **Aaron Boyd**. Supertone 9320 as by **Harry Farr**. Conqueror 7255 as by **Amos Baker**.

Acc. Doc Roberts, md-1; Asa Martin, g.

Richmond, IN			Thursday, August 29, 1929
15526	Just Before The Last Fierce Charge	Ge rejected	
15527	The Hanging Of Edward Hawkins	Ge rejected	
15531,-A	The Girl I Left In Kentucky	Ge rejected	
15532-A	The Wreck Of Number 4 -1	Chg 425	
15533,-A	Goin' To The West Next Fall -1	Ge rejected	
15534	Shut Up In Coal Creek Mine	Chg 425	
15535,-A	The Soldier's Sweetheart	Ge rejected	

Challenge 425 as by **Dick Bell**.

Matrix 15532 was originally logged as *The Wreck Of No. 4 And The Death Of John Daily*.
Matrices 15528/29 are by Merl E. McGinnis; 15530 is by Asa Martin & James Roberts.

JIM BAIRD

Pseudonym on Montgomery Ward, Victor, and Zonophone for Bill Elliott.

AMOS BAKER

Pseudonym on Conqueror for Green Bailey.

BILL BAKER

See Bob Miller.

BUDDY BAKER

This artist's real name is Ernest Baker.

Buddy Baker, v; acc. own g.

Chicago, IL	Thursday, June 21, 1928

45948-1,-2	I Want My Mammy	Vi unissued
45949-1	Penitentiary Blues	Vi 21549
45950-2	Box Car Blues	Vi 21549
45951-1	Alimony Blues	Vi V-40017
45952-1	Matrimonial Intentions	Vi V-40017
45953-1	Nobody Knows What's On My Mind Blues	Vi unissued

Victor 21549 as by **"Buddy" Baker**.

Chicago, IL   Friday, June 22, 1928

| 45954-1 | My Baby's Back In town | Vi unissued |
| 45955-1 | Razor Jim | Vi unissued |

Camden, NJ   Wednesday, June 5, 1929

50896-1,-2	It's Tough On Everybody	Vi unissued
50897-1,-2	The Rambling Cowboy	Vi unissued
50898-1,-2	Friends Of Yesterday	Vi unissued
50899-1,-2	Mother's Lullaby	Vi unissued

CHARLES BAKER (THE WYOMING COWBOY)

Charles Baker, v; acc. prob. own h/g.

Richmond, IN   Monday, August 15, 1932

| 18694 | Just Plain Folks | Ch S-16614 |

Richmond, IN   Wednesday, August 17, 1932

| 18695 | Apple Blossoms | Ch S-16614 |

Richmond, IN   Tuesday, January 16, 1934

19447	Tender Recollections	Ch 16737, 45044, MeC 45044, MW 4929
19448	Curly Joe	Ch 16737, 45044, MeC 45044, Min M-14044
19449	Utah Carroll	Ch 16724, 45052, MeC 45052
19450	The Dying Boy's Prayer	Ch 16724, 45052, MeC 45052, MW 4929, Min M-14038

Champion 16724, 16737 as by **The Wyoming Cowboy**. Revs: Minerva M-14038 by Asa Martin, M-14044 by Cliff Carlisle.

CLEM BAKER

Pseudonym on Supertone for Miller Wikel.

DICK BAKER

Pseudonym on Madison and Van Dyke for Bob Miller.

ELDON BAKER & HIS BROWN COUNTY REVELERS

Charlie Linville, f; Bronson "Barefoot Brownie" Reynolds, h-1/sb/v-2; Harry Adams, lg; Wade Baker, g/v-3; Floyd Baker, g/v-4; prob. Eldon Baker, v-5.

Chicago, IL   Saturday, June 4, 1938

C-2252-1	Come Along Down To The Old Plantation -3	Vo 04441, Cq 9111
C-2253-1,-2	You Can't Do Wrong And Get By -3	Vo unissued
C-2254-1	Lost John -1, 2	Vo 04217
C-2255-1,-2	Choking The Reeds -1	Vo unissued
C-2256-1,-2	I Know There Is Somebody Waiting -3, 4, 5	Vo unissued
C-2257-1,-2	When The Roses Bloom In Dixieland -3, 4, 5	Vo unissued
C-2258-1,-2	Plodding Along -3	Vo unissued

Charlie Linville, f-1; Bronson "Barefoot Brownie" Reynolds, h-2/sb; Harry Adams, lg/v-3; Wade Baker, g/v-4; Floyd Baker, g/v-5; prob. Eldon Baker, v-6.

Chicago, IL   Sunday, June 5, 1938

C-2259-1,-2	Ramblin' Boy -1, 4, 5, 6	Vo unissued
C-2260-1,-2	Don't Lay Me On My Back -1, 4, 5, 6	Vo unissued
C-2261-1	It's Hard -1, 2, 4, 5	Vo 04217
C-2262-1,-2	Froggie Went A-Courtin' -1, 4, 5, 6	Vo unissued
C-2263-1	Don't You Want To Go (To That Happy Home On High) -4, 5, 6	Vo 04279
C-2264-1	I Will Meet You -4, 5, 6	Vo 04279
C-2265-1	Happy Cowboy -1, 4	Vo 04355
C-2266-1	Roll Along, Jordon -1, 4, 5, 6	Vo 04355
C-2267-1	One Eyed Sam -1, 3	Vo unissued: Co C4K47911 (CD)
C-2268-1	Dear Old Dixieland -1, 4	Vo 04441, Cq 9111
C-2269-1,-2	In The Hills Over There -1, 4, 5, 6	Vo unissued

| C-2270-1,-2 | Sittin' Round The Fireside -1, 4? | Vo unissued |
| C-2271-1,-2 | Little Bonnie -1, 4, 5, 6 | Vo unissued |

Only one guitar is used on matrices C-2263/64.

MR. & MRS. J.W. BAKER

J.W. (Jim) Baker, Flora Baker, v duet; acc. J.E. Green, f; J.H. Holbrook, bj; Flora Baker, ah; Jim Baker, g.
Bristol, TN   Wednesday, August 3, 1927

| 39765-2 | The Newmarket Wreck | Vi 20863 |
| 39766-1 | On The Banks Of The Sunny Tennessee | Vi 20863 |

BAKER BOYS

Pseudonym on Aurora for Archie Lee and others. See The Chumbler Family & Associated Groups.

BAKER'S WHITLEY COUNTY SACRED SINGERS

Prob. vocal group, poss. including A.G. Baker, v; acc. unknown.
Knoxville, TN   Wednesday, August 28, 1929

| TK-125 | When I Take My Vacation In Heaven | Vo rejected |
| TK-126 | Jesus Is Getting Us Ready For That Great Day | Vo rejected |

LUKE BALDWIN

Pseudonym on Champion for Bill Cox.

A.J. BALL

See Elmer Bird and associated artists.

RAY BALL [& HIS GUITAR]

Pseudonym on various Plaza/ARC labels and derivatives for Frank Marvin.

WILBUR BALL

Wilbur Ball Of WLAP, v; acc. Cliff Carlisle, sg/y; own g.
Richmond, IN   Tuesday, February 25, 1930

| 16321-A | My Carolina Sunshine Girl | Ge 7153, Spt 9651 |

Supertone 9651 as by **Amos Greene**. Rev. Gennett 7153, Supertone 9651 by Cliff Carlisle.

Wilbur Ball, v; acc. Cliff Carlisle, sg; own g.
Richmond, IN   Tuesday, December 8, 1931

| 18243 | I'm Paying The Price | Ge unissued |

Wilbur Ball also partnered Cliff Carlisle on many of his recordings in 1930-31.

WOLFE BALLARD [& CLAUDE SAMUELS]

Pseudonym on Paramount for Vernon Dalhart [& Carson Robison].

C.L. BALLEN & AMOS BALLEN

C. L. Ballen, f; Amos Ballen, g.
Atlanta, GA   Saturday, January 31, 1925

| 140313- | Spring Place Reel | Co unissued |
| 140314- | I Got Mine | Co unissued |

JOHN BALTZELL

John Baltzell, f; acc. John F. Burckhardt, p.
New York, NY   Friday, September 7, 1923

| 9144-A,-C | Money Musk Medley | Ed 51354 |
| 9145-A,-B,-C | Durang Hornpipe Medley | Ed 51236, 4918 |

New York, NY   Saturday, September 8, 1923

| 9148-A,-B,-C | Old Red Barn Medley Quadrille | Ed 51236, 4914 |
| 9149-A,-B | Buckeye Medley Quadrille | Ed 51354 |

New York, NY   Monday, September 10, 1923

| 9150-A,-B,-C | Farmer's Medley Quadrille | Ed 51548 |
| 9151-A,-B,-C | Drunken Sailor Medley | Ed 51548, 5454 |

Acc. "Mr. Shields" (poss. Roy Shield), p.
New York, NY   Thursday, June 19, 1924

| | Sand Class Reel | Vi unissued trial recording |
| | Pearl Quadrille | Vi unissued trial recording |

| | | Ada's Quadrille | Vi unissued trial recording |
| | | Levison Reel | Vi unissued trial recording |

These trial recordings were "made on approval", and no matrices were assigned. Two takes of each tune were made.

John Baltzell, f solo.
New York, NY   June/July 1924

| 72613-A | John Baltzell's Reel | OK 40206, PaE E3094 |
| 72614-A | Mandylyn Quadrille Medley | OK 40206, PaE E3094 |

John Baltzell, f; acc. John F. Burckhardt, p.
New York, NY   Thursday, March 24, 1927

| 11606-A | Electric Light Schotische | Ed 51995 |

New York, NY   Friday, March 25, 1927

| 11607-B | London Polka | Ed 51995 |
| 11608-A | Gilderoy's Reel | Ed 52022 |

New York, NY   Tuesday, March 29, 1927

11609-A	Clinton Quadrille	Ed 52022
11610-	Tramp Waltz	Ed 5411
11611-	Mocking Bird	Ed 5362
11612-	Sand Reel	Ed unissued
11613-	New Century Hornpipe	Ed unissued

John Baltzell, f solo.
New York, NY   c. late March 1927

7134-	The Arkansas Traveler	Ba 2159, Do 0195, Htd 16496, Or 917, Re 8392, Pm 3015, Bwy 8051
7135-2	Turkey In The Straw	Ba 2151, Do 0179, Htd 16492, Or 945, Re 8303, Pm 3015, Bwy 8052, Cq 7741
7136-	Sailor's Hornpipe	Ba 2159, Do 0195, Htd 16492, Or 945, Re 8392, Pm 3017, Bwy 8051
7137-1	The Girl I Left Behind	Ba 2151, Do 0179, Htd 16496, Or 917, Re 8303, Pm 3017, Bwy 8052, Cq 7741

Homestead 16492, 16496, Oriole 917, 945 as by **Hiram Jones**. Broadway 8051, 8052 as by **John Barton**.
Some pressings of Broadway 8052 and Conqueror 7741 use Doc Roberts' ARC recordings of the tunes, still credited to **John Barton** (Broadway) or **John Baltzell** (Conqueror). The Domino issue cited for matrices 7134 and 7136 is speculative.
Controls appear on various issues instead of, or as well as, the matrices, as follows: 7134 = 885-1,-2; 7136 = 946-2.

John Baltzell, f; acc. Samuel C. Shults, calls-1.
New York, NY   Monday, April 9, 1928

18378-A	Ginger Ridge Quadrille -1	Ed 52450, 5672
N-172-A,-B	Ginger Ridge Quadrille -1	Ed rejected
18379-A	Soldier's Joy Hornpipe -1	Ed 52370, 5634
N-173-A,-B	Soldier's Joy Hornpipe -1	Ed rejected
18380-B	S.J. Rafferty Reel	Ed 52450
N-174-A,-B	S.J. Rafferty Reel	Ed rejected
18381-A	Hills Quadrille	Ed 52370
N-175-A,-B	Hills Quadrille	Ed rejected
18382-B	Flowers At Edinburgh	Ed 52313
N-176-A,-B	Flowers At Edinburgh	Ed rejected
18383-B	Wooten Quadrille	Ed 52425
N-177-A,-B	Wooten Quadrille	Ed rejected
18384-A	Emmett Quadrille -1	Ed 52281, 5562
N-178-A,-B	Emmett Quadrille -1	Ed rejected

Acc. Samuel C. Shults, f-1/calls-2.
New York, NY   Tuesday, April 10, 1928

18385-C	Arkansas Traveler -2	Ed 52294, 5538
N-179-A,-B	Arkansas Traveler -2	Ed rejected
18386-B	Scotch Reel -1	Ed 52395, 5521
N-180-A,-B	Scotch Reel -1	Ed rejected
18387-A	Paddy Ryan's Favorite Irish Jig -1	Ed 52313, 5633
N-181-A,-B	Paddy Ryan's Favorite Irish Jig -1	Ed rejected
18388-B	Kenion Clog	Ed 52281, 5522
N-182-A,-B	Kenion Clog	Ed rejected

Unacc.
New York, NY   Wednesday, April 11, 1928

| 18391-B | Highland Fling | Ed 52395 |
| N-183-A,-B | Highland Fling | Ed rejected |

18392-B	Starlight Waltz	Ed 52425, 5703
N-184-A,-B	Starlight Waltz	Ed rejected
18393-A	Pandora Waltz	Ed 52294
N-185-A,-B	Pandora Waltz	Ed rejected

Matrices 18389/90 are untraced but evidently not by Baltzell.

HENRY L. BANDY

Henry L. Bandy, v; acc. own f.
   Richmond, IN   Wednesday, October 17, 1928

14359	Five Up	Ge unissued: *MS 45005* (LP); *Yz 2200-2* (CD)
14360	Going Across The Sea	Ge rejected: *MS 45004* (LP); *Yz 2200-7* (CD)
14361	Sail Away Ladies	Ge rejected: *MS 45004* (LP); *Yz 2200-4* (CD)
14362	Monkey Show	Ge rejected: *MS 45005* (LP)

KENT BANE

Kent Bane, v; acc. prob. own bj.
   Richmond, IN   Thursday, April 16, 1931

| 17680 | Ship That Never Returned | Ge rejected |

Acc. prob. own bj; Duke Clark, g/poss. v-1.
   Richmond, IN   Wednesday, November 2, 1932

| 18878 | Good Bye My Charming Bessie -1 | Ge rejected |
| 18879 | I Got Mine | Ge rejected |

Matrix 18878 is logged as by **Kent Bane & Duke Clark**.

BANG BOYS

See Roy Acuff.

BANJO JOE

Pseudonym on Columbia for Willard Hodgin. (Records on Paramount under this name are by Gus Cannon; see *B&GR*.)

JACK BANKEY

(Ray) Jack Bankey, v; acc. prob. Tony Lombardo, ac; prob. own g.
   Richmond, IN   Monday, December 17, 1928

| 14589-B | I've Still Got A Place In My Heart For You | Ch 15670, MW 4962 |
| 14590 | The Dearest Pal Is My Mother | Ch 15670, MW 4962 |

Champion 15670 as by **Lee Denton**.

See also Jack & Tony.

EMMETT BANKSTON & RED HENDERSON

Emmett Bankston, v/bj; Red Henderson, v/g.
   Atlanta, GA   Monday, July 30, 1928

402004-	Dollar A Week Furniture Man	OK unissued
402005-	Back To The Farm	OK unissued
402006-B	Six Nights Drunk – Part 1	OK 45292
402007-B	Six Nights Drunk – Part 2	OK 45292

Red Henderson also recorded solo, and both Bankston and Henderson recorded with Earl Johnson.

BAR-X COWBOYS

Ben Christian, f; Elwood B. "Elmer" Christian, f/poss. v-1; Moat Bartley, tbj; Chuck Keeshan, g/v-2; Lynn Henderson, g; Johnny Cuttiette, sb; band v-3.
   Dallas, TX   Tuesday, December 14, 1937

63051-A	Lies -2	De 5482
63052-A	Drifting And Dreaming (Sweet Paradise) -1, 2	De 5510, MeC 45257
63053-A	In A Shanty In Old Shantytown -2	De rejected
63054-A	Underneath The Sun -3	De 5537
63055-A	There Is A Tavern In The Town -2, 3	De 5537
63056-A	That Little Boy Of Mine -2	De rejected
63057-A	Smile, Darn Ya, Smile -2	De 5524, MeC 45265
63058-A	I'd Love To Live In Loveland (With A Girl Like You) -2	De 5482
63059-A	Rockdale Rag	De 5524, MeC 45265
63060-A	When Your Hair Has Turned To Silver (I Will Love You Just The Same) -2	De 5510, MeC 45257

Ben Christian, f; Buddy Ray, f; Ted Daffan, esg; Moat Bartley, tbj; Chuck Keeshan, g/v-1; Buddy Duhon, g/v-2; Elmer Christian, v-3.
    Dallas, TX   Tuesday, February 13, 1940

047697-1	I'm Just An Outcast -1	BB B-8440, MW M-8648, RZ ME59, RZAu G24443, RZIr IZ1338
047698-1	My Dark Eyed Sweetheart -1	BB B-8440, MW M-8648, RZ ME59, RZAu G24443, RZIr IZ1338
047699-1	Sunset Valley -1, 3	BB B-8546, MW M-8659, RZAu G24915
048000-1	Blue Bonnet Governor -2	BB B-8487, MW M-8660
048001-1	Blue Steele Blues	BB B-8487, MW M-8660
048002-1	South	BB B-8546, MW M-8659
048003-1	Houston Shuffle	BB B-8577, MW M-8661
048004-1	When Mama Goes Out The Maid Comes In -3	BB B-8577, MW M-8661

Bill Kruger, f; Ted Daffan, esg; Moat Bartley, tbj; Chuck Keeshan, g/v-1; Elmer Christian, sb.
    Dallas, TX   Tuesday, April 8, 1941

063048-1	You've Got To Stop Fussin' At Me -1	BB B-8825
063049-1	Just For Tonight -1	BB B-8763
063050-1	Let's Go Honky-Tonkin' Tonight -1	BB B-8723
063051-1	Locket Of Gold -1	BB B-8825, RZAu G24915
063052-1	I Want Somebody Like You -1	BB B-8763
063053-1	Hang Over Blues	BB B-8723
063054-1	Struttin' Around	BB B-8801
063055-1	I Didn't Think I'd Care -1	BB B-8801

Bill Kruger, f; Ernest "Deacon" Evans, esg; Moat Bartley, tbj; Jerry Irby, g/v-1; Elmer Christian, sb/v-2.
    Dallas, TX   Thursday, October 9, 1941

071134-1	Only Time Can Tell -1	BB B-8904, RZAu G25205
071135-1	You're Still My Darling -1, 2	BB B-8904, RZAu G25205
071136-1	Let's All Go Down To Grandpa's -1	BB B-8930
071137-1	I Don't Worry -1	BB B-8994
071138-1	I'm So Sorry -1	BB B-8994
071139-1	Girls...Girls...Girls -1	BB B-8930
071140-1	Why Do I Dream Such Dreams? -1	BB 33-0506
071141-1	Jammin' On The Steel Guitar	BB 33-0506

BARBER & OSBORNE

George Barber, md; Gwyn Osborne, g (or vice versa).
    Richmond, IN   Friday, February 5, 1932

18376	In The Shade Of The Parasol	Ch S-16392
18377	Fallen By The Wayside	Ch S-16392
18378	Carbolic Rag	Ge unissued
18379	He Rambled	Ge unissued

TED BARE

Ted Bare, v/y-1; acc. prob. own md.
    Richmond, IN   Thursday, November 21, 1929

15919,-A	The Bulldog Down In Tennessee	Ge rejected
15920,-A	Hokey, Pokey, Diddle, Run	Ge rejected
15922,-A	The Moonshiner's Dream Of Home -1	Ge rejected
15924	My Blue Ridge Mountain Damsel -1	Ge rejected

Intervening matrices are unrelated.

JOHNNY BARFIELD

Johnny Barfield, v; acc. own g.
    Atlanta, GA   Monday, August 21, 1939

041210-1	Why Don't You Give Me My Memories?	BB B-8318, MW M-8408, RZAu G24178
041211-1	Don't Cry My Darlin'	BB B-8318, MW M-8408, RZAu G24178
041212-1	In A Sleepy Country Town	BB B-8300, MW M-8409, RZAu G24245
041213-1	When Daddy Played The Old Banjo	BB B-8300, MW M-8409, RZAu G24245
041214-1	Boogie-Woogie	BB B-8272, MW M-8407
041215-1	Everybody's Tryin' To Be My Baby	BB B-8272, MW M-8407

Acc. Ralph Pleasant, f-1; own g.
    Atlanta, GA   Monday, February 5, 1940

047512-1	Gonna Ride Till The Sun Goes Down -1	BB B-8395, MW M-8653, RZAu G24725
047513-1	My Poodle Doodle Dog -1	BB B-8415, MW M-8656, HMVIn NE637

047514-1	That Little Shirt My Mother Made For Me -1	BB B-8506, MW M-8656
047515-1	Ain't I Right? -1	BB B-8486, MW M-8657
047516-1	Long Tongue Women -1	BB B-8486, MW M-8657
047517-1	Old Fiddler Joe -1	BB B-8395, MW M-8653, RZAu G24725
047518-1	Love Me Only -1	BB B-8447, MW M-8654, RZAu G24761
047519-1	Don't Take My Memories -1	BB B-8447, MW M-8654, RZAu G24761
047520-1	The New "Boogie Woogie"	BB B-8506, MW M-8655
047521-1	It Ain't No Good	BB B-8415, MW M-8655, HMVIn NE637

Atlanta, GA   Tuesday, October 8, 1940

054544-1	In The Heart Of The City	BB B-8586, MW M-8840
054545-1	Desert Lullaby	BB B-8636, MW M-8841, RZAu G24904
054546-1	True To The One I Love -1	BB B-8691, MW M-8842, RZAu G25251
054547-1	Heartaches And Tears -1	BB B-8636, MW M-8840, RZAu G24904
054548-1	Sleep Darlin' Sleep On -1	BB B-8586, MW M-8441
054549-1	Pretty Little Naponee -1	BB B-8691, MW M-8842
054550-1	You'll Want Me To Want You Someday -1	BB B-8782, MW M-8843, RZAu G25156
054551-1	It's A Long Lane That Doesn't Have A Turning -1	BB B-8782, MW M-8843, RZAu G25156
054552-1	Highway Hobo -1	BB B-8830, MW M-8844, RZAu G25251
054553-1	Berry Pickin' Time -1	BB B-8830, MW M-8844

Acc. own g.
Atlanta, GA   Monday, September 29, 1941

071022-1	Ice Man Blues	BB unissued
071023-1	Please Pull Down Your Curtain	BB B-8917
071024-1	I Can't Help It, I Still Love You	BB B-8917
071025-1	Won't You Come Back To Me My Precious Darling	BB unissued
071026-1	The Numbers Blues	BB B-8850
071027-1	It's All Over Now I'm Glad We're Through	BB B-8850

Bluebird B-8850 as by **Johnnie Barfield**.

Johnny Barfield also recorded with Bert Layne and after 1942.

R.L. BARKSDALE

R.L. Barksdale, v; acc. unknown.
Atlanta, GA   Thursday, March 31, 1927

143838-	No Longer Lonely	Co unissued
143839-	One Night As I Lay Dreaming	Co unissued

HILLMAN BARNARD

See Vaughan Quartet & Associated Groups.

BARNARD, McCOY, WALBERT & PACE

See Vaughan Quartet & Associated Groups.

BILL [& CHARLOTTE] BARNES

Pseudonyms on Grey Gull and Radiex for Bob (& Charlotte) Miller.

BILL BARNES & JOEY RAY

Pseudonyms on Grey Gull, Radiex, and Bellbird for Bob Miller & Barnet Burnett.

FRANKIE BARNES

Frankie Barnes, v/y; acc. prob. own g.
Richmond, IN   Friday, October 23, 1931

18127	Hokey Pokey	Ch S-16366, Spr 2746
18128	A Nervy Bum	Ch S-16366, Spr 2746

Matrices 18127/28 were logged as by **Yodeling Frankie Barnes**, and Superior 2746 may have been so credited.

H.M. BARNES & HIS BLUE RIDGE RAMBLERS

Fred Roe, f; Jim E. Smith, f; Frank E. "Dad" Williams, f; Frank Wilson, sg; Lonnie Austin, p; prob. Harry Brown, md; poss. Jack Reedy, bj; Henry Roe, g.
New York, NY   Monday, January 28, 1929

E-29091-	Golden Slippers	Br 313, Spt S2094
E-29092-	Old Joe Clark	Br 313
E-29093-	Repasz Band March	Br 361, Me M18022
E-29094-	Lineman's Serenade	Br 327

Supertone S2094 as by **Smoky Mountain Boys**. Melotone M18022 as by **Le Orchestre Cartier**; matrix E-29093 is titled *La Marche Mt. Laurier* on that issue. Matrix E-29094 may have been recorded on January 29. Rev. Supertone S2094 by Al Hopkins (see The Hill Billies).

Frank Wilson, sg; Lonnie Austin, p; Henry Roe, g; band v.
 New York, NY   Monday, January 28, 1929
 E-29095-   Who Broke The Lock On The Hen-House Door?   Br 310, BrAu 310, BrE1027, Spt S2052, PanAu P12208

Supertone S2052 as by **Smoky Mountain Ramblers** or, on later pressings, **Smoky Mountain Boys**. Matrix W-29095 is titled *Who Broke The Lock On The Hen House Door* on Panachord P12208.

Fred Roe, f; Jim E. Smith, f; Dad Williams, f; Frank Wilson, sg; Lonnie Austin, p; prob. Harry Brown, md; poss. Jack Reedy, bj; Henry Roe, g; band v-1.
 New York, NY   Tuesday, January 29, 1929
 E-29096-   Blue Ridge Ramblers' Rag   Br 346, Spt S2093
 E-29097-   The Flop-Eared Mule   Br 346, Spt S2093
 E-29098-   She'll Be Comin' Round The Mountain When She Comes -1   Br 310, BrAu 310, BrE 1027, Spt S2052, PanAu P12208
 E-29099-   Goin' Down The Road Feelin' Bad -1   Br 327

Supertone S2052 as by **Smoky Mountain Ramblers** or, on later pressings, **Smoky Mountain Boys**; S2093 as by **Smoky Mountain Boys**.

Prob.: Russell Jones, sg; Lonnie Austin, p-1; Henry Roe, g.
 New York, NY   Tuesday, January 29, 1929
 E-29250-   Honolulu Stomp -1   Br 463
 E-29251-   Three O'Clock In The Morning   Br 463

Harry Brown, md; prob. Henry Roe, g.
 New York, NY   Tuesday, January 29, 1929
 E-29252-   Echoes Of Shenandoah Valley   Br 397, 52079

Brunswick 52079 as by **Les Joyeux Montrealais**; matrix E-29252 is titled *Les Echos De St Laurent* on that issue.

Fred Roe, f; Jim E. Smith, f; Dad Williams, f; Frank Wilson, sg; Lonnie Austin, p; prob. Harry Brown, md; poss. Jack Reedy, bj; Henry Roe, g.
 New York, NY   Wednesday, January 30, 1929
 E-29253-   Our Director March   Br 361, Me M18022

Melotone M18022 as by **Le Orchestre Cartier**; matrix E-29253 is titled *La Marche De Notre Directeur* on that issue.

Harry Brown, md; prob. Henry Roe, g.
 New York, NY   Wednesday, January 30, 1929
 E-29254-   Mandolin Rag   Br 397, 52079

Brunswick 52079 as by **Les Joyeux Montrealais**; matrix E-29254 is titled *La Marche Quebecoise* on that issue.

Brunswick files refer to this combination as '10 men', possibly including non-playing vocalists, or additional instrumentalists not audible. The lineups suggested above may not be entirely accurate for each item; for instance, a banjo cannot be discerned on several, and all three fiddlers may not have played throughout.

THE BARNSTORMERS

Recordings by this group on Gennett-group labels fall outside the scope of this book.

BARNYARD STEVE

Barnyard Steve, sp/laughing/v eff (howling dogs, barking dogs, cow, bull, hog, hog-killing, mule, mockingbird).
 Dallas, TX   Wednesday, June 26, 1929
 402724-A   Out On The Farm   OK 45366

Barnyard Steve, jh solo/calls.
 Dallas, TX   Wednesday, June 26, 1929
 402725-A   Arkansas Bill Green   OK 45366

BARR BROTHERS

No details.
 Atlanta, GA   Monday, April 16, 1928
 146100-   Medley Of Southern Songs   Co unissued
 146101-   Mary Anna Brown   Co unissued

ROBERT BARRINGER

The Arkansas Minstrel, v; acc. prob. own g.
 Chicago, IL   Wednesday, August 7, 1929
 TC-4001-   The Mountain Ain't No Place For A Bad Man   Br/Vo unissued trial recording

Robert Barringer, h solo.
   Chicago, IL   Wednesday, August 7, 1929
      TC-4002-   Classic Medley   Br/Vo unissued trial recording

BUDDY BARTLETT

This pseudonym was used on the Canadian label-group Apex/Crown/Domino/Sterling for various artists: sometimes Frank Luther, sometimes Frank Marvin, in one instance (Plaza matrix 8628, *Waiting For The Train*) Ed (Jake) West, but as often as not for popular singers like Irving Kaufman and others.

E.M. BARTLETT GROUPS

Eugene M. Bartlett organized the Hartford Music Company. He was definitely associated with the recordings of the Murphree Hartford Quartette, and probably also with those of the Hartford Quartet. All the sessions listed below are likely to have been by the same group, in which Bartlett himself may have sung.

Hartford Quartet, v quartet; acc. unknown.
   Memphis, TN   Friday, February 21, 1930
      MEM-783   I Am Going Home   Vo 5431
      MEM-784   March Along With The Christ   Vo 5431

Bartlett's Gospel Four, v quartet, directed by Eugene M. Bartlett; acc. unknown, p.
   Grafton, WI   c. May 26, 1930
      L-327-1   He Is King   Pm 3244
      L-333-1   Work In The Harvest Field   Pm 3244
      L-335-1   The Bumble Bee   Pm 3245
      L-336-2   My Nose   Pm 3245
                  The New Sensation   Pm 3250
                  Swing Out On The Premises   Pm 3250

Paramount 3245 as by **Bartlett's Boosters**.
Intervening matrices are untraced but at least some are probably by this group.

Murphree Hartford Quartette, v quartet, directed by Eugene M. Bartlett; acc. Burgess Bell, p-1.
   Richmond, IN   Wednesday, May 28, 1930
      16686   Make His Praises Ring -1   Ge 7249, Spt 9700
      16687   It Won't Be Very Long   Ge 7317, Ch 16056
      16688   I Know My Lord Will Keep Me -1   Ge 7272, Ch 16056, Spt 9730
      16689   Sing Of His Goodness Forever -1   Ge 7317, Spt 9730
      16692   The Men Will Wear Kimonos Bye And Bye   Ge 7293
      16693   I'm Always Out Of Luck   Ge 7245, Ch 16074
      16694   Take A 'Tater And Wait   Ge 7245
      16696-A   Oh How It Hurt   Ge 7268, Ch 16033
      16697-A   That's What Ruined Me   Ge 7268, Ch 16033
      16698   You Can't Keep A Good Man Down   Ge 7293, Ch 16074

Supertone 9730 as by **The Memphis Gospel Quartette**.
Matrices 16690/91 are by Jimmie Mattox; 16695, 16699 by Odas H. Mattox (popular).

Acc. Burgess Bell, p.
   Richmond, IN   Thursday, May 29, 1930
      16700   I Am Waiting With Jesus   Ge 7272
      16701   Riding To Eternity   Ge 7249, Spt 9700

BARTLETT'S BOOSTERS
BARTLETT'S GOSPEL FOUR

See E.M. Bartlett Groups.

BEN BARTON & HIS ORCHESTRA

An item by this group appeared in the Columbia Old Familiar Tunes series (15744-D) but is outside the scope of this work.

JOHN BARTON

Pseudonym on Broadway for John Baltzell (or, on later ARC-Broadway issues, Doc Roberts).

DEWEY & GASSIE BASSETT

Dewey Bassett, Gassie Bassett, v duet; acc. Dewey Bassett, g; poss. Gassie Bassett, g-1.
   Rock Hill, SC   Wednesday, September 28, 1938
      027610-1   Silent Church On The Hill -1   BB B-7876, MW M-7729
      027611-1   Back Water Blues   BB B-8682, MW M-7730
      027612-1   Just Make My People Think You Care   BB B-8235, MW M-7731

027613-1	Blue Moon	BB B-8682, MW M-7730
027614-1	Do You Love Me, Mother Darling?	BB B-7975, MW M-7731
027615-1	Will You Miss Me, Darling, Miss Me?	BB B-7876, MW M-7729
027616-1	Down In New Orleans	BB B-8214, MW M-7732
027617-1	He Died In The Little Shirt His Mother Made	BB B-7975, MW M-7733
027618-1	Last Goodbye	BB B-8188, MW M-7733
027619-1	Homesick Boy	BB B-8214, MW M-7734
027620-1	Sympathy	BB B-8235, MW M-7734
027621-1	Good Evening, Mama	BB B-8188, MW M-7732

Dewey Bassett, Gassie Bassett, v duet; or Dewey Bassett, v-1; acc. Dewey Bassett, g; poss. Gassie Bassett, g.
Atlanta, GA   Thursday, February 8, 1940

047615-1	You Gonna Pray	BB B-8497, MW M-8663
047616-1	Rootin' Tootin' Shootin' Cowboy	BB B-8431, MW M-8662
047617-1	Poppa's Gettin' Old	BB B-8431, MW M-8662
047618-1	Jesus Paved The Way	BB B-8497, MW M-8663
047619-1	The Great Final Judgment	BB B-8547, MW M-8664
047620-1	No Deep True Love -1	BB B-8607, MW M-8665
047621-1	There's A Grave In The Wilderness	BB B-8547, MW M-8664
047622-1	One Year Ago Today	BB B-8607, MW M-8665

DR. HUMPHREY BATE & HIS POSSUM HUNTERS

Oscar Stone, f-1/calls-2; W.J. (Bill) Barret, f-3/v-4/calls-5; Dr. Humphrey Bate, h-6/v-7/calls-8; Walter Ligget, bj/v-9/calls-10; Staley Walton, g; Oscar Albright, sb; band v-11; unidentified, calls-12.
Atlanta, GA   Saturday, March 3, 1928

AT-354	Billy In The Low Ground -1, 5	Br 239
AT-358*/59	Eighth Of January -3, 12	Br 239
AT-360/61*	How Many Biscuits Can You Eat -6, 7, 11	Br 232
AT-362*/63	Ham Beats All Meat -6, 7, 11	Vo 5238
AT-364*/65	Goin' Up-Town -1, 8, 10	Br 232
AT-366/67*	Throw The Old Cow Over The Fence -3, 12	Vo 5238
AT-368*/69	Green Backed Dollar Bill -1	Br 275
AT-370/71*	My Wife Died Saturday Night -6, 7	Br 271
AT-372/73*	Dill Pickle Rag -1, 6	Br 243
AT-374/75*	Take Your Foot Out Of The Mud And Put It In The Sand -2, 6	Br 243
AT-376/77*	Old Joe -1, 5, 11	Br 271
AT-378/79*	Run, Nigger, Run -4, 6, 9	Br 275

On some pressings of Brunswick 239, matrix AT-358 is replaced with an unidentified "ethnic" item, though labelled as *Eighth Of January*. Matrices AT-355 to 357 are untraced.

BATEMAN SACRED QUARTET

Vocal quartet; unacc.
Johnson City, TN   Wednesday, October 23, 1929

149244-2	Nothing Like Old Time Religion	Co 15608-D
149245-1	Some Day	Co 15608-D

JOHNNY BAXTER

Pseudonym on Superior for Charles Underwood (see Hack's String Band).

KATHERINE BAXTER & HARRY NELSON

Poss. Catherine Boswell, Harry Charles, v duet; acc. prob. Catherine Boswell, p.
Long Island, NY   c. April 1929

444-A	Dwelling In The Beulah Land	QRS R.9035
445-A	Let The Lower Lights Be Burning	QRS R.9035
452	I Need Thee Every Hour	QRS R.9026
453	God Will Take Care Of You	QRS R.9026

Matrices 448 to 450 are by Peck's Male Quartette; others are untraced.
See also Nelson & Nelson. Harry Nelson is probably also the second party of Davis & Nelson (see Claude (C.W.) Davis).

PHIL BAXTER & HIS ORCHESTRA

Items by this danceband in the Victor Old Familiar Tunes series (V-40160, V-40204) are beyond the scope of this work. (For futher information on the band, which also recorded for OKeh, see *JR*.)

BAXTER & LAYNE
Pseudonym on Superior for Cobb & Underwood (see Hack's String Band).

THE BAXTER FAMILY TRIO
Pseudonym on Superior for The Welling Trio (see John McGhee & Frank Welling).

MUMFORD BEAN & HIS ITAWAMBIANS
Mumford Bean, f; Relder Priddy, md; Morine Little, g.
    Memphis, TN   Friday, February 17, 1928

400256-B	Slow Time Waltz	OK 45303
400257-B	Flow Rain Waltz	OK 45303
400260-	Downfall Of Paris	OK unissued
400261-	A New Coon In Town	OK unissued

Matrices 400258/59 are by "Blue Coat" Tom Nelson and Johnson–Nelson–Porkchop (see B&GR).

BEARD'S QUARTETTE
Vocal quartet; acc. unknown.
    Memphis, TN   Sunday, February 12, 1928

400206-	Southern Medley	OK unissued
400207-	Wonderful City	OK unissued
400208-	The Little Old Hut	OK unissued
400209-	There's A Bridge Over The River	OK unissued
400210-	Love Sick Blues	OK unissued

IRENE BEASLEY
Some of this singer's Victor recordings were issued in the Old Familiar Tunes series (V-40032, V-40092, V-40125, and V-40173.) They are outside the scope of this work. (For a selective listing see JR. Carson Robison occasionally accompanied her.)

PERRY BECHTEL
This Atlanta-based guitarist and banjo player accompanied several artists listed in this work (as well as others listed in B&GR). Of the recordings he made as a bandleader (whether credited or not) some are plainly beyond the scope of this work, but those listed below have some claim to be included.

The Colonels: unknown, cl; poss. Sterling Melvin, sg; Perry Bechtel, g; unknown, g; unknown, v; unknown, v group.
    Atlanta, GA   Monday, April 14, 1930

ATL-8020-	Sweet Evalina My Gal	Br 427
ATL-8021-	Waiting For The Robert E. Lee	Br 427

Perry Bechtel & His Colonels: unknown, cl/ts-1; unknown, s; poss. Sterling Melvin, sg; poss. Taylor Flanagan, p; Perry Bechtel, g; unknown, bb; Dan Hornsby, v-2; unidentified (prob. Dan Hornsby, Sterling Melvin, others), v group-3.
    Atlanta, GA   Tuesday, November 11, 1930

ATL-6605-	Bill Bailey -1, 2	Br 498
ATL-6606-	Go Tell Aunt Tabby -1, 2	Br 498
ATL-6617-	Over On The Other Side Of Glory -3	Br 579
ATL-6618-	Gospel Train -3	Br 579

Intervening matrices are by other artists.

Perry Bechtel & His Orchestra: no details.
    Atlanta, GA   Tuesday, November 3, 1931

152027-1	Rubber Dolly	Co 2622-D
152028-1	Liza Jane	Co 2622-D

Perry Bechtel subsequently recorded for Bluebird, and after 1942.

JERRY BEHRENS (LOUISIANA BLUE YODLER)
Jerry Behrens, v/y-1; acc. own g.
    New Orleans, LA   Tuesday, December 17, 1929

403504-B	Lonesome For Mother And Home -1	OK 45535
403505-A	Drifting Along	OK 45535

Jerry Behrens, v/y-1/wh-2; acc. own g.
    Atlanta, GA   Wednesday, October 28, 1931

405038-1	Pal Of Pals	OK 45554, PaAu A3395
405039-1	My Ohio Shore	OK 45554, PaAu A3395
405040-	You Were Glad You Had Broken My Heart	OK 41562
405041-1	Sweetheart Of The Valley -1, 2	OK 45564

405042-1	Carmelita	OK 41562, PaAu A3515
405043-1	Nobody's Business	OK 45564

The subcredit is given as (**Louisiana Blue Yodeler**) on most issues from this session, but as **The Louisiana Blue Yodeller** (without parentheses) on Parlophone A3515. Rev. Parlophone A3515 by Captain Appleblossom.
Jerry Behrens recorded after 1942.

BEL-CANTO QUARTET

Recordings by this group, issued in the Brunswick popular (6000) series, and in some cases also in Britain on Panachord (as by the Llewellyn Sacred Singers), are believed to be outside the scope of this work.

BELFORD & ROGERS

Pseudonym on Bell for John McGhee & Frank Welling.

DICK BELL

Pseudonym on Challenge for Green Bailey.

EDDIE BELL

Pseudonym on Victor, Bluebird, and Twin for Frank Luther (see Carson Robison).

DOUGLAS BELLAR & KIRBY RILEY

Douglas Bellar, f/v-1; Kirby Riley, ac/v-2.
New Orleans, LA   Wednesday, October 2, 1929

NO-257-	La Valse La Prison -1	Vo 15847
NO-258-	Mon Camon Le Case Que Je Sui Cordane -2	Vo 15847
NO-259-	Jolie Fille Qui Ta Fa Avec Moi -2?	Vo 15853
NO-260-	Je Marche Nuit Et Jour -1	Vo 15853

BILL BENDER (THE HAPPY COWBOY)

Bill Bender, v; acc. prob. own g.
prob. New York, NY   c. fall 1939

US-57-1	Happy Cowboy	Vs 5124, Elite X18
US-58-1	Biscuit Shootin' Susie	Vs 5127
US-59-1	Trail To Mexico	Elite X17
US-60-1	Billy The Kid	Elite X17
US-61-1	Santa Fe Trail	Elite X16
US-62-1	Whoopee Ti Yi Yo	Vs 5153, Elite X18
US-63-1	The Bald Faced Steer	Vs 5141
US-64-1	Cowboy Medley	Vs 5124, Elite X16
US-65-1	His Trade Marks	Vs 5138
US-66-1	The Devil Of The Sierras	Vs 5127
US-67-1	Lane County Bachelor	Vs 5144
US-68-1	Little Old Sod Shanty On My Claim	Vs 5138, Elite X20
US-69-1	Jesse James	Vs 5141, Stinson 410-2, Asch 410-2
US-70-1	The Buffalo Skinner	Vs 5144, Stinson 410-3, Asch 410-3
US-71-1	Dreary Black Hills	Vs 5150
US-72-1	Joe Bowers	Vs 5130
US-73-1	Mustang Gray	Vs 5135, Stinson 410-1, Asch 410-1
US-74-1	Black Outlaw Steer	Vs 5133
US-75-1	Oh Suzanna, Ring The Banjo	Vs 5153, Elite X19
US-76-1	The Tenderfoot	Vs 5148
US-77-1	Utah Carroll	Vs 5150, Elite X20
US-78-1	The Railroad Corral	Vs 5148
US-79-1	Betsy From Pike	Vs 5135, Elite X19, Stinson 410-1, Asch 410-1
US-80-1	Samuel Hall	Vs 5130, Stinson 410-2, Asch 410-2
US-81-1	Jack O'Diamonds	Vs 5133, Stinson 410-3

Matrix US-68 is titled *Little Old Sod Shanty On The Claim* on Elite X20. Matrix US-70 is titled *Buffalo Skinner* on Asch 410-3. Matrix US-73 is titled *Mustang Grey* on Stinson 410-1, Asch 410-1. Matrix US-77 is titled *Utah Trail* on Elite X20. Matrix US-79 is titled *Sweet Betsy From Pike* on Stinson 410-1, Asch 410-1. Matrix US-80 is titled *Sam Hall* on Stinson 410-2, Asch 410-2. Rev. Asch 410-3 by Clayton McMichen.

CLINTON BENNETT

See Boa's Pine Cabin Boys.

HANK BENNETT

Pseudonym on Edison Bell Winner for Gene Autry.

JOHN BENNETT
Pseudonym on Madison for Arthur Fields, Al Bernard, and possibly others.

GEORGE BENSON
Pseudonym on some copies of Broadway 8020 for Vernon Dalhart.

THE BENTLEY BOYS
Unknown, f-1; unknown, bj; unknown, g; unknown, v.
    Johnson City, TN   Wednesday, October 23, 1929
149254-2	Down On Penny's Farm	Co 15565-D
149255-2	Henhouse Blues -1	Co 15565-D

AL BERNARD
Al Bernard recorded prolifically for several companies during the period 1916-31, as a solo act, in duets with such artists as Billy Beard, Ernest Hare, and Frank Kamplain, and as band vocalist with the Original Dixieland Jazz Band, Goofus Five, and other groups. Many of his recordings were in the blackface comedy idiom. As a whole, then, his work is beyond the scope of this book, but a few of his recordings seem to merit inclusion.

Al Bernard, v; acc. Rube Bloom, p; John Cali, bj.
    New York, NY   Wednesday, September 23, 1925
1393/94/95	Old Uncle Bill	Vo 15140
1396/97/98	On A Slow Train Thru Arkansaw	Vo 15140

Acc. Frank Ferera, sg.
    New York, NY   c. October 7, 1925
9757-A	On A Slow Train Through Arkansaw	Ch 15165, Her 75521

Rev. Champion 15165, Herwin 75521 by Vernon Dalhart.
    New York, NY   Wednesday, October 14, 1925
33568-1,-2,-3	On A Slow Train Thru' Arkansaw	Vi unissued

Acc. Bert Hirsch, f; Harry Reser, bj; Carson Robison, g; Chris Chapman, traps; unknown, boat-wh eff-1/train eff-2.
    New York, NY   Wednesday, June 1, 1927
E-23397*/98/99*	Steamboat Bill -1	Br 178, Spt S2044
E-23400/01*/02	Casey Jones -2	Br 178

Acc. prob.: Bert Hirsch, f; Harry Reser, bj; Carson Robison, g; Chris Chapman, traps; unknown, bell/train eff.
    New York, NY   Friday, September 23, 1927
E-24526*/27/28/29	Casey Jones	Br 178, Spt S2044

Acc. the Gully Jumpers: unknown, f; unknown, p; unknown, bj; unknown, bell/animal eff-1/chimes-2.
    New York, NY   Tuesday, November 15, 1927
E-25222/23	On A Good Time Straw-Ride -1	Br 191
E-25224/25	I'm A Twelve O'Clock Feller (In A Nine O'Clock Town) -2	Br 191

Acc. unknown, f; unknown, h; unknown, p; unknown, train eff.
    New York, NY   c. January/February 1928
2701-A,-B	New River Train	GG/Rad 4150, VD 74150, Mad 1918

Madison 1918 as by **John Bennett**. Revs: Grey Gull/Radiex 4150, Van Dyke 74150, Madison 1918 by Arthur Fields (popular).

Acc. unknown, f; unknown, h; unknown, p; unknown, g.
    New York, NY   c. March 1928
2798-C,-G	Cowboy's Lament (The Dying Cowboy)	GG/Rad 4173, VD 74173, Rad/VD 5113

Van Dyke 74173 as by **Buddy Moore**. The parenthesised title of matrix 2798 does not appear on Radiex/Van Dyke 5113; on Van Dyke 74173 it appears as (Dying Cowboy). Rev. all issues by Al Bernard (popular).

Wiggins Brothers: Al Bernard, James O'Keefe, v duet; or **Seth Wiggins**-1: Al Bernard, v; acc. Tony Colucci, g, unknown, wh.
    New York, NY   Tuesday, April 3, 1928
E-27256-A,-B	Times Am Gittin' Hard	Br 260
E-27257-A,-B	My Grandpappy's Gun -1	Br 260

Al Bernard, v; acc. unknown, f; unknown, h; unknown, p; unknown, jh.
    New York, NY   c. April 1928
2868-A,-B	Oh, Dem Golden Slippers	GG/Rad 4209, VD 74209

Van Dyke 74209 as by **Buddy Moore**. Revs: Grey Gull/Radiex 4209, VD 74209 by Al Bernard (popular).

Al Bernard, v/sp-1; acc. unknown, f; Carson Robison, g/sp-1/wh-2.
    New York, NY   Friday, June 22, 1928

| E-27754-A,-B | Bill Bailey Won't You Please Come Home? -2 | Br 312, BrAu 312, Pan 25146 |
| E-27755-A,-B | The Preacher And The Bear -1 | Br 312, BrAu 312, Spt S2057, Pan 25146 |

Rev. Supertone S2057 by Buell Kazee.

Acc. unknown, f; unknown, h-1; unknown, p; unknown, bj; unknown, boat-wh eff-2.
   New York, NY   c. June 1928

| 2976-B | Steamboat Bill -1, 2 | GG/Rad 4177, VD 74177 |
| 2977-A | Pass Around The Bottle | GG/Rad 4210, VD 74210, Mad 5094 |

At least some issues of Van Dyke 74210 are as by **Buddy Moore**.
Revs: Grey Gull/Radiex 4177, 4210, VD 74177, Madison 5094 by Arthur Fields (popular).

Acc. Carson Robison, h/g/wh.
   New York, NY   Monday, July 9, 1928

| 400853-B | Twenty-Five Years From Now | OK 41214, PaAu A2828 |
| 400854-B | Times Am Gittin' Hard | OK 41214, PaAu A2828 |

Acc. unknown, f; unknown, ac; unknown, g; unknown, train-wh eff-1.
   New York, NY   Wednesday, January 23, 1929

| E-29142- | What The Engine Done -1 | Br 4259 |
| E-29143- | Louisiana Susie | Br 4259 |

Hank Smith, v; acc. unknown, f; unknown, t; unknown, g; unknown, train-wh eff-1.
   New York, NY   Wednesday, April 3, 1929

| E-29536- | What The Engine Done -1 | Vo 5318 |
| E-29537- | Eleven Cent Cotton And Forty Cent Meat | Vo 5318 |

THE BROTHERS BERTINI

Pseudonym on Japanese Columbia, Australian Regal and Regal-Zonophone, and English Regal for Len & Joe Higgins.

JOHN H. BERTRAND

John H. Bertrand & Milton Pitre: John H. Bertrand, ac/v-1; Milton Pitre, g.
   Chicago, IL   c. January 1929

21074-1	The Rabbit Stole The Pumpkin	Pm 12730
21075-2,-3	Miserable -1	Pm 12725
21076-1	Cousinne Lilly -1	Pm 12725
21077-5	The Swallows -1	Pm 12730
21078-2	Valse De Gueydan	Pm 12748
21079-1	Upstairs -1	Pm 12748

John H. Bertrand & Roy Gonzales: unknown, f-1; John H. Bertrand, ac-2/v-3; Roy Gonzales, g/v-4.
   Chicago IL   c. March/April 1929

21243-2	La Delaisser -1, 2, 3	Pm 12776
21245-1	Attendre Pour Un Train -2, 4	Pm 12762
21246-2	Je Veux M'Achete Un Fuse Qui Brille -4	Pm 12762
21248-2	La Fille Du Jolier -1, 2, 3	Pm 12763
21251-2	Le Soldat Fatigue -1, 2, 3	Pm 12763
21252-2	Le Pond De Nante -1, 2, 3	Pm 12776

Intervening matrices are untraced but possibly by these artists.
See also Roy Gonzales.

GILBERT BETZ

Gilbert Betz, v; acc. the Arkansas Travelers: unknown, f; unknown, md; unknown, bj; unknown, g.
   Richmond, IN   Thursday, January 12, 1933

| 18963 | Lamp Lighting Time In The Valley | Ge unissued |

BEVERLEY BUCKLE BUSTERS

Pseudonym on English Decca for the Colt Brothers (see Arthur Fields & Fred Hall).

THE BEVERLY HILL BILLIES

Hank Skillet's real name was Harry Blaeholder; Lem Giles's was Aleth Hansen; Chuck Cook's was Charlie Quirk.

Hank Skillet, f; Ezra Paulette, poss. f/v/y-1; Zeke Manners, ac; Tom "Pappy" Murray, g/v.
   Los Angeles, CA.   Friday, April 25, 1930

| LAE-768-A | When The Bloom Is On The Sage | Br 421, Spt S2049, Vo 03164 |
| LAE-769-A | Red River Valley -1 | Br 421, Spt S2049, Vo 03164 |

Supertone S2049 as by **Stone Mountain Boys**.
Matrix LAE-768 is subtitled (*It's Round Up Time In Texas*) on Vocalion 03164.

Hank Skillet, f; Ezra Paulette, poss. f/v; Zeke Manners, ac; Tom "Pappy" Murray, g/v; Lem Giles, g.
   Los Angeles, CA.   Tuesday, May 27, 1930

LAE-804-A	My Pretty Quadroon	Br 441, BrAu 441
LAE-805-A	When It's Harvest Time (Sweet Angeline)	Br 441, BrAu 441

Hank Skillet, f; Zeke Manners, ac; poss. Jad Dees, g/v/y-1; Lem Giles, g; Ezra Paulette, v/y-1.
   Los Angeles, CA.   Wednesday, July 23, 1930

LAE-846-A	By A Window At The End Of The Lane	Br 455, BrAu 455
LAE-847-A	Mellow Mountain Moon -1	Br 455, BrAu 455
LAE-848-	Blue Mountain Shack	Br rejected
LAE-849-	In The Heart Of The Beverly Hills	Br rejected

Matrix LAE-846 is titled *At The End Of The Lane* on Australian Brunswick 455.

"Vocal duet with orchestra" (sic Brunswick files).
   Los Angeles, CA.   Friday, September 5, 1930

LAE-867-B,-A	Back In The Hills Of Colorado	Br rejected
LAE-868-B,-A	Peek-A-Boo	Br rejected

Elton Britt was a member of the group at the time of this session.

Hank Skillet, f; Zeke Manners, ac; Lem Giles, g/poss. v; poss. Jad Dees, g/v; Ezra Paulette, lv; poss. Curt Barrett, y-1.
   Los Angeles, CA.   Wednesday, November 5, 1930

LAE-893-	Back In The Hills Of Colorado	Br 462
LAE-894-	Peek-A-Boo -1	Br 462
LAE-895-A,-B	Bring Your Roses To Her Now	Br rejected

Although Brunswick files indicate that Brunswick 462 used matrices LAE-893 and 894, the rejected matrices LAE-867 and 868 appear in mirror fashion in the wax of that issue.

Hank Skillet, f; Zeke Manners, ac; Lem Giles, g/poss. v; poss. Jad Dees, g/poss. v; Ezra Paulette, lv.
   Los Angeles, CA.   Tuesday, November 18, 1930

LAE-904-B,-A	Bring Your Roses To Her Now	Br unissued
LAE-905-B	My Old Iowa Home	Br 506
LAE-906-A	Wonder Valley	Br 506

Hank Skillet, f; Zeke Manners, ac; Lem Giles, g/v; poss. Jad Dees, g; Ezra Paulette, lv; poss. Jad Dees or Curt Barrett, v-1.
   Los Angeles, CA.   Tuesday, February 10, 1931

LAE-952-A	The Strawberry Roan -1	Br 514, Spt S2263, Pan 25630
LAE-953-A	Everglades	Br 514, Pan 25630

Rev. Supertone S2263 by Marc Williams.

Hank Skillet, f; Ezra Paulette, f-1/lv; Zeke Manners, ac; Lem Giles, g/v; poss. Jad Dees, g/v-1.
   Los Angeles, CA.   Thursday, February 27, 1931

LAE-958-	Prairie Skies -1	Br 519, BrAu 519, PanAu P12145
LAE-959-	She Sleeps Beneath The Daisies	Br 519, BrAu 519, PanAu P12145

Glen Rice & His Beverly Hill Billies: poss. Squeak McKinney, f; prob. Curt Barrett, g/v-1; Chuck Cook, g/v-2/y-3; Shug Fisher, sb-4/poss. v-5; two unknowns, v-6; Glen Rice, dir.
   San Francisco, CA.   September 1932

SF-1	When I Was A Boy From The Mountains (And You Were A Girl From The Hills) -2?, 3?, 4, 6	Br 597, Pan 25355, RZAu G21977
SF-2-A	Swiss Yodel -2, 3	Br 597, Pan 25355, RZAu G21977
SF-3-A	The Big Corral -1 (lead), 4, 6	Br 598, Pan 25374, RZAu G21981
SF-4-A	Whoopie Ti Yi Yo, Git Along Little Dogies -1 (lead), 2, 4, 6	Br 598, Pan 25374, RZAu G21981
SF-6	Gooseberry Pie -5	Br unissued

All inspected pressings of *When I Was A Boy From The Mountains (And You Were A Girl From The Hills)* bear the ARC transfer matrix B-12471; matrix SF-1 is thus hypothetical. Matrix SF-5 is untraced.

Poss. Squeak McKinney, f; prob. Curt Barrett, g/v-1; Chuck Cook, g/v-2; Shug Fisher, sb; two unknowns, v; Glen Rice, dir.
   San Francisco, CA.   Wednesday, September 28, 1932

SF-12-A	Ridge Runnin' Roan -1 (lead)	Br 599, Pan 25611, RZAu G21982
SF-13-A	Alone In Lonesome Valley -1/2	Br 599, Pan 25611, RZAu G21982
SF-14-A	Back In The Old Sunday School -2 (lead)	Br 600, CrC/MeC/Stg/Roy 93071, Pan 25553, RZAu G22169
SF-15- -	Cowboy Joe -1 (lead)	Br 600, CrC/MeC/Stg/Roy 93071, MeC/Min M-14017, Pan 25553, RZAu G22169

Crown/Melotone/Sterling/Royale 93071 as by **Western Hillbillies**. Melotone M14017 as by **Prairie Ramblers**.
All inspected pressings of *Cowboy Joe* bear the ARC transfer matrix B-12515; matrix SF-15 is thus hypothetical. Matrix SF-13 is titled *Lonesome Valley* on Regal-Zonophone G21982. Rev. Melotone/Minerva M-14017 by Reg Perkins (Canadian).

Ezra Of The Beverly Hill Billies: Ezra Paulette, v; acc. Hank Skillet, f; Lem Giles, g.
  prob. Los Angeles, CA.   c. 1934

| 201 | The Last Roundup | Electro Vox unnumbered |
| 202 | Lonesome Road | Electro Vox unnumbered |

The Original Beverly Hillbillies (Ezra, Jad, Hank, Lem & Charlie): Hank Skillet, f; Lem Giles, g/v; Jad Dees, g/v; Charlie Quirk, g/v; Ezra Paulette, v.
  Los Angeles, CA.   Monday, September 17, 1934

| DLA-54-A,-B | Me And My Burro | De rejected |
| DLA-55-A,-B | Winging My Way To Wyoming | De rejected |

Pappy, Zeke, Ezra & Elton: Zeke Manners, ac; Elton Britt, g/v/poss. y-1; Ted "Pappy" Bellow, g/v; Charlie "Ezra" Heatherington, v.
  New York, NY.   Monday, January 28, 1935

| 39283-B | Isle Of Capri -1 | De 5097 |
| 39284-A,-B | Alpine Milk Man | De rejected |

Only one guitar is used but it is uncertain whose.

Zeke Manners, ac; Elton Britt, g/v/y; Ted "Pappy" Bellow, g/v/y; Charlie "Ezra" Heatherington, v/y.
  New York, NY.   Wednesday, January 30, 1935

| 39315-A | Open Up Them Pearly Gates | De 5097 |

Charlie "Ezra" Heatherington, f-1/v; Zeke Manners, ac; Elton Britt, g/v/y; Ted "Pappy" Bellow, g/v.
  New York, NY.   Tuesday, July 23, 1935

| 39744-A | The Lady In Red | De 5126, Pan 25813 |
| 39745-A | In A Little Gypsy Tea Room -1 | De 5126 |

Pappy, Ezra & Elton: Charlie "Ezra" Heatherington, f/v; Elton Britt, g/v/prob. y; Ted "Pappy" Bellow, g/v.
  New York, NY.   Friday, October 18, 1935

| 60079-A | Where The Rhododendron Grows | De 5153 |
| 60080-B | Red Sails In The Sunset | De 5153, Pan 25813 |

Only one guitar is used but it is uncertain whose.

Ezra Paulette & His Beverly Hill Billies: prob.: Hank Skillet, f; Lem Giles, g/v; Jad Dees, g/v; unknown, sb; Ezra Paulette, lv.
  Los Angeles, CA.   Wednesday, October 20, 1937

LA-1474-A	Singing My Hill Billy Song	Vo 04104, Cq 8955
LA-1475-A,-B	The Old Arapahoe Trail	ARC 8-01-53, Vo 03882, Cq 8955
LA-1476-A	When The Wild Flowers Are In Bloom	ARC 8-04-55, Vo/OK 03263, Cq 8956
LA-1477-	My Little Cow Pony And I	Cq 9011
LA-1478-B	Rosalie	ARC 8-01-53, Vo 03882, Cq 8956
LA-1479-A	The Prisoner's Song	ARC 8-04-55, Vo/OK 03263, Cq 9011
LA-1480-A	On The Texas Prairie	Vo 04104, Cq 8954
LA-1481-	Girl Of The Prairie	Cq 8954

Tom Murray and Charlie Quirk also recorded as **Tom & Chuck** and as vocalists with the Hollywood Hillbilly Orchestra. Zeke Manners and Elton Britt recorded in their own names and elsewhere, and Shug Fisher with Hugh & Shug's Radio Pals.

BIG CHIEF HENRY'S INDIAN STRING BAND

Henry Hall, f-1; Harold Hall, bj-2/v-3; Clarence Hall, g.
  Dallas, TX   Tuesday, October 15, 1929

56382--	Bluebird Waltz -1, 2	Vi V-40225
56383-2	Choctaw Waltz -1, 2	Vi V-40225
56384-1	The Indian Tom Tom -1, 3	Vi V-40281
56385-2	The Indian's Dream -1	Vi V-40281
56386-1	Cherokee Rag -2	Vi V-40195
56387-1	On The Banks Of The Kaney -1, 2	Vi V-40195

Victor V-40225 as by **Henry's String Band**.

BIG JOHN & LITTLE FRANK

Pseudonym on Vocalion and English Panachord for John McGhee & Frank Welling.

BERT BILBRO

Bert Bilbro, h solo.
  Atlanta, GA   Thursday, August 2, 1928

| 402041-A | C. & N.W. Blues | OK 45278 |
| 402042-A | Mohana Blues | OK 45278 |

Bert Bilbro, h/v-1; acc. unknown, g; prob. own bird eff-2.
 Atlanta, GA   Thursday, March 14, 1929

402307-A,-B	The Mocking Bird -2	OK unissued
402308-A,-B	The Old Cherry Tree, Sweet Marie	OK unissued
402309-A	Yes, Indeed I Do -1	OK 45357
402310-B	We're Gonna Have A Good Time Tonight -1	OK 45357

D.H. Bilbro, h solo.
 Charlotte, NC   Wednesday, May 27, 1931

69363-1,-2	Locomotive Blues	Vi unissued
69364-2	Chester Blues	Vi 23831

Rev. Victor 23831 by DeFord Bailey.

BUD BILLINGS
BUD & JOE BILLINGS
BUD BILLINGS & CARSON ROBISON
BUD BILLINGS['] TRIO

Pseudonyms on Victor and associated labels for Frank Luther, respectively as a solo, in duet with Carson Robison (**Joe Billings**) and with his trio. For most of these recordings see Carson Robison. Note, however, that **Bud & Joe Billings** on British Regal MR756, MR780 and Indian Twin FT1523, FT1545 are Carson Robison & His Pioneers.

DOUG BINE & HIS DIXIE RAMBLERS

Jimmy Thomason, f/v-1; Cotton Collins, f; Doug Bine, esg; Charlie Bickford, p; Chesley Halbert, tbj; Cooper Bennett, g; Artice Glenn, sb/v-2.
 San Antonio, TX   Thursday, October 22, 1936

02825-1	How Many Times -1	BB B-6847
02826-1	Ramblers Stomp	BB B-6705
02827-1	Yes Sir -1	BB B-6789
02828-1	Wild	BB B-6705
02829-1	Hi-De-Hi -1	BB B-6789
02830-1	Using That Thing -1	BB B-8133
02831-1	Over Sixty -1	BB B-6677
02832-1	Chinese Honeymoon -1	BB B-6677
02833-1	Stay On The Right Side -2	BB B-6847
02834-1	Roseland Waltz	BB B-7039

Revs: Bluebird B-7039 by Phil Napoleon (see *JR*), B-8133 by Tune Wranglers.
See also Dixie Ramblers [IV].

BINGHAM & WELLS (THE BLIND SINGERS)

Virgil Bingham, ——— Wells, v duet; acc. Virgil Bingham, p.
 Chicago, IL   Tuesday, August 1, 1933

75994-1	Lullaby Lady (From Lullaby Lane)	BB B-5154, Eld 2053, MW M-4380, M-4817
75995-1	There's A Little Box Of Pine On The 7:29	BB B-5154, Eld 2053, MW M-4380, M-4817

BINKLEY BROTHERS DIXIE CLODHOPPERS

Gale Binkley, f; Amos Binkley, bj; Tom Andrews, g; Jack Jackson, g/v.
 Nashville, TN   Friday, September 28, 1928

47098-1,-2	Watermelon Hanging On De Vine	Vi unissued
47099-1,-2	Little Old Log Cabin In The Lane	Vi unissued
47100-1,-2	Give Me Back My Fifteen Cents	Vi unissued
47101-1,-2	All Go Hungry Hash House	Vi unissued

 Nashville, TN   Tuesday, October 2, 1928

47098-3	Watermelon Hanging On De Vine	Vi unissued
47099-4	Little Old Log Cabin In The Lane	Vi V-40129, Yorkville K525
47100-4	Give Me Back My Fifteen Cents	Vi V-40048
47101-4	All Go Hungry Hash House	Vi 21758
47106-2	When I Had But Fifty Cents	Vi V-40129
47107-1	It'll Never Happen Again	Vi 21758
47107-2	It'll Never Happen Again	Vi unissued: *RCA CPL2-9507 (LP)*
47108-1,-2	Rock All Our Babies To Sleep	Vi unissued
47109-1	I'll Rise, When The Rooster Crows	Vi V-40048

Victor V-40129 as by **Binkley Bros. Dixie Clodhoppers**. Yorkville K525 as by **Dixie Clodhoppers**. (Matrix 47099 is believed to be the only country item issued on this label, which in 1932-36 licensed Irish material from Victor for sale through the Yorkville Phonograph Shop, 1553 Third Ave., Near 87th St, New York, N.Y.)
Intervening matrices are by Paul Warmack & His Gully Jumpers. Rev. Yorkville K525 by George O'Brien (Irish).

CONNIE BIRD

See Elmer Bird.

ELMER BIRD & ASSOCIATED ARTISTS

Louis Bird & Jack Hicks, v duet; acc. Elmer Bird & His Trio: prob.: two unknowns, md; unknown, g.
Richmond, IN   Monday, July 1, 1929
    15289,-A   Sweet Marie   Ge rejected

Connie Bird, v; acc. Elmer Bird & His Trio: two unknowns, md; unknown, g.
Richmond, IN   Tuesday, July 2, 1929
    15290   Little Mamie   Ge 6929, Ch 15832, Spt 9491
    15291-B   My Mother's Grave   Ge 6929, Ch 15832, Spt 9491

Champion 15832 as by **Wallace Grey**. Supertone 9491 as by **Edward Duncan**.

Louis Bird & Jack Hicks, v duet; acc. Elmer Bird & His Trio: prob.: two unknowns, md; unknown, g.
Richmond, IN   Wednesday, July 3, 1929
    15294,-A   Paradise Alley   Ge rejected

Elmer Bird & His Happy Five: prob.: two unknowns, md; three unknowns, g.
Knoxville, TN   Sunday, September 1, 1929
    K-169   Sweet Marie   Vo rejected
    K-170   Paradise Alley   Vo rejected
    K-171   Ginsang [sic] Blues   Vo rejected
    K-172   Kentucky Blues   Vo rejected

Elmer Bird & Jack Hicks, v duet; acc. Elmer Bird & His Happy Four: two unknowns, md; three unknowns, g.
Richmond, IN   Friday, November 8, 1929
    15866,-A   The Lilly Of The Valley   Ge rejected
    15867,-A,-B   I Would Not Be Denied   Ge rejected

Elmer Bird & His Happy Four: two unknowns, md; three unknowns, g.
Richmond, IN   Friday, November 8, 1929
    15868   Kentucky Stomp   Ge 7064, Ch S-16421, 45168, Spt 9676,
                                                                                        Spr 2598
    15869   Sleepy Creek Wail   Ge 7064, Ch S-16421, 45168, Spt 9676,
                                                                                        Spr 2598

Supertone 9676 as by **The Duncan Boys**.

Jack Hicks & Lewis Bird, poss. v duet; acc. Elmer Bird & His Happy Four: two unknowns, md; three unknowns, g.
Richmond, IN   Friday, November 8, 1929
    15870,-A   Cricket On The Hearth   Ge rejected

Acc. unknown, md; unknown, g.
Richmond, IN   Friday, November 8, 1929
    15871,-A   I Am Sure He Won't Drink It Again   Ge rejected

Jack Hicks & Charlie Dykes, poss. v duet; acc. Elmer Bird & His Happy Four: two unknowns, md; three unknowns, g.
Richmond, IN   Friday, November 8, 1929
    15872,-A   George Collins   Ge rejected

Charlie Dykes, v; acc. Elmer Bird & His Happy Four: two unknowns, md; three unknowns, g.
Richmond, IN   Friday, November 8, 1929
    15873,-A   When The Liquor Flows Again   Ge rejected

Elmer Bird & A.J. Ball, v duet; acc. unknown, f; unknown, g.
Richmond, IN   Tuesday, February 11, 1930
    16251,-A,-B   Sweet Marie   Ge rejected

Louis Bird, v; acc. unknown, f; unknown, g.
Richmond, IN   Tuesday, February 11, 1930
    16252,-A   The Cricket On The Hearth   Ge rejected

Elmer Bird & His String Band: unknown, f; two unknowns, g.
Richmond, IN   Tuesday, February 11, 1930
    16253   East Tennessee Blues   Ge 7182
    16254   Muscle Shoals Blues   Ge 7182

According to Gennett files this was issued in June 1930 and withdrawn on grounds of copyright on October 1, 1930.

Louis Bird, v; acc. unknown, f; two unknowns, g.
Richmond, IN   Tuesday, February 11, 1930
    16255,-A   Paradise Alley   Ge unissued

A.J. Ball, v; acc. unknown, f; unknown, g.
Richmond, IN   Tuesday, February 11, 1930

| 16256,-A | Ain't Gonna Sin No More | Ge unissued |
| 16257,-A | Do Lord Do Remember Me | Ge rejected |

Louis Bird, v; acc. unknown, f; unknown, g.
Knoxville, TN   Friday, April 4, 1930

| K-8082 | It's Funny What Whiskey Will Do | Vo 5428 |
| K-8083- | Nothing Goes Hard With Me | Vo 5428 |

Kentucky Ramblers: unknown, v-1/y-2/v duet-3/v trio-4; acc. unknown, md; unknown, bj; unknown, g.
Grafton, WI   c. September 1930

L-544-2	I'm A Free Little Bird	Pm 3300
L-545-2	Do Not Wait Till I'm Laid Beneath The Clay -3	Pm 3283
L-546-1	A Pretty White Rose -3	Pm 3284
L-547-1	The Prisoners [sic] Sweetheart -4	Pm 3284
L-549-1	With My Mother Dead And Gone -1	Pm 3283
L-550-1	Little Mamie	Pm 3285
L-551-2	Ginseng Blues -1, 2	Bwy 8271
L-552-2	Good Cocaine (Mama Don't Allow It)	Bwy 8271
L-553-1	Give Me That Old Time Religion -1	Bwy 8270
L-554-1	Glory Glory Glory Glory To The Lamb -4	Bwy 8270
L-555-1	The Unfortunate Brakeman -1	Pm 3285
L-556-1	Everybody Works But Father -1	Pm unissued
L-557-1	Whoa Mule -3	Pm unissued
L-558-1	Some Mother's Boy -4	Pm 3300

Similarities in repertoire and instrumentation strongly suggest that these recordings are by a Bird family group.
Matrices L-548, L-559 are untraced but probably by this group.

Bird's Kentucky Corn Crackers: unknown, md/v; Elmer Bird, g/v; Connie Bird, g/v; Charles Dykes, g.
Louisville, KY   Tuesday, June 16, 1931

69444-2	The Ship That's Sailing High	Vi 23608
69445-1,-2	In A Little Town In Old Kentucky	Vi unissued
69446-1,-2	Little Mamie	Vi unissued
69447-2	Crossed Old Jordan's Stream	Vi 23608

Charles Dykes, v; acc. own g.
Louisville, KY   Wednesday, June 17, 1931

| 69456-1,-2 | Charley's Low-Down Weary Blues – Part 1 | Vi unissued |
| 69456-1,-2 | Charley's Low-Down Weary Blues – Part 2 | Vi unissued |

LOUIS [or LEWIS] BIRD

See Elmer Bird.

NAT BIRD & TOM COLLINS

Nat Bird, f; Tom Collins, g.
Dallas, TX   Sunday, October 27, 1929

| DAL-497 | Hornpipe Medley | Br 376, 52082, Me M18026 |
| DAL-498 | Medley Of Old Fiddlers Favorites | Br 376, 52082, Me M18026 |

Brunswick 52082, Melotone M18026 as by **Les Deux Gaspesiens**; matrix DAL-497 is titled *Le Reel De Janvier*, and matrix DAL-498 *Le Potpourri Du Vieux Violoneux*, on these issues.

BIRD'S KENTUCKY CORN CRACKERS

See Elmer Bird.

L.O. BIRKHEAD & R.M. LANE

Ilton O. Birkhead, f; A.E. Ward, f-1; Ralph M. Lane, f-2; Bill Sawyers, g.
Atlanta, GA   Sunday, October 25, 1931

| 151928-1 | Robinson County -1 | Co 15757-D |
| 151929-1 | Cash River Waltz -2 | Co 15757-D |

WM. BIRKHEAD

See George Edgin.

BIRMINGHAM ENTERTAINERS

Pseudonym on Supertone for the Kessinger Brothers.

JASPER BISBEE

Jasper Bisbee, f; acc. unknown, p; unknown, sb-1.
   New York, NY   Friday, November 23, 1923

8794	Money Musk	Ed unissued
8795	Girl I Left Behind Me -1	Ed unissued
8796	College Quadrille -1	Ed unissued

Acc. B. Bisbee-Schula, p; unknown, calls-1.
   New York, NY   Saturday, November 24, 1923

9259-B,-C	Money Musk	Ed 51381
9260-B,-C	Girl I Left Behind Me – Medley	Ed 51381
9261-B,-C	College Hornpipe	Ed 51382
9262-A,-B	McDonald's Reel	Ed 51278, 4916
9263-A,-C	The Devil's Dream	Ed 51382
9264-B,-C	Opera Reel -1	Ed 51278, 4912

BILLY BISHOP

Billy Bishop, h; acc. prob. own g.
   St. Paul, MN   c. June 27, 1927

12885	Medley Of Old Favorites – Part 1 (Intro: Cricket On The Hearth; Shade Of The Pines; White Wings)	Ge 6203, Ch 15331, Spt 9171, Sil 5081, 8184, Chg 308
12889	Medley Of Old Favorites – Part 2 (Intro: Listen To The Mocking Bird; Annie Laurie)	Ge 6203, Ch 15331, Spt 9171, Sil 5081, 8184, Chg 308

LESTER "PETE" BIVINS

Lester "Pete" Bivins, v/y-1; acc. own g.
   Charlotte, NC   Saturday, February 20, 1937

07200-1	Big Fat Gal	BB B-6886, MW M-7228
07201-1	Married Life Blues -1	MW M-7230
07202-1	Knocking On The Hen House Door	BB B-6886, MW M-7228
07203-1	I'm Goin' Back To Coney Isle	BB B-6950, MW M-7229
07204-1	Minor Blues -1	MW M-7230
07205-1	Bull Dog In Tennessee	BB B-6950, MW M-7229
07206-1	Home With Mother And Dad In The West -1	MW M-7231
07207-1	Back In My Home Town	MW M-7231

Lester (The Highway Man), v; acc. own g.
   Charlotte, NC   Thursday, June 9, 1938

64110-A	Morning Blues	De 5659
64111-A	Cotton Mill Blues	De 5559
64112-A	The Highway Man	De 5559
64113-A	I'm Going Back To Caroline	De 5659
64114-A	Maybe Next Week Some Time	De 5591
64115-A	Texas Blues	De 5591

CARROLL BLACK

Carroll Black, v; acc. prob. own g.
   Richmond, IN   Thursday, August 4, 1932

18661	No Telephone In Heaven	Ge unissued
18662	I'm Thinking Tonight Of My Blue Eyes	Ge unissued

HARRY BLACK

Pseudonym on OKeh for Frank Luther (see Carson Robison).

HERMAN BLACK & HIS ORCHESTRA

Pseudonym on Aurora for "Happy" Dixon's Clod Hoppers.

JIMMIE BLACK

Pseudonym on OKeh and English Parlophone for Frank Luther.

REGGIE BLACK

Pseudonym on Regent for Frank Luther (see Carson Robison).

BLACK BROTHERS

Pseudonym on OKeh and English Parlophone for Frank Luther & Carson Robison (see the latter).

DAD BLACKARD'S MOONSHINERS
See Shelor Family.

THE BLACKBERRY DUDES
Prob. vocal or vocal duet; acc. unknown g; unknown, u.
    Richmond, IN   Wednesday, May 20, 1931
    17753   Knee Deep In Cotton   Ge rejected trial recording

AL BLACKBURN
AL & JOE BLACKBURN
Pseudonyms on Melotone and Polk for, respectively, James McCravy and Frank & James McCravy.

CHARLEY BLAKE
Pseudonym on Supertone for Bill Cox.

BLAKE & MILTON
Pseudonym on Superior for The Singing Sweethearts.

BLALOCK & YATES
(Earl?) Blalock, f/v-1; prob. Ira or Eugene Yates, g.
    Johnson City, TN   Monday, October 21, 1929
    149200-2   Morning Star Waltz   Co 15576-D
    149201-2   Pride Of The Ball -1   Co 15576-D

DAN BLANCHARD
Pseudonym on Champion for Frank Luther.

BLANKENSHIP FAMILY
William Pool Blankenship, f-1/bsv; William Walter Blankenship, g/tv-1; Daphna Blankenship, bj-u-1/lv; Darius Blankenship, vc-1/lv.
    Charlotte, NC   Friday, May 29, 1931
    69376-2   Working On The Railroad -1   Vi 23583, Au 407
    69377-2   Jack And Mae   Vi 23583, Au 407

ROY BLEDSOE
Roy Bledsoe, v; acc. unknown.
    Atlanta, GA   Friday, March 22, 1929
    402411-   My Buddy   OK unissued
    402412-   Memories   OK unissued

Matrices 402409/10, blank in OKeh files but known from test-pressings, may be associated with this artist. There may also be a connection with John Dilleshaw, who recorded on matrices 402405 to 402408, but the lead singer on 402409, and only singer on 402410, is certainly not Dilleshaw, and may be Bledsoe. For details of 402409/10 see Unknown Artists [IV].

FRANK BLEVINS & HIS TAR HEEL RATTLERS
Frank Blevins, v; acc. own f; Fred Miller, tbj; Edd Blevins, g.
    Atlanta, GA   Tuesday, November 8, 1927
    145158-2   Sally Aim [sic]   Co 15765-D
    145159-1   I've Got No Honey Babe Now   Co 15765-D
    145160-2   Old Aunt Betsy   Co 15210-D, Ve 7101-V, Cl 5142-C
    145161-   Little Bunch Of Roses   Co unissued
    145162-   Late Last Night When Willie   Co unissued
    145163-2   Fly Around My Pretty Little Miss   Co 15210-D, Ve 7103-V, Cl 5142-C

Rev. Velvet Tone 7101-V, 7103-V by Blue Ridge Highballers.

Frank Blevins, v; acc. own f; Fred Miller, tbj; Edd Blevins, g/v-1.
    Atlanta, GA   Tuesday, April 17, 1928
    146102-   We Have Met And We Have Parted   Co unissued
    146103-   The Drunkard's Doom   Co unissued
    146104-1   Don't Get Trouble In Your Mind   Co 15280-D
    146105-1   Nine Pound Hammer -1   Co 15280-D

RUBYE BLEVINS
This is the true name of Patsy Montana and a few of her recordings were thus credited.

BLEVINS & BLAIR (OF THE WEST VA. MOUNTAINEERS)

Unknown, f; unknown, bj-1; unknown, g-2; unknown, fiddlestick-3; unknown, v-4/y-4.
Richmond, IN   Tuesday, October 16, 1928

14348,-A	Old Wooden Leg -1, 2	Ge rejected
14349,-A	Lost John -1, 3	Ge rejected
14350,-A	The Bald Headed End Of A Broom -2, 3, 4	Ge rejected

BLIND ANDY [or "ANDY"]

See Andrew Jenkins.

THE BLIND SOLDIER

Sometimes used as a subcredit for David Miller, this was employed on Broadway 4062 and Conqueror 7709 as a pseudonym for him.

BUD BLUE

This pseudonym on OKeh usually disguises either Smith Ballew or Fred Rich & His Orchestra. The Bud Blue credited with a release in the OKeh Old Time Tunes series (45254) and with participation in "The Okeh Medicine Show" is most likely to be Smith Ballew, for details of some of whose recordings see JR.

THE BLUE BOYS

One item with this credit was issued in the OKeh Old Time Tunes series (45314). The artists responsible are Nap Hayes, Matthew Prater, and Lonnie Johnson, who are African-Americans; see B&GR.

BLUE DIAMOND SEXTETTE

See S.E. Mullis Blue Diamond Quartette.

BLUE GRASS BOYS

Pseudonym on Herwin for the Kentucky Thorobreds.

BLUE MOUNTAIN RAMBLERS

Pseudonym on Champion for the Virginia Mountain Boomers.

BLUE RIDGE CORN SHUCKERS

See Ernest V. Stoneman.

BLUE RIDGE DUO

See George Reneau.

BLUE RIDGE GOSPEL SINGERS

Buell Kazee, Lester O'Keefe, v duet; acc. Bert Hirsch, f; Bill Wirges, p.
New York, NY   Tuesday, April 19, 1927

| E-22513/14 | On The Hill Over There | Br unissued |

Acc. Bert Hirsch, f; Bill Wirges, p; Carson Robison, g.
New York, NY   Wednesday, April 20, 1927

E-22523/24*	On The Hills Over There	Br 150
E-22525/26*	My Loved Ones Are Waiting For Me	Br 151, Spt S2096
E-22527/28*	I'm Alone In This World	Br 152
E-22529/30*	I'm Going Home To Die No More	Br 152
E-22531*/32	O Why Not To-Night?	Br 151
E-22537/38*/39	'Twill Be Glory Bye And Bye	Br 150, Spt S2101

Matrices E-22533 to E-22536 are by Buell Kazee. Matrices E-22527 to E-22530 are dated April 19 in Brunswick files, but other evidence seems to contradict this, and the date given above is more probable.
Rev. Supertone S2096, S2101 by Old Southern Sacred Singers.
Buell Kazee also recorded in his own name.

BLUE RIDGE HIGHBALLERS

Charley La Prade, f; Arthur Wells, bj; Lonnie Griffith, g.
New York, NY   Tuesday, March 23, 1926

141841-2	Green Mountain Polka	Co 15070-D
141842-2	Skidd More	Co 15168-D
141843-1	Flop Eared Mule	Co 15081-D
141844-2	Darneo	Co 15132-D, Ve 7103-V, Cl 5139-C

141845-2	Soldier's Joy	Co 15168-D
141846-1	Darling Child	Co 15132-D, Ve 7101-V, Cl 5139-C
141847-	Flying Cloud	Co unissued
141848-1	Under The Double Eagle	Co 15070-D
141849-2	Fourteen Days In Georgia	Co 15081-D
141850-2	Sandy River Belle	Co 15089-D
141851-2	Round Town Girls	Co 15089-D
141852-	Hop Light Ladies	Co unissued

Rev. Velvet Tone 7101-V, 7103-V by Frank Blevins & His Tar Heel Rattlers.

New York, NY   Wednesday, March 24, 1926

| 141856-1,-2 | Going Down To Lynchburg Town – Intro: Don't Let Your Deal Go Down | Co 15096-D, Ve 2488-V, Cl 5428-C |

Both takes of matrix 141856 have been reported on Columbia 15096-D; it is not known which take/s is/are used on Velvet Tone 2488-V and Clarion 5428-C. Velvet Tone 2488-V as by **Smoky Blue Highballers**.
Revs: Columbia 15096-D by Luther B. Clarke; Velvet Tone 2488-V, Clarion 5428-C by North Carolina Ramblers (see Charlie Poole).

Charley La Prade, f; John Thomasson, f; Lige Hardy, bj; Lonnie Griffith, g/v.
New York, NY   c. September 1927

2861-2	Red Wing	Pm 3083, Bwy 8159
2865-2	Jule Girl	Pm 3083, Bwy 8159
2867-2	Are You Angry With Me Darling	Pm 3077, Bwy 8185
2868-1	I'm Tired Of Living Here Alone	Pm 3077, Bwy 8185

Matrix 2868-2 has been reported, but it is uncertain on which issue.
Broadway 8159, 8185 as by **Stone Mountain Entertainers**. Intervening matrices are untraced.
The Blue Ridge Highballers also accompanied Luther B. Clarke.

BLUE RIDGE HILL BILLIES (HOMER, SHORTY & MAC)

Homer Sherrill, f; Everett "Shorty" Watkins, g/v; Kinman McMillar, g/v-1.
Charlotte, NC   Monday, June 22, 1936

102808-1	Uncle Noah's Ark -1	BB B-6609
102809-1	Why Don't You Come Back To Me?	BB B-7070
102810-1	That Three Point Two -1	BB B-6609
102811-1	Think Of Me Thinking Of You	BB B-7070
102812-1	Blue Eyes -1	BB B-6786, RZAu G23209, Twin FT8316
102813-1	When I Was A Boy From The Mountains -1	BB B-6541, Twin FT8207
102814-1	Lonesome -1	BB B-6786, RZAu G23209, Twin FT8316
102815-1	I Love You Best Of All -1	BB B-6541

Rev. Twin FT8207 by Fred Kirby & Don White.

BLUE RIDGE MOUNTAIN ENTERTAINERS

Rather than divide this session piecemeal according to individual artist-credits and scatter the items among several entries, it has been judged more convenient to treat it as a single group of recordings under a single band name – which was indeed used on some issues, as well as on other, non-recording, occasions.

Tom Ashley, v; acc. own g; unknown others ("String Band Acc.", according to Art Satherley's files).
New York, NY   Monday, November 30, 1931

| 11035- | There Will Come A Time | ARC unissued |

Ashley & Greene: Clarence Greene, f/v; Gwen Foster, h/g; Tom Ashley, g/v; poss. Walter Davis, g.
New York, NY   Monday, November 30, 1931

| 11036-3 | Penitentiary Bound | Cq 8149 |

Tom Ashley, v; acc. Gwen Foster, h/g; own g.
New York, NY   Monday, November 30, 1931

| 11037-1 | Drunk Man Blues | Ba 32630, Me M12538, Or 8183, Pe 12864, Ro 5183 |

Walter Davis, v; acc. Gwen Foster, h/g; own g.
New York, NY   Monday, November 30, 1931

| 11038-1 | Crooked Creek Blues | Ba 32630, Me M12538, Or 8183, Pe 12864, Ro 5183 |

Ashley & Green: Clarence Greene, f/v; Gwen Foster, h/g; Tom Ashley, g/v; poss. Walter Davis, g.
New York, NY   Monday, November 30, 1931

| 11039-2 | Short Life Of Trouble | Ba 32427, Or 8129, Pe 12800, Ro 5129, Cq 8149 |

Matrix 11039 on Conqueror 8149 as by **Ashley & Greene**.

Ashley & Foster: Clarence Greene, f; Gwen Foster, h/poss. g/v; Tom Ashley, g/v.
 New York, NY   Monday, November 30, 1931
  11040-2   Baby All Night Long   Vo 02780

Blue Ridge Mountain Entertainers: Clarence Greene, f; Gwen Foster, h/g; Tom Ashley, g.
 New York, NY   Tuesday, December 1, 1931
  11041-3   Cincinnati Breakdown   Ba 32432, Or 8134, Pe 12805, Ro 5134
  11042-2   Honeysuckle Rag   Ba 32432, Or 8134, Pe 12805, Ro 5134

Tom Ashley, v/sp; acc. Clarence Greene, f/sp; Gwen Foster, h/g/sp; Will Abernathy, h/ah/sp; own g; Walter Davis, g/sp.
 New York, NY   Tuesday, December 1, 1931
  11043-1   Over At Tom's House   Cq 8103
  11044-2   The Fiddler's Contest   Cq 8103

Blue Ridge Mountain Entertainers: Clarence Greene, f; Gwen Foster, h/g; Will Abernathy, h/ah; Tom Ashley, g.
 New York, NY   Tuesday, December 1, 1931
  11045-1   Washington And Lee Swing   Ba 32356, Or 8116, Pe 12782, Ro 5116, Cq 7942
  11046-2   Goodnight Waltz   Ba 32356, Or 8116, Pe 12782, Ro 5116, Cq 7942

Tom Ashley, v; acc. Gwen Foster, h; own g
 New York, NY   Tuesday, December 1, 1931
  11047-2   My Sweet Farm Girl   Ba 32353, Or 8113, Pe 12779, Ro 5113,
                          Cq 7939, Vo 02780

Ashley & Foster: Clarence Greene, f; Gwen Foster, h/poss. g/v; Tom Ashley, g/v.
 New York, NY   Tuesday, December 1, 1931
  11048-3   I Have No Loving Mother Now   Ba 32478, Me M12425, Or 8152, Pe 12822,
                          Ro 5152

Matrix 11048 on Perfect 12822 (at least) as by **Tom Ashley & Gwin Foster**.

Clarence Greene, v; acc. unknown.
 New York, NY   Wednesday, December 2, 1931
  11049-   Nine Pound Hammer   ARC unissued

Tom Ashley, v; acc. Gwen Foster, h/sp; own g.
 New York, NY   Wednesday, December 2, 1931
  11050-1   Haunted Road Blues   Ba 32353, Or 8113, Pe 12779, Ro 5113,
                          Cq 7939, Bwy 4076

Broadway 4076 as by **Tom Sargent**. Rev. Broadway 4076 by Cliff Carlisle & Wilbur Ball.

Ashley & Abernathy: Clarence Greene, f; Gwen Foster, h/g; Will Abernathy, ah/v; Tom Ashley, g/v; unidentified, v.
 New York, NY   Wednesday, December 2, 1931
  11051-2   Corrina, Corrina   Ba 32427, Or 8129, Pe 12800, Ro 5129

Blue Ridge Mountain Entertainers: Gwen Foster, h/g/v; Will Abernathy, ah/v.
 New York, NY   Wednesday, December 2, 1931
  11052-2   Bring Me A Leaf From The Sea   Ba 32478, Me M12425, Or 8152, Pe 12822,
                          Ro 5152

Tom Ashley, v; acc. the Blue Ridge Mountain Entertainers: no details.
 New York, NY   Wednesday, December 2, 1931
  11053-   Far Across The Deep Blue Sea   ARC unissued

Gwen Foster, v; acc. the Blue Ridge Mountain Entertainers: no details.
 New York, NY   Wednesday, December 2, 1931
  11054-   Ham And Eggs   ARC unissued

BLUE RIDGE MOUNTAIN GIRLS

Evelyn Harding, unknown, v/y-1 duet; acc. unknown, g.
 Richmond, IN   Friday, November 10, 1933
  19359   The First Whippoorwill Song   Ch 16701
  19360   Rock Me In The Cradle Of Kalua   Ch 16701
  19361   She Came Rollin' Down The Mountain   Ch S-16743, 45094, MeC 45094, MW 4934
  19362   Rocking Alone In An Old Rocking Chair -1   Ch S-16715, 45100
  19363   Woman's Answer To 21 Years   Ch S-16715, 45100, MW 4934

Rev. Champion 45094, Melotone 45094 by Sylvia Porter.
 Richmond, IN   Friday, April 6, 1934
  19511   Silver Valley   Ch 16752, 45090
  19512   My Heart Is Where The Mohawk Flows Tonight   Ch 16763, 45077

19513	Depression Medley	Ge unissued
19514	New Answer To Twenty-One Years	Ch 16752, 45090
19515	Little Ranch House On Circle B	Ch 16763, 45077, MW 4985
19516	Memories Of That Silver Haired Daddy -1	Ch 16795, 45083, MeC 45083, MW 4935
19517	Baby's Lullaby	Ge unissued
19518	When It's Prayer Meetin' Time In The Hollow	Ch 16778, 45108, MW 4985
19519	There's A Mother Always Waiting	Ch 16778, 45108, MW 4935
19520	My Vine Covered Home In The Blue Ridge -1	Ch 16795, 45083, MeC 45083

BLUE RIDGE MOUNTAIN SINGERS

Prob.: Amy Barrett, Vella Barrett, v duet; or Amy Barrett, Vella Barrett, Fred Barrett, v trio-1; acc. Fred Barrett, ah; unidentified, g.

Atlanta, GA　　　　　　　　　　　　　　　　　　　　　　　　　　　　　　　　　　Monday, April 21, 1930

150321- ; 194969-1	Give My Love To Nell	Co 15580-D
150322- ; 194965-1	The Engineer's Last Run -1	Co 15647-D
150323- ; 194966-1	Sinful To Flirt -1	Co 15678-D
150324-2	The Letter That Never Came -1	Co 15580-D
150325-2	Mansion Of Aching Hearts -1	Co 15678-D
150326- ; 194967-1	The Tramp Song -1	Co 15647-D
150331-2; 194968-1	Christine Leroy	Co unissued: *Rdr 1029 (LP)*
150332-2; 194970-2	I Wish I'd Never Met You	Co unissued: *Rdr 1029 (LP)*
150333-2	I'll Remember You Love In My Prayers -1	Co 15550-D
150334-2	Lorena	Co 15550-D

Matrices 150327/28 are by Clayton McMichen & Riley Puckett; 150329/30 by Monroe Walker (see *B&GR*).

See Blue Ridge Singers for a possibly associated group.

BLUE RIDGE MOUNTAINEERS

Frank Miller, f; Clarence McCormick, h; Alice McCormick, p; Homer Castleman, bj.

Richmond, IN　　　　　　　　　　　　　　　　　　　　　　　　　　　　　　　Wednesday, April 3, 1929

15001	Old Flannigan	Ge 6870
15002	Old Voile	Ge 6870

BLUE RIDGE PLAYBOYS

See Leon Selph.

BLUE RIDGE RAMBLERS

Pseudonym on Vocalion for the Prairie Ramblers.

BLUE RIDGE SACRED SINGERS

Bob Cranford, A.P. Thompson, Horace Cassterers, Shaffer Cassterers, v quartet; acc. unknown, p.

Richmond, IN　　　　　　　　　　　　　　　　　　　　　　　　　　　　　　　　Saturday, June 15, 1929

15228-A	Where The Soul Never Dies	Ge 6916, Ch 15793, Spt 9501
15229-A	I Want To Love Him More	Ge 6916, Spt 9502
15230	What Is He Worth To The Soul	Ge 6947, Ch 15793
15231	Serving The Master	Ge 6947, Ch 15926, Spt 9501
15232	Jesus Is Mine	Ge 7188, Ch 15926, Spt 9502
15233	Letting Jesus Lead	Ge rejected

Champion 15793, 15926 as by **Ozark Mountain Sacred Singers**. Supertone 9501, 9502 as by **Oak Ridge Sacred Singers**. Rev. Gennett 7188 by Carolina Gospel Singers.

Bob Cranford and A.P. Thompson are members of The Red Fox Chasers.

This credit is also used for an item on OKeh 45281 which is beyond the scope of this work.

BLUE RIDGE SINGERS

Vocal trio (two men, one woman); acc. unknown, h; unknown, ah; unknown, g.

Atlanta, GA　　　　　　　　　　　　　　　　　　　　　　　　　　　　　　　Saturday, November 5, 1927

145120-2	I Want To Go There Don't You	Co 15228-D
145121-1	Glory Is Now Rising In My Soul	Co 15228-D

It seems likely that this group is associated with the Blue Ridge Mountain Singers.

BLUE RIDGE SUNSHINE BOYS

Vocal duet; acc. poss. own g duet.
   Rock Hill, SC   Friday, September 30, 1938

027687-1	Will My Mother Know Me There?	BB B-7941, MW M-7728
027688-1	Village Grave	BB B-7941, MW M-7728

BLUE SKY BOYS

Bill Bolick, tv/md; Earl Bolick, lv/g.
   Charlotte, NC   Tuesday, June 16, 1936

102640-1	I'm Just Here To Get My Baby Out Of Jail	BB B-6621, MW M-7017
102641-1	Sunny Side Of Life	BB B-6457, MW M-5029
102642-1	There'll Come A Time	BB B-6538, MW M-7016
102643-1	Where The Soul Never Dies	BB B-6457, MW M-5029
102644-1	Midnight On The Stormy Sea	BB B-6480, MW M-5033
102645-1	Take Up Thy Cross	BB B-6567, MW M-7018
102646-1	Row Us Over The Tide	BB B-6567, MW M-7018
102647-1	Down On The Banks Of The Ohio	BB B-6480, MW M-5033
102648-1	I'm Troubled, I'm Troubled	BB B-6538, MW M-7016
102649-1	The Dying Boy's Prayer	BB B-6621, MW M-7017

   Charlotte, NC   Tuesday, October 13, 1936

02569-1	No One To Welcome Me Home	BB B-6669, MW M-7158
02570-1,-2	Short Life Of Trouble	BB unissued
02571-1	Didn't They Crucify My Lord	BB B-6764, MW M-7160
02572-1	Only Let Me Walk With Thee	BB B-6669, MW M-7158
02573-1	Can't You Hear That Night Bird Crying	BB B-6854, MW M-7162
02574-1	An Old Account Was Settled	BB B-6901, MW M-7161
02575-1	Sweet Allalee	BB B-6854, MW M-7162, Twin FT8337
02576-1	You Give Me Your Love	BB B-6714, MW M-7159, RZAu G23374
02577-1	I Believe It	BB B-6808, MW M-7085
02578-1	When The Ransomed Get Home	BB B-6764, MW M-7160
02579-1	Fair Eyed Ellen	BB B-6808, MW M-7161
02580--	Somebody Makes Me Think Of You	BB B-6714, MW M-7159

Montgomery Ward M-7085 as by **Bolick Brothers**. Matrix 02570 was scheduled for issue on Bluebird B-6764 but the master was evidently lost, and matrix 02571 was substituted.
Revs: Bluebird B-6901 by Dixon Brothers; Montgomery Ward M-7085 by Mrs. Jimmie Rodgers; Regal-Zonophone G23374 by Wade Mainer & Zeke Morris; Twin FT8337 by Jimmie Revard.

   Charlotte, NC   Monday, August 2, 1937

011800-1	Sweet Evalina	BB B-7348, MW M-7323
011801-1	No Home	BB B-7311, MW M-7323
011802-1	What Have You Done	BB B-7173, MW M-7324
011803-1	Sing A Song For The Blind	BB B-8143, MW M-7324
011804-1	Within The Circle	BB B-7113, MW M-7325
011805-1	They're All Home But One	BB B-7173
011806-1	Hymns My Mother Sang	BB B-7311, MW M-7326
011807-1	Have No Desire To Roam	BB B-7348, MW M-7326
011808-1	No Disappointment In Heaven	BB B-7113, MW M-7325
011809-1	Story Of The Knoxville Girl	BB B-7755, MW M-7327
011810-1	On The Old Plantation	BB B-8128
011811-1	In My Little Home In Tennessee	BB B-8143, MW M-7327

   Charlotte, NC   Tuesday, January 25, 1938

018671-1	Beautiful, Beautiful Brown Eyes	BB B-7755, MW M-7470
018672-1	The Prisoner's Dream	BB B-7411, MW M-7468
018673-1	The Answer To "The Prisoner's Dream"	BB B-7411, MW M-7469
018674-1	When The Stars Begin To Fall	BB B-7472, MW M-7471
018675-1	We Buried Her	BB B-8017, RZ MR3021
018676-1	Heaven Holds All For Me	BB B-7803, MW M-7472
018677-1	Little Bessie	BB B-8017, MW M-7470, RZ MR3021, Twin FT8714
018678-1	I Need The Prayers	BB B-7803, MW M-7472
018679-1	Old Fashioned Meeting	BB B-7472
018680-1	Katie Dear	BB B-7661, MW M-7468
018681-1	Who Wouldn't Be Lonely	BB B-7661, MW M-7469
018682-1	Life Line	BB B-7984, MW M-7471

Regal-Zonophone MR3021 as by **Alabama Barnstormers**. Rev. Twin FT8714 by Herald Goodman.

Rock Hill, SC   Tuesday, September 27, 1938

027739-1	When The Valley Moon Was Low	BB B-8152
027740-1	My Last Letter	BB B-7878, MW M-7568
027741-1	Mother Went Her Holiness Way	BB B-7984
027742-1	Hang Out The Front Door Key	BB B-8110, MW M-7567
027743-1	This Is Like Heaven To Me	BB B-7933, MW M-7566
027744-1	I've Found A Friend	BB B-7933, MW M-7566
027745-1	Asleep In The Briny Deep	MW M-7568
027746-1	Last Night While Standing By My Window	BB B-7878
027747-1	There Was A Time	BB B-8110, MW M-7567
027748-1	Bring Back My Wandering Boy	BB B-8128

Rev. Bluebird B-8152 by Wade Mainer.

Atlanta, GA   Monday, August 21, 1939

041222-1	When The Roses Bloom In Dixieland	BB B-8294, MW M-8410
041223-1	Are You From Dixie?	BB B-8294, MW M-8410
041224-1	Give Me My Roses Now	BB B-8308, MW M-8411
041225-1	The House Where We Were Wed	BB B-8308, MW M-8411
041226-1	There's No Other Love For Me	BB B-8339, MW M-8412
041227-1	God Sent My Little Girl	BB B-8339, MW M-8412
041228-1	Someone's Last Day	BB B-8356, MW M-8413
041229-1	She'll Be There	BB B-8356, MW M-8413
041230-1	The Lightning Express	BB B-8369, MW M-8414
041231-1	The Royal Telephone	BB B-8369, MW M-8414
041232-1	The Convict And The Rose	BB B-8522, MW M-8415, Twin FT8998
041233-1	Father, Dear Father, Come Home	BB B-8522, MW M-8415, Twin FT8998

Atlanta, GA   Monday, February 5, 1940

047500-1	Will The Angels Play Their Harps For Me	BB unissued
047501-1	We Parted By The Riverside	BB B-8482, MW M-8668
047502-1	Only One Step More	BB B-8552, MW M-8670
047503-1	The East Bound Train	BB B-8552, MW M-8670
047504-1	Since The Angels Took My Mother Far Away	BB unissued
047505-1	The Last Mile Of The Way	BB B-8597, MW M-8669
047506-1	She's Somebody's Darling Once More	BB B-8446, MW M-8667
047507-1	I'm S-A-V-E-D	BB B-8401, MW M-8666
047508-1	Whispering Hope	BB B-8401, MW M-8666
047509-1	The Butcher's Boy	BB B-8482, MW M-8668
047510-1	This Evening Light	BB B-8597, MW M-8669
047511-1	Mary Of The Wild Moor	BB B-8446, MW M-8667

According to the session-sheet, matrix 047500 was "broken in transit."

Atlanta, GA   Monday, October 7, 1940

054508-1	Why Not Confess	BB 33-0516, MW M-8846
054509-1	Turn Your Radio On	BB B-8843, MW M-8846
054510-1	Since The Angels Took My Mother Far Away	BB 33-0516, MW M-8847
054511-1	In The Hills Of Roane County	BB B-8693, MW M-8848
054512-1	Kneel At The Cross	BB B-8843, MW M-8847
054513-1	Brown Eyes	BB B-8693, MW M-8848
054514-1	Short Life Of Trouble	BB B-8829, MW M-8849
054515-1	A Picture On The Wall	BB B-8646, MW M-8845
054516-1	Pictures From Life's Other Side	BB B-8646, MW M-8845
054517-1	Don't Say Goodbye If You Love Me	BB B-8829, MW M-8849

The Blue Sky Boys recorded after 1942.

JIM[MY] BOA
BOA'S PINE CABIN BOYS

Boa's Pine Cabin Boys: unknown, f; unknown, md; unknown, bj; unknown, g; unknown, v duet.

New York, NY   Thursday, June 8, 1933

13438-1	Hurry Johnny, Hurry	Vo 02594, Pan 25615

Matrix 13438 is titled *Hurry, Johnny, Hurry* on Panachord 25615.

Jimmy Boa, v; acc. unknown.

New York, NY   Thursday, June 8, 1933

13439-	I'm A Lonesome Cowboy	ARC unissued

Clinton Bennett, v; acc. unknown, f; unknown, md; unknown, bj; unknown, g.
New York, NY   Thursday, June 8, 1933
    13440-   Where The Ozarks Kiss The Sky   CrC/MeC/Stg/Roy 91882

Rev. all issues by Frank Luther.

Boa's Pine Cabin Boys: unknown, f; unknown, md; unknown, bj; unknown, g; unknown, v duet.
New York, NY   Thursday, June 8, 1933
    13441-1   I Like To Go To Back In The Evening (To That   Vo 02594, Pan 25615
                     Old Sweetheart Of Mine)

The vocalists may be different from those on matrix 13438.
The parenthesised part of the title of matrix 13441 does not appear on Panachord 25615.

Micky McMadd, v; acc. **Boa's Pine Cabin Boys**: no details.
New York, NY   Thursday, June 8, 1933
    13442-   Little Old Sweet Lady   ARC unissued

I'm A Lonesome Cowboy on Crown/Melotone/Sterling/Royale 91727, credited to **Jim Boa (The Texas Drifter)**, is believed to be by Goebel Reeves.

BOB & JIMMY

See Bob Palmer & Jimmy White.

BOB & MONTE

See Bob Palmer & Monte Hall.

BOB'S BOYS

Pseudonym on Continental and Varsity for Bob Miller.

LOY BODINE

Loy Bodine, h solo.
Richmond, IN   Tuesday, January 13, 1931
    17432,-A,-B   Fox Chase No. 2   Ge rejected
    17433,-A   The Hobo's Dream   Ge rejected

Loy Bodine, v; acc. prob. Landon Goff, g.
Richmond, IN   Tuesday, January 13, 1931
    17434   Wabash Cannon Ball   Spr 2608
    17435-A   Farmer Gray   Spr 2608

Loy Bodine, v/y-1; acc. prob. own g; Landon Goff, g-2.
Richmond, IN   Tuesday, March 10, 1931
    17587,-A,-B,-C, Everybody Works But Father   Ge rejected
    -D,-E
    17588,-A,-B,-C, Treasures Untold -1, 2   Ge rejected
    -D
    17589,-A,-B   Dissatisfied -1, 2   Ge unissued

Matrix 17588 is logged as by **Bodine & Goff**.

Acc. prob.: Charles Hager, md; Harry Newman, g.
Richmond, IN   Wednesday, February 3, 1932
    18369-A   A Gangster's Warning   Ch S-16402, Spr 2809
    18370   A Mother's Farewell   Ch S-16402
    18371   Tis Sweet To Be Remembered   Ge rejected
    18372   My Old Plantation And You -1   Ch S-16391
    18373   Where The Old Red River Flows -1 Ch S-16391, Spr 2809

Loy Bodine also recorded with Charlie Hager and Howard Keesee.

BODINE & KEESEE

See Howard Keesee.

DOCK BOGGS

"Dock" Boggs, v; acc. own bj; G.H. (Hub) Mahaffey, g-1.
New York, NY   Thursday, March 10, 1927
    E-21795/96*   Country Blues   Br 131
    E-21797/98*   Sammie, Where Have You Been So Long -1   Br 131
    E-21799/800*   Down South Blues -1   Br 118
    E-21801*/02   Sugar Baby -1   Br 118

E-21811/12*	Danville Girl	Br 132
E-21813/14*	Pretty Polly	Br 132, 80090
E-21815*/16	New Prisoner's Song -1	Br 133, Vo 5144
E-21817/18*	Hard Luck Blues -1	Br 133, Vo 5144

Intervening matrices are by Dykes' Magic City Trio. Rev. Brunswick 80090 by Dick Reinhart.

Dock Boggs, v; acc. own bj; Emry Arthur, g.
Chicago, IL   c. September 1929

21403-2	False Hearted Lover's Blues	LA 1
21404-2	Old Rub Alcohol Blues	LA unissued: *Revenant 205* (CD)
21404-3	Old Rub Alcohol Blues	LA 1
21405-1	Will Sweethearts Know Each Other There	LA unissued: *Revenant 205* (CD)
21405-2	Will Sweethearts Know Each Other There	LA 2
21406-2	Lost Love Blues	LA unissued: *Revenant 205* (CD)
21406-3	Lost Love Blues	LA 2

On Revenant 205, tracks 13 and 14, though reportedly derived from unissued takes, are the issued takes 21406-3 and 21405-2 respectively (duplicating tracks 9 and 10 with speed variations). Tracks 15 to 17 are correctly reported as unissued takes, but track 17 is from matrix 21405-1, not, as implied, 21405-2.

Dock Boggs recorded after 1942.

BOLICK BROTHERS

I Believe It by the Blue Sky Boys on Montgomery Ward M-7085 is so credited.

CARL BOLING & HIS FOUR ACES

Carl Boling, h-1/tbj-2/tg-3/v-4; Ralph Miller, md-5/v-6; Ed Stewart, g or tg/v-7; Robert Knight, g or tg/v-8; Ernest Boling, v-9.
Rock Hill, SC   Wednesday, February 1, 1939

031928-1	Why Did You Leave Me -3, 4, 5, 7	BB B-8209
031929-1	Women Of Today -3, 5, 6, 8	BB B-8193
031930-1	Old Virginia Moon -3, 5, 7, 8	BB B-8224
031931-1	Back To Carolin' -3, 5, 7, 8	BB B-8224
031932-1	Hills Of Carolin' -3, 5, 6, 7	BB B-8240
031933-1	Big Fat Gal Of Mine -3, 5, 7	BB B-8209
031934-1	Sweetheart Of The Smokies -1, 5, 7	BB B-8193
031935-1	Home On The Plains -3, 9	BB B-8240
031936-1	Struttin' The Neck -2, 5	BB B-8061
031937-1	Boling Rag -2, 5	BB B-8061

Carl Boling, tbj/tg; Robert Knight, g/v-1; Lawrence Boling, g/v-2; Jimmy McAbee, sb; Ernest Boling, v-3.
Atlanta, GA   Wednesday, February 7, 1940

047577-1	I'm A Tough Shooting Hombre From Texas -2	BB B-8448, MW M-8672
047578-1	China Boy	BB B-8448, MW M-8672
047579-1	Twilight On The Prairie -3	BB B-8541, MW M-8673
047580-1	You Can't Tame Wild Women -2, 3	BB B-8493, MW M-8674
047581-1	Blue Skies Are Gray Skies -2	BB B-8598, MW M-8674
047582-1	My Sweetheart's Letter -2, 3	BB B-8390, MW M-8671, RZAu G25173, HMVIn NE636
047583-1	Please Don't Say We're Through -2	BB B-8598, MW M-8673
047584-1	I Need A Sweetheart -3	BB B-8390, MW M-8671, HMVIn NE636
047585-1	Guitar Blues	BB B-8541, MW M-8675
047586-1	Gonna' Quit My Rowdy Ways -1, 2	BB B-8493, MW M-8675
047587-1	That Old Rockin' Chair -3	BB B-8638, MW M-8676, RZAu G25180
047588-1	Forget Me And Be Happy -2	BB B-8638, MW M-8676, RZAu G25180

Rev. Regal-Zonophone G25173 by Pine Ridge Boys.

JOHNNY BOND

Johnny Bond, v; acc. **His Red River Valley Boys**: Jerry Adler, h; Jimmy Wakely, g; own g; Dick Reinhart, sb/v-1.
Hollywood, CA   Tuesday, August 12, 1941

H-437-1	Those Gone And Left Me Blues -1	OK 06531, Co 37427, 20154
H-438-1	I Won't Stand In Your Way -1	Cq 9868
H-439-1	Down In The Dumps	OK 06408, Cq 9872, Co 37440, 20167
H-440-1	Don't You Weep Anymore Darlin' -1	OK 06470, Cq 9869, Co 37435, 20162
H-441-1	The Road Is Way Too Long -1	OK 06470, Cq 9869, Co 37435, 20162
H-442-1	Baby You're Thru Foolin' Me	OK 06408, Cq 9872, Co 37440, 20167
H-443-1	I'm Poundin' The Rails Again -1	Cq 9868
H-444-1	A Long Lonesome Road -1	OK unissued

    Hollywood, CA   Tuesday, August 19, 1941
        H-466-1   I'm Gonna Be Long Gone (When I Go Away)   OK 06407, Cq 9871
        H-467-1   I've Had The Blues Before   OK 06531, Cq 9870, Co 37427, 20154
        H-468-1   One More Tear -1   Cq 9870
        H-469-1   Now You Care No More For Me -1   OK unissued
        H-470-1   Draftee Blues   OK 06407, Cq 9871
        H-471-1   Help Me Lose The Blues   OK unissued

Acc. Spade Cooley, f; Jerry Adler, h; Paul Sells, p; Doyle Salathiel, g; Jimmy Wakely, g; own g; Dick Reinhart, sb.
    Hollywood, CA   Tuesday, December 2, 1941
        H-585-1   You Brought Sorrow To My Heart   OK 06577, Co 37255, 20102, RZAu G25172
        H-586-1   You Don't Care   OK 06649, 6732, Co 37400, 20127
        H-587-1   After I'm Gone   OK unissued
        H-588-1   How Low Do The Blues Want To Go   OK 06577
        H-589-1   Someday You're Gonna Be Blue   OK 06649
Rev. Regal-Zonophone G25172 postwar.

Acc. Spade Cooley, f; Jack Mayhew, cl; Jerry Adler, h; Dick Roberts, g; own g; Hank Stern, tu.
    Hollywood, CA   Friday, April 3, 1942
        H-784-1   1942 Turkey In The Straw   OK unissued
        H-785-1   We're Gonna Have To Slap The Dirty Little Jap OK unissued
        H-786-1   Mussolini's Letter To Hitler   OK unissued
        H-787-1   Hitler's Reply To Mussolini   OK unissued

Acc. Spade Cooley, f; Lyall W. Bowen, cl; Art Wenzel, ac; Ralph Thomas, p; own g; Hank Stern, sb/tu.
    Hollywood, CA   Friday, July 31, 1942
        H-906-1   I'm A Pris'ner Of War (On A Foreign Shore) OK 6691, CoC C682
        H-907-1   You Let Me Down   OK unissued
        H-908-1   Der Fuehrer's Face   OK 6691, CoC C682
        H-909-1   Love Gone Cold   OK 6732, Co 37400, 20127
Johnny Bond recorded after 1942.

CAPT. M.J. BONNER (THE TEXAS FIDDLER)

Capt. M.J. Bonner, f; acc. Fred Wagoner, harp-g.
    Houston, TX   Tuesday, March 17, 1925
        32102-2   Yearling's In The Canebrake / The Gal On The Log   Vi 19699
        32103-2   Dusty Miller / Ma Ferguson   Vi 19699

BONNIE BLUE EYES

See Bob Atcher.

REV. HORACE A. BOOKER

Rev. Horace A. Booker, v; acc. poss. own h-1/g.
    Richmond, IN   Sunday, October 23, 1929
        15802   The Streets Of That City -1   [Ge] 20358, 20364
        15803   Creole Girl   Ge rejected
        15804   Ring Dem Heavenly Bells -1   Ge rejected
        15805   Dipping In The Golden Sea -1   Ge rejected
        15806   Life's Railway To Heaven   [Ge] 20358
The issued sides probably appeared on a personal label.

    Richmond, IN   Saturday, April 12, 1930
        16475-A   Just As Rich As You -1   [Ge] 20364
This issue probably appeared on a personal label.
See also Cliff Carlisle.

CLAUDE BOONE

See James Scott–Claude Boone, Cliff Carlisle, and Walter Hurdt. Claude Boone also recorded after 1942.

REV. EDWARD BOONE, MRS. EDWARD BOONE & MISS OLIVE BOONE

Rev. Edward Boone & Miss Olive Boone-1/Rev. & Mrs. Edward Boone-2: Edward Boone, v/sp; Miss Olive Boone, v-1; Mrs. Edward Boone, v-2; acc. unknown, p; unknown, ti; unknown, bj; unknown, u-3.
    Richmond, IN   c. June 1929
        15178   In That City That The Bible Calls Four Square -1, 3   Ge 6903
        15179   Will David Play His Harp For Me? -2   Ge 6903

Rev. Edward Boone, v; or **Rev. Edward & Miss Olive Boone**, v duet-1; acc. unknown, p-2; unknown, ti; unknown, g.
    Richmond, IN   Friday, March 28, 1930

16412	Flowers On The Open Grave	Ge 7225
16413	Salvation Is For All	Ge 7248, Ch S-16683, 45127
16414	Ye Must Be Born Again -1	Ge 7208, Ch S-16683, 45127
16415-A	Mother's Missing Now -1	Ge 7225
16416	Springing Up Within My Soul -1	Ge 7208, Ch 15993
16417-A	I Wonder How They Live At Home -1, 2	Ge 7248, Ch 15993

Champion 15993 as by **Rev. Edward & Olive Boone**; Champion S-16683 prob. as by **Rev. Edward Boone**; Champion 45127 as by **Rev. Edw. Boone**.

Rev. Edward Boone & Daughter Olive-1/Rev. Edward Boone & Family-2/Rev. Edward Boone, Wife & Daughter-3: Rev. Edward Boone, v; Miss Olive Boone, v-4; Mrs. Edward Boone, v-5; acc. unknown, h-6; unknown, p-7; unknown, ti-8; unknown, md-9; unknown, g.
    Richmond, IN   Wednesday, July 30, 1930

16856,-A,-B	A Mansion There For Me -1, 4, 9	Ge rejected
16857,-A,-B	Dying On Calvary -2, 4, 5, 7, 9	Ge rejected
16858,-A,-B	He's The Best Friend I Can Find -1, 4, 9	Ge rejected
16859,-A	No Place To Lay His Head -3, 4, 5, 6	Ge rejected
16860,-A	He Answers Prayers Today -3, 4, 5, 6, 9	Ge rejected
16861	The Book That Mother Gave Me -1, 4, 8, 9	Ge rejected

Rev. Edward Boone & Miss Olive Boone-1/Rev. Edward Boone & Mrs. Boone-2/Rev. Edward Boone & Mrs. Boone & Daughter Olive Boone-3: Rev. Edward Boone, v; Miss Olive Boone, v-4; Mrs. Edward Boone, v-5; acc. unknown, h-6; unknown, p-7; unknown, ti-8; unknown, md-9; unknown, g; unknown, ah-10; unknown, bird eff-11.
    Richmond, IN   Friday, October 24, 1930

17196-A	A Mansion There For Me -1, 4, 8, 10, 11	Ge 7321, Ch 16147, Spr 2690
17197	No Place To Lay His Head -2, 5, 6, 10	Ge 7321, Spr 2690
17198	He Answers Prayers Today -3, 4, 5, 6, 9, 10	Ge 7322, Ch 16147
17199-A	Dying On Calvary -2, 5, 7, 9	Ge 7323
17199-B	Dying On Calvary -2, 5, 7, 9	Spr 2583
17200	The Book That Mother Gave Me -1, 4, 8, 9, 10	Ge 7322, Spr 2583
17201	He's The Best Friend I Can Find -1, 4, 6, 8	Ge 7323

Champion 16147 as by **Sunshine Sacred Trio**. Superior 2583 as by **Rev. Charles Wakefield & Family**, 2690 as by **Rev. Charles Wakefield & Miss Mary Wakefield**.

JIMMY BOONE

Pseudonym on Superior for Cliff Carlisle.

BOONE COUNTY ENTERTAINERS

Pseudonym on Supertone 9177 for the Monroe County Bottle Tippers and on 9163, 9181, 9182, and 9492 for The Red Fox Chasers.

BENNY BORG

Benny Borg (The Singing Soldier), v; acc. own h-1/g.
    Atlanta, GA   Saturday, April 2, 1927

143859-2	Picture From Life's Other Side	Co 15183-D, Ve 7108-V, Cl 5141-C
143860-1	I Want A Pardon For Daddy -1	Co 15148-D
143861-2	A Concert Hall On The Bowery	Co 15183-D, Ve 7109-V, Cl 5141-C
143862-1	You're Going To Leave The Old Home Jim Tonight	Co 15148-D, ReAu G20663

Velvet Tone 7108-V, 7109-V, Clarion 5141-C as by **Matt Judson**.
Revs: Velvet Tone 7108-V, 7109-V by Royal Sumner Quartet; Regal G20663 by Walter Morris.

Scotty The Drifter (The Singing Cowboy), v; acc. own h/g.
    New York, NY   Monday, September 9, 1935

39923-A	Is There No Kiss For Me Tonight Love?	De 5143, DeE F6359, DeSA FM5107, DeIr W4006, RexIr U576
39924-A,-B	The Darned Old Mule From Georgia	De unissued
39925-A	Gooseberry Pie	De 5296
39926-A,-B	Burglar Man And Old Man No. 2	De unissued
39927-A	You Tell Her I Stutter	De 5296
39928-A,-B	Sugar Baby	De rejected
39929-A	Just Before The Battle Mother	De 5143
39930-A	Drunkard's Warning	DeE F6359, DeIr W4006, RexIr U576
39931-A,-B	Bye Bye Blues	De unissued

Decca W4006 as by **Scotty The Drifter**. Rev. Decca FM5107 by Carolina Buddys.

Acc. own h-1/g.
 New York, NY   Tuesday, September 10, 1935

39952-B	Our Senator Huey Long -1	De 5136
39953-A	You're Going To Leave The Old Home Tonight	De 5136
39954-A,-B	The Hill-Billy Bride	De unissued
39955-A,-B	The Soldiers Bonus	De unissued
39956-A,-B	Mother's Crazy Quilt	De rejected

GODFREY BORTON

Pseudonym on Bell for David Miller.

KENNETH BORTON
BORTON & LANG
BORTON & THOMPSON

Pseudonyms on Challenge, the first for Marion Underwood, the others for Marion Underwood & Sam Harris (see Taylor's Kentucky Boys).

LEO [or LEE] BOSWELL

Leo Boswell, v; or **Leo & Dewey Boswell**-1, v duet; acc. unknown, f; prob. Leo Boswell, g.
 Atlanta, GA   Saturday, April 14, 1928

146081-2	Two Little Girls In Blue	Co 15290-D, Re/RZAu G20660
146082-2	The Fatal Rose Of Red	Co 15290-D, Re/RZAu G20660
146083-2	A Memory That Time Cannot Erase -1	Co 15469-D
146084-1	I Love You Nellie -1	Co 15469-D

Lee Boswell, v; acc. Curly Hicks, md/v-1; prob. own g.
 Chicago, IL   Saturday, October 6, 1934

C-9566-A	The Cowboy's Meditation	De 5057
C-9567-A	The Yellow Rose Of Texas	De 5057
C-9568-A,-B	The Old Tobacco Mill -1	De unissued
C-9569-A,-B	When The Sun Goes Down Again	De unissued
C-9570-A,-B	The Last Moving For Me	De rejected
C-9571-A,-B	Take Up Thy Cross	De rejected

Leo Boswell also recorded with Merritt Smith.

CHRIS BOUCHILLON

The Bouchillon Trio: Charley Bouchillon, f; Uris Bouchillon, g; Chris Bouchillon, v.
 Atlanta, GA   c. July 7, 1925

9234-A	She Doodle Dooed	OK 45004

Rev. OKeh 45004 by George Walburn & Emmett Hethcox.

Chris Bouchillon, sp/v; acc. poss. Charley Bouchillon, f-1; Uris Bouchillon, g.
 Atlanta, GA   Thursday, November 4, 1926

143060-2	Talking Blues	Co 15120-D, Vo 02977
143061-1	Hannah -1	Co 15120-D, Ve 2498-V, Cl 5438-C, Vo 02977

Velvet Tone 2498-V, Clarion 5438-C as by **Clay Chapman**. Velvet Tone 2498-V, Clarion 5438-C use the transfer matrix 100585.

Acc. Uris Bouchillon, g; unknown, v-1.
 Atlanta, GA   Saturday, March 26, 1927

143771-2	Waltz Me Around Again Willie -1	Co 15244-D, Ve 7104-V, Cl 5144-C
143772-1,-2	Let It Alone	Co 15178-D
143773-1	You Look Awful Good To Me	Co 15244-D, Ve 7105-V, Cl 5144-C
143774-	In A City Far Away	Co unissued

Velvet Tone 7104-V, 7105-V as by **Jean Mendigal**. Clarion 5144-C as by **Jean Mendrigal**.
Rev. Velvet Tone 7104-V, 7105-V by Williams & Williams.

 Atlanta, GA   Tuesday, April 5, 1927

143896-	South Carolina Blues	Co unissued
143897-3	My Fat Girl	Co 15178-D
143898-2	Born In Hard Luck	Co 15151-D, Ve 2498-V, Cl 5438-C
143899-2	The Medicine Show	Co 15151-D

Velvet Tone 2498-V, Clarion 5438-C as by **Clay Chapman**. Velvet Tone 2498-V, Clarion 5438-C use the transfer matrix 100586.

 Atlanta, GA   Thursday, November 10, 1927

145208-2	Chris Visits The Barber Shop	Co 15213-D, ReAu G20264
145209-2	A Bull Fight In Mexico	Co 15213-D, ReAu G20264

145210-	A Week End At Sam Stover's	Co unissued
145211-	Hebrew And Home Brew	Co unissued
145212-	Good Night Run	Co unissued
145213-	Sam Stover And The Clergyman	Co unissued

Chris Bouchillon, sp/v; acc. unknown, bj-1; Uris Bouchillon, g; unknown, wh-2.
Atlanta, GA   Monday, April 16, 1928

146085-1	Old Blind Heck	Co 15262-D
146086-1	New Talking Blues	Co 15262-D
146087-2	I Got Mine -1, 2	Co 15317-D
146088-1	I've Been Married Three Times	Co 15289-D
146089-2	My Wife's Wedding	Co 15289-D
146090-2	Oyster Stew	Co 15317-D

Mr. & Mrs. Chris Bouchillon, sp duet; acc. Chris Bouchillon, g.
Atlanta, GA   Monday, October 29, 1928

147333-2	Adam And Eve – Part 1	Co 15345-D
147334-2	Adam And Eve – Part 2	Co 15345-D
147335-	Adam And Eve – Part 3	Co unissued
147336-	Adam And Eve – Part 4	Co unissued

Chris Bouchillon, sp; acc. own g.
Atlanta, GA   Tuesday, October 30, 1928

147339-2	Speed Maniac	Co 15373-D
147340-1	Ambitious Father	Co 15373-D
147341-2	Girls Of To-day	Co 15508-D
147342-2	Oh Miss Lizzie	Co 15508-D

THE BOUCHILLON TRIO

See Chris Bouchillon.

W.E. BOWDEN

W.E. Bowden, v; acc. prob. own bj.
Richmond, IN   Monday, May 18, 1931

| 17754 | Boil The Cabbage Down | Ge rejected trial recording |

EARL BOWERS

Pseudonym on Superior for Asa Martin.

BOWERS & LEWIS

Pseudonym on Superior for Asa Martin & James Roberts.

CLARENCE BOWLIN

Clarence Bowlin, v/y; acc. prob. own g.
Richmond, IN   Saturday, December 6, 1930

| 17354 | Lonely Since Norma's Gone | Ge rejected |

BOWLIN & VAN WINKLE

Prob.: vocal duet; acc. unknown, g.
Richmond, IN   c. July 1931

| 17888 | Who Could Tell A Mother's Thoughts | Ge rejected |

CHARLIE BOWMAN

Charlie Bowman, f; acc. Al Hopkins, p-1/v-2; Joe Hopkins, g; John Hopkins, u-3.
New York, NY   Saturday, May 1, 1926

| E-2966*/67 | Hickman Rag -1, 3 | Vo 15377, 5118 |
| E-2968*/69 | Possum Up A Gum Stump, Cooney In The Hollow -2 | Vo 15377, 5118 |

Charlie Bowman & His Brothers: Charlie Bowman, f/v; Walter Bowman, bj/v; Frank Wilson, g/v; poss. Elbert Bowman, g.
Johnson City, TN   Tuesday, October 16, 1928

| 147208-2 | Roll On Buddy | Co 15357-D |
| 147209-2 | Gonna Raise The Ruckus Tonight | Co 15357-D |

Charlie Bowman, f/sp-1; Walter Bowman, bj/sp-1; Frank Wilson, g/sp-1; poss. Elbert Bowman, g/sp-1.
New York, NY   Wednesday, February 20, 1929

| 147972-2 | Forky Dear | Co 15387-D |
| 147973-1 | Moonshiner And His Money -1 | Co 15387-D |

Charles Bowman & Fran Trappe: prob.: Charlie Bowman, f; Fran Trappe, ac.
Johnson City, TN Tuesday, October 23, 1929

| 149258- | Wild Horse | Co unissued |
| 149259- | Caroline Moonshine | Co unissued |

Charlie Bowman also recorded with The Hill Billies and Bowman Sisters.

BOWMAN FAMILY

Vocal group; prob. unacc.
Atlanta, GA Tuesday, October 30, 1928

| 147346- | Panting For Heaven | Co unissued |
| 147347- | Sardis | Co unissued |

BOWMAN SISTERS

Pauline Bowman, Jennie Bowman, v duet; acc. unknown, g.
Johnson City, TN Tuesday, October 16, 1928

| 147206-2 | My Old Kentucky Home | Co 15473-D, CoJ JX-24 |
| 147207-2 | Swanee River | Co 15473-D, CoJ JX-24 |

Matrix 147207 is titled *The Old Folks At Home* on Columbia JX-24.

Acc. Charlie Bowman, f; Fran Trappe, ac.
Johnson City, TN Tuesday, October 23, 1929

| 149256-2 | Railroad Take Me Back | Co 15621-D |
| 149257-2 | Old Lonesome Blues | Co 15621-D |

Acc. unknown.
New York, NY Wednesday, April 22, 1931

10575-	Lonesome Blues	ARC unissued
10576-	The Railroad Boomer	ARC unissued
10577-	When The Leaves Turn Green	ARC unissued

AARON BOYD

Pseudonym on Champion for Green Bailey.

BILL BOYD & HIS COWBOY RAMBLERS

Art Davis, f; Walter Kirkes, tbj; Bill Boyd, g/v-1; Jim Boyd, sb/v-2.
San Antonio, TX Tuesday, August 7, 1934

83822-1	I'm Gonna Hop Off The Train -1, 2	BB B-5740
83823-1	The Ramblers' Rag	BB B-5740, MW M-4535
83824-1	The Lost Wagon	BB B-5788, MW M-4535
83825-1	'Way Down In Missouri	BB B-5788
83826-1	Ridin' On A Humpback Mule -1, 2	BB B-5608, Twin FT1795
83827-1	The Broken Man -1	BB B-5819, Twin FT1877
83828-1	The Strawberry Roan -1	BB B-5667, MW M-4778, Twin FT1844
83829-1	When I Find My Dear Daddy Is Waiting -1, 2	BB B-5819
83830-1	On The Texas Plains -1, 2	BB B-5608, Twin FT1795
83831-1	Ridin' Old Paint And Leadin' Old Ball -1, 2	BB B-5667, MW M-4778

Revs: Twin FT1844 by Fleming & Townsend, FT1877 by Riley Puckett.

Art Davis, f; Slomie Creel, p; Walter Kirkes, tbj; Bill Boyd, g/v-1; Jim Boyd, sb/v-2.
San Antonio, TX Sunday, January 27, 1935

87718-1	St. Louis Blues -1, 2	BB B-5828, MW M-4794, Twin FT1879
87719-1	Thousand Mile Blues -1	BB B-5828, MW M-4794, Twin FT1879
87720-1	The Wind Swept Desert (Desert Blues) -1	BB B-5855, B-6235, MW M-4791, Twin FT1893
87721-1	Song Bird Yodel -1, 2	BB B-5894, RZAu G22648, Twin FT1907
87722-1	Watching The World Go By -1, 2	BB B-5923
87723-1	Going Back To My Texas Home -1, 2	BB B-5923, MW M-7029, Twin FT1922
87724-1	Mama Don't Like No Music -1	BB B-5855, B-6235, MW M-4791, Twin FT1893
87725-1	The Train Song	BB B-5945, MW M-4905, Vi 20-2800, ViJ A1423, Jr-40, V-D 115
87726-1	Harvest Time -1, 2	BB B-5894, RZAu G22648, Twin FT1907
87727-1	Under The Double Eagle	BB B-5945, MW M-4905, Vi 20-2068, ViJ A1423, Jr-40

Rev. Twin FT1922 by Dick Hartman's Tennessee Ramblers.

Art Davis, f/md-1/v-2; Sonny Roden, p; Rankin Moulder, tbj; Bill Boyd, g/v-3; Jim Boyd, g-4/sb-5/v-6; J. Fred McCord, g-5/sb-4.
San Antonio, TX Monday, August 12, 1935

Bill Boyd & His Cowboy Ramblers

94436-1	By A Window -3, 4, 6	BB B-6119, B-8246, RZAu G22853, Twin FT8034
94437-1	Evil In You Children -1, 3, 4, 6	BB B-6068
94438-1	Barn Dance Rag -1, 5?	BB B-6177
94439-1	When The Sun Goes Down Again -3, 4, 6	BB B-6085, Twin FT8006
94440-1	On Top Of The Hill -3, 4, 6	BB B-6119, RZAu G22853, Twin FT8034
94441-1	Old-Fashioned Love -3, 5	BB B-6177
94442-1	Boyd's Blues -5?	BB B-6109
94443-1	The Sweetest Girl -1, 5	BB B-6161
94444-1	David Blues -1, 5	BB B-6109
94445-1	Rio Grande Waltz -3, 4, 6	BB B-6161
94446-1	I Can't Tame Wild Women -1, 2, 5	BB B-6068, Twin FT8019
94447-1	Get Aboard That Southbound Train -3, 4, 6	BB B-6085, Twin FT8006

Rev. Twin FT8019 by Dick Hartman's Tennessee Ramblers.

Jesse Ashlock, f/v-1; Wilson "Lefty" Perkins, esg; Jack Hinson, p; Walter Kirkes, tbj; Bill Boyd, g/v-2; Jim Boyd, sb/v-3.
San Antonio, TX   Monday, February 24, 1936

99313-1	Tumbling Tumbleweeds -2, 3	BB B-6346, MW M-4789
99314-1	Eyes Of Texas -2, 3	BB B-6384, MW M-4793
99315-1	When It's Twilight In Sweetheart Lane -2, 3	BB B-6346, MW M-4789, Twin FT8113
99316-1	Oh, No She Don't -1, 3	BB B-6323, MW M-4795, Twin FT8112
99317-1	Cheatin' On Your Baby -2	BB B-6351
99318-1	Hold On Little Doggies -2, 3	BB B-8198, RZAu G24005, Twin FT8874
99319-1	Wah Hoo -3	BB B-6308, MW M-4790, Twin FT8095
99320-1	Floatin' Down -2, 3	BB B-6492, MW M-7030, Twin FT8226
99321-1	Beale Street Blues -1	BB B-6492, MW M-7030
99322-1	Lone Star -3	BB B-6384, MW M-4793, Twin FT8142
99323-1	My Ball And Chain -2	BB B-6308, MW M-4790, Twin FT8142
99324-1	Mama's Getting Hot And Papa's Getting Cold -2	BB B-6323, MW M-4795
99325-1	River Blues -1	BB B-6443, MW M-7046
99326-1	When The Sun Sets On My Swiss Chalet -2, 3	BB B-6599, MW M-7028, Twin FT8245
99327-1	Must I Hesitate? -1	BB B-6351
99328-1	Jesse Blues -1	BB B-6420
99329-1	I Need One Sweet Letter From You -1	BB B-6486
99330-1	That Ramshackle Shack -2	BB B-6523, MW M-4792
99331-1	Hobo's Paradise (Big Rock Candy Mountain) -2	BB B-6523, MW M-7029, Twin FT8204
99332-1	When They Play Rural Rhythm -2, 3	BB B-6420, MW M-4792

Bluebird B-6384 and matrix 99322 on Twin FT8142 as by **Bill Boyd & His Texas Ramblers**. Bluebird B-6443, Montgomery Ward M-7046 as by **Jesse's String Five**.
Revs: Bluebird B-6443, Montgomery Ward M-7046 by Tampa Red (see *B&GR*); Bluebird B-6486 by Bill Barry & His Orchestra (popular); Twin FT8095 by Cliff Carlisle; FT8112 by Dixon Brothers; FT8113 by Fred Kirby; FT8204 by Wade Mainer & Zeke Morris; FT8226 by Dick Hartman's Tennessee Ramblers; FT8245 by Arthur Smith Trio.

Jesse Ashlock, f; Lefty Perkins, esg-1; Jack Hinson, p-2; Walter Kirkes, tbj; Bill Boyd, g; Jim Boyd, sb.
San Antonio, TX   Monday, February 24, 1936

99333-1	Black And Tan Rag	BB B-6328
99334-1	Goofus -1, 2	BB B-6328
99335-1	Saturday Night Rag	BB B-6599, MW M-7028
99336-1	Prickly Heat	BB unissued

Cecil Brower, f; J.R. Chatwell, f; J.C. Way, esg; John B. "Smoky" Wood, p; Johnny Thames, tbj; Bill Boyd, g/v-1/y-2; William "Curly" Perrin, g/v-3/y-4; Clifton "Rip" Ramsey, sb; band v-5.
San Antonio, TX   Tuesday, October 27, 1936

02946-1	Fan It -1, 5	BB B-7128, MW M-7192
02947-1	Somebody's Been Using It -1, 5	BB B-8246
02948-1	You Can't Come In -1	BB B-6772, MW M-7192
02949-1	Deed I Do -1	BB B-7006
02950-1	You're Tired Of Me -3	BB B-6807
02951-1	Way Out There -1, 2, 3, 4	BB B-6670, MW M-7193, Vi 20-2800
02958-1	An Old Water Mill By A Waterfall -1, 3	BB B-6715, MW M-7189, Twin FT8296
02959-1	Draggin' It Around	BB B-6731
02960-1	Ain't She Coming Out Tonight -1, 5	BB B-6694, RZ MR2433, Twin FT8310
02961-1	You Shall Be Free Monah -1, 5	BB B-6694, MW M-7190, RZ MR2433, Twin FT8310
02962-1	Show Me The Way To Go Home -1, 3	BB B-6715, MW M-7190, Twin FT8296
02963-1	Guess Who's In Town -3	BB B-7006
02964-1	Right Or Wrong	BB B-6731, Twin FT8294
02965-1	That Makes Me Give In -1	BB B-8198, Twin FT8874

02966-1	Jennie Lee -1, 3	BB B-6807
02967-1	Put Me In Your Pocket -1, 3	BB B-6670, MW M-7193, Twin FT8277
02968-1	Yellow Rose Of Texas -1, 3	BB B-7088, MW M-7189, Twin FT8519
02969-1	Blues Is Nothing -1	BB B-6772

Matrix 02961 is titled *Oh, Monah (You Shall Be Free)* on Regal-Zonophone MR2433, Twin FT8310.
Intervening matrices are untraced.
Revs: Twin FT8277 by Tune Wranglers; FT8294 by Jack Moser & His Oklahoma Cavaliers; FT8519 by Musical Musketeers.

Cecil Brower, f; Butch Gibson, cl; Jack Hinson, p; Rankin Moulder, tbj; Bill Boyd, g; Curly Perrin, g; Jim Boyd, sb.
San Antonio, TX   Monday, March 1, 1937

| 07415-1 | Beaumont | BB B-6959 |

Cecil Brower, f; J.R. Chatwell, f; Butch Gibson, cl/as; Jack Hinson, p; Rankin Moulder, tbj; Bill Boyd, g/v-1; Curly Perrin, g/v-2; Jim Boyd, sb/v-3; John Boyd, v-4; band v-5.
San Antonio, TX   Monday, March 1, 1937

07416-1	What's The Use	BB B-7004
07417-1	Dance To Those Sobbin' Blues -2, 3	BB B-7053
07418-1	She's Doggin' Me -3	BB B-6889, MW M-7191
07419-1	Van Buren	BB B-6959
07420-1	Pretty Little Dream Girl -2	BB B-7088, Twin FT8494
07421-1	She's Killin' Me -2, 5	BB B-6889, MW M-7191
07422-1	Little Wooden Whistle -2	BB B-7053, RZAu G23442
07423-1	Red Lips -3	BB B-7507, Vi 21-0351
07424-1	I'll Find You -3	BB B-7507
07425-1	Cemetery Sal -3	BB B-7867
07426-1	Madeira	BB B-7004
07427-1	Meant For Me -4	BB B-8100, MW M-8423
07428-1	Mississippi Mud -3, 5	BB B-8125, MW M-8425
07429-1	That's Why I'm Jealous Of You -2, 3	BB B-7435, MW M-8419
07430-1	New Six Or Seven Times -1	BB B-7128

Matrix 07423 is titled *Red Lips Kiss My Blues Away* on Victor 21-0351; this issue is edited to remove the clarinet solo.
Revs: Bluebird B-7867 by Tune Wranglers; Twin FT8494 by Bill & Louis Carlisle.

Carroll Hubbard, f; Kenneth Pitts, f; unknown, f; Lefty Perkins, esg; Muryel "Zeke" Campbell, eg; John "Knocky" Parker, p; Marvin Montgomery, tbj; Bill Boyd, g/v-1; Curly Perrin, g/v-2; Jim Boyd, sb/v-3; unknown, d.
Dallas, TX   Sunday, September 12, 1937

014048-1	Jungle Town -2, 3	BB B-7347, MW M-8418
014049-1	Come Easy, Go Easy -1	BB B-7800, MW M-7813
014050-1	Frosty Mornin' -1	BB B-7800, MW M-7813
014051-1	I Saw Your Face -3	BB B-7260, MW M-8416
014052-1	An Ace -1, 3	BB B-7435, MW M-8419
014053-1	Cross-Eyed Gal On The Hill -1, 2	BB B-7299, MW M-8417, RZAu G23442, Twin FT8540
014054-1	Can't Use Each Other -2	BB B-7347, MW M-8418
014055-1	My Wonderful One -3	BB B-7260, MW M-8416
014056-1	New Steel Guitar Rag	BB B-7691, MW M-7631, Vi 20-1907, Twin FT8633, *V-D 168*
014057-1	Devilish Mary -1, 2	BB B-7299, MW M-8417
014058-1	Sister Lucy Lee -2	BB B-7189
014059-1	Won't You Please Come Home -3	BB B-7910, MW M-7814
014060-1	So Tired Of Waiting Alone -3	BB B-7910, MW M-7814
014061-1	I'm A High Steppin' Daddy -1	BB B-7521
014062-1	If I Can Count On You -3	BB B-7189
014063-1	See Mama Ev'ry Night -1	BB B-7521
014064-1	Alice Blue Gown -3	BB B-8141

Revs: Bluebird B-8141, Twin FT8633 by Jimmie Revard; Twin FT8540 by Bob Skyles.

Carroll Hubbard, f; Kenneth Pitts, f; Butch Gibson, cl; Lefty Perkins, esg; Knocky Parker, ac/p; Marvin Montgomery, tbj; Bill Boyd, g/v-1; Curly Perrin, g/v-2; Jim Boyd, sb/v-3; Gail Whitney, v-4.
San Antonio, TX   Saturday, April 9, 1938

022304-1	Like You -4	BB B-8100, MW M-8423
022305-1	Annie Laurie Swing -4	BB B-7531
022306-1	I'm Jealous Of The Twinkle In Your Eye -2	BB B-7624
022307-1	Someone In Heaven Is Thinking Of You -2, 3	BB B-7754, MW M-8421, RZAu G23666
022308-1	Song Of The Waterfall -3	BB B-8112, MW M-8424
022309-1	Don't Drop A Slug In The Slot -2, 3	BB B-7573, MW M-8420, RZAu G23576
022310-1	When My Dreams Come True -2, 3	BB B-7739, MW M-7811

022311-1	Ridin' On The Old Ferris Wheel -2	BB B-7573, MW M-8420
022312-1	I'm In Love With You Honey -2	BB B-7624
022313-1	You're Just About Right -1	BB B-7531
022314-1	Broadway Mama -1	BB B-7739, MW M-7811
022315-1	Blues When It Rains -2, 3	BB B-7788, MW M-7812
022316-1	Tableau Clog Dance	BB B-7662, RZAu G23629
022317-1	Pedestal Clog Dance	BB B-7662, RZAu G23629
022318-1	Boyd's Tin Roof Blues	BB B-7788, MW M-7812
022319-1	Home In Indiana -3	BB B-8125, MW M-8425
022320-1	I've Got Those Oklahoma Blues -2	BB B-7754, MW M-8421, RZAu G23666
022321-1	Jig	BB B-7691, MW M-7631

Rev. Regal-Zonophone G23576 by Pine State Playboys (see Claude Casey).

Carroll Hubbard, f; Kenneth Pitts, f; John Boyd, esg-1; Muryel "Zeke" Campbell, eg-2; Knocky Parker, p; Marvin Montgomery, tbj; Bill Boyd, g/v-3; Jim Boyd, g or sb/v-4; unknown, g or sb; band v-5/v eff-6.

San Antonio, TX   Sunday, October 30, 1938

028801-1	My Baby Loves Me, I Know -2, 3	BB B-8081, MW M-7816
028802-1	New Spanish Two-Step -1	BB B-7921, MW M-7630, Vi 20-1907
028803-1	Spanish Fandango -1	BB B-7921, MW M-7630
028804-1	I Love My Baby -1, 4	BB B-8013, MW M-7816
028805-1	Singing And Swinging For Me -1, 3	BB B-7971, MW M-7634
028806-1	Tom-Cat Rag -1, 4, 5, 6	BB B-7940, MW M-7634
028807-1	Here Comes Pappy -2, 3, 5	BB B-7940, MW M-7632
028808-1	One Thing At A Time -2, 4	BB B-7971
028809-1	Weeping Blues -1	BB B-7989, MW M-7633
028810-1	Boyd's Kelly Waltz -1	BB B-7989, MW M-7633, RZAu G24005
028811-1	Never Let You Cry Over Me -1, 4	BB B-8013, MW M-7632
028812-1	La Golondrina -1	BB B-8070, MW M-7815
028813-1	Troubles -1, 4	BB B-8112, MW M-8424
028814-1	I Got The Blues For Mammy -1, 3, 4	BB B-8053, MW M-8422
028815-1	I Want To Go Back -1, 4	BB B-8070, MW M-7815
028816-1	Mill Blues	BB B-8053, MW M-8422

Rev. Bluebird B-8081 by Tennessee Ramblers.

Pat Trotter, f/emd; Buck Buchanan, f; Loren Mitchell, p; Jesse "Slick" Robertson, tbj; J. S. (Jess) Williams, g; Jimmie Meek, sb; Bill Boyd, v-1; Jim Boyd, v-2; v trio (prob.: Jim Boyd, Meek, Williams)-3; band v-4/v eff-5.

Dallas, TX   Monday, February 12, 1940

047659-1	The Sunset Trail To Texas -1, 2	BB B-8394, RZ ME64, RZAu G24716, RZIr IZ1349
047660-1	Drink The Barrel Dry -3	BB B-8394, RZAu G24716
047661-1	Pussy, Pussy, Pussy -3, 5	BB B-8414, HMVIn NE634
047662-1	I Wish You Knew The Way I Feel -2	BB B-8458, RZ ME64, RZAu G24943, RZIr IZ1349
047663-1	You Take It	BB B-8458
047664-1	I'll Take You Back Again -1	BB B-8498
047665-1	You Better Stop That Cattin' 'Round -2	BB B-8414, HMVIn NE634
047666-1	I Want A Feller -1, 2	BB B-8498
047667-1	If You'll Come Back -2	BB B-8533
047668-1	The Zenda Waltz	BB B-8409, RZAu G24217, HMVIn NE645
047669-1	Down At Polka Joe's -2, 4	BB B-8409, RZAu G24217, HMVIn NE645
047670-1	There's A Light Shining Bright -1, 2	BB B-8533

Rev. Regal-Zonophone G24943 by Tennessee Ramblers.

Cecil Brower, f; Kenneth Pitts, f; Bob Dunn, esg; Knocky Parker, p; Marvin Montgomery, tbj-1/tg-2/v-3; Bill Boyd, g/v-4; Leon Payne, prob. g/v-5; poss. Ish Erwin, sb; band v-6.

Dallas, TX   Wednesday, April 9, 1941

063074-1	Flower Of Texas -1	BB B-8769
063075-1	I'll Be Back In A Year, Little Darlin' -2, 3, 5	BB B-8721
063076-1	Jitterbug Jive -1, 5, 6	BB B-8787
063077-1	I Can't Forget (No Matter How I Try) -1, 5	BB B-8769
063078-1	They Go Goo-Goo-Ga-Ga-Goofy Over Gobs -1, 3	BB B-8747
063079-1	I Guess You Don't Care Anymore -1, 4, 5	BB B-8787, RZAu G25158

Bill Boyd may not play guitar on all items.

Cecil Brower, f; Kenneth Pitts, f; Bob Dunn, esg; Knocky Parker, p; Marvin Montgomery, tbj/tg; Bill Boyd, poss. g/v-1; Leon Payne, poss. g/v-2; Johnnie Pearson, prob. g/v-3; poss. Ish Erwin, sb; poss. Derwood Brown, v-4; v group (Montgomery, Pitts, poss. Pearson and/or Payne)-5.

Dallas, TX   Thursday, April 10, 1941

063084-1	Swing Steel Swing	BB B-8721
063085-1	Sweethearts Or Strangers -3	BB B-8728
063086-1	Don't Let The Barrel Go Dry -5	BB B-8747
063087-1	Now I Feel The Way You Do -3	BB B-8728, RZAu G25158
063088-1	No Dice -2	BB B-8823
063089-1	Hold On To That Thing-1?, 4 (lead)	BB B-8823

Cecil Brower, f; Kenneth Pitts, f/ac; prob. Curtis Harwell, esg; Marvin Montgomery, tbj; Bill Boyd, g/v-1; unknown, sb; unidentified, v group-2.
  Dallas, TX   Sunday, October 12, 1941

071180-1	Tell Me Why My Daddy Don't Come Home -1	BB B-8910
071181-1	Rollin' Down The Great Divide -1	BB B-8885, RZAu G25177
071182-1	My Birmingham Rose -1	BB B-9014
071183-1	The Letter I Never Did Mail -1	BB B-8910
071184-1	(When I Had) My Pony On The Range -1	BB B-8885, RZAu G25177
071185-1	Jennie Lou -1	BB 33-0501
077186-1	Tumbleweed Trail -1	BB B-9014
071187-1	Put Your Troubles Down The Hatch -2	BB 33-0501
071188-1	Home Coming Waltz	BB B-8900, Vi 20-2069
071189-1	Over The Waves Waltz	BB B-8900, Vi 20-2068

Rev. Victor 20-2069 postwar.

Bill Boyd recorded after 1942.

COLIN J. BOYD

Recordings by this artist appeared in the Brunswick old-time series (533, 534.) He was a fiddler from Cape Breton, and therefore outside the scope of this work. Others of his recordings appeared in the Columbia 33000-F (Irish) and Decca 14000 (Scots) series, and he also recorded after 1942.

JIM BOYD & AUDREY DAVIS (THE KANSAS HILL BILLIES)

Audrey (Art) Davis, v/f; Jim Boyd, v/g.
  Fort Worth, TX   Sunday, September 30, 1934

FW-1148-2	I Hear An Old Train A'Comin'	Vo 02873
FW-1149-1	Get Aboard That South Bound Train	Vo 02873

Both artists recorded with other groups, especially Bill Boyd & His Cowboy Ramblers, and after 1942.

JOHN BOYD & HIS SOUTHERNERS

Unknown, f; poss. Butch Gibson, cl/as; unknown, p; unknown, g; unknown, sb; John Boyd, v-1.
  Dallas, TX   Monday, June 21, 1937

DAL-416-2	Doin' The Raccoon	Vo 03661
DAL-417-2	Somebody Stole My Gal -1	Vo 03661
DAL-418-	My Gal Sal	Vo unissued
DAL-419-	We'll Never Be Sweethearts Again	Vo unissued

THE BOYS FROM WILDCAT HOLLOW

Pseudonym on Champion for the Monroe County Bottle Tippers.

ERNEST BRANCH & BERNICE COLEMAN

Ernest Branch, v; acc. West Virginia Ramblers: Jess Johnston, f; Bernice Coleman, f; own bj; Roy Harvey, g.
  Richmond, IN   Wednesday, June 3, 1931

17791-	Someone Owns A Cottage	Ch 16286, Spr 2688

Superior 2688 as by **Dave Walker**.

  Richmond, IN   Thursday, June 4, 1931

17794-	Lulu Love	Ch 16286
17795-	Little Foot Prints	Spr 2688
17796-	Yellow Rose Of Texas	Ge rejected

Superior 2688 as by **Dave Walker**.

Bernice Coleman, v; acc. West Virginia Ramblers: Jess Johnston, f; own f; Ernest Branch, bj; Roy Harvey, g.
  Richmond, IN   Thursday, June 4, 1931

17797-A	The Only Girl I Ever Loved	Ch 16456
17798-	The Ring My Mother Wore	Ch 16456

Branch and Coleman also recorded as members of the West Virginia Ramblers on other sides made at this session; see Roy Harvey.

Branch & Coleman: Bernice Coleman, f/v; Ernest Branch, bj/v-1; Roy Harvey, g.
  Atlanta, GA   Monday, October 26, 1931

405030-1	My Fickle Sweetheart	OK 45561
405031-1	(I'm So Lonely) Since My Darling Went Away -1	OK 45568
405032-	Mother's Always Waiting	OK unissued
405033-1	Telegraph Shack -1	OK 45561

Bernice Coleman, f/v; Ernest Branch, bj/v-1; Roy Harvey, g/v-2.
    Atlanta, GA   Tuesday, October 27, 1931

405034-	My Sweet Little Clover	OK unissued
405035-1	Some One	OK 45568
405036-1	My Free Wheelin' Baby -1, 2	OK 45556
405037-1	They All Got A Wife But Me -1	OK 45556

BRANCH & COLEMAN

See Ernest Branch & Bernice Coleman.

WILFRED BRANCHEAU

Wilfred Brancheau, h; acc. prob. own g.
    Richmond, IN   Monday, April 21, 1930

16510	Three O'Clock In The Morning	Ge rejected
16511	Hot Time In The Old Town Tonight; Over There	Ge rejected

BRANDON & WELLS

Pseudonym on Champion and Melotone for The Singing Preachers.

THE BREAKDOWNERS FROM BALSAM GAP

Unknown, f; unknown, h-1; unknown, md; unknown, g; unknown, v-2.
    Winston-Salem, NC   Saturday, September 24, 1927

81603-	Liza, Curl Your Hair	OK unissued
81604-	She Might Have Seen Better Days	OK unissued
81605-	Moonshiner's Ball -1	OK unissued
81606-	Over The Waves	OK unissued
81607-	Shoot That Turkey Buzzard -2	OK unissued
81608-	Balsam Gap Jubilee	OK unissued

AMADIE BREAUX, OPHY BREAUX & CLEMO BREAUX
BREAUX FRERES

Amadie Breaux, Ophy Breaux & Clemo Breaux: Ophy Breaux, f; Amadie Breaux, ac/v-1; Cleoma Breaux, g; unknown, tri-2.
    Atlanta, GA   Thursday, April 18, 1929

110558-2	Ma Blonde Est Partie (My Blonde Went Away And Left Me) -1	Co 40510-F, OK 90010
110559-2	Vas Y Carrement (Step It Fast) -2	Co 40510-F, OK 90010
110560-1	Les Tracas Du Hobo Blues -1	Co 40504-F, OK 90004

Rev. Columbia 40504-F, OKeh 90004 by Cleoma Breaux, Joseph Falcon & Ophy Breaux. For that and other sides by combinations of these musicians, see Joseph F. Falcon.

Breaux Freres (Clifford, Ophy et Amedee): Ophy Breaux, f; Amadie Breaux, ac/v-1; Clifford Breaux, g.
    San Antonio, TX   Tuesday, October 9, 1934

SA-1162-2	Crowley Breakdown	Vo 02858
SA-1163-1	La Valse Des Pins (Pinewood Waltz)	Vo 02859
SA-1164-3	Le Blues De Petit Chien (Little Dog Blues)	Vo 03053
SA-1165-3	La Valse Des Yeux Bleus (Blue Eyes Waltz)	Vo 02962
SA-1166-1	One Step A Marie (Mary's One Step) -1	Vo 02859
SA-1167-3	La Valse Du Vieux Temps (The Old Time Waltz)	Vo 03052
SA-1168-1	Tiger Rag Blues	Vo 02857
SA-1169-3	La Valse D'Auguste (August Waltz)	Vo 03053
SA-1170-1	Mazurka De La Louisiane (Louisiana Mazurka)	Vo 02858
SA-1171-1	Fais Do-Do Negre (Go To Sleep Nigger)	Vo 02857
SA-1172-3	T'As Vole Mon Chapeau (You Have Stolen My Hat)	Vo 02961
SA-1173-2	Home Sweet Home	Vo unissued: *Co CK46220 (CD)*
SA-1173-3	Home Sweet Home	Vo 02961
SA-1174-1	Egan One Step	Vo unissued: *Co CK46220 (CD)*
SA-1174-3	Egan One Step	Vo 03227
SA-1175-3	Le Valse D'Utah (Utah Waltz)	Vo 03227

San Antonio, TX   Wednesday, October 10, 1934
SA-1176-4	Le One Step A Martin (Martin's One Step)	Vo 02962
SA-1177-3	La Valse Du Bayou Plaquemine (Plaquemine Bayou Waltz)	Vo 03052

Vocalion files report that take 3s of all the above recordings (and, in the case of matrix SA-1176, take 4 also) were recorded at various dates in January, March, and April 1935. These are technical remasterings. Where an issue shows such a take, it may be presumed to be the same as either take 1 or 2, but it is generally impossible to determine which.

CLEOMA [or CLEMO] BREAUX

Most of this artist's recordings were in partnership with Joseph F. Falcon, her husband (many of them credited **Cleoma Falcon**); see his entry, and also that for Amadie Breaux [etc.].

CLIFFORD BREAUX

Clifford Breaux, v; acc. poss. own f; poss. Cleoma Falcon, sg.
Dallas, TX   Wednesday, December 15, 1937
63091-A	Continuer De Sonner (Keep A' Knockin' (But You Can't Come In))	De 17043
63092-A	Pourquoi Que Tu Laise Moi (Why Are You Leaving Me)	De 17043

HOMER BRIARHOPPER

This artist's real name is Homer Lee Drye.

Homer Briarhopper, v/y-1; acc. unknown, h; own md; unknown, md; unknown, g.
Charlotte, NC   Monday, February 15, 1937
07033-1	Bill Bailey	BB B-6903, MW M-7242
07034-1	If You Ever Had The Blues -1	BB B-6903, MW M-7242
07035-1	Lights In The Valley Outshine The Sun	MW M-7243
07036-1	Beautiful Home Sweet Home	MW M-7243
07037-1	Roses Bloom Again	[MW M-7244]
07038-1	Shall Not Be Moved	[MW M-7244]

Homer Brierhopper, v; acc. Big Bill Davis, f; prob. own md-1; prob. Johnny Macalester, g.
Charlotte, NC   Thursday, June 9, 1938
64106-A	Mr. McKinley -1	De 5588
64107-A	Little Lulie -1	De 5615, Min M-14084
64108-A	I Am Just What I Am -1	De 5588
64109-A	We Parted At The Gate	De 5615, Min M-14084

Homer Briarhopper recorded after 1942.

BRIER HOPPER BROS.

See The Red Headed Brier Hopper.

BAILEY BRISCOE

Bailey Briscoe, v; acc. own bj; others, if any, unknown.
Johnson City, TN   Wednesday, October 17, 1928
147220-	The Joke Song	Co unissued
147221-	Times Are Getting Hard	Co unissued

ELTON BRITT

Items credited to **Wenatchee Mountaineers** are included here because, although some of them feature Elton Britt in a secondary role, others are vocal solos by him, and hardly distinguishable from items issued under his own name.

Wenatchee Mountaineers: Vern Baker, f/v-1; Elton Baker (Britt), g/v-1; ——— Gaylor, v-1.
New York, NY   Tuesday, August 8, 1933
13741-1	Britt's Reel	Ba 32967, Me M12917, Or 8304, Pe 12976, Ro 5304, Cq 8324
13742-1	Texas Rag	Ba 32967, Me M12917, Cq 8304, Pe 12976, Ro 5304, Cq 8324
13743-	Rabbs Creek	ARC unissued
13744-1	Dear Old Southern Moon -1	Ba 32855, Me M12782, Or 8264, Pe 12938, Ro 5264, Cq 8225
13745-1	Listen To The Mocking Bird	Cq 8323

Gaylor & Britt: Elton Britt, ——— Gaylor, v/y duet; acc. Elton Britt, g.
New York, NY   Tuesday, August 8, 1933
13746-1	The Little Rose Covered Shack	Ba 32980, Me M12930, Or 8307, Pe 12979, Ro 5307

Britt Brothers: Elton Britt, poss. Vern Baker, v/y duet; acc. Elton Britt, g; poss. Vern Baker, g.
New York, NY   Tuesday, August 8, 1933
    13747-2   Alpine Milkman Yodel   Ba 33057, Me M13019, MeC 91800, Or 8336,
                                                                               Pe 13005, Ro 5336, Cq 8197, Min M-910

Conqueror 8197 as by **Wenatchee Mountaineers**. Rev. Minerva M-910 by Cliff Carlisle & Wilbur Ball.

Wenatchee Mountaineers: Elton Britt, v/y; acc. own g.
New York, NY   Tuesday, August 8, 1933
    13748-2   Just An Old Fashioned Locket   Cq 8225

Vern Baker, Elton Britt, —— **Gaylor**, v trio; acc. Vern Baker, f-1; Elton Britt, g/y-2.
New York, NY   Tuesday, August 8, 1933
    13749-2   Bring Your Roses To Your Mother   Ba 32980, Me M12930, Or 8307, Pe 12979,
                                                                               Ro 5307, Cq 8196
    13750-1   I Like Mountain Music -1, 2   Ba 32855, Me M12782, MeC 91617, 93041,
                                                                               Or 8264, Pe 12938, Ro 5264, Cq 8194,
                                                                               Min M-921

Rev. Minerva M-921 by Pickard Family.

New York, NY   Wednesday, August 9, 1933
    13751-2   My Southland -1   Ba 32868, Me M12795, Or 8269, Pe 12940,
                                                                               Ro 5269, Cq 8195

Elton Britt, v/y-1; acc. Vern Baker, f-2; own g.
New York, NY   Wednesday, August 9, 1933
    13759-1   Swiss Yodel -1   Ba 33057, Me M13019, Or 8336, Pe 13005,
                                                                               Ro 5336, Cq 8197
    13760-2   I Was Born In The Mountains -2   Ba 33019, Me M12978, MeC 91805, Or 8321,
                                                                               Pe 12990, Ro 5321, Cq 8194

All issues of matrix 13759 as by **Britt Brothers** except Conqueror 8197 as by **Wenatchee Mountaineers**, as is Cq 8194.

Wenatchee Mountaineers: Vern Baker, f-1/v-2; Elton Britt, g/v/y-3; —— Gaylor, v-4.
New York, NY   Wednesday, August 9, 1933
    13761-2   Wait For The Wagon -2, 4   Ba 32868, Me M12795, MeC 93041, Or 8269,
                                                                               Pe 12940, Ro 5269, Cq 8195, Min M-920
    13762-2   By The Sleepy Rio Grande -1, 3   Ba 32888, Me M12833, MeC 91651, Or 8280,
                                                                               Pe 12953, Ro 5280, Cq 8196, Min M-14008

Revs: Minerva M-920 by Dick Robertson, M-14008 by Frank Marvin.

Elton & Vernon Britt: prob.: Vern Baker, f; Elton Britt, g.
New York, NY   Wednesday, August 9, 1933
    13763-   Sweet Beulah Bill   ARC unissued
    13764-   Sweetest Flower   ARC unissued

Wenatchee Mountaineers: Vern Baker, f-1/v-2; unknown, p-3; Elton Britt, g/v-2; —— Gaylor, v-2.
New York, NY   Thursday, August 10, 1933
    13765-1   Blue-Eyed Ellen -2, 3   Ba 32888, Me M12833, Or 8280, Pe 12953,
                                                                               Ro 5280
    13766-1   Wedding Bells Waltz -1   Cq 8323
    13767-1   When It's Harvest Time -1, 2   Ba 33038, Me M13000, Or 8329, Pe 12997,
                                                                               Ro 5329

Elton Britt, v/y-1; acc. Roy Smeck, sg; own g.
New York, NY   Thursday, November 2, 1933
    14410-1   There's A Home In Wyomin' -1   Ba 32930, Me M12873, Or 8292, Pe 12966,
                                                                               Ro 5292, Cq 8178
    14411-1   When It's Harvest Time In Old New England   Ba 32929, Me M12872, Or 8291, Pe 12965,
                                                                               Ro 5291, Cq 8276
    14412-1   Old Fashioned Dipper (That Hangs On A Nail)   Ba 32990, Me M12940, Or 8310, Pe 12982,
                                                                               Ro 5310, Cq 8270, Lucky 1048
    14413-2   My Mother's Tears -1   Ba 32990, Me M12940, Or 8310, Pe 12982,
                                                                               Ro 5310, Cq 8270, Lucky 1048

Acc. Roy Smeck, sg; prob. Bob Miller, p-2; own g.
New York, NY   Tuesday, December 5, 1933
    14418-   Good Night, Little Girl Of My Dreams -1   ARC unissued
    14419-2   Where The Mountains Tiptoe To The Sea -2   Cq 8337

Elton Britt, v; acc. unknown, h-1; Roy Smeck, sg; poss. Bob Miller, o-2/cel-3; own g.
New York, NY   Wednesday, December 6, 1933

| 14420-1 | When You Played The Old Church Organ -2 | Ba 32929, Me M12872, Or 8291, Pe 12965, Ro 5291, Cq 8276 |
| 14421-1 | The Wrong Man And The Wrong Woman (Went Back Together Again) -1, 3 | Ba 33019, Me M12978, MeC 91805, Or 8321, Pe 12990, Ro 5321, Cq 8337 |

Elton Britt, v/y; acc. own g.
New York, NY   Friday, December 15, 1933

| 14418-3 | Good Night, Little Girl Of My Dreams | Ba 32930, Me M12873, Or 8292, Pe 12966, Ro 5292, Cq 8178 |

Britt & Ford: Ezra Ford, v-1/f; Elton Britt, v/g.
New York, NY   Monday, March 5, 1934

| 14885-2 | Dear Old Daddy -1 | Ba 33003, 33038, Me M12954, M13000, MeC 93086, Or 8315, 8329, Pe 12986, 12997, Ro 5315, 5329, ARC 6-02-55, Cq 8288, Min M-14024 |
| 14886-1 | The Answer To Ninety-Nine Years | Ba 33033, Me M12954, MeC 93086, Or 8315, Pe 12986, Ro 5315, ARC 6-02-55, Cq 8288, Min M-14024 |

Matrix 14886 is titled *The Answer To 99 Years* on Romeo 5315, Conqueror 8288.

Ezra Ford, Elton Britt, v/y-1 duet; acc. unknown, f; unknown, f-2; prob. Frank Novak, cl-3/bj-3/x-3; poss. Bob Miller, p; poss. Elton Britt, g-4; unknown, sb-5.
New York, NY   Wednesday, June 20, 1934

15343-2	Heart In The Heart Of Texas -1, 4	ARC 6-05-60, Cq 8664
15344-2	When I'm Four Times Twenty -2, 4	ARC 6-05-60, Cq 8664
15345-1	Take Me Home -1, 5	Ba 33326, Me M13293, Or 8423, Pe 13106, Ro 5423, Lucky 1057, Co-Lucky 60036
15346-1	In The Hills Of Pennsylvania -1, 2, 4	Ba 33116, Me M13083, Or 8358, Pe 13021, Ro 5358
15347-1,2	Free Wheelin' Hobo -3	Ba 33326, Me M13293, Or 8423, Pe 13106, Ro 5423, Cq 8586, Lucky 1057, Co-Lucky 60036
15348-1	Chime Bells -1, 4	Ba 33116, Me M13083, Or 8358, Pe 13021, Ro 5358

Rev. Conqueror 8586 by Lake Howard.

Elton Britt, v; acc. prob. Bob Miller, p; own g.
New York, NY   Saturday, May 23, 1936

| 19318-2 | 1936 Tornado | ARC 6-08-57 |

Elton Britt, v/y; acc. The Rustic Rhythm Trio: Paul Robinson, h; prob. Bob Miller, p-1; Vaughn Horton, md; Roy Horton, g; own g.
New York, NY   Saturday, May 23, 1936

19319-1	In A Little Inn Way Out In Indiana	ARC 6-11-52, Cq 8688
19320-1	Rain On The Roof	ARC 6-08-57
19321-2	The Sod Buster With The Jug Handle Ears -1	ARC 6-11-52, Cq 8688

Acc. unknown, f; unknown, ac; poss. own g.
New York, NY   Tuesday, June 30, 1936

| 19493-2 | It's A Sin To Tell A Lie | ARC 6-09-57, Cq 8687 |
| 19494-2 | Twilight On The Trail | ARC 6-09-57, Cq 8687 |

Elton Britt, v/y-1; or **Britt & Ford**-2: Elton Britt, Ezra Ford, v duet; acc. unknown, f; unknown, p; unknown, sb.
New York, NY   Thursday, September 10, 1936

19838-	My Pipe, My Slippers And You	ARC unissued
19839-2	Sweetheart, Let's Grow Old Together -2	ARC 6-11-68, Cq 8727, Co-Lucky 60478
19840-1	Gladiola Time -1	ARC 6-11-68, Cq 8727, Co-Lucky 60478
19841-	It Will Have To Do Until The Real Thing Comes Along	ARC unissued

Acc. unknown, f; unknown, p; poss. own g.
New York, NY   Wednesday, March 24, 1937

| 20869-1 | New London School Tragedy (In Eastern Texas) | ARC 7-05-65, Cq 8809 |
| 20870-2 | My Best Friend | ARC 7-05-65, Cq 8809 |

Matrix 20869 is titled *New London Texas School Tragedy* on Conqueror 8809.

Elton Britt, v/y-1; acc. own g.
New York, NY   Friday, May 12, 1939

| 036939-1 | Chime Bells -1 | BB B-8166, MW M-8426, Vi 20-3090, ViJ A1431, RZAu G24016 |

036940-1	Patent Leather Boots -1	BB B-8175, MW M-8427, Vi 20-3093, ViJ A1431, Twin FT8793, RZAu G24110
036941-1	They're Burning Down The House (I Was Brung Up In)	BB B-8175, MW M-8427, Vi 20-3092, Twin FT8793
036942-1	Just Because You're In Deep Elem -1	BB B-8166, MW M-8426, RZAu G24015

Victor 20-3090, 20-3092 as by **Elton Britt & The Skytoppers**.

Elton Britt, v; acc. unknown, f; own g; unknown, sb.
New York, NY   Tuesday, July 18, 1939

037083-1	Two More Years (And I'll Be Free)	BB B-8223, MW M-8428, RZAu G24188
037084-1	Driftwood On The River	BB B-8223, MW M-8428, RZAu G24188
037085-1	Mistook In The Woman I Loved	BB B-8245, MW M-8429, RZAu G24016, Twin FT8891
037086-1	Missouri Joe	BB B-8245, MW M-8429, RZAu G24015, Twin FT8891

Elton Britt, v/y-1; acc. own g.
New York, NY   Tuesday, March 12, 1940

047939-1	Why Did You Leave Me Alone?	BB B-8430, MW M-8683, RZAu G24284
047940-1	Over The Trail	BB B-8430, MW M-8683, RZAu G24284
047941-1	Dreamy Land Bay -1	BB B-8461, MW M-8684, RZAu G24205
047942-1	They're Positively Wrong	BB B-8461, MW M-8684, RZAu G24205

Elton Britt, v; acc. unknown, f; own g; unknown, sb.
New York, NY   Wednesday, August 7, 1940

054974-1	Sierra Sue	BB B-8523
054975-1	Darling What Do You Care	BB B-8523
054976-1	Goodbye, Little Darlin', Goodbye	BB B-8511
054977-1	I'll Never Smile Again	BB B-8511

Acc. Bert Hirsch, f; unknown, cl-1; Frank Novak, ac; own g.
New York, NY   Friday, March 7, 1941

062812-1	There's So Much That I Forgot	BB B-8701, RZAu G25150
062813-1	New Worried Mind	BB B-8666
062814-1	I'll Die Before I Tell You	BB B-8701, RZAu G25150
062815-1	The Precious Jewel -1	BB B-8666, Vi 20-3091

Victor 20-3091 as by **Elton Britt & The Skytoppers**.

Acc. Murray Kellner, f; Ralph Colicchio, eg; own g; Gene Traxler, sb; unknown, v trio-1.
New York, NY   Tuesday, June 17, 1941

066215-1	Rocky Mountain Lullaby	BB B-8818
066216-1	Too Many Tears	BB B-8777
066217-1	Everybody Has The Right To Be Screwy (In His Own Way) -1	BB B-8818
066218-1	Darlin', I've Loved Way Too Much	BB B-8777, RZAu G25143

Elton Britt, v/y-1; acc. Bert Hirsch, f; Vaughn Horton, esg; own g; Lester Braun, sb; unknown, v/wh duet-2.
New York, NY   Wednesday, October 29, 1941

068201-1	Will You Wait For Me, Little Darlin'? (Sequel To "I'll Be Back In A Year")	BB B-8912, RZAu G25206
068202-1	I'll Be In The Army For A Stretch -2	BB B-8912
068203-1	Where Are You Now?	BB B-8946, RZAu G25206
068204-1	She Taught Me To Yodel -1	BB B-8946, Vi 20-3092, RZAu G25143

Victor 20-3092 as by **Elton Britt & The Skytoppers**.

Acc. Mac Coppes, f; William Graham, t; Tony Gottuso, g; own g; Lester Braun, sb.
New York, NY   Thursday, March 19, 1942

073623-1	Buddy Boy	BB B-9023, *V-D 44*
073624-1	I Hung My Head And Cried	BB B-9023, Vi 20-2131, *V-D 44*
073625-1	There's A Star Spangled Banner Waving Somewhere	BB B-9000, Vi 20-2131, 20-3093, 21-0381, *V-D 44*
073626-1	When The Roses Bloom Again	BB B-9000, *V-D 44*

Victor 20-3093 as by **Elton Britt & The Skytoppers**. Rev. Regal-Zonophone G25279 by Bill Boyd (postwar).
Elton Britt also recorded with Pappy, Zeke, Ezra & Elton (see The Beverly Hillbillies) and after 1942.

BRITT & FORD
See Elton Britt.

BRITT BROTHERS
See Elton Britt.

MAYNARD BRITTON

Maynard Britton, v/y; acc. own g.
    Richmond, IN   Saturday, November 15, 1930

17259-A	I Don't Want No Woman	Spr 2563
17260,-A	Mother's Dream	Ge rejected
17261,-A	Prohibition Blues	Ge unissued
17262-A	I Love My Woman	Spr 2563

    Richmond, IN   Saturday, February 7, 1931

17510,-A	Dear Mother I'll Think Of You	Ge unissued
17511-C	Sweetest Girl In All The World	Ch 16478, Spr 2624
17512-A	I Wish The Train Would Wreck	Ch 16543, 45051
17513-B	The Drunkard's Hell	Ch 16543, 45051
17514-B	Always Blue, Lonesome Too	Ch 16478, Spr 2624

Maynard Britton also recorded for the Library of Congress in 1937.

THE BROADCAST BOYS

Pseudonym on Varsity for Jim Cole's Tennessee Mountaineers (see Arthur Fields & Fred Hall).

THE BROADWAY RUSTLER

Pseudonym on Broadway for Goebel Reeves.

ALLIE & PEARL BROCK

Allie & Pearl Brock, v duet; acc. unknown, p-1; Hoke Rice, g; or **Mary Jones**-2: Pearl Brock, v; acc. Hoke Rice, g.
    Richmond, IN   Monday, April 15, 1929

15049-B	Broadway Blues	Ge 6857
15052	You Lied About That Woman – Part 1 -2	Ge 6860
15053,-A,-B	Blue Days -1	Ge rejected

Intervening matrices are by Hoke Rice.

    Richmond, IN   Tuesday, April 16, 1929

15056-A	Bring Me Back My Darling -1	Ge 6857
15058	You Lied About That Woman – Part 2 -2	Ge 6860

Matrix 15057 is by Hoke Rice; matrices 15059/60 are by Louie Donaldson & Allie Brock (see the former).

Acc. Louie Donaldson, g.
    Richmond, IN   Wednesday, April 17, 1929

15064,-A,-B	Just To Break My Heart	Ge rejected

Allie Brock & Louie Donaldson, v duet; acc. Louie Donaldson, g.
    Richmond, IN   Wednesday, April 17, 1929

15065,-A,-B	You're As Welcome As The Flowers In May	Ge rejected

Brock Sisters, v duet; acc. two unknowns, p-1; unknown, g-2.
    Chicago, IL   c. early June 1929

21301-3	Broadway Blues -2	Pm 3163
21308-1	Bring Me Back My Darling -1	Pm 3163

Intervening matrices are untraced.

JESSIE BROCK

See Earl McCoy.

BROCK & DUDLEY

Vocal duet; acc. unknown, sg; unknown, g.
    Atlanta, GA   Wednesday, April 23, 1930

150368-1	I'll Remember You Love	Co 15645-D
150369-2	Lonely	Co 15645-D

BROCK SISTERS

See Allie & Pearl Brock.

BROCKMAN SACRED SINGERS

Pseudonym on Supertone for The Eva Quartette.

CHARLES S. BROOK & CHARLIE TURNER

Charles S. Brook, v; Charlie Turner, v-1/sp-2; acc. prob. one of them, g.
    Atlanta, GA   Monday, November 2, 1931

| 152009-1 | Mama I Wish't I'd Listened To You -2 | Co 15756-D |
| 152010-1 | Will You Love Me When I'm Old -1 | Co 15756-D |

BOB BROOKES

Pseudonym on Columbia for Bob McGimsey.

BILLY BROOKS

Billy Brooks, h/sp; unknown, sp-1; unknown, v eff-1.
    Atlanta, GA   Wednesday, April 16, 1930

| 150241-2 | Freight Train Blues | Co 15614-D |
| 150242-2 | Just From College -1 | Co 15614-D |

BOB BROOKS

Pseudonym on Columbia for Bob McGimsey.

CARLYLE BROOKS & MADELINE WARD

No details.
    Atlanta, GA   Saturday, April 2, 1927

| 143879- | It Pays To Serve Jesus | Co unissued |
| 143880- | Sweeter As The Years Go By | Co unissued |

CHARLES BROOKS

Charles Brooks, v; acc. unknown, p.
    Atlanta, GA   Thursday, October 29, 1931

| 151984-1 | My Mammy's Cabin | Co 15733-D |
| 151985-1 | Baby | Co 15733-D |

CLAYTON BROOKS

Pseudonym on Challenge for C.A. West.

REV. GEORGE M. BROOKS

Pseudonym on Champion for Rev. Joseph Callender.

RICHARD BROOKS & REUBEN PUCKETT

Reuben Puckett & Richard Brooks, v duet; acc. unknown, p.
    Atlanta, GA   Thursday, January 29, 1925

| 140296-1 | Always Think Of Mother | Co 15029-D, Ha 5110-H |
| 140297-1 | Down By The Mississippi Shore | Co 15029-D, Ha 5110-H |

Harmony 5110-H as by **Brooks & Powell**.

Richard Brooks–Ruben Puckett, v duet; acc. one of them, f; the other, g; or unacc.-1.
    Atlanta, GA   Wednesday, February 16, 1927

37900-1	When The Flowers Bloom In Springtime	Vi 20541
37901-1	Hello Central, Give Me Heaven	Vi 20542
37902-1	Good Bye, My Blue Bell -1	Vi 20542
37903-2	Something's Going To Happen, Honey -1	Vi 20541

Richard Brooks & Reuben Puckett, v duet; acc. one of them, f; the other, g.
    New York, NY   Tuesday, June 5, 1928

| E-27648- | I'm Coming Back To Dixie And You | Br 317 |
| E-27649- | Railroad Blues | Br 273 |

Vocal duet; or **Richard Brooks**, v-1; acc. one of them, f; the other, g.
    New York, NY   Wednesday, June 6, 1928

E-27650-A,-B	In The Shade Of The Old Apple Tree	Br unissued
E-27651-A,-B	In The Good Old Summer Time	Br unissued
E-27652-A,-B	It's Hard To Kiss Your Sweetheart -1	Br unissued
E-27655-A,-B	When You Know You're Not Forgotten By The Girl You Can't Forget -1	Br unissued
E-27656-	Long Gone	Br 273

Matrices E-27653/54 are popular.

    New York, NY   Thursday, June 7, 1928

E-27657-	She's More To Be Pitied Than Censured	Br 281, Spt S2075
E-27658-	Where The Red Red Roses Grow	Br 281
E-27659-	All In, Down And Out	Br 317

E-27664-A,-B	Meet Me In Dreamland -1	Br unissued
E-27665-A,-B	School Days -1	Br unissued
E-27666-	The Longest Way Home -1	Br 301

Matrices E-27660 to E-27663 are Spanish. Rev. Supertone S2075 by McGhee & Welling

New York, NY   Friday, June 8, 1928

E-27671-	Memories -1	Br 301
E-27672-A,-B	Black Sheep -1	Br unissued
E-27673-A,-B	When You're A Long Long Way From Home -1	Br unissued

Matrices E-27667/68 are popular; E-27669/70 are by Jack Major.

BROOKS & POWELL

Pseudonym on Harmony for Richard Brooks & Reuben Puckett.

BILL BROWN

Bill Brown was a talent scout and occasional supervisor, or assistant supervisor, of recording sessions, who was active in the late '20s and early '30s, chiefly but not exclusively, in the Atlanta, GA area. He is known to have been associated with Columbia, and participates in at least the two items for which he is given label credit, *A Corn Licker Still In Georgia Parts 1 & 2* (15201-D) and *Parts 3 & 4* (15258-D), where he assists members of the Skillet-Lickers.

Subsequently he worked for Brunswick/Vocalion, and he takes speaking roles on numerous recordings on those labels. He receives label credit on *A Bootlegger's Joint In Atlanta Parts 1 & 2* (Brunswick 419), *The Great Hatfield-McCoy Feud Parts 1 & 2* (Brunswick 422) and *Parts 3 & 4* (Brunswick 423), and *A Georgia Barbecue At Stone Mountain Parts 1 & 2* (Vocalion 5454), but he is to be heard, though uncredited, on several other items from the 1930 sessions held in Atlanta and Knoxville, TN.

BOYCE BROWN & EVERETT ECKARD

See The Brown Brothers.

CECIL BROWN

Cecil Brown, v; acc. unknown.
    Richmond, IN   Wednesday, January 27, 1932

| 18339 | I'll Be Thinking Of You Little Girl | Ge unissued |

HERSCHEL BROWN

Hershal Brown & His Washboard Band: unknown, f; poss. L.K. Sentell, g; Herschel Brown, wb/poss. v-1; unidentified, sp-2.
    Atlanta, GA   Friday, February 24, 1928

41956-1	Nobody Loves Me -1	Vi 21403
41956-2	Nobody Loves Me -1	Vi unissued: *Doc DOCD-8001 (CD)*
41957-1	Down Yonder -2	Vi 21403
41958-2	Liberty -2	Vi V-40070
41959-2	Shanghai Rag -2	Vi V-40070

Victor V-40070 as by **Hershall Brown & His Washboard Band**.

Herschel Brown, sp; acc. L.K. Sentell, g.
    Atlanta, GA   Monday, July 30, 1928

| 402000-A | New Talking Blues | OK 45247 |
| 402001-A | Talking Nigger Blues | OK 45247 |

Herschel Brown & His Boys: unknown, h; unknown, p; unknown, bj; Herschel Brown, sp; L.K. Sentell, sp.
    Atlanta, GA   Monday, July 30, 1928

| 402002-B | Corn Shucking Party In Georgia | OK 45250 |
| 402003-B | Home Brew Party | OK 45250 |

Herschel Brown & His Washboard Band: unknown, h; unknown, p; unknown, bj; Herschel Brown, wb.
    Atlanta, GA   Monday, August 6, 1928

402064-B	Soldier's Joy	OK unissued: *Doc DOCD-8001 (CD)*
402065-A	I Wish That Gal Was Mine	OK 45286
402066-A	Rockingham	OK unissued: *Doc DOCD-8001 (CD)*
402067-B	Old Time Tune Medley	OK 45286

Herschel Brown & L.K. Sentell: L.K. Sentell, g; Herschel Brown, spoons.
    Atlanta, GA   Tuesday, March 19, 1929

| 402368-A | Spanish Rag | OK 45484 |
| 402369-B | Kohalo Rag | OK 45484 |

Herschel Brown, sp; acc. L.K. Sentell, g.
    Atlanta, GA   Tuesday, March 19, 1929

| 402370-A | New Talking Blues No. 2 | OK 45337 |
| 402371-A | Nigger Talking Blues No. 2 | OK 45337 |

Herschel Brown & His Happy Five: two unknowns, f; unknown, cl; Mildred ——, p; L.K. Sentell, g; Herschel Brown, wb-1/perc-2.

Atlanta, GA   Tuesday, March 19, 1929

402372-A	Liberty -1	OK unissued: *Cy 544 (LP)*; *Co C4K47911*, *Doc DOCD-8001 (CDs)*
402373-A,-B	Done Gone Crazy	OK unissued
402374-B	Alabama Breakdown -2	OK 45354
402375-B	OKeh Washboard Breakdown -1	OK 45354

Herschel Brown & His Boys: two unknowns, f-1; unknown, cl; Mildred ——, p-2; Herschel Brown, sp/perc-3; L.K. Sentell, sp; unknown, sp.

Atlanta, GA   Tuesday, March 19, 1929

| 402376-B | County Fair – Part 1 -1, 2 | OK 45494 |
| 402377-A | County Fair – Part 2 -3 | OK 45494 |

Herschel Brown, sp; acc. two unknowns, f; unknown, cl; Mildred ——, p; L.K. Sentell, g/sp; own wb.

Atlanta, GA   Tuesday, March 19, 1929

| 402378-A | Barbecue Down In Georgia – Part 2 | OK unissued: *Doc DOCD-8001 (CD)* |
| 402379-A,-B | Barbecue Down In Georgia – Part 1 | OK unissued |

Herschel Brown was also a member of The Spooney Five.

JAMES BROWN, JR. & KEN LANDON GROUPS

The Two Islanders: prob.: James Brown, Jr., sg; Ken Landon, g; unidentified, v-1.

Richmond, IN   between April 20 and 28, 1931

17710	Washington & Lee Swing	Ch 16461, 40064, Spr 2662
17711-B	Waikiki Blues	Ch 16461, 40021, Spr 2727
17712	Honolulu Sweetheart Of Mine -1	Ch 16256
17713	My Missouri Home -1	Ch 16256, Spr 2662

Superior 2662 as by **Mac & Curl(e)y**; 2727 as by **The Keawe Brothers**.

Richmond, IN   between June 11 and 16, 1931

17824-B	Sailing Along To Hawaii	Ch 16293, 40064, Spr 2708
17825	Hawaii Land	Ch 16323, Spr 2708
17826	Hona Hona Hawaii -1	Ch 16507, Spr 2744
17827	My Hula Love	Ch 16323, Spr 2727
17828	Toodle-Oo, So Long, Goodbye -1	Ch 16293, 40021, Spr 2744

Superior 2708, 2744 as by **Keawe Brothers**; 2727 as by **The Keawe Brothers**.

Richmond, IN   between August 17 and 22, 1932

| 18708 | Honolulu Stomp | Ch 16492 |
| 18709 | My Boat Is Sailing | Ch 16492 |

James Brown, Jr., v; acc. own g; Ken Landon, g.

Richmond, IN   between August 17 and 22, 1932

| 18710 | Good Bye Blues | Ch 16486 |
| 18711 | Moonlight On The River | Ch 16486 |

The Two Islanders: prob.: James Brown, Jr., sg; Ken Landon, g.

Richmond, IN   between August 17 and 22, 1932

| 18712 | Aloha Sunset Land | Ch 16507 |

James Brown, Jr.: no details.

Richmond, IN   Thursday, December 22, 1932

18930	Rock-A-Bye Moon	Ch 16535
18931	Dancing To The Rhythm Of My Heart	Ch 16535
18932	How Can I Go On Without You	Ch 16545
18933	Just A Little Home For The Old Folks	Ch 16545

The Two Islanders: prob.: James Brown, Jr., Ken Landon, v duet; or **Ken Landon**-1, v; acc. unknown, f; two or three unknowns, g.

Richmond, IN   Thursday, December 22, 1932

| 18934 | Sweethearts Forever | Ch 16546 |
| 18935 | Are You Lonesome Tonight? -1 | Ch 16562 |

Revs: Champion 16546 Hodshire Brothers (popular); 16562 by Frank Welling (see John McGhee & Frank Welling).

Brown's Happy Four: unknown, f; unknown, md; unknown, g; unknown, g-1.

Richmond, IN   . Thursday, December 22, 1932

| 18936 | Bootlegger's Dream -1 | Ch 16549 |
| 18937 | Robin Hood | Ch 16549 |

The Two Islanders: prob.: James Brown, Jr., sg; Ken Landon, g.
Richmond, IN Thursday, December 22, 1932

| 18938 | Honolulu Rag | Ch 16537 |

Chuck ———, f/v; James Brown, Jr., sg/v; Ken Landon, g/v.
Richmond, IN Thursday, December 22, 1932

| 18939 | A Song To Hawaii | Ch 16537 |

James Brown, Jr.: no details.
Richmond, IN Friday, March 24, 1933

| 19082 | Same Old Moon | Ch 16590 |

Ken, Chuck & Jim: prob.: Chuck ———, f/v; James Brown, Jr., sg/v; Ken Landon, md/v.
Richmond, IN Friday, March 24, 1933

| 19083 | I Like Mountain Music | Ch 16579, 45131 |
| 19084 | Home On The Range | Ch 16579, MW 4988 |

Matrix 19083 was originally logged as by **James Brown, Jr.** Rev. Montgomery Ward 4988 by Jess Hillard.

Prob.: Chuck ———, f; Ken Landon, md; James Brown, Jr., g.
Richmond, IN Saturday, March 25, 1933

| 19085 | Cattlesburg | Ch 16672, 45131 |

Chuck & Jim: prob. Chuck ———, f; James Brown, Jr., g.
Richmond, IN Saturday, March 25, 1933

| 19086 | Fiddlin' The Fiddle | Ch 16672 |

Ken & Jim: prob.: Chuck ———, f; James Brown, Jr., g; Ken Landon, g; unidentified, v.
Richmond, IN Saturday, March 25, 1933

| 19087 | Forget Me Not | Ch 16642 |

Ken, Chuck & Jim: prob.: Chuck ———, f/v; James Brown, Jr., sg/v; Ken Landon, g/v.
Richmond, IN Saturday, March 25, 1933

| 19088 | Aloma | Ch 16596 |

Prob. James Brown, Jr., sg; Ken Landon, g; Chuck ———, u; unidentified, v.
Richmond, IN Saturday, March 25, 1933

| 19089 | Pollo | Ch 16596 |

No details.
Richmond, IN Saturday, March 25, 1933

| 19090 | Hawaiian Chimes Are Calling | Ch 16642 |

Ken Landon, v; acc. prob. Chuck ———, f; James Brown, Jr., g; own g.
Richmond, IN Saturday, March 25, 1933

| 19091 | At The Close Of A Long Long Day | Ch 16590 |

Jim & Ken: James Brown, Jr., Ken Landon, v duet; acc. own g duet.
Richmond, IN Wednesday, August 8, 1934

| 19644 | Play To Me Gypsy | Ch 16800 |

Ken Landon, v; acc. James Brown, Jr., sg or g; own sg or g.
Richmond, IN Wednesday, August 8, 1934

| 19645 | My Little Grass Shack In Kealukekua | Ge rejected |

Jim & Ken: James Brown, Jr., sg; Ken Landon, sg; unidentified, v-1.
Richmond, IN Wednesday, August 8, 1934

| 19646 | Noko-No March -1 | Ch 16799, 40020 |
| 19647 | Lei Ilima | Ch 16799, 40020 |

Jimmy Brown, v; acc. own g; Ken Landon, g.
Richmond, IN Wednesday, August 8, 1934

| 19648 | Keep A Light In Your Window Tonight | Ch 16812, 45074 |

Jim & Ken: James Brown, Jr., Ken Landon, v duet; acc. own g duet.
Richmond, IN Wednesday, August 8, 1934

| 19649 | The Pretty Quadroon | Ch 16812, 45074 |
| 19650 | There's A Home In Wyomin' | Ch 16800 |

JIMMY BROWN

See James Brown, Jr. & Ken Landon groups.

FIDDLER JOE BROWN [& OTHERS]

For details of Vocalion 5432, credited to **Fiddler Joe Brown, Fiddler A.A. Gray, Seven Foot Dilly**, see John Dilleshaw.

MILTON BROWN & HIS [MUSICAL] BROWNIES

Milton Brown & His Musical Brownies: Cecil Brower, f; Fred Calhoun, p; Ocie Stockard, tbj-1/tg-2/v-3; Derwood Brown, g/v-4; Wanna Coffman, sb; Milton Brown, lv-5/sp-6; band v-7

San Antonio, TX   Wednesday, April 4, 1934

82795-1	Brownie's Stomp -1	BB B-5775, Twin FT1891
82796-1	Joe Turner Blues -1	BB B-5775
82797-1	Oh You Pretty Woman! -1, 3, 4, 5	BB B-5444, MW M-4540, HMV N4317
82798-1	My Precious Sonny Boy -1, 5, 6	BB B-5558, MW M-4759, Twin FT1755
82799-1	Swinging On The Garden Gate -1, 3, 4, 5	BB B-5444, MW M-4540, HMV N4317
82800-1	Do The Hula Lou -1, 5	BB B-5485, MW M-4539, M-4756, Twin FT1749
82801-1	Garbage Man Blues -1, 5, 7	BB B-5558, MW M-4759, Twin FT1755
82802-1	Four, Five Or Six Times -2, 5, 7	BB B-5485, MW M-4539, M-4756, Twin FT1749

Some pressings of Bluebird B-5444 as by **The Fort Worth Boys (Milton Brown & His Musical Brownies)**. HMV N4317 as by **The Fort Worth Boys**. Matrix 82797 is titled *Oh! You Pretty Woman!* on that issue. Rev. Twin FT1891 by Dick Hartman's Tennessee Ramblers.

Cecil Brower, f; Ted Grantham, f; Fred Calhoun, p; Ocie Stockard, tbj/v-1; Derwood Brown, g/v-2; Wanna Coffman, sb; Milton Brown, lv-3/sp-4.

San Antonio, TX   Wednesday, August 8, 1934

83860-1	Where You Been So Long, Corrine? -2, 3	BB B-5808, MW M-4755, Twin FT1864
83861-1	Talking About You -1, 2, 3	BB B-5808, MW M-4755, Twin FT1864
83862-1	Just Sitting On Top Of The World -3	BB B-5715, MW M-4758, Twin FT1825
83863-1	Take It Slow And Easy -3	BB B-5654, MW M-4536, Twin FT1842
83864-1	Get Along, Cindy -2, 3	BB B-5654, MW M-4536
83865-1	Trinity Waltz	BB B-5690, RZAu G22668, Twin FT1812
83866-1	Love Land And You -2, 3, 4	BB B-5610, Twin FT1842
83867-1	This Morning, This Evening, So Soon -1, 2, 3	BB B-5610
83868-1	Girl Of My Dreams -3	BB B-5690, RZAu G22668, Twin FT1812
83869-1	Loveless Love -2, 3	BB B-5715, MW M-4758, Twin FT1825

Milton Brown & His Brownies: Cecil Brower, f/v-1; Bob Dunn, esg; Fred Calhoun, p; Ocie Stockard, tbj/v-2; Derwood Brown, g/v-3; Wanna Coffman, sb; Milton Brown, v-4/sp-5; poss. Milton Brown, train-wh eff-6.

Chicago, IL   Sunday, January 27, 1935

C-9691-A	Put On Your Old Grey Bonnet -3, 4	De 5134
C-9692-C	Pray For The Lights To Go Out -3, 4	De 5111
C-9693-A	In El Rancho Grande -1, 3	De 5071, 46000
C-9694-A	Down By The O-H-I-O -2, 3, 4	De 5111
C-9695-A	I Love You -4	De 5091
C-9696-A	Sweet Jennie Lee -3, 4	De 5091
C-9697-A,-B	A Good Man Is Hard To Find -4	De 5070
C-9698-C	St. Louis Blues -4	De 5070, 46001
C-9699-D	The Object Of My Affection -4	De 5072
C-9700-C	Love In Bloom -3	De 5072
C-9701-A	Chinatown My Chinatown -4	De 5166
C-9702-A	Copenhagen	De 5158, 10097
C-9703-A	Brownie Special -5, 6	De 5174
C-9704-A	Some Of These Days -4	De 5134
C-9705-A	Wabash Blues -3, 4	De 5108

Decca 10097 as by **Meliton Y Sus Rancheros**. Matrix C-9702 is titled *Baile En Mi Rancho* on that issue.

Cecil Brower, f; Bob Dunn, esg; Fred Calhoun, p; Ocie Stockard, tbj/v-1; Derwood Brown, g/v-2/calls-3; Wanna Coffman, sb; Milton Brown, v-4/sp-5.

Chicago, IL   Monday, January 28, 1935

C-9716-A	Beautiful Texas -2, 4	De 5071, 46000
C-9717-A	Just A Dream -4	De 5317
C-9718-A	Cheesy Breeze	De 5166
C-9719-A,-AA	When I'm Gone, Don't You Grieve	De rejected
C-9720-A	Who's Sorry Now -4	De 5158
C-9721-A	One Of Us Was Wrong -2, 4	De 5317
C-9722-A	The House At The End Of The Lane -2, 4	De 5194, MeC 45233, BrSA SA1169
C-9723-A	My Mary -5	De 5080, 46001
C-9724-A	You're Tired Of Me -2	De 5080
C-9726-A	I'll Be Glad When You're Dead You Rascal You -1, 2, 4	De 5149, Min M-14166

C-9727-A	Sweet Georgia Brown -2	De 5121
C-9728-A	Shine On, Harvest Moon -2, 4	De 5121
C-9729-A	You're Bound To Look Like A Monkey When You Grow Old -1, 2, 4	De 5108
C-9730-A	Wheezie Anna -1, 2, 4	De 5342
C-9731-A	Taking Off	De 5149
C-9732-A	Darktown Strutters' Ball -2, 4	De 5179
C-9733-A	Crafton Blues	De 5179
C-9734-A	Black And White Rag	De 5129, 10097, Min M-14166
C-9735-A	In The Shade Of The Old Apple Tree -2, 4	De 5129
C-9736-A	Little Betty Brown -3	De 5194, MeC 45233
C-9737-A	Going Up Brushy Fork	De 5174, Min M-14167

Decca 10097 as by **Meliton Y Sus Rancheros**. Matrix C-9734 is titled *Blanco Y Negro* on that issue. Matrix C-9725 is Mexican.

Cecil Brower, f/v-1; Cliff Bruner, f; Bob Dunn, esg; Fred Calhoun, p; Ocie Stockard, tbj/v-2; Derwood Brown, g/v-3; Wanna Coffman, sb; Milton Brown, v-4/sp-5.

New Orleans, LA Tuesday, March 3, 1936

60610-A	Somebody's Been Using That Thing -2, 3, 4	De 5201
60611--	The Sheik Of Araby -3, 4	De 5303
60612-A	Beale Street Mama -4	De 5295
60613-A	Mama Don't Allow It -3, 4	De 5281
60614-A	Our Baby Boy -4	De 5199
60615-A	Mexicali Rose -3, 4	De 5200
60616--	Stay On The Right Side Sister -3	De 5281
60617-A	If You Can't Get Five Take Two -2, 3, 4	De 5211
60618-A	Cielito Lindo (Beautiful Heaven) -1, 3	De 5303, BrSA SA1169
60619--	The Waltz You Saved For Me -3, 4	De 5233, DeAu X1203, BrSA SA1140
60620--	The Eyes Of Texas -3, 4	De 5209, 46071
60621-A	I Had Someone Before I Had You -4	De 5429
60622-A	I've Got The Blues For Mammy -3, 4, 5	De 5199
60623-A	Texas Hambone Blues -4	De 5226, Min M-14167
60624--	Easy Ridin' Papa -2, 3, 4	De 5325
60625-A	Am I Blue? -2, 3, 4	De 5272

Matrix 60620 is titled *Texas University The Eyes Of Texas Are Upon You* on Decca 46071.

New Orleans, LA Wednesday, March 4, 1936

60626-A	The Wheel Of The Wagon Is Broken -4	De 5209
60627--	Memphis Blues -4	De 5382
60628--	Somebody Stole My Gal -4	De 5462
60629--	Under The Double Eagle	De 5429
60630--	Washington And Lee Swing	De 5266, 46071
60631--	When I'm Gone Don't You Grieve -3, 4	De 5273, Min M-14153
60632--	The Sweetheart Of Sigma Chi -4	De 5239, BrSA SA1140
60633--	An Old Water Mill By A Waterfall -4	De 5233, DeAu X1203
60634-A	The Hesitation Blues -2, 3, 4	De 5266
60635--	Avalon	De 5462
60636-A	Sadie Green (The Vamp Of New Orleans) -4	De 5311
60637-A	Show Me The Way To Go Home -3, 4	De 5211
60638	The Yellow Rose Of Texas -3, 4	De 5273, Min M-14153, DeSA FM5417, BrSA SA1202
60639--	The Roseland Melody -4	De 5295, BrSA SA1202
60640-A	My Galveston Gal -4	De 5356
60641-A	Yes Sir! -4	De 5260, DeAu X1266
60642-A	La Golondrina	De 5356
60643--	When I Take My Sugar To Tea -4	De 5201
60644-A	Song Of The Wanderer -3	De 5251
60645--	Right Or Wrong -3, 4	De 5342
60646-A	Chinese Honeymoon -3, 4	De 5244
60647-A	Alice Blue Gown -4	De 5311

Matrix 60630 is titled *Washington And Lee University Washington And Lee Swing* on Decca 46071. Matrix 60641 is titled *Yes Suh!* on Decca X1266. Rev. Decca FM5417 by Jimmie Davis.

New Orleans, LA Thursday, March 5, 1936

60648-A	Fan It -2, 3, 4	De 5244
60649-A	Tired Of The Same Thing All The Time -4	De 5226
60650--	I'll String Along With You -4	De 5239
60651--	Goofus -4	De 5200

60652- -	"Ida" Sweet As Apple Cider -4	De 5325, 46002
60653- -	When It's Harvest Time, Sweet Angeline -4	De 5272
60654- -	Carry Me Back To The Lone Prairie -4	De 5382
60655-A	A Thousand Good Nights -4	De 5255
60656-A	Keep A Knockin' -4	De 5251
60657- -	Baby Keep Stealin' -4	De 5255
60658- -	The Old Gray Mare -3, 4	De 5260, DeAu X1266

Milton Brown died on April 18, 1936. A recording session was held under the leadership of his brother Derwood in the following year. It seems inappropriately pedantic to list this separately.

Brown's Musical Brownies: Robert "Buck" Buchanan, f/v-1; Johnny Borowski, f/oc-2; Wilson "Lefty" Perkins, esg; Fred Calhoun, p; Ocie Stockard, tbj/v-3; Derwood Brown, g/v-4; Wanna Coffman, sb.

Dallas, TX   Friday, February 19, 1937

61866-A	Confessin' (That I Love You) -3	De 5413
61867-A	The One Rose -4	De 5346, MeC 45049, Min M-14068
61868-A	Bring It On Down To My House Honey -1, 3, 4	De 5394, 46002
61869-A	Louise Louise Blues -4	De 5371
61870-A	How Come You Do Me Like You Do -1, 3, 4	De 5486
61875-A	Long Long Ago -3	De 5346, MeC 45049, Min M-14068
61876-A	I Can't Give You Anything But Love -3	De 5443
61877-A	There'll Be Some Changes Made -4	De 5486
61878-A	Rose Room	De 5443
61879-A	Cross Patch -2, 4	De 5413
61880-A	Everybody Loves My Marguerite -4	De 5394
61881-A	I Just Want Your Stingaree -3	De 5371

Decca 46002 as by **Milton Brown & His Brownies**.

Matrices 61871/72 are by Jimmie Davis (accompanied by Brown's Musical Brownies); 61873/74 by Buddy Jones.

Milton Brown also recorded with The Fort Worth Doughboys; see [The] Light Crust Doughboys.

OSCAR BROWN

Pseudonym on Champion for Thomas C. Ashley.

THOMAS BROWN

Thomas Brown, v; acc. unknown, g.

Atlanta, GA   Friday, November 14, 1930

ATL-6666-A	Carry Me Back To Dixie	Br 593
ATL-6667-A	On The Plains Of Texas	Br 593

BROWN & BRADSHAW

Vocal duet; acc. two unknowns, f.

Chicago, IL   c. August/September 1926

2689-2	Tell Mother I'll Be There	Her 75543

Herwin 75543 is likely to have been also released in the Paramount 33000 series, but no such issue has been traced. Rev. Herwin 75543 by Thursday Evening Prayer Meeters.

BROWN & BUNCH

Pseudonym on Supertone for Rutherford & Foster.

THE BROWN BROTHERS (BOYCE BROWN & EVERETT ECKERD)

Boyce Brown, Everett Eckerd, v duet; or Boyce Brown, v-1; acc. own g duet.

Charlotte, NC   Tuesday, June 16, 1936

102634-1	My Little Darling	MW M-7737
102635-1	We Will Not Forget	MW M-7737
102636-1	My Mother And Dear Old Dad	BB B-6623, MW M-7738
102637-1	Son, Please Come Home	BB B-6623, MW M-7738
102638-1	Innocent Of Murder	MW M-7739
102639-1	I'm A Lonely Hobo -1	MW M-7739

Montgomery Wards as by **Boyce Brown & Everett Eckard**.

BROWN'S HAPPY FOUR

See James Brown, Jr. & Ken Landon groups.

BROWN'S MUSICAL BROWNIES

See Milton Brown & His [Musical] Brownies.

— BRUMFIELD

Unknown, f; unknown, bj; unknown, g.
   Richmond, IN   Saturday, January 4, 1930
   16058   Meat House Blues   Ge rejected trial recording

BILL BRUNER

Bill Bruner, v/y; acc. own g.
   New Orleans, LA   Saturday, December 14, 1929

403424-B	My Pal Of Yesterday	OK 45400
403425-B	That's Why I'm All Alone	OK 45400

Acc. unknown, f-1; unknown, t-2; poss. k-3; own g.
   New York, NY   Tuesday, March 18, 1930

403860-B	Just A Little Dream	OK 45463
403861-A	Singing The Blues With My Old Guitar -1, 2, 3	OK 45438
403862-A	A Gal Like You	OK 45463

   New York, NY   Wednesday, March 19, 1930

403865-B	School Day Dreams -1	OK 45497
403866-A	He's In The Jail House Now -2, 3	OK 45438
403867-A	My Old Home Town Girl -1, 2	OK 45497

CLIFF BRUNER

Cliff Bruner's Texas Wanderers: Cliff Bruner, f; Leo Raley, emd/v-1; Fred "Papa" Calhoun, p; Joe Thames, tbj; Randall "Red" Raley, g/v-2; Dickie McBride, g/v-3; Hezzie Bryant, sb; band v-4.
   San Antonio, TX   Friday, February 5, 1937

61636-A	So Tired -3	De 5368
61637-A	Milk Cow Blues -1	De 5334
61638-A	The Right Key (But The Wrong Keyhole) -2	De 5401
61639-A	You Got To Hi De Hi -1, 4	De 5337
61640-A	In The Blue Of The Night -3	De 5401
61640-B	In The Blue Of The Night -3	De unissued: *BF BCD15932* (CD)
61641-A	Shine -3	De 5434
61641-B	Shine -3	De unissued: *BF BCD15932* (CD)
61642-A	Can't Nobody Truck Like Me -1	De 5337
61642-B	Can't Nobody Truck Like Me -1	De unissued: *BF BCD15932* (CD)
61643-A	Bringin' Home The Bacon -3	De 5334
61644-A	Under The Silvery Moon -3	De 5368
61645-A	Corrine Corrina -1, 3	De 5350
61646-A	Four Or Five Times -1	De 5350
61647-A	Oh You Pretty Woman -1	De 5469
61648-A	I Ain't Gonna Give Nobody None O' This Jelly Roll -1	De 5434
61649-A	Old Fashioned Love -3	De 5469

Cliff Bruner, f/v-1; Dickie Jones, f/v-2; Ernest "Deacon" Evans, esg; Leo Raley, emd/v-3; Doc Warren, p; Joe Thames, tbj/v-4; Red Raley, g/v-5; Dickie McBride, g/v-6; Hezzie Bryant, sb; band v-7.
   Dallas, TX   Wednesday, December 8, 1937

62966-A	Oh How I Miss You Tonight -6	De 5515
62967-A	One Sweet Letter From You -1	De 5529
62968-A	Dream Train -3, 6	De 5499
62969-A	Sunbonnet Sue -6	De 5485
62970-A	To-night You Belong To Me -6	De 5582
62971-A	By A Window At The End Of The Lane -4	De 5515
62972-A	Girl Of My Dreams -3	De 5560
62973-A	I Saw Your Face In The Moon -2	De 5474
62974-A	Red Lips – Kiss My Blues Away -3	De 5529
62975-A	You Can Depend On Me -4	De 5543
62976-A	Sugar -5	De 5560
62977-A	My Daddy, My Mother And Me -?3, 6	De 5485
62978-A	Truckin' On Down -3, 7	De 5582
62979-A	River, Stay 'Way From My Door -6	De 5543
62980-A	Baby Won't you Please Come Home -6	De 5499

Decca 5474, 5485 as by **Cliff Bruner & His Boys**.

Ernest "Deacon" Evans, esg; Leo Raley, emd; Doc Warren, p; Joe Thames, tbj; Red Raley, g; Dickie McBride, g; Hezzie Bryant, sb.

    Dallas, TX   Wednesday, December 8, 1937

    62981-A   Beaumont Rag   De 5474

Decca 5474 as by **Cliff Bruner & His Boys**.

Cliff Bruner, f/v-1; Bob Dunn, esg; Leo Raley, emd; Moon Mullican, p/v-2; Joe Thames, tbj; Dickie McBride, g/v-3; Hezzie Bryant, sb.

    San Antonio, TX   Tuesday, September 13, 1938

64500-A	Annie Laurie -3	De 5647
64501-A	Bring It On Home To Grandma -1	De 5619
64502-A	Ease My Worried Mind -1, 2	De 5610
64503-A	Remember -3	De 5647
64504-A	It Makes No Difference Now -3	De 5604, 46011, MeC 45321
64505-A	My Bonnie Lies Over The Ocean -1, 2, 3 (lead)	De 5638
64506-A	Over Moonlit Waters -3	De 5672
64507-A	Draggin' The Bow	De 5610

Cliff Bruner, f/v-1; Bob Dunn, esg; Leo Raley, emd; Moon Mullican, p/v-2; Joe Thames, tbj/v-3; Dickie McBride, g/v-4; Hezzie Bryant, sb.

    San Antonio, TX   Wednesday, September 14, 1938

64508-A	Yearning Just For You -1, 4	De 5638
64509-A	Old Joe Turner Blues -2	De 5660, 46096
64510-A	When You're Smiling (The Whole World Smiles With You) -2	De 5660, 46096
64511-A	I Wish I Could Shimmy Like My Sister Kate -2	De 5624
64512-A	Sittin' On The Moon -3	De 5619
64512-B	Sittin' On The Moon -3	De unissued: BF BCD15932 (CD)
64513-A	Kangaroo Blues -2	De 5624, Coral 64001
64514-A	I'll Keep On Loving You -2	De 5672, Coral 64001
64515-A	I Hate To Lose You -2	De 5604, MeC 45321

Plain takes of matrices 64513 and 64515 may also have been issued.

Cliff Bruner & His Boys: Cliff Bruner, f/v-1; Bob Dunn, esg; Moon Mullican, p/v-2; Johnny Thames, tbj; prob. Dickie McBride, g; Hezzie Bryant, sb.

    Houston, TX   Saturday, August 26, 1939

66300-A	Jessie	De 5769, 10464, 46051
66301-A	Over The Hill -1, 2	De 5785
66302-A	I'll Keep On Smiling -2	De 5808
66303-A	Truck Driver's Blues -1, 2	De 5725
66304-A	I'm Tired Of You -2	De 5725
66305-A	Because -2	De 5819
66306-A	I'll Forgive You (But I Can't Forget) -2	De 5808
66307-A	I'm Still In Love With You -2	De 5819

Decca 10464 as by **Bruno Y Sus Rancheros**. Matrix 66300 is titled *Jesusita* on that issue.

Cliff Bruner, f/v-1; poss. J.R. Chatwell, f-2; Bob Dunn, esg; Moon Mullican, p/v-3; Johnny Thames, tbj; prob. Dickie McBride, g; Hezzie Bryant, sb.

    Houston, TX   Friday, September 1, 1939

66349-A	Star Dust	De 5743
66350-A	The Other Way -2, 3	De 5753
66351-A	Peggy Lou -2	De 5797, 10464
66352-A	Singin' The Low Down Blues Down Low -2, 3	De 5743
66353-A	It's All Over Now (I Won't Worry) -3	De 5785
66354-A	Tell Me Why Little Girl Tell Me Why -2, 3	De 5797
66355-A	The Girl That You Loved Long Ago -2, 3	De 5769
66356-A	Little White Lies -2, 3	De 5753
66356-B	Little White Lies -2, 3	De unissued: BF BCD15932 (CD)
66357-A	Kelly Swing	De 5728
66358-A	San Antonio Rose	De 5728, 46051

Decca 10464 as by **Bruno Y Sus Rancheros**. Matrix 66351 is titled *Maria Luisa* on that issue.

Cliff Bruner, f/tg-1/v-2; Bob Dunn, esg; Moon Mullican, p/v; poss. Tex Conger (Logan Snodgrass) or Hezzie Bryant, sb.

    Houston, TX   Friday, April 5, 1940

92014-A	Take Me Back Again -2	De 5836, MeC 45358
92015-A	You Don't Love Me But I'll Always Care -2	De 5849, DeAu X1945, MeC 45358
92016-A	I'm Headin' For That Ranch In The Sky -1	De 5836, DeAu X1945
92017-A	Over The Trail	De 5849

Cliff Bruner, f/v-1; Bob Dunn, esg; Moon Mullican, p/v-2; prob. Tex Conger (Logan Snodgrass), g-3; poss. Hezzie Bryant, sb-4.

Houston, TX   Monday, April 8, 1940

92052-A	Ten Pretty Girls -3, 4	De 5824, 46098, MeC 45349
92053-A	Sorry (I'll Say I'm Sorry) -2, 3, 4	De 5860, MeC 45371
92053-B	Sorry (I'll Say I'm Sorry) -2, 3, 4	De unissued: BF BCD15932 (CD)
92054-A	Sparkling Blue Eyes -2, 3, 4	De 5824, 46098, MeC 45349
92055-A	New Falling Rain Blues -2	De 5860, MeC 45371
92055-B	New Falling Rain Blues -2	De unissued: BF BCD15932 (CD)
92056-A	I'll Keep Thinking Of You -2, 3, 4	De 5871, 46011, DeSA FM5161, MeC 45381
92057-A	'Neath The Purple On The Hills -1, 3, 4	De 5871, MeC 45381
92057-B	'Neath The Purple On The Hills -1, 3, 4	De unissued: BF BCD15932 (CD)

Rev. Decca FM5161 by Jimmie Davis.

Cliff Bruner, f/etg-1/v-2; Charles Mitchell, esg; Moon Mullican, p/v-3; Bruce Pierce, tbj/v-4; Oliver "Sock" Underwood, g; prob. Hershel Woodal, sb.

Dallas, TX   Monday, April 28, 1941

93707-A	Draft Board Blues -4	De 5953, MeC 45444
93708-A	I'll Be Faithful -2	De 6012, MeC 45481
93709-A	Jessie's Sister	De 5974
93710-A	Let Me Smile My Last Smile At You -1, 2	De 5961
93711-A	Tequilla Rag	De 5953, MeC 45444
93712-A	Red River Rose -2	De 6012, MeC 45481
93713-A	My Time Will Come Someday -1, 2, 3	De 5974
93714-A	The Sun Has Gone Down On Our Love -1, 2	De 5961

Cliff Bruner recorded after 1942.

BRUNO Y SUS RANCHEROS

Decca 10464 (a Mexican issue) by Cliff Bruner & His Boys was issued thus.

THE BRUNSWICK PLAYERS Featuring Sterling Melvin

Sterling Melvin, sp; acc. unknown, cl; poss. Taylor Flanagan, p; unknown (at least two men and two women), sp.

Atlanta, GA   Monday, March 24, 1930

| ATL-8006 | The Shooting Of Dan McGrew – Part 1 | Br 415, Spt S2076 |
| ATL-8007 | The Shooting Of Dan McGrew – Part 2 | Br 415, Spt S2076 |

Supertone S2076 as by **Melvin's Supertone Players**. One of the male speakers is almost certainly John Dilleshaw.

HOYT "SLIM" BRYANT

Hoyt "Slim" Bryant recorded with Clayton McMichen on several occasions in 1930-32, and with Bert Layne & His Georgia Serenaders in 1931, receiving joint or sole label-credit on a number of issues. Details of these recordings will be found in the entries for Bert Layne and Clayton McMichen. See also Bob Miller and Jimmie Rodgers, whom Bryant accompanied as a member of McMichen's band.

BUCK MT. BAND

Van Edwards, f; Wade Ward, bj; Earl Edwards, g/prob. v-1/prob. y-1.

Richmond, VA   Wednesday, October 16, 1929

403138-	Reckless Rambler	OK unissued
403139-	Go And Leave Me If You Wish	OK unissued
403140-A	Yodeling Blues -1	OK 45428, Ve 2358-V, Cl 5292-C
403141-B	Don't Let The Blues Get You Down	OK 45428, Ve 2361-V, Cl 5295-C

Velvet Tone 2358-V, 2361-V, Clarion 5292-C, 5295-C as by **Art, Andy, Bert & Dave**.
Revs: Velvet Tone 2358-V, 2361-V, Clarion 5292-C, 5295-C by Frank Marvin.

BUCKEYE BOYS

Vocal duet; acc. unknown, bj; unknown, g; unknown, u.

Richmond, IN   Thursday, December 11, 1930

17367	That Old Fashioned Photograph	Spr 2616, Ch 45160
17368	The Maple On The Hill	Spr 2616, Ch 45160
17368-A	The Maple On The Hill	CrC/MeC 93083, Min M-14046
17369	Duck Foot Sue	Ch 16168, 45200
17370-C	Thompson's Old Gray Mule	Ch 16168, 45200, Min M-14046

Rev. Crown/Melotone 93083 by Reg Perkins (Canadian artist).

James R. Halsey is named as royalty payee in Champion files and may have been a member of the group.
This artist-credit was also used on Varsity 5101 as a pseudonym for the Tweedy Brothers (matrix 13653) or Archie Porter & His Happy Buckeyes (matrix 19464).

BUFFALO RAGGED FIVE

Vocal quartet; acc. unknown, g.
    Richmond, IN   Friday, November 27, 1931

| 18226 | Reapers | Ch 16428 |
| 18227 | Our Schoolboy Days | Ch 16428 |

Acc. unknown, h-1; unknown, g.
    Richmond, IN   Monday, October 24, 1932

18855-A	All Of My Sins Are Taken Away -1	Ch 16526, 45111
18856	Jesus Leads, I'll Follow On -1	Ch 16526, 45111
18857	Home Beyond The Sunset	Ch 16555
18858	Redeemed	Ch 16555
18859	Give Me Your Hand	Ch 16673
18860	I'm Bound For Home	Ch 16673

A.J. Skeen is named as royalty payee in Champion files and may have been a member of the group.

BUICE BROTHERS [QUARTET]

Buice Brothers: Paul Buice, T. Carl Buice, Luther Buice, Marvin Buice, v quartet; acc. unknown, p.
    Atlanta, GA   Thursday, April 19, 1928

| 146146-2 | The Home-Coming Week | Co 15527-D |
| 146147-2 | I'm His At Last | Co 15527-D |

Buice Brothers Quartet: Paul Buice, T. Carl Buice, Luther Buice, Marvin Buice, v quartet; acc. unknown, p.
    Atlanta, GA   Tuesday, November 11, 1930

| ATL-6615 | Endless Glory | Br 545 |
| ATL-6616 | Oh Declare His Glory | Br 545 |

Buice Brothers: Paul Buice, T. Carl Buice, Luther Buice, Marvin Buice, v quartet; acc. unknown, p.
    Atlanta, GA   Thursday, August 2, 1934

82883-1	Rock Of Ages	BB B-5722
82884-1	Over The Tide	BB B-5753
82885-1	When All The Singers Get Home	BB B-5613
82886-1	Abide With Me	BB B-5722
82887-1	Life's Railway To Heaven	BB B-5613
82888-1	Christ Arose!	BB B-5753

BULL MOUNTAIN MOONSHINERS

Charles McReynolds, f; William McReynolds, bj; Howard Green, g; Charlie Greer, g; Bill Deane, v.
    Bristol, TN   Monday, August 1, 1927

| 39748-1,-2 | Sweet Marie | Vi unissued |
| 39749-2 | Johnny Goodwin | Vi 21141 |

Rev. Victor 21141 by Tenneva Ramblers (see Grant Brothers).

SAMANTHA BUMGARNER

Samantha Bumgarner & Eva Davis: prob.: Samantha Bumgarner, f/v-1; Eva Davis, bj.
    New York, NY   Tuesday, April 22, 1924

81706-1	Cindy In The Meadows -1	Co 167-D, Ha 5097-H, Di 6010-G, Ve 7036-V
81707-2	I Am My Mamma's Darling Child	Co 191-D, Ha 5113-H
81708-	Down The Road	Co unissued
81709-	Mountain-Top	Co unissued
81710-2	Big-Eyed Rabbit -1	Co 129-D, Ha 5093-H

Harmony 5093-H as by **Luella Gardner & Davis**. Harmony 5097-H, 5113-H, Diva 6010-G, Velvet Tone 7036-V as by **Gardner & David**.
Matrix 81706 is incorrectly identified as take 2 on Sony JXK65750.
Matrix 81707 is titled *I Am My Mamma's Child* on Harmony 5113-H.
Revs: Harmony 5093-H, 5097-H, Diva 6010-G, Velvet Tone 7036-V by Eva Davis.

Samantha Bumgarner, bj solo/calls-1.
    New York, NY   Wednesday, April 23, 1924

81713-	Last Gold Dollar	Co unissued
81714-	Every Day Blues	Co unissued
81715-2	Shout Lou -1	Co 146-D, Ha 5094-H

| 81716-1 | Fly Around My Pretty Little Miss -1 | Co 146-D, Ha 5094-H |
| 81717-2 | The Gamblin' Man | Co 191-D, Ha 5113-H |

Harmony 5094-H as by **Luella Gardner**; 5113-H as by **Gardner & David**. Matrix 81716 is titled *Fly Around Miss* on Harmony 5094-H.

Samantha Bumgarner, v; acc. own bj.
   New York, NY   Wednesday, April 23, 1924

| 81718-2 | The Worried Blues | Co 166-D, Ha 5111-H |
| 81719-1 | Georgia Blues | Co 166-D, Ha 5111-H |

Harmony 5111-H as by **Luella Gardner**; matrix 81718 is titled *Worried Blues* on that issue.

Samantha Bumgarner recorded after 1942.

THE BUMS

Pseudonym on Broadway for Fay & Jay Walkers.

ALVIN BUNCH

Pseudonym on Supertone for Ted Chestnut.

CARL BUNCH

Pseudonym on Bell for Aulton Ray.

SAM BUNCH

Pseudonym on Supertone for John Foster.

BUNCH & JENNINGS

Pseudonym on Challenge for Burnett & Rutherford.

JACK & JIM BURBANK
JIM & JACK BURBANK

Pseudonyms on Superior for Merritt Smith & Leo Boswell.

BEN BURD & BILL WHITE

Pseudonym on Australian Sunrise for Bob Miller & Barney Burnett.

JACK BURDETTE & BERT MOSS

Pseudonym on Superior for Melvin Robinette & Byrd Moore (see the latter).

LLOYD BURDETTE

Lloyd Burdette, v; acc. prob. own h-1/g.
   Richmond, IN   Tuesday, July 28, 1931

17897,-A	When I'm Gone You'll Soon Forget	Ge rejected
17898	Coney Island	Ge unissued
17899,-A	The Boarding House Blues -1	Ge unissued

Acc. prob. own h/g.
   Richmond, IN   Thursday, February 11, 1932

18394	We Shall All Be Reunited	Ge unissued
18395	My Wife Has Gone And Left Me	Ge unissued
18396	Take Me Home	Ge unissued

JOHN BURHAM

Pseudonym on Champion for Frank Jenkins.

JAMES BURKE

Pseudonym on Superior for the Arkansas Woodchopper.

[FIDDLIN'] JIM BURKE
JIM BURKE & JESSE COAT

Pseudonyms on Champion, Silvertone, and Supertone for Doc Roberts (& Asa Martin). **Jim Burke** on Silvertone 8156, Supertone 9260 is either Ted Chestnut (matrix 13798) or John D. Foster (matrix GEX-844).

BURKE BROTHERS

Prob.: Joe Kaipo, sg/v; Billy Burke, g/v; Weldon Burke, u/v.
   Dallas, TX   Tuesday, October 22, 1929

| 56451-1 | At Last My Dreams Have Come True | Vi V-40294, Au 229 |
| 56452-2 | Lonesome And Lonely | Vi V-40294, Au 229 |

All three musicians, in various combinations, also recorded with Jimmie Rodgers. While label credits are to Burke, the actual family name is Burkes.

ABNER BURKHARDT
Pseudonym on Champion for Walter C. Peterson.

BARNEY BURNETT
See Bob Miller.

BOB BURNETT
Pseudonym on Bluebird, Electradisk, and Sunrise for Bob Miller.

RICHARD D. BURNETT

Burnett & Rutherford: Leonard Rutherford, f/v-1; Richard D. Burnett, bj-2/g-3/v-4.
Atlanta, GA   Saturday, November 6, 1926

143092-2	Lost John -1, 3	Co 15122-D
143093-2	Little Stream Of Whiskey -1 (lead), 3, 4	Co 15133-D
143094-2	Weeping Willow Tree -1, 3, 4	Co 15113-D
143095-2	I'll Be With You When The Roses Bloom Again -1, 3, 4	Co 15122-D
143096-1	A Short Life Of Trouble -2, 4	Co 15133-D
143097-2	Pearl Bryan -3, 4	Co 15113-D

Leonard Rutherford, f/v-1; Richard D. Burnett, g-2/v-3.
Atlanta, GA   Saturday, April 2, 1927

143873-2	My Sweetheart In Tennessee -2, 3	Co 15187-D
143874-2	Are You Happy Or Lonesome? -1, 2, 3	Co 15187-D
143875-	Assassination Of J.B. Marcum	Co unissued
143876-	Song Of The Orphan Girl	Co unissued

Leonard Rutherford, f/v-1; Richard D. Burnett, bj-2/g-3/v-4/v eff-5/sp-6.
Atlanta, GA   Thursday, November 3, 1927

145084-2	Curley-Headed Woman -2, 4	Co 15240-D, Ve 2496-V, Cl 5436-C
145085-1	Ramblin' Reckless Hobo -1, 2, 4	Co 15240-D, Ve 2496-V, Cl 5436-C
145086-1	Willie Moore -2, 4	Co 15314-D
145087-2	All Night Long Blues -3, 4	Co 15314-D
145088-1	Ladies On The Steamboat -2, 5, 6	Co 15209-D
145089-2	Billy In The Low Ground -2, 5, 6	Co 15209-D

Velvet Tone 2496-V, Clarion 5436-C as by **Clayton & Parker**.

Rutherford & Burnett: Leonard Rutherford, f/v-1; Richard D. Burnett, bj/v-2/veff-3; Byrd Moore, g.
Richmond, IN   Monday, October 29, 1928

14389	She Is A Flower From The Fields Of Alabama -1, 2	Ge 6688, Chg 420
14390	Under The Pale Moonlight -1, 2	Ge 6688, Chg 420
14391	The Spring Roses	Ge rejected
14394	Cumberland Gap -2, 3	Ge 6706, Ch 15653, Spt 9310

Gennett 6706 as by **Moore, Burnett & Rutherford**. Champion 15653 as by **Norton, Bond & Williams**. Supertone 9310 as by **Southern Kentucky Mountaineers**. Challenge 420 as by **Bunch & Jennings**. Matrices 14392/93 are by Taylor, Moore & Burnett; 14395/96 by Rutherford & Moore. Revs: Champion 15653 by Rutherford & Moore; Supertone 9310 by Taylor, Moore & Burnett.

Moore, Burnett & Rutherford: Leonard Rutherford, f; Richard D. Burnett, bj; Byrd Moore, g.
Richmond, IN   Tuesday, October 30, 1928

| 14397 | Sleeping Lula | Ge rejected |

R.D. Burnett & Lynn Woodard: Richard D. Burnett, f-1/bj-2/v-3; Lynn Woodard, g.
Richmond, IN   Saturday, January 5, 1929

14650	Going Around The World -2, 3	Ge unissued: *Rdr 1004* (LP); *Doc DOCD-8025* (CD)
14651	Going Across The Sea -2, 3	Ge unissued: *Rdr 1004* (LP); *Doc DOCD-8025* (CD)
14652	Bonnie Blue Waltz -1	Ge unissued: *Doc DOCD-8025* (CD)
14653	Green Valley Waltz -1	Ge unissued

Burnett & Ruttledge: Richard D. Burnett, f-1/bj-2/v-3; Oscar Ruttledge, g.
Atlanta, GA   Saturday, April 19, 1930

150291-	My Sweetheart Across The Sea -1/2, 3	Co unissued
150292-	The Fatal Wedding Night -1/2, 3	Co unissued
150293- ; 194950-2	Sleeping Lulu -1	Co 15567-D
150294- ; 194901-1	Blackberry Blossom -1	Co 15567-D

150295-	Let Her Go I'll Meet Her -1/2, 3		Co unissued
150296-	Goodbye Sweetheart Goodbye -1/2, 3		Co unissued

BURNETT & MILLER

See Bob Miller.

BURNETT & RUTHERFORD
BURNETT & RUTTLEDGE

See Richard D. Burnett.

BURNETT BROTHERS [or BROS.]

Pseudonym on Victor and Montgomery Ward for Bob Miller & Barney Burnett.

SMILEY [or SMILIE] BURNETTE

Smilie Burnette, v; acc. Roy Smeck, h-1/bj-1/g/jh-1; poss. Bob Miller, p; unknown, g.
   New York, NY   Tuesday, May 29, 1934

15261-1	Mama Don't Like Music -1	Ba 33082, Me M13046, MeC 91844, Or 8344, Pe 13011, Ro 5344, Cq 8387
15263-1	He Was A Traveling Man	Ba 33082, Me M13046, MeC 91844, Or 8344, Pe 13011, Ro 5344, Cq 8387
15265-	The Lone Cowboy	ARC unissued

Intervening matrices are by Gene Autry & Jimmy Long.

Acc. Roy Smeck, bj-1/g-2; unknown, g.
   New York, NY   Thursday, May 31, 1934

15267-1	Peg Leg Jack -1	Ba 33104, Me M13072, MeC91839, Or 8354, Pe 13018, Ro 5354, Cq 8493, Min M-915
15268-2	Matilda Higgins -2	Ba 33104, Me M13072, MeC 91839, Or 8354, Pe 13018, Ro 5354, Cq 8493

Rev. Minerva M-915 by Pickard Family.

Acc. unknown, g.
   New York, NY   Wednesday, January 16, 1935

16579-1	Minnie The Moocher At The Morgue	ARC unissued: *CSP P4-15542 (LP)*
16580-	I Can Do Without You In The Daytime	ARC unissued

Burnette also recorded duets with Gene Autry at this session, for which see the latter.

Smiley "Frog" Burnette & His Tad-Poles: Smiley Burnette, v; acc. unknown.
   Los Angeles, CA   Thursday, May 19, 1938

LA-1641-A	That's How Donkey's [sic] Were Born	ARC unissued
LA-1642-A	I Can Whip Any Man But Popeye	ARC unissued
LA-1643-A	I'm Doomed To Follow The Bugle	ARC unissued
LA-1644-A	Tumbleweed Tenor	ARC unissued
LA-1645-A	Frog Tuplets	ARC unissued

Smiley Burnette, v; acc. unknown, f; unknown, t; unknown, esg; unknown, g; unknown, sb; unknown, v-1.
   Los Angeles, CA   Thursday, December 1, 1938

DLA-1601-A	Steamboat Bill -1	De 5685
DLA-1602-A	Uncle Fraley's Formula	De 5633
DLA-1603-A	Lawyer Skinner	De 5685
DLA-1604-A	Down By The Cane Brake	De 5633

Smiley Burnette recorded after 1942.

DAPHNE BURNS

Daphne Burns, v; acc. unknown, g; one or more unknowns, v.
   Chicago, IL   c. early July 1927

4705-2	Goodbye To My Stepstones	Pm 3032
4706-2	The Weeping Willow Tree	Pm 3032

JEWELL TILLMAN BURNS & CHARLIE D. TILLMAN

Jewell Tillman Burns, Charlie D. Tillman, v duet; acc. Elizabeth Tillman, p.
   Atlanta, GA   Tuesday, January 27, 1925

140282-1	Old Time Power	Co 15024-D, Ha 5154-H
140283-1	Someday, It Won't Be Long	Co 15024-D, Ha 5154-H
140284-2	My Mother's Bible	Co 15025-D
140285-1	Don't Forget The Old Folks	Co 15025-D

Harmony 5154-H as by **Burns & Tillman**.

    Atlanta, GA   Wednesday, January 28, 1925

| 140290-2 | Tell It Again | Co 15026-D |
| 140291-1 | Sometime, Somewhere | Co 15026-D |

See also Charlie D. Tillman & Daughter (who may be the same).

RUBEN BURNS

See Short Creek Trio.

BURNS & TILLMAN

See Jewell Tillman Burns & Charlie D. Tillman.

BURNS BROTHERS

Vocal duet; acc. unknown, sg; unknown, g.
    New York, NY   Friday, April 16, 1937

61938-A	That's When You Broke My Heart	De 5370, DeAu X1447
61949-A	Mother, Look Down And Guide Me	De 5370, DeAu X1447, MW 8040
62132-A	Old Fashioned Locket	De 5884, MW 8040, MeC 45394

Despite the gaps in matrix numbers, Decca files report these items as having all been recorded on the date shown. Rev. Decca 5884, Melotone 45394 by Texas Wanderers.

JOHN BURTON

Pseudonym on Superior for Howard Keesee.

RUSSELL & LOUIS BURTON

Burton Brothers: v or v duet; acc. prob. one of them, bj; the other, g.
    Richmond, IN   Saturday, May 23, 1931

| 17761 | Old Corn Mill | Ge rejected trial recording |

Russell & Louis Burton, v duet; acc. unknown, h-1; prob. one of them, bj-2/g-3; the other, g.
    Richmond, IN   Tuesday, June 16, 1931

17829-A	Down In Tennessee -2	Ch 16454
17830	The Old Corn Mill -1, 2	Ch 16454, Spr 2703
17835-A	While The Band Is Playing Dixie -1, 3	Ch R-16345, Spr 2703
17836,-A	Jack And Mary -1, 3	Ge unissued

Rev. Champion R-16345 by Woody Leftwich & Roy Lilly.

Lewis Burton, v; acc. unknown, h; unknown, g.
    Richmond, IN   Thursday, February 18, 1932

| 18409 | Dying Hobo | Ge rejected |

Russell Burton, v; acc. unknown, h; two unknowns, g.
    Richmond, IN   Thursday, February 18, 1932

| 18410 | I Don't Love Nobody | Ge unissued |

Russell & Lewis Burton, v duet; acc. unknown, h; unknown, g.
    Richmond, IN   Thursday, February 18, 1932

| 18411 | Jack And May | Ge rejected |

THOS. A. BURTON

Thos. A. Burton, v; acc. prob. own k-1/g.
    Richmond, IN.   Tuesday, October 6, 1931

18080	Won't You Be Mine	Ge rejected
18081	School House Dreams	Ge rejected
18082	I'm Returning To My Log Cabin Home	Ge rejected
18083	I Loved Her In The Moonlight	Ge rejected
18084	I Wonder Why -1	Ge rejected
18085	My Little Home In Alabama -1	Ge rejected

BURTON & BODINE

Pseudonym on Superior for Howard Keesee & Loy Bodine.

BURTON & BURDINEZ

Pseudonym on Superior for Howard Keesee & Loy Bodine.

JOHN BUSBY & GILBERT THOMAS

John & Gilbert (Busby & Thomas), v duet; acc. prob. one of them, g; the other, g.
    Augusta, GA   Friday, June 26, 1936

AUG-117-	She's Coming Now	ARC unissued
AUG-118-	Suicide Blues	ARC unissued
AUG-119-	Sleep On	ARC unissued
AUG-120-	Sweetheart Of Yesterday	ARC unissued

NOLAN BUSH & HIS SOUTHERN PLAYBOYS

Skeets Jasper, f; John L. "Tommy" Treme, esg; prob. George Caldwell, p; Don Tyler, g/v-1; Carl Abbott, sb; Nolan Bush, v-2; poss. unidentified, 3rd v-3.
    Dallas, TX   Thursday, April 10, 1941

063080-1	All In Vain -1, 2 (lead), 3	BB B-8789
063081-1	Until You Went Away -2	BB B-8713
063082-1	When I Won You -1	BB B-8789
063083-1	Sunlight And Starlight -2	BB B-8713

BUSH BROTHERS
BUSH FAMILY

Bush Family, v quartet; acc. unknown, o.
    New Orleans, LA.   Tuesday, April 12, 1927

143959-	He Pardoned Me	Co unissued
143960-2	Music In My Soul	Co 15157-D
143961-	Mother Dear Is Waiting	Co unissued
143962-2	On My Way To Jesus	Co 15157-D

Bush Brothers, v quartet; acc. unknown, o.
    New Orleans, LA.   Thursday, October 27, 1927

145029-2	Saved By His Sweet Grace	Co 15203-D
145030-2	He Pardoned Me	Co 15203-D
145031-1	Hallelujah! He Is Mine	Co 15235-D
145032-1	Oh Wonderful Day	Co 15235-D
145033-2	Mother Dear Is Waiting	Co 15368-D
145034-1	Called Home	Co 15368-D

    New Orleans, LA   Thursday, April 26, 1928

146195-	I've Found A Friend	Co unissued
146196-2	When The Gates Of Glory Open	Co 15263-D
146197-2	On The Glory Road	Co 15263-D
146198-	What Love	Co unissued
146203-2	Does Your Path Seem Long	Co 15287-D
146204-1	Complete For All The World	Co 15287-D

Intervening matrices are by Mr. & Mrs. R.N. Grisham.

Acc. unknown, o-1/p-2.
    New Orleans, LA   Tuesday, December 10, 1929

149570-2	Endless Glory To The Lamb -1	Co 15500-D
149571-2	My Happiest Day -1	Co 15500-D
149572-	Happy Pilgrims -1	Co unissued
149573-	The Redeeming Love -1	Co unissued
149574-1	Keep Your Light Shining -2	Co 15524-D
149575-2	The Pathway -2	Co 15524-D

Acc. unknown, p.
    Jackson, MS   Thursday, December 18, 1930

151127-2	A Look Inside The Glory Gate	Co 15649-D
151128-2	I'll Make It My Home	Co 15649-D
151129-2	What Love!	Co 15696-D
151130-2	I'm No Stranger To Jesus	Co 15696-D
151131-	Singing Along The Way	Co unissued
151132-	In A Little While	Co unissued

BUSTER & JACK

See Jack Cawley's Oklahoma Ridge Runners.

DWIGHT BUTCHER

Slim Oakdale, v/y; acc. poss. own h-1/g.
New York, NY   Tuesday, December 13, 1932

| C-1917-2 | Lonesome Road Blues -1 | Cr 3433, Vs 5126, Cont C-3013 |
| C-1918-2 | Mystery Of Old Number Five | Cr 3433, Vs 5126 |

Varsity 5126, Continental C-3013 as by **Slim Tex**. Rev. Continental C-3013 by Frank Marvin.

Dwight Butcher, v/y; acc. Bob Miller, p-1; own g.
New York, NY   Monday, January 9, 1933

74776-1	The Lonesome Cowboy -1	Vi 23772, MW M-4468
74777-1	A New Day Is Comin' Mighty Soon -1	Vi 23794
74778-1	Sweet Old Lady -1	Vi 23810
74779-1	By A Little Bayou -1	Vi 23794
74780-1	I Am A Fugitive From A Chain Gang -1	Vi unissued
74781-1	Frivolous Frisco Fan -1	Vi 23772
74782-1	Frivolous Frisco Fan	BB B-5012, 1826, Sr S-3112
74783-1	Sweet Old Lady	Eld 1946
74786-1	A New Day Is Comin' Mighty Soon	Eld 1946

Bluebird 1826, Electradisk 1946 as by **Slim Dwight**; Bluebird B-5012 as by **Bill Palmer**. Sunrise S-3112 as by **Hank Hall**. Matrices 74784/85 are by other artists.
Revs: Victor 23810 by Gene Autry; Montgomery Ward M-4468 by Carl T. Sprague; Bluebird B-5012, 1826, Sunrise S-3112 by Bob Miller.

"Slim" Oakdale, v/y; acc. Roy Smeck, sg-1/g-2; own g.
New York, NY   Monday, January 30, 1933

C-1983-2	Mother, The Queen Of My Heart -1	Cr 3476, Vs 5019
C-1984-2	No Hard Times -2	Cr 3461, Vs 5028
C-1985-1	Roll Along Kentucky Moon -1	Cr 3476, Vs 5019
C-1986-2	Nobody Knows But Me -1	Cr 3461, Vs 5028

Varsitys as by **Slim Butcher**.

Dwight Butcher, v/y; acc. poss. own h-1/g; Dick Thomas, g.
New York, NY   Sunday, April 14, 1933

76003-1	Oh Mama, Why Didn't I Listen To You?	Vi 23802
76004-1	The Man That Rode A Mule Around The World -1	Vi 23819
76005-1	My Rambling Days Are Over	Vi 23826, HMVIn N4261
76006-1	Pistol Pete	Vi 23819
76007-1	Got A Freight Train On My Mind	Vi 23826, HMVIn N4261
76008-1	Alarm Clock Blues	Vi 23802

"Slim" Oakdale, v/y; acc. Prince Wong, sg; own g; Adrian Schubert, chimes-1.
New York, NY   Friday, May 31, 1933

C-2088-2	When It's Peach Pickin' Time In Georgia	Cr 3529, Vs 5099
C-2089-2	Prairie Lullaby -1	Cr 3529, Vs 5004
C-2090-2	Cowboy's Heaven -1	Cr 3503, Vs 5004

Varsity 5004 as by **Slim Butcher**, 5099 as by **Tex Slim**. Matrix C-2088 is titled *Peach Pickin' Time In Georgia* on Varsity 5099. Rev. Crown 3503 by Bob Miller.

"Slim" Oakdale Trio: Prince Wong, f; Dwight Butcher, v/y/g; Lou Herscher, v.
New York, NY   Thursday, June 13, 1933

| C-2099-1 | When Jimmy Rodgers Said Goodbye | Cr 3516 |
| C-2100-1 | When It's Sunset Time In Sunny Tennessee | Cr 3516, Vs 5099, Cont C-3011 |

Varsity 5099, Continental C-3011 as by **Tex Slim**.
Matrix C-2100 is titled *When It's Sunset Time In Tennessee* on Varsity 5099, Continental C-3011. Rev. Continental C-3011 by Johnny Marvin.

Joe Smith (The Colorado Cowboy), v/y-1; acc. Pete Canova, f; own g.
New York, NY   Monday, May 28, 1934

82554-1	When The Sun Hides Away For The Day	BB B-5651, Twin FT1843
82555-1	Clyde Barrow And Bonnie Parker -1	BB B-5521
82556-1	John Dillinger	BB B-5522
82557-1	Kidnapping Is A Terrible Crime -1	BB B-5522
82558-1	Pining For The Pines In Carolin' -1	BB B-5530, RZAu G22366
82559-1	The Wyoming Trail -1	BB B-5530, RZAu G22366
82560-1	Young Man, You'd Better Take Care -1	BB B-5521
83561-1	That Silver-Haired Mother	BB B-5651

Rev. Twin FT1843 by Jimmie Davis.

Dwight Butcher, v/y; acc. own g.
 New York, NY   Friday, October 4, 1934
  38792-A,-B   Sing Me A Melody Of The Mountains   De rejected
  38793-A   Down In The Lone Star State   Pan 25647
  38794-A   I'm Lonesome For The Lone Range   Pan 25647
  38795-A,-B   Ain't No Tellin'   De rejected

Acc. Pete Canova, f; own g.
 New York, NY   Thursday, February 20, 1936
  60528-A   I'm A Broken Hearted Cowboy   Ch 45187, MeC 45187, Min M-14040
  60529-A   Don't Let Your Mother Know (The Way I Am To   De unissued
                Go)
  60530-   I Left My Heart In Old Kentucky   De rejected
  60531--   Roll Along Prairie Moon   Ch 45187, MeC 45187, Min M-14027

Minerva M-14027 as by **Andy Long**, M-14040 as by **The Texas Drifter**.
Revs: Minerva M-14027 by Jimmie & Eddie Dean, M-14040 (with same credit) by Goebel Reeves.
Dwight Butcher also recorded with the Prairie Ramblers, and after 1942.

SLIM BUTCHER

Pseudonym on Varsity for Dwight Butcher.

BEN BUTLER

Pseudonym on Madison for Arthur Fields.

WALLACE BUTLER'S HOTEL DE SOTA ORCHESTRA

An item by this group appeared in the Columbia Old Familiar Tunes series (15018-D) but is believed to be outside the scope of this work.

COTTON BUTTERFIELD

Cotton Butterfield, v; acc. unknown.
 Richmond, VA   Wednesday, October 16, 1929
  403142-   Prisoner At The Bar   OK unissued
  403143-   It Can't Be Done   OK unissued
  403144-   Letter Edged In Black   OK unissued
  403145-   Lullaby Yodel   OK unissued

CHARLES BUTTS SACRED HARP SINGERS

Vocal group; acc. unknown, p.
 Atlanta, GA   Friday, August 3, 1928
  402051-A   Lenox   OK 45251
  402052-B   I Would See Jesus   OK 45252
  402053-   Pisgah   OK unissued
  402054-A   The Promised Land   OK 45252
  402055-   The Bower Of Prayer   OK unissued
  402056-B   Murillo's Lesson   OK 45251
  402057-A,-B   [unknown title]   OK unissued

EZRA BUZZINGTON'S RUSTIC REVELERS

Buzzington's Rube Band: no details
 Richmond, IN   Thursday, July 16, 1925
  12289-A   Brown Jug Blues   Ge [Personal] 20124
  12290-A   Back To That Dear Old Farm   Ge [Personal] 20124

Ezra Buzzington's Rustic Revelers: unknown, t-1; poss. Art Sorensen, tb; Gabe Ward, cl/bscl; unknown, piccolo; Paul "Hezzie" Trietsch, k-2/sw/wb/perc/j-3; Ezra Buzzington (Mark Schaeffer), bj; Ken Trietsch, bb; unidentified, v trio-4; Max Terhune, sp-5.
 Richmond, IN   Saturday, August 18, 1928
  14153-B   Brown Jug Blues -2, 3, 4   Ge 6575, Ch 15581, 45163, Spt 9039,
                                                             Iragen IG-29-01, MW 8049
  14154-A   Bass Blues -1   Ge 6575, Ch 15581, 45163, Spt 9039,
                                                             Iragen IG-29-01, MW 8049
  14155   Rube Band Rehearsal, Part 1 -5   Ge rejected
  14156   Rube Band Rehearsal, Part 2 -5   Ge unissued

Champion 15581 as by **Josh Simpkins & His Rube Band**; 45163 as by **Paul Coleman & His Band**. Supertone 9039 as by **Sam Perry's Rube Band**. Iragen IG-29-01 ("issued through International Records Agency, Richmond Hill, N.Y.") as by **Buzzington's Rustic Revelers**.

Max Terhune With Ezra Buzzington's Rustic Revelers: Max Terhune, v eff; others unknown.
    Richmond, IN   Saturday, August 18, 1928
    14157   Barnyard Imitations   Ge rejected

Prob. same as or similar to above; Ezra Buzzington (Mark Schaeffer), v-1.
    New York, NY   Tuesday, March 12, 1929
    GEX-2181-A,-B   Back To That Dear Old Farm -1   Ge rejected
    GEX-2182   I'll Never Love You   Ge 6894, Ch 15701, Spt 9384

The title of matrix GEX-2182 has also been reported on Gennett and Champion as *Alfalfa*.
Rev. Champion 15701, Supertone 9384 popular.

Prob. same as or similar to above; Ezra Buzzington (Mark Schaeffer), v; Ken Trietsch, v-1.
    New York, NY   Saturday, March 30, 1929
    GEX-2194   Down In Louisiana -1   Ge 6894
    GEX-2195,-A,-B Rollin' Home   Ge rejected

Test pressings of the above two matrices have been reported bearing the date April 2, 1929.
    New York, NY   Wednesday, April 3, 1929
    GEX-2203   Kansas City Kitty   Ge 6816, Ch 15719, Spt 9380
    GEX-2204   That's The Good Old Sunny South   Spt 9380

Supertone 9380 as by **California Wampus Kittens**.
Rev. Gennett 6816, Champion 15719 popular.

Gabe Ward and the Trietsch brothers later formed the Hoosier Hot Shots.

BUZZINGTON'S RUBE BAND
BUZZINGTON'S RUSTIC REVELERS

See Ezra Buzzington's Rustic Revelers.

GEORGE BYERS

Pseudonym on Electron for Frank Luther (see Carson Robison).

LYSLE BYRD

Lysle Byrd, v; acc. unknown, h-1; unknown, g.
    Richmond, IN   Monday, July 29, 1929
    15397   Little Darling Pal Of Mine -1   Ge rejected
    15398   Passing Policeman   Ge unissued

Lysle Byrd recorded on the same day as the African-American artist John Byrd (see *B&GR*) and may himself have been African-American, but the items above are described in Gennett files as "Old Time Singing".

PAUL BYRD

See Johnson County Ramblers.

C

ALBERT CAIN

Albert Cain, v; acc. own g.
    Atlanta, GA   Thursday, October 29, 1931
    405046-2   Pickin' On The Old Guitar   OK 45557
    405047-2   Runnin' Wild   OK 45567
    405048-1   Blue Monday Morning Blues   OK 45557
    405049-1   Tell Me What's The Matter Now   OK 45567

CALAWAY'S WEST VIRGINIA MOUNTAINEERS

Prob.: Bill Charles or Bill Davis, f; John McGhee, h/g; unknown, calls; prob. Miller Wikel, sp; at least one other man, sp.
    Richmond, IN   Monday, June 25, 1928
    13921   The Corn Shuckers Frolic   Ge 6546, Spt 9177
    13922,-A,-B   Grandpapa's Frolic   Ge rejected

Supertone 9177 as by **The West Virginia Hilltoppers**; matrix 13921 is titled *The Cornshucker's Frolic* on that issue.
Revs: Gennett 6546 by John McGhee; Supertone 9177 by Monroe County Bottle Tippers.

This group probably took its name from the talent-scout W.R. Calaway.

SAM CALDWELL

Pseudonym on Supertone for Herbert Sweet.

CALDWELL & BUNCH

Pseudonym on Superior for Arthur Cornwall & John Gibson.

CALDWELL BROTHERS

Pseudonym on Supertone for the Sweet Brothers.

BOB CALEN (INTERNAT'L RODEO ACE)

Bob Calen, v; acc. prob. own g.
    Dallas, TX   Thursday, June 27, 1929

402754-A	Down On The Banks Of The Yazoo	OK 45372
402755-A	Carolina Rolling Stone	OK 45372

JEFF CALHOUN
JESS CALHOUN

Pseudonyms on Grey Gull, Radiex, Supreme, and Madison for both Vernon Dalhart and Frank Luther.

CALHOUN SACRED QUARTET

Lawrence D. Neal, tv; C. Philip Reeve, tv; C. Ernest Moody, bv; George Pickard, bsv; acc. Jewell Reeve, p.
    Atlanta, GA   Wednesday, February 16, 1927

37904-1,-2	Purer in Heart	Vi unissued
37905-1	Life's Railway To Heaven	Vi 20543, MW M-4350, Au 215
37906-1,-2	Just Outside The Door	Vi unissued
37907-1	The Church In The Wildwood	Vi 20543, MW M-8116, Au 215

Rev. Montgomery Ward M-4350 by Asher & Rodeheaver (sacred); M-8116 by Vaughan's Texas Quartet.

CALIFORNIA AEOLIANS

Vocal quartet; unacc.
    New York, NY   July 1931

151673-2	The Rose Of Sharon	Co 15699-D
151677-2	The Old Rugged Cross	Co 15699-D

Intervening matrices are untraced.

CALIFORNIA WAMPUS KITTENS

Pseudonym on Supertone for Ezra Buzzington's Rustic Revelers.

HOMER CALLAHAN
WALTER CALLAHAN

See Callahan Brothers.

CALLAHAN BROTHERS
CALLAHAN FAMILY

Callahan Brothers: Homer Callahan, Walter Callahan, v/y-1 duet; acc. own g duet; or **Homer Callahan**-2, v/y; acc. own g; or **Walter Callahan**-3, v/y; acc. own g.
    New York, NY   Tuesday, January 2, 1934

14507-2	Once I Had A Darling Mother	Ba 32955, Me M12898, MeC 91725, Or 8300, Pe 12973, Ro 5300, Cq 8275, Vo/OK 04359, Co 37633, 20232
14508-1	Gonna Quit My Rowdy Ways -1	Ba 33004, Me M12955, Or 8316, Pe 12987, Ro 5316, Cq 8334, Min M-900
14509-1	She's My Curly Headed Baby -1	Ba 32955, Me M12898, MeC 91725, Or 8300, Pe 12973, Ro 5300, Cq 8275, Vo/OK 04359, Co 37633, 20232
14510-2	St. Louis Blues -1	Ba 32954, Me M12897, MeC 91724, Or 8299, Pe 12972, Ro 5299, Cq 8274, Vo/OK 04358
14511-1	Asheville Blues -2	Ba 33093, Me M13057, MeC 91843, Or 8348, Pe 13013, Ro 5348, Cq 9145
14512-1	Mean Mama -3	Ba 33093, Me M13057, MeC 91843, Or 8348, Pe 13013, Ro 5348, Cq 8481
14513-	I Would If I Could But I Can't	ARC rejected

Matrix 14512 is mistakenly credited to **Homer Callahan** on Oriole 8348. Matrix 14509 is titled *She's My Curley Headed Baby* on Vocalion/OKeh 04359. Rev. Minerva M-900 by Cliff Carlisle & Wilbur Ball.

New York, NY			Wednesday, January 3, 1934
14520-1		True Lover	Ba 33056, Me M13018, Or 8335, Pe 13004, Ro 5335, Cq 8336
14521-1		I Don't Want To Hear Your Name -1	Ba 32954, Me M12897, MeC 91724, Or 8299, Pe 12972, Ro 5299, Cq 8274, Vo/OK 04358
14524-2		Katie Dear (Silver Dagger)	Ba 33103, Me M13071, Or 8353, Pe 13017, Ro 5353
14525-2		North Carolina Moon -1	Ba 33056, Me M13018, Or 8335, Pe 13004, Ro 5335, Cq 8335

Intervening matrices are by Jack Hylton & His Orchestra (popular).

Callahan Brothers: Homer Callahan, Walter Callahan, v duet; acc. own g duet; or **Walter Callahan**-1, v; acc. Homer Callahan, g; own g.

New York, NY			Friday, January 5, 1934
14531-1		Don't You Remember The Time	Ba 33103, Me M13071, Or 8353, Pe 13017, Ro 5353, Cq 8336
14532-2		Corn Licker Rag	Ba 33373, Me M13340, Or 8443, Pe 13121, Ro 5443, Cq 8335
14533-1,-2		She's Killing Me -1	Ba 33004, Me M12955, Or 8316, Pe 12987, Ro 5316, Cq 8334

Callahan Brothers: Homer Callahan, Walter Callahan, v/y-1 duet; acc. own g duet; or **Callahan Family**-2: Homer Callahan, Walter Callahan, Alma Callahan, v trio; acc. Homer Callahan, g; Walter Callahan, g.

New York NY			Thursday, August 16, 1934
15637-1		Mother, Pal And Sweetheart -2	Ba 33240, Me M13207, MeC 91907, Or 8390, Pe 13071, Ro 5390, Cq 8394
15638-1		I'm Alone Because I Love You -2	Ba 33240, Me M13207, MeC 91907, Or 8390, Pe 13071, Ro 5390, Cq 8394
15639-1		New Birmingham Jail No. 3 -1	Ba 33180, Me M13147, MeC 91878, Or 8376, Pe 13045, Ro 5376, Cq 8384, Vo/OK 04360
15640-2		I'll Be Thinking Of The Days Gone By	ARC 351028, Cq 8584
15660-2		T.B. Blues No. 2 -1	Ba 33414, Me M13381, Or 8458, Pe 13135, Ro 5458, Cq 8501, Vo/OK 04362, Co 37634, 20233
15661-1		If I Could Only Hear My Mother Pray Again -2	Ba 33243, Me M13210, MeC 91910, Or 8393, Pe 13074, Ro 5393, Cq 8404, Vo/OK 04361, Co 37673, 20272
15662-1		Lord I'm Coming Home -2	Ba 33243, Me M13210, MeC 91910, Or 8393, Pe 13074, Ro 5393, Cq 8404, Vo/OK 04361, Co 37673, 20272

Matrix 15661 is titled *If I Could Hear My Mother Pray Again* on Conqueror 8404.

Callahan Brothers: Homer Callahan, Walter Callahan, v/y-1 duet; acc. own g duet; or **Homer Callahan**-2, v/y; acc. own g.

New York, NY			Friday, August 17, 1934
15667-1		My Good Gal Has Thrown Me Down -2	Ba 33308, Me M13275, Or 8414, Pe 13098, Ro 5414, Cq 8429
15668-1		Seventeen Years Ago	ARC 5-11-62
15669-1		Rattlesnake Daddy -2	Ba 33414, Me M13381, Or 8458, Pe 13135, Ro 5458, Cq 8501, Vo/OK 04362, Co 37634, 20233
15670-2		Would If I Could (But I Can't)	Ba 33373, Me M13340, Or 8443, Pe 13121, Ro 5443, Cq 8481
15671-2		On The Banks Of The Ohio	ARC 5-12-60, Cq 8588
15672-1		Mama Why Treat Me That Way -1	Ba 33308, Me M13275, Or 8414, Pe 13098, Ro 5414, Cq 8429
15673-2		Going To Heaven On My Own Expense	ARC 5-12-60, Cq 8588

Matrix 15669 is titled *Rattle Snake Daddy* on Vocalion/OKeh 04362, Columbia 37634, 20233.

New York, NY			Monday, August 20, 1934
15674-2		Little Poplar Log House On The Hill	Ba 33180, Me M13147, MeC 91878, Or 8376, Pe 13045, Ro 5376, Cq 8384, Vo/OK 04360

Callahan Brothers: Homer Callahan, Walter Callahan, v/y-1 duet; acc. own g duet; or **Homer Callahan**-2, v/y; acc. own g; or **Walter Callahan**-3, v/y; acc. own g.

New York, NY			Tuesday, April 9, 1935
17273-1		She's My Curly Headed Baby No. 2 -1	ARC 351028, Cq 8584
17274-1		I've Just Been A Brakeman -2	ARC 6-02-59

17275-2	Take The News To Mother	ARC 6-06-57, Cq 8689, Vo/OK 02973, Co 37601, 20200
17276-1	Drive My Blues Away -2	ARC 351011, Cq 8557, MeC 92094
17277-1,2	Daddy Dear I Can't Forget You-3	ARC rejected

New York, NY — Wednesday, April 10, 1935

| 17278-2 | I've Rode The Southern And The L. & N. -2 | ARC 351011, Cq 8557, MeC 92094 |

New York, NY — Thursday, April 11, 1935

17285-2	When A Man's Lonesome -1	Ba 33486, Me M13453, Or 8490, Pe 13160, Ro 5490
17286-1	Just One Little Kiss -1	Ba 33486, Me M13453, Or 8490, Pe 13160, Ro 5490
17287-2	Goodbye, Sweetheart, Goodbye	ARC 7-09-59, Cq 8948, Vo/OK 03335, Co 37617, 20216
17288-2	Lonesome And Weary Blues -3	ARC 6-04-59, Cq 8627
17289-2	Rounder's Luck -2	ARC 6-02-59
17290-1	Days Are Blue	ARC 5-11-62
17291-1	Brown's Ferry Blues No. 2	ARC 6-04-59, Cq 8627
17292-1	The Price I Had To Pay	Vo 04483, Cq 9144

Matrix 17287 is titled *Goodbye, Sweetheart Goodbye* on Columbia 37617. Homer Callahan does not yodel on matrix 17289.

Homer Callahan, Walter Callahan, v/y-1 duet; acc. own g duet.

New York, NY — Thursday, April 2, 1936

| 18913-2 | Carolina Sweetheart-1 | ARC 6-11-51, Cq 8690 |

New York, NY — Saturday, April 4, 1936

18928-1	Freight Train Blues -1	ARC 6-09-53, Cq 8731, Vo/OK 03171, Co 37613, 20212
18929-2	Maple On The Hill	ARC 6-06-57, Cq 8689, Vo/OK 02973, Co 37601, 20200
18930-1	Greenback Dollar	ARC 6-07-52, Cq 8682, Vo/OK 03108, Co 37608, 20207
18931-2	Gonna Quit Drinkin' When I Die -1	ARC 6-07-51, Cq 8731, Vo/OK 04363

New York, NY — Monday, April 6, 1936

18932-1	Sweet Violets -1	ARC 6-07-51, Cq 8682, Vo/OK 04363
18933-2	Just One Year	ARC 6-07-52, Vo/OK 03108, Co 37608, 20207
18934-1	When It's Lamplighting Time Up In Heaven	ARC 6-11-51, Cq 8690
18938-2	Cowboy Jack	ARC 6-09-53, Vo/OK 03171, Co 37613, 20212

Intervening matrices are by other artists.

Acc. Roy "Shorty" Hobbs, md; own g duet.

New York, NY — Sunday, December 20, 1936

20428-1,-2	Memories Of My Father -1	ARC unissued
20429-2	Away Out There -1	ARC 7-05-59, Cq 8854
20430-2	The Dying Girl's Farewell	Vo 04483, Cq 9144
20431-2	The End Of Memory Lane	ARC 7-06-69
20432-1	I Want To Be Where You Are -1	ARC 7-05-59, Cq 8854

New York, NY — Monday, December 21, 1936

| 20433-1 | Mama Don't Be So Mean To Me -1 | ARC 7-08-61, Cq 8881 |
| 20434-1 | She's My Curly Headed Baby No. 3 -1 | ARC 7-09-59, Cq 8948, Vo/OK 03335, Co 37617, 20216 |

New York, NY — Tuesday, December 22, 1936

20441-2	She Came Rollin' Down The Mountain	ARC unissued: OH OHS90031 (LP)
20442-1	I Don't Want To Hear Your Name No. 2 -1	ARC 7-04-63, Cq 8825
20443-3	She's Just That Kind No. 2 -1	ARC 7-08-61, Cq 8881
20444-1	Freight Train Whistle Blues No. 2	ARC 7-06-69
20445-1	She's Always On My Mind -1	ARC 7-03-64, Cq 8790
20446-2	Somebody's Been Using That Thing -1	ARC 7-03-64, Cq 8790

New York, NY — Wednesday, December 23, 1936

| 20447-2 | Ninety-Nine's My Name | ARC 7-04-63, Cq 8825 |

Acc. own g duet.

Chicago, IL — Thursday, February 16, 1939

C-2501-3	Dovie Darling -1	Vo 04883
C-2502-2	I Got Her Boozy	Vo unissued: OH OHS90031 (LP)
C-2503-3	Oh Lord Show Me The Light	Vo 04883
C-2504-1,-2	A Little Story	Vo unissued

Chicago, IL   Friday, February 17, 1939

C-2505-2	Lonesome Freight Train Blues -1	Vo/OK 04779, Cq 9223, Co 37638, 20237
C-2506-1	The Best Pal I Had Is Gone -1	Vo 04716, Cq 9222
C-2507-1	I Want To Ask The Stars	Vo 04716, Cq 9222
C-2508-1	My Blue Eyed Jane	Vo/OK 04779, Cq 9223, Co 37638, 20237

Homer Callahan, Walter Callahan, v/y-1 duet; or Walter Callahan, v-2; acc. Homer Callahan, h-3/g or sb; Paul Buskirk, md; Walter Callahan, g; unknown, g or sb.

Dallas, TX   Sunday, April 27, 1941

93685-A	They're At Rest Together -1	De 5952
93686-A	John Henry -1, 3	De 5998, 46104
93687-A	Sweet Thing -2	De 5952, 46104
93688-A	My Darling Little Girl	De 6045
93689-A	A Jealous Woman Won't Do	De 5998
93690-A	Now He's In Heaven	De rejected
93691-A	Sad Memories	De 6045

Homer and Walter Callahan later became known as Bill and Joe Callahan respectively. They recorded after 1942.

REV. JOSEPH CALLENDER

Rev. Joseph Callender, v; acc. own g.

Richmond, IN   Friday, June 1, 1928

| 13880 | In The Beautiful Land | Ge 6582 |
| 13881 | God Leads His Dear Children Along | Ge 6582 |

Richmond, IN   Friday, April 5, 1929

15008	In The Garden Of My Heart	Ge 6843
15009,-A,-B	Peace	Ge rejected
15010	It Won't Be Long, It May Be Soon	Ge 6843, Ch 15733
15011-A	The Haven Of Rest	Ch 15733
15012,-A	I'm Glad That Jesus Won	Ge rejected
15013,-A	God Is Still On The Throne	Ge rejected

Champion 15733 as by **Rev. George M. Brooks**.

AARON CAMPBELL'S MOUNTAINEERS

Unknown, h-1; Aaron Campbell, sg-2/g-3/v; prob. Buddy Webber, g-4/sb-5/v-6.

Richmond, IN   Monday, November 6, 1933

19346	The Man On The Flying Trapeze -1, 3, 5	Ch 16689, 45038
19347	Pride Of The Prairie, Mary -1, 3/4, 6	Ch S-16740, 45086, MeC 45086
19348	The Captain With His Whiskers -1, 3, 5	Ch 16689, 45038
19349	Mother's Knee -2, 4, 6	Ch S-16740, 45086, MeC 45086
19350	Daisies Won't Tell -1?, 3?	Ch S-16751, 45008

Rev. Champion S-16751, 45008 by "Ted" Sharp, Hinman & Sharp.

This group also accompanies Irene Sanders.

ORAN CAMPBELL

Pseudonym on Champion and Herwin for David Miller.

CAMPBELL BROTHERS (CECIL & ED)

Cecil Campbell, Ed Campbell, v duet; acc. Cecil Campbell, sg; prob. Harry Blair, g; poss. Happy Morris, g.

Charlotte, NC   Monday, June 22, 1936

| 102806-1 | Last Night I Had A Dream Of Home | BB B-6821 |
| 102807-1 | She Is Waiting For You In That Happy Home | BB B-6821 |

Cecil Campbell sings lead and Ed Campbell tenor.

Cecil Campbell also recorded with Dick Hartman, Tennessee Ramblers [II] and after 1942.

CAMPBELL'S SACRED SINGERS

Pseudonym on Aurora A22034 for Criterion Male Quartet (*Old Rugged Cross*) or Kanawha Singers (*Shall We Gather At The River*), and on A22035 for Old Southern Sacred Singers.

HARMON CANADA

Harmon Canada, sp-1/v-2; acc. Fred Roberts, f-3; own g.

Richmond, IN   Friday, August 9, 1929

15422-A	The Talkin' Blues -1	Ge 6972, Ch 15808, 45173, Spt 9554
15423	Born In Hard Luck -1	Ge 6972, Ch 15808, 45173, Spt 9554
15424	My Little Home In Tennessee -2, 3	Ge 6961, Spt 9495

Champion 15808, 45173 as by **Joe Smith**.

Fred Roberts & Harmon Canada, v duet; acc. Fred Roberts, f; Harmon Canada, g.
   Richmond, IN   Friday, August 9, 1929
     15425   Take Me Back To My Dear Old Georgia Home   Ge 6961, Spt 9495

Supertone 9495 as by **Roberts & Canada**.

JIMMY CANNON

Pseudonym on Domino for Vernon Dalhart.

CANOVA FAMILY

Julietta Canova, v; or **Anna & Julietta Canova**-1, v duet; acc. prob. Pete Canova, f; prob. Zeke Canova, g.
   New York, NY   Monday, September 10, 1928
     28183   I Wish I Was A Single Gal Again   Br 264
     28184   The Frog Went A-Courtin' -1   Br 264

Julietta Canova is better known as Judy Canova.

The Three Crackers: Anne Canova, Judy Canova, Zeke Canova, v trio; acc. prob. Goebel Reeves, g/y.
   New York, NY   c. November 3, 1930
     GEX-2797,-A   Hannah My Love   Ge rejected
     GEX-2798   Reckless Love   Ge rejected

Judy (Cracker) Canova, v; acc. poss. Zeke Canova, p.
   New York, NY   c. November 5, 1930
     GEX-2801   I Ain't Got Nobody   Ge rejected
     GEX-2802   Nobody Cares If I'm Blue   Ge rejected

The Three Crackers: Anne Canova, Judy Canova, Zeke Canova, v trio; acc. unknown, o.
   New York, NY   c. November 5, 1930
     GEX-2803   Jesus Gives Me Peace   Ge unissued
     GEX-2804   Kept For Jesus   Ge unissued

Leon Canova & Judy Canova: no details.
   New York, NY   c. November 5, 1930
     GEX-2807   Whippoorwill/Hog Horse   Ge rejected
     GEX-2808   Meadlowlark/Screech Owl/Raincrow/Mocking Bird   Ge rejected

Matrices GEX-2805/06 are by Goebel Reeves.

The Three Crackers: Anne Canova, Judy Canova, Zeke Canova, v trio; acc. unknown, o-1; Goebel Reeves, g-2/y-3/sp-4.
   New York, NY   c. November 17, 1930
     GEX-2814,-A   O Happy Day -1, 4   Ge rejected
     GEX-2815   No Not One -1   Ge rejected
     GEX-2816   Hannah My Love -2, 3   Ch 16146
     GEX-2817-A   Reckless Love -2, 3   Ch 16146

Champion 16146 as by **The Clemens Family**.

Annie, Judy & Zeke Canova, v trio; acc. Pete Canova, f; Zeke Canova, g.
   New York, NY   Tuesday, December 2, 1930
     10289-   I've Been Hoodooed   ARC unissued
     10290-1   The Poor Little Thing Cried Mammy   Ba 32127, Or 8044, Pe 12685, Ro 5044
     10291-   Where Is My Wandering Boy   ARC unissued

Acc. Pete Canova, f; unknown, h; Zeke Canova, g; Judy Canova, y-1.
   New York, NY   Friday, December 5, 1930
     10303-   There's Not A Friend   ARC unissued
     10304-1,-3   Whoa Back Buck -1   Ba 32126, Or 8043, Pe 12684, Ro 5043
     10305-   Got The Fever In My Bones   ARC unissued

Acc. Pete Canova, f; unknown, h-1; Zeke Canova, g/sp-2; Judy Canova, y-3/prob. sp-3.
   New York, NY   Monday, December 8, 1930
     10306-   Snake Eyed Killing Dude   Ba 32137, Or 8057, Pe 12700, Ro 5057
     10307-1,-2   Reckless Love   Ba 32127, Or 8044, Pe 12685, Ro 5044
     10308-1   Hannah My Love -1, 2, 3   Ba 32126, Or 8043, Pe 12684, Ro 5043
     10309-3   The Fatal Shot   Ba 32137, Or 8057, Pe 12700, Ro 5057, Cq 7724, Bwy 4052

Conqueror 7724 as by **Annie, Judie & Zeke Canova**.
Revs: Conqueror 7724 by Vernon Dalhart; Broadway 4052 by Carson Robison Trio.

The Clemens Family: Anne Canova, Judy Canova, Zeke Canova, v trio; acc. unknown, h-1; prob. Zeke Canova, g.
   New York, NY   c. December 9, 1930
     GEX-2836   I've Been Hoodooed   Ch 16188
     GEX-2837   Poor Little Thing Cried Mammy -1   Ch 16188

This session was logged as by **The Three Crackers** but Champion 16188 was issued as shown.

Three Georgia Crackers: Anne Canova, Judy Canova, Zeke Canova, v trio; acc. Zeke Canova, g.
    New York, NY   Thursday, December 18, 1930

151159-3	I've Been Hoodooed	Co 15630-D, ReE MR457, ReAu G21370
151160-2	Pore Little Thing Cried Mammy	Co 15653-D
151165-2	Whoa, Buck, Whoa	Co 15630-D, ReE MR457, ReAu G21370

Regals as by **The Three Georgian Crackers**.
    New York, NY   Friday, December 19, 1930

151166-	Nothin' But The Blood Of Jesus	Co unissued
151167-2	Why Did They Dig Ma's Grave So Deep?	ReE MR504, ReAu G21428
151168-2	Hannah, My Love	Co 15653-D, ReE MR504, ReAu G21428

Regals as by **The Three Georgian Crackers**.

Anne, Judy & Zeke With Pete: prob.: Anne Canova, Judy Canova, Zeke Canova, v trio; acc. Pete Canova, f; Zeke Canova, g.
    New York, NY   Monday, December 11, 1933

152590-1	Mississippi Waters	OK 45578
152591-2	Don't Let My Mother Know	OK 45578

Anne, Judy & Zeke: Anne Canova, Judy Canova, Zeke Canova, v trio; acc. Pete Canova, f; unknown, h-1; Zeke Canova, g; unknown, sb; unknown, sw-2; unknown, bones-3; prob. Judy Canova, y-4.
    New York, NY   Monday, December 11, 1933

152592-2	When The Sun Goes Down Behind The Hill (And The Moon Begins To Rise)	OK 45576
152593-1	Me And My Still -1, 2, 3, 4	OK 45576

Anne, Judy & Zeke With Pete: prob.: Anne Canova, Judy Canova, Zeke Canova, v trio; acc. Pete Canova, f; Zeke Canova, g.
    New York, NY   Monday, December 11, 1933

152594-	My Old Model T	Co/OK unissued
152595-	Ain't Gonna Grieve My Lord Anymore	Co/OK unissued

Judy Canova, v; acc. Spade Cooley, f; Mischa Russell, f; Paul Sells, pac; Frank Marvin, esg; Johnny Bond, g; Dick Reinhart, sb.
    Hollywood, CA   Monday, December 15, 1941

H-602-	I've Cried My Last Tear Over You	OK unissued
H-603-1	Is It True	OK 6683
H-604-1	Some One	OK 6683
H-605-	I Love You Too Much	OK unissued

Judy Canova recorded after 1942.

CAP, ANDY & FLIP

See Warren Caplinger.

WARREN CAPLINGER

Warren Caplinger's Cumberland Mountain Entertainers: George Rainey, f/sp-1; Willie Rainey, bj; Albert Rainey, g; Andy Patterson, poss. g/v-2/sp-3/calls-4; Warren Caplinger, v-5/sp-6; band v-7/sp-8.
    Ashland, KY   Wednesday, February 8, 1928

AL-150	Nobody's Business -2, 7	Br 224
AL-158	Chicken Reel -1, 3, 4, 6	Vo 5222
AL-167/68*	Jerusalem Mourn -5, 7	Vo 5240
AL-176	G'wine To Raise A Rucas Tonight -2, 7	Vo 5222
AL-178	Big Ball In Town -2, 7, 8	Br 241
AL-179	McDonald's Farm -2, 3, 7, 8	Br 224
AL-181	Saro -2 (lead), 5	Br 241

Intervening matrices are untraced except AL-169 by the All Star Entertainers; some are doubtless unissued takes of the above items, and others may be unissued titles. Rev. Vocalion 5240 by The Hill Billies.

Unidentified v quartet; acc. George Rainey, f; Willie Rainey, bj; Albert Rainey, g; Andy Patterson, g.
    Ashland, KY   Friday, February 10, 1928

AL-200*/01	When The Redeemed Are Gathering In	Vo 5237

Acc. unidentified, md; unidentified, g.
    Ashland, KY   Friday, February 10, 1928

AL-202/203*	Just Over Jordan	Vo 5237

Patterson, Caplinger & The Dixie Harmonizers-1/Warren Caplinger & The Dixie Harmonizers-2/The Dixie Harmonizers-3/Caplinger, Patterson & The Dixie Harmonizers-4: Andy Patterson, f/v-5; unknown, md-6/v-7; Warren Caplinger, g/v; unknown, v-8.
    Richmond, IN   Tuesday, May 21, 1929

15121	My Wife's Gone To The Country -1, 5, 6, 7, 8	Ge 6872, Ch 15770, Spt 9473
15122-A	The Music Man -2	Ge 6915
15123,-A	Mourn, Jerusalem, Mourn -2	Ge rejected
15124-A	Gonna Raise A Ruckus Tonight -1, 5, 6, 7, 8	Ge 6872, Ch 15770, Spt 9473
15125,-A	On The Banks Of The Silvery Stream -3	Ge rejected
15126	Green Valley Waltz -4, 5, 6	Ge 6915
15127,-A	Sugar Plum Blues -3	Ge rejected

Champion 15770 as by **The Kentucky Serenaders**. Supertone 9473 as by **The Georgia Serenaders**.

Andy Patterson, v; acc. prob. own g.
  Richmond, IN   Tuesday, May 21, 1929

15128,-A	All Day Long	Ge rejected
15129,-A	Willis Mabry (In The Hills Of Rowan County)	Ge rejected

Caplinger, Patterson & The Dixie Harmonizers-1/**Andy Patterson**-2: prob.: Andy Patterson, f/v; Warren Caplinger, g/v-3.
  Richmond, IN   Thursday, May 23, 1929

15130,-A	Saro -1, 3	Ge rejected
15131,-A	Cleveland Hospital Disaster -2	Ge rejected

Warren & Everett Caplinger-1/**Patterson & Caplinger**-2/**Everett & Warren Caplinger**-3: Andy Patterson, f/v-4; Warren Caplinger, g/v; Everett Caplinger, v-5.
  Richmond, IN   Monday, September 9, 1929

15572,-A	The Long Tongued Woman -1, 5	Ge rejected
15573-A	On The Banks Of That Silvery Stream -2, 4	Ge 7003, Ch 15855, Spt 9541
15574	The Black Sheep -2, 4	Ge 7003
15575,-A	When I Had But Fifty Cents -3, 5	Ge rejected

Champion 15855 as by **Roland & Young**. Supertone 9541 as by **White & Dawson**.
Revs: Champion 15855 by Walter Smith; Supertone 9541 by Asa Martin & Doc Roberts

Patterson & Caplinger: Andy Patterson, Warren Caplinger, v duet; acc. unknown, md; Warren Caplinger, g.
  Richmond, IN   Monday, June 9, 1930

16743	Advice To Wife Seekers	Spr 2523
16745	Advice To Husband Seekers	Spr 2523

Superior 2523 as by **Dickson & Carroll**.
Matrices 16744, 16746 are by Carolina Gospel Singers.

Acc. Andy Patterson, f-1; unknown, md-2; Warren Caplinger, g.
  Richmond, IN   Monday, June 9, 1930

16747,-A	Roll 'Em Girls, Roll 'Em	Ge rejected
16748,-A	Long Tongue Women -2	Ge rejected
16749,-A	Did You See My Lovin' Henry -1	Ge rejected
16750.-A	I'm Tyin' The Leaves So They Won't Come Down	Ge rejected
16751,-A	Willie Mabery -1	Ge rejected

Andy Patterson, v; acc. prob. own g.
  Richmond, IN   Monday, June 9, 1930

16752,-A,-B	Pumpkin Pies That Mother Used To Make	Ge rejected

Cap, Andy & Flip: Warren Caplinger, Andy Patterson, William A. "Flip" Strickland, v trio; acc. "Flip" Strickland, md; Andy Patterson, g.
  Farimont, WV   ca. 1936-1938

A-100	Starlit Heaven	Universal unnumbered
A-101	I'm Homesick For Heaven	Universal unnumbered

The above two items are coupled.

Warren Caplinger, Andy Patterson, Flip Strickland, v trio; or Andy Patterson, v-1; acc. Flip Strickland, md-2; Andy Patterson, g.
  poss. Charleston, WV   Thursday, November 9, 1939

19996	I'm Taking My Audition To Sing Up In The Sky -2	FM unnumbered
19997	Lover's Message	FM unnumbered
19998	McBeth Mine Explosion -1, 2	FM unnumbered
19999	Television In The Sky -2	FM unnumbered
20000	Nobody Answered Me	FM unnumbered
20001	I'll Be Listening	FM unnumbered

These are Gennett matrices, used for personal recordings issued on the group's Fireside Melodies label, coupled 19996/19997, 19998/19999, and 20000/20001.

Cap, Andy, & Flip: Warren Caplinger, Andy Patterson, Flip Strickland, v trio; or Andy Patterson, v-1; acc. Flip Strickland, md-2; Andy Patterson, g.
  poss. Charleston, WV   late 1940

20061	My Dear Baby Girl -1	FM unnumbered
20062	Remember Me -2?	FM unnumbered
20063	Star-Lit Heaven -2?	FM unnumbered
20064	Shake My Mothers [sic] Hand For Me -2?	FM unnumbered
20065	Yes We Have A Friend In Daddy -2?	FM unnumbered

These are Gennett matrices, used for personal recordings issued on the group's Fireside Melodies label, coupled 19999 (see previous session)/20061, 20062/20064, and 20063/20065.

Warren Caplinger and Andy Patterson recorded after 1942 with their sons Omer and Milt, respectively, as **Cap, Andy, Milt & Omar** [sic].

CAPT. APPLEBLOSSOM

This artist's real name is Lloyd Yarbrough.

Capt. Appleblossom, v; acc. prob. own g.
    Dallas, TX   Thursday, June 27, 1929

402746-A	When Father Put The Paper On The Wall	OK 45416
402747-A	The Book Of Etiquette	OK 45416, PaE R1081, PaAu A3515
402748-A	The Cowboy's Lament	OK 45373
402749-A	Time Table Blues	OK 45373

Parlophone A3515 as by **Captain Appleblossom**. Revs: Parlophone R1081 by Frank Marvin, A3515 by Jerry Behrens.

KEN CARD

Ken Card, v; acc. prob.: Bill Benner, f; Bill Butler, sg; Ray Whitley, g.
    New York, NY   Wednesday, August 28, 1935

39907-A,-B	Will Rogers (Your Friend And My Friend)	De unissued
39908-A,-B	The Last Flight Of Wiley Post	De unissued

Acc. Bill Benner, f; Bill Butler, sg; Ray Whitley, g/v-1.
    New York, NY   Thursday, September 26, 1935

60002-B	The Last Flight Of Wiley Post	Ch 45148, MW 4941, MeC 45148
60003-A	Will Rogers Your Friend And My Friend -1	Ch 45148, MW 4941, MeC 45148

Decca ledgers indicate that matrices 39907/08 were scheduled to be issued on Montgomery Ward 4941, but reported copies of that issue use matrices 60002/03.

IKE CARGILL

Ike Cargill, v; acc. —— Keenan, f; prob. own g.
    Dallas, TX   Friday, September 20, 1935

DAL-100-1	I'm Going Where The Blues Ain't Never Known	Vo 03087, ARC 6-09-63
DAL-101-2	You're Gonna Miss Me Mama	Vo 03105
DAL-102-2	I'm Through With Women Blues	Vo 03163
DAL-120-2	It's All Because That I Love You	Vo 03087, ARC 6-09-63

Matrices DAL-103/04 are by Dallas Jamboree Jug Band (see *B&GR*); DAL-105 through 112 by Light Crust Doughboys.

Ike Cargill, v/y-1; acc. —— Keenan, f; prob. own g.
    Dallas, TX   Saturday, September 21, 1935

DAL-113-1,-2	I've Been Looking For A Sweetheart	ARC unissued
DAL-114-1,-2	Old Fashioned Mother	ARC unissued
DAL-115-2	If I Was Rich By Gum	Vo 03105
DAL-116-1,-2	I Killed My Daddy	ARC unissued
DAL-117-1,-2	Rainbow Lady	ARC unissued
DAL-118-1	I Know I've Got The Meanest Mama -1	Vo 03163
DAL-119-1,-2	Something Eatin' On Me Blues	ARC unissued

CARL & HARTY

See Karl & Harty.

BILL CARLISLE

Bill Carlisle, v/y; acc. own g.
    New York, NY   Monday, July 24, 1933

13626-1	Rattlesnake Daddy	Vo 25020, 04645
13627-1	Virginia Blues	Vo 25020
13627-2	Virginia Blues	Vo 25020, 04645

Bill Carlisle, v/y-1; acc. Cliff Carlisle, sg-2; own g.
    New York, NY   Tuesday, July 25, 1933

13635-2	Lost On Life's Sea -1, 2	Vo 02528
13637-1	The Final Farewell	Vo 25021

Matrix 13636 is by Cliff Carlisle.

New York, NY　　　　　　　　　　　　　　　　　　　　　　　　Wednesday, July 26, 1933

13648-1	The Little Dobie Shack -2	Vo 25021

Bill Carlisle, v; acc. own h-1/g; Cliff Carlisle, sg-2/v eff-3.

New York, NY　　　　　　　　　　　　　　　　　　　　　　　　Monday, July 31, 1933

13689-2	Blue Eyes	Vo 02528
13690-1	Don't Marry The Wrong Woman -2	Vo 02529
13691-1	Barnyard Tumble -1, 3	Vo 02529

Smiling Bill Carlisle, v/y-1; acc. own g.

New York, NY　　　　　　　　　　　　　　　　　　　　　　　　Tuesday, August 28, 1934

15772-1	Duvall County Blues	Vo 02831
15777-1	Sugar Cane Mama	Vo 02797
15778-1,-2	String Bean Mama -1	Vo 02797
15779-1	Copper Head Mama -1	Vo 02831

Matrices 15777/78 were logged as by **Wild Bill Carlisle** but issued as shown. Intervening matrices are by Cliff Carlisle.

Bill Carlisle-1/**Wild Bill Carlisle**-2, v; acc. own g.

New York, NY　　　　　　　　　　　　　　　　　　　　　　　　Wednesday, August 29, 1934

15789-	A Letter To Dad In The Skies -1	Vo unissued
15790-	Let's Dream Of Each Other -2	Vo unissued

Smiling Bill Carlisle, v; acc. own h-1/g.

New York, NY　　　　　　　　　　　　　　　　　　　　　　　　Friday, August 31, 1934

15792-1	Little Wild Rose	Vo 02928, RZAu G22549
15793-2	Beneath The Weeping Willow Tree -1	Vo 02839, RZAu G22402
15794-1	Bachelor's Blues	Vo 02819, RZAu G22337

New York, NY　　　　　　　　　　　　　　　　　　　　　　　　Wednesday, September 4, 1934

15821-2	Penitentiary Blues	Vo 02819, RZAu G22337
15822-2	Cowboy Jack	Vo 02839, RZAu G22402
15829-1	Little Honey Bee -1	Vo 02928, RZAu G22549

Intervening matrices are by Cliff Carlisle or Carlisle Brothers.

Bill Carlisle, v/y-1; acc. own g.

New York, NY　　　　　　　　　　　　　　　　　　　　　　　　Thursday, April 25, 1935

17369-2	There's A Mouse Been Messin' Around -1	Vo 02946, ARC 6-12-56, Cq 8736
17370-1	Bell Clapper Mama -1	Vo 03018
17371-	Heart Broken Blues -1	ARC unissued
17372-1	Jumpin' And Jerkin' Blues	Vo 02984, ARC 7-02-64, Cq 8789
17373-2	Gonna Kill Myself (Good Gracious Me)	Vo 02946, ARC 6-12-56, Cq 8736
17374-1	Sin Has Caused So Many Tears	ARC 7-04-58, Cq 8802
17415-1	When I Grow Too Old To Dream	Vo 02966

ARC and Conqueror issues as by **Bill Carlisle**.

New York, NY　　　　　　　　　　　　　　　　　　　　　　　　Friday, April 26, 1935

17383-1	Shirkin' Mama Blues -1	Vo 03062
17384-	Sparkin' My Gal	ARC unissued
17385-1	Women Please Quit Knocking (At My Door)	Vo 03062
17386-1	She's Gone But I'll Meet Her In Heaven	ARC 7-04-58, Cq 8802
17387-2	Long Legged Daddy Blues	Vo 03018
17388-1	Two Eyes Of Blue -1	Vo 02966

ARC 7-04-58, Conqueror 8802 as by **Bill Carlisle**.

New York, NY　　　　　　　　　　　　　　　　　　　　　　　　Monday, April 29, 1935

17401-	Lonesome In Dreams	ARC rejected
17403-1	House Cat Mama -1	Vo 02894, ARC 7-02-64, Cq 8789

ARC 7-02-64, Conqueror 8789 as by **Bill Carlisle**. Matrix 17402 is by Lake Howard.

Acc. own h-2/g.

New York, NY　　　　　　　　　　　　　　　　　　　　　　　　Tuesday, April 30, 1935

17412-	The Midwest Dust Storm	ARC rejected
17413-	So Lonely So Blue -2	ARC rejected

Bill Carlisle, v/y-1; acc. own g; unknown, g-2; prob. Cliff Carlisle, v-3.

Charlotte, NC　　　　　　　　　　　　　　　　　　　　　　　　Tuesday, June 16, 1936

102664-1	Rattlin' Daddy -1	BB B-6478, MW M-7035
102665-1	I'm Wearin' The Britches Now -2, 3	BB B-6478, MW M-7035

Acc. Cliff Carlisle, sg-2/g-3/v-4; own g; Shannon Grayson, g-5; unknown, jh-6.

Charlotte, NC   Thursday, June 18, 1936

102676-1	Still There's A Spark Of Love -3, 4, 5	BB B-6600, MW M-7036
102677-1	The Heavenly Train -4, 6	BB B-7019
102678-1	Cowgirl Jean -1, 3, 4, 5	BB B-6600, MW M-7036, Twin FT8247
102679-1	You're Just Like A Dollar Bill -1	BB B-6608, MW M-7037, Twin FT8247
102680-1	Seeing My Gal	BB B-6775, MW M-7177
102681-1	So Long, Baby -1	BB B-6775
102682-1	I Done It Wrong	BB B-6568, MW M-7038, Twin FT8227
102683-1	I Want A Gal	BB B-6568, MW M-7038, Twin FT8227
102684-1	Ten Or Twelve Times, Maybe More -3, 5	BB B-6608, MW M-7037, Twin FT8246
102685-1	He Will Be Your Savior Too -2, 4	BB B-7019

Rev. Twin FT8246 by Cliff Carlisle.

Bill & Louis Carlisle, v duet; acc. Bill Carlisle, g.

Charlotte, NC   Tuesday, February 16, 1937

| 07069-1 | Blue Arizona Moon | BB B-7087, MW M-7176, Twin FT8494 |
| 07070-1 | Bye, Bye, My Love | BB B-7087, MW M-7176 |

Montgomery Ward M-7176 as by **Bill Carlisle**. Rev. Twin FT8494 by Bill Boyd.

Bill Carlisle, v; acc. own g.

Charlotte, NC   Tuesday, February 16, 1937

07071-1	I'll Be All Smiles, Love	BB B-6938, MW M-7174
07072-1	Dreamy Eyes	BB B-7414
07073-1	Feet, Don't Fail Me	BB B-7153, MW M-7177
07074-1	A Shack By The Side Of The Road	BB B-7702, MW M-7175, RZAu G23634
07075-1	Still There's A Spark Of Love – Part 2	BB B-6938, MW M-7174
07076-1	Why Did The Blue Skies Turn Grey?	BB B-7702, MW M-7175, RZAu G23634

Acc. Shannon Grayson, md-1/g-2; own g; poss. Louis Carlisle, sb.

Charlotte, NC   Friday, August 6, 1937

013011-1	Drifting Together -2	BB B-7414
013012-1	I'll Always Be Your Little Darling -2	BB B-7613, RZAu G23596
013013-1	I Know What It Means To Be Lonesome -1	BB B-7613, RZAu G23596
013014-1	Bell Clappin' Mama -2	BB B-7153

Bill Carlisle's Kentucky Home Boys: Cliff Carlisle, sg-1; Shannon Grayson, md-2/g-3/v-4; Bill Carlisle, g/v; unknown, g-5.

Charlotte, NC   Saturday, June 11, 1938

64136-A	Are You Goin' To Leave Me Lil -1, 2, 4	De 5554
64137-A	The Girl I Left So Blue -1, 2, 4	De 5554
64138-A	No Drunkard Can Enter That Beautiful Home -1, 2	De 5595
64139-A	Moonlight Blues -1, 2, 4	De 5562
64140-A	If Jesus Should Come -2, 4, 5	De 5686
64141-A	No Letter In The Mail Today -2, 4, 5	De 5626
64142-A	I'm On My Way To The Promised Land -1, 2	De 5595
64143-A	Big At The Little, Bottom At The Top -1, 2	De 5562
64144-A	You Said We'd Always Drift Together -3, 5	De 5583, MeC 45271
64145-A	Will You Miss Your Lover -1, 2	De 5583, MeC 45271, Min M-14099
64146-A	Drifting -1, 3, 5	De 5626
64147-A	I'm Headin' For Home Sweet Home -1, 3, 5	De 5686

Rev. Minerva M-14099 by Jimmie Davis.

Bill Carlisle's Kentucky Boys: Cliff Carlisle, sg-1/v-2; Shannon Grayson, md-3/g-4/v-5; Bill Carlisle, g/v; unknown, g-6; Sonny Boy Tommy Carlisle, v-7.

Charlotte, NC   Tuesday, July 25, 1939

66001-A	Wabash Cannon Ball -1, 6	De 5713, 46045, MeC 45326
66002-A	Sparkling Blue Eyes -2, 4, 6	De 5713, 46045, MeC 45326, Min M-14144
66009-A	Ditty Wah Ditty -3, 4, 7	De 5718
66010-A	Don't Be Ashamed Of Mother -5, 6, 7	De 5762
66012-A	A Mouse Been Messin' Around -1, 4	De 5718

Intervening matrices are by Cliff Carlisle or Carlisle Brothers. Rev. Minerva M-14144 by Jimmie Davis.

Charlotte, NC   Wednesday, July 26, 1939

66017-A	Sally Let Your Bangs Hang Down -1, 4, 5	De 5742
66018-A	I Dreamed I Searched Heaven For You -1, 3, 4	De 5724
66019-A	Roll On Old Troubles Roll On -1, 3	De 5724
66021-A	Little Pal -4, 6	De 5742
66023-A	Life's Troubled Pathway -1, 4, 5	De 5762

Intervening matrices are by Carlisle Brothers.
Bill Carlisle recorded after 1942.

CLIFF CARLISLE

Clifford Carlisle Of WLAP, v/y; acc. own sg; Wilbur Ball, g-1/v-2.
   Richmond, IN   Tuesday, February 25, 1930

16316	T For Texas -1	Ge 7206, Spt 9671
16317-A	Yodeling Them Blues Away -2	Spt 9708

Supertone 9671, 9708 as by **Amos Greene**.

Lullaby Larkers Of WLAP: Cliff Carlisle, v/sg; Wilbur Ball, v/g; Rev. Horace A. Booker, v/u.
   Richmond, IN   Tuesday, February 25, 1930

16318	The Streets Of That City	Ge rejected personal recording

Cliff Carlisle, v/y; acc. own sg; Wilbur Ball, g.
   Richmond, IN   Tuesday, February 25, 1930

16319	Down In The Jail House On My Knees	Ge 7153, Ch 15969, Spt 9651
16320-A	Memphis Yodel	Ge 7206, Ch 15969, Spt 9671, MW 8035

Gennett 7206 as by **Clifford Carlisle Of WLAP**. Supertone 9651, 9671 as by **Amos Greene**.
Rev. Gennett 7153, Supertone 9651 by Wilbur Ball.

Acc. own sg-1; Wilbur Ball, g.
   Richmond, IN   Wednesday, April 9, 1930

16464	Blue Yodel No. 6	Ge 7187, Ch 15992, Spt 9710
16465-A	Desert Blues -1	Ge 7187, Ch 15992, 45155, Spt 9710, De 5531
16466-A	Just A Lonely Hobo -1	Ge 7244, Ch 16028, Spt 9709
16467	Virginia Blues -1	Ge 7244, Ch 16028, 45155, Spt 9709, MW 8035, De 5531

Supertone 9709, 9710 as by **Amos Greene**.

Acc. own sg; Wilbur Ball, g-1/v-2.
   Richmond, IN   Monday, July 21, 1930

16840-B	On My Way To Lonesome Valley	Ge 7288, Ch 16094, Spt 9707, Spr 2775, MW 4974
16841	I'm Lonely And Blue -1	Ge 7288, Ch 16094, Spt 9707, MW 4974, MeC 45005
16842	Never No Mo' Blues	Spt 9708
16843,-A	Hobo Bill's Last Ride -1, 2	Ge rejected
16844,-A	Trainwhistle Blues -1	Ge rejected
16845,-A,-B	Texas Blues -1	Ge rejected

Supertone 9707, 9708 as by **Amos Greene**. Superior 2775 as by **Jimmy Boone**.

Cliff Carlisle, v/y-1; acc. own sg; Wilbur Ball, g/v-2.
   Richmond, IN   Monday, September 22, 1930

17066-A	That's Why I'm Blue -1	Ge rejected
17067-A	Hobo Blues -1	Ch 16140, 45179, Spt 9772, De 5379, MeC 45179
17068	Crazy Blues -1, 2	Ch 16140, Spt 9772, Spr 2661
17069	Brakeman's Blues -1	Ch 16165, 45140, Spr 2661, MeC 45140
17072	My Dear Old Happy Valley Home	Ge rejected

Supertone 9772 as by **Amos Greene**. Superior 2661 as by **Jimmy Boone**.
Matrices 17070/71 are by Barnard & McGuire (popular).

Cliff Carlisle, v/y; acc. own sg; Wilbur Ball, g-1.
   Richmond, IN   Monday, November 24, 1930

17307,-A	Box Car Blues -1	Ge rejected
17308,-A	The Brakeman's Reply	Ge rejected
17309	No Daddy Blues -1	Ch 16165, 45140, Spr 2638, De 5398, MeC 45208
17310,-A	The Written Letter	Ge rejected

Superior 2638 as by **Jimmy Boone**.

Cliff Carlisle, v/y-1; acc. own sg; Wilbur Ball, g.
   Richmond, IN   Friday, February 13, 1931

17527-A	Hobo Jack's Last Ride -1	Ch 16270, Spr 2775, MW 4936
17528-A	The Brakeman's Reply	Ch 16212, 45179, Spr 2638, De 5379, MeC 45179
17531	Box Car Blues -1	Ch 16212, Spr 2698
17533	The Written Letter -1	Ch 16270, MW 4973, MeC 45005

Superiors as by **Jimmy Boone**. Intervening matrices are popular.

Acc. own sg; Wilbur Ball, g/v-2.

Richmond, IN   Saturday, February 14, 1931

17534	Alone And Lonesome -1	Ch 16239, 45139, De 5378, DeAu X1233, MeC 45139
17535	High Steppin' Mama -1	Ch 16239, 45139, Spr 2698, De 5378, MeC 45139
17536	When You Wore A Tulip -2	Ch 16257, 45147, MW 5002, 8018, MeC 45147
17537	Stars & Guitars In Sunny Mexico	Ge unissued

All issues of matrix 17536 as by **Cliff Carlisle & Wilbur Ball**, except Champion 16257 as by **Lullaby Larkers**. Superior 2698 as by **Jimmy Boone**.

Lullaby Larkers: Cliff Carlisle, v/sg; Wilbur Ball, v/g; or **Cliff Carlisle**-1, v; acc. own sg.

Richmond, IN   Friday, April 17, 1931

17689-A	Birmingham Jail	Ch 16295, 45029, MeC 45029
17690-A	Shine On Harvest Moon	Ch 16257, 45147, Spr 2726, MW 5002, 8018, MeC 45147
17691,-A	Rambler's Blues -1	Ge unissued
17692	True And Trembling Brakeman	Ch 16295, 45029, Spr 2669, MW 8036, MeC 45029

Champion 45029, 45147, Melotone 45029, 45147, Montgomery Ward 5002, 8018, 8036 as by **Cliff Carlisle & Wilbur Ball**. Superior 2669, 2726 as by **Jim & Otto Fletcher**.

Cliff Carlisle, v/y; acc. own sg.

Richmond, IN   Saturday, April 18, 1931

| 17693 | The Plea Of A Mother | Ch R-16329, 45134, MW 4973, MeC 45134 |
| 17694 | The Fatal Run | Ge rejected |

Cliff Carlisle & Wilbur Ball, v duet; acc. Cliff Carlisle, sg; Wilbur Ball, g.

Richmond, IN   Saturday, April 18, 1931

| 17695,-A | Down By The Old Millstream | Ge rejected |
| 17695-B | In The Hills Of Old Kentucky | Spr 2669 |

Superior 2669 as by **Otto & Jim Fletcher**.

Lullaby Larkers: Cliff Carlisle, v/y-1/sg; Wilbur Ball, v/y-1/g.

Richmond, IN   Tuesday, September 8, 1931

| 17997 | Columbus Stockade Blues | Ch S-16364, 45186, Spr 2749, MW 8019 |
| 17998 | When The Cactus Is In Bloom -1 | Ch 16322, 45186, Spr 2726, MW 4943, 8019, MeC 45186 |

Champion 45186, Melotone 45186, Montgomery Ward 4943, 8019 as by **Cliff Carlisle & Wilbur Ball**. Superior 2726, 2749 as by **Jim & Otto Fletcher**.

Cliff Carlisle, v/y-1; acc. own sg-2; Wilbur Ball, g; unidentified, wh-3.

Richmond, IN   Tuesday, September 8, 1931

17999,-A	[untitled]	Ge unissued
18000	She's Waiting For Me -1, 2	Ch S-16434, 45042, De 5541, MeC 45042, 45262, Min M-14083
18001-B	The Cowboy Song -1, 3	Ch S-16434, 45042, Spr 2831, MW 4936, De 5541, MeC 45042, 45262, Min M-14044, M-14083
18002	Childhood Dreams -2	Ch 16322, Spr 2749
18003	The Fatal Run -1, 2	Ch 16447, 45162, Spr 2742, De 5398, MeC 45162, 45208
18004	Memories That Make Me Cry -1, 2	Ch 16447, 45162, MW 4937, MeC 45162
18005	Nobody Wants Me -1, 2	Ch R-16329, 45134, Spr 2742, MeC 45134, DeAu X1233

Champion 16322 as by **Carlisle & Ball**. Superior 2742, 2831 as by **Jimmy Boone**; 2749 as by **Jim & Otto Fletcher**. Rev. Minerva M-14044 by Charles Baker.

Cliff Carlisle, v/y-1; acc. own sg-2; Wilbur Ball, g/y-3; or **Cliff Carlisle & Wilbur Ball**-4, v duet; acc. Cliff Carlisle, sg; Wilbur Ball, g.

New York, NY   Thursday, October 22, 1931

10904-1	Columbus Stockade -4	Ba 32470, Me M12434, Or 8144, Pe 12815, Ro 5144, EBW W40
10908-2	Shanghai Rooster Yodel -1, 2, 3	Ba 32352, Me M12385, Or 8112, Pe 12778, Ro 5112, Cq 7937, EBW W40
10909-2	Modern Mama -1	Cq 7970
10910-	The Widow's Son	ARC rejected
10911-2	Memories That Make Me Cry -1, 2	Ba 32467, Me M12435, Or 8141, Pe 12812, Ro 5141, Cq 7968, 8072, Bwy 4048

Broadway 4048 as by **The Lullaby Larkers**. Rev. Broadway 4048 by Martin & Roberts.

Cliff Carlisle, v/y-1; acc. own sg; Wilbur Ball, g; or **Cliff Carlisle & Wilbur Ball**-2, v/y-3 duet; acc. Cliff Carlisle, sg; Wilbur Ball, g.

New York, NY   Friday, October 23, 1931

10905-2	Dear Old Daddy -2	Cq 7968
10912-2	Desert Blues -2, 3	Ba 32471, Me M12431, Or 8145, Pe 12816, Ro 5145
10913-	Red Wing	ARC rejected
10914-1,-2	Childhood Dreams -2, 3	Ba 32467, Me M12435, Or 8141, Pe 12812, Ro 5141, Cq 8072
10915-1,-2	Where Southern Roses Climb -2	Cq 7969, Bwy 4086
10916-3	I Don't Mind -2, 3	Ba 32468, Me M12432, Or 8142, Pe 12813, Ro 5142, Cq 7972
10917-	Cowboy Song -1	CrC/MeC/Roy 91539
10918-2,-3	Lonely Valley -1	Ba 32429, Me M12389, Or 8131, Pe 12802, Ro 5131, Cq 7876, 7973, CrC/MeC/Roy 91321, Min M-910

Conqueror 7968, Crown/Melotone/Royale 91539 as by **Carlisle & Ball**. Broadway 4086 as by **Lullaby Larkers**.
Revs: Broadway 4086 by Martin & Roberts; Crown/Melotone/Royale 91539 by The Arkansas Woodchopper; Minerva M-910 by Elton Britt.

New York, NY   Monday, October 26, 1931

10906-1	Box Car Yodel -2, 3	Ba 32553, Or 8162, Pe 12838, Ro 5162, Cq 7970, Pan 25414
10907-1	Sunny South By The Sea -2, 3	Ba 32469, Me M12433, Or 8143, Pe 12814, Ro 5143, CrC/MeC/Roy 91392, Min M-900
10919-1	Birmingham Jail No. 2 -2	Ba 32471, Me M12431, Or 8145, Pe 12816, Ro 5145, Cq 7971
10920-1,-2	Alone And Lonesome -2, 3	Ba 32553, Or 8162, Pe 12838, Ro 5162, Cq 7969, Bwy 4073
10921-1,-2,-3	My Rocky Mountain Sweetheart -1	Ba 32429, Me M12389, Or 8131, Pe 12802, Ro 5131, Cq 7876, 7973, Bwy 4084, CrC/MeC/Roy 91321, Min M-912
10922-1,-2	Guitar Blues -1	Ba 32430, Me M12382, Or 8132, Pe 12803, Ro 5132, Cq 7974, Bwy 4084, Vo B1
10923-1	Going Back To Alabama -1	Ba 32352, Me M12385, Or 8112, Pe 12778, Ro 5112, Cq 7937, Bwy 4076
10924-1,-2	The Written Letter -1	Ba 32468, Me M12432, Or 8142, Pe 12813, Ro 5142, Cq 7972, Bwy 4081
10925-	When The Moon Comes Over The Mountain -1	ARC rejected
10926-3	My Two-Time Mama -1	Ba 32470, Me M12434, Or 8144, Pe 12815, Ro 5144, Vo 5488

Melotone M12382, Vocalion B1 as by **Carlisle & Ball**. Vocalion 5488 as by **Bob Clifford**. Broadways as by **The Lullaby Larkers**, except 4081 as by **The Lonesome Hobo**.
Revs: Broadway 4073 by Gene Autry, 4076 by Thomas C. Ashley; Minerva M-900 by Callahan Brothers, M-912 by McDonald Quartette.

New York, NY   Tuesday, October 27, 1931

10937-	The Fatal Run -1	ARC rejected
10938-1,-2	Just A Lonely Hobo -2, 3	Ba 32469, Me M12433, Or 8143, Pe 12814, Ro 5143, Cq 7971, Bwy 4081, CrC/MeC/Roy 91392, Pan 25414
10939-2,-3	I Want A Good Woman -1	Ba 32430, Me M12382, Or 8132, Pe 12803, Ro 5132, Cq 7974, Vo B2

Melotone M12382, Vocalion B2 as by **Carlisle & Ball**. Broadway 4081 as by **Lullaby Larkers**.

Cliff Carlisle, v/y-1; acc. own sg; Wilbur Ball, g-2/u-3; or **Lullaby Larkers**-4: Cliff Carlisle, v/y-5/sg; Wilbur Ball, v/y-5/g.

Richmond, IN   Tuesday, December 8, 1931

18244-A	Memories That Haunt Me -1, 3	Ch S-16419, Spr 2831, MW 4937
18245	Mississippi Blues -2	Ge rejected
18246	Left All Alone -4	Ge unissued
18247	The White Rose -4	Ch 16417, MW 8037
18248	My Lonely Boyhood Days -4, 5	Ch 16417, 45132, Spr 2777, MW 4943, 8037, DeAu X1238

Champion 45132, Montgomery Ward 4937, 4943, 8037, Decca X1238 as by **Cliff Carlisle & Wilbur Ball**. Superior 2777 as by **Otto & Jim Fletcher**; 2831 as by **Jimmy Boone**.

Richmond, IN   Wednesday, December 9, 1931
   18249   Come Back Sweetheart -2   Ch 16419
   18250   The Chicken Roost Blues -4   Ch S-16364, 45132, Spr 2777, MW 8036,
                                                               DeAu X1238

Champion 45132, Montgomery Ward 8036, Decca X1238 as by **Cliff Carlisle & Wilbur Ball**. Superior 2777 as by **Otto & Jim Fletcher**.

Cliff Carlisle & Fred Kirby, v duet; acc. Cliff Carlisle, sg; unknown bj.
New York, NY   Thursday, September 22, 1932
   12347-   Innocent Prisoner   ARC rejected
   12348-   My Dear Old Daddy   ARC rejected
   12349-2   Sweet Cider Time   Cq 8140
   12350-   Little White Rose   ARC rejected
   12351-   My Lonely Boyhood Days   ARC rejected

Cliff Carlisle, v/y; acc. own sg.
New York, NY   Friday, September 23, 1932
   12359-2   When It's Roundup Time In Texas   Ba 32667, Me M12600, Or 8194, Pe 12880,
                                                               Ro 5194, Cq 8098, Vo 5499,
                                                               CrC/MeC/Roy 91518, Pan 25641
   12361-1   Roll On Blue Moon   Cq 8098

Vocalion 5499 as by **Bob Clifford**. Matrix 12360 is by Fred Kirby.

Cliff Carlisle, v/y-1; acc. own sg.
New York, NY   Monday, September 26, 1932
   12366-   Come Back Sweetheart   ARC rejected
   12367-1   Tom Cat Blues -1   Vo 5492
   12368-2   Shanghai Rooster Yodel No. 2 -1   Ba 32746, Me M12674, Or 8225, Pe 12905,
                                                               Ro 5225, Vo 5492, Cq 8140

Vocalion 5492 as by **Bob Clifford**. Despite the label, no banjo is audible on matrix 12367.

New York, NY   Tuesday, September 27, 1932
   12381-2   Hobo Jack's Last Ride -1   Vo 5499, Cq 8097
   12382-2   The Brakeman's Reply -1   Cq 8097
   12383-1   Lonesome For Caroline -1   Ba 32667, Me M12600, Or 8194, Pe 12880,
                                                               Ro 5194, CrC/MeC/Roy 91518, Pan 25641
   12384-2   Memories That Haunt Me -1   Ba 32613, Me M12527, Or 8181, Pe 12861,
                                                               Ro 5181, Cq 8069, CrC/MeC/Roy 91521,
                                                               Pan 25523
   12385-   Lonely Graveyard   ARC rejected

Vocalion 5499 as by **Bob Clifford**.

Acc. own sg; Fred Kirby, g-2/v-2.
New York, NY   Wednesday, September 28, 1932
   12347-   Innocent Prisoner   ARC rejected
   12350-   Little White Rose   ARC rejected
   12351-5   My Lonely Boyhood Days -2   Cq 8139
   12387-2   Hobo Blues -1   Ba 32746, Me M12674, Or 8225, Pe 12905,
                                                               Ro 5225
   12388-1   Ash Can Blues   Vo 02910
   12389-3   She Was A Pip   Vo 02740, Pan 25639

Vocalion 02740, 02910, Panachord 25639 as by **Bob Clifford**.
Rev. Vocalion 02740, Panachord 25639 by Carlisle Brothers.

Cliff Carlisle, v; acc. own sg; unknown, bj-1; poss. Fred Kirby, g-2.
New York, NY   Thursday, September 29, 1932
   12386-2   My Little Pal -2   Cq 8139
   12391-   Louisiana Blues   ARC rejected
   12392-1   Seven Years With The Wrong Woman -1   Ba 32613, Me M12527, Or 8181, Pe 12861,
                                                               Ro 5181, Vo 5488, Cq 8069,
                                                               CrC/MeC/Roy 91521, Pan 25523

Vocalion 5488 as by **Bob Clifford**.

New York, NY   Friday, September 30, 1932
   12409-   In The Land Of The Sky   ARC unissued

Cliff Carlisle, v/y-1; acc. own sg; Bill Carlisle, g-2.
New York, NY   Monday, July 24, 1933
   13623-1   Dream A Little Dream Of Me -2   Ba 33117, Me M13084, Or 8359, Pe 13022,
                                                               Ro 5359

| 13624- | I Married The Wrong Woman | ARC rejected |
| 13625-2 | Where Romance Calls -1 | Ba 33071, Me M13035, Or 8341, Pe 13010, Ro 5341, Cq 8332, CrCMeC/Roy 91815 |

Conqueror 8332 as by **Carlisle Brothers**.

Cliff Carlisle, v/y; acc. own sg; Bill Carlisle, g/sp-1/y-1.
New York, NY   Tuesday, July 25, 1933

| 13628-2 | On The Banks Of The Rio Grande | Ba 32841, Me M12770, Or 8259, Pe 12934, Ro 5259, Cq 8229, CrC/MeC/Roy 91628, Min M-914 |
| 13636-1 | Mouses' Ear Blues -1 | Vo 02656, Pan 25631, RZAu G22140 |

All issues of matrix 13636 as by **Bob Clifford**. Crown/Melotone/Royale 91628, Minerva M-914 as by **Carlisle Brothers**.
Matrix 13636 is titled *Mouse's Ear Blues* on Panachord 25631.
Matrices 13629 to 13634 are by Freddie Martin & His Orchestra (popular); 13635, 13637 are by Bill Carlisle.
Rev. Minerva M-914 by Doc Roberts.

Cliff Carlisle, v/y-1; acc. own sg; Bill Carlisle, h-2/g-3.
New York, NY   Wednesday, July 26, 1933

13638-2	Wreck Of No. 52 -3	Ba 32830, Me M12760, Or 8255, Pe 12931, Ro 5255, Cq 8228, Vo B1, CrC/MeC/Roy 91599
13639-1	Gamblin' Dan -1, 3	Ba 32917, Me M12860, Or 8288, Pe 12962, Ro 5288, Cq 8268
13640-2	I'm Glad I'm A Hobo -1, 2	Ba 32917, Me M12860, Or 8288, Pe 12962, Ro 5288, Cq 8268
13641-1	Ramblin' Jack -1, 3	Ba 32830, Me M12760, Or 8255, Pe 12931, Ro 5255, Cq 8228, Vo B2, CrC/MeC/Roy 91599
13643-	Roll On Blue Moon -3	ARC rejected
13647-2	Ringtail Tom -1, 2	Vo 02656, Pan 25631, RZAu G22140
13649-1	Fussin' Mama -1, 3	Ba 33005, Me M12956, Or 8317, Pe 12988, Ro 5317, Cq 8333
13650-1	Longing For You	Ba 33117, Me M13084, Or 8359, Pe 13022, Ro 5359

All issues of matrix 13647 as by **Bob Clifford**. Matrices 13642, 13644 to 13646 are by Carlisle Brothers; 13648 by Bill Carlisle.

Cliff Carlisle, v; acc. unknown, f-1; prob. Bill Carlisle, h-2/v-3; prob. Bob Miller, p-4/cel-5; unknown, g; unknown, sb.
New York, NY   Friday, July 28, 1933

13667-1	Blue Eyes -1	Ba 32841, Me M12770, Or 8259, Pe 12934, Ro 5259, Cq 8229, CrC/MeC/Roy 91628
13668-2	Dang My Rowdy Soul -1, 3	Ba 32842, Me M12771, Or 8260, Pe 12935, Ro 5260, Cq 8200, Pan 25601
13672-	There's A Cabin In The Pines -1, 4	ARC rejected
13673-1	The Vacant Cabin Door -1, 3, 5	Ba 32885, Me M12821, Or 8276, Pe 12949, Ro 5276, Cq 8201
13674-1	Goin' Down The Road Feelin' Bad -2	Ba 32842, Me M12771, Or 8260, Pe 12935, Ro 5260, Cq 8200, Pan 25601

Matrices 13669 to 13671 are by Carlisle Brothers.

Acc. unknown, f-1; own sg-2; unknown, g-1; unknown, sb-1.
New York, NY   Monday, July 31, 1933

13685-1	Don't Marry The Wrong Woman -1	Ba 32885, Me M12821, Or 8276, Pe 12949, Ro 5276, Cq 8201
13685-2	Don't Marry The Wrong Woman -1	ARC unissued
13685-3,-4	Don't Marry The Wrong Woman -2	ARC unissued
13687-	Traveling Man Blues -1	ARC rejected
13688-2	Sunshine And Daisies -1	Ba 33132, Me M13099, Or 8366, Pe 13027, Ro 5366, Cq 8388

Matrix 13686 is by Carlisle Brothers. Rev. Conqueror 8388 by Carlisle Brothers.

Cliff Carlisle, v/y-1; acc. own sg; Bill Carlisle, g-2.
New York, NY   Tuesday, August 28, 1934

15773-	Let's Tie The Knot	ARC unissued
15774-2	Georgia Moon -1	ARC 5-12-61
15775-1	The Girl In The Blue Velvet Band -1	ARC 5-12-61
15776-2	Sugar Cane Mama -1, 2	Ba 33416, Me M13383, Or 8460, Pe 13137, Ro 5460

New York, NY			Wednesday, August 29, 1934
15783-1	Onion Eating Mama		ARC unissued: Co C4K47911 (CD)
15783-2	Onion Eating Mama		Vo 02910
15784-2	Dollar Is All I Crave -1, 2		Ba 33416, Me M13383, Or 8460, Pe 13137, Ro 5460
15791-	Penitentiary Blues		ARC unissued
15797-2	The Bunch Of Cactus On The Wall -1, 2		ARC 6-05-62, Cq 8642
15798-1	Chicken Roost Blues -1, 2		Ba 33226, Me M13193, Or 8385, Pe 13066, Ro 5385, Cq 8393, CrC/MeC/Roy 91929
15799-2	Goodbye Old Pal -1, 2		Ba 33340, Me M13307, Or 8429, Pe 13110, Ro 5429, Cq 8514, CrC/MeC/Roy 91991

Vocalion 02910 as by **Bob Clifford**. Matrices 15785 to 15788 are by Asa Martin & James Roberts; 15789/90, 15792 to 15794 by Bill Carlisle; 15795/96 by Carlisle Brothers. Rev. ARC 6-05-62, Cq 8642 by Carlisle Brothers.

Acc. own sg; Bill Carlisle, g.
New York, NY			Friday, August 31, 1934
15820-2	Casey County Jail		ARC 6-02-61

Cliff Carlisle, v/y-1; acc. own sg; Bill Carlisle, g-2.
New York, NY			Tuesday, September 4, 1934
15823-2	Sweet Nannie Lisle -1, 2		ARC 350910
15827-2	Hen Pecked Man -1		Ba 33226, Me M13193, Or 8385, Pe 13066, Ro 5385, Cq 8393, CrC/MeC/Roy 91929
15828-	Unloaded Gun		ARC unissued
15830-1	So Blue		ARC 6-02-61

Matrices 15824 to 15826 are by Carlisle Brothers; 15829 by Bill Carlisle.

Cliff Carlisle, v/y-1; acc. own sg-2; Bill Carlisle, g/v-3; Sonny Boy Tommy Carlisle, v-4.
Charlotte, NC			Sunday, February 16, 1936
99162-1	Cowboy Johnnie's Last Ride -1, 2		BB B-6439, MW M-4769, RZ MR2602, RZIr IZ783, Twin FT8425
99163-1	Rambling Yodler -1, 2		BB B-6350, MW M-4769, RZ MR2518, RZAu G22967, Twin FT8095
99164-1	A Wild Cat Woman And A Tom Cat Man -1, 2		BB B-6350, MW M-4770, RZ MR2518, RZAu G22967
99165-1	Look Out, I'm Shifting Gears -1		BB B-6292, MW M-4770
99166-1	My Lovin' Kathleen -2, 3, 4		BB B-6405, MW M-4771
99167-1	A Stretch Of 28 Years -2, 3, 4		BB B-6405, MW M-4771
99168-1	In A Box Car Around The World -1, 2, 3		BB B-6439, MW M-4772, RZ MR2602, RZIr IZ783, Twin FT8425
99169-1	Get Her By The Tail On A Down Hill Drag -1, 2		BB B-6292
99170-1	Handsome Blues -2, 3		BB B-6791, MW M-4772

Bluebird B-6405 and possibly Montgomery Ward M-4771 as by **Cliff Carlisle Trio**.
Matrix 99168 is titled *Engine Driver's Yodel* on Regal-Zonophone MR2602, IZ783, Twin FT8425.
Rev. Twin FT8095 by Bill Boyd.

Cliff Carlisle, v/y-1; acc. own sg; Bill Carlisle, g; unknown, g-2; poss. Louis Carlisle, sb-3; Sonny Boy Tommy Carlisle, v-4/y-5; Cliff Carlisle, Bill Carlisle, Louis Carlisle, Sonny Boy Tommy Carlisle, v quartet-6.
Charlotte, NC			Tuesday, June 16, 1936
102650-1	You'll Miss Me When I'm Gone -2, 3		BB B-6458, MW M-5032
102651-1	That Nasty Swing -1, 2, 3		BB B-6631, MW M-7034, Twin FT8252
102652-1	It Ain't No Fault Of Mine -1, 2, 3		BB B-6631, MW M-7034, Twin FT8252
102653-1	My Traveling Night -1, 2, 3		BB B-7031, RZAu G23274
102654-1	Two Little Sweethearts -1, 2, 3		BB B-7290, RZAu G23659
102655-1	Waiting For A Ride -1, 2, 3		BB B-7094, MW M-7032, M-7365, Twin FT8491
102656-1	A Little White Rose -1, 4, 5		BB B-6791, MW M-7031
102657-1	The Flower Of The Valley -1, 3, 4, 5		BB B-6754, MW M-7031, Twin FT8295
102658-1	Shine On Me -3, 6		BB B-6855, Twin FT8334
102659-1	The Blind Child's Prayer -2?, 3, 4		BB B-6830, RZ MR2458, RZIr IZ664, Twin FT8319
102660-1	Just A Song At Childhood -2?, 3, 4		BB B-6830, Twin FT8319
102661-1	They Say It's The End Of The Trail Old Paint -1, 3, 4, 5		BB B-6754, MW M-7178, Twin FT8295
102662-1	When The Evening Sun Goes Down -2?, 3		BB B-6458, MW M-5032, Twin FT8143
102663-1	I'm Savin' Saturday Night For You -1, 2?, 3		BB B-7094, MW M-7032, Twin FT8491

Matrix 102656 on Bluebird B-6791 as by **Cliff Carlisle & Tommy**. Matrix 102658 as by **Cliff Carlisle Quartet**. Bluebird B-6754, Twin FT8295 as by **Cliff & Tommy Carlisle**.
Revs: Regal-Zonophone MR2458, IZ664 by Dixie Reelers; Twin FT8143 by Delmore Brothers, FT8334 by Jimmie Rodgers.

Cliff Carlisle, v/y-1; acc. own sg; Bill Carlisle, g; unknown, g.
    Charlotte, NC   Saturday, June 20, 1936

Matrix	Title	Release
102731-1	When I Feel Froggie, I'm Gonna Hop	BB B-6493, MW M-7033
102732-1	It Takes An Old Hen To Deliver The Goods	BB B-6493, MW M-7033
102733-1	My Rockin' Mama -1	BB B-6647
102734-1	Shufflin' Gal -1	BB B-6524
102735-1	Wigglin' Mama -1	BB B-6524, Twin FT8246
102736-1	When I'm Dead And Gone -1	BB B-6647

Rev. Twin FT8246 by Bill Carlisle.

Cliff Carlisle, v/y-1; or **Cliff Carlisle With Fred Kirby**-2, v duet; acc. unknown, f; Cliff Carlisle, sg/y; Fred Kirby, g; Sonny Boy Tommy Carlisle, v-3.
    Charlotte, NC   Friday, February 19, 1937

Matrix	Title	Release
07156-1	Just A Wayward Boy -3	BB B-6855
07157-1	There's A Lamp In The Window Tonight -3	BB B-6980, MW M-7179
07158-1	Ridin' That Lonesome Train -3	BB B-6980, MW M-7178
07159-1	A Little Bit Of Lovin' From You	BB B-7461, MW M-7180
07160-1	Cowboy's Dying Dream -2	BB B-7790, MW M-7185, RZ MR2946, RZAu G25121, Twin FT8657, CoSs MZ270
07161-1	Pan-American Man -1	BB B-7717, MW M-7185, Twin FT8634
07162-1	Blue Dreams	BB 33-0514, MW M-7823
07163-1	Pay Day Fight	BB B-7031, MW M-7181, RZAu G23274
07164-1	Rocky Road	MW M-7181
07165-1	New Memories Of You That Haunt Me -1	BB B-7740, MW M-7179, RZAu G23659
07166-1	Sweet As The Roses Of Spring	MW M-7180
07167-1	Down In Caroline	BB unissued

Regal-Zonophone MR2946 and probably Twin FT8657 as by **Cliff Carlisle (The Yodling Cowboy) & Fred Kirby**.
Revs: Bluebird B-7461 by Carlisle Brothers; Bluebird B-7717, Regal-Zonophone G25121, Twin FT8634 by Riley Puckett.

Cliff Carlisle: Cliff Carlisle, Claude Boone, v duet; acc. Cliff Carlisle, sg; Claude Boone, g; unknown, sb.
    Charlotte, NC   Wednesday, August 4, 1937

Matrix	Title	Release
011917-1	The Poor Widow	BB B-7817

Claude Boone–Cliff Carlisle: Claude Boone, v; acc. Cliff Carlisle, sg; own g; unknown, sb.
    Charlotte, NC   Wednesday, August 4, 1937

Matrix	Title	Release
011918-1	Shot The Innocent Man	BB B-7817

Cliff Carlisle, v/y-1; or **Cliff Carlisle–Claude Boone**-2, v duet; acc. Cliff Carlisle, sg; Claude Boone, g; unknown, sb; Sonny Boy Tommy Carlisle, v-3.
    Charlotte, NC   Wednesday, August 4, 1937

Matrix	Title	Release
011919-1	Your Saddle Is Empty Tonight -3	BB B-7790, MW M-7365, RZ MR2946, Twin FT8657, CoSs MZ270
011920-1	Lonely -3	BB 33-0514, MW M-7821
011921-1	The Gal I Left Behind -2	BB B-7290
011922-1	Where My Memory Lies	BB B-8220, MW M-7821
011923-1	Ridin' The Blinds To The Call Of The Pines	BB B-7740
011924-1	Rooster Blues -1	BB B-7147, MW M-7822
011925-1	Troubled Minded Blues	BB B-7147, MW M-7822
011926-1	Hobo's Fate	BB B-8220, MW M-7823

Regal-Zonophone MR2946, Columbia MZ270, and probably Twin FT8657 as by **Cliff Carlisle (The Yodling Cowboy) & Little Tommy**.
Matrix 011919 is titled *Riding The Trail (Your Saddle Is Empty Tonight)* on Regal-Zonophone MR2946, Twin FT8657, and Columbia MZ270.

Cliff Carlisle & His Buckle Busters-1/**Cliff Carlisle & Sonny Boy Tommy**-2: Cliff Carlisle, v/y-3; acc. prob. Leon Scott, f-4; unknown, h-5; own sg; prob. Claude Boone, g/v-6; Sonny Boy Tommy Carlisle, v-7.
    Charlotte, NC   Friday, June 3, 1938

Matrix	Title	Release
64000-A	Over By The Crystal Sea -1, 6, 7	De 5549
64001-A	That Great Judgment Day (Is Coming To All) -1, 6, 7	De 5549
64002-A	Flower Of My Dreams -2, 7	De 5652, Min M-14116
64003-B	The Wreck Of Happy Valley -2, 7	De 5558
64004-A	The Old Home Place -2, 7	De 5652, Min M-14115
64005-A	Two Eyes In Tennessee -2, 7	De 5578
64006-A	Nevada Johnnie -1, 3, 4	De 5593, MeC 45269, Min M-14155
64007-A	Trouble On My Mind -1, 3, 4, 5	De 5593, MeC 45269, Min M-14155
64008-A	Where Are The Pals Of Long Ago -1, 3, 4	De 5674, Min M-14111
64009-A	Blue Dreams -1, 4	De 5631, Min M-14154
64010-A	Lonely Little Orphan Child -2, 7	De 5578
64011-A	When The Angels Carry Me Home -2, 7	De 5607

64012-A	Home Of The Soul -2, 7	De 5607
64013-A	I'm Just A Ramblin' Man -1, 3, 4	De 5631, Min M-14154
64014-A	Weary Traveller -1, 4, 5	De 5558
64015-A	When We Meet Again -1, 4	De 5674

Revs: Minerva M-14115, M-14116 by Jimmie Davis.

Cliff Carlisle's Buckle Busters: Cliff Carlisle, v/sg; Bill Carlisle, v/g; unknown, g; Sonny Boy Tommy Carlisle, v.
Charlotte, NC   Tuesday, July 25, 1939

66003-A	Far Beyond The Starry Sky	De 5716, MeC 45329, Min M-14156
66005-A	Shine Your Light For Others	De 5752
66006-A	The Unclouded Day	De 5716, MeC 45329, Min M-14156

Matrix 66004, though logged as by **Cliff Carlisle's Buckle Busters**, was issued as by **Carlisle Brothers**.

Cliff Carlisle, v; acc. own sg; Bill Carlisle, g; unknown, g.
Charlotte, NC   Wednesday, July 26, 1939

66014-A	Makes No Difference What Life May Bring	De 5732, 46105
66015-A	Black Jack David	De 5732

One pressing run of Decca 46105 replaced matrix 66014 with matrix 66104 by Alberta Hunter (see B&GR).

Acc. own sg; Shannon Grayson, md; Bill Carlisle, g/v-1; unknown, g.
Charlotte, NC   Wednesday, July 26, 1939

66016-A	Footprints In The Snow	De 5720, 46105
66025-A	My Little Sadie -1	De 5720, Min M-14111
66026-A	Prepare Me Oh Lord -1	De 5752

Matrices 66017 to 66019, 66021, 66023 are by Bill Carlisle; 66020, 66022, 66024 are by Carlisle Brothers.

See also Carlisle Brothers.

Cliff Carlisle recorded after 1942.

MILTON & MARION CARLISLE

Milton Carlisle, Marion Carlisle, v duet; or Marion Carlisle, v-1; acc. Shannon Grayson, md-2/g-3; prob. Bill Carlisle, g; poss. Louis Carlisle, sb.
Charlotte, NC   Friday, August 6, 1937

013007-1	My Saviour Understands -3	BB B-7627, MW M-7911
013008-1	Feed Your Soul -3	BB B-7627, MW M-7911
013009-1	To Love And Be Loved -2	BB B-7653
013010-1	Kentucky Sweetheart -1, 3	BB B-7653

CARLISLE & BALL

See Cliff Carlisle.

CARLISLE BROTHERS

This entry is confined to recordings issued (or, if not issued, logged) as by **Carlisle Brothers**; any recordings bearing that artist-credit which are not listed below will be found under Cliff Carlisle. All unassigned reverse sides are by Cliff Carlisle.

Cliff Carlisle, Bill Carlisle, v/y duet; acc. Cliff Carlisle, sg; Bill Carlisle, g.
New York, NY   Wednesday, July 26, 1933

13642-1	Louisiana Blues	Ba 33005, Me M12956, Or 8317, Pe 12988, Ro 5317, Cq 8333

All issues except Conqueror 8333 as by **Cliff Carlisle**.

Cliff Carlisle, Bill Carlisle, v duet; acc. Bill Carlisle, h; poss. Cliff Carlisle, g.
New York, NY   Wednesday, July 26, 1933

13644-2	Sal Got A Meatskin	Vo 02740, Pan 25639
13645-2	The Rustler's Fate	Ba 32942, Me M12885, Or 8298, Pe 12970, Ro 5298, Cq 8199
13646-1	The Little Dobie Shack	Ba 32942, Me M12885, Or 8298, Pe 12970, Ro 5298, Cq 8199

Vocalion 02740 as by **Clifford Brothers**. Conqueror 8199 as by **Cliff Carlisle**. Matrix 13643 is by Cliff Carlisle.

Cliff Carlisle, Bill Carlisle, v/y-1 duet; acc. unknown, f; unknown, g; unknown, sb; unknown, perc-2.
New York, NY   Friday, July 28, 1933

13669-1	End Of Memory Lane -1	Ba 32965, Me M12915, Or 8302, Pe 12974, Ro 5302, Cq 8269
13670-1	Looking For Tomorrow	Ba 33132, Me M13099, Or 8366, Pe 13027, Ro 5366, Cq 8332
13671-1	Traveling Life Alone -2	Ba 33071, Me M13035, Or 8341, Pe 13010, Ro 5341, Cq 8388, CrC/MeC/Roy 91815

Conqueror 8388 as by **Cliff Carlisle**.

Revs: Conqueror 8332 (with same credit), 8388 by Cliff Carlisle.
New York, NY   Monday, July 31, 1933
13686-2   Ramshackled Shack On The Hill   Ba 32965, Me M12915, Or 8302, Pe 12974,
                                                          Ro 5302, Cq 8269

Cliff Carlisle, Bill Carlisle, v duet; acc. Cliff Carlisle, sg; Bill Carlisle, g.
New York, NY   Wednesday, August 29, 1934
15795-   When The Blue Bells Bloom   ARC unissued
15796-1   On The Lone Prairie   ARC 6-05-62, Cq 8642

Cliff Carlisle, Bill Carlisle, v duet; or Cliff Carlisle, v-1; acc. Cliff Carlisle, sg; Bill Carlisle, g.
New York, NY   Tuesday, September 4, 1934
15824-2   Valley Of Peace -1   Ba 33340, Me M13307, Or 8429, Pe 13110,
                                                          Ro 5429, Cq 8514, CrC/MeC/Roy 91991
15825-1,-2   Will You Meet Me Just Inside   Ba 33228, Me M13195, Or 8387, Pe 13068,
                                                          Ro 5387, Cq 8486
15826-1   Jesus My All   Ba 33228, Me M13195, Or 8387, Pe 13068,
                                                          Ro 5387, Cq 8486
15831-1   Won't Somebody Pal With Me   ARC 350910

Matrices 15827/28, 15830 are by Cliff Carlisle; matrix 15829 is by Bill Carlisle.

Bill Carlisle, Cliff Carlisle, poss. Byron Smith, v trio; acc. Bill Carlisle, g; poss. Boyce Brown, g.
Charlotte, NC   Thursday, January 27, 1938
018795-1   When The Old Cow Went Dry   BB B-7461

Carlisle Brothers (Cliff & Bill): Cliff Carlisle, sg/v-1; Shannon Grayson, md-2/prob. v-3; Bill Carlisle, g/v-4; Sonny Boy Tommy Carlisle, v-5.
Charlotte, NC   Tuesday, July 25, 1939
66004-A   Traveling Home -1, 4, 5   De 5793
66007-A   Gonna Raise A Ruckus Tonight -1, 2, 4, 5 De 5774, Min M-14158
66008-A   Beneath The Old Pine Tree -1, 5   De 5807, Min M-14157
66011-A   Goin' Down The Valley One By One -2, 3, 4 De 5807, Min M-14157

Cliff Carlisle, sg-1/v-2; Shannon Grayson, md-3/prob. g-4/prob. v-5; Bill Carlisle, g/v-6; unknown, g-7.
Charlotte, NC   Wednesday, July 26, 1939
66013-A   There Is No More That I Can Say -1, 2, 3 De 5774, Min M-14158
66020-A   I'm Sorry That's All I Can Say -1, 6   De 5793
66022-A   Don't Let Me Worry Your Little Mind -2, 3, 5, 6   De 5778
66024-A   Broken Heart -2, 4, 6, 7   De 5778

Decca 5774 as by **Carlisle Brothers**. Intervening matrices are by Cliff or Bill Carlisle.

Cliff Carlisle, sg-1/v-2; Shannon Grayson, md-3/poss. g-4; Bill Carlisle, g/v-5; unknown, g-6; Sonny Boy Tommy Carlisle, v-7.
Charlotte, NC   Monday, September 16, 1940
68102-A   There'll Come A Time -1, 2, 3, 5   De 5881
68103-A   Juanita -1, 2, 3, 5, 7   De 5881
68105-A   I Wonder Who's Sorry Now -1, 3, 5   De 6075, MeC 45547
68106-A   Flag That Train -1, 2, 3, 5   De 5921, MeC 45419
68107-A   I'd Like To Be Your Shadow In The Moonlight -2,   De 6075, MeC 45547
                3, 5, 6
68108-A,-AA   To Love And Be Loved   De unissued
68109-A   Don't Mention Me -1, 2, 4   De 5892
68110-A   Go And Leave If You Wish To -1, 2, 3, 5   De 5921, MeC 45419

Charlotte, NC   Tuesday, September 17, 1940
68104-A   Somewhere Somebody's Waiting For You -1, 3, 5   De 5903, MeC 45405
68111-A,-B   You'll Never Know   De unissued
68112-A   Will You Always Love Me Darling -1, 2, 3, 5   De 5903, MeC 45405
68113-A   Three Women To Every Man -1, 2, 3   De 5913
68114-A   A Dollar's All I Crave -1, 2, 3   De 5913
68115-A   Nobody Cares -1, 2, 3, 5, 7   De 5892

Cliff Carlisle, Bill Carlisle, v duet; or Cliff Carlisle, v-1; or Bill Carlisle, v-2; acc. Cliff Carlisle, sg; Bill Carlisle, g.
Atlanta, GA   Tuesday, September 30, 1941
071042-1   I'm Sorry Now   BB B-8862
071043-1   You'll Never Know   BB B-8862
071044-1   No Wedding Bells -2   BB B-8936
071045-1   Sugar Cane Mama -1   BB B-8996
071046-1   I Believe I'm Entitled To You   BB B-8936
071047-1   She Waits For Me There   BB B-8996

ALFRED CARLSON

Pseudonym on Supertone for W.C. Childers.

JENKINS CARMEN

Jenkins Carmen, prob. v; acc. Marcheta Carmen, prob. v-1; others unknown.
    Richmond, IN   Tuesday, November 12, 1929

15877, -A	Railroad Boomer; Gypsy Lady -1	Ge rejected

This artist, usually known as Jenks "Tex" Carman, recorded after 1942.

CAROLINA BUDDIES

Posey Rorer, f; Buster Carter, bj/tv-1; Lewis McDaniels, g; Walter Smith, lv; prob. Walter Smith, v eff-2; unidentified, sp-3.
    New York, NY   Tuesday, March 25, 1930

150114-1	The Murder Of The Lawson Family -1	Co 15537-D
150115-1	In A Cottage By The Sea -1	Co 15537-D
150116-1	The Story That The Crow Told Me -2	Co 15641-D
150117-1	My Sweetheart Is A Sly Little Miss -1, 3	Co 15641-D

Matrix 150114 on Columbia CS9660 (LP) is reported to be take 2 but is in fact take 1.

Odell Smith, f; Norman Woodlieff, g/v-1; Walter Smith, lv-2.
    New York, NY   Tuesday, February 24, 1931

151340-2	Work Don't Bother Me -1, 2	Co 15663-D
151341-2	He Went In Like A Lion (But Came Out Like A Lamb) -1	Co 15663-D
151342-	No No Positively No	Co unissued
151343-	How I Love Pretty Little Liza	Co unissued
151344-2	My Evolution Girl -2	Co 15770-D
151345-2	Otto Wood The Bandit -2	Co 15652-D
151346-2	Broken Hearted Lover -1, 2	Co 15652-D
151347-2	Mistreated Blues -2	Co 15770-D

CAROLINA BUDDYS (WOMBLE & LOVE)

——— Womble, ——— Love, v duet; acc. prob. own g duet.
    New York, NY   Monday, September 9, 1935

39932-A	Grandfather's Clock	De 5142
39933-A	Shake Hands With Mother	De 5142
39934-A,-B	My Home	De rejected
39935-A,-B	Mid Night On The Stormy Deep	De rejected
39936-A,-B	East Bound Train	De rejected

There is only one guitar on matrix 39933

——— Womble, ——— Love, v/y-1 duet; acc. prob. own g duet.
    New York, NY   Tuesday, September 10, 1935

39947-A,-B	My Little Girl	De rejected
39948-A	Big River Blues	De 5160
39949- -	Mother The Queen Of My Heart	DeSA FM5496
39950-A	Mississippi Valley Blues -1	De 5160, DeSA FM5107
39951-A,-B	The Two Little Orphans	De rejected

Revs: Decca FM5107 by Scotty The Drifter (Benny Borg), FM5496 by Shelton Brothers.

CAROLINA GOSPEL SINGERS

Clyde Parham, tv; J.W. Parham, tv; Dewey James, bv; A.E. Parham, bsv; acc. unknown, p.
    Savannah, GA   Thursday, August 25, 1927

39848-3	Beyond The River	Vi 21140
39849-2	Jesus Paid It All	Vi 21140

Acc. George Horne, p.
    Richmond, IN   Tuesday, September 10, 1929

15580-A	My Redeemer Lives	Ge 6992, Ch 15833
15581	In Gethsemane, Alone	Ge 6992, Ch 15801
15582	My Prayer	Ge 7023, Ch 15833
15583	He Bore It All	Ge rejected

A.E. Parham is named as soloist on matrix 15582.

Richmond, IN		Thursday, September 26, 1929
15686	Will You Meet Me Up There	Ge 7069, Spr 2529
15687	Jesus Paid It All	Ge 7023, Ch 15856, 45177, Spr 2673
15688	The Promise To The Faithful	Ge 7099
15689-A	He Bore It All	Ge 7099, Ch 15901, 45177, Spr 2673
15690,-A	Where Shall I Be	Ge rejected
15691,-A	It Will Not Be Long	Ge rejected

Superior 2529, 2673 as by **Charleston Sacred Quartette**.

J.W. Parham & Clyde Parham, v duet; acc. prob. George Horne, p.

Richmond, IN		Friday, September 27, 1929
15694,-A	What Are They Doing In Heaven	Ge rejected

Carolina Gospel Singers: Clyde Parham, tv; J.W. Parham, tv; Dewey James, bv; A.E. Parham, bsv; acc. George Horne, p.

Richmond, IN		Friday, September 27, 1929
15695	I'll Serve The King Of Glory	Ge 7129, Spr 2529
15696-A	We Will Rise And Shine	Ge 7069, Ch 15856, Spt 9679
15697,-A	With Joy We Sing	Ge unissued
15698	The Glory Way	Ge 7129, Spt 9679
15699	De Sad Moment	Ge 7169
15700	Eblution	Ge 7169
15701	Drifting Too Far From The Shore	Ge 7188

Gennett 7169 possibly as by **Parham's Dixie Quartet**. Supertone 9679 as by **South Carolina Sacred Quartette**. Superior 2529 as by **Charleston Sacred Quartette**. Rev. Gennett 7188 by Blue Ridge Sacred Singers.

J.W. Parham & Evelyn Smith, v duet; acc. Ruth Hall, p.

Richmond, IN		Monday, October 21, 1929
15795,-A	You Never Mentioned Him To Me	Ge rejected

Charleston Sacred Quartette: poss.: Clyde Parham, tv; J.W. Parham, tv; Dewey James, bv; A.E. Parham, bsv; acc. unknown, o.

Richmond, IN		Monday, June 9, 1930
16744-A	The Saviour Said	Spr 2615
16746-B	Turn Away	Spr 2615

Matrix 16745 is by Warren Caplinger.
See also Parham Bros. Quartette.

CAROLINA LADIES QUARTET

Vocal quartet; unacc.

Richmond, IN		Monday, October 21, 1929
15793	My Loved Ones Are Waiting For Me	Ge 7038, Ch 15879, Chg 426
15794,-A	My Jesus I Love Thee	Ge rejected
15796	Don't Put Off Salvation Too Long	Ge 7038, Ch 15879, Chg 426
15797	That Is All I Need To Know	Ge rejected

Challenge 426 as by **Southland's Ladies Quartette**.
Matrix 15795 is by J.W. Parham & Evelyn Smith (see Carolina Gospel Singers).

Acc. unknown, g.

Richmond, IN		Saturday, June 6, 1931
17804,-A	What Shall We Do With Mother	Ge unissued
17805	Under His Wings	Ch 16644
17806	Sitting At The Feet Of Jesus	Ch 16644
17807-A	It Won't Be Long	Ch R-16319
17809	I Got A Home In That Rock	Ch 16662, 45117
17810-B	The Life Boat	Ch R-16319

Matrix 17808 is popular. Rev. Champion 16662, 45117 by Roy Harvey.
Mrs. W.W. Matthews is named as royalty payee in Champion files and may be a member of this group.

CAROLINA MANDOLIN ORCHESTRA

Several unknowns, md; unknown, p.

New York, NY		c. late December 1927
81972-A	Georgia Camp-Meeting	OK 45191, PaE E6018
81973-B	Red Wing	OK 45191, PaE E6018, Ariel 4278

Parlophone E6018, Ariel 4278 as by **Carolina Mandoline Band**. Rev. Ariel 4278 by Ferera & Franchini (Hawaiian).

CAROLINA MANDOLINE BAND
An item by the Carolina Mandolin Orchestra was thus credited on Ariel and Parlophone.

CAROLINA NIGHT HAWKS
Howard Miller, f; Ted Bare, md/v; Donald Thompson, bj; Charles Miller, g.
    Atlanta, GA   Tuesday, April 17, 1928

146116-	Nobody To Love	Co unissued
146117-	Butcher's Boy	Co unissued
146118-	A Stern Old Bachelor	Co unissued
146119-1	Governor Al Smith For President	Co 15256-D

Rev. Columbia 15256-D by Vernon Dalhart.

CAROLINA QUARTETTE
Vocal quartet; unacc.
    Winston-Salem, NC   Tuesday, September 27, 1927

81633-	Crossing The Bar	OK unissued
81634-B	Saved By His Sweet Grace	OK 45175
81635-A	His Name Is Jesus	OK 45189, PaE R3864
81636-	That Wonderful Day	OK unissued
81637-B	Twilight Is Stealing	OK 45189, PaE R3864
81638-A	Is It Well With Your Soul?	OK 45175

CAROLINA RAMBLERS STRING BAND

Steve Ledford & Daniel Nicholson, v duet; acc. **Carolina Ramblers String Band**: Steve Ledford, f; Daniel Nicholson, bj; Audie "Buffalo" Rodgers, g; poss. Taft Ledford, g.
    New York, NY   Wednesday, February 10, 1932

11261-1	Ninety Nine Years	Ba 32371, Or 8118, Pe 12787, Ro 5118, MeC 91283

Melotone 91283 as by **Daniel Nicholson & Steve Ledford**.

Rodgers & Nicholson: Audie Rodgers, Daniel Nicholson, v duet; acc. **Carolina Ramblers String Band**: Steve Ledford, f; Daniel Nicholson, bj; Audie Rodgers, g; poss. Taft Ledford, g.
    New York, NY   Wednesday, February 10, 1932

11262-3	Worried Man Blues	Ba 32371, Or 8118, Pe 12787, Ro 5118, MeC 91283

Melotone 91283 as by **Daniel Nicholson**.

Carolina Ramblers String Band: Steve Ledford, f/v-1; poss. Taft Ledford, f-2 or g-2; Daniel Nicholson, bj or g/v-3; Audie Rodgers, g/v-4.
    New York, NY   Friday, February 12, 1932

11270-	Old Southern Home -1, 2?, 3, 4	ARC unissued
11271-	Bucking Mule -2?	ARC unissued
11272-1	Rubens Train -1	Ba 33083, Me M13047, Or 8345, Pe 13012, Ro 5345
11273-	Leaving North Carolina -1, 2?, 4	ARC unissued
11274-1,-2	The Girl I Left Behind Me -1	ARC unissued

Matrix 11272 was originally logged as *Rambling Hobo Blues*.

Steve Ledford, f/v-1; poss. Taft Ledford, f-2 or g-2; unknown, h-3; Daniel Nicholson, bj or g/v-4; Audie Rodgers, g/v-5; George Ledford, v-6.
    New York, NY   Tuesday, February 16, 1932

11296-2	I Got A Home In The Beulah Land -1, 2?, 4, 5, 6	Ba 32474, Me M12428, Or 8148, Pe 12818, Ro 5148
11297-	All The Good Times Are Past And Gone -1, 2?, 3, 5	ARC unissued
11298-2	Johnson City Hop - 2?, 3	Ba 32476, Me M12426, Or 8150, Pe 12820, Ro 5150, Cq 8241
11299-3	Chinese Breakdown -2?, 3	Ba 33083, Me M13047, Or 8345, Pe 13012, Ro 5345, Cq 8241
11300-	Free Little Bird -5	ARC unissued
11301-	Cumberland Gap -5	ARC unissued
11302-	The Old Grey Mare -1, 2?	ARC unissued
11303-2	Barnyard Frolic -1, 2?	Ba 32476, Me M12426, Or 8150, Pe 12820, Ro 5150
11304-	Going Down The Road Feeling Bad -1, 2?, 4, 5, 6	ARC unissued

Steve Ledford, f/v; poss. Taft Ledford, f or g; unknown, h-1; Daniel Nicholson, bj/v-2; Audie Rodgers, g/v; George Ledford, v-3.

New York, NY   Wednesday, February 17, 1932
  11305-2   That Lonesome Valley -1, 2, 3   Ba 32474, Me M12428, Or 8148, Pe 12818,
                                                             Ro 5148
  11306-   Nobody's Business -2   ARC unissued
  11307-   Bile Dem Cabbage Down   ARC unissued
  11308-   Ole Joe Clark -2   ARC unissued
Steve Ledford also recorded in his own name.

CAROLINA TAR HEELS

Gwen Foster, h/g/v; Dock Walsh, bj/v.
  Atlanta, GA   Saturday, February 19, 1927
  37927-2   There Ain't No Use Workin' So Hard   Vi 20544
  37928-2   Her Name Was Hula Lou   Vi 20545
  37929-2   Bring Me A Leaf From The Sea   Vi 20545
  37930-2   I'm Going To Georgia   Vi 20544

Gwen Foster, h/g/v-1; Dock Walsh, bj/v.
  Charlotte, NC   Thursday, August 11, 1927
  39793-2   Good-bye My Bonnie, Good-bye   Vi 21193
  39794-3   The Bulldog Down In Sunny Tennessee -1   Vi 20941
  39795-2   Shanghai In China -1   Vi 20941

  Charlotte, NC   Monday, August 15, 1927
  39809-1   My Mamma Scolds Me For Flirting   Vi 21193
  39810-3   I Love My Mountain Home -1   Vi 20931
  39811-1   When The Good Lord Sets You Free -1   Vi 20931

Garley Foster, h/g-1/v-2; Dock Walsh, bj/v; Thomas C. Ashley, g.
  Atlanta, GA   Thursday, October 11, 1928
  47159-1   There's A Man Goin' Around Takin' Names -2 Vi V-40053
  47160-2   I Don't Like The Blues No-How -1   Vi V-40053
  47161-3   Lay Down, Baby, Take Your Rest -1   Vi V-40024
  47162-3   Can't You Remember When Your Heart Was Mine? -1 Vi V-40219

Garley Foster, h-1/g; Dock Walsh, bj/v-2/sp-3; Thomas C. Ashley, g/v-4/sp-5.
  Atlanta, GA   Wednesday, November 14, 1928
  47163-2   Roll On, Boys -1, 4   Vi V-40024
  47164-3   You Are A Little Too Small -1, 4   Vi V-40007
  47165-2   Peg And Awl -1, 2, 4   Vi V-40007
  47166-3   I'll Be Washed -2, 3, 5   Vi V-40219

Garley Foster, h/g/v-1/wh-2; Dock Walsh, bj/v-3; Thomas C. Ashley, g/v-4.
  Camden, NJ   Wednesday, April 3, 1929
  51067-2   My Home's Across The Blue Ridge Mountains -1, Vi V-40100
                     2, 3, 4
  51068-2   Hand In Hand We Have Walked Along Together -3 Vi V-40177
  51069-1   The Train's Done Left Me -4   Vi V-40128
  51070-2   Who's Gonna Kiss Your Lips, Dear Darling -1, 2, 3 Vi V-40100
  51071-1   Oh, How I Hate It -3   Vi V-40077
  51072-2   Rude And Rambling Man -4   Vi V-40077
  51073-1, 2   Somebody's Tall And Handsome   Vi unissued

Garley Foster, h/g/v-1/wh; Dock Walsh, bj/v; Thomas C. Ashley, g/v-2.
  Camden, NJ   Thursday, April 4, 1929
  51073-3   Somebody's Tall And Handsome -1   Vi V-40128
  51079-3   The Old Grey Goose -2   Vi V-40177
Matrices 51074 to 51077 are Polish; matrix 51078 is untraced.

Garley Foster, h-1/g/v; Dock Walsh, bj/v-2.
  Memphis, TN   Wednesday, November 19, 1930
  62968-1   Your Low-Down Dirty Ways -2   Vi 23546
  62969-1   Back To Mexico -2   Vi 23611
  62970-1   The Hen House Door Is Locked -2   Vi 23546
  62971-2   Farm Girl Blues -1, 2   Vi 23516
  62972-2   Got The Farm Land Blues -1   Vi 23611
  62973-2   Washing Mama's Dishes -1, 2   Vi 23516
Victor 23611 as by **The Carolina Tar-Heels**.

Original Carolina Tar Heels: Gwen Foster, h/g; Dock Walsh, bj/v.
Atlanta, GA   Thursday, February 25, 1932

71617-1	Times Ain't Like They Used To Be	Vi 23682
71618-1	Why Should I Care	Vi 23671
71619-1	She Shook It On The Corner	Vi 23682
71624-1	Nobody Cares If I'm Blue	Vi 23671

Intervening matrices are by Pinetop & Lindberg (Sparks) (see *B&GR*).

All four of the Carolina Tar Heels recorded in their own names, as well as in other combinations, sometimes with other artists. See Ashley & Foster, Blue Ridge Mountain Entertainers, Fletcher & Foster, Haywood County Ramblers, and Pine Mountain Boys.

Thomas C. Ashley, Garley Foster, and Dock Walsh recorded after 1942.

CAROLINA TWINS

See Fletcher & Foster.

BOYDEN CARPENTER

Boyden Carpenter, v; acc. poss. own or Ernest Thompson, h/g.
Richmond, IN   Wednesday, January 22, 1930

| 16125,-A | Bring Back My Blue Eyed Boy | Ge rejected |
| 16128,-A | Billy Boy | Ge rejected |

Matrix 16126 is untraced; matrix 16127 is by Ernest Thompson.

Acc. prob. own h/g.
Richmond, IN   Tuesday, September 13, 1932

| 18775 | The Old Grey Goose Is Dead | Ch 16519 |
| 18776 | The Hobo's Convention | Ch 16519 |

HARRY CARPENTER

Pseudonym on Madison 1611 for Johnny Marvin.

JOHN CARPENTER

Pseudonym on Bell for Bradley Kincaid.

CARROLL COUNTY REVELERS

Jess Chamblie, f; John Patterson, bj; Henry Chamblie, g/v.
Atlanta, GA   Friday, March 21, 1930

| ATL-971 | Rome Georgia Bound | Vo 5433 |
| ATL-972/73* | Georgia Wobble Blues | Vo 5433 |

ALEC CARSON

Pseudonym on Empire for Carson Robison.

BERT CARSON

Pseudonym on Superior for Lew Childre.

BOB CARSON TRIO

Pseudonym on labels in the Canadian Crown-Domino-Melotone group for the Carson Robison Trio.

CAL CARSON
CAL & GID CARSON

Pseudonyms on Durium Junior for Carson Robison, and Carson Robison & Frank Luther, respectively.

COWBOY CARSON

Pseudonym on Broadway for Edward L. Crain.

EDWARD CARSON

Edward Carson, v; acc. unknown, f; unknown, g.
Richmond, IN   c. March 1928

13665,-A	We Miss You Precious Darling	Ge rejected
13666,-A,-B	My Mother Is Waiting	Ge rejected
13667,-A	Oh, Mary, Don't You Weep	Ge rejected
13668,-A	Don't You Hear Jerusalem Mourn	Ge rejected

Edward J. Carson, v-1; acc. unknown, f; unknown, bj; unknown, g.
Richmond, IN   Monday, December 30, 1929

16039,-A,-B	Then Honey I Will Come Back To You -1	Ge rejected
16040,-A	Scottische [sic]	Ge rejected
16041,-A	The Old Miller's Will -1	Ge rejected
16042,-A	The Old Mule -1	Ge rejected

It seems possible that Edward Carson is associated with Carson Bros. & Sprinkle.

FIDDLIN' JOHN CARSON

Fiddlin' John Carson, v; acc. own f.
Atlanta, GA   c. June 14, 1923

| 8374-B,-C | The Little Old Log Cabin In The Lane | OK 4890 |
| 8375-A,-B | The Old Hen Cackled And The Rooster's Going To Crow | OK 4890 |

An initial pressing without catalog-number is said to have been circulated in the Atlanta area prior to the assignment of a catalog-number, but no such copies have yet been traced.

Fiddlin' John Carson, v-1/sp-2; acc. own f; or f solo-3.
New York, NY   Wednesday, November 7–Thursday, November 8, 1923

72010-B	When You And I Were Young, Maggie -1	OK 40020
72011-B	You Will Never Miss Your Mother Until She Is Gone -1	OK 4994, PaE R3878
72012-A	Be Kind To A Man When He's Down -1	OK 40050
72013-B	Billy In The Low Ground -3	OK 40020
72014-B	Casey Jones -1	OK 40038
72015-A	Old Sallie Goodman -1	OK 40095
72016-B	Fare You Well Old Joe Clark -1	OK 40038
72017-B	The Farmer Is The Man That Feeds Them All -1	OK 40071
72018-A	Papa's Billy Goat -1	OK 4994, PaE R3878
72021-A	The Kickin' Mule -2	OK 40071
72022-B	Nancy Rowland -3	OK 40238
72023-B	Tom Watson Special -1	OK 40050

Matrices 72010 through 72012 were recorded on November 7, 72021 through 72023 on November 8; the intervening matrices may have been recorded on either date. Matrix 72019 is by Lanin Orchestra (popular); 72020 is untraced.

Fiddlin' John Carson, v; acc. own f.
Atlanta, GA   late March/early April 1924

8603-A	Old And In The Way	OK 40181
8605-B	Dixie Boll Weevil	OK 40095
8606-A	When Abraham And Isaac Rushed The Can	OK 40181
8607-A	The Cat Came Back	OK 40119
8608-A,-B	I Got Mine	OK 40119
8609-A	Dixie Cowboy	OK 7004
8610-A	John Henry Blues	OK 7004

OKeh 7004 is a 12-inch issue. Matrix 8604 is untraced.

Fiddlin' John Carson & His Virginia Reelers: Fiddlin' John Carson, f/v-1; unknown, f-2; poss. Land Norris, bj; unknown, g-3.
Atlanta, GA   late March/early April 1924

8613-A	Arkansas Traveler -2, 3	OK 40108
8614-A	Old Aunt Peggy, Won't You Set 'Em Up Again? -1, 2, 3	OK 40108
8615-A	Dixie Division -1, 2, 3	OK 7003
8616-A	Sugar In The Gourd -1	OK 7003

OKeh 7003 is a 12-inch issue. Matrices 8611/12 are untraced.

Fiddlin' John Carson, v; acc. own f; or f solo-1.
Atlanta, GA   Wednesday, August 27, 1924

8705-B	The Lightning Express	OK 7008
8706-A	I'm Glad My Wife's In Europe	OK 40196
8707-A	Turkey In The Straw	OK 40230
8708-A	Jimmie On The Railroad -1	OK 40238
8709-A	Run, Nigger, Run	OK 40230
8710-A	I'm Nine Hundred Miles From Home	OK 40196

OKeh 7008 is a 12-inch issue.

Fiddlin' John Carson & His Virginia Reelers: Fiddlin' John Carson, f/v; unknown, bj; unknown, g.
Atlanta, GA   Wednesday, August 27, 1924

| 8711-A | It Ain't Gonna Rain No Mo' | OK 40204 |
| 8712-A | Alabama Gal (Won't You Come Out Tonight?) | OK 40204 |

Fiddlin' John Carson, v; acc. own f.
  New York, NY   Thursday, December 18, 1924

73034-A	The Baggage Coach Ahead	OK 7006
73035-A	The Orphan Child	OK 7006
73036-A	The Letter Edged In Black	OK 7008
73037-A	Steamboat Bill	OK 40306
73038-A	It Takes A Little Rain With The Sunshine	OK 40343
73039-A	Old Dan Tucker	OK 40263
73040-A	Boil Them Cabbage Down	OK 40306
73041-A	Old Uncle Ned	OK 40263
73042-A	My North Georgia Home	OK 40343

OKeh 7006, 7008 are 12-inch issues.

  Atlanta, GA   Tuesday, April 14, or Wednesday, April 15, 1925

9053-B	The Death Of Floyd Collins	OK 40363
9054-A	Charming Betsy	OK 40363
9055-	Run Along Home With Lindy	OK rejected
9056-	To Welcome The Travelers Home	OK rejected

Acc. own f; Rosa Lee Carson, g-1.
  New York, NY   Wednesday, June 24, 1925

73456-A	Sally Ann -1	OK 40419
73458-A	There's A Hard Time Coming -1	OK 40411
73459-A	The Boston Burglar -1	OK 40419
73463-A	The Honest Farmer	OK 40411
73464-A	To Welcome The Travellers Home -1	OK 45001
73465-A	Run Along Home With Lindy -1	OK 45001

Matrices 73461, 73468 are by Rosa Lee Carson; other intervening matrices are untraced.

Fiddlin' John Carson & His Virginia Reelers: Fiddlin' John Carson, f; Earl Johnson and/or T.M. Brewer, f-1; unknown, bj; poss. Rosa Lee Carson, g-2.
  Atlanta, GA   Wednesday, July 1, 1925

9184-B	Flat-Footed Nigger -1	OK 45018
9185-A	Bully Of The Town -1, 2	OK 40444
9186-A	Hop Light, Lady -1, 2	OK 45011
9187-A	The Hawk And The Buzzard -1, 2	OK 40444
9188-A	Hell Broke Loose In Georgia -1, 2	OK 45018
9189-A	Soldiers' Joy -2	OK 45011

Fiddlin' John Carson, v; acc. own f; or f solo-1.
  New York, NY   late December 1925

73873-A	The Grave Of Little Mary Phagan	OK 45028
73875-A	All Alone By The Sea Side	OK 45028
73876-A	Do Round My Lindy	OK 45032
73877-A	The Batchelors' Hall	OK 45056
73878-A	The Drunkard's Hiccups	OK 45032
73879-A	Liberty -1	OK 45035
73880-A	The Old Frying Pan And The Old Camp Kettle -1	OK 45035

Matrix 73874 is untraced.

Fiddlin' John Carson & His Virginia Reelers: Fiddlin' John Carson, f/v-1; poss. unknown, f-2; unknown, bj-3; unknown, g.
  Atlanta, GA   Thursday, March 11, 1926

9592-A	Cackling Pullet -2	OK 45040
9593-A	Georgia Wagner -2	OK 45040
9596-A	Good-Bye Liza Jane -1, 2, 3	OK 45049
9599-A	If There Wasn't Any Women In The World -1, 3	OK 45049

Intervening matrices are untraced.

Fiddlin' John Carson, v; acc. own f.
  Atlanta, GA   Wednesday, March 17, 1926

9632-A	Everybody Works But Father	OK 45056

Fiddlin' John Carson & His Virginia Reelers: Fiddlin' John Carson, f/v; poss. unknown, f-1; unknown, bj-2; unknown, g.
  Atlanta, GA   Tuesday, November 2, 1926

9845-A	Fire In The Mountain	OK 45068
9846-A	Peter Went Fishing -1	OK 45068
9847-A	When We Meet On That Beautiful Shore	OK 45077

9852-A Long Way To Tipperary -2 OK 45077

Intervening matrices are untraced.

Fiddlin' John Carson, f/v-1; unknown, f-2; unknown, bj; Moonshine Kate (Rosa Lee Carson), g/v-3; prob. T.M. Brewer, v-4.

Atlanta, GA Thursday, March 17, 1927

80549-A,-B	You'll Never Miss Your Mother Until She's Gone -1	OK unissued
80550-B	Be Kind To A Man When He's Down -1, 3	OK 45301
80551-	Welcome The Traveler Home -1	OK unissued
80552-A	In My Old Cabin Home -1, 3, 4	OK 45096
80553-A	Old And In The Way -1	OK 45273
80554-	Papa's Billy Goat -1	OK unissued
80555-	I'm Glad My Wife's In Europe -1	OK unissued
80556-B	It's A Shame To Whip Your Wife On Sunday -1, 3, 4	OK 45122
80557-A	Cotton Eyed Joe -1	OK 45122
80558-A	Jesse James -2	OK 45139
80559-A	Don't Let Your Deal Go Down -1	OK 45096
80560-B	Swanee River -1, 3, 4	OK 45139

Fiddlin' John Carson, f/v; Earl Johnson, f/v-1; T.M. Brewer, bj or g/v-1; Moonshine Kate, bj or g.

Atlanta, GA Monday, October 10, 1927

81726-B	Old Joe Clark -1	OK 45198
81727-A	Gonna Swing On The Golden Gate -1	OK 45159
81728-B	Did He Ever Return?	OK 45176
81729-B	If You Can't Get The Stopper Out Break Off The Neck -1	OK 45167
81730-A	Engineer On The Mogul	OK 45176
81731-C	Hell Bound For Alabama	OK 45159

Atlanta, GA Tuesday, October 11, 1927

81749-B	Turkey In The Hay	OK 45167
81750-A	The Smoke Goes Out The Chimney Just The Same -1	OK 45186
81751-B	Going Down To Cripple Creek -1	OK 45214
81752-B	Quit That Ticklin' Me -1	OK 45186
81753-B	It Won't Happen Again For A Hundred Years Or More -1	OK 45301
81754-A	The Little Log Cabin By The Stream	OK 45198
81755-B	Christmas Time Will Soon Be Over	OK 45273
81756-A	Run Along Home, Sandy -1	OK 45214

Fiddlin' John Carson, v-1/sp-2; acc. own f; Earl Johnson, f-3/sp-4; prob. T.M. Brewer, bj-5/sp-6; Moonshine Kate, g/v-7/sp-8; prob. Bud Blue, sp-9; Lee Banks, sp-10; Lee "Red" Henderson, sp-10.

Atlanta, GA Friday, August 10, 1928

402116-B	Moonshine Kate -3, 8, 9	OK 45290
402117-A,-B	John's Trip To Boston -1, 2, 6	OK unissued
402118-B	John Makes Good Licker -1, 2, 3, 4, 6, 7, 9, 10	OK 45290
402119-A	I'm Going To Take The Train To Charlotte -1, 5	OK unissued: Co C4K47911, Doc DOCD-8018 (CDs)
402120-A	Ain't No Bugs On Me -1, 5	OK 45259
402121-B	The Burglar And The Old Maid -1, 5	OK 45259

Fiddlin' John Carson & Moonshine Kate: Fiddlin' John Carson, f/v/sp-1; Moonshine Kate, g/v-2/sp-3; unidentified, v duet-4.

Atlanta, GA Saturday, March 16, 1929

402337-B	Hawk And Buzzard -4	OK 45338
402338-B	Down South Where The Sugar Cane Grows -2, 4	OK 45338
402339-B	Meet Her When The Sun Goes Down -2	OK 45353
402340-B	My Ford Sedan -4	OK 45353
402341-A	You Can't Get Milk From A Cow Named Ben -1, 3	OK 45321
402342-A	Going To The County Fair -1, 3	OK 45321

Fiddlin' John Carson, f/v/sp-1; T.M. Brewer, bj (or g)/sp-2; Moonshine Kate, g (or bj)/v-3/sp-4; Bud Blue, sp-5.

New York, NY Monday, August 5, 1929

402554-A,-C	Welcome The Travelers Home No. 2 -3	OK 45384
402555-C	You'll Never Miss Your Mother Until She's Gone No. 2 -3	OK 45384
402556-A	John Makes Good Liquor – Part 3 -1, 4, 5	OK 45369

402557-C	John Makes Good Liquor – Part 4 -1, 2, 4, 5	OK 45369
402558-B	She's More Like Her Mother Every Day -1, 4	OK 45402
402559-B	Times Are Not Like They Used To Be -1, 4	OK 45402

OKeh 45384 as by **Fiddlin' John Carson**.

Fiddlin' John Carson, f/v-1/sp; T.M. Brewer, f-2/g/v-1/sp; Moonshine Kate, bj-3/g-4/v-1/sp.
New Orleans, LA   Tuesday, December 17, 1929

403446-B	Pa's Birthday -1, 3	OK 45440
403447-A	Corn Licker & Barbecue – Part 1 -1, 3	OK 45415
403448-B	Corn Licker & Barbecue – Part 2 -1, 3	OK 45415
403449-A	Who's The Best Fiddler? -2, 4	OK 45448
403500-B	Who Bit The Wart Off Grandma's Nose -1, 3	OK 45448
403501-B	Kate's Snuff Box -1, 3	OK 45440

Intervening matrices are by other artists on other dates.

Fiddlin' John Carson, v; acc. own f; Moonshine Kate, bj; T.M. Brewer, g.
New Orleans, LA   Tuesday, December 17, 1929

403502-A	Sunny Tennessee	OK 45434
403503-A	Whatcha Gonna Do When Your Licker Gives Out?	OK 45434

Fiddlin' John Carson & His Virginia Reelers: Fiddlin' John Carson, f; unknown, f-1; unknown, bj-2; Moonshine Kate, g.
Atlanta, GA   Thursday, April 24, 1930

403920-A	The Raccoon And The Possum -1, 2	OK 45445
403921-A	Hen And The Rooster	OK 45445
403922- ; 480003-	Goin' Where The Climate Suits My Clothes -2	OK 45498
403923- ; 480004-	The Dominicker Duck -2	OK 45498

Matrices 403916 to 403919 are by Moonshine Kate.

Fiddlin' John Carson & Moonshine Kate: Fiddlin' John Carson, f/v/sp-1; unknown, bj; Moonshine Kate, g/v-2/sp-3; unidentified, v duet-4.
Atlanta, GA   Thursday, April 24, 1930

403924- ; 480006-	Silver Threads Among The Gold -2, 4	OK 45488
403925- ; 480005-	On The Banks Of Old Tennessee -2	OK 45488
403926-A	You Gotta Let My Dog Alone	OK 45458
403927- ; 480007-A	John In The Army -1, 3	OK 45458
403928- ; 480008-A	The Old Grey Horse Ain't What He Used To Be -1, 3	OK 45471
403929-	You Can't Forget The Day You Was Born	OK unissued

Rev. OKeh 45471 by Moonshine Kate (see Rosa Lee Carson).

Fiddlin' John Carson & His Virginia Reelers: Fiddlin' John Carson, f/v; unknown, bj; Moonshine Kate, g/v-1; poss. unknown, g (on at least some items); unknown, 3rd v-2.
Atlanta, GA   Tuesday, December 9, 1930

404620-B	After The Ball	OK 45569
404621-B	My Home In Dixie-Land -1, 2	OK 45513
404622-B	The Old Ship Is Sailing For The Promised Land -1, 2	OK 45513
404623-	That Woman Don't Treat John Right	OK unissued
404624-B	At The Cross -1, 2	OK unissued: *LC LBC15 (LP); Doc DOCD-8019 (CD)*
404625-B	Take The Train To Charlotte -1, 2	OK 45542
404626-B	Little More Sugar In The Coffee -2	OK 45542
404627-B	Didn't He Ramble -1, 2	OK 45569
404628-	You Gonna Get Something You Don't Expect	OK unissued
404629-	Darktown Strutters Ball	OK unissued

Fiddlin' John Carson & Moonshine Kate: no details.
Atlanta, GA   Wednesday, December 10, 1930

404647-A,-B	Knotty Head Jake	OK unissued

Fiddlin' John Carson: no details.
Atlanta, GA   Wednesday, December 10, 1930

404648-	I've Got A White Man Working For Me	OK unissued
404649-	Nobody Knows My Troubles But Me	OK unissued

Fiddlin' John Carson & Moonshine Kate: Fiddlin' John Carson, f/v; Moonshine Kate, g/v.
    Atlanta, GA   Friday, October 30, 1931
    405073-   I Intend To Make Heaven My Home   OK 45555

Rev. OKeh 45555 by Moonshine Kate (see Rosa Lee Carson).

No details.
    Atlanta, GA   Saturday, October 31, 1931
    405083-   Pole Cat Blues   OK unissued

Fiddlin' John Carson, v/ f; Bill Willard, bj; Moonshine Kate, g/v-1; Marion "Peanut" Brown, g/v-2.
    Camden, NJ   Tuesday, February 27, 1934

Matrix	Title	Release
78995-1	Papa's Billy Goat	BB B-5787
78997-1	Mama's Nanny Goat	BB B-5787
78998-1	I'm Glad My Wife's In Europe	BB B-6247, MW M-4852
78999-1	Be Kind To A Man When He's Down -1	BB B-6022, MW M-4851
82100-1	You'll Never Miss Your Mother Till She's Gone	BB B-6022
82101-1	Since She Took My Licker From Me	BB B-6247, MW M-4852
82102-1	The New "Comin' 'Round The Mountain" -1, 2	BB B-5401
82103-1	I Was Born Four Thousand Years Ago	BB unissued
82104-1	When The Saints Go Marching In -1, 2	BB B-5560
82105-1	The Honest Farmer	BB B-5742, MW M-4849
82106-1	Taxes On The Farmer Feeds Them All -1, 2	BB B-5742, MW M-4849
82107-1	Bear Me Away On Your Snowy White Wings -1, 2	BB B-5560, MW M-4851
82108-1	I Want To Make Heaven My Home -1, 2	BB B-5483
82109-1	Going Where The Sugar Cane Grows -1, 2	BB B-5652
82110-1	Tennessee Wagoner	BB unissued
82111-1	The Storm That Struck Miami	BB B-5483
82112-1	Georgia's Three-Dollar Tag	BB B-5401

Bluebird B-5560, B-5742, B-6022, Montgomery Ward M-4849, M-4851 as by **Fiddlin' John Carson & Moonshine Kate**. Matrix 78996 was not used; matrices 79000 to 82099 are by other artists on other dates.

Fiddlin' John Carson, v/sp-1; acc. own f; Bill Willard, bj-2; Moonshine Kate, g/v-3/y-4/sp-5; Marion "Peanut" Brown, g/v-6/y-7/sp-8.
    Camden, NJ   Wednesday, February 28, 1934

Matrix	Title	Release
82113-1	I'm Old And Feeble -2, 3	BB B-5959, MW M-4850
82114-1	Old And In The Way -2, 3, 6	BB B-5959, MW M-4850
82115-1	Take Your Burdens To The Lord	BB unissued
82116-1	Gonna Raise A Ruckus	BB unissued
82117-1	Stockade Blues -1, 3, 6, 8	BB B-5447, MW M-4848
82118-1	Do You Ever Think Of Me? -1, 3, 4, 5, 6, 7, 8	BB B-5447, MW M-4848
82119-1	Ain't No Bugs On Me -2, 3, 6	BB B-5652

Bluebird B-5447, Montgomery Ward M-4848 as by **Fiddlin' John Carson–Moonshine Kate–Peanut Brown**.

Fiddlin' John Carson also participated in "The OKeh Medicine Show."

ROSA LEE CARSON

Rosa Lee Carson, v; acc. own g.
    New York, NY   Wednesday, June 24, 1925

Matrix	Title	Release
73461-A	Little Mary Phagan	OK 40446
73468-A	The Lone Child	OK 45005

Intervening matrices are by Fiddlin' John Carson or untraced. Rev. OKeh 40446 by Blind Andy Jenkins.

Acc. Fiddlin' John Carson, f; own g.
    Atlanta, GA   Tuesday, July 7, 1925
    9259-A   The Drinker's Child   OK 45005

Moonshine Kate, v/y-1; acc. own g; unknown, g; Fiddlin' John Carson, sp-2.
    Atlanta, GA   Thursday, April 24, 1930

Matrix	Title	Release
403916-; 480009-A	The Last Old Dollar is Gone -2	OK 45471
403917-B	Texas Blues -1	OK 45444
403918-A	Raggedy Riley	OK 45444
403919-	The Dying Hobo	OK unissued

Rev. OKeh 45471 by Fiddlin' John Carson.

Moonshine Kate & Her Pals: unknown, f; unknown, bj-1; unknown, g; Rosa Lee Carson, g/v.
    Atlanta, GA   Tuesday, December 9, 1930
    404642-   The Brave Soldier   OK 45515

404643-B	Are You Going To Leave The Old Home	OK 45547
404644-B	The Poor Girl Story -1	OK 45547
404645-	Texas Bound	OK 45515

Atlanta, GA   Wednesday, December 10, 1930

| 404646- | I Smell Your Hoecake Burning | OK unissued |

Moonshine Kate, v; acc. own g (at least on 405071).
Atlanta, GA   Friday, October 30, 1931

405070-	Log Cabin Home	OK unissued
405071-	My Man's A Jolly Railroad Man	OK 45555
405072-	Daddy Blues	OK unissued

Rev. OKeh 45555 by Fiddlin' John Carson.

Atlanta, GA   Saturday, October 31, 1931

| 405082- | I'm Blue | OK unissued |

Moonshine Kate (as she was known for most of her recording career) also participated in many of her father Fiddlin' John Carson's recordings. All items label-credited to them both are listed under Fiddlin' John Carson, including those on which Moonshine Kate is the vocalist.

CARSON BOYS

Pseudonym on Broadway for Carver Boys.

CARSON BROS. & SPRINKLE

Unknown, f; unknown, bj; unknown, g; unknown, v.
New York, NY   Friday, December 6, 1929

403483-	After The Ball Game Is Over	OK unissued
403484-B	The Old Miller's Will	OK 45398
403485-	Cumberland Gap	OK unissued
403486-	Ida Red	OK unissued
403487-	Climbing Up The Golden Stairs	OK unissued
403488-A	The Highwayman	OK 45398

CARSON BROTHERS

One side of Australian Brunswick 442 by Carson Robison is so credited.

CARSON BROTHERS–SMITH

Vocal duet; acc. unknown, f; unknown, h-1; Roosevelt Smith, ah-2/g.
Asheville, NC   prob. Tuesday, September 1, 1925

9320-A	When The Redeemed Are Gathering In	OK 45023
9321-A	There Will Be A Bright Tomorrow -1	OK 45013
9322-A	Oh! We Miss You -2	OK 45013
9323-A	Don't Grieve Over Me	OK 45023

Roosevelt Smith also recorded as one of the Smith Brothers.

CARSON FAMILY SACRED QUARTETTE

Vocal quartet (three women, one man); acc. unknown, f; unknown, g.
New York, NY   Tuesday, October 19, 1926

80175-A	Just Over The River	OK 45070
80176-	I'm Glad I'm One Of Them	OK unissued
80177-	I'll Live On	OK unissued
80178-	Just Over In The Glory Land	OK unissued
80179-A	I Need Thee All The Time	OK 45070
80180-	The Glory Land Way	OK unissued
80181-	The Great Reaping Day	OK unissued
80182-	I Will Meet You In The Morning	OK unissued

Matrices 80181/82 are logged as by **Carson Family**.

BUSTER CARTER & PRESTON YOUNG

Posey Rorer, f; Buster Carter, bj-1/v-2; Preston Young, g/v-3.
New York, NY   Friday, June 26, 1931

151643-2	It's Hard To Love And Can't Be Loved -1, 3	Co 15690-D
151644-	Wish That Gal Were Mine	Co unissued
151645-1,-2	Swinging Down The Lane (I'd Rather Be Rosy Nell) -1, 2, 3	Co unissued; *Document DOCD-8064* (CD)

151646-	We'll Be Married When The Sun Goes Down	Co unissued
151647-1	It Won't Hurt No More -1, 2, 3	Co 15702-D
151648-2	A Lazy Farmer Boy -2	Co 15702-D
151649-1	What Sugar Head Licker Will Do -1, 2	Co 15758-D
151650-1	Bill Morgan And His Gal -1, 2, 3	Co 15758-D
151651-1	I'll Roll In My Sweet Baby's Arms -1, 2, 3	Co 15690-D
151652-1	She's A Darn Good Gal -1, 3	Co unissued: *Co C4K47911, Document DOCD-8064 (CDs)*

Matrix 151647 was assigned the transfer matrix 130462 when issued.
Matrix 151652 is titled *Darn Good Girl* on Columbia C4K47911.

FLOYD CARTER

Pseudonym on ARC labels for Bob Miller.

HARRY CARTER

Pseudonym on Supertone for Byrd Moore.

SARA & MABEL CARTER

One side of Zonophone 4294 by The Carter Family was apparently issued thus.

TOM CARTER

Pseudonym on Harmony for Gid Tanner.

WILF CARTER (MONTANA SLIM)

This artist's primary issues, on Canadian Bluebird, are generally as by **Wilf Carter (Montana Slim)**, **Wilf Carter "The Yodeling Cowboy"**, or **Wilf Carter "The Yodeling Cowboy" (Montana Slim)**. A few early issues are as by **Wilf Carter** only.
Most Australian and some British issues on Regal-Zonophone are as by **Wilf Carter "The Yodelling Cowboy"** or **Wilf Carter (The Yodelling Cowboy)**.
Many US Bluebird and most Montgomery Ward issues are as by **Montana Slim** or **Montana Slim (The Yodeling Cowboy)**. The latter credit is also used on issues in the Regal-Zonophone ME and HMV MH series, and with slight spelling or punctuation changes on many of the later issues in the English Regal-Zonophone MR series. Indian and Irish Regal-Zonophone issues follow the label credits of their Australian or English co-issues.
Other significant variations are noted.

Wilf Carter, v/y-1; acc. own g.
Montreal, P.Q.   Wednesday, December 20, 1933

7764-1	Swiss Moonlight Lullaby -1	BB B-4966, B-6515, Vi 21-0091, RZAu G23232, CoSs MZ271
7765-1	The Capture Of Albert Johnson	BB B-4966, RZAu G23714

Matrix 7764 is titled *My Swiss Moonlight Lullaby* on Regal-Zonophone G23232.

Montreal, P.Q.   Thursday, January 11, 1934

7766-1	The Hobo's Blues -1	BB B-4968, RZAu G23147
7768-1	Dear Old Daddy Of Mine	BB B-4972
7769-1	Twilight On The Prairie -1	BB B-4969, RZAu G23712
7770-1	The Roundup In The Fall -1	BB B-4972, B-5545, MW M-4500, RZ MR2157, RZAu G23207, HMVAu EA1454, Twin FT1737
7771-1	Sweetheart Of My Childhood Days	BB unissued
7772-1	A Cowboy's Best Friend Is His Pony	BB B-4968, RZAu G23147

Later pressings of Bluebird B-4972 may replace matrix 7768 with matrix 7910. Matrix 7767 is not by Wilf Carter.

Montreal, P.Q.   Friday, January 12, 1934

7773-1	My Montana Sweetheart	BB unissued
7774-1	He Rode The Strawberry Roan	BB B-4974, RZAu G23152
7775-1	My Little Grey Haired Mother In The West	BB B-4976
7776-1	Little Silver Haired Sweetheart Of Mine	BB B-4969, RZAu G23150
7777-1	A Little Log Shack I Can Always Call My Home -1	BB B-4976
7778-1	Trailrider's Lullaby	BB unissued
7779-1	Trail To Home Sweet Home -1	BB unissued
7780-1	Take Me Back To Old Montana -1	BB B-4974, B-5545, MW M-4500, RZAu G23207, HMVAu EA1454, Twin FT1737

Later pressings of Bluebird B-4976 may replace matrices 7775 and 7777 with matrices 7911 and 7912 respectively.

Montreal, P.Q.   Tuesday, October 16, 1934

7815-1	Awaiting The Chair	BB unissued
7816-1	The Life And Death Of John Dillinger	BB unissued
7817-1	Goodbye Little Pal Of My Dreams -1	BB unissued

7818-1	Sway Back Pinto Pete	BB B-4982, RZAu G23155

Matrix 7819 is not by Wilf Carter.

Wilf Carter, v/y; acc. own g.
Montreal, P.Q.   Wednesday, October 17, 1934

7820-1	The Yodeling Trailrider	BB B-4985, RZAu G23152
7821-1	Returning To My Old Prairie Home	BB unissued

Wilf Carter, v/y-1; acc. own g.
Montreal, P.Q.   Thursday, October 18, 1934

7822-1	Cowboy Don't Forget Your Mother	BB B-4979, RZAu G23154
7823-1	Cowboy Blues -1	BB B-4979, RZAu G23154
7824-1	The Smoke Went Up The Chimney Just The Same	BB unissued
7825-1	Moonlight Prison Blues	BB B-4980, RZAu G25107
7826-1	Prairie Blues -1	BB B-4985, RZAu G23150
7827-1	Down The Old Cattle Trail -1	BB B-4988, RZAu G23711
7828-1	I Miss My Swiss -1	BB B-4982
7829-1	The Cowboy's High-Toned Dance -1	BB B-4991, RZAu G22955
7830-1	Pete Knight, The King Of The Cowboys -1	BB B-4989
7831-1	The Hobo's Dream Of Heaven -1	BB B-4986, RZAu G23151
7832-1	My Little Swiss And Me -1	BB B-4600, RZAu G23148
7833-1	Lover's Lullaby Yodel -1	BB B-4980, RZAu G23155

Later pressings of Bluebird B-4989 may replace matrix 7830 with matrix 7902. Matrix 7829 is titled *Cowboy's High-Toned Dance* on Regal-Zonophone G22955.

Montreal, P.Q.   Friday, October 19, 1934

7834-1	The Hobo's Song To The Mounties	BB B-4988, RZAu G24040
7836-1	The Calgary Roundup -1	BB B-4989
7837-1	The Cowhand's Guiding Star	BB B-4986, RZAu G23151
7815-2	Awaiting The Chair	BB B-4983
7816-2	The Life And Death Of John Dillinger	BB B-4983

Later pressings of Bluebird B-4989 may replace matrix 7836 with matrix 7904. Matrix 7837 is titled *The Cowhan's Guiding Star* on Regal-Zonophone G23151. Matrix 7835 is not by Wilf Carter.

Montreal, P.Q.   Saturday, October 20, 1934

7838-1	By The Silv'ry Moonlight Trail	BB B-4991, RZAu G22955
7839-1	The Dying Mother's Prayer	BB B-4995, RZAu G22957
7840-1	I Long For Old Wyoming	BB B-4600, RZAu G23148

New York, NY   Tuesday, January 15, 1935

39246-A,-B	I'm Gonna Ride To Heaven On A Stream Line Train -1	De unissued
39247-A,-B	Hobo's Dream Of Heaven	De unissued
39248-A	How My Yodelling Days Began -1	Pan 25829
39249-A	Hittin' The Trail -1	Pan 25829

Panachord 25829 as by **Wilf Carter (The Yodelling Cowboy)**.

Wilf Carter, v/y; acc. own g.
New York, NY   Tuesday, February 19, 1935

88731-1	Lonesome For My Baby Tonight	BB B-6208, RZAu G22953
88732-1	I'm Gonna Ride To Heaven On A Streamline Train	BB B-5871, MW M-4860, RZAu G23208, HMVAu EA1565,
88733-1	Hillbilly Valley	BB B-6208, RZ MR2062, RZAu G22953, RZIr IZ428

Matrix 88733 is titled *Hill Billy Valley* on Regal-Zonophone issues.
Rev. Regal-Zonophone MR2062, IZ428 by Girls Of The Golden West.

Wilf Carter, v/y-1; acc. own g.
New York, NY   Thursday, February 21, 1935

86384-1	Sundown Blues -1	BB B-6107, RZ MR1943, RZAu G22935, Twin FT1989
86385-1	Cowboy Lullaby -1	BB B-6107, MW M-4858, M-7604, RZ MR1943, RZAu G22935, Twin FT1989
86386-1	Yodeling Hillbilly -1	BB B-4602, B-8389, MW M-7896, RZ ME63, RZAu G23708, RZIr IZ1348, HMVPg MH186
88733-2	Hillbilly Valley -1	BB unissued
86387-1	The Two Gun Cowboy	BB B-5871, MW M-4860, RZAu G23208, HMVAu EA1565

Regal-Zonophone MR1943 as by **Wilf Carter (The New Yodelling Cowboy Star)**.

Matrix 86384 is titled *Sun Down Blues* on Regal-Zonophone MR1943 and probably G22935. Matrix 86386 is titled *Yodeling Hill-Billy* on HMV MH186, and *Yodelling Hillbilly* on on Regal-Zonophone G23708.
Rev. Montgomery Ward M-4858 by Jesse Rodgers.

    Montreal, P.Q.   Wednesday, March 20, 1935

7900-	Returning To My Old Prairie Home -1	BB B-4993, RZAu G22956
7901-1	The Smoke Went Up The Chimney Just The Same	BB B-4997, RZAu G23713
7902-1	Pete Knight, The King Of The Cowboys -1	?BB B-4989, RZAu G22954
7903-1	Cowboy's Mother -1	BB B-4997, RZAu G23149
7904-1	The Calgary Roundup -1	?BB B-4989, RZAu G22954
7905-1	My Little Yoho Lady -1	BB unissued
7906-	Trail To Home Sweet Home -1	BB B-4993, RZAu G22956
7907-1	My Blues Have Turned To Sunshine -1	BB B-4995, RZAu G22957
7910-	Dear Old Daddy Of Mine	?BB B-4972, RZAu G23149
7911-	My Little Grey Haired Mother In The West	?BB B-4976, RZAu G23153
7912-	A Little Log Shack I Can Always Call My Home -1	?BB B-4976, RZAu G23153

Earliest pressings of Bluebird B-4972 probably use matrix 7768; those of B-4976, matrices 7775 and 7777; and those of B-4989, matrices 7830 and 7836. Matrices 7908/09 are untraced.

    New York, NY   Thursday, April 23, 1936

101423-1,-2	The Rescue From Moose River Gold Mine	BB B-4601, B-6380, MW M-5024, RZAu G23714
101424-1,-2	Keep Smiling Old Pal	BB B-4601, B-6380, MW M-5024, RZAu G23709

Wilf Carter, v/sp-1; acc. own g.
    New York, NY   Wednesday, June 17, 1936

102068-1	Don't Let Me Down Old Pal	BB B-4645, MW M-7263, RZAu G24278
102069-1	Won't You Be The Same Old Pal	BB B-4624, MW M-7263, RZAu G24256
102070-1	The Last Ride Down Lariat Trail	BB B-4623, B-8842, MW M-7259, RZAu G23448
102071-1	Rose Of My Heart	BB B-4616, MW M-7264, RZAu G23451
102072-1	Memories Of My Grey Haired Mother In The West	BB B-4608, MW M-7604, RZAu G24705
102073-1	Broken-Down Cowboy	BB B-4603, B-8374, MW M-7259, RZ MR3337, RZAu G23711, RZIn MR20084, RZIr IZ1074, Twin FT8909, HMVPg MH189
102074-1	That Tumbledown Shack By The Trail	BB B-4647, MW M-7605, RZAu G24309
102075-1	Covered Wagon Headin' West	BB B-4622, MW M-7264, RZAu G23449
102076-1	Midnight, The Unconquered Outlaw	BB B-4605, B-6515, MW M-7186, RZAu G23232
102077-1	The Fate Of Old Strawberry Roan -1	BB B-4602, B-8389, MW M-7186, RZAu G23712
102078-1	The Cowboy Wedding In May	BB B-4639, B-8329, MW M-7260, RZAu G24978
102079-1	Sweetheart Of My Childhood Days	BB B-4604, RZAu G24854
102080-1	Ridin' A Maverick	BB B-4646, MW M-7260, RZAu G24697

Some pressings of Regal-Zonophone G24978 mistakenly replace matrix 102078 with matrix 028322 (see October 27, 1938), though retaining the former's title.

Wilf Carter, v/y-1; acc. own g.
    New York, NY   Saturday, June 20, 1936

102250-1	There'll Be No Blues Up Yonder -1	BB B-4642, B-8875, MW M-7265, RZAu G24309
102251-1	Goodbye Little Pal Of My Dreams -1	BB B-4610, MW M-7265, RZAu G23452
102252-1	I Loved Her Till She Done Me Wrong -1	BB B-4627, RZAu G24231
102253-1	Under The Light Of The Texas Moon -1	BB B-4616, MW M-7266, RZAu G23709
102254-1	I'm Still Waiting For You -1	BB B-4639, B-8329, MW M-7266, RZ ME66, RZAu G24294, RZIr IZ1353, HMVIn NE885
102255-1	Longing For My Mississippi Home -1	BB B-4645, RZAu G24114
102256-1	Old Alberta Plains -1	BB B-4624, MW M-7267, RZAu G23448
102257-1	The Cowboy's Heavenly Dream -1	BB B-4646, MW M-7267, RZAu G24626
102258-1	My Old Montana Home -1	BB B-4647, [MW M-7268], RZAu G24294, Vi 27785, P-114
102259-1	Roamin' My Whole Life Away -1	BB B-6827, RZAu G23211, Twin FT8318
102260-1	The Hobo's Yodel -1	BB B-4610, [MW M-7268], RZAu G23452
102261-1	Yodeling Cow-Girl -1	BB B-6827, RZAu G23211, Twin FT8318
102262-1	The Fate Of The Sunset Trail	BB B-4605, MW M-7605, RZAu G24729
102263-1	Prairie Sunset	BB B-6814, RZAu G24040
102264-1	I Just Can't Forget You Old Pal	BB B-6814, RZAu G23932

Matrix 102258 is titled *My Old Montana Blues* on Montgomery Ward M-7268, Victor 27785, P-114. Matrix 102259 was originally logged as *Why Did I Ever Start Roaming*. Matrix 102261 is titled *Yodelling Cow-Girl* on Regal-Zonophone G23211.

    New York, NY   Wednesday, June 24, 1936

102274-1	Roundup Time In Heaven	BB B-4617, B-6826, RZAu G23210, Twin FT8335
102275-1	Put My Little Shoes Away	BB B-4617, B-9032, RZAu G24772
102276-1	When The Bright Prairie Moon Is Rolling By	BB B-4641, MW M-7606, RZAu G24114

102277-1	Roll On Dreamy Texas Moon -1	BB B-4632, B-8241, MW M-7262, RZ MR3375, RZAu G24099, RZIr IZ1074, Twin FT8890
102278-1	The Old Barn Dance -1	BB B-4603, B-8374, MW M-7898, RZ MR3337, RZAu G23710, RZIn MR20084, Twin FT8909, HMVPg MH189
102279-1	Dreamy Prairie Moon -1	BB B-4604, B-6826, RZAu G23210, Twin FT8335
102280-1	Roundup Time In Sunny Old Alberta -1	BB B-4641, MW M-7606, RZAu G24278
102281-1	Roll Along Moonlight Yodel -1	BB B-4608, MW M-7262, RZAu G23456
102282-1	My Faithful Old Pinto Pal -1	BB B-4627, MW M-7261, RZAu G23713
102283-1	The Preacher And The Cowboy -1	BB B-4632, B-8241, MW M-7261, RZ MR3375, RZAu G24256, RZIr IZ1093, Twin FT8890

New York, NY   Thursday, March 11, 1937

06186-1	When The Sun Says Good-Night To The Prairie	BB B-4621, MW M-7895, Vi 27784, RZAu G23710
06187-1	Where Is My Boy To-Night? -1	BB B-4620, B-8157, MW M-7893, RZ MR3088, RZAu G23450, RZIr IZ994, Twin FT8747, HMVPg MH191
06188-1	There's A Love-Knot In My Lariat -1	BB B-4619, B-8111, MW M-7890, RZ MR3106, RZAu G23456, Twin FT8757
06189-1	My Little Yoho Lady -1	BB B-4619, B-8111, MW M-7890, RZ MR3106, RZAu G23451, Twin FT8757
06191--	How My Yodeling Days Began -1	BB B-4622, MW M-7895, RZAu G23449
06192-1	Answer To Swiss Moonlight Lullaby -1	BB B-4620, B-8181, MW M-7896, RZ MR3145, RZAu G23450, Twin FT8786

Matrix 06187 is titled *Where Is My Wandering Boy Tonight?* on all non-North American issues, except some pressings of Regal-Zonophone G23450. Matrix 06191 is titled *How My Yodelling Days Began* on Regal-Zonophone G23449. Matrix 06192 is titled *Answer To The Swiss Moonlight Lullaby* on Regal-Zonophone MR3145. Matrix 06190 is untraced.

New York, NY   Friday, May 7, 1937

07980-1	The Hindenburg Disaster	BB B-4621

Acc. unknown, sg; own g.
New York, NY   Thursday, June 10, 1937

010639-1	Pete Knight's Last Ride	BB B-4623, MW M-8465, Vi 27785, RZAu G24231

Acc. Carl de Vries, sg-2; own g.
Montreal, P.Q.   Friday, November 19, 1937

8288-1	I Wish I Had Never Seen Sunshine	BB B-4636, RZAu G23567
8289-1	Everybody's Been Some Mother's Darling	BB B-4634, RZAu G23551
8290-1	You'll Always Be Mine In My Dreams -1	BB B-4636, RZAu G23567
8291-1	Dusty Trails -1, 2	BB B-4634, RZAu G23551

Acc. unknown, sg; own g.
New York, NY   Tuesday, May 17, 1938

023191-1	By The Grave Of Nobody's Darling	BB B-4642, B-7618, MW M-8465, RZAu G23708
023192-1	What A Friend We Have In Mother	BB B-4648, B-8157, MW M-7893, RZ MR3088, RZIr IZ994, Twin FT8747, HMVPg MH191

Rev. Bluebird B-7618 by Norwood Tew.

Acc. own g.
New York, NY   Tuesday, October 25, 1938

028041-1	The Little Red Patch On The Seat Of My Trousers	BB B-8361, MW M-7900, RZAu G23953
028042-1	Golden Memories Of Mother And Dad	BB B-4663, MW M-7898, RZAu G24812
028043-1	My Honeymoon Bridge Broke Down -1	BB B-4652, B-8313, MW M-7901, RZAu G24151
028044-1	Down The Yodeling Trail At Twilight -1	BB B-4648, B-8181, MW M-7897, RZ MR3145, RZAu G23932, Twin FT8786, CoSs MZ271
028045-1	I'm Only A Dude In Cowboy Clothes -1	BB B-4652, B-8313, MW M-7901, RZAu G24151
028046-1	My Lulu -1	BB B-4676, B-8924, MW M-8464, RZAu G24812
028047-1	Rootin' Tootin' Cowboy -1	BB B-4649, B-8361, MW M-7900, RZ ME51, RZAu G23953
028048-1	I'm Hittin' The Trail -1	BB B-4654, MW M-7899, Vi 27786, RZAu G24011

Matrix 028044 is titled *Down The Yodelling Trail At Twilight* on Regal-Zonophone G23932, Columbia MZ271, and probably Regal-Zonophone MR3145, Twin FT8786.

New York, NY   Thursday, October 27, 1938

028321-1	We'll Meet Again In Peaceful Valley -1	BB B-4650, 33-0505, MW M-7899, RZAu G24055
028041-2	The Little Red Patch On The Seat Of My Trousers	BB B-4649

028322-1	My Brown Eyed Prairie Rose	BB B-4654, MW M-8461, Vi 27786, RZAu G24011
028323-1	I'll Meet You At The Roundup In The Spring -1	BB B-4676, MW M-8461, Vi 27787, RZAu G24978
028324-1	Dawn On The Prairie -1	BB B-4669, MW M-8462, RZAu G24705
028325-1	My Yodeling Sweetheart -1	BB B-4675, MW M-8462, RZAu G24548
028326-1	Yodeling Memories -1	BB B-4658, MW M-8463, RZAu G24099
028327-1	Cowboy's Airplane Ride -1	BB B-4659, MW M-8463, Vi 27784, RZAu G23986
028328-1	Memories Of My Little Old Log Shack -1	BB B-4665, B-8202, MW M-7894, RZAu G24567
028329-1	My Last Old Yodel Song -1	MW M-8464

Matrix 028325 is titled *My Yodelling Sweetheart* on Regal-Zonophone G24548. Matrix 028326 is titled *Yodelling Memories* on Regal-Zonophone G24099.

Acc. Carl De Vries, sg-2; own g.
New York, NY   Friday, November 4, 1938

028904-1	My Yodeling Days Are Through -1	BB B-4677, 55-3209, MW M-8456
028905-1	Headin' For That Land Of Gold -1	BB B-4669, B-8983, MW M-8456, RZAu G24772
028906-1	Wilf Carter Blues -1	BB B-4667, MW M-8457, RZAu G24729
028907-1	Golden Lariat -2	BB B-4656, B-8150, MW M-7892, RZ MR3209, RZAu G23861
028908-1	A Cowboy Who Never Returned -2	BB B-4675, MW M-8457, RZAu G24548
028909-1	When It's Twilight Over Texas -1, 2	BB B-4672, B-8202, MW M-7894, RZAu G24626
028910-1	My Only Romance Is Memories Of You -2	BB B-4667, B-8284, MW M-8458, RZAu G24165
028911-1	When I Say Hello To The Rockies -1, 2	BB B-4663, B-8284, MW M-7897, RZAu G24165
028912-1	When I Bid The Prairie Good-Bye -2	BB B-4665, MW M-8459, Vi 27787, RZAu G24567
028913-1	My Dreams Come True -2	BB B-4659, MW M-8459, RZAu G23986
028914-1	You Left Your Brand On My Heart -1, 2	BB B-4672, MW M-8460, RZAu G24697
028915-1	Yodeling Love Call -1, 2	BB B-4656, MW M-8460, RZAu G25107

Matrix 028915 is titled *Yodelling Love Call* on Regal-Zonophone G25107.

New York, NY   Thursday, December 8, 1938

| 030371-1 | It Makes No Difference Now | BB B-4650, 33-0519, MW M-8458, Vi 20-2071, RZAu G24055 |

Acc. Carl De Vries, sg; own g.
New York, NY   Monday, April 17, 1939

035757-1	What Difference Does It Make?	BB B-4658, B-8150, MW M-7892, RZAu G23861
035758-1	Answer To It Makes No Difference Now	BB B-8149, MW M-7891, RZAu G23844
035759-1	Roll Along Kentucky Moon	BB B-8149, MW M-7891, RZ MR3209, RZAu G23844

Acc. unknown, h-2; own g; unknown, 2nd v-3; unknown, 3rd v-4; unknown, y-5; unknown, wh-6; unknown, train-wh eff-7; unknown, 2nd train-wh eff-8.
New York, NY   Wednesday, March 27, 1940

048450-1	Red River Valley Blues -1, 2, 6	BB B-8441, MW M-8709, RZ MR3439, RZAu G24206, RZIn MR20174, RZIr IZ1111, Twin FT9102
048451-1	When The White Azaleas Start Blooming -6	BB B-4677, B-8456, MW M-8709, RZ MR3523, RZAu G24193, RZIn MR20249, RZIr IZ1150
048452-1	My Ramblin' Days Are Through -6, 7, 8	BB B-4677, B-8456, MW M-8712, RZ ME51, RZAu G24193
048453-1	I Still Think Of You Sweet Nellie Dean -2, 6	BB B-4697, B-8517, MW M-8713, RZE MR3417, RZIn MR20154, RZIr IZ1113, Twin FT8977
048454-1	He Left The One Who Loved Him For Another -6	BB B-8531, MW M-8713, RZ MR3486, RZAu G24384, RZIn MR20217, RZIr IZ1130
048455-1	When It's Roll-Call In The Bunk House -6	BB B-8548, MW M-8711, RZAu G24354
048456-1	My True And Earnest Prayer -6	BB B-4728, B-8517, MW M-8710, RZ MR3417, RZAu G24794, RZIn MR20154, RZIr IZ1113, Twin FT8977
048457-1	Beautiful Girl Of The Prairie -1, 2, 3, 5, 6	BB B-8472, MW M-8710, RZ ME63, RZIr IZ1348, HMVAu MH186
048458-1	It's All Over Now (I Won't Worry) -2, 6	BB B-8425, MW M-8708, RZ ME61, RZAu G24326, RZIr IZ1344, HMVIn NE883
048459-1	Rattlin' Cannonball -7	BB B-8425, MW M-8708, RZ ME61, RZAu G24326, RZIr IZ1344, HMVIn NE883

| 048460-1 | My Old Canadian Home -1, 3, 6 | BB B-4682, B-8566, MW M-8712, RZAu G24588 |
| 048461-1 | I'll Get Mine Bye-And-Bye -1, 3, 4 | BB B-8548, MW M-8711, RZAu G24354 |

Acc. unknown, h-2; own g; unknown, y-3; unknown, wh-4.
New York, NY   Thursday, April 4, 1940

048647-1	Dad's Little Texas Lad -2, 4	BB B-8591, MW M-8868, RZAu G24742
048648-1	Thinking -1, 2, 4	BB B-8591, MW M-8868, RZAu G24742
048649-1	What A Wonderful Mother Of Mine -2, 4	BB B-8491, MW M-8865, RZAu G24447
048650-1	You Are My Sunshine -2, 4	BB B-8491, MW M-8865, RZAu G24447
048651-1	My Texas Sweetheart -4	BB B-4727, B-8616, MW M-8867, RZAu G24766
048652-1	Echoing Hills Yodel Back To Me -1, 3, 4	BB B-4682, B-8616, MW M-8867, RZ MR3523, RZAu G24766, RZIn MR20249, RZIr IZ1150
048653-1	You Were With Me In The Waltz Of My Dreams -1, 2, 4	BB B-8641, MW M-8869, RZAu G24854
048654-1	When That Some Body Else Was You -4	BB B-8641, MW M-8869
048655-1	My Missoula Valley Moon -1, 4	BB B-4695, B-8661, MW M-8870, RZAu G24992
048656-1	Old Chuck Wagon Days -1	BB B-4687, B-8661, MW M-8871, RZAu G24992
048657-1	It's A Cowboy's Night To Howl -1	BB B-8441, MW M-8866, RZ MR3439, RZAu G24206, RZIn MR20174, RZIr IZ1111, Twin FT9102
048658-1	Back Ridin' Old Trails Again -1	BB B-4697, B-8566, MW M-8870, RZAu G24588

Matrix 048658 is titled *Back Ridin' The Old Trails Again* on Bluebird B-8566, Montgomery Ward M-8870, Regal-Zonophone G24588.

Acc. own g.
New York, NY   Monday, April 8, 1940

048744-1	Let's Go Back To The Bible	BB B-4687, B-8875
048745-1	Why Should I Feel Sorry For You Now?	BB B-8472, MW M-8866, RZ ME66, RZIr IZ1353, HMVIn NE885
048746-1	I Bought A Rock For A Rocky Mountain Gal	BB B-8696, MW M-8871, RZAu G24916
048747-1	It's Great To Be Back In The Saddle Again	BB B-8753, RZ MR3570, RZAu G24965, RZIn MR20287, RZIr IZ1178
048748-1	If You Don't Really Care	BB B-4727, B-8924
048749-1	Why Did We Ever Part	BB B-4728, RZAu G25127
048750-1	LaVerne, My Brown Eyed Rose	BB B-8800, MW M-8872
048751-1	The Last Letter	BB B-4695, B-8842
048752-1	Ride For The Open Range -1	BB B-8800, RZAu G25127
048753-1	Call Of The Range -1	BB B-8753, RZ MR3570, RZAu G24794, RZIn MR20287, RZIr IZ1178
048754-1	Streamlined Yodel Song -1	BB B-8696, Vi 21-0091, RZAu G24916
048755-1	My Old Lasso Is Headed Straight For You -1	BB B-8531, MW M-8872, RZ MR3486, RZAu G24384, RZIn MR20217, RZIr IZ1130

New York, NY   Tuesday, December 16, 1941

068647-1	Memories That Never Die	BB B-4740, 33-0539
068648-1	I'm Thinking Tonight Of My Blue Eyes	BB B-4735, B-9032, Vi 20-2071
068649-1	The Prisoner's Song	BB 33-0505, 55-3202
068650-1	I May Be Wrong	BB 33-0539, 55-3209
068651-1	Old Buddies	BB B-4734
068652-1	Sweetheart's Farewell	BB B-4738
068653-1	Sittin' By The Old Corral	BB 33-0510, 55-3202
068654-1	I'll Always Keep Smiling For You	BB B-4738
068655-1	That First Love Of Mine	BB 33-0510, 55-3201
068656-1	Waiting For A Train -1	BB 55-3201
068657-1	West Of Rainbow Trail -1	BB B-4734, B-8983, RZAu G24965
068658-1	Yodeling My Babies To Sleep -1	BB B-4740
068659-1	Just One More Ride -1	BB B-4735, 33-0519

Wilf Carter recorded after 1942.

CARTER & WILSON

Pseudonym on Harmony for Gid Tanner & Riley Puckett.

CARTER BROTHERS & SON

George Carter, f/v; Andrew Carter, f; Jimmie Carter, g.
Memphis TN   Friday, February 24, 1928

| 400331-A | Liza Jane | OK 45202 |
| 400332-B | Give The Fiddler A Dram | OK 45289 |

400333-B	Old Joe Bone	OK 45289
400334-	Bob Christmas	OK unissued
400335-	Old Molly Hare	OK unissued
400336-A	Saddle Up The Grey	OK 45202

George Carter, f/v-1; Andrew Carter, f; Jimmie Carter, g.
Memphis TN   Thursday, November 22, 1928

M-833-	Give Me A Chaw Tobacco -1	Vo 5295
M-834-	Pay Me Back My Fifteen Cents	Vo unissued
M-835-	Nancy Rowland -1	Vo 5349
M-836-	Cotton Eyed Joe -1	Vo 5349
M-837-	Miss Brown -1	Vo 5297
M-838-	Jenny On The Railroad	Vo 5297
M-839-	Leather Breeches -1	Vo 5295

CARTER FAMILY

Sara Carter, Maybelle Carter, A.P. Carter, v trio; or Sara Carter, A.P. Carter, v duet-1; acc. Sara Carter, ah; Maybelle Carter, g.
Bristol, TN   Monday, August 1, 1927

39750-2	Bury Me Under The Weeping Willow	Vi 21074, BB B-6053, MW M-7020, RZAu G22654
39751-2	Little Log Cabin By The Sea -1	Vi 21074, BB B-6271
39752-2	The Poor Orphan Child -1	Vi 20877, MW M-7445
39753-2	The Storms Are On The Ocean	Vi 20937, BB B-6176, MW M-7021

Sara Carter, v; acc. own ah; Maybelle Carter, g.
Bristol, TN   Tuesday, August 2, 1927

| 39754-2 | Single Girl, Married Girl | Vi 20937, MW M-7445 |
| 39755-1 | The Wandering Boy | Vi 20877, MW M-7446 |

Sara Carter, Maybelle Carter, A.P. Carter, v trio; or Sara Carter, A.P. Carter, v duet-1; acc. Sara Carter, ah; Maybelle Carter, sg-2/g-3.
Camden, NJ   Wednesday, May 9, 1928

45020-2	Meet Me By Moonlight, Alone -1, 2	Vi 23731, BB B-5096, Eld 2011, Sr S-3174, MW M-7149
45021-2	Little Darling, Pal Of Mine -1, 2	Vi 21638, BB B-5301, Eld 2172, Sr S-3382, MW M-4427
45022-1	Keep On The Sunny Side -3	Vi 21434, BB 1836, B-5006, Eld 1964, Sr S-3127, MW M-4225, Zo/RZAu EE179, ZoSA 4270
45022-1R	Keep On The Sunny Side -3	BB 33-0537, Vi 20-3259
45023-2	Anchored In Love -1, 3	Vi V-40036, BB B-5406, Sr S-3427, MW M-4740, Zo 5753, Zo/RZAu EE205, ZoSA 4228, RZ ME33, RZAu T5753, HMVSA SAM147, HMVPg MH184, Twin FT1773

Unless noted otherwise, Sara Carter sings lead in the duets and A.P. Carter harmony.
Matrix 45022-1R is a remastering with enhanced bass response, made on March 20, 1933.

Sara Carter, Maybelle Carter, A.P. Carter, v trio; or Sara Carter, A.P. Carter, v duet-1; or Sara Carter, v-2; acc. Sara Carter, ah-3; Maybelle Carter, g.
Camden, NJ   Thursday, May 10, 1928

45024-2	John Hardy Was A Desperate Little Man -2	Vi V-40190, BB B-6033, MW M-4741, ZoSA 4294
45025-1	I Ain't Goin' To Work Tomorrow -2, 3	Vi 21517, MW M-7019
45026-1	Will You Miss Me When I'm Gone? -1	Vi 21638, MW M-4228
45027-2	River Of Jordan -3	Vi 21434, BB B-5058, Eld 1984, Sr S-3143, MW M-4430, Zo/RZAu EE179, ZoSA 4270
45028-2	Chewing Gum -2, 3	Vi 21517, MW M-7019
45029-1	Wildwood Flower -2	Vi V-40000, BB B-5356, Sr S-3437, MW M-4432
45030-2	I Have No One To Love Me (But The Sailor On The Deep Blue Sea) -3	Vi V-40036, BB B-5356, Sr S-3437, MW M-4320, M-4740, Zo 5753, Zo/RZAu EE205, ZoSA 4228, RZ ME28, RZAu T5753, G22465, HMVSA SAM147, HMVPg MH184, Twin FT1773
45031-2	Forsaken Love -1, 3	Vi V-40000, MW M-4734

Zonophone 4294 as by **Sara & Mabel Carter**.
Matrix 45030 is titled *My Lover On The Deep Blue Sea* on Montgomery Ward M-4320, and *I Have No One To Love Me* on Montgomery Ward M-4740.
Rev. Montgomery Ward M-4320 by Floyd County Ramblers.

Sara Carter, Maybelle Carter, A.P. Carter, v trio; or Sara Carter, A.P. Carter, v duet-1; acc. Sara Carter, ah-2/g-3/y-4; Maybelle Carter, sg-5/g-6.

Camden, NJ   Thursday, February 14, 1929

Matrix	Title	Issues
49856-2	Sweet Fern -1, 3, 4, 5	Vi V-40126, BB B-5927, MW M-4437, RZAu G22826
49857-1	My Clinch Mountain Home -1, 3, 4, 5	Vi V-40058, BB B-5301, Eld 2172, Sr S-3382, MW M-4432, Zo 5493, Zo/RZAu EE226, ZoSA 4226, RZ ME27, RZAu T5493, RZIr IZ325, HMVPg MH185
49858-1	God Gave Noah The Rainbow Sign -2, 6	Vi V-40110, BB B-5272, Eld 2146, Sr S-3353, MW M-4427
49859-3	I'm Thinking To-night Of My Blue Eyes -1, 2, 6	Vi V-40089, BB B-5122, Eld 2032, Sr S-3203, MW M-4230
49860-2	Little Moses -2, 6	Vi V-40110, BB B-5924, MW M-5010
49861-2	Lulu Wall -2, 6	Vi V-40126, BB B-5927, MW M-4437, RZAu G22826, ZoSA 4239
49862-2	The Grave On The Green Hillside -3	Vi V-40150, MW M-7021, ZoSA 4249

On matrix 49857 A.P. Carter sings lead and Sara Carter harmony. Matrix 49863 is by Johnny Dodds (see *JR*).
Revs: Zonophone 4239 by Bud & Joe Billings (Frank Luther & Carson Robison), 4249 by Foreman Family.

Sara Carter, Maybelle Carter, A.P. Carter, v trio; or Sara Carter, A.P. Carter, v duet-1; or Sara Carter, v-2; acc. Sara Carter, ah-3/g-4/y-5; Maybelle Carter, sg-6/g-7.

Camden, NJ   Friday, February 15, 1929

Matrix	Title	Issues
49864-2	Don't Forget This Song -1, 4, 6	Vi V-40328, MW M-7022, Zo/RZAu EE263, ZoSA 4347
49865-2	The Foggy Mountain Top -1, 4, 5, 6	Vi V-40058, MW M-4743, Zo 5493, Zo/RZAu EE210, ZoSA 4226, RZ ME27, RZAu T5493, RZIr IZ325, HMVPg MH185
49866-2	Bring Back My Blue-Eyed Boy To Me -3, 7	Vi V-40190, BB B-6271, MW M-4741, ZoSA 4294
49867-2	Diamonds In The Rough -7	Vi V-40150, BB B-6033, MW M-4434, Twin FT1978
49868-2	Engine One-Forty-Three -2, 4, 7	Vi V-40089, BB B-6223, MW M-4743

Matrix 49864 was originally logged with the subtitle (*My Home In Old Virginia*).
Rev. Zonophone/Regal-Zonophone EE210 by McCravy Brothers.

Sara Carter, Maybelle Carter, A.P. Carter, v trio; or Sara Carter, A.P. Carter, v duet-1; acc. Sara Carter, ah; Maybelle Carter, g.

Atlanta, GA   Friday, November 22, 1929

Matrix	Title	Issues
56566-1	The Homestead On The Farm	Vi V-40207, MW M-7023, Zo/RZ Au EE240, ZoSA 4286
56567-3	The Cyclone Of Ryecove	Vi V-40207, MW M-7023, ZoSA 4286
56568-3	Motherless Children -1	Vi 23641, BB B-5924, MW M-5010, Zo/RZAu EE361

Sara Carter, Maybelle Carter, A.P. Carter, v trio; or Sara Carter, A.P. Carter, v duet-1; or Sara Carter, v-2; acc. Sara Carter, ah-3/g-4/y-5; Maybelle Carter, sg-6/g-7.

Atlanta, GA   Sunday, November 24, 1929

Matrix	Title	Issues
56581-2	When The Roses Bloom In Dixieland -3, 7	Vi V-40229, BB B-5716, MW M-4544, Zo/RZAu EE226, ZoSA 4322
56582-2	No Telephone In Heaven -3, 7	Vi V-40229, BB B-5272, Eld 2146, Sr S-3353, MW M-4430, Zo/RZAu EE240, ZoSA 4322
56583-2	Western Hobo -1, 4, 5, 6	Vi V-40255, BB B-6223, MW M-7147
56584-1	Carter's Blues -2, 4, 5, 7	Vi 23716, BB B-6036, MW M-5012, RZAu G22795, Twin FT1992
56585-3	Wabash Cannonball -2, 3, 7	Vi 23731, BB B-8350, MW M-7444, RZAu G24157

Sara Carter, Maybelle Carter, A.P. Carter, v trio; or Sara Carter, A.P. Carter, v duet-1; or Sara Carter, Maybelle Carter, v duet-2; or Sara Carter, v-3; acc. Sara Carter, ah-4/g-5/y-6; Maybelle Carter, sg-7/g-8.

Atlanta, GA   Monday, November 25, 1929

Matrix	Title	Issues
56586-2	A Distant Land To Roam -5, 8	Vi V-40255, BB B-5543, MW M-7020
56587-2	Jimmie Brown The Newsboy -3, 4, 8	Vi 23554, MW M-5027, Zo/RZAu EE297
56588-1	Kitty Waltz -2, 5, 8	Vi V-40277, BB B-5990, MW M-4434, Zo/RZAu EE238, Twin FT1944
56589-2	Fond Affection -1, 5, 6, 7	Vi 23585, BB B-6176, MW M-4744, ZoSA 4364

Sara Carter, Maybelle Carter, A.P. Carter, v trio; or Sara Carter, A.P. Carter, v duet-1; or A.P. Carter, v-2; acc. Sara Carter, ah/y-3; Maybelle Carter, sg-4/g-5.

Memphis, TN   Saturday, May 24, 1930

59979-1	The Cannon-Ball -2, 5	Vi V-40317, BB B-6020, MW M-4742, Twin FT1962
59980-2	The Lovers' Farewell -1, 5	Vi V-40277, BB B-6036, MW M-5012, Zo/RZAu EE238, Twin FT1992
59981-2	There's Someone Awaiting For Me -1, 3, 5	Vi 23554, Zo/RZAu EE297
59982-2	The Little Log Hut In The Lane -5	Vi V-40328, MW M-7022, Zo/RZAu EE263, ZoSA 4347
59983-2	When The Springtime Comes Again -3, 4	Vi V-40293, BB B-5122, Eld 2032, Sr S-3203, MW M-4227, Zo/RZAu EE256
59984-2	When The World's On Fire -1, 4	Vi V-40293, BB 1836, B-5006, 33-0537, Eld 1964, Sr S-3127, MW M-4229, Zo/RZAu EE256
59985-2	I Have An Aged Mother -1, 4	MW M-7446
59986-2	The Dying Soldier -1, 4	Vi 23641, MW M-4735, Zo/RZAu EE361
59987-2	Worried Man Blues -5	Vi V-40317, 27497, BB B-6020, MW M-4742, RZAu G22795, Twin FT1962

On matrices 59980, 59984 A.P. Carter sings lead and Sara Carter harmony.
Matrix 59980 is titled *The Lover's Farewell* on at least some copies of Bluebird B-6036.
Rev. Victor 27497 by Wade Mainer–Zeke Morris.

Sara Carter, Maybelle Carter, A.P. Carter, v trio; acc. Sara Carter, ah; Maybelle Carter, g.
Memphis, TN   Monday, November 24, 1930

64705-2	Lonesome Valley	Vi 23541, BB B-6117, MW M-4735, Zo/RZAu EE295
64706-2	On The Rock Where Moses Stood	Vi 23513, BB B-6055, MW M-4739, RZAu G22617, ZoSA 4739
64707-2	Room In Heaven For Me	Vi 23618, BB B-5993, MW M-4733, RZAu G22827

Sara Carter, Maybelle Carter, A.P. Carter, v trio; or Sara Carter, A.P. Carter, v duet-1; acc. Sara Carter, ah-2/g-3/y-4; Maybelle Carter, sg-5/g-6.
Memphis, TN   Tuesday, November 25, 1930

64714-2	Lonesome Pine Special -3, 4, 6	Vi 23716, MW M-4737
64715-2	No More The Moon Shines On Lorena -2, 6	Vi 23523, MW M-5027, ZoSA 4328
64716-2	On My Way To Canaan's Land -2, 6	BB B-8167
64717-2	Where Shall I Be? -2, 5	Vi 23523, BB B-6055, MW M-4229, RZAu G22617, ZoSA 4328
64718-2	Sow 'Em On The Mountain (Reap 'Em In The Valley) -1, 2, 5	Vi 23585, BB B-5468, MW M-4744
64719-2	Darling Nellie Across the Sea -2, 6	Vi 23513, MW M-4739, ZoSA 4364
64720-2	The Birds Were Singing Of You -3, 6	Vi 23541, BB B-6117, MW M-4226, Zo/RZAu EE295

Matrix 64718 is titled *Sow 'Em On The Mountain* on Montgomery Ward M-4744.

Sara Carter, Maybelle Carter, A.P. Carter, v trio; or Sara Carter, A.P. Carter, v duet-1; acc. Sara Carter, ah-2/g-3; Maybelle Carter, g.
Charlotte, NC   Monday, May 25, 1931

69345-2	Weary Prodigal Son -1, 3	Vi 23626, MW M-7443, Zo/RZAu EE330
69346-2	My Old Cottage Home -1, 3	Vi 23599, BB B-6000, MW M-5011, RZAu G22828
69347-1	When I'm Gone -2	Vi 23569, BB B-6053, MW M-4736, RZAu G22654, Twin FT1978
69348-2	Sunshine In The Shadows -2	Vi 23626, BB B-5468, MW M-7148, Zo/RZAu EE330, ZoSA 4375
69349-2	Let The Church Roll On -2	Vi 23618, MW M-4733

On matrix 69346 A.P. Carter sings lead and Sara Carter harmony.
Charlotte, NC   Tuesday, May 26, 1931

69350-2	Lonesome For You -1	Vi 23599, BB B-6000, MW M-5011, RZAu G22828
69351-2	Can't Feel At Home -2	Vi 23569, BB B-6257, MW M-4736, ZoSA 4366

On matrix 69350 A.P. Carter and Sara Carter sing alternating solo parts.

Jimmie Rodgers & Sara Carter: Jimmie Rodgers, Sara Carter, v/y duet; acc. Maybelle Carter, g; poss. Sara Carter, g.
Louisville, KY   Wednesday, June 10, 1931

69412-1	Why There's A Tear In My Eye	BB B-6698, MW M-7138, RZ ME33, MR2374, MR2429, RZIr IZ616, IZ649, Twin FT8313

| 69412-3 | Why There's A Tear In My Eye | Vi unissued: *RCA LPM2865, RCA(E) RD7644, DPM2047, RCA(J) RA5463, RA5501, RA5645* (LPs); *BF BCD15865* (CD) |
| 69413-2 | The Wonderful City | BB B-6810, MW M-7137, RZ MR2455, RZAu G23184, RZIr IZ662, Twin FT8313 |

Revs: Bluebird B-6698, Regal-Zonophone ME33, MR2429, IZ649 by Mrs. Jimmie Rodgers; others by Jimmie Rodgers.

Jimmie Rodgers (Assisted By The Carter Family): Jimmie Rodgers, v/y/sp; A.P. Carter, v/sp; Sara Carter, v/sp; Maybelle Carter, v/sp; acc. Maybelle Carter, md/g; Sara Carter, g.

Louisville, KY   Thursday, June 11, 1931

69427-1,-2	Jimmie Rodgers Visits The Carter Family	Vi unissued
69427-3	Jimmie Rodgers Visits The Carter Family	Vi unissued: *Franklin Mint 34, 52, RCA(J) RA5645* (LPs); *BF BCD15865* (CD)
69428-1,-2,-3	The Carter Family And Jimmie Rodgers In Texas	Vi unissued: *ACM 11* (LP)

Other LP/CD issues of matrix 69427 use take 4, slightly edited and with the spoken coda dubbed in from take 3.
It is uncertain which of the previously unissued takes 1, 2, and 3 of matrix 69428 is used on ACM 11.

Jimmie Rodgers, v/y/sp; Sara Carter, v/y-1/sp; A. P. Carter, v-2/sp; Maybelle Carter, v-2/sp; acc. Maybelle Carter, md-2/g-2; Jimmie Rodgers, g-1; Sara Carter, g.

Louisville, KY   Friday, June 12, 1931

| 69427-4 | Jimmie Rodgers Visits The Carter Family -2 | Vi 23574, MW M-4720, RZ ME34, MR3164, Zo/RZAu EE369, Twin FT8806, HMVPg MH188 |
| 69428-4 | The Carter Family And Jimmie Rodgers In Texas -1 | BB B-6762, MW M-7137, RZ ME34, MR3164, Twin FT8806, HMVPg MH188 |

Matrix 69428 is titled *The Carter Family Visits Jimmie Rodgers* on Montgomery Ward M-7137.
Revs: Victor 23574, Montgomery Ward M-4720, Zonophone/Regal-Zonophone EE369 by Jimmie Rodgers; Bluebird B-6762 by Monroe Brothers.

The Carter Family: Sara Carter, Maybelle Carter, A.P. Carter, v trio; acc. Sara Carter, ah-1/g-2; Maybelle Carter, g.

Atlanta, GA   Tuesday, February 23, 1932

71609-1	'Mid The Green Fields Of Virginia -1	Vi 23686, BB B-5243, Eld 2126, Sr S-3326, MW M-4737, Zo/RZAu EE350
71610-2	Happiest Days Of All -1	Vi 23701, BB B-6106, MW M-4738, RZAu G23169
71611-1	Picture On The Wall -2	Vi 23686, 20-3259, BB B-5185, Eld 2078, Sr S-3265, MW M-4228, Zo/RZAu EE350
71612-1	Amber Tresses -2	Vi 23701, BB B-5185, Eld 2058, Sr S-3265, MW M-4738, ZoSA 4379

Sara Carter, Maybelle Carter, A.P. Carter, v trio; acc. Sara Carter, g; Maybelle Carter, g.

Atlanta, GA   Wednesday, February 24, 1932

71613-1	I Never Loved But One	Vi 23656, BB B-6257, MW M-4734, ZoSA 4366
71614-1	Tell Me That You Love Me	Vi 23656, BB B-5406, MW M-4230, RZAu G22465
71615-1	Where We'll Never Grow Old	Vi 23672, BB B-5058, Eld 1984, Sr S-3143, MW M-4349, M-4732
71616-2	We Will March Through The Streets Of The City	Vi 23672, BB B-5161, Eld 2058, Sr S-3242, MW M-4336, M-4732

Matrix 71614 was originally logged with the title *The Moon Looked Down On You And Me*.
Revs: Montgomery Ward M-4336 by Frank & James McCravy, M-4349 by Ed McConnell.

Sara Carter, Maybelle Carter, A.P. Carter, v trio; or Sara Carter, v-1; acc. Sara Carter, ah-2/g-3; Maybelle Carter, g.

Camden, NJ   Wednesday, October 12, 1932

59017-1	Sweet As The Flowers In May Time -3	Vi 23761, BB B-5096, Eld 2011, Sr S-3174, MW M-4226, ZoSA 4375, HMV In N4250
59018-1	Will The Roses Bloom In Heaven -3	Vi 23748, BB B-5161, Eld 2058, Sr S-3242, MW M-7149
59019-1,-2	On A Hill Lone And Gray	Vi unissued
59020-2	My Little Home In Tennessee -2	RCA CNV102
59021-2	The Sun Of The Soul -2	Vi 23776, BB B-5543, MW M-7148, RZAu G22470
59022-1	If One Won't Another One Will -1, 3	Vi 23761, MW M-7444
59023-2	The Broken Hearted Lover -2	Vi 23791, MW M-4433

RCA CNV102 and other issues with a CNV prefix below were custom-made by RCA in 1968, from original metal parts, in a limited edition for the English magazine *Country News & Views*.
Rev. HMV N4250 by Jack Erickson (see Bob Miller).

Sara Carter, Maybelle Carter, A.P. Carter, v trio; or Sara Carter, A.P. Carter, v duet-1; or Sara Carter, Maybelle Carter, v duet-2; acc. Sara Carter, ah-3/g-4; Maybelle Carter, g.

Camden, NJ		Thursday, October 13, 1932
59024-1	Two Sweethearts -3	Vi 23791, BB B-6106, MW M-4433, RZAu G23169
59025-1	The Winding Stream -3	Vi 23807, MW M-7443
59026-1	I Wouldn't Mind Dying -1, 4	Vi 23807, MW M-7358
59027-1	The Spirit Of Love Watches Over Me -2, 4	Vi 23748, BB B-5243, Eld 2126, Sr S-3326, MW M-4227
59028-1	The Church In The Wildwood -3	Vi 23776, BB B-5993, MW M-4225, RZAu G22827

On 59026 A.P. Carter sings lead and Sara Carter harmony.
Matrix 59026 is mistitled *See That My Grave Is Kept Green* on at least some copies of Montgomery Ward M-7358.

Sara Carter, Maybelle Carter, A.P. Carter, v trio; or Sara Carter, Maybelle Carter, v duet-1; acc. Sara Carter, ah-2/g-3/y-4; Maybelle Carter, g/y-5.

Camden, NJ		Saturday, June 17, 1933
76278-1	Give Me Roses While I Live -3	Vi 23821, MW M-7356, HMVIn N4260
76279-1	I Never Will Marry -3	BB B-8350, MW M-7356, RZAu G24157
76280-1	On The Sea Of Galilee -3	Vi 23845, MW M-7355
76281-1	Home By The Sea -3, 4, 5	MW M-7146, M-7357, RCA CNV103
76282-1	When The Roses Come Again -3, 4, 5	RCA CNV103
76283-1	I Loved You Better Than You Knew -3	Vi 23835, MW M-7357, HMVIn N4269
76284-1	This Is Like Heaven To Me -3	Vi 23845, MW M-7358
76285-1	See That My Grave Is Kept Green -3	Vi 23835, ZoSA 4379, HMVIn N4269
76286-1	The Old Rugged Cross	Vi rejected
76287-1	Will The Circle Be Unbroken?	Vi rejected
76288-1	Over The Garden Wall -1, 2	MW M-7354
76289-1	Gold Watch And Chain -2	Vi 23821, MW M-7354, HMVIn N4260
76290-1	School House On The Hill -3	RCA CNV101
76291-1	Will My Mother Know Me There? -3	MW M-7355
76292-1	Faded Flowers -3	Vi unissued: *RCA Camden ACL1-0501, RCA(J) RA5648 (LPs); BF BCD15865 (CD)*
76293-1	Poor Little Orphaned Boy -3	RCA CNV101
76701-1	Give Me Roses While I Live	BB unissued
76702-1	I Never Will Marry	BB unissued
76703-1	On The Sea Of Galilee	BB unissued
76704-1	Home By The Sea	BB unissued
76705-1	When The Roses Come Again	BB unissued
76706-1	I Loved You Better Than You Knew	BB unissued
76707-1	This Is Like Heaven To Me	BB unissued
76708-1	See That My Grave Is Kept Green	BB unissued
76709-1	The Old Rugged Cross	BB unissued
76710-1	Will The Circle Be Unbroken?	BB unissued
76711-1	Over The Garden Wall	BB unissued
76712-1	Gold Watch And Chain	BB unissued
76713-1	School House On The Hill	BB unissued
76714-1	Will My Mother Know Me There	BB unissued
76715-1	Faded Flowers	BB unissued
76716-1	Poor Little Orphaned Boy	BB unissued

It is uncertain whether matrices 76701 to 76716 are actual (rather than technical) rerecordings of the titles recorded on matrices 76278 to 76293, or simultaneously recorded duplicates; the balance of the evidence favours the former.
Rev. Victor 27494 by Uncle Dave Macon.

Sara Carter, Maybelle Carter, A.P. Carter, v trio; or Sara Carter, Maybelle Carter, v duet-1; or A.P. Carter, v-2; acc. Sara Carter, ah-3/g-4; Maybelle Carter, g.

Camden, NJ		Tuesday, May 8, 1934
59019-3	On A Hill Lone And Gray -4	BB B-5961, MW M-4545, RZAu G22657
83129-1	Cowboy Jack -1, 4	BB B-8167, MW M-4545
83130-1	I'll Be All Smiles Tonight -4	BB B-5529, MW M-4497
83131-1	Away Out On The Old Saint Sabbeth -3	BB B-5817, MW M-4544
83132-1	The Cuban Soldier	Vi unissued
83133-1	Darling Little Joe -3	RCA CNV102
83134-1	Happy Or Lonesome -3	BB B-5650, MW M-4550, RZAu G22470
83135-1	One Little Word -3	BB B-5771, MW M-4546, RZAu G22482
83136-1	Darling Daisies -1, 3	BB B-5586, MW M-4496, M-7146, RZAu G22469
83137-1	The East Virginia Blues -1, 4	BB B-5650, MW M-4550, Vi 27494
83138-1	What Does The Deep Sea Say?	Vi unissued

83139-1	Lovers Return -4	BB B-5586, MW M-4496, M-7147, RZAu G22469
83140-1	It'll Aggravate Your Soul -2, 4	BB B-5817, MW M-4541
83141-1	Hello Central! Give Me Heaven -1, 4	BB B-5529, MW M-4497
83142-1	I'm Working On A Building -4	BB B-5716, MW M-4541
83143-1	You've Been Fooling Me, Baby -1, 4	BB B-5771, MW M-4548, RZAu G22482

Sara Carter, Maybelle Carter, A.P. Carter, v trio; or Sara Carter, Maybelle Carter, v duet-1; acc. Sara Carter, ah-2/g-3; Maybelle Carter, g.

Camden, NJ   Tuesday, December 11, 1934

87020-1	Longing For Old Virginia -1, 2	BB B-5856, MW M-5018, RZAu G22596, Twin FT1894
87021-1	March Winds Goin' To Blow My Blues All Away -2	BB B-5990, MW M-4548, Twin FT1944
87022-1	There'll Be Joy, Joy, Joy -2	BB B-5911, MW M-4547
87023-1	Home In Tennessee -2	RCA CNV 104
87024-1	Are You Tired Of Me, My Darling? -2	BB B-5956, MW M-4546, RZAu G22658
87025-1	I Cannot Be Your Sweetheart -2	RCA CNV104
87026-1	My Heart's Tonight In Texas -2	BB B-5908, MW M-4549, RZAu G22501, Twin FT1911
87027-1	Be Careful Boys, Don't Go Too Far	Vi unissued
87028-1	My Virginia Rose	Vi unissued
87029-1	There's No Hiding Place Down Here -2	BB B-5961, MW M-4547, RZAu G22657
87030-1	Cowboy's Wild Song To His Herd -1, 2	BB B-5908, MW M-4549, RZAu G22501, Twin FT1911
87031-1	A Lad From Old Virginia	Vi unissued
87032-1	Sad And Lonesome Day	Vi unissued
87033-1	The Evening Bells Are Ringing -3	BB B-5856, MW M-5018, RZAu G22596, Twin FT1894
87034-1	The Little Dobe Shack	Vi unissued
87035-1	The Mountains Of Tennessee -3	BB B-5956, MW M-4542, RZAu G22658
87036-1	Texas Girl	Vi unissued
87037-1	I'll Be Home Some Day -3	BB B-5911, MW M-4543
87038-1	Faded Coat Of Blue -3	BB B-5974, MW M-4543, RZAu G22656
87039-1	Sailor Boy -1, 2	BB B-5974, MW M-4542, RZAu G22656

Sara Carter, Maybelle Carter, A.P. Carter, v trio; acc. Sara Carter, ah-1/g-2; Maybelle Carter, g.

New York, NY   Sunday, May 5, 1935

17476-1	Glory To The Lamb -1	Ba 33465, Me M13432, MeC 92043, Or 8484, Pe 13155, Ro 5484, Vo/OK 03027, Cq 8529, Co 37669, 20268
17477-1	Behind Those Stone Walls -1	ARC 6-03-51, Cq 8633
17478-1	Sinking In The Lonesome Sea -2	ARC unissued: *Time-Life TLCW06* (LP); BF BCD15865 (CD)
17478-2	Sinking In The Lonesome Sea -2	ARC 7-12-63, Vo/OK 03160, Cq 8644, Co 37756, 20333

Sara Carter, Maybelle Carter, A.P. Carter, v trio; acc. Sara Carter, ah; Maybelle Carter, g.

New York, NY   Monday, May 6, 1935

17471-2	He Took A White Rose From Her Hair	Ba 33462, Me M13429, MeC92040, Or 8481, Pe 13152, Ro 5481, Cq 8530
17472-2	Can The Circle Be Unbroken (Bye And Bye)	Ba 33465, Me M13432, MeC 92043, Or 8484, Pe 13155, Ro 5484, Vo/OK 03027, Cq 8529, Co 37669, 20268
17473-2	Let's Be Lovers Again	ARC 35-09-23, Vo/OK 04442, Cq 8539, MeC 92087
17474-1	Your Mother Still Prays (For You Jack)	Ba 33462, Me M13429, MeC 92040, Or 8481, Pe 13152, Ro 5481, Cq 8530
17475-1	Kissing Is A Crime	ARC 6-05-53, Cq 8643

Sara Carter, Maybelle Carter, A.P. Carter, v trio; or Sara Carter, Maybelle Carter, v duet-1; acc. Sara Carter, ah-2/g-3; Maybelle Carter, g.

New York, NY   Tuesday, May 7, 1935

17479-1	Don't Forget Me Little Darling -3	ARC 6-01-59, Vo/OK 04390, Cq 8636, Co 37636, 20235
17480-2	Sad And Lonesome Day -1, 3	ARC 7-04-53, Cq 8735
17481-2	By The Touch Of Her Hand -3	ARC 6-09-59, Cq 8644
17482-2	East Virginia Blues No. 2 -3	Ba 33463, Me M13430, MeC 92041, Or 8482, Pe 13153, Ro 5482, Cq 8535
17483-1	My Old Virginia Home -3	ARC 6-03-51, Cq 8633

17484-2	My Virginia Rose Is Blooming -2	ARC 7-02-58, Vo/OK 05475, Cq 8691, 9663
17489-2	My Texas Girl -3	ARC 6-09-59, Cq 8691
17490-2	No Other's Bride I'll Be -3	ARC 7-08-69, Cq 8733
17491-2	Gathering Flowers From The Hillside -3	ARC 6-01-59, Vo/OK 04390, Cq 8636, Co 37636, 20235
17492-2	Gospel Ship -3	ARC 6-07-56, Cq 8692
17493-1	The Little Black Train -3	ARC 7-07-62, Vo/OK 03112, Cq 8815

Matrices 17485 to 17488 are by Smith Ballew (popular).

Sara Carter, Maybelle Carter, A.P. Carter, v trio; or Sara Carter, v-1; acc. Sara Carter, ah-2/g-3; Maybelle Carter, g.
New York, NY   Wednesday, May 8, 1935

17498-1	Keep On The Sunny Side -2	ARC 6-07-56, Cq 8692
17499-2	River Of Jordan -2	Ba 33466, Me M13433, MeC 92044, Or 8485, Pe 13156, Ro 5485, Cq 8541
17500-1	Lonesome Valley -2	ARC 7-07-62, Vo/OK 03112, Cq 8815
17500-2	Lonesome Valley -2	ARC unissued: *Time-Life TLCW06* (LP); *BF BCD15865* (CD)
17501-1	God Gave Noah The Rainbow Sign -2	ARC 6-11-59, Cq 8693
17502-1	Single Girl, Married Girl -1, 2	ARC 7-04-53, Cq 8733
17502-2	Single Girl, Married Girl -1, 2	ARC unissued: *Time-Life TLCW02* (LP); *BF BCD15865* (CD)
17503-1	The Fate Of Dewey Lee -3	Ba 33463, Me M13430, MeC 92041, Or 8482, Pe 13153, Ro 5482, Cq 8535
17504-2	Wildwood Flower -3	ARC 5-11-65, Cq 8542

Sara Carter, Maybelle Carter, A.P. Carter, v trio; acc. Maybelle Carter, g; Sara Carter, g.
New York, NY   Thursday, May 9, 1935

17505-1	Sea Of Galilee	Ba 33466, Me M13433, MeC 92044, Or 8485, Pe 13156, Ro 5485, Cq 8541
17506-1	Don't Forget This Song	ARC 7-01-54, Cq 8734
17507-1	My Clinch Mountain Home	ARC 7-08-69, Cq 8806
17508-2	The Storms Are On The Ocean	ARC 7-12-63, Vo/OK 03160, Cq 8806, Co 37756, 20333
17509-1	Will You Miss Me When I'm Gone	Ba 33464, Me M13431, MeC 92042, Or 8483, Pe 13154, Ro 5483, Vo/OK 02990, Cq 8540
17510-1	Broken Hearted Lover	Ba 33464, Me M13431, MeC 92042, Or 8483, Pe 13154, Ro 5483, Vo/OK 02990, Cq 8540

Sara Carter, Maybelle Carter, A.P. Carter, v trio; acc. Sara Carter, ah; Maybelle Carter, g.
New York, NY   Friday, May 10, 1935

17519-1,-2	Little Darling Pal Of Mine	ARC 5-11-65, Cq 8542
17520-2	The Homestead On The Farm	ARC 7-02-58, Vo/OK 05475, Cq 8735, 9663, Pe 16-101
17521-1	Cannon Ball Blues	ARC unissued: *Time-Life TLCW06* (LP); *BF BCD15865* (CD)
17521-2	Cannon Ball Blues	ARC 7-05-55, Cq 8816
17522-2	Meet Me By The Moonlight Alone	ARC 7-01-54, Cq 8734
17523-2	On The Rock Where Moses Stood	ARC 6-11-59, Cq 8693
17524-2	Lulu Walls	ARC 6-05-53, Cq 8643
17525-2	I'm Thinking Tonight Of My Blue Eyes	ARC 35-09-23, Vo/OK 04442, Cq 8539, MeC 92087
17526-1	Worried Man Blues	ARC unissued: *Time-Life TLCW06* (LP); *BF BCD15865* (CD)
17526-2	Worried Man Blues	ARC 7-05-55, Cq 8816

Rev. Perfect 16-101 by Roy Acuff.

Sara Carter, Maybelle Carter, A.P. Carter, v trio; or Sara Carter, Maybelle Carter, v duet-1; acc. Sara Carter, ah-2/g-3; Maybelle Carter, g.
New York, NY   Monday, June 8, 1936

61128-A	My Dixie Darling -2	De 5240, 46086, DeAu X1206, MW 8000, MeC 45229
61129-A	Give Me Your Love And I'll Give You Mine -2	De unissued: *BF BCD15865* (CD)
61129-B	Give Me Your Love And I'll Give You Mine -2	De 5318, MW 8001, BrSA SA1136
61130-A	Are You Lonesome Tonight? -2	De 5240, DeAu X1206, MW 8000, MeC 45229, BrSA SA1138
61131-A	The Last Move For Me -2	De 5386, MW 8002
61132-A	The Wayworn Traveler -2	De 5359, MW 8003
61133-A	Just Another Broken Heart -2	De 5254, DeAu X1223, MW 8004, MeC 45230
61134-A	When Silver Threads Are Gold Again -2	De 5304, DeAu X1353, MW 8005, MeC 45230

61135-A	There's No One Like Mother To Me -2	De 5242, DeAu X1325, DeSA FM5139, MW 8006, MeC 45231
61136-A	In A Little Village Churchyard -2	De 5386, MW 8002, BrSA SA1138
61137-A	Jealous Hearted Me -1, 3	De 5241, 46005, MW 8007, MeC 45231
61138-A	My Native Home -1, 3	De 5241, MW 8007, MeC 45260
61139-B	Sweet Heaven In My View -1, 3	De 5318, MW 8001, BrSA SA1137

Bear Family BCD15865 uses take A of matrix 61129 rather than take B as claimed.
Rev. Decca FM5139 by Shelton Brothers.

Sara Carter, Maybelle Carter, A.P. Carter, v trio; or Sara Carter, Maybelle Carter, v duet-1; acc. Maybelle Carter, g; Sara Carter, g.
New York, NY   Tuesday, June 9, 1936

61140-A	No Depression	De 5242, MW 8006, MeC 45260, BrSA SA1137
61141-A	Bonnie Blue Eyes	De 5304, DeAu X1353, MW 8005, MeC 45258
61142-A	My Honey Lou	De 5263, DeAu X1265, MW 8008, MeC 45258
61143-A	In The Shadow Of The Pines	De 5359, MW 8003
61144-A	Answer To Weeping Willow	De 5254, DeAu X1223, MW 8004, MeC 45232, BrSA SA1136
61145-A	You've Been A Friend To Me	De 5283, DeAu X1325, MW 8009, BrSA SA1139
61146-A	Where The Silvery Colorado Wends Its Way	De 5263, DeAu X1265, MW 8008, MeC 45232
61147-A	Lay My Head Beneath The Rose -1	De 5283, 46005, MW 8009, BrSA SA1139

Sara Carter, Maybelle Carter, A.P. Carter, v trio; or Sara Carter, Maybelle Carter, v duet-1; acc. Sara Carter, ah-2/g-3; Maybelle Carter, g.
New York, NY   Thursday, June 17, 1937

62280-A	The Broken Down Tramp -2	De 5518, Cor 64019, MeC 45255
62281-C	Lover's Lane -2	De 5430, MW 8023
62282-A	Hold Fast To The Right -2	De 5494, MW 8028, MeC 45247, Min M-14085
62283-A	Lord I'm In Your Care -2	De 5494, MW 8028, MeC 45247, Min M-14085
62290-C	Funny When You Feel That Way -3	De 5411, MW 8022
62291-C	In The Shadow Of Clinch Mountain -3	De 5430, MW 8023
62292-A	Hello Stranger -1, 2	De 5479, MW 8027, MeC 45250
62293-A	Never Let The Devil Get The Upper Hand Of You -2	De 5479, MW 8027, MeC 45250
62294-A	When This Evening Sun Goes Down -3	De 5467, MW 8026, MeC 45251
62295-A	Jim Blake's Message -3	De 5467, DeSA FM5134, MW 8026, MeC 45251
62296-B	Honey In The Rock -3	De 5452, MW 8024, Cor 64019
62297-A	Look How This World Has Made A Change -3	De 5452, MW 8024

Matrices 62284 to 62287 are by Dick Robertson (popular).

Sara Carter, Maybelle Carter, A.P. Carter, v trio; or Sara Carter, Maybelle Carter, v duet-1; acc. Maybelle Carter, g; Sara Carter, g.
New York, NY   Friday, June 18, 1937

62288-B	The Little Girl That Played On My Knee	De 5677, MeC 45310
62289-A	You Better Let That Liar Alone	De 5518, MeC 45255
62298-A	Farewell Nellie	De 5677, MeC 45310
62299-C	The Only Girl (I Ever Cared About)	De 5411, MW 8022
62300-A	Goodbye To The Plains	De 5532, DeAu X2184, DeSA FM5135, MeC 45264
62301-A	My Home's Across The Blue Ridge Mountains	De 5532, DeAu X2184, DeSA FM5135, MeC 45264
62302-A	Dark Haired True Lover	De 5447, MW 8025
62303-A	He Never Came Back -1	De 5447, MW 8025

Sara Carter, Maybelle Carter, A.P. Carter, v trio; or Sara Carter, Maybelle Carter, v duet-1; acc. Sara Carter, ah-2/g-3; Maybelle Carter, g.
Charlotte, NC   Wednesday, June 8, 1938

64086-A	Happy In The Prison -2	De 5579, MW 8066, MeC 45281
64087-A	Walking In The King's Highway -2	De 5579, MW 8066, MeC 45281
64088-A	St. Regious Girl -1, 2	De 5649, DeSA FM5133, MW 8067
64089-A	Just A Few More Days -2	De 5632, MW 8068, MeC 45292
64090-A	Bring Back My Boy -2	De 5649, DeSA FM5133, MW 8067
64091-A	It Is Better Farther On -2	De 5692
64092-A	Charlie And Nellie -1, 2	De 5702
64093-A	Cuban Soldier -2	De 5662, MW 8069
64094-A	The Heart That Was Broken For Me -2	De 5662, MW 8069
64095-A	You're Nothing More To Me -1, 2	De 5722
64096-A	Stern Old Bachelor -1, 2	De 5565, MW 8070, MeC 45283
64097-A	Little Joe -2	De 5632, MW 8068, MeC 45292

64098-A	Reckless Motorman -1, 3	De 5722
64099-A	You Denied Your Love -1, 3	De 5702
64100-A	Oh, Take Me Back -1, 3	De 5565, MW 8070, MeC 45283
64101-A	You Are My Flower -1, 3	De 5692
64102-A	Who's That Knockin' On My Window -1, 3	De 5612, MW 8071, MeC 45275
64103-A	They Call Her Mother -1, 3	De 5596, MW 8072, MeC 45280
64104-A	Coal Miner's Blues -1, 3	De 5596, 46086, MW 8072, MeC 45280
64105-A	Young Freda Bolt -1, 2	De 5612, DeSA FM5134, MW 8071, MeC 45275

Sara Carter, Maybelle Carter, A.P. Carter, v trio; or Sara Carter, Maybelle Carter, v duet-1; acc. Sara Carter, ah-2/g-3; Maybelle Carter, g.
    Chicago, IL   Thursday, October 3, 1940

C-3349-1	Little Poplar Log House On The Hill -2	OK 06078, Cq 9568, Co 37654, 20253
C-3350-1	The Dying Mother -2	Cq 9569
C-3351-1	Buddies In The Saddle -2	Cq 9570
C-3352-1	Heaven's Radio -2	OK 05931, Cq 9666
C-3353-1	Beautiful Home -2	Cq 9568
C-3354-1	There'll Be No Distinction There -2	OK 05982, Cq 9572
C-3355-1	Give Him One More As He Goes -3	Cq 9664
C-3356-1	Lonesome For You Darling -1, 3	OK 05843, Cq 9575
C-3357-1	Blackie's Gunman -1, 3	OK 06313, Cq 9570

Sara Carter, Maybelle Carter, A.P. Carter, v trio; or Sara Carter, Maybelle Carter, v duet-1; or Sara Carter, v-2; or A.P. Carter, v-3; acc. Sara Carter, ah-4/g-5; Maybelle Carter, g.
    Chicago, IL   Friday, October 4, 1940

C-3358-1	You've Got To Righten That Wrong -5	OK 05982, Cq 9867
C-3359-1	Meeting In The Air -5	OK 05931, Cq 9666
C-3360-1	My Home Among The Hills -5	OK 06078, Cq 9867, Co 37654, 20253
C-3361-1	Black Jack David -5	OK 06313, Cq 9574
C-3362-1	Look Away From The Cross -5	OK 06030, Cq 9572, 9665
C-3363-1	We Shall Rise -4	OK 06030, Cq 9664
C-3364-1	I Found You Among The Roses -3, 5	Cq 9575
C-3365-1	Bear Creek Blues -2, 4	Cq 9574
C-3366-1	I'll Never Forsake You -1, 4	OK 05843, Cq 9569
C-3367-1	Beautiful Isle O'er The Sea -4	Pe 16-102
C-3368-1	It's A Long Long Road To Travel Alone -1, 5	Cq 9665

Rev. Perfect 16-102 by Coon Creek Girls.

Sara Carter, Maybelle Carter, A.P. Carter, v trio; or Sara Carter, Maybelle Carter, v duet-1; or A.P. Carter, v-2; acc. Sara Carter, ah-3/g-4; Maybelle Carter, g.
    New York, NY   Tuesday, October 14, 1941

066780-1	Why Do You Cry, Little Darling? -1, 4	BB 33-0502
066781-1	You Tied A Love Knot In My Heart -1, 4	RCA CNV105
066782-1	Lonesome Homesick Blues -1, 3	BB 33-0502
066783-1	Wabash Cannonball	BB unissued
067991-1	Dark And Stormy Weather -3	BB B-8868
067992-1	In The Valley Of The Shenandoah -3	BB B-8868
067993-1	The Girl On The Greenbrier Shore -1, 3	BB B-8947
067994-1	Something Got A Hold Of Me -2, 3	BB B-8947
067995-1	Fifty Miles Of Elbow Room -3	BB B-9026
067996-1	Keep On The Firing Line -3	BB B-9026
067997-1	The Wave On The Sea -3	BB 33-0512
067998-1	The Rambling Boy -4	BB 33-0512
067999-1	You're Gonna Be Sorry You Let Me Down -4	RCA CNV105

Members of The Carter Family recorded after 1942.

[THE] CARTWRIGHT BROTHERS

Cartwright Brothers: Bernard Cartwright, f; Jack Cartwright, g.
    Dallas, TX   Friday, December 2, 1927

145300-2	Kelley Waltz	Co 15220-D
145301-3	Honeymoon Waltz	Co 15220-D
145302-	Coon Dog	Co unissued
145303-	Sally Johnson	Co unissued

Bernard Cartwright, f-1/v-2; Jack Cartwright, g/v-3.
    Dallas, TX   Thursday, December 6, 1928

147577-2	When The Work's All Done This Fall -1, 2, 3	Co 15346-D
147578-2	On The Old Chisholm Trail -2, 3	Co 15346-D

147579-2	Get Along Little Dogies -1, 2, 3	Co 15410-D
147580-2	Utah Carrol -1, 3	Co 15410-D
147581-	Over The Waves -1	Co 15677-D
147582-	Waltzes Of The South Plains -1	Co unissued

Rev. Columbia 15677-D by Bob Miller.

Bernard Cartwright, f; Jack Cartwright, g-1/v-2.
Dallas, TX   Sunday, August 11, 1929

55334-2	The Dying Ranger -1, 2	Vi V-40198, BB B-5355, MW M-4460
55335-2	Texas Ranger -2	Vi V-40198, BB B-5355, MW M-4460
55336-2	San Antonio -1	Vi V-40147, MW M-4294
55337-2	Zacatecas -1	Vi V-40147, MW M-4294

Montgomery Ward M-4294 as by **Cartwright Bros.**

Bernard Cartwright, Jack Cartwright, v/y-1 duet; acc. Bernard Cartwright, f; Jack Cartwright, g.
Dallas, TX   Wednesday, October 16, 1929

56394-2	Mammy's Little Black-Eyed Boy -1	Vi 23512
56395-2	Pickanniny [sic] Lullaby	Vi 23512
56396-2	Pretty Little Doggies	Vi V-40247, MW M-4287, Au 236
56397-2	The Wandering Cowboy	Vi V-40247, MW M-4287, Au 236

Victor 23512 as by **The Cartwright Brothers**.

Acc. unknown.
San Antonio, TX   Tuesday, October 9, 1934

| SA-Test #2 | Was Willst Du Haben (What Will You Have) | Vo unissued trial recording |

Acc. Bernard Cartwright, md; Jack Cartwright, g.
San Antonio, TX   Wednesday, October 10, 1934

| SA-Test #1 | The Return Of Country Boy | Vo unissued trial recording |

Despite its title, this item is sung in Spanish.

CARVER BOYS

Warner Carver, f-1/h-2/bj-3/lv-4; Noble "Uncle Bozo" Carver, g/tv-5; Robert Carver, g/bsv-6.
Richmond, IN   Friday, September 6, 1929

15543	Simpson County -1	Pm 3233, Bwy 8180, ARC-Bwy 8180
15544	Pop Goes The Weasel -1	Pm unissued
15545	Sleeping Lula -1	Pm 3199
15546	Tim Brook -3, 4, 5	Pm 3199
15550	I'll Be With You When The Roses Bloom Again -1, 2, 5, 6	Pm 3233, Bwy 8180
15551	The Brave Engineer -2, 5, 6	Pm 3198, Bwy 8246, ARC-Bwy 8246
15552	Darling Nellie Gray -2, 4	Pm 3198, Bwy 8246
15553	I've Anchored in Love Divine -4, 5, 6	Pm 3182, Bwy 8241
15554	No One To Welcome Me Home -4, 5, 6	Pm 3182, Bwy 8241
15555	Wang Wang Harmonica Blues -2	Pm 12822, Bwy 8151
15556	Sisco Harmonica Blues -2	Pm 12822, Bwy 8151

Broadway 8151 as by **The Carver Boys**. Broadway 8180, ARC-Broadway 8180 as by **Cramer Boys**. Broadway 8241 as by **Carson Boys**. Broadway 8246, ARC-Broadway 8246 as by **The Carson Boys**.
The attribution of instruments shown above seems the most likely, but Noble Carver played banjo and may do so on matrix 15546, in which case Warner Carver plays guitar. Matrix 15555 is logged as by **Carver Boys & Joshua White**, giving rise to the theory that the African-American guitarist Josh White is present; it has been impossible to confirm or definitely reject this.
According to Noble Carver the recording date was August 14, 1929.
Matrices 15547 to 15549 are by the Hokum Boys (see *B&GR*).
Revs: ARC-Broadway 8180 by Lester McFarland & Robert A. Gardner; ARC-Broadway 8246 by Asa Martin & Doc Roberts.

CLAUDE CASEY

Claude Casey-1/Claude Casey Trio-2/Claude & Sara Casey-3: Claude Casey, v/g; Tex Isley, v-2/g; Sara Casey, v-3.
New York, NY   Friday, July 16, 1937

21397-	Moonshine In The North Carolina Hall [sic] -2	ARC unissued
21398-	We Are Boys From North Carolina -2	ARC unissued
21399-	Memories Of Charley Poole -1	ARC unissued
21400-	Don't Accuse Your Lover -3	ARC unissued
21401-	Forsaken -1	ARC unissued
21402-	A Change In Business -1	ARC unissued

Art Satherley's files give the name of the third musician as Sara Casey, ARC files as Tara Casey. Since Claude Casey professed to recognise neither name, the correct form must remain speculative.

Pine State Playboys: Jimmy Rouse, f; Willie Coates, p; Claude Casey, g/v; Lawrence Boling, g/v-1; Carl Boling, tg.
Charlotte, NC   Wednesday, January 26, 1938

018729-1	Road Weary Hobo -1	BB B-8127, MW M-7710
018730-1	Why Don't You Come Back To Me -1	BB B-7704, MW M-7711
018731-1	I Took It	BB B-7451, MW M-7710
018732-1	Down With Gin -1	BB B-7451, MW M-7709
018733-1	Keep Praying	BB B-8073, MW M-7711
018734-1	The Instalment [sic] Song -1	BB B-7704, MW M-7709
018735-1	A Boy From North Carolina -1	BB B-7535, MW M-7712
018736-1	Don't Say Goodbye If You Love Me -1	BB B-7535, MW M-7712, RZAu G23576

Rev. Regal-Zonophone G23576 by Bill Boyd.

Claude Casey & His Pine State Playboys: Jimmy Rouse, f; Willie Coates, p; Claude Casey, g/v-1; Lawrence Boling, g/v-2; Carl Boling, tg.
Rock Hill, SC   Tuesday, September 27, 1938

027729-1	My Little Precious Sonny Boy -1	MW M-7706
027730-1	All I Do Is Dream -1	BB B-7883, MW M-7706
027731-1	Happy Cowboy -1, 2	BB B-8127, MW M-7657
027732-1	My Memory Lane -1, 2	BB B-7863, MW M-7657, RZAu G23700
027733-1	Kinston Blues -1, 2	BB B-8056, MW M-7707
027734-1	I'm So Lonesome Tonight -2	BB B-8153, MW M-7708, RZAu G23974
027735-1	You're The Only Star In My Blue Heaven -1	BB B-7863, MW M-7658, RZAu G23700
027736-1	My Heart Is Stamped With Your Name -1, 2	BB B-8056, MW M-7658
027737-1	Pine State Honky Tonk	BB B-7883, MW M-7707
027738-1	Old Missouri Moon -1, 2	BB B-8153, MW M-7708, RZAu G23974

Bluebird B-8127, Montgomery Ward M-7675, M-7710, M-7711 as by **Pine State Playboys**.

Clinton Collins, f-1/sb-2/v-3; Kelland "Kid" Clark, ac; Jimmy Colvard, esg-4/sb-5; Claude Casey, g/v-6/y-7.
Atlanta, GA   Thursday, October 10, 1940

054588-1	You're Gonna Be Sorry -1, 3, 4, 6	BB B-8608
054589-1	I'll Always Love You -1, 5, 6, 7	BB B-8608
054590-1	My Heart's In The Heart Of The Blue Ridge - 2, 4, 6?	BB B-8668
054591-1	Lonesome As Can Be -1, 4, 6?	BB B-8668
054592-1	It Doesn't Matter -2, 3, 4, 6	BB B-8697
054593-1	What's Wrong With Me Now? -1, 4, 6?	BB B-8697
054594-1	When I First Met You -2, 4, 6	BB B-8730
054595-1	Little Girl, Go Ask Your Mother -2, 4	BB B-8730

George Heffernan, f; Gilbert Young, sg; Claude Casey, g/v-1/y-2; Tex Martin, sb/v-2/y-2.
Atlanta, GA   Saturday, October 4, 1941

071098-1	Let Me Hear You Say "I Love You" -1	BB B-8958
071099-1	Swinging With Gilbert	BB B-8849
071100-1	Why Did Things Happen This Way? -1, 2	BB B-8958
071101-1	Hottest Little Baby In Town -1	BB B-8849

Claude Casey recorded after 1942.

CASEY'S OLD TIME FIDDLERS

Casey Aslakson, f; unknown, p; A. Cibelli, md/vc; unknown, g.
New York, NY   Wednesday, May 13, 1931

69603-1	Ocean Waves	Vi 23560, ViJ 23560
69604-1	Casey's Old-Time Waltz	Vi 23560, ViJ 23560

ELRY CASH

Elry Cash, v/y-1; acc. prob. own g.
Atlanta, GA   Thursday, April 18, 1929

148348-2	My Old New Hampshire Home -1	Co 15399-D
148349-1	Won't You Come Back To Me -1	Co 15399-D
148350-2	Then My Love Began To Wane	Co 15457-D
148351-2	When You're In The Graveyard And I'm Away Downtown In Jail -1	Co 15457-D

IRV CASPER & HIS WEYMANN FIVE

The item by this group in the Victor Old Familiar Tunes series (V-40033) is outside the scope of this work.

CASS COUNTY BOYS

Freddie Martin, ac/v; Jerry Scoggins, g/v; Bert Dodson, sb/v.
Dallas, TX   Thursday, April 3, 1941
063010-1	Great Grandad	BB B-8824
063011-1	Riding Down The Canyon	BB B-8824
063012-1	Since I Put A Radio Out In The Henhouse	BB B-8806
063013-1	Trail To Mexico	BB B-8806

The Cass County Boys recorded after 1942.

PETE CASSELL

Pete Cassell, v/y-1; acc. own g.
New York, NY   Wednesday, March 12, 1941
68809-A	Freight Train Blues	De 5954, 46084, 46103
68810-A	St. Louis Blues	De 5954, 46084, 46103
68811-A	I Know What It Means To Be Lonesome -1	De 5934, 46106, Coral 64010
68812-A	Why Don't You Come Back To Me -1	De 5934, 46106, DeSA FM5137, Coral 64010
68813-A	I Can't Feel At Home In This World Anymore	De 6077, MeC 45549
68814-A	One Step More	De 6077, MeC 45549

Rev. Decca FM5137 by York Brothers.
Pete Cassell recorded after 1942.

CLYDE & CHESTER CASSITY

Clyde Cassity, Chester Cassity, v duet; acc. poss. own g duet.
Richmond, IN   Monday, May 19, 1930
16632,-A	Yield Not To Temptation	Ge rejected
16633,-A	More About Jesus	Ge rejected

BILLY CASTEEL WITH SILVER SAGE BUCKEROO'S

No details.
Prob. Detroit MI   ca. 1941
Hollywood Mama	Mellow 1614, Hot Wax 1614
Wayne County Blues	Mellow 1614, Hot Wax 1614

THOMPSON CATES

Vocal duet; acc. unknown, f; unknown, g.
Chicago, IL   c. May 1928
20546-1	Curse Of An Aching Heart	Pm 3103, Bwy 8094
20549-2	Will The Angels Play Their Harps For Me	Pm 3103, Bwy 8094

Broadway 8094 as by **Tess & Cass**. Intervening matrices are untraced.

ROLAND CAULEY [& LAKE HOWARD]
CAULEY FAMILY

Roland Cauley, v; acc. Lake Howard, g.
New York, NY   Tuesday, August 7, 1934
15524-	Snap Bean Blues	ARC unissued
15525-	Leaving The Farm	ARC unissued

Cauley Family-1/Roland Cauley & Lake Howard-2: Roland Cauley, f; —— Cauley, bj-3; Lake Howard, g.
New York, NY   Tuesday, August 7, 1934
15526-	Lenoir County Blues -1, 3	ARC unissued
15527-1	Duplin County Blues -1	Ba 33147, Me M13114, MeC 91877, Or 8373, Pe 13033, Ro 5373
15528-1	Grey Eagle -2	ARC 6-04-54, JL100
15529-	East Carolina Waltz -1	ARC unissued

Cauley Family: Roland Cauley, f/v; —— Cauley, bj/v; Lake Howard, g/v.
New York, NY   Wednesday, August 8, 1934
15553-2	Lumberton Wreck	Ba 33146, Me M13113, MeC 91876, Or 8372, Pe 13032, Ro 5372
15554-2	New River Train	Ba 33146, Me M13113, MeC 91876, Or 8372, Pe 13032, Ro 5372

Cauley & Howard-1/Roland Cauley & Lake Howard-2: Roland Cauley, sg/v-3; Lake Howard, g/v-3.

New York, NY   Wednesday, August 8, 1934

15555-	Little Old Log Cabin In The Lane -1, 3	ARC unissued
15556-	Troublesome Blues -1	ARC unissued
15557-2	Medley – Darling Nelly Gray And Little Brown Jug -2	ARC 6-04-54, JL100

Cauley Family: Roland Cauley, f; —— Cauley, bj; Lake Howard, g.

New York, NY   Thursday, August 9, 1934

15562-2	Seaboard Waltz	Ba 33147, Me M13114, MeC 91877, Or 8373, Pe 13033, Ro 5373
15563-	Wayne County Blues	ARC unissued
15564-	Nora Darling	ARC unissued
15565-	Medley – Mississippi Sawyer And Soldiers Joy	ARC unissued
15566-	Ida Red	ARC unissued

Cauley Family & Howard: Roland Cauley, f/v-1; Lake Howard, g/v-2; —— Cauley, v-3.

New York, NY   Thursday, August 9, 1934

| 15567- | I Shall Not Be Moved -1, 2, 3 | ARC unissued |
| 15589- | He Loves Me So -2? | ARC unissued |

Intervening matrices are by other artists.
Lake Howard also recorded in his own name.

JACK CAWLEY'S OKLAHOMA RIDGE RUNNERS

Howard L. Cawley, f-1; Forrest A. Turner, md; Leonard C. Fulwider, g.

Dallas, TX   Thursday, October 10, 1929

56354-2	Oklahoma Waltz -1	Vi V-40254
56355-2	Tulsa Waltz -1	Vi V-40254
56356-1	Fort Worth Rag	Vi V-40175
56357-2	Blue Devil Rag	Vi V-40175

Victor V-40175 as by **Jack Crawley's Oklahoma Ridge Runners**.

Howard L. Cawley, f-1; Buster Elmore, md-2/g-3; Leonard C. Fulwider, g-4; Jack Cawley, g; prob. Clarence Brown, vc; unidentified, v-5.

Memphis, TN   Monday, November 24, 1930

62999-1	White River Stomp -1, 2, 4	Vi 23521
63000-1	My Cute Gal Sal -1, 2, 4, 5	Vi 23570
64701-2	The Vine Covered Cottage -1, 2, 4	Vi 23570
64702-2	The Dawn Waltz -1, 2, 4	Vi 23521
64703-2	Guitar Duet Blues -3	Vi 23257, 23540
64704-2	Slow Guitar Blues -3	Vi 23257, 23540, MW M-4084

Victor 23257, Montgomery Ward M-4084 as by **Buster & Jack**. Matrices 64703/04 are titled *Cross Tie Blues* and *Pouring Down Blues* respectively on Victor 23540. Matrix 64704 is titled *Guitar Blues* on Montgomery Ward M-4084.
Intervening matrices are by other artists on other dates. Rev. Montgomery Ward M-4084 by Bill Simmons.

CECIL & VI

Cecil S. Perrin, v; acc. own g; Vivian Perrin, g-1/v-2.

Dallas, TX   Wednesday, October 8, 1941

071122-1	I'll Always Love You Darlin' -1, 2	BB B-8880
071123-1	Ragged Pat -1	BB B-8880
071124-1	Now I Am Lonesome And Blue	BB unissued
071125-1	My Darling Wife -1, 2	BB B-8929
071126-1	The Prisoners Farewell -1	BB unissued
071127-1	Won't-Cha -1, 2	BB B-8929

CENTRAL MISSISSIPPI QUARTET

It is not certain, but seems likely, that these two groups are the same or similar.

Vocal quartet; acc. unknown, p.

Memphis, TN   Tuesday, February 18, 1930

MEM-744-	Far Away In The South	Vo 5415
MEM-745-	My Heart's In Mississippi	Vo 5415
MEM-746-	Willing? Loyal? Ready?	Vo unissued
MEM-747-	I'll Wear A White Robe	Vo unissued

Jackson, MS   Friday, December 19, 1930

| 404795-A | Safe In the Homeland | OK 45514 |
| 404796-B | Sweetest Mother | OK 45525 |

404797-B	I'll Wear A White Robe	Ok 45525
404798-A	Angels, Please Tell Mother	OK 45534
404799-B	Shake Hands With Mother	OK 45534
404800-B	God's Children Are Gathering Home	OK 45514

CLEVE CHAFFIN

Cleve Chaffin, v; acc. prob. own g.
    Richmond, IN   Wednesday, November 16, 1927

GEX-943,-A	Sweet Bunch Of Daisies	Ge rejected
GEX-944	Aged Mother	Ge rejected
GEX-945	The Night My Mother Died	Ge rejected
GEX-946	Curtain Of Night	Ge rejected
GEX-948	Wreck Of The C&O	Ge rejected
GEX-949	Railroad Bill	Ge rejected

Matrix GEX-947 is by John McGhee.

McClung Brothers & Cleve Chaffin-1/Leader Cleveland & Men's Bible Class-2/Cleve Chaffin & McClung Brothers-3: Emery McClung, f-4/v-5; unidentified, h-6; Cleve Chaffin, bj/v-7; John McClung, g/v-8; unidentified, sp-9.
    Chicago, IL   c. March 1929

21205-2	Trail Blazer's Favorite -1, 4	Pm 3161
21206-2	Alabama Jubilee -1, 4	Pm 3161
21207-2	Way Beyond The Blue -2, 4?, 5, 7, 8	Pm 3160
21208-2	Babylon Is Fallen Down -2, 5/8, 6, 7, 9	Pm 3160
21209-2	Curtains Of Night -3, 4?, 7	Pm 3179
21210-2	Rock House Gamblers -3, 4?, 7	Pm 3179

The McClung Brothers also recorded in their own name.

THE CHALLENGE HARMONY FOUR

Pseudonym on Challenge for the Woodlawn Quartette.

CHALLENGE QUARTET

Pseudonym on Challenge 430 for the McDonald Quartette. Other issues on Challenge with this credit are by the Criterion Quartet, who are beyond the scope of this work.

OSCAR CHANDLER

Oscar Chandler, v; acc. unknown, g.
    Dallas, TX   Wednesday, October 23, 1929

| TD-445 | Hangman Hold Your Rope | Br/Vo cancelled trial recording |
| TD-446 | The Yellow Cat Came Back | Br/Vo cancelled trial recording |

CLAY CHAPMAN

Pseudonym on Velvet Tone and Clarion for Chris Bouchillon.

CHAPMAN QUARTET

Vocal quartet; acc. (if any) unknown.
    Charlotte NC   Friday, June 19, 1936

| 102709-1 | Throw Open Your Door | BB unissued |
| 102710-1 | The Old Home Place | BB unissued |

LEON CHAPPELEAR

Leon Chappelear (The Lone Star Cowboy), v/y-1; acc. own g.
    Richmond, IN   Tuesday, September 13, 1932

18777	The Message From Home -1	Ge unissued
18778	Trifling Mama Blues -1	Ch S-16547, 45167
18779	Moonlight And Skies	Ge unissued
18780	Little Joe The Wrangler	Ch 16497, 45068, MW 4950, MeC 45068, Min M-14039
18781	Cowboy Jack	Ge unissued
18782	I'd Like To Be In Texas For The Round Up In The Spring	Ch 16497, 45068, MW 4950, MeC 45068
18783	I Love You But I Don't Know Why	Ge rejected
18784	Too Good To Be True	Ch S-16547, 45167

Rev. Minerva M-14039 by Tex Ritter.

Leon's Lone Star Cowboys: Leon "Lonnie" Hall, f/v-1; Johnny Harvey, cl; Howard Oliver, tbj; Leon Chappelear, g/v-2; Gene Sullivan, g; Skipper Hawkins, sb.

Chicago, IL   Wednesday, August 14, 1935

90225-A	Mama Don't Allow It -2	Ch 45151, De 5423, MW 8015
90226-A	Ben Wheeler Stomp	De 5928
90227-A	Dinah -1	Ch 45174, De 5361
90228-A	Milenburg Joys	Ch 45196, De 5454
90229-A	Mistreated Blues-2	Ch 45151, De 5423, MW 8015
90230-A	I'm A Do Right Papa -2	Ch 45174, De 5361
90231-A	That Old Sweetheart Of Mine -2	De 5301
90232-A	Truly I Promise To Love You -2	Ch 45195, De 5914, MeC 45195
90233-A	Tiger Rag	De 5928
90234-A	Bugle Call Rag	Ch 45169, De 5396

Matrix 90235 is by Jimmie Davis.

Lonnie Hall, f/v-1; Johnny Harvey, cl; Howard Oliver, tbj; Leon Chappelear, g/v-2; Gene Sullivan, g; Skipper Hawkins, sb.

Chicago, IL   Thursday, August 15, 1935

90236-A	My Gal Sal -2	De 5301
90237-A,-AA	Sweet Georgia Brown -1	De unissued
90238-A	Weary Blues -2	Ch 45165, De 5323
90239-A	Just Forget -2	Ch 45195, De 5914, MeC 45195
90240-A	Sweet Sue – Just You -2	Ch 45152, De 5328
90241-A	No Mama Blues -2	Ch 45196, De 5454
90242-A	I'm Sitting On Top Of The World -2	Ch 45152, De 5328
90243-A	White River Stomp	Ch 45185, De 5433, MeC 45185

Gene Sullivan, lg/v; Leon Chappelear, g; Skipper Hawkins, sb.

Chicago, IL   Thursday, August 15, 1935

90244-A	Kansas City Blues -3	Ch 45169, De 5396, Min M-14168

Lonnie Hall, f/v-1; Johnny Harvey, cl; Howard Oliver, tbj; Leon Chappelear, g/v-2; Gene Sullivan, g; Skipper Hawkins, sb; band v-3.

Chicago, IL   Thursday, August 15, 1935

90245-A	Four Or Five Times -1, 3	De 45165, De 5323
90246-A,-AA	Darktown Strutters Ball -2	De rejected
90247-A	My Little Girl -2	Ch 45185, De 5433, MeC 45185

Lonnie Hall, f; Speck Harrison, cl/as; Howard Oliver, tbj; Leon Chappelear, g/v-1; Gene Sullivan, g/v-2; Slim Harbert, sb.

New Orleans, LA   Friday, March 13, 1936

60715-	31st Street Blues -1	De 5280
60716-A	China Boy	De 5280
60717-	Mr. And Mrs. Is The Name -2	De 5289
60718-A	I'll Never Say "Never Again" Again -2	De 5288
60719-	Texas Plains -1	De 5288, Min M-14168
60720-	I Know I Love You, But I Don't Know Why -1	De 5289
60721-	Prairie Rose -1	De 5530, MeC 45259, Min M-14132

Rev. Minerva M-14132 by Odus & Woodrow.

Lonnie Hall, f; Hugh Berry, cl-1; Carl Rainwater, esg; Howard Oliver, tbj; Leon Chappelear, g/v; Slim Harbert, sb.

Dallas, TX   Sunday, February 14, 1937

61775-A	Just A Blue Eyed Blonde -1	De 5340
61776-A	Trouble In Mind -1	De 5340
61777-A	Too Good To Be True -1	De 5388
61778-A	Baby Won't You Come Along -1	De 5416
61779-A	You're In My Heart To Stay -1	De 5404, Min M-14165
61780-A	Wild Cat Mama (The Answer to Do Right Papa) -1	De 5404, Min M-14165
61781-A	I'm Serving Days -1	De 5449, MeC 45228
61782-A	Who Walks In When I Walk Out -1	De 5377
61783-A	Travelin' Blues -1	De 5416
61784-A	In A Little Red Barn -1	De 5377
61785-A	I Never Knew -1	De 5697
61786-A	Angry -1	De 5388
61787-A	The Empty Cradle	De 5449, MW 8014, MeC 45228
61788-A	The One Rose (That's Left In My Heart) -1	MW 8014

Matrix 61787 on Decca 5449 as by **Leon Chappelear**.

Lonnie Hall, f; J.R. Chatwell, f; Archie Laurent, p; Howard Oliver, tbj; Leon Chappelear, g/v; Hezzie Bryant, sb.
Dallas, TX   Sunday, December 12, 1937

63030-A	Dear Little Girl	De 5481
63031-A	She's Got Me Worried	De 5571
63032-A	New Do Right Dady	De 5481
63033-A	She's Runnin' Around	De 5511
63034-A	Goin' Up To Dallas	De 5551, Min M-14164
63035-A	Toodle-Oo Sweet Mama	De 5697
63036-A	Red Hot Mama From Way Out West	De 5551, Min M-14164
63037-A	You're A Million Miles From Nowhere	De 5511
63038-A	My Mother's Rosary (Ten Baby Fingers And Ten Baby Toes)	De 5530, MeC 45259
63039-A	Sentimental Gentleman From Georgia	De 5571

Leon Chappelear was a member, with the Shelton Brothers, of the Lone Star Cowboys, who recorded in their own name and with Jimmie Davis. He also recorded (as Leon Chappel) after 1942.

C.W. CHARLES

Pseudonym on Broadway for W.C. Childers.

CHARLES BROTHERS

Pseudonym on Paramount for Phil Reeve & Ernest Moody.

THE CHARLESTON ENTERTAINERS

Pseudonym on Superior for The Welling Trio (see John McGhee & Frank Welling).

CHARLESTON SACRED QUARTETTE

Pseudonym on Superior for the Carolina Gospel Singers.

CHARLESTON SACRED TRIO

Pseudonym on Supertone for The Welling Trio (see John McGhee & Frank Welling).

CHEZZ CHASE

Zeke Macon, v/y; acc. Roy Smeck (as Dixie Sam or, on Van Dyke 74281, Oklahoma Joe), g.
New York, NY   c. May 1929

3441-D	Show Boat Blues	GG/Rad 4281, VD 74281, 5122

Van Dyke 74281 as by **Chezz Chase**; 5122 as by **Cezz Chase**.
Rev. all issues by Gene Autry, except Van Dyke 5122 by Mobile Revelers (see JR).

Chezz Chase, v/y-1; acc. prob. Roy Smeck, g.
New York, NY   Monday, June 24, 1929

8831-	Show Boat Blues	Ba 6563, Je 5569, Or 1647, Htd 16050
8832-	Corn Licker Blues (A Delirious Yodel) -1	Pl unissued

Jewel 5669, Oriole 1647, Homestead 16050 as by **Bob Fagan**. Some issues of matrix 8831 use the control 2345-3.
Rev. all issues of matrix 8831 by Frank Luther (see Carson Robison).

Acc. Roy Smeck (as Alabama Joe), h-1/g.
New York, NY   Monday, July 15, 1929

8867-	Little Empty Cradle	Pl unissued
8869-	She Was A Moonshiner's Daughter -1	Ba 6496, Ca 9245, Je 5698, Lin 3272, Or 1681, Ro 1047, Chg 839, Htd 16057
8870-	The Log Cabin Blues	Pl unissued

Cameo 9245, Lincoln 3272, Romeo 1047 as by **Jimmie Price**. Jewel 5698, Oriole 1681, Challenge 839, Homestead 16057 as by **Bob Fagan**.
Some issues of matrix 8869 use the controls 3997 or 2447-3. Matrix 8868 is by Dubin's Demons (popular).
Revs: Cameo 9245, Lincoln 3272, Oriole 1681, Romeo 1047 by Frank Luther (see Carson Robison); Banner 6496, Challenge 839, Homestead 16057, Jewel 5698 by Frank Marvin.

Acc. Roy Smeck (as Alabama Joe), h/g.
New York, NY   Wednesday, August 7, 1929

8867-	Little Empty Cradle	Ba 6466, Ca 9276, Je 5671, Lin 3303, Ro 1078, Htd 16055
8870-	The Log Cabin Blues	Ba 6495, Ca 9277, Je 5697, Lin 3304, Or 1680, Ro 1079, Htd 16060, Pm 3178, Bwy 8125

Jewels, Orioles, and Homesteads as by **Bob Fagan**. Cameos, Lincolns, and Romeos as by **Jimmie Price**.
Some issues of matrix 8867 use the controls 3996 or 2286-5. (The control 2286 on some issues is given as 2386.) Some issues of matrix 8870 use the controls 3998-1 or 2445-3,-6.
Revs: Oriole 1680 by Frank Marvin; all other issues by Frank Luther (see Carson Robison).

Zeke Macon, v/y; acc. Roy Smeck (as Dixie Sam or, on Radiex/Van Dyke 5116, Alabama Joe), h-1/g.
New York, NY
c. September 1929

3636-A	Tennessee Tess Among The Hills	GG/Rad 4277, Rad 5116, VD 5116, 74277
3637-A	Little Empty Cradle -1	GG/Rad 4276, Rad 5114, VD 5114, 74276, Bellbird 136

Van Dyke 74276, 74277 as by **Chezz Chase**. Radiex/Van Dyke 5116 as by **Cezz Chase**.
Revs: Grey Gull/Radiex 4276, 4277, Van Dyke 74276, 74277, Bellbird 136 by Bob Miller; Van Dyke 5114 by Gene Autry; Radiex/Van Dyke 5116 by Carson Robison.
Other recordings by Chezz Chase are beyond the scope of this book.

MONIE CHASTEEN

Monie Chasteen, v; acc. the Hoosier Hawaiians: no details.
Richmond, IN
Tuesday, November 17, 1931

18190	Sugar	Ge unissued
18191	I'm Lonesome Too	Ge unissued

EVERETT CHEETHAM

Everett Cheetham, v; acc. prob. own g.
poss. San Francisco, CA
c. late 1932

MS-1137	Little Joe, The Wrangler	MacGregor & Sollie unnumbered
MS-1138	The Siree Peaks	MacGregor & Sollie unnumbered

These items are coupled.

LOWELL CHEETHAM

Lowell Cheetham, v; acc. prob. own g.
poss. San Francisco, CA
c. late 1932

MS-1135	Home On The Range	MacGregor & Sollie unnumbered
MS-1136	The High Toned Dance	MacGregor & Sollie unnumbered

These items are coupled.

W.B. CHENOWETH

Chenoweth's Cornfield Symphony Orchestra: W.B. Chenoweth, f; poss. Bill Anderson, f/bj-g; poss. D.F. Hyle, bj.
Dallas, TX
c. October 18, 1924

8757-A	The Last Shot Got Him	OK 40246
8758-A	Hot Foot Step And Fetch It	OK 40246

Dallas, TX
c. October 20, 1925

9379-	[unknown title]	OK unissued
9380-A	Arkansaw Wampus Cat	OK 45025

Rev. OKeh 45025 by Ed Hayes.
Chenoweth's Cornfield Symphony Orchestra also accompanied Ed Hayes at this session.

The Texas Fiddlin Wampus Cat & His Kittens: W.B. Chenoweth, f-1/v-2; poss.D.F. Hyle, bj; poss. Bill Anderson, bj-g.
Chicago, IL
c. February 1926

2438-1	Frolic Of The Wampus Cat -1	Pm 33172, Pu 9172
2439-1	You'll Find Your Mother There -2	Pm 33172, Pu 9172

Texas Fiddlin' Wampus Cat: no details.
Chicago, IL
Monday, December 5, 1927

82006-A,-B	[unknown title]	OK unissued
82008-	Texas Possum Trot	OK unissued
82009-	Cotton Patch Serenade	OK unissued

Matrix 82007 is untraced but possibly by this group.

CHEROKEE RAMBLERS

Marion Orr, f; Skinny Anglin, h; Bill Power, bj; Walter Kite, g; Bill Gatins, j/v-1; unknown, wb/spoons.
New York, NY
Wednesday, July 10, 1935

39683-A	Alabama Jubilee -1	De 5123, Min M-14159
39684-A	Bully Of The Town -1	De 5123, Min M-14159
39685-A,-B	Bob Murphy	De unissued
39686-A,-B	New Liberty	De unissued
39687-A,-B	Bollweevil Blues	De unissued
39688-A,-B	House Of David Blues	De unissued
39691-A,-B	Y. Z. Special	De unissued

| 39692-A | Goin' Down The Road Feelin' Bad | De 5138 |

Issued items are subcredited (**With Bill Gatin & His Jug**) [sic]. Decca 5123 was also issued with C takes, which are aurally identical to the A takes. Intervening matrices are by Bill Gatins.

Marion Orr, f-1; Skinny Anglin, h-2; Bill Power, bj; Walter Kite, g; Bill Gatins, j-3/v-4; unknown, wb-5/spoons-5; unidentified, calls-6.
New York, NY   Thursday, July 11, 1935

39700-C	My Little Girl -1, 2, 3, 4	De 5402
39701-C	Back Up And Push -1, 2, 3, 5	De 5402
39702-A	Home Brew Rag -2, 3	De 5138
39703-A,-B	Home On The Range -2	De unissued
39704-A,-B	I Don't Love Nobody -1, 2, 3, 5	De unissued
39705-A	Short'nin' Bread -1, 5, 6	De 5162
39706-A	Magnolia Waltz -1, 3	De 5162

Issued items are subcredited (**With Bill Gatin & His Jug**), except matrix 39702 as (**With Bill Gatin & His Gang**).

CHERRY SISTERS

Patsy Cherry, sg/v; Clara Belle Cherry, md/lv; Margaret Cherry, g/v.
Dallas, TX   Friday, April 4, 1941

063020-1	At The End Of Memory Lane	BB B-8836
063021-1	You Tell Me Your Dream (I'll Tell You Mine)	BB B-8836
063022-1	When You Come To The Rainbow's End	BB B-8770
063023-1	Colorado Memories	BB B-8770
063024-1	Sweet Bunch Of Daisies	BB B-8746
063025-1	When They Ring Those Golden Bells	BB B-8746

CHESTER & ROLLINS

Pseudonym on Aurora for Frank Luther & Carson Robison.

TED CHESTNUT

Ted Chestnut (or Chesnut, as he is always spelled in Gennett sources) first recorded as a member of the Kentucky Thorobreds.

Ted Chestnut, v; acc. Doc Roberts, f; Asa Martin, g.
Richmond, IN   Thursday, May 10, 1928

13798	Knoxville Girl	Sil 8156, Spt 9260
13800	The Rowan County Feud	Ge 6513, Ch 15524
13801-A	The Death Of J.B. Marcum	Ge 6513, Ch 15524
13802	The Letter From Home	Ge 6480, Ch 15544
13803-A	My Mother Was A Lady	Ge 6480, Ch 15544, Spt 9180

Champion 15524, 15544 as by **Cal Turner**. Supertone 9180 as by **Alvin Bunch**; 9260, Silvertone 8156 as by **Jim Burke**. Matrix 13799 is by Doc Roberts & Asa Martin. Rev. Silvertone 8156, Supertone 9260 by John D. Foster.

Richmond, IN   Monday. May 14, 1928

| 13832 | The Dingy Miner's Cabin | Ge 6531, Spt 9178 |

Matrix 13832 was logged and issued on Gennett 6531 as by **Asa Martin**, and on Supertone 9178 as by **Emmett Davenport**. Rev. Gennett 6531, Supertone 9178 by Asa Martin.

Acc. Doc Roberts, f-1; Asa Martin, g.
Richmond, IN   Thursday, August 23, 1928

14168-B	He's Only A Miner Killed In The Ground -1	Ge 6603, Ch 15587, Spt 9180
14169	Bring Back My Boy -1	Ge 6603, Cq 7258
14170	Little Old Log Cabin By The Stream -1	Ge 6673, Ch 15630, Cq 7258
14171-A	Old And Only In The Way	Chg 422
14172	Only A Tramp	Ge 6673, Ch 15587, Cq 7262
14172-A	Only A Tramp -1	Ge unissued
14173	The Drunkard's Doom	Ge 6638, Chg 422

Champion 15587, 15630 as by **Cal Turner**. Supertone 9180 as by **Alvin Bunch**. Challenge 422 as by **Oliver Moore**. Conqueror 7258, 7262 as by **Eli Jenkins**.

Richmond, IN   Friday, August 24, 1928

| 14182 | A Prisoner At 23 -1 | Ge rejected |
| 14183 | By The Silvery Rio Grande | Ge 6638, Ch 15630, Cq 7262 |

Champion 15630 as by **Cal Turner**. Conqueror 7262 as by **Eli Jenkins**.
Matrix 14182 was originally titled *Charlie Brown*, which is crossed out in the ledger and replaced with the title shown.

CHICAGO RHYTHM KINGS

Bluebird B-6397 under the name of this group (for which see JR) couples a genuine Chicago Rhythm Kings item with one, *Sarah Jane*, by the Tune Wranglers.

CHIEF PONTIAC

No details.
    New York, NY   Thursday, September 6, 1928

146959-	Medley Of Old Time Jigs 1. Money Musk; 2. Evoline; 3. Sailors' Hornpipe; 4. Old Hen Cackled; 5. Turkey In The Straw; 6. Money Musk	Co unissued
146960-	Medley Of Two-Steps 1. Carry Me Back To Old Virginny; 2. When You And I Were Young Maggie; 3. Silver Threads Among The Gold; 4. My Old Kentucky Home; 5. 'Way Down Upon The Swanee River	Co unissued

CHIEF SHUNATONA, DOUG McTAGUE & SKOOKUM

See Cowboy Tom's Roundup.

BILL CHILDERS

See W.C. Childers.

W.C. CHILDERS

W.C. Childers, v; acc. unknown.
    San Antonio, TX   Tuesday, March 6, 1928

400398-	When The Work's All Done This Fall	OK unissued

Childers & White: W.C. Childers, Clyde White, v duet; acc. unknown, f; unknown, vla; unknown, p; unknown, vc.
    San Antonio, TX   Wednesday, March 7, 1928

400416-	Your Mother Always Cares For You	OK 45208, PaE R3868
400417-B	Jesus Is All To Me	OK 45213
400418-	Red River Valley	OK 45208, PaE R3868
400419-B	Don't Grieve Your Mother	OK 45213

Bill Childers, v; acc. unknown, f; unknown, vla; unknown, p.
    San Antonio, TX   Wednesday, March 7, 1928

400420-A	When The Work's All Done This Fall	OK 45203
400421-B	Bury Me Not On The Lone Prairie	OK 45203

W.C. Childers, v; acc. own g.
    Richmond, IN   Monday, July 1, 1929

15295,-A,-B	There's A Mother Always Waiting	Ge rejected

    Richmond, IN   Wednesday, July 3, 1929

15299	That Little Old Hut Was A Mansion To Me	Ge 6943, Ch 15898, Spt 9655

Champion 15898 as by **Enos Wanner**. Supertone 9655 as by **Andy Hopkins**.

    Richmond, IN   Tuesday, July 9, 1929

15312-B	Workin' Habits	Ge 7021, Ch 15830, Spt 9490
15313	I'm Not As Good As I Appear	Ge 6973
15314	I'll Smoke My Long Stemmed Pipe	Ge 7113, Spt 9655
15315,-A	Flowers From Mother's Grave	Ge rejected
15316	Over The Hills To The Poorhouse	Ge 6943, Ch 15791, 45166, Spt 9472, MeC 45166
15317	Don't Grieve Your Mother	Ge 6931, Ch 15810, Spt 9561
15318	The Grand Roundup	Ge 6931, Ch 15791, Spt 9472
15319	Put Me Off At Buffalo	Ge 7021, Ch 15830, Spt 9490

Champion 15791, 15810, 15830 as by **Enos Wanner**. Supertone 9490, 9561, 9655 as by **Andy Hopkins**; 9472 as by **Alfred Carlson**.

    Richmond, IN   Wednesday, July 10, 1929

15320	Your Mother's Always Waiting	Ge 6973, Ch 15810, 45166, Spt 9561, MW 4965, MeC 45166
15321	That Little Old Hut Was A Mansion To Me	Ge rejected

Champion 15810 as by **Enos Wanner**. Supertone 9561 as by **Andy Hopkins**.

Acc. own g; poss. Mrs. W.C. Childers, v-1.
    Grafton, WI   c. September 1929

L-4-2	Amber Tresses Tied In Blue	Pm 3181, Bwy 8153
L-5-1	Somewhere Somebody's Waiting -1	Pm 3181, Bwy 8153

Broadway 8153 as by **C.W. Charles**.

W.C. Childers, v/y-1; acc. own g.
   Richmond, IN   Saturday, November 23, 1929
   15943,-A   The Death Of Little Joe   Ge rejected
   15952   Blue Yodel No. 5 -1   Ge rejected
Matrix 15944 is Mexican; 15945/46 are by Duke Clark; 15947 to 15951 are Mexican.
   Richmond, IN   Monday, November 25, 1929
   15954,-A   Blue Yodel No. 6 -1   Ge rejected

Acc. prob.: Ed Showalter, f; Haskell Harkleroad, bj; Grace Kinzele, g.
   Richmond, IN   Monday, November 25, 1929
   15955-B   Too Late You Have Come Back To Me   Ge 7066, Spt 9601
Supertone 9601 as by **Andy Hopkins**.
   Richmond, IN   Wednesday, November 27, 1929
   15957   Crepe On The Little Cabin Door   Ge 7066, Ch 15898, Spt 9601, MW 4965
Champion 15898 as by **Enos Wanner**. Supertone 9601 as by **Andy Hopkins**. Matrix 15956 is by the Richmond Melody Boys.

W.C. Childers & E.F. Showalter, v duet; acc. poss.: Haskell Harkleroad, bj; Grace Kinzele, g.
   Richmond, IN   Wednesday, November 27, 1929
   15960-A,-B   The Picture On The Wall   Ge rejected

W.C. Childers, v; acc. poss.: Haskell Harkleroad, bj; Grace Kinzele, g.
   Richmond, IN   Friday, November 29, 1929
   15965,-A   A Picture From Life's Other Side   Ge rejected

Acc. unknown, o-1; prob. own g-2; Mrs. W.C. Childers, v-3.
   Richmond, IN   Thursday, May 15, 1930
   16608-A   The Fatal Rose Of Red -1   Ge 7223, Spt 9778
   16611   A Mother's Plea -1, 2   Spt 9713, Spr 2525
   16613-A   The Prison Warden's Secret -2   Ge 7292, Ch 16052, Spt 9713
   16614-A   The House At The End Of The Lane -2, 3   Ge 7292, Ch 16098, 33042, Spr 2659
Champion 16052 as by **Enos Wanner**, 16098 as by **Enos Wanner & Mrs. Wanner**. Supertone 9713, 9778 as by **Andy Hopkins**. Superior 2525 as by **George Holmes**, 2659 as by **Mr. & Mrs. George Holmes**. Intervening matrices are by The Scare Crow (see *B&GR*). Rev. Superior 2659 by Asa Martin & James Roberts.
   Richmond, IN   Friday, May 16, 1930
   16617-B   Bring Back My Wandering Boy -1, 2   Ch 16052, Spr 2525
   16618-A   Two Little Girls In Blue -1, 2   Ge 7223, Ch 16098, 33042, Spt 9778
Champion 16052, 16098 as by **Enos Wanner**. Supertone 9778 as by **Andy Hopkins**. Superior 2525 as by **George Holmes**.

Wanner & White: W.C. Childers, Clyde G. White, v duet; acc. prob. W.C. Childers, k/g; prob. Clyde G. White, k.
   Richmond, IN   Monday, July 27, 1931
   17889   That Little Boy Of Mine   Ch 16306, 45188, Spr 2734, MW 4960,
                                                                   MeC 45188
   17893-A   The Pretty Quadroon   Ch 16306, Spr 2713
   17894-A   Little Old Church In The Valley   Ch 16348, 45188, Spr 2734, MW 4960,
                                                                     MeC 45188
Superior 2713 as by **Holmes & Taylor**. Matrices 17890/91 are by Edgar Wilson; 17892 is popular. Revs: Champion 16348, Superior 2713 by Edgar Wilson.

W.C. Childers, v; acc. prob. own k/g.
   Richmond, IN   Tuesday, July 28, 1931
   17900   Strawberry Roan – Part II   Ch 16467, 45103, Spr 2722, MW 4951
   17901   Strawberry Roan – Part I   Ch 16467, 45103, Spr 2722, MW 4951
Superior 2722 as by **Enos Wanner**. Matrices 17900/01 are titled *The Strawberry Roan – Part 2* and *The Strawberry Roan – Pt. 1* respectively on Montgomery Ward 4951.

Wanner Duo: prob.: W.C. Childers, unknown, v duet; acc. unknown.
   Atlanta, GA   Friday, October 23, 1931
   151908-   Too Late   Co unissued
   151909-   Just A Lonely Cowboy   Co unissued
   151910-   Cowboy's Letter From Home   Co unissued
   151911-   My Long Stem Pipe   Co unissued

Wanner & Jenkins: prob.: W.C. Childers, Rev. Andrew Jenkins, v duet; acc. unknown, g.
   Atlanta, GA   Saturday, October 24, 1931
   151922-1   A Sweetheart's Promise   Co 15728-D, ReAu G21558
   151923-1   When The Dew Is On The Rose   Co 15728-D, ReAu G21558

CHILDERS & WHITE

See W.C. Childers.

LEW CHILDRE

Lew Childre, v/y-1; acc. own sg.
Richmond, IN   Monday, March 31, 1930

16428,-A	It Don't Do Nothin' But Rain	Ge rejected
16429,-A	It Can't Be Done	Ge rejected
16430,-A	Wagon Yard -1	Ge rejected
16431,-A	Moonshine Blues -1	Ge rejected
16432-A	My Red-Haired Lady	Spr 2520
16433,-A	Where The River Shannon Flows	Ge rejected
16434,-A,-B	Horsie Keep Your Tail Up	Ge rejected
16435,-A	The Old Grey Mare	Ge rejected
16436,-A	Little Joe The Wrangler	Ge rejected
16437,-A	Jack Of Diamonds	Ge rejected

Superior 2520 as by **Bert Carson**.

Richmond, IN   Thursday, April 10, 1930

| 16470 | Wagon Yard | Ge 7183, Ch 16011 |
| 16471 | Moonshine Blues | Ge 7183, Ch 16011 |

Richmond, IN   Friday, April 11, 1930

16472,-A	The Old Gray Mare	Ge rejected
16473,-A	Jack O' Diamonds	Ge rejected
16474,-A	It Don't Do Nothing But Rain	Ge rejected

Lew Childre, v/y-1; or **Childre & Walker**-2: Lew Childre, prob. Wiley Walker, v duet; acc. prob. Wiley Walker, f; Lew Childre, sg.
Richmond, IN   Thursday, September 11, 1930

17018	I Learned About Women From Her	Spr 2520
17019,-A	It Can't Be Done	Ge rejected
17020,-A	Blue Ridge Mountain Queen -2	Ge rejected
17021	The Old Grey Mare	Ge 7312, Ch 16093, Spt 9773
17022,-A	It Didn't Do Nothing But Rain	Ge rejected
17023-A	Horsie Keep Your Tail Up -1	Ge 7312, Ch 16093, Spt 9773

Superior 2520 as by **Bert Carson**.

Lew Childre, v/y-1; acc. own sg.
Chicago, IL   Monday, March 23, 1936

C-1299-1	Hang Out Your Front Door Key	ARC 6-06-51, Cq 8657
C-1300-1	The Fishing Blues -1	ARC 6-06-51
C-1301-2	My Red Haired Lady -1	ARC 6-08-59
C-1302-1,-2	Under A Southern Moon	ARC unissued
C-1303-1	I'm Savin' Up Coupons (To Get One Of Those)	ARC 6-08-59
C-1304-1,-2	Hog Calling Blues	ARC unissued
C-1305-1,-2	When My Louie Sings His Yodel-Laddy-Hoo -1	ARC unissued

Chicago, IL   Tuesday, March 24, 1936

C-1310-1	When My Louie Sings His Yodel-Laddy-Hoo -1	Cq 8656
C-1311-1,-2	Here's Your Opportunity	ARC unissued
C-1312-1,-2	My Heart Is In The Hills Of Carolina	ARC unissued
C-1313-2	Horsie Keep Your Tail Up	ARC 6-10-52, Cq 8656
C-1314-1,-2	The Answer To Nobody's Darling	ARC unissued
C-1315-1,-2	Moonshine Blues	ARC unissued
C-1316-1,-2	My Mammy	ARC unissued
C-1317-1	Wagon Yard -1	ARC 6-10-52

Chicago, IL   Wednesday, March 25, 1936

| C-1318-1 | It Don't Do Nothing But Rain | Cq 8657 |
| C-1319-1,-2 | My Mary | ARC unissued |

Lew Childre recorded after 1942.

VIRGINIA CHILDS

The majority of Virginia Childs' recordings appear to be on the margin of this book's subject-matter, but they are listed in their entirety.

Virginia Childs, v; acc. unknown, p.
Atlanta, GA   Friday, April 23, 1926

| 142124-1,-2 | I'm A Heart-Broken Mama | Co unissued |
| 142125-1,-2 | Got No Time | Co unissued |

Acc. Roy Smeck, g.
New York, NY   Thursday, August 19, 1926

142540-1,-2	Down-Hearted Blues	Co unissued
142541-1,-2,-3	The St. Louis Blues	Co unissued
142542-1,-2,-3	If You Can't Hold The Man You Love	Co unissued
142543-1,-2	You're Burnin' Me Up (Turnin' Me Down)	Co unissued

Acc. Jack Glogau, p.
New York, NY   Friday, August 20, 1926

142544-1,-2	Six Feet Of Papa	Co unissued
142545-1,-2	I Got A Papa Down In New Orleans	Co unissued
142546-1,-2,-3	Prescription For The Blues	Co unissued
142547-1,-2,-3	Farewell Blues	Co unissued

Daisy Douglas, v; acc. prob. Clayton McMichen or Bert Layne, f-1; Riley Puckett, g.
Atlanta, GA   Wednesday, November 3, 1926

| 143042-1 | Down Hearted Blues | Co 14175-D |
| 143043-2 | The St. Louis Blues -1 | Co 14175-D |

Virginia Childs, v; acc. unknown, p.
Atlanta, GA   Wednesday, November 3, 1926

| 143044-1,-2,-3 | You're Burnin' Me Up (Turnin' Me Down) | Co unissued |
| 143045-1,-2 | If You Can't Hold The Man You Love | Co unissued |

BILL CHITWOOD

Bill Chitwood & Bud Landress: Bill Chitwood, f; Bud Landress, bj/v-1.
New York, NY   Thursday, November 20, 1924

14269/70	Howdy, Bill -1	Br rejected
14271/72	Pa, Ma And Me -1	Br 2884, Sil 3095
14273/74	Over The Sea	Br 2810, Sil 3049
14275/76	Hen Cackle	Br 2811, Sil 3050
14277/78	Johnny, Get Your Gun -1	Br rejected
14279	Fourth Of July -1	?Br 2883

New York, NY   Friday, November 21, 1924

14284	Fourth Of July -1	?Br 2883
14285/86	Jesse James -1	Br unissued
14287/88/89	Whoa Mule	Br 2811, Sil 3050
14290/91	Furniture Man -1	Br 2884, Sil 3095
14292/93	Cynda -1	Br unissued
14294/95	Jerusalem, Mourn -1	Br 2809, Sil 3048
14296/97	I Got Mine -1	Br 2810, Sil 3049

It is uncertain whether Brunswick 2883 uses matrix 14279 or 14284.

New York, NY   Monday, November 24, 1924

| 14298/99 | Howdy, Bill -1 | Br 2809, Sil 3048 |
| 14300/01 | Johnny, Get Your Gun -1 | Br 2883 |

Silvertone 3095 as by **McClelland & Ellis**. Matrices 14298/99 and 14300/01 are remakes of matrices 14269/70 and 14277/78 respectively and it is assumed that they are the ones chosen for issue.

Bill Chitwood & His Georgia Mountaineers: Bill Chitwood, f/v; Bud Landress, bj/v; poss. Clyde Evans, g/v; unknown, g/v.
Atlanta, GA   Wednesday, March 23, 1927

80619-B	How I Got My Wife	OK 45100
80620-A	Smiling Watermelon	OK 45110
80621-A	Preacher Blues	OK 45131
80622-B	I Had But Fifteen Cents	OK 45131
80623-A	It Won't Happen Again For Months	OK 45110
80624-B	Fourth Of July At The Country Fair	OK 45100

Bill Chitwood, f/v/sp-1; poss. Earl Johnson, f; poss. Bud Landress, bj/v; unknown, g/v; poss. unknown, g/v.
Atlanta, GA   Monday, October 3, 1927

81652-A	When Married Folks Are Out Of Cash	OK 45162
81653-	Boys Keep Away From The Girls	OK unissued
81654-A	Raise Rough House Tonight	OK 45236
81655-B	Bill Wishes He Was Single Again	OK 45236

| 81656- | Lula Wall | OK unissued |
| 81657-B | Kitty Hill -1 | OK 45162 |

Lead vocal probably variously by Chitwood and Landress, with group vocal by some or all other musicians.
Bill Chitwood also recorded with the Clyde Evans Band, Georgia Yellow Hammers, Gordon County Quartet, and Turkey Mountain Singers.

AXEL CHRISTENSEN

Monologues by this artist in the Paramount Old Time Tunes series are beyond the scope of this work.

CHRISTIAN HARMONY SINGERS

See John McGhee & Frank Welling.

CHRISTINE

This artist's full name is Christine Endeback.

Christine, v; acc. The Rangers: prob.: Harry Sims, f; Augie Klein, ac; Ozzie Westley, g; Clyde Moffet, sb.
Chicago, IL   Wednesday, March 5, 1941

93552-B	Whispering Friends	De 5935, DeSA FM5140
93553-A	A Message From Home	De 5935
93554-A	Red Rose	De 6081, MeC 45553
93555-A	Peaceful Valley	De 6081, MeC 45553
93556-A	Trailing Arbutus	De 5968
93557-A	A Voice In The Valley	De 5968

Rev. Decca FM5140 by Jimmy Wakely.

HOMER CHRISTOPHER

Homer Christopher & Wife: Homer Christopher, f; Katherine Christopher, g.
Atlanta, GA   April 1926

| 9624-A | Southern Railroad | OK 45041 |
| 9625-A | After The Ball | OK 45041 |

Homer Christopher–Raney Vanvink: Homer Christopher, pac; Raney Vanvink (or Van Vink), g.
Atlanta, GA   Thursday, February 17, 1927

37910-3	Lost Mamma Blues	Vi 20656
37911-1,-2	Sleep, Baby, Sleep	Vi unissued
37912-1	Waiting For The Robert E. Lee	Vi 20656
37913-2	Going Slow	Vi 21128

Rev. Victor 21128 by Alphus McFayden.

Homer Christopher & Raney Van Vink: Homer Christopher, pac; Raney Vanvink (or Van Vink), g.
Atlanta, GA   Friday, March 18, 1927

80569-B	Going Slow	OK 45117
80570-A	Lost Mamma Blues	OK 45097
80571-B	Alabama Jubilee	OK 45138
80572-B	Spartanburg Blues	OK 45117, 16276
80573-A	Hilo March	OK 45138, 16276
80574-B	Red Wing	OK 45097

OKeh 16276 (a Mexican issue) as by **Christopher Y Van Vink**; matrix 80572 is titled *El Payaso*, and matrix 80573 *Hilo Marcha*, on that issue.

Atlanta, GA   Wednesday, October 5, 1927

81681-B	Farewell To Thee	OK 45277
81682-B	Drifting Back To Dreamland	OK 45147
81683-A	Home Town Rag	OK 45147
81684-B	March In "D"	OK 45277
81685-B	Old Fashioned Waltz	OK 45195
81686-B	Sleep, Baby Sleep	OK 45195

CHRISTOPHER Y VAN VINK

This artist-credit was used for a release in the Okeh 16000 Mexican series by Homer Christopher & Raney Van Vink.

CHUCK & JIM

See James Brown, Jr. & Ken Landon groups.

CHUCK WAGON GANG

Rose Carter Karnes, sv; Anna Carter, av; D.P. "Dad" Carter, tv; Ernest "Jim" Carter, bsv; acc. "Jim" Carter, g.
San Antonio, TX   Wednesday, November 25, 1936

SA-2594-1	The Son Hath Made Me Free	ARC 7-04-71, Vo/OK 03472, Cq 8836, Co 37670, 20269
SA-2595-2	We Miss You Mother	ARC unissued: *Ha HL7318, HS11118 (LPs)*
SA-2596-1	Kneel At The Cross	Co 20699
SA-2596-2	Kneel At The Cross	ARC 7-04-71, Vo/OK 03472, Cq 8836, Co 37670, 20269, 20699
SA-2597-1	A Beautiful Life	Vo/OK 04342, Co 37453, 20180, 20698, 54029
SA-2597-2	A Beautiful Life	ARC unissued: *Co FC40152 (LP)*
SA-2598-1	The Church In The Wildwood	Co 20501, 20699, 54010
SA-2598-2	The Church In The Wildwood	ARC 7-09-60, Vo/OK 03028, Co 20501, 20699
SA-2599-1	I'd Rather Have Jesus	ARC 7-09-60, Vo/OK 03028, Co 20501, 20700, 54010
SA-2600-1	Standing Outside	Cq 8837
SA-2600-2	Standing Outside	ARC unissued: *Ha HL7318, HS11118 (LPs)*
SA-2601-1	Will You Meet Me Over Yonder?	Vo/OK 04342, Cq 8837, Co 37453, 20180, 54029
SA-2602-1	Massa's In The Cold, Cold Ground	ARC unissued: *Co BT15905 (Cass); Sony 28910 (CD)*

Matrix SA-2602 was logged as *Massa's In De Cold Ground*.

Rose Carter Karnes, sv; Anna Carter, av; "Dad" Carter, tv-1/bsv-2; Ernest "Jim" Carter, tv-3/bsv-4; acc. "Dad" Carter, md-5; "Jim" Carter, g.
San Antonio, TX   Wednesday, November 25, 1936

SA-2603-2	Take Me Back To Renfro Valley -3, 5	ARC 7-03-70, Vo/OK 03434, Cq 8784, Co 37707, 20285
SA-2604-1	At The Rainbow's End -1, 4	ARC 8-01-62
SA-2605-2	Take Me Back To Col-ler-rad-da Fer To Stay -3, 5	ARC 7-08-55, Vo/OK 02983, Cq 8963
SA-2606-1	Carry Me Back To The Mountains -3, 5	ARC 7-06-73
SA-2607-1	Echoes From The Hills -3, 5	ARC 7-03-58, Vo 03426, Cq 8785
SA-2608-1,-2	Mother Of The Valley -2, 3	ARC unissued
SA-2609-1	Wonder Valley -2, 3, 5	ARC 7-06-73

Rose Carter Karnes, sv; Anna Carter, av; acc. "Dad" Carter, md; "Jim" Carter, g.
San Antonio, TX   Thursday, November 26, 1936

SA-2610-1	I'll Be All Smiles Tonight	ARC 7-03-58, Vo 03426, Cq 8785

Rose Carter Karnes, sv/y-1; Anna Carter, av; Ernest "Jim" Carter, tv; "Dad" Carter, bsv-2; acc. "Dad" Carter, md-3; "Jim" Carter, g.
San Antonio, TX   Thursday, November 26, 1936

SA-2611-1	Put My Little Shoes Away -2	ARC 7-08-55, Vo/OK 02983, Cq 8963
SA-2612-1	Sunny South By The Sea -1, 3	ARC 7-03-70, Vo/OK 03434, Cq 8784, Co 37707, 20285
SA-2613-1,-2	My Wild Irish Rose -2, 3	ARC unissued
SA-2614-1,-2	Where The River Shannon Flows -3	ARC unissued
SA-2615-1	The Engineer's Child -3	Vo/OK 04105

Matrix SA-2612 is titled *Dear Old Sunny South (By The Sea)* on some pressings of OKeh 03434.

Rose Carter Karnes, sv/y-1; Anna Carter, av-2; Ernest "Jim" Carter, tv-3; "Dad" Carter, bsv-4; acc. "Dad" Carter, md-5; "Jim" Carter, g.
Dallas, TX   Friday, June 25, 1937

DAL-470-2	I Want To Be A Real Cowboy Girl -2, 3, 4	ARC 8-04-54, Vo/OK 03224, Cq 8988
DAL-471-1	The Little Green Mound On The Hill -2, 3	ARC 8-01-62
DAL-472-2	Oklahoma Blues -1, 5	ARC 8-04-54, Vo/OK 03224, Cq 8988
DAL-473-1,-2	The New Frontier -2, 3, 5	ARC unissued
DAL-4741-1,-2	Cowboy Yodel -1, 2, 3, 5	ARC unissued
DAL-475-2	Will You Love Me (When My Hair Has Turned To Silver?) -2, 3, 5	Vo/OK 04105
DAL-476-1,-2	Mississippi Valley Blues -2, 3, 4, 5	ARC unissued
DAL-477-2	Texas Star -2, 3, 4	ARC unissued: *Co FC40152 (LP)*

Rose Carter Karnes, sv; Anna Carter Gordon, av; "Dad" Carter, tv; Ernest "Jim" Carter, bsv; acc. "Jim" Carter, g.
Saginaw, TX   Tuesday, April 23, 1940

DAL-1032-1	After The Sunrise	OK 05682, Co 37450, 20177
DAL-1032-2	After The Sunrise	Co 20177, 54009
DAL-1033-1	Higher	Vo/OK 05600, Co 20178
DAL-1033-2	Higher	Co 37451, 20178
DAL-1034-1	I Love To Tell Of His Love	OK 06091, Co 37447
DAL-1034-2	I Love To Tell Of His Love	Co 37447, 20174
DAL-1035-1	Getting Ready To Leave This World	OK 05782

DAL-1035-2	Getting Ready To Leave This World	Co 37449, 20176
DAL-1036-1	Heaven Is My Home	OK 05970
DAL-1036-2	Heaven Is My Home	Co 37448, 20175
DAL-1037-1	We Are Climbing	OK 05682, Co 37450, 20177
DAL-1037-2	We Are Climbing	Co 20177, 54009
DAL-1038-1	Lord, Lead Me On	Vo/OK 05536, Co 37452, 20179
DAL-1038-2	Lord, Lead Me On	Co 37452, 20179
DAL-1038-	Lord, Lead Me On	Co 54034
DAL-1039-1	An Empty Mansion	Vo/OK 05536, Co 37452, 20179
DAL-1039-2	An Empty Mansion	Co 37452, 20179
DAL-1039-	An Empty Mansion	Co 54034
DAL-1040-1	I've Found A Hiding Place	OK 05782
DAL-1040-2	I've Found A Hiding Place	Co 37449, 20176, 20698
DAL-1041-1	Holding To His Hand Of Love	Vo/OK 05600, Co 37451, 20178
DAL-1041-2	Holding To His Hand Of Love	Co 37451, 20178
DAL-1042-1	Sunset Is Coming (But The Sunrise We'll See)	OK 05970, Co 37448, 20175
DAL-1042-2	Sunset Is Coming (But The Sunrise We'll See)	Co 20175
DAL-1043-1	Holy Be Thy Great Name	OK 06091, Co 37447, 20174
DAL-1043-2	Holy Be Thy Great Name	Co 20174

It is not known which takes of matrices DAL-1038/39 were used for Columbia 54034.

Rose Carter Karnes, sv; Anna Carter Gordon, av; "Dad" Carter, tv; Ernest "Jim" Carter, bsv; acc. "Jim" Carter, g.
Fort Worth, TX   Saturday, March 8, 1941

DAL-1245-1	He Set Me Free	OK 06596, Co 37444, 20171
DAL-1245-2	He Set Me Free	Co 37444, 20171, 54028
DAL-1246-1	Wonderful	OK 06302, Co 20173
DAL-1246-2	Wonderful	Co 37446
DAL-1247-1	Love Is The Key	OK 06551, Cq 9882, Co 37445, 20172
DAL-1248-1	Coming	Cq 9884, Co 20521, 54030
DAL-1250-1	I'll Be No Stranger There	OK 06596, Cq 9882, Co 37444, 20171
DAL-1250-2	I'll Be No Stranger There	Co 20171
DAL-1250-	I'll Be No Stranger There	Co 54028

It is not known which take of matrix DAL-1250 was used for Columbia 54028.

Rose Carter Karnes, sv; Anna Carter Gordon, av; "Dad" Carter, tv; Ernest "Jim" Carter, bsv; acc. "Jim" Carter, g.
Fort Worth TX   Sunday, March 9, 1941

DAL-1249-1	We Shall Have Glory Afterwhile	OK 06302, Co 20173
DAL-1249-2	We Shall Have Glory Afterwhile	Co 37446
DAL-1257-1	O Rock Of Ages Hide Thou Me	Co 20521, 54030
DAL-1258-2	He's Coming Again	Cq 9885, Co 20460, 54015
DAL-1259-1	I Love My Savior, Too	Cq 9883, Co 37989, 20392, 54035, CoC C999
DAL-1260-2	On The Jericho Road	Cq 9885, Co 37989, 20392, 54035, CoC C999
DAL-1261-2	Jesus Hold My Hand	Cq 9883, Co 20460, 54015
DAL-1262-1	Mighty Close To Heaven	OK 06551, Cq 9884, Co 37445, 20172

Matrices DAL-1257 and DAL-1261 were scheduled for OKeh 6678, but this was not released.
Intervening matrices are by the Sunshine Boys.
The Chuck Wagon Gang recorded after 1942.

CHUMBER, COKER & RICE

Misspelling on Broadway 8234 for Chumbler, Coker & Rice.

CHUMBLER, COKER & RICE

See The Chumbler Family & Associated Groups.

THE CHUMBLER FAMILY & ASSOCIATED GROUPS

Chumbler, Coker & Rice: Howard Coker, f; William Archer Chumbler, md; Hoke Rice, g.
Long Island City, NY   c. April 1929

| 397-B | Alabama Square Dance – Part 1 | QRS R.9017, Bwy 8234 |
| 398 | Alabama Square Dance – Part 2 | QRS R.9017, Bwy 8234 |

Broadway 8234 as by **Chumber, Coker & Rice**.

Chumbler's Breakdown Gang: prob.: Howard Coker, f; William Archer Chumbler, md; Hoke Rice, g/v.
Long Island City, NY   c. April 1929

| 405-A | Brown Mule Slide | QRS R.9019, Pm 3309 |

Paramount 3309 as by **Davis–Rice–Thomas**.

Aurally Chumbler's Breakdown Gang sound very like Davis, Rice & Thomas (see Claude (C.W.) Davis), but in the absence of firmer data the item above is listed according to the label-credit on its primary issue. Chumbler's Breakdown Gang was also used on QRS R.9016 as a pseudonym for, or misidentification of, The Highlanders (see Charlie Poole).
Revs: QRS R.9019, Paramount 3309 by Davis, Rice & Thomas (see Claude (C.W.) Davis).

The Chumbler Family: William Archer Chumbler, ah/v-1; George Elmo Chumbler, g/prob. v-2; Irene Chumbler, v-3; Laura Chumbler, v-4; —— Thompson, v-5; unidentified, wh-6.

Atlanta, GA — Monday, November 4, 1929

149358-	The Hallelujah Side	Co unissued
149359-2	Sailing To Glory -3, 4, 5	Co 15481-D
149360-2	Jacobs [sic] Ladder -2, 3, 4	Co 15481-D
149361-	In A Garden -4	Co unissued
149362-2	I'm Going Home To My Wife -1, 3, 4, 6	Co 15513-D
149363-1	If He Should Come Again -3/4, 5	Co 15513-D

Archie Lee, Bill Brown, "Pops" Melvin, Hoke Rice, Pink Lindsey, Judge Lee: prob. Pink Lindsey, f/sp; Hoke Rice, g/v/sp; William Archer "Archie Lee" Chumbler, v/sp; Bill Brown, sp; Sterling "Pops" Melvin, sp; George Elmo "Judge Lee" Chumbler, sp.

Atlanta, GA — Thursday, March 20, 1930

ATL-961/62/63/64*	A Bootlegger's Joint In Atlanta – Pt. 1	Br 419, Au A22019
ATL-965/66*/67	A Bootlegger's Joint In Atlanta – Pt. 2	Br 419, Au A22019

Aurora A22019 as by **Baker Boys**.
Pts. 3 & 4 of this sketch were by a somewhat different personnel; see John Dilleshaw.

Lee Brothers: William Archer "Archie Lee" Chumbler, v; acc. unknown.

Atlanta, GA — Friday, March 21, 1930

ATL-982-	Work Don't Bother Me	Br/Vo rejected

Lee Brothers Trio: William Archer "Archie Lee" Chumbler, ah/v; poss. George Elmo "Judge Lee" Chumbler, g; poss. Hoke Rice, g.

Atlanta, GA — Friday, November 14, 1930

ATL-6668-	You Can't Ride My Mule	Br 501
ATL-6669-	Cotton Mill Blues	Br 501

William Archer and George Elmo Chumbler were probably also members of Jim King & His Brown Mules.

CHUMBLER'S BREAKDOWN GANG

See The Chumbler Family & Associated Groups.

CLAGG & SLIGER

It seems likely that Clagg & Sliger and The Hymn Time Boys are identical, and all their known recordings are listed together below on that supposition.

Clagg & Sliger-1/**The Hymn Time Boys**-2, v duet; acc. —— Davis, g; —— Ramsey, g.

Richmond, IN — Thursday, March 27, 1930

16403,-A	Dear To The Heart Of The Shepherd -2	Ge rejected
16405,-A	There's Sunshine In My Soul -2	Ge rejected
16407,-A	She Was Bred In Old Kentucky -1	Ge rejected

Richmond, IN — Friday, March 28, 1930

16409,-A	Just Plain Folks -1	Ge rejected
16410,-A	Love Lifted Me -2	Ge rejected
16411,-A	Bring Them In -2	Ge rejected

Intervening matrices are by Philippine artists.

SUNNY CLAPP & HIS BAND O' SUNSHINE

One coupling by this danceband was issued in the Victor Old Familiar Tunes series (V-40152). It is beyond the scope of this work. (Further information on the band, which recorded a number of items for Victor and Okeh, may be found in JR.)

GENE CLARDY & STAN CLEMENTS

Gene Clardy, f; Stanley Clements, g.

Memphis, TN — Tuesday, February 18, 1930

MEM-748-	Sleeping Time Waltz	Vo 5462
MEM-749-	Black Mustache	Vo 5418, Me M12176, M18030, MeC 93130, Min M-14013
MEM-750-	Harvest Home Waltz	Vo 5462
MEM-751-	Moonlight Clog	Vo 5418, Me M12176, M18030, MeC 93130

Melotone M18030 as by **Clardy et Clement**; matrix MEM-749 is titled *La Moustache Noire*, and MEM-751 *Clair De La Lune*, on that issue. Rev. Minerva M-14013 by Stripling Brothers.

Stanley Clements also recorded under his own name.

CLARDY ET CLEMENT

One release by Gene Clardy & Stan Clements, on Melotone M18030, was issued thus.

DUKE CLARK

Duke Clark, v; acc. own g.
 Richmond, IN   Saturday, November 23, 1929

15945,-A	1199 Blues	Ge rejected
15946,-A,-B	Lonesome Road Blues	Ge rejected

 Richmond, IN   Tuesday, April 28, 1931

17715	The Wreck Of The F.F.V.	Spr 2687
17716	1199 Blues	Spr 2687

 Richmond, IN   Thursday, July 16, 1931

17879,-A	Somebody's Waiting For Me	Ge rejected
17880,-A	Belle Of The Ball	Ge rejected
17881	Don't Send My Boy To Prison	Ge rejected
17882	Little Indian Napanee	Ge rejected

Acc. Jess Johnston, f-1/p-2; own g.
 Richmond, IN   Friday, October 9, 1931

18094	Abdul Abubul Amir -1	Ge rejected
18095	The Life Time Man -1	Ge rejected
18096-A	Old Deacon Johnson -2	Ch 16445

Rev. Champion 16445 by Jess Hillard.

Duke Clark & Harry Hillard, v duet; acc. own g duet.
 Richmond, IN   Thursday, July 14, 1932

18597	Kentucky Days	Ge unissued
18598	When The Dew Is On The Rose	Ge rejected
18600	I Had A Girl	Ge rejected

Matrix 18599 is by Harry Hillard; 18601 is by Frank James (see *B&GR*).

Duke Clark, v; acc. own g; Harry Hillard, g.
 Richmond, IN   Thursday, July 14, 1932

18602	Make A Change In Business	Ch 16470
18603	Belle Of The Ball	Ch 16470

Jess Hillard & Duke Clark, v duet; acc. own g duet; Jess Hillard, y.
 Richmond, IN   Friday, August 26, 1932

18741	I'll Get Mine Bye And Bye	Ch 16617

Rev. Champion 16617 by Jess Hillard.

Acc. own g duet.
 Richmond, IN   Saturday, August 27, 1932

18744	Jess & Duke's Salty Gob [sic]	Ch 16491

Rev. Champion 16491 by Jess Hillard.

Duke Clark, v; acc. own g.
 Richmond, IN   Saturday, August 27, 1932

18746	11:99 Blues	Ch 16624

Duke Clark, v/y-1; acc. own g.
 Richmond, IN   Wednesday, February 1, 1933

18994	There Is Somebody Waiting For Me	Ch S-16565
18995	Back Biting Blues -1	Ge unissued
18996	K.C. Whistle Blues -1	Ge unissued
18997	They Call Her Hula Lou	Ge unissued
18998	30 Minutes Behind The Time	Ch S-16565
18999	Lifetime Prisoner	Ch 16624

FRANK CLARK

Pseudonym on Champion for J.P. Ryan.

JOHN CLARK

Pseudonym on Champion for Herbert Sweet (see Sweet Brothers).

ORLA CLARK

Clark & Edans-1/**Orla Clark**-2: —— Edans, h-3/g-4; Orla Clark, g/v.
Richmond, IN　　　　　　　　　　　　　　　　　　　　　　　　　　　　　　c. March 1928

13625,-A,-B	Wabash Cannonball -1, 4	Ge rejected
13626,-A	Portland Maine -1, 4	Ge rejected
13627-A	I Want Some Home Brew -2, 4	Ge 6464, Cq 7261
13646-A	Joe Turner Blues -2, 3	Cq 7261
13647-A	Little Brown Head -1, 3	Ge 6497

Conqueror 7261 as by **Frank Jones**. Intervening matrices are by other artists.
Revs: Gennett 6464 by H.K. Hutchison, 6497 by Cranford, Thompson & Miles (see The Red Fox Chasers).

THEO. & GUS CLARK

Theo Clark, f; Gus Clark, g.
Atlanta, GA　　　　　　　　　　　　　　　　　　　　　　　　　　　Tuesday, March 12, 1929

402285-	Careless Love	OK unissued
402286-	Take Me Home To My Wife	OK unissued
402287-B	Wimbush Rag	OK 45339
402288-B	Barrow County Stomp	OK 45339

WALTER CLARK

Pseudonym on Australian Melotone for Vernon Dalhart.

CLARK & CLARE

Pseudonym on Grand Pree for Vernon Dalhart & Carson Robison.

CLARK & EDANS

See Orla Clark.

CLARK & HOWELL

Pseudonym on Supertone for Melvin Robinette & Byrd Moore.

CLARK BROTHERS

Pseudonym on Champion for Sweet Brothers.

LUTHER B. CLARKE

This artist's full name is Luther Bernard Clarke.

Luther B. Clarke, v; acc. Blue Ridge Highballers: Charley La Prade, f; Arthur Wells, bj; Lonnie Griffith, g.
New York, NY　　　　　　　　　　　　　　　　　　　　　　　　Wednesday, March 24, 1926

141853-2	Bright Sherman Valley	Co 15069-D
141854-1	I'll Be All Smiles To-night Love	Co 15069-D
141855-2	Wish To The Lord I Had Never Been Born	Co 15096-D

Rev. Columbia 15096-D by Blue Ridge Highballers.

CLASSIC CITY QUARTET

Vocal quartet; acc. unknown, p.
Atlanta, GA　　　　　　　　　　　　　　　　　　　　　　　Wednesday, November 6, 1929

149389-2	I'll Be Singing 'Round The Throne Someday	Co 15566-D
149390-2	Hold Thou To Me	Co 15566-D

AL CLAUSER & HIS OKLAHOMA OUTLAWS

Albert "Slim" Phillips, f; Larry Brandt, ac; Don Austin, bj-1/g-2/v; Al Clauser, g/v; Harry "Tex" Hoepner, sb/v.
Los Angeles, CA　　　　　　　　　　　　　　　　　　　　　Wednesday, March 17, 1937

LA-1278-A	The West, A Nest, And You -2	ARC 7-05-77, Cq 8838
LA-1279-B	Sunrise On The Guinea Farm -2	MacGregor 984
LA-1280-B	I'm Goin' Back To My Little Mountain Shack -2	MacGregor 985
LA-1281-B	The Death Of Jesse James -1	ARC 7-11-63, MacGregor 986
LA-1282-A,-B	Little Black Bronc -1	ARC 7-08-63, Cq 8840, MacGregor 987
LA-1283-A,-B	As We Ride Down The Old Prairie Trail -2	ARC 7-06-72, MacGregor 988
LA-1284-	Lonesome Trail -2	ARC unissued
LA-1285-A,-B	Trail Of The Mountain Rose -2	ARC 7-05-77, Cq 8838, MacGregor 990
LA-1286-B	I'm Ridin' Down The Trail To Albuquerque -2	ARC 7-06-72, Cq 8839, MacGregor 991
LA-1287-	When It's Springtime In The Blue Ridge Mountain -2	ARC unissued
LA-1288-A,-B	Whoa, Mule, Whoa -1	ARC 7-08-63, Cq 8840, MacGregor 993
LA-1289-A,-B	Rocky Mountain Express -2	ARC 7-11-63, Cq 8839, MacGregor 994

MacGregors as by **Dude Martin & Cowboy Group**. Other items on MacGregor with that artist-credit are actually by Dude Martin, including some that appeared on the reverse sides of some of the above issues. The items shown as unissued may have been issued on MacGregor, but if so are untraced. (MacGregor 983 and 989 are by Martin.)

Al Clauser recorded after 1942.

BOB CLAYTON

Pseudonym on ARC-Broadway for Gene Autry.

CLAYTON & GREENE

Pseudonym on ARC-Broadway for Gene Autry & Jimmy Long.

CLAYTON & HIS MELODY MOUNTAINEERS

Clayton Schultz, f; unknown, f; unknown, sg-1/g-2; unknown, md or bj.
    Knoxville, TN   Friday, April 4, 1930
    K-8064-   Lookout Valley Waltz -2   Vo 5434
    K-8065-   June Wedding Waltz -1   Vo 5434

Matrix K-8065 was originally logged as *April Shower Waltz*.

CLAYTON & PARKER

Pseudonym on Velvet Tone for Burnett & Rutherford (see Richard D. Burnett).

HARMON CLEM & PRINCE ALBERT HUNT

See Prince Albert Hunt.

THE CLEMENS FAMILY

Pseudonym on Champion for The Three Crackers (see Canova Family).

STANLEY CLEMENTS

Stanley Clements, v; acc. own g.
    Atlanta, GA   Friday, October 23, 1931
    405000-1   The Terrible Marriage   OK 45562
    405001-1   The Habit I Never Have Had   OK 45562

Stanley Clements also recorded with Gene Clardy, and after 1942.

CLIFF CLICK

See the Short Creek Trio.

CLIFF & RAY

See Clifford Gross.

BOB CLIFFORD
CLIFFORD BROTHERS

Pseudonyms on Vocalion, English Panachord, and Australian Regal-Zonophone for Cliff Carlisle and Carlisle Brothers respectively.

CLINCH MOUNTAIN SINGERS

Vocal group; acc. unknown.
    Altanta, GA   Friday, April 18, 1930
    150277-   Clinch Mountain   Co unissued
    150278-   To Be Named   Co unissued

CLINCH VALLEY BOYS

Pseudonym on Challenge for Taylor's Kentucky Boys, and on Champion, Silvertone, and Supertone for Marion Underwood & Sam Harris (see Taylor's Kentucky Boys).

GEORGE CLINE & HIS BOYS

Pseudonym on Challenge for Tommy Dandurand & His Gang.

CLOVER LEAF OLD TIME FIDDLIN' TEAM

Two or three unknowns, f; poss. unknown, p; unknown, g; unknown, v.
    Atlanta, GA   Thursday, August 9, 1928
    402109-A, -B   [Come Be My Rainbow]   OK unissued
    402110-   Where The Morning Glories Grow   OK unissued
    402111-   Somewhere, Someone Is Waiting   OK unissued

JESSIE COAT
Pseudonym on Champion for Asa Martin.

JESSIE COAT & JOHN BISHOP
Pseudonym on Champion for Asa Martin & James Roberts.

COATS SACRED QUARTETTE
James B. Coats, av; Buford Jefcoats, tv; Chealous Sumrall, bv; Glaston Hilbun, bsv; acc. James B. Coats, p.
    Jackson, MS   Thursday, October 17, 1935

JAX-181-3	I Am Feeling Love Waves	Vo/OK 05525
JAX-182-	Oh What A Joy To Sing	Vo 03129
JAX-183-	On The Royal Glory Road	Vo 03129
JAX-184-	Won't We Be Happy	Vo/OK 05451
JAX-185-1	We'll Soon Be Done With Troubles And Trials	ARC 7-04-59, Cq 8801
JAX-186-	Just Wear A Smile	Vo/OK 05451
JAX-187-1	I'd Rather Have Jesus	ARC 7-04-59, Cq 8801
JAX-188-3	Heaven For Me	Vo/OK 05525

CLARENCE COBB & AUBREY PROW
See Madisonville String Band.

GENE "HONEY GAL" COBB & JACK "SMOKE" GRAY
Recordings by these artists for Gennett are blackface sketches and the like, and outside the scope of this work.

COBB & UNDERWOOD
See Hack's String Band.

NED COBBEN
Pseudonym on Harmony, Velvet Tone, and Diva for, possibly, Arthur Fields.

COFER BROTHERS
Paul Cofer, f/v; Leon Cofer, g/v; Ben Evans, wh-1.
    Atlanta, GA   Saturday, March 19, 1927

80581-A	Where The Morning Glories Grow	OK 45137
80582-A	The Great Ship Went Down	OK 45137
80583-	Nothing From Nothing Leaves You	OK unissued
80584-B	The All Go Hungry Hash House	OK 45099
80585-	Down In Arkansas	OK unissued
80586-A	The Georgia Hobo -1	OK 45099

Paul Cofer, f/v/sp-1; Leon Cofer, g/v/sp-2.
    Atlanta, GA   Wednesday, March 13, 1929

402299-	We Will Outshine The Sun	OK unissued
402300-B	Because He Loved Her So	OK unissued: *Marimac 9110 (Cass); Doc DOCD-8021 (CD)*
402301-	Little Janie Green	OK unissued
402302-A	Keno, The Rent Man -1, 2	OK 45486
402303-B	Rock That Cradle Lucy -2	OK unissued: *Cy 544 (LP); Doc DOCD-8021 (CD)*
402304-B	How Long?	OK 45486

See also Georgia Crackers.

ART COFFEE
Pseudonym on Challenge for Otto Gray's Oklahoma Cowboy Band.

OSCAR L. COFFEY
Oscar Coffey, v; acc. own bj.
    Richmond, IN   Wednesday, February 8, 1928

13428	Stay All Night And Don't Go Home	Ge rejected

    Richmond, IN   Wednesday, May 9, 1928

13787,-A	The Bold Knights Of Labor	Ge rejected
13788,-A	He Never Came Back	Ge rejected
13789,-A	I'll Be All Smiles Tonight	Ge rejected
13790,-A	Amber Tresses Tied In Blue	Ge rejected
13791,-A,-B	Flitting Away	Ge rejected
13792-B	Poor But A Gentleman Still	Ge 6496, Spt 9306

13793,-A	That Little Black Mustache	Ge rejected
13794	Far Back In My Childhood	Ge 6481
13795	My Dear Old Mountain Home	Ge 6481, Ch 15523, Spt 9306, 9325
13796-A	Six Feet Of Earth Makes Us All One Size	Ge 6496, Ch 15523, Spt 9325

Champion 15523 as by **Barney Dunroe**. Supertone 9306 as by **Dick Meeks**, 9325 as by **Oscar Fox**. Matrix 13792 is titled *Poor, But A Gentleman Still* on Supertone 9306. Matrix 13796 is titled *Six Feet Of Earth Makes Us All Of One Size* on Champion 15523, Supertone 9325. Of matrix 13787 the Gennett ledger notes "correct title: The Heathen Chinese."

ALLEN D. COLE

Allen D. Cole, f; acc. unknown, bj.
    Richmond, IN   Friday, February 14, 1930

| 16273,-A | Stoney Creek Rag | Ge rejected |

Allen D. Cole also recorded at this session with Byrd Moore.

GRADY & HAZEL COLE

Grady Cole, Hazel Cole, v duet; acc. Elmer Hicks, ac-1; Curley Hicks, g.
    Atlanta, GA   Thursday, August 24, 1939

041302-1	Will You Think Of Me?	BB B-8285, MW M-8431
041303-1	Brother, Be Ready For That Day	BB B-8285, MW M-8431
041304-1	You Can Be A Millionaire With Me -1	BB B-8262, MW M-8430
041305-1	I'm Building Me A Home, Sweet Home -1	BB B-8305, MW M-8432
041306-1	The Tramp On The Street -1	BB B-8262, MW M-8430
041307-1	I Want To Live Like Daddy -1	BB B-8305, MW M-8432

Grady Cole, Hazel Cole, v duet; or Grady Cole, v-1; acc. unknown, g.
    Atlanta, GA   Tuesday, February 6, 1940

047571-1	Shattered Love	BB B-8536
047572-1	Precious Thoughts Of Mother	BB B-8536
047573-1	Forbidden Love -1	BB B-8573
047574-1	What A Change One Day Can Make	BB B-8573
047575-1	I'm On My Way To A Holy Land	BB B-8442
047576-1	A Beautiful Dream	BB B-8442

JAMES COLE STRING BAND

This group had one release on Vocalion (5226). On aural and other evidence it seems certain to be an African-American group. See James Cole in *B&GR*.

JIM COLE'S TENNESSEE MOUNTAINEERS

See Arthur Fields & Fred Hall.

REX COLE MOUNTAINEERS

See Arthur Fields & Fred Hall.

RILEY COLE QUARTET

Vocal quartet; acc. unknown.
    Atlanta, GA   Thursday, November 1, 1928

| 147370- | I Am Happy With My Saviour | Co unissued |
| 147371- | That City Of Rest | Co unissued |

SAM COLE & HIS CORN HUSKERS

See Arthur Fields & Fred Hall.

BERNICE COLEMAN

See the joint entry for Ernest Branch & Bernice Coleman.

DUTCH COLEMAN

Dutch Coleman, v/y-1; acc. own g; or **Red Whitehead & Dutch Coleman**-2: Red Whitehead, h; Dutch Coleman, g.
    Chicago, IL   Wednesday, December 11, 1929

C-5014½	The Clayton Case	Vo 5408
C-5016	New Ground Blues	Vo 5391
C-5017-A,-B	Lonesome Blues -1	Vo unissued
C-5018	Lonesome Blues -1	Vo unissued
C-5019	Gonna Raise Some Bacon At Home	Vo 5467
C-5020	Gonna Raise Some Bacon At Home	Vo unissued
C-5021	Booneville Stomp -2	Vo 5414

C-5023	Granny Get Your Hair Cut	Vo 5391
C-5024	In That Home Beyond The Sky	Vo 5408
C-5025	Dad's Getting Fuzzy -2	Vo 5414
C-5026	It's More Than I Can Bear -1	Vo 5467
C-5027-A,-B	There's No Use Denying (A Woman's As Good As A Man) -1	Vo unissued

Matrices C-5017/18, C-5027 carry a file note "Transf. to Melotone" but no issue has been traced on that label.
Matrices C-5015, C-5022 are untraced.
Dutch Coleman recorded (as Brother Dutch Coleman) after 1942.

PAUL COLEMAN & HIS BAND

Pseudonym on Champion for Ezra Buzzington's Rustic Revelers.

THE COLLIER TRIO

Otto Collier, md; William Collier, bj; Alsey Collier, g.
New Orleans, LA   c. November 9/10, 1928

NOR-765-	The Bluebird Waltz	Br 289, 52076
NOR-766-	Irene Waltz	Br 289, 52076
NOR-767-	Over The Waves	Br 288
NOR-768-	Ben Hur March	Br 288

Brunswick 52076 as by **Les Joyeux Montrealais**; matrix NOR-765 is titled *Valse De L'Oiseau Bleu*, and matrix NOR-766 *La Valse D'Irene*, on that issue.

New Orleans, LA   Friday, November 28, 1930

NO-6739-	After The Ball	Br 507
NO-6740-	When You And I Were Young, Maggie	Br 507
NO-6741-	Happy Home Waltz	Br 550
NO-6742-	Napoleon March	Br 550

AL COLLINS

Pseudonym on Paramount for the Gentry Brothers.

BILL COLLINS

The coupling issued with this artist credit on Victor 20673 (*When The Moon Shines Down Upon The Mountain/Mountaineer Song (Cindy)*) is by the popular singer Gene Austin.

EDITH & SHERMAN COLLINS

Edith Collins, Sherman Collins, v/y-1 duet; acc. Sherman Collins, g; Orville ———, g.
New York, NY   Friday, March 11, 1938

63399-A	The Convict And The Rose	De 5513
63400-A	Brown Eyes	De 5573
63401-A	What Is Home Without Love	De 5526
63402-A	Jealous Hearted Me No. 2	De 5513
63403-A	What Will You Take In Exchange (For Your Soul)	De 5635, 46010
63404-A	I Can't Feel At Home In This World Anymore	De 5635
63405-A	Jesus, The Holy Child	De 5504, 46010
63406-A	This Old Dirty Jail	De 5526
63407-A	I Wanna Be Loved	De 5542
63408-A,-B	I Thought I Was Dreaming	De rejected
63409-A	I Want You By My Side	De 5573
63410-A,-B	When It's Lamplightin' Time In The Valley	De rejected
63411-A	Curley Headed Baby No. 3 -1	De 5542

New York, NY   Saturday, March 12, 1938

63412-A,-B	Will The Circle Be Unbroken	De unissued
63413-A,-B	Little Mother Of The Hills	De unissued
63414-A	What Would You Give In Exchange No. 5	De 5504
63415-A	You're A Flower Blooming In The Wildwood	De 5503
63416-A	You Blotted My Happy School Days	De 5503

POP COLLINS (OLD TIMBER) & HIS BOYS

Pseudonym on Edison for Arthur Fields.

ROY COLLINS

See Vaughan Quartet & Associated Groups.

UNCLE TOM COLLINS

Uncle Tom Collins, v; acc. own bj.
    Atlanta, GA   Thursday, June 2, 1927

80955-A	Little Brown Jug	OK 45132
80956-A	Every Race Has A Flag But The Coons	OK 45140
80957-	Two Little Girls In Blue	OK unissued
80958-	Down On The Farm	OK unissued
80959-A	The Four Sons-Of-A-Gun	OK 45119
80960-B	'Tain't No Lie	OK 45132
80961-B	Every Day Will Be Sunday Bye And Bye	OK 45119
80962-A	Chicken, You Can't Roost Too High For Me	OK 45140

COLLINS BROTHERS THE PRIDE OF KENTUCKY

Pseudonym on Paramount for the Gentry Brothers.

THE COLONELS

See Perry Bechtel.

COLT BROTHERS

See Arthur Fields & Fred Hall.

COLUMBIA BAND

One side of Columbia 15728-D was assigned this artist-credit; it is believed to be outside the scope of this work. (For the other side of this record, credited to Bob Ferguson, see Bob Miller.)

HITER COLVIN

Hiter Colvin, f; acc. Herb Sherrill, g.
    Dallas, TX   Monday, October 21, 1929

56435-2	Monroe Stamp	Vi V-40239
56436-1	Old Lady Blues	Vi V-40271
56437-1	Hiter's Favorite Waltz	Vi 23815
56438-1	Dixie Waltz	Vi V-40271
56439-2	Rabbit Up The Gum Stump	Vi V-40239, MW M-8148
56440-1	Indian War Whoop	Vi 23815

Victor V-40271 as by **Hyter Colvin**. Matrix 56439 is titled *Rabbit In The Pea Patch* on Montgomery Ward M-8148. Rev. Montgomery Ward M-8148 by Vernon Dalhart.

GEORGIA COMPTON'S REELERS

Mack Compton, f; others unknown.
    Atlanta, GA   Friday, August 10, 1928

402122-	My Blue Heaven	OK unissued
402123-	Yes, Sir, That's My Baby	OK unissued
402124-	American Eagle	OK unissued
402125-	No Nance	OK unissued

CONLEY & LOGAN

Pseudonym on Challenge for Walter Smith & Norman Woodlieff.

PETER J. CONLON

One item by this Irish-American button accordion player was issued on OKeh 45030.

CARL CONNER

Carl Conner, v; acc. prob. own h/g.
    Atlanta, GA   Friday, April 23, 1926

142092-1	Jones And Bloodworth Case	Co 15076-D
142093-3	Story Of Gerald Chapman	Co 15076-D

ADLER CONNOR & JULIAN GRADER

One of them, f; the other, ac; one of them, v.
    New Orleans, LA   Tuesday, October 1, 1929

TNO-232-	Valse De Boscoville	Br 371
TNO-233-	Lake Arthur Two-Step	Br 371

Brunswick files also give the second party's surname as Crader, but the label-credit is as shown.

GEORGE CONWAY

Pseudonym on Madison and Van Dyke for Arthur Fields (and for other, popular, artists).

HERB COOK

Herb Cook, v; acc. unknown, p.
    Atlanta, GA   Tuesday, October 27, 1931

151962-2	Arkansaw Sweetheart	Co 15729-D
151963-1	I Wonder Why	Co 15778-D
151964-2	Lou'siana	Co 15729-D
151965-1	Just A Little Happiness	Co 15778-D

Herb Cook also recorded popular material in the ARC TO- (trial recordings) series in April 1935.

JOE COOK (THE SWEET SINGER OF SWEET SONGS)

Joe Cook, v; acc. unknown, f; unknown, sg; unknown, g.
    Charlotte, NC   Friday, February 19, 1937

07168-1	A Sweet Little Girl In Blue	BB B-6884, MW M-7245
07169-1	Daddy In The Hills	MW M-7246
07170-1	When I Come To The End Of The Trail	MW M-7188
07171-1	Lonely Memories	MW M-7246
07172-1	I Will See You Tonight In My Dreams	BB B-6884, MW M-7245
07173-1	My Old Blackie	MW M-7188

Acc. two unknowns, g; unknown, sb.
    Charlotte, NC   Wednesday, August 4, 1937

011927-1	So Now You Come Back To Me	BB unissued
011928-1	In The Hills Of Caroline	BB unissued
011929-1	Nobody Knows My Name	BB B-7362
011930-1	Since I Left The City	BB unissued

Rev. Bluebird B-7362 by Zeke Morris.

A singer of this name recorded for Brunswick in 1926, but there is no evidence to connect him with the above artist.

ROBERT COOK'S OLD TIME FIDDLERS

Two unknowns, f; unknown, md or bj; unknown, g.
    Dallas, TX   c. October 23, 1928

DAL-712-	Medley Of Old Time Fiddlers' Favorites – No. 1 (Mississippi Sawyer–Cowboy's Quickstep–Soldiers' Joy–Hop Light Ladies–Arkansaw Traveller)	Vo 5265
DAL-713-	Medley Of Old Time Fiddlers' Favorites – No. II (Sallie Johnson–Sheep And The Hog Walking Through The Pasture–Turkey In The Straw–Billy In The Low Ground–Leather Breeches)	Vo 5265

TOM COOK

Pseudonym on Madison and Van Dyke for Vernon Dalhart, Arthur Fields, or Frank Luther, and possibly other artists.

ADELE COOMBER

Pseudonym on Summit for Adelyne Hood.

WALTER COON

Walter Coon, v; acc. **The Joy Boys**: unknown, h; unknown, g.
    Richmond, IN   Thursday, September 19, 1929

15632	The Boys [sic] Best Friend	Ge 7005, Ch 15831, Cq 7272
15633-A	Come Home Father	Ge 7005, Ch 15831, Cq 7272

Champion 15831 as by **Ray Elkins**. Conqueror 7272 as by **Charley Vaughn**.
Matrix 15632 is titled *The Boys Faithful Friend* on Conqueror 7272.

Walter Coon & His Joy Boys: unknown, h/jh; unknown, g; unknown, bones.
    Richmond, IN   Thursday, September 19, 1929

15636-A	Huskin' Bee	Ge 7002, Ch 15828, Spt 9543, Spr 2671
15637-A	Louisiana Hop	Ge 7002, Ch 15828, Spt 9543

Champion 15828 as by **Uncle George Green & His Boys**. Supertone 9543 as by **Sandy Creek Wood Choppers**. Superior 2671 as by **Stanton's Joy Boys**. Matrices 15634/35 are by J.P. Ryan.

Walter Coon, v; acc. unknown, h; unknown, g.
    Richmond, IN   Friday, December 6, 1929

15977	Fly Away Birdie To Heaven	Ge 7097, Cq 7271
15978	Father's A Drunkard And Mother Is Dead	Ge 7097, Cq 7271

Conqueror 7271 as by **Charley Vaughn**.

Walter Coon & His Joy Boys: unknown, h/jh; unknown, g; unknown, bones.
    Richmond, IN   Friday, December 6, 1929

15979	Goodbye Summer, Hello Winter	Ge 7079, Ch 15896, Spt 9680
15980	Polly Wolly Doodle	Ge 7079, Ch 15896, Spt 9680, Spr 2671

Champion 15896 as by **Uncle George Green & His Boys**. Supertone 9680 as by **Sandy Creek Wood Choppers**. Superior 2671 as by **Stanton's Joy Boys**.
Matrix 15979 is titled *Good Bye Summer, Hello Winter*, and matrix 15980 *Polly Wally Doodle*, on Supertone 9680.

Walter Coon, v; acc; unknown, h; unknown, g.
    Richmond, IN   Friday, December 6, 1929

15981,-A	Damaged Goods	Ge rejected
15982,-A	Goldstine And Lavinskie	Ge rejected

    Richmond, IN   Tuesday, September 2, 1930

16981-B	Poor Old Dad	Spr 2544
16982-B	On The Banks Of The Ohio	Spr 2544
16983	The Club Had A Meeting	Ge rejected
16984	On A Tom Thumb Golf Course	Ge rejected
16985	Fond Affection	Spr 2521
16986	Creole Girl	Spr 2521
16987,-A	When The Autumn Leaves Are Turning To Gold	Ge rejected
16988,-A	Good Bye Step Stone	Ge rejected

Superiors as by **Frank Stanton**.
Walter Hamacker and Louis Bawmbach are named as royalty recipients, with Coon, in Superior ledgers in respect of the above session, and probably perform on it.

COON CREEK GIRLS

Lily May Ledford, f-1/bj-2/v; Esther "Violet" Koehler, md-3; Rosie Ledford, g/v-4; Evelyn "Daisy" Lange, sb-5; unidentified, v-6.
    Chicago, IL   Monday, May 30, 1938

C-2237-1	Sowing On The Mountain -2, 4, 5, 6	Vo/OK 04278, Cq 9113
C-2238-1	Old Uncle Dudy (Keep Fiddling On) -1, 3, 4, 5, 6	Vo/OK 04278, Cq 9113
C-2243-1	Banjo Pickin' Girl -2, 4, 5, 6	Vo/OK 04413
C-2244-1	The Soldier And The Lady -4	Vo 04504
C-2245-1,-2	Give Me The Roses While I Live	Vo unissued
C-2246-2	Lulu Lee -4, 5	Vo 04504
C-2247-1	Pretty Polly -2, 5	Vo/OK 04659, Pe 16-102
C-2248-1	Flowers Blooming In The Wildwood -2, 4, 5, 6	Vo/OK 04659, Cq 9231
C-2249-1	Little Birdie -2, 5	Vo/OK 04413, Cq 9231

Matrices C-2239 to C-2242 are by A'nt Idy Harper & The Coon Creek Girls. Rev. Pe 16-102 by Carter Family.
The Coon Creek Girls, in various lineups, recorded after 1942.

COON HOLLOW BOYS

Pseudonym on Champion for the Smoky Mountain Boys.

FORREST COPELAND & JOHNNY BRITTON

Forrest Copeland, f; Johnny Britton, g.
    Dallas, TX   Sunday, October 27, 1929

DAL-521	Brilliancy	Br/Vo rejected trial recording
DAL-522	Killie-Cranky	Br/Vo rejected trial recording

COPELAND CHORUS
COPELAND QUARTET

Copeland Chorus: two unknowns, tv; two unknowns, av; two unknowns, bv; unknown, bsv; unacc.
    Dallas, TX   Friday, October 18, 1929

56422-1,-2	My Precious Bible	Vi unissued
56423-1,-2	Sing Old Hymns To Me	Vi unissued

Copeland Quartet, v quartet; unacc.
    Dallas, TX   Monday, October 21, 1929

56443-1,-2	Songs Of Adoration	Vi unissued
56444-1,-2	The Riches Of Love	Vi unissued

COPPERHILL MALE QUARTET

Clinton Painter, tv; Elvin Harper, sv; W.V. "Dick" Johnson, bv; Lee Pless, bsv; acc. Ms Wofford, p.
 Atlanta, GA   Wednesday, April 6, 1927
  143925-2   There Is A Fountain Filled With Blood   Co 15164-D
  143926-   Crossing The Bar   Co unissued
Rev. Columbia 15164-D by The Happy Four.

WALTER COQUILLE

Walter Coquille, sp; others, sp.
 New Orleans, LA   Tuesday, March 5, 1929
  NO-130-   Mayor Of Bayou Pom Pom Part I   Br 319
  NO-131-   Mayor Of Bayou Pom Pom Part II   Br 319
Matrix NO-130 is titled *Mayor Of Bayou Mom Pom Part I* on some copies of Brunswick 319.
 New Orleans, LA   Saturday, September 29, 1929
  NO-230-   The Mayor Of Bayou Pom Pom – Pt. 5   Br cancelled
  NO-231-   The Mayor Of Bayou Pom Pom – Part III (On Traffic)   Br 359
  NO-254-   The Mayor Of Bayou Pom Pom – Part IV (On Hunting & Fishing In The Bayou)   Br unissued
  NO-255-   The Mayor Of Bayou Pom Pom – Pt. 6   Br cancelled
  NO-256-   The Mayor Of Bayou Pom Pom – Part IV (On Hunting & Fishing In The Bayou)   Br 359
Intervening matrices are by other artists.
 New Orleans, LA   Thursday, November 20, 1930
  NO-6711-   The Re-election Of The Mayor Of Bayou Pom Pom – Part 1   Br 494
  NO-6712-   The Re-election Of The Mayor Of Bayou Pom Pom – Part 2   Br 494
 New Orleans, LA   Friday, November 21, 1930
  NO-6723-A   The Surprise Party Of The Mayor Of Bayou Pom Pom – Part 1   Br 591
  NO-6724-A   The Surprise Party Of The Mayor Of Bayou Pom Pom – Part 2   Br 591

THE CORLEY FAMILY

Vocal group; acc. unknown, g.
 Dallas, TX   Wednesday, December 4, 1929
  149518-2   He Keeps My Soul   Co 15495-D
  149519-2   When Jesus Comes   Co 15495-D
  149520-1   The Way To Glory Land   Co 15574-D
  149521-2   Give The World A Smile   Co 15574-D

CORN COB CRUSHERS

Unknown, f; unknown, md; unknown, bj; unknown, g.
 Richmond, IN   Wednesday, December 23, 1931
  18267   Lonesome Road Blues   Ch 16449, 45178, MeC 45178
  18268   Rag Time Annie   Ch S-16373, 45178, Spr 2794, MeC 45178
  18269   Kamona March   Ge unissued
  18270   Dill Pickle Rag   Ch S-16373, Spr 2794
Superior 2794 as by **West Virginia Ridge Runners**. Rev. Champion 16449 by West Virginia Ramblers (see Roy Harvey).

Loren Abram is named as royalty payee in Champion files and is likely to have been a member of the group, as also is Arnold Frazier. See Loren H. Abram.

ARTHUR CORNWALL (CAROLINA'S LYRIC TENOR)

Arthur Cornwall, v; or **Arthur Cornwall & John Gibson**, v duet-1; acc. unknown, p; unknown, k-2; unknown, bj; unknown, g.
 Richmond, IN   Monday, December 7, 1931
  18232,-A   I Had But Fifty Cents -2   Ge unissued
  18233   Gonna Quit Drinkin' When I Die -1, 2   Ge unissued
  18234   Ain't Gonna Do It No More -1, 2   Ch 16429
  18235,-A   Yes Indeed I Do -1, 2   Ge unissued
  18236-A   Walking The Highway -1, 2   Ch 16429

18237	Get Your Head In Here -1, 2	Ge rejected
18238,-A	The Tiny Shoe	Ge unissued
18239	It's All Gone Now -1, 2	Ge rejected
18240	Bessie's Monkey -1, 2	Ge unissued
18241	My Bones Is Gonna Rise Again -1, 2	Ch S-16379, Spr 2791
18242	Gonna Have A Good Time Tonight -1, 2	Ch S-16379, Spr 2791

Superior 2791 as by **Caldwell & Bunch**.

ARTHUR CORNWALL & WILLIAM CLEARY

Arthur Cornwall, William Cleary, v duet; acc. unknown, f; unknown, sg; unknown, p.
New York, NY   Wednesday, July 9, 1930

9851-1,-3	Rock Of Ages	Ba 0763, Do 4621, Je 6014, Or 2014, Pe 12638, Re 10069, Cq 7714
9852-3	Old Rugged Cross	Ba 0717, Cq 7714, Htd 16108
9853-	Absent	Ba 0763, Do 4605, Je 6014, Or 2014, Pe 12634, Re 10069, Cq 7594

Revs: Banner 0717, Homestead 16108 by E.R. Nance Singers; Conqueror 7594 by Frank & James McCravy; others untraced.

New York, NY   Friday, July 11, 1930

9861-	What A Friend We Have In Jesus	Pe 167, Cq 7797
9862-1	Where We Never Grow Old	Ba 32092, Do 4714, Je 20027, Or 8027, Pe 12654, Re 10293, Ro 5027, ARC-Bwy 8127, Cq 7796, Htd 16093, 23032
9863-3	When They Ring Those Golden Bells	Ba 32092, Do 4714, Je 20027, Or 8027, Pe 12654, Re 10293, Ro 5027, Cq 7796, Htd 16093, 23032

Matrix 9862 is titled *Where We'll Never Grow Old* on ARC-Broadway 8127. Rev. ARC-Broadway 8127 by Gentry Brothers.

New York, NY   Thursday, July 17, 1930

9876-	Sunshine In My Soul	ARC unissued
9877-	In The Garden	ARC unissued
9878-	Beautiful Isle	ARC unissued
9879-	Pass It On	Pe 167, Cq 7797

COTTLE BROTHERS

No details.
Dallas, TX   Wednesday, December 4, 1929

149516-	Texas Waltz	Co unissued
149517-	Cottle Waltz	Co unissued

COTTON & BARFIELD

No details.
Atlanta, GA   Wednesday, November 9, 1927

145176-	Railroad Bill	Co unissued
145177-	Whistling Rufus	Co unissued

According to the son of Johnny Barfield, the second party is "Coot" Barfield, Johnny's uncle.

COTTON MILL WEAVERS

No details.
Atlanta, GA   Wednesday, April 18, 1928

146120-	My Own Iona	Co unissued
146121-	Picture On The Wall	Co unissued

JIM COUCH

Jim Couch, h solo.
Asheville, NC   prob. August 31 or September 1, 1925

9314-A	Medley: Dill Pickle–Turkey In The Straw–Swanee River	OK 40467
9315-A	St. Louis Tickle	OK 40467

WALTER COUCH & WILKS RAMBLERS

Walter Couch, f; Bonson Couch, bj; Kelly Couch, g; unidentified, v-1.
Charlotte, NC   Wednesday, February 17, 1937

07112-1	Fourteen Days In Georgia	BB B-7252, MW M-7136

07113-1	Lonesome Trail -1	BB B-7095, MW M-7135, Twin FT8474
07114-1	Want My Black Baby Back -1	BB B-7095, MW M-7135
07115-1	Chesapeake Bay	BB B-7252, MW M-7136

Montgomery Wards as by **Mainer's Mountaineers**. Rev. Twin FT8474 by Shep Fields (popular).

COURVILLE & McGEE

See Dennis McGee.

COUSIN LEVI WITH HIS CAROLINA BLUEBIRDS

Vocal duet; or vocal trio-1; acc. unknown, f-2; unknown, md; two unknowns, g.
Charlotte, NC   Friday, January 28, 1938

018803-1	Dad's Vacant Chair -1, 2	BB B-7522
018804-1	Somebody's Waiting -2	BB B-7522
018805-1	I'm Not Turning Back	BB unissued
018806-1	I Found The Way	BB unissued
018807-1	Homesick And Blue	BB unissued

The Bluebird session-sheet also lists washboard in the collective instrumentation but appears to exclude it from each item.

RAY COVERT

Ray Covert, v; acc. prob. own h/g.
St. Paul, MN   c. June 30, 1927

| 12898 | Billy Boy | Ge 6204, Her 75564 |

Revs: Gennett 6204 by Vernon Dalhart; Herwin 75564 by David Miller.

COWBOY JOE

Pseudonym on Sunrise for Stuart Hamblen.

COWBOY PIONEERS

Unknown instrumental group.
Dallas, TX   Thursday, February 18, 1937

| 61836-A | Davis Rag | De unissued |

This group recorded during sessions by Jimmie Davis and Buddy Jones and may involve their accompanists.

COWBOY TOM'S ROUNDUP WITH CHIEF SHUNATONA, DOUG McTAGUE & SKOOKUM

Doug McTague, v/y/g; Chief Shunatona, v/sp/tomtom; Skookum, v/sp; Cowboy Tom, sp; unidentified, v eff/train eff.
New York, NY   Monday, September 19, 1932

| 152300-1 | Cowboy Tom's Roundup Part 1 Get Along Little Doggies; The Dawn; Cowboy's Trademarks | Co 15781-D |
| 152301-1 | Cowboy Tom's Roundup Part 2 Red River Valley; Tom Tom Dance; Going Back To Texas | Co 15781-D |

BILL COX

Bill Cox, v/y-1; acc. own h-2/g.
Richmond, IN   Thursday, July 11, 1929

15328	In The Big Rock Candy Mountain No. 2 -1, 2	Spt 9556
15329	California Blues -1	Ge 6928, Ch 15853, 45157, Spt 9534
15330	Nigger Loves A Watermellon [sic] -2	Ge 7004, Ch 15829, Spt 9559
15331	The Moonshine In The Hills -2	Ge 7037, Ch 15853, Spt 9489
15332	Jackson County -2	Ge 6928, Spt 9559
15333-A	Daddy And Home -1	Ge 6946, Ch 15811, Spt 9476

Champion 15811, 15829, 15853 as by **Luke Baldwin**. Supertone 9476 as by **Jim Morgan**; 9489, 9534, 9559 as by **Charley Blake**.

Richmond, IN   Friday, July 12, 1929

15334-A	My Old Pal -1	Ge 6946, Ch 15811, Spt 9476
15335-A	Back Home In Tennessee -2	Ge 7037, Spt 9489
15336	Go Long Mule (Parody) -2	Spt 9540
15337-A	When We Meet On The Beautiful Shore	Ge 7004, Ch 15792, Spt 9540
15338	She'll Be Comin' 'Round The Mountain No. 2 -2	Ge 6974, Spt 9556
15339	Hungry Hash House Blues -2	Ge 6974, Ch 15792, Spt 9534

Champion 15792, 15811 as by **Luke Baldwin**. Supertone 9476 as by **Jim Morgan**; 9489, 9534, 9540, 9556 as by **Charley Blake**. Matrix 15338 is titled *She'll Be Coming Round The Mountain No. 2* on Supertone 9556.

Richmond, IN   Monday, October 28, 1929

| 15815 | The Death Of Frank Bowen -2 | Ge 7052 |
| 15816 | When We Sing Of Home -1, 2 | Ge 7052, Ch 15945 |

15817,-A,-B	The Old Axe Shop	Ge rejected
15818	I Love The Jailer's Daughter -2	Ge 7155, Ch 15945, Spt 9641
15819	Guitar Blues -1	Ge 7080, Ch 15877, 45021, Spt 9600
15820	Alabama Blues -2	Ge 7080, Ch 15877, 45021, Spt 9600
15821,-A	In All My Dreams	Ge rejected
15822,-A	We're Riding On The Dummy Dummy Line	Ge rejected
15823	It Won't Happen Again	Ge 7155, Ch 16142, Spt 9641

Champion 15877, 15945, 16142 as by **Luke Baldwin**. Supertone 9600, 9641 as by **Charley Blake**.

Richmond, IN   Tuesday, October 29, 1929

15824,-A	Down In Arkansas -2	Ge rejected
15825,-A	Bring Back The Sunshine And Roses	Ge rejected
15826	Please Stay Home Tonight	Ge rejected
15827,-A	You Can't Give Your Kisses To Somebody Else	Ge rejected
15828,-A	The Dollar And The Devil	Ge rejected
15829,-A	My Old Carolina Home -1, 2	Ge rejected
15830,-A,-B	Clouds Gwine Roll Away -2	Ge rejected

Richmond, IN   Monday, April 28, 1930

16544	My Rough And Rowdy Ways -1	Ge 7226, Ch 16009, Spt 9724
16545	My Old Log Cabin Home -2	Ge 7266, Spt 9714, Spr 2558
16546-B	Since We Landed Over Here -2	Spt 9724
16547	The Yodeling Cowboy -1	Ge 7226, Ch 16009, Spt 9722
16549,-A	My High Silk Hat And Gold Top Walking Cane -1	Ge rejected
16550,-A	The Hell Bound Train	Ge rejected
16551	Cause All My Good Times Are Taken Away -2	Ch 16142
16552,-A	[untitled]	Ge rejected
16553	The Hand Car Yodel -1	Ge 7266, Ch 16075, Spt 9722, Spr 2636

Champion 16009, 16075, 16142 as by **Luke Baldwin**. Supertone 9714, 9722, 9724 as by **Charley Blake**. Superior 2558, 2636 as by **Clyde Ashley**. Matrix 16548 is unrelated.

Richmond, IN   Tuesday, April 29, 1930

16554-A	Down In Arkansas -2	Ch 16075, Spt 9714, Spr 2558

Champion 16075 as by **Luke Baldwin**. Supertone 9714 as by **Charley Blake**. Superior 2558 as by **Clyde Ashley**.

Richmond, IN   Friday, November 21, 1930

17292	Got Them Drunken Blues -2	Ch 16186, Spr 2636
17293	When The Roses Bloom In Dixie -1, 2	Ch 16254
17294-A	The Bootlegger's Plea -1	Ch 16186, Spr 2711
17295	The Ramblin' Railroad Boy -1	Ch 16232, Spr 2605
17296-A	Where The Red Red Roses Grow	Ch 16254
17297-A	Aint'cha Comin' Out Tonight -2	Ch 16162, Spr 2676
17298,-A	Woman Suffrage -1	Ge unissued
17299-A	High Silk Hat And Gold Top Walking Cane -1	Gh 16232, Spr 2676
17300,-A	Bury Me In The Tennessee Mountains -1	Ge unissued
17301	Pray For The Lights To Go Out -1, 2	Spr 2605
17302	Don't Ever Marry A Widow -2	Ch 16162, 45157, Spr 2711
17303,-A	Song Of The Bandits -2	Ge rejected

Champion 16162, 16186, 16232, 16254 as by **Luke Baldwin**. Superior 2605, 2636, 2676, 2711 as by **Clyde Ashley**.

Richmond, IN   Monday, August 17, 1931

17929-A	Travelin' Blues -1, 2	Ch S-16343, 45141, Spr 2778, De 5509
17930	Leaving Town Blues -2	Ch S-16313, 45141, Spr 2723, De 5509
17931	Married Life Blues -2	Ch S-16313, 45007
17932	Are You Tired Of Me, Darling? -1	Ch S-16317, 45092, Spr 2751, De 5497
17933	In 1992 -1	Ch 16443, 45092, Spr 2833, De 5497
17934	Alimony Woman -1	Ch S-16317, 45007, Spr 2778
17935	I Found You Among The Roses -2	Ch 16443, 45106, Spr 2833, MW 4942, MeC 45106
17936	Blue Ridge Mountain Blues -2	Ch 45106, MeC 45106
17936-A	Blue Ridge Mountain Blues -2	Ch S-16343, Spr 2723
17937-A	My Alabama Home -1	Spr 2751
17938,-A	I'm Lonesome Too	Ge unissued

Champion S-16313, S-16317, S-16343, 16443 as by **Luke Baldwin**. Superior 2723, 2751, 2778, 2833 as by **Clyde Ashley**. Rev. Montgomery Ward 4942 by Jimmy Long.

New York, NY   Wednesday, August 30, 1933

13897-2	Midnight Special -2	Ba 32891, Me M12797, MeC 91653, Or 8271, Pe 12942, Ro 5271, Cq 8230, Pan 25626

13898-1	N.R.A. Blues -2	Ba 33280, Me M13247, Or 8406, Pe 13090, Ro 5406, Cq 8392
13899-1	Ramblin' Hobo -1	Ba 33045, Me M13007, MeC 91802, Or 8331, Pe 13001, Ro 5331, Cq 8330
13900-1	Alimony Woman -1	Ba 32891, Me M12797, MeC 91653, Or 8271, Pe 12942, Ro 5271, Cq 8230, Pan 25626
13901-2	Brown Eyes -1	Ba 33094, Me M13058, Or 8349, Pe 13014, Ro 5349, Cq 8330
13902-1	Lay My Head Beneath The Rose -1	Ba 32892, Me M12798, Or 8272, Pe 12943, Ro 5272, Cq 8202, Pan 25605
13915-1	East Cairo Street Blues -1	ARC 350909, MeC 92088
13916-2	New Mama -2	Ba 32941, Me M12884, Or 8297, Pe 12969, Ro 5297, Cq 8362
13917-1	The Best Friend I Ever Had -1	Ba 32916, Me M12859, Or 8287, Pe 12961, Ro 5287, Cq 8232
13918-1	I Got Those Drunken Blues -2	Ba 32991, Me M12941, Or 8311, Pe 12983, Ro 5311, Cq 8362

Matrix 13901 is titled *My Brown Eyes* on Conqueror 8330.
Intervening matrices are by popular or blues artists on other dates.

Bill Cox, v; acc. own h/g.
New York, NY   Thursday, August 31, 1933

13923-1	Blue Ridge Mountain Blues	Ba 32941, Me M12884, Or 8297, Pe 12969, Ro 5297, Cq 8232
13924-1	Just As The Sun Went Down	Cq 8331, MeC 91729
13925-1	We'll Sow Righteous Seed	Cq 8331
13926-2	The Jailer's Daughter	Ba 33045, Me M13007, MeC 91802, Or 8331, Pe 13001, Ro 5331, Cq 8203
13927-2	When The Women Get In Power	Ba 32991, Me M12941, Or 8311, Pe 12983, Ro 5311, Cq 8231
13928-	A Nigger Loves A Watermelon	ARC unissued

Acc. own h-1/g.
New York, NY   Saturday, September 2, 1933

13939-	The Golden State Limited -1	ARC unissued
13940-1	Where The Red Red Roses Grow -1	Ba 32892, Me M12798, MeC 91729, Or 8272, Pe 12943, Ro 5272, Cq 8202, Pan 25605
13941-1	Barefoot Boy With Boots On -1	Ba 33094, Me M13058, Or 8349, Pe 13014, Ro 5349, Cq 8231
13942-2	Bring Back The Sunshine And Roses	Ba 32916, Me M12859, Or 8287, Pe 12961, Ro 5287, Cq 8203

Bill Cox, v/y-1; acc. own h-2/g.
New York, NY   Tuesday, September 4, 1934

15850-2	Sugar Daddy Blues -1	ARC 5-12-56, Cq 8589
15851-1	Browns Ferry Blues -1	Ba 33194, Me M13161, Or 8380, Pe 13049, Ro 5380, Cq 8469
15852-1	Home In Sunlit Valley -2	Cq 8402
15853-2	The Gangster's Yodel -1	Ba 33227, Me M13194, MeC 91930, Or 8386, Pe 13067, Ro 5386, Cq 8391, Min M-906
15854-1,-2	Sweet Kentucky Lou -2	Ba 33371, Me M13338, Or 8441, Pe 13119, Ro 5441, Cq 8495
15855-1,-2	Rollin' Pin Woman -2	Ba 33324, Me M13291, Or 8421, Pe 13104, Ro 5421, Cq 8496
15856-1	Long Chain Charlie Blues -2	Ba 33194, Me M13161, Or 8380, Pe 13049, Ro 5380, Cq 8469
15857-2	Georgia Brown Blues -1, 2	ARC 6-04-60, Cq 8666
15858-	Railroad Under The Sea -2	ARC unissued
15864-1,-2	Hard Luck Blues -2	Ba 33280, Me M13247, Or 8406, Pe 13090, Ro 5406, Cq 8392

Rev. Minerva M-906 by Red Foley.

Bill Cox, v/y-1; acc. own h/g.
New York, NY   Wednesday, September 5, 1934

15859-	For The Sake Of Days Gone By -1	ARC unissued
15860-	My Blue Ridge Sweetheart	ARC unissued
15861-1	The Clouds Gwine Roll Away	ARC 6-04-60, Cq 8666
15862-	One Night Of Heaven With You	ARC unissued

15863-1	Down In Dixie Land	Ba 33371, Me M13338, Or 8441, Pe 13119, Ro 5441, Cq 8495
15865-2	It's Killing Me	ARC 350909, MeC 92088
15866-1	Blue Eyed Sally -1	ARC 5-11-55
15867-2	Star Boarder Blues -1	Ba 33324, Me M13291, Or 8421, Pe 13104, Ro 5421, Cq 8496

ARC and Conqueror issues are subcredited (**The Dixie Songbird**).

Bill Cox, v; acc. own h/g.
New York, NY   Friday, September 7, 1934

15869-1	My Gamblin' Days	Ba 33227, Me M13194, MeC 91930, Or 8386, Pe 13067, Ro 5386, Cq 8391
15870-	The Moonshiner's Daughter And I	ARC unissued
15871-	Shake Hands With Mother Again	ARC unissued
15872-1	The Model Church	Cq 8402

New York, NY   Tuesday, February 26, 1935

| 16927-3 | The Trial Of Bruno Richard Hauptmann – Part I | Ba 33377, Me M13344, MeC 91959, Or 8446, Pe 13123, Ro 5446, Cq 8454 |
| 16938-3 | The Trial Of Bruno Richard Hauptmann – Part II | Ba 33377, Me M13344, MeC 91959, Or 8446, Pe 13123, Ro 5446, Cq 8454 |

Bill Cox, v/y-1; acc. own h-2/g.
New York, NY   Wednesday, February 27, 1935

16929-2	I Long For Your Love Each Day -2	ARC 5-11-55
16930-	Roamin' In Wyomin' -2	ARC rejected
16931-	When The Roses Bloom In Dixie -2	ARC rejected
16932-	When The Snow Flakes Fall Again -2	ARC rejected
16933-1	The Golden Train	ARC 7-12-62, Vo/OK 03253, Cq 8934
16935-2	Memphis Mama Blues -1	Ba 33430, Me M13397, Or 8465, Pe 13140, Ro 5465, Cq 8515
16936-	Six Women Done Me Wrong -1	ARC unissued

ARC 5-11-55, Melotone M13397, and Conqueror 8515 are subcredited (**The Dixie Songbird**).

New York, NY   Thursday, February 28, 1935

16934-	The Land Of The Sweet Bye And Bye -2	ARC rejected
16951-1	You'll Never Make No Lovin' Wife -2	Ba 33430, Me M13397, Or 8465, Pe 13140, Ro 5465, Cq 8515
16952-	My Shack By The Track -1	ARC rejected

Bill Cox (The Dixie Songbird), v; acc. own h/g.
New York, NY   Friday, August 30, 1935

18035-1,-2	The Fate Of Will Rogers And Wiley Post	ARC 5-11-54, Cq 8543, MeC 92070, Min M-933
18036-	My Long Lost Pal	ARC rejected
18037-1	Married Life Blues	ARC 5-12-56, Cq 8589

Rev. Minerva M-933 by Red Foley.

Bill Cox, v/y-1; acc. own h/g.
New York, NY   Tuesday, September 3, 1935

18038-2	Will And Wiley's Last Flight	ARC 5-11-54, Cq 8543, MeC 92070
18039-1	When Once Again We'll Go Home	ARC 6-02-60
18040-	The Mansion Of Aching Hearts	ARC unissued
18041-	A Miner's Life	ARC rejected
18042-2	Sweethearts And Kisses	ARC 6-02-60
18043-	My Alabama Rose -1	ARC unissued
18044-	Just Try To Picture Me Down In Tennessee	ARC unissued

Bill Cox & Cliff Hobbs (The Dixie Songbirds), v duet; acc. Bill Cox, h/g/y-1; Cliff Hobbs, g.
New York, NY   Tuesday, November 17, 1936

20263-4	Gonna Make Whoopee Tonight	ARC 7-02-62, Vo/OK 03043, Cq 8772, Co 37700, 20279
20264-4,-5	Train Whistle Blues -1	ARC 7-07-67, Cq 8962
20265-4	Lonesome For You -1	OK 05726
20266-4	There's More Good Woman [sic] Gone Wrong	ARC 7-03-69, Cq 8783

ARC files report that matrix 20264 was remade on July 6, 1937, and matrices 20265/66 on November 25, 1936. The former is certainly a technical remastering; it seems likely that the others are also.
The subcredit (**The Dixie Songbirds**) does not appear on all issues of the recordings made in November 1936.

New York, NY   Wednesday, November 18, 1936

20279-5	Runaway Train Blues -1	ARC 7-11-53, Cq 8961
20280-3	Fiddling Soldier	ARC 7-08-70, Vo/OK 03161, Cq 8883
20281-4	Hot Lip Baby	ARC 7-03-69, Cq 8783
20282-3	Sally Let Your Bangs Hang Down -1	ARC 7-08-70, Vo/OK 03161, Cq 8883
20283-4	Oozlin' Daddy Blues -1	ARC 7-05-76
20283-5	Oozlin' Daddy Blues -1	ARC unissued: Co C2K47466, Co(E) 472886 (CDs)

ARC files report that matrices 20279/80, 20282/83 were remade on November 27, 1936, matrix 20279 was remade again on September 15, 1937, and matrix 20283 was remade again on July 8, 1937. The last two are certainly and the others probably technical remasterings.

Acc. Bill Cox, h-1/g/y-2; Cliff Hobbs, g/y-3.
New York, NY   Friday, November 20, 1936

20298-4	Kansas City Blues -1	ARC 7-05-76
20299-3,-5	Little Red Shoes -1, 2	ARC 7-07-67, Cq 8962
20300-2	Blue Eyed Sailor -2	OK 05726
20301-1,-2,-3	Two Little Children	ARC unissued
20302-4	Horse Neck Daddy	ARC 7-11-53, Cq 8961
20303-4	I Wanna Be Loved -2, 3	ARC 7-02-62, Vo/OK 03043, Cq 8772, Co 37700, 20279
20304-3	Just As The Sun Went Down	ARC 7-04-77, Cq 8331, 8817
20305-3	The Great Reunion -1	ARC 7-04-77, Cq 8817

Only one guitar is used on matrix 20298.
ARC files report that matrices 20298/99 and 20301 to 20305 were remade on November 27-28, 1936, and matrix 20299 remade again on July 6, 1937. The last is certainly and the others probably technical remasterings.

Acc. Bill Cox, h/g; Cliff Hobbs, g.
New York, NY   Saturday, November 28, 1936

| 20338-2 | Franklin Roosevelt's Back Again | ARC 7-02-61, OK 05896, Cq 8771 |
| 20339-1 | The Democratic Donkey (Is In His Stall Again) | ARC 7-02-61, OK 05896, Cq 8771 |

Matrix 20339 on OKeh 05896 as by **Bill Cox**.

Acc. Bill Cox, h-1/g/y-2; Cliff Hobbs, g.
New York, NY   Monday, October 18, 1937

21901-1	The Whole Dam Family	ARC 8-03-52, Vo 03380, Cq 8986
21902-1	Answer To What Would You Give In Exchange For Your Soul	ARC 7-12-62, Vo/OK 03253, Cq 8934
21903-2	Drift Along Pretty Moon	OK 04235
21904-2	Sparkling Brown Eyes -2	Vo/OK 04341, Cq 9104
21905-2	Heart Broken Prisoner -1	Vo 04148, Cq 9005
21912-2	Crepe On The Door -1	Vo 04148, Cq 9005

Acc. Bill Cox, h-1/g; Cliff Hobbs, g.
New York, NY   Tuesday, October 19, 1937

21910-1	Mollie Rinktum	Vo 04077, Cq 9004
21911-	Dear Mother Has Taught Me The Way	ARC unissued
21913-2	My Wife And Sweetheart -1	Vo 04641
21914-1	Blue Eyed Blonde -1	Vo 04235
21915-1	Don't Make Me Go To Bed (I'll Be Good) -1	Vo/OK 04454, Cq 9094
21916-1	Chittlin' Cookin' Time In Cheatham County	ARC 8-03-52, Vo 03380, Cq 8986
21917-1	I Still Write Your Name In The Sand	Vo/OK 04454, Cq 9094

Acc. Bill Cox, h-1/g/y-2; Cliff Hobbs, g/y-3.
New York, NY   Wednesday, October 20, 1937

21921-2	Filipino Baby -1	Vo/OK 04341, Cq 9104
21922-	Highway Man	ARC unissued
21923-1	Banjo Joe -2, 3	Vo 04641
21924-2	Jazz Baby -1	Vo 04077, Cq 9004

Only one guitar is used on matrix 21924.

Billy Cox & Cliff Hobbs, v/y-1 duet; acc. Bill Cox, g; Cliff Hobbs, g-2.
Chicago, IL   Sunday, April 2, 1939

WC-2534-A	Lovers' Leap	Vo/OK 04989, Cq 9353
WC-2535-A	Bury Me In The Hill Billy Way -2	Vo 05055, Cq 9353
WC-2536-A	Didi Wa Didi -1	Vo 05191, Cq 9219
WC-2537-A	Blue For My Blue Eyes -2	Vo 04869
WC-2538-A	When Our Wonderful Savior Comes Down	Vo unissued
WC-2539-A	The Hobo's Lullaby -1	Vo 04924, Cq 9221, 9352
WC-2540-A	The Battle Axe And The Devil -2	Vo 04811, Cq 9220
WC-2541-A	Dang My Pop-Eyed Soul -1, 2	Vo 04811, Cq 9220

WC-2542-A	Electric Chair Blues -1	Vo 04924, Cq 9352
WC-2543-A	Lover's Farewell -2	Vo 05285
WC-2544-A	Old Pinto And Me -2	Vo 05055, Cq 9221
WC-2545-A	Blue Mountain Shack -2	Vo 05191
WC-2546-A	I've Found My Love -1	Vo 05285, Cq 9218
WC-2547-A	Oh Sweet Mama -2	Vo 04869, Cq 9219
WC-2548-A	The Last Letter -2	Vo/OK 04989, Cq 9218

Bill Cox & Cliff Hobbs, v duet; or **Bill Cox**-1, v; acc. Bill Cox, h-2/g.
Chicago, IL   Wednesday, September 25, 1940

WC-3323-A	Darling, Do You Know Who Loves You -2	OK 05929
WC-3324-A	The Angel Of The Shore	OK unissued
WC-3325-A	Can't We Make Up Again	OK 06185
WC-3326-A	Why Not Confess -2	OK 05929
WC-3327-A	My Love Divine	OK unissued
WC-3328-A	Will There Be Any Flowers -2	OK 05994
WC-3329-A	Little Blossom -1	OK 06043
WC-3330-A	Smiling Through Tears -2	OK 06043
WC-3331-A	The Night I Fell In Love	OK 06079
WC-3332-A	Hitch Hiking Blues -2	OK 05879
WC-3333-A	Liquor Bowl Blues -2	OK 05832
WC-3334-A	When Night Comes On -2	OK 05832
WC-3335-A	Darling Rose Marie -2	OK 06079
WC-3336-A	Don't Tell Me Goodbye (If You Love Me)	OK 06185
WC-3337-A	The Spreading Maple	OK unissued
WC-3338-A	Oh That Nasty Raid	OK unissued
WC-3339-A	My Tootsie Wootsie Gal -2	OK 05879
WC-3340-A	Yes Good Lord -2	OK 05994

Bill Cox recorded after 1942.

RICHARD COX

Cox & Henson: prob.: Richard Cox, Bernard F. Henson, g duet.
Richmond, IN   Friday, July 29, 1932

18638	National Blues	Ch S-16694
18639	Beech Fork Blues	Ch S-16694

Richard Cox & His National Fiddlers: Richard Cox, f or g; Bernard F. Henson, f or g; unknown, h-1; Frank Welling, g.
Richmond, IN   Saturday, July 30, 1932

18640	East Tennessee Blues	Ch 16563
18641	Downfall Of Adam	Ch 16563
18642	Sleeping Lulu -1	Ch 16475
18643	Honeysuckle Blues	Ch 16475

Richard Cox, v; acc. own g; prob. Bernard F. Henson, g-1.
Richmond, IN   Saturday, July 30, 1932

18644	It Ain't So Good -1	Ch S-16693, 45040
18645	Chewing Chawin' Gum	Ch S-16693, 45040

Bernard F. Henson, v; acc. prob. own g.
Richmond, IN   Saturday, July 30, 1932

18646	I Know What It Means To Be Lonely	Ge unissued

COX & CAMPBELL

Pseudonym on Broadway for Frank & James McCravy.

COX & HENSON

See Richard Cox.

EDWARD L. CRAIN

Cowboy Ed Crane, v; acc. own g.
New York, NY   Thursday, July 16, 1931

10737-	The Old Gray Haired Man	ARC unissued

New York, NY   Thursday, July 23, 1931

10737	The Old Gray Haired Man	ARC unissued
10740-2	Bandit Cole Younger	Cq 8010, Bwy 4055
10741-	Little Blossom – Part 1	ARC unissued
10742-	Little Blossom – Part 2	ARC unissued

10743-1	Starving To Death On A Government Claim	Cq 8013, Bwy 4056
10744-2	Cowboy's Home Sweet Home	Cq 8010

Broadway 4055, 4056 as by **Cowboy Carson**. Revs: Broadway 4055 by Frank Luther, 4056 by Carson Robison.

New York, NY   Friday, July 24, 1931

10745-3	Arkansas Wanderer	Cq 8013
10746-	Boys In Blue	ARC unissued

Edward L. Crain (The Texas Cowboy), v; acc. own g.

New York, NY   Monday, August 17, 1931

151729-	Little Blossom – Part 1	Co unissued
151730-	Little Blossom – Part 2	Co unissued
151731-2	Bandit Cole Younger	Co 15710-D
151732-	Starving To Death On A Government Claim	Co unissued
151733-2	Cowboy's Home Sweet Home	Co 15710-D
151734-	The Old Gray Haired Man	Co unissued

Acc. prob. own h-1; own g.

New York, NY   c. October 1931

1529-2	Cowboy's Home Sweet Home -1	Cr 3250, Vs 5034, MW M3017, CrC/MeC/Stg/Roy 93027
1530-1	God Pity The Life Of A Cowboy -1	Cr 3250, Vs 5034, MW M3016, CrC/MeC/Stg/Roy 93027
1531-2	Bury Me Out On The Prairie	Cr 3239, Htd 22991, Vs 5043, MW M3019
1532-2	Little Joe The Wrangler	Cr 3239, Htd 22991, Vs 5043, MW M3019
1533-2	Whoopee Ti-Yi-Yo, Git Along Little Dogies	Cr 3275, Htd 23003
1542-1	Twenty One Years -1	Cr 3238, Htd 22990
1543-2	Poor Boy	Cr 3238, Htd 22990, Vs 5037
1551-3	The Old Chisholm Trail	Cr 3275, Htd 23003, Vs 5044, MW M3020

No subcredit on Crown 3238. Crown 3239 as by **(Edward L. Crain) The Texas Cowboy**. Montgomery Wards as by **Bob Star (The Texas Ranger)**. Varsitys as by **Cowboy Rodgers**.
The Homestead catalogue numbers were also allocated to issues by Slim Smith (22990), Crockett's Mountaineers (22991), and Jack Kaufman or Frank Marvin (23003).
Matrix 1530 is titled *Pity The Life Of A Cowboy* on all issues except Crown 3250. Matrix 1531 is titled *Bury Me Out On The Lone Prairie* on Varsity 5043, Montgomery Ward M3019. Matrix 1532 is titled *Little Joe, The Wrangler* on Varsity 5043, Montgomery Ward M3019. Matrix 1551 is titled *Old Chisholm Trail* on Homestead 23003, Varsity 5044, Montgomery Ward M3020.
Intervening matrices are popular or untraced.
Revs: Montgomery Ward M3016 by Johnny Marvin, M3017 by Frank Marvin, M3020 by Clayton McMichen; Varsity 5037 by Bob Miller, 5044 (with same credit) by Clayton McMichen.

AL CRAMER

Pseudonym on Broadway for the Gentry Brothers.

CRAMER BOYS

Pseudonym on Broadway for the Carver Boys.

CRAMER BROTHERS

Pseudonym on Broadway for the Gentry Brothers. (One side of Broadway 8061 uses this artist credit as a pseudonym for Vernon Dalhart & Carson Robison.)

COWBOY ED CRANE

See Edward L. Crain.

BOB CRANFORD
CRANFORD & THOMPSON
CRANFORD, THOMPSON & MILES

See The Red Fox Chasers.

AL CRAVER

Pseudonym on Columbia for Vernon Dalhart.

CHARLIE CRAVER (ARKANSAS CHARLIE)

Arkansas Charlie, v; acc. unknown, f; unknown, h-1; unknown, g.

Chicago, IL   Wednesday, October 3, 1928

C-2383-	Goodbye Old Paint -1	Vo 5270
C-2384-	The Texas Trail -1	Vo 5292

| C-2385- | The Little Shirt My Mother Made For Me | Vo 5270 |
| C-2386-A,-B | When I Had But Fifty Cents -1 | Vo unissued |

Acc. unknown, f-1; unknown, h-1; unknown, p-2; unknown, g-1.
    Chicago, IL   Thursday, October 4, 1928

C-2396-	Little Mary Jane -1	Vo 5278
C-2397-	The Two Old Soldiers -1	Vo 5292
C-2398-	That Old Brown Derby -2	Vo unissued

Rev. Vocalion 5278 by Frank Luther.

Acc. unknown, f-1; unknown, h-2; unknown, g.
    New York, NY   Friday, January 11, 1929

| E-28967- | Take Me Back To Collerradda Fer To Stay -2 | Vo 5298 |
| E-28968- | He Was A Travellin' Man -1 | Vo 5298 |

Acc. unknown, h; unknown, g; or **Craver & Tanner**-1: Charlie Craver, Elmo Tanner, v duet; acc. unknown, h; unknown, g.
    Chicago, IL   Monday, July 1, 1929

| C-3757- | The Poor Fish | Vo 5355 |
| C-3758- | Goin' Down To Town -1 | Vo 5355 |

    Chicago, IL   Wednesday, July 3, 1929

C-3770-	The Bum's Rush -1	Vo 5342
C-3771-	The Little Old Sod Shanty -1	Vo 5342
C-3774-A,-B	The Cowboy's Dream	Vo rejected
C-3775-	We All Grow Old In Time	Vo 5367
C-3778-	Little Alice Summers	Vo 5367

Matrices C-3776/77 are by Junie Cobb (see *JR*).

Acc. unknown, f; unknown, g; or **Craver & Tanner**-1: Charlie Craver, Elmo Tanner, v duet; acc. unknown, f; unknown, g.
    Chicago, IL   Saturday, July 6, 1929

| C-3787-A,-B | The Sheriff And The Robber -1 | Vo unissued |
| C-3788-A,-B,-C | Old Zip Coon | Vo rejected |

Acc. unknown, f-1; unknown, h-2; unknown, g.
    Chicago, IL   Saturday, July 20, 1929

C-3910-	The Sheriff And The Robber -1	Vo 5401
C-3911-	Old Zip Coon -1	Vo 5384
C-3912-	That Old Go Hungry Hash House Where We Board -2	Vo 5401

Matrix C-3910 as by **Craver & Tanner**, erroneously. Rev. Vocalion 5384 by Luke Highnight & His Ozark Strutters.

Acc. unknown, h-1; unknown, g.
    Chicago, IL   Saturday, July 27, 1929

C-3955-A,-B	You'll Get "Pie" In The Sky When You Die -1	Vo rejected
C-3956-A,-B	If I Had My Druthers -1	Vo rejected
C-3957-A,-B	The Hobo's Spring Song	Vo rejected

    Chicago, IL   Tuesday, August 13, 1929

| C-4037-A,-B | The Hobo's Spring Song | Br rejected |
| C-4038-A,-B | If I Had My Druthers | Br rejected |

    Chicago, IL   Thursday, August 15, 1929

| C-4039-A,-B | You'll Get Pie In The Sky When You Die -1 | Vo rejected |

Charlie Craver, v; acc. unknown, f; unknown, h; unknown, g.
    New York, NY   Tuesday, November 26, 1929

| E-31489- | At Father Power's Grave | Br 4638 |
| E-31490- | The Shrine At The Miracle Grave | Br 4638 |

Acc. unknown, h; unknown, g.
    New York, NY   Wednesday, November 27, 1929

| E-31491- | The Hobo's Spring Song | Br 449, BrAu 449, Spt S2059 |
| E-31492- | If I Had My Druthers | Br 449, BrAu 449 |

Rev. Supertone S2059 by Bill Baker & Bob Miller's Hinky Dinkers (see Bob Miller).

Acc. unknown, f; unknown, h-1; unknown, g.
    New York, NY   Thursday, December 12, 1929

| E-31516- | Oh, Jailer Bring Back That Key -1 | Br 392 |
| E-31517- | You'll Get "Pie" In The Sky When You Die | Br 392 |

Acc. unknown, f; unknown, h; unknown, bj; unknown, g.
   New York, NY   Friday, February 14, 1930

E-32038-	I've Been To The Pen And I'm Goin' Again (Gosh Darn My Rowdy Soul)	Br 457, Spt S2067
E-32039-A,-B	On A Tennessee Trail	Br/Vo rejected

Supertone S2067 as by **Martin Craver**. Revs: Brunswick 457 by Frank Marvin; Supertone S2067 by Frank Luther & Carson Robison.

Acc. unknown, f; unknown, h; unknown, md-1/bj-2; unknown, g.
   New York, NY   Friday, February 28, 1930

E-32060-A,-B	My Lulu Gal -2	Br/Vo rejected
E-32061-	Then The World Began -2	Br 410
B-32062-	Oh Christofo Columbo -1	Br 410

MARTIN CRAVER

Pseudonym on Supertone for Charlie Craver or Frank Marvin.

OSCAR CRAVER

Pseudonym on Conqueror for Byrd Moore.

CRAVER & TANNER

See Charlie Craver.

ALVIN CRAWFORD

Pseudonym on Superior for C.A. West.

CRAWFORD & MILTON

Pseudonym on Supertone for Cranford & Thompson (see The Red Fox Chasers).

JACK CRAWLEY'S OKLAHOMA RIDGE RUNNERS

Victor V-40175 by Jack Cawley's Oklahoma Ridge Runners was mistakenly credited thus.

CRAZY HILLBILLIES BAND

"Shorty" Fincher, f-1; poss. Chad (?) Rowell (?), bj-2; Hamilton "Rawhide" Fincher, g/v-3; Sue Fincher, v-4; unknown, sb-5.
   New York, NY   Friday, January 12, 1934

152680-	Going Down The Road Feeling Bad -1, 2, 5	OK 45579
152681-	Leaving On The New River Train -1, 2, 5	OK 45579
152682-2	Falling Leaf -3, 4	OK 45577
152683-1	She's A Flower From The Fields Of Alabama -3, 4	OK 45577
152684-2	Danced All Night With A Bottle In My Hand; Old Waggoner -1, 2, 5	OK 45575
152685-2	Too Young To Get Married; Flatwood -1, 2, 5	OK 45575

OKeh 45577 as by **Sue & Rawhide Acc. By The Crazy Hillbillies Band**.
The band, with announcer Jack D. Brinkley, also recorded 20 15-minute radio shows at the studio on January 8, 9, and 12.

JOE CREDUER–ALBERT BABINEAUX

Joe Creduer, ac/v; Albert Babineaux, tri.
   New Orleans, LA   Tuesday, November 12, 1929

56524-1	Tu Va Partir Seul (When You Are Gone Alone)	Vi 22367
56525-2	Petit Ou Gros, Donne Moi Le (Little Or Big, Give It To Me)	Vi 22367
56526-1	Ma Cherie (My Cherie)	Vi 22577
56527-1	La Fille Que J'Aime (The Girl I Love)	Vi 22577

ANATOLE CREDURE

Anatole Credure, v; acc. unknown, f; unknown, ac; unknown, g.
   Dallas, TX   Friday, November 1, 1929

DAL-557-	Lake Charles Waltz	Br 382
DAL-558-	Gasport One Step	Br 382
DAL-559-	Lacassine Waltz	Br 383
DAL-560-	Black Bayou One Step	Br 383

CROCKER & CANNON

Pseudonym on Challenge for Rutherford & Foster.

ALBERT CROCKETT
"DAD" CROCKETT
ELNORA CROCKETT
JOHNNY CROCKETT
JOHNNY & ALBERT CROCKETT
JOHNNY CROCKETT & HIS KENTUCKY MOUNTAINEERS
JOHNNY CROCKETT & TRIO

See the entry headed Crockett [Family] Mountaineers.

CROCKETT [FAMILY] MOUNTAINEERS
CROCKETT'S KENTUCKY MOUNTAINEERS

Crockett Family Mountaineers: John Crockett Sr, f; George Crockett, f; Johnny Crockett, bj; Clarence Crockett, g; Albert Crockett, tg; Alan Crockett, bones.
  Los Angeles, CA   Monday, November 12, 1928
  LAE-334-   Medley Of Old-Time Dance Tunes – Part I (Husk-   Br 291, Spt S2088
              ing Bee–Old Molly Hare–Wild Horse–Soldier's
              Joy–Arkansas Traveler)
  LAE-335-   Medley Of Old-Time Dance Tunes – Part II (Sour-   Br 291, 80094, Spt S2088
              wood Mountain–Sally In The Garden–Sally
              Goodin)

Matrix LAE-335 is titled (1) *Sourwood Mountain* (2) *Sally In The Garden* (3) *Sally Goodin* on Brunswick 80094.
Rev. Brunswick 80094 by Uncle Dave Macon.

Johnny Crockett, Albert Crockett, v duet; acc. Johnny Crockett, g.
  Los Angeles, CA   Monday, November 12, 1928
  LAE-336-   Hard Cider Song   Br 290

Johnny Crockett, v/wh; acc. George Crockett, f; own g.
  Los Angeles, CA   Monday, November 12, 1928
  LAE-337-   Rosalee   Br 290

Johnny & Albert Crockett: Johnny Crockett, g; Albert Crockett, tg.
  Chicago, IL   Friday, August 9, 1929
  C-4015   Fresno Blues   Br 372

"Dad" Crockett: John Crockett Sr, v; acc. George Crockett, bj.
  Chicago, IL   Friday, August 9, 1929
  C-4016   Sugar Hill   Br 372, 80093

Rev. Brunswick 80093 by Bradley Kincaid.

Crockett's Kentucky Mountaineers: George Crockett, f; John Crockett Sr, f-1; Clarence Crockett, h-2/jh-3/v-4; Johnny Crockett, g/lv-5; Albert Crockett, v-6.
  Chicago, IL   Friday, August 9, 1929
  C-4017   Kitty Ki -2, 4, 5, 6   Br 353
  C-4018   Bonaparte's Retreat -1, 3   Br 353

John Crockett Sr, f-1; George Crockett, f-2; Johnny Crockett, bj-3/g-4/v-5; Albert Crockett, g or tg-6/v-7; prob. Clarence Crockett, g-8; Alan Crockett, bones-9/v-10.
  New York, NY   Monday, November 25, 1929
  E-31485-   In The Shade Of The Old Apple Tree -1, 2, 4, 5, 7, Br 394, BrAu 394, PanAu 12299
              10
  E-31486-A,-B On The Road To Tennessee -4, 5   Br rejected
  E-31487-A,-B Uncle Booker's Hoedown (Buffalo Gal) -1, 2, 3, 6, Br rejected
              8, 9
  E-31488-   After The Ball -1, 2, 4?, 6?   Br 394, BrAu 394, PanAu 12299

John Crockett Sr, f-1/bj-2; George Crockett, f-3; Alan Crockett, f-4/bones-5; Clarence Crockett, h-6/jh-7/g-8/v-9; Johnny Crockett, bj-10/g-11/v-12; Albert Crockett, tg-13/v-14/calls-15.
  New York, NY   January/February 1931
  1145-3   Bile Dem Cabbage Down -1, 3, 4, 5, 6, 9, 11, 12,   Cr 3101, Htd 23040, *Vs 5046, MW M3021*
              14
  1146-1   I Was Born About 10,000 Years Ago -1, 3, 4, 8,   Cr 3101, Htd 23040, *Vs 5088, MW M3024,*
              11, 12, 13   *JDs 3506*
  1147-1   Lightnin' Express -1, 3, 8, 11, 12, 13, 14   Cr 3074, *Vs 5078, MW M3024*
  1148-2   Cripple Creek -2, 3, 5, 7, 8, 11, 12, 13, 14   Cr 3172, *Vs 5046, MW M3021*
  1149-   The Blind Man's Lament -3, 4, 11, 12   Cr 3143, Pm 3278, Bwy 8310
  1152-2   Granny's Old Arm-Chair -1, 3, 8, 9, 11, 12, 13, 14 Cr 3188, Pm 3277, *Vs 5078, MW M3026*
  1153-2   My Blue-Eyed Girl And I -1, 3, 4, 8, 11, 12, 14   Cr 3074, Pm 3277, *Vs 5058, MW M3023*
  1154-   Sweet Betsy From Pike -3, 4, 8, 11, 12, 13   Cr 3121, Htd 22991

1155-1	Sugar In My Coffee -1, 5, 8, 10, 13, 15	Cr 3075, Htd 23039, *Vs 5058, MW M3023*
1156-3	Convict's Lament -3, 4, 8, 11, 12	Cr 3143, Pm 3278, Bwy 8310
1157-2	Buffalo Gal's Medley -1, 3, 5, 8, 10, 13	Cr 3075, Htd 23039, *Vs 5088, MW M3026, JDs 3506*
1158-	I Knowed I'd Settle Down -3, 8, 9, 11, 12, 14	Cr 3121, Htd 22991, Pm 3302

Crown 3074 as by **Johnny & Albert Crockett**; 3075 as by **Johnny Crockett & His Kentucky Mountaineers**; 3101 as by **Crockett's Kentucky Mountaineers** (matrix 1145)/**Johnny Crockett** (matrix 1146); 3143 prob. as by **Johnny Crockett**; 3188 as by **Johnny Crockett & Trio**. Paramount 3278, Broadway 8310 as by **Johnny Crockett**. Montgomery Wards as by **Harlan Miners Fiddlers**. Varsity 5046 as by **Crockett Mountaineers**; 5058 as by **Kentucky Kernals**; 5088 as by **Hale's Kentucky Mountaineers**. Joe Davis 3506 as by **Kentucky Mountaineers**. All other issues as by **Crockett's Kentucky Mountaineers**. Homestead 22991 was also allocated to an issue by Edward L. Crain.
Matrix 1146 is titled *I Was Born 10,000 Years Ago* on Varsity 5088, Joe Davis 3506, or *Born Ten Thousand Years Ago* on Montgomery Ward M3024. Matrix 1147 is subtitled *(Please Mr Conductor, Don't Put Me Off Of The Train)* on Crown 3024. Matrix 1153 is titled *Blue Eyed Gal* on Varsity 5058. Matrix 1157 is titled *Buffalo Gals* on Varsity 5088, Montgomery Ward M3026, Joe Davis 3506.
Matrices 1150/51 are by The High Steppers (popular).

John Crockett Sr, f-1/bj-2; George Crockett, f; Alan Crockett, f-3/jh-4; Clarence Crockett, h-5/jh-6/g-7; Johnny Crockett, bj-8/g-9/v-10; Albert Crockett, tg-11/v-12; Elnora Crockett, v-13.
    New York, NY   May 1931

1343-2	Skip To My Lou -1, 3, 6, 7, 8, 12, 13	Cr 3188, *Vs 5082, MW M3025, Cont C-3012*
1345-1	Shoo Fly -1, 3, 5, 9, 10, 12	Cr 3159, Htd 23041, *Vs 5049, MW M3022, JDs 3505*
1346-2	Roving Gambler -1, 9, 10	Cr 3159, Htd 23041, Pm 3302, *Vs 5082, MW M3025, Cont C-3012*
1348-2	Little Rabbit And Rabbit Where's Your Mammy -2, 4, 9, 11	Cr 3172, *Vs 5049, MW M3022, JDs 3505*

Crown 3159 probably as by **Crockett's Kentucky Mountaineers** (matrix 1345)/**Johnny Crockett** (matrix 1346); 3188 as by **Elnora Crockett**. Montgomery Wards as by **Harlan Miners Fiddlers**. Varsity 5049, Joe Davis 3505 as by **Crockett Mountaineers**. Varsity 5082, Continental C-3012 as by **Pete Daley's Arkansas Fiddlers**. All other issues as by **Crockett's Kentucky Mountaineers**.
Matrix 1346 is titled *The Roving Gambler* on Montgomery Ward M3025. Matrix 1348 is titled *Little Rabbit* on Joe Davis 3505. Intervening matrices are untraced.
Members of the Crockett Family recorded after 1942.

CROMWELL BROTHERS

Vocal duet; acc. unknown, f-1; unknown, g; unknown, g-2.
    Richmond, IN   Tuesday, September 30, 1930

17118,-A	Meet Me In Honeysuckle Time -2	Ge rejected
17119,-A	We Have Met And We Have Parted	Ge rejected
17120	Always In The Way	Ge rejected
17121	The Irishman And The Barber -1	Ge rejected

C.A. CRONIC
CRONIC BROTHERS

Cronic Brothers-1, v duet; or C.A. Cronic-2, v; acc. unknown.
    Atlanta, GA   Thursday, April 19, 1928

146138-	Take This Letter To My Mother -1	Co unissued
146139-	Careless Love -2	Co unissued

C.A. Cronic is likely to be the Clarence Cronic who recorded with Smith's Sacred Singers. The other brother may be J.C. Cronic, who recorded with the Sheffield Male Quartet.

CROOK BROTHERS STRING BAND

Matthew H. Crook, h; Herman M. Crook, h; Thomas J. Givans, bj; George R. Miles, g/calls; Hick Burnett, g.
    Nashville, TN   Friday, October 5, 1928

47140-2	My Wife Died On Friday Night	Vi V-40020
47141-2	Going Across The Sea	Vi V-40099, Au 223
47142-1	Jobbin Gettin' There [sic]	Vi V-40020, MW M-8137
47830-2	Love Somebody	Vi V-40099, Au 223

Victor V-40020 as by **Crook Brothers' String Band**. Montgomery Ward M-8137 as by **Crook Brother's String Band**; matrix 47142 is titled *Barn Dance On The Mountain Part 1* on that issue. Intervening matrices are by other artists.
Rev. Montgomery Ward M-8137 by Mellie Dunham's Orchestra.

BALLARD CROSS

See Hugh Cross.

HUGH CROSS

Cross & McCartt: Hugh Cross, Luther McCartt, v duet; acc. Luther McCartt, md; Hugh Cross, g.
Atlanta, GA Thursday, April 7, 1927

| 143931-1 | When The Roses Bloom Again | Co 15143-D, CoE 19006 |
| 143932-2 | Sweet Rosie O'Grady | Co 15143-D, CoE 19006, ReAu G20668 |

Hugh Cross, v; acc. Luther McCartt, md-1; own g.
Atlanta, GA Thursday, April 7, 1927

| 143933-1 | The Parlor Is A Pleasant Place To Sit In Sunday Night -1 | Co 15182-D |
| 143934-2 | I'm Going Away From The Cotton Fields | Co 15182-D |

Acc. own g.
Atlanta, GA Wednesday, November 2, 1927

145069-	Last Night Was The End Of The World	Co unissued
145070-1	Down Where The Cotton Blossoms Grow	Co 15231-D
145071-2	The Mansion Of Aching Hearts	Co 15231-D
145072-	Where The Morning Glories Twine Around The Door	Co unissued

Hugh Cross & Riley Puckett, v/wh-1 duet; or **Hugh Cross**-2, v; acc. Clayton McMichen, f-3; Riley Puckett, g-4; Hugh Cross, g.
Atlanta, GA Thursday, November 3, 1927

145091-2	Red River Valley -1, 4	Co 15206-D, CoE 19012
145092-1	When You Wore A Tulip -3, 4	Co 15206-D, CoE 19012, ReAu G20668
145093-	Lorena -2	Co unissued
145094-	In The Evening -2	Co unissued

Mr. & Mrs. Hugh Cross: Hugh Cross, Mary Cross, v duet; or **Hugh Cross**-1, v; acc. Hugh Cross, g.
Atlanta, GA Wednesday, April 11, 1928

146008-2	I Love You Best Of All	Co 15259-D
146009-1	You're As Welcome As The Flowers In May	Co 15259-D
146010-2	If I Had Only Had A Home Sweet Home	Co 15613-D
146011-2	My Little Home In Tennessee -1	Co 15613-D

Hugh Cross & Riley Puckett, v/wh-1 duet; acc. Riley Puckett, g.
Atlanta, GA Thursday, April 12, 1928

146026-2	Tuck Me To Sleep In My Old Kentucky home	Co 15421-D
146027-2	Gonna Raise Ruckus Tonight	Co 15455-D, ReE MR56
146028-2	Where The Morning Glories Grow -1	Co 15266-D
146029-1	My Wild Irish Rose	Co 15266-D

Regal MR56 as by **The Alabama Barn Stormers**. Rev. Regal MR56 (with same credit) by Ira & Eugene Yates.

Atlanta, GA Monday, October 22, 1928

| 147244-2 | Call Me Back Pal O' Mine | Co 15337-D |

Hugh Cross, v/y-1; acc. own g.
Atlanta, GA Tuesday, October 23, 1928

| 147259-2 | In The Hills Of Tennessee | Co 15365-D |
| 147260-1 | Never No More Blues -1 | Co 15365-D |

Hugh Cross & Riley Puckett, v duet; acc. Riley Puckett, g.
Atlanta, GA Tuesday, October 23, 1928

147265-2	Clover Blossoms	Co 15337-D
147266-1	Smiles	Co 15478-D
147267-2	Tell Me	Co 15478-D

Mr. & Mrs. Hugh Cross: Hugh Cross, Mary Cross, v duet; acc. Hugh Cross, g.
Atlanta, GA Monday, April 8, 1929

148204-2	Dearest Sweetest Mother	Co 15395-D
148205-2	Mother's Plea	Co 15395-D
148206-2	Down Where The Swanee River Flows	Co 15458-D
148207-2	Pretty Little Blue-Eyed Sally	Co 15458-D

Atlanta, GA Tuesday, April 9, 1929

| 148216- | Back Home In Tennessee | Co unissued |
| 148217- | In 1960 You'll Find Dixie Looking Just The Same | Co unissued |

Hugh Cross, v/y; acc. own g.
Atlanta, GA Tuesday, April 9, 1929

| 148218-2 | I'll Climb The Blue Ridge Mountains Back To You | Co 15439-D |
| 148219-1 | Wabash Cannon Ball | Co 15439-D |

Hugh Cross & Riley Puckett, v duet; acc. Riley Puckett, g.
   Atlanta, GA   Wednesday, April 10, 1929

   148229-1   I'm Going To Settle Down   Co 15455-D, CoSA DE505
   148230-1   Go Feather Your Nest   Co 15421-D

Rev. Columbia DE505 by James Johnson.

Ballard Cross, v; acc. own g.
   Knoxville, TN   Thursday, August 29, 1929

   K-142-   Old Black Crow In The Hickory Nut Tree   Vo 5359
   K-143-   My Poodle Dog   Vo 5359

   Knoxville, TN   Saturday, August 31, 1929

   K-146-   The Wabash Cannon Ball   Vo 5377
   K-147-   Lorrainna   Vo 5377
   K-154-   Down Where The Swanee River Flows   Vo 5402
   K-155-   Won't You Waltz Home Sweet Home With Me   Vo 5402

Matrices K-144/45 are by Cumberland Mountain Fret Pickers; matrices K-148/49 by the University of Tennessee Trio; matrices K-150 through 153 by Cal Davenport & His Gang.

Mr. & Mrs. Hugh Cross: Hugh Cross, Mary Cross, v duet; acc. Hugh Cross, g.
   Atlanta, GA   Tuesday, October 29, 1929

   149284-2   My Old Cabin Home   Co 15504-D
   149285-1   When The Flowers Bloom Again In The Ozarks   Co 15504-D
   149286-   When The Golden Rod Is Blooming   Co unissued
   149287-   I'd Love To Fall Asleep   Co unissued
   149291-2   There's A Mother Old And Gray   Co 15575-D

Matrix 149288 is by Bill Helms & Riley Puckett; matrices 149289/90 are by Clayton McMichen & Riley Puckett.

   Atlanta, GA   Wednesday, October 30, 1929

   149292-1   When The Bees Are In The Hive   Co 15575-D

Hugh Cross, v; acc. own g.
   Atlanta, GA   Wednesday, October 30, 1929

   149293-   Daddy   Co unissued
   149294-   Back To Old Kentucky   Co unissued

Bob Nichols & Hugh Cross: Clayton McMichen, Hugh Cross, v duet; acc. unknown, f-1; unknown, g-2; prob. different unknown, g-3.
   Atlanta, GA   Friday, November 1, 1929

   149334-2   Corrine Corrina -2   Co 15480-D
   149335-2   I Left My Gal In The Mountains -1, 3   Co 15480-D

Mr. & Mrs. Hugh Cross: Hugh Cross, Mary Cross, v duet; acc. Hugh Cross, g.
   Atlanta, GA   Saturday, November 2, 1929

   149336-   Carolina's Callin'   Co unissued
   149337-   Are You Happy Or Lonesome   Co unissued

Ballard Cross, v; prob. acc. own g.
   Knoxville, TN   Thursday, April 3, 1930

   K-8076-   An Old-Fashioned Cottage   Br/Vo rejected
   K-8077-   Old Daddy Dear   Br/Vo rejected

These titles were originally logged as by **Heavy Martin**. Under that pseudonym Cross also participates in recordings at this session by Smoky Mountain Ramblers, Lowe Stokes, and Tennessee Farm Hands.

Bob Nichols & Hugh Cross: Clayton McMichen, Hugh Cross, v duet; acc. Clayton McMichen, f-1; Hugh Cross, g.
   Atlanta, GA   Wednesday, April 16, 1930

   150236- ;   When I Lived In Arkansas -1   Co 15698-D
   130461-1
   150237-2   In The Hills Of Old Virginia   Co 15556-D

   Atlanta, GA   Monday, April 21, 1930

   150320-2;   When It's Peach Picking Time In Georgia -1   Co 15698-D
   130469-1

   Atlanta, GA   Tuesday, April 22, 1930

   150343-2   Smoky Mountain Home -1   Co 15556-D

Hugh & Shug's Radio Pals: Ted Grantham, f; Lennie Aleshire, poss. f; Buddy Ross, ac; Shug Fisher, sb/prob. v-1; Hugh Cross, v/y-2.
   New York, NY   Friday, July 16, 1937

   62398-A   Honeymoon Stream -1   De 5407
   62399-A   Union County   De 5439

62400-A	On A Green Mountainside In Virginia -1	De 5534
62401-A	That's My Paradise	De 5439
62402-A	Weeping Willow Lane -1	De 5506
62403-A	Sugar Babe	De 5407
62404-A	The Little Girl Dressed In Blue -2	De 5428
62405-A	Where The Golden Poppies Grow -1	De 5406, MeC 45224
62406-A	What's The Reason (I'm Not Pleasin' You)	De 5506
62407-A	There's A Blue Sky Over Yonder -1	De 5466
62408-A	Back To Old Smoky Mountain -1	De 5466
62409-A	Nobody's Sweetheart	De 5534
62410-A	Are You From Dixie?	De 5451, Coral 64009
62411-A	Moonlight And Roses	De 5406, MeC 45224
62412-A	When You Wore A Tulip	De 5428
62413-A	Five Foot Two, Eyes Of Blue (Has Anybody Seen My Girl?)	De 5451, Coral 64009

See also Riley Puckett.

CROSS & McCARTT

See Hugh Cross.

FRANK & PHIL CROW
PHIL CROW TRIO

The brothers Frank and Phil Luther occasionally recorded using their real name, Crow; the trio credit was used when they were joined by Carson Robison, under whose name these items are listed.

CROWDER BROTHERS
CROWDER FAMILY

Crowder Brothers: Clovis Crowder, f-1/bsv-2; Warren Crowder, md-3; Olfa Crowder, g/lv/y-4; Ortive Crowder, g/tv/y-4.

Augusta, GA   Wednesday, July 1, 1936

AUG-145-3	Depot Blues	ARC 6-10-60, Cq 8718
AUG-146-3	Blonde Headed Baby -4	ARC 6-10-60, Cq 8718
AUG-147-3	Worried Blues -4	ARC 6-12-65, Cq 8755
AUG-148-	Trusting My Sweetheart	ARC unissued
AUG-150-1,-2	The Sailing Ship -1, 2	ARC unissued
AUG-159-	We All Love Mother -1, 2, 3	ARC unissued
AUG-160-	My Courtin' Days Are Over	ARC unissued
AUG-161-	Augusta Georgia Blues	ARC unissued
AUG-162-	Darling Little Sweetheart -3	ARC unissued
AUG-163-	North Asheville Blues -3	ARC unissued
AUG-164-	North Carolina Blues -3	ARC unissued
AUG-165-3	I Don't Let The Girls Worry My Mind	ARC 6-12-65, Cq 8755
AUG-166-	Aged Mother	ARC unissued

Matrices AUG-150, 159, and 166 were logged as by **Crowder Family**. Matrix AUG-149 is by Charlie Mitchell; matrices AUG-151 to 158 are by Piano Red (see B&GR).

Clovis Crowder, f-1/bsv-2; Olfa Crowder, g/lv; Ortive Crowder, g/tv.

Chicago, IL   Tuesday, December 8, 1936

C-1696-2	New Maple On The Hill -1, 2	ARC 7-02-63, Cq 8782
C-1697-2	The Sailing Ship -1, 2	ARC 7-02-63, Cq 8782
C-1698-2	Lonesome Lost Gal Blues	ARC 7-04-70
C-1699-1,-2	Worst Old Blues	ARC unissued
C-1700-1,-2	Got No Use For The Women	ARC unissued
C-1701-1,-2	My Courting Days Are Over	ARC unissued
C-1702-1,-2	We All Love Mother -1, 2	ARC unissued
C-1703-1,-2	The One Who Set You Free -1, 2	ARC unissued
C-1704-2	Leave Me Darling I Don't Mind	ARC 7-04-70
C-1705-1,-2	Trusting My Sweetheart	ARC unissued
C-1706-1,-2	Darling Little Sweetheart	ARC unissued
C-1707-1,-2	Buncombe County Blues	ARC unissued
C-1708-1,-2	Take Me Home Boys Tonight (Take Me Home)	ARC unissued
C-1709-2	I'll Journey On	ARC 7-03-71

Chicago, IL   Wednesday, December 9, 1936

C-1710-2	Our Mansion Is Ready -2	ARC 7-03-71
C-1711-1,-2	All My Sins Been Taken Away -2	ARC unissued
C-1712-1,-2	Sales Tax Blues	ARC unissued
C-1713-1,-2	North Carolina Blues	ARC unissued

Chicago, IL   Thursday, December 10, 1936
    C-1714-1,-2   The Strawberry Roan -1, 2   ARC unissued
    C-1715-1,-2   Farewell My Loved Ones -2   ARC unissued
    C-1716-1,-2   Our Friend -2   ARC unissued
    C-1717-1,-2   My Sweetheart Has Gone And Left Me   ARC unissued

Clovis Crowder, f-1/bsv-2; unknown, sg-3; Olfa Crowder, g/lv/y-4; Ortive Crowder, g/tv/y-4.
New York, NY   Wednesday, September 22, 1937
    21720-   I'm Happy In Prison -1, 2, 3   ARC unissued
    21721-   Will The Lighthouse Shine On Me -1, 2   ARC unissued
    21722-   When Father Is Gone -1, 2   ARC unissued
    21723-   Land Of Liberty And Love -1, 2   ARC unissued
    21724-   We All Love Mother -1, 2, 3   ARC unissued
    21725-2   Answer To Blonde Headed Baby -3, 4   ARC 7-11-60, Cq 8894
    21726-2   Wild West Rambler -3   ARC 7-11-60, Cq 8894
    21727-2   Old Chain Gang -1, 2, 3   ARC 8-03-57, Vo 03030
    21728-   Aged Mother -1, 2   ARC unissued
    21729-   Oh Little Children   ARC unissued
    21730-1   Ridin' My Jenny   ARC 7-12-52, Cq 8943
    21735-2   My Soul Is Lost   Cq 8899

Matrices 21731 to 21734 are by Fletcher Henderson & His Orchestra (see *JR*).

New York, NY   Thursday, September 23, 1937
    21736-2   My Courting Days Are Gone -4   Cq 8898
    21737-   Daddy Is Gone   ARC unissued
    21738-1,-2   Guitar Runaway   ARC unissued
    21739-1   Got No Use For Women   ARC 8-03-57, Vo 03030, Cq 8943
    21740-1   Dying In Ashville [sic] Jail   Cq 8899
    21741-1   Sweet Little Girl Of Mine   Cq 8898
    21748-1,-2   My Sweetheart's Gone And Left Me   ARC unissued
    21749-   Buncombe County Blues   ARC unissued
    21750-1,-2   Sales Tax Blues   ARC unissued
    21751-1,-2   Worst Old Blues (I Ever Had)   ARC unissued
    21752-   Trusting My Sweetheart -1, 2   ARC unissued

Matrices 21742 to 21747 are popular.

New York, NY   Friday, September 24, 1937
    21753-2   Night Time Is The Right Time -1,2   ARC 7-12-52
    21754-   Life's Railway To Heaven -1, 2   ARC unissued
    21755-   Our Friend Is Gone   ARC unissued
    21756-1,-2   One Year Ain't Long   ARC unissued
    21757-   North Carolina Blues   ARC unissued
    21758-   Farewell My Loved One   ARC unissued

FRANK CRUMIT

Despite having one coupling issued in the Victor Old Familiar Tunes series (V-40214), and recording other items of considerable peripheral interest, Frank Crumit does not fall within the scope of this work. (For details of his recordings see Rust, *The Complete Entertainment Discography*.)

PAUL CRUTCHFIELD & JOHN CLOTWORTHY

Paul & John (The Disciples of Harmony): Paul Crutchfield, John Clotworthy, v duet; acc. unknown.
Atlanta, GA   Friday, April 20, 1928
    146153-   Have Thine Own Way, Lord   Co unissued
    146154-   Nothing Between   Co unissued

Paul & John, v duet; acc. unknown, f; unknown, p; unknown, vc.
Atlanta, GA   Saturday, August 4, 1928
    402058-A,-B   [I'm Going Back To The Farm]   OK unissued

Sp duet; acc. unknown, p.
Atlanta, GA   Saturday, August 4, 1928
    402059-   [unknown title]   OK unissued

Acc. unknowns, brass band.
Atlanta, GA   Saturday, August 4, 1928
    402062-B   Band Rehearsal For Old Settler's Reunion – Part 1   OK 45280
    402063-B   Band Rehearsal For Old Settler's Reunion – Part 2   OK 45280

Paul Crutchfield, v/sp; acc. unknown, g.
Atlanta, GA   Tuesday, August 7, 1928

| 402078-A | Uncle Hiram's Trip To The City – Part 1 | OK 45266 |
| 402079-A | Uncle Hiram's Trip To The City – Part 2 | OK 45266 |

Paul & John, sp duet; acc. unknown, g.
Atlanta, GA   Tuesday, August 7 or Wednesday, August 8, 1928
| 402081- | [unknown title] | OK unissued |

Crutchfield (Paul) & Clotworthy (John), v duet; acc. two unknowns, f; unknown, g.
Atlanta, GA   Wednesday, August 8, 1928
402088-	[There's A Land Beyond The Starlight]	OK unissued
402089-A	Death's River	OK 45261
402090-A	Sweet, The Memory Of My Mother	OK 45261

CRUTHERS BROTHERS

Smith Ballew, Saxie Dowell, v duet; acc. two unknowns, f; unknown, g.
New York, NY   Tuesday, February 19, 1929
| 401624-B | Carolina Moon | OK 45307 |
| 401625-C | Wednesday Night Waltz | OK 45307 |

CRYSEL BOYS WITH ALLEN BULLARD

Allen Bullard, f; Curtis Crysel, md; Jack Crysel, g/v; unknown, g.
Birmingham, AL   Tuesday, April 6, 1937
| B-88-1 | My Gal Kate | ARC 7-07-68 |
| B-89-1 | Crazy Blues | ARC 7-07-68 |

CRYSTAL SPRINGS RAMBLERS

Joe Holley, f; Link Davis, f; Earl Driver, as; Loren Mitchell, p; Morris Deason, tbj or g/v-1; J.B. Brinkley, g; Jimmy McAdoo, sb.
Dallas, TX   Wednesday, June 9, 1937
DAL-240-1	Swingin' And Truckin' -1	Vo 03856
DAL-241-2	Swingin' To Glory -1	Vo 03646
DAL-242-1,-2	When Somebody Thinks You're Wonderful	Vo unissued

Joe Holley, f; Link Davis, f/v-1; Earl Driver, as; Loren Mitchell, p; Morris Deason, tbj or g/v-2; J.B. Brinkley, g/v-3; Jimmy McAdoo, sb; band v-4.
Dallas, TX   Saturday, June 19, 1937
DAL-370-	My Texas Home	Vo unissued
DAL-371-2	Tired Of Me -1	Vo 03707
DAL-372-	Mr. Deep Blue Sea	Vo unissued
DAL-373-	Springtown Shuffle	Vo unissued
DAL-374-2	Down In Arkansas -4	Vo 03856
DAL-375-2	Fort Worth Stomp -2	Vo 03646
DAL-376-1	Tell Me Pretty Mama -3	Vo 03707

CUMBERLAND MOUNTAIN FRET PICKERS

No details.
Knoxville, TN   Thursday, August 29, 1929
| TK-144 | Call Of The Cumberlands | Br/Vo rejected trial recording |
| TK-145 | Little Blue Haird [sic] Boy | Br/Vo rejected trial recording |

CUMBERLAND RIDGE RUNNERS

Homer "Slim" Miller, f; Karl Davis, md/v; Hartford Taylor, g/v; prob. Red Foley, sb/poss. v; John Lair, v; poss. Linda Parker, v.
Chicago, IL   Tuesday, April 11, 1933
| C-534-1 | Sally's Not The Same Old Sally | Cq 8161 |
| C-534-4 | Sally's Not The Same Old Sally | Ba 32773, Me M12702, Or 8235, Pe 12914, Ro 5235 |

Homer "Slim" Miller, f/poss. v-1; Karl Davis, md/v-2; Hartford Taylor, g/v-2; Red Foley, sb/v-1.
Chicago, IL   Wednesday, April 12, 1933
C-539-3	Goofus	Ba 33022, Me M12981, Or 8324, Pe 12993, Ro 5324, Cq 8160
C-540-1	Ridin' On A Humped Backed Mule -1, 2	Cq 8162
C-541-2	Ole Rattler -1, 2	Ba 32773, Me M12702, Or 8235, Pe 12914, Ro 5235, Cq 8161

C-542-1	Nobody's Darling -2	Cq 8162
C-543-2	Roundin' Up The Yearlings	Ba 33022, Me M12981, Or 8324, Pe 12993, Ro 5324, Cq 8160

For Conqueror 8310 with this artist credit see Karl & Harty.

CUMBERLAND STRING BAND
Pseudonym on Superior for Hack's String Band.

JAMES CUMMINGS
Pseudonym on Madison for Vernon Dalhart.

M. HOMER CUMMINGS & SON HUGH

M. Homer Cummings, Hugh Cummings, v duet; acc. Gladys Eary, p.
Richmond, IN   Monday, August 20, 1934

19665	Gloom And Darkness Precede The Dawn	Ch 16821, 45115
19666	Someone Will Welcome You	Ch 16821, 45115
19667	It Will Matter But Little At Last	Ge unissued
19668	Only The Best	Ch 16810, 45122
19669	I Need Thee Every Hour	Ch 16810, 45122

DAVE CUTRELL

Dave Cutrell, v; acc. prob. own g.
St. Louis, MO   May 1926

9650-A	Pistol Pete's Midnight Special	OK 45057

Despite the label-credit to McGinty's Oklahoma Cow Boy Band as accompanists, the instrumentation is as shown. Rev. OKeh 45057 by McGinty's Oklahoma Cow Boy Band (see Otto Gray).

D

DACA

Daca, v; acc. prob. own g.
New York, NY   Monday, October 15, 1934

38849-A	Hell In Texas	De unissued
38850-A,-B	My Little Mohee	De unissued

The *US Catalogue of Copyright Entries* lists several compositions, including one of those above, associated with 'Daca, the cowsongboy, of U.S.' All were published by Harry Payne Reeves, whose identity the soubriquet may conceal.

TED DAFFAN'S TEXANS

Harry Sorensen, ac; Ted Daffan, esg/v-1; Ralph C. Smith, p; Sidney "Buddy" Buller, lg; Charles W. "Chuck" Keeshan, g/v-2; Elwood B. "Elmer" Christian, sb.
Saginaw, TX   Thursday, April 25, 1940

DAL-1058-2	Worried Mind -2	OK 05668, Cq 9563, 9699, Co 37013, 20039
DAL-1059-2	Crying The Blues Again -2	OK 05741
DAL-1060-2	Let Her Go -2	OK 05796, Cq 9700, Co 37651, 20250
DAL-1061-1	Where The Deep Water Flows -1	OK 05741
DAL-1062-2	Rainy Day Blues -1	OK 05796, Cq 9700. Co 37651, 20250
DAL-1063-2	I'm Sorry I Said Goodbye -2	OK 05855, Cq 9701
DAL-1064-1	I'm A Fool To Care -2	Vo/OK 05573, Cq 9697, Co 37648, 20247
DAL-1065-1	Blue Steel Blues	OK 05668, Cq 9699, Co 37013, 20039
DAL-1066-2	Grey Eyed Darling -1	OK 05855, Cq 9698
DAL-1067-2	She Goes The Other Way -1	OK 05918, Cq 9698
DAL-1068-2	Put Your Little Arms Around Me -2	Vo/OK 05573, Cq 9697, Co 37648, 20247
DAL-1069-2	I Told You So -2	OK 05918, Cq 9701

Rev. Conqueror 9563 by Brownie McGhee (see *B&GR*).

Fort Worth, TX   Friday, February 21, 1941

DAL-1148-1	Car Hop's Blues -2	OK 06452, Co 37438, 20165
DAL-1149-1	Down Hilo Way -2	OK 06126
DAL-1150-1	Breakin' My Heart Over You -1	OK 06452, Co 37438, 20165
DAL-1151-2	I'll Travel Alone -2	OK 06504, Co 37431, 20158
DAL-1152-1,-2	Take Me Back Again -1, 2	OK unissued
DAL-1153-1	You're On My Mind -2	OK 06383
DAL-1154-1,-2	I'm Losing My Mind Over You -2	OK unissued

DAL-1155-2	Weary Worried And Blue -1	OK 06253, Co 37661, 20260
DAL-1156-2	Too Late, Little Girl, Too Late -1	OK 06253, Co 37661, 20260
DAL-1157-1,-2	West Wind Blues	OK unissued

Fort Worth, TX   Saturday, February 22, 1941

DAL-1158-1,-2	Don't Be Blue For Me -2	OK unissued
DAL-1159-1	Laura Lou -2	OK 06383
DAL-1160-1	Strip Tease Swing	OK 06126
DAL-1161-1,-2	Just Fooling Around -2	OK unissued
DAL-1162-1	Because -2	OK 06172, Co 37657, 20256
DAL-1163-1	I Lost My Sunshine -2	OK 06504, Co 37431, 20158
DAL-1164-1,-2	Snow White Roses -1, 2	OK unissued
DAL-1165-2	Always Alone -1, 2	OK 06311, Co 37662, 20261
DAL-1166-1	Those Blue Eyes Don't Sparkle Anymore -2	OK 06172, Co 37657, 20256
DAL-1167-1	Weary Steel Blues	OK 06311, Co 37662, 20261

Leonard Seago, f/v-1; Freddy Courtney (Ralph Courtney Hawkins), ac; Ted Daffan, esg/v-2; Ralph C. Smith, p; Buddy Buller, lg; Chuck Keeshan, g/v-3; Johnny Johnson, sb; Lindley "Spike" Jones, d.

Hollywood, CA   Friday, February 20, 1942

H-652-	Sweetheart Rose -1	OK unissued
H-653-	Just Drifting -1, 3	OK unissued
H-654-	Gonna Get Tight Tonight -1	OK unissued
H-655-1	Born To Lose -1	OK 6706, Co 37667, 20266, 21400, CoC C712, V-D 240, V-D Navy 20
H-656-	Poor Mistreated Me -1	OK unissued
H-657-	Troubled Heart Of Mine -1	OK unissued
H-658-1	Bluest Blues -2	OK 6719, Co 37033, 20058, V-D 459, V-D Navy 239
H-659-1	No Letter Today -1, 3	OK 6706, Co 37667, 20266, 21400, CoC C712, V-D 240, V-D Navy 20
H-660-1	Time Won't Heal My Broken Heart -1	OK 6729, Co 37038, 20063
H-661-1	Long John	Co 37823, 20358
H-662-1	Look Who's Talkin' -1	OK 6719, Co 37033, 20058, V-D 459, V-D Navy 239
H-663-	Lonesome Steel Guitar	OK unissued

Rev. Columbia 37823, 20358 postwar.

Freddy Courtney, ac; Ted Daffan, esg; Ralph C. Smith, p; Buddy Buller, lg; Chuck Keeshan, g/v-1; Johnny Johnson, sb; Leonard Seago, v-2; unknown woman, v-3.

Hollywood, CA   Saturday, February 21, 1942

H-664-	Only You -1	OK unissued
H-665-	Locket Of Gold -1	OK unissued
H-666-	Rose Of Santa Fe -1	OK unissued
H-667-1	You're Breaking My Heart -3	OK 6729, Co 37038, 20063
H-668-	A Letter To A Soldier -3	OK unissued
H-669-	I'll Keep On Smiling -1	OK unissued
H-670-	After You Left Me Alone -1	OK unissued
H-671-	You Didn't Mind Saying Goodbye -1	OK unissued
H-672-	Just Thinking Of You -1	OK unissued
H-673-	Blues On My Mind -1	OK unissued
H-674-	I Think That I've Been Fair -2	OK unissued
H-675-	You Can't Make Me Worry Anymore -1	OK unissued

Matrices H-664 to 666, H-668 to 675 were logged as by **Boys Of The Rio Grande** but are identified in the Satherley files as by a Daffan group. Matrix H-667 was logged and issued as by **Ted Daffan's Texans**.

Ted Daffan recorded after 1942.

PETE DALEY'S ARKANSAS FIDDLERS

Pseudonym on Varsity and Continental for Crockett's Kentucky Mountaineers.

VERNON DALHART

Vernon Dalhart (his real name was Marion Try Slaughter, but he never used it professionally) began his long recording career in 1915. For almost a decade he was engaged around the New York studios to record popular material – songs from musicals and operettas of the day, standard numbers, coon-songs, comic pieces, etc. Then, on May 14, 1924, he recorded for Edison *The Wreck On The Southern Old 97*. The success of this song, which he also recorded for numerous other labels, played a large part in determining the course of his career. Although he continued to record popular material from time to time, the greater part of his work after that date was directed at the market for Southern (old time, hillbilly) songs.

That greater part is the subject of this discography. All recordings predating the May 1924 Edison session have been excluded, as have the relatively few later sessions wholly devoted to popular material. It may be that some of Dalhart's popular work has nonetheless slipped into this listing: it has been impossible to hear everything, and in any case the line between the categories is not always easy to draw.

The discography includes all Dalhart's vocal duets with Carson Robison, even those for which Robison received primary label-credit. His vocal duets with Adelyne Hood are also included here, but see her entry for a few other recordings in which Dalhart participated.

Vernon Dalhart, v; acc. own h; Frank Ferera, g.
New York, NY					Wednesday, May 14, 1924

| 9514-B,-C | The Wreck On The Southern Old 97 | Ed 51361, 4898 |

Rev. Edison 51361 by Ernest Hare (popular).

Acc. Lou Raderman, f-1/vla-2; own h-3; Nat Shilkret, p-4; Carson Robison, g/wh-5; unknown, train-wh eff-6.
New York, NY					Wednesday, August 13, 1924

30632-1,-3	Wreck Of The Old 97 -3, 5, 6	Vi 19427
30633-2	The Prisoner's Song -2	Vi 19427
30634-1,-2	Way Out West In Kansas -1, 4	Vi unissued

Further takes of matrices 30632/33 were recorded on March 18, 1926.

Acc. prob. own h; unknown, g.
New York, NY					c. August 1924

| (1)5552-1,-2 | The Wreck Of The '97 | Ba 1531, Bell 340, 355, Clover 1694, Do 3501, DoC 21121, Em 7348, Or 375, Re 9829, Sil 2701, Cq 7067, Apex 8259, 8428, Leo 10040, Mc 22004, St 10040 |

Domino 3501 as by **Bob White**. Oriole 375 as by **Dick Morse**. Microphone 22004 as by **Fred King**.
Bell 355 exists in two versions, coupling *My Darling Nellie Gray/After The Ball Is Over* and *Wreck Of The '97/My Darling Nellie Gray*.
Matrix 5552 is titled *Wreck Of The '97* on Bell 340, 355, Domino 3501, Emerson 7348, Oriole 375, Regal 9829, or *Wreck Of The 97* on Apex 8259.
Rev. Apex 8259 by Arthur Hall (popular).

Acc. own h; unknown, bj.
New York, NY					c. August 1924

| 5590- | Go 'Long Mule | Ba 1416, Bell P-297, Do 396, DoC 21006, Or 259, Re 9711, Sil 2409, GG/Rad 2164, Pm 20347, Pu 11347, Bwy/Hudson/Lyratone/Mitchell/Triangle 11418, Pennington 1418, Apex 8249, St 8249 |

Banner 1416, Bell P-297, Regal 9711, Apex 8249 as by **Bob White**. Domino 396 as by **Fred King**. Oriole 259 as by **Dick Morse**. Silvertone 2409 as by **Harry Raymond**. Grey Gull/Radiex 2164 as by **Josephus Smith**.
Matrix 5590 is titled *Go Long Mule* on Bell P-297, Grey Gull/Radiex 2164, Broadway/Hudson/Lyratone/Mitchell/Triangle 11418, Pennington 1418.
Some issues use one or more of the controls 11076, 3019, 234, 297A-W, 597-L.
Revs: Banner 1416, Oriole 259, Apex 8249 by Vernon Dalhart (popular); Regal 9711 by Billy Jones (popular); Grey Gull/Radiex 2164 by Steve Porter (popular); Lyratone/Mitchell 11418, Pennington 1418 (and probably associated issues) by Eddy Clark (popular).

Sid Turner, v; acc. prob. own h; unknown, g.
New York, NY					c. August 1924

| 105510-1 | Wreck Of The Southern No. 97 | Pat 032068, Pe 12147, Hmg 970, Je 20050, Or 8050, Ro 5050 |
| 105511-1 | Go 'Long, Mule | Pat 032068, Pe 12147, Hmg 970, Je 20050, Or 8050, Ro 5050, PAE 10750 |

Rev. Pathé Actuelle 10750 by Vernon Dalhart (popular).

Vernon Dalhart, v; acc. Lou Raderman, f; prob. own h; Jack Shilkret, p; Carson Robison, g.
New York, NY					Friday, September 26, 1924

| 30863-3 | De Clouds Are Gwine To Roll Away | Vi 19486 |
| 30864-1,-2,-3 | Ain't You Coming Out To-night | Vi unissued |

Rev. Victor 19486 by Aileen Stanley (popular).

Acc. unknown, s; unknown, bj.
New York, NY					c. September 1924

5628-2	Oh You Can't Fool An Old Hoss Fly	Ba 1415, Do 394, Re 9714, Apex 8261, St 8261
5629	It Ain't Gonna Rain No More	Ba 1417, Do 398, Or 248, Re 9714
5638	Doodle Doo Doo	Ba 1420, Do 399, DoC 21000, Re 9718, Apex 8261, St 8261

Banner 1415, 1417, 1420, Regal 9714, 9718 as by **Bob White**. Domino 394, 398, 399 as by **Fred King**. Oriole 248 as by **Dick Morse**.

Some issues use controls, as follows: 5628 = 12014; 5629 = 3056; 5638 = 12025.
Intervening matrices are by other artists.
Revs: Banner 1415 by Arthur Fields (popular), 1417 by Billy Jones (popular).

Vernon Dalhart & Co.: Vernon Dalhart, v; acc. unknown, f; prob. own h-1; Frank Ferera, g.
   New York, NY   Thursday, October 16, 1924

9789-A,-B,-C	The Prisoner's Song	Ed 51459, 4954
9790-A,-B,-C	Way Out West In Kansas -1	Ed 51459, 4955
9791-C	Ain't You Coming Out To-night?	Ed 51430, 4951

Rev. Edison 51430 by Billy Jones & Ernest Hare (popular).

Vernon Dalhart, v; acc. unknown, f; two unknowns, cl; own h; unknown, p; Carson Robison, g.
   New York, NY   Thursday, October 23, 1924

30864-5	Ain't You Coming Out Tonight	Vi 19667

Acc. unknown, f/vla-1; own h-2; unknown, g.
   New York, NY   c. October 28, 1924

9147	The Prisoner's Song -1	Ge 3030, 5588, Ch 15073, Sil 3030, 5588, Chg 163, 319, Her 75505, Bu 8013, WS 20174
9148-A,-B	Way Out West In Kansas	Ge unissued
9149	The Wreck Of The Southern Old '97 -2	Ge 3019, 5588

Matrix 9149 was later replaced by matrix 9617 (see note on session of c. June 23, 1925).

Acc. unknown, f/vla-1; own h-2; unknown, g.
   New York, NY   c. October 1924

105625-1,-2	The Prisoner's Song -1	Pat 032085, Pe 12164, PAE 11346, GP 18537
105626-1	Way Out West In Kansas -2	Pat 032087, Pe 12166, Aj 17084, Apex 679, St 679

Pathé 032087, Perfect 12166 as by **Guy Massey**. Pathé Actuelle 11346 as by **Albert Gordon**. Grand Pree 18537 as by **Paul Adams**. Ajax 17084, Apex 679 as by **Lou Hayes**.
Matrix 105626 is titled *Way Out West In Kansas* on Ajax 17084.
Revs: Pathé 032085, Perfect 12164 by Frank Bessinger (popular); Pathé 032087, Perfect 12166, Ajax 17084, Apex 679 by Art Gillham (popular); Grand Pree 18537 unascertained.

Acc. unknown, f; own h; Frank Ferera, g.
   New York, NY   c. October 1924

5699-2	Way Out West In Kansas	Ba 1450, Re 9744, Sil 2439, DoC 21024

Revs: Regal 9744 by Billy Jones & Ernest Hare; Silvertone 2439 by Ernest Hare (both popular).

Acc. unknown, f; own h-1; Frank Ferera, g.
   New York, NY   Thursday, November 13, 1924

140136-	The Prisoner's Song	Co unissued
140137-2	Ain't-Ya Comin' Out To-night? -1	Co 257-D

   New York, NY   Tuesday, November 25, 1924

140136-6	The Prisoner's Song	Co 257-D
140137-	Ain't Ya Comin' Out Tonight	Co unissued
140150-2	De Clouds Are Gwine To Roll Away -1	Co 267-D, Ha 5107-H, Ve 7031-V, Di 6001-G

Harmony 5107-H, Diva 6001-G as by **Mack Allen**.
Matrices 140136/37 were later replaced on Columbia 257-D by matrices 141748 and 141751 (see March 3, 1926).
Matrix 140150 is titled *Clouds Are Gwine To Roll* on Harmony 5107-H.

Guy Massey, v; acc. unknown, f; own h-1; unknown, g.
   New York, NY   c. November 1924

105659-1	De Clouds Are Gwine To Roll Away	Pat 032091, Pe 12170, Apex 680, St 680, PAE 10998, GP 18461
105660-1	Ain't Ya Comin' Out To-night -1	Pat 032091, Pe 12170, PAE 10998, GP 18461

Grand Pree 18461 as by **Paul Adams**.
Revs: Apex 680, Starr 680 by Fred Thomas (popular).

Vernon Dalhart, v; acc. unknown, f; unknown, g.
   New York, NY   ?November/December 1924

2606	Ain't Ya Comin' Out Tonight	Em 10850
2607-3; 5830-1	The Prisoner's Song	Em 10850, Ba 1496, Do 3466, Or 355, Re 9795

Domino 3466 as by **Bob White**. Oriole 355 as by **Dick Morse**.
Emerson matrix 2607-3 was acquired by Plaza and assigned the matrix 5830-1, from which all issues above except Emerson 10850 are derived. Plaza matrix 5830-2, a c. January 1925 rerecording of the same title, replaces the Emerson-derived matrix on later pressings of the Plaza-group issues.

Acc. own h/jh; unknown, p; Anthony Franchini, g.
   New York, NY   Friday, December 19, 1924
   140196-2   I'm Doin' The Best I Can   Co 267-D, Ha 5107-H, Ve 7031-V, Di 6001-G
Harmony 5107-H, Diva 6001-G, and some issues of Velvet Tone 7031-V as by **Mack Allen**.
Matrix 140196 is titled *I'm Doing The Best I Can* on Harmony 5107-H.

Guy Massey, v; acc. own h; unknown, p-1; unknown, bj-2; unknown, g.
   New York, NY   Friday, January 16, 1925
   105790-1   Doin' The Best I Can -1   Pat 032104, Pe 12183
   105791-1   The Time Will Come -2   Pat 032104, Pe 12183

Vernon Dalhart, v; acc. own h; Anthony Franchini, g; unknown, u.
   New York, NY   Tuesday, January 27, 1925
   140364-2,-3   The Time Will Come   Co 299-D, Ha 5115-H, Ve 7035-V, Di 6005-G
   140365-2,-3   He Sure Can Play A Harmonica (It's The Second   Co 299-D, Ha 5115-H, Ve 7035-V, Di 6005-G
                            Best Thing That He Does)
Harmony 5115-H, Diva 6005-G as by **Mack Allen**.
Matrix 140364 is titled *Time Will Come* on Harmony 5115-H; the subtitle of matrix 140365 is omitted on that issue.

Acc. unknown, f; own h-1; unknown, g/wh-2.
   New York, NY   c. January 1925
   5830-2,-B,-C   The Prisoner's Song   Ba 1496, Bell 340, 1142, Do 3466, DoC 21121,
                                                                                  Em 3013, 7162, Or 355, Re 9795,
                                                                                  GG/Globe/Rad/Supreme 4070, Mad 1601,
                                                                                  Aj 17115, Apex 8314, 8428, Leo 10040,
                                                                                  Mc 22004, St 10040
   5831-2   Doin' The Best I Can -1, 2   Ba 1496, Do 3466, Or 355, Re 9795
Domino 3466 as by **Bob White**. Oriole 355 as by **Dick Morse**. Madison 1601 as by **James Cummings**. Microphone 22004 as by **Fred King**.
Matrix 5830-1 was assigned to an earlier recording of the same title acquired from Emerson (see session of ?November/December 1924) and also used for some of the issues above. Despite the use of 2, B, and C "takes," all inspected copies of issues above are identical. A transfer matrix or control number 43024 appears only on Emerson 3013.
Matrix 5830 is titled *Prisoner's Song* on Bell 340, Madison 1601.
The Prisoner's Song on Banner 0826, Cameo 0426, Domino 4643, Jewel 6076, Oriole 2076, Perfect 12644, Regal 10132, Romeo 1440, and Challenge 784, using matrices 5830-3 or 15830-1, is a later electrical recording, possibly from the session of September 10, 1930.
Revs: Grey Gull 4070 by Francis Herold (popular); Globe/Radiex/Supreme 4070 by Stellar Quartet (popular); Madison 1601 by Henry Gray (popular); Ajax 17115 by Bert Lewis (popular).

Acc. unknown, f; unknown, vla-1; prob. own h-2; unknown, p-3; Carson Robison, g.
   New York, NY   Wednesday, February 4, 1925
   31906-1,-2   The Chain Gang Song -2   Vi unissued
   31907-1,-2   I Will Ne'er Forget My Mother And My Home -1, 3   Vi unissued
Matrix 31906-1 was scheduled for Victor 19658 but this was never issued.

Acc. prob. Murray Kellner, f-1; own h-2; Anthony Franchini, g.
   New York, NY   Thursday, February 5, 1925
   140320-3   The Chain Gang Song -2   Co 334-D, Ha 5128-H
   140321-1,-2   Mother And Home -1   Co 334-D, Ha 5128-H
Harmony 5128-H as by **Mack Allen**.

Acc. unknown, f; unknown, g.
   New York, NY   c. February 26, 1925
   9364-A   A Boy's Best Friend Is His Mother   Ge 3030, 5675, Ch 15155, Sil 3030, Chg 161,
                                                                               322, Her 75505
   9365   In The Baggage Coach Ahead   Ge unissued

Acc. unknown, f; unknown, p-1; Carson Robison, g-2; unknown, traps-3; Ed Smalle, humming-4.
   New York, NY   Thursday, February 26, 1925
   31907-3   I Will Ne'er Forget My Mother And My Home -1,   Vi 19627
                              2, 3, 4
   32016-1,-2   In The Baggage Coach Ahead -2   Vi unissued
   32016-3,-4   In The Baggage Coach Ahead -3   Vi unissued

Bob Massey, v; acc. unknown, f-1; own h-2; unknown, g.
   New York, NY   c. February 1925
   105827-1   Mother And Home -1   Pat 032111, Pe 12190
   105828-1,-2   Chain Gang Song -2   Pat 032111, Pe 12190

Vernon Dalhart, v; acc. poss.: Murray Kellner, f; Carson Robison, g.
New York, NY   Monday, March 2, 1925

| 140407- | In The Baggage Coach Ahead | Co unissued |
| 140408- | A Boy's Best Friend Is His Mother | Co unissued |

These items were rerecorded (electrically) on April 6, 1925.

Acc. Lou Raderman, f; own h-1; Jack Shilkret, p-2; Carson Robison, h-3/g; May Singhi Breen, u; Joe Green, traps-4.
New York, NY   Wednesday, March 4, 1925

32053-4	The Time Will Come -1	Vi 19637
32054-1,-2,-3	The Runaway Train -2, 4	Vi unissued
32055-2	He Sure Can Play The Harmonica -3	Vi 19667

Matrix 32054-2 was scheduled for Victor 19658 but this was never issued.
Rev. Victor 19637 by Gene Austin & Carson Robison (popular).

Acc. unknown, f; unknown, g.
New York, NY   c. March 5, 1925

| 9365-A | In The Baggage Coach Ahead | Ge 3019, 5675, Ch 15155, Chg 162, 311, Her 75503 |

Tobe Little, v; acc. unknown, f-1; own h-2; unknown, g.
New York, NY   c. first week of March 1925

| 73221-B | The Prisoner's Song -1 | OK 40328 |
| 73222-A | Chain Gang Song -2 | OK 40328 |

Vernon Dalhart, v; acc. unknown, f-1; own h; unknown, p-2; Carson Robison, g.
New York, NY   Monday, March 16 or Tuesday, March 17, 1925

10257-A	The Chain Gang Song	Ed 51597, 5176
10258-B,-C	The Time Will Come -1	Ed 51541, 5015
10259-A,-B,-C	Doin' The Best I Can -1, 2	Ed 51541, 5016

Acc. unknown, f; prob. Carson Robison, g; Elliott Shaw, Franklyn Baur, Wilfred Glenn, v trio.
New York, NY   Thursday, March 19, 1925

| 32226-3 | In The Baggage Coach Ahead | Vi 19627 |

Bob Massey, v; acc. unknown, f; unknown, g.
New York, NY   c. March 1925

| 105930-1 | Baggage Coach Ahead | Pat 032120, Pe 12199 |
| 105931-1 | A Boy's Best Friend Is His Mother | Pat 032120, Pe 12199, Ca 703 |

Some issues of Cameo 703 use matrix 105931; others use Cameo matrix 1386 (see below).

Vernon Dalhart, v; acc. prob.: Murray Kellner, f; unknown, g.
New York, NY   c. March 1925

| 1385-A,-B | The Prisoner's Song | Ca 703, Lin 2335, Ro 241, Tremont 0536 |
| 1386-A,-C | A Boy's Best Friend Is His Mother | Ca 703, Lin 2335, Tremont 0536 |

Tremont 0536 as by **Vernon Dell**. Some issues of Cameo 703 use Pathé matrix 105931 (see above) rather than Cameo matrix 1386. Rev. Romeo 241 by Buddy Gravelle (popular).

Acc. own h; unknown, bj-md-1; unknown, bj-2; unknown, g-3/wh-4.
New York, NY   Wednesday, April 1, 1925

5900-1,-2	He Sure Can Play The Harmonica -3	Ba 1611, Do 3582, Re 9914, Sil 2744, Cq 7066, Apex 8339, St 10008, Leo 10008
5911-1,-2	The Chain Gang Song -3	Ba 1531, Do 3501, Or 421, Re 9829, Apex 8358, Mc 22021, St 10025, Leo 10025
5912-1,-2	There's One Born Every Minute -1, 3, 4	Ba 1529, Do 3496, Re 9826, Apex 8358, St 10026, Leo 10026
5913-2	Christofo Colombo -1, 3, 4	Ba 1529, Do 3498, Or 428, Re 9826, Sil 2536
5937-	Time Will Come -3	Ba 1560, Do 3532, Re 9860
5938-1,-3	Dear, Oh Dear -2	Ba 1560, Do 3532, Or 375, Re 9860, Apex 8380, Leo 10042, Mc 22038, St 10042

Banner 1560, Dominos, Regal 9860 as by **Bob White**. Oriole 375, 421, 428 as by **Dick Morse**.
Matrix 5938 is titled *Dear, Oh, Dear* on Oriole 375.
Revs: Silvertone 2536 by Sidney Mitchell (popular); Leonora 10026, Starr 10026 by Arthur Hall & John Ryan (popular); other Leonora and Starr issues unknown.

Acc. own h; unknown, bj; Carson Robison, g; unknown, eff-1.
New York, NY   Saturday, April 4, 1925

| 140496-3 | Dear, Oh Dear | Co 351-D |
| 140497-3 | The Runaway Train -1 | Co 351-D |

Acc. prob.: Murray Kellner, f; Carson Robison, g.
New York, NY   Monday, April 6, 1925

| 140407-4 | In The Baggage Coach Ahead | Co 15028-D |
| 140408-3 | A Boy's Best Friend Is His Mother | Co 15028-D, ReE G8571 |

Regal G8571 as by **Herbert Vernon**.

Vernon Dalhart & Co.: Vernon Dalhart, v; acc. prob.: Murray Kellner, f; Carson Robison, g.
New York, NY   Monday, April 13, 1925

| 10315-A,-C | In The Baggage Coach Ahead | Ed 51557, 5011 |

Vernon Dalhart, v; acc. unknown, f-1; own h-2; prob. Carson Robison, g; unknown, eff-3.
New York, NY   c. April 22-24, 1925

| 9473-A | Mother And Home -1 | Ge 3051, Sil 4018, Chg 163, Her 75511 |
| 9474-A | The Runaway Train -2, 3 | Ge 3051, Ch 15017, Sil 4018, Chg 162, 311, Her 75511 |

The plain take of matrix 9473 was logged as *I Will Never Forget My Mother And My Home*.

Vernon Dalhart & Co.: Vernon Dalhart, v; acc. prob. Murray Kellner, f; own h-1; prob. Carson Robison, g.
New York, NY   Thursday, April 30, 1925

| 10343-A,-B,-C | Many, Many Years Ago | Ed 51557, 5013 |
| 10344-A | The Runaway Train -1 | Ed 51584, 5028 |

Vernon Dalhart, v; acc. unknown, f; prob. Carson Robison, g.
New York, NY   c. April 1925

5971-1,-2	In The Baggage Coach Ahead	Ba 1549, Bell 348, Clover 1694, Do 3519, DoC 21416, 181104, Em 7348, Or 421, Re 9847, Sil 2701, Cq 7067, Apex 8345, CrC/Roy 81104, Stg 281104, MeC/Min M-902, Fo 9847
5972-1	A Boy's Best Friend Is His Mother	Ba 1549, Do 3519, Or 490, Re 9847, Sil 2683, Cq 7068, Apex 8345
5973-	My Mother's Humming Lullaby	Re 9859

Dominos (except some issues of 3519) as by **Bob White**. Oriole 421 as by **Dick Morse**, 490 as by **Frank Evans**.
Matrix 5972 is titled *A Boy's Best Friend* on Conqueror 7068, Silvertone 2683.
In The Baggage Coach Ahead on Banner 0826, Cameo 0426, Domino 4643, Jewel 6076, Lincoln 1520, Oriole 2076, Perfect 12644, Regal 10132, Romeo 1440, and Challenge 784, using matrix 15971-2 or -3, is a later electrical recording, possibly from the session of September 10, 1930.

Acc. Carson Robison, h/g.
New York, NY   Tuesday, May 12, 1925

| 31906-3 | The Chain Gang Song | Vi 19684, HMV BD379, Zo/RZAu EE35 |

Rev. HMV BD379 by Harry "Mac" McClintock.

Acc. unknown, f; Carson Robison, g.
New York, NY   Wednesday, May 13, 1925

| 140595-3 | The Picture That Is Turned Toward The Wall | Co 15030-D, Re/RZAu G20724 |
| 140596-2 | After The Ball | Co 15030-D, ReE G8571 |

Regal G8571 as by **Herbert Vernon**.

Acc. own h; Carson Robison, g; Chris Chapman, wh-1/anvil eff-2.
New York, NY   Thursday, May 14, 1925

| 15723/24/25 | The Runaway Train -1 | Br unissued? |
| 15726/27/28 | The Chain Gang Song -2 | Br unissued? |

Acc. Lou Raderman, f-1/vla-2; Carson Robison, h-3/g; Franklyn Baur, Wilfred Glenn, Elliott Shaw, v trio-4; unknown, eff-5.
New York, NY   Tuesday, May 19, 1925

32054-6	The Runaway Train -1, 3, 5	Vi 19684, ZoAu EE35
32706-1,-2	The Boston Burglar -1, 3	Vi unissued
32707-2	Many, Many Years Ago -2, 4	Vi 19681
32708-1	A Boy's Best Friend Is His Mother -1, 4	Vi 19681, 24281, ZoSA 4251

Acc. B. Altschuler, vla-1; own h-2; Carson Robison, g; Chris Chapman, wh-3/bells-3.
New York, NY   Thursday, May 21, 1925

E-15765*/66/67	Prisoner's Song -1	Br 2900, BrAu 2900, Spt S2000
E-15768*/69	The Letter Edged In Black -1	Br 2900, BrAu 2900, 2911, Spt S2000, Au A22028
E-15770/71*	The Runaway Train -2, 3	Br 2911, BrE 2911, BrA 2900, Spt S2004
E-15772*/73	Chain Gang Song -2, 3	Br 2911, BrE 2911, BrAu 2911, Spt S2006

Australian Brunswick 2900 exists in two versions, coupling *The Prisoner's Song/The Runaway Train* and *The Prisoner's Song/The Letter Edged In Black*.
Rev. Aurora A22028 by Frank & James McCravy.

Al Craver, v; acc. own h; Carson Robison, g.
New York, NY   Wednesday, May 27, 1925
   140627-3   The Death Of Floyd Collins   Co 15031-D
   140628-1   Little Mary Phagan   Co 15031-D

Vernon Dalhart, v; acc. unknown, vla-1; own h-2; prob. Carson Robison, g; unknown, eff-3.
New York, NY   Friday, May 29, 1925
   E-15910*/11   Rovin' Gambler -1, 2, 3   Br 2923, Spt S2014
   E-15912/13/14 The New River Train -1   Br unissued
   E-15915/16   (Who's It Who Loves You) Who's It, Huh? -2   Br unissued
   E-15917/18   The Sneeze Song – If You'll Ker-Ker-Chooey Me Br unissued
                        (Then I'll Ker-Chooey You) -2

Guy Massey, v; acc. own or Carson Robison, h; Carson Robison, g; unknown, eff-1.
New York, NY   c. May 1925
   106049-1   Dear, Oh! Dear   Pat 032128, Pe 12207
   106050-1   The Runaway Train -1   Pat 032128, Pe 12207, GP 18607

Grand Pree 18607 as by **David Adams**.

Vernon Dalhart, v; acc. poss. own h; Carson Robison, g/wh-1.
New York, NY   Thursday, June 4, 1925
   140646-2   The Sinking Of The Titanic   Co 15032-D
   140647-1   New River Train -1   Co 15032-D

Al Craver, v; acc. own h/jh; Carson Robison, g.
New York, NY   Saturday, June 6, 1925
   140656-2   The Rovin' Gambler   Co 15034-D

Vernon Dalhart & Co.: Vernon Dalhart, v; acc. prob. Murray Kellner, f; own h/jh-1; Carson Robison, g.
New York, NY   Tuesday, June 9, 1925
   10424-A   Rovin' Gambler -1   Ed 51584, 5027
   10425   New River Train   Ed 51597, 5032

Vernon Dalhart, v; acc. own h; Carson Robison, g/wh-1.
New York, NY   Friday, June 12, 1925
   32895-1,-2,-3,-4 Who's It Who Loves You, Who's It, Huh?   Vi unissued
   32896-1,-2,-3   The Sneeze Song   Vi unissued
   33007-1   Dear Oh Dear -1   Vi 19717

Acc. unknown, f; prob. Carson Robison, g.
New York, NY   Monday, June 15, 1925
   6051-3,-4   After The Ball   Ba 1578, Bell 355, 1162, Do 3549, DoC 21008,
                                                                         Em 7162, Or 658, Re 9879, Apex 8395,
                                                                         St 10057
   6052-2,-3   In A Mansion Of Aching Hearts   Ba 1578, Do 3549, Re 9879

Oriole 658 as by **Dick Morse**.
Bell 355 exists in two versions, coupling *My Darling Nellie Gray/After The Ball Is Over* and *Wreck Of The '97/My Darling Nellie Gray*. Matrix 6051 is titled *After The Ball Is Over* on Bell 355, 1162, Emerson 7162.

Acc. own h/jh-1; unknown, g; unknown, eff-2.
New York, NY   Tuesday, June 16, 1925
   6053-1,-3   The Runaway Train -2   Ba 1580, Do 3550, DoC 21416, Or 454, Re 9878,
                                                                         Apex 8380, Leo 10041, Mc 22021, St 10041
   6054-4   Casey Jones -1   Ba 1580, Do 3550, Or 454, Re 9878

Domino 3550 as by **Bob White**. Oriole 454 as by **Dick Morse**.
Revs: Leonora 10041, Starr 10041 by Happiness Boys (popular).

Acc. Ed Thiele, f-1; Bert Borodkin, vla-2; own h-3; Carson Robison, g; Chris Chapman, wh eff-4.
New York, NY   Thursday, June 18, 1925
   E-15999/6000   The New River Train -2, 3, 4   Br unissued
   E-16001/02   Many Many Years Ago -1   Br unissued
   E-16003/04   After The Ball -1   Br unissued
   E-16005/06   Boston Burglar -3   Br unissued

Al Craver, v; acc. own h/jh; Carson Robison, g.
New York, NY   Monday, June 22, 1925
   140708-1   The Wreck Of The 1256 (On The Main Line Of Co 15034-D
                        The C. & O.)

Vernon Dalhart, v; acc. unknown, f; own h-1; prob. Carson Robison, g; unknown, train-wh eff-2.
New York, NY   c. June 23-27, 1925

9615	The New River Train -1	Ge 3084, Sil 3084, Chg 165, 321, Her 75506
9616	The Little Rosewood Casket	Ge 3084, Ch 20323, Sil 3084, Chg 164, 322, Her 75506, Apex 386, CrC/MeC 81032, DoC 21152, St 9632, Stg 281032
9617	The Wreck Of The Southern Old '97 -1, 2	Ge 3019, 5588, Ch 15121, Sil 5588, Chg 161, 320, Her 75503, Bu 8013

Some pressings of Apex 386 and possibly other Canadian issues replace Gennett matrix 9616 with Plaza matrix 7398 (= Pathé matrix 106332) (see c. November 1925 session).

Matrix 9617 replaced matrix 9149 (see c. October 28, 1924 session) and was itself replaced by matrix GEX-1254-A (see c. May 22, 1928 session).

Acc. poss. Ed Thiele, f-1; poss. Bert Borodkin, vla-2; own h-3; Carson Robison, g; Chris Chapman, wh eff-4.
New York, NY   Wednesday, June 24, 1925

E-16048/49/50	New River Train -2, 3, 4	Br 2923
E-16051/52	The Dying Girl's Message -1, 2	Br 2927, Spt S2010
E-16053/54	Many Times I've Wandered -1, 2	Br 2927
E-16055*/56; E-1977/78W	Boston Burglar -3	Br 2942, Vo 15216, 5085, Spt S2005, Au A22029

Acc. own h/jh-1; Carson Robison, g.
New York, NY   Thursday, June 25, 1925

32895-5	Who's It, Who Loves You – Who's It, Huh?	Vi 19717
33043-2	Casey Jones -1	Vi 20502, MW M-8246, ZoAu EE47, Twin FT1786
	Strummin' My Blues Away	Vi unissued

Strummin' My Blues Away was recorded on approval and not assigned a matrix.
Matrix 33043 is titled *Brave Engineer* on Montgomery Ward M-8246.
Revs: Victor 20502, Twin FT1786 by Ernest Rogers; Zonophone EE47 by Billy Murray (popular).

Acc. poss. Ed Thiele, f-1; poss. Bert Borodkin, vla-2; own h-3, Carson Robison, g.
New York, NY   Monday, June 29, 1925

E-16064/65*/66	Wild And Reckless Hobo -3	Br 2942, Spt S2005, Au A22029
E-16067/68/69	Many, Many Years Ago -1, 2	Br 2924
E-16070/71/72	The Picture That Is Turned Toward The Wall -1	Br unissued?
E-16073/74*	After The Ball -1, 2	Br 2924, Au A22018

Rev. Aurora A22018 by Richard Brooks & Reuben Puckett.

Acc. unknown, f; unknown, g.
New York, NY   ?c. June 1925

	I'll Ne'er Forget My Mother And My Home	Bell 348, Em 7374
	My Darling Nellie Gray	Bell 355, Em 7355
	Just Break The News To Mother	Bell 364

Most Bell issues by Dalhart appear to have been leased from Plaza, but no Plaza recordings of these titles by Dalhart have been traced. The suggested date is very speculative, and the items may not have been recorded at one session. Bell 355 exists in two versions, coupling *My Darling Nellie Gray/After The Ball Is Over* and *Wreck Of The '97/My Darling Nellie Gray*.

Acc. unknown.
New York, NY   Wednesday, July 1, 1925

| 6051- | After The Ball Is Over | Pl unissued |

Acc. poss.: Murray Kellner, f; Carson Robison, g.
New York, NY   Wednesday, July 8, 1925

6054-	Casey Jones	Pl unissued
6090-	Meet Me Tonight In Dreamland	Pl unissued
6091-2	Many Many Years Ago	Ba 1594, Do 3565, Re 9895

Acc. poss. Murray Kellner, f-1; prob. own h-2; prob. Carson Robison, g.
New York, NY   c. July 9, 1925

| 1519-C | The Chain Gang Song -2 | Ca 766, Lin 2374, Ro 329 |
| 1520-B | In The Baggage Coach Ahead -1 | Ca 766, Lin 2374, Ro 330 |

Acc. poss. Murray Kellner, f; Carson Robison, g.
New York, NY   Friday, July 10, 1925

| 140679-3 | The Santa Barbara Earthquake | Co 15037-D |
| 140680-1 | The John T. Scopes Trial | Co 15037-D |

Vernon Dalhart & Company: Vernon Dalhart, v; acc. poss.: Murray Kellner, f; Carson Robison, g.
New York, NY   Thursday, July 16, 1925

| 10493-A,-B | After The Ball | Ed 51610, 5144 |
| 10494-B | The Picture That Is Turned Toward The Wall | Ed 51607, 5147 |

Acc. prob. own h; unknown, p-1; prob. Carson Robison, g.
   New York, NY   Friday, July 17, 1925

| 10503-B | Dear, Oh Dear -1 | Ed 51605 |
| 10504-A,-B,-C | I Wish I Was A Single Girl Again | Ed 51610, 5154 |

Vernon Dalhart, v; acc. prob. own h; Carson Robison, g.
   New York, NY   c. July 18-22, 1925

| 9669 | I Wish I Was A Single Girl Again | Ge 3107, Ch 15035, Her 75504 |
| 9670 | The Sneezing Song | Ge 3107 |

Revs: Champion 15035 by Jack Kaufman (popular); Herwin 75504 by David Miller.

Vernon Dalhart & Company: Vernon Dalhart, v; acc. prob. Murray Kellner, f; own h-1/jh-2; prob. Carson Robison, g.
   New York, NY   Friday, July 24, 1925

| 10516-C | Casey Jones -1, 2 | Ed 51611, 5599 |
| 10517-B,-C | The Little Rosewood Casket | Ed 51607, 5062 |

Rev. Edison 51611 by Gene Austin (popular).

Vernon Dalhart, v; acc. poss. Murray Kellner, f; own h; Carson Robison, g.
   New York, NY   Thursday, July 30, 1925

| 140795-2 | The Sidewalks Of New York (East Side, West Side) | Co 437-D, 15256-D |
| 140796-1 | The Girl I Left Behind Me | Co 437-D |

Columbia 15256-D as by **Al Craver**. The subtitle of matrix 140795 is omitted on that issue.
Rev. Columbia 15256-D by Carolina Night Hawks.

Acc. unknown, f; own h-1/jh-2; prob. Carson Robison, g/wh-3.
   New York, NY   c. July 1925

106127-3,-4,-5	Many Many Years Ago	Pat 32144, Pe 12223
106128-2,-4	The New River Train -1, 3	Pat 032133, Pe 12212
106129-2,-3	The Rovin' Gambler -1, 2	Pat 032133, Pe 12212, PAE 11346

Pathé 032133, Perfect 12212 as by **Guy Massey**. Pathé Actuelle 11346 as by **Albert Gordon**.

Vernon Dalhart & Company: Vernon Dalhart, v; acc. poss. Murray Kellner, f; own h; prob. Carson Robison, g.
   New York, NY   Monday, August 3, 1925

10539-C	She's Comin' 'Round The Mountain	Ed 51608, 5052
10540-A	The Boston Burglar	Ed 51608, 5129
10541-B,-C	The Sneeze Song (If You'll Ker-Ker-Chooey Me)	Ed 51605

Matrix 10541 was scheduled for Edison 5061 but this was never issued.

Vernon Dalhart, v; acc. unknown, f; own h-1; poss. Carson Robison, g.
   New York, NY   Saturday, August 8, 1925

| 6124 | Blue Ridge Mountain Blues -1 | Ba 1611, Do 3582, Or 486, 513, Re 9914, Pm 3045, Bwy 8061, Her 75501 |
| 6125-1,-2 | Lightning Express | Ba 1594, Do 3565, DoC 181178, 21088, Or 473, Re 9895, Apex 8395, CrC/Roy 81178, Mc 22038, St 10057 |

Oriole 473, 486 as by **Frank Evans**. Broadway 8061 as by **Cramer Brothers**.
Some issues of Herwin 75501 use Gennett matrix 9703-A instead of Plaza matrix 6124.
Some issues of matrix 6124 use the controls 775 or 809.

Acc. poss.: Murray Kellner, f; Carson Robison, g.
   New York, NY   Monday, August 10, 1925

| 140831-3 | William Jennings Bryan's Last Fight | Co 15039-D |
| 140832-1 | Many, Many, Years Ago | Co 15039-D |

Acc. unknown, f-1; unknown, oboe-2; own or Carson Robison, h-3; own jh-4; Carson Robison, g.
   New York, NY   Wednesday, August 26, 1925

33347-1	The Convict And The Rose -1, 2	Vi 19770, Zo/RZAu EE45, ZoSA 4269
33348-2	Little Rosewood Casket -1, 2	Vi 19770, MW MW-4338, ZoSA 4269
33349-2	Blue Ridge Mountain Blues -1, 3	Vi 19811, MW M-8061
33350-1	She's Comin' 'Round The Mountain -3, 4	Vi 19811, MW M-8148

Revs: Montgomery Ward M-4338 by Johnny Marvin, M-8148 by Hiter Colvin.

Acc. unknown, f; own h-1; poss. Carson Robison, g.
   New York, NY   c. August 28-31, 1925

| 9702-A | The Lightning Express | Ge 3129, Ch 15017, Sil 3129, Chg 165, 320, Her 75501 |
| 9703-A | Blue Ridge Mountain Blues -1 | Ge 3129, Sil 3129, Chg 164, 314, Her 75501 |

Some issues of Herwin 75501 use Plaza matrix 6124 instead of Gennett matrix 9703-A, and replace Dalhart's matrix 9702-A with the Paramount matrix 2176 of *The Lightning Express* by Arthur Tanner.

Acc. poss. Murray Kellner, f; own h-1; poss. Carson Robison, g; unknown, train eff-2.
  New York, NY   August/September 1925
    1597-B   The Runaway Train -1, 2   ?Ca 814, Lin 2431
    1598-A   Just Tell Them That You Saw Me   Ca 805, Lin 2412
    1599-A   The John T. Scopes Case   Ca 792, Lin 2397
    1600-A   Bryan's Last Fight   Ca 792, Lin 2397
  Revs: Cameo 805, Lincoln 2412 by Gloria Geer (popular); ?Cameo 814, Lincoln 2431 by Al Bernard (popular).

Vernon Dalhart & Company: Vernon Dalhart, v; acc. poss.: Murray Kellner, f; Carson Robison, g.
  New York, NY   Wednesday, September 2, 1925
    10555-B   The John T. Scopes Trial (The Old Religion's Better   Ed 51609, 5059
                    After All)
    10556-A,-B,-C The Death Of Floyd Collins   Ed 51609, 5049

Vernon Dalhart, v; acc. Lou Raderman, f-1/vla; own h-2; Carson Robison, g; Vernon Dalhart, Carson Robison, wh duet-3; unknown, train-wh eff-4.
  New York, NY   Wednesday, September 9, 1925
    33372-2   The Wreck Of The 1256 -2, 3, 4   Vi 19812
    33373-3   Wreck Of The Shenandoah -1   Vi 19779
    33374-2,-3   Death Of Floyd Collins -2   Vi 19779, 19821
    33375-2   Mother's Grave   Vi 19812
  Victor 19779 was withdrawn shortly after release.

Jep Fuller, v; acc. Ted Thiele, f; Carson Robison, g.
  New York, NY   Thursday, September 10, 1925
    1322/23/24W   The Wreck Of The Shenandoah   Vo 15125, 5074
    1325/26/27W   The Santa Barbara Earthquake   Vo 15125, 5074

Vernon Dalhart, v; acc. unknown, f; prob. Carson Robison, g.
  New York, NY   c. September 11-14, 1925
    9714   The John T. Scopes Trial   Ge 3134, Ch 15025, Sil 3134, Chg 166
    9715   Bryan's Last Fight   Ge 3134, Ch 15025, Sil 3134, Chg 166
    9716   Just Tell Them That You Saw Me   Ge 3143, Ch 20323, Sil 4012, Chg 167, 310,
                                                             Her 75507
    9717-A   Jesse James   Ge 3143, Sil 4012, Chg 503, Her 75507

Acc. poss. Murray Kellner, f; own h-1; prob. Carson Robison, g.
  New York, NY   Friday, September 11, 1925
    140929-1,-2   The Wreck Of The Shenandoah   Co 15041-D
    140930-1   Stone Mountain Memorial   Co 15041-D
    140931-2   Frank Dupree -1   Co 15042-D
    140932-1   Mother's Grave   Co 15048-D, Re/RZAu G20724

Acc. unknown, f; own h; unknown, g.
  New York, NY   c. September 12, 1925
    6193-1,-2   The Death Of Floyd Collins   Ba 1613, Bell 364, Do 3584, DoC 21142, 21487,
                                                             Em 7364, Or 490, Re 9916, Sil 2683,
                                                             Cq 7068, Pm 3012, Bwy 8047, Apex 8466,
                                                             Leo 10131, St 10131
Takes 1 and 2 of matrix 6193 are different; the latter was used on Oriole 490 and possibly other issues. The matrix is shown on some issues as 16193 or 36193.
Oriole 490 as by **Frank Evans**.
Matrix 6193 is titled *Death Of Floyd Collins* on Bell 364.
The control 3037 is believed to have been assigned only to Bell 364 and Emerson 7364. Some other issues use the control 614.
Revs: Banner 1613, Regal 9916, and possibly other issues by Billy Burton (popular).

Tobe Little, v; acc. unknown, f; own h-1/jh-2; prob. Carson Robison, g.
  New York, NY   Monday, September 14, 1925
    73606-B   The Fate Of The Shenandoah -1   OK 40459
    73607-B   The Rescue Of The PN-9   OK 40460
    73608-A   The Wreck Of The Shenandoah   OK 40460
    73609-B   The Picture Turned To The Wall   OK 40459
    73610-D   Stone Mountain Memorial   OK 40479
    73611-D,-E   Rovin' Gambler -1, 2   OK 40479

Vernon Dalhart & Company: Vernon Dalhart, v; acc. poss. Murray Kellner, f; own h-1/jh-2; prob. Carson Robison, g.
  New York, NY   Tuesday, September 15, 1925
    10572-A,-B,-C Wreck Of The 1256 -1, 2   Ed 51620, 5127
    10573-C,-F,-H Wreck Of The Shenandoah   Ed 51620, 5078

Vernon Dalhart, v; acc. own h/jh-1; Carson Robison, g.
New York, NY   Saturday, September 19, 1925

140966-2	The Curse Of An Aching Heart	Co 15048-D, ReAu G20771
140967-2	Sydney Allen	Co 15042-D
141018-1	Little Birdie -1	Co 15044-D
141019-	When I'm With You	Co unissued

Columbia 15044-D as by **Al Craver**. Intervening matrices are by other artists.
Rev. Regal G20771 by Michael Ahern (popular).

Guy Massey, v; acc. unknown, f; own h-1/jh-2; poss. Carson Robison, g.
New York, NY   c. September 21, 1925

| 106269-2 | Wreck Of The 12:56 On The C. And O. -1, 2 | Pat 32139, Pe 12218 |
| 106270-2 | Wreck Of The Shenandoah | Pat 32139, Pe 12218 |

Vernon Dalhart & Company: Vernon Dalhart, v; acc. poss.: Murray Kellner, f; Carson Robison, g.
New York, NY   Tuesday, September 22, 1925

| 10585-B,-C | Jesse James | Ed 51621, 5057 |
| 10586-B | The Ship That Never Returned | Ed 51621, 5175 |

Tobe Little, v; acc. unknown, f; own h-1; Carson Robison, g/bird eff-2.
New York, NY   Thursday, October 1, 1925

| 73668-B | Dreams Of The Southland -2 | OK 40488 |
| 73669-B | Little Rosewood Casket -1 | OK 40488, PaAu A3489, A3528 |

Parlophone A3489, A3528 as by **Paul Taylor**.
Rev. Parlophone A3528 by Morgan Denmon.

Vernon Dalhart, v; acc. Benny Posner, f; Carson Robison, g/bird eff-1.
New York, NY   Monday, October 5, 1925

33286-1,-2,-3	Goodness Me! Holy Gee!	Vi unissued
33287-2	Stone Mountain Memorial	Vi 19810
33288-2	Dreams Of The Southland -1	Vi 19810
33289-1,-2,-3	I'm Satisfied With You	Vi unissued

Acc. poss. Murray Kellner, f; own h-1; Carson Robison, g.
New York, NY   Tuesday, October 7, 1925

1650-C	The Convict And The Rose	Ca 810, Lin 2427, Ro 329, Electron 5008, 5074, PmAu 2511
1651-C	Mother's Grave	Ca 812, Lin 2429, Ro 333
1652-B	The Wreck Of The Shenandoah	Ca 809, Lin 2426, Ro 331
1653-B	Little Mary Phagan -1	Ca 811, Lin 2428, Ro 332
1654-B	The Letter Edged In Black -1	Ca 809, Lin 2426, Ro 331

Revs: Electron 5008, 5074 by Walter Remick (popular); Paramount 2511 by The Crooning Cavaliers (popular).

Acc. unknown, f; own h; poss. Carson Robison, g.
New York, NY   Friday, October 9, 1925

73696-B	The Dream Of The Miner's Child	OK 40498, PaAu A3489
73697-B	The Sailor Boy's Farewell	OK 40487
73698-B	When The Whole World Turns You Down (Go Back To Your Mother And Home)	OK 40487

Parlophone A3489 as by **Paul Taylor**. Matrix 73696 is titled *Dream Of The Miner's Child* on that issue.

Al Craver, v; acc. own h; Carson Robison, g.
New York, NY   Friday, October 9, 1925

| 141099-2 | Sinking Of The Submarine S-51 | Co 15044-D |

Vernon Dalhart, v; acc. poss. Murray Kellner, f; poss. Del Staigers, c-1; own h-2/jh-3; prob. Carson Robison, g.
New York, NY   c. October 13, 1925

9766	The Convict And The Rose	Ge 3168
9767-A-	The Wreck of "1256" - 1, 2, 3	Ge 3158, Sil 3812, Chg 231, 502, Bu 8012
9768	The Wreck Of The Shenandoah	Ge 3158, Ch 15048, Sil 3812, Chg 506

Matrix 9767 is titled *The Wreck Of The "256"* on Buddy 8012.
Rev. some issues of Champion 15048 by George Ake (see note to c. November 24, 1925 session).

Vernon Dalhart & Company: Vernon Dalhart, v; acc. poss.: Murray Kellner, f; Carson Robison, g.
New York, NY   Tuesday, October 13, 1925

| 10631-A | Stone Mountain Memorial | Ed 51637, 5080 |
| 10632-A,-C | Dreams Of The Southland | Ed 51637 |

Vernon Dalhart, v; acc. poss.: own h; Carson Robison, g.
New York, NY   Wednesday, October 14, 1925

| 106319-3 | The Death Of Floyd Collins | Pat 32144, Pe 12223 |

Vernon Dalhart-1/**Al Craver**-2, v; acc. poss. Murray Kellner, f; Del Staigers, c-3; own h-4; Carson Robison, g.
New York, NY   Saturday, October 17, 1925

141149-1	The Fatal Wedding -1	Co 15051-D, CoAu 01890
141150-1	The Dying Girl's Message -1, 4	Co 15051-D, CoAu 01890
141151-1	The Convict And The Rose -2, 3	Co 15046-D
141152-1,-2	The Dream Of The Miner's Child -2, 3, 4	Co 15046-D

Vernon Dalhart, v; acc. Murray Kellner, f; own h; Carson Robison, g.
New York, NY   Tuesday, October 20, 1925

33587-3	Dream Of A Miner's Child	Vi 19821, Zo/RZAu EE45

Acc. unknown, f; prob. Del Staigers, c-1; own h-2; prob. Carson Robison, g/wh-3.
New York, NY   Thursday, October 22, 1925

106332-1	Little Rosewood Casket -2	Ba 6044, Do 0199, 0234, Or 978, Pat 32149, Pe 12228, Re 8431, 8551, Cq 7175, 7750, Apex 386
106333-2	The Convict And The Rose -1	Pat 32150, Pe 12229
106334-1	The Dream Of The Miner's Child -2, 3	Pat 32150, Pe 12229
106335-1	Mother's Grave -1	Pat 32149, Pe 12228
106336-1	Dreams Of The Southland -3	Pat 32153, Pe 12232
106337-2	Stone Mountain Memorial	Pat 32153, Pe 12232

Oriole 978 as by **Frank Evans**.
Matrix 106332 was assigned, in c. June 1927, the Plaza matrix 7398, from which all the issues shown are derived except Pathé 32149, Perfect 12228. Some issues of matrix 106332 use the control 1012.
Some issues of Apex 386 use instead Gennett matrix 9616 (see c. June 23–27, 1925).
Revs: Banner 6044, Oriole 978 by Harold Lambert (popular).

Acc. unknown, f; poss. Del Staigers, c-1; poss. own h-2; poss. Carson Robison, g.
New York, NY   Friday, October 23, 1925

6253-2,-3	The Wreck Of The Shenandoah	Ba 1652, Bell 374, Do 3623, Em 7364, Or 511, Re 9958
6254-1,-2	Mother's Grave -1	Ba 1652, Bell 374, Do 3623, Em 7374, Or 545, Re 9958, Sil 2704, Cq 7070, Pm 33176, Pu 9176
6255-2	The Convict And The Rose -1	Ba 1653, Do 3624, Re 9959, Sil 2706, Chg 560, Cq 7069, Apex 8417, Leo 10088, St 10088
6256-2	The Letter Edged In Black -2	Ba 1653, Bell 396, Do 3624, DoC 21131, Em 7355, Or 511, Re 9959, Sil 2705, Chg 560, Cq 7074, Pm 3012, Bwy 8048, Her 75516, Apex 8417, CrC 81060, Leo 10088, Mc 22073, St 10088

Oriole 511 as by **Dick Morse**, 545 as by **Frank Evans**.
Paramount 33176 and Puritan 9176 issues of matrix 6254 show the Paramount matrix and control numbers 2581 and 330.
Other issues of matrix 6254 use the control 126; some issues of matrix 6256 use the control 615.
Some issues of Herwin 75516 use Gennett matrix 9898 (see c. December 15–18, 1925).
Revs: Bell 396 by Henry Irving (popular); Broadway 8048 by Kentucky Thorobreds; Crown 81060 by Frank Luther.

Acc. poss. Murray Kellner, f; own h-1; Carson Robison, g/wh-2; unknown, train eff-3.
New York, NY   Monday, October 26, 1925

1674-B	Little Rosewood Casket	Ca 811, Lin 2428, Ro 333
1675-A,-B	The Dream Of The Miner's Child -1	Ca 812, Lin 2429, Ro 332
1676-B	The Runaway Train -1, 3	Ca 814, Lin 2431
1677-B	Rovin' Gambler -1, 2	Ca 810, Lin 2427, Ro 330
1678-C	Stone Mountain Memorial	Ca 813, Lin 2430
1679-C	Sidney Allen -1	Ca 813, Lin 2430

Revs: Cameo 814, Lincoln 2431 by Al Bernard (popular).

Vernon Dalhart & Company: Vernon Dalhart, v; acc. poss.: Murray Kellner, f; Carson Robison, g.
New York, NY   Tuesday, October 27, 1925

10654	Convict And The Rose	Ed 51643, 5081
10655	Mother's Grave	Ed 51643, 5096

Vernon Dalhart, v; acc. unknown, f; unknown, vla-1; prob. Carson Robison, g.
New York, NY   c. October 27, 1925

73740-A	Mother's Grave -1	OK 40498, PaAu A2884
73741-A	The Convict And The Rose	OK 40506, PaAu A2884

Parlophone A2884 as by **Frank Hutchinson**.

Acc. Murray Kellner, f; own h-1; Carson Robison, g.
New York, NY   Friday, October 30, 1925
    33829-3   Zeb Turney's Gal -1   Vi 19867
    33830-3   The Letter Edged In Black -1   Vi 19837, MW M-8048, Zo/RZAu EE36
    33831-2   The Lightning Express   Vi 19837, Zo/RZAu EE36, ZoSA 4251
Rev. Montgomery Ward M-8048 by Charles Harrison (popular).

Al Craver, v; acc. prob. Murray Kellner, f; own h; Carson Robison, g.
New York, NY   Wednesday, November 4, 1925
    141239-1   The Letter Edged In Black   Co 15049-D
    141240-3   Zeb Turney's Gal   Co 15049-D

Vernon Dalhart & Company: Vernon Dalhart, v; acc. prob. Murray Kellner, f; own h; Carson Robison, g.
New York, NY   Friday, November 6, 1925
    10667-A,-B   The Dream Of The Miner's Child   Ed 51649, 5085
    10668-A,-C   The Letter Edged In Black   Ed 51649, 5088
An excerpt of matrix 10668 was used on Sample Advertising Record #2.

Vernon Dalhart, v; acc. unknown, f; prob. Carson Robison, g.
New York, NY   c. November 7, 1925
    9807   Stone Mountain Memorial   Ge 3179, Sil 3827, Chg 506, Her 75524
    9808-A   Mother's Grave   Ge 3179, Sil 3827, Chg 167, 312, Her 75523

Acc. unknown, f; own h; prob. Carson Robison, g.
New York, NY   Tuesday, November 17, 1925
    73756-B   Zeb Turney's Gal   OK 40506
    73757-B   The Life Of Tom Watson   OK 40510
    73758-B   The Faded Letter   OK 40510

Vernon Dalhart & Company: Vernon Dalhart, v; acc. prob. Murray Kellner, f; own h; Carson Robison, g.
New York, NY   Monday, November 23, 1925
    10689-A   Zeb Turney's Gal   Ed 51656, 5091
    10690-B   Sydney Allen   Ed 51729, 5110
Rev. Edison 51656 by Al Bernard (popular).

Vernon Dalhart, v; acc. unknown, f; own h; prob. Carson Robison, g.
New York, NY   c. November 24, 1925
    9853-A   The Dream Of The Miner's Child   Ge 3197, Chg 505, Her 75502
    9854-A   The Death Of Floyd Collins   Ge 3197, Ch 15048, Chg 160, 315?, 318, Her 75502
Matrix 9854-A was replaced, after July 13, 1928, by matrix GEX-1257-A. A later issue of Champion 15048 replaced matrix 9854-A with *Sand Cave* (matrix 12229) by George Ake as by **Edward Johnson**.

Al Craver, v; acc. prob. Murray Kellner, f; Del Staigers, c-1; own h-2; Carson Robison, g.
New York, NY   Tuesday, November 24, 1925
    141311-1,-2   Sentenced To Life Behind These Gray Walls -2   Co 15060-D
    141312-2   My Little Home In Tennessee -1   Co 15056-D
    141313-2   Naomi Wise -1   Co 15053-D
    141314-2   Thomas E. Watson -2   Co 15053-D

Vernon Dalhart, v; acc. poss. Murray Kellner, f; own h-1; prob. Carson Robison, g/wh-2.
New York, NY   Wednesday, November 25, 1925
    6307-1,-2   Zeb Turney's Gal -1   Ba 1671, Do 3643, Re 9979, Sil 2705, Cq 7074, Pm 3013, Bwy 8050
    6308-1   Dream Of The Miner's Child -1, 2   Ba 1672, Do 3642, Or 545, Re 9978, Pm 33176, Pu 9176, Apex 386, St 9632
    6309-2   Stone Mountain Memorial   Ba 1671, Do 3643, Re 9978, Pm 3046
    6310-2   Sydney Allen -1   Ba 1672, Do 3642, Re 9979, Pm 3047, Bwy 8063
Oriole 545 as by **Frank Evans**.
Paramount 33176 and Puritan 9176 issues of matrix 6308 show the Paramount matrix and control numbers 2580 and 329. Other issues use controls as follows: 6307 = 617; 6308 = 125; 6309 = 782, 812; 6310 = 784, 814.

Acc. Murray Kellner, f; Del Staigers, c-1; own h-2/wh-3; Carson Robison, g/wh-4.
New York, NY   Tuesday, December 1, 1925
    34105-2   Behind These Gray Walls -1, 2   Vi 19999, MW M-8061, ZoAu EE23
    34106-3   My Little Home In Tennessee -4   Vi 19918
    34107-3   Naomi Wise -3, 4   Vi 19867
    34108-2   Unknown Soldier's Grave -1   Vi 19918, ZoAu EE23

Al Craver-1/**Vernon Dalhart**-2, v; acc. prob.: Murray Kellner, f; Del Staigers, c-3 or t -3; Carson Robison, g.
New York, NY   Tuesday, December 8, 1925

141363-2	The Unknown Soldier's Grave -1, 3	Co 15056-D
141364-2	Mollie Darling -2, 3	Co 15054-D
141365-3	I'll Be With You When The Roses Bloom Again -2	Co 15054-D

Vernon Dalhart & Company: Vernon Dalhart, v; acc. prob. Murray Kellner, f; own h-1; Carson Robison, g.
New York, NY   Thursday, December 10, 1925

10718-A,-B,-C	My Little Home In Tennessee	Ed 51670
10719-A,-B,-C	The Unknown Soldier's Grave	Ed 51670, 5102
10720-B	Behind These Gray Walls -1	Ed 51669, 5099
10721-B	Naomi Wise -1	Ed 51669, 5098

Tobe Little-1/**Vernon Dalhart**-2, v; acc. unknown, f; poss. Del Staigers, t-3; own h-4; poss. Carson Robison, g.
New York, NY   Friday, December 11, 1925

73826-A	Behind These Gray Walls -1, 3, 4	OK 40532
73827-A	The Unknown Soldier's Grave -1, 3	OK 40532
73828-B	The Drunkard's Hell -2, 4	OK 40565
73829-A	The Drunkard's Lone Child -2, 4	OK 40581

Vernon Dalhart, v; acc. unknown, f; poss. Del Staigers, c-1; own h-2; poss. Carson Robison, g.
New York, NY   c. December 15-18, 1925

9896	The Unknown Soldier's Grave -1	Ge 3238, Ch 15073, Chg 157, 323, Her 75517
9897-B	Behind Those Gray Walls	Ge 3222, Sil 3856, Chg 230, 502, Her 75516
9898-A	The Letter Edged In Black -2	Ge 3222, Chg 160, 319, Her 75516

Some pressings of Herwin 75516 use instead Plaza matrices 6370 (see January 6, 1926) and 6256 (see October 23, 1925) respectively.

Acc. prob. Murray Kellner, f; poss. Del Staigers, c-1; own h-2; prob. Carson Robison, g/wh-3.
New York, NY   Thursday, December 17, 1925

1734-B	Behind These Gray Walls -2	Ca 863
1735-B	The Unknown Soldier's Grave -1	Ca 863
1736-B	Thomas E. Watson -2	Ca 869
1737-B	The Wreck Of The 1256 -2, 3	Ca 869

Acc. Murray Kellner, f; own h; unknown, p-1; Carson Robison, g.
New York, NY   Monday, December 21, 1925

33645-2	The Jealous Lover Of Lone Green Valley	Vi 19951
33646-1	Oh Captain, Captain Tell Me True	Vi 19951
33647-3	Kitty Wells	Vi 20058
33648-1	Nellie Dare And Charley Brooks	Vi 20058
33649-2	Putting On The Style	Vi 19919
33650-2	The Little Black Moustache -1	Vi 19919

Matrix 33647 was logged as *Kitty Wells: The Moonshiner's Lament* but issued as shown.

Acc. poss. Murray Kellner, f; poss. Del Staigers, c-1; own h-2; Carson Robison, g.
New York, NY   Wednesday, January 6, 1926

6370-	Behind These Gray Walls -1, 2	Ba 1689, Do 3659, Re 9995, Pm 3045, Bwy 8061, Her 75516, Apex 8455, Leo 10117, Mc 22073, St 10117
6371-1	The Unknown Soldier's Grave	Ba 1688, Do 3660, DoC 21131, Re 9996, Sil 2744, Cq 7066, Apex 8455, Leo 10117, St 10117
6372-2	Naomi Wise -2	Ba 1689, Do 3659, Re 9996, Sil 2735
6373-	Dreams Of The Southland	Ba 1688, Do 3660, DoC 21169, Re 9995, Apex 8499, Leo 10167, LS 24033, Mc 22119, St 10167

Domino 21169 as by **Norman Hart**.
Some issues of Herwin 75516 use instead Gennett matrix 9897 (see c. December 15–18, 1925).
Matrix 6370 is titled *Behind These Grey Walls* on Broadway 8061.
Some issues of matrix 6370 use the controls 779 or 810.

Acc. poss. Murray Kellner, f; poss. Del Staigers, c-1; own h-2; Carson Robison, g/wh-3.
New York, NY   Tuesday, January 12, 1926

106523-1,-2	Behind These Gray Walls -2	Pat 32160, Pe 12239
106524-2	Unknown Soldier's Grave -1	Pat 32159, Pe 12238
106525-1	Naomi Wise -1, 2	Pat 32159, Pe 12238
106526-1,-2	The Letter Edged In Black -2	Pat 32160, Pe 12239
106535-2	Thomas E. Watson -2, 3	Pat 32162, Pe 12241
106536-2; 2983	The Altoona Freight Wreck -2	Ca 8218, Pat 32162, Pe 12241, Ro 598

Matrix 106536 is titled *Altoona Freight Wreck* on Romeo 598.
Intervening matrices are by other artists.

Acc. Murray Kellner, f; Del Staigers, c-1; own h-2; Carson Robison, g.
New York, NY   Thursday, January 14, 1926
    E-2127/28/29   The Convict And The Rose -1   Vo 15217, 5086
    E-2130/31/32   The Unknown Soldier's Grave -1   Vo 15282, 5089
    E-2133/34/35   The Dream Of The Miner's Child -2   Vo 15217, 5086
    E-2136/37/38   The Ship That Never Returned -2   Vo 15216, 5085

Al Craver-1/**Vernon Dalhart**-2, v; acc. prob. Murray Kellner, f; own h-2/jh-3; Carson Robison, g/wh-4.
New York, NY   Friday, January 15, 1926
    141495-1,-2   The Engineer's Dying Child -1   Co 15060-D, CoAu 01891
    141496-2   The Freight Wreck At Altoona -1, 2, 3   Co 15065-D
    141497-2   Down On The Farm -2, 4   Co 15062-D, ReAu G21470
    141498-2   My Mother's Old Red Shawl -2   Co 15062-D, ReAu G21470
Rev. Columbia 01891 by Miner Hawkins.

Vernon Dalhart, v; acc. prob. Murray Kellner, f; own h; prob. Carson Robison, g.
New York, NY   c. January 26-28, 1926
    9947   Life Of Tom Watson   Ge 3238, Sil 3856, Chg 505, Her 75517
    9948   Zeb Turney's Gal   Ge 3251, Chg 157, 316, Her 75525
    9949-A   Sydney Allen   Ge 3251, Chg 231, Her 75525

Vernon Dalhart & Co.: Vernon Dalhart, v; acc. prob. Murray Kellner, f; own h/jh-1; prob. Carson Robison, g; unknown, g-2.
New York, NY   Thursday, January 28, 1926
    10800   The Engineer's Child   Ed rejected
    10801-A,-B   Frank Dupre -1, 2   Ed 51693, 5117
    10802-A   Thomas E. Watson   Ed 51693, 5101
    10803-A,-C   The Freight Wreck At Altoona   Ed 51718, 5122
An extract of matrix 10803 was used on Sample Advertising Record #6.

Vernon Dalhart, v; acc. Murray Kellner, f; own h-1/jh-2; Frank Franchini, g.
New York, NY   Wednesday, February 3, 1926
    E-2336/37/38   Zeb Turney's Gal -1   Vo 15280, 5087
    E-2339/40/41   Sydney Allen -1, 2   Vo 15280, 5087
    E-2342/43/44   Naomi Wise -1   Vo 15281, 5088
    E-2345/46/47   Mother's Grave   Vo 15281, 5088
    E-2348/49/50   Behind These Gray Walls -1   Vo 15282, 5089

Acc. prob. Murray Kellner, f; own h/jh-1; prob. Carson Robison, g.
New York, NY   Saturday, February 6, 1926
    E-2377/78/79W   The Engineer's Child   Vo 15283, 5090
    E-2380/81/82W;   My Little Home In Tennessee   Vo 15284, 5091, Br 102, Spt S2003
    E-21937/38/39
    E-2383/84/85W   The Altoona Wreck -1   Vo 15283, 5090
    E-2386/87/88W   Frank Dupre -1   Vo 15284, 5091

Acc. prob.: Murray Kellner, f; Carson Robison, g.
New York, NY   c. February 8, 1926
    9959   Behind The Clouds (Are Crowds And Crowds Of   Ge 3254
                          Sunbeams)
    9960-A   You're Always A Baby To Mother   Ge 3254

Vernon Dalhart-1/**Tobe Little**-2, v; acc. unknown, f-3; own h/jh-4; prob. Carson Robison, g/wh-5.
New York, NY   c. February 10, 1926
    73998-A   The Altoona Freight Wreck -1, 4, 5   OK 40581
    73999-B   The Death Of Floyd Collins -1, 3   OK 40568
    74000-B   Little Mary Phagan -2, 3, 5   OK 40568
    74001-B   Kinnie Wagner -1, 3, 4, 5   OK 40565

Dalhart's Texas Panhandlers: prob. Murray Kellner, f; Vernon Dalhart, h/jh-1/v; Carson Robison, g/wh-2.
New York, NY   Tuesday, February 16, 1926
    141636-1   Better Get Out Of My Way -1   Co 15064-D
    141637-1   The Death Of Floyd Collins (Waltz) -2   Co 15064-D

Al Craver, v; acc. prob. Murray Kellner, f; own h/jh; Carson Robison, g.
New York, NY   Tuesday, February 16, 1926
    141638-1,-2   Kinnie Wagner   Co 15065-D

Vernon Dalhart, v; acc. poss. Murray Kellner, f; unknown, o.
New York, NY   Tuesday, February 16, 1926
    141639-2   Where Is My Wandering Boy To-night   Co 15072-D
    141640-2   He Will Lead Me Home   Co 15072-D

Acc. unknown, f; own h-1/jh-2; poss. Carson Robison, g; unknown, clock eff-3.
   New York, NY   Thursday, February 18, 1926

6445-2	The Freight Wreck At Altoona -1, 2	Ba 1741, Do 3712, DoC 21169, Re 8051, Sil 2704, Cq 7070, Pm 3047, Bwy 8062, Apex 8499, Leo 10167, LS 24033, St 10167
6446-2	The Engineer's Child	Ba 1741, Do 3712, DoC 21156, Re 8051, Sil 2706, Cq 7069, Apex 8472, Leo 10140, Mc 22099, St 10140
6447-2	The Governor's Pardon -3	Ba 1724, Do 3694, DoC 21152, Re 8032, Sil 2735, Pm 33177, Pu 9177, Her 75520, Apex 8472, Leo 10144, Mc 22089, St 10144

Some copies of Domino 3712 as by **Bob White**. Domino 21169 as by **Norman Hart**.
Matrix 6445 is titled *The Freight Wreck Of Altoona* on Broadway 8062.
Some issues of matrix 6445 use the controls 813 or 783.
Paramount 33177 and Puritan 9177 show the Paramount matrix and control numbers 2578 and 331.

Acc. prob. Murray Kellner, f; own h-1/jh-2; Carson Robison, g.
   New York, NY   Friday, February 19, 1926

106648-3	Sydney Allen -1, 2	Pat 32167, Pe 12246
106649-1	Zeb Turney's Gal -1	Pat 32167, Pe 12246
106650-1	The Engineer's Child	Pat 32171, Pe 12250
106651-1	Gold Star Mothers	Pat 32171, Pe 12250

Acc. prob. Murray Kellner, f; own h-1; Carson Robison, g.
   New York, NY   c. February 23, 1926

9989	The Engineer's Child	Ge 3260, Ch 15076, Chg 155, 230, 313, Her 75523
9990	The Freight Wreck At Altoona -1	Ge 3260, Ch 15076, Chg 156, 317, Her 75524, Bu 8012

Vernon Dalhart & Co.: Vernon Dalhart, v; acc. Murray Kellner, f; own h; prob. Carson Robison, g.
   New York, NY   Monday, March 1, 1926

10800-F,-H	The Engineer's Child	Ed 51718, 5135

Dalhart's Texas Panhandlers: Murray Kellner, f; Vernon Dalhart, h/jh-1/v; prob. Carson Robison, g.
   New York, NY   Monday, March 1, 1926

10857-C	Better Get Out Of My Way -1	Ed 51714, 5345
10858-A,-C	Floyd Collins Waltz	Ed 51714, 5148

Vernon Dalhart, v; acc. Murray Kellner, f; own h-1/jh-2; Carson Robison, g/wh-3; unknown, clock eff-4.
   New York, NY   Tuesday, March 2, 1926

34662-2	Floyd Collins Waltz -1, 3	Vi 19997
34663-3	Better Get Out Of My Way -1, 2	Vi 19997
34664-2	The Engineer's Child	Vi 19983, Zo 2748, ZoAu 2748, RZ T2748
34665-1	The Freight Wreck At Altoona -1	Vi 19999, MW M-8062
34666-2	The Governor's Pardon -4	Vi 19983, Zo 2748, ZoAu 2748, RZ T2748
34667-	Guy Massey's Farewell	Vi unissued

Victor 19997 as by **Vernon Dalhart Trio**.

Acc. prob. Murray Kellner, f; own h-1; Carson Robison, g; unknown, clock eff-2.
   New York, NY   Wednesday, March 3, 1926

141748-1	The Prisoner's Song	Co 257-D
141749-1,-2,-3	Guy Massey's Farewell	Co 15066-D
141750-1,-2	The Prison Clock (The Governor's Pardon) -2	Co 15066-D
141751-1	Ain't-Ya Comin' Out To-night? -1	Co 257-D

Matrices 141748 and 141751 replaced matrices 140136/37 (see November 13, 1924) on Columbia 257-D. The subtitle of matrix 141750 appears on issues of take 2 only.

Dalhart's Texas Panhandlers: Murray Kellner, f; Vernon Dalhart, h/jh-1/v; Carson Robison, g/wh-2.
   New York, NY   Tuesday, March 9, 1926

E-18279/80/81; E-2605/06/07W	Floyd Collins' Waltz -2	Vo 15303, 5092
E-18282/83; E-2608/09W	Better Get Out Of My Way -1	Vo 15303, 5092

Vernon Dalhart, v; acc. Murray Kellner, f; Carson Robison, g.
   New York, NY   Tuesday, March 9, 1926

E-18284/85; E-2610/11W	Guy Massey's Farewell	Vo 15304, 5093
E-18286/87/88; E-2612/13/14W	The Governor's Pardon	Vo 15304, 5093

Dalhart's Texas Panhandlers: Murray Kellner, f; Vernon Dalhart, h/jh-1/v; prob. Carson Robison, g/wh-2.
New York, NY   Tuesday, March 9, 1926

| 74026- | Better Get Out Of My Way -1 | OK 40584 |
| 74027- | Floyd Collins Waltz -2 | OK 40584 |

Vernon Dalhart, v; acc. unknown, f; poss. Carson Robison, g.
New York, NY   Wednesday, March 10, 1926

| 6468-1 | Guy Massey's Farewell | Ba 1724, Do 3694, DoC 21142, 21487, Re 8032, Sil 2734, Pm 33177, Pu 9177, Her 75520, Apex 8466, Leo 10131, Mc 22089, St 10131 |

Paramount 33177 and Puritan 9177 show the Paramount matrix and control numbers 2579 and 332.
Rev. Silvertone 2734 by Irving Combs (popular).

Vernon Dalhart-1/Texas Panhandlers-2: Vernon Dalhart, v; acc. prob. Murray Kellner, f; own h-3/jh-4; Carson Robison, g; unknown, clock eff-5.
New York, NY   c. March 1926

106722-2	The Death Of Floyd Collins – Waltz -2, 3?	Pat 36434, Pe 14615
106723-2	Guy Massey's Farewell -1	Pat 32178, Pe 12257
106724-1	Better Get Out Of My Way -2, 3?, 4?	Pat 36434, Pe 14615, PAE 11142
106725-2	The Governor's Pardon (The Clock Song) -1, 5	Pat 32178, Pe 12257

Vernon Dalhart, v; acc. poss. Lou Raderman, vla-1; own h-2; Carson Robison, g; unknown, train-wh eff-3.
New York, NY   Thursday, March 18, 1926

30632-4	Wreck Of The Old 97 -2, 3	Vi 19427, 119427, 27-0016, BB B-5335, Sr S-3416, MW M-4477
30632-	Wreck Of The Old 97 -2, 3	BB B-10578
30633-6	The Prisoner's Song -1	Vi 19427, 119427, 24281, 27-0016, *BB B-10578*

Bluebird B-10578 uses technical remakes, made on December 13, 1939; that of matrix 30632, carrying no take-number, is different from 30632-4, but that of matrix 30633, reportedly take 4, is identical with take 6. Victor 119427 is a Canadian issue.
Revs: Bluebird B-5335, Sunrise S-3416, Montgomery Ward M-4477 by The Vagabonds.

Acc. prob.: Murray Kellner, f; Carson Robison, g; unknown, clock eff-1.
New York, NY   Thursday, March 18, 1926

| 1870-E | The Governor's Pardon -1 | Ca 913 |
| 1871-E | Guy Massey's Farewell | Ca 913 |

Vernon Dalhart & Co.: Vernon Dalhart, v; acc. prob.: Murray Kellner, f; Carson Robison, g.
New York, NY   Thursday, March 25, 1926

| 10893-C | Lightning Express (Please, Mr. Conductor) | Ed 51735, 5150 |
| 10894-C | Governor's Pardon | Ed 51729, 5151 |

Rev. Edison 51735 by Charles Harrison (popular).

Vernon Dalhart, v; acc. prob. Murray Kellner, f; own h/jh; Carson Robison, g/wh-1.
New York, NY   Monday, April 5, 1926

141913-	I'm Satisfied With You	Co unissued
141914-2	Goin' To Have A Big Time To-night -1	Co 15082-D
141915-1,-3	Putting On The Style	Co 15082-D

Acc. prob. Murray Kellner, f; own h/jh-1; unknown, p-2; Carson Robison, g.
New York, NY   Tuesday, April 13, 1926

| 141956-2 | The Little Black Mustache -2 | Co 15077-D, CoAu 01892 |
| 141957-2 | Old Bill Moser's Ford -1 | Co 15077-D, Re/RZAu G20664 |

Matrix 141956 is titled *The Little Black Moustache* on Columbia 01892.

Acc. Murray Kellner, f; own h-1/jh-2; Carson Robison, g.
New York, NY   Saturday, April 17, 1926

E-2782/85W	Putting On Style -1, 2	Vo 15327, 5102
E-2783/84/86W	Goin' To Have A Big Time Tonight -2	Vo 15328, 5103
E-2787/88W	Kinnie Wagner -1, 2	Vo 15327, 5102
E-2789/90/91W	The Little Black Mustache -1	Vo 15328, 5103

Acc. prob. Murray Kellner, f; own h-1/jh-2; unknown, p-3; prob. Carson Robison, g; unidentified, wh-4.
New York, NY   Monday, April 19, 1926

106816-1	Little Black Mustache -1, 3	Pat 32183, Pe 12262
106817-1	Puttin' On Style -1, 2	Pat 32183, Pe 12262
106818-1	I'm Satisfied With You -4	Pat 32187, Pe 12266

Revs: Pathé 32187, Perfect 12266 by Billy Jones & Ernest Hare (popular).

Acc. prob. Murray Kellner, f; own h-1/jh-2; unknown, p-3; prob. Carson Robison, g.
New York, NY   Monday, April 19, 1926

1929-A,-B	Puttin' On The Style -1, 2	Ca 982, Lin 2546, Ro 242
1930-A	The Little Black Moustache -3	Ca 982, Lin 2546, Ro 242

Acc. unknown, f; own h-1/jh-2; unknown, g; unknown, traps.
New York, NY   Wednesday, April 21, 1926

74131-B	Puttin' On The Style -1, 2	OK 40616
74132-B	Old Bill Moser's Ford -1, 2	OK 40616
74133-A	Guy Massey's Farewell	OK 40608
74134-B	The Governor's Pardon	OK 40608

Acc. prob.: Murray Kellner, f; Carson Robison, g; unknown, clock eff-1.
New York, NY   c. April 24-26, 1926

X-84,-A	I'm Satisfied With You	Ge unissued
X-85-A	Guy Massey's Farewell	Ge 3304, Her 75520
X-86-B	The Governor's Pardon -1	Ge 3304, Her 75520

Acc. unknown, f; own h-1; prob. Carson Robison, g.
New York, NY   Wednesday, April 28, 1926

74149-A	The Jones And Bloodworth Execution -1	OK 40623
74150-A	Floyd Collins' Dream -1	OK 40623
74151-	The Little Black Moustache	OK 40638
74152-	Goin' To Have A Big Time To-night	OK 40638

OKeh 40638 has also been reported as using a recording of *Goin' To Have A Big Time To-night* with the matrix 80017, but this is an unissued recording of the title by Land Norris.

Vernon Dalhart & Co.: Vernon Dalhart, v; acc. prob. Murray Kellner, f; own h; prob. Carson Robison, g.
New York, NY   Tuesday, May 4, 1926

10957-A,-C	The Jealous Lover Of Lone Green Valley	Ed 51749, 5171

New York, NY   Friday, May 7, 1926

10958-A,-C	The Drunkard's Lone Child	Ed 51749, 5170

Vernon Dalhart, v; acc. prob. Murray Kellner, f; own h; prob. Carson Robison, g.
New York, NY   c. May 14-17, 1926

X-111	The Great Titanic	Ge 3311, Ch 15121, Sil 3828, Chg 155, 317, Her 75518
X-112-A	The Ship That Never Returned	Ge 3311, Sil 3828, Chg 156, 315?, 318, Her 75518

Matrix X-111 was replaced after July 13, 1928 by matrix GEX-1278-A (see c. May 23, 1928).

Vernon Dalhart & Carson Robison, v duet; acc. Murray Kellner, f; Carson Robison, g; Lucien Schmit, vc.
New York, NY   Wednesday, June 16, 1926

E-3241/42/43W; E-19608/09/10*	Just A Melody	Br 3232, BrAu 3232, Vo 5145
E-3244/45/46W; E-19611/12/13*	When You're Far Away	Br 3232, BrAu 3232

Vernon Dalhart & Carson J. Robison, v duet; acc. poss. Murray Kellner, f; Carson Robison, g; unknown, vc.
New York, NY   Thursday, June 17, 1926

142310-2	Just A Melody	Co 847-D, ReAu G20025
142311-2	When You're Far Away	Co 847-D, ReAu G20025

Vernon Dalhart, v; or Vernon Dalhart, Carson Robison, v duet-1; acc. Murray Kellner, f; Carson Robison, g.
New York, NY   Thursday, June 17, 1926

35696-3	We Sat Beneath The Maple On The Hill -1	Vi 20109, ZoSA 4296
35697-2	The Old Fiddler's Song	Vi 20109, Zo/RZAu EE58

Rev. Zonophone 4296 by Shannon Quartet (popular).

Acc. Murray Kellner, f; John Cali, lute.
New York, NY   Saturday, June 19, 1926

E-19618/19*/20*	The Old Fiddler's Song	Br 3234, BrAu 3234, Spt S2011
E-19621/22/23*	Lay My Head Beneath A Rose	Br 3234, BrAu 3234, Spt S2010

Acc. prob.: Murray Kellner, f; Carson Robison, g.
New York, NY   Tuesday, June 22, 1926

6621-1	Lay My Head Beneath A Rose	Ba 1790, Do 3760, DoC 21192, 181178, Or 697, Re 8097, Pm 33179, Pu 9179, Bwy 8019, Apex 8516, CrC/Roy 81178, Leo 10174, LS 24041, Mc 22119, Min M-14002, St 10174, Beeda 116
6622-2	The Old Fiddler's Song	Ba 1790, Do 3760, DoC 21187, Or 658, Re 8097, Sil 2807, Pm 3046, Apex 8516, Leo 10174, LS 24046, St 10174, Beeda 116

Some copies of Domino 3760 as by **Bob White**. Oriole 658, 697 as by **Frank Evans**. Silvertone 2807 as by **Fern Holmes**. Lucky Strike 24046 as by **Albert Vernon**.
Some issues use controls, as follows: 6621 = 355, 411-3; 6622 = 811, 780.
Rev. Oriole 697 by Harry Crane (popular).

Acc. prob. Murray Kellner, f; own h-1; prob. Carson Robison, g.
New York, NY   June 23-25, 1926

106932-1; 2985	The Old Fiddler's Song	Ca 8219, Pat 32197, Pe 12276, Ro 599
106933-1	Lay My Head Beneath A Rose	Pat 32197, Pe 12276
106934-1	I Wished I Was A Single Girl Again -1	Pat 32195, Pe 12274
106935-1	The Jones And Bloodworth Execution -1	Pat 32195, Pe 12274

Al Craver, v; acc. poss. John Cali, lute.
New York, NY   Friday, June 25, 1926

| 142346-2,-3 | John The Baptist | Co 15086-D |
| 142347-2 | The Tramp | Co 15086-D |

Vernon Dalhart, v; acc. prob.: Murray Kellner, f; Carson Robison, g.
New York, NY   Saturday, June 26, 1926

| 142348-2 | I Wish I Was Single Again | Ve 7039-V, Di 6013-G, Sil 3263 |
| 142349-1 | It's Sinful To Flirt | Ve 7039-V, Di 6013-G, Sil 3263 |

Diva 6013-G, Silvertone 3263 as by **Tom Watson**.
Matrix 142349 is titled *It's Simple To Flirt* on Diva 6013-G, Silvertone 3263.

New York, NY   Tuesday, June 29, 1926

| 142357-1,-3 | The Old Fiddler's Song | Co 15087-D |
| 142358-2,-3 | Lay My Head Beneath A Rose | Co 15087-D |

Acc. prob. Murray Kellner, f; own h-1/jh-2; prob. Carson Robison, g.
New York, NY   c. July 12, 1926

| X-208 | The Old Fiddler's Song | Ge 3350, Ch 15137, Sil 3829, Chg 154, 316, Her 75522, Bu 8066 |
| X-209 | Puttin' On Style -1, 2 | Ge 3364, Chg 150, 314 |

Acc. prob. Murray Kellner, f; prob. Carson Robison, g.
New York, NY   c. July 15, 1926

| X-220 | Lay My Head Beneath A Rose | Ge 3350, Ch 15137, Sil 3829, Her 75522, Bu 8066 |

Acc. prob. Murray Kellner, f; own h; prob. Carson Robison, g.
New York, NY   Thursday, July 15, 1926

| 74228-A | Pardon Of Sidna [sic] Allen | OK 40657 |
| 74229-B | The Picnic In The Wildwood | OK 40657 |

Vernon Dalhart & Carson Robison, v duet; acc. unknown.
New York, NY   Friday, July 16, 1926

| 80072- | Just A Melody | OK 40711 |
| 80073- | When You're Far Away | OK 40711 |

Acc. unknown, f; prob. Carson Robison, g; unknown, vc.
New York, NY   Monday, July 26, 1926

| 11122-A | Just A Melody | Ed 51807 |
| 11123-C | When You're Far Away | Ed 51807 |

An excerpt of matrix 11123 was used on Sample Advertising Record #11.

Vernon Dalhart, v/sp-1; acc. prob.: Murray Kellner, f; own h-2; Carson Robison, g.
New York, NY   Wednesday, August 4, 1926

| 142499-2 | The Picnic In The Wildwood -2 | Co 15092-D |
| 142507-3 | On That Dixie Bee Line -1 | Co 15092-D |

Intervening matrices are by other artists.

Vernon Dalhart, v; acc. prob.: Murray Kellner, f; own h-1; Carson Robison, g.
New York, NY   c. August 23-24, 1926

| X-230-A | Put My Little Shoes Away -1 | Ge 3364, Sil 3857, Chg 154, Her 75521 |
| X-232 | Papa's Billy Goat | Ge 3365, Ch 15147, Sil 3857, Chg 150, 313, Her 75531 |

Revs: Gennett 3365 by Murray Kellner; Champion 15147 by John Hammond; Herwin 75521 by Al Bernard.

Will Terry-1/Vernon Dalhart-2, v; acc. prob. Murray Kellner, f; poss. Carson Robison, g.
New York, NY   Thursday, August 26, 1926

| 107050-1,-2 | There's A New Star In Heaven To-night Rudolph Valentino -1 | Pat 32203, Pe 12282, GP 18607 |

107051-1,-2   An Old Fashioned Picture -2   Pat 32203, Pe 12282, GP 18607
Grand Pree 18607 as by **Arthur Reeves**.

Vernon Dalhart, v; acc. prob. Murray Kellner, f; poss. Carson Robison, g.
   New York, NY   Friday, August 27, 1926
   142578-2,-3   There's A New Star In Heaven Tonight – Rudolph   Co 718-D, ReAu G20005
                      Valentino
   142579-3   I Lost A Wonderful Pal (When I Lost You)   Co 718-D, CoAu 01307, Re/RZAu G21303
Revs: Columbia 01307 by Franklyn Baur; Regal G20005 by Ruth Etting; Regal/Regal-Zonophone G21303 by Maurice Gunsky (all popular).

   New York, NY   Friday, August 27, 1926
   80082-B   There's A New Star In Heaven Tonight (Rudolph   OK 40678, PaAu A2124, Capitol 4400
                      Valentino)
   80083-A   An Old Fashioned Picture   OK 40678, PaAu A2124
Capitol 4400 (an Australian issue) as by **Alan Thomas**. Matrix 80082 is titled *There's A New Star In Heaven To-night* on that issue. Rev. Capitol 4400 popular.

   New York, NY   c. late August 1926
   6708-1,-3,-5 There's A New Star In Heaven Tonight – Rudolph   Ba 1810, Do 3782, DoC 21192, Or 656, Re 8119,
                      Valentino   Sil 2816, Pm 33179, Pu 9179, Bwy 8019,
                                                                            Apex 8532, Leo 10193, LS 24046, Mc 22130,
                                                                            St 10193
   6709-3   Meet Me At Twilight   Ba 1830, Do 3797, Re 8136, Pm 33181, Pu 9181,
                                                                            Bwy 8020, 8163
   418-1   Meet Me At Twilight   Or 656
Matrix 418-1 is different from matrix 6709-3 and may not have been recorded at this session.
Some issues of Domino 3782, Regal 8119 as by **Bob White**. Oriole 656 as by **Frank Evans**. Silvertone 2816 as by **Fern Holmes**. Paramount 33179, 33181, Broadway 8019, 8020, 8163 as by **Wolfe Ballard**, except some copies of Broadway 8020 as by **George Benson**. Apex 8532 as by **Bob White**. Lucky Strike 24046 as by **Albert Vernon**.
Matrix 6708 is titled *There's A New Star In Heaven Tonight (Rudolph Valentino)* on Puritan 9179, Broadway 8019.
Some issues use controls, as follows: 6708 = 354, 417-4; 6709 = 364.
Revs: Banner 1810, Domino 3782 by Billy Burton (popular); Regal 8119 by Franklyn Baur (popular); Silvertone 2816 by Arthur Fields.

Acc. unknown, f; prob. Carson Robison, g.
   New York, NY   late August 1926
   74314-B   Pictures From Life's Other Side   OK 40696
   74315-B   The Picture That Is Turned To The Wall   OK 40696

   New York, NY   c. late August/early September 1926
   6744-3   An Old Fashioned Picture   Ba 1834, Do 3805, DoC 21213, Re 8144,
                                                                            Pm 3048, Bwy 8062, 8162, Apex 8535,
                                                                            Leo 10199, LS 24064, Mc 22137, St 10199
   6745-3   Stars Are The Windows Of Heaven   Ba 1830, Do 3797, Or 749, Re 8136
Oriole 749 as by **Frank Evans**.
Some issues use controls, as follows: 6744 = 815, 785; 6745 = 523.
Rev. Broadway 8162 by Frank Luther.

Acc. Murray Kellner, f; Roy Smeck, g.
   New York, NY   Thursday, September 2, 1926
   36092-3   There's A New Star In Heaven To-night (Rudolph   Vi 20193, Zo 2849, Zo/RZAu RZ EE21
                      Valentino)
   36093-2   An Old-Fashioned Picture   Vi 20193, MW M-8062, Zo 2849, Zo/RZAu EE58
Matrix 36092 is subtitled *(Rudolph Valentino Memorial Song)* on Zonophone/Regal-Zonophone EE21.
Rev. Zonophone/Regal-Zonophone EE21 by Henry Burr & James Stanley (popular).

Acc. prob. Murray Kellner, f; unknown, g.
   New York, NY   c. September 4-10, 1926
   X-251-A   There's A New Star In Heaven Tonight (Rudolph   Ge 3370, Ch 15139, Chg 188, Her 75526
                      Valentino)
   X-252   An Old Fashioned Picture   Ge 3370, Ch 15139, Chg 149, 309, Her 75526
Rev. Challenge 309 by Ernest Stoneman.

Acc. prob. Murray Kellner, f; Carson Robison, g.
   New York, NY   Tuesday, September 7, 1926
   11179-C   An Old Fashioned Picture   Ed 51827, 5240
   11180-B   There's A New Star In Heaven To-night (Rudolph   Ed 51827, 5239
                      Valentino)

An excerpt of matrix 11180 was used on Sample Advertising Record #12.

Acc. prob. Murray Kellner, f; own h; prob. Carson Robison, g.
New York, NY   Saturday, September 11, 1926

80102-B	Kinnie Wagner's Surrender	OK 40685
80103-B	Billy Richardson's Last Ride	OK 40685

Al Craver, v; acc. own h; prob. Carson Robison, g.
New York, NY   Tuesday, September 14, 1926

142616-3	Kinnie Wagner's Surrender	Co 15098-D
142617-3	Billy Richardson's Last Ride	Co 15098-D

Vernon Dalhart, v; acc. unknown.
New York, NY   Wednesday, September 22, 1926

80129-	Stars (Are The Windows Of Heaven)	OK 40692
80130-	Miami Storm	OK 40692

Acc. unknown, f; prob. Carson Robison, g; unknown, train-wh eff-1.
New York, NY   Wednesday, September 22, 1926

107105-1,-3	The Miami Storm	Pat 32209, Pe 12288
107106-2	Billy Richardson's Last Ride -1	Pat 32209, Pe 12288

Acc. unknown, f; prob. Carson Robison, g/wh-1.
New York, NY   Wednesday, September 22, 1926

6784-2	The Miami Storm	Ba 1834, Do 3805, DoC 21539, Or 715, Re 8144, Pm 33181, Pu 9181, Bwy 8020, Apex 8541, Leo 10203, LS 24517, St 10203
6785-2	I Want A Pardon For Daddy -1	Ba 1855, Do 3827, DoC 21213, Or 715, Re 8166, Pm 33182, Pu 9182, Bwy 8021, Her 75545, Apex 8541, Leo 10203, St 10203

Oriole 715 as by both **Dick Morse** and **Frank Evans**. Paramount 33181, 33182, Broadway 8020, 8021, Herwin 75545 as by **Wolfe Ballard**, except some copies of Broadway 8020 as by **George Benson**. Lucky Strike 24517 as by **Albert Vernon**.
Matrix 6784 is titled *Miami Storm* on Paramount 33181.
Matrix 6785 is titled *I Want A Pardon For My Daddy* on Broadway 8021, Herwin 75545.
Some issues use controls, as follows: 6784 = 363, 455; 6785 = 387, 456.
Rev. Domino 21539 by Frank Austin (popular).

Acc. prob.: Murray Kellner, f; Carson Robison, g.
New York, NY   Thursday, September 23, 1926

142683-1,-3	The Miami Storm	Co 15100-D
142684-1,-4	An Old Fashioned Picture	Co 15100-D, CoAu 01897

Rev. Columbia 01897 by Jack Mathis.

Acc. unknown, f; own h-1; prob. Carson Robison, g.
New York, NY   c. September 28, 1926

GEX-279-A	The Miami Storm	Ge 3378, Ch 15165, Sil 3839, 3851, Chg 188, 323, 369, 503, Her 75527, HGS 2005
GEX-280-A	Billy Richardson's Last Ride -1	Ge 3378, Sil 3839, 3851, Chg 149, 310, Her 75527, HGS 2005

Rev. Champion 15165 by Al Bernard.
New York, NY   Tuesday, September 28, 1926

E-3864/65*	The Miami Storm	Vo 5000
E-3866/67*	Kinnie Wagner's Surrender -1	Vo 5000

Acc. Abe Essig, f; Roy Smeck, g.
New York, NY   Wednesday, September 29, 1926

36364-3	The Miami Storm	Vi 20239
36365-3	A Handful Of Earth From Mother's Grave	Vi 20239

Acc. unknown.
New York, NY   Friday, October 1, 1926

11230	The Miami Storm	Ed rejected

Jep Fuller, v; acc. Murray Kellner, f; own h-1; Carson Robison, g.
New York, NY   Tuesday, October 5, 1926

E-3900*/01	The Crepe On The Old Cabin Door -1	Vo 5015
E-3902*/03*	Pearl Bryan	Vo 5015

Vernon Dalhart, v; acc. prob.: Murray Kellner, f; Carson Robison, g.
New York, NY   Thursday, October 14, or Friday, October 15, 1926

11230-H	The Miami Storm	Ed 51856, 5237
11231-C	Billy Richardson's Last Ride	Ed 51856, 5232

An excerpt of matrix 11230 was used on Sample Advertising Record #13.

Acc. poss. Murray Kellner, f; own h-1; prob. Carson Robison, g; unknown, train-wh eff-2.

New York, NY   Monday, October 18, 1926

6832-1	We Will Meet At The End Of The Trail	Ba 1855, Do 3827, DoC 21222, Or 769, Re 8166, Apex 8553, Leo 10216, LS 24069, St 10216
6850-2	The Crepe On The Old Cabin Door -1	Ba 1879, Do 3850, DoC 21222, Re 8190, Sil 2910, Pm 33182, Pu 9182, Bwy 8021, Her 75545, Apex 8553, Leo 10216, LS 24355, Mc 22355, St 10216
6851-1	Billy Richardson's Last Ride -1, 2	Ba 1879, Do 3850, DoC 21624, Re 8190, Pm 3048, Bwy 8063, Apex 26064, LS 24576, Mc 22581

Oriole 769 as by **Frank Evans**. Silvertone 2910 as by **Fern Holmes**. Paramount 33182, Broadway 8021, Herwin 75545 as by **Wolfe Ballard**.

Some issues use controls, as follows: 6832 = 563; 6850 = 388; 6851 = 816, 786.

Acc. Murray Kellner, f; Carson Robison, g.

New York, NY   Tuesday, October 19, 1926

E-20445/46*; E-4162/63W	We Will Meet At The End Of The Trail (A Tribute To Rudolph Valentino)	Vo 15491, Br 3358, BrAu 3358
E-20447/48	Long Ago	Br/Vo unissued

Acc. unknown.

New York, NY   Wednesday, October 20, 1926

80183-	I'd Like To Be In Texas (When They Round Up In The Spring)	OK 40706
80184-	The Crepe On The Little Cabin Door	OK 40706
80185-	We Will Meet At The End Of The Trail	OK unissued

Vernon Dalhart, v; or Vernon Dalhart, Carson Robison, v duet-1; acc. Murray Kellner, f; Vernon Dalhart, h-2; Carson Robison, g.

New York, NY   Wednesday, October 20, 1926

36848-2	The Crepe On The Old Cabin Door -2	Vi 20387, MW M-8021
36849-	We Will Meet At The End Of The Trail (A Tribute To Rudolph Valentino) -1	Vi unissued

Rev. Montgomery Ward M-8021 by Henry Burr & James Stanley (popular).

Vernon Dalhart, v; or Vernon Dalhart, Carson Robison, v/wh duet-1; acc. poss. Murray Kellner, f; Vernon Dalhart, h-2; Carson Robison, g; unknown, vc-3.

New York, NY   Friday, October 22, 1926

107162	Just A Melody -1, 3	Pat 32279, Pe 12358
107163-1,-2	When You're Far Away -1, 3	Pat 32220, Pe 12299
107164-2	The Crepe On The Old Cabin Door -2	Pat 32216, Pe 12295
107165-1,-2	We Will Meet At The End Of The Trail	Pat 32216, Pe 12295

Revs: Pathé 32220, Perfect 12299 by George Morbid (popular); Pathé 32279, Perfect 12358 by Ernest Stoneman.

Vernon Dalhart, v; acc. prob. Murray Kellner, f; own h-1; prob. Carson Robison, g.

New York, NY   Saturday, October 23, 1926

142866-3	The Crepe On The Little Cabin Door -1	Co 15107-D, CoE 19032, Re/RZAu G20664
142867-1	We Will Meet At The End Of The Trail (A Tribute To Rudolph Valentino)	Co 15107-D, CoE 19032

Vernon Dalhart-1/**Al Craver**-2, v; acc. prob. Murray Kellner, f; own h; Carson Robison, g/wh-3.

New York, NY   Monday, November 1, 1926

142895-2,-3	I'd Like To Be In Texas When They Round Up In The Spring -1, 3	Co 15131-D
142896-2	Pearl Bryan -2	Co 15169-D

Al Craver, v; or **Al Craver & Charlie Wells**-1: Vernon Dalhart, Carson Robison, v duet; acc. prob. Murray Kellner, f; Vernon Dalhart, h-2; Carson Robison, g.

New York, NY   Monday, November 8, 1926

142922-3	The Fate Of Kinnie Wagner -2	Co 15109-D, ReAu G20096
142923-2	We Sat Beneath The Maple On The Hill -1	Co 15109-D, ReAu G20096

Vernon Dalhart, v; acc. Murray Kellner, f; own h-1; Carson Robison, g.

New York, NY   Wednesday, November 10, 1926

E-4056/57*W	Don't Let Your Deal Go Down -1	Vo 5045
E-4058/59*W: E-21936	Billy Richardson's Last Ride -1	Vo 5045, Br 102, Spt S2003

| E-4060/61W | I'd Like To Be In Texas (When They Round Up In The Spring) -1 | Vo 5044 |
| E-4062/63W | We Sat Beneath The Maple On The Hill | Vo 5044 |

Vernon Dalhart, v; or **Vernon Dalhart & Carson Robison**-1, v duet; acc. prob. Murray Kellner, f; Vernon Dalhart, h; Carson Robison, g.
New York, NY   Wednesday, November 17, 1926

11312-A,-B	The Dying Girl's Message	Ed 51883, 5267
11313-A,-B,-C	If I Could Hear My Mother Pray Again -1	Ed 51883, 5265
11314-A	Don't Let The Deal Go Down	Ed 51949, 5260

Vernon Dalhart–Carson Robison, v duet; acc. unknown.
New York, NY   c. November 19-20, 1926

| GEX-349-A | Just A Melody | Ge rejected |
| GEX-350-A,-B | When You're Far Away | Ge rejected |

Vernon Dalhart, Carson Robison, v/wh-1 duet; acc. two unknowns, f; Roy Smeck, sg-2; Carson Robison, g; unknown, vc.
New York, NY   Friday, November 19, 1926

| 36949-1,-2,-3,-4 | Far Away In Hawaii -2 | Vi unissued |
| 36950-2 | Just A Melody -1 | Vi 20369, Zo 2927, HMVAu EA147 |

Rev. HMV EA147 by The Revellers (popular).

Vernon Dalhart, v; acc. Murray Kellner, f; Carson Robison, g.
New York, NY   Monday, November 29, 1926

| E-20836/37*; E-4160/61W | Long Ago | Vo 15491, Br 3358, BrAu 3358 |

Acc. prob.: Murray Kellner, f; Carson Robison, g.
New York, NY   c. November 1926

| 2203-A | Rags | Ca 1052 |
| 22040-A | If You Can't Tell The World She's A Good Little Girl (Just Say Nothing At All) | Ca 1052 |

Vernon Dalhart–Carson Robison, v duet; acc. two unknowns, f; Roy Smeck, sg; Carson Robison, g.
New York, NY   Wednesday, December 1, 1926

| 36949-7 | Far Away In Hawaii | Vi 20369, Zo 2927, HMVAu EA295 |

Vernon Dalhart, v; acc. Murray Kellner, f; own h-1; Carson Robison, g.
New York, NY   Wednesday, December 1, 1926

| 36987-1 | A Lonesome Boy's Letter Back Home | Vi 20536, ZoAu EE69 |
| 36988-2 | The Sad Lover -1 | Vi 20387 |

Rev. Zonophone EE69 by Henry Burr (popular).

Acc. prob.: Murray Kellner, f; own h-1/jh-2; Carson Robison, g.
New York, NY   Tuesday, December 14, 1926

| 11370 | I'm The Man That Rode The Mule Around The World -2 | Ed 51901, 5278 |
| 11371 | Can I Sleep In Your Barn Tonight, Mister? -1 | Ed 51901, 5283 |

Edison 5283 was possibly never issued.

Vernon Dalhart & Carson Robison, v duet; acc. unknown, f; prob. Carson Robison, g; unknown, vc.
New York, NY   c. December 15-20, 1926

| GEX-386-B | Just A Melody | Ge 6012, Ch 15197, Sil 5007, 25007, 8011, Chg 224, Her 75533, HGS 2018, Vo XA18024 |
| GEX-387-A | When You're Far Away | Ge 6012, Ch 15197, Sil 5007, 25007, 8011, Chg 224, Her 75533, HGS 2018 |

Vernon Dalhart, v; acc. Murray Kellner, f; poss. own h; Carson Robison, g.
New York, NY   Monday, December 20, 1926

| 37157-3 | On The Dixie Bee Line | Vi 20538 |
| 37158-3 | Billy Richardson's Last Ride | Vi 20538, MW M-8063 |

Rev. Montgomery Ward M-8063 by Newton Gaines.

Al Craver-1/**Vernon Dalhart**-2, v; acc. prob. Murray Kellner, f; own h; prob. Carson Robison, g.
New York, NY   Friday, January 14, 1927

143308-3	The Wreck Of Number Nine -1	Co 15121-D
143309-2	The Wreck Of The Royal Palm Express -1	Co 15121-D
143310-2	The Sad Lover -2	Co 15131-D

Vernon Dalhart, v; acc. prob. Murray Kellner, f; own h-1; prob. Carson Robison, g.
    New York, NY   c. January 1927

6986-1	There's A Spark Of Love Still Burning (In The Embers Of My Heart)	Ba 1919, Do 3890, Je 5047, Or 808, Re 8235
6987-4	My Sweetheart, My Mother And Home -1	Ba 1919, Do 3890, DoC 21367, Or 811, Re 8235, Sil 2910, Htd 111, 16334, Apex 8713, LS 24187, Mc 22265, St 8713

Jewel 5047, Oriole 808, 811 as by **Frank Evans**. Silvertone 2910 as by **Fern Holmes**. Homestead 111 as by **Frank Thompson**.
The subtitle of matrix 6986 is omitted on Jewel 5047, Oriole 808.
Some issues use controls, as follows: 6986 = 642-1; 6987 = 648-5.
Revs: Oriole 808, 811 popular; Homestead 111 by Jerome Mason (popular).

Vernon Dalhart-1/Tobe Little-2, v; or **Vernon Dalhart & Carson Robison**-3, v duet; acc. prob. Murray Kellner, f; Vernon Dalhart, h; Carson Robison, g.
    New York, NY   Tuesday, February 1, 1927

80370-A	The Wreck Of The Royal Palm -1	OK 45086
80371-B	The Wreck Of The No. 9 -1	OK 45086
80372-	The Halls-Mills Case	OK unissued
80373-B	Pearl Bryan -2	OK 45090
80374-B	The Sad Lover -1	OK 45085
80375-A	My Carolina Home -3	OK 45085

Vernon Dalhart, v; or **Vernon Dalhart–Carson Robison**-1, v duet; acc. Murray Kellner, f; unknown, f; Vernon Dalhart, h-2; Carson Robison, g.
    New York, NY   Wednesday, February 2, 1927

37594-3	The Wreck Of The Royal Palm -2	Vi 20528
37595-2	Three Drowned Sisters -2	Vi 20528
37596-2	I Know There Is Somebody Waiting (In The House At The End Of The Lane) -1	Vi 20536

Al Craver-1/**Mack Allen**-2, v; or **Vernon Dalhart & Charlie Wells**-3: Vernon Dalhart, Carson Robison, v duet; acc. prob. Murray Kellner, f; Vernon Dalhart, h-4; Carson Robison, g.
    New York, NY   Thursday, February 3, 1927

143384-3	The Three Drowned Sisters -1, 4	Co 15126-D
143385-3	Barbara Allen -1, 4	Co 15126-D
143386-2,-3	I Know There Is Somebody Waiting (In The House At The End Of The Lane) -3	Co 15162-D, CoAu 01893, ReE G9370
143389-3	Muddy Water (A Mississippi Moan) -2	Ha 351-H, Ve 1351-V, Di 2351-G
143390-3	Long Ago -2	Ha 417-H, Ve 1417-V, Di 2417-G
143391-2	Song Of The Wanderer (Where Shall I Go?) -2	Ha 351-H, Ve 1351-V, Di 2351-G

Regal G9370 as by **Sam Peters & Harry Jones**.
Velvet Tone 1351-V, 1417-V, Diva 2351-G, 2417-G may also have been issued as by **Vernon Dalhart**.
Matrices 143387/88 are by The Xylo-Rimba Orchestra (popular).

Vernon Dalhart, v; acc. prob. Murray Kellner, f; own h-1; Carson Robison, g.
    New York, NY   c. February 7, 1927

GEX-501-A	Wreck Of The Royal Palm -1	Ge 6051, Ch 15232, Sil 5005, 8139, 25005, Spt 9236, Chg 243, Her 75540, Vo XA18019
GEX-502-A	Wreck Of The Number 9 -1	Ge 6051, Ch 15232, Sil 5005, 8139, 25005, Spt 9236, Chg 243, 321, Her 75540, Vo XA18019, Gaiety P122
GEX-503,-A	Sad Lover	Ge rejected

Matrix GEX-502 is titled *The Wreck Of Number Nine* on Supertone 9236.

Acc. prob. Murray Kellner, f; own h; prob. Carson Robison, g.
    New York, NY   Monday, February 7, 1927

11506-A	Bury Me Not On The Lone Prairie	Ed 51949, 5315
11507-B,-C	Kennie Wagner's Surrender	Ed 52020, 5313

    New York, NY   c. February 7, 1927

2333-B	Billy Richardson's Last Ride	Ca 1143
173-A	Billy Richardson's Last Ride	Ro 350, Vri 5059
2334-A; 108301-	The Wreck Of The Royal Palm	Ca 1143, Pat 32380, Pe 12459
174-A	The Wreck Of The Royal Palm	Ro 350, Vri 5059

Revs: Pathé 32380, Perfect 12459 by Ernest Stoneman.

Acc. prob. Murray Kellner, f; own h; prob. Carson Robison, g; unknown, train-wh eff-1.
    New York, NY   Saturday, February 12, 1927

7056-2,-3	The Wreck Of The Number Nine -1	Ba 1990, Do 3959, DoC 21264, Or 897, Re 8322, Pm 3021, Bwy 8054, Apex 8596, CrC/MeC 81032, LS 24094, Mc 22169, MeC/Min M-902, Roy 381032, Stg 281032
7057-3	The Wreck Of The Royal Palm	Ba 1957, Do 3927, DoC 21264, Or 860, Re 8280, Pm 3016, Bwy 8050, Apex 8596, LS 24094, Mc 22169

Oriole 860, 897 as by **Frank Evans**.
Some issues use controls, as follows: 7056 = 668, 820; 7057 = 625, 746.
Rev. Banner 1957 by Lambert & Hillpot (popular).

Acc. Murray Kellner, f; own h; Carson Robison, g.
New York, NY   Tuesday, February 15, 1927

E-21503*/04/05; E-4661/62/63W	The Wreck Of The Royal Palm	Br 3470, 101, BrE 3470, Vo 5138, Spt S2001
E-21506/07/08*; E-4658/59/60W	The Wreck Of The Number Nine	Br 3470, 101, Vo 5138, Spt S2001
E-21509*/10; E-4654*/55W	The Three Drowned Sisters	Br 3469, 100, Vo 5137, Spt S2004
E-21511*/12; E-4656*/57W	Billy, The Kid	Br 3469, 100, Vo 5137, Spt S2006

Brunswick 3469 and 3470 were released on February 25, 1927 and cancelled on April 18, 1927, being transferred to Brunswick 100 and 101, the first issues in the new Songs From Dixie series.

Vernon Dalhart-1/**Tobe Little**-2, v; or **Vernon Dalhart & Carson Robison**-3, v duet; acc. prob. Murray Kellner, f; Carson Robison, g.
New York, NY   Monday, February 21, 1927

80450-B	Billy The Kid -1	OK 45102
80451-B	Barbara Allen -2	OK 45090
80452-B	Song Of The Wanderer (Where Shall I Go?) -1	OK 45091
80453-A	The Shadow Song -3	OK 45091

Acc. prob. Murray Kellner, f; own h-1; prob. Carson Robison, g.
New York, NY   c. February 1927

107400-C	Hand Me Down My Walking Cane -1	Pat 32248, Pe 12327
107401-C; 2989	Gypsy's Warning -1	Ca 8221, Lin 2826, Pat 32251, Pe 12330, Ro 601
107402-B; 2991	The Butcher's Boy	Ca 8222, Lin 2827, Pat 32251, Pe 12330, Ro 602
107403-C	Can I Sleep In Your Barn To-Night, Mister? -1	Pat 32248, Pe 12327

Some issues of Banner 1993 replace Ernest Stoneman's *Hand Me Down My Walking Cane* (Plaza matrix 7222) with a Dalhart recording of the title, probably matrix 107400, but retain Stoneman's label-credit.
Matrix 107401 is titled *The Gypsy's Warning* on Pathé 32251, Perfect 12330.

Jeff Calhoun, v; acc. prob. Murray Kellner, f; own h/jh-1; Carson Robison, g.
New York, NY   ?c. February/March 1927

2342-B	May I Sleep In Your Barn Tonight Mister?	GG 4118, ?Globe 4118, Rad 4118, ?Supreme 4118, VD 74118, Mad 1912
2343-B,-E	Wreck Of The Old 97	GG 4131, ?Globe 4131, Rad 4131, ?Supreme 4131, Pm 3018, Bwy 8053
2344-A	Jesse James	GG 4133, ?Globe 4133, Rad 4133, ?Supreme 4133, VD 74133
2345-A	Rovin' Gambler -1	GG 4135, ?Globe 4135, Rad 4135, ?Supreme 4135, VD 74135, Pm 3018, 3302, Bwy 8053, Her 75532

Van Dyke 74118, 74135 as by **Martin Dixon**. Madison 1912 as by **James Ahearn**. Paramount 3018, Broadway 8053 (which replace matrices 2343, 2345 with the controls 629, 628 respectively and were issued about May 1927) as by **Vernon Dalhart**. Some issues of matrix 2345 use the control 206.
Some issues of Paramount 3302 by Crockett's Kentucky Mountaineers replace their Crown recording of *Rovin' Gambler*, and some issues of Herwin 75532 by Welby Toomey replace his Gennett recording of the same title, with Dalhart's Grey Gull matrix 2345-A.
Later issues of Grey Gull/?Globe/Radiex/?Supreme 4118, Van Dyke 74118 use the same title in a recording (matrix 2342-E) by Frank Luther, in his own name or as by **Jeff Calhoun**.
Later issues of Grey Gull/?Globe/Radiex/?Supreme 4131 use the same title in a recording (matrix 2511-A,-B) by Arthur Fields, in his own name or as by **Jeff Calhoun** or **Mr. X** or **Vel Veteran**.
Later issues of Grey Gull/?Globe/Radiex/?Supreme 4133, Van Dyke 74133 use the same title in a recording (matrix 3032-A) by, and as, Frank Luther.
Later issues of Grey Gull/?Globe/Radiex/?Supreme 4135, Van Dyke 74135 use the same title in a recording (matrix 2345-C) by Frank Luther as by **Jeff Calhoun**.

Revs: Grey Gull/?Globe/Radiex/?Supreme 4118, Van Dyke 74118 by Francis Herold (popular); Grey Gull/?Globe/Radiex/ ?Supreme 4135, Van Dyke 74135 by Kenneth Calvert (popular); Madison 1912 by Jack Ryan (popular); Paramount 3302 by Crockett's Kentucky Mountaineers; Herwin 75532 by Welby Toomey. For revs of Grey Gull/?Globe/Radiex/?Supreme 4131, 4133 see note to Grey Gull session of c. May 1927.

Al Craver, v; or **Vernon Dalhart & Charlie Wells**-1: Vernon Dalhart, Carson Robison, v/wh-2 duet; acc. prob. Murray Kellner, f; Vernon Dalhart, h-3/jh-4; Carson Robison, g/wh-5.

New York, NY   Tuesday, March 1, 1927

143554-2	Billy The Kid -3	Co 15135-D
143555-3	The Wreck Of C. & O. Number 5 -3	Co 15135-D
143556-3	Death's Shadow Song -1, 5	Co 15152-D, CoAu 01894
143557-3	My Blue Ridge Mountain Home -2, 3, 4	Co 15152-D, CoAu 01893

Vernon Dalhart–Carson Robison, v duet; acc. Murray Kellner, f; Vernon Dalhart, h; William Carlino, bj; Carson Robison, g.

New York, NY   Wednesday, March 9, 1927

38150-2	My Blue Ridge Mountain Home	Vi 20539, MW M-4053, HMVAu EA295
38151-2	Golden Slippers	Vi 20539, BB B-6406, HMVAu EA226, Twin FT8144

Matrix 38150 is titled *My Blue Mountain Home* on some copies of Victor 20539, HMV EA295. Matrix 38151 is titled *O Dem Golden Slippers* on HMV EA226.
Revs: Bluebird B-6406, Twin FT8144 by Frank Luther & Carson Robison; HMV EA226 by Frank Crumit (popular).

Vernon Dalhart: Vernon Dalhart, Carson Robison, v/wh-1 duet; acc. unknown, f; Carson Robison, g; unknown, vc.

New York, NY   Friday, March 11, 1927

2387-A	Just A Melody -1	Ca 1157, Lin 2637, Ro 376, Vri 5069, PmAu 2558, Regent R1029
2388-A	I Know There Is Somebody Waiting (In The House At The End Of The Lane)	Ca 1157, Lin 2637, Ro 376, Vri 5069

Regent R1029 as by **Bob Hillman**.
Some issues of matrix 2388 use the control 215.
Rev. Regent R1029 (with same credit) popular.

Vernon Dalhart, v; or **Vernon Dalhart & Carson Robison**-1, v/wh duet; acc. Murray Kellner, f; Vernon Dalhart, h-2/ jh-3; Carson Robison, g.

New York, NY   Saturday, March 12, 1927

E-22016/17*; E-4670/71*W	The Wreck Of C. & O. No. 5 -2	Vo 5140, Br 117, Spt S2002
E-22018*/19; E4672*/73W	Barbara Allen -2	Vo 5140, Br 117, Spt S2002
E-22020/21; E-4674/75*W	The House At The End Of The Lane -1	Vo 5139, Br 121, BrAu 3839, Spt S2015
E-22022/23; E-4676/77*W	My Blue Ridge Mountain Home -1, 2, 3	Br 121, 3839, BrAu 3839, Vo 5145, Spt S2015

Vernon Dalhart, v; acc. prob.: Murray Kellner, f; own h; Carson Robison, g.

New York, NY   Tuesday, March 15, 1927

11573-C	Pretty Little Dear	Ed 51974, 5322
11574-C	Get Away, Old Man, Get Away	Ed 51974, 5321

Dalhart & Robison, v/wh-1 duet; or **Vernon Dalhart**-2, v; acc. prob. Murray Kellner, f; Vernon Dalhart, h-3/jh-4; Carson Robison, g/wh-5.

New York, NY   Friday, March 18, 1927

80641-B	I Know There's Somebody Waiting -5	OK 45190, PaE R3865
80642-A	My Blue Ridge Mountain Home -1, 3, 4	OK 45107, 45190, PaE R3865
80643-B	Wreck Of The C. And O. No. 5 -2	OK 45102

Vernon Dalhart, v; acc. prob. Murray Kellner, f; own h-1/jh-2; Carson Robison, g.

New York, NY   Tuesday, March 22, 1927

143700-3	Get Away, Old Man, Get Away -1, 2	Co 969-D, CoE 19026
143701-2	Oh Bury Me Not On The Lone Prairie (The Dying Cowboy)	Co 969-D

Rev. Columbia 19026 by Dan Hornsby.

Acc. Bert Hirsch, f-1; own h-2; Bill Wirges, o-3/p-4; Carson Robison, g.

New York, NY   Wednesday, March 23, 1927

E-22083/84	The Gipsy's Warning -1, 3	Br unissued
E-22085*/86	The Gipsy's Warning -1, 2	Br 122, Spt S2011
E-22087/88*	Let Me Call You Sweetheart (I'm In Love With You) -4	Br 3523

Acc. Murray Kellner, f; own h/jh-1; Carson Robison, g.
   New York, NY   Wednesday, March 23, 1927
   E-4754/55/56W;   Get Away, Old Man, Get Away -1   Br 123
     E-22157*/58/59
   E-4757/58/59W;   Pretty Little Dear   Br 123
     E-22160/61*/62

Acc. Murray Kellner, f; own h; Carson Robison, g.
   New York, NY   Thursday, March 24, 1927
   E-22089/90*/91   Molly Darling   Br 122

Vernon Dalhart, v; or **Dalhart & Robison**-1, v/wh duet; acc. prob. Murray Kellner, f; Vernon Dalhart, h/jh-2; Carson Robison, g/wh-3.
   New York, NY   Thursday, March 24, 1927
   107436-1   My Blue Ridge Mountain Home -1   Pat 32254, Pe 12333, PAE 11475, GP 18669
   107437-1   Get Away Old Man – Get Away -2   Pat 32254, Pe 12333, PAE 11475,
                                                   Broadcast Twelve 3369, GP 18662
   107438-1   Pretty Little Dear   Pat 32257, Pe 12336
   107439-1   The Wreck Of Number Nine -3   Pat 32257, Pe 12336
Grand Pree 18662 as by **Paul Adams**, 18669 as by **Adams & Morris**.
Matrix 107437 is titled *Get Away – Old Man – Get Away* on Broadcast Twelve 3369.
Revs: Broadcast Twelve 3369 by Carson Robison; Grand Pree 18662 by Brown & Allen (popular).

Mack Allen, v; acc. prob. Murray Kellner, f; Carson Robison, g/wh-1.
   New York, NY   Monday, March 28, 1927
   143715-1   Can't Yo' Heah Me Callin' Caroline -1   Ha 506-H, Ve 1506-V, Di 2506-G
   143716-3   Mighty Lak' A Rose   Ha 506-H, Ve 1506-V, Di 2506-G
   143717-   Some Of These Days   Co unissued
Velvet Tone 1506-V, Diva 2506-G may also have been issued as by **Vernon Dalhart**.

Vernon Dalhart, v; or **Dalhart & Robison**-1, v duet; acc. prob. Murray Kellner, f; Vernon Dalhart, h/jh-2; Carson Robison, g/wh-3.
   New York, NY   c. March 30-April 2, 1927
   GEX-547-A   My Blue Ridge Mountain Home -1, 2, 3   Ge 6076, Ch 15246, Sil 5087, 8143, 25087,
                                                        Spt 9230, Chg 271, 730, Her 75544, BP 8028
   GEX-548-A   Get Away Old Man Get Away -2   Ge 6076, Ch 15260, Sil 5016, 8131, 25016,
                                                        Spt 9228, Chg 271, 730, Her 75546,
                                                        Vo XA18024
   GEX-549-A   Barbara Allen   Ge 6136, Ch 15246, Sil 5016, 8131, 25016,
                                                        Spt 9228, Chg 268, Her 75544, BP 8028
Matrix GEX-547 on Champion 15246 as by **Vernon Dalhart & Carson Robison**, on Challenge 730 as by **Vernon Dalhart**. Another issue of Herwin 75546 exists: see note to c. May 14–16, 1927 session.
Matrix GEX-548 is titled *Get Away, Old Man, Get Away* on Supertone 9228, Challenge 730, or *Get Away Old Man, Get Away* on Vocalion XA18024.
Rev. Champion 15260 by Chubby Parker.

Vernon Dalhart, v; acc. prob. Murray Kellner, f; own h-1; Carson Robison, g.
   New York, NY   Saturday, April 2, 1927
   E-22227*/28   The Return Of Mary Vickery -1   Br 139
   E-22229/30*   The Miner's Doom -1   Br 139, Spt S2014
   E-22231*/32* A Home On The Range -1   Br 137, Spt S2009
   E-22233*/34* The Dying Cowboy (Bury Me Not On The Lone   Br 137, Spt S2009
                   Prairie) -1
   E-22235*/36* Cowboy's Herding Song (Lay Down, Dogies)   Br 138, Spt S2007
Matrix E-22235/36 was originally logged as *Lay Down, Dogies (Cowboy's Night Song)*. It is titled *Cowboy's Evening Song (Lay Down, Dogies)* on Supertone S2007.

Vernon Dalhart, v; or Vernon Dalhart, Carson Robison, v duet-1; acc. prob. Murray Kellner, f; Vernon Dalhart, h-2; unknown, p-3; Carson Robison, g.
   New York, NY   Monday, April 4, 1927
   E-22237/38*   Cowboy's Evening Song (Goin' Home) -1, 2   Br 138, Spt S2007
   E-22239/40*   Till We Meet Again -3   Br 140, Spt S2013
   E-22241/42*   Meet Me To-night In Dreamland -1, 3 Br 140, Spt S2013
   E-22243*/44   Someday Sweetheart -3   Br 3523, BrAu 3523
Matrix E-22237/38 was originally logged as *Goin' Home (Cowboy Song)*. It is titled *Cowboy's Herding Song (Goin' Home)* on Supertone S2007.

Vernon Dalhart, v; acc. Murray Kellner, f; own h-1; Carson Robison, g.
   New York, NY   Tuesday, April 12, 1927

38455-1	Lay Down, Doggies	Vi V-40114, ZoSA 4254
38456-1	The Gypsy's Warning -1	Vi 20795
38457-2	Jesse James -1	Vi 20966
38458-2	Billy The Kid -1	Vi 20966

Rev. Zonophone 4254 by Kelly Harrell.

Acc. prob. Murray Kellner, f; own h-1; Carson Robison, g.
New York, NY　　　　　　　　　　　　　　　　　　　　　　　　　　　　　Monday, April 18, 1927

E-22465*/66*	Down On The Farm	Vo 5139, Br 142, BrAu 142, Spt S2008, Au A22027
E-22467/68*	My Mother's Old Red Shawl	Br 142, BrAu 142, Spt S2008, Au A22027
E-22469*/70*	The Jealous Lover Of Lone Green Valley -1	Br 143, Spt S2012
E-22471*/72	Nellie Dare And Charlie Brooks -1	Br 143

Acc. Samuel Raitz, f; own h-1; Nat Shilkret, o-2; Andy Sannella, g.
New York, NY　　　　　　　　　　　　　　　　　　　　　　　　　　　　Wednesday, April 27, 1927

38494-3	I'll Be With You When The Roses Bloom Again	Vi 20611, MW M-4331, Zo/RZAu EE55
38495-2	The Mississippi Flood -1, 2	Vi 20611, Zo/RZAu EE55

Rev. Montgomery Ward M-4331 by Frank Luther.

Acc. Sam Raitz, f; own h; Carson Robison, g.
New York, NY　　　　　　　　　　　　　　　　　　　　　　　　　　　　　Thursday, April 28, 1927

E-22761/62*/63*; E-4903/04/05W	The Mississippi Flood	Vo 5141, Br 153
E-22772*/73*/74*; E-4906/07/08W	The Engineer's Dream	Vo 5141, Br 153, Spt S2012

Al Craver, v; acc. poss. Murray Kellner, f; own h; prob. Carson Robison, g.
New York, NY　　　　　　　　　　　　　　　　　　　　　　　　　　　　　　Monday, May 2, 1927

144075-2	The Mississippi Flood	Co 15146-D
144076-1,-2	The Engineer's Dream	Co 15146-D

Vernon Dalhart, v; or **Dalhart & Robison**-1, v/wh duet; acc. poss. Murray Kellner, f; Vernon Dalhart, h; Carson Robison, g.
New York, NY　　　　　　　　　　　　　　　　　　　　　　　　　　　　　　Monday, May 2, 1927

107526-1	The Mississippi Flood	Pat 32261, Pe 12340
107527-1	The Engineer's Dream	Pat 32261, Pe 12340
107528-1	Goin' Home -1	Ca 9067, Lin 3096, Pat 32277, Pe 12356, Ro 871
107529-	Lay Down Doggies (Cowboy's Night Song)	Ca 9069, Lin 3098, Pat 32277, Pe 12356, Ro 873

Matrix 107529 (3627) on Cameo 9069, Lincoln 3098 as by **Vernon Dalhart Trio**.
Matrix 107529 is titled *Cowboy's Night Song (Lay Down Doggies)* on Cameo 9069, and *Cowboy's Night Song (Lay Down, Doggies)* on Romeo 873.
Some issues use controls or transfer matrices, as follows: 107528 = 3624; 107529 = 3627.

Vernon Dalhart, v; acc. poss. own h; prob. Carson Robison, g.
New York, NY　　　　　　　　　　　　　　　　　　　　　　　　　　　　　　Tuesday, May 3, 1927

11678-C	The Crepe On The Old Cabin Door	Ed 52020, 5337
11679	My Horses Ain't Hungry	Ed 52077, 5348

Acc. unknown, f; own h-1; prob. Carson Robison, g.
New York, NY　　　　　　　　　　　　　　　　　　　　　　　　　　　　　　Friday, May 6, 1927

7209-1	The Mississippi Flood -1	Ba 1990, Do 3959, DoC 21271, Re 8322, Pm 3020, Her 75546, Apex 8611, Mc 22167
7210-	The Engineer's Dream	Je 5031, Or 912, Pm 3020, Her 75546, Apex 8611, DoC 21271, Mc 22167

Jewel 5031, Oriole 912 as by **Frank Evans**.
Another issue of Herwin 75546 is derived from Gennett: see note to c. May 14–16, 1927 session.
Some issues use controls, as follows: 7209 = 650; 7210 = 651, 850.

Acc. poss. Murray Kellner, f; own h; prob. Carson Robison, g.
New York, NY　　　　　　　　　　　　　　　　　　　　　　　　　　　　　Saturday, May 7, 1927

81069-A,-C	The Mississippi Flood	OK 45107
81070-	When The Roses Bloom Again	OK unissued

Acc. poss. Murray Kellner, f; own h-1/jh-2; prob. Carson Robison, g; unknown, train-wh eff-3.
New York, NY　　　　　　　　　　　　　　　　　　　　　　　　　　　　Wednesday, May 11, 1927

2452-B	The Mississippi Flood -1	Ca 1160
250-A	The Mississippi Flood	Ro 389, Vri 5073
2453-B	The Engineer's Dream -1	Ca 1160

251-A	The Engineer's Dream -3	Ro 389, Vri 5073
2454-B	Get Away, Old Man, Get Away -1, 2	Ca 1174, 9073, Lin 2669, 3102, Ro 399, 877, GP 18716
252-A	Get Away, Old Man, Get Away -1, 2	Ro 399, Vri 5086
2455-B	The Little Old Log Cabin In The Lane	Ca 1174, 9073, Lin 2669, 3102, Ro 399, 877, Electron 5007, StgAu 1132
253-A	The Little Old Log Cabin In The Lane	Lin 2669, Ro 399, Vri 5086

Grand Pree 18716 as by **Paul Adams**.
Most issues of Romeo 399 appear to use matrices 252/253, but some use 2454/2455. Lincoln 2669 usually couples matrices 2454/2455 but was also issued with 2455/253. Similar variations may occur on other issues.
Revs: Grand Pree 18716 by Louis Young (popular); Electron 5007, though credited to Dalhart, by Marjorie Harcum (popular).

Vernon Dalhart & Carson Robison, v duet; acc. two unknowns, f; Carson Robison, g.
New York, NY   Thursday, May 12, 1927

| 38743-2 | My Carolina Home | Vi 20795 |
| 38744-1,-2,-3 | The Heroes' Last Flight | Vi unissued |

Matrix 38744-3 was approved for issue but never issued.

Vernon Dalhart, v; or **Dalhart & Robison**-1, v/wh duet; acc. poss. Murray Kellner, f; Vernon Dalhart, h-2; Carson Robison, g.
New York, NY   Friday, May 13, 1927

107536-1	I'll Be With You When The Roses Bloom Again -2	Pat 32264, Pe 12343
107537-1	My Carolina Home -1	Pat 32264, Pe 12343, PAE 11475, GP 18669
107538-	The Last Flight	Pat 32270, Pe 12349, Chg 733
107539-1	The Wreck Of The C. And O. No. 5 -2	Ca 8218, Lin 2873, Pat 32270, Pe 12349, Ro 598, Chg 733

Grand Pree 18669 as by **Adams & Morris**.
Matrix 107539 is titled *Wreck Of The C. & O. #5* on Romeo 598.
Some issues of matrix 107539 use the control or transfer matrix 2984.

Vernon Dalhart, v; acc. poss. Murray Kellner, f; own h; prob. Carson Robison, g.
New York, NY   c. May 14-16, 1927

GEX-650-B	The Mississippi Flood	Ge 6136, Ch 15278, Sil 5063, 25063, Chg 268, Her 75546, BP 8027
GEX-651	The Engineer's Dream	Ge 6204, Ch 15355, Sil 5090, 8136, 25090, Spt 9234
GEX-652	Sad Lover	Ge 6169, Ch 15355, Sil 5090, 8136, 25090, Spt 9234, BP 8027, Gaiety P122

Another issue of Herwin 75546 replaces GEX-650 and GEX-548 (see above) with Plaza matrices 7209 and 7210 (whose Paramount controls are 650 and 651).
Revs: Gennett 6204 by Ray Covert; Champion 15278 by Chubby Parker.

Mack Allen, v; acc. prob.: Murray Kellner, f; Carson Robison, g.
New York, NY   Thursday, May 19, 1927

| 144179-3 | The Mississippi Flood Song (On The Old Mississippi Shore) | Ha 417-H, Ve 1417-H, Di 2417-G |

It is uncertain whether Velvet Tone 1417-V and Diva 2417-G were issued as shown or as by **Vernon Dalhart**.

Vernon Dalhart, v; acc. unknown, f; prob. Carson Robison, g.
New York, NY   c. May 20, 1927

| 2472-A,-B,-C,-D | Lucky Lindy | Ca 1162, Lin 2638, Ro 390, Vri 5074 |
| 2473-A,-B,-C,-D | "Lindbergh" (The Eagle Of The U.S.A.) | Ca 1162, Lin 2638, Ro 390, Vri 5074 |

Acc. Sam Raitz, f; own h; Carson Robison, g.
New York, NY   Saturday, May 21, 1927

| E-23282/83 | The Lost French Flyers (Captains Nungesser & Coli) | Br unissued |
| E-23284*/85 | Jim Blake | Br 173 |

Brunswick 173 was probably never issued.

Acc. unknown, vn; unknown, c; unknown, cl; unknown, p; unknown, g; unknown, bb; unknown, vc; unknown, d.
New York, NY   Monday, May 23, 1927

| 38826-2 | Lindbergh (The Eagle Of The U.S.A.) | Vi 20674, ZoAu EE61 |

Revs: Victor 20674, Zonophone EE61 by Vaughn De Leath (popular).

Vernon Dalhart-1/**Al Craver**-2, v; acc. poss. Murray Kellner, f; own h-3; prob. Carson Robison, g.
New York, NY   Tuesday, May 24, 1927

144210-2	The Airship That Never Returned -1, 3	Co 15162-D
144211-1,-3	The Death Of Lura Parsons -2, 3	Co 15169-D
144212-1,-2	Lucky Lindy -1	Co 1000-D

Vernon Dalhart, v; acc. unknown orch.
   New York, NY   Tuesday, May 24, 1927
   144213-2,-3   Lindbergh (The Eagle Of The U.S.A.)   Co 1000-D

Acc. unknown, f; prob. Carson Robison, g.
   New York, NY   Wednesday, May 25, 1927
   2480-A   The Heroes' Last Flight   Ca 1163, Ro 391
Revs: Cameo 1163, Romeo 391 by Leroy Montesanto (popular).

Acc. Sam Raitz, f; unknown, t-1; own or Carson Robison, h-2; Carson Robison, g; unknown, traps-3.
   New York, NY   Thursday, May 26, 1927
   E-23323*/24*/25; Lucky Lindy -1, 3   Br 3572, BrAu 3572, Vo 5168
     E-6010/11/12W
   E-23326*/27*;   The Lost French Flyers (Captains Nungesser &   Br 3572, BrAu 3572, Vo 5168
     E-6013/14W   Coli)
   E-23328/29/30* The Death Of Lura Parsons -2   Br 173
Brunswick 173 was probably never issued.

Acc. unknown orch.
   New York, NY   Friday, May 27, 1927
   11715-C   Lindbergh (The Eagle Of The U.S.A.)   Ed 52029, 5362
   11716-A,-C   Lucky Lindy   Ed 52029, 5356

Acc. poss. Murray Kellner, f; prob. Carson Robison, g.
   New York, NY   c. May 31, 1927
   GEX-661-B,-C   Lindbergh (The Eagle Of The U.S.A.)   Ge 6169, Ch 15286, Sil 5087, 8144, 25087,
                                                                                   Spt 9238, Chg 369, Her 75555
Matrix GEX-661 is titled *Lindbergh, The Eagle Of The U.S.A.* on Silvertone 8144.
Revs: Champion 15286 by Walter Lyboult (popular); Herwin 75555 by Ben Jarrell (see Da Costa Woltz).

   New York, NY   c. May 1927
   7268-1   Like An Angel You Flew Into Everyone's Heart   Ba 1995, Do 3966, Re 8327
                            (Lindbergh)
   874-2,-3   Like An Angel You Flew Into Everyone's Heart   Or 923
                            (Lindbergh)
Oriole 923 as by **Frank Evans**.
Revs: Banner 1995 by Arthur Fields (popular); Oriole 923 by Hugh Donovan (popular).

Jeff Calhoun, v; acc. prob. Murray Kellner, f; own h; Carson Robison, g.
   New York, NY   c. May 1927
   2396-A   Wreck Of The Titanic   GG 4131, ?Globe 4131, Rad 4131, 04131,
                                                                 ?Supreme 4131
   2397-A   The Butcher Boy   GG 4133, ?Globe 4133, Rad 4133,
                                                                ?Supreme 4133
   2398-A   I Wish I Was Single Again   GG 4141, ?Globe 4141, Mad 1918, Rad 4141,
                                                                ?Supreme 4141
   2399-B   Wild And Reckless Hobo   GG 4140, ?Globe 4140, Mad 5073, Rad 4140,
                                                                ?Supreme 4140, VD 5073
Madison/Van Dyke 5073 as by **Richard Eustis**.
Matrix 2396 is titled *The Wreck Of The Titanic* on Radiex 4131.
Another issue of Grey Gull 4131, Radiex 4131 couples Dalhart's matrix 2396-A not with his earlier matrix 2343, *Wreck Of The Old 97* (see c. February/March 1927 session), but with a recording of the latter title by Arthur Fields (matrix 2511), in his own name or as by **Jeff Calhoun** or **Mr. X**. Some such issues are as by **Jess Calhoun**. Later issues of Grey Gull 4131, Radiex 4131 use the same title in a recording (matrix 3128-B) by Frank Luther, in his own name or as by **Jeff Calhoun**.
Later issues of Grey Gull/?Globe/Radiex/?Supreme 4133, Van Dyke 74133 use the same title in a recording (matrix 3031-C) by, and as, Frank Luther.
Later issues of Grey Gull/?Globe/Radiex/?Supreme 4141 use the same title in a recording (matrix 3017,-B) by Frank Luther, in his own name or as by **Jeff Calhoun**.
Revs: Grey Gull/?Globe/Radiex/?Supreme 4140 by Arthur Hall (popular), 4141 by Francis Herold (popular); Madison/Van Dyke 5073 by Frank Luther.

Vernon Dalhart & Carson Robison, v duet; acc. Murray Kellner, f; Bill Wirges, p; Carson Robison, g/wh-1.
   New York, NY   Friday, June 3, 1927
   E-23448*/49/50   A Memory That Time Cannot Erase -1   Br 3577, Me M12017, Po P9074, PanAu P12017
   E-23451/52*/53   I Wonder If You Still Remember   Br 3577, Me M12017, Po P9074, PanAu P12017
Melotone M12017, Polk P9074, Panachord P12017 as by **The Jones Brothers**.

Vernon Dalhart, v; acc. unknown, f; prob. Carson Robison, g/wh-1.
   New York, NY   Saturday, June 11, 1927

| 144268-2 | Chamberlin And Lindy (Our Hats Are Off To You) | Co 1025-D |
| 144269-3 | Charlie Boy (We Love You) -1 | Co 1025-D |

New York, NY mid-June 1927

| 2500-A,-B,-C | Chamberlin And Lindy (Our Hats Are Off To You) | Ca 1175, Ro 392 |
| 2501- | Charley Boy (We Love You) | Ca 9096, Lin 3123, Ro 898 |

Revs: Cameo 1175, Romeo 392 by The Happiness Boys (popular); Cameo 9096 by Harry Smith (popular).

Acc. unknown, f; Carson Robison, g/wh-1; own wh-2.
New York, NY c. June 1927

107598-	Charlie Boy -1, 2	Pat 32273, Pe 12352
107599-	Chamberlin And Lindy (Our Hats Are Off To You)	Pat 32273, Pe 12352
	Lindbergh, The Eagle Of U.S.A.	Pat 32266, Pe 12345
	Lucky Lindy	Pat 32266, Pe 12345

Vernon Dalhart, v; or **Vernon Dalhart & Carson Robison**-1, v/wh-2 duet; acc. poss. Adelyne Hood, f; Vernon Dalhart, h-3; unknown, p-4; Carson Robison, g-5.
New York, NY Tuesday, July 12, 1927

10672-	Why Ain't I Happy At All -1, 5	Pat 32281, Pe 12360
107673-2	I Know There Is Somebody Waiting -1, 2, 5	Pat 32290, Pe 12369, Spt 32290
107674-2	A Memory That Time Cannot Erase -1, 2, 4	Pat 32290, Pe 12369, Spt 32290
107675-	Put My Little Shoes Away -1, 3, 5	Ca 9069, Lin 3098, Pat 32285, Pe 12364, Ro 873
107676-	Bury Me Not On A Lone Prairie -5	Ba 0531, Ca 0131, ?Do 4477, DoC 183039, Je 5784, 20048, Or 1783, 8048, Pat 32282, Pe 12361, ?Re 8922, Ro 5048, Cq 7467, Bwy 4099, CrC/MeC 83039, MeC 12143, Stg 283039
107677-1	The Three Drowned Sisters -3, 5	Ca 9068, Lin 3097, Pat 32285, Pe 12364, Ro 872
107678-2	The Cowboy's Lament -3, 5	Ba 0531, Ca 0131, 8219, ?Do 4477, Je 5784, 20048, Or 1783, 8048, Pat 32282, Pe 12361, ?Re 8922, 9017, 10017, Ro 599, 5048, Cq 7467, 7724, Bwy 4099, DeE F2506
107679-1	Barbara Allen -3, 5	Ca 8222, Lin 2827, Pat 32281, Pe 12360, Ro 602
107680-1	Bad Companions -5	Ca 8221, Lin 2826, Pat 32286, Pe 12365, Ro 601
107681-1	When The Work's All Done This Fall -5	Ca 9111, Lin 3138, Pat 32286, Pe 12365, Ro 913

Matrix 107672 on Perfect 12360 and matrix 107675 on Cameo 9069, Perfect 12364, Romeo 873 as by **Dalhart & Robison**.
Matrices 107676 and 107678 were assigned, on November 22, 1929, the Plaza matrices 9174 and 9175 (sometimes shown as 19174 and 19175) respectively, from which all the issues shown are derived except Pathé 32282 and Perfect 12361.
Melotone 12143, which couples matrices 9174 and 7470, was so issued only in Canada; the US issue bearing this number contains the same titles in versions by Frank & Phil Luther.
Matrix 107676 is titled *Bury Me Not On The Lone Prairie* on Jewel 20048, Oriole 8048, Perfect 12361, Romeo 5048.
Matrix 107678 is titled *Cowboy's Lament* on Conqueror 7724, or *The Dying Cowboy* on Decca F2506.
Some issues use controls or transfer matrices, as follows: 107675 = 3628; 107676 = 9174-2; 107677 = 3625; 107678 = 2986, 9175; 107679 = 2992; 107680 = 2990; 107681 = 3725.
Revs: Cameo 9111, probably Lincoln 3138, Regal 9017, 10017, Romeo 913 by Frank Marvin; Conqueror 7724 by the Canova Family; Decca F2506 by Ben Alley (popular).

Vernon Dalhart–Carson Robison, v/wh-1 duet; acc. Adelyne Hood, p; Carson Robison, g.
New York, NY Thursday, July 21, 1927

| 39692-2 | If Your Love Like The Rose Should Die -1 | Vi 21094 |
| 39693-2 | A Memory That Time Cannot Erase | Vi 21094 |

Vernon Dalhart, v; acc. prob. Adelyne Hood, f; own h-1; Carson Robison, g.
New York, NY July 1927

| 2546-B | The Cowboy's Dream -1 | Ca 1203, Lin 2666, Ro 431 |
| 2547-B | Bury Me Not On The Lone Prairie | Ca 1203, Lin 2666, Ro 431 |

Acc. prob. Adelyne Hood, f; own h/jh-1; Carson Robison, g/wh-2.
New York, NY Wednesday, August 3, 1927

| 11835-B | The Wreck Of Number Nine -1, 2 | Ed 52088, 5394 |
| 11836-C | The Mississippi Flood | Ed 52088, 5395 |

Acc. Adelyne Hood, f; Carson Robison, g/wh-1.
New York, NY Wednesday, August 10, 1927

| 39950-2 | Where The Coosa River Flows | Vi 20888 |
| 39951-1 | My Boy's Voice -1 | Vi 20888 |

Vernon Dalhart, v; or **Dalhart & Robison**-1, v duet; acc. prob. Adelyne Hood, f; Vernon Dalhart, h-2/jh-3/wh-4; unknown, bj-5; Carson Robison, g/wh-6.
New York, NY Wednesday, August 24, 1927

7469-2	When The Moon Shines Down Upon The Mountain -2, 3, 4, 6	Ba 6090, Do 0192, DoC 21334, Je 5115, Or 1026, Re 8409, Cq 7737, Chg 682, Htd 16158, 23031, Bwy 4049, Apex 8673, LS 24133, Mc 22210
7470-1,-2	When The Work's All Done This Fall	Ba 6086, Do 0192, DoC 21334, 181028, Je 5114, Or 1020, Re 8409, Cq 7737, Chg 688, Apex 8673, CrC/MeC/Roy/Stg 81028, MeC 12143, LS 24133, Mc 22210, Roy 381028, Stg 281028, Min M-904
7471-1,-2	Golden Slippers -1, 2, 3, 5	Ba 6090, Do 0193, DoC 21309, Je 5115, Or 1026, Re 8408, Sil 1526, 21526, Chg 682, Cq 7062, Htd 16158, 23031, Pm 3055, Bwy 8036, Apex 8656, CrC/MeC 81034, LS 24123, Mc 22200, Min M-922, Ruby 71034, Stg 281034
7472-3	My Blue Ridge Mountain Home -1, 2, 4, 5, 6	Ba 6086, Do 0193, DoC 21309, 181172, Je 5114, Or 1020, Re 8408, Sil 1526, 21526, Chg 688, Cq 7062, Pm 3055, Bwy 8036, 4053, Apex 8656, CrC/Roy 81172, LS 24123, Mc 22200, Stg 281172

Matrix 7471 on Banner 6090, Crown 81034 as by **Vernon Dalhart & Carson J. Robison**.
Jewel 5114, 5115, Oriole 1020, 1026, Homestead 16158 as by **Frank Evans** (matrices 7469, 7470) or **Evans & Clark** (matrices 7471, 7472). Paramount 3055, Broadway 8036 as by **Wolfe Ballard & Claude Samuels**.
Matrix 7469 was assigned, on October 23, 1933, ARC matrix 14206, which appeared on Broadway 4049.
Melotone 12143, which couples matrices 7470 and 9174, was so issued only in Canada; the US issue bearing this number contains the same titles in recordings by Frank & Phil Luther.
Matrix 7471 is titled *Oh! Dem Golden Slippers* on Minerva M-922.
Some issues use controls, as follows: 7469 = 1114,-2,-3; 7470 = 1070-1; 7471 = 1113-1, 872; 7472 = 1069-3, 871.
Revs: Broadway 4049 by the Colt Brothers (see Arthur Fields & Fred Hall), 4053 by the Arkansas Woodchopper; Minerva M-904 by Red Foley.

Vernon Dalhart, v; or **Vernon Dalhart & Carson Robison**-1, v duet; acc. Adelyne Hood, f/v-2; Vernon Dalhart, h-3/jh-4; unknown, cel-5; unknown, bj-6; Carson Robison, g/wh-7.
    New York, NY   Friday, August 26, 1927

107743-1	Jim Blake -3	Ca 8223, Lin 2828, Pat 32301, Pe 12380, Ro 603
107744-1,-2	Lura Parsons	Ca 8223, Lin 2828, Pat 32301, Pe 12380, Ro 603
107745-1	Picture From Life's Other Side	Ca 9067, Lin 3096, Pat 32296, Pe 12375, Ro 871
	I Wonder If You Still Remember -1, 5	Pat 32307, Pe 12386
	Cindy -3, 4	Pat 32307, Pe 12386
107749-1	When The Moon Shines Down Upon The Mountain -3, 4, 7	Pat 32295, Pe 12374, Chg 732
107750-1	Golden Slippers -1, 3, 4, 6	Pat 32295, Pe 12374, Chg 732
107752-2	Where We Never Grow Old -1, 2, 5	Ca 9068, Lin 3097, Pat 32296, Pe 12375, Ro 872

Matrix 107750 on Challenge 732 as by **Dalhart & Robison**. Matrix 107752 on Perfect 12375 as by **Vernon Dalhart–Carson Robison–Adelyne Hood**, and on Romeo 872 as by **Vernon Dalhart Trio**.
The items with unknown matrices may account for two of the matrices 107746/47/48/51.
Some issues use controls or transfer matrices, as follows: 107743 = 2993; 107744 = 2994; 107745 = 3623; 107752 = 3626.

Vernon Dalhart, v; or **Vernon Dalhart & Charlie Wells**-1: Vernon Dalhart, Carson Robison, v duet; acc. prob. Adelyne Hood, f; Vernon Dalhart, h/jh; unknown, bj; Carson Robison, g.
    New York, NY   Monday, August 29, 1927

144588-	Where The Coosa River Flows	Co unissued
144589-2	When The Moon Shines Down Upon The Mountain	Co 15181-D, CoE 19009, CoAu 01895
144590-2	Golden Slippers -1	Co 15181-D, CoE 19009, CoAu 01892

Rev. Columbia 01895 by Dan Hornsby.

Vernon Dalhart, v; or **Vernon Dalhart & Carson Robison**-1, v duet; acc. prob. Adelyne Hood, f; Vernon Dalhart, h/jh; unknown, bj; Carson Robison, g.
    New York, NY   Wednesday, September 7, 1927

11873-B	My Blue Ridge Mountain Home -1	Ed 52095, 5414
11874-A	When The Moon Shines Down Upon The Mountain	Ed 52095, 5413

Vernon Dalhart, v; or **Dalhart & Robison**-1, v duet; acc. prob. Adelyne Hood, f/p-2; Vernon Dalhart, h-3/jh-4/wh-5; unknown, bj-6; Carson Robison, g/wh-7.
    New York, NY   Friday, September 9, 1927

2599-B	Crepe On The Old Cabin Door	Ca 1248, Lin 2713, Ro 468, Ang 3077, PmAu 2510, StgAu 1132

2600-B	Wreck Of The No. 9 -3, 4	Ca 1247, Lin 2712, Ro 478
2601-A	Hand Me Down My Walking Cane -3	Ca 1237, Lin 2702, Ro 465
2602-A	Wish I Was A Single Girl Again -3, 4	Ca 1237, Lin 2702, Ro 465
2603-A	My Carolina Home -1, 5, 7	Ca 1246, Lin 2711, Ro 477, GP 18718
2604-A	My Blue Ridge Mountain Home -1, 2, 3, 4, 5, 6, 7	Ca 1236, 9074, Lin 2701, 3103, Ro 464, 878, GP 18718
2605-B	Golden Slippers-1, 3, 4, 6	Ca 1236, 9074, Lin 2701, 3103, Ro 464, 878

Grand Pree 18718 as by **Wood & Turner**.
Matrix 2599 is mistitled *A Memory That Time Cannot Erase* on Angelus 3077, Paramount 2510, and Sterling 1132.
Matrix 2600 is titled *Wreck Of The #9* on some issues of Romeo 478.
Revs: Angelus 3077 (though credited to Dalhart), Paramount 2510 by Wm Robyn (popular).

Vernon Dalhart, v; or **Vernon Dalhart & Carson Robison**-1, v duet; acc. prob. Adelyne Hood, f; Vernon Dalhart, h-2/jh-3; unknown, p-4; Carson Robison, g-5/wh-6.
New York, NY   c. September 12-17, 1927

GEX-861	When The Moon Shines Down Upon The Mountain -2, 5, 6	Ge 6374, Ch 15375, Sil 5062, 8140, 25062, Spt 9237, Spr 347, Her 75569, Bell 1170
GEX-862-A	Cindy -2, 3, 5	Ge 6289, Ch 15393, Sil 5062, 8140, 25062, Spt 9237, Chg 405, Spr 347, Her 75569
GEX-863-A	My Boy's Voice -5, 6	Ge 6289, Ch 15375, Sil 5063, 8133, 25063, Spt 9231, Her 75571
GEX-864	If Your Love Like The Rose Should Die -1, 4	Sil 5063, 25063

Matrix GEX-864 on Silvertone 5063, 25063 was replaced in May 1928 by matrix GEX-650-B.
Matrix GEX-861 is titled *When The Moon Shines Down Upon The Mountains* on Supertone 9237.
Revs: Gennett 6374 by Chubby Parker; Bell 1170 by David Miller.

Vernon Dalhart-1/**Al Craver**-2, v; acc. own h-3; Carson Robison, g.
New York, NY   Thursday, September 15, 1927

144675-	My Boy's Voice -1	Co unissued
144676-3	The Fate Of Mildred Doran -2, 3	Co 15192-D
144677-3	Jim Blake -2, 3	Co 15192-D

Vernon Dalhart, v; or **Dalhart & Robison**-1, v duet; acc. prob. Adelyne Hood, f-2/p-3; Vernon Dalhart, h-4/jh-5/wh; Carson Robison, g/wh.
New York, NY   c. September 15, 1927

2613-B,C	When The Moon Shines Down Upon The Mountain -2, 4, 5	Ca 1246, Lin 2711, Ro 477
2614-B,C	A Memory That Time Cannot Erase -1, 3	Ca 1248, Lin 2713, Ro 468
2615-C	If Your Love Like The Rose Should Die -1, 3	Ca 1247, Lin 2712, Ro 478

No details (prob. as for next session).
New York, NY   Monday, September 26, 1927

7524-	I Know There Is Somebody Waiting	Pl unissued
7525-	My Boy's Voice	Pl unissued
7526-	Wreck Of The C. & O. No. 5	Pl unissued
7527-	Mildred Doran's Last Flight	Pl unissued

Vernon Dalhart, v; or **Dalhart & Robison**-1, v duet; acc. prob. Adelyne Hood, f; Vernon Dalhart, h-2/wh-3; Carson Robison, g/wh-4.
New York, NY   Monday, October 10, 1927

7524-4	I Know There Is Somebody Waiting -1, 3, 4	Ba 6114, 7102, Do 0198, DoC 21346, Je 5283, Or 1053, Re 8430, Chg 557, Cq 7059, Apex 8689
7525-5	My Boy's Voice -4	Ba 6113, Chg 558, Cq 7059, Do 0198, Je 5137, Or 1054, Re 8430
7526-3	Wreck Of The C. & O. No. 5 -2, 4	Ba 6113, Chg 558, Cq 7071, 7169, Do 0209, Je 5137, Or 1053, Re 8469, Apex 8689, Do 21356
7527-3	Mildred Doran's Last Flight -2	Ba 6114, Chg 557, Do 0199, Or 1054, Re 8431

Banner 6114, Jewel 5283, Apex 8689 as by **Vernon Dalhart & Carson J. Robison**. Jewel 5137, Oriole 1053, 1054 as by **Frank Evans**, except matrix 7524 on Oriole 1053 as by **Evans & Clark**.
Matrix 7527 is titled *The Fate Of Mildred Doran* on Banner 6114.
Some issues use controls, as follows: 7524 = 1165-4; 7525 = 1163-6; 7526 = 1164-3; 7527 = 1166.

Vernon Dalhart, v; acc. prob. Adelyne Hood, f; own h/jh; unknown, p-1; prob. Carson Robison, g.
New York, NY   Saturday, October 15, 1927

11958-C	The Little Black Mustache -1	Ed 52118, 5433
11959-C	Puttin' On The Style	Ed 52118, 5434

Vernon Dalhart, Carson Robison, Adelyne Hood, v trio; acc. Vernon Dalhart, h; Adelyne Hood, p; Carson Robison, g.
New York, NY   Tuesday, October 18, 1927
    40188-1,-2,-3   Old Plantation Melodies   Vi unissued

Adelyne Hood also recorded at this session in her own name.

Vernon Dalhart & Carson Robison & Adelyne Hood, v trio; acc. Adelyne Hood, f; Vernon Dalhart, h; unknown, cel; Carson Robison, g.
New York, NY   Wednesday, October 26, 1927
    11984-C   When The Sun Goes Down Again   Ed 52134, 5438
    11985-C   Sing On Brother, Sing!   Ed 52134, 5439

Vernon Dalhart, v; acc. unknown, vn; unknown, p; unknown, marimba-1; unknown, wh.
New York, NY   Wednesday, October 26, 1927
    144912-2   Our American Girl   Co 1175-D
    144913-3   The Whole World Is Waiting (For Dreams To   Co 1175-D, ReAu G20123
                         Come True) -1

Rev. Regal G20123 by Elliot Shaw (popular).

Vernon Dalhart, v; or **Dalhart & Robison**-1, v/wh-2 duet; or **Dalhart, Robison & Hood**-3, v trio; acc. Adelyne Hood, f; Vernon Dalhart, h-4/jh-5; unknown, bj-6; Carson Robison, g.
New York, NY   Thursday, October 27, 1927
    7587-2   Oh Susanna -3, 4, 5, 6   Ba 6137, Do 4068, DoC 21346, Je 5159,
                                                                      Or 1083, Re 8450, Chg 559, Cq 7063,
                                                                      Pm 3075, Bwy 8066, Apex 8688,
                                                                      CrC/MeC 81034, LS 24152, Mc 22230,
                                                                      Ruby 71034, Stg 281034
    7588-2   When The Sun Goes Down Again -1, 2   Ba 2180, Do 0208, DoC 21356, Je 5187,
                                                                      Or 1112, Re 8470, Cq 7073, Apex 8688,
                                                                      LS 24152, Mc 22230
    7589-3   Sing On, Brother, Sing -3, 4   Ba 6138, Do 4068, DoC 21382, Je 5165,
                                                                      Or 1082, Re 8450, Chg 562, Cq 7063,
                                                                      Pm 3075, Bwy 8066, Apex 8699, LS 24170,
                                                                      Mc 22248
    7590-2   Shine On, Harvest Moon -1   Ba 2181, Do 0213, DoC 21417, Je 5186,
                                                                      Or 1113, Re 8488, Sil 1610, 21610, Chg 556,
                                                                      Cq 7060, 7722, Htd 16512, Apex 8713,
                                                                      LS 24170, Mc 22248

Jewel 5159, 5165 as by **The Jewel Trio**. Jewel 5186, 5187, Oriole 1112, 1113, Homestead 16512 as by **Evans & Clark**. Oriole 1082, 1083 as by **The Oriole Trio**. Conqueror 7722 possibly as by **Vernon Dalhart** only. Crown 81034, and possibly Melotone 81304, Sterling 281034, as by **Dalhart Robison Hood**.
Matrix 7589 was assigned, on October 23, 1933, ARC matrix 14205, for projected release in (probably) the Broadway 4000 series, but no such release was made. Matrix 7587 is titled *Oh Susanna!* on unidentified issues.
Some issues use controls, as follows: 7587 = 1234-2,-3, 965; 7588 = 1291-2; 7589 = 1237-1, 966; 7590 = 1293.

Vernon Dalhart Trio: Vernon Dalhart, Carson Robison, Adelyne Hood, v trio; acc. Adelyne Hood, f; Carson Robison, g.
New York, NY   Friday, October 28, 1927
    81581-B   When The Sun Goes Down Again   OK 45164
    81582-A   Sing On, Brother, Sing   OK 45164

Dalhart & Robison, v duet; acc. Adelyne Hood, f; Carson Robison, g/wh.
New York, NY   c. October 1927
    107850-   When The Sun Goes Down Again   Pat 32323, Pe 12402

Vernon Dalhart, v; acc. Adelyne Hood, f; unknown, p-1; Carson Robison, g-2/wh-3.
New York, NY   Wednesday, November 9, 1927
    18023-B   The Whole World Is Waiting (For Dreams To   Ed 52144, 5452
                         Come True) -1, 3
    18024-C   Where The Coosa River Flows -2   Ed 52144

Acc. Adelyne Hood, f; Carson Robison, g/wh-1.
New York, NY   Thursday, November 10, 1927
                         Down Where The Coosa River Flows   Pat 32318, Pe 12397
                         My Boy's Voice -1   Pat 32318, Pe 12397

Vernon Dalhart–Carson Robison, v duet; or **Vernon Dalhart–Carson Robison–Adelyne Hood**-1, v trio; acc. Adelyne Hood, f; Vernon Dalhart, h-2/jh-3; William Carlino, bj-4; Carson Robison, g/wh-5; unknown, bells-6.
New York, NY   Tuesday, November 15, 1927
    40576-2   Sing On, Brother, Sing -1, 2   Vi 21083, Zo 5447, HMVAu EA294
    40577-2   Hear Dem Bells -2, 4, 6   Vi 21083, Zo 5447, HMVAu EA286

40578-2	Oh! Susanna -1, 2, 3, 4	Vi 21169, Zo 5126, HMVAu EA309
40579-2	When The Sun Goes Down Again -5	Vi 21169, Zo 5126, HMVAu EA309

Zonophone 5447 as by **Vernon Dalhart, Carson Robison & Adelyne Hood** (matrix 40756)/**Vernon Dalhart & Carson Robison** (matrix 40577).
Revs: HMV EA286 by Whiteman's Rhythm Boys (popular), EA294 by Frank Crumit (popular).

Vernon Dalhart, v; acc. unknown.
New York, NY   Friday, November 18, 1927

2696-	Where The Coosa River Flows	Ca 1273, Lin 2738, Ro 507
2697-	My Boy's Voice	Ca 1273, Lin 2738, Ro 507

Acc. Adelyne Hood, f; own h-1/jh-2; unknown, p-3; Carson Robison, g-4/wh-5.
New York, NY   Wednesday, November 23, 1927

7629-3	Where The Coosa River Flows -4	Ba 6138, Do 4069, Je 5165, Or 1083, Re 8449, Chg 562
7630-3	The Whole World Is Waiting For Dreams To Come True -3, 5	Ba 6137, Do 4069, Je 5159, Or 1082, Re 8449, Chg 559
7639-2	The Old Grey Mare -1, 2, 4	Ba 2180, Do 0209, DoC 21367, Je 5187, Or 1112, Re 8469, Cq 7071, 7169, Apex 8699, CrC 81033, Stg 81033, 281033, LS 24187, Mc 22265, MeC/Min M-901

Jewel 5165 as by **The Jewel Trio**. Jewel 5187, Oriole 1082, 1083, 1112 as by **Frank Evans**.
Some issues use controls, as follows: 7629 = 1236-3; 7630 = 1235-1; 7639 = 1290-1,-2.
Rev. Minerva M-901 by Frank Marvin.

Vernon Dalhart & Carson Robison, v duet; or **Vernon Dalhart, Carson Robison & Adelyne Hood**-1, v trio; acc. Adelyne Hood, f; Bert Hirsch, f-2; Vernon Dalhart, h-3/jh-4/wh-5; Carson Robison, g/wh-6.
New York, NY   Monday, November 28, 1927

E-25316/17*/18*; E-7105/06W	Sing On, Brother, Sing -1, 3	Br 149, 3743, BrAu 3743, Vo 5214, PanAu P12173
E-25319*/20*; E-7107/08W	Old Plantation Melody -2, 6	Br 126, 3742, BrAu 3742, Vo 5213, Spt S2016
E-25321/22*; E-7109/10W	When The Moon Shines Down Upon The Mountain -3, 4, 6	Br 149, 3743, BrAu 3743, Vo 5213, Spt S2016, PanAu P12173
E-25323*/24*; E-7111/12W	When The Sun Goes Down Again -5, 6	Br 126, 3742, BrAu 3742, Vo 5214

Dalhart–Robison–Hood, v trio; acc. Carson Robison, g.
New York, NY   c. November 1927

107888-	Sing On Brother Sing	Pat 32323, Pe 12402

Vernon Dalhart & Company: Vernon Dalhart, Carson Robison, v duet; acc. prob. Adelyne Hood, f; Vernon Dalhart, h; Carson Robison, g.
New York, NY   Thursday, December 15, 1927

18107-C	My Carolina Home	Ed 52174, 5459
18108-B	O! Dem Golden Slippers	Ed 52174, 5460

Dalhart, Robison & Hood, v trio; acc. Adelyne Hood, f; poss. William Carlino, bj; Carson Robison, g.
New York, NY   Tuesday, December 20, 1927

7686-3	Old Plantation Melody	Ba 7047, Do 0212, DoC 31004, Je 5229, Or 1146, Re 8489, Chg 570, Apex 8795

Jewel 5229 as by **The Jewel Trio**. Oriole 1146 as by **The Oriole Trio**.
Some issues use the control 1349-3.

Dalhart–Robison–Hood, v trio; or Vernon Dalhart, v-1; or **Dalhart & Robison**-2, v/wh-3 duet; acc. Adelyne Hood, f; Vernon Dalhart, h-4/jh-5; poss. William Carlino, bj-6; Carson Robison, g; unknown, bell eff-7.
New York, NY   Tuesday, December 20, 1927

107966-2	I'll Meet Her When The Sun Goes Down -1, 4, 5	Pat 32326, Pe 12405
107967-1	Oh, Susanna -4, 6	Pat 32326, Pe 12405, PeE P420
107985	Heah Dem Bells -4, 6, 7	Pat 32330, Pe 12409, Sr 32330
107988	Shine On Harvest Moon -2, 3	Pat 32330, Pe 12409, PeE P420, Sr 32330
	Where Is My Mama? -2	Pat 32335, Pe 12414
	Mobile Bay -6	Pat 32335, Pe 12414

Perfect P420 as by **Dalhart, Robison & Hood**.

Vernon Dalhart, v; or Vernon Dalhart, Carson Robison, v duet-1; or Vernon Dalhart, Carson Robison, Adelyne Hood, v trio-2; acc. Adelyne Hood, f-3; Vernon Dalhart, h-4/jh-5/wh-6; poss. William Carlino, bj-7; Carson Robison, g/wh-8.
New York, NY   Tuesday, December 20, 1927

2748-B	I'll Meet Her When The Sun Goes Down -3, 4, 5	Ca 8107, Lin 2761, Ro 530, PmAu 2558
2749-B	Oh Susanna -2, 3, 4, 5, 7	Ca 8116, Lin 2770, Ro 539

2750-B	Sing On Brother Sing -2	Ca 8107, Lin 2761, Ro 530
2751-B	When The Sun Goes Down Again -1, 3, 6, 8	Ca 8148, Lin 2802, Ro 571
2752-A	Among My Souvenirs -2, 3, 8	Ca 8106, Lin 2760, Ro 529, Electron 5005, PmAu 2507

Rev. Electron 5005 by Lawrence Henry (popular).

Vernon Dalhart, v; or **Vernon Dalhart & Carson Robison**-1, v duet; acc. Adelyne Hood, f; Vernon Dalhart, h-2/jh-3; Carson Robison, g/wh-4.

New York, NY   Wednesday, December 21, 1927

7672-	Hear Dem Bells -1	Ba 2181, Do 0208, Je 5186, Or 1113, Re 8470, Chg 556, Cq 7073, Htd 16512, Apex 26090
7684-6	I'll Meet Her When The Sun Goes Down -2, 3	Ba 7020, Do 0213, DoC 21453, Je 5205, Or 1146, Re 8488, Sil 1610, 21610, Cq 7060, 7722, Apex 8795
7685-7	Where Is My Mama? -1, 4	Ba 7020, Do 0212, Je 5205, Or 1148, Re 8489

Jewel 5186, 5205, Oriole 1113, Homestead 16512 as by **Evans & Clark**, except matrix 7684 on Jewel 5205 as by **Frank Evans**. Oriole 1146 as by **Frank Evans**, 1148 as by **Evans & Clarke**. Conqueror 7722 possibly as by **Vernon Dalhart** only. Some issues use controls, as follows: 7672 = 1292; 7684 = 1345-7; 7685 = 1346-6, -7.
Rev. Apex 26090 by Harry Stride (popular).

Vernon Dalhart, v; or Vernon Dalhart, Carson Robison, Adelyne Hood, v trio-1; acc. Adelyne Hood, f; Vernon Dalhart, h-2; Carson Robison, g.

New York, NY   Tuesday, January 3, 1928

| 145463-2 | I'll Meet Her When The Sun Goes Down | Ha 612-H, Ve 1612-V, Di 2612-G |
| 145464-2 | Sing On, Brother, Sing -1, 2 | Ha 566-H, Ve 1566-V, Di 2566-G |

Harmony 566-H, 612-H as by **Mack Allen**.

Vernon Dalhart & Carson Robison, v/wh-1 duet; or Vernon Dalhart, Carson Robison, Adelyne Hood, v trio-2; acc. Adelyne Hood, f; Vernon Dalhart, h-3; poss. William Carlino, bj-4; Carson Robison, g; unknown, eff-5/bell-6.

New York, NY   Wednesday, January 4, 1928

145472-3	When The Sun Goes Down Again -1, 4, 5	Ha 612-H, Ve 1612-V, Di 2612-G
145473-3	Hear Dem Bells -2, 3, 4, 6	Ha 566-H, Ve 1566-V, Di 2566-G
145474-1	Where Is My Mama	Co 15218-D

Harmony 566-H as by **Mack Allen**, 612-H as by **Mack Allen & Gil Parker**. Velvet Tone 1612-V, Diva 2612-G as by **Vernon Dalhart & Gil Parker**. Columbia 15218-D as by **Al Craver & Charlie Wells**.

Al Craver, v; acc. Adelyne Hood, f; Carson Robison, g.

New York, NY   Thursday, January 5, 1928

| 145475-3 | Little Marion Parker | Co 15218-D |

Vernon Dalhart: Vernon Dalhart, Carson Robison, v duet; or Vernon Dalhart, Carson Robison, Adelyne Hood, v trio-1; acc. Adelyne Hood, f; poss. William Carlino, bj-2; Carson Robison, g/wh-3; Vernon Dalhart, wh-4; unknown, bells-5.

New York, NY   Friday, January 6, 1928

2784-A	Hear Dem Bells -1, 2, 5	Ca 8116, Lin 2770, Ro 539
2785-A	On Mobile Bay -1, 2	Ca 8114, Lin 2768, Ro 537
2786-A	Where Is My Mama? -3	Ca 8148, Lin 2802, Ro 571
2787-A	Shine On Harvest Moon -3, 4	Ca 8115, Lin 2769, Ro 538, GP 18710, Electron 5006, PmAu 2507, Golden Tongue CW111, MeAu FG10012

Grand Pree 18710 as by **Paul Adams**. Golden Tongue CW111 as by **Arthur Hillman**. Melotone FG10012 as by **Fred Laurie & Chas King**.
Revs: Cameo 8114, 8115, Lincoln 2768, 2769, Romeo 537, 538 by Jack Kaufman (popular); Electron 5006 by Lawrence Henry (popular); Golden Tongue CW111 unknown; Melotone FG10012 by Roderic Newman (popular).

Vernon Dalhart & Company: Vernon Dalhart, v; acc. unknown (but prob. similar to that on the session of February 17, 1928).

New York, NY   Thursday, January 12, 1928

| 18165 | Old Plantation Melody | Ed unissued |
| 18166 | A Memory That Time Cannot Erase | Ed unissued |

Vernon Dalhart, v; or **Vernon Dalhart & Carson J. Robison**-1, v duet; acc. prob. Adelyne Hood, f; unknown, t-2; Vernon Dalhart, h-3/jh-4; Carson Robison, g; several unidentifieds, sp-5/laughing-5.

New York, NY   Friday, January 20, 1928

| 7741-2 | Lone Eagle (Lindy To Mexico) -2 | Ba 7026, Do 0216, Je 5209, Or 1148, Re 8495, Sil 1611, 21611, Cq 7061 |
| 7742-2 | That Old Wooden Rocker -1 | Ba 7074, Do 0216, 0234, DoC 21399, Je 5253, Or 1166, Re 8495, 8551, Sil 1611, 21611, Cq 7061, 7175, 7750, Bwy 4063, Apex 8732, LS 24190, Mc 22268 |

| 7743-2 | The Little Brown Jug -3, 4, 5 | Ba 7026, 7102, Do 0224, DoC 21399, Je 5209, 5283, Or 1194, Re 8527, Cq 7173, Apex 8732, CrC 81033, LS 24190, Mc 22268, Min M-922, Stg 81033, 281033 |

Jewel 5209, Oriole 1148 as by **Frank Evans**. Jewel 5253, Oriole 1166 as by **Evans & Clarke**. Silvertone 1611, Conqueror 7061, Broadway 4063, and probably Silvertone 21611 as by **Dalhart & Robison**. Conqueror 7750 as by **Vernon Dalhart**. Some issues use controls, as follows: 7741 = 1359-2; 7742 = 1397-2; 7743 = 1360-2.
Rev. Broadway 4063 by (Asa) Martin & (James) Roberts.

Al Craver, v; or **Al Craver & Charlie Wells**-1: Vernon Dalhart, Carson Robison, v duet; acc. prob. Adelyne Hood, f; Vernon Dalhart, h-2; poss. William Carlino, bj; Carson Robison, g.
New York, NY   Wednesday, January 25, 1928

| 145581-2 | That Good Old Country Town -1, 2 | Co 15223-D |
| 145582-1 | Henry's Made A Lady Out Of Lizzie | Co 15223-D |

Dalhart & Robison, v duet; or **Dalhart, Robison & Hood**-1, v trio; acc. Adelyne Hood, f; Vernon Dalhart, h-2/jh-3; poss. William Carlino, bj-4; Carson Robison, g/wh-5.
New York, NY   Wednesday, February 8, 1928

7773-2	Sweet Elaine -1, 5	Ba 7046, Do 0221, Je 5228, Or 1167, Re 8508, Chl 569, Cq 7172
7774-2	Bring Me A Leaf From The Sea -2, 3, 4	Ba 7046, Do 0220, DoC 181028, Je 5228, Or 1167, Re 8509, Chg 569, Cq 7058, Apex 8739, CrC 81028, MeC 81028, 181028, Roy 381028, Stg 81028, 281028
7775-2	That Good Old Country Town -2, 3, 4	Ba 7047, Do 0221, Je 5229, Or 1166, Re 8508, Chg 570, Cq 7172, Pm 3088, Bwy 8076

Jewel 5228 as by **The Jewel Trio** (7773)/**Evans & Clarke** (7774), 5229 as by **Evans & Clarke**. Oriole 1166 as by **Evans & Clarke**, 1167 as by **The Oriole Trio** (7773)/**Evans & Clark** (7774). Conqueror 7058 and matrix 7775 on Conqueror 7172 as by **Vernon Dalhart & Carson Robison**. Paramount 3088, Broadway 8076 as by **Wolfe Ballard & Claude Samuels**. Some issues use controls, as follows: 7773 = 1404-1; 7774 = 1403-2; 7775 = 1405-2, 1004.
Revs: Regal 8509, Conqueror 7058, Paramount 3088 by Irving Kaufman (popular).

Vernon Dalhart–Carson Robison, v duet; or **Vernon Dalhart**-1, v; acc. Adelyne Hood, f; Vernon Dalhart, h-2; William Carlino, bj; Carson Robison, g/wh.
New York, NY   Monday, February 13, 1928

| 42438-2 | That Good Old Country Town -2 | Vi 21306 |
| 42439-2 | You Can't Blame Me For That -1 | Vi 21306 |

Vernon Dalhart & Co.: Vernon Dalhart, Carson Robison, v duet; or Vernon Dalhart, Carson Robison, Adelyne Hood, v trio-1; acc. Adelyne Hood, f; unknown, p; Carson Robison, g/wh.
New York, NY   Friday, February 17, 1928

| 18165-G | Old Plantation Melody -1 | Ed 52229, 5488 |
| 18166-C | A Memory That Time Cannot Erase | Ed 52229, 5495 |

Vernon Dalhart & Co.: Vernon Dalhart, v; or **Vernon Dalhart & Carson Robison**-1, v duet; acc. Adelyne Hood, f; Vernon Dalhart, h/jh; William Carlino, bj; Carson Robison, g/wh.
New York, NY   Friday, February 17, 1928

| 18245-A | That Good Old Country Town -1 | Ed 52248, 5498 |
| 18246-A | You Can't Blame Me For That | Ed 52248, 5499 |

Vernon Dalhart, v; or **Vernon Dalhart & Carson Robison**-1, v duet; acc. Adelyne Hood, f; Vernon Dalhart, h/jh-2; William Carlino, bj-3; Carson Robison, g/wh-4.
New York, NY   February 1928

108058-1	You Can't Blame Me For That -2	Pat 32345, Pe 12424
108059-1	Little Brown Jug -2, 3	Pat 32342, Pe 12421
108060-2	Old Gray Mare -3	Pat 32342, Pe 12421
108064-2	That Good Old Country Town -1, 2, 3	Pat 32345, Pe 12424
108065-2	Bring Me A Leaf From The Sea -1, 2, 3	Pat 32351, Pe 12430

Intervening matrices are untraced.

Vernon Dalhart, v; or **Vernon Dalhart Trio**-1: Vernon Dalhart, Carson Robison, v duet; acc. Adelyne Hood, f; Vernon Dalhart, h-2/jh; William Carlino, bj; Carson Robison, g/wh-3.
New York, NY   February 1928

2900-A,-B	You Can't Blame Me For That -2, 3	Ca 8169, Lin 2824, Ro 592, GP 18715, PmAu 2557, MeAu 10017
2901-A	The Little Brown Jug -2	Ca 8168, Lin 2823, Ro 591
2902-A	The Old Grey Mare -2	Ca 8169, Lin 2824, Ro 592
2907-A	That Good Old Country Town -1, 3	Ca 8168, Lin 2823, Ro 591
2908-A	Bring Me A Leaf From The Sea -1, 2	Ca 8199, Lin 2854, Ro 629

Grand Pree 18715 as by **Wood & Turner**. Paramount 2557 as by **Gene Hall**. Melotone 10017 as by **Walter Clark**. Intervening matrices are untraced.

Revs: Grand Pree 18715 by Albert Lee (popular); Paramount 2557 (with same credit) by unidentified popular artist; Melotone 10017 by Laurie & King (popular).

Vernon Dalhart, v; or **Dalhart, Robison & Hood**-1, v trio; acc. Adelyne Hood, f; Carson Robison, g.
New York, NY　　　　　　　　　　　　　　　　　　　　　　　　　　　　　Thursday, March 1, 1928

| 108... - | The Miner's Prayer | Pat 32359, Pe 12438 |
| 108... - | Old Plantation Melody -1 | Pat 32359, Pe 12438 |

Vernon Dalhart–Carson Robison–Adelyne Hood, v trio; or **Vernon Dalhart & Carson Robison**-1, v duet; acc. Murray Kellner, f; Adelyne Hood, f; Carson Robison, g; Vernon Dalhart, wh-2.
New York, NY　　　　　　　　　　　　　　　　　　　　　　　　　　　　　Thursday, March 8, 1928

| 43336-3 | In The Hills Of Old Kentucky -2 | Vi 21488 |
| 43337-2 | Drifting Down The Trail Of Dreams -1 | Vi 21488 |

Vernon Dalhart & Carson J. Robison, v duet; or **Vernon Dalhart**-1, v; acc. prob. Adelyne Hood, f; prob. Murray Kellner, f-2; Vernon Dalhart, h-3; Carson Robison, g/wh-4.
New York, NY　　　　　　　　　　　　　　　　　　　　　　　　　　　　　Friday, March 9, 1928

7831-3	Drifting Down The Trail Of Dreams -2, 4	Ba 7073, Do 0228, Je 5252, Or 1195, Re 8543, Cq 7174
7832-2,-3	Six Feet Of Earth -3	Ba 7098, Do 0225, DoC 21423, Je 5278, Or 1219, Re 8526, Chg 587, Cq 7730, Pm 3091, Bwy 8067, Apex 8762
7833-3	I'm Drifting Back To Dreamland -2	Ba 7073, Do 0224, DoC 21432, Je 5252, Or 1195, Re 8527, Cq 7173, Apex 8744, LS 24343, Mc 22343
7834-3	Little Marian Parker -1, 3	Ba 7074, Do 0225, DoC 21417, 181104, Je 5253, Or 1194, Re 8526, Cq 7730, Pm 3091, Bwy 8067, Apex 8779, CrC/Roy 81104, Stg 281104, LS 24206, Mc 22284

Jewel 5253, Oriole 1194 as by **Frank Evans**. Matrix 7832 on Conqueror 7730 as by **Dalhart & Robison**, on Paramount 3091 as by **Dalhart–Robison**, and on Broadway 8067 as by **Vernon Dalhart**.
Matrix 7834 is titled *Little Marion Parker* on Broadway 8067, Sterling 281104.
Some issues use controls, as follows: 7831 = 1452-2; 7832 = 1463-2, 1013, 1113; 7833 = 1451-2; 7834 = 1410,-3, 1014, 1114.

Vernon Dalhart, v; or **Vernon Dalhart & Carson Robison**-1, v/wh duet; or **Dalhart–Robison–Hood**-2, v trio; acc. Adelyne Hood, f; prob. Murray Kellner, f-3; Carson Robison, g.
New York, NY　　　　　　　　　　　　　　　　　　　　　　　　　　　　Wednesday, March 14, 1928

108089-	Drifting Down The Trail Of Dreams -1, 3	Pat 32354, Pe 12433
108090-1	In The Hills Of Old Kentucky -2, 3	Pat 32351, Pe 12430
108091-	Song Of The Failure	Pat 32354, Pe 12433

Vernon Dalhart Trio: Vernon Dalhart, v; or Vernon Dalhart, Carson Robison, v duet-1; acc. Adelyne Hood, f; Carson Robison, g.
New York, NY　　　　　　　　　　　　　　　　　　　　　　　　　　　　　c. mid-March 1928

2960-A	Drifting Down The Trail Of Dreams -1	Ca 8214, Lin 2869, Ro 644, GP 18703, PmAu 2539, Golden Tongue CW116
2961-	In The Hills Of Old Kentucky	Ca unissued
2962-A	Song Of The Failure	Ca 8199, Lin 2854, Ro 629, GP 18710, PmAu 2539

Grand Pree 18703 as by **Clark & Clare The Joy Boys**, 18710 as by **Paul Adams**. Golden Tongue CW116 as by **The Joy Boys**.
Matrix 2961 is hypothetical.
Revs: Grand Pree 18703, Golden Tongue CW116 popular.

Vernon Dalhart & Carson J. Robison, v duet; or **Vernon Dalhart, Carson J. Robison & Adelyne Hood**-1, v trio; or **Vernon Dalhart**-2, v; acc. Adelyne Hood, f; poss. Murray Kellner, f; Carson Robison, g.
New York, NY　　　　　　　　　　　　　　　　　　　　　　　　　　　　　Tuesday, March 20, 1928

7863-	A Memory That Time Cannot Erase	Ba 7099, Do 4140, Je 5279, Or 1220, Re 8544, Chg 588, Pm 3101, Bwy 8072
7864-	In The Hills Of Old Kentucky -1	Ba 7099, Do 0228, DoC 21453, Je 5279, Or 1220, Re 8543, Chg 588, Pm 3092, Bwy 8075, Apex 8779
7865-3	Song Of The Failure -2	Ba 7098, Do 4140, Je 5278, Or 1219, Re 8544, Chg 587, Pm 3092, Bwy 8075, Apex 8853, LS 24355, Mc 22355

Matrix 7864 on Broadway 8075 as by **Dalhart–Robison–Hood**. Matrix 7864 is titled *The Hills Of Old Kentucky* on that issue. Some issues use controls, as follows: 7863 = 1502-2; 7864 = 1501-2, 1025, 1125; 7865 = 1462-3, 1024, 1124.

Vernon Dalhart, v; or Vernon Dalhart, Carson Robison, v/wh duet-1; acc. Adelyne Hood, f; Vernon Dalhart, h-2; Carson Robison, g.
New York, NY   Tuesday, March 20, 1928

43159-1	Song Of The Failure	Vi 21331
43160-1,-2	Where Is My Mama? -1	Vi unissued
43161-1	The Miner's Prayer -2	Vi 21331

Matrix 43160-1 was approved for issue but not issued.

Vernon Dalhart, v; or Vernon Dalhart, Carson Robison, Adelyne Hood, v trio-1; acc. Adelyne Hood, f; Carson Robison, g.
New York, NY   Wednesday, March 21, 1928

| 145788- | Song Of The Failure | Co unissued |
| 145789- | In The Hills Of Old Kentucky -1 | Co unissued |

Vernon Dalhart, v; or **Vernon Dalhart & Carson Robison**-1, v duet; acc. prob. Adelyne Hood, f; Vernon Dalhart, h; Carson Robison, g.
New York, NY   Thursday, March 22, 1928

| 108107-1 | Little Marion Parker | Pat 32350, Pe 12429 |
| 108108-2 | Six Feet Of Earth -1 | Pat 32350, Pe 12429 |

Jeff Calhoun, v; or **Jeff Calhoun & Bob Andrews**-1: Vernon Dalhart, Carson Robison, v/wh duet; acc. prob. Adelyne Hood, f; Vernon Dalhart, h/jh-2; poss. William Carlino, bj-3; Carson Robison, g.
New York, NY   Tuesday, March 27, 1928

2821-B	Wreck Of The Number Nine	GG 4172, Rad 4172
2822-A	Wreck Of The 1256 -2	GG 4226, Rad 4226, Sr 33051
2823-A,-B	Freight Wreck At Altoona -2	GG 4172, Rad 4172
2824-A	My Blue Ridge Mountain Home -1, 2, 3	GG 4180, Rad 4180, VD 74180, Sr 33051

Van Dyke 74180 as by **Martin Dixon & Bob Andrews**. Sunrise 33051 as by **Joseph Sears**.
Revs: Grey Gull/Radiex 4180, Van Dyke 74180 by Westell Gordon (popular).

Vernon Dalhart, v; or **Vernon Dalhart Trio**-1: Vernon Dalhart, Carson Robison, v duet; acc. prob. Adelyne Hood, f; Carson Robison, g.
New York, NY   March 1928

3002-A	Little Marian Parker	Ca 8191, Lin 2846, Ro 621
3003-A	Six Feet Of Earth -1	Ca 8191, Lin 2846, Ro 621
3004	The Miner's Prayer	Ca 8214, Lin 2869, Ro 644, GP 18704

Grand Pree 18704 as by **Paul Adams**.
Rev. Grand Pree 18704 by Albert Lee (popular).

Vernon Dalhart, v; acc. prob. Adelyne Hood, f; own h-1; Carson Robison, g.
New York, NY   Tuesday, April 3, 1928

| 145897-2 | Song Of The Failure | Ha 634-H, Ve 1634-V, Di 2634-G |
| 145898-2 | The Miner's Prayer -1 | Ha 634-H, Ve 1634-V, Di 2634-G |

Harmony 634-H as by **Mack Allen**.

Al Craver-1, v; or **Vernon Dalhart & Carson Robison**-2/**Al Craver & Charlie Wells**-3, v duet; acc. prob.: Murray Kellner, f; Adelyne Hood, f; Vernon Dalhart, h-4/jh-5; Carson Robison, g/wh-6.
New York, NY   Thursday, April 5, 1928

145963-2	The Hanging Of The Fox (Edward Hickman – Slayer Of Little Marion Parker) -1, 4	Co 15251-D, CoE 19017
145964-3	Drifting Down The Trail Of Dreams -2, 6	Co 15282-D, ReAu G21469
145965-3	Bring Me A Leaf From The Sea -2, 4, 5	Co 15282-D, ReAu G21469
145966-3	Six Feet Of Earth -3, 4	Co 15251-D, CoE 19017, CoAu 01894

Only one fiddle is heard on matrices 145963, 145966.

Vernon Dalhart, v; acc. unknown, f; prob. own h-1; unknown, g.
New York, NY   Thursday, April 12, 1928

| 43561-3 | Tired Of Mother – Part 1 | Vi 21369 |
| 43562-3 | Tired Of Mother – Part 2 -1 | Vi 21369 |

Vernon Dalhart, Adelyne Hood & Carson J. Robison, v trio; or **Vernon Dalhart & Carson J. Robison**-1, v duet; acc. Adelyne Hood, f; prob. Murray Kellner, f; Vernon Dalhart, h-2/jh-3; unknown, bj-4; Carson Robison, g.
New York, NY   Wednesday, April 18, 1928

| 7923-4 | Climbing Up De Golden Stairs -2, 3, 4 | Ba 7126, Do 0239, DoC 181172, Or 1243, Re 8567, Cq 7176, Apex 8774, CrC/Roy 81172, Stg 281172 |
| 7924-3 | The Little Green Valley -1 | Ba 7103, Do 0239, Je 5284, Or 1225, Re 8567, Ro 1173, Chg 631, Cq 7176, Bwy 4053 |

Matrix 7924 on Conqueror 7176 possibly as by **Dalhart & Robison**.
Some issues use controls, as follows: 7923 = 1554; 7924 = 1508-3.
Rev. Romeo 1173 by Frank Luther (see Carson Robison).

Vernon Dalhart–Carson Robison, v duet; or Vernon Dalhart, Carson Robison, Adelyne Hood, v trio-1; acc. Adelyne Hood, f; prob. Murray Kellner, f; William Carlino, bj-2; Carson Robison, g; unknown, steam-wh eff-3.
    New York, NY   Monday, April 23, 1928

43599-3	The Little Green Valley	Vi 21457, MW M-4053, Zo 5212, HMVAu EA382, Twin FT1280
43900-3	Steamboat -2, 3	Vi 21644
43901-2	There's A Whippoorwill A'Calling	Vi 21644
43902-1,-2,-3	Climbin' Up De Golden Stairs -1, 2	Vi unissued

Zonophone 5212 as by **Vernon Dalhart & Carson Robison**. Twin FT1280 as by **Dalhart & Robison**.

Vernon Dalhart, v; acc. unknown, f; own h; prob. Carson Robison, g.
    New York, NY   Thursday, April 26, 1928

7940-2	The West Plains Explosion	Ba 7125, Do 0241, Je 5307, Or 1243, Re 8568, Chg 626, Cq 7177, Pm 3097, Bwy 8074
7941-3	The Hanging Of Charles Birger	Ba 7126, Do 0241, Or 1244, Re 8568, Cq 7177, Pm 3097, Bwy 8074

Some issues use controls, as follows: 7940 = 1551-3, 1043, 1143; 7941 = 1553-3, 1044, 1144.

Acc. poss. Adelyne Hood, f; own h-1; Carson Robison, g.
    New York, NY   Friday, April 27, 1928

7942-3	The Death Of Floyd Bennett	Ba 7103, Do 0235, DoC 21423, Je 5284, Or 1225, Re 8552, Chg 631, Cq 7099, Pm 3101, Bwy 8072, Apex 8762, LS 24206, Mc 22284
7943-2	The Empty Cradle -1	Ba 7125, Do 0235, Je 5307, Or 1244, Re 8552, Chg 626, Cq 7099

Some issues use controls, as follows: 7942 = 1507-1,-3; 7943 = 1552-3.

Vernon Dalhart Trio (Ca/Lin/Ro)/**Vernon Dalhart & Carson Robison** (Pat/Pe), v duet/trio-1; acc. Adelyne Hood, f; prob. Murray Kellner, f; Vernon Dalhart, h-2/jh-3; poss. William Carlino, bj-4; Carson Robison, g; unknown, steamboat wh eff-5.
    New York, NY   Friday, April 27, 1928

108157-2; 3101-A	The Little Green Valley	Ca 8267, Lin 2915, Pat 32364, Pe 12443, PeE P407, Ro 690
108158- ; 3102-A	There's A Whip-poor-will A-Calling	Ca 8268, Lin 2916, Pat 32369, Pe 12448, Ro 691
108159-2; 3103-A	Steamboat Keep Rockin' -4, 5	Ca 8268, Lin 2916, Pat 32364, Pe 12443, PeE P407, Ro 691
108160- ; 3104-A	Climbing Up De Golden Stairs -1, 2, 3, 4	Ca 8267, Lin 2915, Pat 32369, Pe 12448, Ro 690

Matrix 108160 on Pathé 32369, Perfect 12448 as by **Dalhart–Robison–Hood**. Perfect P407 as by **Dalhart & Robison**.
Matrix 108158/3102 is titled *There's A Whippoorwill A-Calling* on Cameo 8268.
Matrix 108159/3103 is titled *Steamboat, Keep Rockin'* on Romeo 691.

Vernon Dalhart, v; acc. Adelyne Hood, f; own h-1; Carson Robison, g.
    New York, NY   Monday, April 30, 1928

400637-B	The Hanging Of Charles Birger -1	OK 45215
400638-A	The West Plains Explosion -1	OK 45215
400639-B	The Death Of Floyd Bennett -1	OK 45218
400640-B	The Empty Cradle	OK 45218

Acc. Adelyne Hood, f; own h; Carson Robison, g.
    New York, NY   Tuesday, May 1, 1928

43690-1,-2,-3	The Empty Cradle	Vi unissued
43691-1,-2,-3	The Death Of Floyd Bennett	Vi unissued

Matrix 43690-3 was approved for issue but not issued.

Vernon Dalhart Trio (Ca/Lin/Ro)/**Vernon Dalhart** (Pat/Pe): Vernon Dalhart, v; acc. Adelyne Hood, f; own h-1; Carson Robison, g.
    New York, NY   Wednesday, May 2, 1928

108... - ; 3113-A	The West Plains Explosion -1	Ca 8269, Lin 2917, Pat 32373, Pe 12452, Ro 692
108... - ; 3114-A	The Hanging Of Charles Birger -1	Ca 8269, Lin 2917, Pat 32373, Pe 12452, Ro 692
108... - ; 3115-A	The Empty Cradle	Ca 8224, Lin 2872, Pat 32361, Pe 12440, Ro 647
108... - ; 3116-A	The Death Of Floyd Bennett	Ca 8224, Lin 2872, Pat 32361, Pe 12440, Ro 647

Jeff Calhoun, v; or **Jeff Calhoun & Bob Andrews**-1: Vernon Dalhart, Carson Robison, v duet; acc. prob. Adelyne Hood, f; Vernon Dalhart, h/jh-2; poss. William Carlino, bj-3; Carson Robison, g; unknown, train eff-4.

New York, NY   Friday, May 4, 1928

2903-A	Billy Richardson's Last Ride -2	GG 4226, Rad 4226
2904-B	Six Feet Of Earth -1	GG 4224, Rad 4224
2905-A	Climbing Up Those Golden Stairs -1, 2	GG 4227, Rad 4227
2906-A	Casey Jones -2, 3, 4	GG 2412, 4174, Rad 2412, 4174, VD 74174, 5085, Mad 1923, 5085

Some issues of Grey Gull 4174, Radiex 4174 as by **Jeff Fuller**. Van Dyke 74174 as by **Martin Dixon**. Madison 1923 as by **James Ahearn**.
Some issues of matrix 2906 use the control 304.
Revs: Grey Gull/Radiex 2412 by Jack Kaufman (popular), 4174 by Vel Veteran (Irving Kaufman?) (popular), 4224 by Westell Gordon (popular), 4227 by Al Bernard (popular); Van Dyke 74174 by Hal Evans (Irving Kaufman?) (popular); Van Dyke/Madison 5085, and possibly Madison 1923, by Arthur Fields.

Vernon Dalhart & Company: Vernon Dalhart, v; acc. unknown.

New York, NY   Wednesday, May 9, 1928

18480-A	The Empty Cradle	Ed 52307, 5540
N-241-A,-B	The Empty Cradle	Ed unissued
18481-A	The Death Of Floyd Bennett	Ed 52307, 5541
N-242-A,-B	The Death Of Floyd Bennett	Ed rejected

Vernon Dalhart, v; acc. prob. Adelyne Hood, f; own h; Carson Robison, g.

New York, NY   c. May 22, 1928

GEX-1254-A	Wreck Of The Old Southern 97	Ge 6654, Ch 15121, Sil 8141, Spt 9241
GEX-1255	The Prisoner's Song	Sil 8138, Spt 9235
GEX-1256	Wreck Of The 12:56	Sil 8142, Spt 9239
GEX-1257-A	Death Of Floyd Collins	Ch 15048, Sil 8134, Spt 9227
GEX-1258	The Engineer's Child	Sil 8135, Spt 9233
GEX-1259-A	Wreck Of The C. & O. No. 5	Ch 15907, Sil 8145, Spt 9240
GEX-1260	The Convict And The Rose	Sil 8135, Spt 9233

From July 13, 1928, matrix GEX-1254-A replaced matrix 9617 on Champion 15121, and GEX-1257-A replaced matrix 9854 on Champion 15048. (But see note to c. November 24, 1925 session.)

Vernon Dalhart, v; or **Vernon Dalhart & Carson Robison**-1, v/wh-2 duet; acc. prob. Adelyne Hood, f; Vernon Dalhart, h/jh-3; prob. William Carlino, bj-4; Carson Robison, g.

New York, NY   c. May 23, 1928

GEX-1273-A	The Little Rosewood Casket	Ch 15906, 45076, Sil 8133, Spt 9231, MW 4952
GEX-1274-A	A Letter Edged In Black	Ch 15906, 45076, Sil 8134, Spt 9227
GEX-1275	Jim Blake	Ch 15546, Sil 8145, Spt 9240
GEX-1276-A	Just Tell Them That You Saw Me	Ge 6512, Ch 15583, Sil 8132, Spt 9229
GEX-1277-A	Jesse James	Ch 15546, Sil 8132, Spt 9229
GEX-1278-A	Sinking Of The Great Titanic	Ch 15121, Sil 8137, Spt 9232
GEX-1279	The Ship That Never Returned	Ch 15907, Sil 8137, Spt 9232
GEX-1284-A	Oh Dem Golden Slippers -1, 3, 4	Ge 6512, Ch 15567, 33005, Sil 8143, Spt 9230
GEX-1285	When The Sun Goes Down Again -1, 2, 3, 4	Ch 15583, Sil 8144, Spt 9238, Spr 2546

Champion 15583, Silvertone 8144, Supertone 9230, 9238 as by **Dalhart & Robison**. Superior 2546 as by **Robison & Dalhart**.
From July 13, 1928, matrix GEX-1278-A replaced matrix X-111 on Champion 15121.
Intervening matrices are by other artists.
Revs: Superior 2546 by Carson Robison & Frank Luther; Montgomery Ward 4952 by Welling & McGhee.

Vernon Dalhart–Carson Robison–Adelyne Hood, v trio; acc. Adelyne Hood, f; Vernon Dalhart, h/jh; William Carlino, bj; Carson Robison, g.

New York, NY   Wednesday, May 23, 1928

43902-6	Climbin' Up De Golden Stairs	Vi 21457, Zo 5212, HMVAu EA382, Twin FT1280

Zonophone 5212 as by **Vernon Dalhart, Carson Robison & Adelyne Hood**. Twin FT1280 as by **Dalhart, Robison & Hood**.

Vernon Dalhart, v; acc. prob. Adelyne Hood, f; own h; Carson Robison, g.

New York, NY   c. May 25, 1928

GEX-1286	Wreck Of The Shenandoah	Ch 15048, Sil 8142, Spt 9239
GEX-1287-B	A Boy's Best Friend Is His Mother	Ge 6654, Ch 15648, 45031, Sil 8138, Spt 9235
GEX-1288-A	In The Baggage Coach Ahead	Ch 15648, 45031, Sil 8141, Spt 9241
GEX-1289	Can't You Hear Me Calling, Caroline?	Sil 8255, Spt 9154

From July 13, 1928, matrix GEX-1286 replaced matrix 9768 on Champion 15048.
Rev. Supertone 9154 by Harrison & Hollinshead (popular).

Vernon Dalhart: Vernon Dalhart, Carson Robison, Adelyne Hood, v trio; or **Vernon Dalhart & Carson Robison**-1, v duet; acc. Adelyne Hood, f; prob. Murray Kellner, f; Vernon Dalhart, h-2/jh-3; William Carlino, bj; Carson Robison, g; unknown, steamboat wh eff-4.

New York, NY   Saturday, June 2, 1928

| 146382-3 | Climbing Up De Golden Stairs -2, 3 | Co 15265-D, ReAu G21476, *Vo 02968* |
| 146383-2 | Steamboat Keep Rockin' -1, 4 | Co 15265-D, ReAu G21476, *Vo 02968* |

Vocalion/OKeh 02968 use the ARC transfer matrices 17423 and 17341 respectively, made on April 26, 1935.

Vernon Dalhart, v; acc. prob. Adelyne Hood, f; own h; Carson Robison, g.

New York, NY   Monday, June 4, 1928

| 146384-1 | The Song Of The Shut-In | Ha 664-H, Ve 1664-V, Di 2664-G, Apex 26125, DoC 21688, LS 24613, Mc 22613 |
| 146385-2 | Since Mother's Gone | Ha 664-H, Ve 1664-V, Di 2664-G |

Harmony 664-H as by **Mack Allen**.

Vernon Dalhart & Company: Vernon Dalhart, v; acc. poss. Adelyne Hood, f; own h; Carson Robison, g.

New York, NY   Monday, June 4, 1928

18560	The West Plains Explosion	Ed 52335, 5558
N-287-B	The West Plains Explosion	Ed 11002
18561	The Hanging Of Charles Birger	Ed 52335, 5559
N-288-B	The Hanging Of Charles Birger	Ed 11002

Vernon Dalhart, v; or **Vernon Dalhart & Carson Robison**-1, v duet; acc. prob. Adelyne Hood, f; Vernon Dalhart, h/jh; poss. William Carlino, bj; Carson Robison, g; several unidentifieds, laughing-2.

New York, NY   Monday, June 11, 1928

146421-	The Old Gray Mare	Co unissued
146422-2	The Little Brown Jug -2	Ve 7042-V, Di 6016-G
146423-	My Blue Ridge Mountain Home -1	Co unissued
146424-	Them Golden Slippers -1	Co unissued

New York, NY   Wednesday, June 20, 1928

| 146421-4 | The Old Gray Mare | Ve 7042-V, Di 6016-G |

Acc. unknown, f; unknown, o; unknown, bells.

New York, NY   Wednesday, June 27, 1928

| 146586-3 | A Choir Boy Sings All Alone To-night | Ha 685-H, Ve 1685-V, Di 2685-G |

Harmony 685-H as by **Mack Allen**.

Acc. two unknowns, f; unknown, g.

New York, NY   Wednesday, June 27, 1928

| 146587-2 | Floral Wreaths | Ha 685-H, Ve 1685-V, Di 2685-G |

Harmony 685-H as by **Mack Allen**.

Acc. poss. Adelyne Hood, f; own h/jh; poss. William Carlino, bj; unknown, g.

New York, NY   Thursday, June 28, 1928

| 146595-3 | My Blue Ridge Mountain Home | Ve 7043-V, Di 6017-G, Puritone 1070 |
| 146596-1 | Them Golden Slippers | Ve 7043-V, Di 6017-G, Puritone 1070 |

Acc. prob. Adelyne Hood, f; unknown, g.

New York, NY   Friday, July 20, 1928

| 146752-2 | The Faded Knot Of Blue | Ha 805-H, Ve 1805-V, Di 2805-G, Apex 26125, DoC 21689, LS 24613, Mc 22613 |

Harmony 805-H as by **Mack Allen**.

Acc. poss. Adelyne Hood, f; own h; unknown, p; poss. William Carlino, bj.

New York, NY   Friday, July 20, 1928

| 146753-2 | The Ohio River Blues | Ha 707-H, Ve 1707-V, Di 2707-G |

Harmony 707-H as by **Mack Allen**.

Acc. prob. Adelyne Hood, f; own h; poss. William Carlino, bj; unknown, g.

New York, NY   Tuesday, July 24, 1928

| 146789-2 | The Ohio River Blues | Co 15343-D |
| 146790-3 | 'Er Somethin' | Co 15343-D |

Acc. prob. Adelyne Hood, f; own jh; poss. William Carlino, bj; unknown, g.

New York, NY   Wednesday, July 25, 1928

| 146795- | 'Er Somethin' | Ha/Ve/Di unissued |
| 146796-1 | Polly Woddle Doodle | Ha 707-H, Ve 1707-V, Di 2707-G |

Harmony 707-H as by **Mack Allen**.

Acc. own h-1; unknown, g; Adelyne Hood, sp-2.

New York, NY   Monday, July 30, 1928

| 146821-1,-2 | Hallelujah! I'm A Bum -1 | Co 1488-D, CoJ J708, ReAu G20361 |
| 146822-1,-3 | The Bum Song -2 | Co 1488-D, CoJ J708, ReAu G20361 |

Matrices 146821/22 are retitled *Hallelujah! I'm A Bum (I'm A Tramp)* and *The Bum Song (The Song Of The Tramp)* respectively on Regal G20361.

Acc. prob.: unknown, f; unknown, p.
New York, NY   Tuesday, August 21, 1928

| 146866- | Treasure Untold | Ha/Ve/Di unissued |
| 146867- | Mother Was A Lady | Ha/Ve/Di unissued |

Acc. unknown, o.
New York, NY   Tuesday, August 28, 1928

| 146912-2 | A Warning To Boys | Ha 729-H, Ve 1729-V, Di 2729-G |
| 146913-3 | A Warning To Girls | Ha 729-H, Ve 1729-V, Di 2729-G |

Harmony 729-H as by **Mack Allen**.

Acc. unknown, f; unknown, p.
New York, NY   Thursday, August 30, 1928

| 146866-4 | Treasure Untold | Ha 721-H, Ve 1721-V, Di 2721-G |
| 146867-4 | Mother Was A Lady Or, If Jack Were Only Here | Ha 721-H, Ve 1721-V, Di 2721-G, Apex 26136, Cr/MeC 83013, DoC 21695, 183013, LS 24620, Mc 22620, Stg 283013 |

Harmony 721-H as by **Mack Allen**.
Matrix 146867 is titled *Mother Was A Lady (Or, If Jack Were Only Here)* on unidentified issues.

Acc. Adelyne Hood, f/sp-1; own h-2/jh-3/sp-4; poss. William Carlino, bj; unknown, g.
New York, NY   Tuesday, September 11, 1928

| 146980-2 | The Bully Song – Part 1 -1, 2, 4 | Co 15302-D, CoAu 01873 |
| 146981-3 | The Bully Song – Part 2 -3 | Co 15302-D, CoAu 01873 |

Acc. Adelyne Hood, f/sp-1; own h-2/jh-3; poss. William Carlino, bj; unknown, g.
New York, NY   Friday, September 21, 1928

| 147025-2 | The Bully Song – Part 1 -1, 2 | Ha 741-H, Ve 1741-V, Di 2741-G |
| 147026-1 | The Bully Song – Part 2 -2, 3 | Ha 741-H, Ve 1741-V, Di 2741-G |

Harmony 741-H as by **Mack Allen**.

Al Craver, v; or **Vernon Dalhart & Adelyne Hood**-1, v duet; acc. prob. Adelyne Hood, f-2; Vernon Dalhart, h-3; unknown, md-4; poss. William Carlino, bj-5; unknown, g.
New York, NY   Monday, September 24, 1928

147051-1	Conversation With Death (By A Blind Girl) -2, 4	Co 15585-D, Re/RZAu G21566
147052-2	The Old Bureau Drawer -2, 4	Co 15585-D, Re/RZAu G21566
147053-1	Sing Hallelujah -1, 3, 5	Co 15306-D
147054-3	The Frog Song -1, 5	Co 15306-D
147055-	The Frog Song	Co unissued
147056-	Sing Hallelujah	Co unissued

Vernon Dalhart, v; acc. poss. Adelyne Hood, f-1; own h-2; unknown, p-3; unknown, g.
New York, NY   Saturday, September 29, 1928

| 147088-3 | Who Said I Was A Bum? | Co 1585-D, ReAu G20377 |
| 147089-3 | Wanderin' -1, 2, 3 | Co 1585-D, ReAu G20377 |

Vernon Dalhart, Adelyne Hood, v duet; acc. Vernon Dalhart, h-1; poss. William Carlino, bj; unknown, g.
New York, NY   Thursday, October 4, 1928

| 147055-5 | The Frog Song | Ha 783-H, Ve 1783-V, Di 2783-G |
| 147056-4 | Sing Hallelujah -1 | Ha 783-H, Ve 1783-V, Di 2783-G |

Harmony 783-H as by **Mack Allen**.

Vernon Dalhart, v; acc. Adelyne Hood, f; unknown, g; unknown, eff.
New York, NY   Thursday, October 4, 1928

| 147104-2 | Santa Claus, That's Me! | Ha 754-H, Ve 1754-V, Di 2754-G |
| 147105-2 | Hooray For St. Nick | Ha 754-H, Ve 1754-V, Di 2754-G |

Harmony 754-H as by **Mack Allen**.

Vernon Dalhart & Company: Vernon Dalhart, v; acc. prob. Adelyne Hood, f; unknown, g.
New York, NY   Monday, October 8, 1928

18789	The Choir Boy Sings All Alone Tonight	Ed 52423, 5629
N-487	The Choir Boy Sings All Alone Tonight	Ed unissued
18790	The Old Bureau Drawer	Ed 52423, 5630
N-488	The Old Bureau Drawer	Ed unissued

Vernon Dalhart, v; acc. Adelyne Hood, f; unknown, g; unknown, eff.
New York, NY   Tuesday, October 9, 1928

| 147116-3 | Santa Claus, That's Me! | Co 15320-D |
| 147117-3 | Hooray For St. Nick | Co 15320-D |

Vernon Dalhart & Company: Vernon Dalhart, v; or **Vernon Dalhart & Adelyne Hood**-1, v duet; acc. Adelyne Hood, f; unknown, g.

New York, NY　　　　　　　　　　　　　　　　　　　　　　　　　　　Monday, October 15, 1928

18804	Ohio River Blues	Ed 52434
N-501-A	Ohio River Blues	Ed rejected
N-501-B	Ohio River Blues	Ed unissued
18805	Sing Hallelujah -1	Ed 52434
N-502-A	Sing Hallelujah -1	Ed rejected
N-502-B	Sing Hallelujah -1	Ed unissued

Vernon Dalhart, v; acc. prob. Adelyne Hood, f; own h-1; unknown, p-2; unknown, bj-3/g.

New York, NY　　　　　　　　　　　　　　　　　　　　　　　　　　　Tuesday, October 23, 1928

| 147134-2 | Watching The Trains Come In | Ha 767-H, Ve 1767-V, Di 2767-G |
| 147135-2 | Wanderin' -1, 2, 3 | Ha 767-H, Ve 1767-V, Di 2767-G |

Harmony 767-H as by **Mack Allen**.

Acc. prob. Adelyne Hood, f; own h-1; unknown, p-2; poss. William Carlino, bj-3; unknown, g; unknown, wh-4.

New York, NY　　　　　　　　　　　　　　　　　　　　　　　　　　Tuesday, November 13, 1928

147455-2	'Leven Cent Cotton -1, 2, 3	Ha 821-H, Ve 1821-V, Di 2821-G, Puritone 1062-S
147456-3	My Tennessee Mountain Home -1, 4	Ha 821-H, Ve 1821-V, Di 2821-G, Puritone 1062-S
147457-2	Sweet Little Old Lady	Ha 805-H, Ve 1805-V, Di 2805-G

Harmony 805-H, 821-H, Puritone 1062-S as by **Mack Allen**.

Acc. prob. Adelyne Hood, f; own h-1/jh-2; unknown, p-3; poss. William Carlino, bj-4; unknown, g.

New York, NY　　　　　　　　　　　　　　　　　　　　　　　　　　Friday, November 16, 1928

| 147467-2 | Hillbilly Love Song -1 | Ha 797-H, Ve 1797-V, Di 2797-G |
| 147468-3 | Sippin' Cider -2, 3, 4 | Ha 797-H, Ve 1797-V, Di 2797-G |

Harmony 797-H as by **Mack Allen**.

Vernon Dalhart & Company: Vernon Dalhart, v; acc. prob. Adelyne Hood, f; own h/jh; poss. William Carlino, bj; unknown, g.

New York, NY　　　　　　　　　　　　　　　　　　　　　　　　　　Monday, November 19, 1928

18879-B	Polly-Wolly-Doodle	Ed 52457, 5641
N-574-B	Polly-Wolly-Doodle	Ed 20001
18880-B	Eleven Cent Cotton	Ed 52457, 5640
N-575-B	Eleven Cent Cotton	Ed 20001

Vernon Dalhart, v; acc. prob. Adelyne Hood, f; own h-1/jh-2; poss. William Carlino, bj; unknown, g.

New York, NY　　　　　　　　　　　　　　　　　　　　　　　　　Wednesday, December 5, 1928

49229-1,-2,-3	The Ohio River Blues	Vi unissued
49230-1	Polly Wolly Doodle -1, 2	Vi V-40132, BB B-8406, Zo 5779, RZ T5779, RZAu T5779
49231-1,-2	Hill-Billy Love Song	Vi unissued
49232-1,-2	Sippin' Cider	Vi unissued

Matrix 49230-1 was technically remade on April 4, 1940.

Vernon Dalhart & Company: Vernon Dalhart, v; acc. unknown.

New York, NY　　　　　　　　　　　　　　　　　　　　　　　　　Wednesday, December 12, 1928

18938-B	The Big Rock Candy Mountains	Ed 52472, 5652
N-629-A	The Big Rock Candy Mountains	Ed 20003
18939-B	The Bum Song No. 2	Ed 52472, 5653
N-630-C	The Bum Song No. 2	Ed 20003

Edison 20003 was probably not issued.

Vernon Dalhart, v; acc. prob. Adelyne Hood, f-1; unknown, p-2; unknown, bj/g; unknown, g; own jh-3/v eff-4; unknown, perc-5.

New York, NY　　　　　　　　　　　　　　　　　　　　　　　　　　Monday, December 17, 1928

| 147708-2 | A Gay Caballero -2, 5 | Ha 812-H, Ve 1812-V, Di 2812-G |
| 147709-3 | The Mule Song -1, 3, 4 | Ha 812-H, Ve 1812-V, Di 2812-G |

Harmony 812-H as by **Mack Allen**.

Acc. unknown, f; unknown, p; unknown, bj.

New York, NY　　　　　　　　　　　　　　　　　　　　　　　　　　Tuesday, December 18, 1928

| 147714-3 | Summer Time In Old Kentucky | Ha 868-H, Ve 1868-V, Di 2868-G |

Harmony 868-H as by **Mack Allen**.

Acc. two unknowns, f; unknown, g.
 New York, NY   Tuesday, December 18, 1928
  147715-3   Fiddler Joe   Ha 868-H, Ve 1868-V, Di 2868-G

Harmony 868-H as by **Mack Allen**.

Vernon Dalhart, v; or **Vernon Dalhart & Adelyne Hood**-1, v duet; acc. Adelyne Hood, f; others unknown.
 New York, NY   Friday, December 21, 1928
  18958   Where Is My Wandering Boy Tonight   Ed 52487, 5662
  N-649-A,-B   Where Is My Wandering Boy Tonight   Ed rejected
  18959   The Ninety And Nine -1   Ed unissued
  N-650-A,-B   The Ninety And Nine -1   Ed rejected

Matrix 18959 was remade on February 25, 1929 and it is assumed that the issue was derived from that recording.

Vernon Dalhart, v; acc. prob. Adelyne Hood, f-1; own h-2/jh-3; unknown, p-4; unknown, bj-5; unknown, g-6; unknown, sb-7; unknown, eff-8.
 New York, NY   Thursday, January 16, 1929
  147789-2   Wreck Of The N & W Cannon Ball -1, 2, 6, 8   Co 15378-D
  147790-3   Low Bridge Everybody Down (Or Fifteen Years On   Co 15378-D
     The Erie Canal) -3, 4, 5, 7
  147791-3   Sippin' Cider -1, 2, 3, 5, 6   Co 1712-D, ReAu G20437
  147792-2   The Mule Song -1, 2, 3, 6   Co 1712-D, ReE G9370, ReAu G20437

Regal G9370 as by **Sam Peters**.

 New York, NY   Tuesday, January 21, 1929
  147865-2   Wreck Of The N & W Cannon Ball -1, 2, 6, 8   Ha 831-H, Ve 1831-V, Di 2831-G
  147868-1   Low Bridge Everybody Down (Or Fifteen Years On   Ha 831-H, Ve 1831-V, Di 2831-G
     The Erie Canal) -3, 4, 5, 7

Harmony 831-H as by **Mack Allen**.
Intervening matrices are by Jan Garber (popular).

Acc. prob. Adelyne Hood, f; own h-1/jh-2; unknown, g.
 New York, NY   Wednesday, January 22, 1929
  147873-   The Letter Edged In Black   Ve 7044-V, Di 6018-G
  147874-3   I Wish I Was A Single Girl Again -1, 2   Ve 7046-V, Di 6020-G
  147875-3   The Cowboy's Lament -1   Ve 7045-V, Di 6019-G, Cl 5241-C, Apex 26136,
       CrC/MeC 83013, DoC 21695, 183013,
       LS 24620, Mc 22620, Min M14002,
       Stg 283013

 New York, NY   Thursday, January 23, 1929
  147878-2   Can I Sleep In Your Barn Tonight Mister -1   Ve 7046-V, Di 6020-G, CrC/MeC 83039,
       DoC 183039, Stg 283039
  147879-2   When The Work's All Done Next Fall   Ve 7045-V, Di 6019-G, Cl 5241-C
  147880-   In The Baggage Coach Ahead   Ve 7044-V, Di 6018-G

Vernon Dalhart, v; or **Vernon Dalhart–Adelyn Hood**-1, v duet; acc. unknown, f-2; Adelyne Hood, f-3/p-4; Vernon Dalhart, h-5/jh-6; unknown, bj-7; unknown, g; unknown, wh-8.
 New York, NY   Monday, February 11, 1929
  48350-1   Sing Hallelujah -1, 5, 7   Vi V-40050, ZoAu EE204
  48351-2   Eleven Cent Cotton -2, 5, 6, 7   Vi V-40050, *BB B-8406*, ZoAu EE204
  48352-3   Summer Time In Old Kentucky -2, 4, 7, 8   Vi V-40064
  48353-2   Fiddler Joe -2, 3   Vi V-40064
  49232-4   Sippin' Cider -2, 5, 6, 7   Vi V-40132

Matrix 48350 on Zonophone EE204 as by **Vernon Dalhart & Adelyne Hood**.
Matrix 48351 is titled *Eleven Cent Cotton And Forty Cent Meat* on Bluebird B-8406.
Matrix 48351-2 was technically remade on April 4, 1940.

Vernon Dalhart & Company: Vernon Dalhart, v; acc. prob. Adelyne Hood, f -1/p-2; own h-3/jh-4; unknown, bj-5; unknown, g-6.
 New York, NY   Wednesday, February 20, 1929
  19058-B   Low Bridge! – Everybody Down (Fifteen Years On   Ed 52533, 5679
     The Erie Canal) -2, ?3, 4, 5
  N-749-A   Low Bridge! – Everybody Down (Fifteen Years On   Ed rejected
     The Erie Canal) -2, ?3, 4, 5
  19059-B   The Wreck Of The N & W Cannonball -1, 3, 6   Ed 52533, 5680
  N-750-A,-B   The Wreck Of The N & W Cannonball -1, 3, 6   Ed rejected

Vernon Dalhart & Adelyne Hood, v duet; acc. Adelyne Hood, f; unknown, o.
 New York, NY   Monday, February 25, 1929
  18959-B   The Ninety And Nine   Ed 52487

Vernon Dalhart, v; acc. two unknowns, f; unknown, g.
   New York, NY   Tuesday, March 19, 1929
   148102-3   Roll On River   Ha 879-H, Ve 1879-V, Di 2879-G
   148103-   We Never Speak As We Pass By   Ha unissued
Harmony 879-H as by **Mack Allen**.

Acc. unknown, f; own h-1; unknown, bj-2; unknown, g; unknown, train-wh eff-3.
   New York, NY   Thursday, March 21, 1929
   148117-1   The Yazoo Train On The Arkansas Line -1, 2, 3   Ha 893-H, Ve 1893-V, Di 2893-G
   148118-2   Little Red Caboose -1   Ha 893-H, Ve 1893-V, Di 2893-G
   148119-2   The Alabama Flood   Ha 879-H, Ve 1879-V, Di 2879-G
Harmony 879-H, 893-H as by **Mack Allen**.

Acc. unknown, f; Adelyne Hood, f-1/p-2; own h-3; unknown, g.
   New York, NY   Tuesday, March 26, 1929
   49791-3   Roll On, River -1   Vi V-40075
   49792-1,-2   Alabama Flood Song -1   Vi unissued
   49793-1   Flood Song -3   Vi V-40075
   49794-1,-2   Plucky Lindy's Lucky Day -2   Vi unissued

Vernon Dalhart & Company: Vernon Dalhart, v; acc. unknown, f; poss. Adelyne Hood, f; unknown, p; unknown, bj.
   New York, NY   Wednesday, March 27, 1929
   19127-A,-B   Alabama Flood   Ed rejected
   N-820-A   Alabama Flood   Ed unissued
   N-820-B   Alabama Flood   Ed rejected
   19128-B   Roll On River   Ed 52566, 5696
   N-821-A   Roll On River   Ed unissued
   N-821-B   Roll On River   Ed rejected
   N-821-C   Roll On River   Ed unissued

Acc. unknown, f; unknown, p-1; unknown, bj; unknown, g-2; unknown, castanets-3; unknown, wh-4.
   New York, NY   Thursday, March 28, 1929
   19131-B   Plucky Lindy's Lucky Day -1, 2, 3   Ed 52558, 5695
   N-824-A,-B,-C Plucky Lindy's Lucky Day -1, 2, 3   Ed unissued
   19132-B   Summertime In Old Kentucky -4   Ed 52558
   N-825-A,-B,-C Summertime In Old Kentucky -4   Ed rejected
Matrices 19129/30 are by Billy Murray (popular).

Vernon Dalhart, v; acc. unknown, f; Adelyne Hood, f/p-1; own h-2; unknown, bj-3/g.
   New York, NY   Thursday, March 28, 1929
   148143-3   The Alabama Flood -2   Co 15386-D
   148144-2   Roll On River -1, 3   Co 15386-D

Vernon Dalhart & Company: Vernon Dalhart, v; or Vernon Dalhart, Adelyne Hood, v duet-1; acc. unknown, f; Vernon Dalhart, h-2; Adelyne Hood, p-3; unknown, bj-4/g-5.
   New York, NY   Thursday, April 11, 1929
   19127-G   Alabama Flood -2, 5   Ed 52566, 5697
   N-820   Alabama Flood -2, 5   Ed unissued
   19153-B   Ain't Gonna Grieve My Mind -1, 3, 4   Ed 52599
   N-852-A   Ain't Gonna Grieve My Mind -1, 3, 4   Ed unissued
   N-852-B   Ain't Gonna Grieve My Mind -1, 3, 4   Ed rejected
   N-852-C   Ain't Gonna Grieve My Mind -1, 3, 4   Ed unissued

Vernon Dalhart, v; or Vernon Dalhart, Adelyne Hood, v duet-1; acc. prob.: unknown, f; Adelyne Hood, p; unknown, bj; unknown, wh-2.
   New York, NY   Tuesday, April 16, 1929
   148443-1   Ain't Gonna Grieve My Mind Any More -1   Ha 903-H, Ve 1903-V, Di 2903-G
   148444-1   King Of Borneo -2   Ha 903-H, Ve 1903-V, Di 2903-G
Harmony 903-H as by **Mack Allen**.

Acc. prob. Adelyne Hood, f; own h; unknown, g.
   New York, NY   Thursday, April 18, 1929
   148448-3   Custer's Last Fight   Ha 916-H, Ve 1916-V, Di 2916-G
   148449-1   Buffalo Bill   Ha 916-H, Ve 1916-V, Di 2916-G
Harmony 916-H as by **Mack Allen**.

Vernon Dalhart, v; or Vernon Dalhart, Adelyne Hood, v duet-1; acc. unknown, f; Adelyne Hood, f; Vernon Dalhart, h-2; unknown, bj-3; unknown, g.
   New York, NY   Monday, April 29, 1929
   49794-4   Plucky Lindy's Lucky Day -3   Vi V-40086

51935-3	Ain't Gonna Grieve My Mind -1, 3	Vi V-40086, Zo 5779, ZoSA 4234, RZ T5779, RZAu T5779
51936-1	Hoe Down -2, 3	Vi V-40114
51937-1	I Long To See The One I Left Behind	Vi V-40094
51938-2	Many Years Ago	Vi V-40094

Vernon Dalhart, v; or Vernon Dalhart, Adelyne Hood, v duet-1; acc. unknown, f; Adelyne Hood, p; unknown, bj; Vernon Dalhart, jh-2; unknown, wh-3.
New York, NY   Thursday, May 9, 1929

| 148478-3 | Ain't Gonna Grieve My Mind -1 | Co 15405-D, CoJ J1145 |
| 148488-2 | Poor Old Mare -2, 3 | Co 15405-D, CoJ J1145 |

Intervening matrices are by other artists.

Vernon Dalhart & Company: Vernon Dalhart, v; acc. prob. own h; poss. Adelyne Hood, p; unknown, bj.
New York, NY   Friday, May 24, 1929

19215	Sing Fa-Da-Riddle, Sing Dey	Ed 52599
N-919-A	Sing Fa-Da-Riddle, Sing Dey	Ed unissued
N-919-B	Sing Fa-Da-Riddle, Sing Dey	Ed rejected
N-919-C	Sing Fa-Da-Riddle, Sing Dey	Ed unissued

Vernon Dalhart, v; or Vernon Dalhart, Adelyne Hood, v duet-1; acc. Adelyne Hood, f; Vernon Dalhart, h-2/jh-3; unknown, bj; unknown, g.
New York, NY   Tuesday, May 28, 1929

| 148636-2 | Sing Fa-Da Riddle, Sing Dey (Or Poor Old Mare) -3 | Ha 935-H, Ve 1935-V, Di 2935-G |
| 148637-3 | Razor's In De Air -1, 2 | Ha 935-H, Ve 1935-V, Di 2935-G |

Harmony 935-H as by **Mack Allen**.

Vernon Dalhart, v; acc. unknown, f; Adelyne Hood, f-1/p-2; unknown, bj-3/g-4.
New York, NY   Wednesday, May 29, 1929

| 148645-2 | Dixie Way -2, 3 | Ha 946-H, Ve 1946-H, Di 2946-G |
| 148646-1 | I'm Just Going Down To The Gate Dear Ma -1, 4 | Ha 946-H, Ve 1946-H, Di 2946-G |

Harmony 946-H as by **Mack Allen**.

Vernon Dalhart, v; or **Adelyne Hood & Vernon Dalhart**-1, v duet; acc. Adelyne Hood, f; Vernon Dalhart, h/jh-2; unknown, bj; unknown, g.
New York, NY   Thursday, June 6, 1929

| 148660-1 | Razor's In De Air -1, 2 | Co 15417-D, ReAu G20642 |
| 148661-2 | Dixie Way | Co 15417-D, ReAu G20642 |

Matrix 148660 on Regal G20642 as by **Vernon Dalhart & Adelyn Hood**.

Vernon Dalhart, v; acc. poss. Adelyne Hood, f; poss. Murray Kellner, f; unknown, g.
New York, NY   Monday, July 1, 1929

| 148764-3 | What Does The Deep Sea Say | Ha 960-H, Ve 1960-V, Di 2960-G |
| 148765-1 | If I Could See Mother Tonight | Ha 960-H, Ve 1960-V, Di 2960-G |

Harmony 960-H as by **Mack Allen**.

Acc. poss. Adelyne Hood, f; own h/jh-1; unknown, bj; unknown, g.
New York, NY   Tuesday, July 2, 1929

| 148769-1 | Who Is That A-Comin' Down The Mountain -1 | Ha 971-H, Ve 1971-V, Di 2971-G |
| 148770-3 | Gimme Good Old Sorghum Any Old Time | Ha 971-H, Ve 1971-V, Di 2971-G |

Harmony 971-H as by **Mack Allen**.

Vernon Dalhart & Company, v; or **Vernon Dalhart & Adelyne Hood**-1, v duet; acc. unknown.
New York, NY   Wednesday, July 17, 1929

19299	Dixie Way	Ed 52628
N-1023	Dixie Way	Ed 20010
19300	Razors In De Air -1	Ed 52628
N-1024	Razors In De Air -1	Ed 20010

Edison 20010 as by **Vernon Dalhart & Adelyne Hall**.

Vernon Dalhart, v; acc. poss. Adelyne Hood, f; own h; unknown, bj; unknown, g.
New York, NY   Monday, July 22, 1929

| 148836-3 | The Old Kitty Kate (On The Mississippi Line) | Co 15440-D |
| 148837-3 | Going Down To New Orleans | Co 15440-D |

Acc. poss. Adelyne Hood, f; own h-1; unknown, bj; unknown, g; unknown, steam-wh eff-2.
New York, NY   Tuesday, July 23, 1929

| 148840-3 | Going Down To New Orleans -1, 2 | Ha 982-H, Ve 1982-V, Di 2982-G |
| 148841-2 | My Kentucky Mountain Girl | Ha 982-H, Ve 1982-V, Di 2982-G, ReAu G20641 |

Harmony 982-H as by **Mack Allen**.

Rev. Regal G20641 by Malcolm Legette (popular).

New York, NY Thursday, August 15, 1929
148881-2	Farm Relief Song -1	Ha 992-H, Ve 1992-V, Di 2992-G
148882-3	The Crow Song Caw-Caw-Caw	Ha 992-H, Ve 1992-V, Di 2992-G, Cl 5164-C

Harmony 992-H as by **Mack Allen**.

New York, NY Monday, August 19, 1929
148890-3	In The Town Where I Was Born	Ha 1004-H, Ve 2004-V, Cl 5163-C
148891-3	Hello Bill Brown	Ha 1004-H, Ve 2004-V

Harmony 1004-H as by **Mack Allen**.

Al Craver, v; acc. poss. Adelyne Hood, f; own h-1; unknown, bj; unknown, g.

New York, NY Thursday, August 22, 1929
148913-2	Farm Relief Song -1	Co 15449-D
148914-3	The Crow Song Caw-Caw-Caw	Co 15449-D

Vernon Dalhart, v; acc. poss. Adelyne Hood, f; own h-1/jh-2; unknown, bj-3/g-4; unknown, g.

New York, NY Thursday, August 29, 1929
148946-1	Johnny Long, The Engineer -1, 2, 3	Ha 1013-H, Ve 2013-V, Cl 5163-C
148947-1,-3	Swinging In The Lane -4	Ha 1013-H, Ve 2013-V, Cl 5162-C, ReE MR23, ReAu G20741, RZIr IZ342

Harmony 1013-H, Regals as by **Mack Allen**.
Revs: Regal MR23, Regal-Zonophone IZ342 by James J. Mullan (Irish); Regal G20741 by Jack Mathis.

Acc. poss.: Adelyne Hood, f; own h; unknown, bj; unknown, g.

New York, NY Monday, September 23, 1929
149034-3	In The Hills Of Tennessee	Ha 1037-H, Ve 2037-V, Cl 5162-C
149035-2	Blue Ridge Sweetheart	Ha 1037-H, Ve 2037-V

Harmony 1037-H as by **Mack Allen**.

New York, NY Tuesday, September 24, 1929
149036-3	Roll Dem Cotton Bales	Ha 1167-H, Ve 2167-V, Cl 5161-C
149037-1	Mobile – Alabam	Ha 1167-H, Ve 2167-V, Cl 5161-C

Harmony 1167-H as by **Mack Allen**.

Acc. poss. Adelyne Hood, f; poss. Murray Kellner, f; own h-1/jh-2; unknown, sg-3; unknown, bj-4; unknown, g; Bob MacGimsey, wh-5; unknown, eff-6.

New York, NY Friday, October 4, 1929
56749-1	The Farm Relief Song -1, 2, 4	Vi V-40149, MW M-8144
56750-1	The Crow Song Caw-Caw-Caw -4, 6	Vi V-40149, MW M-8144
56751-1	Whippoorwill -3, 5	Vi V-40162
56752-1	Blue Ridge Sweetheart -3, 5	Vi V-40162, ZoSA 4323

Acc. poss. Adelyne Hood, f; own h/jh-1; unknown, bj; unknown, g.

New York, NY Tuesday, October 22, 1929
149166-2	I'll Get Along Somehow -1	Ha 1054-H, Ve 2054-V, Cl 5056-C
149167-3	Out In The Great North West	Ha 1071-H, Ve 2071-V, Cl 5160-C

Harmony 1054-H, 1071-H as by **Mack Allen**.

New York, NY Wednesday, October 23, 1929
149171-1	Home In The Mountains	Ha 1071-H, Ve 2071-V, Cl 5160-C
149172-2	The Golden West	Ha 1217-H, Ve 2059-V, 2217-V, Cl 5159-C

Harmony 1071-H, 1217-H as by **Mack Allen**.
Matrix 149172 was later replaced on Velvet Tone 2059-V by matrix 149426 (see November 14, 1929).

Acc. poss. Adelyne Hood, f; poss. Murray Kellner, f; unknown, sg-1; unknown, bj-2; unknown, g.

New York, NY Thursday, October 24, 1929
149177-2	Home In The Mountains -2	Co 15475-D, CoJ J1231
149178-2	Blue Ridge Sweetheart -1	Co 15475-D, CoJ J1231

Acc. poss. Adelyne Hood, f; own h-1/jh-2; unknown, bj; unknown, g; unknown, wh-3.

New York, NY Thursday, November 7, 1929
149474-1	Barnacle Bill The Sailor No. 2	Ha 1304-H, ReE MR37
149475-3	The Whistle Song -1, 2, 3	Ha 1059-H, Ve 2059-V, Cl 5159-C, ReAu G20688

Harmony 1059-H, 1304-H, Regal G20688 as by **Mack Allen**. Regal MR37 as by **The Regal Rascals**.
Matrix 149474 is titled *The Return Of Barnacle Bill* on Regal MR37.
Rev. Regal MR37 (with same credit) by Billy Jones & Ernest Hare (popular).

New York, NY   Thursday, November 14, 1929
   149425-3   A Tale Of A Ticker   Ha 1054-H, Ve 2054-V
   149426-2   The Return Of The Gay Caballero   Ha 1059-H, Ve 2059-V, ReE MR118,
                                                              ReAu G20688

Harmony 1054-H, 1059-H, Regal MR118, G20688 as by **Mack Allen**.

Acc. Adelyne Hood, f-1; unknown, t; Ross Gorman, cl-2; own h-3/jh-4; unknown, o-5; John Cali, bj-6; unknown, g-7.
New York, NY   Wednesday, November 20, 1929
   57545-2   Eleven Months And Ten Days More -1, 2, 3, 4, 6, 7   Vi V-40194
   57546-2   I'll Get Along Somehow -1, 2, 3, 4, 6, 7   Vi V-40194, ZoSA 4323
   57547-1   At Father Power's Grave -5   Vi V-40179
   57548-1   Be Careful What You Say -1, 7   Vi V-40179

Matrix 57545 was originally logged as *Eleven More Months And Ten More Days*, and matrix 57546 as *Got A Horse And Cow (I'll Get Along Somehow)*.

Acc. prob. Adelyne Hood, f-1; unknown, c; unknown, o-2; unknown, g-3.
New York, NY   Thursday, November 21, 1929
   149450-3   At Father Power's Grave -2   Ha 1058-H, Ve 2058-V, ReE MR135
   149479-3   Be Careful What You Say -1, 3   Ha 1058-H, Ve 2058-V, Cl 5158-C

Harmony 1058-H, Regal MR135 as by **Mack Allen**.
Rev. Regal MR135 by Frank Quinn (Irish).

Acc. prob. Adelyne Hood, f; unknown, c; unknown, g; unknown, sb-1.
New York, NY   Saturday, November 30, 1929
   149657-3   Song Of The Condemned -1   Co 2061-D, ReAu G20754
   149658-3   Be Careful What You Say   Co 2061-D, ReAu G20754

Acc. Adelyne Hood, f-1/v-2/sp-3; prob. Ross Gorman, cl/bscl; unknown, bj; unknown, g; own jh-4/sp-5.
New York, NY   Wednesday, December 18, 1929
   149603-3   Calamity Jane (From The West) -2, 3, 5   Ha 1080-H, Ve 2080-V, Cl 5158-C
   149604-1   There'll Be One More Fool In Paradise -1, 4 Ha 1080-H, Ve 2080-V, Cl 5164-C, ReE MR260

Matrix 149603 on Harmony 1080-H as by **Mack Allen & Adelyne Hood**, and on Velvet Tone 2080-V, Clarion 5158-C as by **Vernon Dalhart & Adelyne Hood**. Matrix 149604 on Harmony 1080-H, Regal MR260 as by **Mack Allen**.

Adelyne Hood & Vernon Dalhart: Adelyne Hood, v/sp; Vernon Dalhart, sp; acc. prob. Ross Gorman, cl/bscl; unknown, bj; unknown, g.
New York, NY   Thursday, December 26, 1929
   149618-3   Calamity Jane (From The West)   Co 2102-D, CoAu 01929, CoJ J932

Vernon Dalhart, v; acc. Adelyne Hood, f; prob. Ross Gorman, cl/bscl; unknown, bj; unknown, g; own jh.
New York, NY   Thursday, December 26, 1929
   149619-3   Out In The Great North West   Co 2102-D, CoAu 01929, CoJ J932

Vernon Dalhart–Adelyn Hood: Vernon Dalhart, v-1/sp-2; Adelyne Hood, v-3/sp-4; or **Vernon Dalhart**-5, v; acc. Adelyne Hood, f-6; Ross Gorman, bscl/s-7; Vernon Dalhart, h-8/jh-9; Roy Smeck, bj; Joe Biondi, g.
New York, NY   Monday, January 20, 1930
   58396-1   Calamity Jane -2, 3, 4   Vi V-40224
   58397-2   Hallelujah, There's A Rainbow In The Sky -1, 3, 6   Vi V-40227
   58398-1   There'll Be One More Fool In Paradise Tonight -5,   Vi V-40227
                 6, 7, 8, 9
   58399-1   Out In The Great Northwest -1, 6, 9   Vi V-40224

Vernon Dalhart, v; acc. prob. Adelyne Hood, f; own h/jh; unknown, bj; unknown, g.
New York, NY   Tuesday, January 21, 1930
   149785-2   Squint Eyed Cactus Jones   Ha 1164-H, Ve 2164-V, ReE MR118,
                                                              ReAu G20900
   149786-1   The Tariff Bill Song   Ha 1164-H, Ve 2164-H

Harmony 1164-H, Re MR118 as by **Mack Allen**.
Matrix 149785 is titled *Squint-Eyed Cactus Jones* on Velvet Tone 2164-V. Rev. Regal G20900 untraced.

Vernon Dalhart, v; or **Vernon Dalhart & Adelyne Hood**-1, v duet; acc. Adelyne Hood, f; prob. Ross Gorman, cl/bscl; unknown, bj; unknown, g; unknown, sb.
New York, NY   Wednesday, January 22, 1930
   149791-3   Eleven More Months And Ten More Days   Ha 1095-H, Ve 2095-V, Cl 5027-C,
                                                              ReAu G21102
   149792-3   Hallelujah! There's A Rainbow In The Sky -1 Ha 1095-H, Ve 2095-V, 2154-V, Cl 5076-C,
                                                              ReE MR177

Matrix 149791 on Harmony 1095-H, Regal G21102 as by **Mack Allen**. Matrix 149792 on Harmony 1095-H as by **Mack Allen & Adelyne Hood**.

There may be no guitar on matrix 149791.
Rev. Regal G21102 by Marvin Thompson.

Al Craver, v; acc. prob. Adelyne Hood, f; prob. Ross Gorman, cl/bscl; own h-1/jh-2; unknown, bj; unknown, g.
New York, NY   Wednesday, January 29, 1930

| 149925-3 | Eleven More Months And Ten More Days | Co 15512-D |
| 149926-2 | Squint Eyed Cactus Jones -1, 2 | Co 15512-D |

Vernon Dalhart, v; acc. prob. Adelyne Hood, f-1; prob. Ross Gorman or Frank Novak, bscl; unknown, md-2/bj-3; unknown, g; own jh-4; unknown, castanets-5.
New York, NY   Wednesday, February 26, 1930

| 150019-1 | Just An Old Spanish Custom -2, 5 | Ha 1124-H, Ve 2124-V, Cl 5156-C |
| 150020-1 | And The Wise Old Owl Said Hoo -1, 3, 4 | Ha 1204-H, Ve 2204-V, Cl 5156-C, ReE MR260 |

Harmony 1124-H, 1204-H, Regal MR260 as by **Mack Allen**.
Matrix 150020 is titled *And The Wise Old Owl Said 'Hoo'* on Regal MR260.

Acc. poss. Adelyne Hood, f; prob. Ross Gorman or Frank Novak, cl/bscl; own h-1/jh-2; unknown, bj; unknown, g.
New York, NY   Thursday, February 27, 1930

| 150026-1 | My Mary Jane -1, 2 | Ha 1204-H, Ve 2204-V, Cl 5157-C |
| 150029-3 | In 1992 | Ha 1124-H, Ve 2124-V, Cl 5056-C |

Harmony 1124-H, 1204-H as by **Mack Allen**.
Intervening matrices are by Buddy Rogers (popular).

Al Craver, v; acc. poss. Adelyne Hood, f; unknown, md-1/g-2; unknown, g.
New York, NY   Thursday, March 6, 1930

| 150068-2 | The Hanging Of Eva Dugan -1 | Co 15530-D |
| 150069-3 | Pappy's Buried On The Hill -2 | Co 15530-D |

Vernon Dalhart, v; acc. unknown, f; poss. Frank Novak, f-1/cl-2; unknown, md-3/g-4; unknown, g.
New York, NY   Thursday, March 27, 1930

| 150127-2,3 | Since Mother's Gone From The Old Home -2, 3 | Ha 1154-H, Ve 2154-V, Di 3154-G, Cl 5157-C |
| 150133-2 | The Call Of Mother Love -1, 4 | Ha 1154-H, Ve 2154-V, Di 3154-G, Cl 5076-C |

Harmony 1154-H as by **Mack Allen**.
Some pressings of Velvet Tone 2154-V couple matrices 150127 and 149792 rather than as above.
Matrices 150128 to 150130 are by Ann Cass (popular); 150131/32 are by Bessie Smith (see *B&GR*).

Acc. poss. Adelyne Hood, f; prob. Ross Gorman or Frank Novak, cl-1/bscl; own h-2/jh-3; unknown, bj; unknown, g.
New York, NY   Friday, March 28, 1930

| 150143-2 | When I Bought That Wedding Ring -2, 3 | Ha 1259-H, Ve 2259-V, Cl 5066-C, ReE MR295 |
| 105144-2 | For The First Time In Twenty-Four Years -1 | Ha 1259-H, Ve 2259-V, ReE MR295, ReAu G21044 |

Harmony 1259-H, Regal MR295, G21044 as by **Mack Allen**.
Rev. Regal G21044 by Fields & Hall.

Al Craver-1/**Vernon Dalhart**-2, v; or **Vernon Dalhart & Adelyne Hood**-3, v duet; acc. Adelyne Hood, f-4; prob. Ross Gorman or Frank Novak, cl-5/bscl; unknown, p-6; unknown, bj; unknown, g.
New York, NY   Monday, March 31, 1930

150149-2	For The First Time In Twenty-Four Years -1, 4	Co 15546-D
150150-1	In 1992 -1, 4, 5	Co 15546-D
150151-3	Hallelujah! There's A Rainbow In The Sky -3, 6	Co 15542-D, CoJ J1070
150152-1	You Ain't Been Living Right -2, 4, 5, 6	Co 15542-D, CoJ J1070

Vernon Dalhart, v; acc. prob. Adelyne Hood, f; prob. Ross Gorman or Frank Novak, cl/bscl/s-1; unknown, bj; unknown, g; own jh-2.
New York, NY   Monday, April 28, 1930

| 150495-2 | Roll Them Clouds Away -2 | Ha 1244-H, Ve 2244-V, ReAu G20943 |
| 150496-1 | Oh! Adam Had 'Em -1 | Ha 1244-H, Ve 2244-V, ReAu G20943 |

Harmony 1244-H, Regal G20943 as by **Mack Allen**.

Vernon Dalhart, v/sp-1; acc. Adelyne Hood, f-2/v-3/sp-4; prob. Ross Gorman or Frank Novak, s-5; unknown, bj; unknown, g; several unknowns, sp-6.
New York, NY   Wednesday, April 30, 1930

| 150510-4 | Yukon Steve And Alaska Ann -1, 3, 4, 6 | Ha 1184-H, Ve 2184-V, Cl 5027-C, ReE MR243 |
| 150511-3 | The Pony Express -2, 5 | Ha 1184-H, Ve 2184-V, Cl 5028-C |

Harmony 1184-H as by **Mack Allen**. Regal MR243 as by **The Regal Rascals**; matrix 150510 is titled *Yukon Steve And Brick Top Alaska Ann* on that issue.
Rev. Regal MR243 (with same credit) by Arthur Fields & Fred Hall.

Vernon Dalhart, v; acc. Adelyne Hood, f/v-1; prob. Ross Gorman or Frank Novak, cl-2/bscl; own h-3/jh-4; unknown, bj; unknown, g.
New York, NY   Wednesday, May 14, 1930

150413-2	Matrimony Bill -2	Ha 1193-H, Ve 2193-V, Cl 5066-C, ReAu G20830
150414-2	Don't Marry A Widow -3, 4	Ha 1193-H, Ve 2193-V, Cl 5028-C, ReAu G20830
150415-2	My Oklahoma Home -2	Ha 1217-H, Ve 2217-V
150416-	You Remind Me Of The Girl That Used To Go To School With Me -1	Ha 1304-H

Harmony 1193-H, 1217-H, 1304-H, Regal G20830 as by **Mack Allen**.

Al Craver-1/**Vernon Dalhart**-2, v; or **Vernon Dalhart & Adelyne Hood**-3, v duet; acc. Adelyne Hood, f; prob. Ross Gorman or Frank Novak, cl-4/bscl; Vernon Dalhart, h-5/jh-6; unknown, bj-7/g-8; unknown, g.

New York, NY   Friday, May 16, 1930

150433-3	The Tariff Bill Song -1, 5, 6, 7	Co 15561-D
150434-3	My Mary Jane -2, 5, 6, 7	Co 15610-D
150435-3	The Deacon's Prayer -3, 4, 7	Co 15610-D, ReE MR177
150436-3	My Oklahoma Home -1, 4, 8	Co 15561-D

Vernon Dalhart, v; acc. poss. Adelyne Hood, f; prob. Ross Gorman or Frank Novak, cl-1/bscl-1; own h/jh-2; unknown, bj; unknown, g.

New York, NY   Wednesday, June 4, 1930

9781-1,-3	Tariff Bill Song -2	Ba 0745, Ca 0345, Do 4584, Je 5996, Or 1996, Pe 12624, Re 10051, Cq 7573
9782-1,-3	Don't Marry A Widow -1	Ba 0745, Ca 0345, Do 4583, Je 5996, Or 1996, Pe 12622, Re 10051, Cq 7572, Bwy 4059

Revs: Domino 4583, Perfect 12622, 12624, Conqueror 7572, 7573, Broadway 4059 by Carson Robison.

Acc. poss. Adelyne Hood, f; poss. Frank Novak, cl/bscl-1/sb-2; own h-3/jh-4; unknown, bj; unknown, g.

New York, NY   Wednesday, July 16, 1930

9870-1,-2	Roll Dem Cotton Bales -2, 3, 4	Ba 0772, Ca 0372, Do 4600, Je 6022, Or 2022, Pe 12631, Re 10078, Ro 1385, Cq 7591
9871-1,-2,-3	Mobile – Alabam -1	Ba 0772, Ca 0372, Do 4604, Je 6022, Or 2022, Pe 12633, Re 10078, Ro 1385, Cq 7593

Revs: Perfect 12631, Conqueror 7591 by Frank Marvin; Perfect 12633, Conqueror 7593 by Carson Robison.

Acc. unknown, f; own h-1; unknown, g.

New York, NY   Wednesday, September 10, 1930

(1)5830-1,-3	The Prisoner's Song	Ba 0826, Ca 0426, Do 4643, Je 6076, Or 2076, Pe 12644, Re 10132, Ro 1440, Chg 784
(1)5971-2,-3	In The Baggage Coach Ahead	Ba 0826, Ca 0426, Do 4643, Je 6076, Li 1520, Or 2076, Pe 12644, Re 10132, Ro 1440, Chg 784
10014-3	Barbara Allen	MeC 91306, Stg 91306
10015-2	Oh Bury Me Out On The Prairie -1	Ba 0843, Ca 0443, Je 6093, Or 2093, Re 10149, Ro 1457, Chg 786, Cq 7729, Bwy 4060, MeC 91306, Stg 91306
10016-2,-3	When They Changed My Name To A Number	Ba 0824, Ca 0424, Do 4642, Je 6075, Or 2075, Pe 12643, Re 10131, Ro 1439, Chg 783, Cq 7631

Matrices (1)5830 and (1)5971 were electric recordings of the titles on the earlier acoustic matrices 5830 and 5971 (see sessions of c. January and c. April 1925 respectively). On aural evidence it seems likely that they were made at this session.
Matrix 10015 is titled *Bury Me Out On The Lone Prairie* on Broadway 4060.
Revs: Banner 0843, Jewel 6093, Oriole 2093, Romeo 145, Challenge 786, Conqueror 7729 by The Pickard Family; Broadway 4060 and all issues of matrix 10016 by Carson Robison.

Acc. prob. Adelyne Hood, f-1/p-2; own h/jh-3; unknown, bj-4/g-5.

New York, NY   poss. early 1931

5029-A	Rovin' Gambler -1, 3, 5	Durium 9-1
5030-A	Letter Edged In Black -1, 5	Durium 9-2
5031-A	Hand Me Down My Walking Cane -2, 4	Durium 9-3
5032-A	Golden Slippers -2, 4	Durium 9-4

Acc. Adelyne Hood, f/v-1; unknown, ts-2; unknown, ac; own h-3/jh-4; Len Fillis, sg-5/g-6; unknown, sb-7; unknown, train-wh eff-8.

London, England   Wednesday, April 1, 1931

AR-593-2	The Runaway Train -3, 4, 6, 8	ReE MR346, RZ MR3817, Re/RZAu G21106, RZIr IZ1359
AR-594-	River Stay Away From My Door -6	ReE MR332
AR-595-2	Get Away, Old Man, Get Away -2, 3, 4, 6, 7	ReE MR346, RZ MR3817, Re/RZAu G21106, RZIr IZ1359

AR-596-	It's Time To Say Aloha To You -1, 5	ReE MR332

London, England   Thursday, April 2, 1931

AR-597-	When The Bloom Is On The Sage	Re rejected
AR-598-	Mountains Ain't No Place For Bad Men	Re rejected
AR-599-	Rock Me To Sleep In My Rocky Mountain Home	Re rejected
AR-600	Rabbit In The Pea Patch	Re rejected

Acc. Adelyne Hood, f; own h-1; Bobby Gregory, pac-2; prob. Roy Smeck, sg-3/bj-4/g-5; unknown, p/cel; unknown, sb-6.

New York, NY   Thursday, May 5, 1932

1709-2	That Old Faded Rose -5	Cr 3323, Htd 23084, Vs 5107, Broadcast International B-103
1710-2	I'm Writing A Letter To Heaven -3	Cr 3323, Htd 23084, Vs 5113, Broadcast International B-103
1711-1	Hoopy Scoopy -1, 2, 4, 6	Cr 3356, Htd 23086, Vs 5085

Varsity 5107, 5113 as by **Bill Vernon**.
Matrix 1709 is titled *Faded Rose* on Varsity 5107. Matrix 1710 is titled *A Letter To Heaven* on Varsity 5113. Matrix 1711 is titled *Hoopee Scoopee* on Varsity 5085.

Acc. Adelyne Hood, f-1/p-2; own h-3; poss. Roy Smeck, bj-4/g-5.

New York, NY   Thursday, June 2, 1932

1747-2	Oh, It's Great To Be A Doctor -2, 3, 4	Cr 3356, Htd 23086, Vs 5085
1748-2	Wreck Of The Circus Train -1, 3, 5	Cr 3340, Htd 23085, Vs 5113
1749-2	A Rope Around My Picture -1, 5	Cr 3340, Htd 23085, Vs 5107

Varsity 5107, 5113 as by **Bill Vernon**.
Matrix 1747 is titled *It's Great To Be A Doctor* on Varsity 5085. Matrix 1748 is titled *The Wreck Of The Circus Train* on Varsity 5113. Matrix 1749 is titled *There's A Rope Around My Picture* on Varsity 5107.

Acc. unknown (prob. same as next session).

New York, NY   Monday, April 2, 1934

15029-	The Letter Edged In Black	Br unissued?
15030-	The Prisoner's Song	Br unissued?

Vernon Dalhart, v; or **Vernon Dalhart With Adelyn Hood**-1, v duet; acc. Adelyne Hood, f; unknown, sg-2; unknown, p-3; unknown, g.

New York, NY   Wednesday, April 25, 1934

15029-A	The Letter Edged In Black	Br 6799, DeE F5006
15030-A	The Prisoner's Song	Br 6799, DeE F5006
15120-A	In The Valley Of Yesterday -1	Br 6901, DeE F5070, RZAu G22121
15121-A	The Old Covered Bridge -2, 3	Br 6901, DeE F5070, RZAu G22121

Vernon Dalhart & His Big Cypress Boys: Vernon Dalhart, v; acc. Bert Hirsch, f; poss. own h-1; Charles Magnante, pac-2; unknown, bj-3; John Cali, g; Hank Stern, tu-4/sb-5.

New York, NY   Monday, May 1, 1939

036628-1	You'll Never Take Away My Dreams -1, 3, 4	BB B-8170, MW M-8433, RZAu G23952
036629-1	(Don't Forget Me) Dear Little Darling -2, 5	BB B-8229, MW M-8435, RZAu G24036
036630-1	Lavender Cowboy -1, 2, 3, 4	BB B-8229, MW M-8435, RZAu G24036
036631-1	Johnnie Darlin' -2, 5	BB B-8170, MW M-8433, RZAu G23952
036632-1	Don't Cry, Little Sweetheart, Don't Cry -2, 5	BB B-8191, MW M-8434, RZAu G24070
036633-1	My Mary Jane -2, 3, 4	BB B-8191, MW M-8434, RZAu G24070

DALHART'S TEXAS PANHANDLERS

See Vernon Dalhart.

BILLY DALTON

Pseudonym on Madison 5006, and probably Madison 50006, Van Dyke 5006, for Jack Weston (but elsewhere for other, popular, artists).

WALTER DALTON [& HIS GUITAR]

Pseudonym on Pathé and Perfect for Frank Marvin.

TOMMY DANDURAND & HIS GANG

Tommy Dandurand, f; poss. Rube Tronson, f; poss. Chubby Parker, bj; unknown, g (on some items); Ed Goodreau, calls.

Chicago, IL   c. March 24, 1927

12650-A	Haste To The Wedding	Ge 6088, Ch 15354, Sil 5014, 25014, 8125, Spt 9158, Her 75547
12651	Big Town Fling	Ge 6088, Ch 15262, Sil 5039, 25039, 8186, Spt 9156, Her 75547

12652-A	Campbells Are Coming	Ge 6121, Ch 15354, Sil 5014, 25014, 8125, Spt 9158, Chg 406, Her 75551
12653-A	Devil's Dream	Ge 6121, Ch 15280, Sil 5015, 25015, 8130, Spt 9162, Her 75551
12654-A	Two Step Quadrille	Ge 6101, Ch 15262, Sil 5015, 25015, 8130, Spt 9162
12655-A	Larry O'Gaff	Ge 6101, Ch 15280, Sil 5039, 25039, 8186, Spt 9156

Gennetts and Herwins as by **Uncle Steve Hubbard & His Boys**. Champions as by **George Thomas & His Music**. Silvertone 5014, 5015 as by **Tommy Dandurand & His Gang Of W.L.S.** Silvertone 5039 as by **Tommy Dandurand & His Barn Dance Fiddlers**. Supertones as by **Dandurand & His Barn Dance Fiddlers**. Challenge 406 as by **George Cline & His Boys**. Matrix 12653 is titled *Devils Dream* on Champion 15280.

Tommy Dandurand, f; poss. Rube Tronson, f; poss. Chubby Parker, bj; Ed Goodreau, calls.
Chicago, IL   c. August 1, 1927

12952	The Irish Washerwoman	Ge 6351, Ch 15410, Sil 5058, 25058, 8127, Spt 9160, Spr 321
12953-A	McLeod's Reel	Ge 6351, Ch 33002, Sil 5059, 25059, 8126, Spt 9159
12954-A	Leather Breeches	Ge 6273, Ch 15410, Sil 5059, 25059, 8126, Spt 9159, Chg 406, Spr 321
12955-A	Over The Ocean Waves	Ge 6436, Sil 5060, 25060, 8128, Spt 9161
12956-A	Soldier's Joy	Sil 5060, 25060, 8128, Spt 9161

Gennett 6436 as by **Uncle Steve Hubbard & His Boys**. Champion 15410 as by **George Thomas & His Music**; 33002 artist credit untraced. Supertones as by **Dandurand & His Barn Dance Fiddlers**. Challenge 406 as by **George Cline & His Boys**. Superior 321 artist credit untraced. Rev. Gennett 6436 by Grayson & Whitter.

Chicago, IL   c. August 13, 1927

12988-A	Buffalo Girl	Ge 6273, Sil 5061, 25061, 8124, Spt 9157
12992-A	Medley Of Old Time Waltzes	Sil 5058, 25058, 8127, Spt 9160
12993	The Beau Of Oak Hill	Sil 5061, 25061, 8124, Spt 9157

Supertone 9157, 9160 as by **Dandurand & His Barn Dance Fiddlers**. Intervening matrices are by African-American artists.

JOHN W. DANIEL

John W. Daniel, f solo.
Camden, NJ   Saturday, July 17, 1926

35928-1,-2	The Charleston Hornpipe	Vi unissued
35929-1,-2	Cottage Hornpipe	Vi unissued
35930-1,-2	Turkey In The Straw	Vi unissued
35931-1,-2	Forkied [sic] Deer	Vi unissued

DANIELS–DEASON SACRED HARP SINGERS

Vocal quartet (three men, one woman); unacc.
Atlanta, GA   Wednesday, October 24, 1928

147280-2	Primrose Hill	Co 15323-D
147281-2	Coronation	Co 15323-D
147282-1	Hallelujah	Co unissued: *Co C4K47911 (CD)*
147283-	Pryel's Hymn	Co unissued

TOM DARBY & JIMMIE TARLTON

Darby & Tarlton: Tom Darby, Jimmie Tarlton, v duet; acc. Jimmie Tarlton, sg; Tom Darby, g.
Atlanta, GA   Tuesday, April 5, 1927

143902-2	Down In Florida On A Hog	Co 15197-D
143903-1	Birmingham Town	Co 15197-D

Atlanta, GA   Thursday, November 10, 1927

145202-2	Birmingham Jail	Co 15212-D
145203-2	Columbus Stockade Blues	Co 15212-D
145204-2	Gamblin' Jim	Co 15684-D
145205-2	Lonesome In The Pines	Co 15684-D

Columbia 15684-D as by **Tom Darby & Jimmie Tarlton**.

Tom Darby, Jimmie Tarlton, v duet; or Jimmie Tarlton, v-1; acc. Jimmie Tarlton, sg; Tom Darby, g.
Atlanta, GA   Thursday, April 12, 1928

146042-2	After The Ball	Co 15254-D
146043-2	I Can't Tell Why I Love You	Co 15254-D
146044-2	The Irish Police	Co 15293-D

146045-2	The Hobo Tramp	Co 15293-D
146046-2	Alto Waltz -1	Co 15319-D
146047-	Sleeping In The Manger	Co unissued
146048-	Daddy Won't Have No Easy Rider Here	Co unissued
146049-2	Mexican Rag -1	Co 15319-D

Tom Darby & Jimmie Tarlton, v duet; or Jimmie Tarlton, v-1; or Tom Darby, v-2; acc. Jimmie Tarlton, sg/humming-3; Tom Darby, g/y-4/sp-5/humming-3.
Atlanta, GA   Wednesday, October 31, 1928

147358-2	Birmingham Jail No. 2	Co 15375-D
147359-2	The Rainbow Division	Co 15360-D
147360-2	Country Girl Valley -2	Co 15360-D
147361-2	Lonesome Railroad -1, 3	Co 15375-D
147366-1	If You Ever Learn To Love Me -1	Co 15388-D
147367-2	If I Had Listened To My Mother	Co 15388-D
147368-1	Traveling Yodel Blues -4	Co 15330-D
147369-1	Heavy Hearted Blues -1, 5	Co 15330-D

Intervening matrices are by Red Mountain Trio.

Tom Darby, Jimmie Tarlton, v-1/sp-2 duet; or Jimmie Tarlton, v-3/y-4; or Tom Darby, v-5/y-6; acc. Jimmie Tarlton, sg; Tom Darby, g.
Atlanta, GA   Monday, April 15, 1929

148293-2	The New York Hobo -1	Co 15452-D
148294-1	All Bound Down In Texas -1	Co 15477-D
148295-2	Touring Yodel Blues -5, 6	Co 15419-D
148296-2	Slow Wicked Blues -3, 4	Co 15419-D
148297-2	Black Jack Moonshine -1	Co 15452-D
148298-2	Ain't Gonna Marry No More -3	Co 15477-D
148303-2	Down In The Old Cherry Orchard -1	Co 15403-D
148304-1	Where The Bluebirds Nest Again -1	Co 15403-D
148305-2	Beggar Joe -3, 4	Co 15624-D
148306-2	When You're Far Away From Home -1, 4/6	Co 15624-D
148307-2	Birmingham Rag -2	Co 15436-D
148308-2	Sweet Sarah Blues -3, 4	Co 15436-D

Matrices 148299/300 are by Thrasher Family; 148301/02 are by Freeman & Ashcraft.

Tom Darby, Jimmie Tarlton, v duet; or Jimmie Tarlton, v-1/y-2; or Tom Darby, v-3; acc. Jimmie Tarlton, sg/wh-4; Tom Darby, g/wh-4/sp-5.
Atlanta, GA   Thursday, October 31, 1929

149308-	Where The River Shannon Flows	Co unissued
149309-1	Little Bessie	Co 15492-D, ReE MR70, RZ ME30, RZAu G21659
149310-2	I Left Her At The River -3	Co 15492-D
149311-2	Jack And May -1, 2	Co 15528-D
149312-1	Captain Won't You Let Me Go Home	Co 15528-D
149313-	The Blue And The Gray	Co unissued
149322-1	Going Back To My Texas Home	Co 15715-D
149323-2	The Whistling Songbird -3, 4	Co 15511-D, ReE MR119
149324-2	Freight Train Ramble -1, 2, 5	Co 15511-D
149325-3	Lonesome Frisco Line	Co unissued: *FV FV12504* (LP); *Co C4K47911, BF BCD15764* (CDs)
149326-1	Down Among The Sugar Cane	Co 15715-D
149327-	What Is Home Without Love	Co unissued

Regal MR70, Regal-Zonophone ME30, G21659 as by **The Alabama Barn Stormers**; Regal MR119 as by **The Regal Rascals**. Intervening matrices are by other artists.
Revs: Regal MR70, Regal-Zonophone ME30, G21659 by Elzie Floyd & Leo Boswell; Regal MR119 popular.

Tom Darby, Jimmie Tarlton, v duet; or Jimmie Tarlton, v-1/y-2; or Tom Darby, v-3; acc. Jimmie Tarlton, sg; Tom Darby, g.
Atlanta, GA   Wednesay, April 16, 1930

150247-2	The Black Sheep	Co 15674-D
150248-1	Little Ola	Co 15591-D, Vo 03077
150249- ; 194998-2	Once I Had A Sweetheart -3	Co 15674-D
150250-1	The Maple On The Hill -1	Co 15591-D, Vo 03077
150251-2	My Father Died A Drunkard -1, 2	Co 15552-D, ReE MR146, RZAu G21864
150252-1	Frankie Dean	Co 15701-D

Regal MR146, Regal-Zonophone G21864 as by **Tom Darby**. Rev. Regal MR146 by Frank & James McCravy.

    Atlanta, GA   Thursday, April 17, 1930

Matrix	Title	Issue
150263- ; 194997-1	Pork Chops	Co 15611-D
150264-2	On The Banks Of A Lonely River -3	Co 15572-D
150265-2	Faithless Husband -1, 2	Co 15552-D, RZAu G21864
150266- ; 194995-1	Hard Time Blues -3	Co 15611-D
150267- ; 194994-1,-2	Rising Sun Blues -1, 2	Co 15701-D
150268-2	My Little Blue Heaven -1	Co 15572-D

Regal-Zonophone G21864 as by **Tom Darby**.

Jimmie Tarlton & Tom Darby, v duet; acc. Jimmie Tarlton, sg; Tom Darby, g.
    Atlanta, GA   Sunday, February 28, 1932

71627-1	13 Years In Kilbie Prison	Vi 23680, MW M-4335

    Atlanta, GA   Monday, February 29, 1932

71628-2	Once I Had A Fortune	Vi 23680, MW M-4335

Matrices 71629 through 71632 are by Jimmie Tarlton.

Jimmy Tarlton & Tom Darby, v duet; or **Jimmy Tarlton**, v-1; acc. Jimmie Tarlton, sg; Tom Darby, g.
    New York, NY   Wednesday, June 7, 1933

Matrix	Title	Issue
13432-1	Let's Be Friends Again	Ba 32810, Me M12743, MeC 91601, Or 8249, Pe 12926, Ro 5249, Cq 8170
13433-	I Long For The Pines	ARC unissued
13434-	Hitch Hike Bums -1	ARC unissued
13435-2	By The Old Oaken Bucket, Louise -1	Ba 32810, Me M12743, MeC 91601, Or 8249, Pe 12926, Ro 5249
13436-	Baby I Can't Use You -1	ARC unissued
13437	Black Sheep	ARC unissued

Rev. Conqueror 8170 by Frank Luther.
Darby sings lead and Tarlton harmony on their duets.
Solo recordings by Jimmie Tarlton are listed under his name. Tom Darby also recorded with the Georgia Wild Cats. Jimmie Tarlton recorded after 1942.

MOUNTAIN DEW DARE

Pseudonym on OKeh for Willard Hodgin.

CHUCK DARLING

Chuck Darling, h; acc. Hervey Hoskins, g.
    Hollywood, CA   Friday, October 17, 1930

Matrix	Title	Issue
61043-1	Harmonica Rag	Vi V-40330, BB B-5285, Eld 2158, Sr S-3366, MW M-4911
61044-2	Blowin' The Blues	Vi V-40330, BB B-5285, Eld 2158, Sr S-3366, MW M-4911

DENVER DARLING

Denver Darling & His Texas Cowhands: Denver Darling, v; acc. poss. Slim Duncan, f; unknown, cl; unknown, ac; own g; poss. Eddie Smith, sb.
    New York, NY   Thursday, November 6, 1941

Matrix	Title	Issue
69917-A	Don't Let Your Sweet Love Die (Like Flowers In The Fall)	De 6005
69918-A	It's Your Worry Now	De 6058
69919-A	Silver Dollar	De 6058
69920-A	I'm Thinking Tonight Of My Blue Eyes	De 6005

Denver Darling, v; acc. own g.
    New York, NY   Monday, December 22, 1941

70084-A	Cowards Over Pearl Harbor	De 6008, MeC 45486
70085-A	I'll Pray For You	De 6008, MeC 45486

Denver Darling & His Texas Cowhands: Denver Darling, v; acc. unknown, f; unknown, cl; unknown, ac; unknown, esg; unknown, g; unknown, sb; band v.
    New York, NY   Wednesday, February 18, 1942

70340-A	We're Gonna Have To Slap The Dirty Little Jap (And Uncle Sam's The Guy Who Can Do It)	De 6027

70341-A	Get Your Gun And Come Along (We're Fixin' To Kill A Skunk)	De 6027
70342-A	Mussolini's Letter To Hitler	De 6028
70343-A	Hitler's Reply To Mussolini	De 6028

Acc. unknown, f-1; poss. Vaughn Horton, esg; own g; poss. Eddie Smith, sb.
    New York, NY   Monday, March 9, 1942

70452-A	How Low Do The Blues Want To Go	De 6036
70453-A	Live And Let Live -1	De 6033
70454-A	You Brought Sorrow To My Heart	De 6036
70455-A	Branded Wherever I Go	De 6033

Acc. unknown, f-1; unknown, esg-2/bj-3; own g; poss. Eddie Smith, sb.
    New York, NY   Thursday, April 2, 1942

70608-A	There Was A Time -2	De 6050
70609-A	Cherokee Maiden -2	De 6050
70610-A	1942 Turkey In The Straw -1, 3	De 6043
70611-A	The Devil And Mr. Hitler -2	De 6043

Acc. unknown, f; poss. Vaughn Horton, eg; own g; poss. Eddie Smith, sb; band v-1.
    New York, NY   Tuesday, July 14, 1942

71046-A	I'm A Pris'ner Of War (On A Foreign Shore)	De 6061
71047-A	Modern Cannon Ball	De 6063
71048-A	The Little Brown Jug Goes Modern -1	De 6061
71049-A	Care Of Uncle Sam	De 6063

Denver Darling recorded after 1942.

DAVE & HOWARD

See David McCarn.

CAL DAVENPORT & HIS GANG

Prob.: Hubert Davenport, h; Cal Davenport, bj; Malcolm Davenport, g; Bill Brown, g; unidentified, v-1.
    Knoxville, TN   Saturday, August 31, 1929

K-150	Double Eagle March	Vo 5394
K-151	Broken Hearted Lover -1	Vo 5371
K-152	Little Rosewood Casket -1	Vo 5371
K-153	Blue Ridge Mountain Blues -1	Vo 5398

There is possibly only one guitar on matrix K-153.
Revs: Vocalion 5394, 5398 by Tennessee Ramblers.

EMMETT DAVENPORT

Pseudonym on Supertone for Asa Martin.

HOMER DAVENPORT

Homer Davenport, bj solo.
    Richmond, IN   Wednesday, April 22, 1925

12219	Down In Tennessee Blues	Ge 5715, 3022, Sil 4009, Chg 110

Challenge 110 as by **The Three Howard Boys**. Revs: Gennett 5715, Silvertone 4009, Challenge 110 by Homer Davenport & Young Brothers; Gennett 3022 by John Hammond.
For recordings credited to **Homer Davenport & Young Brothers** see Jess Young.

DAVENPORT & TRACY

Pseudonym on Supertone for (Asa) Martin & (James) Roberts.

EVA DAVID

Pseudonym on Diva, Velvet Tone, and Harmony for Eva Davis.

CHARLIE DAVIS

Pseudonym on Timely Tunes and Aurora for Claude (C.W.) Davis.

CLAUDE [C.W.] DAVIS

Jewell Davis: Claude Davis, v; or **Davis & Layne**: Claude Davis, Bert Layne, v duet-1; acc. Bert Layne, f; unknown, f-2; Claude Davis, g.
    Winston-Salem, NC   Wednesday, September 21, 1927

81361-B	Thinking Of The Days I've Done Wrong -2	OK 45152
81362-B	When Maple Leaves Are Falling	OK 45152

81363-	Give Me Your Heart	OK unissued
81364-	When The Flowers Bloom In Springtime	OK unissued
81365-	Bury Me Beneath The Willow -1	OK unissued
81366-	Sleep On Brown Eyes -1	OK unissued

C.W. Davis, v; or **C.W. Davis–Bert Layne**, v duet-1; acc. Bert Layne, f; own g.
    Atlanta, GA   Friday, February 24, 1928

41964-1	When The Flowers Bloom In The Springtime	Au 36-107
41964-2	When The Flowers Bloom In The Springtime	TT C-1559
41965-2	Down In A Southern Town	TT C-1559, Au 36-107
41966-2	Sleep On, Brown Eyes -1	Vi 21370
41967-2	Give Me Your Heart	Vi 21370

Timely Tunes C-1559, Aurora 36-107 as by **Charlie Davis**.

Acc. Lowe Stokes, f; Bert Layne, f; own g.
    Richmond, IN   Saturday, June 23, 1928

13911	Thinking Of The Days I Did Wrong	Ge rejected
13912	Sweet Bunch Of Daisies	Ge 6637
13913	Travelling Coon	Ge 6548

Davis, Stokes & Layne: Lowe Stokes, f/v; Bert Layne, f/v; Claude Davis, g/v.
    Richmond, IN   Saturday, June 23, 1928

| 13914-A | Way Down In Alabam' | Ge 6548 |

Monroe County Bottle Tippers: Lowe Stokes, f/sp; Claude Davis, g/sp; Bert Layne, sp.
    Richmond, IN   Saturday, June 23, 1928

| 13915 | The Fiddlin' Bootleggers – Part I | Ge 6585, Ch 15633, 45010, Spt 9177 |
| 13916-A | The Fiddlin' Bootleggers – Part II | Ge 6585, Ch 15633, 45010 |

Champion 15633, 45010 as by **The Boys From Wildcat Hollow**. Supertone 9177 as by **The Boone County Entertainers**; matrix 13915 is titled *Fiddlin' Bootleggers* on that issue. Rev. Supertone 9177 by Calaway's West Virginia Mountaineers.

C.W. Davis & Lowe Stokes, v duet; acc. Lowe Stokes, f; Bert Layne, f; Claude Davis, g.
    Richmond, IN   Saturday, June 23, 1928

| 13917 | Sweet William | Ge 6637, Spt 9314 |

Supertone 9314 as by **Harper & Page**. Rev. Supertone 9314 by Asa Martin & James Roberts.

Lookout Mountain Revelers: Lowe Stokes, f/v-1/sp-2; Bert Layne, f/v-3/sp-4; Claude Davis, g/v-5/sp-6.
    Chicago, IL   c. June 1928

20627-2	Dreaming Of Mother -3, 5	Pm 3123, Bwy 8200
20628-2	Oh Wasn't I Getting Away -3, 5	Pm 3123, Bwy 8200
20629-1	Pussycat Rag -1, 3, 5	Pm 3111, Bwy 8140
20630-1	Bury Me Beneath The Willow -1, 3, 5	Pm 3143, Bwy 8213
20631-2	I Ain't Got No Sweetheart -1, 3, 5	Pm 3111, Bwy 8140
20632-2	Barn Dance On The Mountain Part I -2, 4, 5, 6	Pm 3105, Bwy 8137
20633-1	Down In Atlanta -5	Pm 3164, Bwy 8285
20634-2	When The Maple Leaves Are Falling -5	Pm 3164, Bwy 8285
20635-2	Barn Dance On The Mountain Part II -2, 4, 6	Pm 3105, Bwy 8137

Paramount 3143 as by **Lookout Mountain Singers**; 3164 as by **Lookout Mountain Boys**. Broadways as by **Great Gap Entertainers**. *Sleeping In A Box Car*, composed by "Lane and Davis", which was copyrighted by Chicago Music on November 30, 1928, may have been recorded at this session. Rev. Paramount 3143, Broadway 8213 by Red Brush Singers.

Claude Davis & Bob Nichols: Claude Davis, Clayton McMichen, v/y-1 duet; acc. Clayton McMichen, f; Bert Layne, f; Claude Davis, g.
    Atlanta, GA   Tuesday, April 9, 1929

| 148220-1 | We Were Pals Together | Co 15397-D, CoSA DE504 |
| 148221-2 | Down In A Southern Town -1 | Co 15397-D, CoSA DE504 |

    Atlanta, GA   Thursday, April 11, 1929

| 148249-1 | Underneath The Southern Moon | Co 15446-D |
| 148250-2 | Meet Me Tonight In Dreamland | Co 15446-D |

Davis & Nelson: Claude Davis, Harry (?) Nelson, v duet; acc. prob. Claude Davis, md; prob. Harry (?) Nelson or unknown, g.
    Long Island City, NY   c. April 1929

394	Charming Betsy	QRS R.9011, Pm 3227, Bwy 8177
395	When The Flowers Bloom In The Spring	QRS R.9011, Pm 3227, Bwy 8177
399-A	Every Little Bit Added To What You Got	QRS R.9018, Pm 3187, Bwy 8195
400	I Don't Bother Work	QRS R.9018, Pm 3187, Bwy 8195

Broadway 8177, 8195 as by **Drake & Norman**. Harry (?) Nelson may in fact be Harry Charles. Matrix 396 is untraced; matrices 397/98 are by Chumbler, Coker & Rice.

Davis Trio-1/Davis, Rice & Thomas-2: poss. Henry Thomas, f; Claude Davis, md; Hoke Rice, g.
Long Island City, NY   c. April 1929

402-A	The Only Way -1	QRS R.9013, Pm 3238, Bwy 8191
403-A	Sleepy Hollow -1	QRS R.9013, Pm 3238, Bwy 8191
404	Circus Day Rag -2	QRS R.9019, Pm 3309

Paramount 3309 as by **Davis–Rice–Thomas**. Broadway 8191 as by **Drake Trio**. Matrix 401 is by Hoke Rice. Rev. QRS R.9019, Paramount 3309 by Chumbler's Breakdown Gang (on latter issue as **Davis–Rice–Thomas**).

Davis & Nelson: Claude Davis, Harry (?) Nelson, v duet; acc. unknown, f-1; prob. Claude Davis, md-2; Harry (?) Nelson or unknown, g; unknown, wh-3.
Long Island City, NY   c. April 1929

410	I Don't Want Your Greenback Dollar -2, 3	QRS R.9014, Pm 3188, Bwy 8243
411	Meet Me Tonight In Dreamland -2	QRS R.9014, Pm 3188, Bwy 8243
414-A	I Shall Not Be Moved -1	QRS R.9023, Pm 3186, Bwy 8189
421-A	Death Is No More Than A Dream -2	QRS R.9023, Pm 3186, Bwy 8189

Broadway 8189, 8243 as by **Drake & Norman**. Matrices 412/13, 417/18 are by Hoke Rice; 415/16 by Nelson & Nelson; 419/20 untraced.

Claude Davis, v; acc. unknown, cl-1; own g.
Atlanta, GA   Monday, November 10, 1930

ATL-6601-	Over The Hills In Caroline -1	Br 503
ATL-6602-	When The Flowers Bloom In The Springtime	Br 503

Claude Davis Trio: prob.: Clyde Kiser, h/g; Claude Davis, v/g; Rudle Kiser, v/y/wh-1.
Atlanta, GA   Monday, November 2, 1931

152005-1	Standing By The Highway -1	Co 15740-D
152006-1	I Don't Want Your Gold Or Silver	Co 15740-D, Re/RZAu G21557
152007-	Wish Me Good Luck On My Journey	Co unissued
152008-	Give Me Your Heart	Co unissued

Rev. Regal/Regal-Zonophone G21557 by Johnnie Gates.
Claude Davis also recorded with the Gibbs Brothers.

EVA DAVIS

Eva Davis, v; acc. own or Samantha Bumgarner, bj.
New York, NY   Tuesday, April 22, 1924

81711-2	Wild Bill Jones	Co 129-D, Ha 5093-H
81712-2	John Hardy	Co 167-D, Ha 5097-H, Ve 7036-V, Di 6010-G

Harmony 5093-H, 5097-H, Velvet Tone 7036-V, Diva 6010-G as by **Eva David**.
Rev. all issues by Samantha Bumgarner & Eva Davis (see the former).

JEWELL DAVIS

Pseudonym on OKeh for Claude (C.W.) Davis.

JIMMIE DAVIS

Jimmie Davis, v/y-1; acc. James Enloe, p.
Chicago, IL   July/August 1928

5204-2	Ramona	Doggone unnumbered
5205-2	You'd Rather Forget Than Forgive	Doggone unnumbered
5206-2	Think Of Me Thinking Of You	Doggone unnumbered
5207-2	Way Out On The Mountain -1	Doggone unnumbered

These were custom recordings by Paramount for station KWKH, Shreveport, LA. They were coupled 5204-2/5206-2 and 5205-2/5207-2.

Jimmie Davis, v/y; acc. Allen Dees, g.
Dallas, TX   Tuesday, December 4, 1928

147558-	Nobody's Business	Co unissued
147559-	Out Of Town Blues (Dallas)	Co unissued

Acc. Prentis Dumas, sg.
Memphis, TN   Thursday, September 19, 1929

55545-2	The Barroom Message	Vi V-40154
55546-2	The Baby's Lullaby	Vi V-40154, ZoSA 4362
55547-1	Out Of Town Blues	Vi V-40215
55548-2	Home Town Blues	Vi V-40215

Acc. poss. Prentis Dumas, sg; unknown, g.
Memphis, TN   Monday, May 19, 1930

59940-2	Settling Down For Life	Vi V-40332

59941-2	My Dixie Sweetheart	Vi V-40302, BB B-7071
59942-1	You're The Picture Of Your Mother	Vi V-40332, ZoSA 4362

Acc. poss. Prentis Dumas, sg; unknown, g-1.
Memphis, TN Tuesday, May 20, 1930

59949-1	Doggone That Train	Vi V-40286
59949-2	Doggone That Train	Vi unissued: *BF BFX15285 (LP)*
59950-2	My Louisiana Girl -1	Vi V-40302, MW M-7360
59951-1	Cowboy's Home Sweet Home -1	Vi 23718, MW M-7359

Rev. Victor 23718 by Bob Miller.

Acc. prob.: Ed Schaffer, sg; Oscar Woods, g.
Memphis, TN Tuesday, May 20, 1930

59952-1	She's A Hum Dum Dinger (From Dingersville)	Vi unissued: *BF BFX15285 (LP)*
59952-2	She's A Hum Dum Dinger From Dingersville	Vi V-40286, BB 1835, B-5005, Eld 1963, Sr S-3128, MW M-4283

Matrix 59952 is titled *She's A Hum Dum Dinger* on at least some secondary issues.

Acc. prob.: Ed Schaffer, sg-1; unknown, sg-2; Oscar Woods, g-3; unknown, g-4.
Memphis, TN Saturday, November 29, 1930

64752-1	Before You Say Farewell -2, 4	Vi unissued: *BF BCD15943 (CD)*
64752-2	Before You Say Farewell -2, 4	Vi 23559, BB B-5698, Twin FT1827
64753-2	Where The Old Red River Flows -2, 4	Vi 23525
64754-2	Penitentiary Blues -2, 4	Vi 23544, ZoSA 4367
64755-2	Arabella Blues -1, 3	Vi 23517, BB B-5496
64756-2	In Arkansas -2, 4	Vi 23525
64757-2	Lonely Hobo -2, 4	Vi 23648, Au 414, BB B-4955
64758-1	I'll Be Happy Today -2, 4	Vi unissued: *BF BCD15943 (CD)*
64758-2	I'll Be Happy Today -2, 4	Vi 23559, BB B-5806, MW M-7361, Twin FT1863
64759-1	A Woman's Blues -1	Vi 23544
64759-2	A Woman's Blues -1	Vi unissued: *BF BFX15285 (LP); BF BCD16216 (CD)*
64760-2	Bear Cat Mama From Horner's Corners -1, 3	Vi 23517, BB 1835, B-5005, Eld 1963, Sr S-3128, MW M-4283
64761-2	My Arkansas Sweetheart -2, 4	Vi 23648, Au 414, BB B-4955, B-5806, MW M-7360, HMVIn N4280

Matrix 64760 is titled *Bear Cat Mama* on Montgomery Ward M-4283.
Revs: HMV N4280 by Frank Marvin; Twin FT1863 by Asher Sizemore; Zonophone 4367 by Dick Robertson.

Acc. Eddie "Snoozer" Quinn, g-1, Buddy Jones, g.
Charlotte, NC Tuesday, May 26, 1931

69352-2	Hobo's Warning -1	Vi unissued: *BF BCD15943 (CD)*
69353-1,-2	Bury Me In Old Kentucky -1	Vi unissued
69354-1,-2	The Gambler's Return -1	Vi unissued
69355-1	Wild And Reckless Hobo	Vi 23628, ZoAu EE331

Jimmie Davis, v/sp; acc. Buddy Jones, h/g/sp; unknown, train-wh eff.
Charlotte, NC Tuesday, May 26, 1931

69356-2	The Davis Limited	Vi 23601, BB B-6249

Jimmie Davis, v; acc. Snoozer Quinn, g; Buddy Jones, g.
Charlotte, NC Wednesday, May 27, 1931

69357-2	She Left A Runnin' Like A Sewing Machine	Vi 23587

Jimmie Davis, v/sp-1; acc. "Dizzy Head" (Ed Schaffer), sg/v-2; Snoozer Quinn, g-3.
Charlotte, NC Wednesday, May 27, 1931

69358-1	Down At The Old Country Church -1, 2	Vi unissued: *BF BCD15943 (CD)*
69358-2	Down At The Old Country Church -1, 2	Vi 23628, MW M-7361, ZoAu EE331
69359-1	She's A Hum-Dum Dinger – Part 2 (From Dingersville) -3	Vi 23587, BB B-5751
69359-2	She's A Hum-Dum Dinger – Part 2 (From Dingersville) -3	Vi unissued: *BF BFX15285 (LP)*
69360-1	Market House Blues -3	Vi 23620
69361-1	Get On Board, Aunt Susan -3	Vi 23620, BB B-5319, Sr S-3400
69362-1	Midnight Blues -3	Vi 23601, BB B-6249, HMVIn N4399

Rev. HMV N4399 by Girls Of The Golden West.

Jimmie Davis, v; acc. "Dizzy Head" (Ed Schaffer), sg-1; Snoozer Quinn, g.
Charlotte, NC Thursday, May 28, 1931

| 69367-1 | There's Evil In Ye Children, Gather 'Round -1 | Vi 23573, BB B-5319, Sr S-3400 |
| 69368-1 | Pea Pickin' Papa | Vi 23573 |

Acc. Jack Davis, sg; Jack Barnes, g/v-1; Ruth White, sb/v-1.
    Dallas, TX   Saturday, February 6, 1932

| 70651-1 | I'll Get Mine Bye And Bye -1 | Vi 23674, BB B-5697, Twin FT1811 |
| 70652-1 | Barnyard Stomp | Vi 23659 |

Acc. poss. Jack Barnes, g; Ausie B. Grigg, sb-1.
    Dallas, TX   Sunday, February 7, 1932

70653-1	I Wonder (If She Is Blue) -1	Vi unissued: *BF BCD15943 (CD)*
70654-1	1982 Blues	Vi 23688
70655-1	High Behind Blues	Vi 23703, BB B-5699

Matrix 70654 was logged, but not issued, with the parenthesised title (*Davis' Last Day Blues*).

Acc. Ed Schaffer, sg; Oscar Woods, g-1/v-2/sp-3.
    Dallas, TX   Monday, February 8, 1932

70656-1	Saturday Night Stroll -2	Vi 23688, MW M-7363
70657-1	Sewing Machine Blues -1	Vi 23703, BB B-5751
70658-1	Red Nightgown Blues -1	Vi 23659, BB B-5699
70659-1	Davis' Salty Dog -1, 2, 3	Vi 23674

Matrices 70660/61 are by Eddie (Schaffer) & Oscar (Woods) (see *B&GR*).

Acc. unknown, h-1; poss. Ed Davis, g; unknown, g-2.
    Camden, NJ   Thursday, November 3, 1932

59056-1	You Can't Tell About The Women Nowadays -2	Vi 23746, BB B-5697, Twin FT1811
59057-1	The Shotgun Wedding	Vi 23746, BB B-5496, Twin FT1809
59058-1	Hold 'Er, Newt -1	Vi 23752, BB B-6437, HMVIn N4409
59059-2	Yo Yo Mama -2	Vi 23793, BB B-6437, HMVIn N4409
59060-1	Tom Cat And Pussy Blues	Vi 23763, BB B-6272, Twin FT8096
59061-1	Organ-Grinder Blues	Vi 23763, BB B-6272
59062-1	Rockin' Blues	Vi unissued: *BF BFX15125 (LP); BF BCD15943 (CD)*
59063-1	Wampus Kitty Mama -2	Vi unissued: *BF BFX15285 (LP); BF BCD15943 (CD)*

Revs: Victor 23752 by Dick Robertson, 23793 by Fleming & Townsend; Twin FT1809 by Harold & Hazel, FT8096 by Tune Wranglers.

Acc. Rubye Blevins, f/v-1/y; unknown h; poss. Ed Davis, g/v-1; unknown, g/v-1.
    Camden, NJ   Friday, November 4, 1932

59064-1	Bury Me In Old Kentucky -1	Vi 23749
59065-1	Jealous Lover	Vi 23778, MW M-4327
59066-1	Gambler's Return	Vi 23778, MW M-4327
59067-1	Home In Caroline -1	Vi 23749, BB B-5698, MW M-7363, Twin FT1827

Acc. Joe Attlesey (Shelton), md; Leon Chappelear, g; Bob Attlesey (Shelton), u-1/j-2.
    Chicago, IL   Friday, August 4, 1933

76862-1	It's All Coming Home To You -1	BB B-5156, Eld 2055, Sr S-3237, MW M-4449, M-7362
76863-1	I Wonder If She's Blue -1	BB B-5187, Eld 2080, Sr S-3267, MW M-4388, M-7362
76864-1	When It's Round-Up Time In Heaven -1	BB B-5187, Eld 2080, Sr S-3267, MW M-4388, M-7359
76865-1	Would You -2	BB B-5359, Sr S-3440, MW M-4485
76866-1	You've Been Tom Cattin' Around -2	BB B-5425, HMVIn N4303
76867-1	Alimony Blues -1	BB B-5425, HMVIn N4303

Acc. Joe Attlesey (Shelton), md; Leon Chappelear, g; Bob Attlesey (Shelton), u.
    Chicago, IL   Saturday, August 5, 1933

76872-1	The Keyhole In The Door	BB B-5156, Eld 2055, Sr S-3237, MW M-4449
76873-1	Beautiful Texas	BB unissued: *BF BCD15943 (CD)*
76873-2	Beautiful Texas	BB B-5394, HMV N4333
76874-1	Triflin' Mama Blues	BB B-5635, Twin FT1843
76875-1	I Want Her Tailor-Made	BB B-5359, Sr S-3440, MW M-4485
76876-1	Alimony Blues	BB B-5635
76877-1	There Ain't Gonna Be No Afterwhile	BB B-5570, HMVIn N4350

Revs: Bluebird B-5394, HMV N4333 by Girls Of The Golden West; Twin FT1843 by Joe Smith.

Acc. Leon Chappelear, g.
  Chicago, IL   Saturday, August 5, 1933
    76878-1   Easy Rider Blues   BB B-5570, HMVIn N4350

Acc. Warren Pottinger, sg; Loyce (Bud) "Tex" Swaim, g; Bill Parker, g.
  Chicago, IL   Friday, September 21, 1934
    9494-A   Nobody's Darlin' But Mine   De 5090, 46003, DeSA FM5110, BrSA SA1052
    9495-A   When It's Round-Up Time In Heaven   De 5090
    9496-A   Good Time Papa Blues   De 5032
    9497-A   Shirt Tail Blues   De 5032
Rev. Decca FM5110, Brunswick SA1052 by Norman Phelps.
  Chicago, IL   Monday, September 24, 1934
    9506-A   It's Been Years (Since I've Seen My Mother)   De 5031
    9507-A   Beautiful Mary   De 5031
    9508-A   My Brown Eyed Texas Rose   De 5104, 46004
    9509-A   Moonlight And Skies (No. 2)   De 5104
    9510-A   Jellyroll Blues   De 5064
    9511-A   Graveyard Blues   De 5064

Acc. poss. Buddy Jones, g/v-1; poss. unknown others.
  Chicago, IL   Sunday, August 11, 1935
    90213-A,-AA,-B I Wish I Had Never Seen Sunshine   De unissued
    90214-A,-AA   Bed Bug Blues -1   De unissued

Jimmie Davis, v; or **Jimmie Davis & Buddy Jones**, v duet-1; acc. poss. Joe Shelton, md; prob. Buddy Jones, g;
unknown, g-2.
  Chicago, IL   Monday, August 12, 1935
    90215-A,-AA   Deep Mississippi Blues   De rejected
    90216-A,-AA   Will You Love Me When I'm Old   De rejected
    90217-A   Are You Tired Of Me Darling? -1   De 5155
    90218-A   Red River Blues -1, 2   De 5155
    90219-A,-B,-BB Corn Fed Mama   De rejected
    90220-A,-AA,-B I Ain't Gonna Let Satan Turn Me 'Round -1 De rejected
Matrix 90221 was used for an advertisement.
  Chicago, IL   Tuesday, August 13, 1935
    90222-A,-AA   Come On Over To My House (Ain't Nobody Home   De rejected
                      But Me) -1?
    90223-A,-AA   In My Cabin Tonight -1?   De rejected

Jimmie Davis, Buddy Jones, v duet; acc. unknown.
  Chicago, IL   Wednesday, August 14, 1935
    90235-A,-AA   'Twill Be Sweet When We Meet   De rejected

Jimmie Davis, v; acc. prob.: Bill Harper, f; Charles Mitchell, esg; Tex Swaim, g; Ova Mitchell, u; Hershel Woodal, sb.
  New Orleans, LA   Thursday, March 19, 1936
    60822-A   The Answer To Nobody's Darling But Mine De 5203, DeE F6358, RexIr U575
    60823-A   In My Cabin Tonight   De 5231, MeC 45236
    60824-A,-B   When A Boy From The Mountains (Weds A Girl De 5203
                      From The Valley)

Acc. poss. Curly Fox, f; poss. Buddy Jones, g; Hershel Woodal, sb.
  New Orleans, LA   Thursday, March 19, 1936
    60825-A   Come On Over To My House (Ain't Nobody Home   De unissued: *BF BCD15943 (CD)*
                      But Me)

Acc. prob.: Bill Harper, f; Charles Mitchell, esg; Tex Swaim, g; Ova Mitchell, u; Hershel Woodal, sb.
  New Orleans, LA   Thursday, March 19, 1936
    60832-A   Don't Say Goodbye If You Love Me   De 5270, DeAu X1275
    60832-B   Don't Say Goodbye If You Love Me   De unissued: *BF BCD16216 (CD)*
Matrices 60826 to 60829 are by Roy Shaffer; 60830/31 are by Rex Griffin; 60833/34 are by Paradise Entertainers.
  New Orleans, LA   Saturday, March 21, 1936
    60835-A   I Wish I Had Never Seen Sunshine   De 5231, 46004, DeE F6358, MeC 45236,
                                                               RexIr U575

Acc. poss. Curly Fox, f; Buddy Jones, g/v-1/y/sp; Hershel Woodal, sb.
  New Orleans, LA   Saturday, March 21, 1936
    60836-A   High Geared Mama   De 5206
    60837-A   Bed Bug Blues -1   De 5206

Jimmie Davis & Buddy Jones, v duet; acc. Buddy Jones, g; poss. Ova Mitchell, u-1.
New Orleans, LA   Saturday, March 21, 1936

| 60845-A | I Ain't Gonna Let Ol' Satan Turn Me 'Round | De 5235 |
| 60846-A | 'Twill Be Sweet When We Meet -1 | De 5235 |

Matrices 60838 to 60841 are by Joe Robechaux (see JR); 60842 to 60844 are by Sharkey Bonano (see JR).

Jimmie Davis, v; acc. unknown, f; unknown, cl; Charles Mitchell, esg; Tex Swaim, g; poss. Ova Mitchell, u; unknown, sb.
Los Angeles, CA   Monday, June 1, 1936

DLA-377-A	My Blue Bonnet Girl	De 5238, DeAu X1204, MeC 45238
DLA-377-B	My Blue Bonnet Girl	De unissued: *BF BCD16216* (CD)
DLA-378-A	Ridin' Down The Arizona Trail	De 5238, DeAu X1204, MeC 45238, Min M-14072
DLA-378-B	Ridin' Down The Arizona Trail	De unissued: *BF BCD16216* (CD)
DLA-379-A	Mama's Getting Hot And Papa's Getting Cold	De 5249
DLA-379-B	Mama's Getting Hot And Papa's Getting Cold	De unissued: *BF BCD16216* (CD)
DLA-380-A	When It's Peach Pickin' Time In Georgia	De 5270, DeAu X1275

Acc. unknown, cl; Tex Swaim, h/g; poss. Ova Mitchell, u; unknown, sb.
Los Angeles, CA   Monday, June 1, 1936

| DLA 381-A | Come On Over To My House (Ain't Nobody Home But Me) | De 5249 |

Acc. Bill Harper, f; Charles Mitchell, esg; Tex Swaim, g; Ova Mitchell, u; Hershel Woodal, sb.
Dallas, TX   Tuesday, February 16, 1937

61811-A	That's Why I'm Nobody's Darling	De 5336, MeC 45220, Min M-14073
61812-A	Do You Ever Think Of Me?	De 5400, 46159, DeSA FM5112
61813-A	Prairie Of Love	De 5336, MeC 45221, Min M-14075
61814-A	Sweet Lorene	De 5465, DeAu X1574, MeC 45246, Min M-14069

Matrix 61812 is titled *Do You Ever Think Of Me* on Decca 46159, FM5112.

Dallas, TX   Wednesday, February 17, 1937

61815-A	Just Forgive And Forget	De 5415, DeAu X1572, MeC 45244, Min M-14072, M-14129
61816-A	Pal Of Long Ago	De 5363, DeAu X1390, MeC 45220
61817-A	If I Cry You'll Never Know	De 5465, DeAu X1574, DeSA FM5112, MeC 45246, Min M-14079, Pan 25967
61818-A	Sweetheart Of West Texas	De 5415, DeAu X1572, MeC 45244, Min M-14129

Matrix 61817 is titled *If I Ever Cry You'll Never Know* on Decca FM5112.

Acc. Buster Jones, esg; Tex Swaim, g; Ova Mitchell, u; Hershel Woodal, sb; unknown, d.
Dallas, TX   Wednesday, February 17, 1937

| 61819-A | Ten Tiny Toes | De 5349, MeC 45221 |

Matrices 61820 to 61828 are by Shelton Brothers.

Acc. Bill Harper, f; Charles Mitchell, esg; Tex Swaim, g; Ova Mitchell, u; Hershel Woodal, sb; unknown, d-1.
Dallas, TX   Wednesday, February 17, 1937

61829-A	I Wonder Where You Are	De 5435, MeC 45245, Min M-14069
61830-A	In The West Where Life Is Free	De 5477, DeAu X1591, MeC 45241
61831-A	You'll Be Comin' Back Some Day -1	De 5380

Acc. "Jake" (poss. Jack Davis), esg; poss. Leon Chappelear, g-1; Tex Swaim, g; Ova Mitchell, u; Hershel Woodal, sb; unknown, d.
Dallas, TX   Wednesday, February 17, 1937

| 61832-A | Hard Hearted Mama | De unissued: *BF BCD15943* (CD) |
| 61833-A | Jimmie's Travelin' Blues -1 | De 5435, MeC 45245, Min M-14079 |

Acc. Bill Harper, f; Charles Mitchell, esg-1; "Jake" (poss. Jack Davis), esg-2; Tex Swaim, g; Ova Mitchell, u; Hershel Woodal, sb.
Dallas, TX   Thursday, February 18, 1937

| 61834-A | I Wonder Who's Kissing Her Now -1 | De 5363, DeAu X1390, MeC 45222, Min M-14075 |
| 61835-A | Pi-Rootin' Around -2 | De 5380 |

Acc. Brown's Musical Brownies: Robert "Buck" Buchanan, f; Johnny Borowski, f; Wilson "Lefty" Perkins, esg; Fred "Papa" Calhoun, p; Ocie Stockard, tbj; Derwood Brown, g; Wanna Coffman, sb.
Dallas, TX   Friday, February 19, 1937

| 61871-A | High Geared Daddy | De 5349, MeC 45222 |
| 61872-A | Honky Tonk Blues | De 5400, 46137 |

Acc. Lani McIntire & His Hawaiians: poss. Bob Nichols, esg; Lani McIntire, g; George Kainapu, u; Al McIntire, sb; band v-1.
   New York, NY   Sunday, October 17, 1937

62688-A	Nobody's Darling But Mine -1	De 1504
62689-A	One, Two, Three, Four -1	De 1505, DeSA FM5129
62690-A	Have You Ever Been In Heaven?	De 1504, Pan 25980
62691-A	The Greatest Mistake In My Life	De 1505

Acc. Charles Mitchell, esg; unknown, p; unknown, tbj; unknown, g; unknown, sb; unknown, woodblocks-1.
   Dallas, TX   Thursday, December 9, 1937

62992-A	(Sweetheart) Please Be True To Me -1	De 5492, MeC 45249, Min M-14080
62993-A	By The Grave Of Nobody's Darling (My Darling's Promise)	De 5477, DeAu X1591, MeC 45241, Min M-14073
62994-A	Shackles And Chains	De 5492, 46159, MeC 45249
62995-A	Call Me Back Pal O' Mine -1	De 5525, MeC 45253
62996-A	Just A Girl That Men Forget -1	De 5539, MeC 45263, Min M-14090
62997-A	All Alone In This World -1	De 5525, MeC 45253
62997-B	All Alone In This World -1	De unissued: BF BCD16216 (CD)

Jimmie Davis, v/wh-1; acc. Charles Mitchell, esg-2; Buster Jones, esg-3; unknown, p; unknown, tbj; unknown, g; unknown, sb; unknown, woodblocks-4; band v-5.
   Dallas, TX   Friday, December 10, 1937

62998-A	I Think I'll Turn Your Damper Down	De rejected
62999-A	Goodbye Old Booze -2, 3, 5	De 5505, MeC 45248, Min M-14080, Pan 25980
63000-A	My Mama Told Me	De unissued
63001-B	You're As Welcome As The Flowers In May -2	De 5867, MeC 45377, Min M-14126
63002-A	I Saw Your Face In The Moon -1, 2, 4	De 5473, DeAu X1575
63005-A	I Love Everything That You Do -3	De 5539, MeC 45263
63006-A	Hard Hearted Mama -3	De 5505, MeC 45248

Matrix 62999 is titled *Goodbye, Old Booze* on Panachord 25980. Matrices 63003/04 are by Exie Louise Brown and Texas Tommy respectively (see B&GR). Rev. Minerva M-14126 by Texas Wanderers.

Jimmie Davis, v; acc. Charles Mitchell, esg; unknown, g; unknown, sb.
   Dallas, TX   Thursday, December 16, 1937

63102-A	There's A Gold Mine In The Sky	De 5473, DeAu X1575, Pan 25967

Acc. Charles Mitchell's Texans (or Charles Mitchell & His Texans): Bill Harper, f/vc-1; Charles Mitchell, esg; Tex Swaim, g; Ova Mitchell, u; Hershel Woodal, sb; band v-2.
   San Antonio, TX   Thursday, September 22, 1938

64562-A,-B,-C	Nobody's Lonesome For Me	De 5642, DeAu X1792, DeSA FM5117, MeC 45294, Min M-14100
64562-B	Nobody's Lonesome For Me	Min M-14100
64563-A	Meet Me Tonight In Dreamland -1	De 5616, DeAu X1792, DeSA FM5117, MeC 45274, Min M-14094, Pan 26019
64564-A	There's A Ranch In The Rockies	De 5605, DeAu X1739, MeC 45279, Min M-14091, Pan 26010
64569-A	Headin' Home -2	De 5616, MeC 45274, Min M-14095, Pan 26019
64570-A	Farewell To The Range	De 5605, DeAu X1739, MeC 45279, Min M-14092, Pan 26010
64571-A	I'm Drifting Back To Dreamland	De 5642, 46211
64572-A	Memories -1	De 5675, DeSA FM5144, MeC 45311, Min M-14115

Matrices 64569 to 64572 may have been recorded on September 21.
Revs: Minerva M-14091, M-14092 by Odus & Woodrow; M-14094, M-14095 by Buddy Jones; M-14115 by Cliff Carlisle.
   San Antonio, TX   Friday, September 23, 1938

64565-A	I'm Waiting For Ships That Never Come In	De 5867, MeC 45377

Acc. Rudy Sooter's Ranchmen: Frank Liddel, f; Jack Hogg, esg; Rudy Sooter, g; Lloyd Perryman, sb.
   Los Angeles, CA   Sunday, November 6, 1938

DLA-1551-A	It Makes No Difference Now	De 5620, DeAu X1703, DeIr W4502, DeSA FM5118, MeC 45286, Pana 26041
DLA-1552-A	The Curse Of An Aching Heart	De 5620, DeAu X1703, DeIr W4502, DeSA FM5118, MeC 45286, Pan 26041
DLA-1553-A	You Tell Me Your Dream I'll Tell You Mine	De 5627, DeAu X1729, DeIr W4416, Pan 26023
DLA-1554-A	Don't Break Her Heart Boy	De 5627, DeAu X1729, DeIr W4416, Pan 26023

Acc. Charles Mitchell's Texans (or Charles Mitchell & His Texans): prob. Lonnie Hall, f; Charles Mitchell, esg; Tex Swaim, g; Ova Mitchell, u; Hershel Woodal, sb.
   Houston, TX   Sunday, March 5, 1939

65140-A	I've Tried So Hard To Forget You	De 5687, MeC 45305, Min M-14108
65141-A	What Good Will It Do	De 5666, DeIr W4473, DeSA FM5143, Min M-14090, M-14099, Pan 26039
65142-A,-B	The Same Old Moon Is Shining	De 5666, DeIr W4473, Min M-14100, Pan 26039
65143-A	I'm Wondering Now	De 5675, DeSA FM5144, MeC 45311, Min M-14116
65144-A	Dream Of Love	De 5715, MeC 45328, Min M-14119
65145-A	If Tomorrow Never Comes	De 5687, MeC 45305, Min M-14108
65152-A	When You Know You're Not Forgotten By The Girl You Can't Forget	De unissued: *MCA MCAD-10087, BF BCD16216* (CDs)
65153-A	Some Must Win – Some Lose	De 5698, DeAu X2067
65154-A	Down At The End Of Memory Lane	De 5698, DeAu X2067
65155-A	In My Heart You'll Always Be Mine	De 5715, DeAu X2168, DeSA FM5143, MeC 45328, Min M-14119, M-14144

Intervening matrices are by Shelton Brothers. Revs: Minerva M-14099, M-14144 by Bill Carlisle; M-14116 by Cliff Carlisle.

Acc. Charles Mitchell's Texans (or Charles Mitchell & His Texans): prob. Lonnie Hall, f; poss. Bob Dunn, tb-1; Charles Mitchell, esg; Tex Swaim, g; Hershel Woodal, sb.
Houston, TX   Saturday, September 2, 1939

66367-A	The Last Letter	De 5726, MeC 45334, Min M-14104
66368-A	Born To Be Blue -1	De 5726, MeC 45334, Min M-14105
66368-B	Born To Be Blue -1	De unissued: *BF BCD16216* (CD)
66369-A	Never Break A Promise -1	De 5750
66370-A	What Else Can I Do -1	De 5794
66371-A	Why Should I Care	De 5799
66372-A	It's Hard But It's True -1	De 5847, DeAu X1933
66373-A	Last Trip Of The Old Ship -1	De 5737, MeC 45337, Min M-14104
66374-A	Why Do you Treat Me Like Dirt Under Your Feet	De 5766
66375-A	Walls of White	De 5766
66376-A	I'm Still A Fool Over You	De 5794
66377-A	My Blue Heaven -1	De 5779
66377-B	My Blue Heaven	De unissued: *BF BCD16216* (CD)

Acc. unknown, cl; unknown, p; unknown, g; unknown, sb.
New York, NY   Tuesday, September 19, 1939

| 66615-A | Two More Years (And I'll Be Free) | De 5750 |

Acc. Charles Mitchell, esg; unknown, p; unknown, g; unknown, sb.
New York, NY   Friday, September 22, 1939

| 66644-A | Leanin' On The Old Top Rail | De 5737, MeC 45337, Min M-14105 |

Acc. Charles Mitchell's Orchestra: unknown, t; unknown, cl; Charles Mitchell, esg; unknown, p; Leon Chappelear, g; unknown, sb.
New York, NY   Monday, February 5, 1940

67157-A	You Are My Sunshine	De 5813, MeC 45388
67158-A	Your Promise Was Broken	De 5803
67159-A	I'd Love To Call You Sweetheart	De 5803
67160-A	Old Timer	De 5813, MeC 45388
67160-B	Old Timer	De unissued: *BF BCD16216* (CD)
67161-A	Baby Your Mother (Like She Babied You)	De 5820, MeC 45346
67162-A	Roll Along, Kentucky Moon	De 5820, MeC 45346

Acc. Charles Mitchell's Texans: unknown, f-1; Charles Mitchell, esg-2; Buster Jones, esg-3; Tex Swaim, g; Hershel Woodal, sb.
Houston, TX   Wednesday, April 10, 1940

92071-A	There's A Chill On The Hill Tonight -1, 2	De 5830
92071-B	There's A Chill On The Hill Tonight -1, 2	De unissued: *BF BCD16216* (CD)
92072-A	Write A Letter To Your Mother -1, 2	De 5838, MeC 45369
92073-A	My Mother's Bible -1, 2	De 5830, DeSA FM5125
92074-A	Why Should I Be To Blame -3	De 5847, DeAu X2168
92074-B	Why Should I Be To Blame -3	De unissued: *BF BCD16216* (CD)
92075-A	I Feel The Same As You -1, 3	De 5858, DeAu X1933, MeC 45369

Rev. Decca FM5125 by Rice Brothers Gang.

Acc. Charles Mitchell's Orchestra: poss. Bill Graham, t; unknown, esg; unknown, p; unknown, g; unknown, sb.
New York, NY   Monday, September 16, 1940

| 68097-A | You're My Darling | De 5889, DeAu X2082, DeSA FM5142, MeC 45397 |

68098-A	On The Sunny Side Of The Rockies	De 5902, DeAu X1977, DeSA FM5129, MeC 45448
68099-A	The Love I Have For You	De 5889, DeAu X2082, DeSA FM5142, MeC 45397
68100-A	Sweethearts Or Strangers	De 5902, 46003, DeAu X1977, DeSA FM5161, MeC 45448
68101-A	Some Other Man	De 5926

Rev. Decca FM5161 by Cliff Bruner.

Acc. poss. Bill Graham, t; unknown, esg; unknown, p; unknown, g; unknown, sb.
New York, NY   Thursday, February 20, 1941

68724-A	I'm Sorry Now	De 5926
68725-A	The Prisoner's Song	De 5966, DeSA FM5136, MeC 45455
68726-A	My Mary	De 5955
68727-A	There's An Old Fashioned House On A Hillside	De 5940, MeC 45433
68728-A	Too Late	De 5940, MeC 45433

Acc. Jim Hewlett, t; Charles Mitchell, esg; Aubrey "Moon" Mullican, p; Cliff Bruner, etg; Tex Swaim, g; poss. Hershel Woodal, sb.
Dallas, TX   Friday, May 2, 1941

93750-A	I'm Knocking At Your Door Again	De 5989, MeC 45469
93750-B	I'm Knocking At Your Door Again	De unissued: BF BCD16216 (CD)
93751-A	What More Can I Say	De unissued: BF BCD16216 (CD)
93751-B	What More Can I Say	De 6025
93752-A	I Told You So	De 5966, DeSA FM5136, MeC 45455
93753-A	I Hung My Head And Cried	De 5978, DeSA FM5491
93753-B	I Hung My Head And Cried	De unissued: BF BCD16216 (CD)
93754-A	I'll Be True To The One I Love	De 5955
93754-B	I'll Be True To The One I Love	De unissued: BF BCD16216 (CD)
93755-A	Just Because (Of You Little Girl)	De 5978
93755-B	Just Because (Of You Little Girl)	De unissued: BF BCD16216 (CD)

Acc. Bill Graham, t; Vaughn Horton, esg; Frank Signorelli, p; Tony Gottuso, g; Haig Stephens, sb.
New York, NY   Wednesday, September 17, 1941

69752-A	You're Breaking My Heart ('Cause You Don't Care)	De 6044
69753-A	I Loved You Once	De 5999, MeC 45476
69754-A	Pay Me No Mind	De 5989, MeC 45469
69755-A	Won't You Forgive Me?	De 5999, MeC 45476

New York, NY   Tuesday, December 2, 1941

69984-A	I'm Thinking Tonight Of My Blue Eyes	De 6006, MeC 45484
69985-A	You Told Me A Lie	De 6062
69986-A	The End Of The World	De 6044
69987-A	You'll Be Sorry	De 6025

New York, NY   Thursday, December 4, 1941

69997-A	Sweetheart Of The Valley	De 6006, MeC 45484
69998-A	I'm The One	De unissued: BF BCD16216 (CD)
69999-A	Tears On My Pillow	De 6009, MeC 45487
70000-A	I Wish I Had A Sweetheart (Like That Old Sweetheart Of Mine)	De 6009, 46211, MeC 45487
70001-A,-AA	Just A Rollin' Stone	De unissued
70002-A	I Dreamed Of An Old Love Affair	De 6070

Acc. Don Linder, t; Dick Roberts, esg; Al Mack, p; Johnny Bond, g; Jimmy Wakely, sb.
Los Angeles, CA   Friday, May 15, 1942

DLA-2985-A	I've Got My Heart On My Sleeve	De 6053
DLA-2986-A	Don't You Cry Over Me	De 6062
DLA-2987-A	Live And Let Live	De 6053
DLA-2987-B	Live And Let Live	De unissued: BF BCD16216 (CD)
DLA-2988-AA	All Because You Said Goodbye	De 46039

Acc. unknown, t; Charles Mitchell, esg; Moon Mullican, p; unknown, g; unknown, sb.
New York, NY   Monday, July 27, 1942

71215-A	What's The Matter With You, Darling	De 46038, DeSA FM5198
71216-A	A Sinner's Prayer	De 6070
71217-A	Where Is My Boy Tonight	De 6065
71218-A	Columbus Stockade Blues	De 6083, 46137, MeC 45555
71219-A	Plant Some Flowers By My Grave	De 6065, 46085, DeSA FM5417, FM5491

71220-A	Walkin' My Blues Away	De 6083, MeC 45555
71225-A	What Happened	De 46038
71226-A,-AA	I'll Never Say Goodbye (Just So Long)	De unissued

Matrices 71221 to 71224 are by Sonny Boy Williams (see *B&GR*).
Revs: Decca FM5198 apparently postwar, FM5417 by Milton Brown.
Jimmie Davis recorded after 1942.

KARL DAVIS

See Karl & Harty.

STAN DAVIS

Stan Davis, v; acc. prob. own g.
New York, NY   Tuesday, November 12, 1929

403257-A	The Body In The Bag	OK 45401, PaE R567
403258-B	The Boy Who Stuttered And The Girl Who Lisped	OK 45401, PaE R567

WALTER DAVIS

See Blue Ridge Mountain Entertainers.

DAVIS & NELSON

See Claude (C.W.) Davis.

DAVIS–RICE–THOMAS

See Claude (C.W.) Davis.

DAVIS, STOKES & LAYNE

See Claude (C.W.) Davis.

DAVIS TRIO

See Claude (C.W.) Davis.

DAVE DAWSON'S STRING BAND

Pseudonym on Superior for Green's String Band.

JACK DAWSON

Jack Dawson, v/sp; acc. prob. own g.
New York, NY   Thursday, July 7, 1938

64273-A	I'm Waiting For Ships That Never Come In	De 5584
64274-A	Too Many Parties And Too Many Pals	De 5584

J.W. DAY

J.W. Day, f/v-1/sp-2; acc. Carson Robison, g.
New York, NY   Monday, February 27, 1928

42483-1	Forked Deer	Vi 21407
42484-1	Marthis Campbell	Vi 21353
42485-1	The Wild Wagoner	Vi 21353
42486-1	Billy In The Lowland	Vi 21407
42487-1	The Wild Horse On Stoney Point	Vi V-40025
42488-1	Black-Eyed Susie	Vi V-40127, Au 225
42489-1	Grand Horn Pipe	Vi V-40127, Au 225
42490-1	Little Boy Working On The Road	Vi V-40025
42491-1	Way Up On Clinch Mountain (Drunken Hiccough Song) -1	Vi 21635
42492-1	The Arkansaw Traveler -2	Vi 21635

All issues except Aurora 225 and some copies of Victor 21353 as by **Jilson Setters (J.W. Day)**. On copies of Victor 21353 with the fuller artist-credit, matrix 42484 is titled *Marthie Campbell*.
James William Day also recorded (as Jilson Setters) for the Library of Congress in 1937.

ROY DEAL

Pseudonym on Conqueror for John McGhee or (matrix 16032 on Conqueror 7273) Frank Welling.

THE DEAL FAMILY

Vocal quartet; acc. unknown, o.
Atlanta, GA   Thursday, March 31, 1927

143832-2	Everybody Will Be Happy Over There	Co 15147-D

143833-2	Working And Singing	Co 15176-D
143834-2	A Wonderful Time	Co 15191-D
143835-2	Be A Daniel	Co 15176-D
143836-1	The Sinless Summerland	Co 15191-D
143837-1	I'm A Rolling	Co 15147-D

Atlanta, GA   Saturday, November 5, 1927

145124-1	Beautiful Home Somewhere	Co 15214-D
145125-2	'Twill Be All Glory Over There	Co 15248-D
145126-2	Oh! Come	Co 15359-D
145127-2	I'm On My Way To Glory	Co 15359-D
145128-2	He's Coming Again	Co 15214-D
145129-2	Joy Among The Angels	Co 15248-D

Atlanta, GA   Saturday, April 14, 1928

146070-2	Jesus Paid It All	Co 15285-D
146071-2	God Shall Wipe Our Tears Away	Co 15285-D
146072-	Shouting In The Air	Co unissued
146073-	His Way Is Best	Co unissued
146074-	The Old Account Was Settled Long Ago	Co unissued
146075-	Just A Little While	Co unissued

Acc. unknown, o-1; unknown, g-2.
Atlanta, GA   Friday, April 19, 1929

148365-2	You Must Unload -2	Co 15412-D
148366-1	Give Me Your Hand -2	Co 15412-D
148367-2	The Glory Train -2	Co 15451-D
148368-1	The Home Coming Week -1	Co 15670-D
148369-2	Where Shall I Be -1	Co 15670-D
148370-2	Rocking On The Waves -1	Co 15451-D

EDDIE DEAN
JIMMIE & EDDIE DEAN

Eddie Dean, v; prob. acc. own g.
Chicago, IL   Monday, July 9, 1928

C-2042-	Bare Foot Days	Vo unissued trial recording

Jimmie & Eddie Dean, v duet; acc. one of them, g.
Chicago, IL   Monday, September 10, 1934

C-9446-	Tell Mother I'll Be There	De 5023
C-9447-	(There's) No Disappointment In Heaven	De 5023
C-9448-	There Shall Be Showers Of Blessing	De 5024, DeE F5340, RexIr U248
C-9449-	Happy In Him	De 5024
C-9450-A	There's No Friend Like Jesus	DeE F5340, RexIr U248
C-9455-A,-B	God Will Take Care Of You	De unissued

Intervening matrices are by Jesse Crawford (popular).
Chicago, IL   Friday, November 2, 1934

C-776-1	My Last Moving Day	Ba 33295, Me M13262, Or 8412, Pe 13095, Ro 5412, Cq 8438
C-777-1	The Soldier's Story	?Me M13339?, ?Or 8442, Pe 13095, ?Ro 5442, Cq 8438

Chicago, IL   Tuesday, November 13, 1934

C-834-1	When I Move To That New Range	Ba 33295, Me M13262, Or 8412, Pe 13095, Ro 5412, Cq 8439
C-835-1	The Old Mill Wheel	ARC unissued
C-836-1	Since My Mother's Dead And Gone	ARC unissued

Chicago, IL   Thursday, November 15, 1934

C-836-2	Since My Mother's Dead And Gone	ARC 7-02-57, Cq 8439
C-853-1	End Of A Bandit's Trail	ARC unissued

Chicago, IL   Monday, January 7, 1935

C-777-2,-3	The Soldier's Story	ARC unissued
C-853-2,-3	End Of A Bandit's Trail	ARC unissued

Chicago, IL   Thursday, January 24, 1935

C-777-4	The Soldier's Story	Ba 33372, ?Me M13339, ?Or 8442, ?Ro 5442
C-853-4	End Of A Bandit's Trail	Ba 33372, Me M13339, Or 8442, Pe 13120, Ro 5442, Cq 8471

Rev. Conqueror 8471 by Fleming & Townsend.

   Chicago, IL   Tuesday, October 29, 1935

C-1123-2	My Herdin' Song	Cq 8598
C-1124-1	Get Along Little Dogies	Cq 8598
C-1125-1,-2	Barefoot Days	ARC unissued

   Chicago, IL   Wednesday, October 30, 1935

C-1139-2	That Little Boy Of Mine	ARC 6-12-55, Cq 8597, 8753
C-1140-1,-2	Who's That Calling?	ARC unissued
C-1141-2	The Oregon Trail	ARC 6-02-53, Cq 8596
C-1142-1	We're Saying Goodbye	ARC 6-05-54
C-1143-1	Seven More Days	ARC 6-05-54

Rev. Conqueror 8753 by Steelman Sisters.

   Chicago, IL   Friday, November 1, 1935

C-1147-1	Red Sails In The Sunset	ARC 6-02-53, Cq 8599, Min M-14027
C-1148-2	There's An Old Family Album In The Parlor	ARC 7-02-57, Cq 8599
C-1149-1	Roll Along Prairie Moon	Cq 8596
C-1150-2	Golden Barefoot Days	ARC 6-12-55, Cq 8597

Minerva M-14027 as by **The Texas Rangers**. Rev. Minerva M-14027 by Dwight Butcher.

Eddie Dean, v; acc. Jack Statham, ac; Gus Snow, g; C. Martin Kob, sb.

   Los Angeles, CA   Thursday, September 4, 1941

DLA-2718-A	Little Grey Home In The West	De 6026
DLA-2719-A	On The Banks Of The Sunny San Juan	De 5988, MeC 45468
DLA-2720-A	When It's Harvest Time In Peaceful Valley	De 5988, MeC 45468
DLA-2721-A	Where The Silv'ry Colorado Wends Its Way	De 6026

Acc. Paul Sells, pac; Frank Marvin, esg; own g; Herb Kratoska, g; Budd Hatch, sb.

   Los Angeles, CA   Wednesday, February 25, 1942

DLA-2914-A	Back In The Saddle Again	De 6034
DLA-2915-A	Sleepy-Time In Caroline	De 6034, 46135
DLA-2916-A	How Can You Say You Love Me?	De 6086, 46135, MeC 45558
DLA-2917-A	I'm Comin' Home Darlin'	De 6086, MeC 45558
DLA-2918-	The Land Where The Roses Never Fade	DeSA FM5518
DLA-2919-	Don't Forget That Jesus Loves You	DeSA FM5518

Eddie Dean recorded after 1942.

HENRY DECKER

Pseudonym on Challenge for Ruben Burns (see Short Creek Trio).

LOYAL DECKER

See The Deckers.

UNCLE NICK DECKER

No details.

   Johnson City, TN   Tuesday, October 16, 1928

| 147194- | Parody On Home Sweet Home | Co unissued |
| 147195- | She Never Came Back | Co unissued |

WAYNE DECKER

See The Deckers.

THE DECKERS

Wayne Decker, Loyal Decker, v duet; acc. unknown, sg; unknown, g; unknown, sb.

   Grafton, WI   c. December 1931

| L-1295-1 | When It's Night Time In Nevada | Pm 3281, Bwy 8312 |
| L-1296-1 | When The Moon Comes Over The Mountain | Pm 3281, Bwy 8312 |

Wayne Decker, v; acc. unknown, sg; unknown, g; unknown, sb.

   Grafton, WI   c. December 1931

| L-1297-2 | When I Take My Vacation In Heaven | Bwy 8321 |

Loyal Decker, v; acc. unknown, sg; unknown, g; unknown, sp; two unknowns, humming.

   Grafton, WI   c. December 1931

| L-1298-2 | Down The Trail To Home Sweet Home | Bwy 8321 |

The Deckers: Wayne Decker, Loyal Decker, v duet; acc. unknown, sg; unknown, md; unknown, g; unknown, sb.

   Grafton, WI   c. December 1931

L-1299-	The Gangster's Warning	Pm 3276
L-1300-	Thirteen More Steps	Pm 3276
L-1302-2	That Little Boy Of Mine	Pm 3323

Matrix L-1301 is untraced but probably by these artists.

Unknown (female), v; acc. unknown, sg; unknown, g; unknown, sb.
Grafton, WI   c. December 1931
| L-1303-2 | Little Mother Of Mine | Pm 3323 |

ALBERT E. DELL

No details.
New York, NY   Monday, May 14, 1934
| TO-1411 | Wagon Wheels | ARC unissued trial recording |

GEORGIA DELL

See the McClendon Brothers.

VERNON DELL

Pseudonym on Tremont for Vernon Dalhart.

ROSCOE & SAMUEL DELLINGER
DELLINGER FAMILY

Roscoe & Samuel Dellinger: unidentified v; acc. unknown, md; two unknowns, g.
Charlotte, NC   Tuesday, February 16, 1937
07077-1	Telling The Stars About You	BB B-6868, MW M-7247
07078-1	Swinging In The Lane	BB B-6868, MW M-7247
07079-1	Ship That Never Returned	MW M-7248
07080-1	Snowflakes	BB B-6852, MW M-7248

Dellinger Family: unidentified, v duet; acc. unknown, md; unknown, g.
Charlotte, NC   Saturday, February 20, 1937
| 07218-1 | The Ohio River Flood | BB B-6852 |

DELMORE BROTHERS

Alton Delmore, Rabon Delmore, v duet; acc. Alton Delmore, g; Rabon Delmore, tg.
Atlanta, GA   Wednesday, October 28, 1931
| 151976-1 | Got The Kansas City Blues | Co 15724-D |
| 151977-1 | Alabama Lullaby | Co 15724-D |

Chicago, IL   Wednesday, December 6, 1933
77218-1	I Ain't Got Nowhere To Travel	BB B-5467, HMVIn N4334
77219-1	Ramblin' Minded Blues	BB B-5467, HMVIn N4334
77220-1	Smoky Mountain Bill And His Song	BB B-5589
77221-1	Gonna Lay Down My Old Guitar	BB B-5299, Eld 2170, Sr S-3380, MW M-4420
77222-1	Lonesome Yodel Blues	BB B-5299, Eld 2170, Sr S-3380, MW M-4420
77223-1	I Ain't Gonna Stay Here Long	BB B-5653, Twin FT1829
77224-1	Brown's Ferry Blues	BB B-5403, MW M-4750, HMVIn N4324
77225-1	I'm Mississippi Bound	BB B-5653
77226-1	I'm Goin' Back To Alabama	BB B-5358, Sr S-3439, MW M-4459
77227-1	I'm Leavin' You	BB B-5358, Sr S-3439, MW M-4459
77228-1	I've Got The Big River Blues	BB B-5531, HMVIn N4349
77229-1	The Girls Don't Worry My Mind	BB B-5589, Twin FT1810

Revs: Bluebird B-5403, Montgomery Ward M-4750, HMV N4324 by Allen Brothers; Twin FT1810, FT1829 by Riley Puckett.

Chicago, IL   Thursday, December 7, 1933
77252-1	Bury Me Out On The Prairie	BB B-5338, Sr S-3419, MW M-4060, M-4458
77253-1	The Frozen Girl	BB B-5338, Sr S-3419, MW M-4458
77254-1	Lonesome Jailhouse Blues	BB B-5741, Twin FT1862
77255-1	Blue Railroad Train	BB B-5531, HMVIn N4349
77256-1	By The Banks Of The Rio Grande	BB B-5741, Twin FT1862

Matrix 77252 is titled *Oh Bury Me Out On The Prairie* on Montgomery Ward M-4060.
Rev. Montgomery Ward M-4060 by Bud Billings (Frank Luther) & Carson Robison.

New Orleans, LA   Tuesday, January 22, 1935
87660-1	Don't Let Me Be In The Way	BB B-6120, Twin FT8024
87661-1	When It's Summertime In A Southern Clime	BB B-5957
87662-1	Hey Hey, I'm Memphis Bound	BB B-5857, MW M-4553
87663-1	I Guess I've Got To Be Goin'	BB B-6002

87664-1	Blow Yo' Whistle, Freight Train	BB B-5925
87665-1	Down South	BB B-6034, MW M-4751, Twin FT1979
87666-1	Brown's Ferry Blues – Part 2	BB B-5893, MW M-4553, Twin FT1906
87667-1	I Got The Kansas City Blues	BB B-6002
87668-1	I Know I'll Be Happy In Heaven	BB B-6120, Twin FT8024
87669-1	Keep The Camp Fires Burning	BB B-6019, MW M-4752, RZAu G22791
87670-1	Alabama Lullaby	BB B-6034, MW M-4751, Twin FT1979
87671-1	The Fugitive's Lament	BB B-6019, MW M-4752, RZAu G22791, Twin FT1961
87672-1	I Believe It For My Mother Told Me So	BB B-5857, MW M-4552
87673-1	I'm Going Away	BB B-5853, Twin FT1906
87674-1	I Long To See My Mother	BB B-5957, MW M-4552
87675-1	Lorena, The Slave	BB B-5925, Twin FT1941

Revs: Twin FT1941 by Eddie Bell (Frank Luther), FT1961 by 'Lasses & Honey.

Acc. Arthur Smith, f-1; Alton Delmore, g; Rabon Delmore, tg.
Charlotte, NC   Monday, February 17, 1936

99171-1	The Nashville Blues	BB B-6312, MW M-4753, Twin FT8111
99172-1	The Lover's Warning	BB B-6522
99173-1	I'm Worried Now	BB B-6349, MW M-4754
99174-1	Take Away This Lonesome Day	BB B-6998
99175-1	Promise Me You'll Always Be Faithful	BB B-8637, RZAu G24925
99176-1	Don't You See That Train?	BB B-6522
99177-1	It's Takin' Me Down	BB B-6312, MW M-4753, Twin FT8111
99178-1	That Yodelin' Gal – Miss Julie	BB B-8687
99179-1	I'm Gonna Change My Way	BB B-6349, MW M-4754
99180-1	Gamblin' Yodel	BB unissued
99181-1	Happy Hickey – The Hobo	BB B-6386, Twin FT8143
99182-1	Lonesome Yodel Blues No. 2	BB B-6386
99183-1	Put Me On The Trail To Carolina -1	BB B-6401, Twin FT8165
99184-1	Carry Me Back To Alabama -1	BB B-6401, Twin FT8165
99185-1	My Smokey Mountain Gal -1	BB B-7778, MW M-7849
99186-1	Take Me Back To The Range -1	BB B-8687

Rev. Twin FT8143 by Cliff Carlisle.

Charlotte, NC   Wednesday, February 17, 1937

07087-1	No Drunkard Can Enter There	BB B-6915, MW M-7150
07088-1	Southern Moon	BB B-6841, MW M-7151
07089-1	False Hearted Girl	BB B-6949, MW M-7153, Twin FT8400
07090-1	The Budded Rose -1	BB B-7262, MW M-7154
07091-1	Blind Child	BB B-6915, MW M-7153
07092-1	Are You Marching With The Savior?	BB B-7029, MW M-7154, RZAu G23273
07093-1	I Don't Know Why I Love Her	BB B-6841, MW M-7151
07094-1	Don't Forget Me Darling	BB B-7029, MW M-7152, RZAu G23273
07116-1	Memories Of My Carolina Girl	BB B-6949, MW M-7152
07117-1	No One	BB B-6998, MW M-7150

Intervening matrices are by other artists. Rev. Twin FT8400 by Three Tobacco Tags.
For Montgomery Ward M-7155 to M-7157, credited to the Delmore Brothers, see Arthur Smith.

Charlotte, NC   Tuesday, August 3, 1937

011885-1	Lead Me	BB B-7337, MW M-7318
011886-1	I Need The Prayers Of Those I Love	BB B-7672, MW M-7318
011887-1	I've Got The Railroad Blues	BB B-7300, MW M-7319
011888-1	The Weary Lonesome Blues	BB B-7300, MW M-7319
011889-1	Heavenly Light Is Shining On Me	BB B-7337, MW M-7317
011890-1	Wonderful There	BB B-7672, MW M-7317
011891-1	The Farmer's Girl	BB B-7383, MW M-7320
011892-1	Singing My Troubles Away	BB B-7129, MW M-7320
011893-1	They Say It Is Sinful To Flirt	BB B-7192, MW M-7321
011894-1	Till The Roses Bloom Again	BB B-7192, MW M-7321
011895-1	When We Held Our Hymn Books Together	BB B-7192, MW M-7322
011896-1	Hi De Ho Baby Mine -1	BB B-7129
011897-1	Look Up, Look Down The Lonesome Road -1	BB B-7383, MW M-7322

Acc. Alton Delmore, g; Rabon Delmore, tg.
Charlotte, NC   Tuesday, January 25, 1938

018713-1	Ain't It Hard To Love	BB B-7560, MW M-7853
018714-1	Bury Me Under The Weeping Willow	BB B-7741, MW M-7853
018715-1	Brother Take Warning	BB B-7741, MW M-7475

018716-1	Alcatraz Island Blues	BB B-7778, MW M-7849
018717-1	Goodbye Booze	BB B-7436
018718-1	There's A Lonesome Road	BB B-8052, MW M-7475

Charlotte, NC   Wednesday, January 26, 1938

018754-1	Cause I Don't Mean To Cry When You're Gone	BB B-7496, MW M-7474
018755-1	Careless Love (Bring My Baby Back)	BB B-7436, MW M-7473
018756-1	In That Vine Covered Chapel In The Valley	BB B-7496, MW M-7473, Twin FT8571
018757-1	Big Ball In Texas	BB B-7560, MW M-7474

Rev. Twin FT8571 by Wiley, Zeke & Homer.
For Montgomery Ward M-7477 to M-7479, credited to the Delmore Brothers, see Arthur Smith.
Acc. Chuck Maudlin, f; Alton Delmore, g; Smiley O'Brien, g/v-1; Rabon Delmore, tg; Joe Zinkan, sb.

Rock Hill, SC   Thursday, September 29, 1938

027642-1	Leavin' On That Train	BB B-7913, MW M-7677
027643-1	The Cannon Ball	BB B-7991, MW M-7677
027644-1	My Home's Across The Blue Ridge Mountains	BB B-8247, MW M-7678
027645-1	15 Miles From Birmingham	BB B-8031, MW M-7678
027646-1	I'm Alabama Bound	BB B-8264, MW M-7695
027647-1	Nothing But The Blues	BB B-8247, MW M-7695
027648-1	Some Of These Days You're Gonna Be Sad	BB B-7957, MW M-7696
027649-1	Where Is My Sailor Boy	BB B-7957, MW M-7679
027671-1	Heart Of Sorrow	BB B-8637, MW M-7696
027672-1	Quit Treatin' Me Mean	BB B-8031, MW M-7697
027673-1	Just The Same Sweet Thing To Me	BB B-8290, MW M-7698
027674-1	The Only Star	BB B-7991, MW M-7679
027675-1	A Better Range Is Home -1	BB B-8290, MW M-7698
027676-1	Git Along	BB B-7913, MW M-7697

Matrices 027650 to 027653 are by Smith's Crackerjacks; 027654 to 027670 are by Walter Hurdt.

Rock Hill, SC   Sunday, February 5, 1939

032669-1	Don't Let My Ramblin' Bother Your Mind	BB B-8177, MW M-7852
032670-1	Baby You're Throwing Me Down	BB B-8177, MW M-7852
032671-1	Gonna Lay Down My Old Guitar – Part 2	BB B-8215, RZAu G24087
032672-1	Brown's Ferry Blues – Part 3	BB B-8230
032673-1	I Loved You Better Than You Knew	BB B-8215, MW M-7851, RZAu G24087
032674-1	Goin' Back To Georgia	BB B-8264, MW M-7850
032675-1	Home On The River	BB B-8052, MW M-7851
032676-1	Gamblers Yodel	BB B-8230
032677-1	Wabash Blues	BB B-8204, MW M-7850
032678-1	Go Easy Mabel -1	BB B-8204, MW M-7850

Matrix 032671 is titled *Gonna Lay Down My Old Guitar* on Regal-Zonophone G24087.
Acc. Ted Brooks, esg-1; Alton Delmore, g; Rabon Delmore, tg.

Atlanta, GA   Tuesday, February 6, 1940

047551-1	The Wabash Cannon-Ball Blues -1	BB B-8404, MW M-8685
047552-1	Over The Hills -1	BB B-8451, MW M-8686, RZAu G24925
047553-1	The Dying Truckdriver -1	BB B-8451, MW M-8686
047554-1	Scatterbrain Mama -1	BB B-8404, MW M-8685
047555-1	Happy On The Mississippi Shore	BB B-8613, MW M-8687
047556-1	That's How I Feel, So Goodbye	BB B-8557, MW M-8688
047557-1	Rainin' On The Mountain	BB B-8557, MW M-8688
047558-1	See That Coon In A Hickory Tree	BB B-8418, MW M-8687
047559-1	The Storms Are On The Ocean	BB B-8613, MW M-8689
047560-1	Back To Birmingham	BB B-8418, MW M-8689
047561-1	The Eastern Gate	BB B-8488, MW M-8690
047562-1	God Put A Rainbow In The Clouds	BB B-8488, MW M-8690

Acc. Alton Delmore, g; Rabon Delmore, tg.

New York, NY   Wednesday, September 11, 1940

68069-A	There's Trouble On My Mind Today	De 5878
68070-A	Silver Dollar	De 5878
68071-A	Old Mountain Dew	De 5890, MeC 45398
68072-A	In The Blue Hills Of Virginia	De 5890, MeC 45398
68073-A	Make Room In The Lifeboat For Me	De 5897
68074-A	When It's Time For The Whip-Poor-Will To Sing	De 5925, DeAu X2209, MeC 45423
68075-A	Will You Be Lonesome Too?	De 5925, DeAu X2209, MeC 45423
68076-A	Broken Hearted Lover	De 5907
68077-A	She Won't Be My Little Darling	De 5907
68078-A	Gathering Flowers From The Hillside	De 5897

Acc. unknown, bj-1; Alton Delmore, g; Rabon Delmore, tg; poss. Herman "Zeke" Phillips, sb.
New York, NY   Wednesday, July 16, 1941

69508-A	I Now Have A Bugle To Play	De 6000, MeC 45477
69509-A	Last Night I Was Your Only Darling -1	De 6000, MeC 45477
69510-A	Baby Girl	De 6051
69511-A	New False Hearted Girl	De 6080, MeC 45552
69512-A	I Wonder Where My Darling Is Tonight	De 6051
69513-A	Precious Jewel	De 5970, 46049
69514-A	Gospel Cannon Ball	De 5970, 46049
69515-A	I'll Never Fall In Love Again -1	De 6080, MeC 45552
69516-A	Honey I'm Ramblin [sic] Away	De 46043
69517-A	I'm Leavin' You	De 46043
69518-A	You Ain't Got Nothin' I Can't Do Without	De unissued

The Delmore Brothers recorded after 1942.

THE DELTA TWINS

No details.
Jackson, MS   Friday, October 18, 1935

JAX-189-	The Lonesome Road	ARC unissued

Jackson, MS   Saturday, October 19, 1935

JAX-190-	When The Sun Goes Down	ARC unissued

DEMPSEY QUARTETTE

Vocal quartet; acc. unknown.
Atlanta, GA   Thursday, April 12, 1928

146034-	With Joy We Sing	Co unissued
146035-	Face To Face	Co unissued

MORGAN DENMON

Morgan Dennan, v; acc. prob. own g.
Atlanta, GA   Thursday, October 28, 1926

9827-A	Down Among The Hills Of Tennessee	OK 45075
9828-A	Naomi Wise	OK 45075

Morgan Dennon-1/**Morgan Denmon**-2, v; acc. prob. own g.
Atlanta, GA   Monday, March 14, 1927

80517-A	My Little Rambling Rose -2	OK 45306
80518-B	The Girl I Loved In Sunny Tennessee -1	OK 45105
80519-B	The Two Drummers -2	OK 45306
80520-B	I've Still Got Ninety Nine -1	OK 45105
80521-A,-B	[Just Forget]	OK unissued

Matrix 80522 is probably an unidentified item by this artist.

Morgan Denmon, v; acc. prob. own g.
Atlanta, GA   Wednesday, March 13, 1929

402291-	Lullaby Yodel	OK unissued
402292-A	Drunkard's Dream	OK 45327, PaAu A3528
402293-A	The Wild And Reckless Hobo	OK 45327, Ve 2366-V, Cl 5300-C
402294-	Lonesome Valley	OK unissued

Velvet Tone 2366-V, Clarion 5300-C as by **Emmett McWilliams**. Parlophone A3528 as by **Robert Harris**. Matrix 402292 is titled *The Drunkard's Dream* on Parlophone A3528. Rev. Velvet Tone 2366-V, Clarion 5300-C by Frank Hutchison; Parlophone A3528 by Vernon Dalhart.

MORGAN DENNAN
MORGAN DENNON

See Morgan Denmon (which has been assumed to be the correct spelling of this artist's name).

DENSON–PARRIS SACRED HARP SINGERS

Delilah Denson, S. Whitt Denson, Owel W. Denson, Oren A. Parris, v quartet; acc. unknown, p; or unacc.-1.
Atlanta, GA   Friday, August 3, 1934

82896-1	Fillmore	BB B-5597
82897-1	New Britain	BB B-5597
82898-1	Ragan	BB B-5976
82899-1	Raymond	BB B-5976
83800-1	The Heavenly Port	BB B-5598

83801-1	Conversion	BB B-5598
83802-1	Blooming Youth -1	BB B-5599
83803-1	The Good Old Way -1	BB B-5599
83804-1	Calvary -1	BB B-5670
83805-1	Vain World, Adieu -1	BB B-5670
83806-1	Mount Zion	BB B-5977
83807-1	The Christian's Hope	BB B-5977
83808-1	Sing To Me Of Heaven	BB B-5978
83809-1	Concord	BB B-5978
83810-1	Resurrected -1	Bb B-5979
83811-1	Reverential Anthem -1	BB B-5979
83812-1	Passing Away -1	BB B-5980
83813-1	Exhortation -1	BB B-5980

Denson Trio: Delilah Denson, S. Whitt Denson, Owel W. Denson, v trio; or Delilah Denson, S. Whitt Denson, Owel W. Denson, R.E. (Bob) Denson, v quartet-1; acc. unknown, p.
Atlanta, GA   Friday, August 3, 1934

| 83814-1 | Jesus, Hold My Hand | BB unissued |
| 83815-1 | Soon We'll Pass Away -1 | BB unissued |

THE DENSON QUARTET

R.E. (Bob) Denson, tv; S. Whitt Denson, av; J.C. Brown, bsv; Mrs Nancy Brown, v; unacc.
Atlanta, GA   Monday, October 29, 1928

| 147331-2 | Christian Soldier | Co 15526-D |
| 147332-2 | I'm On My Journey Home | Co 15526-D |

DENSON TRIO

See Denson–Parris Sacred Harp Singers.

DENSON'S SACRED HARP SINGERS OF ARLEY, ALABAMA

Vocal group, prob. including S. Whitt Denson; acc. unknown, p-1.
Birmingham, AL   Tuesday, November 13, or Wednesday, November 14, 1928

BIRM-788-	Ninety Fifth -1	Br 287
BIRM-789-	The Christians Hope	Br 287
BIRM-790-	The Happy Sailor	Br 302
BIRM-791-	Protection	Br 302

LEE DENTON

Pseudonym on Champion for Jack Bankey.

THE DESMOND DUO

Pseudonym on Australian Embassy for Lester McFarland & Robert A. Gardner.

DICK DEVALL

Dick Devall, v; unacc.
Dallas, TX   Sunday, October 13, 1929

| 56372-2 | Tom Sherman's Barroom | TT C-1563, Au 36-115 |
| 56373-2 | Out On The Lone Star Cow Trail | TT C-1563, Au 36-115 |

BUDDY DEWITT (THE SINGING MOUNTAINEER)

Buddy DeWitt, v/y-1; acc. own g.
Richmond, IN   Monday, July 17, 1933

19251	A Broken Hearted Mother	Ch 16680
19252	Rose Of Mother's Day -1	Ch 16680
19253	My Kentucky Cabin	Ch 16658
19254	The Sad, Sad Story	Ch 16825, 45101, MeC 45101
19255	Our Last Good-Bye	Ch 16658
19256	Young Brothers	Ch 16637

Revs: Champion 16637 by Kenneth Houchins; Champion 16825, 45101, Melotone 45101 by Don Weston.

CHAS. M. DEWITTE (THE VAGABOND YODELER)

Unlike Gennett files, copyright registration books spell this artist's last name DeWitt.

Chas. M. DeWitte, v/y-1; acc. own g.
Richmond, IN   Monday, August 10, 1931

| 17913 | Little Maiden Of The Mountain | Ch 16759, Spr 2721 |

17914	The Girl I Met In Bluefield -1	Ch 16759, Spr 2721
17915,-A	The Dying Hobo's Prayer	Ge rejected
17916,-A	Far Away On The Sleepy Rio Grande	Ge rejected

Superiot 2721 as by **The Vagabond Yodeler**.

Richmond, IN — Sunday, November 29, 1931

18228	Just A Stranger	Ch 16444
18229	Vagabond Yodel -1	Ch S-16371, Spr 2793
18230	No More To Ride The Rails	Ch S-16371, Spr 2793

Superior 2793 as by **The Vagabond Yodeler**.

Chas. M. DeWitte, v/y; acc. own g.
Richmond, IN — Tuesday, December 1, 1931

| 18231 | Vagabond Yodel No. 2 | Ch 16444 |

Richmond, IN — Saturday, December 19, 1931

| 18252 | I Was A Pal To Daddy | Ge rejected |

AL DEXTER

Al Dexter, v; acc. Bobby Symons, esg/eg; Luke Owens, g; Jack True, sb.
San Antonio, TX — Saturday, November 28, 1936

SA-2640-1	New Jelly Roll Blues	ARC 7-03-65, Vo 03435
SA-2641-1	Honky Tonk Blues	ARC 7-03-65, Vo 03435
SA-2642-1	If We Can't Be Sweethearts Why Can't We Be Pals	ARC 7-07-61, Vo 03569
SA-2643-1	Little Sod Shanty	ARC 7-04-64, Vo 03461
SA-2644-1	Whisper Again That You Love Me	ARC 7-07-61, Vo 03569
SA-2645-2	Mother Mine	ARC 7-04-64, Vo 03461

Dallas, TX — Tuesday, June 15, 1937

DAL-330-2	Dusty Road	Vo 03988
DAL-331-1	Car Hoppin' Mama	ARC 7-09-62, Vo 03636
DAL-332	One More Day In Prison	ARC unissued
DAL-333-1,-2	Waiting Old Pal For You	ARC unissued

Acc. Bobby Symons, esg/eg; Luke Owens, g/v-1; Jack True, sb.
Dallas, TX — Thursday, June 17, 1937

DAL-344-1	Honky Tonk Baby	ARC 7-12-56, Vo 03719
DAL-345-1	Broken Hearted Blues	ARC 7-09-62, Vo 03636
DAL-346-2	Don't Cry For Me When I'm Gone	ARC 7-12-56, Vo 03719
DAL-347-2	The Calico Rag	ARC 7-10-61, Vo 03676
DAL-348-	Stealing Through The Shadows	ARC unissued
DAL-349-1	You've Got Love In Your Heart	ARC 8-02-64, Vo 03927
DAL-350-2	In A Little Green Valley	Vo 03988
DAL-351-2	Sweet Lips (Kiss My Blues Away)	ARC 7-10-61, Vo 03676
DAL-352-2	I'm Leaving My Troubles Behind	ARC 8-02-64, Vo 03927
DAL-353-	In The Days Of Yesterday -1	ARC unissued

Acc. Bobby Symons, esg/eg; Luke Owens, g; Jack True, sb.
Dallas, TX — Wednesday, May 11, 1938

DAL-493-1	She's The Sunshine Of Moonshine Valley	Vo 04327
DAL-494-1	Bring It On Home To Me	Vo 04327
DAL-495-1	The Day You Came Along	Vo unissued
DAL-496-1	Dreaming Of You	Vo unissued
DAL-497-1	My Baby Loves Me	Vo 04277
DAL-498-1	One More Day In Prison	Vo 04405
DAL-499-1	Blue Eyed Baby	Vo unissued
DAL-500-1,-2	She Can't Be Satisfied	Vo unissued
DAL-501-2	I'm Happy When You're Happy	Vo 04405
DAL-502-1	In Days Of Yesterday	Vo 04174

Dallas, TX — Thursday, May 12, 1938

| DAL-503-1 | Gypsy Swing | Vo 04277 |
| DAL-504-1 | Answer To "Honky Tonk Blues" | Vo 04174 |

Al Dexter & His Troopers: Al Dexter, v; acc. poss. Leaford Hall, f-1; Aubrey Gass, h-2/wb-3/v-4; poss. Jack Lee, esg; unknown, eg; Mabel Ogden, p; own md-5/g.
Dallas, TX — Tuesday, June 13, 1939

DAL-785-3	Daddy's In The Dog House Now -1, 3, 5	Vo 05121, Cq 9330
DAL-786-3	Diddy, Wah, Diddy With A Blah! Blah! -2	Vo/OK 05255
DAL-787-3	Jelly Roll Special -1, 3	Vo/OK 04988, Co 37641, 20240

DAL-788-1	My Troubles Don't Trouble Me No More-1, 2, 5	Vo 05042
DAL-789-1	My Blue Eyes Are Not My Blue Eyes Now -1, 3, 5	Vo 05042
DAL-790-3	Why Do I Think Of Someone -1, 3	Vo/OK 05255
DAL-791-3	Bar Hotel -1, 3	Vo 05121, Cq 9330
DAL-792-1	Sunshine -1, 3, 4, 5	Vo/OK 04988, Co 37641, 20240

Acc. Cecil Brower, f; Aubrey Gass, h-1/wb; unknown, esg; own md-2/g; unknown, g; poss. Joe Ferguson, sb.
Saginaw, TX   Tuesday, April 23, 1940

DAL-1044-2	There's No Use In Loving You -2	OK 05680
DAL-1045-2	When We Go A Honky Tonkin' -2	Vo/OK 05572, Cq 9731
DAL-1046-1	Let Me Join The C.C.C. -1	OK 05906
DAL-1047-2	Walking In My Sleep	OK 05680
DAL-1048-2	Wine, Women And Song	Vo/OK 05572, Cq 9731
DAL-1049-2	Poor Little Honky Tonk Girl	OK 05906

Acc. Cecil Brower, f; unknown, esg; own eg-1/g-2; unknown, g; poss. Joe Ferguson, sb.
Saginaw, TX   Wednesday, April 24, 1940

DAL-1050-1,-2	Things That Might Have Been -1	OK unissued
DAL-1051-1	Come Back To Me My Darling -1	OK 05783, Cq 9732
DAL-1052-1	You May Be Sorry -2	OK 05783, Cq 9732
DAL-1053-1,-2	Rainbow Trail -2	OK unissued

Cecil Brower, f; Ted Daffan, esg; Al Dexter, eg/md-1/v-2; J.B. Brinkley, g; Joe Ferguson, sb; Aubrey Gass, wb/traps.
Fort Worth, TX   Tuesday, March 4, 1941

DAL-1215-1	Down At The Roadside Inn -1, 2	OK 06127
DAL-1216-2	It's Too Late To Say You're Sorry Now -2	OK 06287
DAL-1217-1	Meet Me Down In Honky Tonk Town -2	OK 06483, Co 37434, 20161
DAL-1218-1	You Will Always Be My Darling -2	OK 06287
DAL-1219-1	The Money You Spent Was Mine -2	OK 06206
DAL-1220-1	Alimony Blues -2	OK 06206
DAL-1221-1	Darling, It's All Over Now -2	OK 06397, Co 37441, 20168
DAL-1222-1,-2	Sweet Talkin' Mama -2	OK unissued
DAL-1223-1	New Soldier's Farewell -2	OK 06127
DAL-1224-1,-2	Spanish Rose -1	OK unissued
DAL-1225-1	Honky Tonk Chinese Dime -2	OK 06604, Co 37417, 20144

Cecil Brower, f; Ted Daffan, esg; Al Dexter, eg/v-1; J.B. Brinkley, g; Joe Ferguson, sb; Aubrey Gass, wb/traps; band v-2.
Fort Worth, TX   Wednesday, March 5, 1941

DAL-1226-1	All I Want Is You -1	OK 06483, Co 37434, 20161
DAL-1227-1	Who's Been Here? -1, 2	OK 06397, Co 37441, 20168
DAL-1228-1	Sundown Polka	OK 06604, Co 37417, 20144

Al Dexter, v; acc. Wilmot "Holly" Hollinger, t; Paul Sells, pac; Frank Marvin, esg; own eg; Johnny Bond, g; Fred Whiting, sb.
Hollywood, CA   Wednesday, March 18, 1942

H-735-1	It's Up To You	Co 37062, 20073, CoC C830
H-736-1	So Long Pal	OK 6718, Co 37404, 20131, CoC C736, *V-D 400*
H-737-1	Too Late To Worry	OK 6718, Co 37404, 20131, CoC C736
H-738-1	Rosalita	OK 6708, Co 37668, 20267, CoC C713, *V-D 400*
H-739-1	Remember You're Mine	OK unissued
H-740-1	My Blue Eyes	OK unissued

Rev. all issues of matrix H-735 postwar.

Acc. Wilmot "Holly" Hollinger, t; Paul Sells, pac; Dick Roberts, esg; own eg; Dick Reinhart, g; Fred Whiting, sb.
Hollywood, CA   Friday, March 20, 1942

H-741-1	Pistol Packin' Mama	OK 6708, Co 37668, 20267, M737, CoC C713, *V-D 26*
H-742-1	Why Did It Have To Be	Co 37880, 20365
H-743-1	I'll Wait For You Dear	OK 6727, Co 37037, 20062
H-744-1	There'll Come A Time	Co 20593

Rev. all issues of matrices H-742, H-744 postwar.

Carl Cotner, f; Paul Sells, pac; Frank Marvin, esg; Al Dexter, eg/v-1; Dick Reinhart, g; Fred Whiting, sb.
Hollywood, CA   Saturday, March 21, 1942

H-745-1	Maybe, Baby It's Me -1	Co 37538, 20184
H-746-1	Guitar Polka	Co 36898, 20010, CoC C776
H-747-1	What Is Life Lived Alone	OK unissued
H-748-1	I'm Losing My Mind Over You -1	OK 6727, Co 37037, 20062

Rev. all issues of matrices H-745, H-746 postwar.

Al Dexter recorded after 1942.

LOIS DEXTER
See Patt Patterson.

THE DEZURIK SISTERS (CAROLINE & MARY JANE)

Caroline Dezurik, Mary Jane Dezurik, v/y duet; acc. own g duet.
Chicago, IL   Friday, December 16, 1938

C-2407-1	I Left Her Standin' There (With A Doo-Dad In Her Hair)	Vo/OK 04616, Cq 9253, RZ MR3368, RZAu G23802, RZIn MR20112, RZIr IZ1091
C-2408-1	Sweet Hawaiian Chimes	Vo/OK 04704, Cq 9252
C-2409-2	Guitar Blues	Vo/OK 04704, Cq 9252
C-2410-1	The Arizona Yodeler	Vo/OK 04616, Cq 9253, RZ MR3368, RZAu G23802, RZIn MR20112, RZIr IZ1091
C-2411-1	Birmingham Jail	Vo/OK 04781, Cq 9251
C-2412-2	Go To Sleep My Darling Baby	Vo/OK 04781, Cq 9251

The DeZurik Sisters recorded after 1942 as The Cackle Sisters.

DIAMOND D BOYS

No details.
Los Angeles, CA   Friday, March 15, 1935

| LA-368- | When Old Age Pension Check Comes To Our Door | ARC unissued |
| LA-369- | Chuck Wagon Blues | ARC unissued |

HARRY DICK
Pseudonym on Varsity for Dick Robertson.

TOM DICKEY SHOW BOYS

Tom Dickey, f-1; Emil "Bash" Hofner, esg-2/g-3; Bert Ferguson, p; Adolph Hofner, g/v-4; Bill Dickey, sb/v-5; band v-6.
San Antonio, TX   Thursday, October 27, 1938

028729-1	It Makes No Difference Now -1, 2, 4	BB B-7920, MW M-7627, RZAu G23719
028730-1	She's Got Everything At Her Command -1, 3, 4	BB B-7997
028731-1	I Thank You, Mister Moon -1, 2, 4	BB B-7997, MW M-7628
028732-1	Schottische -1, 3	BB B-7946, MW M-7627, RZAu G23752
028733-1	Fifteen Dollars A Week -1, 3, 5, 6	BB B-7920, MW M-7629
028734-1	This Crazy Thing -1, 2, 4	BB B-7980, MW M-7629
028735-1	That's All I Want To Know -1, 3, 4	BB B-7946, MW M-7628, RZAu G23752
028736-1	I Wish You Well -2, 4	BB B-7980

Rev. Regal-Zonophone G23719 by Arthur Smith.
Tom Dickey recorded after 1942.

BOB DICKSON
Pseudonym on various labels for Dick Robertson.

DICKSON & CARROLL
Pseudonym on Superior for Andy Patterson & Warren Caplinger (see the latter).

M.S. DILLEHAY

M.S. Dillehay, v; acc. unknown, sg; own g.
El Paso, TX   Wednesday, July 10, 1929

| 55216-1 | Mexican Beans | Vi V-40155 |
| 55220-1 | Mother-In-Law | Vi V-40155 |

Intervening matrices are Spanish.

JOHN DILLESHAW

John Dilleshaw & The String Marvel: prob. Pink Lindsey, f-1/md-2/g-3; John Dilleshaw, g/v-4.
Atlanta, GA   Friday, March 22, 1929

402405-A	[Where The River Shannon Flows] -1,4	OK unissued: *Doc DOCD-8002 (CD)*
402406-B	[Bad Lee Brown] -1, 4	OK unissued: *LC LBC9 (LP); Doc DOCD-8002 (CD)*
402407-B	Spanish Fandango -3	OK 45328
402408-A	Cotton Patch Rag -2	OK 45328

Matrices 402405/06 are uncredited and untitled in OKeh files; the titles given here are hypothetical, and the takes derived from test-pressings.

Seven Foot Dilly, Pink Lindsey, Shorty Lindsey, Bill Kiker: Harry Kiker, f/poss. sp; Shorty Lindsey, tbj/sp; John Dilleshaw, g/sp; Pink Lindsey, sb/sp.
    Atlanta, GA   Wednesday, March 19, 1930
    ATL-914*/15/16/   The Square Dance Fight On Ball Top Mountain –   Vo 5419
        17   Part 1

Fiddler Joe Brown, Fiddler A.A. Gray, Seven Foot Dilly: Joe Brown, f; A.A. Gray, f; John Dilleshaw, sp; Archer Lee "Archie Lee" Chumbler, sp; Hoke Rice, sp; several unknowns, sp.
    Atlanta, GA   Wednesday, March 19, 1930
    ATL-922   A Fiddler's Tryout In Georgia – Part 1   Vo 5432
    ATL-925   A Fiddler's Tryout In Georgia – Part 2   Vo 5432
Matrices ATL-918/19 are by The Morris Family; 920/21 by Hoke Rice; 923/24 by The Morris Family.

Seven Foot Dilly, Pink Lindsey, Shorty Lindsey, Bill Kiker: Harry Kiker, f/poss. sp; Shorty Lindsey, tbj/sp; John Dilleshaw, g/sp; Pink Lindsey, sb/sp.
    Atlanta, GA   Wednesday, March 19, 1930
    ATL-926/27/28/   The Square Dance Fight On Ball Top Mountain –   Vo 5419
        29*   Part 2

Seven Foot Dilly, Pink Lindsey, Shorty Lindsey, Fiddler Gray, Bill Brown: A.A. Gray, f; Harry Kiker, f; Shorty Lindsey, tbj/sp; John Dilleshaw, g/sp/v-1; Pink Lindsey, sb/sp; Bill Brown, sp.
    Atlanta, GA   Wednesday, March 19, 1930
    ATL-989/90   A Georgia Barbecue At Stone Mountain – Part 1   Vo 5454
    ATL-993/94/95   A Georgia Barbecue At Stone Mountain – Part 2   Vo 5454
Matrices ATL-991/92 are by Melton & Minter.

A.A. Gray & Seven Foot Dilly: A.A. Gray, f; John Dilleshaw, g/sp.
    Atlanta, GA   Thursday, March 20, 1930
    ATL-951   Tallapoosa Bound   Vo 5430
    ATL-952   Streak O'Lean – Streak O' Fat   Vo 5430

Dilly & His Dill Pickles: Harry Kiker, f; Shorty Lindsey, tbj/sp-1; John Dilleshaw, g/sp; Pink Lindsey, sb/sp-1.
    Atlanta, GA   Saturday, March 22, 1930
    ATL-974   Georgia Bust Down   Vo 5436
    ATL-975   Pickin' Off Peanuts -1   Vo 5436
    ATL-976   Lye Soap   Vo 5446
    ATL-977   Hell Amongst The Yearlings   Vo 5446

A.A. Gray & Seven Foot Dilly: A.A. Gray, v/f-1; John Dilleshaw, v/g.
    Atlanta, GA   Saturday, March 22, 1930
    ATL-983   Nigger Baby -1   Vo 5458
    ATL-984   The Old Ark's A'Moving   Vo 5458

Dilly & His Dill Pickles: Harry Kiker, f; Shorty Lindsey, tbj; John Dilleshaw, g/sp; Pink Lindsey, sb.
    Atlanta, GA   Saturday, March 22, 1930
    ATL-985   Sand Mountain Drag   Vo 5421
    ATL-986   Bust Down Stomp   Vo 5421

John Dilleshaw, sp; acc. own g.
    Atlanta, GA   Monday, March 24, 1930
    ATL-8002   Farmer's Blues   Vo 5459
    ATL-8003   Walkin' Blues   Vo 5459

Seven Foot Dilly & His Dill Pickles: no details.
    Atlanta, GA   Monday, November 10, 1930
    ATL-6295   Down The River We Go   Br unissued
    ATL-6296   She Had A Little Pig   Br unissued

Seven Foot Dilly, Bill Kiker, Fiddler A.A. Gray, Pink Lindsey, Shorty Lindsey, Bill Brown, Dan Tucker: no details.
    Atlanta, GA   Monday, November 10, 1930
    ATL-6297   Aunt Mandy's Barn Dance – Part 1   Br rejected
    ATL-6298   Aunt Mandy's Barn Dance – Part 2   Br rejected

Seven Foot Dilly & His Dill Pickles: Lowe Stokes, f; poss. A.A. Gray or Harry Kiker, f; poss. Shorty Lindsey, tbj; John Dilleshaw, g; prob. Pink Lindsey, sb.
    Atlanta, GA   Monday, November 10, 1930
    ATL-6299   Kenesaw Mountain Rag   Br 575
    ATL-6600   Bibb County Hoe Down   Br 575
Matrices ATL-6295/96 and 6299/600 are credited in Brunswick files both to **Seven Foot Dilly & His Dill Pickles** (as on Brunswick 575) and to **Seven Foot Dilly & His Pot Lickers**.

John Dilleshaw, v; poss. acc. own g.
   Atlanta, GA   Wednesday, November 12, 1930

| ATL-6672 | The Warning Dream | Br unissued |
| ATL-6673 | Plant Sweet Flowers On My Grave | Br unissued |

Seven Foot Dilly, Dan Tucker, Archie Lee, Lowe Stokes, "Pops" Melvin: Lowe Stokes, f; unknown, bj; John Dilleshaw, g/sp; unidentified, v-1; band v-2; Archer Lee "Archie Lee" Chumbler, Sterling Melvin, unidentified others, sp.
   Atlanta, GA   Friday, November 14, 1930

| ATL-6658/59 | A Bootlegger's Joint In Atlanta – Part 3 -1 | Br 489 |
| ATL-6676/77 | A Bootlegger's Joint In Atlanta – Part 4 -2 | Br 489 |

Intervening matrices are by other artists.

DILLY & HIS DILL PICKLES

See John Dilleshaw.

DIX & WILSON

See Tom & Don.

DIXIE CLODHOPPERS

Pseudonym on Yorkville for Binkley Brothers Dixie Clodhoppers.

DIXIE CRACKERS

Gus Boaz, f; unknown, g; unknown, v; band v.
   Chicago, IL   January 1929

| 21131-1 | The Old Bell Cow | Pm 3151 |
| 21138-1,-2 | Bile Them Cabbage Down | Pm 3151 |

Matrices 21132/33 are by Blind Lemon Jefferson (see *B&GR*); 21136/37 are by the North Georgia Four, with which this group is associated and which may supply some of the chorus voices.

This group is also associated with the Moody Bible Sacred Harp Singers and Phil Reeve–Ernest Moody.

DIXIE DEMONS

Unknown, f; unknown, cl; unknown, poss. piccolo; unknown, sw; poss. another unknown, sw; unknown, g; unknown, sb; unknown, wb; unknown, v; unknown, v-1/sp-2.
   New York, NY   Wednesday, September 11, 1935

39957-A	After You've Gone	De 5141
39958-A	Shine -1	De 5171
39959-A	Ain't She Sweet	De 5141
39960-A	Yes Sir, That's My Baby -1, 2	De 5163
39961-A	Runnin' Wild -2	De 5140

   New York, NY   Thursday, September 12, 1935

39968-A	Casey Jones	De 5140
39969-A	Old Fashioned Love -2	De 5171
39970-A	From Monday On	De 5148
39971-A	Me And My Shadow	De 5148
39972-A	Sweet Sue – Just You	De 5163

DIXIE GIRLS

Vocal duet; acc. prob. own g duet.
   Chicago, IL   September/October 1927.

| 4897-2 | Tuck Me To Sleep | May's K.M.A. 20303 |
| 4900- | Bells Of Hawaii | May's K.M.A. 20303 |

These are Paramount matrices, custom-made for this Iowa label.

THE DIXIE HARMONIZERS

See Warren Caplinger.

THE DIXIE MOUNTAINEERS

See Ernest V. Stoneman.

DIXIE RAMBLERS [1]

Posey Rorer, f; Buster Carter, bj; Lewis McDaniels, g; unidentified calls-1.
   New York, NY   Thursday, March 27, 1930

| 9515-2 | Green Mountain Polka -1 | Pe 143 |

9516-1,-2	Long Eared Mule	Je 20003, Or 8003, Ro 5003

New York, NY   Friday, March 28, 1930

9529-1,-2	Sandy River Bells -1	Je 20003, Or 8003, Pe 142, Ro 5003
9530-	Old Virginia Breakdown	ARC unissued

Revs: Perfect 142, 143 untraced.
At this session this group also accompanied Walter Smith.

DIXIE RAMBLERS [II]

Hector Duhon, f; Hector Stutes, f; unknown, sg; Jesse Duhon, g; Willie Vincent, g/sb/v-1.

New Orleans, LA   Saturday, August 10, 1935

94386-1	Dixie's Hottest	BB B-6086
94387-1	I've Got A Gal -1	BB B-6118
94388-1	Put On Your Old Grey Bonnet -1	BB B-6248
94389-1	Barroom Blues -1	BB B-6118
94390-1	Cottage On The Hill -1	BB B-6179
94391-1	Loveless Love -1	BB B-6248
94392-1	I Took It	BB B-6086
94393-1	Under The Moon With You -1	BB B-6179

The Dixie Ramblers: Hector Duhon, f; Hector Stutes, f-1; unknown, sg-2; Jesse Duhon, g; Willie Vincent, sb-3/v-4.

New Orleans, LA   Wednesday, February 19, 1936

99218-1	Lalita -1, 2, 3, 4	BB B-2181
99219-1	Blue Waltz -1, 2, 3, 4	BB B-6442
99220-1	The Death Of Oswald -1, 2, 3, 4	BB B-2181
99221-1	La Musique Encore, Encore -1, 2, 3, 4	BB B-2180, MW M-4881
99222-1	A Beautiful Lady In Blue -2, 4	BB B-6387
99223-1	The Waltz You Saved For Me -1, 2, 3, 4	BB B-6352, RZAu G23004
99224-1	Dixie Ramblers Waltz -3	BB B-6352, B-2500, RZAu G23004

Bluebird B-6387 as by **Smoky Mt Fiddler Trio**. Bluebird B-2500 (a Mexican issue) as by **El Violinista Campestre**; matrix 99224 is titled *Vals Dixie* on that issue.
Revs: Bluebird B-2180, Montgomery Ward M-4881 by Falcon Trio (see Joseph F. Falcon); Bluebird B-2500 Mexican; B-6387, B-6442 by Arthur Smith.

DIXIE RAMBLERS [III]

Oscar Stockton, f; Willie Duboise, bj; Wallace K. Wimberly, tbj; Henry C. Lowery, g/v-1; Joe Lowery, g/v-1; unknown African-American, sb.

Birmingham, AL   Monday, March 29, 1937

B-47-	That Little Shack I Call My Home Sweet Home-1	ARC unissued
B-48-2	Franklin County Blues	ARC 7-06-63
B-49-	Flat Footed Nigger	ARC unissued
B-50-2	Ridin' In An Old Model "T"	ARC 7-06-63
B-51-	Jefferson County Blues	ARC unissued
B-52-	Let Us Try My Dream -1	ARC unissued

DIXIE RAMBLERS [IV]

Jimmy Thomason, f/v-1; Buddy Woody, ac; Doug Bine, esg; Jake Kolinek, g; Cooper Bennett, sb/v-2.

Dallas, TX   Saturday, October 11, 1941

071168-1	I'm A Dog House Daddy -1	BB B-8898
071169-1	I Wonder What's The Matter -1	BB B-8978
071170-1	I'm Putting You Out Of My Mind -2	BB B-9035
071171-1	I Hope You're Happy Now -2	BB B-9035
071172-1	He's An Army Man -1	BB B-8898
071173-1	Dance Away Polka	BB B-8978

Doug Bine & His Dixie Ramblers are an associated group.

DIXIE REELERS

Ollie Bunn, v/f-1; Daddy John Love, v-2/g-3; Clarence Todd, v-4/g-5.

Charlotte, NC   Saturday, June 20, 1936

102717-1	What A Friend We Have In Mother -2, 3, 4, 5	BB B-6461, MW M-5030, Twin FT8205
102718-1	My Heart Is Broken For You -2, 3, 5	BB B-6461, MW M-5030, Twin FT8205
102719-1	Answer To Maple On The Hill – Part 2 -2, 4, 3/5	BB B-6713, MW M-7099
102720-1	Lonesome Valley – Part 2 -2, 4, 3/5	BB B-6713, MW M-7099
102721-1	Walkin' in My Sleep -1, 3, 4, 5	BB B-6831, MW M-7101
102722-1	Father, Dear Father -1, 2, 3, 4, 5	BB B-6831, MW M-7101, RZ MR2458
102723-1	I Shall Not Be Moved -2, 3, 4, 5	BB B-7958, MW M-7100

| 102724-1 | Do You Want To See Mother Again? -1, 4, 3/5 | BB B-6738, MW M-7100 |

Regal-Zonophone MR2458 as by **The Alabama Barnstormers**.
Matrix 102719 is titled *Maple On The Hill – Part 3*, and matrix 102720 is titled *I've Got To Walk That Lonesome Valley*, on Montgomery Ward M-7099. Matrix 102722 is titled *Father, Dear Father, Come Home* on Regal-Zonophone MR2458. Revs: Bluebird B-6738, B-7958 by Mainer's Mountaineers; Regal-Zonophone MR2458 by Cliff Carlisle.

DIXIE SACRED QUARTETTE

Pseudonym on Champion for The Eva Quartette.

DIXIE SACRED SINGERS

Pseudonym on Challenge, Silvertone, and Supertone for the Eva Quartette. This credit was also used for sacred recordings by Uncle Dave Macon and associates.

DIXIE SACRED TRIO

See John McGhee & Frank Welling.

DIXIE STRING BAND

Poss.: J.M. Mitchell or Dr. W.M. Powell, f; A.M. Bean, tbj; Charles S. Brook, g.
    Atlanta, GA   Thursday, November 3, 1927

| 145095-2 | Dixie Waltz | Co 15273-D |
| 145096-2 | Aldora Waltz | Co 15273-D |

This artist credit is also used for Paramount recordings (and derivatives) by Arthur Tanner.

DIXIELAND FOUR

Arthur Herbert, Alex Mason, Neil Evans, Jesse Phillips, v quartet; acc. Bill Wirges, p.
    New York, NY   Friday, May 13, 1927

| E-23132/33/34 | Put On Your Old Grey Bonnet | Br 3559, 4114, Spt S2105 |
| E-22135/36/37 | Down By The Old Mill Stream | Br 3559, 4114, Spt S2105, Au A22014 |

Supertone S2105 as by **Harmony Quartet**. Aurora A22014 as by **Archie Ruff's Singers**. Rev. Aurora A22014 by Buell Kazee. The same lineup recorded as the Kanawha Singers.

DIXIELAND SWINGSTERS

Dave Durham, f-1/t-2; Karl "Buck" Houchens, cl/ts/v-3; Jerry Collins, p; Larry Downing, g; Cliff Stier, sb; band v-4.
    Charlotte, NC   Monday, August 2, 1937

011853-1	Swingsters Lullaby -2	BB B-7109
011854-1	Blue Skies -2	BB B-7258
011855-1	Nagasaki -2	BB B-7258
011856-1	Love Me Or Leave Me -2	BB B-7160
011857-1	Fiddleobia -1	BB B-7160
011858-1	Touched In The Head -2, 3, 4	BB B-7109

Dave Durham, t/k-1; Buck Houchens, ts/v-2; Jerry Collins, p; Larry Downing, g/v-3; Cliff Stier, sb; band v-4.
    Rock Hill, SC   Monday, September 26, 1938

026973-1	Ferdinand, The Bull -2, 4	BB B-7857, MW M-7535
026974-1	The Widow's Daughter -2, 4	BB B-7857, MW M-7535
026975-1	Bring Back The Greenback Dollar	BB B-7882, MW M-7725
026976-1	Blue Eyes	BB B-7882, MW M-7725
026977-1	Don't Try To Cry Your Way Back To Me -3	BB B-7899, MW M-7726
026978-1	Sing A Little Swing Song -2, 3, 4	BB B-7899, MW M-7726
026979-1	Bennie, The Bumble Bee, Feels Bum -2, 4	BB B-7948, MW M-7727
026980-1	East Tennessee Quiver -1	BB B-7948, MW M-7727

This session was originally logged as by **Dave Durham & Dixieland Swingsters** and Bluebird B-7857, B-7899 are so credited.

Dave Durham, t-1/bj-2; Buck Houchens, cl/ts-3/v-4; Jerry Collins, p; Larry Downing, g/v-5; Cliff Stier, sb; band v-6.
    Rock Hill, SC   Thursday, February 2, 1939

031946-1	An Old Rockin' Chair -1, 4	BB B-8090
031947-1	It's A Lonely Trail -1, 5	BB B-8079
031948-1	Story Of John Hardy -1, 4	BB B-8079
031949-1	My Pretty Quadroon -1, 5	BB B-8109
031950-1	A New Dress For Ida Red -2, 3	BB B-8054
031951-1	Now And Forever -1, 3, 5	BB B-8126
031952-1	Shut The Door -1, 4, 6	BB B-8126
031953-1	Wander Down The Valley -1, 3, 5	BB B-8090
031954-1	Five Man Blues -1, 3	BB B-8054
031955-1	On The Prairie -1, 3, 5	BB B-8109

DORSEY & BEATRICE DIXON
DIXON BROTHERS

Dixon Brothers (Howard & Dorsey), v duet; acc. Howard Dixon, sg; Dorsey Dixon, g.
Charlotte, NC   Wednesday, February 12, 1936

94674-1	Weave Room Blues	BB B-6441, MW M-7024
94675-1	Two Little Rosebuds	BB B-6441, MW M-7015
94676-1	Sales Tax On The Women	BB B-6327, MW M-4823
94677-1	Intoxicated Rat	BB B-6327, MW M-4823, Vi 27495, P78, Twin FT8112
94678-1	Not Turning Back	BB B-6901, MW M-7857
94679-1	White Flower For You	BB B-6630, MW M-7014

Revs: Bluebird B-6901, Twin FT8112 by Bill Boyd; Victor 27495 by Arthur Smith.

Vocal duet; or Howard Dixon, v-1; or Dorsey Dixon, v-2; acc. Howard Dixon, sg; Dorsey Dixon, g; Mutt Evans, v-3/g-3.
Charlotte, NC   Tuesday, June 23, 1936

102816-1	Answer To Maple On The Hill – Part 1	BB B-6462, MW M-5025
102817-1	Answer To Maple On The Hill – Part 2	BB B-6630, MW M-7014
102818-1	Greenback Dollar – Part 1 -1	BB B-6462, MW M-5025
102819-1	Spinning Room Blues -2	MW M-7024
102820-1	My Girl In Sunny Tennessee -3	BB B-6582, MW M-7015
102821-1	A Wonderful Day -3	MW M-7025
102822-1	Are You Sure? -3	BB B-7263, MW M-7025
102823-1	That Old Vacant Chair -3	BB B-6582

Vocal duet; or Howard Dixon, v-1; acc. Howard Dixon, sg; Dorsey Dixon, g.
Charlotte, NC   Tuesday, October 13, 1936

02561-1	I'm Just Here To Get My Baby Out Of Jail – Part 2	BB B-6691, MW M-7089
02562-1	Never To Be Sweethearts Again	MW M-7173
02563-1	Bonnie Blue Eyes – Part 2	BB B-6691, MW M-7089
02564-1	Ocean Of Life	BB B-7374
02565-1	Rambling Gambler -1	BB B-6809
02566-1	Dark Eyes -1	BB B-6809, MW M-7173
02567-1	Easter Day	MW M-7090
02568-1	That Old True Love	BB B-6867, MW M-7090

Matrix 02563 is titled *Hush Little Bonnie* on Montgomery Ward M-7089.

Vocal duet; acc. Howard Dixon, sg; Dorsey Dixon, g; Beatrice Dixon, v-1/poss. g-2.
Charlotte, NC   Thursday, February 18, 1937

07135-1	Answer To Maple On The Hill – Part 4	BB B-6867, MW M-7170
07136-1	Beautiful Stars -1, 2	BB B-6979, MW M-7172
07137-1	I Will Meet My Precious Mother -1	BB B-6979, MW M-7172
07138-1	Weaver's Life	BB B-7802, MW M-7170
07139-1	Darling Do You Miss Me	BB B-7020, MW M-7171
07140-1	Little Bessie	MW M-7171
07150-1	How Can A Broke Man Be Happy	BB B-7674, MW M-7854
07151-1	The School House Fire	BB B-7020, MW M-7854
07152-1	She Tickles Me	MW M-7855
07153-1	Fisherman's Luck	MW M-7855

Intervening matrices are by other artists.

Charlotte, NC   Thursday, August 5, 1937

011972-1	I Won't Accept Anything For My Soul	BB B-7374, MW M-7335
011973-1	What Can I Give In Exchange	MW M-7336
011974-1	What Would You Give In Exchange – Part 5	BB B-7263, MW M-7335
011975-1	The Girl I Left In Danville	BB B-7674, MW M-7337
011976-1	Two Little Boys	MW M-7336
011977-1	The Lonely Prisoner	MW M-7337
011978-1	The Old Home Brew	BB B-7802, MW M-7857

Dorsey & Beatrice Dixon, v duet; acc. prob. own g duet.
Charlotte, NC   Thursday, August 5, 1937

011979-1	Always Waiting For You	BB B-7152
011980-1	When Jesus Appears	BB B-7640
011981-1	Satisfied At Last	BB B-7152
011982-1	Shining City Over The River	BB B-7640

Charlotte, NC   Tuesday, January 25, 1938

| 018655-1 | Promise In Store | BB unissued |
| 018656-1 | Anywhere Is Home | BB B-7599 |

018657-1	Beneath An Old Maple	BB unissued
018658-1	Fields On Fire	BB unissued
018659-1	The Blood Of Jesus Saved Me	BB unissued
018660-1	Where Shall I Be	BB B-7599
018661-1	Promise In The Book Of Life	BB unissued
018662-1	Broken Hearted Girl	BB unissued

Dixon Brothers (Howard & Dorsey), v duet; acc. Howard Dixon, sg; Dorsey Dixon, g.
   Charlotte, NC   Tuesday, January 25, 1938

018683-1	Down With The Old Canoe	BB B-7449, MW M-7489
018684-1	I Didn't Hear Anybody Pray	BB B-7449, MW M-7489
018685-1	Glorious Light Is Dawning	BB B-7767, MW M-7492
018686-1	Have Courage To Only Say No	BB B-7767, MW M-7492
018687-1	A Mother, A Father, A Baby	MW M-7490
018688-1	A Church At The Foot Of The Hill	MW M-7490
018689-1	By Himself	MW M-7491
018690-1	Tempted And Tried	MW M-7491

   Rock Hill, SC   Sunday, September 25, 1938

026955-1	Time For Me To Go	MW M-7577
026956-1	Beyond Black Smoke	MW M-7578
026957-1	When Gabriel Blows His Trumpet For Me	MW M-7579
026958-1	Speak Evil Of No Man	MW M-7579
026959-1	Jimmie And Sallie	MW M-7578
026960-1	The Story Of George Collins	MW M-7580
026961-1	The Light Of Homer Rogers	MW M-7580
026962-1	After The Ball	MW M-7577

Howard Dixon also recorded with Frank Gerald as the Rambling Duet and in their own names. Dorsey Dixon recorded after 1942.

"HAPPY" DIXON'S CLOD HOPPERS

This group, which played hillbilly tunes in popular-danceband settings, is beyond the scope of this work.

THE DIZZY TRIO

Carson Robison, h/g; Roy Smeck, bj/jh; Borrah Minevitch, p.
   Camden, NJ   Tuesday, August 5, 1924

30546-3	Hayseed Rag	Vi 19421, Zo 3805

Revs: Victor 19421 by International Novelty Orchestra; Zonophone 3805 untraced.

BONNIE DODD & MURRAY LUCAS

Bonnie Dodd, Murray Lucas, v duet; acc. Bonnie Dodd, sg; prob. Murray Lucas, g.
   Hot Springs, AR.   Saturday, March 6, 1937

HS-30-	Are You Sorry, Are You Blue	ARC unissued
HS-31-1	So I'll Have Part Of You	Cq 8843
HS-32-1	I Have Kept My Promise, Darling	ARC 7-07-69, Cq 8843
HS-33-1	Ozark Mountain Rose	ARC 7-07-69

   Hot Springs, AR.   Saturday, March 13, 1937

HS-51-	Poor Little Doggie	ARC unissued
HS-52-	I'm Dreaming Of Someone I Love	ARC unissued

   Hot Springs, AR.   Tuesday, March 16, 1937

HS-68-	Would You Care	ARC unissued
HS-69-	I Have Hung My Old Guitar On The Wall	ARC unissued

JOHNNY DODDS

Pseudonym on OKeh & Australian Parlophone for Gene Autry.

TINY DODSON'S CIRCLE-B BOYS

Tiny Dodson, f; Jack Shelton, lv/g; Curly Shelton, tv/g.
   Charlotte, NC   Tuesday, June 7, 1938

64072-A	Unfriendly World	De 5563
64073-A	Two Little Rosebuds	De 5563
64074-A	I'd Rather Have Jesus	De 5656
64075-A	There Is Power In The Blood	De 5656
64076-A	Girl I Love Don't Pay Me No Mind	De 5586
64077-A	Katy Dear	De 5586

Decca 5586 as by **Tiny Dodson's (Circle-B Boys)**.

DOMINO GEORGE

Pseudonym on Champion for Loren H. Abram.

LOUIE DONALDSON

Louie Donaldson & Allie Brock, v duet; acc. Louie Donaldson, g.
Richmond, IN   Tuesday, April 16, 1929

| 15059,-A | I Love You Best Of All | Ge rejected |
| 15060,-A,-B | When The Morning Glories Grow | Ge rejected |

Louie Donaldson & Hoke Rice: Louie Donaldson, v/g; Hoke Rice, g.
Richmond, IN   Wednesday, April 17, 1929

| 15061 | The Gang's All Here | Ge 6885, Chg 427 |
| 15062 | Bogey Alley | Ge 6885 |

Challenge 427 as by **Maines & Hodge**. Rev. Challenge 427 by Melvin Robinette & Byrd Moore (see the latter).
See also Allie & Pearl Brock.

RUTH DONALDSON & HELEN JEPSEN

Ruth Donaldson, Helen Jepsen, v duet; acc. one of them, sg; the other, ti.
St. Paul, MN   c. June 3, 1927

| 12822,-A | Mother Still Prays For You Jack | Ge rejected |
| 12823,-A | I Saw My Mother Kneeling | Ge rejected |

Acc. one of them, ti.
St. Paul, MN   c. June 8, 1927

| 12829,-A | When I Take My Vacation In Heaven | Ge rejected |
| 12830,-A | Glory To God He's Come Home | Ge rejected |

Acc. one of them, sg; the other, ti.
St. Paul, MN   c. June 15, 1927

| 12842,-A | Mother Still Prays For You | Ge rejected |
| 12843 | I Saw My Mother Kneeling | Ge 6192, Ch 15336, Spt 9264, Sil 5074, 8168, Chg 403 |

Champion 15336 as by **Donaldson & Jepsen**. Silvertone 5074, 8168, Supertone 9264 as by **Jepsen & Donaldson**. Challenge 403 as by **Ruth & Wanda Wallace**.

St. Paul, MN   c. June 16, 1927

| 12851 | Leave It There | Ge 6241, Ch 15353, Chg 341 |
| 12852,-A | I Want To Go There | Ge rejected |

Champion 15353 as by **Donaldson & Jepsen**. Challenge 341 as by **Jepsen & Donaldson**.

Acc. prob. own ti duet.
St. Paul, MN   c. June 23, 1927

12874	Glory To God He's Come Home	Ge 6241, Ch 15336, Spt 9264, Sil 5074, 8168, Chg 403
12875	When I Take My Vacation In Heaven	Ge 6192, Ch 15353, Chg 341
12876,-A	I'm Going Higher Someday	Ge unissued
12877,-A	You Must Unload	Ge rejected

Champion 15336 as by **Donaldson & Jepsen**. Silvertone 5074, 8168, Supertone 9264, Challenge 341 as by **Jepsen & Donaldson**. Challenge 403 as by **Ruth & Wanda Wallace**.

Jepsen & Donaldson, v duet; acc. one of them, sg-1/ti-2; the other, ti; unknown, g-3.
Richmond, IN   Tuesday, July 14, 1931

17864-A	No Disappointments In Heaven -2, 3	Ch 16460
17865,-A	When We're Traveling Thru The Air -2	Ge rejected
17866,-A	Jesus Filled My Life With Sunshine -2	Ge unissued
17867,-A,-B	A Better Home -2	Ge unissued
17868-B	He Just Makes Us Willing -2	Ch 16448, Spr 2834
17869	Jesus Has Lifted Me -1	Ch 16448, Spr 2834
17870,-A	I Believe The Good Old Bible -1	Ge unissued
17871	Lift Up The Standard -2	Ch 16460
17872	I Saw My Mother Kneeling -1	Ch S-16304, Spr 2707
17873	The Devil's No Relation -2	Ch 16298, Spr 2766
17874	I'm Going Home -2	Ch 16298, Spr 2707
17875-A	I'm Going Higher Some Day -2	Ch S-16304, Spr 2735
17876-A	Keep On Keeping On -2	Ch 16354
17877-A	I'd Like To Hear Elijah Pray Again -2	Ch 16354, Spr 2766
17878-A	When I Take My Vacation In Heaven -2	Spr 2735

Superiors, except 2834, as by **Donaldson & Jepsen**.

DONALDSON & JEPSEN

See Ruth Donaldson & Helen Jepsen.

OSCAR [SLIM] DOUCET

Slim Doucet, v; acc. own ac; Chester Hawkins, g.
    Atlanta, GA   Wednesday, March 20, 1929

| 402382-B | Chere Yeux Noirs | OK 45333 |
| 402383-B | Waxia Special | OK 45333 |

Oscar Doucet–Alius Soileau: Alius Soileau, f; Oscar Doucet, ac/v.
    New Orleans, LA   Thursday, November 7, 1929

56516-1	When I Met You At The Gate	BB B-2085
56517-2	Oh Baby!	Vi 22366
56518-2	Bayou Courtebleau	BB B-2085
56519-2	Slim's Blues	Vi 22366

REV. & MRS C.A. DOUGHERTY

Rev. C.A. Dougherty, Mrs C.A. Dougherty, v duet; acc. unknown, p.
    Atlanta, GA   Wednesday, October 27, 1926

| 9822-A | No Disappointment In Heaven | OK 45076 |
| 9823-A | Just An Old Fashioned Gospel Is Needed Today | OK 45076 |

DOC DOUGHERTY & HIS ORCHESTRA

Two couplings by this danceband were issued in the Victor Old Familiar Tunes series (V-40111, V-40119) but are beyond the scope of this work. (For further information see JR under Doc Daugherty & His Orchestra. Frank Luther is the vocalist on the latter coupling and other Victor items by this band.)

EVAN DOUGLAS & NATE SMITH

Pseudonym on Champion for Kirk McGee & Blythe Poteet (see McGee Brothers).

DRAKE & NORMAN

Pseudonym on Broadway for Davis & Nelson (see Claude (C.W.) Davis).

DRAKE TRIO

Pseudonym on Broadway for the Davis Trio (see Claude (C.W.) Davis).

THE DRUM QUARTET

Male vocal quartet; acc. unknown, p.
    Atlanta, GA   Saturday, October 12, 1940

056542-1	When Jesus Comes	BB B-8601, MW M-8850
056543-1	Where Is God?	BB B-8601, MW M-8850
056544-1	Lead Me Gently Home, Father	BB B-8651, MW M-8851
056545-1	The Last Mile Of The Way	BB B-8651, MW M-8851
056546-1	Wonderful	BB B-8683, MW M-8852
056547-1	No Tears In Heaven	BB B-8683, MW M-8852

FRANK DUDGEON

Frank Dudgeon, v; acc. own g.
    Richmond, IN   Thursday, October 20, 1932

| 18853 | I Hate To Be Called A Hobo | Ch 16532 |
| 18854 | Atlanta Bound | Ch 16532 |

    Richmond, IN   Wednesday, March 8, 1933

19072	When It's Lamp Lightin' Time In The Valley	Ch 16575, 45104, MW 4948
19073	The Crime I Didn't Do	Ch 16580
19074	11 More Months And 10 More Days Part 2	Ch 16580
19075	Rattler	Ch 16602
19076	Birmingham Jail No. 2	Ch 16602
19077	Sweet Betsy From Pike	Ch 16575

Rev. Champion 45104 by Chick Bullock (popular); Montgomery Ward 4948 by Harry Hillard.
Frank Dudgeon recorded after 1942.

ARTHUR DUHON

Arthur Duhon, v/y-1; acc. unknown, sg; poss. own g.
    Dallas, TX   Wednesday, September 25, 1935

DAL-150-1	Just Like You	Vo 03088
DAL-151-2	No Path Of Sunshine -1	Vo 03207
DAL-154-2	My Star Of The Sky	Vo 03088

Intervening matrices are by the Dallas Jamboree Jug Band (see *B&GR*).

Arthur Duhon, v; or **Arthur Duhon & Don McCord**, v duet-1; acc. unknown, sg; poss. Arthur Duhon, g.
Dallas, TX   Thursday, September 26, 1935

DAL-155-1,-2	My Ladder Of Dreams -1	Vo unissued
DAL-156-1	Pretty Blue Eyes	Vo 03207
DAL-159-1,-2	Blue Bonnet Yodelling Blues -1	Vo unissued

Intervening matrices are by the Dallas Jamboree Jug Band (see *B&GR*).

Lonesome Buddy (Arthur Duhon), v; acc. own g.
Dallas, TX   Monday, April 7, 1941

063044-1	What Caused Me To Roam	BB B-8729
063045-1	My Little Ranch Home	BB B-8764
063046-1	Answer To My Precious Darlin'	BB B-8729
063047-1	Your Heart Has Turned To Stone	BB B-8764

FRANK DUNBAR

Pseudonym on Superior for Raymond Render.

EDWARD DUNCAN

Pseudonym on Supertone for Connie Bird (see Elmer Bird & Associated Artists).

LULA DUNCAN

See Duncan Sisters Trio.

THE DUNCAN BOYS

Pseudonym on Supertone for Elmer Bird & His Happy Four.

DUNCAN SISTERS (VERNA LEE & LOTTIE JO)

Verna Lee Duncan, Lottie Jo Duncan, v duet; acc. unknown, p.
Atlanta, GA   Monday, October 26, 1931

151948-	Hard Luck Mamma	Co unissued
151949-1	Dusty Roads	Co 15745-D

Rev. Columbia 15745-D by Sawyer Sisters.

DUNCAN SISTERS TRIO

Duncan Sisters Trio, v trio; acc. unknown, p.
Chicago, IL   Monday, September 16, 1935

C-90326-A,-B,-C	The Hem Of His Garment	De unissued
C-90327-A,-B,-C	A Message To Mother	De unissued
C-90328-A,-B	Jesus You Taught Me How To Smile	De rejected
C-90329-A,-B	I Will Never Move Again	De unissued

Lula Duncan, v; acc. unknown, f; unknown, p.
Chicago, IL   Monday, September 16, 1935

C-90330-A,-AA	The Last Mile Of The Way	De rejected
C-90331-A,-AA	When We Rise To Meet Our Friend	De unissued

UNCLE ECK DUNFORD

Uncle Eck Dunford, v; acc. Hattie Stoneman, f/v-1; Ernest V. Stoneman, h/g/v-2; own g; Iver Edwards, u.
Bristol, TN   Wednesday, July 27, 1927

39716-1	The Whip-Poor-Will's Song -1	Vi 20880
39717-2	What Will I Do, For My Money's All Gone -1	Vi 21578
39718-2	Skip To Ma Lou, My Darling -2	Vi 20938
39719-1	Barney McCoy -3	Vi 20938

Matrix 39717 as by **Uncle Eck Dunford–Hattie Stoneman**; matrix 39719 as by **Uncle Eck Dunford–Ernest Stoneman**. Rev. Victor 20880 by Ernest Stoneman (with Dunford and others).

Uncle Eck Dunford, sp; acc. Ernest V. Stoneman, bj.
Atlanta, GA   Saturday, October 22, 1927

40334-1	Sleeping Late	Vi 21244
40335-1	My First Bicycle Ride	Vi 21131
40336-1	The Taffy-Pulling Party	Vi 21244
40337-2	The Savingest Man On Earth	Vi 21131

Uncle Eck Dunford, v; acc. prob. own f-1; George Stoneman, bj/v-2; Ernest V. Stoneman, g.
Atlanta, GA   Wednesday, February 22, 1928
    41940-1,-2   Uncle Joe -1   Vi unissued
    41941-2   Sweet Summer Has Gone Away -1, 2   Vi 21578
    41942-1,-2   Tell Me Where My Eva's Gone -1?, 2   Vi unissued
    41943-1,-2   Old Uncle Jessie -1   Vi unissued

Matrix 41941 as by **Uncle Eck Dunford–Ernest Stoneman**. There may no vocal on matrices 41940 and 41943.

Acc. Hattie Stoneman, f-1/md-2; Ernest V. Stoneman, h; Bolen Frost, bj; own g.
Bristol, TN   Tuesday, October 30, 1928
    47254-2   Angeline, The Baker -2   Vi V-40060
    47255--   Old Shoes And Leggin's -1   Vi V-40060

Eck Dunford also recorded with Ernest V. Stoneman and Fields Ward, and for the Library of Congress in 1937.

MELLIE DUNHAM'S ORCHESTRA

Mellie Dunham, f; Cherrie Noble, p; M.A. Noble, vc/calls-1.
New York, NY   Tuesday, January 19, 1926
    34338-1   Chorus Jig -1   Vi V-40131
    34339-2   Lady Of The Lake -1   Vi 19940
    34340-3   Mountain Rangers -1   Vi 19940
    34341-1   Hull's Victory   Vi V-40131
New York, NY   Wednesday, January 20, 1926
    34344-1,-2,-3,-4   Boston Fancy -1   Vi unissued
Camden, NJ   Tuesday, January 26, 1926
    34344-7   Boston Fancy -1   Vi 20001, MW M-8137
    34440-2   Rippling Waves Waltz   Vi 20001

Victor 20001, Montgomery Ward M-8137 as by **Mellie Dunham & His Orchestra**. Matrix 34344 is titled *Barn Dance On The Mountain – Part 2* on Montgomery Ward M-8137. Rev. Montgomery Ward M-8137 by the Crook Brothers.

New York, NY   Wednesday, February 3, 1926
    34389-4   Medley Of Reels   Vi 20537
Camden, NJ   Wednesday, February 3, 1926
    34528-4   Medley Of Reels   Vi 20537

JACK DUNIGAN

Jack Dunigan, v; acc. own g.
Richmond, IN   Tuesday, August 25, 1931
    17954   Just For A Girl   Ge rejected trial recording

Jack Dunigan is also a member of Clayton McMichen's Georgia Wildcats.

BOB DUNN'S VAGABONDS

Bob Dunn, esg/v-1; Leo Raley, emd/v-2; Mancel Tierney, p; Hezzie Bryant, sb; Frederick "Fritz" Kehm, d; Aubrey "Moon" Mullican, v-3.
Houston, TX   Thursday, March 2, 1939
    65100-B   Mama's Gone, Goodbye   De 5667
    65101-B   Too Long -3   De 5667
    65102-A   It Must Be Love -3   De 5694
    65103-B   Blue Skies -3   De 5676
    65104-B   Mean Mistreater Blues -3   De 5694
    65105-A   Toodle-Oodle-Oo -3   De 5676
    65106-A   When Night Falls -1   De 5684
    65107-A   You'll Pay Some Day -3   De 5733
    65108-A   You Don't Know My Mind -3   De 5684
    65109-A   Graveyard Blues -2   De 5707
    65110-A   I Want The Whole World To Know I Love You -3   De 5707

One Decca source gives March 3 as a date for matrices 65101 and 65107/08.

Bob Dunn, esg/v-1; Leo Raley, emd; Moon Mullican, p; poss. Aubrey "Red" Greenhaw or Dickie McBride, g; Hezzie Bryant, sb; Sybil Hopkins, v-2; Chuck Keeshan, v-3.
Houston, TX   Tuesday, September 5, 1939
    66415-A   Basin Street Blues -2   De 5733
    66416-A   Was That All I Meant To You -2 De 5746
    66419-A   Meet Me Tonight In Dreams -3   De 5789
    66420-A   Stompin' At The Honky Tonk   De 5772

66421-A	Wednesday Rag	De 5772
66422-A	I'll Tell The World (She's A Good Little Girl) -1	De 5789
66423-A	Sweet Bunch Of Daisies	De 5746

Matrices 66417/18 are by Leon Selph's Blue Ridge Playboys.

Poss. Rudy Rivera, cl; Bob Dunn, esg/v-1; Mancel Tierney, p/v-2; Sam Jones, etg; unknown, g; Hezzie Bryant, sb; band v-3.

Houston, TX   Thursday, April 11, 1940

92082-A	I'll Forget Dear (That I Ever Loved You) -1	De 5828
92083-A	Juke Box Rag	De 5828
92084-A	I Found You Out When I Found You In (Somebody Else's Arms) -1	De 5848
92085-A	I'll Get By (As Long As I Have You) -2	De 5868, MeC 45378
92086-A	'Round Her Neck She Wears A Yeller Ribbon (For Her Love Who Is Fur, Fur, Away) -1, 3	De 5868, MeC 45378
92087-A	Marcheta	De 5848

TEX DUNN & HIS ARIZONA COWBOYS

Tex Dunn, v; or Tex Dunn, unknown, v-1/y-2 duet; acc. poss. Fiddlin' Jack ———, f; poss. Happy Wilson, g; Tex Dunn, g; poss. Shorty Dunn, sb.

Charlotte, NC   Monday, August 2, 1937

011845-1	Away Out There -1, 2	BB B-7112, MW M-7371
011846-1	Little Texas Cowgirl -1	BB B-7112, MW M-7371
011847-1	Prairie Darling -1	MW M-7368
011848-1	In The Pines -1, 2	MW M-7368
011849-1	Cowboy's Lullaby	MW M-7369
011850-1	Arizona Trail -1	MW M-7369
011851-1	Rainbow's End -1	MW M-7370
011852-1	Arizona Moon	MW M-7370

Tex Dunn recorded after 1942.

BARNEY DUNROE

Pseudonym on Champion for Oscar L. Coffey.

DUO DE VIOLIN Y GUITARRA

Pseudonym on OKeh 16604 and 16679 for W.T. Narmour & S.W. Smith.

DUO INSTRUMENTAL

Pseudonym on OKeh 16714, 16740 for W.T. Narmour & S.W. Smith.

DUO ROBLES

Pseudonym on OKeh 16731 for Hugh Roden.

MELVIN DUPREE

Dupree's Rome Boys: Bill Shores, f; Frank Locklear, md; Melvin Dupree, g.

Atlanta, GA   Friday, March 15, 1929

402321-B	Wedding Bells Waltz	OK 45320
402322-B	Underneath The Mellow Moon	OK 45320
402323-A	Cat Rag	OK 45356
402324-B	12th Street Blues	OK 45356

Dupree & Locklear: Frank Locklear, md; Melvin Dupree, g; or **Melvin Dupree**-1, g solo.

Richmond, IN   Tuesday, April 2, 1929

14991	Norfolk Flip	Ge 6988
14992	Augusta Rag -1	Ge 6988
14993,-A	Kileau March	Ge rejected

Dupree and Locklear were also members of Shores Southern Trio, which recorded at this session.

Melvin Dupree also recorded with the Georgia Organ Grinders (see Gid Tanner), Georgia Yellow Hammers, Uncle Bud Landress, Bill Shores, and Gid Tanner.

DUPREE & LOCKLEAR
DUPREE'S ROME BOYS

See Melvin Dupree.

DAVE DURHAM & DIXIELAND SWINGSTERS

See the Dixieland Swingsters.

SLIM DWIGHT
Pseudonym on Bluebird and Electradisk for Dwight Butcher.

DYE'S SACRED HARP SINGERS
Vocal group; acc. unknown, p.
    Richmond, IN   Thursday, December 13, 1928

14566,-A	Confidence	Ge rejected
14567	New Hosanna	Ge 6827
14568	Amazing Grace	Ge 6889
14569-A	Victoria	Ge 6764
14570-A	Heavenly Armor	Ge 6779
14571,-A	Animation	Ge rejected

    Richmond, IN   Friday, December 14, 1928

14572	Olney	Ge 6827
14573,-A	Sons Of Sorrow	Ge rejected
14574-A	How Firm A Foundation	Ge 6889
14575,-A	I'm On My Journey Home	Ge rejected
14576	Return Again	Ge rejected
14577,-A	Florida	Ge rejected
14578	Pleyel's Hymn	Ge 6779

    Richmond, IN   Saturday, December 15, 1928

14579-A	Bethel	Ge 6764
14580	Calvary	Ge 6736, Spt 9532
14581,-A,-B	Ortonville	Ge rejected
14582-A	Land Of Beulah	Ge 6736
14583,-A	Florence	Ge rejected
14584,-A	Duane Street	Ge rejected
14585,-A	Resurrected	Ge rejected

Rev. Supertone 9532 untraced.

John Marion Dye and his son Homer S. Dye, both of whom played piano, are probably members of this group.

CHARLES DYKES
See Elmer Bird & Associated Artists.

DYKES' MAGIC CITY TRIO
John Dykes, f/v-1; Myrtle Vermillion, ah/v-2; G.H. "Hub" Mahaffey, g/v.
    New York, NY   Wednesday, March 9, 1927

E-21803/04*	Frankie	Br 127, Vo 5143
E-21805/06*	Poor Ellen Smith	Br 127, Vo 5143
E-21807/08*	Cotton Eyed Joe	Br 120
E-21809/10*	Twilight Is Stealing -1, 2	Br 130

John Dykes, f; Myrtle Vermillion, ah; G.H. "Hub" Mahaffey, g/v-1/calls-2.
    New York, NY   Thursday, March 10, 1927

E-21831/32*	Tennessee Girls -2	Br 120
E-21833/34*	Huckleberry Blues -2	Br 129
E-21835/36*	Free Little Bird -1	Br 129
E-21837*/38	Shortening Bread -1, 2	Br 125
E-21839/40*	Ida Red -1	Br 125
E-21841*/42	Callahan's Reel -2	Vo 5181, BrC 126
E-21843/44*	Red Steer -2	Vo 5181, BrC 126

John Dykes, f/v-1; Myrtle Vermillion, ah/v-2; G.H. "Hub" Mahaffey, g/v.
    New York, NY   Friday, March 11, 1927

E-21845*/46/47	Golden Slippers	Br 128
E-21848*/49	Hook And Line	Br 128
E-21850/51*/52	Far Beyond The Blue Sky -1, 2	Br 130

E

EARL & JOE
See Earl B. Zaayer.

EAST TEXAS SERENADERS

Daniel H. Williams, f; John Munnerlyn, tbj; Cloet Hamman, g; Henry Bogan, vc.
    Dallas, TX   Friday, December 2, 1927

145310-2	Sweetest Flower	Co 15229-D
145311-2	Combination Rag	Co 15229-D

    Dallas, TX   Thursday, October 25, 1928

DAL-720-	Acorn Stomp	Br 282
DAL-721-	Shannon Waltz	Br 282
DAL-722-	Deacon Jones	Br 298
DAL-723-	Aldeline Waltz	Br 298, Me M18019

Melotone M18019 as by **Les Serenadeurs Du Lac St. Jean**; matrix DAL-723 is titled *La Valse Chicoutimi* on that issue. Rev. Melotone M18019 (with same credit) by Kessinger Brothers.

    Dallas, TX   Sunday, October 27, 1929

DAL-533-	Dream Shadows	Br 453
DAL-534-	Babe	Br 453
DAL-535-	Meadow Brook Waltz	Br 379
DAL-536-	Three In One Two-Step	Br 379
DAL-537-	McKinney Waltz	Br 429
DAL-538-	Before I Grew Up To Love You	Br 429

    Dallas, TX   Friday, November 28, 1930

DAL-6767-	Louisa Waltz	Br 538
DAL-6768-	Gulf Breeze Waltz	Br 562
DAL-6769-	Ozark Rag	Br 538
DAL-6770-	Mineola Rag	Br 562

Daniel H. Williams, f; Henry Lester (or Henry Russell?), f; Shorty Lester, tbj; Cloet Hamman, g; Henry Bogan, vc.
    Dallas, TX   Saturday, February 20, 1937

61882-A	Del Rio Waltz	De 5347, MeC 45053
61883-A	Beaumont Rag	De 5408
61884-A	Serenaders' Waltz	De 5408
61885-A	Fiddlin' The Fiddle	De rejected
61886-A	Say A Little Prayer For Me	De 5458
61887-A	East Texas Drag	De 5347, MeC 45053
61888-A	German Waltz	De rejected
61889-A	Sweetest Flower Waltz	De 5458
61890-A	Arizona Stomp	De 5375
61891-A	Shannon Waltz	De 5375

GARNER ECKLER & ROLAND GAINES

The Yodeling Twins (Garner Eckler & Roland Gaines), v/y-1 duet; acc. Guy Blakeman, f-2; Garner Eckler, g; Roland Gaines, g.
    Richmond, IN   Thursday, February 1, 1934

19470	Moonlight And Skies -1, 2	Ch 16747, 45043, MW 4930
19471	One Little Kiss -1	Ch 16723, 45087, DeAu X1240
19472	Mountain Ranger's Lullaby -2	Ch 16723, 45087, MW 4930, DeAu X1240
19473	Single Life Is Good Enough For Me (Crooning Bachelor) -2	Ch 16747, 45043

Champion 45043, 45087, Montgomery Ward 4930, Decca X1240 as by **Garner Eckler & Roland Gaines (The Yodeling Twins)**. Decca X1240 erroneously shows matrix 19491 instead of 19471.

EDGEWATER SABBATH SINGERS

Vocal group; acc. unknown.
    poss. Chicago, IL   c. April 1927

	Golden Slippers	Pm 3000
	Just A Little While	Pm 3000
	I'm Going To Leave The Old Home	Pm 3005
	Heavenly Sunshine	Pm 3005

GEORGE EDGIN

George Edgin, v; acc. own g.
    Richmond, IN   Wednesday, November 27, 1929

15959,-A	Old Sweethearts Of Mine	Ge rejected

George Edgin & Wm. Birkhead: George Edgin, f; William Birkhead, g.
Richmond, IN   Monday, December 16, 1929
| 16002 | Good Night Waltz | Ge rejected |

George Edgin, v; acc. own f; William Birkhead, g.
Richmond, IN   Monday, December 16, 1929
| 16003,-A | The Unknown Soldier | Ge rejected |

Wm. Birkhead, v; acc. George Edgin, g.
Richmond, IN   Wednesday, December 18, 1929
| 16004 | Jail House Now | Ge rejected trial recording |

George Edgin, v; acc. own g.
Richmond, IN   Wednesday, January 8, 1930
| 16063,-A,-B | Bring Back My Buddie | Ge rejected |
| 16064,-A | The Unknown Soldier | Ge rejected |

Earl Wright & The Arkansas Corndodgers: George Edgin, f; Earl Wright, g/v; unknown, g.
Richmond, IN   Tuesday, January 26, 1932
18332-A	My Ozark Mountain Home	Ch S-16382, Spr 2822
18333	Cold Penitentiary Blues	Ge unissued: *CARS unnumbered (Vol. 3) (CD)*
18334	My Little Old Southern Home By The Sea	Ge rejected
18335	Take Me Home To My Mother	Ch S-16382, Spr 2822
18336	Make Me A Pallet On The Floor	Ge unissued

Superior 2822 as by **Sam Weber**.

Richmond, IN   Tuesday, February 2, 1932
18365	The Arkansas Hotel	Ge unissued
18366	The Broken Hearted Vow	Ge unissued
18367	The Canyon Song	Ge rejected

George Edgin, v; acc. own g.
Richmond, IN   Tuesday, February 2, 1932
| 18368 | Those Out Of Town Girls | Ge rejected |

George Edgin's Corn Dodgers With Earl Wright & Brown Rich: George Edgin, f; Earl Wright, g/v; Brown Rich, vc; unidentified, v eff-1.
New York, NY   Friday, March 18, 1932
152148-1	My Ozark Mountain Home	Co 15754-D
152149-	Take Me Home To My Mother	Co unissued
152150-	The Heart Broken Vow	Co unissued
152151-	The Unknown Soldier	Co unissued
152152-	Make Me A Pallet	Co unissued
152153-1	Corn Dodger No. 1 Special -1	Co 15754-D
152154-	Southern Moon Waltz	Co unissued
152155-	Blue Mountain Sally Goodin	Co unissued

The Ozarkers: George Edgin, f; Earl Wright, g/v; Brown Rich, vc.
New York, NY   Friday, March 18, 1932
405172-	99 Years	OK unissued
405173-A	The Arkansas Hotel	OK unissued: *LC LBC11 (LP); CARS unnumbered (Vol. 3) (CD)*
405174-	Dear Old Sunny South (By The Sea)	OK 45573
405175-	East Bound Train	OK unissued
405176-	Green Valley Waltz	OK unissued
405177-	There's More Pretty Girls Than One	OK 45573

George Edgin recorded after 1942.

DAVE EDWARDS & HIS ALABAMA BOYS

Cotton Thompson, f/v-1; Lewis Tierney, f; Carl Rainwater, esg/j-2; Mancel Tierney, p; Bud McDonald, g/v-3; Harley Huggins, g; Darrell Jones, sb; Keith Payne, d.
Dallas, TX   Thursday, December 16, 1937
63093-A	Jig Time -1	De 5522
63094-A	Josephine	De rejected
63095-A	Smiles -3	De 5478
63096-A	Sailing On The Robert E. Lee -1	De 5507
63097-A	You're No Good Anymore -1, 3	De 5470
63098-A	Oh By Jingo! (Oh By Gee, You're The Only Girl For Me) -1	De 5564

63099-A	Missouri Waltz -1, 3	De 5564
63100-A	Sigh And Cry Blues	De 5470
63101-A	Down In Jungle Town -1, 3	De 5507
63103-B	Minnie The Moocher -1	De 5536
63104-A	Done Sold My Soul To The Devil -1	De 5493
63105-A	Blue Man's Blues	De 5478
63106-A	Down In Arkansas -1, 2	De 5536
63107-A	Baby (You're As Sweet As Honey To Me) -1	De 5522
63108-A	Hula Lou -1	De 5493

Matrix 63102 is by Jimmie Davis.
Dave Edwards was the band's business manager.

JACK EDWARDS

Pseudonym on Supertone for Jack Golding.

EL PELIRROJO ARMONICO

Pseudonym on Mexican Bluebird for Syd "Willie (Red)" Newman; see Jack Pierce.

EL VIOLINISTA CAMPESTRE

One side of Bluebird B-2500 (a Mexican release), with this artist credit, is by the Dixie Ramblers [II].

ODIS ELDER

Odis Elder, v; acc. poss. Frank Novak, cl-1/x-2; unknown, h-3; prob. Bob Miller, p; poss. own or Ray Whitley, g.
    New York, NY   Monday, September 17, 1934

15957-1	Rain	Ba 33231, Me M13198, Or 8389, Pe 13070, Ro 5389, Cq 8405, Lucky 1038
15958-2	Little Hill Billy Heart Throb -1, 3	Ba 33220, Me M13187, MeC 91868, Or 8383, Pe 13064, Ro 5383, Cq 8390
15959-2	I'm Lonesome For You Caroline	Ba 33231, Me M13198, Or 8389, Pe 13070, Ro 5389, Cq 8405, Lucky 1038
15960-1	Silvery Prairie Moon -2	Ba 33220, Me M13187, MeC 91868, Or 8383, Pe 13064, Ro 5383, Cq 8390

Acc. unknown.
    New York, NY   Friday, October 5, 1934

| 16038- | Worthy | ARC unissued |

At both these sessions Odis Elder recorded duets with Ray Whitley, for which see the latter.

ELK CREEK TRIO

Pseudonym on Champion for the Gibson String Trio or Workman, Ramsey & Wolfe (evidently the same group).

RAY ELKINS

Pseudonym on Champion for Walter Coon.

ELKINS STRINGED STEPPERS

Unknown, s; unknown, md; unknown, bj; unknown, g.
    Atlanta, GA   Thursday, November 4, 1926

| 9871-A | Since You Called Me Sweetheart | OK 45079 |
| 9872-A | Speed | OK 45079 |

JOSSIE ELLERS

Jossie Ellers, v; acc. the Cedar Crest Singers: unidentified, bj-1; unidentified, g; Emry Arthur, v/sp; William Rexroat, v.
    Chicago, IL   Tuesday, January 8, 1929

| C-2767- | Dying For Someone To Love Me -1 | Vo 5294 |
| C-2768- | The Old Maid's Song | Vo 5294 |

Josie (Of The Cumberland Ridge Runners), v; acc. Karl Davis, md/v/sp; Harty Taylor, g/v.
    Chicago, IL   Friday, November 1, 1935

| C-1160-1 | The Old Maid | ARC 6-02-54, Cq 8616 |

Rev. ARC 6-02-54, Conqueror 8616 by Karl Davis (see Karl & Harty).
Jossie Ellers is probably a member of William Rexroat's Cedar Crest Singers.

ELLINGTON SACRED QUARTETTE

Pseudonym on Challenge 402 for The Eva Quartette (*Bringing In The Sheaves*)/McDonald Quartette (*While The Years Roll On*).

BILL ELLIOTT

Bill Elliott, v; acc. Bob Mitchell, o.
   Camden, NJ   Friday, February 5, 1932

70563-1	When The Oriole Sings Again	Vi 23652
70564-1	Pals Of The Little Red School	Vi 23652
70565-1	Hills Of Idaho	Vi 23646
70566-1	When It's Springtime In The Blue Ridge Mountains	Vi 23646
70567-1	Lonesome Valley	Vi 23658, MW M-4337
70568-1	Good Old Times (Are Coming Back Again)	Vi 23649, Zo 6119
70569-1	The Funny Old World Rolls Along	Vi 23649, Zo 6119
70570-1	Eleven More Months And Ten More Days – Part 1	Vi 23658
70571-1	Eleven More Months And Ten More Days – Part 2	Vi 23670, MW M-4328

Victor 23649, Montgomery Ward M-4328, M-4337, Zonophone 6119 as by **Jim Baird**.
Revs: Victor 23670 by Graham Brothers; Montgomery Ward M-4328 by Dick Robertson, M-4337 by Bob Miller.

JERRY ELLIS

Pseudonym on Champion for Jack Golding.

ELM CITY QUARTET

Vocal quartet; unacc.
   Richmond, IN   c. October 1934

19726	Twenty Five Years From Now	Ch 16827, 45109
19727	The Tree Song	Ch 16827, 45109

ELMER & JUD[D]

Alternative credit on several labels for the Hobbs Brothers. ARC-Broadway 8052, as **Elmer & Jud**, is by Doc Roberts.

BUGGS EMERICK

Buggs Emerick, v; acc. prob. own bj.
   Richmond, IN   Wednesday, April 3, 1929

15003	My Little Home In Tennessee	Ge rejected

TOM EMERSON'S MOUNTAINEERS

Unknown, f; unknown, ac; unknown, g; unknown, sb; Polly Shaffer, v-1; Lem Saunders & Gang, v-2.
   New York, NY   Tuesday, October 31, 1939

043251-1	Rhythm In The Hills -1	BB B-8346, MW M-8692
043252-1	(Honey I've Got) Everything But You -1	BB B-8346, MW M-8692
043253-1	Hurry Johnny Hurry -2	BB B-8320, MW M-8691
043254-1	You Gotta Take Off Your Shoes (To Sing A Hillbilly Song) -1	BB B-8320, MW M-8691

EMERSON SACRED QUARTET

Pseudonym on Supertone for the McDonald Quartette.

EMMETT & AIKEN STRING BAND

Prob.: Oscar Aiken, f; Dewey Emmett, bj; Roy Emmett, g; R.L. Emmett, vc.
   Atlanta, GA   c. July 7, 1925

9232-A	Dance In The Light Of The Moon	OK 45022

Matrix 9231 is untraced but possibly also by this group. Rev. OKeh 45022 by Clayton McMichen.

EMORY'S MALE QUARTET

Pseudonym on Broadway for Peck's Male Quartette.

FLOY ENGLAND

Floy England, v; acc. unknown.
   Dallas, TX   Friday, December 7, 1928

147589-	Zebra Dunn (Cowboy Song)	Co unissued
147590-	The Ranchman's Daughter	Co unissued

Columbia files note that this artist was Deputy Sheriff of Runnells County, Texas.

JACK ERICKSON

See Bob Miller.

ETOWAH QUARTET

Vocal quartet; acc. unknown, p.
  Atlanta, GA   Wednesday, April 18, 1928

146128-1	For Me	Co 15635-D
146129-1	Who Is That?	Co 15635-D

  Knoxville, TN   Sunday, April 6, 1930

K-8096-	Walking With My Lord	Vo 5466
K-8097-	Back In The Years	Vo 5466

EUCLID QUARTETTE

Vocal quartet; acc. unknown.
  Knoxville, TN   Saturday, August 31, 1929

K-158-	Kneel At The Cross	Vo rejected
K-159-	Jesus Paid It All	Vo rejected

THE EVA QUARTETTE

Vocal quartet; acc. unknown, o.
  Birmingham, AL   c. July 13, 1927

GEX-710	They Crucified My Savior	Ge 6335, Ch 15411, Sil 5209, 8172, Spt 9268, Chg 404, Spr 322
GEX-711	While The Years Roll On	Sil 8175, Spt 9271
GEX-712	Rock Of Ages	Ge rejected
GEX-713	Bringing In The Sheaves	Ge 6335, Ch 15448, Sil 8175, 8261, Spt 9271, Chg 402, Spr 365, Bell 1180, Her 75567

Champion 15411, 15448 as by **Dixie Sacred Quartette**. Silvertone 5209, 8172, 8175, Supertone 9268 possibly, and Challenge 404 definitely, as by **Dixie Sacred Singers**. Silvertone 8261 as by **Hamlin Quartette**. Supertone 9271 as by **Brockman Sacred Singers**. Challenge 402 as by **Ellington Sacred Quartette**. Superior 322, 365, Herwin 75567 credits uncertain. Revs: Champion 15411, Superior 322, Herwin 75567 by Woodlawn Quartette; Silvertone 5209 untraced; Silvertone 8172, 8261, Supertone 9268, Challenge 402, Superior 365 by McDonald Quartette.

Eva Quartette With W.J. Smith: v quartet (or quintet?); acc. unknown, o.
  Birmingham, AL   c. August 11, 1927

GEX-792-A	You Can't Make A Monkey Out Of Me	Ge 6239, Ch 15431, Sil 5072, 8169, Spt 9265, Chg 404, Her 75575
GEX-793,-A	Jesus Is Over All	Ge rejected
GEX-794	How Wonderful Heaven Must Be	Ge 6239, Sil 5076, 8171, Spt 9267, Bell 1180, Her 75573
GEX-795	Nearer My God To Thee	Ge 6420, Ch 15448, Sil 5072, 8169, Spt 9265, Chg 339

Champion 15431, 15448 as by **Dixie Sacred Quartette**. Silvertone 5072, 5076, 8169, 8171 possibly, Supertone 9265, 9267, Challenge 339, 404 definitely, as by **Dixie Sacred Singers**. Herwin credits untraced. Revs: Gennett 6420, Silvertone 5076, 8171, Supertone 9267, Challenge 339, Herwin 75573 by Woodlawn Quartette; Champion 15431 by McDonald Quartette; Herwin 75575 by Short Creek Trio.

CLYDE EVANS BAND

Prob.: Bill Chitwood, f; C. Philip Reeve, g; Clyde Evans, g/poss. v; band v-1.
  Atlanta, GA   Monday, November 4, 1929

149365-2	How I Got My Gal	Co 15597-D
149366-2	All Gone Now -1	Co 15597-D

Clyde Evans also recorded with the Georgia Yellow Hammers, Moody Quartet, Turkey Mountain Singers, and possibly Bill Chitwood.

FRANCIS EVANS

Pseudonym on Plaza-group labels for Vernon Dalhart or Frank Luther.

FRANK EVANS

Pseudonym on Plaza-group labels for Vernon Dalhart or Frank Luther.

JOHN B. EVANS

John B. Evans, v; acc. own g.
  Ashland, KY   early February 1928

AL-141/42*	The Kicking Mule	Br 237, Au A22020
AL-143*/44	Three Nights Experience	Br 237, Au A22020

| AL-145*/46 | The Last Mile Of The Way | Br 276 |
| AL-147/48* | Mother's Grave | Br 276, Spt S2051 |

Aurora A22020 as by **Mike Long**. Rev. Supertone S2051 by Marc Williams.

ROY EVANS
This artist, though appearing in old-time series, is outside the scope of this work.

EVANS & CLARK[E]
Pseudonym on Jewel and Oriole for Vernon Dalhart & Carson Robison.

EVANS' OLD TIMER
Pseudonym on Champion for Frank Welling (see John McGhee & Frank Welling).

CLAY EVERHART
See North Carolina Cooper Boys.

EZRA OF THE BEVERLY HILL BILLIES
See The Beverly Hill Billies.

F

BOB FAGAN
Pseudonym on Challenge, Homestead, Jewel, and Oriole for Chezz Chase.

CLEOMA FALCON
See Joseph F. Falcon.

JOSEPH FALCON

Joseph F. Falcon, v; acc. own ac; Cleoma Breaux, g.
New Orleans, LA   Friday, April 27, 1928

| 146216-2 | The Waltz That Carried Me To My Grave (La Valce Qui Ma Portin D Ma Fose) | Co 15275-D, OK 90018 |
| 146217-2 | Lafayette (Allon A Luafette) | Co 15275-D, OK 90018 |

Joseph F. Falcon & (or With) Clemo Breaux: Joseph F. Falcon, ac/v-1/sp-2; Cleoma Breaux, g/v-3.
New York, NY   Monday, August 27, 1928

146904-1	Fe Fe Ponchaux -1	Co 15301-D
146905-2	A Cowboy Rider -1	Co 40502-F, OK 90002
146906-1	Vieux Airs (Old Tunes)	Co 15325-D
146907-1	Marie Buller -3	Co 40502-F, OK 90002
146908-1	Le Vieux Soulard Et Sa Femme (The Old Drunkard And His Wife) -2, 3	Co 15301-D
146909-2	La Marche De La Noce (Wedding March) -1	Co 15325-D

Matrices 146907/08 as by **Clemo Breaux & (or With) Joseph F. Falcon**.

Cleoma Breaux With Joe (or Joseph) Falcon & Ophy Breaux: Ophy Breaux, f; Joseph Falcon, ac; Cleoma Breaux, g/v.
Atlanta, GA   Thursday, April 18, 1929

| 110550-2 | Prenez Courage (Take Courage) | Co 40503-F, OK 90003 |
| 110551-1 | C'Est Si Triste Sans Lui (It Is So Blue Without Him) | Co 40508-F, OK 90008 |

Joseph Falcon With Clemo & Ophy Breaux: Ophy Breaux, f; Joseph Falcon, ac/v; Cleoma Breaux, g.
Atlanta, GA   Thursday, April 18, 1929

| 110552-2 | Poche Town | Co 40506-F, OK 90006 |
| 110553-2 | Osson | Co 40506-F, OK 90006 |

Joseph Falcon & Cleoma Breaux: Joseph Falcon, ac/v; Cleoma Breaux, g.
Atlanta, GA   Thursday, April 18, 1929

| 110554-2 | Elle M'A Oublie (She Has Forgotten Me) | Co 40508-F, OK 90008 |

Joseph Falcon With Clemo & Ophy Breaux: Ophy Breaux, f; Joseph Falcon, ac/v; Cleoma Breaux, g.
Atlanta, GA   Thursday, April 18, 1929

| 110555-2 | Quand Je Suis Partis Pour Le Texas (When I Left Home For Texas) | Co 40503-F, OK 90003 |

Joseph Falcon, v; acc. Ophy Breaux, f; own ac; Cleoma Breaux, g; unknown, tri.
Atlanta, GA   Friday, April 19, 1929

| 110556-2 | Aimer Et Perdre (To Love And Lose) | Co 40513-F, OK 90013 |
| 110557-2 | Arcadian One Step | Co 40513-F, OK 90013 |

Cleoma Breaux With Joe (or **Joseph**) **Falcon & Ophy Breaux**: Ophy Breaux, f; Joseph Falcon, ac; Cleoma Breaux, g/v.
Atlanta, GA   Friday, April 19, 1929

| 110561-2 | Mon Couer T'Appelle (My Heart Aches For You) | Co 40504-F, OK 90004 |

Intervening matrices are by Amadie Breaux, Ophy Breaux & Clemo Breaux.
Rev. Columbia 40504-F, OKeh 90004 by Amadie Breaux, Ophy Breaux & Clemo Breaux.

Jos. Falcon, ac/v-1; Cleoma Breaux Falcon, g/v-2
San Antonio, TX   Wednesday, August 8, 1934

83850-1	Le Valse De Mon Reve (Waltz Of My Dream)	BB B-2188
83851-1	Vous Etes Si Doux (You Are So Sweet) -1	BB B-2188
83852-1	La Fille A Oncle Elair (Uncle Elair's Daughter)	BB B-2191
83853-1	Ils La Volet Mon Trancas -2	BB B-2191

Joseph Falcon, v; or **Cleoma Falcon**, v-1; acc. Joseph Falcon, ac; Cleoma Breaux Falcon, g.
New Orleans, LA   Saturday, December 22, 1934

39185-A	La Valse De Madame Sosten (Mrs. Sosten Waltz)	De 17000
39186-A	Mes Yeux Bleus (My Blue Eyes) -1	De 17000
39187-A	Au Revoir Cherie (Bye Bye Sweetheart)	De 17001
39188-A	Ouvrez Grand Ma Fenetre (Raise My Window High) -1	De 17001
39189-A	Rayne Special	De 17006
39190-A	Ma Valse Preferee (My Favorite Waltz) -1	De 17005
39191-A	La Jolie Fille N'En Veut Plus De Moi (The Nice Girl Don't Want Me Any More)	De 17011
39192-A	Buvez Plus Jamais (Never Drink No More)	De 17011
39193-A	Vous Etes Gentille (You're Sweet)	De 17005
39194-A	La Valse Crowley (The Waltz Crowley) -1	De 17006
39207-A	Blues Negres (Niggar Blues) -1	De 17004
39208-A	Soucis Quand J'Etais Gamin (Troubles When I Was A Boy)	De 17004

Falcon Trio: Moise Morgan, f; Joseph F. Falcon, ac/v-1; Cleoma Breaux Falcon, g/v-2.
New Orleans, LA   Thursday, February 20, 1936

99225-1	The Waltz I Love (La Valse J'Aime) -2	BB B-2182, MW M-4879
99226-1	On My Way Back Home (En Route Chez Moi) -1	BB B-2182, MW M-4879
99227-1	My Old Used To Be (Mon Vieux D'Autrefois) -1	BB B-2185
99228-1	Poor Boy (Pauvre Garcon) -1	BB B-2185
99229-1	Raise Your Window -2	BB B-2183
99230-1	Prize Winner -1	BB B-2183
99231-1	Catahoula Stomp -2	BB B-2186
99232-1	My Favorite (Mon Favori) -2	BB B-2180, MW M-4881

Revs: Bluebird B-2180, Montgomery Ward M-4881 by Dixie Ramblers [II]; Bluebird B-2186 by Hackberry Ramblers.

Joseph Falcon, v; or **Cleoma Falcon**, v-1; acc. Moise Morgan, f; Joseph Falcon, ac-2; Cleoma Breaux Falcon, g; or **Joseph & Cleoma Falcon**-3: Joseph Falcon, ac; Cleoma Breaux Falcon, g.
New Orleans, LA   Thursday, March 12, 1936

NO-60701-A	Quand Je Quite Ta Maison (When I Leave Your Home) -2	De 17022
NO-60702-A	La Valse De Baldwin -2	De 17018
NO-60703-A	You Are Hard To Please -2	De 17019
NO-60704-	I Can't Do Without You -1, 2	De 17019
NO-60705-B	Le Vieux Breakdown (The Old Breakdown) -3	De 17022
NO-60706-A	Frisco One-Step -1, 2	De 17018
NO-60707-	L'Amour Indifferent (Careless Love) -1, 2	De 17024
NO-60708-	Pin Solitaire (Lonesome Pine) -1, 2	De 17024
NO-60709-A	Jeuste Parcque (Just Because) -1	De 17015
NO-60710-A	Pas La Belle De Personne Que Moi (Nobody's Darlin' But Mine) -1	De 17015

Joseph Falcon, ac/v-1; acc. Cleoma Breaux Falcon, g; or **Cleoma Falcon**, v-2; acc. unknown, f-3; Joseph Falcon, ac; own g.
Dallas, TX   Sunday, February 21, 1937

| 61902-A | Le Nouveau Lafayette (New Lafayette) -1 | De 17025 |

61903-A	The Waltz That Carried Me To My Grave -1	De 17048
61904-A	La Nuit De Samedi (Saturday Night Waltz) -1	De 17025
61905-A	C'Est Tard Et Le Temps Partir (It's Late And Time To Go) -1	De 17034
61906-A	Prairie De Pin (Pine Prairie)	De 17028
61907-A	Step On It -1	De 17030
61908-A	Hand Me Down My Walking Cane -2, 3	De 17059
61909-A	Bonnie Blues Eyes -2	De 17034
61910-A	C'Est Mauvais De Dire Un Mensonge (It's A Sin To Tell A Lie) -2	De 17028
61911-A	Lulu's Back In Town -2	De 17030

Joseph Falcon, v; acc. unknown, f; own ac; Cleoma Breaux Falcon, g.
Dallas, TX   Wednesday, December 15, 1937

63083-A	Blues De Leebou	De 17050
63084-A	Je Suis Se Seul (I Am So Lonely)	De 17044
63085-A	Your Last Chance	De 17059
63086-A	Louisiana Special	De 17038

Decca files give the original title of matrix 63086 as *Rayne Special*.

Cleoma Falcon, v; acc. unknown, f; Joseph Falcon, ac-1; own g.
Dallas, TX   Wednesday, December 15, 1937

63087-A	Je Suis Laissee Seule (I'm Left All Alone) -1	De 17050
63088-B	Je Suis Parti Sous Le Grand Chemin Tres Dissatisfe (I Left The Highway Very Dissatisfied) -1	De 17048
63089-A	Je Serais Vrai A Quelqu'un J'Aime (I'll Be True To The One I Love)	De 17038
63090-A	Lettres D'Amour Dans Le Sable (Love Letters In The Sand)	De 17044

Joseph Falcon recorded after 1942.

FALCON TRIO

See Joseph F. Falcon.

J.D. FARLEY

J.D. Farley, v; acc. unknown, sg; unknown, g.
San Antonio, TX   Monday, July 29, 1929

| 55291-2 | I'm A Lone Star Cowboy | Vi V-40269, MW M-4300 |
| 55292-2 | Bill Was A Texas Lad | Vi V-40269, MW M-4300 |

THE FARM HANDS

Unknown, f-1/h-2/ac-3; unknown, bj-4; unknown, g-5.
Grafton, WI   c. March 1931

L-828-2	Chicken Reel -1, 4, 5	Pm 3293
L-831-1	Speed The Plow -1, 4, 5	Pm 3293
L-833-1	The Old Hayloft Waltz -3, 4	Pm 3294
L-835-1	Bury Me Out On The Prairie -2, 5	Pm 3294

Intervening matrices are untraced but probably by this group.

FARMER SISTERS (THE TENNESSEE HARMONY GIRLS)

Vocal duet; acc. prob. one of them, g.
Jackson, MS   Friday, October 11, 1935

JAX-108-	In Lover's Lane	ARC unissued
JAX-109-	When The Roses Wave In Dixie	ARC unissued
JAX-110-	Little Green Valley	ARC unissued
JAX-111-	Louisiana Moon	ARC unissued
JAX-112-	Mississippi Valley Blues	ARC unissued

Jackson, MS   Saturday, October 12, 1935

JAX-121-1	The Maple On The Hill	Vo 03104
JAX-122-	I Know There Is Somebody Waiting	ARC unissued
JAX-123-	My Old Pal Of Yesterday	ARC unissued
JAX-124-1	You're As Welcome As The Flowers In May	Vo 03153
JAX-125-1	I Love You Best Of All	Vo 03153
JAX-126-	Little Mother Of The Hills	ARC unissued
JAX-127-	Goin' Back To Texas	ARC unissued
JAX-128-	Beautiful Texas	ARC unissued

JAX-129-	The Picture On The Wall	ARC unissued
JAX-130-	I Am Bound For That City	ARC unissued
JAX-131-	My Carolina Home	ARC unissued
JAX-132-2	Little Home in Tennessee	Vo 03104

HARRY FARR
HARVEY FARR

Pseudonyms on Supertone for Green Bailey.

DUDLEY & JAMES FAWVOR

Dudley Fawvor, James Fawvor, v duet; acc. prob. one of them, ac; the other, g.
New Orleans, LA   Monday, December 17, 1928

147660-2	T'Est Petite A Ete T'Est Meon (You Are Little And You Are Cute)	Co 40505-F, OK 90005
147661-1	La Valse De Creole (The Creole Waltz)	Co 40505-F, OK 90005

Matrix 147661 is mistitled *La Vals De Breole* on OKeh 90005.

FAY & THE JAY WALKERS

Unidentified, sg; Alex Hood, bj; Dick Parman, g; Elmer Snyder, v; Faye Cole, v-1.
Chicago, IL   Monday, April 2, 1928

20432-2	Longing For Home	Pm 3156, Bwy 8236
20433-1	Those Dark Eyes I Love So Well -1	Pm 3156, Bwy 8236

Dick Parman, v/y; acc. unknown, p.
Chicago, IL   Monday, April 2, 1928

20436-2	Rock All Our Babies To Sleep	Pm 3100, Bwy 8093

Unidentified, sg; Alex Hood, bj; Dick Parman, g; Elmer Snyder, v.
Chicago, IL   Monday, April 2, 1928

20439-1	My Baby Don't Love Me	Pm 3100, Bwy 8093

Broadway 8093 as by **The Bums**.
The listed four names were remembered by Dick Parman as the members of the group. The distribution of vocal and instrumental roles is conjectural. The steel guitar was presumably played by Snyder or Cole. Intervening matrices are untraced.

FRANK FERERA

Of this Hawaiian guitarist's many recordings, two were issued in the Paramount Old Time Tunes series (3133); they are beyond the scope of this work.

JOHN FERGUS

Pseudonym on Silvertone 4019 for David Miller.

BOB FERGUSON [& HIS SCALAWAGGERS]

Pseudonym on Columbia for Bob Miller.

JOHN FERGUSON

Pseudonym on Challenge for Welby Toomey, on Silvertone for George Ake, and on Supertone for David Miller.

FERGUSON & CLARK

Pseudonym on Clarion and Velvet Tone for Elzie Floyd & Leo Boswell.

FIDDLER JOE & HIS BOYS

See Joseph Samuels.

ARTHUR FIELDS & FRED HALL

Arthur Fields (whose real name was Abe Finkelstein) was a vocalist in great demand, and Fred Hall a busy contractor, pianist, vocalist, and bandleader, in the New York recording studios of the late '20s and early '30s. Much of their work is outside the boundaries of this book; some of it is documented, under both names, in JR. However, in 1928-32 they recorded a good deal of hillbilly-styled material, mostly written by them and often accompanied by a circle of musicians with whom they also broadcast regularly as the Rex Cole Mountaineers. Of the groups listed below, Jim Cole's Tennessee Mountaineers, Rex Cole Mountaineers, Sam Cole & His Corn Huskers, Fred "Sugar" Hall & His Sugar Babies, Buck Wilson & His Rangers, and Eddie Younger & His Mountaineers all appear to be drawn from this pool of musicians (but note that Fred "Sugar" Hall & His Sugar Babies were also credited with numerous novelty or hot dance recordings).
The other artist credits denote Fields & Hall, or Fields as a soloist, with generally smaller groups of probably different musicians. Fields recorded very prolifically for Grey Gull/Radiex; the items listed below are some, but quite likely not all, of those that fall within the scope of this work.

Arthur Fields, v; acc. unknown f; unknown, p.
New York, NY   c. May 1927

| 2392-C,-D | The Terrible Mississippi Flood | GG/Rad 2334 |
| 2393-F | The End Of The Shenandoah | GG/Rad 2334 |

Acc. unknown, f; unknown, h-1; unknown, g.
New York, NY   c. June 1927

| 2444-C | The Little Black Mustache -1 | GG/Rad 4144 |
| 2445-A | The Pickwick Club Tragedy | GG/Rad 4086, Globe 4086, Supreme 4086 |

Grey Gull 4086, Radiex 4086, and possibly Globe 4086, Supreme 4086 as by **Bob Thomas**.
Rev. Grey Gull/Radiex 4144 by Arthur Fields (popular).

Acc. unknown, f; unknown, g; unknown, wh; unknown, train-wh eff.
New York, NY   c. June/July 1927

| 2511-A,-B,-C | Wreck Of The Old '97 | GG/Rad 4131, Globe 4131, Supreme 4131, VD/Mad 5085 |

Grey Gull/Radiex (etc.) 4131 was issued in several forms. Issues using Fields' matrix 2511 were variously credited to **Arthur Fields**, **Jeff** (or **Jess**) **Calhoun**, **Mr. X**, and **Vel Veteran**; but note that **Jeff** (or **Jess**) **Calhoun** was also used for a Vernon Dalhart recording of *Wreck Of The Old 97* (matrix 2343-E) on an earlier issue of Grey Gull/Radiex (etc.) 4131.
Van Dyke/Madison 5085 as by **Vel Veteran**. The control 309 appears on some issues.
Revs: Grey Gull/Radiex (etc.) 4131 by Vernon Dalhart or Frank Luther; Van Dyke/Madison 5085 by Frank Luther.

Acc. unknown.
New York, NY   c. January/February 1928

| 2702-A | Girl I Left Behind Me | GG/Rad 4153 |

Rev. Grey Gull/Radiex 4153 by Arthur Fields (popular).

Acc. unknown, cl; unknown, o.
New York, NY   c. February 1928

| 2733-A,-B | Floyd Collin's [sic] Fate | GG/Rad 4086, Globe 4086, Supreme 4086, Mad 1607 |

Grey Gull/Radiex 4086 (etc?) as by **Bob Thomas**. Madison 1607 as by **James Cummings**. A later issue of Grey Gull 4086 replaces matrix 2733 with matrix 3819 (see below).

Acc. unknown, f; poss. unknown, h; unknown, g.
New York, NY   c. February 1928

| 2738-A,-B | In The Baggage Coach Ahead | GG/Rad 4090, Globe 4090, Supreme 4090, Sr 33015 |

Sunrise 33015 as by **Jack Ramsey**.
Rev. Grey Gull/Radiex (etc.) 4090 by John Ryan (popular).
Recordings of *In The Baggage Coach Ahead* using matrix 2738-F on Van Dyke/Madison 5074 as by **Harry Conway**, or matrix 2738-G on Grey Gull 4268 as by **Jerry White** and Van Dyke 74268 as by **Ben Litchfield**, are believed not to be by Fields.

Acc. unknown, f; unknown, ac-1; unknown, sg-1; unknown, g; unknown, bell-2.
New York, NY   c. June 1928

2965-A	The Drunkard's Lone Child -1	GG/Rad 4200, ?VD 74200
2966-B	The Picture That's Turned To The Wall	GG/Rad 2409, 4185, ?VD 74185
2967-B	The Fatal Wedding -2	GG/Rad 4208, ?VD 74208, VD/Mad 5078
2968-B	Just Before The Battle, Mother	GG/Rad 4201, ?VD 74201
2969-A,-B	The Vacant Chair	GG/Rad 4205, ?VD 74205
2970-A,-B	Break The News To Mother	GG/Rad 4178, ?VD 74178, VD/Mad 5074
2971-A,-B	Mother's Old Red Shawl	GG/Rad 4205, ?VD 74205

Van Dyke/Madison 5074, 5078 as by **George French**.
Revs: Grey Gull/Radiex 4178 (etc.) by Arthur Fields (popular); 2409, 4185, 4201 by John Ryan (popular); 4200 by Frank Luther; Van Dyke/Madison 5074 popular, 5078 by Vernon Dalhart or Frank Luther.

Henry Williams: prob. Arthur Fields, v; acc. unknown.
New York, NY   ?c. June/July 1928

| 31304-2 | The Wreck Of The '97 | Marathon 043 |
| 31305-2 | The Train That Never Arrived | Marathon 043 |

Arthur Fields, v; acc. unknown, f; unknown, h; unknown, g.
New York, NY   c. July 1928

| 2996-A,-B | The Engineer's Dying Child | GG/Rad 4208, ?VD 74208 |

Later issues of (at least) Grey Gull 4208 use take D by Frank Luther, credited to either **Frank Luther** or **Tom Cook**. This D take is believed to be the only one used on Madison (and possibly Van Dyke) 5077, also as by **Tom Cook**.

Pop Collins (Old Timber) & His Boys: prob. Arthur Fields, v; acc. unknown, f; unknown, ac (or o?); unknown, g.
New York, NY   Monday, August 20, 1928

| 18665-A | A Mother's Dying Wish | Ed 52426, 5619 |

N-373-	A Mother's Dying Wish	Ed unissued
18666-A	The Train That Never Arrived	Ed 52426
N-374-	The Train That Never Arrived	Ed unissued

Edison files comment on the N- masters: N-373 "A – OK," N-374 "B – OK"

Arthur Fields, v; acc. unknown, g.
New York, NY   c. August 1928

3062-A	Hallelujah I'm A Bum	GG/Rad 2418, 4228, ?VD 74228, Mad 1642
3062-C	Hallelujah I'm A Bum	GG/Rad 2418, 4228, ?VD 74228, Mad 1938
3063-B	The Bum Song	GG/Rad 2417

Madison 1642 as by **John Bennett**, 1938 as by **George French**.
Revs: Grey Gull/Radiex 2417 by Honey Duke & His Uke (Johnny Marvin), 2418 by Al Bernard (popular); Madison 1642 untraced, 1938 by Frank Kamplain (popular).

Arthur Fields, v; acc. unknown, f; prob. unknown, as; unknown, p.
New York, NY   c. September 1928

| 3143-A,-B | The Dying Hobo | GG/Rad 4228, ?VD 74228 |

Vel Veteran: prob. Arthur Fields, v; acc. unknown, f; unknown, g.
New York, NY   c. September 1928

| 3157-B | The Murder Of Little Marion Parker | GG/Rad 4237, ?VD 74237 |

New York, NY   c. October/November 1928

| 3193-A | The Pardon Came Too Late | GG/Rad 4237, ?VD 74237 |

Acc. unknown, f; unknown, h; unknown, g; unknown, jh; unknown, v-1.
New York, NY   c. November 1928

3220-B	Barbara Allen	GG/Rad 4239, ?VD 74239
3221-A	O Bury Me Not On The Lone Prairie	GG/Rad 4239, ?VD 74239
3222-A	Common Bill -1	GG/Rad 4232, ?VD 74232

Some issues of matrix 3220 as by **Jeff Calhoun**.
Rev. Grey Gull/Radiex 4232 popular.

Pop Collins (Old Timber) & His Boys: prob. Arthur Fields, v; acc. unknown, f; unknown, ac (or o?); unknown, g.
New York, NY   Wednesday, January 16, 1929

19011-B	I'd Like To Send A Message Up To Heaven	Ed 52507
N-702-A,-B	I'd Like To Send A Message Up To Heaven	Ed rejected
19012-A,-B	Pappy's Buried On The Hill	Ed 52507
N-703-A,-B	Pappy's Buried On The Hill	Ed rejected

Ned Cobben: poss. Arthur Fields, v; acc. unknown.
New York, NY   Wednesday, February 27, 1929

| 147998-2 | Barnacle Bill The Sailor | Ha 861-H, Ve 1861-V, Di 2861-G |
| 147999-3 | Mountains Ain't No Place For Bad Men | Ha 861-H, Ve 1861-V, Di 2861-G |

Ned Cobben has been taken to be a pseudonym for Vernon Dalhart, but the weight of expert opinion supports the case for Arthur Fields. Another possible candidate is the popular singer Irving Kaufman.

Vel Veteran: prob. Arthur Fields, v; acc. unknown, s (?); unknown, h; unknown, p; unknown, jh.
New York, NY   c. February/March 1929

| 3277-D | Rock Candy Mountain | GG/Rad 4225, ?VD 74225 |
| 3277-E | Rock Candy Mountain | Mad 1934 |

Madison 1934 as by **Ben Butler**.
Revs: Grey Gull/Radiex 4225 by Al Bernard (popular); Madison 1934 by Frank Kamplain (popular).

Ned Cobben: poss. Arthur Fields, v; acc. unknown, f; unknown, g; unknown, wh duet-1.
New York, NY   Friday, March 22, 1929

| 148122-1 | The Copper And The Gunman | Ha 883-H, Ve 1883-V, Di 2883-G, Puritone 1090-S |
| 148123-2 | The Utah Trail -1 | Ha 883-H, Ve 1883-V, Di 2883-G, Puritone 1090-S |

Matrices 148122/23 were logged as by **Ned Cobbin** but issued as shown.

Poss. Arthur Fields, v/wh; acc. unknown, f; unknown, g.
New York, NY   Thursday, April 18, 1929

| 148450-3 | Red River Valley | Ha 901-H, Ve 1901-V, Di 2901-G, Puritone 1089-S |
| 148451-1 | My Carolina Home | Ha 901-H, Ve 1901-V, Di 2901-G, Puritone 1089-S |

Eddie Powers: Arthur Fields, v; acc. unknown, f; unknown, ac; unknown, g.
New York, NY   Thursday, May 9, 1929

148491-2	The Story Of The Gambler	Ha 927-H, Ve 1927-V, Di 2927-G
148492-1	The Train That Never Arrived	Ha 927-H, Ve 1927-V, Di 2927-G
148493-	Oh Gee, There Ain't No Justice	Ha unissued
148494-	The Shoes We Have Left Are All Right	Ha unissued

Matrix 148493 was logged as by **Arthur Fields**.

New York, NY   Thursday, July 11, 1929

148800-2	A Mother's Dying Wish	Ha 972-H, Ve 1972-V, Di 2972-G
148801-1	Pappy Is Buried On The Hill	Ha 994-H, Ve 1994-V, Di 2994-G
148802-3	I'd Like To Take An Aeroplane To Heaven	Ha 994-H, Ve 1994-V, Di 2994-G
148803-1	The Warden's Secret	Ha 972-H, Ve 1972-V, Di 2972-G

Arthur Fields & Fred Hall, v/sp duet; acc. poss. Philip D'Arcy, f; unknown, md; poss. Al Russo, g; poss. Joseph Mayo, gong; several men, v/sp.

New York, NY   Wednesday, November 27, 1929

| 149643-2 | Song Of The Condemned | Ha 1079-H, Ve 2079-V, Di 3079-G, CoE DB112, CoAu DO182 |

Arthur Fields, v/sp; **Fred Hall**, sp; acc. poss. Philip D'Arcy, f; unknown, f; poss. Al Russo, g; unknown woman, sp.

New York, NY   Wednesday, November 27, 1929

| 149644-1 | The Song Of The Blind Man | Ha 1079-H, Ve 2079-V, Di 3079-G, CoE DB112, CoAu DO182 |

Bob Thomas: Arthur Fields, v; acc. unknown, f; unknown, o.

New York, NY   December 1929/January 1930

| 3819-A | Floyd Collins' Fate | GG 4086 |

Matrix 3819 replaced matrix 2733-A on later (blue and gold label) pressings of Grey Gull 4086, though still coupled with matrix 2445-A.

Lem Green (The Singing Rambler): prob. Arthur Fields, v; acc. unknown.

New York, NY   Monday, January 6, 1930

| 403586- | The Whistle Song | OK unissued |
| 403587- | I'm On The Chain Gang Now | OK unissued |

Eddie Younger & His Mountaineers: poss.: Philip D'Arcy, f/h; Leo McConville, t; Eddie Grosso, cl; Charles Magnante, ac; Fred Hall, p; unknown, jh; unknown, j; Arthur Fields, v.

New York, NY   Thursday, January 9, 1930

| 149748-3 | I Love Virginia | Ve 7062-V, Di 6036-G, Cl 5165-C |
| 149749-2 | Down At The Bottom Of The Mountain | Ve 7062-V, 7077-V, Di 6036-G, Cl 5047-C |

Regarding Velvet Tone 7077-V, see note to May 26, 1930 session.

Joe & Zeb Gaunt: Arthur Fields, Fred Hall, v duet; acc. poss.: Philip D'Arcy or Tom Vodola, f; Charles Magnante, ac; Al Russo, poss. bj/g; unknown, jh-1.

New York, NY   Thursday, January 9, 1930

| 149750-1; 403761-A | Jew's Harp Bill -1 | Ha 1091-H, Ve 2091-V, Di 3091-G, Cl 5165-C, OK 45418, PaE E6357, PaAu A3061, ReE MR243, ReAu G21044, Ariel Z4673 |
| 149751-3 | I'll Think Of You Sweetheart | Ha 1091-H, Ve 2091-V, Di 3091-G |

OKeh 45418, Parlophone A3061, E6357, prob. Ariel Z4673 as by **Greene Brothers**. Regal MR243, G21044 as by **The Regal Rascals**.
Revs: Parlophone A3061 by Gene Autry, E6357, prob. Ariel Z4673 by Pete Wiggins (Frank Luther); Regal MR243, G21044 by Vernon Dalhart.

Lem Greene: prob. Arthur Fields, v; acc. poss.: Charles Magnante, ac; Al Russo, g.

New York, NY   Tuesday, January 28, 1930

| 403696-A | Eleven Months And Ten More Days | OK 45418 |

Eddie Younger & His Mountaineers: poss.: Philip D'Arcy or Tom Vodola, f; Leo McConville, t; Eddie Grosso or Philip D'Arcy, h; Charles Magnante, ac; poss. Andy Sannella, sg-1; Fred Hall, p; unknown, jh; unknown, j; Arthur Fields, v; unknown, y-2.

New York, NY   Thursday, February 6, 1930

149966-2; 404027-	Maw And Paw And Me	Ve 7069-V, Di 6043-G, Cl 5020-C, OK 45450
149967-2	The Apple Song	Ve 7069-V, Di 6043-G, Cl 5108-C, ReE MR209, RZAu G22150
149968-2; 404028-	Georgia Home -1	Ve 7065-V, Di 6039-G, Cl 5039-C, OK 45450
149969-3; 403975-	The Waltz Of The Hills -2	Ve 7065-V, Di 6039-G, Cl 5021-C, OK 45439, ReE MR209, RZAu G22150

OKehs as by **Fred "Sugar" Hall & His Sugar Babies**. Regal MR209, Regal Zonophone G22150 as by **Alabama Barnstormers**. Leo McConville may not be present on all items.

Buck Wilson & His Rangers: poss.: Philip D'Arcy, f/h-1; Tom Vodola, f; Leo McConville, t; Charles Magnante, ac; Al Russo, g; unknown, j; Arthur Fields, v.
    New York, NY   Friday, March 21, 1930

150107-2	When It's Springtime In The Rockies -1	Ha 1129-H, Ve 2129-V, Di 3129-G, Cl 5004-C
150108-3; 403976-	In Dear Old Tennessee (Where Someone Waits For Me)	Ha 1129-H, Ve 2129-V, 7127-V, Di 3129-G, Cl 5085-C, OK 45439

Clarion 5085-C, Velvet Tone 7127-V as by **Eddie Younger & His Mountaineers**. OKeh 45439 as by **Fred "Sugar" Hall & His Sugar Babies**. Rev. Clarion 5004-C by Jerry Mason & His Californians (popular).

Fields & Hall, v duet; acc. unknown.
    New York, NY   c. March 26, 1930

GEX-2650	The Whistle Song	Ge rejected

Matrices GEX-2647 to 2649 are by Tin Pan Paraders with vocal(s) by Fields (& Hall).

Arthur Fields, v; acc. unknown, f; unknown, g.
    New York, NY   ?c. March 1930

	The Warden's Secret	QRS 1034
	Story Of The Gambler	QRS 1034

Buck Wilson & His Rangers-1/Eddie Younger & His Mountaineers-2: poss.: Philip D'Arcy, f; Tom Vodola, f; Leo McConville, t; Charles Magnante, ac; Al Russo, g; unknown, jh; Arthur Fields, v.
    New York, NY   Monday, April 7, 1930

150176-2	They Cut Down The Old Pine Tree-1	Ha 1142-H, Ve 2142-V, Di 3142-G
150177-1	The Lonesome Trail -1	Ha 1142-H, Ve 2142-V, Di 3142-G
150178-	I'm Looking Ahead -2	Ve 7085-V, Di 6059-G, Cl 5166-C
150179-	I'm In Heaven -2	Ve 7085-V, Di 6059-G, Cl 5167-C

Arthur Fields & His Trio: Arthur Fields, v; acc. poss. Al Russo, g; poss. Joseph Mayo, gong; unknown, v trio.
    New York, NY   Thursday, April 24, 1930

150487-3	Temperance Is Coming	Ha 1159-H, Ve 2159-V, Di 3159-G
150488-	Tom Noonan (Bishop Of Chinatown)	Ha 1153-H, Ve 2153-V, Di 3153-G
150489-	You Can't Win	Ha 1153-H, Ve 2153-V, Di 3153-G

Accompaniment details are known only for matrix 150487.

Mopey Dick: prob. Arthur Fields, v; acc. unknown, g.
    New York, NY   Friday, April 25, 1930

(1)9643-1,-2	I'm Glad I'm A Bum	Ba 0742, Ca 0342, Do 4582, Je 5992, Or 1992, Pe 12623, Re 10047, Ro 1355, Cq 7567, 7836
(1)9644-1	I'll Get Along Somehow	Ba 0738, Ca 0338, Je 5989, Or 1989, Pe 12623, Ro 1353, Cq 7567, 7836

Rev. all issues of matrix 9643, except Perfect 12623, Conqueror 7567, 7836, by Frank Marvin. Rev. all issues of matrix 9644, except Perfect 12623, Conqueror 7567, 7836, by Billy Murray & Walter Scanlan (popular).

Arthur Fields, v; acc. poss.: Charles Magnante, ac; Al Russo, g.
    New York, NY   Friday, May 2, 1930

150499-2	Good News From Home	Ha 1159-H, Ve 2159-V, Di 3159-G

Fred "Sugar" Hall & His Sugar Babies: poss.: Philip D'Arcy or Tom Vodola, f; Eddie Grosso, cl; Charles Magnante, ac; Al Russo, g; unknown, vc(?); unknown, jh; Arthur Fields, v.
    New York, NY   Monday, May 19, 1930

150441- ; 404043-C	Bury Me In The Tennessee Mountains	OK 41425
150442- ; 404044-A	When I Look To The West (I Think Of You)	OK 41425
150443-	When It's Winter In The Ozarks	Co unissued
150444-	The Mosquito Song	Co unissued

This session was logged by Columbia as by **Fields & Hall**, but OKeh 41425 was issued as shown.

Eddie Younger & His Mountaineers: poss.: Philip D'Arcy, f/h-1; Tom Vodola, f; Leo McConville, t; Eddie Grosso, cl-2; Charles Magnante, ac; Fred Hall, p (if present); unknown, jh-3; Arthur Fields, v; unknown, v duet-4.
    New York, NY   Monday, May 26, 1930

150533-2	Rocky Mountain Sal	Ve 7077-V, Di 6051-G, Cl 5021-C
150534-2	Where The Colorado's Flowing	Ve 7077-V, Di 6051-G, Cl 5047-C
150535-2	Down By The Old Cabin Door -2, 3, 4	Ve 7084-V, Di 6058-G, Cl 5039-C
150536-2	Long, Lean, Lanky Lew -1, 2, 3	Ve 7084-V, Di 6058-G, Cl 5020-C

Velvet Tone 7077-V was issued in two forms, coupling matrices 150533/34 or matrices 150534/149749 (for the latter matrix see January 9, 1930 session).

Sam Cole & His Corn Huskers: poss.: Philip D'Arcy, f; Tom Vodola, f; Leo McConville, t; Eddie Grosso or Philip D'Arcy, h-1; Charles Magnante, ac; Fred Hall, p; Al Russo, g; unknown, jh-2; Arthur Fields, v.
    New York, NY   c. June 15, 1930

9804-2	Down At The Bottom Of The Mountain -2	Ba 0770, Ca 0370, Do 4602, Je 6023, Or 2023, Pe 11303, Re 10077, Ro 1386, Cq 7595, 7738
9806-1	In 1992 -1, 2	Ba 0770, Ca 0370, Do 4622, Je 6023, Or 2023, Re 10077, Ro 1386, Cq 7611, 7751
9807-2,-3	Rocky Mountain Sal	Ba 0799, Ca 0399, Do 4602, Je 6049, Or 2049, Pe 11303, Re 10105, Ro 1414, Cq 7595, 7738
9808-1,-2,-3	In Dear Old Tennessee	Ba 0799, Ca 0399, Do 4622, Je 6049, Or 2049, Re 10105, Ro 1414, Cq 7611, 7751

Matrix 9805 is by Chick Bullock (popular).

Eddie Younger & His Mountaineers: poss.: Tom Vodola, f; Leo McConville, t; Eddie Grosso, cl-1; Philip D'Arcy, h; Charles Magnante, ac; Al Russo, g; unknown, jh; Arthur Fields, v.
    New York, NY   Monday, August 25, 1930

150726-2	After The Old Barn Dance -1	Ve 7089-V, Di 6063-G, Cl 5067-C
150727-1	Me And My Brother Joe	Ve 7091-V, Di 6065-G, Cl 5067-C
150728-	She Cost Two Dollars And Seventy Cents	Ve 7091-V, Di 6065-G, Cl 5166-C
150729-1	On The Old Hay Ride In The Mornin' -1	Ve 7089-V, 7127-V, Di 6063-G, Cl 5085-C

Joe & Zeb Gaunt: Arthur Fields, Fred Hall, v duet; acc. poss.: Tom Vodola, f; Eddie Grosso, cl; Al Russo, g.
    New York, NY   Wednesday, October 8, 1930

150867-1	That Goes On For Days And Days	Ha 1238-H, Ve 2238-V, Di 3238-G, Cl 5183-C
150868-2	Those Were The Very Last Words He Said	Ha 1238-H, Ve 2238-V, 2285-V, Di 3238-G, Cl 5184-C

Clarion 5183-C, 5184-C, Velvet Tone 2285-V as by **Hall Brothers**.
Rev. Clarion 5183-C, 5184-C by Sammy Fain (popular).

Eddie Younger & His Mountaineers: poss.: Philip D'Arcy, f/poss. oc-1; Tom Vodola, f; Leo McConville, t; Eddie Grosso, cl; Eddie Grosso or Philip D'Arcy, h; Charles Magnante, pac; Al Russo, g; Al Morse or Gus Helleberg, sb (if present); unknown, jh; Arthur Fields, v; band v-2.
    New York, NY   Monday, October 20, 1930

150886-1	Back In The Old Green Hills	Ve 7119-V, 7125-V, Cl 5168-C
150887-3	If You See My Little Mountain Girl -2	Ve 7119-V, Cl 5167-C
150888-2	He Would Hum A Little Tune All Day Long -1	Ve 7122-V, Cl 5108-C
150889-2	Gonna Buy Me A Brand New Suit	Ve 7122-V, 7125-V, Cl 5168-C

Rex Cole Mountaineers: poss.: Philip D'Arcy, f/piccolo-1; Tom Vodola, f; Leo McConville, t; Eddie Grosso or Philip D'Arcy, h-2; Charles Magnante, pac; poss. Andy Sannella, sg-3; Fred Hall, p; Al Russo, bj; Al Morse or Gus Helleberg, sb; unknown, jh-4; Arthur Fields, v.
    New York, NY   Friday, November 7, 1930

E-35275-A	She's Too Good For Me -2, 4	Me 12036, Po P9070, Au 22022, Pan 25006, PanAu P12036, DeE F5951
E-35276-B	I Laughed So Hard I Nearly Died -1, 2, 4	Me 12036, Po P9070, Au 22022, Pan 25006, PanAu P12036, DeE F5951
E-35277-	Wilderness -3	Me M12055, Po P9060, PanAu P12055
E-35278-	I'm Pining For The Pines And Caroline -3	Me M12055, Po P9060, PanAu P12055

Aurora A22022 as by **Rocky Mountaineers**.

Sam Cole & His Corn Huskers: poss.: Tom Vodola, f; Philip D'Arcy, f/piccolo/wh-1; Leo McConville, t; Eddie Grosso, cl-2; Eddie Grosso or Philip D'Arcy, h; Charles Magnante, pac; Fred Hall, p; Al Russo, g; unknown, jh; Arthur Fields, v.
    New York, NY   Monday, December 29, 1930

10337-3	Ma And Pa And Me	Ba 32149, Pe 15458, Re 10328, Cq 7757
10338-2	The Whistle Song -1	Ba 32149, Pe 15458, Re 10328, Cq 7757
10339-3	On The Old Hay Ride In The Morning -2	Ba 32085, Je 6206, Or 2206, Pe 15420, Re 10263, Ro 1571, Cq 7703
10340-2	After The Old Barn Dance	Ba 32085, Je 6206, Or 2206, Pe 15420, Re 10263, Ro 1571, Cq 7703

Matrices 10337/38 are believed to have been issued on Oriole and Romeo, and possibly Jewel, but no issue-numbers have been traced.

Rex Cole Mountaineers: poss.: Tom Vodola, f; Philip D'Arcy, f-1/h-2; Leo McConville, t; Charles Magnante, pac; Andy Sannella, sg-3/g-4; Al Morse or Gus Helleberg, sb; Arthur Fields (logged as "Long Tom"), v; Frank Kamplain, y-5.
    New York, NY   Friday, January 16, 1931

E-35803-	Dancing 'Round The Apple Tree -2, 4	Me M12281, Po P9090
E-35804-	Yazoo, Mississippi -2?, 4	Me M12281, Po P9090
E-35805-	The Waltz Of The Hills -1, 3, 5	Me M12085, Po P9019, PanAu P12085
E-35806-	There's A Blue Sky Out Yonder -1, 3	Me M12085, Po P9019, PanAu P12085

Eddie Younger & His Mountaineers: poss.: Tom Vodola or Philip D'Arcy, f; Leo McConville, t-1; Eddie Grosso, cl-2/h-3; Charles Magnante, pac; Al Russo, g; Al Morse or Gus Helleberg, sb; unknown, oc; unknown, jh; Arthur Fields, v.
New York, NY   Friday, January 23, 1931

151240-	The Old Family Album	Ve 2337-V, Cl 5271-C
151241-	Hang It In The Hen House	Ve 2337-V, Cl 5271-C
151242-2	Empty Barrels -1, 2	Ve 2410-V, Cl 5346-C
151243-1	She Lives 'Round The Bend A Ways -2, 3	Ve 2410-V, Cl 5346-C

Colt Brothers: Arthur Fields, Fred Hall, v duet; acc. Rex Cole Mountaineers: poss.: unknown, f; Eddie Grosso, cl; Charles Magnante, pac; unknown, bj; Al Russo, g.
New York, NY   Thursday, February 5, 1931

| E-36025- | Eleven More Months And Ten More Days Pt 1 | Me M12106, Pan 25029, PanAu P12106, Mayfair G2000 |
| E-36026- | Eleven More Months And Ten More Days Pt 2 | Me M12106, Pan 25029, PanAu P12106, Mayfair G2000 |

Mayfair G2000 as by **Al & Pete Livingstone With Original Buckle Busters**.

Gunboat Billy & The Sparrow: Arthur Fields, Fred Hall, v duet; or **The Sparrow**: Arthur Fields, v-1/sp-2; acc. poss. Eddie Grosso, cl-3/h-4; poss. Charles Magnante, ac-5; poss. Al Russo, bj-6/g-7; unknown woman, sp-8.
New York, NY   c. February 1931

1191-1	Eleven More Months And Ten More Days -3, 5, 6	Cr 3077, Vs 5063
1192-1	Oh For The Life Of A Hobo -1, 2, 4, 7, 8	Cr 3077, Vs 5100
1193-2	I Hate To Be Called A Hobo -1, 4, 5, 7	Cr 3097, CrC/MeC 93015, Stg 293015, Roy 393015, Vs 5100
1194-1 (1975)	Eleven More Months And Ten More Days – Part 2 -3, 5, 6	Cr 3097, Pm 3273, Bwy 8254, CrC/MeC 93015, Stg 293015, Roy 393015, Vs 5063, Lyric 3371, Summit Z116

Varsitys as **Fields & Hall**. Summit Z116 as **Sundy & Mundy**.
The title of matrix 1194 omits – Part 2 on Lyric 3371.
Some issues of matrix 1194 use the control 1975.
Revs: Paramount 3273, Broadway 8254, Lyric 3371 by Luther Brothers (see Carson Robison); Summit Z116 by Adelyne Hood.

Mopey Dick: prob. Arthur Fields, v; acc. poss. Eddie Grosso, h; poss. Al Russo, g; Rosaline Greene, sp-1.
New York, NY   Monday, March 16, 1931

| E-36475-A | Oh! For The Life Of A Hobo -1 | Me M12136, Pan 25277 |
| E-36476- | I Hate To Be Called A Hobo | Me M12136, Pan 25277 |

Jim Cole's Tennessee Mountaineers: poss.: Tom Vodola, f; Eddie Grosso, cl; Charles Magnante, pac; Andy Sannella, sg; Al Russo, g; Arthur Fields, v.
New York, NY   c. March 1931

1252-	I'm Pining For The Pines And Caroline	Cr 3102, Summit Z146
1253-	Lonesome Road	Cr 3102
	Rocky Mountain Sal	Cr 3122
	Oh Bury Me Beneath The Willow	Cr 3122

Rev. Summit Z146 by Jay Wilbur (popular).

Poss.: Tom Vodola, f; Leo McConville, t; Eddie Grosso, h-1; Charles Magnante, pac; Andy Sannella, sg-2; Al Russo, bj-3/g-4; Gus Helleberg, tu; unknown, oc; unknown, jh; Arthur Fields, v; Fred Hall, v-5; unknown, y-6.
New York, NY   c. April 1931

1304-2	Old Folks Dance Medley – Part 1 -1, 3	Cr 3158, CrC/MeC 93024, Vs 5042
1305-2	Old Folks Dance Medley – Part 2 -3	Cr 3158, CrC/MeC 93024, Vs 5042
1306-2	Waltz Of The Hills -2, 4, 6	Cr 3142
1307-2	Down In The Valley -2, 4, 5	Cr 3142

Crown/Melotone 93024 as by **Jim Cole's Mountaineers**. Varsity 5042 as by **The Broadcast Boys**.
Matrix 1304 is titled *Home Folk Songs*, and matrix 1305 *Sourwood Mountain*, on Varsity 5042.

Rex Cole Mountaineers: Arthur Fields, Fred Hall, v duet; acc. unknown.
New York, NY   Wednesday, June 10, 1931

| 365017- | Dancing 'Round The Apple Tree | Ve 2418-V, Cl 5354-C |

Acc. poss.: Philip D'Arcy, f/piccolo (or oc)/h-1; Leo McConville, t; Charles Magnante, pac; Al Russo, g; unknown, jh-2; unknown, bones-3.
New York, NY   Wednesday, June 17, 1931

365018-2	Cousin Cindy's Wedding	Ve 2437-V, Cl 5373-C
365019-	I'll Marry May In June	Ve 2418-V, Cl 5354-C
365020-2	Henry, Did You Weed The Cabbage Patch ("Yes, Pappy, Yes")	Ve 2437-V, Cl 5373-C

| 365021-1 | I Don't Need No 'Lasses To Sweeten Liza Jane | Ve 2449-V, Cl 5385-C |
| 365022-2 | Our Happy Little Cabin Home -1, 2, 3 | Ve 2449-V, Cl 5385-C |

Colt Brothers: Arthur Fields, Fred Hall, v/sp duet; acc. Rex Cole Mountaineers: poss.: Tom Vodola or Adelyne Hood, f-1; Eddie Grosso, cl-2; Charles Magnante, pac; Al Russo, bj-3/g-4.

New York, NY   Monday, January 18, 1932

11136-	Eleven More Months And Ten More Days Pt 3 -2, 3	Me M12314, Pan 25166
11137-	Eleven More Months And Ten More Days Pt 4 -2, 3	Me M12314, Pan 25166
11138-A	That Goes On For Days And Days Pt 1 -1, 4	Me M12333, Pan 25204, DeE F3129

Panachord 25204 as by **The Colt Brothers**. Decca F3129 as by **Beverley Buckle Busters**; Pt 1 is omitted from the title of matrix 11138 on that issue. The accompaniment credit to Rex Cole Mountaineers is omitted on Melotone M12333.

Acc. Rex Cole Mountaineers: poss.: Adelyne Hood, f-1; Eddie Grosso, cl-2/h-3; Charles Magnante, pac; Al Russo, g.

New York, NY   Thursday, February 25, 1932

11355-A	That Goes On For Days And Days Pt 2 -1, 3	Me M12333, Pan 25204
11356-A	I Laughed So Hard I Nearly Died -3	Me M12449, DeE F3129
11357-A	Hang It In The Hen-house -2	Me M12348, Pan 25325
11358-A	Down At The Bottom Of The Mountain -3	Me M12348, Bwy 4049, Pan 25575
11359-A	In Nineteen Ninety-Two -2	Me M12449, Pan 25325

Panachord 25204 as by **The Colt Brothers**. Decca F3129 as by **Beverley Buckle Busters**.
The accompaniment credit to Rex Cole Mountaineers is omitted on Melotone M12333.
Rev. Broadway 4049 by Vernon Dalhart.

Acc. Rex Cole Mountaineers: poss.: Eddie Grosso, cl; Charles Magnante, pac; Adelyne Hood or Fred Hall, p; Al Russo, bj.

New York, NY   Monday, March 28, 1932

| 11592-A | That Funny Old World Goes Rolling Along | Me M12483, Pan 25246 |
| 11593- | It Must Have Been Something I Et | Me M12483, Pan 25246 |

Lucy Gray With The Colt Brothers: Adelyne Hood, v; Arthur Fields, Fred Hall, poss. others, sp; acc. poss.: Eddie Grosso, cl; Charles Magnante, pac; Adelyne Hood or Fred Hall, p; Al Russo, bj.

New York, NY   Monday, March 28, 1932

| 11594-A | Calamity Jane | Me M12423, Pan 25276 |
| 11595- | The Lady That's Known As Lou | Me M12423, Pan 25276 |

Colt Brothers: Arthur Fields, Fred Hall, v duet; acc. Rex Cole Mountaineers: poss.: Eddie Grosso, cl; Charles Magnante, pac; Adelyne Hood or Fred Hall, p; Al Russo, bj.

New York, NY   Monday, March 28, 1932

| 11596- | Our Home Town Mountain Band | Me unissued |

Gunboat Billy & The Sparrow: Arthur Fields, Fred Hall, v duet ; acc. poss. Philip D'Arcy, f/h-1; poss. Al Russo, g.

New York, NY   Friday, May 13, 1932

72576-1	I Don't Want To Get Married	Vi 23698
72577-1	Oh For The Life Of A Hobo -1	Vi 24024, ZoAu EE338
72578-1	I'm Glad I'm A Bum -1	Vi 23698
72579-1	I Hate To Be Called A Hobo -1	Vi 24024, ZoAu EE338
72580-1	Four Stone Walls And A Ceiling	Vi 23714
72581-1	That Goes On For Days And Days	Vi 23714

Colt Brothers: Arthur Fields, Fred Hall, v duet; acc. poss. Tom Vodola, f; Eddie Grosso, cl/h; Charles Magnante, pac; Al Russo, bj/g; unknown, bones; poss. unknown, v.

New York, NY   Friday, July 15, 1932

| 12090-A | After The Old Barn Dance | Me M12506, Pan 25575 |

Acc. poss.: Eddie Grosso, cl; Charles Magnante, pac; Al Russo, g; unknown, jh.

New York, NY   Wednesday, July 20, 1932

12091-A	If You See My Little Mountain Gal (Tell Her I'm Coming Back)	Me M12506, Pan 25575
12092-A	Our Home Town Mountain Band Pt 1	Me M12458, Pan 25257
12093-A	Our Home Town Mountain Band Pt 2	Me M12458, Pan 25257

Arthur Fields & Fred Hall: prob. Arthur Fields, v; acc. unknown, o; unknown, p; unknown, d; The Piedmont Quartet, v quartet.

New York, NY   Friday, August 12, 1932

12184-	Arthur And Freddie (Part I) (Thank You For Your Information)	Br 6415, Pan 25354
12185-	Arthur And Freddie (Part II) (Thank You For Your Information)	Br 6415, Pan 25354
12186-A	Temperance Is Coming (Part I)	Br 6367, DeE F3200
12187-A	Temperance Is Coming (Part II)	Br 6367, DeE F3200

Colt Brothers: Arthur Fields, Fred Hall, v duet; acc. poss.: Andy Sannella, sg; Al Russo, g.
    New York, NY   Monday, December 12, 1932

12712-A	That's Why I Left The Mountains	Pan 25613
12713-	Four Stone Walls And A Ceiling	Pan 25433
12714-	Those Were The Very Last Words He Said	Me M12601, Pan 25433

Acc. unknown, f; unknown, cl; unknown, piccolo or oc; unknown, h; unknown, g; unknown, jh.
    New York, NY   Wednesday, December 14, 1932

12715-A	I'll Get Along Somehow	Me M12601, Pan 25613

All the instruments except the guitar may be played by one musician. This instrumentation may also apply to matrices 12713/14.

Fields & Hall (The Sunday Drivers): Arthur Fields, Fred Hall, v duet; or Arthur Fields, v-1; acc. poss.: Philip D'Arcy, f/h-2; Charles Magnante, pac; poss. Fred Hall, p; unknown, tu; unknown, oc-3; unknown, jh-4; unknown, spoons; band v-5.
    New York, NY   c. June 1940

US-1733-1	Kethcup -1, 2, 4	Vs 5146
US-1734-	Gonna Buy Me A Brand New Suit	Vs 5147
US-1735-1	Yes, Pappy, Yes -1, 2, 4, 5	Vs 5149, Elite X11
US-1736-1	It Looks Like Lucy -1, 3, 5	Vs 5151, Elite X11
US-1737-	Every Jack Must Have A Jill	Vs 5152
US-1738-1	The Smoking Habit	Vs 5149, Elite X12
US-1739-1	Turpentine -2, 3, 4	Vs 5146
US-1740-1	Dancing 'Round The Apple Tree	Vs 5147, Elite X12
US-1741-	I'm In Heaven	Vs 5151
US-1742-	Cousin Cindy's Wedding	Vs 5152

Elites as by **Arthurs Camp Boys**.
Matrix US-1735 is titled *Yes Pappy Yes*, and matrix US-1736 is titled *Looks Like Lucy*, on Elite X11.

Arthur Fields, v; acc. unknown orch.
    New York, NY   Summer, 1942

W212-	There's A Star Spangled Banner Waving Somewhere	Hit 7021
W213-	I Found A Peach In Orange, New Jersey	Hit 7021
W218-1	Der Fuehrer's Face	Hit 7023
W219-1	Gee, But It's Great To Meet A Friend (From Your Home Town)	Hit 7023

Intervening matrices are untraced.

G.W. FIELDS

G.W. Fields, v; acc. prob. own bj.
    Richmond, IN   Friday, October 11, 1929

15758	The Little Brown Jug	Ge rejected trial recording

DARRELL FISCHER & HIS "LOG-JAMMERS"

Recordings on Standard by this band are beyond the scope of this work.

FREDDIE FISHER & HIS BAND

Recordings by this band in the Decca Hill Billy series are beyond the scope of this work. (The leader was known as Freddy "Schnicklefritz" Fisher. The band works in a novelty polka idiom.)

JOE FISHER CONCERTINA ORCHESTRA

This is a polka band, and its recordings issued in the Decca Hill Billy series are beyond the scope of this work.

TAYLOR FLANAGAN & HIS TRIO

Prob. Dan Hornsby, Sterling Melvin, unknown, v trio; acc. Taylor Flanagan, p; Perry Bechtel, bj.
    Atlanta, GA   Sunday, November 16, 1930

ATL-6696-A	Little Brown Jug	Br 573
ATL-6697-A	Li'l Liza Jane	Br 573

Taylor Flanagan also recorded with Perry Bechtel and Dan Hornsby.

FLANNERY SISTERS (BILLIE & ALLIE)

Violet "Billie" Flannery, Alene "Allie" Flannery, v/y-1 duet; acc. Allie Flannery, g.
    Chicago, IL   Wednesday, August 29, 1934

C-9376-	Lullaby Baby -1	De 5000
C-9377-	Springtime In The Blue Ridge Mountains	DeSA FM5104

| C-9378-A | Carry Me Back To The Mountains -1 | De 5000, DeSA FM5104 |
| C-9379-A,-B | Cumberland Mountains | De unissued |

Chicago, IL   Friday, April 19, 1935

| C-9932-A | I'm Drifting Back To Dreamland | DeSA FM5495 |
| C-9933-A | Where The Beautiful Red River Flows -1 | DeSA FM5495 |

Chicago, IL   Friday, May 22, 1936

90740-A	Wild Western Moonlight	De 5284, BrSA SA1204
90741-A	Columbus Stockade (Go And Leave Me If You Wish To) -1	De 5256
90742-A	Come Back To The Hills	De 5256, BrSA SA1204
90743-A	I Know There Is Somebody Waiting	De 5284

FLAT CREEK SACRED SINGERS

Shellie Propes Mundy, sv; Benjamin Propes, tv; James Bagwell, bv; James Marlowe Propes, bsv; acc. unknown, o; Rev. A.H. Holland, sp-1.

Atlanta, GA   Thursday, March 1, or Friday, March 2, 1928

AT-326 ½/27½*	When We Go To Glory-Land	Vo 5232
AT-328/29½*	Mother Tell Me Of The Angels	Br 236, Spt S2098
AT-330/31*	Is It Far?	Vo 5232
AT-332/33*	Look Away To Calvary -1	Br 236, Spt S2098
AT-334/35*	Prepare To Meet Thy God -1	Br 294
AT-338/39*	Love Keeps Me Singing	Br 294
AT-340/41*	Old-Fashioned Hill	Vo 5223
AT-344/45*	He Loved Me So	Vo 5223
AT-346/47*	Home On The Banks Of The River	Br 265
AT-348/49*	Tell It Everywhere You Go	Br 265

Matrices AT-336/37, 342/43 are probably also by this group.
See also Propes Quartet for a probably associated group.

FLEMING & TOWNSEND

Reece Fleming, Respers Townsend, v/y duet; acc. Respers Townsend, h/k-1; Reece Fleming, g.

Memphis, TN   Friday, June 6, 1930

62595-1	Little Home Upon The Hill	Vi V-40321, BB B-5874
62596-2	I'm Blue And Lonesome -1	Vi V-40321, BB 1832, B-5002, Eld 1960, Sr S-3106, MW M-4280
62597-2	She's Just That Kind -1	Vi V-40297, BB 1832, B-5002, Eld 1960, Sr S-3106, MW M-4280
62598-1	Just One Little Kiss -1	Vi V-40297

Acc. Respers Townsend, h/md-1; Reece Fleming, g.

Memphis, TN   Thursday, November 20, 1930

62978-2	Something's Got To Change Somewhere	Vi 23520, BB B-5186, Eld 2079, Sr S-3266, MW M-4440
62979-2	I'll Tell You About The Women	Vi 23520, BB B-5378, Sr S-3459
62980-1	The Ramblin' Boy -1	Vi 23557, BB B-5470, Twin FT1736
62981-2	Drifting On	Vi 23543, BB B-5821, Twin FT1878

Victor 23520 as by **Fleming–Townsend**. Rev. Bluebird B-5470, Twin FT1736 by Allen Brothers.

Memphis, TN   Tuesday, November 25, 1930

64710-2	(Mama) What Makes You That Way?	Vi 23509, BB B-5186, Eld 2079, Sr S-3266, MW M-4440
64711-2	She's Always On My Mind	Vi 23509, BB B-5106, Eld 2022, Sr S-3189
64712-2	Gonna Quit Drinkin' When I Die	Vi 23543, BB B-5106, Eld 2022, Sr S-3189
64713-2	Me, The Moon And My Gal -1	Vi 23557, BB B-5695, Twin FT1826

Acc. Respers Townsend, h/k-1; Reece Fleming, g.

Charlotte, NC   Monday, May 18, 1931

69301-2	Blowin' The Blues	Vi 23635
69302-2	I'm Leavin' This Town -1	Vi 23563, BB B-5378, Sr S-3459
69303-1	Lookin' For A Mama -1	Vi 23563, BB B-5696
69304-2	Wanna Be A Man Like Dad -1	Vi 23604, BB B-5874
69305-2	Pretty Mama, You're Doin' Wrong-1	Vi 23575, BB B-5497
69306-1	I Wanta Be Where You Are -1	Vi 23594, BB B-5696

Acc. Respers Townsend, h-1/sg-2; Reece Fleming, g.

Charlotte, NC   Tuesday, May 19, 1931

69307-1	I Feel So Blue -1	Vi 23625, BB B-5426
69308-2	A Drunkard's Resolution -1	Vi 23635
69309-1	My Baby Can't Be Found -1	Vi 23625, BB B-5821, Twin FT1878
69310-1	Sweet Daddy From Tennessee -1	Vi 23575, BB B-5256, Eld 2136, Sr S-3339, MW M-4441
69311-2	How Can You Be Mean To Me -1	Vi 23594, BB B-5256, Eld 2136, Sr S-3339, MW M-4441
69312-1	Come And Drift With Me -2	Vi 23604, BB B-5695, Twin FT1826

Acc. Respers Townsend, h-1/md-2; Reece Fleming, g.
Atlanta, GA   Thursday, February 18, 1932

61391-2	Yes, I Got Mine -1	Vi 23676, BB B-5566
61392-2	Bad Reputation -2	Vi 23694, BB B-5566, Twin FT1794
61393-2	Oh That Cow -1, 2	Vi 23676, BB B-5694, Twin FT1844
61394-2	Cottonfield Blues -1, 2	Vi 23710, BB B-5426, HMVIn N4304

Revs: Twin FT1794 by Dick Robertson; FT1844 by Bill Boyd; HMV N4304 by Riley Puckett.

Acc. Respers Townsend, h-1/k-2/md-3; Reece Fleming, g.
Atlanta, GA   Friday, February 19, 1932

61399-2	She's Just That Kind – No. 2 -1, 2	Vi 23666, BB B-5497
61400-2	First Time In Jail -1, 2, 3	Vi 23666, BB B-5634
71601-2	That Lonesome Train -1	Vi 23710, BB B-5634
71602-1	Unlucky Me -2, 3	Vi 23694

Acc. Respers Townsend, h/k; Reece Fleming, g.
Camden, NJ   Monday, December 12, 1932

74838-1	Do-Do-Daddling Thing	Vi 23793
74839-1	Dreamy Moon Of Tennessee	Vi unissued

Rev. Victor 23793 by Jimmie Davis.

Acc. Respers Townsend, k-1/md-2/g-3; Reece Fleming, g.
Camden, NJ   Tuesday, December 13, 1932

74840-1	I Love You Sweetheart, I Love You -3	Vi 23771
74841-1	The Picture On My Dresser -3	Vi 23789
74842-1	The Blues Have Gone -3	Vi 23758
74843-1	The Memory That Lingers -1	Vi unissued
74844-1	The Gambler's Advice -1	Vi 23829
74845-1	When It's Hottest Time Down South -3	Vi 23771

Rev. Victor 23829 by Harry (Mac) McClintock.

Acc. Respers Townsend, h-1/k-2/md-3/g-4; Reece Fleming, g.
Camden, NJ   Wednesday, December 14, 1932

74856-1	I'll Never See Her Again	Vi 23789
74857-1	Right Always Wins -1, 2, 3	Vi 23814
74858-1	Look What You Done -1, 2, 3	Vi unissued
74859-1	My City Girl -4	Vi unissued
74860-1	Lonesome (I Need You)-1, 3	Vi 23758
74861-1	Longing For Mother -4	Vi 23814

Acc. Respers Townsend, k-1/sg-2/g-3; Reece Fleming, g; unidentified, v solo-4.
New York, NY   Monday, September 24, 1934

15995-1	When I'm Gone You'll Be Blue -2	ARC 35-10-13, Cq 8567
15996-1	Hey Hey Pretty Mama -1, 3, 4	Ba 33357, Me M13324, Or 8436, Pe 13116, Ro 5436, CrC/MeC/Roy/Stg 91971
15997-1,-2	Longing For Hawaii -2	ARC unissued
15998-1,-2	The Orphan Child -3	ARC unissued
15999-1,-2	Happy And Gay -1, 3	ARC unissued
16000-2	The Untrue Lover -3	ARC 5-12-62, Cq 8587

Acc. Respers Townsend, h/k-1; Reece Fleming, g.
New York, NY   Tuesday, September 25, 1934

16051-1,-2	Our President And The Farmers -1	ARC unissued
16052-1	What You Gonna Do (This Year My Friend) -1	Ba 33431, Me M13398, Or 8466, Pe 13141, Ro 5466
16053-2	I'll Get Along	Ba 33264, Me M13231, Or 8399, Pe 13084, Ro 5399
16054-1	Little Shack By The Maple	ARC 5-12-62, Cq 8587
16055-1,-2	Springtime In The Mountains	ARC unissued

Respers Townsend, v; acc. prob. own g.
    New York, NY   Tuesday, September 25, 1934
    16056-1,-2   Southern Jane   ARC unissued

Fleming & Townsend, v/y duet; acc. Respers Townsend, h; Reece Fleming, g.
    New York, NY   Tuesday, September 25, 1934
    16057-1,-2   Years Ago I Had A Lover   ARC unissued
    16058-2   Gonna Quit Drinking When I Die   Ba 33357, Me M13324, Or 8436, Pe 13116,
                                                              Ro 5436, Cq 8471, CrC/MeC/Roy/Stg 91971

Rev. Conqueror 8471 by Jimmie & Eddie Dean.

Acc. Respers Townsend, h/k-1; Reece Fleming, g.
    New York, NY   Wednesday, September 26, 1934
    16017-1   The Gambler's Confession -1   ARC 35-10-13, Cq 8567
    16018-2   She's Just That Kind   Ba 33264, Me M13231, Or 8399, Pe 13084,
                                                              Ro 5399
    16019-1,-2   Little Home On The Hill   ARC unissued
    16020-2   Blue And Lonesome   Ba 33431, Me M13398, Or 8466, Pe 13141,
                                                              Ro 5466

Reece Fleming, Respers Townsend, v/y duet; or Reece Fleming, v-1; acc. Respers Townsend, h-2/sg-3/md-4/g-5; Reece Fleming, g.
    New York, NY   Monday, August 16, 1937
    62527-A   Triflin' Mama From Dixie -4   De 5463
    62528-A   Old Coon Dog Blue -2   De 5419
    62529-B   If I Had Somebody -4   De 5427, MeC 45212, Min M-14063
    62530-A   Banana Peeling Mama -2   De 5419
    62531-A   A Rambling Gambling Rounder -1, 5 De 5516
    62532-A   Ride Along Little Gal   De 5445, MeC 45226
    62533-A   A Longing For You- 3   De 5516
    62534-A   Just At Twilight -3   De 5487
    62535-A   The Criminal's Fate -2   De 5427, MeC 45212, Min M-14062
    62536-A   That's When You Take The Blues -1, 4 De 5463
    62537-A   Tell My Baby I'm Gone -1, 4   De 5487
    62538-A   Weary Mind Blues -1   De 5445, MeC 45226

Revs: Minerva M-14062 by Shelton Brothers, M-14063 by Roy Shaffer.

JIM & OTTO FLETCHER

Pseudonym on Superior for Cliff Carlisle & Wilbur Ball.

JOE FLETCHER & ARTHUR HIGGINS

Pseudonym on Velvet Tone and Clarion for Earl Shirkey & Roy Harper.

OTTO & JIM FLETCHER

Pseudonym on Superior for Cliff Carlisle & Wilbur Ball.

TEX FLETCHER

This artist's real name is Jerry Bisceglia.

Tex Fletcher, v; acc. own g.
    New York, NY   Wednesday, November 8, 1933
    14278-   I'm A Wandering Ranger   ARC unissued
    14279-   St. Regis Valley   ARC unissued
    14280-   The Tenderfoot   ARC unissued
    14281-   Windy Bill   ARC unissued

Matrices 14280/81 were logged as by **Texas Fletcher**.

    New York, NY   Monday, November 16, 1936
    61415-A   Ridge Runnin' Roan   De 5302, MeC 45010
    61416-A   The Zebra Dun   De 5302, MeC 45010
    61417-A   The Border Affair (Mi Amor Mi Corazon) De 5300, DeAu X1333, MeC 45011
    61418-A   I'm Goin' Back To Red River Valley   De 5300, DeAu X1333, MW 8011, MeC 45011

Montgomery Ward 8011 as by **Tack Foster**.

Tex Fletcher, v/y-1; acc. own g.
    New York, NY   Friday, December 18, 1936
    61494-A   I'm Here To Get My Baby Out Of Jail De 5312, MW 8011
    61495-A,-B   Cowman's Lament   De unissued
    61496-A   Still There's A Spark Of Love -1   De 5312

Montgomery Ward 8011 as by **Tack Foster**.

Acc. unknown, f; own g.
   New York, NY   February 1937

61587-A	I Lost My Love In The Ohio Flood	De 5332, MW 8010
61588-A	A Song For Mother	De 5332, MW 8010

Montgomery Ward 8010 as by **Tack Foster**.

Tex Fletcher, v; or **Tex Fletcher & Joe Rogers**, v duet-1; acc. unknown, f; unknown, md; prob. Tex Fletcher, g.
   New York, NY   Wednesday, June 2, 1937

62237-A	Mistook In The Woman I Loved	De 5391, MeC 45206
62238-A	Seven More Days -1	De 5403
62239-A	The Girl In The Blue Velvet Band -1	De 5403
62240-A	The Poor Blind Child	De 5391, MeC 45206, Min M-14076

Rev. Minerva M-14076 by Roy Shaffer.

Tex Fletcher's Lonely Cowboys: unknown, f; unknown, ac; unknown, sg; unknown, g; unknown, sb; Tex Fletcher, v.
   New York, NY   Friday, October 8, 1937

62670-A	Wondering	De 5441, MW 8045
62671-A	Yodel Lady	De 5450
62672-A	Little Sweetheart Of The Ozarks	De 5450
62673-A	My Ole Dog And Me	De 5441, MW 8045

Some copies of Decca 5450 couple matrix 62672 with matrix C-91122 by Sally Foster.

Two unknowns, f; unknown, ac; unknown, sg; unknown, g; unknown, sb; Tex Fletcher, v.
   New York, NY   Friday, February 11, 1938

63273-A	Highways Are Happy Ways (When They Lead The Way To Home)	De 5520
63274-A	Shine On, Rocky Mountain Moonlight	De 5489
63275-A	I Get The Blues When It Rains	De 5520
63276-A	Ain't She Sweet	De 5489
63277-A	Meet Me Tonight In The Cowshed	De 5500
63278-A	Down On The Old Plantation	De 5500

Tex Fletcher recorded after 1942.

FLETCHER & FOSTER

Carolina Twins: Gwen Foster, h/g/v/y-1; David O. Fletcher, g/v/y-2.
   Atlanta, GA   Monday, February 20, 1928

41920-2	The Boarding House Bells Are Ringing	Vi 21575
41921-2	One Dark And Rainy Night	Vi 21575
41922-2	Your Wagon Needs Greasing	Vi 21363
41923-2	Off To The War I'm Going -1, 2	Vi 21363

   Bristol, TN   Friday, November 2, 1928

47281-2	Where Is My Mamma?	Vi V-40044
47282-2	When You Go A'Courtin'	Vi V-40044
47283-2	I Sat Upon The River Bank -1, 2	Vi V-40098

   Bristol, TN   Saturday, November 3, 1928

47285-1	New Orleans Is The Town I Like Best -2	Vi V-40123
47286-2	She Tells Me That I Am Sweet	Vi V-40123
47287-1	Mr. Brown, Here I Come -1, 2	Vi V-40098

David Fletcher, v; acc. own g.
   Richmond, IN   c. August 14, 1929

15444	Change In Business	Ge rejected trial recording

Carolina Twins: Gwen Foster, h/g-1/v-2/sp-3/wh-4; David Fletcher, g/v/sp-3/wh-4.
   Atlanta, GA   Thursday, November 28, 1929

56621-1	Who's Going To Love Me -2, 4	Vi V-40310
56622-2	Southern Jack -2, 3	Vi V-40310
56623-1	Since My Baby's Gone Away -1, 2	Vi 23502
56624-1	I Want My Black Baby Back -1, 2, 4	Vi 23502
56625-1	Gal Of Mine Took My Licker From Me -1, 2	Vi V-40243
56626-2	A Change In Business All Around	Vi V-40243

Matrix 56621 is titled *Who'se Going To Love Me* on some pressings.

Fletcher & Foster: Gwen Foster, h-1/g; David Fletcher, g.
   Atlanta, GA   Friday, November 29, 1929

56627-2	Charlotte Hot Step -1	Vi V-40232
56628-2	Red Rose Rag	Vi V-40232

Despite the labels, the harmonica is heard on matrix 56627, not 56628.

Gwen Foster, h/g/v; David Fletcher, g/v.
   Richmond, IN   Tuesday, September 23, 1930

17074	Working So Hard	Ch 16121
17075	Travelin' North	Ch 16121
17076	Going A Courtin'	Spr 2537

Superior 2537 as by **Saxton Bros.**
Rev. Superior 2537 by Johnson Brothers.

TIM FLORA & RUFUS LINGO

One of them, v; acc. prob. one of them, f; the other, g.
   Memphis, TN   Friday, February 24, 1928

400321-B	Stuttering Billy	OK 45311
400322-	My Horses Ain't Hungry	OK unissued
400323-	Leather Briches [sic]	OK unissued
400324-	Portland Belle	OK unissued
400325-A	A Lonely Tramp	OK 45311
400326-	Creole Belle	OK unissued

FLORIDA WALTZ ORCHESTRA

This credit on the English Mayfair label was assigned to an item (*Many Happy Returns Of The Day*) by Lester McFarland & Robert A. Gardner.

ELZIE FLOYD & LEO BOSWELL

Elzie Floyd, Leo Boswell, v duet; or Elzie Floyd, v-1; acc. Leo Boswell, h-2/md; Elzie Floyd, g.
   Atlanta, GA   Saturday, March 26, 1927

143763-2	She's Only A Bird In A Gilded Cage	Co 15150-D, Ve 2489-V, Cl 5429-C, ReAu G20355
143764-	Birdie Darling	Co unissued
143765-	Old Black Sheep	Co unissued
143766-1	Lonesome Valley	Co 15167-D, Ve 2489-V, Cl 5429-C
143767-1	The Two Orphans	Co 15167-D, Ve 2491-V, Cl 5431-C, ReE/RZ MR70, RZ ME30, RZAu G21659
143768-2	Nellie Dare -1, 2	Co 15150-D

Velvet Tones and Clarions as by **Ferguson & Clark**. Regal/Regal-Zonophone issues except Regal G20355 as by **Alabama Barnstormers**.
Revs: Velvet Tone 2491-C, Clarion 5431-C by Earl Shirkey & Roy Harper; Regal/Regal-Zonophone MR70, Regal-Zonophone ME30, G21659 by Darby & Tarlton; Regal G20355 by Ford & Glenn (popular).

Floyd & Boswell, v duet; acc. unknown.
   Atlanta, GA   Friday, November 11, 1927

145222-	Oh Captain, Captain Tell Me True	Co unissued
145223-	I Love You Nellie	Co unissued

Leo Boswell also recorded in his own name.

FLOYD COUNTY RAMBLERS

Banks McNeil, f; Walter Boone, h/tv-1; Sam McNeil, bj; J.W. (Will) Boone, g/lv-1.
   New York, NY   Friday, August 29, 1930

63610-3	The Story Of Frieda Bolt -1	Vi V-40307
63611-1	Step Stone -1	Vi V-40331, BB B-5107, Eld 2023, Sr S-3190, ZoSA 4325
63612-2	Ragtime Annie	Vi 23759, TT C-1561, Au 36-113
63613-2	Sunny Tennessee -1	Vi V-40307, MW M-4320
63614-2	Granny Will Your Dog Bite?	Vi 23759, TT C-1561, Au 36-113
63615-1	Aunt Dinah's Quilting Party -1	Vi V-40331, BB B-5107, Eld 2023, Sr S-3190, ZoSA 4325

Timely Tunes C-1561, Aurora 36-113 as by **Virginia Ramblers**.
Rev. Montgomery Ward M-4320 by Carter Family.

DAVID FOLEY

Pseudonym on Challenge for G.B. Grayson & Henry Whitter.

RED FOLEY

Rambling Red Foley, v/y; acc. Cumberland Ridge Runners: Homer "Slim" Miller, f; Karl Davis, md; Hartford Taylor, g.
   Chicago, IL   Tuesday, April 11, 1933

C-535-1	The Lone Cowboy	Ba 32783, Me M12718, MeC 91597, M-908, Or 8237, Pe 12918, Ro 5237, Vo 5501, Cq 8163, Min M-908, RZAu G22934

| C-538-2 | Single Life Is Good Enough For Me | Ba 32783, Me M12718, MeC 91597, Or 8237, Pe 12918, Ro 5237, Vo 5501, Cq 8163, Min M-904, RZAu G22934 |

Intervening matrices are by Linda Parker.
Rev. Minerva M-904 by Vernon Dalhart; Melotone 908, Minerva M-908 by George Gobel.

Red Foley, v/y-1; acc. Cumberland Ridge Runners: Homer "Slim" Miller, f; Karl Davis, md; Hartford Taylor, g.
Chicago, IL   Monday, November 20, 1933

| C-666-1,-2 | Blonde Headed Girl -1 | Ba 33021, Me M12980, MeC 91762, Or 8323, Pe 12992, Ro 5323, Cq 8198 |
| C-667-2 | The Dying Rustler | Ba 33021, Me M12980, MeC 91762, Or 8323, Pe 12992, Ro 5323, Cq 8198 |

Conqueror 8198 as by **Red Foley**.

Chicago, IL   c. March 21, 1934

CP-1008-	I Traced Her Little Footsteps In The Snow	Cq 8304
CP-1009-1	Seven Long Years -1	Ba 33134, Me M13101, MeC 91881, Or 8368, Pe 13029, Ro 5368, Cq 8303, Min M-933
CP-1010-3	Just One Little Kiss -1	Ba 33134, Me M13101, MeC 91881, Or 8368, Pe 13029, Ro 5368, Cq 8303, Min M-932
CP-1011-1	Echoes Of My Plantation Home	Ba 33035, Me M12994, MeC 91804, Or 8328, Pe 12996, Ro 5328, Cq 8285
CP-1016-2	I Got The Freight Train Blues-1	Ba 33035, Me M12994, MeC 91804, Or 8328, Pe 12996, Ro 5328, Cq 8285, Min M-906
CP-1021-	In My Childhood Days -1	Cq 8304

Matrices CP-1012 through 1015 are by The Westerners (Massey Family); 1017/18 by Linda Parker; 1019/20 by (Harty) Taylor & (Karl) Davis.
Revs: Minerva M-906, M-933 by Bill Cox; M-932 by Jack Fulton (popular).

Red Foley & Lulu Belle: Red Foley, Lulu Belle (Myrtle Cooper), v/y-1 duet; acc. Red Foley, g.
Chicago, IL   c. March 24, 1934

CP-1050-1,-2	Hi Rinkum Inktum Doodle	Cq 8316
CP-1051-1	Going Out West This Fall	Cq 8316
CP-1051-3	Going Out West This Fall -1	Cq 8316

Lulu Belle also recorded in her own name, accompanied by Foley, at this session.

Red Foley, v/y-1; acc. own g.
Chicago, IL   Monday, December 9, 1935

C-1178-1	Old Shep	ARC 6-03-53, Cq 8631
C-1179-2	Yodeling Radio Joe -1	Cq 8659
C-1180-1	Headin' Back To Texas -1	Cq 8659
C-1181-2	Sing Me A Hill-Billy Ballad	ARC 6-03-53, Cq 8631

Chicago, IL   Tuesday, March 31, 1936

C-1336-1	The 1936 Floods	ARC 6-06-59, Cq 8676
C-1337-1,-2	My Renfro Valley Home -1	ARC unissued
C-1338-1,-2	An Old Fashioned Shack -1	ARC unissued
C-1339-2	The Mailman's Warning	ARC 6-06-59, Cq 8676

Red Foley, v; acc. prob.: Harry Sims, f; Augie Klein, ac; Ozzie Westley, g; Clyde Moffett, sb.
Chicago, IL   Tuesday, March 4, 1941

93538-A	Old Shep	De 5944, MeC 45438
93539-A	A Rose And A Prayer	De 5962, MeC 45452
93540-A	Ridin' On A Rainbow	De 5936
93541-A	Montana Moon	De 5932, MeC 45428
93542-A	It Makes No Never Mind	De 5932, MeC 45428
93543-B	Nobody	De 5981, 29494, MeC 45464
93544-A	I Don't Care Anymore	De 5944, MeC 45438
93545-A	Ridin' Home	De 5981, MeC 45464

Chicago, IL   Tuesday, March 25, 1941

| 93606-A | I'll Be Back In A Year (Little Darlin') | De 5937, MeC 45430 |
| 93607-A | Where The Mountains Meet The Moon | De 5937, MeC 45430 |

Chicago, IL   Wednesday, March 26, 1941

| 93604-A | Be Honest With Me | De 5936 |
| 93605-A | I Ain't Lazy I'm Just Dreamin' | De 5962, MeC 45452 |

Chicago, IL   Friday, November 14, 1941

93777-A	Chiquita	De 6010
93778-A	Pals Of The Saddle	De 6069
93779-A	Is It True	De 6048
93780-A	I'm Looking For A Sweetheart (Not A Friend)	De 6048
93781-A	Someday Somewhere Sweetheart	De 6069
93782-A	Will You Wait For Me, Little Darlin' (Sequel To I'll Be Back In A Year)	De 6010

Red Foley recorded after 1942.

OSCAR FORD

Ford & Grace: Oscar Ford, v; acc. own f; Dewey Grace, g (or vice versa).
Atlanta, GA   Tuesday, October 4, 1927

81664-B	Down In The Old Home Town	OK 45157
81665-	Georgia Is My Home	OK unissued
81666-A	Hide Away	OK 45237
81667-B	Kiss Me, Cindy	OK 45157
81668-B	Old Folks Get In Bed	OK 45237

Oscar Ford, v; acc. poss. own f; Riley Puckett, g.
Atlanta, GA   Thursday, April 11, 1929

148240-1	Henry Ford's Model A	Co 15437-D
148241-2	Married Life Blues	Co 15437-D

Oscar Ford, v/y-1; acc. Lowe Stokes, f; Bert Layne, f; Riley Puckett, g.
Atlanta, GA   Thursday, April 17, 1930

150253-2	Me And My Gal	Co 15554-D
150254-2	Riding In A Chevrolet Six	Co 15554-D
150255-2	Sweetest Girl In Town -1	Co 15599-D
150256-2	The Farmer's Dream	Co 15599-D

Oscar Ford, v; acc. Clayton McMichen, f; poss. Bert Layne, f-1; Riley Puckett, g.
Atlanta, GA   Friday, December 5, 1930

151045-2	The Girl I Love In Tennessee	Co 15673-D
151046-2	Little Nan	Co 15673-D
151047-2	Race Between A Ford And Chevrolet -1	Co 15634-D
151048-1	Georgia Is My Home -1	Co 15634-D

Oscar Ford also participates in sketch recordings by the "Skillet-Licker circle;" see Clayton McMichen.

FORD & GRACE

See Oscar Ford.

THE FOREMAN FAMILY

Vocal group; acc. unknown, g; unknown, u.
Dallas, TX   Wednesday, October 16, 1929

56398-2	The Poor Old Slave	Vi V-40165
56399-2	The Dying Nun	Vi V-40165, ZoSA 4249
56400-1,-2	The Faithless Husband	Vi unissued
56401-1,-2	Too Late	Vi unissued

Rev. Zonophone 4249 by Carter Family.

FORMAN SISTERS

Vocal trio; acc. unknown, f; unknown, c; unknown, tb; unknown, p; Carson Robison, g.
New York, NY   Thursday, December 12, 1929

57767-1	Oh! Bright Home	Vi V-40192
57768-1	Let Me Rest	Vi 23558
57769-1	Oh, I Want To See Him	Vi 23558
57770-1	Keep Straight Ahead	Vi V-40192

THE FORT WORTH BOYS (MILTON BROWN & HIS MUSICAL BROWNIES)

Some copies of Bluebird B-5444, and probably all copies of HMV N4317, by Milton Brown & His Musical Brownies were issued with this credit.

FORT WORTH DOUGHBOYS

See Light Crust Doughboys.

FORTNER FAMILY MIXED QUARTETTE

Vocal quartet; acc. unknown.
    Atlanta, GA   Wednesday, August 1, 1928

402028-	Rocking On The Waves	OK unissued
402030-	Kneel At The Cross	OK 45255
402031-	Sometime You Will Pray	OK 45255
402032-	Jesus Is True	OK unissued
402033-	Hand In Hand With Jesus	OK unissued

Matrix 402029 is untraced but probably by this group.

JOE FOSS & HIS HUNGRY SAND-LAPPERS

Unknown, f; unknown, bj; unknown, g; unknown, v/y-1.
    Atlanta, GA   Thursday, April 12, 1928

| 146030-2 | Wee Dog Waltz -1 | Co 15268-D, ReAu G20670 |
| 146031-1 | Oh! How She Lied | Co 15268-D, ReAu G20670 |

GARLEY FOSTER

Garley Foster, v; acc. own g.
    Charlotte, NC   Saturday, May 30, 1931

| 69396-1,-2 | Imitating The Birds On The Mountain – Part 1 | Vi unissued |
| 69397-1,-2 | Imitating The Birds On The Mountain – Part 2 | Vi unissued |

Garley Foster is a member of the Carolina Tar Heels.

GWEN FOSTER

Gwen Foster, h; acc. own g.
    Charlotte, NC   Thursday, August 11, 1927

| 39796-1 | Black Pine Waltz | Vi 20934 |

Gwen Foster, h solo.
    Charlotte, NC   Monday, August 15, 1927

| 39812-2 | Wilkes County Blues | Vi 20934 |

Gwen Foster, v; acc. unknown, f-1; own h-2; unknown, bj-3; unknown (poss. own), g; unknown, g; unknown, sb.
    Rock Hill, SC   Sunday, February 5, 1939

| 032663-1 | How Many Biscuits Can I Eat? -1, 2, 3 | BB B-8082, MW M-7859 |
| 032665-1 | Side-Line Blues | BB B-8082, MW M-7859 |

Intervening and surrounding matrices are by Three Tobacco Tags, who probably constitute some or all of the accompanying musicians.

Gwen (or Gwyn) Foster also recorded with Thomas C. Ashley, Blue Ridge Mountain Entertainers, Carolina Tar Heels, and Fletcher & Foster (Carolina Twins).

JOHN D. FOSTER

John D. Foster & Jesse James: Jesse James, md/v-1; John D. Foster, g/v-2.
    Birmingham, AL   c. July 28, 1927

| GEX-753-A | Good Bye, My Darlin' -2 | Ge 6434 |
| GEX-754,-A,-B | There's More Purty Gals Than One -1 | Ge rejected |

J.D. Foster & J.D. James: Jesse James, md/v-1; John D. Foster, g/v-2.
    Birmingham, AL   c. August 17, 1927

GEX-843	Green Valley	Ge rejected
GEX-844	When I Was Single My Pockets Would Jingle -1/2	Ge 6434, Ch 33014, Sil 8156, Spt 9260
GEX-845	Little Log Cabin In The Lane	Ge rejected

Silvertone 8156, Supertone 9260 as by **Jim Burke**.
Vocal attributions are unknown except for matrix GEX-844, which is a vocal solo by one or the other.
Revs: Champion 33014 untraced; Silvertone 8156, Supertone 9260 by Ted Chestnut.

Foster & James: Jesse James, md/v; John D. Foster, g/v.
    Atlanta, GA   Sunday, November 10, 1927

| 145218- | She's A Flower From The Fields Of Alabama | Co unissued |
| 145219- | Don't Ask Me Why I'm Weeping | Co unissued |

Vocal attributions are unknown.

Rutherford & Foster: Leonard Rutherford, f/v-1; John Foster, g/v-2.
    Richmond, IN   Monday, January 14, 1929

14683	Six Months Ain't Long -1, 2	Ge 6807, Ch 15750, Spt 9352
14684	I'm As Free A Little Birdie As Can Be -1, 2	Ge 6746, Spt 9352
14685	Let Her Go I'll Meet Her -1, 2	Ge 6746, Ch 15691, Spt 9375
14686-A	She's Only A Bird In A Gilded Cage -1, 2	Ge 6777, Ch 15691, Spt 9375
14687	There's No One Like The Old Folks -1, 2	Ge 6777
14688	Bloody War -1	Ge 6807
14689	My Sarah Jane -2	Ge 6791, Spt 9372
14690	Little Streams Of Whiskey -1, 2	Ge rejected
14691	Storms May Rule The Ocean -1	Ge 6791
14692	Taylor's Quickstep	Ge 6913, Spt 9406
14693	All Night Long Blues	Ge rejected

Champion 15691, 15750 as by **Marlow & Young**. Supertone 9352 as by **Taylor & Bunch**; 9372 as by **Sam Bunch**; 9375 as by **Brown & Bunch**; 9406 as by **Fox & Davis**. Matrix 14692 is titled *Monroe County Quickstep* on Supertone 9406. Gennett files report, probably erroneously, that Rutherford plays guitar on matrix 14693.
Revs: Champion 15750 by Melvin Robinette & Byrd Moore (see the latter); Supertone 9372 by Green Bailey; 9406 by Virginia Mountain Boomers.

Richmond, IN   Wednesday, April 10, 1929

15018	My Carolina Home -1, 2	Ge 6873, Ch 15732, Spt 9443, Spr 2640
15019	Two Faithful Lovers -1, 2	Chg 423
15024,-A	In The Land Of Beginning Again -1/2	Ge rejected
15025,-A	Broken Promises -1/2	Ge rejected
15026-A	Meet Me In The Moonlight -1, 2	Ge 6873, Spt 9443
15031	These Bones Gwine Rise Again -1, 2	Ge 6976, Cq 7276

Champion 15732 as by **Marlow & Young**. Supertone 9443 as by **Brown & Bunch**. Challenge 423 as by **Crocker & Cannon**. Conqueror 7276 as by **Rankin Brothers**.
Matrix 15023 is popular; other intervening matrices are by Melvin Robinette & Byrd Moore (see the latter). Rev. Champion 15732 by Byrd Moore.

Richmond, IN   Thursday, April 11, 1929

15032	Richmond Blues-2	Ge 6976, Cq 7276
15033,-A	Jonah's Scriptural Submarine-2?	Ge rejected
15037	There's More Pretty Girls Than One -1, 2	Chg 423
15038	The Girl I Left Behind Me -1	Ge rejected
15039,-A	Waggoner	Ge unissued
15040	Sally Johnson	Ge 6913

Challenge 423 as by **Crocker & Cannon**. Conqueror 7276 as by **Rankin Brothers**. Matrices 15038/39 were logged as by **Leonard Rutherford**. Matrices 15034/35 are popular; 15036 is by Melvin Robinette & Byrd Moore (see the latter).

J.D. Foster, v; or **Rutherford & Foster**, v duet-1; acc. Leonard Rutherford, f; John Foster, g.
Richmond, IN   Friday, July 5, 1929

15300,-A	Blue Ridge Mountain Blues	Ge rejected
15301,-A	Are You Happy Or Lonesome -1	Ge rejected
15302	I'm Drifting Back To Dreamland -1	Ge rejected

Rutherford & Foster, v duet; or **John Foster**-1/**J.D. Foster**-2, v; acc. Leonard Rutherford, f-3; John Foster, g.
Richmond, IN   Wednesday, November 6, 1929

15854,-A	Missouri Waltz -3	Ge rejected
15855,-A	Kentucky Moonshiner -3	Ge rejected
15856,-A	Do Not Ask Me Why I'm Weeping -1, 3	Ge rejected
15857,-A	Are You Happy Or Lonesome? -3	Ge rejected
15858,-A	A Short Life Of Trouble -3	Ge rejected
15859,-A	Send This Letter To My Mother -1, 3	Ge rejected
15860,-A	Dry, Dry, Dry -1, 3	Ge rejected
15861,-A	Everybody's Blues -1, 3	Ge rejected
15862,-A	My Favorite Blues -1, 3	Ge rejected
15863,-A	They've All Got A Wife But Me -2	Ge rejected
15864,-A,-B	Lips That Touch Liquor Shall Never Touch Mine -3	Ge rejected
15865,-A	Drifting Back To Dreamland -1	Ge rejected

Leonard Rutherford, John Foster, v duet; acc. Leonard Rutherford, f; John Foster, g.
Atlanta, GA   Friday, November 14, 1930

ATL-6664-	The Cabin With The Roses At The Door	Br 490
ATL-6665-	Six Months Ain't Long	Br 490

Atlanta, GA   Saturday, November 15, 1930

ATL-6670-A	My Boyhood Happy Days	Br 581
ATL-6671-A	The Faithful Lovers	Br 581

Foster & Young: T.S. Young, md/tv; John Foster, g/lv.
Richmond, IN
Tuesday, February 13, 1934

19490	Some Day I'll Wander Back Again	Ch 16753, 45102, MW 4953
19491	We Can Only Have One Mother	Ch 16753, 45102, MW 4953
19492-A	My Boyhood Happy Days	Ch S-16733, 45037

Willard & Young: John Foster, ——— Willard, v duet; acc. John Foster, g.
Richmond, IN
Tuesday, February 13, 1934

| 19493 | Cabin With Roses At The Door | Ch S-16733, 45037 |

Leonard Rutherford also recorded in his own name and with Richard D. Burnett.

SALLY FOSTER

This artist's real name is Louise Rautenberg.

Sally Foster, v; acc. prob. own g.
Chicago, IL
Thursday, May 21, 1936

| C-90736-A | Woman's Answer To Nobody's Darling | De 5229, BrSA SA1153 |
| C-90737-A | We Buried Her Beneath The Willow | De 5229, BrSA SA1153 |

Acc. **The Travelers**: Rene "Zeb" Hartley, f-1/sb-2; Ted "Otto" Morse, t; George "Bill" Thall, cl-3/sb-4; Art Wenzel, ac; Ted "Buddy" Gilmore, g.
Chicago, IL
Tuesday, December 8, 1936

C-91025-A,-B	The Cradle And The Music Box -2, 3	De unissued
C-91026-B	Ma! (He's Making Eyes At Me) -2, 3	De 5387
C-91027-A,-B	When The White Azaleas Start Blooming	De unissued
C-91028-A	Betty Brown -1, 4	De 5308
C-91029-A,-B	Don't Take The Sweet Out Of Sweetheart	De unissued
C-91030-A	Why Must You Leave Me My Darling -2, 3	De 5308

Acc. **The Travelers**: Otto Morse, t; Bill Thall, cl; Art Wenzel, ac; Buddy Gilmore, g; Zeb Hartley, sb.
Chicago, IL
Friday, January 29, 1937

C-91118-A	The Cradle And The Music Box	De 5387
C-91119-A	When The White Azaleas Start Blooming	De 5352
C-91120-A	Don't Take The Sweet Out Of Sweetheart	De 5333, DeAu X1374
C-91122-A	I Only Want A Buddy Not A Sweetheart	De 5352, 5450

Some pressings of Decca 5450 by Tex Fletcher's Lonely Cowboys couple matrix 62672 by that group and matrix C-91122 by Sally Foster.

Acc. **The Travelers**: Zeb Hartley, f; Otto Morse, t; Art Wenzel, ac; Buddy Gilmore, g; Bill Thall, sb.
Chicago, IL
Saturday, January 30, 1937

| C-91121-A | In Berry Pickin' Time | De 5333, DeAu X1374 |

Sally Foster recorded after 1942.

TACK FOSTER

Pseudonym on Montgomery Ward for Tex Fletcher.

FOSTER & YOUNG

See John D. Foster.

FOUNDATION QUARTETTE

Vocal quartet; acc. unknown, f; unknown, p; unknown, vc.
Atlanta, GA
Monday, August 6, 1928

402068-A	No One Knows	OK 45293
402069-A	When They Ring Those Golden Bells For You And Me	OK 45293
402070-A	Sweet And Low	OK 45271, PaE R3876
402071-B	When The Sunset Turns The Ocean Blue To Gold	OK 45309
402072-B	Softly And Tenderly Jesus Is Calling	OK 45271, PaE R3876
402073-B	I Love To Tell The Story	OK 45309

THE FOUR ACES

Decca recordings credited to **The Four Aces With Leo Soileau** are listed under Leo Soileau. The sessions below are by an at least partly different group without Soileau. (Other groups of this name are in the popular field.)

Boyce Jones, f; prob. Bobby Thibodeaux, p; Floyd Shreve, g; Bill "Dewey" Landry, g; Tony Gonzales, d; unidentified, v-1.
New Orleans, LA
Saturday, April 2, 1938

| 022050-1 | Honey Does You Love Your Man -1 | BB B-7548, MW M-7723 |
| 022051-1 | I Got Mine -1 | BB B-7548, MW M-7723 |

022052-1	Tu-N'As Laisser Seul (You Left Me Alone) -1	BB B-2039
022053-1	Porquoi Es-Tu Triste? (Why Are You Sad) -1	BB B-2039
022054-1	Aces Breakdown	BB B-2045
022055-1	Second Street Blues -1	BB B-2045
022056-1	Beautiful Mary -1	BB B-7765, MW M-7724, RZAu G23664
022057-1	More To Pity -1	BB B-7765, MW M-7724, RZAu G23664

New Orleans, LA　　　　　　　　　　　　　　　　　　　　　　　　Sunday, October 23, 1938

028511-1	Je Vous Jamise Kete Braie -1	BB B-2058
028512-1	Leleaux Breakdown	BB B-2058
028513-1	Vous Me Fois Espere -1	BB B-2067
028514-1	Que Ces Que Ma Chere -1	BB B-2067
028515-1	Vous Avez Quitte Avec Que Unde Dotre -1	BB B-2061
028516-1	Lake Charles Waltz	BB B-2061
028517-1	Whatcha Gonna Do -1	BB B-2080
028518-1	Deserted Lover-1	BB B-2080
028519-1	There's Always A Welcome At Home -1	BB unissued
028520-1	Our Dreams Come Drifting Back -1	BB unissued

THE FOUR ANDERSONS

Pseudonym on Bell for the Woodlawn Quartette.

THE FOUR BUZZ SAWS

See Jimmy Yates Groups.

THE FOUR HORSEMEN

Unknown, f; unknown, bj; two unknowns, g.
Richmond, IN　　　　　　　　　　　　　　　　　　　　　　　　　　Friday, June 13, 1930

16763	St. Louis Blues	Ge rejected
16764	The Hoosier Rag	Ge rejected

FOUR NOVELTY ACES

Mixed quartet; acc. unknown, p.
Chicago, IL　　　　　　　　　　　　　　　　　　　　　　　　　Monday, December 4, 1933

77184-1	Drifting In A Lover's Dream	BB unissued
77185-1	Standin' In Need Of Prayer	BB B-5561
77186-1	Get Away Jordan	BB B-5561
77187-1	Honey	BB unissued

FOUR PICKLED PEPPERS

Hamon Newman, tbj; Esmond Harris, g; Norman Woodlieff, g/v-1; Dallas Hubbard, bones-2/v-3.
Rock Hill, SC　　　　　　　　　　　　　　　　　　　　　　　Friday, September 30, 1938

027689-1	The Woman I Love -1, 3	MW M-7754
027690-1	Somebody's Darling, Not Mine -1	BB B-8618, MW M-7753
027691-1	My Little Nappanee -1	BB B-8618, MW M-7654
027692-1	Four Leaf Clover -2, 3	BB B-8642, MW M-7753
027693-1	Thirteen Steps -1	BB B-8642, MW M-7754
027694-1	Poor Old Jane -2, 3	BB B-8231, MW M-7755
027695-1	Come Along Children, Come Along -1, 3	BB B-8231, MW M-7755
027696-1	When I Was A Baby -2, 3	BB B-7894, MW M-7756
027697-1	Bungalow Big Enough For Two -2, 3	BB B-7894, MW M-7756
027698-1	Jolly Group Of Cowboys -1	BB B-8016, MW M-7654, RZAu G24076

Rev. Bluebird B-8016, Regal-Zonophone G24076 by Girls Of The Golden West.

Lonnie Austin, f; Hamon Newman, tbj; Earl Taylor, g; Norman Woodlieff, g/v-1; Dallas Hubbard, v-2.
Atlanta, GA　　　　　　　　　　　　　　　　　　　　　　　　Tuesday, August 22, 1939

041244-1	I'll Remember You, Love, In My Prayers -1, 2	BB B-8293, MW M-8436
041245-1	I'm Not Angry With You, Darling -1, 2	BB B-8293, MW M-8436
041246-1	Long Lost Sweetheart -1, 2	BB B-8326, MW M-8437, RZAu G24621
041247-1	When The Golden Moon Is Shining -1, 2	BB B-8326, MW M-8437, RZAu G24621
041248-1	From Broadway To Heaven -1, 2	BB B-8355, MW M-8438
041249-1	That Wabash Rag -1	BB B-8355, MW M-8438
041250-1	Dill Pickle Rag -2	BB B-8518, MW M-8439
041251-1	Baby Chile -1	BB B-8518, MW M-8439
041252-1	Ramblin' John -2	BB B-8543, MW M-8440
041253-1	She's A Cousin Of Mine -1	BB B-8543, MW M-8440

FOUR VIRGINIANS

Richard Bigger, f; Leonard Jennings, ti; Elvin Bigger, g/v-1; Fred Richards, g; unidentified, calls-2.
    Winston-Salem, NC   Wednesday, September 21, 1927

81367-A	Swing Your Partner -2	OK 45181
81368-B	Promenade All -2	OK 45201
81369-B	New Coon In Town -2	OK 45181
81370-	Chasing Squirrels	OK unissued
81371-B	One Is My Mother -1	OK 45163
81372-A	Two Little Lads -1	OK 45163

Rev. OKeh 45201 by Scottdale String Band.

CODY FOX & HIS YELLOW JACKETS

See The Yellow Jackets [II].

CURLEY FOX

Curley Fox, f; prob. acc. Joe Shelton, g.
    Chicago, IL   Monday, August 19, 1935

C-90250-A,-AA	Listen To The Mocking Bird	De rejected
C-90253-A,-AA	Fifty Years Ago Waltz	De rejected

Intervening matrices are by Shelton Brothers.

Curley Fox, sp; acc. own g.
    Chicago, IL   Tuesday, August 20, 1935

C-90259-A,-AA	Talking Blues	De rejected

Curley Fox, v; acc. prob. Bob Shelton, md; prob. own g.
    Chicago, IL   Wednesday, August 21, 1935

C-90267-A,-AA	Loveless Love	De rejected

Curley Fox, f/sp; acc. Joe Shelton, g/sp.
    New York, NY   Tuesday, December 17, 1935

60238-A	One Eleven Special	De 5169, Min M-14162

Curley Fox, f; acc. Joe Shelton, g.
    New York, NY   Wednesday, December 18, 1935

60239-A	Listen To The Mocking Bird	De 5213, Min M-14161
60240-A	Fifty Years Ago Waltz	De 5213, Min M-14161
60241-A	Tennessee Roll	De 5169, Min M-14162

Curley Fox, sp; acc. own g.
    New York, NY   Thursday, December 19, 1935

60260-A	Curley's New Talkin' Blues	De 5185

Curley Fox, v; acc. Bob Shelton, md; Joe Shelton, g.
    New York, NY   Friday, December 20, 1935

60266-A	Yum Yum Blues	De 5185

Curley Fox recorded after 1942.

GLEN FOX & JOE WILSON

Pseudonym on Vocalion and Australian Regal-Zonophone for Asa Martin & James Roberts.

OSCAR FOX

Pseudonym on Supertone for Oscar L. Coffey.

FOX & DAVIS

Pseudonym on Supertone for Rutherford & Foster (see John D. Foster).

THE FOX CHASERS

Unknown, f; unknown, bj; unknown, g; unknown, bones.
    San Antonio, TX   Wednesday, June 11, 1930

404163-A	Red Wing	OK 45477

    San Antonio, TX   Thursday, June 12, 1930

404164-A	New Broom	OK 45477
404165-A	Forked Deer	OK 45496
404166-A	Eighth Of January	OK 45496

JACK FOY

Jack Foy, v; acc. prob. own g.
   Richmond, IN   Saturday, November 30, 1929
    15970,-A   My Little Lady   Ge rejected
    15971,-A   Root Hog Or Die   Ge rejected

Jack Foy, v/y-1; acc. prob. own g.
   Richmond, IN   Tuesday, December 24, 1929
    16011,-A   Everybody Does It In Hawaii -1   Ge rejected
    16012,-A   Root Hog Or Die   Ge rejected

DUEL FRADY

According to Victor files this artist's first name is Euel, but his record is credited as shown.

Duel Frady, v; acc. J.D. Stephens, bj; own g (or vice versa).
   Charlotte, NC   Monday, August 15, 1927
    39733-1   Poor Boy   Vi 20930
    39734-1   Leavenworth   Vi 20930

JACK FRALIA

See Jack & Bill.

FRANKIE & JOHNNY

Pseudonym on ARC labels and Conqueror for John McGhee & Frank Welling.

LEYLAND FRANKLIN

Pseudonym on Piccadilly for Carson Robison.

FRANKY & JOHNNY

Pseudonym on ARC labels and Conqueror for John McGhee & Frank Welling.

ART FRAZIER

See Wyzee Hamilton.

LEE FRAZIER

Lee Frazier, v/y-1; acc. prob. own g.
   Richmond, IN   Tuesday, May 23, 1933
    19184   The Ice Man Blues   Ch S16626
    19185   Turned Around Blues -1   Ch S16626

FREDRICKSBURG FUTURE FARMERS

Unknown, f; seven unknowns, h; two unknowns, ac; five unknowns, g.
   San Antonio, TX   Wednesday, February 26, 1936
    99392-1   Hi Lee Hi Lo   BB unissued
    99393-1   Isle Of Capri   BB unissued

FREEMAN & ASHCRAFT

Jack Freeman, Zeamond Ashcraft, v duet; acc. one of them, g; one of them, y.
   Atlanta, GA   Monday, April 15, 1929
    148301-2   I'll Still Write Your Name In The Sand   Co 15442-D

One of them, h; acc. the other, g.
   Atlanta, GA   Monday, April 15, 1929
    148302-1   Alabama Rag   Co 15442-D

FREEMAN QUARTETTE

Vocal quartet; acc. unknown, p.
   Birmingham, AL   Monday, November 12, 1928
    BIRM-773-   With Joy We Sing   Vo 5276
    BIRM-774-   Jesus Knows How   Vo 5276
    BIRM-775-   I'm Only On A Visit Here   Vo 5289
    BIRM-776-   My Troubles Will Be Over   Vo 5289
    BIRM-777-   Walking With My Savior   Vo 5316
Rev. Vocalion 5316 by Uncle Dave Macon.

Chicago, IL   Monday, August 19, 1929

C-4136-	Right Will Win	Vo 5376
C-4137-	I'll Ride On The Clouds With My Lord	Vo 5376
C-4138-	The Master Of The Storm	Vo 5429
C-4139-	I'm On The Right Side Now	Vo 5429
C-4140-	The King I Love	Vo 5368
C-4141-	All Praise Our King	Vo 5416

Chicago, IL   Tuesday, August 20, 1929

C-4142-	We Shall Reach Home	Vo 5461
C-4143-	It's Just Like Heaven	Vo 5461
C-4144-	I Want My Life To Testify	Vo 5357
C-4145-	O Blessed Day	Vo 5357
C-4146-	A Happy Song Of Praise	Vo 5416
C-4147-	Sing Hallelujah And Hozanna	Vo 5400
C-4152-	Living For Jesus	Vo 5400
C-4153-	Fly Away And Sing	Vo 5368
C-4154-	O Lights Of Home	Vo 5449
C-4155-	My Glorious Saviour	Vo 5449

Intervening matrices are Spanish.

THE FREENY HARMONIZERS

Prob.: Ira Ellis, f/v-1; S. Carlton Freeny, tbj; Neal Babb, g/v-2.
Jackson, MS   Sunday, October 20, 1935

JAX-204-	Roll On, Mississippi, Roll On	ARC unissued
JAX-206-1	Podunk Toddle	Vo 03140
JAX-207-1	Travellin' Blues -2	Vo 03140
JAX-208-	Ain't She Sweet	ARC unissued
JAX-209-	How Come You Do Me Like You Do? -1	ARC unissued
JAX-210-	It's Tight Like That	ARC unissued

Matrix JAX-205 is by The Mississippi Moaner (see B&GR).

FREENY'S BARN DANCE BAND

Leslie Freeny, f; Hendrix Freeny, f; Cleveland Freeny, md; S. Carlton Freeny, tbj; Fonzo Cannon, g/v-1/calls-2.
Jackson, MS   Tuesday, December 16, 1930

404736-B	Don't You Remember The Time	OK 45508
404737-B	The Leake County Two Step	OK 45524
404738-B	Sullivan's Hollow	OK 45508
404739-B	Croquet Habits -1	OK 45524
404740-B	Mississippi Square Dance – Part 1 -2	OK 45533
404741-B	Mississippi Square Dance – Part 2 -2	OK 45533

GEORGE FRENCH

Pseudonym on Madison and Van Dyke for Arthur Fields (and possibly for other, popular, artists).

CHARLES FRESHOUR & THE LONELY EAGLES

One side of Paramount 3247 and Broadway 8264 was thus credited (the other to Wilmer Watts & The Lonely Eagles); see Wilmer Watts.

MAX FRIEDMAN

Max Friedman, v; acc. unknown, f; unknown, p.
New York, NY   Saturday, February 23, 1929

401648-B	I Wish I Had Died In My Cradle (Before I Grew Up To Love You)	OK 45316
401649-B	In The Heart Of Kentucky	OK 45316

SAM & FRED FRIEND (THE FRIEND BROTHERS)

Sam Friend, Fred Friend, v duet; acc. prob. one of them, md; the other, g.
Hot Springs, AR.   Wednesday, March 17, 1937

HS-72-	Ozark Mountain Queen	ARC unissued
HS-73-	If I Could Drift Back There Again	ARC unissued
HS-74-	Dreaming Of The Old Homestead	ARC unissued
HS-75-	Blue Eyed Sally	ARC unissued

FRIENDSHIP FOUR
FRIENDSHIP QUARTETTE

Friendship Four: Mrs. N.R. York, sv; Mrs. L.T. Lasiter, av; A.W. Harwell, tv; —— Sherman, bsv; acc. unknown, p-1.
Memphis, TN   Saturday, February 4, 1928

| 41844-2 | Amazing Grace -1 | Vi 21287 |
| 41845-2 | Pearly White City | Vi 21287 |

Friendship Quartette: prob.: Mrs. N.R. York, sv; Mrs. L.T. Lasiter, av; A.W. Harwell, tv; —— Sherman, bsv; acc. unknown, p-1.
Memphis, TN   Thursday, February 23, 1928

400308-B	Lead Me Gently Home, Father -1	OK 45204
400309-A	I Surrender All -1	OK 45204
400310-B	The Great Judgment Morning -1	OK 45233
400311-A	Abide With Me	OK 45233
400312-B	Jesus Saviour Pilot Me	OK 45265
400313-B	Lead Me Saviour	OK 45265

COLUMBUS FRUGE

Columbus Fruge, v; acc. own ac.
Memphis, TN   Wednesday, September 18, 1929

55540-2	The Toad (Saut' Crapaud)	Vi 22184
55541-2	Pleur Plus'	Vi 22206
55542-2	Bayou Teche	Vi 22184
55543-2	Point Clear Blues	Vi 22206

WILFRED FRUGE–LEO SOILEAU

Leo Soileau, f; Wilfred Fruge, ac/v.
New Orleans, LA   Friday, November 8, 1929

56512-1,-2	Returning Home	Vi unissued
56513-1,-2	My Sweetheart Was Discouraged	Vi unissued
56514-1,-2	Mama's Crying For Me	Vi unissued
56515-1,-2	Calcasieu	Vi unissued

FRUIT JAR GUZZLERS (STEVENS & BOLAR)

Unidentified, v/v duet-1/v trio-2/sp-3; acc. unidentified, f-4; unidentified, bj; unidentified, g.
Chicago, IL   c. March 1928

20443-1	Wild Horse -4?	Pm 3095
20444-3	Old Joe Clark -4	Pm 3148
20445-1	Sourwood Mountain -4?	Pm 3095
20447-3	Fox In The Mountain -4?	Pm 3106, Bwy 8138
20448-1	C. & O. Whistle -4	Pm 3148
20449-2	The Black Sheep Of The Family	Pm 3099
20451-2	Kentucky Bootlegger -1	Pm 3113, Bwy 8139
20452-2	Cool Penitentiary -2	Pm 3113, Bwy 8139
20453-1	Steel Driving Man	Pm 3121, Bwy 8199
20454-2	Stack-O-Lee	Pm 3121, Bwy 8199
20455-2	Pity The Tramp	Pm 3099
20456-1	Cripple Creek -4	Bwy 8108
20456-2	Cripple Creek -4	Pm 3116
20457-2	Cackling Hen -3, 4	Pm 3116, Bwy 8108
20461-3	Yes I'm Free	Pm 3106, Bwy 8138

Broadways as by **The Pan Handle Boys**, except 8108 as by **Stone & Butler**.
Matrix 20457 is titled *Cacklin' Hen* on Broadway 8108.
Matrices 20446, 20450, 20458 to 20460 are untraced but probably by this group.

L.C. FULENWIDER

L.C. Fulenwider, prob. v; acc. unknown.
New York, NY   May/June 1924

| 91482-2 | Cradle Song | Co Personal unnumbered |

Columbia files note: "shipped June 14 1924"
This artist is included on the supposition that he may be the same as Leonard C. Fulwider (below).

JEP FULLER

Pseudonym on Vocalion for Vernon Dalhart.

LEONARD C. FULWIDER

Leonard C. Fulwider, v; acc. Cawley's Oklahoma Ridge Runners: Howard L. Cawley, f; Forrest A. Turner, md; own g.
    Dallas, TX   Thursday, October 10, 1929

    56358-1   Dalton Round-Up   Vi V-40270, Au 238

Acc. own g.
    Dallas, TX   Thursday, October 10, 1929

    56359-2   Whoa, Mule, Whoa   Vi V-40270, Au 238

Leonard C. Fulwider was a member of Jack Cawley's Oklahoma Ridge Runners.

J.B. FUSLIER & HIS MERRYMAKERS

This artist's full and correct name is Jean Batiste Fuselier.

J.B. Fuslier, v; acc. own f; Preston Manuel, g; prob. M.J. Achten, g; unidentified, v-1/v eff-1/sp-1.
    New Orleans, LA   Saturday, April 2, 1938

    022042-1   Ma Chere Jolite   BB B-2036
    022043-1   Ma Chere Catain   BB B-2036
    022044-1   Ma Chere Vieux Maison Dan Swet   BB B-2041
    022045-1   Ma Chere Joui Rouge   BB B-2041
    022046-1   Two Step De La Tell   BB B-2050
    022047-1   La Valse Du La Compaign   BB B-2050
    022048-1   Redell Breakdown   BB B-2052
    022049-1   Ma Chere Basett -1   BB B-2052

J.B. Fuslier, v; acc. own f; unknown, tbj; Preston Manuel, g; prob. M.J. Achten, g; unidentified, v-1/v eff-1.
    New Orleans, LA   Saturday, October 22, 1938

    027847-1   La Valse De Rebot (Drunkard's Waltz) -1   BB B-2055
    027848-1   Ponce A Moi (Think Of Me) -1   BB B-2055
    027849-1   La Robe Barre (Striped Dress)   BB B-2063
    027850-1   Chere Te Te (Honey Child)   BB B-2063
    027851-1   La Valse A Columbus (Columbus Waltz)   BB B-2071
    027852-1   Gueydon Two-Step -1   BB B-2071
    027853-1   La Fille De La Compaigne (Country Girl)   BB B-2068
    027854-1   Two-Step De Le Momou   BB B-2079
    027855-1   Ma Chere Bouclett (My Curly Headed Girl)   BB B-2068
    027856-1   Vien Don Ma Reguin (Come And Meet Me)   BB B-2079

J.B. Fuslier also recorded with Miller's Merrymakers and after 1942.

G

RAY GADDIS

Ray Gaddis, v; acc. unknown, f; unknown, g.
    Richmond, IN   Friday, February 20, 1931

    17543,-C   Drunken Hiccoughs   Ge rejected

NEWTON GAINES

Newton Gaines, v; acc. own g.
    Dallas, TX   Saturday, October 12, 1929

    56368-2   The Wreck Of The Six Wheeler   TT C-1564, Au 36-116
    56369-2   For Work I'm Too Lazy   TT C-1564, Au 36-116
    56370-2   A Walkin' The Streets Of Laredo   Vi V-40253, Au 237
    56371-2   Barbara Allen   Vi V-40253, Au 237

Timely Tunes C-1564, Aurora 36-116 as by **Jim New**.

Newton Gaines had earlier (1908-10) made cylinder recordings for John A. Lomax.

CLARENCE GANUS
CLAUDE GANUS
GANUS BROTHERS
GANUS BROTHERS [JUNIOR] QUARTET[TE]

Ganus Brothers Quartet: prob.: Clarence Ganus, bv; Claude Ganus, v; Cecil Ganus, v; Clyde Ganus, bsv; acc. Clarence Ganus, g.
    Atlanta, GA   Saturday, October 27, 1928

| 147314-2 | Have A Sunny Smile | Co 15390-D |
| 147315-1 | Rejoice In God | Co 15390-D |

Ganus Brothers: prob.: Clarence Ganus, Claude Ganus, v duet; acc. Clarence Ganus, g.

Atlanta, GA   Saturday, October 27, 1928

| 147316-2 | Sometime We'll Say Goodbye | Co 15331-D |
| 147317-2 | Wondrous Love | Co 15331-D |

Ganus Brothers Quartettte: prob.: Clarence Ganus, bv; Claude Ganus, v; Cecil Ganus, v; Clyde Ganus, bsv; acc. unknown, p.

Birmingham, AL   Tuesday, November 13, 1928

BIRM-782-	There We'll Spend Eternity	Vo 5271
BIRM-783-	Jesus Knows The Way	Vo 5271
BIRM-784-	Cast Thy Bread Upon The Water	Vo 5324
BIRM-785-	Beautiful City Of Zion	Vo 5324

Clarence Ganus, v; acc. prob. own g.

Birmingham, AL   Thursday, November 15, 1928

| BIRM-806- | Down In Indiana | Vo 5284, Me M12142, Po P9073, Pan 25053 |
| BIRM-807- | All Night Long | Vo 5284, Me M12142, Po P9073, Pan 25053 |

Clarence & Claude Ganus, v duet; acc. unknown, f-1; prob. Cecil Ganus, md; prob. Clarence Ganus, g; Claude Ganus, g.

Birmingham, AL   Thursday, November 15, 1928

BIRM-808-	Memories Of Floyd Collins -1	Vo 5272
BIRM-809-	Sometime You'll Pray -1	Vo 5272
BIRM-810-	Just The Thought Of Mother	Vo 5312
BIRM-811-	Row Us Over The Tide	Vo 5312

Clarence Ganus, v; acc. two unknowns, f; unknown, p; prob. own g.

Chicago, IL   Wednesday, October 16, 1929

C-4649-	Won't The Angels Let Mama Come Home	Vo 5452
C-4650-	Lay Me Where My Mother's Sleeping	Vo 5452
C-4651-	The Dying Soldier	Vo 5396

Rev. Vocalion 5396 by Emry Arthur.

Acc. prob. own g.

Chicago, IL   Wednesday, October 16, 1929

| C-4652- | Take A Tater And Wait | Vo 5409 |

Chicago, IL   Thursday, October 17, 1929

C-4653-	I'm Going Away (Cause You Don't Treat Me Right)	Vo 5417
C-4654-	My Girl With Auburn Hair	Vo 5417
C-4655-	My Sunny Alabama Home	Vo 5409

Clarence Ganus, v/y-1; acc. unknown, cl-2; prob. own g.

Chicago, IL   Friday, October 18, 1929

C-4666-	I Love Nobody But You -1	Vo 5385
C-4667-3	This Morning – This Evening So Soon -2	Vo 5386
C-4668-	Sleeping At The Foot Of The Bed	Vo 5386

Rev. Vocalion 5385 by Emry Arthur.

Ganus Brothers Junior Quartet: prob.: Clarence Ganus, bv; Claude Ganus, v; Cecil Ganus, v; Clyde Ganus, bsv; acc. unknown.

Atlanta, GA   Friday, November 14, 1930

ATL-6660-	Beautiful Land Of Glory	Br rejected
ATL-6661-	Why Stay Outside	Br rejected
ATL-6662-	All Praise The Lord	Br rejected
ATL-6663-	I'm Gonna Rise Up	Br rejected

Clarence, Claude, Cecil, and Clyde Ganus were brothers. Their father Walter P. Ganus is reported to have participated in Columbia and Vocalion sessions, but in what capacity is unknown.

LUELLA GARDNER [& DAVIS]
GARDNER & DAVID

Pseudonyms on Diva, Harmony, and Velvet Tone for Samantha Bumgarner & Eva Davis.

GARLAND BROTHERS & GRINSTEAD

Vocal trio; acc. unknown, f; unknown, g; unknown, vc.

Johnson City, TN   Thursday, October 18, 1928

| 147234-1 | Just Over The River | Co 15679-D |
| 147235-2 | Beautiful | Co 15679-D |

CLEM GARNER
See Earl McCoy.

R.C. GARNER
GARNER BROS.

Garner Bros., v duet; acc. R.C. Garner, sg; Etha K. Thomas, p.
   Richmond, IN   Saturday, November 1, 1924

| 12061 | From Jerusalem To Jericho | JGS 20077 |
| 12062-B | I'm Over The Jordan Tide | JGS 20077 |

These and subsequent recordings were custom-made by Gennett for the Jubilee Gospel Singers label.

   Richmond, IN   Friday, January 9, 1925

| 12119 | Take This Message To My Mother | Ge rejected |
| 12120 | Do Lord, Do Remember Me | JGS 20089 |

   Richmond, IN   Friday, January 24, 1925

12130	Jim & Me	JGS 20088
12131-B	The Papal Anthem A 100% Song	JGS 20088
12132-A	Take This Message To My Mother	JGS 20089

R.C. Garner, v; acc. Etha K. Thomas, p; own g; or R.C. Garner, sg solo-1; or Garner Bros.-2, v duet; acc. R.C. Garner, sg; Etha K. Thomas, p.
   Richmond, IN   Monday, April 13, 1925

12203-A	You're Going To Leave The Old Home Jim	JGS 20104
12204-A	Two Robes -2	JGS 20102
12205-A	I'm On My Way To Heaven -1	JGS 20104
12206-A	The Bright Fiery Cross -2	JGS 20102

BLIND UNCLE GASPARD

Blind Uncle Gaspard, v; acc. own g; Delma Lachney, g-1.
   Chicago, IL   c. January 26, 1929

C-2869-	Assi Dans La Fenetre De Ma Chambre (Sitting In The Window Of My Room)	Vo 5280
C-2870-	Mercredi Soir Passé (Last Wednesday Night)	Vo 5281
C-2876-	Marksville Blues -1	Vo 5320

Intervening matrices are by Delma Lachney. Rev. all issues by Delma Lachney.

   New Orleans, LA   Tuesday, March 5, 1929

| NO-122- | Natchitocheo (French Town) | Vo 5333 |
| NO-123- | Sur Le Borde De L'Eau (On The Riverside) | Vo 5333 |

Blind Uncle Gaspard also recorded with Delma Lachney.

JOHNNIE GATES (THE SAW MILL YODLER)

Johnnie Gates, v/y; acc. own g.
   New York, NY   Monday, June 2, 1930

150541-2	Saw Mill Blues No. 1	Co 15573-D
150542-1	Don't Leave Mother Alone	Co 15573-D, Re/RZAu G21557
150543-2	Saw-Mill Blues No. 2	Co 15661-D
150544-3	The Little Pale Face Girl	Co 15661-D

Columbia 15661-D is subcredited (**The Saw-Mill Yodler**); Regal/Regal-Zonophone G21557 is subcredited (**The Saw Mill Yodeler**). Rev. Regal/Regal -Zonophone G21557 by Claude Davis Trio.

BILL GATIN

This artist's name is correctly spelled Bill Gatins.

Bill Gatin, sp; acc. Marion Orr, g.
   New York, NY   Wednesday, July 10, 1935

| 39689-C | Talkin' Blues | De 5122 |

Bill Gatin, v/y; acc. Marion Orr, f; Walter Kite, g.
   New York, NY   Wednesday, July 10, 1935

| 39690-C | I Don't Work For A Livin' | De 5122 |

Bill Gatins also recorded with the Cherokee Ramblers.

GATWOOD SQUARE DANCE BAND

Unknown, f; unknown, md; unknown, g; Allen Rainey, calls.
   New Orleans, LA   Saturday, December 15, 1928

| 147646-2 | Third Party | Co 15363-D |
| 147647-1 | Shear The Sheep Bobbie | Co 15363-D |

This group may be associated with the Rainey Old Time Band.

JOE & ZEB GAUNT
See Arthur Fields & Fred Hall.

DAVID GAUTHIER

David Gauthier, v; acc. prob. own g.
 Grafton, WI   c. late October 1931

| L-1208-1 | Cowboy's Meditation | Bwy 8325 |
| L-1210-1 | The Orphan Girl | Bwy 8325 |

Matrix L-1209 is untraced but probably by this artist.
 Grafton, WI   c. April 1932

| L-1456-2 | The Texas Cowboy | Pm 581 |
| L-1457-1 | The Bright Mohawk Valley | Pm 581 |

RED GAY & JACK WELLMAN
RED GAY'S BROWN JUG BAND

Red Gay & Jack Wellman: Red Gay, f/sp; Jack Wellman, g/sp.
 Atlanta, GA   Thursday, November 13, 1930

| ATL-6652- | Flat Wheel Train Blues – No. 1 | Br 523 |
| ATL-6653- | Flat Wheel Train Blues – No. 2 | Br 523 |

Red Gay's Brown Jug Band: no details.
 Atlanta, GA   Friday, November 14, 1930

| ATL-6654 | Good Morning Waltz | Br unissued |
| ATL-6655 | Golden Waltz | Br unissued |

WHIT GAYDON

Whit Gaydon, v-1/sp-2/v eff; acc. own f.
 Memphis, TN   Tuesday, September 17, 1929

| 55527-2 | Tennessee Coon Hunt -2 | Vi V-40315 |
| 55528-2 | Hen Cacklin' Piece -1 | Vi V-40315 |

NORMAN GAYLE

Pseudonym on Champion for G.B. Grayson & Henry Whitter.

GENE & GLENN

Recordings by this duet, whose full names are Gene Carroll and Glenn Rowell, seem not quite to fit within the scope of this book. Glenn Rowell also recorded with Ford Rush (in Columbia's popular series, as **Ford & Glenn**).

GENTRY BROTHERS

Lester McFarland, f-1/v; George Reneau, h-2/g/v.
 New York, NY   c. June 14, 1927

7316-2	A Picture From Life's Other Side -1, 2	Ba 6041, Do 0186, Htd 16494, Or 974, Re 8370, Chg 667, Cq 7731, Apex 8722
7317-2	Where We Never Grow Old	Ba 2164, Do 0186, Je 5116, Or 1001, Re 8370
7318-	If I Could Hear My Mother Pray Again -2	Ba 2165, Or 1000, Pm 3039, Bwy 8058

Banner 2164, 2165, 6041, Challenge 667 as by **Lonesome Pine Twins**. Domino 0186, Regal 8370, Conqueror 7731 as by **Smoky Mountain Twins**. Jewel 5116, Oriole 974, 1000, 1001, Homestead 16494 as by **Halliday Brothers**. Paramount 3039 as by **Collins Brothers/The Pride Of Kentucky**. Broadway 8058 as by **Cramer Brothers**.
Controls are used on some issues as follows: 7316 = 1005; 7317 = 1058-2; 7318 = 1055-2, 753.

Lester McFarland, f-1/v; George Reneau, h-2/g/v-3.
 New York, NY   Wednesday, June 15, 1927

7322-1	You'll Never Miss Your Mother 'Till She's Gone -1, 2, 3	Ba 2164, Do 0196, Je 5116, Or 1001, Re 8414, Cq 7072, Apex 8722
7323-2	I Was Born Four Thousand Years Ago -1, 2, 3	Do 0191, Re 8390, Pm 3041, Bwy 8059, Cq 8065
7324-	Love Always Has Its Way -2	Ba 6040, Do 0190, Or 975, Re 8389, Pm 3039, Bwy 8058, Chg 660
7325-	Midnight On The Stormy Deep	Pl unissued
7326-	On Top Of Old Smokey -1, 2, 3	Pm 3040, Bwy 8071

7327-	Put My Little Shoes Away -1, 2, 3	Do 0190, Re 8389, Pm 3040, Bwy 8071
7330-2	Sara Jane -1, 2, 3	Do 0191, Re 8390, Pm 3041, Bwy 8059, Cq 7065
7331-	John Henry Blues	Pl unissued
7332-	When The Work's Done This Fall -1	Pm 3042, Bwy 8060

Banner 2164, 6040 as by **Lonesome Pine Twins**. Challenge 660 as by **John Sackett**. Domino 0190, 0191, 0196, Regal 8389, 8390, 8414, Conqueror 7065, 7072 as by **Smoky Mountain Twins**. Oriole 975 as by **Fred Halliday**; 1001 as by **Halliday Brothers**. Paramounts as by **Collins Brothers/The Pride Of Kentucky**, except 3039 as by **Al Collins**. Broadways as by **Cramer Brothers**, except 8060 as by **Al Cramer**.

Matrix 7322 is titled *You'll Never Miss Your Mother Till She's Gone* on Banner 2164, Oriole 1001. Matrix 7323 is titled *I Was Born 4000 Years Ago* on Domino 0191.

Controls are used on some issues, as follows: 7322 = 1057-1; 7323 = 758; 7324 = 1008-2, 754; 7330 = 757; 7332 = 760.

Lester McFarland, v; acc. own g; unidentified, train-wh eff.
    New York, NY   Thursday, June 16, 1927

7335-	K. C. Whistle	Ba 2165, Or 1000

Banner 2165 as by **John Sackett**. Oriole 1000 as by **Fred Halliday**. Unspecified issues of matrix 7335 use the control 1056-2.

Lester McFarland, f/v; George Reneau, h-1/g/v.
    New York, NY   Thursday, June 16, 1927

7336-3	In The Good Old Summer Time -1	Ba 6040, Do 0187, Or 975, Re 8369, Pm 3042, Bwy 8060, Chg 660
7337-1	There's No Disappointment In Heaven	Ba 6041, Do 0196, Htd 16494, Je 5116, Or 974, Re 8414, Chg 667, Cq 7072, ARC-Bwy 8127

Banner 6040, 6041, Challenge 660 as by **Lonesome Pine Twins**. Domino 0187, 0196, Regal 8369, 8414, Conqueror 7072 as by **Smoky Mountain Twins**. Jewel 5116, Oriole 974, 975, Homestead 16494 as by **Halliday Brothers**. Paramount 3042 as by **Collins Brothers/The Pride Of Kentucky**. Broadway 8060, ARC-Broadway 8127 as by **Cramer Brothers**.

Broadway 8127 uses the same titles as ARC-Broadway 8127, but from Paramount matrices by XC Sacred Quartette.

Controls are used on some issues, as follows: 7336 = 1007-1, 759; 7337 = 1006.

Revs: Domino 0187, Regal 8369 by Ernest V. Stoneman; ARC-Broadway 8127 by Cornwall & Cleary.

Lester McFarland and George Reneau also recorded in their own names, the former generally in partnership with Robert A. Gardner.

GENTRY FAMILY

Leonard Gentry, tv; Giles Gentry, tv; Paul Gentry, bv; Wade Gentry, bsv; unacc.
    Nashville, TN   Wednesday, October 3, 1928

47126-1	You Can't Make A Monkey Out Of Me	Vi V-40013
47127-1,-2	Hop Along, Sister Mary	Vi unissued

    Nashville, TN   Saturday, October 6, 1928

47155-1	Jog Along, Boys	Vi V-40013
47156-1,-2	In The Evening Take Me Home	Vi unissued
47157-1,-2	Jesus Paid It All	Vi unissued
47158-1,-2	The Church In The Wildwood	Vi unissued

GEORGE & HENSON

——— George, v-1; Russell Henson, v-2; acc. prob. one of them, f; the other, bj-3/g-4.
    Richmond, IN   Friday, January 10, 1930

16066,-A	I Wonder If You Love Me -1?, 4	Ge rejected
16067,-A	Sweet William -2, 3	Ge rejected

——— George, Russell Henson, v duet; acc. prob. one of them f; the other, g.
    Richmond, IN   Tuesday, January 21, 1930

16116,-A,-B	My Tennessee Sweetheart	Ge unissued
16117	The Reckless Hobo	Ge rejected trial recording

GEORGIA CRACKERS

Paul Cofer, f/v; Leon Cofer, bj/v; Ben Evans, g/poss. v-1.
    Atlanta, GA   Monday, March 21, 1927

80593-A	Riley The Furniture Man	OK 45111
80594-	Railroad Bill	OK unissued
80595-B	Coon From Tennessee -1	OK 45098
80596-B	The Georgia Black Bottom	OK 45111
80597-B	Diamond Joe	OK 45098
80598-	Dance All Night With A Bottle In Your Hand	OK unissued

Paul Cofer, f/prob. v; Leon Cofer, bj; Ben Evans, g.
Atlanta, GA   Wednesday, October 12, 1927
81757-	Bright Lights In The Graveyard	OK unissued
81758-B	I've Got A Gal In Baltimore	OK 45192
81759-	Bad Mule	OK unissued
81760-	Climbing Up The Golden Stairs	OK unissued
81761-A	Stockade Blues	OK 45192
81762-	Year Of Jubilo	OK unissued

See also Cofer Brothers. The Georgia Crackers who recorded after 1942 are connected with the Newman Brothers (Hank & Slim).

GEORGIA MELODY BOYS

Pseudonym on Broadway for the Golden Melody Boys.

THE GEORGIA ORGAN GRINDERS

Clayton McMichen, f; Bert Layne, f; Lowe Stokes, o; Fate Norris, bj; Melvin Dupree, g; Dan Hornsby, v-1.
Atlanta, GA   Tuesday, April 9, 1929
148222-2	Back Up And Push	Co 15394-D
148223-2	Smoke Behind The Clouds -1	Co 15394-D
148224-	Sweet Sixteen Next Sunday	Co unissued

Matrix 148224 was logged as by **Lowe Stokes & His Organ Grinders**.

Clayton McMichen, f/v-1; Bert Layne, f; Lowe Stokes, f-2/o-3; Fate Norris, bj; Melvin Dupree, g; Dan Hornsby, v-4; unidentified, v-5/v duet-6; band v-7.
Atlanta, GA   Wednesday, April 10, 1929
148227-2	Four Thousand Years Ago -3, 4, 7	Co 15445-D
148228-2	Georgia Man -2, 6	Co 15445-D
148231-2	Skip To My Lou My Darling -2, 5, 7	Co 15415-D
148232-2	Charming Betsy -1, 2, 7	Co 15415-D

Intervening matrices are by Hugh Cross & Riley Puckett.

GEORGIA PEACHES

No details.
Atlanta, GA   Tuesday, March 25, 1930
| ATL-8014 | I'll Be Back Home | Br/Vo rejected trial recording |
| ATL-8015 | Those Old Time Days | Br/Vo rejected trial recording |

GEORGIA POT LICKERS

See Lowe Stokes.

GEORGIA SACRED HARP QUARTET

Vocal quartet; prob. unacc.
Atlanta, GA   late August 1924
| 8735- | Windham | OK 40195 |
| 8738- | Wondrous Love | OK 40195 |

Intervening matrices are untraced.

THE GEORGIA SERENADERS

Pseudonym on Supertone for Warren Caplinger & The Dixie Harmonizers.

GEORGIA WILDCATS

Jesse Pitts, bj/v; Tom Darby, g/v.
Charlotte, NC   Wednesday, May 27, 1931
| 69365-1 | She's Waiting For Me (Fort Benning Blues) | Vi 23640 |

Charlotte, NC   Friday, May 29, 1931
69378-1,-2	The Bootlegger Song	Vi unissued
69379-1,-2	The Monkey Song	Vi unissued
69380-1	Goin' Down That Lonesome 'Frisco Line	Vi 23640

Charlotte, NC   Saturday, May 30, 1931
| 69398-1,-2 | Broke Man Blues | Vi unissued |
| 69399-1,-2 | High Sheriff From Georgia | Vi unissued |

Tom Darby also recorded under his own name with Jimmie Tarlton. Jesse Pitts is possibly a member of Hinson, Pitts & Coley.

GEORGIA YELLOW HAMMERS

Bill Chitwood, f/v-1/bsv-2/sp-1; Bud Landress, bj/lv-2; C. Philip Reeve, g/v-2; Elias Meadows, g/tv-3.
    Atlanta, GA   Friday, February 18, 1927

37919-1	Pass Around The Bottle -2, 3	Vi 20550, MW M-8054
37920-2	Going To Ride That Midnight Train -2	Vi 20549
37921-1	Johnson's Old Grey Mule -1	Vi 20550
37922-2	Fourth Of July At A Country Fair -2, 3	Vi 20549

Rev. Montgomery Ward M-8054 by Bud Billings (Frank Luther).

Bud Landress, f/lv; C. Ernest Moody, bj-u/v; Phil Reeve, g/v; Clyde Evans, g/v.
    Charlotte, NC   Tuesday, August 9, 1927

39777-2	Tennessee Coon	Vi 21073
39778-2	All Old Bachelors Are Hard To Please	Vi 21073
39779-2	Mary, Don't You Weep	Vi 20928
39780-2	Going To Raise A Rucus Tonight	Vi 20928
39781-1	I'm S-A-V-E-D	Vi 21195
39782-2	The Picture On The Wall	Vi 20943

Andrew Baxter, f; Ernest Moody, bj-u; Phil Reeve, g; Clyde Evans, g; Bud Landress, sp.
    Charlotte, NC   Tuesday, August 9, 1927

39783-2	G Rag	Vi 21195

Bud Landress, f/lv; Ernest Moody, bj-u/v; Phil Reeve, g/v; Clyde Evans, g/v.
    Charlotte, NC   Wednesday, August 10, 1927

39787-2	My Carolina Girl	Vi 20943

Bud Landress, f/lv/sp-1; Ernest Moody, bj-u/v-2; Phil Reeve, g/v-2; Clyde Evans, g/v-2.
    Atlanta, GA   Tuesday, February 21, 1928

41924-2	Song Of The Doodle Bug -2	Vi 21362
41925-1	The Moonshine Hollow Band -2	Vi 21626-2
41926-2	My Eyes Are Growing Dimmer Every Day -2	Vi 21486
41927-1	The Running Blues -1	Vi 21626
41928-1	When The Birds Begin Their Singing In The Trees -2	Vi 21362

    Atlanta, GA   Wednesday, February 22, 1928

41945-1	The Old Rock Jail Behind The Old Iron Gate	Vi 21486

Bill Chitwood, f/v-1/sp-2; Bud Landress, bj/lv/sp-2; Ernest Moody, g/v-3/sp-2; Phil Reeve, g/v-4/sp-2.
    Atlanta, GA   Thursday, October 18, 1928

47189-3	Big Ball In Memphis -1, 3, 4	Vi V-40138
47190-2	Come Over And See Me Sometime -1, 3, 4	Vi V-40091, ZoSA 4235
47191-1	Sale Of Simon Slick – Part 1 -2, 3, 4	Vi V-40069
47192-3	Sale Of Simon Slick – Part 2 -1, 2, 3, 4	Vi V-40069
47193-3	Kiss Me Quick -1, 3, 4	Vi V-40091, ZoSA 4235
47194-3	Black Annie	Vi V-40138
47195-2	Warhorse Game -1, 3, 4	Vi V-40004
47196-3	The Deacon's Calf -3/4	Vi V-40004

Bill Chitwood, f/v-1; Ernest Moody, poss. f-2/u-3/v-1; Phil Reeve, g/v-1; Melvin Dupree, g.
    Atlanta, GA   Wednesday, November 27, 1929

56613-1	Childhood Days -1, 3	Vi 23542
56614-2	No One To Welcome Me Home -1, 2	Vi 23542
56615-1	White Lightning -3	Vi 23683, BB B-5126, Sr S-3207, Au 406
56616-1	Peaches Down In Georgia -3	Vi 23683, BB B-5126, Sr S-3207, Au 406

See also Bill Chitwood, Clyde Evans Band, (Uncle) Bud Landress, Phil Reeve–Ernest Moody. Members of this circle also participate in recordings by the following groups: Calhoun Sacred Quartet, Charles Brothers, Dixie Crackers, Gordon County Quartet, Moody Bible Sacred Harp Singers, The Moody Quartet, North Georgia Four, North Georgia Quartette, Turkey Mountain Singers. (For a collective discography of these recordings see Old Time Music 25 [Summer 1977] 17-21.)

FRANK GERALD & HOWARD DIXON

Frank Gerald, Howard Dixon, v duet; acc. Howard Dixon, sg; Frank Gerald, g.
    Charlotte, NC   Thursday, February 18, 1937

07154-1	At Twilight Old Pal Of Yesterday	MW M-7856
07155-1	Call Me Pal Of Mine	MW M-7856

Montgomery Ward M-7856 as by **Dixon Brothers**.

The Rambling Duet (Frank Gerald–Howard Dixon), v/y-1 duet; acc. Howard Dixon, sg; Frank Gerald, g.
    Charlotte, NC   Thursday, August 5, 1937

011983-1	Honey It's Just Because	BB B-7131
011984-1	Back To My Wyoming Home -1	BB B-7131
011985-1	I Can't Tell Why I Love You	BB B-7233
011986-1	Under The Old Cherry Tree	BB B-7233

Bluebird B-7233 is subcredited (**Frank Gerald–H. Dixon**).

Charlotte, NC   Tuesday, January 25, 1938

018663-1	Woman's Answer To "What Is Home Without Love"	BB B-7450, MW M-7465
018664-1	Hobo Jack The Rambler	BB B-7534, MW M-7466
018665-1	More Pretty Girls Than One – Part 3	BB B-7484, MW M-7464
018666-1	There's A Place In My Home For Mother	BB B-7574, MW M-7465
018667-1	Bootlegger's Story	BB B-7484, MW M-7467
018668-1	Wonder Who's Kissing Her – Part 2	BB B-7534, MW M-7466
018669-1	Prisoner's Plea	BB B-7574, MW M-7467
018670-1	Faithless Husband	BB B-7450, MW M-7464

Frank Gerald–Howard Dixon, v duet; acc. Howard Dixon, sg; Frank Gerald, g.

Rock Hill, SC   Sunday, September 25, 1938

026963-1	'Twas Only A Dream	BB B-8055
026964-1	Answer To Broken Engagement	BB B-8151
026965-1	The Old Apple Tree	BB unissued
026966-1	By The Old Oaken Bucket, Louise	BB B-8151
026967-1	I Told The Stars About You	BB unissued
026968-1	That Old Sweetheart Of Mine	BB unissued

Frank Gerald–Howard Dixon–Mutt Evans, v trio; acc. unidentified, md; unidentified, bj; unidentified, g.

Rock Hill, SC   Sunday, September 25, 1938

026969-1	Honey Baby Mine	BB B-7895
026970-1	My Trundle Bed	BB B-8055
026971-1	New Trouble	BB B-7895
026972-1	Trial Testing Time	BB unissued

Howard Dixon also recorded with Dorsey Dixon as the Dixon Brothers.

HUGH GIBBS STRING BAND

James William Jackson, f; Bob Gibbs, tbj; Hugh Gibbs, harp-g; Joe Gibbs, g; unidentified, v-1; Harry Charles v-2; Samuel Spencer, v-3.

Chicago, IL   c. March 1927

4391-1	Swinging In The Lane -1	Pm 3001
4395-2	I'm Goin [sic] Crazy -1	Pm 3001
4401-3	Lord I'm Coming Home -2	Pm 3002
4405-2	My Little Girl -3	Pm 3004
4407-3	Almost Persuaded -3	Pm 3002
4408-2	In The Good Old Summer Time	Pm 3004
	Chicken Reel	Pm 3003
	Double Eagle March	Pm 3003

Intervening matrices are untraced, but two are doubtless accounted for by Paramount 3003, and some, if not all, of the others are likely to be by this group also. According to Jackson, further titles recorded at this session included *When The Roses Bloom Again*, *I Don't Love Nobody*, and *Bully Of The Town*.

GIBBS & WATSON

Pseudonym on Harmony and Silvertone for Gid Tanner & Riley Puckett (see both).

GIBBS BROTHERS WITH CLAUDE DAVIS

Hugh Gibbs, sg; Bob Gibbs, md; Joe Gibbs, g; Claude Davis, v; unidentified, v-1.

Knoxville, TN   Tuesday, April 1, 1930

K-8058-	Goodbye Dixie Dear	Vo 5469
K-8059-	Do You Think That You Could Love Me	Vo 5469
K-8060-	You Left Me Last Night Broken Hearted	Vo 5464
K-8061-	Strolling Home With Jenny -1	Vo 5464
K-8062-	I Love My Toodlum-Doo	Vo 5447
K-8063-	I Wandered Away From Home	Vo 5447

GIBSON STRING TRIO

W.C. Pitman, Jr, md; unidentified, md; unidentified, g.

Richmond, IN   Thursday, August 30, 1928

| 14219 | Silvery Bell | Ge 6618, Ch 15584, Spt 9308, 9312 |
| 14220 | Persian Lamb | Ge 6618, Spt 9312 |

Champion 15584 as by **Elk Creek Trio**. Supertone 9308 as by **Scott County Trio**.
The unidentified musicians are named in Gennett files as J.A. Ramsey and Louis Wolf, but it is not known who plays which instrument.

Workman, Ramsey & Wolfe: unidentified, f; unidentified, bj; unidentified, g.
Richmond, IN   Thursday, August 30, 1928

| 14221 | The South Solon Quadrille | Ge 6659, Spt 9308 |
| 14222-A | St. James | Ge 6659, Ch 15584 |

Champion 15584 as by **Elk Creek Trio**. Supertone 9308 as by **Scott County Trio**.
The musicians are identified in Gennett files as Dan Workman, J.A. Ramsey, and Louis Wolf [sic], but it is not known who plays which instrument.

The Gibson String Trio: unknown, md; unknown, bj; unknown, g.
Richmond, IN   Thursday, October 25, 1928

14377,-A	Banjo Rag	Ge 6793
14378,-A	On Desert Sands	Ge rejected
14379,-A,-B	Peacock Strut	Ge rejected
14380,-A	Dixie Moonbeam	Ge rejected
14381,-A	Sassafras Rag	Ge 6793
14382,-A	Butterscotch Rag	Ge rejected

It is not known which takes of matrices 14377 and 14381 are used on Gennett 6793.

GIDDENS SISTERS

Vocal trio; acc. unknown, md-1; unknown, g.
Atlanta, GA   Wednesday, June 1, 1927

80949-A	Standing On The Promises Of God	OK 45120
80950-	Stand Up For Jesus	OK unissued
80951-B	Don't Sell Pa Any More Rum -1	OK 45143
80952-A	Where Is My Wandering Boy To-night? -1	OK 45143
80953-	Jesus Is Calling	OK unissued
80954-A	There Is A Fountain Filled With Blood	OK unissued: LC LBC15 (LP); WHAA WH-1017 (CD)

Unacc.
Atlanta, GA   Thursday, June 2, 1927

80963-	[unknown title]	OK unissued
80964-A	Where We'll Never Grow Old	OK 45165
80965-	[unknown title]	OK unissued

Unacc.-1; or acc. unknown, g-2.
Atlanta, GA   Friday, June 3, 1927

80968-A	Asleep In Jesus -1	OK 45165
80969-A	I'm Going Home To Die No More -2	OK 45120
80970-	O Why Not Tonight -2	OK unissued

THE GILBERT FAMILY

Pseudonym on Canadian Crown, Domino, Sterling, and possibly Melotone for the Pickard Family.

CLARENCE GILL

Clarence Gill, v; acc. unknown.
Richmond, IN   Thursday, January 6, 1927

12590,-A	The L&N Brakeman	Ge rejected
12592,-A	It Ain't No Place For Me	Ge rejected
12593,-A	Little Cory	Ge rejected

Matrix 12591 is by John Hammond.

HENRY C. GILLILAND–A.C. (ECK) ROBERTSON

See A.C. (Eck) Robertson.

GIRL O' YESTERDAY (KATHRYN PARSONS)

Kathryn Parsons, v; acc. unknown, p.
New York, NY   between September 24 and October 26, 1930

| GEX-2782 | Oldtime Medley | Ge rejected trial recording |
| GEX-2783 | The Baggage Coach Ahead | Ge rejected trial recording |

These items are described in Gennett's files as "Old Time Vocal", but with a note: "Artist not H.B. [i.e. hillbilly]."

THE GIRLS OF THE GOLDEN WEST

Professionally known as Mildred and Dorothy Good, these artists' real surname was Goad.

Mildred Good, Dorothy Good, v/y duet; acc. Dorothy Good, g.

Chicago, IL   Friday, July 28, 1933

75961-1	Started Out From Texas	BB B-5155, Eld 2054, Sr S-3236, MW M-4384, HMVIn N4405
75962-1	Colorado Blues	BB B-5155, Eld 2054, Sr S-3236, MW M-4384, HMVIn N4405
75963-1	That Silver-Haired Daddy Of Mine	BB B-5167, Eld 2064, Sr S-3248, MW M-4455, HMVIn N4407, Twin FT9118
75964-1	Put Away My Little Shoes	BB B-5226, Eld 2112, Sr S-3309, MW M-4404, Twin FT8128
75965-1	Hi O, Hi O (Night Herding Song)	BB B-5189, Eld 2082, Sr S-3269, MW M-4412, Twin FT8187
75966-1	You Get A Line And I'll Get A Pole	BB B-5167, Eld 2064, Sr S-3248, MW M-4455
75967-1	Tumble Down Shack In My Dreams	BB B-5283, Eld 2157, Sr S-3364, RZ ME32, MR2099, Twin FT8074
75968-1	Listen To The Story Of Sleepy Hollow Bill	BB B-5189, Eld 2082, Sr S-3269, MW M-4412, Twin FT8187
75969-1	Baby's Lullaby	BB B-5226, Eld 2112, Sr S-3309, MW M-4404, Twin FT8128

Matrix 75967 is titled *Tumble Down Shack Of My Dreams* on Regal-Zonophone ME32, MR2099.
Rev. all issues of matrix 75967 by Lone Star Cowboys.

Chicago, IL   Tuesday, December 5, 1933

77194-1	My Little Old Nevada Home	BB B-6004, RZAu G23168, HMVIn N4382
77195-1	Home Sweet Home In Texas	BB B-5318, Sr S-3399, MW M-4417, RZAu G22369, HMVIn N4407, Twin FT9118
77196-1	When The Bees Are in The Hive	BB B-5427, MW M-4486, HMVIn N4347
77209-1	Lonely Cowgirl	BB B-6054, RZAu G22669, HMVIn N4385
77210-1	Little Old Cabin In The Lane	Vi 23857, BB B-5737, RZ ME31, MR1597, RZAu G22550, HMVIn N4288
77211-1	The Cowgirl's Dream	Vi 23857, BB B-5318, Sr S-3359, MW M-4417, RZAu G22369, HMVIn N4288
77212-1	Sing Me A Song Of The Mountains	BB B-6004, RZAu G23168, HMVIn N4382
77213-1	Round-Up Time In Texas	BB B-5382, Sr S-3463, MW M-4461, HMVIn N4404
77214-1	The Dying Cowboy On The Prairie	BB B-5382, Sr S-3463, MW M-4461, HMVIn N4404
77215-1	The Tramp's Mother	BB B-5394, MW M-4486, HMVIn N4333
77216-1	Old Pal of Yesterday	BB B-5427, HMVIn N4347
77217-1	The Roamer's Memories	BB B-6054, RZAu G22669, HMVIn N4385

Matrices 77197/98 are by Whiskey Bottle Boys; 77199 to 77201 by Duke Ellington (see *JR*); 77202 to 77208 by Ted Weems (see *JR*). Rev. Bluebird B-5394, HMV N4333 by Jimmie Davis.

Chicago, IL   Tuesday, October 9, 1934

80839-1	Will There Be Any Yodelers In Heaven?	BB B-8587, RZAu G24817
80840-2	Going Back To Mississippi	BB B-8587, RZAu G24817
80841-1	Ride–Ride–Ride	BB B-5719, MW M-7203, Twin FT1845
80842-1	Old Chisholm Trail	BB B-5718, RZ ME31, MR1597, RZAu G22550, Twin FT1845,
80843-1	We'll Meet At The End Of The Trail	BB B-8473, RZ MR3401, Twin FT8958
80844-1	Cowboy Jack	BB B-5719, HMVIn N4370
80845-1	Whoopee Ti-Yi-Yo Git Along Little Doggies	BB B-5718, HMVIn N4370
80846-1	Two Cowgirls On The Lone Prairie	BB B-8562, RZAu G24359
80847-1	Lonesome Valley Sally	BB B-8562, RZAu G24359
80848-1	Round-Up In Cheyenne	BB B-8473, RZ MR3401, Twin FT8958

Chicago, IL   Wednesday, October 31, 1934

80951-1	I'm Lonesome For You Caroline	BB B-5737, HMVIn N4373
80952-1	Bucking Broncho	BB B-5752, MW M-7204, RZAu G22480, HMVIn N4408, Twin FT9119
80953-1	By The Silvery Rio Grande	BB B-5752, MW M-7204, RZAu G22480, HMVIn N4408, Twin FT9119

Rev. HMV N4373 by Jesse Rodgers.

Chicago, IL			Monday, November 4, 1935
96266-1	My Dear Old Arizona Home	BB B-6255, MW M-7202, RZAu G22830, HMVIn N4398	
96267-1	I Want To Be A Real Cowboy Girl	BB B-6164, MW M-4802, RZAu G22770, HMVIn N4393	
96268-1	On Treasure Island	BB B-6163, MW M-4980, RZAu G22770, HMVIn N4392	
96269-1	Take Me Back To My Boots And Saddle	BB B-6164, MW M-4802, RZAu G22761, HMVIn N4393	
96270-1	Let Me Sleep On The Edge Of The Prairie	BB B-6255, MW M-7203, RZAu G22832, HMVIn N4399	
96271-1	My Cross-Eyed Beau	BB B-6205, RZ MR2062, RZAu G22883, RZIr IZ428, HMVIn N4396	
96272-1	Red Sails In The Sunset	BB B-6163, MW M-4980, RZAu G22761, HMVIn N4392	

Revs: Regal-Zonophone MR2062, IZ428 by Wilf Carter; HMV N4399 by Jimmie Davis.

Chicago, IL			Tuesday, November 5, 1935
96273-1	Roll Along, Prairie Moon	BB B-6178, MW M-4801, RZAu G22829, Twin FT8037	
96274-1	The Oregon Trail	BB B-6178, MW M-4801, RZAu G22829, Twin FT8037	
96275-1	Cowboy's Heaven	BB B-6205, RZAu G22883, HMVIn N4396	
96276-1	Carry Me Back To The Mountains	BB B-8016, MW M-7202, RZAu G24076	
96277-1	There's An Empty Cot In The Bunk House Tonight	BB B-6226, MW M-4820, HMVIn N4398	

Revs: Bluebird B-6226, Montgomery Ward M-4820 by Dick Hartman's Tennessee Ramblers; Bluebird B-8016, Regal-Zonophone G24076 by Four Pickled Peppers.

Chicago, IL			Monday, November 25, 1935
96512-1	Take Me Back To Renfro Valley	BB B-6259, MW M-4803, Vi Z-354, RZAu G22830, HMVIn N4401	

Chicago, IL			Thursday, December 12, 1935
96475-2	Faded Love Letters Of Mine	BB B-6259, MW M-4803, Vi Z-354, RZAu G22832, HMVIn N4401	

Acc. Dorothy Good, g; Bill McCluskey, v-1.

Chicago, IL			Monday, February 28, 1938
C-2129-1	The Roundup In Cheyenne	Vo/OK 04292, Cq 9010, Co 37724, 20301	
C-2130-1	There's A Silver Moon On The Golden Gate	Vo/OK 04147, Cq 8998, Co 37721, 20298	
C-2131-1,-2	What You Gonna Do – What You Gonna Say	Vo unissued	
C-2132-1	Roamin' In The Gloamin' -1	Vo/OK 04373, Cq 9115, RZAu G23746	
C-2133-2	Cowboy Love Call	Vo/OK 04103, Cq 9114, Co 37720, 20297	
C-2134-1	Barn Dance Of Long Ago	Vo/OK 04234, Co 37723, 20300	
C-2135-1	I Want To Be A Real Cowboy Girl	Vo/OK 04234, Cq 9010, Co 37723, 20300	
C-2136-1	Oh Darling You're Breakin' My Heart	Vo/OK 04022, Cq 8998, Co 37719, 20296	
C-2137-1	Only One Step More	Vo/OK 04053, Cq 8997, Co 37758, 20335	
C-2138-1	Will There Be Any Yodeling In Heaven?	Vo/OK 04053, Cq 8997, Co 37758, 20335	
C-2139-1	Texas Moon	Vo/OK 04373, Cq 9115, 9696, RZAu G23746	
C-2140-1,-2	Give Me A Straight Shooting Cowboy	Vo unissued	
C-2141-1	I Love Her Just The Same	Vo/Ok 04147, Cq 9114, Co 37721, 20298	
C-2142-1	On The Sunny Side Of The Rockies	Vo/OK 04103, Cq 9009, Co 37720, 20297	
C-2143-1	Ragtime Cowboy Joe	Vo/OK 04292, Cq 9696, Co 37724, 20301	
C-2144-1	By The Grave Of Nobody's Darling (My Darling's Promise)	Vo/Ok 04022, Cq 9009, Co 37719, 20296	

The Girls Of The Golden West, and Dorothy Good (as Dolly Good), recorded after 1942.

GLAD TIDINGS SACRED FOUR

Pseudonym on Broadway and Paramount for the Paramount Sacred Four.

J.C. GLASSCOCK

J.C. Glasscock, f; acc. unknown, o; unknown, bj.

Birmingham, AL			c. July 13, 1927
GEX-714	Hop Light Lady	Ge rejected	
GEX-715	Peek-A-Boo	Ge rejected	

LONNIE GLOSSON

Lonnie Glosson, h solo/v eff-1; acc. unknown, sp-2/eff-2.
Grafton, WI   c. December 1931
   L-1314-2   The Fox Chase -1   Bwy 8333
   L-1316-2   Fast Train Blues -2   Bwy 8333

Matrix L-1315 is by Renfro Valley Boys (see Karl & Harty).

Lonnie Glosson, h solo/v eff.
Chicago, IL   Thursday, October 8, 1936
   C-1542-1   Lonnie's Fox Chase   Cq 8732

Lonnie Glosson, v; acc. own g.
Chicago, IL   Thursday, October 8, 1936
   C-1543-1   Arkansas Hard Luck Blues   Cq 8732

Lonnie Glosson, h solo/v eff.
Chicago, IL   Friday, October 9, 1936
   C-1544-1   Lost John   ARC unissued

Lonnie Glosson, v; acc. own g.
Chicago, IL   Friday, October 9, 1936
   C-1545-1   Lonnie's Hard Luck   ARC unissued

Lonnie Glosson recorded after 1942.

SHORTY GODWIN

Shorty Godwin, v; acc. prob. own g.
Atlanta, GA   Friday, April 12, 1929
   148262-2   Jimbo Jambo Land   Co 15411-D
   148263-2   Turnip Greens   Co 15411-D

Bill "Shorty" Godwin later performed as "Hiram Hayseed."

GEORGE GOEBEL

George Goebel, v; acc. prob. Gene Autry, g-1; own u-2.
Chicago, IL   Wednesday, April 12, 1933
   C-544-1   Berry Picking Time -1   Cq 8156
   C-545-1   Billy Richardson's Last Ride -1 Cq 8156
   C-546-2   A Cowboy's Best Friend Is His Horse -1   Cq 8157, MeC 91727, M-908, Min M-908
   C-547-2   Night Herding Song -2   Cq 8157

Revs: Melotone 91727 by Goebel Reeves; Melotone M-908, Minerva M-908 by Red Foley.

George Goebel recorded after 1942.

DAN GOLDEN

Pseudonym on Champion for H.K. Hutchison.

DEWEY GOLDEN & HIS KENTUCKY BUZZARDS

No details.
Johnson City, TN   Thursday, October 18, 1928
   147236-   Big Sandy Valley   Co unissued
   147237-   Going Down To Carbin [sic] Town   Co unissued

THE GOLDEN ECHO BOYS (OF GOD'S BIBLE SCHOOL)

Vocal group; prob. unacc.
Richmond, IN   Friday, December 12, 1930
   17373,-A   One Night As I Lay Dreaming   Ge rejected
   17374,-A   Calvary   Ge rejected
   17375,-A   Jesus Paid It All   Ge rejected
   17376,-A   Redeemed   Ge rejected
   17377,-A   What A Wondrous Love   Ge rejected
   17378,-A   I Ain't Goin' To Study War No More   Ge rejected

Acc. unknown, g; unknown, g-1.
Richmond, IN   Friday, June 10, 1932
   18539   Every Time I Feel The Spirit -1   Ge unissued
   18540   Great Change Since I've Been Born Ge unissued
   18541   City Of Gold   Ge unissued

18542	Shall We Meet	Ge unissued
18543	Rock Of Ages	Ge unissued
18544	Will The Circle Be Unbroken	Ge unissued

Matrix 18539 was logged as by **The Echo Boys**; matrices 18541 to 18544 as by **Golden Echo Boys Quartette**.

GOLDEN HOUR MIXED QUARTETTE

Vocal quartet; acc. unknown.
New York, NY   October 1927

81573-	Joy To The World!	OK 40924
81574-	O! Little Town Of Bethlehem	OK 40924

GOLDEN MELODY BOYS

Phil Featherstone's surname was originally Featherston(e)haugh.

Phil Featherstone, md; Dempsey Jones, ti/v.
Chicago, IL   c. October 1927

20111-4	The Old Tobacco Mill	Pm 3068, Bwy 8089
20115-2	I Wonder Why Nobody Cares For Me	Pm 3074, Bwy 8120
20121-2	The Cross Eyed Butcher	Pm 3068, Bwy 8089
20128-1	When The Golden Rod Is Blooming Once Again	Pm 3081, Bwy 8119
20129-2	Would You Ever Think Of Me	Pm 3074, Bwy 8120
20130-2	Cabin Home	Pm 3081, Bwy 8119

Broadway 8089, 8119, 8120 as by **Georgia Melody Boys**.
Matrices 20112, 20123 are by Blind Blake (see *B&GR*); 20114 is by Lucius Hardy (see *B&GR*); 20116 to 20120 are by Wisconsin Roof Orchestra (popular); others are untraced.

Golden Melody Boys (Demps & Phil): Phil Featherstone, md; Dempsey Jones, ti/v-1.
Chicago, IL   c. January 1928

20303-1	Sabula Blues	Pm 3107
20304-1	Jack And May -1	Pm 3124, Bwy 8211
20305-2	Freak Medley	Pm 3107
20306-2	Gonna Have 'Lasses In De Mornin' -1	Pm 3087, Bwy 8134
20307-2	Way Dow [sic] In Arkansas -1	Pm 3087, Bwy 8134
20308-1	Maybe Some Lucky Day -1	Pm 3124, Bwy 8211

Broadway 8134, 8211 as by **Georgia Melody Boys**.

Phil Featherstone, h-1/md-2/v-3/sp-4; Dempsey Jones, ti-5/g-6/v-7/sp-4.
Chicago, IL   c. October 1928

20935-2	Blushing Bride -2, 5, 7	Pm unissued: Yz 2048 (CD)
20936-2	When The Lilac Blooms -2, 3, 5, 7	Pm 3137, Bwy 8207
20937-1	Uncle Abner And Elmer At The Rehearsal, Part I -1, 4, 5	Pm 3153
20938-2	Uncle Abner And Elmer At The Rehearsal, Part II -2, 3, 4, 5, 7	Pm 3153
20939-2	No One's Going To Miss Me When I'm Gone -2, 3, 5, 7	Pm 3137, Bwy 8207
20945-3	Guitar Rag -2, 6	Pm 3169

Broadway 8207 as by **Georgia Melody Boys**. Matrices 20940 and 20942 to 20944 are by Blind Joe Taggart (see *B&GR*); 20941 is untraced. Rev. Paramount 3169 by William Haid (popular).

Dempsey Jones, v; acc. own g.
Richmond, IN   Thursday, November 19, 1931

18192	The Old Tobacco Mill	Ch 16356, Spr 2824
18193	The Cross Eyed Butcher	Ch 16356, Spr 2824
18194	I Wonder Why Nobody Cares For Me	Ch 16416, Spr 2832
18195	Cabin Home	Ch 16697
18196	Jack And May	Ch 16416, Spr 2832
18197	The Sinking Of The Vestris	Ge unissued

Superior 2824, 2832 as by **Dan Martin**. Rev. Champion 16697 by Frank Welling (see John McGhee & Frank Welling).

GOLDEN ROD & RED HAT OF WSAI

Comic dialogue.
Richmond, IN   Saturday, August 4, 1928

14127-A	Always Wrong, Part 1	Ge 6579, Ch 15563
14128,-A	Always Wrong	Ge rejected
14129-A	Always Wrong, Part 2	Ge 6579, Ch 15563

JACK GOLDING

Jack Golding, v; acc. unknown, bj; unknown, g-1.
    Richmond, IN   Wednesday, November 14, 1928

14418	Sunny Land	Ge rejected
14419	Wondering -1	Ge rejected

Acc. unknown, g.
    Richmond, IN   Thursday, November 22, 1928

14449,-A	Wondering	Ge rejected
14450,-A	When Polly Walk Thru The Hollyhock [sic]	Ge unissued

    Richmond, IN   Tuesday, December 11, 1928

14552	Me And The Man In The Moon	Ge 6727, Ch 15642
14553	That Old Sweetheart Of Mine	Ge rejected
14554	In The Big Rock Candy Mountains	Ge 6715, Ch 15646, Spt 9342
14555-A	Bum Song No. 2	Ge 6715, Ch 15646, Spt 9342

Champion 15642, 15646 as by **Jerry Ellis**. Supertone 9342 as by **Weary Willie**.
Rev. Champion 15642 by Jack Bankey.

    Richmond, IN   Thursday, January 24, 1929

14725	Mrs. Murphy's Chowder	Ge 6744, Ch 15664, Spt 9356

Champion 15664 as by **Jerry Ellis**. Supertone 9356 as by **Jack Edwards**.

Acc. unknown, ac; unknown, g.
    Richmond, IN   Saturday, January 26, 1929

14737-A	A Gay Caballero	Ge 6744, Ch 15664, Spt 9356

Champion 15664 as by **Jerry Ellis**. Supertone 9356 as by **Jack Edwards**.

Acc. unknown, ac.
    Richmond, IN   Friday, February 8, 1929

14785-A	I Wonder If You Miss Me Tonight	Ge 6756, Ch 15682
14786	Rhythm King	Ge 6756

Champion 15682 as by **Jerry Ellis**.

Acc. unknown, p; unknown, bj.
    Richmond, IN   Friday, March 1, 1929

14849	I Found You Out (When I Found You In Somebody Else's Arms)	Ch 15682

Champion 15682 as by **Jerry Ellis**.

Acc. unknown, p.
    Richmond, IN   Thursday, March 14, 1929

14910	[unknown title]	Ge rejected

Acc. unknown, u.
    Richmond, IN   Saturday, March 16, 1929

14925	She's Got A Great Big Army Of Friends	Ge rejected

Acc. unknown, ac; unknown, p.
    Richmond, IN   Saturday, July 27, 1929

15389,-A	Longing For Home	Ge rejected
15390,-A	When You're Nobody's Boy But Your Mothers' [sic]	Ge rejected

Acc. unknown, f; unknown, ac; unknown, g.
    Richmond, IN   Saturday, August 10, 1929

15426	Longing For Home	Ge 6986, Ch 15805, Spt 9558
15427	When You're Nobody's Boy But Your Mothers [sic]	Ge 6986, Ch 15805, Spt 9558

Champion 15805 as by **Jerry Ellis**. Supertone 9558 as by **Jack Edwards**.

Acc. unknown, g.
    Richmond, IN   Thursday, May 1, 1930

16567,-A	In The Shade Of The Old Apple Tree	Ge rejected
16568,-A	Daisies Won't Tell	Ge rejected

    Richmond, IN   Thursday, July 3, 1930

16809,-A	I Had But Fifty Cents	Ge rejected
16810,-A,-B	The Tramp	Ge rejected

    Richmond, IN   Friday, July 18, 1930

16837	I Had But Fifty Cents	Ge 7263, Ch 16072, Spt 9711
16838-B	The Tramp	Ge 7263, Ch 16072, Spt 9711

Champion 16072 as by **Jerry Ellis**. Supertone 9711 as by **Jack Edwards**.

Rettig & Golding, prob. v duet; acc. unknown.
Richmond, IN   Friday, July 18, 1930
    16839   [unknown title]   Ge unissued trial recording

Jack Edwards, v; acc. unknown, g; unknown, g-1.
Richmond, IN   Thursday, August 14, 1930
    16912-B   I Learned About Women From Her -1   Spt 9737
    16913   That Little Black Mustache   Spt 9737

It may be guessed, correctly, that this artist is barely within the scope of this work. Gennett files indicate that some of his material was made expressly as "popular vocal," some for the hillbilly catalogue.

ROY GONZALES

Roy Gonzales, v/y-1; acc. own g.
Richmond, IN   Saturday, July 13, 1929
    15349-A   Attendre Pour Un Train -1   Pm 12807
    15350-A   Un Fussi Qui Brille -1   Pm 12807
    15351,-A   Dor Mon Enfant Dor   Pm rejected
    15352,-A   Ma Maison Aupres De L'Eau   Pm rejected
    15353-A   Anuiant Et Bleue -1   Pm 12832
    15354-A   Choctaw Beer Blues -1   Pm 12832

The data is as given in Gennett's files; however, Paramount 12807 mistakenly shows matrix 15348-A for *Attendre Pour Un Train* and 15349-A for *Un Fussi Qui Brille*. Similarly, Paramount 12832 is reported as showing matrix 15352-A for *Anuiant Et Bleue* and 15353-A for *Choctaw Beer Blues*.
See Leo Soileau for adjacent recordings.
Roy Gonzales also recorded with John H. Bertrand.

GOOD'S BOX WHITTLERS

See Buell Kazee.

HERALD GOODMAN & HIS TENNESSEE VALLEY BOYS

Howard "Howdy" Forrester, f; Arthur Smith, f; Virgil Atkins, bj; Billy Byrd, g; Joe Forrester, sb; Herald Goodman, v-1.
Rock Hill, SC   Monday, September 26, 1938
    027719-1   Tell Me -1   BB B-8033, MW M-7684
    027720-1   The Old Mountain Man -1   BB B-8065, MW M-7680, RZAu G23937
    027721-1   Is Your Name Written There -1   BB B-8065, MW M-7682
    027722-1   Tennessee Swing -1   BB B-7868, MW M-7683
    027723-1   The Great Shining Light -1   BB B-7999, MW M-7681
    027724-1   That'll Do Now, That'll Do -1   BB B-8033, MW M-7684
    027725-1   New Lamp Lighting Time In The Valley -1 BB B-7999, MW M-7681, Twin FT8714
    027726-1   The Lamplighter's Dream -1   BB B-7935, MW M-7682, RZAu G23720
    027727-1   Dad's Little Boy -1   BB B-7935, MW M-7680, RZAu G23720
    027728-1   Banjo Rag   BB B-7868, MW M-7683, RZAu G23937

Rev. Twin FT8714 by Blue Sky Boys.

GOODMAN SACRED SINGERS

Pseudonym on Champion, Challenge, and Herwin for the McDonald Quartette.

PRICE GOODSON

See Da Costa Woltz's Southern Broadcasters.

GOOSE CREEK GULLY JUMPERS

Pseudonym on Superior for Nicholson's Players.

ALBERT GORDON

Pseudonym on Actuelle for Vernon Dalhart.

ALEX GORDON

Pseudonym on Conqueror for Frank Jenkins' Pilot Mountaineers.

TOMMY GORDON & HIS CORN HUSKERS

Pseudonym on Superior for Lonesome Luke & His Farm Boys.

GORDON COUNTY QUARTET

Prob.: Phil Reeve, lv; Ernest Moody, tv; Bud Landress, bv; Tom Chitwood, bsv; acc. Bill Chitwood, f; unknown, p.
Atlanta, GA   Friday, April 18, 1930

150281-2	Walking In The King's Highway	Co 15713-D
150282-2	Beyond The Clouds Is Light	Co 15713-D

JOE GORE & OLIVER PETTREY

Joe Gore, Oliver Pettrey, v duet; acc. own g duet.
   Richmond, IN   Monday, April 20, 1931

17698	I'll Not Be Your Sweetheart	Ch 16271
17699	Good-Bye Sweetheart	Ch 16271
17700,-A	Now I Am All Alone	Ge rejected
17702,-A	My Name Is Johnny Brown	Ge rejected

Matrix 17701 is popular.

Oliver Pettrey, v/y; acc. Joe Gore, g; own g.
   Richmond, IN   Monday, April 20, 1931

17703	The Young Rambler	Ge unissued

THE GOSPEL FOUR

Pseudonym on Champion and Melotone for The Singin' Preachers.

GOSPEL SANCTIFIED SINGERS

Vocal group; acc. unknown.
   Chicago, IL   Tuesday, July 2, 1929

C-3767-	When He Calls Me I Will Answer	Br/Vo rejected
C-3768-	It Is Well	Br/Vo rejected
C-3769-	Shine On Me	Br/Vo rejected

THE GOSPEL SINGER

Pseudonym on Champion for Frank Welling (see John McGhee & Frank Welling).

FRED & GERTRUDE GOSSETT

Vocal duet; acc. prob. one of them, g.
   Atlanta, GA   Wednesday, April 16, 1930

150232-1	All The Good Times Are Passed And Gone	Co 15596-D
150233-1	Go Bury Me	Co 15596-D

TED GOSSETT'S BAND

Ted Gossett, f; Pete Woods, bj; Earl Nossinger, g; Enos Gossett, g.
   Richmond, IN   Tuesday, September 16, 1930

17041	Eight of January	Ch 16160, Spt 9776, Spr 2655
17042-A	Fox Chase	Ge 7308, Ch 16116, Spt 9738, Spr 2655, Vs 5090
17043-A	Wild Geese	Ge 7308, Ch 16116, Spt 9738, Vs 5090
17045	Bow Legged Irishman	Ch 16310, Spr 2731
17046	Rocky Mountain Goat	Spr 2731
17049	House Of David Blues	Ge rejected

Supertone 9738 as by **Marvin's String Band**; 9776 as by **The Lee County String Band**. Superior 2655, 2731 as by **Buddy Young's Kentuckians**. Intervening matrices are by Tommy Whitmer's Band.
Revs: Champion 16160, Supertone 9776 by Tommy Whitmer's Band; Champion 16310 by Earl & Joe.

ROMAN GOSZ OLD TIME BAND

This group had several releases in the Decca Hill Billy series but is a polka band and outside the scope of this book. (Gosz also recorded for numerous labels after 1942.)

THE GRADY FAMILY

Unknown, f-1; unknown, sg-2; unknown, md; unknown, g; unknown, sb.
   Atlanta, GA   Saturday, December 6, 1930

151073-1	Gold Diggers -2	Co 15633-D
151074-	Buttercup	Co unissued
151075-1	Carolina's Best -1	Co 15633-D
151076-	Cliffside Rag	Co unissued

HENRY GRAHAM

Pseudonym on Bell for John McGhee.

[THE] GRAHAM BROTHERS

The Graham Brothers, v trio; acc. unknown, f; unknown, g.
   New York, NY   Tuesday, February 23, 1932

| 71884-1 | Ninety-Nine Years – Part 1 | Vi 23654 |
| 71885-1 | Ninety-Nine Years – Part 2 | Vi 23654 |

Grant Trio, v trio; acc. one of them, p.
New York, NY   Wednesday, March 3, 1932

| 71912-1 | I Hear The Voice Of An Angel | Vi 23743 |
| 71913-1 | Say A Prayer For Mother's Baby | Vi unissued |

These items were logged as by **The Graham Brothers**. They were originally scheduled for Victor 23657, which was not issued. Rev. Victor 23743 by Bob Miller.

Graham Brothers, v trio; acc. Frank Novak, f/cl-1/bscl-2/ac-3; unknown, p; unknown, bj-4; John Cali, g.
New York, NY   Wednesday, March 17, 1932

71966-1	Under The Old Umbrella -1, 3	Vi 23667
71967-1	It Ain't No Fault Of Mine -1, 2, 3, 4	Vi 23667, Zo 6149
71968-1	Gene, The Fighting Marine	Vi 23664
71969-1	Bobby Boy -1, 3, 4	Vi 23664, Zo 6149
71970-1	Bobby Boy – Part 2 -1, 3, 4	Vi 23690
71971-1	Don't Hang Me In The Morning	Vi 23670, Zo/RZAu EE317

Victor 23664 as by **Graham Bros**. Victor 23667 and matrix 71967 on Zonophone 6149 as by **Grant Trio**.
Matrix 71972 by these artists is with orchestral accompaniment and is beyond the scope of this work.
Revs: Victor 23670 by Bill Elliott; 23690 by Harry (Mac) McClintock; Zonophone/Regal-Zonophone EE317 by Solemn & Gay (popular).

Acc. one of them, p.
New York, NY   Wednesday, March 24, 1932

| 72208-1 | Spring's Tornado | Vi 23668 |
| 72209-1 | Embers | Vi 23668 |

LEW GRANT

Pseudonym on Van Dyke 82526 and Goodson 183 for Carson Robison.

GRANT BROTHERS

Tenneva Ramblers: Jack Pierce, f; Jack Grant, bj-md; Claude Slagle, bj; Claude Grant, g/v.
Bristol, TN   Thursday, August 4, 1927

39770-2	The Longest Train I Ever Saw	Vi 20861
39771-2	Sweet Heaven When I Die	Vi 20861
39772-2	Miss 'Liza, Poor Gal	Vi 21141

Rev. Victor 21141 by Bull Mountain Moonshiners.

Jack Pierce, f; Jack Grant, bj-md; Claude Slagle, bj-1; Claude Grant, g/v.
Atlanta, GA   Saturday, February 18, 1928

41908-2	Darling, Where Have You Been So Long? -1	Vi 21645
41909-1	If I Die A Railroad Man -1	Vi 21406
41909-2	If I Die A Railroad Man -1	Vi unissued: RCA LPV532, RD7870 (LPs)
41910-2	I'm Goin' To Georgia -1	Vi 21645
41911-1	The Curtains Of Night	Vi 21289
41912-2	The Lonely Grave	Vi 21289
41913-1	Seven Long Years In Prison -1	Vi 21406

Grant Brothers & Their Music: Jack Pierce, f/v; Jack Grant, bj-md/v; Claude Slagle, bj; Claude Grant, g/v.
Johnson City, TN   Monday, October 15, 1928

147178-1	When A Man Is Married	Co 15332-D, Ve 7111-V, Cl 5147-C
147179-1	Goodbye My Honey – I'm Gone	Co 15460-D
147180-2	Tell It To Me	Co 15332-D, Ve 7102-V, Cl 5147-C
147181-2	Johnson Boy	Co 15460-D

Jack Grant is the lead vocalist on matrix 147181.
Revs: Velvet Tone 7102-V by Atco Quartet, 7111-V by Stroup Quartet.

GRANT TRIO

See [The] Graham Brothers.

GRAPEVINE COON HUNTERS

Unknown, f; unknown, bj-m or tbj; prob. two unknowns, g.
Dallas, TX   Friday, November 28, 1930

| DAL-6765-A | The Grapevine Waltz | Br 584 |
| DAL-6766-A | The Droan Waltz | Br 584 |

A.A. GRAY

A.A. Gray, f solo.
    Atlanta, GA   Thursday, March 20, or Friday, March 21, 1924

| 8591-A | Bonaparte's Retreat | OK 40110 |
| 8592-A | Merry Widow Waltz | OK 40110 |

A.A. Gray & Seven Foot Dilly: A.A. Gray, f; John Dilleshaw, g/sp.
    Atlanta, GA   Thursday, March 20, 1930

| ATL-951- | Tallapoosa Bound | Vo 5430 |
| ATL-952- | Streak O' Lean – Streak O' Fat | Vo 5430 |

A.A. Gray, John Dilleshaw, v duet; acc. A.A. Gray, f-1; John Dilleshaw, g.
    Atlanta, GA   Saturday, March 22, 1930

| ATL-983- | Nigger Baby -1 | Vo 5458 |
| ATL-984- | The Old Ark's A'Moving | Vo 5458 |

See also John Dilleshaw.

CURLY GRAY

Curly Gray, v; or **Grace & Curly Gray**, v duet-1; acc. unknown, bj-md; unknown, g.
    Dallas, TX   Thursday, June 24, 1937

DAL-461-1	Hard Luck Blues	Vo 03664
DAL-462-1	Pretty Little Girl	Vo 03720
DAL-463-1	Big Dallas Blues	Vo 03664
DAL-464-	Little Joe The Hobo -1	Vo unissued
DAL-465-	Huntsville Blues -1	Vo unissued
DAL-466-1	Comin' Down The River -1	Vo 03720

JACK "SMOKE" GRAY

See Gene Cobb & Jack Gray.

LESLIE GRAY

Pseudonym on Simcha for Frank Luther, or Carson Robison & Frank Luther (see Carson Robison).

LUCY GRAY

See Arthur Fields & Fred Hall.

"MOMMIE" [MRS. OTTO] GRAY

See Otto Gray.

OTTO GRAY

McGinty's Oklahoma Cow Boy Band (Otto Gray, Director): unknown, f; unknown, bj; poss. Dave Cutrell, g; unknown, bell; poss. unknown, vc; poss. other unknowns, other instruments; unknown, v eff.
    St. Louis, MO   May 1926

| 9648-A | Cow Boy's Dream | OK 45057 |

Billy McGinty organized and possibly financed this group but may not have been one of the musicians. Rev. OKeh 45057 by Dave Cutrell.

Owen Gray, v; acc. **Otto Gray's Oklahoma Cowboy Band**: poss. "Chief" Sanders, f; poss. Wade "Hy"' Allen, bj; own g; poss. Lee "Zeke" Allen, vc.
    Richmond, IN   Tuesday, January 17, 1928

| 13365-A | It Can't Be Done | Ge 6376, Ch 15446, Sil 8147, Spt 9242, Fast 2632 |
| 13366 | Adam And Eve | Ge 6376, Ch 15482, Sil 8147, Spt 9242, Chg 396 |

Champion 15446, 15482 as by **McGinty's Oklahoma Cowboy Band**. Silvertone 8147, Supertone 9242 as by **Otis Stewart**. Challenge 396 as by **Art Coffee**. Rev. Challenge 396 by Maple City Four.

Fred Wilson, v; acc. **Otto Gray's Oklahoma Cowboy Band**: poss. "Chief" Sanders, f; poss. Wade "Hy"' Allen, bj; Owen Gray, g; poss. Lee "Zeke" Allen, vc.
    Richmond, IN   Tuesday, January 17, 1928

| 13367 | Lone Prairie | Ge unissued |

Mrs. Otto Gray, v; acc. **Otto Gray's Oklahoma Cowboy Band**: poss. "Chief" Sanders, f; Owen Gray, g; poss. Lee "Zeke" Allen, vc.
    Richmond, IN   Tuesday, January 17, 1928

| 13368-A | Your Mother Still Prays For You, Jack | Ge 6387, Ch 15446, Sil 8159, Spt 9244 |

Champion 15446 as by **McGinty's Oklahoma Cowboy Band**. Silvertone 8159, Supertone 9244 as by **Grace Means**. Matrix 13368 is titled *Your Mother Still Prays For You* on Supertone 9244.

    Richmond, IN   Wednesday, January 18, 1928
| 13369,-A | Drunkard's Lone Child | Ge rejected |
| 13370,-A | Blind Child | Ge rejected |

Owen Gray, v; acc. **Otto Gray's Oklahoma Cowboy Band**: poss. "Chief" Sanders, f; poss. Wade "Hy" Allen, bj; own g/sp-1; poss. Lee "Zeke" Allen, vc.

    Richmond, IN   Saturday, January 28, 1928
| 13407 | It Can't Be Done -1 | Ch 15446, Sil 8147, Spt 9242, Spr 346, Bell 1169, Fast 2632 |
| 13408 | Adam And Eve | Ge unissued |

For pseudonyms used on issues of matrix 13407 see above for matrix 13365-A, except Bell 1169 as by **Will Pickett**. It is uncertain whether matrix 13365-A and matrix 13407 were both issued on all the labels shown.

Fred Wilson, v; acc. **Otto Gray's Oklahoma Cowboy Band**: poss. "Chief" Sanders, f; poss. Wade "Hy" Allen, bj; Owen Gray, g; poss. Lee "Zeke" Allen, vc.

    Richmond, IN   Saturday, January 28, 1928
| 13409 | Bury Me On The Lone Prairie | Ge 6405, Ch 15482, Sil 8159, Spt 9244, Spr 346, Bell 1169 |

Champion 15482 as by **McGinty's Oklahoma Cowboy Band**. Silvertone 8159, Supertone 9244 as by **Gus Link**. Bell 1169 as by **George Talbot**.

Mrs. Otto Gray, v; acc. **Otto Gray's Oklahoma Cowboy Band**: poss. "Chief" Sanders, f; poss. Wade "Hy" Allen, bj; Owen Gray, g; poss. Lee "Zeke" Allen, vc.

    Richmond, IN   Saturday, January 28, 1928
13409-A,-B	Bury Me On The Lone Prairie	Ge unissued
13410	Your Mother Still Prays For You, Jack	Ge rejected
13411	Drunkards Lone Child	Ge 6405
13412	In The Baggage Coach Ahead	Ge 6387

Otto Gray & His Oklahoma Cowboy Band: poss. Wade "Hy" Allen, bj; poss. Owen Gray, g; unidentified, v.

    Richmond, IN   Wednesday, May 9, 1928
| 13785,-A,-B | From Hell To Arkansas | Ge rejected |
| 13786,-A | Coon Hunt | Ge rejected |

Otto Gray & His Cowboy Band: poss. "Chief" Sanders, f-1; unknown, sg-2; poss. Wade "Hy" Allen, bj-3; prob. Owen Gray, g/v; unknown, g; unidentified, v-4/y-4.

    Chicago, IL   Monday, September 17, 1928
C-2317-	It Can't Be Done -1, 3	Vo 5250
C-2318-	Adam And Eve -3	Vo 5250
C-2319-	Tom Cat Blues -2, 4	Vo 5267

Two unidentifieds, sp/v eff; unacc.

    Chicago, IL   Monday, September 17, 1928
| C-2320- | Coon Hunt | Vo 5267 |

Poss. "Chief" Sanders, f; Owen Gray, g/v-1; poss. unknown, g-2; poss. Lee Allen, vc-3; Mrs. Otto Gray, v-4.

    Chicago, IL   Saturday, October 13, 1928
C-2435-	Your Mother Still Prays For You, Jack -3, 4	Vo 5301
C-2436-	Be Home Early Tonight My Dear Boy -3, 4	Vo 5301
C-2437-	Barefoot Boy With Boots On -1, 2	Vo 5256
C-2438-	I Had But Fifty Cents -1	Vo 5256

Poss. "Chief" Sanders, f; poss. Wade Allen, bj; prob. Owen Gray, g/v/sp; unknown, sp-1.

    Chicago, IL   Tuesday, March 12, or Wednesday, March 13, 1929
C-3108-	Plant A Watermelon On My Grave -1	Vo 5327
C-3109-	The Terrible Marriage -1	Vo 5327
C-3110-	I Can't Change It	Vo 5337
C-3111-	Midnight Special	Vo 5337

"Mommie" Gray, v; acc. **Otto Gray's Oklahoma Cowboy Band**: no details.

    Richmond, IN   Tuesday, May 20, 1930
| 16635-B | Down Where The Swanee River Flows | Ge 7222, Ch 16027 |
| 16636-B | Gathering Up The Shells From The Sea Shore | Ge 7222, Ch 16027 |

Otto Gray & His Oklahoma Cowboys: "Chief" Sanders, f-1/v-2; Wade Allen, bj-3/v-4; poss. Owen Gray, g-5; unknown, g-6; Lee Allen, vc-7/v-8.

    New York, NY   Monday, February 16, 1931
| E-35856- | Who Stole The Lock -1, 3, 5, 7, 8 | Me M12182, Po P9017, Min M-14001, Pan 25449 |

E-35857-	Cat Came Back -1, 2, 5, 7	Me M12127, Po P9047, PanAu P12126
E-35858-	Suckin' Cider -3, 5, 6, 7, 8	Me M12127, Po P9047, Pan 25040, PanAu P12127
E-35859-	When You Come To The End Of The Day -1, 3, 4	Me M12223, PanAu P12223
E-35860-	4000 Years Ago -1, 2, 3, 5	Me M12182, Po P9017, Min M-14001, Pan 25449
E-35861-	Mammy's Little Coal Black Rose -1, 3, 4	Me M12223, PanAu P12223

Polk P9047 possibly as by **Otto Gray & His Oklahoma Outlaws**. Matrix E-35856 is titled *Who Stole The Lock From The Hen House Door?*, and matrix E-35860 is titled *Four Thousand Years Ago*, on Panachord 25449.
Although the matrix sequence would suggest a date in January 1931, examination of Brunswick files leads to the conclusion that the given date is correct.
Revs: Panachord 25040 by Pickard Family; P12126, P12127 by Frank Marvin.

OWEN GRAY
See Otto Gray.

GRAY & NELSON
Pseudonym on Supertone for Doc Roberts & Asa Martin.

REV. C.M. GRAYSON
Sermons.
Memphis, TN   Friday, February 3, 1928

41834-1	Judas Sold Christ	Vi 21290
41835-2	God's Indictment	Vi 21290

G.B. GRAYSON & HENRY WHITTER

G.B. Grayson, f/v/sp; Henry Whitter, g/sp-1.
New York, NY   early October 1927

GEX-903-A	Nobody's Darling -1	Ge 6304, Ch 15395
GEX-904	I'll Never Be Yours -1	Ge 6373, Ch 15447, Sil 8160, Spt 9247, Chg 393
GEX-905	Handsome Molly -1	Ge 6304, Ch 15629
GEX-906-A	Shout Lula -1	Ge 6373, Ch 15501
GEX-907	You Never Miss Your Mother Until She's Gone	Ge 6320, Ch 15395, Sil 8160, Spt 9247, Chg 394
GEX-908-A	Train No. 45 -1	Ge 6320, Ch 15447, Chg 397
GEX-909,-A	John Henry The Steel Driving Man	Ge rejected
GEX-910,-A,-B	He's Coming To Us Dead	Ge rejected

Gennett 6320, 6373, Champion 15629 as by **Henry Whitter & G.B. Grayson**. Champion 15395 as by **Greyson Thomas & Will Lotty**; 15447, 15501 as by **Norman Gayle**. Silvertone 8160, Supertone 9247 as by **Dillard Sanders**. Challenges as by **David Foley**. Revs: Challenge 393 by Marion Underwood & Sam Harris; 394 by Roy Harvey.

G.B. Grayson–Henry Whitter: G.B. Grayson, f/v/sp-1; Henry Whitter, g-2/sp-2.
Atlanta, GA   Tuesday, October 18, 1927

40302-1	Handsome Molly -2	Vi 21189
40303-1	He Is Coming To Us Dead -2	Vi 21139
40304-2	Don't Go Out Tonight, My Darling -2	Vi 21139
40305-2	Rose Conley -2	Vi 21625
40306-1	Ommie Wise	Vi 21625
40307-2	Train 45 -1, 2	Vi 21189, BB B-5498

Victor 21625 as by **Grayson & Whitter**.

Henry Whitter: G.B. Grayson, f/v/sp/calls-1; Henry Whitter, g/v-2/sp-3.
New York, NY   Tuesday, February 21, 1928

GEX-1091	Sally Gooden	Ge 6733, Ch 15501
GEX-1092	Mine Is For Mary -3	Ge unissued: *DU DU33033 (LP); Doc DOCD-8054 (CD)*
GEX-1093	She's Mine, All Mine -2, 3	Ge 6656, Ch 15465
GEX-1094	Sweet Rosie O'Grady -3	Ge 6418
GEX-1094-A	Sweet Rosie O'Grady -3	Ge unissued: *Doc DOCD-8054 (CD)*
GEX-1095,-A	I've Always Been A Rambler	Ge rejected
GEX-1096-A	Red Or Green	Ge 6418, Ch 15465, Chg 397
GEX-1097	Cluck Old Hen -3	Ge 6656, Ch 15629
GEX-1098	Old Jimmy Sutton -1, 3	Ge 6436

Gennett 6436 as by **Whitter & Grayson**. Champion 15465, 15501 as by **Norman Gayle**; 15629 as by **Henry Whitter & G.B. Grayson**. Challenge 397 as by **David Foley**. Matrix GEX-1092 is titled *My Mind Is To Marry* on Davis Unlimited 33033, Document DOCD-8054. The date shown is taken from the label of a test pressing.
Revs: Gennett 6436 by Tommy Dandurand, 6733 by Ernest V. Stoneman.

G.B. Grayson–Henry Whitter: G.B. Grayson, f/v/sp-1; Henry Whitter, g/v-2/sp-3.
New York, NY   Tuesday, July 31, 1928

46630-2	The Red And Green Signal Lights	Vi V-40063
46631-2	Joking Henry	Vi V-40038
46632-1,-2	There's A Man Goin' 'Round Takin' Names	Vi unissued
46633-2	The Nine-Pound Hammer -1, 2, 3	Vi V-40105
46634-2	Short Life Of Trouble -2	Vi V-40105
46635-2	I've Always Been A Rambler	Vi V-40324
46636-1	Where Are You Going, Alice? -1	Vi V-40135
46637-1	A Dark Road Is A Hard Road To Travel	Vi V-40063

Victor V-40135, V-40324 as by **Grayson & Whitter**.

G.B. Grayson, f/v/sp; Henry Whitter, g/sp-1.
New York, NY   Wednesday, August 1, 1928

| 46638-2 | Barnyard Serenade -1 | Vi V-40038 |
| 46639-2 | Little Maggie With A Dram Glass In Her Hand | Vi V-40135, BB B-7072 |

Victor V-40135 as by **Grayson & Whitter**.

Grayson & Whitter: G.B. Grayson, f/v-1/sp-2; Henry Whitter, g/sp-3.
Memphis, TN   Monday, September 30, 1929

56309-2	On The Banks Of Old Tennessee -1, 2	Vi V-40235, BB B-7072, ZoSA 4329
56310-2	Never Be As Fast As I Have Been -1, 2, 3	Vi 23565
56311-2	I Have Lost You Darling, True Love -1, 2	Vi V-40268
56312-2	Tom Dooley -1	Vi V-40235
56313-1	Going Down The Lee Highway -2, 3	Vi 23565, BB B-5498

Rev. Zonophone 4329 by Bill Simmons.

G.B. Grayson, f/v/sp; Henry Whitter, g.
Memphis, TN   Tuesday, October 1, 1929

56322-1	I Saw A Man At The Close Of Day	Vi V-40324
56323-1,-2	The Coal Creek Mines	Vi unissued
56324-2	What You Gonna Do With The Baby	Vi V-40268

GRAYSON COUNTY RAILSPLITTERS
See Fields Ward.

GREAT GAP ENTERTAINERS
Pseudonym on Broadway for the Lookout Mountain Boys/Revelers/Singers (see Claude (C.W.) Davis).

CLARENCE GREEN [& WISE BROTHERS]
See Clarence Greene.

UNCLE GEORGE GREEN & HIS BOYS
Pseudonym on Champion for Walter Coon & His Joy Boys.

GREEN & RUSSELL
Pseudonym on Supertone for Leonard Rutherford & Byrd Moore.

GREEN'S STRING BAND

A. Judson Green, f; Herman Green, f; Ila Bassett, g; Preston Green, sb.
Richmond, IN   Monday, September 15, 1930

17030-B	Gray Eagle	Ch 16249, Spr 2575
17031-A	Glide Waltz	Ge 7307, Ch 16115
17032,-A	Wedding Of The Winds	Ge rejected
17033-A	Zenda Waltz	Ge 7307, Ch 16115, Spr 2517
17034-A	Steward Long Bow	Ch 16249
17035-A	The Widow Hayse	Ch 16489
17036	Rickett's Hornpipe	Ch 16489
17037,-A	Dixie Schottische	Ge unissued
17038	Over The Waves	Spr 2517
17039-A	Repasz Band March	Spr 2575
17040-A	Pickaway	Ch 16503

Superiors as by **Dave Dawson's String Band**. Matrix 17033-A is titled *Sea Shore Waltz* on Superior 2517. Rev. Champion 16503 by Madisonville String Band.

AMOS GREENE
Pseudonym on Supertone for Cliff Carlisle.

CLARENCE GREENE

Clarence Green, v; acc. Will Abernathy, h/ah; own g.
Atlanta, GA   Saturday, November 5, 1927
| 145122-2 | On The Banks Of The Ohio | Co 15311-D |
| 145123-2 | Fond Affection | Co 15311-D |

Clarence Green & Wise Brothers: Clarence Greene, f; Bee Wise, bj; Omer Wise, Sr., g.
Johnson City, TN   Monday, October 15, 1928
| 147188-2 | Pride Of The Ball | Co 15680-D |
| 147189-1 | Kitty Waltz | Co 15680-D |

Clarence Green, v; acc. own g.
Johnson City, TN   Monday, October 15, 1928
147190-1	Johnson City Blues	Co unissued: Co C4K47911, C2K47466, Co(E) 472886 (CDs)
147190-2	Johnson City Blues	Co 15461-D
147191-1	Ninety-Nine Years In Jail	Co 15461-D

Clarence Greene, v; acc. own g.
Bristol, TN   Tuesday, October 30, 1928
| 47250-2 | Good-Night Darling | Vi V-40141 |
| 47251-1 | Little Bunch Of Roses | Vi V-40141 |

Moore & Green: Clarence Greene, f; Byrd Moore, g; or **Fiddlin' Green & Byrd Moore**-1, v duet; acc. Clarence Greene, f; Byrd Moore, g.
Richmond, IN   Thursday, February 13, 1930
16258,-A	Lay Down Baby Blues	Ge rejected
16259	Cincinnati Rag	Ch 16357, Spr 2838
16260	Pig Angle	Ch 16357, Spr 2838
16261	Pride Of The Ball	Ge rejected
16262,-A	In The Hills Of Tennessee -1	Ge rejected

Superior 2838 as by **Moss & Long**.

Fiddlin' Green & Byrd Moore, v duet; acc. Clarence Greene, f; Byrd Moore, g.
Richmond, IN   Friday, February 14, 1930
| 16265,-A | The Lonesome Valley | Ge rejected |
| 16267,-A | Frankie Silver's Confession | Ge unissued |

Matrix 16266 is by Walter Taylor (see *B&GR*).
Clarence Greene is also a member of the Blue Ridge Mountain Entertainers and Byrd Moore & His Hot Shots.

LEM GREENE
See Arthur Fields & Fred Hall.

GREENE BROTHERS
See Arthur Fields & Fred Hall.

GREENSBORO BOYS QUARTET

Vocal quartet; unacc.
Johnson City, TN   Tuesday, October 16, 1928
| 147198-1 | Sing Me A Song Of The Sunny South | Co 15507-D |
| 147199-2 | Sweet Little Girl Of Mine | Co 15507-D |

GREENVILLE TRIO

No details.
Atlanta, GA   Thursday, November 4, 1926
| 143058- | Tipperary Moonlight | Co unissued |
| 143059- | Bulldog | Co unissued |

This group may be associated with Chris Bouchillon.

PROFESSOR & MRS. GREER

Professor I.G. Greer, Mrs. Greer, v duet; acc. Mrs. Greer, du.
poss. New York, NY   c. October 1929
GEX-2435-	Black Jack Davy – Part I	Pm 3195
GEX-2436-	Black Jack Davy – Part II	Pm 3195
GEX-2437-	Sweet William And Fair Ellen – Part 1	Pm 3236

GEX-2438-	Sweet William And Fair Ellen – Part 2	Pm 3236
GEX-2439-	The Three Babes	Pm unissued
GEX-2440-	Hay Tank Toodle All Day	Pm 3255
GEX-2441-	As The Train Rattled On	Pm unissued
GEX-2442-	The Fellow That Looks Like Me	Pm 3255
GEX-2443-	Battleship Maine	Pm unissued
GEX-2444-	The Darling Mustache	Pm unissued
GEX-2445-	The House Carpenter – Part 1	Pm unissued
GEX-2446-	The House Carpenter – Part 2	Pm unissued

It is not certain that all the unissued items are by these artists, since the data were derived from a source deficient in artist credits, but several of them are known to have been in their repertoire. Matrix GEX-2440 is also reported titled *Hey Dey Diddle All The Day* and GEX-2442 titled *Fellow That Looks Like Me*.

Professor & Mrs. Greer also recorded for the Library of Congress.

BOBBY GREGORY

Bobby Gregory, v; acc. own pac; unknown, g.
    New York, NY   Monday, February 4, 1929

401586-A	The Convict's Song	OK 45350
401587-A	The Run-A-Way Boy	OK 45350
401588-B	Who Threw Mush In Grandpa's Whiskers?	OK 45473, PaE R1131, PaAu A3408
401589-B	Hoopee Scoopee	OK 45473, PaE R1131, PaAu A3408

Bobby Gregory, pac; acc. unknown, g.
    New York, NY   Monday, March 4, 1929

| 401686-A | Little Pal Of Mine | OK 45500 |
| 401687-A | Medley Of Old Time Waltzes | OK 45500 |

No details.
    New York, NY   c. late December 1929

| 3789- | Yodeling Bill | GG/Rad 4310, VD 84310 |

Rev. all issues by Gene Autry.

Bobby Gregory recorded after 1942.

WALLACE GREY

Pseudonym on Champion for Connie Bird (see Elmer Bird).

REX GRIFFIN

Rex Griffin, v/y; acc. Johnny Motlow, bj; own g.
    Chicago, IL   Monday, March 25, 1935

C-9867-A	Why Should I Care If You're Blue	De 5118
C-9868-A	Blue Eyes Lullaby	De 5089
C-9869-A	Just For Old Times' Sake	De 5147
C-9870-A	Love Call Yodel	De 5088

    Chicago, IL   Tuesday, March 26, 1935

C-9871-A	I Don't Love Anybody But You	De 5089
C-9872-A	The Trail To Home Sweet Home	De 5088
C-9873-A	Let Me Call You Sweetheart Again	De 5147
C-9874-A	Mean Woman Blues	De 5118
C-9875-	Dixieland Sweetheart	De unissued: BF BCD15911 (CD)
C-9876-	Down In Old Alabama	De unissued: BF BCD15911 (CD)

It is not known which takes of matrices C-9875/76 are used on Bear Family BCD15911.

Rex Griffin, v/y-1; acc. own g.
    New Orleans, LA   Monday, March 2, 1936

NO-60600-A	Everybody's Tryin' To Be My Baby -1	De 5294
NO-60601-A	If You Call That Gone, Good Bye	De 5250
NO-60602-A	The Yodeling Cowboy's Last Song -1	De 5395, MeC 45207, Min M-14064
NO-60603-A	I Love You Nellie -1	De 5250
NO-60604-A	I'm Just Passin' Through -1	De 5202
NO-60605-A	I'm Ready To Reform -1	De 5294
NO-60606-A	The Walkin' Blues -1	De 5227
NO-60607-A	An Old Faded Photograph	De 5269
NO-60608-A	Sittin' On The Old Settee -1	De 5202
NO-60609-A	Sweet Mama Hurry Home -1	De 5395, MeC 45207

Rev. Minerva M-14064 by Tex Ritter.

Acc. unknown, sg-2; own g; unknown, g-3.
New Orleans, LA   Thursday, March 19, 1936
    NO-60830-   Would You Leave Me Alone Little Darling -3   De 5227, BrSA SA1101
    NO-60831-A   The Last Love Call Yodel -1, 2   De 5269

Rev. Brunswick SA1101 by Roy Shaffer.

Acc. own g.
New York, NY   Thursday, May 13, 1937
    62194-A   The Last Letter   De 5383, MeC 45204, Min M-14106,
                                                                       Coral 64007
    62195-A   Over The River -1   De 5383, MeC 45204, Min M-14107

Acc. own g; Ted Brooks, g-2/v-3; Smitty Smith, sb-4/v-5.
New York, NY   Monday, September 25, 1939
    66650-B   Answer To The Last Letter   De 5745, Min M-14106
    66651-A   My Hill Billy Baby   De 5770
    66652-A   I Think I'll Give Up (It's All Over Now)   De 5814
    66653-A   Beyond The Last Mile   De 5764
    66654-A   Just Partners   De 5745, Min M-14107
    66655-A   The Lovesick Blues -1   De 5770, Coral 64007
    66656-A   I Love You As Before   De 5814
    66657-A   I'll Never Tell You That I Love You -2, 3, 4, 5 De 5786
    66658-A   Nobody Wants To Be My Baby -2, 3, 4, 5   De 5786
    66659-A   Maybe You'll Think About Me -2   De 5798
    66660-A   You Got To Go To Work -1, 2   De 5798
    66661-A   An Old Rose And A Curl -2, 4   De 5764

Decca 5786 as by **Rex Griffin With Ted & Smitty**.
Rex Griffin recorded after 1942.

GRINNELL GIGGERS

Ben Tinnon, f; Melvin Paul, bj; Grover Grant, g.
Memphis, TN   Friday, May 30, 1930
    62555-2   Ruth's Rag   Vi V-40275, BB B-5284, B-8182, Sr S-3365,
                                                                       MW M-4473
    62556-1   The Giggers Waltz   Vi V-40275, BB B-5284, Sr S-3365, MW M-4473

Ben Tinnon, f; Melvin Paul, md; Grover Grant, g.
Memphis, TN   Wednesday, November 26, 1930
    64725-2   Gigger Waltz No. 2   Vi 23511
    64726-2   Duck Shoes Rag   Vi 23511, BB B-8182
    64727-1   Cotton Pickers' Drag   Vi 23632
    64728-2   Sunset Waltz   Vi 23632
    64729-2   Plow Boy Hop   Vi 23675
    64730-1   Uncle Ned's Waltz   Vi 23675

MR. & MRS. R.N. GRISHAM
GRISHAM'S QUARTET

Mr. & Mrs. R.N. Grisham, v duet; acc. prob. Miss Grisham, o.
New Orleans, LA   Wednesday, April 13, 1927
    143965-1   Reaching To You   Co 15177-D
    143966-2   We'll Be At Home Again   Co 15177-D

Mr. & Mrs. R.N. Grisham & Daughter, v trio; acc. prob. Miss Grisham, p.
New Orleans, LA   Monday, October 24, 1927
    145004-2   Angels Tell My Mother I'll Be There   Co 15255-D
    145005-1   'Tis Wonderful   Co 15255-D

Mr. & Mrs. R.N. Grisham, v duet; acc. prob. Miss Grisham, p.
New Orleans, LA   Monday, October 24, 1927
    145006-   'Twill All Be Glory Over There   Co unissued
    145007-   I'll Be A Friend To Jesus   Co unissued

Mr. & Mrs. R.N. Grisham & Daughter, v trio; acc. prob. Miss Grisham, o.
New Orleans, LA   Thursday, April 26, 1928
    146199-1   Just Beyond The Gates   Co 15305-D
    146200-2   We're Drifting On   Co 15379-D

Mr. & Mrs. R.N. Grisham, v duet; acc. prob. Miss Grisham, o.

New Orleans, LA   Thursday, April 26, 1928
  146201-2   The Heart That Was Broken For Me   Co 15379-D
  146202-2   I'll Be A Friend To Jesus   Co 15305-D

Grisham's Quartet: ——— Carpenter, tv; Mrs. R.N. Grisham, av; R.N. Grisham, bv; ——— Bush, bsv; acc. prob. Miss Grisham, p.
  Atlanta, GA   Saturday, November 23, 1929
  56575-1   When The Mighty Trumpet Sounds   Vi V-40295, BB B-5271, Eld 2145, Sr S-3352
  56576-2   Redeeming Star   Vi V-40295, BB B-5271, Eld 2145, Sr S-3352
  56577-1   My Prayer   Vi V-40238, BB B-5405
  56578-1   Some Day We'll Meet Our Mother   Vi V-40238, BB B-5405

Mr. & Mrs. R.N. Grisham, v duet; acc. Miss Grisham, p.
  Atlanta, GA   Saturday, November 23, 1929
  56579-   I Hear A Voice   BB B-5538
  56580-   Can I Forget?   BB B-5538

CLIFFORD GROSS

Clifford Gross & Muryel Campbell: Clifford Gross, f; Muryel Campbell, g.
  Dallas, TX   Sunday, June 13, 1937
  DAL-286-1   Sally Goodin   ARC 7-10-52, Vo 03650
  DAL-287-   Leather Breeches   ARC unissued
  DAL-288-   Devil's Dream   ARC unissued
  DAL-289-1   Houchins Waltz   ARC 7-10-52, Vo 03650
  DAL-290-   Goin' Up The Country   ARC unissued
  DAL-291-   Run Them Coons In The Ground   ARC unissued
  DAL-292-1   Waggoner   ARC 7-12-57, Vo/OK 03721, Cq 9753
  DAL-293-1   Green River Waltz   ARC 7-12-57, Vo/OK 03721, Cq 9756
  DAL-294-   Tableau Clog   ARC unissued

Rev. Conqueror 9756 by Light Crust Doughboys.

  Dallas, TX   Sunday, June 20, 1937
  DAL-393-   Money Musk   ARC unissued

Cliff & Ray: Clifford Gross, f; Ramon (Ray) DeArman, g.
  Dallas, TX   Wednesday, May 18, 1938
  DAL-592-1   Seaside Schottische   Vo/OK 04743
  DAL-593-1,-2   Sleepin' Lula   Vo unissued
  DAL-594-1,-2   Stony Point   Vo unissued
  DAL-595-1   Bear Creek Hop   Vo 04293
  DAL-596-1   Tableau Clog   Vo 04293
  DAL-597-1   Rocky Mountain Goat   Vo/OK 04204, Cq 9753
  DAL-598-1   Rustic Schottische   Vo/OK 04204, Cq 9754
  DAL-599-1   Southern Flower Waltz   Vo/OK 04743

Rev. Conqueror 9754 by Prairie Ramblers.

BIXY GUIDRY–PERCY BABINEAUX

See Percy Babineaux–Bixy Guidry.

GUIDRY BROTHERS

Unidentified, f; unidentified, ac; unidentified, g; unidentified, v/y-1.
  New Orleans, LA   Tuesday, October 1, 1929
  NO-242-   Le Garcon Chez Son Pere   Vo 15854
  NO-243-   La Valse Du Mariage -1   Vo 15854
  NO-244-   Le Garcon Negligent   Vo 15849
  NO-245-   Homme Abondonne   Vo 15849
  NO-246-   Le Recommendation Du Soulard   Vo 15844
  NO-247-   Ie Mes Beaux Yieux   Vo 15844

DELIN T. GUILLORY–LEWIS LAFLEUR

Lewis Lafleur, f; Delin T. Guillory, ac/v.
  New Orleans, LA   Thursday, November 7, 1929
  56508-2   Ma Petite Blonde (My Little Blonde)   Vi 22209
  56509-1   Quelqun Est Jalous (Somebody Is Jealous)   Vi 22209
  56510-1   Alone At Home   BB B-2082
  56511-1   Stop That   BB B-2082

GUNBOAT BILLY & THE SPARROW
See Arthur Fields & Fred Hall.

WOODY GUTHRIE

Woody Guthrie, v; acc. own h-1/g.
New York, NY   Friday, April 26, 1940

050145-1	The Great Dust Storm	Vi 26622
050146-1	Talkin' Dust Bowl Blues	Vi 26619
050147-1	Pretty Boy Floyd -1	Vi unissued: *RCA LPV502, PL12099, Rdr 1040, RCA(E) RD7642* (LPs); *BMG/RCA-Cam(E) 74321317742, BMG/Buddah 74465-99724-2* (CDs)
050148-1	Dusty Old Dust	Vi 26622
050149-1	Dust Bowl Blues -1	Vi unissued: *RCA LPV502, PL12099, Rdr 1040, RCA(E) RD7642* (LPs); *BMG/RCA-Cam(E) 74321317742, BMG/Buddah 74465-99724-2* (CDs)
050150-1	Blowin' Down The Road -1	Vi 26619
050151-1	Tom Joad – Part 1 -1	Vi 26621
050152-1	Tom Joad – Part 2 -1	Vi 26621
050153-1	Do Re Mi	Vi 26620
050154-1	Dust Bowl Refugee -1	Vi 26623
050155-1	I Ain't Got No Home In This World Anymore -1	Vi 26624
050156-1	Vigilante Man -1	Vi 26624

New York, NY   Friday, May 3, 1940

050600-1	Dust Can't Kill Me -1	Vi 26620
050601-1	Dust Pneumonia Blues	Vi 26623

Victor 26619/20/21 were issued in Victor album P27 (*Dust Bowl Ballads – Vol. 1*), and Victor 26622/23/24 in Victor album P28 (*Dust Bowl Ballads – Vol. 2*).

Woody Guthrie also recorded for the Library of Congress and after 1942.

H

E.E. HACK STRING BAND
HACK'S STRING BAND

E.E. Hack String Band: Virgil "Cricket" Garrett, f; James Brown, f; Melvin "Slats" Bethel, md; Walter Cobb, bj; Bill Brown, g; Gene Garrett, sb; Eugene "Buster" Hack, jazzhorn-1.
Atlanta, GA   Wednesday, April 17, 1929

148334-2	Black Lake Waltz	Co 15466-D
148335-2	Waltz Of Dreams	Co 15466-D
148336-2	Too Tight Rag -1	Co 15418-D
148337-2	West Kentucky Limited	Co 15418-D

Hack's String Band: Cricket Garrett, f-1; James Brown, f-1; Slats Bethel, md; Walter Cobb, bj; Bill Brown, g; Charles Underwood, g; Gene Garrett, sb; or **Cobb & Underwood Acc. Hack's String Band**-2: Walter Cobb, Charles Underwood, v duet with same acc.; or **Charles Underwood Acc. Hack's String Band**-3: Charles Underwood, v/y-4 with same acc.
Richmond, IN   Monday, September 29, 1930

17093,-A,-B	Hauthan Waltz -1	Ge rejected
17095,-A	The D Waltz -1	Ge rejected
17096	Banjo Marmolo	Ch 16292, 33026
17097	Kentucky Plow Boy's March	Ch 16292, Spr 2536
17099	Black Sheep Blues -2	Ge 7311, Ch 16144, 45146
17100	I Want My Rib -3	Ch R-16362, Spr 2811, *Vs 5092*
17101	Crawdad Song -2	Ch R-16362, 45146, Spr 2811
17102	Black Snake Moan -3	Ge 7311, Ch 16144
17103	Wink The Other Eye -1	Ch 16326, 45149, Spr 2536
17104	Pretty Little Girl -1	Ch 16326, 45149
17105,-A	I Want To Waltz With You Honey -1	Ge rejected
17106,-A	Queen's Waltz -1	Ge rejected
17107,-A	Henpecked Papa -3, 4	Ge unissued

Champion 45149 as by **Hacks' String Band**. Superior 2536 as by **Cumberland String Band**; 2811 as by **Johnny Baxter** (matrix 17100)/**Baxter & Layne** (matrix 17101). Varsity 5092 as by **Red's Dixie Ramblers**.
Matrix 17097 is titled *Plow Boy's March* on Superior 2536. Matrices 17094, 17098 are Hawaiian.
Rev. Champion 33026 untraced; Varsity 5092 by Red Perkins & His Dixie Ramblers (see *JR*).

HACKBERRY RAMBLERS

Luderin Darbone, f; Lonnie Rainwater, sg; Floyd Rainwater, g/v-1; Lennis Sonnier, g/v-2; band v-3.
New Orleans, LA   Saturday, August 10, 1935

94384-1	Tickle Her	BB B-2173
94385-1	Crowley Waltz	BB B-2173
94394-1	Just Because -3	BB B-6069, MW M-4816
94395-1	Bonnie Blue Eyes -1	BB B-6069, MW M-4816
94396-1	You've Got To Hi-De-Hi -2, 3	BB B-6136
94397-1	Nobody Like You	BB B-6110
94398-1	'Neath The Weeping Willow Tree -1, 3	BB B-6181
94399-1	Louisiana Moon -3	BB B-6181
94400-1	My Little Girl -3	BB B-6136
94401-1	Hackberry Trot	BB B-6110

Intervening matrices are by Dixie Ramblers [II].

Luderin Darbone, f; Floyd Rainwater, g/v-1/y-2; Lennis Sonnier, g/v-3; Johnnie Puderer, sb; band v-4.
New Orleans, LA   Wednesday, February 19, 1936

99206-1	Bring It Down To The Jailhouse, Honey -1	BB B-2002
99207-1	Green Valley Waltz -1, 4	BB B-2002
99208-1	Mama Don't Allow No Hanging Around -1	BB B-2187
99209-1	Sonny Boy -1	BB B-6368
99210-1	Don't Ever Trust A Friend -1, 4	BB B-6368
99211-1	Blue Eyes -1	BB B-6289, MW M-4812
99212-1	On Top Of The World -1, 2	BB B-2010
99213-1	Leave Me If You Wish -1?	BB B-2186
99214-1	High Mountain Blues -1	BB B-2187
99215-1	A Little Rendezvous In Honolulu -1	BB B-6289, MW M-4812
99216-1	Su Charin -3?	BB B-2179
99217-1	Te Ma Pris De La Maison -3?	BB B-2179

Rev. Bluebird B-2186 by Joseph F. Falcon.

New Orleans, LA   Saturday, October 17, 1936

02662-1	Jolie Blonde -3	BB B-2003
02663-1	Jai Passe Devonde Ta Parte -3	BB B-2007
02664-1	Mermentan Stomp -3	BB B-2003
02665-1	Te Petite Et Te Meon -3	BB B-2005
02666-1	Jai Pas Bien Fey -3	BB B-2007
02667-1	Vinton High Society	BB B-2005
02668-1	Over The Teacups -3	BB B-2009
02669-1	Just Once More	BB B-2009
02670-1	The Wandering Man -1, 2	BB B-2019
02671-1	Dobie Shack -1	BB B-2019
02672-1	Ramblin' -1, 2	BB B-2010
02673-1	Carolina Home -1	BB unissued

Luderin Darbone, f; Joe Werner, h-1/g; Lennis Sonnier, g/v-2.
New Orleans, LA   Monday, February 22, 1937

07219-1	Jolie Petite Fille -2	BB B-2011
07220-1	Louisiana Breakdown -1	BB B-2011
07221-1	Cajun Crawl -1, 2	BB B-2013
07222-1	Ma Chere Belle -1, 2	BB B-2015
07223-1	Darbone's Breakdown -1	BB B-2015
07224-1	Se Pas La Pan -1, 2	BB B-2017
07225-1	Rice City Stomp -1, 2	BB B-2017
07226-1	Jai Pres Parley -2	BB B-2013

Riverside Ramblers: Luderin Darbone, f; Joe Werner, h/g/v; Lennis Sonnier, g.
New Orleans, LA   Monday, February 22, 1937

07227-1	Wondering	BB B-6926, MW M-7338
07228-1	Dissatisfied	BB B-6926, MW M-7338
07229-1	Stay In Your Own Back Yard	BB B-7063, MW M-7339
07230-1	Drifting Along	BB B-7063, MW M-7339

Hackberry Ramblers: Luderin Darbone, f; Lennis Sonnier, g/v-1; Floyd Shreve, g; Johnnie Puderer, sb.
New Orleans, LA   Friday, September 10, 1937

014000-1	Quitter La Maison -1	BB B-2021
014001-1	Te Ma Faite Kite -1	BB B-2023
014002-1	Shreve Breakdown	BB B-2023
014003-1	Darbone's Creole Stomp	BB B-2025

014004-1	Church Point Breakdown -1	BB B-2025
014005-1	Jai Maitritte Pas Sa -1	BB B-2027
014006-1	Vie Vals -1	BB B-2027
014007-1	Pas Aller Vita	BB B-2021

Riverside Ramblers: Luderin Darbone, f/v-1; Floyd Shreve, g/v-2; Lennis Sonnier, g; Johnnie Puderer, sb.
New Orleans, LA   Friday, September 10, 1937

014008-1	Louisiana Sweetheart - 2	BB B-7251, MW M-7340
014009-1	Ain't Satisfied -2	BB B-7202, MW M-7341
014010-1	The Old Fiddle Blues -2	BB B-7251, MW M-7340
014011-1	Ain't Gonna Give You None -1	BB B-7202, MW M-7341

Hackberry Ramblers: Luderin Darbone, f/v-1; Floyd Shreve, g; Danny Shreve, g; Pete Duhon, sb.
New Orleans, LA   Friday, April 1, 1938

022020-1	Oh Josephine, My Josephine -1	BB B-2035
022021-1	Et La Bas -1	BB B-2040
022022-1	Chere Tite Fille -1	BB B-2044
022023-1	Cherie A You Toi Te? -1	BB B-2044
022024-1	Faux Pas Tu Bray Cherie -1	BB B-2048
022025-1	La Breakdown A Pete	BB B-2035
022026-1	Mon Cour Me Fais Ci Mal -1	BB B-2048, B-2088
022027-1	Fais Pas Ca -1	BB B-2040, B-2090

Revs: Bluebird B-2088, B-2090 by Happy Fats & His Rayne-Bo Ramblers.

Riverside Ramblers: Luderin Darbone, f/v-1; Floyd Shreve, g/v-2; Danny Shreve, g/v-3; Pete Duhon, sb.
New Orleans, LA   Friday, April 1, 1938

022028-1	Little Acadian Girl -1	BB B-7846, MW M-7672
022029-1	Was It Tears -2	BB B-7974, MW M-7672
022030-1	Longing For You -2	BB B-7974, MW M-7673
022031-1	There'll Come A Time -3	BB B-7846, MW M-7673

Hackberry Ramblers: Luderin Darbone, f/v-1; Floyd Shreve, g/v-2; Danny Shreve, g; Pete Duhon, sb/v-3; band v-4.
New Orleans, LA   Saturday, October 22, 1938

027857-1	Dans Le Grand Bois (In The Forest) -3	BB B-2059
027858-1	Jolie Fille (Pretty Girl) -3	BB B-2065
027859-1	La Valse Du Vieux Temp (Old-Time Waltz) -1	BB B-2065
027860-1	One Step De L'Amour -1, 4	BB B-2056
027861-1	Une Pias Ici Et Une Pias La Bas -1, 4	BB B-2056
027862-1	J'Vas Tamey Camaime (I Love You) -1, 2 (lead)	BB B-2066
027863-1	La Valse De La Prison (Waltz Of The Prison) -2	BB B-2066
027864-1	French Two-Step	BB B-2059

Riverside Ramblers: Luderin Darbone, f/v-1; Floyd Shreve, g/v-2; Danny Shreve, g/v-3; Pete Duhon, sb.
New Orleans, LA   Saturday, October 22, 1938

027865-1	Let's Go Fishing -1	BB B-7942, MW M-7674
027866-1	She's One Of Those -2	BB B-7942, MW M-7674
027867-1	Right Or Wrong -2	BB B-8000, MW M-7675
027868-1	One Sweet Letter -3	BB B-8000, MW M-7675

The Hackberry Ramblers recorded after 1942.

CHARLIE HAGER

Hager & Bodine: Charlie Hager, Loy Bodine, v duet; or **Charlie Hager**, v-1; acc. Charlie Hager, md; Loy Bodine, g.
Richmond, IN   Wednesday, February 3, 1932

| 18374 | She's More To Be Pitied Than Censured | Ge unissued |
| 18375 | Black Sheep Blues -1 | Ge rejected |

See also Loy Bodine.

JACK HAGWOOD

Jack Hagwood & Boys: Jack Hagwood, v; acc. several unknowns, g.
Richmond, IN   Wednesday, January 14, 1931

| 17436 | [unknown title] | Ge rejected trial recording |

Gennett files note "Hawaiian guitars" but do not say how many.

Jack Hagwood (The Radio Jack), v; acc. poss. own g.
Richmond, IN   Wednesday, January 14, 1931

| 17437,-A | I'm Glad I'm A Bum | Ge rejected |
| 17438,-A | My Wife's Done Gone And Left Me | Ge rejected |

WILLIAM HAID

This banjoist, though featured on one side of Paramount 3169 (as well as several other recordings entirely his own), is beyond the scope of this work.

EWEN HAIL (THE COWBOY MINSTREL)

Ewen Hail, v; acc. Bert Hirsch, f-1; Carson Robison, g/wh-2.
    New York, NY   Thursday, March 31, 1927

Matrix	Title	Issues
E-22202/03	Cowboy's Lament -2	Br/Vo unissued
E-22204*/05	Cowboy's Lament -1	Vo 5146, Br 141, BrC 433, BrAu 141, Spt S2043
E-22206	Lavender Cowboy -2	Br/Vo unissued
E-22207/08*	Lavender Cowboy -1	Vo 5146, Br 141, BrC 433, BrAu 141

Rev. Supertone S2043 by Buell Kazee.

Ewen Hail also recorded popular material in the Vocalion 15000 series.

THERON HALE & DAUGHTERS

Theron Hale, f; Mamie Ruth Hale, f-1/md-2; Elizabeth Hale, p.
    Nashville, TN   Wednesday, October 3, 1928

Matrix	Title	Issues
47118-1	Listen To The Mocking Bird -1	Vi V-40019
47119-1	Turkey Gobbler -1	Vi V-40019
47120-3	Beautiful Valley -1	Vi V-40046
47121-1,-2,-3	Kiss Waltz	Vi unissued
47122-	Jolly Blacksmith -2	Vi V-40046
47123-1,-2,-3	Wink The Other Eye	Vi unissued
47124-2	Hale's Rag -2	Vi V-40046
47125-1,-2	The Old Race Horse	Vi unissued

Victor V-40046 was issued in two forms, coupling matrices 47120/47122 and 47122/47124.

Theron Hale recorded after 1942.

TRAVIS B. HALE–E.J. DERRY JR.

Travis B. Hale, E.J. Derry Jr, v duet; acc. E.J. Derry Jr, md; Travis B. Hale, bj; or **Travis B. Hale**-1, v; acc. own bj.
    Chicago, IL   Monday, June 6, 1927

Matrix	Title	Issues
38631-2	The Dying Hobo	Vi 20796
38632-3	Long Gone	Vi 20866
38633-1	Oh Bury Me Out On The Prairie (The Cowboy's Lament) -1	Vi 20796, MW M-4040
38634-2	Can't You Hear Me Say I Love You	Vi 20866

Rev. Montgomery Ward M-4040 by Bud Billings (Frank Luther) & Carson Robison (see the latter).

HALE'S KENTUCKY MOUNTAINEERS

Pseudonym on Varsity for Crockett's Kentucky Mountaineers.

AMBROSE HALEY & HIS OZARK RAMBLERS

Wade Ray, f; Monte Rhine, lg; Ambrose Haley, tg/v; Sonny Haley, sb.
    Chicago, IL   Wednesday, May 26, 1937

Matrix	Title	Issues
C-1892-2	I Can't Lose That Longing For You	ARC 7-11-66, Vo 03709
C-1893-1	I'm So Alone With The Crowd	ARC 7-08-52, Vo 03590
C-1894-1,-2	Down Sunshine Lane	ARC unissued
C-1895-2	When A Lady Meets A Gentleman Down South	ARC 7-11-66, Vo 03709
C-1898-1,-2	Ozark Stomp	ARC unissued

Wade Ray, f; Monte Rhine, lg; Ambrose Haley, tg/v; Sonny Haley, sb; or **Ozark Ramblers Trio**-1: prob. v trio with same acc.
    Chicago, IL   Thursday, May 27, 1937

Matrix	Title	Issues
C-1896-1,-2	Kansas City Kitty	ARC unissued
C-1897-1	It Looks Like Rain In Cherry Blossom Lane	ARC 7-08-52, Vo 03590
C-1899-1	I Wouldn't Trade The Silver In My Mother's Hair (For All The Gold In The World)	ARC 7-10-54, Vo/OK 03648, Cq 8888
C-1900-1,-2	I Ought To Break Your Neck	ARC unissued
C-1901-1	How's Your Folks And My Folks (Down In Norfolk Town)	ARC 7-10-54, Vo/OK 03648, Cq 8888
C-1902-1,-2	Ridin' The Trail Back Home -1	ARC unissued
C-1903-1,-2	Plain Old Me	ARC unissued
C-1904-1,-2	In A Shanty In Old Shanty Town	ARC unissued

C-1905-1,-2	Sally's Not The Same Old Sally	ARC unissued
C-1906-1,-2	We'll Rest At The End Of The Trail -1	ARC unissued
C-1907-1,-2	Any Time	ARC unissued

Ambrose Haley recorded after 1942.

ARTY HALL & HIS RADIO RUBES

Arty Hall, two unknowns, v trio; or Arty Hall, sp-1; acc. unknown, f; unknown, ac; unknown, g.
New York, NY   Wednesday, August 11, 1937

21492-1	Down In The Old Home Town	ARC 7-10-59, Cq 8884
21493-2	The Story Of Seven Roses	ARC 7-10-59, Cq 8884
21494-1	I Wish I Had Died In My Cradle (Before I Grew Up To Love You)	Cq 8885
21495-1	Conversation With A Mule -1	ARC 7-12-54
21496-1	Maple On The Hill No. 4	ARC 7-11-52
21497-1	By The Stump Of The Old Pine Tree	ARC 7-11-52, Cq 8885

Arty Hall, two unknowns, v trio; acc. unknown, f; unknown, ac; unknown, h-1/jh-1; unknown, g.
New York, NY   Friday, October 8, 1937

21825-	Turkey Hash	ARC unissued
21826-	I'm Getting Ready To Go	ARC unissued
21827-	Study War No More	ARC unissued
21828-	Drifting Too Far From The Shore	ARC unissued
21829-	Where We Never Grow Old	ARC unissued
21830-2	Sara Jane -1	ARC 7-12-54

DON HALL TRIO

Recordings by this group on Victor, Bluebird, and associated labels are beyond the scope of this work.

FRED "SUGAR" HALL & HIS SUGAR BABIES

Most of the recordings so credited are outside the scope of this work (for comment and a selective discography see *JR*), but see Arthur Fields & Fred Hall.

GENE HALL

Pseudonym on Australian Paramount for Vernon Dalhart.

HANK HALL

Pseudonym on Sunrise for Dwight Butcher.

LEAFORD HALL & HIS TEXAS VAGABONDS

Leaford Hall, f; Bill Vitovsky, esg; Mabel Ogden, p; prob. Frances Hooten, tbj; Aldan "Wimpy" Hutson, g; Liston Weaver, sb; unknown, v-1; Jean Ogden, v-2.
Dallas, TX   Tuesday, April 29, 1941

93715-A	Wednesday Night	De 5951
93716-A	After My Laughter Came Tears -2	De 6015
93717-A	Why Did I	De rejected
93718-A	Blue Man	De 6015
93719-A	Take Me Back To Texas -1, 2	De 5951
93720-A,-B	Gee But I Hate To Go Home Alone	De rejected

Jean Ogden was Mabel's daughter.

ROY HALL & HIS BLUE RIDGE ENTERTAINERS

Tommy Magness, f-1/sp-2; unknown, md-3; Clato Buchanan, tbj-4; Roy Hall, g/v-5/sp-2; Talton Aldridge, g/v-6; Bob Hopson, g/sp-2.
Columbia, SC   Monday, November 7, 1938

SC-84-1	Come Back Little Pal -1, 3, 4, 5, 6	Vo/OK 04842
SC-85-	Look On And Cry	Vo unissued
SC-86-	Crying Holy	Vo unissued
SC-87-	Lay Me Where My Mother Is Sleeping	Vo unissued
SC-88-1	Good For Nothing Gal -5, 6	Vo 04627
SC-89-1	The Lonely Blues -5, 6	Vo 04627
SC-90-1	Where The Roses Never Fade -1, 3, 4, 5	Vo/OK 04771, Cq 9184
SC-91-1	Answer To Great Speckled Bird -1, 3, 4, 5	Vo/OK 04771, Cq 9184
SC-92-	When The Sun Sets Someday -5, 6	Vo unissued
SC-93-	Orange Blossom Special -1, 2, 3, 4	Vo unissued: *Sony JXK65750 (CD)*
SC-94-	Stranger Blues	Vo unissued
SC-95-1	Sunny Tennessee -1, 3, 4, 5, 6	Vo/OK 04842

SC-96-	She Was Only Flirting	Vo unissued
SC-97-1	The Lonesome Dove -1, 3, 4, 5	Vo/OK 04717, Cq 9230
SC-98-	Shed Your Tears Upon Me	Vo unissued
SC-99-	No Never Alone	Vo unissued
SC-100-	Oh Those Tombs	Vo unissued
SC-101-1	Wabash Cannon Ball -1, 3, 4, 5	Vo/OK 04717, Cq 9230

One guitar is absent on matrices SC-88/89.

Tommy Magness, f-1/md-2; Bill Brown, esg; Clayton Hall, bj/v-3; Roy Hall, g/v-4; Saford Hall, g/v-5; Wayne Watson, sb.

Atlanta, GA   Tuesday, October 9, 1940

054572-1	New "San Antonio Rose" -1, 4	BB B-8561
054573-1	She's Winkin' At Me -2, 3, 4	BB B-8702
054574-1	I'd Die Before I'd Cry Over You -1, 4	BB B-8561
054575-1	Your Heart Should Belong To Me -2, 3, 4	BB B-8702
054576-1	Don't Let Your Sweet Love Die -1, 3, 4	BB B-8656
054577-1	Can You Forgive -2, 3, 4	BB B-8656
054578-1	Loving You Too Well -2, 3, 4	BB B-8676
054579-1	I Played My Heart And Lost -1, 3, 4	BB B-8676
054580-1	Rubber Dolly -1, 3, 4, 5	BB B-8617
054581-1	Bye Bye, Baby, Bye Bye -1, 3, 4	BB B-8617
054582-1	Little Sweetheart Come And Kiss Me -1, 3, 5	BB B-8794, RZAu G25164
054583-1	'Neath The Bridge At The Foot Of The Hill -1, 3, 4	BB B-8794, RZAu G25164

Tommy Magness, f; Bill Brown, sg; Clayton Hall, bj/v-1; Roy Hall, g/v-2; Wayne Watson, sb; Jim Eanes, v-3.

Atlanta, GA   Wednesday, October 1, 1941

071048-1	Until I Return To You -1, 2	BB B-8906
071049-1	Natural Bridge Blues -3	BB B-8863
017050-1	I Wonder If The Moon Is Shining? -1, 2	BB B-8959
071051-1	I Wonder Where You Are Tonight? -1, 2, 3	BB B-8959
071052-1	I'm Glad We Didn't Say Goodbye -2	BB 33-0515
071053-1	My Sweet Mountain Rose -2	BB B-8906
071054-1	The Best Of Friends Must Part -1, 2	BB 33-0515
071055-1	Polecat Blues	BB B-8863

Roy Hall also recorded with the Hall Brothers.

RUFUS HALL & THE PLAINSMEN

Pseudonym on Broadway for the North Carolina Ramblers & Roy Harvey (see Roy Harvey).

HALL BROTHERS

Roy Hall, Jay Hugh Hall, v duet; or Roy Hall, v-1; acc. own g duet.

Charlotte, NC   Tuesday, February 16, 1937

07039-1	When It Gets Dark	BB B-6925, MW M-7236
07040-1	McDowell Blues	BB B-7363, MW M-7238
07041-1	Whistle, Honey, Whistle	BB B-6925, MW M-7236
07042-1	Never Alone	BB B-7801, MW M-7239
07043-1	Spartanburg Jail	BB B-7363, MW M-7238
07044-1	Hitch Hike Blues -1	BB B-7801, MW M-7239
07045-1	Little Mo-Hee	BB B-6843, MW M-7237
07046-1	Way Out There	BB B-6843, MW M-7237
07047-1	Little Girl You've Done Me Wrong	BB B-7103, [MW M-7240]
07048-1	My Girl Has Gone And Left Me	BB B-7103, [MW M-7240]
07049-1	I'll Remember You, Love, In My Prayers	[MW M-7241]
07050-1	Kingdom Land	[MW M-7241]

Montgomery Ward issues as by **Hall Brothers (Roy & Jay)**.

Acc. Steve Ledford, f-2; own g duet.

Charlotte, NC   Thursday, January 27, 1938

018773-1	It Was Only A Dream	BB B-7462
018774-1	An Old Man's Story	BB B-8923
018775-1	Alcatraz Prisoner	BB B-7462
018776-1	Your Love Was Not True -2	BB B-7728
018777-1	Constant Sorrow -2	BB unissued
018778-1	The Wrong Road -1, 2	BB B-7728

Rock Hill, SC   Monday, September 26, 1938

| 027703-1 | The Great Speckled Bird | BB unissued |
| 027704-1,-2 | Waiting The Boatman | BB unissued |

027705-1,-2	Don't Go Away Unsaved	BB unissued
027706-1	Lovers Goodbye	BB unissued
027707-1,2	Alcatraz Prisoner Part 2	BB unissued
027708-1	The Elevated Railroad In The City	BB B-8923

Roy Hall subsequently recorded with his Blue Ridge Entertainers.
This artist credit was also used as a pseudonym on Clarion and Velvet Tone for Joe & Zeb Gaunt (see Arthur Fields & Fred Hall).

HALL COUNTY SACRED SINGERS

Vocal group; acc. unknown, p.
    Atlanta, GA   Tuesday, March 18, 1930

ATL-907-	You Can't Do Wrong And Get By	Vo 5420
ATL-908-	He Knows How	Vo 5420
ATL-909-	When Jesus Came My Way	Vo 5438
ATL-910-	I'm Free	Vo 5438
ATL-911-	I Am Bound For Home	Vo 5444
ATL-912-	O Glorified City	Vo 5444

HALL FAMILY

Unknown, md; unknown, g; Marjorie Hall, v.
    Richmond, VA   Thursday, October 17, 1929

| 403165- | Little Stranger | OK unissued |
| 403166- | Molly Bland | OK unissued |

These items were logged, evidently incorrectly, as by **Hall Family & Bertha Hewlett**, as were matrices 403167/68, for which see Bertha Hewlett. The musicians are likely to be Marjorie Hall's parents.

FRED HALLIDAY
HALLIDAY BROTHERS

Pseudonyms on Homestead, Jewel, and Oriole for the Gentry Brothers.

STUART HAMBLEN

Stuart Hamblen, v/y-1; acc. own g.
    Camden, NJ   Thursday, June 6, 1929

49424-1	The Boy In Blue	Vi V-40109, BB B-5242, Eld 2125, Sr S-3325, MW M-4303, Au 230
49425-2	Drifting Back To Dixie	Vi V-40319, ZoAu EE258
49426-1	When The Moon Shines Down Upon The Mountain -1	Vi V-40109, BB B-5242, Eld 2125, Sr S-3325, MW M-4303, M-4308, Au 230
49427-1	The Big Rock Candy Mountains – No. 2	Vi V-40319, ZoAu EE258
49427-2	The Big Rock Candy Mountain	Vi unissued: *RCA (SP) DMM4-0343 (LP)*

Victor V-40109, V-40319, Zonophone EE258 are subcredited "**Cowboy Joe**." Sunrise S-3325 as by **Cowboy Joe**. Rev. Montgomery Ward M-4308 by Frank Luther.

Stuart Hamblen, v/y/wh-1; acc. own g.
    Culver City, CA   Friday, March 21, 1930

| 54736-1 | Wrong Keyhole | Vi V-40242 |
| 54737-2 | I Gotta Feelin' -1 | Vi V-40242 |

Stuart Hamblen, v; acc. unknown, sg; own g; unknown, u.
    Culver City, CA   Monday, May 5, 1930

| 54781-1 | Hawaii | Vi V-40306 |
| 54782-1 | Standin' On The Pier In The Rain | Vi V-40306 |

Acc. unknown, f; own g; unknown, g.
    Hollywood, CA   Thursday, August 21, 1930

| 61014-2 | By The Sleepy Rio Grande | Vi V-40311 |
| 61015-2 | Sailor's Farewell | Vi V-40311 |

Acc. Ted Dahl & His Orchestra: two unknowns, f; three unknowns, c; unknown, tb; three unknowns, s; unknown, p; unknown, bj; unknown, vc; unknown, sb; unknown, d.
    Hollywood, CA   Friday, November 13, 1931

| 68334- | Golden River | BB B-8468 |
| 68335- | Dream Book Of Memories | BB B-8468 |

Acc. two unknowns, f; unknown, ac; unknown, g; unknown, sb.
    Hollywood, CA   Friday, November 13, 1931

| 68336-1 | My Brown-Eyed Texas Rose | Vi 23685, MW M-4312 |
| 68337-1 | My Mary | Vi 23685 |

Rev. Montgomery Ward M-4312 by Frank Luther & Carson Robison (see the latter).

Stuart Hamblen & His Covered Wagon Jubilee: no details.
    Los Angeles, CA   Wednesday, April 18, 1934

| L-162-1,-2 | Where The Blue Grass Grows | ARC unissued |
| L-163-1,-2 | Across The Great Divide | ARC unissued |

Stuart Hamblin & His Covered Wagon Jubilee: Stuart Hamblen, v; acc. Len Dossey, f; Norman Hedges, f; Vince Engel, ac/p; "Herman the Hermit" Snyder, bj; own g; Ace Spriggins, g; poss. Skipper Hawkins, sb.
    Los Angeles, CA   Friday, August 3, 1934

DLA-1-A	Poor Unlucky Cowboy	De 5001, Pan 25714
DLA-2-A	Texas Plains	De 5001
DLA-3-A	Riding Old Paint Leading Old Bald	De 5145, Pan 25714
DLA-4-A,-B	Little Rag Doll	De rejected
DLA-5-A	Lopez The Bandit	De 5145

Matrix DLA-3 is titled *Ridin' Old Paint Leading Old Bald* on Panachord 25714.

Acc. poss. Len Dossey, f; unknown, cel; own g; unknown, g; Skipper Hawkins, sb.
    Los Angeles, CA   Saturday, February 23, 1935

DLA-104-A	Sunshine Alley	De 5077
DLA-105-A	Lola Lee	De 5077
DLA-106-A	Be Just Like Your Daddy	De 5109
DLA-107-A	Poor Boy	De 5109

Stuart Hamblen recorded after 1942.

PAUL HAMBLIN

Paul Hamblin, v; acc. own g.
    Culver City, CA   Friday, March 21, 1930

54732-2	The Strawberry Roan	Vi V-40260
54733-1	Prairie Maiden	Vi V-40280, Au 240
54734-1	Fallen Leaf	Vi V-40280, Au 240
54735-2	Under Dakota's Cross	Vi V-40260

WYZEE HAMILTON

Wyzee, Tucker & Lecroy: Wyzee Hamilton, f; ———Tucker, bj; ——— Lecroy, g.
    Chicago, IL   January 1927

| 4173-3 | Fifty Years Ago | Pm 33186, Her 75542 |
| 4174-1 | Hamilton's Special Breakdown | Pm 33186, Her 75542 |

Lecroy may play banjo and Tucker guitar.

Wyzee Hamilton, v; acc. **Hamilton's Harmonians**: own f; Frank Nichols, f; Art Frazier, tbj/v; Luther Patrick, g.
    Birmingham, AL   c. July 8, 1927

| GEX-700 | Old Sefus Brown | Ge rejected |

Wyzee Hamilton, v; acc. **Hamilton's Harmonians**: own f; Frank Nichols, f; Art Frazier, tbj/v-1; Luther Patrick, g; or Art Frazier-2, v; acc. Wyzee Hamilton, f; Frank Nichols, f; own tbj; Luther Patrick, g.
    Birmingham, AL   c. July 9, 1927

GEX-699	She's More To Be Pitied Than Censured	Ge rejected
GEX-700-A	Old Sefus Brown -1	Ge 6272, Ch 15376, Chg 336
GEX-701	Because He Was Only A Tramp -2	Ge rejected
GEX-702	Fifty Years Ago	Ge rejected

Champion 15376 as by **Davie Meek & His Boys**. Challenge 336 as by **Reuben White**.
Revs: Gennett 6272, Champion 15376, Challenge 336 by Short Creek Trio.

    Birmingham, AL   c. August 15, 1927

GEX-808,-A	She's More To Be Pitied Than Censured	Ge rejected
GEX-809,-A	Fifty Years Ago	Ge rejected
GEX-810,-A	Old Sefus Brown -1?	Ge rejected
GEX-811,-A	Because He Was Only A Tramp -2	Her 75571

Rev. Herwin 75571 by Vernon Dalhart.

Luther Patrick, sp; acc. Wyzee Hamilton, f; Frank Nichols, g.
    Birmingham, AL   c. August 30, 1927

| GEX-859-A | Grandfather's Liver (Ain't Whut It Used To Wuz) | Ge 6448 |
| GEX-860 | Cornbread | Ge 6448 |

Hamilton appears in Gennett's files variously as Wyzee and Y.Z. Hamilton, and his group as Hamilton's Harmonians or Hamilton Harmonicons.

HAMLIN MALE QUARTET[TE]
Pseudonym on Silvertone and Supertone for Woodlawn Quartette.

[THE] HAMLIN QUARTETTE
Pseudonym on Champion and possibly Herwin for Woodlawn Quartette. One side of Silvertone 8261, credited to **Hamlin Quartette**, is in fact by The Eva Quartette.

HAMLIN SACRED QUARTETTE
Pseudonym on Challenge for Woodlawn Quartette.

TONY HAMMES

Tony Hammes, h solo.
    unknown location.   unknown date

	Red Wing	Bwy 8231
	Golden Slippers	Bwy 8231

These items were probably also issued on Paramount and/or QRS, but no such issues have been traced.

JOHN HAMMOND

John Hammond, v; acc. own bj.
    Richmond, IN   Wednesday, April 8, 1925

12196	Little Birdie	Ge 5697, 3022, Sil 3859, 5697, Chg 168, Bu 8014
12197-A	Purty Polly	Ge 5697, 3021, Ch 15147, Sil 3859, 5697, Chg 168, Bu 8014

Champion 15147 as by **Abe Morris**. Challenge 168 as by **Levi Stanley**.
Gennett ledgers appear to report that the A take of matrix 12196 is by Albert Rose.
Revs: Gennett 3021 by Homer Davenport & Young Brothers (see Jess Young), 3022 by Homer Davenport; Champion 15147 by Vernon Dalhart.

    Richmond, IN   Thursday, January 6, 1927

12589,-A	Johnny's Gone To Cuba	Ge rejected
12591,-A	I'm As Pretty Little Bird As I Can Be	Ge rejected

Matrix 12590 is by Clarence Gill.

    Richmond, IN   Saturday, September 17, 1927

13028-A	Purty Polly	Sil 5070, 8149, Spt 9249
13029	Little Birdie	Ge 6256, Ch 15356, Sil 5070, 8149, Spt 9249, Chg 332
13030	My Mama Always Talked To Me	Ge 6256
13031	As Free A Little Bird As Can Be	Chg 332

Challenge 332 as by **William Price**. Rev. Champion 15356 by Holland Puckett.

SID HAMPTON (THE YODELIN' MAN FROM DIXIE LAND)

Sid Hampton, v/y; acc. own g.
    New York, NY   Saturday, May 3, 1930

150432-2	The Hills Of Tennessee	Co 15583-D
150500-2	I'll Be With You Mother	Co 15583-D
150501-	Waiting For A Train	Co unissued
150502-2	Swanee Sweetheart	Co 15555-D
150503-1	Kicking Mule	Co 15555-D
150504-	A Sailor's Plea	Co unissued
150505-	A Moonshiner's Daughter	Co unissued

Intervening matrices are by other artists on other dates.

DICK HANDLEY
Pseudonym on Challenge for Dick Parman.

REV. J.O. HANES & MALE CHOIR

Rev. J.O. Hanes, sermons with singing; with male choir.
    Chicago, IL   c. September 1927

20000-1	Abounding Sin And Abounding Grace	Pm 3057
20001-1	Sin And The Remedy	Pm 3058
20002-1	Sowing And Reaping	Pm 3069
20003-1	A Symphony Of Calls	Pm 3057
20004-2	The Great Transactions Done	Pm 3058

20005-1	Weighed And Found Wanting	Pm 3069
20006-2	A Sermon To Men	Pm 3056
20007-2	A Message Of Faith	Pm 3056

Paramount 3056 as by **Rev. J.O. Hanes**.

HOWARD HANEY

Howard Haney, v; acc. prob. own g.

Chicago, IL
Tuesday, December 20, 1927

| C-1402/03* | Mother's Prayers For Jack | Vo 5204 |
| C-1404/05* | Sunset Gates Of Gold | Vo 5204 |

Matrices C-1402/03 were remastered as E-7031/32W, and C-1404/05 as E-7033/34W.

Chicago, IL
Wednesday, December 21, 1927

C-1406*/07	Keep On The Firing Line	Br 204
C-1408*/09	If Jesus Leads This Army	Br 204
C-1410/11*	The Wandering Boy	Vo 5203
C-1412/13*	The Dying Boy's Message	Vo 5203

Matrices C-1410/11 were remastered as E-7027/28W, and C-1412/13 as E-7029/30W.

HANK, THE YODELING RANGER

See Hank Snow.

"POP" HANKS & HIS BOYS

See Joseph Samuels.

WILLIAM HANSON

William Hanson, v; acc. own g.

Atlanta, GA
Thursday, December 11, 1930

404673-A	Stop And Listen Blues	OK 45506
404674-B	Sitting On Top Of The World	OK 45506
404675-	Gambling On The Sabbath Day	OK 45523
404676-	The Little White Washed Cabin	OK 45523

HAPPINESS BOYS

The recordings of this popular team – the duet of Billy Jones and Ernest Hare – do not fall within the scope of this work, but their name was used on one occasion as a pseudonym, on the Australian label Worth, for a Carson Robison group.

HAPPY FATS & HIS RAYNE–BO RAMBLERS

Rayne-Bo Ramblers: Norris Savoy, f; Warnest Schexnyder, g; Leroy "Happy Fats" LeBlanc, g/v-1.

New Orleans, LA
Saturday, August 10, 1935

94402-1	Le Fille De St. Martin -1	BB B-2172
94403-1	La Valse De L'Amour -1	BB B-2172
94404-1	Rayne Breakdown	BB B-2176
94405-1	Dor, Baby, Dor -1	BB B-2176
94406-1	Chere 'Tite Fille	BB B-2175
94407-1	Mon Cuore Et Pour Toit -1	BB B-2175

Moise Sonnier, f; Louis Arceneaux, f/wb; Roy Romero, sg; Leroy "Happy Fats" LeBlanc, g/v; two unknowns, g.

New Orleans, LA
Friday, September 10, 1937

014012-1	La Place Mon Couer Desire	BB B-2022
014013-1	Les Crepes A'Nasta	BB B-2026, B-2092
014014-1	Valse De Maria Bueller	BB B-2026
014015-1	Tu M'a Quite Dans La Misere	BB B-2029
014016-1	Noveau Grand Gueyan	BB B-2024
014017-1	Vain Ton Don A Ma Mort	BB B-2028, B-2092
014018-1	Oublies Mois Jamais Petite	BB B-2028
014019-1	Les Blues De Bosco	BB B-2022

Matrix 014013 is titled *Les Crepa A'Nasta*, and matrix 014017 is titled *Vain Ton Don A Mar Mar*, on Bluebird B-2092. The Bluebird session-sheet also lists harmonica, but it is uncertain where, or if, it is to be heard.
Revs: Bluebird B-2024, B-2029 Mexican.

Happy Fats & Rayne Bo Ramblers: Oran "Doc" Guidry, f; Roy Romero, sg; Robert Thibodeaux, p; Ray Guidry, tbj; Leroy "Happy Fats" LeBlanc, g/v; Nathan Guidry, sb; unidentified, v-1.

New Orleans, LA
Saturday, April 2, 1938

| 022032-1 | Les Ecrivis Dan Platin -1 | BB B-2034, B-2091 |
| 022033-1 | Dans Le Chere De La Lune | BB B-2042, B-2090 |

022034-1	Ta Oblis De Vernier	BB B-2042
022035-1	Ma Belle Mellina	BB B-2046
022036-1	Se Mallereux -1	BB B-2046, B-2089
022037-1	Dellaide	BB B-2049
022038-1	Jus Pasque	BB B-2037, B-2091
022039-1	Le Reponse De Blues De Bosco	BB B-2049, B-2088
022040-1	Aux Long Du Bois	BB B-2034
022041-1	Te Jolie Te Petite	BB B-2037

Matrix 022039 is titled *Le Reponse De Blus De Bosco* on Bluebird B-2088.
Revs: Bluebird B-2088, B-2089, B-2090 by Hackberry Ramblers.

Doc Guidry, f; Willie Vincent, sg; poss. Ray Guidry, tbj; Leroy "Happy Fats" LeBlanc, g/v-1/sp-2; Nathan Guidry, sb; unidentified, v-2.

New Orleans, LA Sunday, October 23, 1938

027887-1	My Little Cajun Girl -1	BB B-2057, B-2087
028500-1	Chan Se Tige -1	BB B-2062
028501-1	La Vieux Two Step Francais -1	BB B-2074
028502-1	Trakas En Ede -2	BB B-2062
028503-1	La Nouvelle Marche De Marris -1	BB B-2057
028504-1	Aux Bal Se Te Maurice -1	BB B-2074
028505-1	Mabelle Tete Catin -1	BB B-2072, B-2087
028506-1	Est-ce Que Tu M'Aimes -1	BB B-2070
028507-1	Memoire De Mom -1	BB B-2070
028508-1	Le Mellaige -1	BB B-2072
028509-1	Give My Baby My Old Guitar -1	BB B-8105
028510-1	Going Home To Mother -1	BB B-8105

Happy Fats & His Rayne-Bo Ramblers: Harry Choates, f-1/eg-2/v-3; Ray Clark, esg-4/v-5; Harold "Popeye" Broussard, p/v-6; Joseph M. "Pee Wee" Broussard, tbj; Sandy Lormand, g/v-7; Leroy "Happy Fats" LeBlanc, sb/v-8.

Dallas, TX Wednesday, February 14, 1940

048005-1	O.S.T. Gal -1, 4, 8	BB B-8537, MW M-8693
048006-1	A Little High Chair -1, 4, 8	BB B-8648, MW M-8695
048007-1	The Old Ice Man -1, 4, 6	BB B-8537, MW M-8693
048008-1	I Know You Feel The Way I Do -1, 4, 8	BB B-8623, MW M-8694
048009-1	Lake Charles Shuffle -1, 4	BB B-8623, MW M-8694
048010-1	I've Grown So Lonely For You -2, 5	BB B-8648, MW M-8695
048011-1	Gran Prairie -1, 4, 8	BB B-2081
048012-1	La Polka A Gilbent -1, 4	BB B-2083
048013-1	La Veuve De La Coulee -1, 4, 8	BB B-2081
048014-1	Les Tete Fille Lafayette -1, 3, 4, 7	BB B-2083

Ambrose Thibodeaux, f; Julius "Papa Cairo" Lamperez, esg/v-1; Pee Wee Broussard, tbj/v-2; Bradley "Sleepy" Stutes, g/v-3; Leroy "Happy Fats" LeBlanc, sb/v-4.

Dallas, TX Wednesday, October 8, 1941

071114-1	Su Parti A La Maison (I Am Going Home) -2	BB unissued
071115-1	Joilie Schvr Rouge (Pretty Red Hair) -4	BB unissued: *CMF 017-D* (CD)
071116-1	Alon's Rendezvous (Let's Go To The Rendezvous) -4	BB unissued
071117-1	Te Kaplan (Little Kaplan) -4	BB unissued
071118-1	In The House At The End Of The Road -1, 4	BB B-8879
071119-1	When The Weeping Willow Smiles -4	BB B-8879
071120-1	I'm Not Sorry Now -3	BB B-8928
071121-1	If I Ever Leave The South -4	BB B-8928

Happy Fats recorded after 1942.

THE HAPPY FOUR

Jeff Chastain, lv; Lee Campbell, tv; Jess Ballew, bv; —— Thompson, bsv; acc. Lee Campbell, h; Jess Ballew, g.

Atlanta, GA Wednesday, April 6, 1927

| 143924-2 | He Knows How | Co 15164-D |

Rev. Columbia 15164-D by Copperhill Male Quartet.

Atlanta, GA Friday, November 11, 1927

| 145220-2 | Come And Dine | Co 15225-D |
| 145221-2 | Climbing Up The Golden Stairs | Co 15225-D |

THE HAPPY-GO-LUCKY BOYS (CLYDE, STEVE & HUGH)

Steve Ledford, f-1; Clyde Moody, md-2/g/v-3; Jay Hugh Hall, g/v-4.

Atlanta, GA Monday, February 5, 1940

047522-1	Darling, I'm Still In Love With You -2, 3, 4	BB B-8528, MW M-8719
047523-1	No Letter In The Mail Today -1, 3, 4	BB B-8467, MW M-8719
047524-1	Come Back, Sweetheart -1, 3, 4	BB B-8467, MW M-8720
047525-1	I Hope She's Satisfied -1, 3, 4	BB B-8528, MW M-8720
047526-1	Happy-Go-Lucky Breakdown -1	BB B-8391, MW M-8718
047527-1	What-Cha Gonna Do With The Baby? -1, 3, 4	BB B-8391, MW M-8718

THE HAPPY HAYSEEDS

Ivan Laam, f; Fred Laam, bj; Bill Simmons, g.
   Culver City, CA   Monday, March 4, 1930

54653-2	Tail Of Halley's Comet	Vi 23722
54654-1,-2	Mills' Waltz	Vi unissued

   Culver City, CA   Tuesday, March 5, 1930

54664-1	Ladies' Quadrille	Vi 23722
54665-1	Cottonwood Reel	Vi 23774, TT C-1562, Au 36-114

Timely Tunes C-1562, Aurora 36-114 as by **The Tennessee Fiddlers**.

   Culver City, CA   Wednesday, March 6, 1930

54671-1	Home Sweet Home	Vi 23774, TT C-1562, Au 36-114
54672-1,-2	Mocking Bird	Vi unissued
54673-1	Rattlesnake	Vi unissued

Timely Tunes C-1562, Aurora 36-114 as by **The Tennessee Fiddlers**.

HAPPY HOLLOW HOODLUMS

Gomer Cool, f-1; Paul Sells, ac; Herb Kratoska, g; Clarence Hartman, sb.
   Chicago, IL   Saturday, April 6, 1935

C-9904-A	Down Home Rag -1	De 5098
C-9905-A	Panama	De 5098

HAPPY HOOSIERS

Prob.: unknown, f; unknown, h; unknown, bj; unknown, g.
   Richmond, IN   Friday, September 9, 1932

18771	Scottish Bag Pipe	Ge unissued
18772	Nigger In The Woodpile	Ge unissued

At this session this group also accompanies Fern Harris, who may be a member of the band.

HAPPY JACK

This artist's last name may be Burns.

Happy Jack, v; acc. unknown, sg; unknown, g.
   Atlanta, GA   Tuesday, October 27, 1931

151960-1	I'm Only Suggesting This	Co 15720-D
151961-1	The Wooden Wedding	Co 15720-D

THE HAPPY VALLEY BOYS

Gerry Byrd, sg; Ernie Cornelison, g/v-1.
   Atlanta, GA   Wednesday, October 9, 1940

054564-1	Homecoming Time In Happy Valley -1	BB B-8592, [MW M-8853]
054565-1	I'll Never Leave Old Dixieland Again -1	BB B-8592, [MW M-8853]
054566-1	You Don't Love Me -1	BB B-8703, [MW M-8854]
054567-1	Weeping Willow Valley -1	BB B-8703, [MW M-8854]
054568-1	Renfro Valley Home -1	BB B-8657, [MW M-8855]
054569-1	Hop Along Peter -1	BB B-8657, [MW M-8855]
054570-1	My Little Grass Shack In Kealakekua, Hawaii	BB B-8776, [MW M-8856]
054571-1	Sophisticated Hula	BB B-8776, [MW M-8856]

Gerry Byrd recorded as Jerry Byrd, and Ernie Cornelison as Ernie Lee, after 1942.

HAPPY VALLEY FAMILY

Jo Taylor, Alma Taylor, Jack Taylor, v trio; acc. Chick Hurt, md; Jack Taylor, g.
   Chicago, IL   Monday, October 28, 1935

C-1118-2	Going Down The Valley	ARC 6-03-54, Vo/OK 04484, Cq 8604, Co 37761, 20338
C-1119-1	The Royal Telephone	ARC 6-05-55, Vo/OK 04251, Cq 8663

Chicago, IL   Tuesday, October 29, 1935

C-1126-2	Shake Hands With Mother Again	ARC 6-03-54, Vo/OK 04484, Cq 8603, Co 37761, 20338
C-1127-2	Lily Of The Valley	ARC 6-05-55, Vo/OK 04251, Cq 8663
C-1128-1,-2	Down Among The Budding Roses	ARC 6-08-53, Vo 04296, Cq 8603

Jo or Alma Taylor, Jack Taylor, v duet; acc. Chick Hurt, md; Jack Taylor, g; Jo or Alma Taylor, y.
Chicago, IL   Thursday, October 31, 1935

C-1146-2	My Clinch Mountain Home	ARC 6-08-53, Vo 04296, Cq 8604

Only one of the women sings on matrix C-1146, while the other yodels.

Jo and Alma Taylor also recorded as **Jo & Alma**. Chick Hurt and Jack Taylor are members of the Prairie Ramblers.

SLIM HARBERT & HIS OKEH BOYS

Grundy C. "Slim" Harbert, v; acc. Jimmy Thomason, f; Dave Frazier, eg; Aubrey "Moon" Mullican, p; Bruce Pierce, tbj; own sb.
Hollywood, CA   Tuesday, March 3, 1942

H-710-	Fruit Wagon Gal	OK unissued
H-711-	I've Got Enough Of Your Foolin'	OK unissued
H-712-	Lulu Lou	OK unissued
H-713-1	Brown Bottle Blues	OK unissued: *Ep EG37324 (LP); ABM ABMMCD1098, Acrobat ACRCD158 (CDs)*
H-714-	Rosey Lee	OK unissued
H-715-	I'm Gonna Cook Your Goose	OK unissued
H-716-	Honey This Time I'm Gone	OK unissued
H-717-	Around The Corner At Smokey Joe's	OK unissued
H-718-	You're All The World To Me	OK unissued
H-719-	Don't Check Out On Me	OK unissued
H-720-	Who Comes In At My Back Door	OK unissued
H-721-	You Brought Sorrow To My Heart	OK unissued
H-722-	Can't We Start All Over	OK unissued
H-723-	Look Who's Squawkin'	OK unissued

Matrix H-713 as by **Slim Harbert & His Boys** on Epic EG37324, ABM ABMMCD1098, Acrobat ACRCD158.

Slim Harbert is a member of the Sunshine Boys, under whose name this session was originally logged. He recorded after 1942 with his daughter, as Mallie Anne & Slim.

TEX HARDIN

Tex Hardin, v; acc. prob. own h/g.
Richmond, IN   Monday, January 16, 1933

18970	The Old Chisholm Trail	Ch S-16552, MW 4954
18971	The Trail To California	Ch S-16552, MW 4954

HARDIN & GRINSTAFF

No details.
Johnson City, TN   Tuesday, October 16, 1928

147200-	Single Girl – Married Girl	Co unissued
147201-	Seven Years	Co unissued

The first party may be John Hardin and may play fiddle.

CLARENCE HARDING

Clarence Harding, v; acc. prob. own g.
Richmond, IN   Friday, November 10, 1933

19364	Granny's Old Arm Chair	Ge rejected
19365	Great Grandad	Ge rejected

Richmond, IN   Friday, April 6, 1934

19521	Home Coming Time In Happy Valley	Ge unissued
19522	What Does The Deep Sea Say	Ge unissued

Clarence Harding is presumably related to Evelyn Harding, associated with the Blue Ridge Mountain Girls, whose sessions are adjacent to his.

ERNEST HARE

The bulk of this artist's work was in the popular field, but his recordings under the pseudonyms "Hobo" Jack Turner and Earl Harris, and a few in his own name, seem worth including here.

"Hobo" Jack Turner, v; acc. poss. own g.
New York, NY   Tuesday, July 31, 1928

| 146823-3 | The Bum Song | Ha 705-H, Ve 1705-V, Di 2705-G, Puritone 1015-S |
| 146824-3 | Hallelujah! I'm A Bum | Ha 705-H, Ve 1705-V, Di 2705-G, Puritone 1015-S |

New York, NY   Tuesday, September 4, 1928

| 146943-6 | The Bowery Bums | Ha 740-H, Ve 1740-V, Di 2740-G, Re/RZAu G20415 |
| 146944-5 | The Bums Rush | Ha 740-H, Ve 1740-V, Di 2740-G, Re/RZAu G20415 |

New York, NY   Tuesday, December 11, 1928

| 147414-2,-4 | The Big Rock Candy Mountains | Ha 807-H, Ve 1807-V, Di 2807-G |
| 147415-2 | She Waits And Waits | Ha 807-H, Ve 1807-V, Di 2807-G, Cl 5170-C |

New York, NY   Monday, February 4, 1929

| 147916-1 | In The Jail House Now | Ve 7047-V, Di 6021-G |
| 147917-2 | Oklahoma Blues | Ve 7047-V, Di 6021-G |

New York, NY   Tuesday, June 25, 1929

| 148752-4 | The Squire And The Deacon | Ha 956-H, Ve 1956-V, Di 2956-G |
| 148753-2 | A High Silk Hat And A Walking Cane | Ha 956-H, Ve 1956-V, Di 2956-G |

New York, NY   Tuesday, October 8, 1929

| 149113-3 | Only A Bum | Ha 1038-H, Ve 2038-V, Di 3038-G |
| 149114-2 | In A Graveyard On The Hill | Ha 1038-H, Ve 2038-V, Di 3038-G |

New York, NY   Monday, November 25, 1929

| 149488-3 | The Tramp Song | Ha 1070-H, Ve 2070-V, Di 3070-G |
| 149489-1 | I Don't Work For A Living | Ha 1070-H, Ve 2070-V, Di 3070-G |

New York, NY   Monday, January 13, 1930

| 149752-2 | Everybody Does It In Hawaii | Ha 1089-H, Ve 2089-V, Di 3089-G |
| 149753-3 | A Hobo's Life Is A Happy Life | Ha 1089-H, Ve 2089-V, Di 3089-G, Cl 5169-C |

New York, NY   Wednesday, March 19, 1930

150094-3	Panhandle Jack	Ha 1180-H, Ve 2180-V, Di 3180-G, Cl 5169-C
150095-1	When It's Springtime In The Rockies	Ha 1128-H, Ve 2128-V, Di 3128-G, Cl 5046-C, CoE DB218
150096-3	I'm Glad I'm A Bum	Ha 1228-H, Ve 2128-V, Di 3128-G, Cl 5024-C

Rev. Columbia DB218 by Ruth Etting (popular).

New York, NY   Tuesday, June 10, 1930

150576-1	I Don't Want To Get Married	Ha 1187-H, Ve 2187-V, Di 3187-G, Cl 5046-C
150577-1	Seven Days From Now	Ha 1187-H, Ve 2187-V, Di 3187-G, Cl 5024-C
150578-1	The Waltz Of The Hills	Ha 1180-H, Ve 2180-V, Di 3180-G, Cl 5170-C

Ernest Hare, v; acc. poss. Frank Novak, f; poss. own g.

New York, NY   Friday, January 15, 1932

| 152067-3 | New Twenty One Years | Co 2602-D, Re/RZAu G21332 |
| 150268-3 | Fifty Years Repentin' | Co 2602-D, Re/RZAu G21332 |

Matrix 152067 is titled *Twenty One Years (Pt. 2)* on Regal/Regal-Zonophone G21332.

"Hobo" Jack Turner, v; acc. poss. own g.

New York, NY   Friday, January 15, 1932

| 365053- | New Twenty One Years | Ve/Cl unissued |
| 365054- | Fifty Years Repentin' | Ve/Cl unissued |

New York, NY   Thursday, January 21, 1932

| 365053-3 | New Twenty One Years | Ve 2513-V, Cl 5453-C |
| 365054-2 | Fifty Years Repentin' | Ve 2513-V, Cl 5453-C |

Acc. unknown.

New York, NY   Tuesday, February 2, 1932

| 365061- | Them Good Old Times (Are Comin' Back Again) | Ve 2528-V, Cl 5468-C |

New York, NY   Wednesday, February 3, 1932

| 365062- | Gene The Fighting Marine | Ve 2528-V, Cl 5468-C |

Ernest Hare-1/**Earl Harris**-2, v; acc. prob. Frank Novak, f-3/bscl-4/ac; poss. own g.

New York, NY   Wednesday, February 3, 1932

| 152100-1 | Them Good Old Times (Are Comin' Back Again) -1, 3, 4 | Co 15742-D |
| 152101-1 | Gene The Fighting Marine -1 | Co 15742-D |

405136-A	Them Good Old Times (Are Comin' Back Again) -2, 3, 4	OK 45566
405137-A	Gene The Fighting Marine -2	OK 45566

Matrices 152100/01 are also assigned in Columbia files the controls or transfer matrices 130720 and 130719 respectively.

FRANK HARKINS & MELVIN OWENS

Pseudonym on Broadway for Owen Mills (David Miller) & Frank Welling.

GEORGE HARKINS

Pseudonym on Broadway for Sid Harkreader & Grady Moore.

HARKINS & MORAN

Pseudonym on Broadway usually for Sid Harkreader & Grady Moore but sometimes for John McGhee & Frank Welling, or Frank Welling alone.

HARKINS & PERRY

Pseudonym on Broadway for Sid Harkreader & Blythe Poteet.

SID HARKREADER

Sid Harkreader, v; acc. own g.
New York, NY   Monday, April 13, 1925

677/78	The Dying Girl's Message	Vo 15075, 5066
681*/82	Dark Eyes	Vo 15366, 5114

Acc. own g/wh-1.
New York, NY   Tuesday, April 14, 1925

687/88	New River Train	Vo 15035, 5063
689/90	Where Is My Boy Tonight	Vo 15075, 5066
691/92	I Wish I Was A Single Girl Again	Vo 15035, 5063
693/94	Many Times With You I Wandered	Vo 15100, 5070
697/98	Southern Whistling Coon -1	Vo 15063, 5065
701/02	Struttin' 'Round	Vo 15193, 5082

New York, NY   Wednesday, April 15, 1925

715/16	Blue Ridge Mountain Blues	Vo 15193, 5082
717/18	Little Sweetheart	Vo unissued

Intervening (and surrounding) matrices are by Uncle Dave Macon. For recordings with Macon see the latter.
Revs: Vocalion 15063, 15100, 5065, 5070 by Uncle Dave Macon; 15366, 5114 by George Reneau.

Harkreader & Moore: Sid Harkreader, f-1/g-2/v-3/sp-4; Grady Moore, f-5/sg-6/g-7/v-8/sp-9.
Chicago, IL   June 1927

4590-1,-2	The Bully Of The Town -1, 3, 7	Pm 3022, Bwy 8056
4591-1,-2	Hand Me Down My Walking Cane -2, 3, 6, 8	Pm 3022, Bwy 8055
4592-2	Old Joe -1, 4, 7, 9	Pm 3023, Bwy 8114
4593-1	John Henry -1, 3, 7	Pm 3023, Bwy 8114, Her 75532
4596-2	Don't Reckon It'll Happen Again -2, 3, 7	Pm 3044
4597-2	There's A Little Rosewood Casket -2, 3, 6	Pm 3024, Bwy 8115
4598-3	The Gambler's Dying Words -1, 3, 7, 8	Pm 3025, Bwy 8115, ARC-Bwy 8115
4599-2	A Picture From Life's Other Side -1, 3, 7, 8	Pm 3024, Bwy 8055
4600-1	The Land Where We Never Grow Old -1, 3, 7, 8	Pm 3052, 3296, Bwy 8081
4604-2	Where The River Shannon Flows	Pm 3035
4605-2	Kitty Wells -1, 3, 7	Pm 3043, Bwy 8157
4606-3	Way Down In Jail On My Knees -2, 3, 6, 8	Pm 3025, Bwy 8115
4610-2	My Little Home In Tennessee -1, 3, 7	Pm 3043, Bwy 8157
4611-2	Only As Far As The Gate	Pm 3035
4612-2	Bits Of Blues -2, 3, 7	Pm 3044
4613-1	I Love The Hills Of Tennessee -5, 8	Pm 3033
4614-2	Mocking Bird Breakdown	Pm 3033
4616-1	In The Sweet Bye And Bye -1, 3, 7, 8	Pm 3061, Bwy 8117
4617-1	The Old Rugged Cross -1, 3, 7, 8	Pm 3061, Bwy 8117
4618-2	A Trip To Town -4, 7	Pm 3063, Bwy 8065
4620-2	It Looks To Me Like A Big Time Tonight -1, 3, 7, 8	Pm 3054, Bwy 8217
4621-1	Will There Be Any Stars In My Crown -1, 3, 7, 8	Pm 3052, 3296, Bwy 8081
4622-1	Lazy Tennessee -1, 7	Pm 3063, Bwy 8064
4623-2	Run Nigger Run -1, 3, 7	Pm 3054, Bwy 8217

Paramount 3052, 3054, 3061, 3063 as by **Sid Harkreader & Grady Moore**. Matrix 4613 on Paramount 3033 as by **G.D. Moore & His Violin**. Broadways as by **Harkins & Moran**, except 8065 as by **George Harkins**. Matrix 4593 on Herwin 75532 as by **McBridge & Wright**, titled *Death Of John Henry*. (Other pressings of Herwin 75532 replace matrix 4593 with

Gennett matrix 12572, *The Death Of John Henry* by Welby Toomey.) Intervening matrices are untraced.
Revs: Broadway 8064, 8065 by Kentucky Thorobreds; ARC-Broadway 8115 by David Miller.

Harkreader & Poteet: Sid Harkreader, f-1/v-2; Blythe Poteet, g/v-3.
   Chicago, IL   c. April 1928

20471-2	Red River Valley -1, 2, 3	Pm 3141, Bwy 8202
20474-1	It Won't Be Long Now -1, 2	Pm 3141, Bwy 8202
20478-2	Life's Railway To Heaven -1, 2, 3	Pm 3094, Bwy 8129
20479-2	He'll Find No Girl Like Me -1, 2, 3	Pm 3112
20480-1	Sweet Bird-1, 2, 3	Pm 3112
20481-2	Drink Her Down -1, 2	Pm 3118
20484-2	Take Me Back To My Carolina Home -1, 2, 3	Pm 3104, Bwy 8219
20485-1	Wang Wang Blues -1	Pm 3118
20486-2,-3	Where Is My Mama -1, 2, 3	Pm 3094, Bwy 8129
20487-2	Traveling Coon -3	Pm 3104, Bwy 8219
20488-2	Chin Music -2	Pm 3183
20489-1	On The Bowery -1, 2	Pm 3183

Paramount 3104 as by **Sid Harkreader & Blythe Poteet** (matrix 20484)/**Blythe Poteet** (matrix 20487). Matrix 20488 on Paramount 3183 as by **Sid Harkreader**. Broadway 8129 as by **Harkins & Perry**; 8202 as by **Harkins & Moran**; 8219 as by **Philip Perry**.
A copy of Paramount 3118 has been reported bearing matrix 20485 in the wax and on the label but playing *Take Me Back To My Carolina Home*.
Sid Harkreader also recorded with Uncle Dave Macon.

HARKREADER & MOORE
HARKREADER & POTEET

See Sid Harkreader.

HARLAN MINERS FIDDLERS

Pseudonym on Montgomery Ward for Crockett's Kentucky Mountaineers.

HARMONICA BILL

William B. Russell, v; acc. own h; unknown, g.
   Richmond, IN   Wednesday, February 17, 1932

18399-A	The Volunteer Organist	Ch S-16393
18400	Darling Chloe	Ch 16425
18401,-A	Noah's Ark	Ge unissued

   Richmond, IN   Thursday, February 25, 1932

18422	Georgia The Dear Old State I Love	Ch 16425, Spr 2806
18423	Blue Grass Hayseed	Ge rejected
18424	The Prisoner's Radio	Ch S-16393, Spr 2789
18425-A	Answer To The Gypsy's Warning	Ch S-16399, Spr 2789
18426	Great Grandad And Grandma	Ch S-16399, Spr 2806

Superiors as by **Harmonica Jim**.

HARMONICA JIM

Pseudonym on Superior for Harmonica Bill.

HARMONY FOUR

Vocal quartet; acc. unknown, p.
   Dallas, TX   Thursday, November 28, 1929

403368-	I Have To Raise My Voice In Song	OK 45441
403369-	I Hold His Hand	OK 45441
403370-A	My Friend Divine	OK 45419
403371-A	I'll Know Him	OK 45419
403372-B	I'm Sailing On	OK 45399
403373-B	He's A Wonderful Savior To Me	OK 45399

Gennett recordings with this artist-credit, or as by **Harmony Quartette**, are by an African-American group.

HARMONY QUARTET

Pseudonym on Supertone S2105 for the Dixieland Four, or on S2110 for the Ritz Quartet (popular).

RICHARD HAROLD

Richard Harold, v; acc. prob. Fred Pendleton, f-1; own g.
   Johnson City, TN   Tuesday, October 16, 1928

147202-2	The Battleship Maine	Co 15586-D
147203-1	The Fisher's Maid	Co 15586-D
147204-1	Sweet Bird -1	Co 15426-D
147205-1	Mary Dear	Co 15426-D

HAROLD & HAZEL

Hazel ——, v/y-1; acc. poss. own f-2; Harold Maus, g.
Chicago, IL   Monday, December 4, 1933

77174-1	Texas -1, 2	BB B-5469, MW M-4489
77175-1	Pack My Things -2	BB B-5975, Twin FT1942
77176-1	Wait For Me	BB B-5975, Twin FT1942
77177-1	With My Guitar -1, 2	BB B-5469, MW M-4489, Twin FT1809

Rev. Twin FT1809 by Jimmie Davis.

A'NT IDY HARPER

This artist's real name is Margaret Lillie.

A'nt Idy Harper & The Coon Creek Girls: A'nt Idy Harper, v; acc. Lily May Ledford, f; Esther "Violet" Koehler, md; Rosie Ledford, g; Evelyn "Daisy" Lange, sb; unidentified, v trio-1.
Chicago, IL   Monday, May 30, 1938

C-2239-1	The Old Apple Tree	Vo 04203, Cq 9065
C-2240-1	Poor Naomi Wise	Vo 04354
C-2241-1	Sweet Fern -1	Vo 04354
C-2242-1	Lulu Wall	Vo 04203, Cq 9065

JACK HARPER

Pseudonym on Vocalion for Billy Vest.

OSCAR & DOC HARPER
OSCAR HARPER'S TEXAS STRING BAND

Oscar Harper's Texas String Band: Oscar Harper, f; Doc Harper, g.
San Antonio, TX   Thursday, March 8, 1928

400431-A	Ragtime Annie	OK unissued
400432-B	Kelly Waltz	OK 45227
400433-A	Bouquet Waltz	OK 45227

Dallas, TX   Saturday, October 26, 1929

| DAL-487- | She Gave Up | Vo 5403 |
| DAL-488- | Sally Johnson | Vo 5403 |

Oscar & Doc Harper: Oscar Harper, f; Doc Harper, g.
Dallas, TX   Wednesday, November 27, 1929

403344-A	Dallas Bound	OK 45420
403345-A	Twinkle Little Star	OK 45485
403346-A	Terrell Texas Blues	OK 45420
403347-B	Bitter Creek	OK 45485
403348-A	Beaumont Rag	OK 45397
403349-A	Billy On The Low Ground	OK 45397

ROY HARPER & EARL SHIRKEY

See Earl Shirkey. (Roy Harper is Roy Harvey.)

ROY R. HARPER

Roy R. Harper, h; acc. own md.
Atlanta, GA   c. March 15, 1924

| 8580-A | Jenny Lind Polka | OK unissued |
| 8581-A | Rockingham | OK unissued |

A test pressing of these items survives. On its label the title of matrix 8581 has been emended, possibly by the artist, to *Cindy Or Rockingham*.

WM. HARPER & NELSON HALL

Pseudonym on Superior for John McGhee & Frank Welling.

HARPER & HALL
HARPER & HILL

Pseudonyms on Superior for John McGhee & Frank Welling.

HARPER & PAGE
Pseudonym on Supertone for Claude (C.W.) Davis & Lowe Stokes (see the former).

HARPER & TURNER
Pseudonym on Silvertone and Supertone for John McGhee & Frank Welling.

HARPER BROTHERS
Pseudonym on Brunswick for Frank Luther & Carson Robison, or on Supertone for Lester McFarland & Robert A. Gardner.

HARPER FAMILY TRIO
Pseudonym on Supertone for John & Alma McGhee & Frank Welling.

KELLY HARRELL

Kelly Harrell, v; acc. unknown, f-1; Carson Robison, h-2/g; unknown, train eff-3.
New York, NY   Wednesday, January 7, 1925

31584-2	New River Train -1, 2, 3	Vi 19596
31585-2	Rovin' Gambler -1, 3	Vi 19596
31586-2	I Wish I Was A Single Girl Again -2	Vi 19563
31587-3	Butcher's Boy -1	Vi 19563

Acc. Henry Whitter, h/g.
Asheville, NC   Tuesday, August 25, 1925

9270-A	I Was Born About 10,000 Years Ago	OK 40486
9271-A	Wild Bill Jones	OK 40486
9272-A	Peg And Awl	OK 40544
9273-A	I Want A Nice Little Fellow	OK unissued
9274-A	I Was Born In Pennsylvania	OK 40544
9275-A	Little Mohee	OK unissued
9276-A	I'm Going Back To North Carolina	OK 40505
9277-A	Be At Home Soon Tonight, My Dear Boy	OK 40505
9279-A	The Wreck On The Southern Old 97	OK 7010
9280-A	Blue Eyed Ella	OK 7010

OKeh 7010 is a 12-inch disc. Matrix 9278 is by R.B. Smith–S.J. Allgood.

Acc. unknown, f-1; Carson Robison, h-2/g; unknown, train eff-3.
New York, NY   Tuesday, June 8, 1926

31584-6	New River Train -1, 2, 3	Vi 20171
31585-6	Rovin' Gambler -1, 3	Vi 20171, MW M-4367
31586-6	I Wish I Was A Single Girl Again -2	Vi 20242
31587-5	Butcher's Boy -1	Vi 20242

Rev. Montgomery Ward M-4367 by Masters' Hawaiians (see Kelly Brothers).

Acc. unknown, f; Carson Robison, h-1/g.
New York, NY   Wednesday, June 9, 1926

35667-3	O! Molly Dear Go Ask Your Mother	Vi 20280
35668-3	Broken Engagement -1	Vi 20280
35669-2	Dying Hobo -1	Vi 20527
35670-3	Beneath The Weeping Willow Tree	Vi 20535
35671-3	My Horses Ain't Hungry	Vi 20103, ZoSA 4254
35672-4	Bright Sherman Valley -1	Vi 20527

Rev. Zonophone 4254 by Vernon Dalhart.

Acc. unknown, f; Carson Robison, h-1/g; unknown, cuckooo eff-2.
New York, NY   Thursday, June 10, 1926

35673-3	The Cuckoo She's A Fine Bird -2	Vi V-40047
35674-3	Hand Me Down My Walking Cane	Vi 20103, MW M-4330
35675-2	Bye And Bye You Will Forget Me -1	Vi 20535

Rev. Montgomery Ward M-4330 by Frank Luther.

Acc. Posey Rorer, f; R.D. Hundley, bj; Alfred Steagall, g.
Camden, NJ   Tuesday, March 22, 1927

38231-2	Oh, My Pretty Monkey	Vi V-40047
38232-1	I Love My Sweetheart The Best	Vi 20867
38233-2	Henry Clay Beattie	Vi 20797
38234-1	I Want A Nice Little Fellow	Vi 20867

Kelly Harrell, v/poss. wh-1; acc. Posey Rorer, f; R.D. Hundley, bj; Alfred Steagall, g; unidentified, v-2.
Camden, NJ   Wednesday, March 23, 1927

38235-2	My Name Is John Johannah -1	Vi 21520
38236-2	In The Shadow Of The Pine	Vi 20657
38237-2	Charles Giteau [sic] -2	Vi 20797
38238-1	I'm Nobody's Darling On Earth	Vi 20657
38239-2	My Wife, She Has Gone And Left Me	Vi 21520

Victor 21520 as by **Kelly Harrell (Virginia String Band)**.

Kelly Harrell–Henry Norton, v duet; acc. Virginia String Band: Lonnie Austin, f; R.D. Hundley, bj; Alfred Steagall, g.
Charlotte, NC   Friday, August 12, 1927

| 39800-2 | Row Us Over The Tide | Vi 20935 |
| 39801-2 | I Have No Loving Mother Now | Vi 20935 |

Kelly Harrell, v; acc. Virginia String Band: Lonnie Austin, f; R.D. Hundley, bj; Alfred Steagall, g.
Charlotte, NC   Friday, August 12, 1927

| 39807-3 | For Seven Long Years I've Been Married | Vi 21069 |
| 39808-2 | Charley, He's A Good Old Man | Vi 21069 |

Matrices 39802 to 39806 are by Red Patterson's Piedmont Log Rollers.

Acc. —— Gorodetzer, f-1; Alfred Steagall, g.
Camden, NJ   Monday, February 18, 1929

| 49869-1,-2 | Are You Going To Leave Your Old Home Today? -1 | Vi unissued |
| 49870-2 | The Henpecked Man | Vi 23689 |

Acc. Sam Freed, f; Roy Smeck, h-1/jh-1; Alfred Steagall, g.
Camden, NJ   Tuesday, February 19, 1929

49873-2	She Just Kept Kissing On -1	Vi V-40095
49874-2	All My Sins Are Taken Away -1	Vi V-40095
49875-2	Cave Love Has Gained The Day	Vi 23689
49876-1	I Heard Somebody Call My Name	Vi 23747

Rev. Victor 23747 by Bob Miller.

ZEB HARRELSON & M.B. PADGETT

Unidentified, f; unidentified, h; unidentified, g; unidentified, v-1.
Atlanta, GA   Thursday, October 28, 1926

| 9824-A | Soldier's Joy | OK 45078 |
| 9825-A | Finger Ring -1 | OK 45078 |

HARRINGTON–LANDRY & STEWARD

Unidentified, f; unidentified, ac; poss. Sydney Landry, g; unidentified, v-1.
New Orleans, LA   Monday, December 16, 1929

| 403444-B | Tu Aura Regret -1 | OK 45411 |
| 403445-A | La Stompe Clreole [sic] | OK 45411 |

CARL HARRIS
Pseudonym on Challenge for Doc Roberts.

CHIC HARRIS
Pseudonym on Lucky Strike 24347 for Frank Luther (see Carson Robison).

EARL HARRIS
Pseudonym on OKeh for Ernest Hare.

FERN HARRIS

Fern Harris, v; acc. the Happy Hoosiers: unknown, f-1; unknown, h-1; unknown, p-2; unknown, bj; unknown, g-1.
Richmond, IN   Friday, September 9, 1932

| 18773 | ABC Of Religion -1 | Ge unissued |
| 18774 | Clouds Gonna Roll Away -2 | Ge unissued |

The Happy Hoosiers also recorded at this session in their own name.

GEORGE E. HARRIS

George E. Harris, v; acc. own g.
Richmond, IN   Tuesday, October 9, 1928

14306,-A	Since I've Grown So Used To You	Ge rejected
14307,-A	That's My Blue Heaven	Ge rejected
14308,-A	Black Bottle Blues	Ge rejected
14309,-A	Dear Old Texas Blues	Ge rejected

George Harris, v; acc. own h/g.
    Chicago, IL   Tuesday, October 16, 1928
    C-2444-A,-B   Since I've Grown So Used To You   Vo rejected
    C-2445-A,-B   That's The Blue Heaven For Me   Vo rejected
    C-2446-A,-B   Black Bottle Blues   Vo rejected
    C-2447-A,-B   Dear Old Texas Blues   Vo rejected

George E. Harris, v; acc. own h/g.
    New York, NY   Wednesday, February 12, 1930
    149814-2   That's The Blue Heaven For Me   Co 15543-D
    149815-2   Since I've Grown So Used To You   Co 15543-D
    149816-   Dear Old Texas Blues   Co unissued
    149817-   Black Bottle Blues   Co unissued

ELDER GOLDEN P. HARRIS

Golden P. Harris, v; acc. own f.
    New York, NY   Thursday, March 19, 1931
    E-36489   No Sorrow There   Me M12178
    E-36490   I'll Lead A Christian Life   Me M12178

Elder G.P. Harris, v; acc. own f.
    New York, NY   unknown date, probably early 1930s
    149-1   My God The Spring Of All My Joys   Harris 101
    150-1   My Christian Friends In Bonds Of Love   Harris 101

This is a custom recording by the Consolidated Recording Corp., New York. Some copies, or perhaps an entire later pressing, replace the titles shown with *Dunlap* and *Bottomley* respectively, the tune-titles for these items as customarily used in Sacred Harp circles.

J.D. HARRIS

J.D. Harris, f; acc. Ernest Helton, bj-1/g-2; unidentified (prob. Harris), calls-3.
    New York, NY   November/December 1924
    1958   The Grey Eagle   Bwy B-1958
    1963   The Bucking Mule -1   Bwy A-1963
    1964   Whip The Devil Around The Stump -1, 3   Bwy A-1964
    1965   The Blackberry Rag -1   Bwy B-1965
    1969   Jeff Davis -2   Bwy A-1969

J.D. Harris, v; acc. Ernest Helton, bj.
    New York, NY   November/December 1924
    1971   Lone And Sad   Bwy B-1971

The above items are coupled as follows: A-1964/B-1958; A-1963/B-1971; A-1969/B-1965. Intervening matrices are untraced but at least some are likely to be by Harris.

J.D. Harris, f solo.
    Asheville, NC   prob. Friday, August 28 or Saturday, August 29, 1925
    9307-A   The Cackling Hen   OK 45024

Harris may have recorded other items at this session. Rev. OKeh 45024 by George Walburn & Emmett Hethcox.

ROBERT HARRIS

Pseudonym on Australian Parlophone for Morgan Denmon.

SIM HARRIS

Pseudonym on Homestead and Oriole for Ernest V. Stoneman.

HARRIS QUARTET
HARRIS SACRED QUARTETTE

Pseudonyms on Supertone for the McDonald Quartette.

HAPPY BUD HARRISON

Happy Bud Harrison, v/y; acc. own g.
    New Orleans, LA   c. February 1929
    NO-100-   Hush-A-Bye Baby Blues   Vo 5328
    NO-101-   Long Tall Mama Blues   Vo 5328
    NO-102-   New Orleans Mama Blues   Vo 5305
    NO-103-   My Buddy   Vo 5305

Acc. unknown, t; unknown, cl; own g.
Chicago, IL   Wednesday, May 29, 1929
C-3551-	Levee Breaking Blues – Part I	Vo 5332
C-3552-	Levee Breaking Blues –Part II	Vo 5332
C-3553-	Mail Man Blues – Part I	Vo 5344
C-3554-	Mail Man Blues – Part II	Vo 5344

Acc. own g; unknown, train-wh eff-1.
Chicago, IL   Friday, May 31, 1929
C-3565-	Homesick Daddy	Vo 5370
C-3566-	Ball And Chain Blues	Vo 5370
C-3567-	I'm Glad I'm Free	Vo 5350
C-3568-	The Wreck Of The G. & S.I. -1	Vo 5350

Acc. unknown, sg; unknown, sb.
Chicago, IL   Wednesday, August 14, 1929
| C-4077- | You Came My Way | Vo 5405 |
| C-4078- | Mama Don't Allow No Easy Riders Here | Vo 5405 |

PETE HARRISON'S BAYOU BOYS
Pseudonym on Velvet Tone and Clarion for Charlie Poole & the North Carolina Ramblers.

CHARLES HART
The real name of a prolific recording artist in the popular idiom in the 1920s, this was also used as a pseudonym, on the Australian label Angelus, for Frank Luther (see Carson Robison.)

JIMMY HART & HIS MERRYMAKERS
Earl Caruthers, f/v-1; Tiny Moore, emd/v-2; Jimmy Hart, p/poss. v-3; Kenny Taylor, g; Byron "Barney" Youngblood, sb.
Dallas, TX   Friday, April 4, 1941
063014-1	Teeny Weeny	BB B-8793
063015-1	It's Kinda Late To Be Sorry -3	BB B-8719
063016-1	Let's Start All Over Again -2	BB B-8751
063017-1	Cheatin' On Me -2	BB B-8719
063018-1	After Thinking It Over -1	BB B-8793
063019-1	Little Hula Girl -1	BB B-8751

An associated lineup recorded as Port Arthur Jubileers for Decca and as The Jubileers for Bluebird.

JOHNNY HART
Pseudonym on Clarion and Velvet Tone for Frank Marvin.

NORMAN HART
Pseudonym on Canadian Domino for Vernon Dalhart.

HART & CATES
Sam Hart, Toney Cates, v duet; acc. unknown, f; unknown, g.
Chicago, IL   Tuesday, December 11, 1928
402212-	The Prodigal Son	OK unissued
402213-B	Old Home Nest	OK 45499
402214-A	In The Valley Of Broken Hearts	OK 45499

Matrix 402215, blank in OKeh files, is possibly also by these artists.

HART & OGLE
—— Hart, —— Ogle, v duet; acc. prob. one of them, g.
Grafton, WI   c. October 1931
L-1178-4	They Cut Down The Old Pine Tree	Pm 3297
L-1179-1	Round Up Time In Texas	Pm 3297, ARC-Bwy 3297
L-1180-1	Power's Crimes	Bwy 8299, 8304
L-1181-1	Casey Jones	Bwy 8303
L-1182-1	Seeing Nellie Home	Bwy 8303
L-1183-1	Two Locks Of Hair	Bwy 8299, 8304

Rev. ARC-Broadway 3297 by Carson Robison.

HART BROTHERS
Vocal duet; acc. prob. one of them, g.
Chicago, IL   c. January 1929
| 21099-1 | The Miner's Prayer | Pm 3162, 3262 |

Chicago, IL c. June 1929
21324-1	The Prodigal Son	Pm 3176, 3265
21325-2	Lamp Lighting Time In The Valley	Pm 3162, 3262
21326-1,-2	The Empty Cradle	Pm 3176, 3265

There is a possible connection with Sam Hart of Hart & Cates, and conceivably with the first party of Hart & Ogle.

HARTFORD CITY TRIO

Unknown, h; unknown, bj; unknown, g.
Richmond, IN Friday, November 15, 1929
15887,-A	At The Cross	Ge rejected
15888,-A	Brighten The Corner	Ge rejected
15889,-A	Down In The Cane Break	Ge rejected
15890,-A	Billie Gray	Ge rejected

HARTFORD QUARTET

See E.M. Bartlett Groups.

DICK HARTMAN'S TENNESSEE RAMBLERS
HARTMAN'S HEART BREAKERS

Dick Hartman's Tennessee Ramblers: Kenneth "Pappy" Wolfe, f-1; prob. Jack Gillette, f-2/v-3; Dick Hartman, h-4/tg-5/v-6; unknown, p-7; Cecil "Curly" Campbell, sg-8/bj-9/g-10/v-11/y-12; Harry Blair, g-13/v-14/sp-15; v trio (Blair, lv; Wolfe, tv; Campbell, bv) -16; unidentified, clapping-17.
New York, NY Thursday, January 3, 1935
87238-1	When I Take My Vacation In Heaven -1, 2, 10, 13, 16	BB B-5796, MW M-4857
87239-1	Silver Threads -1, 2, 10, 13, 16	BB B-5796, MW M-4857
87240-1	Wolfe's Trail -1, 5, 9, 13	BB B-5797
87241-1	From The Palms Of Hawaii -5, 8, 13	BB B-5962, ViJ Jr-42
87242-1	March Of The Roses -5, 8, 13	BB B-5962, ViJ Jr-42
87243-1	Still Talkin' -13, 15	BB B-5992
87244-1	Long, Long Ago -1, 2, 13, 14	BB B-5992, HMVIn N4381
87245-1	I Got The Carolina Blues -1, 10, 11, 12, 13	BB B-5909, Twin FT1922
87246-1	Take This Message To Mother -1, 2, 10, 13, 16	BB B-5891
87247-1	My Little Hut In Carolina -1, 2, 10, 13, 16	BB B-6003
87248-1	Pappy's Breakdown -1, 5, 9, 13	BB B-5797
87249-1	She's Long She's Tall -1, 10, 11, 12, 13	BB B-5909
87250-1	Beautiful Heaven Must Be -1, 2, 10, 13, 16	BB B-6003
87251-1	She's My Curly Headed Baby -5?, 10, 13, 16	BB B-5891
87252-1	Loveless Love -1, 2, 10, 13, 16	BB B-5876
87253-1	When It's Harvest Time In Peaceful Valley -1, 2, 10, 13, 16	BB B-5837
87254-1	Dad's Favorite Waltz -1, 2, 5, 9, 13	BB B-5876
87255-1	South Bound Train -1, 2, 10, 13, 16	BB B-5837, Twin FT1891
87256-1	Hot Time -1, 3, 6, 7, 10, 13	BB B-5875
87257-1	Don't Go 'Way, Doggone Ya -4, 7, 9, 13, 17	BB B-5875

Victor Jr-42 as by **Mountain Ramblers**. Revs: HMV N4381 by Jimmie Rodgers; Twin FT1891 by Milton Brown; FT1922 by Bill Boyd.

Kenneth "Pappy" Wolfe, f-1/v-2; Dick Hartman, h-3/tg-4/v-5; Cecil "Curly" Campbell, sg-6/bj-7/g-8/v-9; Harry Blair, g/v-10; Fred "Happy" Morris, g/sb-11/v-12; v trio (Blair, lv; Wolfe, tv; Campbell, bv) -13.
Atlanta, GA Sunday, August 4, 1935
94300-1	Mountain Dew Blues -8, 12	BB B-6105
94301-1	Back To Old Smoky Mountain -1, 2, 8, 9	BB B-6105, Twin FT8019
94302-1	New Red River Valley -1, 2, 8, 9	BB B-6162
94303-1	Beautiful Texas -1, 2, 3, 8, 9, 12	BB B-6226, MW M-4820
94304-1	New How-Do-You-Do -1, 2, 3, 5, 8, 9	BB B-6089, Twin FT8021
94305-1	Little Green Valley -1, 8, 13	BB B-6180, Twin FT8038
94306-1	'Dis Train-1, 8, 13	BB B-6135
94307-1	Little Sweetheart Of The Mountain -1, 6, 13	BB B-6180, Twin FT8038
94308-1	Give Me Back My Texas Home -1, 8, 9	BB unissued
94309-1	New River Train -1, 8, 9	BB B-6162
94310-1	Dese Bones Gonna Rise Again -1, 3, 8, 13	BB B-6089, Twin FT8021
94311-1	Step Light Ladies	BB unissued
94312-1	Melody Of Hawaii	BB unissued
94313-1	Birmingham Jail -2, 4, 6, 9	BB B-6207, MW M-4814
94314-1	Pennsylvania Hop -1, 4, 7, 11	BB B-6122
94315-1	Kentucky Jig -1, 4, 7, 11	BB B-6122

Revs: Bluebird B-6226, Montgomery Ward M-4820 by Girls Of The Golden West; Twin FT8019 by Bill Boyd.

Kenneth "Pappy" Wolfe, f-1/v-2; Dick Hartman, h-3/tg-4/v-5; unknown, p-6; Cecil "Curly" Campbell, bj-7/g-8/v-9; Harry Blair, g; Fred "Happy" Morris, sb/v-10; v trio (Blair, lv; Wolfe, tv; Campbell, bv) -11.

Atlanta, GA   Monday, August 5, 1935

94318-1	Who Broke The Lock? -1, 2, 5, 8, 9, 10	BB B-6207, MW M-4814, Twin FT8059
94319-1	Ramblers' Rag -1, 4, 7	BB B-6274
94320-1	Leechburg Polka -1, 4, 7	BB B-6274
94321-1	Goin' Down The Road -1, 3, 7, 11	BB B-6135, Twin FT8035
94322-1	Memories of Old -1, 4, 7	BB B-6227
94323-1	Dick's Hoedown -3, 6, 7	BB B-6227

Revs: Twin FT8035 by Jesse Rodgers; FT8059 by Pink Lindsey.

Washboard Wonders: Elmer Warren, f/k; Dick Hartman, md/bj/tg; unknown, md; Harry Blair, g/v; Fred "Happy" Morris, sb; Kenneth "Pappy" Wolfe, wb/eff/v-1.

Charlotte, NC   Wednesday, June 17, 1936

102666-1	Feather Your Nest -1	BB B-6495
102667-1	Oh, My Goodness	BB B-6455, RZ MR2193, Twin FT8147
102668-1	You've Gotta Eat Your Spinach, Baby	BB B-6455, RZ MR2193, Twin FT8147
102669-1	Cheatin' On Me	BB B-6495
102670-1	It Ain't Right	BB B-6464
102671-1	I Take To You	BB B-6464

Hartman's Heart Breakers: Elmer Warren, f; Cecil "Curly" Campbell, bj; Harry Blair, g; unknown, g; Dick Hartman, tg; Fred "Happy" Morris, sb; Kenneth "Pappy" Wolfe, traps/sw; Betty Lou, v; band sp.

Charlotte, NC   Monday, June 22, 1936

102770-1	Fetch It On Down To My House	BB B-6494
102771-1	Give It To Me, Daddy	BB B-6542, Twin FT8206
102772-1	Let Me Play With It	BB B-6481
102773-1	Oh Sweet Daddy, Oh Pshaw	BB B-6494
102774-1	Please, Mr. Moon, Don't Tell On Me	BB B-6516
102775-1	Grandma And Grandpa	BB B-6516
102776-1	Feels Good	BB B-6481
102777-1	No Huggin' Or Kissin'	BB B-6542, Twin FT8206

Dick Hartman's Tennessee Ramblers: Kenneth "Pappy" Wolfe, f/v-1; Elmer Warren, f; Cecil "Curly" Campbell, sg/v-2; Dick Hartman, md/tg; Harry Blair, g/v-3; Fred "Happy" Morris, g/sb/v-4.

Charlotte, NC   Monday, June 22, 1936

102796-1	The White House On The Hill -1, 3	BB B-6566, MW M-7108, Twin FT8226
102797-1	I Want To Walk In The Heavenly Way -1, 3	MW M-7110
102798-1	Hold Fast To The Right -1, 3	MW M-7110
102799-1	What Is Home Without Baby -1, 3	BB B-6622, MW M-7109
102800-1	Give My Love To Nell -2, 4	BB B-6622, MW M-7109
102801-1	Are You Tired Of Me, Darling? -3	BB B-6566, MW M-7108

Rev. Twin FT8226 by Bill Boyd.

Washboard Wonders: Elmer Warren, f/k-1; Dick Hartman, bj; Harry Blair, g/v; Fred "Happy" Morris, g/sb; unknown, g/sb; Kenneth "Pappy" Wolfe, wb/eff.

Charlotte, NC   Monday, June 22, 1936

102802-1	Meet Me At The Ice-House -1	BB B-6526
102803-1	And Still No Luck With You -1	BB B-6463
102804-1	All Is Quiet On The Old Front Porch Tonight -1	BB B-6463
102805-1	Down Yonder (In The Valley)	BB B-6526

Hartman's Heart Breakers: Elmer Warren, f; Cecil "Curly" Campbell, bj; Harry Blair, g; Dick Hartman, tg; Fred "Happy" Morris, sb; Kenneth "Pappy" Wolfe, wb/sw; Betty Lou, v; band sp.

Charlotte, NC   Sunday, October 11, 1936

02500-1	Susan Brown	BB unissued
02501-1	Blue For A Red Headed Daddy	BB unissued
02502-1	Cuban Appetizer	BB unissued
02503-1	A Night In Carolina	BB B-6656
02504-1	My Southern Movements	BB B-6656
02505-1	Jazz Mad Man	BB unissued
02514-1	I'll Be Down	BB unissued
02515-1	Darkness All Around Me	BB unissued
02516-1	You Met A Gal	BB unissued
02517-1	Dick And I	BB unissued
02518-1	If You Have The Blues	BB unissued
02519-1	I Want It	BB unissued

Intervening matrices are untraced.

Washboard Wonders: Elmer Warren, f-1/k-2; Dick Hartman, bj; Harry Blair, g/v-3; Fred "Happy" Morris, g/sb/v-4; unknown, g/sb; Kenneth "Pappy" Wolfe, wb/eff/v-5.
    Charlotte, NC   Sunday, October 11, 1936

02520-1	Let's Incorporate -1, 2, 3	BB B-6761
02521-1	Follow The Bugle -1, 4	BB B-8165
02522-1	You're Everything Sweet -1, 2, 3	BB B-6737
02523-1	She Takes Her Time -1, 3	BB B-6671
02524-1	Roll Your Own -1, 3	BB B-6671
02525-1	Sailor's Sweetheart -1, 3	BB B-6737
02526-1	Breeze (Blow My Baby Back To Me) -1, 2, 5	BB B-6761
02527-1	Apple Tree – Part 2 -1, 3	BB B-6648
02528-1	Apple Tree – Part 1 -2, 3	BB B-6648
02529-1	Margie -1, 2, 3	BB B-8165

Members of this group continued to record after the departure of Dick Hartman as Tennesee Ramblers.

BOB HARTSELL

Bob Hartsell, v/y; acc. unknown, md-1; unknown, g.
    Charlotte, NC   Monday, February 15, 1937

07005-1	I'm A Handsome Man -1	BB B-7439, MW M-7169
07006-1	Rambling Freight Train Yodel	BB B-7439, MW M-7169

Montgomery Ward M-7169 as by **Three Tobacco Tags**.

Bob Hartsell, v; acc. unknown, md; two unknowns, g.
    Charlotte, NC   Tuesday, January 25, 1938

018705-1	Round-Up Time In Dreamland	BB B-7473
018706-1	Rock Me To Sleep In My Rocky Mountain Home	BB B-7473

HARTWIC BROTHERS

Vocal duet; acc. unknown, p.
    Dallas, TX   Sunday, October 27, 1929

DAL-513-	Sailing On	Vo 5399
DAL-514-	Jesus Is My Headlight	Vo 5399

JOE HARVEY (AMERICA'S YODELING COWBOY)

Joe Harvey, v/y; acc. prob. own g.
    Los Angeles, CA   Wednesday, August 8, 1934

DLA-14-A	Yodeling Joe	De rejected
DLA-15-A	Cactus Bill	De rejected

UNCLE JOHN HARVEY'S OLD TIME DANCE ORCHESTRA

Pseudonym on Herwin for Tommy Dandurand & His Gang or, on 75519, Tom Owens Barn Dance Trio.

ROY HARVEY

Roy Harvey, v; acc. **North Carolina Ramblers**: Posey Rorer, f; Charlie Poole, bj; own g.
    New York, NY   Friday, September 17, 1926

142639-	Minstrel Hall	Co unissued
142640-2	The Brave Engineer	Co 15174-D

Roy Harvey & Posey Rorer: Posey Rorer, f; Roy Harvey, g/v.
    New York, NY   Wednesday, May 11, 1927

144122-	Blue Eyes	Co unissued
144123-1	Dark Eyes	Co 15714-D
144124-	San Antonio	Co unissued
144125-	Blue-Eyed Ella	Co unissued
144126-	Walking On The Streets Of Glory	Co unissued
144127-	Learning McFadden To Waltz	Co unissued
144128-2	Willie, Poor Boy	Co 15714-D

    New York, NY   Thursday, May 12, 1927

144129-	Jack And May	Co unissued
144130-	What Is Home Without Love	Co unissued
144131-1	When The Bees Are In The Hive	Co 15155-D
114138-	Sweet Sunny South	Co unissued
144139-2	Daisies Won't Tell	Co 15155-D

Intervening matrices are by jazz or popular artists.

Roy Harvey, v; acc. **North Carolina Ramblers**: Posey Rorer, f; Bob Hoke, bj-md; Charlie Poole, bj; own g.
    New York, NY   Tuesday, July 26, 1927

144520-2	The Wreck Of Virginian No. 3	Co 15174-D

Roy Harvey, v; or **Roy Harvey & Bob Hoke**-1/**North Carolina Ramblers**-2, v duet; acc. Posey Rorer, f; Bob Hoke, bj-md; Roy Harvey, g.
    New York, NY   c. September 26-28, 1927

GEX-880	Please Papa Come Home -1	Ge 6303, Ch 15394, Sil 8161, Spt 9251, Chg 390
GEX-881	The Old Clay Pipe -1	Ge 6303
GEX-882-C	Write A Letter To My Mother	Ge 6288, Ch 15394, Sil 8161, Spt 9251, Chg 390
GEX-883	Poor Little Joe	Ge 6288, Ch 15414, Chg 394, Spr 325
GEX-884-A	We Will Outshine The Sun-1	Ge 6350, Sil 5182, 8173, Spt 9269
GEX-885	Walking On The Streets Of Glory -1	Ge 6350, Ch 15412, Sil 5182, 8173, Spt 9269, Chg 401, Spr 323
GEX-886	I Cannot Call Her Mother -2	Sil 5181, 8147, Spt 9246
GEX-887	Pearl Bryant -2	Sil 5181, 8147, Spt 9246

Matrices GEX-880/81, 886/87 were logged as by **The North Carolina Ramblers** but issued as shown. Champion 15394 as by **Geo. Runnels & Ed Sawyer**; 15412 as by **Geo. Runnels & Howard Hall**; 15414 as by **Geo. Runnels**. Silvertones and Supertones as by **The Three Kentucky Serenaders**, except Supertone 9251 as by **The Kentucky Serenaders**. Challenges as by **James Ragan** or (items suffixed -1 or -2) **James Ragan & Oliver Beck**. Revs: Champion 15412, 15414, Challenge 401 by John McGhee & Frank Welling; Challenge 394 by Grayson & Whitter.

North Carolina Ramblers & Roy Harvey: Posey Rorer, f; Bob Hoke, bj-md/v-1; Roy Harvey, g/v-2.
    Chicago, IL   October 1927

20078-2	Take Back The Ring -1, 2	Pm 3064, Bwy 8118
20079-1	Willie My Darling -1, 2	Pm 3064, Bwy 8118
20080-2	Give My Love To Nell -1, 2	Pm 3065, Bwy 8080
20081-2	My Mother And My Sweetheart -1, 2	Pm 3065, Bwy 8080
20082-2	She Is Only A Bird In A Gilded Cage -1, 2	Pm 3079, Bwy 8183
20083-1,-2	Bill Mason -2	Pm 3079, Bwy 8183
20084-2	Kitty Blye -1, 2	Pm 3072, Bwy 8158
20085-	Maggie Dear, I'm Called Away -2?	Pm unissued
20086-1,-2	I'm Glad I'm Married -1	Pm 3136, Bwy 8206
20087-1,-2	Sweet Sunny South -2	Pm 3136, Bwy 8206
20088-	Three Leaves Of Shamrock -2?	Pm unissued
20089-2	Blue Eyes -1, 2	Pm 3072, Bwy 8158

Paramount 3136 as by **North Carolina Ramblers/Roy Harvey**. Broadway 8080, 8158 as by **Wilson Ramblers**; 8118 as by **The Plainsmen & Rufus Hall**; 8183 as by **Rufus Hall & The Plainsmen**; 8206 as by **The Plainsmen**. Some copies of Broadway 8158 credit matrix 20084 to **Stone Mountain Entertainers**.

Roy Harvey & North Carolina Ramblers: Posey Rorer, f; Bob Hoke, bj-md/v-1; Roy Harvey, g/v.
    Ashland, KY   Thursday, February 16, 1928

AL-268	The Bluefield Murder -1	Br 250
AL-271	I'll Be There, Mary Dear -1	Br 234, Au A22032
AL-275	What Is Home Without Love -1	Br 268
AL-276/77*	As We Parted At The Gate -1	Br 234, Au A22032
AL-279	There's A Mother Old And Gray Who Needs Me Now -1	Br 223
AL-280	There'll Come A Time	Br 223
AL-282/3	Sweet Refrain	Vo 5243
AL-285	Budded Roses -1	Br 268
AL-288/89	Take Me Back To Home And Mother -1	Vo 5243
AL-290	George Collins -1	Br 250

Aurora A22032 as by **Roy Harvey's Ramblers**.

Fred Newman, v; acc. Odell Smith, f; Lonnie Austin, f; Lucy Terry, p; Charlie Poole, bj; own g.
    New York, NY   May 8, 9 or 10, 1929

2913-2	San Antonio	Pm 3177, 3267, Bwy 8288
2914-2	What Is A Home Without Babies	Pm 3177, 3267, Bwy 8288

Other sides from this session, logged and issued as by The Highlanders, are listed under Charlie Poole.

Roy Harvey & Leonard Copeland, g duet; Roy Harvey, sp-1.
    Johnson City, TN   Tuesday, October 22, 1929

149216-2	Just Pickin'	Co 15514-D
149217-2	Beckley Rag	Co 15514-D
149218-2	Underneath The Sugar Moon	Co 15582-D
149219-2	Lonesome Weary Blues -1	Co 15582-D

New York, NY   Tuesday, April 22, 1930

150337-2; 194946-	Greasy Wagon	Co 15637-D
150338-2; 194947-	Mother's Waltz	Co 15637-D
150339-	Monroe County Blues	Co unissued
150340-2; 194973-2	Back To The Blue Ridge	Co unissued: Cy 523 (LP); Co C4K47911, Cy CD3512, Doc DOCD-8052 (CDs)

Roy Harvey, v; acc. own g.
New York, NY   Tuesday, April 22, 1930

150354-	Lamplighting Time In The Valley	Co unissued
150355-	There's A Mother Old And Gray	Co unissued

Matrices 150341 to 150353 are by Earl Shirkey & Roy Harper (i.e. Roy Harvey) (see the former), or by other artists.

Acc. Odell Smith, f; own g/sp-1.
New York, NY   Tuesday, September 9, 1930

150781-2	Just Good-Bye I Am Going Home	Co 15609-D
150782-1	The Lilly Reunion -1	Co 15609-D

Acc. Jess Johnston, f/v-1; own g.
Richmond, IN   Wednesday, December 3, 1930

17337-B	Hobo's Pal	Ch 16187, Spr 2658
17338	There'll Be A Change In Business	Ge rejected
17339	Wreck Of The C&O Sportsman	Ge rejected
17340	The Lilly Reunion	Ge rejected
17341-A	No Room For A Tramp	Ch 16187
17342-A	Little Seaside Village	Ch 16213, Spr 2658
17343	Milwaukee Blues	Spr 2626
17344	When It's Lamp Lighting Time In The Valley -1	Ge rejected
17345	My Smoky Mountain Home -1	Ge rejected
17346-A	When The Bees Are In The Hive	Ch 16213, MW 4947

Superior 2626, 2658 as by **John Martin**.

Jess Johnston, f/v-1; Roy Harvey, g/v-2.
Richmond, IN   Thursday, December 4, 1930

17347	The Dying Brakeman -1	Ch 16255
17348	Railroad Blues -2	Ch 16255, Spr 2626

Superior 2626 as by **John Martin**.

Harvey & Johnson: Roy Harvey, Jess Johnston, g/sp-1 duet.
Richmond, IN   Thursday, December 4, 1930

17349-A	Jefferson Street Rag	Ch 16781, 45011
17350-B	Guitar Rag -1	Ch 16781, 45011

Roy Harvey, v; or **Roy Harvey & Jess Johnson**-1, v duet; acc. **West Virginia Ramblers**: Jess Johnston, f; Bernice Coleman, f; Ernest Branch, bj; Roy Harvey, g.
Richmond, IN   Wednesday, June 3, 1931

17782-A	By A Cottage In The Twilight -1	Ch 16780, Spr 2684
17783	Goodbye Maggie, Goodbye Darling -1	Ch 16331, 45035
17784	Blue Eyes -1	Ch 16294, Spr 2779
17785	Goodbye Sweetheart Goodbye -1	Ch 16294, Spr 2684
17786-A	Gambling Blues	Ch 16281
17787	John Hardy Blues	Ch 16281
17788	California Murderer	Ge rejected
17789-A	The Great Reaping Day -1	Ch 16662, 45117
17790	You're Bound To Look Like A Monkey -1	Ch 16331, Spr 2779

Rev. Champion 16662, 45117 by Carolina Ladies Quartet.

West Virginia Ramblers: Jess Johnston, f; Bernice Coleman, f; Ernest Branch, bj; Roy Harvey, g.
Richmond, IN   Wednesday, June 3, 1931

17792	O Dem Golden Slippers	Ch 16757, 45017
17793	Birdie	Ch 16449

Matrix 17791 is by Ernest Branch. Revs: Champion 16449 by Corn Cob Crushers; 16757, 45017 by Lexington Red Peppers.

Roy Harvey, v; or **Roy Harvey & Jess Johnson**-1, v duet; acc. **West Virginia Ramblers**: Jess Johnston, f; Bernice Coleman, f; Ernest Branch, bj; Roy Harvey, g.
Richmond, IN   Thursday, June 4, 1931

17799	Where The Whippoorwill Is Whispering Good-Night	Ch R-16312, Spr 2701, MW 4947

17800	Called To Foreign Fields	Ch R-16312
17801	My Mother And My Sweetheart -1	Ch 16780, 45035
17802	Flowers Now -1	Ge rejected
17803	Wreck Of The C&O Sportsman	Spr 2701

Champion R-16312 as by **Roy Harvey Acc. By Jess Johnson's Ramblers**. Superior 2701 as by John Martin. Matrices 17794 to 17798 are by Ernest Branch & Bernice Coleman.

Roy Harvey also recorded with Charlie Poole, Ernest Branch & Bernice Coleman, and Weaver Brothers. His duets with Earl Shirkey are listed under the latter's name.

HARVEY & HOKE

See Roy Harvey.

HARVEY & JOHNSON

See Roy Harvey.

THE HARVEY FAMILY

Pseudonym on Microphone and Sterling for the Pickard Family.

THE HARWOOD ENTERTAINERS

Vocal duet; acc. unknown, p; unknown, md; unknown, g.
    Dallas, TX   Thursday, November 27, 1930

| DAL-6755 | The Sheriff's Sale | Br/Vo rejected |
| DAL-6756 | On Her Wedding Morn | Br/Vo rejected |

DELLA HATFIELD

See Emry Arthur.

OVERTON HATFIELD

Pseudonym on Columbia for Gene Autry.

HATTON BROTHERS

Vertner Hatton, f/sp-1; Jess Hatton, bj; Asa Martin, g-2/sp/calls.
    Richmond, IN   Tuesday, April 4, 1933

| 19120 | Hook And Line -1 | Ch 16628 |
| 19121 | Wish I Had My Time Again -2 | Ch 16628 |

The Hattons also recorded with Charlie Wilson & His Gang.

HAUULEA ENTERTAINERS

Unknown, sg; unknown, g; unknown, u; unknown, v trio-1.
    San Antonio, TX   Sunday, June 15, 1930

404312-B	Twelfth Street Rag	OK 45461
404313-B	Ellis March	OK 45461
404314-B	Railroad Blues -1	OK 45490, PaE F1075
404315-A	Right Or Wrong -1	OK 45490, PaE F1075

HAWAIIAN PALS

Ollie Humphries, sg/tv; Lewis McDaniels, g/lv.
    Charlotte, NC   Thursday, May 21, 1931

| 69333-1 | If You'll Be Mine | Vi 23588, Au 408 |
| 69334-1 | It's Awful What Whiskey Will Do | Vi 23588, Au 408 |

Lewis McDaniels also recorded in his own name and with the Carolina Buddies and Walter Smith.

THE HAWAIIAN SONGBIRDS (TED & ROY)

Ted Broughton, sg/v-1; Roy Rodgers, g/v-1; one of them, y-1.
    Dallas, TX   c. October 25, 1928

| DAL-696-A | Songbird Yodel -1 | Br 4164, BrAu 4164, Pe 11342, Ba 32536, Me M12469, Pan 25393 |
| DAL-697-A | Happy Hawaiian Blues | Br 4164, BrAu 4164, Pe 11342, Ba 32536, Me M12469, Pan 25393 |

Panachord 25393 as by **Hawaiian Songbirds** with no subcredit.

These recordings were remastered by ARC on July 29, 1932 and assigned the matrices 12134 and 12135 respectively; it is from these transfers that the Banner, Melotone, and Panachord issues are derived.

Hawaiian Song Birds: no details.
    Dallas, TX   Sunday, November 30, 1930

DAL-6793-	Sometime	Br rejected
DAL-6794-	Arkansaw Sweetheart	Br rejected

A Roy Rodgers, possibly the same man, recorded with Hugh Roden.

HAWAIIAN TRIO

Pseudonym on Broadway for the Westbrook Conservatory Entertainers.

UNCLE BEN HAWKINS [& HIS BOYS or GANG]

Pseudonym on Champion, Silvertone, Supertone, and Challenge for Ernest V. Stoneman.

UNCLE BILLY HAWKINS

Pseudonym on Champion for William B. Houchens.

UNCLE JIM HAWKINS

This pseudonym was used on Challenge as follows:
    101 Murray Kellner (*Hell Broke Loose In Georgia*); Doc Roberts (*And The Cat Came Back The Very Next Day*)
    109 William B. Houchens
    111 Doc Roberts
    112 Doc Roberts
    301 William B. Houchens
    304 Murray Kellner
It was also used on Champion for Fiddlin' Sam Long.

MINER HAWKINS

Miner Hawkins, v; acc. unknown, h-1; unknown, g.
    New York, NY   Tuesday, March 9, 1926

141779-2	A Coal Miner's Dream	Co 15067-D
141779-3	A Coal Miner's Dream	CoAu 01891
141780-2	The Song Of The Sea -1	Co 15067-D

Rev. Columbia 01891 by Vernon Dalhart.

TED HAWKINS

Ted Hawkins Mountaineers: prob. Lowe Stokes, f; Ted Hawkins, md; poss. Riley Puckett, g; poss. others.
    Atlanta, GA   Friday, December 5 or Saturday, December 6, 1930

151059-	Sanford Barnes	Co unissued
151060-	Mandolin Rag	Co unissued

Unknown, f; Ted Hawkins, md; unknown, g; Johnnie Tallent, v.
    Atlanta, GA   Monday, November 2, 1931

152001-1	Roamin' Jack	Co 15752-D
152002-1	When The Lillies Bloom Again (In Old Kentucky)	Co 15752-D
152003-	Hawkins Rag	Co unissued
152004-	Memories Of Mother	Co unissued

Ted Hawkins–Riley Puckett: Ted Hawkins, md; Riley Puckett, g.
    San Antonio, TX   Thursday, March 29, 1934

82688-1	Tokio Rag	BB B-5656, ViJ Jr-68
82689-1	Texas Hop	BB B-5473
82690-1	Raindrop Waltz	BB B-5473, RZAu G22555
82691-1	Rainbow Waltz	BB B-5656, RZAu G22555, ViJ Jr-68

Regal-Zonophone G22555 as by **Ted Hawkins & Riley Puckett**. RCA 8416-2-R (CD) claims to use matrix 82688-2 but the item is identical to the issued take 1.

Gid Tanner, f; Gordon Tanner, f; Ted Hawkins, f/v-1; Riley Puckett, g/v-1.
    San Antonio, TX   Friday, March 30, 1934

82717-1	Down In The Valley -1	BB B-5691, RZAu G22464
82718-1	Zelma	BB B-5691, RZAu G22464

Regal-Zonophone G22464 as by **Ted Hawkins & Riley Puckett**; matrix 82717 is titled *Down In The Valley Waltz*, and matrix 82718 is titled *Zelma Waltz*, on that issue.

Ted Hawkins, md; Riley Puckett, g.
    San Antonio, TX   Friday, March 30, 1934

82726-1	Kimball House	BB B-5514
82727-1	Hop Light Ladies	BB B-5514

Matrices 82719 to 82725 are by Gid Tanner.

HAWKINS BROTHERS

Bert Hirsch, f; Tony Colucci, g.
   New York, NY   Friday, December 7, 1928

| E-28901-A,-B | Sassafras Blues | Br/Vo unissued trial recording |

DEWEY HAYES

Selma & Dewey Hayes, v duet; acc. prob. Dewey Hayes, g.
   Charlotte, NC   Thursday, May 20, 1931

| 69323-1 | Your Chestnut Hair Is Dimmed With Snow | Vi 23629, Au 411 |
| 69324-1 | Broken Heart | Vi 23629, Au 411 |

Dewey Hayes (The Carolina Troubadour), v; prob. acc. own g.
   Atlanta, GA   Friday, October 22, 1931

151900-	Deep River Blues	Co unissued
151901-	I'm A Rambler	Co unissued
151902-1	Bring Back The One I Love	Co 15753-D
151903-1	Cowboy's Prayer	Co 15753-D

ED HAYES

Ed Hayes, v; acc. **Chenoweth's Cornfield Symphony Orch.**: W.B. Chenoweth, f; poss. Bill Anderson, f /bj-g; poss. D.F. Hyle, bj.
   Dallas, TX   c. October 19, 1925

| 9369- | [unknown title] | OK unissued |
| 9370-A | The Big White Rooster And The Little Brown Hen | OK 45025 |

Rev. OKeh 45025 by Chenoweth's Cornfield Symphony Orchestra.

LOU HAYES

Pseudonym on Ajax and Apex for Vernon Dalhart.

NAP HAYES & MATTHEW PRATER

Although appearing in the OKeh Old Time Tunes series (45231), these are African-American artists; see *B&GR*.

SELMA & DEWEY HAYES

See Dewey Hayes.

HAYES & JENKINS

Pseudonym on Superior for the Johnson Brothers or, on *Goin' A Courtin'* (2537), for Fletcher & Foster.

GACE HAYNES & EUGENE BALLENGER

No details.
   Knoxville, TN   Wednesday, August 28, 1929

| K-140 | The Blues | Br/Vo rejected |
| K-141 | Tennessee Go-By | Br/Vo rejected |

These may be African-American artists.

BILLY HAYS & HIS ORCHESTRA

The Victor recordings by this band were all issued in the Old Familiar Tunes series (V-40055, V-40056, V-40087, V-40103, and V-40113) but are outside the scope of this work. It may be noted, however, that Carson Robison and Frank Luther participated in some items; see *VMB*.

THE HAYSEEDS

Pseudonym on Canadian Sterling for the Hobbs Brothers.

HAYWIRE MAC

See Harry (Mac) McClintock.

HAYWOOD COUNTY RAMBLERS

Prob.: Garley Foster, h/g/v; Vaughn Medford, md; Dock Walsh, bj/v.
   Charlotte, NC   Friday, May 28, 1931

69369-2	All Bound Down	Vi 23779, MW M-4332
69370-1,-2	Short Life In Trouble	Vi unissued
69371-2	Buncombe Chain Gang	Vi 23779, MW M-4332

LUTHER E. HEATWOLE

See Vaughan Quartet & Associated Groups.

HEINIE & THE GRENADIERS

This is a polka band, "from WTMJ, the Milwaukee Journal Station" (thus Decca files). Its releases in the Decca Hill Billy series (5119, 5120, 5146) are beyond the scope of this work.

HARMON E. HELMICK

Harmon E. Helmick, v; or **Mr. & Mrs. H.E. Helmick**-1, v duet; acc. prob. Harmon E. Helmick, g.
   Richmond, IN   Friday, May 29, 1931

17769-A	Bound For The Promised Land	Ch 16744, 45112
17770	Keep On The Sunny Side Of Life	Ch R-16705, 45126, De 5498
17771	Little Moses -1	Ch R-16705, 45126, De 5498
17772	The Little Black Train	Ch 16744, 45112

Champion 45112 as by **Harmon E. Hemlick**. Matrix 17771 on Decca 5498 as by **Mr. & Mrs. Harmon E. Hemlick**.

BILL HELMS & HIS UPSON COUNTY BAND

Bill Helms, f; Grady Owens, f; John Hogan, bj; Ty Cobb Hogan, g.
   Atlanta, GA   Thursday, February 23, 1928

41950-1	Thomastown [sic] Breakdown	Vi 21649
41951-2	Georgia Blues	Vi 21649
41952-1	Rosco Trillion	Vi V-40079, Au 221, MW M-8234
41953-1	Alabama Jubilee	Vi V-40079, Au 221, MW M-8234

Issues of Montgomery Ward M-8234 with the red-and-yellow label carry the original Victor titles of matrices 41952/53, but those with the black label are retitled *Alabama Square Dance – Part 1* and *Alabama Square Dance – Part 2* respectively.

Bill Helms recorded with the Home Town Boys and Riley Puckett.

ED HELTON SINGERS

Vocal group; acc. unknown, md; unknown, g.
   Johnson City, TN   Thursday, October 18, 1928

147232-1	A Storm On The Sea (The Sinking Of The Steam-ship Vestris)	Co 15327-D
147233-2	My Old Cottage Home	Co 15327-D

ERNEST HELTON

Ernest Helton, bj solo.
   Asheville, NC   prob. Friday, August 28 or Saturday, August 29, 1925

9311-A	Royal Clog	OK 45010

Rev. OKeh 45010 by R.B. Smith–S.J. Allgood.

Ernest Helton recorded with J.D. Harris. He also made cylinder recordings for Robert W. Gordon of the Library of Congress in November 1925.

OSEY HELTON

Osey Helton, f solo.
   poss. New York, NY   unknown date

5118-	Cumbling [sic] Gap	Bwy 5118
5119-	Asheville	Bwy 5119
5122-1	Rocky Road To Dublin	Bwy 5122
5123-1	Green River	Bwy 5123

These items are coupled as Broadway 5118/5119 and 5122/5123. Intervening matrices are untraced but possibly by this artist.

HARMON E. HEMLICK

Champion 45112 by Harmon E. Helmick was mistakenly credited thus.

RED HENDERSON

Red Henderson, sp; acc. prob. Emmett Bankston, bj.
   Atlanta, GA   Thursday, August 2, 1928

402043-A	Automobile Ride Through Alabama – Part 1	OK 45283
402044-A	Automobile Ride Through Alabama – Part 2	OK 45283

HENDERSON BROTHERS (THE WANDERING COWBOYS)

Larry Henderson, —— Henderson, v duet; acc. prob. one of them, md; the other, g.
   Jackson, MS   Friday, October 18, 1935

JAX-191-	Roll On Freight Train	ARC unissued

JAX-192-	Better Quit Your Rowdy Ways	ARC unissued
JAX-193-2	Way Out West	Vo 03128
JAX-194-2	The Grave Beneath The Pines	Vo 03128

HENDERSONVILLE DOUBLE QUARTET

Vocal octet; acc. unknown, p.
Atlanta, GA   Tuesday, April 16, 1929

| 148313-2 | Onward Ye Soldiers | Co 15443-D |
| 148314-2 | I Want My Life To Testify | Co 15443-D |

HENDERSONVILLE QUARTET

Earl T. Brown, tv; John T. Wilkins, tv; Roy C. Bennett, bv; A. Farry Barber, bsv; unacc.
Atlanta, GA   Saturday, November 23, 1929

56571-1	Under His Wings	Vi V-40250
56572-1	Blue Galilee	Vi V-40250
56573-1	Take Time To Be Holy	Vi V-40213
56574-2	That Beautiful Land	Vi V-40213

FISHER HENDLEY

Fisher Hendley, v; acc. own bj.
Asheville, NC   prob. Thursday, August 27 or Friday, August 28, 1925

| 9297-A | Nigger, Will You Work? | OK 45012 |
| 9298-A | Let Your Shack Burn Down | OK 45012 |

Whitter–Hendley–Small: Fisher Hendley, bj/v/sp; Marshall Small, bj; Henry Whitter, g/sp.
Memphis, TN   Friday, November 28, 1930

64742-1,-2	Mah Yaller Gal	Vi unissued
64743-1	A Pretty Gal's Love	BB B-6555
64744-1	Another Man's Wife	BB B-6555
64745-1,-2	The Possum Hunt	Vi unissued

Fisher Hendley, bj/sp-1; Marshall Small, bj-2; Henry Whitter, g/sp-1.
Memphis, TN   Saturday, November 29, 1930

64748-1	Shuffle, Feet, Shuffle -2	Vi 23528
64749-1	Tar And Feathers -2	Vi 23528
64750-1	Pretty Little Girl	Vi unissued
64751-1	Whitter's Rabbit Hunt -1	Vi unissued

Victor 23528 as by **Hendley & Small**.

Fisher Hendley & His Carolina Tar Heels: unknown, f; Fisher Hendley, bj; unknown, g.
New York, NY   Friday, August 11, 1933

13772-1	Medley – Cindy, Soldier's Joy And Mississippi Sawyer	Vo 02612
13773-	Katie Cline	ARC unissued
13774-	Roosters Comb	ARC unissued
13775-1	Going Down Town	Vo 02612
13776-1	Greasy Possum	Vo 02530
13777-1	Peek-A-Boo	Vo 02530
13778-1	Under The Double Eagle	Vo 02679
13779-1	Hook And Line	Vo 02679

Fisher Hendley, v; acc. own bj; unknown, g.
New York, NY   Friday, August 11, 1933

| 13780-1 | Answer To Big Rock Candy Mountain | Vo 02543, RZAu G22174 |
| 13781-2 | Work In 1930 | Vo 02543 |

Rev. Regal-Zonophone G22174 by Gene Autry & Jimmie Long.

Fisher Hendley & His "Aristocratic Pigs": Sam Poplin, f/v-1; prob. Ezra Roper, ac-2; Fisher Hendley, bj-3; "Little Boy Blue" (Hampton Bradley), g/v-4; "Baby Ray" (Dixon Stewart), sb-5/v-6.
Columbia, SC   Monday, October 31, 1938

SC-31-1	My Family Circle -2, 4, 5	Vo/OK 04881
SC-32-	Memories In The Moonlight -2, 4, 5, 6	Vo unissued
SC-33-1	Darling, Do You Know Who Loves You? -2, 4, 5	Vo/OK 04516, Cq 9190
SC-34-1	Won't Somebody Tell My Darling -2, 4, 5	Vo/OK 04937
SC-35-1	My Angel Sweetheart -2, 4, 6	Vo/OK 05016
SC-36-	I'm Thinking Tonight Of You Dear -2, 5, 6	Vo unissued
SC-37-1	Brown Eyes -2, 3, 4, 5	Vo/OK 04556
SC-38-	When I Was Born -2, 4, 5	Vo unissued

SC-39-	Down By The Moss Covered Spring -1, 2, 4, 5	Vo unissued
SC-40-1	You Make My Heart Go Boom -1, 2, 4, 5	Vo/OK 05016
SC-41-1	I'm Going Back To The Mountains -1, 2, 4, 5	Vo 05095
SC-42-1	To Leave You Would Break My Heart -1, 4, 5	Vo/OK 04556

Sam Poplin, f; prob. Ezra Roper, ac-1; unknown, md-2; Fisher Hendley, bj-3; "Little Boy Blue", g/v-4; "Baby Ray", sb-5/v-6; unidentified, v duet-7; unidentified, sp/crying-8.
    Columbia, SC   Tuesday, November 1, 1938

SC-43-1	She'll Be There -1, 4, 5	Vo 04658
SC-44-1	Blue Eyes -2, 6, 8	Vo/OK 04718, Cq 9228
SC-45-1	Walking In The Shoes Of John -2, 3, 5, 7	Vo 05216
SC-46-1	Push Them Clouds Away -2, 3, 5, 7	Vo 05216

Sam Poplin, f-1/v-2; prob. Ezra Roper, ac-3; unknown, md-4; Fisher Hendley, bj-5/v-6; "Little Boy Blue", g/v-7; "Baby Ray", sb-8/v-9; unidentified, v duet-10/trio-11.
    Columbia, SC   Wednesday, November 2, 1938

SC-50-1	I'll Meet My Precious Mother -4, 5, 8, 10	Vo 05095
SC-51-1	Blind Child's Prayer -1, 3, 6, 7, 8	Vo 04658
SC-52-1	Hop Along Peter -1, 4, 5, 8, 11	Vo 04780, Cq 9227
SC-53-1	Come Back To The Hills -2, 3, 7, 8	Vo/OK 04718, Cq 9228
SC-54-1	If It Wasn't For Mother And Dad -1, 4, 7, 9	Vo/OK 04881

Sam Poplin, f; prob. Ezra Roper, ac; "Little Boy Blue", g/v; "Baby Ray", sb.
    Columbia, SC   Friday, November 11, 1938

SC-142-1	It Makes No Difference Now	Vo/OK 04516, Cq 9190

Sam Poplin, f; "Little Boy Blue", g; unidentified, g; "Baby Ray", sb.
    Columbia, SC   Saturday, November 12, 1938

SC-163-2	The Raindrop Waltz	Vo/OK 04937

Fisher Hendley, v; acc. own bj.
    Columbia, SC   Saturday, November 12, 1938

SC-164-1	Weave Room Blues	Vo 04780, Cq 9227

HENDLEY & SMALL

See Fisher Hendley.

TED (STRAW) HENLEY

Ted (Straw) Henley, v; acc. unknown.
    Chicago, IL   Saturday, August 29, 1931

C-7975-	The Fate Of Walter Harris	Br custom recording
C-7976-	Since The Angels Carried My Mother Home To Glory	Br custom recording

Brunswick session-sheets categorize these recordings as "priv[ate]" and note that the artist's fee was "paid to Brunswick Radio Corp."

TAL HENRY & HIS NORTH CAROLINIANS

This danceband recorded for Victor and Bluebird and some of its items for the former were issued in the Old Familiar Tunes series (V-40034, V-40035, V-40133); they are beyond the scope of this work. (For further information on the band's Victor recordings see JR.)

HENRY COUNTY FOUR

Pseudonym on Challenge for the Maple City Four.

HENRY COUNTY TRIO

Pseudonym on Bell for the Short Creek Trio.

HENRY'S STRING BAND

See Big Chief Henry's Indian String Band.

LARRY HENSLEY

See Walker's Corbin Ramblers.

HENSLEY & TAYLOR
HENSLEY, TAYLOR & WALKER

See Walker's Corbin Ramblers.

BERNARD F. HENSON

See Richard Cox.

RUSSELL HENSON

Russell Henson, v; acc. unknown, f; unknown, bj.
    Richmond, IN   Friday, January 10, 1930
    16067,-A   Sweet William   Ge rejected

See also George & Henson.

CHARLIE HERALD

Numerous recordings by this artist were issued in the Canadian Bluebird (B-4900) series, and it is believed that Herald was chiefly active in Canada and thus outside the scope of this work. He also had a single release in the Decca Hill Billy series (5058, as Charlie Herald & His Roundup Rangers).

DIDIER HERBERT

This artist's last name is correctly spelled Hebert.

Didier Hebert, v; acc. own g.
    New Orleans, LA   Tuesday, December 10, 1929
    111390-1   I Woke Up One Morning In May   Co 40517-F, OK 90017

Rev. Columbia 40517-F, OKeh 90017 by E. Segura & D. Herbert (see Segura Bros.).

WILLIE (RED) HERMAN

Pseudonym, or erroneous credit, on Bluebird and Montgomery Ward for Syd "Willie (Red)" Newman; see Jack Pierce.

HERMAN BROTHERS

Pseudonym on Broadway for the Hobbs Brothers.

HERNANDEZ BROTHERS

This group made numerous records for Victor's Mexican series. Although one coupling appeared in the company's Old Familiar Tunes series (V-40081), it is outside the scope of this work.

PETE HERRING

Pete Herring, v; acc. own g.
    Memphis, TN   Wednesday, May 28, 1930
    62525-1,-2   I've Got A House In Chicago   Vi unissued
    62526-1,-2   Take A 'Tater And Wait   Vi unissued

This artist is a member of the Mississippi 'Possum Hunters.

OLLIE HESS

Ollie Hess, v/y; acc. prob. own g.
    Grafton, WI   c. March 1932
    L-1369-1   Mammy's Lullaby   Bwy 8322
    L-1371-1   Sleep Baby Sleep   Bwy 8322

Matrix L-1370 is untraced. This is a female artist.

BERTHA HEWLETT

Holland Wilkerson, v; acc. Bertha Hewlett, p.
    Richmond, VA   Thursday, October 17, 1929
    403167-   My Redeemer   OK unissued
    403168-   I Shall Not Be Moved   OK unissued

Although Bertha Hewlett appears to play an accompanying role, these items are logged under her name only.

THE HI-FLYERS

The Texas High Flyers: prob. Clifford Gross, f; poss. Claude Davis, md; Ocie Stockard, tg; poss. Herman Arwine, g.
    Dallas, TX   Friday, November 28, 1930
    DAL-6759-   Crafton Blues   Br/Vo rejected
    DAL-6760-   The Blue Bonnet Waltz   Br/Vo rejected

The Hi-Flyers: Darrell Kirkpatrick, f; "Butch" Gibson, cl; Billy Briggs, esg; Landon Beaver, p; Elmer Scarborough, tbj/tg; Willie Wells, g/v-1; Darrell Kirkpatrick, Billy Briggs or Willie Wells, sb.
    Dallas, TX   Sunday, June 13, 1937
    DAL-280-1,-2   Lady, Be Good   ARC unissued
    DAL-281-1,-2   Vision Of Deams   ARC unissued
    DAL-282-1,-2   He's A Curbstone Cutie (They Call Him Jelly Bean)   ARC unissued
    DAL-283-1,-2   Razz Ma Tazz Stomp   ARC unissued
    DAL-284-2   The Five Piece Band -1   Vo 03964

DAL-285-2	Honolulu Flapper Gal	Vo 03964
DAL-295-1,-2	You Can Depend On Me	ARC unissued
DAL-296-1	You're The One I Care For -1	ARC 7-12-65, Vo 03764
DAL-297-2	Jealous -1	ARC 7-12-65, Vo 03764
DAL-298-2	Under The Double Eagle	ARC 7-11-56, Vo/OK 03684, Co 37711, 20288
DAL-299-1	Making A Baby From Georgia -1	ARC 7-10-55, Vo 03647
DAL-300-1	Joe Turner Blues	ARC 7-10-55, Vo 03647

Intervening matrices are by Clifford Gross & Muryel Campbell.

Darrell Kirkpatrick, f-1/lg-2; "Butch" Gibson, cl; Billy Briggs, esg; Landon Beaver, p/v-3; Elmer Scarborough, tbj/tg; Willie Wells, g/v-4; Zack Hurt, sb/v-5.

    Dallas, TX   Friday, June 18, 1937

DAL-354-2	Down The Trail -2, 3 (lead), 4, 5	Vo/OK 04011
DAL-355-1	Home On The Range -1, 3, 4, 5 (lead)	Vo/OK 04011
DAL-356-	Eleven More Months And Ten More Days	ARC unissued
DAL-357-	The Night Wind	ARC unissued
DAL-358-1	Old Tobacco Mill -1, 5	Vo 04093
DAL-359-1	(Pin A Bluebonnet On Your New Bonnet) Bluebonnet -1, 4	ARC 7-09-55, Vo 03619
DAL-360-2	There's A Little Green Mill (By A Little Green Hill) -1, 4	ARC 7-09-55, Vo 03619
DAL-361-2	Hi-Flyer Stomp -1	ARC 7-11-56, Vo/OK 03684, Co 37711, 20288
DAL-362-1	Static Stomp -1	Vo 04093

Darrell Kirkpatrick, f/v-1; Wilson "Lefty" Perkins, esg; Landon Beaver, p; Steve Wooden, g/v-2; Elmer Scarborough, tg; prob. Ernest Hackworth, sb; unknown, wh-3.

    Dallas, TX   Tuesday, December 6, 1938

DAL-737-1	Answer To It Makes No Difference Now -2	Vo/OK 04703, Cq 9244
DAL-738-1	Dragging The Bow	Vo/OK 04671
DAL-739-	Out Near The Rainbow's End -2, 3	Vo unissued
DAL-740-1	Razz Ma Tazz Stomp	Vo/OK 04589
DAL-741-1	He's A Curbstone Cutie (They Call Him Jelly Bean) -1	Vo/OK 04589
DAL-742-1	Don't Say Goodbye -2	Vo/OK 04671
DAL-743-1	Lonesome Mama Blues -5	Vo/OK 05346
DAL-744-1	In A Land Where The Sun Goes Down -2	Vo unissued
DAL-745-1	You Can Depend On Me -1	Vo/OK 04703, Cq 9244
DAL-746-1	My Bonnie Lies Over The Ocean -2	Vo/OK 05346

Darrell Kirkpatrick, f/ac; Sleepy Johnson, f; Andrew Schroeder, esg/v-1; Landon Beaver, p; Buster Ferguson, g/v-2; Elmer Scarborough, tg; Sleepy Johnson or Andrew Schroeder, sb (where present).

    Dallas, TX   Saturday, June 24, 1939

DAL-938-1	Honky Tonk Mama -2	Vo/OK 05054
DAL-939-1	I'll Get By -2	Vo/OK 05176
DAL-940-1	Unlock This Doghouse Door -2	Vo/OK 05054
DAL-941-1	Let's Spend The Night In Hawaii -1	Vo/OK 05000, RZAu G24004
DAL-942-1	That's Why I Sigh And Cry -2	Vo/OK 05000, RZAu G24004
DAL-943-1	I'll Never Let You Cry -2	Vo/OK 05176

Darrell Kirkpatrick, f/ac/emd; Sleepy Johnson, f-1/sb-2; Andrew Schroeder, esg/v-3; Landon Beaver, p; Buster Ferguson, g/v-4; Elmer Scarborough, tg; prob. Dick Reinhart, sb-5.

    Fort Worth, TX   Monday, April 22, 1940

DAL-1021-1	The Honky Tonky Jump -2, 4	OK 05623, Co 37748, 20325
DAL-1022-1	Get Hot Or Go Home -2, 4	OK 05723
DAL-1023-1	Dark Bedroom Blues -2, 3	OK 05784
DAL-1024-1	Roadside Rag -2	OK 05623, Cq 9737, Co 37748, 20325
DAL-1025-1	I'm Sorry Now -1, 4, 5	OK 05723, Cq 9737
DAL-1026-	We Both Were Wrong -2, 4	Vo unissued
DAL-1027-1	You'll Never Admit You're Sorry -2, 4	OK 05784
DAL-1028-2	Barn Yard Romp -1, 4, 5	Vo/OK 05560
DAL-1029-1	Why Did You Teach Me To Love You -2, 3, 4	OK 05679
DAL-1030-2	Osage Indian Girl -2, 4	OK 05679
DAL-1031-1	Sleepy Waltz -1, 5	Vo/OK 05560

The Hi-Flyers also recorded as Universal Cowboys with Dick Reinhart on April 21.

Darrell Kirkpatrick, f/ac/emd; Andrew Schroeder, esg; Sheldon Bennett, eg; Landon Beaver, p; Buster Ferguson, g/v; Elmer Scarborough, tg; prob. Wayne Benson, sb.

    Fort Worth, TX   Sunday, March 9, 1941

DAL-1279-1	There's Another One Waiting	OK 06491

Darrell Kirkpatrick, f/ac/emd; Andrew Schroeder, esg; Sheldon Bennett, eg/v-1; Landon Beaver, p; Buster Ferguson, g/v-2; Elmer Scarborough, tg; prob. Wayne Benson, sb.
    Fort Worth, TX   Monday, March 10, 1941

DAL-1275-1	Mable Ain't Able -1	OK 06396
DAL-1276-1	Juke Box Jump	OK 06396
DAL-1277-1	Our Last Goodnight -2	OK 06252, Cq 9874
DAL-1278-1	Watcha Gonna Do -2	OK 06312
DAL-1280-1	You've Broken My Heart Dear -2	OK 06491, Cq 9875
DAL-1281-1	Beer Parlor Jive	OK 06559
DAL-1282-1	The Day You Left Me -2	OK 06252, Cq 9874
DAL-1283-1,-2	I'm Doing It Too -2	OK unissued
DAL-1284-1	Alamo Polka	OK 06559
DAL-1285-1	Reno Street Blues	OK 06183, Cq 9873
DAL-1286-1	The Night We Said Goodbye -2	OK 06312
DAL-1287-1,-2	You Can't Do That To Me -2	OK unissued

Darrell Kirkpatrick, f/ac/emd; Andrew Schroeder, esg/v-1; Sheldon Bennett, eg/v-2; Landon Beaver, p; Buster Ferguson, g/v-3; Elmer Scarborough, tg; prob. Wayne Benson, sb.
    Fort Worth, TX   Tuesday, March 11, 1941

DAL-1288-1	What Do I Do Now -1	Cq 9875
DAL-1289-1	Low Blues -1	OK 06137
DAL-1290-1	I Thought You Meant It -1	Cq 9876
DAL-1291-1,-2	I Know The Reason Why -3	OK unissued
DAL-1292-1	The Wise Old Owl -2	OK 06137
DAL-1293-1	I'll Carry On -3	Cq 9876
DAL-1294-1	Blonde-Headed Woman -3	OK 06183, Cq 9873

HI NEIGHBOR BOYS

Cecil "Tex" Wilson, f-1; Harold Compton, ac-2; Eddy Grishaw, g/v-3; Woodrow Wilson "Slim" Wofford, v-4.
    Columbia, SC   Friday, November 11, 1938

SC-145-1	Keep Truckin' -1, 2, 4	Vo 04555
SC-146-1	Honky Tonk Mamma -1, 2, 4	Vo 04691
SC-147-1	I'm Through With You Little Girl -1, 2, 3	Vo 04895
SC-148-	Prairie Moon -1?, 2?, 3	Vo unissued
SC-149-1	Zeb Terney's Stomp -1, 2	Vo unissued: Ep EG-37324 (LP); ABM ABMMCD1098, Acrobat ACRCD158 (CDs)
SC-150-1	Down Among The Faded Roses -3, 4	Vo 04895
SC-151-1	You Took My Sunshine -2, 3, 4	Vo/OK 04773
SC-152-1	On Your Way -1, 2, 3	Vo/OK 04773
SC-153-1	Are You Lonesome For Me (Tonight Old Pal) -4	Vo 04555
SC-154-1	Guitar Fantasy	Vo 04691

Matrix SC-149 is titled *Zeke Terney's Stomp* on Epic EG37324, ABM ABMMCD1098, Acrobat ACRCD158.
Eddie Grishaw recorded after 1942 as Zeb Turner (with his brother James Grishaw as Zeke Turner).

HIBBARD SISTERS

Vocal trio; acc. unknown, g.
    New York, NY   Tuesday, November 29, 1932

TO-1229	Seven Years With The Wrong Man	ARC unissued trial recording

THE HICKORY NUTS

Perry Propst, f-1; Julius Plato "Nish" McClured, bj/v; Horace Propst, g/v.
    Winston-Salem, NC   Saturday, September 24, 1927

81609-A	There'll Be No Liars There -1	OK 45220
81610-B	I'm Going Away To Leave You -1	OK 45220
81611-	I'm Going Away And You Can't Bring Me Back	OK unissued
81612-A	The Louisville Burglar -1	OK 45169
81613-B	I'll Tell You What I Saw Last Night	OK 45169
81614-	Downfall Of Paris -1?	OK unissued

HARRY HICKOX

Harry Hickox, v; acc. own g.
    El Paso, TX   Friday, July 12, 1929

55241-1,-2	Monkey Song	Vi unissued

JACK HICKS

See Elmer Bird.

RHODA HICKS

Rhoda Hicks, v; acc. prob. own g.
  Richmond, IN   Thursday, June 26, 1930

    16792,-A   O How She Lied   Ge unissued?

Acc. prob. own g; unknown, g.
  Richmond, IN   Monday, July 18, 1932

    18605   In A Shanty In Old Shanty Town   Ch 16466
    18606-A   My Silent Love   Ch 16466

Rhoda Hicks also recorded with the Tate Brothers.

LUTHER HIGGINBOTHAM

No details.
  Chicago, IL   Tuesday, October 3, 1933

    152519-1,-2   Duval County Blues   Co unissued
    152520-1   Thirty Years   Co unissued

Luther Higginbotham was associated with Three Floridians.

JOSEPH & PETER HIGGINS

Joseph Higgins, Peter Higgins, v duet; acc. unknown, o.
  Chicago, IL   Thursday, January 16, 1930

    C-5241-   Where He Leads Me   Vo 5404
    C-5242-   The Way Of The Cross Leads Home   Vo 5404

LEN & JOE HIGGINS

One of them, bj; the other, g.
  New York, NY   Friday, February 24, 1928

    145683-2   Kentucky Wedding Chimes   Co 15243-D, CoSA DE501, CoJ J967, ReE MR55,
                                                                            Re/RZAu G20819
    145684-3   Medley Of Old Southern Melodies (1) Massa's In   Co 15243-D, CoSA DE501, CoJ J967, ReE MR55,
                              De Cold, Cold Ground; (2) Old Dog Tray –   Re/RZAu G20819
                              Hard Times; (3) Swanee River; (4) Old Black Joe;
                              (5) In My Old Kentucky Home

Columbia J967, Regal MR55, Regal/Regal-Zonophone G20819 as by **The Brothers Bertini**. Matrix 145683 is titled *Wedding Chimes*, and matrix 145684 *Medley Of Stephen Foster Songs/Intro: Massa's In De Cold, Cold Ground; Old Dog Tray; Hard Times; Swanee River; Old Black Joe; In My Old Kentucky Home; Oh, Susanna*, on Regal MR55, Regal/Regal-Zonophone G20819.

  New York, NY   Wednesday, October 17, 1928

    147123-3   The Old White Mule   Co 15354-D
    147124-1   Slippery Elm Tree   Co 15354-D

THE HIGHLANDERS

Like the Allegheny Highlanders (with which group its personnel was identical) this was essentially a Charlie Poole band, and its recordings for Paramount are listed under his name.

E. HIGHLEY

This pseudonym was used on one side of Broadway 8327 for – possibly – the popular singer Leroy Montesanto.

THE HIGHLEYS

Vocal duet; acc. unknown, p.
  Richmond, IN   Tuesday, February 25, 1930

    16322,-A   Six Feet Of Earth   Ge rejected
    16323,-A   In The Garden   Ge rejected

  Richmond, IN   Wednesday, February 26, 1930

    16326,-A   Calling The Prodigal   Ge rejected
    16327,-A   There Is Glory in My Soul   Ge rejected
    16329   My Sheep Know My Voice   Ge rejected
    16331   They Are Calling Me Over The Tide   Ge rejected

Matrices 16328, 16330 are by Mansfield Patrick.

Acc. unknown, g.
  Grafton, WI   c. October 1931

    L-1185-4   God Is Still On The Throne   Bwy 8320
    L-1186-4   You Go To Your Church I'll Go To Mine   Bwy 8320

LUKE HIGHNIGHT

This artist's surname is correctly spelled Hignight.

Luke Hignight, v; acc own bj.
Memphis, TN   Saturday, February 25, 1928

| 400341- | Run, Johnny, Run | OK unissued |

Luke Highnight & His Ozark Strutters: Frank Gardner, f; Luke Hignight, h/bj; Hubert Tucker, g.
Memphis, TN   Thursday, November 22, 1928

M-827-	Bailey Waltz	Vo 5325
M-828-	There's No Hell In Georgia	Vo 5325
M-829-	Love Somebody	Vo unissued
M-830-	Sailing On The Ocean	Vo 5384
M-831-	Fort Smith Breakdown	Vo 5339
M-832-	Walk Along John	Vo 5339

Rev. Vocalion 5384 by Arkansas Charlie (Charlie Craver).

BOB HILL

Pseudonym on Victor for Bob Miller.

EZRA HILL & HENRY JOHNSON

Pseudonym on Champion for Melvin Robinette & Byrd Moore (see the latter).

FRANK HILL

Pseudonym on Supertone for Frank Welling (see John McGhee & Frank Welling).

PEGGY HILL

Items by this singer issued in the Victor Old Familiar Tunes series (V-40042, V-40134), for details of which see *JR*, are outside the scope of this work.

THE HILL BILLIES

Alonzo Elvis "Tony" Alderman, f; Albert Green (Al) Hopkins, p-1/v; John Rector, bj; Joe Hopkins, g.
New York, NY   Thursday, January 15, 1925

73117-A	Old Joe Clark	OK 40376
73118-A	Silly Bill -1	OK 40294
73119-A	Cripple Creek -1	OK 40336
73120-A	Whoa! Mule -1	OK 40376
73121-A	Sally Ann -1	OK 40336
73122-A	Old Time Cinda -1	OK 40294

Matrices 73115/16 may be unknown titles by this group.

Tony Alderman, f; Charles Bowman, f-1/bj-2; Elmer Hopkins, h-3; Al Hopkins, p/v-4; Joe Hopkins, g/v-5; John Hopkins, u/v-6.
New York, NY   Friday, April 30, 1926

E-2938*/39W	Mountaineer's Love Song -2, 3, 4 (lead), 5, 6, 7	Vo 15367, 5115
E-2940/41W	Goin' Down The Road -4, 5, 6	Vo unissued
E-2942/43W	Old Joe Clark -2, 4	Vo 15369, 5117
E-2944/45W	Silly Bill -2, 4	Vo 15369, 5117
E-2946/47W	Going To The Wedding Sally Ann -5	Vo unissued
E-2948*/49W	Long Eared Mule -1, 6	Vo 15368, 5116
E-2950*/51W	Cripple Creek -2, 3, 4	Vo 15367, 5115
E-2952/53*W	Mississippi Sawyer -1, 3	Vo 15368, 5116

Charlie Bowman, f; acc; Al Hopkins, p-1/v-2; Joe Hopkins, g; John Hopkins, u-3.
New York, NY   Saturday, May 1, 1926

| E-2966*/67W | The Hickman Rag -1, 3 | Vo 15377, 5118 |
| E-2968*/69W | Possum Up A Gum Stump, Cooney In The Hollow -2 | Vo 15377, 5118 |

The Hill Billies (Vocalion)/**Al Hopkins & His Buckle Busters** (Brunswick/Supertone): Tony Alderman, f-1; Charles Bowman, f-2; Al Hopkins, p-3/v-4/sp-5; Henry Roe, g-6; Joe Hopkins, g-7; John Hopkins, u-8; unidentified, v eff-9.

New York, NY   Thursday, October 21, 1926

E-3972*/73W	Fisher's Hornpipe -1, 3, 6/7, 8	Vo 5017
E-3974/75W	Cackling Hen -2, 3, 4, 5, 6/7, 8, 9	Vo 5020
E-3976/77W; 21940/41	East Tennessee Blues -2, 3, 6, 7, 8	Vo 5016, Br 103
E-3978/79W; 21954/55	Governor Alf Taylor's Fox Chase -2, 4	Vo 5016, Br 106, Spt S2094

Rev. Supertone S2094 by H.M. Barnes & His Blue Ridge Ramblers.

Tony Alderman, f-1; Fred Roe, f-2; Charles Bowman, bj-3; Al Hopkins, p-4/v-5/calls-6; Henry Roe, g-7; Joe Hopkins, g-8; John Hopkins, u-9.
    New York, NY   Friday, October 22, 1926

E-3980/81W	Walking In The Parlor -1, 2, 3, 4, 6, 7, 9	Vo 5024
E-3982*/83W	Blue Eyed Girl -1, 2, 3, 4, 5, 7/8, 9	Vo 5017
E-3984/85W; 21948/49*	Cinda -1, 2, 3, 4, 5, 7/8, 9	Vo 5025, Br 105
E-3986/87W; 21946*/47	Bristol Tennessee Blues -2, 7	Vo 5025, Br 104
E-3988/89W; 21942/43	Round Town Girls -1, 3, 4, 5, 7, 8, 9	Vo 5023, Br 103
E-3990/91W; 21944/45	Buck-Eyed Rabbits -1, 3, 4, 5, 7/8, 9	Vo 5023, Br 104
E-3992/93W	Cumberland Gap -1/2, 4, 5, 7/8	Vo 5024
E-3994*/95W	Sourwood Mountain -1/2, 5, 7/8	Vo 5022
E-3996*/97W	Ragged Annie -1, 2, 4, 7/8, 9	Vo 5022
E-3998/99W	Texas Gals -1, 2, 4, 7/8, 9	Vo 5021

Tony Alderman, f-1; Fred Roe, f-2; Charles Bowman, f-3/bj-4; unknown, h-5; Al Hopkins, p/v-6; Joe Hopkins, g/v-7; Henry Roe, g-8; John Hopkins, u-9/v-10.
    New York, NY   Saturday, October 23, 1926

E-4000/01W	Going Down The Road Feeling Bad -1, 2, 4, 6, 7, 8, 9, 10	Vo 5021
E-4002*/03*W; 21950/51	Sally Ann -1, 4, 6, 9	Vo 5019, Br 105
E-4004*/05W	Betsy Brown -1, 5, 6	Vo 5018
E-4006/07W	Kitty Wells -1, 5, 6	Vo 5018
E-4008/09W; 21952/53	Kitty Waltz -3	Vo 5019, Br 106

Charles Bowman, f; Al Hopkins, sp.
    New York, NY   Saturday, October 23, 1926

E-4010/11W	Donkey On The Railroad Track	Vo 5020

Tony Alderman, f/v; Charles Bowman, f/v; Elbert Bowman, g; John Hopkins, u/v; Al Hopkins, v.
    New York, NY   Thursday, May 12, 1927

E-23110/11*	Blue Ridge Mountain Blues	Br 180

Tony Alderman, f/v-1; Charles Bowman, f-2/g-3/v-4; Jack Reedy, bj-5; Elbert Bowman, g-6/hammer eff-7; John Hopkins, u/v-8; Al Hopkins, v/y-9/calls-10; band v-11.
    New York, NY   Friday, May 13, 1927

E-23116/17*	Sweet Bunch Of Daisies -1, 4, 6, 8	Vo 5178, Br 174
E-23118*/19	Daisies Won't Tell -6	Vo 5178, Br 174
E-23120*/21	Down To The Club -3	Br 184
E-23122/23*	Sleep Baby Sleep -3, 9	Vo 5186, Br 185
E-22124/25*	Black Eyed Susie -1, 2, 4, 5, 6, 8, 11	Vo 5179, Br 175, 80095
E-23126*/27	Cluck Old Hen -2, 5	Vo 5179, Br 175, 80095
E-23128*/29	The Nine Pound Hammer -3, 5, 7, 10	Br 177
E-23130*/31	Whoa, Mule -1, 4, 5, 6, 8	Br 179

Tony Alderman, Charles Bowman, Al Hopkins, John Hopkins, v quartet; acc. James O'Keefe, p.
    New York, NY   Saturday, May 14, 1927

E-23145/46*/47	Echoes Of The Chimes	Br 180

Tony Alderman, f; Charles Bowman, f-1/bj-2; Jack Reedy, bj; Elbert Bowman, g; Al Hopkins, v/calls-3.
    New York, NY   Saturday, May 14, 1927

E-23148/49*	Boatin' Up Sandy -1, 3	Br 182
E-23150/51*	Johnson Boys -2	Br 179

Tony Alderman, f-1/v-2; Charles Bowman, f-3/bj-4/v-5; Jack Reedy, bj-6/bells-7; Elbert Bowman, g; John Hopkins, u-8/v-9; Al Hopkins, v/y-10/sp-11/calls-12; band sp-13.
    New York, NY   Monday, May 16, 1927

E-23169/70*; E-6427/28W	Hear Dem Bells -1, 2, 3, 5, 6, 7, 9	Vo 5173, Br 181, 189, Spt S2040
E-23171*/72	Georgie Buck -2, 4, 5, 9	Vo 5182, Br 183
E-23173/74*	The Feller That Looked Like Me -1, 2, 3, 5, 8, 9	Br 184
E-23175/76*	C.C. & O. No. 558 -1, 2, 3, 5, 7, 8, 9, 11	Br 177
E-23177/78*	Darling Nellie Gray -1, 2, 4, 5, 6, 8, 9, 12	Vo 5186, Br 185
E-23179*/80	She'll Be Comin' 'Round The Mountain- 1, 2, 3, 5, 6, 8, 9	Vo 5240, Br 181

E-23181/82*	Ride That Mule -1, 3, 6, 11, 13	Br 186

Revs: Vocalion 5173, Brunswick 189, Supertone S2040 by Kanawha Singers; Vocalion 5240 by Warren Caplinger.

Tony Alderman, f-1/v-2; Charles Bowman, f-3/bj-4/g-5/v-6; Jack Reedy, bj-7; Elbert Bowman, g; John Hopkins, u/v-8; Al Hopkins, v/y-9/calls-10.
New York, NY   Tuesday, May 17, 1927

E-23183*/84	Bug In The Taters -3, 7, 10	Br 182
E-23185/86*	Baby Your Time Ain't Long -1, 2, 4, 6, 7, 8	Vo 5182, Br 183
E-23187*/88	Oh Where Is My Little Dog Gone? -1, 5, 9	Vo 5183, Br 187
E-23189*/90	Wasn't She A Dandy -1, 7	Vo 5183, Br 187
E-23191/92*	Roll On The Ground -2, 3, 4, 6, 7, 8	Br 186
E-23193/94	Daisies Won't Tell	Vo/Br unissued

Al Hopkins, v; acc. Carson Robison, g/wh-1.
New York, NY   Saturday, May 21, 1927

E-23286*/87	When You Were Sweet Sixteen	Br 176
E-23288/89*	Down The Old Meadow Lane -1	Br 176

Al Hopkins & His Buckle Busters: Tony Alderman, f-1; Ed Belcher, f-2; Frank Wilson, sg-3; unknown, bj-4; Walter Hughes, g; John Hopkins, u-5; Al Hopkins, v-6; band v-7.
New York, NY   Thursday, December 20, 1928

E-28916-A,-B	Lynchburg Town -1	Br unissued
E-28917-A,-B	Oh Didn't He Ramble	Br unissued
E-28918-	Gideon's Band -1/2, 5, 6, 7	Br 295
E-28919-	Old Dan Tucker -2, 4, 5, 6, 7	Br 295
E-28920-	Old Uncle Ned -1, 2, 3, 6, 7	Br 300
E-28921-A	West Virginia Gals -1	Br 318
E-28922-	Blue Bell -1, 3, 5, 6, 7	Br 300
E-28923-A	Carolina Moonshiner -1/2, 4, 6	Br 318

Tony Alderman, f-1; Ed Belcher, f-2; Frank Wilson, sg-3; unknown, bj-4; Walter Hughes, g; John Hopkins, u-5; Al Hopkins, v-6/sp-7.
New York, NY   Friday, December 21, 1928

E-28924-A	Polka Medley/Intro: Rocky Road To Dublin, Jenny Lind -2, 3, 5	Br 321, Vo 8525
E-28925-A	Marsovia Waltz -1/2, 3, 5	Br 321, Vo 8525
E-28926-A	Wild Hoss -1, 2, 4, 6	Br 335
E-28927-A	Medley Of Old Time Dance Tunes/Intro: Soldier's Joy–Turkey Buzzard–When You Go A-Courtin' -1, 2, 4, 6, 7	Br 335

Vocalion 8525 (a Mexican issue) as by **Los Alegres**; matrix E-28924 is titled *De Todas Un Poco*, and matrix E-28925 *Marsovia*, on that issue.

HILL BROTHERS

Dewey Hill, h/g/v; Sam Hill, ah/v; Helen Nance, v.
New York, NY   Monday, April 28, 1930

9649-	Little Darling Pal Of Mine	ARC unissued
9650-	My Dream	ARC unissued

Dewey Hill, h/g/v; Sam Hill, ah/v.
New York, NY   Tuesday, April 29, 1930

9659-	Hallelujah To The Lamb	ARC unissued

New York, NY   Wednesday, April 30, 1930

9675-	The Wild And Reckless Hobo	ARC unissued
9676-	Jack And Joe	ARC unissued

Hill Brothers With Willie Simmons: Bill Hill, f-1/ah-2/v-3; Dewey Hill, h-4/g/v; Willie Simmons, v.
Charlotte, NC   Friday, August 6, 1937

013015-1	Just Over In The Glory Land -2	BB B-7223, MW M-7372
013016-1	I'm Glad I Counted The Cost -2	MW M-7372
013017-1	I Am On My Way To Heaven -2	BB B-7223, MW M-7373
013018-1	Looking To My Prayer -3, 4	MW M-7373
013019-1	Sweetheart, I Have Grown So Lonely -1	MW M-7374
013020-1	In The Hills Of Old Virginia -4	MW M-7374

Montgomery Wards as by **Hill Brothers & W. Simmons**.
The Hill Brothers also accompany the Nance Singers at the April 1930 ARC session.

HILL'S VIRGINIA MOUNTAINEERS

Pseudonym on Silvertone and Supertone for Taylor's Kentucky Boys.

HARRY HILLARD

Harry Hillard, v; acc. poss. own g.
   Richmond, IN   Saturday, March 28, 1931
    17650   [unknown title]   Ge rejected trial recording

Harry Hillard, v/y-1; acc. Duke Clark, g.
   Richmond, IN   Tuesday, April 28, 1931
    17714-B   Nobody Knows But Me   Spr 2663
    17717-A   The Myster [sic] Of No. 5 -1   Spr 2663, MW 4968

Matrix 17717 is titled *The Mystery Of No. 5* on Montgomery Ward 4968. Matrices 17715/16 are by Duke Clark.
Rev. Montgomery Ward 4968 by Frank Welling (see John McGhee & Frank Welling).

Harry Hillard, v/y; acc. the Hoosier Hawaiians: A.J. McNew, sg; prob. Lloyd Wright, sg; two unknowns, g.
   Richmond, IN   Monday, September 28, 1931
    18055-A   Blue Yodel No. 9   Ch 16337, Spr 2733, MW 4948
    18056-A   I'm Looking For A Brand New Mama   Ch 16337

Superior 2733 as by **Jack Logan**. Revs: Superior 2733 by Jess Hillard; Montgomery Ward 4948 by Frank Dudgeon.

Harry Hillard, v; acc. unknown, g; unknown, g-1.
   Richmond, IN   Friday, March 11, 1932
    18443   Chicago Blues -1   Ge rejected
    18444   99 Years   Ge rejected

Duke Clark & Harry Hillard, v duet; or **Harry Hillard**-1, v/y; acc. prob. own g duet.
   Richmond, IN   Thursday, July 14, 1932
    18597   Kentucky Days   Ge unissued
    18598   When The Dew Is On The Rose   Ge rejected
    18599   Gambling Polka Dot Blues -1   Ch 16476
    18600   I Had A Girl   Ge rejected

Rev. Champion 16476 by Kenneth Houchins.

JESS HILLARD

Jesse Hillard, v; acc. own g.
   Richmond, IN   Thursday, April 16, 1931
    17679   Pride Of The Prairie Blues   Ge rejected trial recording

Jess Hillard, v/y-1; acc. own g.
   Richmond, IN   Thursday, May 21, 1931
    17758   The Rambler's Blues -1   Ch 16398, 45091, Spr 2695
    17759   The New River Train   Spr 2805

Superior 2805 as by **Burt Shaw**.

Acc. own g; unknown, g.
   Richmond, IN   Friday, June 19, 1931
    17838-A   Penitentiary Blues -1   Ch R-16368, 45047, Spr 2695

Acc. own g; poss. Jess Johnston, g-2.
   Richmond, IN   Friday, September 11, 1931
    18009-A   A Woman Blues -1, 2   Ch 16347, 45095, MeC 45095
    18010,-A   There's Evil In Your Children   Ge unissued
    18011-A   She's A Hum Dum Dinger   Ch 16445

Rev. Champion 16445 by Duke Clark.

Jess Hillard & His Aces: prob. Jess Johnston, f; poss. Nelson Hillard, md; Jess Hillard, g/calls.
   Richmond, IN   Friday, September 11, 1931
    18012   Cackling Hen   Ch 16333, 45001
    18013   Arkansas Traveler   Ch 16333, 45001, MW 4988

Rev. Montgomery Ward 4988 by Ken, Chuck & Jim (see James Brown, Jr. & Ken Landon Groups).

Jess Hillard, v; acc. poss. Jess Johnston, p-1/g-2; own g-3.
   Richmond, IN   Friday, September 11, 1931
    18014-A   Pea Picking Papa -2, 3   Ch 16347, 45095, MeC 45095, Spr 2733
    18015-A   Don't Let Your Deal Go Down -1   Spr 2760

Superior 2733 as by **Burt Shaw**; 2760 as by **Bert Shaw**. Rev. Superior 2733 by Harry Hillard.

Jess Hillard, v/y; acc. own g; unknown, g.
   Richmond, IN   Friday, November 25, 1931
    18222   Dog Gone Them Blues   Ch R-16368, 45047, Spr 2760

Superior 2760 as by **Bert Shaw**. Matrix 18222 is titled *Doggone Them Blues* on Champion 45047.

Jess Hillard, v; acc. own g.
   Richmond, IN   Thursday, February 25, 1932
    18421   That'll Make A Change In Business   Ge rejected

Jess Hillard, v/y-1; acc. Nelson Hillard, md; own g.
   Richmond, IN   Monday, March 14, 1932
    18447   Ninety-Nine Years   Ch 16398, 45091, Spr 2805
    18449   From Now On Make Your Whoopee At Home -1   Ge rejected

Superior 2805 as **Burt Shaw**. Matrix 18448 is by Nelson Hillard.

Jess Hillard, v/y-1; acc. own g; or **Jess Hillard & Duke Clark**, v duet-2; acc. own g duet; Jess Hillard, y.
   Richmond, IN   Friday, August 26, 1932
    18740   My Time Ain't Long -1   Ch 16491
    18741   I'll Get Mine Bye And Bye -2   Ch 16617
    18742   99 Years Blues   Ch 16617
    18743   Barnyard Stomp -1   Ge rejected

Jess Hillard, v; acc. own g; or **Jess Hillard & Duke Clark**-1, v duet; acc. own g duet.
   Richmond, IN   Saturday, August 27, 1932
    18744   Jesse And Duke's Salty Gob [sic] -1   Ch 16491
    18745   Red Night Gown Blues   Ch 16525

Jess Hillard, v/y-1; acc. own g.
   Richmond, IN   Friday, December 2, 1932
    18922   Little White Washed Chimney At The End   Ge unissued
    18923   Blue Yodel No. 10 -1   Ch 16525

   Richmond, IN   Thursday, January 19, 1933
    18974   Mother, The Queen Of My Heart   Ge rejected
    18975   Mississippi Moon -1   Ch 16564
    18976   Little Whitewashed Chimney At The End   Ch 16564

Jess Hillard, v/y; acc. own g; prob. Duke Clark, g-1.
   Richmond, IN   Wednesday, February 1, 1933
    19000   Barnyard Stomp -1   Ch 16571, 45026
    19001   Seven Years With The Wrong Woman   Ch 16571, 45026

Jess Hillard, v/y-1; acc. own g; prob. Duke Clark, g-2.
   Richmond, IN   Thursday, February 9, 1933
    19009   Don't Forget Me Little Darling   Ge unissued
    19010   Out Of Town Blues -1, 2   Ge rejected
    19011   Walking The Last Mile -1, 2   Ge unissued
    19012   Let Me Be Your Side Track -1, 2   Ge unissued

Jess Hillard's West Va. Hillbillies: prob. Jess Johnston, f; unknown, md; Jess Hillard, g; unknown, g.
   Richmond, IN   Thursday, February 9, 1933
    19013   Spring Heel Hornpipe   Ge unissued

Jess Hillard & His West Va. Hillbillies: Jess Johnston, f; —— Neal, md; Jess Hillard, g.
   Richmond, IN   Friday, July 14, 1933
    19242   Austin Breakdown   Ch S-16651, 45003
    19243   Make Down The Bed And We'll All Sleep Together   Ch S-16651, 45003

Champion 45003 as by **Jess Hillard & His West Virginia Hillbillies**.

Jess Hillard, v; acc. own g.
   Richmond, IN   Friday, July 14, 1933
    19244   Tall Mamma Blues   Ch 16639
    19245   Mother, The Queen Of My Heart   Ch 16639

Jess Hillard & His West Va. Hillbillies: Jess Johnston, f; —— Neal, md; Jess Hillard, g.
   Richmond, IN   Friday, July 14, 1933
    19246   Rollin' River   Ch S-16670
    19247   Dixie Rag   Ch S-16670
    19248   Wild Goose Waltz   Ch S-16638
    19249   Hell Up Flat Rock   Ch S-16638
    19250   Knock Around The Kitchen   Ch 16691

Rev. Champion 16691 by Hoosier Rangers.

NELSON HILLARD

Nelson Hillard, v; acc. unknown, g.
   Richmond, IN   Monday, March 14, 1932
    18448   Don't Let Your Deal Go Down   Ge unissued

ARTHUR HILLMAN

Pseudonym on Australian Golden Tongue for Vernon Dalhart.

BOB HILLMAN

Pseudonym on Australian Regent for Vernon Dalhart.

THE HILLTOPPERS (TOM, DON & ERNIE)

Doyne "Don" Wilson, esg/v; Jimmy Atkins ("Tom Tanner"), g/v; Ernie Newton, sb/v.
Chicago, IL   Friday, November 1, 1935

C-1151-2	Me And My Burro	ARC 6-03-57, Cq 8637
C-1152-1	Mountain Boy	ARC 6-06-54, Cq 8747
C-1155-1	'Tis Sweet To Be Remembered	ARC 6-06-54, Cq 8747
C-1156-1	Following The Stars	ARC 6-03-57, Cq 8637

Intervening matrices are by Christine Smith.

"Wee Wee Three": Doyne "Don" Wilson, esg/v-1; Jimmy Atkins ("Tom Tanner"), g/v-1; Ernie Newton, sb/v-1; unidentified, v solo-2.
Chicago, IL   Thursday, October 8, 1936

C-1537-2	Sing, Sing, Sing (With A Swing) -1	Vo 03356
C-1538-1	Flamin' Mamie -2	Vo 03383
C-1539-1	Organ Grinder's Swing -1	Vo 03356
C-1540-2	My Old Maid (In The Shade Of The Old Apple Tree) -2	Vo 03383
C-1541-1,-2	Take Me Home Boys Tonight -1	ARC unissued

Don Wilson also recorded with Tom Dix as Tom & Don.

MRS. LEON HINKLE

Mrs. Leon Hinkle, v; acc. unknown.
Richmond, IN   Wednesday, July 13, 1932

18588	Face To Face	Ge unissued
18589	Beautiful Isle	Ge unissued
18590	Shepherd Show Me How To Go	Ge unissued
18591	Come Ye Disconsolate	Ge unissued
18592	Homeland	Ge unissued
18593	Gentle Presence	Ge unissued
18594	Saved By Grace	Ge unissued
18595	Sometime We'll Understand	Ge unissued

These recordings were made for Chapel but it is not known if they were issued on that label.

THE HINKY DINKERS

See Bob Miller.

HINSON, PITTS & COLEY

Guy Hinson, g-1/v-2; Jesse D. Pitts, g-3/v-4; David Coley, g-5/v-6.
Charlotte, NC   Monday, January 24, 1938

018612-1	Jealous Lover -1, 3, 4, 5, 6	BB unissued
018613-1	Whoa, Mule, Whoa -1, 2, 3, 5, 6	BB B-7438, RZ MR2793, Twin FT8584
018614-1	Central, Hello -1, 2, 3, 5, 6	BB B-7611
018615-1	Mother And Home- 1?, 2, 3?, 4, 5?	BB unissued
018616-1	In Old Wyoming -3?, 4	BB B-7611
018617-1	Drunkards Warning -3?, 4	BB unissued
018618-1	Spinning Room Blues -3, 5, 6	BB unissued
018619-1	Farmer Grey -1, 3, 5,6	BB B-7438, RZ MR2793, Twin FT8584
018620-1	In The Moonlight -5?, 6	BB unissued
018621-1	Blue Days -1?, 2	BB unissued

Regal-Zonophone MR2793, Twin FT8584 as by **The Rodeo Boys**.
Only two guitars are used on matrix 018615, but it is not known whose.
A Jesse Pitts recorded earlier with Tom Darby.

W.A. HINTON

W.A. Hinton, bj solo.
San Antonio, TX   Saturday, January 31, 1931

| 67129-1 | Little Brown Jug | Vi unissued |
| 67130-1 | Downfall Of Paris | Vi unissued |

| 67131-1 | Leather Britches | Vi 23555 |
| 67132-1 | Shortenin' Bread | Vi unissued |

Rev. Victor 23555 by David McCarn.

HOBBS BROTHERS

Artist credits on several labels imply that these are Elmer and Jud (or Judd) Hobbs, but it is not known who plays which instrument.

Unidentified, f; unidentified, g; unidentified, calls-1.
New York, NY   Wednesday, November 7, 1928

1898-1	Turkey In The Straw -1	Ba S6224, Je 5458, Or 1414
8298-2	Turkey In The Straw -1	Do 4311, Htd 16516, Re 8759, Cq 7332, Pm 3224, Bwy 8165, QRS R.9003, Apex 8918, CrC/MeC 81065, DoC 181065, StgC 281065, MeC/Min M-14015
8299-2	Hell Among The Yearlings	Do 4330, Htd 16516, Cq 7350, Pm 3224, Bwy 8165, QRS R.9003, Apex 8918, CrC/MeC 81065, DoC 181065, StgC 281065, MeC/Min M-14016
1899-3	Hell Among The Yearlings	Ba S6224, Je 5458, Or 1414

Jewel 5458, Homestead 16516 as by **Elmer & Jud**. Paramount 3224 as by **Hobbs Brothers (Elmer & Jud)**. Broadway 8165 as by **Herman Brothers**. Apex 8918, Crown/Melotone 81065, Domino 181065, Melotone/Minerva M-14015, M-14016 as by **Elmer & Judd**. Sterling 281065 as by **The Hayseeds**.

Although the 1898/99 matrices do not appear to be genuine, it seems likely that the recordings bearing them are not from another session but alternative takes of matrices 8298 and 8299 respectively.

New York, NY   Thursday, March 7, 1929

| 8596-2 | Devil's Dream -1 | Ba S6435, Do 4330, Je 5644, Cq 7350, Pm 3219, Bwy 8161, 1762, QRS R.9008, Apex 8959, CrC 81074, DoC 181074, StgC 281074, MeC/Min M-14015, ImpIr A538 |
| 8597-2 | Patty On The Turnpike | Ba S6435, Do 4311, Je 5644, Re 8759, Cq 7332, Pm 3220, Bwy 8161, 1762, QRS R.9008, Apex 8959, CrC 81074, DoC 181074, StgC 281074, MeC/Min M-14016, ImpIr A538 |

Jewel 5644 possibly as by **Elmer & Jud**. Paramount 3220 and probably Paramount 3219, QRS R.9008 as by **Hobbs Brothers (Elmer & Jud)**. Broadway 8161 as by **Herman Brothers**. Apex 8959, Crown 81074, Domino 181074, Melotone/Minerva M-14015, M-14016 as by **Elmer & Judd**. Sterling 281074 credit unknown.
Matrix 8596 is titled *The Devil's Dream* on Imperial A538. Revs: Paramount 3219, 3220 by Claude (C.W.) Davis.

HOBO JIM
"HOBO SAM"

It seems likely that both these pseudonyms cloak the identity of the songwriter Ben Samberg.

Hobo Jim, v; acc. own g.
New York, NY   c. January 5, 1931

| GEX-2864,-A | King Of The Hobos | Ge rejected |
| GEX-2865,-A | Once A Bum Always A Bum | Ge rejected |

"Hobo Sam", v; acc. prob. own h/g.
prob. New York, NY   c. late 1936

| 302-A | Once A Bum, Always A Bum | Novelty 302 |
| 302-B | Horses Work, Not Me! | Novelty 302 |

GEORGE HOBSON

Pseudonym on Silvertone for George Reneau.

HODGERS BROTHERS
HODGERS QUARTET

Hodgers Brothers: prob.: Ernest Hodges, f; Johnny Blainer, tbj; Ralph Hodges, g; poss. others; unidentified, v.
Johnson City, TN   Wednesday, October 17, 1928

| 147216- | Dog-Gone Mule | Co unissued |
| 147217- | What Are You Going To Do With Baby | Co unissued |

Hodgers Quartet: Dick Parman and poss. some of the above, v quartet; acc. unknown.
Johnson City, TN   Wednesday, October 17, 1928

| 147218- | I'll Go Flipping Through The Pearly Gates | Co unissued |
| 147219- | You Can't Make A Monkey Out Of Me | Co unissued |

This group was organized by the father of Ernest and Ralph Hodges.

ALMOTH HODGES
See Bob Miller.

RALPH HODGES & HIS DIXIE VAGABONDS
Red Aldridge, f; Frankie Ray, f; Bob Barker, cl; Ralph Hodges, g/v; Ameril Dobias, sb.
    Chicago, IL   Monday, December 7, 1936

91015-A	Moonlight On The Mountain	De 5309
91016-A	Nobody Cares For Me	De 5351
91017-B	His Last Words (Tell Me Sweetheart That You Love Me)	De 5535, DeSA FM5141

Rev. Decca FM5141 by Jimmy Wakely.

    Chicago, IL   Tuesday, December 8, 1936

91018-A	Roll Along Kentucky Moon	De 5351
91019-	She'll Be There	BrSA SA1256
91020-B	Old Kentucky Dew	De 5309
91021-A	The Pine Tree On The Hill	De 5321, DeAu X1372, BrSA SA1256
91022-A	Mother The Queen Of My Heart	De 5535
91023-A,-B	Poor Lonesome Boy (The Unfaithful Lover)	De unissued
91024-A	Where The Morning Glories Twine Around The Door	De 5321, DeAu X1372

Ralph Hodges is not the artist of that name who recorded with the Hodgers Brothers.

WILLARD HODGIN[S]

Willard Hodgin, v; acc. unknown.
    New York, NY   Monday, January 17, 1927

| 143313- | Echoes From Around The Old Cabin Door | Co unissued |

Acc. own bj.
    New York, NY   Wednesday, May 18, 1927

| E-23227 | Uncle Ned | Br unissued trial recording |
| E-23228 | The Kingdom Comin' | Br unissued trial recording |

Mountain Dew Dare, v/wh; acc. own bj.
    New York, NY   c. Friday, November 18, 1927

| 81831-B | Courtin' The Widow | OK 45170 |
| 81833-B | Don't Love A Smiling Sweetheart | OK 45170 |

Matrix 81832 is untraced.

Willard Hodgin, v; acc. own bj.
    New York, NY   Monday, January 23, 1928

| 18184-B | Don't Love A Smiling Sweetheart | Ed 52204, 5477 |
| 18185-B | Courtin' The Widow | Ed 52204, 5478 |

Banjo Joe, v; acc. own bj; unknown, train-wh eff-1.
    New York, NY   Wednesday, February 29, 1928

| 145696-2 | Engineer Joe | Co 15238-D |
| 145697-2 | I'm Just A Ramblin' Gambler | Co 15238-D |

Willard Hodgin, v; acc. own bj.
    New York, NY   Saturday, March 3, 1928

| 18280-C | The Girl That Lived On Polecat Creek | Ed 52243, 5504 |

    New York, NY   Monday, March 5, 1928

| 18279-B | A Red-Headed Widow Was The Cause Of It All | Ed 52243, 5503 |

Willard Hodgins, v/wh-1; acc. own bj-2/g-3; unknown, train-wh eff-4.
    New York, NY   late March 1928

7869-2	The Engineer's Hand Was On The Throttle -1, 2	Ba 7152, Do 0240, Re 8569, Cq 7178
7870-	I Can Remember The Kind Things Mother Did -2	Ba 7124, Je 5305, Or 1242
7871-2	She Waves As His Train Passes -1, 2, 4	Ba 7124, Do 0240, Je 5305, Re 8569, Cq7178
7872-	Don't You Think Of Sister And Brother -3	Ba 7152, Or 1242

Banner 7124 as by **William** (or poss. **Willard**) **Randolph**, 7152 as by **Willard Randolph**. Jewel 5305, Oriole 1242 as by **Kit Nelson**. Controls are used on Oriole 1242 as follows: 7870 = 1550-4; 7872 = 1562-3.

Willard Hodgin, v; acc. own bj.
    New York, NY   Monday, April 2, 1928

| 18356 | Quit Knockin' On The Jail House Door | Ed 52278, 5518 |

N-160-A,-B	Quit Knockin' On The Jail House Door	Ed unissued
18357	The Judge Done Me Wrong	Ed 52278, 5517
N-161-A,-B	The Judge Done Me Wrong	Ed unissued

Willard Hodgin (Banjo Joe), v; acc. own bj.
Camden, NJ   Monday, May 7, 1928

45013-1,-2,-3	The Girl That Lived On Polecat Creek	Vi unissued
45014-1	A Red-Headed Widow Was The Cause Of it All	Vi 21485
45015-1,-2	Love Is A Ticklish Thing	Vi unissued
45016-1	Don't Get One Woman On Your Mind	Vi 21485

Willard Hodgin, v; acc. own bj.
New York, NY   Monday, May 28, 1928

18540-B	Love Is A Ticklish Thing	Ed 52332, 5570
N-278-A	Love Is A Ticklish Thing	Ed rejected
N-278-B	Love Is A Ticklish Thing	Ed unissued
18541-B	An Ugly Gal's Got Something Hard To Beat	Ed 52332, 5557
N-279-A	An Ugly Gal's Got Something Hard To Beat	Ed unissued
N-279-B	An Ugly Gal's Got Something Hard To Beat	Ed rejected

Acc. unknown.
New York, NY   c. March 5, 1930

| GEX-2620 | I Walk Backwards To Keep From Goin' Straight | Ge rejected |

HOFFNER BROS.

Bluebird B-2575, by Jimmie Revard & His Oklahoma Playboys, was issued thus.

ADOLPH HOFNER

Adolph Hofner & His Texans: Johnny Williams, f; Olan "Smiley" Whitley, esg; Cecil Hogan, eg; Bill Pennington, p; Emil "Bash" Hofner, tbj; Adolph Hofner, g/v-1; Gordon K. "Buck" Wheeler, sb; unidentified, v trio-2.
San Antonio, TX   Tuesday, April 5, 1938

022122-1	Better Quit It Now -1	BB B-7597
022123-1	Someday Soon -1	BB B-7701
022124-1	I Never Felt So Blue -1	BB B-7833
022125-1	Someone Thinks Of Someone -1, 2	BB B-7641
022126-1	How I Miss You Tonight -1	BB B-7597
022127-1	Ride Along -2	BB B-7900
022128-1	Night Time Down South -1	BB B-7833
022129-1	A Hole In The Wall -1	BB B-7641
022130-1	Our Little Romance Is Through -1	BB B-7701
022131-1	Tonight I'm Blue And Lonely -1	BB B-7752, Twin FT8637
022132-1	Come On And Swing Me -1	BB B-7900
022133-1	Brown Eyed Sweet -1	BB B-7752, Twin FT8637

Tom Dickey, f; Beal Ruff, cl; Emil "Bash" Hofner, esg/v-1; Gilbert "Bert" Ferguson, p; Adolph Hofner, g/v; Bill Dickey, sb; unidentified, v trio-2.
San Antonio, TX   Tuesday, October 25, 1938

028581-1	Swing With The Music -1	BB B-7931
028582-1	So Tired Of Waiting	BB B-8030
028583-1	I'll Keep My Old Guitar	BB B-7931, MW M-7669
028584-1	Dreaming	BB B-8071, MW M-7669, RZAu G24043
028585-1	That Honky-Tonky Rhythm	BB B-8071
028586-1	It's Best To Behave	BB B-7955
028587-1	It's All My Fault	BB B-7988, MW M-7671
028588-1	Am I Happy? -2	BB B-7988
028589-1	I Guess You're Laughing Now	BB B-8030
028590-1	Someone Is Alone	BB B-8024, MW M-7671, RZAu G23790
028591-1	That Little Town	BB B-7955, MW M-7670
028592-1	Little Brown-Eyed Lady	BB B-8024, MW M-7670, RZAu G23790

Regal-Zonophone G24043 as by **The Texans**. Rev. Regal-Zonophone G24043 by Tune Wranglers.

Leon Seago, f/emd-1; Johnny Williams or Johnny Rives, f; Emil "Bash" Hofner, esg/v-2; Bert Ferguson, p; Adolph Hofner, g/v-3; Buck Wheeler, sb; poss. Johnny Rives, d-4.
Dallas, TX   Tuesday, February 13, 1940

047671-1	You're Always On My Mind -1, 3, 4	BB B-8628
047672-1	Kitty Clyde	BB unissued
047673-1	Why Should I Cry Over You? -3, 4	BB B-8421, MW M-8696
047674-1	Because I Have Lost You -3, 4	BB B-8421, MW M-8696, RZAu G24304

047675-1	Strashidlo (The Ghost) -2, 3, 4	BB B-8463, MW M-8697
047676-1	Dis Ja Liebe Spim -2, 3	BB B-8463, MW M-8697
047677-1	Joe Turner Blues -1, 4	BB B-8508, MW M-8698
047678-1	Sam, The Old Accordian Man -3, 4	BB B-8508, MW M-8698
047679-1	Maria Elina -3, 4	BB B-8416, MW M-8699, RZAu G24304
047680-1	Spanish Two Step -4	BB B-8416, MW M-8699

Regal-Zonophone G24304 as by **The Texans**. Matrix 047672 is noted in Bluebird files as "broken in transit."
Rev. Bluebird B-8628 by Wade Mainer.

Adolph Hofner & His San Antonians: J.R. Chatwell, f; Johnny Rives, f/d; Emil "Bash" Hofner, esg/etg-1/v-2; Bert Ferguson, p/wh-3; Adolph Hofner, g/v-4/sp-5/calls-6; Buck Wheeler, sb.

Fort Worth, TX   Friday, February 28, 1941

DAL-1195-1	South Texas Swing	OK 06350
DAL-1196-1	Alamo Rag	OK 06139, Co 37656, 20255
DAL-1197-1	Cotton-Eyed Joe -1	OK 06184, Co 37658, 20257
DAL-1198-1	Until We Meet Again -4	OK 06264
DAL-1199-1	Sometimes -1, 2, 4	OK 06614, Co 37415, 20142
DAL-1200-1	Waiting Dear, For You -1, 4	OK 06614, Co 37415, 20142
DAL-1201-1	Jessie Polka	OK 06350, Co 20455
DAL-1202-1	I Was So Happy -1, 4	OK 06264
DAL-1203-1	You Don't Love Me Anymore -1, 4	OK 06492, Co 37433, 20160
DAL-1204-1	Will You Think Of Me -1, 4	OK 06492, Co 37433, 20160
DAL-1205-1	There's A Star In The Heavens -4	OK 06139, Co 37656, 20255
DAL-1206-1	Paul Jones (Arkansas Traveler) -3, 5, 6	OK 06184, Co 37658, 20257

J.R. Chatwell, f-1; Johnny Rives, f-2/d; Walter Kleypas, ac-3/p; Emil "Bash" Hofner, esg-4/eg-5/v-6; Adolph Hofner, g/v-7; Atlee Frazier, sb.

Hollywood, CA   Saturday, February 28-Sunday, March 1, 1942

H-690-1	Sage Brush Shuffle -1, 4	Co 37241, 20100
H-691-1	Tickle Toe -1, 3, 4, 5	Co 20455
H-692-	I Guess You Forgot -1, 4, 5, 7	Co unissued
H-693-	For The One I Love Is You -1, 4, 7	Co unissued
H-694-1	Alamo Steel Serenade -1, 4	Co 37817, 20356
H-695-	Rose Of The Alamo -1, 4, 7	Co unissued
H-696-	Let's Count The Stars Together -1, 4, 7	Co unissued
H-697-1	Sweetheart This Is Goodbye -1, 4, 5, 7	Co 37241, 20100
H-698-1	Swing With The Music -1, 4, 5, 6, 7	Co 37817, 20356
H-699-	With You Still In My Heart -1, 4, 7	Co unissued
H-700-	Training Camp Shuffle -1, 4	Co unissued
H-701-	Dratenik The Tinker Polka -1, 4	Co unissued
H-702-	Red Handkerchief -3, 4, 6, 7	Co unissued
H-703-	Barbara Polka -2, 3, 6, 7	Co 319-F
H-704-	At The Spring -3, 4, 6, 7	Co 319-F
H-705-1	Gulf Coast Special -1, 4	Co unissued: Ep EG37324 (LP)
H-706-	There's A Palace Down In Dallas -1, 2, 4, 7	Co unissued
H-707-1	Farewell To Prague -1, 2, 3, 4, 5, 7	Co 321-F
H-708-1	Svestkova Alej (The Prune Song) -1, 2, 3, 6, 7	Co 321-F
H-709-	Wabash Blues -1, 4	Co unissued

Columbia 319-F, 321-F as by **Adolph Hofner & His Bohemians**.
In Columbia's ledgers several of the above matrices, both issued and unissued, are assigned 1A takes and described as "remakes"; this probably denotes technical rather than actual rerecordings.

Adolph Hofner also recorded with the Tom Dickey Show Boys and Jimmie Revard & His Oklahoma Playboys, and after 1942.

CHARLES HOGG

Charles Hogg, v; acc. unknown.

New York, NY   Tuesday, September 20, 1938

TO-1715	Gold Mine In The Sky	ARC unissued trial recording
TO-1716	Music Maestro Please	ARC unissued trial recording
TO-1717	Cathedral In The Pines	ARC unissued trial recording
TO-1718	Ride Tenderfoot Ride	ARC unissued trial recording

Matrix TO-1714 is a *Script Reading Test* by this artist.

ROBERT HOKE & VERNAL WEST

Prob.: Robert Hoke, v/bj; Vernal Vest, v/u; poss. others.

Johnson City, TN   Wednesday, October 17, 1928

| 147222- | In The Shadow Of The Pines | Co unissued |

| 147223- | Bye And Bye You Will Forget Me | Co unissued |

Robert Hoke also recorded with Roy Harvey, and Vernal Vest with Fred Pendleton.

REV. WALT HOLCOMB, D.D.

Sermons; acc. unknown, p
   Atlanta, GA   Wednesday, August 8, 1928

402101-	[unknown title]	OK unissued
402102-A	House of Prayer	OK 45262
402103-A	Safety First	OK 45262
402104-	Hearts Aglow	OK unissued

E.B. HOLDEN QUARTET

Vocal quartet; acc. Hovah Grissom, p.
   Richmond, IN   Wednesday, March 5, 1930

16351,-A	Led By The Lord Of All	Ge rejected
16352	He Keeps My Soul	Ge rejected
16353	The Master Needs You	Ge rejected
16354	I'm Only On A Visit Here	Ge rejected

GEORGE HOLDEN

Pseudonym on Challenge for John McGhee.

THE HOLINESS SINGERS

No details.
   Johnson City, TN   Thursday, October 18, 1928

| 147238- | Mother Dear Has Gone Away | Co unissued |
| 147239- | Mother Is Gone | Co unissued |

DR. D.D. HOLLIS

Dr. D. Dix Hollis, f solo.
   New York, NY   c. June 1924

1790-1	Turkey In De Straw	Pm 33153
1791-1	Walking In The Parlor	Pm 33153
1795-1	None Greater Than Lincoln	Pm unissued: *Doc DOCD-8032 (CD)*
1796-1	Lone Indian	Pm unissued: *Doc DOCD-8032 (CD)*
1797-1	Dixie And Yankee Doodle	Sil 3513
1798-1	The Girl Slipped Down	Sil 3513
1799-1	Glory On The Big String	Pm unissued: *Doc DOCD-8032 (CD)*
1800-1	Whistlebee	Pm unissued: *Doc DOCD-8032 (CD)*

Intervening matrices are untraced but are likely to be by this artist.

HOLLYWOOD HILLBILLY ORCHESTRA

Three unknowns, f; unknown, c; three unknowns, s; unknown, sg; unknown, p; unknown, g; unknown, sb; unknown, d; unknown, marimba; Chuck Cook, Tom Murray, v duet.
   Hollywood, CA   Saturday, July 26, 1930

| 61001-3 | Mellow Mountain Moon | Vi 22503, Au 203 |
| 61002-3 | When The Bloom Is On The Sage | Vi 22503, Au 203 |

Aurora 203 as by **Mountain Hillbilly Orchestra**.

Chuck Cook and Tom Murray also recorded on their own as **Tom & Chuck**, and with The Beverly Hill Billies.

HOLMAN & ROBINSON

Vocal duet; acc. Mrs. W.E. Robinson, p.
   Atlanta, GA   Friday, November 29, 1929

| 56629- | Take Time To Be Holy | TT C-1565, Au 36-117 |
| 56630-1 | Nailed To The Cross | TT C-1565, Au 36-117 |

FERN HOLMES

Pseudonym on Silvertone for Vernon Dalhart.

[MR. & MRS.] GEORGE HOLMES

Pseudonym on Superior for [Mr. & Mrs.] W.C. Childers.

SALTY HOLMES

See Prairie Ramblers.

HOLMES & TAYLOR

Pseudonym on Superior for W.C. Childers & Clyde G. White.

REV. CALBERT HOLSTEIN & SISTER BILLIE HOLSTEIN

Rev. Calbert Holstein, Sister Billie Holstein, v duet; acc. prob. one of them, g.
   Ashland, KY   c. mid-February 1928

AL-299/300*	Zions Hill	Br 246
AL-301*/02	Garden Of My Heart	Br 246
AL-303*/04	Yes I Know	Br 270
AL-305*/06	Ring The Bells Of Freedom	Br 270

HOME FOLK FIDDLERS
HOME FOLKS

See Small Town Players.

THE HOME TOWN BOYS

Bill Helms, f/v-1; Gid Tanner, bj/v-2; Riley Puckett, g/v-3.
   Atlanta, GA   Monday, October 26, 1931

151942-1	Raccoon On A Rail	Co 15762-D
151943-1	Home Town Rag	Co 15762-D
151944-1	Still Write Your Name In The Sand -1, 3	Co 15736-D
151945-1	Still Got 99 -1, 2, 3	Co 15736-D

STEVE HOMESLEY & HIS ALABAMA BOYS

No details.
   Atlanta, GA   Wednesday, April 18, 1928

146136-	Old Coon	Co unissued
146137-	Mayflowers	Co unissued

HONEY DUKE & HIS UKE

Pseudonym, on various labels, for Johnny Marvin.

HONEYBOY & SASSAFRAS[S]

Honeyboy & Sassafrass: George Fields, v/poss. sp; ——— Welsh, v/poss. sp; acc. unknown.
   Dallas, TX   Sunday, December 9, 1928

147616-	Crow [sic] Dad Song	Co unissued
147617-	Counting The Fords Pass By	Co unissued

Honeyboy & Sassafrass (Fields & Welsh): George Fields, v/sp; ——— Welsh, v/sp; acc. unknown, g.
   Dallas, TX   Sunday, October 27, 1929

DAL-539-	Krawdad [sic] Song	Br 417
DAL-540-	The Lighthouse Song	Br 417

Honeyboy & Sassafras (Fields & Welsh): George Fields, v/sp; ——— Welsh, v/sp; acc. poss. Daniel H. Williams, f-1; unknown, h-2; unknown, g; poss. Henry Bogan, vc-3; band sp-4.
   Dallas, TX   Friday, November 28, 1930

DAL-6757-	The Chicken Sermon -1, 3, 4	Br 509
DAL-6758-	The Hard Luck Boy	Br rejected
DAL-6761-A	Some Family -2	Br 585
DAL-6762-A	Preacher And The Bear	Br 585
DAL-6763-	The Cafe Song	Br rejected
DAL-6764-	She's My Honey Bee	Br 509

Matrices DAL-6759/60 are by Texas High Flyers (see The Hi-Flyers).

HONOLULU STROLLERS

It seems almost certain that the two groups who used this name are not associated.

Unknown, sg; unknown, g; unknown, u; unknown, v trio; unknown, y-1.
   San Antonio, TX   Wednesday, March 7, 1928

400410-A	My Wild Irish Rose	OK 45226, PaE E3570, PaAu A2636
400411-B	Mighty Lak A Rose -1	OK 45239, PaE E6255, PaAu A2554
400412-B	Red Wing	PaAu A2554
400413-B	Old Oaken Bucket	OK 45226, PaE E3570
400415-A	My Isle Of Golden Dreams	OK 45239

Matrix 400414, blank in OKeh files, may also be by this group.
Revs: Parlophone A2636 by Kalama's Quartette (Hawaiian), E6255 by Frank Luther (see Carson Robison).

Sweeny Prosser, sg; unknown, bj; unknown, g; unknown, u; unknown, v-1.
    Charlotte, NC   Friday, May 22, 1931
    69335-1   Don't Say No -1   Vi 23600, HMVIn N4204
    69336-1   Hula Nights   Vi 23600, ZoSA 4369, HMVIn N4204
Rev. Zonophone 4369 by Walter Kolomoku's Honoluluans.

ADELYNE HOOD

Adelyne Hood, v; acc. Vernon Dalhart, h/v-1; own p; Carson Robison, g/v-2.
    New York, NY   Tuesday, October 18, 1927
    40188-1,-2,-3   Old Plantation Melodies -1, 2   Vi unissued
    40189-1,-2,-3   Alligator Song   Vi unissued

Adelyne Hood & Vernon Dalhart: Adelyne Hood, v/sp; Vernon Dalhart, sp; acc. prob. Ross Gorman, bscl; unknown, bj; unknown, g.
    New York, NY   Thursday, December 26, 1929
    149618-3   Calamity Jane (From The West)   Co 2102-D, CoAu 01929, CoJ J932
Revs: Columbia 2102-D, 01929, J932 by Vernon Dalhart.

Vernon Dalhart–Adelyn Hood: Vernon Dalhart, v-1/sp-2; Adelyne Hood, v/sp-3; acc. Adelyne Hood, f-4; Ross Gorman, bscl; Roy Smeck, bj; Joe Biondi, g.
    New York, NY   Monday, January 20, 1930
    58396-1   Calamity Jane -2, 3   Vi V-40224
    58937-2   Hallelujah, There's A Rainbow In The Sky -1, 4   Vi V-40227
For matrices 58398/99 see Vernon Dalhart.
Revs: Victor V-40224, V-40227 by Vernon Dalhart.

Adelyne Hood, v; acc. prob. Ross Gorman, bscl; poss. Roy Smeck, bj; unknown, g; John I. White, sp.
    New York, NY   Wednesday, February 5, 1930
    9340-2   Calamity Jane   Ba 0645, Ca 0245, Do 4510, Je 5900, Or 1900,
                                                                           Pe 12594, Re 8955, Ro 1261, Cq 7500,
                                                                           Summit Z116, Lyric 3400

Summit Z116 as by **Adele Coomber**.
Revs: Domino 4510, Perfect 12594, Regal 8955, Conqueror 7500, Lyric 3400 by Chick Bullock (popular); Summit Z116 by Gunboat Billy & The Sparrow (Arthur Fields & Fred Hall); others by Murray & Scanlan (popular).

Adelyne Hood, v/sp; acc. unknown, f; prob. Ross Gorman or Frank Novak, bscl; unknown, p; poss. Vernon Dalhart, sp; unknown, telephone eff-1.
    New York, NY   Wednesday, February 26, 1930
    150018-1   Madam Queen-1   Ve 7067-V, Di 6041-G, Cl 5171-C
    New York, NY   Thursday, February 27, 1930
    150025-2   He's On The Chain Gang Now   Ve 7067-V, Di 6041-G, Cl 5172-C

Acc. unknown (prob. similar to March 26, 1930 session).
    New York, NY   Wednesday, March 5, 1930
    9409-   He's On The Chain Gang Now   ARC unissued
    9413-   Madam Queen   ARC unissued
Intervening matrices are by popular artists.

Acc. unknown, f; prob. Ross Gorman or Frank Novak, bscl-1; unknown, p; unknown, g; prob. Vernon Dalhart, sp.
    New York, NY   Thursday, March 6, 1930
    150070-3   Madam Queen   Co 2158-D
    150071-3   He's On The Chain Gang Now -1   Co 2158-D

Acc. unknown, f; prob. Ross Gorman or Frank Novak, bscl; unknown, p; unknown, g; unknown man (not Vernon Dalhart), sp.
    New York, NY   Wednesday, March 26, 1930
    9409-5,-6   He's On The Chain Gang Now   Ba 0682, Ca 0282, Chg 884, Do 454-, Je 5935,
                                                                           Or 1935, Pe 12606, Re 8993, Ro 1298
    9413-   Madam Queen   ?Ba 0677, ?Ca 0277, Do 454-, Je 5930, Or 1930,
                                                                           Pe 12606, Re 8993, Ro 12--
Revs: all issues of matrix 9409 except Domino 454-, Perfect 12606, Regal 8993 by John I. White; all issues of matrix 9413 except Domino 454-, Perfect 12606, Regal 8993 by The Radio Imps (popular).

Acc. unknown.
    New York, NY   Thursday, March 27, 1930
    150126-2   I'm The Lady That's Known As Lou   Ve 7074-V, Di 6048-G, Cl 5171-C
    New York, NY   Friday, March 28, 1930
    150142-   The Day Has Come   Ve 7074-V, Di 6048-G, Cl 5173-C

Edie Clark, v; acc. unknown.
New York, NY   c. April 1930
    4011-B   Calamity Jane   GG/Rad 4308, VD 74308

This is not confirmed as an Adelyne Hood item. The artist credit is taken from Van Dyke 74308; it is not known if Grey Gull/Radiex 4308 use the same credit. Rev. all issues popular.

Adelyne Hood, v; acc. unknown, f-1; prob. Ross Gorman or Frank Novak, bscl-2; poss. Roy Smeck, bj-3/u-4; unknown, g; several unknowns, sp; unknown, sound-eff.
New York, NY   Thursday, May 15, 1930
    150425-3   Clementine (The Bargain Queen) -2, 3, 4   Ve 7080-V, Di 6054-G, Cl 5173-C
    150426-2   Song Of The Old Ding Dong -1   Ve 7080-V, Di 6054-G, Cl 5172-C

Betsy White, v; acc. unknown.
New York, NY   Wednesday, June 4, 1930
    9783-2   I'm The Lady That's Known As Lou   Ro 1412, Htd 16148

New York, NY   Wednesday, July 16, 1930
    9872-1   Clementine The Bargain Queen   Ro 1412, Htd 16148

Adelyne Hood, v; acc. prob. Ross Gorman or Frank Novak, bscl; poss. Roy Smeck, bj; unknown, g; Vernon Dalhart, other unknown men, sp-1.
New York, NY   Tuesday, October 28, 1930
    150905-2   Westward Ho For Reno   Ve 2350-V, Cl 5284-C
    150906-2   The Daughter Of Calamity Jane -1   Ve 2350-V, Cl 5284-C

Adelyne Hood also recorded in duet with Vernon Dalhart, in trio with Dalhart and Carson Robison (see Vernon Dalhart), with Arthur Fields & Fred Hall, and as Betsy White on NBC Thesaurus transcriptions.

ALEX HOOD & HIS RAILROAD BOYS

Emory Mills, f; John Walker, md; Alex Hood, bj/sp-1; Bert Earls, g; Clyde Whittaker, g; Bill Brown, sp.
Knoxville, TN   Tuesday, April 8, 1930
    K-8108-   L. And N. Rag -1   Vo 5463
    K-8109-   Corbin Slide   Vo 5463

HOOSIER DUO

Vocal duet; acc. unknown, p.
Richmond, IN   Saturday, December 26, 1931
    18280   The Sweetest Story Ever Told   Ge rejected
    18281   The Church By The Side Of The Road   Ge rejected

THE HOOSIER HAWAIIANS

McNew & Wright (Hoosier Hawaiians): prob.: A.J. McNew, g/v; Lloyd Wright, g/v; unknown, g.
Richmond, IN   Friday, July 31, 1931
    17904   Utah Trail   Ge rejected trial recording

The Hoosier Hawaiians: A.J. McNew, sg; Lloyd Wright, sg; unknown, g; poss. another unknown, g; poss. Harry Hillard, unknown, v duet.
Richmond, IN   Monday, September 28, 1931
    18057-A   The Utah Trail   Ch 16336, Spr 2740, MW 4956
    18058   When The Bloom Is On The Sage   Ch 16336, Spr 2740, MW 4956

Superior 2740 as by **Weber & Brooks**. Montgomery Ward 4956 as by **Wright & McNew**.

Prob.: unidentified, v or v duet; acc. unidentified, g.
Richmond, IN   Friday, February 12, 1932
    18397   My Rose Of Tennessee   Ge rejected

The Hoosier Hawaiians also accompanied Monie Chasteen and Harry Hillard. See also Lloyd Wright.

HOOSIER HOT SHOTS

Otto "Gabe" Ward, cl/v; Ken Trietsch, g/v; Frank Kettering, sb/v; Paul "Hezzie" Trietsch, wb/perc/sw/motor horn/v. Throughout this entry, the spoken introductions that occur on most items are by Ken and Hezzie Trietsch and sometimes other members.
Chicago, IL   Tuesday, November 13, 1934
    C-826-2   Sentimental Gentleman From Georgia   Ba 33403, Me M13370, Or 8455, Pe 13133,
                                                                                   Ro 5455, Vo/OK 03726, Cq 8494, Rex 8745,
                                                                                   ImpSd 17031
    C-827-2   Hoosier Stomp   Ba 33358, Me M13325, Or 8437, Pe 13117,
                                                                                   Ro 5437, Vo/OK 03725, Cq 8480, Co 37713,
                                                                                   20290

C-828-2	Yes She Do – No She Don't	Ba 33420, Me M13387, Or 8464, Pe 13138, Ro 5464, Vo/OK 03727, Cq 8513
C-829-1	Whistlin' Joe From Ko Ko Mo	Ba 33312, Me M13279, Or 8418, Pe 13102, Ro 5418, Vo/OK 03724, Cq 8445
C-830-2	Four Thousand Years Ago	Ba 33312, Me M13279, Or 8418, Pe 13102, Ro 5418, Vo/OK 03724, Cq 8445
C-831-1	Farmer Gray	Ba 33403, Me M13370, Or 8455, Pe 13133, Ro 5455, Vo/OK 03726, Cq 8494
C-832-1	Oakville Twister	Ba 33358, Me M13325, Or 8437, Pe 13117, Ro 5437, Vo/OK 03725, Cq 8480, Co 37713, 20290
C-833-2	I'm Looking For A Girl	Ba 33420, Me M13387, Or 8464, Pe 13138, Ro 5464, Vo/OK 03727, Cq 8513

Imperial 17031 possibly as by **America's Hill-Billy Aces, The Original Hoosier Hot Shots**.

Gabe Ward, cl/v-1; Ken Trietsch, g/lv-2/v-1; Frank Kettering, sb/v-1; Paul "Hezzie" Trietsch, wb/perc/sw/motor horn/v-1.

Chicago, IL   Friday, June 14, 1935

C-1000-A	You May Belong To Somebody Else, But I Love You Just The Same -1?	ARC unissued
C-1001-B	Black Eyed Susan Brown -1	ARC 5-12-55, Vo/OK 03730, Co 37714, 20291, MeC 41255
C-1002-A	This Is The Chorus -1, 2	ARC 350914, Vo 03728, Cq 8665
C-1003-B	Down In The Valley -1	ARC 35-10-30, Vo/OK 03729, Cq 8555
C-1004-B	Ha-Cha-Nan (The Daughter Of San) -1, 2	ARC 350914, Vo 03728, Cq 8601
C-1005-A	Shake Your Feet	ARC unissued
C-1006-A	Meet Me By The Ice House Lizzie -1	ARC 35-10-30, Vo/OK 03729, Cq 8555, Rex 8745, ImpSd 17031
C-1007-A	Back In Indiana -1	ARC 5-12-55, Vo/OK 03730, Co 37714, 20291, MeC 41255

Imperial 17031 possibly as by **America's Hill-Billy Aces, The Original Hoosier Hot Shots**.

Gabe Ward, cl/v; Ken Trietsch, g/v; Frank Kettering, sb/v; Paul "Hezzie" Trietsch, wb/perc/sw/motor horn/v.

Chicago, IL   Monday, October 28, 1935

C-1111-1	Limehouse Blues	Vo 05013, Cq 8601
C-1112-	I Can't Give You Anything But Love	Cq 8592
C-1113-2	San	ARC 6-02-62, Vo/OK 03731, Cq 8645, Rex 8744, ImpSd 17030
C-1114-1	Everybody Stomp	ARC 7-04-62, Vo/OK 03742, Cq 8803, Co 37716, 20293
C-1115-2	Bow Wow Blues	ARC 6-05-57, Vo/OK 03733, Cq 8645
C-1116-2	Them Hill-Billies Are Mountain-Williams Now	ARC 6-06-62, Vo/OK 03731, Cq 8635, Rex 8744, ImpSd 17030
C-1117-1	Virginia Blues	Vo 03949

Imperial 17030 possibly as by **America's Hill-Billy Aces, The Original Hoosier Hot Shots**.

Gabe Ward, cl/v; Ken Trietsch, g/v; Frank Kettering, sb/v; Paul "Hezzie" Trietsch, wb/perc/sw/motor horn/v; Uncle Ezra (Patrick Barrett), v-1.

Chicago, IL   Saturday, November 2, 1935

C-1163-1	I Like Bananas, Because They Have No Bones	ARC 6-04-58, Vo/OK 03732, Cq 8592, Rex 8797
C-1164-1,-2	Jam Making Time	ARC unissued
C-1165-2	Ida! (Sweet As Apple Cider)	ARC 6-04-58, Vo/OK 03732, Cq 8665
C-1166-1	Where You Going Honey	ARC 6-09-51, Vo/OK 03735, Cq 8694
C-1167-2	They Go Wild, Simply Wild Over Me -1	Cq 8615
C-1168-1	At The Old Maids Ball -1	Cq 8615

Conqueror 8615 as by **Uncle Ezra & The Hoosier Hot Shots**.
According to Art Satherley's files, Ken Trietsch is absent on matrix C-1164.

Gabe Ward, cl/lv-1/v-2; Ken Trietsch, g/lv-3/v-2; Frank Kettering, sb/v-2; Paul "Hezzie" Trietsch, wb/perc/sw/motor horn/jh-4/v-2.

Chicago, IL   Wednesday, February 26, 1936

C-1281-1	Wah-Hoo!	ARC 6-06-57, Vo/OK 03733, Cq 8635, Rex 8797
C-1282-1	At The Darktown Strutters' Ball -2, 3	ARC 6-07-53, Vo/OK 03734, Cq 8661
C-1283-1	Nobody's Sweetheart -2, 3	ARC 6-07-53, Vo/OK 03734, Cq 8694, Rex 8835
C-1284-1,-2	Stay Out Of The South -2?	ARC unissued
C-1285-2	I Like Mountain Music -1, 2, 4	ARC 8-01-55, Vo/OK 03853, Cq 8965, Co 37717, 20294, CoC C978

| C-1286-2 | You're Driving Me Crazy (What Did I Do) -2 | ARC 7-01-68, Vo/OK 03739, Cq 8661, Co 20632, CoC C1403, Co-Lucky 60230, LX-6 |

Each member of the group takes the lead vocal in turn, and one yodels, on matrix C-1281.

Chicago, IL Monday, March 30, 1936

| C-1335-1 | Hold 'Er Eb'ner -2?, 3? | ARC 6-11-67, Vo/OK 03737, Cq 8717 |

Gabe Ward, cl/lv-1/v-2; Ken Trietsch, g/v-2; Frank Kettering, sb/v-2; Paul "Hezzie" Trietsch, wb/perc/sw/motor horn/v-2.

Chicago, IL Monday, June 15, 1936

C-1401-1	Take Me Out To The Ball Game -2	ARC 6-10-51, Vo/OK 03736, Cq 8745, Co 20432, CoC C1092
C-1402-2	Bye Bye Blues -2	ARC 6-10-51, Vo/OK 03736, Cq 8745, Co 20432, CoC C1092
C-1403-1,-2	Somebody Loves Me -2?	ARC unissued
C-1404-2	I'll Soon Be Rolling Home -2	ARC 7-02-51, Vo/OK 03740, CoC C501
C-1405-1	Ain't She Sweet -2	ARC 7-08-51, Vo/OK 03745
C-1406-1	Is It True What They Say About Dixie? -2	ARC 6-09-51, Vo/OK 03735, Rex 8835
C-1407-1	I Wish I Could Shimmy Like My Sister Kate -2	ARC 7-09-61, Vo/OK 03644, Cq 8886
C-1408-2	It Ain't Nobody's Biz'ness What I Do -1, 2	ARC 8-02-56, Vo/OK 03901
C-1409-2	No More -2	ARC 8-02-56, Vo/OK 03901
C-1410-1	Some Of These Days	ARC 6-11-67, Vo/OK 03737, Cq 8717

Matrix C-1404 was scheduled for OKeh 05895, but this was not released.

Chicago, IL Monday, August 3, 1936

| C-1444-1,-2,-3 | Ah Woo! Ah Woo! To You -2? | ARC unissued |

Chicago, IL Monday, October 5, 1936

C-1518-2	That's What I Learned In College -2	ARC 6-12-72, Vo/OK 03738, Cq 8743
C-1519-1	Margie -2	ARC 7-03-63, Vo/OK 03741, Cq 8792, Co 37715, 20292
C-1520-1	Alexander's Ragtime Band -2	ARC 7-03-63, Vo/OK 03741, Cq 8792, Co 37715, 20292
C-1521-1	Hot Lips -2	ARC 7-06-60, Vo/OK 03744
C-1522-1	Shake Your Dogs	ARC 6-12-72, Vo/OK 03738, Cq 8743
C-1523-2	Sweet Sue – Just You -2	ARC 7-06-60, Vo/OK 03744, Cq 9169
C-1524-1	Toot, Toot, Tootsie, Goo'bye -1, 2	ARC 7-01-68, Vo/OK 03739, CoC C1403, Co-Lucky 60230

Matrix C-1523 on Columbia CK52735, reportedly take 1, is identical to the issued take 2.
Rev. Conqueror 9169 by Bob Wills.

Chicago, IL Tuesday, November 17, 1936

| C-1679-3 | Jingle Bells -2 | ARC 7-02-51, Vo/OK 03740, Cq 9248, CoC C501, Co-Lucky LX-6 |

Matrix C-1679 was scheduled for OKeh 05895, but this was not released.

Chicago, IL Friday, November 20, 1936

| C-1679-4 | Jingle Bells -2 | ARC unissued |

Chicago, IL Friday, November 27, 1936

| TI-35 | Pick That Bass | ARC unissued trial recording |

Chicago, IL Wednesday, January 20, 1937

C-1755-2	Pick That Bass -2	ARC 7-04-62, Vo/OK 03742, Cq 8803, Co 37716, 20293
C-1756-1,-2	Indiana -2?	ARC unissued
C-1757-1	I Ain't Got Nobody (And Nobody Cares For Me) -2	Vo/OK 03949
C-1758-1	The Coat And Pants Do All The Work -2	ARC unissued: Co CK52735 (CD)
C-1758-2	The Coat And Pants Do All The Work (And The Vest Gets All The Gravy) -2	ARC 7-05-51, Vo/OK 03743, Cq 8810
C-1759-1,-2	The Kid In The Three Cornered Pants -2?	ARC unissued
C-1760-2	Breezin' Along With The Breeze -2	ARC 7-09-61, Vo/OK 03644, Cq 8886
C-1761-1	I Want A Girl (Just Like The Girl That Married Dear Old Dad) -2	ARC 8-01-55, Vo/OK 03853, Cq 8965, Co 37717, 20294, CoC C978
C-1762-1	I've Got A Bimbo Down On The Bamboo Isle -1?, 2	ARC 7-08-51, Vo/OK 03745, Cq 8900

Chicago, IL Friday, January 29, 1937

| C-1804-1 | Goofus -2 | ARC 7-11-54, Vo/OK 03683, Cq 8900, Co 37710, 20287, CoC C914 |
| C-1805-2 | When You Wore A Tulip (And I Wore A Big Red Rose) -2 | ARC 7-05-51, Vo/OK 03743, Cq 8810 |

| C-1806-2 | Runnin' Wild | ARC 7-11-54, Vo/OK 03683, Co 37710, 20287, CoC C914 |

Gabe Ward, cl/lv-1/v-2; Ken Trietsch, g/v-2; Frank Kettering, bb-3/sb-4/v-2; Paul "Hezzie" Trietsch, wb/perc/sw/motor horn/v-2.

Chicago, IL   Tuesday, February 15, 1938

C-2094-3	Farewell Blues -2, 3	Vo 04024
C-2095-1	Down Home Rag -4	Vo/OK 04090
C-2096-1	Meet Me Tonight In The Cowshed -2, 4	Vo/OK 04090, Cq 9064
C-2097-2	Etiquette Blues -1, 2, 4	Vo 04024
C-2098-	Virginia Blues -2, 4	Vo 03949?

Gabe Ward, cl/v-1; Ken Trietsch, g/v-1; Frank Kettering, sb/v-1; Paul "Hezzie" Trietsch, wb/perc/sw/motor horn/v-1.

Chicago, IL   Friday, June 3, 1938

| C-2250-1 | After You've Gone | Vo/OK 04215 |
| C-2251-1 | Tit Willow -1 | Vo/OK 04481, CoC C296 |

Chicago, IL   Monday, June 6, 1938

C-2272-1	Oh By Jingo! -1	Vo/OK 04614
C-2273-1	You Said Something When You Said Dixie -1	Vo/OK 04215, Cq 9064
C-2274-	How'Ya Gonna Keep 'Em Down On The Farm -1	Vo/OK 04352, Cq 9063
C-2275-1	Red Hot Fannie	Vo/OK 04289
C-2276-1	Swinging With Dora	Vo/OK 04289
C-2277-	Milenberg Joys	Vo/OK 04352, Cq 9063
C-2278-1	Wabash Blues	Vo/OK 04614, Cq 9041
C-2279-1,-2	Rosedale, Everyone's Home Town -1	Vo unissued?

Chicago, IL   Wednesday, September 14, 1938

C-2314-2	The Sheik Of Araby -1	Vo/OK 04481, CoC C296
C-2315-1,-2	Down In Jungle Town	Vo unissued?
C-2316-1	A Hot Dog, A Blanket And You -1	Vo/OK 04426, Cq 9154
C-2317-1,-2	You're A Horse's Neck -1?	Vo unissued
C-2318-1,-2	I'll Make A Ring Around Rosie -1?	Vo unissued
C-2319-1	The Flat Foot Floogee -1	Vo/OK 04426, Cq 9154, 9401

Chicago, IL   Monday, October 24, 1938

| C-2318-4 | I'll Make A Ring Around Rosie -1? | Vo unissued |

Gabe Ward, cl/v; Ken Trietsch, g/v; Frank Kettering, sb/v; Paul "Hezzie" Trietsch, wb/perc/sw/motor horn/v.

Chicago, IL   Friday, October 28, 1938

| C-2368-1 | The Man With The Whiskers | Vo/OK 04502, Cq 9248 |
| C-2369-1 | The Girl Friend Of The Whirling Dervish | Vo/OK 04502, 04571 |

Chicago, IL   Tuesday, November 15, 1938

C-2385-1	When Paw Was Courtin' Maw	Vo/OK 04554, Cq 9191
C-2386-	Toy-Town Jamboree	Vo 04541, 04571
C-2387-1,-2,-3	Ferdinand The Bull	Vo unissued
C-2388-1,-2	Beale Street Mama	Vo unissued

Chicago, IL   Friday, December 2, 1938

| C-2387-4,-5 | Ferdinand The Bull | Vo 04541, Vo/OK 04554, Cq 9191 |

It has been assumed that issues are derived from these rather than earlier takes.

Chicago, IL   Thursday, February 2, 1939

C-2434-2	Where Has My Little Dog Gone?	Vo 04688, Cq 9247
C-2435-	When You're Smiling	Vo 04893
C-2436-2	Like A Monkey Likes Cocoanuts	Vo 04688, Cq 9247
C-2437-1	Moving Day In Jungle Town	Vo/OK 04946
C-2437-2	Moving Day In Jungletown	Vo unissued: Co CK52735, CoE 472203 (CDs)

Matrix C-2436 on Columbia CK52735, 472203, reportedly take 1, is identical to the issued take 2.

Gabe Ward, cl/v-1; Ken Trietsch, g/v-1; Frank Kettering, sb/v-1; Paul "Hezzie" Trietsch, wb/perc/sw/motor horn/v-1; Skip Farrell, v-2.

Chicago, IL   Wednesday, February 8, 1939

C-2473-	Skeedee-Waddle-Dee-Waddle-Do -2	Vo 04893?
C-2474-2	Annabelle -2	Vo/OK 04697
C-2475-	Avalon -2	Vo/OK 04823
C-2476-1	It's A Lonely Trail (When You're Travelin' All Alone) -2	Vo/OK 04697?
C-2477-1	Ever So Quiet -1	Vo unissued?

Matrices C-2475 and C-2477 were scheduled for Vocalion 04808, but this was not released.

Gabe Ward, cl/v; Ken Trietsch, g/v; Frank Kettering, sb/v; Paul "Hezzie" Trietsch, wb/perc/sw/motor horn/v.
   Chicago, IL   Thursday, March 9, 1939

| C-2476-3 | It's A Lonely Trail | Vo 04697? |

   Chicago, IL   Tuesday, March 28, 1939

| C-2473-4 | Skeedee-Waddle-Dee-Waddle-Do | Vo 04893? |
| C-2477-4 | Ever So Quiet | Vo/OK 04824 |

   Chicago, IL   Saturday, April 22, 1939

WC-24599-1	From The Indies To The Andes In His Undies	Vo/OK 04946
WC-24600-2	Three Little Fishes	Vo/OK 04823, Cq 9246
WC-24601-2	Look On The Right Side	Vo 05013
WC-24602-2	Beer Barrel Polka (Roll Out The Barrel)	Vo/OK 04824, Cq 9246, 9402, 9529

Rev. Conqueror 9529 by Globe Trotters (polka band).
   Chicago, IL   Thursday, September 14, 1939

WC-2716-1	The Merry-Go-Round Up	Vo/OK 05119, Cq 9328
WC-2717-1	Willie, Willie, Will You?	Vo/OK 05119, Cq 9328, 9659
WC-2718-1	The Martins And The Coys	Vo/OK 05214
WC-2719-1	Rural Rhythm	Vo/OK 05214, Cq 9659

Gabe Ward, cl/v-1; Ken Trietsch, g/v-1; Frank Kettering, sb/v-1; Paul "Hezzie" Trietsch, wb/perc/sw/motor horn/v-1; Skip Farrell, v-2.
   Chicago, IL   Thursday, September 21, 1939

WC-2747-A	(Ho-dle-ay) Start The Day Right -2	Vo/OK 05145, Cq 9329
WC-2748-A	Are You Havin' Any Fun -2	Vo/OK 05145, Cq 9329
WC-2749-1	Put On Your Old Red Flannels -1	Vo/OK 05132
WC-2750-1	Sam, The College Leader Man -1	Vo/OK 05132

Gabe Ward, cl/v; Ken Trietsch, g/v; Frank Kettering, sb/v; Paul "Hezzie" Trietsch, wb/perc/sw/motor horn/v.
   Chicago, IL   Friday, December 8, 1939

WC-2838-A	The Pants That My Pappy Gave To Me	Vo/OK 05485, Cq 9657
WC-2839-A	He'd Have To Get Under, Get Out And Get Under	Vo/OK 05345, Cq 9396
WC-2840-A	Oh! You Beautiful Doll	Vo/OK 05345, Cq 9396
WC-2841-A	Okay Baby	OK 05809

Gabe Ward, cl/v-1; Ken Trietsch, g/v-1; Frank Kettering, sb/v-1; Paul "Hezzie" Trietsch, wb/perc/sw/motor horn/v-1; Skip Farrell, v-2.
   Chicago, IL   Tuesday, December 12, 1939

WC-2854-A	Careless -2	Vo/OK 05295, Cq 9399
WC-2855-A	In An Old Dutch Garden (By An Old Dutch Mill) -2	Vo/OK 05295, Cq 9399
WC-2856-A	There Are Just Two I's In Dixie -1	Vo unissued
WC-2857-A	Connie's Got Connections In Connecticut -1	Vo/OK 05437

Gabe Ward, cl/v-1; Ken Trietsch, g/v-1; Frank Kettering, sb/v-1; Paul "Hezzie" Trietsch, wb/perc/sw/motor horn/v-1; unknown, vb; Skip Farrell, v-2.
   Chicago, IL   Tuesday, January 9, 1940

WC-2858-A	Everything I Do, I Sure Do Good -2	Vo/OK 05584, Cq 9582
WC-2859-A	What Is So Rare -2	Vo/OK 05485
WC-2860-A	I Don't Care (Life's A Jamboree) -2	Vo/OK 05584, Cq 9582
WC-2861-A	Shirley -1	OK 05622

Gabe Ward, cl/v; Ken Trietsch, g/v; Frank Kettering, sb/v; Paul "Hezzie" Trietsch, wb/perc/sw/motor horn/v.
   Chicago, IL   Monday, January 29, 1940

WC-2908-A	Ma, She's Making Eyes At Me	Vo/OK 05390, Cq 9395
WC-2909-A	Big Noise From Kokomo	OK 05754, Cq 9584, CoC C87
WC-2910-A	Swanee	Vo/OK 05437
WC-2911-A	I'm Just Wild About Harry	Vo/OK 05390, Cq 9395

   Chicago, IL   Thursday, April 11, 1940

WC-3024-A	Who's Sorry Now?	OK 05745, Cq 9398, 9402, CoC C87
WC-3025-A	No, No Nora	Vo/OK 05547, Cq 9398
WC-3026-A	(Down By The) O-H-I-O	Vo/OK 05547, Cq 9397, 9581
WC-3027-A	Phil The Fluter's Ball	OK 05622, Cq 9397, 9658

   Chicago, IL   Friday, June 14, 1940

WC-3122-A	My Wife Is On A Diet	Cq 9583, CoC C67
WC-3123-A	Diga Diga Do	OK 05665, CoC C48
WC-3124-A	Poor Papa (He's Got Nothing At All)	Cq 9583, CoC C67
WC-3125-A	The Kitten With The Big Green Eyes	OK 05665, CoC C48

Chicago, IL   Tuesday, August 6, 1940
WC-3219-A   Everybody Loves My Baby (But My Baby Don't   OK 06017
             Love Nobody But Me)
WC-3220-A   The Guy Who Stole My Wife   OK 06217, Cq 9917
WC-3221-A   The Poor Little Country Maid   OK 05809, Cq 9584
WC-3222-A   Tiger Rag   OK 06017, Cq 9917, CoC C231

Chicago, IL   Wednesday, October 2, 1940
WC-3341-A   Noah's Wife (Lived A Wonderful Life)   OK 05891, CoC C163
WC-3342-A   Way Down In Arkansaw   OK 05891, Cq 9581, CoC C163
WC-3343-A   I Just Wanna Play With You   OK 05942, CoC C188
WC-3344-A   That's Where I Met My Girl   OK 05942, Cq 9658, CoC C188
WC-3345-A   When There's Tears In The Eyes Of A Potato   OK 05853, CoC C187
WC-3346-A   Beatrice Fairfax, Tell Me What To Do   OK 05853, CoC C187
WC-3347-A   How Come You Do Me Like You Do   OK unissued
WC-3348-A   St Louis Blues   OK 06217

Chicago, IL   Tuesday, January 21, or Wednesday, January 22, 1941
C-3543-1   Keep An Eye On Your Heart   OK 06065
C-3544-1   With A Twist Of The Wrist   OK 06065
C-3545-1   Let's Not And Say We Did   OK 06114
C-3546-1   Swing Little Indians Swing   OK 06713, Cq 9657

Chicago, IL   Monday, January 27, 1941
C-3581-1   There'll Be Some Changes Made   OK 06114
C-3582-1   My Bonnie   OK unissued: *Co CK52735, CoE 472203* (CDs)
C-3583-1   Dude Cowboy   OK 06503
C-3584-1   The Streets Of New York   OK 06713

Chicago, IL   Thursday, June 5, 1941
C-3847-1   No Romance In Your Soul   Cq 9918
C-3848-1   Windmill Tillie   OK 06348
C-3849-1   The Band Played On   OK 06273
C-3850-1   Since We Put A Radio Out In The Hen House   OK 06425, Cq 9916, CoC C482
C-3851-1   He's A Hillbilly Gaucho   OK 06348
C-3852-1   Lazy River   Cq 9918

Chicago, IL   Monday, June 9, 1941
C-3861-1   Rhyme Your Sweetheart   OK 06599
C-3862-1   Bull Frog Serenade   OK 06503
C-3863-1   There's A Tavern In The Town   OK unissued
C-3864-1   Blues (My Naughty Sweetie Gives To Me)   OK 06599
C-3865-1   When The Lightning Struck The Coon Creek Party OK 06425, Cq 9916, CoC C482
             Line
C-3866-1   The Hut-Sut Song (A Swedish Serenade)   OK 06273

Chicago, IL   Tuesday, January 20, 1942
C-4155-1   One-Eyed Sam   OK unissued: *Co CK52735, CoE 472203* (CDs)
C-4156-1   She's Got A Great Big Army Of Friends   OK 06613
C-4157-1   Cuddle Up A Little Closer, Lovey Mine   OK unissued
C-4158-1   She Was A Washout In The Blackout   OK 06613
C-4159-1   The Covered Wagon Rolled Right Along   OK unissued
C-4160-1   They Go Googoo, Gaga, Goofy Over Gobs   OK unissued
C-4161-1   My Little Girl   OK unissued
C-4162-1   You'd Be Surprised   OK unissued

The Hoosier Hot Shots recorded after 1942. For earlier recordings by an associated group see Ezra Buzzington's Rustic Revelers.

THE HOOSIER RANGERS

See Clyde Martin & His Hoosier Rangers.

AL HOPKINS [& HIS BUCKLE BUSTERS]

See The Hill Billies.

ANDY HOPKINS

Pseudonym on Supertone for W.C. Childers.

DOC HOPKINS

Doc Hopkins, v; acc. own g.
    Chicago, IL   Friday, July 17, 1931

| TC-7907- | Sweet Betsy From Pike | Me unissued |
| TC-7908- | Sugar Babe | Me unissued |

Although described on the Brunswick session-sheets as test, i.e. trial, recordings, these are also shown as having been designated for the Melotone M12000 series.

Grafton, WI   c. November 1931

L-1218-2	Sugar Babe	Bwy 8306
L-1219-1	Sweet Betsie From Pike	Bwy 8306
L-1220-2	Barbara Allen	Bwy 8307
L-1221-2	The Little Old Log Cabin In The Lane	Bwy 8305
L-1222-2	Gooseberry Pie	Bwy 8307
L-1224-1	Down On The Old Plantation	Bwy 8305

Broadway 8306 shows L-1218 on the label, L-1418 (erroneously) in the wax. Matrix L-1223 is untraced.

Grafton, WI   c. April 1932

L-1461-2	Twenty One Years	Pm 577
L-1462-2	Old Joe Clark	Pm 577
L-1466-2	Little Joe	Bwy 8337
L-1471-1	Methodist Pie	Bwy 8337

Matrices L-1465, L-1468 are by Little Georgie Porgie; other intervening matrices are untraced.

Acc. prob. Slim Miller, f-1; unknown, sg-2; own g; unknown, sb-3.

Chicago, IL   Monday, January 20, 1936

C-1201-1,-2	Old Fiddler Joe -1, 3	ARC unissued
C-1204-1,-2	Ducky Daddy -2	ARC unissued
C-1206-1,-2	Empty Cradle	ARC unissued
C-1207-1	The Range In The Sky	ARC unissued
C-1208-1	Fourteen Little Puppies	ARC unissued
C-1209-1	On The Hills Over There	ARC unissued
C-1210-1	The Old Cross Roads	ARC unissued

Intervening matrices are by Karl & Harty.

No details.

Chicago, IL   Wednesday, March 4, 1936

| C-1289-1,-2 | Nobody's Darling But Mine | ARC unissued |
| C-1290-1,-2 | Cabin Just Over The Hill | ARC unissued |

Acc. own g.

Chicago, IL   Friday, October 9, 1936

C-1546-1	The Church Of Long Ago	Cq 8749
C-1547-1	The Range In The Sky	ARC unissued
C-1548-1	The Plush Covered Album	ARC unissued
C-1549-1	The Pal That Is Always True	Cq 8748
C-1550-1	The Black Sheep	ARC unissued
C-1551-1	Asleep In The Briny Deep	ARC unissued
C-1552-1	Mother The Queen Of My Heart	Cq 8748
C-1553-1	Cabin Just Over The Hill	ARC unissued
C-1554-1	The Great Judgment Morning	Cq 8749

Acc. Karl Davis, md/poss. v; Harty Taylor, g/poss. v; poss. own g.

Chicago, IL   Monday, January 25, 1937

| C-1766-1,-2 | The Old Chain Gang | ARC unissued |
| C-1767-1,-2 | The Hound Dog Blues | ARC unissued |

ARC files assign these items to Karl & Harty, but Art Satherley's ledgers report them as by Doc Hopkins.

Acc. own g.

Chicago, IL   Wednesday, March 5, 1941

93546-A	Bad Companions	De 5983, MeC 45464
93547-A	Wreck Of The Old Thirty-One	De 6039
93548-A	Wreck Between New Hope And Gethsemane	De 6039
93549-A	Kitty Wells	De 5983, MeC 45464
93550-A	Fate Of The Battleship Maine	De 5945
93551-A	My Little Georgia Rose	De 5945

Doc Hopkins recorded after 1942.

DAN HORNSBY

Although some of the items below fall strictly outside the scope of this book, other items and Dan Hornsby's associations with other artists seem to justify an unselective entry.

Dan Hornsby Trio: prob.: Sterling Melvin or Perry Bechtel, sg/v; Taylor Flanagan, p/tv; Dan Hornsby, lv.

Atlanta, GA   Tuesday, November 8, 1927

145168-1	Dear Old Girl	Co 15769-D
145169-	The Banquet In Misery Hall	Co unissued
145170-1	Cubanola Glide	Co 1268-D, ReAu G20240
145171-2	O, Susanna!	Co 1268-D, ReAu G20240

Taylor Flanagan, p/tv; Perry Bechtel, bj/bv; Dan Hornsby, lv.
Atlanta, GA   Friday, April 20, 1928

146165-2	On Mobile Bay	Co 15276-D
146166-2	I Want A Girl (Just Like The Girl That Married Dear Old Dad)	Co 15276-D, CoE 19026, CoAu 01895
146167-	Goodbye Alexander	Co unissued
146168-	Oceana Roll	Co unissued

Rev. Columbia 19026, 01895 by Vernon Dalhart.

Dan Hornsby, v; acc. prob. Clayton McMichen or Bert Layne, f; Riley Puckett, g.
Atlanta, GA   Tuesday, October 23, 1928

| 147270-2 | The Story Of C.S. Carnes | Co 15321-D |
| 147271-2 | The Shelby Disaster | Co 15321-D |

Dan Hornsby Trio: poss. Sterling Melvin, sg/bsv; Perry Bechtel, g/bv; Dan Hornsby, lv.
Atlanta, GA   Thursday, November 1, 1928

| 147373-2 | She Was Bred In Old Kentucky | Co 15381-D |
| 147374-2 | Can't Yo' Heah Me Callin' Caroline | Co 15381-D |

Dan Hornsby Novelty Quartet: poss. Sterling Melvin, sg/bsv; Taylor Flanagan, p/tv; Perry Bechtel, g/bv; Dan Hornsby, lv.
Atlanta, GA   Thursday, November 1, 1928

| 147375-2 | Oh! By Jingo | Co 1637-D, ReAu G20406 |
| 147376-1 | Has Anybody Here Seen Kelly? | Co 1637-D, ReAu G20406 |

Dan Hornsby, v; acc. poss. Sterling Melvin, sg; Taylor Flanagan, p; Perry Bechtel, g.
Atlanta, GA   Thursday, November 1, 1928

| 147377-1 | Just A Baby's Prayer At Twilight | Co 15578-D |
| 147378-1 | I'm Sorry I Made You Cry | Co 15578-D |

Dan Hornsby Novelty Quartet: poss. Sterling Melvin, sg/bsv; Perry Bechtel, g/bv; Dan Hornsby, lv; Taylor Flanagan, tv.
Atlanta, GA   Sunday, April 14, 1929

148276-	The Vamp	Co unissued
148277-1	Take Me Out To The Ball Game	Co 15444-D
148278-2	Hinky Dinky Dee	Co 15444-D

Matrix 148276 is logged as by **Dan Hornsby's Novelty Qt**.

Dan Hornsby Novelty Orchestra: no details.
Atlanta, GA   Wednesday, April 17, 1929

| 148325-2 | All Alone | Co 15769-D |

Dan Hornsby, v; acc. unknown, g.
prob. New York, NY   Friday, December 12, 1930

| 151133-1 | History In A Few Words | Co 15628-D |
| 151134-2 | The Lunatic's Lullaby | Co 15628-D |

Dan Hornsby & His Lion's Den Trio: Dan Hornsby, v; acc. poss. Bob Miller, p-1; prob. Perry Bechtel, g/bv; prob. Taylor Flanagan, tv; prob. Sterling Melvin, bsv.
Atlanta, GA   Tuesday, November 3, 1931

152015-	Katinka	Co unissued
152016-1	A Sailor's Sweetheart	Co 15771-D, ReE MR549, ReAu G21509
152017-1	Three Blind Mice -1	Co 15771-D, ReE MR549, ReAu G21509
152018-	So This Is Venice	Co unissued

Matrices 152015, 152018 are logged as by **Dan Hornsby & Trio**.

Dan Hornsby also recorded with Perry Bechtel, Taylor Flanagan & His Trio, Georgia Organ Grinders, Clayton McMichen (with whom he participated in "rural drama" items as Tom Dorsey), Gid Tanner, and Jess Young's Tennessee Band. He later made children's records for Bluebird as Uncle Ned.

JAMES HORTON & FAMILY

Pseudonym on Superior for the E.R. Nance Family.

HORTON & MOORE

Pseudonym on Broadway for the Carver Boys (8000 series) or Asa Martin & James Roberts (4000 series).

WILLIAM B. HOUCHENS

Wm. B. Houchens, f; acc. Saloma Dunlap, p.

Richmond, IN — Monday, September 18, 1922

11190-C	Arkansaw Traveler	Ge 4974, 3262, Ch 15084, Cd 537, Chg 109, 301, Apex 407
11191	Liverpool Hornpipe; Durang's Hornpipe	Ge 5066, St 9381
11192-B	Turkey In The Straw	Ge 4974, 5240, 3262, Ch 15084, Chg 109, Apex 407

Champion 15084 as by **Uncle Billy Hawkins**. Challenges as by Uncle **Jim Hawkins**.
Gennett 5240 carries a special Christmas Greetings label.
Revs: Gennett 5240 by Kin Hubbard (popular comic); Cardinal 537 by Harry Reser (popular); Challenge 301 by Fiddlin' Sam Long.

Richmond, IN — Monday, February 26, 1923

11326-B	(A) Dance Wid A Gal, Hole In Her Stocking (B) Leather Breeches (C) Big Eared Mule	Ge 5070, Ch 15085, Sil 4005
11327	Devil's Dream; Money Musk	Ge 5066, St 9381
11328-A	(A) Irish Washerwoman (B) Kitty Clyde	Ge 5070, Ch 15085, Sil 4005
11329-A	(A) Bob Walker (B) When You And I Were Young Maggie (C) Collin's Reel	Ge 5516, Cx 40360, Sil 4007
11330-B	(A) College Hornpipe (B) Hel'n Georgia	Ge 5516, Cx 40360, Sil 4007

Champion 15085 as by **Fiddlin' Ike Pate**.

Acc. unknown.

Richmond, IN — Monday, May 28, 1923

11472	Morris Dance	Ge unissued
11473	Torch Dance	Ge unissued
11474	Old Kentucky Home	Ge unissued

Acc. Saloma Dunlap, p-1; unknown, g-2.

Richmond, IN — Monday, September 15, 1924

12014	Wagner -2	Sil 4015
12015	Fisher's Hornpipe And Opera Reel -2	Sil 4056
12016-B	Cincinnati Hornpipe And Devine's Hornpipe -1	Sil 4015
12017	Miller's Reel/Old Sport Reel -1	Sil 4055
12018	Turnpike Reel/Farrell O'Gar's Favorite -1	Sil 4055
12019	Temperance Reel/Reilly's Reel -1, 2	Sil 4056

KENNETH HOUCHINS

Kenneth Houchins, v/y-1; acc. own g.

Richmond, IN — Thursday, July 28, 1932

18613	There's A Good Gal In The Mountains -1	Ch 16473
18614	Fancy Nancy	Ch 16473
18615	Our Old Family Album	Ch S-16695
18616	Puttin' On The Style	Ch 16476
18617	Them Old Hitch Hiking Blues -1	Ch 16619
18618	Bay Rum Blues	Ch 16619
18619	Tennessee Blues	Ch 16501
18620	That Yodeling Gal Of Mine -1	Ch 16501, MW 4971
18621	Do Right Daddy Blues -1	Ch 16484
18622	Low Down Woman Blues -1	Ch 16484
18623	The Fate Of The Lindbergh Baby	Ge unissued

Rev. Champion 16476 by Harry Hillard.

Richmond, IN — Tuesday, January 24, 1933

18980	Mean Old Ball And Chain Blues	Ch 16603
18981	The Yodeling Drifter -1	Ch 16584, MW 4946
18982	Lonesome Downhearted And Blue	Ge rejected
18983	Why Should I Feel So Lonely?	Ch S-16553
18984	Wanderer's Warning	Ch S-16553, MeC 45006
18985	Get Along Little Doggies	Ch 16584
18986	The Prisoner's Child	Ch 16603, MW 4946, MeC 45006

Richmond, IN — Tuesday, July 18, 1933

19257	The Old Missouri Moon -1	Ch 16637
19258	Little Farm House Upon The Hill	Ch 16679
19259	When The Golden Rods Are Waving	Ch S-16650, MW 4971
19260	Little Sweetheart, Little Pal Of Mine -1	Ch S-16695, 45078

19261	I'm Just A Yodeling Rambler -1	Ch 16636
19262	The Wandering Hobo's Song -1	Ch 16636
19263	Back To Old Smoky Mountain -1	Ch S-16650, 45078
19264	Cowboy's Meditation	Ch S-16669, 45028, MW 4972, Min M-14042
19265	Behind These Gray Walls	Ch S-16669, 45028, MW 4972, Min M-14043
19266	Homesick For Heaven	Ch 16679
19267	I've Got These Oklahoma Blues -1	Ge unissued

Revs: Champion 16637 by Buddy DeWitte; Minerva M-14042 by Prairie Serenaders, M-14043 by Asa Martin.

Ken Houchins & Slim Cox, v duet; acc. Slim Cox, f; Ken Houchins, g.
Richmond, IN   Tuesday, April 10, 1934

| 19528 | Down The Old Ohio River Valley | Ch 16755, 45049 |
| 19529 | Louisiana Moon | Ch 16755, 45049 |

Ken Houchins, v; acc. Slim Cox, f-1; own g.
Richmond, IN   Tuesday, April 10, 1934

19530	My Silver Haired Mom	Ch S-16775, 45088, MeC 45088
19531	My Little Ozark Mountain Home	Ch S-16775, 45088, MeC 45088
19532	The Innocent Convict -1	Ge unissued

At least some copies of Melotone 45088 are uncredited.

Ken Houchins & Slim Cox: Slim Cox, f; Kenneth Houchins, g.
Richmond, IN   Tuesday, April 10, 1934

| 19533 | The Deal | Ge rejected |
| 19534 | The Fun's All Over | Ge rejected |

Kenneth Houchins, v/y-1; acc. own g.
Richmond, IN   Monday, June 4, 1934

19591	Blue Ridge Lullaby -1	Ch 16783, 45030, DeAu X1242
19592	The Gangster's Brother	Ch 16807, 45054, MeC 45054
19593	Ramshackled Shack On The Hill -1	Ch 16783, 45030, DeAu X1242
19594	The End Of Memory Lane -1	Ch 16807, 45054, MW 4926, MeC 45054, DeAu X1235
19595	When Jimmie Rodgers Said "Goodbye" -1	Ch 16793, 45062, MW 4926
19596	Good Luck Old Pal -1	Ch 16793, 45062, DeAu X1235

Ken Houchins, v/y-1; acc. own g.
Chicago, IL   Thursday, August 8, 1935

| C-1084-A,-B | Little Old Farm House Upon The Hill | ARC unissued trial recording |
| C-1085-A,-B | That Yodeling Gal Of Mine -1 | ARC unissued trial recording |

H.P. HOUSER

H.P. Houser, v; acc. own g.
Memphis, TN   Monday, May 26, 1930

| Test-325-1 | The Laughing Song | Vi unissued trial recording |
| Test-326-1 | The Second Class Hotel | Vi unissued trial recording |

It is impossible to ascertain the nature of these sides, but they appear to be within the scope of this work.

JOHN & EDDIE HOWARD

Pseudonym on Velvet Tone and Clarion for Charlie & Bud Newman.

JOHN HENRY HOWARD

John Henry Howard, v; acc. own h/g.
Richmond, IN   Wednesday, August 12, 1925

12302	Black Snake	Ge 3124
12303,-A	Round Town Blues	Ge rejected
12304	Do Lord Do Remember Me	Ge 3117
12305	I've Started For The Kingdom	Ge 3117
12306	Gonna Keep My Skillet Good & Greasy	Ge 3124
12307	The Old Grey Goose	Ge rejected
12308	Lonesome Road Blues	Ge rejected
12309	Where Have You Been My Pretty Little Girl	Ge rejected
12310	Little Brown Jug	Ge rejected

LAKE HOWARD

Lake Howard, v; acc. own g.
New York, NY   Tuesday, August 7, 1934

| 15523-1 | Lover's Farewell | Ba 33281, Me M13248, Or 8407, Pe 13091, Ro 5407 |

New York, NY   Thursday, August 9, 1934

15558-2	New Chattanooga Mama	Ba 33145, Me M13112, Or 8371, Pe 13031, Ro 5371
15559-1	Get Your Head In Here	Ba 33145, Me M13112, Or 8371, Pe 13031, Ro 5371
15560-1	Don't Let Your Deal Go Down	Ba 33281, Me M13248, Or 8407, Pe 13091, Ro 5407
15561-2	Chewing Chewing Gum	Ba 33388, Me M13355, Or 8449, Pe 13128, Ro 5449

New York, NY   Friday, August 10, 1934

| 15590-2 | Love Me, Darling, Love Me | Ba 33388, Me M13355, Or 8449, Pe 13128, Ro 5449 |

New York, NY   Monday, April 29, 1935

17402-	I'll Remember Your Love (In My Prayers)	ARC unissued
17404-2	Forsaken Love	ARC 5-11-57
17405-1	I Have No One To Love Me (But The Sailor On The Deep Blue Sea)	Ba 33469, Me M13426, Or 8478, Pe 13151, Ro 5478

Matrix 17403 is by Bill Carlisle.

Lake Howard & Bill Wakefield, v duet; acc. own g duet.

New York, NY   Tuesday, April 30, 1935

| 17410-2 | Walking In The Light (Of The Lord) | ARC 6-01-55 |

Lake Howard, v; acc. own g.

New York, NY   Tuesday, April 30, 1935

17411-2	Streamlined Mama	ARC 350924, Cq 8586, CrC/MeC/Roy/Stg 92086
17414-1	It's None Of Your Business	Ba 33469, Me M13426, Or 8478, Pe 13151, Ro 5478
17416-1	I've Lost My Love	ARC 350924, CrC/MeC/Roy/Stg 92086
17417-2	Little Annie	ARC 5-11-57

Intervening matrices are by Bill Carlisle. Rev. Conqueror 8586 by Elton Britt.

New York, NY   Wednesday, May 1, 1935

17402-	I'll Remember Your Love (In My Prayers)	ARC unissued
17451-	Village By The Sea	ARC unissued
17452-	The Orphan Child	ARC unissued

Lake Howard & Bill Wakefield, v duet; acc. own g duet.

New York, NY   Wednesday, May 1, 1935

| 17453-1 | Within My Father's House | ARC 6-01-55 |

See also Cauley Family.

THE HOWARD BOYS

Pseudonym on Velvet Tone, Clarion, and Australian Regal/Regal Zonophone for the Scottdale String Band.

HOWARD-PEAK (THE BLIND MUSICIANS)

James Howard, f/v; Charles Peak, g/v.

Bristol, TN   Tuesday, October 30, 1928

| 47246-2 | I Cannot Be Your Sweetheart | Vi V-40189 |
| 47247-2 | Three Black Sheep | Vi V-40189 |

J.H. HOWELL

J.H. Howell's Union County Band: "Bootsie", bj/v; Julius H. Howell, g/v.

Charlotte, NC   Saturday, February 20, 1937

| 07208-1 | The Book Of Life | BB unissued |
| 07209-1 | Come Along Little Children | BB unissued |

J.H. Howell, h solo.

Charlotte, NC   Saturday, February 20, 1937

| 07210-1 | Howell's Railroad | BB B-7162 |
| 07211-1 | Lost John | BB B-7162 |

J.H. Howell's Carolina Hillbillies: "Cebe", "Bill", v duet; acc. own g duet.

Charlotte, NC   Saturday, January 29, 1938

018826-1	My Sweetheart Has Gone And Left Me	BB B-7509, MW M-7757
018827-1	Lonesome Life Of Worry	BB B-8236
018828-1	Burning Of Cleveland School	BB B-7509
018829-1	Father Alone	MW M-7757

"Boots", J.H. Howell, v duet; acc. unknown, f; two unknowns, g.
   Charlotte, NC   Saturday, January 29, 1938

| 018830-1 | Girl That Worries My Mind | BB B-8219, MW M-7758 |

"Boots", v; acc. own bj; unknown, g.
   Charlotte, NC   Saturday, January 29, 1938

| 018831-1 | Mollie Married A Travelin' Man | BB B-8219, MW M-7758 |

Unknown, f; two unknowns, g; unknown, hollering; unknown, sp-1.
   Charlotte, NC   Saturday, January 29, 1938

| 018832-1 | Rock City Blues -1 | BB B-8236 |
| 018833-1 | Charlotte Rag | BB destroyed |

ROBERT HOWELL

Pseudonym on Herwin for Holland Puckett.

UNCLE STEVE HUBBARD & HIS BOYS

Pseudonym on Gennett and Herwin for Tommy Dandurand & His Gang.

HUFF'S QUARTETTE

Leonard D. Huffstutler, three unknowns, v quartet; acc. unknown, p.
   Dallas, TX   Sunday, October 27, 1929

DAL-529-	Hail To The King	Vo 5383
DAL-530-	I Found This Love On Calvary	Vo 5383
DAL-531-	I'm Led By Love	Vo 5410
DAL-532-	Wonderful King	Vo 5410

HUGGINS & PHILIPS SACRED HARP SINGERS

Vocal group; unacc.
   Birmingham, AL   Wednesday, November 14, 1928

BIRM-793-	Blooming Youth	Vo 5273
BIRM-794-B,-A	Blooming Youth	Br/Vo unissued
BIRM-795-	Lover Of The Lord	Vo 5273
BIRM-796-B,-A	Murillas [sic] Lesson	Br/Vo unissued
BIRM-797-B,-A	Sherburne	Br/Vo unissued
BIRM-798-B,-A	Jesus Died For Me	Br/Vo unissued
BIRM-799-B,-A	Not Made With Hand	Br/Vo unissued

HUGH & SHUG'S RADIO PALS

See Hugh Cross.

LESLIE HUGHES

Leslie Hughes, v; acc. unknown.
   Atlanta, GA   Monday, November 7, 1927

| 145142- | There Is A New Name Written Down In Glory | Co unissued |
| 145143- | Jesus Is Coming | Co unissued |

DAN HUGHEY

Pseudonym on Champion for Bradley Kincaid.

DAVE HUGHS AND BAND

Dave Hughs, v; acc. own ac; Curly Nichols, g; Ted Walls, sb; Clifford Kendrick, d.
   San Antonio, TX   Monday, April 4, 1938

022080-1	I Ain't Got No Gal	BB B-7789
022081-1	Any Time	BB B-7638
022082-1	When The Circus Came To Town	BB B-7638
022083-1	Tell Me Why	BB B-7831
022084-1	Accordion Joe	BB B-7789
022085-1	End Of The Road	BB B-7831

This band was drawn from the personnel of Bob Skyles & His Skyrockets.

THE HUMBARD FAMILY

Clement Humbard, as-1/esg-2/md-3/v-4; Ruth Humbard, ac/v; Rex Humbard, g/v; Leona Humbard, sb/v-5.
    Saginaw, TX   Tuesday, April 16, 1940

DAL-983-	No Longer Lonely -2, 4, 5	Vo/OK 05562
DAL-984-2	I Love My Savior Too -2, 4, 5	OK 06006
DAL-985-	What A Wonderful Feeling -1, 4, 5	OK 05624
DAL-986-2	The Meeting In The Air -3	OK 05739

Clement Humbard, as-1/md-2/tbj-3/v-4; Ruth Humbard, ac-5/v; Rex Humbard, g/v-6; Leona Humbard, sb/v-7.
    Saginaw, TX   Wednesday, April 17, 1940

DAL-987-2	Christ Is Keeping My Soul -1, 2, 5, 6	OK 06006
DAL-988-2	Heavenly Sunshine -1, 4, 5, 6, 7	OK 05739
DAL-989-	Sweetest Mother -4, 5, 6, 7	Vo/OK 05562
DAL-990-1	Driftwood -2, 6	OK 06055
DAL-991-2	Keep On The Firing Line -1, 3, 5, 7	OK 06055
DAL-992-1	I'll Fly Away -2, 6	OK 05624
DAL-992-2	I'll Fly Away -2, 6	OK unissued: *Co C4K47911 (CD)*

The guitar may not be present on all items.
The Humbard Family recorded after 1942.

HUMPHRIES BROTHERS

Jess Humphries, f; Cecil Humphries, g.
    San Antonio, TX   Tuesday, June 10, 1930

404119-	Ragged Ann Rag	OK 45489
404120-B	Black And White Rag	OK 45464, 16729
404121-B	What Made The Wild Cat Wild	OK 45501
404122-B	St. Louis Tickle	OK 45464, 16729
404123-A,-B	Sweet Bunch Of Daisies	OK 45501
404124-	Good Old Summer Time	OK 45489
404125-A	After The Ball	OK 45478, 16736
404126-A	Over The Waves	OK 45478, 16736

DAVE HUNT

Pseudonym on Champion for Willie Stoneman.

PRINCE ALBERT HUNT

Prince Albert Hunt's Texas Ramblers: Archie "Prince" Albert Hunt, f/v-1; unknown, g.
    San Antonio, TX   Thursday, March 8, 1928

400434-B	Katy On Time	OK 45230
400435-A	Blues In A Bottle -1	OK 45230
400436-A	Traveling Man -1	OK 45446

Harmon Clem & Prince Albert Hunt: Harmon Clem, f; Prince Albert Hunt, g.
    Dallas, TX   Wednesday, June 26, 1929

402726-A	Canada Waltz	OK 45360
402727-A	Oklahoma Rag	OK 45360

Prince Albert Hunt's Texas Ramblers: Prince Albert Hunt, f/sp-1; Harmon Clem, g/poss. sp-1; poss. unknown, g.
    Dallas, TX   Wednesday, June 26, 1929

402728-A	Wake Up Jacob	OK 45375
402729-	Ragtime Annie	OK unissued
402730-B	Waltz Of Roses	OK 45375
402731-A	Houston Slide -1	OK 45446

DALE HUNTER

Dale Hunter, v; acc. unknown.
    Chicago, IL   Friday, January 31, 1936

C-1221-1	The Prisoner's Letter	ARC unissued
C-1222-1	Two-Time Mama Blues	ARC unissued

WALTER HURDT

Walter Hurdt, v/y; acc. prob. own g.
    Charlotte, NC   Friday, February 19, 1937

07176-1	Double Trouble Blues	MW M-7277
07177-1	Goodbye Mama Blues	MW M-7277
07178-1	Engineer Blues	BB unissued

| 07179-1 | Two Timing Mama Blues | MW M-7278 |
| 07180-1 | Traveling Along Blues | MW M-7278 |

Walter Hurdt, Cliff Carlisle, v duet; acc. own g duet.
Charlotte, NC   Friday, February 19, 1937

| 07181-1 | Just A Cottage | BB unissued |

Walter Hurdt–Claude Boone, v duet; acc. own g duet; Walter Hurdt, y-1.
Charlotte, NC   Friday, February 19, 1937

| 07182-1 | I'm Ridin' Now | BB B-7008 |
| 07183-1 | The Hobo Blues -1 | BB B-7008 |

Walter Hurdt & His Singing Cowboys: prob. Smoky Wiseman or Chuck Wiseman, f; Leroy "Slim" Johnson, g; Walter Hurdt, g; prob. Curly Burleson, sb.
Rock Hill, SC   Thursday, September 29, 1938

027654-1	Fiddle And Guitar Runnin' Wild	BB B-8370, MW M-7600
027655-1	Playing Around	BB B-8309, MW M-7601
027656-1	Fox Hunter's Luck	BB B-8330, MW M-7600

Montgomery Ward M-7600, M-7601 as by **Walter Hurdt & Boys**. Rev. Montgomery Ward M-7601 by Leroy Johnson.

Walter Hurdt, prob. Leroy "Slim" Johnson, prob. Curly Burleson, v trio; or unidentified, v duet-1; acc. prob. Smoky Wiseman or Chuck Wiseman, f-2; Leroy "Slim" Johnson, g; Walter Hurdt, g; prob. Curly Burleson, sb.
Rock Hill, SC   Thursday, September 29, 1938

027657-1	Hold Him Down Cowboy -2	BB B-8008, MW M-7597
027658-1	I'm A Straight Shooting Cowboy -2	BB B-8008, MW M-7597
027659-1	Riding By The Rio Grande -2	MW M-7598
027660-1	Mississippi Home -2	BB unissued
027661-1	When The Rent Man Comes Around -2	BB B-8183
027662-1	To The End Of The Trail -2	BB B-8330, MW M-7599
027663-1	My Brave Buckaroo -2	BB B-8462, MW M-7598
027664-1	Down The Arizona Trail -2	BB B-8370, MW M-7599
027667-1	I'm Through With Women -1	BB B-7915
027668-1	I've Always Loved My Old Guitar -1	BB B-7959
027669-1	My Skinny Sarah Jane -1, 2	BB B-7915
027670-1	Carry Me Back To The Blue Ridge -1	BB B-7959

Matrices 027665/66 are by Leroy Johnson.

Prob. Smoky Wiseman or Chuck Wiseman, f; Leroy "Slim" Johnson, g; Walter Hurdt, g; Curly Burleson, g.
Rock Hill, SC   Thursday, February 2, 1939

| 031956-1 | Lost Dog | BB B-8063, MW M-7858 |
| 031957-1 | Train Special | BB B-8063, MW M-7858 |

Prob. Walter Hurdt, prob. Leroy "Slim" Johnson, prob. Curly Burleson, v trio; or Leroy "Slim" Johnson, Curly Burleson, v duet-1; acc. Smoky Wiseman or Chuck Wiseman, f-2; Leroy "Slim" Johnson, g; Walter Hurdt, g; prob. Curly Burleson, g.
Rock Hill, SC   Thursday, February 2, 1939

031962-1	Honey, What's The Matter Now? -2	BB B-8041, MW M-7873
031963-1	She's Got The Habit -2	BB B-8041, MW M-7873
031964-1	Think Of Me -2	BB B-8134, MW M-7876
031965-1	No Matter How He Done It -2	BB B-8084, MW M-7875
031966-1	She's Anybody's Gal -1	BB unissued
031967-1	She Won't Pay Me No Mind -2	BB B-8183
031968-1	I'm Drinking My Troubles Down -1	BB B-8309
031969-1	Cause My Baby's Gone -1	BB B-8462
031970-1	I Told Them All About You -1, 2	BB B-8074, MW M-7874
031971-1	No Fooling -1, 2	BB B-8074, MW M-7874
031972-1	She's Got Rhythm Now -2	BB B-8134, MW M-7876
031973-1	She Can't Be Satisfied -2	BB B-8084, MW M-7875

Bluebird B-8063, Montgomery Ward M-7858 as by **Walter Hurdt**. Bluebird B-8074 as by **Johnson & Burleson**. Smoky Wiseman or Chuck Wiseman may replace Hurdt in the vocal trio on matrix 031967. Matrices 031958 to 031961 are by Leroy Johnson.
See also Leroy Johnson.

RIP HURLEY & BOB

Pseudonym on Velvet Tone for Earl Shirkey & Roy Harper.

ZACK HURT

See Zack & Glenn.

JOHN HUTCHENS
Pseudonym on Champion, Montgomery Ward, and Decca for John McGhee.

JOHN HUTCHENS & JAMES ALSTON
Pseudonym on Champion, Decca, and Montgomery Ward for McGhee & Cogar (see John McGhee & Frank Welling).

HUTCHENS BROTHERS
Pseudonym on Champion, Decca, and Montgomery Ward for John McGhee & Frank Welling.

[THE] HUTCHENS['] FAMILY [TRIO]
Pseudonym on Champion, Decca, and Montgomery Ward for John & Alma McGhee & Frank Welling (see John McGhee & Frank Welling).

FRANK HUTCHINSON
Pseudonym on Australian Parlophone for Vernon Dalhart.

TOM HUTCHINSON
Pseudonym on Challenge for Thomas C. Ashley.

CARL HUTCHISON
Pseudonym on Conqueror for J.P. Ryan.

FRANK HUTCHISON

Frank Hutchison, v; acc. own g.
New York, NY   Tuesday, September 28, 1926
| 80143-A | Worried Blues | OK 45064 |
| 80144-A | Train That Carried The Girl From Town | OK 45064 |

Frank Hutchison, h; acc. own g.
New York, NY   Friday, January 28, 1927
80350-B	Stackalee	OK 45106
80351-	The Wild Horse	OK 45093
80352-	Long Way To Tipperary	OK 45089

Frank Hutchison, v; prob. acc. own g.
New York, NY   Friday, January 28, 1927
| 80353- | The Gospel Ship | OK unissued |

Frank Hutchison, g solo.
New York, NY   Friday, January 28, 1927
| 80354- | The West Virginia Rag | OK 45083 |

Frank Hutchison, sp; acc. own h.
New York, NY   Friday, January 28, 1927
| 80355- | C&O Excursion | OK 45089 |

Frank Hutchison, v; acc. own h-1/g.
New York, NY   Friday, January 28, 1927
80356-	Coney Isle	OK 45083
80357-	Old Rachel	OK 45093, Ve 7106-V, Cl 5131-C
80358-A	Lightning Express	OK 45144
80359-A	Stackalee -1	OK 45106

Rev. Velvet Tone 7106-V by Frank & James McCravy.

St. Louis, MO   Thursday, April 28, 1927
| 80776- | Old Rachel | OK rejected |
| 80777- | Lonesome Valley | OK rejected |

Frank Hutchison, g solo.
St. Louis, MO   Thursday, April 28, 1927
| 80778-A | Logan County Blues | OK 45121 |

Frank Hutchison, v; acc. own g.
St. Louis, MO   Friday, April 29, 1927
80782-A	Worried Blues	OK 45114, Ve 7107-V, Cl 5131-C
80783-B	The Train That Carried The Girl From Town	OK 45114
80784-B	The Last Scene Of The Titanic	OK 45121
80785-B	All Night Long	OK 45144
80786-	Over The Waves	OK unissued

Rev. Velvet Tone 7107-V by Frank & James McCravy.

Sherman Lawson & Frank Hutchison: Sherman Lawson, f; Frank Hutchison, g.
New York, NY   Monday, September 10, 1928

401102-	Cluck Old Hen	OK unissued
401103-	Old Corn Liquor	OK unissued
401104-	Sally Gooden	OK unissued

Frank Hutchison, v; acc. Sherman Lawson, f; own h-1/g.
New York, NY   Monday, September 10, 1928

| 401105-B | Alabama Girl, Ain't You Comin' Out Tonight? | OK 45313 |
| 401106-B | Hell Bound Train -1 | OK 45452, Ve 2366-V |

Velvet Tone 2366-V as by **Billy Adams**. Rev. Velvet Tone 2366-V by Morgan Denmon.

Sherman Lawson & Frank Hutchison: Sherman Lawson, f; Frank Hutchison, g/v.
New York, NY   Monday, September 10, 1928

| 401108-A | Wild Hogs In The Red Brush | OK 45274 |

Matrix 401107 is by Sherman Lawson.

Frank Hutchison, v; acc. unknown.
New York, NY   Monday, September 10, 1928

| 401109-A,-B | Boston Burglar | OK unissued |

Acc. own g; or g solo-1.
New York, NY   Tuesday, September 11, 1928

401110-B	The Burglar Man	OK 45313
401111-B	Back In My Home Town	OK 45258
401112-B	The Miner's Blues	OK 45258
401113-B	Hutchison's Rag -1	OK 45274

Acc. own g.
New York, NY   Tuesday, July 9, 1929

402504-B	The Boston Burglar	OK 45425
402505-	Down In Lone Green Valley	OK unissued
402506-B	The Chevrolet Six	OK 45378
402507-B	Cumberland Gap	OK 45570
402508-B	The Deal	OK 45570
402509-B	Railroad Bill	OK 45425
402510-B	Johnny And Jane – Part 1	OK 45361
402511-B	Johnny And Jane – Part 2	OK 45361
402512-B	Cannon Ball Blues	OK 45378

Frank Hutchison, sp; acc. own g.
New York, NY   Tuesday, July 9, 1929

| 402513-B | K.C. Blues | OK 45452 |

Frank Hutchison also participated in The OKeh Medicine Show.

H.K. HUTCHISON

H.K. Hutchison, v; acc. J.S. Ross, h/g.
Richmond, IN   Tuesday, April 3, 1928

13632,-A	My Lindy Dear	Ge rejected
13633	Good Old Turnip Greens	Ge 6464, Ch 15525, Spt 9184
13634,-A	Down By The Weeping Willow Tree	Ge rejected
13635,-A	The Death Of Laura Parson [sic]	Ge rejected

Champion 15525 as by **Dan Golden**. Supertone 9184 as by **David Neal**.
Revs: Gennett 6464 by Orla Clark; Champion 15525 by Thomas C. Ashley; Supertone 9184 by Byrd Moore.

THE HYMN TIME BOYS

See Clagg & Sliger.

I

JOE IKEOLE & SOL NAWAHINE

Though one item by these Hawaiian artists was issued in the Paramount Old Time Tunes series (3132) they are outside the scope of this work.

IMPERIAL QUARTET

Vocal quartet; acc. unknown.
Richmond, VA   Thursday, October 17, 1929

403153-	Old Time Medley	OK unissued
403154-	Lawd, I Want To Be Right	OK unissued
403155-	Gwine Up	OK unissued
403156-	Mister Chicken	OK unissued

HARVEY IRWIN

Harvey Irwin, v; acc. own g.
Asheville, NC   prob. Friday, August 28 or Saturday, August 29, 1925

9303-A	Sunny Tennessee	OK 45052
9304-A	I Have No Mother Now	OK 45014
9305-A	The Blind Child	OK 45014
9306-A	They Always Pick On Me	OK 45052

BURL IVES

Burl Ives, v; acc. own g.
Richmond, IN   Tuesday, July 23, 1929

| 15380 | Behind The Clouds | Ge rejected trial recording |

According to Gennett files this recording was destroyed on August 6, 1929.

Burl Ives recorded after 1942.

J

JACK & BILL

Jack Fralia, Bill ——, v duet, or Jack Fralia, v-1; acc. poss. one of them, p.
Dallas, TX   Thursday, June 27, 1929

402750-	Melon Time In Dixieland	OK unissued
402751-	I'm Waiting For Ships That Never Come In -1	OK unissued
402752-A	The Lonesome Road	OK 45368
402753-B	What A Wonderful Mother You'd Be	OK 45368

JACK & JEAN (THE SWEETHEARTS OF THE MOUNTAINS)

Jack ——, Jean ——, v duet; acc. poss. one of them, bj-md; poss. one of them, g.
Rock Hill, SC   Wednesday, September 28, 1938

027777-1	I'm Mighty Blue	MW M-7713
027778-1	He's Waiting For Me	MW M-7714
027779-1	I'm Going Back	MW M-7713
027780-1	In The Evening	MW M-7714
027781-1	Bring Back My Darling	MW M-7715
027782-1	Once You Were My Little Darling	MW M-7716
027783-1	Golden Sunset	MW M-7717
027784-1	We'll Meet At The Foot Of The Hill	MW M-7715
027785-1	Smoky Mt Blues	MW M-7716
027786-1	Let Him Lead You	MW M-7717

JACK & LESLIE

Jack Hilliard, Leslie Palmer, v duet; or Jack Hilliard, v-1; acc. Leslie Palmer, sg; Jack Hilliard, g.
Charlotte, NC   Friday, June 10, 1938

64120-A	I'm In The Glory Land Way	De 5555
64121-A	Where The Soul Of Man Never Dies	De 5589
64122-A	The Last Mile Of The Way	De 5589, Coral 64008
64123-A	The Great Speckled Bird	De 5555, Coral 64008
64124-A	If It Wasn't For Mother And Dad	De 5575
64125-	Somebody's Waiting For Me	De 5671, MeC 45298
64126-A	She's Killin' Me	De 5602
64127-A	She's A Hum Ding Mama -1	De 5602
64128-A	There's A Mother Old And Gray (Who Needs Me Now) -1	De 5671, MeC 45298
64129-A	Now You're Gone I Can't Forget You	De 5623
64130-A	Will Your Heart Ache When I'm Gone	De 5655
64131-A	Poor Orphan Boy	De 5655
64132-A	Mississippi River Blues	De 5561
64133-A	Trouble In Mind No. 3	De 5561

| 64134-A | Old Shep | De 5575 |
| 64135-A | Darling Think Of What You've Done | De 5623 |

Jack Hilliard sings lead, and Leslie Palmer tenor, on the vocal duets.

JACK & TONY

Ray Jack Bankey, v; acc. Tony Lombardo, h-1/ac-2/vb-3; own g-4.
New York, NY   Tuesday, January 14, 1930

403623-A	I Still Have A Place In My Heart For You -2, 4	OK 45422
403624-A	Since I Gave My Heart To You -3, 4	OK 45421
403625-A	You're My Old Fashioned Sweetheart -2	OK 45421
403626-B	The Burial Of The Miner's Child -1, 4	OK 45422

At this session and on January 13 these artists (who were associated with station KQV in Pittsburgh, PA) also recorded instrumentals issued by OKeh and Columbia in Polish and Italian series (see *EMOR*).

Jack Bankey also recorded for Gennett under his own full name.

THE JACK HARMONICA PLAYER

Pseudonym on Vocalion for Emry Arthur.

HAPPY JACKSON

Pseudonym on Herschel Gold Seal 2021 for Frank Luther (*Who Said I Was A Bum?*) or Carson Robison (*Goin' To Have A Big Time Tonight*) (Cameo masters).

JACK JACKSON

Jack Jackson, v/y-1; acc. own g.
Johnson City, TN   Monday, October 21, 1929

149202-2	Flat Tire Blues -1	Co 15662-D
149203-1	My Alabama Home -1	Co 15662-D
149206-2	In Our Little Home Sweet Home	Co 15497-D
149207-2	I'm Just A Black Sheep	Co 15497-D

Matrices 149204/05 are by George Wade & Francum Braswell.

Jack Jackson also recorded with Binkley Brothers Dixie Clodhoppers.

MELFORD JACKSON

Melford Jackson, v; or Melford Jackson & Cecil Kite, v duet-1; acc. unknown, bj; two unknowns, g.
Richmond, IN   Saturday, September 28, 1929

15702-A,-B	[unknown title]	Ge rejected
15703	Down Where The Swanee River Flows -1	Ge rejected
15704,-A	Can't You Hear Me Calling Caroline -1	Ge rejected
15705,-A,-B	Shian, Crenbells, Tony Boy	Ge rejected

AUNT MOLLY JACKSON

Aunt Molly Jackson, v/sp; acc. poss. own g.
New York, NY   Thursday, December 10, 1931

| 150240-1 | Kentucky Miner's Wife – Part 1 (Ragged Hungry Blues) | Co 15731-D |
| 150241-1 | Kentucky Miner's Wife – Part 2 (Ragged Hungry Blues) | Co 15731-D |

New York, NY   Tuesday, December 15 or Wednesday, December 16, 1931

| 152046- | Poor Miners Farewell | Co unissued |
| 150247- | I Love Coal Miners | Co unissued |

JACKSON COUNTY BARN OWLS

Pseudonym on Champion for the Jackson County Ramblers [with E.W. McClain & J.O. Harpold].

JACKSON COUNTY RAMBLERS

Unknown, h; unknown, bj; unknown, g.
Richmond, IN   Saturday, May 17, 1930

16619	Letart Isle	Ch 16284
16620,-A	The Greasy String	Ge unissued
16621	Carolina Girl	Ch 16284

E.W. McClain & J.O. Harpold, v duet; or E.W. McClain, v-1; acc. the Jackson County Ramblers: unknown, h; unknown, bj; unknown, g.
Richmond, IN   Saturday, May 17, 1930

16626-A	I Wonder How The Old Folks Are At Home	Ge 7224, Ch 16031, Spt 9716, MW 4964
16629	Bake That Chicken Pie	Ge 7224, Ch 16031, Spt 9716
16630	The Man Behind The Plow -1	Ge unissued

Champion 16031, Montgomery Ward 4964 as by **Jackson County Barn Owls**. Supertone 9716 as by **McClain & Harpold**. Matrices 16222 through 16225 are by The Scare Crow (see *B&GR*); 16627/28 are popular.
Rev. Montgomery Ward 4964 by Bob Miller.

WALTER JACOBS & LONNIE CARTER
WALTER JACOBS & THE CARTER BROTHERS

Items with these credits in the Okeh Old Time Tunes series (45436 with the former, 45468 and 45482 with the latter) are by Walter Vinson, Lonnie Chatman, and Bo Chatman (or the first two only). These were African-American musicians: in these formations, in effect, the Mississippi Sheiks; see *B&GR*.

JAKE & CARL

Carl Swanson, md/tv/y; Jake Watts, g/lv/y; acc. Bob Miller, p-1.
New York, NY   Wednesday, November 24, 1937

22063-	There Are Just Two I's In Dixie (Two Blue Eyes That Mean The World To Me) -1	ARC unissued
22064-	(I'm A) Hillbilly Boy From The Mountains	ARC unissued
22065-	Dear Little Darling -1	ARC unissued
22066-1	Susie Brown	ARC 8-02-53, Cq 8987
22067-2	What Would You Give (In Exchange For Your Mother-In-Law) -1	ARC 8-02-53, Cq 8987
22068-	When It's Prayer-Time On The Prairie -1	ARC unissued

Jake & Carl (The Original Nightherders): Carl Swanson, md/tv/y; Jake Watts, g/lv/y.
New York, NY   Wednesday, September 6, 1939

042642-1	Old Wishing Well	BB B-8299, MW M-8442
042643-1	Hill Billy Boy From The Mountains	BB B-8274, MW M-8441, RZAu G24702, Twin FT8892
042644-1	When The White Azaleas Start Blooming	BB B-8274, MW M-8441, RZAu G24702
042645-1	Please Don't Love Nobody When I'm Gone	BB B-8299, MW M-8442, RZAu G24990

Matrix 042643 is titled *Hillbilly Boy From The Mountains* on Regal-Zonophone G24702 and Twin FT8892.
Revs: Regal-Zonophone G24990 by Texas Jim Robertson; Twin FT8892 by Riley Puckett.
Jake Watts also recorded with Don Sullivan as the Ozark Boys. Both he and Carl Swanson recorded, separately, after 1942.

BEN JARRELL

See Da Costa Woltz's Southern Broadcasters.

LE ROY JARVIS

Pseudonym on Supertone for Jimmy Long.

JARVIS & JUSTICE

Reese Jarvis, f; Dick Justice, g/sp-1.
Chicago, IL   Monday, May 20, 1929

C-3517-	Guian Valley Waltz	Br 333
C-3518-	Poor Girl's Waltz -1	Br 333
C-3519-	Poca River Blues	Br 358, 52083, Me M18010
C-3520-	Muskrat Rag	Br 358, 52083, Me M18010

Melotone M18010 as by **Les Deux Gaspesiens**.
Matrix C-3519 is titled *La Danse De La Rivier Bleue*, and C-3520 is titled *Le Reel A Quatre*, on Brunswick 52083.
Dick Justice also recorded under his own name.

ANDREW JENKINS

Blind "Andy", v; acc. own g.
Atlanta, GA   Monday, April 13, 1925

9046-A	The Country Church Yard	OK 40393
9047-A	Frank Du Pree [sic]	OK 40446

Rev. OKeh 40446 by Rosa Lee Carson.
New York, NY   c. early June 1925

73413-B	Just As The Sun Went Down	OK 40416
73415-B	Floyd Collins In Sand Cave	OK 40393
73416-A	Break The News To Mother	OK 40416

Matrix 73414 is untraced but probably by Andrew Jenkins.

Atlanta, GA   c. July 1, 1925
9192-A   A Dream Of Home   OK 45007
9193-A   The Little Newsboy   OK 45007

Blind "Andy", v; or Blind "Andy" & Mary Eskew, v duet-1; acc. unknown, f; unknown, h; unknown, g.
Atlanta, GA   Thursday, March 11, 1926
9600-A   Charming Billy (Billy Boy) -1   OK 45043
9602-A   Short Dresses And Bobbed Hair   OK 45043
Matrix 9601 (and matrix 9603) is untraced.

"Goodby" Jenkins, v; acc. own f.
Atlanta, GA   Tuesday, October 26, 1926
9812-A   Georgia Girl   OK 45088
9813-A   Papa's Got A Home   OK 45088

"Gooby" Jenkins, v; acc. own f; unknown, g.
Atlanta, GA   Wednesday, October 27, 1926
9816-A   The Kennesaw Mountain Blues   OK 45082
9817-A   The Prisoner's Dream   OK 45082
9818-A   Fiddlin' Bill   OK 45069
9819-A   Gypsy's Warning   OK 45069
OKeh 45069 is subcredited **(The Blind Fiddler)**.
Matrices 9810/11, 9814/15, and 9820/21 are blank in OKeh files; of these at least 9814/15 may be by Andrew Jenkins.

Acc. poss. own h/g/wh.
Atlanta, GA   Friday, June 3, 1927
80966-A   Gruver Meadows   OK 45115
80967-A   Hopefull [sic] Walter Booth   OK 45115

Blind Andy, v; acc. two unknowns, f; unknown, p; unknown, vc.
Memphis, TN   Monday, February 20, 1928
400275-D   The Fate Of Edward Hickman   OK 45197
400276-C   Little Marian Parker   OK 45197

Andrew Jenkins & Carson Robison, v duet; acc. two unknowns, f; unknown, g; unknown, bell eff-1.
New York, NY   Tuesday, June 19, 1928
400799-B   Only A Tear   OK 45481
400800-B;   On The Banks Of The Old Omaha   OK 45232, Ve 2392-V, Cl 5326-C,
  100537   Re/RZAu G21102
400802-B   The Sidewalks Of New York (East Side, West Side)   OK 45232
400803-B;   My Dixie Home   OK 45264, Ve 2396-V, Cl 5330-C
  100541
400804-A   Just Tell Them That You Saw Me   OK 45246, PaE R3872, PaAu A2706
400805-B   The Little Flower Girl   OK 45481
400806-B;   I Hear Dem Bells -1   OK 45264, Ve 2392-V, Cl 5326-C, PaE E6400,
  100538   R3875, Ariel Z4725, Re/RZAu G21094

OKeh 45264, ParlophoneR3875 as by **Jenkins & Robison.** Velvet Tone 2392-V, 2396-V, Clarion 5326-C, 5330-C, Regal/Regal-Zonophone G21094, G21102 as by **Marvin Thompson.** Parlophone A2706 as by **Andrew J. Jenkins & Carson Robison.** Parlophone E6400 as by **The Sanctified Singers.** Ariel Z4725 as by **Sacred Singers.** Matrix 400801 is untraced but probably by these artists.
Revs: Velvet Tone 2396-V, Clarion 5330-C by Frank Marvin; Regal/Regal-Zonophone G21094 by Carson Robison, G21102 by Vernon Dalhart; Parlophone E6400, Ariel Z4725 (with same credits) by Frank & James McCravy.

Andrew Jenkins & Carson Robison, v duet; or **Andrew Jenkins,** v solo-1; acc. unknown, f; unknown, f (or poss. vla-2); unknown, g; unknown, train-wh eff-3; Andrew Jenkins, sp-4.
New York, NY   Wednesday, June 20, 1928
400807-B   In The Baggage Coach Ahead -3   OK 45234
400808-B   Silver Threads Among The Gold -2, 4   OK 45246, PaE R3872, PaAu A2706
400809-   The Mansion Of Aching Hearts -1   OK unissued
400810-A   The Mansion Of Aching Hearts -1   OK 45234
Parlophone A2706 as by **Andrew J. Jenkins & Carson Robison.**

Blind Andy, v/wh; acc. unknown, h-1; unknown, g.
Atlanta, GA   Friday, March 15, 1929
402325-C   Stone Mountain Tank Explosion -1   OK 45343
402330-B   Tragedy On Daytona Beach   OK 45343
Intervening matrices are by McMichen's Harmony Boys.

Blind Andy, v/y; acc. prob. own g.
Atlanta, GA   Saturday, March 16, 1929

402343-B	Tennessee Yodel Man Blues	OK 45347, Ve 2367-V
402344-A	Rambling Yodel Sam	OK 45347, Ve 2367-V

Velvet Tone 2367-V as by **Marvin Thompson**.

Jenkins & Whitworth: Andrew Jenkins, —— Whitworth, v duet; acc. unknown f; unknown, g.
Atlanta, GA   Saturday, March 16, 1929

402345-	The Little Old Cabin In The Mountain	OK 45331
402346-	I'll Be All Smiles Tonight	OK 45331

Blind Andy, v; acc. unknown, vla; unknown, g; Mary Lee Spain, v-1.
Atlanta, GA   Thursday, March 21, 1929

402395-C	The Alabama Flood -1	OK 45319
402396-A	The Fate Of Elba, Alabama	OK 45319

Acc. unknown, f; unknown, h; unknown, g; poss. own sp.
New York, NY   Wednesday, March 5, 1930

403814-B,-C	Hello World Song (Don't You Go 'Way)	Hello World Dog Gone 001

This is an OKeh custom recording for W.K. Henderson and station KWKH, Shreveport, LA. Rev. by W.K. Henderson.

Blind Andy, v; or **Andrew Jenkins & Frank Hicks**, v/sp duet-1; acc. two unknowns, f-2; unknown, g; unidentified, wh-3.
Atlanta, GA   Wednesday, April 23, 1930

403908-A	In The Valley Where The Bluebonnets Grow -2	OK 45454
403909-A	Stop And Look For The Train -2	OK 45454
403910-A	The Old Account Was Settled Long Ago -1, 3	OK 45443
403911-A	Don't Stop Praying -1, 3	OK 45443

For recordings credited to Wanner & Jenkins see W.C. Childers. Andrew Jenkins was also a member of the Jenkins Family, and recorded after 1942.

ELI JENKINS

Pseudonym on Conqueror for Ted Chestnut.

FRANK JENKINS

Oscar Jenkins' Mountaineers: Frank Jenkins, f; Oscar Jenkins, bj; Ernest V. Stoneman, g/v.
Chicago, IL   c. August 1929

21381-2	Burial Of Wild Bill	Pm 3240, Bwy 8249
21382-1,-2	The Railway Flagman's Sweetheart	Pm 3240, Bwy 8249

Frank Jenkins' Pilot Mountaineers: Frank Jenkins, f; Oscar Jenkins, bj; Ernest V. Stoneman, g/v-1.
Richmond, IN   Thursday, September 12, 1929

15589	The Railroad Flagman's Sweetheart-1	Cq 7269
15590,-A	The Murder Of Nellie Brown -1	Ge rejected
15591	When The Snowflakes Fall Again -1	Cq 7270
15592-A	The Burial Of Wild Bill -1	Cq 7270
15593,-A	I Will Be All Smiles Tonight -1	Ge rejected: *Old Homestead OHCS 199* (LP)
15594,-A	In The Year Of Jubilo -1	Ge rejected
15595	A Message From Home Sweet Home -1	Cq 7269
15596-A	Sunny Home In Dixie	Ge 7034, Spt 9677
15597-A	Old Dad	Ge 7034, Spt 9677

Supertone 9677 as by **Riley's Mountaineers**. Conqueror 7269, 7270 as by **Alex Gordon**.

"GOOBY" [or "GOODBY"] JENKINS

See Andrew Jenkins.

JESS JENKINS

Pseudonym on Challenge for Walter C. Peterson.

OSCAR JENKINS' MOUNTAINEERS

See Frank Jenkins.

JENKINS & ROBISON
JENKINS & WHITWORTH

See Andrew Jenkins.

[THE] JENKINS FAMILY
[THE] JENKINS SACRED SINGERS

The Jenkins Family: Andrew Jenkins, Irene Spain, Mary Lee Spain, v trio; acc. Irene Spain, o.
Atlanta, GA   c. August 28, 1924

8724-A	If I Could Hear My Mother Pray Again	OK 40214
8725-A	Farewell	OK 40248
8726-A	The Church In The Wildwood	OK 40214
8727-A	I Got Mine	OK 40247
8728-A	The Silver Lining	OK 40249
8729-A	Sail On	OK 40249
8730-A	Nobody Cares	OK 40248
8731-A	Make Jesus Your Choice	OK 40247

Acc. unknown, md; poss. Andrew Jenkins, g; unidentified, v duet (rather than trio) -1.
Atlanta, GA   c. January 8–9, 1925

8835-A	Will There Be Any Stars In My Crown -1	OK 40331
8836-A	The Old Rugged Cross	OK 40287
8837-A	Jesus Is Coming Back Again -1	OK 40331
8838-A	Shout And Shine For Jesus	OK 40359
8844-A	Jesus Is Calling	OK 40359
8845-A	There Shall Be Showers Of Blessing	OK 40377
8846-A	Sing It And Tell It	OK 40287
8855-A	Milk And Honey	OK 40390

Matrices 8839 to 8843 are untraced; 8847/48 by Roba Stanley; 8849 to 8851 untraced; 8852 by Roba Stanley; 8853/54 by Vic Meyers' Atlanta Melody Artists (popular).

Andrew Jenkins, Irene Spain, v duet; acc. Irene Spain, o; Andrew Jenkins, sp.
Atlanta, GA   c. January 10, 1925

| 8856-A | Old Time Southern Revival | OK 7007 |
| 8857-A | Georgia Camp Meeting | OK 7007 |

OKeh 7007 is a 12-inch issue.

No details (poss. from above session).
Atlanta, GA   c. January 10, 1925

| | Memories Of Sam P. Jones | OK 7012 |
| | Revival Meeting In Dixie | OK 7012 |

OKeh 7012 is a 12-inch issue.

Andrew Jenkins, Irene Spain, Mary Lee Spain, v trio; acc. Irene Spain, o-1/p-2.
Atlanta, GA   Monday, April 13, 1925

9048-A	Safe In The Arms Of Jesus -1	OK 40390
9049-A	That Old, Old Story -1	OK 40407
9051-A	Whiter Than Snow -2	OK 40407

Matrix 9050 is by Vic Meyers' Atlanta Melody Artists (popular); 9052 is untraced.

Acc. unknown, md; poss. Andrew Jenkins, g.
Atlanta, GA   c. mid-April 1925

| 9062-A | That Lonesome Valley | OK 40377 |

Matrices 9063 to 9067 are untraced, but at least some of them may be by the Jenkins Family.

Acc. Irene Spain, o-1/p-2.
Atlanta, GA   early July 1925

| 9239-A | I'll Go Where You Want Me To Go -1 | OK 45002 |
| 9255-A | I Choose Jesus -2 | OK 45002 |

Matrices 9235 to 9238, 9240, 9245/46, 9248, 9251/52, 9256 to 9258 are untraced; 9241/42 are by Kimo Kalohi (Hawaiian); 9243/44 by Catherine Henderson (see B&GR); 9247, 9249/50, 9253/54 by Jack Linx (popular). At least some of the untraced matrices may be by the Jenkins Family.

Acc. unknown, f; poss. Irene Spain, p.
Atlanta, GA   Friday, March 12, 1926

9614-A	Beulah Land	OK 45055
9615-A	Trusting My Redeemer	OK 45038
9616-A	I'm So Glad That Jesus Found Me	OK 45038
9617-A	He Leads Me Home	OK 45050
9618-A	On Christ The Solid Rock I Stand	OK 45050
9619-A	Land Where We'll Never Grow Old	OK 45055

Acc. poss. Irene Spain, o.
Atlanta, GA   c. October 26, 1926

9802-A	Beautiful Garden Of Prayer	OK 45071
9803-A	Work, For The Night Is Coming	OK 45071
9804-A	The Promised Land	OK 45087
9805-A	The Haven Of Rest	OK 45067
9806-A	The Railroad Of Life	OK 45067

9807-A	Crossing The Tide	OK 45087
9808-A	What About You?	OK 45080
9809-A	Drive Away Your Troubles With A Song	OK 45080

Jenkins' Sacred Singers: Andrew Jenkins, unknown man, Irene Spain, Mary Lee Spain, v quartet; unacc.; or acc. two unknowns, g-1.

Atlanta, GA   Tuesday, March 15, 1927

80530-B	The Wages Of Sin Is Death	OK 45367
80531-A	How Will It Be With Your Soul?	OK 45367
80532-B	Pictures From Life's Other Side -1	OK 45134
80533-	The Glory Land Way -1	OK 40795
80534-	When I See The Blood -1	OK 40795
80535-	Mother And Dad	OK unissued

The Jenkins Family: Andrew Jenkins, Irene Spain, Mary Lee Spain, v trio; or unidentified, v duet-1; acc. Irene Spain, o-2/p-3; unknown, md-4; poss. Andrew Jenkins, g-5.

Atlanta, GA   Monday, March 21, 1927

80587-A	Let The Lower Lights Be Burning -4, 5	OK 45104
80588-B	Only A Prayer -2	OK 45134
80589-B	Jesus I Come -2	OK 45104
80590-B	Be Of Good Cheer -2	OK 45470
80591-B	Gather The Golden Sheaves -1, 3	OK 45180
80592-B	God Will Take Care Of You -1, 3	OK 45180

OKeh 45104 as by **Jenkins Family**, 45134 as by **Jenkins' Sacred Singers**.

The Jenkins Sacred Singers: Andrew Jenkins, Irene Spain, Mary Lee Spain, v trio; acc. Irene Spain, o; unknown, bell-1.

Atlanta, GA   Wednesday, March 23, 1927

| 80661-C | The Church In The Wildwood -1 | OK 45113 |
| 80662-A | If I Could Hear My Mother Pray Again | OK 45113 |

The Jenkins Family: Andrew Jenkins, Irene Spain, Mary Lee Spain, v trio; acc. unknown, cl; unknown, p.

Atlanta, GA   Saturday, August 11, 1928

402131-A	His Way With Thee	OK 45470
402133-A,-B	Swing Low Sweet Chariot	OK unissued
402134-A,-B	I'm Gwine To Heaven When I Die	OK unissued

Matrix 402132, blank in OKeh files, is probably also by the Jenkins Family.

Jenkins Family: Andrew Jenkins, Irene Spain or Mary Lee Spain, v duet; acc. two unknowns, f; poss. Andrew Jenkins, g.

Atlanta, GA   Wednesday, April 23, 1930

| 403906-A | That Little Old Hut | OK 45563 |
| 403907-A,-B | Two Log Cabin Orphans | OK unissued |

Acc. unknown, md; poss. Andrew Jenkins, g.

Atlanta, GA   Wednesday, April 23, or Thursday, April 24, 1930

403912-B	When We All Get To Heaven	OK 45460
403913-B	Under The Blood Of Jesus	OK 45460
403914-A,-B	I'm On My Way To Heaven	OK unissued
403915-B	I'm On The Sunny Side	OK 45563

Andrew Jenkins, Irene Spain, Mary Lee Spain, v trio; or Andrew Jenkins, Irene Spain or Mary Lee Spain, v duet-1; acc. unknown, md; poss. Andrew Jenkins, g.

Atlanta, GA   Monday, July 30, 1934

82810-1	Death Is Only A Dream -1	BB B-5625
82811-1	The Glory Land Way	BB B-5743
82812-1	When We All Get To Heaven	BB B-5655
82813-1	The Haven Of Rest	BB B-5822
82814-1	Jesus Is All The World To Me	BB B-5692
82815-1	I Will Sing Of My Redeemer	BB B-5655
82816-1	Dying From Home, And Lost	BB B-5776
82817-1	We Are Going Down The Valley	BB B-5692
82818-1	Under The Blood	BB B-5776
82819-1	When I See The Blood	BB B-5822
82820-1	Jesus, I Come	BB B-5743
82821-1	Eat At The Welcome Table -1	BB B-5625

Andrew Jenkins also recorded under his own name. See also The Irene Spain Family.

HERB JENNINGS

Pseudonym on Champion for Welby Toomey.

JENNINGS BROTHERS
Pseudonym on Champion for the Tweedy Brothers.

JEPSEN & DONALDSON
See Ruth Donaldson & Helen Jepsen.

BEN JERRELL
Ben Jarrell was thus mistakenly credited on some issues. See Da Costa Woltz's Southern Broadcasters.

FRED L. JESKE [& LOUIS ROEN]

Fred L. Jeske & Louis Roen, prob. v duet; acc. unknown.
  Grafton, WI   c. February 1931
  L-778-   Fresh Eggs   Bwy 1440
  L-781-   I'm Doin' That Thing   Bwy 1440
Matrices L-779/80 are untraced.

Fred L. Jeske, v; acc. prob. own g.
  Grafton, WI   c. April 1931
  L-930-   That Little Boy Of Mine   Bwy 1451
  L-933-2   The Waltz You Saved For Me   Bwy 1452, Ang 3346, Lyric 3401
  L-934-2   Blue Pacific Moonlight   Bwy 1450
  L-939-1   Grandfather's Clock   Pm 3288
  L-940-1   A Little Yeller Dog   Pm 3288
Matrices L-931/32 are popular; L-935 to L-938 are untraced.
Revs: Broadway 1450, 1452 by Luther Brothers (see Carson Robison), 1451 by Frank Crandall (popular); Angelus 3346, Lyric 3401 untraced.

JESSE'S STRING FIVE
Pseudonym on Bluebird B-6443 for Bill Boyd & His Cowboy Ramblers.

JIM & BOB (THE GENIAL HAWAIIANS)

Bob Kaai, sg-1/u-2/v-3; Jim Holstein, g/v-4.
  Chicago, IL   Tuesday, December 12, 1933
  77323-1   Coffee In The Morning, Kisses In The Night -1, 4   BB B-5294, Eld 2165, Sr S-3375
  77324-1   Chimes -1   BB B-5295, Eld 2166, Sr S-3376, MW M-4476
  77325-1   Goodnight Taps -1   BB B-5295, Eld 2166, Sr S-3376, MW M-4476
  77326-1   Sweet Georgia Brown -2   BB B-5944
  77327-1   Rome Wasn't Built In A Day -1, 4   BB B-5294, Eld 2165, Sr S-3375
  77328-1   Aloma -1, 3, 4   BB B-5407
  77329-1   St. Louis Blues -1   BB B-5316, Sr S-3397, MW M-4424
  77330-1   Calling Aloha To Me -1, 3, 4   BB B-6056
  77331-1   The Hula Blues -1, 3, 4   BB B-5407
  77332-1   The Song Of The Range -1   BB B-5316, Sr S-3397, MW M-4424
  77333-1   By The Waters Of Minnetonka -1   BB B-5944
  77334-1   There's A Little Grey Mother Dreaming -1, 3, 4   BB B-6056

JIM & CHARLIE

Unidentified, v; acc. unknown, f; unknown, g.
  Richmond, IN   Wednesday, April 8, 1931
  17660,-C   Happy Days Of Yore   Ge rejected
  17661,-C   Good Bye Booze   Ge rejected

JIM & KEN
See James Brown, Jr. & Ken Landon groups.

JO & ALMA (THE KENTUCKY GIRLS)

Jo Taylor, Alma Taylor, v duet; acc. Chick Hurt, mandola; Salty Holmes, g; Jack Taylor, sb; band v-1.
  Chicago, IL   Wednesday, February 23, 1938
  C-2116-1   Little Moses   Vo 04248
  C-2117-2   You Have Learned To Love Another   Vo 04173, Cq 9116
  C-2118-2   Trav'ling On The Glory Road -1   Vo 04248
  C-2119-1   Plant Sweet Flowers On My Grave   Vo 04313, Cq 9117
  C-2120-1   Lorena   Vo 04313, Cq 9117
  C-2121-1   When The Bees Are In The Hive   Vo 04173, Cq 9116

| C-2122-1,-2 | Broken Engagement | ARC unissued |
| C-2123-1,-2 | The Lifeboat | ARC unissued |

Conqueror 9116, 9117 as by **Happy Valley Family**.

Jo and Alma Taylor were also members of the Happy Valley Family.

JOE'S ACADIANS

See Joe Werner.

WHITEY JOHN

Pseudonym on labels in the Plaza group for John I. White.

JOHNNIE & JACK
JOHNNIE & MACK

Johnnie & Mack: one of them, md; the other, g.
   Richmond, IN   c. early February 1930

| 16226 | Life Is But A Dream | Ge unissued |
| 16228 | School Days | Ge rejected |

Matrix 16227 is popular.

Johnnie & Jack: one of them, md; the other, g.
   Richmond, IN   Monday, March 3, 1930

| 16345 | Sweet Evelina; Peggy O'Neil | Ge rejected |

JOHNNY & SLIM

Pseudonym on Superior for Johnny Barfield and Hoyt "Slim" Bryant as vocalists with Bert Layne & His Georgia Serenaders; see Bert Layne.

WHITEY JOHNS

Pseudonym on Plaza-group labels and derivatives for John I. White.

CHARLES JOHNSON

See the Johnson Brothers.

DALTON JOHNSON & WALLACE DANGFIELD

One of them, h; the other, g.
   Richmond, IN   Wednesday, February 24, 1932

18417	The Girl I Left Behind Me	Ge rejected
18418	Jay Bird	Ge rejected
18419	He Lives On High	Ge rejected
18420	In The Garden	Ge rejected

EARL JOHNSON

Earl Johnson & His Dixie Entertainers: Earl Johnson, f/v/sp-1; Emmett Bankston, bj/v-2; Byrd Moore, g/v-3.
   New York, NY   Monday, February 21, 1927

80460-	Hand Me Down My Walking Cane	OK unissued
80461-B	Ain't Nobody's Business -2, 3	OK 45092, PaE R3859
80462-B	Dixie -2, 3	OK 45129
80463-A	Hen Cackle -2	OK 45123
80464-	Bully Of The Town -3	OK unissued: *Cy 543(LP); Doc DOCD-8005 (CD)*
80465-B	I'm Satisfied -2	OK 45129
80466-A	Three Night's Experience -2	OK 45092, PaE R3859
80467-B	Johnson's Old Grey Mule -1	OK 45123

Earl Johnson, f/v; Emmett Bankston, bj/v; Byrd Moore, g/v.
   Atlanta, GA   Wednesday, March 23, 1927

80625-A	Boil Dem Cabbage Down	OK 45112
80626-C	John Henry Blues	OK 45101
80659-A	I Don't Love Nobody	OK 45101
80660-A	Shortenin' Bread	OK 45112

Moore sings lead vocal rather than Johnson on matrix 80659. Intervening matrices are by other artists.

Earl Johnson & His Clodhoppers: Earl Johnson, f/v-1/sp-2; Emmett Bankston, bj/v-3; Lee "Red" Henderson, g/v-4/sp-5.
   Atlanta, GA   Friday, October 7, 1927

| 81705-B | I Get My Whiskey From Rockingham -1, 3 | OK 45183 |
| 81706-B | Red Hot Breakdown -1 | OK 45209 |

81707-B	I've Got A Woman On Sourwood Mountain -1, 3, 4	OK 45171
81708-A	All Night Long -1, 3	OK 45383
81709-A	Old Grey Mare Kicking Out Of The Wilderness -1	OK 45183
81710-A	They Don't Roost Too High For Me -1, 2, 5	OK 45223, PaE R3869
81711-A	Mississippi Jubilee	OK 45223, PaE R3869
81712-B	Leather Breeches -1	OK 45209

Atlanta, GA   Tuesday, October 11, 1927

81743-A	Poor Little Joe -1, 3, 4	OK 45406
81744-B	The Little Grave In Georgia -1, 3	OK 45194
81745-A	In The Shadow Of The Pine -1	OK 45194
81746-A	Johnnie, Get Your Gun -1	OK 45171
81747-B	Earl Johnson's Arkansaw Traveler -2, 5	OK 45156
81748-A	Twinkle Little Star -2, 5	OK 45156

Earl Johnson, f; unknown, f; prob. Emmett Bankston, bj; prob. Lee "Red" Henderson, g; unidentified, v-1; unknown, laughing-2.

Atlanta, GA   Thursday, August 2, 1928

402036-A,-B	Weeping Willow -1	OK unissued
402037-C	Nigger On The Wood Pile -2	OK 45269
402038-C	Nigger In The Cotton Patch -2	OK 45383

Earl Johnson, f; unknown, f; prob. Emmett Bankston, bj; prob. Lee "Red" Henderson, g; unknown, laughing-1.

Atlanta, GA   Thursday, August 9, 1928

402112-A	Alabama Girl, Ain't You Comin' Out To-Night? -1	OK 45300
402113-B	Laughin' Rufus -1	OK 45406
402114-A	G. Rag -1	OK 45300
402115-A	Wire Grass Drag	OK 45269

Earl Johnson & His Dixie Entertainers: Earl Johnson, f/v-1; Emmett Bankston, bj; Lee "Red" Henderson, g.

Atlanta, GA   Friday, November 22, 1929

56560-1	Rocky Palace	Vi V-40304
56561-2	Green Mountain	Vi V-40304
56562-2	Fiddlin' Rufus	Vi V-40212
56563-2	Mississippi Sawyer	Vi V-40212
56564-1	He's A Beaut -1	Vi 23638, Au 405
56565-1	I Lost My Girl -1	Vi 23638, Au 405

Victor 23638, Aurora 405 as by **Earl Johnson's Dixie Entertainers**.

Earl Johnson, f/v; Bill Henson, g/v-1; Lula Bell (Mrs. Earl) Johnson, v-2.

Atlanta, GA   Wednesday, December 3, 1930

404614-A	When The Roses Bloom Again For The Bootlegger -1, 2	OK 45545
404615-A	Buy A Half Pint And Stay In The Wagon Yard -1	OK 45528
404616-B	Take Me Back To My Old Mountain Home -1	OK 45528
404617-B	There's No Place Like Home	OK 45545
404618-B	Bringing In The Sheaves -1, 2	OK 45512
404619-A	I Know That My Redeemer Liveth -1, 2	OK 45512

Henson sings lead vocal rather than Earl Johnson on matrix 404616.

Earl Johnson, f/v; unknown, g; poss. another unknown, g.

Atlanta, GA   Thursday, October 29, 1931

405044-1	Close Your Bright Eyes	OK 45559
404045-1	Way Down In Georgia	OK 45559

Earl Johnson's first recordings were with Arthur Tanner and others in 1925 and are listed under Arthur Tanner.

EDWARD JOHNSON

Pseudonym on Champion 15048 for George Ake.

ERNEST JOHNSON

Pseudonym on Harmony for Ernest Thompson.

GENE JOHNSON

Pseudonym on Timely Tunes and Aurora for Gene Autry.

HENRY JOHNSON

Pseudonym on Champion for Byrd Moore.

JAMES JOHNSON

James Johnson, v; acc. prob. own h/g.
    Atlanta, GA   Monday, October 22, 1928

147249-	The Tie That Binds	Co unissued
147250-1	Put On Your Old Grey Bonnet	Co 15453-D, CoSA DE505
147251-2	Papa Please Buy Me An Airship	Co 15453-D
147252-	In The Village By The Sea	Co unissued

Rev. Columbia DE505 by Hugh Cross & Riley Puckett.

JESS JOHNSON

See Jess Johnston.

JIMMY JOHNSON'S STRING BAND

Les Smitha, f; Jake Shucks, bj; Basil Martin, g; Jimmy Johnson, g-1/calls-2/clapping-3.
    Richmond, IN   Thursday, November 12, 1931

18167	Glee Club March -1	Ch 16430
18168	Ching Chow -1	Ch 16430
18169	Step Lively -1, 2, 3	Ch S-16389, Spr 2821
18170	Washington Quadrille -2	Ch S-16389, Spr 2821

Superior 2821 as by **Jimmie Johnson's String Band**.

Andy Palmer, v; acc. Jimmy Johnson's String Band: own f; Bill Mulligan, bj; Basil Martin, g; or **Jimmy Johnson's String Band**-1: Andy Palmer, f; Bill Mulligan, bj; Basil Martin, g.
    Richmond, IN   Monday, August 22, 1932

18726	Getting Tired Of Railroading	Ch 16506
18727	Shipping Port -1	Ch S-16559
18728	Soap In The Wash Pan -1	Ch 16516
18729	Drink More Cider	Ch 16516
18730	Old Blind Dog	Ch 16541
18731	Gate To Go Through	Ch 16541
18732	Jennie Baker -1	Ch S-16559
18733	Bury Me On The Prairie	Ch 16506

JULIAN JOHNSON & LEON HYATT

Julian Johnson, v-1; Leon Hyatt, v-2; acc. prob. one of them, md-3; the other, g.
    Charlotte, NC   Thursday, January 27, 1938

018782-1	Little Paper Boy -1, 2	BB B-7510, MW M-7740
018783-1	My Little Darling -1, 2	MW M-7740
018784-1	That Little Girl Of Mine -1, 2	MW M-7741
018785-1	I Love Only You -1, 2	MW M-7741
018786-1	I Love You I Do -1	MW M-7742
018787-1	Death Has Caused Me To Ramble -1, 3	MW M-7742
018788-1	TB Killed My Daddy -1, 3	BB B-7510, MW M-7743
018789-1	I'm Thinking Tonight Of Mother -2	MW M-7743

LELAND JOHNSON (THE TALKING BARITONE)

Leland Johnson, v; acc. unknown.
    Dallas, TX   Saturday, October 26, 1929

DAL-477	Too Many Parties And Too Many Pals	Br/Vo cancelled
DAL-478	The Lonesome Road	Br/Vo cancelled

LEROY [SLIM] JOHNSON

Leroy Johnson, g; acc. prob. Walter Hurdt, g; poss. Smoky or Chuck Wiseman, g; prob. Curly Burleson, sb.
    Rock Hill, SC   Thursday, September 29, 1938

027665-1	Rhythm In E	BB B-7860
027666-1	Guitar Rag	BB B-7860, MW M-7601

Montgomery Ward M-7601 as by **Walter Hurdt & Boys**. Rev. Montgomery Ward M-7601 by Walter Hurdt.

Acc. prob. Walter Hurdt, g; poss. Curly Burleson, g.
    Rock Hill, SC   Thursday, February 2, 1939

031958-1	Wild Indian	BB B-8124
031959-1	Syncopated Swing	BB B-8075
031960-1	Texas Sand	BB B-8075
031961-1	Time Rhythm	BB B-8124

Leroy Johnson also recorded at both the above sessions as a member of Walter Hurdt & His Singing Cowboys. For items credited to **Johnson & Burleson** (Bluebird B-8074, Montgomery Ward M-7874) see Walter Hurdt.

Slim Johnson & The Singing Cowboys: prob.: Smoky Wiseman, f; Chuck Wiseman, f; Leroy (Slim) Johnson, g; Curly Burleson, sb; unidentified (poss. Johnson and Smoky Wiseman), v duet-1.

Atlanta, GA   Tuesday, February 6, 1940

047563-1	Blue Skies Above -1	BB B-8643, MW M-8701
047564-1	Fisherman's Daughter -1	BB B-8471, MW M-8700
047565-1	The Old Gulf Coast -1	BB B-8471, MW M-8700
047566-1	Courtin' In The West Virginia Hills -1	BB B-8643, MW M-8701
047567-1	Truck Drivers' Blues -1	BB B-8563, MW M-8702
047568-1	What If My Dreams Don't Come True? -1	BB B-8563, MW M-8702
047569-1	Tell Me With Your Blue Eyes -1	BB B-8658, MW M-8703
047570-1	Honeysuckle Blues	BB B-8658, MW M-8703

Only one fiddle is audible on some items.

NELLIE JOHNSON

Pseudonym on Harmony for Connie Sides.

PAUL [& CHARLES] JOHNSON

See the Johnson Brothers. Paul Johnson on Perfect and associated labels is a pseudonym for, probably, Jack Kaufman.

R.N. JOHNSON

R.N. Johnson, v; acc. unknown, f; unknown, g.

Richmond, IN   c. March 1928

13636,-A,-B	Unclouded Day	Ge rejected
13637,-A,-B	Mother's Gone	Ge rejected

Conceivably this artist may be the Roland N. Johnson who recorded with Ernest Phipps.

RALPH E. JOHNSON

Ralph E. Johnson, v; acc. unknown, f; unknown, t; unknown, p.

Richmond, IN   Saturday, October 20, 1928

14374	Where The Roses Never Fade	Ge rejected

Richmond, IN   Friday, November 2, 1928

14404,-A,-B	In The Land Where The Roses Never Fade	Ge rejected
14405,-A,-B	Keep Smiling Thru'	Ge rejected

SLIM JOHNSON & THE SINGING COWBOYS

See Leroy [Slim] Johnson.

SMILIN' TUBBY JOHNSON

Pseudonym on Champion for Chubby Parker.

JOHNSON & BURLESON

See Walter Hurdt.

JOHNSON & LEE

Vocal/yodelling-1 duet; acc. prob. one of them, g; unknown, train-wh eff-2.

Hattiesburg, MS   Saturday, July 18, 1936

HAT-127-	Log Cabin On The Hill	ARC unissued
HAT-128-3	Let's Go	ARC 6-12-64
HAT-129-3	Goodbye Little Darling -1, 2	ARC 6-12-64
HAT-130-	She's A Hot Shot Baby	ARC unissued
HAT-131-	Stephensville Blues	ARC unissued
HAT-132-	When I'm In A Far Away Land	ARC unissued
HAT-137-	Mississippi Bound -1	ARC unissued

Matrix HAT-137 may have been recorded on July 20. Intervening matrices are by Rajah Evans (see B&GR).

JOHNSON BROTHERS

Paul Johnson, v/sg; Charles Johnson, v-1/g; unidentified, k-2; unidentified, wh solo-3/duet-4.

Camden, NJ   Thursday, May 12, 1927

38902-1,-2,-3	Henry Judd Gray	Vi unissued
38903-2	Down In Happy Valley -1, 4	Vi 20661
38904-1	Careless Love	Vi 20940
38905-1	Wings Of An Eagle	Vi 20661

| 38906-1,-2 | Dream Of The Miner's Child | Vi unissued |
| 38907-1 | Alecazander -2, 3 | Vi 20662 |

Charles Johnson, v; acc. own g; Sam Roberts Jr., barking.
  Camden, NJ   Thursday, May 12, 1927

| 38908-2 | Sweet Nellie Brown | Vi 20662 |

Johnson Brothers: Paul Johnson, v; acc. El Watson, h-1/bones-2; own sg-3/bj-4; Charles Johnson, g.
  Bristol, TN   Thursday, July 28, 1927

39722-3	Two Brothers Are We -2, 3	Vi 21243
39723-1	The Jealous Sweetheart -3	Vi 21243
39723-2	The Jealous Sweetheart -3	Vi unissued: *CMF-011-L (LP); 011-D (CD)*
39724-2	A Passing Policeman -2, 3	Vi unissued: *CMF-011-L (LP); 011-D (CD)*
39729-3	The Soldier's Poor Little Boy -1, 4	Vi 20891
39730-2	Just A Message From Carolina -3	Vi 20891
39731-2	I Want To See My Mother (Ten Thousand Miles Away) -2, 3	Vi 20940

Matrices 39722, 39729 as by **Johnson Brothers With Tennessee Wildcats**. Intervening matrices are by Blind Alfred Reed.

Paul Johnson, v-1/sg-2/bj-3; Charles Johnson, v-4/sp-5/g.
  Camden, NJ   Thursday, May 24, 1928

45200-1,-2	My Old Virginia Home -1, 2, 4	Vi unissued
45201-2	Old Timer From Caroliner -1, 2	Vi 21532
45202-2	Baby, Come Kiss Your Honey -4, 5	Vi 21532
45203-1,-2	The Dutchman's Daughter -1, 2	Vi unissued
45204-1,-2	Broken-Hearted Wife -1, 2	Vi unissued
45205-2	Smoky Mountain Far Away -1, 2, 4	Vi 21646, MW M-8071
45206-2	Crime Of The D'Autremont Brothers -1, 3	Vi 21646

Matrix 45205 is titled *On Top Of Old Smokey* on Montgomery Ward M-8071.
Rev. Montgomery Ward M-8071 by Vaughn's Happy Two.

Paul & Charles Johnson, v duet; or **Paul Johnson**, v-1/y-2; acc. Paul Johnson, sg-3/bj-4; Charles Johnson, g.
  Richmond, IN   Thursday, September 4, 1930

16991-A	I Played On My Spanish Guitar -3	Ge 7313, Spr 2537
16993-B	Wild Cat Hollow -1, 3	Ge 7313, Spr 2612
16994	Yadkin River -1, 3	Ge unissued
16997	Rose Of Heaven -1, 3	Spr 2612
17000,-A	My Ashville [sic] Home In Caroline -1, 4	Ge unissued
17003-A	Out On The Western Plains -1, 2	Ge rejected

Superior 2537 as by **Hayes & Jenkins**.
Matrices 16992, 16995, 17002 are by Clara Burston; 16996, 16998/99, 17001 by Walter Cole (see *B&GR* for both).
Rev. Superior 2537 by Fletcher & Foster.

JOHNSON BROTHERS' BAND FROM SAND MOUNTAIN

Dan Johnson, f; W.H. Johnson, f/hv-1; Leo Johnson, f/v-2; Ras Johnson, g/lv-3/v solo-4; Adous Johnson, sb.
  Atlanta, GA   Wednesday, August 1, 1928

402022-A,-B	Murilla's Lesson – Intro. What A Friend We Have In Jesus -1, 2, 3	OK unissued
402023-A,-B	Holy Manna -1, 2, 3	OK unissued
402024-A,-B	Daisies Won't Tell -4	OK unissued
402025-A,-B	Silver Moon	OK unissued
402027-A,-B	Everybody Works But Father -2, 3	OK unissued

Matrix 402026, blank in OKeh files, is probably by this group.

JOHNSON BROTHERS QUARTETTE

Vocal quartet; acc. unk. p.
  Birmingham, AL   Wednesday, November 14, 1928

| BIRM-800- | Oh, Declare His Glory | Vo 5283 |
| BIRM-801- | Living In Glory Divine | Vo 5283 |

JOHNSON COUNTY RAMBLERS

Paul Byrd, Talmadge Pollard, v duet; acc. own g duet; or **Paul Byrd**-1, v; acc. own k-2/g; or **Talmadge Pollard**-3, v; acc. own k-4/g.
  Charlotte, NC   Friday, August 6, 1937

013038-1	Where He Leads Me I'll Follow	MW M-7744
013039-1	He Will Set Your Fields On Fire	MW M-7745
013040-1	Shouting On The Hills	MW M-7745

013041-1	Beautiful Louisiana	MW M-7744
013042-1	Don't You Love Your Daddy Too	MW M-7746
013043-1	Tie Me To Your Apron Strings Again	MW M-7746
013044-1	Going Crazy -1	BB B-7372, MW M-7747
013045-1	Never Had Such A Time In My Life -1, 2	BB B-7372, MW M-7747
013046-1	Love That Lies -3, 4	BB B-7176, MW M-7748
013047-1	Mind Your Own Business -3	BB B-7176, MW M-7748

JOHNSON SISTERS TRIO

Unknown, f; unknown, bj; unknown, g; unknown, v duet-1.
    Hot Springs, AR   Monday, March 8, 1937

HS-34-	East Tennessee Blues	ARC unissued
HS-35-	Mama Grows Hot, Papa Grows Cold -1	ARC unissued

JESS JOHNSTON

This artist recorded on numerous occasions in an accompanying or, at least, secondary role; for these recordings see the artists listed at the end of the entry. The session given in full here is the only one in which he appears to have been given nominal priority. His surname is always misspelled Johnson.

Jess Johnston, v; acc. prob. own f-1/g-2; Bert Froste, g-3/v-4.
    Richmond, IN   Wednesday, November 4, 1931

18150,-A	George Collins -2, 3	Ge unissued
18151,-A	In The Hills Of Tennessee -2, 3, 4	Ge rejected
18152,-A	Separation Blues -2, 3	Ge unissued
18153	A Rose With A Broken Stem -2	Ge rejected
18154	Rubin -1, 3	Ge unissued

Matrix 18152 is not logged as by Johnston and Froste, but acc. is given as two guitars and there is a strong implication that it belongs here. Gennett files also note, of this item, "Can Use Race Another Name."
See also Duke Clark, Roy Harvey, Jess Hillard, Ted Lunsford, Byrd Moore.

JOLLY BOYS OF LAFAYETTE

Leon "Crip" Credeur, f/v-1; Joseph Fabacher, ac-2; Francis "Red" Fabacher, g; unknown, d-3.
    Dallas, TX   Sunday, February 21, 1937

61912-A	Cata Houla Breakdown -2	De 17029
61913-A	La Valse A Papa	De 17026
61914-A	Tant Que Tu Est Avec Moi (As Long As You're With Me) -1, 2, 3	De 17036
61915-A	High Society -2, 3	De 17036
61916-A	Old Man Crip -1, 2, 3	De 5431
61917-A	There'll Come A Time -1, 2, 3	De 5431
61918-A	Abbeville	De 17026
61919-A	La Valse De La Lafayette -3	De 17029
61920-A	Jolly Boys' Breakdown	De 17032
61921-A	Jolie (Brunette) -1	De 17032

BILL & LOUIS JONES

Louis Jones, v-1; or Bill Jones, v-2; acc. unknown, f; two unknowns, g.
    Richmond, IN   Friday, February 17, 1933

19028	Bill Johnson -1	Ch S-16567
19029	Slim Gal -2	Ch S-16567

See Lane's Old Time Fiddlers for a possibly associated group.

BUDDY JONES

Buddy Jones' first recordings were duets with Jimmie Davis; see the latter.

Buddy Jones, v/y-1; acc. poss. Buster Jones, esg; own g; poss. Hershel Woodal, sb; unknown, v-2.
    Dallas, TX   Thursday, February 18, 1937

61837-A	Mean Old Lonesome Blues -1	De 5372
61838-A	The Women ('Bout To Make A Wreck Out Of Me) -1	De 5345
61858-A,-B	My Pal – Jimmie Davis	De rejected
61859-A	Drunkard's Blues -1	De 5414
61860-A	Rambler's Blues -1	De 5414
61861-A	My Home In The Hills Of Caroline -2	De 5345

Matrices 61839 to 61849 are by Shelton Brothers; 61850/51 by Blind Norris; 61852 to 61855 by Alex Moore; 61856/57 by Andrew Hogg (for the last three artists see *B&GR*).

Buddy Jones, sp; acc. own g.
    Dallas, TX   Friday, February 19, 1937

61873-A	Huntin' Blues	De 5372
61874-A	Butcher Man Blues	De 5372

Buddy Jones, v/y-1; acc. Doc Massey, f-2; Buster Jones, esg; own g; unknown, sb; unknown, woodblocks; band v-3.
    Dallas, TX   Saturday, December 11, 1937

63009-A	Ragged But Right -2	De 5476
63010-A	When The Cactus Is In Bloom -1, 2	De 5521
63011-A	(It's Mighty Cold) When The Sun Goes Down -2, 3	De 5521
63012-A	Small Town Mama -2	De 5476
63013-A	Shreveport County Jail Blues -1, 2	De 5490
63014-A	My Home, My Baby And Me -1, 2	De 5600, MeC 45267, Min M-14094
63015-A	Streamlined Mama -2	De 5538
63016-A	I'm Your Real And True Friend -1	De 5600, MeC 45267, Min M-14095
63017-A	Tomcattin' Around -1, 2	De 5490
63018-A	Evil Stingaree -1, 2	De 5538

Revs: Minerva M-14094, M-14095 by Jimmie Davis.

Buddy Jones, v; acc. poss. Lonnie Hall, f-1; Buster Jones, esg; unknown, tbj; own g; unknown, sb; band v-2.
    San Antonio, TX   Wednesday, September 21, 1938

64558-A	Carry The Good Work On -1	De 5637
64559-A	I'll Get Mine Bye And Bye -1, 2	De 5654
64560-A	Small Town Mama No. 2	De 5613
64561-A	Easy Rollin' Sue -1	De 5654
64566-A	She's Sellin' What She Used To Give Away	De 5613
64567-A	I Ain't Goin' Your Way -2	De 5637
64568-A	Old Fashioned Sweetheart	De 5693

Intervening matrices are by Jimmie Davis.

Acc. Bob Dunn, esg-1; Leo Raley, emd; Joe Thames, tbj; Dickie McBride, g; Hezzie Bryant, sb; band v-2.
    Houston, TX   Friday, March 3, 1939

65123-A	Easy Rider – Easy Rider -1	De 5682
65124-A	Ease My Troubled Mind	De 5673
65125-A	I'm In The Doghouse Now -2	De 5682
65126-A	Oklahoma City Blues	De 5693
65127-A,-B	She's Selling What She Used To Give Away No. 2	De rejected
65128-A	She's Got Her Jinx On Me	De 5673
65129-A	The Roughest Gal In Town	De 5703

Acc. Cliff Bruner, f; Bob Dunn, esg; Leo Raley, emd-1; Joe Thames, tbj; Dickie McBride, g; Hezzie Bryant, sb; band v-2.
    Houston, TX   Saturday, March 4, 1939

65138-A	I'll Get Mine Bye And Bye No. 2 -1, 2	De 5711
65139-A	You Cannot Take It With You	De 5711

Acc. Buster Jones, esg; Leo Raley, emd; Moon Mullican, p; own g; Hezzie Bryant, sb; band v-1.
    Houston, TX   Wednesday, August 30, 1939

66333-A	Hold It A Little Longer	De 5731
66334-A	I Can't Be Bothered	De 5788
66335-A	I Can't Use You Anymore	De 5816
66336-A	I'll Get Mine Bye And Bye No. 3 -1	De 5816
66337-A	Boog-A-Boo Baby	De 5744
66338-A	Like The Doctor Said	De 5788
66339-A	Tend To Your Business -1	De 5809
66340-A	Alice From Dallas	De 5744
66341-A	Rockin' Rollin' Mama	De 5731
66342-A	You'll Miss Me Some Sweet Day	De 5821
66343-A	Settle Down Blues	De 5821
66344-A	I'm In The Doghouse Now No. 2 -1	De 5773
66345-A	She's Got The Best In Town -1	De 5773
66346-A	I Wish I'd Never Met You	De 5757
66347-A	Action Speaks Louder Than Words	De 5757
66348-A	I Think I'll Turn Your Damper Down	De 5809

Acc. poss. own or Dickie McBride, g.
    Houston, TX   Saturday, September 2, 1939

66378-A,-B	Garbage Man	De rejected
66379-A	Big Mama Blues	De rejected

Acc. Buster Jones, esg; Moon Mullican, p; own g; Buddy Ray or Bill Mounce, sb. (Ray and Mounce each played on one 1940 session, but it is not known which.)

Houston, TX   Sunday, April 7, 1940
92042-A	Mean Old Sixty Five Blues	De 5850
92043-A	I'll Come Back Dear (If You're Still In Love With Me)	De 5850
92044-A	Going Back To Louisiana Lou	De 5896
92045-A	Taxicab Driver's Blues	De 5861, MeC 45372

Houston, TX   Monday, April 8, 1940
92046-A	Waiting For A Train	De 5827
92047-A	Dear Old Sunny South By The Sea	De 5840, MeC 45362
92048-A	I Won't Miss You When You Go Away	De 5827
92049-A	Any Old Time	De 5840, MeC 45362
92050-A	I'm Going Back To Sadie	De 5861, 46079, MeC 45372
92051-A	Sailing Blues	De 5896

Acc. Cliff Bruner, f-1/etg-2; Bill Vitovsky, esg; Moon Mullican, p; Bruce Pierce, tbj; own g; Oliver "Sock" Underwood, g; prob. Herschel Woodal, sb.

Dallas, TX   Tuesday, April 29, 1941
93722-A	Don't Ever Leave Me Alone -1, 2	De 5950
93723-A	Honey, Don't Turn Me Down -1	De 5984
93724-A	You've Got Just What It Takes -1	De 6013
93725-B	Red Wagon -2	De 5950

Acc. Cliff Bruner, f; Bill Vitovsky, esg; Moon Mullican, p; Bruce Pierce, tbj; own g; Oliver "Sock" Underwood, g; prob. Herschel Woodal, sb.

Dallas, TX   Wednesday, April 30, 1941
93726-A	What Is Life Lived Alone	De 5984, 46079
93727-A	Gonna Change My Business All Around	De 5967, MeC 45456
93728-A	If I'm Wrong, I'm Sorry	De 6013
93729-A	Mean Hangover Blues	De 5967, MeC 45456

Acc. Cliff Bruner, f; Vaughn Horton, esg; Joe Moresco, p; Dave Wallace, tbj; own g; Harry Patent, sb.

New York, NY   Wednesday, September 17, 1941
69748-A	She's A Hum-Dum Dinger	De 6049
69749-B	Don't Say Goodbye If You Love Me	De 6030
69750-A	I'm Going To Get Me A Honky Tonky Baby	De 6049
69751-A	Every Day Blues	De 6030

CARL JONES

Carl Jones, v/y-1; acc. prob. own g.

Atlanta, GA   Thursday, December 11, 1930
404670-A	How Well I Remember	OK 45516
404671-B	My Tennessee Girl -1	OK 45540
404672-B	The Wild Man Of Borneo	OK 45516

Rev. OKeh 45540 by Hugh Roden & Roy Rodgers.

COLON JONES
See Riley Puckett.

DEMPSEY JONES
See the Golden Melody Boys.

FLOYD JONES
Recordings by this artist in the Paramount Old Time Tunes series (3029, 3030) and on Vocalion are believed to be outside the scope of this work.

FRANK JONES
Pseudonym on Conqueror for Orla Clark.

HIRAM JONES
Pseudonym on Homestead and Oriole for John Baltzell.

L.V. JONES & HIS VIRGINIA SINGING CLASS

Vocal group, directed by Levi Vincen Jones; unacc.

Winston-Salem, NC   Tuesday, September 27, 1927
81627-B	In That Crowning Day	OK 45187

81628-	Keep On Climbing	OK unissued
81629-	My Beautiful Home	OK unissued
81630-A	Will My Mother Know Me There?	OK 45187
81631-	I'm Glory Bound	OK unissued
81632-	Come And Be Saved	OK unissued

LOUIS JONES

See Bill & Louis Jones.

MARY JONES

Pseudonym on Gennett for Pearl Brock (see Allie & Pearl Brock).

ROY JONES

Roy Jones, v/y; acc. poss. own g.
    Atlanta, GA   Thursday, April 12, 1928

| 146036-2 | Southern Yodel Blues | Co 15428-D, Ve 2495-V, Cl 5435-C |
| 146037-2 | Farmer John's Yodel | Co 15428-D, Ve 2495-V, Cl 5435-C |

Velvet Tone 2495-V as by **Roy Evans**. Velvet Tone 2495-V, Clarion 5435-C use the transfer matrices 100580 and 100578 respectively.

This artist may be Roy Evans, who recorded yodel songs in his own name and is outside the scope of this work (see JR).

JONES & BILLINGS

Pseudonym on Clarion and Velvet Tone for W.T. Narmour & S.W. Smith.

THE JONES BROTHERS

Pseudonym on Melotone, Polk, and Panachord for Vernon Dalhart & Carson Robison, or Carson Robison & Frank Luther, or the Carson Robison Trio.

THE JONES BROTHERS TRIO

Vocal trio; acc. unknown, pac.
    Atlanta, GA   Sunday, October 12, 1940

056548-1	I've Changed My Mind	BB B-8622, MW M-8858
056549-1	I'm Gonna Sail Away	BB B-8622, MW M-8858
056550-1	Rock Of Ages Keep My Soul	BB B-8576, MW M-8857
056551-1	I'm A Gonna Be In That Glad Band	BB B-8667, MW M-8859
056552-1	Victory In Jesus	BB B-8576, MW M-8857
056553-1	Have A Little Talk With Jesus	BB B-8667, MW M-8859
056554-1	The Cross On The Hill	BB B-8707, [MW M-8860]
056555-1	My Soul Will Shout Hallelujah	BB B-8707, [MW M-8860]

JONES COUNTY BOYS

No details.
    New Orleans, LA   Friday, December 14, 1928

| 147640- | Coon Hunting Blues | Co unissued |
| 147641- | Jones County Blues | Co unissued |

BILLY JORDAN

Pseudonym on Champion for Doc Roberts.

JERRY JORDAN

Pseudonym on Supertone for Walter Smith.

JORDAN & RUPERT

Pseudonym on Supertone for Walter Smith & Norman Woodlieff.

JORDAN BROTHERS (THOMAS, CHALMERS & HERSHEL)

Thomas Jordan, md/v; Chalmers Jordan, g/v; Hershel Jordan, g/v; unidentified, y-1.
    Charlotte, NC   Monday, August 2, 1937

011837-1	Georgia Mountain Home	BB B-7123
011838-1	Goin' Back Home	BB B-7235
011839-1	When We Put On An Old Pair Of Shoes	BB B-7235
011840-1	Dear Old Dixie	BB unissued
011841-1	An Answer To Birmingham Jail	BB B-7123, MW M-7655
011842-1	Along Life's Journey	BB unissued
011843-1	Riding & Roping -1	MW M-7655
011844-1	Saw Mill Blues -1	BB unissued

JERRY JORDON
Pseudonym on Supertone for Walter Smith.

JOSIE (OF THE CUMBERLAND RIDGE RUNNERS)
See Jossie Ellers.

THE JUBILEERS
Tiny Moore, f/emd/v-1; unknown, f; A.C. Peveto, esg; Jesse Tyler, p; Don Tyler or Billy Parker, g; unknown, sb.
    Dallas, TX   Tuesday, October 7, 1941

071108-1	Boogie Woogie Johnson	BB B-8972
071109-1	My Heart Makes A Monkey Out Of Me -1	BB unissued
071110-1	Start A Little Rainbow In My Heart -1	BB B-8874
071111-1	San Antonio Moonlight	BB B-8874
071112-1	The Right String But The Wrong Yo-Yo -1	BB B-8972
071113-1	Ain't You Sorry Now -1	BB unissued

For associated lineups see Jimmy Hart & His Merrymakers and Port Arthur Jubileers.

WALTER JUDD
Walter Judd, v; acc. two unknowns, g.
    Richmond, IN   Thursday, October 8, 1931

18092,-A	Reno Valley	Ge unissued

JUDIE & JULIE
Judie Jones, Julie Jones, v duet; acc. prob. one of them, g.
    Atlanta, GA   Wednesday, August 23, 1939

041260-1	A Letter To Mother	BB B-8345, MW M-8443
041261-1	She Thinks First Of You	BB B-8345, MW M-8443
041262-1	Sittin' On The Old Settee	BB B-8324, MW M-8444, RZAu G24460
041263-1	Little Bunch Of Roses	BB B-8324, MW M-8444, RZAu G24460
041264-1	Gathering Buds	BB B-8386, MW M-8445
041265-1	My Old Pal Of Yesterday	BB B-8278, MW M-8446
041266-1	There's A Bridle Hanging On The Wall	BB B-8278, MW M-8446
041289-1	Rockin' Alone In An Old Rockin' Chair	BB B-8411, MW M-8447
041290-1	When The Bees Are In The Hive	BB B-8411, MW M-8447
041291-1	Drifting Too Far From The Shore	BB B-8386, MW M-8445

Matrices 041267 to 041274 are by Morris Brown Quartet (see B&GR); 041275 to 041284 by Riley Puckett; 041285 to 041288 by Rev. J.M. Gates (see B&GR).

Judie & Julie recorded, as the Jones Sisters, after 1942.

MATT JUDSON
Pseudonym on Clarion and Velvet Tone for Benny Borg.

DICK JUSTICE
Dick Justice, v; acc. own g.
    Chicago, IL   Monday, May 20, 1929

C-3513-	Old Black Dog	Br 395
C-3514-	Little Lulie	Br 336
C-3515-	Brown Skin Blues	Br 336
C-3516-	Cocaine	Br 395

    Chicago, IL   Tuesday, May 21, 1929

C-3521-	Henry Lee	Br 367
C-3522-	One Cold December Day	Br 367
C-3523-A	K.C. Brown	Br unissued
C-3524-A	West Virginia Girl	Br rejected

See also Jarvis & Justice.

K

BOB KACKLEY [& BEN WEAVER]
Pseudonym on ARC labels and OKeh for Bob Miller [& Barney Burnett].

BOB KACKLY
Pseudonym on Crown for Bob Miller.

CHARLES KAMA & M.T. SALAZAR

Despite releases in Victor's Old Familar Tunes series (23655, 23734) and their accompaniments to Jimmie Rodgers, these artists' Hawaiian recordings are beyond the scope of this work.

KANAWHA SINGERS

Arthur Herbert, Alex Mason, Neil Evans, Jesse Phillips, v quartet; acc. Bill Wirges, p.
New York, NY   Friday, April 29, 1927

| E-22775/76/77* | West Virginia Hills | Br 158, Vo 5142 |
| E-22778*/79/80 | Hail West Virginia | Br 158, Vo 5142 |

Acc. Sam Raitz, f; Vernon Dalhart, h/v; John Cali, tbj; Carson Robison, g.
New York, NY   Saturday, August 13, 1927

| E-24213/14/15/16 | Golden Slippers | Br 189, Vo 5173, Spt S2040 |

Rev. all issues by Al Hopkins.

Acc. two unknowns, f; poss. Bill Wirges, p; unknown, tbj.
New York, NY   Friday, January 13, 1928

| E-26002/03* | Indiana | Br 255 |
| E-26004/05* | On The Banks Of The Wabash Far Away | Br 255 |

Acc. unknown orch. (five musicians); Carson Robison, g added on some takes.
New York, NY   Tuesday, January 24, 1928

| E-26257/58* | Swing Low, Sweet Chariot | Br 205, 3801, BrAu 3801, BrE 3798, Spt S2125, Au A22026 |
| E-26259/60* | Climbing Up De Golden Stairs | Br 205, 3801, BrAu 3801, BrE 3798, Spt S2125, Au A22026 |

Brunswick 3798 as by **The Kanawha Singers**. Aurora A22026 as by **Archie Ruff's Singers**.

Acc. unknown orch.
New York, NY   Friday, May 18, 1928

| E-27567- | Goodbye My Lover Goodbye | Br 242, 3991, BrAu 242, 3991, Spt S2074 |
| E-27568- | That Good Old Country Town (Where I Was Born) | Br 242, 3991, BrAu 242, 3991 |

Rev. Supertone S2074 by Bob Miller.

Acc. unknown.
New York, NY   Thursday, April 4, 1929

| E-29540- | Climb Up, Ye Chillun, Climb | Br rejected |
| E-29541- | Ella Ree | Br rejected |

Acc. unknown, f; unknown, tbj; unknown, g.
New York, NY   c. April 30, 1929

| E-29698- | De Camptown Races | Br 337, BrAu 337 |
| E-29699- | Keep In De Middle Of De Road | Br 337, BrAu 337 |

Australian Brunswick 337 as by **Kanwha Singers**.

Acc. unknown, o.
New York, NY   Tuesday, June 11, 1929

E-30053-	Brighten The Corner Where You Are	Br 328, BrAu 328
E-30054-	Shall We Gather At The River	Br 328, BrAu 328, Au A22034
E-30055-	God Be With You	Br unissued

Aurora A22034 as by **Campbell's Sacred Singers**. Rev. Aurora A22034, with same credit, by Criterion Male Quartet.

New York, NY   Friday, June 28, 1929

E-30303-	Rescue The Perishing	Br unissued
E-30304-	There's Sunshine In My Soul Today	Br 472, BrAu 472
E-30305-	If Your Heart Keeps Right	Br 472, BrAu 472

Acc. unknown, f; unknown, p; unknown, tbj; unknown, g; unknown, wh.
New York, NY   Thursday, July 18, 1929

| E-30402- | Mountains Ain't No Place For Bad Men | Br 347, Spt S2068 |
| E-30403- | A High Silk Hat And A Walking Cane | Br 347, Spt S2050 |

Revs: Supertone S2050 by Frank Marvin, S2068 by Pickard Family.

Acc. unknown, p; unknown, tbj.
New York, NY   Tuesday, August 27, 1929

E-30513-	Ella Ree (Carry Me Back To Tennessee)	Br 459, PanAu P11984
E-30514-	Climb Up, Ye Chillun, Climb	Br 459, PanAu P11984
E-30515-	Early In The Mornin'	Br 365
E-30516-	The Gospel Train	Br 365

The same lineup also recorded as the Dixieland Four.

KARL & HARDY
See Karl & Harty.

KARL & HARTY

Renfro Valley Boys: prob. John Lair, h; Karl Davis, md/v; Hartford Taylor, g/v.
Grafton, WI   c. December 1931

L-1315-2	My Renfro Valley Home	Pm 3315
L-1317-2	The Old Grey Goose Is Dead	Pm 3315
L-1320-2	I'm Thinking Tonight Of My Blue Eyes	Pm 3316
L-1321-1	Twenty One Years	Pm 3311, Bwy 8318
L-1322-1	I Wonder How The Folks Are At Home	Pm 3311, Bwy 8318, ARC-Bwy 3311
L-1323-1	The Yellow Rose Of Texas	Pm 3316
L-1324-1	Loreena	Pm 3321, Bwy 8334
L-1325-1	Who's Gonna Shoe Your Pretty Little Feet	Pm 3321, Bwy 8334

Matrix L-1324 is titled *Lorrenna* on Broadway 8334. Matrix L-1316 is by Lonnie Glosson; matrices L-1318/19 are untraced.
Rev. ARC-Broadway 3311 by Carson Robison.

Taylor & Davis: Karl Davis, Harty Taylor, v duet; acc. Karl Davis, md; Harty Taylor, g.
Chicago, IL   Thursday, March 22, 1934

CP-1019-1	I'm Here To Get My Baby Out Of Jail	Ba 33118, Me M13085, Or 8360, Pe 13023, Ro 5360, Cq 8310
CP-1020-1	I Dreamed I Searched Heaven For You	Ba 33118, Me M13085, Or 8360, Pe 13023, Ro 5360, Cq 8310

Conqueror 8310 as by **Cumberland Ridge Runners**.

Karl & Hardy (Of The Cumberland Ridge Runners): Karl Davis, Harty Taylor, v duet; or Karl Davis, v-1; acc. prob. Homer "Slim" Miller or Tex Atchison, f-2; Karl Davis, md; Harty Taylor, g.
Chicago, IL   Friday, November 1, 1935

C-1157-1	There'll Come A Time	ARC unissued
C-1158-1	Two Babes	ARC unissued
C-1159-1	There's A Beautiful Home -2	ARC 6-02-52, Cq 8605
C-1161-1	My Blue Eyed Boy -1, 2	ARC 6-02-54, Cq 8616
C-1162-1	Friendless And Sad	ARC 6-02-52, Cq 8605

ARC 6-10-54 as by **Karl Davis Acc. by the Cumberland Ridge Runners**. Conqueror 8605, 8616 as by **Karl & Hardy**. Matrix C-1160 is by Josie (see Jossie Ellers).
Revs: ARC 6-02-54, Conqueror 8616 by Josie (see Jossie Ellers).

Acc. prob. Homer "Slim" Miller or Tex Atchison, f-2; Karl Davis, md; Harty Taylor, g; poss. Red Foley, sb-3.
Chicago, IL   Monday, January 20, 1936

C-1202-1	No Place To Pillow My Head -2	ARC 6-04-61, Cq 8626
C-1203-1	We Buried Her Beneath The Willow (Ridge Runners' Tribute To Linda Parker) -2	ARC 6-04-61, Cq 8626
C-1205-2	I'm S-A-V-E-D -1, 2, 3	ARC 6-10-54, Cq 8660
C-1211-1	Song Of The Blind	ARC unissued
C-1212-1	I Need The Prayers Of Those I Love	ARC unissued

ARC 6-10-54 as by **Karl Davis Acc. by the Cumberland Ridge Runners**. Conqueror 8660 as by **Karl Davis (Of The Cumberland Ridge Runners)**. Matrices C-1204, C-1206 to C-1210 are by Doc Hopkins.

Chicago, IL   Wednesday, March 4, 1936

C-1202-2,-3	No Place To Pillow My Head	ARC unissued
C-1203-3,-4	We Buried Her Beneath The Willow (Ridge Runners' Tribute To Linda Parker)	ARC unissued
C-1212-3	I Need The Prayers Of Those I Love	ARC 6-10-54, Cq 8660

ARC 6-10-54 as by **Taylor & Davis Acc. by the Cumberland Ridge Runners**. Conqueror 8660 as by **Harty Taylor & Karl Davis (Of The Cumberland Ridge Runners)**.

Carl & Harty, v duet; acc. Karl Davis, md; Harty Taylor, g.
Chicago, IL   Friday, July 10, 1936

C-1525-2	The Prisoner's Dream	ARC 7-01-53, Cq 8728
C-1526-2	The House Where We Were Wed	ARC 7-04-57, Cq 8728
C-1527-1	I'm Going Home This Evening	ARC 7-04-57, Cq 8833
C-1528-1	The Hymns My Mother Sang	ARC 7-05-60, Cq 8729
C-1529-2	They Are All Going Home But One	ARC 7-01-69, Cq 8729
C-1530-2	Our Partner's Phonograph Record (Song Our Partner Sang)	Cq 8730
C-1531-1	The Holiness Mother	ARC unissued
C-1532-1	Tombigbee River Farewell	ARC 7-01-69

C-1533-1	Darling Think Of What You've Done	ARC 7-01-53, Cq 8730
C-1534-1	I Am Just What I Am	ARC unissued?

Chicago, IL   Monday, January 25, 1937

C-1763-1	Answer To The Prisoner's Dream	ARC 7-05-60, Cq 8833
C-1764-1,-2	From A Cabin In Kentucky	ARC unissued
C-1765-1,-2	We Are Drifting Down The Rugged Stream Of Time	ARC unissued
C-1766-1,-2	The Old Chain Gang	ARC unissued
C-1767-1,-2	The Hound Dog Blues	ARC unissued

Acc. poss. Alan Crockett, f; Karl Davis, md; Harty Taylor, g.
Chicago, IL   Monday, February 19, 1940

WC-2927-A	She Did Not Get Her Baby Out Of Jail	Vo/OK 05439, Cq 9408
WC-2928-A	Read The Bible	OK 05640
WC-2929-A	I Didn't Hear Anyone Pray	Vo/OK 05439, Cq 9408, 9796
WC-2930-A	Holiness Mother	OK 05640

Karl Davis, Harty Taylor, v duet; or Karl Davis, v-1; acc. poss. Alan Crockett, f; Karl Davis, md; Harty Taylor, g.
Chicago, IL   Thursday, February 20, 1940

WC-2935-A	Little Sweetheart, I'm In Prison	Vo/OK 05549, Cq 9406, 9796
WC-2936-A	Two-Faced Preacher	Vo/OK 05549, Cq 9406, 9687
WC-2937-A	Seven Beers With The Wrong Woman -1	Vo/OK 05500, Cq 9407, 9687, CoC C25
WC-2938-A	Don't Monkey 'Round My Widder -1	Vo/OK 05500, Cq 9407, CoC C25

Karl & Harty, v duet; or Karl Davis, v-1; acc. unknown, f; Karl Davis, md; Harty Taylor, g; unknown, g; unknown, sb; band v-2.
Chicago, IL   Friday, January 24, 1941

C-3559-1	Look What Those Blue Eyes Did To Me	OK 06163, Cq 9688, Co 38139, 20414
C-3560-1	Gospel Cannon Ball	OK 06207, Cq 9689
C-3561-1	Let's All Have Another Beer -2	OK 06066, Cq 9690
C-3562-1	Sweet Mama Put Him In Low	OK 06066, Cq 9842
C-3563-1	Kentucky	OK 06163, Cq 9688, Co 38139, 20414
C-3564-1	Fifty-One Beers -1	OK 06115, Cq 9690
C-3565-1	I Heard The Wicked Pray	OK 06207, Cq 9689
C-3566-1	You Didn't Want A Sweetheart	OK 06115, Cq 9842

Acc. unknown, f-2; Karl Davis, md-3; Harty Taylor, g; unknown, g; band v-4.
Chicago, IL   Sunday, June 8, 1941

C-3853-1	Hymns They Sang (At Mother's Grave)	OK unissued
C-3854-1	Don't Be Blue, Little Pal, Don't Be Blue -2, 3	OK 06301, Cq 9841
C-3855-1	Angel Of East Tennessee -2, 3	OK 06385, Cq 9840
C-3856-1	I'll Always Love You -2, 3	OK 06301, Cq 9841
C-3857-1	Training Camp Blues -2, 3, 4	OK 06385, Cq 9840
C-3858-1	He's A Ring Tail Tornado -1, 2, 3	OK 06586, Cq 9843, CoC C600
C-3859-1	Some Girls Do And Some Girls Don't -1	OK 06586, Cq 9843, CoC C600
C-3860-1	Concertina Waltz	OK unissued

Acc. unknown, f; Karl Davis, md; Harty Taylor, g.
Chicago, IL   Tuesday, January 27, 1942

C-4171-1	I Hide My Face And Cry	OK unissued: *Time-Life TLCW-05* (LP)
C-4172-	Girls, Don't Refuse To Kiss A Soldier	OK unissued
C-4173-1	You Let Me Down	OK 06622, Co 37414, 20141
C-4174-	Tears In My Beer	OK unissued
C-4175-	I Get The Same Old Story	OK unissued
C-4176-1	Truck Drivers' Sweetheart	OK 06622, Co 37414, 20141
C-4177-	Stepping Stones To Heaven	OK unissued
C-4178-	When I Laid My Bible Down	OK unissued

Matrices C-4172 and C-4174 were scheduled for OKeh 06666 but this was never issued.

Karl Davis and Hartford Taylor also recorded as members of the Cumberland Ridge Runners and with Josie (see Jossie Ellers), and after 1942.

ALFRED G. KARNES

Alfred G. Karnes, v; acc. own harp-g.
Bristol, TN   Friday, July 29, 1927

39738-1	Called To The Foreign Field	Vi V-40327
39739-1	I Am Bound For The Promised Land	Vi 20840
39740-2	Where We'll Never Grow Old	Vi 20840
39741-1,-2	When I See The Blood	Vi unissued

| 39742-2 | When They Ring The Golden Bells | Vi 20933, MW M-4348 |
| 39743-1 | To The Work | Vi 20933 |

Rev. Montgomery Ward M-4348 by Gene Arnold.

Bristol, TN   Sunday, October 28, 1928

47231-1,-2,-3	The Sinner Sinks In Sad Despair	Vi unissued
47232-1	Do Not Wait 'Till I'm Laid 'Neath The Clay	Vi V-40327
47233-2	The Days Of My Childhood Plays	Vi V-40076
47234-2	We Shall All Be Reunited	Vi V-40076

Bristol, TN   Monday, October 29, 1928

47235-1,-2	That's Why The Boys Leave The Farm	Vi unissued
47236-1,-2	Clouds Of Glory	Vi unissued
47242-1,-2	The City Of Gold	Vi unissued

Matrices 47237 to 47241 are by Ernest Phipps.

JACK KAUFMAN

One release by this artist appeared in the Paramount Old Time Tunes series (3209), but his work as a whole was in the popular field. This name was also a pseudonym for Frank Luther on the Australian labels Angelus and Starr.

BUELL KAZEE

Buell Kazee, v; acc. own bj.

New York, NY   Tuesday, April 19, 1927

E-22493*/94	John Hardy	Br 144
E-22495*/96	Roll On, John	Br 144
E-22497/98*	Rock Island	Br 145
E-22499/500*	Old Whisker Bill, The Moonshiner	Br 145

New York, NY   Wednesday, April 20, 1927

| E-22533*/34* | Darling Cora | Br 154 |
| E-22535*/36 | East Virginia | Br 154 |

Acc. Bert Hirsch, f; unknown, p-1; Carson Robison, g/wh-2.

New York, NY   Thursday, April 21, 1927

E-22553/54/55	Mandy Lee -1	Br unissued
E-22556/57	Just Tell Them That You Saw Me -1, 2	Br unissued
E-22558/59	When The Harvest Days Are Over (Jessie Dear) -1, 2	Br unissued
E-22560/61	Where The Sweet Magnolias Grow -1	Br unissued
E-22562*/63	The Ship That's Sailing High	Br 155
E-22564/65*	If You Love Your Mother (Meet Her In The Skies)	Br 155

Acc. own bj; Carson Robison, g-1/wh-1.

New York, NY   Thursday, April 21, 1927

E-22566*/67	The Roving Cowboy	Br 156, BrC 436, Spt S2043
E-22568*/69	The Little Mohee -1	Br 156, BrC 436
E-22570*/71/72	The Old Maid -1	Br 157, Spt S2082, Au A22021
E-22573*/74	The Sporting Bachelors	Br 157, Spt S2082, Au A22021
E-22575/76	The Frog Went A Courtin' -1	Br unissued

Aurora A22021 as by **Ray Lyncy**. Rev. Supertone S2043 by Ewen Hail.

Acc. own bj-1/g-2.

New York, NY   Monday, January 16, 1928

E-26031/32*	The Butcher's Boy (The Railroad Boy) -1	Br 213, BrC 437
E-26033/34*	Lady Gay -1	Br 212, 80089
E-26035*/36	The Orphan Girl -1	Br 211, Spt S2045, DeF F3789, DeIr W4083, RexIr U251
E-26037/38*	Poor Boy Long Ways From Home -1	Br 217
E-26039/40	Little Bessie -1	Br 215, Vo 5231
E-26041*/42	My Mother -2	Br 215, Vo 5231
E-26043*/44	Poor Little Orphan Boy -2	Br 211, DeE F3789, DeIr W4083, RexIr U251
E-26045*/46	The Cowboy's Farewell -2	Br 212, Spt S2046
E-26047/48*	Gambling Blues -2	Br 218, DeIr W4330, RexIr U585

Revs: Supertone S2046 by Marc Williams, Brunswick 80089 by Bascom Lamar Lunsford.

New York, NY   Tuesday, January 17, 1928

E-26049*/50	A Married Girl's Troubles -2	Br 218, Spt S2047, DeIr W4330, RexIr U585
E-26051*/52	You Are False But I'll Forgive You -2	Br 217, Spt S2047, Au A22017
E-26053/54	A Short Life Of Trouble -1	Br unissued: *Yz 2030, 2200-6 (CDs)*

E-26055*/56*	Don't Forget Me, Little Darling -2	Br 206, BrAu 3802, PanAu P12179, DeE F3872, DeE F18003, DeSA FM5177, DeIr W4088, RexIr U252

Aurora A22017 as by **Miller Brothers**. Matrix E-26053/54 was scheduled for Brunswick 214 but not issued; a file copy survives.
Rev. Aurora A22017 (with same credit) by Lester McFarland & Robert A. Gardner.

Acc. Bert Hirsch, f; unknown, p; Carson Robison, g.
    New York, NY   Wednesday, January 18, 1928

E-26061/62*	The Faded Coat Of Blue	Br 206, BrAu 3802, Spt S2045, Au A22014, PanAu P12179, DeE F3872, DeE F18003, DeSA FM5177, DeIr W4088, RexIr U252

Aurora A22014 as by **Archie Ruff's Singers**. Rev. Aurora A22014 (with same credit) by Dixieland Four.

Acc. own bj.
    New York, NY   Wednesday, January 18, 1928

E-26063/64*	The Wagoner's Lad (Loving Nancy)	Br 213, BrC 437
E-26065/66	The Dying Soldier (Brother Green)	Br unissued: *Yz 2028, 2200-1 (CDs)*

Matrix E-26065/66 was scheduled for Brunswick 214 but not issued; a file copy survives.

Buell Kazee, v; or **Buell Kazee & Sookie Hobbs**-1: Buell Kazee, Carson Robison, v duet; acc. Bert Hirsch, f; Carson Robison, g/wh-2.
    New York, NY   Thursday, January 19, 1928

E-26073/74	Snow Deer -2	Br unissued
E-26075/76*	Red Wing -1, 2	Br 210, Spt S2057, DeIr W4331, RexIr U586
E-26077*/78	Snow Deer -1, 2	Br 210, DeIr W4331, RexIr U586
E-26089/90*	In The Shadow Of The Pines -2	Br 216, Vo 5221
E-26091*/92	You Taught Me How To Love You Now Teach Me To Forget	Br 216, Vo 5221

Decca W4331 and prob. Rex U586 as by **Buell Kazee**.
Rev. Supertone S2057 by Al Bernard.

Acc. unknown, sg; own bj; A.L. Walker, g; John Richards, sound-eff-1/bells-2.
    Chicago, IL   Wednesday, June 12, 1929

C-3587-	The Hobo's Last Ride	Br 330, Spt S2056
C-3588-	Steel A Goin' Down -1	Br 330
C-3590-	Toll The Bells -2	Br 351

Matrix C-3589 is by Lee Sims (popular). Rev. Supertone S2056 by Frank Luther.

Acc. unknown, sg-1; own bj; A.L. Walker, g-2.
    Chicago, IL   Thursday, June 13, 1929

C-3591-A,-B	I Am Lonely -1, 2	Br unissued
C-3592-	The Cowboy Trail	Br 481
C-3593-	The Blind Man	Br 351
C-3596-	I'm Rolling Along -1, 2	Br 481
C-3597-A,-B	The New Jail	Br unissued
C-3598-A,-B	The Empty Cell	Br unissued

Matrices C-3594/95 are by Tampa Red (see *B&GR*).

Acc. unknown, sg; own bj; A.L. Walker, g.
    Chicago, IL   Friday, June 14, 1929

C-3599-A,-B	Fifteen Years Ago	Br unissued

Buell Kazee, v/sp; acc. own bj; Jack Kapp, sp.
    Chicago, IL   Friday, June 14, 1929

C-3600-A,-B	A Mountain Boy Makes His First Record – Part I	Br unissued
C-3603-	A Mountain Boy Makes His First Record – Part II	Br 338, Spt S2084

Brunswick 338 is credited to **Buell Kazee Assisted by John Richards**. Richards was a member of the Brunswick staff (see June 12, 1929 session above), whose name was here used to hide the identity of Brunswick's recording supervisor, Jack Kapp.
Matrices C-3601/02 are unrelated.

    Chicago, IL   Monday, July 1, 1929

C-3756-	A Mountain Boy Makes His First Record – Part I	Br 338, Spt S2084

See the note to the previous session.

Goods Box Whittlers: Buell Kazee, Elmo Tanner, prob. Jack Kapp, prob. John Richards, sp.
    Chicago, IL   Monday, July 1, 1929

C-3759-A,-B,-C	Election Day In Kentucky – Part 1	Vo unissued
C-3760-A,-B	Election Day In Kentucky – Part 2	Vo unissued

Matrices C-3757/58 are by Charlie Craver.

Buell Kazee, v/sp; acc. unknown, f; own bj; unknown, g; two unknown men, v/sp.
Chicago, IL   Wednesday, July 24, 1929
| C-3934- | Election Day In Kentucky – Part I | Vo 5352 |
| C-3935- | Election Day In Kentucky – Part II | Vo 5352 |

Matrices C-3934/35 were logged as by **Soap Box Whittlers** but issued as shown.

Buell Kazee was also a member of the Blue Ridge Gospel Singers. He recorded after 1942.

[THE] KEAWE BROTHERS

Pseudonym on Superior for The Two Islanders (see James Brown, Jr. & Ken Landon groups).

HANK KEENE

Hank Keene & His Connecticut Hill Billies: unknown, f; Hank Keene, prob. p/v; unknown, bj; unknown, g.
New York, NY   Thursday, February 12, 1931
| E-36066- | The "Run-A-Way Boy" | Br 516, Pan 25089 |
| E-36067- | Little Sweetheart Of The Prairie | Br 516 |

Rev. Panachord 25089 by Bert Peck.

Hank Keene, v/y-1; acc. unknown, f; unknown, pac; own p; unknown, bj.
New York, NY   Friday, October 27, 1933
78285-1	The Last Round-Up -1	BB B-5241, Eld 2124, Sr S-3324, MW M-4397
78286-1	Home On The Range -1	BB B-5241, Eld 2124, Sr S-3324, MW M-4397
78287-1	Let's Go Down To The Old State Fair -1	BB B-5254, Eld 2134, Sr S-3337, MW M-4447
78288-1	Yodelling Blues -1	BB B-6035, MW M-4448, Twin FT1963
78289-1	Hank Keene's Song Of The Crow	BB B-5254, Eld 2134, Sr S-3337, MW M-4447
78290-1	I'm Goin' West -1	BB B-5339, Sr S-3420, MW M-4446
78291-1	I've Got A Gal In The Mountains -1	BB B-6035, MW M-4448, Twin FT1963
78292-1	After The Round-Up -1	BB B-5339, Sr S-3420, MW M-4446
78293-1	Little Green Mound On The Hillside	BB unissued

Hank Keene & His Radio Gang: unknown, f; unknown, pac; Hank Keene, p/v; unknown, bj; unknown, sb-1; unknown, castanets-2; unknown, eff-3.
New York, NY   Monday, May 20, 1935
17625-	The Runaway Boy	ARC unissued
17626-2	The Little Ragamuffin -1	Ba 33487, Me M13454, Or 8491, Pe 13161, Ro 5491
17627-	Who Stole The Cherries Off Aunt Minnie's Bonnet	ARC unissued
17628-	She Fell For The Villian's [sic] Moustache	ARC unissued
17629-1	Farmer's Holiday -2, 3	Ba 33487, Me M13454, Or 8491, Pe 13161, Ro 5491
17630-	The Little Empty Crib	ARC unissued

HOWARD KEESEE

Howard Keesee, v/y; acc. own g.
Richmond, IN   Monday, October 14, 1929
| 15773 | You And My Old Guitar | Ge 7035, Ch 15875, Spt 9627 |
| 15774 | My Little Lady | Ge 7035, Ch 15875, Spt 9627 |

Champion 15875 as by **Andy Marlow**. Supertone 9627 as by **Jimmy Reese**.

Acc. unknown, bj-1; own g.
Richmond, IN   Monday, December 16, 1929
15998-B	My Dear Old Sunny South By The Sea -1	Ge 7113, Ch 15899, Spt 9613
15999-B	Blue Yodel No. 5 -1	Ge 7082, Ch 15899, Spt 9613
16000	My Little Home Down In New Orleans -1	Ge 7082, Spr 2618
16001,-A	I'm Sorry We Met	Ge rejected

Champion 15899 as by **Andy Marlow**. Supertone 9613 as by **Jimmy Reese**. Superior 2618 as by **John Burton**.

Acc. unknown, bj; own g.
Richmond, IN   Monday, February 24, 1930
| 16313,-A | A Sailor's Plea | Ge rejected |
| 16314-A | Long Lonesome Road | Ge 7166, Spr 2573 |

Superior 2573 as by **John Burton**.

Richmond, IN   Tuesday, February 25, 1930
| 16315-A | Memphis Special Blues | Ge 7166, Spr 2573 |

Superior 2573 as by **John Burton**.

Richmond, IN   Monday, June 23, 1930

16781,-A	Texas Blues	Ge rejected
16782,-A	Proving My Love	Ge rejected
16783,-A	I Don't Want You Mama	Ge rejected
16784	Going Down In Georgia	Ge rejected
16785,-A	Careless Love	Ge rejected

Keesee may not play g on matrix 16782.

Acc. own g.
Richmond, IN   Thursday, July 3, 1930

16802,-A	I Don't Want You Mama	Ge rejected
16803	Proving My Love	Ge rejected
16804,-A	Careless Love	Ge rejected
16805,-A	Going Down In Georgia	Ge rejected
16806	I'm Sorry We Met	Ge rejected
16807,-A	A Sailor's Plea	Ge rejected

John Burton, v; or **Keesee & Bodine**-1: Howard Keesee, Loy Bodine, v duet; acc. Howard Keesee, g.
Richmond, IN   Tuesday, August 19, 1930

16928-A	Proving My Love	Spr 2618
16929	I Don't Want You Mama	Spr 2522
16930	Going Down In Georgia	Spr 2522
16932-A	A Sailor's Plea -1	Ge 7315, Ch 16097
16933	Indiana Pal Of Mine -1	Ge 7315, Ch 16097

Matrix 16931 is unrelated.

Howard Keesee, v; or **Bodine & Keesee**-1: Howard Keesee, Loy Bodine, v duet; acc. Howard Keesee, g.
Richmond, IN   Wednesday, April 29, 1931

17718-A	The Mystery Of No. 5	Ch 16260
17719-A	Nobody Knows But Me	Ch 16260
17720-A	My Dixie Home -1	Ch 16305, Spr 2672
17721	I Still Got Ninety-Nine -1	Ch 16305
17722	Treasures Untold -1	Spr 2672

Superior 2672 as by **Burton & Burdinez**.

Keesee & Bodine: Howard Keesee, Loy Bodine, v duet; acc. prob. own g duet; unknown, u; Howard Keesee, y.
Richmond, IN   Thursday, July 30, 1931

17902	Pal Of My Sunny Days	Ge rejected
17903	Beside The Ocean Blue	Ge rejected

Acc. unknown, h-1; Howard Keesee, g/y-2; Loy Bodine, y-3.
Richmond, IN   Wednesday, October 7, 1931

18086	The Longest Train I Ever Saw -1	Ch S-16374, Spr 2823
18087	Little Bunch Of Roses	Ch 16446, Spr 2823
18088	Pal Of My Sunny Days -2	Ch 16446, Spr 2810
18089	Beside The Ocean Blue -2, 3	Ch S-16374, Spr 2810

Superior 2810, 2823 as by **Burton & Bodine**.

Howard Keesee, Loy Bodine, v duet; or Howard Keesee, v-1/y-1; acc. unknown, h-2; Howard Keesee, g.
Richmond, IN   Thursday, September 29, 1932

18810	Sleepy Hollow -2	Ge unissued
18811	When It's Harvest Time Sweet Angeline -2	Ge unissued
18812	Let Me Be Your Side Track -1	Ge unissued
18813	The Unmarked Grave -2	Ge unissued

KEESEE & BODINE

See Howard Keesee.

M.O. KELLER

M.O. Keller, h solo.
New York, NY   Wednesday, August 3, 1927

E-24161	Two Little Girls In Blue	Br 188
E-24162	In The Shadow Of The Pine	Br 188

KELLER SISTERS & LYNCH

Vocal trio (two women and one man); acc. prob. one of them, g; —— Lynch, y.
New York, NY   Thursday, December 15, 1932

TO-1241	My Pretty Quadroon	ARC unissued trial recording

Acc. unknown, p.
New York, NY   Wednesday, January 25, 1933
    TO-1255   The Sad Song   ARC unissued trial recording

The Keller Sisters & Lynch also recorded popular material for Brunswick.

MURRAY KELLNER

Murray Kellner (The Fiddlin' Cowboy), f; acc. Vernon Dalhart, h/jh; poss. Carson Robison, g.
New York, NY   c. August 23-24, 1926
    X-231   Hell Broke Loose In Georgia   Ge 3365, Chg 101, 304, Her 75531

Challenge 101, 304 as by **Uncle Jim Hawkins**.

Revs: Gennett 3365, Herwin 75531 by Vernon Dalhart; Challenge 101 by Doc Roberts, 304 by Homer Davenport & Young Brothers.

Murray Kellner accompanied Vernon Dalhart on many recordings, and other artists, but the item above is believed to be his only recording under his own name. An artist of that name recorded after 1942.

BUD KELLY

This pseudonym was used on Broadway 8323, 8331 for Rex Kelly (see Buck Nation), and on Paramount 3279, 3304 for, probably, the popular singer Leroy Montesanto. The sides thus credited on Paramount 3303 may be by different artists.

R.D. KELLY & JULIUS DUNN

One of them, md/v-1; the other, g/v-1.
Atlanta, GA   Monday, December 1, 1930
    404600-B   Down The River Of Golden Dreams -1   OK 45510
    404601-B   Moonlight On The Colorado -1   OK 45510
    404602-A   Harem Scarem   OK 45543
    404603-B   Auto Club March   OK 45543

REX KELLY

Buck Nation's first recordings, for Paramount, were issued under this, believed to be his real name.

KELLY BROTHERS
THE KELLY FAMILY

Masters Hawaiians: Ralph Masters, sg; Kelly Masters, bj-1/g-2.
Camden, NJ   Thursday, July 2, 1931
    68249-1   Military March Medley -2   Vi 23610, HMVIn N4213
    68250-1   Military March Medley -2   TT unissued
    68251-1   Hawaiian Star Dust -2   TT unissued
    68252-1   Hawaiian Star Dust -2   Vi 23581, ZoAu EE290
    68253-1   Chimes Of Hawaii -2   Vi 23610, HMVIn N4213
    68254-1   Chimes Of Hawaii -2   TT unissued
    68255-1   Lion Rag -1   Vi 23639, HMV B4286, HMVIn N4211,
                                                              ZoAu EE362
    68256-1   Lion Rag -1   TT unissued

Zonophone EE290, HMV B4286 as by **Masters' Hawaiians**.
Rev. HMV N4211 by Charles Kama & M.T. Salazar.

Camden, NJ   Friday, July 3, 1931
    68257-1   Lonesome Without My Baby -1   Vi 23639, HMV B4286, ZoAu EE362
    68258-1   Lonesome Without My Baby -1   TT unissued
    68259-1   My South Sea Sweetheart -1   Vi 23624, HMV B4287, ZoAu EE314
    68260-1   My South Sea Sweetheart -1   TT unissued
    68261-1   Blue Sparks -1   TT unissued
    68262-1   Blue Sparks -1   Vi 23624, HMV B4287, ZoAu EE314
    68263-1   Memory Waltz -2   TT unissued
    68264-1   Memory Waltz -2   Vi 23581, MW M-4360, ZoAu EE290

This and the previous day's session were logged as by **Kelly Bros**. but issued as shown. Matrix prefixes on the session-sheets indicate that the alternative version of each title was made for release on Timely Tunes.
Montgomery Ward M-4360, Zonophone EE290, EE314, HMV B4286, B4287 as by **Masters' Hawaiians**. Rev. Montgomery Ward M-4360 by Walter Kolomoku.

Kelly Brothers: prob.: Ramon Kelly, sg/v-1; Jerry Kelly, g/v-2; unknown, g. Ramon Kelly is likely to be the "Ralph Masters", and Jerry Kelly the "Kelly Masters", of the foregoing sessions.
New York, NY   Wednesday, June 7, 1933
    76393-1   Tears I've Shed Over You -2   Vi 23849
    76395-1   I'm Drifting Back To Dreamland   Vi 23853

76397-1	Stormy Hawaiian Weather	Vi 23853, HMVIn N4275
76399-1	Hawaiian Hurricane	Vi unissued
76400-1	Tropical Isle Of Somewhere	Vi unissued
76405-1	South Sea Serenade	Vi 23833
76407-1	Always Remember -2	Vi 23833, HMVIn N4262
76392-1	Tears I've Shed Over You -2	BB B-5222, Eld 2108, Sr S-3305
76394-1	I'm Drifting Back To Dreamland	Bb B-5095, Eld 2010, Sr S-3173
76396-1	Stormy Hawaiian Weather	BB B-5101, Eld 2018, MW M-4429
76398-1	Hawaiian Hurricane	BB B-5095, Eld 2010, Sr S-3173
76404-1	Tropical Isle Of Somewhere	BB B-5101, Eld 2018, MW M-4429
76406-1	South Sea Serenade	BB B-5158, Eld 2057, Sr S-3239
76408-1	Always Remember -2	BB B-5158, Eld 2057, Sr S-3239
76409-1	I Like Mountain Music -1	Vi unissued
76411-1	After You've Gone	Vi 23822, HMVIn N4248
76413-1	Red Hot Town -1, 2	Vi 23828
76415-1	Floating Down A River -1	Vi 23828
76417-1	Hot Hula Lips	Vi 23822, HMVIn N4248
76410-1	I Like Mountain Music -1	BB B-5191, Eld 2084, Sr S-3271, MW M-4367
76412-1	After You've Gone	BB B-5121, Eld 2031, Sr S-3202, MW M-7060
76414-1	Red Hot Town	BB B-5222, Eld 2108, Sr S-3305
76416-1	Floating Down A River -1	BB B-5191, Eld 2084, Sr S-3271
76418-1	Hot Hula Lips	BB B-5121, Eld 2031, Sr S-3202, MW M-7060

All Bluebird, Electradisk, Sunrise, and Montgomery Ward issues as by **Masters Hawaiians**, with the vocalists, where present, identified as Ramon Masters and Jerry Masters.
The out-of-matrix-sequence recording order is attested by the Victor session-sheets.
Revs: Montgomery Ward M-4367 by Kelly Harrell; HMV N4262 by Harry (Mac) McClintock, N4275 by Charles Kama & M.T. Salazar.

Prob.: Ramon Kelly, sg/v-1; Jerry Kelly, g/v-2.
New York, NY   Tuesday, September 18, 1934

38680-A	China Boy	De rejected
38681-A	Sweet Georgia Brown	De rejected
38682-A	Precious One	De 5027
38683-	Tiger Rag -1, 2	De 5027

The Kelly Family: prob. : Ramon (or Raymond) Kelly, sg/v; Jerry Kelly, g/v-1.
New York, NY   Tuesday, October 2, 1934

38768-A	Out On The Desert -1	De 5324, DeSA FM5105
38769-A	Can I Sleep In Your Barn To-night, Mister? -1	De 5054
38770-	I Left My Gal In The Mountains -1	De 5053
38771-B	A Picture From Life's Other Side -1	De 5054
38772-A	The Daughter Of Moonshine Bill -1	De rejected
38773-A	Hawkin Sisters -1	De 5324
38774-A	Carrie, Sarrie And Me -1	De 5053, Pan 25649
38775-A	The Crosseyed Butcher	Pan 25649

Rev. Decca FM5105 by Tex Owens.

KEN & JIM
KEN, CHUCK & JIM

See James Brown, Jr. & Ken Landon groups.

KENTUCKY BAY RUM BOTTLERS

No details.
Richmond, IN   Saturday, April 13, 1929

15047	Rummy	Ge rejected trial recording

KENTUCKY COON HUNTERS

Unknown, f; unknown, md/v; unknown, g/v; unknown, g.
Louisville, KY   Wednesday, June 17, 1931

69454-1,-2	Ain't Goin' To Grieve My Lord No More	Vi unissued
69455-1,-2	Ain't Goin' To Lay My Armour Down	Vi unissued

The session-sheet credits the arrangements of these items to Edd Hayes, who may be one of the group.

THE KENTUCKY GIRLS

Mrs. H.S. Berry, Helena Berry Edmonson, v duet; acc. poss. one of them, g; poss. the other, u.
Dallas, TX   Thursday, December 6, 1928

147583-2	Old And Only In The Way	Co 15364-D
147584-1	Sweet Golden Daisies	Co 15364-D

Helena Berry Edmonson was Mrs. H.S. Berry's daughter.

KENTUCKY HOLINESS SINGERS

Vocal group; acc. unknown, md; unknown, bj; two unknowns, g.
    Knoxville, TN   Friday, March 28, 1930

K-8030-	I'm On My Way	Vo 5439
K-8031-	I Will Not Be Removed	Vo 5439

This may be an Elmer Bird group.

KENTUCKY KERNELS

Pseudonym on Varsity for Crockett's Kentucky Mountaineers.

KENTUCKY MOUNTAIN BOYS

Pseudonym on Supertone for Lester McFarland & Robert A. Gardner.

KENTUCKY MOUNTAIN CHORISTERS

Vocal group (prob. three men), acc. unknown, f; two unknowns, g.
    Richmond, IN   Tuesday, February 5, 1929

14770-A	The Great Reaping Day	Ge 6888
14771	We'll Understand It Better Bye And Bye	Ge 6888
14772,-A,-B	Fill My Way Every Day With Love	Ge rejected
14773,-A	When The Saints Go Marching In	Ge rejected

There may be some connection between this group and B.L. Reeves.

KENTUCKY MOUNTAINEERS

Pseudonym on Joe Davis for Crockett's Kentucky Mountaineers.

KENTUCKY RAMBLERS

See Elmer Bird & Associated Artists. **The Kentucky Ramblers** was used as a pseudonym on Australian Panachord for Jack Reedy & His Walker Mountain String Band.

THE KENTUCKY SERENADERS

Pseudonym on Champion for the Dixie Harmonizers (see Warren Caplinger), and on Supertone for Roy Harvey (& Bob Hoke).

KENTUCKY STRING TICKLERS

Rogers Bros. & Burgher: Silas Rogers, f; Oddis J. Burgher, bj; Charlie Rogers, g; or **Silas Rogers**-1, v with same acc.; or **Rogers Bros.**-2: prob. Silas Rogers, Charlie Rogers, v duet with same acc.
    Richmond, IN   Friday, August 29, 1930

16953	Traveler's Rest	Ge rejected
16954	Stove Pipe Blues	Ge rejected
16955	Gabe	Ge rejected
16956	Hot Corn – Cold Corn -1	Ge rejected
16957	Railroad Blues -2	Ge rejected

    Richmond, IN   Saturday, August 30, 1930

16959	Chicken Sneeze -2	Ge rejected

Matrix 16958 is unrelated.

Kentucky String Ticklers: Silas Rogers, f; Bunk Lane, p; Oddis J. Burgher, bj.
    Richmond, IN   Wednesday, March 1, 1933

19065	Tipple Blues	Ch S-16577
19066	Stove Pipe Blues	Ch S-16577
19067	Georgia Bust Down	Ch S-16581
19068	Crooked John	Ch S-16581
19069	Leaving Here Blues	Ch 16681, 45014
19070	Richmond Polka	Ch 16681, 45014

KENTUCKY THORO[UGH]BREDS

Kentucky Thoroughbreds: Doc Roberts, f-1/md-2/v-3; Dick Parman, g/v-4; Ted Chestnut, v-5.
    Chicago, IL   Wednesday, April 13–Thursday, April 14, 1927

4453-2	I Love You Best Of All -1, 4, 5	Pm 3010, Bwy 8047
4454-2	Drunk Man's Blues -1	Pm 3008, Bwy 8045

4455-2	Cumberland Blues -1	Pm 3009, Bwy 8046
4456-1	Rocky Mountain Goat -1	Pm 3008, Bwy 8046
4457-2	Wagoner -1	Pm 3009, Bwy 8045
4459-1	If I Only Had A Home Sweet Home -1, 4, 5	Pm 3010, Bwy 8048
4461-2	In The Shade Of The Old Apple Tree -2, 4, 5	Pm 3036, Bwy 8128, Her 75566
4463-1	Mother's Advice -2, 4, 5	Pm 3011
4464-2	Preacher And The Bear -2, 4, 5	Pm 3036, Bwy 8128, Her 75566
4465-2	Room For Jesus -1, 3, 4, 5	Pm 3014
4466-2	This World Is Not My Home -1, 3, 4, 5	Pm 3014
4467-1	I Left Because I Loved You -1, 4, 5	Pm 3011

Paramount 3008, 3009 as by **Quadrillers**. Broadway 8045, 8046 as by **Lone Star Fiddlers**; 8047, 8048, 8128 as by **Old Smoky Twins**. Herwin 75566 as by **Blue Grass Boys**.
Titles also recorded at this session were *My Carolina Home* and *Tom Sherman's Barroom*, and possibly also *Phil Roberts Blues* and *Durkin Blues*.
Matrices 4458, 4460 are untraced but probably by this group; 4462, 4468 are by Blind Blake (see B&GR).

Kentucky Thorobreds: Doc Roberts, f-1/md-2; Ted Chestnut, bj-md/v; Dick Parman, g/v.
Chicago, IL   Monday, September 19–Wednesday, September 21, 1927

20051-3	I've Waited Long For You -2	Pm 3071, Bwy 8070
20052-1	Only A Miner -2	Pm 3071, Bwy 8070
20054-3	He Cometh -1	Pm 3059, Bwy 8064, 8218
20055-1	'Till We Meet Again -2	Pm 3059, Bwy 8065, 8218
20056-2	I'll Not Marry At All -1	Pm 3080, Bwy 8184
20059-2	Shady Grove -1	Pm 3080, Bwy 8184

Broadway 8064, 8065, 8070, 8184, 8218 as by **Old Smoky Twins**. Matrix 20055 is titled *Till We Meet Again* on Broadway issues.
Titles also recorded at this session were *Old Man Brown*, *New Money*, *My Baby Don't Love Me*, *Jim And Me*, *Wouldn't Take Nothing For My Journey*, *Bring Back My Wandering Boy*, and *The Hallelujah Side*.
Matrices 20053, 20057/58 are untraced but probably by this group.

BOB KERBY & GEORGE BARTON

No details.
Dallas, TX   Friday, November 1, 1929

| DAL-561 | Crap Shooter | Br/Vo cancelled trial recording |
| DAL-562 | F Waltz | Br/Vo cancelled trial recording |

KESSINGER BROTHERS (CLARK & LUCHES)

Clark Kessinger, f; Luches Kessinger, g; Ernest Legg, calls-1.
Ashland, KY   Friday, February 10, 1928

AL-204*/05	Chicken In The Barnyard -1	Br 256, Spt S2087
AL-206/07*	Forked Deer	Br 247, Spt S2089
AL-208/09*	Hell Among The Yearlings -1	Br 235, Spt S2090
AL-210*/11	Patty On The Turnpike -1	Vo 5248

Supertone S2087, S2089, S2090 as by **Birmingham Entertainers**. Rev. Supertone S2087 by Tennessee Ramblers.
Ashland, KY   Saturday, February 11, 1928

AL-212/13*	Devil's Dream -1	Br 256
AL-214*/15	Wild Horse -1	Vo 5248
AL-216*/17	Wednesday Night Waltz	Br 220, 52086, BrAu 220
AL-218/19*	Goodnight Waltz	Br 220, 52086, BrAu 220
AL-220*/21	Garfield March	Br 238
AL-222*/23	Kanawha March	Br 238
AL-224/25*	Sixteen Days In Georgia	Br 267
AL-226*/27	The Girl I Left Behind Me -1	Br 267
AL-228*/29	Arkansas Traveller	Br 247, Spt S2086, Me M18020
AL-230*/31	Turkey In The Straw -1	Br 235, Spt S2086

Supertone S2086 as by **Birmingham Entertainers**. Brunswick 52086 as by **Les Deux Gaspesiens**. Melotone M18020 as by **Les Deux Paroissiens**.
Matrix AL-216/17 is titled *La Valse De Musicien* and AL-218/19 *La Valse Des Amoureux* on Brunswick 52086. Matrix AL-228/29 is titled *Le Reel Des Voyageurs* on Melotone M18020.

New York, NY   Monday, February 4, 1929

E-29259-	Old Jake Gillie	Br 323
E-29260-A,-B	Durang's Hornpipe	Br rejected
E-29261-A,-B	Hot Foot	Br rejected
E-29262-	Sally Johnson	Me M12161, MeC 93132, Po P9016, Vo 02704, Min M-14088

E-29263-A,-B	Over The Waves Waltz	Br rejected
E-29264-A,-B	Black Hawk Waltz	Br rejected
E-29265-	Portsmouth	Me M12161, MeC 93132, Po P9016, Vo 02704, Min M-14088
E-29266-A,-B	Little Brown Jug	Br rejected
E-29267-A,-B	Three Forks Of Sandy	Br unissued
E-29275-	Sally Goodin	Br 308, Au A22039

All issues of matrices E-29262 and E-29265 as by **Wright Brothers**. Aurora A22039 as by **Arnold Brothers**.
Rev. Aurora A22039 by Tennessee Ramblers.

New York, NY   Tuesday, February 5, 1929

E-29157-	Wild Goose Chase	Br 331, Spt S2089
E-29158-	Dill Pickles Rag	Br 315
E-29159-	Tug Boat	Br 315
E-29160-A,-B	Salt River	Br rejected
E-29161-A	Johnny Bring The Jug 'Round The Hill	Br 311, Spt S2090
E-29270-	Birdie	Br 323
E-29271-	Mississippi Sawyer	Br 309, 52077
E-29272-	Richmond Polka	Be 309, 52077
E-29273-	Soldier's Joy	Br 341, 52081
E-29274-	Chinky Pin	Br 396, 52080

Supertone S2089, S2090 as by **Birmingham Entertainers**. Brunswick 52077, 52080, 52081 as by **Les Joyeux Montrealais**.
Matrix E-29271 is titled *Le Reel Gaspesien*, and E-29272 *Le Reel De Richmond*, on Brunswick 52077. Matrix E-29273 is titled *Set Americain – 3ie Partie* on Brunswick 52081, and E-29274 *Set Americain – 2ie Partie* on Brunswick 52080.
Matrices E-29268/69 are untraced.

New York, NY   Wednesday, February 6, 1929

E-29276-	Sourwood Mountain	Br 308, Au 22039
E-29277-	Long-Eared Mule	Br 341, 52081
E-29278-	Done Gone	Br 396, 52080

Brunswick 52080, 52081 as by **Les Joyeux Montrealais**. Aurora A22039 as by **Arnold Brothers**.
Matrix E-29277 is titled *Set Americain – 4ie Partie* on Brunswick 52081, and E-29278 *Set Americain – 1er Partie* on Brunswick 52080. These three items may have been recorded on Tuesday, February 5.

New York, NY   Monday, June 24, 1929

E-30119-A	Brownstown Girl	Vo 02565, DeE F3862, RexIr U390
E-30120-A	Josh And I	Vo 02565, DeE F3862, RexIr U390
E-30121-	Bully Of The Town	Br unissued
E-30122-A	Boarding House Bells Are Ringing Waltz	Br 352, 52085, Spt S2091
E-30123-A	Rat Cheese Under The Hill	Br 458, Spt S2091
E-30180-A	Durang Hornpipe	Br 364
E-30181-	Hot Foot	Me M12272, Po P9086, Vo 5481
E-30182-A	Over The Waves Waltz	Br 344, 52078, Au A22038
E-30183-A	Black Hawk Waltz	Br 344, 52078, Au A22038
E-30184-	Three Forks Of Sandy	Vo 02567

Supertone S2091 as by **Birmingham Entertainers**. Melotone M12272, Polk P9086 as by **Wright Brothers**. Brunswick 52078, 52085 as by **Les Joyeux Montrealais**. Aurora A22038 as by **Arnold Brothers**. Decca F3862 as by **The Kessinger Brothers**.
Matrix E-30119 is titled *Brownstown Gal* on Decca F3862. Matrix E-30122 is titled *Valse De La Vieille Maison* on Brunswick 52085. Matrix E-30183 is titled *Sur Les Vagues*, and E-30183 *La Valse De L'Epervier*, on Brunswick 52078.
Decca F3862 was erroneously pressed so that the side labelled *Brownstown Gal* plays *Josh And I* and vice versa. This may also be true of Rex U390. Vocalion 02567 may not have been issued.

New York, NY   Tuesday, June 25, 1929

E-30187-A	West Virginia Special	Vo 02566, DeE F3863, RexIr U391
E-30188-	Salt River	Me M12272, Po P9086, Vo 5481
E-30189-A	Kanawha County Rag	Vo 02566, DeE F3863, RexIr U391
E-30190-	Going Up Brushy Fork	Br 458, Me M18019
E-30191-A	McCloud's Reel	Br 580, MeC 93072, Min M-14020
E-30192	Liza Jane	Br 521
E-30193-	Whistling Rufus	Br 521
E-30194-A	Don't Let The Deal Go Down	Br 411
E-30195-A,-B	Shortenin' The Bread	Br unissued
E-30196-A	Sopping The Gravy	Br 411

Melotone M12272, Polk P9086 as by **Wright Brothers**. Melotone M18019 as by **Les Serenadeurs Du Lac St Jean**. Melotone 93072, Minerva M-14020 as by **The Oldtimers**. Decca F3863 as by **The Kessinger Brothers**.
Matrix E-30190 is titled *Reel De Roberval* on Melotone M18019. Decca F3863 was erroneously pressed so that the side labelled *West Virginia Special* plays *Kanawha County Rag* and vice versa.
Rev. Melotone M18019 (with same credit) by East Texas Serenaders.

New York, NY			Wednesday, June 26, 1929
E-30197-A	Polka Four	Br 468	
E-30198-A	Midnight Serenade Waltz	Br 352, 52085	
E-30199-A	Gippy Get Your Hair Cut	Br 364	
E-30300-	Rockingham	Vo 02567	
E-30301-A	Little Brown Jug	Br 468	
E-30302-A	Little Betty Brown	Br 580, MeC 93072, Min M-14020	

Brunswick 52085 as by **Les Joyeux Montrealais**. Melotone 93072, Minerva M-14020 as by **The Oldtimers**.
Matrix E-30198 is titled *Serenade De Minuit* on Brunswick 52085. Vocalion 02567 may not have been issued.

New York, NY			Monday, September 15–Thursday, September 18, 1930
E-34409-A	Wildflower Waltz	Br 484, PanAu P11996	
E-34410-A	Ragtime Annie	Br 540	
E-34411-A,-B	Irish Wash Woman	Br unissued	
E-34412-A	Chicken Reel	Br 480, Me M18020	
E-34413-A	Mary Jane Waltz	Br 484, PanAu P11996	
E-34414-	Under The Double Eagle March	Br 592	
E-34415-	Steamboat Bill	Br 563	
E-34416-A,-B	Virginia Mann Schottische Polka	Br rejected	
E-34417-	Marching Through Georgia	Br 518	
E-34421-	Dixie	Br 518	
E-34422-A	Lauterbach Waltz	Br 567	
E-34423-A	Lonesome Road Blues	Br 540	
E-34424-A	Pop Goes The Weasel	Br 480	
E-34434-	Regal March	Br 592	
E-34435-A	Mexican Waltz	Br 567	
E-34475-A,-B	Seaside Polka	Br rejected	
E-34476-	Neapolitan Two Step	Br 563	
E-34477-A	Everybody To The Punchin'	Br 554	
E-34478-A	Shoo! Fly	Br 554	

Melotone M18020 as by **Les Deux Paroissiens**. Panachord P11996 as by **Old Fashioned Boys**.
Matrix E-34412 is titled *Le Reel Des Poulets* on Melotone M18020.
Brunswick files date the above recordings to 15, 16, and 18 September but differ as to which items were recorded on each day.
Clark Kessinger recorded after 1942.

PERRY KIM & EINAR NYLAND

Perry Kim, Einar Nyland, v duet; acc. one of them, md; the other, g.
  Chicago, IL   unknown date

431	I Will Sing Of My Redeemer	Rainbow 1018, OK 40489
432	Keep Me On The Firing Line	Rainbow 1018, OK 40489

  poss. Chicago, IL   unknown date

891	He Touched Me And Made Me Whole	Rainbow 1065
894	Speak My Lord	Rainbow 1065

Intervening matrices are untraced.

  poss. Chicago, IL   unknown date

5061	No Disappointment In Heaven	Rainbow 1066
5062	He Keeps Me Singing	Rainbow 1066

Kim & Nyland, v duet; acc. one of them, md; the other, g.
  poss. Chicago, IL   poss. late 1924 or early 1925

8038	Heaven In My Soul	Rainbow 1097
8039-1	I Was There When It Happened	Rainbow 1097
8045-1	I Will Shout His Praise In Glory	Rainbow 1100
8046	Your Mother Wonders Where You Are Tonight	Rainbow 1100
8050	The Prodigal Son – Part 1	Rainbow 1099
8051	The Prodigal Son – Part 2	Rainbow 1099

Intervening matrices are untraced.

Perry Kim & Einar Nyland, v duet; acc. one of them, md; the other, g.
  Chicago, IL   Saturday, September 18, 1926

36261-1,-2	It Was For Me	Vi unissued
36262-1,-2,-3	It Cleanseth Me	Vi unissued
36263-1,-2	No Disappointment In Heaven	Vi unissued
36264-1,-2	I Will Sing Of My Redeemer	Vi unissued

  Chicago, IL   Sunday, September 26, 1926

36412-1,-2	An Old Account Settled	Vi unissued
36413-1,-2,-3	The Hallelujah	Vi unissued

Kim & Nyland, v duet; acc. one of them, mandola; the other, g.
Chicago, IL   Wednesday, June 22, 1927
39049-1,-2	The Suffering Redeemer	Vi unissued
39050-2	The Old Account Settled Long Ago	Vi 20868
39051-1	It Was For Me	Vi 20868
39052-1,-2	Keep Me On The Firing Line Jesus	Vi unissued

B.F. KINCAID

Benjamin F. Kincaid, v; acc. own g.
Richmond, IN   Thursday, February 27, 1930
16333,-A,-B	She Was Bred In Old Kentucky	Ge rejected
16334,-A	I'm Longing For My Old Kentucky Home	Ge rejected
16335,-A	Live Anyhow Till I Die	Ge rejected
16336,-A	Goo-Goo Eyes	Ge rejected
16337,-A	On The Banks Of The Wabash	Ge rejected
16338,-A	In The Shade Of The Old Apple Tree	Ge rejected

Richmond, IN   Monday, September 29, 1930
17108,-A	Just As The Sun Went Down	Ge rejected

Richmond, IN   Tuesday, September 30, 1930
17109,-A	Save My Mother's Picture From The Fire	Ge rejected
17111	Just Because She Made Them Goo Goo Eyes	Ge 7309, Spr 2574
17113	Lane County Bachelor	Ge 7309, Spr 2574
17114	Dying For Some One To Love Me	Spr 2530
17115	We Parted By The Riverside	Spr 2530
17116	My Old Sweetheart	Ge rejected
17117,-A	On The Banks Of The Wabash	Ge rejected

Superior 2530, 2574 as by **Martin King**. In Gennett files matrices 17108/09 are subcredited (**The Brier Hopper Of WFIW**). Matrices 17110 and 17112 are unrelated trial recordings.

BRADLEY KINCAID

Bradley Kincaid, v; acc. own g.
Chicago, IL   c. December 19, 1927
13312	The Fatal Wedding	Ge 6363, Ch 15428, Sil 5186, 8217, Spt 9211, Spr 366, Bell 1178
13313-A	Sweet Kitty Wells	Ge 6363, Ch 15502, Sil 5187, 8218, Spt 9208, MeC 45008

Champion 15428, 15502 as by **Dan Hughey**. Bell 1178 as by **John Carpenter**. The subcredit (**WLS Artist**) appears on all Silvertone and Supertone issues of recordings made in 1927–28.
After October 22, 1929 matrix 13313 was replaced by matrix 15746.
Revs: Champion 15428 by Holland Puckett; 15502 by David Miller.

Chicago, IL   c. February 27, 1928
13472	Barbara Allen	Sil 5187, 8217, Spt 9211
13473	Methodist Pie	Ge 6417, Ch 15631, Sil 5189, 8220, Spt 9210
13474	Froggie Went A-Courting	Ge 6462, Ch 15466, Sil 5188, 8219, Spt 9209

Champion 15466, 15631 as by **Dan Hughey**. Matrix 13473 is titled *An Old Camp Meeting* on Champion 15631.

Chicago, IL   c. February 28, 1928
13478-A	Sourwood Mountain	Ge 6417, Ch 15631, Sil 5189, 8220, Spt 9210, Spr 366, Bell 1178
13479	The Swapping Song	Ge 6462, Ch 15466, Sil 5188, 8219, Spt 9209
13480	Bury Me On The Prairie	Sil 5187, 8218, Spt 9208, Spr 2588

Champion 15466, 15631 as by **Dan Hughey**. Bell 1178 as by **John Carpenter**. Superior 2588 as by **Harley Stratton**.

Chicago, IL   c. March 9, 1928
13520	Paper Of Pins	Ge rejected
13521	The Turkish Lady	Ge rejected
13522	The Two Sisters	Sil 5190, 8221, Spt 9212
13523	Fair Ellen	Sil 5190, 8221, Spt 9212

Chicago, IL   c. March 20, 1928
13575	The Little Rosewood Casket	Ge rejected
13578,-A	The Ship That Never Returned	Ge rejected

Matrices 13576/77 are by WLS Radio Artists; 13579/80 are popular.

Chicago, IL   c. March 23, 1928
13581,-A	Barney McCoy	Ge rejected
13582,-A	Don't Put Me Off The Train	Ge rejected

Chicago, IL c. July 12, 1928

14028	Pearl Bryan	Ge rejected
14029	Rip Van Winkle	Ge rejected
14030	Liza Up In The Sim'mon Tree	Ge rejected
14031-A	Cuckoo Is A Pretty Bird	Ge rejected
14032	Four Thousand Years Ago	Ge rejected
14033	Don't Put Me Off The Train	Ge rejected
14034	Soldier, Soldier, Will You Marry Me	Ge rejected
14035	Little Mohee	Ge rejected
14036	Butcher Boy	Ge rejected
14037	I Loved You Better Than You Knew	Ge rejected
14038	Billy Boy	Ge rejected
14039	Fair Ellen	Ge rejected
14040	Two Sisters	Ge rejected
14041	Paper Of Pins	Ge rejected
14042	Red River Valley	Ge rejected
14043	The Orphan Girl	Ge rejected

Richmond, IN Monday, January 28, 1929

14738	Four Thousand Years Ago	Ge 6761, Ch 15687, 45057, Spt 9362, Spr 2656, MeC 45057
14739	When The Work's All Done This Fall	Ge 6989
14740	Give My Love To Nell	Ge 7020, Spt 9350
14741-B	In The Streets Of Laredo	Ge 6790, Spt 9404
14742-B	Wreck On The C. & O. Road	Ge 6823, Ch 15710, 45098, Spt 9350, MeC 45057
14743	Pearl Bryan	Ge 6823, Ch 15731, Spt 9404
14744-B	The Little Mohee	Ge 6856, Ch 15731, Spt 9402
14745	The Red River Valley	Ge 6790, Ch 15710, 45098, Spt 9403, Spr 2588
14746	Liza Up In The 'Simmon Tree	Ge 6761, Ch 15687, 45057, Spt 9362
14747	The Little Rosewood Casket	Ge 6989, Spt 9403
14748	A Paper Of Pins	Ge 6856, Spt 9402

It is uncertain which take of matrix 14742 was used on Supertone 9350, and which of matrix 14746 on Supertone 9362. Champion 15687, 15710, 15731 as by **Dan Hughey**. Superior 2588 as by **Harley Stratton**. Matrix 14742 is titled *The Wreck On The C. & O. Road* on Champion 15710.

Richmond, IN Friday, June 7, 1929

15163-A	Happy Days Long Ago	Ge 6944, Ch 15787, Spt 9471, MeC 45022
15168	Little Old Log Cabin In The Lane	Ge 6958, Ch 15923, Spt 9505, MeC 45022
15169	Will The Angels Play Their Harps For Me	Ge 6900, Ch 15771, 45130, Spt 9452, MeC 45130, Min M-14059
15170	Charlie Brooks	Ge 6958, Ch 16029, 45039, Spt 9648, Spr 2788
15171	Angels In Heaven Know I Love You	Ge 6900, Ch 15771, 45130, Spt 9452, MeC 45130, Min M-14059
15172	Let That Mule Go Aunk! Aunk!	Ge 6944, Ch 15787, Spt 9471, Spr 2656
15173	Old Number Three	Ge 7020, Ch 15923, Spt 9505, Spr 2788
15174,-A	Billy Boy	Ge rejected

Champion 15771, 15787, 15923, 16029 as by **Dan Hughey**. Matrix 15170 is titled *Charley Brooks* on Supertone 9648. Intervening matrices are by other (African-American) artists.

Richmond, IN Friday, October 4, 1929

15734-A	Cindy	Ge 7112, Ch 15851, Spt 9568, Spr 2770
15735-A	My Little Home In Tennessee	Ch 15851, Spt 9568
15736	On Top Of Old Smoky	Ge 7053, Ch 16029, 45039, Spt 9566, Spr 2770, MW 4984
15737	And So You Have Come Back To Me	Ge rejected
15738-A	After The Ball	Ge 7081, Ch 15876, Spt 9648, MeC 45002
15739-A	I Will Be All Smiles Tonight	Ge 7053, Ch 15876, Spt 9566, MeC 45002
15740	Pretty Little Pink	Spt 9666
15741	The Blind Girl	Ge 7081, Ch 15968, Spt 9565
15741-A	The Blind Girl	MW 4984, MeC 45008
15742	De Ladies Man	Ge rejected
15743-A	Mary Wore Three Links Of Chain	Spt 9666
15744	I Could Not Call Her Mother	Ge 7112, Ch 15968, Spt 9565
15745	Two Little Orphans	Ge rejected
15746	Sweet Kitty Wells	Spt 9208, MeC 45008

Champion 15851, 15876, 15968, 16029 as by **Dan Hughey**.
Take A of matrix 15741 was used after April 15, 1930; presumably before that date the plain take was employed.

Chicago, IL		Friday, November 22, 1929
C-4732-A,-B,-C	Give My Love To Nell	Br rejected
C-4733-A,-B	The Blind Girl	Br rejected
C-4734-A,-B	Methodist Pie	Br rejected
C-4735-A,-B	Sweet Kitty Wells	Br rejected
C-4736-A,-B	When The Work's All Done This Fall	Br rejected
C-4737-A,-B	Barbara Allen	Br rejected
C-4738-A,-B	Streets Of Laredo	Br rejected
Chicago, IL		Friday, January 24, 1930
C-5302	When The Work's All Done This Fall	Br 403, Spt S2017
C-5303	Give My Love To Nell	Br 403, Spt S2017
C-5304	Methodist Pie	Br 420, Spt S2018
C-5305-A	Barbara Allen	Me M12349, Vo 02685, Cq 7982, Pan 25633, DeIr W4148
C-5306-A	The Blind Girl	Me M12349, Vo 02685, Cq 7983, Bwy 4085, Pan 25633, DeIr W4148
C-5307	Sourwood Mountain	Br 420, Spt S2018, Cq 8090

Broadway 4085 as by **George McKinley**.

Chicago, Il.		Wednesday, March 12, 1930
C-5558	Cindy	Br 464, 80093
C-5559	Pretty Little Pink	Br 464
Chicago, IL		Wednesday, October 8, 1930
C-6426	I Wish I Had Someone To Love Me	Me M12372, Vo 02686, RZAu G22216
C-6427	Old Joe Clark	Br 485, 80096, Cq 8090
C-6428	Old Coon Dog	Br 485
C-6429	The Innocent Prisoner	Me M12372, Vo 02686, RZAu G22216

Rev. Brunswick 80096 by Tennessee Ramblers.

Chicago, IL		Friday, January 2, 1931
C-6865	Somewhere, Somebody's Waiting For You	Me M12262, Vo 02705, Po P9079, Cq 7984, RZAu G22218
C-6866	The Fatal Derby Day	Me M12315, Vo 02684, Pan 25917, RZAu G22215
C-6867-A	The Red River Valley	Me M12183, Vo 5476, 04647, ARC 7-06-71, Po P9050, PanAu P12183, DeIr W4475
C-6868-A	A Picture Of Life's Other Side	Me M12183, Vo 5476, 04647, ARC 7-06-71, Po P9050, Cq 7983, PanAu P12183, DeIr W4475
C-6869	Two Little Girls In Blue	Me M12291, Vo 5475, Po P9093, CrC/MeC/Stg 91316, Pan 25199, DeIr W4456
C-6870	Gooseberry Pie	Me M12291, Vo 5475, Po P9093, CrC/MeC/Stg 91316, Pan 25199, DeIr W4456
C-6871-A	The Fatal Wedding	Me M12315, Vo 02684, Cq 7982, Bwy 4085, Pan 25917, RZAu G22215

Broadway 4085 as by **George McKinley**. Rev. Regal-Zonophone G22218 by Frank Marvin.

Chicago, IL		Saturday, January 3, 1931
C-6872-B	Bury Me Out On The Prairie	Me M12332, Vo 5474, Cq 8091, ARC 7-06-70, RZAu G22575
C-6873-A	The True And Trembling Brakeman	Me M12184, Vo 02683, Po P9064, Cq 8091, Pan 25901
C-6874-A	The Lightning Express	Me M12184, Vo 02683, Po P9064, Pan 25901, RZAu G22211
C-6875	For Sale, A Baby	Me M12262, Vo 02705, Po P9079, RZAu G22211
C-6876-A	After The Ball	Me M12332, Vo 5474, Cq 7984, ARC 7-06-70

Matrix C-6874 is titled *Please, Mr. Conductor, Don't Put Me Off The Train* on Regal-Zonophone G22211.

New York, NY		Thursday, September 14, 1933
77659-1	Some Little Bug Is Goin' To Get You Some Day	BB B-5179, Eld 2085, Sr S-3276, MW M-4379
77660-1	Long, Long Ago	BB B-5179, Eld 2085, Sr S-3276, MW M-4379
77661-1	The First Whippoorwill Song	BB B-8478
77662-1	Two Little Orphans	BB B-4906
77663-1	In The Little Shirt That Mother Made For Me	BB B-5321, Sr S-3402, MW M-4421, RZAu G22367
77664-1	Three Wishes	BB B-4906
77665-1	Mammy's Precious Baby	BB B-8478

77666-1	Sweet Betsy From Pike	BB B-5321, Sr S-3402, MW M-4421
77667-1	The House Carpenter (An Old English Ballad)	BB B-5255, Eld 2135, Sr S-3338
77668-1	Dog And Gun (An Old English Ballad)	BB B-5255, Eld 2135, Sr S-3338
77669-1	The Old Wooden Rocker	BB B-5201, Eld 2091, Sr S-3282, MW M-4405
77670-1	My Mother's Beautiful Hands	BB B-5201, Eld 2091, Sr S-3282, MW M-4405

New York, NY   Wednesday, February 14, 1934

81383-1	Somebody's Waiting For You	BB B-8410, RZAu G24913
81384-1	The Letter Edged In Black	BB B-5895, RZAu G22499, Twin FT1908
81385-1	Little Rosewood Casket	BB B-5895, RZAu G22499, Twin FT1908
81386-1	The Ship That Never Returned	BB B-5569, RZAu G22339
81387-1	Jimmie Rodgers' Life	BB B-5377, Sr S-3458
81388-1	The Death Of Jimmie Rodgers	BB B-5377, Sr S-3458
81389-1	Mrs. Jimmie Rodgers' Lament	BB B-5423, MW M-4457, RZAu G22367
81390-1	Life Is Like A Mountain Railroad	BB B-8501
81391-1	Little Joe	BB B-5423, MW M-4457
81392-1	The Blind Girl	BB B-8501, RZAu G24913
81393-1	I'll Take You Home Again, Kathleen	BB B-5569, RZAu G22339
81394-1	Zeb Tourney's Gal (Feud Song)	BB B-8410

New York, NY   Monday, May 7, 1934

82388-1	The Death Of Jimmie Rodgers	BB B-5486, MW M-4456
82389-1	The Life Of Jimmie Rodgers	BB B-5486, MW M-4456
82390-1	In The Hills Of Old Kentucky	BB B-5971, RZAu G22554, HMVIn N4380
82391-1	Just Plain Folks	BB B-5971, RZAu G22554, HMVIn N4380

Matrix 82389 is titled *Jimmie Rodgers' Life* on Montgomery Ward M-4456.

New York, NY   Thursday, September 13, 1934

38649-A	Darlin' Clementine	Pan 25986, DeIr W4271
38650-A	In The Hills Of Old Kentucky	De rejected
38651-A	My Mother's Beautiful Hands	De 5026, DeIr W4271, Pan 25986
38652-A	The Old Wooden Rocker	De 5026, DeIr W4372, Pan 26004
38653-	Ain't We Crazy	De 5025
38654-A	In The Little Shirt That Mother Made For Me	De 5025, DeIr W4372, Pan 26004

Acc. Irma F. Kincaid, p-1; own g-2/y-3.

New York, NY   Friday, November 30, 1934

39105-A	Down By The Railroad Track -1	De 12035
39121-A,-B	Water Under The Bridge -1	De rejected
39122-B	Sweet Inniscarra -1	De 12035
39123-	The Foggy Dew -1	De 12024
39124-A	That Tumble-Down Shack In Athlone -1	De 12024
39125-A	When Irish Eyes Are Smiling -2	De 12053
39126-	The Cowboy's Dream -2	De 5048
39143-	Red River Valley -2	De 5048
39144-B	I'd Like To Be In Texas -2, 3	De 12053

Intervening matrices are by other artists.

Bradley Kincaid recorded after 1942.

REV. CLYDE D. KING

Rev. Clyde D. King, v; acc. Reg Peel, p.
   Chicago, IL   c. March 23, 1928

13596	The Ninety And Nine	Ge rejected

Rev. Clyde D. King was a member of The Singing Preachers.

FRANK KING (BLACK FRANK)

Items by this artist in the Vocalion old-time series (5308, 5309) are reported to be accordion solos, and from their titles and place of recording (San Antonio, TX) it seems likely that they are Bohemian material; see *EMOR*.

FRED KING

Pseudonym on Domino and Microphone for Vernon Dalhart.

GENE KING

Gene King, v; acc. poss. own g.
   Richmond, IN   Friday, September 9, 1932

18768	Ohio Sweetheart	Ge rejected
18769	Always In Dreams You're A Pal	Ge rejected

JIM KING & HIS BROWN MULES

No details.
    Atlanta, GA   Saturday, April 14, 1928

146062-	I Want A Sweetheart	Co unissued
146063-	Brown Mule Slide	Co unissued

This group is believed to have included two Thomases — one of them probably Henry Thomas, who was associated with Hoke Rice and Claude (C.W.) Davis — and two Chumblers, presumably William Archer Chumbler and George "Elmo" Chumbler.

JOHN (DUSTY) KING & HIS RANGE BUSTERS

John (Dusty) King, v; acc. Jesse Ashlock, f; Fred Tony Travers, pac; Rudy Sooter, g; Rufus Cline, sb.
    Hollywood, CA   Thursday, January 22, 1942

072052-1	Deep In The Heart Of Texas	BB B-8952
072053-1	I Hung My Head And Cried	BB B-9038
072054-1	Promise To Be True While I'm Away	BB B-8952
072055-1	Someday You'll Know You Did Wrong	BB B-9038

MARTIN KING

Pseudonym on Superior for B.F. Kincaid.

FRED KIRBY

Fred Kirby, v; acc. poss. Cliff Carlisle, sg; prob. own g.
    New York, NY   Friday, September 23, 1932

12360-	Old Fashioned Sweetheart	ARC unissued

    New York, NY   Wednesday, September 28, 1932

12390-	Mother And Dad	ARC unissued

    New York, NY   Thursday, September 29, 1932

12393-	Cottage By The Wayside	ARC unissued
12394-	Darling Nell	ARC unissued

During the sessions listed above, Fred Kirby recorded duets with Cliff Carlisle, listed under the latter.

Fred Kirby, v/y-1; acc. own g.
    Charlotte, NC,   Wednesday, February 12, 1936

94667-1	My Man -1	BB unissued
94668-1	I'm A Gold Diggin' Papa -1	BB B-6419, Twin FT8149
94669-1	Lonesome Lullaby -1	BB B-6419, MW M-4855, Twin FT8149
94670-1	I'm Lonesome, Sad And Blue -1	BB B-6325, MW M-4853, Twin FT8113
94671-1	In The Shade Of The Old Pine Tree	BB B-6325, MW M-4853
94672-1	Cottage By The Wayside	MW M-4854
94673-1	My Old Fashioned Sweetheart	BB unissued

Rev. Twin FT8113 by Bill Boyd.

Fred Kirby, v; acc. own g; or **Fred Kirby–Bob Phillips**-1, v/y-2 duet; acc. own g duet.
    Charlotte, NC   Thursday, February 13, 1936

94673-	My Old Fashioned Sweetheart	MW M-4854
94680-1	My Little Texas Town	MW M-4855
94681-1	Roll On, Roll On -1	BB B-6367, MW M-7027, RZ MR2132, Twin FT8108
94682-1	My Darling Nell -1	BB B-7056, MW M-4856, RZAu G23271
94683-1	Round-Up Time In Heaven -1, 2	BB B-6367, MW M-7027, RZ MR2132, Twin FT8108
94684-1	My Carolina Sweetheart -1, 2	BB B-7056, MW M-4856, RZAu G23271

Regal-Zonophone MR2132 as by **Fred Kirby & Bob Phillips, The Yodelling Evangelists**.

Fred Kirby, v/y-1; or **Fred Kirby–Don White**-2, v duet; or **Fred Kirby–Cliff Carlisle**-3, v duet; acc. Don White, sg-4/ g-5; Fred Kirby, g.
    Charlotte, NC   Friday, June 19, 1936

102700-1	My Old Saddle Horse Is Missing -2	BB B-6540, Twin FT8207
102701-1	That Good Old Utah Trail -3, 4	BB B-6540
102702-1	My Man -1, 5	BB B-6597
102703-1	I Got A Red Hot Mama -1, 5	BB B-7190
102704-1	My Heavenly Sweetheart -1	BB B-6597

Rev. Twin FT8207 by Blue Ridge Hill Billies.

Fred Kirby, v; acc. unknown, f; prob. Don White, g; unknown, g; own g; unknown, sb.
    Charlotte, NC   Monday, October 12, 1936

02549-1	Song Of The Golden West	BB B-6763, MW M-7183, Twin FT8356
02550-1	Wagon Train Keep Rollin' Along	BB B-6763, MW M-7183, Twin FT8356
02551-1	Get Along, Old Paint	BB B-7009, MW M-7182, Twin FT8420
02552-1	Underneath The Texas Moonlight	BB B-7310, Twin FT8554
02553-1	Where The Longhorn Cattle Roam	BB B-7009, MW M-7182, Twin FT8420
02554-1	I'm The Roughest And Toughest	BB B-7310, Twin FT8554

Fred Kirby, v/y-1; or Fred Kirby, Don White, v duet-2; acc. unknown, f-3; Don White, poss. f-4/esg-5/g-6; prob. Fred Kirby, g-7; unknown, u-8; unknown, sb; unknown, v-9.

Charlotte, NC   Saturday, August 7, 1937

013048-1	Night Time On The Prairie -5, 7, 8	BB B-7164, MW M-7364, RZ MR2655, Twin FT8487
013049-1	Home (Answer To "Home On The Range") -3, 4, 7	BB B-7164, MW M-7364, RZ MR2655, Twin FT8487
013050-1	Yes, My Mother Comes From Ireland -3, 6	BB B-7261
013051-1	My Sweet Little Mother Of The Range -2, 3, 6	BB B-7261, RZAu G23438
013052-1	Hello My Baby -1, 2, 3, 6, 9	BB B-7190

Matrix 013051 on Bluebird B-7261 as by **Fred Kirby–Don White**.
Rev. Regal-Zonophone G23438 by Jesse Rodgers.

Fred Kirby's Carolina Boys: prob. Tiny Dodson, f; Cliff Carlisle, sg-1/v-2; prob. Don White, esg-3/g-4/v-5; Fred Kirby, g/v; unidentified (poss. Dodson), v-6.

Charlotte, NC   Tuesday, June 7, 1938

64068-A	Precious Jesus I'll Be There -4, 5	De 5594, 46083
64069-A	Birmingham Jail -1, 2, 4	De 5576
64070-A	God's Love Will Shine -4, 5, 6	De 5594
64071-A	Prayer Meetin' Time In The Mountain -3, 5, 6	De 5611

Prob. Don White, esg-1/g-2/v-3; unknown, md-4/v-5; Fred Kirby, g/v.

Charlotte, NC   Tuesday, June 7, 1938

64078-A	Hello My Baby	De rejected
64079-A	You're The Only Star In My Blue Heaven -1	De 5557, MeC 45284, Min M-14096, M-14138
64080-A	Calling Ole Faithful -1	De 5557, MeC 45284, Min M-14097
64081-A	Deep Sea Blues -2	De 5708
64082-A	Columbus Stockade Blues -2, 3	De 5576
64083-A	Find My Precious Home -2, 3, 4	De 5680, 46083, MeC 45307, Min M-14120
64084-A	Change In Business	De rejected
64085-A	My Carolina Home -3, 4, 5	De 5611

Decca 5557, Melotone 45284 as by **Fred Kirby**. Matrices 64072 to 64077 are by Tiny Dodson's Circle-B Boys.
Rev. Minerva M-14138 by Ray Whitley.

Fred Kirby, v; acc. prob. Don White, esg; own g.

Charlotte, NC   Wednesday, June 15, 1938

| 64166-A | Cathedral In The Pines | De 5548, MeC 45285, Min M-14097 |
| 64167-A | Every Day Is Mother's Day To Me | De 5548, MeC 45285, Min M-14096 |

Fred Kirby's Carolina Boys: Fred Kirby, prob. Don White, v duet; acc. own g duet.

Charlotte, NC   Wednesday, June 15, 1938

| 64168-A | Bury Me Beneath The Roses | De 5708 |
| 64169-A | Life's Railway To Heaven | De 5680, MeC 45307, Min M-14120 |

Fred Kirby recorded after 1942.

KITTS BROS.

Zeke Kitts, Bill Kitts, v duet; acc. unknown, g.

Dallas, TX   Sunday, August 11, 1929

| 55342-1 | O Beautiful Land | Vi V-40171 |
| 55343-1 | 'Twill Not Be Long | Vi V-40171 |

FRANK KNAPP

Pseudonym for Frank Kamplain, whose recordings are beyond the scope of this work.

THE KNIGHT SISTERS

Vocal duet; acc. unknown.

Richmond, IN   Wednesday, January 27, 1932

| 18337 | The Bright Mohawk Valley | Ge unissued |
| 18338 | I Once Loved A Girl | Ge unissued |

KNIPPERS BROS. & PARKER

Ottis J. Knippers, tv; John Raymond Parker, 2nd tv; Cecil Christopher Knippers, bv; acc. John Raymond Parker, p.
Richmond, IN   Tuesday, April 17, 1934

19542	The Grand Old Story	Ch 16760, 45116, De 5502
19543	The Sunshine Train	Ch 16760, 45116, De 5502
19544	Happy Am I	Ch 16771, 45118
19545	How Beautiful Heaven Must Be	Ch 16777, 45119, De 5366, MeC 45119
19546	Resting In The Current Of His Love	Ch 16777, 45119, De 5366, MeC 45119
19547	Soon We'll Be Going Home	Ch 16794, 45120, De 5365
19548	That Little Old Hut	Ch 16771, 45118
19549	I Dreamed I Searched Heaven For You	Ch 16794, 45120, De 5365
19550	Won't It Be Wonderful There	Ch 16829, 45128
19551	What A Wonderful Time That Will Be	Ch 16829, 45128

BERT KNOWLES

Pseudonym on Clarion and Velvet Tone for Goebel Reeves.

VANCE KNOWLES–RED LAY

Vance Knowles, Red Lay, v/y-1 duet; acc. prob. own g duet.
Charlotte, NC   Saturday, June 20, 1936

| 102737-1 | A Thousand Miles From Texas -1 | BB B-6585 |
| 102738-1 | Two Chairs On The Porch For You And Me | BB B-6585 |

WALTER KOLOMOKU'S HONOLULUANS

This Hawaiian group recorded numerous sides for Victor, of which two were issued in the Old Familiar Tunes series (V-40085), perhaps because of the nature of the tunes (*Wednesday Night Waltz* and *My Wild Irish Rose/In The Good Old Summer Time/Sweet Rosie O'Grady*). The group and its work as a whole are beyond the scope of this work.

A. KOTOFF

Though appearing once in the Paramount Old Time Tunes series (3090), this artist is a performer of Russian music, associated with the Native Russian Troupe With Greisha Haitewich, and well beyond the scope of this work.

DAN KUTTER

Pseudonym on Challenge for David Miller.

KAY KYSER & HIS ORCHESTRA

This band's earliest recordings, for Victor, were issued in the Old Familiar Tunes series (V-40028, V-40222, and V-40258) but are outside the scope of this work. (For details of some of them see *JR*.)

L

PIERRE LA DIEU

Pierre La Dieu, v; acc. unknown, f; unknown, p.
New York, NY   Tuesday, July 3, 1928

| 146619-2 | The Shanty-Man's Life | Co 15278-D |
| 146620-3 | Driving Saw-Logs On The Plover | Co 15278-D |

DELMA LACHNEY

Delma Lachney & Blind Uncle Gaspard: Delma Lachney, f; Blind Uncle Gaspard, g; or **Delma Lachney**-1, v; acc. own f; Blind Uncle Gaspard, g.
Chicago, IL   c. January 26, 1929

C-2867-	Riviere Rouge (Red River)	Vo 5281
C-2868-	Baoille -1	Vo 5280
C-2872-	La Danseuse (The Dancer)	Vo 5303
C-2873-	Le Bebe Et Le Gambleur (The Baby And The Gambler) -1	Vo 5303
C-2874-	Cher Ami Ma Vie Est Ruini (Dear Friend My Life Is Ruined) -1	Vo 5302
C-2875-	La Louisiana (Louisiana)	Vo 5302
C-2877-	Baltimore Waltz	Vo 5320

Matrices C-2869/70 and C-2876 are by Blind Uncle Gaspard; C-2871 is untraced.

Delma Lachney, v; acc. own f; Blind Uncle Gaspard, g; or **Blind Uncle Gaspard & Delma Lachney**-1: Delma Lachney, f; Blind Uncle Gaspard, g.

New Orleans, LA   Tuesday, March 5, 1929

NO-124-	L'Aurevoir D'Une Mere (Mother's Farewell)	Vo 5347
NO-125-	Je Me Trouve Une Dolie Fille (I Find A Pretty Girl)	Vo 5347
NO-126-	Avoyelles (Parish Name) -1	Vo 5314
NO-127-	Je M'En Vas Dans Le Chemin (Going Down The Road) -1	Vo 5314

HENRI LACROIX

This French-Canadian harmonica and jew's-harp player recorded prolifically for several labels in their French-Canadian series. Three items made for the Brunswick 52000 and Melotone M18000 series were also issued in the Brunswick old-time series (342, one side of 343).

DENVER LAKE

See Lake & Cavanagh.

SLIM LAKE

Pseudonym on Superior for Hoyt "Slim" Bryant (see Bert Layne).

LAKE & CAVANAGH

Lake & Cavanagh: prob.: ——— Cavanagh, f; Denver Lake, g; or **Denver Lake**-1, v; acc. own g.

Richmond, IN   Wednesday, April 23, 1930

16519,-A	Cincinnati Hornpipe; Rickett's Hornpipe; Fairy Dance	Ge rejected
16521,-A	Opera Reel; Hell's Poppin' In The Barnyard	Ge rejected
16522,-A	The Farmer Took Another Load Away -1	Ge rejected

Matrix 16520 is Hawaiian.

BELA LAM

Bela Lam's full name was Zandervon Obeliah Lam.

Bela Lam & His Greene County Singers: Bela Lam, tv/bj; Alva Lam, lv/g; Rosa Lam, av; John Paul Meadows, bsv.

New York, NY   Thursday, July 7, 1927

81140-	Two Little Girls In Blue	OK unissued
81141-A	On The Resurrection Morning We Shall Rise	OK 45145
81142-A	Row Us Over The Tide	OK 45126
81143-B	Poor Little Bennie	OK 45136
81144-	Listen To The Mocking Bird	OK unissued
81145-B	When The Roll Is Called Up Yonder	OK 45228
81146-B	Follow Jesus	OK 45228
81147-B	Little Maud	OK 45177
81148-B	The Sweet Story Of Old	OK 45145
81149-B	May Dearest May	OK 45136

New York, NY   Friday, July 8, 1927

| 81150-A | See That My Grave Is Kept Green | OK 45126 |
| 81151-A | Sweet Bye And Bye | OK 45177 |

Richmond, VA   Tuesday, October 15, 1929

403124-B	Tell It Again	OK 45456
403125-A	If To-night Should End The World	OK 45456
403126-B	Glory Bye And Bye	OK 45407
403127-A	Crown Him	OK 45407
403128-	I Had A Darling Little Girl	OK unissued
403129-	Watermelon Smiling On The Vine	OK unissued

OKeh 45456 as by **Bela Lam & His Green County Singers**. Matrices 403126/27 were logged as by **Bela Lam Family**.

SLIM LAMAR & HIS SOUTHERNERS

The bulk of this danceband's recordings for Victor was issued in the Old Familiar Tunes series (V-40005, V-40049, V-40093, V-40130, and V-40146) but is outside the scope of this work. (For further information, see JR. The occasional vocalist Bob Nolan was not the man later known as a founder-member of the Sons of the Pioneers.)

LAMBERT & HILLPOT

Items by these artists, even that issued in the Paramount Old Time Tunes series (one side of 3013), are outside the scope of this work.

G.E. LANCASTER

G.E. Lancaster, v/y; acc. two unknowns, g.
    Richmond, IN   Saturday, April 5, 1930
      16448   Tennessee Yodel   Spr 2538

Rev. Superior 2538 by Raymond Render.

KEN LANDON

See James Brown, Jr. & Ken Landon groups.

LEE LANDON

Pseudonym on Champion for Hoke Rice.

UNCLE BUD LANDRESS

Uncle Bud Landress, v; acc. own bj.
    Atlanta, GA   Thursday, February 23, 1928
      41948-1   Coon-Hunting In Moonshine Hollow   Vi 21354
      41949-1   Visiting Sal's House In Moonshine Hollow   Vi 21354

Uncle Bud Landress With The Georgia Yellow Hammers: Uncle Bud Landress, v; acc. own f; Frank Locklear, md/v-1; Melvin Dupree, g/v-2.
    Atlanta, GA   Thursday, November 21, 1929
      56551-1   Rubber Doll Rag   Vi V-40252
      56552-2   Rip Van Winkle Blues   Vi V-40252
      56553-1,-2   The Picture Of Mother's Love   Vi unissued
      56554-1,-2   My Heart Is Broken -1, 2   Vi unissued

Uncle Budd Landress, v; acc. Frank Locklear, md-1; Melvin Dupree, g; Mrs. Mary Landress, v-2.
    Atlanta, GA   Friday, November 22, 1929
      56569-1   The Daddy Song – Part 1 -1   Vi 23606
      56570-1   The Daddy Song – Part 2 -2   Vi 23606

Uncle Bud Landress was a regular member of the Georgia Yellow Hammers and recorded with several associated groups; for a complete list see the endnote to the Georgia Yellow Hammers entry.

JOS. P. LANDRY

Joseph P. Landry, sp.
    New Orleans, LA   Saturday, November 16, 1929
      56540-1   Jack Lafiance On De Crawfish   Vi 22212
      56541-1   Jack Lafiance At The Telephone   Vi 22212

SYDNEY LANDRY

Sydney Landry, v/y; acc. own g.
    New Orleans, LA   Monday, December 9, 1929
      111382-2   Confession D'Amour (Confession Of Love)   Co 40516-F, OK 90016
      111383-2   La Blouse Francaise (French Blues)   Co 40516-F, OK 90016

DUKE LANE

Pseudonym on Supertone for Hoke Rice.

LANE'S OLD TIME FIDDLERS

Unknown, f; two unknowns, g.
    Richmond, IN   Monday, February 17, 1933
      19030   Chicken In The Barn Lot   Ge unissued
      19031   Slow Buck Reel   Ge unissued

See Bill & Louis Jones for possibly associated artists.

BOB LARKAN & FAMILY
FIDDLING BOB LARKIN & HIS MUSIC MAKERS

Fiddling Bob Larkin & His Music Makers: Bob Larkin, f/v-1; Forrest "Bob" Larkin, p; Alice Sherbs, g; William Holden Sherbs, g.
    Memphis, TN   Wednesday, February 22, 1928
      400285-B   Beautiful Belle -1   OK 45229
      400286-   Ain't She Sweet -1   OK unissued: *CARS unnumbered (Vol. 2) (CD)*
      400287-   Under The Double Eagle   OK unissued: *CARS unnumbered (Vol. 2) (CD)*

400288-A	The Higher Up The Monkey Climbs -1	OK 45205
400289-B	Saturday Night Waltz	OK 45229
400290-A	The Women Wear No Clothes At All -1	OK 45349
400291-B	Kansas City Reel	OK 45205
400292-A	Paddy, Won't You Drink Some Good Old Cider?	OK 45349

Bob Larkan & Family: Bob Larkin, f; Forrest "Bob" Larkin, p; Alice Sherbs or William Holden Sherbs, g.
    Memphis, TN   Wednesday, November 21, 1928

M-820-	Little Nellie's Waltz	Vo 5277
M-821-	Saturday Night Waltz	Vo 5277
M-822-	Prairie County Waltz	Vo 5329
M-823-	Arkansas Waltz	Vo 5329

    Memphis, TN   Thursday, November 22, 1928

M-824-	Silver Nail	Vo 5313
M-825-	McLeods Reel	Vo 5313
M-826	Saturday Night Waltz	Vo unissued

'LASSES & HONEY ('LASSES WHITE & HONEY WILDS)

'Lasses White, v/sp-1; acc. Honey Wilds, g-2/v-3/sp-4; Curt Poulton, g-5.
    Chicago, IL   Tuesday, April 23, 1935

85878-1	One-Eyed Sam -1, 4, 5	BB B-5940, Twin FT 1924
85879-1	Cumberland Valley -5	BB B-6018, RZAu G22796, Twin FT1961
85880-1	Taxi Jim -1, 2, 3, 4, 5	BB B-5940, Twin FT1924
85881-1	Jimmy Bone -2, 5	BB B-6018, RZAu G22796
85882-1	Radio Mama -2, 5	BB B-6742
85883-1	Alabamy Bound -2, 5	BB B-6742
85884-1,-2	Nigger Blues -2, 5	BB unissued
85885-1	Galloping Dominoes -1, 4	BB B-6197, Twin FT8056
85886-1,-2	The Prize Fighter	BB unissued
85887-1	Going To The Ball -1, 4	BB B-6197, Twin FT8056

Bluebird B-6197 as by **Lasses & Honey**. Rev. Twin FT1961 by Delmore Brothers.

'Lasses White recorded earlier for Columbia, but that material is beyond the scope of this work. Honey Wilds recorded after 1942 with Bunny Biggs as Jamup & Honey.

LAUREL FIREMEN'S QUARTET
THE LAUREL (MISSISSIPPI) FIREMEN'S QUARTETTE

There is likely to be a connection between these two groups, though they are not, on aural evidence, identical. Despite being listed in early editions of *B&GR*, they are white.

Laurel Firemen's Quartet: prob.: Bartie Odom, lv; Vol Summerall, tv; Jug Matthews, bsv; Millard Pridgen, v; Algia Holifield, v; acc. Vol Summerall, g.
    New Orleans, LA   Monday, December 16, 1929

403438-B	Jesus Is The Light	OK 45426
403439-B	My Friend Divine	OK 45437
403440-B	He's Calling All	OK 45426
403441-A	Because I Love Him	OK 45437
403442-B	Give The World A Smile	OK 45404
403443-B	When I Reach Home	OK 45404

The Laurel (Mississippi) Firemen's Quartette, v quartet; acc. unknown, g.
    Hattiesburg, MS   Friday, July 17, 1936

HAT-117-	Lot In Canaan Land	ARC unissued
HAT-118-	Inside The Gate	ARC unissued
HAT-119-3	What A Change	ARC 6-12-68
HAT-120-3	The Great Redeemer	ARC 6-12-68, Cq 8746
HAT-121-2	You Gotta Live Your Religion Every Day	ARC 6-11-60, Cq 8746
HAT-122-1	I Won't Have To Cross Jordan Alone	ARC 6-11-60
HAT-123-	While Ages Roll Away	ARC unissued
HAT-124-	Hallelujah In My Soul	ARC unissued

CHARLIE LAWMAN

Pseudonym on Crown for the popular singer Leroy Montesanto.

BRIAN LAWRANCE & HIS HOT FIVE

This popular danceband had two releases in the Decca Hill Billy series (5925, 5930), drawn from the British Decca catalogue. The musicians were British, except for the violin-playing leader, who was Australian. The records are beyond the scope of this work.

ZORA LAYMAN

Zora Layman, v; acc. unknown, f; unknown, p; unknown, md.
New York, NY   Tuesday, January 31, 1933
12998-1   Seven Years With The Wrong Man   Ba 32702, Me M12633, Or 8212, Pe 12889,
                                                          Ro 5212, Vo 5485, Cq 8101,
                                                          CrC/MeC/Roy/Stg 91516, Pan 25621
12999-   Young Man   ARC unissued

Vocalion 5485 as by **Zora Luther**. Rev. all issues of matrix 12998 by Frank Luther Trio.

Acc. two unknowns, f; poss. unknown, cl; unknown, p; unknown, g; unknown, sb; prob. Frank Luther, sp.
New York, NY   Friday, February 10, 1933
13055-2   The Answer To 21 Years   Ba 32722, Me M12651, Or 8216, Pe 12898,
                                                          Ro 5216, CrC/MeC/Roy/Stg 91524

Matrix 13056, logged as by **Zora Layman & Frank Luther** but issued as by **Frank Luther Trio**, is listed under Frank Luther. Rev. all issues by Frank Luther.

Acc. unknown, cl; unknown, sg; unknown, p; unknown, g; unknown, sb.
New York, NY   Saturday, September 15, 1934
38674-A   All Night Long   De 6087

Acc. unknown, f; unknown, sg-1; unknown, p; unknown, g; unknown, lute-2; unknown, sb-3.
New York, NY   Wednesday, September 26, 1934
38740-   Poor Lone Girl -1   De 5034
38741-   Fair Young Lover -1   De 5034
38743-A   I've Got Man Trouble -3   De 5033
38744-   The Wrong Man And The Wrong Woman -1, 2   De 5033, Pan 25679

Matrix 38742 (and 38745) is by Frank Luther. Rev. Panachord 25679 by Frank Luther.

Acc. unknown.
New York, NY   Friday, October 5, 1934
38797-A   My Old Flame   De 244, DeE F5329
38798-A   Troubled Waters   De 244, DeE F5329

Doreen O'Dare, v; acc. unknown.
New York, NY   Wednesday, November 14, 1934
39017-A   That Old Wooden Rocker   De 12044

This and the first three items recorded at the next session were issued in Decca's Irish (12000) series.

Acc. unknown, f; unknown, ac; unknown, p.
New York, NY   Friday, November 16, 1934
39026-A   Great Grandma   De 12022
39127-A   Granny's Old Armchair   De 12022
39128-A   My Mother's Old Red Shawl   De 12044
39129-A   Hurray, I'm Single Again   De 6087

Decca 6087 as by **Zora Layman**. Intervening matrices are by other artists on other dates.

Zora Layman, v; acc. unknown, f; unknown, vla; unknown, sg; unknown, p.
New York, NY   Tuesday, February 12, 1935
39353-A,-B   The Cowboy's Best Friend   De unissued

Zora & The Hometowners: Zora Layman, v; acc. unknown, f; unknown, g; unknown, sb; unknown, male v group.
New York, NY   Tuesday, November 23, 1937
62804-A   When The Organ Played O' Promise Me   De 5459, MeC 45252, Pan 25992
62805-A   In The Mission By The Sea   De 5459, MeC 45252, Rex 9222
62806-A   Old Cowboy   De 5572, Pan 25992
62807-A   When The Curtains Of Night Are Pinned Back By   De 5460, Rex 9222
              The Stars
62808-A   Handsome Texas Buckaroo   De 5688
62809-A   I'll Be Hanged (If They're Gonna Hang Me)   De 5460, Pan 26005

Decca 5688, Rex 9222 as by **Zora Layman & The Hometowners**. Panachord 25992, 26005 as by **Zora Layman & His** [sic] **Hometowners**.

Zora Layman, v; acc. unknown orch.
New York, NY   Wednesday, July 6, 1938
64262-   Don't Go In The Lion's Cage Tonight   De 2089, Rex 9509
64263-   The Beautiful Bearded Lady   De 2089, Rex 9509
64264-A   Handsome Texas Buckaroo   De rejected
64265-A   Cowboys Ain't Stupid Like Cupid   De 5688

Rex 9509 as by **Zora Layman & The Hometowners**.

Acc. unknown, f; unknown, g; unknown, sb.
New York, NY Wednesday, July 6, 1938

    64266-A   Cowboy's Best Friend   De 5572, Pan 26005

Decca 5572 as by **Zora & The Hometowners**. Panachord 26005 as by **Zora Layman & His** [sic] **Hometowners**.

Zora Layman recorded duets with her husband Frank Luther and as a member of his Trio; see his entry. She also recorded standard songs not listed above, and after 1942.

BERT LAYNE

Bert Layne's Melody Boys: Bert Layne, f; unknown, md-1; Claude (C.W.) Davis, g.
Atlanta, GA Thursday, November 13, 1930

ATL-6651-	Nights Of Gladness	Br unissued
ATL-6656-	Nights Of Gladness	Br 502
ATL-6657-	Sparklets Waltz -1	Br 502

Matrices ATL-6652 to 6655 are by Red Gay groups.

Bert Layne, f/v; prob. Lowe Stokes, f; Claude (C.W.) Davis, g.
Atlanta, GA Saturday, November 15, 1930

ATL-6682-	Sailing On The Robert E. Lee	Br rejected
ATL-6683-	Caroline Train	Br rejected

Bert Layne, f; Claude (C.W.) Davis, g/v.
Atlanta, GA Tuesday, November 18, 1930

ATL-6649-B	I Ain't Got No Sweetheart	Br 582
ATL-6650-A	Give Me Your Heart	Br 582

Johnny Barfield & Hoyt Bryant Acc by Bert Layne & His Georgia Serenaders: Johnny Barfield, Hoyt "Slim" Bryant, v duet; acc. Bert Layne, f; Hoyt "Slim" Bryant, g; Johnny Barfield, g; or **Hoyt Bryant**-1: Hoyt Bryant, v solo with same acc.; or **Bert Layne & His Georgia Serenaders**-2: Bert Layne, f/v/sp; Hoyt "Slim" Bryant, g/v/sp; Johnny Barfield, g/v/sp.
Richmond, IN Friday, November 13, 1931

18174-A	On The Banks Of The Old Ohio	Ch 16406, Spr 2752
18175	Back To My Georgia Home	Ch 16406, Spr 2752
18176	Yum Yum Blues -1	Ch 16407, Spr 2819
18177	Peach Picking Time In Georgia -1	Ch 16407, Spr 2819
18178	The Rabbit Hunt – Part 1 -2	Ch 16346, Spr 2812
18179	The Rabbit Hunt – Part 2 -2	Ch 16346, Spr 2812

Superior 2752 as by **Johnny & Slim**, 2812 as by **Hoyt "Slim" Bryant & His Riversiders**, 2819 as by **Slim Lake**.

Johnny Barfield Acc. By Bert Layne's Serenaders: Johnny Barfield, v; acc. Bert Layne, f; unknown, f; Hoyt "Slim" Bryant, g; own g; or **Johnny Barfield**-1: Johnny Barfield, v; acc. own g.
Richmond, IN Sunday, November 15, 1931

18180	Sweet Florine	Ch S-16415, Spr 2839
18181	Highway Hobo -1	Ch S-16415, Spr 2839

Superior 2839 as by **Johnny Miller**.

Bert Layne recorded on several occasions with Claude (C.W.) Davis; their joint work is listed under the latter. Layne was also a frequent member of Gid Tanner & His Skillet-Lickers and recorded with various associated groups; see Clayton McMichen.

'LAZY' LARRY

Pseudonym on Cameo-group labels and derivatives for Frank Luther.

ANGELAS LE JEUNNE

Angelus Le Jeunne, ac/v-1; acc. Denus McGee, f; Ernest Fruge, f.
New Orleans, LA Monday, September 30, 1929

NO-224-	La Valse De Church Point -1	Br 368
NO-225-	Petit Tes Canaigh -1	Br 368
NO-226-	Perrodin Two Step	Br 369
NO-227-	Valse De La Louisianne -1	Br 369
NO-228-	Valse De Pointe Noire -1	Br 370
NO-229-	Bayou Pom Pom One Step -1	Br 370

Le Jeunne & Fruge: Angelas La Jeunne, v; acc. Ernest Fruge, f; own ac.
New Orleans, LA Wednesday, November 19, 1930

NO-6700-	Le Petit One Step	Br 558, Me M18052
NO-6701-	La Valse De La Veuve	Br 558, Me M18052
NO-6706-	La Valse Du Bayou Sauvage	Br 493
NO-6707-	One Step De Chataignier	Br 493
NO-6708-	One Step Du Maraist Bouler	Br 511
NO-6709-	La Valse A Tidom Hanks	Br 511

NO-6715-	One Step A Cain	Br 530
NO-6716-	La Valse Du Texas	Br 530
NO-6727-	La Valse A Aristil Creduer	Br 577
NO-6728-	Madam Donnez Moi Les	Br 577

Matrices NO-6702, 6705, 6725/26 are by Patrick (Dak) Pellerin; NO-6703/04, 6713/14 are by Denus McGee & Ernest Fruge; NO-6710 is by Mr. & Mrs. Ed Lindsey; NO-6711/12, 6723/24 are by Walter Coquille; NO-6717 to NO-6722 are by McGee & Ardoin (see Amedie Ardoin).

LE JEUNNE & FRUGE

See Angelas Le Jeunne.

LE ORCHESTRE CARTIER

Pseudonym on Melotone M18022 for H.M. Barnes & His Blue Ridge Ramblers. (Also used on M18021 for Whoopee John Wilfahrt's Concertina Orchestra, which is outside the scope of this work.)

LEADER CLEVELAND & MEN'S BIBLE CLASS

Pseudonym on Paramount for Cleve Chaffin & the McClung Brothers (see the latter).

LEAKE COUNTY REVELERS

Will Gilmer, f/v-1; R.O. Mosley, bj-md; Jim Wolverton, bj; Dallas Jones, g; unidentified, v-2.
New Orleans, LA   Wednesday, April 13, 1927

143967-2	Johnson Gal -1	Co 15149-D, *Vo 02959*
143968-2	Leather Breeches -2	Co 15149-D, *Vo 02959*
143969-1	Wednesday Night Waltz	Co 15189-D, *Vo 02920, Co 20199, 37600*
143970-1	Good Night Waltz	Co 15189-D, *Vo 02920, Co 20199, 37600*

Will Gilmer, f; R.O. Mosley, bj-md; Jim Wolverton, bj; Dallas Jones, g/v-1; v trio (usually Jones, lv; Gilmer, tv; Wolverton, bsv)-2; unidentified, wh-3.
Atlanta, GA   Thursday, October 25, 1927

145012-2	My Wild Irish Rose -2	Co 15776-D
145013-1	My Bonnie Lies Over The Ocean -2	Co 15227-D, CoAu 01896
145014-2	In The Good Old Summertime -2	Co 15227-D, CoAu 01896, Ve 2494-V, Cl 5434-C
145015-2	Listen To The Mocking Bird -1, 3	Co 15776-D
145016-2	The Old Hat -1	Co 15205-D
145017-2	Monkey In The Dog Cart	Co 15205-D

Velvet Tone 2494-V, Clarion 5434-C as by **Texarkana Melody Boys**.
Rev. Velvet Tone 2494-V, Clarion 5434-C by McMichen's Melody Men.

Will Gilmer, f; R.O. Mosley, bj-md; Jim Wolverton, bj; Dallas Jones, g/v-1; unidentified, v duet-2; unidentified, v eff-3.
New Orleans, LA   Friday, April 27, 1928

146208-2	Been To The East – Been To The West -1	Co 15318-D
146209-3	Crow Black Chicken -2, 3	Co 15318-D
146210-2	Make Me A Bed On The Floor -2	Co 15264-D
146211-2	Merry Widow Waltz	Co 15264-D
146212	Julia Waltz	Co unissued
146213-2	They Go Wild Simply Wild Over Me -1	Co 15292-D
146214-2	Put Me In My Little Bed -1	Co 15292-D
146215-	Coon, Coon, Coon	Co unissued

Will Gilmer, f; R.O. Mosley, bj-md; Jim Wolverton, bj; Dallas Jones, g; unidentified, v.
New Orleans, LA   Wednesday, December 12, 1928

| 147624-2 | Bring Me A Bottle | Co 15380-D |

Will Gilmer, f; R.O. Mosley, bj-md; Jim Wolverton, bj; Dallas Jones, g/v-1/y-2.
New Orleans, LA   Thursday, December 13, 1928

147625-2	Birds In The Brook	Co 15625-D, Re/RZAu G21139
147626-2	Rockin' Yodel -1, 2	Co 15353-D
147627-2	Memories	Co 15767-D
147628-2	Magnolia Waltz	Co 15625-D, Re/RZAu G21139
147629-1	Julia Waltz	Co 15353-D
147630-	Texas Kickin' Maud	Co unissued
147631-2	Molly Put The Kettle On -1	Co 15380-D

Regal/Regal-Zonophone G21139 as by **The Alabama Barnstormers**.

Will Gilmer, f; R.O. Mosley, bj-md; Jim Wolverton, bj; Dallas Jones, g/v-1/y-2; v trio (usually Jones, lv; Gilmer, tv; Wolverton, bsv)-3; unidentified, wh duet-4.
Atlanta, GA   Tuesday, April 16, 1929

148315-2	Memories Waltz -1	Co 15427-D
148316-1,-2	Bonnie Blue Eyes -3	Co unissued
148317-1	Where The Silv'ry Colorado Wends Its Way -1	Co 15427-D
148318-	In The Shadow Of The Pines	Co unissued
148319-2	Georgia Camp Meeting	Co 15409-D
148320-2	I'm Gwine Back To Dixie -3	Co 15409-D
148321-2	Dry Town Blues	Co 15441-D
148322-2	Saturday Night Breakdown	Co 15470-D
148323-2	Good Fellow -2, 3, 4	Co 15441-D
148324-2	Uncle Ned -2, 3	Co 15470-D, ReE G9458, Re/RZAu G20753

Regal G9458, Regal/Regal-Zonophone G20753 as by **The Alabama Barn Stormers**.
Rev. Regal G9458, Regal/Regal-Zonophone G20753 by McCartt Brothers & Patterson.

Will Gilmer, f; R.O. Mosley, bj-md; Jim Wolverton, bj; Dallas Jones, g.
New Orleans, LA   Tuesday, December 10, 1929

149582-2	Leake County Blues	Co 15520-D
149583-1	Lonesome Blues	Co 15520-D
149584-	Leake County Breakdown	Co unissued
149585-	Smith's March (New Orleans)	Co unissued
149586-2	Sweet Rose Of Heaven	Co 15501-D
149587-2	Beautiful Bells	Co 15501-D
149588-2	Mississippi Moon Waltz	Co 15569-D
149589-2	Courtin' Days Waltz	Co 15569-D

Will Gilmer, f; R.O. Mosley, bj-md; Jim Wolverton, bj; Dallas Jones, g/v-1/y-2; unidentified, v duet-3; v trio (usually Jones, lv; Gilmer, tv; Wolverton, bsv)-4.
Jackson, MS   Thursday, December 18, 1930

151119-2	Thirty-First Street Blues -2, 3	Co 15668-D
151120-2	Picture No Artist Can Paint -4	Co 15691-D, Re/RZAu G21475
151121-1	When It's Springtime In The Rockies -1	Co 15648-D
151122-2	Texas Fair	Co 15691-D
151123-2	Mississippi Breakdown	Co 15668-D
151124-1	Lazy Kate	Co 15767-D
151125-2	Jungle Waltz	Co 15648-D
151126-	Gilmar [sic] Waltz	Co unissued

Regal/Regal-Zonophone G21475 as by **The Alabama Barnstormers**; matrix 151120 is titled *A Picture No Artist Can Paint* on that issue. Rev. Regal/Regal-Zonophone G21475 by McMichen's Melody Men.

LEATHERMAN SISTERS (LUCILLE & LILLIAN)

Lucille Leatherman, Lillian Leatherman, v/y-1 duet; acc. own g duet.
Charlotte, NC   Wednesday, June 17, 1936

102672-1	Curly-Headed Baby – Part 2 -1	BB B-6490
102673-1	Lonesome For You, Darling	BB B-6490
102674-1	Just A Little While	BB B-6598
102675-1	Home Coming Week	BB B-6598

STEVE LEDFORD

Steve Ledford & The Mountaineers: Steve Ledford, v; acc. own f; Wade Mainer, bj; Clyde Moody, g/v-1; Jay Hugh Hall, g/v-2; poss. unidentified, v-3.
Charlotte, NC   Thursday, January 27, 1938

018766-1	Since I Met My Mother-In-Law	BB B-7742, MW M-7483
018779-1	Bachelor Blues	BB B-7626
018780-1	Only A Broken Heart -1, 2, 3	BB B-7626
018781-1	Happy Or Lonesome -1, 2, 3	BB B-7742

Montgomery Ward M-7483 as by **Steve Ledford**.
Matrices 018767 to 018772 are by Wade Mainer; 018773 to 018778 are untraced. Rev. Montgomery Ward M-7483 by Wade Mainer.
See also Wade Mainer.

ARCHIE LEE [& OTHERS]

See The Chumbler Family & Associated Groups.

POWDER RIVER JACK–KITTY LEE

Powder River Jack Lee, v; acc. own h/g; Kitty Lee, g.
Hollywood, CA   Monday, November 3, 1930

61049-1	Tying A Knot In The Devil's Tail	Vi 23527, MW M-4462, ZoSA 4326
61050-	The Old Black Steer (Old Cowboy Song)	BB B-5298, Eld 2169, Sr S-3379
61051-	My Love Is A Cowboy (Old Cowboy Song)	BB B-5298, Eld 2169, Sr S-3379
61052-2	Powder River, Let 'Er Buck	Vi 23527, MW M-4462

Bluebird B-5298, Electradisk 2169, Sunrise S-3379 as by **"Powder River" Jack Lee**.
Possibly only one guitar is used on matrix 61050.
Rev. Zonophone 4326 by Frank Marvin.

Probably the same.
   Chicago, IL   Thursday, December 10, 1936

C-91042-A	The Santa Fe Trail	De unissued
C-91043-A	The Cowboy's Farewell	De unissued

LEE BROTHERS [TRIO]

See The Chumbler Family & Associated Groups.

THE LEE COUNTY STRING BAND

Pseudonym on Supertone for Ted Gossett's Band.

WOODY LEFTWICH

Woody Leftwich, v; acc. own g.
   Richmond, IN   Thursday, July 20, 1933

19269	Pal Of Mine, Please Come Home	Ge rejected
19270	I'm Riding Around Them Cattle	Ge unissued
19271	It's Funny When You Feel That Way	Ge rejected
19272	Looking For A Gal	Ge rejected
19273	My Own Blues	Ge rejected
19274	My Mammy's Yodel Song	Ge rejected

See also Fred Pendleton.

MALCOLM LEGETTE

Malcolm Legette, v; acc. poss. own g.
   Atlanta, GA   Monday, October 29, 1928

147327-2	Life On An Ocean Wave	Co 15424-D
147328-1	Song Of The Tramp	Co 15424-D, Re/RZAu G20641

Rev. Regal/Regal-Zonophone G20641 by Vernon Dalhart.

FRED LEHMAN

Fred Lehman, v; acc. poss. own g.
   Richmond, IN   Saturday, September 1, 1928

14225	Dan O'Brien's Raffle	Ge rejected
14226	Sweet Bunch Of Daisies	Ge rejected

JOE LEIGH

Pseudonym on Eclipse and Unison for Frank Luther (see Carson Robison).

LEM'S DOWN HOME BOYS

Lem Paschal, unknown, v duet; or Lem Paschal, two unknowns, v trio-1; acc. unknown, f; unknown, g.
   New York, NY   Monday, September 14, 1936

61259-A	I Love The Life Of A Cowboy -1	De 5290, DeAu X1334, Min M-14163
61260-A	Ball And Chain	De 5276
61261-A	No Other Fellow's Sweetheart	De 5290, DeAu X1334, Min M-14163, BrSA SA1203
61262-A	I Know There'll Be Music In Heaven	De 5276, BrSA SA1203

LEON'S LONE STAR COWBOYS

See Leon Chappelear.

LES DEUX GASPESIENS

Pseudonym on Brunswick and Melotone for various artists, as follows:
Br 52082, Me M18026 Nat Bird & Tom Collins
Br 52083, Me M18010 Jarvis & Justice
Br 52084, Me M18029 The Red Headed Fiddlers
Br 52085, 52086 Kessinger Brothers

LES DEUX PAROISSIENS

Pseudonym on Melotone for the Kessinger Brothers.

LES FRERES BOISVERT

Pseudonym on Melotone for the Stripling Brothers, except on one side of M18025 (*Polka Classique*), which is by the Polish artists Ignacy Podgorski and Josef Pawlak.

LES JOYEUX MONTREALAIS

Pseudonym used on Brunswick as follows: on 52076 for the Collier Trio; on 52077/78, 52080/81, and 52085/86 for the Kessinger Brothers; and on 52079 for H.M. Barnes & His Blue Ridge Ramblers.

LES SERENADEURS DU LAC ST. JEAN

Melotone M18019, with this artist credit, couples items by the Kessinger Brothers (E-30190) and the East Texas Serenaders (DAL-723).

BOB LESTER & BUD GREEN

Pseudonym on Melotone, Polk, and English/Australian Panachord for Lester McFarland & Robert A. Gardner.

JOE LESTER

Pseudonym on Superior for Jimmy Long.

JOE LESTER & DICK MOSS

Pseudonym on Superior for Jimmy Long & Cliff Keiser.

JOE & MARY [or MAY] LESTER

Pseudonym on Superior for Jimmy & Beverly Long. On Superior 2754, *By And By You Will Forget Me*, credited to **Joe & Mary Lester**, is in fact by Fred Pendleton & West Virginia Melody Boys.

LESTER (THE HIGHWAY MAN)

See Lester "Pete" Bivins.

AL LEWIS

Pseudonym on Challenge for Asa Martin.

CHARLES LEWIS

Harmony 5145-H by Charles Lewis Stine was credited thus.

E. ARTHUR LEWIS

Evangelist Lewis, v; acc. own "mandola-mandolin".
Richmond, IN   Tuesday, April 17, 1923

11407,-A	The Wondrous Story	[Lewis] 10	
11408,-A	Mother Now Your Saviour Is My Saviour Too	[Lewis] 10	
11409,-A,-B	And The Very God Of Peace Sanctify You Wholly	[Lewis] rejected	
11410,-A,-B	But The World Treats Real Salvation In Such A Funny Way	[Lewis] rejected	
11411,-A	I Am Looking Daily For My Saviour	[Lewis] rejected	

These and subsequent recordings were custom-made by Gennett.
Issued recordings are on an unnamed personal label bearing the artist's photograph and credited thus: "Sung by Evangelist Lewis/Playing His Special Make Instrument/Mandola-Mandolin/E. Arthur Lewis/341 W. Marquette Rd./Chicago, Ill."

Richmond, IN   Thursday, April 19, 1923

11412,-A	Jonah	[Lewis] unissued?	
11413,-A	Religious – Swanee River Song	[Lewis] unissued?	
11414,-A	What You Need Now Is Sanctification	[Lewis] unissued?	
11415-A	I Will Live For My Saviour	[Lewis] 6	
11416-A	Let's Have The Old Time Ring	[Lewis] 5	
11417,-A	The Time That Used To Be In Front	[Lewis] 7?	

Matrix 11415 was remade as matrix 12258, matrix 11416 as matrix 12506, and matrix 11417 as matrix 12507 (see below); presumably later pressings of [Lewis] 6, 5, and 7 use the later matrices.

Richmond, IN   Friday, April 20, 1923

11418,-A	Scatter Seeds Of Kindness	[Lewis] 8	
11419	O Wand'rer On Life's Troubled Sea	[Lewis] 6	
11420-A	I Will Sing Of My Saviour	[Lewis] 12	
11421,-A	The Carnal Mennagerie [sic]	[Lewis] unissued?	

| 11422,-A | I Have Entered The Land Of Corn And Wine | [Lewis] unissued? |
| 11423 | Good Old Time Religion Is A Million Miles Ahead | [Lewis] unissued |

Matrix 11418 was remade as matrix 12505, and matrix 11419 as matrix 12257 (see below); presumably later pressings of [Lewis] 8 and 6 use the later matrices.

Richmond, IN   Thursday, May 3, 1923
11453,-A,-B	The Carnal Mennagerie [sic]	[Lewis] unissued?
11454	That Good Old Time Religion Is A Million Miles Ahead	[Lewis] 5
11455	This Is God's Will	[Lewis] unissued?
11456,-A	Religious – Swanee River Song	[Lewis] unissued

Richmond, IN   Friday, June 15, 1923
| 11511 | Where My Saviour Leads Me I'll Follow All The Way | [Lewis] 12 |

E. Arthur Lewis, v; acc. own "mandola-mandolin."
Richmond, IN   Friday, March 20, 1925
| 12176 | Kept On The Firing Line | [Lewis] 14 |
| 12177-B | Keep Me On The Firing Line Jesus | [Lewis] 14 |

E. Arthur Lewis & His Mandola-Mandolin, v; acc. own "mandola-mandolin."
Richmond, IN   Thursday, May 28, 1925
12253	Swanee River	[Lewis] 8
12254	Farwell [sic] Father I Am Dying	[Lewis] 17
12255	How Tedious And Tasteless The Hours	[Lewis] 17
12256	Scatter The Seeds Of Kindness	[Lewis] rejected
12257	Oh Wanderer On Life's Troubled Sea	[Lewis] 6
12258	I Will Live For My Savior	[Lewis] 6

A note in the Gennett ledger on matrices 12253 and 12256 to 12258 reads: "remake; chg [charge] remake." Matrix 12256, though assigned the issue number [Lewis] 8, is described in the ledger as "rejected by Lewis; master ord[ered] destroyed June 15," and it seems probable that the issued recording is matrix 12505. Concerning matrices 12257/58, see the notes to the sessions of April 19-20, 1923.

Richmond, IN   Thursday, April 22, 1926
12502	Coming Soon I Know You'll Take Me	[Lewis] unissued?
12503	If I Came From A Monkey	[Lewis] unissued?
12504	River Shannon Second Blessing	[Lewis] unissued?
12505	Scatter Seeds Of Kindness	[Lewis] 8
12506	Let's Have The Old Time Ring	[Lewis] 5
12507	The Line That Used To Be In Front	[Lewis] 7
12508	And The Very God Of Peace	[Lewis] 9
12509	The World Treats Real Salvation	[Lewis] 11

A note in the Gennett ledger on matrices 12505 to 12509 reads: "remake; not charged."
Revs: [Lewis] 7, 9, 11 are untraced but presumably by Lewis.

Evangelist Lewis, v; acc. own "mandola-mandolin"; Chicago Aeolian Ladies Quartet, v quartet.
Chicago, IL   1926
| 642 | Keep Me On The Firing Line, Jesus | Rodeheaver Special 3 |

Acc. own "mandola-mandolin."
Chicago, IL   1926
| 890 | In Our Hearts The Bells Of Heaven Sweetly Chime | Rodeheaver Special 3 |

E.M. LEWIS

E.M. Lewis, h/ah.
Richmond, IN   Friday, March 21, 1930
| 16388,-A | The Tramp's Dream; Koots Town; The Mountain Man | Ge rejected |
| 16389,-A | The Woodchuck On The Hill; King's Head; Nigger Stays At Home | Ge rejected |

EVANGELIST LEWIS

See E. Arthur Lewis.

FRANK LEWIS

Pseudonym on Sterling for Frank Luther (see Carson Robison).

TEXAS JIM LEWIS

Texas Jim Lewis & His Lone Star Cowboys: Andrew "Cactus" Soldi, f; Walter "Shorty" Fulkersin, ac; Eugene "Smokey" Rogers, bj-1/g-2; Curly Engel, tg/v-3/y-4; Texas Jim Lewis, sb/hootin' nanny-5/v-6; band v-7.

New York, NY   Friday, September 24, 1937

21759-1	12th Street Rag -1, 5	Vo/OK 03977
21760-1	There's A Love Knot In My Lariat -2, 3, 4	ARC 8-02-63, Vo/OK 03915
21761-2	Who Broke The Lock (On The Hen House Door) -2, 3, 6	ARC 7-12-55, Vo/OK 03754
21762-2	'Way Down Upon The Swanee River -1, 3, 6	Vo/OK 03977
21763-2	Crawdad Song -2, 7	ARC 7-12-55, Vo/OK 03754
21764-1	I'll Be Thinking Of You Little Girl -2, 3, 4	ARC 8-02-63, Vo/OK 03915

Cactus Soldi, f; Larry "Pedro" DePaul, ac; Jack Rivers, g/v-1; Pete Wray, g; Texas Jim Lewis, sb/hootin' nanny-2/v-3; Cindy Walker, v-4.

Los Angeles, CA   Friday, August 23, 1940

DLA-2082-A	Seven Beers With The Wrong Man -4	De 5874, MeC 45383
DLA-2083-A	Seven Beers With The Wrong Woman -3	De 5874, MeC 45383
DLA-2084-A,-B	Rock And Rye Polka -1	De 5875, 46021, MeC 45384
DLA-2085-A	Wine, Women And Song -2, 3	De 5875, 46021, MeC 45384

Jack Rivers Lewis, Texas Jim Lewis's half-brother, legally changed his name to Jack Rivers, but it is uncertain when this occurred. Pete Wray was a professional name of Loman Landell. An AFM Local 47 contract gives a recording date of August 18.

Carl LaMagna, f; Larry DePaul, ac/v-1; Jack Rivers, g/v-2; Buddy Hayes, sb; Texas Jim Lewis, v-3; Cindy Walker, v-4.

Los Angeles, CA   Wednesday, September 11, 1940

DLA-2147-A	Love Has Been The Ruin Of A Many Young Maid -4	De 5905, MeC 45407
DLA-2148-A	Love Has Been The Ruin Of A Many Young Man -3	De 5894, MeC 45401
DLA-2149-A	The Covered Wagon Rolled Right Along -1, 2, 3 (lead)	De 5894, 46053, MeC 45401
DLA-2150-A	Hill Billy Bill -1, 2, 4 (lead)	De 5912, MeC 45412

Matrix DLA-2147 is titled *Love Has Been The Ruin Of Many A Young Maid* on Melotone 45407, and matrix DLA-2148 is titled *Love Has Been The Ruin Of Many A Young Man* on Melotone 45401.

An AFM Local 47 contract gives a recording date of September 10.

Spade Cooley, f; Larry DePaul, solovox/v-1; Jack Rivers, g/v-2; Pete Wray, g/v-3; Texas Jim Lewis, sb.

Los Angeles, CA   Friday, November 8, 1940

DLA-2235-A	New San Antonio Rose -3	De 5901, 46097, MeC 45404
DLA-2236-A	South	De 5905, MeC 45407
DLA-2237-A	Mary, The Prairie And I -1, 2, 3	De 5912, MeC 45412
DLA-2238-A	Worried Mind -3	De 5901, 46097, MeC 45404

Pinky Tomlin, v; acc. Texas Jim Lewis & His Band: Carl LaMagna, f; Larry DePaul, ac; Jack Rivers, g; poss. Pete Wray, g; Texas Jim Lewis, sb.

Los Angeles, CA   Tuesday, December 17, 1940

DLA-2278-A	The Object Of My Affection	De 3649
DLA-2279-A	I Did It And I'm Glad	De 3649
DLA-2280-A	What's The Reason (I'm Not Pleasin' You)	De 3811, 25333
DLA-2281-	The Love Bug Will Bite You (If You Don't Watch Out)	De 3811

Rev. Decca 25333 by Pinky Tomlin (popular).

Texas Jim Lewis & His Lone Star Cowboys: Carl LaMagna, f; Larry DePaul, ac/v-1; Jack Rivers, g/v-2; Eugene Dan Walsh, g/v-3; Texas Jim Lewis, hootin' nanny-4/v-5; Buddy Hayes, sb.

Los Angeles, CA   Friday, August 15, 1941

DLA-2643-A	Beaver Creek -1, 2, 5 (lead)	De 6001, 46063, MeC 45478
DLA-2644-A	Pretty Quadroon -2, 3 (lead), 5	De 5990, MeC 45470
DLA-2645-B	Just A While -3	De 6056
DLA-2646-A	Hootin' Nannie Annie -4, 5	De 6001, MeC 45478

Vernon "Junior" Greenlaw, f; Larry DePaul, ac/v-1; Jack Rivers, g/v-2; Eugene Dan Walsh, g/v-3; Texas Jim Lewis, hootin' nanny-4/v-5; Buddy Hayes, sb.

Los Angeles, CA   Monday, August 25, 1941

DLA-2681-A	Old Fashioned Hoedown -1, 2, 4, 5 (lead)	De 5990, MeC 45470
DLA-2682-A	Molly Darling -3	De 6020
DLA-2683-A	If It Hadn't Been For You -3	De 6020
DLA-2684-A	My Bear Cat Mountain Gal -5	De 6031

Junior Greenlaw, f; poss. Ray Foster, t/v-1; Ernest "Skeeter" Hubbert, poss. t/g; Larry DePaul, ac/v-2; Jack Rivers, g/v-3; Texas Jim Lewis, sb/v-4; Dan Walsh, v-5.

Los Angeles, CA   Friday, February 27, 1942

DLA-2924-A,-AA	When There's Tears In The Eyes Of A Potato	De unissued
DLA-2925-A	Rose Of The Border -3?, 4?, 5 (lead)?	De 6056
DLA-2926-A,-B	The Old Man Of The Mountain -1/5	De unissued
DLA-2927-A	Big Bad Bill (From The Badlands) -2, 3, 4 (lead)	De 6031

Decca files assign the vocal on matrix DLA-2926 to Ray Foster, but Lewis, Rivers, and DePaul reject this and credit Dan Walsh. AFM files list Foster on trumpet, but others suggest Hubbert. Ray Foster was apparently the professional name of Ray Robbins; his association with the band is unclear.

William H. (Billy) Hill, f; Skeeter Hubbert, t/g; Larry DePaul, ac/v-1; Jack Rivers, g/v-2; Texas Jim Lewis, sb/hootin' nanny-3/v-4; Pete Wray, v-5.
Los Angeles, CA   Saturday, June 27, 1942

L-3071-A,-AA	My Little Prairie Flower -5	De unissued
L-3072-B	Midnight Flyer -3, 4	De 6078, MeC 45550
L-3073-A,-AA,-B	I've Found Somebody New -2	De unissued
L-3074-A	Hitch Old Dobbin To The Shay Again -1, 2, 4 (lead)	De 6085, MeC 45557

The train effects on matrix DLA-3072 were made by DePaul, accordion, and Lewis, hootin' nanny.

Spade Cooley, f; Larry DePaul, ac/v-1; Jack Rivers, g/v-2; Dan Walsh, g/v-3; Texas Jim Lewis, sb/v-4.
Los Angeles, CA   Thursday, July 23, 1942

L-3118-A	You Gotta Go -2	De 6085, MeC 45557
L-3119-A	Tweedle O'Twill -4	De 6064
L-3120-A	Dusty Skies -1, 2, 3 (lead)	De 6064
L-3121-A,-AA	Just Wait And See	De unissued
L-3122-A	My Little Prairie Flower -2	De 6078, MeC 45550

Texas Jim Lewis recorded after 1942.

LUMMIE LEWIS & HIS MERRYMAKERS

George Hutinger, f; Carl Highsmith, cl/ts; Mac Register, p; Aldan "Wimpy" Hutson, tbj; Columbus "Lummie" Lewis, g/v-1/prob. y-2; Dick Haltom or Pinky Dawson, sb; Shelly Lee Alley, v-3; unidentified, v-4; band v-5.
Dallas, TX   Wednesday, June 23, 1937

DAL-448-1	It Worries Me -4, 5	Vo 03696
DAL-449-2	Those Mean Mama Blues -2, 3	Vo 03855
DAL-450-2	Save It For Me -3	Vo 03632
DAL-451-1	Travelin' Blues -1	Vo 03696
DAL-452-2	Sweetheart Of Mine -3	Vo 03855
DAL-453-1	Merrymakers Stomp	Vo 03632

LEWIS BROTHERS

Dempson Lewis, f; Denmon Lewis, g.
El Paso, TX   Thursday, July 11, 1929

55227-2	Bull At The Wagon	Vi V-40172, Au 400
55228-2	Sally Johnson	Vi V-40172, MW M-4345, Au 400
55229-2	When Summer Comes Again	Vi V-40187
55230-2	Caliope	Vi V-40187

Victor V-40172 as by **Lewis Bros**. Rev. Montgomery Ward M-4345 by Rodeo Trio.

THE LEWIS TRIO

Pseudonym on Lyric for the Carson Robison Trio.

LEXINGTON RED PEPPERS

Unknown, f; unknown, bj-md; unknown, g.
Richmond, IN   Friday, May 29, 1931

| 17773-A | Pride Of The Ball | Ch 16757, 45017 |

Rev. Champion 16757, 45017 by West Virginia Ramblers (see Roy Harvey).

[THE] LIGHT CRUST DOUGHBOYS

Fort Worth Doughboys: Bob Wills, f/v eff-1; Derwood Brown, g/v-2; C.G. "Sleepy" Johnson, tg; Milton Brown, v.
Dallas, TX   Tuesday, February 9, 1932

| 70670-1 | Nancy Jane -1, 2 | Vi 23653, BB B-5257, Eld 2137, Sr S-3340, MW M-4416, M-4757, Au 415 |
| 70671-1 | Sunbonnet Sue | Vi 23653, BB B-5257, Eld 2137, Sr S-3340, MW M-4416, M-4757, Au 415 |

Montgomery Ward M-4757 as by **Milton Brown & His Musical Brownies**.

[The] Light Crust Doughboys

W. Lee O'Daniel & His Light Crust Doughboys: Clifford Gross, f-1; Sleepy Johnson, f-2/tbj-3; Leon McAuliffe, sg-4; Leon Huff, g/v-5; Herman Arnspiger, lg; Ramon DeArman, sb; W. Lee O'Daniel, ldr; v quartet (Huff, lv; DeArman, tv; Johnson, bv; Gross, bsv)-6; unidentified, v-7.

Chicago, IL   Tuesday, October 10, 1933

Matrix	Title	Issue
C-621-1,-2	Beautiful Texas -1, 2, 4, 5, 6	Vo 02621
C-622-1	Blue Bonnet Waltz -1, 3, 4	Vo 02621, RZAu G22095
C-623-2	Your Own Sweet Darling Wife -1, 2, 4, 5, 6	Vo 02695, Pan 25634, RZAu G22217
C-624-2	On To Victory Mr. Roosevelt -1, 3, 4, 5, 6	Vo 02604
C-625-1	I Want Somebody To Cry Over Me -3, 5, 7	Vo 02605, Pan 25622
C-626-2	Put Me In Your Pocket -1, 2, 4, 5, 6	Vo 02731
C-627-1	Texas Breakdown -1, 3	Vo 02633

Take 1 of matrix C-621 is believed to have been used only on later pressings, while take 2 may appear only on the original issue.
Leon Huff may not play guitar on all of the recordings during his tenure with the Light Crust Doughboys.
Rev. Regal-Zonophone G22095 by Carter's Orchestra (popular).

Clifford Gross, h; Sleepy Johnson, tbj; Herman Arnspiger, g; Leon Huff, v; W. Lee O'Daniel, ldr/sp; band v.

Chicago, IL   Wednesday, October 11, 1933

Matrix	Title	Issue
C-628-1	In The Fall Of '29	Vo 02604

Clifford Gross, f-1; Sleepy Johnson, f-2/tbj-3; Leon McAuliffe, sg-4; Leon Huff, g/v-5/y-6; Herman Arnspiger, lg; Ramon DeArman, sb; W. Lee O'Daniel, ldr; v quartet (Huff, lv; prob.: DeArman, Johnson, McAuliffe)-7.

Chicago, IL   Wednesday, October 11, 1933

Matrix	Title	Issue
C-629-2	Please Come Back To Me -1, 3, 5	Vo 02695, Pan 25634, RZAu G22217
C-630-1	Memories Of Jimmy [sic] Rodgers -3, 4, 5, 6	Vo 02605, Pan 25622, RZAu G22177
C-631-1	Roll Up The Carpet -1, 3, 5	Vo 02842
C-632-	One More River To Cross	Vo unissued
C-633-1	That City For Shut-Ins -1, 2, 5, 7	Vo 02929
C-634-1	Doughboy Rag -1, 3	Vo 02633

Rev. Regal-Zonophone G22177 by Asa Martin & Doc Roberts.

Clifford Gross, f; Sleepy Johnson, f-1/tbj-2; Leon Huff, g/v-3/y-4; Herman Arnspiger, lg; Ramon DeArman, g; Leon McAuliffe, sb; W. Lee O'Daniel, ldr.

San Antonio, TX   Saturday, April 7, 1934

Matrix	Title	Issue
SA-2140-B	The Gangster's Moll -1, 3, 4	Vo 02731
SA-2141-B	My Brown Eyed Texas Rose -1, 3, 4	Vo 02726, Pan 25640, RZAu G22311
SA-2142-B	Alamo Waltz -2	Vo 02769, RZAu G22255
SA-2143-A,-B	Texas Centennial Waltz -2	Vo unissued

Clifford Gross, f; Sleepy Johnson, tbj; Leon Huff, g/lv; Herman Arnspiger, lg; Ramon DeArman, g; Leon McAuliffe, sb; W. Lee O'Daniel, ldr; band v.

San Antonio, TX   Saturday, April 7, or Sunday, April 8, 1934

Matrix	Title	Issue
	Doughboys Theme Song #1	ARC unissued: *Co C4K47911 (CD)*
	Doughboys Theme Song #2	ARC unissued: *Co C4K47911 (CD)*

These items, originally logged as *Opening Doughboys Theme* and *Closing Doughboys Theme* respectively, were pressed on one side of a test-pressing designated SA Test #4.

Clifford Gross, f; Sleepy Johnson, f-1/tbj-2; Leon Huff, g/v-3; Herman Arnspiger, lg; Ramon DeArman, g; Leon McAuliffe, sb; W. Lee O'Daniel, ldr; v trio (Huff, lv; DeArman, tv; Johnson, bv)-4.

San Antonio, TX   Sunday, April 8, 1934

Matrix	Title	Issue
SA-2144-A	Saturday Night Rag -2	Vo 02842
SA-2145-A	Kelly Waltz -2	Vo/OK 02727
SA-2145-B	Kelly Waltz -2	Vo 02727, RZAu G22249
SA 2146-A	Killem -2	Vo 02892
SA-2147-B	Bill Cheatum -2	Vo 02892
SA-2148-A	Rochester Schottische -2	Vo/OK 02727
SA-2148-B	Rochester Schottische -2	Vo 02727, RZAu G22249
SA-2149-A	Heel And Toe - Polka -2	Vo 02769, RZAu G22255
SA-2150-B	How Beautiful Heaven Must Be -1, 4	Vo 02929
SA-2151-B	She's Still That Old Sweetheart Of Mine -2, 3	Vo 02726, Pan 25640, RZAu G22311

Clifford Gross, f; Sleepy Johnson, f-1/tbj-2; Leon Huff, g/v-3; Ramon DeArman, g/v-4; Leon McAuliffe, sb/v-5; W. Lee O'Daniel, ldr.

Fort Worth, TX   Monday, October 1, 1934

Matrix	Title	Issue
FW-1150-1	When We Reach Our Happy Home -1, 3, 4	Vo 02832
FW-1151-1	When It's Round-Up Time In Heaven -1, 3, 4	Vo 02832
FW-1152-	That Silver Haired Mother	Vo unissued
FW-1153-1	Ridin' Ole Paint And Leadin' Old Bald -2, 3, 4	Vo 02851
FW-1154-	The Morro Castle Disaster	Vo unissued

| FW-1155-1 | My Mary -1, 3 | Vo 02872 |
| FW-1156-1 | When They Baptized Sister Lucy Lee -2, 5 | Vo 02916 |

Clifford Gross, f; Sleepy Johnson, f-1/tbj-2/g-3; Leon Huff, g/v-4/y-5; Ramon DeArman, g/y-6; Leon McAuliffe, sb; W. Lee O'Daniel, ldr; v quartet (Huff, lv; DeArman, tv; Johnson bv; Gross, bsv)-7; unidentified, v-8; unidentified, sp-9.
Fort Worth, TX   Saturday, October 6, 1934

FW-1157-1	Texas Plains -1, 4, 5	Vo 02851
FW-1158-2	There's A Little Gray Mother Dreaming -3, 4, 7	Vo 02872
FW-1159-1	Thirty First Street Blues -2, 6, 7?, 8, 9	Vo 02916
FW-1160-1	Texas Centennial March -2, 4	Vo 02863
FW-1161-1	The Governor's Ball -1, 4	Vo 02863

The Light Crust Doughboys: Clifford Gross, f; Kenneth Pitts, f; Leon Huff, g/v-1/y-2; Doc Eastwood, tbj-3; Ramon DeArman, g; Herbert Barnum, sb; W. Lee O'Daniel, ldr; v trio (Huff, lv; Pitts, bv; Gross, bsv)-4.
Fort Worth, TX,   Monday, April 22, 1935

FW-1182-3	Milenberg Joys -3	Vo 03032
FW-1183-	West Texas Stomp	Vo unissued
FW-1184-	Business In "F"	Vo unissued
FW-1185-3	Prairie Lullaby -1, 2, 3	Vo/OK 03017
FW-1186-1	Carry Me Back To The Lone Prairie -1, 4	Vo 03044
FW-1187-	When You Hear Me Call	Vo unissued
FW-1188-	Some Of These Days	Vo unissued

Only one fiddle is present on some sides.

Clifford Gross, f; Kenneth Pitts, f; Leon Huff, g/v-1/y-2; Doc Eastwood, tbj-3; Ramon DeArman, g/v-4; Herbert Barnum, sb; W. Lee O'Daniel, ldr.
Fort Worth, TX   Tuesday, April 23, 1935

FW-1196-	Copenhagen	Vo unissued
FW-1197-	Oh By Jingo	Vo unissued
FW-1198-2	There's An Empty Cot In The Bunkhouse Tonight -1, 2	Vo/OK 02992
FW-1199-1	My Million Dollar Smile -1, 3	Vo 02975
FW-1200-	I Don't Wanna Go To School	Vo unissued
FW-1201-2	Old Joe Clark -1, 3, 4	Vo 02975

Vocalion 02975 as by **W. Lee O'Daniel & His Light Crust Doughboys**.

Clifford Gross, f; Kenneth Pitts, f-1; Leon Huff, g/v-2; Doc Eastwood, tbj; Ramon DeArman, g/v-3; Herbert Barnum, sb; W. Lee O'Daniel, ldr.
Fort Worth, TX   Wednesday, April 24, 1935

FW-1207-3	Ragtime Annie	Vo 03032, Cq 9756
FW-1208-	Tug Boat	Vo unissued
FW-1209-	Rocky Mountain Goat	Vo unissued
FW-1210-	Waggoner	Vo unissued
FW-1211-3	El Rancho Grande -1, 2, 3	Vo/OK 03017
FW-1212-	My Old Dog Tray	Vo unissued
FW-1213-	Bury Me 'Neath The Weeping Willow	Vo unissued
FW-1214-1	My Pretty Quadroon -1, 2, 3	Vo/OK 02992

Rev. Conqueror 9756 by Clifford Gross & Muryel Campbell.

Clifford Gross, f; Kenneth Pitts, f; Leon Huff, g/v-1; Doc Eastwood, tbj; Ramon DeArman, g/v-2; Herbert Barnum, sb; W. Lee O'Daniel, ldr; v quartet (Huff, lv; DeArman, tv; Pitts, bv; Gross, bsv) -3.
Fort Worth, TX   Thursday, April 25, 1935

FW-1215-	Fort Worth Rag	Vo unissued
FW-1216-	Doughboy Hop	Vo unissued
FW-1217-1	The Old Rugged Cross -3	Vo 03064
FW-1218-1	There's No Disappointment In Heaven -1, 2	Vo 03064
FW-1219-	In The Garden	Vo unissued
FW-1220-	Whisper Your Mother's Name	Vo unissued
FW-1221-1	The Cowboy's Dream -3	Vo 03044

Only one fiddle is present on some sides.

Clifford Gross, f; Kenneth Pitts, f; Doc Eastwood, tbj; Curly Perrin, g/v-1; Ramon DeArman, g; Herbert Barnum, sb; v trio (DeArman, lv; Perrin, tv; Pitts, bv) -2.
Dallas, TX   Friday, September 20, 1935

DAL-105-2	My Blue Heaven -1	Vo/OK 03141
DAL-106-1,-2	My Buddy	Vo unissued
DAL-107-2	Nobody's Darling But Mine -1	Vo/OK 03065, Co 37604, 20203
DAL-108-1,-2	My Carolina Mountain Rose	Vo unissued

DAL-109-1	My Melancholy Baby -1	Vo/OK 03141
DAL-110-2	Rural Rhythm -2	Vo 03069
DAL-111-1	In A Little Gypsy Tea Room -1	Vo 03069
DAL-112-1	The Waltz You Saved For Me -1	Vo/OK 03065, Co 37604, 20203

Clifford Gross, f; Kenneth Pitts, f; Muryel Campbell, lg; Marvin Montgomery, tbj; Dick Reinhart, g/v-1; Bert Dodson, sb; v trio (prob. Dodson, lv; Reinhart, tv; Pitts, bv) -2; group v (with successive lv by Dodson (twice), Pitts, Montgomery, Reinhart)-3.

Fort Worth, TX,   Saturday, April 4, 1936

FW-1250-3	I'm A Ding Dong Daddy (From Dumas) -1	Vo 03239
FW-1251-	My Buddy -2	Vo unissued
FW-1252-3	I Like Bananas (Because They Have No Bones) -3	Vo 03238
FW-1253-	The Wheel Of The Wagon Is Broken -1	Vo unissued

Clifford Gross, f; Kenneth Pitts, f; Muryel Campbell, lg; Marvin Montgomery, tbj; Dick Reinhart, g/prob. v; Bert Dodson, sb.

Fort Worth, TX,   Sunday, April 5, 1936

| FW-1254- | Little Hillbilly Heart Throb | Vo unissued |

Kenneth Pitts, f/sp; Muryel Campbell, lg; Marvin Montgomery, tbj/lv/sp; Dick Reinhart, g; Bert Dodson, sb/sp; v quartet (Dodson, lv; Reinhart, tv; Pitts, bv; Clifford Gross, bsv).

Fort Worth, TX,   Sunday, April 5, 1936

| FW-1255-3 | Did You Ever Hear A String Band Swing | Vo 03239 |

Kenneth Pitts, f; Clifford Gross, f-1; Muryel Campbell, lg; Marvin Montgomery, tbj-2/tg-3; Dick Reinhart, g; Bert Dodson, sb/v.

Fort Worth, TX   Sunday, April 5, 1936

FW-1256-	Tonight I Have A Date -2	Vo unissued
FW-1257-3	Saddle Your Blues To A Wild Mustang -1	Vo 03238
FW-1258-	Gloomy Sunday -1, 3	Vo unissued
FW-1259-	Memories	Vo unissued

Clifford Gross, f; Kenneth Pitts, f; Muryel Campbell, lg; Dick Reinhart, md-1/g-2/v-3; Marvin Montgomery, tbj-4/tg-5; Bert Dodson, sb/v-6; v trio (Dodson, lv; Reinhart, tv; Pitts, bv)-7.

Los Angeles, CA   Tuesday, May 26, 1936

LA-1121-A	Little Hill-Billy Heart Throb -2, 3, 4	Vo 03403
LA-1122-A	My Buddy -1, 5, 7	Vo 03433
LA-1123-A	The Wheel Of The Wagon Is Broken -2, 3, 5	Vo 03257
LA-1124-A	Tonight I Have A Date -2 ,4, 6	Vo unissued
LA-1125-	Lost -2, 5, 6	Vo 03257

Kenneth Pitts, f; Clifford Gross, f-1; Muryel Campbell, lg; Marvin Montgomery, tbj-2/tg-3/v-4; Dick Reinhart, g/v-5; Bert Dodson, sb/v-6.

Los Angeles, CA   Friday, May 29, 1936

LA-1126-A	Uncle Zeke -2	Vo 03310
LA-1127-A	All My Life -1, 3, 6	Vo 03282
LA-1128-A	Jig In G -1, 2	Vo unissued
LA-1129-A	When The Moon Shines On The Mississippi Valley -1, 2, 5	Vo 03403
LA-1130-A	I Have Found A Honey -2, 6	Vo 03433
LA-1131-A	It's Been So Long -2, 6	Vo 03282
LA-1132-A	Cross-Eyed Cowboy From Abilene -2, 4	Vo 03310

Kenneth Pitts, f/ac-1; Clifford Gross, f; Muryel Campbell, lg; Marvin Montgomery, tbj; Dick Reinhart, g/v-2; Bert Dodson, sb/v-3; v trio (Dodson, lv; Reinhart, tv; Pitts, bv) -4; v quartet (Dodson, lv; Reinhart, tv; Pitts, bv; Gross, bsv) -5.

Fort Worth, TX   Thursday, September 10, 1936

FW-1262-	I'd Love To Live In Loveland (With A Girl Like You) -2, 3	Vo unissued
FW-1263-3	Happy Cowboy -3, 4	Vo 03345
FW-1264-	Blue Guitar	Vo unissued
FW-1265-	A Mug Of Ale	Vo unissued
FW-1266-	Sweet Georgia Brown	Vo unissued
FW-1267-3	Oh! Susanna -1, 3, 5	Vo 03345
FW-1268-	The Strawberry Roan	Vo unissued
FW-1269-	The Big Corral	Vo unissued
FW-1270-	I Want A Girl (Just Like The Girl That Married Dear Old Dad) -2	Vo unissued
FW-1271-	When You Wore A Tulip (And I Wore A Big Red Rose) -2	Vo unissued

[The] Light Crust Doughboys

Kenneth Pitts, f-1/ac-2/p-3; Clifford Gross, f-4; Muryel Campbell, eg; John W. "Knocky" Parker, ac-5/p; Marvin Montgomery, tbj; Dick Reinhart, g/v-6; Ramon DeArman, sb/v-7; v quartet (DeArman, lv; Reinhart, tv; Pitts, bv; Gross, bsv) -8.

Dallas, TX   Saturday, June 12, 1937

DAK-267-	Theme Song, etc. [sic]	Vo unissued
DAL-268-1	Emmaline -1, 6	Vo 03718
DAL-269-1,2	Let Me Ride By Your Side In The Saddle	Vo unissued
DAL-270-1,2	Tom Cat Rag	Vo unissued
DAL-271-1	Blue Guitars -1	Vo/OK 03610
DAL-272-1	Dusky Stevedore -3, 4, 5, 6, 7 (lead)	Vo 03867
DAL-273-1	If I Don't Love You (There Ain't A Cow In Texas) -3, 4, 5, 6	Vo 03718
DAL-274-2	Roll Along Jordan -2, 4, 5, 7, 8	Vo 03867
DAL-275-1,2	One Sweet Letter From You	Vo unissued
DAL-276-1,2	Song Of The Saddle	Vo unissued
DAL-277-1,2	Anna Lou	Vo unissued
DAL-278-1	Avalon -3, 4, 5	Vo/OK 03610
DAL-279-1,2	Little Girl Dressed In Blue	Vo unissued

On matrix DAL-278 the second-chorus piano solo is played by both Parker and Pitts, sitting at the treble and bass ends respectively.

Dallas, TX   Sunday, June 20, 1937

DAL-385-2	Gig-A-Wig Blues -3, 5	Vo 03926
DAL-386-1	In A Little Red Barn -1, 4, 7	Vo 03645
DAL-387-1	Beaumont Rag -4	Vo 03645
DAL-388-1	The Eyes Of Texas -1, 4, 8	Vo/OK 03660, Co 37626, 20225
DAL-389-1	Washington And Lee Swing -2, 4	Vo/OK 03660, Co 37626, 20225
DAL-390-	Stay On The Right Side Sister	Vo unissued
DAL-391-2	Just Once Too Often -1, 6	Vo 03926
DAL-392-	Stay Out Of The South (If You Want To Miss Heaven On Earth) -1, 4, 6	Vo unissued

Light Crust Doughboys: Kenneth Pitts, f-1/p-2/g-3; Clifford Gross, f-4; Dick Reinhart, esg-5/eg-6/g-7/v-8; Muryel Campbell, eg-9/g-10; Knocky Parker, ac-11/p; Marvin Montgomery, tbj-12/tg-13; Ramon DeArman, sb/v-14; Charles Burton, v-15; v trio (DeArman, lv; Reinhart, tv; Pitts, bv)-16; v quartet (DeArman, lv; Reinhart, tv; Pitts, bv; Gross, bsv)-17; v/humming quartet (DeArman, lv; Reinhart, tv; Pitts, bv; Parker Willson, bsv)-18.

Dallas, TX   Saturday, May 14, 1938

DAL-529-1	Sitting On Top Of The World -1, 6, 8, 10, 12	Vo/OK 04261
DAL-530-1	Weary Blues -1, 7, 9, 12	Vo 04921
DAL-531-1	Gulf Coast Blues -1, 7, 8, 9, 12	Vo 04921
DAL-532-1	The Budded Rose -1, 4, 7, 9, 12, 14	Vo/OK 04825
DAL-533-1	I'll Get Mine -1, 4, 7, 8, 9, 12, 17	Vo 04468
DAL-534-1	Blue Hours -1, 4, 5, 10, 11, 13	Vo 04326, Cq 9062
DAL-535-1	Three Shif-less Skonks -1, 4, 7, 9, 12, 14, 17	Vo/OK 04261
DAL-536-1,2	Kalua Loha	Vo unissued
DAL-537-1	Slow Down Mr. Brown -1, 7, 8, 9, 12	Vo 04468
DAL-538-1	Beautiful Ohio -1, 4, 7, 9, 12, 15	Vo/OK 04158, Co 37722, 20299
DAL-539-1	Waiting For The Robert E. Lee -2, 4, 7, 8, 9, 11, 12	Vo/OK 04216, Cq 9061
DAL-540-1	The Hills Of Old Wyomin' -1, 7, 9, 12, 15, 18	Vo/OK 04158, Co 37722, 20299
DAL-541-1	Tom Cat Rag -1, 7, 9, 12, 14, 16	Vo/OK 05473
DAL-542-1,2	Gig-A-Wig Blues -1, 4, 7, 9, 12	Vo unissued?
DAL-543-1	Knocky-Knocky -1, 7, 9, 12	Vo 04403
DAL-544-1	The Birth Of The Blues -1, 4, 7, 8, 9, 12	Vo/OK 04216, Cq 9061
DAL-545-1	Rockin' Alone (In An Old Rockin' Chair)	Vo unissued
DAL-546-2	Pretty Little Dear -1, 4, 7, 8, 9, 12, 14	Vo/OK 05413, Cq 9411
DAL-547-1	Sweeter Than An Angel -1, 7, 8, 9, 12	Vo 04403
DAL-548-1	Stumbling -1, 3, 7, 10, 13	Vo 04326, Cq 9062
DAL-549-2	Clarinet Marmalade -1, 7, 9, 12	Vo/OK 05473

Matrix DAL-542 has been reported as replacing matrix DAL-385 on later pressings of Vocalion 03926, but no pressing in this form has been traced.

Kenneth Pitts, f; Robert "Buck" Buchanan, f-1; John Boyd, esg-2; Muryel Campbell, eg-3/g-4; Knocky Parker, p; Marvin Montgomery, k-5/tbj-6/tg-7; Jim Boyd, g-8/sb-9/v-10; Ramon DeArman, g-9/sb-8; humming trio (DeArman, lv; Boyd, tv; Pitts or Parker Willson, bv) -11.

Dallas, TX   Wednesday, November 30, 1938

| DAL-641-1 | It Makes No Difference Now -1, 2, 3, 7, 8, 10 | Vo/OK 04559, Cq 9172 |
| DAL-642-2 | Blue-Eyed Sally -1, 3, 6, 8, 10 | Vo 04702 |

DAL-643-1	You're The Only Star (In My Blue Heaven) -1, 4, 7, 8, 10	Vo 04702
DAL-644-1	Baby, Give Me Some Of That -1, 3, 6, 8, 10	Vo/OK 04638, Cq 9195
DAL-645-1	Dirty Dish Rag Blues -3, 6, 8, 10	Vo 04701
DAL-646-1	(New) Jeep's Blues -1, 3, 6, 8	Vo 04701
DAL-647-1	Zenda Waltz Song -1, 3, 7, 8	Vo/OK 04825
DAL-648-1,2	Grey Skies -1, 3, 6, 8, 10	Vo unissued
DAL-649-1	Thousand Mile Blues -1, 3, 5, 6, 8, 10	Vo 04770
DAL-650-1	Gin Mill Blues -1, 3, 7, 9	Vo/OK 04560, Cq 9254
DAL-651-1,-2	Yancey Special -1, 3, 6, 8	Vo unissued
DAL-652-1	The Farmer's Not In The Dell -1, 3, 6, 8, 10	Vo/OK 04638, Cq 9195
DAL-653-1	Foot Warmer -1, 3, 6, 9	Vo 04770
DAL-654-1	Troubles -1, 3, 6, 8, 10, 11	Vo/OK 04559, Cq 9172

Robert "Buck" Buchanan, f; Muryel Campbell, eg; Knocky Parker, p; Marvin Montgomery, tbj/v/sp; Ramon DeArman, g/v/sp/v eff; Jim Boyd, sb/v; Kenneth Pitts, v.
Dallas, TX   Wednesday, November 30, 1938

DAL-655-1	Pussy, Pussy, Pussy	Vo/OK 04560, Cq 9254, RZAu G23970

The speakers on this item are Montgomery, taking the "female" role, and DeArman, and the cat effects are by DeArman.
Rev. Regal-Zonophone G23970 by Bob Wills.

Cecil Brower, f; Kenneth Pitts, f-1/p-2/v-3; Muryel Campbell, eg; Knocky Parker, ac-4/p; Marvin Montgomery, tbj-5/tg-6/v-7/sp-8; Ramon DeArman, g/v-9/sp-10/v eff-11; Jim Boyd, sb/v-12/v eff-13; Charles Burton, v-14; Parker Willson, v-15/sp-16/v eff-17; v trio (DeArman, lv; Boyd, tv; Willson, bsv)-18; v quartet (DeArman, lv; Boyd, tv; Pitts, bv; Willson, bsv)-19.
Dallas, TX   Wednesday, June 14, 1939

DAL-803-1	Let's Make Believe We're Sweethearts -1, 5, 12	Vo 05269, Cq 9527
DAL-804-1	Thinking Of You -2, 4, 5, 9	Vo 04974, Cq 9350
DAL-805-1	If I Didn't Care -1, 6, 14	Vo 04965
DAL-806-1	Mary Lou -1, 6, 14	Vo 04965
DAL-807-1	In Ole' Oklahoma -1, 6, 15	Vo 05308
DAL-808-1	She Gave Me The Bird -1, 3, 5, 7, 8, 9, 11, 12, 13, 15, 17	Vo 05039
DAL-809-1	Three Naughty Kittens -3, 7, 9, 12, 15, 16, 17	Vo 05269, Cq 9527
DAL-810-1	We Must Have Beer -1, 4, 5, 19	Vo 04973
DAL-811-1	Tea For Two -1, 6	OK 06016
DAL-812-3	Little Rock Getaway -1, 6	OK 06016
DAL-813-1	We Found Her Little Pussy Cat -1, 3, 6, 7, 8, 9, 10, 11, 12, 15, 17	Vo/OK 05092
DAL-814-1,-2	Old November Moon-1, 5, 12	Vo unissued
DAL-815-1	The Cattle Call -1, 5, 12, 18	Vo/OK 05413, Cq 9411
DAL-816-1	Texas Song Of Pride -1, 5, 19	Vo/OK 05308

Montgomery takes the "female" speaking part on matrices DAL-808, DAL-813; Willson contributes the bird effects on matrix DAL-808.
According to Vocalion files, take 3 of matrix DAL-812 was recorded on July 13, 1939. If that was a genuine rather than technical rerecording, it would have been made at the Burrus Mill Studio in Saginaw, TX.

Cecil Brower, f; Kenneth Pitts, f-1; Muryel Campbell, eg; Knocky Parker, p; Marvin Montgomery, k-2/tbj; Ramon DeArman, g-3/sb-4/v-5; Jim Boyd, g-4/sb-3/v-6.
Dallas, TX   Thursday, June 15, 1939

DAL-827-1	Two More Years (And I'll Be Free) -1, 3, 6	Vo 04974, Cq 9350
DAL-828-3	Mama Won't Let Me -1, 3	Vo 04973
DAL-829-1	All Because Of Lovin' You -1, 3, 5	OK 05867
DAL-830-3	Oh Baby Blues (You Won't Have No Mama At All) -1, 3, 6	Vo/OK 05201, Cq 9409, Co 37737, 20314
DAL-831-3	Beer Drinkin' Mama -1, 4, 6	Vo/OK 05201, Cq 9409, Co 37737, 20314
DAL-832-1	Mama Gets What She Wants -3, 6	Vo 05039
DAL-833-1	My Gal's With My Pal Tonight -1, 3, 6	OK 05968
DAL-834-1	I Had Someone Else Before I Had You (And I'll Have Someone After You're Gone) -1, 3, 6	OK 05968
DAL-835-1	You Got What I Want -1, 3, 6	Vo/OK 05092
DAL-836-1	Jazzbo Joe -1, 2, 3, 6	Vo/OK 05357
DAL-837-1	If I Had My Way -1, 3, 6	OK 05867

Cecil Brower, f; Kenneth Pitts, f-1; Muryel Campbell, eg-2/g-3; Marvin Montgomery, tbj; Ramon DeArman, g-4/sb-5/v-6; Jim Boyd, g-5/sb-4/ v-7.
Saginaw, TX   c. early September 1939

25317-1	I'll Keep On Loving You -1, 2, 4, 6	Vo/OK 05120, Co 37736, 20313
25318-1	Little Rubber Dolly -3, 5, 6 (lead), 7	Vo/OK 05120, Cq 9306, Co 37736, 20313

Cecil Brower, f; Kenneth Pitts, f/bv-1; Muryel Campbell, eg; Knocky Parker, p; Marvin Montgomery, tbj; Jim Boyd, g/v/ horse eff-2; Ramon DeArman, sb/v-3; Parker Willson, bsv-4.

Saginaw, TX c. late October 1939

| 25525-1 | Horsie! Keep Your Tail Up! (Keep The Sun Out Of My Eyes) -1, 2, 3 (lead), 4 | Vo/OK 05227, Cq 9349, Co 20452, CoC C1137 |
| 25526-1 | Truck Driver's Blues | Vo/OK 05227, Cq 9349, Co 20452, CoC C1137 |

Cecil Brower, f; Kenneth Pitts, f-1/p-2/bv-3; Muryel Campbell, sg-4/eg-5/g-6; Knocky Parker, ac-7/p; Marvin Montgomery, tbj-8/tg-9; Jim Boyd, g/v; Ramon DeArman, sb/v-10.

Saginaw, TX c. early December 1939

25594-1	Green Valley Trot -3, 5, 8, 10	Vo/OK 05357, Cq 9410
25595-1	Marinita -2, 6, 7, 9	Vo/OK 05307
25596-1	Careless -1, 4, 5, 8	Vo/OK 05307
25597-1	Listen To The Mocking Bird -4, 8/9, 10 (lead)	Vo unissued

Cecil Brower, f; Leroy Millican, eg; Babe Wright, p; Marvin Montgomery, tbj; Paul Waggoner, g; Joe Ferguson, sb/v-1; Ramon DeArman, v-2; Kenneth Pitts, bv-3.

Saginaw, TX Wednesday, April 24, 1940

DAL-1054-2	Goodbye Little Darling -1, 2 (lead), 3	Vo/OK 05535, Co 37745, 20322
DAL-1055-1	I Want A Feller -2	OK 05653
DAL-1056-2	Rainbow	Vo/OK 05610, Co 37746, 20323
DAL-1057-2	Alice Blue Gown -1	Vo/OK 05535, Co 37745, 20322

Cecil Brower, f; Leroy Millican, eg; Babe Wright, p; Marvin Montgomery, tbj; Paul Waggoner, g; Joe Ferguson, sb/v-1; Ramon DeArman, v-2; Kenneth Pitts, bv-3; Parker Willson, bsv-4.

Saginaw, TX Friday, April 26, 1940

DAL-1070-2	South	Vo/OK 05610, Co 37746, 20323
DAL-1071-1	She's Too Young (To Play With The Boys) -1, 2 (lead), 3, 4	OK 05821
DAL-1072-2	Mean Mean Mama (From Meana) -1	OK 05752
DAL-1073-1	Cripple Creek -1, 2, 3, 4	OK 05653
DAL-1074-2	Little Honky Tonk Headache -1	OK 05752
DAL-1075-2	Good Gracious Gracie! -1	OK 05821
DAL-1076-2	If You'll Come Back -2	OK 05696
DAL-1077-1	Snow Deer	OK 05696

Cecil Brower, f; Kenneth Pitts, f/v-1; Ted Daffan, esg-2; Muryel Campbell, eg; Frank Reneau, p; Marvin Montgomery, tbj; J.B. Brinkley, g/v-3; Joe Ferguson, sb/v-4; Parker Willson, v-5.

Fort Worth, TX Thursday, February 27, 1941

DAL-1184-1	Too Late -2, 3 (lead), 4	OK 06113, Cq 9865
DAL-1185-1	The Little Bar Fly -3	OK 06621, *V-D 280, V-D Navy 60*
DAL-1186-1	It's Your Worry Now -3	OK 06443
DAL-1187-1	Zip Zip Zipper -1, 3, 4, 5	OK 06594, *V-D 439, V-D Navy 219*
DAL-1188-1	The Bartender's Daughter -3	OK 06621, *V-D 280, V-D Navy 60*
DAL-1189-1	Don't Lie To An Innocent Maiden -4	OK 06216
DAL-1190-1,-2	Little Honky Tonk Heart-throb -3	OK unissued
DAL-1191-1	Five Long Years -2, 3	OK 06286, Cq 9866
DAL-1192-1	Sweet Sally -3	OK 06594, *V-D 439, V-D Navy 219*
DAL-1193-1	Slufoot On The Levee	OK 06161
DAL-1194-1	Honky Tonk Shuffle	OK 06216

Matrix DAL-1190 was scheduled for OKeh 06665 but this was never issued.
Rev. V-Disc 280, probably V-D Navy 60 by Bill Gale (polka band).

Cecil Brower, f; Kenneth Pitts, f-1/bv-2; Muryel Campbell, eg; Frank Reneau, p; Marvin Montgomery, tbj-3/tg-4/v-5; J.B. Brinkley, g/v-6; Joe Ferguson, sb/v-7; Parker Willson, v-8; Dolores Jo Clancy, v-9.

Fort Worth, TX Monday, March 3, 1941

DAL-1207-1	Be Honest With Me -1, 3, 6	OK 06113, Cq 9865
DAL-1208-1	Bear Creek Hop -2, 3, 6, 7, 8	OK 06349
DAL-1209-1	It's Funny What Love Will Make You Do -1, 3, 6	OK unissued: *Co C4K47911 (CD)*
DAL-1210-1,-2	Do You Ever Miss Me	OK unissued
DAL-1211-1	Won't You Wait Another Year -1, 3, 6	OK 06286, Cq 9866
DAL-1212-1	I Want A Waitress -1, 2, 3, 5 (lead), 6, 7, 8	OK 06349
DAL-1213-1	Can't Ease My Evil Mind -1, 3, 6	OK 06161
DAL-1214-1	After You Said You Were Leaving -1, 4, 9	OK 06443

Matrix DAL-1210 was scheduled for OKeh 06665 but this was never issued.

Cecil Brower, f; Kenneth Pitts, f/bv-1; Muryel Campbell, eg; Frank Reneau, p; Marvin Montgomery, tbj; J.B. Brinkley, g/v-2; Joe Ferguson, sb/v-3; Parker Willson, bsv-4.

Fort Worth, TX Thursday, March 6, 1941

DAL-1229-1,-2	Big House Blues -1, 2, 3, 4	OK unissued
DAL-1230-1,-2	We Just Can't Get Along -2	OK unissued
DAL-1231-1	Have I Lost Your Love Forever (Little Darling) -3	OK 06521
DAL-1232-1	Why Did You Lie To Me -2	OK 06521
DAL-1233-1,-2	I'll Never Say Goodbye -2	OK unissued

Light Crust Doughboys Sacred Quartet: J.B. Brinkley, lv; Joe Ferguson, tv; Kenneth Pitts, bv; Parker Willson, bsv; acc. Frank Reneau, p.

Fort Worth, TX   Thursday, March 6, 1941

DAL-1234-1,-2	Salvation Has Been Brought Down	OK unissued
DAL-1235-1,-2	I Shall See Him Bye And Bye	OK unissued
DAL-1236-1	I Know I'll See My Mother Again	Cq 9887
DAL-1237-2	Beyond The Clouds	Cq 9886

Fort Worth, TX   Friday, March 14, 1941

DAL-1323-1	This Life Is Hard To Understand	OK 06560, Cq 9886
DAL-1324-1	In The Morning	OK 06560, Cq 9887

The Light Crust Doughboys recorded after 1942.

W.A. [ADD] LINDSAY [or LINDSEY]

Add Lindsay, h; acc. unknown, mandola-1; Alvin Conder, bj; poss. Harold Weems, g; unidentified, v.

Memphis, TN   Wednesday, February 1, 1928

41819-2	Turnip Greens	Vi 21401
41820-1,-2	Ragtime Man	Vi unissued
41823-1,-2	Old Rabbit -1	Vi unissued
41824-2	Whoah Mule -1	Vi 21401

Matrices 41821/22 are by Frank Stokes (see B&GR).

W.A. Lindsey & Alvin Conder: W.A. Lindsey, h; acc. Alvin Conder, bj; prob. own g; unidentified, v.

Memphis, TN   Thursday, February 23, 1928

400303-	Good Old Turnip Greens	OK 45346

Memphis, TN   Friday, February 24, 1928

400316-B	Boll Weevil	OK 45346
400317-A,-B	Had Nothing Else To Do	OK unissued
400318-	Down The Road	OK unissued
400319-B	I Surely Am Living A Ragtime Life	OK unissued: LC LBC11 (LP)
400320-	In That War	OK unissued

MR. & MRS. ED LINDSEY

Vocal duet; acc. unknown.

New Orleans, LA   Thursday, November 20, 1930

NO-6710	The Corpse At The Express Office	Br/Vo rejected

PINK LINDSEY

Pink Lindsey & His Boys: no details.

Atlanta, GA   Saturday, April 13, 1929

148274-	Love Ship	Co unissued
148275-	For Old Times Sake	Co unissued

Pink Lindsey & His Bluebirds: unknown, f; unknown, tbj; Marion "Peanut" Brown, g/v-1; Pink Lindsey, sb.

Atlanta, GA   Tuesday, August 6, 1935

94334-1	12th Street Rag	BB B-6221, MW M-4824
94335-1	The Story Of Adam -1	BB B-6221, MW M-4824, Twin FT8059

Rev. Twin FT8059 by Dick Hartman's Tennessee Ramblers.

Pink Lindsey also recorded with John Dilleshaw.

GUS LINK

Pseudonym on Supertone for Fred Wilson with Otto Gray's Oklahoma Cowboy Band (see Otto Gray).

TOBE LITTLE

Pseudonym on OKeh for Vernon Dalhart.

LITTLE BROWN CHURCH QUARTET

Vocal quartet; acc. Olga Sandor, p.

Chicago, IL   Wednesday, February 15, 1928

13436	Abide With Me	Ge rejected trial recording

Acc. John Brown, p.
Chicago, IL   Tuesday, March 13, 1928
13541,-A	The Church In The Wildwood	Ge rejected
13542,-A	Jesus, Lover Of My Soul	Sil 8235
13543,-A	I Need Thee Every Hour	Sil 8235

It is uncertain which takes of matrices 13542/43 are used on Silvertone 8235.

LITTLE GEORGIE PORGIE BREAKFAST FOOD BABY OF THE AIR

George "Little Georgie Porgie" Savage, v; acc. Doc Hopkins, g.
Grafton, WI   c. April 1932
L-1458-1	Medley Of Kiddie Rhymes	Pm 573
L-1460-2	The Ring Song	Pm 573
L-1465-1	The Cross Eyed Boy And School Days	Pm 572
L-1468-1	Boyhood Days Down On The Farm	Pm 572

Matrices L-1461/62 and L-1466 are by Doc Hopkins; matrices L-1459, L-1463/64, and L-1467 are untraced.

AL & PETE LIVINGSTONE WITH ORIGINAL BUCKLE BUSTERS

Pseudonym on Mayfair for the Colt Brothers (see Arthur Fields & Fred Hall).

DOCTOR LLOYD & HOWARD MAXEY

Howard Maxey, f/sp-1; Dr Lloyd, g/sp-1; one of them, v-2.
Winston-Salem, NC   Thursday, September 22, 1927
81379-B	Western Union -1	OK 45150
81380-A,-B	Bright Sherman Valley	OK unissued
81381-A,-B	As Far As The Gate	OK unissued
81382-	Darling's Black Mustache	OK unissued
81383-	Jordan Is A Hard Road To Travel	OK unissued
81384-A	The Girl I Left Behind Me -2	OK 45150

[THE] LOG CABIN BOYS

Log Cabin Boys: Freddie Owen, Frankie More, v duet; acc. prob. one of them md-1/bj-2; the other, g; unidentified, jh-3.
Chicago, IL   Friday, October 13, 1933
C-635-2	Ole Bill Jackson Brown -2, 3	Ba 32903, Me M12844, Or 8284, Pe 12958, Ro 5284, Cq 8226, Pan 25628
C-636-1	I'm Livin' On The Mountain -2	Ba 32903, Me M12844, Or 8284, Pe 12958, Ro 5284, Cq 8226, Pan 25628
C-637-1	Tell Me You'll Always Remember -1	Ba 33020, Me M12979, MeC 91763, Or 8322, Pe 12991, Ro 5322, Cq 8227
C-638-1	Please Papa Come Home -1	Cq 8227
C-638-2	Please Papa Come Home -1	Ba 33020, Me M12979, MeC 91763, Or 8322, Pe 12991, Ro 5322

Matrix C-636 is titled *I'm Living On The Mountain* on Panachord 25628.

The Log Cabin Boys: Freddie Owen, Frankie More, v duet; acc. prob. one of them md-1; the other, g.
Chicago, IL   Thursday, September 20, 1934
C-9502-A	I Will Sing Of My Redeemer -1	De 5036
C-9503-C	I'm Tying The Leaves So They Won't Come Down -1	De 5035
C-9504-A	Answer To Twenty-One Years -1	De 5035
C-9505-A	Where Is My Wandering Boy Tonight	De 5036

Acc. poss. one of them, sg; the other, g.
Chicago, IL   Monday, May 6, 1935
C-9994-A	New Brown's Ferry Blues	De 5103
C-9995-A	New Crawdad Song	De 5013

Chicago, IL   Tuesday, May 7, 1935
C-9996-A	That Silver-Haired Daddy Of Mine	De 5110
C-9997-A	When It's Prayer Meetin' Time In The Hollow	De 5110

GEORGE E. LOGAN

Pete The Hired Man (George E. Logan), v; acc. prob. own h/g.
Richmond, IN   Thursday, June 14, 1934
19607	By The Ozark Trail	Ch 16786, 45036, MW 4986
19608	Hobo Life	Ch 16786, 45036
19609	Grave Of Rosa Lee	Ch 16792, 45004
19610	Will The Roses Bloom In Heaven?	Ch 16792, 45004, MW 4986, DeAu X1269

Champion 45004, 45036, Montgomery Ward 4986 as by **Geo. E. Logan (Pete The Hired Man)**.
Rev. Decca X1269 by Jimmy & Beverly Long.

JACK LOGAN

Pseudonym on Challenge for Norman Woodlieff, or on Superior for Harry Hillard.

LOGAN COUNTY TRIO

Pseudonym on Challenge, Silvertone, and Supertone for the Short Creek Trio. Matrix GEX-547 on Silvertone 25003, with this credit, is by Ernest V. Stoneman.

LONE STAR COWBOYS

Joe Attlesey, md/v; Leon Chappelear, g/v; Bob Attlesey, u/v.
    Chicago, IL   Friday, August 4, 1933

76868-1	Hang Out The Front Door Key	Vi 23846, BB B-6001
76869-1	Deep Elm Blues	Vi 23846, BB B-6001, HMVIn N4278
76870-1	Will There Be Any Cowboys In Heaven?	Vi 23850, HMVIn N4283
76871-1	Wonderful Child	Vi 23850, HMVIn N4283

Rev. HMV N4278 by The Vagabonds.

Joe Attlesey, md/v/sp-1; Leon Chappelear, g/v/sp-1; Bob Attlesey, u-2/j-3/v/sp-1.
    Chicago, IL   Saturday, August 5, 1933

76879-1	Crawdad Song -1, 3	BB B-6052, Vi 20-2941, HMVIn N4384
76880-1	Who Wouldn't Be Lonely? -2	BB B-5283, Eld 2157, Sr S-3364, RZ ME32, MR2099, Twin FT8074
76881-1	Just Because -1, 3	BB B-6052, Vi 20-2941, HMVIn N4384

Regal-Zonophone ME32, MR2099, Twin FT8074 as by **The Lone Star Rangers**.
Rev. all issues of matrix 76880 by Girls Of The Golden West.

The Lone Star Cowboys in this formation also accompanied Jimmie Davis. They later parted company, Leon Chappelear to form Leon's Lone Star Cowboys (see Leon Chappelear) and the Attlesey brothers to become known as the Shelton Brothers, under which name their subsequent recordings are listed.

THE LONE STAR COWBOYS

Prob.: Paul Gray, f; Jimmy Walker, g/v; Joe Stout, g/v-1.
    Richmond, IN   Wednesday, August 1, 1934

19640	The Golden Sunset Trail	Ch 16790, 45046
19641	Dillinger's Warning -1	Ch 16790, 45046

Matrix 19640 is titled *Golden Sunset Trail* on Champion 45046.

LONE STAR FIDDLERS

Pseudonym on Broadway for the Kentucky Thorobreds.

[THE] LONE STAR RANGER

Pseudonym on many labels for John I. White.

THE LONE STAR RANGERS

Pseudonym on Regal-Zonophone and Twin for the Lone Star Cowboys.

THE LONESOME COWBOY [I]

Pseudonym on several labels for John I. White.

THE LONESOME COWBOY [II]
THE LONESOME COWGIRL

One of these artists is named Buerl Sisney.

The Lonesome Cowgirl, v/y-1; acc. own u; or **The Lonesome Cowboy**-2, v/y-3; acc. own g; or **The Lonesome Cowboy & Girl**-4, v duet; acc. prob. The Lonesome Cowboy, g.
    Richmond, IN   Wednesday, March 18, 1931

17610-C,-D	Jim Blake -2	Ge unissued
17611-A	Anniversary Blue Yodel No. 7 -1	Spr 2631
17612-A	Livin' In The Mountains -1	Spr 2631
17613	The Yodeling Cowboy -2, 3	Spr 2652
17614,-A	Left My Gal In The Mountains -4	Ge rejected
17616-A	My Mother Was A Lady -4	Spr 2652
17617	Lonesome Cowboy -1	Ch S-16767, 45080
17618	Memphis Gal -2, 3	Ch S-16767, 45080

Champion 45080 as by **The Lonesome Cowgirl** on both sides. Superior 2652 as by **The Lonesome Cowgirl & Cowboy**. Matrix 17615 is unrelated.

LONESOME HOBO

Pseudonym on Broadway (4000 series) for Cliff Carlisle.

LONESOME LUKE & HIS FARM BOYS

Luke Decker, f; Ira Decker, bj; C.W. Johnson, g; Lee Day, g/calls; band sp-1.
    Richmond, IN   Thursday, February 12, 1931

17522	Beaver Valley Breakdown	Ch 16269, Spr 2614
17524-B	Half Way To Arkansas	Ch 16269, Spr 2614
17525-B	Wid Hog In The Woods -1	Ch 16229, Spr 2712
17526-B	Dogs In The Ash Can	Ch 16229, Spr 2712

Superior 2614, 2712 as by **Tommy Gordon & His Corn Huskers**.
Gennett files give the original title of matrix 17522 as *Chicago Breakdown*. Matrix 17523 is popular.

LONESOME PINE TWINS

Pseudonym on Banner and Challenge for the Gentry Brothers.

THE LONESOME SINGER (LANIER STEWART)

Lanier Stewart, v; acc. unknown, g.
    New York, NY   Wednesday, June 14, 1939

037361-1	Unwanted Sweetheart	BB B-8259, RZAu G24148
037362-1	(I Keep Lying, Lying) Little White Lies	BB B-8259, RZAu G24148

ANDY LONG

Pseudonym on one side of Minerva M-14027 for Dwight Butcher.

BEVERLY LONG
BEVERLY & JIMMY LONG

See Jimmy Long.

CLAY LONG & HIS LONGHORNS

Clay Long, v; acc. Bob Symons, esg; Bob Burgess, g; Jack True, sb.
    Dallas, TX   Wednesday, November 30, 1938

DAL-636-1	The Birmingham Prisoner	Vo 04812
DAL-637-1,-2	The Man From Memphis	Vo unissued
DAL-638-1,-2	Till Your Returning	Vo unissued
DAL-639-1	Alabama Moon	Vo 04731
DAL-640-1	Answer To Disappointed Love	Vo 04602

Clay Long, v/sp-1; acc. Bob Symons, esg; Bob Burgess, g; Jack True, sb.
    Dallas, TX   Thursday, December 1, 1938

DAL-656-1	I'm Gonna Ride -1	Vo 04812
DAL-657-1	Captain Tell Me True	Vo 04731
DAL-658-1	I Love You Best Of All	Vo 04602

GEORGE LONG & HIS SINGERS

Vocal group (five men, two women); unacc.
    Memphis, TN   Tuesday, March 1, 1927

37969-1,-2	In That Happy Home Over Yonder	Vi unissued
37970-1	What Shall Our Answer Be	Vi 20567
37971-1,-2	Murillo's Lesson	Vi unissued
37972-1	I'm Going Home To Die No More	Vi 20567

JIMMY LONG

Jimmie Long, v/y; acc. own g.
    New York, NY   before March 5, 1930

GEX-2621	Hobo Yodel	Ge rejected
GEX-2622	Missouri Is Calling	Ge rejected

Jimmy Long, v; acc. poss. own g.
    New York, NY   Wednesday, March 5, 1930

| 150066-1 | Watching The Clouds Roll By | Ve 7087-V, Di 6061-G |
| 150067-2 | When Father Was A Boy | Ve 7087-V, Di 6061-G |

Jimmy Long, v/y; acc. own sg.
Richmond, IN   Wednesday, April 30, 1930

16558	Lonely And Blue Pining For You	Ge rejected
16560,-A	My Cannibal Maiden	Ge rejected
16561,-A	Watching The Clouds Roll By	Ge rejected
16562,-A	That's Why I Left The Mountains	Ge rejected
16563,-A	Hobo Yodel	Ge rejected
16564,-A	Missouri Is Calling	Ge rejected

Matrix 16559 is by Odas H. Mattox.

Jimmy Long, v-1/y-2; or **Jimmy Long & Cliff Keiser**, v duet-3; acc. Jimmy Long, sg.
Richmond, IN   Thursday, August 21, 1930

16934-A	Watching The Clouds Roll By -1, 2	Ch 16117
16935	Hobo Yodel No. 2 -1, 2	Ch 16164
16936-A	Blue Pining For You -1, 2	Ge 7287, Spt 9775
16937	Missouri Is Calling -2, 3	Ge 7314, Ch 16099, Spr 2654
16938-A	I'm Always Dreaming Of You -3	Ge 7314, Ch 16099, Spr 2632, MW 4942
16939-A	That's Why I Left The Mountains -1, 2	Ge 7287, Ch 16117, Spt 9775, Spr 2675
16940-A	My Alabama Home -1, 2	Ch 16164

Supertone 9775 as by **Le Roy Jarvis**. Superior 2632, 2654 as by **Joe Lester & Dick Moss**; 2675 as by **Joe Lester**. Rev. Montgomery Ward 4942 by Bill Cox.

Jimmy Long, v/y-1; acc. own g; or **Jimmy & Beverly Long**, v duet-2; acc. unknown, p.
Richmond, IN   Monday, December 1, 1930

17325	Saved By Grace -2	Ch 16214
17326,-A	The Shepherd Of Love -2	Ge rejected
17327	Listen To The Voice -2	Ch 16214
17328-A	Mississippi Valley Blues	Ch 16233, 45084, Spr 2683
17329	Yodel Your Troubles Away -1	Ch 16233, 45084, Spr 2675

Superior 2675, 2683 as by **Joe Lester**. Matrix 17328 is titled *Mississippi Blues* on Superior 2683.

Jimmy Long, v-1/y-2; or **Jimmy Long & Cliff Keiser**, v duet-3; acc. Jimmy Long, sg.
Richmond, IN   Tuesday, December 2, 1930

17330	My Old Pal Of Yesterday -3	Ch 16190, 45089, Spr 2654
17331	That Silver Haired Daddy Of Mine -3	Ch 16190, 45089, Spr 2632
17332-A	My Dreaming Of You -3	Spr 2606
17333-A	My Old Cottage Home -3	Spr 2606
17334,-A	Falsefying [sic] Mamma -1, 2	Ge rejected
17335	Dog Gone Blues -1, 2	Ch 16296
17336,-A	When Father Was A Boy -1, 2	Ge rejected

Superior 2632, 2654 as by **Joe Lester & Dick Moss**.

Jimmy & Beverly Long, v/y-1 duet; acc. unknown, p-2/g-3; Jimmy Long, g.
Richmond, IN   Monday, June 1, 1931

17774-A	Have You Found Someone Else To Love You -1, 3	Ch 16280, Spr 2754
17775-A	By The Ozark Trail -3	Ch 16311, Spr 2702
17776,-A	My Sweetheart In The Moon -1, 3	Ge rejected
17777-A	What Does It Matter As Long As I Have You -3	Ch 16280, Spr 2702
17778-A	Saviour Lead Them (Orphans) -2	Ch 16487

Superior 2702, 2754 as by **Joe & Mary Lester**.

Beverly Long, v; or **Jimmy Long**-1, v/y; acc. Jimmy Long, g; unknown, g-2.
Richmond, IN   Tuesday, June 2, 1931

17779-A	The Heart That Was Broken For Me -2	Ch 16487, 45007
17780-A	Let's Get Together -1, 2	Ch 16311
17781	Down And Out Blues -1	Ch 16296, Spr 2683

Superior 2683 as by **Joe Lester**.

Long Family Trio: Jimmy Long, Beverly Long, Ina Mae Spivey, v trio; acc. unknown, p.
Richmond, IN   Wednesday, March 16, 1932

18456	I'm So Glad Trouble Don't Last Always	Spr 2796
18457	Swinging On The Golden Gate	Ge rejected
18458	The Little Old Church In The Valley	Ge unissued
18459	Alone With My Sorrow	Ge rejected
18460	Beautiful Isle Of Sorrow	Chapel 503

Superior 2796 as by **Raymond Adams**.

    Richmond, IN   Thursday, March 17, 1932

18461	Abide With Me	Chapel 503
18462	Nearer My God To Thee	Chapel 504
18463	Jesus Savior Pilot Me	Chapel 504
18465	Rock Of Ages	Chapel 505
18466	God Will Take Care Of You	Chapel 505

Matrix 18464 is blank in Gennett files.

Jimmy Long, v/y-1; acc. own g.
    New York, NY   Thursday, June 30, 1932

73050-1	Lonely And Blue, Pining For You	Vi 23724, MW M-4321
73051-1	Down And Out Blues	Vi 23724, MW M-4321
73052-1	Yodel Your Troubles Away -1	Vi 23705, MW M-4315, M-8130
73053-1	Doggone Blues	Vi 23705, MW M-4316
73056-1	In The Cradle Of My Dreams	Vi 23824
73057-1	Alone With My Sorrows	Vi 23824

Matrix 73052 is titled *Yodeling Them Blues Away* on Montgomery Ward M-8130.
Matrices 73054/55 are by Gene Autry.
Revs: Montgomery Ward M-4315, M-4316 by Jimmie Rodgers, M-8130 by Carson Robison & Frank Luther.

Jimmy & Beverly Long, v/y-1 duet; or **Beverly Long**, v-2; acc. Jimmy Long, g.
    Richmond, IN   Wednesday, June 21, 1933

19207	The Answer To 21 Years	Ch 16632, 45023
19208-A	Alone With My Sorrows -1	Ch 16690, 45022
19209	Cowboy's Heaven -1	Ch 16690, 45022
19210	Seven More Days	Ch 16632, 45023, DeAu X1269
19211	Two Little Orphans -2	Ch 16659
19212	The Old Folks Back Home	Ch 16663
19213	The Old Church Choir	Ch 16663

Decca X1269 as by **Jimmie & Beverly Long**.
Rev. Decca X1269 by George E. Logan.

Jimmy & Beverly Long, v/y-1 duet; or **Beverly Long**, v-2; or **Jimmy Long**-3, v/y; acc. Jimmy Long, g.
    Richmond, IN   Thursday, June 22, 1933

19214	If I Could Bring Back My Buddy	Ge unissued
19215	In The Cradle Of My Dreams	Ge unissued
19216	If I Had You -1	Ch S-16671
19217	The Soldier's Sweetheart -2	Ch 16659
19218	My Catalina Mountain Rose -1	Ch S-16671
19219	Gosh I Miss You All The Time -3	Ch 16641
19220	Hang It In The Hen House -3	Ch 16641

Beverly & Jimmy Long, v/y-1 duet; acc. Jimmie Dale, sg; Jimmy Long, g.
    Chicago, IL   Monday, July 31, 1933

75983-1	Have You Found Someone Else? -1	BB B-5188, Eld 2081, Sr S-3268, MW M-4410
75984-1	In The Cradle Of My Dreams -1	BB B-5188, Eld 2081, Sr S-3268, MW M-4410
75985-1	The Old Folks Back Home	BB B-5157, Eld 2056, Sr S-3238, MW M-4387
75986-1	Buddy	BB B-5157, Eld 2056, Sr S-3238, MW M-4387
75987-1	Seven More Days	BB B-5139, Eld 2045, Sr S-3220, MW M-4381
75988-1	The Old Church Choir	BB B-5139, Eld 2045, Sr S-3220, MW M-4381

Jimmy Long also recorded with Gene Autry.

MIKE LONG

Pseudonym on Aurora for John B. Evans.

FIDDLING SAM LONG OF THE OZARKS

Fiddling Sam Long, f; acc. Roy Kastner, g.
    Richmond, IN   c. January/February 1926

12460	Seneca Square Dance	Ge 3284, Ch 15098, Chg 102, 301, Bu 8019
12461	Echoes Of The Ozarks	Ge 3284, Chg 103, Bu 8018
12462	Listen To The Mockingbird	Ge 3255, Chg 102, Bu 8018
12463,-A,-B	The Rights Of Man	Ge rejected
12464	Sandy Land	Ge 3255, Ch 15098, Chg 103, Bu 8019
12465,-A	Stoney Point And Mule Skinner's Delight	Ge unissued

Champion 15098 as by **Uncle Jim Hawkins**. Challenge 102, 103, 301 as by **Fiddlin' Dave Neal**.
Rev. Challenge 301 by William B. Houchens.

WESLEY LONG

An artist of this name appears in advertisements in African-American newspapers of the 1920s and '30s, and it is possible that the Paramount session below is by this – presumably – African-American performer. The Bluebird artist, though issued with that name, appears on the session-sheet as Wesley Jones. His recordings come at the end of a session by the Sain Family and he probably participated in that group's recordings.

Wesley Long, v; acc. prob. own jazz horn/u.
Grafton, WI   c. December 1929

| L-207-3 | Down On The Farm | Pm 12932 |
| L-208-2 | Nobody's Sweetheart Now | Pm 12932 |

Wesley Jones, v; acc. prob. own g.
Charlotte, NC   Friday, February 19, 1937

| 07190-1 | They Are Wild Over Me | BB B-6891 |
| 07191-1 | Old Deacon Jones | BB B-6891 |

LONG & MILES

Pseudonym on Supertone for (Asa) Martin & (James) Roberts.

LONG BROTHERS

See Gene Autry.

LONG FAMILY TRIO

See Jimmy Long.

LOOKOUT MOUNTAIN BOYS
LOOKOUT MOUNTAIN REVELERS
LOOKOUT MOUNTAIN SINGERS

See Claude (C.W.) Davis.

LOS ALEGRES

Pseudonym on Vocalion 8525 (a Mexican issue) for Al Hopkins & His Buckle Busters (see The Hill Billies).

LOS CHICOS DE LAS PRADERAS

Pseudonym on Mexican Bluebird for [The] Prairie Ramblers.

LOS FRONTERIZOS (THE BORDER BOYS)

Pseudonym on Mexican Bluebird for Jack Pierce & the Oklahoma Cowboys.

LOUISIANA BOYS

Vocal trio; acc. unknown, f; unknown, p; unknown, sb; unknown, vc; unknown, d.
New Orleans, LA   Wednesday, January 23, 1935

| 87696-1 | Every Man A King | BB B-5840 |
| 87697-1 | Follow Long (The Louisiana Song) | BB B-5840 |

LOUISIANA LOU

Louisiana Lou's real name was Eva Mae Greenwood; at the time of these recordings her married name is believed to have been Conn.

Louisiana Lou, v; acc. own g.
Chicago, IL   Monday, December 4, 1933

77178-1	Her Black Sheep Is In The Fold	BB B-5749
77179-1	When The Moon Shines Down Upon The Mountains	BB B-5636
77188-1	The Lover Who Loved Me Last Spring	BB B-5484
77189-1	Sinful To Flirt	BB B-5424, MW M-4487
77190-1	The Export Gal	BB B-5424, MW M-4487
77191-1	A Package Of Love Letters	BB B-5484, MW M-4488
77192-1	With My Banjo On My Knee	Vi 23858, BB B-5636, MW M-4488
77193-1	Go 'Long, Mule	Vi 23858, BB B-5749

Matrices 77180/81 are untraced; matrices 77182/83 are by Harold Maus; matrices 77184 to 77187 are by Four Novelty Aces.

LOUISIANA PETE

This pseudonym was used on some issues in the Bluebird B-2000 Cajun series for the Mexican accordionist Narciso Martinez, the recordings concerned having been originally issued in the B-3000 Mexican series.

LOUISIANA RAMBLERS

Recordings by this group in the Decca Hill Billy series are outside the scope of this work.

LOUISIANA ROUNDERS

See Joe Werner.

LOUISIANA STROLLERS

Unknown, f; two unknowns, g; unknown, sb; unknown v-1/v duet-2.
    New Orleans, LA   Wednesday, March 18, 1936

NO-60814-A	Sleepy Rio Grande -2	De 5282, DeAu X1304, MW 8042
NO-60815-A	Dancing With My Shadow -2	Ch 45199, MeC 45199
NO-60816-	Strollers Waltz	Ch 45199, MeC 45199
NO-60817-	Marsovia Waltz	De 5282, DeAu X1304, MW 8042
NO-60818-	Kansas City Kitty -1	De 5287
NO-60819-	I'm Looking Over A Four Leaf Clover -1	De 5298
NO-60820-	The Unexplained Blues -1	De 5298
NO-60821-A	Married Woman's Blues -1	De 5287

DADDY JOHN LOVE

Daddy John Love, v; acc. own g.
    Atlanta, GA   Tuesday, August 6, 1935

94336-1	Broken Hearted Blues	BB B-6090, MW M-4715, Twin FT8023
94337-1	Green Back Dollar	BB B-6090, MW M-4715, Twin FT8023
94343-1	Searching For A Pair Of Blue Eyes	BB B-6194, MW M-4716

Montgomery Ward M-4715, M-4716 as by **Mainer's Mountaineers**.
These items were recorded during a session by J.E. Mainer's Mountaineers, of whom Love was a member.
Revs: Bluebird B-6194, Montgomery Ward M-4716 by J.E. Mainer's Mountaineers.

Daddy John Love & Hilliard Bros.: Daddy John Love, v; acc. —— Hilliard, f; —— Hilliard, g; —— Hilliard, g; own g.
    Charlotte, NC   Friday, February 14, 1936

99104-1	Mean Old Jailhouse Blues	BB B-6366
99105-1	I Went To See My Sweetheart	BB unissued

Daddy John Love, v; acc. own g; unknown, train-wh eff-1.
    Charlotte, NC   Friday, February 14, 1936

99106-1	My Wife Went Away And Left Me	BB B-6294, MW M-4813
99107-1	Railroad Blues -1	BB B-6624, Twin FT8249
99108-1	Triflin' Woman Blues	BB B-6366
99109-1	Over The Hills In Carolina	BB B-6675, MW M-7102
99110-1	Budded Roses	BB B-6675, MW M-7102
99111-1	What Makes Him Do It?	BB B-6624, Twin FT8249
99112-1	My Little Red Ford	BB B-6294, MW M-4813

    Charlotte, NC   Saturday, June 20, 1936

102725-1	I Am Dreaming Of Mother	BB B-6583
102726-1	Cotton Mill Blues	BB B-6491
102727-1	Blue Days	BB B-6583
102728-1	No Place Like Home	BB B-6491
102729-1	Homeless Child	BB B-8199, MW M-7103
102730-1	Where Is My Mama?	BB B-8199, MW M-7103

Daddy John Love was also a member of the Dixie Reelers, and recorded after 1942.

LOVELESS TWINS QUARTET

Herman Loveless, Harmon Loveless, Lela Loveless, Lola Loveless, v quartet; unacc.
    Camden, NJ   Monday, November 28, 1927

40739-	Only Waiting	Vi 21519
40740-2	Guide Me, O Thou Great Jehovah	Vi 21242
40741-	Still Still With Thee	Vi 21519
40742-2	Lead Kindly Light	Vi 21242

HOMER LOVELL

Homer Lovell, f; acc. unknown, g.
    Richmond, IN   Tuesday, April 24, 1928

13728	The Mocking Bird	Ge rejected

ROMAINE LOWDERMILK

Romaine Lowdermilk, v/y; acc. unknown.
    Chicago, IL   Tuesday, May 25, 1937
    CTO-5   Cowboy Yodel   ARC unissued trial recording

RAMBLIN' RED LOWERY

Ramblin' Red Lowery's real name was Earl L. Winchester.

Ramblin' Red Lowery, v; acc. own g.
    New York, NY   Sunday, January 14, 1934
    14603-1   Bum On The Bum   Vo 02631, Cq 8287

Ramblin' Red Lowery, v/y; acc. own g.
    New York, NY   Monday, January 15, 1934
    14600-1   Ramblin' Red's Memphis Yodel No. 2   Vo 02665
    14601-1   Ramblin' Red's Memphis Yodel No. 1   Vo 02631, Cq 8338, Pan 25643
    14602-   Ramblin' Red's Memphis Yodel No. 3   ARC unissued

Matrix 14601 is titled *Ramblin' Red's Memphis Yodel* on Conqueror 8338, Panachord 25643.

Ramblin' Red Lowery, v; or **Ramblin' Red Lowery & Mother**, v duet-1; acc. Ramblin' Red Lowery, g.
    New York, NY   Tuesday, January 16, 1934
    14623-   The Ramblin' Red Head   ARC unissued
    14624-   Who Will Be My Friend   ARC unissued
    14625-   No One To Kiss Me Good-night -1   ARC unissued
    14626-1   Take Me Back To Tennessee   Vo 02641, Cq 8287, Pan 25637
    14627-   Love Is No Pleasure   ARC unissued

Matrix 14626 is subtitled *(Ramblin' Red's Theme Song)* on Panachord 25637.

Red Lowery, v/y; or **Ramblin' Red Lowery & Mother**, v duet-1; acc. Ramblin' Red Lowery, g.
    New York, NY   Wednesday, January 17, 1934
    14632-2   He's A Ramblin' Man   Ba 33341, Me M13308, Or 8430, Pe 13111,
                                                         Ro 5430
    14633-   The Sighing Winds -1   ARC unissued

Ramblin' Red Lowery, v/y-1; or **Ramblin' Red Lowery & Mother**, v duet-2; acc. Ramblin' Red Lowery, g.
    New York, NY   Thursday, January 18, 1934
    14645-   Molly Darling   ARC unissued
    14646-2   Mother, Pal And Sweetheart   Vo 02641, Cq 8338, Pan 25637
    14647-   Memphis Yodel No. 4 -1   ARC unissued
    14648-2   Lonesome Weary Blues -1   Ba 33341, Me M13308, Or 8430, Pe 13111,
                                                         Ro 5430
    14649-   Curtains Of Night -2   ARC unissued
    14650-1   Cross-Eyed Sue   Vo 02665, Pan 25643

All issues of matrix 14648 as by **Red Lowery**.

LUBBOCK TEXAS QUARTET

Vocal quartet; acc. unknown, g.
    Dallas, TX   Friday, December 6, 1929
    149554-1   Turn Away   Co 15510-D
    149555-2   O Mother How We Miss You   Co 15510-D

FRANK LUCKER

Pseudonym on Piccadilly 552 for Frank Luther, or Carson Robison & Frank Luther (see Carson Robison).
(**Lucker & Ford** on Piccadilly 570 are Al Bernard & Frank Kamplain, and outside the scope of this work.)

[THE] LULLABY LARKERS

See Cliff Carlisle.

LULU BELLE & SCOTTY

Lulu Belle's given name was Myrtle Eleanor Cooper; Scotty's was Scott Wiseman. They married in 1934.

Lulu Belle, v/y; acc. Ramblin' Red Foley, g.
    Chicago, IL   c. March 24, 1934
    CP-1052-1   Daffy Over Taffy   Cq 8315
    CP-1053-1   Little Black Moustache   Cq 8315

Lulu Belle also recorded duets with Red Foley at this session.

Lulu Belle & Scotty, v/y-1 duet; or **Lulu Belle Wiseman**, v/y solo-2; acc. Scott Wiseman, h-3/bj-4/g-5;
Lulu Belle Wiseman, g-6.
    Chicago, IL   Wednesday, October 30, 1935

C-1129-2	Sugar Babe -1, 4, 6	ARC 6-08-58, Cq 8595
C-1130-1	Tildy Johnson -3, 5	ARC 6-08-58, Cq 8595
C-1131-2	Madam I've Come To Marry You -1, 3, 5	ARC 6-06-53, Cq 8593
C-1132-1	Get Along Home Cindy -4, 6	ARC 6-03-59, Cq 8594
C-1133-2	The Farmer's Daughter -2, 5	ARC 6-06-53, Cq 8593
C-1134-1	Prisoner At The Bar -5	ARC 6-03-59, Cq 8594

Matrix C-1133 on Conqueror 8593 as by **Lulu Belle**. Matrix C-1131 is titled *Madame I've Come To Marry You* on Conqueror 8593.

Lulu Belle Wiseman, Scott Wiseman, v/y-1 duet; or Lulu Belle Wiseman, v-2/y-3; acc. Alan Crockett, f; Scott Wiseman, bj-4; Floyd "Salty" Holmes, g; Jack Taylor, sb.

Chicago, IL　　　　　　　　　　　　　　　　　　　　　　　　　　　　　　　　Thursday, February 2, 1939

C-2428-2	When I Yoo Hoo In The Valley -1	Vo/OK 04690, Cq 9249
C-2429-1	This Train -4	Vo/OK 04910
C-2430-1	Wish I Was A Single Girl Again -2, 4	Vo/OK 04772, Cq 9189
C-2431-1	Never Take No For An Answer -2, 3, 4	Vo/OK 04772, Cq 9189
C-2432-1	Mountain Dew -4	Vo/OK 04690, Cq 9249
C-2433-2	Turn Your Radio On -4	Vo/OK 04910

Lulu Belle Wiseman, Scott Wiseman, v duet; acc. Alan Crockett, f; Scott Wiseman, bj-1/wh-2; Salty Holmes, g; Jack Taylor, sb.

Chicago, IL　　　　　　　　　　　　　　　　　　　　　　　　　　　　　　　　Friday, February 10, 1939

C-2496-1	It Ain't Nobody's Bizness -1	Vo/OK 04962, Cq 9250
C-2497-2	Prisoner's Dream -2	Vo/OK 04841, Cq 9250
C-2498-1	There's A Little Pine Log Cabin	Vo/OK 04962
C-2499-1	From Jerusalem To Jericho	OK 05958, Cq 9695
C-2500-3	The Old Red Cradle	Vo/OK 04841

Lulu Belle Wiseman, Scott Wiseman, v duet; or Scott Wiseman, v-1; acc. prob. Alan Crockett, f; Scott Wiseman, bj-2; Salty Holmes, g; Jack Taylor, sb.

Chicago, IL　　　　　　　　　　　　　　　　　　　　　　　　　　　　　　Tuesday, September 24, 1940

WC-3311-A	Did You Ever Go Sailing?	OK 05833, Cq 9694
WC-3312-A	The Wampus Cat	OK 06054, Cq 9587
WC-3313-A	That Crazy War -1, 2	OK 06103
WC-3314-A	Remember Me	OK 05833, Cq 9694
WC-3315-A	The Empty Stocking	Cq 9586
WC-3316-A	There's No Hiding Place Down There -2	OK 05958, Cq 9695
WC-3317-A	Be Careful Girls	OK 06103, Cq 9586
WC-3318-A	I'd Like To Go Back	OK 06005, Cq 9693
WC-3319-A	Row Us Over The Tide	OK unissued
WC-3320-A	Whoa Back Buck -1, 2	OK 06054, Cq 9587
WC-3321-A	The Wandering Boy	OK 06005, Cq 9693
WC-3322-A	Down In The Diving Bell	OK unissued

Matrix WC-3317 is titled *Be Careful Girl* on Conqueror 9586.

Lulu Belle also recorded with Red Foley. Scott Wiseman also recorded solo as Skyland Scotty and under that name with the Prairie Ramblers. Lulu Belle & Scotty recorded after 1942.

BASCOM LAMAR LUNSFORD

Bascom Lamar Lunsford, v; acc. own bj.

Atlanta, GA　　　　　　　　　　　　　　　　　　　　　　　　　　　　　　　Saturday, March 15, 1924

| 8578-A | Jesse James | OK 40155 |
| 8579-A | I Wish I Was A Mole In The Ground | OK 40155 |

Bascom Lamar Lunsford–Blackwell Lunsford: Blackwell Lunsford, f; Bascom Lamar Lunsford, bj/v.

Asheville, NC　　　　　　　　　　　　　　　　　　　　　　　　　　　　　　August 27, 28 or 29, 1925

| 9292-A | Fate Of Santa Barbara | OK 45008 |
| 9293-A | Sherman Valley | OK 45008 |

Matrices 9291 and 9294 to 9296 are untraced. From a contemporary press account it appears probable that these were all by the Lunsfords and that the items were, or included some of, *The Last Battle, Mountain Dew, Nollpros Nellie*, and an unidentified dance tune (see *Old Time Music* 31, pp 7, 10).

Bascom Lamar Lunsford "The Minstrel Of The Appalachians", v; acc. own bj.

Ashland, KY　　　　　　　　　　　　　　　　　　　　　　　　　　　　　　　Monday, February 6, 1928

AL-117/18*	Lost John Dean	Br 227, Vo 5246
AL-119*/20	Get Along Home Cindy	Br 228
AL-121/22*	Mountain Dew	Br 219
AL-123*/24	"Nol Pros" Nellie	Br 230

AL-125*/26	Lulu Wall	Br 229, Vo 5252
AL-127*/28	Darby's Ram	Br 228, 80089
AL-129/30*	Stepstone	Br 231, 314
AL-131/32*	I Wish I Was A Mole In The Ground	Br 219
AL-133-34*	Kidder Cole	Br 230
AL-135/36*	Italy	Br 227, Vo 5246
AL-137/38*	Little Turtle Dove	Br 229, Vo 5252
AL-139/40*	Dry Bones	Br 231, 314

Rev. Brunswick 80089 by Buell Kazee.

Bascom Lunsford, v-1/sp-2; acc. Bert Layne, f; poss. own bj; Fred Stanley, g; unknown, sp-3.
   Atlanta, GA   Tuesday, April 15, 1930

150220-	Take Me Home Little Birdie -1	Co unissued
150221-	I Wish I Was A Mole In The Ground -1	Co unissued
150228-2	Speaking The Truth -2	Co 15595-D
150229-1	A Stump Speech In The 10th District -2, 3	Co 15595-D

Intervening matrices are by other artists.

Bascom Lamar Lunsford recorded very prolifically and on numerous occasions for the Archive of American Folk Song at the Library of Congress, and also commercially after 1942.

TED LUNSFORD

Theodore Lunsford, v; acc. prob. own g.
   Richmond, IN   Thursday, April 16, 1931

17681	Gambler's Blues	Ge rejected trial recording

Ted Lunsford (The Missouri Brakeman), v/y; acc. unknown, md; prob. own g.
   Richmond, IN   Thursday, May 21, 1931

17760-A	Mississippi River Blues	Ch 16287, Spr 2689

Superior 2689 as by **Tom Ward**.

Acc. prob own g; unknown, g.
   Richmond, IN   Thursday, June 11, 1931

17818-A	The Hobo's Return	Ch 16287, Spr 2689

Superior 2689 as by **Tom Ward**.

Tommy Ward, v/y; acc. unknown, md; prob. own g.
   Richmond, IN   Thursday, June 25, 1931

17848-B	My Blue Eyed Jane	Spr 2709
17849-A	Jimmie The Kid	Spr 2709

Ted Lunsford, v/y-1; acc. Jess Johnston, f-2/p-3; prob. own g; unknown, g.
   Richmond, IN   Friday, October 2, 1931

18075,-A	Give Me Back My Heart -2	Ge rejected
18076,-A	Arabella Blues -2	Ge rejected
18077,-A	I'm Lonesome Too -2	Ge rejected
18078,-A	Bear Cat Mama From Horner's Corner -2	Ge rejected
18079	Blue Yodel No. 9 -1, 3	Ge rejected

LUNSFORD BROS.

Prob.: Carl Stewart, f-1 ; Eddie Smith, h-2; Jesse Carpenter, esg; Paul Lunsford, g/v-3; Leaford Lunsford, sb/v-3.
   Charlotte, NC   Monday, June 30, 1941

CHAR-25; 30925-1	Thinking Only Of You -1, 3	OK 06541
CHAR-26; 30926-1	No Matter What Happens -1, 3	OK 06417
CHAR-27; 30927-1	They Drew My Number (Goodbye My Darling) -1, 3	OK 06417
CHAR-28; 30928-1	Steel Guitar Wobble -2	OK 06541
CHAR-29; 30929-1	Boo Hoo Blues -2	OK 06650
CHAR-30; 30930-1	I Love No One But You -1, 3	OK 06650
CHAR-31; 30931-	Please Come Back -1, 3	OK unissued
CHAR-32; 30932-	Just Remember -1, 3	OK unissued

FRANCIS LUTHER

See Frank Luther (under Carson Robison).

FRANK LUTHER

Until mid-1932 most of Frank Luther's country recordings were in close collaboration with Carson Robison. Consequently all his work up to that date is listed under Robison, even those recordings in which Robison may not have participated.

Bud Billings, v; acc. prob. Frank Novak, f-1/cl-2/ac-3; unknown, p; two unknowns, g-4; unknown, wh-eff-5.
New York, NY   Thursday, July 14, 1932

73108-1	When The White Azaleas Start Blooming -1, 3, 4	Vi 23709, ZoSA 4380, HMVIn N4238
73109-1	Grandmother's Bible -3, 4	Vi 23706, MW M-4346, HMVAu EA1391, HMVIn N4227
73110-1	Nobody To Love -4	Vi 23706, HMVIn N4226
73111-1	I Wonder If He's Singing To The Angels To-night -3	Vi 23725, MW M-4314
73112-1	Reformatory Blues -2, 4, 5	Vi 23709, MW M-4306, ZoSA 4380, HMVIn N4238
73113-1	Hang On, Brother -4	Vi 23715

Revs: Victor 23715, Montgomery Ward M-4306 by Bob Miller; Victor 23725 by Gene Autry; Montgomery Ward M-4314 by McCravy Brothers, M-4346 by Ed McConnell; HMV N4226 by Carson Robison & Frank Luther.

Frank Luther, v; or **Frank Luther Trio**-1: Frank Luther, Zora Layman, Leonard Stokes, v trio; acc. Frank Novak, f-2/cl-3/s-4/ac-5/x-6; unknown, h-7; John Cali, sg-8/bj-9/g-10; Bill Wirges, p; own oc-11/bells-12/v eff-13.
New York, NY   Wednesday, September 28, 1932

73595-1	Buck Jones Rangers' Song -4, 6, 8, 9, 12	Eld 1903, MW M-4325
73596-1	A Chew Of Tobacco And A Little Drink -2, 3, 7, 11	Eld 1920, MW M-4309
73597-1	He's Too Far Gone -3, 10	Eld 1920, MW M-4310
73598-1	In The Blue Hills Of Virginia -	Eld 1918
73599-1	When The Leaves Turn Red And Fall -1	Eld 1918
73600-1	Old River Valley -1, 2, 5, 12, 13	BB 1823, B-5009, Eld 1903, Sr S-3109, MW M-4325, HMVAu EA1391
73701-1	A Little Street Where Old Friends Meet	Vi unissued

Electradisk 1920 as by **Leonard Stokes**. Revs: Bluebird 1823, B-5009, Sunrise S-3109 by Bob Miller; Montgomery Ward M-4309 by Jimmie Rodgers, M-4310 by Robison & Luther.

Acc. Frank Novak, f-2/cl-3/s-4/ac-5/x-6; John Cali, sg-7/bj-8/g-9; Bill Wirges, p; own bells-10.
New York, NY   Saturday, October 1, 1932

73701-2	A Little Street Where Old Friends Meet -	Vi 23732, HMVAu EA1243, HMVIn N4319
73732-1	When The Leaves Turn Red And Fall -1, 4, 6, 7	Vi 23735, MW M-4331
73733-1	The Circle Has Been Broken -	Vi 23732, MW M-4330, HMVAu EA1243, ZoSA 4373
73734-1	In The Blue Hills Of Virginia -2, 7, 10	Vi 23735, MW M-4308, ZoSA 4373
73735-1	You're The World's Sweetest Girl -3, 5, 6, 8, 9	Vi 23737
73736-1	Sweetest Of All My Dreams -3, 6	Vi 23737, MW M-4318

Victor 23737, Montgomery Ward M-4318 as by **Luther–Stokes Trio**. Montgomery Ward M-4330, M-4331, Zonophone 4373, HMV N4319 as by **Bud Billings Trio**.
Revs: Montgomery Ward M-4308 by Stuart Hamblen, M-4318 by Frank Marvin, M-4330 by Kelly Harrell, M-4331 by Vernon Dalhart.

Bud Billings' Trio: Frank Luther, Zora Layman, Leonard Stokes, v trio; acc. Frank Novak, f-1/cl-2/ac-3/x-4; unknown, f-5; John Cali, sg-6/bj-7/g-8; Bill Wirges, p.
New York, NY   Friday, October 21, 1932

73849-1	I'll Meet You In Loveland -3?, 6/7/8	Vi 23744
73850-1	Going Back To The One I Love -2, 4, 6, 8	Vi 23741, HMVIn N4240
73851-1	My Ivy Covered Cabin Home -1, 2, 5, 8	Vi 23740, HMVIn N4244
73852-1	I Wouldn't Trade The Silver In My Mother's Hair -2, 4, 7, 8?	Vi 23741, ZoSA 4381, HMVIn N4240
73853-1	Just Around The Bend -1, 2, 4, 5, 6	Vi 237340, HMVIn N4244
73854-1	Silver-Haired Mother -3?, 6/7/8	Vi 23744

Victor 23741, Zonophone 4381, HMV N4240 as by **Luther–Stokes Trio**.
Rev. Zonophone 4381 by Gene Autry.

Buddy Spencer Trio: Frank Luther, Zora Layman, Leonard Stokes, v trio; acc. Frank Novak, f-1/cl-2/x-3; poss. John Cali, sg-4/md-5; prob. Bob Miller, p.
New York, NY   Wednesday, November 2, 1932

12525-1	When The Leaves Turn Red And Fall -2, 3	Ba 32632, Me M12560, Or 8185, Pe 12867, Ro 5185, Cq 8141, CrC/MeC/Stg/Roy 91465, Pan 25620
12526-1	The Circle Has Been Broken -2	Ba 32632, Me M12560, Or 8185, Pe 12867, Ro 5185, Cq 8141, CrC/MeC/Stg/Roy 91465, Pan 25620
12527-2	Rockin' Alone (In An Old Rockin' Chair) -1, 2, 5	Ba 32629, Me M12536, Or 8182, Pe 12863, Ro 5182, Vo 5487, Cq 8099, CrC/MeC/Stg/Roy 91456, Pan 25399, Co-Lucky 60222
12528-1	When The Mellow Moon Is Shining -3, 4	Ba 32629, Me M12536, Or 8182, Pe 12863, Ro 5182, Vo 5491, Cq 8099, CrC/MeC/Stg/Roy 91456, Pan 25399, Co-Lucky 60222

Vocalion 5487, 5491, Conqueror 8099, 8141 as by **Frank Luther Trio**.

New York, NY — Monday, November 21, 1932

12622-1	The New Twenty-One Years -5	Ba 32679, Me M12602, Or 8198, Pe 12884, Ro 5198, Vo 5491, Cq 8100
12623-3	Ivy Covered Cabin Home -	Ba 32633, Me M12561, Or 8186, Pe 12868, Ro 5186, Cq 8142, CrC/MeC/Stg/Roy 91466, Pan 25638
12624-	From Cradle Bars To Prison Bars	ARC unissued
12625-2	The Old Ladies Home -	Ba 32633, Me M12561, Or 8186, Pe 12868, Ro 5186, Cq 8142, CrC/MeC/Stg/Roy 91466, Pan 25638

Vocalion 5491, Conqueror 8100, 8142 as by **Frank Luther Trio**.

Frank Luther's Trio: Frank Luther, Zora Layman, Leonard Stokes, v trio; acc. prob. Frank Novak, ac; poss. John Cali, g.

New York, NY — Monday, December 5, 1932

1923-2	When The Wandering Boy Comes Home	Cr 3415, MW M3001, Vs 5002
1924-1	Seven Years With The Wrong Woman	Cr 3431, Vs 5105
1925-2	At The Close Of A Long Long Day	Cr 3415, MW M3001, Vs 5002
1926-2	From Cradle Bars To Prison Bars	Cr 3431, Vs 5083

Montgomery Ward M3001 as by **Carson Robison & Frank Luther**. Varsity 5002, 5083 as by **Frank Luther Trio**. Matrix 1925 is titled *At The Close Of A Long Day* on Montgomery Ward M3001, Varsity 5002.
Rev. Varsity 5083 by Carson Robison.

Buddy Spencer Trio: Frank Luther, Zora Layman, Leonard Stokes, v trio; acc. prob. Frank Novak, ac-1/sb-2; poss. Bob Miller, p; poss. John Cali, g; unknown, wh-3.

New York, NY — Thursday, December 8, 1932

12700-2	The Beer Song -1, 3	Ba 32646, Me M12587, Or 8192, Pe 12876, Ro 5192, Vo 5487, Cq 8102
12701-2	When The White Azaleas Start Blooming -2	Ba 32650, Me M12573, Or 8187, Pe 12871, Ro 5187, Cq 8238, CrC/MeC/Stg/Roy 91476, Pan 25604
12702-1	Tie Me To Your Apron Strings Again -2	Ba 32650, Me M12573, Or 8187, Pe 12871, Ro 5187, Cq 8143, CrC/MeC/Stg/Roy 91476, Pan 25604
12703-2	Fifty Years From Now -1	Ba 32646, Me M12587, Or 8192, Pe 12876, Ro 5192, Cq 8102

Vocalion 5487, Conqueror 8102, 8143, 8238 as by **Frank Luther Trio**. Matrix 12701 may be titled *When The White Sage Starts Blooming* on Panachord 25604.

Acc. unknown, f; unknown, g.

New York, NY — Tuesday, January 3, 1933

12624-3	From Cradle Bars To Prison Bars	Ba 32884, Me M12820, Or 8275, Pe 12948, Ro 5275, Cq 8210, CrC/MeC/Stg/Roy 93090
12818-2	Peaceful Valley	Ba 32966, Me M12916, Or 8303, Pe 12975, Ro 5303, Cq 8273, CrC/MeC/Stg/Roy 93092
12819-	Beatrice Snipes	ARC unissued
12820-	I'm A Fugitive From A Chain Gang	ARC unissued

All issues of matrix 12624 except Crown/Melotone/Sterling/Royale 93090 as by **Frank Luther Trio**.
Revs: Crown/Melotone/Sterling/Royale 93090 by Goebel Reeves, 93092 by Asa Martin.

Frank Luther Trio: Frank Luther, Zora Layman, Leonard Stokes, v trio; or Frank Luther, v-1; acc. unknown, f; unknown, h-2; unknown, g.

New York, NY — Saturday, January 14, 1933

12902-1	It Seems I've Always Held Your Hand	Ba 32734, Me M12663, Or 8221, Pe 12902, Ro 5221, Cq 8238, CrC/MeC/Stg/Roy 91719
12903-2	Innocent Prisoner -1, 2	Ba 32679, Me M12602, Or 8198, Pe 12884, Ro 5198, Vo 5485, Cq 8100, CrC/MeC/Stg/Roy 91720
12904-1	Down By The Old Rustic Well	Ba 32734, Me M12663, Or 8221, Pe 12902, Ro 5221, Cq 8143, CrC/MeC/Stg/Roy 91719

All issues of matrix 12903 except Vocalion 5485, Conqueror 8100 as by **Buddy Spencer Trio**.
Rev. Vocalion 5485 by Zora Layman.

Frank Luther's Trio: Frank Luther, Zora Layman, Leonard Stokes, v trio; acc. Frank Novak, cl-1/bscl-2/ac-3/sb-4; unknown, h-5; unknown, p-6; unknown, g; prob. Frank Luther, oc-7/wh-8; unknown, oc-9/wh-9.

New York, NY   Tuesday, January 24, 1933

1967-1	Fifty Years From Now -2, 3, 7	Cr 3459, Gem 3459, Vs 5020
1968-1	Good Old Beer -1, 3, 7, 8, 9	Cr 3459, Gem 3459, Vs 5020
1969-2	Down By The Old Rustic Well -4, 5, 6	Cr 3445, Vs 5013

Varsity 5013, 5020 as by **Frank Luther**. Matrix 1969 is titled *Down By The Old Rustic Mill* on Varsity 5013.
Acc. unknown, h; unknown, g.

New York, NY   Wednesday, January 25, 1933

| 1976-2 | When It's Lamp Lightin' Time In The Valley | Cr 3445, Vs 5013 |

Varsity 5013 as by **Frank Luther**.

Buddy Spencer Trio: Frank Luther, Zora Layman, Leonard Stokes, v trio; acc. poss. Frank Novak, f; poss. Bob Miller, p; poss. John Cali, md; unknown, sb.

New York, NY   Tuesday, January 31, 1933

| 12996- | The Forsaken Girl | CrC/MeC/Stg/Roy 91720 |
| 12997-2 | Unwanted Children | Ba 32702, Me M12633, Or 8212, Pe 12889, Ro 5212, Cq 8101, CrC/MeC/Stg/Roy 91516, Pan 25621 |

All issues of matrix 12997 as by **Frank Luther Trio**. No take is shown on Melotone 91720.
Zora Layman sings lead on matrix 12997.
Rev. all issues of matrix 12997 by Zora Layman.

Frank Luther Trio: Frank Luther, Zora Layman, v duet; acc. unknown, f; unknown, h; unknown, g; unknown, sb.

New York, NY   Friday, February 10, 1933

| 13056-1 | Valley Of Memories | Ba 32722, Me M12651, Or 8216, Pe 12898, Ro 5216, Cq 8237, CrC/MeC/Stg/Roy 91524 |

Rev. all issues of matrix 13056 except Conqueror 8237 by Zora Layman.

Frank Luther, v; acc. unknown, f; unknown, h; unknown, g.

New York, NY   Monday, April 10, 1933

| 13218-2 | The Akron Disaster | Ba 32748, Me M12676, MeC 91532, Or 8227, Pe 12907, Ro 5227, Cq 8151 |
| 13219-2 | When The Goldenrods Are Waving | Ba 32748, Me M12676, MeC 91532, Or 8227, Pe 12907, Ro 5227, Cq 8151 |

Frank Luther Trio: Frank Luther, Zora Layman, Leonard Stokes, v trio; acc. unknown, f; unknown, ac-1; unknown, ah-2; unknown, g.

New York, NY   Wednesday, May 24, 1933

13382-1	Ten Hours A Day – Six Days A Week -1	Ba 32808, Me M12741, Or 8247, Pe 12924, Ro 5247, Vo 5503, Cq 8169, CrC/MeC/Stg/Roy 91639, Rex 8139, RZAu G22168
13383-2	When The Wild, Wild Roses Bloom -1	Cq 8237, CrC/MeC/Stg/Roy 91728
13384-1	When Jesus Beckons Me Home -2	Cq 8211

Acc. unknown, f; unknown, h-1; unknown, g; unknown, sb; prob. Frank Luther, oc-2/wh-3; unknown (poss. Leonard Stokes), oc-4.

New York, NY   Wednesday, May 31, or Thursday, June 1, 1933

13411-1	The Lie He Wrote Home -2, 4	Ba 32884, Me M12820, Or 8275, Pe 12948, Ro 5275, Cq 8210
13412-1	On The Colorado Trail -3	Ba 32808, Me M12741, Or 8247, Pe 12924, Ro 5247, Cq 8169, CrC/MeC/Stg/Roy 91639
13413-1	When I Take My Vacation In Heaven -1	Ba 32809, Me M12742, Or 8248, Pe 12925, Ro 5248, Cq 8170, CrC/MeC/Stg/Roy 91640

Rev. Conqueror 8170 by Darby & Tarlton.

Acc. unknown, f; unknown, g; unknown, sb; prob. Frank Luther, oc-1; unknown (poss. Leonard Stokes), oc-2.

New York, NY   Wednesday, June 7, 1933

| 13429-1 | Way Up There -1, 2 | Ba 32809, Me M12742, Or 8248, Pe 12925, Ro 5248, Vo 5502, Cq 8211, CrC/MeC/Stg/Roy 91640, RZAu G22167 |
| 13430- | Sweetheart Lane - | ARC 5-12-63, Cq 8585, CrC/MeC/Stg/Roy 91728 |

Buddy Spencer Trio: Frank Luther, Zora Layman, Leonard Stokes, v trio; acc. two unknowns, f; unknown, g.
New York, NY   Wednesday, June 7, 1933

| 13431-1 | All The Glory Is Gone | Ba 32979, Me M12929, Or 8306, Pe 12978, Ro 5306, Cq 8272, CrC/MeC/Stg/Roy 91704 |

Zora Layman sings lead on matrix 13431. This item was logged as by **Bob Miller**.

Acc. unknown, f; unknown, h-1; prob. Frank Novak, ac-2/sb-3/x-4; unknown, g.
New York, NY   Wednesday, June 21, 1933

13482-2	Every Sunday Night Back Home -3	Ba 32890, Me M12835, Or 8282, Pe 12955, Ro 5282, Vo 5503, Cq 8209, CrC/MeC/Stg/Roy 91652, Pan 25632, RZAu G22168
13483-1	Home On The Range -1, 4	Ba 32966, Me M12916, Or 8303, Pe 12975, Ro 5303, Cq 8273
13484-1	Shepherd Of The Air -2	Ba 32890, Me M12835, Or 8282, Pe 12955, Ro 5282, Vo 5502, Cq 8209, CrC/MeC/Stg/Roy 91652, Pan 25632, RZAu G22167

Vocalion 5502, 5503, Conqueror 8209, Crown/Melotone/Sterling/Royale 91652 as by **Frank Luther Trio**.
In ARC files matrix 13484 is subtitled (*Dedicated to Father Coughlin Pastor Of Shrine Of Little Flower*), but this does not appear on any known issue.

Frank Luther Trio: Frank Luther, Ray Whitley, v duet; or Frank Luther, Zora Layman, Ray Whitley, v trio-1; acc. prob.: Roy Smeck, sg; Bill Mitchell, md-2; Ray Whitley, g; Frank Novak, sb; Frank Luther, bells.
New York, NY   Friday, January 26, 1934

| 14700-1 | Swaller-Tail Coat -1 | Ba 33034, Me M12993, Or 8327, Pe 12995, Ro 5327, Cq 8284, Rex 8139 |
| 14701-1 | The Last Of The 21 Year Prisoner -2 | Ba 33263, Me M13230, MeC 91882, Or 8398, Pe 13083, Ro 5398, Cq 8395 |

Matrix 14701 is titled *The 21 Year Prisoner Is Dead* on Melotone 91882.
Rev. Melotone 91882 by Boa's Pine Cabin Boys.

Frank Luther, Ray Whitley, v duet; acc. prob.: Frank Novak, f; Roy Smeck, h; John Cali, g; Ray Whitley, g; Frank Luther, bells.
New York, NY   Monday, January 29, 1934

| 14720-1 | The Old Spinning Wheel | Ba 32979, Me M12929, Or 8306, Pe 12978, Ro 5306, Cq 8272, CrC/MeC/Stg/Roy 91704 |

Frank Luther, Ray Whitley, v/y duet; acc. prob. Frank Novak, f/sb; Bill Mitchell, md; poss. John Mitchell, md; Ray Whitley, g.
New York, NY   Wednesday, February 28, 1934

| 14871-1 | In The Valley Of Yesterday | Ba 32999, Me M12960, Or 8314, Pe 12985, Ro 5314, Cq 8284, CrC/MeC/Stg/Roy 91730 |

Frank Luther, Zora Layman, Ray Whitley, v trio; acc. poss. Roy Smeck, g; poss. Frank Novak, sb.
New York, NY   Thursday, March 1, 1934

| 14873-2 | Wagon Wheels | Ba 32999, Me M12960, Or 8314, Pe 12985, Ro 5314, Cq 8283, CrC/MeC/Stg/Roy 91730, Min M-923 |

Rev. Minerva M-923 by Patt Patterson & Lois Dexter.

Acc. poss.: Roy Smeck, sg; Bill Mitchell, md; John Mitchell, md; Ray Whitley, g.
New York, NY   Thursday, March 1, 1934

| 14874-1 | The Tree That Father Planted For Me | Ba 33034, Me M12993, Or 8327, Pe 12995, Ro 5327, Cq 8283 |

Rocky Mountain Rangers: Frank Luther, Zora Layman, unknown, v trio; acc. unknown, f; unknown, f-1; prob. Roy Smeck, sg-2/md-3; unknown, g; poss. Frank Novak, sb-4; Frank Luther, y-5; unknown, wh-6.
New York, NY   Thursday, May 3, 1934

15157-B	Seven Years With The Wrong Woman -2, 3	Br 6908, RZAu G22122
15158-B	Ridin' Down That Old Texas Trail -3, 4, 5	Br 6907, RZAu G22123
15159-A	That Silver Haired Daddy Of Mine -1, 6	Br 6907, RZAu G22123
15160-B	Seven Years With The Wrong Man -3, 4	Br 6908, RZAu G22122

Regal-Zonophone G22122, G22123 as by **Frank Luther's Rocky Mountain Rangers**.

Frank Luther Trio: Frank Luther, Ray Whitley, v/y duet; acc. prob. John Mitchell, tbj; Frank Novak, sb.
New York, NY   Friday, July 6, 1934
    15396-1   In A Little Red Barn On A Farm Down In Indiana   Ba 33115, Me M13082, Or 8357, Pe 13020,
                                                                                                 Ro 5357, Cq 8389, CrC/MeC/Stg/Roy 91842

Frank Luther, Ray Whitley, v duet; acc. prob.: Roy Smeck, sg; Bob Miller, p; Ray Whitley, g; Frank Novak, sb.
New York, NY   Friday, July 6, 1934
    15397-1   Buffalo Range   Ba 33115, Me M13082, Or 8357, Pe 13020,
                                                                                                   Ro 5357, Cq 8389, CrC/MeC/Stg/Roy 91842

Acc. prob.: Roy Smeck, sg; Ray Whitley, g; Frank Novak, sb; Frank Luther, bells-1.
New York, NY   Wednesday, July 11, 1934
    15415-   Clyde Barrow And Bonnie Parker   ARC unissued
    15416-   The Little Grey Church In The Valley -1   ARC 5-12-63, Cq 8585
    15417-1   The Old Family Doctor   Ba 33263, Me M13230, Or 8398, Pe 13083,
                                                                                  Ro 5398, Cq 8395, CrC/MeC/Stg/Roy 91882

Prob. Frank Luther, v/y; acc. prob.: Roy Smeck, sg; Ray Whitley, g; Frank Novak, sb.
New York, NY   Wednesday, July 11, 1934
    15418-1,-2   Courtin' Cowboy   ARC unissued

Frank Luther, v; acc. poss. Frank Novak, f; unknown, h; prob. Ray Whitley, g.
New York, NY   Thursday, July 26, 1934
    15457-1   Crime Does Not Pay   Ba 33123, Me M13090, Or 8364, Pe 13024,
                                                                                    Ro 5364, Cq 8385, CrC/MeC/Stg/Roy 91822
    15458-2   Outlaw John Dillinger   Ba 33123, Me M13090, Or 8364, Pe 13024,
                                                                                    Ro 5364, Cq 8385, CrC/MeC/Stg/Roy 91822

Frank Luther, v; acc. unknown, f; unknown, g; unknown, sb.
New York, NY   c. August 26, 1934
    38434-   A Little Girl Dressed In Blue   De 5008
    38435-   They Cut Down The Old Pine Tree   De 5009

Frank Luther Trio: Frank Luther, Zora Layman, Leonard Stokes, v trio; acc. unknown, sg; unknown, g; unknown, sb.
New York, NY   c. August 26, 1934
    38436-   Wonder Valley   De 5002
    38437-B   When The Bloom Is On The Sage   De 5002
    38438-   When I Was A Boy From The Mountains And You De 5009
                   Were A Girl From The Hills

Frank Luther, v; acc. poss. Frank Novak, ac; unknown, g; unknown, sb.
New York, NY   Wednesday, August 29, 1934
    38465-A   Peg-Leg Jack   De 5037, DeE F5259
Matrix 38465 is titled *Peg Leg Jack* on Decca F5259.

Frank Luther & Zora Layman, v duet; acc. unknown, sg; poss. Frank Luther, cel-1; poss. John Cali, md-2; unknown, g; unknown, sb.
New York, NY   Wednesday, August 29, 1934
    38466-   Carolina Moon   De 5005
    38467-   Somebody Loves You -1   De 5005
    38468-A   When Your Hair Has Turned To Silver (I Will Love De 5007
                   You Just The Same) -1, 2
    38469-A   Good Night Little Girl Of My Dreams -1   De 5007

Frank Luther Trio: Frank Luther, Zora Layman, Leonard Stokes, v trio; acc. unknown, sg; unknown, g; unknown, sb.
New York, NY   Friday, August 31, 1934
    38510-A   Somewhere In Old Wyoming   De 5004
    38511-   In The Valley Of The Moon   De 5038
    38512-   Keep A Light In Your Window Tonight   De 5003
    38513-   It's Time To Say Aloha   De 5003

Frank Luther & Zora Layman, v duet; acc. unknown, f; unknown, g; unknown, bs; unknown, jh.
New York, NY   Friday, August 31, 1934
    38514-A   A Hill Billy Wedding In June   De 5008

Frank Luther Trio: Frank Luther, Zora Layman, Leonard Stokes, v trio; acc. poss. John Cali, sg-1/lute-2; poss. Frank Luther, cel-3; unknown, g; unknown, sb.
New York, NY   Tuesday, September 4, 1934
    38536-A   Mellow Mountain Moon -1, 3   De 5004
    38537-   A Little Street Where Old Friends Meet -2 De 5006
    38538-   Rock Me To Sleep In My Rocky Mountain Home De 5006
                 -1, 3

Acc. unknown, f; unknown, ac; unknown, g; unknown, eff-1.
 New York, NY   Tuesday, September 4, 1934
  38539-   Barnacle Bill The Sailor   De 151, DeE F5346
  38540-A   The Return Of Barnacle Bill -1   De 151

Frank Luther, v; acc. prob. Frank Novak, bscl; unknown, g; unknown, sb; own oc; unknown (poss. Leonard Stokes), oc; unknown, jh.
 New York, NY   Saturday, September 15, 1934
  38666-   I Know Everything   De 5055, Pan 25679

Rev. Panachord 25679 by Zora Layman.

Frank Luther & Zora Layman, v duet; acc. poss. John Cali, sg-1/lute-2; unknown, g; unknown, sb.
 New York, NY   Saturday, September 15, 1934
  38667-   I'll Be With You When The Roses Bloom Again -1   De 5028
  38668-A   The Bright Sherman Valley -2   De 5028

Frank Luther, v; acc. unknown, f; poss. Frank Novak, cl/alto cl; unknown, p; unknown, g; unknown, sb; prob. own oc.
 New York, NY   Saturday, September 15, 1934
  38675-A   The Ladies' Man (Or A Devil With The Women)   De 5322, DeAu X1373

Frank Luther Trio: Frank Luther, Zora Layman, Leonard Stokes, v trio; acc. prob. Frank Novak, ac-1/sb-2; unknown, h-3; poss. John Cali, sg-4/g-5/lute-6; poss. Frank Luther, cel-7; unknown, g.
 New York, NY   Friday, September 21, 1934
  38701-   A Picture From Life's Other Side -2, 3, 4   De 5039
  38702-   Where We'll Never Grow Old -1, 6, 7   De 5039
  38703-   Moonlight And Roses (Bring Mem'ries Of You) -2, 4, 7   De 5038
  38704-A   I Wonder Will My Mother Be On That Train? -2, 5   De 5189, MeC 45216

Frank Luther, v; acc. unknown, f; unknown, g; unknown, sb; unknown, eff-1.
 New York, NY   Wednesday, September 26, 1934
  38742-A   Empty Pocket Blues   De 5055
  38745-A   I'm Popeye The Sailor Man -1   De 5037, DeE F5259

Matrices 38743/44 are by Zora Layman.

Frank Luther Trio: Frank Luther, Zora Layman, Leonard Stokes, v trio; acc. unknown, sg; unknown, sb; unknown, tomtoms.
 New York, NY   Tuesday, October 16, 1934
  38851-   Your Enemy Cannot Harm You   De 5050

Frank Luther Quartet-1/Frank Luther Quartette-2: Frank Luther, Zora Layman, Leoard Stokes, unknown, v quartet; acc. unknown, g; unknown, sb; unknown, tomtoms.
 New York, NY   Tuesday, October 16, 1934
  38852-A   The Lord's Prayer -1   De 1103, 5052, DeE F6207
  38853-   My Lord's Gonna Move This Wicked Race -2   De 5051

Frank Luther, v; acc. unknown, temple block/tomtom/jungle drum.
 New York, NY   Tuesday, October 16, 1934
  38854-A   Rhythmatism   De unissued

Frank Luther Trio: Frank Luther, Zora Layman, Leonard Stokes, v trio; acc. unknown, h-1; prob. Frank Novak, ac-2; poss. John Cali, sg-3; unknown, g; unknown, sb.
 New York, NY   Tuesday, November 13, 1934
  39013-A   Sun Of My Soul -2   De 5189, MeC 45216
  39014-A   When The Saints Go Marching Home -1, 3   De 5051

Acc. prob. Frank Novak, ac-1; unknown, p-2; unknown, g; unknown, sb.
 New York, NY   Wednesday, November 14, 1934
  39015-   You Better Let That Liar Alone -2   De 5050
  39016-A   The Lord Is My Shepherd -1   De 1103, 5052, DeAu F6207

Frank Luther, v; acc. unknown, f; prob. Frank Novak, ac.
 New York, NY   Friday, November 16, 1934
  39023-A   The Letter Edged In Black   De 435, 12023
  39024-A   In The Baggage Coach Ahead   De 435, 12023
  39025-A   The Little Lost Child   De unissued

Decca 12023 as by **Dennis O'Leary**.

Acc. unknown, f; prob. Frank Novak, cl; unknown, p; unknown, sb.
 New York, NY   Tuesday, February 12, 1935
  39354-A   Who Stole The Lock Off The Henhouse Door?   De 5322, DeAu X1373
  39355-A,-B   Return To The Prairie   De unissued

Frank & Buddy Ross: Frank Luther, Fred Rose, v duet; acc. unknown, g.
New York, NY   Wednesday, April 7, 1937

62111-A	Plant A Weeping Willow On My Grave (When I Go)	De 5360
62112-A	I'll Be True To The One I Love	De 5357
62113-A	There's An Old Easy Chair By The Fireplace	De 5357, DeAu X1392
62114-A	Oh How I Need My Mother	De 5360, DeAu X1392

Acc. unknown, h; unknown, g.
New York, NY   Thursday, April 29, 1937

62164-A	There's A Picture On The Easel In The Parlor	De 5376
62165-A	Pray For Me Mother	De 5412, DeSA FM5115, BrSA SA1453
62166-A	The Pretty Little Girl With A Smile	De 5376
62167-A	Will I Ever Find My True Love	De 5412

Rev. Decca FM5115, Brunswick SA1453 by Shelton Brothers.

Frank Luther & Zora Layman, v duet; acc. unknown, f; unknown, ac; unknown p.
New York, NY   Thursday, May 20, 1937

62211-A	Nearer, My God, To Thee	De 1469, Rex 9147, BrSA SA1339
62212-A	In The Sweet Bye And Bye	De 1469, Rex 9147, BrSA SA1339

Frank Luther With The Luther Trio: Frank Luther, Zora Layman, Leonard Stokes, v trio; acc. unknown, f; unknown, g; unknown, sb.
New York, NY   Friday, June 25, 1937

62314-B	Home On The Range – Part 1	De 1427, DeE F6823, DeAu X1465
62315-A	Home On The Range – Part 2	De 1427, DeE F6823, DeAu X1465
62316-A	Home On The Range – Part 3	De 1428, DeE F6824, DeAu X1466
62317-A	Home On The Range – Part 4	De 1428, DeE F6824, DeAu X1466
62318-A	Home On The Range – Part 5	De 1429, DeE F6825, DeAu X1467
62319-A	Home On The Range – Part 6	De 1429, DeE F6825, DeAu X1467

Decca F6823 to F6825 as by **Frank Luther & Company**.
The above items are titled *Selection Of Cowboy Songs Parts 1–6* on Decca X1465 to X1467.
Decca 1427 to 1429 were issued in an album titled *Home On The Range Parts 1–6*.

Frank Luther & The Luther Trio: Frank Luther, Zora Layman, Leonard Stokes, v trio; acc. prob.: unknown, f; unknown, g; unknown, sb.
New York, NY   Thursday, March 3, 1938

63367-A,-B	Comin' 'Round The Mountain – No. 2 1. Golden Slippers; 2. Roving Gambler; 3. In The Baggage Coach Ahead; 4. Old Dan Tucker	De unissued
63368-A,-B	Comin' 'Round The Mountain – No. 1 1. She'll Be Coming 'Round The Mountain; 2. Can I Sleep In Your Barn Tonight Mister; 3. When The Roses Bloom Again; 4. Turkey In The Straw	De unissued
63369-A,-B	Comin' 'Round The Mountain – Part 4 1. Ida Red; 2. Bully Of The Town; 3. Down In The Valley; 4. Sourwood Mt. [sic]	De unissued

Frank Luther With The Luther Trio: Frank Luther, Zora Layman, Leonard Stokes, v trio; acc. unknown, f; unknown, g; unknown, sb.
New York, NY   Friday, May 13, 1938

63768-A	1. She'll Be Comin' 'Round The Mountain; 2. When The Roses Bloom Again; 3. Can I Sleep In Your Barn Tonight, Mister?; 4. Turkey In The Straw	De 2137, DeAu X1677
63769-A	1. Oh, Dem Golden Slippers; 2. Rovin' Gambler; 3. In The Baggage Coach Ahead; 4. Ole Dan Tucker	De 2137, DeAu X1677
63770-A	1. Billy Boy; 2. Barbara Allen; 3. I Was Born 4000 Years Ago	De 2138, DeAu X1678
63771-A	1. Ida Red; 2. Bully Of The Town; 3. Down In The Valley; 4. Sourwood Mountain	De 2138, DeAu X1678
63772-A	1. Buffalo Gals; 2. Butcher Boy; 3. East Bound Train	De 2139, DeAu X1679
63773-A	1. Hand Me Down My Walking Cane; 2. My Horses Ain't Hungry; 3. Little Brown Jug	De 2139, DeAu X1679

The above items are titled *Old Time Songs Medley No. 1, No. 2,* and *No. 3* respectively on Decca X1677, X1678, and X1679. See also the note following the next session.

New York, NY   Tuesday, June 14, 1938

63970-A	1. Pass Around The Bottle; 2. Put My Little Shoes Away; 3. Boston Burglar; 4. Skip To My Lou	De 2140, DeAu X1699
63971-A	1. Little Rosewood Casket; 2. Pretty Polly; 3. Arkansas Traveler	De 2140, DeAu X1699
63972-A	1. Maple On The Hill; 2. When I Was Single; 3. Blue Eyed Ellen	De 2141, DeAu X1680
63973-A	1. New River Train; 2. Letter Edged In Black; 3. Goodbye, My Lover, Goodbye	De 2141, DeAu X1680

The above items are titled *Old Time Songs Medley No 4* and *No 5* respectively on Decca X1680 and X1699. Decca 2137 to 2141 were issued in an album titled *American Folk Songs* (Decca Album 25).

Frank Luther–Zora Layman–Leonard Stokes, v trio; acc. unknown, ac; unknown, g; unknown, sb.
New York, NY   Tuesday, June 21, 1938

64170-B	Colorado Sunset	De 1903
64171-A	The Grass Is Just As Green	De 1954
64172-A	(Take Me Back To) The Wide Open Places	De 1954
64173-A	Chimes Of Arcady	De 1903

From this point Frank Luther recorded almost exclusively songs and stories for children and medleys of standard songs. (He had already recorded in those idioms, but that material has not been included above.) He continued to record after 1942.

PHIL & FRANK LUTHER

See Carson Robison.

ROBINSON LUTHER

This credit was used, either as a pseudonym or in error, on the Australian labels Angelus and Lyric for Frank Luther, possibly with Carson Robison (see the latter).

ZORA LUTHER

Zora Layman's married name was used on Vocalion 5485.

LUTHER BROTHERS

This credit was used on Crown and associated labels for Carson Robison & Frank Luther (see the former).

THE LUTHER FAMILY

Pseudonym on Microphone for the Pickard Family.

LUTHER–STOKES TRIO

See Frank Luther.

RAY LYNCY

Pseudonym on Aurora A22021 for Buell Kazee.

ROY LYONS & THE JUSTICE BROTHERS

Roy Lyons, v; acc. unidentified, md; unidentified, bj; unidentified, g.
Richmond, IN   Wednesday, July 24, 1929

| 15383,-A,-B | Forsaken Love | Ge rejected |
| 15384,-A | Slighted Sweetheart | Ge rejected |

LYRIC QUARTETTE

Vocal quartet; acc. unknown, p.
Atlanta, GA   Thursday, October 8, 1940

054538-1	Somebody Loves Me	BB B-8698
054539-1	I Can Tell You The Time	BB B-8698
054540-1	Do You Know Him?	BB B-8663
054541-1	I'm On My Way To Glory	BB B-8627
054542-1	Living On The Glory Side	BB B-8663
054543-1	For The Soul That's Redeemed	BB B-8627

"MAC" (HARRY McCLINTOCK)
MAC'S HAYWIRE ORCHESTRA

See Harry "Mac" McClintock.

MAC & BOB
Pseudonym on several labels for Lester McFarland & Robert A. Gardner.

MAC & CURL[E]Y
Pseudonym on Superior for The Two Islanders (see James Brown, Jr. & Ken Landon groups).

PALMER McABEE
Palmer McAbee, h solo.
   Atlanta, GA   Tuesday, February 21, 1928

41929-2	Lost Boy Blues	Vi 21352
41930-2	McAbee's Railroad Piece	Vi 21352

This artist is speculatively included in *B&GR*, but the recordings are described on the Victor session-sheet as "Hillbilly".

W.W. MACBETH
W.W. Macbeth, h solo.
   Dallas, TX   c. October 20, 1925

9381-A	Listen To The Mocking Bird	OK 40509
9382-A	Carry Me Back To Old Virginny	OK 40509

W.W. Macbeth & Tom Collins: W.W. Macbeth, h; Tom Collins, g.
   Dallas, TX   c. October 23, 1928

DAL-714-	My Wild Irish Rose	Vo 5282
DAL-715-	Listen To The Mocking Bird/Intro: Turkey In The Straw	Vo 5282

W.W. Macbeth, h; acc. unknown, g.
   Dallas, TX   Wednesday, October 30, 1929

DAL-549-	Red Wing	Br 443, BrAu 443, Spt S2092, PanAu P12175
DAL-550-	Dixie Medley	Br 373
DAL-551-	Over The Waves	Br 443, BrAu 443, Spt S2092, PanAu P12175
DAL-552-	Southern Melodies	Br 373

   Dallas, TX   Sunday, November 30, 1930

DAL-6795-A	Darling Nellie Gray	Br 571
DAL-6796-A	Missouri Waltz	Br 571
DAL-6797-	After The Ball	Br unissued

DICKIE McBRIDE
Dickie McBride, v; acc. Grady Hester, f; J.D. Standlee, esg; Anthony Scanlin, p; Aubrey "Red" Greenhaw, g; Hezzie Bryant, sb.
   Houston, TX   Tuesday, September 5, 1939

66395-A	To Tell The Truth (I Told A Lie)	De 5734, Min M-14117
66396-A	I'm Dreaming Tonight Of The Old Folks	De 5734, Min M-14117
66397-A	You'll Be Sorry Bye And Bye	De 5754
66398-A	I've Nothing To Live For Now	De 5767
66399-A	If You Cared (You'd Have Spared Me This Trouble)	De 5754
66400-B	I'm Counting On The Mountain Moon	De 5767
66401-A	I'm Grievin' For Believin' In A Lie	De 5791
66402-A,B	This Night Is Mine	De 5791

Dickie McBride & The Village Boys: Dickie Jones, f; Buddy Ray, f/v-1; Bob Dunn, esg; Mancel Tierney, p/v-2; "Red" Greenhaw, g; Dickie McBride, g/v-3; Hezzie Bryant, sb.
   Dallas, TX   Thursday, May 1, 1941

93742-A	I Don't Want Anyone But You -3	De 6002, MeC 45479
93743-A	Tulsa Twist	De 5949
93744-A	(I'm Gonna Get High And Say) Goodbye To The Blues -1	De 5965, MeC 45454
93745-A	I'll Miss You When I'm Gone -3	De 6052
93746-A	New It Makes No Difference Now -3	De 5949
93747-A	Out Where West Winds Blow -1 (lead), 2, 3	De 6002, MeC 45479
93748-A	Tell Me Dear (Don't You Care) -3	De 6052
93749-B	Singin' Steel Blues (The Waco Wail)	De 5965, MeC 45454

Dickie McBride recorded after 1942.

ED McBRIDE
Ed McBride, v/y; acc. prob. own g.
   New York, NY   Friday, June 4, 1937

62241-A,-B	The Old Ladies' Home	De unissued
62242-A,-B	If Mothers Could Live On Forever	De unissued

McBRIDGE & WRIGHT

Pseudonym on Herwin 75532 for Sid Harkreader & Grady Moore.

DAVID McCARN

David McCarn, v; acc. own g.
   Memphis, TN   Monday, May 19, 1930

59943-2	Everyday Dirt	Vi V-40274
59944-2	Cotton Mill Colic	Vi V-40274

Acc. own h-1/g.
   Memphis, TN   Wednesday, November 19, 1930

62974-1	Hobo Life -1	Vi 23532
62975-1	The Bashful Bachelor -1	Vi 23532
62976-2	Poor Man, Rich Man (Cotton Mill Colic No. 2) -1	Vi 23506
62977-2	Take Them For A Ride	Vi 23506

David McCarn, h/g.
   Memphis, TN   Thursday, November 20, 1930

62982-1,-2	Mexican Rag	Vi unissued
62983-1	Gastonia Gallop	Vi 23555

Rev. Victor 23555 by W.A. Hinton.

Dave & Howard: David McCarn, h-1/g/v; Howard Long, k-2/v.
   Charlotte, NC   Tuesday, May 19, 1931

69315-2	My Bone's Gonna Rise Again -1	Vi 23577
69316-1	Fancy Nancy (Every Day Dirt No. 2)	Vi 23566
69317-1	Bay Rum Blues -1	Vi 23566
69318-2	Serves 'Em Fine -1, 2	Vi 23577

McCARTHY BROTHERS

Recordings with this artist credit in the Decca Hill Billy series (5092/3) are by Hermanos Moreno y Coro, a Mexican accordion/guitar duet (see EMOR).

McCARTT BROTHERS & PATTERSON

Luther McCartt, f/y-1; Barney McCartt, md/y-1; Andy Patterson, g/v-2/y-1.
   Johnson City, TN   Thursday, October 18, 1928

147242-2	Green Valley Waltz -1, 2	Co 15454-D, ReE G9458, Re/RZAu G20753
147243-2	Over The Sea Waltz	Co 15454-D

Regal G9458, Regal/Regal-Zonophone G20753 as by **The Alabama Barn Stormers**.
Matrix 147242 is titled *Green Valley, – Waltz* on Regal G9458.
Rev. Regal G9458, Regal/Regal-Zonophone G20753 (with same credit) by Leake County Revelers.

E.W. McCLAIN & J.O. HARPOLD

See the Jackson County Ramblers.

McCLELLAND & ELLIS

Pseudonym on Silvertone for Bill Chitwood & Bud Landress.

McCLENDON BROTHERS [WITH GEORGIA DELL]

McClendon Brothers With Georgia Dell: Rupert McClendon, f-1/v-2; prob. Buster McClendon, g; Georgia Dell, v-3.
   Charlotte, NC   Sunday, October 11, 1936

02506-1	Heaven Bound Gold -2	BB B-6961
02507-1	The Story Of Love Divine -3	BB B-6740
02508-1	My Little Mountain Lady, Queen Of Alabam' -1, 2, 3	BB B-6961
02509-1	Gamblin' On The Sabbath -3	BB B-6740
02510-1	Corns On My Feet -1, 2	BB B-7832
02511-1	Free As I Can Be -1, 3	BB B-7339
02512-1	Who's Goin' To Shoe Your Pretty Little Feet -1, 3	BB unissued
02513-1	Goin' To Have A Big Time Tonight -1, 2	BB B-7832

Bluebird B-7832 as by **McClendon Brothers**. Rev. Bluebird B-7339 by Mrs. Jimmie Rodgers.

Rupert McClendon, f-1/v-2; prob. Buster McClendon, g; Jesse Bassett, prob. g/v-3; Georgia Dell, poss. g/v-4.
   Rock Hill, SC   Wednesday, September 28, 1938

027796-1	Will There Be Any Fiddlers Up There? -1, 2?, 4?	MW M-7751
027797-1	Alabama Hills -1, 2, 4	BB B-8375
027798-1	Careless Soul -3, 4	MW M-7751
027799-1	Where The Love Light Never Dies -1, 2?, 4?	MW M-7752
027600-1,2	Handy Man Blues -3	BB unissued
027601-1	Unwanted Dream -1, 2?, 4?	BB unissued

Bluebird B-8375 as by **McClendon Brothers**.

McClendon Brothers: Jesse Bassett, v; acc. own g.
Rock Hill, SC   Wednesday, September 28, 1938

027602-1	Love Hunting Blues	BB B-8192

McClendon Brothers With Georgia Dell: Rupert McClendon, f-1/v-2; prob. Buster McClendon, g; Jesse Bassett, prob. g/v-3; Georgia Dell, poss. g/v-4; Ernest McClendon, v-5.
Rock Hill, SC   Wednesday, September 28, 1938

027603-1	Don't You Love Your Daddy Too? -3, 4, 5	BB B-8922, MW M-7752
027604-1	Red Roses, Sweet Violets So Blue -4	BB B-7914, MW M-7749
027605-1	Keep Your Love Letters, I'll Keep Mine -4	BB B-7914, MW M-7749
027606-1	Precious Love, Please Come Home -1, 2?, 4?	MW M-7750
027607-1	Plant Some Flowers By My Grave -1, 4	BB B-8922, MW M-7750

Bluebird B-7914, Montgomery Ward M-7749 as by **Georgia Dell**.

McClendon Brothers: Buster McClendon, h/v-1; acc. unidentified, g.
Rock Hill, SC   Wednesday, September 28, 1938

027608-1	Goodbye, Baby, Goodbye -1	BB B-8192
027609-1	Down Home	BB B-8375

Rupert and Ernest McClendon recorded after 1942.

HARRY "MAC" McCLINTOCK

"Mac" (Harry McClintock), v; acc. Virgi Ward, f-1; own g.
Oakland, CA   Thursday, March 1, 1928

42041-2	Get Along, Little Doggies -1	Vi V-40016, MW M-4469
42042-2	Cowboy's Lament -1	Vi 21761, Au 422
42043-1,-2	Good-Bye Old Paint -1	Vi unissued
42044-1	The Texas Rangers -1	Vi 21487, MW M-4784
42045-2	Sam Bass	Vi 21420

Montgomery Ward M-4784 as by **Radio Mac**.

Acc. own g.
Oakland, CA   Saturday, March 10, 1928

42073-2	Jesse James	Vi 21420
42074-1,-2	The Trail To Mexico	Vi unissued
42075-2	Sweet Betsy From Pike	Vi 23704, MW M-4324
42076-1,-2	Billy Venero	Vi unissued
42077-2	My Dad's Dinner Pail	Vi 21521

Victor 23704, Montgomery Ward M-4324 as by **Radio Mac**.
Revs: Victor 23704 by Bob Miller; Montgomery Ward M-4324 by Jimmie Rodgers.

Acc. own g; H. O'Neill, sp-1.
Oakland, CA   Friday, March 16, 1928

42094-2	The Bum Song -1	Vi 21343, BB B-11083, ZoAu EE120
42095-2	The Man On The Flying Trapeze	Vi 21567
42096-1	Jerry, Go Ile That Car	Vi 21521

Matrix 42094 is titled *The "Bum" Song* on Zonophone EE120.

Acc. **His Haywire Orchestra/Orchestry**-1: prob. Asa "Ace" Wright, f; unknown, h; own g.
Oakland, CA   Thursday, March 22, 1928

42113-4	The Old Chisholm Trail	Vi 21421
42114-1	My Last Old Dollar	Vi 23690
42115- -	Bald Top Mountain -1	Vi 23829, HMVIn N4262

Victor 23690 as by **Radio Mac (Harry McClintock)**. HMV N4262 as by **Radio Mac & His Haywire Orchestry**.
Revs: Victor 23690 by Graham Brothers, 23829 by Fleming & Townsend; HMV N4262 by Kelly Brothers.

Oakland, CA   Friday, March 23, 1928

42119-1,-2	Cowboy's Lament	Vi unissued
42120-3	Goodbye, Old Paint	Vi 21761, Au 422
42121-2	The Trail To Mexico	Vi V-40016, MW M-4469

Oakland, CA   Tuesday, March 27, 1928

| 42128-2 | Red River Valley | Vi 21421, MW M-4058 |

Montgomery Ward M-4058 as by **Mac's Haywire Orchestra**. Rev. Montgomery Ward M-4058 by Jimmie Rodgers.

Acc. **His Haywire Orchestra**: prob. Asa "Ace" Wright, f; unknown, s-1; unknown, h; own g; Buck Buckholtz, d-1.
Oakland, CA   Saturday, March 31, 1928

42076-3	Billy Venero	Vi 21487, MW M-4465
42129-1	The Circus Days -1	Vi 21567
42137-2	Hallelujah! I'm A Bum	Vi 21343, BB B-11083, ZoAu EE120

Matrix 42137 is titled *Hallelujah! I'm A "Bum"* on Zonophone EE120. Matrices 42130 to 42136 are by other artists.
Rev. Montgomery Ward M-4465 by Carl T. Sprague.

Harry McClintock "Radio Mac", v; acc. own g.
Hollywood, CA   Wednesday, September 5, 1928

| | Fifty Cents | Vi unissued trial recording |
| 46452-1 | Ain't We Crazy? | Vi V-40101, ZoSA 4241 |

Revs: Victor V-40101 by Peg Moreland; Zonophone 4241 by Vernon Dalhart.

"Mac" (Harry McClintock), v; acc. own g; Dorothy Ellen Cole, sp-1.
Hollywood, CA   Thursday, September 6, 1928

| 46453-2 | The Bum Song No. 2 -1 | Vi 21704, ZoAu EE125 |
| 46454-2 | The Big Rock Candy Mountains | Vi 21704, MW M-8121, HMV BD379, ZoAu EE125 |

Matrix 46453 is titled *The "Bum" Song – No. 2* on Zonophone EE125.
Revs: Montgomery Ward M-8121 by Jimmie Rodgers; HMV BD379 by Vernon Dalhart.

Hollywood, CA   Tuesday, April 30, 1929

50878-1	Hobo's Spring Song	Vi 22003
50878-2	Hobo's Spring Song	Vi V-40112
50879-1	If I Had My Druthers	Vi 22003, V-40112
50880-1,-2	The Broken Tambourine	Vi unissued
50881-2	His Parents Haven't Seen Him Since	Vi 23586, MW M-4490

Victor 23856, V-40112 as by **Radio Mac**.

Radio Mac, v; acc. Mac's Haywire Orchestra/Orchestry-1: Asa "Ace" Wright, f; Waite "Chief" Woodall, f; own h/g; Jerry Richard, bj; Cecil "Rowdy" Wright, g; Cleo "Doc" Shahan, g.
Culver City, CA   Friday, December 13, 1929

54531-2	He Sure Can Play A Harmoniky	Vi 23586, MW M-4490
54532-1	Homespun Gal -1	Vi 23510
54533-2	Can I Sleep In Your Barn? -1	Vi V-40264, ZoSA 4291

Montgomery Ward M-4490 as by **"Mac" (Harry McClintock)**. Rev. Victor 23510 by Peg Moreland.

Culver City, CA   Sunday, December 15, 1929

54534-2	Roamin' -1	Vi V-40264, ZoSA 4291
54535-1	Fireman Save My Child	Vi V-40234, Au 228, MW M-4298
54536-1	The Trusty Lariat	Vi V-40234, Au 228, MW M-4298, M-4784

Harry McClintock, v-1/sp-2; acc. unknown.
prob. San Francisco, CA   c. 1930

| 367 | Schwartz Gingerale Song -1 | Flexo unnumbered |
| 368 | Schwartz Gingerale Commercial -2 | Flexo unnumbered |

These matrices are coupled on a 4½-inch disc. There is no artist credit.

"Mac" (Harry McClintock), v; acc. Waite "Chief" Woodall, f; Frank Gilmore, ac; Buck Buckholtz, traps.
San Francisco, CA   Thursday, October 15, 1931

| 68325-2 | Fifty Years From Now | Vi 22845, 23614 |
| 68326-1 | When It's Time To Shear The Sheep I'm Coming Back | Vi 22845, 23614 |

Haywire Mac (Harry McClintock), v; acc. own g.
Hollywood, CA   Wednesday, December 14, 1938

DLA-1657-A	The Bum Song	De 5640
DLA-1658-A	The Bum Song No. 2	De 5689
DLA-1659-A	Hallelujah! I'm A Bum	De 5640
DLA-1660-A	The Big Rock Candy Mountains	De 5689

Harry "Mac" McClintock recorded after 1942.

JOHN & EMERY McCLUNG (McCLUNG BROTHERS)

Emery McClung, f/v-1; John McClung, g/v-2/wh-3; Carson Robison, wh-4.
New York, NY   Monday, March 7, 1927

E-21762/63/64*	Standin' In The Need Of Prayer -1, 2, 4	Br 119, Spt S2072
E-21765/66/67*	Walk The Streets Of Glory -1, 2	Br 119, Spt S2072
E-21768*/69/70	Chicken -2, 3	Br 135
E-21771/72*/73	Liza Jane -2	Br 135
E-21774*/75/76	Birdie -4	Br 134
E-21777/78/79*	The Fun Is All Over -4	Br 134
E-21780*/81/82	It's A Long Way To Tipperary -1, 2	Br 136
E-21783/84*/85	When You Wore A Tulip And I Wore A Big Red Rose -1, 2	Br 136

Supertone S2072 and some pressings of Brunswick 119 as by **The West Virginia Snake Hunters (John & Emery McClung)**.
For recordings credited to **McClung Brothers & Cleve Chaffin** see the latter.

[SMILIN'] ED McCONNELL
ED & GRACE McCONNELL
ED McCONNELL & FAMILY

Ed McConnell's full name is James Edwin McConnell.

Ed McConnell, v; or **Ed & Grace McConnell**, v duet-1; acc. Ed McConnell, p; Lambdin Kay, sp-2.
Atlanta, GA   Thursday, January 29, 1925

140306-2	Tote Your Load -1, 2	Co 314-D
140307-	I'll Never Let The Devil Win	Co unissued
140308-1	The Klucker Blues	Co 314-D

Matrix 140306 is subcredited **Announced by Lambdin Kay of WSB**.

Ed McConnell, v/sp-1; or **Ed & Grace McConnell**, v duet-2; acc. Ed McConnell, o.
Atlanta, GA   Friday, October 2, 1925

141076-	Orlando	Co unissued
141077-	Sunbonnet Gal -2	Co unissued
141078-1	Elder Bigby's Discourse Part 2 -1	Co 733-D
141079-1	Elder Bigby's Discourse Part 1 -1	Co 733-D

Acc. Ed McConnell, p.
Atlanta, GA   Monday, April 4, 1927

143892-2	Bye And Bye -2	Co 1681-D
143893-2	The Devil Song	Co 1681-D
143894-1	Walking In The Light -2	Co 15780-D
143895-3	Leaving Smiles -2	Co 15780-D

Ed McConnell, v/sp-1; or **Ed & Grace McConnell**, v duet-2; or **Ed McConnell & Family**, v group-3; acc. Ed McConnell, o.
Atlanta, GA   Wednesday, April 18, 1928

146124-2	I Want To Be Like Jesus -2	Co 15291-D
146125-2	My Loving Brother (Rock Of Ages) -3	Co 15291-D
146126-3	Elder Jackson's Sermon – Part 1 -1	Ha 677-H, Ve 1677-V, Di 2677-G, Cl 5022-C
146127-2	Elder Jackson's Sermon – Part 2 -1	Ha 677-H, Ve 1677-V, Di 2677-G, Cl 5022-C

"Smiling" Ed McConnell, v; acc. own p.
Richmond, IN   Saturday, January 3, 1931

17407-A	The Hell Bound Train	Ch 16209, 45137
17408	The Devil Song	Ch 16209, 45137
17409-A	The Royal Telephone	Ch 16263
17410-A	Leave It There	Ch 16263

Smilin' Ed McConnell, v; acc. own o-1/p-2.
Chicago, IL   Wednesday, May 3, 1933

75498-1	Tiny Toys -2	BB B-5105, Eld 2021, Sr S-3188
75499-1	That Little Boy Of Mine -2	BB unissued
75500-1	The Royal Telephone -2	BB B-8194
75801-1	The Church Of Long Ago -2	BB unissued
75802-1	The Hell-Bound Train -2	BB B-5140, Eld 2046, Sr S-3221
75803-1	I'll Never Let The Devil Win -2	BB B-5140, Eld 2046, Sr S-3221
75804-1	Life's Railway To Heaven -2	BB B-8194
75805-1	Don't Forget The Old Folks -2	BB B-5105, Eld 2021, Sr S-3188
75806-1	When Jesus Beckons Me Home -1	BB B-5075, Eld 1998, Sr S-3156
75807-1	The Old Rugged Cross -1	BB B-5075, Eld 1998, Sr S-3156
75808-1	When The World Forgets -1	BB B-5200, Eld 2090, Sr S-3281
75809-1	Leave It There -1	BB B-5275, Eld 2149, Sr S-3356
75810-1	In A Friendly Sort Of Way -1	BB B-5275, Eld 2149, Sr S-3356
75811-1	Where Is My Boy Tonight -1	BB B-5200, Eld 2090, Sr S-3281
75812-1	Tiny Toys -2	Vi 23808

75813-1	That Little Boy Of Mine -2	Vi 23808
75814-1	The Royal Telephone -2	Vi 23812
75815-1	The Church Of Long Ago -2	Vi 23823, MW M-4349
75816-1	The Hell-Bound Train -2	Vi unissued
75817-1	I'll Never Let The Devil Win -2	Vi unissued
75818-1	Life's Railway To Heaven -2	Vi 23823
75819-1	Don't Forget The Old Folks -2	Vi 23812, MW M-4346
75820-1	When Jesus Beckons Me Home -1	Vi 23844
75821-1	The Old Rugged Cross -1	Vi 23844
75822-1	When The World Forgets -1	Vi 23848, MW M-4386
75823-1	Leave It There -1	Vi 23848
75824-1	In A Friendly Sort Of Way -1	Vi 23825
75825-1	Where Is My Boy Tonight? -1	Vi 23825, MW M-4386

Revs: Montgomery Ward M-4346 by Frank Luther, M-4349 by Carter Family.

EARL McCOY & JESSIE BROCK
EARL McCOY, ALFRED MENG & CLEM GARNER

Earl McCoy & Jessie Brock, v duet; acc. prob. Earl McCoy, sg; poss. Jessie Brock, g.
Atlanta, GA   Tuesday, November 5, 1929

| 149393-1 | Cotton Mill Girl | Co 15499-D |

Atlanta, GA   Wednesday, November 6, 1929

149394-1	Are You Tired Of Me Darling	Co 15499-D
149395-2	If I Could Hear My Mother Pray Again	Co 15604-D
149396-2	Off To War	Co 15604-D

Earl McCoy, Alfred Meng & Clem Garner: unidentified, v duet; acc. prob. Earl McCoy, sg; unidentified, g.
Atlanta, GA   Wednesday, April 23, 1930

| 150370-2 | John Henry The Steel Drivin' Man | Co 15622-D |
| 150371-1 | Forty Per Cent | Co 15622-D |

SHORTY McCOY & HIS SOUTHERN PLAYBOYS

Ransom Barnett, f; Dennis Woodall, sg; Paul Lunsford, g; Leaford Lunsford, sb; Shorty McCoy, calls.
Chicago, IL   Friday, September 12, 1941

064878-1	Buffalo Gals	BB 33-0511
064879-1	The Big Eared Mule (The Two Bit Whirl)	BB B-8948
064880-1	Arkansas Traveler (Step Right Back And Watch Her Smile)	BB B-8948
064881-1	Cindy	BB 33-0511

WILLIAM McCOY

Though appearing in the Columbia Old Familar Tunes series, this is an African-American artist (see *B&GR*).

FRANK & JAMES McCRAVY
McCRAVY BROTHERS

Frank McCravy–James McCravy, v duet; acc. Justin Ring Trio: unknown, f; unknown, p; unknown, vc.
New York, NY   February 1925

73187-B	One Of God's Days	OK 40319
73188-B	Nailed To The Cross	OK 40345
73189-A	The Promised Land	OK 40371
73192-B	We'll Understand It Better Bye And Bye	OK 40319
73193-B	In The Hour Of Trial	OK 40345
73194-B	Drifting	OK 40371

Intervening matrices are untraced.

Frank & James McCravy, v duet; acc. unknown, f; unknown, p; unknown, bj; James McCravy, g; Nat Shilkret, dir.
New York, NY   Friday, July 8, 1927

38638-2	Bye And Bye	Vi 20817, ZoSA 4271
39639-3	These Bones G'wina Rise Again	Vi 20869, Zo/RZ 5340
39640-2	Jacob's Ladder	Vi 21188
39641-1	Six Feet Of Earth	Vi 20869, MW M-4336, Zo/RZ 5340
39642-2	Only A Rosebud	Vi 20817, ZoSA 4271

Zonophone 4271 as by **McCravy Brothers**.
Revs: Victor 21188 by Phil Reeve & Ernest Moody; Montgomery Ward M-4336 by Carter Family.

Acc. unknown, f; unknown, p-1/cel-2; poss. James McCravy, g-3; unknown, wh-4.
New York, NY   Sunday, July 10, 1927

81155-A	Jacob's Ladder -1, 3	OK 45128, Ve 7107-V, Cl 5134-C, PaE E6400, R3862, Ariel Z4725
81156-A	Hello Central, Give Me Heaven -2, 3	OK 45135, PaE R3863
81157-A	In The Shade Of The Old Apple Tree -2, 3, 4	OK 45135, Ve 2395-V, Cl 5329-C, PaE R3863, ReAu G21090
81158-B	I Want To Be There -1	OK 45128, Ve 7106-V, Cl 5134-C, PaE R3862

Parlophone E6400 as by **The Sanctified Singers**. Ariel Z4725 as by **Sacred Singers**.
Velvet Tone 2395-V, Clarion 5329-C, and probably Regal G21090 use the transfer matrix 100539.
Revs: Velvet Tone 2395-V, Clarion 5329-C, Regal G21090 by Scottdale String Band; Velvet Tone 7106-V, 7107-V by Frank Hutchison; Parlophone E6400, Ariel Z4725 (with same credits) by Andrew Jenkins & Carson Robison.

Acc. unknown, f; unknown, p; unknown, bj; unknown, g.
New York, NY   Wednesday, December 7, 1927

| E-25463/64 | Jacob's Ladder | Br unissued |
| E-25465/66 | I Shall Not Be Moved | Br unissued |

Acc. two unknowns, f; unknown, p; unknown, vc; unknown, bells-1.
New York, NY   Friday, December 9, 1927

E-25493/94*; E-6899/900W	In The Gloaming	Vo 5195, Me M12045, Po P9056, PanAu P12045
E-25495/96*	Silver Threads Among The Gold -1	Br 197, 3785, BrAu 3785, Spt S2025, DeE F3874, RexIr U430
E-25497/98*	When You And I Were Young, Maggie	Br 197, 3785, BrAu 3785, Spt S2025, DeE F3874, Pan P12065, RexIr U430

Melotone M12045, Polk P9056, Panachord P12045 as by **Al & Joe Blackburn**. Supertone S2025 as by **Lonesome Pine Twins**. Rev. Panachord P12065 untraced.

Acc. unknown, f; unknown, p; unknown, vc.
New York, NY   Saturday, December 10, 1927

E-25507/08*	Bye And Bye	Vo 5193, Me M12116, Po P9063, PanAu P12116
E-25509/10*	I Want To Go There	Br 192, 3777, BrAu 3777
E-25511/12*	Six Feet Of Earth	Br 193, 3778, BrAu 3778, Spt S2020, DeSA FM5190

Melotone M12116, Polk P9063, Panachord P12116 as by **Al & Joe Blackburn**. Supertone S2020 as by **Lonesome Pine Twins**.

Acc. unknown, f; unknown, p; unknown, g-1.
New York, NY   Tuesday, December 13, 1927

E-25560*/61	Jacob's Ladder -1	Br 192, 3777, BrAu 3777
E-25562/63*	I Shall Not Be Moved	Br 196, 3784, DeE F3875, RexIr U431
E-25564*/65; E-6843/44W	Leave It There -1	Vo 5193, Me M12116, Po P9063, PanAu P12116

Melotone M12116, Polk P9063, Panachord P12116 as by **Al & Joe Blackburn**.

Acc. two unknowns, f; unknown, p; unknown, vc; unknown, chimes.
New York, NY   Tuesday, December 13, 1927

| E-25578/79* | Mandy Lee | Br 198, 3786 |

Acc. unknown orch. (six men), incl. Joe Green, vb.
New York, NY   Wednesday, December 14, 1927

E-25610/11	Good-bye, Little Girl, Good-bye	Br 467, 3807, BrAu 467, PanAu P12294
E-25612/13*; E-6901/02W	Love's Old Sweet Song	Vo 5195, Me M12045, Po P9056, PanAu P12045
E-25614/15	Just As The Sun Went Down	Br/Vo unissued

Melotone M12045, Polk P9056, Panachord P12045 as by **Al & Joe Blackburn**.

Acc. unknown, f; unknown, p; Carson Robison, g.
New York, NY   Wednesday, December 14, 1927

E-25592*/93; E-6849/50W	One Night As I Lay Dreaming	Vo 5194, Me M12038, Po P9020, PanAu P12038
E-25594/95*	Will The Circle Be Unbroken	Br 194, 3779, BrAu 3779, Spt S2019, DeE F3749, RexIr U428
E-25596*/97	When They Ring The Golden Bells	Br 194, 3779, BrAu 3779, Spt S2019, DeE F3749, RexIr U428

Melotone M12038, Polk P9020, Panachord P12038 as by **Al & Joe Blackburn**. Supertone S2019 as by **Lonesome Pine Twins**.

Frank McCravy, James McCravy, v duet; or **James McCravy**, v-1; acc. unknown, f; unknown, p; unknown, bj-2; unknown, g.
New York, NY   Monday, December 19, 1927

E-25676/77*	De's Bones Gwine Rise Again -2	Br 193, 3778, Spt S2020, DeSA FM5190
E-25678/79*	When The Saints Go Marching Home	Br 196, 3784, Spt S2023, DeE F3875, RexIr U431
E-25680*/81; E-6847/48W	What Are They Doing In Heaven Today -1	Vo 5194, Me M12038, Po P9020, PanAu P12038

Melotone M12038, Polk P9020, Panachord P12038 as by **Al Blackburn**. Supertone S2020, S2023 as by **Lonesome Pine Twins**.

Frank McCravy, v/sp; acc. Chris Chapman, eff.
New York, NY   Tuesday, December 20, 1927

| E-25702/03 | The Balking Mule | Br/Vo unissued |

Frank McCravy, James McCravy, v duet; acc. unknown orch. (five men).
New York, NY   Tuesday, December 20, 1927

| E-25704/05 | The Church Bells Are Ringing For Mary | Br/Vo unissued |
| E-25706/07 | Old Fashioned Locket | Br/Vo unissued |

Acc. unknown orch. (six men), incl. Frank Black, cel.
New York, NY   Thursday, December 22, 1927

E-25722/23*	The Trail Of The Lonesome Pine	Br 198, 3786
E-25724/25*	The Sweetest Story Ever Told	Vo 5196
E-25726*/27	Won't You Come Over To My House (Intro. "Daddy")	Vo 5196

Acc. unknown, f; unknown, p; unknown, g.
New York, NY   Monday, July 30, 1928

| E-27924- | So May You | Br 465 |
| E-27925- | Haven Of Rest | Br 504 |

Acc. unknown, f; unknown, p; unknown, bj-1; unknown, g-2.
New York, NY   Tuesday, July 31, 1928

E-27928-	Ring Dem Heavenly Bells -1	Br 4191, BrAu 4191, Me M12270, Po P9084, Spt S2023
E-27929-	Dip Me In The Golden Sea -1, 2	Br 4195, BrE 3958, BrAu 4195
E-27930-	No Hiding Place Down There (Sister Lucy) -1, 2	Br 4195, BrE 3958, BrAu 4195
E-27931-	Hide Away -1, 2	Br 4191, BrAu 4191, Me M12270, Po P9084
E-27932-A	Stand By Me -2	Br 504

Melotone 12270, Polk P9084 as by **Al & Joe Blackburn**. Supertone S2023 as by **Lonesome Pine Twins**.

Acc. unknown, f; unknown, p; unknown, g.
New York, NY   Wednesday, August 1, 1928

E-27938-	The Old Rugged Cross	Vo 5293
E-27939-	No More Dying	Br 444, BrAu 444
E-27940-	Looking This Way	Vo 5255
E-27941-	The Pearly White City	Br 465
E-27942-	When I Get To The End Of The Way	Br 444, BrAu 444

Acc. unknown, f; unknown, p; unknown, bj-1/g.
New York, NY   Thursday, August 2, 1928

E-27951-	One Of God's Days	Vo 5293
E-27952-	Look For Me -1	Br 380, DeE F3879
E-27953-	The Two Lives	Br 452
E-27954-	The Bird With The Broken Pinion	Br 4455, BrAu 4455, Spt S2022, PanAu P12214

Supertone S2022 as by **Lonesome Pine Twins**.

Acc. unknown, f; unknown, p; unknown, g.
New York, NY   Friday, August 3, 1928

E-27963-	When My Life Work Is Ended	Br 452
E-27964 1/2-	The Vacant Chair	Br 4455, BrAu 4455, Spt S2024, Au A22028, PanAu P12214
E-27972-	Beautiful City Of God	Br 380, DeE F3879
E-27973-	Trundle Bed	Vo 5255

Supertone S2024 as by **Lonesome Pine Twins**. Intervening matrices are unrelated.
Rev. Aurora A22028 by Vernon Dalhart.

New York, NY   Tuesday, December 4, 1928

E-28786-	We'll Never Say Good-bye	Br 406
E-28787-A,-B	Can A Boy Forget His Mother?	Br unissued
E-28788-A,-B	My Mother's Bible	Br unissued
E-28789-A,-B	Sing The Old Hymns To Me	Br unissued

Acc. unknown, f; unknown, p; unknown, bj-1/g.
   New York, NY   Wednesday, December 5, 1928

E-28790-	The Beautiful Garden Of Prayer	Br 406
E-28791-A,-B	Susan Jane -1	Br unissued
E-28792-	Cradle's Empty (Baby's Gone)	Br 4485, BrAu 4485
E-28793-	Daddy	Br 4485, BrAu 4485

Acc. unknown orch.
   New York, NY   Thursday, December 6, 1928

E-28794-	Just As The Sun Went Down	Br 467, BrAu 467
E-28795-A,-B	Sweet Marie	Br unissued
E-28796-	A Bird In A Gilded Cage	Br 4335, BrAu 4335, Spt S2022
E-28797-	Sweet Genevieve	Br 4391, BrAu 4391
E-28798-	Let Me Hear The Songs My Mother Used To Sing	Br 4391, BrAu 4391, Spt S2024
E-28799-	Sweet Adeline (You're The Flower Of My Heart)	Br 4335, BrAu 4335

Supertone S2022, S2024 as by **Lonesome Pine Twins**.

Acc. unknown, f; unknown, p; unknown, bj.
   New York, NY   Friday, December 7, 1928

E-28900-A,-B	Keep In The Middle Of The Road	Br unissued trial recording

McCravy Brothers (Frank & James), v duet; acc. unknown, f; Carson Robison, h; unknown, bj.
   New York, NY   Monday, December 17, 1928

46395-2	Dip Me In The Golden Sea	Vi V-40026, Zo/RZ 5528, Zo/RZAuEE210, ZoSA 4229
46396-2	Ring Them Heavenly Bells	Vi V-40026, Zo/RZ 5528, ZoSA 4229

Zonophone 4229 and possibly other Zonophone/Regal-Zonophone issues as by **McCravy Brothers** only.

Acc. unknown, f; Roy Smeck, h-1/g/jh; unknown, bj.
   New York, NY   Tuesday, December 18, 1928

46397-2	Trundle Bed	Vi V-40074, Zo/RZ 5576, ZoSA 4238
46398-1	Hide Away -1	Vi V-40104, Zo/RZ 5576, ZoSA 4237
46399-2	Sister Lucy -1	Vi V-40104, ZoSA 4237

Victor V-40074 as by **Frank & James McCravy**. Victor V-40104 and probably all Zonophone/Regal-Zonophone issues as by **McCravy Brothers** only.
Rev. Zonophone 4238 by Vaughan Quartet.

Acc. unknown, f; unknown, cl; unknown, bj.
   New York, NY   Tuesday, December 18, 1928

49000-2	Old-Fashioned Photograph Of Mother	Vi V-40074, ZoSA 4233

Victor V-40074 as by **Frank & James McCravy**.
Rev. Zonophone 4233 by Stamps Quartet.

Acc. unknown, f; unknown, t; Carson Robison, h/g; unknown, p; unknown, bj; Leonard Joy, dir.
   New York, NY   Monday, July 15, 1929

55610-1	The Dollar And The Devil	Vi V-40312
55611-1	Keep In The Middle Of The Road	Vi V-40312
55612-2	What Are They Doing In Heaven?	Vi V-40120

Victor V-40312 as by **McCravy Brothers** only.

Acc. two unknowns, f; unknown, c; unknown, p; Leonard Joy, cel; unknown g.
   New York, NY   Wednesday, July 17, 1929

53926-1	Sweet Marie	Vi V-40180, ZoSA 4293
53927-2	Prepare To Meet Your Mother	Vi V-40151, ZoSA 4250
53928-2	Can A Boy Forget His Mother?	Vi V-40120, MW M-4314

Victor V-40151, V-40180, and probably Zonophone 4293, 4250 as by **McCravy Brothers** only.
Rev. Montgomery Ward M-4314 by Frank Luther.

McCravy Brothers, v duet; acc. unknown, f; unknown, c; unknown, p; unknown, bj; unknown, g; Leonard Joy, dir.
   New York, NY   Thursday, July 18, 1929

53931-1	She Was Bred In Old Kentucky	Vi V-40203, ZoSA 4289
53932-1	Down Where The Cotton Blossoms Grow	Vi V-40203, ZoSA 4289
53933-1,-2	My Old Rose	Vi unissued

Acc. two unknowns, f; unknown, c; unknown, p; unknown, g; Leonard Joy, dir.
   New York, NY   Friday, July 19, 1929

53933-3	My Old Rose	Vi V-40180, ZoSA 4293
53938-1,-2	O Think Of The Home Over There	Vi unissued
53939-1,-2	Till We Meet Again (God Be With You)	Vi unissued
53940-2	Tell It Again	Vi V-40151, ZoSA 4250

Intervening matrices are unrelated.

New York, NY — Monday, December 16, 1929

57778-2	I Feel Like Going On	Vi V-40218, ZoSA 4330
57779-1	My Mother's Old Bible Is True	Vi V-40265, MW M-4254, M-4301, M-8204, ZoSA 4320
57780-1	He Cares For Our Souls, Not Our Sighs	Vi V-40218, ZoSA 4330
57781-1	I'll Be There	Vi V-40265, MW M-4301, ZoSA 4320

Rev. Montgomery Ward M-8204 by Criterion Quartet.

Frank & James McCravy, v duet; acc. two unknowns, f; unknown, p; unknown, bj.

New York, NY — Tuesday, March 11, 1930

9425-2,-3	The Better Home	Ba 0650, Ca 0250, Do 4605, Je 5907, Or 1907, Pe 12634, Re 10080, Ro 1270, Chg 876, Cq 7594, Htd 16063, 23036, Apex 41244, CrC/MeC 81462
9426-2,-3	Will The Circle Be Unbroken	Ba 0650, Ca 0250, Do 4527, Je 5907, Or 1907, Pe 12601, Re 8974, Ro 1270, Chg 876, Cq 7794, Htd 16063, 23036, ARC-Bwy 8194, Apex 41244, CrC/MeC 81462
9427-1,-2,-3	The Resurrection Morning	Ba 0679, Ca 0279, Do 4527, Je 5934, Or 1934, Pe 12601, Re 8974, Ro 1301, Cq 7794, Htd 16126, 23037

Matrix 9426 on ARC-Broadway 8194 (as by **Austin Brothers**) replaces the same title on Broadway 8194 by Westbrook Conservatory Entertainers (Gennett matrix GEX-2399-A).
Matrix 9427 is mistitled *The Ressurection Morning* on Homestead 16126.
Revs: Banner 0679, Cameo 0279, Jewel 5934, Oriole 1934, Romeo 1301, Homestead 16126, 23037 by The Pickard Family; ARC-Broadway 8194 by Westbrook Conservatory Entertainers.

Acc. unknown, f; unknown, g.

New York, NY — Thursday, March 20, 1930

E-32396-A,-B	The Resurrection Morning	Br cancelled
E-32397-A,-B	The Better Home	Br cancelled

Acc. unknown, f; unknown, g; unknown vc.

New York, NY — Monday, March 24, 1930

403877-A	When The Saints Go Marching Home	OK 45435, Ve 2296-V, Cl 5218-C, PaE R1069
403878-B	The Two Lives	OK 45466
403879-B	Can A Boy Forget His Mother	OK 45466

Velvet Tone 2296-V, Clarion 5218-C as by **McCravy Brothers**. Parlophone R1069 as by **The Sanctified Singers**.
Velvet Tone 2296-V, Clarion 5218-C use the transfer matrix 100467.

New York, NY — Wednesday, March 26, 1930

403850-	The Better Home	OK 45435, PaE R1189
403851-E	Will The Circle Be Unbroken	OK 45433, Ve 7095-V, Cl 5132-C
403852-D	The Resurrection Morning	OK 45433, Ve 7095-V, Cl 5132-C

OKeh 45433, Parlophone R1189 as by **McCravy Brothers**.

New York, NY — Friday, March 28, 1930

150145-1	The Better Home	Co 15617-D
150146-3	The Great Judgement Morning	Co 15544-D
150147-2	The Dollar And The Devil	Co 15544-D, ReE MR208
150148-1	No More Dying	Co 15617-D, ReE MR146, RZAu G21843

Revs: Regal MR146 by Tom Darby & Jimmie Tarlton, MR208 by Frank Luther; Regal-Zonophone G21843 by The Hillbilly Singers (Australian).

Acc. unknown orch.

New York, NY — Wednesday, April 2, 1930

150163-3	I Love You In The Same Old Way (Darling Sue)	Co 15764-D, RZAu G22060
150164-1	Don't Forget To Drop A Line To Mother	Co 15764-D, RZAu G22060

Acc. two unknowns, f; unknown, g.

New York, NY — Wednesday, April 23, 1930

403977-B	Leave It There	OK 45447, Ve 2297-V, Cl 5219-C, RZ MR1223, RZAu G22130
403978-B	Stand By Me	OK 45447, Ve 2296-V, Cl 5218-C, RZ MR1223, RZAu G22130
403979-B	I'm Homesick For Heaven	OK 45457, PaE R1189
403980-A	Swinging On The Golden Gate	OK 45457, Ve 2297-V, Cl 5219-C, PaE R1069, ReE MR433

Velvet Tone 2296-V, 2297-V, Clarion 5218-C, 5219-C, Parlophone R1189, Regal-Zonophone MR1223, G22130 as by **McCravy Brothers**. Parlophone R1069 as by **The Sanctified Singers**.
Velvet Tone 2296-V, Clarion 5218-C use the transfer matrix 100469; Velvet Tone 2297-V, Clarion 5219-C use the transfer matrix 100468.
Rev. Regal MR433 by Carson Robison & Frank Luther.

Acc. unknown, f; unknown, p-1; unknown, g.
   New York, NY   Thursday, April 24, 1930

E-32622-	The Dollar And The Devil	Br 424, Spt S2021
E-32623-	Good Lord Takin' Care Of The Poor Folks -1	Br 424, Spt S2021

Supertone S2021 as by **Lonesome Pine Twins**.

Acc. unknown, f; unknown, p; unknown, g.
   New York, NY   Thursday, September 4, 1930

9983-3	Jacob's Ladder	Ba 0830, Ca 0430, Do 4644, Je 6080, Or 2080, Pe 12645, Re 10136, Ro 1444, Cq 7795
9984-2	Dip Me In The Golden Sea	Ba 0831, Ca 0431, Do 4645, Je 6081, Or 2081, Pe 12646, Re 10137, Ro 1445, Cq 7859
9985-2	The Two Lives	Cq 7848
9986-1	The Dollar And The Devil	Ba 0831, Ca 0431, Do 4645, Je 6081, Or 2081, Pe 12646, Re 10137, Ro 1445, Cq 7859
9987-2	Des'e Bones Gwine Rise Again	Ba 32243, Or 8089, Pe 12741, Ro 5089, Cq 7847
9988-3	I Want To Go There	Ba 0830, Ca 0430, Do 4644, Je 6080, Or 2080, Pe 12645, Re 10136, Ro 1444, Cq 7795
9989-1	Bye And Bye	Ba 32355, Or 8115, Pe 12781, Ro 5115, Cq 7834, 7946
9990-3	What Are They Doing In Heaven Today	Cq 7848

Acc. unknown, f-1; unknown, 2nd f-2; unknown, sg-3; unknown, p-4; unknown, bj-5; unknown, g-6.
   New York, NY   Friday, September 5, 1930

9991-2	I Shall Not Be Moved -1, 2, 4	Ba 32308, Or 8103, Pe 12764, Ro 5103
9992-1	Don't Forget To Drop A Line To Mother -1, 4, 6	Ba 32084, Je 6174, Or 2174, Pe 12679, Re 10262, Ro 1550, Cq 7700
9993-2	Swinging On The Golden Gate -1, 4, 5	Ba 32243, Or 8089, Pe 12741, Ro 5089, Cq 7847
9994-3	No More Dying -	Ba 32209, Or 8078, Pe 12730, Ro 5078, Cq 7858
9995-1	Can A Boy Forget His Mother -1, 3, 4	Ba 32084, Je 6174, Or 2174, Pe 12679, Re 10262, Ro 1550, Cq 7700, Bwy 4061
9996-2	Hello Central Give Me Heaven -	Cq 7834
9997-2	I'm Homesick For Heaven Tonight -1, 6	Ba 32089, Je 6173, Or 2173, Pe 12678, Re 10289, Ro 1549, Cq 7799, CrC/Roy/Stg 91085
9998-1	Stand By Me -	Ba 32209, Or 8078, Pe 12730, Ro 5078, Cq 7858
9999-3	One Night As I Lay Dreaming -1, 4, 6	Ba 32088, Je 20040, Or 8040, Pe 12672, Re 10288, Ro 5040, Cq 7705, CrC/Roy/Stg 91084
10000-1,-2	Down By The Window Where My Mother Used To Pray -1, 4, 6	Ba 32088, Je 20040, Or 8040, Pe 12672, Re 10288, Ro 5040, Cq 7705, Bwy 4061, CrC/Roy/Stg 91084
10001-3	Look For Me -4, 5	Ba 32089, Je 6173, Or 2173, Pe 12678, Re 10289, Ro 1549, CrC/Roy/Stg 91085
10002-1	Leave It There -	Ba 32355, Or 8115, Pe 12781, Ro 5115, Cq 7946

Broadway 4061 as by **Austin Brothers**.
Revs: all issues of matrix 9991 by Gene Autry; Conqueror 7799 by Famous Garland Jubilee Singers (see *B&GR*).

Acc. two unknowns, f; unknown, p; unknown, g.
   New York, NY   Tuesday, September 9, 1930

10009-2,-3	It Came Upon The Midnight Clear	Ba 0872, Ca 0472, Do 4675, Je 6119, Or 2119, Pe 12655, Re 10178, Ro 1484, Cq 7992, Vo/OK 04491
10010-1,-2	Oh, Little Town Of Bethlehem	Ba 0872, Ca 0472, Do 4675, Je 6119, Or 2119, Pe 12655, Re 10178, Ro 1484, Cq 7992, Vo/OK 04491

Vocalion/OKeh 04491 as by **Frank & James McGravy**.

Acc. unknown, f-1; unknown, g; unknown, sb-2; unknown, chimes-3.
   New York, NY   c. November 10, 1930

1078-1	Jacob's Ladder -1	Cr 3078, *Vs 5048, Ge/JDs 3503, Davis DA20-1*
1079-1	Will The Circle Be Unbroken -1	Cr 3040, *Vs 5040, Ge/JDs 3500, Davis DA20-4*
1080-1	The Old Rugged Cross -	Cr 3041, *Vs 5040, Ge/JDs 3500*

1081-	The Two Lives -	Cr 3173, Htd 23028
1082-	No More Dying -	Cr 3173, Htd 23028
1083-2	I Shall Not Be Moved -1, 2	Cr 3041, Vs 5055, Ge/JDs 3504, Davis DA20-6
1084-2	When They Ring The Golden Bells -1, 3	Cr 3040, Pm 3274, Bwy 8255, Vs 5048, Ge/JDs 3503, Davis DA20-3
1085-1	Can A Boy Forget His Mother -1	Cr 3120, Htd 23030, Pm 3274, Bwy 8255, Vs 5074, Ge/JDs 3501
1088-1	I Want To Go There – Don't You? -1, 2	Cr 3078, Vs 5055, Ge/JDs 3504, Davis DA20-8

Varsity 5074 as by **McCravy Brothers**. Matrices 1086/87 are untraced.

Al & Joe Blackburn, v duet; acc. unknown, f; unknown, sg-1/g-2; unknown, o-3/p-4.
New York, NY   Thursday, December 18, 1930

E-35571-A,-B	While The Days Are Going By -1, 3	Me unissued
E-35572-	While The Days Are Going By -1, 4	Me M12074, Po P9057
E-35573-	The Life Boat -1, 4	Me M12185, Po P9058
E-35574-	The Great Judgement Morning -2, 4	Me M12137, Po P9059
E-35825-	I Have Read Of A Beautiful City -2, 4	Me M12074, Po P9057
E-35826-	Down By The Window Where My Mother Used To Pray -2, 4	Me M12137, Po P9059

Frank & James McCravy, v duet; acc. unknown, f; unknown, sg-1/bj-2/g-3; unknown, p.
New York, NY   Friday, December 19, 1930

E-35763-	I'm Going Through -2	Br 515, DeE F3896, RexIr U433
E-35764-	Is My Name Written There -3	Br 535, DeE F3864, RexIr U429
E-35765-	Sweeter Than All -3	Me M12185, Po P9058
E-35766-	My Father Is Rich In House And Lands (The Child Of A King) -3	Br 528
E-35767-	Shadows -1	Br 535, DeE F3864, RexIr U429
E-35768-	When The Shadows Flee Away -1	Br 515, DeE F3896, RexIr U433
E-35769-	Where We'll Never Grow Old -3	Br 528

Melotone M12185, Polk P9058 as by **Al & Joe Blackburn**.

Acc. unknown, f-1; unknown, g.
New York, NY   c. January 1931

1105-2	Dip Me In The Golden Sea	Cr 3205, Htd 23029, Pm 3292, Bwy 8250, Vs 5061, Ge/JD 3502, Davis DA20-2
1106-2	We Will Understand It Better Bye And Bye	Cr 3205, Htd 23029, Pm 3292, Bwy 8250, Vs 5061, Ge/JD 3502, Davis DA20-5
1107-2	One Night As I Lay Dreaming -1	Cr 3120, Htd 23030, Vs 5074, Ge/JD 3501, Davis DA20-7

Varsity 5074 as by **McCravy Brothers**.
Matrix 1106 is titled *Bye And Bye* on Paramount 3292, Broadway 8250, Varsity 5061, Gennett/Joe Davis 3502, Davis DA20-5; some of these issues use the control 1990.

Acc. unknown, f; unknown, p-1/cel-2; unknown, g.
New York, NY   Wednesday, October 28, 1931

E-37329-A	Over Yonder -2	Pan 25472
E-37330-	Remember Your Mother -1	Br 566, Pan 25576
E-37331-	We Shall Meet Bye And Bye -1	Pan 25171
E-37332-A	Does This Train Go To Heaven? -1	Br 572, Pan 25273
E-37324-	Wonderful Peace	Br unissued
E-37375-A	Sweet Peace, The Gift Of God's Love -1	Pan 25472
E-37376-	Softly And Tenderly -1	Br 566, Pan 25576
E-37377-	That Beautiful Land -1	Pan 25171

Despite the numerical irregularity, these matrices are listed in the order given in Brunswick files.

Acc. unknown, f-1; unknown, sg-2/g-3; unknown, p-4/cel-5.
New York, NY   Thursday, October 29, 1931

E-37336-	Sometime -2, 5	Me M12296, Po P9094, MeC/Roy 91317, Pan 25598
E-37337-A	Cast Thy Bread Upon The Waters -1, 3, 4	Me M12369, Pan 25358
E-37338-	Sunrise -1, 2, 3, 4	Me M12296, Po P9094, MeC/Roy 91317, Pan 25598
E-37339-	Sometime We'll Understand -1, 3, 4	Me unissued

Melotone M12296, M12369, Polk P9094 as by **Al & Joe Blackburn**.

Acc. unknown, f-1/vla-2; prob. Frank Novak, cl-3/ac-4/x-5; unknown, sg-6/bj-7/g-8; unknown, p; unknown, eff-9.
New York, NY   Friday, October 30, 1931

| E-37340-A | The Glorious Gospel Train -7, 9 | Br 572, Pan 25273 |

E-37341-	Nobody's Little Girl -1, 3, 8	Me M12325
E-37342-A	Just Tell Them That You Saw Me -1, 3, 8	Me M12325, Pan 25358
E-37343-	I've Grown So Used To You -1, 3, 8	Me M12507
E-37344-	The Girl I Loved In Sunny Tennesse -1, 4, 8	Me M12507
E-37345-A	I Want To Dream By The Old Mill Stream -2, 5, 6	Br 589, DeE F3876, RexIr U432
E-37346-A	The Sinner And The Song -1, 4, 8	Me M12369

Melotone M12325, M12369, M12507 as by **Al & Joe Blackburn**.

Acc. unknown, f; prob. Frank Novak, f-1/cl-2/ac-3/sb-3; unknown, p; unknown, bj-4/g-5.
New York, NY   Monday, November 2, 1931

E-37385-A	Why Can't We Be Sweethearts (Once Again?) -2, 5	Br 589, Pan 25170, DeE F3876, RexIr U432
E-37386-	(You Are Mine) 'Til The End Of The Waltz -2, 5	Me M12279, Po P9088, Pan 25170
E-37348-	When The Rest Of The Crowd Goes Home (I Always Go Home Alone) -1, 2, 5	Me M12279, Po P9088, Pan 25169
E-37349-	When I Wore My Daddy's Brown Derby -3, 4	Pan 25169

Melotone M12279, Polk P9088 as by **Al & Joe Blackburn**.
Matrix E-37348 is titled *When The Rest Of The Crowd Go Home* on Panachord 25169.
Matrices are listed in the order given in Brunswick files.

Mack Bros., v duet; acc. unknown f; unknown, 2nd f-1; unknown, sg-2/md-3; unknown, g.
New York, NY   Tuesday, January 29, 1935

39286-A	Get Away, Old Man, Get Away -2	De 5073
39287-A,-B	By The Old Swinging Bridge Across The Rim -3	De unissued
39288-A	Only A Rose Bud -3	De 5125
39289-A	On The Good Old Santa Fe -3	De 5073
39290-A,-B	That Silver Haired Daddy Of Mine -1, 3	De unissued
39291-A	Just Around The Bend (From The Rainbow's End) -3	De 5125

Acc. unknown, o.
New York, NY   Tuesday, January 29, 1935

| 39296-A | When I Take My Vacation In Heaven | De 5086 |
| 39297-A | My Mother's Evening Prayer | De 5086 |

Matrices 39292 to 39295 are popular.

CARL McCRAY

Carl McCray, v; acc. unknown.
Richmond, VA   Friday, October 18, 1929

| 403171- | When Grape Juice Turns To Wine | OK unissued |
| 403172- | Where Is My Mother? | OK unissued |

Carl McCray was a member of the Salem Highballers.

L.W. McCREIGHT
L.W. McCREIGHTON

See Dr. Claude Watson.

LEWIS McDANIELS

Roy Martin & His Guitar: Lewis McDaniels, v; acc. own g.
New York, NY   Thursday, March 27, 1930

| 9525-1,-2 | My Father Doesn't Love Me | Je 20004, Or 8004, Ro 5004, Htd 16116 |
| 9526- | The Hard Luck Soldier | ARC unissued |

Lewis McDaniels, v/y-1; acc. own g.
New York, NY   Friday, March 28, 1930

| 9537- | North Carolina Blues -1 | Je 20006, Or 8006, Pe 144, Ro 5006 |
| 9538-1,-2 | Down Among The Budding Roses | Je 20004, Or 8004, Pe 144, Ro 5004, Htd 16116 |

Revs: Jewel 20006, Oriole 8006, Romeo 5006 by Walter Smith.
At this session McDaniels also accompanied Walter Smith and participated in recordings by Dixie Ramblers [I].

Roy Martin: Lewis McDaniels, v; acc. own g.
New York, NY   Monday, May 5, 1930

| 9710- | The Drunkard's Child | ARC unissued |

New York, NY   Tuesday, May 6, 1930

9711-	Behind The Hen House	ARC unissued
9712-	Whisper Your Mother's Name	ARC unissued
9713-	Desert Blues	ARC unissued
9719-	Bye And Bye You Will Forget Me	ARC unissued

Matrix 9714 was logged as by Walter Smith, but see the note thereto in the latter's entry. Matrices 9715 to 9718 are by dancebands.
At this session McDaniels also accompanied and sang duets with Walter Smith.

Lewis McDaniel–Gid Smith, v duet; or Lewis McDaniels, v-1/y-2; or Walter Smith, v-3; acc. Walter Smith, h-4; Patt Patterson, sg-5; Lois Dexter, tbj-6; Lewis McDaniels, g.
   New York, NY   Monday, May 12, 1930

62220-2	I've Loved You So True -5, 6	Vi 23505
62221-2	It's Hard To Leave You, Sweet Love -5, 6	Vi V-40287
62222-2	I Went To See My Sweetheart -1, 5, 6	Vi 23505
62223-2	One More Kiss Before I Go -2, 3, 4	TT C-1560, Au 36-108
62224-2	We'll Talk About One Another	Vi V-40287
62225-2	My Father Doesn't Love Me -1, 2	TT C-1560, Au 36-108

Timely Tunes C-1560, and possibly Aurora 36-108, as by **Louis McDaniel–Gid Smith**.

Lewis McDaniels (as his name is correctly spelled) also recorded with the Carolina Buddies and Hawaiian Pals, and possibly with Patt Patterson.

McDEARIS STRING BAND

Prob. Owen McDearis, f; others unknown.
   Atlanta, GA   Thursday, April 19, 1928

146142-	Southern Seas	Co unissued
146143-	Dreams Of Love	Co unissued

JOHN A. McDERMOTT

John A. McDermott Pioneer Fiddler and Caller, f/calls; acc. Floyd Stanton, p.
   Chicago, IL   Friday, July 2, 1926

TC-EX1047/48 (EX19988*/90)	Virginia Reel Medley – Part I (Miss McLeod's Reel–Tramp, Tramp, Tramp, The Boys Are Marching–Virginia Reel–The Girl I Left Behind Me)	Br 20050, BrAu 20050

Australian Brunswick 20050 as by **John A. McDermott/Fiddler and Caller**. Matrix TC-EX1047/48 is titled *Virginia Reel Medley – Part I (Miss McLeod's Reel–Tramp, Tramp, Tramp, The Boys Are Marching)* on Australian Brunswick 20050. These are 12-inch issues.

   Chicago, IL   Saturday, July 3, 1926

TC-XE1050/49 (XE19989*/91)	Virginia Reel Medley – Part II (Miss McLeod's Reel–Tramp, Tramp, Tramp, The Boys Are Marching–Virginia Reel–The Girl I Left Behind Me)	Br 20050, BrAu 20050

Australian Brunswick 20050 as by **John A. McDermott/Fiddler and Caller**. Matrix TC-XE1050/49 is titled *Virginia Reel Medley – Part II (Virginia Reel–The Girl I Left Behind Me)* on Australian Brunswick 20050. These are 12-inch issues.

   Chicago, IL   Thursday, December 30, 1926

EX-TC1051 (EX21084)	Happy Bill Daniel's Quadrille (Part I)	Br 20053
EX-TC1052 (EX21085)	Happy Bill Daniel's Quadrille (Part II)	Br 20053

Brunswick 20053 is a 12-inch issue.

McDONALD BROTHERS

Vocal duet; acc. unknown, g.
   Dallas, TX   Wednesday, October 30, 1929

DAL-547-	Jack And Joe	Vo 5406
DAL-548-	Poor Little Joe	Vo 5406

McDONALD QUARTET[TE]

McDonald Quartette: Alvin McDonald, lv; Harold McDonald, tv; Ralph McDonald, bv; W.E. Smithmire, bsv; acc. unknown, p.
   Birmingham, AL   c. August 8, 1927

GEX-781-A	Working For The Master	Ge 6269, Ch 15330, Sil 5176, 8261, Spt 9140, Chg 342, Spr 365, Her 75581
GEX-782-A	Love Enough For Me	Ge 6269, Ch 15431, Sil 5209, 8172, Spt 9268, Chg 342, Spr 365, Her 75581

Champion 15330, 15431, Challenge 342, Herwin 75581 as by **Goodman Sacred Singers**. Supertone 9140 as by **Harris Quartet**, 9268 credit uncertain. Superior 365 credit uncertain.

540 McDonald Quartet[te]

Revs: Champion15330, Supertone 9140 by Woodlawn Quartette; Champion 15431, Supertone 9268, Superior 365 by Eva Quartette.

Richmond, IN   Tuesday, May 1, 1928

13730	On My Way With Jesus	Ge 6498
13731	That Beautiful Land	Ge 6466, Ch 15504
13732-A	Over In The Glory Land	Ge 6465
13733	Rocking On The Waves	Ge 6466, Ch 15547
13734-A	I Am Redeemed At Last	Ge 6465, Ch 15547
13735-A	Going Home	Ge 6581
13736	One At Last	Ge 6705
13737-A	Give The World A Smile	Ge 6581, Ch 15612
13738	He Knows How	Ge 6623
13739-A	Oh Declare His Glory	Ge 6467, Ch 15504
13740	Coming	Ge 6467
13741-A	Jesus Lead Me There	Ge 6515
13742-A	He'll Tell Us All About It	Ge 6498, Ch 15612
13743	What A Day That Will Be	Ge 6623
13744-A	Keep The Sunlight In Your Sky	Ge 6605
13745-A	I'm His At Last	Ge 6605
13746-A	My Happy Song	Ge 6563
13747	The Holy Trinity	Ge 6640
13748-A	Living On The Love Of God	Ge 6515
13749-A	Come On	Ge 6563
13750-A	While The Years Roll On	Ge 6468, Chg 402
13751	My Troubles Will Be Over	Ge 6468
13752-A	Glory Now Is Rising In My Soul	Ge 6705, Ch 15673
13753	Nearing My Long Sought Home	Ge 6640, Ch 15673

Champion 15504, 15547, 15612, 15673 as by **Goodman Sacred Singers**. Challenge 402 as by **Ellington Sacred Quartette**. Rev. Challenge 402 (with same credit) by Eva Quartette.

Lovelle McDonald, lv; Harold McDonald, tv; Ralph McDonald, bv; W.E. Smithmire, bsv; acc. unknown, p.

Richmond, IN   Thursday, December 6, 1928

14523	Do Your Best – Then Wear A Sunny Smile	Ge 6765, Ch 15713, 45150, Spt 9354, Chg 430, MW 4991
14524-A	I Love To Tell His Love	Ge 6917
14525-A	City Of Rest	Ge 6765
14526-A	The Gospel Tide Is Rolling On	Ge 6780
14527-A	Living For Christ Each Day	Ge 6962

Champion 15713, 45150 as by **Goodman Sacred Singers**. Supertone 9354 as by **Emerson Sacred Quartet**. Challenge 430 as by **Challenge Quartet**.

Richmond, IN   Friday, December 7, 1928

14528-A	Right Will Always Win	Ge 6962, Ch 15878, Spt 9504
14529-A	I Heard His Voice	Ge 6859
14530-A	I'm Happy With My Savior	Ge 7054, Ch 15878, Spt 9504
14531	Singing On The Journey Home	Ch 16100
14532-A	Keep Holding On	Ge 6859, Ch 15773, 45124, Spt 9354
14533	The Home Coming Week	Ge unissued
14535-A	Reapers Be True	Ge 7007
14536-A	Wonderful	Ge 7054
14537	Riding On The Glory Waves	Ge 6780, Ch 15713, 45150, Spt 9401, Chg 430, MW 4991
14538-A	A Happy Band	Ge 6917, Ch 15813
14539	The Glory Land Way	Ge 7007, Ch 16100, Spt 9503

Champion 15713, 15773, 15813, 15878, 16100, 45124, 45150 as by **Goodman Sacred Singers**. Supertone 9354 as by **Emerson Sacred Quartet**, 9503, 9504 as by **Harris Sacred Quartette**. Challenge 430 as by **Challenge Quartet**. Matrix 14534 is unrelated.

Richmond, IN   Saturday, December 8, 1928

14540	He's With Me All The Way	Ge 6811, Spt 9401
14541	Where We'll Never Grow Old	Ge 6811, Ch 15773, 45124, Spt 9503
14542-A	Love	Ge 6735
14543-A	Hallelujah! He's Mine	Ge 6735, Ch 15813

Champion 15773, 15813, 45124 as by **Goodman Sacred Singers**. Supertone 9503 as by **Harris Sacred Quartette**.

McDonald Quartet: Lovelle McDonald, lv; Harold McDonald, tv; Ralph McDonald, bv; Ancil Matthews, bsv; acc. unknown, p.

Atlanta, GA   Saturday, December 13, 1930

404701-	Christ Is Mine, Forever Mine	OK 45517
404702-B	Living For Jesus	OK 45538
404703-B	Singing To Victory	OK 45503
404704-A	The Glad Bells	OK 45503
404705-	The Precious Memories	OK 45517
404706-A	My Friend	OK 45538
404707-B	I'm No Stranger To Jesus	OK 45530
404708-B	He Keeps My Soul	OK 45530

McDonald Quartette: R.F. McDonald, W.H. Riggins, S.M. Harbuck, L.P. Nichols, v quartet; acc. unknown, p.

New York, NY   Thursday, September 15, 1932

12298-2	Working For The Master	Ba 32591, Me M12519, Or 8173, Pe 12851, Ro 5173, Cq 8008
12299-	Love Enough For Me	Ba 32869, Me M12796, Or 8270, Pe 12941, Ro 5270, Cq 8050
12300-2	Rocking On The Waves	Ba 33342, Me M13309, Or 8431, Pe 13112, Ro 5431, Cq 8053, 8502
12301-1	Give The World A Smile	Ba 32668, Me M12597, Or 8195, Pe 12881, Ro 5195
12302-1	Gypsy Love Song (Slumber On, My Little Gypsy Sweetheart) (Gypsy Yodel)	Ba 32590, Me M12517, MeC 91523, Or 8172, Pe 12850, Ro 5172, Cq 8065, Min M-912
12303-1	Way Down In Georgia	Ba 32589, Me M12518, Or 8171, Pe 12849, Ro 5171, Cq 8064, Broadcast International 111
12304-1	My Faith Is Clinging To Thee	Cq 8052, Bwy 4115
12305-2	Precious Memories	Ba 32592, Me M12520, Or 8174, Pe 12852, Ro 5174, Cq 8009

Broadcast International 111 as by **McDonald's Male Quartet**.
Revs: Minerva M-912 by Cliff Carlisle & Wilbur Ball; Broadcast International 111 by Carson Robison & Frank Luther.

New York, NY   Friday, September 16, 1932

12308-1	We'll Reap What We Sow	Cq 8053
12309-2	Love Lifted Me	Ba 32592, Me M12520, Or 8174, Pe 12852, Ro 5174, Cq 8009
12316-	My Redeemer Lives	Cq 8050
12317-1	We'll Never Say Goodbye	Ba 32869, Me M12796, Or 8270, Pe 12941, Ro 5270, Cq 8052
12318-1	Living For Jesus	Ba 33342, Me M13309, Or 8431, Pe 13112, Ro 5431, Cq 8502
12319-	Trying To Be Happy	Cq 8051

Intervening matrices are by popular artists on other dates.

New York, NY   Saturday, September 17, 1932

12320-1	Grandmother's Bible	Ba 32668, Me M12597, Or 8195, Pe 12881, Ro 5195, Cq 8051, Bwy 4115
12321-	The Blue Hills Of Virginia	ARC unissued
12322-	Nobody To Love	ARC unissued

New York, NY   Monday, September 19, 1932

12328-2	Roll On Blue Moon	Ba 32590, Me M12517, Or 8172, Pe 12850, Ro 5172, Cq 8065
12329-	By A Little Bayou	ARC unissued
12330-	Singing An Old Hymn	ARC unissued
12331-1	Happy With Him	Ba 32591, Me M12519, Or 8173, Pe 12851, Ro 5173, Cq 8008

New York, NY   Tuesday, September 20, 1932

12336-	Birmingham	ARC unissued
12337-	McDonald's Farm	ARC unissued
12338-1	Hurrah For Arkansas (In The Hills Of Arkansas)	Ba 32589, Me M12518, Or 8171, Pe 12849, Ro 5171, Cq 8064

The McDonald Quartet recorded after 1942.

McDONALD'S MALE QUARTET

This credit was used on Broadcast International for the McDonald Quartette.

OTIS McDONNELL

Otis McDonnell, v; acc. poss. own g.

Richmond, IN   Tuesday, August 25, 1931

| 17953 | Long Time Ago | Ge rejected trial recording |

MacDOWELL SISTERS

MacDowell Sisters "Sweethearts Of The Air": Edith MacDowell, Grace MacDowell, v duet; acc. one of them, sg; the other, g or u.
   poss. Kansas City, MO [unknown date]

256	In The Garden	Unity 402
258	God Is Love	Unity 402

Unity 402, pressed on a dark green flexible material, was produced for the Unity School of Christianity, Kansas City, MO.
Edith & Grace MacDowell also recorded for Victor in 1924 ("for personal use only," according to Victor files) and for Edison, but all these recordings are believed to be in the Hawaiian idiom.

MACEDONIA QUARTET

Fred McPhail, tv; Floyd Inman, tv; Spencer Smith, bv; C.E. Henderson, bsv; unacc.
   Memphis, TN   Monday, February 6, 1928

41848-1	Sweet Little Girl Of Mine	Vi 21293
41849-1	The House By The Side Of The Road	Vi 21293
41850-1	Who'll Be To Blame?	Vi 21576
41851-2	I Have Been Redeemed	Vi 21576

LESTER McFARLAND & ROBERT A. GARDNER

Lester McFarland, Robert A. Gardner, v duet; acc. Lester McFarland, h/md; Robert A. Gardner, g.
   New York, NY   Wednesday, October 13, 1926

E-3924*/25*W;	When The Roses Bloom Again	Vo 5027, Br 111, Spt S2028, Ba 32523, Or 8155,
E-21967*/68		Pe 12832, Ro 5155, Cq 8006

Supertone S2028 as by **Kentucky Mountain Boys**. ARC issues as by **Bob & Mac**.

Lester McFarland, v; acc. own h/g.
   New York, NY   Wednesday, October 13, 1926

E-3926W	Many Many Years Ago	Vo 5027

Lester McFarland, Robert A. Gardner, v duet; acc. Lester McFarland, f-1/md-2; Robert A. Gardner, g.
   New York, NY   Wednesday, October 13, 1926

E-3927/28*W;	Bully Of The Town -1	Vo 5026, Br 116
E-21932/33*		
E-3929W;	Pretty Polly -1	Vo 5026, Br 116
E-21934		
E-3930W;	There's No Disappointment In Heaven -2	Vo 5123, Br 111, Spt S2028
E-21969		
E-3931W	If I Could Hear My Mother Pray Again -2	Vo 5123

Supertone S2028 as by **Kentucky Mountain Boys**.

Acc. Lester McFarland, h-1/md; Robert A. Gardner, g.
   New York, NY   Thursday, October 14, 1926

E-3932W	When I Was Single	Vo 5122
E-3933W	Sarah Jane -1	Vo 5122
E-3934W;	Hand Me Down My Walking Cane -1	Vo 5028, Br 107, Spt S2032
E-21956		
E-3935W;	I Was Born Four Thousand Years Ago -1	Vo 5028, Br 110, Spt S2033, Au A22017
E-21966		
E-3936W;	I Will Sing Of My Redeemer	Vo 5124, Br 160, DeE F3873, RexIr U401
E-25682		
E-3937W;	When Our Lord Shall Come Again	Vo 5124, Br 160, DeE F3873, RexIr U401
E-25683		

Supertone S2032, S2033 as by **Kentucky Mountain Boys**. Aurora A22017 as by **Miller Brothers**. Decca F3873, Rex U401 as by **Mac & Bob**.
Rev. Aurora A22017 (with same credit) by Buell Kazee.

Lester McFarland & Robert A. Gardner, v duet; acc. Lester McFarland, h-1/md; Robert A. Gardner, g; or **Lester McFarland**-2, v; acc. own g; or **Robert A. Gardner**-3, v; acc. own g.
   New York, NY   Saturday, October 16, 1926

E-3950W	Midnight On The Stormy Deep	Vo 5125
E-3951W	Careless Love -1	Vo 5125
E-3952W	Casey's Whistle -2	Br/Vo unissued
E-3953*/54W	Clover Blossom -3	Vo 5126
E-3955/56W;	Down By The Riverside	Vo 5127, Br 108
E-21959/60		

E-3957W	The Lonesome Valley -1	Vo 5127
E-3958W; E-21962	Are You Tired Of Me, Darling?	Vo 5128, Br 109, BrC 432, Spt S2039
E-3959W; E-21961	You're As Welcome As The Flowers In May -2	Vo 5128, Br 108, Spt S2037, Au A22012
E-3960W; E-21963	You Give Me Your Love And I'll Give You Mine -2	Vo 5129, Br 109, BrC 432, Spt S2039
E-3961W	Don't You Remember The Time -1	Vo 5129
E-3962W	Somebody Knows -3	Vo 5130
E-3963W	Love Always Has Its Way -2	Vo 5130

Supertone S2037, S2039 as by **Kentucky Mountain Boys**. Aurora A22012 as by **Miller Brothers**.
Matrix E-3959W is titled *You're As Welcome As The Flower In May* on Supertone S2037.

Lester McFarland & Robert A. Gardner, v duet; acc. Lester McFarland, md; Robert A. Gardner, g; or **Lester McFarland**-1, v; acc. own g.

New York, NY   Friday, December 10, 1926

E-4208*/09*W; E-21964/65*	Knoxville Girl	Vo 5121, Br 110
E-4210/11W	Chattanooga Blues -1	Vo 5121
E-4212*/13*W	Old Black Sheep	Vo 5120
E-4214*/15*W; E-21957*/58	My Carolina Home	Vo 5120, Br 107
E-4220/21W	St. Louis Blues -1	Br/Vo unissued
E-4222/23W	Tennessee Jail Bird	Br/Vo unissued

Matrix E-4208/09W is titled *Knoxville Gal* on Brunswick 110.
Intervening matrices are by the Old Southern Sacred Singers, of whom McFarland and Gardner were part.

Lester McFarland & Robert A. Gardner, v duet; or Robert A. Gardner, v-1; acc. Lester McFarland, f-2/h-3/md; one of them, k-4; Robert A. Gardner, g.

New York, NY   Tuesday, May 3, 1927

E-22880*/81/82; E-6594/95/96W	He Carved His Mother's Name Upon The Tree -1	Vo 5188, Br 171, Spt S2029, Au A22033
E-22883/84; E-6555/66-W	The Texas Ranger -1, 2	Vo 5177, Br 168
E-22885/86/87; E-6446/47/48W	The Bright Sherman Valley -3	Vo 5174, Br 169, Spt S2031
E-22888/89*; E-6606/07W	The Blind Child's Prayer	Vo 5184, Br 167
E-22890/91*; E-6591W	Three Leaves Of Shamrock -3	Vo 5187, Br 170, Me M12075, M12608, Po P9053, Ba 32680, Or 8199, Pe 12885, Ro 5199, Cq 8061, Bwy 4089, DeE F3664, RexIr U601
E-22892/93*; E-6592/93W	Gentle Anna -1	Vo 5187, Br 170, Me M12075, Po P9053, Bwy 4088
E-22894/95*; E-6597/98W	'Tis Home Because Mother Is There -3	Vo 5188, Br 171, Spt S2029, Au A22033
E-22896/97*; E-6545/46W	I'll Be All Smiles Tonight	Br 164, DeE F3929, RexIr U406
E-22898/99	Dublin Bay -1, 4	Br/Vo unissued

Supertone S2029, S2031 as by **Kentucky Mountain Boys**. Me M12075, Po P9053 as by **Bob Lester & Bud Green**. Banner 32680, Melotone M12608, Oriole 8199, Perfect 12885, Romeo 5199, Conqueror 8061, Decca F3664, Rex U601 as by **Mac & Bob**. Broadway 4088, 4089 as by **Parsons & Kent**. Aurora A22033 as by **Miller Brothers**. Vocalion 5188 may not have been issued.

Lester McFarland & Robert A. Gardner, v duet; acc. Lester McFarland, h-1/md; Robert A. Gardner, g; or Lester McFarland-2, v; acc. own h-3/g/sp-4; Robert A. Gardner, sp-4; unknown, train-wh eff-5.

New York, NY   Friday, May 6, 1927

E-23027/28*; E-6608/09W	The Letter That Came Too Late -2, 3	Vo 5184, Br 167
E-23029/30*; E-6115/16W	Casey's Whistle -2, 5	Vo 5126, Br 163
E-23031/32*; E-6553/54W	Joe Turner's Blues -2, 4	Vo 5177, Br 168
E-23033/34	Can You, Sweetheart, Keep A Secret?	Br/Vo unissued
E-23035*/36; E-6547/48W	I'm Free Again -1	Br 164, DeE F3929, RexIr U406
E-23037*/38	The Tennessee Jail Bird	Br 163

| E-23039/40*;
E-6449/50W | The East Bound Train | Vo 5174, Br 169, Spt S2032 |

Matrices E-23030, E-23032 (but not E-23028) as by **Lester McFarland**. Supertone S2032 as by **Kentucky Mountain Boys**. DeE F3929, RexIr U406 as by **Mac & Bob**.

Lester McFarland & Robert A. Gardner, v duet; acc. Lester McFarland, h-1/md; Robert A. Gardner, g.

New York, NY — Wednesday, December 7, 1927

E-25453/54; E-6907/08W	Where Is My Mamma	Vo 5197
E-25455/56; E-6909/10W	Don't Grieve Your Mother -1	Vo 5197
E-25467/68; E-7330/31W	The Baggage Coach Ahead	Vo 5200, Br 200, 3788, BrC 326, Au A22013
E-25469/70; E-7332/33W	The Lightning Express -1	Vo 5200, Br 200, 3788, BrC 326, Au A22013
E-25471*/72	The Two Orphans -1	Br 202, 3790, Spt S2026
E-25473*/74	You'll Never Miss Your Mother Till She's Gone -1	Br 202, 3790, Spt S2026

Supertone S2026 as by **Kentucky Mountain Boys**. Aurora A22013 as by **Miller Brothers**. Intervening matrices are by other artists.

New York, NY — Thursday, December 8, 1927

E-25475*/76	Weeping Willow Tree -1	Br 199, 3787, BrAu 3787, PanAu P12180
E-25477/78*	Seeing Nellie Home (Quilting Party) -1	Br 199, 3787, BrAu 3787, PanAu P12180
E-25479*/80; E-6859/60W	Sweet Allalee -1	Vo 5199
E-25481/82; E-6857/58W	Whispering Hope	Vo 5192

Panachord P12180 as by **McFarland & Gardner**.

New York, NY — Friday, December 9, 1927

E-25487*/88; E-6915/16W	Lay My Head Beneath The Rose -1	Vo 5199
E-25489/90; E-6919/20W	I'll Remember You Love In My Prayers	Br/Vo unissued
E-25491/92; E-6921/22W	Can You, Sweetheart, Keep A Secret	Br/Vo unissued

Acc. unknown, f; unknown, p; Lester McFarland, md; Robert A. Gardner, g.

New York, NY — Saturday, December 10, 1927

E-25517/18*	The Old Rugged Cross	Br 190, 3781, BrAu 3781, Pan 25180
E-25519/20; E-6855/56W	Beautiful Isle Of Somewhere	Vo 5192
E-25521/22*	In The Garden	Br 201, 4055, BrAu 4055, Spt S2118, DeE F3928, RexIr U405

Supertone S2118 as by **Perry Brothers**. Decca F3928, Rex U405 as by **Mac & Bob**. Panachord 25180 as by **McFarland & Gardner**.
Rev. Supertone S2118 by Homer Rodeheaver (sacred).

Acc. Lester McFarland, h-1/md; Robert A. Gardner, g.

New York, NY — Tuesday, December 13, 1927

E-25580*/81: E-6853*/54W	My Wild Irish Rose	Vo 5191, Me M12175, Cq 8060
E-25582*/83; E-6851*/52W	Where The River Shannon Flows	Vo 5191, Me M12175, M12608, Ba 32680, Or 8199, Pe 12885, Ro 5199, Cq 8060, Bwy 4089, DeE F3664, RexIr U601
E-25584*/85*	The Drunkard's Dream	Br 203, 3791, Spt S2027
E-25586*/87	May I Sleep In Your Barn, Tonight, Mister? -1	Br 203, 3791, Spt S2027
E-25588/89; E-6923/24W	When I'm Gone You'll Soon Forget	Vo 5201
E-25590/91*	Sweet Hour Of Prayer	Br 201, 4055, BrAu 4055, DeE F3928, RexIr U405

Supertone S2027 as by **Kentucky Mountain Boys**. Melotone M12175 as by **Bob Lester & Bud Green**. Banner 32680, Melotone M12608, Oriole 8199, Perfect 12885, Romeo 5199, Conqueror, Decca F3664, Rex U601 as by **Mac & Bob**. Broadway 4089 as by **Parsons & Kent**.

New York, NY — Thursday, December 15, 1927

| E-25616/17;
E-6925/26W | When You're Gone I Won't Forget | Vo 5201 |
| E-25618/19;
E-6911/12W | Where Is My Boy, Tonight? | Vo 5198 |

E-25620-21; E-6913/14W	If You Love Your Mother (Meet Her In The Skies) -1	Vo 5198
E-25622/23; E-6929/30W	Give My Love To Nell, O! Jack -1	Vo 5202
E-25624/25; E-6927/28W	The Broken Engagement	Vo 5202

Acc. unknown, f; unknown, p; Lester McFarland, md; Robert A. Gardner, g-1.
New York, NY   Thursday, December 15, 1927

E-25632/33*	Rock Of Ages	Br 190, 3781, BrAu 3781, Spt S2117, Pan 25180
E-25634/35*	Let The Rest Of The World Go By -1	Br 195, 3780, BrAu 3780
E-25636*/37	I'm Forever Blowing Bubbles -1	Br 195, 3780, BrAu 3780
E-25638/39	Call Me Back, Pal, O'Mine -1	Br/Vo unissued

Supertone S2117 as by **Perry Brothers**. Australian Brunswick 3780 as by **L. McFarland & R.A. Gardner**. Australian Brunswick 3781, Panachord 25180 as by **McFarland & Gardner**. Rev. Supertone S2117 by Old Southern Sacred Singers.

Acc. Lester McFarland, h-1/md; Robert A. Gardner, g.
New York, NY   Monday, August 13, 1928

E-28046-	The Last Mile Of The Way	Vo 5285
E-28047-	Call Me Back, Pal O' Mine	Vo 5364
E-28048-	Call Me Back Again	Vo 5285
E-28049-	The Kentucky Bride's Fate -1	Br 305, Spt S2035

Supertone S2035 as by **Kentucky Mountain Boys**.

New York, NY   Tuesday, August 14, 1928

E-28062-	Little Nell	Br 286
E-28063-	Nobody's Darling -1	Vo 5381
E-28064-	Go And Leave Me If You Wish To -1	Br 293
E-28065-	In The Shadow Of The Pines -1	Vo 5364
E-28066-	The Murder Of J. B. Markham [sic] -1	Br 305, Spt S2035
E-28067-	Soldier Boy In Blue	Vo 5259

Supertone S2035 as by **Kentucky Mountain Boys**.

Lester McFarland, Robert A. Gardner, v duet; or **Robert A. Gardner**-1, v; acc. Lester McFarland, h/md; Robert A. Gardner, g.
New York, NY   Wednesday, August 15, 1928

E-28085-	The Old Village Church	Br 286, Spt S2038
E-28086-	The Dollar And The Devil	Vo 5322
E-28087-	Tennessee Jail Bird	Br 316
E-28088-	In Kansas -1	Vo 5411
E-28089-	Rosenthal's Goat	Vo 5322
E-28094-	While I Was In Arkansas	Vo 5411
E-28095-	Shivering in The Cold	Vo 5381
E-28096-	The Drunkard's Own Child	Vo 5307

Supertone S2038 as by **Kentucky Mountain Boys**.
Intervening matrices are unrelated.

New York, NY   Thursday, August 16, 1928

E-28097-	Hold Fast To The Right	Vo 5259
E-28098-	Birmingham Jail	Br 293, Spt S2031
E-28099-	Woman Suffrage	Br 316

Supertone S2039 as by **Kentucky Mountain Boys**.

Acc. Lester McFarland, h-1/md; Robert A. Gardner, g.
New York, NY   Monday, February 18, 1929

E-29350-	I Love You The Best Of All -1	Br 339
E-29351-	The Orphan Girl -1	Vo 5369
E-29352-A	The Drunkard's Child's Plea -1	Br 570, DeE F3784, RexIr U399
E-29353-	The Dying Girl's Message -1	Vo 5369
E-29354-	There's No One Like Mother To Me -1	Br 332, BrAu 332, Au A22012, Pan 25274, PanAu P12187, DeE F3894, RexIr U402
E-29355-	The Old Cottage Home	Br 332, BrAu 332, Pan 25274, DeE F3894, RexIr U402

Aurora A22012 as by **Miller Brothers**. Panachord 25274, P12187 as by **McFarland & Gardner**. Decca F3784, F3894, Rex U399, U402 as by **Mac & Bob**.

New York, NY   Tuesday, February 19, 1929

| E-29356-A,-B | The Reply To The Weeping Willow -1 | Br unissued |
| E-29357- | The City Of Sighs And Tears -1 | Vo 5392 |

E-29358-	On The Road To Happiness -1	Br 339
E-29359-A	You're Going To Leave The Old Home Jim (There's A Mother Waiting You At Home Sweet Home)	Br 311, Spt S2037, DeE F3908, RexIr U404
E-29360-	Put My Little Shoes Away -1	Br 322, Spt S2038
E-29361-	The Dying Girl's Farewell -1	Vo 5307
E-29362-	She's The Tie That Binds -1	Br 322

Supertone S2037, S2038 as by **Kentucky Mountain Boys**. Decca F3908, Rex U404 as by **Mac & Bob**.

Acc. Lester McFarland, h/md; Robert A. Gardner, g.
New York, NY   Wednesday, February 20, 1929

E-29363-A	Just Plain Folks	Br 311, Spt S2033, DeE F3908, RexIr U404
E-29364-A	The Orphan Boy	Br 570, DeE F3784, RexIr U399
E-29365-A,-B	Mary Of The Wild Moor	Br unissued

Supertone S2033 as by **Kentucky Mountain Boys**. Decca F3784, F3908, Rex U399, U404 as by **Mac & Bob**.

Acc. Lester McFarland, h-1/md; Robert A. Gardner, g.
New York, NY   Thursday, February 21, 1929

E-29366-	Carolina Moon	Br 307, BrAu 307, DeSA FM5188
E-29367-	Always In The Way -1	Vo 5392
E-29368-	I Wish I Had Died In My Cradle (Before I Grew Up To Love You)	Br 307, BrAu 307, PanAu P12187, DeSA FM5188

Panachord P12187 as by **McFarland & Gardner**; the parenthesised part of the title of matrix E-29368 is omitted on that issue.

New York, NY   Monday, June 17, 1929

E-30044-A	A Picture No Artist Can Paint	Br 350, BrAu 350, Spt S2036, Au A22024, DeE F3785, PanAu P12245, RexIr U400
E-30045-	My Old New Hampshire Home -1	Br 409, BrAu 409
E-30046-	In The Valley Of Kentucky -1	Br 366, PanAu P11994
E-30047-	Sunny Tennessee -1	Br 409, BrAu 409
E-30048-	Old And Only In The Way	Br rejected
E-30049-	The Hut On The Back Of The Lot	Br rejected
E-30150-A,-B	The Songs My Mother Used To Sing -1	Br rejected
E-30151-	Home Sweet Home In Tennessee	Br 366, PanAu P11994
E-30152-A,-B	'Tis Sweet To Be Remembered -1	Br rejected

Supertone S2036 as by **Kentucky Mountain Boys**. Aurora A22024 as by **Miller Brothers**. Decca F3785, Rex U400 as by **Mac & Bob**. Panachord P11994 as by **The Radio Duo**, P12245 as by **McFarland & Gardner**.

New York, NY   Tuesday, June 18, 1929

E-30153-	The Tramp -1	Br 398, Spt S2030
E-30154-A,-B	The Death Of My Mother-In-Law -1	Br rejected
E-30155-A,-B	A Woman's Tongue Will Never Rest -1	Br rejected
E-30156-A,-B	Will You Love Me When I'm Old -1	Br rejected
E-30157-A,-B	Man, Poor Man -1	Br rejected
E-30158-	The Cross On The Prison Floor	Br 398, Spt S2030
E-30159-A,-B	Don't Fall Too Deep In Love -1	Br rejected
E-30160-A,-B	When The Leaves Begin To Fall	Br rejected
E-30161-A,-B	I Took It -1	Br rejected

Supertone S2030 as by **Kentucky Mountain Boys**.

Acc. Lester McFarland, h/md-1/bj-2; Robert A. Gardner, g.
New York, NY   Wednesday, June 19, 1929

E-30162-	When The Harvest Days Are Over -1	Br 356
E-30163-	The Romance Ended -1	Br 356
E-30164-A,-B	Loreina -2	Br rejected
E-30165-A	Little Log Cabin In The Lane -2	Br 350, BrAu 350, Spt S2036, Au A22024, DeE F3785, RexIr U400

Supertone S2036 as by **Kentucky Mountain Boys**. Aurora A22024 as by **Miller Brothers**. Decca F3785, Rex U400 as by **Mac & Bob**.

Acc. Lester McFarland, md; Robert A. Gardner, g.
New York, NY   Saturday, June 22, 1929

| E-30178- | Pagan Love Song | Br 334, BrAu 334 |
| E-30179- | Blue Hawaii | Br 334, BrAu 334 |

Acc. Lester McFarland, h/md; Robert A. Gardner, g.
Knoxville, TN   Sunday, March 30, 1930

| K-8046- | Where The Sweet Magnolias Bloom | Br 426, BrAu 426 |
| K-8047- | My Little Georgia Rose | Br 426, BrAu 426 |

Acc. Lester McFarland, h-1/md; Robert A. Gardner, g.

Knoxville, TN — Thursday, April 3, 1930

Matrix	Title	Issues
K-8068-A	I've Grown So Used To You -1	Vo 02781, RZAu G22312
K-8069-	If I Only Could Blot Out The Past	Br unissued
K-8070-	The Prisoner Is My Son	Br rejected
K-8071-	Twenty One Years Is A Long Time	Br rejected
K-8072-B	The Unmarked Grave -1	Br 548, DeE F3895, PanAu P12251, RexIr U403
K-8073-B	The Mansion Of Aching Hearts	Br 548, DeE F3895, PanAu P12251, RexIr U403
K-8074-	Will The Roses Bloom In Heaven -1	Br 461, DeE F3930, RexIr U407
K-8075-	Asleep At The Switch	Br 461, DeE F3930, RexIr U407

Vocalion 02781, Regal-Zonophone G22312, Panachord P12251 as by **McFarland & Gardner**. Decca F3895, F3930, Rex U403, U407 as by **Mac & Bob**.

New York, NY — Monday, June 16, 1930

Matrix	Title	Issues
E-32973-A	The Prisoner Is My Son -1	Br 578
E-32974-A	Hello, Central! Give Me Heaven	Br 479, BrAu 479, Me M12273, PanAu P12273
E-33125-A,-B	And A Little Child Shall Lead Them -1	Br unissued
E-33126-A	On The Banks Of The Wabash -1	Br 479, BrAu 479, Me M12273, PanAu P12273
E-33128-A	Send The Light -1	Pan 25606
E-33129-A	When I Take My Vacation In Heaven -1	Pan 25606
E-33130-A,-B	Only Flirting -1	Br rejected
E-33131-A,-B	(I Said Goodbye To Everything) When I Said Goodbye To You -1	Br unissued
E-33132-A	The Hills Of Carolina -1	Br 466, BrAu 466

Melotone M12273 probably as by **Bob Lester & Bud Green**. Panachord 25606, P12273 as by **McFarland & Gardner**. Matrix E-32974 is titled *Hello, Central! Give Me Heaven* (*Hello Central – Give Me Heaven*) on Australian Brunswick 479.

New York, NY — Tuesday, June 17, 1930

Matrix	Title	Issues
E-33127-A	Carry Me Back To Old Virginny -1	Br 475, BrAu 475, DeE F3732, DeIr W4159, RexIr U398
E-33133-A,-B	I Left Ireland And Mother	Br unissued
E-33134-B	Does True Love Live Today? -1	Me M12233, Cq 8003, Bwy 4092, Pan 25103, PanAu P12233
E-33135-A	Two Little Girls Loved One Little Boy	Me M12233, Cq 8003, Bwy 4091, Pan 25103, PanAu P12233
E-33136-A,-B	The Spider And The Fly	Br unissued
E-33137-A	What Does The Deep Sea Say -1	Br 483, BrAu 483, Ba 32523, Or 8155, Pe 12832, Ro 5155, Cq 8006
E-33138-A	There's Somebody Waiting For Me -1	Vo 02760, RZAu G22274
E-33139-A	Sadie Ray -1	Me M12271, Po P9085, Bwy 4090

Melotone, Polk, and Panachord issues as by **Bob Lester & Bud Green**. ARC issues of matrix E-33137 as by **Bob & Mac**. Vocalion 02760, Regal-Zonophone G22274 as by **McFarland & Gardner**. Broadway 4090, 4091, 4092 as by **Parsons & Kent**. Decca F3732, W4159, Rex U398 as by **Mac & Bob**.
Matrix E-33135 is titled *Two Little Girls Love One Little Boy* on Panachord P12233.
Intervening matrices are by other artists.

New York, NY — Wednesday, June 18, 1930

Matrix	Title	Issues
E-32515-A	When You Know You're Not Forgotten, By The Girl You Can't Forget	Br 586
E-32516-A	Home Sweet Home	Br 475, BrAu 475, DeE F3732, DeIr W4159, PanAu P12294, RexIr U398
E-33143-A	Diamonds And Roses	Me M12271, Po P9085, Cq 8061, Bwy 4092
E-33144-A	I'm Tying The Leaves So They Won't Come Down	Br 586
E-33145-A,-B	Perished In The Snow -1	Br rejected
E-33146-A	Simple To Flirt -1	Br 578
E-33147-A,-B	The Royal Telephone -1	Br rejected

Melotone M12271, Polk P9085 as by **Bob Lester & Bud Green**. Broadway 4092 as by **Parsons & Kent**. Decca F3732, W4159, Rex U398 as by **Mac & Bob**.
Rev. Panachord P12294 by McCravy Brothers.

New York, NY — Thursday, June 19, 1930

Matrix	Title	Issues
E-33148-A,-B	When It's Springtime In The Rockies	Br unissued
E-33149-	When It's Springtime In The Rockies	Br 439, BrAu 439, Spt S2034, PanAu P12216
E-33150-A,-B	Will It Pay -1	Br unissued
E-33151-A,-B	She's More To Be Pitied Than Censured -1	Br rejected
E-33152-A,-B	Out In The Cold World	Br rejected
E-33153-A,-B	A Comical Ditty -1	Br rejected

Supertone S2034 as by **Kentucky Mountain Boys**. Panachord P12216 as by **McFarland & Gardiner**.

New York, NY   Friday, June 20, 1930

E-33154-A,-B	In Kentucky -1	Br unissued
E-33155-A,-B	Love's Ship	Br rejected
E-33156-	Dancing With Tears In My Eyes	Br 439, BrAu 439, BrSA 454, PanAu P12216
E-33157-	Somewhere In Old Wyoming	Br 438, BrAu 438, BrSA 454, Spt S2034
E-33158-A,-B	Lazy Lou'siana Moon	Br unissued
E-33159-A	Lazy Lou'siana Moon	Br 438, BrAu 438

Supertone S2034 as by **Kentucky Mountain Boys**. Panachord P12216 as by **McFarland & Gardiner**.
Matrix E-33159 is titled *Lazy Louisiana Moon* on Australian Brunswick 438.
Brunswick 454 was pressed in the U.S. for export to South Africa.

New York, NY   Monday, June 23, 1930

| E-33160-A | By The Honeysuckle Vine | Br 551, Pan 25110, PanAu P12252 |
| E-33161-A | Where The Ozarks Kiss The Sky | Br 551, Pan 25110, PanAu P12252 |

Panachord 25110, P12252 as by **McFarland & Gardner**.

New York, NY   Tuesday, June 24, 1930

E-33167-A,-B	Old And Only In The Way -1	Br rejected
E-33168-A,-B	The Death Of My Mother-In-Law -1	Br rejected
E-33228-	Melancholy Moon	Br 451
E-33229-B	Down The River Of Golden Dreams	Br 466, BrAu 466

Acc. Lester McFarland, h-1/md; unknown or McFarland, bj-2; Robert A. Gardner, g.

New York, NY   Wednesday, June 25, 1930

E-33169-	My Heart Belongs To The Girl Who Belongs To Somebody Else	Br 451
E-33170-A	Twenty-One Years -1	Br 483, BrAu 483, DeE F3117, DeIr W4155, PanAu P12174
E-33171-A	Loreina -1, 2	Pan 25617
E-33172-B	Will You Love Me When I'm Old? -1	Pan 25617

Panachord 25617, P12174 as by **McFarland & Gardner**. Decca F3117, W4155 as by **Mac & Bob**; matrix E-33170 is titled *Twenty-One Years – Part 1* on those issues.
Rev. Panachord P12174 by Carson Robison.

Atlanta, GA   Thursday, November 13, 1930

ATL-6619-	Love's Ship	Br 527
ATL-6620-A	She's More To Be Pitied Than Censured	Me M12241, Cq 8004, Bwy 4090, Pan 25182
ATL-6621-A	'Tis Sweet To Be Remembered	Me M12241, Cq 8004, Bwy 4091, Pan 25182
ATL-6622-	When The Leaves Begin To Fall	Br 561
ATL-6623-	Old And Only In The Way	Br unissued
ATL-6624-	Only Flirting	Br unissued
ATL-6625-A	The Hut On The Back Of The Lot -1	Vo 02781, RZAu G22312
ATL-6626-	Perished In The Snow	Br 561
ATL-6627-	The Royal Telephone	Br 537
ATL-6628-	Don't Fall Too Deep In Love	Br unissued
ATL-6629-	Out In The Cold World	Br 568, Pan 25473
ATL-6630-	The Songs My Mother Used To Sing	Br 568, Pan 25473
ATL-6639-	Alabama Lullaby	Br 499
ATL-6640-	Come Back Tonight In My Dreams	Br 492
ATL-6641-	Gee, But I'm Lonesome Tonight	Br 527
ATL-6642-	I'm Alone Because I Love You	Br 492
ATL-6643-	When Your Hair Has Turned To Silver (I Will Love You Just The Same)	Br 499
ATL-6644-	It Pays To Serve Jesus	Br 537

Vocalion 02781, Regal-Zonophone G22312, Panachord 25473 as by **McFarland & Gardner**. Melotone M12241, Panachord 25182 as by **Bob Lester & Bud Green**. Conqueror 8004 as by **Mac & Bob**. Broadway 4090, 4091 as by **Parsons & Kent**. Intervening matrices are by other artists on November 12.

Acc. unknown, f; Lester McFarland, md; Robert A. Gardner, g.

New York, NY   Thursday, March 5, 1931

E-36275-	Tears	Br 520, Spt S2259
E-36276-	Rocky Mountain Rose	Br 525, PanAu P11986
E-36277-	Little Sweetheart Of The Mountains	Br 520, Spt S2259, S2262, PanAu P12245

Supertone S2259 as by **Harper Brothers**; this issue may have been withdrawn shortly after release. Supertone S2262 as by **Kentucky Mountain Boys**. Panachord P11986 as by **The Radio Duo**, P12245 as by **McFarland & Gardner**.

New York, NY   Saturday, March 7, 1931

| E-36286-A | The Little Old Church In The Valley | Br 524, Spt S2261 |
| E-36287- | You'll Be Mine In Apple Blossom Time | Br 524, PanAu P11983, P11986 |

E-36288- Shine On Harvest Moon Br 525, Spt S2262

Supertone S2261, S2262 as by **Kentucky Mountain Boys**. Panachord P11983, P11986 as by **The Radio Duo**.
Rev. Panachord P11983 popular.

Acc. Lester McFarland, md; Robert A. Gardner, g.
    Chicago, IL   Wednesday, May 13, 1931
    C-7816-A   When It's Nightime In Nevada   Br 541, Spt S2261, Pan 25110

Supertone S2261 as by **Kentucky Mountain Boys**. Panachord 25110 as by **McFarland & Gardner**.
    Chicago, IL   Friday, June 12, 1931
    C-7865-   Don't Lay Me On My Back (In My Last Sleep)   Br 541
    Chicago, IL   Wednesday, August 19, 1931
    C-7960-B   When The Moon Comes Over The Mountain   Br 553, Spt S2260, Pan 25107, PanAu P11980,
                                                                Embassy E145
    C-7961-A   Many Happy Returns Of The Day   Br 553, Spt S2260, Pan 25107, PanAu P11980,
                                                                 Mayfair G2061, Embassy E143

Supertone S2260 as by **Kentucky Mountain Boys**. Panachord 25107 as by **McFarland & Gardner**, P11980 as by **The Radio Duo**. Mayfair G2061 as by **Florida Waltz Orchestra**. Embassy E143, E145 as by **The Desmond Duo**.
Revs: Mayfair G2061, Embassy E143, E145 popular.

    Chicago, IL   early March 1932
    JC-8495-A   An Old Fashioned Home In New Hampshire   Br 594
    JC-8496-A   When It's Springtime In The Blue Ridge Mountains   Br 594
    Chicago, IL   Tuesday, March 15, 1932
    JC-8530-A   Ninety-Nine Years – Part I   Br 588, DeE F3251
    JC-8531-A   Ninety-Nine Years – Part II   Br 588, DeE F3251
    JC-8532-   Little Home Of Long Ago   DeE F3391
    JC-8533-   Little Girl In Carolina   MeC 93074, DeE F3391

Decca F3251, F3391 as by **Mac & Bob**.

    Chicago, IL   Monday, May 9, 1932
    JC-8621-1   That Little Boy Of Mine   DeE F3166
    JC-8622-1,-2   When We Carved Our Hearts On The Old Oak   Vo 02760, RZAu G22274, DeE F3166
                                Tree

Vocalion 02760, Regal-Zonophone G22274 as by **McFarland & Gardner**. Decca F3166 as by **Mac & Bob**.

Mac & Bob, v duet; acc. Lester McFarland, md; Robert A. Gardner, g.
    Chicago, IL   Wednesday, May 25, 1932
    JC-8637-1   That Silver Haired Daddy Of Mine   Me M12404, Cq 8005, DeE F3081, RexIr U609
    JC-8638-1   When I Was A Boy From The Mountains (And You   Me M12404, Cq 8005, Bwy 4088, DeE F3081,
                                Were A Girl From The Hills)   RexIr U609

Broadway 4088 as by **Parsons & Kent**.

    Chicago, IL   Thursday, May 26, 1932
    C-8643-2   Twenty-One Years – Part 2   Br 596, DeE F3117, DeIr W4155
    C-8644-2   There's No Light In The Window (Of The House   Br 596
                              On The Hill)

McFarland & Gardner, v duet; acc. Lester McFarland, md; Robert A. Gardner, g.
    Chicago, IL   Tuesday, January 17, 1933
    C-510-   Broadway Moon   ARC unissued
    C-511-   Mammy's Precious Baby   ARC unissued
    C-512-   I'll Go On Loving You   ARC unissued
    C-513-1   I Told The Stars About You   Ba 32692, Me M12623, Or 8211, Pe 12886,
                                                      Ro 5211, Cq 8137, DeE F3487, RexIr U610

Conqueror 8137, Decca F3487, Rex U610 as by **Mac & Bob**.

Acc. unknown, f; Lester McFarland, md; Robert A. Gardner, g.
    Chicago, IL   Wednesday, January 18, 1933
    C-514-   When It's Lamp Lightin' Time In The Valley   Ba 32692, Me M12623, Or 8211, Pe 12886,
                                                        Ro 5211, Cq 8137, DeE F3487, RexIr U610
    C-515-1   Only Childhood Sweethearts   DeE F3609
    C-516-2   Schoolhouse Dreams   Vo 02749, RZAu G22273

Conqueror 8137, Decca F3487, F3609, Rex U610 as by **Mac & Bob**.
Matrix C-514 was assigned the transfer matrix B-12995-A.

    Chicago, IL   Monday, January 23, 1933
    C-517-1   Lonesome And Blue   DeE F3686
    C-522-1   The Pal That Is Always True   DeE F3609

C-523-1	When The Candle Lights Are Gleaming	Vo 02749, DeE F3542, RZAu G22273
C-524-1	A White House Of Our Own	DeE F3686
C-525-1	Seven Years With The Wrong Woman	DeE F3542

Decca F3542, F3609, F3686 as by **Mac & Bob**.
Intervening matrices are by other artists.

Mac & Bob (McFarland & Gardner), v duet; acc. Lester McFarland, md; Robert A. Gardner, g.
    New York, NY   Thursday, April 25, 1935

17375-1	Under The Old Umbrella	ARC 5-12-52, Cq 8583, CrC/MeC/Stg/Roy 93084, Min M-14026
17376-1	Keep A Light In Your Window Tonight	ARC 35-10-29, Cq 8568, CrC/MeC/Stg/Roy 92091, Me/Min M-935
17377-1	Paint A Rose On The Garden Wall	Ba 33458, Me M13425, Or 8477, Pe 13150, Ro 5477, Cq 8534
17378-1	Just A Kerosene Lamp	Ba 33458, Me M13425, Or 8477, Pe 13150, Ro 5477, Cq 8534

Rev. Melotone/Minerva M-935 by Gene Autry.

    New York, NY   Friday, April 26, 1935

17389-1	Please Let Me Broadcast To Heaven	ARC 35-10-29, Cq 8568, CrC/MeC/Stg/Roy 92091, Min M-14031
17390-	Little Home Of Long Ago	Cr/Me/Stg/Roy 93074, Min M-14019
17391-1	Down Where The Roses Go To Sleep	ARC 350908, Cq 8564, CrC/MeC/Stg/Roy 92090
17392-1	When The Candle Lights Are Gleaming	ARC 5-12-52, Cq 8583, CrC/MeC/Stg/Roy 93084, Min M-14026

Revs: Minerva M-14019 by Jack Elliott (Canadian), M-14031 by Goebel Reeves.

    New York, NY   Wednesday, May 1, 1935

| 17454- | There Must Be A Bright Tomorrow (For Each Yesterday Of Tears) | ARC unissued |
| 17455- | Mother Wants To See You | ARC unissued |

    New York, NY   Friday, May 3, 1935

17464-2	Swinging Down The Old Orchard Lane	ARC 350908, Cq 8564, CrC/MeC/Stg/Roy 92090
17465-	Finger Prints (Upon The Window Pane)	ARC unissued
17466-	An Old Sweet Song (For A Sweet Old Lady)	ARC unissued

Mac & Bob, v duet; acc. unknown, f; Lester McFarland, md; Robert A. Gardner, g; unknown, sb.
    Chicago, IL   Wednesday, February 21, 1940

WC-2943-A	He Left The One Who Loved Him For Another	Vo/OK 05427, Cq 9421
WC-2944-A	I've Nothing To Live For Now	Vo/OK 05427, Cq 9421
WC-2945-A	What A Friend We Have In Mother	Vo/OK 05613, Cq 9418, CoC C984
WC-2946-A	There Must Be A Bright Tomorrow (For Each Yesterday Of Tears)	Vo/OK 05613, Cq 9418, CoC C984
WC-2947-A	Take Up Thy Cross	Vo/OK 05488, Cq 9420
WC-2948-A	I Heard My Mother Call My Name In Prayer	Vo/OK 05488, Cq 9420
WC-2949-A	Down The Lane Of Memory	Vo/OK 05537, Cq 9419
WC-2950-A	Under The Old Sierra Moon	Vo/OK 05537, Cq 9419

McFarland & Gardner recorded after 1942.

J.D. McFARLANE & DAUGHTER

J.D. McFarlane, f; acc. ———— McFarlane (?), p.
    Asheville, NC   prob. Thursday, August 27, or Friday, August 28, 1925

| 9299-A | Devil In The Woodpile | OK 45027 |
| 9300-A | Whistlin' Rufus | OK 45027 |

ALPHUS McFAYDEN

This artist's last name is, correctly, McFadyen.

Alphus McFayden, g solo.
    Atlanta, GA   Tuesday, October 18, 1927

| 40301-2 | 1. Turkey In The Straw. 2. Arkansas Traveler | Vi 21128 |

Rev. Victor 21128 by Homer Christopher & Raney Vanvink.

DENUS McGEE

Dennis McGee, v; acc. own f; Sady D. Courville, f.
    New Orleans, LA   early March 1929

| NO-108- | Madame Young Donnez Moi Votre Plus Jole Blonde (Madam Young, Give Me Your Sweetest) | Vo 5319 |

NO-109-	Mon Chere Bebe Creole (My Creole Sweet Mama)	Vo 5319
NO-110-	Myself	Vo 5348
NO-111-	Vous M'Avez Donne Votre Parole (You Gave Me Your Word)	Vo 5348
NO-112-	Allon A Tassone (Let's Go To Tassone)	Vo 5334
NO-113-	Disez Goodbye A Votre Mere (Tell Your Mother Goodbye)	Vo 5334

Courville & McGee: Dennis McGee, Sady D. Courville, f duet.
  New Orleans, LA early March 1929

| NO-114- | Courville And McGee Waltz | Vo 5315 |
| NO-115- | Happy | Vo 5315 |

Dennis McGee, v; acc. own f; Ernest Fruge, f.
  New Orleans, LA Wednesday, October 2, 1929

NO-234-	Valse Du Puit D'Huile	Vo 15846
NO-235-	One Step De Mamou	Vo 15846
NO-236-	Valse Du La Penitencier	Vo 15851
NO-237-	One Step De Chupic	Vo 15851
NO-248-	Valse Des Vachers	Vo 15848
NO-249-	Jeunes Gens Campagnard	Vo 15848
NO-250-	La Valse Des Reid	Vo 15850
NO-251-	Adieu Rosa	Vo 15850

Matrices NO-238/39 are untraced; matrices NO-240/41 are by Hal Jordy (see JR); matrices NO-242 to NO-247 are by Guidry Brothers.

Dennis McGee & Ernest Fruge: Dennis McGee, f/v; Ernest Fruge, f.
  New Orleans, LA Wednesday, November 19, 1930

| NO-6703- | La Valse De Lange Au Paille | Br 496 |
| NO-6704- | Two Step Du Grand Maraist | Br 496 |

Dennis McGee, Ernest Fruge, f duet; Walter Coquille, calls/sp.
  New Orleans, LA Thursday, November 20, 1930

| NO-6713- | La Rille Cajen | Br 512 |
| NO-6714- | La Danse Carre | Br 512 |

Dennis McGee, f/v; Ernest Fruge, f.
  New Orleans, LA Friday, November 21, 1930

NO-6729-	Lanse Des Belaire	Br 557
NO-6730-	Les Blues Du Texas	Br 557
NO-6731-	La Valse De Rosalie (Rosalie Waltz)	Br 590, Me M18051
NO-6732-	One Step Des McGee (McGee's One Step)	Br 590, Me M18051
NO-6733-	Valse A Pap	Br 532
NO-6734-	Two Step De La Ville Platte	Br 532

Denus McGee also recorded with Amede Ardoin and Angelas Le Jeunne, and after 1942.

JOHN & ALMA McGEE & FRANK FLEMING

Pseudonym on Angelus 3321, Clifford 5321 for John & Alma McGhee & Frank Welling (see John McGhee & Frank Welling).

KIRK McGEE [& BLYTHE POTEET]

See McGee Brothers.

SAM McGEE

See McGee Brothers.

McGEE & ARDOIN

See Amedie Ardoin.

McGEE BROTHERS

Sam McGee, g solo/sp.
  New York, NY Wednesday, April 14, 1926

| E-2767/68 | Buck Dancer's Choice | Vo 15318, 5094 |
| E-2769/70 | The Franklin Blues | Vo 15318, 5094 |

Sam McGee, v; acc. own g; or Sam McGee, g solo-1.
  New York, NY Saturday, April 17, 1926

| E-2794/95 | In A Cool Shady Nook | Vo 15325, 5104 |
| E-2796/97 | If I Could Only Blot Out The Past | Vo 15326, 5101 |

| E-2798/99 | Knoxville Blues -1 | Vo 15326, 5101 |

Revs: Vocalion 15325, 5104 by Uncle Dave Macon.
Sam McGee also accompanied Uncle Dave Macon on his recordings of April 14-17.

McGee Brothers: Kirk McGee, f-1/md-2/bj-3/v-4; Sam McGee, g/v-5; or **McGee Brothers & Todd**-6: Mazy Todd, f; Kirk McGee, f-1/bj-3/v-4; Uncle Dave Macon, bj-7; Sam McGee, g/v-5.

New York, NY   Wednesday, May 11, 1927

E-5014*/15	Old Master's Runaway -3, 4, 6	Vo 5167
E-5016/17*	Charming Bill -1, 4, 6, 7	Vo 5166
E-5018*/19	A Flower From My Angel Mother's Grave -2, 4	Vo 5166
E-5020/21*	C-h-i-c-k-e-n Spells Chicken -1, 4, 5	Vo 5150
E-5022/23*	Salty Dog Blues -1, 4	Vo 5150
E-5024*/25	Salt Lake City Blues -1, 4	Vo 5169
E-5026*/27	Rufus Blossom -3, 4, 5, 6	Vo 5170
E-5028*/29	Ragged Jim -2, 4	Vo 5170
E-5030/31*	Someone Else May Be There While I'm Gone -1, 4	Vo 5167
E-5032*/33	Hannah Won't You Open The Door? -3, 4	Vo 5169
E-5034/35*	My Family Has Been A Crooked Set -3, 5	Vo 5171
E-5036/37*	The Tramp -2, 5	Vo 5171

The McGee brothers also recorded with Uncle Dave Macon as the Dixie Sacred Singers, and accompanied him as His Fruit Jar Drinkers (in both cases with Mazy Todd), on recordings made on May 7-11.

Sam McGee, v; acc. own bj-g-1/g-2.

Chicago, IL   Wednesday, July 25, 1928

C-2132-	Easy Rider -1	Vo 5254
C-2133	Chevrolet Car -1	Vo 5254
C-2136-	As Willie And Mary Strolled By The Seashore -2	Vo 5310
C-2137-	The Ship Without A Sail -2	Vo 5310

Intervening and surrounding matrices are by Uncle Dave Macon, generally accompanied by Sam McGee.

Kirk McGee & Blythe Poteet, v duet; or **Blythe Poteet**, v-1/wh-2; acc. Kirk McGee, f-3/md-4/g-5; Blythe Poteet, g.

Richmond, IN   Monday, November 26, 1928

14462-A	If I Only Had A Home -5	Ge 6704, 15711
14463	A Flower From My Angel Mother's Grave -4	Ge unissued
14464-A	Love Always Has Its Way -1, 4	Ge 6778
14465-B	No One Else Can Take Your Place -4	Ge 6731
14466	The House At The End Of The Lane -5	Ge rejected
14467	The Red River Valley -5	Ge rejected
14469	Southern Whistling Coon -1, 2, 3	Ge rejected
14470-A	Kickin' Mule -3	Ge 7022, Cq 7257
14471	Way Down In Arkansas -3	Ge rejected
14472	C-H-I-C-K-E-N Spells Chicken -3	Ge 7022, Cq 7257

Champion 15711 as by **Evan Douglas & Nate Smith**. Conqueror 7257 as by **Rogers & Picket**. Matrix 14468 is popular.

Kirk McGee & Blythe Poteet, v duet; or **Kirk McGee**, v-1; acc. Kirk McGee, f-2/md-3/bj-4; Blythe Poteet, g.

Richmond, IN   Tuesday, November 27, 1928

14473	Home Ain't Nothin' Like This -2	Ge rejected
14474	Where Is My Mama? -3	Ge rejected
14475-B	Only A Step To The Grave -3	Ge 6778, Ch 15711, Spt 9373
14476-A	If I Could Hear My Mother Pray Again -3	Ge 6731, Ch 15651, 45069, Spt 9318
14477	My Mother's Hands -3	Ge rejected
14778-A	If I Could Only Blot Out The Past -3	Ge 6704, Ch 15651, 45069, Spt 9373
14479	My Wife Left Me -1, 3	Ge 6960
14480	My Girl Is A High Born Lady -4	Ge rejected
14481	Shoo Fly Don't Bother Me -4	Ge rejected

Champion 15651, 15711, 45069 as by **Evan Douglas & Nate Smith**. Supertone 9318 as by **McMann & Roberts**, 9373 as by **Rand & Foster**. Rev. Supertone 9318 by Dick Parman.

Kirk & Sam McGee, v duet; acc. Kirk McGee, bj; Sam McGee, g.

Richmond, IN   Tuesday, August 14, 1934

| 19655 | Brown's Ferry Blues | Ch S-16804, 45033, De 5348 |

Champion 45033 possibly as by **Sam & Kirk McGee**.

Kirk McGee, v; acc. own g; Sam McGee, g.

Richmond, IN   Wednesday, August 15, 1934

| 19658 | Tune In On Heaven | Ge unissued |

Sam McGee, v; acc. own g.

Richmond, IN   Wednesday, August 15, 1934

| 19660 | Railroad Blues | Ch S-16804, 45033, De 5348 |

Intervening and surrounding matrices are by Uncle Dave Macon, generally accompanied by the McGee brothers.
Sam and Kirk McGee recorded both together and individually after 1942.

JOHN McGHEE & FRANK WELLING

Most of the recordings by these artists are collaborations, under a variety of credits, sometimes with McGhee's name first, sometimes Welling's. For the sake of clarity all their work is listed below: joint, individual, and in duets or trios with McGhee's daughter Alma and Welling's wife Thelma. Also included are recordings by one or the other of them with different partners.

John McGhee, v; acc. prob. own h/g.
Richmond, IN   Wednesday, November 16, 1927

| GEX-947-A | The Preacher And The Bear | Ge 6403, Ch 15414, 33014, Sil 5212, 8162, Spt 9256, Chg 392, Spr 325 |

Champion 15414 as by **John Hutchens**; 33014 credit untraced. Silvertone 5212, 8162, Supertone 9256 as by **Jess Oakley**. Challenge 392 as by **George Holden**.
Revs: Champion 15414 by Roy Harvey, 33014 untraced; Challenge 392 by David Miller.

John McGhee & Frank Welling, v duet; acc. John McGhee, h-1/g-2; Frank Welling, sg-3/g-4.
Richmond, IN   Wednesday, November 16, 1927

GEX-950-A	He Keeps Me Singing -2, 3	Ge 6334, Ch 15412, Sil 8166, Spt 9262, Chg 399, Spr 323
GEX-951	I'm Gonna Ride In Elijah's Chariot	Ge rejected
GEX-952-A	I've Been Redeemed -1, 4	Ge 6334
GEX-953,-A	When We All Get To Heaven	Ge rejected

Champion 15412 as by **Hutchens Brothers**. Silvertone 8166, Supertone 9262 as by **Harper & Turner**. Challenge 399 as by **Markham Brothers**.
Possibly only one guitar is used on some items. Matrices GEX-948/49 are by Cleve Chaffin.
Rev. Champion 15412 by Roy Harvey.

John McGhee, v; acc. prob. own g.
Richmond, IN   Wednesday, November 16, 1927

| GEX-954,-A | I Got Mine | Ge rejected |

Acc. prob. own h/g.
Chicago, IL   c. December 30, 1927

13329-A	The Sinking Of The Submarine S-4	Ge 6362, Ch 15427, Sil 5203, 8163, Spt 9257, Chg 385, 389, Spr 367, Bell 1177
13330	The Wreck Of Virginian Train No. 3	Ch 15467, Sil 5203, 8163, Spt 9257, Chg 389, Spr 344, Bell 1167
13331	Aged Mother	Ge 6419, Ch 15483, Sil 8158, Spt 9243

Champion 15427, 15467, 15483 as by **John Hutchens**. Silvertone 8158, 8163, Supertone 9243, 9257 as by **Jesse Oakley**. Silvertone 5203 as by **Jess Oakley**. Challenge 385, 389 as by **George Holden**. Bell 1167, 1177 as by **Henry Graham**.
Revs: Silvertone 8158 by Holland Puckett; Bell 1177 by David Miller.

Chicago, IL   c. December 31, 1927

| 13333-A | The Marian Parker Murder | Ge 6362, Ch 15427, Chg 385, Spr 344, Bell 1167 |
| 13334 | I Got Mine | Ge 6403, Ch 15503, Sil 5212, 8162, Spt 9256, Chg 391 |

Champion 15427, 15503 as by **John Hutchens**. Silvertone 5212, 8162, Supertone 9256 as by **Jesse Oakley**. Challenge 385, 391 as by **George Holden**. Bell 1167 as by **Henry Graham**.
Rev. Challenge 391 by Thomas C. Ashley.

Welling & McGhee, v duet; or prob. Frank Welling, v-1; acc. John McGhee, h-2/g; Frank Welling, sg-3.
Chicago, IL   December 1927 / January 1928

20248-3	At The Cross -3	Pm 3115, Bwy 8212
20249-2	There Is A Fountain Filled With Blood -3	Pm 3115, Bwy 8212
20250-3	The Haven Of Rest -3	Pm 3093, Bwy 8135
20251-1	Knocking At The Door -2	Pm 3093, Bwy 8135
20252-1	My Mother's Bible -3	Pm 3108, Bwy 8204
20253-1	In The Garden -3	Pm 3084, Bwy 8198
20254-2	There Is Sunshine In My Soul -3	Pm 3084, Bwy 8198
20256-1	Are You Washed In The Blood -2, 3	Pm 3102, Bwy 8136
20257-1	What A Friend We Have In Jesus -2, 3	Pm 3102, Bwy 8136
20258-2	When The Roll Is Called Up Yonder -3	Pm 3108, Bwy 8204
20261-2	There's A Spark Of Love Still Burning -1	Pm 3157, Bwy 8215

Broadway 8135, 8136 as by **Wilkins & Moore**, 8198, 8204 as by **Wilkins & Sharon**, 8212, 8215 as by **Harkins & Moran**.
Matrix 20255 is by Tony Prince (popular); 20259/60 are untraced.

John McGhee & Frank Welling, v duet; or **Frank Welling**, v-1; acc. John McGhee, h-2/g-3; Frank Welling, sg-4/g-5.
Richmond, IN   Wednesday, January 18, 1928

13371-A	Constantly Abiding -3, 4	Chg 400
13372	I Surrender All -3, 4	Ge rejected
13373	Praise The Lord It's So -2, 5	Ge 6389, Ch 15464, Sil 5206, 8170, Spt 9266, Chg 400, Spr 345, Bell 1168
13374	I'm On The Sunny Side -2, 5	Ge 6389, Ch 15485, Sil 8166, Spt 9262, Chg 401, Spr 383, Bell 1185
13375	Meet Me There -2, 5	Ge 6435, Ch 15464, Sil 5206, 8170, Spt 9266, Spr 383, Bell 1184
13376	I Am Resolved -2, 5	Ge 6435, Ch 15485, Chg 399, Spr 345, Bell 1168
13377	I Feel Like Traveling On -2, 5	Ge rejected
13378	Get A Transfer -5	Ge rejected
13379	Daddy Blues -1, 3, 4	Ge rejected

Champion 15464, 15485 as by **Hutchens Brothers**. Silvertone 5206, 8166, 8170, Supertone 9262, 9266 as by **Harper & Turner**. Challenge 399, 400, 401 as by **Markham Brothers**. Bell 1168, 1184, 1185 as by **Belford & Rogers**.
Revs: Challenge 401 by Roy Harvey; Bell 1184, 1185 by Woodlawn Quartette.

Richmond, IN   Thursday, January 19, 1928

13380	I'se Goin' From The Cotton Fields -3, 4	Ge rejected
13381	Stepping In The Light -3, 4	Ge rejected
13382	Where The Gates Swing Outward Never -5	Ge rejected

J.L. McGhee & Frank Welling, v duet; acc. John McGhee, h-1/g-2; Frank Welling, sg-3/g-4/u-5.
Ashland, KY   Sunday, February 12, 1928

AL-234*/35; E-7442W	God's Love -2, 3	Vo 5241
AL-236/37*; E-7435W	Whosoever Meaneth Me -2, 3	Vo 5251
AL-238/39*	There Is Power In The Blood -2, 3	Br 251
AL-240*/41; E-7436W	The Lily Of The Valley -1, 4	Vo 5251
AL-242/43*	I Would Not Be Denied -2, 3	Br 251
AL-244*/45; E-7438W	Go By The Way Of The Cross -1, 4	Vo 5299
AL-246/47; E-7439/40W	The Eastern Gate -4	Vo 5299
AL-248/49*	The Old Account Was Settled Long Ago -1, 2, 5	Br 258, Spt S2075
AL-250*/51	Dwelling In Beulah Land -2, 3	Br 258

Rev. Supertone S2075 by Richard Brooks & Reuben Puckett.

Acc. John McGhee, h-1/g-2; Frank Welling, sg-3/g-4; "opening prayer by Rev. Jos. W. Hagin"-5.
Ashland, KY   Monday, February 13, 1928

AL-252*/53; E-7441W	The Hallelujah Side -1, 4	Vo 5241
AL-254*/55	He Abides -2/4, 5	Br 222
AL-258*/59	Hide Me -2, 3	Br 222
AL-260*/61	I Am Coming Home -1, 4	Br 272
AL-262/63*	Have Thine Own Way Lord -2, 3	Br 272
AL-264; E-7444W	The Nearer The Sweeter -2, 3	Vo 5263
AL-265; E-7445W	Shouting Hallelujah All The Way -1, 4	Vo 5263

Matrices AL-256/57 are untraced but probably by these artists.

John McGhee, v; acc. prob. own o; Frank Welling, g.
Richmond, IN   early to mid-April 1928

13615-B	Breaking Of The St. Francis Dam	Ge 6419, Ch 15467, Spr 367

Champion 15467 as by **John Hutchens**.

McGhee & Welling, v duet; acc. John McGhee, h/g; Frank Welling, u.
Richmond, IN   early to mid-April 1928

13616	I'm Free Again	Ge 6533, Ch 15588
13617-A	Climbing Up The Golden Stairs	Ch 15567
13618	I Want To Go There, Don't You	Ge 6533

Champion 15567, 15588 as by **Hutchens Brothers**.
Rev. Champion 15567 by Vernon Dalhart & Carson Robison.

Frank Welling, v; acc. John McGhee, o; own g.
Richmond, IN   early to mid-April 1928

13619	The Lonely Village Churchyard	Ge rejected

John L. McGhee, v; acc. prob. own o-1; Frank Welling, g; unknown, bell-1.
Richmond, IN   early to mid-April 1928
    13620-A   The Volunteer Organist -1   Ge 6450, Ch 15483
    13621   Bring Back The Old Time Music   Ge 6450

Champion 15483 as by **John Hutchens**.

Mr. & Mrs. Frank Welling: Frank Welling, Thelma Welling, v duet; acc. Frank Welling, g.
Richmond, IN   early to mid-April 1928
    13622   He Hideth My Soul   Ge rejected
    13623   The Bible Is Good Enough For Me   Ge rejected

Frank Welling, v; acc. own sg or g; John McGhee, g.
Richmond, IN   early to mid-April 1928
    13624   Are You From Dixie   Ge rejected

McGhee & Welling, v duet; or **John McGhee**-1, v; acc. John McGhee, h-2/g-3; Frank Welling, sg-4/g-5.
Richmond, IN   Tuesday, April 24, 1928
    13699   Get A Transfer -5   Ge 6657
    13700   Stepping In The Light -2, 3, 4   Ge 6657, Ch 15588
    13704   I Feel Like Traveling On -5   Ge rejected
    13705-A   Bill Bailey, Won't You Please Come Home -1, 2, 3/   Ge 6479
                             5
    13706-A   Bill Bailey, Ain't That A Shame -1, 2, 3/5   Ge 6479, Ch 15503
    13707   These Bones Gonna Rise Again -2, 5   Ge rejected

Champion 15503 as by **John Hutchens**, 15588 as by **Hutchens Brothers**.
Matrices 13701 to 13703 are by Bryant's Jubilee Quartet (see B&GR).

John McGhee, v; acc. prob. own o.
Richmond, IN   Wednesday, May 9, 1928
    13797   A Suffering Child Made Happy   Ge 6587

With prob. own h/g.
Richmond, IN   Friday, June 1, 1928
    13882-A   Hard Luck Jim   Ge 6546, Ch 15751, Cq 7260
    13883-A   Life Ain't Worth Living When You're Broke   Ge 6960, Ch 15751, Cq 7260

Champion 15751 as by **John Hutchens**. Conqueror 7260 as by **Roy Deal**.
Matrix 13883 is titled *Life Ain't Worth Livin' When You're Broke* on Conqueror 7260.
Revs: Gennett 6546 by Calaway's West Virginia Mountaineers, 6960 by Kirk McGee.

Acc. West Virginia Mountaineers: no details, but poss. incl. ——— Blevins, ——— Blair, one playing f and the other bj or g.
Richmond, IN   Wednesday, August 15, 1928
    14146-A   Hatfield-McCoy Feud   Ge 6587
    14147   Just Plain Folks   Ge rejected

Frank Welling, v/y; acc. own sg; John McGhee, g.
Richmond, IN   Wednesday, August 15, 1928
    14149-B   Yodelin' Daddy Blues   Ge 6616, Ch 15582, Spt 9083

Gennett 6616 as by **Frank Welling Of The West Virginia Mountaineers**. Champion 15582 as by **Clarence Young**.
Matrix 14148 is by West Virginia Mountaineers.
Revs: Gennett 6616 by Fred Wingate (popular); Champion 15582 by Hollinshead & Harrison (popular); Supertone 9083 by Willie Stoneman.

Frank Welling, v/y-1; acc. Bill Davies or Miller Wikel, f-2; own sg-3/g-4; prob. John McGhee, g-5/v-6.
Chicago, IL   c. August/September 1928
    20795-2   She's My Mama And I'm Her Daddy -1, 3, 5   Pm 3125, Bwy 8201
    20800-2   I Want To Go Back To My Old Mountain Shack   Pm 3125, Bwy 8201
                            -1, 4
    20804-2   Lead Me Higher Up The Mountain -2, 3, 5, 6   Pm 3119, Bwy 8205
    20805-2   The Last Mile -2, 3, 5, 6   Pm 3119, Bwy 8205
    20808-   Too Many Parties And Too Many Pals -4   Pm 3157

Paramount 3119 as by **Frank Welling & Red Brush Rowdies**. Broadway 8201, 8205 as by **Frank Wilkins**.
Later pressings of Paramount 3157 probably replace matrix 20808 with matrix 21171 (see c. February 1929 session).
Matrix 20800 is titled *I Want To Get Back To My Old Mountain Shack* on Broadway 8201.
Matrices 20796 to 20798, 20802/03, 20807 are by Red Brush Rowdies; Welling sang on 20807 but was not credited.

McGhee & Welling: John McGhee, v/humming; acc. Frank Welling, g/y/sp.
Richmond, IN   Sunday, October 14, 1928
    14339-A   I Wants My Lulu   Ge 6671, Ch 15671, 45184, Spt 9353

Champion 15671, 45184 as by **Hutchens Brothers**. Supertone 9353 as by **Harper & Turner**.

Frank Welling, John McGhee, v duet; or Frank Welling, v-1/y-1; acc. John McGhee, h-2/g-3; Frank Welling, sg or g; one of them, sp-4.
    Richmond, IN   Monday, October 15, 1928

14340	The Hand That Rocks The Cradle -1	Ge rejected
14341-B	Nothing To Do, But -1	Ge 6671
14342	At The Battle Front -	Ge 6749, Ch 15753
14343-B	Will There Be Any Stars In My Crown? -	Ge 6874
14344-A	My Savior First Of All -3	Ge 6749, Ch 15693, Spt 9316
14345	Why Not Tonight -2, 4	Ge 6690, Ch 15693, Spt 9391
14346-A	I Love To Tell The Story -3, 4	Ge 6874, Ch 15753, Spt 9391
14347	Drifting Down -3	Ge rejected

Champion 15693, 15753 as by **Hutchens Brothers**. Supertone 9316, 9391 as by **Harper & Turner**.

Frank Welling, John McGhee, v duet; or Frank Welling, v-1/y-2; or John McGhee, v-3; acc. John McGhee, h-4/g-5/humming-6; Frank Welling, sg or g; one of them, sp-7.
    Richmond, IN   Tuesday, October 16, 1928

14351	Lullaby Land -1, 2, 5?, 6	Ge 6719, Ch 15671, Spt 9353
14352	I Feel Like Traveling On -4, 7	Ge 6690, Ch 15632, Spt 9316
14353	Just Plain Folks -3, 5?	Ge rejected
14354	Lonely Village Churchyard -1, 5?	Ge 6719, Ch 15650, Spt 9319
14355	My Redeemer -5?	Ge rejected
14356	Let The Song Ring Out -5?, 7	Ch 15632

Champion 15632, 15671 as by **Hutchens Brothers**, 15650 as by **Clarence Young**. Supertone 9316, 9353 as by **Harper & Turner**, 9319 as by **Frank Hill**.
Matrices 14348 to 14350 are by Blevins & Blair (of the West Virginia Mountaineers).
Rev. Supertone 9319 by Dick Parman.

Welling & Shannon Successors To Welling & McGhee: Frank Welling, William Shannon, v duet; acc. Frank Welling, g; one of them, sp-1.
    Chicago, IL   c. November 1928

20957-2	I'm A Child Of The King	Pm 3134, Bwy 8155
20962-2	Must Jesus Bear The Cross Alone -1	Pm 3142
20965-2	Brighten The Corner Where You Are	Pm 3134, Bwy 8155
20967-2	S.O.S. Vestris	Pm 3127
20969-2	Are You A Christian -1	Pm 3142

Paramount 3127 as by **Welling & Schannen**. Broadway 8155 as by **Wilkins & Sharon**.
Intervening matrices are untraced but possibly by these artists.
Rev. Paramount 3127 by Ozark Warblers.

McGhee & Cogar: John McGhee, Thomas Cogar, v duet; acc. Thomas Cogar, f; John McGhee, g.
    Richmond, IN   Monday, December 3, 1928

14503	The Vestris Disaster	Ge 6703, Ch 15650, Spt 9326
14504-A	My Old Cottage Home	Ge 6703, Spt 9326
14505	My Redeemer	Ge rejected
14506	The Song Of Wonderful Love	Ge rejected
14507	On Jordan's Stormy Bank	Ge rejected

Champion 15650 as by **John Hutchens & James Alston**. Supertone 9326 as by **Rand & Foster**.

Acc. Thomas Cogar, f; John McGhee, g; one of them, y-1.
    Richmond, IN   Tuesday, December 4, 1928

14508-A	I Want To Be A Worker For The Lord	Ge 6721, Spt 9313
14509	My Savior First Of All	Ge rejected
14510	Calling The Prodigal	Ge 6932
14511	Burial Of The Miner's Child	Ge rejected
14512	There's Glory In My Soul	Ge 6932
14513-A	He Included Me	Ge 6795, Ch 15649
14514	Where The Gates Swing Outward Never	Ge 6721, Ch 15649, Spt 9313
14515	Leaning On The Everlasting Arms	Ge 6795
14516	The Hand That Rocks The Cradle -1	Ge rejected

Champion 15649 as by **John Hutchens & James Alston**. Supertone 9313 as by **Rand & Foster**.

Welling & McGhee, v duet; acc. John McGhee, h/g; Frank Welling, sg.
    Chicago, IL   c. February 1929

21166-2	Pass Me Not Oh Gentle Saviour	Pm 3175
21170-2	I Love To Walk With Jesus	Pm 3175

Several of the surrounding matrices are by David Miller accompanied by Welling & McGhee.

Frank Welling, v; acc. own g.
    Chicago, IL   c. February 1929

| 21171-2 | Too Many Parties And Too Many Pals | Pm 3157, Bwy 8215 |

Broadway 8215 as by **Harkins & Moran**.

Dixie Sacred Trio: Frank Welling, John McGhee, poss. Alma McGhee, v trio; acc. Frank Welling, sg; John McGhee, g.
New York, NY   c. October 1929

| GEX-2417-A | There's A Guiding Star | Pm 3215, Bwy 8242 |
| GEX-2418-A | We Are Marching Home | Pm 3215, Bwy 8242 |

Frank Welling, John McGhee, unknown man, v trio; acc. Frank Welling, sg; John McGhee, g.
New York, NY   c. October 1929

| GEX-2419-A | Shall It Be You | Pm 3228 |

Frank Welling, unknown man, v duet; acc. Frank Welling, g; John McGhee, sp.
New York, NY   c. October 1929

| GEX-2420-A | Don't You Want To Go | Pm 3228 |

Martin Brothers: Frank Welling, John McGhee, v duet; acc. John McGhee, h-1/g; Frank Welling, sg-2.
New York, NY   c. October 1929

GEX-2425-A	The Marion Massacre -2	Pm 3194
GEX-2426-A	The North Carolina Textile Strike -1, 2	Pm 3194
GEX-2427-A	Don't Marry A Man If He Drinks -2	Pm 3248, Bwy 8265
GEX-2428	Will They Deny Me When They're Men	Pm 3248, Bwy 8265
GEX-2429-A	Climbing Up Dem Golden Stairs -	Pm 3217
GEX-2430-A	Whistling Rufus -	Pm 3217

Possibly only one guitar is used on some items.

Frank Welling, v/sp; acc. prob. own g.
New York, NY   c. October 1929

| GEX-2431 | A Plea To Young Wives | Pm 3216 |
| GEX-2432 | A Dedication To Mother | Pm 3216 |

Christian Harmony Singers: prob.: Frank Welling, John McGhee, Alma McGhee, v trio; acc. unknown, o.
New York, NY   c. October 1929

GEX-2447	Come Thou Fount	Pm 3204
GEX-2448	The Royal Diadem	Pm 3204
GEX-2449	Sweet Happy Home	Pm 3241
GEX-2450	Way Over In The Promised Land	Pm 3241
GEX-2451	The Model Church – Part I	Pm 3196
GEX-2452	The Model Church – Part II	Pm 3196

Billie Whoop: John McGhee, v; acc. own h/g.
New York, NY   c. October 1929

| GEX-2453 | Just Kiss Yourself Goodbye | Pm 3230, Bwy 8190 |
| GEX-2454 | Why Don't You Go | Pm 3230, Bwy 8190 |

Broadway 8190 as by **Billy Wheeler**.

John McGhee, v; acc. own h-1/g; Frank Welling, sg; prob. W.K. Henderson, sp.
Grafton, WI   c. October 1929

| L-93-4 | Hello World Doggone | KWKH/KWEA [unnumbered] |
| L-93-? | Hello World Doggone -1 | KWKH/KWEA [unnumbered] |

These are special pressings for the radio stations named.
Matrices L-91/92 may also be by McGhee & Welling.
Revs are blank.

Welling–McGhee–Teter: unidentified v duet; acc. prob. Frank Welling, sg; Jack Teter or John McGhee, g.
Grafton, WI   c. October 1929

| L-94-1 | Back To The Harbor Of Home Sweet Home | Pm 3223, Bwy 8262 |
| L-95-2 | Don't Sing Aloha When I Go | Pm 3223, Bwy 8262 |

McGhee & Welling, v duet; acc. Frank Welling, sg-1/g-2; John McGhee, g.
Richmond, IN   Friday, December 27, 1929

16020-A	What A Gathering That Will Be -1	Ge 7114, Ch 15971, 45125, Spt 9678, Spr 2799
16021-A	Whosoever Surely Meaneth Me -1	Ge 7156, Ch 16101, Spt 9726
16022-A	Beautiful Garden Of Prayer -1	Ge 7083, Spt 9726
16023-A	When We All Get To Heaven -2	Ge 7083, Ch 15900, Spt 9658
16024-A	No Never Alone -1	Ge 7114, Ch 15900, Spt 9678

Champion 15900, 15971, 16101, 45125 as by **Hutchens Brothers**. Supertone 9658, 9678, 9726 as by **Harper & Turner**. Superior 2799 as by **Harper & Hall**.

Frank Welling-1, v; acc. own g; or **John McGhee**-2, v; acc. own h/g.
Richmond, IN   Saturday, December 28, 1929

| 16026 | Little Pal -1 | Ge rejected |

16027	Southwest Mine Disaster -2	Ge rejected
16028	Picture From Life's Other Side -1	Ge 7096, Ch 15924, Spt 9612, Spr 2585
16029	The Great Airplane Crash -2	Ge 7096, Cq 7273
16030-A	Let Me Down Easy -1	Ge 7142, Ch 15991
16031	Hello World Doggone You -2	[Ge] 20362
16032	Moundsville Prisoner -1	Spr 2585, Cq 7273
16033	That's A Plenty -1	Ge 7142, Ch 15991
16034	I Wish They'd Do It Now -2	Ge rejected

Champion 15924, 15991 as by **Clarence Young**. Supertone 9612 as by **Frank Hill**. Superior 2585 as by **Walter Regan**. Conqueror 7273 as by **Roy Deal** (matrix 16029)/**Joe Summers** (matrix 16032).
[Gennett] 20362 is a personal issue, possibly not with a standard Gennett label.

McGhee & Welling, v duet; acc. John McGhee, h-1/g-2; Frank Welling, sg-3/g-4.
    Richmond, IN   Saturday, December 28, 1929

16035	Down The Lane To Home Sweet Home -2, 3/4	Ge rejected
16036	The Half Has Never Yet Been Told -2, 3/4	Ge rejected
16037	Sweet Adeline At The Still -1, 4	Ge unissued
16038	Then I Got Drunk Again -2/4	Ge rejected

McGhee & Welling, v duet; or **Frank Welling**-1, v; or **John McGhee**-2, v; acc. John McGhee, h-3/g-4; Frank Welling, sg-5/g-6/sp-7.
    Richmond, IN   Saturday, January 11, 1930

16068,-A	O&C Railroad Wreck -2, 3, 4	Ge rejected
16069	You're As Welcome As The Flowers In May -2, 4	Ge rejected
16070	Don't Grieve Your Mother -4/6	Ge unissued
16071	A Flower From My Angel Mother's Grave -4/6	Ge rejected
16072	Picture On The Wall -4/6	Ge rejected
16073	She Rests By The Swanee River -2, 4	Ge rejected
16074,-A	When The Harvest Days Are Over, Jessie Dear -4, 5/6	Ge rejected
16075	Where Is My Mama -4, 5/6	Ge rejected
16076	There Is A Vacant Chair At Home For You -4, 5/6	Ge rejected
16077	I'm Drifting Back To Dreamland -4, 5/6	Ge rejected
16078-A	I'll Not Forget You Daddy -1, 6	Ge 7111, Spt 9612
16079	Somebody's Darling Astray -4, 5/6	Ge rejected
16080	Little Pal -1, 5, 7	Ge 7111, Ch 15924
16081	Down The Lane To Home Sweet Home -4, 5/6	Ge rejected
16082	Sweet Adeline At The Still -4, 5/6	Ge rejected
16083	Burning Kisses -4, 5/6	Ge rejected
16084	Running Wild -4/6	Ge rejected
16085	Life's Railway To Heaven -4/6	Ge rejected

Champion 15924 as by **Clarence Young**. Supertone 9612 as by **Frank Hill**.

John McGhee, v; acc. Frank Welling, sg-1; own g; Alma McGhee, humming.
    Richmond, IN   Monday, February 3, 1930

| 16188-A | You're As Welcome As The Flowers In May | Ge 7168, Ch 15967, Spt 9674, MW 4966 |
| 16189 | When The Harvest Days Are Over Jessie Dear -1 | Ge 7168, Ch 15967, Spt 9674, MW 4966 |

Champion 15967 as by John Hutchens. Supertone 9674 as by **Jesse Oakley**. Montgomery Ward 4966 as by **John & Alma McGhee**.

John & Alma McGhee & Frank Welling, v trio; acc. Frank Welling, sg; John McGhee, g.
    Richmond, IN   Monday, February 3, 1930

16190-A	Picture On The Wall	Ge 7185, Ch 16032, 45096, Spt 9649, Spr 2641, MW 4927
16191	A Flower From My Angel Mother's Grave	Ge 7316, Ch 15989, 45158, Spt 9649, Spr 2641, MW 4952, MeC 45158, DeAu X1237
16192-A	Where Is My Mamma	Ge 7185, Ch 15989, 45158, Spt 9656, MeC 45158, DeAu X1237

Champion 15989, 16032, 45096, 45158, Montgomery Ward 4927, 4952, Decca X1237 as by **Hutchens Family Trio**. Supertone 9649, 9656 as by **Harper Family Trio**. Superior 2641 as by **The Mitchell Family Trio**.
Matrix 16192 is titled *Where Is My Mamma?* on Champion 45158, Decca X1237.
Rev. Montgomery Ward 4952 by Vernon Dalhart.

McGhee & Welling, v duet; acc. Frank Welling, sg; John McGhee, g.
    Richmond, IN   Monday, February 3, 1930

| 16195 | Down The Lane To Home Sweet Home | Ge 7247, Ch 16122, Spt 9626, Spr 2678, MW 4928, MeC 45023 |
| 16196 | I'm Drifting Back To Dreamland | Ge 7247, Ch 16122, Spt 9626, Spr 2678, MW 4928, MeC 45023 |

| 16198 | I Surrender All | Ge 7294, Ch 16101, Spt 9725 |
| 16199-A | Life's Railway To Heaven | Ge 7156, Ch 15971, 45125, Spt 9658, Spr 2799 |

Champion 15971, 16101, 16122, Montgomery Ward 4928, Melotone 45023 as by **Hutchens Brothers**. Supertone 9626, 9658, 9725 as by **Harper & Turner**. Superior 2678 as by **Harper & Hall**, 2799 as by **Harper & Hill**.
Matrices 16193/94, 16197 are Mexican.

John & Alma McGhee & Frank Welling, v trio; acc. Frank Welling, sg; John McGhee, g.
Richmond, IN   Monday, February 3, 1930

| 16200 | We Shall See The King Someday | Ge 7143, Ch 15948, Spt 9645 |

Champion 15948 as by **Hutchens Family Trio**. Supertone 9645 as by **Harper Family Trio**.

Richmond, IN   Tuesday, February 4, 1930

| 16203-A | He'll Understand | Ge 7143, Ch 15948, Spt 9645 |

Champion 15948 as by **Hutchens Family Trio**. Supertone 9645 as by **Harper Family Trio**.
Matrices 16201/02 are Mexican.

McGhee & Welling, v/sp-1 duet; acc. Frank Welling, sg-2/g-3; John McGhee, g-4; one of them, wh-5.
Richmond, IN   Tuesday, February 4, 1930

16204-A	Old Kentucky Dew -2, 4	Ge 7128, Ch 15944, 45184, Spt 9640
16205	Sweet Adeline At The Still -1, 3/4	Ge 7128, Ch 15944, Spt 9640
16206-B	There's A Vacant Chair At Home Sweet Home -2, 4, 5	Ge 7269, Ch 16032, 45096, Spt 9656, Spr 2678, MW 4927, DeAu X1270

Champion 15944, 16032, 45096, 45184, MW 4927 as by **Hutchens Brothers**. Supertone 9640, 9656 as by **Harper & Turner**. Superior 2678 as by **Harper & Hall**.
Rev. Decca X1270 by Don Weston.

John McGhee, v; acc. prob. own g.
Richmond, IN   Tuesday, February 4, 1930

| 16207 | Hello World Doggone | Ge rejected |

John & Alma McGhee & Frank Welling, v trio; acc. John McGhee, h; Frank Welling, sg-1 or g-1/u-2.
Richmond, IN   Monday, April 7, 1930

| 16449 | Down By The Old Mill Stream -2 | Ge rejected |
| 16450 | Springtime In The Rockies -1 | Ge rejected |

McGhee & Welling, v duet; acc. Frank Welling, sg; John McGhee, g.
Richmond, IN   Tuesday, April 8, 1930

| 16458 | Nailed To The Cross | Spr 2602, MeC 45009, Min M-14058 |
| 16459 | Going Down The Valley | Ge 7294, Spt 9725, Spr 2602, MeC 45009, Min M-14058 |

Supertone 9725 as by **Harper & Turner**. Superior 2602 as by **Wm. Harper & Nelson Hall**.
Matrix 16459 may be titled *Goin' Down The Valley One By One* on Melotone 45009, Minerva M-14058.

John & Alma McGhee & Frank Welling, v trio; acc. John McGhee, h-1/g-2; Frank Welling, sg-3/g-4; unknown, cel-5; unidentified, wh-6.
Richmond, IN   Tuesday, April 8, 1930

16460	I Will Praise Him Hallelujah -1, 4	Ge 7228, Ch 16013, Spt 9729
16461	Sweeping Through The Gates -1, 4	Ge 7228, Ch 16013, Spt 9729
16462-A	Till We Meet Again -2, 3, 5, 6	Ge 7269, Ch 16076, Spt 9720, Ang 3321, Clifford 5321
16463-A	I'm Forever Blowing Bubbles -2, 3, 5	Ge 7316, Ch 16076, Spt 9720, Ang 3321, Clifford 5321

Champion 16013, 16076 as by **Hutchens Family Trio**. Supertone 9720, 9729 as by **Harper Family Trio**. Angelus 3321, Clifford 5321 as by **Murphee Hartford Quartette** (matrix 16462)/**John & Alma McGee & Frank Fleming** (matrix 16463). Matrices 16462/63 were probably also issued on Lyric 3321, but no copy has yet been traced.

John McGhee, v; acc. prob. own h/g; poss. own perc-1.
Grafton, WI   c. April 1930

L-290-4	Columbus Prison Fire	Pm 3234, Bwy 8188
L-292-2	The Prisoner's Child	Pm 3234, Bwy 8188
L-298-2	Fall In Behind -1	Pm 3253, Bwy 8269
L-299-1	Since I Married That Actor Man -1	Pm 3253, Bwy 8269

Paramount 3253, Broadway 8269 as by **Billy Whoop**. Broadway 8188 as by **John Moore**.
Matrix L-291 is by John Byrd (see *B&GR*); other intervening matrices are untraced.

The Welling Trio: Frank Welling, John McGhee, Thelma Welling, v trio; or **Mr. & Mrs. Frank Welling**-1, v duet; acc. Frank Welling, sg; John McGhee, g.
Richmond, IN   Monday, May 26, 1930

| 16659 | Wait Till The Sun Shines Nellie | Ge 7291, Ch 16054, Spt 9718 |
| 16660 | School Days | Ch 16120, 45171, Spt 9719 |

16661	Let The Rest Of The World Go By	Ch 16054, Spt 9719
16662-A	I Love To Walk With Jesus	Spt 9728, Spr 2557
16663	Hallelujah All The Way	Ch 16078, Spt 9728
16664	I Am Coming Home	Ge 7271, Ch 16078, Spt 9727, Spr 2557
16665	The Last Mile Of The Way	Ge rejected
16666	Just Inside The Eastern Gate	Ge 7271, Ch 16035, 45123, Spt 9727
16667-A	Will The Circle Be Unbroken	Ch 16035, 45123
16668	Sweet Peace, Gift Of God's Love -1	Ge unissued
16669	Constantly Abiding -1	Ge rejected
16670	Old Time Power	Ge unissued

Supertone 9718, 9719 as by **The Charleston Entertainers**, 9727, 9728 as by **Charleston Sacred Trio**. Superior 2557 as by **The Baxter Family Trio**. Matrix 16670 was logged as by **Welling's Sacred Singers**.

Frank Welling, v/sp; acc. own g.
Richmond, IN   Monday, May 26, 1930

16671	Just As Your Mother Was	Spr 2524
16672	O How I Miss You Tonight	Spr 2524
16672-X	It's Nobody's Business But My Own	Ge rejected

Superior 2524 as by **Walter Regan**.

Acc. own g; John McGhee, g.
Richmond, IN   Tuesday, May 27, 1930

16673	The Darktown Strutter's [sic] Ball	Ge rejected
16674	Money Won't Make Everybody Happy	Ge rejected
16675	I Told You That I Would Never Forget You	Ge rejected

The Welling Trio: Frank Welling, John McGhee, Thelma Welling, v trio; acc. Frank Welling, sg; John McGhee, g.
Richmond, IN   Tuesday, May 27, 1930

| 16676-A | Tie Me To Your Apron Strings Again | Ge 7291, Ch 16120, 45171, Spt 9718 |

Supertone 9718 as by **The Charleston Entertainers**.

Frank Welling, v/sp; acc. own g.
Richmond, IN   Monday, October 20, 1930

| 17173 | Too Many Parties And Too Many Pals | Ge unissued |

Wellings & McGhee Trio: prob.: Frank Welling, John McGhee, Thelma Welling, v trio; or Frank Welling, John McGhee, v duet-1; acc. John McGhee, h-2/g-3; Frank Welling, sg-4/g-5.
New York, NY   Wednesday, November 5, 1930

10210-2	In The Garden -3, 4	Ba 32135, Or 8055, Pe 12698, Re 10313, Ro 5055, Cq 7712, ARC-Bwy 8198
10211-2	He Keeps Me Singing -1, 3, 4	Cq 7977
10212-2	Whosoever Surely Meaneth Me -3, 4	Cq 7977
10213-2	Are You Washed In The Blood? -3/5	Ba 32135, Or 8055, Pe 12698, Re 10313, Ro 5055, Cq 7712
10214-	I Will Praise Him Hallelujah	ARC unissued
10215-2	There Is Sunshine In My Soul -2, 3/5	Ba 32125, Me M12388, Or 8047, Pe 12688, Ro 5047, Cq 7731, ARC-Bwy 8198, Pan 25367
10216-1	I'm On The Sunny Side -1, 2, 3/5	Ba 32354, Me M12387, Or 8114, Pe 12780, Ro 5114, Cq 7945
10217-1	Praise The Lord It's So -2, 3/5	Ba 32208, Or 8077, Pe 12729, Ro 5077, Cq 8133, Pan 25447
10218-1,-2	The Picture On The Wall -2, 3/5	Ba 32124, Or 8046, Pe 12687, Ro 5046, Cq 7873

Some issues may be as by **Welling & McGhee Trio**. Conqueror 7731 as by **Wellings & McGhee**, 7873 as by **Frank Welling & John McGhee** (later pressings as by **Wellings & McGhee Trio**). Perfect 12780, Conqueror 7945, 7977 as by **Welling & McGhee**. ARC-Broadway 8198 as by **Walker Brothers**.
Rev. Conqueror 7731 by Gentry Bros.

New York, NY   Thursday, November 6, 1930

10219-	I Feel Like Traveling On	ARC unissued
10220-	When We All Get To Heaven	ARC unissued
10221-2	I Am Resolved -2, 3, 4	Ba 32208, Or 8077, Pe 12729, Ro 5077, Cq 8133, Pan 25447
10222-2	Don't Grieve Your Mother -3, 4	Ba 32265, Or 8096, Pe 12752, Ro 5096, Cq 7830
10223-2,-3	A Flower From My Angel Mother's Grave -2, 3/5	Ba 32265, Or 8096, Pe 12752, Ro 5096, Cq 7830
10224-2	Where Is My Mama? -3, 4	Ba 32124, Or 8046, Pe 12687, Ro 5046, Cq 7873
10225-1	In A Lonely Village Churchyard -2, 3/5	Ba 32136, Or 8056, Pe 12699, Ro 5056, Cq 7713
10226-1	I'm Free Again -2, 3, 4	Ba 32136, Or 8056, Pe 12699, Ro 5056, Cq 7713
10227-	When The Roll Is Called Up Yonder	ARC unissued

Conqueror 7873 as by **Frank Welling & John McGhee**; later pressings as by **Wellings & McGhee Trio**.

    New York, NY   Friday, November 7, 1930

10228-2	The Haven Of Rest -1, 3, 4	Ba 32125, Me M12388, Or 8047, Pe 12688, Ro 5047, Pan 25367
10229-2	The Old Account Was Settled Long Ago -1, 2, 3/5	Cq 7978
10235-1	Where Is My Boy Tonight? -3, 4	Cq 7747, 7841, ARC-Bwy 8160
10236-2	Sweeping Through The Gates -1, 2, 3/5	Cq 7978
10237-1	Sweet Bunch Of Daisies -3, 4	Cq 7841
10238-	What A Gathering That Will Be	ARC unissued

Conqueror 7978 as by **Welling & McGhee**. ARC-Broadway 8160 as by **Walker Brothers**.
Intervening matrices are popular.
Revs: Conqueror 7747 by James Roberts; ARC-Broadway 8160 by Nelson & Nelson.

Mr. & Mrs. Frank Welling & John McGhee: Frank Welling, Thelma Welling, John McGhee, v trio; acc. Frank Welling, sg; unknown, sg; John McGhee, g.

    Richmond, IN   Thursday, November 13, 1930

17241	Hide Me	Ch 16191, Spr 2700
17242-A	Pass Me Not O Gentle Savior	Ch 16169, Spr 2776
17243-A	Must Jesus Bear The Cross Alone	Ch 16283
17244-A	The Old Rugged Cross	Ch 16169, Spr 2657

Champion 16169, 16191 as by **The Hutchens Family Trio**, 16283 as by **Hutchens Family Trio**. Superior 2657, 2700 as by **The Mitchell Family Trio**, 2776 as by **The Mitchell Family**.

Acc. John McGhee, h-1/g; Frank Welling, sg; unknown, sg.

    Richmond, IN   Friday, November 14, 1930

17245	In The Garden	Ch 16235
17246-A	There Is Sunshine In My Soul Today	Ch 16191, Spr 2657, De 5514
17247	Brighten The Corner Where You Are	Ge unissued
17248	There Is Power In The Blood	Ch 16283, Spr 2776, De 5514
17249	When You're Gone I Won't Forget -1	Ge unissued
17250	There's A Girl In The Heart Of Maryland -1	Ge rejected
17252	Smiles	Ch 16145
17253	He Abides	Ge unissued
17254-B	The Lily Of The Valley	Ch 16235, Spr 2700
17255	The Nearer The Sweeter	Ge unissued
17256	Since I Have Been Redeemed	Ge rejected
17257	Sweet Peace, Gift Of God's Love	Ge unissued
17258	That's How I Need You	Ch 16145

Champion 16191 as by **The Hutchens Family Trio**, 16145, 16235, 16283 as by **Hutchens Family Trio**. Superior 2657, 2700 as by **The Mitchell Family Trio**, 2776 as by **The Mitchell Family**. Decca 5514 as by **Hutchens' Family Trio**.
Only one steel guitar is used on matrix 17254.
Matrix 17251 is untraced but possibly by these artists.

Frank Welling–John McGhee–Alma McGhee, v trio; or **Frank Welling**-1, v; acc. John McGhee, h-2/g/sp-3; Frank Welling, sg-4/g-5/sp-6.

    Grafton, WI   c. February 1931

L-767-1	Don't You Grieve Your Mother -4	Pm 3286
L-768-	Money Won't Make Everybody Happy	Pm unissued
L-769-2	Where Is My Mama -4	Pm 3286
L-770-2	Picture On The Wall -4	Pm 3287
L-773-	We'll Bust Them Trucks	Pm unissued
L-774-	The Brotherhood	Pm unissued
L-775-2	Busted Bank Blues -1, 5	Pm 3287
L-786-1	I'm On The Sunny Side -2	Pm 3310
L-788-2	Almost Persuaded -3/6, 4	Pm 3310

Paramount 3310 as by **Frank Welling & John McGhee**.
Matrices L-778, L-781 are by Fred L. Jeske & Louis Roen; other intervening matrices are untraced but at least some are probably by the above artists.

Frankie & Johnny-1/**Welling & McGhee**-2: John McGhee, h/g/v-3; unknown, k-4; Frank Welling, sg-5/g/v-6; unknown, bj.

    New York, NY   Wednesday, November 4, 1931

10956-2	Beech Fork Special -1	Ba 32593, Me M12521, Or 8175, Pe 12853, Ro 5175, Cq 7976
10957-	Birdie -2	ARC unissued
10958-2	Red Wing -1, 3, 4, 5, 6	Ba 32593, Me M12521, Or 8175, Pe 12853, Ro 5175, Cq 7976
10959-2	Maybe Next Week Sometime -1, 3, 4, 5, 6	Ba 32351, Or 8111, Pe 12777, Ro 5111, Cq 7990

Welling & McGhee, v duet; acc. John McGhee, h-1/g-2; Frank Welling, sg-3/g-4.
   New York, NY   Wednesday, November 4, 1931

10960-1,-2	My Little Mountain Home -1, 2/4	Ba 32333, Or 8108, Pe 12769, Ro 5108, Cq 7940, Bwy 4077, CrC/MeC/Stg/Roy 91239
10961-1	The Maple On The Hill -1, 2/4	ARC 5-12-59, Cq 7966, 8638
10962-	Wait Till The Sun Shines Nellie -2, 3/4	ARC unissued

Broadway 4077 as by **Walker Brothers**. Crown/Melotone/Sterling/Royale 91239 as by **John McGhee**.
Rev. Broadway 4077 by Carson Robison.

   New York, NY   Thursday, November 5, 1931

10963-2	The Crime At Quiet Dell -2, 3	Ba 32333, Or 8108, Pe 12769, Ro 5108, Cq 7940, CrC/MeC/Stg/Roy 91239

Frankie & Johnny-1/**Big John & Little Frank**-2, v duet; acc. John McGhee, h; unknown, bj-3; Frank Welling, g.
   New York, NY   Thursday, November 5, 1931

10964-1	Old Kentucky Dew -1	Ba 32555, Or 8164, Pe 12840, Ro 5164, Cq 8014
10965-1	Sweet Adeline At The Still -1	Ba 32555, Or 8164, Pe 12840, Ro 5164, Cq 8014
10966-	Roll It Down -2, 3	Vo 02544
10967-1	Take Your Time Papa -1, 3	Ba 32351, Or 8111, Pe 12777, Ro 5111, Cq 7990
10968-1	I Got Some Of That -2, 3	Vo 02544, Pan 25616

Rev. Panachord 25616 by Ashley & Foster (see Thomas C. Ashley).

Welling & McGhee: Frank Welling, v; acc. John McGhee, h-1; own g.
   New York, NY   Thursday, November 5, 1931

10969-	Money Can't Make Everybody Happy -1	ARC unissued
10970-	Bank Bustin' Blues	ARC unissued

John McGhee, v; acc. Frank Welling, sg; own g.
   New York, NY   Thursday, November 5, 1931

10971-1,-2	You Are As Welcome As Flowers In May	ARC 5-12-59, Cq 7966, 8638

Matrix 10971 as by **John McGhee** on Conqueror 7966, 8638.
Matrix 10971 is titled *You Are As Welcome As Flowers* on Conqueror 7966.

Frank Welling, John McGhee, v duet; acc. John McGhee, h-1/g-2; Frank Welling, sg-3/g-4.
   New York, NY   Friday, November 6, 1931

10972-	There Is A Fountain Filled With Blood -1, 4	ARC unissued
10973-1	Sweet Hour Of Prayer -2, 3	Ba 32428, Or 8130, Pe 12801, Ro 5130, Cq 7979, Bwy 4121, CrC/MeC/Stg/Roy 91320
10974-2	I'm Bound For The Promised Land -1, 4	Ba 32354, Me M12387, Or 8114, Pe 12780, Ro 5114, Cq 7945, Bwy 4121
10975-1	The Beautiful Garden Of Prayer -2, 3	Ba 32428, Or 8130, Pe 12801, Ro 5130, Cq 7979, CrC/MeC/Stg/Roy 91320

Broadway 4121 as by **Walker Brothers**. Crown/Melotone/Sterling/Royale 91320 as by **Frank Welling & John McGhee**.

Frank Welling, v; acc. poss. Richard Cox, f-1; unknown, h-2; unknown, k-3; unknown, cel-4; poss. Bernard F. Henson, g-5; own g.
   Richmond, IN   Thursday, July 28, 1932

18624-A	The Voice In The Village Choir	Ch 16474, MW 4961
18625-A	My Little Mountain Home -1, 4	Ch 16474, MW 4961
18626	Maybe Next Week Sometime -2, 3	Ch 16500
18627	No Low Down Hanging Around -1, 2, 3, 5	Ch 16709
18628	Slide Daddy Slide	Ch 16709
18629	Roll It Down Baby	Ch 16618

Champion 16500, 16709 as by **Evans' Old Timer**.
Matrix 18624 is titled *The Voice In The Old Village Choir* on Montgomery Ward 4961.
Matrix 18628 may have been recorded on July 29.

   Richmond, IN   Friday, July 29, 1932

18630	T-Bone Steak -2	Ge unissued
18631	My Mother-In-Law -2	Ch 16500
18632	Sing Me A Song Of The South -1, 2	Ch 16512
18633	Honeysuckle Time -1, 2	Ch 16512
18634	Willie After The Ball -1, 2, 5	Ch 16618
18635	The Old Fashioned Faith	Ch 16531
18636	Money Won't Make Everybody Happy	Ge rejected
18637	The Old Elm Tree	Ch 16531

Champion 16500, 16512, 16431 as by **Evans' Old Timer**.

Welling & McGhee, v duet; acc. John McGhee, h-1; Frank Welling or John McGhee, g.
   Richmond, IN   Friday, August 12, 1932

18676	I Am Thine O Lord -1	Ch 16511
18677	Leaning On The Everlasting Arms -1	Ch 16511
18678	He Abides	Ch 16542
18679	Just Over In The Glory Land	Ch 16542
18680	This World Is Not My Home -1	Ch 16585
18681	The Hallelujah Side -1	Ch 16585
18682	There's A Great Day Coming -1	Ch S-16479
18683	Nothing But The Blood -1	Ch S-16598, 45121, MeC 45121
18684	Go By The Way Of The Cross -1	Ch S-16569
18685	Standing On The Promises -1	Ch S-16569
18686	My Burdens Rolled Away -1	Ch S-16479

Champion S-16479, 16511, 16542 as by **McGhee & Welling**, 45121 as by **Frank Welling & John McGhee**.

Frank Welling, John McGhee, v duet; or **Frank Welling**-1, v; acc. John McGhee, h-2/g-3; Frank Welling, sg-4/g-5.
   Richmond, IN   Saturday, August 13, 1932

18687	Ring The Bells Of Heaven -2, 3/5	Ch 16660, 45114
18688	I Heard My Mother Call My Name In Prayer -3, 4	Ch S-16598, 45121, MeC 45121
18689	Face To Face -3, 4	Ch 16660, 45114
18690	His Promise To Me -3, 4/5	Ge unissued
18691	I Would Not Be Denied -3, 4/5	Ge rejected
18692	I Can't Think Of Everything -1, 5	Ch 16562

Champion 45114, 45121 as by **Frank Welling & John McGhee**.
Rev. Champion 16562 by Ken Landon (see James Brown, Jr. & Ken Landon groups).

Frank Welling, v/sp-1; acc. own sg-2/g-3; Harry Sayre, p.
   Richmond, IN   Thursday, April 13, 1933

19132-A	The Ill-Fated Akron -3	Ch 16588
19133-A	The Old Man's Story -3	Ch 16588
19134	Back In The Old Sunday School -3	Ch 16594
19135	Little Old Cross Road Store -3	Ch 16594
19136	I Wouldn't Trade The Silver In My Mother's Hair -2	Ch 16609, MW 4968
19137	Shake Hands With Mother Again -3	Ch 16609
19138	Daddy's Lullaby -1, 3	Ch 16652
19139	Daddy And Son	Ch 16697

Matrix 19136 is titled *I Wouldn't Trade The Silver In My Mother's Hair (For All The Gold In The World)* on Montgomery Ward 4968.
Revs: Champion 16697 by Dempsey Jones (see Golden Melody Boys); Montgomery Ward 4968 by Harry Hillard.

Frank Welling-1/**The Gospel Singer**-2, v/sp-3; acc. Harry Sayre, p.
   Richmond, IN   Friday, April 14, 1933

19140	Mother And Son -1, 3	Ch 16652
19141	The Rock That's Higher Than I -2	Ch S-16633
19142	Sunrise -2	Ch S-16633
19143	A Poor Wayfaring Stranger -2	Ge unissued
19144	A Charge To Keep I Have -2	Ch 16608
19145	An Evening Prayer -1	Ch 16608

Matrices 19141/42, 19144 may have been issued as by **The Gospel Singers**.

McGhee and/or Welling also accompanied David Miller and Miller Wikel and participated in recordings by Calaway's West Virginia Mountaineers and the Red Brush Rowdies. Frank Welling recorded (as Uncle Si) after 1942.

McGHEE & COGAR
McGHEE & WELLING

See John McGhee & Frank Welling.

BOB McGIMSEY

Bob McGimsey was chiefly known for his whistling, which he performed on numerous recordings both in his own name and by other artists. Most of his work was in the popular idiom, but a few items fall within the scope of this book.

Bob McGimsey, v; acc. unknown, f; unknown, p; unknown, g; unknown, vc; Eli Oberstein, dir.
   New York, NY   Wednesday, May 13, 1931

69605-	Shadrach	Vi 23562, RZAu G23693
69606-	Religion Ain't Nothing To Play With	Vi 23562, RZAu G23693

Bob Brookes, v; acc. unknown, f; unknown, g; unknown, sb.
   New York, NY   Monday, May 18, 1931

151555-3	Shadrach	Co 15676-D
151556-1	Wandering Lamb	Co 15676-D

Bob McGimsey, v-1/wh-2; acc. Barney Burnett, g.
New York, NY   Wednesday, June 17, 1931

69949-1	Bob's Medley -1	Vi 23584, ZoAu EE326
69950-1	Whistling Bob -1, 2	Vi 23584, ZoAu EE326
69951-1	Whistling Bob -1, 2	Vi unissued
69952-1	Zeb's Gal Susanna -1	Vi unissued
69957-1	Southern Melodies – Part 1 -2	Vi 23612
69958-1	Southern Melodies – Part 2 -2	Vi 23612

Matrix 69951 was intended for issue on Timely Tunes as by **Bob Brooks**.
Matrices 69953 to 69956 are by Victor Orchestra (popular).

Bob Brooks, v/wh; acc. unknown, g.
New York, NY   Friday, June 19, 1931

151619-3	Red River Valley	Co 15689-D
151620-2	Lonesome Cowboy	Co 15689-D
151621-	Clover Blossoms	Co unissued

MERLE McGINNIS (THE JOY KID)

Merle McGinnis, v; acc. poss. own g.
Richmond, IN   Thursday, August 29, 1929

| 15528-A | (There's No Use) Knocking On The Blinds | Ge 6990 |
| 15529-A | Highway Blues | Ge 6990 |

McGINTY'S OKLAHOMA COW BOY BAND (OTTO GRAY, DIRECTOR)

See Otto Gray.

FRANK & JAMES McGRAVY

Vocalion/OKeh 04491 by Frank & James McCravy is erroneously credited thus.

LEON McGUIRE

Leon McGuire, v; acc. own g.
Dallas, TX   Sunday, October 27, 1929

| DAL-553- | When The Blue Eyes Met The Brown | Vo 5393 |
| DAL-554- | Be Home Early Tonight | Vo 5393 |

MACK BROS.

Pseudonym on Decca for Frank & James McCravy.

GEORGE McKINLEY

Pseudonym on Broadway (4000 series) for Bradley Kincaid.

CAPT. McKINNEY & E.L. GRAHAM

No details.
Dallas, TX   Friday, June 27, 1929

402742-	Give Me Back The Fifteen Cents	OK unissued
402743-	Soap Suds Over The Fence	OK unissued
402744-	Evening Star	OK unissued
402745-	Kiss Waltz	OK unissued

At least one of these musicians almost certainly plays fiddle.

McKINNEY BROTHERS

Vocal duet; acc. prob. one of them, md; the other, g.
Richmond, IN   Tuesday, September 25, 1934

19698	Kentucky Is Calling Me	Ge unissued
19699	Memories Of Long Ago	Ge unissued
19700	Old Uncle Joe	Ch 16830, 45041
19701	Coney Island Baby	Ch 16830, 45041
19702	Goin' Down The Road – Feelin' Bad	Ge unissued
19703	Four O'Clock Blues	Ge unissued

There may be no vocal on matrices 19702/03.

McLAUGHLIN'S OLD TIME MELODY MAKERS

Unknown, f; unknown woman, p; Dr. —— McLaughlin, bj; unknown, g; unknown, sb; Druce Rude ("Barney Mills"), v-1.

Memphis, TN			Tuesday, February 14, 1928
41900-1	Whistling Rufus -1	Vi V-40117, Au 224	
41901-2	Take Your Foot Out Of The Mud -1	Vi V-40117, Au 224	
41902-1	Georgia Camp Meeting -1	Vi 21286	
41903-1	Dill Pickles Rag	Vi 21286	

Unknown, f; unknown woman, p; Dr. —— McLaughlin, bj; unknown, g; unknown, sb; Druce "Barney" Rude, v-1; unidentified, laughing-2.

Memphis, TN			Wednesday, November 21, 1928
M-816-	Old Days Medley -1	Vo 5296	
M-817-	Mississippi Shadows -1	Vo 5296	
M-818-	Hilarious Zeb -2	Vo 5330	
M-819-	Raisin' 'Ell -1	Vo 5330	

According to Druce Rude, the personnel of this group was the same for both sessions. This group is very probably the same as, or related to, Raggedy Ann's Melody Makers.

GRACE & SCOTTY MacLEAN

Grace & Scotty MacLean, v duet; acc. unknown, pac; unknown, p.

New York, NY			Monday, November 15, 1937
22027-1	When Your Old Wedding Ring Was New	ARC 8-03-53, Vo 03058	
22028-	Sunday On The Farm	ARC unissued	

New York, NY			Tuesday, December 14, 1937
22028-	Sunday On The Farm	ARC unissued	

Acc. unknown, h; unknown, pac; unknown, p.

New York, NY			Thursday, December 30, 1937
22236-1	When Rhododendrons Bloom Again	ARC 8-03-53, Vo 03058	

Acc. unknown, pac; unknown, p.

New York, NY			Thursday, February 10, 1938
22413-1	Just An Old Birthday Present (From An Old Sweetheart Of Mine)	ARC 8-04-61, Vo 03113	

New York, NY			Friday, February 11, 1938
22414-1	Shine On, Rocky Mountain Moonlight	ARC 8-04-61, Vo 03113	

AL McLEOD'S COUNTRY DANCE BAND

Unknown , f; unknown, ac; unknown, tbj; unknown, sb; Ed Durlacher, calls.

New York, NY			Friday, March 21, 1941
68848-A	She'll Be Comin' 'Round The Mountain When She Comes	De 15053, 29210, 40142	
68849-A	Billy Boy, Billy Boy	De 15053, 29210, 40142	
68850-A	Cowboy's Dream	De 15055, 29212, 40144	
68851-A	Mademoiselle From Armentieres	De 15055, 29212, 40144	
68852-A	Dip And Dive	De 15054, 29211, 40143	
68853-A	The Grapevine Twist	De 15054, 29211, 40143	

Matrix 68849 is titled *Billy Boy* on Decca 29210.
Decca 15053/54/55 were grouped in album A-229, 29210/11/12 in album A-474, and 40142/43/44 in album DU-734.

MICKEY McMADD

See Boa's Pine Cabin Boys.

McMANN & ROBERTS

Pseudonym on Supertone for Kirk McGee & Blythe Poteet (see McGee Brothers).

CLAYTON McMICHEN

McMichen's Home Town Band: Clayton McMichen, f; Robert Stephens, Jr., cl; Robert Stephens, bj; Lowe Stokes, g.

Atlanta, GA			Tuesday, July 7, 1925
9227-A	Bully Of The Town	OK 45034	
9228-A	Sweet Bunch Of Daisies	OK 40445	
9229-A	Silver Bell	OK 40445	
9230-A	Alabama Jubilee	OK 45022	

Revs: OKeh 45022 by Emmett & Aiken String Band, 45034 by Dr. Claud E. Watson & L.W. McCreight.

Riley Puckett & Bob Nichols, v duet; acc. Clayton McMichen, f; unknown, f; Riley Puckett, g.

Atlanta, GA			Thursday, April 22, 1926
142085-1	My Carolina Home	Co 15095-D, Vo 02947, RZAu G22591	

Here and on subsequent Columbia recordings Bob Nichols is a pseudonym for Clayton McMichen. Other recordings made at this session, though McMichen participated in them, were credited to Riley Puckett.

Bob Nichols & Gid Tanner: no details.
Atlanta, GA   Thursday, November 4, 1926
   143046-   The Drunkard's Hic-cups   Co unissued

McMichen's Melody Men: Clayton McMichen, f; K.D. Malone, cl; Riley Puckett, g/v-1.
Atlanta, GA   Thursday, November 4, 1926
   143056-2   Let Me Call You Sweetheart -1   Co 15111-D, Ve 2494-V, Cl 5434-C
   143057-1   Sweet Bunch Of Daisies   Co 15111-D

Velvet Tone 2494-V, Clarion 5434-C as by **Carey Taylor & His 'Ginny Boys**.
Revs: Velvet Tone 2494-V, Clarion 5434-C by Leake County Revelers.

Atlanta, GA   Saturday, November 6, 1926
   143090-1   House Of David Blues -1   Co 15130-D, Vo 02919
   143091-2   Down Yonder   Co 15130-D, Vo 02919

Bob Nichols & Riley Puckett, v duet; acc. Clayton McMichen, f; Riley Puckett, g.
Atlanta, GA   Saturday, November 6, 1926
   143098-2   Ring Waltz   Co 15136-D
   143099-1   Underneath The Mellow Moon   Co 15136-D
   143100-1   Don't You Remember The Time   Co 15114-D
   143101-2   My Isle Of Golden Dreams   Co 15114-D

Clayton McMichen, f solo.
Atlanta, GA   Saturday, March 26, 1927
   143769-1   St. Louis Blues   Co 15190-D
   143770-1   Fiddlin' Medley (Old Time Fiddlers' Medley)   Co 15190-D

Bob Nichols & Riley Puckett: Clayton McMichen, f/v-1; prob. Bert Layne, f; Riley Puckett, g/v.
Atlanta, GA   Wednesday, March 30, 1927
   143813-1   Let The Rest Of The World Go By -1   Co 15198-D, Re/RZAu G20665
   143814-2   Till We Meet Again -1   Co 15161-D, Re/RZAu G20665
   143815-2   I'm Forever Blowing Bubbles   Co 15161-D
   143816-   My Old Kentucky Home   Co unissued

Rev. Columbia 15198-D by Riley Puckett.

Atlanta, GA   Thursday, March 31, 1927
   143831-   Three O'Clock In The Morning   Co unissued

Clayton McMichen & His Singing Sisters: no details.
Atlanta, GA   Thursday, March 31, 1927
   143840-   Old Black Joe   Co unissued
   143841-   Mister Moon   Co unissued

Clayton McMichen, Gid Tanner, Riley Puckett, Bob Nichols, Fate Norris & Bert Layne: Clayton McMichen, f/sp; Gid Tanner, f/hv-1/sp; Bert Layne, f/sp; Fate Norris, bj/sp; Riley Puckett, g/lv-2/sp; Ezra (Ted) Hawkins, calls-3.
Atlanta, GA   Friday, April 1, 1927
   143848-1   A Fiddlers' Convention In Georgia – Part 1 -1, 2   Co 15140-D
   143849-2   A Fiddler's [sic] Convention In Georgia – Part 2 -3   Co 15140-D

Riley Puckett & Clayton McMichen: Clayton McMichen, f; Riley Puckett, g/v/wh-1.
Atlanta, GA   Saturday, April 2, 1927
   143867-2   Cindy   Co 15232-D
   143868-2   Little Brown Jug -1   Co 15232-D
   143869-   Alcoholic Blues   Co unissued
   143870-   Down Hearted Blues   Co unissued

McMichen's Melody Men: Clayton McMichen, f; poss. Lowe Stokes, f; poss. K.D. Malone, cl-1; Riley Puckett, g/v.
Atlanta, GA   Tuesday, November 1, 1927
   145059-1   When You And I Were Young Maggie   Co 15247-D, CoE 19016, Re/RZAu G20667
   145060-1   Silver Threads Among The Gold   Co 15247-D, CoE 19016, Re/RZAu G20667
   145061-2   Ain't She Sweet? -1   Co 15310-D

Clayton McMichen, Riley Puckett, Gid Tanner, Lowe Stokes, Fate Norris, Bob Nichols & Bill Brown: Clayton McMichen, f/sp; Lowe Stokes, f/sp; Gid Tanner, f/sp; Fate Norris, bj/sp; Riley Puckett, g/sp/v; Bill Brown, sp-1.
Atlanta, GA   Tuesday, November 1, 1927
   145066-3   A Corn Licker Still In Georgia Part 1   Co 15201-D
   145067-2   A Corn Licker Still In Georgia Part 2 -1   Co 15201-D

Bob Nichols & Riley Puckett, v duet; acc. Clayton McMichen, f; Riley Puckett, g.
Atlanta, GA   Tuesday, November 1, 1927
   145068-1   My Blue Ridge Mountain Queen   Co 15216-D, CoE 19013

McMichen's Melody Men: Clayton McMichen, f/v; poss. Lowe Stokes, f; Riley Puckett, g/v.
Atlanta, GA   Wednesday, November 2, 1927
145077-2	My Carolina Home	Co 15224-D

Bob Nichols & Riley Puckett, v duet; acc. Clayton McMichen, f; Riley Puckett, g.
Altanta, GA   Wednesday, November 2, 1927
145082-	'Neath The Old Apple Tree	Co unissued
145083-2	The Trail Of The Lonesome Pine	Co 15304-D

Atlanta, GA   Thursday, November 3, 1927
145090-3	In The Shade Of The Old Apple Tree	Co 15216-D, CoE 19013

McMichen's Melody Men: Clayton McMichen, f; poss. Lowe Stokes, f; poss. K.D. Malone, cl-1; Riley Puckett, g/v-2.
Altanta, GA   Friday, November 4, 1927
145099-1	Aloha Oe (Farewell To Thee)	Co 15202-D
145100-2	The Missouri Waltz	Co 15202-D
145101-2	Darling Nellie Gray -1, 2	Co 15310-D, Re/RZAu G21475
145102-1	Fifty Years Ago -1	Co 15224-D

Regal/Regal-Zonophone G21475 as by **Alabama Barnstormers**. Rev. Regal/Regal-Zonophone G21475 by Leake County Revelers.

Bob Nichols & Riley Puckett, v duet; acc. Clayton McMichen, f; poss. Lowe Stokes, f; Riley Puckett, g.
Atlanta, GA   Wednesday, April 11, 1928
146024-2	When The Maple Leaves Are Falling	Co 15350-D
146025-3	Dear Old Dixieland	Co 15350-D

Clayton McMichen, Riley Puckett, Gid Tanner, Lowe Stokes, Fate Norris, Bob Nichols & Bill Brown: Clayton McMichen, f/sp/v-1; Lowe Stokes, f/sp; Gid Tanner, f/hv-2/sp; Fate Norris, bj/sp; Riley Puckett, g/sp/v; Bill Brown, sp-3; several unidentified, laughing.
Atlanta, GA   Thursday, April 12, 1928
146032-1	A Corn Licker Still In Georgia Part 3 -1	Co 15258-D
146033-2	A Corn Licker Still In Georgia Part 4 -2, 3	Co 15258-D

Clayton McMichen & Dan Hornsby, dialog; acc. Clayton McMichen, f; unknown, f-1.
Atlanta, GA   Thursday, April 12, 1928
146038-1	The Original Arkansas Traveler Part 1	Co 15253-D
146039-3	The Original Arkansas Traveler Part 2 -1	Co 15253-D

Gid Tanner, Clayton McMichen, Riley Puckett, Lowe Stokes & Fate Norris: Clayton McMichen, f/sp-1; Gid Tanner, f/sp; Lowe Stokes, f/sp; Fate Norris, bj/sp; Riley Puckett, g/sp; unidentified, horn eff-2/dog eff-3/hog eff-4.
Atlanta, GA   Friday, April 13, 1928
146056-3	Possum Hunt On Stump House Mountain – Part 1 -1, 2, 3	Co 15298-D
146057-1	Possum Hunt On Stump House Mountain – Part 2 -1, 3	Co 15298-D
146058-3	Hog Killing Day – Part 1 -4	Co 15468-D
146059-2	Hog Killing Day – Part 2	Co 15468-D

McMichen's Melody Men With Riley Puckett: Clayton McMichen, f; prob. K.D. Malone, cl; Riley Puckett, g/v.
Atlanta, GA   Saturday, April 14, 1928
146076-2	Where The River Shannon Flows	Co 15288-D, CoE 19024
146077-1	Home Sweet Home	Co 15288-C, CoE 19024

Slight variations of the artist credit appear on the labels of some copies of Columbia 15288-D.

Riley Puckett & Clayton McMichen: Clayton McMichen, f; Riley Puckett, g/v.
Atlanta, GA   Saturday, April 14, 1928
146078-2	Slim Gal	Co 15295-D
146079-2	Old Molly Hare	Co 15295-D

Bob Nichols & Riley Puckett, v duet; acc. Clayton McMichen, f; Riley Puckett, g.
Atlanta, GA   Saturday, April 14, 1928
146080-1	'Neath The Old Apple Tree	Co 15304-D

McMichen–Layne String Orchestra: Clayton McMichen, f/v-1; Bert Layne, f; prob. K.D. Malone, cl; Riley Puckett, g/v; unknown, sb.
Atlanta, GA   Tuesday, October 23, 1928
147261-1	Little Blue Ridge Girl	Co 15464-D
147262-3	The Dying Hobo -1	Co 15464-D
147272-	Sailing On The Robert E. Lee	Co unissued

Some copies of Columbia 15464-D give the artist-credit as **McMichen–Layne String Orch**.
Intervening matrices are by other artists.

Atlanta, GA   Wednesday, October 24, 1928
   147274-2   Down On The Ozark Trail -1   Co 15356-D

Clayton McMichen, Riley Puckett, Gid Tanner, Lowe Stokes & Fate Norris: Clayton McMichen, f/sp; Gid Tanner, f/v/sp; Lowe Stokes, f/sp; Fate Norris, bj/sp; Riley Puckett, g/v/sp; Bill Brown, sp-1; gunshot eff-2.
Atlanta, GA   Wednesday, October 24, 1928
   147275-3   Corn Licker Still In Georgia – Part 5   Co 15366-D
   147276-3   Corn Licker Still In Georgia – Part 6 -1, 2   Co 15366-D

McMichen's Melody Men: Clayton McMichen, f/v; prob. K.D. Malone, cl; Riley Puckett, g.
Atlanta, GA   Wednesday, October 24, 1928
   147277-2   When You're Far From The Ones Who Love You   Co 15391-D

Fate Norris, Gid Tanner, Hugh Cross, Lowe Stokes, Clayton McMichen & K.D. Malone: Clayton McMichen, f; Gid Tanner, f/v/sp; Lowe Stokes, f/poss. sp; K.D. Malone, cl-1; Fate Norris, bj-2/hv-3/sp; Hugh Cross, g-4/sp; unidentified, sp; unidentified, pig eff.
Atlanta, GA   Wednesday, October 24, 1928
   147278-2   A Day At The County Fair – Part 1 -1, 4   Co 15332-D
   147279-3   A Day At The County Fair – Part 2 -2, 3   Co 15332-D

McMichen's Melody Men: Clayton McMichen, f; K.D. Malone, cl; Perry Bechtel, g; Dan Hornsby, v.
Atlanta, GA   Wednesday, October 24, 1928
   147284-2   Wabash Blues   Co 15340-D
   147285-2   Lonesome Mama Blues   Co 15340-D

Atlanta, GA   Thursday, October 25, 1928
   147286-2   Sailing On The Bay Of Tripoli   Co 15391-D

Riley Puckett & Clayton McMichen: Clayton McMichen, f; Riley Puckett, g/v.
Atlanta, GA   Friday, October 26, 1928
   147297-2   Bill Johnson   Co 15358-D
   147298-2   Farmer's Daughter   Co 15686-D
   147299-1   Paddy Won't You Drink Some Cider   Co 15358-D
   147300-2   The Arkansas Sheik   Co 15686-D

Columbia 15686-D as by Clayton **McMichen & Riley Puckett**.

McMichen-Layne String Orchestra: Clayton McMichen, f; Bert Layne, f; Riley Puckett, g/v; unknown, sb.
Atlanta, GA   Friday, October 26, 1928
   147308-2   The Blind Child's Prayer Part 1   Co 15333-D
   147309-3   The Blind Child's Prayer Part 2   Co 15333-D
   147310-2   Daisies Won't Tell   Co 15356-D
   147311-   Ramblin' Boy   Co unissued

McMichen's Melody Men: no details.
Atlanta, GA   Thursday, April 11, 1929
   148238-   Back In Tennessee   Co unissued
   148239-   Last Night Broken Hearted   Co unissued

Clayton McMichen, Riley Puckett, Gid Tanner, Lowe Stokes, Fate Norris & Tom Dorsey: Clayton McMichen, f/sp; Lowe Stokes, f/sp; Gid Tanner, f/sp; Fate Norris, bj/sp; Riley Puckett, g/sp; Dan Hornsby, sp; band v.
Atlanta, GA   Friday, April 12, 1929
   148266-3   Corn Licker Still in Georgia Part 7   Co 15432-D
   148267-3   Corn Licker Still in Georgia Part 8   Co 15432-D

Clayton McMichen & Riley Puckett: Clayton McMichen, f/sp; Riley Puckett, g/v-1.
Atlanta, GA   Tuesday, October 29, 1929
   149289-2   McMichen's Reel   Co 15521-D
   149290-2   Rye Straw -1   Co 15521-D

McMichen's Melody Men: no details.
Atlanta, GA   Wednesday, October 30, 1929
   149304-   I Don't Care What You Used To Be   Co unissued
   149305-   Down The Lane To Home Sweet Home   Co unissued

Clayton McMichen, f/v; poss. Bert Layne, f; unknown, sg.
Atlanta, GA   Thursday, October 31, 1929
   149316-1   Honolulu Moon   Co 15540-D, Re/RZAu G21593
   149317-2   When Clouds Have Vanished   Co 15540-D, Re/RZAu G21593

Regal/Regal-Zonophone G21593 as by **Regal Hill-Billy Singers**.

Clayton McMichen, Riley Puckett, Gid Tanner, Lowe Stokes, Fate Norris & Tom Dorsey: Clayton McMichen, f/sp; Lowe Stokes, f/sp; Gid Tanner, f/sp; Fate Norris, bj/sp; Riley Puckett, g/sp; Dan Hornsby, sp-1; band v-2.
Atlanta, GA   Friday, November 1, 1929

| 149328-2 | Corn Licker Still In Georgia Part 9 | Co 15531-D |
| 149329-2 | Corn Licker Still In Georgia Part 10 -1, 2 | Co 15531-D |

Bob Nichols & Hugh Cross, v duet; acc. Clayton McMichen, f-1; Hugh Cross, g.
Atlanta, GA   Friday, November 1, 1929

| 149334-2 | Corrine Corrina | Co 15480-D |
| 149335-2 | I Left My Gal In The Mountains -1 | Co 15480-D |

Hugh Cross, Clayton McMichen, Riley Puckett, Gid Tanner, Fate Norris & Lowe Stokes: Clayton McMichen, f/sp-1; Lowe Stokes, f/sp-2; Gid Tanner, f/v eff-3/sp-4; Fate Norris, bj/sp; Riley Puckett, g/sp; Hugh Cross, sp.
Atlanta, GA   Saturday, November 2, 1929

| 149338-3 | Kickapoo Medicine Show – Part 1 -1, 2, 4 | Co 15482-D |
| 149339-3 | Kickapoo Medicine Show – Part 2 -3 | Co 15482-D |

Clayton McMichen, Riley Puckett, Lowe Stokes, Fate Norris, Bert Layne, Uncle Fuzz & Tom Dorsey: Clayton McMichen, f/sp; Lowe Stokes, f/sp; Bert Layne, f/sp; Fate Norris, bj/sp; Riley Puckett, g/sp; Dan Hornsby, v-1/sp; prob. Frank Walker, sp-2; band v-3.
Atlanta, GA   Saturday, November 2, 1929

| 149340-1 | A Night In A Blind Tiger – Part 1 | Co 15503-D |
| 149341-1 | A Night In A Blind Tiger – Part 2 -1, 2, 3 | Co 15503-D |

Clayton McMichen, Riley Puckett, Gid Tanner, Lowe Stokes, Fate Norris: Clayton McMichen, f/sp; Gid Tanner, f/sp; Lowe Stokes, f/sp; Fate Norris, poss. bj/sp; Riley Puckett, g/sp; unidentified, bee eff.
Atlanta, GA   Monday, November 4, 1929

| 149369-3 | A Bee Hunt On Hill For Sartin Creek – Part 1 | Co 15700-D |
| 149370-1 | A Bee Hunt On Hill For Sartin Creek – Part 2 | Co 15700-D |

Bob Nichols, v; acc. poss. own g.
Atlanta, GA   Tuesday, April 15, 1930

| 150218-3 | The Killing Of Tom Slaughter | Co 15590-D |
| 150219-3 | The Grave In The Pines | Co 15590-D |

Bob Nichols & Hugh Cross, v duet; acc. Clayton McMichen, f-1; Hugh Cross, g.
Atlanta, GA   Wednesday, April 16, 1930

150236- ;	When I Lived In Arkansas -1	Co 15698-D
130461-1		
150237-2	In The Hills Of Old Virginia	Co 15556-D

Clayton McMichen: no details.
Atlanta, GA   Wednesday, April 16, 1930

| 150238- | Allen Vane | Co unissued |

Clayton McMichen, Riley Puckett, Gid Tanner, Lowe Stokes, Bert Layne, Fate Norris, Oscar Ford & Tom Dorsey: Clayton McMichen, f/v-1/sp; Gid Tanner, f/sp; Lowe Stokes, f/sp; Bert Layne, f/sp; Fate Norris, bj/sp; Riley Puckett, g/sp; Oscar Ford, v-2/sp; Dan Hornsby, sp; unidentified, dog eff-3.
Atlanta, GA   Thursday, April 17, 1930

150271-3;	Taking The Census – Part 1 -1, 3	Co 15549-D
194881-2		
150272-1;	Taking The Census – Part 2 -2	Co 15549-D
194882-2		

Clayton McMichen, Riley Puckett, Gid Tanner, Lowe Stokes, Bert Layne, Oscar Ford & Tom Dorsey-1/Clayton McMichen, Riley Puckett, Gid Tanner, Lowe Stokes, Bert Layne, Oscar Ford, Uncle Fuzz & Tom Dorsey-2: Clayton McMichen, f/sp; Gid Tanner, f/sp; Lowe Stokes, f/sp; Bert Layne, f/sp; Riley Puckett, g/v-3/sp; Oscar Ford, sp; Dan Hornsby, sp; unknown (prob. Frank Walker) , sp-4.
Atlanta, GA   Saturday, April 19, 1930

150299- ;	Jeremiah Hopkins' Store At Sand Mountain – Part 1 -1, 3	Co 15598-D
194902-2		
150300- ;	Jeremiah Hopkins' Store At Sand Mountain – Part 2 -2, 4	Co 15598-D
194903-2		

Clayton McMichen, v/y; acc. poss. own g.
Atlanta, GA   Monday, April 21, 1930

| 150319-2; | Prohibition Blues | Co unissued: *Co C2K47466, Co(E) 472886 (CDs)* |
| 194949-1 | | |

Bob Nichols & Hugh Cross, v duet; acc. Clayton McMichen, f; Hugh Cross, g.
Atlanta, GA   Monday, April 21, 1930

| 150320-2; | When It's Peach Picking Time In Georgia | Co 15698-D |
| 130469-1 | | |

The labels of some copies spell the title *When Its Peach Picking Time In Georgia*.

Clayton McMichen & Riley Puckett: Clayton McMichen, f; Riley Puckett, g.
   Atlanta, GA   Monday, April 21, 1930
   150327-2   Done Gone   Co 15594-D
   150328-2   Cumberland Valley Waltz   Co 15594-D

Clayton McMichen, Riley Puckett, Gid Tanner, Lowe Stokes, Fate Norris & Tom Dorsey: Clayton McMichen, f/sp; Lowe Stokes, f/sp; Gid Tanner, f/sp; Fate Norris, bj/sp; Riley Puckett, g/v-1/sp; Dan Hornsby, sp-2; band v-3.
   Atlanta, GA   Monday, April 21, 1930
   150335- ;   Corn Licker Still In Georgia Part 11   Co 15618-D
   130026-1
   150336- ;   Corn Licker Still In Georgia Part 12 -1, 2, 3   Co 15618-D
   130027-1

Bob Nichols & Hugh Cross, v duet; acc. Clayton McMichen, f; Hugh Cross, g.
   Atlanta, GA   Tuesday, April 22, 1930
   150343-2   Smoky Mountain Home   Co 15556-D

Clayton McMichen & Riley Puckett: Clayton McMichen, f; Riley Puckett, g.
   Atlanta, GA   Thursday, December 4, 1930
   151028-   Lover's Waltz   Co unissued

Clayton McMichen & Hugh Bryant: Clayton McMichen, f; Hoyt "Slim' " Bryant, g; prob. one or both, v.
   Atlanta, GA   Sunday, December 7, 1930
   151081-   Where The Bloom Is On The Sage   Co unissued

Clayton McMichen, Riley Puckett, Lowe Stokes, Bert Layne & Tom Dorsey: Clayton McMichen, f/v-1/sp; Lowe Stokes, f/sp; Bert Layne, f/sp; Riley Puckett, g/v-2/sp; Dan Hornsby, v-3/sp.
   Atlanta, GA   Monday, December 8, 1930
   151098-3   Prohibition – Yes Or No – Part 1 -1, 2, 3   Co 15632-D
   151099-1   Prohibition – Yes Or No – Part 2   Co 15632-D

Clayton McMichen, Riley Puckett, Gid Tanner, Lowe Stokes, Bert Layne, Bob Nichols & Tom Dorsey: Clayton McMichen, f/sp; Gid Tanner, f/sp; Lowe Stokes, f/sp; Bert Layne, f/sp; Riley Puckett, g/v-1/sp-2; poss. Ted (Ezra) Hawkins, v-3; Dan Hornsby, sp; unidentified, sp.
   Atlanta, GA   Monday, December 8, 1930
   151100-3   Fiddlers' Convention – Part 3 -3   Co 15667-D
   151101-2   Fiddlers' Convention – Part 4 -1, 2   Co 15667-D

Clayton McMichen, Riley Puckett, Gid Tanner, Lowe Stokes, Bert Layne & Tom Dorsey: Clayton McMichen, f/v-1/sp; Lowe Stokes, f/sp; Bert Layne, f/sp; Gid Tanner, bj/sp; Riley Puckett, g/v/sp; Dan Hornsby, sp-2; band v; unidentified, laughing-3.
   Atlanta, GA   Monday, December 8, 1930
   151102-1   Corn Licker Still In Georgia Part 13   Co 15703-D
   151103-3   Corn Licker Still In Georgia Part 14 -1, 2, 3   Co 15703-D

Clayton McMichen & Hoyt Bryant: Clayton McMichen, f; Hoyt "Slim" Bryant, g; prob. one or both, v.
   Atlanta, GA   Monday, December 8, 1930
   151104-   You Brought A New Kind Of Love To Me   Co unissued

McMichen's Georgia Wildcats With Slim Bryant: Clayton McMichen, f/v-1; Hoyt "Slim" Bryant, g/v.
   Atlanta, GA   Monday, October 26, 1931
   151932-1   When The Bloom Is On The Sage -1   Co 15723-D
   151933-1   Yum Yum Blues   Co 15723-D

McMichen & Puckett: Clayton McMichen, f; Riley Puckett, g.
   Atlanta, GA   Monday, October 26, 1931
   151934-   Devil's Dream   Co unissued
   151935-   Durna [sic] Hornpipe   Co unissued

Bob Nichols & Puckett: prob.: v duet; acc. Clayton McMichen, f; Riley Puckett, g.
   Atlanta, GA   Monday, October 26, 1931
   151936-   Longest Train I Ever Seen   Co unissued
   151937-   That's No Business Of Mine   Co unissued

Clayton McMichen's Georgia Wildcats: Clayton McMichen, f/v-1/sp-2; poss. Bert Layne, f; Hoyt "Slim" Bryant, g/v-3.
   Atlanta, GA   Wednesday, October 28, 1931
   151966-1   Wild Cat Rag -2   Co 15775-D
   151967-   Carolina Train   Co unissued
   151968-   On The Banks Of The Ohio   Co unissued
   151969-   Back To My Georgia Home   Co unissued
   151970-   The Golden Wedding Ring   Co unissued
   151971-1   Sweet Floreine -1, 3   Co 15775-D

McMichen & Puckett: prob.: Clayton McMichen, f; Riley Puckett, g.
Atlanta, GA   Friday, October 30, 1931

| 151988- | Hog Face Blues | Co unissued |
| 151989- | No Name Blues | Co unissued |

Clayton McMichen's Georgia Wildcats-1/Clayton McMichen & "Slim" Bryant-2/"Slim" Bryant-3: Clayton McMichen, f/v-4/calls-5; Oddie McWinders, bj/v-6; Hoyt "Slim" Bryant, g/v-7.
New York, NY   Friday, August 26, 1932

1811-2	Georgia Wildcat Breakdown -1, 4	Cr 3385, Htd 23091, MeC 93029, Vs 5010, JDs 3512, Davis DA-19-4
1812-1	Hog-Trough Reel -1, 5	Cr 3385, Htd 23091, MeC 93029, Min M-14012, Vs 5016, Ge 7011, Beacon 7011, Davis DA-19-1
1813-3	Wreck Of The Old '97 -3, 7	Cr 3384, Htd 23090, Vs 5029, Asch 410-3
1814-3	Singing An Old Hymn -1, 4, 6, 7	Cr 3384, Htd 23090, Vs 5110
1815-3	'Way Down In Caroline -2, 4, 7	Cr 3386, Htd 23092, Vs 5052
1816-3	Back In Tennessee -3, 7	Cr 3386, Htd 23092, Vs 5052

Some Crown and possibly other issues may be as by **Clayton McMichen Georgia Wildcats**. Varsity 5110 as by **Clayton McMichen**. Gennett 7011, Beacon 7011 as by **Clayton McMichen & His Georgia Wildcats**. Davis DA-19-1, DA-19-4 as by **Clayton McMichen & His Wildcats**. Asch 410-3 as by **Clayton McMichen & Orchestra**.
Matrix 1812 is titled *Hog Trough Reel* on Varsity 5016, Gennett 7011, Beacon 7011, Davis DA-19-1. Matrix 1813 is titled *Wreck Of The 97* on Varsity 5029. Matrix 1815 is titled *Way Down In Carolina* on Varsity 5052.
Rev. Asch 410-3 by Bill Bender.

Clayton McMichen's Georgia Wildcats-1/Clayton McMichen & "Slim" Bryant-2/"Slim" Bryant-3/Joe & Bob Nichols-4/Oddie McWinders-5/Bud Thompson-6: Clayton McMichen, f-7/v-8/calls-9/sp-10; Oddie McWinders, bj-11/v-12; Hoyt "Slim" Bryant, g/v-13/sp-14; Bob Miller (as Bud Thompson), v-15.
New York, NY   Tuesday, August 30, 1932

1823-2	Arkansas Traveler -1, 7, 9, 11	Cr 3397, MeC 93031, Vs 5010, Ge 7011, Beacon 7011, Davis DA-19-2
1824-1	The Old Hen Cackled -1, 7, 10, 11, 14	Vs 5064, JDs 3510
1825-2	Give The Fiddler A Dram -1, 7, 10, 11, 14	Vs 5011, JDs 3510
1826-2	Ider Red -1, 7, 8, 10, 11, 14	Cr 3397, MeC 93031, Min M-14012, Vs 5011, JDs 3511, Davis DA-19-5
1827-2	The Blue Hills Of Virginia -4, 7, 8, 13	Cr 3447, Htd 23096, Vs 5030
1828- -	Down The Ozark Trail -7, 8, 12, 13	Vs 5044, MW M-3020
1830-1	Countin' Cross Ties -6, 7, 11, 15	Cr 3432, Htd 23097, Vs 5075
1831-1	Log Cabin In The Lane -4, 8, 13	Cr 3447, Htd 23096, Vs 5026, JDs 3513, Davis DA-19-7
1832-1	Where The Skies Are Always Blue -4, 7, 8, 11, 13	Cr 3399, Htd 23094, Vs 5097
1833-1	Bummin' On The I.C. Line -6, 7, 11, 15	Cr 3432, Htd 23097, Vs 5097
1834-1	Red Wing -4, 7, 8, 11, 13	Cr 3419, Htd 23098, Vs 5016, JDs 3513, Davis DA-19-8
1835-1	Down In Old Kentucky -5, 7, 11, 12	Cr 3398, Htd 23093, Vs 5026
1836-1	All I've Got Is Gone -5, 11, 12	Cr 3398, Htd 23093, Vs 5025
1837-1	Yum Yum Blues -3, 7, 11, 13	Cr 3418, Htd 23099, Vs 5025
1838-1	Smoky Mountain Home -4, 7, 8, 11, 13	Cr 3399, Htd 23094, Vs 5030, JDs 3512, Davis DA-19-3
1839-1	I Don't Love Nobody -1, 7, 9, 11	Cr 3416, Htd 23095, Vs 5064
1840-1	Old Joe Clarke -1, 7, 8, 11	Cr 3416, Htd 23095, Vs 5029, JDs 3511, Davis DA-19-6
1842-1	When The Bloom Is On The Sage (Round-Up Time In Texas) -2, 7, 8, 11, 13	Cr 3419, Htd 23098

Varsity 5044 as by **Cowboy Rodgers**, 5075 as by **Clayton McMichen & Georgia Wildcats**, 5097, 5110 as by **Clayton McMichen**. Joe Davis 3510 as by **Clayton McMichen & His Georgia Wildcats**, 3511 as by **Clayton McMichen & His Wildcats**. Davis DA-19-1 to DA-19-8 as by **Clayton McMichen & His Wildcats**; these four discs were issued as an album set.
Matrices 1829, 1841 are by Bob Miller.
Revs: Crown 3418, Homestead 23099, Varsity 5075, 5097, 5110 by Bob Miller; Varsity 5044 (with same credit), Montgomery Ward M3020 by Edward L. Crain.

Clayton McMichen's Georgia Wildcats: Clayton McMichen, f/v-1; Ken Newton, f/v-2/wh-3; Jerry Wallace, bj/g; Hoyt "Slim" Bryant, g/v-4; Raymond "Loppy" Bryant, sb; v trio (usually Newton, "Slim" Bryant, and "Loppy" Bryant; sometimes McMichen, Newton, and "Slim" Bryant)-5; unidentified, y-6.
New York, NY   Thursday, July 22, 1937

62422-A	Farewell Blues	De 5436, MeC 45225
62429-A	In The Pines -5	De 5448, MeC 45227
62430-A	Chicken Don't Roost Too High -1, 5	De 5491
62431-A	I Want My Rib -1, 5	De 5424
62432-A	Georgiana Moon -2, 3	De 5491
62433-A	Bile Dem Cabbage Down -1, 5	De 5436, MeC 45225

62434-A	Sweet Bunch Of Daisies -4	De 5418
62435-A	Frankie And Johnnie -1	De 5418, 46072
62436-A	Under The Old Kentucky Moon -3, 5, 6	De 5448, MeC 45227
62437-A	Yum Yum Blues -4	De 5424

Intervening matrices are unrelated.

Clayton McMichen, f/v-1; Ken Newton, f/v-2/wh-3; Carl Cotner, f; Jerry Wallace, bj/g; Hoyt "Slim" Bryant, g/v-4; Raymond "Loppy" Bryant, sb/v-5; v trio (usually Newton, "Slim" Bryant, and "Loppy" Bryant; sometimes McMichen, Newton, and "Slim" Bryant)-6; unidentified, wh-7.

New York, NY   Tuesday, August 2, 1938

64376-A	Please Don't Sell My Pappy No More Rum -6	De 5601, 6091
64377-A	The Wang Wang Blues	De 5646
64378-A	St. Louis Woman (Got Her Diamond In The Hock Shop Now) -1	De 5614
64379-A	Anna From Indiana -6	De 5574
64380-A	Is There Still Room For Me ('Neath The Old Apple Tree) -6	De 5577
64381-1	The Trail Of The Lonesome Pine (In The Blue Ridge Mountains Of Virginia) -6	De 5634
64384-A	Whispering -2, 3, 7	De 5634
64385-C	Just An Old Chimney Stack -4, 5	De 5670

Clayton McMichen, f/v-1; Ken Newton, f/v-2; Carl Cotner, f; Jerry Wallace, bj/g; Hoyt "Slim" Bryant, g; Raymond "Loppy" Bryant, sb/v-3; v trio (usually Newton, "Slim" Bryant, and "Loppy" Bryant; sometimes McMichen, Newton, and "Slim" Bryant)-4.

New York, NY   Wednesday, August 3, 1938

64382-A	I'm Gonna Learn To Swing -1	De 5614
64383-A	Downhearted Blues -1	De 5646
64386-A	I Gotta Ketch Up With My Settin' -4	De 5592
64387-B	Put Your Arms Around Me, Honey (I Never Knew Any Girl Like You) -4	De 5670, 6091
64388-A	Only A Faded Rose -2	De 5592
64389-A	Mary Lou -1, 2	De 5601
64390-A	I'm Free A Little Bird As I Can Be -1, 2, 3, 4	De 5574
64391-A	Alexander's Ragtime Band -4	De 5577, 46072

Clayton McMichen, f; Ken Newton, f/v-1/wh-2; Carl Cotner, f; Jerry Wallace, bj/g; Hoyt "Slim" Bryant, g; Raymond "Loppy" Bryant, sb/v-3; unknown, vb-4; v trio (usually Newton, "Slim" Bryant, and "Loppy" Bryant; sometimes McMichen, Newton, and "Slim" Bryant)-5.

New York, NY   Monday, May 29, 1939

65665-A	I Wonder Who's Kissing Her Now -1, 2, 4	De 5705
65666-A	Free A Little Bird As I Can Be, No. 2 -3, 5	De 5701
65667-A	My Gal's A Lulu -5	De 5701
65668-A	Dream Trail -5	De 5710, MeC 45324
65669-A	Misery On My Mind -1	De 5727
65670-A	Old Fashioned Locket -1	De 5780
65671-A	The Lily That Bloomed For Me -1	De 5765

Clayton McMichen, f; Ken Newton, f/v-1/wh-2; Carl Cotner, f; Jerry Wallace, bj/g; Hoyt "Slim" Bryant, g; Raymond "Loppy" Bryant, sb/v-3; v trio (usually Newton, "Slim" Bryant, and "Loppy" Bryant; sometimes McMichen, Newton, and 'Slim' Bryant)-4.

New York, NY   Wednesday, May 31, 1939

65681-A	I Cannot Tell A Lie -4	De 5705
65682-A	What Good Will It Do -1	De 5699
65683-A	Jesse James -3, 4	De 5710, MeC 45324
65684-A	Just Tell Them That You Saw Me -3, 4	De 5765
65685-A	All Through The Night -2	De 5699
65686-A	Rose Of Shenandoah Valley -4	De 5721, MeC 45332, DeSA FM5145
65687-A	Little Darling, I'll Be Yours -1	De 5721, MeC 45332, DeSA FM5145

Clayton McMichen, f/v-1; Ken Newton, f/v-2/wh-3; Carl Cotner, f; Jerry Wallace, bj/g; Hoyt "Slim" Bryant, g/v-4; Raymond "Loppy" Bryant, sb; v trio (usually Newton, "Slim" Bryant, and "Loppy" Bryant; sometimes McMichen, Newton, and "Slim" Bryant)-5.

New York, NY   Thursday, June 1, 1939

65704-A	I'm Ridin' The Trail Back Home -5	De 5714
65705-A	I Could Tell By The Look On His Face -4, 5	De 5727
65706-A	Don't Trouble Me -2, 3	De 5714
65707-A	Put On Your Old Grey Bonnet -1, 5	De 5780

Clayton McMichen, f; acc. Jerry Wallace, bj-1; Hoyt "Slim" Bryant, g-2.
New York, NY   Thursday, June 1, 1939

65708-A	1. Turkey In The Straw 2. Old Hen Cackle 3. Fiddler's Dram -2	De 2647, 27306
65709-A	1. Old Joe Clark 2. Pretty Little Widder 3. Shortenin' Bread -2	De 2647, 27306
65710-A	1. Fire In The Mountain 2. Ida Red 3. Sally Goodin -1, 2	De 2648, 27307
65711-A	1. Soldier's Joy 2. Arkansas Traveler 3. Mississippi Sawyer -1	De 2648, 27307
65712-A	1. Sourwood Mountain 2. Peter Went A Fishin' 3. Sugar In The Gourd -1	De 2649, 27308
65713-A	1. Devil's Dream 2. Rickett's Hornpipe 3. Fisher's Hornpipe -1, 2	De 2649, 27308

The third tune on matrix 65708 is titled *Fiddler's Dream* on some copies.

Clayton McMichen also recorded, uncredited, with artists in the "Skillet-Licker circle" and others, and after 1942.

McMICHEN–LAYNE STRING ORCHESTRA

See Clayton McMichen.

McMICHEN'S GEORGIA WILDCATS

See Clayton McMichen.

McMICHEN'S HARMONY BOYS

Elmer McMichen, f/v-1; Hoyt Newton, f; ——— Woods, bj; Hoyt "Slim" Bryant, g/v.
Atlanta, GA   Friday, March 15, 1929

402326-B	Ain't She Sweet?	OK 45330
402327-	Hand Me Down My Walking Cane	OK unissued
402328-B	Sweetheart Days -1	OK 45330
402329-	In The Shade Of The Old Apple Tree	OK unissued

McMICHEN'S HOME TOWN BAND

See Clayton McMichen.

McMICHEN'S MELODY MEN

See Clayton McMichen.

McMILLAN QUARTET

Vocal quartet; acc. unknown, p.
Atlanta, GA   Saturday, April 2, 1927

| 143863-2 | Glory Is Coming | Co 15194-D |
| 143864-2 | No Stranger Yonder | Co 15194-D |

Atlanta, GA   Friday, April 20, 1928

| 146157-1 | I Love To Tell His Love | Co 15681-D |
| 146158-2 | Singing On The Journey Home | Co 15681-D |

McMillian Sacred Singers: prob. similar personnel; acc. unknown, p.
Atlanta, GA   Monday, March 24, 1930

| ATL-8004- | Glory For The Faithful | Vo 5473 |
| ATL-8005- | Our Watchword | Vo 5473 |

McMILLIAN SACRED SINGERS

See McMillan Quartet.

UNCLE DAVE MACON

Uncle Dave Macon, v; acc. own bj.
New York, NY   Tuesday, July 8, 1924

13330/31*/32	Keep My Skillet Good And Greasy	Vo 14848, 5041
13333/34*/35	Hill Billie Blues	Vo 14904, 5051
13336/37/38	Old Maid's Last Hope (A Burglar Song)	Vo 14850, 5043
13339/40*	All I've Got's Gone	Vo 14904, 5051
13341/42*	The Fox Chase	Vo 14850, 5043

New York, NY   Wednesday, July 9, 1924

| 13343*/44 | Papa's Billie Goat | Vo 14848, 5041 |

13345/46	Muskrat Medley; Intro: Rye Strawfields	Vo rejected
13347/48	Old Ship Of Zion	Vo rejected
13349/50	Just From Tennessee	Vo rejected
13351/52	That High Born Gal Of Mine	Vo rejected

Acc. own bj; or **Uncle Dave Macon & Sid Harkreader**-1/**Sid Harkreader**-2: Sid Harkreader, f; Uncle Dave Macon, bj/v-3.

New York, NY   Thursday, July 10, 1924

13353/54*	The Little Old Log Cabin In The Lane -1, 3	Vo 14864, 5046
13355/56*/57	(She Was Always) Chewing Gum	Vo 14847, 5040
13358/59*	Jonah And The Whale -1, 3	Vo 14864, 5046
13360/61*	I'm Going Away To Leave You, Love	Vo 14847, 5040
13362*/63	Love Somebody -2	Vo 14887, 5047
13364*/65	Soldier's Joy -2	Vo 14887, 5047

Vocalion 14887 is subcredited **Uncle Dave Macon**.

New York, NY   Friday, July 11, 1924

| 13375*/76 | Bile Them Cabbage Down | Vo 14849, 5042 |
| 13377/78 | Down By The River | Vo 14849, 5042 |

New York, NY   Monday, April 13, 1925

667/68*	Run, Nigger, Run	Vo 15032, 5060
669/70	Old Dan Tucker	Vo 15033, 5061
671/72	Station Will Be Changed After A While	Vo 15341, 5109
673/74	Rooster Crow Medley	Vo 15101, 5071
675/76	Going Across The Sea	Vo 15192, 5081
679/80	Just From Tennessee	Vo 15143, 5075

Matrices 677/78, 681/82 are by Sid Harkreader.

New York, NY   Tuesday, April 14, 1925

683/84	Watermelon Smilin' On The Vine	Vo 15063, 5065
685/86	All-Go-Hungry Hash House	Vo 15076, 5067
695/96	From Jerusalem To Jericho	Vo 15076, 5067
699/700	I Tickled Nancy	Vo 15341, 5109

Matrices 687 to 694, 697/98, 701/02 are by Sid Harkreader.
Rev. Vocalion 15063 by Sid Harkreader.

Acc. own bj; or **Uncle Dave Macon & Sid Harkreader**-1: Sid Harkreader, f-2/g-3/v-4; Uncle Dave Macon, bj/g-5/v.

New York, NY   Wednesday, April 15, 1925

703/04	Arkansas Travelers -1, 3	Vo 15192, 5081
705/06	The Girl I Left Behind Me -1, 2, 5	Vo 15034, 5062
707/08	Muskrat Medley	Vo 15101, 5071
709/10	Old Ship Of Zion -1, 3	Vo 15033, 5061
711/12	Down In Arkansaw -1, 4	Vo 15034, 5062
713/14	Down By The Old Mill Stream -1, 3	Vo 15143, 5075

New York, NY   Thursday, April 16, 1925

| 719/20 | I Don't Reckon It'll Happen Again | Vo 15032, 5060 |
| 721/22 | Save My Mother's Picture From The Sale | Vo 15100, 5070 |

Acc. own bj-1; Sam McGee, g.

New York, NY   Wednesday, April 14, 1926

E-2751*/52*	Rise When The Rooster Crows -1	Vo 15321, 5097
E-2753*/54	Way Down The Old Plank Road -1	Vo 15321, 5097
E-2755/56	The Bible's True -1	Vo 15322, 5098
E-2757*/58*	He Won The Heart Of My Sarah Jane -1	Vo 15322, 5098
E-2759*/60	Last Night When My Willie Came Home	Vo 15319, 5095
E-2761/62	I've Got The Mourning Blues	Vo 15319, 5095
E-2763*/64	Death Of John Henry (Steel Driving Man) -1	Vo 15320, 5096, Br 112, 80091
E-2765*/66	On The Dixie Bee Line (In That Henry Ford Of Mine) -1	Vo 15320, 5096, Br 112

Matrix E-2763/64 is titled *The Death Of John Henry* on Brunswick 80091.

Acc. own bj; Sam McGee, g.

New York, NY   Friday, April 16, 1926

E-2774*/75	Whoop 'Em Up, Cindy	Vo 15323, 5099
E-2776*/77*	Only As Far As The Gate, Dear Ma	Vo 15323, 5099
E-2778/79	Just Tell Them That You Saw Me	Vo 15324, 5100
E-2780/81	Poor Sinners, Fare You Well	Vo 15324, 5100

New York, NY Saturday, April 17, 1926
E-2792/93 Old Ties Vo 15325, 5104

Revs: Vocalion 15325, 5104 by Sam McGee.

Acc. own bj; or bj solo-1.
New York, NY Wednesday, September 8, 1926
E-3686*/87	We Are Up Against It Now	Vo 15447, 5009
E-3688/89*	Uncle Dave's Beloved Solo -1	Vo 15439, 5001
E-3690*/91	The Old Man's Drunk Again	Vo 15441, 5003
E-3692/93*	I Ain't Got Long To Stay	Vo 15447, 5009
E-3694*/95	Ain't It A Shame To Keep Your Honey Out In The Rain	Vo 15448, 5010
E-3696*/97	Stop That Knocking At My Door	Vo 15444, 5006
E-3698/99*	Sassy Sam	Vo 15444, 5006
E-3700*/01	Shout, Mourner, You Shall Be Free	Vo 15445, 5007
E-3702/03	I Don't Care If I Never Wake Up	Vo 15446, 5008
E-3704/05*	In The Good Old Summer Time	Vo 15441, 5003
E-3706*/07	Something's Always Sure To Tickle Me	Vo 15442, 5004
E-3708*/09	Sourwood Mountain Medley	Vo 15443, 5005
E-3710/11*	Deliverance Will Come	Vo 15439, 5001
E-3712/13*	Wouldn't Give Me Sugar In My Coffee	Vo 15440, 5002

New York, NY Thursday, September 9, 1926
E-3718*/19	Kissin' On The Sly	Vo 15452, 5013
E-3720*/21*	Hold On To The Sleigh	Vo 15451, 5012, Br 114, Spt S2042
E-3722*/23	In The Good Old Days Of Long Ago	Vo 15442, 5004
E-3724/25*	My Girl's A High Born Lady	Vo 15445, 5007
E-3726*/27*	The Cross Eyed Butcher And The Cackling Hen	Vo 15453, 5014, Br 114, Spt S2041
E-3728/29*	In The Old Carolina State (Where The Sweet Magnolias Bloom)	Vo 15443, 5005
E-3730*/31	Never Make Love No More	Vo 15453, 5014, Br 113
E-3732/33*	Arcade Blues	Vo 15440, 5002
E-3734/35*	Them Two Gals Of Mine	Vo 15446, 5008
E-3736/37*	Diamond In The Rough	Vo 15451, 5012, Br 113
E-3738*/39	Tossing The Baby So High	Vo 15452, 5013
E-3740/41*	Sho' Fly, Don't Bother Me	Vo 15448, 5010
E-3742/43*	Uncle Ned	Vo 15450, 5011
E-3744*/45	Braying Mule	Vo 15450, 5011

Matrix E-3720 is used on Brunswick 114, matrix E-3721 on Supertone S-2042; it is uncertain which take is used on the Vocalion issues.

Uncle Dave Macon & His Fruit Jar Drinkers: Uncle Dave Macon, v; acc. Kirk McGee, f/v-1; Mazy Todd, f; own bj; Sam McGee, g/v-2.
New York, NY Saturday, May 7, 1927
E-4923*/24	Bake That Chicken Pie -1, 2	Vo 5148
E-4925*/26	Rock About My Sara Jane -1, 2	Vo 5152, Br 80091
E-4927*/28	Tell Her To Come Back Home	Vo 5153
E-4929/30*	Hold That Wood-Pile Down -1, 2	Vo 5151
E-4931/32*	Carve That Possum -1, 2	Vo 5151
E-4933*/34	Hop High Ladies, The Cake's All Dough	Vo 5154
E-4935/36*	Sail Away Ladies -1, 2	Vo 5155, Br 80094

Matrix E-4925/26 is titled *Rock About, My Saro Jane* on Brunswick 80091; matrix E-4935/36 is titled *Sail Away, Ladies* on Brunswick 80094. Rev. Brunswick 80094 by The Crockett Family.

Acc. Kirk McGee, f-1/md-2/v-3; Mazy Todd, f-4; own bj/sp-5/calls-6/laughing-7/v eff-8; Sam McGee, g/v-9.
New York, NY Monday, May 9, 1927
E-4944/45*	I'm A-Goin' Away In The Morn -1, 3, 4, 9	Vo 5148
E-4946*/47	Sleepy Lou -1, 4, 5, 6	Vo 5156
E-4948/49*	The Gray Cat On The Tennessee Farm -1, 4	Vo 5152
E-4950/51*	Walk, Tom Wilson, Walk	Vo 5154
E-4952*/53	I'se Gwine Back To Dixie -2	Vo 5157
E-4954/55*	Take Me Home, Poor Julia -2, 4	Vo 5157
E-4956/57*	Go Along Mule -1, 3, 4, 5, 7, 8, 9	Vo 5165
E-4958/59*	Tom And Jerry -1, 4, 5, 6	Vo 5165
E-4960*/61	The Rabbit In The Pea Patch -1, 4	Vo 5156
E-4962*/63	Jordan Is A Hard Road To Travel -1, 4	Vo 5153
E-4967/68	Pickaninny Lullaby Song -1	Vo 5155

Matrices E-4964 to E-4966 are untraced.

Dixie Sacred Singers-1/**Uncle Dave Macon & McGee Brothers**-2: Kirk McGee, f-3/md-4/v; Mazy Todd, f-5; Uncle Dave Macon, bj/v; Sam McGee, g/v; or **Uncle Dave Macon**-6, v with same acc.

    New York, NY   Tuesday, May 10, 1927

E-4969/70*	Are You Washed In The Blood Of The Lamb -1, 4, 5	Vo 5158
E-4971/72*	The Maple On The Hill -1, 4, 5	Vo 5158
E-4973/74*	Poor Old Dad -2, 4, 5	Vo 5159
E-4975/76*	Walking In The Sunlight -1, 4, 5	Vo 5160
E-4977*/78	O Bear Me Away On Your Snowy Wings -1, 4, 5	Vo 5160
E-4979/80*	The Mockingbird Song Medley -3, 6	Vo 5161
E-4981/82*	Shall We Gather At The River -1, 4	Vo 5162
E-4983/84	When The Roll Is Called Up Yonder -1, 3	Vo unissued
E-4985*/86	In The Sweet Bye And Bye -1, 4, 5	Vo 5162
E-4987/88	God Be With You 'Till We Meet Again -1, 4	Vo unissued

Uncle Dave Macon, v; acc. own bj.

    New York, NY   Tuesday, May 10, 1927

E-4989/90*	In The Shade Of The Old Apple Tree	Vo 5149
E-4991/92*	Molly Married A Travelling Man	Vo 5159
E-4993/931/2*	When Reubin Comes To Town	Vo 5163
E-4994/95*	Got No Silver Nor Gold Blues	Vo 5164
E-4996/97*	Heartaching Blues	Vo 5161
E-4998/99*	Roe Rire Poor Gal	Vo 5163

Uncle Dave Macon & McGee Brothers-1/**Uncle Dave Macon & Sam McGee**-2: Uncle Dave Macon, v/sp; acc. own bj; Sam McGee, g-3/v-4; Kirk McGee, v-5.

    New York, NY   Wednesday, May 11, 1927

E-5038*/39	You've Been A Friend To Me -1, 4, 5	Vo 5172
E-5040/41*	Backwater Blues -2, 3	Vo 5164

Matrices E-5014 to E-5037 are by McGee Brothers.

Uncle Dave Macon, v; acc. own bj.

    New York, NY   Wednesday, May 11, 1927

E-5042*/43	More Like Your Dad Every Day	Vo 5172
E-5044/45*	I'll Never Go There Any More (The Bowery)	Vo 5149

    Indianapolis, IN   c. June 23, 1928

IND-666-	Jesus, Lover Of My Soul	Vo 5316

Rev. Vocalion 5316 by Freeman Quartette.

Uncle Dave Macon, v/sp; acc. own bj; Sam McGee, bj-g-1/v-2; or Uncle Dave Macon, Sam McGee, bj duet-3.

    Chicago, IL   Wednesday, July 25, 1928

C-2125-	From Earth To Heaven -1	Br 329
C-2126-	The Coon That Had The Razor -1	Vo 5261
C-2127-	Buddy Won't You Roll Down The Line -1, 2	Br 292
C-2128-	Worthy Of Estimation -1	Br 266
C-2129-	I'm The Child To Fight -1, 2	Br 292
C-2130-	Over The Road I'm Bound To Go -1	Br 329
C-2131-A,B	Uncle Dave's Banjo Medley (She's The Only Girl I Love/Don't Love Nobody/Sweet Violets/Devil's Dream) -3	Br rejected
C-2134-A,-B	The Dying Thief	Br rejected
C-2135-A,-B	Uncle Dave's Favorite Religious Melodies (Nearer My God To Thee/Sweet Hour Of Prayer/Sweet Bye And Bye) -3	Br rejected
C-2138-	The New Ford Car	Vo 5261

Matrices C-2132/33, C-2136/37 are by Sam McGee.

Acc. own bj; Sam McGee, g-1; or **Uncle Dave Macon & Sam McGee**-2, v duet with same acc.

    Chicago, IL   Thursday, July 26, 1928

C-2139-	The Gal That Got Stuck On Everything She Said	Br 266
C-2140-	Comin' Round The Mountain -1, 2	Br 263, BrC 425
C-2141-	Governor Al Smith -1	Br 263

Rev. Brunswick 425 by Frank Luther & Carson Robison (see the latter).

Acc. own bj; or **Uncle Dave Macon & Sid Harkreader**-1; Uncle Dave Macon, bj/v; Sid Harkreader, g/v-2.

    Chicago, IL   Thursday, June 20, 1929

C-3657-	Darling Zelma Lee -1, 2	Vo 5380
C-3658-	Put Me In My Little Bed -1, 2	Vo 5397

C-3659-	Life And Death Of Jesse James -1, 2	Vo 5356
C-3660-	Man That Rode The Mule Around The World -1, 2	Vo 5356
C-3661-	Tennessee Jubilee -1, 2	Br 355
C-3662-	New Coon In Town -1	Br 340
C-3664-	For Goodness Sakes Don't Say I Told You -1	Vo 5374
C-3665-	We Need A Change In Business All Around -1	Vo 5374
C-3666-	Susie Lee	Vo 5380
C-3667-	Mister Johnson -1	Vo 5341
C-3668-	Farm Relief	Vo 5341
C-3669-	Uncle Dave's Travels – Part III (In And Around Nashville)	Br 355

Matrix C-3663 is Mexican.

Uncle Dave Macon & Sid Harkreader: Uncle Dave Macon, bj; Sid Harkreader, g.
    Chicago, IL   Thursday, June 20, 1929

| C-3670- | Uncle Dave And Sid On A Cut-Up | Br rejected |
| C-3671- | Select Banjo Waltz | Br rejected |

Uncle Dave Macon, v/sp; acc. own bj; Sid Harkreader, g-1; or **Uncle Dave Macon & Sid Harkreader**-2/Sid Harkreader & Uncle Dave Macon-3; Uncle Dave Macon, bj/v; Sid Harkreader, g/v-4.
    Chicago, IL   Friday, June 21, 1929

C-3675-A	Since Baby's Learned To Talk	Br 362, Spt S2041
C-3676-A	Uncle Dave's Travels – Part IV (Visit At The Old Maid's)	Br 362, Spt S2042
C-3677-A,-B	Cumberland Mountain Deer Race -1	Br rejected
C-3678-A,-B	Nobody's Darling On Earth -3, 4	Br rejected
C-3679-	Over The Mountain -2, 4	Br 349
C-3680-	Hush Little Baby Don't You Cry	Vo 5397
C-3681-A,-B	Darby Ram -1	Br unissued
C-3682-A,-B	Eli Green's Cake Walk -1	Br unissued
C-3687-	Uncle Dave's Travels – Part 1 (Misery In Arkansas) -1	Br 340
C-3688-A,-B	Flitting Away -2, 4	Br unissued
C-3689-A,-B	Traveling Down The Road -2, 4	Br unissued
C-3690-	Uncle Dave's Travels – Part 2 (Around Louisville, Ky.)	Br 349
C-3691-	Children I Must Go -2	Br unissued
C-3692-	When First I Fell In Love -2	Br unissued
C-3693-A,-B	Railroadin' And Gamblin' -2, 4	Br unissued
C-3694-A,-B	That's Where My Money Goes -2, 4	Br unissued

Matrix C-3683 is by Jimmie Noone (see *JR*); matrix C-3684 is by Hattie Mae Smith (see *B&GR*); matrices C-3685/86 are by Tampa Red (see *B&GR*).

Acc. own bj; or **Uncle Dave Macon & Son**-1: prob.: Uncle Dave Macon, v; acc. own bj; Dorris Macon, g.
    Knoxville, TN   Monday, March 31, 1930

K-8048	Little Sally Waters	Br/Vo rejected
K-8049	Let's All Go Home	Br/Vo rejected
K-8052	Trade With Your Home Man	Br/Vo rejected
K-8053	I Wish I Had My Whiskey Back -1	Br/Vo rejected
K-8054	Going To The Mill -1	Br/Vo rejected
K-8055	Possum Pie -1	Br/Vo rejected
K-8056	Leave The Old Sheep Alone -1	Br/Vo rejected
K-8057	I Used To Love Somebody -1	Br/Vo rejected

Matrices K-8050/51 are untraced.

Acc. own bj; Sam McGee, bj-g.
    Jackson, MS   Wednesday, December 17, 1930

404754-A	Tennessee Red Fox Chase	OK 45507
404755-B	The Wreck Of The Tennessee Gravy Train	OK 45507
404756-	Oh Baby, You Done Me Wrong	OK 45552
404757-B	She's Got The Money Too	OK 45552
404758-A	Oh Lovin' Babe	OK unissued: *Rdr 1028 (LP)*
404759-	Mysteries Of The World	OK 45522
404760-	Round Dice Reel	OK unissued
404761-	Come On Buddie, Don't You Want To Go	OK unissued: *Rdr 1028 (LP)*
404762-	Go On, Nora Lee	OK unissued: *Rdr 1028 (LP)*
404763-	Was You There When They Took My Lord Away	OK 45522

It is assumed that the issued take of matrix 404757 is B, since it differs from the unissued take A.

Uncle Dave Macon-1/**Uncle Dave Macon & McGee Brothers**-2: Uncle Dave Macon, v; acc. own bj; Kirk McGee, bj-3/g-4/v-5; Sam McGee, g-6.
    Richmond, IN   Tuesday, August 14, 1934

19651	Thank God For Everything -2, 4, 6	Ch 16805, 45105, De 5373
19652	When The Train Comes Along -2, 3, 5, 6	Ch 16805, 45105, De 5373
19653	The Train Done Left Me And Gone -2, 3, 6	Ge unissued
19654	You've Been A Friend To Me -1	Ge unissued
19656	There's Just One Way To The Pearly Gates -2, 3, 6	Ge unissued
19657	The Grey Cat -1, 3, 6	Ge unissued

Decca 5373 and probably Champion 45105 as by **Uncle Dave Macon & Kirk & Sam McGee**. Matrix 19655 is by McGee Brothers.

Acc. own bj-3; Kirk McGee, bj-4/g-5/v-6; Sam McGee, g.
    Richmond, IN   Wednesday, August 15, 1934

19659	Tennessee Tornado -1, 5	Ge unissued
19661	Eli Green's Cake Walk -1	Ge unissued
19662	The Good Old Bible Line -2, 3, 5	Ge unissued
19663	Don't Get Weary Children -2, 3, 4, 6	Ch 16822, 45048, MW 8029, De 5369
19664	He's Up With The Angels Now -2, 3, 4	Ch 16822, 45048, MW 8029, De 5369

Montgomery Ward 8029, Decca 5369, and probably Champion 45048 as by **Uncle Dave Macon & Kirk & Sam McGee**. Matrices 19658, 19660 are by McGee Brothers.

"Uncle Dave" Macon (The Dixie Dewdrop), v; acc. own bj; Alton Delmore, g-1/v-1; Rabon Delmore, g-1/v-1.
    New Orleans, LA   Tuesday, January 22, 1935

87684-1	Over The Mountain -1	BB B-5926, Twin FT1923
87685-1	When The Harvest Days Are Over -1	BB B-5842, MW M-4819
87686-1	One More River To Cross -1	BB B-5842, MW M-4819
87687-1	Just One Way To The Pearly Gates -1	BB B-5926, Twin FT1923
87688-1	I'll Tickle Nancy	BB B-5873
87689-1	I'll Keep My Skillet Good And Greasy	BB B-5873

Uncle Dave Macon, v; acc. unknown, f-1; own bj; unknown, g-2/v-3; unknown, 2nd g-4.
    Charlotte, NC   Tuesday, August 3, 1937

011910-1	All In Down And Out Blues -2, 3	BB B-7350, MW M-7347
011911-1	Honest Confesson Is Good For The Soul -2, 3	BB B-7174, MW M-7348
011912-1	Fame Apart From God's Approval	BB B-7385, MW M-7348
011913-1	The Bum Hotel -1	BB B-7350, MW M-7347
011914-1	From Jerusalem To Jericho -2, 3, 4	BB B-7174, MW M-7349
011915-1	Two-In-One Chewing Gum	BB B-7234, MW M-7350
011916-1	Travelin' Down The Road -1	BB B-7234, MW M-7350

Revs: Bluebird B-7385 by Monroe Brothers; Montgomery Ward M-7349 by Southern Melody Boys (as by **Uncle Dave Macon**).

Acc. own bj; "Smoky Mountain" Glenn Stagner, g-1/v-2.
    Charlotte, NC   Monday, January 24, 1938

018644-1	Country Ham And Red Gravy -1	BB B-7951, MW M-7458
018645-1	Summertime On The Beeno Line -1, 2	BB B-7779, MW M-7461
018646-1	He Won The Heart Of Sarah Jane -1	BB B-7549, MW M-7458
018647-1	Peek-A-Boo -1	BB B-7779, MW M-7462
018648-1	Working For My Lord -1, 2	BB B-8279, MW M-7459
018649-1	She's Got The Money Too	BB B-7549, MW M-7884
018650-1	Wait Till The Clouds Roll By -1, 2	BB B-8341, MW M-7460
018651-1	Things I Don't Like To See -1	BB B-8279, MW M-7459
018652-1	They're After Me	BB B-8422, MW M-7460
018653-1	My Daughter Wished To Marry	BB B-8422, MW M-7461
018654-1	Beautiful Love	BB B-8341, MW M-7462

Issues of matrices 018645 and 018650 as by **Uncle Dave Macon & Smoky Mt. Glenn**.

Acc. unknown, f-1; own bj.
    Charlotte, NC   Wednesday, January 26, 1938

018758-1	Give Me Back My Five Dollars	BB B-8325, MW M-7884
018759-1	Railroadin' And Gamblin'	BB B-8325, MW M-7463
018760-1	Cumberland Mountain Deer Race	BB B-7951, MW M-7463, Vi 27494
018761-1	Johnny Grey -1	BB B-8379, MW M-7885
018762-1	The Gayest Old Dude That's Out	BB B-8379, MW M-7885

Rev. Victor 27494 by Carter Family.

Uncle Dave Macon also made personal and home recordings both before and (chiefly) after 1942. Some airshots were also recorded by listeners.

ZEKE MACON

Pseudonym on Radiex (and probably other associated labels) and Bellbird for Chezz Chase.

MACON QUARTET

Vocal quartet; unacc.-1; or acc. unknown, p-2.
    Atlanta, GA   Monday, March 28, 1927

143787-1	Uncle Joe -1	Co 15211-D
143788-2	Yodel -2	Co 15211-D

MACON STRING TRIO

No details.
    Atlanta, GA   Monday, November 7, 1927

145138-	The Burning Of The Kimball House	Co unissued
145139-	The Texas Ranger	Co unissued

WHITEY McPHERSON

Whitey McPherson's recordings were made with a group known as The Rhythm Wreckers. Recordings by that band without McPherson (as well as some of the sessions below) are listed in JR.

The Rhythm Wreckers: Muggsy Spanier, c; Ben Kanter, cl; unknown, p; Danny Stewart, sg; Francis Palmer, sb; Ben Pollack, d; Whitey McPherson, v/y-1/poss. g.
    Los Angeles, CA   Saturday, March 27, 1937

LA-1290-A	Never No Mo' Blues -1	Vo 3523, BrG A81214, 602080, Co-Lucky 60521
LA-1291-A	St. Louis Blues	Vo 3566, Co-Lucky 60309, LX7
LA-1292-A	Blue Yodel No. 2 (My Lovin' Gal Lucille) -1	Vo 3566, Co-Lucky 60433

Matrix LA-1290 is titled *Never No More Blues* on Columbia-Lucky 60521. Matrix LA-1291 is titled *St. Lewis Blues* on Columbia-Lucky 60309, LX7.
Revs: Vocalion 3523, Brunswick A81214, 602080, Columbia-Lucky 60309, LX7 by The Rhythm Wreckers without McPherson.

Muggsy Spanier, c; Ben Kanter, cl; unknown, p; Danny Stewart, sg; Francis Palmer, sb; Ben Pollack, d; Whitey McPherson, v/y/poss. g.
    Los Angeles, CA   Wednesday, June 9, 1937

LA-1346-A	Red-Headed Music Maker	Vo 3670, Co-Lucky 60334
LA-1347-B	Blue Yodel No. 1	Vo 3642, Co-Lucky 60334, CoJ M294

Rev. Columbia M194 popular.

    Los Angeles, CA   Thursday, June 17, 1937

LA-1349-A	Blue Yodel No. 3	Vo 3670, Co-Lucky 60521
LA-1350-A	Desert Blues	Vo 3642, Co-Lucky 60433

Matrices LA-1348, 1351 are by The Rhythm Wreckers with other (popular) vocalists.

Whitey McPherson, v/y; acc. **The Rhythm Wreckers:** unknown, t; unknown, cl; Danny Stewart, sg; unknown, p; poss. own g; unknown, sb; unknown, tu; Ben Pollack, d.
    Los Angeles, CA   Tuesday, November 9, 1937

LA-1518-A	Brakeman Blues	Vo/OK 03937
LA-1519-A	Old Fashioned Love	Vo/OK 03937
LA-1520-A	Meanest Thing Blues	ARC 8-01-64, Vo 03883
LA-1521-A	Little Lady	ARC 8-01-64, Vo 03883

Whitey McPherson, v/y-1; acc. The Rhythm Wreckers: unknown, f; unknown, t; unknown, cl; unknown, sg; unknown, p; unknown, sb; unknown, d; two unidentified, v eff-2.
    Los Angeles, CA   Saturday, April 2, 1938

LA-1620-B	Am I Blue?	Vo 04339
LA-1621-B	Blue Ridge Mountain Blues -2	Vo/OK 04245
LA-1623-B	Trouble In Mind -1	Vo/OK 04245
LA-1624-A	Blue Yodel No. 5 -1	Vo 04339

Matrix LA-1622 is by Jerry Colonna (popular).

McQUEEN QUARTET

Vocal quartet; acc. (if any) unknown.
    New Orleans, LA   Saturday, December 15, 1928

147644-	Lovesick Blues	Co unissued
147645-	Liza Jane	Co unissued

McVAY & JOHNSON

Ancil L. McVay, Roland N. Johnson, unknown, v trio; acc. Roland N. Johnson, f; unknown, bj-md; Ancil L. McVay, g.
    Johnson City, TN   Wednesday, October 17, 1928

| 147224-1 | Ain't Going To Lay My Armor Down | Co 15370-D |
| 147225-2 | I'll Be Ready When The Bridegroom Comes | Co 15370-D |

These artists recorded with Ernest Phipps & His Holiness Singers.

EMMETT McWILLIAMS

Pseudonym on Clarion and Velvet Tone for Morgan Denmon.

ODDIE McWINDERS

Oddie McWinders was a member of Clayton McMichen's Georgia Wildcats for their Crown session and some items therefrom were issued in his name. See Clayton McMichen. (McWinders also participated, with others of the Wildcats, in a Jimmie Rodgers session shortly beforehand.) See also **Robert Walton & McWinders**.

EDDIE MADDEN

Pseudonym on Velvet Tone for Marvin Williams.

MADDEN COMMUNITY BAND

Prob.: George Gilmer or Thurman Ware, f; Cooney Vaughan, p; unknown, md; poss. Grady Russell or Grover Russell, g; unknown, v.
Hattiesburg, MS   Friday, July 24, 1936
| HAT-166- | Going Down Town | ARC unissued |
| HAT-167- | Pallet On The Floor | ARC unissued |

MADDUX FAMILY

Unknown, f; unknown, md; unknown, g.
Dallas, TX   Sunday, February 21, 1937
| 61922-A | College Hornpipe | De 5393 |
| 61923-A | Stone Rag | De 5393 |

MADISONVILLE STRING BAND

Clarence Cobb, f/v-1; Houston Tucker, md-2; Aubrey Prow, g/v-3; Noah Tucker, sb.
Richmond, IN   Friday, October 3, 1930
17132-A	B Flat Rag -2	Ch 16462, 45005, Spr 2756, De 5437
17134-A	Italian Dream Waltz -2	Ch 16462, 45005, Spr 2756, De 5437
17135,-A,-B	Floreene Waltz -2	Ge rejected
17136,-A	Whippoorwill Waltz	Ge rejected
17137	My Pretty Snow Dear -1, 2, 3	Ch 16167
17138	Good-bye Little Sweetheart Forever -1, 2, 3	Ch 16167
17139-A	Next To Your Mother Who Do You Love -2	Ch 16503

Champion 16167 as by **Cobb & Prow Acc. By Madisonville String Band**.
Matrix 17133 is by Mr. & Mrs. Homer Taylor. Rev. Champion 16503 by Green's String Band.

JAP MAGEE

Jap Magee & Banjo: Jap Magee, v; acc. own bj.
Dallas, TX   Saturday, October 27, 1928
| DAL-742-A | Right Or Wrong | Br 4267 |
| DAL-743-A | Barrel House Blues | Br 4267 |

Jap Magee, v; acc. own g.
Dallas, TX   Wednesday, October 23, 1929
| TD-443 | Ersula I Love You | Br unissued |
| TD-444 | Leaving You Blues | Br unissued |

These items were intended for release in the Brunswick hillbilly series.

THE MAGNOLIA TRIO

Vocal trio; acc. unknown, sg; unknown, g; unknown, u.
Jackson, MS   Friday, December 19, 1930
404791-B	'Neath The Old Pine Tree At Twilight	OK 45521
404792-A	My Carolina Sweetheart	OK 45505
404793-A	When The Violets Bloom Again In The Springtime	OK 45521
404794-A	Moonlight On Biscayne Bay	OK 45505

JACK MAHONEY

Jack Mahoney, v; acc. poss. own g.
New York, NY   Monday, June 15, 1931

151608-2	The Convict And The Bird	Co 15685-D
151609-1	The Hobo And The Pie	Co 15685-D

Acc. poss. Bob Miller, cel; poss. own g.
    New York, NY   Wednesday, July 15, 1931

151684-1	The Convict's Return	Co 15712-D
151685-1	Woodman Spare That Tree	Co 15712-D

Acc. unknown.
    New York, NY   c. December 12, 1931

152042-	The Prisoners [sic] Love Letters	Co unissued
152043-	Our Blue Haired Boy	Co unissued

    New York, NY   mid-December 1931

365050-	Our Blue Haired Boy	VT/Cl unissued
365051-	The Prisoners [sic] Love Letters	VT/Cl unissued

Matrices 365050/51, undated in Columbia files but made at some time between December 10 and 18, seem likely to be transfers of the Columbia matrices 152043/42.

J.E. MAINER'S MOUNTAINEERS

Joseph Emmett Mainer, f/v-1; Wade Mainer, bj/v-2; Zeke Morris, g/v-3; Daddy John Love, g/v-4.
    Atlanta, GA   Tuesday, August 6, 1935

94328-1	Ship Sailing Now -2, 3	BB B-6088, MW M-4714
94329-1	This World Is Not My Home -3	BB B-6088, MW M-4714
94330-1	Maple On The Hill -2, 3	BB B-6065, MW M-4969, Vi 20-3241, DJ606, RZAu G22837
94331-1	Take Me In The Lifeboat -2, 3	BB B-6065, MW M-4969, RZAu G22837
94332-1	Seven And A Half -1	BB B-6792, MW M-7009
94333-1	New Curly Headed Baby -2, 3	BB B-6104, MW M-4970
94338-1	Let Her Go God Bless Her -1, 3, 4	BB B-6104, MW M-4970
94339-1	City On The Hill -1, 2, 3, 4	BB B-6160, MW M-4711
94340-1	The Longest Train -1, 3, 4	BB B-6222, MW M-7005
94341-1	Write A Letter To Mother -1, 2, 3, 4	BB B-6194, MW M-4716
94342-1	Lights In The Valley -1, 2, 3, 4	BB B-6160, MW M-4711, Vi 20-3241

Montgomery Wards, except M-4969, M-4970, as by **Mainer's Mountaineers**. Regal-Zonophone G22837 as by **The Melody Mountaineers**.
Matrices 94334/35 are by Pink Lindsey & His Bluebirds; matrices 94336/37 (and 94343) are by Daddy John Love.
Revs: Bluebird B-6194, Montgomery Ward M-4716 by Daddy John Love; B-6222 by Smith's Sacred Singers; Montgomery Ward M-7005 by Wade Mainer & Zeke Morris; Victor DJ606 by Hank Snow (postwar).

J.E. Mainer, f-1/v-2; Ollie Bunn, f-3/bj-4/g-5/v-6; Clarence Todd, f-7/bj-8/g-9/v-10; Howard Bumgardner, g-11/v-12; band sp-13.
    Charlotte, NC   Friday, February 14, 1936

99113-1	Goin' Back West In The Fall -1, 2, 4/8, 5/9, 6, 10, 11, 12	BB B-6440, MW M-7002
99114-1	New Lost Train Blues -3/7, 5/9	BB B-6424, MW M-7003
99115-1	Number 111 -1, 5, 9, 13	BB B-6424, MW M-7003
99116-1	I Am Walking In The Light -2, 4/8, 5/9, 6, 10, 11	BB B-6385, MW M-7001
99117-1	Don't Cause Mother's Hair To Turn Grey -4/8, 5/9, 6, 10, 11	BB B-6324, MW M-4712
99118-1	When I Reach My Home Eternal -1, 2, 6, 11	BB B-6385, MW M-7001
99119-1	Fatal Wreck Of The Bus -2, 6, 11	BB B-6290, MW M-4717
99120-1	Behind The Parlor Door -1, 2, 6, 11	BB B-6440, MW M-7002
99121-1	Satisfied -1, 2, 6, 10, 11, 12	BB B-6324, MW M-4712
99122-1	One To Love Me -1, 4/8, 5/9, 6, 10	BB B-6290, MW M-4717

Montgomery Ward issues as by **Mainer's Mountaineers**.

J.E. Mainer, f/v-1; Junior Misenheimer, bj; Harold Christy, g; Beacham Blackweller, g/v-2; Wade Mainer, v-3; Zeke Morris, v-4.
    Charlotte, NC   Monday, June 15, 1936

102600-1	On A Cold Winter Night -3	BB B-6629, MW M-7008, Vi 27496
102601-1	John Henry Was A Little Boy -1, 2, 3	BB B-6629, MW M-7008
102602-1	The Old And Faded Picture -1, 3, 4	BB B-6479, MW M-5035
102603-1	Take Me Home To The Sweet Sunny South -3	BB B-6479, MW M-5035
102604-1	Walk That Lonesome Valley -1, 3, 4	BB B-6596, MW M-7007
102605-1	Got A Home In That Rock -1, 3, 4	BB B-6539, MW M-7004
102606-1	Johnson's Old Grey Mule -1, 3, 4	BB B-6584, MW M-7006
102607-1	Won't Be Worried Long -1, 3, 4	BB B-6738, MW M-7009
102608-1	Goin' Down The River Of Jordan -1, 3, 4	BB B-6539, MW M-7004

102609-1	Why Do You Bob Your Hair, Girls? -1	BB B-6792, MW M-7131
102610-1	Down Among The Budded Roses -1	BB unissued
102611-1	Watermelon On The Vine -1, 3, 4	BB B-6584, MW M-7006

Montgomery Ward issues as by **Mainer's Mountaineers**.
Revs: Bluebird B-6738 by Dixie Reelers; Montgomery Ward M-7007, M-7131 by Wade Mainer & Zeke Morris; Victor 27496 by Gid Tanner.

J.E. Mainer, f-1; Leonard Stokes, md/v; DeWitt "Snuffy" Jenkins, bj-2; George Morris, g/v; band v-3.
Charlotte, NC   Thursday, August 5, 1937

011987-1	We Can't Be Darlings Anymore	BB B-7151, MW M-7300
011988-1	Tell Mother I'll Meet Her	BB B-7222, MW M-7300
011989-1	In A Little Village Churchyard	BB B-7222, MW M-7301
011990-1	Carry Your Cross With A Smile	BB B-7523, MW M-7302
011991-1	Swing The Door Of Your Heart Open Wide	BB B-7401, MW M-7302
011992-1	Answer To "Greenback Dollar"	BB B-7151, MW M-7301
011993-1	There's A Green Hill Far Away	BB B-7401, MW M-7303
011994-1	Miss Me When I'm Gone	BB B-7349, MW M-7304
011995-1	Floating Down The Stream Of Time -1, 2, 3	BB B-7523, MW M-7303
011996-1	Don't Go Out -1, 2	BB B-7349, MW M-7304
011997-1	Don't Get Trouble In Your Mind -1, 2	BB B-7289, MW M-7305
011998-1	Kiss Me Cindy -1, 2	BB B-7289, MW M-7305

Matrices 011991 and 011994 on Bluebird as by **Leonard Stokes–George Morris**.
Montgomery Ward issues as by **Mainer's Mountaineers**.

Leonard Stokes, George Morris, v duet; or Leonard Stokes, v-1; acc. Leonard Stokes, md; George Morris, g; or George Morris, v-2; acc. own g.
Charlotte, NC   Sunday, January 23, 1938

018600-1	Your Best Friend Is Always Near	BB B-7586, MW M-7453
018601-1	Lamp Lighting Time In Heaven	BB B-7412, MW M-7452
018602-1	When The Light's Gone Out In Your Soul	BB B-7586, MW M-7453
018603-1	I Once Loved A Young Man	BB B-7659, MW M-7456
018604-1	Somebody Cares	BB B-7659, MW M-7455
018605-1	I'm Living The Right Life Now	BB B-7412, MW M-7452
018606-1	Just Over In The Glory Land	BB B-7730, MW M-7454
018607-1	I'm In The Glory Land Way	BB B-7730, MW M-7454
018608-1	If I Lose, Let Me Lose	BB B-7471, MW M-7456
018609-1	Great Reaping Day	BB B-7958, MW M-7455
018610-1	Oh Why Did I Ever Get Married -1	BB B-7471, MW M-7457
018611-1	Back To Johnson City -2	BB B-7845, MW M-7457

Montgomery Ward issues as by **Mainer's Mountaineers**.
Revs: Bluebird B-7845 by Wade Mainer, B-7958 by Dixie Reelers.

J.E. Mainer, f/v-1; Clyde Moody, g/v-1; Jay Hugh Hall, g/v-1.
Rock Hill, SC   Saturday, February 4, 1939

032635-1	Drunkard's Hiccoughs -1	BB B-8400, MW M-7881
032636-1	Country Blues	BB B-8187, MW M-7881
032637-1	I'm A Poor Pilgrim -1	MW M-7880
032638-1	Concord Rag	BB B-8187, MW M-7880

Matrix 032635 is titled *Drunkard's Hiccups* on Montgomery Ward M-7881.
Rev. Bluebird B-8400 by Hal Davis & His Orchestra (popular).

For Montgomery Ward M-7135, M-7136 as by **Mainer's Mountaineers** see Walter Couch & Wilks Ramblers. For *Sleep On, Departed One* on Montgomery Ward M-7134 with the same credit see The Tennessee Hill Billy With Ruth & Leo West.
J.E. Mainer recorded after 1942.

WADE MAINER

Wade Mainer–Zeke Morris, v duet; acc. Wade Mainer, h-1/bj; Zeke Morris, g; or Zeke Morris, v-2; acc. own g.
Charlotte, NC   Friday, February 14, 1936

99133-1	Come Back To Your Dobie Shack -1	BB B-6551, MW M-4719
99134-1	Just As The Sun Went Down -2	BB B-6383, MW M-4718
99135-1	What Would You Give In Exchange	BB B-8073, MW M-7134
99136-1	A Leaf From The Sea -1	BB B-6347, MW M-4713
99137-1	Brown Eyes	BB B-6347, MW M-4713

Montgomery Ward issues as by **Mainer's Mountaineers**. Canadian pressings of Bluebird B-6383 as by **Zeke Morris**.
Revs: Bluebird B-8073 by Claude Casey; Montgomery Ward M-7134 by The Tennessee Hill Billy (as by **Mainer's Mountaineers**).

Charlotte, NC   Saturday, February 15, 1936

99138-1	Maple On The Hill – Part 2 (Driftin' To That Happy Home)	BB B-6293, MW M-4710
99139-1	Going To Georgia -1	BB B-6423, MW M-4719
99140-1	Nobody's Darling But Mine	BB B-6423
99141-1	Mother Came To Get Her Boy From Jail	BB B-6383, MW M-4718
99142-1	Where The Red, Red Roses Grow -1	BB B-6293, MW M-4710, Twin FT8094

Montgomery Ward issues as by **Mainer's Mountaineers**.
Rev. Twin FT8094 by Riley Puckett.

Wade Mainer, Zeke Morris, v duet; or Wade Mainer, Zeke Morris, Norwood Tew, v trio-1; acc. Wade Mainer, bj; Zeke Morris, g.
    Charlotte, NC   Monday, June 15, 1936

102612-1	Cradle Days -1	BB B-6489, MW M-5031
102613-1	Gathering Flowers From The Hills	BB B-6489, MW M-5031
102614-1	My Mother Is Waiting	BB B-6551, MW M-7005
102615-1	If I Could Hear My Mother	BB B-6460, MW M-5028
102616-1	Nobody's Darling On Earth	BB B-6460, MW M-5028, Twin FT8204
102617-1	Shake Hands With Mother	BB B-6596, MW M-7007

Montgomery Ward issues as by **Mainer's Mountaineers**.
Revs: Bluebird B-6596, Montgomery Ward M-7005, M-7007 by J.E. Mainer's Mountaineers; Twin FT8204 by Bill Boyd.

Wade Mainer, Zeke Morris, v duet; or **Wade Mainer–Zeke Morris–Homer Sherrill**-1, v trio; acc. Homer Sherrill, f; Wade Mainer, bj; Zeke Morris, g.
    Charlotte, NC   Monday, October 12, 1936

02530-1	They Said My Lord Was A Devil	BB B-6653, MW M-7091
02531-1	Won't Somebody Pal With Me? -1	BB B-6704, MW M-7092
02532-1	Hop Along Peter -1	BB B-6752, MW M-7131
02533-1	Just One Way To The Pearly Gates -1	BB B-6784, MW M-7132
02534-1	Dear Daddy, You're Gone	BB B-6752, MW M-7133, RZAu G23374
02535-1	Been Foolin' Me, Baby -1	BB B-6704, MW M-7092
02536-1	I'll Be A Friend Of Jesus -1	BB B-6784, MW M-7132
02537-1	Cowboy's Pony In Heaven	BB B-6653, MW M-7091
02548-1	[Commercial - Old Sams Soda] -1	BB unissued: Old Homestead OHCS124 (LP)

Montgomery Ward issues as by **Mainer's Mountaineers**.
The LP issue of matrix 02548 is derived from a shellac test pressing whose label carries the title *The Good Southern Soda*. Intervening matrices are by Monroe Brothers. Rev. Regal-Zonophone G23374 by Blue Sky Boys.

Wade Mainer, Zeke Morris, v duet; acc. Wade Mainer, bj; Zeke Morris, g; or Wade Mainer, v-1; acc. Zeke Morris, g; or Zeke Morris, v-2; acc. own g.
    Charlotte, NC   Tuesday, February 16, 1937

07051-1	Little Birdie	BB B-6840, MW M-7127
07052-1	Always Been A Rambler	BB B-6890, MW M-7129
07053-1	Starting Life Anew With You	BB B-6840, MW M-7130
07054-1	Little Rosebuds	BB B-6993, MW M-7127, Twin FT8419
07055-1	Train Carry My Girl Back Home -1	BB B-6890, MW M-7129
07056-1	In The Land Beyond The Blue -2	BB B-6936, MW M-7128
07057-1	A Change All Around	BB B-6993, MW M-7130, Twin FT8419
07058-1	Short Life And It's Trouble	BB B-6936, MW M-7128

Montgomery Ward issues as by **Mainer's Mountaineers**.
    Charlotte, NC   Monday, August 2, 1937

011812-1	Dying Boy's Prayer	BB B-7165, MW M-7306
011813-1	Free Again	BB B-7114, MW M-7306, Twin FT8492
011814-1	Answer To "Two Little Rosebuds"	BB B-7114, MW M-7307, Twin FT8492
011815-1	I'm Not Turning Backward	BB B-7165, MW M-7308

Montgomery Ward issues as by **Mainer's Mountaineers**.

Wade Mainer–Zeke Morris, v duet; or **Wade Mainer–Zeke Morris–Steve Ledford**-1: Steve Ledford, v; or Wade Mainer, v-2; acc. Steve Ledford, f/v-3; Wade Mainer, bj; Zeke Morris, g.
    Charlotte, NC   Monday, August 2, 1937

011820-1	Riding On That Train Forty-Five -1	BB B-7298, Vi 27493
011821-1	Little Maggie -3	BB B-7201, MW M-7309
011822-1	Little Pal	BB B-7201, MW M-7309
011823-1	Down In The Willow -2	BB B-7298, MW M-7307, Vi 27497

Montgomery Ward issues as by **Mainer's Mountaineers**. Matrices 011816 to 011819 are untraced.
Revs: Victor 27493 by Monroe Brothers, 27497 by Carter Family.

Zeke Morris, v; acc. Steve Ledford, f; own g.
    Charlotte, NC   Monday, August 2, 1937

011824-1	Garden Of Prayer	BB B-7362, MW M-7308

Montgomery Ward M-7308 as by **Mainer's Mountaineers**.
Rev. Bluebird B-7362 by Joe Cook.

Wade Mainer & His Little Smilin' Rangers: Wade Mainer, h-1/bj/v; unknown, sg-2; Zeke Morris, g; Robert "Buck" Banks, g; Morris "Buddy" Banks, v-3.

Charlotte, NC   Monday, August 2, 1937

011825-1	Ramshackle Shack -1, 2, 3	BB B-7274, MW M-7310
011826-1	Memory Lane -2	BB B-7274, MW M-7310, RZ MR2687, Twin FT8504
011827-1	Wild Bill Jones	BB B-7249, MW M-7311
011828-1	I Want To Be Loved -3	BB B-7249, MW M-7311

Montgomery Ward issues as by **Mainer's Mountaineers**. Regal-Zonophone MR2687, Twin FT8504 as by **The Smiling Rangers**. Revs: Regal-Zonophone MR2687, Twin FT8504 popular.

Morris "Buddy" Banks, md/v; Wade Mainer, bj; Robert "Buck" Banks, g/v; Zeke Morris, g.

Charlotte, NC   Tuesday, August 3, 1937

011816-1	What Are You Going To Do Brother?	BB B-7384
011817-1	Companions Draw Nigh	BB B-7384
011818-1	Mountain Sweetheart	BB B-7587
011819-1	Don't Forget Me, Little Darling	BB B-7587

Wade Mainer & Sons Of The Mountaineers: Steve Ledford, f; Wade Mainer, bj-1/v-2; Clyde Moody, g; Jay Hugh Hall, g/hv-3; Julia "Princess" Mainer, v-4/y-4; or **Steve Ledford & The Mountaineers**-5: Steve Ledford, v with same acc.; or Wade Mainer-6, v/sp; acc. own bj; Julia "Princess" Mainer, sp.

Charlotte, NC   Thursday, January 27, 1938

018763-1	Lonely Tomb -1, 2, 3	BB B-7424, MW M-7480
018764-1	Pale Moonlight -1, 2, 3	BB B-7483, MW M-7481
018765-1	All My Friends -1, 2	BB B-7424, MW M-7480
018766-1	Since I Met My Mother-In-Law -1, 5	BB B-7742, MW M-7483
018767-1	Don't Get Too Deep In Love -1, 2	BB B-7483, MW M-7481
018768-1	Don't Leave Me Alone -1, 2, 3	BB B-7561, MW M-7482
018769-1	I Won't Be Worried -1, 2, 3	BB B-7561, MW M-7482
018770-1	Where Romance Calls -4	BB B-7753, MW M-7483
018771-1	Another Alabama Camp Meetin' -6	BB B-7753, MW M-7484
018772-1	Mitchell Blues -1	BB B-7845, MW M-7484

Revs: Bluebird B-7742 by Steve Ledford, B-7845 by J.E. Mainer's Mountaineers.

Steve Ledford, f-1/lv-2; Wade Mainer, bj-3/lv-4; Clyde Moody, g/lv-5; Jay Hugh Hall, g; unidentified (but poss. sometimes including Dan Hornsby and Frank Walker), v duet or trio; unidentified, y duet-6.

Rock Hill, SC   Monday, September 26, 1938

026981-1	Farther Along -1, 5	BB B-8023, MW M-7560
026982-1	Dear Loving Mother And Dad -1, 5	BB B-8152, MW M-7561
026983-1	Can't Tell About These Women -1, 3, 4	BB B-7965, MW M-7562
026984-1	That Kind -4	BB B-7861, MW M-7562
026985-1	If I Had Listened To Mother -1, 2, 3	BB B-8137, MW M-7561
026986-1	She Is Spreading Her Wings For A Journey -3, 4	BB B-8023, MW M-7559
026987-1	The Same Old You To Me -1, 2, 3	BB B-7924, MW M-7564
026988-1	Life's Ev'nin' Sun -3, 4	BB B-8007, MW M-7559, Twin FT8716
026997-1	Mother Still Prays For You Jack -1, 3, 4	BB B-8137, MW M-7563
026998-1	You're Awfully Mean To Me -3, 4, 6	BB B-7861, MW M-7565
026999-1	Home In The Sky -4	BB B-8007, MW M-7560, Twin FT8716
027700-1	A Little Love -4	BB B-7924, MW M-7563
027701-1	North Carolina Moon -4	BB B-8628, MW M-7564
027702-1	More Good Women Gone Wrong -1, 2, 3	BB B-7965, MW M-7565

Bluebird B-7924 as by **Wade Mainer & His Blue Ridge Buddies**. Intervening matrices are by other artists.
Revs: Bluebird B-8152 by Blue Sky Boys, B-8628 by Adolph Hofner.

Steve Ledford, f-1/sb-2; Wade Mainer, bj-3/v-4; Clyde Moody, g/v-5; Jay Hugh Hall, g/v-6; unidentified (but poss. sometimes including Dan Hornsby and Frank Walker), v duet or trio; unidentified, y duet-7.

Rock Hill, SC   Saturday, February 4, 1939

032625-1	Sparkling Blue Eyes -5, 6	BB B-8042, MW M-7882, Vi 20-2159, *V-D 168*
032626-1	We Will Miss Him -5, 6	BB B-8042, MW M-7882
032627-1	I Left My Home In The Mountains -1, 3, 4	BB B-8091, MW M-7883
032628-1	I Met Her At A Ball One Night -2, 3, 4	BB B-8091, MW M-7883
032629-1	You May Forsake Me -1, 3, 4	BB B-8120
032630-1	Look On And Cry -1, 3, 4	BB B-8120
032631-1	One Little Kiss -4, 7	BB B-8145
032632-1	Mama, Don't Make Me Go To Bed -4, 5	BB B-8145

032633-1	Crying Holy -1, 3, 4	BB B-8203
032634-1	Heaven Bells Are Ringing -3, 4	BB B-8203

Wade Mainer, Clyde Moody, Jay Hugh Hall, v trio; or unidentified (a minister friend of Mainer), v-1; or Wade Mainer, v-2; or Wade Mainer, Clyde Moody, Dan Hornsby, v trio-3; acc. Wade Mainer, bj; Clyde Moody or Jay Hugh Hall, g.

Atlanta, GA   Monday, August 21, 1939

041200-1	Sparkling Blue Eyes No. 2	BB B-8249, MW M-8448
041201-1	The Poor Drunkard's Dream -1	BB B-8273, MW M-8449
041202-1	Were You There? -1	BB B-8273, MW M-8449
041203-1	The Gospel Cannon Ball -2	BB B-8249, MW M-8448
041204-1	The Great And Final Judgment	BB B-8288, MW M-8450
041205-1	What A Wonderful Saviour Is He -1	BB B-8288, MW M-8450
041206-1	Why Not Make Heaven Your Home -1	BB B-8340, MW M-8451
041207-1	Mansions In The Sky -3	BB B-8340, MW M-8451
041208-1	Not A Word Of That Be Said	BB B-8359, MW M-8452
041209-1	Drifting Through An Unfriendly World	BB B-8359, MW M-8452

Wade Mainer, Curley Shelton, Jack Shelton, v trio; or Wade Mainer, v-1; acc. Curley Shelton, md-2; Wade Mainer, bj-3; Jack Shelton, g.

Atlanta, GA   Monday, September 29, 1941

071014-1	Shake My Mother's Hand For Me -2	BB B-8848
071015-1	Anywhere Is Home -2	BB B-8965
071016-1	I Can Tell You The Time -2, 3	BB B-8965
071017-1	He Gave His Life -2	BB B-8887
071018-1	Ramblin' Boy -1, 3	BB B-8990
071019-1	The Precious Jewel	BB B-8887, Vi 20-2159
071020-1	Old Ruben -1, 3	BB B-8990
071021-1	Precious Memories	BB B-8848

Wade Mainer also recorded with his brother J.E. Mainer, and after 1942.

C. MAINES

Pseudonym on Challenge for Hoke Rice.

MAINES & HODGE

Pseudonym on Challenge for Louie Donaldson & Hoke Rice.

MAJESTIC [MALE] QUARTET

Majestic Male Quartet, v quartet; acc. unknown, p.

Charlotte, NC   Thursday, February 13, 1936

94698-1	Coming	BB B-6833
94699-1	Jesus Hold My Hand	BB B-6580
99100-1	Troubles All Will End	BB unissued
99101-1	Harmonies Of Heaven	BB unissued
99102-1	I Love To Raise My Voice	BB B-6833
99103-1	Jericho Road	BB B-6580

Majestic Quartet, v quartet; acc. unknown, p.

Rock Hill, SC   Saturday, February 4, 1939

032617-1	In The Shadow Of The Cross	BB B-8051
032618-1	Oh, Happy Day	BB B-8051
032619-1	Who?	BB unissued
032620-1	Living On The Sunny Side	BB unissued
032621-1	I'll Meet You In The Morning	BB B-8255
032622-1	Holy Be Thy Name	BB B-8255
032623-1	He Said If I Be Lifted Up	BB B-8154
032624-1	A Little Talk With Jesus	BB B-8154

JACK MAJOR

Jack Major, v/y; acc. unknown, p.

New York, NY   Thursday, July 7, 1927

144434-3	Silver Moon	Co 15362-D
144435-3	My Kentucky Mountain Sweetheart	Co 15362-D
144436-3	Indian Dawn	Co 1073-D
144439-	At Dawning (I Love You)	Co unissued
144440-1	(Oh, The Whippoorwill Sings In The Sycamore) Just The Same	Co 1073-D

Matrices 144437/38 are popular.

New York, NY   Wednesday, August 3, 1927
 144531- Two Little Pretty Birds Co unissued
 144532-3 The Spell O' The Moon Co 1151-D
 144533- Hush My Baby Hush My Honey Gal Co unissued

Rev. Columbia 1151-D by Billy "Uke" Carpenter (popular).

Acc. unknown, f; unknown, p; prob. own g.
 New York, NY Friday, June 8, 1928
 27669- Melancholy Yodel Blues Br 252, BrAu 252, Spt S2065
 27670- Tennessee Mountain Gal Br 252, BrAu 252, Spt S2065

Jack Major, v/y-1/wh-2; acc. orch; William F. Wirges, dir.
 New York, NY Saturday, June 9, 1928
 27677-A,-B Good Night -1 Br unissued
 27678-A,-B I Tore Up Your Picture When You Said Goodbye Br unissued
  (But I've Put It Together Again) -2

These items were recorded for the popular series.

Acc. unknown, f; unknown, p; prob. own g.
 Chicago, IL c. November 1928
 C-2518- Meet Me Tonight In Dreamland Br 279
 C-2519- I'm Sorry I Made You Cry Br 279

Jack Major "The Voice Of The Southland", v; acc. two unknowns, f; unknown, p; unknown, 2nd p-1; unknown, cel-2; unknown, g-3; unknown, wh-4.
 Chicago, IL Saturday, October 12, 1929
 C-4645- Climbing The Stairs -3, 4 Vo rejected
 C-4646- Perhaps -1, 2 Vo rejected

These items were recorded for the popular series.

Jack Major, v; acc. prob. own g.
 Chicago, IL Saturday, May 9, 1936
 90713-A Country Doctor (Doc. Brown Has Moved Upstairs) – De 5230
  Part 1
 90714-A Country Doctor (Doc. Brown Has Moved Upstairs) – De 5230
  Part 2

BLIND JOE MANGUM–FRED SHRIBER

Blind Joe Mangrum, f; Fred Shriver, pac. (These are apparently the correct spellings of their names.)
 Nashville, TN Saturday, October 6, 1928
 47151-1,-2,-3 Mammoth Cave Waltz Vi unissued
 47152-1,-2,-3 The Rose Waltz Vi unissued
 47153-3 Bacon And Cabbage Vi V-40018
 47154-3 Bill Cheatam Vi V-40018
 47816-1 Cradle Song Vi unissued

ZEKE MANNERS

Zeke Manners & His Swing Billies: Zeke Manners, pac-1; unknown, esg; unknown, g; unknown, sb; unknown, oc-2; unknown, bazooka or slide-wh; poss. unknown, x-3; poss. unknown, wb-4; unknown, traps-5; unknown, bell-6; unknown, train-wh eff-7; band v/sp-8; poss. Elton Britt, y-9.
 New York, NY March 1937
 M-240-1 Mr. Ghost Goes To Town -1, 2, 3, 4, 5, 9 Vri VA 536
 M-241-1 Leave It Up To Uncle Jake -1, 4, 9 Vri VA 536
 M-242-1 Organ Grinder's Swing -1, 3, 5, 8 Vri VA 640
 M-243-1 Blow The Whistle -2, 4, 6, 7, 8 Vri VA 640

Members of the band are addressed on matrix M-242 as Ed, Hank, Bob, Bill, and Ace. Hank appears to play the bazooka or slide-whistle, and Ed may play electric steel guitar.

Zeke Manners & His Gang: Mac Ceppos, f; Harry Duncan, cl; Zeke Manners, pac/v; Denver Darling, g; Lester Braun, sb; Arthur Maratti, traps.
 New York, NY Wednesday, March 4, 1942
 073359-1 I Betcha My Heart I Love You BB B-9041, Vi 20-2130
 073360-1 The Fightin' Son-Of-A-Gun BB B-9020
 073361-1 When My Blue Moon Turns To Gold Again BB B-9020, Vi 20-2130
 073362-1 That's Why I Waited So Long BB B-9041

Zeke Manners recorded after 1942.

MANSFIELD & HALL
See Mansfield Patrick.

MAPLE CITY FOUR
Fritz Meissner, tv; Pat Petterson, v; Art Janes, v; Al Rice, v; acc. unidentified, oc; unidentified, wb; several unidentified, other instruments; or unknown, p-1.

Chicago, IL   Thursday, April 13, 1933

C-548-3	Tiger Rag	Ba 32770, Me M12699, Or 8232, Pe 15774, Ro 5232, Cq 8167, Pan 25612, Rex 8053
C-549-2	Oh Mo-nah	Ba 32770, Me M12699, Or 8232, Pe 15774, Ro 5232, Cq 8167, Pan 25612, Rex 8053
C-550-	Two Little Pretty Birds	Cq 8166
C-551-	Will The Angels Play Their Harps For Me	Ba 32774, Me M12703, Or 8236, Pe 12915, Ro 5236, Cq 8166
C-552-2	Tell My Mother I'm In Heaven	Ba 32774, Me M12703, Or 8236, Pe 12915, Ro 5236, Cq 8165
C-553-2	Rockin' Alone In An Old Rockin' Chair -1	Cq 8165

Rex 8053 as by **Washboard Novelty Quartette**. Matrix C-549 is titled *Oh! Monah* on Panachord 25612.

Acc. unknown.
Chicago, IL   Friday, March 23, 1934

CP-1038-	Angry	Cq 8302
CP-1039-	Take Me Back To Col-ler-rad-da Fer To Stay	Cq 8302

Acc. unknown, o-1/p-2.
Chicago, IL   Monday, March 26, 1934

CP-1074-	The Old Wooden Rocker -1	Cq 8301
CP-1075-	Beautiful Isle Of Somewhere -1	Cq 8301
CP-1077-	Bobby Boy, Oh Boy, Oh Boy -2	ARC unissued
CP-1078-	Zettie Zum Zum On The Zither -2	ARC unissued

Matrix CP-1076 is by Gene Autry.
The Maple City Four's earlier (1927-1928) recordings for Gennett are beyond the scope of this work.

MARKHAM BROTHERS
Pseudonym on Challenge for John McGhee & Frank Welling.

TED MARKLE
Ted Markle, f; acc. Roy Shield, p.
New York, NY   Friday, August 14, 1925

33312-1,-2,-3	Reel Of Old Tunes	Vi unissued
33313-1,-2,-3	Long Horn Pipes [And] Reels	Vi unissued
33314-1	Indian Dance	Vi unissued

ANDY MARLOW
Pseudonym on Champion for Howard Keesee.

MARLOW & YOUNG
Pseudonym on Champion for Leonard Rutherford & John Foster.

ALBERT MARQUES
Pseudonym on Australian Panachord for Maury Pearson.

ROY MARSH
Roy Marsh, v; acc. unknown.
New York, NY   Wednesday, March 28, 1928

145926-	Ozark Trail	Co 1388-D
145927-	Don't Lie To Me	Co 1388-D
145928-	Mean Papa Blues	Co unissued
145929-	County Boy Blues	Co unissued

CHARLIE MARSHALL
Charlie Marshall's Mavericks Band: unknown, f; unknown, h; unknown, ac; Charlie Marshall, g/v.
Hollywood, CA   Tuesday, September 25, 1934

79383-1	Leanin' On The Hitchin' Rail	Vi unissued
79384-1	What Makes Your Head So Red?	Vi unissued

Charlie Marshall, v; acc. unknown, f; unknown, h; unknown, ac; own g; band v-1.
   San Francisco, CA   Friday, April 5, 1935

SF-201-	Take Me Back To Col-ler-rad-da Fer To Stay	Vo 02967
SF-202-	The Mowin' Machine	Vo 03045
SF-203-	The Santa Fe Trail -1	Vo 02967
SF-204-1	Tom Bigbee River -1	Vo 03019
SF-205-1	What Makes Your Head So Red?	Vo 03019
SF-206-	The Old Hitchin' Rail	Vo 03045

Charlie Marshall recorded after 1942.

ASA MARTIN

Asa Martin, v; acc. Doc Roberts, f; own g.
   Richmond, IN   Monday, May 14, 1928

13830	Second Love	Ge 6762
13831	Lost Love	Ge 6531

The vocal on matrix 13832, *The Dingy Miner's Cabin*, issued as by **Asa Martin** on Gennett 6531, and as by **Emmett Davenport** (a common Martin pseudonym) on Supertone 9178, was actually by Ted Chestnut; see his entry.

Asa Martin, v; or **Asa Martin & Jimmie Roberts**-1: Asa Martin, James Roberts, v duet; acc. Doc Roberts, md; Asa Martin, g.
   Richmond, IN   Thursday, August 23, 1928

14166-A	The Old New Hampshire Village -1	Ge 6601, Ch 15585, Spt 9314
14166-C	The Old New Hampshire Village	Ge unissued
14167-A	Friends Of Long Ago -1	Ge 6601
14167-B	Friends Of Long Ago	Spt 9179, Ch 15611, 45175, MeC 45175

Champion 15585 as by **Jesse Coat & John Bishop**, 15611 as by **Jesse Coat**. Supertone 9179 as by **Emmett Davenport**, 9314 as by **Long & Miles**.
Rev. Supertone 9314 by C.W. Davis.

Asa Martin, v; or Asa Martin, James Roberts, v duet-1; acc. Asa Martin, h/g; Doc Roberts, md.
   Richmond, IN   Friday, August 24, 1928

14184	East Bound Train -1	Ch 15585, 33045
14184-A	East Bound Train	Ge 6621, Spt 9178
14185-A	The Dying Girl's Message	Ge 6621, Ch 15611, 45175, Spt 9179, MeC 45175, Min M-14038

Champion 15585 as by **Jesse Coat & John Bishop**, 15611 as by **Jesse Coat**. Champion 33045 credit unknown. Supertone 9178, 9179 as by **Emmett Davenport**.
Revs: Champion 33045 unknown; Supertone 9178 (with same credit) by Ted Chestnut (see note to May 14, 1928 session); Minerva M-14038 by Charles Baker.

Acc. own g.
   Richmond, IN   Saturday, December 1, 1928

14498,-A	Always In The Way	Ge rejected
14499	Bad Companions	Ge 6762, Chg 421

Challenge 421 as by **Al Lewis**. Rev. Challenge 421 by Dick Parman.

Acc. Doc Roberts, md; own g.
   Richmond, IN   Saturday, March 16, 1929

14923	There Is No Place Like Home For A Married Man	Ge 6808, Ch 15712, Spt 9388
14924-A	She Ain't Built That Way	Ge 6808, Ch 15712, 45129, Spt 9388

Champion 15712 as by **Jesse Coat**. Supertone 9388 as by **Emmett Davenport**.

Asa Martin, v; or **Asa Martin & James Roberts**-1, v duet; acc. Doc Roberts, md-2/v-3; Asa Martin, g.
   Richmond, IN   Thursday, August 29, 1929

15522	When The Roses Bloom Again For The Bootlegger -2	Ge 6975, Ch 15854, Spt 9539
15523	The Virginia Moonshiner -2	Ge 6975, Ch 15854, Spt 9539
15524	The Fellow That Looks Like Me -2	Ge 7050, Ch 15922, 45129, Spt 9642
15525-A	Gwine Down To Town	Ge 7050
15530	Down On The Farm -1	Ge 7068, Spt 9541
15536,-A	An Old Fashioned Picture Of Mother -1, 3	Ge rejected
15537,-A,-B	Guide Me Oh My Saviour Guide	Ge rejected
15538,-A	The Model Church	Ge rejected

Gennett 7068 as by **Asa Martin & Doc Roberts**. Champion 15854, 15922 as by **Jesse Coat**. Supertone 9539, 9642 as by **Emmett Davenport**, 9541 as by **Potter & James**.
Matrices 15526/27, 15531 to 15535 are by Green Bailey; matrices 15528/29 are by Merle McGinnis.
Revs: Gennett 7068 by Byrd Moore; Supertone 9541 by Warren Caplinger.

Asa Martin, James Roberts, v duet; acc. Asa Martin, h/g.
    Richmond, IN   Monday, January 13, 1930
        16089,-A   Sweet Evalina, Dear Evalina   Ge rejected

Asa Martin, v; acc. Doc Roberts, md-1; poss. James Roberts, md-2; own g.
    Richmond, IN   Tuesday, January 14, 1930
        16096,-A,B   Lilly Dale   Ge rejected
        16097   Johnny The Drunkard -1   Ge 7207, Ch 15922, Spt 9642
        16100,-A   [unknown title] -2   Ge rejected

Champion 15922 as by **Jesse Coat**. Supertone 9642 as by **Emmett Davenport**.
Intervening matrices are by Doc Roberts.

Asa Martin, v; or Asa Martin, James Roberts, v duet-1; acc. Doc Roberts, md; Jerry Wallace, md-2; Asa Martin, g.
    Richmond, IN   Thursday, April 24, 1930
        16523   Barefoot Boy With Boots On -1   Spr 2526
        16524   I Tickled Her Under The Chin   Ge 7207, Spr 2526
        16525-A   Put On Your Old Gray Bonnet -1, 2   Ge 7242, Ch 16049, Spt 9774, Spr 2659
        16526,-A   Maggie Dear I'm Called Away -1   Ge rejected
        16527,-A   That's Home Sweet Home To Me   Ge rejected
        16528-B   The Old Fashioned Picture Of Mother   Ge 7242, Ch 16049, 33060, Spt 9774, MW 4944

Matrix 16525 on Gennett 7242, Champion 16049 as by **Asa Martin & James Roberts**. Champion 33060 credit unknown.
Supertone 9774 as by **Davenport & Tracy** (matrix 16525)/**Emmett Davenport** (matrix 16528). Superior 2526 as by **Earl Bowers**, 2659 as by **Bowers & Lewis**.
Revs: Champion 33060 unknown; Superior 2659 by W.C. Childers; Montgomery Ward 4944 by Manhattan Quartette (popular).

Asa Martin & Roy Hobbs: Roy Hobbs, md; Asa Martin, g/v-1.
    Richmond, IN   Friday, April 25, 1930
        16531,-A   San Antonio -1   Ge rejected
        16532,-A   Little Black Moustache -1   Ge rejected
        16533,-A   Lee County Rag   Ge rejected
        16534,-A   Scottdale Stomp   Ge rejected

Asa Martin, v; acc. Ed Lewis, ah-1; own g.
    Richmond, IN   Thursday, January 15, 1931
        17439   The Little Old Jail House -1   Ge rejected
        17440   The Contented Hobo   Ch 16299, Spr 2607
        17441   That's Home Sweet Home To Me   Ch 16299, Spr 2607
        17442   It's Funny When You Feel That Way   Ch S-16769, 45067

Superior 2607 as by **Earl Bowers**.

Asa Martin, h-1/g/v-2; Ed Lewis, ah-3.
    Richmond, IN   Friday, January 16, 1931
        17443   Mind Your Own Business -2   Ch 16272
        17444   A Socker On The Kisser -1, 2, 3   Ch 16272
        17445   My Cabin Home Among The Hills -2, 3   Ch S-16769, 45067
        17446,-A   My Lost Lover On The Sea -2, 3   Ge rejected
        17447   Medley Of Old Time Waltzes -1, 3   Ge rejected
        17448   Gentle Annie -1, 2, 3   Ch S-16568
        17449   Medley Of Old Time Melodies -1, 3   Ge rejected

Asa Martin & James Roberts, v duet; acc. Doc Roberts, f; Asa Martin, g.
    New York, NY   Thursday, March 5, 1931
        10467-2   Sunny Tennessee   Ba 32306, Or 8101, Pe 12762, Ro 5101,
                                                                    Cq 7965, Bwy 4080
        10468-2   Good Bye Betty   Ba 32204, Or 8073, Pe 12725, Ro 5073,
                                                                    Cq 7941, Bwy 4047
        10469-2   The Pine Tree On The Hill   Ba 32246, Me M12391, MeC 91541, Or 8092,
                                                                    Pe 12744, Ro 5092, Cq 7745, Bwy 4063,
                                                                    Min M-905
        10470-2   Darling Nellie Gray   Ba 32306, Or 8101, Pe 12762, Ro 5101,
                                                                    Cq 7965, ARC-Bwy 8246

Broadway 4047, 4063, 4080, ARC-Broadway 8246 as by **Horton & Moore**.
Earlier issues of Broadway 8246 use the Carver Boys' Paramount matrix of *Darling Nellie Gray* (as by **The Carson Boys**).
Revs: Broadway 4063 by Vernon Dalhart & Carson Robison; Melotone 91541 by Arkansas Woodchopper; Minerva M-905 by Gene Autry.

Asa Martin, v; or **Asa Martin & James Roberts**-1, v duet; acc. Doc Roberts, md-2; Asa Martin, g.
New York, NY   Friday, March 6, 1931

10472-2	The Contented Hobo -2	Ba 32177, Or 8064, Pe 12710, Ro 5064, Cq 7746
10473-2	The Wandering Hobo -2	Ba 32177, Or 8064, Pe 12710, Ro 5064, Cq 7746
10474-2	The Little Old Jail House -2	Ba 32307, Me M12393, Or 8102, Pe 12763, Ro 5102, Cq 7844, Bwy 4070
10477-2	The Rovin' Moonshiner	Ba 32307, Me M12393, Or 8102, Pe 12763, Ro 5102, Cq 7844
10478-1	Knoxville Girl -1	Ba 32178, Or 8065, Pe 12711, Ro 5065, Cq 7837, Bwy 4087
10479-3	My Lover On The Deep Blue Sea -1	Ba 32204, Or 8073, Pe 12725, Ro 5073, Cq 7941, Bwy 4080

Conqueror 7844 as by **Asa Martin & James Roberts**. Broadway 4070, 4080, 4087 as by **Horton & Moore**.
Matrix 10478 is titled *The Knoxville Girl* on Broadway 4087. Intervening matrices are by James Roberts.
Rev. Broadway 4070 by Gene Autry.

Asa Martin, v; acc. James Roberts, md-1; own g.
New York, NY   Saturday, March 7, 1931

10480-2	East Bound Train	Ba 32178, Or 8065, Pe 12711, Ro 5065, Cq 7837, Bwy 4086
10481-2	Give My Love To Nellie, Jack -1	Ba 32246, Me M12391, Or 8092, Pe 12744, Ro 5092, Cq 7745

Broadway 4086 as by **Horton & Moore**.
Matrix 10481 is titled *Give My Love To Nell* on some issues.
Rev. Broadway 4086 by Cliff Carlisle.

Asa Martin & James Roberts-1/**Martin & Roberts**-2: Asa Martin, James Roberts, v duet; acc. Doc Roberts, md-3; James Roberts, md-4/g-5; Asa Martin, g.
New York, NY   Thursday, March 24, 1932

11565-1	My Blue Eyed Boy -2, 3, 5	Ba 32651, Me M12569, Or 8188, Pe 12782, Ro 5188, Cq 8146, CrC/MeC/Roy/Stg 91477
11566-2	When The Roses Bloom In Dixie -1, 3/4	Ba 32477, Me M12424, Or 8151, Pe 12821, Ro 5151, Cq 8070, Bwy 4087
11567-2	Ninety-Nine Years (Is Almost For Life) -2, 3/4	Ba 32426, Me M12436, Or 8128, Pe 12799, Ro 5128, Vo 5486, Cq 7967, Bwy 4048, CrC/MeC/Roy/Stg 91318
11568-1,-4	Prisoner No. 999 -2, 3/4	Ba 32426, Me M12436, Or 8128, Pe 12799, Ro 5128, Cq 7967, Bwy 4047, CrC/MeC/Roy/Stg 91318

Vocalion 5486 as by **Glen Fox & Joe Wilson**. Broadway 4047, 4048, 4087 as by **Horton & Moore**. Crown/Melotone/Royale/Sterling 91318 as by **Asa Martin & James Roberts**.
Rev. Broadway 4048 by Cliff Carlisle.

Asa Martin & James Roberts-1/**Martin & Roberts**-2: Asa Martin, James Roberts, v duet; acc. Doc Roberts, md; Asa Martin, g; James Roberts, g.
New York, NY   Friday, March 25, 1932

11570-	Keep On The Sunny Side	ARC unissued
11571-2	Rycove Cyclone -1	Ba 32554, Or 8163, Pe 12839, Ro 5163, Cq 8068
11572-	Aggravating Lula Love	ARC unissued
11573-1	Aged Mother -2	Ba 32651, Me M12569, Or 8188, Pe 12872, Ro 5188, Cq 8146, CrC/MeC/Roy/Stg 91477
11574-2	Bury Me 'Neath The Weeping Willow -2	Ba 32522, Me M12497, Or 8154, Pe 12831, Ro 5154, Cq 8011, CrC/MeC/Roy/Stg 91402
11575-1	The Ship That Never Returned -1	Ba 32554, Or 8163, Pe 12839, Ro 5163, Cq 8068
11576-2	Dying Cowboy -1	Ba 32522, Me M12497, Or 8154, Pe 12831, Ro 5154, Cq 8011, CrC/MeC/Roy/Stg 91402

Matrices 11570, 11572 were logged as by **Doc Roberts Trio**.
Matrix 11576 is titled *The Dying Cowboy* on Conqueror 8011.

Asa Martin, v; acc. prob. Doc Roberts, md; own g.
New York, NY   Friday, March 25, 1932

11581-1	She Ain't Built That Way	Ba 32475, Me M12427, Or 8149, Pe 12819, Ro 5149, Cq 8012

Matrix 11577 is by James Roberts; matrices 11578 to 11580 are by Doc Roberts.

Asa Martin & James Roberts-1/**Fiddling Doc Roberts Trio**-2: Asa Martin, James Roberts, v duet; or **Asa Martin**-3, v; acc. Doc Roberts, f-4; Doc Roberts or James Roberts, md-5; Asa Martin, g.
New York, NY   Saturday, March 26, 1932

11586-3	My Rocky Mountain Queen -1, 5	Ba 32477, Me M12424, Or 8151, Pe 12821, Ro 5151, Cq 8070, Bwy 4069
11588-2	Ninety-Nine Years -2, 4	Ba 32609, Me M12522, Or 8176, Pe 12857, Ro 5176, Cq 8078
11589-1	I Tickled Her Under The Chin -3, 5	Ba 32475, Me M12427, Or 8149, Pe 12819, Ro 5149, Cq 8012

Broadway 4069 as by **Horton & Moore**.
Matrix 11587 is by Doc Roberts.
Revs: all issues of matrix 11588 by Doc Roberts; Broadway 4069 by Carson Robison Trio.

Asa Martin & Roy Hobbs, v duet; acc. Roy Hobbs, md-1/g-2; Asa Martin g.
Richmond, IN   Wednesday, October 19, 1932

18840	The Lonely Drifter -1	Ch 45065
18840-A	The Lonely Drifter -1	Ch 16520
18841	Hot Corn -1	Ch 16520, 45065
18842	All I've Got's Gone -1	Ch 16539
18843-A	The Little Old Jail House -2	Ch 16539
18844	Down The Hobo Trail To Home -1	Ch 16529
18845	Prisoner No. 999 -1	Ch 16529, 45176, MeC 45176, Min M-14041

Champion 16520, 45065 as by **Asa Martin & Ray Hobbs**. Minerva M-14041 as by **Martin & Hobbs**.
Matrix 18845 is titled *Prisoner No. 949* on Champion 45176, Melotone 45176, Minerva M-14041.
Rev. Minerva M-14041 by Walton West.

Martin & Hobbs: Roy Hobbs, md; Asa Martin, g.
Richmond, IN   Wednesday, October 19, 1932

| 18846 | Havana River Glide | Ch 16536 |
| 18847 | Wild Cat Rag | Ch 16536 |

Asa Martin, v; or Asa Martin, Roy Hobbs, v duet-1; acc. Roy Hobbs, md; Asa Martin, g.
Richmond, IN   Wednesday, October 19, 1932

18848	Good-Bye Betty	Ch S-16557
18849	The Rovin' Moonshiner	Ch S-16557
18852	I Must See My Mother -1	Ch S-16568, 45176, MeC 45176, Min M-14043

Champion 45176, Melotone 45176 as by **Asa Martin & Roy Hobbs**. Minerva M-14043 as by **Martin & Hobbs**.
Rev. Minerva M-14043 by Kenneth Houchins.

Martin & Roberts: Asa Martin, James Roberts, v duet; acc. Doc Roberts, md-1; James Roberts, md-2/g-3; Asa Martin, g.
New York, NY   Thursday, February 2, 1933

13011-	San Antonio -2	ARC unissued
13012-1	Shadows And Dreams -1/2	ARC 6-01-51, Cq 8062
13013-1	Hang Down Your Head And Cry -1, 3	Ba 32831, Me M12761, Or 8256, Pe 12932, Ro 5256, Cq 8207

Martin & Roberts: Asa Martin, James Roberts, v duet; or **Asa Martin**-1, v; acc. Doc Roberts, md-2; James Roberts, md-3/g-4; Asa Martin, g.
New York, NY   Friday, February 3, 1933

13015-1	Bronco Bill -2/3	Ba 32747, Me M12675, Or 8226, Pe 12906, Ro 5226, Cq 8206
13016-1	There's Someone Waiting For You -2/3	Cq 8233
13017-2	Low Down Hanging Around -1, 4	Ba 32831, Me M12761, Or 8256, Pe 12932, Ro 5256, Cq 8207
13018-1	A Letter From Home Sweet Home -2/3	Ba 32703, Me M12634, MeC 91517, Or 8213, Pe 12890, Ro 5213, Cq 8145
13019-2	When It's Lamp Lightin' Time In The Valley -2/3	Ba 32712, Me M12642, MeC 91522, Or 8214, Pe 12894, Ro 5214, Vo 5490, Co-Lucky 60301
13020-1	My Dixie Home -2/3	Ba 32703, Me M12634, MeC 91517, Or 8213, Pe 12890, Ro 5213, Vo 5490
13021-1	Message Of A Broken Heart -2/3	Ba 32772, Me M12701, MeC 91578, Or 8234, Pe 12913, Ro 5234, Vo 5496, Cq 8233, RZAu G22177
13022-1	My Old Homestead By The Sea -2/3	Ba 32712, Me M12642, MeC 91522, Or 8214, Pe 12894, Ro 5214, Vo 5486
13023-1	The Roundup In The Spring -2/3	Ba 32747, Me M12675, Or 8226, Pe 12906, Ro 5226, Vo 5496, Cq 8206, RZAu G22247
13024-	That Little Boy Of Mine -2/3	ARC unissued
13025-1	There's No Place Like Home -1, 2/3	Ba 32931, Me M12874, Or 8293, Pe 12967, Ro 5293, Cq 8145
13026-	Barefoot Boy With Boots -1, 2/3	MeC 93092

All issues of matrix 13017 as by **Martin & Roberts**.
Vocalion 5486, 5490, 5496, Regal-Zonophone G22177, 22247, Columbia-Lucky 60301 as by **Glen Fox & Joe Wilson**.
Revs: Regal-Zonophone G22177 by W. Lee O'Daniel, G22247 by Tex Ritter; Melotone 93092 by Buddy Spencer Trio (see Frank Luther); Columbia-Lucky 60301 by Original Yellow Jackets (see JR).

Martin & Roberts: Asa Martin, James Roberts, v duet; or **Asa Martin**-1, v; acc. James Roberts, g; Asa Martin, g.
New York, NY   Saturday, February 4, 1933

13029-2	Where's My Sweetie Now -1	Ba 32931, Me M12874, Or 8293, Pe 12967, Ro 5293
13030-1	The Old Covered Bridge	Vo 5495

Vocalion 5495 as by **Glen Fox & Joe Wilson**.

Martin & Roberts: Asa Martin, James Roberts, v duet; acc. James Roberts, md; Asa Martin, g.
New York, NY   Monday, February 6, 1933

13031-1	There's A Little Box Of Pine On The 7:29	Ba 32772, Me M12701, MeC 91578, Or 8234, Pe 12913, Ro 5234, Vo 5495, Cq 8062, RZAu G22176
13032-	When It's Lamp Lighting Time In The Valley	ARC unissued

Vocalion 5495, Regal-Zonophone G22176 as by **Glen Fox & Joe Wilson**.
Matrix 13031 is titled *There's A Little Box Of Pine On The 7.29* on Regal-Zonophone G22176.
Rev. Regal-Zonophone G22176 by Gene Autry.

Asa Martin & Roy Hobbs, v duet; or **Asa Martin**-1, v; acc. Roy Hobbs, md; Asa Martin, g.
Richmond, IN   Tuesday, April 4, 1933

19114	Red River Valley Rose	Ch 16589, 45133
19115	I'm On My Way Back	Ch 16589, 45133
19116	The Girl By The Rio Grande	Ch S-16597
19117	Shadows And Dreams	Ch S-16597
19118	Gamblin' Cowboy -1	Ch S-16611
19119	Down In Old Kentucky -1	Ch S-16611

Champion 45133 as by **Asa Martin & Ray Hobbs**.
Matrix 19115 is titled *I'm On My Way Back* on Champion 45133.
Matrices 19120/21 are by Hatton Brothers with Asa Martin and Roy Hobbs (see Charlie Wilson).

Roy Hobbs, md; Asa Martin, g/v-1.
Richmond, IN   Wednesday, April 5, 1933

19122	Jake Walk Papa -1	Ch S-16627, 45034
19123	Bronco Bill -1	Ch S-16627, 45034
19126	Wolf County Blues	Ch S-16610
19127	Medley Of Breakdowns	Ch S-16610

Champion S-16610 as by **Martin & Hobbs**.
Matrices 19124/25 are by Charlie Wilson.

Martin & Rose: Asa Martin, Arthur Rose, v duet; acc. Doc Roberts, md; Asa Martin, g; James Roberts, g.
New York, NY   Tuesday, August 15, 1933

13795-	My Homestead On The Farm	Cq 8341
13796-2	It's Hard To Be Bound Down In Prison	Cq 8339
13797-	Springtime And Flowers	ARC unissued

Acc. Doc Roberts or James Roberts, md; Asa Martin, g.
New York, NY   Tuesday, August 15, 1933

13798-1	Ragtime Chicken Joe	ARC 35-10-12, Cq 8339, 8566, MeC 92093

ARC 35-10-12, Conqueror 8566, Melotone 92093 as by **Fiddling Doc Roberts Trio**.

Arthur Rose, v; acc. Asa Martin, g; James Roberts, g.
New York, NY   Tuesday, August 15, 1933

13799-	Lu Lu Gal	ARC unissued

Asa Martin, James Roberts, v duet; or Asa Martin, Arthur Rose, v duet-1; acc. Doc Roberts, md; Asa Martin, g; James Roberts, g.
New York, NY   Wednesday, August 16, 1933

13804-1	Put My Little Shoes Away	Cq 8208
13812-	Take Me Home To My Grandma -1	Cq 8341
13819-	Treasures Untold	ARC unissued

Conqueror 8208 as by **Fiddling Doc Roberts Trio**.
Matrices 13805 to 13808, 13811 are by Doc Roberts; matrices 13809/10, 13813 to 13818 are popular.

Asa Martin, James Roberts, v duet; or Asa Martin, Arthur Rose, v duet-1; acc. Doc Roberts, f-2/md-3; James Roberts, md-4/g-5; Asa Martin, g.
New York, NY   Thursday, August 17, 1933

13823-1	In The Shadow Of The Pines -3/4	ARC 35-10-12, Cq 8208, 8566, MeC 92093, Min M-14032

13824-1	School Day Sweetheart -1, 3, 5	Cq 8340
13825-	Days Are Blue -1?, 3, 5	ARC unissued
13826-2	Many Years Ago -2	Cq 8340

All issues of matrix 13823 as by **Fiddling Doc Roberts Trio**.
Matrices 13820/21 are by James Roberts & Arthur Rose (see the former).
Rev. Minerva M-14032 by Goebel Reeves.

Asa Martin With James Roberts: Asa Martin, v; or Asa Martin, James Roberts, v duet-1; acc. Asa Martin, g; James Roberts, g.

New York, NY   Tuesday, August 28, 1934

| 15745-1 | Crawling And Creeping | Ba 33400, Me M13367, Or 8452, Pe 13130, Ro 5452, Cq 8509 |
| 15746- | Going Back To Alabama -1 | ARC unissued |

Conqueror 8509 as by **Asa Martin**.
Rev. all issues of matrix 15745 by James Roberts.

Martin & Roberts: Asa Martin, James Roberts, v duet; acc. Doc Roberts, md-1; James Roberts, md-2/g-3; Asa Martin, g.

New York, NY   Wednesday, August 29, 1934

15780-1	Little Shack Around The Corner -1/2	Ba 33279, Me M13246, MeC 91993, Or 8405, Pe 13089, Ro 5405, Cq 8508
15781-1	Sweet Florine -3	Ba 33181, Me M13148, Or 8377, Pe 13046, Ro 5377
15782-1	Crawdad Song -3	Ba 33181, Me M13148, Or 8377, Pe 13046, Ro 5377
15785-2	Careless Love -1, 3	ARC 5-11-63
15786-1	Budded Roses -1, 3	Ba 33279, Me M13246, MeC 91993, Or 8405, Pe 13089, Ro 5405, Cq 8508, MeC/Min M-931

Matrices 15783/84 are by Cliff Carlisle. Rev. Melotone/Minerva M-931 by Prairie Ramblers.

Acc. Doc Roberts, md-1; James Roberts, g; Asa Martin, g.

New York, NY   Thursday, August 30, 1934

15805-2	Lillie Dale	ARC 5-11-63
15806-2	Hot Corn -1	ARC 6-03-52
15807-1	Down On The Farm	ARC 6-01-51

Rev. ARC 6-03-52 by Doc Roberts.

Asa Martin & His Kentucky Hillbillies: Asa Martin, v; acc. Joe Dedry, f-1; Glen Carpenter, h-2; own h-3/g; Don Weston, sg-4/g-5/v-6.

Columbia, SC   Thursday, November 10, 1938

SC-130-1	I'll Be Here A Long, Long Time -1, 3, 5, 6	Vo 04673
SC-131-1	Low And Blue -1, 2/3, 5, 6	Vo 04529
SC-132-1	Way Down On The Farm -1, 2/3, 5, 6	Vo 04673
SC-133-1	Jennie Barn Bound -1, 2/3, 5, 6	Vo 04529
SC-134-1	Red River Valley Rose -1, 5, 6	Vo 04569
SC-135-1	Roadside Drifter -1, 5	Vo 04759, Cq 9242
SC-136-1	Quit Hanging Around, Baby -1, 4	Vo 04759, Cq 9242
SC-137-1	Knock-Kneed Susie Jane -1, 2, 5, 6	Vo 04827
SC-138-1	Lonesome, Broke And Weary -4	Vo 04894
SC-139-1	Harlan Town Tragedy -4	Vo 04894
SC-140-1	Hot Sausage Mama -5	Vo 04827
SC-141-1	Chums For Fifty Years -1, 5, 6	Vo 04569

Asa Martin also recorded in partnership with Doc Roberts and accompanied James Roberts on most of the items listed under his name. He also recorded after 1942.

CLYDE MARTIN & HIS HOOSIER RANGERS

Unknown f; unknown, p; unknown, md; unknown, g.

Richmond, IN   Tuesday, November 10, 1931

18161	Ride 'Em Cowboy	Ch 16691
18164	Little Brown Jug; White River Bottom	Ch 16409
18165	Shuber's Hoe Down	Ch 16409
18166	Nobody's Business	Ge unissued

Champion 16691 as by **The Hoosier Rangers**. Matrices 18162/63 are unrelated. Rev. Champion 16691 by Jess Hillard.

DAN MARTIN

Pseudonym on Superior for Dempsey Jones (see Golden Melody Boys).

DUDE MARTIN & COWBOY GROUP

Pseudonym employed by the MacGregor transcription company for Al Clauser & His Oklahoma Outlaws on some 10-inch discs for radio use. Martin was a known performer who recorded for MacGregor in his own name, and it is not known why the firm used it in conjunction with the sides Al Clauser cut for ARC, most of which were released by MacGregor.

HEAVY MARTIN

Pseudonym on Vocalion for Hugh Cross.

JOHN MARTIN

Pseudonym on Superior for Roy Harvey.

JOHNNY MARTIN

Pseudonym on Supertone for Jimmie Mattox.

ROY MARTIN & HIS GUITAR

Pseudonym on ARC labels for Lewis McDaniels.

TROY MARTIN & ELVIN BIGGER

Troy Martin, Elvin Bigger, v duet; acc. prob. one of them, g.
   New York, NY   Saturday, May 16, 1936

19265-	Meet Me In The Moonlight	ARC unissued
19266-	Give Me Flowers While I'm Living	ARC unissued
19267-	Can't Blame Me For That	ARC unissued
19270-	Heartbroken Girl	ARC unissued
19271-1	I'm Going Home	ARC 6-10-53
19272-2	You'll Never Miss Your Mother Till She's Gone	ARC 6-10-53, Cq 7072

Conqueror 7072 as by **Smoky Mountain Family**. Earlier issues of Conqueror 7072 use a recording of the same song by the Gentry Brothers (Plaza matrix 7322), as by **Smoky Mountain Twins**.
Matrices 19268/69 are popular.
Rev. Conqueror 7072 (with same credit) by Peck's Male Quartette.

Elvin Bigger was a member of the Four Virginians.

MARTIN & HOBBS
MARTIN & ROBERTS
MARTIN & ROSE

See Asa Martin. (For **Martin & Roberts** on Supertone, however, see Doc Roberts.)

MARTIN BROTHERS

Pseudonym on Paramount and Broadway for John McGhee & Frank Welling.

MARTIN MELODY BOYS

Unknown, f; unknown, bj-md; unknown, g; unknown, v duet-1; unknown, y-1.
   Atlanta, GA   Tuesday, April 16, 1929

148309-	I'd Love To Live In Loveland	Co unissued
148310-2	An Old Sweetheart Of Mine -1	Co 15413-D
148311-1	The Donald Rag	Co 15413-D
148312-	Twinkle Little Star	Co unissued

FRANK[IE] MARVIN

Frank Marvin also recorded popular repertoire with his own ukulele accompaniment. This entry excludes those recordings but is believed to be otherwise complete.

Frank Marvin, v; acc. unknown, h; unknown, g.
   New York, NY   c. July 1927

2526-B	The Bully Of The Town	GG/Rad 4149

Rev. Grey Gull/Radiex 4149 by Bob Blake (popular).

Acc. unknown.
   New York NY   c. April 1928

2861-A,-B	Show Me The Way To Go Home	GG/Rad 4199

Rev. Grey Gull/Radiex 4199 by Arthur Hall (popular).

Frankie Wallace & His Guitar, v/y; acc. own sg.
   New York, NY   Wednesday, June 13, 1928

8038-1,-2,-3	Blue Yodel No. 1	Ba 7180, Do 0251, Je 5349, Or 1297, Re 8604, Chg 901, Cq 7163, Htd 16508, 23005, Pm 3272, 12659, Bwy 3272, 8083, ImpE 2124

Paramount 12659 as by **Louis Warfield**. Broadway 3272, 8083 as by **Johnnie Moore**. Imperial 2124 as by **Frank Luther**. Matrix 8038 is titled *Jimmy Rodgers Blue Yodel* on Broadway 3272, 8083, Paramount 3272, 12659, or *Blue Yodel* on Imperial 2124.
Some issues use the controls 1675-1, 1069.

Frank Marvin, v/y-1; acc. own sg.
   New York, NY   Monday, June 18, 1928

8042-1	Way Out On The Mountain -1	Ba 7179, Do 0251, Je 5351, Or 1299, Re 8604, Chg 691, Cq 7163, Pm 3272, 12659, Bwy 3272, 4051, 8083
8043-3	In The Jail House Now	Ba 7180, Do 0253, Je 5349, Or 1299, Re 8605, Chg 901, Cq 7164, Htd 16508, 23005

Paramount 12659 as by **Louis Warfield**. Broadway 3272, 8083 as by **Johnnie Moore**. Broadway 4051 as by **Jack West**.
Controls appear on some issues as follows: 8042 = 1673-3, 1070; 8043 = 1676-3.
Rev. Broadway 4051 by Carson Robison.

   New York, NY   Thursday, June 21, 1928

8053-	Blue Yodel No. 2 -1	Pl unissued

Frank Marvin, v/y; acc. own sg.
   New York, NY   Wednesday, June 27, 1928

E-27781-	Blue Yodel	Br 248, 3979, BrAu 3979, BrSA SA248
E-27782-	Away Out On The Mountain	Br 248, 3979, BrAu 3979, BrSA SA248
E-27783-	Blue Yodel Number 2	Br 249, 3985, BrAu 3985, BrSA SA249
E-27784-	In The Jail House Now	Br 249, 3985, BrAu 3985, BrSA SA249

Frankie Wallace & His Guitar, v/y; acc. own sg.
   New York, NY   Thursday, June 28, 1928

8061-4	The Soldier's Sweetheart	Ba 7205, Do 0256, Je 5374, Or 1327, Re 8623, Chg 544, Cq 7165
8062-2	Sleep, Baby, Sleep	Ba 7206, Do 0256, Je 5375, Or 1326, Re 8623, Cq 7165, Htd 16510

Some issues of matrix 8061 use the control 1732-4.

Frankie Wallace With His Guitar, v/y; acc. own sg.
   New York, NY   Friday, June 29, 1928

18598-B	Blue Yodel	Ed 52356, 5571
N-310-A	Blue Yodel	Ed 11006
18599-B	Way Out On The Mountain	Ed 52356, 5587
N-311-B	Away Out On The Mountain	Ed 11006

Edison 11006 as by **Frank Marvin**.

Frankie Wallace & His Guitar, v/y; acc. own sg.
   New York, NY   c. June 1928

3233-A; 108254-	Blue Yodel	Ca 8284, Lin 2932, Pat 32376, Pe 12455, Ro 707
3234-A; 108255-	Way Out On The Mountain	Ca 8288, Lin 2936, Pat 32376, Pe 12455, Ro 711

Pathé 32376, Perfect 12455 as by **Walter Dalton & His Guitar**.
Controls appear on various issues instead of, or as well as, the matrices, as follows: 3233/108254 = 1069; 3234/108255 = 1070.
Revs: Cameo 8284, 8288, Lincoln 2932, 2936, Romeo 707, 711 by Carson Robison.

   New York, NY   Thursday, July 5, 1928

8053-6	Blue Yodel No. 2	Ba 7206, Do 0257, Je 5375, Or 1327, Re 8622, Cq 7167, Htd 16510, Pm 3139, Bwy 8121
8074-3	The Brakeman's Blues	Ba 7205, Do 0257, Je 5374, Or 1326, Re 8622, Chg 544, Cq 7167
8075-2	Ben Dewberry's Final Run	Ba 7179, Do 0253, Je 5351, Or 1297, Re 8605, Chg 691, Cq 7164

Paramount 3139, Broadway 8121 as by **Louis Warfield**.
Controls appear on various issues instead of, or as well as, the matrices, as follows: 8053 = 1733-6, 1151; 8074 = 1731-3; 8075 = 1674-2.
Rev. Paramount 3139, Broadway 8121 by Frank Luther.

George White, v/y; acc. own sg.
   New York, NY   Wednesday, July 11, 1928

400861-B	Drowsy Moonlight	OK 45241, PaE E6245
400862-B	Swanee Blue Jay	OK 45241

Parlophone E6245 as by **Frank Marvin**.
Rev. Parlophone E6245 by Ralph Richardson.

Frankie Wallace & His Guitar, v/y; acc. own sg.
New York, NY   c. July 11, 1928
    GEX-2000-A   Blue Yodel No. 2   Ge 6562, Ch 15562, Spt 9082
    GEX-2001   Away Out On The Mountain   Ge 6562, Ch 15562, 33058, Spt 9082

Matrices GEX-2000/01 were logged as shown but issued thus: Gennett 6562 as by **Francis Wallace**; Champion 15562 as by **Yodelin' Jimmy Warner**; Supertone 9082 as by **Frankie Wallace**. Champion 33058 credit unknown. Rev. Champion 33058 by Fred Wingate (popular).

Frank Marvin & His Guitar, v/y; acc. own sg.
New York, NY   Wednesday, July 18, 1928
    E-27854-   Ben Dewberry's Final Run   Br 253, Spt S2055
    E-27855-   The Brakeman's Blues   Br 253, Spt S2055

Supertone S2055 as by **The Texas Ranger**.

Frank Wallace, v/y; acc. J. C. Johnson, p.
New York, NY   Saturday, July 21, 1928
    146763-2   Drowsy Moonlight   Ha 696-H, Ve 1696-V, Di 2696-G
    146764-1   Swanee Blue Jay   Ha 696-H, Ve 1696-V, Di 2696-G

Frank Wallace & His Guitar, v/y; acc. unknown, f; own g.
New York, NY   Monday, August 20, 1928
    18663-A   Drowsy Moonlight   Ed 52387
    N-371-   Drowsy Moonlight   Ed rejected
    18664-C   Swanee Blue-Jay   Ed 52387, 5603
    N-372-   Swanee Blue Jay   Ed 11023

Frankie Wallace: v/y; acc. unknown, f; unknown, g.
New York, NY   Wednesday, August 29, 1928
    8161-   Treasure Untold   Ba 7234, Do 0261, Or 1354, Re 8642, Chg 916, 946

Some issues use the control 1784-3.
Revs: Banner 7234, Oriole 1354, Challenge 916, 946 by Carson Robison and/or Frank Luther (see the former).

Frankie Wallace & His Guitar, v; acc. own sg.
New York, NY   Wednesday, August 29, 1928
    8162-   If Brother Jack Were Here   Ba 7233, Do 0261, Or 1353, Re 8642

Matrix 8162 is titled *If Brother Jack Were Only Here or Mother Was A Lady* on Oriole 1353.
Some issues use the control 1782-2.
Revs: Banner 7233, Oriole 1353 by Carson Robison & Frank Luther.

George White, v/y; acc. unknown, f; own sg.
New York, NY   Thursday, August 30, 1928
    401089-B   Dixie Shadows   OK 45257, Kismet K723
    401090-D   Treasure Untold   OK 45257, Kismet K723

Kismet K723 as by **Frankie Marvin**.

Frank Wallace & His Guitar, v/y; acc. unknown, f; poss. own h-1; own sg.
New York, NY   Tuesday, September 18, 1928
    18733-A,-B,-C   Oklahoma Blues   Ed rejected
    N-438-A,-B   Oklahoma Blues   Ed rejected
    18734-A   Watermelon Smilin' On The Vine -1   Ed 52451, 5620
    N-439-   Watermelon Smilin' On The Vine -1   Ed 11023

Frankie Wallace, v/y; acc. own sg-1/g-2.
New York, NY   September/October 1928
    3323-; 108347-   Oklahoma Blues -1   Ca 8328, Lin 2976, Pat 32395, Pe 12474, Ro 751
    3324-; 108348-   In The Jail House Now -1   Ca 8328, Lin 2976, Pat 32395, Pe 12469, Ro 751
    3325-1; 108349-3   Mother Was A Lady -1   Ca 8378, Lin 3026, Pat 32390, Pe 12469, Ro 801
    3330-A; 108355-   Watermelons Smiling On The Vine -2   Ca 8361, Lin 3009, Pat 32395, Pe 12474, Ro 784
    3331-1; 108356-1   Don't Send My Boy To Prison -1   Ba 32058, Ca 8378, Do 4705, Je 6180, Lin 3026, Or 2180, Pat 32396, Pe 12475, Re 10238, Ro 801, 1545, Cq 7704, 7735, CrC 91054, Stg 291054, Roy 391054

Pathé 32390, Perfect 12469 as by **Walter Dalton**; Pathé 32395, 32396, Perfect 12474, 12475 as by **Walter Dalton & His Guitar**.
Matrix 3325/108349 is titled *If Brother Jack Were Here* on Pathé 32390, Perfect 12469.
Revs: Banner 32058, Domino 4705, Jewel 6180, Oriole 2180, Pathé 32396, Perfect 12475, Regal 10238, Romeo 1545, Conqueror 7735 by Carson Robison; Conqueror 7704 by Gene Autry.

Frankie Marvin & His Guitar, v/y; acc. unknown, f-1; own g.
   New York, NY   Tuesday, October 16, 1928

18812-B	In The Jailhouse Now -1	Ed 52436, 5628
N-509-B	In The Jailhouse Now -1	Ed 20002
18813-A	Barber's Blues -1	Ed 52451
N-510-A,-B	Barber's Blues -1	Ed rejected
18814-B	Ben Dewberry's Final Run	Ed 52436, 5627
N-511-A	Ben Dewberry's Final Run	Ed 20002

Frankie Wallace, v/y; acc. own sg-1/g-2.
   New York, NY   October/November 1928

3403-; 108465-	Blue Yodel No. 2 -2	Ca 8362, Lin 3010, Pat 32405, Pe 12484, Ro 785
3404-; 108471-	Barbers' Blues -1	Ca 8362, Lin 3010, Pat 32410, Pe 12489, Ro 785
3405-; 108472-1	Poor Man's Blues -1	Ca 8361, Lin 3009, Pat 32410, Pe 12489, Ro 784

Pathé 32405, 32410, Perfect 12484, 12489 as by **Walter Dalton & His Guitar**.
Rev. Pathé 32405, Perfect 12484 by Carson Robison.

Frank Marvin & His Guitar, v/y; acc. unknown, f; own g.
   New York, NY   Friday, November 23, 1928

18895-A	The Song Of Sorrow	Ed 52460
N-590-A,-B	The Song Of Sorrow	Ed rejected
18896-A	Walking Down The Railroad Track	Ed 52460, 5645
N-591-A,-B	Walking Down The Railroad Track	Ed rejected

Frank Marvin, v/y; acc. own g.
   New York, NY   Wednesday, November 28, 1928

E-28780-	Oklahoma Blues	Br 278
E-28781-	Walkin' Down The Railroad Track	Br 278, Spt S2050

Supertone S2050 as by **The Texas Ranger**.
Rev. Supertone S2050 by Kanawha Singers.

George White & His Guitar, v/y; acc. unknown, f/md-1; own sg.
   New York, NY   Friday, November 30, 1928

401415-A	Oklahoma Blues	OK 45287
401416-A	Walkin' Down The Railroad Track -1	OK 45287, Ve 2362-V, Cl 5296-C

Velvet Tone 2362-V, Clarion 5296-C as by **Johnny Hart**. Those issues use the transfer matrix 100524.

Frankie Wallace & His Guitar, v/y-1; acc. unknown, f-2; own sg.
   New York, NY   c. November 1928

3481-; 108482-2	The Song Of Sorrow -1, 2	Ca 9016, Lin 3045, Pat 32453, Pe 12532, Ro 820
3482-A; 108483-	Walkin' Down The Railroad Track -2	Ca 9019, Lin 3048, Pat 32414, Pe 12493,
		Ro 823, Ang 3078, Gracelon 4022,
		MeAu 10084, StAu 726
3483-; 108484-	Blue Yodel No. 3 -1	Ca 9016, Lin 3045, Pat 32414, Pe 12493, Ro 820

Pathé 32414, 32453, Perfect 12493, 12532 as by **Walter Dalton**. Romeo 820, 823, Angelus 3078, Gracelon 4022, Melotone 10084, Starr 726 as by **Frankie Wallace**.
Revs: Cameo 9019, Lincoln 3048, Pathé 32453, Perfect 12532, Romeo 823, Angelus 3078, Gracelon 4022, Melotone 10084, Starr 726 by Frank Luther (see Carson Robison).

Frankie Marvin & His Guitar, v/y; acc. unknown, f; own g.
   New York, NY   Tuesday, December 11, 1928

18934-A	My Dreaming Of You	Ed 52490
N-625-A,-B	My Dreaming Of You	Ed rejected
18935-A	Poor Man's Blues	Ed 52490
N-626-A,-B	Poor Man's Blues	Ed rejected

Frank Marvin, v; acc. unknown.
   New York, NY   Tuesday, January 22, 1929

401551-	Riding On The Elevated Railroad	OK unissued
401552-	My Mammy's Yodel Song	OK unissued

Frankie Marvin & His Guitar, v/y; acc. unknown, f; own sg/v eff.
   New York, NY   Tuesday, February 5, 1929

19027-A	Riding On The Elevated Railroad	Ed 52523, 5692
N-718-A,-B,-C	Riding On The Elevated Railroad	Ed rejected

   New York, NY   Wednesday, February 6, 1929

19034-B	My Mammy's Yodel Song	Ed 52523
N-725-A,-B,-C	My Mammy's Yodel Song	Ed rejected

Frank Marvin & His Guitar, v/y; acc. own g.
　New York, NY   Saturday, February 23, 1929
　E-29371-   Riding On The Elevated Railroad   Br 303, Spt S2078
　E-29372-   Oklahoma Blues No. 2   Br 303
Supertone S2078 as by **The Texas Ranger**.

Frankie Marvin & His Guitar, v/y; acc. own sg-1/g-2.
　New York, NY   Wednesday, February 27, 1929
　148000-3   The Big Rock Candy Mountains -2   Co 1753-D
　148001-3   Riding On The Elevated Railroad -1   Co 1753-D, ReAu G20491
Rev. Regal G20491 by Pearce Brothers (popular).

Frankie Wallace & His Guitar, v/y-1; acc. own sg-2/g-3.
　New York, NY   c. February 1929
　3665-; 108673-   Riding On The Elevated Railroad -3   Ca 9111, Lin 3138, Pat 32448, Pe 12527, Ro 913
　3666-; 108674-   Oklahoma Blues No. 2 -1, 2   Ca 9091, Lin 3118, Pat 32448, Pe 12527, Ro 893
Pathé 32448, Perfect 12527 as by **Walter Dalton**.
Revs: Cameo 9091, Lincoln 3118, Romeo 893 by Carson Robison; Cameo 9111, Lincoln 3138, Romeo 913 by Vernon Dalhart.

George White, v/y; acc. own sg-1/g-2.
　New York, NY   Monday, March 11, 1929
　401707-A   The Two Gun Cowboy -2   OK 45335, Ve 2361-V, Cl 5295-C
　401708-A   Oklahoma Blues No. 2 -1   OK 45335, Ve 2360-V, Cl 5294-C
Velvet Tone 2360-V, 2361-V, Clarion 5294-C, 5295-C as by **Johnny Hart**. Those issues use transfer matrices, as follows:
401707 = 100521; 401708 = 100520. Rev. Velvet Tone 2361-V, Clarion 5295-C by Buck Mt. Band.

Frankie Wallace & His Guitar, v/y; acc. own sg.
　New York, NY   early March 1929
　3709-A; 108927-   My Mammy's Yodel Song   Ca 9110, Lin 3137, Pat 32476, Pe 12555, Ro 912
　3710-B   My Hulu Girl   Ca 9110, Lin 3137, Ro 912
Pathé 32476, Perfect 12555 as by **Walter Dalton & His Guitar**.
Rev. Pathé 32476, Perfect 12555 by Dad Pickard (see The Pickard Family).

Frankie Marvin & His Guitar, v/y; acc. unknown.
　New York, NY   Thursday, April 4, 1929
　19143   Oklahoma Blues   Ed 52576
　N-836-A   Oklahoma Blues   Ed unissued
　N-836-B,-C   Oklahoma Blues   Ed rejected
　19144   The Two Gun Cowboy   Ed 52576, 5705
　N-837-A,-B,-C   The Two Gun Cowboy   Ed unissued

Frankie Wallace & His Guitar, v/y; acc. own sg; poss. own wh or v eff -1.
　New York, NY   April 1929
　3782; 108754-2   The Two Gun Cowboy -1   Ca 9150, Lin 3177, Pat 32458, Pe 12537, Ro 952
　3783; 108755-1   Blue Yodel No. 4   Ca 9150, Lin 3177, Pat 32458, Pe 12537, Ro 952
Pathé 32458, Perfect 12537 as by **Walter Dalton & His Guitar**.

Frank Marvin & His Guitar, v/y-1/v eff; acc. own g; poss. own wh-2.
　New York, NY   c. April 1929
　E-29612-   My Lulu   Br 320
　E-29613-   The Two-Gun Cowboy -1, 2   Br 320, Spt S2079
Supertone S2079 as by **The Texas Ranger**.

Frankie Wallace & His Guitar, v/y-1; acc. own sg-2/g-3.
　New York, NY   April/May 1929
　3884-3; 108845-   Lullaby Yodel -1, 2   Ca 9192, Lin 3219, Pat 32467, Pe 12546, Ro 994
　3885-A; 108846-   It's Funny When You Feel That Way -2   Ca 9196, Lin 3223, Pat 32467, Pe 12546, Ro 998
　3886-; 108847-   A High Silk Hat And A Walking Cane -2   Ca 9196, Lin 3223, Pat 32468, Pe 12547, Ro 998
　3887-; 108848-   Mountains Ain't No Place For Bad Men -3 Ca 9197, Lin 3224, Pat 32468, Pe 12547, Ro 999
Pathé 32467, 32468, Perfect 12546, 12547 as by **Walter Dalton & His Guitar**.
Revs: Cameo 9192, Lincoln 3219, Romeo 994 by Carson Robison; Cameo 9197, Lincoln 3224, Romeo 999 (all as by **Jimmie Price**) by Dad Pickard (see The Pickard Family).

Frankie Marvin, v/y-1; acc. own sg-2/g-3; poss. own v eff -4.
　New York, NY   Tuesday, May 21, 1929
　148603-2   My Mammy's Yodel Song -1, 2   Co 1889-D
　148604-2   It's Funny When You Feel That Way -3, 4 Co 1889-D

The Marvin Family: unknown, f; Frank Marvin, sg/sp; Thelma Marvin, calls.
　New York, NY   Tuesday, May 21, 1929

148605-2	Life On The Ocean Wave	Co 15474-D

George White, v/y-1; acc. own sg-2/g-3.
New York, NY   Monday, May 27, 1929

401990-A	My Mammy's Yodel Song -1, 2	OK 45351
401991-B	It's Funny When You Feel That Way -3	OK 45351, Ve 2396-V, Cl 5330-C

Velvet Tone 2396-V, Clarion 5330-C as by **Johnny Hart**.
Those issues use the transfer matrix 100542.
Rev. Velvet Tone 2396-V, Clarion 5330-C by Andrew Jenkins & Carson Robison.

Frank Marvin & His Guitar, v; acc. own g.
New York, NY   Monday, June 3, 1929

19232	A High Silk Hat And A Walking Cane	Ed 52607
N-936-A,-B,-C	A High Silk Hat And A Walking Cane	Ed unissued
19233	It's Funny When You Feel That Way	Ed 52607
N-937-A	It's Funny When You Feel That Way	Ed unissued
N-937-B,-C	It's Funny When You Feel That Way	Ed rejected

Matrix 19232 was scheduled for Edison cylinder 5723 but never issued thus.

Frankie Marvin, v/y; acc. own sg.
New York, NY   Friday, June 14, 1929

148703-2	Yodeling Them Blues Away	Co 15474-D

Frank Marvin, v/y-1; acc. unknown, f; own g; poss. own v eff -2.
New York, NY   Wednesday, July 3, 1929

19274	Blue Yodel – No. 4 -1, 2	Ed 52650
N-998-A,-B,-C	Blue Yodel – No. 4 -1	Ed rejected
19275	She's Old And Bent (But She Just Keeps Hoofin' Along)	Ed 52650
N-999-A,-B,-C	She's Old And Bent (But She Just Keeps Hoofin' Along)	Ed rejected

Johnny & Frank Marvin, v duet; acc. own sg duet.
New York, NY   Monday, July 8, 1929

53909-1,-2	Sweetheart, You're In My Dream	Vi unissued
53910-1,-2	She's Old And Bent (But She Just Keeps Hoofin' Along)	Vi unissued

Frank Marvin & His Guitar, v/y-1; acc. unknown, c; poss. own sg-2/g-3; unknown, bj-4.
New York, NY   Monday, July 15, 1929

E-30341-	My Mammy's Yodel Song -1, 2	Br 345, BrAu 345, Spt S2080, Au A22025
E-30342	She's Old And Bent But She Gets There Just The Same -3, 4	Br 345, BrAu 345, Spt S2080, Au A22025

Australian Brunswick 345 as by **Marvin & His Guitar**. Supertone S2080 as by **The Texas Ranger**. Aurora A22025 as by **Joe Wright & His Guitar**.
Matrix E-30342 is titled *She's Old And Bent, But She Gets There Just The Same* on Australian Brunswick 345.

Frankie Marvin, v/y-1; acc. unknown, t; own sg; unknown, bj-2/g-3.
New York, NY   Tuesday, July 23, 1929

148838-3	A Happy Go Lucky Boy -3	Co 1941-D, ReAu G20590
148839-3	Oklahoma Land Of The Sunny West -1, 2	Co 1941-D

Rev. Regal G20590 by Charles Hamp (popular).

Walter Dalton & His Guitar, v/v eff; acc. own g.
New York, NY   Wednesday, August 7, 1929

8909-2	A High Silk Hat And A Walking Cane	Ba 6496, Do 4398, Je 5698, Or 1680, Re 8843, Chg 839, Cq 7410, Htd 16057

Though logged as shown, this item was issued on Domino 4398, Regal 8843, Conqueror 7410 as by **Frankie Wallace & His Guitar**, and on other issues as by **Ray Ball & His Guitar**.
Some issues of matrix 8909 use the control 2446.
Revs: Banner 6496, Jewel 5698, Oriole 1680, Challenge 839, Homestead 16057 by Chezz Chase; Domino 4398, Regal 8843, Conqueror 7410 by Frank Luther (see Carson Robison).

Frankie Wallace & His Guitar, v/y-1; acc. unknown, t; own sg.
New York, NY   Wednesday, August 21, 1929

8941-; 108897-3; 3981	Oklahoma, Land Of The Sunny West	Ba 6534, Ca 9239, Do 4418, Lin 3266, Or 1716, Pat 32487, Pe 12566, Re 8865, Ro 1041, Cq 7424
8942-1; 108898-2; 3982	She's Old And Bent (But She Just Keeps Hoofin' Along)	Ba 6534, Ca 9321, Do 4417, Lin 3344, Or 1716, Pat 32487, Pe 12566, Re 8864, Ro 1118, Cq 7423, Apex 41037, Cr 81175, Do 181175, Stg 281175

```
            8943-1; 10889-2;  Yodeling Them Blues Away -1              Ba 6533, Ca 9239, Do 4418, Je 5722, Lin 3266,
               3983                                                       Or 1714, Pat 32485, Pe 12564, Re 8865,
                                                                          Ro 1041, Cq 7424, Htd 16058, 23006,
                                                                          Pm 3180, Bwy 8130
```

Banner, Jewel, Oriole issues as by **Ray Ball & His Guitar**. Pathé 32485, 32487, Perfect 12564, 12566 as by **Walter Dalton & His Guitar**. Apex 41037 as by **Frankie Wallace**. Crown 81175, Domino 181175 as by **Buddy Bartlett**. Sterling 281175 as by **Fred Wallace**.
The parenthesised part of the title of matrix 8942 is omitted on Oriole 1716.
Matrix 8943/108899/3983 is titled *Yodelin' Them Blues Away* on Perfect 12564.
Controls appear on various issues instead of, or as well as, the matrices, as follows: 8941 = 2520-2; 8942 = 2521-2, 9118; 8943 = 2492, 1370.
Revs: Banner 6533, Jewel 5722, Oriole 1714, Pathé 32485, Perfect 12564, Regal 8864, Conqueror 7423, Homestead 16058, 23006 by Frank Luther (see Carson Robison); Cameo 9321, Lincoln 3344, Romeo 1118 by John I. White; Paramount 3180, Broadway 8130 by Carson Robison; Crown 81175, Domino 181175, Sterling 281175 by Billy Murray (popular).

Frankie Wallace, v/y; acc. unknown, t; unknown, bj-1; own g.
    New York, NY   Thursday, September 19, 1929
```
        9030-; 4086-C    Miss Moonshine -1                        Ba 6560, Ca 9290, Do 4439, Je 5745, Lin 3317,
                                                                     Or 1750, Re 8882, Ro 1092, Cq 7435,
                                                                     Htd 16059, 23007, Pm 3190, Bwy 8132
        9031-; 4087-C    Dust-Pan Blues                           Ba 0530, Ca 0130, Do 4439, Je 5782, Or 1781,
                                                                     Pat 32491, Pe 12570, Re 8882, Ro 1144,
                                                                     Cq 7435, Htd 16067
```
Banner 6560, Homestead 23007, and possibly other issues of matrix 9030 as by **Ray Ball & His Guitar**. Jewel 5745, Homestead 16059 as by **Ray Ball**. Pathé 32491, Perfect 12570 as by **Walter Dalton**.
Controls or transfer matrices appear on various issues instead of, or as well as, the matrices, as follows: 9030/4086 = 2546; 9031/4087 = 109034.
Revs: Banner 6560, Jewel 5745, Oriole 1750, Homestead 16059, 23007 by Frank Luther (see Carson Robison); Pathé 32491, Perfect 12570, Paramount 3190, Broadway 8132 by John I. White.

George White, v/y/v eff; acc. unknown, t; own sg.
    New York, NY   Wednesday, September 25, 1929
```
        402990-A     Dust Pan Blues                              OK 45382, PaE R1081
        402991-B     Miss Moonshine                              OK 45382
```
Rev. Parlophone R1081 by Capt. Appleblossom.

Frankie Wallace & His Guitar, v; acc. unknown, cl; poss. Roy Smeck, sg-1/g-2; own g; poss. own v eff-3.
    New York, NY   Wednesday, September 25, 1929
```
        9040-        Slu Foot Lou -2, 3                          Ba 0530, Ca 0130, Do 4462, Je 5782, Or 1781,
                                                                    Pat 32498, Pe 12577, Re 8906, Ro 1144,
                                                                    Cq 7452, Htd 16067
        9041-        Stay Away From My Chicken House -1          Ca 9290, Do 4462, Lin 3317, Pat 32498,
                                                                    Pe 12577, Re 8906, Ro 1092, Chg 877,
                                                                    Cq 7452, 7727, Apex 41037
```
Pathé 32498, Perfect 12577 as by **Walter Dalton & His Guitar**. Apex 41037 as by **Frankie Wallace**.
Controls or transfer matrices appear on various issues instead of, or as well as, the matrices, as follows: 9040 = 4096; 9041 = 4098.
Revs: Challenge 877, Conqueror 7727 by John I. White.

Frankie Marvin & His Oklahoma Hounds: N. Weiner, t?; John Cali, bj?; Frank Marvin, poss. g/v.
    New York, NY   Thursday, September 26, 1929
```
        N-1158          She's Old And Bent                       Ed 20011
        N-1159          Oklahoma, Land Of The Sunny West         Ed 20011
        N-1160-A,-B,-C  A Happy Go Lucky Boy                     Ed unissued
```

Frankie Marvin, v/y/v eff; acc. unknown, t; prob. own g.
    New York, NY   Friday, September 27, 1929
```
        149070-2        Dust Pan Blues                           Co 15518-D, CoJ J933
        149071-3        Miss Moonshine                           Co 15518-D, CoJ J933
```

Frank Marvin & His Guitar, v/y; acc. unknown, t; unknown, bj-1; poss. own g.
    New York, NY   Monday, September 30, 1929
```
        E-31085-        Oklahoma, Land Of The Sunny West -1      Br 374, Spt S2070
        E-31086-        Dust Pan Blues                           Br 360
        E-31087-        Miss Moonshine                           Br 360
```
Supertone S2070 as by **The Texas Ranger**.

    New York, NY   Thursday, October 24, 1929
```
        E-31298-        Slu-Foot Lou                             Br 384
        E-31299-        Yodeling The Blues Away                  Br 384, Spt S2077
```

E-31300-   Stay Away From My Chicken House -1   Br 374, Spt S2070

Supertone S2070, S2077 as by **The Texas Ranger**.

Frankie Wallace, v/y-1; acc. unknown, cl; unknown, ac; unknown, sg; unknown, g.
New York, NY   Thursday, October 24, 1929

9099-3   I'm Riding The Blinds On A Train Headed West -1   Ba 0529, Ca 0129, Do 4459, Je 5783, Or 1782, Pat 32495, Pe 12574, Re 8903, Ro 1143, Cq 7449, Htd 16006, 23003, Pm 3202, Bwy 8142

Pathé 32495, Perfect 12574 as by **Walter Dalton**.
Some issues use the control 1633.
Revs: Banner 0529, Cameo 0129, Jewel 5783, Oriole 1782, Romeo 1143, Homestead 16006, 23003 by Jack Kaufman (popular); Paramount 3202, Broadway 8142 by John I. White.

Acc. unknown, ac; unknown, md.
New York, NY   Thursday, October 24, 1929

9100-2,-3   I Don't Work For A Living   Ba 0527, Ca 0127, Do 4459, DoC 181250, Je 5781, Or 1779, Pat 32495, Pe 12574, Re 8903, Ro 1145, Cq 7449, Htd 16068, 23004, Pm 3209, Bwy 8145, Apex 41070, Cr 81250, Stg 281250

Pathé 32495, Perfect 12574 as by **Walter Dalton**. Crown 81250, Domino 181250, Sterling 281250 as by **Buddy Bartlett**.
Some issues use the control 1676.
Revs: Banner 0527, Cameo 0127, Jewel 5781, Oriole 1779, Romeo 1145, Homestead 16068, 23004, Paramount 3209, Broadway 8145, Apex 41070 by Jack Kaufman (popular); Crown 81250, Domino 181250, Sterling 281250 (all with same credit) by Frank Luther (see Carson Robison).

Frankie Marvin, v/y-1; acc. unknown, f; unknown, c; unknown, ac; unknown, bj; own g; unknown, g.
New York, NY   Monday, October 28, 1929

57029-1   Oklahoma, Land Of The Sunny West -1   Vi V-40159, ZoSA 4290
57030-2   Old Family Album   Vi V-40159, ZoSA 4290

Zonophone 4290 as by **Frank Marvin**.

Acc. unknown, f-2; unknown, t; unknown, cl; prob. own g.
New York, NY   Wednesday, January 8, 1930

149744-3   I Don't Work For A Living -2   Co 2091-D, CoJ J956, ReAu G20713
149745-3   Slue Foot Lou -1   Co 2091-D, CoJ J956

Rev. Regal G20713 by Four Provinces Orchestra (Irish).

Frankie Wallace, v/y; acc. own sg-1; unknown, tg(?)-1.
New York, NY   Monday, January 13, 1930

9280-1,-3   Blue Yodel No. 5 -1   Ba 0583, Ca 0183, Do 4493, DoC 181336, Je 5839, Or 1839, Pat 32509, Pe 12588, Re 8937, Ro 1205, Cq 7481, Htd 16138, 23012, Pm 3211, Bwy 8147, CrC 81336, Stg 281336

9281-2   Our Old Family Album -   Ba 0618, Ca 0218, Do 4493, DoC 181336, Je 5875, Or 1875, Pat 32509, Pe 12588, Re 8937, Ro 1237, Cq 7481, Pm 3211, Bwy 8147, CrC 81336, Stg 281336

Pathé 32509, Perfect 12588 possibly also issued as by **Walter Dalton**.
Revs: all Banner, Cameo, Jewel, Oriole, Romeo, Homestead issues by John I. White.

Frank Marvin & His Guitar, v/y; acc. unknown, f-1; unknown, t; poss. own g; unknown, v eff -2/train eff-3.
New York, NY   Wednesday, January 15, 1930

E-31876   Frankie And Johnnie (You'll Miss Me In The Days To Come)   Br 400, BrAu 400, Spt S2077
E-31877   I Don't Work For A Living -2   Br 401, Spt S2081
E-31878   I'm Riding The Blinds On A West Bound Train -3   Br 400, BrAu 400, Spt S2078
E-31879   Our Old Family Album -1   Br 401

Matrix E-31878 on Australian Brunswick 400 as by **Frank Marvin**. Supertone S2077, S2078, S2081 as by **The Texas Ranger**.

Frankie Marvin, v/y; acc. unknown, f; Johnny Marvin, sg; unknown, g.
New York, NY   Tuesday, January 21, 1930

59102-2   Mother's Song Of Love   Vi V-40233
59103-1   The Girl I Left Behind   Vi V-40233, MW M-8052
59104-1   Slue-Foot Lou   Vi V-40278, Zo 5898, ZoSA 4326, Twin FT1825
59105-1   The Wild And Woolly West   Vi V-40278, Zo 5898, Twin FT1825

Matrix 59104 is titled *Slu-Foot Lou* on Zonophone 5898.

Revs: Montgomery Ward M-8052 by Rodeo Trio; Zonophone 4326 by Powder River Jack & Kitty Lee.

Frankie Wallace, v/y; acc. unknown, sg; unknown, g.
   New York, NY   Thursday, January 23, 1930
   9304-2,-3   Everybody Does It In Hawaii   Ba 0617, Ca 0217, Do 4511, Je 5873, Or 1873,
                                                                Pe 12595, Re 8956, Ro 1235, Cq 7501,
                                                                Htd 16153, 23016
Revs: Banner 0617, Cameo 0217, Jewel 5873, Oriole 1873, Romeo 1235, Homestead 16153, 23016 by John I. White; Domino 4511, Perfect 12595, Regal 8956, Conqueror 7501 by Carson Robison.

Acc. unknown, h; unknown, jh; unknown, g.
   New York, NY   Thursday, January 23, 1930
   9305-1,-2   Oh For The Wild And Woolly West   Ba 0703, Ca 0303, Do 4529, DoC 181354,
                                                                Je 5963, Or 1963, Pe 12598, Re 8973,
                                                                Ro 1326, Cq 7509, Apex 41170,
                                                                CrC/MeC 81354, Stg 281354, Min M-901
Matrix 9305 is titled *Oh! For The Wild And Woolly West* on Apex 41170, Crown/Melotone 81354, Domino 181354, Sterling 281354, Minerva M-901, or *Oh! For The Wild And Wooly West* on Perfect 12598.
Revs: Domino 4529, Perfect 12598, Regal 8973, Conqueror 7509, Crown/Melotone 81354, Domino 181354, Sterling 281354 by John I. White; Minerva M-901 by Vernon Dalhart.

Frank Marvin & His Guitar, v/y; acc. unknown, f-1; own g.
   New York, NY   Monday, March 17, 1930
   E-32384-   Livin' In The Mountains -1   Br 413, BrE 1091, Spt S2081
   E-33285-   Oh! For The Wild And Woolly West   Br 413, BrE 1091, Spt S2079
Supertone S2079, S2081 as by **The Texas Ranger**.

George White, v/y; acc. unknown, f-1; unknown, t-2; unknown, bj-3; prob. own g.
   New York, NY   Monday, March 17, 1930
   403855-B   Livin' In The Mountains -2   OK 45432, Ve 2362-V, Cl 5296-C
   403856-B   Oh! For The Wild And Wooly West -1, 3   OK 45432, Ve 2358-V, Cl 5292-C
Velvet Tone 2358-V, Clarion 5292-C as by **Andy Anderson**. Velvet Tone 2362-V, Clarion 5296-C as by **Johny Hart**. Those issues use transfer matrices, as follows: 403855 = 100523; 403856 = 100515.
Rev. Velvet Tone 2358-V, Clarion 5292-C by Buck Mt. Band.

Frankie Marvin, v/y; acc. unknown, f; unknown, t-1; prob. own g.
   New York, NY   Tuesday, March 18, 1930
   150090-3   Oh, For The Wild And Woolly West   Co 15568-D
   150091-2   Livin' In The Mountains -1   Co 15568-D

Frankie Wallace & His Guitar, v/y; acc. poss. own h-1; Gene Autry, g.
   New York, NY   Thursday, April 3, 1930
   9562-2,-4   Livin' In The Mountains -1   Ba 0681, Ca 0281, Do 4548, Je 5933, Or 1933,
                                                                 Pe 12609, Re 8994, Ro 1297, Chg 883,
                                                                 Cq 7537
   9563-2,-3   Blue Yodel No. 6   Ba 0680, Ca 0280, Do 4548, Je 5937, Or 1937,
                                                                Pe 12609, Re 8994, Ro 1296, Cq 7537,
                                                                Htd 16140, 23013
Revs: Banner 0680, 0681, Cameo 0280, 0281, Jewel 5933, 5937, Oriole 1933, 1937, Romeo 1296, 1297, Homestead 16140, 23013 by Carson Robison.

Frank Marvin, v/y-1; acc. poss. own h-2; unknown, bj; own g; unknown, jh-3.
   New York, NY   Tuesday, April 29, 1930
   9671-1,-2,-3   Yodeling Cowboy -1   Ba 0703, Ca 0303, Do 4568, Je 5963, Or 1963,
                                                                Pe 12619, Re 9017, Ro 1326, Cq 7558,
                                                               Bwy 4058, CrC/MeC/Stg/Roy 91247
   9672-2   Over At The Old Barn Dance -2, 3   Ba 0742, Ca 0342, Do 4568, Je 5992, Or 1992,
                                                                Pe 12619, Re 10047, Ro 1355, Cq 7558,
                                                               CrC/MeC/Stg/Roy 91247
Broadway 4058 as by **Jack West**.
Revs: Banner 0742, Cameo 0342, Jewel 5992, Oriole 1992, Regal 10047, Romeo 1355 by Mopey Dick (see Arthur Fields & Fred Hall); Regal 9017 by Vernon Dalhart; Broadway 4058 by Carson Robison.

Frank Marvin & His Guitar, v/y; acc. unknown, f; unknown, h; unknown, bj; unknown, g; unknown, jh.
   New York, NY   Monday, May 26, 1930
   E-32927   Mother's Song Of Love   Br unissued
   E-32928   The Girl I Left Behind   Br rejected
   E-32929   Over At The Old Barn Dance   Br 457, Spt S2066
Supertone S2066 as by **Martin Craver**.
Revs: Brunswick 457 by Charlie Craver; Supertone S2066 by Frank Luther & Carson Robison.

Frankie Marvin, v; acc. unknown.
New York, NY   late May 1930
    150539-   Out On An Island   Co unissued
    150540-   Over At The Old Barn Dance   Co unissued

Frank Marvin & His Guitar, v/y; acc. unknown, cl-1; unknown, sg-2; unknown, g; unknown, u.
New York, NY   Wednesday, July 9, 1930
    E-33321   Out On An Island -2   Br 448
    E-33322   I'm Looking For A Gal -1   Br 448

Frankie Wallace & His Guitar, v/y; acc. unknown, sg-1; own g; poss. unknown, u-2.
New York, NY   Friday, July 11, 1930
    9859-3   Out On An Island -1, 2   Do 4600, Pe 12631, Cq 7591, Cr 91054,
                                              Stg 291054, Roy 391054
    9860-1,-3   Hobo Bill's Last Ride   Ba 0773, Ca 0373, Do 4601, Je 6024, Or 2024,
                                              Pe 12632, Re 10079, Ro 1388, Chg 785,
                                              Cq 7592

Revs: Domino 4600, Perfect 12631, Conqueror 7591 by Vernon Dalhart; all issues of matrix 9860 by Carson Robison.

Frank Marvin, v; acc. unknown.
New York, NY   Wednesday, October 1, 1930
    E-34657-   My Baby Just Cares For Me   Br rejected

Frank Marvin & His Guitar, v/y; acc. poss own h-1/g.
New York, NY   Thursday, October 2, 1930
    E-34660-   Hobo Bill's Last Ride -1   Br 474
    E-34661-   I'm Just A Gambler   Br 474

Frank Marvin, v; acc. unknown.
New York, NY   Friday, October 10, 1930
    E-34831/32*   My Baby Just Cares For Me   Br 4949, BrAu 4949
    E-34833-   You're Simply Delish   Br 4949, BrAu 4949

Frankie Wallace, v; acc. unknown, cl; unknown, h-1; prob. own u/v eff-2.
New York, NY   Tuesday, October 28, 1930
    10181-1   Making Little Ones Out Of Big Ones -1   Ba 32034, Do 4693, Je 6154, Or 2154, Pe 12663,
                                              Re 10212, Ro 1518
    10182-1   I'm Looking For A Gal -2   Ba 32034, Do 4693, Je 6154, Or 2154, Pe 12663,
                                              Re 10212, Ro 1518

Frankie Marvin & His Guitar, v/y; acc. own or poss. Carson Robison, g.
New York, NY   c. October/November 1930
    1032-2   Blue Yodel No. 7   Cr 3028, Htd 22993, *MW M3005, Vs 5038*
    1033-1   Yodelling Cowboy   Cr 3028, Htd 22993, *MW M3005, Vs 5038*

Montgomery Ward M3005 as by **Frank Luther & Carson Robison**. Varsity 5038 as by **Frank Marvin & Carson Robison**.
Matrix 1032 is titled *Blue Yodel*, and matrix 1033 *Yodeling Cowboy*, on Varsity 5038.

Frankie Marvin, v/y; acc. prob. Gene Autry, g.
New York, NY   c. October/November 1930
    1058-3   I'm In The Jail House Now – No. 2   Cr 3026, Htd 22992, *Vs 5039*, ImpE 2607
    1059-2   Hobo Bill's Last Ride   Cr 3026, Htd 22992, *Vs 5039*

Varsity 5039 as by **Frank Marvin**. Imperial 2607 as by **Frankie Marvin & His Guitar**.
Matrix 1058 is titled *I'm In The Jailhouse Now* on Varsity 5039, or *I'm In The Jail House Now* on Imperial 2607.

Frank Marvin & His Guitar, v/y-1; acc. unknown, sg-2; own g; prob. own v eff-3.
New York, NY   Friday, November 21, 1930
    E-35430   A Yodeling Hobo -1   Br unissued
    E-35431-A   Makin' Little Ones Out Of Big Ones -3   Br 517, DeE F3747, RexIr U602
    E-35432-A   I'll Be Thinking Of You Little Gal -2   Br 517, DeE F3747, RexIr U602

Matrix E-35432 is titled *I'll Be Thinking Of You, Little Gal* on Decca F3747.

George White, v/y; acc. own sg-1/g-2.
New York, NY   Wednesday, December 3, 1930
    404564-A   Making Little Ones Out Of Big Ones -1   OK 45502, Ve 2360-V, Cl 5294-C
    404565-A   I Am Just A Gambler -2   OK 45502, Ve 2359-V, Cl 5293-C

Velvet Tone 2359-V, 2360-V, Clarion 5293-C, 5294-C as by **Johnny Hart**. Those issues use transfer matrices, as follows:
404564 = 100519; 404565 = 100518.
Rev. Velvet Tone 2359-V, Clarion 5293-C by Charlie & Bud Newman.

Frankie Marvin & His Guitar, v/y-1; acc. own h-2/g; Roy Smeck, g-3.
New York, NY   c. January 1931

| 1121-1 | Blue Yodel No. 8 -1, 3 | Cr 3058, Htd 22994, Bwy 8235, Vs 5131 |
| 1122-2 | True Blue Bill -2 | Cr 3058, Htd 22994, Bwy 8235, Vs 5109 |

Varsity 5109 as by **Frankie Marvin**, 5131 as by **Frank Marvin & Roy Smeck**.
Matrix 1121 is titled *Blue Yodel* on Varsity 5131.
Some issues use control numbers, as follows: 1121 = 1956; 1122 = 1955.

Frank Marvin, v; acc. unknown, f; unknown, f-1; unknown, t-2; prob. Frank Novak, cl-3 or bscl-3/ac-4; unknown, g.
New York, NY   Friday, February 27, 1931

E-36197-A	When The Moon Comes Over The Mountain -1	Me M12170, Po P9054
E-36198-A	On The Ozark Mountain Trail -1	Me M12170, Po P9054, Min M-14008
E-36199-	Bear Cat Papa -2, 3	Me M12126, Po P9051, PanAu P12126
E-36200-	True Blue Bill -1, 4	Me M12126, Po P9051, PanAu P12127

Revs: Minerva M-14008 by Wenatchee Mountaineers (see Elton Britt); Panachord P12126, P12127 by Otto Gray.

Frankie Marvin & His Guitar, v; acc. Roy Smeck, sg; unknown, g; unknown, u.
New York, NY   c. February 1931

| 1189-2 | Frankie And Johnny | Cr 3076, Htd 22999, MW 1015, Vs 8056 |
| 1190-3 | Those Gambler's Blues | Cr 3076, Htd 22999, MW 1015, Vs 8056, John Ryan Record 301 |

Montgomery Ward 1015 as by **Roy Smeck Hawaiian Orchestra**. Varsity 8056 as by **Roy Smeck Trio**. John Ryan Record 301 is uncredited.
Homestead 22999 was also assigned to a Carson Robison issue.
Matrix 1189 is titled *Frankie And Johnnie* on Varsity 8056. Matrix 1190 is titled *Gambler's Blues* on John Ryan Record 301.
Rev. John Ryan Record 301 by John Ryan (popular).

Frank Marvin, v; acc. unknown, f; unknown, sg-1; poss. own g.
New York, NY   Tuesday, March 31, 1931

| E-36435-A | They Cut Down The Old Pine Tree | Me M12139, Vo 02682, Po P9071, Pan 25052, PanAu P12139, Rex 9970 |
| E-36436-A | Come Back To The Hills -1 | Me M12139, Vo 02682, Po P9071, Pan 25642, PanAu P12139, RZAu G22218 |

Revs: Panachord 25642 by Gwyn Foster (see Thomas C. Ashley); Regal-Zonophone G22218 by Bradley Kincaid.

Acc. own h-1/g-2; Gene Autry, g-3/v-4.
New York, NY   Wednesday, April 1, 1931

68856-2	Old Man Duff -1, 3	Vi 23553, ZoAu EE296
68857-1	Old Man Duff -1, 3	TT C-1553
68858-2	I'm A Truthful Fellow (True Blue Bill) -1, 3	Vi 23553, MW M-8235, ZoAu EE296
68859-1	I'm A Truthful Fellow -1, 3	TT C-1554
68860-1	Valley In The Hills -2	TT C-1555, Au 36-104
68861-1	Valley In The Hills -2	Vi unissued
68862-1	She's Just That Kind -1, 3	TT C-1553
68863-1	She's Always On My Mind -2, 3, 4	Eld 1932, TT C-1554
68864-1	I'm Blue And Lonesome -2, 3, 4	Eld 1932, TT C-1555, Au 36-104

Timely Tunes issues, Aurora 36-104, and possibly Electradisk 1932 as by **Gene Autry & Frankie Marvin**.
Matrix 68858 is titled *True Blue Bill* on Montgomery Ward M-8235.
Matrix 68860-2 is a solo version of *Valley In The Hills* by Gene Autry.
Rev. Montgomery Ward M-8235 by Jimmie Rodgers.

Frankie Marvin & His Guitar, v; acc. Roy Smeck, sg; own g.
New York, NY   c. April 1931

| 1299-2 | A Gangster's Warning | Cr 3125, Htd 23000, Pm 3276, Vs 5137 |
| 1300-2 | 13 More Steps | Cr 3125, Htd 23000, Pm 3276, Vs 5131 |

Varsity 5131 as by **Frank Marvin & Roy Smeck**, 5137 as by **Roy Smeck's Trio**.
Matrix 1299 is titled *The Gangster's Warning* on Paramount 3276. Matrix 1300 is titled *Thirteen More Steps* on Paramount 3276, Varsity 5131.
Some issues use controls, as follows: 1299 = 2035; 1300 = 2036.
Rev. Varsity 5137 by Roy Smeck (popular).

Frank Marvin, v; acc. unknown, f; A. Cibelli, md/vc; unknown, p; unknown, g; Bob McGimsey, wh.
New York, NY   Wednesday, May 13, 1931

| 69602-2 | When It's Night-Time In Nevada | Vi 23561, MW M-4318, HMVIn N4280 |

Revs: Victor 23561 by Gene Autry; Montgomery Ward M-4318 by Frank Luther; HMV N4280 by Jimmie Davis.

Frank Marvin, v/y; acc. two unknowns, f; unknown, s; unknown, p; unknown, g; unknown, tu; unknown, d.
New York, NY   Monday, May 19, 1931

| E-36709- | I'm Gonna Yodel My Way To Heaven | Me M12224, Po P9069, CrC/MeC 93014, Min M-14006, Stg 293014, Pan 25052, PanAu P12224, Rex 9970 |

Acc. unknown, f; poss. own g.
   New York, NY   Monday, May 19, 1931

| E-36710- | Old Man Duff | Me M12224, Po P9069, Pan 25064, PanAu P12224 |

Acc. poss. Frank Novak, f/ac-1; poss. Roy Smeck, h-2/g.
   New York, NY   c. May 1931

| 1331-2 | Mountain Boy -2 | Cr 3157, Htd 23023, Vs 5071, CrC/MeC/Roy 93014, Min M-14006, Stg 293014, Summit Z145 |
| 1332-2 | I'm Gonna Yodel My Way To Heaven -1 | Cr 3157, Htd 23023, Vs 5071, ImpE 2607, Summit Z145, Lyric 3421 |

Varsity 5071 as by **Frankie Marvin With Roy Smeck Trio**. Imperial 2607 as by **Frankie Marvin & His Guitar**. Lyric 3421 as by **Gene Arnold**.
Rev. Lyric 3421 by Carson Robison.

With unknown, f; poss. Frank Novak, bscl-1/s-2/ac; unknown, g.
   New York, NY   Wednesday, June 17, 1931

E-36862-	Rambling Cowboy -1, 2	Me M12240, Pan 25064
E-36863-A	Yodeling Cowboy	Me M12213, Vo 5478, Po P9015, Min M-14007
E-36864-A	Cowboy Yodel -1	Me M12213, Vo 5478, Po P9015, Min M-14007
E-36865-	Cowboy's Heaven	Me M12240

Matrix E-36862 is titled *Yodeling Rambling Cowboy* on Panachord 25064.

Frankie Marvin & His Guitar, v/y; acc. unknown, f-1; unknown, fl-1; unknown, h-1; own g; unknown, vc-1.
   New York, NY   c. June/July 1931

| 1400-3 | The Strawberry Roan | Cr 3174, Htd 23024, MW M3017, Vs 5036, Cont C-3013 |
| 1401-4 | Ramblin' Cowboy -1 | Cr 3174, Htd 23024, MW M3018, Vs 5036 |

Montgomery Ward M3017, M3018 as by **Bob Star (The Texas Ranger)**. Varsity 5036 as by **Cowboy Rodgers**. Continental C-3013 as by **Cowboy Rogers**.
Matrix 1400 is titled *Strawberry Roan* on Montgomery Ward M3017, Varsity 5036, Continental C-3013.
Revs: Montgomery Ward M3017 (with same credit) by Edward L. Crain, M3018 (with same credit) by Johnny Marvin; Continental C-3013 by Dwight Butcher.

Acc. own g.
   New York, NY   c. August 1931

| 1449-2 | T.B. Blues | Cr 3204, Htd 23056, Pm 3275, Vs 5032 |
| 1450-2 | Travellin' Blues | Cr 3204, Htd 23056, Pm 3275, Vs 5032 |

Frank Marvin, v/y; acc. unknown, f; prob. Frank Novak, f-1/t-2/cl-3/bscl-4/ac-5/bj-6; poss. own g; unknown, sp-7.
   New York, NY   Thursday, September 3, 1931

E-37122-A	The Cowboy's Sweetheart -1, 3	Me M12261, Pan 25109
E-37123-A	There's Gold In Them Thar Hills -3, 4, 5, 6, 7	Me M12261, Pan 25109
E-37124-	Blue Yodel – No. 9 -4	Me M12250, Po P9080, Pan 25104, BrSA SA107
E-37175-	T.B. Blues -2, 3, 4	Me M12250, Po P9080, Pan 25104, BrSA SA107

Matrix E-37124 is titled *Blue Yodel* on Brunswick SA107.
Brunswick files state that only three musicians were present.
Intervening matrices are unrelated.

Frankie Marvin & His Guitar, v/y-1; acc. poss. Roy Smeck, sg-2; own g.
   New York, NY   Thursday, March 2, 1933

2005-2	Sheriff's Sale -2	Cr 3474, Vs 5095
2006-1	Cuddled In My Mammy's Arms -1	Cr 3475, Vs 5095
2007-2	One Thousand Miles Away From Home -1	Cr 3475, Vs 5109

Varsity 5095, 5109 as by **Frankie Marvin**.
Matrix 2007 is titled *A Thousand Miles Away From Home* on Varsity 5109.

   New York, NY   Friday, March 3, 1933

| 2008-2 | The Answer To 21 Years | Cr 3474, Vs 5105 |

Rev. Varsity 5105 by Frank Luther.
Frank Marvin also accompanied Gene Autry and Johnny Marvin and recorded after 1942.

JOHNNY MARVIN

The majority of the recordings by this singer, guitarist, and ukulele-player were in the popular idiom and are listed in Rust's *Complete Entertainment Discography*, as well as selectively in *JR*. The items listed below, however, fall within the scope of this work.

Honey Duke & His Uke, v; acc. own u.
    New York, NY   c. February/March 1927
    2308-A   Get Away Old Man Get Away   GG/Rad 2323, 2417, Mad 1611
Madison 1611 as by **Harry Carpenter**.
Revs: Grey Gull/Radiex 2323 by Al Bernard (popular), 2417 by Arthur Fields; Madison 1611 by James Wylie (popular).
    New York, NY   c. March/April 1927
    2360-B   Hand Me Down My Walking Cane   GG/Rad 4119
Later pressings of Grey Gull/Radiex 4119 use take E by Frank Luther (as **Tom Cook**).
Rev. Grey Gull/Radiex 4119 by Arthur Fields.
    New York, NY   c. June 1927
    31148   Get Away Old Man Get Away   Bell 523, Em 3153
Emerson 3153 as by **Jimmy May**.
Revs: Bell 523 by Henry Irving; Emerson 3153 by Bob Reardon (both popular).

Johnny Marvin, v/y; acc. Joe Venuti, f; own g.
    New York, NY   Tuesday, August 21, 1928
    46923-2   Watermelon Smilin' On The Vine   Vi 21653
Rev. Victor 21653 by Peg Moreland.

Johnny Marvin, v; acc. unknown, vn; unknown, s; unknown, p; unknown, g; unknown, sb; Frank Marvin, v-1; Leonard Joy, dir.
    New York, NY   Wednesday, February 25, 1931
    67470-1   Little Sweetheart Of The Prairie   Vi 22649, MW M-8253, HMV B3903, HMVAu EA897
    67471-2   Little Sweetheart Of The Mountains -1   Vi 22649, MW M-8253, HMV B3904, HMVAu EA897
Matrix 67471 on HMV B3904 as by **Johnny & Frankie Marvin**; on HMV EA897 as by **Frankie & Johnny Marvin**.
Rev. HMV B3903 untraced.

Acc. two unknowns, vn; unknown, tb; unknown, s; unknown, p; unknown, g; unknown, sb; Leonard Joy, dir.
    New York, NY   Tuesday, March 31, 1931
    53003-1   Would You Take Me Back Again?   Vi 22666, HMV B3904, HMVAu EA917
    53004-1   Rocky Mountain Rose   Vi 22666, HMVAu EA917

Johnny Marvin, v/y; acc. prob. Frank Novak, f-1/bscl-2; unknown, bj-3; two unknowns, g; unknown, sb-4; poss. own k or v eff-5.
    New York, NY   Monday, February 29, 1932
    1643-1   Atlanta Bound -3, 4, 5   Cr 3292, Htd 22985, *Vs 5015*
    1644-2   Jail House Blues -1, 4   Cr 3293, *Vs 5015*
    1645-2   Seven Come Eleven -1, 4, 5   Cr 3293, *Vs 5021*
    1646-3   Our Old Grey Mare (She's Old And Bent) -2, 3   Cr 3292, Htd 22985, *Vs 5115*, ImpE 2743
Varsity 5015, 5021 as by **Johnnie Marvin**.
Matrix 1644 is titled *Jailhouse Blues* on Varsity 5015.
Matrix 1645 is titled *7-11* on Varsity 5021.
Matrix 1646 is titled *The Old House And Old Grey Mare* on Varsity 5115.
Rev. Imperial 2743 by Jack Feeney (popular).

Johnny Marvin, v/y-1; acc. poss. Frank Novak, f-2/cl-3; unknown, t-4; unknown, p; poss own g/v eff; unknown, v duet-5; Norman Brokenshire, sp-6.
    New York, NY   Wednesday, March 2, 1932
    152112-1; 365067 Seven Come Eleven -3   Co 15750-D, Ve 2535-V, Cl 5475-C, Re/RZAu G21498
    152114-1; 365068 Yodelin' My Way To Heaven -1, 2, 4   Co 15750-D, Ve 2535-V, Cl 5475-C, Re/RZAu G21498
    152115-   Medley – Part 1 (Intro. Bend Down, Sister/Take Your Girlie To The Movies/Take It Slow And Easy/Old Grey Mare) -3?, 4?, 5, 6   Co 2655-D
    152116-   Medley – Part 2 (Intro. They're Wearing 'Em Higher In Hawaii/So's Your Old Lady/Etiquette/Seven Come Eleven) -3?, 4?, 6   Co 2655-D
Velvet Tone 2535-V, Clarion 5475-C as by **Honey Duke & His Uke**.
Matrix 152114 is titled *I'm Gonna Yodel My Way To Heaven* on Regal/Regal-Zonophone G21498.
Matrix 152113 is by Ben Selvin (popular).

Johnny Marvin & Johnny Amendt, v/y duet; acc. unknown, f; two unknowns, g; unknown, sb.
    New York, NY   Thursday, March 24, 1932

| 1678-2 | Ma And Pa (Send Their Sweetest Love) | Cr 3310, Vs 5067 |
| 1679-2 | The Mississippi Valley Blues | Cr 3309, Htd 22988, Vs 5021 |

Varsity 5021 as by **Johnnie Marvin**. Matrix 1679 is titled *Mississippi Blues* on Varsity 5021.

Johnny Marvin, v/y-1; acc. unknown, f-2; prob. Frank Novak, bscl-3; unknown, p-o-4; poss. own g.
New York, NY   Thursday, March 24, 1932

| 1680-2 | Home On The Range -2, 4 | Cr 3310, 3370, Htd 23088, MW M3016, Vs 5008 |
| 1681-1 | The Yodeling Hobo -1, 3 | Cr 3309, Htd 22988, MW M3018, Vs 5008 |

Montgomery Ward M3016, M3018 as by **Bob Star (The Texas Ranger)**. Varsity 5008 as by **The Texas Ranger**.
Revs: Crown 3370, Homestead 23088 by Dick Robertson; Montgomery Ward M3016 by Edward L. Crain, M3018 by Frank Marvin.

Johnny Marvin, v/y; acc. own g.
New York, NY   Tuesday, May 31, 1932

72825-1	When You Hear Me Call	Vi 23691, MW M-4339, Zo/RZAu EE384, HMVIn N4282
72826-1	Jack And Jill	Vi 23728, HMVIn N4241
72827-1	The Man With The Big Black Mustache	Vi 23708, MW M-4338, HMVIn N4232
72828-1	Go Along Bum And Keep On Bumming Along	Vi 23728, HMVIn N4241
72829-1	Seven Come Eleven	Vi 23708, HMVIn N4232
72830-1	I'm Gonna Yodel My Way To Heaven	Vi 23691, MW M-4339, Zo/RZAu EE384, HMVIn N4282

Rev. Montgomery Ward M-4338 by Vernon Dalhart.

Johnny Marvin, v/y-1; or **Johnny Marvin & Johnny Amendt**-2, v duet; acc. prob. Frank Novak, bscl-3/bj-4; two unknowns, g; poss. Johnny Marvin, u-5/v eff-6.
New York, NY   Tuesday, June 14, 1932

1755-2	When I Hear You Call O-Le-O-La-E -1, 4, 6	Cr 3341, Vs 5115
1756-1	The Voice In The Old Village Choir -2	Cr 3339, Vs 5022
1757-2	In A Shanty Down In Shanty Town -2	Cr 3339, Vs 5022
1758-2	When I Kissed That Girl Good-Bye -3, 5, 6	Cr 3341, Vs 5067, Cont C-3011

Varsity 5022 as by **Johnnie Marvin**.
Matrix 1755 is titled *When You Hear Me Call* on Varsity 5115.
Matrix 1757 is titled *In A Shanty In Old Shanty Town* on Varsity 5022.
Matrix 1757 is titled *When You Kiss That Gal Goodbye* on Varsity 5067, Continental C-3011.
Rev. Continental C-3011 by Dwight Butcher.

Acc. Roy Smeck, sg-1/bj-2; own g.
New York, NY   Thursday, July 28, 1932

| 12130-2 | I'm The Man That's Been Forgotten No. 1 -1 | Ba 32528, Me M12460, Or 8160, Pe 12833, Ro 5160, Cq 8066, CrC/MeC/Stg/Roy 91428 |
| 12131-1 | I'm The Man That's Been Forgotten No. 2 -2 | Ba 32528, Me M12460, Or 8160, Pe 12833, Ro 5160, Cq 8066, CrC/MeC/Stg/Roy 91428 |

Johnny Marvin, v/y; acc. Frank Marvin, sg; own g/v eff.
New York, NY   Tuesday, December 11, 1934

| 38997-A | I Want My Boots On When I Die | De 5056, Pan 25682 |

Johnny & Frankie Marvin, v duet; acc. Frank Marvin, h; Johnny Marvin, g/y/v eff.
New York, NY   Tuesday, December 11, 1934

| 39005-A | Lazy Texas Longhorns | De 5056, Pan 25682 |

Panachord 25682 as by **Frankie & Johnnie Marvin**.
Matrices 38998 to 39004 are by John McGettigan (Irish).

Johnny Marvin, v; acc. Frank Marvin, sg-1; own g.
New York, NY   Monday, February 18, 1935

39368-A	The Last Mile	Pan 25973
39369-A	Beneath A Bed Of Daisies -1	Pan 25973
39370-A,-B	Grandma's Rockin' Chair	De rejected
39371-A,-B	My Big Swiss Cheese	De rejected

Acc. Joe Krechter, cl; Paul Sells, pac; Frank Marvin, esg; own g; Jimmy Wakely, g; Dick Reinhart, sb; unknown, wh-1.
Los Angeles, CA   Wednesday, September 11, 1940

DLA-2151-A	We Like It	De 5891
DLA-2152-B	Me And My Shadow -1	De 5891
DLA-2153-A	No One To Kiss Me Goodnight	De 5904, MeC 45406
DLA-2154-A	As Long As I Live	De 5904, MeC 45406

See also Frank Marvin.

MARVIN & HIS GUITAR
Pseudonym on Australian Brunswick for Frank Marvin.

THE MARVIN FAMILY
See Frank Marvin.

MARVIN'S STRING BAND
Pseudonym on Supertone for Ted Gossett's Band.

DIXIE MASON

Dixie Mason, v; acc. prob. own g.
    Chicago, IL   Thursday, April 27, 1933
      75485-1   The Little Old Church In The Valley   Vi 23798
      75486-1   In The Gloaming   Vi 23798

PAUL MASON

Paul Mason, v; acc. unknown, pac/p; unknown, g.
    New York, NY   Friday, April 11, 1930
      403898-A   They Cut Down The Old Pine Tree   OK 45479
      403899-A   The True And Trembling Brakeman   OK 45479

MASSANUTTEN MILITARY ACADEMY QUARTET
Though appearing in the Columbia Old Familiar Tunes series, this group is outside the scope of this work.

BOB MASSEY
Pseudonym on Pathé and Perfect for Vernon Dalhart.

CURT MASSEY
See The Massey Family.

DAD MASSEY
See The Massey Family.

GUY MASSEY
Pseudonym on Pathé and Perfect for Vernon Dalhart.

HAPPY MASSEY

Happy Massey, v; acc. poss. own g.
    Richmond, IN   Saturday, February 22, 1933
      19040   Somebody Waiting For You   Ge unissued
      19041   Bad Companions   Ge unissued

LOUISE MASSEY
See The Massey Family.

[THE] MASSEY FAMILY (THE WESTERNERS)

Dott Curtis Massey, f/v-1; Larry Wellington, ac; Louise Massey, prob. p-2; Allen Massey, g; Milt Mabie, sb; group v-3.
    Chicago, IL   Friday, October 13, 1933
      C-639-   The Cowboy's Dream   ARC unissued
      C-640-2   New River Train -3   Cq 8204
      C-641-   Trail To Mexico   ARC unissued
      C-642-2   The Big Corral -1, 2, 3   Cq 8205

The Massey Family: Curt Massey, f; Larry Wellington, ac; Allen Massey, g/lv-1; Milt Mabie, sb; group including Louise Massey, v.
    Chicago, IL   Tuesday, November 21, 1933
      C-668-2   The Cowboy's Dream -1   Cq 8204
      C-669-2   The Trail To Mexico   Cq 8205

The Westerners (Massey Family): Curt Massey, f; Larry Wellington, ac; Allen Massey, g/v-1; Milt Mabie, sb; Louise Massey, v-2; group v-3.
    Chicago, IL   Tuesday, March 20 – Wednesday, March 21, 1934
      CP-1001-3   There's An Empty Cot In The Bunkhouse Tonight -3   Cq 8291
      CP-1002-1,2   Ridin' Down That Old Texas Trail -3   Ba 33044, Me M13006, Or 8330, Pe 13000,
                                                                        Ro 5330, OK 05740, Cq 8286, Co 37650,
                                                                        20249, CrC/MeC/Stg/Roy 91801, Min M-916

CP-1003-1	Goin' Down To Santa Fe Town -3	Ba 33044, Me M13006, Or 8330, Pe 13000, Ro 5330, OK 05740, Cq 8292, Co 37650, 20249, CrC/MeC/Stg/Roy 91801
CP-1004-1	When The White Azaleas Start Blooming -2	Ba 33339, Me M13306, Or 8428, Pe 13109, Ro 5428, Vo/OK 04221, Cq 8294, Co 37631, 20230, Co-Lucky 60408
CP-1005-	Old Pinto-	Cq 8294
CP-1006-1	When It's Prayer Meetin' Time In The Hollow -2	Ba 33374, Me M13341, Or 8444, Pe 13122, Ro 5444, Cq 8291, CrC/MeC/Stg/Roy 91990
CP-1007-2	Rounded Up In Glory -1, 3	Ba 33069, Me M13033, Or 8339, Pe 13008, Ro 5339, Cq 8293, CrC/MeC/Stg/Roy 91813

All issues of matrix CP-1004 as by **Louise Massey Acc. By The Westerners**. Conquerors, and all issues of matrix CP-1006, as by **The Westerners**.
Revs: Minerva M-916 by Tex Ritter; Columbia-Lucky 60408 by Carson Robison.

Curt Massey, f/v-1; Larry Wellington, ac; Allen Massey, g/v-2; Milt Mabie, sb; group including Louise Massey, v-3.
Chicago, IL   Thursday, March 22, 1934

CP-1012-3	Carry Me Back To The Lone Prairie -1, 3	Ba 33133, Me M13100, Or 8367, Pe 13028, Ro 5367, Cq 8293, CrC/MeC/Stg/Roy 91880
CP-1013-3	The Cowboy's Dream -2, 3	Ba 33069, Me M13033, Or 8339, Pe 13008, Ro 5339, CrC/MeC/Stg/Roy 91813
CP-1014-1	A Roundup Lullaby-	Cq 8286
CP-1015-3	Out On Loco Range -3	Ba 33133, Me M13100, Or 8367, Pe 13028, Ro 5367, Cq 8292, CrC/MeC/Stg/Roy 91880

Conquerors as by **The Westerners**.

Curt Massey, f/v-1; Larry Wellington, ac; Allen Massey, g/v-2; Milt Mabie, sb; Louise Massey, v-3; group v-4.
Chicago, IL   Tuesday, November 6, 1934

C-786-1	Shorty's Nightmare -2, 4	ARC 6-01-54, Cq 8460, CrC/MeC/Stg/Roy 93087
C-787-1	Beautiful Texas -4	Cq 8437
C-788-1	Nobody To Love -3	Ba 33339, Me M13306, Or 8428, Pe 13109, Ro 5428
C-789-1	Rancho Grande -1, 4	Ba 33446, Me M13413, Or 8472, Pe 13146, Ro 5472, Vo/OK 04223, CrC/MeC/Stg/Roy 92027
C-790-1	Buckaroo Stomp	Cq 8459
C-791-1	Mr. Rhythm	ARC unissued

All issues of matrix C-788 as by **Louise Massey Acc. By The Westerners**. Conquer 8459 as by **The Westerners**.
Later pressings of Melotone M13306 replace matrix C-788 with matrix 19415, but it is uncertain whether later pressings (if any) of Banner 33339, Oriole 8428, Perfect 13109, and Romeo 5428 do likewise.

Curt Massey, f/t-1/v-2/laughing-3; Larry Wellington, ac-4/p-5; poss. Louise Massey, p-6; Allen Massey, g/v-7; Milt Mabie, sb; group v-8/laughing-9.
Chicago, IL   Thursday, November 8, 1934

C-808-1	My Gal On The Rio Grande -2, 4, 8	Ba 33446, Me M13413, Or 8472, Pe 13146, Ro 5472, Vo/OK 04223, Cq 8434, CrC/MeC/Stg/Roy 92027
C-809-1	The Santa Fe Trail -4, 7, 8	ARC 6-03-58, Cq 8434, CrC/MeC/Stg/Roy 93089, Min M-14029
C-810-1	Brown Skin Gal (Down The Lane) -3, 4/5, 9	Vo 02882
C-811-1	Honeysuckle Schottische -5	Ba 33328, Me M13295, Or 8425, Pe 13108, Ro 5425, Vo/OK 04222, Co 37632, 20231, M-450, Lucky 1047
C-812-1	Round-Up Time In Heaven -2, 4, 8	Ba 33374, Me M13341, Or 8444, Pe 13122, Ro 5444, Cq 8437, CrC/MeC/Stg/Roy 91990
C-813-1	Hot Romance -1, 4, 6	Vo 02882

Vocalion 02882 as by **The Massey Family**. All issues of matrix C-811 as by **The Westerners (The Massey Family)**.

The Westerners (The Massey Family): Curt Massey, f/v-1; Larry Wellington, ac; Allen Massey, g/v-2; Milt Mabie, sb; group including Louise Massey, v-3.
Chicago, IL   Wednesday, November 14, 1934

C-837-1	Pretty Boy Floyd -1	Vo 02850, Cq 8444
C-838-1	If Jesse James Rode Again -3	Vo 02850, Cq 8444
C-839-1	I Wonder If She's Blue	ARC unissued
C-840-1	Twinkle Twinkle Little Star	Cq 8459
C-841-1	Old Rose Waltz	ARC 7-10-51, Vo/OK 04310, Cq 8896
C-842-1	Varsovienna	Co 37632, 20231, M-450
C-842-2	Varsovienna	Ba 33328, Me M13295, Or 8425, Pe 13108, Ro 5425, Vo/OK 04222, Lucky 1047

610 [The] Massey Family (The Westerners)

    C-843-1   Gol-Darn Wheel -2   ARC 6-01-54, CrC/MeC/Stg/Roy 93087,
                                                                          Min M-14025
    C-844-1   Song Of The Lariat -3   ARC 6-03-58, Cq 8460, CrC/MeC/Stg/Roy 93089,
                                                                           Min M-14029

Matrix C-837 on Vocalion 02850 as by **Dot Massey**, and on Conqueror 8444 as by **The Westerners/Massey Family**.
Rev. Minerva M-14025 is untraced.

Curt Massey, f/v; Allen Massey, g; Milt Mabie, sb; group including Louise Massey, v.
    Chicago, IL   Wednesday, January 23, 1935
    C-812-2   Round-Up Time In Heaven   Cq 8437

Curt Massey, f-1/t/v-2; Larry Wellington, ac; Allen Massey, g; Milt Mabie, sb; Louise Massey, v-3.
    Chicago, IL   Tuesday, June 18, 1935
    C-1013-B   The Little Wooden Whistle Wouldn't Whistle -1, 2   ARC 6-10-59, Vo 02993, Vo/OK 04414,
                                                                                       Cq 8716, Co 37726, 20303
    C-1014-B   Sweet Mama Tree Top Tall -2   ARC 7-01-65, Vo 02993
    C-1015-B   Where The Morning Glories Grow -1, 3   Vo 03063, Cq 8895
    C-1016-A   Dragging The Bow -1   ARC 7-01-65, Vo 03063

Vocalion 03063 as by **The Massey Family (The Westerners)**.

Dad Massey & His Family (The Westerners): Henry A. "Dad" Massey, f/sp; Curt Massey, f-1; Larry Wellington, ac; Allen Massey, g; Joe ———, g; Milt Mabie, sb; Louise Massey, sp; band, laughing-2.
    New York, NY   Monday, June 8, 1936
    19404-1   Tugboat And Pineywoods   ARC 7-03-53
    19405-1   Dixie Medley -1, 2   ARC 7-03-53

The Westerners (The Massey Family): Curt Massey, f/v-1; Larry Wellington, ac; Allen Massey, g/v-2; Milt Mabie, sb; Louise Massey, v-3; group v-4.
    New York, NY   Monday, June 8, 1936
    19406-1   Is It True What They Say About Dixie -1, 3   ARC 6-08-62, Cq 8714
    19407-1   Partner, It's The Parting Of The Way -3   ARC 6-08-62, Cq 8714
    19408-1   My Herdin' Song -2   ARC 6-09-52, Cq 8715
    19409-2   Good Old Turnip Greens -1, 4   ARC 6-10-59, Vo/OK 04414, Cq 8716,
                                                                                       Co 37726, 20303

Dad Massey & His Family (The Westerners): Henry A. "Dad" Massey, f; Curt Massey, f-1; Larry Wellington, ac; Allen Massey, g; Joe ———, g; Milt Mabie, sb; unidentified, calls-2.
    New York, NY   Monday, June 8, 1936
    19410-1   Durang's Hornpipe -1, 2   ARC 6-11-53, Cq 8738, 9755
    19411-1   Ragtime Annie   ARC 6-11-53, Cq 8738
    19412-   Done Gone   ARC unissued
    19413-   Sailor's Hornpipe   ARC unissued

Rev. Conqueror 9755 by Prairie Ramblers.

The Westerners (The Massey Family): Curt Massey, f; Larry Wellington, ac; Allen Massey, g; Milt Mabie, sb; Louise Massey, v-1; group v-2.
    New York, NY   Monday, June 8, 1936
    19414-1   Texas Star (Dedicated To The Texas Centennial) -2 ARC 6-09-52, Cq 8715
    19415-1   Nobody To Love -1   Ba 33339(?), Me M13306, Or 8428(?),
                                                                                  Pe 13109(?), Ro 5428(?), Vo/OK 04221,
                                                                                  Co 37631, 20230

Regarding matrix 19415, see note following session of November 6, 1934.

Curt Massey, f/v-1; Larry Wellington, ac; Allen Massey, g/v-2; Milt Mabie, sb; Louise Massey, v-3; group v-4/sp-5.
    New York, NY   Thursday, March 11, 1937
    20784-1   My Little Buckaroo -1, 3, 4   ARC 7-05-68, Cq 8807, Co-Lucky 60330
    20785-1   Everybody Kiss Your Partner (The Whistle Song)   Cq 8829
                              -1, 2, 3, 4, 5
    20786-1   Life's Evening Sun Is Sinking Low -1, 2   ARC 7-06-51, Vo/OK 02957, Cq 8807
    20787-   Putting On The Style   ARC unissued
    20788-2   Play Me That Single Time Jazz -1   ARC 7-07-51, Cq 8829
    20789-1   Wanderers (My Lop-Eared Mule, My Broken-Down   ARC 7-05-68, Co-Lucky 60330
                               Horse 'N' Me) -1, 3, 4

Curt Massey, f/v-1; Larry Wellington, ac-2/p-3; Allen Massey, g; Milt Mabie, sb; Louise Massey, v-4; group v-5.
    New York, NY   Wednesday, March 24, 1937
    20873-2   When The Poppies Bloom Again -2, 4   ARC 7-05-75, Cq 8812, Co M-417
    20874-2   When My Dream Boat Comes Home -2, 4   ARC 7-05-75, Cq 8812, Co M-417
    20875-2   Falling Leaves -2, 5   ARC 7-08-62, Cq 8820

20876-2	Broken Engagement -2, 5	ARC 7-08-62, Cq 8820
20877-1	Raggin' The Blues (At The Old Piano) -1, 3	ARC 7-07-51, Cq 8895
20878-2	Carry Me Over The Warm Desert Sands -2, 5	ARC 7-10-51, Vo/OK 04310, Cq 8896

Curt Massey, f/v; Larry Wellington, ac; Allen Massey, g/v; Milt Mabie, sb.
New York, NY   Wednesday, April 7, 1937

20961-2	What Would You Give In Exchange For Your Soul No. 2	ARC 7-06-51, Vo/OK 02957, Cq 8820, 9669

Rev. Conqueror 9669 by Prairie Ramblers.

Louise Massey & The Westerners: Curt Massey, f/t/v-1; Larry Wellington, ac; Allen Massey, g; Milt Mabie, sb; Louise Massey, v-2; group v.
Chicago, IL   Monday, September 25, 1939

WC-2757-A	South Of The Border (Down Mexico Way) -2	Vo/OK 05147, Cq 9320, Co 37645, 20244
WC-2758-A	A Gay Ranchero (Las Altenitas) -1	Vo/OK 05147, Cq 9320, Co 37645, 20244
WC-2759-A	Dude Cowboy	Vo/OK 05271, Cq 9680
WC-2760-A	Bunkhouse Jamboree -1	Vo/OK 05146, Cq 9680, Co 37644, 20243

Curt Massey, f/t/v-1; Larry Wellington, ac; Allen Massey, g/v-2; Milt Mabie, sb; Louise Massey, v-3; group v-4.
Chicago, IL   Tuesday, September 26, 1939

WC-2765-A	I Only Want A Buddy – Not A Sweetheart -1	Vo/OK 05271, Cq 9321
WC-2766-A	Wildflower Indian Maid -3	Vo/OK 05230
WC-2767-A	Ragtime Cowboy Joe -4	Vo/OK 05146, Cq 9321, Co 37644, 20243
WC-2768-A	A Golden Tomorrow Ahead -1, 2	Vo/OK 05230

Curt Massey, f/t/v-1; Larry Wellington, ac; unknown, eg; Allen Massey, g/v-2; Milt Mabie, sb; Louise Massey, v-3; group v-4.
Chicago, IL   Saturday, December 9, 1939

WC-2846-A	Billie Boy -1, 2, 3, 4	Vo/OK 05358, Cq 9600
WC-2847-A	Polly Wolly Doodle -2, 4	Vo/OK 05296
WC-2848-A	Listen To The Mocking Bird -3	Vo/OK 05358, Cq 9600
WC-2849-A	Billy -3	Vo/OK 05296

Henry A. Massey (Dad of The Westerners), f; acc. prob. Larry Wellington, ac/p; Allen Massey, g; Milt Mabie, sb.
Chicago, IL   Saturday, December 9, 1939

WC-2850-A	Kasoos Hornpipe	Vo unissued
WC-2851-A	Rochester Schottische	Vo unissued
WC-2852-A	El Capitan	Vo unissued
WC-2853-A	New Roswell Schottische	Vo unissued

Louise Massey & The Westerners: Louise Massey, v/sp-1; acc. Curt Massey, f/t; Larry Wellington, ac; unknown, eg; Allen Massey, g; Milt Mabie, sb; unknown, d; unknown, vb; group v.
Chicago, IL   Tuesday, February 20, 1940

WC-2931-A	Pop Goes The Weazel	Vo/OK 05462, Cq 9383, 9414
WC-2932-A	Go In And Out The Window	Vo/OK 05561
WC-2933-A	Mary Had A Little Lamb -1	Vo/OK 05462, Cq 9414
WC-2934-A	Lil Liza Jane	Vo/OK 05561, Cq 9682

Louise Massey, v; acc. Curt Massey, f/t; prob. Bill Thall, cl/as; Larry Wellington, ac; Allen Massey, g; Milt Mabie, sb; Bobby Christian, d/vb; group v-1.
Chicago, IL   Thursday, February 22, 1940

WC-2951-A	Rock And Rye Polka	Vo/OK 05511, Cq 9412, Co 37744, 20321, CoC C56, C979
WC-2952-A	Little Brown Jug	Vo/OK 05425, Cq 9413, Co 37646, 20245
WC-2952-3B	Little Brown Jug	Co 52007
WC-2953-A	Put Your Little Foot Right Out -1	Vo/OK 05425, Cq 9413, Co 37646, 20245, 52007
WC-2954-A	Ye Olde Rye Waltz	Vo/OK 05511, Cq 9412, Co 37744, 20321, CoC C56, C979

Matrix WC-2952-3B may be an edited dubbing of matrix WC-2952-A.

Acc. Curt Massey, f; Larry Wellington, ac; Allen Massey, g; Milt Mabie, sb.
Chicago, IL   Saturday, June 8, 1940

WC-3076-A	I'll Get By Somehow	OK 05795, Cq 9602
WC-3077-A	Lonely Rose	OK 05651

Louise Massey, v; or **Curt Massey & The Massey Family**-1: Curt Massey, v; acc. Curt Massey, f; Larry Wellington, ac; Allen Massey, g; Milt Mabie, sb.
Chicago, IL   Monday, June 10, 1940

WC-3078-AA	Lonesome, That's All	OK 05795, Cq 9602
WC-3079-A	Way Up There -1	OK 05722

[The] Massey Family (The Westerners)

Louise Massey & The Westerners: Louise Massey, v; or group v-1/sp-2; acc. Curt Massey, f/t; Larry Wellington, ac-3/p-4; George Barnes, eg; Allen Massey, g; Milt Mabie, sb.
Chicago, IL   Tuesday, June 11, 1940

WC-3084-A	Tennessee Fish Fry -1, 3	OK 05650, Cq 9599
WC-3085-A	What You Gonna Do When The Rent Comes 'Round (Rufus Rastus Johnson Brown) -1, 2, 3	OK 05650, Cq 9599
WC-3086-A	It's A Lovely Day Tomorrow -4	OK 05651

Curt Massey & The Massey Family: Curt Massey, v; acc. own f/t; Larry Wellington, ac; George Barnes, eg; Allen Massey, g; Milt Mabie, sb.
Chicago, IL   Tuesday, June 11, 1940

WC-3087-A	Old Timer	OK 05722, Cq 9383

Louise Massey & The Westerners: Curt Massey, f/t/v-1; unknown, cl/s; Larry Wellington, ac-2/p-3; unknown, sg; Allen Massey, g; Milt Mabie, sb; Louise Massey, v-4.
Chicago, IL   Friday, October 11, 1940

C-3415-1	Beer And Skittles -2	OK 05916, Cq 9682, Co 37754, 20331
C-3416-1	Bagatelle -2	OK 06194
C-3417-1	Biarritz -2	OK 05941, Cq 9685
C-3418-1	Waltz Time Melody (Varso-Vienna) -3	OK 05941, Cq 9685, Co 20508, CoC C1198
C-3419-1	Las Gaviotas (Seagulls) -2	OK 06194
C-3420-1	Quiera Mi Jesusita -2	OK 05916, Co 37754, 20331
C-3421-1	Old Pioneer -1, 2	OK 05865, Cq 9585
C-3422-1	Goodnight Mother -1, 2	OK 05865, Cq 9585
C-3423-1	Tears On My Pillow -2, 4	OK 05992, Cq 9683, Co 37653, 20252
C-3424-1	We Never Dream The Same Dream Twice -2, 4	OK 05904, Cq 9684
C-3425-1	Dream Valley -2, 4	OK 05904, Cq 9684
C-3426-1	Mistakes -2, 4	OK 05992, Cq 9683, Co 37653, 20252

Curt Massey, f/t; unknown, cl/s; Larry Wellington, ac; Allen Massey, g; Milt Mabie, sb.
Chicago, IL   Thursday, January 23, 1941

C-3551-1	Army Rookie Polka	OK 06042, Cq 9679
C-3552-1	Sailor Boy	OK 06042, Cq 9679
C-3553-1	La Fiesta	OK 06251, CoC C376
C-3554-1	Ciribiribin	OK 06251, CoC C376

Louise Massey, v; acc. Curt Massey, f; Larry Wellington, ac; unknown, sg; Allen Massey, g.
Chicago, IL   Monday, January 27, 1941

C-3577-1	Since You Said Goodbye To Me	OK 06125, Cq 9686
C-3578-1	I Left My Heart In Texas	OK 06077, Cq 9681
C-3579-1	My Adobe Hacienda	OK 06077, Cq 9681, Co 37332, 20117, 52006, CoC C879
C-3580-1	Though We Never Meet Again	OK 06125, Cq 9686

Curt Massey, f/t/v-1; unknown, cl; Larry Wellington, ac-2/p-3; unknown, sg; Allen Massey, g; Milt Mabie, sb; Louise Massey, v-4; group v-5.
Chicago, IL   Thursday, May 29, 1941

C-3815-1	Answer To I'll Be Back In A Year, Little Darlin' (I'll Be Waiting For You, Darlin') -2, 4	OK 06337, Cq 9834, CoC C423
C-3816-1	I Used To Love You (But It's All Over Now) -2, 4	OK 06337, Cq 9834, CoC C423
C-3817-1	My Sister And I -2, 4	OK 06262, CoC C382
C-3818-1	The Band Played On -3, 4	OK 06262, CoC C382
C-3819-1	Nellie Bly -2, 4, 5	OK 06558, Cq 9838, Co C583
C-3820-1	Ridin' High -1, 2, 4, 5	OK 06502, Cq 9837
C-3821-1	Huckleberry Picnic -1, 2, 4, 5	OK 06502, Cq 9838
C-3822-1	Mama Inez (Oh! Mom-E-Nez) -1, 2	OK 06558, Cq 9837, Co C583

Curt Massey, f/v-1; unknown, cl; Larry Wellington, ac; unknown, sg; Allen Massey, g; Milt Mabie, sb; Louise Massey, v-2; group v-3.
Chicago, IL   Tuesday, June 3, 1941

C-3831-1	It Was Wonderful Then (And It's Wonderful Now) -1	OK 06275, Cq 9835
C-3832-1	Where The Mountains Meet The Moon -1	OK 06275, Cq 9835
C-3833-1	Don't Be Blue For Me -1	OK 06462, Cq 9836
C-3834-1	Always Alone -1	OK 06462, Cq 9836
C-3835-1	Lazy Acres -1, 3	OK 06406
C-3836-1	You Don't Love Me (But I'll Always Care) -1	Cq 9839
C-3837-1	With So Many Reasons -2	Cq 9839
C-3838-1	Nothing Matters Anymore -2	OK 06406

Curt Massey, f/t/v-1; unknown, cl; Larry Wellington, ac; unknown, sg; Allen Massey, g; Milt Mabie, sb; Louise Massey, v-2.

  Chicago, IL   Thursday, January 22, 1942
  C-4147-1   There'll Come A Day -2   OK 06612, Co 37416, 20143
  C-4148-1   I'm Human Too   OK unissued
  C-4149-1   Rancho Pillow   OK unissued
  C-4150-1   Gals Don't Mean A Thing (In My Young Life) -1   OK 6687, Co 37408, 20135

Matrix C-4149 was scheduled for OKeh 06656 but never issued.

Curt Massey, f/v-1; unknown, cl; Larry Wellington, ac; unknown, sg; Allen Massey, g; Milt Mabie, sb; Louise Massey, v-2.
  Chicago, IL   Monday, January 26, 1942
  C-4163-1   The Ghost Of Robert E. Lee   OK unissued
  C-4164-1   I'm Thinking Tonight Of My Blue Eyes -2   OK 06612, Co 37416, 20143
  C-4165-1   How Foolish Of Me   OK unissued
  C-4166-1   The Honey Song (Honey, I'm In Love With You) -1   OK 6687, Co 37408, 20135, V-D 26
  C-4167-1   Somewhere West Of Heaven   OK unissued
  C-4168-1   Squeeze Box Polka   Co 20508, CoC C1198
  C-4169-1   Starlight Schottische   Co 37332, 20117, CoC C879
  C-4170-   'Long The Rio Grande   OK unissued

Matrix C-4163 was scheduled for OKeh 06656 but never issued.
Matrix C-4166 is titled *Honey, I'm In Love With You* on some pressings of OKeh 6687.
Members of The Massey Family recorded after 1942.

MASTERS' HAWAIIANS

See the Kelly Brothers.

[BLIND] JACK MATHIS

Jack Mathis, v; acc. own g.
  Dallas, TX   Monday, December 3, 1928
  147554-2   Your Mother Still Prays For You   Co 15344-D, CoAu 01897
  147555-2   When The Roses Come Again   Co 15344-D

Rev. Columbia 01897 by Vernon Dalhart.

  Dallas, TX   Sunday, December 9, 1928
  147620-1   Charming Bessie Lee   Co 15450-D, CoSA DE503
  147621-1   Annie Dear I'm Called Away   Co 15450-D, CoSA DE503, ReAu G20741

Rev. Regal G20741 by Vernon Dalhart.

Blind Jack Mathis, v; acc. own g.
  Dallas, TX   Friday, October 18, 1929
  56418-2   Those Dark Eyes   Vi V-40262
  56419-1   Are You Tired Of Me, Darling?   Vi 23593, BB B-4956, Au 417
  56420-1,-2   Annie Dear, I'm Called Away   Vi unissued
  56421-2   Your Love And Mine   Vi V-40262

Revs: Victor 23593, Bluebird B-4956, Aurora 417 by Peg Moreland.

JIMMIE MATTOX

Jimmie Mattox, v/y; acc. own g.
  Richmond, IN   Wednesday, May 28, 1930
  16690   Good Bye Mama   Ge 7227, Ch 16053, Spt 9721
  16691   Sweet Wimmin'   Ge 7227, Ch 16053, Spt 9721

Supertone 9721 as by **Johnny Martin**.

HAROLD MAUS

Harold Maus, g solo.
  Chicago, IL   Monday, December 4, 1933
  77182-1   Guitar March   BB B-5304, Eld 2174, Sr S-3385, MW M-4474
  77183-1   Guitar Medley   BB B-5304, Eld 2174, Sr S-3385, MW M-4474

Harold Maus is also the first party of Harold & Hazel.

BILLIE MAXWELL (THE COW GIRL SINGER)

Billie Maxwell, v; acc. E.G. Maxwell, f; own g.
  El Paso, TX   Tuesday, July 2, 1929
  53294-2   Billy Venero – Part 1   Vi V-40148
  53295-2   Billy Venero – Part 2   Vi V-40148

Acc. own g.
 El Paso, TX   Thursday, July 11, 1929
   55231-2   The Arizona Girl I Left Behind Me   Vi V-40188
   55232-2   The Cowboy's Wife   Vi V-40188
   55233-1   Where Your Sweetheart Waits For You, Jack   Vi V-40241, Au 234
   55234-1   Haunted Hunter   Vi V-40241, Au 234

Victor V-40188 as by **Billy Maxwell**. Both Victor V-40188 and V-40241 are subcredited (**The Cowgirl Singer**).
Billie Maxwell was also a member of the White Mountain Orchestra.

JIMMY MAY

Pseudonym on Emerson 3153 for Johnny Marvin.

D.T. MAYFIELD

D.T. Mayfield, v; acc. unknown.
 Atlanta, GA   Thursday, November 10, 1927
   145214-   Never Alone   Co unissued
   145215-   I Surrender All   Co unissued

KEN MAYNARD

Ken Maynard, v; acc. own g.
 Hollywood, CA   Monday, April 14, 1930
   149830-   Fannie Moore   Co unissued: *Yz 2028 (CD)*
   149831-2   The Cowboy's Lament   Co 2310-D, CoJ J1123
   149832-2   The Lone Star Trail   Co 2310-D, CoJ J1123
   149833-   Sweet Betsy From Pike   Co unissued
   149834-   A Prisoner For Life   Co unissued
   149835-   When The Round Up's Done This Fall   Co unissued
   149836-   Jessie James   Co unissued
   149837-2   Home On The Range   Co unissued: *CSP P4-15542 (LP); Yz 2023 (CD)*

Columbia 2310-D as by **Ken Maynard (The American Boy's Favorite Cowboy)**.

MAZE & JONES

Prob. v duet; acc. prob. one of them, g.
 Richmond, IN   Wednesday, July 13, 1932
   18596   Silver Haired Daddy Of Mine   Ge rejected trial recording

CLYDE MEADOWS

Clyde Meadows, v; acc. poss. own h/g.
 Richmond, IN   Monday, January 14, 1929
   14694   Take This Letter To My Mother   Ge rejected trial recording

See also Fred Pendleton, and possibly the West Virginia Coon Hunters.

GRACE MEANS

Pseudonym on Supertone for Mommie Gray with Otto Gray's Oklahoma Cowboy Band.

DAVIE MEEK & HIS BOYS

Pseudonym on Champion for Wyzee Hamilton.

DICK MEEKS

Pseudonym on Supertone for Oscar L. Coffey.

MELITON Y SUS RANCHEROS

Decca 10097 (a Mexican issue) by Milton Brown & His Brownies was issued thus.

THE MELODY BOYS

Vocal trio; or v solo-1; acc. poss. own g trio; unidentified, y-2.
 Rock Hill, SC   Sunday, September 25, 1938
   026927-1   One Little Kiss -2   MW M-7690
   026928-1   Working On The Railroad -2   MW M-7690
   026929-1   My Wild Irish Rose   MW M-7691
   026930-1   Wait Till The Sun Shines, Nellie   BB B-8172, MW M-7692
   026931-1   Why Should It End This Way?   MW M-7691
   026932-1   My Mother's Prayer -1   MW M-7692
   026933-1   What You Mean To Me -1   MW M-7693

026934-1	Beautiful Isle	MW M-7693
026935-1	I'm Glad For Your Sake -1	MW M-7694
026936-1	Some Day Sweetheart -1	BB B-8172, MW M-7694

Matrix 026930 is titled *Wait Till The Sun Shines* on Montgomery Ward M-7692.

THE MELODY MOUNTAINEERS

Pseudonym on Australian Regal-Zonophone for Mainer's Mountaineers.

MELTON & MINTER

Male vocal duet; acc. prob. one of them, g.
 Atlanta, GA   Monday, March 17, 1930

| ATL-903 | Old Bay Mule Of Mine | Vo rejected |
| ATL-904 | Paddy's Irish Pup | Vo rejected |

 Atlanta GA   Saturday, March 22, 1930

| ATL-991 | Let Me Call You Sweetheart | Vo 5435 |
| ATL-992 | Let The Rest Of The World Go By | Vo 5435 |

 Atlanta, GA   Tuesday, March 25, 1930

| ATL-8012 | Meet Me Tonight In Dreamland | Vo rejected |
| ATL-8013 | Till We Meet Again | Vo rejected |

MELTON & WAGGONER

Male vocal duet; acc. poss. one of them, ah; the other, g.
 Atlanta, GA   Tuesday, October 30, 1928

| 147337-2 | In The Hills Of Old Kentucky (My Mountain Rose) | Co 15423-D, CoSA DE502 |
| 147338-2 | Underneath The Cotton Moon | Co 15423-D, CoSA DE502 |

Melton may be the first party in the previous entry; Waggoner may be Bruce Waggoner.

MELVIN'S SUPERTONE PLAYERS

Pseudonym on Supertone for The Brunswick Players.

MEMPHIS BOB

See Bob Miller.

THE MEMPHIS GOSPEL QUARTETTE

Pseudonym on Supertone for the Murphree Hartford Quartette (see E.M. Bartlett Groups).

JEAN MENDIGAL

Pseudonym on Velvet Tone for Chris Bouchillon.

JEAN MENDRIGAL

Pseudonym on Clarion for Chris Bouchillon.

MERIDIAN HUSTLERS

Unknown, f; unknown, bj; unknown, g; unknown, v-1.
 Chicago, IL   c. June 1929

| 21314-1 | I'd Rather Stay Out In The Rain -1 | Pm 3173, Bwy 8239 |
| 21316-1 | Queen City Square Dance | Pm 3173, Bwy 8239 |

On Broadway 8239 the matrices are reversed, both on the labels and in the wax, and the former title is given as *I'd Rather Be Out In The Rain*. Matrix 21315 is untraced.

MERT'S HOMETOWN SERENADERS

Mert's Hometown Serenaders Featuring Merton Bories & Doc Johnson: unidentified, v duet; acc. unknown, h; unknown, p.
 Los Angeles, CA   Wednesday, June 12, 1929

| LAE-537 | We Gotta Look Into This | Vo 5338 |
| LAE-538 | Topsy Turvy | Vo 5338 |

METHODIST MINISTERS QUARTET

Vocal quartet; prob. unacc.
 Chicago, IL   c. March 14, 1928

| 13547 | I Want My Life To Tell For Jesus | Ge unissued trial recording |

MIDKIFF, SPENCER & BLAKE

Unidentified, f; unidentified, g; unidentified, u.
   Richmond, IN   Monday, August 18, 1930

16926,-A	Dunbar-Midkiff Jig; Fun's All Over	Ge rejected
16927,-A,-B	Ragtime Annie; Dillpickle Rag; Barnyard Hymn	Ge rejected

ARTHUR MILES

Arthur Miles, v/y/wh/v eff; acc. prob. own g.
   Dallas, TX   Thursday, August 8, 1929

55305-1	Lonely Cowboy – Part 1	Vi V-40156, Au 232
55306-2	Lonely Cowboy – Part 2	Vi V-40156, Au 232

PAUL MILES [& THE RED FOX CHASERS]

See The Red Fox Chasers.

MILES & THOMPSON

See The Red Fox Chasers.

MILES, CRANFORD & THOMPSON

See The Red Fox Chasers.

BOB MILLER

This listing does not include band recordings by Bob Miller & His Orchestra.

Bob Miller, v; acc. own p.
   New York, NY   Friday, August 17, 1928

146851-1	Eleven Cent Cotton Forty Cent Meat – Part 1	Co 15297-D
146852-2	Eleven Cent Cotton Forty Cent Meat – Part 2	Co 15297-D
146853-	Little Red Caboose (Behind The Train)	Co unissued
146854-	Missouri Joe	Co unissued

Columbia 15297-D as by **Bob Ferguson**.

Acc. unknown.
   New York, NY   Monday, August 27, 1928

46953-1,-2	The Girl That You Betrayed	Vi unissued
46954-1,-2	Skeeter And Bumble-Bee	Vi unissued

Bob Kackley: Bob Miller, v; acc. unknown.
   New York, NY   Friday, September 28, 1928

8213-	Sweet Little Old Lady	ARC unissued
8214-	The Girl That You Betrayed	ARC unissued

The Hinky Dinkers: no details, but prob. similar to next session.
   New York, NY   Wednesday, May 29, 1929

8783-	Duck Foot Sue	ARC unissued
8784-	Hurry Johnny Hurry	ARC unissued

Bob Miller Trio: unknown, h-1; Bob Miller, p/v; prob. Barney Burnett, bj; unknown, g; unknown, jh; unknown, eff.
   New York, NY   Thursday, May 30, 1929

E-30007	Hurry Johnnie Hurry -1	Br 4431, BrAu 4431
E-30008	Duck Foot Sue	Br 4431, BrAu 4431

Australian Brunswick 4431 as by **Bob Miller & His Hinky Hinkers**.
Barney Burnett could play both banjo and guitar and, on this and subsequent sessions where both are heard, may play either – or sometimes, by doubling, both.

Miller's Bullfrog Tutters: Bob Miller, p/v; prob. Barney Burnett, bj/v; unknown, g; unknown, jh; unknown, eff-1.
   New York, NY   Monday, June 3, 1929

402414-	Hurry, Johnny, Hurry	OK 45348, Ve 2357-V, Cl 5291-C
402415-B	Duck Foot Sue -1	OK 45348, 45541, Ve 2356-V, Cl 5290-C

OKeh 45541 as by **Miller & Burnett**. Velvet Tone 2356-V, 2357-V, Clarion 5290-C, 5291-C as by **Sherman & Lee**. Velvet Tone 2356-V, Clarion 5290-C use the transfer matrix 100511; Velvet Tone 2357-V, Clarion 5291-C use the transfer matrix 100514.

Bob Miller & His Hinky Dinkers: no details.
   New York, NY   Monday, July 1, 1929

E-30092	Missouri Joe	Br rejected
E-30093	Missouri Mule	Br rejected

Bob Ferguson & His Scalawaggers: Bob Miller, p/v; prob. Barney Burnett, bj/v; unknown, g; unknown, jh.

New York, NY		Wednesday, July 3, 1929
148779-2	Keep On Keepin' On	Co 15433-D
148780-1	Toodle Lolly Day	Co 15433-D

Miller's Bullfrog Entertainers: Bob Miller, p/v/sp; Barney Burnett, bj/v/sp; Charlotte Miller, v/sp; unknown, g; unknown, jh; unknown, eff.

New York, NY		Friday, July 5, 1929
402493-A	Jennie's Strawberry Festival – Part 1	OK 45358, PaE R1218
402494-B	Jennie's Strawberry Festival – Part 2	OK 45358, PaE R1218

Parlophone R1218, subtitled *"Music of All Nations Series, No. 9 & 10"*, as by **Bob Miller's Bull Frog Entertainers**; matrices 402493/94 are titled *A Hill-Billy Party/Jennie's Strawberry Feast Parts 1 & 2* on that issue.

Bob Miller & His Hinky Dinkers: Bob Miller, p/v/sp; Barney Burnett, bj/v/sp; Charlotte Miller, v/sp; unknown, g; unknown, jh; unknown, eff.

New York, NY		Wednesday, July 10, 1929
E-30332	Jenny's Strawberry Festival – Part 1	Br 4494
E-30333	Jenny's Strawberry Festival – Part 2	Br 4494

Bob Ferguson & His Scalawaggers: Bob Miller, p/v/sp; prob. Barney Burnett, bj/v/sp; unknown, harp-1; unknown, eff-2.

New York, NY		Monday, July 22, 1929
148832-1	Golden Wings -1	Co 15529-D
148833-2	Missouri Joe -2	Co 15529-D

Bob Miller, v; acc. unknown.

New York, NY		Thursday, August 1, 1929
E-30425	Those Campaign Lyin' Sugar Coated Ballot-Coaxin' Farm Relief Blues	Br rejected
E-30426	The Dry Votin', Wet Drinkin' Better-Than-Thou Hypocritical Blues	Br rejected

These items were remade as matrices E-30519/20 with abbreviated titles and altered artist credit (see below).

Bob Miller & His Hinky Dinkers: Bob Miller, p/v; prob. Barney Burnett, bj-1/v; unknown, g-2; unknown, harp-3; unknown, sp-4.

New York, NY		Friday, August 2, 1929
E-30431	When I Put On My Long White Robe -1, 2	Br 4553, BrAu 4553
E-30432	Golden Wings -3, 4	Br 4553, BrAu 4553

No details.

New York, NY		Monday, August 12, 1929
E-30433	Missouri Mule	Br rejected
E-30434	Missouri Joe	Br rejected

Bill Barnes & Joey Ray: Bob Miller, Barney Burnett, v duet; acc. Bob Miller, p; Barney Burnett, bj; unknown, train-wh eff-1.

New York, NY		August/September 1929
3638-A	'Leven Cent Cotton	GG/Rad 4276, VD 74276, Sr 33027
3639-B	Duck Foot Sue -1	GG/Rad 4277, VD 74277, 5071, Mad 5071, Bellbird 135

Van Dyke 74276, 74277 as by **Bob Miller & Barney Burnett**. Van Dyke 5071 as by **Joe Adams & James Clark**. Madison 5071 as by **Smith & James**. Sunrise 33027 as by **Ben Burd & Bill White**.
Revs: Grey Gull/Radiex 4276, 4277, Van Dyke 74276, 74277 by Chezz Chase; Sunrise 33027 untraced.

Bob Miller & His Hinky Dinkers: prob.: Bob Miller, p/v; Barney Burnett, bj/v; unknown, g; Charlotte Miller, v.

New York, NY		Sunday, September 1, 1929
E-30519	Farm Relief Blues	Br 4529, BrAu 4529
E-30520	Dry Votin' Wet Drinkers	Br 4529, BrAu 4529

Matrices E-30519/20 are dated August 1 in Brunswick files, probably in error for September 1.

Miller's Bullfrog Entertainers: Bob Miller, p/v; prob. Barney Burnett, bj/v; unknown, jh; unknown, eff.

New York, NY		Monday, September 16, 1929
402951-C	Missouri Joe	OK 45386, Ve 2357-V, Cl 5291-C
402952-B	Missouri Mule	OK 45386, Ve 2356-V, Cl 5290-C, PaE R1154

Velvet Tone 2356-V, 2357-V, Clarion 5290-C, 5291-C as by **Sherman & Lee**. Parlophone R1154 as by **Bob Miller Trio**.
Velvet Tone 2356-V, Clarion 5290-C use the transfer matrix 100512; Velvet Tone 2357-V, Clarion 5291-C use the transfer matrix 100513.

Bob Ferguson & His Scalawaggers: Bob Miller, p/v; prob. Barney Burnett, g/v-1; unknown, g-2.

New York, NY		Monday, October 21, 1929
149161-2	The Farmers Letter To The President -2	Co 15476-D
149162-2	Dry Votin' Wet Drinkers -1	Co 15476-D

Bob Miller & His Hinky Dinkers: Bob Miller, p/v; prob. Barney Burnett, g; unknown, g-1; unknown, jh-1; unknown, v duet-1.

 New York, NY   Wednesday, October 23, 1929

 E-31294   Keep On, Keepin' On -1   Br 4636
 E-31295-A   The Farmer's Letter To The President   Br 4636, Spt S2060

Bill Barnes & Joey Ray: Bob Miller, v; acc. unknown, f; own p; Barney Burnett, g; unknown, train-wh eff-1.

 New York, NY   November/December 1929

 3753-B   Little Red Caboose -1   GG/Rad 4286, VD 74286, 5012, Mad 5012,
                        50012, Sr 33038, Bellbird 135
 3754-A   The Farmer's Letter To The President   GG/Rad 4286, VD 74286, Bellbird 136

Van Dyke 74286 as **Bob Miller & Barney Burnett**. Van Dyke/Madison 5012, Madison 50012 as by **Dick Baker**. Sunrise 33038 as by **Ben Burd & Bill White**.
Madison 50012 has also been reported as 10012.
Matrix 3753 may be titled *The Little Red Caboose (Behind The Train)* on some issues.
Some issues of matrix 3753 use the control 130-B.
Revs: Bellbird 136 by Chezz Chase; Sunrise 33038 untraced.

Joe Adams & James Clark: Bob Miller, Barney Burnett, v duet; acc. unknown, f; Bob Miller, p; Barney Burnett, g-1; several unknowns, sp-2.

 New York, NY   c. November/December 1929

 203-A; 212   Dry Voters And Wet Drinkers -2   VD/Mad 5028, Mad 50028
 205-B; 3945-B   Twenty-One Years -1   VD/Mad 5076
 216-A   Farm Relief Blues -1   Rad/VD/Mad 5044, Mad 50044
 217-A   'Leven Cent Cotton And Forty Cent Meat -1 Rad/VD/Mad 5044, Mad 50044

It is uncertain whether the above items were recorded, as shown, at a single session, and even whether the matrices are genuine matrices at all, rather than controls. Some of these items may prove to be identical to similarly-titled items on Grey Gull/Radiex/Van Dyke (see surrounding sessions), but matrix 203, for example, is not.

Barney Burnett, v/y; acc. **Bob Miller's Hinky Dinkers**: unknown, f; unknown, h; two unknowns, gazoom; Barney Burnett, bj/g; unknown, wh; unknown, train-wh eff.

 New York, NY   Thursday, December 19, 1929

 E-31680   The Little Red Caboose Behind The Train   Br 466, Spt S2074

Rev. Supertone S2074 by Kanawha Singers.

Bill Baker, v; acc. **Bob Miller's Hinky Dinkers**: two unknowns, gazoom-1; Bill Baker, g; unknown, v duet-2; unknown, eff-3.

 New York, NY   Thursday, December 19, 1929

 E-31681   The Wild And Reckless Hobo -1, 3   Br 445, Spt S2059
 E-31682   In The Hills Of Arkansas -2   Br 446
 E-31683-A   Hard Times In Arkansas -1   Br 445, Spt S2060

Rev. Supertone S2059 by Charlie Craver.

Bob Miller & His Hinky Dinkers: unknown, f; poss. Almoth Hodges, h/sp; unknown, gazoom; poss. Bill Baker, g/sp; one or two unknowns, sp.

 New York, NY   Friday, December 20, 1929

 E-31734   Practice Night At Chicken Bristle – Part I   Br 404, Spt S2085
 E-31735   Practice Night At Chicken Bristle – Part II   Br 404, Spt S2085

Almoth Hodges, v; acc. **Bob Miller's Hinky Dinkers**: unknown, f; poss. Almoth Hodges, h; poss. Bill Baker, g.

 New York, NY   Friday, December 20, 1929

 E-31736   The Hobo From The T & P Line – Part I   Br 399, BrAu 399
 E-31737   The Hobo From The T & P Line – Part II   Br 399, BrAu 399

Australian Brunswick 399 as by **Hodges, Miller's Hinky Dinkers**. Matrices E-31736/37 are titled *The Hobo From T. & P. Line – Part 1/Part 2* on that issue.

Bob Miller & Barney Burnett, v/sp-1 duet; acc. Bob Miller, p; Barney Burnett, bj-2/g-3; unidentified, wh-1; unidentified, eff-1.

 New York, NY   January 1930

 3839-B   Missouri Joe -1, 2   GG/Rad/VD 4293, VD 84293, 5027, Mad 5027,
                        50027
 3840-B   Dry Voters And Wet Drinkers -3   GG/Rad 4292, VD 84292

Van Dyke 4293, 5027, Madison 5027, 50027 as by **Joe Adams & James Clark**.
Revs: Grey Gull/Radiex 4292, 4293, Van Dyke 84292, 84293 by Jack Weston; Van Dyke/Madison 5027, Madison 50027 by Al Bernard.

Bob Ferguson & His Scalawaggers: unknown, t; unknown, k; Bob Miller, p/v-1; prob. Barney Burnett, g/prob. y-2; prob. Bill Baker, v-3.

 New York, NY   Friday, January 31, 1930

| 149947-2 | Wild And Reckless Hobo -3 | Co 15616-D |
| 149948-3 | Little Red Caboose -1, 2 | Co 15616-D |

Miller & Burnett, v duet; acc. unknown, f-1; unknown, gazoom-2; Bob Miller, p; Barney Burnett, bj-3/g-4.
New York, NY   c. March 24, 1930
GEX-2641-A	Long White Robe -2, 3	Ge 7220, Ch 15985, 45081, Spr 2764
GEX-2642-A	Twenty-One Years -1, 4	Ge 7220, Ch 15985, 45081, Spr 2764, MW 4964
GEX-2643-A	Missouri Joe -2, 3	Ge 7164, Ch 15963, 33054

Superior 2764 as by **Burnett & Miller**.
Revs: Champion 33054 by Gene Autry; Montgomery Ward 4964 by Jackson County Barn Owls.

Charlotte Miller, v; acc. unknown (prob. similar to that above).
New York, NY   c. March 24, 1930
| GEX-2644 | Dangerous Nan McGrew | Ge 7164, Ch 15963, 33069 |

Bob Miller, v; acc. unknown, f; own p; Barney Burnett, bj-1/g-2/v; prob. Charlotte Miller, v.
New York, NY   March 1930
| 3944-A | Long White Robe -1 | GG 4300, 5072, Rad 4300, VD 84300, 5072, Mad 5072 |
| 3945-B | Twenty-One Years -2 | GG/Rad 4300, VD 84300, 5076, Mad 5076 |

Grey Gull/Van Dyke/Madison 5072, Van Dyke/Madison 5076 as by **Joe Adams & James Clark**.
See note on Van Dyke/Madison session of c. November/December 1929.
Revs: Grey Gull/Van Dyke/Madison 5072 by The Virginians (see B&GR); Van Dyke/Madison 5076 by Frank Luther (see Carson Robison).

Charlotte & Bob Miller: no details.
New York, NY   March/April 1930
| 3975-C | Dangerous Nan McGrew | GG/Rad 4305, VD 84305 |
| 3976-B | Poker Alice | GG/Rad 4305, VD 84305 |

Charlotte Miller & Bob Ferguson, v/sp duet; acc. unknown, f; unknown, k-1; Bob Miller, p; prob. Barney Burnett, g/v.
New York, NY   Wednesday, April 16, 1930
| 150471-2 | Poker Alice -1 | Co 15558-D |
| 150472-2 | Dangerous Nan McGrew | Co 15558-D |

Bob Ferguson & His Scalawaggers: unknown, f; Bob Miller, p/v/sp; prob. Barney Burnett, g/sp; unknown, sp-1; unknown, telephone eff-2.
New York, NY   Wednesday, April 16, 1930
| 150473-2 | They're Hanging Old Jonesy Tomorrow -1 | Co 15553-D |
| 150474-2 | Prisoner's Letter To The Governor -2 | Co 15553-D |

Miller & Miller: Bob Miller, Charlotte Miller, v duet; or **Miller & Burnett**-1: Bob Miller, Barney Burnett, v duet; acc. unknown, f; Bob Miller, p; Barney Burnett, g; unknown, vc.
New York, NY   Thursday, April 24 or Friday, April 25, 1930
| 403981-C | The Ohio Prison Fire | OK 45442 |
| 403982-B | Twenty One Years -1 | OK 45442, 45541, PaE R1154 |

Charlotte & Bob Miller, v/sp duet; acc. unknown, f; Bob Miller, p-1; Barney Burnett, g/v-2; unknown, bell-3.
New York, NY   c. April 29, 1930
| GEX-2689-B | The Ohio Prison Fire | Ge 7201, Ch 16008 |
| GEX-2690-C | Poker Alice -1, 2, 3 | Ge 7201, Ch 16008, 33069 |

Matrix GEX-2689 was remade as matrix GEX-2696 (see below); both versions are believed to have been issued.

Bob Miller, v; or **Charlotte & Bob Miller**-1, v duet; acc. two unknowns, f; Bob Miller, p; Barney Burnett, g; several unknown men, sp-2; two unknown men, sp-3.
New York, NY   April/May 1930
4038-A	The Ohio Prison Fire -1	GG/Rad 4311, VD 84311, 5111
4039-B	They're Hanging Old Jonesy Tomorrow -2	GG/Rad 4315, VD 84315, 5075, Mad 5075
4040-B	The Prisoner's Letter To The Governor -3	GG/Rad 4314, VD 84314, 5071, Mad 5071
4041-B	Little Red Lantern	GG/Rad 4316, VD 84316, 5112
4042-B	Captain Dan's Last Trip -1	VD 5111

Grey Gull/Radiex 4311 as by **Bill & Charlotte Barnes**. Van Dyke/Madison 5071, 5075 as by **Joe Adams**.
Revs: Grey Gull/Radiex 4311 by Frank Luther; 4314, Van Dyke 84314 by Gene Autry; 4315, Van Dyke 84315 by Al Bernard (popular); 4316 by Steve Porter (popular); Van Dyke 84316 by Floyd Reeves (popular); Van Dyke/Madison 5075 by Jerry White (popular); Van Dyke 5112 by Frank Luther (see Carson Robison).

Charlotte Miller, v; acc. **Bob Miller & His Hinky Dinkers**: unknown, f; Bob Miller, p; prob. Barney Burnett, g.
New York, NY   Monday, May 19, 1930
| E-32805 | Dangerous Nan McGrew | Br 428, BrE 1156 |

Bob Miller & His Hinky Dinkers: unknown, f; Bob Miller, p/v/sp; prob. Barney Burnett, g/sp; prob. another man, sp.

New York, NY   Monday, May 19, 1930
E-32806	They're Hanging Old Jonesy Tomorrow	Br 428, BrE 1156
E-32807	Five Cent Glass Of Beer	Br unissued trial recording
E-32808	Page Mister Volstead	Br unissued trial recording

Bob Miller, v; acc. unknown, f; own p; prob. Barney Burnett, g; two unidentifieds, sp-1.
New York, NY   c. May 20, 1930
GEX-2694-A	Five Cent Glass Of Beer -1	Ge 7239, Ch 16024
GEX-2695-B	Page Mr. Volstead	Ge 7239, Ch 16024
GEX-2696-	The Ohio Prison Fire	Ge 7201, Ch 16008

Regarding matrix GEX-2696, see c. April 29, 1930 session.

Bob Miller & His Hinky Dinkers: no details.
New York, NY   Tuesday, July 15, 1930
| E-33432 | Chain Store Blues – Part 1 | Br rejected |
| E-33433 | Chain Store Blues – Part 2 | Br rejected |

Bob Miller, v; acc. unknown, f; prob. Barney Burnett, g.
New York NY   Thursday, August 28, 1930
| 404386-B | Four Cent Tobacco And Forty Cent Meat | OK 45475 |
| 404387-C | Little Cotton Mill Girl | OK 45475 |

Acc. unknown, f; poss. Frank Novak, cl-1/s-1; unknown, ac; prob. own p; prob. Barney Burnett, g; unknown, v duet-2.
New York, NY   Tuesday, November 11, 1930
| 404541-A | Nebuchudneezer | OK 45495 |
| 404542-B | Pretzels -1, 2 | OK 45495 |

Acc. unknown, f; prob. Frank Novak, cl/bscl-1/bss-1; unknown, ac; prob. Barney Burnett, g; unknown, v duet-2.
New York, NY   Thursday, November 13, 1930
| E-35254 | Nebuchadneezar | Me M12033 |
| E-35255 | Pretzels -1, 2 | Me M12033 |

Bob Ferguson & His Scalawaggers: Bob Miller, p/v; prob. Benny Nawahi, sg; unknown, g.
New York, NY   Wednesday, February 25, 1931
| 151351-3 | 1930 Drought | Co 15664-D |
| 151352-3 | Bank Failures | Co 15664-D |

Bob Miller, v; acc. prob. Benny Nawahi, sg; two unknowns, g.
New York, NY   Monday, March 9, 1931
| E-36289-A,B | Bank Failures | Br rejected |
| E-36291 | Corn Pone And Pot Licker Crumbled Or Dunked | Br 529 |

Matrix E-36290 is an unrelated trial recording.

Bob Ferguson & Charlotte Miller, v/sp duet; acc. prob. Benny Nawahi, sg; unknown, g.
New York, NY   Monday, March 9, 1931
| 151409-3 | Corn Pone And Pot Likker (Crumbled Or Dunked) – Part 1 | Co 15657-D |
| 151410-3 | Corn Pone And Pot Likker (Crumbled Or Dunked) – Part 2 | Co 15657-D |

Bob Miller, v; acc. unknown, f; prob. Barney Burnett, g.
New York, NY   Monday, March 23, 1931
| E-36268 | I Took My Time Agoin' (But, Oh! How I Hurried Back) | Br 529 |

Bob Sherman-1/Bob Kackley & Ben Weaver-2/Bob Kackley-3/Bob Ferguson-4: Bob Miller, v; or Bob Miller, Barney Burnett, v duet-5; acc. Bob Miller, p; Barney Burnett, g.
New York, NY   Wednesday, May 20, 1931
365009-2	Little Sweetheart Of The Prairie -1, 5	Ve 2400-V, Cl 5336-C
404920-B	Little Sweetheart Of The Prairie -2, 5	OK 45531
365010-2	The Strawberry Roan -1	Ve 2400-V, Cl 5336-C
404921-B	The Strawberry Roan -3	OK 45531
151557-1	The Strawberry Roan -4	Co 15677-D

Matrices 365009/10 were logged as by **Bob Ferguson** but issued as shown.
Despite the different matrices, all recordings of each title are believed to be identical.
Rev. Columbia 15677-D by Cartwright Brothers.

Bob Ferguson, v; acc. unknown, g.
New York, NY   Wednesday, July 15, 1931
| 151686-1 | Clover Blossoms | Co 15704-D |
| 151687-1 | Anna-May | Co 15704-D |

Acc. unknown.
   New York, NY   Tuesday, December 1, 1931
     151895-   The Pardon Of Tom Mooney   Co unissued
     151896-   Sweet Pal   Co unissued

Bob Ferguson & His Scalawaggers: unknown, f; Bob Miller, p/v; prob. Barney Burnett, g.
   New York, NY   Tuesday, December 1, 1931
     151897-2   The Crime Of Harry Powers   Co 15727-D

Uncle Bud & His Plow Boys: unknown, f; Bob Miller, p/v.
   New York, NY   Tuesday, December 1, 1931
     365042-2   Twenty-One Years   Ve 2478-V, Cl 5418-C
     365043-2   What Does The Deep Sea Say   Ve 2478-V, Cl 5418-C, Co 15727-D

Columbia 15727-D as by **Bob Ferguson & His Scalawaggers**.

Bob Ferguson & His Scalawaggers: Bob Miller, cel/v; unknown, g.
   New York, NY   Thursday, December 10, 1931
     152039-1   The Unmarked Grave   Co 15732-D

Bob Stuckeley: Bob Miller, v; acc. unknown, f; own p; unknown, g.
   New York, NY   Thursday, December 10, 1931
     365046-   Crime Of Harry Powers   Ve/Cl unissued
     365047-1   The Unmarked Grave   Ve 2504-V, Cl 5444-C

Matrices 365046/47 were logged as by **Bob Stukeley** but matrix 365047 was issued as shown.

Bob Stukeley & Ben Weaver: prob. Bob Miller, Barney Burnett, v duet; acc. unknown, f; Bob Miller, p.
   New York, NY   Friday, December 18, 1931
     365052-   The Death Of Jack "Legs" Diamond   Ve/Cl unissued

Bob Ferguson & His Scalawaggers: prob.: unknown, f; Bob Miller, p/v.
   New York, NY   prob. December 18, 1931
     152050-   The Death Of Jack "Legs" Diamond   Co unissued

Bob Stukeley & Ben Weaver: prob. Bob Miller, Barney Burnett, v duet; acc. unknown, f; Bob Miller, p.
   New York, NY   Wednesday, December 23, 1931
     365052-3   The Death Of Jack "Legs" Diamond   Ve 2504-V, Cl 5444-C

Bob Ferguson & His Scalawaggers: unknown, f; Bob Miller, p/v.
   New York NY   prob. December 23, 1931
     152050-4   The Death Of Jack "Legs" Diamond   Co 15732-D

Memphis Bob, v; acc. unknown, f; own p.
   New York, NY   Thursday, December 31, 1931
     152055-1   Little Marian McLean   Co 15735-D
     152056-1   Beyond Prison Walls   Co 15735-D

Bob Ferguson & His Scalawaggers: unknown, f; Bob Miller, p/v.
   New York, NY   Wednesday, January 20, 1932
     152084-1   "New" Twenty-One Years   Co 15739-D
     152085-3   Fifty Years Repentin'   Co 15739-D

Bud Skidmore: poss. Bob Miller, v; acc. unknown, cl; unknown, g.
   New York, NY   Wednesday, May 4, 1932
     152183-1   Behind The Big White House   Co 15761-D

The Shelby Singers: Bob Miller, two unknowns, v trio; acc. unknown, ac; Bob Miller, cel; unknown, g-1.
   New York, NY   Wednesday, May 4, 1932
     152184-1   Nobody To Love -1   Co 15760-D
     152185-1   The Voice In The Old Village Choir   Co 15760-D

Matrices 152184/85 were originally logged as by **Bob Ferguson & His Scalawaggers** but issued as shown.

Bud Skidmore: poss. Bob Miller, v; acc. unknown, ac; unknown, g.
   New York, NY   Wednesday, May 4, 1932
     152186-1   The Sad Song   Co 15761-D

Bob Ferguson, v; acc. unknown, f; unknown, g.
   New York, NY   Friday, May 13, 1932
     152197-1   Charles A. Lindbergh, Jr.   Co 15759-D
     152198-1   There's A New Star Up In Heaven (Baby Lindy Is Up There)   Co 15759-D

Bob Miller, v; acc. prob. Barney Burnett, g; unknown, g.
   New York, NY   Thursday, June 9, 1932

72858-1	Little Red Caboose Behind The Train	Vi 23693, MW M-4337
72859-1	The Mule Song (Missouri Mule)	Vi 23697, MW M-4234
72860-1	In The Hills Of Arkansas	Vi 23723
72861-1	Twenty-One Years – Part 2	Vi 23693, MW M-4235
72862-1	Things That Might Have Been	Vi 23697, MW M-4237
72863-1	Song Of The Brown Family	Vi 23704

Victor 23697, 23704 as by **Bob Ferguson**, 23723 as by **Bill Palmer**.
Revs: Victor 23704 by "Mac" (Harry McClintock); Montgomery Ward M-4337 by Jim Baird.

Acc. prob. Barney Burnett, g/v-1; unknown, g/v-1.
New York, NY   Thursday, July 28, 1932

73136-1	The Rich Man And The Poor Man	Vi 23719, MW M-4236
73137-1	The Poor Forgotten Man -1	Vi 23723
73138-1	The Big-Mouthed Elephant And The Long-Eared Mule	Vi 23712
73139-1	Keep On Keeping On -1	Vi 23715
73140-1	I Can't Go To The Poorhouse	Vi 23719, MW M-4236
73141-1	Five Cent Cotton	Vi unissued
73142-1	The Happy Warrior	Vi 23712
73143-1	He Was A Good Man (But He's Dead And Gone)	Vi 23718

Victor 23715 as by **Bob Ferguson**, 23718 as by **Bob Hill**, 23723 as by **Bill Palmer**.
Revs: Victor 23715 by Frank Luther, 23718 by Jimmie Davis.

Uncle Bud & His Plow Boys: unknown, h-1; prob. Barney Burnett, bj-2/g-3; unknown, g; Bob Miller, v.
New York, NY   Tuesday, August 9, 1932

12163-1	Five Cent Cotton -2	Ba 32588, Me M12516, Or 8170, Pe 12848, Ro 5170, Cq 8063
12164-2	Them Good Old Times -1, 2	Ba 32588, Me M12516, Or 8170, Pe 12848, Ro 5170, Cq 8063
12165-	He Was A Good Man (But He's Dead And Gone) -3	ARC unissued

Prob. Barney Burnett, bj-1/g-2; unknown, g; Bob Miller, v.
New York, NY   Wednesday, August 10, 1932

12168-	The Rich Man And The Poor Man -2	ARC unissued
12169-	I Can't Go To The Poorhouse -2	ARC unissued
12170-	Poor Forgotten Man -1	ARC unissued

Bud Thompson: Bob Miller, v; acc. Clayton McMichen, f; Oddie McWinders, bj; Slim Bryant, g.
New York, NY   Friday, August 26, 1932

1814-1	Singing An Old Hymn	Cr unissued

Miller's role on this take is deduced from a test pressing. The issued take 3 has a trio vocal by McMichen, McWinders, and Bryant (see Clayton McMichen).

Acc. Clayton McMichen, f; Oddie McWinders, bj; Slim Bryant, g; band v-1.
New York, NY   Tuesday, August 30, 1932

1829-1	Free Wheelin' Hobo	Vs 5075, Cont C-3016
1830-1	Countin' Cross Ties -1	Cr 3432, Htd 23097, Vs 5075
1833-1	Bummin' On The I.C. Line	Cr 3432, Htd 23097, Vs 5097
1841-1	Five Cent Cotton	Cr 3418, Htd 23099, Vs 5122

Varsity 5075, Continental C-3016 as by **Clayton McMichen & Georgia Wildcats**; Varsity 5097 as by **Clayton McMichen**, 5122 as by **Bob's Boys**.
Matrix 1841 is titled *Eleven Cent Cotton, Forty Cent Meat* on Varsity 5122.
Intervening matrices are by Clayton McMichen.
Revs: Crown 3418, Homestead 23099, Varsity 5097 by Clayton McMichen.

Bob Miller–Barney Burnett, v duet; or Bob Miller, v-1; acc. Frank Novak, f-2/ac-3; poss. Barney Burnett, g.
New York, NY   Friday, September 16, 1932

73508-1	Singing An Old Hymn -3	BB 1827, B-5013, Eld 1907, Sr S-3113, MW M-4401
73509-1	Singing An Old Hymn -1, 3	Vi 23727
73510-1	Free Wheelin' Hobo -1, 3	BB 1824, B-5010, Eld 1908, Sr S-3110
73511-1	Baby, Please Come Back -1, 2	BB 1823, B-5009, Eld 1908, Sr S-3109, MW M-4233
73512-1	Baby, Please Come Back -3	Vi 23730
73513-1	Countin' Cross Ties -3	Eld 1917
73514-1	Countin' Cross Ties -3	Vi 23730, BB 1824, B-5010, Sr S-3110
73515-1	Yazoo Red -1, 3	El 1917, MW M-4232
73516-1	New Twenty-One Years -1, 2	BB 1827, B-5013, Eld 1907, Sr S-3113, MW M-4233

73517-1	From Cradle Bars To Prison Bars -3	Vi 23733, MW M-4237
73518-1	Prisoner No. 999 -1, 2	Vi 23733, MW M-4306
73519-1	Old Shoes A-Draggin' -1, 3	Vi 23727

Victor 23727, 23730 as by **Burnett Brothers**. Bluebird 1823, 1824, B-5009, B-5010, Electradisk 1908, 1917, Sunrise S-3109, S-3110 as by **Bill Palmer**. Bluebird 1827, B-5013, Sunrise S-3113 as by **Palmer Trio**. Montgomery Ward M-4232, M-4306 as by **Bob Miller**, M-4233 as by **Bob Miller** (matrix 73511)/**Bob Miller Trio** (matrix 73516).
Matrix 73511 is titled *Baby Please Come Back* on Electradisk 1908.
Rev. Montgomery Ward M-4306 by Frank Luther.

Bill Palmer's Trio: Bob Miller, p-1/v; Barney Burnett, bj/v-2; A. Sirillo, g.
New York, NY   Thursday, November 3, 1932

73910-1	Duck Foot Sue -1	Vi 23742
73911-1	Duck Foot Sue -1	BB 1825, B-5011, Eld 1938, Sr S-3111
73912-1	Rockin' Alone (In An Old Rockin' Chair) -1, 2	Vi 23745
73913-1	Rockin' Alone (In An Old Rockin' Chair) -1, 2	Eld 1937
73914-1	Seven Years (With The Wrong Woman) -1	Vi 23745
73915-1	What Does The Deep Sea Say? -1, 2	Vi 23747
73916-1	When The Mellow Moon Is Shining -2	Vi 23743
73917-1	Hurry, Johnny, Hurry -1	Vi 23742
73918-1	Seven Years (With The Wrong Woman) -1, 2	BB B-5034, Eld 1919, Sr S-3132, MW M-4232
73919-1	What Does The Deep Sea Say? -1, 2	BB B-5034, Eld 1919, Sr S-3132, MW M-4401
73920-1	When The Mellow Moon Is Shining -1, 2	Eld 1937, MW M-4235
73921-1	Hurry, Johnny, Hurry -1	Eld 1938

Victor 23743, 23745 as by **Burnett Bros.**, 23747 as by **Bob Miller Trio**. Montgomery Ward M-4232, M-4235, M-4401 as by **Bob Miller Trio**, except the first pressing (with red-and-yellow label) of M-4235 as by **Burnett Bros**.
Revs: Victor 23743 by Graham Brothers, 23747 by Kelly Harrell.

Barney Burnett's Trio: Barney Burnett, Bob Miller, unknown, v trio; or **Bud Thompson**-1: Bob Miller, v; acc. Barney Burnett, g; unknown, g.
New York, NY   Friday, December 23, 1932

1940-1	Keep On Keeping On	Cr 3460, Vs 5139, Cont C-8002
1941-1	In The Hills Of Arkansas	Cr 3446, Vs 5121, Cont C-3016
1942-1	Don't Forget Me Little Darling	Cr 3446, MW M3013, Vs 5018, 5145, Cont C-3014
1943-1	Walking The Last Mile -1	Cr 3430, Vs 5134, Cont C-8000
1944-2	I'm A Fugitive From A Chain Gang -1	Cr 3430, Vs 5134, Cont C-8000
1945-2	Behind The Big White House	Cr 3460, Vs 5017
1946-	Free Wheeling Hobo	Vs 5139

Montgomery Ward M3013 as by **Bob Miller & His Boys**. Varsity 5017 as by **Back Home Boys**, 5018 as by **Hal Monroe**, 5121 as by **Bob's Boys**, 5134 as by **Bob Miller**, 5139, 5145 as by **Bob Miller Boys**. Continental C-3014 as by **Hal Monroe**, C-3016 as by **Bob's Boys**, C-8000 as by **Bob Miller**, C-8002 as by **Bob Miller Boys**.
Matrix 1941 is titled *Hills Of Arkansas* on Varsity 5121, Continental C-3016.
Matrix 1942 is titled *Don't Forget Me, Little Darling* on Varsity 5018.
Matrix 1943 is titled *Walking That Last Mile* on Continental C-8000.
Matrix 1944 is titled *Fugitive From A Chain Gang* on Varsity 5134, Continental C-8000.
Matrix 1945 is titled *The Little White House Behind The Big White House* on Varsity 5017.
Rev. Continental C-3014 by Frank Luther & Carson Robison (see the latter).

Bob Miller Trio: Bob Miller, p-1/cel-2/v-3; A. Sirillo, bj/v-4; Barney Burnett, g/v-5; unknown, g-6; Jack Erickson, v-7; unidentified (poss. Burnett), humming-8.
New York, NY   Thursday, December 29, 1932

74741-1	Taking Those Last Steps -3	Vi 23768, MW M-4231
74742-1	Beatrice Snipes -1, 3	Vi 23768
74743-1	The Prisoner's Letter To The Governor -3	Vi 23775, MW M-4231
74744-1	Down By The Old Rustic Well -1, 2, 4, 5, 7, 8	Vi 23770
74745-1	A Fugitive From A Chain Gang -7	Vi 23770
74746-1	Don't Forget Me, Little Darling -1, 3	Vi 23775
74747-1	Down By The Old Rustic Well -1, 4, 5, 7	MW M-4323
74748-1	Taking Those Last Steps -3, 6	Eld 1940
74749-1	They're Hanging Old Jonesy Tomorrow -3, 6	BB 1825, B-5011, Eld 1940, Sr S-3111
74750-1	Good Old Beer -1, 3	BB 1826, B-5012, Sr S-3112, MW M-4234
74751-1	The House Where Love Had Died -1, 3	Eld 1947
74752-1	Don't Forget Me, Little Darling -1, 3	Eld 1947

Victor 23768 as by **Bob Miller**, 23770 as by **Jack Erickson**. All issues of matrix 74749 as by **Bob Burnett**. Bluebird 1826, B-5012 as by **Bill Palmer**. Electradisk 1947 as by **Bill Palmer Trio**. Sunrise S-3112 as by **Slick Palmer**. Montgomery Ward M-4231 as by **Bob Miller** (matrix 74741)/**Bob Miller Trio** (matrix 74743), M-4323 as by **Jack Erickson**.
Revs: Bluebird B-1826, B-5012, Sunrise S-3112 by Dwight Butcher; Montgomery Ward M-4323 by Carter Family.

Bob Ferguson, v; acc. unknown, f; unknown, g.
   New York, NY   Wednesday, April 5, 1933
   152386-2   The Crash Of The Akron   Co 15782-D
Rev. Columbia 15782-D by Columbia Band (popular).

Barney Burnett's Trio: Bob Miller, Barney Burnett, unknown, v trio; or **Bud Thompson**-1: Bob Miller, v; acc. unknown, f; Bob Miller, cel-2; Barney Burnett, g/humming-3.
   New York, NY   Tuesday, April 25, 1933
   2045-2   When The Wild, Wild Roses Bloom -2   Cr 3488, *MW M3014*, *Vs 5027*
   2046-2   When The White Azaleas Start Blooming -1, 3   Cr 3502, *MW M3014*, *Vs 5027*
   2047-2   Little Mother Of The Hills -2   Cr 3488, *MW M3015*, *Vs 5037*
   2048-2   The House Where Love Has Died -1   Cr 3503, *Vs 5145*
   2049-1   The Lie He Wrote Home -1   Cr 3489, *Vs 5069*
   2050-1   My Valley Of Memories -3   Cr 3502, *Vs 5069*
   2051-1   Rockin' Alone (In An Old Rocking Chair) -1   Cr 3489, *MW M3013*, *Vs 5018*

Montgomery Ward M3013, M3014, M3015 as by **Bob Miller & Boys**. Varsity 5018 as by **Hal Monroe**, 5027, 5037 as by **Hal Monroe Trio**, 5069 as by **Bob Miller Trio**, 5145 as by **Bob Miller Boys**.
Matrix 2045 is titled *When The Wild Wild Roses Bloom* on Montgomery Ward M3014, Varsity 5027. Matrix 2051 is titled *Rocking Along In An Old Rocking Chair* on Varsity 5018.
Revs: Crown 3503 by Dwight Butcher; Montgomery Ward M3015 (with same credit), Varsity 5037 by Edward L. Crain.

Barney Burnett's Trio: Bob Miller, Barney Burnett, v duet; or **Bud Thompson**-1: Bob Miller, v; acc. unknown, f; Barney Burnett, g.
   New York, NY   Thursday, June 22, 1933
   2113-1   In The Little White Church On The Hill   Cr 3513, *Vs 5093*
   2114-1   Every Sunday Night Back Home   Cr 3513, *Vs 5017*
   2115-1   When I Take My Vacation In Heaven   Cr 3515, *MW M3012*, *Vs 5007*
   2116-1   Way Up There   Cr 3515, *MW M3012*, *Vs 5007*
   2117-1   Little Old Sweet Lady -1   Cr 3530, *Vs 5093*
   2118-1   Where The Ozarks Kiss The Sky -1   *Vs 5104*
   2119-1   Colorado Trail -1   *Vs 5104*
   2120-1   All The Glory Is Gone -1   Cr 3530

Montgomery Ward M3012 as by **Bob Miller & His Boys**. Varsity 5007 as by **Hal Monroe**, 5017 as by **Back Home Boys**, 5093 as by **The Miller Boys**, 5104 as by **Bob Miller**.
Matrix 2113 is titled *Little White Church On The Hill*, and matrix 2117 *Sweet Lady*, on Varsity 5093.

Bob Miller, Barney Burnett, unknown, v trio; or Bob Miller, v-1; acc. Barney Burnett, bj-2/g-3; unknown, g; unknown, bell-4.
   New York, NY   Monday, July 24, 1933
   2141-1   Shepherd Of The Air -3   Cr 3531, *Vs 5118*
   2142-1   When You Played The Organ -3, 4   *Vs 5118*
   2143-1   Where The Silvery Sea (Meets The Golden Shore) -3   *Vs 5121*, *Cont C-8002*
   2144-1   The Dying Girl -3   *Vs 5128*
   2145-1   Hurray Johnnie Hurray -2   *Vs 5111*, *Cont C-3018*, *C-8001*
   2146-1   Tell My Mother I'm In Heaven -1, 3   Cr 3531, *Vs 5110*, *5128*
   2147-1   A Hill Billy Wedding In June -1, 2   Cr 3532, *Vs 5111*, *Cont C-8001*
   2148-1   Keep A Light In Your Window Tonight -1, 3   Cr 3532, *Vs 5122*

Crown 3531 as by **Barney Burnett Trio** (matrix 2141)/**Bud Thompson** (matrix 2146), 3532 as by **Barney Burnett's Trio**. Varsity 5110 as by **Clayton McMichen**, 5111 as by **Bob Miller Trio**, 5118, 5121, 5122 as by **Bob's Boys**, 5128 as by **Bob Miller's Boys**. Cont C-8001 as by **Bob Miller Trio**, C-8002 as by **Bob's Boys**.
Matrix 2145 is titled *Hurry Johnnie Hurry* on Continental C-8001. Matrix 2147 is titled *Hill Billy Wedding* on Varsity 5111, or *Hillbilly Wedding* on Continental C-8001.
Rev. Varsity 5110 by Clayton McMichen.

Bob Miller, v; acc. own p; Elton Britt, g/v/y; Ezra Ford, v/y.
   New York, NY   Wednesday, June 20, 1934
   TO-1435-1,-2,-3   Take Me Home Boys   ARC unissued trial recording
Acc. unknown.
   New York, NY   Saturday, October 27, 1934
   TO-1472   Pretty Boy Floyd   ARC unissued trial recording

Floyd Carter: Bob Miller, v; acc. **Prairie Ramblers**: Tex Atchison, f; Chick Hurt, mandola; Salty Holmes, g; Jack Taylor, sb.
   New York, NY   Thursday, February 21, 1935
   16909-   The Flemington Kidnapping Trial   ARC unissued
   16910-1   Finger-Prints (Upon The Window Pane)   Ba 33378, Me M13345, MeC 91954, Or 8447,
                                                                                  Pe 13124, Ro 5447, Cq 8464

Conqueror 8464 as by **Bob Miller**. Matrix 16910 is titled *Finger Prints (Upon The Window Pane)* on that issue.

New York, NY Thursday, March 7, 1935
16909-4 The Flemington Kidnapping Trial Ba 33378, Me M13345, MeC 91954, Or 8447,
Pe 13124, Ro 5447, Cq 8464

Conqueror 8464 as by **Bob Miller**.
Bob Miller & His Trio: Bob Miller, v; unknown, v trio; acc. Prairie Ramblers: Tex Atchison, f; Chick Hurt, mandola; Salty Holmes, g; Jack Taylor, sb.
New York, NY Tuesday, March 26, 1935
17192-2 Long White Robe Cq 8489
17193-2 Down In The Old Home Town Cq 8490

Matrices 17192/93 were originally logged as by **Floyd Carter With Prairie Ramblers**.

Bob Miller, v; unknown, v trio-1; acc. Prairie Ramblers: Tex Atchison, f; Chick Hurt, mandola; Salty Holmes, g; Jack Taylor, sb; band sp-2.
New York, NY Wednesday, March 27, 1935
17194-1 The Woman Who Done Me Wrong -2 Cq 8489
17195-1 May Days And Grey Days -1 Cq 8490

Matrices 17194/95 were originally logged as by **Floyd Carter With Prairie Ramblers**.

Floyd Carter: Bob Miller, v; acc. unknown.
New York, NY Monday, April 8, 1935
17261- A Story Of A Dear Old Lady ARC unissued
17262- When I Dream Of My Red River Home ARC unissued
17263- The Brother Of Missouri Joe ARC unissued
17264- Down Where The Roses Go To Sleep ARC unissued
17265- Under The Old Umbrella ARC unissued
17266- When A Man Get's [sic] Over Sixty ARC unissued

Bob Miller, v; acc. unknown, g.
New York, NY Wednesday, August 21, 1935
TO-1574 Tragedy Of Will Rogers And Wiley Post ARC unissued trial recording
TO-1575 Wiley Wills [sic] Last Flight ARC unissued trial recording

Acc. unknown.
Chicago, IL Thursday, November 5, 1936
TI-21 Duchess Had The Duke For Dinner ARC unissued trial recording
TI-22 When It's Prayer-Time On The Prairie ARC unissued trial recording
TI-23 Wild And Woolly Willie ARC unissued trial recording
TI-24 There Are Just Two 'I's In Dixie ARC unissued trial recording
TI-25 Tears ARC unissued trial recording
TI-26 Who's Gonna Bite Your Ruby Lips ARC unissued trial recording
TI-27 Nobody's Business ARC unissued trial recording

Acc. unknown.
Chicago, IL Wednesday, February 17, 1937
TI-45 Mistook In The Woman I Found ARC unissued trial recording
TI-46 Trotting Along The Road ARC unissued trial recording

These are uncredited in ARC ledgers but seem likely to have been by Miller.

Acc. unknown.
Chicago, IL Friday, April 23, 1937
TI-50 Mistook In The Woman I Love ARC unissued trial recording
TI-51 Trottting Along The Road ARC unissued trial recording

Bob Miller supervised numerous other artists' ARC and Victor sessions, and sometimes played on them.

CHARLOTTE MILLER

See Bob Miller. (This artist, whose given name was Charlotte Thompson, was Bob Miller's first wife.)

DAVE MILLER

Silvertone 8154 and Supertone 9258 by David Miller were credited thus.

DAVEY MILLER

Conqueror 7839 and ARC-Broadway 8115 by David Miller were credited thus.

DAVID MILLER

David Miller, v; acc. Cecil Adkins, bj; own g.
Cincinnati, OH c. December 16, 1924
12104 Lonesome Valley Ge unissued

| 12105 | Little Old Log Cabin In The Lane | Ge 3062, Sil 4019, Her 75504 |

Silvertone 4019 as by **John Fergus**.
Revs: Gennett 3062, Silvertone 4019 by George Ake; Herwin 75504 by Vernon Dalhart.

Acc. own g.
Richmond, IN   May 1927

12790	That Bad Man Stacklee	Ge 6188, Ch 15334, Chg 327, Her 75561
12791	My Little Indian Napanee	Her 75564
12792	Two Little Orphans	Ge 6188, Ch 15317, Sil 5094, 8154, Spt 9258, Chg 326, Her 75558, Spr 384, Bell 1187
12793	Don't Forget Me Little Darling	Ge 6175, Ch 15298, Sil 5094, 8154, Spt 9258, Chg 326, Her 75558, Spr 384, Bell 1186
12794	The Lonesome Valley	Ge 6175, Ch 15317, Chg 327, Her 75557

Silvertone 8154, Supertone 9258 as by **Dave Miller**. Silvertone 5094 possibly as by **John Ferguson**. Challenge 326, 327 as by **Dan Kutter**. Herwins as by **Oran Campbell**. Bell 1186, 1187 as by **Godfrey Borton**.
Revs: Champion 15298 by Chubby Parker, 15334 by Holland Puckett; Herwin 75557 by Holland Puckett, 75561 by Ben Jarrell (see Da Costa Woltz's Southern Broadcasters), 75564 by Ray Covert; Bell 1186 by Aulton Ray (see Taylor's Kentucky Boys).

Richmond, IN   Friday, November 4, 1927

13200,-A	Don't Take My Darling Boy Away	Ge rejected
13201	Sweet Floetta	Ge 6333, Ch 15413, Chg 386, Spr 324
13202	Many Times With You I've Wandered	Ge 6333, Ch 15429
13203	A Little Child Shall Lead Them	Ge 6349, Ch 15413, Chg 395, Spr 324, Bell 1187
13204	Give My Love To Nellie, Jack	Ge 6388, Ch 15502, Chg 392, Spr 368, Bell 1177
13205	Down Where The Swanee River Flows	Ge 6388, Sil 5204, 8164, Spt 9259, Chg 395
13206,-A	My Little Girl	Ge rejected
13207	You'll Find Her With The Angels	Ge 6349, Ch 15429, Sil 5204, 8164, Spt 9259, Chg 386, Spr 368, Bell 1170
13208,-A	Uncle Sammy	Ge rejected

Champions as by **Oran Campbell**. Silvertone 5204, 8164, Supertone 9259 as by **John Ferguson**. Challenge 386, 392, 395 as by **Don Kutter**. Bell 1170, 1177, 1187 as by **Godfrey Borton**.
Revs: Champion 15502 by Bradley Kincaid; Challenge 392 by John McGhee; Bell 1170 by Vernon Dalhart, 1177 by John McGhee.

Owen Mills & Frank Welling-1/Owen Mills & Welling & McGhee-2/Owen Mills Acc. by Welling & McGhee-3:
David Miller, v; acc. John McGhee, h/g; Frank Welling, sg.
Chicago, IL   c. February 1929

21163-1	Since Mother's Gone -1	Pm 3155, Bwy 8214
21164-1	At The Old Church Door -2	Pm 3158, Bwy 8237
21165-2	A Mother's Plea -1	Pm 3155, Bwy 8214
21172-2	Don't Forget Me Darling -2	Pm 3158, Bwy 8237
21179-1,-2	It's Hard To Be Shut Up In Prison -3	Pm 3159
21180-2	The Faded Coat Of Blue -3	Pm 3159

Broadway 8214 as by **Frank Harkins & Melvin Owens**, 8237 as by **Wilkins & Moore**.
McGhee may not be present on matrix 21165.
Matrices 21166, 21170/71 are by John McGhee and Frank Welling; other intervening matrices may also be by those artists.

Davie Miller, v; acc. prob. John McGhee, h-1; own g.
Richmond, IN   Monday, April 7, 1930

16451	Little Indian Napanee	Ge rejected
16452	But I Do You Know I Do	Ge rejected
16453	Back To The Harbor Of Home Sweet Home -1	Ge rejected
16454	Since Dear Old Mother's Gone -1	Ge rejected
16455	A Mother's Plea	Ge rejected
16456	A Spanish Cavalier -1	Ge rejected

The Blind Soldier (David Miller), v; acc. own g.
New York, NY   Thursday, January 22, 1931

10384-	Many Times With You I've Wandered	ARC unissued
10385-	Two Little Orphans	ARC unissued
10386-	Don't Forget Me Little Darling	ARC unissued
10387-3	My Sweet Floetta	Cq 7839
10388-2	It's Hard To Be Shut Up In Prison	Ba 32134, Or 8054, Pe 12697, Ro 5054, Cq 7709, Bwy 4062
10389-	There'll Come A Time	ARC unissued

Conqueror 7839 as by **Davey Miller**.
Rev. Broadway 4062 by Gene Autry.

New York, NY   Friday, January 23, 1931

10390-	Give My Love To Nellie	ARC unissued
10391-2	Way Down In Jail On My Knees	Ba 32134, Or 8054, Pe 12697, Ro 5054, Cq 7709, ARC-Bwy 8115
10392-2	My Pretty Little Indian Napanee	Cq 7839
10393-	The Gypsies Warning	ARC unissued
10394-	The Spanish Cavalier	ARC unissued

Conqueror 7839, ARC-Broadway 8115 as by **Davey Miller**.
Rev. ARC-Broadway 8115 by Harkreader & Moore.

David Miller, g solo.
   New York, NY   Friday, January 23, 1931

10395-3	Jailhouse Rag	Ba 32202, Or 8071, Pe 12723, Ro 5071
10396-2	Cannon Ball Rag	Ba 32202, Or 8071, Pe 12723, Ro 5071

David Miller, v; acc. own g.
   New York, NY   Friday, January 23, 1931

10397-	My Little Girl	ARC unissued
10398-	A Little Child Shall Lead Them	ARC unissued

   New York, NY   Saturday, January 24, 1931

10399-	Lonesome Valley	ARC unissued

EMMETT MILLER

This artist's work was chiefly in a minstrel style, often with jazz accompaniment, and was usually issued in the OKeh 40000 popular series, but one coupling did appear in the OKeh Old Time Tunes series (45546). Miller's name also headed the roster of artists on the OKeh Medicine Show sequence (45380, 45391, 45413); for that set of recordings see the entry for The OKeh Medicine Show. The bulk of Miller's work is listed in *JR*.

JOHNNY MILLER

Pseudonym on Superior for Johnny Barfield; see Bert Layne.

RUSSELL MILLER

Russell Miller, f; acc. D.W. Brundage, p.
   Richmond, IN   Tuesday, October 21, 1924

12055-B	(a) Golden Tresses Clog (b) Wilson Clog (c) Rustic Clog	Miller 20079
12056-B	(a) My Old Kentucky Home (b) Missouri Stuff	Miller 20079

These items were custom-recorded by Gennett.

STANLEY MILLER

Pseudonym on Champion for Price Goodson (see Da Costa Woltz's Southern Broadcasters).

TONY MILLER & THE COW-BOYS

Pseudonym on English Plaza for Carson Robison.

MILLER & BURNETT

See Bob Miller.

MILLER & MILLER

See Bob Miller.

THE MILLER BOYS

Artist credit used on Varsity for a Bob Miller group.

MILLER BROTHERS

Pseudonym on Aurora for Lester McFarland & Robert A. Gardner or, on one side of A22017 (*You Are False But I'll Forgive You*), Buell Kazee.

MILLER'S BULLFROG ENTERTAINERS
MILLER'S BULLFROG TUTTERS

See Bob Miller.

MILLER'S MERRYMAKERS

J.B. Fuselier, f/v-1; Bethoven Miller, g/v-2; unknown, g.
   New Orleans, LA   Saturday, October 17, 1936

02674-1	Merrymakers' Hop -1	BB B-2004
02675-1	Te Ma Lessa Jolie Blonde -1	BB B-2006
02676-1	Pine Island -1	BB B-2006
02677-1	Lake Arthur Waltz -1	BB B-2004
02678-1	My Love Shall Never Fail -2	BB B-2008
02679-1	Anna Mae	BB B-2008
02680-1	It's The Top Of Everything -2	BB B-2020
02681-1	Over The Waves	BB B-2020

J.B. Fuselier, f/v-1; Bethoven Miller, g; unknown, g.
   New Orleans, LA   Monday, February 22, 1937

07231-1	Lake Arthur Stomp -1	BB B-2012
07232-1	Chere Tu Tu -1	BB B-2012
07233-1	Elton Two Step -1	BB B-2016
07234-1	Chere Te Mon -1	BB B-2018
07235-1	Round-Up Hop -1	BB B-2014
07236-1	Ma Julie Noir So (My Pretty Black Eyes) -1	BB B-2014
07237-1	Cajun Breakdown	BB B-2016
07238-1	Old Time Breakdown	BB B-2018

J.B. Fuselier also recorded in his own name and after 1942.

MR. & MRS. E.C. MILLS

Vocal duet; acc. unknown.
   Chicago, IL   Monday, April 29, 1929

| TC-3396 | Row Us Over The Tide | Vo unissued trial recording |

OWEN MILLS

Pseudonym on Paramount for David Miller.

MILNER & CURTIS WITH THE MAGNOLIA RAMBLERS

Luke Milner, f; Luke Curtis, f; Homer Ellis, md; Leo Ellis, g.
   Memphis, TN   Tuesday, February 18, 1930

MEM-752-	Sunshine And Paradise	Vo rejected
MEM-753-	Everybody Knows It!	Vo rejected
MEM-754-	Evening Shade Waltz	Vo 5426
MEM-755-	Northeast Texas	Vo 5426

MILO TWINS

Edward Milo, Edwin Milo, v/y-1 duet; acc. own g duet.
   Houston, TX   Friday, September 1, 1939

66359-A	Weary Lonesome Blues	De 5748
66360-A	I'm Worried Now -1	De 5790
66361-A	It's Sinful To Flirt	De 5832
66362-A	Quit Treatin' Me Mean -1	De 5729
66363-A	Blow Your Whistle Freight Train -1	De 5832
66364-A	Singing My Troubles Away	De 5748
66365-A	Fugitive's Lament	De 5790
66366-A	Ain't It Hard (To Love One That Don't Love You) -1	De 5729

Edward Milo sings lead and Edwin Milo harmony.

The Milo Twins recorded after 1942.

BILLY MILTON & HIS ONE MAN BAND

Billy Milton, h; acc. own g; several unknowns, calls/shouting.
   St. Paul, MN   c. September 29, 1927

13103	The Old Fashioned Square Dance	Ge 6318, Chg 407
13106,-A	Medley Of Old Time Jigs And Reels Part 1	Ge rejected
13107,-A	Medley Of Old Time Jigs And Reels Part 2	Ge rejected

Challenge 407 as by **Uncle John Stuart (The One Man Band)**. Matrices 13104/05 are unrelated.
Rev. Challenge 407 by Da Costa Woltz's Southern Broadcasters.

Acc. own g.
   St. Paul, MN   c. October 6, 1927

| 13102 | Dill Pickles | Ge 6318 |

FLOYD MING & HIS PEP STEPPERS

Hoyt Ming, f; Troy Ming, md; Rozelle Ming, g; A.D. Coggin, calls-1.
   Memphis, TN   Monday, February 13, 1928

41896-1	Indian War Whoop	BB B-5195, Sr S-3275
41896-2	Indian War Whoop	Vi 21294
41897-1	Old Red -1	BB B-5195, Sr S-3275
41897-2	Old Red -1	Vi 21294
41898-2	White Mule -1	Vi 21534
41899-1	Tupelo Blues	Vi 21534

Hoyt and Rozelle Ming recorded after 1942.

MINTONS OZARK STRING BAND

Luke Hignight, h/bj/v; others unknown.
   Memphis, TN   Saturday, February 25, 1928

400337-	Dreams Of The Ozarks	OK unissued
400338-	Rhode Island Red	OK unissued
400339-	Shoesole Rag	OK unissued
400340-	The Irish Frolic	OK unissued

MISSISSIPPI JUVENILE QUARTETTE

Vocal quartet; acc. unknown, p.
   Memphis, TN   Sunday, February 26, 1928

400351-	Hush! Somebody's Calling My Name	OK unissued
400352-	Massa's In The Cold, Cold Ground	OK unissued
400353-A	Memories Of Galilee	OK 45216
400354-B	Wandering Child, Oh, Come Home	OK 45216

MISSISSIPPI MUD STEPPERS

Items with this credit in the OKeh Old Time Tunes series (45504, 45519, 45532) are by the African-American artists Charlie McCoy and (probably) Walter Vinson; see *B&GR*.

MISSISSIPPI 'POSSUM HUNTERS

Lonnie Ellis, f; Pete Herring, g; John M. Holloway, vc.
   Memphis, TN   Wednesday, May 28, 1930

62523-2	Mississippi Breakdown	Vi 23595, BB B-4951, Au 403
62524-2	'Possum On The Rail	Vi 23595, BB B-4951, Au 403

John M. Holloway, f; Lonnie Ellis, md; Pete Herring, g.
   Memphis, TN   Wednesday, May 28, 1930

62533-2	The Last Shot Got Him	Vi 23644
62534-2	Rufus Rastus	Vi 23644

Matrices 62525/26 are by Pete Herring; matrices 62527 to 62530 are by Wheeler & Lamb; matrices 62531/32 are by Ray Brothers.

MISSOURI PACIFIC LINES BOOSTER QUARTET

L.S. Spann, tv; B.M. Gibson, tv; E.L. Hunt, bv; L.L. Gibson, bsv; unacc.
   Memphis, TN   Thursday, September 20, 1928

47068-2	One At Last	Vi V-40051
47069-2	When The Home Gates Swing Open	Vi V-40051

ARTELUS MISTRIC

Artelus Mistric, v; acc. own h.
   New Orleans, LA   Thursday, November 7, 1929

56506-2	Belle Of Point Claire	Vi 22208
56507-2	You Belong To Me	Vi 22208

CHARLES MITCHELL & HIS ORCHESTRA

Cliff Bruner, f/v-1; Jim Hewlett, t; Charles Mitchell, esg; Moon Mullican, p/v-2; Tex Swaim, g; Hershel Woodal, sb.
   Dallas, TX   Friday, April 11, 1941

063090-1	Jersey Side Jive	BB B-8716
063091-1	Rainbow Island -1, 2	BB B-8736
063092-1	Broken Hearted -2	BB B-8757
063093-1	My Island Reverie -2	BB B-8799

063094-1	The Sun Has Gone Down On Our Love -2	BB B-8716
063095-1	I Still Believe In You -2	BB B-8757
063096-1	Faithful Little Cowboy -2	BB B-8799
063097-1	You Don't Love Me Any More (Little Darling) -2	BB B-8736

Cliff Bruner, f; Jim Hewlett, t; Charles Mitchell, esg; Moon Mullican, p/v-1; Tex Swaim, g; Hershel Woodal, sb; unknown, d; Leon Huff, v-2; prob. Charles Burton, v-3.
    Dallas, TX   Friday, October 10, 1941

071160-1	Little Star Of Heaven -2	BB B-8935
071161-1	Too Late To Start All Over -3	BB B-8892
071162-1	Monita	BB B-8892
071163-1	I Dreamed Of An Old Love Affair -3	BB B-8935
071164-1	If It's Wrong To Love You -2	BB 33-0508
071165-1	Let's Go Dreaming -2	BB B-9002
071166-1	Mean Mama Blues -1	BB 33-0508
071167-1	Where An Angel Waits For Me -1	BB B-9002

CHARLIE MITCHELL & HIS KENTUCKY RIDGE RUNNERS

Unknown, f; unknown, bj-1; unknown, g; unknown, sb; unknown, v; two unknown women, v-2
    Augusta, GA   Monday, June 29, 1936

AUG-142-3	She's A High Geared Mama -1	ARC 6-10-57, Cq 8719
AUG-143-3	Bring It On Down To My House -1	ARC 6-10-57, Cq 8719
AUG-144-3	What A Friend We Have In Mother -2	ARC 6-12-67, Cq 8737
AUG-149-3	Apple Blossom Time -2	ARC 6-12-67, Cq 8737

Intervening matrices are by Crowder Brothers.

MITCHELL BROTHERS (SUNSHINE RAMBLERS)

Vocal duet; acc. prob. one of them, f/md-1; the other, g.
    Birmingham, AL   Thursday, April 8, 1937

B-97-1	I'll Think Of You -1	ARC 7-06-62
B-98-2	No One Left To Love Me -1	ARC 7-09-53
B-99-1	All For The Sake Of Her	ARC 7-06-62
B-100-1	Ragged But Right	ARC 7-09-53

THE MITCHELL FAMILY [TRIO]

Pseudonym on Superior for John McGhee & Frank Welling groups.

MOATSVILE STRING TICKLERS

Prob. Cecil Frye, f; Gordon Frye, f; poss. Brooks Ritter, bj-1 or bj-md-1, or Zell Frye, tbj-1; poss. Marshall Summers, Doyle Shaffer, or Floyd Frye, g; poss. Harold Ritter, sb-2; unidentified, v quartet-3.
    Johnson City, TN   Tuesday, October 22, 1929

149232-1	The West Virginia Hills -1, 3	Co 15491-D
149233-2	Moatsville Blues -2	Co 15491-D
149234-	Lost Waltz	Co unissued
149235-	Goodbye My Lover, Goodbye	Co unissued

[THE] MODERN MOUNTAINEERS

Modern Mountaineers: J.R. Chatwell, f-1; Hal Hebert, cl-2/ts-3/v-4; J.C. Way, esg; Johnny Thames, tbj; Smoky Wood, g/v-5; Lefty Groves, g; Rip Ramsey, sb; band v-6.
    San Antonio, TX   Monday, March 1, 1937

07431-1	Gettin' That Low Down Swing -1, 3, 5	BB B-7047
07432-1	Sweet Little Girl Of Mine -1, 3, 5	BB B-6997
07433-1	Who's Cryin' Sweet Papa Now -1, 3, 5	BB B-6911
07434-1	Everybody's Truckin' -1, 3, 5, 6	BB B-6911
07435-1	Drifting Along -1, 3, 5	BB B-6976
07436-1	Dirty Dog Blues -1, 2, 5	BB B-6976
07437-1	I'm A Swingin' Hill Billie Singer	BB unissued
07438-1	Mississippi Sandman -4	BB B-6997
07439-1	Loud Mouth -1, 3, 5	BB B-7047, Vi 20-2132

Rev. Victor 20-2132 by Allen Brothers.

Tommy Dunlap, esg; Red Oglesby, p; Johnny Thames, tbj; Buddy Ray, g; Cooper Bennett, g; poss. Jimmy Thomason, g; Lew Frisby, sb; J.R. Chatwell, v.
    San Antonio, TX   Saturday, September 18, 1937

| 014300-1 | Never Slept Last Night | BB B-7323 |

J.R. Chatwell, f/v-1; Jimmy Thomason, f/g/v-2; Tommy Dunlap, esg; Red Oglesby, p/v-3; Johnny Thames, tbj/v-4; Buddy Ray, g/v-5; Cooper Bennett, g; Lew Frisby, sb.

San Antonio, TX   Saturday, September 18, 1937

014301-1	End Of The Lane -1, 2	BB B-7470
014302-1	Some Day -5	BB B-7323
014303-1	Working At The Wrong Keyhole -2	BB B-7423
014304-1	Gypsy Lady -5	BB B-7247
014305-1	Moonlight Waters -5	BB B-7423
014306-1	You Gotta Know How To Truck & Swing -1, 4	BB B-7247
014307-1	Bad Blues -1, 2, 5	BB B-7671
014308-1	Modern	BB B-7671
014309-1	Dixieland -3	BB B-7470

There is only one fiddle on some items, probably Chatwell's; in those instances Thomason may play guitar.

The Modern Mountaineers: Buddy Ray, f/v-1; J.D. Standlee, esg; Moon Mullican, p/v-2; Johnny Thames, bj; Aubrey "Red" Greenhaw, g; Bill Mounce, sb.

Dallas, TX   Tuesday, February 13, 1940

047689-1	Rackin' It Back	BB B-8437, MW M-8704
047690-1	It's All Over Now -1	BB B-8437, MW M-8704
047691-1	Remember -2	BB B-8558, MW M-8705
047692-1	Someday -1	BB B-8558, MW M-8705
047693-1	Pipe Liner's Blues -2	BB B-8593, MW M-8706
047694-1	When You're Gone -2	BB B-8527, MW M-8707
047695-1	When My Baby Comes To Town -2	BB B-8593, MW M-8706
047696-1	There Ain't No Use In Cryin' -1?	BB B-8527, MW M-8707

The line-up on this and the following session is that of the contemporary Texas Wanderers.

Buddy Ray, f/v-1; George Ogg, ts/v-2; Ernest "Deacon" Evans, esg; Ralph Smith, p; Johnny Thames, tbj; Arthur "Buddy" Duhon, g/v-3; unknown, sb.

Dallas, TX   Monday, April 7, 1941

063038-1	Don't Leave Me Now -2, 3	BB B-8724
063039-1	I'm Gonna Say Goodbye To The Blues -1	BB B-8775
063040-1	Honky-Tonk Gal -1	BB B-8811
063041-1	Trying To Be True -1	BB B-8811
063042-1	Dry Those Tears Little Darlin' -3	BB B-8724
063043-1	Sunshine In Dixie -3	BB B-8775

Grady Hester, f; Bob Dunn, esg; Johnny Thames, tbj; Jerry Irby, g/v-1; prob. Bill Mounce, sb; band v-2.

Dallas, TX   Saturday, October 11, 1941

071174-1	Mary Jane -1	BB B-8982
071175-1	We're Happy In The U.S.A. -1	BB B-8960
071176-1	Takin' Off	BB B-8960
071177-1	I Still Think Of You -1	BB B-9029
071178-1	Baby You've Let Me Down -1, 2	BB B-8982
071179-1	A Prisoner's Adieu -1	BB B-9029

BILL MONROE & HIS BLUE GRASS BOYS

Tommy Magness, f; Clyde Moody, md; Bill Monroe, g/v/y; Willie "Cousin Wilbur" Wesbrooks, sb.

Atlanta, GA   Monday, October 7, 1940

054518-1	Mule Skinner Blues	BB B-8568, MW M-8861, Vi 20-3163

Tommy Magness, f; Bill Monroe, md/v; Clyde Moody, g/v; Willie "Cousin Wilbur" Wesbrooks, sb.

Atlanta, GA   Monday, October 7, 1940

054519-1	No Letter In The Mail	BB B-8611, MW M-8862

Bill Monroe, md/tv; Clyde Moody, g/lv; Tommy Magness, bv; Willie "Cousin Wilbur" Wesbrooks, bsv.

Atlanta, GA   Monday, October 7, 1940

054520-1	Cryin' Holy Unto My Lord	BB B-8611, MW M-8862

Tommy Magness, f; Bill Monroe, md/v-1/y-2; Clyde Moody, g/v-3; Willie "Cousin Wilbur" Wesbrooks, sb.

Atlanta, GA   Monday, October 7, 1940

054521-1	Six White Horses -3	BB B-8568, MW M-8861
054522-1	Dog House Blues -1, 2	BB B-8692, MW M-8863
054523-1	I Wonder If You Feel The Way I Do -1, 3	BB B-8813, MW M-8864
054524-1	Katy Hill	BB B-8692, MW M-8863, Vi 20-3295
054525-1	Tennessee Blues	BB B-8813, MW M-8864

Bill Monroe, md/lv-1/tv-2; Pete Pyle, g/lv-2/tv-1; Art Wooten, bv; Willie "Cousin Wilbur" Wesbrooks, bsv.

Atlanta, GA   Thursday, October 2, 1941

| 071070-1 | Shake My Mother's Hand For Me -2 | BB B-8953 |
| 071071-1 | Were You There? -1 | BB B-8953 |

Art Wooten, f/sp-1; Bill Monroe, md/v-2/y-3/sp-1; Pete Pyle, g/v-4/sp-1; Willie "Cousin Wilbur" Wesbrooks, sb/v-5/sp-1.

Atlanta, GA   Thursday, October 2, 1941

071072-1	Blue Yodel No. 7 -2, 3	BB B-8861, Vi 20-3163
071073-1	The Coupon Song -5	BB B-8893
071074-1	Orange Blossom Special -1, 2, 4	BB B-8893
071075-1	Honky Tonk Swing	BB B-8988
071076-1	In The Pines -2, 5	BB B-8861
071077-1	Back Up And Push	BB B-8988, Vi 20-3295

See also Monroe Brothers. Bill Monroe recorded after 1942.

(CHARLIE) MONROE'S BOYS

Zeke Morris, md/hv-1; Charlie Monroe, g/lv; Bill Calhoun, g/hv.

Rock Hill, SC   Thursday, September 29, 1938

027632-1	Once I Had A Darling Mother	BB B-7949, MW M-7573
027633-1	No Home, No Place To Pillow My Head	BB B-7922, MW M-7573
027634-1	Farther Along	BB B-7922, MW M-7574
027635-1	When The World's On Fire – Part 2	BB B-7990, MW M-7574
027636-1	Take Me Back To The Valley	BB B-8015, MW M-7575
027637-1	Happy Spirit	BB B-7990, MW M-7576
027638-1	The Great Speckled Bird	BB B-7862, MW M-7572
027639-1	Tell Him To Come Back Sweet Fern	BB B-8015, MW M-7575
027640-1	Every Time I Feel -1	BB B-7862, MW M-7572
027641-1	You're Gonna Miss Me When I'm Gone	BB B-7949, MW M-7576

Some issues of Bluebird B-7862 as by **The Monroe Boys**.

Zeke Morris, md/hv; Charlie Monroe, g/lv.

Rock Hill, SC   Sunday, February 5, 1939

032651-1	Oh Death	BB B-8092, MW M-7888
032652-1	Guided By Love	BB B-8050, MW M-7886
032653-1	If You See My Saviour	BB B-8092, MW M-7888
032654-1	From Shore To Shore	BB B-8118, MW M-7889
032655-1	Is She Praying There?	BB B-8050, MW M-7886
032656-1	Joy Bells In My Soul	BB B-8118, MW M-7889
032657-1	Just One Year	BB B-8064, MW M-7887
032658-1	Black Sheep	BB B-8064, MW M-7887

Charlie Monroe also recorded with his brother Bill as the Monroe Brothers, and after 1942.

HAL MONROE [TRIO]

Pseudonym on Continental and Varsity for Bob Miller.

THE MONROE BOYS

Some issues of Bluebird B-7862 by (Charlie) Monroe's Boys are credited thus.

MONROE BROTHERS (CHARLIE & BILL)

Bill Monroe, Charlie Monroe, v/y-1 duet; acc. Bill Monroe, md; Charlie Monroe, g.

Charlotte, NC   Monday, February 17, 1936

99193-1	My Long Journey Home	BB B-6422, MW M-4747
99194-1	What Is Home Without Love	BB B-6363, MW M-4746
99195-1	What Would You Give In Exchange?	BB B-6309, MW M-4745
99196-1	Little Red Shoes	BB B-6645, MW M-4748
99197-1	Nine Pound Hammer Is Too Heavy	BB B-6422, MW M-4747
99198-1	On Some Foggy Mountain Top -1	BB B-6607, MW M-4749
99199-1	Drifting Too Far From The Shore	BB B-6363, MW M-4746
99200-1	In My Dear Old Southern Home -1	BB B-6607, MW M-4749
99201-1	New River Train	BB B-6645, MW M-4748
99202-1	This World Is Not My Home	BB B-6309, MW M-4745

Some Montgomery Ward issues as by **Monroe Brothers** only.

Charlotte, NC   Sunday, June 21, 1936

102739-1	Watermelon Hangin' On That Vine	BB B-6829, MW M-7010
102740-1	On The Banks Of The Ohio	BB B-7385, MW M-7010
102741-1	Do You Call That Religion?	BB B-7055, MW M-7143
102742-1	God Holds The Future In His Hands	BB B-6477, MW M-5026

102743-1	You've Got To Walk That Lonesome Valley	BB B-6477, MW M-5026
102744-1	Six Months Ain't Long	BB B-6512, MW M-7012
102745-1	Just A Song Of Old Kentucky	BB B-6552, MW M-7011
102746-1	Don't Forget Me	BB B-6552, MW M-7011
102747-1	I'm Going	BB B-7055, MW M-7143
102748-1	Darling Corey	BB B-6512, MW M-7012, Vi 27493

Rev. Victor 27493 by Wade Mainer–Zeke Morris–Steve Ledford.

Charlotte, NC   Monday, October 12, 1936

02538-1	My Saviour's Train	BB B-6729, MW M-7086
02539-1	I Am Thinking Tonight Of The Old Folks	BB B-6773, MW M-7141
02540-1	Dreamed I Searched Heaven For You	BB B-6729, MW M-7086
02541-1	The Old Crossroad	BB B-6676, MW M-7087
02542-1	The Forgotten Soldier Boy	BB B-6829, MW M-7140
02543-1	We Read Of A Place That's Called Heaven	BB B-6676, MW M-7087
02544-1	Will The Circle Be Unbroken?	BB B-6820, MW M-7142
02545-1	The Saints Go Marching In	BB B-6820, MW M-7142
02546-1	Roll In My Sweet Baby's Arms	BB B-6773, MW M-7145
02547-1	Where Is My Sailor Boy?	BB B-6762, MW M-7140

Rev. Bluebird B-6762 by Jimmie Rodgers & Carter Family.

Charlotte, NC   Monday, February 15, 1937

07019-1	I Am Ready To Go	BB B-6866, MW M-8453
07020-1	What Would The Profit Be?	BB B-6912, MW M-8454
07021-1	Some Glad Day	BB B-6866, MW M-8453
07022-1	I Have Found The Way	BB B-6912, MW M-8454
07023-1	I Am Going That Way	BB B-7007, MW M-7141
07024-1	Katy Cline	BB B-6960, MW M-8455
07025-1	Roll On, Buddy	BB B-6960, MW M-8455
07026-1	Weeping Willow Tree	BB B-7093, MW M-7145
07027-1	I'll Live On	BB B-7007, MW M-7144
07028-1	Oh, Hide You In The Blood	BB B-7093, MW M-7144

Charlotte, NC   Tuesday, August 3, 1937

011875-1	What Would You Give In Exchange? – Part 2	BB B-7122, MW M-7312
011876-1	On That Old Gospel Ship	BB B-7273, MW M-7312
011877-1	What Would You Give In Exchange? – Part 3	BB B-7122, MW M-7313
011878-1	Let Us Be Lovers Again	BB B-7191, MW M-7316
011879-1	All The Good Times Are Passed And Gone	BB B-7191, MW M-7316
011880-1	What Would You Give In Exchange? – Part 4	BB B-7326, MW M-7314
011881-1	On My Way To Glory	BB B-7145, MW M-7313
011882-1	My Last Moving Day	BB B-7273, MW M-7314
011883-1	He Will Set Your Fields On Fire	BB B-7145, MW M-7315
011884-1	Sinner You Better Get Ready	BB B-7326, MW M-7315

Charlotte, NC   Friday, January 28, 1938

018808-1	Have A Feast Here Tonight	BB B-7508, MW M-7447
018809-1	Goodbye Maggie	BB B-7508, MW M-7447
018810-1	Rollin' On	BB B-7598, MW M-7451
018811-1	The Old Man's Story	BB B-7425, MW M-7448
018812-1	I've Still Got Niney-Nine	BB B-7425, MW M-7448
018813-1	Little Joe	BB B-7598, MW M-7451
018814-1	A Beautiful Life	BB B-7562, MW M-7450
018815-1	Pearly Gates	BB B-7460, MW M-7449
018816-1	On My Way Back Home	BB B-7460, MW M-7449
018817-1	When Our Lord Shall Come Again	BB B-7562, MW M-7450

Charlie Monroe sings lead and Bill Monroe tenor.
Charlie and Bill Monroe also recorded in their own names, and after 1942.

MONROE COUNTY BOTTLE TIPPERS

See Claude (C.W.) Davis.

MONROE QUARTETTE

Vocal quartet; acc. unknown, p.

Atlanta, GA   Friday, March 18, 1927

80561-	Beautiful Land	OK 40794
80562-	Whispering Hope	OK 40794
80563-B	Just Before The Battle Mother	OK 45133

80564-B	Old Folks At Home	OK 45133
80565-A	Bruddah Brown	OK 45141
80566-B	The Bulldog	OK 45141

PATSY MONTANA

Patsy Montana (born Ruby [which she later spelled Rubye] Blevins) made most of her pre-1942 recordings with the Prairie Ramblers. Listed here are those for which she received primary or joint label-credit; see the Prairie Ramblers entry for other items in which she participated.

Patsy Montana, v/y; acc. Ed Davis, g.
Camden, NJ   Friday, November 4, 1932

59068-1	Montana Plains	Vi unissued
59069-1	Sailor's Sweetheart	Vi unissued
59070-1	I Love My Daddy Too	Vi 23760, MW M-4322
59071-1	When The Flowers Of Montana Were Blooming	Vi 23760, MW M-4322

Although this session was logged as by **Rubye Blevins**, both issues were as by **Patsy Montana**. She also recorded on this date with Jimmie Davis.

Rubye Blevins, v/y; Acc. By The Prairie Ramblers: Tex Atchison, f; own f-1/own g-2; Chick Hurt, mandola-3/g-4; Salty Holmes, g; Jack Taylor, sb-5; unknown, wh-6.
Chicago, IL   Wednesday, December 6, 1933

77247-1	Homesick For My Old Cabin -2, 3	BB B-5973
77248-1	Home Corral -2, 3	BB B-5973
77249-2	Montana Plains -1, 4, 5	BB B-5404, MW M-4484, RZ MR1956, HMVIn N4325
77250-2	Waltz Of The Hills -1, 4, 5, 6	BB B-5404, MW M-4484, RZ MR1956, HMVIn N4325

Regal-Zonophone MR1956 is subcredited (**The Montana Yodelling Cowgirl**).

Patsy Montana & (or With) The Prairie Ramblers: Patsy Montana, v/y; acc. Tex Atchison, f; Chick Hurt, mandola; Salty Holmes, g; Jack Taylor, sb.
New York, NY   Thursday, February 14, 1935

| TO-1510 | I Want To Be A Cowboy's Sweetheart | ARC unissued trial recording |

Acc. Tex Atchison, f; Chick Hurt, mandola; Salty Holmes, g; Jack Taylor, sb; band v-1/y-2.
New York, NY   Friday, August 16, 1935

17966-1,-2	I Wanna Be A Cowboy's Sweetheart	ARC 5-11-56, Vo/OK 03010, Cq 8575
17967-2	Ridin' Old Paint -1	ARC 5-11-56, Vo/OK 03010, Cq 8575
17969-2	Old Black Mountain Trail -2	ARC 6-07-55, Cq 8695
17970-1	Gold Coast Express	ARC 6-08-52, Vo/OK 04469, Cq 8709

Matrix 17968 is by Prairie Ramblers.

Chicago, IL   Tuesday, January 21, 1936

C-1213-1	Sweetheart Of The Saddle	ARC 6-04-53, Cq 8630
C-1214-1,-2	Where The Sage Brush Billows Roll	ARC unissued
C-1218-2	The She Buckaroo	ARC 6-04-53, Cq 8630

Intervening matrices are by Prairie Ramblers.

Chicago, IL   Wednesday, March 25, 1936

C-1320-2	The Wheel Of The Wagon Is Broken	ARC 6-06-58, Vo/OK 04518, Cq 8654
C-1321-2	Lone Star	ARC 6-07-55, Cq 8695
C-1322-1	Give Me A Home In Montana	ARC 6-06-58, Vo/OK 04518, Cq 8654

Patsy Montana, v; acc. Tex Atchison, f; Chick Hurt, mandola; Salty Holmes, g; Jack Taylor, sb.
Chicago, IL   Wednesday, May 13, 1936

| C-1375-2 | Woman's Answer To Nobody's Darling | ARC 6-08-52 |

Chicago, IL   Tuesday, May 26, 1936

| C-1375-4 | Woman's Answer To Nobody's Darling | ARC unissued |

Patsy Montana, v/y-1; acc. Tex Atchison, f; Chick Hurt, mandola; Salty Holmes, g; Jack Taylor, sb.
Chicago, IL   Thursday, May 28, 1936

C-1375-6	Woman's Answer To Nobody's Darling	ARC 6-08-52, Vo/OK 04469, Cq 8709
C-1391-2	Blazin' The Trail -1	ARC 6-09-58, Cq 8711
C-1392-1	Montana -1	ARC 6-09-58, Cq 8711

Patsy Montana, v/y; acc. Tex Atchison, f; Chick Hurt, mandola; Ken Houchins, g; Jack Taylor, sb.
Chicago, IL   Tuesday, October 13, 1936

C-1558-1	I'm An Old Cowhand (From The Rio Grande)	ARC 7-01-52, Cq 8744
C-1559-1	Your Own Sweet Darling Wife	ARC 7-03-60, Cq 8826
C-1560-2	My Baby's Lullaby	ARC 7-03-60, Cq 8826

| C-1561-2 | Echoes From The Hills | ARC 7-01-52, Cq 8744 |
| C-1562-1 | Goin' Back To Old Montana | ARC 7-02-52, Cq 8827 |

    Chicago, IL   Thursday, October 22, 1936

| C-1601-2 | Chuck Wagon Blues | ARC 7-02-52, Cq 8827 |

Acc. Tex Atchison, f; Chick Hurt, mandola; Ken Houchins, g; Jack Taylor, sb; unidentified, y-1; band v-2.

    Chicago, IL   Tuesday, January 26, 1937

C-1772-1,-2	There's A Ranch In The Sky	ARC unissued
C-1773-1,-2	Pride Of The Prairie	ARC unissued
C-1774-2	I Wanna Be A Cowboy's Sweetheart No. 2 (I've Found My Cowboy Sweetheart) -1	ARC 7-05-74, Vo/OK 03268, Cq 8853, 9778
C-1775-1,-2	A Cowboy's Honeymoon	ARC unissued
C-1776-1	I'm A Wild And Reckless Cowboy (From The West Side Of Town) -2	ARC 7-04-69, Vo/OK 03135, Cq 8786

All issues of matrix C-1776 as by **Prairie Ramblers &** (or **With**) **Patsy Montana**.
Matrix C-1774 may be titled *I've Found My Cowboy Sweetheart* on Conqueror 8853.

Patsy Montana, v; acc. Tex Atchison, f; Salty Holmes, h-1/j-2; Chick Hurt, tbj; Ken Houchins, g; Jack Taylor, sb; band v-3.

    Chicago, IL   Thursday, January 28, 1937

C-1787-1,-2	I Only Want A Buddy	ARC unissued
C-1788-1,-2	Out On The Lone Prairie	ARC unissued
C-1789-1	With A Banjo On My Knee -1, 2, 3	ARC 7-04-69, Vo/OK 03135, Cq 8786
C-1789-2	With A Banjo On My Knee -2, 3	ARC unissued: *Co FC38909 (LP)*

All issues of matrix C-1789-1 as by **Prairie Ramblers &** (or **With**) **Patsy Montana**.

Patsy Montana, v/y; acc. Tex Atchison, f; Chick Hurt, mandola; Ken Houchins, g; Jack Taylor, sb; unidentified, y.

    Chicago, IL   Thursday, March 11, 1937

| C-1775-4 | A Cowboy Honeymoon | ARC 7-05-74, Vo/OK 03268, Cq 8853 |

Acc. Tex Atchison, f; Chick Hurt, mandola; Ken Houchins, g; Jack Taylor, sb.

    Chicago, IL   Monday, May 24, 1937

C-1773-4	Pride Of The Prairie	ARC 7-08-54, Vo/OK 03292, Cq 8893
C-1787-3,-4	I Only Want A Buddy (Not A Sweetheart)	ARC 7-08-54, Vo/OK 03292, Cq 8893
C-1788-3,-4	Out On The Lone Prairie	ARC unissued
C-1886-1,-2	Ridin' The Sunset Trail	ARC unissued

    Chicago, IL   Tuesday, May 25, 1937

| C-1772-3,-4 | There's A Ranch In The Sky | ARC unissued |

Acc. Tex Atchison, f; Chick Hurt, mandola; Salty Holmes, g; poss. Ken Houchins, g; Jack Taylor, sb.

    Chicago, IL   Friday, October 1, 1937

C-1775-5	There's A Ranch In The Sky	ARC 7-12-51, Vo/OK 03377, Cq 8887
C-1788-5	Out On The Lone Prairie	ARC 8-03-56, Vo/OK 03422, Cq 8980
C-1886-4	Ridin' The Sunset Trail	ARC 7-12-51, Vo/OK 03377, Cq 8887

Rev. ARC 8-03-56 by Prairie Ramblers.

Patsy Montana, v/y-1; acc. Tex Atchison, f; Chick Hurt, mandola; Salty Holmes, g; Jack Taylor, sb.

    Chicago, IL   Wednesday, February 16, 1938

| C-2102-1 | Big Moon | Vo 04135 |
| C-2103-1 | My Dear Old Arizona Home -1 | Vo/OK 04247, Cq 8979 |

Patsy Montana, v/y; acc. Tex Atchison, f; Chick Hurt, mandola; Salty Holmes, g; Jack Taylor, sb; unidentified, y-1.

    Chicago, IL   Thursday, February 17, 1938

C-2104-1	Cowboy Rhythm -1	Vo unissued: *Co FC38909 (LP)*
C-2104-2	Cowboy Rhythm -1	Vo/OK 04023
C-2105-1	Little Sweetheart Of The Ozarks	Vo/OK 04023, Cq 8981
C-2107-1	Rodeo Sweetheart	Vo/OK 04076, Cq 9003, Cq 9778

Matrix C-2106 is by Prairie Ramblers.

Patsy Montana, v/y-1; acc. Tex Atchison, f; Chick Hurt, mandola; Salty Holmes, g; Jack Taylor, sb.

    Chicago, IL   Monday, February 21, 1938

C-2109-1	Little Rose Of The Prairie -1	Vo/OK 04247, Cq 8979
C-2111-1	Someone To Go Home To	Vo 04291, Cq 8980
C-2112-1	The Waltz Of The Hills -1	Vo/OK 04076, Cq 9003
C-2114-2	Shine On, Rocky Mountain Moonlight -1	Vo 04135, Cq 8981

Intervening matrices are by Prairie Ramblers. Rev. Vocalion 04291 by Prairie Ramblers.

Patsy Montana, v; acc. Alan Crockett, f; Salty Holmes, h-1/g; Chick Hurt, mandola; Bob Long, g; Jack Taylor, sb; band v-2.

    Chicago, IL   Monday, October 17, 1938

C-2362-1	I'm A-Ridin' Up The Old Kentucky Mountain -1	Cq 9118
C-2363-2	High Falutin' Newton -2	Vo unissued: Co FC38909 (LP)
C-2364-1	You'll Have To Wait Till My Ship Comes In	Cq 9119
C-2365-1,-2,-3	The Strawberry Roan -2	Vo unissued
C-2366-1,-2	Give Me A Straight Shooting Cowboy	Vo unissued
C-2367-1,-2	An Old Saddle For Sale -2	Vo unissued

Acc. Alan Crockett, f; Chick Hurt, mandola; Salty Holmes, g; Bob Long, g; Jack Taylor, sb; band v-1.
   Chicago, IL   Thursday, October 27, 1938

C-2363-4	High Falutin' Newton -1	Vo/OK 04482, Cq 9119
C-2365-4	The Strawberry Roan -1	Vo/OK 04482, Cq 9118
C-2366-4	Give Me A Straight Shooting Cowboy	Cq 9120
C-2367-4	An Old Saddle For Sale -1	Cq 9120

Patsy Montana, v/y-1; acc. Alan Crockett, f; Chick Hurt, mandola; Salty Holmes, g; Bob Long, g; Jack Taylor, sb.
   Chicago, IL   Thursday, December 1, 1938

C-2396-1	That's Where The West Begins -1	Vo 04568, Cq 9192
C-2397-1	You're The Only Star (In My Blue Heaven)	Vo 04568, Cq 9192

   Chicago, IL   Tuesday, December 6, 1938

C-2399-1,-2	In Ole' Oklahoma	Vo unissued
C-2400-1,-2	Little Old Locket Of Gold	Vo unissued
C-2402-1,-2	I've Got A Silver Haired Sweetheart In The Golden West	Vo unissued
C-2403-1,-2	Lone Star Lullaby	Vo unissued

Matrix C-2401 is by Prairie Ramblers.

Patsy Montana, v/y-1; acc. Alan Crockett, f; Chick Hurt, mandola; Salty Holmes, g; Bob Long, g; Jack Taylor, sb.
   Chicago, IL   Wednesday, February 1, 1939

C-2423-1	Han'some Joe (From The Land Of The Navaho)	Vo 04742
C-2424-2	A Rip Rip Snortin' Two Gun Gal -1	Vo/OK 04689, Cq 9263
C-2425-2	I'm Goin' West To Texas	Vo/OK 05081
C-2426-1	I'm A-Ridin' Up The Old Kentucky Mountain	Vo 04742
C-2427-1	Singin' In The Saddle	Vo/OK 04689, Cq 9263

Rev. Vocalion/OKeh 05081 by Prairie Ramblers.

Acc. Alan Crockett, f; poss. Augie Klein, ac; George Barnes, eg; Chick Hurt, mandola; Salty Holmes, g; Bob Long, g; Jack Taylor, sb.
   Chicago, IL   Monday, September 25, 1939

WC-2761-A	I Wanna Be A Western Cowgirl -1	Vo/OK 05217, Cq 9322
WC-2762-A	Old Nevada Moon	Vo/OK 05164, Cq 9678
WC-2763-A	My Million Dollar Smile	Vo/OK 05164, Cq 9323
WC-2764-A	My Poncho Pony	Vo/OK 05334, Cq 9422

Acc. Alan Crockett, f; Chick Hurt, mandola; Salty Holmes, g; Bob Long, g; Jack Taylor, sb.
   Chicago, IL   Friday, September 29, 1939

WC-2769-A	Back On Montana Plains	Vo/OK 05334, Cq 9323
WC-2770-A	The Moon Hangs Low (On The Ohio)	Vo/OK 05284, Cq 9422
WC-2771-A	My Song Of The West	Vo/OK 05217, Cq 9678
WC-2772-A	I'd Love To Be A Cowboy (But I'm Afraid Of Cows)	Vo/OK 05284, Cq 9322

Acc. Alan Crockett, f; Chick Hurt, md; Salty Holmes, g; Bob Long, g; Jack Taylor, sb.
   Chicago, IL   Tuesday, February 20, 1940

WC-2939-A	Swing Time Cowgirl	Vo/OK 05426, Cq 9424
WC-2940-A	Leanin' On The Ole Top Rail	Vo/OK 05426, Cq 9424
WC-2941-A	I Wanta Be A Cowboy's Dreamgirl -1	Vo/OK 05474, Cq 9423
WC-2942-A	Shy Little Ann From Cheyenne	Vo/OK 05474, Cq 9423

Patsy Montana & Her Pardners: Patsy Montana, v/y-1; acc. Cecil Brower, f; J.B. Brinkley, eg; Marvin Montgomery, tg; Joe Ferguson, sb.
   Dallas, TX   Thursday, April 24, 1941

93651-A	I'll Be Waiting For You Darlin'	De 5947
93652-A,-B	Gallopin' To Gallup (On The Santa Fe Trail)	De 6024
93653-A	I'll Keep On Wishing For You	De 5956, MeC 45447
93654-A	Blanket Me With Western Skies	De 6024
93655-A	Rodeo Queen	De unissued
93656-A	Shy Anne From Old Cheyenne -1	De 5947
93657-A	Sunny San Antone	De 5972, MeC 45459
93658-A	I Want To Be A Cowboy's Sweetheart -1	De 5956, MeC 45447
93721-A	I'm Gonna Have A Cowboy Weddin'	De 5972, MeC 45459

Matrix 93721 was transferred from matrix 93650.

Acc. Hugh Farr, f; Karl Farr, lg; Gene Haas, g; Pat Brady, sb; unidentified, v duet-2.
   Los Angeles, CA   Friday, February 27, 1942

DLA-2920-A	Deep In The Heart Of Texas -1, 2	De 6032
DLA-2921-A,-B	Boogie Woogie Cowboy	De unissued
DLA-2922-A	I'll Wait For You -1	De 6032
DLA-2923-A,-B	I'll Be True While You're Gone	De unissued

Patsy Montana recorded after 1942.

MONTANA SLIM

See Wilf Carter.

BARTMON MONTET–JOSWELL DUPUIS

The former's correct first name is believed to be Berthmost.

Bartmon Montet, ac/v; Joswell Dupuis, g.
   New Orleans, LA   Saturday, November 9, 1929

56520-1	L'Abandonner (The Abandoned Waltz)	Vi 22211
56521-1	Je M'En Suis Alle (I'm Going Away)	Vi 22211
56522-2	L'Eau Haute (High Water Waltz)	Vi 22562
56523-2	Nina One-Step	Vi 22562

REV. C.D. MONTGOMERY

Although issued in the Columbia Old Familiar Tunes catalogue (15023-D), this artist is African-American.

PHIL MONTGOMERY

Pseudonym on Superior for Dick Parman.

MONTGOMERY QUARTET

Vocal quartet; acc. unknown, o.
   New York, NY   Tuesday, August 21, 1934

38355-A	Life's Railway To Heaven	De 146, DeAu X1128
38356-A	The Old Rugged Cross	De 146
38357-	The Little Brown Church	De 147, DeAu X1128
38358-	In The Garden	De 147

MOODY BIBLE INSTITUTE TRIO (W.M.B.I. ANNOUNCERS' TRIO)

Wendell P. Loveless, tv; Howard A. Hermansen, bv-1; William E. King, bsv; acc. Howard A. Hermansen, p.
   Chicago, IL   Wednesday, June 20, 1928

45932-1	I Cannot Get Beyond His Love -1	Vi V-40015
45933-1	In My Heart There Rings A Melody -1	Vi 23615
45934-1	He Will Never Cast You Out -1	Vi 21624
45935-1	Grace Greater Than Our Sins -1	Vi V-40015
45936-1	Precious Hiding Place	Vi 21628
45937-1	Wonderful Story Of Love -1	Vi 21628
45938-1	Saved! -1	Vi 23615
45939-1	How Firm A Foundation -1	Vi 21624

This group was originally named **WMBI Announcers' Trio** on the Victor session-sheet. Station WMBI, Chicago was owned by the Moody Bible Institute.

MOODY BIBLE SACRED HARP SINGERS

Poss.: C. Philip Reeve, C. Ernest Moody, R.E. Worsham, C.C. Harper, v quartet; acc. Gus Boaz, f; Ira Mashburn, o; unknown, g.
   Chicago, IL   January 1929

21121-2	Liberty	Pm 3152
21123-2	In That Morning	Pm 3152

Matrix 21122 is untraced.

This group is associated with the Dixie Crackers, North Georgia Four/Quartette, and Phil Reeve & Ernest Moody.

THE MOODY QUARTET

Frank Harmon, lv; Lawrence Neal, tv; C. Ernest Moody, bv; Clyde Evans, bsv; acc. unknown, o.
   Atlanta, GA   Wednesday, March 19, 1930

TATL-933	Kneel At The Cross	Vo 5448
TATL-934	I Believe In God	Vo 5448

These items are described in Brunswick files as trial recordings, made for Brunswick but transferred, in July 1930, to Vocalion.

Lawrence Neal and C. Ernest Moody were members of the Calhoun Sacred Quartet; Moody was also a member of the Georgia Yellow Hammers and associated groups, and recorded with Phil Reeve. Clyde Evans recorded in his own name and with the Georgia Yellow Hammers.

MOONSHINE DAVE

Pseudonym on Champion for Sunshine Pritchard.

MOONSHINE HARRY

Pseudonym on Supertone for Sunshine Pritchard.

MOONSHINE KATE

See Rosa Lee Carson.

THE MOONSHINERS

Two unknowns, f; two unknowns, g.
New York, NY   Tuesday, February 4, 1930
59146-1	Fulton County	Vi V-40223
59147-1	Shelby County	Vi V-40223
59148-1	Sweetheart Waltz	Vi V-40284
59149-1	Midnight Waltz	Vi V-40284

Matrices 59146/47 were originally titled *Birmingham – Part 1* and *Birmingham – Part 2* respectively on the Victor session-sheet.

BILL MOORE

Pseudonym on Sunrise for Frank Luther (see Carson Robison).

BYRD MOORE

Byrd Moore, v; acc. Marion Underwood, bj-1; own g.
Richmond, IN   Friday, June 22, 1928
13901	Mamma Toot Your Whistle -1	Ge 6586, Spt 9399
13902	The Bully Of The Town -1	Ge 6763, Spt 9399
13903-A	All Night Long -1	Ge 6686, Cq 7259
13904,-A,-B	How I Got My Wife -1	Ge rejected
13905,-A	Way Down In Florida On A Bum -1	Ge rejected
13906	Harvey Logan	Ge 6549
13907	Bed Bugs Makin' Their Last Go Round	Ge 6586, Cq 7259
13908-A	Hobo's Paradise -1	Ge 6549, Spt 9184
13909	Careless Lover -1	Ge 6991
13910,-A	On The Banks Of The Old Tennessee -1	Ge rejected

Supertone 9184, 9399 as by **Harry Carter**. Conqueror 7259 as by **Oscar Craver**.
Rev. Supertone 9184 by H.K. Hutchison.

Richmond, IN   Tuesday, October 30, 1928
14400	Snatch 'Em Back Blues	Ge 6763
14401	Back Water Blues	Ge 6686

Byrd Moore, v; or **Robinette & Moore**-1: Melvin Robinette, Byrd Moore, v duet; acc. Melvin Robinette, f/sp-2; Byrd Moore, g/sp-2.
Richmond, IN   Wednesday, April 10, 1929
15020	Birmingham Jail -1	Ge 6841, Ch 15750, Spt 9536, Spr 2640
15021	Good Bye Sweetheart -1	Ge 7068, Spt 9536
15022	When The Snowflakes Fall Again -2	Ge 6841, Ch 15732, Spt 9560
15027	Mama Don't Allow No Low Down Hangin' Around	Ge 6991

Champion 15732 as by **Henry Johnson**, 15750 as by **Ezra Hill & Henry Johnson**. Supertone 9536 as by **Clark & Howell**, 9560 as by **Harry Carter**.
Matrix 15023 is popular; matrices 15024 to 15026 are by Rutherford & Foster (see John D. Foster).
Revs: Gennett 7068 by Asa Martin & Doc Roberts; Champion 15732, 15750, Superior 2640 by Rutherford & Foster (see John D. Foster); Supertone 9560 by Dick Parman.

Melvin Robinette, f/sp-1; Byrd Moore, g/sp-1.
Richmond, IN   Wednesday, April 10, 1929
15028	Flop Eared Mule -1	Ge 6884, Spt 9500
15029	Favorite Two Step	Ge 6957
15030	That Old Tiger Rag -1	Ge 6957, Chg 427, Spr 2696

Supertone 9500 as by **Clark & Howell**. Superior 2696 as by **Jack Burdette & Bert Moss**. Challenge 427 as by **Robinson & Evans**.
Matrix 15028 is titled *Flop Ear Mule* on Supertone 9500.
Rev. Challenge 427 by Louie Donaldson & Hoke Rice.

Richmond, IN   Thursday, April 11, 1929

    15036   Last Days In Georgia -1   Ge 6884, Spt 9500, Spr 2696

Supertone 9500 as by **Clark & Howell**. Superior 2696 as by **Jack Burdette & Bert Moss**.
Matrices 15031 to 15033 are by Rutherford & Foster (see John D. Foster); matrices 15034/35 are popular.

Byrd Moore & His Hot Shots: Clarence Greene, f/tv; Clarence Ashley, g/lv; Byrd Moore, g/bv.
   Johnson City, TN   Wednesday, October 23, 1929

    149240-1   Frankie Silvers   Co 15536-D
    149241-1   The Hills Of Tennessee   Co 15536-D
    149242-1,-2   Careless Love   Co 15496-D
    149243-2   Three Men Went A Hunting   Co 15496-D

Moore & Green: Clarence Greene, f; Byrd Moore, g.
   Richmond, IN   Thursday, February 13, 1930

    16258,-A   Lay Down Baby Blues   Ge rejected
    16259   Cincinnati Rag   Ch 16357, Spr 2838
    16260   Pig Angle   Ch 16357, Spr 2838
    16261   Pride Of The Ball   Ge rejected

Superior 2838 as by **Moss & Long**.

Fiddlin' Green & Byrd Moore, v duet; acc. Clarence Greene, f; Byrd Moore, g.
   Richmond, IN   Thursday, February 13, 1930

    16262,-A   In The Hills Of Tennessee   Ge rejected

Superior 2838 as by **Moss & Long**.

Byrd Moore & Allen D. Cole: Allen D. Cole, f; Byrd Moore, g.
   Richmond, IN   Thursday, February 13, 1930

    16263,-A   West Virginia Sally Ann   Ge rejected

Byrd Moore, v; acc. Clarence Greene or Allen D. Cole, f; own g.
   Richmond, IN   Friday, February 14, 1930

    16264,-A   Eagle Rock Blues   Ge rejected

Fiddlin' Green & Byrd Moore, v duet; acc. Clarence Greene, f; Byrd Moore, g.
   Richmond, IN   Friday, February 14, 1930

    16265,-A   The Lonesome Valley   Ge rejected
    16267,-A   Frankie Silver's Confession   Ge unissued

Matrix 16266 is by Walter Taylor (see *B&GR*).

Byrd Moore & Allen Cole: Allen D. Cole, f; Byrd Moore, g.
   Richmond, IN   Friday, February 14, 1930

    16269,-A   Boatman's Dance   Ge rejected

Matrix 16268 is by Walter Taylor (see *B&GR*).

Byrd Moore, v/y-1; acc. unknown, bj-2; own g-3.
   Richmond, IN   Friday, February 14, 1930

    16274   The Up North Blues -2   Ge rejected
    16276   Got The Guitar Blues -1, 3   Spr 2559

Superior 2559 as by **Bert Moss**.
Matrix 16270 is by Walter Taylor (see *B&GR*); matrices 16271, 16273 are by Allen D. Cole; matrix 16272 is by Rev. Emmett Dickinson (see *B&GR*).

Byrd Moore & Jess Johnson: Jess Johnston, f; Byrd Moore, g/sp-1.
   Richmond, IN   Saturday, September 27, 1930

    17087-A   Killin' Blues   Ch 16469, Spr 2539
    17089   My Trouble Blues -1   Ch 16469, Spr 2539

Superior 2539 as by **Bert Moss & Joe Long**.
Matrix 17088 is by Tommie Bradley (see *B&GR*).

Byrd Moore, v/y-1; acc. own g.
   Richmond, IN   Saturday, September 27, 1930

    17091   Jake Leg Blues -1   Spr 2559
    17092,-A   Lovin' Blues   Ge rejected

Superior 2559 as by **Bert Moss**.
Matrix 17090 is by Tommie Bradley (see *B&GR*).

Acc. Jess Johnston, f; own g.
   Richmond, IN   Friday, October 10, 1930

    17166   Root Hog Or Die   Ge unissued

Jesse Johnson & Byrd Moore, v duet; acc. Jess Johnston, f; Byrd Moore, g.
   Richmond, IN   Friday, October 10, 1930
   17167   It Might Have Been Worse   Ge rejected

Byrd Moore & His Hot Shots: Byrd Moore, g/v; —— McKinney, C.C. Johnson, —— Henry, unknown instruments.
   Richmond, IN   Thursday, August 25, 1932
   18736   Take A Circle Around The Moon   Ge unissued
   18737   When I Walk Into Your Parlor   Ge unissued
   18738   Spring Roses   Ch 16498
   18739   O Take Me Back   Ch 16498

Byrd Moore also recorded with Richard D. Burnett & Leonard Rutherford, and probably accompanied Allen D. Cole on items under the latter's name.

CARRIE MAE MOORE–FAYE BARRES

Carrie Mae Moore, Faye Barres, v/y-1 duet; acc. prob. James Andrew Boyett, g.
   New York, NY   Wednesday, July 3, 1940
   051751-1   Why Did You Leave Me Alone?   BB B-8507, RZAu G24995
   051752-1   The Everglades Blues -1   BB B-8532
   051753-1   I Thought I'd Forgotten You   BB B-8507, RZAu G24995
   051754-1   There's A Reason Why I Love You More   BB B-8532

Regal-Zonophone G24995 as by **Carrie Mae Moore & Faye Barres**.

CHARLES MOORE

Pseudonym on Ariel for Frank Luther (see Carson Robison).

G.D. MOORE & HIS VIOLIN

See Sid Harkreader.

JACK MOORE

Jack Moore, v; acc. prob. own u.
   Richmond, IN   Monday, June 22, 1931
   17844   In The Hills Of Tennessee   Ge rejected

JOHN MOORE

Pseudonym on Broadway for John McGhee.

JOHNNIE MOORE

Pseudonym on Broadway for Frank Marvin.

LOWELL MOORE

Lowell Moore, v; acc. unknown.
   Richmond, IN   Tuesday, December 29, 1931
   18282   Final Ride Of Jimmie Bryan   Ge rejected
   Richmond, IN   Thursday, January 28, 1932
   18341   Jimmie Bryan's Final Ride   Ge rejected
   18342   The Return Of A Wandering Boy   Ge rejected

OLIVER MOORE

Pseudonym on Challenge for Ted Chestnut.

SAM MOORE

Recordings by this artist in the Vocalion Old Southern Tunes series with Sam Freed (5131, 5132), Roy Smeck (one side of 5133), and Horace Davis (the other side of 5133) are, like his other recordings, outside the scope of this work.

MOORE & GREEN

See Byrd Moore.

MOORE, BURNETT & RUTHERFORD

See Richard D. Burnett.

MOORE SISTERS

Vocal duet; acc. poss. one of them, sg; poss. the other, g-1/u-2.
   Atlanta, GA   Thursday, October 6, 1927
   81687-B   Daisies Won't Tell -2   OK 45149

81688-B	Memories -1	OK 45149
81689-	There's A Warm Spot In My Heart For Tennessee	OK unissued
81690-	Drifting	OK unissued
81691-	When Dreams Come True	OK unissued
81692-	How Can I Leave Thee	OK unissued

MOPEY DICK

See Arthur Fields & Fred Hall.

"PEG" MORELAND

"Peg" Moreland, v; acc. own g.
    Chicago, IL   Tuesday, July 3, 1928

46047-1	The Old Step Stone	Vi V-40008
46048-1	He Never Came Back	Vi V-40101
46049-1	Over The Hills To The Poorhouse	Vi 21548
46050-2	Going Back To Dixie	Vi 21653
46051-1	Stay In The Wagon Yard	Vi unissued

Victor 21653 as by **Peg Moreland**.
Matrix 46048 was originally titled *When We Meet On That Beautiful Shore*.
Revs: Victor 21653 by Johnny Marvin, V-40101 by Harry "Mac" McClintock.

    Chicago, IL   Thursday, July 5, 1928

46051-2	Stay In The Wagon Yard	Vi V-40008
46052-1	The Maple In The Lane	Vi 21724
46053-1	Clover Blossoms	Vi 21724
46054-1	The Prisoner At The Bar	Vi 21548

Peg Moreland, v; acc. own g.
    Dallas, TX   Monday, August 12, 1929

55351-1	You're Gonna Miss Me, Hon!	Vi V-40137
55352-1	I'm Saving Up Coupons	Vi V-40137
55353-1	Make Me A Cowboy Again	Vi V-40272, Au 239

    Atlanta, GA   Wednesday, November 20, 1929

56542-1	When I Had But Fifty Cents	Vi V-40209
56543-2	You'll Want Someone To Love You When You're Old	Vi V-40272, Au 239
56544-1	Cowboy Jack	Vi 23593, BB B-4956, Au 417
56545-2	That's A Habit I Never Had	Vi V-40209

Revs: Victor 23593, Bluebird B-4956, Aurora 417 by Blind Jack Mathis.

    Memphis, TN   Friday, May 16, 1930

59929-1	When It's Moonlight On The Prairie	Vi V-40296
59930-2	In Berry Picking Time	Vi 23539

Rev. Victor 23539 by Bud Billings (Frank Luther).

    Memphis, TN   Saturday, May 17, 1930

59936-2	I Got Mine	Vi 23510
59937-1	In The Town Where I Was Born	Vi V-40296

Rev. Victor 23510 by Radio Mac (Harry "Mac" McClintock).

E.F. MORGAN

E.F. Morgan, v; acc. unknown.
    Richmond, IN   Saturday, September 12, 1931

18016	[unknown title]	Ge rejected trial recording

Acc. poss. own g.
    Richmond, IN   Thursday, October 1, 1931

18073	The Drunkard	Ge rejected
18074	Cheyenne	Ge rejected

This artist may be Everett Morgan.

EDWARD MORGAN

Edward Morgan, v; acc. unknown, f; unknown, p; unknown, g.
    Richmond, IN   Saturday, June 30, 1928

13951	Flee As A Bird	Ge rejected

This item was made as a personal recording and is described in Gennett files as "sacred vocal."

EVERETT MORGAN

Everett Morgan, v; acc. prob. own g.
   Richmond, IN   Thursday, February 2, 1933

19004	The Old Musicians Harp	Ch 16583
19005	Old Time Melodies	Ch 16583
19006	Texas Home	Ch 16616
19007	Cheyenne	Ch 16616

JIM MORGAN

Pseudonym on Supertone for Bill Cox.

SUE MORGAN

Sue Morgan, v; acc. Paul Garde, p.
   Chicago, IL   c. early December 1927

| 13273 | Just Plain Folks | Ge rejected |
| 13274 | The Ridge Of Sighs | Ge rejected |

Acc. Olive Ingram, p.
   Chicago, IL   c. February 16, 1928

| 13437,-A,-B | Just Plain Folks | Ge rejected |
| 13438,-A | The Picture That Is Turned Toward The Wall | Ge rejected |

THE MORGANTON TRIO

Fred Denton, bj; others unknown.
   Atlanta, GA   Monday, November 7, 1927

| 145152- | The Fate Of Gladys Kincaid | Co unissued |
| 145153- | Two Little Girls In Blue | Co unissued |

ABE MORRIS

Pseudonym on Champion for John Hammond.

FRANK MORRIS OF RADIO STATION W.T.A.S. VILLA OLIVA, ELGIN, ILL.

Frank Morris, v; acc. unknown, u.
   Chicago, IL   c. May 1925

| 2118-2 | Stand Up And Sing For Your Father | Pm 3070, Pu 11402 |
| 2119-1 | The Old Brown Pants | Pm 3070, Pu 11402 |

WALTER MORRIS

Walter Morris, v/sp-1; acc. unknown, f-2; unknown, g.
   Atlanta, GA   Thursday, April 22, 1926

142080-1	Take Back Your Gold	Co 15101-D, Ve 2497-V, Cl 5437-C, Re/RZAu G20663
142081-1	The Railroad Tramp	Co 15101-D, Ve 2497-V, Cl 5437-C
142082-1	Crazy Coon -1, 2	Co 15079-D
142083-2	Betsey Brown -2	Co 15079-D

Rev. Regal/Regal-Zonophone G20663 by Benny Borg.
   Atlanta, GA   Thursday, November 4, 1926

| 143066- | Crazy Cracker | Co unissued |
| 143067-1 | Sweet Marie | Co 15115-D, Ve 7099-V, Cl 5136-C |

Rev. Velvet Tone 7099-V by Sunshine Four.
   Atlanta, GA   Saturday, November 6, 1926

| 143108-2 | Lulu Walsh | Co 15115-D, Ve 7100-V, Cl 5136-C |
| 143109- | Marsha Run Away | Co unissued |

Rev. Velvet Tone 7100-V by Sunshine Four.
   Atlanta, GA   Wednesday, April 6, 1927

143911-1	Mother's Face I Long To See -2	Co 15186-D
143912-2	In The Time Of Long Ago -2	Co 15186-D
143913-	Barney McCoy	Co unissued
143914-	I'll Never Leave Old Dixie Again	Co unissued

ZEKE & GEORGE MORRIS

Zeke Morris, George Morris, v duet; acc. own g duet.
   Charlotte, NC   Monday, June 15, 1936

102622-1	I Miss My Mother And Dad	MW M-7133
102623-1	They Said My Lord's The Devil	BB unissued

Montgomery Ward M-7133 as by **Wade Mainer & Zeke Morris**. Rev. Montgomery Ward M-7133 by Wade Mainer & Zeke Morris.

MORRIS BROTHERS (WILEY & ZEKE)

Wiley, Zeke & Homer (The Smilin' Rangers): Homer Sherrill, f; Zeke Morris, md-1/g-2/v; Wiley Morris, g/v.
Charlotte, NC   Wednesday, January 26, 1938

018737-1	Understand It Better Bye-And-Bye -2	BB B-7497, MW M-7488
018738-1	Answer To "Blue Eyes" -2	BB B-7426, MW M-7485
018739-1	Someone To Love You When You're Old -2	BB B-7497, MW M-7486
018740-1	I Will Never Turn Back -2	BB B-7572, MW M-7488
018741-1	Greenback Dollar – Part 3 -1	BB B-7426, MW M-7486
018742-1	It Is Love -2	BB B-7572, MW M-7487
018743-1	Under The Old Kentucky Moon -2	BB B-7628, MW M-7485
018744-1	The Eastern Gate -2	BB B-7628, MW M-7487

Morris Brothers (Wiley & Zeke): Wiley Morris, Zeke Morris, v duet; or Wiley Morris, v-1; or Zeke Morris, v-2; acc. Wiley Morris, g; Zeke Morris, g.
Rock Hill, SC   Thursday, September 29, 1938

027622-1	Darling Think What You Have Done	BB B-7967
027623-1	Does Jesus Care	BB B-8103
027624-1	The Story Of Charlie Lawson -1	BB B-7903
027625-1	Riding To See The Sun Go Down	BB B-8136
027626-1	The Great Speckled Bird (New Version)	BB B-7903
027627-1	Don't Say Goodbye If You Love Me	BB B-8136
027628-1	Let Me Be Your Salty Dog	BB B-7967
027629-1	There's A Trail That's Winding -2	BB B-8025
027630-1	I Love The Silver In Your Hair -1	BB B-8025
027631-1	Will The Circle Be Unbroken Bye And Bye	BB B-8103

Wiley Morris, Zeke Morris, v duet; or Wiley Morris, v-1; or Zeke Morris, v-2/y-3; acc. Zeke Morris, md-4/g-5; Wiley Morris, g.
Rock Hill, SC   Sunday, February 5, 1939

032639-1	If You Love Your Mother -4	BB B-8677, MW M-8469
032640-1	Now She's Gone (I'm Sittin' On Top Of The World) -4	MW M-8470
032641-1	Just How Pretty You Smile -4	BB B-8043
032642-1	Blessed Jesus, Hold My Hand -4	BB B-8567, MW M-8471
032643-1	Farewell Kentucky -1, 5	BB B-8653, MW M-8472
032644-1	I Will Meet My Precious Mother -4	BB B-8677, MW M-8469
032645-1	Married Woman Blues -2, 5	BB B-8043
032646-1	Telephone To Glory -4	BB B-8567, MW M-8471
032647-1	Dream Of The Miner's Child -4	BB B-8841
032648-1	Old Covered Bridge -2, 3, 5	BB B-8653, MW M-8472
032649-1	Little Nellie -4	BB B-8841
032650-1	Last Letter -1, 5	MW M-8470

Wiley Morris, Zeke Morris, v duet; or Wiley Morris, v-1; or Eunice Ayers, v-2; or Wiley Morris, Zeke Morris, Eunice Ayers, v trio-3; acc. prob. Tiny Dodson, f-4; unknown, g; unknown, sb-5.
Atlanta, GA   Thursday, August 24, 1939

041308-1	One Little Word -4, 5	BB B-8252, MW M-8466
041309-1	Wabash Cannon Ball No. 2 -1, 4, 5	BB B-8252, MW M-8466
041310-1	My Lord Will Come For Me -3	BB B-8269, MW M-8467
041311-1	It's Blues -4	BB B-8314, MW M-8468
041312-1	Gabriel's Trumpet -2	BB B-8314, MW M-8468
041313-1	He'll Set Your Fields On Fire -3	BB B-8269, MW M-8467

Matrix 041312 as by **Morris Brothers – Little Eunice, Vocalist**.
The Morris Brothers recorded after 1942.

THE MORRIS FAMILY

Unknown, ah-1; Rev. Frank Morris, md/v; Girlie Jean Morris, bj/v; Fanny Lou Morris Ringeisen, g/v.
Atlanta, GA   prob. Wednesday, March 19, 1930

ATL-918-	Will It Be You	Vo 5424
ATL-919-	A Dream Of Home	Vo 5424
ATL-923-	Dark Eyes	Vo 5442
ATL-924-	Oh Mary Don't You Weep	Vo 5465

| ATL-931- | He Rose Unknown -1 | Vo 5465 |
| ATL-932- | Blue Eyed Boy | Vo 5442 |

Matrices ATL-920/21 are by Hoke Rice; matrices ATL-922, ATL-925 are by Fiddler Joe Brown & Fiddler A.A. Gray (see John Dilleshaw); matrices ATL-926 to 929 are by John Dilleshaw; matrix ATL-930 is untraced.

MORRISON TWIN BROTHERS STRING BAND

Abbie Morrison, f; Apsie Morrison, f; Claude Morrison, g; Lawson Morrison, g.
Memphis, TN   Tuesday, June 3, 1930

| 62567-1 | Dry And Dusty | Vi V-40323 |
| 62568-2 | Ozark Waltz | Vi V-40323 |

DICK MORSE

Pseudonym on Oriole for Vernon Dalhart.

MORTON & CRANE

Pseudonym on Supertone for Thompson & Miles (see The Red Fox Chasers).

ARNOLD MOSELEY

This artist, who had one release in the Victor Old Familiar Tunes series (V-40220), is believed to be beyond the scope of this work.

JACK MOSER & HIS OKLAHOMA CAVALIERS

Bob Kendrick, f/v-1; Freddy Loveland, eg; unknown, p; Allan Moser, g/v-2; Jack Moser, d; unidentified, sp-3.
San Antonio, TX   Monday, October 26, 1936

02921-1	Goin' 'Round And 'Round This World -1, 2	BB B-6728
02922-1	Oklahoma -2	BB B-6751, Twin FT8294
02923-1	I Mean Corrina -1, 3	BB B-6728
02924-1	Why Shouldn't I -2	BB B-6751

Rev. Twin FT8294 by Bill Boyd.

BERT MOSS

Pseudonym on Superior for Byrd Moore.

BERT MOSS & JOE LONG

Pseudonym on Superior for Byrd Moore & Jess Johnston.

MOSS & LONG

Pseudonym on Superior for Byrd Moore & Clarence Greene.

OTIS & TOM MOTE

Otis Mote, v; acc. own h/g.
Richmond, VA   Thursday, October 17, 1929

| 403157-A | Tight Like That | OK 45389 |
| 403158-A | Railroad Bill | OK 45389 |

Otis & Tom Mote, v duet; acc. Otis Mote, h/g.
Richmond, VA   Thursday, October 17, 1929

| 403159- | Church Of God Is Right | OK 45429 |
| 403160- | Home In The Rock | OK 45429 |

Otis Mote, v; acc. own h-1/g.
Richmond, IN   Tuesday, January 10, 1939

19986	Will You Love Me When My Carburetor Is Busted -1	Husk O'Hare unissued?
19987	I Can't Get Her Started	Husk O'Hare unnumbered
19988	I Got A Girl In Mexico -1	Husk O'Hare unissued?
19989	Thinking Tonight Of My Sweetheart -1	Husk O'Hare unnumbered

These are custom recordings by Gennett for the promoter Husk O'Hare.

MOULTRIE GEORGIA QUARTET

Vocal quartet; acc. unknown.
Atlanta, GA   Monday, November 1, 1926

| 143000- | 'Tis The Old Time Religion | Co unissued |
| 143001- | Rock Of Ages | Co unissued |

BILL MOUNCE & THE SONS OF THE SOUTH

Tony Sepolio, f; Bob Dunn, esg; Pete Burke, Sr., p; Oliver "Sock" Underwood, g-1/v-2; Jerry Irby, g-3/v-4; Bill Mounce, sb; band v-5.

Dallas, TX   Tuesday, April 8, 1941

063056-1	I Don't Get It -1, 2, 5	BB B-8745
063057-1	From The Start (And To The End) -1, 2	BB B-8745
063058-1	It's Just My Imagination -1, 2	BB B-8807
063059-1	Adios -1	BB B-8718
063060-1	Kickin' It Off -1, 2	BB B-8718
063061-1	Do We Have To Be Apart -3, 4	BB B-8807

Bob Dunn, esg; Jimmy Wyble, eg; Arvin Ercil Shanks, p; "Sock" Underwood, g/v-1; Bill Mounce, sb.

Dallas, TX   Thursday, October 9, 1941

071148-1	I've Found A New Baby	BB B-8869
071149-1	I'm Sorry That You've Gone -1	BB B-8869
071150-1	18 Months, Little Darlin' -1	BB B-8916
071151-1	What's Bob Done	BB B-8976
071152-1	I Thought About You -1	BB B-8976
071153-1	I've Been Drafted -1	BB B-8916

MOUNT VERNON MIXED QUARTET

Vocal quartet (two men, two women); unacc.

Atlanta, GA   Thursday, March 20, 1930

| TATL-955 | What A Day That Will Be | Br 546 |
| TATL-956 | Let Me Go Home | Br 546 |

MOUNT VERNON QUARTET

Vocal quartet; acc. unknown, o.

Atlanta, GA   Saturday, April 2, 1927

| 143865-2 | The New Jerusalem Way | Co 15245-D |
| 143866-1 | Tenting Tonight On The Old Camp Ground | Co 15245-D |

The following recordings may be by a different group.

Vocal quartet; acc. unknown, p.

Atlanta, GA   Thursday, August 2, 1934

82879-1	I'd Rather Be An Old-Time Christian	BB B-5614
82880-1	Sweet Bye-And-Bye	BB B-5693
82881-1	In The Happy Over Yonder	BB B-5614
82882-1	When I Take My Vacation On Heaven's Bright Shore	BB B-5693

MOUNTAIN HILLBILLY ORCHESTRA

Pseudonym on Aurora for the Hollywood Hillbilly Orchestra.

MOUNTAIN RAMBLERS

Pseudonym on Japanese Victor for Dick Hartman's Tennessee Ramblers.

THE MOUNTAIN SINGERS MALE QUARTET

Vocal quartet; acc. unknown.

New York, NY   Tuesday, February 19, 1929

401626-	Bringing In The Sheaves	OK 45315
401627-	Throw Out The Life Line	OK 45315
401628-	Jerusalem Morn	OK unissued

Acc. unknown, o; unknown, cel-1/p-2; unknown, chimes.

New York, NY   Tuesday, July 2, 1929

| 402487-A | Stand Up For Jesus -1 | OK 45364 |
| 402488-B | Whosoever Meaneth Me -2 | OK 45364 |

MOUNTAIN VIEW QUARTET

Vocal quartet; acc. unknown.

Atlanta, GA   Wednesday, April 18, 1928

| 146122- | On The Glory Road | Co unissued |
| 146123- | Willing Workers | Co unissued |

THE MOUNTAINEERS
Pseudonym on Broadway for The Highlanders (see Charlie Poole).

MOUTH ORGAN BAND
Pseudonym on Australian Regal and Regal-Zonophone for the Murphy Brothers Harp Band.

ERNEST MULL
Ernest Mull, v; acc. prob. own h-1/g.
    Richmond, IN   Thursday, May 29, 1930

16703	Old Rattler -1	Ge rejected
16704	Me And My Wife's Wedding	Ge rejected

    Richmond, IN   Monday, June 2, 1930

16705,-A	Been Married Three Times	Ge rejected
16706,-A	Me And My Wife's Wedding	Ge rejected
16707,-A	Ground Hog Blues	Ge rejected
16708,-A	Rub Alcohol Blues -1	Ge rejected
16709,-A	Old Rattler -1	Ge rejected
16710,-A	Nobody's Business	Ge rejected

S.E. MULLIS BLUE DIAMOND QUARTETTE
Vocal sextet (poss. four men, two women), unacc.
    Richmond, IN   Tuesday, March 1, 1932

18431	Let The Church Roll On	Ch 16424
18432	God Shall Wipe All Tears Away	Ge rejected
18433	Were You There	Ge rejected
18434	Dis Train	Ch 16424

This session was logged in Gennett files as by **Blue Diamond Sextette** but Champion 16424 was issued as shown.

ARTURO MUÑIZ
Pseudonym on Mexican Bluebird for Arthur Smith.

MURPHEE HARTFORD QUARTETTE
Pseudonym (or erroneous credit) on Angelus 3321, Clifford 5321 for John & Alma McGhee & Frank Welling (see John McGhee & Frank Welling).

MURPHREE HARTFORD QUARTETTE
See E.M. Bartlett Groups.

MURPHY BROTHERS [HARP BAND]
Murphy Brothers Harp Band: two unknowns, h; two unknowns, g; unknown, v trio-1.
    Atlanta, GA   Thursday, December 4, 1930

151020-2	Boat Song March	Co unissued: Cy 549 (LP)
151021-	Kiss Me Waltz	Co unissued
151022-2	Little Bunch Of Roses -1	Co 15646-D, Re/RZAu G21147
151023-1	Downfall Of Paris	Co 15646-D, Re/RZAu G21147

Regal/Regal-Zonophone G21147 as by **Mouth Organ Band**.

Murphy Brothers, v duet; or unidentified, v-1/y-1; acc. unknown, h; two unknowns, g.
    Richmond, IN   Thursday, June 11, 1931

17819	When Katie Comes Down To The Gate	Ch 16455, Spr 2716
17820-A	A Little White Rose	Ch 16455, Spr 2716
17821,-A	Bashful Beau -1	Ge unissued

Superior 2716 as by **Murphy Bros. Harp Band**.

MURPHY SACRED SINGERS
Vocal group; unacc.
    Atlanta, GA   Thursday, October 6, 1927

81693-A	That Beautiful Home	OK 45172
81694-	Joy For The Redeemed	OK unissued
81695-	The Rock Amid The Waves	OK unissued
81696-A	I'll Be Ready	OK 45172
81697-	Thou Art Gone	OK unissued
81698-	Is It Far	OK unissued

MUSTARD & GRAVY (DIXIE'S TASTIEST COMBINATION)

Frank Rice, Ernest Stokes, v duet; acc. prob. one of them, bj-1/g-2; the other, g-3; one of them, spoons-4.
Rock Hill, SC   Wednesday, September 28, 1938

027787-1	Circus Parade -2, 3	BB B-7859
027788-1	Sister Jackson -2/3, 4	BB B-7859
027789-1	Five Nights' Experience -2, 3	BB B-7905
027790-1	The Whale Did, I Know He Did -2, 3	BB B-7905
027791-1	Ain't Goin' To Be Treated This Way -1, 3	BB B-8161
027792-1	Rooster On The Limb -1, 3	BB B-8161
027793-1	Mother's Dream -2, 3	BB unissued
027794-1	Mother's Picture On The Old Cabin Wall -2, 3	BB unissued
027795-1,-2	Lay Down My Sword And Shield -2, 3	BB unissued

Mustard & Gravy recorded after 1942.

CHRISTINE MUSZAR

Christine Muszar & Petrick (Dak) Pellerin, v duet; acc. unknown, p.
Atlanta, GA   Wednesday, March 20, 1929

402385-A	Z' Amours Marianne	OK 45376

Rev. OKeh 45376 by Patrick (Dak) Pellerin.

Christine Muszar, v; acc. unknown, p.
Atlanta, GA   Wednesday, March 20, 1929

402386-A	Au Clair De La Lune (By The Light Of The Moon)	OK 45334
402387-B	La Chanson D'Evangeline (Evangeline's Song)	OK 45334

HINKEY MYERS

Hinkey Myers, v; acc. unknown.
Atlanta, GA   Friday, October 30, 1931

151986-	I'll See You Again	Co unissued
151987-	I'm Tying The Leaves	Co 15725-D

Rev. Columbia 15725-D by Peggy Parker.

N

CHARLES NABELL

Charles Nabell, v; acc. own g.
St. Louis, MO   Friday, November 28, 1924

8759-A	The Preacher Made Us One	OK 40262
8760-A	While The Leaves Came Drifting Down	OK 40262
8761-A	The Letter From Home Sweet Home	OK 40252
8762-A	The Great Round Up	OK 40252

St. Louis, MO   March 1925

9007-A	Little Joe	OK 40418
9008-A	There's A Mother Always Waiting You At Home Sweet Home	OK 40418
9009-A	The Sheriff Sale	OK 40389
9010-A	Flower From My Angel Mother's Grave	OK 40362
9011-A	Nobody's Business	OK 40389
9012-A	Write A Letter To My Mother	OK 40362
9013-B	Utah Carl	OK 7009
9014-A	Follow The Golden Rule	OK 7009

OKeh 7009 is a 12-inch issue.

St. Louis, MO   November 1925

9391-A	The Hills Of Old Kentucky	OK 45031
9392-A	Would You Care?	OK 45031
9393-A	Memories Of The South Before The War	OK 45039
9394-A	After The War Is Over	OK 45021
9395-A	Scope's [sic] Trial	OK 45039
9396-A	When The Whole World Turns You Down	OK 45021

[E.R.] NANCE FAMILY
THE [E.R.] NANCE SINGERS

The Nance Singers: Helen Nance, av; Madie Nance, sv; Valena Jolly, sv; Rita Jolly, tv/sp-1; Earl Nance, bsv; acc. Helen Nance, o-2/p-3.

New York, NY   Monday, April 28, 1930

9645-	The King Needs Workers -2	ARC unissued
9646-	His Death Was Not In Vain -3	ARC unissued
9647-	Lend Your Aid -3	ARC unissued
9648-	Tell It With Joy -3	ARC unissued
9651-	Old Hymns Are Best -1	ARC unissued

Matrices 9649/50 are by Hill Brothers & Helen Nance.

Helen Nance, av; Madie Nance, sv; Valena Jolly, sv; Rita Jolly, tv; Earl Nance, bsv; acc. Dewey Hill, h-1/g-2; Helen Nance, p-3; Samuel Hill, ah-4.

New York, NY   Tuesday, April 29, 1930

9652-	Sail Away Home -3	ARC unissued
9653-	The Time Is Now -3	ARC unissued
9654-	Happy Am I -3	ARC unissued
9658-	The Place Prepared For Me -3	ARC unissued
9660-	Looking To My Prayer -1, 2, 4	ARC unissued
9661-1,2	On The Sea Of Life -1, 2	Ba 0717, Je 20018, Or 8018, Ro 5018, Htd 16108
9662-	Watching You -3	ARC unissued

All issues of matrix 9661 as by **The E.R. Nance Singers**. Matrices 9655 to 9657 are by Carson Robison & Frank Luther; 9659 by Hill Brothers. Rev. some pressings of Banner 0717, Homestead 16108 by Arthur Cornwall & William Cleary.

Helen Nance, av; Madie Nance, sv; Valena Jolly, sv; Rita Jolly, tv; Earl Nance, bsv-1; acc. Helen Nance, o-2; Rita Jolly, o-3; Dewey Hill, g-4.

New York, NY   Wednesday, April 30, 1930

9663-1	The Old Rugged Cross -1, 3	Ba 0717, Je 20018, Or 8018, Ro 5018, Htd 16108
9664-	The House Upon A Rock -1, 2	ARC unissued
9665-	That Will Be A Happy Moment -1, 3	ARC unissued
9666-	Is It Well With Your Soul? -1	ARC unissued
9667-	I'd Like To Live There With You	ARC unissued
9677-	In Heaven -1, 4	ARC unissued

All issues of matrix 9663 as by **The E.R. Nance Singers**. Matrix 9665 is titled *That Will Be A Happy Morning* in Art Satherley's files. Some pressings of Banner 0717, Romeo 5018, and Homestead 16108 (and probably also of Jewel 20018 and Oriole 8018) replace matrix 9663 with a recording of *The Old Rugged Cross* by Arthur Cornwall & William Cleary (ARC matrix 9852). Matrices 9668/70/73/74 are popular; 9671/72 are by Frank Marvin; 9675/76 are by Hill Brothers.

Helen Nance, av; Madie Nance, sv; Valena Jolly, sv; Rita Jolly, tv; Earl Nance, bsv-1; acc. Helen Nance, o-2; Rita Jolly, o-3.

New York, NY   Friday, May 2, 1930

9678-	When They Ring Those Golden Bells -1, 3	ARC unissued
9679-	What A Friend We Have In Jesus	ARC unissued
9685-	If I Could Hear My Mother Pray Again -1, 2	ARC unissued
9686-	Everybody's Happy There -1, 2	ARC unissued
9687-	When God's Singers Reach Glory -1, 2	ARC unissued
9688-	The Speckled Peas -1	ARC unissued
9689-	The Barnyard Conference -1	ARC unissued

Matrices 9680 to 9684 are unrelated.

Nance Family With Traphill Twins: Helen Nance, av; Madie Nance; sv; Earl Nance, bsv; acc. Byron Bryan, bj; Sam Hallbrook, g.

New York, NY   Tuesday, April 14, 1931

E-36575-	Sweet Freedom	Br 565
E-36576-	The Lawson Murder	Br 542
E-36577-	Mother's Advice	Br 542
E-36578-	I'm On My Way To Heaven	Br 565

E.R. Nance "Booneville Singers": Helen Nance, av; Madie Nance, sv; Earl Nance, bsv; unacc.

Richmond, IN   Thursday, April 16, 1931

17682	The Lot In Canaan's Land	Ge rejected trial recording

E.R. Nance Family With Clarence Dooley-1/Nance Family & Clarence Dooley-2/Nance Family With Clarence Dooley -3: Helen Nance, av; Madie Nance, sv; Clarence Dooley, tv; Earl Nance, bsv; acc. Helen Nance, p-4/md-5; Clarence Dooley, g-6.

Richmond, IN   c. August 26, 1931

17955	Good Bye To My Stepstone -2, 5, 6	Ch S-16316
17956	A Mother's Advice -2, 5, 6	Ch S-16316
17957	The Lot In Canaan's Land -1, 5, 6	Ch S-16410, Spr 2720
17958	Sweet Freedom -1, 5, 6	Ch S-16410, Spr 2813
17959	I Am On My Way To Heaven -1, 5, 6	Ch S-16330, 45138, Spr 2750
17960	The Time Is Now -3, 4	Ch S-16418
17961	All Will Be Well When The Night Is Past -1, 4	Ch S-16369, Spr 2813

Champion 45138 as by **E.R. Nance Family & Clarence Dooley**. Superior 2720, 2750, 2813 as by **James Horton & Family**. Matrix 17959 is titled *I'm On My Way To Heaven* on Champion 45138.

Richmond, IN c. August 29, 1931

17962	Somebody's Knocking At Your Door -1	Ch S-16369, Spr 2750
17963	I Want To Go – I Want To Go -3	Ch S-16418
17964	Do You Think I'll Make A Soldier -1, 4	Ch S-16330, 45138, Spr 2720

Champion 45138 as by **E.R. Nance Family & Clarence Dooley**. Superior 2720, 2750 as by **James Horton & Family**. Dewey and Samuel Hill also recorded in their own names, sometimes assisted by Helen Nance.

W.T. NARMOUR & S.W. SMITH

William T. Narmour, f; Shell W. Smith, g.
Memphis, TN Wednesday, February 15, 1928

400231-B	Captain George, Has Your Money Come?	OK 45242, Ve 2390-V, Cl 5324-C
400232-B	Whistling Coon	OK 45263
400233-B	The Sunny Waltz	OK 45242, RZAu G22885
400234-B	Who's Been Giving You Corn?	OK 45263
400235-B	Heel And Toe	OK 45276, Ve 2390-V, Cl 5324-C
400236-B	Little Star	OK 45276

Velvet Tone 2390-V, Clarion 5324-C as by **Jones & Billings**. Regal-Zonophone G22885 as by **Narmour & Smith**.

Atlanta, GA Monday, March 11, 1929

402269-B	Charleston No. 1	OK 45317, 16679, Ve 7097-V, Cl 5129-C
402270-B	Kiss Me Waltz	OK 45344, 16615
402271-B	Gallop To Georgia	OK 45344, 16679
402272-A	Midnight Waltz	OK 45329, 16604, Vo 03283, RZAu G23003
402273-A	Carroll County Blues	OK 45317, 16615, Ve 7098-V, Cl 5129-C
402274-B	Someone I Love	OK 45329, 16604, Vo 03283, RZAu G23003

OKeh 16604, 16679, and possibly 16615 as by **Duo De Violin Y Guitarra**. (These are issues in OKeh's Mexican series.) Velvet Tone 7097-V, 7098-V, Clarion 5129-C as by **Jones & Billings**. Regal-Zonophone G23003 as by **Narmour & Smith**. Matrix 402270 is titled *Besame Vals*, and matrix 402273 *Estristecido*, on OKeh 16615. Matrix 402272 is titled *Vals De Media Noche*, and matrix 402274 *Alquien Que Amo*, on OKeh 16604.
Revs: Velvet Tone 7097-V, 7098-V by Scottdale String Band.

New York, NY Monday, September 23, 1929

402982-A	Charleston No. 2	OK 45377
405983-B	Carroll County Blues No. 2	OK 45377
402984-B	Avalon Blues	OK 45414
402985-A	Winona Echoes	OK 45414

New York, NY Wednesday, September 25, 1929

402993-A	Dry Gin Rag	OK 45390
402994-B	Mississippi Waves Waltz	OK 45424
402995-B	Sweet Milk And Peaches	OK 45424

S.W. Smith, f; W. T. Narmour, g.
New York, NY Wednesday, September 25, 1929

| 402996-A | Rose Waltz | OK 45390 |

Narmour & Smith also participated in The OKeh Medicine Show recorded on September 24-25.

Narmour & Smith: W. T. Narmour, f; S.W. Smith, g.
San Antonio, TX Friday, June 6, 1930

404064-A	Take Me As I Am	OK 45548
404065-B	Texas Breakdown	OK 45492, 16756
404066-B	Limber Neck Blues	OK 45548
404067-A	Jake Leg Rag	OK 45469, 16732
404068-A	Carroll County No. 3	OK 45459, 16714
404069-A	Charleston No. 3	OK 45459, 16714

OKeh 16714, and possibly 16732 and 16756, as by **Duo Instrumental**.
Matrix 40467 is titled *En El Campo* on OKeh 16732. Matrix 404068 is titled *El Distrito De Carroll*, and matrix 404069 *El Charleston Num. 3*, on OKeh 16714.

San Antonio, TX   Saturday, June 7, 1930
404082-A	Avalon Quick Step	OK 45469, 16732
404083-A	Bouquets Of June Waltz	OK 45480, 16740, RZAu G22885
404084-A	Where The Southern Crosses The Dog	OK 45480, 16740
404085-A	Texas Shuffle	OK 45536
404086-B	Tequila Hop Blues	OK 45536
404087-B	Mississippi Breakdown	OK 45492, 16756

OKeh 16740 and possibly 16732 and 16756 as by **Duo Instrumental**.
Matrix 40482 is titled *Tiempo Alegre* on OKeh 16732. Matrix 404083 is titled *Ramilletes De Junio Vals*, and matrix 404084 *El Cruce*, on OKeh 16740. Matrix 404087 is titled *El Baile Mississippi* on OKeh 16756.

W.T. Narmour, f; S.W. Smith, g; or S.W. Smith, f-1; W.T. Narmour, g-1.
Atlanta, GA   Monday, July 30, 1934
82822-1	The New Charleston – No. 1	BB B-5615, MW M-4525
82823-1	The New Charleston – No. 2	BB B-5720, B-6234, MW M-4529
82824-1	The New Charleston – No. 3	BB B-5810
82825-1	The New Carroll County Blues – No. 1	BB B-5615, MW M-4525
82826-1	The New Carroll County Blues – No. 2	BB B-5720, B-6234, MW M-4529
82827-1	The New Carroll County Blues – No. 3	BB B-5810
82828-1	Midnight Waltz	BB B-5637
82829-1	Someone I Love	BB B-5637
82830-1	Gallop To Georgia	BB B-5669
82831-1	Kiss Me	BB B-5823
82832-1	The Dry Gin Rag	BB B-5669
82833-1	Mississippi Wave Waltz	BB B-5823
82834-1	The Rose Waltz -1	BB B-5754, RZAu G22481
82835-1	Winona Echoes	BB B-5754, RZAu G22481
82836-1	Sweet Milk And Peaches	BB B-5616
82837-1	Avalon Blues	BB B-5616

LEN NASH AND HIS COUNTRY BOYS

Prob. Len Nash, v; acc. Hugh Farr, f; Karl Farr, g.
Los Angeles, CA   c. early 1929
LTR-91	On The Road To California	Br 354, Spt S2069

Len Nash, v; acc. Hugh Farr, f; unknown, ac-1; Karl Farr, g.
Los Angeles, CA   Friday, July 19, 1929
LAE-547-	"The Trail To Mexico"	Br 354, Spt S2069
LAE-548-	Orphan Girl -1	Br 387
LAE-549-	The Ozark Trail	Br 387
LAE-550-B,-A	On The Road To California	Br rejected

Hugh Farr, f; unknown, bj-1; Karl Farr, g; unknown, sb; Len Nash, v-2; several unknowns, v-3/sp-3.
Los Angeles, CA   Tuesday, June 3, 1930
LAE-810-B,-A	Mr. Frog Went A-Courtin'	Br rejected
LAE-811-B,-A	Crazy About Women	Br rejected
LAE-812-A,-B	In The Good Old Days (Part 1)	Br rejected
LAE-813-A,-B	In The Good Old Days (Part 2)	Br rejected
LAE-814-A	Goin' Down To Town -1, 2, 3	Br 440, BrAu 440
LAE-815-A	Kelley Waltz	Br 440, BrAu 440

Accompaniment details are unknown for matrices LAE-810 to 813.

BUCK NATION

This artist's real name is believed to be Rex Kelly or Kelley.

Rex Kelly, v; acc. own g.
Grafton, WI   c. January/February 1932
L-1381-2	Strawberry Roan	Pm 569, Bw 8331
L-1382-2	Down By The Railroad Track	Pm 569, 3319
L-1388-2	Berry Picking Time	Pm 3319
L-1389-2	Susan Van Duzan	Bwy 8331
L-1390-1	Bronco Mustang	Bw 8323
L-1391-2	Cowboy's Lament	Bw 8323

Broadway 8323, 8331 as by **Bud Kelly**. Intervening matrices are untraced.

Buck Nation & Ray Whitley, v/y duet; acc. prob.: Bill Benner, f; Jake Watts, h-1; Bill Butler, sg; Buck Nation and/or Ray Whitley, g.
New York, NY   Thursday, January 17, 1935

39254-A	End Of Memory Lane	BrSA SA879
39254-B	End Of Memory Lane	De 5065, DeSA FM5494
39255-A	Ramshackled Shack On The Hill -1	De 5065, DeSA FM5494, BrSA SA879

Buck Nation, v; acc. prob. Bill Benner, f; poss. own g.
New York, NY   Friday, January 18, 1935

| 39262-A,-B | By The Old Oaken Bucket, Louise | De rejected |
| 39263-A,-B | Bruno Hauptmann's Fate | De unissued |

Buck Nation, v/y-1; acc. prob.: Bill Benner, f; Jake Watts, h-2; Bill Butler, sg; own or Ray Whitley, g.
New York, NY   Tuesday, January 22, 1935

39273-A	The Kidnapper's Story	De 5172, MeC 45213
39274-A	The Ill-Fated Morro Castle	De rejected
39275-A	Blue Ridge Mountain Sweetheart -1	De 5066
39276-A	The Church Bells Told -2	De 5066, Pan 25742

Buck Nation, v; acc. prob.: Bill Benner, f; Jake Watts, h; own or Ray Whitley, g.
New York, NY   Monday, February 11, 1935

39262-C,-D	By The Old Oaken Bucket, Louise	De unissued
39351-A	Twelve Cent Cotton Rollin' In Wealth	De 5081
39352-A	Granddad's Cuspidor	De 5081, Pan 25742

Buck Nation & Ray Whitley, v duet; acc. prob.: Bill Benner, f; Jake Watts, h-1; Bill Butler, sg; Buck Nation and/or Ray Whitley, g.
New York, NY   Friday, February 15, 1935

| 39366-A | Vine Covered Church | De 5114, BrSA SA915 |
| 39367-A | Newly Moulded Mound -1 | De 5114, BrSA SA917 |

Revs: Brunswick SA915 by Frank Luther, SA917 by Stuart Hamblen.

Buck Nation, v; acc. prob.: Bill Benner, f; Jake Watts, h; Bill Butler, sg; own or Ray Whitley, g.
New York, NY   Tuesday, February 19, 1935

| 39263-C | Bruno Hauptmann's Fate | De 5075 |
| 39372-A | The End Of Public Enemy Number One | De 5075 |

Acc. prob.: Bill Benner, f; Bill Butler, sg; own or Ray Whitley, g.
New York, NY   Thursday, February 21, 1935

39382-A	Rocking Chair Lullaby	De 5105
39383-A	The Old Mill Wheel	De 5105
39384-A	Sunset Trail	De 5124
39385-A	The Trail's End	De 5172, MeC 45213, Min M-14065
39386-A	Take Me Back To My Home On The Plains	De 5124

Rev. Minerva M-14065 by Tex Ritter.

Acc. unknown orch.
New York, NY   Monday, February 25, 1935

| 39389-A,-B | Lazy River | De rejected |

This item was made for the popular series.

Buck Nation was also a member of the Airport Boys.

NATIONAL BARN DANCE ORCHESTRA

Two unknowns, f; unknown, md-1 or bj-1; two unknowns, g; unknown, calls.
Chicago, IL   Friday, October 6, 1933

78106-1	Barn Dance – Part 1 -1	BB B-5212, Eld 2098, Sr S-3293, MW M-4389
78107-1	Barn Dance – Part 2 -1	BB B-5212, Eld 2098, Sr S-3293, MW M-4389
78108-1	Polka Quadrille	BB B-5213, Eld 2099, Sr S-3294, MW M-4390
78109-1	Cotillion – Part 1 -1	BB B-5214, Eld 2100, Sr S-3295, MW M-4391
78110-1	Cotillion – Part 2 -1	BB B-5214, Eld 2100, Sr S-3295, MW M-4391
78111-1	The Virginia Reel -1	BB B-5213, Eld 2099, Sr S-3294, MW M-4390
78112-1	Balance Six Quadrille -1	BB B-5215, Eld 2101, Sr S-3296, MW M-4392
78113-1	Waltz Quadrille – Part 1 -1	BB B-5216, B-4705, Eld 2102, Sr S-3297, MW M-4393
78114-1	Waltz Quadrille – Part 2 -1	BB B-5216, B-4705, Eld 2102, Sr S-3297, MW M-4393
78115-1	Square Dance – Part 1 -1	BB B-5217, B-4709, Eld 2103, Sr S-3298, MW M-4394
78116-1	Square Dance – Part 2 -1	BB B-5217, B-4709, Eld 2103, Sr S-3298, MW M-4394
78117-1	"Fishing Time" Square Dance -1	BB B-5215, Eld 2101, Sr S-3296, MW M-4392

NATIONS BROTHERS (SHELTON & MARSHALL)

Shelton Nations, f; Marshall Nations, g.
    Jackson, MS   Sunday, October 13, 1935

Matrix	Title	Issue
JAX-133-1	Bankhead Blues	ARC 6-11-54, Vo 03118
JAX-134-1	Magnolia One Step	ARC 6-11-54, Vo 03118
JAX-135-2	Railroad Blues	Vo 03152
JAX-136-1	Negro Supper Time	ARC 7-05-78
JAX-137-1	Lincoln County Blues	Vo 03184
JAX-138-1	Sales Tax Toddle	Vo 03184
JAX-139-	Whistlin' Coon	ARC unissued
JAX-140-1	Honeymoon Waltz	ARC 7-05-78
JAX-141-	Sunny Waltz	ARC unissued
JAX-142-1	The Little Black Mustache	Vo 03152

The subcredit is omitted on ARC 7-05-78.

NATIVE RUSSIAN TROUPE WITH GREISHA HAITEWICH

Though released in the Paramount Old Time Tunes series, records by this group (3089/90) are of Russian balalaika music and are beyond the scope of this work.

AMOS NEAL

Pseudonym on Champion for Dick Parman.

FIDDLIN' DAVE NEAL

Pseudonym on Challenge for Fiddlin' Sam Long.

DAVID NEAL

Pseudonym on Supertone for H.K. Hutchison.

FRANK NEAL & HIS BOYS

Pseudonym on Challenge for Da Costa Woltz's Southern Broadcasters.

PLEAMAN S. NEAL'S HARMONY THREE

Vocal trio; acc. unknown.
    Dallas, TX   Sunday, October 27, 1929

Matrix	Title	Issue
DAL-501	Beneath The Stars	Br unissued
DAL-502	On A Summer's Day	Br unissued

These items were intended for issue in the Brunswick 100 Hillbilly series.

RUTH NEAL & WANDA NEAL

Ruth Neal, Wanda Neal, v duet; acc. unknown, bj; unknown, g.
    Atlanta, GA   Friday, June 3, 1927

Matrix	Title	Issue
80971-	Death of Floella	OK unissued
80972-B	The Two Orphans	OK 45124, PaE R3861
80973-	Never Alone	OK unissued
80974-	I Gave My Life For Thee	OK unissued
80975-	Silent Night	OK unissued
80976-	In A Home Far Away	OK unissued
80977-	Sweet Bunch Of Daisies	OK unissued
80978-	Put My Little Shoes Away	OK unissued

Ruth Neal, Wanda Neal, v duet; or **Wanda Neal**, v-1; acc. unknown, bj; unknown, g.
    Atlanta, GA   Saturday, June 4, 1927

Matrix	Title	Issue
80979-	Way Down South	OK unissued
80980-A	Round Town Girls -1	OK 45124, PaE R3861
80981-	Smiling Sea	OK unissued
80982-	Peaceful Sleep	OK unissued

Acc. poss. Bert Layne, f; unknown, f; poss. Claude (C.W.) Davis, g.
    Winston-Salem, NC   Tuesday, September 20, 1927

Matrix	Title	Issue
81351-	Death Of Flo Ella	OK unissued
81352-	Down On The Farm	OK unissued
81353-	Just Over The Smiling Sea	OK unissued
81354-	No Never Alone	OK unissued

FIDDLIN' FRANK NELSON

Pseudonym on Challenge and Superior for Doc Roberts.

KIT NELSON

Pseudonym on Jewel and Oriole for Willard Hodgin.

MORRIS NELSON

Morris Nelson, v; acc. poss. own p.
    Atlanta, GA   Wednesday, February 22, 1928
    41931-1,-2   My Alpine Yodelling Sweetheart   Vi unissued

The Victor session-sheet carries the description "(Hillbilly)".

NELSON & NELSON

Harry Charles, another, v duet; acc. unknown, f-1; unknown, md-2; unknown, g.
    Long Island City, NY   c. April 1929
    415   Oh Where Is My Wandering Boy Tonight -1   QRS R.9021
    415-A   Oh, Where Is My Wandering Boy Tonight -1   Pm 3219, Bwy 8160
    416-A   Work For The Night Is Coming -1, 2   QRS R.9021, Pm 3220, Bwy 8160,
                                                                 ARC-Bwy 8160

Paramount 3219, 3220, Broadway 8160 as by **Norman & Norman**.

Revs: Paramount 3219, 3220 by Hobbs Brothers; ARC-Broadway 8160 by John McGhee & Frank Welling.

Harry Charles also recorded at this session (as Harry Nelson) with Katherine Baxter (who is possibly Catherine Boswell), and probably with Claude (C.W.) Davis (as Davis & Nelson). The unidentified vocalist above may in fact be Davis.

NELSTONE'S HAWAIIANS

Hubert A. Nelson, sg/v-1; James D. Touchstone, g/v.
    Memphis, TN   Friday, September 21, 1928
    47074-1   Adam And Eve -1   Vi V-40011, MW M-4492
    47075-1,-2   Just Lonesome -1   Vi unissued
    47076-2   North-Bound Train -1   Vi V-40065, ZoSA 4232
    47077-   You'll Never Find A Daddy Like Me   Vi V-40011, MW M-4492

Revs: Victor V-40065 by Jimmy Yates, Zonophone 4232 by Frank Luther & Carson Robison (see the latter).

James D. Touchstone, h-1/g/v-2/sp-3; Hubert A. Nelson, sg/v-4/sp-3.
    Atlanta, GA   Saturday, November 30, 1929
    56636-2   Mobile County Blues -1, 3   Vi V-40273
    56637-1   Just Because -1, 2, 4   Vi V-40273
    56638-2   Village School -2, 4   Vi V-40193
    56639-2   Fatal Flower Garden -2, 4   Vi V-40193

J.P. NESTER

James Preston Nester, v; acc. Norman Edmonds, f; own bj.
    Bristol, TN   Monday, August 1, 1927
    39744-2   Train On The Island   Vi 21070
    39745-1   Georgia   Vi unissued
    39746-1   John My Lover   Vi unissued
    39747-1   Black-Eyed Susie   Vi 21070

NETTLE BROTHERS STRING BAND

See Bill Nettles.

BILL NETTLES

Bill Nettles & His Dixie Blue Boys: Doc Massey, f; Bill Nettles, md/v-1; Norman Nettles, g/v-2; Luther Nettles, sb.
    Dallas, TX   Tuesday, June 22, 1937
    DAL-420-1   Shake It And Take It -1   ARC 7-09-64, Vo 03634
    DAL-421-1   My Cross-Eyed Nancy Jane -1   ARC 7-09-64, Vo 03634
    DAL-422-   A Mother's Last Prayer   ARC unissued
    DAL-423-2   A Prisoner's Farewell -1   Vo 04075
    DAL-424-2   No Daddy Blues -1   ARC 7-10-63, Vo 03662
    DAL-425-2   Just A Little Lovin' -1   ARC 7-10-63, Vo 03662
    DAL-426-2   Oxford (Miss.) Blues -1   ARC 7-11-57, Vo 03694
    DAL-427-1   Lazy River Moon -2   ARC 8-01-57, Vo 03857
    DAL-428-1   I Miss The Girl (That Misses Me) -1   ARC 7-11-57, Vo 03694

DAL-429-2	A Heart That Is Broken For You -1, 2	ARC 8-01-57, Vo 03857
DAL-430-2	Where The Sweet Magnolias Bloom -1, 2	Vo 04012
DAL-431-	The Return To Red River Valley	ARC unissued

San Antonio, TX   Sunday, October 31, 1937

SA-2849-1,-2	Living And Loving In Style	ARC unissued
SA-2850-1,-2	Swingin' On That New River Train	ARC unissued
SA-2851-1,-2	My Louisiana Sweetheart	ARC unissued
SA-2852-1,-2	If You'll Take Me Back	ARC unissued
SA-2854-1	She's Runnin' Wild -2	Vo 04075
SA-2855-1	The Answer To "Wondering" -1	ARC 8-02-54, Vo 03903
SA-2856-2	Early Morning Blues -1	Vo 04012

Matrix SA-2853 is by Kitty Gray (see *B&GR*).

Bill & Norman Nettles, v duet; acc. Bill Nettles, md; Norman Nettles, g.

San Antonio, TX   Monday, November 1, 1937

| SA-2857-1,-2 | The Coming Of The King | ARC unissued |
| SA-2858-1,-2 | When The Book Of Life Is Opened | ARC unissued |

Bill Nettles & His Dixie Blue Boys: Doc Massey, f; Bill Nettles, md/v; Norman Nettles, g; Luther Nettles, sb.

San Antonio, TX   Monday, November 1, 1937

SA-2859-1	Answer To Blue Eyes	Vo 03952
SA-2860-1,-2	The Hottest Mama In Town	ARC unissued
SA-2861-1	When We Kissed And Said Good-bye	ARC 8-02-54, Vo 03903
SA-2862-1	Louisiana Moon	Vo 03952

Prob.: Criss Herrington, f; Larry Nola, cl-1/ts-2; Spec Harrison or Harry O'Shea, ac; Bill Nettles, md/v-3; Norman Nettles, g/v-4; Luther Nettles, sb.

Dallas, TX   Sunday, December 4, 1938

DAL-697-1,-2	After You've Said Goodbye -4	Vo unissued
DAL-698-1,-2	I'll Always Be True To You -4	Vo unissued
DAL-699-1	She's Selling What She Used To Give Away -1, 3	Vo/OK 04655, Cq 9188, Co 37732, 20309
DAL-708-1,-2	Red Hot Mama -4	Vo unissued
DAL-709-1	Why Do The Men Love The Women? -4	Vo 04757
DAL-710-1,-2	She's The Treasure Of Them All -4	Vo unissued
DAL-711-1	High Steppin' Mama -2, 4	Vo 04615
DAL-712-1	Big Shot Daddy Blues -2, 3	Vo 04615
DAL-713-1	Sugar Baby Blues -1, 2, 3	Vo/OK 04655, Cq 9188, Co 37732, 20309

Intervening matrices are by Kitty Gray and Buddy Woods (see *B&GR* for both).

Dallas, TX   Monday, December 5, 1938

| DAL-714-1 | Turn About Swing -1, 3 | Vo 04757 |

Nettles Brothers String Band: Lonnie Hall, f; Jimmy King, esg; Bill Nettles, md/v-1; Norman Nettles, g/v-2; Reginald Ward, sb.

Dallas, TX   Thursday, April 3, 1941

063000-1	Fannin' *[sic]* Street Blues -1	BB B-8720
063001-1	Howdy Do Blues -1	BB B-8819
063002-1	Small Town Blues -1	BB B-8819
063003-1	Dan, The Banana Man -1	BB B-8720
063004-1	I'll Never Worry Over You -2	BB B-8805
063005-1	You Go Your Way, I'll Go Mine -2	BB B-8805

Bluebird B-8720 as by **Nettle Brothers String Band**. All the items from this session were remastered, on various dates in May 1941. Most issues seem to have been from these dubbed masters, but at least some issues of matrix 063000 use the (presumably original) take 1.

Lonnie Hall, f/v-1; Jody Pilliod, esg; Mahlon Reynolds, bj; Norman Nettles, g/v-2; Joe Grady Thomas, sb; Bill Nettles, v-3.

Dallas, TX   Wednesday, October 8, 1941

071128-1	I Feel The Draft Coming On -3	BB B-8911
071129-1	She's Runnin' Wild -2	BB B-8881
071130-1	There's No Use To Worry Now -3	BB B-8911
071131-1	Beautiful Hawaiian Shores -1, 2	BB 33-0504
071132-1	Shift Gears Truck And Go -3	BB B-8881
071133-1	When I Go A Courtin' My Best Gal -2	BB 33-0504

Bill Nettles recorded after 1942.

NETTLES BROTHERS STRING BAND

See Bill Nettles.

JIM NEW

Pseudonym on Timely Tunes and Aurora for Newton Gaines.

NEW ARKANSAS TRAVELERS

Victor recordings with this credit (of which 21288 was the only issued coupling) feature what is apparently an English music-hall singer, one A. Bishop, with unknown accompanists (2h, g). Although these accompanists may possibly have been American country musicians, the performances must be (reluctantly) judged to be outside the scope of this work.

NEW DIXIE DEMONS

Art ———, cl; unknown, piccolo; unknown, k; Davy ———, g; poss. Buddy Valentine, sb; unknown, wb; unknown, sw; band v.

Chicago, IL   Saturday, July 18, 1936

| 90798-A | It Ain't Right | De 5253, DeE F6245 |
| 90799-A | Za-Zoo-Za | De 5253 |

This session was originally logged as by **The Prairie Plowboys**.

Chicago, IL   Thursday, August 13, 1936

C-90829-A	I'm A Rootin' Shootin' Tootin' Man From Texas	De 5264, DeE F6213
C-90830-A	Was I Drunk?	De 5257
C-90831-A	Toot Toot Tootsie Goodbye	De 5264
C-90832-A	Ace In The Hole	De 5257
C-90833-A	Bye Bye Baby	De 5259
C-90834-A	Everybody Kiss Your Partner	De 5259, DeE F6444

Chicago, IL   Saturday, September 19, 1936

C-90872-A	I'm Afraid Of Bees	De 5292, DeE F6212
C-90873-A	Oh! You Rogue (You Stole My Heart)	De 5271
C-90874-A	Piles Of It	De 5277, DeE F6213
C-90875-A	'Tain't A Fit Night Out For Man Or Beast	De 5271, DeE F6212
C-90876-A	The Preacher And The Bear	De 5277, DeE F6245
C-90877-A	Man Man What A Band!	De 5292

Matrices C-90875/76 were "remade" on October 9, 1936; it is presumed that these were technical remasterings.

Chicago, IL   Tuesday, December 8, 1936

| C-91033-A,-B | Sweet Potato Bill | De rejected |

Chicago, IL   Wednesday, December 9, 1936

C-91034-A	Pick That Bass	De 5314, DeE F6344
C-91035-B	Maybe	De 5362
C-91036-A	Oh! What I Know About Roscoe	De 5314
C-91037-A	They're Off	De 5320, DeE F6344

Chicago, IL   Wednesday, December 16, 1936

C-91061-A,-B	No, No, Nora	De rejected
C-91062-A	I Would If I Could But I Can't	De 5392
C-91063-A	They Go Wild Simply Wild Over Me	De 5320

Chicago, IL   Thursday, January 28, 1937

C-91097-A	Don't Bring Lulu	De 5343
C-91098-A	You Can Tell She Comes From Dixie	De 5343, DeE F6444
C-91099-A	Looking At The World Thru Rose Colored Glasses	De 5362
C-91100-A	Coquette	De 5392

CHARLIE [& BUD] NEWMAN

Charlie Newman, v/y-1; acc. prob. own g.

Atlanta, GA   Thursday, October 28, 1926

| 9831-A | Sweet Bunch Of Daisies | OK 45072 |
| 9832-A | Rock All Our Babies To Sleep -1 | OK 45072 |

Atlanta, GA   Tuesday, March 15, 1927

80537-A	Get Away, Old Man, Get Away	OK 45095, PaE R3860
80538-B	Blue Ridge Mountain Blues	OK 45184
80539-B	Pretty Little Dear	OK 45095, PaE R3860
80540-B	Susie Ann	OK 45116
80541-B	Sleep, Baby, Sleep -1	OK 45184
80542-A	The Fellow That's Just Like Me	OK 45116

Charlie & Bud Newman, v duet; acc. two unknowns, f-1; prob. own g duet; prob. Charlie Newman, y-2.
Memphis, TN   Saturday, February 11, 1928

400200-A	My Blue Ridge Mountain Queen -1	OK 45200
400201-	Grady's Daughter	OK unissued
400202-B	The Old Traveling Man	OK 45431, Ve 2359-V, Cl 5293-C
400204-C	Sweet Bunch Of Daisies -1	OK 45200
400205-B	Rock All Of Our Babies To Sleep -2	OK 45431

Velvet Tone 2359-V, Clarion 5293-C as by **John & Eddie Howard**. Matrix 400203 is blank in OKeh files but probably by these artists. Rev. Velvet Tone 2359-V, Clarion 5293-C by Frank Marvin.

FRED NEWMAN

Pseudonym on Paramount and Broadway for Roy Harvey.

HANK & SLIM NEWMAN

These artists' real names were Henry J. and Marion Alonzo Newman respectively.

Hank & Slim (The Newman Brothers), v/y-1 duet; acc. Hank Newman, g.
New York, NY   Thursday, September 6, 1934

15832-2	How Beautiful Heaven Must Be	Vo 02808
15833-2	When I Take My Vacation In Heaven	Vo 02808
15834-1	Mississippi River Blues	Vo 02807
15835-1	Moonlight And Skies -1	Vo 02852
15836-1	Good Old Country Town	Vo 02852
15837-2	When The Sun Goes Down Again	Vo 02807
15838-2	Dear Old Mother	Vo 02840, RZAu G22401
15839-2	Three Pictures Of Life's Other Side	Vo 02840, RZAu G22401

Hank & Slim Newman recorded after 1942.

ROY NEWMAN & HIS BOYS

Art Davis, f/v-1; prob. Thurman Neal, f; Roy Newman, p; Walker Kirkes, tbj; Jim Boyd, g/v-2; Ish Erwin, sb; unidentified 3rd v-3.
Fort Worth, TX   Sunday, September 30, 1934

FW-1140-2	Messin' Around	Vo 02906
FW-1141-1	Tiger Rag -1, 2, 3	Vo 02906
FW-1142-1	Weary Blues	Vo 02864
FW-1143-	Red Wing -1, 2	Vo unissued
FW-1144-1	Drag Along Blues	Vo 02864
FW-1145-1	Chicken Reel	Vo 02883
FW-1146-	'Way Down Yonder In Carolina -1, 2	Vo unissued
FW-1147-1	Git Along Home Cindy -1, 2 (lead)	Vo 02883

Art Davis, f/v-1; Thurman Neal, f; Holly Horton, cl/v-2/sp-3; Roy Newman, p; Walker Kirkes, tbj; Jim Boyd, g/v-4; Randall "Buddy" Neal, g; Ish Erwin, sb; Ramon DeArman, sp-3; band v-3.
Fort Worth, TX   Thursday, June 27, 1935

FW-1222-B	Tin Roof Blues -2	Vo 02994
FW-1223-B	Garbage Man Blues -1, 3	Vo 02994
FW-1224-A	Somebody Loves Me -4	Vo 03000
FW-1225-A	Barn Dance Rag	Vo 03000

Art Davis, f/md-1; Thurman Neal, f; Holly Horton, cl; Roy Newman, p; Walker Kirkes, tbj; Jim Boyd, eg-2/g-3; Earl Brown, g/v-4; Randall "Buddy" Neal, g; Ish Erwin, sb; Ray Lackland, v-5; Buddy Harris, v-6; band v-7.
Dallas, TX   Friday, September 27, 1935

DAL-172-1	Rhythm Is Our Business -2, 5, 7	Vo 03103
DAL-173-1	Dinah -3, 6	Vo 03183
DAL-174-1	I Can't Dance (Got Ants In My Pants) -3, 4, 7	Vo/OK 03117, Co 37611, Co 20210
DAL-175-1	Slow And Easy -1, 2, 4	Vo 03103

Earl Brown may play string bass (rather than Erwin?) on some items.

Art Davis, f/md-1; Thurman Neal, f; Holly Horton, cl; Roy Newman, p; Walker Kirkes, tbj; Jim Boyd, eg-2/g-3/v-4; Earl Brown, g/v-5; Randall "Buddy" Neal, g; Ish Erwin, sb; Ray Lackland, v-6; band v-7.
Dallas, TX   Saturday, September 28, 1935

DAL-178-1	Hot Dog Stomp -2	Vo 03371
DAL-179-1	The Lonesome Road -3, 6	Vo 03212
DAL-180-2	Shine On, Harvest Moon -3, 6, 7	Vo 03272
DAL-181-1	Corrine, Corrina -1, 3, 4, 5	Vo/OK 03117, Co 37611, Co 20210

Earl Brown may play string bass (rather than Erwin?) on some items.

Art Davis, f/v-1; Thurman Neal, f; Holly Horton, cl; Roy Newman, p; Walker Kirkes, tbj; Jim Boyd, g; Earl Brown, g/v-2; Randall "Buddy" Neal, g; Ish Erwin, sb; Ray Lackland, v-3.
    Dallas, TX   Tuesday, October 1, 1935

DAL-191-1	How Many Times -1	Vo 03151
DAL-192-2	Sadie Green (The Vamp Of New Orleans) -2	Vo 03151
DAL-193-1	Rock-A-Bye Moon -3	Vo 03272
DAL-194-1	A Good Man Is Hard To Find -2	Vo 03325
DAL-195-1	Some Of These Days -3	Vo 03183
DAL-196-1	There'll Be Some Changes Made -2	Vo 03325

Art Davis, f; Thurman Neal, f; Holly Horton, cl; Roy Newman, p; Walker Kirkes, tbj; Jim Boyd, eg-1/g-2/v-3; Earl Brown, g/v-4; Randall "Buddy" Neal, g; Ish Erwin, sb; unidentified, v-5.
    Dallas, TX   Friday, October 4, 1935

DAL-201-3	Birmingham Jail -2, 3, 5	Vo 03212
DAL-202-1	(What Did I Do To Be So) Black And Blue -2, 4	Vo 03240
DAL-203-2	12th Street Rag -1	Vo 03240
DAL-204-1	Wonderful One -2, 4	Vo 03371

According to ARC files, takes 1 and 2 of matrix DAL-201 were recorded on October 4, 1935 and take 3 on March 26, 1936. It is assumed that take 3 is a technical rerecording.

Thurman Neal, f; prob. Cecil Brower, f; Holly Horton, cl; unknown, esg; Roy Newman, p; Walker Kirkes, tbj; Jim Boyd, g/v-1; Earl Brown, g; poss. Randall "Buddy" Neal, g; Ish Erwin, sb; Charlie Lockhart, v-2.
    Fort Worth, TX   Sunday, November 8, 1936

FW-1278-	Hot Potato Stomp	Vo unissued
FW-1279-	Everybody's Blues -1	Vo unissued
FW-1280-	There's A Silver Moon On The Golden Gate -2	Vo unissued
FW-1281-	Too Busy! -2	Vo unissued

Cecil Brower, f; Holly Horton, cl-1; Bob Dunn, esg; Roy Newman, p; Walker Kirkes, tbj; Jim Boyd, g/v-2; Earl Brown, g/v-3; Ish Erwin, sb; Charlie Lockhart, v-4.
    Dallas, TX   Sunday, June 6, 1937

DAL-205-1,-2	I Love My Baby (My Baby Loves Me)	Vo unissued
DAL-206-1,-2	Long, Long Ago	Vo unissued
DAL-207-2	When You And I Were Young Maggie -1, 3	Vo 03598
DAL-208-1	We'll Meet By The Bend In The River -1, 4	Vo 03598
DAL-209-2	Everybody's Blues -1, 2	Vo 03878
DAL-210-2	She's Doggin' Me -3	Vo 03672
DAL-211-1,-2	Match Box Blues	Vo unissued

Cecil Brower, f; Holly Horton, cl-1; Bob Dunn, esg-2; Roy Newman, p-3; Walker Kirkes, tbj; Jim Boyd, g/v-4; Earl Brown, g/v-5/v eff-6; Ish Erwin, sb; Charlie Lockhart, v-7; band v-8.
    Dallas, TX   Monday, June 14, 1937

DAL-308-2	Takin' Off -1, 2, 3	Vo 04025
DAL-309-1	Who Calls You Sweet Mama Now? -1, 2, 3, 5	Vo 03631
DAL-310-1	The Night That You Nestled In My Arms -2, 3, 7	Vo 03631
DAL-311-	Drifting And Dreaming (Sweet Paradise)	Vo unissued
DAL-312-1	Mississippi Mud -5, 6, 8	Vo 04025
DAL-313-1	When There's Tears In The Eyes Of A Potato -1, 2, 3, 4	Vo 03878
DAL-314-	Cemetery Sal	Vo unissued
DAL-315-1	Dust Off That Old Piano -1, 2, 3, 7	Vo 03938
DAL-316-1	Mary Lou -1, 2, 3, 4	Vo/OK 03752
DAL-317-	Railroad Blues	Vo unissued

Cecil Brower, f-1; Holly Horton, cl-2; Bob Dunn, esg-3; Roy Newman, p; Walker Kirkes, tbj; Jim Boyd, g/v-4; Earl Brown, g/v-5/v eff-6; Ish Erwin, sb.
    Dallas, TX   Friday, June 18, 1937

DAL-363-2	I'm Saving Saturday Night For You -1, 2, 3, 5	Vo/OK 03752
DAL-364-1	Catch On And Let's Go -1, 2, 3	Vo 03672
DAL-365-1	Back In Your Own Back Yard -1, 2, 3, 4	Vo 03938
DAL-366-2	Graveyard Blues -2, 5	Vo 03963
DAL-367-1	Better Get Off Your High Horse Baby -1, 2, 3, 4, 5	Vo 03963
DAL-368-1	Everywhere You Go -1, 2, 3, 5	Vo 03999
DAL-369-1	Tamiami Trail -1, 5, 6	Vo 03999

Carroll Hubbard, f; unknown, f; Holly Horton, cl; Bill Staton, ac; Roy Newman, p; Walker Kirkes, tbj; Julian Akins, lg; Earl Brown, g/v; Gene Sullivan, g; Ish Erwin, sb.
    Dallas, TX   Thursday, December 1, 1938

DAL-660-1	Down Hearted Blues	Vo/OK 04959, Co 37734, 20311

Bill Staton, ac; Walker Kirkes, tbj; Julian Akins, lg; Gene Sullivan, g/v; Earl Brown, g; Ish Erwin, sb.
    Dallas, TX   Thursday, December 1, 1938

| DAL-661-1 | Kansas City Blues | Vo/OK 04959, Co 37734, 20311 |

Carroll Hubbard, f; unknown, f; Holly Horton, cl; Bill Staton, ac; Roy Newman, p; Walker Kirkes, tbj; Julian Akins, lg; Earl Brown, g; Gene Sullivan, g; Ish Erwin, sb.
    Dallas, TX   Thursday, December 1, 1938

| DAL-662-1,-2 | Nagasaki | Vo unissued |

Carroll Hubbard, f; Julian Akins, lg; Gene Sullivan, g; Earl Brown, v.
    Dallas, TX   Thursday, December 1, 1938

| DAL-663-1 | Match Box Blues | Vo/OK 04578, Co 37729, 20306 |

Carroll Hubbard, f; unknown, f; Holly Horton, cl; Bill Staton, ac; Roy Newman, p; Walker Kirkes, tbj; Julian Akins, lg/v-1; Earl Brown, g/v-2; Gene Sullivan, g; Ish Erwin, sb.
    Dallas, TX   Thursday, December 1, 1938

DAL-664-1	I Cried For You -2	Vo 04792, Cq 9245
DAL-665-1	Texas Stomp	Vo 04866, Cq 9271
DAL-666-1	Take Me Back To My Home In The Mountains -1	Vo 05486, Cq 9429
DAL-667-1	My Baby Rocks Me (With One Steady Roll) -2	Vo 04578, Co 37729, 20306
DAL-668-1	I've Got It	Vo 04639, Cq 9351

Carroll Hubbard or unknown, f; Holly Horton, cl; Bill Staton, ac; George Bell, p; Walker Kirkes, tbj; Julian Akins, lg; Gene Sullivan, g/v; Earl Brown, g; Ish Erwin, sb.
    Dallas, TX   Thursday, December 1, 1938

| DAL-669-1 | Everybody's Trying To Be My Baby | Vo/OK 04866, Cq 9271 |

Carroll Hubbard, f; unknown, f; Holly Horton, cl-1; Bill Staton, ac; Roy Newman, p; Walker Kirkes, tbj; Julian Akins, lg/v-2; Earl Brown, g/v-3; Gene Sullivan, g/v-4; Ish Erwin, sb.
    Dallas, TX   Monday, December 5, 1938

DAL-722-1	Eleven Pounds Of Heaven -1, 3	Vo/OK 04792, Cq 9245
DAL-723-1	I Don't Love Anyone But You -4	Vo/OK 04740
DAL-724-1	I Used To Love You (But It's All Over Now) -1, 3	Vo/OK 04639, Cq 9351
DAL-725-1	Where The Morning Glories Grow -2, 4 (lead)	Vo 05379
DAL-726	Cemetery Sal -1, 3	Vo unissued
DAL-727-1	I Love My Baby (My Baby Loves Me) -1, 3	Vo/OK 05486, Cq 9429
DAL-728-1	Boog-A-Boo Baby -1, 3	Vo/OK 04740

Cecil Brower, f; Carroll Hubbard, f; poss. Kenneth Pitts or Gar Austin, f; Holly Horton, cl-1; Harry Sorensen, ac; Roy Newman, p; Julian Akins, lg; Earl Brown, g/v-2; Gene Sullivan, g/v-3; Ish Erwin, sb; band v-4.
    Dallas, TX   Monday, June 19, 1939

DAL-856-1	The Devil With The Devil -1, 2, 4	Vo 05066
DAL-857-1	Blues, Why Don't You Let Me Alone? -1, 2	Vo 05320
DAL-858-1	Round The World On A Dime -1	Vo 05066
DAL-859-1	I've Got The Walkin' Blues -1, 3	Vo 05379
DAL-860-1	Kentucky, Sure As You're Born -2	Vo/OK 05242
DAL-861-1	If I Ever Get To Heaven -1, 3	Vo 05014
DAL-862-1	I'm Tired Of Everything But You -1, 3	Vo 05014

Cecil Brower, f; Carroll Hubbard, f; poss. Kenneth Pitts or Gar Austin, f; Holly Horton, cl-1; Harry Sorensen, ac; Roy Newman, p; Julian Akins, lg/v-2; Earl Brown, g/v-3; Gene Sullivan, g; Ish Erwin, sb.
    Dallas, TX   Tuesday, June 20, 1939

DAL-871-1	Don't Let Me Stand In Your Way -3	Vo 05320
DAL-872-1,-2	Out Of Place	Vo unissued
DAL-873-1	Love Burning Love -1, 2	Vo 05175
DAL-874-1	Everything Is Peaches 'Neath The Old Apple Tree -1, 3	Vo/OK 05242
DAL-875-1	I Ought To Break Your Neck (For Breakin' My Heart) -1, 3	Vo 05175

WILLIE (RED) NEWMAN

See Jack Pierce.

NEWTON COUNTY HILL BILLIES

Alvis L. Massengale, f; Marcus Harrison, md; Andrew Harrison, g.
    Jackson, MS   Tuesday, December 16, 1930

404742-A	The Little Princess Footsteps	OK 45549
404743-	Happy Hour Breakdown	OK 45520
404744-B	Nine O'Clock Breakdown	OK 45544

404745-A	Going To The Wedding To Get Some Cake	OK 45549
404746-B	Give Me A Bottle Of I Don't Care What	OK 45544
404747-	The Quaker Waltz	OK 45520

BOB NICHOLS

Pseudonym on Columbia for Clayton McMichen.

JOE & BOB NICHOLS

This pseudonym was used for some vocal duets by Clayton McMichen and Hoyt "Slim" Bryant recorded at the Crown session by Clayton McMichen's Georgia Wildcats. See Clayton McMichen.

NICHOLS BROTHERS

Claude Nichols, f/v; Lawrence Nichols, g-1/v-2/y-3; Stanton Nichols, tg/v-4/y-5.
    Charlotte, NC   Thursday, May 28, 1931

69366-1	She's Killing Me -1	Vi 23582
69372-1	Dear Old Tennessee -1, 2, 3, 5	Vi 23596
69373-2	I'm Lonely Since Mother's Gone -2, 4, 5	Vi 23596

Matrices 69367/68 are by Jimmie Davis; 69369 to 69371 by Haywood County Ramblers.
Rev. Victor 23582 by Pine Mountain Boys.

W.J. NICHOLSON
NICHOLSON, FLOYD & SPURGEON

See Nicholson's Players.

NICHOLSON'S PLAYERS

Prob.: ——— Floyd, f; ——— Ashabraner, h; Will J. Nicholson, bj; Glen Spurgeon, g; unknown, jh.
    Richmond, IN   Thursday, January 23, 1930

| 16133 | Irish Washerwoman; My Bonnie; Oh Susanna | Ge 7151, Ch 15942, 33001, Spt 9644, Spr 2738 |

Supertone 9644 as by **Armstrong's Players**. Superior 2738 as by **Goose Creek Gully Jumpers**.
Rev. Champion 33001 by Doc Roberts.

Prob.: ——— Floyd, f; ——— Ashabraner, h; Will J. Nicholson, bj; Glen Spurgeon, g; unknown, j-1.
    Richmond, IN   Friday, January 24, 1930

16135	Turkey In The Straw–Old Folks At Home–Big Eared Mule -1	Ge 7125, Ch 16137, Spt 9644, Spr 2738
16137-A	Sweet Bunch Of Daisies	Ge 7151, Ch 16007, 45193, MeC 45193, Spt 9661
16138	Muskakatuck Waltz	Ge 7125, Ch 15942, Spt 9733, Spr 2639

Supertone 9644, 9661, 9733 as by **Armstrong's Players**. Superior 2639, 2738 as by **Goose Creek Gully Jumpers**.
Matrices 16134, 16136 are Mexican.

W.J. Nicholson, bj; acc. prob. Glen Spurgeon, g.
    Richmond, IN   Friday, January 24, 1930

| 16140 | My Lady | Spr 2533 |

Matrix 16139 is popular.
Rev. Superior 2533 by Mansfield Patrick.

Nicholson, Floyd & Spurgeon: ——— Floyd, f; Will J. Nicholson, bj; Glen Spurgeon, g.
    Richmond, IN   Friday, January 24, 1930

| 16142 | My Honey | Ge 7241, Ch 16137, Spt 9733 |

Champion 16137 as by **Nicholson's Players**. Supertone 9733 as by **Armstrong's Players**. Matrix 16141 is Mexican.

Ashabraner & Spurgeon: ——— Ashabraner, h; Glen Spurgeon, g.
    Richmond, IN   Friday, January 24, 1930

| 16143 | Let Me Call You Sweetheart | Ge 7241, Ch 16007, 45193, MeC 45193, Spt 9661, Spr 2639 |

Champion 16007, 45193, and probably Melotone 45193 as by **Nicholson's Players**. Supertone 9661 as by **Armstrong's Players**. Superior 2639 as by **Goose Creek Gully Jumpers**.

Glen Spurgeon, v/y; acc. own g.
    Richmond, IN   Friday, January 24, 1930

| 16144 | Daddy And Home | Ge rejected |

THE NITE OWLS

Bob Symons, esg/eg; Luke Owens, g/v-1; Jack True, sb/v-2.
    Dallas, TX   Wednesday, June 16, 1937

DAL-334-	I'll Never Cry Over You	ARC unissued
DAL-335-2	I'm Just As Happy (As I've Ever Been) -2	ARC 7-10-60, Vo 03675, Cq 8951
DAL-336-2	Yum-Yum Blues -2	ARC 7-11-64, Vo/OK 03706
DAL-337-	Back Yard Stomp	ARC unissued
DAL-338-	(I'm Crying 'Cause I Know I'm) Losing You	ARC unissued
DAL-339-2	Get Hot (For Your Loving Daddy) -1	ARC 7-11-64, Vo/OK 03706
DAL-340-1	I've Lost You So Why Should I Care -1	ARC 7-09-54, Vo 03621, Cq 8947
DAL-341-1	Coquette -1	ARC 7-09-54, Vo 03621, Cq 8947
DAL-342-	Sweet Thing	ARC unissued

Bob Symons, eg/g; Luke Owens, g/v; Jack True, sb.
Dallas, TX   Thursday, June 17, 1937

DAL-343-1	Nine Miles Out O' Town	ARC 7-10-60, Vo 03675, Cq 8951

Bob Symons, esg/eg; Luke Owens, g/v-1; Jack True, sb/v.
San Antonio, TX   Monday, November 1, 1937

SA-2863-1	Ma! (She's Making Eyes At Me) -1	Vo/OK 03987
SA-2864-1,-2	Take Me Back To Your Heart	ARC unissued
SA-2865-1,-2	My Brown Eyed Texas Girl	ARC unissued
SA-2866-1,-2	Headin' For The Texas Plains	ARC unissued

Bob Symons, esg/eg; Luke Owens, g/v-1; Jack True, sb/v-2; Helen Hunt, v-3.
San Antonio, TX   Tuesday, November 2, 1937

SA-2867-1,-2	I Had Someone Else Before I Had You (And I'll Have Someone After You're Gone) -2	ARC unissued
SA-2868-1,-2	There'll Be Some Changes Made -2	ARC unissued
SA-2869-1	I Lost My Gal Again -2	Vo 04853
SA-2870-1	I Wish You Were Jealous Of Me -2	Vo 04853
SA-2871-1	Papa's Gone -2	Vo/OK 04517
SA-2872-1	Married Man Blues -3	Vo/OK 03987, Co 37718, 20295
SA-2873-1	Egyptian Ella -2	Vo 04064
SA-2874-1,-2	Get Along, Little Pony, Get Along	ARC unissued
SA-2875-1	I Saw Your Face In The Moon -1	ARC 8-01-61, Vo/OK 03879
SA-2876-1	Do You Ever Think Of Me -1	ARC 8-01-61, Vo/OK 03879, Co 37718, 20295
SA-2877-2	All That I'm Asking Is Sympathy -1	Vo/OK 03951
SA-2878-1,-2	Get It Ready -1	ARC unissued
SA-2879-2	Rosie -1	Vo/OK 03951
SA-2880-1	Ain't That Too Bad -1	Vo 04118

Unknown, h-1; Bob Symons, esg/eg/v-2; Luke Owens, g/v-3; Jack True, sb.
San Antonio, TX   Monday, November 15, 1937

SA-3015-1	Loud Mouth -1, 3	ARC 8-02-55, Vo/OK 03905
SA-3016-1	Chinatown, My Chinatown -3	ARC unissued
SA-3017-1	Jealous -3	Vo 04064
SA-3018-1	What's Yo' Name -3	ARC 8-02-55, Vo/OK 03905
SA-3019-1	(I Wanna Go Where You Go, Do What You Do) Then I'll Be Happy -3	Vo/OK 04517
SA-3020-1	You Fooled Around And Waited Too Long -3	Vo 04118
SA-3021-1,-2	You Oughta See My Fanny Dance -2	ARC unissued

Bob Symons, esg/eg; Luke Owens, g/v-1; Jack True, sb/v-2.
Dallas, TX   Thursday, May 12, 1938

DAL-505-1	Eight Ball Blues -2	Vo 04233, Cq 9069
DAL-506-1	Memphis Blues -1	Vo 04312
DAL-507-1	Beale Street Blues -1	Vo/OK 05203
DAL-508-1	Here Comes Your Pappy (With The Wrong Kind Of Load) -2	Vo 04233, Cq 9069
DAL-509-1,-2	Hop-Head Joe -2	Vo unissued
DAL-510-1	Think It Over -2	Vo 04935
DAL-511-1,-2	If You Won't Be Mean To Me -1	Vo unissued
DAL-512-1,-2	Frankie And Johnny (You'll Miss Me In The Days To Come) -1	Vo unissued
DAL-513-1	Rancho Grande (My Ranch) -1	Vo/OK 04372, Co 37635
DAL-514-1	Cielito Lindo (Beautiful Heaven) -1	Vo/OK 04372, Co 37635
DAL-515-1,-2	I Cried For You (Now It's Your Turn To Cry Over Me) -1	Vo unissued
DAL-516-1	Mistakes -2	Vo 04452

Bob Symons, esg/eg/v-1; Luke Owens, g/v; Jack True, sb/v-2.

Dallas, TX			Friday, May 13, 1938
DAL-517-2	Blue Hawaiian Moonlight	Vo/OK 04159	
DAL-518-1	If I Had My Way	Vo 04452	
DAL-519-1	In The Royal Hawaiian Hotel -1, 2	Vo/OK 04159	
DAL-520-1	Get It Ready -1, 2 (lead)	Vo 04312	

Bob Symons, esg/eg; Bob Burgess or Luke Owens, g; Jack True, sb/v-1; Bob Burgess, v-2.

Dallas, TX			Friday, December 2, 1938
DAL-670-1	It's A Lonesome Old Town (When You're Not Around) -1	Vo 04935	
DAL-671-1	I Got Worry On My Mind -1	Vo 04626	
DAL-672-1	High And Dry Blues -1	Vo 04794	
DAL-673-1	Please Don't Do That -1	Vo 04715	
DAL-674-1	I'm Sorry I Made You Cry -1	Vo 04626	
DAL-675-1	I'm Getting Absent Minded Over You -1	Vo 04715	
DAL-676-1	Who's Sorry Now? -2	Vo/OK 05203	
DAL-677-1	Come A Little Closer -1	Vo 04794	

The Nite Owls accompanied Al Dexter on his 1936–38 sessions.

FLORA NOLES

Flora Noles, v; acc. unknown, f; unknown, h; unknown, g.

Atlanta, GA			March 1926
9609-A	Little Mohee	OK 45037	
9610-A	Sailor Boy's Farewell	OK 45037	

GEORGE A. NORMAN

George A. Norman, v; acc. prob. own g.

Richmond, IN			Saturday, November 1, 1930
17223	Moonshine In The West Virginia Hills	Ge rejected	

NORMAN & NORMAN

Pseudonym on Paramount and Broadway for Nelson & Nelson.

BO NORRIS & HIS BUFFALO BOYS

Unknown, cl; unknown, p; unknown, g; unknown, sb; Byron Smith, v; band v-1.

Charlotte, NC			Thursday, January 27, 1938
018793-1,-2	When The Old Cow Went Dry -1	BB unissued	
018794-1,-2	One Horse Shay	BB unissued	

CHARLIE NORRIS

Pseudonym on Clarion and Velvet Tone for Gid Tanner & His Skillet-Lickers, except on Clarion 5425-C and Velvet Tone 2485-V for Riley Puckett.

FATE NORRIS

Fate Norris & The Tanner Boys: Gid Tanner, f/v; Arthur Tanner, bj/v; Fate Norris, g/v.

Atlanta, GA			Thursday, November 4, 1926
143047-2	New Dixie	Co 15124-D	
143048-	Hungry Hash House	Co unissued	
143049-2	I Don't Reckon That'll Happen Again	Co 15124-D	

Fate Norris & His Play Boys: prob. Clayton McMichen, f/v; prob. Gid Tanner, f/v; Fate Norris, bj/v; Riley Puckett, g/v.

Atlanta, GA			Friday, April 12, 1929
148254-2	Roll 'Em On The Ground	Co 15435-D	
148255-2	Johnnie Get Your Gun	Co 15435-D	

Fate Norris also recorded with Gid Tanner, and was a frequent member of Gid Tanner & His Skillet-Lickers. He also participated in many of the sketch recordings by the "Skillet-Licker circle;" see Clayton McMichen.

LAND NORRIS

Land Norris, v; acc. own bj.

Atlanta, GA			early April 1924
8619-A	Yellow Gal	OK 40096	
8620-A	Groundhog	OK 40096	

Atlanta, GA			c. August 26, 1924
8700-A	Cumberland Gap	OK 40212	
8701-A	You Ought To Be Arrested And Put In Jail	OK 40374	
8702-A	Kitty Puss	OK 40212	
8073-A	Fox Chase In Georgia	OK 40374	

Atlanta, GA			c. April 22, 1925
9083-A	Gambling Man	OK 40404	
9084-A	Muskrat	OK 40404	
9086-A	Charming Betsy	OK 45033	

Matrix 9085 is untraced but probably by this artist.

Atlanta, GA			c. July 2, 1925
9194-A	Dogwood Mountain	OK 40433	
9195-A	Pat That Butter Down	OK 45017	
9196-A	Little Birdie	OK 45006	
9197-A	Dinah	OK 45017	
9199-A	I Love Somebody	OK 45033	
9200-A	Ida Red	OK 45006	
9201-A	Red Creek	OK 40433	

Matrix 9198 is untraced but probably by this artist.

New York, NY			Wednesday, April 27, 1926
80009-A	The Old Grey Mare	OK 45047	
80010-A	Johnnie	OK 45047	
80011-	The Old Jim Crow	OK unissued	
80012-A	Bum-Dalay	OK 45058	

New York, NY			Thursday, April 28, 1926
80013-	A Pilgrim's Song	OK unissued	
80014-	Some Sweet Day Bye And Bye	OK unissued	
80015-	I've Wandered To The Village Tom	OK unissued	
80016-A	Getting Into Trouble	OK 45058	
80017-	Goin' To Have A Big Time To-night	OK unissued	

LYMON NORRIS

Lymon Norris, v/y-1; acc. prob. own g.

Richmond, IN			Thursday, October 29, 1931
18134,-A	Reckless Hobo	Ge rejected	
18135	In A Lonely Jail -1	Ch 16431, 45070	
18136	I'll Never Get Drunk Anymore	Ch 16431, 45070	

NORRIS BROTHERS

Pseudonym on Supertone for Walter Smith & Norman Woodlieff.

THE NORRIS QUARTET

Vocal quartet; acc. unknown.

New Orleans, LA			Friday, December 14, 1928
147638-	I've Been Redeemed	Co unissued	
147639-	Precious Memories	Co unissued	

NORTH CANTON QUARTET

Vocal quartet; acc. unknown, p.

Atlanta, GA			Wednesday, April 23, 1930
150366-2	I'm Bound For Home	Co 15643-D	
150367-2	I Want To Live Beyond The Grave	Co 15643-D	

NORTH CAROLINA COOPER BOYS

Robert Dewey Cooper, f; Henry Clay Everhart, bj; Thomas Franklin Cooper, g; unidentified, v-1/v duet-2.

Winston-Salem, NC			Wednesday, September 28, 1927
81645-	Give My Love To Nell	OK unissued	
81646-	Kittie Wells	OK unissued	
81647-	Pictures Tonight	OK unissued	
81648-A	Daniel In The Den Of Lions -2	OK 45174	
81649-B	Red Rose Of Texas -1	OK 45174	
81650-	I Used To Wear A White Hat	OK unissued	

Clay Everhart & North Carolina Cooper Boys: Robert Dewey Cooper, f; Henry Clay Everhart, bj; Thomas Franklin Cooper, g; unidentified, v duet-1.

Atlanta, GA Tuesday, October 27, 1931

151950-1	Standing By A Window -1	Co 15737-D
151951-	Nobody's Darling On Earth	Co unissued
151952-1	The Rose With A Broken Stem -1	Co 15737-D
151953-	Down Among The Shady Woodland	Co unissued

NORTH CAROLINA FOX CHASERS

Pseudonym on Supertone for The Red Fox Chasers.

NORTH CAROLINA HAWAIIANS

Unknown, sg; unknown, g; unknown, u.

Atlanta, GA Tuesday, August 7, 1928

402082-B	Wednesday Night Waltz	OK 45248, PaE R3873
402083-B	Soldiers' Joy	OK 45248, PaE R3873
402084-B	Bully Of The Town	OK 45297
402085-A	Hand Me Down My Walking Cane	OK 45297
402086-B	Pass Around The Bottle	OK 45405
402087-A	Chinese Breakdown	OK 45405

NORTH CAROLINA RAMBLERS (LED BY POSEY RORER)

See Charlie Poole. For items credited to **North Carolina Ramblers** (Gennett) or to **North Carolina Ramblers & Roy Harvey** (Paramount) see Roy Harvey.

NORTH CAROLINA RIDGE RUNNERS

Elmer Elliott, f/v; Willie Fugate, bj; Gleason "Dock" Miller, g.

Atlanta, GA Tuesday, April 17, 1928

| 146106-1 | Nobody's Darling | Co 15650-D |
| 146107-1 | Be Kind To A Man When He's Down | Co 15650-D |

NORTH GEORGIA FOUR
NORTH GEORGIA QUARTETTE

North Georgia Quartette-1/North Georgia Four-2: poss.: R.E. Worsham, J.H. Cook, J.H. Harper, C.C. Harper, v quartet; acc. poss. Gus Boaz, f; unknown, g ; or unacc.-3.

Chicago, IL mid-July 1928

20694-2	How Beautiful Heaven Must Be -1	Pm 3114, Bwy 8209
20695-1	Each Day I'll Do A Golden Deed -1	Pm 3120, Bwy 8222
20698-1	I Can, I Do, I Will -2	Pm 3135
20701-1	Wandering Child Come Home -2, 3	Pm 3135
	Amazing Grace -2	Pm 3149
	Redeemed -2	Pm 3149

Broadway 8209 as by **Alabama Four**, 8222 as by **Phillips Brothers**.
Intervening matrices are untraced, but two of them probably apply to Paramount 3149.
Revs: Broadway 8209, 8222 (under same credit) by Phil Reeve & Ernest Moody.

North Georgia Four: poss.: Phil Reeve, C. Ernest Moody, R.E. Worsham, C.C. Harper, v quartet; or unidentified, v-1/y-1; acc. Gus Boaz, f; unknown, g.

Chicago, IL January 1929

| 21136-2 | Bye Bye Mama -1 | Pm 3174 |
| 21137-1 | She Was A Lulu | Pm 3174 |

This group was associated with the Dixie Crackers, Moody Bible Sacred Harp Singers (possibly much the same lineup as the 1929 group above), and Phil Reeve & Ernest Moody.

THE NORTHLANDERS

See Jimmy Yates groups.

HENRY NORTON

For duets with Kelly Harrell see the latter. Henry Norton was also a member of Red Patterson's Piedmont Log Rollers.

NORTON & BOND

Pseudonym on Champion for Leonard Rutherford & Byrd Moore (see the latter).

NORTON, BOND & THOMAS

Pseudonym on Champion for Taylor, Moore & Burnett.

NORTON, BOND & WILLIAMS
Pseudonym on Champion for Moore, Burnett & Rutherford (see Richard D. Burnett).

O

OAK MOUNTAIN FOUR
Pseudonym on Champion for Ray Sand's Harmony Four.

OAK RIDGE SACRED SINGERS
Pseudonym on Supertone for the Blue Ridge Sacred Singers.

SLIM OAKDALE [TRIO]
Pseudonym on Crown for Dwight Butcher.

JESS[IE] OAKLEY
Pseudonym on Silvertone and Supertone for John McGhee.

CHARLIE OAKS
THE OAKS FAMILY

Charlie Oaks, v; acc. own h/g.
  New York, NY   Monday, August 3, 1925
    1001*/02-W   A Boy's Best Friend Is His Mother   Vo 15343, 5110
    1003/04*-W   Ginger Blue   Vo 15344, 5111
    1005/06-W   The Drunkard's Dream   Vo 15195, 5084
  New York, NY   Tuesday, August 4, 1925
    1007/08/09*-W   Home Of The Soul   Vo 15345, 5112
    1010/11-W   Moonshine   Vo 15195, 5084
    1012*/13-W   Just Before The Battle, Mother   Vo 15345, 5112
    1014/15-W   The Kaiser And Uncle Sam   Vo 15104, 5073
    1016/17-W   Marching Through Flanders   Vo 15104, 5073
    1018*/19-W   Who Will Care For Mother Now   Vo 15346, 5105
    1020/21-W   Poor Little Joe   Vo 15103, 5072
  New York, NY   Wednesday, August 5, 1925
    1022/23*-W   Old Cottage Home   Vo 15346, 5105
    1024*/25-W   The Old Musician And His Harp   Vo 15344, 5111
    1026/27-W   I Have No Mother Now   Vo 15103, 5072
    1028/29*-W   Darling Nellie Grey   Vo 15343, 5110
    1030/31-W   The Broken Engagement   Vo 15144, 5076
    1032/33-W   The Fatal Wedding   Vo 15144, 5076
    1034*/35-W   Boll Weevil   Vo 15342, 5113
  New York, NY   Thursday, August 6, 1925
    1036/37*-W   Adam And Eve   Vo 15342, 5113

Charlie Oaks, h; acc. own g.
  New York, NY   Thursday, August 6, 1925
    1038/39-W   Medley 1. Ring The Bell, Watchman 2. Soldier's   Vo unissued
                    Dream
    1040/41-W   Over The Waves   Vo unissued

Charlie Oaks, v; acc. own h/g.
  New York, NY   Friday, August 7, 1925
    1061/62/63-W   The Death Of Williams Jennings Bryan   Vo 15094, 5068
    1064/65/66-W   The John T. Scopes Trial   Vo 15094, 5068
    1072/73/74-W   Mary Phagan   Vo 15099, 5069
    1075/76/77-W   The Death Of Floyd Collins   Vo 15099, 5069
Intervening matrices are untraced.

Charley Oakes, v; acc. own h/g; unknown, g.
  Birmingham, AL   c. July 18, 1927
    GEX-738,-A   Mary Of The Wild Moor   Ge rejected
    GEX-739,-A,-B,-C   The Blind Girl   Ge rejected

Oaks Family: Charlie Oaks, h/g/v; Mrs. Oaks, ah/k/v.
  Memphis, TN   Wednesday, June 4, 1930

62575-2	Wake Up, You Drowsy Sleeper	Vi 23795
62576-1	Since My Dear Old Mother's Gone	Vi 23832
62577-1	I Know His Voice	Vi 23795
62578-	Will It Pay?	BB B-5807
62579-	You'll Miss Me When I'm Gone	BB B-5807
62580-1	The Picture Of My Home	Vi 23832

WYOMING JACK O'BRIEN

Wyoming Jack O'Brien, v/y; acc. prob. own g.
   New York, NY   Monday, April 8, 1935

TO-1535	I Wish I Stayed In The Wagonyard	ARC unissued trial recording

JOHNNY O'BRIEN

Johnny O'Brien, h; acc. unknown bj; unknown, g.
   New York, NY   c. February 25, 1929

147993-1	The "St. Louis Blues"	Co 1749-D
147994-1	Wabash Blues	Co 1749-D

W. LEE O'DANIEL & HIS HILLBILLY BOYS

Darrell Kirkpatrick, f; Ray Lunday, sg; Clifford Wells, tbj; Leon Huff, g/v-1; June Whalin, g/hv-2; Connie "Pancho" Galvan, sb; W. Lee O'Daniel, ldr.
   Dallas, TX   Thursday, September 26, 1935

DAL-160-1	Hillbilly Stomp	Vo 03089
DAL-161-1	In That Vine Covered Chapel (In The Valley) -1, 2	Vo 03162
DAL-162-2	Mother's Crazy Quilt -1, 2	Vo 03162
DAL-163-1	Our Little Dream House In Lullaby Lane -1	Vo 03196, Co-Lucky 60207
DAL-164-1,2	I Like Bananas (Because They Have No Bones)	Vo unissued
DAL-165-3	A Jug Of Wine And You -1	Vo 03089

Take 3 of matrix DAL-165 is a technical remastering, made on October 24, 1935, of either take 1 or take 2 recorded on September 26.

Darrell Kirkpatrick, f; Ray Lunday, sg; Clifford Wells, tbj; Leon Huff, g/v-1/y-2; June Whalin, g/v-3/hv-4; Pancho Galvan, sb; W. Lee O'Daniel, ldr.
   Dallas, TX   Monday, September 30, 1935

DAL-182-1	I Never Knew -1	Vo 03127
DAL-183-1	Chinatown, My Chinatown -1	Vo 03127, Co-Lucky 60510
DAL-184-1	In An Old Log Cabin (By An Old Log Fire) -1, 4	Vo 03297
DAL-185-1	Who's Sorry Now? -1	Vo 03248
DAL-186-1	Peach Pickin' Time In Georgia -1, 2	Vo 03196, Co-Lucky 60207
DAL-187-1	San Antonio -1, 3	Vo 03248
DAL-188-1	Someone In Heaven Is Thinking Of You -1, 4	Vo 03297

Labels of DAL-187/88 give June Whalin's first name as Jerry, possibly a nickname.
Rev. Columbia-Lucky 60510 by Louis Prima (popular).

Carroll Hubbard, f; Wilson "Lefty" Perkins, esg; Pat O'Daniel, tbj; Leon Huff, g/v-1; William "Curly" Perrin, g; Wallace Griffin, sb; W. Lee O'Daniel, ldr.
   San Antonio, TX   Saturday, November 21, 1936

SA-2562-2	Rhythm And Romance -1	Vo 03412
SA-2563-1,-2	When -1	Vo unissued
SA-2564-2	We'll Rest At The End Of The Trail -1	Vo/OK 03538
SA-2565-2	An Old Water Mill By A Waterfall -1	Vo 03442
SA-2566-1	Get Hot	Vo 03471
SA-2567-2	Ida, Sweet As Apple Cider -1	Vo unissued: Co C4K47911 (CD)
SA-2568-1,-2	Runnin' Wild -1	Vo unissued
SA-2569-1,-2	Black Eyed Susan Brown -1	Vo unissued
SA-2570-2	Yours And Mine -1	Vo 03494
SA-2571-2	My Wishing Song -1	Vo 03494
SA-2572-2	My Cotton Pickin' Darling -1	Vo 03413
SA-2573-1	Smile For Me -1	Vo 03568

Carroll Hubbard, f; Lefty Perkins, esg; Pat O'Daniel, tbj; Leon Huff, g/v-1; Curly Perrin, g/poss. v-2; Wallace Griffin, sb; W. Lee O'Daniel, ldr.
   San Antonio, TX   Sunday, November 22, 1936

SA-2574-2	Keep A Light In Your Window Tonight -1	Vo/OK 03538
SA-2575-2	Don't Let The Deal Go Down	Vo 03471
SA-2576-1	The Old Spring Of Love -1	Vo 03442
SA-2577-1	Everybody Kiss Your Partner (The Whistle Song) -1	Vo 03412, Cq 8829

| SA-2578-1 | Back To Old Smoky Mountain -1, 2 | Vo 03568 |
| SA-2579-1 | The House At The End Of The Lane -1 | Vo 03413 |

Carroll Hubbard, f; Mike O'Daniel, f; Pat O'Daniel, tbj; Leon Huff, g/v/y-1; Curly Perrin, g/v-2; Wallace Griffin, sb; unidentified, v-3; band v-4; W. Lee O'Daniel, ldr.

Dallas, TX   Thursday, June 10, 1937

DAL-243-1	Confessin' (That I Love You)	Vo 03633
DAL-244-1	There'll Be Some Changes Made	Vo/OK 03902
DAL-245-2	Congratulate Me	Vo 04542
DAL-246-2	Coquette -2, 3	Vo 03674
DAL-247-1	On A Chinese Honeymoon -2	Vo 03986
DAL-248-1	Ev'ryone's Out – So Let's Stay In To-Night	Vo 03633
DAL-249-1	Cross Patch	Vo 03986
DAL-250-1,-2	Sing Cowboy Sing	Vo unissued
DAL-251-1	When You Hear Me Call -1	Vo 03674
DAL-252-1,-2	My Ole Dog And Me -4	Vo unissued

Dallas, TX   Friday, June 11, 1937

DAL-253-3	I Can't Give You Anything But Love	Vo 03753
DAL-254-2	Thank You Mr. Moon	Vo 03753
DAL-255-1	There's Evil In Ye Children -4	Vo 03950
DAL-256-1	Tuck Away My Lonesome Blues	Vo 04102
DAL-257-2	Bear Cat Mama	Vo 03950
DAL-258-2	Devilism [sic] Mary	Vo 04102
DAL-259-1	Mellow Mountain Moon -2	Vo/OK 04049
DAL-260-2	Yodeling Ranger -1	Vo 04388
DAL-261-1	Yes-Suh -4	Vo/OK 03902
DAL-262-1	I Don't Mind -1	Vo 04542
DAL-263-2	Dirty Hangover Blues	Vo 04440, Cq 9167
DAL-264-1	Million Dollar Smile	Vo unissued
DAL-265-1	Beautiful Texas	Vo unissued
DAL-266-1	Put Me In Your Pocket -2	Vo/OK 04049
DAL-267-1	Mr. W. Lee O'Daniel And His Hillbilly Boys (Theme Song)	Vo unissued

Take 3 of matrix DAL-253 is a technical remastering, made on October 8, 1937, of either take 1 or take 2 recorded on June 11.

Mike O'Daniel, f; Bundy Bratcher, ac; Kermit Whalin, esg; Pat O'Daniel, tbj; Leon Huff, g/v-1; Curly Perrin, g/v-2; Wallace Griffin, sb; Kitty "Texas Rose" Williamson, v-3/y-4; band v-5; W. Lee O'Daniel, ldr.

Dallas, TX   Sunday, May 15, 1938

DAL-550-1	Long, Long Ago -1	Vo/OK 04185, Co 37630, 20229
DAL-551-1	Dear Evalina, Sweet Evalina -1, 2	Vo 04440, Cq 9167
DAL-552-1	Everything Is Lovely Down In Dixie Land -1	Vo 04388
DAL-553-1,-2	I Got The Spring Fever Blues -3	Vo unissued
DAL-554-1	Baby Won't You Please Come Home -3	Vo 04353
DAL-555-1	Lonesome Road Blues -1	Vo/OK 04311, Cq 9087
DAL-556-2	I'm Drifting Back To Dreamland -1, 2	Vo 04244
DAL-557-1	All I Do Is Dream Of You -1	Vo 04244
DAL-558-1	Alabama Jubilee -5	Vo/OK 04311, Cq 9087
DAL-559-1	I've Got The Blues -3, 4	Vo 04353
DAL-560-1,-2	I Wanna Be A Cowboy's Sweetheart -3, 4	Vo unissued
DAL-561-1	Beautiful Texas -1, 2	Co 20229
DAL-561-2	Beautiful Texas -1, 2	Vo/OK 04185, Co 37630

Mike O'Daniel, f; Bundy Bratcher, ac; Kermit Whalin, esg; Pat O'Daniel, tbj; Leon Huff, g/v-1; Curly Perrin, g; Wallace Griffin, sb; Kitty "Texas Rose" Williamson, v-2; band v-3; W. Lee O'Daniel, ldr.

Dallas, TX   Saturday, December 3, 1938

DAL-685-1	High Falutin' Newton -1	Vo/OK 04588, Co 37730, 20307
DAL-686-1	Roll On, Mississippi, Roll On -1	Vo 04852
DAL-687-1	That Old Fashioned Way -1	Vo 04656
DAL-688-1	Please Pass The Biscuits, Pappy (I Like Mountain Music) -1	Vo/OK 04727, Cq 9229
DAL-689-1,-2	Who's Sorry Now? -2	Vo unissued
DAL-690-1	So Tired Of Dreaming -1	Vo 04778
DAL-691-1	Someday Sweetheart -1	Vo 04852
DAL-692-1	Old Yazoo -1	Vo 04778
DAL-693-1	Have You Ever Been Lonely? (Have You Ever Been Blue) -1	Vo/OK 04588, Co 37730, 20307
DAL-694-1,-2	Who Calls You Sweet Daddy Now? -2	Vo unissued

| DAL-695-2 | Song Of Hawaii -3 | Vo 04656 |
| DAL-696-1 | One Sweet Letter From You -1 | Vo/OK 04727, Cq 9229 |

For recordings credited to **W. Lee O'Daniel & His Light Crust Doughboys**, see Light Crust Doughboys.

DOREEN O'DARE

Pseudonym for Zora Layman, used on items issued in Decca's Irish (12000 series) catalogue.

ODUS & WOODROW

Southern Melody Boys: Odus Maggard, bj/v; Woodrow Roberts, g/v-1.
Charlotte, NC   Wednesday, February 17, 1937

07100-1	Down In Baltimore -1	BB B-7057, MW M-7225
07101-1	Dividing Line -1	MW M-7223
07102-1	Lonesome Scenes Of Winter	MW M-7227
07103-1	Tribulation Days -1	BB B-6883, MW M-7222, M-7349
07104-1	If You See My Saviour -1	BB B-6883, MW M-7222
07105-1	When The Autumn Leaves Fall	MW M-7225
07106-1	Carry Me Over The Tide -1	MW M-7223
07107-1	Wind The Little Ball Of Yarn	BB B-7057, MW M-7227
07108-1	Lonely And Sad -1	MW M-7226
07109-1	Sweet Locust Blossoms	MW M-7224
07110-1	I'll Remember You, Love, In My Prayer -1	MW M-7224
07111-1	Back In California	MW M-7226

Bluebird B-7057 as by **Southern Melody Boys (Odus Maggard & Woodrow Roberts)**. Montgomery Ward M-7349 as by **Uncle Dave Macon**.
Rev. Montgomery Ward M-7349 by Uncle Dave Macon.

Odus & Woodrow: Odus Maggard, bj/v; Woodrow Roberts, g/v-1/sp-2.
Charlotte, NC   Thursday, June 9, 1938

64116-A	When The Spring Roses Are Blooming -1	De 5570
64117-A	I Been Here A Long, Long Time -2	De 5603, MeC 45266, Min M-14091
64118-A	Waiting For The Boatman (To Guide Us O'er) -1	De 5570
64119-A	I Told The Stars About You	De 5603, MeC 45266, Min M-14092, M-14132

Revs: Minerva M-14091, M-14092 by Jimmie Davis, M-14132 by Leon's Lone Star Cowboys.

HAL O'HALLORAN'S HOOLIGANS

Unknown, f; unknown, cl; two unknowns, k-1; unknown, g; unknown, sb; unknown, wb; unknown, j; unknown, v-2/v duet-3/v trio-4/y-5/y duet-6.
New York, NY   Friday, January 10, 1936

60320-A	She's 'Way Up Thar -2	De 5175
60321-A	By The Sea -1, 4	De 5188, MeC 45234
60322-A	Corrine Corrina -3, 6	De 5188, MeC 45234
60323-A	Tie Me To Your Apron Strings Again -4	De 5176
60324-A	Sleepy Time Gal -2	De 5176
60325-A	The Music Goes 'Round And Around -2, 5	De 5175

THE OKEH ATLANTA SACRED HARP SINGERS

Vocal group, conducted by W.A. Malone; unacc.
Atlanta, GA   Friday, March 15, 1929

402331-	Sweet River	OK unissued
402332-	Ragan	OK unissued
402333-	Mean	OK unissued
402334-	Sweet Prospect	OK unissued
402335-	Corinth	OK unissued
402336-	Bound For Canaan	OK unissued

Atlanta, GA   Monday, March 18, 1929

402359-B	Penick	OK 45323
402360-A	Return Again	OK 45323
402361-B	Edom	OK 45324
402362-A	Parting Hand	OK 45324
402363-A	Ortonville	OK 45325
402364-A	Ninety-Fifth	OK 45325

THE OKEH MEDICINE SHOW

Although it would be more consistent to list these items under the leading name on the labels, namely Emmett Miller, they are probably best known to many users of this book as "The OKeh Medicine Show." The participants are listed not in conventional discographical sequence but in the order of their appearance.

Emmett Miller – Narmour & Smith, Fiddlin' John Carson, Moonshine Kate, Bud Blue, Frank Hutchison, Black Brothers, Martin Malloy: Emmett Miller, v/sp; W.T. Narmour, f; S.W. Smith, g; Fiddlin' John Carson, f/v/sp; Moonshine Kate, g/sp; Bud Blue, p; Frank Hutchison, g/v/sp; Black Brothers: Carson Robison, Frank Luther, v/sp duet; acc. unknown, f; unknown, g; Martin Malloy, sp.
    New York, NY   Tuesday, September 24, 1929

402988-B	The Medicine Show – Act I	OK 45380
402989-C	The Medicine Show – Act II	OK 45380

Emmett Miller – Narmour & Smith, Fiddlin' John Carson, Moonshine Kate, Frank Hutchison, Bud Blue, Black Brothers, Martin Malloy: Emmett Miller, v/sp; W.T. Narmour, f; S.W. Smith, g; Fiddlin' John Carson, f/v/sp; Moonshine Kate, g/v/sp; Bud Blue, p/sp; Frank Hutchison, g/v/sp; Black Brothers: Carson Robison, Frank Luther, v/sp duet; acc. unknown, h; unknown, jh; unknown, g; Martin Malloy, sp.
    New York, NY   Wednesday, September 25, 1929

402992-B	The Medicine Show – Act III	OK 45391
402997-C	The Medicine Show – Act V	OK 45413
402998-C	The Medicine Show – Act IV	OK 45391
402999-B	The Medicine Show - Act VI	OK 45413

The personnel and instrumentation given for Acts III to VI are collective; Bud Blue speaks only on Act IV and plays piano, if at all (accompanying Emmett Miller), on Act VI; the Black Brothers appear on Act III only; and there are other minor variations. Matrices 402993 to 402996 are by W.T. Narmour & S.W. Smith.

[THE] OKLAHOMA COWBOYS (DIRECTED BY JACK PIERCE)

See Jack Pierce.

THE OKLAHOMA SWEETHEARTS

Jean Leeper, Jane Leeper, v duet; "with string acc." (thus the Art Satherley files).
    Charlotte, NC   Saturday, June 7, 1941

CHAR-13	While You Are Out Cheatin' On Me	OK unissued
CHAR-14	You're Going To Be Sorry	OK unissued
CHAR-15	Darling Do You Know Who Loves You	OK unissued
CHAR-16	The Last Goodbye	OK unissued

The Oklahoma Sweethearts recorded after 1942.

OLD FASHIONED BOYS

Pseudonym on Australian Panachord for the Kessinger Brothers.

OLD HENRY'S MUSICIANS

Recordings under this credit, evidently of a studio group playing standard old-time tunes, are beyond the scope of this work.

OLD QUEBEC TRIO

One side of Brunswick 343 was thus credited. It was originally issued on Melotone M18032 as by **Trio du Vieux Quebec**, and as French-Canadian material is beyond the scope of this work.

THE OLD SETTLERS

Vocal quartet; acc. unknown, f-1; prob. Frank Novak, cl-2/bscl-3; unknown, h-4; poss. unknown, o; unknown, g; unknown, sb; unknown, oc-5; several unknowns, sp-6/wh-6/laughing-6.
    New York, NY   Thursday, January 17, 1935

16651-1,-2	Take Me Home	ARC unissued
16652-1,-2	If I Knew Where I Was Going To Die -1, 2, 4, 5, 6	ARC unissued
16653-	Take Your Pack On Your Back And Go Back To Your Shack (In The Carolinas) -2	ARC unissued
16658-	I Wish I Had My First Wife Back -1, 3	ARC unissued

Intervening matrices are by Abe Lyman Orchestra (popular).

THE OLD SEXTON

Pseudonym on Plaza-group labels for John I. White.

OLD SMOKY TWINS

Pseudonym on Broadway for the Kentucky Thorobreds.

OLD SOUTHERN SACRED SINGERS

Lester McFarland, Robert A. Gardner, Vernon Dalhart, Wilfred Glenn, v quartet; acc. Lester McFarland, md; Robert A. Gardner, g.
    New York, NY   Friday, December 10, 1926

E-4216/17*	Where We Never Grow Old	Vo 5119, Br 115, Spt S2095
E-4218*/19	'Tis A Picture From Life's Other Side	Vo 5119, Br 115, Spt S2095

These items were transferred, respectively, to matrices E-21930/31 and E-21928/29. Brunswick 115 uses the controls B-12070-A, B-12069-A respectively, possibly in error for E-21070-A, E-21069-A.
Vocalion 5119 as by **Smoky Mountain Sacred Singers**.
McFarland and Gardner sing the verses, augmented by Dalhart and Glenn on the choruses, on matrix E-4216/17; Gardner sings lead, augmented by the other three on the choruses, on matrix E-4218/19.

Lester McFarland, Robert A. Gardner, Vernon Dalhart, Wilfred Glenn, v quartet; acc. Bill Wirges, o-1; Frank Black, o-2.
    New York, NY   Wednesday, May 4, 1927

E-22921/22*/23	The Old-Time Religion -1	Br 161
E-22924/25*/26	I Am Bound For The Promised Land -1	Br 161, Spt S2096
E-22927/28/29*	The Home Over There -1	Br 172, Spt S2117, DeE F3877, RexIr U476
E-22930/31*	What A Friend We Have In Jesus -2	Br 172, Au A22035, DeE F3877, RexIr U476
E-22932*/33	Take The Name Of Jesus With You (The Precious Name) -2	Vo 5176, Br 162, Me M12076
E-22934/35*	Will There Be Any Stars In My Crown? -2	Vo 5176, Br 162, Me M12076

Vocalion 5176 as by **Smoky Mountain Sacred Singers**. Melotone M12076 as by **Olympic Quartet**. Aurora A22035 as by **Campbell's Sacred Singers**. Rev. Supertone S2117 by McFarland & Gardner.

Acc. Bill Wirges, o-1; Lester McFarland, md-2; Robert A. Gardner, g-2; Carson Robison, g-2.
    New York, NY   Thursday, May 5, 1927

E-22959/60*	Just Break The News To Mother -2	Br 165, Spt S2097
E-22961/62/63	Just Before The Battle Mother -2	Br/Vo unissued
E-22964/65	There Is A Fountain -1	Br/Vo unissued
E-22966/67	Nothing Between -1	Br 159, DeE F3931, RexIr U477
E-22968/69/70*	The Unclouded Day -1	Vo 5185
E-22971/72	Safe In The Arms Of Jesus -1	Br 159, Spt S2100, Au A22035, DeE F3931, RexIr 0477
E-22973/74*	My Mother's Prayers Have Followed Me -1	Br 165, Spt S2097

Vocalion 5185 as by **Smoky Mountain Sacred Singers**. Aurora A22035 as by **Campbell's Sacred Singers**.

Lester McFarland, Robert A. Gardner, Lester O'Keefe, Wilfred Glenn, v quartet; acc. Bill Wirges, o.
    New York, NY   Friday, May 6, 1927

E-23019½*/20	Soul Winner For Jesus	Vo 5185
E-23021/22*/23	Going Down The Valley One By One	Br 166, Spt S2102, DeE F3786, RexIr U474
E-23024/25/26*	Onward, Christian Soldiers	Br 166, Spt S2100, DeE F3786, RexIr U474

Vocalion 5185 as by **Smoky Mountain Sacred Singers**.

Same or similar v quartet; acc. unknown, o.
    New York, NY   Thursday, June 20, 1929

E-30166-A,-B	Softly And Tenderly	Br unissued
E-30167-A,-B	I Must Tell Jesus	Br unissued
E-30168-A	Nothing But The Blood Of Jesus	Br 389
E-30169-A	Precious Name (Take The Name Of Jesus With You)	Br 389
E-30170-A	'Tis So Sweet To Trust In Jesus	Br 486, DeE F3741, RexIr U472
E-30171-A	Only Trust Him	Br 471, DeE F3748, RexIr U473
E-30172-A	Will There Be Any Stars In My Crown	Br 390
E-30173-A	Where The Gates Swing Outward Never	Br 357, Spt S2102, DeE F3787, RexIr U475
E-30174-A	Will My Mother Know Me There?	Br 357, Spt S2101, DeE F3787, RexIr U475
E-30175-A	Lord, I'm Coming Hom	Br 390
E-30176-A	I'll Go Where You Want Me To Go	Br 471, DeE F3748, RexIr U473
E-30177-B	I'll Live On	Br 486, DeE F3741, RexIr U472

Rev. Supertone S2101 by Blue Ridge Gospel Singers.

OLD TIME DANCE ORCHESTRA

This credit was used on Gennett 0112 for The Red Fox Chasers.

THE OLDTIMERS

Pseudonym on Canadian Melotone and Minerva for the Kessinger Brothers.

OLIVER & ALLEN (THE BLIND SINGERS)

Vocal duet; acc. prob. one of them, g.
    Charlotte, NC   Thursday, August 5, 1937

011999-1	My Little Buckaroo	BB B-7124, MW M-7376
013000-1	Blue Hawaii	BB B-7124, MW M-7377
013001-1	Let's Be Sweethearts Again	BB B-7175, MW M-7375
013002-1	Greenville Blow	BB B-7402, MW M-7376

013003-1	Darling The Sunshine Grows Brighter	BB B-7175, MW M-7377
013004-1	In The Hills Of Old Kentucky	BB B-7327, MW M-7375
013005-1	Meetin' Time In The Hollow	BB B-7327, MW M-7378
013006-1	Alone Because I Love You	BB B-7402, MW M-7378

OLYMPIC QUARTET

Pseudonym on Melotone for the Old Southern Sacred Singers.

ORIGINAL CAROLINA TAR HEELS

See Carolina Tar Heels.

THE ORIGINAL SACRED HARP CHOIR

Vocal group; prob. unacc.
New York, NY   c. June/July 1922

8358-	Penick	Br 5146
8359-	The Christian Warfare	Br 5146
8364-	Antioch	Br 5147
8365-	Easter Anthem	Br 5147
8402-	Canaan's Land	Br 5150
8418-	New Britain	Br 5150
	Soft Music	Br 5151
	Pleyel's Hymn	Br 5151

ORIGINAL STAMPS QUARTET[TE]

See Stamps Quartet.

ORQUESTA DE CUERDA DEL SUR

Pseudonym on OKeh 16391 for Scottdale String Band.

BOB OSBORNE

Bob Osborne, v; acc. own g; or g solo-1.
Richmond, IN   Thursday, October 30, 1930

17220	My Son Joshua	Ge rejected
17221	Guitar Lullaby -1	Ge unissued
17222	Hot Pepper -1	Ge unissued

G.C. OSBORNE [& GEORGE WILLIAMS]

G.C. Osborne (The World's Wonder Banjoist), bj; acc. unknown, md; unknown, bj; poss, George Williams, g.
Richmond, IN   c. April 1928

| 13661 | Token In Blues | Ch 15507 |

In Gennett files the description "Old Time Playin' " has been crossed out and a note appended: "use as race inst."
Rev. Champion 15507 by Jimmy Blythe & W.E. Burton (see *JR*).

G.C. Osborne & George Williams: G.C. Osborne, bj; George Williams, g.
Richmond, IN   c. April 1928

| 13663 | Rattlesnake Rag | Bonham 20322 |

Bonham 20322 is a Gennett personal recording. Matrix 13662 is by George Williams.
Rev. Bonham 20322 by George Williams.

OTIS & ELEANOR

Eleanor [?Clements], ac/v-1; Otis Clements, g/v/y-2.
Atlanta, GA   Thursday, February 8, 1940

047623-1	My Home On The Prairie -2	BB B-8632, MW M-8716, RZAu G24889
047624-1	Weddin' In The Wildwood -2	BB B-8632, MW M-8716, RZAu G24889
047625-1	El Rancho Grande	BB B-8542, MW M-8715
047626-1	Cielito Lindo	BB B-8542, MW M-8715
047627-1	The Little Home Down In The Valley -2	BB B-8436, MW M-8714
047628-1	'Way Fer Down In The Holler -1	BB B-8652, MW M-8717
047629-1	Panhandle Blues -2	BB B-8436, MW M-8714
047630-1	'Tain't No Use	BB B-8652, MW M-8717

OWEN BROTHERS & ELLIS

The Stamps Quartet (Owens Brothers & Ellis): Arch Owen, lv; Aubrey Owen, tv; Herbert "Hub" Owen, bv; Oglesby Lonnie Ellis, bsv; acc. Crawford D. "Babe" Owen, g.

	Dallas, TX		Friday, December 2, 1927
145308-2	In The City Where There Is No Night	Co 15242-D	
145309-1	I Am Going Over There	Co 15242-D	

The Stamps Quartet: Arch Owen, lv; Babe Owen, joint lv-1; Aubrey Owen, tv; Hub Owen, bv; Oglesby Lonnie Ellis, bsv; acc. Babe Owen, g.

	Dallas, TX		Monday, December 3, 1928
147550-2	Coming	Co 15347-D	
147551-2	Go On, We'll Soon Be There	Co 15347-D	

Owens Brothers: Hub Owen, f/bv-1; Babe Owen, g; Aubrey Owen, sb-2/tv-1; Arch Owen, lv-1; Oglesby Lonnie Ellis, bsv-1; unidentified, v eff-1.

	Dallas, TX		Monday, December 3, 1928
147552-2	If You Don't Like My Ford Coupe, Don't You Cadillac Me -1	Co 15416-D	
147553-2	Golden Memories Waltz -2	Co 15416-D	

The Stamps Quartet: Arch Owen, lv; Aubrey Owen, tv; Hub Owen, bv; Oglesby Lonnie Ellis, bsv; acc. Babe Owen, g.

	Dallas, TX		Tuesday, December 4, 1928
147556-2	Delighting In The Love Of God	Co 15434-D	
147557-2	Working For The King Of Kings	Co 15434-D	

Owens Brothers & Ellis (A Stamps Quartet): Arch Owen, lv; Aubrey Owen, tv; Hub Owen, bv; Oglesby Lonnie Ellis, bsv; acc. Babe Owen, g.

	Dallas, TX		Wednesday, December 4, 1929
149522-2	I Worship The Lord	Co 15502-D	
149523-2	I Am O'ershadowed By Love	Co 15655-D	
149524-2	I Want To Do My Best	Co 15502-D	
149525-2	He's Calling All	Co 15655-D	
149528-2	You Shall Reap What You Sow	Co 15560-D	
149529-2	He's Calling You	Co 15560-D	

Matrix 149529 is titled *He's Calling All* on some pressings of Columbia 15560-D.
Matrices 149526/27 are blank in Columbia files.

Owen Brothers & Ellis: Arch Owen, lv; Aubrey Owen, tv; Hub Owen, bv; Oglesby Lonnie Ellis, bsv; acc. Babe Owen, g.

	Memphis, TN		Tuesday, May 27, 1930
62517-2	Wonderful Voice Of Jesus	Vi V-40309, BB B-5773	
62518-2	The Harvest Field	Vi V-40309, BB B-5773	
62519-2	I'm Walking In The Light	Vi V-40283	
62520-	Life's Ocean Waves Are Rolling On	BB B-5539	
62521-2	Right Upon The Firing Line	Vi V-40283	
62522-	Look On The Bright, Beautiful Side	BB B-5539	

E.B. OWENS

E.B. Owens, v/y; acc. prob. own g.

	Atlanta, GA		Thursday, April 18, 1929
148352-1	Sweet Carlyle	Co 15414-D	
148353-2	Goodbye Forever, Darling	Co 15414-D	

TEX OWENS

Tex Owens, v/y-1/wh-2; acc. prob. own g.

	Chicago, IL		Tuesday, August 28, 1934
C-9355-A	Cattle Call	De 5015, 46133	
C-9356-A	Two Sweethearts -1	De 5187, MeC 45215	
C-9357-A	Rocking Alone In An Old Rocking Chair -2	De 5187, 46133, DeSA FM5105	
C-9358-A	Pride Of The Prairie -1	De 5015, BrSA SA846	

Revs: Melotone 45215 by Shelton Brothers; Decca FM5105 by Kelly Family; Brunswick SA846 by Pie Plant Pete.

Tex Owens – "The Texas Ranger", v; acc. own g.

	Chicago, IL		Wednesday, September 23, 1936
01308-1/1A	The Cattle Call	BB unissued	
01309-1/1A	I'm Going Back To Old Texas	BB unissued	
01310-1/1A	Lonesome Train Whistling Blues	BB unissued	
01311-1/1A	My Old Dog And Me	BB unissued	
01312-1/1A	Night Herdin' Lullabye	BB unissued	
01313-1/1A	Pals Of The Prairie	BB unissued	
01314-1/1A	Ride Beneath The Texas Moon	BB unissued	
01315-1/1A	Will The Circle Be Unbroken	BB unissued	

| 01316-1 | Never Grow Old | BB unissued |
| 01317-1/1A | My Mothers [sic] Call | BB unissued |

Tex Owens recorded after 1942.

TOM OWENS BARN DANCE TRIO

Poss. Tommy Dandurand, f; unknown, g; Tom Owens, calls.
Richmond, IN   Tuesday, February 23, 1926

12468-B	Ocean Waves	Ge 3303, Sil 3104, Chg 104, 306
12469-B	Kings Head	Sil 3104, Chg 105
12470-B	Stoney Point	Ge 3303, Sil 3105, Chg 106
12471-B	Buffalo Girls	Sil 3105, Chg 104, 306
12472	Buckwheat Batter	Ge 3292, Sil 3106, Chg 107, Her 75519
12473-A	The Irish Washerwoman	Sil 3106, Chg 105
12474-B	Hell On The Wabash	Ge 3292, Sil 3107, Chg 106, Her 75519
12475	McLeod's Reel	Sil 3107, Chg 107

Silvertone and Challenge issues, except Challenge 306, as by **Tom Owens WLS Barn Dance Trio**. Herwin 75519 as by **Uncle John Harvey's Old Time Dance Orchestra**.

OWENS BROTHERS (& ELLIS)

See Owen Brothers & Ellis.

OZARK BOYS (JAKE & DON)

Jake Watts, Don Sullivan, v/y-1 duet; acc. prob. Jake Watts, h-2; prob. one of them, g; prob. Don Sullivan, wh-3.
New York, NY   Tuesday, January 21, 1941

68601-A	All The Good Times Are Past And Gone -2, 3	De 5929, MeC 45426
68602-A	Chime Bells -1, 2, 3	De 5919
68603-A	Everybody Gets A Letter But Me	De 5919
68604-A	I Hear The Ozark Mountains Calling Me -2	De 5929, MeC 45426

Jake Watts also recorded with Carl Swanson as Jake & Carl, and after 1942.

OZARK MOUNTAIN SACRED SINGERS

Pseudonym on Champion for the Blue Ridge Sacred Singers.

OZARK RAMBLER

Recordings with this credit on Paramount appear all to be by the popular singer Leroy Montesanto. One side thus credited on Broadway 8327 may be by a different, unidentified artist.

OZARK WARBLERS

Vocal duet; acc. unknown, f; unknown, g; unknown, jh.
Chicago, IL   c. October 1928

| 20934-2 | Memories Of Floyd Collins | Pm 3127 |

Rev. Paramount 3127 by Welling & Schannen (see John McGhee & Frank Welling).

THE OZARKERS

See George Edgin.

P

ROBERT N. PAGE

Robert N. Page, v; acc. own g.
Charlotte, NC   Tuesday, August 16, 1927

| 39817-1 | Ride And Shine On The Dummy Line | Vi 21067 |
| 39818-2 | I'm Gonna Move Further Down The Road | Vi 21067 |

ANDY PALMER

See Jimmy Johnson's String Band.

BILL PALMER
BILL PALMER'S TRIO
BILL PALMER TRIO

Pseudonyms on Victor, Bluebird, Electradisk, and Sunrise for Bob Miller. One side of Bluebird B-5012 (*Frivolous Frisco Fan*), as by **Bill Palmer**, is actually by Dwight Butcher.

BOB PALMER & MONTE HALL

Bob & Monte: Bob Palmer, Monte Hall, v duet; acc. unknown, f; Bob Palmer, p.

Los Angeles, CA   Monday, October 22, 1928

| LAE-302-B,-A | The Tumble-Down Shack In Dixieland | Br unissued trial recording |
| LAE-303-A,-B | When It's Springtime In The Rockies | Br unissued trial recording |

These were trial recordings for the Brunswick 4000 popular series.

Acc. Bob Palmer, p.

Los Angeles, CA   Tuesday, January 15, 1929

| LAE-388-B | The Utah Trail | Vo 5279 |
| LAE-389-A | When It's Springtime In The Rockies | Vo 5279, Me M12174 |

Rev. Melotone M12174 by Frank Luther (see Carson Robison).

Bob Palmer & Monte Hall, v duet; acc. prob. Bob Palmer, p.

New York, NY   Thursday, January 17, 1929

| 147810- | The Utah Trail | Co unissued |
| 147811- | The Tumble Down Shack In Dixieland | Co unissued |

Bob & Monte, v duet; acc. unknown orch.-1; or prob. Bob Palmer, p; unknown, g; unknown, u.

Los Angeles, CA   Wednesday, July 17, 1929

LAE-541-	Old Virginny Lullaby -1	Vo 5343
LAE-542-	The Tumbled Down Shack In Dixie Land	Vo cancelled
LAE-543-	The Tumbled Down Shack In Dixie Land	Vo cancelled
LAE-544-	When We Turn Out The Old Town Band -1	Vo 5343
LAE-545-	Back To Hawaii And You	Vo 5373
LAE-546-	Pals	Vo 5373

The orchestra is described on the labels of Vocalion 5343 as **Studio Trio** on matrix LAE-541, **Band** on matrix LAE-544.

Acc. unknown.

Los Angeles, CA   Tuesday, October 29, 1929

LAE-646-	When The Sun Goes Down	Vo rejected
LAE-647-	From The Heart Of The West	Vo rejected
LAE-648-	Ivy	Vo cancelled

Acc. two unknowns, f; unknown, p.

Los Angeles, CA   Wednesday, November 20, 1929

| LAE-669-A | When The Sun Goes Down | Vo 5387 |
| LAE-670-A | From The Heart Of The West (Came You) | Vo 5387 |

BOB PALMER & JIMMY WHITE

Bob & Jimmy: Bob Palmer, Jimmy White, v duet; acc. Bob Palmer, p; Jimmy White, g.

Hollywood, CA   Thursday, August 21, 1930

| 61016-1,-2 | Where The Golden Poppies Grow | Vi unissued |
| 61017-1,-2 | When The Raindrops Pattered On Our Old Tin Hats | Vi unissued |

Hollywood, CA   Wednesday, August 27, 1930

| 61016-4 | Where The Golden Poppies Grow | Vi 22522 |
| 61017-3,-4 | When The Raindrops Pattered On Our Old Tin Hats | Vi 22522 |

Hollywood, CA   Monday, February 9, 1931

| 61071-1 | Beautiful Northwest Country | Vi 23529 |
| 61072-2 | Blue Mountain Home In The West | Vi 23529 |

SLICK PALMER

Pseudonym on Sunrise for Bob Miller.

PALMER SISTERS

Hue Tokah Palmer, sv; Sudie Belle Palmer, av; Alice Palmer, tv; acc. D.M. Brock, p.

Bristol, TN   Friday, November 2, 1928

47275-2	We'll Sing On That Shore	Vi V-40037
47276-2	Singing The Story Of Grace	TT C-1566, Au 36-118
47277-2	Help Me To Find The Way	TT C-1566, Au 36-118
47278-3	He'll Be With Me	Vi V-40037

PALMER TRIO

Pseudonym on Bluebird and Sunrise for Bob Miller.

PALMETTO MALE QUARTETTE

Vocal quartet; acc unknown, p.
   Richmond, IN   Thursday, April 9, 1931

17663,-A	It's Just Like Heaven To Me	Ge rejected
17664,-A	Lights Along The Shore	Ge unissued
17665,-A	O'ershadowed By God's Love	Ch 16250
17666,-A	I'm Not Satisfied Here	Ch 16250
17667-A	I Love To Raise My Voice In Song	Ch 16731
17668-A	God's Love	Ch 16731
17669,-A	Where Is God?	Ge unissued

L.F. Crocker is listed in Champion files as a royalty payee and may be a member of this group.

PAN HANDLE BOYS

Pseudonym on Broadway for the Fruit Jar Guzzlers.

PANHANDLE PETE

This artist's real name is Howard Nash.

Panhandle Pete, v; acc. own h/g.
   Charlotte, NC   Saturday, June 4, 1938

64026-A	The Gambler's Dying Words	De 5599, MeC 45268
64027-A	This World Of Sorrow	De 5599, MeC 45268
64028-A	(Gonna Quit My Ramblin') Some Of These Days	De 5567
64029-A	Goodbye My Honey I'm Gone	De 5567
64030-A	Blue Weary And Lonesome	De 5683
64031-A	I'm On My Way To Canaan's Land	De 5683

PAPPY, EZRA & ELTON
PAPPY, ZEKE, EZRA & ELTON

See The Beverly Hill Billies.

PARADISE ENTERTAINERS

Unknown, f; unknown, sg; unknown, g; unknown, u.
   New Orleans, LA   Saturday, March 21, 1936

NO-60833-	Golden Wedding Anniversary Waltz	De 5221, BrSA SA1074
NO-60834-A	Alamo March	De 5221, BrSA SA1103

Revs: Brunswick SA1074 by Stripling Brothers, SA1103 by Ray Kinney (Hawaiian).

PARADISE JOY BOYS

Felix St Clair, f; prob. Cy McNally, g/v.
   Dallas, TX   Thursday, October 18, 1928

DAL-682-A	Cemetary Sal	Br 4268
DAL-683-A	Graveyard Blues	Br 4268
DAL-686-A	Match-Box Blues	Br 4265
DAL-687-A	It Keeps On Raining	Br 4265

Matrices DAL-684/85 are by Billy & His Uke (The Texas Joy Boy), who, despite his nickname, was apparently not a member of the Paradise Joy Boys.

PARAMOUNT QUARTET

Vocal quartet; unacc.
   Atlanta, GA   Friday, January 30, 1925

140309-2	What Did He Do?	Co 15020-D
140310-2	Heaven Is My Home	Co 15020-D

PARAMOUNT SACRED FOUR

Vocal quartet; acc. unknown, p.
   Chicago, IL   c. September 1927

20013-1	Right Will Always Win	Pm 3066, Bwy 8105
20014-2	Echoes From The Glory Shore	Pm 3066, Bwy 8105
20015-2	The Beautiful Land	Pm 3078, 3306, Bwy 8182
20016-2	The Unclouded Day	Pm 3078, 3306, Bwy 8182
20019-2	Near The Cross	Pm 3060, Bwy 8087
20020-1	Jesus Has Pardoned Me	Pm 3082
20021-1	How Wonderful Heaven Must Be	Pm 3073, Bwy 8133

20022-2	Riding The Billows For Home	Pm 3073, Bwy 8133
20023-2	I've Waited Too Long To Prepare	Pm 3082
20024-	Death Is No More Than A Dream	Pm 3060, Bwy 8087
20025-	Heaben	Pm 12557
20026-	Get Away Jordan	Pm 12557

Paramount 3306, Broadway 8182 as by **Glad Tidings Sacred Four**. Broadway 8087, 8105, 8133 as by **Star Sacred Singers**. Intervening matrices are untraced.

PARHAM BROS. QUARTETTE

Vocal quartet; acc. unknown.
Richmond, IN   Monday, January 4, 1926

12452-A	We'll Love Each Other Over There	[Ge] 20164
12453-A	The Man Of Galilee	[Ge] 20164

These are personal recordings and may not bear standard Gennett labels.

It is at least possible that this group is associated with the Carolina Gospel Singers.

PARHAM'S DIXIE QUARTET

See Carolina Gospel Singers.

GEORGE R. PARISEAU'S ORCHESTRA

No details, but prob. similar instrumentation to that of the following session.
Richmond, IN   Friday, March 22, 1929

14949,-A	Lovers Dream	Ge unissued
14950-A	Waggoner's Hornpipe	Ge 6899
14951-A	Fisher's Hornpipe	Ge 7033
14952-A	Money Musk And Little Reel	Ge 6899
14953-A	Flowers Of Edinburgh And Sandy Bottom	Ge 7033

Unknown, f; unknown, c; unknown, p; unknown, tbj.
Richmond, IN   Saturday, March 29, 1930

16418	Pretty Pond Lillies	Ch 16802, 45009
16419	Falling Leaf	Ch 16802, 45009
16420	Little Fairy	Ge 7203, Ch 15987, Spt 9750, Spr 2691
16421	Moonshiner's Serenade	Ge 7203, Ch 15987, Spt 9750, Spr 2691

Supertone 9750 as by **Sutton's Southern Serenaders**.

BYRON PARKER & HIS MOUNTAINEERS

Homer Sherrill, f-1/bv-2; Leonard Stokes, md-3/g-4/v-5; DeWitt "Snuffy" Jenkins, bj-6; Clyde Robbins, g/tv-7; Byron Parker, bsv-8.
Atlanta, GA   Friday, February 9, 1940

047637-1	Little Pal -1, 4, 5, 6, 7	BB B-8521, MW M-8723, RZAu G24892
047638-1	I'm Sorry, That's All I Can Say -3, 5, 7	BB B-8521, MW M-8723, RZAu G24892
047639-1	The Family Circle -1, 4, 6, 8	BB B-8476, MW M-8722
047640-1	A Beautiful Life -1, 2, 4, 5, 6, 7, 8	BB B-8476, MW M-8722
047641-1	We Shall Rise -1, 2, 4, 5, 6, 7, 8	BB B-8551, MW M-8724
047642-1	Oh Darling Come Back -3, 5, 7	BB B-8551, MW M-8724
047643-1	Carroll County Blues -1, 4, 6	BB B-8432, MW M-8721
047644-1	Up Jumped The Devil -1, 4, 6	BB B-8432, MW M-8721

Homer Sherrill, f; Snuffy Jenkins, bj; Leonard Stokes, g/v-1; Clyde Robbins, g/tv-2; band sp-3.
Atlanta, GA   Thursday, October 10, 1940

054596-1	C & N.W. Railroad Blues	BB B-8673, [MW M-8874]
054597-1	Peanut Special -3	BB B-8673, [MW M-8874]
054598-1	The Letter That Went To God -1, 2	BB B-8633, [MW M-8873]
054599-1	Tell Her Not To Wait For Me -1	BB B-8708, [MW M-8875]
056500-1	I Love My Saviour -1, 2	BB B-8633, [MW M-8873]
056501-1	He Is My Friend And Guide -1, 2	BB B-8771, [MW M-8876]
056502-1	That's Why I'm Blue -1, 2	BB B-8771, [MW M-8876]
056503-1	Married Life Blues -1	BB B-8708, [MW M-8875]

Byron Parker groups recorded after 1942.

C.W. PARKER

C.W. Parker, v; acc. poss. own g.
Richmond, IN   Monday, October 24, 1932

18861	Take This Letter To My Mother	Ge unissued

CHARLIE PARKER

Charlie Parker & Mack Woolbright, v duet; acc. Charlie Parker, bj; Mack Woolbright, g; or **Charlie Parker**-1, bj solo/sp; or **Charlie Parker Trio**-2: prob.: Charlie Parker, Mack Woolbright, unknown, v trio; acc. Charlie Parker, bj; Mack Woolbright, g.

Atlanta, GA　　　　　　　　　　　　　　　　　　　　　　　　　　　　　　　Wednesday, April 6, 1927

143918-2	Give That Nigger Ham	Co 15154-D
143919-2	Rabbit Chase -1	Co 15154-D
143920-	Where Shall I Be -2	Co unissued
143921-	While Eternal Ages Roll	Co unissued

Atlanta, GA　　　　　　　　　　　　　　　　　　　　　　　　　　　　　Thursday, November 10, 1927

145194-1	The Man Who Wrote Home Sweet Home Never Was A Married Man	Co 15236-D
145195-1	Ticklish Reuben	Co 15236-D
145196-2	The Old Arm Chair	Co 15694-D
145197-1	Will, The Weaver	Co 15694-D

CHUBBY PARKER

This artist's real name was Frederick R. Parker.

Chubby Parker, v; acc. own tbj.

Chicago, IL　　　　　　　　　　　　　　　　　　　　　　　　　　　　　　　c. February 26, 1927

12601-A	Nickety Nackety Now Now Now	Ge 6077, Ch 15247, Sil 5011, 25011, Spt 9189
12602,-A	Little Brown Jug	Ge rejected
12603,-A	Whoa Mule Whoa	Ge rejected
12604,-A	Oh Susanna	Ge rejected
12605	I'm A Stern Old Bachelor	Ge 6097, Ch 15247, Sil 4001, 5012, 25012, Spt 9188, Her 75548
12606	Bib-A-Lollie Boo	Ge 6077, Sil 4001, 5012, 25012, Spt 9188

Champion 15247 as by **Smilin' Tubby Johnson**. Matrix 12601 is titled *Nickity Nackity Now Now Now* on Supertone 9189. Later pressings of Supertone 9188, 9189 reportedly use rerecordings of the titles; see note to October 21, 1930 session.

Chubby Parker, v/wh-1; acc. own tbj.

Chicago, IL　　　　　　　　　　　　　　　　　　　　　　　　　　　　　　　c. April 2, 1927

12676,-A	Whoa Mule Whoa	Ge rejected
12677	Oh Suzzana -1	Ge 6097, Ch 15278, Sil 5013, 25013, Spt 9191, Her 75548
12688	The Little Brown Jug -1	Ge 6120, Ch 15298, Sil 5013, 25013, Spt 9191

Champion 15278, 15298 as by **Smilin' Tubby Johnson**.
Matrix 12677 is titled *O, Suzanna* on Silvertone 5013, 25013 and *Oh, Susanna* on Champion 15278, Supertone 9191, and Herwin 75548. Matrix 12688 is titled *Little Brown Jug* on Silvertone 5013, 25013.
Later pressings of Supertone 9191 reportedly use rerecordings of the titles; see note to October 21, 1930 session.
Intervening matrices are by other artists. Revs: Champion 15278 by Vernon Dalhart, 15298 by David Miller.

Chicago, IL　　　　　　　　　　　　　　　　　　　　　　　　　　　　　　　c. April 1927

12735-A	Whoa Mule Whoa	Ge 6120, Ch 15260, Sil 5011, 25011, Spt 9189

Matrix 12735 is titled *Whoa, Mule, Whoa* on Supertone 9189.
Later pressings of Supertone 9189 reportedly use a rerecording of the title; see note to October 22, 1930 session.

St. Paul, MN　　　　　　　　　　　　　　　　　　　　　　　　　　　　　　c. September 17, 1927

13088	A Rovin' Little Darky	Ge 6374, Ch 15430, Sil 5102, 25102, Spt 9190
13089	Uncle Ned	Ge 6287, Ch 15393, Sil 5103, 25103, Spt 9192
13090	Darling Nellie Gray	Sil 5101, 25101, Spt 9187
13091	Oh-Dem Golden Slippers	Ge 6287, Ch 15430, Sil 5102, 25102, Spt 9190
13092	His Parents Haven't Seen Him Since	Ge 6319, Sil 5101, 25101, Spt 9187
13093-A	My Little Sod Shanty On The Claim	Ge 6319, Sil 5103, 25103, Spt 9192

Champion 15430 as by **Smilin' Tubby Johnson**.
Matrix 13088 is titled *A Rovin' Little Darkey* on Champion 15430, Silvertone 5102, 25102. Matrix 13090 is titled *Darling Nelly Gray* in Gennett files and probably on Supertone 9187. Matrix 13093 is titled *My Little Old Sod Shanty On The Claim* on Silvertone 5103 and probably 25103.
Later pressings of Supertone 9187, 9190, and 9192 reportedly use rerecordings of the titles; see notes to October 21-22, 1930 sessions.
Rev. Champion 15393 by Vernon Dalhart.

"Chubby" Parker & His Old-Time Banjo, v/wh; acc. own tbj.

New York, NY　　　　　　　　　　　　　　　　　　　　　　　　　　　　　Thursday, August 23, 1928

146878-2	Down On The Farm	Co 15296-D
146879-2	King Kong Kitchie Kitchie Ki-Me-O	Co 15296-D

Chubby Parker, v/wh-1; acc. own h-2/tbj.
Richmond, IN
Tuesday, October 21, 1930

17176	King Kong Kitchie Kitchie Ki-Me-O -2	Ch 16211, Spt 9731
17177-A	Get Away Old Maids Get Away	Ch 16211, Spt 9723, MW 4945
17178	In Kansas -1	Spt 9723
17179	Grandfather's Clock	Ch 16163, Spt 9732
17180-A	The Old Wooden Rocker -1	Ch 16163, Spt 9732, MW 4945
17181	You'll Hear The Bells In The Morning -2	Ch 16143, Spt 9731
17182	Nickety Nackety Now Now Now	Ge unissued
17183,-A	Whoa Mule Whoa	Spt 9189
17184,-A	Bib-A-Lollie-Boo	Spt 9189
17185	I'm A Stern Old Bachelor	Ch 16143, Spt 9188
17186	A Rovin' Little Darkey -2	Spt 9190
17187	Uncle Ned -2	Spt 9192

Matrix 17180 is titled *Old Wooden Rocker* on Montgomery Ward 4945.
The Supertone issues of matrices 17182 to 17187 are reported in Gennett files as replacing the issues derived from 1927 matrices.

Chubby Parker, v; acc. own h-1/tbj.
Richmond, IN
Wednesday, October 22, 1930

17188	Oh Susanna	Spt 9191
17189,-A	Oh Dem Golden Slippers -1	Spt 9190
17190	Little Brown Jug -1	Spt 9191
17191	My Little Old Sod Shanty On The Claim -1	Spt 9192
17192,-A	Darling Nellie Gray -1	Spt 9187
17193	His Parents Haven't Seen Him Since	Spt 9187
17194	Long Long Ago -1	Ge unissued
17195	The Bright Little Valley	Ge rejected

The Supertone issues of matrices 17188 to 17193 are reported in Gennett files as replacing the issues derived from 1927 matrices.

Chubby Parker & His Little Old-Time Banjo, v/wh-1; acc. own tbj.
New York, NY
Wednesday, October 14, 1931

10876-2	Nickety Nackety Now Now Now	Cq 7889
10877-2	Bib-A-Lollie-Boo -1	Cq 7891
10878-3	A Rovin' Little Darkey -1	Cq 7897
10879-1	The Year Of Jubilo -1	Cq 7897
10880-2	I'm A Stern Old Bachelor	Ba 32611, Me M12524, Or 8178, Pe 12859, Ro 5178, Cq 7888, Pan 25416
10881-2	Get Away, Old Maids Get Away -1	Ba 32611, Me M12524, Or 8178, Pe 12859, Ro 5178, Cq 7888, Pan 25416
10882-2	Whoa Mule Whoa	Cq 7892
10883-3	The Kissing Song -1	Cq 7891

Matrix 10881 is titled *Get Away Old Maids, Get Away* on Panachord 25416.

Acc. own h-2/tbj.
New York, NY
Thursday, October 15, 1931

10884-2	In Kansas -1	Cq 7894
10885-1,-2	My Little Old Sod Shanty On The Claim -1	Cq 7894
10886-3	His Parents Haven't Seen Him Since	Cq 7895
10887-1	The Irish Christening	Cq 7896
10888-1	And That Was Irish Too -2	Cq 7896
10889-1	See The Black Clouds A Breakin' Over Yonder -2	Cq 7890
10890-1	You'll Hear The Bells In The Morning -2	Cq 7890
10891-1	Bingo Was His Name -1	Cq 7892

New York, NY
Friday, October 16, 1931

10892-3	King Kong Kitchie Kitchie Ki-Me-O -2	Cq 7889
10893-1,-3	Little Brown Jug -2	Cq 7893
10894-2	Drill, Ye Tarriers, Drill -1	Cq 7893
10895-2	Davey Crockett -2	Cq 7895

DAN PARKER
DAN & BILL PARKER

Pseudonym on Crown and associated labels for Dick Robertson (**Dan Parker**) or Dick Robertson and possibly Bob Miller (**Dan & Bill Parker**).

LINDA PARKER

Linda Parker's real name at the time of her death on August 12, 1935 was Jeanne Muenich Janes.

Linda Parker, v; acc. the **Cumberland Ridge Runners**: Homer "Slim" Miller, f-1; Karl Davis, md; Hartford Taylor, g; Red Foley, sb-2.
Chicago, IL   Tuesday, April 11, 1933

C-536-2	Take Me Back To Renfro Valley -1, 2	Cq 8164
C-537-2	I'll Be All Smiles Tonight	Cq 8164

Acc. the **Cumberland Ridge Runners**: Homer "Slim" Miller, f; Karl Davis, md; Hartford Taylor, g; Red Foley, sb; unidentified (prob. Karl Davis, Hartford Taylor, Red Foley), v/y trio-1.
Chicago, IL   Thursday, March 22, 1934

CP-1017-1	Lonesome Valley Sally -1	Cq 8311
CP-1018-1	My Ozark Mountain Home	Cq 8311

PEGGY PARKER

This artist's sole release in the Columbia Old Familiar Tunes series (one side of 15725-D) is beyond the scope of this work.

PARKER & DODD

——— Parker, ——— Dodd, v duet; acc. unknown.
New York, NY   Thursday, September 29, 1932

12395-	I Still Write Your Name In The Sand	ARC unissued

Acc. unknown, bj-1; unknown, g/tg-2; unknown, g.
New York, NY   Friday, September 30, 1932

12404-	Sad And Lonely Mountain Boy	ARC unissued
12405-1	Blue Eyed Jane -2	Ba 32817, Me M12745, Or 8250, Pe 12928, Ro 5250
12406-	Peaceful Valley	ARC unissued
12407-1	Sail Away Lady -1	Ba 32817, Me M12745, Or 8250, Pe 12928, Ro 5250
12408-	Bile Dem Cabbage Down	ARC unissued

Acc. unknown, sg; unknown g.
New York, NY   Monday, October 3, 1932

12412-	Seven Years With The Wrong Woman	ARC unissued
12413-2	Walking The Last Mile	Ba 32606, Me M12525, MeC 91448, Or 8179, Pe 12856, Ro 5179, Cq 8077
12414-	The Circle Has Been Broken	ARC unissued
12415-1	Near The Cross	Cq 8132

Acc. unknown, sg-1; unknown, bj-2; unknown, g.
New York, NY   Tuesday, October 4, 1932

12417-2	Don't Forget Me Little Darling -2	Ba 32606, Me M12525, MeC 91448, Or 8179, Pe 12856, Ro 5179, Cq 8077
12420-3	Jesus Is Tenderly Calling -1	Ba 32724, Me M12653, Or 8218, Pe 12900, Ro 5218, Cq 8131
12421-1	God Will Take Care Of You -1	Cq 8132
12422-2	Back To The Harbor Of Home Sweet Home -1	Ba 32612, Me M12526, Or 8180, Pe 12860, Ro 5180, Cq 8076
12423-	Ivy Covered Cabin	ARC unissued

All issues of *Jesus Is Tenderly Calling* are believed to be derived from matrix 12420 rather than 12436 (see below). Matrices 12418/19 are by other artists.

New York, NY   Wednesday, October 5, 1932

12436-	Jesus Is Tenderly Calling	ARC unissued
12437-1	Many Times With You I've Wandered -2	Ba 32612, Me M12526, Or 8180, Pe 12860, Ro 5180, Cq 8076
12438-	My Sweet Floetta	ARC unissued
12439-2	Bringing In The Sheaves	Ba 32724, Me M12653, Or 8218, Pe 12900, Ro 5218, Cq 8131

Matrix 12439 is titled *Bring In The Sheaves* on Perfect 12900.

PARKER QUARTETTE

Vocal quartet; or Joe Carey, v solo-1; acc. unknown, p.
New York, NY   Tuesday, August 27, 1935

39889-A	Look For The Rainbow	De 5144
39890-B	You Got To Live Your Religion Every Day	De 5144

39891-A	Play On, Little David	De 5164
39892-A	Naturalized For Heaven	De 5164
39893-A	Victory Is Coming	De 5355
39894-A	Swing Wide Yo' Golden Gate	De 5355
39895-A	His Coming Draweth Nigh	De 5886
39896-A	My Home Sweet Home	De 5886
39897-A	He Rescued Me	De 5911
39898-A	It Won't Be Long	De 5911
39899-	We're Living For Jesus	De 5931
39900-A	After The Rain	De 5931
39901-A	What A Happy Time	De 5297
39902-A	I'll Find A Sweet Rest	De 5297
39903-A	We'll Understand It Better -1	De 5186, MeC 45217
39904-A	No Stranger Yonder -1	De 5186, MeC 45217
39905-A	Don't Be Knockin'	De 5214
39906-A	It's Just Like Heaven	De 5214

DICK PARMAN

Parman & Snyder: Dick Parman, Elmer Snyder, v duet; acc. unknown, bj-1; Dick Parman, g.
Memphis, TN   Monday, February 20, 1928

400269-	[Polly Wolly Woodle] -1	OK unissued
400270-A,- B	[Are You From Dixie?]	OK unissued
400271-B	Blue Bell	OK 45302
400272-	Don't You Love Your Daddy	OK unissued
400273-B	She'll Be Coming Around The Mountain	OK 45302
400274-	Whoa, Mule, Whoa	OK unissued

Parman Of Kentucky (The Mountain Poet), v; acc. prob. own g.
Chicago, IL   c. October/November 1928

| 20953-2 | We've Been Chums For Fifty Years | Pm 3138, 3261 |
| 20954-1 | The Old Covered Bridge | Pm 3138, 3261 |

Dick Parman, v; acc. Doc Roberts, f-1; prob. own g.
Richmond, IN   Friday, November 30, 1928

| 14486-B | That Old Covered Bridge | Ge 6718, Spt 9319, Spr 2542 |
| 14488 | Seven Long Years Of Trouble -1 | Ge 6792, Chg 421 |

Supertone 9319 as by **Dave Turner**. Superior 2542 as by **Phil Montgomery**. Challenge 421 as by **Dick Handley**.
Matrix 14487 is by Green Bailey.
Revs: Supertone 9319 by Frank Welling; Challenge 421 by Asa Martin.

Dick Parman, v/y-1; acc. Asa Martin, h-2; prob. own g.
Richmond, IN   Saturday, December 1, 1928

14491-A	Many Troubles Blues -1	Ge 6747, Spt 9374
14492-A	Rock All Our Babies To Sleep -1	Ge 6747, Ch 15692, 45099, Spt 9374
14493-B	We've Been Chums For Fifty Years -2	Ge 6792, Spt 9560
14494-A	She'll Be Coming 'Round The Mountain -2	Ge 6718, Ch 15692, 45099, Spt 9318

Champion 15692 as by **Amos Neal**, 45099 as by "**Doc**" **Roberts**. Supertone 9318, 9374, 9560 as by **Dave Turner**.
Champion 45099 has what is inscribed in the wax as the plain take of matrix 14494 but is identical with the take issued elsewhere, apparently A. Matrix 14494 is titled *She'll Be Comin' 'Round The Mountain* on Supertone 9318. Matrices 14489/90 are by Green Bailey.
Revs: Supertone 9318 by Kirk McGee & Blythe Poteet, 9560 by Byrd Moore.

Dick Parman, v; or **Dick Parman & Lowell Smith**-1, v duet; acc. Lowell E. Smith, p-2; Dick Parman, g-3.
Richmond, IN   Saturday, January 25, 1930

16147,-A	The Trail Of The Lonesome Pine -2	Ge rejected
16149,-A,-B	In The Hills Of Old Kentucky -2	Ge rejected
16152-A	Dark Eyes -1, 2	Ge 7127
16154	Are You From Dixie -3	Ge 7127

Matrices 16148, 16150 are Hawaiian; matrices 16151, 16153 are Spanish/Mexican.

Acc. own g; Lowell Smith, u-2.
Richmond, IN   Saturday, April 26, 1930

16538-A	I Love You Best Of All -1	Ge 7204, Ch 16010, 45189
16539-A	If I Only Had A Home Sweet Home -1	Ge 7204, Ch 16010, 45189
16540-A	I've Waited Long For You -1	Ge rejected
16541,-A	I Wonder Who's Kissing Her Now -1	Ge rejected
16542,-A	It Takes A Long Tall Brownskin Gal -2	Ge rejected
16543,-A	Old Fashioned Locket -2	Ge rejected

Champion 16010, 45189 as by **Parman & Smith**.

Richmond, IN   Wednesday, July 16, 1930

16829,-A	Old Fashioned Locket -2	Ge rejected
16830,-A	In The Hills Of Old Kentucky -1	Ge rejected
16831-B	The Trail Of The Lonesome Pine -1	Ge 7267, Ch 16055, Spt 9715
16832,-A	I Wouldn't Take Nothing For My Journey -2	Ge rejected
16833,-A	It Takes A Long Tall Brownskin Gal -1	Ge rejected
16834,-A	For Me And My Gal -1	Ge rejected
16835-A	I've Waited Honey, Waited Long For You -1	Ge 7267, Ch 16055, Spt 9715
16836	I Wonder Who's Kissing Her Now	Ge rejected

Champion 16055 as by **Parman & Smith**. Supertone 9715 as by **Dave & Alice Taylor**.

Dick Parman, v; acc. own g.
Richmond, IN   Thursday, October 2, 1930

17126,-A	In The Hills Of Old Kentucky	Ch 16300, MeC 45014
17127-A	Just An Old Fashioned Locket	Ch 16300, Spr 2542, MeC 45014
17128,-A	What I Saw In Havana	Ge unissued
17129,-A	Charming Betsy	Ge rejected
17130,-A	When I Get You Alone Tonight	Ge rejected
17131	In The Shade Of The Old Apple Tree	Ge rejected

Superior 2542 as by **Phil Montgomery**.

PARMAN & SMITH
PARMAN & SNYDER
PARMAN OF KENTUCKY

See Dick Parman.

HAPPY JIM PARSONS & THE BOYS OF COMPANY "B"

Happy Jim Parsons, v; acc. unknown, f; unknown, cl; unknown, h; unknown, ac; unknown, g; unknown, sb; band v.
?New York, NY   ?c. February/March 1942

Johnny Private	Standard T-2060
The Saga Of Susie Brown (Ril-A-Ral-A-Ree)	Standard T-2060

PARSONS & KENT

Pseudonym on Broadway (4000 series) for Lester McFarland & Robert A. Gardner.

PAT–HALLEY–JARDINE

Two of them, bj; one of them, g.
Richmond, IN   Wednesday, February 15, 1933

19032	Tamiami Trail	Ch 16566
19033	Egyptian Ella	Ch 16566

Matrix 19032 is described in Gennett files as "old-time playing." On the face of it, however, these items seem likely to be outside the scope of this work.

FIDDLIN' IKE PATE

Pseudonym on Champion for William B. Houchens.

FIDDLIN' JIM PATE

Fiddlin' Jim Pate, f; acc. Tom Pate, g.
Dallas, TX   Wednesday, October 16, 1929

56392-2	Prisoner Boy	Vi V-40170
56393-2	Texas Farewell	Vi V-40170

JOE PATEK'S BOHEMIAN ORCHESTRA

One record by this group was issued in the Decca Hill Billy series, but it is outside the scope of this work.

LUTHER PATRICK

See Wyzee Hamilton.

MANSFIELD PATRICK

Mansfield Patrick, g solo.
Richmond, IN   Wednesday, February 26, 1930

16328,-A	Try And Play It	Ge rejected

Mansfield & Hall: Mansfield Patrick, Herman Hall, bj duet.

Richmond, IN   Wednesday, February 26, 1930
16330-A   Crazy Joe   Spr 2533

Matrix 16329 is by The Highleys.
Rev. Superior 2533 by W.J. Nicholson (see Nicholson's Players).

COLONEL JOHN A. PATTEE

Col. John A. Pattee, f; acc. unknown, p; unknown, calls.
   New York, NY   Saturday, September 6, 1924
    81976-1   Old Gatville Quadrille   Co 231-D, Ha 5013-H
    81977-1   Old Money Musk Quadrille   Co 231-D, Ha 5013-H
    81978-   Virginia Reel   Co unissued
    81979-   Old Zip Coon Medley   Co unissued

Harmony 5013-H as by **Colonel Pattee**.

ANDY PATTERSON

See Warren Caplinger. (This artist also recorded as part of the McCartt Brothers & Patterson.)

PATT PATTERSON

This artist's full name is James Arthur Patterson.

Pat Patterson & His Champion Rep Riders: Pat Patterson, sg-1/v-2; Lois Dexter, tbj; unknown, g; unknown, calls-3.
   New York, NY   Wednesday, May 14, 1930
    9735-   The Roundup In The Spring -2?   ARC unissued
    9736-   The Dry Landers -2?   ARC unissued
    9737-   The Old Black Steer -2?   ARC unissued
    9738-1,-2   The Cat's Whiskers -1   Je 20024, Or 8024, Pe 164, Ro 5024, Htd 16092
    9739-1   Sagebrush Dance -3   Je 20024, Or 8024, Ro 5024, Htd 16092

Matrix 9738 is titled *The Cats' Whiskers* on Oriole 8024.

Pat Patterson, sg-1/g-2/v/y-3; Lois Dexter, tbj/v-4; poss. Lewis McDaniels, g; unknown, male v-5.
   New York, NY   Tuesday, May 20, 1930
    9748-1,-2   The Wandering Cowboy -1, 3   Ba 32901, Je 20021, Or 8021, Ro 5021,
                                                                    Htd 16102, 23011
    9749-2   On The Red River Shore -1, 4   Ba 0870, Ca 0470, Do 4673, Je 20022,
                                                                    Me M12386, Or 8022, Pe 12650, Re 10176,
                                                                    Ro 5022, Bwy 4101, Cq 7711, Htd 16091,
                                                                    23008, CrC/MeC 81499, Stg 281499,
                                                                    Min M-923
    9750-2   The Old Chisholm Trail -2, 4, 5   Ba 32091, Je 20021, Or 8021, Pe 164, Ro 5021,
                                                                    Htd 16102, 23011
    9751-2   Tidy Up And Down The Old Brass Wagon -2   Ba 32090, Je 20031, Or 8031, Pe 168, Ro 5031,
                                                                    Cq 7701

All issues of matrix 9749 are as by **Patt Patterson & Lois Dexter**. McDaniels (if it is he) may not be present on all items. Matrix 9750 is titled *The Old Chisolm Trail* on some issues of Jewel 20021. Rev. Minerva M-923 by Frank Luther Trio.

Pat Patterson & Lois Dexter, v duet; or **Patt Patterson**-1, v; acc. Patt Patterson, sg; Lois Dexter, tbj; poss. Lewis McDaniels, g.
   New York, NY   Thursday, May 22, 1930
    9757-2,-3   A Home On The Range   Ba 0870, Ca 0470, Do 4673, Je 20022,
                                                                    Me M12386, Or 8022, Pe 12650, Re 10176,
                                                                    Ro 5022, Cq 7711, Htd 16091, 23008,
                                                                    Apex 41268, CrC/MeC 81499, Stg 281499,
                                                                    Min M-919
    9758-2   The Cowboy's Love Song   Ba 32090, Je 20031, Or 8031, Pe 168, Ro 5031,
                                                                    Bwy 4101, Cq 7701
    9759-   Jack O' Diamonds -1   ARC unissued

Some issues of Conqueror 7711 are erroneously pressed with ARC matrix 19757, an organ instrumental by George C. Crook. Rev. Minerva M-919 by Frank Luther & Carson Robison (see the latter).

Patt James, v; acc. prob. Lois Dexter, tbj; poss. own g.
   New York, NY   Thursday, October 16, 1930
    TE-34019   The Wandering Cowboy   Vo rejected trial recording
    TE-34020   Old Chisolm [sic] Trail   Vo rejected trial recording

Patt Patterson & Lois Dexter, v duet; acc. prob.: Patt Patterson, sg; Lois Dexter, tbj.
   New York, NY   Saturday, February 14, 1931
    10423-   Snow Covered Face   ARC unissued

10424-	Beneath A Sheltering Pine	ARC unissued
10425-	I'se Born In A Texas Town	ARC unissued

New York, NY   Monday, February 16, 1931

10426-	Thirteen More Steps	ARC unissued
10427-	Blue Eyed Girl	ARC unissued

The accompaniment is confirmed as above for matrix 10426.

New York, NY   Thursday, February 26, 1931

10426-	Thirteen More Steps	ARC unissued

Patt Patterson (Acc. by Champion Rep Riders), v; acc. own sg; unknown, g-1.

New York, NY   Friday, March 13, 1931

10424-	Beneath A Sheltering Pine	ARC unissued
10426-12	Thirteen More Steps -1	Ba 32206, Or 8075, Pe 12727, Ro 5075, Cq 7756
10495-	Make Me A Cowboy Again For A Day	ARC unissued

Lois Dexter, v; acc. unknown.

New York, NY   Saturday, March 14, 1931

10496-	A Gal Like Me	ARC unissued

New York, NY   Monday, March 23, 1931

10529-	Rose Of Sante Fe	ARC unissued
10530-	The Lone Driftin' Riders	ARC unissued

Patt Patterson & Lois Dexter, v duet; acc. Patt Patterson, sg; Lois Dexter, tbj; unknown, g.

New York, NY   Friday, April 10, 1931

10423-7	Snow Covered Face	Ba 32206, Or 8075, Pe 12727, Ro 5075, Cq 7756
10425-	I'se Born In A Texas Town	ARC unissued
10562-	Oklahoma Sunshine	ARC unissued

Patterson and Dexter also accompanied Lewis McDaniels and Walter Smith.

RED PATTERSON'S PIEDMONT LOG ROLLERS

Percy Setliff, f; John Fletcher "Red" Patterson, bj/v; Dick Nolen, tbj; Lee Nolen, g; Henry Norton, tv-1; band v-2.

Charlotte, NC   Friday, August 12, 1927

39797-2	My Sweetheart Is A Shy Little Fairy -1	Vi 21187
39798-2	Don't Forget Me, Little Darling	Vi 21187
39799-3	Down On The Banks Of The Ohio	Vi 35874
39802-2	The White Rose -1	Vi 21132
39803-2	The Battleship Of Maine	Vi 20936
39804-2	Poor Little Joe	Vi 35874
39805-2	The Sweet Sunny South	Vi 21132
39806-2	I'll Never Get Drunk Anymore -2	Vi 20936

Victor 21187, 35874 as by **Piedmont Log Rollers**. Victor 35874 is a 12-inch issue. Matrices 39800/01 are by Kelly Harrell.

PATTERSON & CAPLINGER
PATTERSON, CAPLINGER & THE DIXIE HARMONIZERS

See Warren Caplinger.

PAUL & JOHN

See Paul Crutchfield & John Clotworthy.

EZRA PAULETTE & HIS BEVERLY HILL BILLIES

See The Beverly Hill Billies.

JACKSON PAVEY & HIS CORN SHUCKERS

Pseudonym on Clarion and Velvet Tone for Gid Tanner & His Skillet-Lickers.

PHIL PAVEY

Phil Pavey, v/y; acc. poss. Spencer Williams, p; unknown, bj-1.

New York, NY   Friday, February 15, 1929

401613-B	Arizona Blues	OK 45355
401614-A	Prairie Blues	OK 45308, PaE E6207
401615-A	Utah Mormon Blues	OK 45355
401616-A	Broncho Bustin' Blues -1	OK 45308, PaE E6207

LEON PAYNE

Leon Payne, v; acc. own g.

Dallas, TX   Saturday, April 5, 1941

063026-1	'Neath An Indian Summer Moon	BB B-8788
063027-1	Down Where The Violets Grow	BB B-8735
063028-1	Arizona Lullaby	BB B-8812
063029-1	'Neath The Old Pine Tree	BB B-8837, RZAu G25165
063030-1	When The Sun Sets On The Sierra	BB B-8788
063031-1	Let It End This Way	BB B-8837, RZAu G25165
063032-1	Teach Me To Forget	BB B-8812
063033-1	Ten Thousand Tomorrows	BB B-8735

Leon Payne also recorded with Bill Boyd, and after 1942.

PEACEFUL VALLEY FOLK[S]

Peaceful Valley Folks, v trio; acc. unknown, f; unknown, g.
New York, NY   Monday, October 14, 1935

60059-A	The Oregon Trail	De 5154
60060-A	Take Those Mountains Out Of My Way	De 5154, Pan 25834
60061-A	Take Me Back To My Boots And Saddle	De 5150, Pan 25816
60062-A	It's Spring In The Rockies Again	De 5150, Pan 25834

New York, NY   Monday, November 18, 1935

60152-A	On Treasure Island	De 5159, Pan 25821
60153-A	The Wheel Of The Wagon Is Broken	De 5159

New York, NY   Tuesday, November 26, 1935

60176-E	The Maple On The Hill	De 5165, DeAu X1121, Pan 25816
60177-B	The Passing Of Little Joe	De 5165, DeAu X1121, Pan 25821

At least some issues of Panachord 25816 and 25821 are as by **Peaceful Valley Folk**.

MAURY PEARSON

Maury Pearson, v; acc. Ernest C. Daulton, p.
New York, NY   Wednesday, March 14, 1928

E-26973/74*	Blessed Redeemer	Br 280
E-26975*/76	Hiding In The Shadow Of The Rock	Br 233, Spt S2073, PanAu P11999
E-26977*/78	I Am Praying For You	Br 296
E-26979/80*	Though Your Sins Be As Scarlet	Br 261, Spt S2099
E-26981/82*	I Know That My Redeemer Lives	Vo 5239
E-26983*/84	What Will You Do With Jesus?	Br 261, Spt S2099

Panachord P11999 as by **Albert Marques**.

Acc. unknown, f; Ernest C. Daulton, p.
New York, NY   Thursday, March 15, 1928

E-26997/98*	When I Can Read My Title Clear	Br 296
E-26999*/7000	It Is You, Just You, Jesus Needs	Br 280
E-27001*/02	Some One Is Praying For You	Br 233, Spt S2073, PanAu P11999
E-27003/04*	'Tis Jesus	Vo 5239
XE-27005/06	The Holy City	Br/Vo unissued
XE-27007/08	The Ninety And Nine	Br/Vo unissued

Panachord P11999 as by **Albert Marques**. Matrices XE-27005/06, XE-27007/08 were intended for a 12-inch issue.

BERT PECK

Bert Peck, v; acc. unknown, sg; unknown, g.
Dallas, TX   Thursday, November 27, 1930

DAL-6753-	The Maiden's Plea	Br 522, Pan 25089
DAL-6754-	Over The Hills To The Poorhouse	Br 522

Rev. Panachord 25089 by Hank Keene.

PECK'S MALE QUARTETTE

Poss.: C.P. Sheffield, tv; J.C. Cronic, tv; H.D. Wallace, poss. bv; Emory Peck, bsv; acc. Catherine Boswell, p.
Long Island City, NY   c. April 1929

430-A	Because I Love Him	QRS R.9027
431-A	The Uncloudy Day	QRS R.9024
432	How Beautiful Heaven Must Be	QRS R.9024
433-A	Happy All The Time	QRS R.9027
434-A	Everybody Will Be Happy Over There	QRS R.9025, Bwy 8196
435-A	Do Your Best And Wear A Smile	QRS R.9028, Pm 3189, Bwy 8244

436	Eternity	QRS R.9028, Pm 3189, Bwy 8244
442	Sing Of His Word	QRS R.9029, Pm 3207, Bwy 8259
443-A	There Is Sunshine In My Soul Today	QRS R.9025, Bwy 8196
448-A	The Home Over There	QRS R.9029, Pm 3207, Bwy 8259
449-A	There Is Power In The Blood	QRS R.9030, Pm 3307
450-A	Since Jesus Came Into My Heart	QRS R.9030, Pm 3307
454-A	When Jesus Comes	QRS R.9032, Pm 3191
456-A	Working For The King Of Kings	QRS R.9032, Pm 3191
457-A	The Way To Glory Land	QRS R.9033, Pm 3192
459-A	Cheer Along The Way	QRS R.9033, Pm 3192
	Pressing Along	Pm 3193, 3263
	A Wonderful Time	Pm 3193, 3263

Broadway 8196 as by **Emory's Male Quartet**.
Matrices 437 to 441 are by Biddleville Quintette (see *B&GR*); matrices 444/45 are by Katharine Baxter & Harry Nelson. Matrices 446/47, 451 to 453, 455, 458 are untraced, but some at least are probably by this group, and two of them almost certainly account for the titles on Paramount 3193, 3263.

Vocal quartet (prob. the same as or similar to the above); acc. Catherine Boswell, p.
    New York, NY   Wednesday, September 24, 1930

10080-2	Drifting Down	Je 20038, Or 8038, Pe 12670, Ro 5038
10081-2	There's No Disappointment In Heaven	Cq 7072
10082-2	Going Down The Valley	Ba 32100, Je 20029, Or 8029, Pe 166, Ro 5029, Cq 7798
10083-	One Of These Days	ARC unissued
10084-	The Love Of Jesus Covers The World	ARC unissued
10085-1	Oh I Want To See Him	Ba 32100, Je 20029, Or 8029, Pe 166, Ro 5029, Cq 7798
10086-	Shall We Gather At The River	ARC unissued
10087-	It Will Always Be Wonderful There	ARC unissued
10088-	Don't Be Knocking	ARC unissued

Conqueror 7072 as by **Smoky Mountain Family**. Earlier issues of Conqueror 7072 use a recording of the same song by the Gentry Brothers (Plaza matrix 7337), as by **Smoky Mountain Twins**.
Rev. Conqueror 7072 (with same credit) by Troy Martin & Elvin Bigger.

    New York, NY   Thursday, September 25, 1930

10089-	What A Friend	ARC unissued
10090-	Bloom Brightly Sweet Roses	ARC unissued
10091-	I Love To Tell The Story	ARC unissued
10092-	Wandering Child Oh Come Home	ARC unissued
10093-2	Sometime Somewhere	Je 20038, Or 8038, Pe 12670, Ro 5038
10094-1	The Uncloud Day	Ba 32097, Je 20039, Or 8039, Pe 12671, Ro 5039
10095-2	No Stranger Yonder	Ba 32097, Je 20039, Or 8039, Pe 12671, Ro 5039
10096-	Crown Him Lord Of All	ARC unissued
10097-	Take The Name Of Jesus With You	ARC unissued

PELICAN WILDCATS

Willie Ross Mayes, f; Dolphus Hill, md; Kenneth Mayes, g.
    Atlanta, GA   Tuesday, October 27, 1931

151956-1	Walkin' Georgia Rose	Co 15755-D
151957-	Love Flower Waltz	Co unissued

Rev. Columbia 15755-D by Charles B. Smith (see Bernard (Slim) Smith).

PATRICK (DAK) PELLERIN

Patrick (Dak) Pellerin, v; acc. prob. own bj.
    Atlanta, GA   Wednesday, March 20, 1929

402380-B	Cinque Pieds Deux	OK 45332
402381-B	Grand Galle Li Fils A Moncre Pierre	OK 45332
402384-B	Ah! Suzette Chere	OK 45376

Matrices 402382/83 are by Oscar (Slim) Doucet.
Rev. OKeh 45376 by Christine Muszar & Patrick (Dak) Pellerin (see the former).

Acc. Mina Stubbs, p.
    New Orleans, LA   Sunday, December 15, 1929

403426-	Dex Yeux De Goo Goo	OK 45409
403427-B	Because	OK 45410

	403428-B	Je Jais Pos C Cannye (Ain't Misbehavin')	OK 45410	
	403429-	New Orleans	OK 45409	

Acc. prob. own bj.
    New Orleans, LA   Wednesday, November 19, 1930

	NO-6702-	Mamie Que J'Aime Tant (Mamie I Love So Much)	Br 510
	NO-6705-	Le Garcon Boulanger (The Baker Boy)	Br 510

Matrices NO-6703/04 are by Denus McGee & Ernest Fruge.

    New Orleans, LA   Friday, November 21, 1930

	NO-6725-	C'Ist Je Pourez Et Avec Toi Ce Soir (If I Could Be With You)	Br 560
	NO-6726-	Na Pas Des Mouche Sur Moi (There Ain't No Flies On Me)	Br 560

FRED PENDLETON

Fred Pendleton–Clyde Meadows: Fred Pendleton, f/v; Clyde Meadows, g.
    Bristol, TN   Saturday, November 3, 1928

	47284-1,-2	The Last Farewell	Vi unissued
	47887-1,-2	The Young Rambler	Vi unissued

Intervening matrices are by other artists on the same and other dates.

Fred Pendleton & The West Virginia Melody Boys: Fred Pendleton, f; Basil Selvey, md; Richard Harold, g; L. Vernal Vest, u; unidentified, v (if any).
    Richmond, IN   Wednesday, August 6, 1930

	16891,-A	The West Virginia Blues	Ge rejected
	16892,-A	Ebenezer	Ge rejected

Fred Pendleton, v; or **Fred Pendleton & Basil Selvey**, v duet-1; acc. Fred Pendleton, f; Basil Selvey, md; Richard Harold, g; L. Vernal Vest, u.
    Richmond, IN   Thursday, August 7, 1930

	16893,-A	I Wish I Was In Tennessee	Ge rejected
	16894,-A	Willie And Kate -1	Ge rejected
	16895,-A	Lonesome Railroad Blues	Ge rejected
	16896,-A	She's Sleeping 'Neath The Maple -1	Ge rejected

Fred Pendleton, f-1/v-2; Basil Selvey, md-3/v-4; Richard Harold, g; L. Vernal Vest, v-5.
    Richmond, IN   Tuesday, April 7, 1931

	17656	By And By You Will Forget Me -1, 2, 3	Ch 16248, Spr 2754
	17657	Come Take A Trip In My Airship -3, 5	Ch 16457, Spr 2647
	17658	Down By The Hawthorn Tree -1, 2, 3	Ch 16457
	17659-A	The Wreck Of The Westbound Air Liner -1, 4, 5	Ch 16248, Spr 2647

Superior 2647 as by **Red River Coon Hunters**, 2754 as by **Joe & Mary Lester**.

Fred Pendleton, v; acc. unknown, h; Lundy Akers, bj; Woody Leftwich or Roy Lilly, g.
    Richmond, IN   Tuesday, May 26, 1931

	17765,-A	Bull Dog Down In Tennessee	Ge unissued

Woody Leftwich & Roy Lilly, v duet; acc. Fred Pendleton, f; Lundy Akers, bj; Woody Leftwich or Roy Lilly, g.
    Richmond, IN   Tuesday, May 26, 1931

	17766	Lonesome Road Blues	Ch 16345

Lundy Akers, v; acc. Fred Pendleton, f; own bj; Woody Leftwich, g; Roy Lilly, g.
    Richmond, IN   Tuesday, May 26, 1931

	17767,-A	Good Bye Booze	Ge unissued

Fred Pendleton also recorded with the West Virginia Night Owls.

JACK PENEWELL

Recordings by this artist and his "Twin Six guitar" on Paramount and Broadway are outside the scope of this work.

BESS PENNINGTON

Bess Pennington, v; acc. prob. own g.
    Knoxville, TN   Saturday, April 5, 1930

	K-8090-	If You Think I'm Not Worthy	Vo 5423
	K-8091-	Jack And May	Vo 5423

HANK PENNY & HIS RADIO COWBOYS

Sheldon Bennett, f/v-1; Sammy Forsmark, sg; Louis Dumont, tbj; Hank Penny, g/v-2; Carl Stewart, sb/v-3.
    Columbia, SC   Wednesday, November 9, 1938

SC-116-1	Back Up A Little Bit -2	Vo 04640
SC-117-1	They're All Just The Same To Me -2	Vo 04922
SC-118-1	Sweet Talkin' Mama -2	Vo 04543
SC-119-1	Flamin' Mamie -2	Vo 04543
SC-120-	One Sweet Letter From You -1	Vo unissued
SC-121-	Riding On The Old Ferris Wheel -2	Vo unissued
SC-122-1	Cowboy's Swing	Vo/OK 05438, Cq 9392
SC-123-1	Blue Melody -2	Vo 04826
SC-124-1	She's Just That Kind -2	Vo/OK 04741, Co 37733, 20310
SC-125-1	Mama's Getting Young -2	Vo 04826
SC-126-1	Cheatin' On You Baby -1	Vo/OK 04741, Co 37733, 20310
SC-127-1	Hesitation Blues -1, 2	Vo 04922
SC-128-	When I Take My Sugar To Tea -3	Vo unissued
SC-129-1	I've Got The Right Key Baby -2	Vo 04640

Sheldon Bennett, f/v-1; Boudleaux Bryant, f; Noel Boggs, esg; Louis Dumont, tbj; Hank Penny, g/v-2; Carl Stewart, sb/v-3.

Memphis, TN   Monday, July 3, 1939

MEM-20-1	Hot Time Mama -2	Vo 05380
MEM-21-1	Red Hot Papa -2	Vo 05321, Cq 9391, Co 37740, 20317
MEM-22-1	I Want My Rib -2	Vo 05026
MEM-23-1	Chill Tonic	Vo unissued:*Epic EG37324 (LP); ABM ABMMCD1098, Acrobat ACRCD158 (CDs)*
MEM-24-	I Hate To Lose You -1	Vo unissued
MEM-25-	Walking Home From An Old Country School -2	Vo unissued
MEM-26-1	All Night And All Day Long -2	Vo 05215
MEM-27-1	Take It Slow And Easy -2	Vo 05270
MEM-28-1	The Last Goodbye -2	Vo/OK 05148, Cq 9711
MEM-29-1	Black Eyed Susie -3	Vo 05270
MEM-30-1	You're So Different -2	Vo 05215
MEM-31-1	Tonight You Belong To Me -2	Vo/OK 05148, Cq 9711
MEM-32-1	I Told Them All About You -2	Vo 05321, Cq 9391, Co 37740, 20317

Sheldon Bennett, f/v-1; Boudleaux Bryant, f; Noel Boggs, esg; Louis Dumont, tbj/v-2; Hank Penny, g/v-3; Carl Stewart, sb.

Memphis, TN   Tuesday, July 4, 1939

MEM-33-2	It Ain't Gonna Rain No Mo' -3	Vo 05067, Cq 9332
MEM-34-1	Yankee Doodle -1, 2	Vo 05067, Cq 9332
MEM-35-1	I Like Molasses -3	Vo 05380
MEM-36-1	Mississippi Muddle	Vo 05026
MEM-37-1	Won't You Ride In My Little Red Wagon -3	Vo/OK 05438, Cq 9392

Hank Penny, v; acc. Boudleaux Bryant, f; Eddie Duncan, esg; Louis Dumont, tbj; own g; Carl Stewart, sb.

Chicago, IL   Monday, June 10, 1940

WC-3088-A	Just A Message	OK 05654
WC-3089-A	Just For Old Time's Sake	OK 06004
WC-3090-A	I Don't Love Anybody But You	OK 05957
WC-3091-A	Rose's Sister	OK 05844, Cq 9708

Boudleaux Bryant, f; Eddie Duncan, esg; Louis Dumont, tbj; Hank Penny, g/v-1; Carl Stewart, sb.

Chicago, IL   Tuesday, June 11, 1940

WC-3092-A	Just Forget -1	OK 05844, Cq 9708
WC-3093-A	Oh Yes? Take Another Guess -1	OK 05654
WC-3094-A	Peach Tree Shuffle	OK 05724, Cq 9710, Co 37750, 20327
WC-3095-A	Steel Guitar Hula	OK 05724, Cq 9710, Co 37750, 20327

Boudleaux Bryant, f; Eddie Duncan, esg; Louis Dumont, tbj/v-1; Hank Penny, g/v-2; Carl Stewart, sb.

Chicago, IL   Wednesday, June 12, 1940

WC-3096-A	Hawaiian Honeymoon -2	OK 05797, Cq 9709
WC-3097-A	Looking For Somebody To Love -1	OK 05957
WC-3098-A	Tobacco State Swing	OK 05797, Cq 9709
WC-3099-A	One Of Us Was Wrong -2	OK 06004

Carl Stewart, f/sb; Eddie Smith, h; Kelland Clark, ac; Jimmie Colvard, esg; unknown (poss. Clark doubling), p; Hank Penny, g/v-1.

Charlotte, NC   Sunday, June 29, 1941

CHAR-17; 30918-	Blue Ridge Blues	Cq 9846
CHAR-18; 30933-	Midnight Blues -1	Cq 9847

CHAR-19; 30919-	Standin' Neath The Old Pine Tree -1	Cq 9846
CHAR-20; 30920-1	Why Did I Cry? -1	OK 06522, Cq 9844, Co 37666, 20265
CHAR-21; 30921-1	Army Blues -1	OK 06426, Cq 9845
CHAR-22; 30922-	Off To Honolulu -1	Cq 9847
CHAR-23; 30923-1	Somebody -1	OK 06426, Cq 9845
CHAR-24; 30924-1	Lonesome Train Blues -1	OK 06522, Cq 9844, Co 37666, 20265

Two sets of matrices were assigned to the recordings made at this session: the CHAR- numbers at the time of recording, and the 30000 numbers later in New York. Only the latter appear on the discs.

Hank Penny recorded after 1942.

OLD HANK PENNY

This artist's real name is Roger Johnson. He is not associated with the preceding Hank Penny.

Old Hank Penny, v; acc. prob. own g.
    New York, NY   Friday, June 3, 1932

| 152203-1 | My Blue Ridge Mountain Bride | Co 15766-D |
| 152204-1 | When It's Apple Blossom Time Up In The Berkshires | Co 15766-D |

PHILIP PERRY

Pseudonym on Broadway for Sid Harkreader & Blythe Poteet.

SAM PERRY'S RUBE BAND

Pseudonym on Supertone for Ezra Buzzington's Rustic Revelers.

PERRY BROTHERS

Unknown, md; unknown, tbj; unknown, g.
    New York, NY   Sunday, April 14, 1935

39476-A	Under The Double Eagle	De 5095, 10059
39477-A	Napoleon's March	De 5115, 10059
39478-A	Ben Hur	De 5094
39479-A	Over The Waves	De 5094, 10058
39480-A	My Hero	De 5095
39481-A	Skater's Waltz	De 5115, 10058

Decca 10058, 10059 (Mexican-series issues) as by **Trio Gonzales**.
Matrix 39476 is titled *Bajo La Aguila Doble*, and matrix 39477 *Marcha Napoleonica*, on Decca 10059. Matrix 39479 is titled *Sobre Las Olas*, and matrix 39481 *Los Patinadores*, on Decca 10058.
This artist-credit is also used on Supertone S2117, S2118 for Lester McFarland & Robert A. Gardner, the Old Southern Sacred Singers, or Homer Rodeheaver.

PERRY COUNTY MUSIC MAKERS

Henry Bone, h; Nonnie Smith Presson, zither/v/y-1; Bulow Smith, g/v/y-1.
    Knoxville, TN   Friday, March 28, 1930

K-8026	I'm Sad And Blue	Vo 5425
K-8027-	Maudaline	Vo 5425
K-8028-	Got A Buddy I Must See -1	Vo 5443
K-8029-	By The Cottage Door	Vo 5443

The harmonica is inaudible throughout, but Bone's presence at the session was confirmed by the other members of the group.
The Perry County Music Makers recorded after 1942.

PETE THE HIRED MAN

See George E. Logan.

SAM PETERS [& HARRY JONES]

Pseudonym on English Regal for Vernon Dalhart [& Carson Robison].

WALTER C. PETERSON (THE KENTUCKY WONDER BEAN)

Walter C. Peterson, h/g.
    Chicago, IL   c. April/May 1924

| 1752-2 | Old Time Melodies – Part I (After The Ball, My Wild Irish Rose, In The Good Old Summer Time) | Pm 33150, Pu 9150, Sil 3512, Bwy 8013 |
| 1753-2 | Old Time Melodies – Part II (My Little Girl, I Want A Girl, Turkey In The Straw) | Pm 33150, Pu 9150, Sil 3512, Bwy 8013 |

Chicago, IL   c. March 14, 1927

12631	Medley Old Time Favorites (Part II): After The Ball; Peek A Boo; In The Good Old Summertime; The Kentucky Bean With His Double Barreled Shot Gun	Ge 6078, Ch 15261, 45000, Sil 4002, 5009, 25009, 8204, Spt 9196, Spr 349, Bell 1172, MW 4989, MeC 45000
12632	Over The Waves	Ge 6102, Ch 15279, 45018, Sil 5126, 8206, Spt 9198, Spr 349, Chg 409, Bell 1172
12633	Medley Old Time Favorites (Part I): Sidewalks Of New York; Let Me Call You Sweetheart; Sweet Rosie O'Grady	Ge 6078, Ch 15279, 45018, Sil 4002, 5009, 25009, 8204, Spt 9196, Chg 408
12634	Red Wing; My Little Girl; Turkey In The Straw	Ge 6102, Ch 15261, 45000, Sil 5126, 8206, Spt 9198, Chg 408, MW 4989, MeC 45000

Champion 15261, 15279 as by **Abner Burkhardt**. Challenge 408, 409 as by **Jess Jenkins**. Bell 1172 as by **Uncle Frank Templeton**. Minor variations abound in the spelling of the tune-titles in the medleys, and in the artist credit; no attempt has been made to document these.

Chicago, IL   c. August 3, 1927

| 12961 | Pony Boy; Down In Jungle Town; The Old Gray Bonnet | Ge 6221, Ch 15357, Sil 5124, 25124, 8207, Spt 9199 |
| 12962 | On A Sunday Afternoon; Just One Girl; My Wild Irish Rose | Ge 6221, Ch 15377, Sil 5123, 25123, 8205, Spt 9197, Chg 409 |

Champion 15357, 15377 as by **Abner Burkhardt**. Challenge 409 as by **Jess Jenkins**.

Chicago, IL   c. September 1927

13002	Mariechen Walzer	Sil 5125, 25125, 8203, Spt 9195
13003	Bummelpetuss [sic]	Sil 5125, 25125, 8203, Spt 9195
13004	My Irish Molly O; Tipperary; Good Morning Mr. Zip, Zip, Zip	Ge 6274, Ch 15377, Sil 5123, 25123, 8205, Spt 9197
13005	One-Two-Three-Four	Ge 6274, Ch 15357, Sil 5124, 25124, 8207, Spt 9199

Champion 15357, 15377 as by **Abner Burkhardt**.

Chicago, IL   c. November 28, 1927

13243,-A	Highways Are Happy Ways; A Night In June	Ge rejected
13244,-A	Rock A Bye Baby; Sleep Baby Sleep	Ge rejected
13245-A	Where The River Shannon Flows	Ge 6463, Ch 15669, Sil 5197, 8201, Spt 9201
13246-A	Marching Through Georgia	Ge 6406, Sil 5197, 8201, Spt 9201
13247	On Wisconsin; Hail Hail The Gang's All Here; Big Night Tonight	Ge 6406, Sil 5196, 8200, Spt 9200
13248,-A	Old Gal Of Mine; When You Wore A Tulip	Ge unissued

Champion 15669 as by **Abner Burkhardt**.

Chicago, IL   c. December 7, 1927

13292,-A,-B	The Story Book Call; The Darktown Strutters Ball	Ge rejected
13293	Little Annie Rooney; Two Little Girls In Blue	Ge 6674, Sil 5198, 8202, Spt 9194
13294	School Days; Ring Around The Rosy	Ge 6463, Sil 5196, 8200, Spt 9200
13295	Old Time Favorites Medley (Lazy Old Mary Will You Get Up; Animal Fair; Mary Had A Little Lamb; Yankee Doodle; Farmer In The Dell; London Bridge)	Ge 6674, Ch 15669, Sil 5198, 8202, Spt 9194

Champion 15669 as by **Abner Burkhardt**.

Walter C. Peterson, v; acc. own h/g.

Chicago, IL   c. February 12, 1928

| 13433 | My Blue Ridge Mountain Home | Ge rejected trial recording |

OLIVER PETTREY

See Joe Gore.

EARL & WILLIE PHELPS
NORMAN PHELPS' VIRGINIA ROUNDERS
WILLIE PHELPS

Norman Phelps' Virginia Rounders: Earl Phelps, f/v-1; Ken Card, bj; Willie Phelps, g/v-2; William Lloyd "Stubby" Stubb, sb; Norman Phelps, d; unidentified, y-3/wh-4/dog eff-5; band v-6.
New York, NY   Monday, February 24, 1936

60548-A	Lulu's Back In Town -1	De 5193
60549-A	Roll Along Prairie Moon -1	De 5192
60550-A	You Gotta See Mama Every Night -1	De 5212
60551-	I'm Gonna Sit Right Down And Write Myself A Letter -1	De 5193
60552-	It's Tight Like That -1, 6	De 5191
60553-	Skunk In The Collard Patch -5	De 5252
60554-	Bear's Gap	De 5307
60555-	Black Eyed Susan Brown -1	De 5268
60556-B	Sweet Violets -1, 6	De 5191
60557-A	Talkin' 'Bout You -1	De 5237
60561-A	Minnie The Mermaid -1	De 5286
60562-A	The Rose In Her Hair -1	De 5192
60563-	Margie -1	De 5245, BrSA SA1069
60564-	I Like Mountain Music -1	De 5252
60565-	Nobody's Business But My Own -1, 6	De 5237
60569-A,-B	Since You Left Me All Alone	De unissued
60570-	Swing Low Sweet Chariot -1	De 5245
60571-	My Mother -2, 3	De 5204, DeAu X1177, DeSA FM5110, BrSA SA1052
60572-	Nobody's Darlin' But Mine -2, 4	De 5204, DeAu X1177

There are minor variations of the artist-credit on some issues. Matrices 60558 to 60560 were not used; 60566 to 60568 are by Marc Williams. Revs: Decca FM5110, Brunswick SA1052 by Jimmie Davis; Brunswick SA1069 by Don Rietto & His Accordion Band (English popular).

Earl & Willie Phelps, v/y duet; acc. Earl Phelps, f; Ken Card, bj; Willie Phelps, g; Stubby Stubb, sb.
New York, NY   Monday, February 24, 1936

60573-A	Mother And Dad	De 5220, MeC 45209, Min M-14077, BrSA SA1075
60574-	Please Take Me Back To My Darling	De 5220, MeC 45209, Min M-14077, BrSA SA1075

Norman Phelps' Virginia Rounders: Earl Phelps, f/v; Ken Card, bj; Willie Phelps, g; Stubby Stubb, sb; Norman Phelps, d; unidentified, v trio-1.
New York, NY   Monday, February 24, 1936

60575-A	Honeysuckle Rose	De 5307
60576-	When I Wore My Daddy's Brown Derby -1	De 5286
60577-	Bye Bye Blues	De 5268
60578-	Atlanta Blues	De 5212

Earl Phelps, f/sw-1/v-2; Ken Card, bj; Willie Phelps, g/v-3; Stubby Stubb, sb; Norman Phelps, d-4; band v-5.
New York, NY   Friday, May 8, 1936

61094-A	I Like Bananas (Because They Have No Bones) -1, 2, 4, 5	De 5224
61095-A	The Terrible Tupelo Storm -3	De 5223
61096-A	The Moose River Mine Song (The Glitter Of Gold) -2	De 5223
61097-A	My Baby's Hot -1, 2, 4	De 5224
61098-A	On A Road That Winds Down To The Sea -2, 4	De 5225, BrSA SA1100
61099-A	A Beautiful Lady In Blue -2, 4	De 5225, BrSA SA1100

Decca 5223 as by **Willie Phelps Accompanied By The Virginia Rounders**.
Willie Phelps recorded after 1942.

COLONEL PHILLIPS
Pseudonym on Paramount and Broadway for Obed (Dad) Pickard (see The Pickard Family).

GUY PHILLIPS
Pseudonym on Herwin for Arthur Tanner.

PORTER PHILLIPS

Porter Phillips, v; acc. poss. own g.
Richmond, IN   Thursday, February 2, 1933

19002	On The 14th Of November	Ge unissued

| 19003 | Lexington Blues | Ge unissued |

T.H. PHILLIPS

T.H. Phillips, v; acc. E.E. Akins, f; poss. own g.
Birmingham, AL   c. July 22-23, 1927
| GEX-740,-A,-B | Devilish Mary | Ge rejected |

PHILLIPS BROTHERS

Pseudonym on Broadway for the Charles Brothes (see Phil Reeve & Ernest Moody) or the North Georgia Quartette.

PHILYAW BROTHERS

Myrl Philyaw, James Philyaw, v duet; acc. own g duet.
New York, NY   Tuesday, September 7, 1937
21639-1	Take Me Back Little Darling	ARC 7-11-51, Vo 02974, Cq 8952
21640-1	The Prisoner's Last Song	ARC 7-12-53, Vo 02997, Cq 8889
21641-1	Mother I'm Coming Back Someday	Cq 8889

New York, NY   Wednesday, September 8, 1937
21650-1	Pretty Little Girls Are Made To Marry	ARC 8-01-60, Vo 03011, Cq 8890
21651-1	There's No Other Friend Like Mother	ARC 7-12-53, Vo 02997
21652-	When The Saints Go Marching In	ARC unissued
21655-2	Ain't Never Comin' Back	Vo 04065
21656-1	A True Sweetheart	ARC 8-01-60, Vo 03011, Cq 8890
21657-	What Is Home Without Love	ARC unissued
21658-	On My Way To Canaan Land	ARC unissued

Matrices 21653/54 are by Emery Deutsch & His Orchestra (popular).

New York, NY   Thursday, September 9, 1937
21660-3	Just Forgive And Forget	ARC 7-11-51, Vo 02974, Cq 8952
21661-	Didn't They Crucify My Lord	ARC unissued
21662-	Somebody's Wrong About The Bible	ARC unissued

New York, NY   Thursday, December 16, 1937
22180-2	I Wish I Had Never Seen Sunshine	ARC 8-02-60, Vo 03111
22181-1,-2	Just One Time	ARC 8-04-53, Vo 03419, Cq 9006
22182-2	Mama Take Your Time	ARC 8-04-53, Vo 03419, Cq 9006
22183-1	Lonely Sweetheart	Vo 04314
22184-	Those Memories Break My Heart	ARC unissued
22185-2	Bring Back My Blue Eyed Sweetheart	Vo 04186
22186-	On The Banks Of The Ohio	ARC unissued
22187-1	Lonesome Lovesick Prisoner	Vo 04314

New York, NY   Friday, December 17, 1937
22196-2	There Our Love Won't End This Way	ARC 8-02-60, Vo 03111
22197-2	It's Hard To Please Your Mind	Vo 04119
22198-1	Daddy, You Are Too Late	Vo 04119
22199-2	Some Day You Are Gonna Be Sorry	Vo 04065
22200-2	Are You Ready My Friend	ARC 8-02-61, Vo/OK 03379, Cq 8984
22201-	Where Shall I Be	ARC unissued
22202-2	What Would You Give In Exchange For Your Soul No. 5	ARC 8-02-61, Vo/OK 03379, Cq 8984

New York, NY   Saturday, December 18, 1937
| 22203-2 | Brown's Ferry Blues, No. 4 | Vo 04186 |
| 22206- | You Can't Stop Me From Dreaming | ARC unissued |

Matrices 22204/05 are by Floyd Council (see B&GR).

ERNEST PHIPPS

Ernest Phipps & His Holiness Quartet: prob. A.G. Baker, poss. Ernest Phipps, v duet; acc. prob. Ernest Phipps, f; two unknowns, g.
Bristol, TN   Tuesday, July 26, 1927
39710-1	I Want To Go Where Jesus Is	Vi 20834, BB B-5273, Eld 2147, Sr S-3354
39711-2	Do, Lord, Remember Me	Vi 20927
39712-2	Old Ship Of Zion	Vi 20927
39713-3	Jesus Getting Us Ready For That Great Day	Vi 21192

| 39714-2 | Happy In Prison | Vi 21192 |
| 39715-2 | Don't Grieve After Me | Vi 20834 |

Ernest Phipps & His Holiness Singers: A.G. Baker, Minnie Phipps, Nora Byrley, unidentified others, v group; acc. Ernest Phipps, f; Roland N. Johnson, f; Ethel Baker, p; Ancil L. McVay, md; Eula Johnson, bj; Shirley Jones, g; Alfred G. Karnes, unidentified others, clapping.

Bristol, TN   Monday, October 29, 1928

47237-3	If The Light Has Gone Out In Your Soul	Vi V-40010
47238-3	Went Up In The Clouds Of Heaven	Vi V-40106
47239-1,-2	The Firing Line	Vi unissued
47240-2	I Know That Jesus Set Me Free	Vi V-40106
47241-	Shine On Me	BB B-5540

Matrix 47242 is by Alfred G. Karnes.

Bristol, TN   Tuesday, October 30, 1928

47243-3	Bright Tomorrow	Vi V-40010, BB B-5273, Eld 2147, Sr S-3354
47244-1,-2,-3	Cloud And Fire	Vi unissued
47245-	A Little Talk With Jesus	BB B-5540

Bluebird B-5273 and probably Electradisk 2147, Sunrise S-3354 as by **Ernest Phipps & His Holiness Quartet**.

ROY PICK

Roy Pick, v; acc. two unknowns, g.

Richmond, IN   Tuesday, January 28, 1930

| 16167,-A,-B | The Death Of Dr. Snook | Ge rejected |
| 16168,-A | The Ozark Mystery | Ge rejected |

Richmond, IN   Tuesday, February 11, 1930

| 16247,-A,-B | The Ozark Mystery | Ge rejected |

DAD PICKARD
OBED PICKARD

See The Pickard Family.

THE PICKARD FAMILY

Obed Pickard Of Station WSM, Nashville, TN.: Obed "Dad" Pickard, v/sp-1; acc. unknown, g-2; own jh-3.

Atlanta, GA   Thursday, March 31, 1927

143827-1	Bury Me Not On The Lone Prairie -2	Co 15141-D
143828-1	Kitty Wells -2	Co 15141-D
143829-2	Walking In The Parlor -1, 3	Co 15246-D
143830-1	The Old Gray Horse -1, 3	Co 15246-D

The title of matrix 143829 is misspelled *Walking In The Palor* on some pressings of Columbia 15246-D.

No details.

Atlanta, GA   Wednesday, November 2, 1927

| 145080- | The Music Of The Old Cow Bell | Co unissued |
| 145081- | Chinese Blues | Co unissued |

The Pickard Family: Dad Pickard, h/jh/v; Mom Pickard, p; Bubb Pickard, g; Ruth Pickard, v.

New York, NY   Thursday, December 13, 1928

8398-1,-4,-5	She'll Be Comin' 'Round The Mountain	Ba 6311, Do 0270, Je 5535, Or 1502, Re 8716, Chg 992, Cq 7251, Pm 3213, Bwy 8148, Apex 8886, Mc 22388, MeC 91467, Min M-921, BwyE 1740
8399-5	Rabbit In The Pea Patch	Ba S-6283, Do 4286, Je 5508, Or 1502, Re 8734, Chg 993, Cq 7313, Htd 16518, Pm 3213, Bwy 8148, BwyE 1740
8400-4	Down In Arkansas	Ba S-6283, Do 0270, Je 5508, Or 1472, Re 8716, Chg 993, Cq 7251, Htd 16518, Pm 3214, Bwy 8149, QRS R.9002
8401-4	Get Away From That Window	Ba 6311, Do 4286, DoC 181057, Je 5535, Or 1472, Re 8734, Chg 992, Cq 7313, Pm 3214, Bwy 8149, QRS R.9002, Apex 8886, Mc 22388, CrC/MeC 81057, Stg 281057, Roy 381057

Paramount 3213, 3214, Broadway 8148, 8149 as by **Pleasant Family**. Crown 81057, possibly Melotone 81057, Domino 181057, Royale 381057 as by **The Gilbert Family**. Microphone 22388, Sterling 281057 as by **The Harvey Family**. Plaza files indicate that the above matrices were remade on December 28, 1928. It is not certain whether this denotes a technical remake or a genuine session at which further takes of these matrices were made; if the latter, takes 4 and 5 would presumably have been made at the later session.

Controls appear on various issues instead of, or as well as, the matrices, as follows: 8398 = 2079-1, 1740, 501; 8399 = 2023-4, 1741, 502; 8400 = 2022-4, 1743, 504; 8401 = 2030-4, 1742, 503.

Revs: Melotone 91467 by McDonald Quartette; Minerva M-921 by Wenatchee Mountaineers.

Dad Pickard, h/jh-1/v; Mom Pickard, p-2; Bubb Pickard, g; Ruth Pickard, v-3.
New York, NY   Thursday, January 31, 1929

8513-	Good-Bye My Honey I'm Gone -1, 2, 3	Ba 6343, Do 4305, Je 5562, Or 1532, Re 8753, Chg 990, Cq 7326, Mc 22419
8514-	Buffalo Gals -1, 2, 3	Ba 6371, Ca 9278, Do 4305, Je 5590, Lin 3305, Or 1562, Re 8753, Ro 1080, Cq 7326
8515-1	The Little Red Caboose Behind The Train	Ba 6371, Ca 9278, Do 4328, Do 181057, Je 5590, Lin 3305, Or 1562, Re 8776, Ro 1080, Cq 7349, 7736, Pm 3231, Bwy 8179, ARC-Bwy 8179, QRS R.9006, Apex 8916, Mc 22419, CrC/MeC 81057, Stg 281057, Roy 381057
8516-	In The Shade Of The Old Apple Tree	Pl unissued

Paramount 3231, Broadway 8179 as by **Pleasant Family**. ARC-Broadway 8179 as by **Pickard Family**. Crown 81057, possibly Melotone 81057, Domino 181057, Royale 381057 as by **The Gilbert Family**. Microphone 22419, Sterling 281057 as by **The Harvey Family**.

Matrix 8513 is titled *Goodbye My Honey, I'm Gone* on Oriole 1532, Challenge 990. Matrix 8514 is titled *Buffalo Gal* on Romeo 1080. Matrix 8515 is titled *The Little Red Caboose* on Conqueror 7736.

Matrix 8516 was remade on February 18, 1929; it is uncertain whether this was a technical remake or a genuine rerecording, but in any case no takes were issued.

Controls appear on various issues instead of, or as well as, the matrices, as follows: 8513 = 2143-1; 8514 = 2207, 4066; 8515 = 2206, 1809, 4065, 513.

Dad Pickard, h/jh/v; Mom Pickard, p; Bubb Pickard, g; Ruth Pickard, v.
New York, NY   Monday, February 18, 1929

8554-2	Thompson's Old Gray Mule	Ba 6343, Do 4328, Je 5562, Or 1532, Re 8776, Chg 990, Cq 7349, 7736, Pm 3231, Bwy 8179, ARC-Bwy 8179, QRS R.9006, Mc 22453

Paramount 3231, Broadway 8179 as by **Pleasant Family**. ARC-Broadway 8179 as by **Pickard Family**. Microphone 22453 as by **The Luther Family**.

Matrix 8554 is titled *Thompson's Old Grey Mule* on Paramount 3231, Broadway 8179, ARC-Broadway 8179.

Controls appear on various issues instead of, or as well as, the matrix, as follows: 2144-2, 1810, 514.

Rev. Microphone 22453 by Billy Murray (popular).

Dad Pickard, v; acc. own h/jh-1; Mom Pickard, p.
New York, NY   Friday, April 5, 1929

8664-1	Birmingham Jail	Ba 6401, Ca 9197, Do 4349, DoC 181171, Je 5617, Lin 3224, Or 1594, Pat 32476, Pe 12555, Re 8792, Ro 999, Cq 7363, Htd 16052, Pm 12784, Bwy 8123, Apex 41025, CrC 81171, Stg 281171
8665-2	Behind The Parlor Door	Ba 6434, Do 4349, Je 5643, Or 1620, Re 8792, Cq 7363
8666-1	My Old Boarding House	Ba 6401, Do 4365, DoC 181171, Je 5617, Or 1594, Re 8810, Cq 7378, Htd 16052, Apex 41025, CrC 81171, Stg 281171, Min M-915
8667-1	Sally Goodin -1	Ba 6434, Do 4365, Je 5643, Or 1620, Re 8810, Cq 7378

Paramount 12784, Broadway 8123 as by **Colonel Phillips**. Cameo 9197, Lincoln 3224, Romeo 999 as by **Jimmie Price**. Pathé 32476, Perfect 12555 as by **Harry "Rocky" Wilson**. Crown 81171, Domino 181171, Sterling 281171 as by **The Gilbert Family**. Matrix 8664 is titled *Sweet Thing* on Paramount 12784, Broadway 8123.

Controls appear on various issues instead of, or as well as, the matrices, as follows: 8664 = 2271, 3899-C, 1263; 8665 = 2324; 8666 = 2272; 8667 = 2325.

Revs: Paramount 12784, Broadway 8123 by Frank Luther (see Carson Robison); Cameo 9197, Lincoln 3224, Pathé 32476, Perfect 12555, Romeo 999 by Frank Marvin; Minerva M-915 by Smiley Burnette.

The Pickard Family (Dad, Mother, Bubb & Ruth): Dad Pickard, h/jh/v; Mom Pickard, p; Bubb Pickard, g/poss. v; Ruth Pickard, poss. g/v.
Chicago, IL   Friday, July 26, 1929

C-3948-A/B	Rabbit In The Pea Patch	Br 348, Spt S2071
C-3949-B/A	Down In Arkansas	Br 348, Spt S2071

Second guitar, where present, may be by Ruth Pickard; third vocal, where present, is by Bubb Pickard.

Dad Pickard, h/jh-1/v; Mom Pickard, p; Bubb Pickard, g/poss. v; Ruth Pickard, poss. g/v.
   Chicago, IL   Monday, September 16, 1929

C-4416-B/A	Behind The Parlor Door	Br 363
C-4417-B/A	Buffalo Gals -1	Br 363

The Pickard Family: Dad Pickard, h/jh-1/v; Bubb Pickard, g/v-2; Ruth Pickard, v-3.
   Chicago, IL   Tuesday, October 29, 1929

C-4696-A/B	Get Me Out Of This Birmingham Jail	Br 385, Spt S2068, Au A22023
C-4697-B/A	I'll Meet Her When The Sun Goes Down -1, 2, 3	Br 385, Au A22023

Aurora A22023 as by **Arnold Brothers**. Rev. Supertone S2068 by Kanawha Singers.

Pickard Family (Dad, Mother, Bubb & Ruth): Dad Pickard, h/v; Bubb Pickard, g; unknown, g; Ruth Pickard, v; poss. Mom Pickard, v.
   Chicago, IL   Wednesday, December 4, 1929

C-4793-A,-B,-C	Get Away From That Window	Br rejected
C-4794-A,-B,-C	Thompson's Old Gray Mule	Br rejected

   Chicago, IL   Monday, January 20, 1930

C-5190-1,-2,-3	Get Away From That Window	Br rejected
C-5191-1,-2,-3	Thompson's Old Gray Mule	Br rejected

The Pickard Family: unknown, f-1; Dad Pickard, h/v; Mom Pickard, p; Bubb Pickard, g/v.
   New York, NY   Thursday, February 6, 1930

9345-3	Down In The Cane Break	Do 4585, Pe 12625, Cq 7574
9346-1,-2	On The Dummy Line -1	Ba 0744, Ca 0344, Do 4585, Je 5995, Or 1995, Pe 12625, Re 10049, Ro 1357, Chg 882, Cq 7574, Pm 3218, Bwy 8150
9347-2	Good-Bye Mr. Greenback	Do 4547, Pe 12607, Re 8992, Cq 7529
9348-	When You Wore A Tulip	ARC unissued

Some issues of matrix 9346 use the control 1755.
Revs: Paramount 3218, Broadway 8150 by John I. White.

Unknown, f-1; Dad Pickard, h/v; Bubb Pickard, g/v-2; unknown, g-3; Ruth Pickard, v-4.
   New York, NY   Tuesday, February 11, 1930

9354-1,-3	Blind Boy's Lament -1	Ba 0843, Ca 0443, Je 6093, Or 2093, Re 10149, Ro 1457, Chg 786, Cq 7729, MeC 93062
9355-1,-2	Kitty Wells -2, 3, 4	Ba 0648, Ca 0248, Do 4528, Je 5905, Or 1905, Pe 12600, Re 8972, Ro 1267, Cq 7517, Htd 16064
9356-2,-3	The Old Gray Goose Is Dead -1, 2, 4	Ba 0744, Ca 0344, Do 4528, Je 5995, Or 1995, Pe 12600, Re 8972, 10049, Ro 1357, Chg 882, Cq 7517

Matrix 9354 is titled *The Blind Boy's Lament* on Conqueror 7729. Matrix 9356 is titled *The Old Grey Goose Is Dead* on some unidentified issues. Rev. all issues of matrix 9354, except Melotone 93062, by Vernon Dalhart.

Dad Pickard, Bubb Pickard, Ruth Pickard, poss. Mom Pickard, v group; acc. unknown, o.
   New York, NY   Friday, February 14, 1930

9360-	The Church In The Wildwood	ARC unissued
9361-1,-2	Life's Railway To Heaven	Ba 0679, Ca 0279, Je 5934, Or 1934, Ro 1301, Htd 16126, 23037, MeC 93062

Rev. all issues of matrix 9361, except Melotone 93062, by Frank & James McCravy.

Dad Pickard, h/v; Bubb Pickard, g/v; Ruth Pickard, v.
   New York, NY   Friday, February 14, 1930

9362-1,-2	He Never Came Back	Ba 0648, Ca 0248, Do 4547, Je 5905, Or 1905, Pe 12607, Re 8992, Ro 1267, Cq 7529, Htd 16064

Dad Pickard, h/v; Bubb Pickard, g/v; Ruth or Mom Pickard, v.
   Chicago, IL   Friday, June 6, 1930

C-5825-	The Old Grey Goose Is Dead	Me M12129, Po P9049
C-5826-	She Never Came Back	Me M12129, Po P9049, Pan 25040

Rev. Panachord 25040 by Otto Gray.

   Chicago, IL   Thursday, June 12, 1930

C-5828-	Good Bye Liza Jane	Br rejected

The Pickard Family recorded after 1942.

JACK PICKELL

Jack Pickell, v; acc. unknown, f; unknown, p.
   Atlanta, GA   Tuesday, September 29, 1925

141008-2	The Old Rugged Cross	Co 15052-D
141009-2	When They Ring The Golden Bells	Co 15061-D
141010-2	That's Why I Love Him So	Co 15052-D
141011-1	Memories (Mothers' Song)	Co 15061-D

Acc. unknown, f-1; Forest Traylor, p.
Atlanta, GA   Wednesday, April 21, 1926

142072-1	If I Could Hear My Mother Pray Again -1	Co 15117-D
142073-2	Don't You Love Your Daddy Too?	Co 15117-D
142074-1,-2	Is It Well With Your Soul?	Co 15083-D
142075-2	The Last Mile Of The Way	Co 15083-D
142076-2	The Lily Of The Valley	Co 15603-D
142077-1	My Task	Co 15603-D

PEARL PICKENS

This vocalist member of Carson Robison's Pioneers received primary label-credit on at least one of the group's recordings for the English label Broadcast Twelve. See Carson Robison.

WILL PICKETT

Pseudonym on Bell for Owen Gray with Otto Gray's Oklahoma Cowboy Band (see the latter).

PIE PLANT PETE

This artist's real name is Claude W. Moye.

Pie Plant Pete, h; acc. own g.
Richmond, IN   Friday, January 25, 1929

| 14726 | Ben Tucker Reel | Ge 6776, Ch 15709, Spt 9405 |

Pie Plant Pete, v; acc. own h/g.
Richmond, IN   Friday, January 25, 1929

14727	The Ocean Waves	Ge 6776, Spt 9652
14728	Asleep At The Switch	Ge 6810, Ch 15709, Spt 9405, MeC 45003
14729-A	The Letter That Never Came	Ge 6810, Ch 15752, Spt 9363, MeC 45003
14730-B	Boston Burglar	Ge 6748, Ch 15752, Spt 9351
14731-A	Hand Me Down My Walking Cane	Ge 6748, Ch 15688, 33043, 45064, Spt 9363, Spr 2677, Me 4987, MeC 45064
14732	Wreck Of The No. 9	Ge rejected
14733-A	When The Work's All Done This Fall	Ch 15688, 45064, Spt 9351, Spr 2677, MW 4987, MeC 45064

Champion 15688, 15709, 15752 as by **Asparagus Joe**. Superior 2677 as by **Jerry Wallace**.
Parts of matrices 14727 and 14726 (in that order) were used to create matrix 15089 by Smoky Mountain Boys.
Rev: Champion 33043 by the Sweet Brothers.

Pie Plant Pete, v/y-1; acc. own h/g; or h-2; acc. own g.
Richmond, IN   Tuesday, March 11, 1930

16370-A	Waiting For The Railroad Train -1	Ge 7167, Ch 15970, 45093, Spt 9668, Spr 2577, MeC 45093
16371	The Farmer Song	Ge 7167, Spt 9669
16372	Medley Of Old Familiar Tunes, Part I -2	Ch S-16770, 45015, Spt 9667
16373-A	Sand Will Do It	Ch 16012, Spt 9669
16374	Nutty Song -1	Ge 7205, Ch 16012, Spt 9652, Spr 2577

Champion 15970, 16012 as by **Asparagus Joe**. Superior 2577 as by **Jerry Wallace**.
Matrix 16372 is titled *Medley Of Old Familiar Tunes Part 1* on Champion 45015.

Richmond, IN   Wednesday, March 12, 1930

16375-A	Medley Of Old Familiar Tunes, Part II -2	Ch S-16770, 45015, Spt 9667
16377,-A,-B	Round'n-Around'n-Around	Ge rejected
16381	O Jailer Bring Back That Key -1	Ge 7205, Ch 15970, 45093, Spt 9668, Spr 2643, MeC 45093

Champions, except S-16770, 45015, as by **Asparagus Joe**. Superior 2643 as by **Jerry Wallace**.
Matrix 16375 is titled *Medley Of Old Familiar Tunes Part 2* on Champion 45015.
Matrices 16376, 16378 are popular; matrices 16379/80 are by Rev. H.L. Shumway.

Richmond, IN   Friday, August 8, 1930

16898-A	Lakes Of Pontchartrain	Spt 9717
16899-A	Good Old Turnip Greens	Ch 16118, 45063, Spt 9712, MeC 45063
16900	Roving Gambler	Ch 16118, 45063, Spt 9712, Spr 2643, MeC 45063
16901-A	You'll Find Her With The Angels	Ge 7289, Ch 16071, Spt 9701

16902,-A	Potato Song -1	Ge rejected
16903,-A,-B	Be Kind To A Man When He's Down	Ge rejected
16904-A	Little Brown Jug	Spt 9717
16905,-A	Oh Susanna	Ge rejected
16906-A	The Lightning Express	Ge 7289, Ch 16071, Spt 9701

Champions, except 45063, as by **Asparagus Joe**. Superior 2643 as by **Jerry Wallace**.

Chicago, IL   Monday, September 10, 1934

C-9468-A	I'll Remember You Love In My Prayers	De 5014
C-9469-A	Goodbye My Lover Goodbye	De 5014
C-9470-	Goin' Down The Road	De 5030, BrSA SA846
C-9471-A,-B	Go And Leave Me If You Wish	De unissued
C-9472-	Rosalee	De 5030
C-9473-A,-B	If I Only Had A Home Sweet Home	De unissued

Matrix C-9469 is titled *Goodby My Lover Goodbye* on some pressings of Decca 5014. Rev. Brunswick SA846 by Tex Owens.

Chicago, IL   Thursday, November 1, 1934

C-766-1	Somewhere Somebody's Waiting For You	Ba 33311, Me M13278, Or 8417, Pe 13101, Ro 5417, Cq 8440
C-767-1	She Lived Down By The Firehouse	Ba 33311, Me M13278, Or 8417, Pe 13101, Ro 5417, Cq 8440
C-768-1	Little Mohee	ARC 35-10-14, CrC/MeC/Stg/Roy 93094, Min M-14030
C-769-2	Boston Burglar	Cq 8435
C-770-3	Stay On The Farm	Ba 33310, Me M13277, Or 8416, Pe 13100, Ro 5416, Cq 8446
C-771-1	Did You Ever Hear A Goldfish Sing?	Ba 334115, Me M13382, Or 8459, Pe 13136, Ro 5459

Chicago, IL   Friday, November 2, 1934

C-772-1	Don't Try It, It Can't Be Done	Ba 33310, Me M13277, Or 8416, Pe 13100, Ro 5416, Cq 8446
C-773-1	The Sailor's Plea	ARC unissued
C-774-1,-2	Oh Jailer Bring Back That Key	Ba 33415, Me M13382, Or 8459, Pe 13136, Ro 5459, Cq 8435
C-775-1	The Lake Of Ponchatrain	ARC 35-10-14, CrC/MeC/Stg/Roy 93094, Min M-14030

Matrix C-774 is titled *Old Jailer Bring Back That Key* on Conqueror 8435.

Chicago, IL   Monday, June 17, 1935

C-1012-1	Prairie Moon	ARC 6-06-52, Cq 8653

Chicago, IL   Tuesday, June 18, 1935

C-1017-1	Think Of Mother All The Time	ARC 6-06-52, Cq 8653
C-1018-1	Farming By The Fire	ARC 6-01-52
C-1019-1	I'm Going Back To 'Tucky -1	ARC 6-01-52

Pie Plant Pete recorded after 1942.

PIEDMONT LOG ROLLERS

See Red Patterson's Piedmont Log Rollers.

JACK PIERCE

Jack Pierce & His Boys: Jack Pierce, f; Syd "Willie (Red)" Newman, h/k-1; Orville "Rex" Mitchell, lg; Debs "Slim" Mays, g; Earl Carr, sb/v-2.

New York, NY   Thursday, August 20, 1936

19722-2	Oklahoma Blues -1	Vo 03326, ARC 7-03-72
19723-2	Monday Morning Blues -2	Vo 03382

Jack Pierce, f/v-1; Willie (Red) Newman, h/k-2/perc-3/flexatone-4; Rex Mitchell, lg/v-5; Slim Mays, g/v-6; Earl Carr, sb; prob. Jack Pierce, Rex Mitchell, Slim Mays, v trio-7.

New York, NY   Monday, August 24, 1936

19738-1	Mountain Rhythm -1, 3, 6	Vo 03362
19739-2	South Of The Mason Dixon Line -7	Vo 03326, ARC 7-03-72
19740-1	Lookin' For A Hill Billy Bride -1, 6	Vo 03309
19741-2	Where The Western Horizon Begins -4, 5	Vo 03362
19742-1	In The Golden West With You -4, 7	Vo 03382
19743-2	Sweet Georgia Brown -2, 6	Vo 03309

Vocalion 03309 as by **Jack Pierce & His Cowboys**.

Jack Pierce & The Oklahoma Cowboys: Jack Pierce, f/v-1; Willie (Red) Newman, h; Rex Mitchell, lg/v-2; Slim Mays, g/v-3; Earl Carr, sb; prob. Jack Pierce, Rex Mitchell, Slim Mays, v trio-4.

New York, NY   Wednesday, September 9, 1936

0500-1	Hill Billy Shack In The Valley -4	BB B-6822, Twin FT8317
0501-1	Spooning 'Neath A Western Sky -4	BB B-6785
0502-1	Keep On Shining, Colorado Moon -2	BB B-6646, RZ MR2329, Twin FT8216
0503-1	If You Don't Believe I'm Leavin' -1, 3	BB B-6610, Twin FT8248
0504-1	My Home On The Western Plains -2	BB B-6646, RZ MR2329, Twin FT8216
0505-1	My Dad -3	BB B-6822
0506-1	The Blue Ridge Home I Love -1, 3	BB B-6632

Regal-Zonophone MR2329 as by **Oklahoma Cowboys Directed By Jack Pierce**. Twin FT8216 as by **The Oklahoma Cowboys**.
Rev. Twin FT8317 by Tune Wranglers.

Willie (Red) Herman-1/Willie (Red) Newman-2, h; acc. prob. Slim Mays, g; Earl Carr, sb.

New York, NY   Wednesday, September 9, 1936

0507-1	Sweetheart, Let's Grow Old Together -1	BB B-6572, MW M-7055
0508-1	(Trouble Ends) Out Where The Blue Begins -1	BB B-6572, MW M-7055
0509-1	Shine On, Harvest Moon -2	BB B-6625, B-2509, MW M-7054
0510-1	St. Louis Blues -2	BB B-6625, B-2509, MW M-7054

Bluebird B-2509 (a Mexican issue) as by **El Pelirrojo Armonico**.

Slim-1/Slim Jim-2: Slim Mays, v-2/sp-1; acc. own g; Jack Pierce, sp-1.

New York, NY   Wednesday, September 9, 1936

0511-1	Slim's Talkin' Blues Part 1 -1	BB B-7782
0512-1	Slim's Talkin' Blues Part 2 -1	BB B-7782
0513-1	Soap Box Blues -2	BB B-6603
0514-1	Rabbit Blues -2	BB B-6603

Jack Pierce & The Oklahoma Cowboys: Jack Pierce, f; Rex Mitchell, g; Slim Mays, g; Earl Carr, sb.

New York, NY   Wednesday, September 9, 1936

0515-1	Wild Flower Waltz	BB unissued
0516-1	Sing Nightingale	BB unissued
0517-1	Spanish Waltz	BB B-2508
0518-1	Jack's Polka	BB B-2507
0519-1	Jill's Polka	BB B-2507

Bluebird B-2507, B-2508 (Mexican-series issues) as by **Los Fronterizos (The Border Boys)**.
Matrix 0518 is titled *La Polka De Juanito*, and matrix 0519 *La Polka De Jill*, on Bluebird B-2507.
Rev. Bluebird B-2508 by Netty y Jesus Rodriguez (Mexican).

Earl Carr, f; Rex Mitchell, g-1; Slim Mays, g.

New York, NY   Wednesday, September 9, 1936

0520-1	Helena	BB unissued
0521-1	Driftwood	BB B-3186, Vi V-21139
0522-1	Mountain Goat -1	BB B-3186, Vi V-21139
0523-1	Oklahoma Medley -1	BB unissued
0524-1	Frontier Breakdown -1	BB unissued

Blueird B-3186 (a Mexican issue) as by **Violinistas**. Victor V-21139 (a Ukrainian-series issue) as by **Wijskowa Orkestra**.
Matrix 0521 is titled *Lena Acarreada Por Al Agua* on Bluebird B-3186, and *Dobra Horilka (Fine Brandy)* on Victor V-21139.
Matrix 0522 is titled *Cabra* on Bluebird B-3186, and *Nad Richkoju (At The River)* on Victor V-21139.

Willie (Red) Newman, h; Rex Mitchell, g/v; Slim Mays, g; Earl Carr, sb.

New York, NY   Wednesday, September 9, 1936

0525-1	Dust Pan Blues	BB unissued

Jack Pierce, f/v-1; Willie (Red) Newman, h/k-2; Rex Mitchell, lg; Slim Mays, g/v; Earl Carr, sb; band sp-3.

New York, NY   Wednesday, September 9, 1936

0526-1	Wabash Blues -1	BB B-6632
0527-1	Wang Wang Blues -1	BB unissued
0528-1	Has Anybody Seen My Gal -2, 3	BB B-6610, Twin FT8248
0529-1	If I Had My Way -1	BB B-6785

Jack Pierce also recorded with the Smyth County Ramblers and Tenneva Ramblers, and Syd Newman with the Five Harmaniacs.

PINE KNOB SERENADERS

Pseudonym on Superior for The Yellow Jackets [1].

THE PINE MOUNTAIN BOYS

Garley Foster, h-1/k-2/g/v-3; Dock Walsh, bj/v.
    Charlotte, NC   Saturday, May 30, 1931

69391-2	The Gas Run Out -3	Vi 23592
69392-2	She Wouldn't Be Still -1, 2	Vi 23582
69393-2	Roll On, Daddy, Roll On -1, 2, 3	Vi 23605, Au 410
69394-2	The Apron String Blues -1	Vi 23605, Au 410
69395-2	Wild Women Blues -1, 3	Vi 23592

Rev. Victor 23582 by Nichols Brothers.

PINE MOUNTAIN RAMBLERS

Pseudonym on Champion for the Sweet Brothers.

THE PINE RIDGE BOYS

Marvin Taylor, Douglas Spivey, v/y-1 duet; acc. own g duet.
    Atlanta, GA   Tuesday, August 22, 1939

041254-1	You Are My Sunshine -1	BB B-8263, MW M-8473, Vi 20-2403
041255-1	Farther Along	BB B-8263, MW M-8473
041256-1	The Convict And The Rose	BB B-8360, MW M-8474, RZAu G24184
041257-1	Where The Old Red River Flows -1	BB B-8360, MW M-8474, RZAu G24184
041258-1	When Mother Prayed For Me	BB B-8331, MW M-8475, RZAu G25173
041259-1	The Clouds Will Soon Roll By	BB B-8331, MW M-8475

Rev. Regal-Zonophone G25173 by Carl Boling.

The Pine Ridge Boys (**Marvin Taylor & Douglas Spivey**), v/y-1 duet; acc. Douglas Spivey, g; Marvin Taylor, g-2.
    Atlanta, GA   Friday, October 11, 1940

056518-1	I Won't Care -1, 2	BB B-8671, [MW M-8877]
056519-1	Railroad Boomer -1, 2	BB B-8671, [MW M-8877]
056520-1	Mississippi River Blues -2	BB B-8556, [MW M-8878]
056521-1	Old Shep -2	BB B-8556, [MW M-8878], Vi 20-2403
056522-1	Little Darlin' I'll Be Yours -2	BB B-8626, [MW M-8879]
056523-1	Whitehouse Blues -2	BB B-8626, [MW M-8879]
056524-1	When You Have No One To Love You -2	BB B-8741, [MW M-8880], RZAu G25114
056525-1	Wind -1	BB B-8741, [MW M-8880]
056526-1	When It's Tooth Pickin' Time In False Teeth Valley -2	BB B-8795, [MW M-8882]
056527-1	There's A Mother Always Waiting You At Home -2	BB B-8831, [MW M-8881]
056528-1	Crooning Bachelor -1, 2	BB B-8795, [MW M-8882], RZAu G25114
056529-1	Just Tell Me That You Love Me Yet -2	BB B-8831, [MW M-8881]

The subcredit is shown as (**Marvin Taylor–Douglas Spivey**) on Regal-Zonophone issues.
Spivey is the solo vocalist heard during most of matrix 056521.

Pine Ridge Boys (**Marvin Taylor–Douglas Spivey**), v/y-1 duet; acc. Douglas Spivey, g; Marvin Taylor, g-2.
    Atlanta, GA   Monday, September 29, 1941

071008-1	Answer To "You Are My Sunshine" -1	BB B-8854
071009-1	No Matter What Happens	BB B-8854
071010-1	Put Your Arms Around Me, Honey -2	BB B-8940
071011-1	This Means Our Last Goodbye	BB B-8977
071012-1	You'll Be Sorry, Dear, You'll Pay	BB B-8977
071013-1	Lonesome For You Annabelle	BB B-8940

PINE RIDGE RAMBLERS

Lil, Happy, Eva, v trio; acc. three unidentifieds, g.
    Charlotte, NC   Monday, January 24, 1938

018636-1	Song Of The Saddle	MW M-7656
018637-1	Hittin' The Trail	MW M-7656

Lil, Happy, v duet; acc. two unidentifieds, g.
    Charlotte, NC   Monday, January 24, 1938

018638-1	When Winter Weaves Its Silver In Our Hair	BB B-7818
018639-1	Parents I Left Alone	BB B-7818

Happy, v/y; acc. two unidentifieds, g.
    Charlotte, NC   Monday, January 24, 1938

018640-1,2	Moonshine Blues	BB unissued
018641-1	Fifteen Years Ago Today	BB unissued

Lee, Ray, v duet-1/Ray, v-2; acc. two unidentifieds, g.
   Charlotte, NC   Monday, January 24, 1938
   018642-1   The Dying Brakesman -1   BB unissued
   018643-1   Burglar Man -2   BB unissued

PINE STATE PLAYBOYS
See Claude Casey.

THE PIONEER TRIO
The group's last names may be Vogt, Haskell, and Bush.

Vocal trio; acc. unknown.
   Los Angeles, CA   Thursday, October 16, 1930
   LTR-335   When It's Harvest Time In Peaceful Valley   Br unissued trial recording

PIPERS GAP RAMBLERS
Hasten Lowe, f; Ike Lowe, bj; Josh Hanks, g/v; Walter Hanks, tambourine-1/v.
   Winston-Salem, NC   Monday, September 26, 1927
   81621-   Cold Icy Floor   OK unissued
   81622-   Judgement Morning   OK unissued
   81623-A   I Ain't Nobody's Darling   OK 45185
   81624-A   Yankee Doodle -1   OK 45185
   81625-   Katie Kline   OK unissued
   81626-   I Won't Never Get Drunk Anymore   OK unissued

RUTH PIPPIN & THELMA DAVENPORT
Prob. vocal duet; acc. unknown.
   Knoxville, TN   Tuesday, August 27, 1929
   K-119   In The Garden   Br/Vo rejected
   K-120   How Beautiful Heaven Must Be   Br/Vo rejected

THE PLAINSMEN [& RUFUS HALL]
Pseudonym on Broadway for the North Carolina Ramblers & Roy Harvey (see the latter).

PLANTATION BOYS (OLAN & KENNETH SMITH)
Olan Smith, Kenneth Smith, v duet; acc. prob. one of them, g.
   San Antonio, TX   Friday, October 23, 1936
   02856-1   My Home In Arkansas   BB B-6678, MW M-7104, Twin FT8274
   02857-1   Dreams Of Days Gone By   MW M-7107
   02858-1   My Hillside Kentucky Home   MW M-7107
   02859-1   The Hut In The Cotton Fields   MW M-7106
   02860-1   Will There Be A Great Judgment Morning   BB unissued
   02861-1   Wish I Had Never Met You   BB B-6678, MW M-7104, Tw FT8274
   02862-1   My Old Plantation Home   BB unissued
   02863-1   Wonder Valley   MW M-7105
   02864-1   No Home   BB B-6981, MW M-7106
   02865-1   You're The Only Star In Heaven   BB B-6981, MW M-7105
   02866-1   When It's Moonlight On The Meadow   BB unissued
   02867-1   In An Old Southern Home   BB unissued

PLEASANT FAMILY
Pseudonym on Broadway for The Pickard Family.

PLYMOUTH VERMONT OLD TIME BARN DANCE ORCH. WITH UNCLE JOHN WILDER
Uncle John Wilder, f; Lewis Carpenter, f; Clarence Blanchard, cl; Cassie Cady, p; Linn Cady, d; Herbert L. Moore, calls.
   New York, NY   Monday, October 25, 1926
   80193-A   Portland Fancy   OK 45073
   80194-B   Lady Washington Reel   OK 45073

TALMADGE POLLARD
See Johnson County Ramblers.

CHARLIE POOLE [WITH THE NORTH CAROLINA RAMBLERS]
Charlie Poole, v; acc. the North Carolina Ramblers: Posey Rorer, f; own bj; Norman Woodlieff, g.
   New York, NY   Monday, July 27, 1925

140786-1	The Girl I Left In Sunny Tennessee	Co 15043-D
140787-1	I'm The Man That Rode The Mule 'Round The World	Co 15043-D
140788-2	Can I Sleep In Your Barn Tonight Mister	Co 15038-D
140789-1	Don't Let Your Deal Go Down Blues	Co 15038-D

North Carolina Ramblers Led By Posey Rorer-1/North Carolina Ramblers-2: Posey Rorer, f; Charlie Poole, bj; Roy Harvey, g.

New York, NY — Thursday, September 16, 1926

142627-1	Flyin' Clouds -1	Co 15106-D, Ve 2488-V, Cl 5428-C
142631-1,-2	Wild Horse -2	Co 15279-D
142632-1	Forks Of Sandy -1	Co 15106-D
142633-2	Mountain Reel -2	Co 15279-D

Velvet Tone 2488-V, Clarion 5428-C as by **Smoky Blue Highballers**. Intervening matrices are popular.
Rev. Velvet Tone 2488-V, Clarion 5428-C by Blue Ridge Highballers.

Charlie Poole With The North Carolina Ramblers: Charlie Poole, v; acc. Posey Rorer, f; own bj; Roy Harvey, g.

New York, NY — Friday, September 17, 1926

| 142637-1 | Good-Bye Booze | Co 15138-D |
| 142638-1 | Monkey On A String | Co 15099-D |

Matrices 142639/40 are by Roy Harvey with the North Carolina Ramblers.

North Carolina Ramblers Led By Posey Rorer: Posey Rorer, f; Charlie Poole, bj; Roy Harvey, g.

New York, NY — Saturday, September 18, 1926

142641-1	Too Young To Marry	Co 15127-D
142642-1	Ragtime Annie	Co 15127-D
142643-	Little Dog Waltz	Co unissued
142644-1	A Kiss Waltz	Co unissued: Hi HLP8005, Cy 540 (LPs); Cy CD-3508 (CD)

Charlie Poole With The North Carolina Ramblers: Charlie Poole, v; acc. Posey Rorer, f; own bj; Roy Harvey, g.

New York, NY — Saturday, September 18, 1926

| 142645-2 | Leaving Home | Co 15116-D |
| 142646-1 | Budded Rose | Co 15138-D |

New York, NY — Monday, September 20, 1926

142657-3	There'll Come A Time	Co 15116-D, Ve 2492-V, Cl 5432-C
142658-2	White House Blues	Co 15099-D
142659-1,-2	The Highwayman	Co 15160-D
142660-1	Hungry Hash House	Co 15160-D, Ve 2492-V, Cl 5432-C

Velvet Tone 2492-V, Clarion 5432-C as by **Pete Harrison's Bayou Boys**.

New York, NY — Monday, July 25, 1927

144509-1	If I Lose, I Don't Care	Co 15215-D
144510-	On The Battle Fields Of Belgium	Co unissued
144511-1	You Ain't Talkin' To Me	Co 15193-D
144512-2	Coon From Tennessee	Co 15215-D
144513-	When I Left My Good Old Home	Co unissued
144514-3	The Letter That Never Came	Co 15179-D
144515-1	Take A Drink On Me	Co 15193-D
144516-1,-2	Falling By The Wayside	Co 15179-D

Charlie Poole, bj; acc. Lucy Terry, p.

New York, NY — Tuesday, July 26, 1927

144517-	Down In Georgia	Co unissued
144518-1	Sunset March	Co 15184-D
144519-	Teasin' Fritz	Co unissued
144521-2	Don't Let Your Deal Go Down Medley	Co 15184-D

Matrix 144520 is by Roy Harvey.

Charlie Poole With The North Carolina Ramblers: Charlie Poole, v/sp-1; acc. Lonnie Austin, f; own bj; Roy Harvey, g/sp-1; unidentified, wh-2.

New York, NY — Monday, July 23, 1928

146767-2	A Young Boy Left His Home One Day	Co 15584-D
146768-2	My Wife Went Away And Left Me	Co 15584-D
146769-2	I Cannot Call Her Mother	Co 15307-D
146770-2	I Once Loved A Sailor	Co 15385-D
146771-2	Husband And Wife Were Angry One Night	Co 15342-D
146772-1	Hangman, Hangman, Slack The Rope	Co 15385-D

146773-1	Ramblin' Blues -2	Co 15286-D
146774-2	Took My Gal A-Walkin'	Co 15672-D
146775-1	What Is Home Without Babies	Co 15307-D
146776-2	Jealous Mary	Co 15342-D
146778-1	Old And Only In The Way	Co 15672-D
146779-2	Shootin' Creek -1	Co 15286-D

Matrix 146777 is popular.

New York, NY — Monday, May 6, 1929

148469-3	Bill Mason	Co 15407-D
148470-1	Good-Bye Mary Dear	Co 15456-D
148471-1	Leaving Dear Old Ireland	Co 15425-D
148472-1	Baltimore Fire	Co 15509-D

New York, NY — Tuesday, May 7, 1929

148474-1	The Wayward Boy	Co 15456-D
148475-2	Sweet Sunny South	Co 15425-D
148476-2	He Rambled	Co 15407-D
148477-1	The Mother's Plea For Her Son	Co 15509-D

Matrix 148473 is classical.

The Highlanders: Lonnie Austin, f; Odell Smith, f; Lucy Terry, p; Charlie Poole, bj/v-1; Roy Harvey, g; band sp-2.

New York, NY — May 8, 9, or 10, 1929

2909-1	Under The Double Eagle	Pm 3184, Bwy 8152
2910-2	Richmond Square -2	Pm 3184, Bwy 8152
2911-2	Flop Eared Mule -2	Pm 3171
2912-1	Lynchburg Town	Pm 3171
2915-1	Tennessee Blues -1	Pm 3200, Bwy 8146, QRS R.9016
2916-1	May I Sleep In Your Barn Tonight Mister -1	Pm 3200, Bwy 8146, QRS R.9016

Broadway 8146 as by **The Tennessee Mountaineers**, 8152 as by **The Mountaineers**. QRS R.9016 as by **Chumbler's Breakdown Gang**. Matrices 2913/14 are by Roy Harvey.

Allegheny Highlanders: Lonnie Austin, f/sp; Odell Smith, f/sp; Lucy Terry, p; Charlie Poole, bj/v/sp; Roy Harvey, g/v/sp.

New York, NY — Saturday, May 11, 1929

E-29798-	A Trip To New York (Part I)	Br 324
E-29799-	A Trip To New York (Part II)	Br 324
E-29900-	A Trip To New York (Part III)	Br 325
E-29901-	A Trip To New York (Part IV)	Br 325

Charlie Poole With The North Carolina Ramblers: Charlie Poole, v; acc. Odell Smith, f; own bj; Roy Harvey, g.

New York, NY — Thursday, January 23, 1930

149900-1	Sweet Sixteen	Co 15519-D
149901-2	My Gypsy Girl	Co 15519-D
149902-1	The Only Girl I Ever Loved	Co 15711-D
149903-	I Left My German Home	Co unissued
149904-2	Write A Letter To My Mother	Co 15711-D
149905-	When I'm Far Away	Co unissued
149906-1	If The River Was Whisky	Co 15545-D
149907-1	It's Movin' Day	Co 15545-D

Charlie Poole & Roy Harvey: Odell Smith, f-1/sp-2; Charlie Poole, bj/sp-3; Roy Harvey, g/sp.

New York, NY — Thursday, January 23, 1930

| 149908-1 | Southern Medley -3 | Co 15615-D |
| 149909-3 | Honeysuckle -1, 2 | Co 15615-D |

Charlie Poole With The North Carolina Ramblers: Charlie Poole, v; acc. Odell Smith, f; own bj-1; Roy Harvey, g.

New York, NY — Tuesday, September 9, 1930

150773-1	Good-Bye Sweet Liza Jane -1	Co 15601-D
150774-2	Look Before You Leap -1	Co 15601-D
150775-2	One Moonlight Night -1	Co 15668-D
150776-	Little Doctor Fell In The Well -1?	Co unissued
150777-2	Just Keep Waiting Till The Good Time Comes -1	Co 15636-D
150778-2	Mother's Last Farewell Kiss	Co unissued:Hi HLP8005, Cy 540 (LPs); Cy CD-3508 (CD)
150779-2	Milwaukee Blues -1	Co 15688-D
150780-2	Where The Whippoorwill Is Whispering Good-Night	Co 15636-D

THE POOLE FAMILY

No details.
    Atlanta, GA   Wednesday, April 17, 1929

148330-	Schotische [sic] Dance	Co unissued
148331-	Rickett's Hornpipe	Co unissued

The following items are anonymous in Columbia files. They may be further recordings by The Poole Family.
    Atlanta, GA   Wednesday, April 17, 1929

148332-	Smoky Mountain	Co unissued
148333-	Dixie Darling	Co unissued

MURRELL POOR DUO

Despite Murrell Poor's involvement with country music acts in West Virginia during the 1930s, the two instrumental selections he and another recorded in 1928, though issued in the OKeh Old Time Tunes series (45245), are beyond the scope of this work.

POPE'S ARKANSAS MOUNTAINEERS

John H. Chism, f; J.W. (Joe) McKinney, bj/v; John Sparrow, g/high tv; Wallace Chism, g/low tv; Lee F. "Tip" McKinney, v.
    Memphis, TN   Monday, February 6, 1928

41852-2	Cotton-Eyed Joe	Vi 21469
41853-2	Get Along Home, Miss Cindy	Vi 21577
41854-1	George Washington	Vi 21469

Tip McKinney, sp; acc. John Chism, f.
    Memphis, TN   Monday, February 6, 1928

41855-1,-2	Arkansas Stump Speech (Marry A Widow)	Vi unissued
41856-1,-2	Arkansas Stump Speech (Bring Me A Load Of Corn In The Fall)	Vi unissued

John Chism, f; Joe McKinney, bj/v; John Sparrow, g/high tv; Wallace Chism, g/low tv; Tip McKinney, v.
    Memphis, TN   Monday, February 6, 1928

41857-2	Birmingham	Vi 21295
41858-2	Hog Eye	Vi 21295
41859-1	Jaw Bone	Vi 21577

POPLIN–WOODS TENNESSEE STRING BAND

W.E. Poplin, f/v-1; Louise Woods, p; Jack Woods, md/v eff-2; Francis Woods, g/v-3.
    Nashville, TN   Thursday, October 4, 1928

47132-1,-2	Sally, Let Me Chaw Your Rosin Some -1	Vi unissued
47133-1,-2	Flop-Eared Mule -2	Vi unissued
47134-2	Dreamy Autumn Waltz	Vi V-40080, Au 222, ZoSA 4368
47135-1,-2	Lovers' Call Waltz	Vi unissued
47136-1,-2	Pray For The Lights To Go Out -1, 3	Vi unissued
47137-1	Are You From Dixie? -1, 3	Vi unissued
47137-2	Are You From Dixie? -1	Vi V-40080, Au 222
47138-1,-2	Honey, Honey, Honey -3	Vi unissued
47139-1,-2	Robert E. Lee	Vi unissued

Aurora 222, Zonophone 4368 as by **Tennessee String Band**.
Rev. Zonophone 4368 by Taylor's Louisiana Melody Makers.

PORT ARTHUR JUBILEERS

Dick Jones, f/v-1; Earl Caruthers, f/emd-2/v-3; Jimmy Hart, ac-4/p-5; Alton Bailey, tbj; Toby Kelley, g/v-6; Byron "Barney" Youngblood, sb.
    Houston, TX   Wednesday, April 3, 1940

92000-A	Jones Stomp -2, 5	De 5854
92001-A	Jeep's Blues -4	De 5854
92002-A	Roses In The Sunset -1, 3 (lead), 5	De 5839, MeC 45361
92003-A	When You're Thinking Of The One That You Forgot -2, 5, 6	De 5822, MeC 45347
92004-A	Texas Star -2, 5	De 5839, MeC 45361
92005-A	Pussywillow -2, 5	De 5822, MeC 45347, Min M-14122

Rev. Minerva M-14122 by Rice Brothers Gang.

An associated lineup recorded as Jimmy Hart & His Merrymakers and The Jubileers.

ARCHER [or ARCHIE] PORTER

Archer Porter, h; acc. own g.
    Chicago, IL   c. October 1925

2310-1	Medley Of Old Time Tunes (Soldier's Joy–Massa's In The Cold, Cold Ground–Turkey In The Straw –Johnny Get Your Gun)	Pm 33169, Pu 9169, EBW 4536
2314-1	Medley Of Old Time Waltzes (Lauterbach–Peek-A-Boo)	Pm 33169, Pu 9169, EBW 4536

Matrices 2312/13 are by Joseph Chadwick (popular); 2311 is untraced.

Sylvia Porter "The Happy Buckeye", v; acc. Archie Porter, h/g.
    Richmond, IN   Wednesday, January 31, 1934

19462	Old Bill Mosher's Ford	Ch S-16743, 45094, MeC 45094

Rev. all issues by Blue Ridge Mountain Girls.

Archie Porter, h/g/v-1; or **Archie Porter & His Happy Buckeyes**-2: Archie Porter, h/g; unknown, ac; unknown, sg.
    Richmond, IN   Wednesday, January 31, 1934

19463	When I Had But Fifty Cents -1	Ge unissued
19464	Medley Of Old Timers -2	Ch 16729, *Vs 5101*
19465	Medley Of Old Timers -2?	Ge unissued
19466	Log Cabin Call	Ch 16729
19467	Ocean Waves Call	Ge unissued

Varsity 5101 as by **Buckeye Boys**. Matrix 19464 is titled *Medley Of Old Time Tunes* on Varsity 5101. Rev. Varsity 5101 (with same credit) by Tweedy Brothers.

DICK PORTER

Pseudonym on Microphone for Frank Luther (see Carson Robison).

SYLVIA PORTER "THE HAPPY BUCKEYE"

See Archer (or Archie) Porter.

BLYTHE POTEET

Blythe Poteet recorded with Sid Harkreader for Paramount and with Kirk McGee for Gennett. See Harkreader and McGee (the latter under McGee Brothers) for details of these sessions, including the few items credited to Poteet only.

POTTER & JAMES

Pseudonym on Supertone for Asa Martin & James Roberts.

EARL POWELL

Earl Powell, v; acc. own g.
    New York, NY   Tuesday, October 27, 1936

20133-	Jack The Yodeling Mule	ARC unissued
20134-	I Won't Be Blue No More	ARC unissued
20135-	The Old Virginia Rambler	ARC unissued
20136-	I Don't Care If You Never Come Round	ARC unissued
20137-	Low Down Jail House Blues	ARC unissued
20138-	Everybody's Knocking At My Door	ARC unissued

HARVEY POWELL

Harvey Powell, v; acc. poss. own g.
    Richmond, IN   Saturday, November 15, 1930

17263	Highway Man	Ge rejected

    Richmond, IN   Friday, April 10, 1931

17670,-A,-B,-C	It's Hard To Love And Can't Be Loved	Ge rejected
17671	Three Perished In The Snow	Ge rejected

JACK & JOHNNIE POWELL

Jack Powell, v/prob. sg.; Johnnie Powell, v/prob. g.
    Atlanta, GA   Wednesday, November 20, 1929

56550-1	You Ain't Talking To Me	Vi V-40259
56555-1,-2	My Dear Old Southern Home	Vi unissued

Intervening matrices are by Uncle Bud Landress.

Johnnie Powell, v/sg-1/g-2; Jack Powell, v-3/md.
    Atlanta, GA   Thursday, November 21, 1929

56556-2	Ridin' On Down That Road -1, 3	Vi V-40259
56557-2	By The Old Garden Gate -2	Vi 23568

Victor 23568 as by **Johnnie Powell**. Rev. Victor 23568 by Mason Stapleton.

WILLIAM H. POWELL

William H. Powell, v; acc. unknown, bj; unknown, g.
Richmond, IN   Tuesday, August 20, 1929
15469	41 Days In Jail	Ge rejected trial recording

EDDIE POWERS

Pseudonym on Harmony, Velvet Tone, and Diva for Arthur Fields.

FIDDLIN' POWERS & FAMILY

James Cowan Powers, f; Orpha Powers, md; Charlie Powers, bj; Carrie Powers, g; Ada Powers, u; unidentified, v (if any).
New York, NY   Monday, August 11, 1924
	Way Down In Georgia	Vi unissued trial recording

James Cowan Powers, f; Orpha Powers, md; Charlie Powers, bj; Carrie Powers, g; Ada Powers, u; Carson Robison, v-1.
New York, NY   Monday, August 18, 1924
30578-1,-2	Brown's Dream	Vi unissued
30579-1,-2	Old Swinnie	Vi unissued
30580-1,-2	Three Forks Of Kentucky River	Vi unissued
30581-1	The Little Old Cabin In The Lane -1	Vi 19448
30582-2	Old Joe Clark -1	Vi 19434
30583-1	Sour Wood Mountains -1	Vi 19448

New York, NY   Tuesday, August 19, 1924
30584-1,-2	Cumberland Gap	Vi unissued
30585-1,-2	Buck Creek Girls	Vi unissued
30588-1,-2	Billy In The Low Ground	Vi unissued
30589-1,-2	Birdie	Vi unissued
30590-2	Patty On The Turnpike	Vi 19450
30591-1,-2	Sally Goodin	Vi unissued
30592-2	Callahan's Reel	Vi 19450
30595-1,-2	Rocky Road To Dinah's House	Vi unissued
30596-2	Sugar in The Gourd	Vi 19449
30597-1	Cripple Creek	Vi 19449
30598-2	Ida Red -1	Vi 19434

Intervening matrices are by other artists.

James Cowan Powers, f; Orpha Powers, md; Charlie Powers, bj/v; Carrie Powers, g; Ada Powers, u.
New York, NY   Friday, October 2, 1925
10612-B	Old Joe Clark	Ed 51662, 5076
10613-A,-B	Sour Wood Mountains	Ed 51789, 5123

James Cowan Powers, f; Orpha Powers, md/v-1; Charlie Powers, bj/v-2; Carrie Powers, g; Ada Powers, u.
New York, NY   Saturday, October 3, 1925
10614-B	Ida Red -2	Ed 51662, 5094
10615	Pretty Fair Miss -1	Ed unissued
10616-A	Cripple Creek -2	Ed 51789, 5219

Matrix 10615 was scheduled for release on Edison cylinder 5417 but never issued.

James Cowan Powers, f; Orpha Powers, md; Charlie Powers, bj/v; Carrie Powers, g; Ada Powers, u.
New York, NY   Tuesday, October 6, 1925
10620-B	Cluck Old Hen	Ed 52083, 5246
10621	Rocky Road To Dinah's House	Ed 5421

James Cowan Powers, f; Orpha Powers, md; Charlie Powers, bj/v-1; Carrie Powers, g; Ada Powers, u.
New York, NY   Wednesday, October 7, 1925
10622	Little Old Log Cabin In The Lane	Ed unissued
10623-A	Sugar In The Gourd -1	Ed 52083, 5134

It has been reported, apparently from Edison files, that matrix 10621 was scheduled for release on Edison cylinder 5327 but never issued. This may be erroneous and in fact apply to matrix 10622.

C. Powers: Charlie Powers, v; acc. own g.
New York, NY   Wednesday, October 7, 1925
10624	Wild And Reckless Hobo	Ed 5131

Fiddlin' Powers & Family: James Cowan Powers, f; John L. "Steamboat" Porter, h; Orpha Powers, md; Charlie Powers, bj; Carrie Powers, g; Ada Powers, u; band v-1/sp-2.

Winston-Salem, NC   Wednesday, September 28, 1927

81639-	Shady Tree	OK unissued
81640-B	Did You Ever See The Devil, Uncle Joe? -1	OK 45268
81641-B	Old Molly Hair -1	OK 45268
81642-	Charlie Karo	OK unissued
81643-A	Old Virginia Reel – Part 1 -2	OK 45154
81644-A	Old Virginia Reel – Part 2 -2	OK 45154

PRAETORIAN QUARTET

Vocal quartet; unacc.

Dallas, TX   Sunday, December 9, 1928

147618-1	Is It Well With Your Soul	Co 15384-D
147619-2	At Sunset I'm Going Home	Co 15384-D

[THE] PRAIRIE RAMBLERS

No attempt has been made to differentiate **Prairie Ramblers** issues from those designated **The Prairie Ramblers**.

Shelby "Tex" Atchison, f; Charles "Chick" Hurt, mandola; Floyd "Salty" Holmes, g/v-1; Jack Taylor, sb.

Chicago, IL   Wednesday, December 6, 1933

77238-1	Go Easy Blues -1?	Vi 23856, BB B-5320, Eld 2186, Sr S-3401, MW M-4418
77239-1	Rollin' On -1	BB B-5395, Sr S-3476, MW M-4483, HMVIn N4357
77240-1	Next Year -1	Vi 23856, BB B-5395, Sr S-3476, MW M-4483, HMVIn N4357
77241-1	De Blues	BB B-5320, Eld 2186, Sr S-3401, MW M-4418

Salty Holmes, h; acc. Tex Atchison, f; Chick Hurt, g; Jack Taylor, sb.

Chicago, IL   Wednesday, December 6, 1933

77242-1	I Want My Mama Blues	Vi 23859, BB B-5303, Eld 2173, Sr S-3384, MW M-4423
77243-1	Kentucky Blues	Vi 23859, BB B-5303, Eld 2173, Sr S-3384, MW M-4423

Victor 23859 as by **Prairie Ramblers**.

Prairie Ramblers: Tex Atchison, f; Chick Hurt, mandola-1/tbj-2; Salty Holmes, g/v-3; Jack Taylor, sb; unidentified, v eff-4/perc eff-4; band v-5.

Chicago, IL   Wednesday, December 6, 1933

77244-1	Tex's Dance -2	BB B-5302, B-2439, Sr S-3383, MW M-4472
77245-1	Blue River -1, 4	BB B-5302, B-2439, Sr S-3383, MW M-4472
77246-1	Shady Grove My Darling -2, 3, 5	BB B-5322, Sr S-3403, MW M-4471
77251-1	Gonna Have A Feast Here Tonight -1, 5	BB B-5322, Sr S-3403, MW M-4471

Bluebird B-2439 (a Mexican issue) as by **Los Chicos De Las Praderas**. Matrix 77244 is titled *Danza De Texas*, and matrix 77245 *Rio Azul*, on that issue. RCA 8416 2 R claims to use take 2 of matrix 77246 but this is identical to take 1. Matrices 77247 to 77250 are by Patsy Montana (with the Prairie Ramblers).

Blue Ridge Ramblers: Tex Atchison, f; Salty Holmes, h-1/g/j-1; Bob Miller, p-2; Chick Hurt, mandola/v-3; Jack Taylor, sb/v-4; unidentified, v-5/calls-6.

New York, NY   Thursday, February 14, 1935

16859-	Ridin' Down The Canyon -5	ARC unissued
16860-1	Texas Plains -5	Vo 02911
16861-1	Uncle Noah's Ark	Vo 02976
16862-1	Jug Rag -1	Vo 02999, ARC 6-12-58, Cq 8754
16863-1	Hurry, Johnny, Hurry -2, 3, 4	Vo 02976, Vo/OK 03402, Co 37621, 20220
16864-1	Lefty's Breakdown -6	Vo 03033
16865-1	De Blues	Vo 02911

ARC 6-12-58, Conqueror 8754 as by **Prairie Ramblers**. Vocalion 03402, Columbia 37621, 20220 as by **Sweet Violet Boys**.

Tex Atchison, f; Chick Hurt, mandola; Salty Holmes, g; Jack Taylor, sb; unidentified, v-1.

New York, NY   Thursday, February 21, 1935

16908-1	Big Ball In Texas	Vo 02918
16911-1	Strut Your Material	Vo 03033
16912-1	Ole Faithful -1	Vo 02918

Matrices 16909/10 are by Bob Miller (with the Prairie Ramblers).

Prairie Ramblers: Tex Atchison, f/lv; Chick Hurt, mandola/v; Salty Holmes, g; Jack Taylor, sb/v.

New York, NY   Thursday, March 7, 1935

| TO-1520 | Just A Kerosene Lamp | ARC unissued trial recording |

Tex Atchison, f/v-1; Chick Hurt, mandola/v-2; Salty Holmes, g/v-3/y-4; Jack Taylor, sb/v-5.
New York, NY   Thursday, March 28, 1935

17210-	Snowflakes -2, 5	ARC unissued
17211-1	That Old Home Town Of Mine (Is Still Alive) -1	Ba 33445, Me M13412, Or 8471, Pe 13145, Ro 5471, Cq 8516, CrC/MeC/Stg/Roy 92026
17212-1	That Old Home Town Of Mine (Is Still Alive)	Vo 02999, ARC 6-12-58, Cq 8754
17213-1	I'm Rollin' On -3, 4	ARC 350925, CrC/MeC/Stg/Roy 92085

Vocalion 02999 as by **Blue Ridge Ramblers**.

Tex Atchison, f/v-1; Chick Hurt, mandola/v-2; Salty Holmes, g; Jack Taylor, sb/v-3; band, v-4.
New York, NY   Tuesday, April 2, 1935

17231-1,-2	Just A Kerosene Lamp -1 (lead), 2, 3	ARC unissued
17232-1	We Parted By The River Side -2, 3	ARC 6-10-58, Cq 8713
17233-	This World Is Not My Home -3 (solo), 4	ARC unissued
17234-	Do Lord Remember Me -4	ARC unissued

Tex Atchison, f; Chick Hurt, mandola/v; Jack Taylor, prob. g/v.
New York, NY   Monday, April 15, 1935

| 17210-4 | Snowflakes | ARC 7-06-53 |

Tex Atchison, f/v-1; Chick Hurt, mandola/v-2; Salty Holmes, g; Jack Taylor, sb/v-3; band v-4.
New York, NY   Monday, April 15, 1935

17231-3	Just A Kerosene Lamp -1 (lead), 2, 3	Ba 33474, Me M13441, Or 8486, Pe 13158, Ro 5486, Co-Lucky 60349
17233-4	This World Is Not My Home -3 (solo), 4	Ba 33449, Me M13416, Or 8475, Pe 13147, Ro 5475, Vo/OK 03100, Cq 8503, CrC/MeC/Stg/Roy 92028, MeC/Min M-934
17234-3	Do Lord Remember Me -4	Ba 33449, Me M13416, Or 8475, Pe 13147, Ro 5475, Vo/OK 03100, Cq 8503, CrC/MeC/Stg/Roy 92028, MeC/Min M-934
17293-2	Jack-Of-All-Trades -1, 4	ARC 350925, CrC/MeC/Stg/Roy 92085

It is possible that the above remakes of matrices 17210, 17231, 17233, and 17234 are technical rather than, as is assumed here, genuine rerecordings.

Tex Atchison, f-1/v-2; Chick Hurt, mandola/v-3/sp-4; Salty Holmes, g/v-5; Jack Taylor, sb/v-6/sp-7; band v-8; unidentified, eff-9.
New York, NY   Tuesday, April 16, 1935

17306-1	Jim's Windy Mule -1, 2, 3, 4, 5, 7, 8, 9	ARC 6-05-61, Vo/OK 03587, Cq 8646, Co 37764, 20341
17307-2	Back To My Mountain Home -2 (solo), 3, 6	ARC 7-01-64, Cq 8759
17308-2	Paint A Rose On The Garden Wall -1, 3, 6	ARC 7-07-65, Cq 8891

Vocalion/OKeh 03587, Columbia 37764, 20341 as by **Sweet Violet Boys**.

Tex Atchison, f; Salty Holmes, h/j/v-1; Chick Hurt, mandola/v-2; Jack Taylor, g/v-3; unidentified, v-4.
New York, NY   Thursday, April 18, 1935

17351-1,-2	Gonna Have A Feast Here Tonight -1, 2, 3	Ba 33445, Me M13412, Or 8471, Pe 13145, Ro 5471, Cq 8516, CrC/MeC/Stg/Roy 92026
17352-	I Just Had Fifteen Cents -4	ARC unissued
17353-	Coal Miners' Blues -4	ARC unissued
17354-	The Ghost And The Graveyard -1	ARC unissued

Tex Atchison, f; Chick Hurt, mandola; Salty Holmes, g; Jack Taylor, sb; Roland Gaines, v/y.
New York, NY   Monday, May 13, 1935

17530-2	Isle Of Capri	Ba 33457, Me M13424, Or 8476, Pe 13148, Ro 5476, Cq 8536, CrC/MeC/Stg/Roy 92029, MeC/Min M-931
17531-1	When I Grow Too Old To Dream	Ba 33474, Me M13441, Or 8486, Pe 13158, Ro 5486, Cq 8536, Co-Lucky 60349
17532-2	Put On An Old Pair Of Shoes	Ba 33457, Me M13424, Or 8476, Pe 13148, Ro 5476, Cq 8556, CrC/MeC/Stg/Roy 92029

Rev. Melotone/Minerva M-931 by Asa Martin.

Tex Atchison, f/v-1; George "Bill" Thall, cl; poss. Bob Miller, p-2/chimes-3; Chick Hurt, mandola-4/tbj-5/v-6; Salty Holmes, g; Jack Taylor, sb/v-7; band v-8; unidentified, eff-9.
New York, NY   Thursday, August 15, 1935

17958-2	Nobody's Darling But Mine -3, 4, 8	ARC 5-11-52, Vo/OK 03085, Cq 8573, Co 37606, 20205
17959-2	Just Because -1, 2, 5, 6	ARC 5-11-51, Cq 8580
17960-1	Yip, Yip Yowie, I'm An Eagle -5, 6, 9	Vo/OK 03218

| 17961-2 | Truckin' (Truck-Truck-Truckin' Along) -1, 2, 5 | ARC 5-11-64, Cq 8609 |
| 17963-2 | Deep Elem Blues -4, 7, 8 | ARC 5-11-51, Cq 8580 |

Vocalion 03218 as by **Sweet Violet Boys**.

Tex Atchison, f/v-1; Bill Thall, cl; poss. Bob Miller, p-2; Chick Hurt, mandola-3/tbj-4/v-5; Salty Holmes, g/v-6; Jack Taylor, sb/v-7; band v-8; unidentified, v-9.

New York, NY   Friday, August 16, 1935

17962-1	Hop Pickin' Time In Happy Valley -1, 2, 4, 8	Vo/OK 03219, Cq 8556
17964-2	Jesus Hold My Hand -1, 3, 6, 7	Vo/OK 03115, ARC 6-11-70, Cq 8726, Co 37610, 20209
17965-1	If The Stork Comes To Our House -1, 4, 5, 6, 7	ARC 6-05-61, Cq 8628
17968-2	Swinging Down The Old Orchard Lane -4, 5, 9	ARC 5-11-64

Vocalion 03219 as by **Sweet Violet Boys**. Matrices 17966/67, 17969/70 are by Patsy Montana.

Tex Atchison, f/v-1; Bill Thall, cl/v-2; poss. Bob Miller, p; Chick Hurt, tbj/v-3; Salty Holmes, g; Jack Taylor, sb; unidentified, v-4.

New York, NY   Saturday, August 17, 1935

17971-1	I'll Never Say "Never Again" Again -1, 3	ARC 5-11-53, OK 06243, CoC C593
17972-1	You Look Pretty In An Evening Gown -4	ARC 5-11-52, Vo/OK 03085, Cq 8573, Co 37606, 20205
17973-2	The Lady In Red -2	ARC 5-11-53, OK 06243, CoC C593

Tex Atchison, f-1/v-2; Bill Thall, cl/v-3; John Brown, p; Chick Hurt, mandola/v-4; Salty Holmes, g/v-5; Jack Taylor, sb/v-6.

Chicago, IL   Monday, October 28, 1935

C-1120-3	Take Me Back To My Boots And Saddle -2 (solo), 4, 5, 6	ARC 6-02-51, Cq 8602, Min M-14023, Co-Lucky 60286
C-1121-2	Down By The Old Mill Stream -1, 2, 3, 4, 5, 6	Vo/OK 03256, Cq 8600, Co 37615, 20214
C-1122-1	The Oregon Trail -1, 2	ARC 6-01-53, Cq 8576, Min M-14023

All issues of matrix C-1121 except Conqueror 8600 as by **Sweet Violet Boys**.
Rev. Columbia-Lucky 60286 by Gene Autry.

Tex Atchison, f/v-1; Bill Thall, cl/v-2; Chick Hurt, mandola/v-3; Salty Holmes, g/v-4; Jack Taylor, sb/v-5; band, v-6/sp-7.

Chicago, IL   Wednesday, October 30, 1935

C-1135-2	Roll Along Prairie Moon -1	ARC 6-01-53, Cq 8609
C-1136-1	Red Sails In The Sunset -1, 3, 4, 5	Cq 8576
C-1137-1	Ridin' Down The Canyon When The Desert Sun Goes Down -1, 3, 4, 5	ARC 6-08-56, Cq 8710
C-1138-1	Sweet Violets- -2, 6, 7	Vo/OK 03110, Co 37609, 20208, CoC C976

All issues of matrix C-1138 as by **Sweet Violet Boys**.

Tex Atchison, f/v; Bill Thall, cl; Chick Hurt, mandola; Salty Holmes, g; Jack Taylor, sb; band v-1.

Chicago, IL   Thursday, October 31, 1935

| C-1144-1 | On Treasure Island | ARC 6-02-51, Cq 8602 |
| C-1145-2 | Put On Your Old Grey Bonnet -1 | Vo/OK 03110, Cq 8600, Co 37609, 20208, CoC C976 |

All issues of matrix C-1145 except Conqueror 8600 as by **Sweet Violet Boys**.

Tex Atchison, f/v-1; Chick Hurt, mandola/v-2; Salty Holmes, g/v-3/sp-4; Jack Taylor, sb/v-5; Patsy Montana, sp-6; band v-7; unidentified, v-8.

Chicago, IL   Tuesday, January 21, 1936

C-1214-1,-2	Where The Sage Brush Billows Roll -8	ARC unissued
C-1215-2	The Music Goes 'Round And Around -1, 2, 3, 5	ARC 6-04-51, Cq 8628
C-1216-1,-2	Weary Little Pony -8	ARC unissued
C-1217-2	Just Come On In -4, 5, 6, 7	ARC 6-04-51, Cq 8646
C-1219-1,-2	Precious Sonny Boy -3	ARC unissued

Matrix C-1218 is by Patsy Montana.

Sweet Violet Boys: Tex Atchison, f/v-1; Bill Thall, cl-2/v-3; John Brown, p-4; Chick Hurt, mandola-5/tbj-6/v-7; Salty Holmes, g/v-8; Jack Taylor, sb/v-9; band v-10.

Chicago, IL   Monday, March 23, 1936

C-1295-3	Sweet Violets #2 -3, 4, 10	Vo/OK 03256, Co 37615, 20214
C-1296-2	Sweet Birds -1, 2, 7, 8, 9 (solo)	Vo/OK 03218
C-1297-2	She Come Rolling Down The Mountain -1, 2, 4, 6	Vo/OK 03219
C-1298-1,-2	Old Rocket -2, 5, 7, 8, 9	ARC unissued

Matrix C-1298 logged as by **Prairie Ramblers**.

Prairie Ramblers: Tex Atchison, f; John Brown, p; Chick Hurt, mandola; Salty Holmes, g/v-1; Jack Taylor, sb; unidentified, v-2.

    Chicago, IL   Wednesday, March 25, 1936

    C-1323-2   Put On An Old Pair Of Boots (And Saddle Up   ARC 6-07-54, Cq 8655
                          Your Horse) -1
    C-1324-1,-2   Woman's Answer To Nobody's Darling -2   ARC unissued

Matrix C-1323 on Conqueror 8655 as by **Salty Holmes With The Prairie Ramblers**.

Bill Thall, cl; Chick Hurt, mandola/v; Salty Holmes, g/v; Jack Taylor, sb/v; Tex Atchison, v.
    Chicago, IL   Wednesday, April 29, 1936
    C-1324-3   Woman's Answer To Nobody's Darling   ARC 6-07-54, Cq 8655

Tex Atchison, f/v; Chick Hurt, mandola; Salty Holmes, g; Jack Taylor, sb.
    Chicago, IL   Thursday, May 28, 1936
    C-1390-1   I'm Looking For The Bully Of The Town   ARC 6-08-56, Cq 8710

Chick Hurt, mandola/v; Jack Taylor, g/v.
    Chicago, IL   Friday, June 26, 1936
    C-1411-1   What Would You Give In Exchange For Your   ARC 6-09-60, Vo/OK 03061, Cq 8712,
                          Soul?   Co 37603, 20202
    C-1414-1   Maple On The Hill – Part 2 (Drifting To That   ARC 6-09-60, Vo/OK 03061, Cq 8712,
                          Happy Home)   Co 37603, 20202

Intervening matrices by Washboard Sam (see *B&GR*).

Sweet Violet Boys: Tex Atchison, f; Bill Thall, cl/v; John Brown, p; Chick Hurt, mandola; Salty Holmes, g; Jack Taylor, sb; band v.
    Chicago, IL   Friday, July 3, 1936
    C-1417-2   Hinky Dinky Parley Voo Part 1   Vo/OK 03281, Cq 9067, Co 37704, 20283

Take 3 of matrix C-1417, recorded on August 7, 1936, is almost certainly a technical remake.

Prairie Ramblers: Tex Atchison, f/v-1; Chick Hurt, mandola/v-2; Salty Holmes, g; Jack Taylor, sb/v-3; band v-4.
    Chicago, IL   Friday, July 17, 1936
    C-1438-1   How Beautiful Heaven Must Be -1, 2   ARC 6-11-70, Vo/OK 03115, Cq 8726,
                                                                               Co 37610, 20209
    C-1439-1   There's No Disappointment In Heaven -3, 4   Cq 8811
    C-1440-2   There's More Pretty Girls Than One -1, 2, 3   ARC 6-10-58, Cq 8713

Sweet Violet Boys: Tex Atchison, f; Bill Thall, cl/v-1; John Brown, p; Chick Hurt, mandola; Salty Holmes, g; Jack Taylor, sb; band v-2/sp-3.
    Chicago, IL   Friday, July 17, 1936
    C-1441-1   Medley Of Bar-Room Songs -1 (solo), 2, 3   Vo/OK 03281, Co 37704, 20283
    C-1442-1   Down On The Farm -1, 3   Vo/OK 03327, Co 37705, 20284
    C-1443-2   Hinky Dinky Parley Voo No. 2 -1, 2   Vo/OK 03327, Co 37705, 20284

Prob. same or similar.
    Chicago, IL   Sunday, August 9, 1936
    TI-8   I Haven't Got A Pot To Cook   ARC unissued trial recording
    TI-9   I Went To Honolulu To Get A Lei   ARC unissued trial recording

These are uncredited in ARC ledgers but seem likely to have been by the Sweet Violet Boys.

Prairie Ramblers: Tex Atchison, f; Chick Hurt, mandola/v; Ken Houchins, g; Jack Taylor, sb/v.
    Chicago, IL   Tuesday, October 13, 1936
    C-1555-2   Life Is A Mighty Long Time   ARC 7-01-64, Cq 8759

Sweet Violet Boys: Tex Atchison, f; Bill Thall, cl/v-1; Chick Hurt, tbj; Ken Houchins, g; Jack Taylor, sb; unidentified, v-2.
    Chicago, IL   Tuesday, October 13, 1936
    C-1556-2   I Haven't Got A Pot To Cook In -1   Vo/OK 03402, Co 37621, 20220
    C-1557-1,-2   I Went To Honolulu Just To Get Myself A Lei -2   ARC unissued

Prairie Ramblers: Tex Atchison, f; Bill Thall, cl; Chick Hurt, mandola; Ken Houchins, g/v; Jack Taylor, sb; band v-1.
    Chicago, IL   Thursday, October 22, 1936
    C-1602-2   Are You From Dixie ('Cause I'm From Dixie Too) -1   ARC 7-02-56
    C-1603-2   The Preacher And The Bear   ARC 7-02-56

Tex Atchison, f; Chick Hurt, mandola/v; Ken Houchins, g; Jack Taylor, sb/v.
    Chicago, IL   Friday, November 13, 1936
    C-1673-1   Somebody's Darling Not Mine   ARC 7-05-67, Cq 8832

Tex Atchison, f; Chick Hurt, mandola/v-1; Ken Houchins, g/v-2; Jack Taylor, sb/v-3; band v-4.
    Chicago, IL   Thursday, January 28, 1937
    C-1790-1,-2   Little Joe -1, 3   ARC unissued
    C-1791-1,-2   Will I Ride The Range In Heaven -1, 4   ARC unissued
    C-1792-2   Cactus Blossoms -2, 4   ARC 8-03-56, Vo 03422, Cq 8892

Revs: ARC 8-03-56, Vocalion 03422 by Patsy Montana.

Tex Atchison, f; Chick Hurt, mandola/v; Ken Houchins, g; Jack Taylor, sb/v-1; band v-2.
 Chicago, IL   Tuesday, March 9, 1937
C-1790-3	Little Joe -1	ARC 7-05-67
C-1791-4	Will I Ride The Range In Heaven -2	ARC 7-09-51, Vo/OK 03332, Cq 8811

Tex Atchison, f; Chick Hurt, mandola; Ken Houchins, g; Jack Taylor, sb; unidentified, calls-1.
 Chicago, IL   Tuesday, March 9, 1937
C-1838-2	Raise The Roof In Georgia -1	ARC 7-08-60, Cq 8830
C-1839-1	Bacon Rind -1	ARC 7-08-60, Cq 8830
C-1840-1	Kansas City Rag	ARC 7-11-61, Cq 8831
C-1841-2	Smoky Mountain Schottische	ARC 7-11-61, Cq 8831, 9754

Take 3 of matrix C-1839, recorded on July 17, 1937, is almost certainly a technical remake.
Rev. Conqueror 9754 by Cliff & Ray (see Clifford Gross).

Tex Atchison, f; Chick Hurt, mandola; Ken Houchins, g; Jack Taylor, sb; Skyland Scotty (Scott Wiseman), v.
 Chicago, IL   Thursday, March 11, 1937
C-1850-2	In The Dog House Now	ARC 7-06-53, Cq 8832

Tex Atchison, f; Chick Hurt, mandola/v-1; Ken Houchins, g; Jack Taylor, sb/v-2; unidentified, v-3.
 Chicago, IL   Monday, May 24, 1937
C-1881-2	Maple On The Hill No. 4 -1, 2	ARC 7-09-51, Vo/OK 03332, Cq 8892, 9669
C-1882-2	I'll Be True To The One I Love -1, 2	ARC 7-07-65
C-1883-1,-2	Story Of The Seven Roses -3	?ARC unissued

Matrix C-1881 is titled *Maple On The Hill* on OKeh 03332 and *Maple On The Hill #4* on Conqueror 9669.
Rev. Conqueror 9669 by The Massey Family.

Sweet Violet Boys: Tex Atchison, f; Bill Thall, cl/v-1; Chick Hurt, mandola/v-2; Ken Houchins, g/v-3; Jack Taylor, sb; unidentified v-4; band v-5.
 Chicago, IL   Monday, May 24, 1937
C-1884-2	Round And Round (Yas, Yas, Yas) -2, 5	Vo/OK 03663, Co 37767, 20344
C-1885-2	Sweet Violets No. 3 -1, 5	Vo/OK 03587, Cq 9067, Co 37764, 20341
C-1887-1,-2	Gee, But It's Great To Meet A Friend (From Your Home Town) -4	ARC unissued
C-1889-1	They're Burning Down The House I Was Brung Up In -3, 5	Vo/OK 03663, Co 37767, 20344

Matrix C-1886 is by Patsy Montana.
 Chicago, IL   Tuesday, May 25, 1937
C-1888-1,-2	There's A Man That Comes To Our House (Every Single Day) -3	ARC unissued

Prairie Ramblers: Tex Atchison, f; Chick Hurt, mandola; Ken Houchins, g; Jack Taylor, sb; unidentified v.
 Chicago, IL   Tuesday, May 25, 1937
C-1890-1,-2	Uncle Eph's Got The Coon	ARC unissued
C-1891-1,-2	Mistook In The Woman I Love	ARC unissued

Tex Atchison, f; Chick Hurt, mandola/v; Ken Houchins, g; Jack Taylor, sb/v.
 Chicago, IL   Tuesday, July 6, 1937
C-1882-3	I'll Be True To The One I Love	Cq 8891

Tex Atchison, f; Chick Hurt, mandola/v-1; Ken Houchins, g; Jack Taylor, sb/v-2; unidentified v-3.
 Chicago, IL   Wednesday, July 14, 1937
C-1881-3	Maple On The Hill No. 4 -1, 2	ARC unissued
C-1883-3,-4	Story Of The Seven Roses -3	?ARC 7-09-52

It is uncertain whether any of the above takes of matrices C-1881 and C-1883 could be technical remakes of the recordings made on May 24, 1937.

Sweet Violet Boys: Tex Atchison, f; poss. Bill Thall, cl; Chick Hurt, mandola; Ken Houchins, g; Jack Taylor, sb; unidentified v.
 Chicago, IL   Wednesday, July 14, 1937
C-1887-3,-4	Gee, But It's Great To Meet A Friend (From Your Home Town)	ARC unissued

It is uncertain whether the above takes of matrix C-1887 could be technical remakes of the recordings made on May 24, 1937.

Tex Atchison, f/v; Chick Hurt, mandola/v; Salty Holmes, g/v; poss. Ken Houchins, g; Jack Taylor, sb/v.
 Chicago, IL   Friday, October 1, 1937
C-1887-5	Gee But It's Great To Meet A Friend (From Your Home Town)	ARC 7-09-52, Vo/OK 03766, Cq 9066, 9443, Co 37768, 20345

Prairie Ramblers: Tex Atchison, f/v-1; poss. Bill Thall, cl; Chick Hurt, mandola; Salty Holmes, g; poss. Ken Houchins, g; Jack Taylor, sb/v-2; band v-3.
    Chicago, IL   Friday, October 1, 1937

C-1890-4	Uncle Eph's Got The Coon -2, 3	ARC 8-01-54, Cq 8935
C-1891-4	Mistook In The Woman I Love -1, 3	ARC 8-01-54, Cq 8935

Matrix C-1890 is titled *Uncle Oph's Got The Coon* on some issues of ARC 8-01-54.

Sweet Violet Boys: Tex Atchison, f; Bill Thall, cl; Chick Hurt, mandola; Salty Holmes, g; Ken Houchins, poss. g/v; Jack Taylor, sb; band v.
    Chicago, IL   Thursday, October 7, 1937

C-1888-4	There's A Man That Comes To Our House (Every Single Day)	Vo/OK 03766, Cq 9066, 9443, Co 37768, 20345

Prairie Ramblers: Tex Atchison, f/v-1; Chick Hurt, mandola; Salty Holmes, g/v-2; Jack Taylor, sb; band v-3; unidentified, v-4.
    Chicago, IL   Monday, February 14, 1938

C-2086-2	I Wish I Had Never Seen Sunshine -1, 3	Cq 8975
C-2087-2	On The Sunny Side Of The Rockies -1, 3	Cq 8976
C-2088-1	High, Wide, And Handsome -2	Vo 04039, Cq 8977
C-2089-1	Old Cowboy -1, 3	Vo 04291, Cq 9024
C-2090-1,-2	'Deed We Do -4	ARC unissued

Take 3 of matrix C-2087, recorded on April 1, 1938, is almost certainly a technical remake of take 1 or 2 recorded on this date.
Rev. Vocalion 04291 by Patsy Montana.

Tex Atchison, f/v-1; Chick Hurt, mandola; Salty Holmes, g/v-2; Jack Taylor, sb/v-3; unidentified, v-4.
    Chicago, IL   Tuesday, February 15, 1938

C-2091-3	Ten Little Miles -1, 2, 3	Cq 8976
C-2092-1,-2	There's A Bridle Hangin' On The Wall -4	ARC unissued
C-2093-1	Headin' For The Rio Grande -2	Vo 04039, Cq 8977

Take 3 of matrix C-2091, recorded on April 1, 1938, is almost certainly a technical remake of take 1 or 2 recorded on this date.

Tex Atchison, f/v-1; Bill Thall, cl-2/v-3; Chick Hurt, mandola/v-4; Salty Holmes, g/v-5; Jack Taylor, sb/v-6.
    Chicago, IL   Wednesday, February 16, 1938

C-2099-1	Nobody Loves My Soul -1, 4, 5 (solo), 6	Vo/OK 04134, Cq 8978, Co 37759, 20336
C-2100-1	Does Jesus Care? -1, 4, 5, 6 (solo)	Vo/OK 04134, Cq 8978, Co 37759, 20336
C-2101-1	Sixty-Seven Gals In Savannah -2, 3	Vo 04218

Tex Atchison, f; Chick Hurt, mandola/v-1; Salty Holmes, g/v-2; Jack Taylor, sb/v-3; band v-4.
    Chicago, IL   Thursday, February 17, 1938

C-2106-1	Fetch Me Down My Trusty 45 -1, 2	Vo 04092, Cq 9024
C-2108-1	He Was A Traveling Man -3, 4	Vo 04092, Cq 9002

Matrix C-2107 is by Patsy Montana.

Tex Atchison, f/v-1; Chick Hurt, mandola/v-2; Salty Holmes, g/v-3; Jack Taylor, sb/v-4; band v-5.
    Chicago, IL   Monday, February 21, 1938

C-2110-1	By The Grave Of Nobody's Darling (My Darling's Promise) -1, 2, 4	ARC 8-04-59, Vo/OK 03469, Cq 8975
C-2113-1	I'll Be Hanged (If They're Gonna Hang Me) -1 (lead), 2, 3, 5	Vo 04218, Cq 9002
C-2115-1	I Hope You Have Been True -2, 3	ARC 8-04-59, Vo/OK 03469

Vocalion 03469 was issued considerably later than its number would imply; it is in fact a reissue of that number, which had been used earlier (as 3469) for a popular item. Intervening matrices are by Patsy Montana.

Sweet Violet Boys: Tex Atchison, f; Bill Thall, cl/v-1; Chick Hurt, mandola-2/tbj-3/v-4; Salty Holmes, g; Jack Taylor, sb; band v-5.
    Chicago, IL   Friday, February 25, 1938

C-2124-1,-2	Brother Of Old Missouri Joe -1	ARC unissued
C-2125-1	What Would You Give In Exchange For Your Mother-In-Law -1, 3, 5	Vo 04010
C-2126-1	Walkin' In My Sleep -2, 4, 5	Vo 04010

Prairie Ramblers: Tex Atchison, f; Bill Thall, cl/v-1; Chick Hurt, mandola/tbj; Salty Holmes, g; Jack Taylor, sb; unidentified, v-2.
    Chicago, IL   Friday, February 25, 1938

C-2127-1,-2	When I Need Lovin' -1	ARC unissued
C-2128-1,-2	I'll Take Care Of Your Cares -2	ARC unissued

Tex Atchison, f/v-1; Chick Hurt, mandola/v-2; Salty Holmes, g/v-3; Bob Long, g; Jack Taylor, sb/v-4; band v-5; unidentified, v-6.

Chicago, IL   Tuesday, September 13, 1938
C-2308-1   Mountain Home -1, 5   Vo 04601, Cq 9109
C-2309-2   Poor Ole Davy -1, 3, 5   Cq 9110
C-2310-1   Somebody Knows -6   Cq 9109
C-2311-1   The Lonesome Trail Ain't Lonesome Anymore -1,   Vo 04427, Cq 9153
              2, 3, 4, 5
C-2312-1   Monkeys Is The Cwaziest People! -1, 3, 5   Vo unissued: *Co FC38909 (LP)*
C-2313-2   Somebody's Smile -1, 5   Cq 9110

Sweet Violet Boys: Tex Atchison, f; Bill Thall, cl-1/v; Chick Hurt, mandola; Salty Holmes, g; Bob Long, g; Jack Taylor, sb; band v-2.
Chicago, IL   Wednesday, September 14, 1938
C-2320-1   You Oughta See My Fannie Dance -1   Vo/OK 04528, Co 37773, 20350
C-2321-1   We're The Sweet Violet Boys -2   Vo/OK 04428, Cq 9099
C-2322-1   Back Yard Stomp -1   Vo/OK 04528, Co 37773, 20350
C-2323-1   I Wish I'd Never Been Born -1   Vo/OK 04428, Co 9099

Prairie Ramblers: Tex Atchison, f/v-1; Chick Hurt, mandola; Salty Holmes, g; Bob Long, g; Jack Taylor, sb; band v-2; unidentified, v-3.
Chicago, IL   Thursday, September 15, 1938
C-2328-2   I've Got A Pocketful Of Dreams -1, 2   Vo 04427, Cq 9153
C-2329-1,-2   Living On Easy Street -3   Vo unissued

Sweet Violet Boys: Alan Crockett, f; Salty Holmes, h/g; Chick Hurt, mandola/tbj; Bob Long, g; Jack Taylor, sb; unidentified, v.
Chicago, IL   Thursday, November 17, 1938
C-2389-1,-2,-3 Chiselin' Daddy   Vo unissued
C-2390-1,-2   I Married A Mouse Of A Man   Vo unissued

Prairie Ramblers: Alan Crockett, f; Chick Hurt, mandola; Salty Holmes, g/v-1; Bob Long, g; Jack Taylor, sb; unidentified, v-2.
Chicago, IL   Thursday, November 17, 1938
C-2391-1   Weary Troubled Me -1   Vo 04601
C-2392-1,-2   Please Come Home -2   Vo unissued
C-2393-1,-2   An Empty Stall -2   Vo unissued

Alan Crockett, f; Chick Hurt, mandola; Salty Holmes, g/v-1; Bob Long, g/v-2; Jack Taylor, sb; band v-3; unidentified, v-4; unidentified, v eff-5.
Chicago, IL   Tuesday, December 6, 1938
C-2398-1,-2   Watermelon Smiling On The Vine -4   Vo unissued
C-2401-1,-2   Crockett's Reel   Vo unissued
C-2404-1   Lucy Long -2, 3   Vo unissued: *CSP P4-15542 (LP)*
C-2405-1,-2   Old California   Vo unissued
C-2406-1   Ghost In The Graveyard -1, 2, 5   Vo unissued: *CSP P4-15542 (LP)*

Intervening matrices are by Patsy Montana.

Sweet Violet Boys: Alan Crockett, f; Chick Hurt, mandola; Salty Holmes, g; Bob Long, g; Jack Taylor, sb; Lucille Lee (Lucille Overstake), v.
Chicago, IL   Thursday, January 26, 1939
C-2413-1,-2   Chiselin' Daddy   Vo unissued
C-2414-1,-2   I Married A Mouse Of A Man   Vo unissued

Prairie Ramblers: Alan Crockett, f/v-1; Salty Holmes, bazooka-2/g; Chick Hurt, mandola; Bob Long, g; Jack Taylor, sb; band v.
Chicago, IL   Thursday, January 26, 1939
C-2415-1,-2   The Funny Old Hills -1   Vo unissued
C-2416-3   Hitch Up The Horse And Buggy -1, 2   Vo 04868, Cq 9272
C-2417-3   I Wonder If You Feel The Way I Do   Vo/OK 04672

Alan Crockett, f/v-1; Chick Hurt, mandola; Salty Holmes, g; Bob Long, g; Jack Taylor, sb/v-2; band v-3; unidentified, v-4.
Chicago, IL   Tuesday, January 31, 1939
C-2418-1   Please Come Home -2, 3   Vo/OK 05231
C-2419-2   Somebody's Smile -1, 3   Vo/OK 04672
C-2420-1,-2   Happy Cowboy -1, 3   Vo unissued
C-2421-1,-2   They're Burning Down The House I Was Brung Up   Vo unissued
              In -4
C-2422-1,-2   I Still Love You -4   Vo unissued

Sweet Violet Boys: Alan Crockett, f; Bill Thall, cl; Chick Hurt, mandola; Salty Holmes, g; Bob Long, g; Jack Taylor, sb; Lucille Lee (Lucille Overstake), v.

    Chicago, IL   Tuesday, February 7, 1939
    C-2413-3   Chiselin' Daddy   Vo/OK 04714, Cq 9225
    C-2414-3   I Married A Mouse Of A Man   Vo/OK 04714, Cq 9225

Prairie Ramblers: Alan Crockett, f/v-1; Salty Holmes, h-2/g-3; Chick Hurt, mandola; Bob Long, g; Jack Taylor, sb; band v-4; unidentified, v-5.
    Chicago, IL   Tuesday, February 7, 1939
    C-2467-1   Down The Lane Of Memory -1, 3, 4   Vo 05002
    C-2468-1,-2   Somebody Knows -5   Vo unissued
    C-2469-1,-2   Gram-pa Snazzy Fryin' Eggs -5   Vo unissued
    C-2470-1   They Can't Shoot Me In The Morning -1, 3, 4   Vo 04729, Cq 9265
    C-2471-1   Please Send Me To Jail, Judge! -1, 2, 4   Vo 04729, Cq 9265

Salty Holmes, v; acc. own or Bob Long, g.
    Chicago, IL   Tuesday, February 7, 1939
    C-2472-1   Sour Dough Dan   Vo 04868, Cq 9272

Sweet Violet Boys: Alan Crockett, f/v-1; Bill Thall, cl; George Barnes, eg; Chick Hurt, mandola; Salty Holmes, g; Bob Long, g; Jack Taylor, sb; Gale Ryan, v-2; band v-3.
    Chicago, IL   Friday, February 17, 1939
    C-2512-1   Fly, Butterfly! -1, 3   Vo/OK 04756, Cq 9224
    C-2513-1,-2   Take Your Hand Off My Can -2   Vo unissued
    C-2514-1   The Stamp Collector -1   Vo/OK 04756, Cq 9224
    C-2515-3   I'm Gonna Fix Your Wagon -2   Vo 05412

Prairie Ramblers: Alan Crockett, f/v-1; Chick Hurt, mandola; Salty Holmes, g; Bob Long, g; Jack Taylor, sb; band v-2; unidentified, v-3.
    Chicago, IL   Friday, February 17, 1939
    C-2516-1   The Lord Is Watching Over Me -3   Vo/OK 04796, Cq 9264, Co 37762, 20339
    C-2517-2   Only One Step More -1, 2   Vo/OK 04796, Cq 9264, Co 37762, 20339

Alan Crockett, f/v-1; Chick Hurt, mandola/v-2; Salty Holmes, g; Bob Long, g; Jack Taylor, sb/v-3; band v-4.
    Chicago, IL   Tuesday, May 23, 1939
    WC-2598-A   I'm Just A Poor Hillbilly Looking Fer A Hill -1, 4   Vo 05231
    WC-2599-A   Back In '67 -1, 4   Vo 04936, Cq 9327
    WC-2600-A   Gotta Hit That Texas Trail Tonight -1, 4 Vo/OK 05081
    WC-2601-A   Who Will Love You When I'm Gone? -1, 4 Vo 05002
    WC-2602-A   You Can't Break The Heart Of A Farmer -2, 3 Vo 04936, Cq 9327
    WC-2603-A   Just Because You're In Deep Elem -2, 3 Vo 04899, Cq 9326
    WC-2604-A   I Just Don't Care Anymore -2, 3   Vo 04899, Cq 9326
    WC-2605-1,-2 Beaumont Rag   Vo unissued
Rev. Vocalion/OKeh 05081 by Patsy Montana.

Sweet Violet Boys: Alan Crockett, f/v-1; Bill Thall, cl; George Barnes, eg; Chick Hurt, mandola; Salty Holmes, g; Bob Long, g/v-2; Jack Taylor, sb; Lucille Lee (Lucille Overstake), v-3; band v-4.
    Chicago, IL   Friday, September 22, 1939
    WC-2751-A   Boy, Take Your Time -3   Vo/OK 05162
    WC-2752-A   The Widow's Lament -3   Vo 05283
    WC-2753-A   Chiselin' Mama -3   Vo/OK 05229, Co 37774, 20351
    WC-2754-A   Sally Let Your Bangs Hang Down -1, 4   Vo/OK 05229, Co 37774, 20351
    WC-2755-A   I Love My Fruit -1, 4   Vo/OK 05162
    WC-2756-A   You're A Dog -1   Vo 05283

Alan Crockett, f/v (as Papaya Pete) -1; Willie Thall, cl-2/s-3; Augie Klein, ac; Chick Hurt, md-4/tbj-5; Salty Holmes, g; Bob Long, g; Jack Taylor, sb; Gale Ryan, v-6; band v-7.
    Chicago, IL   Thursday, January 18, 1940
    WC-2866-A   Show Me A Man That Won't -2, 4, 6   Vo/OK 05368, Cq 9446, Co 37775, 20352
    WC-2867-A   I Give In So Easy -3, 5, 6   Vo/OK 05368, Cq 9446, Co 37775, 20352
    WC-2868-A   Princess Poo-poo-ly Has Plenty Papaya -1, 2   Vo unissued
    WC-2869-A   On Mexico's Beautiful Shore -1, 3, 4, 7   Vo 05412

Alan Crockett, f/v-1; Augie Klein, ac; George Barnes, eg; Chick Hurt, md; Salty Holmes, g; Bob Long, g; Jack Taylor, sb; Gale Ryan, v-2; Dwight Butcher, v-3; band v-4.
    Chicago, IL   Thursday, February 15, 1940
    WC-2915-1,-A Ja-Da (Ja-da, Ja-da, Jing-Jing-Jing) -2, 4   Vo unissued
    WC-2916-A   You've Got To See Mamma Ev'ry Night (Or You   Vo/OK 05498
                        Can't See Mamma At All) -2
    WC-2917-A   Goodbye To Old Mexico -3   Vo unissued: *Co FC38909 (LP)*
    WC-2918-1   Lula From Honolulu -1   Vo/OK 05498
Matrix WC-2917 was logged as by **Prairie Ramblers**.

Alan Crockett, f/v-1/sp-2; Willie Thall, cl-3/s-4; Augie Klein, ac; Chick Hurt, md; Salty Holmes, g; Bob Long, g; Jack Taylor, sb; Gale Ryan, v-5; band v-6.
    Chicago, IL   Friday, February 16, 1940

WC-2919-1,-A	She's A Wants Everything Takes Anything Gal -1, 3, 6	Vo unissued
WC-2920-A	Father Put The Cow Away -3, 5, 6	Vo/OK 05461, Cq 9445
WC-2921-A	Let's All Get Good And Drunk -1, 2, 3, 6	OK 06482, CoC C534
WC-2922-A	Fly, Butterfly! #2 -1, 4, 6	Vo/OK 05461, Cq 9445

Alan Crockett, f/v-1; Willie Thall, cl-2/s-3; Augie Klein, ac; Chick Hurt, md; Salty Holmes, g; Bob Long, g; Jack Taylor, sb; band v-4; unidentified, v-5.
    Chicago, IL   Wednesday, May 29, 1940

WC-3072-A	Your Lonesome Daddy Loved You All The Time -2, 5	OK unissued
WC-3073-A	The Scarecrow Song -1, 2	OK 05681
WC-3074-A	She Was The Daughter Of A Butterfly And He Was The Son Of A Bee -1, 2	OK unissued
WC-3075-A	I'm Wastin' My Time -1, 3, 4	OK 05681

Prairie Ramblers: Alan Crockett, f/v-1; George Barnes, eg; prob. John Brown, p; Chick Hurt, md/v-2; Salty Holmes, g; Jack Taylor, sb/v-3; Gale Ryan, d or traps; band v-4.
    Chicago, IL   Monday, October 7, 1940

C-3369-1	Sugar Hill -1, 4	OK 05878, Cq 9588
C-3370-1	Dese Bones Gwine Rise Again -2, 4	Cq 9717
C-3371-1	Wine, Women And Song -3, 4	OK 05878, Cq 9717
C-3372-1	Little Turtle Dove -1, 4	Cq 9727
C-3373-1	Get Hot Or Go Home -1	OK 05854, Cq 9588, Co 37752, 20329
C-3374-1	Booley Wooger -1, 4	OK 05854, Cq 9724, Co 37752, 20329
C-3375-1	Good Old Fashioned Hoe Down -1, 4	OK 05892, Cq 9724, CoC C174
C-3376-1	Beaver Creek -1, 4	OK 05892, Cq 9927, CoC C174

Alan Crockett, f/v-1; Dale "Smokey" Lohman, esg or "vib-a-chord;" prob. John Brown, p; Chick Hurt, md/v-2; Salty Holmes, g; Jack Taylor, sb/v-3; band v-4; unidentified, v-5.
    Chicago, IL   Tuesday, October 8, 1940

C-3393-1	Since I Lost My Darling -2, 3	OK 06028, Cq 9590
C-3394-1	The Mountains Will See Her Face No More -2, 3	OK 05943, Cq 9726
C-3395-1	Be Honest With Me -5	OK 06028, Cq 9590
C-3396-1	My Darling Of The Valley -2, 3	OK 05943, Cq 9827
C-3397-1	I'll Come Back To You -2, 3	OK 05969, Cq 9726
C-3398-1	All I Ever Do Is Wait -1, 4	OK 05969, Cq 9723

Alan Crockett, f/v-1; Dale "Smokey" Lohman, esg or "vib-a-chord;" prob. John Brown, p; Chick Hurt, md/v-2; Salty Holmes, g; Jack Taylor, sb/v-3; band v-4.
    Chicago, IL   Wednesday, January 22, 1941

C-3547-1	Lonesome For You Annabelle -1, 4	OK 06149, Cq 9827
C-3548-1	I'll Be Back In A Year (Little Darlin') -2, 3	OK 06053, Cq 9725, Co 20800
C-3549-1	I Won't Mind -2, 3	OK 06149, Cq 9723
C-3550-1	Old Mississippi Moon -1, 4	OK 06053, Cq 9722

Alan Crockett, f/v-1; prob. John Brown, p; Chick Hurt, md/v-2; Salty Holmes, g/v-3; Jack Taylor, sb; poss. Gale Ryan, d or traps; band v-4.
    Chicago, IL   Tuesday, January 28, 1941

C-3585-1	I've Got A Gal In Ev'ry State -1 (lead), 2	OK 06230, Cq 9725
C-3586-1	Sing It Fast And Hot -1, 4	OK 06230, Cq 9722
C-3587-1	Double-Crossing Mama -1	OK 06102, Cq 9727, CoSs MZ244
C-3588-1	Rollin' Along -1, 3, 4	OK 06102, Cq 9927, CoSs MZ244

Alan Crockett, f/v-1; Reggie Cross, h; prob. John Brown, p; Chick Hurt, md/v-2; Rusty Gill, g/v-3; Salty Holmes, g; Jack Taylor, sb/v-4; band v-5; unidentified, v-6.
    Chicago, IL   Monday, June 2, 1941

C-3823-1	Darling, Do You Love Another -2, 4	OK 06576, Cq 9830
C-3824-1	Sergeant! Can You Spare A Girl -3	OK 06436, Cq 9825
C-3825-1	Smiles Thru Tear Drops -6	Cq 9830
C-3826-1	You Were Right And I Was Wrong -3, 5	OK 06628, Cq 9831
C-3827-1	Don't Say Goodbye Little Darling -2, 4	OK 06436, Cq 9825
C-3828-1	I'll Love You Till I Die -2, 4	OK 06576, Cq 9831
C-3829-1	There's No Place For The Devil In My Home -4, 5	Cq 9832
C-3830-1	An Old Revival Meetin' -1, 5	Cq 9832

Alan Crockett, f/v-1; Rusty Gill, h; John Brown, p; Chick Hurt, md-2/tbj-3/v-4; Salty Holmes, g/j/v-5; Jack Taylor, sb; Gale Ryan, v-6.
    Chicago, IL   Tuesday, June 10, 1941

C-3867-1	Double Crossin' Daddy -2, 6	OK 06285, Cq 9826
C-3868-1	Pool Playin' Papa -2, 6	OK 06361
C-3869-1	It Makes No Never Mind -2, 6	OK 06361
C-3870-1	I'll Be Waiting For You Darling -2, 6	OK 06285, Cq 9826, Co 20800
C-3871-1	Nellie's Not The Same Nell Now -1, 3	OK 06628, Cq 9828
C-3872-1	Tell Me Little Gal, Ain't I Your Feller? -1, 4, 5	OK 06532, Cq 9829
C-3873-1	My Head Went Round And Round -1 (lead), 5	OK 06482, Cq 9828, CoC C534
C-3874-1	Don't Think Anymore About Me -1, 4	OK 06532, Cq 9829

OKeh 06482, Columbia C534, and matrix C-3873 on Conqueror 9828 as by **Sweet Violet Boys**. Matrix C-3870 is titled *Answer To I'll Be Back In A Year Little Darlin' (I'll Be Waiting For You, Little Darlin')* on Conqueror 9826 and Columbia 20800.
The Prairie Ramblers also accompanied Lulu Belle & Scotty and Patsy Montana, and recorded after 1942.
This credit was also used as a pseudonym on Melotone/Minerva M-14017 for The Beverly Hill Billies.

PRAIRIE SERENADERS

Issues so credited on Champion 45164, 45190, Decca 5923, and Melotone 45421 are derived from the English Panachord label. The Prairie Serenaders are in fact The Hill Billies, an English group that recorded prolifically for the local Regal-Zonophone label.

CHARLIE PRESCOTT

Pseudonym on Challenge for Aulton Ray.

FRANK PRESTAGE

Frank Prestage, v/y; acc. poss. own g.
    Richmond, IN   Tuesday, July 15, 1930

16828	[unknown title]	Ge rejected trial recording

LEW PRESTON & HIS MEN OF THE RANGE

Darrell Kirkpatrick, f-1/ac; unidentified, h-2; Andy Schroeder, esg; Jasper "Jake" Wright, g/v; Lew Preston, prob. g/lv; Joseph E. "Elmer" Crenshaw, prob. sb/v.
    Saginaw, TX   Saturday, April 20, 1940

DAL-1003-2	There Ain't Gonna Be No Me (To Welcome You)	OK 05710
DAL-1004-1	I've Got The Blues In My Heart	OK 05868
DAL-1005-1	Goodbye, Little Blue Eyes, Don't Cry	Vo/OK 05586
DAL-1006-1	Honey Baby Mine -1	Vo/OK 05586
DAL-1007-1	Hawaiian Skies	OK 05768
DAL-1008-1	Isles Across The Sea	OK 05768
DAL-1009-1	We've Said Our Last Goodbye	OK 05710
DAL-1010-2	Doin' Things On The Farm -1, 2	OK 05868

Darrell Kirkpatrick, f; poss. Foy Willingham, esg; Lew Preston, g/lv; Jake Wright, g/v-1; Elmer Crenshaw, sb/v-1.
    Fort Worth, TX   Tuesday, March 11, 1941

DAL-1295-1	Doin' It Right	OK 06362
DAL-1296-1	Troubled Mind	OK 06162
DAL-1297-1	Sad And Lonely -1	Cq 9862
DAL-1298-1,-2	Darling Little Girl -1	OK unissued
DAL-1299-1,-2	Little Darling -1	OK unissued
DAL-1300-1	Some Glad Day -1	OK 06362

Darrell Kirkpatrick, f; poss. Foy Willingham, esg; Lew Preston, g/lv-1; Jake Wright, g/v-2; Elmer Crenshaw, sb/v-2.
    Fort Worth, TX   Wednesday, March 12, 1941

DAL-1301-1,-2	The Faded Rose	OK unissued
DAL-1302-1	Convict's Prayer -1, 2	Cq 9682
DAL-1303-1	Soldier Boy Stomp	OK 06162
DAL-1304-1	Rose Of Santa Fe -1	OK 06241
DAL-1305-1	Maid Of Mexico -1, 2	OK 06241
DAL-1306-1,-2	Rose Of Mexico	OK unissued

Lew Preston recorded after 1942.

BESS & TEE PREWITT (THE DAY DREAMERS)

Bess Prewitt, Tee Prewitt, v duet; acc. poss. one of them, g.
    Birmingham, AL   Saturday, April 10, 1937

B-115-	How Beautiful Heaven Must Be	ARC unissued
B-116-	Back In The Old Sunday School	ARC unissued

JIMMIE PRICE

This pseudonym was used on Plaza/ARC issues usually for John I. White but occasionally also for Chezz Chase, and once for The Pickard Family.

WILLIAM PRICE

Pseudonym on Challenge for John Hammond.

PRICE FAMILY SACRED SINGERS

Vocal group; acc. unknown, f; unknown, o; unknown, g.
    Atlanta, GA   Tuesday, March 22, 1927

80605-B	We Are Journeying On	OK 45222
80606-A	I Went Down Into The Garden	OK 40796
80608-B	Ship Of Glory	OK 40796
80610-B	He Pardoned Me	OK 45222

Matrices 80607 and 80609, blanks in OKeh files, are probably unissued items by this group.

PRICE–PROSSER–TEASLEY

Sweeny Prosser, sg; Harold M. Teasley, sg; Cecil Price, u.
    Charlotte, NC   Monday, August 15, 1927

39815-2	Meet Me In Hawaii	Vi 21018
39816-1	Wabash Blues	Vi 21018

Sweeny Prosser was also a member of the Honolulu Strollers.

TONY PRINCE

Although he had one record issued in the Paramount Old Time Tunes series (3085), this accordionist is beyond the scope of this work.

B.L. PRITCHARD

See Scottdale String Band.

"SUNSHINE" PRITCHARD

"Sunshine" Pritchard, v; acc. prob. own g.
    Richmond, IN   Tuesday, June 11, 1929

15189-A	Biscuit Jim	Ch 15789, Spt 9553
15190,-A	Stockade Blues	Ge rejected
15191-A	Son Of A Gun	Ge 6902, Ch 15789, Spt 9553

Champion 15789 as by **Moonshine Dave**. Supertone 9553 as by **Moonshine Harry**.

    Richmond, IN   Wednesday, June 12, 1929

15196-A	Our Little Blue Haired Boy	Ge 6902

PROPES QUARTET

Male vocal quartet; acc. unknown, p.
    Atlanta, GA   Wednesday, August 1, 1934

82870-1	Rocking On The Waves	BB B-5612, MW M-4805
82871-1	On The Jericho Road	BB B-5612, MW M-4805
82872-1	Overshadowed By His Love	BB B-5672
82873-1	Springtime In Glory	BB B-5672

PROXIMITY STRING QUARTET

Unknown, md or bj-md; two unknowns, g; unknown, v; band v-1.
    Johnson City, TN   Tuesday, October 16, 1928

147196-2	Lindy -1	Co 15533-D
147197-1	Louise	Co 15533-D

HOLLAND PUCKETT

This artist's real name may be Hartsell Watson.

Holland Puckett, v; acc. own h-1/g.
    Richmond, IN   c. April 1927

12771-A	Put On Your Old Gray Bonnet -1	Ge 6144, Ch 15299, Chg 270, 329, Her 75554
12772	Weeping Willow Tree -1	Ge 6144, Ch 15334, Sil 8158, Spt 9243, Chg 270, 330, Bell 1179

12784	He Lives On High	Ge 6206, Ch 15333, Sil 5075, 8167, Spt 9263
12785	A Mother's Advice	Ge 6163, Ch 15299, Chg 330, Her 75556
12786	The Dying Cowboy	Ge 6271, Ch 15428, Sil 5065, 25065, 8152, Spt 9253, Her 75557
12789	Chas. A Brooks	Ge 6163, Her 75556

Champion 15299, 15333, 15334, 15428, Silvertone 8158, Supertone 9243, 9263, Challenge 270, 329, 330 as by **Harvey Watson**. Supertone 9253 as by **Si Puckett**. Herwin 75554, 75556, 75557 as by **Robert Howell**. Bell 1179 as by **Riley Wilcox**.
Intervening matrices are by Da Costa Woltz's Southern Broadcasters.
Revs: Champion 15333 by Ben Jarrell, 15334 by David Miller, 15428 by Bradley Kincaid; Silvertone 8158, Supertone 9243 by John McGhee, 9263 by Ben Jarrell; Herwin 75554 by Da Costa Woltz's Southern Broadcasters, 75557 by David Miller.

Richmond, IN   c. May 1927

12814	Drunken Hiccoughs	Ge 6189, Ch 15356, Chg 328
12815	The Broken Engagement	Ge 6189, Her 75562
12815-B	The Broken Engagement	Bell 1179
12816	The Bright Sherman Valley	Ge 6433, Sil 5064, 25064, 8153, Spt 9254, Chg 329, Her 75562
12817	I'll Remember You Love In My Prayers	Ge 6206, Her 75559
12818	The Key Hole In The Door -1	Ge 6271, Sil 5064, 25064, 8153, Spt 9254, Chg 328
12819	Little Birdie -1	Her 75563
12820	Come And Kiss Me, Baby Darling	Ge 6433, Sil 5065, 25065, 8152, Spt 9253, Her 75563

Champion 15356, Challenge 328, 329 as by **Harvey Watson**. Supertone 9253, 9254 as by **Si Puckett**. Herwin 75559, 75562, 75563 as by **Robert Howell**. Bell 1179 as by **Riley Wilcox**.
Matrix 12818 is titled *The Keyhole In The Door* on Supertone 9254.
Revs: Champion 15356 by John Hammond; Herwin 75559 by Ben Jarrell.

Richmond, IN   Friday, May 11, 1928

13804,-A	The Jail Bird	Ge rejected
13805-A	The Old Cottage Home	Ge 6532, Spt 9324
13806,-A	Sadie Ray	Ge rejected
13807,-A,-B	The Scolding Wife	Ge rejected
13808,-A	Too Late, Too Late	Ge rejected
13809	The Maple On The Hill -1	Ge 6532, Spt 9186
13810	Faded Bunch Of Roses -1	Ge 6720, Spt 9186
13811,-A	Leaf By Leaf The Roses Fall	Ge rejected
13812,-A	Old Virginia Rambler	Ge rejected
13813	Little Bessie	Ge 6720, Spt 9324
13814,-A	Red White And Blue	Ge rejected

Supertone 9186 as by **Si Puckett**.

REUBEN PUCKETT

See Richard Brooks.

RILEY PUCKETT

Riley Puckett, v; acc. Gid Tanner, f-1; own g.
New York, NY   Friday, March 7, 1924

81600-2	Little Old Log Cabin In The Lane -1	Co 107-D, Ha 5116-H
81601-	Knoxville Girl -1	Co rejected
81602-1	Johnson's Old Grey Mule	Co 150-D, Ha 5095-H
81603-3	Old Joe Clark	Co 15033-D, Ha 5146-H
81605-1	Casey Jones	Co 113-D, Ha 5118-H

Columbia 107-D, 113-D, 150-D originally as by **George Riley Puckett**; later pressings of those, and all pressings of Columbia 15033-D, as by **Riley Puckett**. Harmonys as by **Fred Wilson**. Matrix 81602 is titled *Johnson's Mule* on Harmony 5095-H. Matrix 81604 is by Gid Tanner.

Riley Puckett, v/y-1; acc. Gid Tanner, f-2; own g.
New York, NY   Saturday, March 8, 1924

81626-1	Steamboat Bill	Co 113-D, Ha 5118-H
81628-1	1. Chicken Don't Roost Too High For Me - 2 [2. I Don't Love Nobody]	Co 150-D, Ha 5095-H
81629-	Devilish Mary -2?	Co unissued
81631-	Lightning Express -2?	Co rejected
81632-1	Strawberries -1	Co 220-D
81633-1	Rock All Our Babies To Sleep -1	Co 107-D, Ha 5116-H

Columbia 107-D, 113-D, 150-D originally as by **George Riley Puckett**; later pressings, and all pressings of Columbia 220-D, as by **Riley Puckett**. The second tune on matrix 81628 (here parenthesised) is by Gid Tanner alone and so credited. Matrix 81628 (first tune) on Harmony 5095-H as by **Gibbs & Watson**; this item is titled *1. Chicken Roost* (and the second tune *2. I Don't Love*) on that issue.

Matrices 81606 to 81625 are by other artists; 81627, 81630, 81634/35, 81638 are by Gid Tanner; 81636/37 are untraced but probably not by Puckett (or Tanner).

Riley Puckett, v/y-1; acc. Gid Tanner, f-2; own bj-3/g-4.
New York, NY   Thursday, September 11, 1924

140006-2	You'll Never Miss Your Mother 'Till She's Gone -4	Co 240-D, Ha 5126-H
140007-1	Just As The Sun Went Down -4	Co 240-D, Ha 5126-H
140008-1	Sleep Baby Sleep -1, 4	Co 220-D
140009-	Ring Waltz -4	Co unissued
140010-1	We'll Sow Righteous Seed For The Reaper -4	Co 15004-D, Ha 5148-H, Sil 3260
140011-2	Where Is My Wandering Boy Tonight -4	Co 15004-D, Ha 5148-H, Sil 3260
140012-1	Blue Ridge Mountain Blues -2, 4	Co 254-D, Ha 5127-H
140013-	Darling Nellie Gray -2, 4	Co unissued
140014-2	Old Black Joe -2, 4	Co 15005-D, Ha 5133-H, Sil 3259, ReE G8411, ReAu G8411
140015-	Papa's Billy Goat -2, 4	Co unissued
140016-1	Jesse James -4	Co 15033-D, Ha 5146-H
140017-	I Am Going Down The Road Feeling Bad -2, 4	Co unissued
140018-1	Liza Jane -2, 3	Co 15014-D, Ha 5140-H, Sil 3261
140020-	Going Along Downtown -2, 3	Co unissued
140021-2	Whoa Mule -2, 3	Co 15040-D, Ha 5147-H, Sil 3258
140022-1	Bile Dem Cabbage Down -2, 3	Co 254-D, Ha 5127-H
140023-2	Railroad Bill -2, 3	Co 15040-D, Ha 5147-H, Sil 3258
140024-2	O! Susanna -3	Co 15014-D, Ha 5140-H, Sil 3261
140025-	Nobody's Business If I Do -4	Co unissued
140026-	When You And I Were Young Maggie -4	Co 15005-D, Ha 5133-H, Sil 3259

Harmonys as by **Fred Wilson**. Silvertone 3260, 3262 as by **Tom Watson**. Matrix 140019 is by Gid Tanner. Revs: Harmony 5144-H, Silvertone 3262 by Gid Tanner.

Riley Puckett, v; acc. own g.
New York, NY   Friday, September 12, 1924

140027-2	Swanee River	Co 15003-D, Ha 5132-H, ReE G8411, ReAu G8411
140028-1	When I Had But Fifty Cents	Co 15015-D, Ha 5141-H
140029-2	Burglar Man	Co 15015-D, Ha 5141-H
140030-1	Spanish Cavalier	Co 15003-D, Ha 5132-H

Harmony 5132-H, 5141-H as by **Fred Wilson**. Matrices 140031, 140045/46 are by Gid Tanner (with Riley Puckett).

New York, NY   Monday, June 15, 1925

140668-2	Just Break The News To Mother	Co 15035-D
140669-2	The Drunkard's Dream	Co 15035-D
140670-3	I Wish I Was Single Again	Co 15036-D

New York, NY   Tuesday, June 16, 1925

140681-	Down By The Old Mill Stream	Co unissued
140682-	It's Hard To Be Bound Down In Prison	Co unissued
140683-	Send Back My Wedding Ring	Co unissued
140684-	Hello Central, Give Me Heaven	Co unissued
140685-	Long Tongue Women	Co unissued
140686-	Just Bumming A Railroad Train	Co unissued
140687-1,-2	Wait Till The Sun Shines Nellie	Co 15073-D, Ve 2485-V, Cl 5425-C, Re/RZAu G20662
140688-	To Wed You In The Golden Summer Time	Co unissued
140689-1	Silver Threads Among The Gold	Co 405-D
140690-2	It's Simple To Flirt	Co 15036-D
140691-	Won't You Come Over To My House	Co unissued
140692-	When I'm Gone You'll Soon Forget	Co unissued
140693-	When You're Gone I Won't Forget	Co unissued
140694-	The Preacher And The Bear	Co unissued
140695-	Throw Out The Life-Line	Co unissued
140696-	Press Along To Glory Land	Co unissued

Velvet Tone 2485-V, Clarion 5425-C as by **Charlie Norris**.
Matrix 140687 is titled *Wait Till The Sun Shines, Nellie* on Regal/Regal-Zonophone G20662.

New York, NY   Wednesday, June 17, 1925
    140697-1   Let Me Call You Sweetheart   Co 405-D
Atlanta, GA   Wednesday, September 30, 1925
    141061-3   The Preacher And The Bear   Co 15045-D
    141062-1   Long Tongue Women   Co 15045-D
    141063-1   To Wed You In The Golden Summertime Co 15068-D
    141064-2   Won't You Come Over To My House   Co 15058-D
    141065-2   Down By The Old Mill Stream   Co 15058-D
    141066-1   When You're Gone I Won't Forget   Co 15055-D
    141067-1   When I'm Gone You'll Soon Forget   Co 15055-D
Atlanta, GA   Friday, October 2, 1925
    141080-1   Send Back My Wedding Ring   Co 15073-D, Ve 2487-V, Cl 5427-C,
                                                       Re/RZAu G20662
    141081-2   The Boston Burglar   Co 15050-D
    141082-1   The Orphan Girl   Co 15050-D
    141083-2   Hello Central Give Me Heaven   Co 15068-D
    141084-   In The Good Old Summer Time   Co unissued
    141085-1   You'd Be Surprised   Co 15063-D
    141086-2   I'll Never Get Drunk Any More   Co 15063-D
Velvet Tone 2487-V, Clarion 5427-C as by **Will Taylor**.
Atlanta, GA   Tuesday, April 20, 1926
    142054-1   Wal I Swan   Co 15078-D
    142055-2   Rock-A-Bye Baby   Co 15088-D
    142056-1,-2   Sauerkraut   Co 15088-D, Ve 2485-V, Cl 5425-C
    142057-1   Everybody Works But Father   Co 15078-D, Ve 2487-V, Cl 5427-C
    142058-2   Jack And Joe   Co 15139-D
    142059-2   Put My Little Shoes Away   Co 15125-D
Velvet Tone 2485-V, Clarion 5425-C as by **Charlie Norris**. Velvet Tone 2487-V, Clarion 5427-C as by **Will Taylor**.

Acc. Clayton McMichen (as Bob Nichols), f; own g.
    Atlanta, GA   Thursday, April 22, 1926
    142084-1   I'm Drifting Back To Dreamland   Co 15095-D, *Vo 02947*, RZAu G22951

Riley Puckett & Bob Nichols: Riley Puckett, Clayton McMichen, v duet; acc. Clayton McMichen, f; Bert Layne, f; Riley Puckett, g.
    Atlanta, GA   Thursday, April 22, 1926
    142085-1,-2   My Carolina Home   Co 15095-D, *Vo 02947*, RZAu G22951

Riley Puckett, v; acc. prob. Bill Shores, f; own g.
    Atlanta, GA   Thursday, April 22, 1926
    142086-2   Sally Goodwin   Co 15102-D, *Vo 02940*
    142087-1,-2   Ida Red   Co 15102-D, *Vo 02940*
    142088-1   Down In Arkansas   Co 15139-D
    142089-1,-2   I'll Take You Home Again Kathleen   Co unissued

Bob Nichols & Riley Puckett, v duet; acc. Clayton McMichen, f; Riley Puckett, g.
    Atlanta, GA   Saturday, November 6, 1926
    143098-2   Ring Waltz   Co 15136-D
    143099-1   Underneath The Mellow Moon   Co 15136-D
    143100-1   Don't You Remember The Time   Co 15114-D
    143101-2   My Isle Of Golden Dreams   Co 15114-D

Riley Puckett, v; acc. own g.
    Atlanta, GA   Saturday, November 6, 1926
    143102-2,-3   My Poodle Dog   Co 15196-D
    143103-2   Take Me Back To My Old Carolina Home Co 15125-D
    143104-1,-2   Somebody's Waiting For You   Co unissued
    143105-2   My Puppy Bud   Co 15196-D

Bob Nichols & Riley Puckett, v duet; or Riley Puckett, v-1; acc. Clayton McMichen, f; prob. Bert Layne, f; Riley Puckett, g.
    Atlanta, GA   Wednesday, March 30, 1927
    143813-1   Let The Rest Of The World Go By   Co 15198-D, Re/RZAu G20665
    143814-2   Till We Meet Again   Co 15161-D, Re/RZAu G20665
    143815-2   I'm Forever Blowing Bubbles -1   Co 15161-D
    143816-1,-2   My Old Kentucky Home   Co unissued

Atlanta, GA   Thursday, March 31, 1927
  143831-1,-2   Three O'Clock In The Morning   Co unissued

Riley Puckett, v; acc. Clayton McMichen, f; own g.
Atlanta, GA   Friday, April 1, 1927
  143854-D   That Old Irish Mother Of Mine   Co 15198-D
  143855-2   Fire On The Mountain   Co 15185-D
  143856-2   Alabama Gal   Co 15185-D
  143857-2   Sleep Baby Sleep   Co 15171-D
  143858-1   Little Log Cabin In The Lane   Co 15171-D
Columbia 15198-D as by **Bob Nichols & Riley Puckett**.

Atlanta, GA   Saturday, April 2, 1927
  143867-2   Cindy   Co 15232-D
  143868-2   Little Brown Jug   Co 15232-D
  143869-1,-2   Alcoholic Blues   Co unissued
  143870-1,-2   Down Hearted Blues   Co unissued
Columbia 15232-D as by **Riley Puckett & Clayton McMichen**.

Riley Puckett, g solo/sp.
Atlanta, GA   Saturday, April 2, 1927
  143871-2   Fuzzy Rag   Co 15163-D
  143872-1   The Darkey's Wail   Co 15163-D

Riley Puckett, v; acc. own g.
Atlanta, GA   Monday, October 31, 1927
  145043-2   Red Wing   Co 15226-D, CoE 19014, Re/RZAu G20666
  145044-2   I'm Going Where The Chilly Winds Don't Blow Co 15392-D
  145045-2   Come Be My Rainbow   Co 15226-D, CoE 19014

Bob Nichols & Riley Puckett, v duet; acc. Clayton McMichen, f; Riley Puckett, g.
Atlanta, GA   Tuesday, November 1, 1927
  145068-1   My Blue Ridge Mountain Queen   Co 15216-D, CoE 19013

Atlanta, GA   Wednesday, November 2, 1927
  145082-1,-2   'Neath The Old Apple Tree   Co unissued
  145083-2   The Trail Of The Lonesome Pine   Co 15304-D

Atlanta, GA   Thursday, November 3, 1927
  145090-3   In The Shade Of The Old Apple Tree   Co 15216-D, CoE 19013

Hugh Cross & Riley Puckett, v duet; acc. Clayton McMichen, f-1; Riley Puckett, g.
Atlanta, GA   Thursday, November 3, 1927
  145091-2   Red River Valley   Co 15206-D, CoE 19012
  145092-1   When You Wore A Tulip -1   Co 15206-D, CoE 19012, Re/RZAu G20668
Rev. Regal/Regal-Zonophone G20668 by Cross & McCartt (see Hugh Cross).

Riley Puckett, v; acc. own g.
Atlanta, GA   Friday, November 4, 1927
  145109-1,-2   Breeze   Co unissued
  145110-2   All Bound 'Round With The Mason Dixon Line Co 15250-D
  145111-1   M-O-T-H-E-R   Co 15250-D

Riley Puckett, v/y-1; acc. own g.
Atlanta, GA   Wednesday, April 11, 1928
  146012-1   Mama Won't Allow No Low Down Hanging   Co 15261-D
                     Around
  146013-2   Blue Yodel -1   Co 15261-D
  146014-1,-2   The Leaves Of Shamrock   Co unissued
  146015-1,-2   Meet Me Tonight In Dreamland   Co unissued

Bob Nichols & Riley Puckett, v duet; acc. Clayton McMichen, f; unknown, f; Riley Puckett, g.
Atlanta, GA   Wednesday, April 11, 1928
  146024-2   When The Maple Leaves Are Falling   Co 15350-D
  146025-3   Dear Old Dixieland   Co 15350-D

Hugh Cross & Riley Puckett, v/wh-1 duet; acc. Riley Puckett, g.
Atlanta, GA   Thursday, April 12, 1928
  146026-2   Tuck Me To Sleep (In My Old Kentucky Home) Co 15421-D
  146027-2   Gonna Raise Ruckus Tonight   Co 15455-D, ReE MR56

146028-2	Where The Morning Glories Grow -1	Co 15266-D	
146029-1	My Wild Irish Rose	Co 15266-D	

Regal MR56 as by **The Alabama Barn Stormers**. Rev. Regal MR56 by Ira & Eugene Yates.

Riley Puckett, v; acc, own g.
Atlanta, GA   Saturday, April 14, 1928

146068-2	Little Maumee	Co 15277-D	
146069-2	Breeze	Co 15277-D	

Riley Puckett & Clayton McMichen: Clayton McMichen, f; Riley Puckett, g/v.
Atlanta, GA   Saturday, April 14, 1928

146078-2	Slim Gal	Co 15295-D	
146079-2	Old Molly Hare	Co 15295-D	

Bob Nichols & Riley Puckett, v duet; acc. Clayton McMichen, f; Riley Puckett, g.
Atlanta, GA   Saturday, April 14, 1928

146080-1	'Neath The Old Apple Tree	Co 15304-D	

Hugh Cross & Riley Puckett, v duet; acc. Riley Puckett, g; one of them, humming.
Atlanta, GA   Monday, October 22, 1928

147244-2	Call Me Back Pal O' Mine	Co 15337-D	

Riley Puckett, v/y-1/wh-1; acc. own g.
Atlanta, GA   Monday, October 22, 1928

147257-2	Don't Try It For It Can't Be Done	Co 15392-D	
147258-2	Away Out On The Mountain -1	Co 15324-D, CoE 19025	

Hugh Cross & Riley Puckett, v duet; acc. Riley Puckett, g; one of them, humming-1.
Atlanta, GA   Tuesday, October 23, 1928

147265-2	Clover Blossoms -1	Co 15337-D	
147266-1	Smiles	Co 15478-D	
147267-2	Tell Me	Co 15478-D	

Riley Puckett, v/y-1/wh-2; acc. own g.
Atlanta, GA   Tuesday, October 23, 1928

147268-2	On The Other Side Of Jordan -2	Co 15374-D	
147269-2	The Moonshiner's Dream -1	Co 15324-D, CoE 19025	
147273-1	I'm Going To Georgia -2	Co 15374-D	

Matrices 147270/71 are by Dan Hornsby; matrix 147272 is by McMichen–Layne String Orch.

Riley Puckett & Clayton McMichen: Clayton McMichen, f/sp-1; Riley Puckett, g/v.
Atlanta, GA   Friday, October 26, 1928

147297-2	Bill Johnson	Co 15358-D	
147298-2	Farmer's Daughter	Co 15686-D	
147299-1	Paddy Won't You Drink Some Cider -1	Co 15358-D	
147300-2	The Arkansas Sheik	Co 15686-D	

Columbia 15686-D as by **Clayton McMichen & Riley Puckett**.

Hugh Cross & Riley Puckett, v duet; acc. Riley Puckett, g.
Atlanta, GA   Wednesday, April 10, 1929

148229-1	I'm Going To Settle Down	Co 15455-D	
148230-1	Go Feather Your Nest	Co 15421-D	

Riley Puckett, v; acc. prob. Clayton McMichen, f; prob. Bert Layne, f; own g.
Atlanta, GA   Wednesday, April 10, 1929

148233-2	Waiting For A Train	Co 15408-D	
148234-2	Carolina Moon	Co 15393-D	
148235-2	Will You Ever Think Of Me	Co 15393-D	

Acc. own g.
Atlanta, GA   Thursday, April 11, 1929

148242-2	Don't Let Your Deal Go Down	Co 15448-D	
148243-1	McKinley	Co 15448-D	
148244-2	I'm Up In The Air About Mary	Co 15408-D	

Arthur Tanner & Riley Puckett, v duet; acc. Arthur Tanner, bj; Riley Puckett, g.
Atlanta, GA   Friday, April 12, 1929

148264-1	Bring Back My Blue-Eyed Boy	Co 15577-D	

Rev. Columbia 15577-D by Arthur Tanner.

Bill Helms & Riley Puckett: Bill Helms, f; Riley Puckett, g/v.
Atlanta, GA   Tuesday, October 29, 1929

149288-2	Lost Love	Co 15774-D	

Clayton McMichen & Riley Puckett: Clayton McMichen, f/sp; Riley Puckett, g/v.
Atlanta, GA   Tuesday, October 29, 1929
  149290-2   Rye Straw   Co 15521-D

Riley Puckett, v; acc. own g.
Atlanta, GA   Wednesday, October 30, 1929
  149295-1   Dissatisfied   Co 15505-D

Colon Jones & Riley Puckett, v duet; acc. unknown, f; Riley Puckett, g.
Atlanta, GA   Wednesday, October 30, 1929
  149303-2   That Saxophone Waltz   Co 15774-D

Riley Puckett, v; prob. acc. own g.
Atlanta, GA   Thursday, October 31, 1929
  149314-   It's Only An Old Fashioned Cottage   Co unissued
  149315-   Sunny Tennessee   Co unissued

Acc. Clayton McMichen, f; own g.
Atlanta, GA   Monday, November 4, 1929
  149364-1   Frankie And Johnny (You'll Miss Me In The Days   Co 15505-D
                     To Come)

Acc. own g.
Atlanta, GA   Monday, April 14, 1930
  150208-2   Waitin' For The Evening Mail   Co 15605-D
  150209-2   Ramblin' Boy   Co 15605-D

Atlanta, GA   Wednesday, April 16, 1930
  150243-2   Nine Hundred Miles From Home   Co 15563-D
  150244-2   There's A Hard Time Coming   Co 15708-D
  150245-2   Paw's Old Mule   Co 15708-D
  150246-2   Dark Town Strutters Ball   Co 15563-D

Atlanta, GA   Friday, December 5, 1930
  151049-1,-2   Moonlight On The Colorado   Co 15631-D
  151050-2   The Cat Came Back   Co 15656-D

Atlanta, GA   Monday, December 8, 1930
  151094-1,-2   Somewhere In Old Wyoming   Co 15631-D
  151095-1   Beaver Cap   Co 15656-D
  151096-   I Wish I Were A Single Girl Again   Co unissued
  151097-   Dark Eyes   Co unissued

Bob Nichols & Puckett, v duet; acc. Clayton McMichen, f; Riley Puckett, g.
Atlanta, GA   Monday, October 26, 1931
  151936-   Longest Train I Ever Saw   Co unissued
  151937-   That's No Business Of Mine   Co unissued

Riley Puckett, v; acc. own g.
Atlanta, GA   Thursday, October 29, 1931
  151978-1   East Bound Train   Co 15747-D
  151979-1   Careless Love   Co 15747-D
  151980-1   Twenty-One Years   Co 15719-D
  151981-1   All Bound Down In Prison   Co 15719-D

Tanner & Puckett: Gid Tanner, f/poss. v; Riley Puckett, g/poss. v.
Atlanta, GA   Thursday, October 29, 1931
  151982-   No. 2 Schottiche [sic]   Co unissued
  151983-   Parody On Home Sweet Home   Co unissued

Riley Puckett, v; acc. Ted Hawkins, md-1; own g.
San Antonio, TX   Thursday, March 29, 1934
  82695-1   Careless Love   BB B-5532, MW M-4507
  82696-1   Waitin' For The Evenin' Mail   BB B-5432, MW M-4981
  82697-1   Chain Gang Blues   BB B-5818, Twin FT1877
  82698-1   George Collins -1   BB B-5818, MW M-4551
  82699-1   I'm Gettin' Ready To Go   BB B-5587, MW M-4506
  82700-1   Ragged But Right -1   BB B-5587, MW M-4506, Twin FT1810
  82700-2   Ragged But Right -1   BB unissued: *RCA 8416-2 (CD)*

Revs: Twin FT1810 by Delmore Brothers, FT1877 by Bill Boyd.

Acc. Gid Tanner, f-1; Gordon Tanner, f-1; Ted Hawkins, md-2; own g.

San Antonio, TX   Friday, March 30, 1934
82711-1	K.C. Railroad (Going Down The Road Feeling Bad)	BB B-5471, MW M-4508, M-7042
82712-1	Four Day Blues	BB B-5786, Twin FT1892
82713-1	Just As We Used To Do	BB B-5786, Twin FT1892
82714-1	I'm Drifting Back To Dreamland -2	BB B-5532, MW M-4507
82715-1	My Carolina Home -1, 2	BB B-5471, MW M-4508, M-7042, Twin FT1748
82716-1	The Old Spinning Wheel -2	BB B-5432, MW M-4981, HMVIn N4304

Revs: HMV N4304 by Fleming & Townsend; Twin FT1748 by Tom & Don.

For recordings with Gid Tanner & The Skillet-Lickers, including duets with members thereof, made at the March 1934 Bluebird session, see Ted Hawkins and Gid Tanner.

Riley Puckett, v; or **Riley Puckett–Red Jones**-1, v duet; acc. unknown, f-2; Riley Puckett, g.
Atlanta, GA   Tuesday, July 31, 1934
82848-1	Wednesday Night Waltz -2	BB B-5607, MW M-4498, M-4818
82849-1	Renfro Valley Home	BB B-5607, MW M-4498, M-4818, Twin FT1829
82850-1	I Only Want A Buddy (Not A Sweetheart)	BB B-5666, MW M-4505
82851-1	Lost Love -1	BB B-5666, MW M-4505
82852-1	Saxophone Waltz -1	BB B-5738
82853-1	Puckett Blues	BB B-5738, MW M-4551

Rev. Twin FT1829 by Delmore Brothers.

Acc. Ted Hawkins, md-1; own g.
Atlanta, GA   Thursday, August 8, 1935
94368-1	The Isle Of Capri	BB B-6064, MW M-4982
94369-1	My Buddy	BB B-6067, MW M-4815
94370-1	Caroline Sunshine Girl	BB B-7373
94371-1	Put On An Old Pair Of Shoes	BB B-6103, RZAu G22936, Twin FT8004
94372-1	Blue Ridge Mountain Blues	BB B-6196, Twin FT8055
94373-1	Don't Let Your Deal Go Down	BB B-6067, MW M-4815
94374-1	Curly-Headed Baby	BB B-6134, RZAu G22936
94375-1	Nobody's Business	BB B-6103, Twin FT8022
94376-1	Roll Back The Carpet	BB B-6064, MW M-4982, Twin FT8004
94377-1	What's The Reason (I'm Not Pleasin' You) -1	BB B-6134, Twin FT8022

Rev. Bluebird B-6196, Twin FT8055 by Jesse Rodgers.

Acc. Charles Smith, f-1; own g.
Charlotte, NC   Friday, February 14, 1936
99123-1	In A Little Gypsy Tea Room	BB B-6291, MW M-4760
99124-1	When I Grow Too Old To Dream -1	BB B-6291, MW M-4760
99125-1	Old Maids' Brown [sic] Ferry Blues	BB B-7717, Twin FT8634
99126-1	Riley's Hen-House Door -1	BB B-7373
99127-1	Back To My Home In Smokey Mountain -1	BB B-6348, RZAu G22966
99128-1	Santa Fé Folks Fiesta -1	BB B-6313, MW M-4761
99129-1	Bury Me 'Neath The Willow Tree -1	BB B-6348, RZAu G22966
99130-1	Ole Faithful -1	BB B-6313, MW M-4761, Twin FT8094
99131-1	I Want To Wander In The Cumberland Mountains -1	BB B-6404, Twin FT8166
99132-1	My Old Mule -1	BB B-6404

Revs: Bluebird B-7177, Twin FT8634 by Cliff Carlisle; Twin FT8094 by Wade Mainer & Zeke Morris, FT8166 by Tune Wranglers.

Riley Puckett, v; or **Riley Puckett & Red Jones**-1, v duet; acc. Riley Puckett, g.
New York, NY   Tuesday, September 28, 1937
62621-A	Poor Boy -1	De 5455
62622-A	There's More Pretty Girls Than One – Part 1 -1	De 5438
62623-A	There's More Pretty Girls Than One – Part 2 -1	De 5438
62624-A	Short Life Of Trouble	De 5442
62625-A	The Longest Train	De 5523
62626-A	Somebody's Waiting For Me	De 5523
62627-A	Moonlight On The Colorado -1	De 5540

New York, NY   Wednesday, September 29, 1937
62628-A	The Broken Engagement -1	De 5540
62629-A	Gulf Coast Blues	De 5472
62630-A	Take Me Back To My Carolina Home	De 5472
62631-A	Altoona Freight Wreck	De 5455
62632-A	The Cat Came Back	De 5442

    Rock Hill, SC   Wednesday, February 1, 1939

031916-1	Can't Put That Monkey On My Back	BB B-8037, MW M-7902
031917-1	Though You're Not Satisfied With Me	BB B-8119, RZAu G24318
031918-1	Let My Peaches Be	BB B-8037, MW M-7902
031919-1	Moonlight, Shadows And You	BB B-8066, MW M-7903
031920-1	The Old Apple Tree	BB B-8104, MW M-7906
031921-1	Story Of The Preacher And The Bear	BB B-8083, MW M-7904
031922-1	That Old Irish Mother Of Mine	BB B-8144, MW M-7905
031923-1	When Irish Eyes Are Smiling	BB B-8144, MW M-7905
031924-1	I Wish I Was Single Again	BB B-8066, MW M-7903
031925-1	Boots And Saddle	BB B-8119
031926-1	I Wish I Was A Single Girl Again	BB B-8083, MW M-7904
031927-1	The Longest Train I Ever Saw	BB B-8104, MW M-7906

Riley Puckett, v/y-1; acc. unknown, pac-2; unknown, md; own g.
    Atlanta, GA   Wednesday, August 23, 1939

041275-1	Tie Me To Your Apron Strings -2	BB B-8371, MW M-8477
041276-1	I Get The Blues When It Rains -2	BB B-8371, MW M-8477
041277-1	Dream Train -2	BB B-8258, MW M-8476
041278-1	Little Sir Echo -2	BB B-8258, MW M-8476
041279-1	New "Givin' Everything Away" -2	BB B-8277, MW M-8478
041280-1	Frankie And Johnnie -2	BB B-8277, MW M-8478
041281-1	When I'm Gone, You'll Soon Forget Me	BB B-8295, MW M-8479, RZAu G24318
041282-1	'Way Out There -1	BB B-8354, MW M-8480, RZ ME55, RZAu G25121
041283-1	Back On The Texas Plains -1	BB B-8354, MW M-8480, RZ ME55
041284-1	How Come You Do Me, Like You Do?	BB B-8295, MW M-8479
041292-1	I Told Them All About You	BB B-8335, MW M-8481
041293-1	Red River Valley	BB B-8335, MW M-8481

Intervening matrices are unconnected. Rev. Regal-Zonophone G25121 by Cliff Carlisle & Fred Kirby.

Riley Puckett, v; acc. unknown, pac-1; unknown, md; own g.
    Atlanta, GA   Monday, February 5, 1940

047529-1	South Of The Border	BB B-8399, MW M-8726
047530-1	Red Sails In The Sunset	BB B-8399, MW M-8726
047531-1	Whistle And Blow Your Blues Away	BB B-8452, MW M-8728
047532-1	Margie	BB B-8452, MW M-8728
047533-1	Oh, Johnny, Oh	BB B-8384, MW M-8725
047534-1	Take Me Back To My Boots And Saddle	BB B-8384, MW M-8725
047535-1	When I Grow Too Old To Dream -1	BB B-8483, MW M-8727
047536-1	It's A Sin To Tell A Lie -1	BB B-8483, MW M-8727

Acc. unknown woman, md; own g.
    Atlanta, GA   Friday, October 11, 1940

056504-1	Ma! (He's Making Eyes At Me)	BB B-8578, MW M-8883
056505-1	Walking My Baby Back Home	BB B-8578, MW M-8883
056506-1	Get Out And Get Under The Moon	BB B-8596, MW M-8884
056507-1	When I'm Back In Tennessee	BB B-8596, MW M-8884
056508-1	Nobody's Business	BB B-8621, MW M-8885
056509-1	Playmates	BB B-8621, MW M-8885

Pete Pyle, who recorded immediately after Puckett on this date, remembered the mandolinist as a woman.

Acc. unknown, md; own g.
    Atlanta, GA   Thursday, October 2, 1941

071078-1	Where The Shy Little Violets Grow	BB B-8989
071079-1	In A Little Garden	BB 33-0500
071080-1	Tuck Me To Sleep In My Old Kentucky Home	BB B-8954
071081-1	When It's Peach Pickin' Time In Georgia	BB B-8954
071082-1	Old Fashioned Locket	BB 33-0500
071083-1	Railroad Boomer	BB B-8989

Riley Puckett was a regular, and usually credited, member of Gid Tanner & His Skillet-Lickers, and recorded with many artists associated with that group. See Hugh Cross, Ted Hawkins, The Home Town Boys, Clayton McMichen, Lowe Stokes, Arthur Tanner, Gid Tanner.

SI PUCKETT

Pseudonym on Supertone for Holland Puckett.

PUCKETT & JONES

See Riley Puckett.

PETE PYLE

Pete Pyle, v/y-1; acc. Edward Crowe, md; own g.
Atlanta, GA   Friday, October 11, 1940
056510-1	Home Sweet Home In The Rockies -1	BB B-8672, MW M-8887, RZAu G25222
056511-1	Don't You Worry 'Bout Me When I'm Gone	BB B-8672, MW M-8886, RZAu G25222
056512-1	You've Broken Your Promise	BB B-8602, MW M-8888
056513-1	I Don't Care	BB B-8602, MW M-8888
056514-1	I Guess You'll Soon Forget	BB B-8711, MW M-8889
056515-1	It's So Hard To Be Just A Pal To You	BB B-8581, MW M-8889
056516-1	I Just Can't Say Goodbye	BB B-8711, MW M-8887
056517-1	Little Blue Eyed Blonde, Goodbye	BB B-8581, MW M-8886

Atlanta, GA   Tuesday, September 30, 1941
071034-1	Why Don't You Leave Me Alone	BB B-8905
071035-1	Beer Drinkin' Blues	BB B-8971
071036-1	All Over A Smile	BB B-8905
071037-1	Please Don't Fool Me	BB B-8856, RZAu G25154
071038-1	I Made A Mistake	BB B-8971
071039-1	Wasted Tears	BB B-9001
071040-1	I'll Be Gone For Awhile	BB B-8856
071041-1	Love's A Game That Two Can Play	BB B-9001, RZAu G25154

Pete Pyle recorded after 1942.

Q

QUADRILLERS
See the Kentucky Thorobreds.

THE QUEEN TRIO

No details.
Johnson City, TN   Tuesday, October 22, 1929
149224-	Sunday Morning Blues	Co unissued
149225-	The June Bug	Co unissued

FRANK QUINN
One side by this artist appeared in the Okeh Old Time Tunes series (45030). Quinn was an American Irish musician, and his recordings are thus beyond the scope of this work.

R

THE RADIO DUO
Pseudonym on Australian Panachord for Lester McFarland & Robert A. Gardner.

THE RADIO IMPS
This credit, generally used by a popular group, was applied to the Carson Robison Trio on one side of Imperial 2510.

RADIO MAC
See Harry (Mac) McClintock.

RADIO RUBES

Harry Duncan, f/v-1; unknown, esg; unknown, g; unknown, sb; Eddie Smith, v-2; unidentified, v trio-3.
New York, NY   Tuesday, October 24, 1939
043223-1	I'm Glad It's Over Now -2	BB B-8319, MW M-8729
043224-1	The Lie He Wrote Home -3	BB B-8349, MW M-8730, RZAu G24203
043225-1	You're On The Right Side Of The Ocean -3	BB B-8319, MW M-8729
043226-1	The Big Little Family Of The Hills -1	BB B-8349, MW M-8730, RZAu G24203

JAMES RAGAN [& OLIVER BECK]
Pseudonym(s) on Challenge for Roy Harvey [& Bob Hoke].

RAGGEDY ANN'S MELODY MAKERS

Unknown, f; unknown, p; unknown, bj; unknown, g; unknown, v.
Memphis, TN   Tuesday, February 21, 1928

400281-	Smokey Mokes	OK unissued
400282-	Raising 'Ell	OK unissued
400283-B	Zends [sic] Waltz	OK 45235
400284-A	Waltz Medley	OK 45235

This group is very probably the same as, or related to, McLaughlin's Old Time Melody Makers.

THE RAILROAD BOYS

Pseudonym on Superior for Roy Harvey & Jess Johnston with the West Virginia Ramblers (see Roy Harvey).

THE RAINBOW QUARTETTE

Vocal quartet; acc. unknown.
    Atlanta, GA   Friday, April 13, 1928

| 146060- | When Jesus Comes | Co unissued |
| 146061- | When The Sweet Bye And Bye Is Ended | Co unissued |

    Atlanta, GA   Monday, November 4, 1929

| 149367- | Don't Be Knocking | Co unissued |
| 149368- | 'Twas Love Devine [sic] | Co unissued |

R.L. RAINES

R.L. Raines, v; acc. unknown, bj; unknown, g.
    Richmond, IN   Saturday, December 6, 1930

| 17351 | Save My Mother's Picture From The Sale | Ge rejected |
| 17352 | The Old Arm Chair | Ge rejected |

R.L. Raines & Son, v duet; acc. unknown, bj; unknown, g.
    Richmond, IN   Saturday, December 6, 1930

| 17353,-A | $10,000 Reward For The Chicken (That Roosts Too High For me) | Ge rejected |

R.L. Raines's son may have been Sherman Raines.

SHERMAN RAINES

Sherman Raines, v; acc. poss. own g.
    Richmond, IN   Saturday, December 6, 1930

| 17355 | My Fat Gal | Ge rejected |

BUD RAINEY

Bud Rainey, v; acc. unknown.
    New York, NY   Wednesday, July 15, 1936

| 61204-A,-B | If I Had My Way | De unissued |
| 61205-A,-B | Ace In The Hole | De unissued |

RAINEY OLD TIME BAND

Two unknowns, f; unknown, md or bj-md; unknown, g; unknown, sp-1.
    New Orleans, LA   Saturday, December 15, 1928

| 147648-2 | Engineer Frank Hawk -1 | Co 15675-D |
| 147649-1 | Crawford March | Co 15675-D |

Matrices 147646/47 are by the Gatwood Square Dance Band, which included Allen Rainey; there may be some connection between the two groups.

RALEY BROTHERS

Unidentified, v/y-1; acc. prob. Adrian Raley, sg; —— Raley, g.
    Charlotte, NC   Thursday, February 18, 1937

07146-1	Hen Pecked Man -1	BB unissued
07147-1	Chicken Roost Blues -1	BB B-7062
07148-1,-2	When The Shanghai Takes His Ride	BB unissued
07149-1	I Want A Woman	BB B-7062

THE RAMBLING DUET (FRANK GERALD & HOWARD DIXON)

See Frank Gerald & Howard Dixon.

THE RAMBLING KID & THE PROFESSOR

Ovie Davis, Arnold Davis, v duet; acc. prob. one of them, h; prob. the other, g.
    Birmingham, AL   Friday, April 9, 1937

B-101-1	The Evergreen Tree By The River	ARC 7-07-54
B-102-	The Little White House	ARC unissued
B-103-2	In My Little Home In Tennessee	ARC 7-07-54
B-104-1	The Boy The Ladies Saved From Jail	ARC 7-08-71
B-105-1	When The Stars Begin To Fall	ARC 7-08-71
B-106-	When My Saviour Calls Me Home	ARC unissued

RAMBLING RANGERS

Curtis Streets, Edward Conway, Norwood Conway, v trio; or Edward Conway, Norwood Conway, v duet-1; or Curtis Streets, v-2; acc. prob. one of them, g.

Charlotte, NC   Thursday, February 18, 1937

07141-1	Wyoming For Me	BB B-6914, MW M-7366
07142-1	Memory Lane	BB B-6914, MW M-7366
07143-1	Where Is My Mama -1	BB unissued
07144-1	Train No. 52 -2	BB unissued
07145-1	If You'll Let Me Be Your Sweetheart -2	BB unissued

THE RAMBLING RANGERS

Harold Whatley, sg; Oliver Warren, g/v; Sammy Stalsby, g.

Dallas, TX   Thursday, December 1, 1938

| DAL-659-1 | Gittin' Tired | Vo 04949 |

Harold Whatley, sg/v-1; Oliver Warren, g/lv; Sammy Stalsby, g/v-2.

Dallas, TX   Friday, December 2, 1938

DAL-678-1	Tired Of Ramblin' -2	Vo 04758
DAL-679-1,-2	Good Bye Old Booze -2	Vo unissued
DAL-680-1	Jesus, Lover Of My Soul -1, 2	Vo 04628
DAL-681-1,-2	Sad And Lonely	Vo unissued
DAL-682-1	When The Sun Goes Down -1, 2	Vo 04758
DAL-683-1	No One -1, 2	Vo 04949
DAL-684-1	Oh Lord -2	Vo 04628

[JOE] RAMER FAMILY

Pseudonym on Broadway for the Joe Reed Family.

JACK RAMSEY

Pseudonym on Sunrise for Arthur Fields.

THE RANCH BOYS

Jack Ross, Joe "Curley" Bradley, Ken "Shorty" Carson, v trio; acc. Ken Carson, g.

Chicago, IL   Friday, September 7, 1934

C-9416-A	The Last Round-Up	De 5017, Pan 25955
C-9417-B	The Old Spinning Wheel	De 5017
C-9418-B	Tumbling Tumbleweeds	De 5040, Pan 25999
C-9419-A	When It's Springtime In The Rockies	De 5016, Pan 25990

Chicago, IL   Tuesday, September 11, 1934

C-9438-A	The Utah Trail	De 5016, Pan 25990
C-9439-A	Ragtime Cowboy Joe	De 5074, Pan 25713
C-9440-A,-B	The Dying Mountaineer	De rejected
C-9441-A	Wonder Valley	De rejected

Chicago, IL   Friday, September 28, 1934

| C-9534-A | Where The Mountains Kiss The Sky | De 5040, Pan 25955 |

Chicago, IL   Friday, October 19, 1934

C-9580-A	Cowboy's Lament	De 5061, Pan 25907
C-9581-A	Strawberry Roan	De 5074, Pan 25970
C-9582-A	A Home On The Range	De 5045, Pan 26038
C-9583-A	Red River Valley	De 5045, Pan 25999

Chicago, IL   Monday, October 29, 1934

| C-9598-A | Carry Me Back To The Lone Prairie | De 5046, Pan 26038 |
| C-9599-A | You're Just A Flower From An Old Bouquet | De 5046, Pan 25713 |

Chicago, IL   Monday, December 31, 1934

| C-9625-A | Ole Faithful | De 5061 |

The Ranch Boys

Chicago, IL   Tuesday, January 8, 1935

C-9630-A	Cowboy's Lament	De 5061
C-9631-A,-B,-C	In An Old Log Cabin	De rejected

Matrix C-9630 replaced matrix C-9580 on later pressings of Decca 5061.

Chicago, IL   Tuesday, April 16, 1935

C-9926-C	Roll Along Covered Wagon	De 5113
C-9927-C	Ridin' The Range	De 5113, Pan 25907

Acc. unknown, f; Ken Carson, g.

Chicago, IL   Wednesday, April 24, 1935

C-9948-A	Missouri Waltz	De 5167, DeE F5633
C-9949-A	Just An Evening At Home	De 5167, Pan 25946
C-9950-A	Me And My Burro	De 5128, Pan 25946
C-9951-A	Beautiful Ohio	De 5128, DeE F5633

Matrix C-9950 was also issued, coupled with matrix 9492 by Happy Jack Turner, on a Decca pressing numbered 9950/9492.

Chicago, IL   Wednesday, March 4, 1936

C-90676-	Lone Star	Pan 25940, BrSA SA1102
C-90677-	The Old Oak Tree	Pan 25940, BrSA SA1102

Chicago, IL   Wednesday, May 27, 1936

C-90756-A,-B	Twilight On The Trail	De unissued
C-90757-A,-B	Prairie Moonlight And You	De unissued
TC-90758-A	Mexican Medley	De rejected

Chicago, IL   Tuesday, June 16, 1936

C-90756-D	Twilight On The Trail	De 5234, MeC 45237
C-90757-D	Prairie Moonlight And You	De 5234, MeC 45237, Min M-14074

Chicago, IL   Friday, July 31, 1936

C-90810-A	Hidden Valley	De 5258, DeAu X1268, MeC 45240
C-90811-A,-B	We'll Rest At The End Of The Trail	De rejected
C-90812-A	The Old Corral	De 5258, DeAu X1268, MeC 45240, Pan 25970

Chicago, IL   Saturday, December 12, 1936

C-91051-B	Wanderers (My Lop Eared Mule, My Broken Down Horse And Me)	De 5319, DeAu X1371, MeC 45242, Pan 25915
C-91052-A	Little Ah Sid	De 5319, DeAu X1371, MeC 45242, Min M-14070, Pan 25915
C-91053-A,-B	Bury Me Out On The Prairie (I Got No Use For The Women)	De rejected
C-91054-A,-B	Little Old Sod Shanty On The Claim	De rejected

Chicago, IL   Friday, January 29, 1937

C-91108-A	Bury Me Out On The Prairie	De 5341, DeAu X1364, MeC 45243, Min M-14070, Pan 25936
C-91109-A	Little Old Sod Shanty On The Claim	De 5341, DeAu X1364, MeC 45243, Min M-14074, Pan 25936

Chicago, IL   Saturday, March 20, 1937

C-91140-A	My Little Buckaroo	De 5354, DeAu X1356, MeC 45223
C-91141-A	Ole Pardner	De 5354, DeAu X1356, MeC 45223, Pan 25921

New York, NY   Friday, October 28, 1938

64713-A,-B	1. Cowboy's Dream 2. Strawberry Roan	De unissued
64714-A	1. Chisholm Trail. 2. Yellow Rose Of Texas	De 2642
64715-A	Clementine: Little Ah Sid	DeE F7364
64716-A,-B	1. Little Old Sod Shanty On The Claim 2. Good Bye Old Paint	De unissued
64717-A,-B	1. Buffalo Gals 2. Cowboy Dance	De unissued
64718-A,-B	1. Git Along Little Dogies 2. Little Joe The Wrangler	De unissued
64719-A	1. Bury Me Out On The Prairie 2. Cowboy's Lament	DeE F7366
64720-A	1. Cowboy Jack 2. Red River Valley	De 2645
64721-C	1. Big Corral 2. Sweet Betsy From Pike	De 2646, DeE F7367
64722-C	Home On The Range	De 2646, DeE F7367, Vo 55027

New York, NY   Saturday, October 29, 1938

64723-A	They Cut Down The Old Pine Tree	DeE F7739
64724-A	The West, A Nest And You	De unissued

64725-A	Let The Rest Of The World Go By	De rejected
64726-A	The Prisoner's Song	DeE F7739

    New York, NY   Wednesday, April 5, 1939

64713-C	1. Cowboy's Dream 2. Strawberry Roan	De 2642, DeE F7363, Vo 55028
64714-D	1. The Chisholm Trail 2. The Yellow Rose Of Texas	De 2642, DeE F7363, Vo 55028
64715-C	1. Clementine 2. Little Ah Sid	De 2643, Vo 55027
64716-C	1. Little Old Sod Shanty On The Claim 2. Goodbye, Old Paint	De 2643, DeE F7364
64718-D	1. Git Along Little Dogies 2. Little Joe The Wrangler	De 2644, DeE F7365, RexIr R5039

Matrix 64713 is titled *Cowboy's Dream; The Strawberry Roan*, and matrix 64714 is titled *The Chisholm Trail; The Yellow Rose Of Texas*, on Decca F7363. Matrix 64716 is titled *The Little Old Sod Shanty On The Claim: Good-Bye, Old Paint* on Decca F7364.

    New York, NY   Sunday, April 16, 1939

64717-C,-D	1. Buffalo Gals 2. Cowboy Dance	De 2644, DeE F7365, RexIr R5039

These takes of matrices first recorded on October 28, 1938 were presumably recorded at one or the other of the April 1939 sessions above, or at about that time.

64719-C	1. Bury Me Out On The Prairie 2. Cowboy's Lament	De 2645, DeIr W5070
64719-D	1. Bury Me Out On The Prairie 2. Cowboy's Lament	De 2645, Vo 55029
64720-C	1. Cowboy Jack 2. Red River Valley	De 2645, DeE F7366, DeIr W5070, Vo 55029

Matrix 64719 is titled *Bury Me Out On The Prairie: Cowboy's Lament*, and matrix 64720 is titled *Cowboy Jack: Red River Valley*, on Decca W5070.

Decca 2642 to 2646 were collected in Decca album 65, and Vocalion 55027 to 55029 in Vocalion album VP-2.

    Chicago, IL   Friday, March 7, 1941

93558-A	In The Chapel In The Moonlight	De 3852, 24930
93559-A	Wagon Wheels	De 3849, 24929
93560-A	The Last Round-Up	De 24928
93560-B	The Last Round-Up	De 3848
93561-A	There's A Home In Wyomin'	De 3849, 24929
93562-A	The Old Spinning Wheel	De 3852, 24930
93563-A	The Call Of The Canyon	De 3850, 24931
93564-A	Lights Out	De 3851, 24931
93565-A	All Ashore	De 3851
93566-A	Empty Saddles	De 3848, 24928
93567-A	Colorado Memories	De 3850

Decca 3848 to 3852 were collected in Decca album 237, and 24928 to 24931 in Decca album 754.

THE RANCHERS

Two unknown men, unknown woman, v trio; acc. unknown, g.

    Chicago, IL   Tuesday, April 20, 1937

TO-1672	I Only Want A Buddy Not A Sweetheart	ARC unissued trial recording

RAND & FOSTER

Pseudonym on Supertone 9313, 9326 for McGhee & Cogar (see John McGhee & Frank Welling), and on Supertone 9373 for Kirk McGee & Blythe Poteet (see McGee Brothers).

WILLARD RANDOLPH
WILLIAM RANDOLPH

Pseudonyms on Banner for Willard Hodgin.

THE RANGE RIDERS

Poss. Jelly Green, f; prob. Spec Harrison, cl-1/as-2; unknown, p; unknown, g; Harold "Little Willie" Roberts, sb/v-3; unknown, tu; Ruth Byles, v-4; unidentified, v-5.

    Hot Springs, AR.   Monday, March 1, 1937

HS-1-1	The Range Riders' Stomp -1, 2	Vo 03579
HS-2-	Put It Down -5	ARC unissued
HS-3-2	No Foolin' -2, 4	Vo 03579
HS-4-	Full House Blues -5	ARC unissued
HS-5-1	Who Calls You Sweet Mama Now? -1, 2, 3	ARC 7-05-69, Vo 03503
HS-6-	Afraid -5	ARC unissued
HS-7-2	It Don't Mean A Thing -1, 2, 3	Vo 03548
HS-8-	Muddy Moon Blues -5	ARC unissued

HS-9-1	How Come You Do Me Like You Do -1, 3	ARC 7-05-69, Vo 03503
HS-10-2	Five Foot Two, Eyes Of Blue -1, 2, 3	Vo 03548

Bill Barnes, a salesman at KWKH, receives composer-credit for matrix HS-1 and probably worked with the group in a management capacity.

FRANK RANGER

Pseudonym on Rex 8056 for John I. White (*11 More Months And 10 More Days*) or Frank Luther (*Will The Angels Play Their Harps For Me*).

[THE] RANGERS QUARTET[TE]

Rangers Quartet: Vernon Hyles, lv; Denver Crumpler, tv; Walter Leverett, bv; Arnold Hyles, bsv; acc. Vernon Hyles, g.

New York, NY · Friday, September 22, 1939

66451-A	I've Found A Hiding Place	De 5735, 46055
66452-A	You Got To Be Holy	De 5735
66453-A	Holy Be Thy Great Name	De 5736
66454-A	He Bore It All	De 5736, 46331
66455-A	I'm In The King's Highway	De 5768, 46056
66456-A	What Would You Give	De 5768, 46056
66457-A	In The Shadow Of The Cross	De 5781, 46055
66458-A	Through This World I Sadly Roam	De 5781
66459-A	Just A Little Talk With Jesus	De 5749
66460-A	I've Been Listening In On Heaven	De 5749
66461-A	I Shall Go Home In The Morning	De 5802, 46331
66462-A	I Dreamed I Met Mother And Daddy	De 5802

The Rangers Quartette: Vernon Hyles, lv; Denver Crumpler, tv; Walter Leverett, bv; Arnold Hyles, bsv; acc. Vernon Hyles, g.

Charlotte, NC · Thursday, June 26, 1941

CHAR-1; 30906-1	Goodbye Sin	OK 06513, Cq 9878
CHAR-2; 30907-1	The Glory Special	OK 06578, Cq 9878
CHAR-3; 30908-1	Beyond The Clouds	OK 06569, Cq 9879
CHAR-4; 30909-1	Mighty The Lord	OK 06569, Cq 9879
CHAR-5; 30910-	Where He Leads Me	Cq 9880
CHAR-6; 30911-	An Old Log Cabin For Sale	OK unissued
CHAR-7; 30912-1	I've Changed My Mind	OK 06513
CHAR-8; 30913-1	Keep A Happy Heart	OK 06445, Cq 9877
CHAR-9; 30914-1	If Heaven's Any Better	OK 06578, Cq 9881
CHAR-10; 30915-1	I Will Slip Away Home	Cq 9881
CHAR-11; 30916-	Somebody Knows	Cq 9880
CHAR-12; 30917-1	Let Jesus Convoy You Home	OK 06445, Cq 9877

Matrices 30910 and 30915 were scheduled for OKeh 6658, but this was never issued.

RANKIN BROTHERS

Pseudonym on Conqueror for Leonard Rutherford & John Foster (see the former).

GROVER RANN

Grover Rann & Harry Ayers, v duet; acc. one of them, g.

Atlanta, GA · Wednesday, April 23, 1930

| 150372-2 | They Tell Me Love's A Pleasure | Co 15600-D |
| 150373-2 | Little Dolly Driftwood | Co 15600-D |

Grover Rann & His Lookout Mountaineers: Grover Rann, Harry Ayers, v duet; acc. Grover Rann, f-1/g-2; Harry Ayers, g.

Atlanta, GA · Saturday, December 6, 1930

151067-	Wayward Traveller	Co unissued
151068-	I Know There Is Somebody Waiting	Co unissued
151069-	Nobody's Darling	Co unissued
151070-2	Don't Stay After Ten -2	Co 15638-D
151071-	Song Of The Harvest	Co unissued
151072-1	I'se Gwine Back To Dixie -1	Co 15638-D

AULTON RAY

See Taylor's Kentucky Boys.

RAY BROTHERS

Will E. Ray, f; S. Vardaman Ray, g.
Memphis, TN   Wednesday, May 28, 1930

62531-2	Honeysuckle Waltz	Vi V-40313
62532-2	Choctaw County Rag	Vi V-40313
62535-2	Jake Leg Wobble	Vi V-40291
62536-	Friday Night Waltz	Vi V-40291

Victor V-40291 as by **The Ray Brothers**.
Matrices 62533/34 are by the Mississippi 'Possum Hunters.

Will E. Ray, f; S. Vardaman Ray, g/v-1.
Memphis, TN   Friday, November 21, 1930

62984-2	Tuscaloosa Waltz	Vi 23552
62985-2	Mississippi Echoes	Vi 23552
62986-2	Home Town Waltz	Vi 23713, BB B-5789, RZAu G22597
62987-2	Winona Rag	Vi 23713, BB B-5789
62988-2	Got The Jake Leg Too -1	Vi 23508
62989-2	The Folks Back Home -1	Vi 23508

Rev. Regal-Zonophone G22597 by Arthur Smith.

HARRY RAYMOND

Pseudonym on Silvertone for Vernon Dalhart.

RAYNE-BO RAMBLERS

See Happy Fats & His Rayne-Bo Ramblers.

REAVES WHITE COUNTY RAMBLERS

Isaac "Ike" Reaves, f-1; Ira Reaves, f-2/straw-beating-3; Lloyd Reaves, o/v-4; Ed Rumble, g/calls-5.
Chicago, IL   Friday, April 27, 1928

C-1893	Down In Arkansas -1, 2	Vo 5224
C-1894	Pope Waltz -1, 2	Vo 5224
C-1895	Strawberry Blues -2, 4	Vo 5217
C-1896	Hesitation Blues (Oh! Baby Must I Hesitate) -2, 4	Vo 5217
C-1897	Arkansas Pullet -1, 4	Vo 5260
C-1898	Reaves Waltz -1	Vo 5260
C-1899	Rattler Tree'd A 'Possum -1, 4	Vo 5219
C-1900	Shortening Bread -1, 2, 4	Vo 5218
C-1901	Ten Cent Piece -1, 3, 5	Vo 5218
C-1902	Arkansas Wagner -1	Vo 5219
C-1903	Drunkard's Hiccoughs -1, 3	Vo 5247
C-1904	Flying Engine -1, 2?, 5	Vo 5247

THE RECORD BOYS

Recordings by this group, which is believed to have included Al Bernard and Frank Kamplain, were issued in the Vocalion Old Southern Tunes series (5136) but are outside the scope of this work.

RECTOR TRIO

John Rector, f; unknown, bj; unknown, g; unknown, v-1.
Atlanta, GA   Wednesday, December 3, 1930

151006-2	Skyland Rag	Co 15658-D
151007-1	Mount Pisgah Blues -1	Co 15658-D
151008-	Pretty Little Indian Napanee	Co unissued
151009-	Them Thirty Nines Of Mine	Co unissued

This is not the John Rector associated with The Hill Billies, nor the musician who recorded for the Library of Congress Archive of American Folk-Song at Galax, VA in 1937.

RED BRUSH ROWDIES

Poss. Bill Davies, f; poss. Miller Wikel, f; unknown, bj-1; Frank Welling, g-2; prob. John McGhee, g; unidentified, wh-3.

Chicago, IL　　　　　　　　　　　　　　　　　　　　　　　　　　　　　　　　c. August/September 1928

20796-2	No One's Hard Up But Me -1?, 2?	Pm 3140
20797-2	The Third Of July -1?, 2?	Pm 3140
20798-2	Tuck Me In -1, 2	Pm 3122
20802-1	Harbor Of Home Sweet Home -1, 2	Pm 3150
20803-1	Midnight Serenade -1, 2, 3	Pm 3150

Poss. Bill Davies or Miller Wikel, f; unknown, bj-1; Frank Welling, sg-2/lv; prob. John McGhee, g/v-3.

Chicago, IL　　　　　　　　　　　　　　　　　　　　　　　　　　　　　　　　c. August/September 1928

20804-2	Lead Me Higher Up The Mountain -2, 3	Pm 3119, Bwy 8205
20805-2	The Last Mile -2, 3	Pm 3119, Bwy 8205
20807-1	Hatfield-McCoy Feud -1	Pm 3122

Paramount 3119 as by **Frank Welling & Red Brush Rowdies**. Broadway 8205 as by **Frank Wilkins**. There may be only one guitar on matrix 20807, which may be played by either Welling or McGhee. Matrices 20795, 20800 are by Frank Welling; others are untraced.

RED BRUSH SINGERS

Vocal duet or trio; acc. unknown, f; unknown, bj.

Chicago, IL　　　　　　　　　　　　　　　　　　　　　　　　　　　　　　　　c. March 1928

20462-2	Beyond The Starry Plane	Pm 3143, Bwy 8213

Rev. Paramount 3143, Broadway 8213 by Lookout Mountain Revelers.
This group may be the same as, or associated with, the Fruit Jar Guzzlers.

THE RED FOX CHASERS

Paul Miles & The Red Fox Chasers-1/Cranford, Thompson & Miles-2/Miles, Cranford & Thompson-3/Cranford & Thompson-4: Guy Brooks, f; Bob Cranford, h/v-5; Paul Miles, bj/v-6; A.P. Thompson, g/v-7.

Richmond, IN　　　　　　　　　　　　　　　　　　　　　　　　　　　　　　　Wednesday, April 4, 1928

13638	Turkey In The Straw -1	Ge 6516, 0112, Ch 15522, 33046, Spt 9163
13639	The Arkansas Traveler -1	Ge 6516, Spt 9163
13640	Wreck On The Mountain Road -5, 7	Ch 15484, Cq 7256
13641-B	Two False Lovers -2, 5, 6, 7	Ge 6497, Ch 15484
13642	We Shall Meet On That Beautiful Shore -3, 5, 6, 7	Ge 6449
13643-A	Looking To My Prayer -4, 5, 7	Ge 6449
13644	Under The Double Eagle -1	Ge 6461
13645	Did You Ever See The Devil, Uncle Joe? -1	Ge 6461, Ch 15522

Gennett 0112 as by **Old Time Dance Orchestra**. Champion 15484 as by **The Virginia Possum Tamers**, 15522 as by **The Virginia Possum Tamers**. Supertone 9163 as by **The Boone County Entertainers**. Conqueror 7256 as by **Thomas & Jordan**.
Parts of matrices 13645, 13639, and 13638 were used (in that order) to create matrix 15089 by the Smoky Mountain Boys.
Revs: Gennett 6497 by Clark & Edans (see Orla Clark); Champion 33046 by Doc Roberts.

Paul Miles & The Red Fox Chasers-1/Thompson, Cranford & Miles-2/Cranford & Thompson-3: Guy Brooks, f/v-4; Bob Cranford, h/v-5; Paul Miles, bj/v-6; A.P. Thompson, g/v-7.

Richmond, IN　　　　　　　　　　　　　　　　　　　　　　　　　　　　　　　Thursday, June 28, 1928

13936-C	Mountain Sweetheart -3, 5, 7	Ge 6636, Ch 15609, Spt 9322
13937-B	Something Wrong With My Gal -3, 5, 7	Ge 6672, Ch 15672, Spt 9182
13938	Twinkle Little Star -1	Ge 6568
13939	Honeysuckle Time -3, 5, 7	Ge 6672, Spt 9181
13940-B	The Blind Man And His Child -2, 5, 6, 7	Ge 6602, Ch 15609, Spt 9181
13941-B	Tell Mother I'll Meet Her -2, 5, 6, 7	Ge 6602, Ch 15566, MW 4963
13942	Mississippi Sawyer -1	Ge 6568
13943	When The Redeemed Are Gathering In -4, 5, 6, 7	Ge rejected

Champion 15566, 15609, 15672, Montgomery Ward 4963 as by **The Virginia Possum Tamers**. Supertone 9181, 9182 as by **The Boone County Entertainers**, 9322 as by **The North Carolina Fox Chasers**.

Paul Miles & The Red Fox Chasers-1/Cranford & Thompson-2: Guy Brooks, f/v-3; Bob Cranford, h/v; Paul Miles, bj/v-4; A.P. Thompson, g/v.

Richmond, IN　　　　　　　　　　　　　　　　　　　　　　　　　　　　　　　Friday, June 29, 1928

13944-B	Stolen Love -2	Ge 6636, Ch 15672, Cq 7256
13945	May I Sleep In Your Barn Tonight, Mister -1	Ge 6547, Spt 9182
13946	Weeping Willow Tree -1	Ge 6547, Ch 15566, Spt 9322
13947	Hallelujah We Shall Rise -3, 4	Ge unissued

Champion 15566, 15672 as by **The Virginia Possum Tamers**. Supertone 9182 as by **The Boone County Entertainers**, 9322 as by **The North Carolina Fox Chasers**. Conqueror 7256 as by **Thomas & Jordan**.

Paul Miles & The Red Fox Chasers: Guy Brooks, f/sp; Bob Cranford, h/sp; Paul Miles, bj/sp; A.P. Thompson, g/sp.
    Richmond, IN   Wednesday, June 12, 1929

15192-A	The Red Fox Chasers Makin' Licker Part I	Ge 6886, Ch 15769, Spt 9456
15193	The Red Fox Chasers Makin' Licker Part II	Ge 6886, Ch 15769, Spt 9456
15194-A	The Red Fox Chasers Makin' Licker Part 3	Ge 6912, Ch 15809
15195-A	The Red Fox Chasers Makin' Licker Part 4	Ge 6912, Ch 15809

Champion 15769, 15809 as by **The Virginia Possum Tamers**. Supertone 9456 as by **The Stone Mountain Boys**. The above items are titled *The Virginia Possum Tamers Makin' Licker Part I/II/III/IV* on Champion 15769 and 15809. Matrices 15192/93 are titled *Makin' Likker In North Carolina Part I/II* on Supertone 9456.

Cranford & Thompson-1/Bob Cranford-2/Miles & Thompson-3/Thompson & Miles-4/Paul Miles-5: Guy Brooks, f; Bob Cranford, h/v-6; Paul Miles, bj/v-7; A.P. Thompson, g/v-8.
    Richmond, IN   Thursday, June 13, 1929

15199-A	Naomi Wise -1, 6, 8	Ge 6945
15200	What Is Home Without Babies -1, 6, 8	Ge 6901, Ch 15925, Spt 9492
15201	Back To The Hills Of Carolina -8	Ge rejected
15202-A	Little Sweetheart Pal Of Mine -1, 6, 8	Ge 6901, Ch 15790, 45079, Spt 9535
15203	I Wonder If 'Twas Very Wrong -6, 8	Ge rejected
15204	Virginia Bootleggers -5, 7	Ge 6930, Ch 15790, 45079, Spt 9492
15205	Devilish Mary -2, 6	Ge 6945
15206	The Girl I Loved In Sunny Tennessee -4, 7, 8	Ge 6930, Spt 9497
15207-B	Put My Little Shoes Away -3, 7, 8	Ge 6914, Ch 15925, Spt 9535, MW 4963
15208	Bring Me A Leaf From The Sea -1, 6, 8	Ge 6959
15209-A	How I Love My Mabel -1, 6, 8	Ge 6959
15210-A	Budded Roses -4, 7, 8	Ge 6914, Spt 9497

Champion 15790, 15925, 45097, Montgomery Ward 4963 as by **Virginia Possum Tamers**. Supertone 9492 as by **Boone County Entertainers**, 9497 as by **Morton & Crane**, 9535 as by **Crawford & Milton** (matrix 15202)/**Morton & Crane** (matrix 15207).

Cranford & Thompson, v duet; acc. Bob Cranford, h; unknown, md-1; A.P. Thompson, g.
    Richmond, IN   Monday, January 26, 1931

17479	Good Bye Little Bonnie	Ch S-16676, 45061, Spr 2594
17480-A	Two Babes In The Woods	Ch S-16768
17481-A	Katy Cline -1	Ch S-16676, 45061, Spr 2594
17482-A	The Murder Of The Lawson Family	Ch 16261
17483	Jim And Me	Ch S-16768
17484-A	Lula Wall	Ch 16243
17485,-A	Henry Clay Beattie	Ge unissued

Superior 2594 as by **Cal Turner & Bud Parkins**.
    Richmond, IN   Tuesday, January 27, 1931

17486	Otto Wood	Ch 16261
17487,-A	The Life Of A Tramp	Ge rejected
17489	Pretty Polly	Ch 16490, 45097, Spr 2625, MeC 45097
17490	Sweet Fern	Ch 16490, 45097, Spr 2625, MeC 45097
17491	That Sweetie Of Mine	Ch 16243

Superior 2625 as by **Turner & Parkins**. Matrix 17488 is unrelated.

Paul Miles recorded for the Library of Congress Archive of American Folk-Song in 1940.

[THE] RED HEADED BRIER HOPPER

This artist's real name is Lonnie Edward Anderson.

Red Headed Brier Hopper, v; acc. own g.
    Richmond, IN   Wednesday, February 22, 1933

19038	Gooseberry Pie	Ch S-16578
19039	Don't Be Angry With Me Darling	Ch S-16578

The Red Headed Brier Hopper, v; or **Brier Hopper Bros.-1**: Lonnie Anderson, unknown, v duet; acc. Lonnie Anderson, g.
    Richmond, IN   Friday, July 21, 1933

19275-C	I'm Sitting Sad And Lonely -1	Ch S-16692, 45032, De 5385
19276-C	Bring Back My Blue Eyed Boy -1	Ch S-16692, 45032, De 5385
19277	Lorena -1	Ch S-16708, 45066
19278	The Fatal Derby Day	Ch 16678, 45045
19279	Three Wishes	Ch S-16668

19280	Dear Old Mother	Ch 16678, 45045
19281	That Little Old Shirt That Mother Made For Me	Ch S-16668
19282	The Pine Tree On The Hill	Ch 16648, 45024, DeAu X1239
19283	Is There No Chance For Me Tonight Love	Ch S-16708, 45066
19284	Answer To 99 Years	Ch 16648, 45024, DeAu X1239

Champion 45024, 45032, 45045, 45066, Decca X1239 as by **Le Roy Anderson (The Red Headed Brier Hopper)**.

The Red Headed Brier Hopper, v; or **Red & Son Raymond**-1: Lonnie Anderson, Raymond Anderson, v duet; acc. Lonnie Anderson, g.

Richmond, IN   Friday, August 24, 1934

19675	End Of Twenty One Years	Ch 16811, 45055
19676	The Wrong Man And The Wrong Woman	Ch S-16797, 45085
19677	A Mother's Wayward Son	Ch 16811, 45055
19678	Mother's Beautiful Hands -1	Ch S-16797, 45085
19679	Little Bessie	Ch S-16820, 45059
19680	Gambling On The Sabbath	Ch S-16820, 45059

Champion 45055, 45059, 45085 as by **Le Roy Anderson (The Red Headed Brier Hopper)**, except matrix 19678 on Champion 45085 as by **Red & Son Raymond**.

THE RED HEADED FIDDLER[S]

The Red Headed Fiddlers (A.L. Steeley & J.W. Graham): A.L. "Red" Steeley, f; J. Warner "Red" Graham, bj.

Dallas, TX   Thursday, October 18, 1928

| DAL-688- | Never Alone Waltz | Br 285, 52084, Me M18029 |
| DAL-689- | Texas Quickstep | Br 285, 52084, Me M18029 |

Brunswick 52084, Melotone M18029 as by **Les Deux Gaspesiens**.
Matrix DAL-688 is titled *La Valse D'Un Soir*, and DAL-689 *Le Reel De St. Urbain*, on those issues.

"Red" Steeley, f; —— Wisrock, md; "Red" Graham, g; Albert Wisrock, g.

Dallas, TX   Sunday, October 27, 1929

DAL-489-A	Texas Waltz	Br 388
DAL-490-A	Rag-Time Annie	Br 388
DAL-491-	St. Jobe's Waltz	Br 460
DAL-492-	Fatal Wedding	Br 460

'Red' Steeley, f; 'Red' Graham, bj.

Dallas, TX   Sunday, October 27, 1929

| DAL-493- | Cheat 'Em | Br 470 |
| DAL-494- | Far In The Mountain | Br 470 |

The Red Headed Fiddler: "Red" Steeley, f; Mildred Steeley, g.

Dallas, TX   Saturday, November 29, 1930

DAL-6781-	Paddy On The Hand Car	Br 526
DAL-6782-	Wagoner's Hornpipe	Br unissued
DAL-6783-	The Steeley Rag	Br 526
DAL-6784-	Johnson Grass Rag	Br unissued

RED MOUNTAIN TRIO

See Jimmy Yates Groups.

RED RIVER COON HUNTERS

Pseudonym on Superior for Fred Pendleton & the West Virginia Melody Boys.

RED RIVER DAVE (DAVE McENERY)

Red River Dave, v; acc. Vaughn Horton, esg; own g; Roy Horton, sb.

New York, NY   Thursday, January 18, 1940

67071-A	When They Changed My Name To A Number	De 5806
67072-A	Down Del Rio Way	De 5799
67073-A	Where Is My Mama	De 5806
67074-A	When You're A Long Long Way From Home	De 5799

New York, NY   Wednesday, May 8, 1940

67690-A	When It's Springtime In The Rockies	De 5853, Coral 64013
67691-A	Things That Might Have Been	De 5842, DeAu X1935
67692-A	Stars Over Laredo	De 5842, DeAu X1935, Coral 64013
67693-A	My Red River Valley Home	De 5853

New York, NY   Monday, June 24, 1940

67881-A,-B	Goodbye, Little Darlin', Goodbye	De 5863
67882-A	Would You Care	De 5863
67883-A	Sierra Sue	De 5864, MeC 45374
67884-A	Her Name Was Rosita	De 5864, MeC 45374

Red River Dave, v/wh-1; acc. own g.
  New York, NY   Monday, July 22, 1940

67942-A	Daddy And Home	De 5869, MeC 45379
67943-A	My Old Pal -1	De 5869, MeC 45379

Red River Dave recorded after 1942.

RED & SON RAYMOND

See The Red Headed Brier Hopper.

RED'S DIXIE RAMBLERS

Varsity 5092, with this artist credit, couples one item by Red Perkins & His Dixie Ramblers (for whom see JR) and one (I Want My Rib) by Cobb & Underwood (see E.E. Hack String Band).

BLIND ALFRED REED

Blind Alfred Reed, v; acc. own f; poss. Arthur Wyrick, g-1.
  Bristol, TN   Thursday, July 28, 1927

39725-1	The Wreck Of The Virginian	Vi unissued: *RCA LPV532, RCA(E) RD7870* (LPs)
39725-2	The Wreck Of The Virginian	Vi 20836
39726-1	I Mean To Live For Jesus -1	Vi 20939
39727-1	You Must Unload -1	Vi 20939
39728-1	Walking In The Way With Jesus -1	Vi unissued: *CMF-011-L* (LP); *011-D* (CD)
39728-2	Walking In The Way With Jesus -1	Vi 20836

Acc. own f; Arville Reed, g.
  Camden, NJ   Monday, December 19, 1927

40790-2	Explosion In The Fairmount Mines	Vi 21191
40791-2	Fate Of Chris Liveley And Wife	Vi 21533
40792-2	Why Do You Bob Your Hair, Girls	Vi 21360
40793-2	Always Lift Him Up And Never Knock Him Down	Vi 21360, BB B-5882
40794-2	The Prayer Of The Drunkard's Little Girl	Vi 21191

Rev. Victor 21533 by West Virginia Night Owls.

Acc. own f; Arville Reed, g/v-1.
  New York, NY   Tuesday, December 3, 1929

57571-2	Woman's Been After Man Ever Since	Vi V-40196
57572-2	Why Don't You Bob Your Hair Girls – No. 2	Vi V-40196
57573-2	There'll Be No Distinction There -1	Vi 23550, BB B-5882
57574-2	We've Got To Have 'Em, That's All -1	Vi V-40290
57575-1	Beware -1	Vi 23550
57576-1,-2	The Railroader -1	Vi unissued

Victor 23550 as by **Blind Alfred & Orville Reed**.
  New York, NY   Wednesday, December 4, 1929

57742-2	The Old-Fashioned Cottage -1	Vi 23650
57743-1	How Can A Poor Man Stand Such Times And Live	Vi V-40236
57744-1	Black And Blue Blues	Vi V-40290
57745-1,-2	Bonnie Little Girl -1	Vi unissued
57746-1	You'll Miss Me -1	Vi 23650
57747-2	Money Cravin' Folks	Vi V-40236

Victor 23650 as by **Blind Alfred & Orville Reed**.

BILL & BELLE REED

Bill Reed, Belle Reed, v duet; or Bill Reed, v-1; acc. prob. one of them, g.
  Johnson City, TN   Wednesday, October 17, 1928

147210-2	You Shall Be Free	Co 15336-D
147211-2	Old Lady And The Devil -1	Co 15336-D

See also The Reed Children, The Reed Family.

HARRY REED & WM. F. WYNN

One of them, h; the other, g.
  Richmond, IN   Thursday, October 11, 1928

14326	Chicken Reel	Ge rejected

Richmond, IN   Saturday, October 13, 1928
14338   Norwegian Waltz And Chicken Reel   Ge rejected

JOE REED FAMILY

Vocal group; acc. unknown, md; unknown, g.
Chicago, IL   c. June 1928
20619-2   I Will Tell A Wondrous Story   Pm 3117, Bwy 8221
20623-1   Little David Play On Your Harp   Pm 3109, Bwy 8106
20624-1   Jesus Is Getting Us Ready   Bwy 8106
20624-2   Jesus Is Getting Us Ready   Pm 3109
20626-2   Two Little Children   Pm 3117, Bwy 8221

Broadway 8106 as by **Joe Ramer Family**, 8221 as by **Ramer Family**.
Intervening matrices are untraced.

ORVILLE REED

This artist's correct name is Arville Reed.

Orville Reed, v; acc. own g.
Camden, NJ   Monday, December 19, 1927
40795-2   The Telephone Girl   Vi 21190

Rev. Victor 21190 by West Virginia Night Owls.
See also Blind Alfred Reed, West Virginia Night Owls.

THE REED CHILDREN

Vocal group; acc. unknown, g.
Johnson City, TN   Wednesday, October 17, 1928
147212-2   I'll Be All Smiles Tonight   Co 15525-D
147213-2   I Once Did Have A Sweetheart   Co 15525-D

THE REED FAMILY

No details.
Johnson City, TN   Wednesday, October 17, 1928
147214-   A Few More Years   Co unissued
147215-   Bright And Golden Lights   Co unissued

REED QUARTETTE

Pseudonym on Broadway for the Riley Quartette.

L.K. REEDER

L.K. Reeder, v; acc. unknown, h; prob. own g.
St. Louis, MO   c. October 26, 1925
9415-A   Falling Leaf   OK 45026
9416-A   Will You Love Me When I'm Old?   OK 45026

JACK REEDY

This artist's given name is Weldon Reedy.

Jack Reedy & His Walker Mountain String Band: Fred Roe, f/sp-1; Frank Wilson, sg-1/sp-1; Jack Reedy, bj/sp-1; Henry Roe, g/sp-1; Walter "Sparkplug" Hughes, g/sp-1; unidentified, v-2; band v-2.
Ashland, KY   mid-February 1928
AL-293   Chinese Breakdown -1   Br 221, PanAu P11995
AL-296   Ground Hog -2   Br 221, PanAu P11995

Panachord P11995 as by **The Kentucky Ramblers**.
Intervening matrices are untraced but probably by this group.

Jack Reedy & His River Boys: no details, except Jack Reedy, sp; Walter "Sparkplug" Hughes, sp.
Knoxville, TN   Monday, April 7, 1930
K-8102-   Seven Mile Ford Rag   Br/Vo rejected
K-8103-   Fox Chase Stomp   Br/Vo rejected

Jack Reedy also recorded with The Hill Billies and Smyth County Ramblers.

JIMMY REESE

Pseudonym on Supertone for Howard Keesee.

PHIL REEVE & ERNEST MOODY

Phil Reeve-Ernest Moody, v duet; acc. Phil Reeve, g; Ernest Moody, g-1/u-2; one of them, y.
    Atlanta, GA   Thursday, February 17, 1927

37908-2	Down Where The Watermelon Grows -2	Vi 20540
37909-1,-2,-3	Rock All Our Babies To Sleep -1	Vi unissued

Rev. Victor 20540 by Ernest Stoneman & Kahle Brewer.

Acc. Phil Reeve, g; Ernest Moody, g; Clyde Watts, g-1; Phil Reeve or Ernest Moody, y-2.
    Charlotte, NC   Wednesday, August 10, 1927

37909-5	Rock All Our Babies To Sleep -2	Vi 20929
39788-1,-2	Never Alone -1	Vi unissued
39789-2	Bees Are Humming Around The Flowers -2	Vi 20929
39790-2	Sweet Evelina -2	Vi 21188

Victor 21188 as by **Reeve & Moody**. Rev. Victor 21188 by Frank & James McCravy.

Acc. Phil Reeve, g/y; Ernest Moody, u.
    Atlanta, GA   Thursday, February 23, 1928

41946-1,-2	I Want You Every Day	Vi unissued
41947-1,-2	Miss Lucy Long	Vi unissued

Charles Brothers (Philip & Ernest), v duet; acc. unknown, f; unknown, g.
    Chicago, IL   c. June 1928

20690-2	Oh How I Love Jesus	Pm 3120, Bwy 8222
20693-1	Looking This Way	Pm 3114, Bwy 8209

Broadway 8209 as by **Alabama Four**, 8222 as by **Phillips Brothers**.
Intervening matrices are untraced.
Rev. all issues by the North Georgia Quartette.

Reeve and Moody may have participated in recordings made at the last session above by the North Georgia Quartette (or Four), and probably were involved in later Paramount recordings by the Moody Bible Sacred Harp Singers and North Georgia Four. They were also members of the Georgia Yellow Hammers and several associated groups.

ARTHUR REEVES

Pseudonym on Grand Pree for Vernon Dalhart.

B.L. REEVES

B.L. Reeves, v; acc. unknown, f-1; unknown, g-1; poss. own g.
    Richmond, IN   Thursday, February 5, 1929

14774	Why Have You Left Me Lonely	Ge rejected
14775	Midnight On The Stormy Deep -1	Ge rejected

GOEBEL REEVES

This artist's full name is Goebel Leon Reeves.

Goebel Reeves, v/y-1; acc. own g.
    Dallas, TX   Tuesday, June 25, 1929

402714-B	The Tramp's Mother -1	OK 45381
402715-B	I Learned About Women From Her	OK 45381
402716-A	The Drifter – Part 1 -1	OK 45365
402717-B	The Drifter – Part 2 -1	OK 45365

Goebel Reeves (The Texas Drifter), v/y; acc. own g.
    New York, NY   Friday, January 3, 1930

403579-B	When The Clock Struck Seventeen	OK 45408
403580-B	Blue Undertaker's Blues	OK 45408
403581-A	Blue Undertaker's Blues – Part 2	OK 45427
403582-A	Fortunes Galore	OK 45449

    New York, NY   Monday, January 6, 1930

403588-A	My Mountain Gal	OK 45427, Ve 2355-V, Cl 5289-C
403589-B	A Song Of The Sea	OK 45491
403590-B	In The Land Of The Never Was	OK 45491
403591-	Blue Undertaker's Blues – Part 3	OK unissued
403592-	Blue Undertaker's Blues – Part 4	OK unissued
403593-A	The Texas Drifter's Warning	OK 45449

Velvet Tone 2355-V, Clarion 5289-C as by **Bert Knowles**. Those issues use the transfer matrix 100510.
Revs: Velvet Tone 2355-V, Clarion 5289-C by Carson Robison.

George Riley (The Yodeling Rustler), v/y-1; acc. own g.
New York, NY   Monday, July 21, 1930

9885-2	At The End Of The Hobo's Trail -1	Ba 32131, Je 20051, Or 8051, Pe 12694, Re 10309, Ro 5051, Cq 7706, CrC 91114, Stg 291114, Roy 391114
9886-1	The Last Letter -1	Ba 32099, Je 20037, Or 8037, Pe 12669, Re 10305, Ro 5037, Cq 7742
9887-2	The Grave By The Whispering Pine -1	Ba 32098, Je 20032, Or 8032, Pe 165, 12668, Re 10304, Ro 5032, Cq 7707, Bwy 4045, MeC/Stg/Roy 93090
9888-1,-2	The Tramp's Mother -1	Ba 0871, Ca 0471, Do 4674, Je 20023, Or 8023, Pe 12653, Re 10177, Ro 5023, Bwy 4098
9889-	Mother-In-Law Blues	ARC unissued
9890-	I Learned About Women From Her	ARC unissued
9891-1,-2	The Texas Drifter's Warning -1	Ba 0871, Ca 0471, Do 4674, Je 20023, Or 8023, Pe 12653, Re 10177, Ro 5023, Bwy 4045
9892-1	My Mississippi Home -1	Ba 32131, Je 20051, Or 8051, Pe 12694, Re 10309, Ro 5051, Cq 7706, CrC 91114, Stg 291114, Roy 391114
9893-2	The Cowboy's Dream	Ba 32099, Je 20037, Or 8037, Pe 12669, Re 10305, Ro 5037, Cq 7742, Bwy 4098, CrC 81450, DoC 181450, Stg 281450, Roy 381450
9894-3	The Railroad Bum	Ba 32098, Je 20032, Or 8032, Pe 165, 12668, Re 10304, Ro 5032, Cq 7707

The above session was logged as by **The Yodeling Rustler**, except matrices 9886 and 9893 as by **George Riley, The Yodeling Rustler**, but all or most of the primary ARC issues were as shown. Conqueror 7742 as by **George Riley (The Yodeling Cowboy)**; other Conquerors probably as by **Goebel Reeves (The Yodeling Rustler)**. Broadways as by **The Broadway Rustler**. Crown 81450, Domino 181450, Sterling 281450, Royale 381450 as by **The Yodeling Rustler**.
Revs: Crown 81450, Domino 181450, Sterling 281450, Royale 381450 by Carson Robison & Frank Luther; Melotone/Sterling/Royale 93090 by Buddy Spencer Trio (see Frank Luther).

Goebel Reeves, v/y; acc. own g.
New York, NY   c. September 24, 1930

GEX-2781	At The End Of The Hobo's Trail	Ge rejected

The Texas Drifter (Goebel Reeves), v/y/sp-1; acc. own g.
New York, NY   Wednesday, October 15, 1930

E-34013-A	The Drifter – Part 1	Me M12016, Po P9018, Vo 5484, Au A22016, Pan 25229
E-34014-A	The Drifter – Part 2	Me M12016, Po P9018, Vo 5484, Au A22016, Pan 25229
E-34015-A	At The End Of The Hobo's Trail -1	Me M12047, Po P9065, Au A22031, Pan 25198, PanAu P12047
E-34016-	The Oklahoma Kid -1	Me M12047, Po P9065, Au A22031, Min M-14003, Pan 25198, PanAu P12047

Aurora A22016, A22031 as by **Louis Acker**. Panachord 25198, 25229, P12047, Minerva M-14003 as by **The Texas Drifter**. Rev. Minerva M-14003 by Gene Autry.

Goebel Reeves, v/y; acc. own g.
New York, NY   c. October 16, 1930

GEX-2784-B	At The End Of The Hobo's Trail	Ch 16139
GEX-2785-A	The Hobo's Grave	Ch 16139
GEX-2786	The Drifter – Part 1	Ch 16234
GEX-2787,-A	The Drifter – Part 2	Ge rejected

Champion 16139 as by **The Texas Drifter (Goebel Reeves)**.

New York, NY   c. October 22, 1930

GEX-2792	Station H.O.B.O.	Ch 16189
GEX-2793,-A	The Hobo's Last Letter	Ge rejected

Champion 16189 as by **The Texas Drifter (Goebel Reeves)**.

New York, NY   c. November 5, 1930

GEX-2805,-A	The Land Of The Never Was	Ge rejected
GEX-2806-A	I Learned About Women From Her	Ch 16234, 45194, MeC 45194

Matrix GEX-2806 was logged as *The Loves Of A Drifter*.

New York, NY   c. November 17, 1930

   GEX-2818-A   The Hobo's Last Letter   Ch 16189, 45194, MeC 45194

Champion 16189 as by **The Texas Drifter (Goebel Reeves)**.

The Texas Drifter, v/y-1/sp-2; acc. own g.

   Los Angeles, CA   Tuesday, April 14, 1931

Matrix	Title	Issues
LA-993-A	Hobo's Last Letter -1	Br 539
LA-994-A	Station H.O.B.O. -2	Br 539, Pan 25313
LA-995-	Land Of The Never Was	Me M12186, Po P9066
LA-996-A	Railroad Boomer -1	Me M12242, Pan 25105, PanAu P12242,
LA-996-B	Railroad Boomer -1	MeC M12242
LA-997-B,-A	The Tramp's Mother	Me M12242, Pan 25108, PanAu P12242,
LA-998-A	Cowboy's Dream	Me M12214, Po P9067
LA-999-A	Mother-In-Law Blues	Me M12232, Pan 25108
LA-1025- -	Fortunes Galore -1	Me M12232, Pan 25105
LA-1026-A	Bright Sherman Valley	Me M12186, Po P9066
LA-1027-A	Little Joe, The Wrangler	Me M12214, Po P9067, Pan 25313

Brunswick 539 as by **Goebel Reeves**.
At least one copy exists of Canadian Melotone 12242 on which matrix ATL-996 (shown in wax as ALT-996) by The Four Buzz Saws (see Jimmy Yates Groups) is pressed in error for matrix LA-996.
Matrix LA-994 is titled *H.O.B.O. Calling* on Panachord 25313. Intervening matrices are by other artists on other dates.

The Texas Drifter (Goebel Reeves), v/y; acc. own g.

   Chicago, IL   Friday, October 30, 1931

Matrix	Title	Issues
C-8257-	I'm A Lonesome Cowboy	Me M12302, MeC/Stg/Roy 91727
C-8258-	The Cowboy's Secret	Me M12302
C-8259-A	John Law And The Hobo	Me M12290, MeC M-913, Po P9092, MeC/Stg/Roy 91315, Pan 25250
C-8260-A,-B	The Prisoner's Song	Me M12290, MeC M-913, Po P9092, MeC/Stg/Roy 91315, Pan 25250

Matrix C-8260-A is used on Panachord 25250, C-8260-B on Royale 91315; it is uncertain which takes are used on other issues.
Melotone/Sterling/Royale 91315, Panachord 25250 as by **The Texas Drifter**. Melotone/Sterling/Royale 91717 as by **Jim Boa (The Texas Drifter)**.
Matrix C-8260 is titled *The Texas Drifter's Prison Song* on Melotone M-913, Melotone/Sterling/Royale 91315.
Rev. Melotone/Sterling/Royale 91717 by George Goebel.

Goebel Reeves, The Texas Drifter, v/y-1; acc. own g.

   San Francisco, CA   Monday, August 13, 1934

Matrix	Title	Issues
5-B	The Cowboy's Prayer -	Vo 02828, RZAu G22363
6-A	Hobo's Lullaby -	Vo 02828, RZAu G22363
8-A	The Wandering Boy -1	ARC 35-09-11, Cq 8565, MeC/Stg/Roy 92092, Min M-14031
9-B	The Hobo And The Cop -1	Vo 02806, RZAu G22336
11-A	Where The Mississippi Washes	Ba 33402, Me M13369, Or 8454, Pe 13132, Ro 5454, Cq 8517
12-	The Cowboy's Lullaby	Vo 02806, RZAu G22336
13-A	It's True I'm Just A Convict	ARC 35-09-11, Cq 8565, MeC/Stg/Roy 92092, Min M-14032
14-	I'm Just A Lonesome Cowboy	ARC unissued

Regal-Zonophone G22336, G22363 as by **Goebel Reeves**.
Intervening matrices were not used.
Revs: Minerva M-14031 by Lester McFarland & Robert A. Gardner, M-14032 by Doc Roberts.

The Texas Drifter, v/y/sp-1; acc. own g.

   Chicago, IL   Friday, August 31, 1934

Matrix	Title	Issues
C-9363-A	Cowboy's Lullabye	De 5021, Pan 25663
C-9364-A	Hobo's Lullaby	Ch 45181, MeC 45181, DeE F5264, BrSA SA830
C-9365-A	The Drifter's Buddy (A True Story) -1	Ch 45181, MeC 45181, Min M-14040, Pan 25848, DeAu X1226
C-9366-A	The Cowboy's Prayer	Pan 25848, DeAu X1226
C-9367-A	Happy Days (I'll Never Leave Old Dixieland Again)	DeE F5264, BrSA SA830
C-9368-A	The Wayward Son	Pan 25768
C-9369-A	Reckless Tex	De 5020, Pan 25768
C-9370-A	The Soldier's Return	Pan 25991, DeIr W5125
C-9371-A	Miss Jackson Tennessee	Pan 25991, DeIr W5125
C-9372-A	My Mountain Girl	Pan 26018, DeIr W5127
C-9373-A	Cold And Hungry	Pan 26018, DeIr W5127

C-9374-A	Meet Me At The Crossroads, Pal	De 5021, Pan 26042, RexIr R5034
C-9375-A	The Yodelin' Teacher -1	De 5020, Pan 25663

Decca 5020, 5021, Champion 45181 as by **The Texas Drifter (Goebel Reeves)**.
Matrix C-9363 is titled *Cowboy's Lullaby*, and matrix C-9375 is titled *The Yodellin' Teacher*, on Panachord 25663.
Matrix C-9364 is titled *Hobo's Holiday* on Brunswick SA830. Matrix C-9365 is titled *The Drifter's Prayer* on an unidentified issue.
Rev. Minerva M-14040 by Dwight Butcher.

Goebel Reeves "The Texas Drifter", v/y/sp-1; acc. own g.
    Chicago, IL   Wednesday, November 14, 1934

C-845-1	The Big Rock Candy Mountain -1	Ba 33309, Me M13276, Or 8415, Pe 13099, Ro 5415, Cq 8470
C-846-1	The Soldier's Return	ARC unissued
C-847-1	I Have My Dog	ARC unissued
C-848-1	Stars With Stripes	ARC unissued
C-849-1	Reckless Tex From Texas	Ba 33402, Me M13369, Or 8454, Pe 13132, Ro 5454, Cq 8443, 8517
C-850-1	The Bar None Ranch	Cq 8443
C-851-1	The Hobo's Prayer	Cq 8442
C-852-1	Cold And Hungry	Cq 8442

    Chicago, IL   Thursday, November 15, 1934

C-854-1	The Hobo's Sweetheart	ARC unissued
C-855-1	The Convict's Soul	ARC unissued
C-856-5	The Cowboy's Dizzy Sweetheart	Ba 33309, Me M13276, Or 8415, Pe 13099, Ro 5415, Cq 8470
C-857-1	The Luckiest Man In Love	ARC unissued

The Texas Drifter, v/y; acc. own g.
    Chicago, IL   Monday, January 14, 1935

C-9648-A	The Kidnapped Baby	Pan 26042, RexIr R5034

Goebel Reeves also recorded with the Canova Family and made many recordings in the mid-1930s for the MacGregor transcription company.

JOE REEVES

Pseudonym on Conqueror for Miller Wikel, or on later pressings of Conqueror 7765 for James Roberts.

REEVES FAMILY

Vocal duet; acc. poss. one of them, md; poss. the other, g.
    Birmingham, AL   Monday, April 5, 1937

B-85-	We Got A Home In The Heavenly Sky	ARC unissued
B-86-	Shake Hands With Mother Again	ARC unissued

REGAL HILL-BILLY SINGERS

Pseudonym on Australian Regal and Regal-Zonophone for Merritt Smith & Leo Boswell (G21556) or McMichen's Melody Men (G21593).

THE REGAL RASCALS

Pseudonym used on English Regal, and Australian Regal and Regal-Zonophone, as follows:
MR37 Billy Jones & Ernest Hare (popular) (147727) / Vernon Dalhart (149474)
MR119 Tom Darby & Jimmie Tarlton (149323) / Frank Luther & Carson Robison (150023)
MR243 Joe & Zeb Gaunt (Arthur Fields & Fred Hall) (149750) / Vernon Dalhart (150510).
G21044 Joe & Zeb Gaunt (Arthur Fields & Fred Hall) (149750)

WALTER REGAN

Pseudonym on Superior for Frank Welling (see John McGhee & Frank Welling).

SAM REID

See Reid Bros. Band From Greene Mountain.

REID BROS. BAND FROM GREENE MOUNTAIN

Unknown, f; prob. Sam Reid, bj; unknown, g; unknown, v-1.
    Winston-Salem, NC   Friday, September 23, 1927

81391-	Oh Mary, Don't You Weep	OK unissued
81392-	Old Time Religion	OK unissued
81393-	John Brown	OK unissued
81394-	Penitentiary Blues -1	OK unissued

Sam Reid, v; acc. own bj.
   Winston-Salem, NC   Friday, September 23, 1927

81395-	Applejack	OK unissued
81396-	Shake Little Lula	OK unissued

DICK REINHART

Dick Reinhart, v; acc. own g.
   Dallas, TX   Sunday, October 27, 1929

DAL-483-	Rambling Lover	Br 386
DAL-484-B	Always Marry Your Lover	Br 386, 80090

Matrix DAL-484 is titled *The Girl I Left Behind* on Brunswick 80090.
Rev. Brunswick 80090 by Dock Boggs.

Dick Reinhart & His Universal Cowboys: Dick Reinhart, v; acc. Darrell Kirkpatrick, ac/emd-1; Andrew Schroeder, esg; Landon Beaver, p; Elmer Scarborough, tbj/tg; own or Buster Ferguson, g; Sleepy Johnson, sb.
   Saginaw, TX   Sunday, April 21, 1940

DAL-1011-1	I'm In The Doghouse Again	OK 05666
DAL-1012-1	Baby Be On Your Way	OK 05666
DAL-1013-1	Little Brown Eyed Girl	OK 05742, Cq 9712
DAL-1014-2	Ruck Tuckin' Baby -1	Vo/OK 05611, Co 37747, 20324
DAL-1015-1,-2	I'm Satisfied In Loving You -1	Vo/OK unissued
DAL-1016-2	Just A Honky Tonk Gal -1	Vo/OK 05548, Cq 9716
DAL-1017-1,-2	Hash House Hattie	Vo/OK unissued
DAL-1018-2	It Won't Do You No Good -1	Vo/OK 05548, Cq 9716
DAL-1019-2	I Trusted You Once Too Often -1	Vo/OK 05611, Co 37747, 20324
DAL-1020-1	Don't Ever Say Adieu	OK 05742, Cq 9712

Acc. Carl Cotner, f; Frank Marvin, esg; Paul Sells, p; Johnny Bond, g; Jimmy Wakely, g; own sb; unidentified, v-1.
   Los Angeles, CA   Wednesday, August 28, 1940

LA-2342-A	Hey Toots	OK 05917, Cq 9714
LA-2343-A	You're The Red Red Rose Of My Heart	Cq 9713
LA-2344-A	No One To Kiss Me Goodnight	Cq 9713
LA-2345-A	Won't You Remember	OK 06029, Cq 9860
LA-2346-A	I Trusted You Once Too Often	OK 05981, Cq 9859
LA-2347-A	My Heart Belongs To An Angel	OK 06029, Cq 9860
LA-2348-A	Little Sweetheart I Miss You	OK 05981, Cq 9859
LA-2349-A	Wooly Booger -1	OK 05917, Cq 9714

Dick Reinhart & His Lone Star Boys: Dick Reinhart, v; or Dick Reinhart, Vera Woods, v duet-1; or Vera Woods, v-2; acc. Carl Cotner, f; Jack Mayhew, cl; Paul Sells, pac; Johnny Bond, g; Fred Whiting, sb; Spike Jones, d.
   Hollywood, CA   Monday, August 4, 1941

H-409-1	Midnight Patrol	OK 06641
H-410-1	Be My Darlin' -1	OK 06471, Cq 9853
H-411-1	Fort Worth Jail -1	OK 06373, Cq 9857
H-412-1	Little Girl Of My Dreams -1	OK 06471, Cq 9853
H-413-1	Rooky Toody	OK 06595, Cq 9852
H-414-1	Why Don't We Do This More Often -2	OK 06372, Cq 9858
H-415-1	I Don't Care -1	OK 06595, Cq 9852
H-416-1	Cherokee Rose -1	OK 06372, Cq 9858

   Hollywood, CA   Monday, August 11, 1941

H-427-1	You Never Can Tell -1	Cq 9856
H-428-1	Don't Think It Ain't Been Charmin' -1	Cq 9856
H-429-1	I Know What You're Thinkin' -1	OK 06539, Cq 9855
H-430-1	Stop And Fix It	OK 06641
H-431-1	One Kiss -1	Cq 9855
H-432-1	Don't Make Me Wait Too Long	OK 06539, Cq 9854
H-433-1	Don't Break My Heart	Cq 9854
H-434-1	Truck Drivers' Coffee Stop	OK 06373, Cq 9857

Dick Reinhart, v; acc. Jack Mayhew, cl; Paul Sells, p; own g; Herb Kratoska, g; Fred Whiting, sb.
   Hollywood, CA   Monday, March 23, 1942

H-749-1	Will I See You Again	OK unissued
H-750-1	Darling Ease My Worried Mind	OK unissued
H-751-1	Traveling Man's Blues	OK unissued
H-752-1	Cross My Heart	OK unissued
H-753-1	Darling You Know	OK unissued
H-754-1	Go Your Way	OK unissued

Conqueror 9715, issued as by **Dick Reinhart & His Universal Cowboys**, comes from a session logged and otherwise issued as by **Universal Cowboys**; see Universal Cowboys.

Dick Reinhart also recorded with the Light Crust Doughboys, Three Virginians, and The Wanderers, and after 1942.

RAYMOND RENDER

No details.
Richmond, IN   Friday, June 27, 1930
16796	[unknown title]	Ge rejected trial recording

Raymond Render, v/y-1; acc. unknown, g.
Richmond, IN   Monday, July 7, 1930
16811,-A	Does He Ever Think Of Me	Ge rejected
16812	Nobody's Darling On Earth -1	Spr 2538

Superior 2538 as by **Frank Dunbar**.
Rev. Superior 2538 by G.E. Lancaster.

Ray Render, v/y-1; acc. unknown, g.
Richmond, IN   Tuesday, October 28, 1930
17212	Daddy's Wonderful Pal	Ge rejected
17213	My Old Mountain Home -1	Ge rejected
17214	Does She Ever Think Of Me?	Ge rejected
17215	Are You Tired Of Me Darling?	Ge rejected

GEORGE RENEAU

George Reneau The Blind Musician Of The Smoky Mountains, h/g; acc. Gene Austin, v/calls.
New York, NY   April 1924
13054	The Wreck On The Southern 97	Vo 14809, 5029
13058	Lonesome Road Blues	Vo 14809, 5029
13061	Little Brown Jug	Vo 14812, 5031
13069	You Will Never Miss Your Mother Until She Is Gone	Vo 14811, 5030
13072	Turkey In The Straw	Vo 14812, 5031
13076	Life's Railway To Heaven	Vo 14811, 5030
13079	Casey Jones	Vo 14813, 5032

Intervening matrices are almost certainly unissued takes of the above items, but an entirely unissued item may have been recorded between matrices 13061 and 13069.

New York, NY   April 1924
13112	Susie Ann	Vo 14815, 5034
13114	Blue Ridge Blues	Vo 14815, 5034
13116	When You And I Were Young, Maggie	Vo 14814, 5033
13120	Here, Rattler, Here (Calling The Dog)	Vo 14814, 5033
13122	Arkansas Traveler	Vo 14813, 5032

New York, NY   Wednesday, September 10, 1924
13666*/67	Red Wing	Vo 14896, 5049

New York, NY   Friday, September 12, 1924
13677/78*	Jesse James	Vo 14897, 5050
13679/80*	Birmingham	Vo 14946, 5055
13681*/82	The New Market Wreck	Vo 14930, 5054, Sil 3052

Silvertone 3052 as by **George Hobson**.

New York, NY   Saturday, September 13, 1924
13683/84	Cindy	Vo unissued
13685/86	Sweet Bye And Bye	Vo unissued

New York, NY   Monday, September 15, 1924
13687*/88	Smoky Mountain Blues	Vo 14896, 5049
13689/90/91*	The Baggage Coach Ahead	Vo 14918, 5052, Sil 3047

Silvertone 3047 as by **George Hobson**.

New York, NY   Tuesday, September 16, 1924
13698*/99	The C & O Wreck	Vo 14897, 5050
13700/01	Little Nigger Baby	Vo unissued

New York, NY   Wednesday, September 17, 1924
13702*/03	The Bald-Headed End Of The Broom	Vo 14930, 5054, Sil 3052
13704*/05	My Redeemer	Vo 15046, 5064

Silvertone 3052 as by **George Hobson**.

George Reneau, h; acc. poss. Charles Bates, p.
New York, NY   Wednesday, September 17, 1924
   13706/07/08*   I've Got The Railroad Blues   Vo 14946, 5055

George Reneau, h/g; acc. Gene Austin, v/calls.
New York, NY   Wednesday, September 17, 1924
   13718*/19   Softly And Tenderly   Vo 14918, 5052, Sil 3047
                     We're Floating Down The Stream Of Time   Vo 15046, 5064

Silvertone 3047 as by **George Hobson**. It is not certain that *We're Floating Down The Stream Of Time* was recorded on this date, but it is likely to have been made about this time.

The Blue Ridge Duo Gene Austin & George Reneau: George Reneau, h/g; Gene Austin, v/calls.
New York, NY   Monday, September 22, 1924
   9727-B   Lonesome Road Blues   Ed 51515, 4975
   9728-C   Blue Ridge Blues   Ed 51515, 4976
   9729-A,-C   Turkey In The Straw   Ed 51502, 4977
New York, NY   Tuesday, September 23, 1924
   9730-A,-B   Little Brown Jug   Ed 51422, 4973
   9731-A   You'll Never Miss Your Mother Untill [sic] She Has   Ed 51498, 4961
                        Gone
   9732-A,-C   Arkansas Traveler   Ed 51422, 4936
New York, NY   Wednesday, September 24, 1924
   9735-B,-C   Life's Railway To Heaven   Ed 51498, 4968
   9736-B,-C   Susie Ann   Ed 51502, 4978

Matrices 9733/34 are by the Georgia Melodians.

George Reneau The Blind Musician Of The Smoky Mountains, h/g/v-1; acc. Gene Austin, v-2.
New York, NY   Tuesday, February 24, 1925
   410/11/12W   Little Rosewood Casket -2   Vo 14997, 5057, Sil 3044
   413/14/15W;   The Prisoner's Song -1   Vo 14991, 5056, Sil 3045
   15219/20
   416/17/18W   Woman's Suffrage -1   Vo 14999, 5059
   419/20/21W   Wild And Reckless Hoboes -1   Vo 14999, 5059
   422/23/24W   The Lightning Express -2   Vo 14991, 5056, Sil 3045
   425/26/27W   Rock All Our Babies To Sleep -2   Vo 14997, 5057, Sil 3044
   428/29W   Wild Bill Jones -2   Vo 14998, 5058, Sil 3046
   430/31W   The Letter Edged In Black -2   Vo 14998, 5058, Sil 3046

Silvertones as by **George Hobson**.

George Reneau, v; acc. own h/g.
New York, NY   Wednesday, October 14, 1925
   1447/48/49W   The Sinking Of The Titanic   Vo 15148, 5077
   1450/51/52W   Rovin' Gambler   Vo 15148, 5077
   1453/54/55W   Railroad Lover   Vo 15194, 5083
   1456/57/58W   Gambling On The Sabbath Day   Vo 15149, 5078
   1459/60*/61W   Old Man On The Hill   Vo 15347, 5106
   1462/63/64W   Bad Companions   Vo 15150, 5079
New York, NY   Thursday, October 15, 1925
   1465/66*/67W   The Weeping Willow Tree   Vo 15349, 5108
   1468/69/70W   May I Sleep In Your Barn To-night, Mister   Vo 15149, 5078
   1471/72*/73W   Love Always Has Its Way   Vo 15347, 5106
   1479/80/81*W   When I Shall Cross Over The Dark Rolling Tide   Vo 15348, 5107
   1482/83*/84W   On Top Of Old Smoky   Vo 15366, 5114
   1485/86W   When The Work's All Done This Fall   Vo 15150, 5079
   1487/88*W   Old Rugged Cross   Vo 15348, 5107

Matrices 1474W to 1478W are by Harry Reser (popular).
Revs: Vocalion 15366, 5114 by Sid Harkreader.

New York, NY   Friday, October 16, 1925
   1489/90/91W   The Hand Of Fate   Vo 15182, 5080
   1492/93/94W   Jack And Joe   Vo 15182, 5080
   1495/96/97W   I'm Glad My Wife's In Europe   Vo 15194, 5083
   1498/99/1500W   The Fatal Wedding   Vo unissued?
   1501/02/03*W   Two Orphans   Vo 15349, 5108

George Reneau also recorded with Lester McFarland as the Gentry Brothers.

RENFRO VALLEY BOYS
See Karl & Harty.

THE REUBENS
No details, exc. Chas. Heck, calls-1.
Richmond, IN   Sunday, January 20, 1924
   30008,-A,-B,-C   The Reubens Special -1   Ge unissued?
   30009,-A   Morning Star (Waltz)   Ge unissued?

JIMMIE REVARD & HIS OKLAHOMA PLAYBOYS

Ben McKay, f/v-1; Emil "Bash" Hofner, esg; Eddie Whitley, p/v-2; Cotton Cooper, tbj; Adolph Hofner, g/v-3; Jimmie Revard, sb/v-4; band sp-5.

San Antonio, TX   Thursday, October 22, 1936

02801-1	Ride 'Em Cowboy -2	BB B-6739, RZ MR2409
02802-1	Holding The Sack -4	BB B-6992, Twin FT8418
02803-1	Cake Eatin' Man -4	BB B-6753
02804-1	Triflin' Gal -2	BB B-6739, RZ MR2409
02805-1	Swing Me -2	BB B-6712, RZ MR2377
02806-1	A Little Prayer For Me -3	BB B-7085
02807-1	Dirty Dog -3	BB B-6992, Twin FT8418
02808-1	Fox And The Hounds -5	BB B-6753
02809-1	Blues In The Bottle -2	BB B-6842
02810-1	She's All Mine -3	BB B-6842
02835-1	What's The Use -3	BB B-6823
02836-1	Since You Left Me, Hon -4	BB B-6823
02837-1	Big String Band -1, 5	BB B-6654

Bluebird B-6654, B-6679, Regal-Zonophone MR2377, MR2409 as by **Jimmie Revard & His Oklahoma Cowboys**.
Matrix 02801 is titled *Ride 'Em, Cowboy* on Regal-Zonophone MR2409.
Matrices 02811 to 02824 are Spanish; matrices 02825 to 02834 are by Doug Bine.

Ben McKay, f/v-1; Emil "Bash" Hofner, esg/v-2; Eddie Whitley, p/v-3; Cotton Cooper, tbj/v-4; Adolph Hofner, g/v-5; Jimmie Revard, sb/v-6.

San Antonio, TX   Monday, October 26, 1936

02936-1	She Is My Gal -6	BB B-7297
02937-1	Crafton Blues	BB B-6712
02938-1	Oklahoma Rounder -1	BB B-6654
02939-1	After Hours Blues -3	BB B-6774
02940-1	Big Daddy Blues -3	BB B-6774
02941-1	Star Kovarna -2, 5	BB B-2575
02942-1	Na Marjanse -2, 5	BB B-2575
02943-1	It Ain't No Good -4	BB B-6679
02944-1	Naughty, Naughty -4	BB B-6679, RZ MR2377
02945-1	Just Refined -5	BB B-7061

Bluebird B-2575 as by **Hoffner Bros**. Regal-Zonophone MR2377 as by **Jimmie Revard & His Oklahoma Cowboys**.
Rev. Bluebird B-7297 by Hal Davis (popular).

Ben McKay, f/v-1; Emil "Bash" Hofner, esg; Art Francis, p; Cotton Cooper, tbj; Adolph Hofner, g/v-2; Curly Williams, g or sb/v-3; Jimmie Revard, g or sb/v-4.

San Antonio, TX   Friday, February 26, 1937

07351-1	Playboy's Breakdown	BB B-7371, Vi 20-2987
07352-1	Tulsa Waltz	BB B-7371, Vi 20-2987
07353-1	I've Got Trouble In Mind -3	BB B-6935
07354-1	Lose Your Blues And Laugh At Life -3	BB B-7028
07355-1	You're Mean To Me -4	BB B-6935, Twin FT8376
07356-1	My Little Girl I Love You -3	BB B-6877, Vi 20-3117, DJ564, Twin FT8337
07357-1	It's My Time Now -3	BB B-6877
07358-1	Riding Down The Canyon -1, 3	BB B-8141
07359-1	That's My Gal -3	BB B-7028
07360-1	Thinking -4	BB B-7172
07361-1	Pickin' Cotton Blues -3	BB B-7172
07362-1	Spanish Medley Of Waltzes -2, 3	BB B-8117
07363-1	I Want A Girl -3	BB B-7085, Twin FT8475
07364-1	Daddy's Got The Deep Elm Blues -2	BB B-7061

Revs: Bluebird B-8141 by Bill Boyd; Victor DJ564 by Cecil Campbell; Twin FT8337 by Blue Sky Boys, FT8376 by Tune Wranglers, FT8475 by Bob Skyles.

Bob Belmard, f; Cal Callison, ac; Emil "Bash" Hofner, esg; George Timberlake, p; Chet Carnes, tbj/v-1; Adolph Hofner, g/v-2; Curly Williams, g or sb/v-3; Jimmie Revard, g or sb/v-4; unidentified, v trio-5.
   San Antonio, TX   Tuesday, September 14, 1937

Matrix	Title	Release
014135-1	Come Up And See Me Some Day -4	BB B-7248
014136-1	Bound To Look Like A Monkey -3	BB B-7481
014137-1	We Played A Game -2	BB B-7309
014138-1	At The End Of The Lane -5	BB B-7370
014139-1	We'll Ride The Tide Together -2	BB B-7199
014140-1	Papa's Gettin' Mad -3	BB B-7520
014141-1	Does My Baby Love Me, Yes Sir! -2	BB B-7199
014142-1	Let Me Live And Love You -3	BB B-7248
014143-1	Gee! But It's Great Walking Back Home -2	BB B-7309
014144-1	Cats Are Bad Luck -1	BB B-7520
014145-1	Am I Blue -2	BB B-7481
014146-1	It's All So Sweet -2	BB B-7370

Bob Belmard, f; Leon Seago, f/v-1; Cal Callison, ac; Emil "Bash" Hofner, esg/v-2; George Timberlake, p; Joe Malloy (or Malloie), g/v-3; Curly Williams, g or sb/v-4; Jimmie Revard, g or sb; unidentified, v-5; band v-6.
   San Antonio, TX   Monday, April 4, 1938

Matrix	Title	Release
022086-1	Everything's Gonna Be All Right -4, 6	BB B-7559
022087-1	Goodness Gracious Gracie -4	BB B-7658
022088-1	I'm Waitin' Mabel -3	BB B-7610
022089-1	You're As Pretty As A Picture -2, 3	BB B-7727, Twin FT8633
022090-1	Old Waterfall -4	BB B-7911
022091-1	Is There Still Room For Me -3	BB B-7610
022092-1	My Ozark Mountain Home -3	BB B-7776
022093-1	There's A Picture In My Heart -3	BB B-7727
022094-1	The Bees Are In The Hive -1, 3 (lead), 4, 5	BB B-7658
022095-1	Baby Your Mother -3	BB B-7911
022096-1	Tell Me, Little Coquette -4	BB B-7559
022097-1	Someone Else You Care For -4	BB B-7776

Rev. Twin FT8633 by Bill Boyd.

Leon Seago, f/v-1; Jimmie Revard, cl-2/v-3; Emil "Bash" Hofner, esg; George Timberlake, p; Adolph Hofner or Curly Williams, g; poss. Buck Wheeler, sb; Edmond Frankie, traps.
   San Antonio, TX   Tuesday, October 25, 1938

Matrix	Title	Release
028605-1	Hill Billy Swing -1, 2	BB B-7964
028606-1	A Bundle Of Old Southern Sunshine -2, 3	BB B-8005, MW M-7666
028607-1	I'm Gettin' Nowhere -2, 3	BB B-8039, MW M-7666
028608-1	Oh! Swing It -2, 3	BB B-8005
028609-1	All Dolled Up -1, 2	BB B-8062
028610-1	If I Only Could Blot Out The Past -2, 3	BB B-7939, MW M-7668
028611-1	Little Picture Playhouse -1, 2	BB B-8117
028612-1	It's A Long, Long Way To Tipperary -3	BB B-8088
028613-1	An Old-Time Westerner -2, 3	BB B-7964, MW M-7667
028614-1	Cheatin' -3	BB B-8039
028615-1	Totten' The Poke -3	BB B-7939, MW M-7668
028616-1	Smiles -1, 2	BB B-8088, MW M-7667

Rev. Bluebird B-8062 by Tennessee Ramblers.

Leon Seago, f-1/v-2; unknown, f-1; Emil "Bash" Hofner, esg; Bert Ferguson, p; Adolph Hofner, g/v-3; Buck Wheeler, sb; poss. Edmond Frankie or Johnny Rives, d; Jimmie Revard, v-4; band v-5.
   Dallas, TX   Monday, February 13, 1940

Matrix	Title	Release
047681-1	Don't Waste Your Tears Over Me, Little Girl -1, 4	BB B-8405, MW M-8731
047682-1	Just A Good Time Gal -1, 4	BB B-8405, MW M-8731
047683-1	I'll Take Her Back -1, 4	BB B-8513, MW M-8734
047684-1	The Sidewalk Waltz -4	BB B-8419, MW M-8732, RZAu G24350
047685-1	Mistakes -1, 3	BB B-8419, MW M-8732, RZAu G24350
047686-1	Under The Moon -4	BB B-8453, MW M-8733
047687-1	If They String Me Up -1, 2, 5	BB B-8453, MW M-8733, RZAu G24523
047688-1	Ja-Da -1, 4	BB B-8513, MW M-8734

Matrix 047685 is titled *Mistakes Waltz* on Regal-Zonophone G24350.
Rev. Regal-Zonophone G24523 by Bob Dyer (Australian).
Jimmie Revard recorded after 1942.

REX QUARTETTE

Pseudonym on Broadway for the Riley Quartette.

WILLIAM REXROAT'S CEDAR CREST SINGERS

Prob.: William Rexroat, Emry Arthur, Jossie Ellers, v trio; acc. unidentified, bj; prob. William Rexroat, g; Emry Arthur, g.

Chicago, IL   Tuesday, January 8, 1929

C-2761-A,-B	Swinging In The Lane	Vo unissued
C-2762-	Build Me A Bungalow	Vo 5323
C-2763-	What Kind Of Shoes You Gwine To Wear	Vo 5345
C-2764-	We Shall Wear A Crown	Vo 5345
C-2765-A,-B	Listen To The Mocking Bird	Vo unissued

One guitar is absent on matrix C-2765.
Rev. Vocalion 5323 by Emry Arthur & William Rexroat (see the former).

Acc. prob. William Rexroat or Emry Arthur, g.

Chicago, IL   Tuesday, January 8, 1929

C-2770-	Fading Away	Vo 5290
C-2771-	The Outcast	Vo 5290

Matrices C-2766, C-2769 are by Emry Arthur & William Rexroat; matrices C-2767/68 are by Jossie Ellers.

HAMP REYNOLDS' SACRED HARP SINGERS

W.A. Owen, treble v; Hamp Reynolds, tv; H.A. Jackson, bsv; acc. Mrs. Dora Burton, p.

Atlanta, GA   Friday, October 19, 1928

47205-1,-2	Hallelujah!	Vi unissued
47206-1,-2	Soft Music	Vi unissued
47207-1,-2	Return Again	Vi unissued
47208-1,-2	Fillmore	Vi unissued

DUSTY RHODES & HIS GUITAR

Dusty Rhodes, v; acc. own g.

Dallas, TX   between October 19 and 25, 1928

DAL-710-	Shanghai Rooster	Br 283
DAL-711-	Mike The Turk	Br 283

Dallas, TX   Monday, October 28, 1929

DAL-511-	Chinaman's Song	Vo cancelled
DAL-512-	Chicken Pie	Vo cancelled

RHUBARB RED

Les Paul, v; acc. own h/g.

Chicago, IL   Wednesday, May 20, 1936

C-90732-A	Just Because	MW 8012
C-90733-A	Answer To Just Because	MW 8013
C-90734-A	Deep Elem Blues #2	MW 8013
C-90735-A	Deep Elem Blues	MW 8012

Les Paul (whose real name is Lester William Polfuss) recorded after 1942.

THE RHYTHM WRECKERS

Some of the recordings by this band are beyond the scope of this work and are included in JR. For others, see Whitey McPherson.

EDD RICE

Edd Rice, v; acc. prob. own g.

Chicago, IL   Saturday, January 14, 1928

C-1484/85*	Over The Hills To The Poorhouse	Vo 5212
C-1486*/87	There's A Mother Old And Gray Who Needs Me Now	Vo 5212

Matrices C-1484/85 were remastered as E-6931/32W, and C-1486/87 as E-6933/34W.

Chicago, IL   Thursday, April 5, 1928

C-1875-	The Fate Of Edward Hickman	Vo 5216
C-1876-	The Breaking Of The St. Francis Dam	Vo 5216

Chicago, IL   Friday, April 6, 1928

C-1883-	Cricket On The Hearth	Vo 5220
C-1884-	In The Harbor Of Home Sweet Home	Vo 5220

GLEN RICE & HIS BEVERLY HILL BILLIES
See The Beverly Hill Billies.

HOKE RICE

Hoke Rice & His Southern String Band: poss. Howard Coker, f; poss. William Archer Chumbler, md; Hoke Rice, g/sp.
    Long Island City, NY   c. April 1929

391	Chinese Breakdown	QRS R.9010, Pm 3229, 3308, Bwy 8178
392	Macon, Georgia Breakdown	QRS R.9010, Pm 3229, 3308, Bwy 8178

Paramount 3308 as by **Hoke Rice & Capitol String Band**. Broadway 8178 as by **Hoke Rice & His Capitol String Band**. Matrix 392 is titled *Macon, Ga. Breakdown* on Paramount 3308.

Hoke Rice, v/y; acc. own g.
    Long Island City, NY   c. April 1929

393	Waiting For A Train	QRS R.9012

Hoke Rice & His Southern String Band: poss. Howard Coker, f; poss. William Archer Chumbler, md; Hoke Rice, g.
    Long Island City, NY   c. April 1929

396	Down Yonder	QRS unissued

Hoke Rice, v/y; acc. poss. William Archer Chumbler, md-1; own g.
    Long Island City, NY   c. April 1929

401	Lullaby Yodel	QRS R.9012
412	Way Down South By The Sea -1	QRS R.9022, Pm 3212, Bwy 8164
413	I'm Lonely And Blue	Pm 3212, Bwy 8164
413-A	I'm Lonely And Blue	QRS R.9022
417-A	Ain't That Kind Of A Cat Yodel	QRS R.9015, Pm 3239, Bwy 8192
418-A	Down In A Southern Town Yodel	QRS R.9015, Pm 3239, Bwy 8192

Matrix 418 is titled *Down In A Southern Town* on Broadway 8192.
Matrices 394/95, 399/400, 402 to 404, 410/11, 414 are by Claude (C.W.) Davis groups; matrix 397 is by Chumbler, Coker & Rice; matrix 405 is by Chumbler's Breakdown Gang; matrices 415/16 are by Nelson & Nelson; others are untraced.

Slim Barton & Eddie Mapp; or **Slim Barton & James Moore**-1: Eddie Mapp, h-2; James Moore, h-3; Hoke Rice, g-4/v-5/humming-6.
    Long Island City, NY   c. April 1929

469-A	I'm Hot Like That -2, 4	QRS R.7088
470-A	Careless Love -2, 4	QRS R.7088
471	Wicked Treatin' Blues -2, 5, 6	QRS unissued
471-A	Wicked Treatin' Blues -2, 5, 6	QRS R.7089, Pm 13114
472	It's Tight Like That -2, 4	QRS R.7081
473	Poor Convict Blues -1, 3, 4, 6	QRS R.7081
477	Fourth Avenue Blues -2, 3, 4	QRS R.7089, PM 13114

Matrix 474 is by Curley Weaver; matrices 475/76 are by Eddie Mapp and James Moore (see *B&GR* for all).

Hoke Rice & His Guitar: Hoke Rice, v/y-1; acc. own g.
    Long Island City, NY   c. April 1929

478	The Dirty Hangout Where I Stayed - Part 1	QRS R.9037
479	The Old Concert Hall In The Bowery	QRS unissued
480	At The End Of The Sunset Trail -1	QRS unissued
481	The Dirty Hangout Where I Stayed - Part 2	QRS R.9037

Hoke Rice also recorded at these c. April 1929 sessions in groups nominally headed by William Archer Chumbler and Claude (C.W.) Davis, and with Catherine Boswell.

Hoke Rice, v/y; acc. own g.
    Richmond, IN   Monday, April 15, 1929

15048	Waitin' For A Train	Ge 6839, Ch 15767, Spt 9496
15050	Blue Yodel No. 3	Ge 6855, Ch 15727, Spt 9425
15051	Blue Yodel No. 4	Ge 6855, Ch 15727, Spt 9425

Champion 15727, 15767 as by **Lee Landon**. Supertone 9425, 9496 as by **Duke Lane**.
Matrix 15049 is by Allie & Pearl Brock.

Hoke Rice, v/y-1; acc. own g.
    Richmond, IN   Tuesday, April 16, 1929

15054	Unexplained Blues	Ge 7067, Chg 424
15055	Oh Sweet Mama Blues	Ge 7067, Chg 424
15057-B	Lullaby Yodel -1	Ge 6839, Ch 15767, Spt 9496

Champion 15767 as by **Lee Landon**. Supertone 9496 as by **Duke Lane**. Challenge 424 as by **C. Maines**.
Matrices 15052/53, 15056 are by Allie & Pearl Brock.

Hoke Rice, v/y; acc. own g.
  Richmond, IN   Wednesday, April 17, 1929
    15063,-A,-B   I'm Gonna Live On High   Ge rejected
Matrix 15058 is by Allie & Pearl Brock; matrices 15059 to 15062 are by Louie Donaldson (15061/62 with Hoke Rice).

Hoke Rice & His Hoky Poky Boys: Tom ———, cl; prob. William Archer Chumbler, md/v-1; Hoke Rice, g/v-2/sp-3; unidentified, sp-4.
  Atlanta, GA   Tuesday, March 18, 1930
    ATL-905   I Don't Love Nobody -2, 3, 4   Br 482
    ATL-906   Georgia Gal -1, 3   Br 482
    ATL-920   Brown Mule Slide -2, 3   Br 416
    ATL-921   Georgia Jubilee -2, 3   Br 416
    ATL-936   Put On Your Old Grey Bonnet -2   Br 473
    ATL-937   Wabash Blues -1, 2   Br 473

Hoke Rice, v; acc. unknown.
  Atlanta, GA   Friday, March 21, 1930
    ATL-913   The Death Of Clark, The Bandit   Br rejected
    ATL-935   The Beggar's Daughter   Br rejected
    ATL-980/81   The Girl From Natchez   Br rejected

Hoke Rice & Harry Stark, v/humming-1 duet; acc. unknown, f-2; Hoke Rice, g.
  Atlanta, GA   Wednesday, November 12, 1930
    ATL-6635   Mammy's Pickaninny -2   Br 552
    ATL-6636   Floating Down To Cotton Town -1   Br 552

Hoke Rice also recorded with Lowe Stokes and The Swamp Rooters, and participated in the sketch *A Bootlegger's Joint In Atlanta – Parts 1 & 2* (Brunswick 419) (see The Chumbler Family & Associated Groups). He was later joint leader with his brother Paul of the Rice Brothers' Gang.

RICE BROTHERS' GANG

Johnny Gorman, as-1/esg-2; Warren Sykes, h-3; Hoke Rice, eg/v-4; Paul Rice, g/v-5; Mike Eargle, sb.
  Charlotte, NC   Monday, June 13, 1938
    64148-A   King Cotton Stomp -3   De 5552
    64149-A   I Love My Saviour -2, 4, 5   De 5553, 46065
    64150-B   On The Jericho Road -2, 4, 5   De 5553, 46065
    64151-A   Marie -1, 4   De 5556
    64152-A   On The Sunny Side Of The Street -1, 3   De 5590, 46069
    64153-A   Sweet Someone -2, 4, 5   De 5552
    64154-A   Cheatin' On Your Baby -1, 3, 5   De 5636
    64155-A   Mood Indigo -1, 4, 5   De 5569

Warren Sykes, h/spoons-1; Hoke Rice, eg/v-2; Paul Rice, g/v-3; Mike Eargle, sb.
  Charlotte, NC   Wednesday, June 15, 1938
    64156-A   Be Careful With Those Eyes -2   De 5569
    64157-A   Hold Me -3   De 5598
    64158-A   When I'm Walking With My Sweetness -2, 3   De 5622
    64159-A   You Tell Her Cause I Stutter -2, 3   De 5598
    64160-A   My Idea Of Heaven -2   De 5590
    64161-A   You Got That Thing -2   De 5650
    64162-A   China Boy -1   De 5622
    64163-A   Ain't That Too Bad -2   De 5636
    64164-A   Do Something -2, 3   De 5650
    64165-A   Sugar Blues -2   De 5556, 46069

Prob. Johnny Gorman, cl-1; Warren Sykes, h-2; prob. Billy Galloway, esg; Hoke Rice, g/v-3; Paul Rice, g/v-4; probably Mike Eargle, sb.
  New York, NY   Monday, September 13, 1939
    66424-A   Japanese Sandman -1, 2   De 5777
    66425-A   Nagasaki -1, 2   De 5805
    66426-A   Lovelight In The Starlight -2, 3, 4   De 5763
    66427-A   Down Yonder -1, 2   De 5751
    66428-A   Alabama Jubilee -1, 2, 3, 4   De 5738
    66429-A   They Cut Down The Old Pine Tree -1, 2, 3, 4 De 5751
    66430-A   I Cried For You -1, 2, 4   De 5792
    66431-A   I Wish You Were Jealous Of Me -1, 4   De 5777
    66432-A   You Are My Sunshine -2, 4   De 5763
    66433-A   Is It True What They Say About Dixie -1, 2, 3 De 5804
    66434-A   Sweetheart Wait For Me   De unissued

66435-A	Won't You Come Back To Me -3, 4	De 5738
66436-A	It Made You Happy When You Made Me Cry -2, 3	De 5815
66437-A	Girl Of My Dreams -1, 2, 3	De 5893
66438-A	Oh Susannah -1, 2, 3	De 5804
66439-A	You've Got To See Daddy Ev'ry Night -1, 2, 3	De 5805
66440-A	In A Shanty In Old Shantytown -1, 2, 4	De 5815
66441-A	At The Close Of A Long Long Day -4	De 5792

Pete Hardin, f; Eddie Hurd, cl; Hoke Rice, g/v/y-1; Paul Rice, g/v-2/y-1; Reggie Ward, sb.
Houston, TX   Saturday, April 6, 1940

92018-A	No Matter What Happens, My Darling	De 5837, DeAu X1902, MeC 45359
92019-A	Sally Do You Love Me	De 5823
92020-A	Below The Rio Grande	De 5837, DeAu X1902, MeC 45359
92021-A	I Won't Have Any Troubles Anymore -2	De 5893
92022-A	Hurry Johnny Hurry -1, 2	De 5859, MeC 45370
92030-A	Yes! We Have No Bananas -2	De 5852, MeC 45366
92031-A	Mary Lou	De 5870, MeC 45380
92032-A	My Sweetheart Darling	De 5870, MeC 45380
92033-A	Sweetheart Wait For Me	De 5823, Min M-14122
92034-A	You'll Only Have One Mother -2	De 5859, DeSA FM5125, MeC 45370
92035-A	When It's Blossom Time In Old Caroline -2	De 5852, MeC 45366

Matrices 92023 to 92029 are by the Shelton Brothers.
Revs: Minerva M-14122 by Port Arthur Jubileers; Decca FM5125 by Jimmie Davis.

Cliff Bruner, f/etg-1; unknown, cl; Hoke Rice, eg/v-2; Paul Rice, g/v-3.
Dallas, TX   Sunday, April 27, 1941

93679-A	Little Girl, I'm So Blue Without You -1, 3	De 6004
93680-A	You Don't Love Me Anymore (Little Darlin') -1, 2	De 5959, DeSA FM5138, MeC 45451
93681-A	Ridin' Down The Canyon -1, 2, 3	De 6004
93682-A	Linda May Polka -1	De 6019
93683-A	My Troubled Mind	De unissued
93684-A	Do You -2	De 5971, MeC 45458
93692-A	I'll Always Love You (Should I Live A Thousand Years) -2, 3	De 6088
93693-A	Dry Your Eyes, Little Girl -2	De 6019
93694-A	Please Don't Stay Away -2	De 6088
93695-A	Railroad Boomer -2, 3	De 5971, MeC 45458
93696-A	My Carolina Sunshine Girl -3	De 5959, DeSA FM5138, MeC 45451

Matrices 93685 to 93691 are by the Callahan Brothers.

Hoke Rice also recorded in his own name.

RENUS RICH & CARL BRADSHAW

Renus Rich, Carl Bradshaw, v/y duet; acc. prob. one of them, f; prob. the other, g.
Johnson City, TN   Monday, October 15, 1928

| 147186-2 | Goodbye Sweetheart | Co 15341-D |
| 147187-1 | Sleep Baby Sleep | Co 15341-D |

EDNA RICHARDS & EDNA DAVIS

Edna Richards, Edna Davis, v duet; acc. unknown, g.
Richmond, IN   Friday, September 12, 1930

| 17024 | [unknown title] | Ge rejected trial recording |

FRED RICHARDS

Fred Richards, v/y; acc. own g.
Johnson City, TN   Wednesday, October 23, 1929

149246-2	My Katie	Co 15483-D
149247-2	Danville Blues	Co 15483-D
149248-	Women Rule The World	Co unissued
149249-	Old Pal	Co unissued

Richmond, IN   Friday, June 19, 1931

| 17840 | [unknown title] | Ge rejected trial recording |

New York, NY   Tuesday, May 23, 1933

| 13378- | Freight Wreck of No. 52 | ARC unissued |
| 13379- | Carolina Sunshine | ARC unissued |

| 13380- | Hobo's Yodel | ARC unissued |
| 13381- | Watching The Moon | ARC unissued |

CHAS. RICHARDSON & O.S. GABEHART

Chas. Richardson, O.S. Gabehart, v duet; acc. unknown, g.
New York, NY   Wednesday, August 7, 1929

402568-B	My Redeemer	OK 45476
402569-B	God Is Still On The Throne	OK 45371
402570-B	Take Up Thy Cross	OK 45403
402571-B	I Want My Life To Count For Jesus	OK 45392

Acc. unknown, f; unknown, p; unknown, vc.
New York, NY   Wednesday, August 7, 1929

402572-A	The Heart That Was Broken For Me	OK 45476
402573-B	Reaching To You	OK 45392
402574-A	The Unclouded Day	OK 45371
402575-A	The Ninety And Nine	OK 45403

RALPH RICHARDSON

Ralph Richardson, v/y; acc. unknown, f; unknown, p; unknown, vc.
Atlanta, GA   Tuesday, July 31, 1928

402019-	Love's Old Sweet Song	OK unissued
402020-B	Sauerkraut Is Bully	OK 45267, PaAu A2733
402021-A	Little Dog Yodel	OK 45267, PaE E6245, PaAu A2733

Rev. Parlophone E6245 by Frank Marvin.

RICHMOND MELODY BOYS

Prob.: Ed Showalter, f; Haskell Harkleroad, bj; Grace Kinzele, g.
Richmond, IN   Monday, November 25, 1929

| 15956 | Wild Flowers | Ge rejected |

The Richmond Melody Boys accompanied W.C. Childers at this session.

Texas Cowboy Trio: Ed Showalter, f; Haskell Harkleroad, bj; Grace Kinzele, g.
Richmond, IN   Monday, March 10, 1930

16363	New Harmony Waltz	Spt 9673
16364	Pine Tree	Ge rejected: Yz 2200-5 (CD)
16365	Eighth Of January	Ge rejected
16366	The Boston Waltz	Spt 9673

Matrices 16363 to 16366 were logged as by **The Kentucky Woodchoppers** but issued as shown.

Richmond, IN   Monday, April 21, 1930

16506,-A	Devil's Serenade	Ge unissued
16507,-A	Sailor's Dream	Ge unissued
16508,-A	Kelly Waltz	Ge unissued
16509,-A	Wild Flowers	Ge unissued

BOBBIE & RUBY RICKER

Bobbie Ricker, v/y-1; acc. poss. own g; or **Bob & Ruby Ricker**-2, v duet; acc. poss. Bobbie Ricker, g; or **Bobbie Ricker & Marion**-3: unidentified, v/y; acc. poss. own g duet.
Augusta, GA   Sunday, June 28, 1936

AUG-124-	Women Will Talk	ARC unissued
AUG-125-	C.C.C. Lament	ARC unissued
AUG-136-	On Top Of Old Smoky -3	ARC unissued
AUG-137-3	I Know There Is Somebody Waiting -2	ARC 6-12-66
AUG-138-	True Love Is A Blessing -2	ARC unissued
AUG-139-3	The Texas Ranger-1	ARC 6-12-66
AUG-140-1,-2	Reply To Nobody's Darling	ARC unissued
AUG-141-	If You Want To See A Girl That's [sic] -2	ARC unissued

Matrices AUG-126/27 are by Smith & Harper; matrices AUG-128 to AUG-135 are by Dennis Crumpton & Robert Summers (see B&GR for both).

RIDGEL'S FOUNTAIN CITIANS

Leroy Ridgel, f; Charles Ancil Ridgel, md/v; Millard Whitehead, g/v; Carthel Ridgel, g.
Knoxville, TN   Saturday, August 27, 1929

| K-115- | Hallelujah To The Lamb | Vo 5363 |
| K-116- | Be Ready | Vo 5363 |

| K-117- | Free Little Bird | Vo 5389 |
| K-118- | Little Bonnie | Vo 5389 |

Leroy Ridgel, f; Charles Ancil Ridgel, md; Millard Whitehead, g; Carthel Ridgel, g; unidentified, v/v duet-1; prob. Bill Brown, sp; "Heavy Martin" (Hugh Cross), sp.

Knoxville, TN   Thursday, April 3, 1930

K-8078-	The Bald Headed End Of The Broom	Vo 5455
K-8079-	The Nick Nack Song	Vo 5455
K-8080-	Baby Call Your Dog Off	Vo 5427
K-8081-	Gittin' Upstairs -1	Vo 5427

GEORGE RILEY (THE YODELING RUSTLER)

Pseudonym on ARC labels for Goebel Reeves. On Conqueror 7742 the subcredit is changed to (**The Yodeling Cowboy**).

RILEY QUARTETTE

Vocal quartet; acc. John Marion Dye, p.

Chicago, IL   c. August 1927

4748-1	Wonderful Story Of Love	Pm 3053, Bwy 8208
4749-2	Saviour Lead Me Lest I Stray	Pm 3053, Bwy 8208
4754-1	The Church In The Wildwood	Pm 3049, Bwy 8116
4757-2	Hallelujah He Is Mine	Pm 3062
4758-2	The Master Of The Storm	Pm 3049, Bwy 8116
4759-2	My Faith Is Clinging To Thee	Pm 3076, Bwy 8156
4760-2	Wonderful Love	Pm 3062
4762-2	How Beautiful Heaven Must Be	Pm 3076, Bwy 8156
4768-2	There Is A Name	Pm 3067, Bwy 8088
4769-2	God Holds The Future In His Hands	Pm 3067, Bwy 8088

Broadway 8088, 8156 as by **Reed Quartette**; 8116, 8208 as by **Rex Quartette**.
Intervening matrices are untraced except 4752/53 by Rev. Stephenson & Male Choir.
John Marion Dye was associated with Dye's Sacred Harp Singers.

RILEY'S MOUNTAINEERS

Pseudonym on Supertone for Frank Jenkins & His Pilot Mountaineers.

HARRY RING'S SOUTHERN MELODY ARTISTS

One coupling by this group was issued in the Okeh Old Time Tunes series (45285) but it is outside the scope of this work.

TEX RITTER

This artist's full name is Maurice Woodward Ritter.

Tex Ritter, v; acc. own g.

New York, NY   Friday, September 2, 1932

| 152293-1 | (A) A 'Ridin' Old Paint (B) Git Along Little Doggies | Co unissued: BF BCD16260 (CD) |
| 152294-1 | Rye Whiskey | Co unissued: BF BCD16260 (CD) |

New York, NY   Monday, October 31, 1932

| 12518- | Cowboys Christmas Ball | ARC unissued |

New York, NY   Wednesday, March 15, 1933

13155-1	A Ridin' Old Paint	ARC unissued: BF BCD16260 (CD)
13155-2	A Ridin' Old Paint	ARC unissued: BF BCD16260 (CD)
13156-1	Every Day In The Saddle	ARC unissued
13157-1	Good-bye, Old Paint	Ba 32735, Me M12664, MeC 91761, Or 8222, Pe 12903, Ro 5222, Vo 5493, 04911, Cq 8073, Co 37640, 20239, CoC C1075, EBW W21, Pan 25538, RZAu G22247
13157-2	Goodbye, Old Paint	ARC unissued: BF BCD16260 (CD)
13158-1	Rye Whiskey	ARC unissued: BF BCD16260 (CD)
13158-2	Rye Whiskey, Rye Whiskey	Ba 32735, Me M12664, MeC 91761, Or 8222, Pe 12903, Ro 5222, Vo 5493, 04911, Cq 8144, Co 37640, 20239, CoC C1075, EBW W21, Pan 25538

Rev. Regal-Zonophone G22247 by (Asa) Martin & Roberts.

Acc. unknown, f; own g.

New York, NY   Friday, April 14, 1933

| 13155-3 | A Riding Old Paint | Ba 32992, Me M12942, MeC 91760, Or 8312, Pe 12984, Ro 5312, Cq 8144, EBW W53 |

| 13156-3 | Everyday In The Saddle | Ba 32992, Me M12942, MeC 91760, Or 8312, Pe 12984, Ro 5312, Cq 8073, Min M-916, EBW W53 |

Rev. Minerva M-916 by The Westerners.

Acc. own g.
New York, NY   Monday, January 21, 1935

| 39271-A | Sam Hall | De 5076, Pan 25741 |
| 39272-A | Get Along Little Dogie | Ch 45191, MeC 45191 |

Acc. prob.: Bill Benner, f; Jake Watts, h-1/poss. g-2; Bill Butler, sg; Buck Nation, g.
New York, NY   Tuesday, February 5, 1935

39328-A	Thirty Three Years In Prison -1	De 5112, MeC 45035, Min M-14049
39329-A	Lady Killin' Cowboy -1	De 5076, Pan 25741
39330-A	I'm A Do Right Cowboy -1	De 5112, MeC 45035, Min M-14066, Pan 25795
39331-B	Bill The Bar Fly -2	Ch 45191, De 5305, DeAu X1336, MW 8031, MeC 45191, Pan 25795

Matrix 39332 is titled *Bill, The Bar Fly* on Panachord 25795.

Acc. prob.: Bill Benner, f; Jake Watts, h-1; Bill Butler, sg; Buck Nation, g; unknown, sb-2.
New York, NY   Wednesday, October 16, 1935

60067-A	Nobody's Darling But Mine -1, 2	Ch 45153, De 12084, MeC 45153, Min M-14053
60068-A	My Brown Eyed Texas Rose	Ch 45153, De 12084, MeC 45153
60069-A	(Take Me Back To My) Boots And Saddle	Ch 45154, MW 4967, MeC 45154, Pan 25802
60070-A	The Oregon Trail	Ch 45154, MW 4967, MeC 45154, Pan 25802

Matrix 60068 was scheduled for release on Panachord 26047 but never issued.

Acc. prob.: Bill Benner, f; Bill Butler, esg; Buck Nation, g; own wh-1.
New York, NY   Friday, April 17, 1936

61057-A	Answer To Nobody's Darling But Mine	Ch 45197, MW 8020, MeC 45197, Min M-14053
61061-A	A Melody From The Sky	Ch 45198, De 5922, MeC 45420
61062-A	The Hills Of Old Wyomin' -1	Ch 45198, De 5922, MeC 45420
61063-A	We'll Rest At The End Of The Trail	Ch 45197, MW 8020, MeC 45197, Min M-14039

Matrices 61058/59 are by Louis Armstrong (see *JR*); matrix 61060 is an unrelated radio advertisement.
Rev. Minerva M-14039 by Leon Chappelear.

Acc. Frank Liddel, f-1; Bill Murray, ac-2; Jack Hogg, sg; Rudy Sooter, g; Lloyd Perryman, sb.
Los Angeles, CA   Wednesday, December 2, 1936

DLA-645-A	High, Wide And Handsome -1, 2	De 5315, DeAu X1370, MeC 45034, Min M-14049, Pan 26022
DLA-646-A	Headin' For The Rio Grande -1, 2	De 5306, DeAu X1341, DeIr W5126, MW 8032, Pan 26012
DLA-647-A	Out On The Lone Prairie -1, 2	De 5305, DeAu X1336, MW 8031, Pan 25954
DLA-648-A	Arizona Days -1, 2	De 5315, DeAu X1370, MeC 45034, Min M-14067, Pan 26022
DLA-649-A,-B	My Sweet Chiquita	De rejected
DLA-650-A	Jailhouse Lament	De 5306, DeAu X1341, DeIr W5126, MW 8032, Pan 26012

Acc. F. Clint, f; Harley Luse, ac; Charles Sargent, g; Clyde Wilson, sb; Frank Sanucci, ldr.
Los Angeles, CA   Monday, May 17, 1937

DLA-794-A	Hittin' The Trail	De 5405, DeAu X1398, MeC 45201, Min M-14066, Pan 25954
DLA-795-A	I'm A Natural Born Cowboy	De 5389, DeAu X1389, MeC 45205, Min M-14064, Pan 26034
DLA-796-A	Ride, Ride, Ride	DeAu X1398
DLA-797-A	Ridin' Down The Trail To Albuquerque	De 5405, DeAu X1389, X1397, MeC 45201, Min M-14067
DLA-798-A	Sing Cowboy Sing	DeAu X1389
DLA-799-A	Down The Colorado Trail	De 5389, DeAu X1397, MeC 45205, Min M-14065, Pan 26034

Matrix DLA-797-A was scheduled for release on Panachord 26047 but never issued.
Revs: Minerva M-14064 by Rex Griffin, M-14065 by Buck Nation.

Acc. his Texans: M.L. "Rocky" Stone, f; Gene Fleenor, g; Happy Perryman, g; Jack Thornhill, sb; Slim Davis, Happy Perryman, Jack Thornhill, v trio.
Los Angeles, CA   Wednesday, January 4, 1939

| DLA-1697-A | When It's Lamp Lightin' Time In The Valley | De 5648, DeAu X1738, DeIr W5130, Pan 26040 |
| DLA-1698-A | Singin' In The Saddle | De 5639, DeAu X1738, DeIr W5131, Pan 26046 |

| DLA-1699-A | Sundown On The Prairie | De 5648, DeIr W5130, Pan 26040 |
| DLA-1700-A | Viva Tequila | De 5639, DeIr W5131, Pan 26046 |

Acc. his Texans: Charlie Linville, f; Paul Sells, pac; Frank Marvin, sg-1/eff-2/prob. v-3; Johnny Bond, g/v-3; Cliffie Stone, sb/prob. v-3.

Hollywood, CA — Thursday, June 11, 1942

26-A	Jingle Jangle Jingle -2, 3	Cap 110
27-A	Someone -1	Cap 132
28-A	Goodbye My Little Cherokee -1	Cap 110
29-A	I've Done The Best I Could -1	Cap 132

Tex Ritter recorded after 1942.

RIVERSIDE RAMBLERS

This credit is used for recordings by the Hackberry Ramblers with English rather than French vocals. See Hackberry Ramblers.

RIVERSIDE STRING BAND

Unknown, f; poss. another unknown, f; unknown, h; unknown, md; unknown, g; poss. another unknown, g; unknown, v-1/v duet-2.

Atlanta, GA — Saturday, April 19, 1930

| 150297-1; 194948-2 | Hang Out Your Front Door Key -2 | Co unissued |
| 150298-2; 194898-2 | Just Married -1 | Co unissued: *Rdr 1035 (LP)* |

ROANE COUNTY RAMBLERS

Jimmy McCarroll, f; John Kelly, md; Howard Wyatt, bj; Luke Brandon, g.

Johnson City, TN — Monday, October 15, 1928

147182-2	Home Town Blues	Co 15328-D
147183-2	Southern No. 111	Co 15328-D
147184-1	Step High Waltz	Co 15377-D
147185-1	Tennessee Waltz	Co 15377-D

Atlanta, GA — Monday, April 15, 1929

148279-2	McCarroll's Breakdown	Co 15438-D
148280-2	Green River March	Co 15438-D
148281-	Green Valley Waltz	Co unissued
148282-	Bird Dog Waltz	Co unissued
148283-2	Roane County Rag	Co 15398-D
148284-1	Everybody Two Step	Co 15398-D

Jimmy McCarroll, f; John Kelly, md; Howard Wyatt, bj; Luke Brandon, g; Arnum "Curly" Fox, g.

Johnson City, TN — Monday, October 21, 1929

149208-1	Free A Little Bird – 1930 Model	Co 15498-D
149209-2	Johnson City Rag	Co 15498-D
149210-2	Callahan Rag	Co 15570-D
149211-2	Alabama Trot	Co 15570-D
149212-	Big Footed Nigger	Co unissued
149213-	Smoky Mountain Waltz	Co unissued

Howard Wyatt and Luke Brandon also recorded as a duet.

ROANOKE JUG BAND

Billy Altizer, f/v-1; Richard Mitchell, md; Walter Keith, bj; Ray Barger, g; Mahlon B. Overstreet, g; unidentified, calls-2; band sp-3.

Richmond, VA — Friday, October 18, 1929

403177-A	Johnny Lover -2	OK 45423
403178-A	Stone Mountain Rag	OK 45423
403179-A	Triangle Blues	OK 45393
403180-B	Home Brew Rag -1, 3	OK 45393

Despite the group's name, no jug was used.

GEORGE [SHORTBUCKLE] ROARK

George Roark, v; acc. own bj.

Johnson City, TN — Thursday, October 18, 1928

| 147230-1 | I Ain't A Bit Drunk | Co 15383-D |
| 147231-1 | My Old Coon Dog | Co 15383-D |

Shortbuckle Roark & Family: George Roark, Sr., George Roark, Jr., Robert Roark, Oda Roark, v quartet; acc. George Roark, Sr., bj.
    Bristol, TN   Sunday, November 4, 1928

47288-1,-2	Broken-Hearted	Vi unissued
47289-1	I Truly Understand, You Love Another Man	Vi V-40023
47290-1,-2	Terrible Day	Vi unissued
47291-2	My Mother's Hands	Vi V-40023

George Roark Sr., v; acc. own bj.
    Bristol, TN   Sunday, November 4, 1928

47292-1,-2	I Ain't A Bit Drunk	Vi unissued
47293-1,-2	Hook And Line	Vi unissued

George Roark recorded for the Library of Congress in 1938.

LEROY ROBERSON

Leroy Roberson, v; acc. unknown.
    Dallas, TX   Friday, November 1, 1929

TDA-575-	Chicago Bound Blues	Br rejected
TDA-576-	Life In The City	Br rejected

Brunswick files note that these items were originally scheduled for the 7000 ("race") series.

Leroy Roberson, v/y; acc. own g.
    Memphis, TN   Saturday, May 31, 1930

62563-1	Early, Early In The Morning	Vi 23522
62564-2	My Beaumont Mama Blues	Vi 23522

DOC ROBERTS

Listed below are all sides for which Doc Roberts receives sole or primary label-credit, except those which feature the vocals of his partner Asa Martin and son James Roberts, usually credited to **Martin & Roberts** but occasionally to **Fiddling Doc Roberts Trio**. A few items with the latter billing are actually by Martin and Arthur Rose, and are listed under the former, or are solos by James Roberts.

Dock Roberts & Edgar Boaz: Doc Roberts, f; Edgar Boaz, g.
    Richmond, IN   Thursday, October 1, 1925

12358-A	Martha Campbell	Ge 3152
12359	All I've Got Is Done Gone	Ge 3162, Chg 111, 501
12360	My Baby Loves Shortenin' Bread	Ge 3162, Chg 112
12361	Dixie ('Way Down South In Dixie)	Ge 3152, Chg 111

Challenge 111, 112 as by **Uncle Jim Hawkins**.

    Richmond, IN   Friday, November 13, 1925

12418-A	And The Cat Came Back The Very Next Day	Ge 3235, Chg 101, 501
12419	Billy In The Low Grounds [sic]	Ge 3235, Chg 112, Bu 8017

Challenge 101, 112 as by **Uncle Jim Hawkins**, 501 as by **Dock Roberts**. Buddy 8017 as by **Fiddlin' Dock Roberts**. Revs: Challenge 101 (with same credit) by Murray Kellner; Buddy 8017 by Jess Young.

Dock Roberts, v; acc. Edgar Boaz, g.
    Richmond, IN   c. October 1926

12575	In The Shadow Of The Pine	Ge 6025, Ch 15209, Sil 5006, 8151, Spt 9252, Chg 229, Her 75534

Champion 15209 as by **Billy Jordan**. Silvertone 8151, Supertone 9252 as by **Doc Roberts**. Challenge 229 as by **Carl Harris**. Rev. all issues by Welby Toomey.

Fiddlin' Doc Roberts, f; acc. John Booker, g.
    Richmond, IN   Friday, August 26, 1927

13038	Arkansas Traveler	Sil 5079, 8185, Spt 9172
13039	Buck Creek Gal	Ch 15500, Sil 5077, 8180, Spt 9164, Chg 307
13040	Black Eyed Susie	Ge 6257, Ch 15396, Sil 5077, 8180, Spt 9164, Spr 386
13041	Old Buzzard	Ge 6336, Ch 15449, Sil 5079, 8185, Spt 9172, Chg 303
13042	Waynesburgh	Ge 6257, Ch 15449, Sil 5078, 8182, Spt 9168
13043	Cripple Creek	Ge 6336, Ch 15396, Sil 5078, 8182, Spt 9168, Chg 303, Spr 348, Bell 1171

Champion 15396, 15449, 15500, Silvertone 5077, 5078, 5079 as by **Fiddlin' Jim Burke**. Silvertone 8180, 8182, 8185, Supertone 9164, 9168, 9172 as by **Jim Burke**. Challenge 303, 307, Superior 386, and possibly 348 as by **Fiddlin' Frank Nelson**. Bell 1171 as by **Fiddlin' Bob White**.
Matrix 13040 is titled *Black-Eyed Susie* on Silvertone 8180.

Acc. Joe Booker, g.
  Richmond, IN   Saturday, August 27, 1927
    13054   Billy In The Low Ground   Ge 6390, Ch 15500, Sil 8178, Spt 9176, Spr 386,
                                                            Bell 1188
    13055   And The Cat Came Back   Ge 6390, Sil 8179, Spt 9165, Chg 307, Spr 348,
                                                            Bell 1171

Champion 15500 as by **Fiddlin' Jim Burke**. Silvertone 8178, 8179, Supertone 9165, 9176 as by **Jim Burke**. Challenge 303, 307, Superior 386, and possibly 348 as by **Fiddlin' Frank Nelson**. Bell 1171 as by **Fiddlin' Bob White**, 1188 as by **Bob White**.
Revs: Silvertone 8178, Supertone 9176, Bell 1188 by Short Creek Trio; Silvertone 8179, Supertone 9165 by Taylor's Kentucky Boys.

Acc. Asa Martin, g.
  Richmond, IN   Thursday, May 10, 1928
    13799,-A   Dance With A Girl With A Hole In Her Stocking,   Ge rejected
                  Leather Breeches, Big-Eared Mule

  Richmond, IN   Monday, May 14, 1928
    13825,-A,-B   The Irish Washerwoman, Kitty Clyde   Ge rejected
    13826,-A   Sal's Got A Meat Skin Laid Away   Ge rejected
    13827,-A   Sailor's Hornpipe   Ge rejected
    13828   My Old Coon Dog   Ge 6588
    13829   Smoky Row   Ge 6588, Ch 15564

Champion 15564 as by **Fiddlin' Jim Burke**.

  Richmond, IN   Tuesday, May 15, 1928
    13833   Old Zip Coon And Medley Reels   Ge 6495, Ch 15564, 33046
    13834,-A   Old Eliza Jane   Ge rejected
    13835-B   Dance With A Gal With Hole In Her Stocking   Ge 6495, Sil 8176, Spt 9169
    13836   Leather Breeches, Big Eared Mule, Irish Washer- Sil 8176, Spt 9169
                  woman

Champion 15564 as by **Fiddlin' Jim Burke**. Silvertone 8176, Supertone 9169 as by **Jim Burke**. Champion 33046 credit unknown.
Matrix 13835 is titled *Dance Wid A Gal With Hole In 'Er Stocking* on Silvertone 8176, and *Dance Wid A Gal With A Hole In 'Er Stocking* on Supertone 9169.
Rev. Champion 33046 by The Red Fox Chasers.

  Richmond, IN   Friday, August 24, 1928
    14174-A   Shippin' Sport   Ge 6689, Spt 9355
    14175   Brick Yard Joe   Ge 6635, Ch 15608, Spt 9173
    14176-A   New Money   Ge 6775, Spt 9355
    14177   I've Got A Girl Named Susie   Ge 6635, Ch 15668, 45136, Spt 9311
    14178   Run Smoke Run   Ge 6689, Ch 15608, 45136, Spt 9311
    14179   Shoot That Turkey Buzzard   Ge 6775, Ch 15668, Spt 9173
    14180-A   Farewell Waltz   Ge 6717, Spt 9377
    14181   Good Bye Waltz   Ge 6717

Champion 15608, 15668, Supertone 9173, 9311, 9355 as by **Fiddlin' Jim Burke**. Supertone 9377 as by **Gray & Nelson**.
Rev. Supertone 9377 by Byrd Moore.

Doc Roberts & Asa Martin: Doc Roberts, md; Asa Martin, g.
  Richmond, IN   Friday, August 24, 1928
    14186   Mandolin Rag   Ge 6750, Spt 9309
    14187   Take Those Lips Away   Ge 6750, Ch 15690, 45142, Spt 9309, De 5444

Champion 15690 as by **Jim Burke & Jesse Coat**, 45142 as by **Asa Martin**. Supertone 9309 as by **Gray & Nelson**.
Matrices 14182/83 are by Ted Chestnut; matrices 14184/85 are by Asa Martin.

Fiddlin' Doc Roberts, f; acc. Asa Martin, g/v-1/calls-2.
  Richmond, IN   Friday, March 15, 1929
    14911-B   Martha Campbell -2   Spt 9397
    14912   Waltz The Hall -2?   Spt 9670
    14913   The Girl I Left Behind Me -1, 2   Ge 6826, Ch 33001, Spt 9397
    14914   Who's Been Here Since I've Been Gone?   Ge 6826, Spt 9670
    14915   Honeymoon Waltz   Ge 7017, Ch 15749
    14916   Jacks Creek Watlz   Ge 7017, Ch 15749, 45142, De 5444
    14917   Rocky Mountain Goat   Ge 6942, Ch 15873, Spt 9390
    14918   The Devil In Georgia   Ge 6942, Ch 15788, Spt 9390
    14919   Johnny Inchin' Along   Ge 7049, Ch 15873
    14920   Deer Walk   Ge 7049, Ch 15788

Gennett 6826 as by **Doc Roberts & Asa Martin**. Champion 15749 as by **Jim Burke & Jesse Coat**; 15788, 15873, Supertone 9390 as by **Fiddlin' Jim Burke**. Champion 33001 credit unknown. Champion 45142 as by **Asa Martin**. Supertone 9397 as by **Martin & Roberts**, 9670 as by **Gray & Nelson**. Decca 5444 as by **Asa Martin & Doc Roberts**.
Matrix 14916 is titled *Jack's Creek Waltz* on Decca 5444.
Rev. Champion 33001 by Nicholson's Players.

Roberts & Martin: Doc Roberts, md; Asa Martin, g.
   Richmond, IN   Saturday, March 16, 1929
   14921   My Baby Don't Love Me   Ge 7094, Spt 9498
   14922   Shamrock Schottische   Ge 7094, Spt 9498

Supertone 9498 as by **Gray & Nelson**.

Fiddlin' Doc Roberts, f-1/md-2; acc. Asa Martin, h-3/g.
   Richmond, IN   Monday, January 13, 1930
   16086   Rye Straw -1   Ge 7221, Ch 16026
   16087,-A   Callahan -1   Ge rejected
   16090,-A   Sailor On The Deep Blue Sea -2   Ge rejected
   16091   Sally Gooden -1, 3   Ge 7221, Ch 15921, Spr 2762
   16092   Chicken Reel -1, 3   Ge 7110, Ch 15921, Spt 9659
   16093,-A   Maneater -1, 3   Ge unissued
   16094   Hawk's Got A Chicken -1   Ge 7110, Ch 16026, Spt 9659, Spr 2762
   16095,-A   Old Fashioned Picture Of Mother -1/2, 3   Ge rejected

Matrix 16086 on Gennett 7221 as by **Doc Roberts & Asa Martin**. Champion 15921, 16026, Supertone 9659 as by **Fiddlin' Jim Burke**.
Intervening matrices are by Asa Martin.

Doc Roberts, f; acc. Asa Martin, g.
   Richmond, IN   Tuesday, January 14, 1930
   16098   All That I've Got's Done Gone   Ch 16208, 45135
   16099   The Drunken Man's Dream   Ch 16208, 45135

Champion 16208 as by **Fiddlin' Jim Burke**.

Fiddling Doc Roberts Trio: Doc Roberts, f; Asa Martin, g.
   New York, NY   Thursday, March 5, 1931
   10462-2   The Waggoner   Ba 32309, Or 8104, Pe 12765, Ro 5104, Cq 7975
   10463-1,-2   Did You Ever See The Devil, Uncle Joe   Ba 32203, Me M12390, Or 8072, Pe 12724,
                                                             Ro 5072, Cq 8136
   10464-1   Shortenin' Bread   Ba 32309, Or 8104, Pe 12765, Ro 5104, Cq 7975
   10465-2   Sally Ann   Ba 32176, Or 8063, Pe 15467, Ro 5063, Cq 7766
   10466-2   Farewell Waltz   Ba 32176, Or 8063, Pe 15467, Ro 5063, Cq 7766

   New York, NY   Friday, March 6, 1931
   10471-1   Wednesday Night Waltz   Ba 32203, Me M12390, Or 8072, Pe 12724,
                                                             Ro 5072, Cq 8136

Doc Roberts, f; Asa Martin, g; James Roberts, g.
   New York, NY   Friday, March 25, 1932
   11578-1   Turkey In The Straw   Ba 32818, Me M12746, Or 8251, Pe 12929,
                                                               Ro 5251, Cq 7741, ARC-Bwy 8052
   11579-2   I Don't Love Nobody   Ba 32818, Me M12746, Or 8251, Pe 12929,
                                                              Ro 5251, Cq 8239
   11580-1   Over The Waves   Ba 32609, Me M12522, Or 8176, Pe 12857,
                                                              Ro 5176, Cq 8078

Conqueror 8239 as by **Fiddlin' Doc Roberts Trio**.
Regarding Conqueror and ARC-Broadway issues of matrix 11578, see the note following the next session.
Rev. all issues of matrix 11580, though credited to **Fiddling Doc Roberts Trio**, by Asa Martin & James Roberts (see the former).

Doc Roberts, f; Asa Martin, g.
   New York, NY   Saturday, March 26, 1932
   11587-2   The Girl I Left Behind Me   Cq 7741, ARC-Bwy 8052

Conqueror 7741 as by **John Baltzell**, ARC-Broadway 8052 as by **John Barton or Elmer & Jud**.
Earlier issues of Conqueror 7741 and Broadway 8052 (the latter as by **John Barton**) use John Baltzell's Plaza masters of the same tunes.

Doc Roberts, f; Asa Martin, g; James Roberts, g.
   New York, NY   Friday, February 3, 1933
   13027-1   Carroll County Blues   Ba 32713, Me M12641, MeC 91718, Or 8215,
                                                             Pe 12895, Ro 5215, Cq 8104

| 13028-1 | Charleston Number 1 | Ba 32713, Me M12641, MeC 91718, Or 8215, Pe 12895, Ro 5215, Cq 8104 |

Conqueror 8104 as by **Fiddlin' Doc Roberts Trio**.
New York, NY   Wednesday, August 16, 1933

13805-1	Cumberland Gap	Cq 8239
13806-	All I Got's Done Gone	ARC unissued
13807-2	Cumberland Blues	Ba 32889, Me M12834, Or 8281, Pe 12954, Ro 5281, Cq 8240
13808-	Sourwood Mountain	ARC unissued
13811-2	Down Yonder	Ba 32889, Me M12834, Or 8281, Pe 12954, Ro 5281, Cq 8240

Conqueror 8239, 8240 as by **Fiddlin' Doc Roberts Trio**. Matrices 13809/10 are popular.

Fiddlin' Doc Roberts Trio: Doc Roberts, md; Asa Martin, g; James Roberts, g.
New York, NY   Thursday, August 17, 1933

| 13822-1 | Honeymoon Stomp | Cq 8240 |

Fiddling Doc Roberts Trio: Doc Roberts, f-1/md-2; Asa Martin, g; James Roberts, g.
New York, NY   Tuesday, August 28, 1934

15741-1	Pickin' And Playin' -2	ARC 6-03-52
15742-	Spit Devil Rag -1	ARC unissued
15747-1	Blue Grass Rag -1	Ba 33242, Me M13209, MeC 91909, Or 8392, Pe 13073, Ro 5392, Cq 8510
15748-1	'Way Down South -1	Ba 33488, Me M13455, Or 8492, Pe 13162, Ro 5492
15749-1	Coal Tipple Blues -1	Ba 33242, Me M13209, MeC 91909, Or 8392, Pe 13073, Ro 5392, Cq 8510
15750-	Down Home Rag -1	ARC unissued

Matrices 15743/44 are by James Roberts; matrices 15745/46 are by Asa Martin.
Revs: ARC 6-03-52 by Asa Martin; all issues of matrix 15748 (with same credit) by James Roberts.
Doc Roberts recorded after 1942.

FRANK ROBERTS, BUD ALEXANDER & FIDDLIN' SLIM SANDFORD

Frank Roberts, Bud Alexander & Fiddlin' Slim Sampson-1/**Frank Roberts, Bud Alexander & Fiddlin' Slim Sandford**-2: prob.: Fiddlin' Slim Sandford, f; Bud Alexander, md; Frank Roberts, g.
Richmond, IN   Wednesday, September 25, 1929

15676	Sixty Six -1	Pm unissued
15677	Billboard -1	Pm unissued
15678	Kawanha [sic] Waltz -2	Pm unissued
15679	Alabama Dream -2	Pm unissued

Sandford & Roberts-1/**Slim Sandford**-2/**Slim Sandford & Frank Roberts**-3: prob.: Fiddlin' Slim Sandford, f; Frank Roberts, g-4.
Richmond, IN   Wednesday, September 25, 1929

15680	So Long -1, 4	Pm unissued
15681	Traveling Train -2, 4?	Pm unissued
15682	Traveling Preacher -2, 4?	Pm unissued
15683	Fry St. Blues -3, 4	Pm unissued

Frank Roberts, Bud Alexander & Fiddlin' Slim Sandford: prob.: Fiddlin' Slim Sandford, f; Bud Alexander, md; Frank Roberts, g.
Richmond, IN   Wednesday, September 25, 1929

| 15684 | Key Hole Blues | Pm unissued |
| 15685 | See See Ryder | Pm unissued |

Matrices 15676 to 15685 were recorded by Gennett for Paramount. In Gennett files matrices 15680 to 15685 are described as "blues," and there is a strong possibility that these artists are African-Americans, though the files do not, as they customarily would, add the description "race."

[FRED] ROBERTS & [HARMON] CANADA

See Harmon Canada.

JAMES ROBERTS

Most of James Roberts's recordings were vocal duets with Asa Martin and are listed under the latter's name. The following are his recordings as a vocal soloist, or duettist with Arthur Rose.

James Roberts, v; acc. Asa Martin, h/g.
Richmond, IN   Monday, January 13, 1930

| 16088,-A | Long Long Ago | Ge rejected |

Acc. Roy Hobbs, md; Asa Martin, g.
   Richmond, IN   Friday, April 25, 1930
   16530,-A   The Butcher Boy   Ge rejected

Acc. own g.
   New York, NY   Friday, March 6, 1931
   10475-1   May I Sleep In Your Barn Tonight, Mister?   Ba 32205, Or 8074, Pe 12726, Ro 5074, Cq 7765
   10476-2   Crepe On The Cabin Door   Ba 32205, Or 8074, Pe 12726, Ro 5074, Cq 7747
Conqueror 7765 as by **Joe Reeves**. The version of *May I Sleep In Your Barn Tonight, Mister?* on Conqueror 7254, with the same credit, is a Gennett master by Miller Wikel.
Revs: Conqueror 7747 by John McGhee & Frank Welling, 7765 by Gene Autry.

Acc. own or Doc Roberts, md; Asa Martin, g.
   New York, NY   Friday, March 25, 1932
   11577-   Blue Ridge Mountain Blues   ARC unissued

Roberts & Rose: Arthur Rose, v; acc. Doc Roberts, md; Asa Martin, g; James Roberts, g.
   New York, NY   Wednesday, August 16, 1933
   13820-1   Mother, Queen Of My Heart   Ba 32855, Me M12783, MeC 91629, Or 8265,
                                                         Pe 12939, Ro 5265, Cq 8234, Min M-914
Melotone 91629, Conqueror 8234, Minerva M-914 as by **Fiddlin' Doc Roberts Trio**.
Rev. Minerva M-914 by Carlisle Brothers.

James Roberts, Arthur Rose, v duet; acc. Doc Roberts, md; Asa Martin, g; James Roberts, g.
   New York, NY   Thursday, August 17, 1933
   13821-1   Little Mother Of The Hills   Ba 32855, Me M12783, MeC 91629, Or 8265,
                                                          Pe 12939, Ro 5265, Cq 8234
Melotone 91629, Conqueror 8234 as by **Fiddlin' Doc Roberts Trio**.
Matrix 13826, recorded at this session, though issued as by **Martin & Rose** (and therefore listed under Asa Martin), may have featured James Roberts as vocal soloist.

James Roberts, v/y; acc. own g; Asa Martin, g.
   New York, NY   Tuesday, August 28, 1934
   15743-1   A Good Man Is Waiting For You   Ba 33488, Me M13455, Or 8492, Pe 13162,
                                                          Ro 5492
   15744-1   Down And Out Blues   Ba 33325, Me M13292, Or 8422, Pe 13105,
                                                          Ro 5422
All issues of matrix 15743 as by **Fiddling Doc Roberts Trio**.
Rev. all issues of matrix 15743 by Doc Roberts.

James Roberts, v; acc. own g; Asa Martin, g; unidentified, train-wh eff-1.
   New York, NY   Wednesday, August 29, 1934
   15787-2   String Bean Mama   Ba 33325, Me M13292, Or 8422, Pe 13105,
                                                          Ro 5422
   15788-2   Duval County Blues -1   Ba 33400, Me M13367, Or 8452, Pe 13130,
                                                          Ro 5452, Cq 8509
All issues of matrix 15788 as by **James Roberts With Asa Martin**.
Rev. all issues of matrix 15788 by Martin & Roberts (see Asa Martin).
James Roberts recorded after 1942, often with his then wife as James & Martha Carson.

JOHNNY ROBERTS

Johnny Roberts, v; acc. own g.
   Chicago, IL   Sunday, August 11, 1935
   C-90211-   Little Darling   Ch unissued
   C-90212-   When You Were A Boy On My Knee Ch unissued
   New York, NY   mid-November 1935
   60146-B   Memories Of Huey Long   De personal recording
   60147-B   When We Cross That Great Divide   De personal recording
   60148-A   Poor Man's Friend No. 1   De personal recording
   60149-A   Poor Man's Friend No. 2   De personal recording
These unnumbered issues, which are coupled 60146/47 and 60148/49, bear the wording "Sung and Composed by Johnny Roberts/Bossier City, La./Dedicated to the/Share Our Wealth Society/Huey P. Long, Founder."
   New York, NY   Thursday, November 21, 1935
   18290   Put On Your Old Blue Dress   ARC unissued
   18291   My Dear Little Mother   ARC unissued
   18292   I Wish I Had Never Seen Sunshine   ARC unissued
   18293   In That Old Fashioned Buggy   ARC unissued

Acc. unknown, f; own g.
Dallas, TX   Saturday, December 11, 1937
| 63020-A | Put On Your Old Blue Dress | De 5651 |
| 63021-A | I Wish You Were With Me Tonight | De 5651 |

ROBERTS & CANADA
See Harmon Canada.

ROBERTS & MARTIN
See Doc Roberts.

ROBERTS & ROSE
See James Roberts.

A.C. (ECK) ROBERTSON
This artist's full name is Alexander Campbell Robertson.

Henry C. Gilliland–A.C. (Eck) Robertson, f duet.
New York, NY   Friday, June 30, 1922
26660-2	Arkansaw Traveler	Vi 18956
26661-1,-2	Apple Blossom	Vi unissued
26662-1,-2	Forked Deer	Vi unissued
26663-2	Turkey In The Straw	Vi 19149

A.C. (Eck) Robertson, f; acc. Nat Shilkret, p-1.
New York, NY   Saturday, July 1, 1922
26664-1	Sallie Gooden	Vi 18956
26665-1,-2	Brilliancy And Cheatum -1	Vi unissued
26666-1	Sallie Johnson And Billy In The Low Ground -1	Vi 19372
26667-2	Ragtime Annie	Vi 19149
26668-1,-2	1. General Logan 2. Dominion Hornpipe -1	Vi unissued
26669-1	Done Gone -1	Vi 19372

A.C. (Eck) Robertson & Family: A.C. (Eck) Robertson, f; Dueron Robertson, tbj; Nettie Robertson, g; Daphne Robertson, tg.
Dallas, TX   Monday, August 12, 1929
55346-2	Texas Wagoner	Vi V-40145
55347-1	There's A Brown Skin Girl Down The Road Somewhere	Vi V-40145
55348-1	Amarillo Waltz	Vi V-40298
55349-1	Brown Kelly Waltz – Part 1	Vi V-40334, BB B-5777, MW M-4908, RZAu G22483
55350-1	Brown Kelly Waltz – Part 2	Vi V-40334, BB B-5777, MW M-4908, RZAu G22483

Victor V-40145 as by **Eck Robertson**, V-40298 as by **Eck Robertson & Family**.
Nettie Robertson was A.C.'s wife, and Dueron and Daphne their son and daughter.

Eck Robertson–Dr. J.B. Cranfill, f duet; acc. Dueron Robertson, tbj; Nettie Robertson, g; Daphne Robertson, tg.
Dallas, TX   Thursday, October 10, 1929
| 56360-1 | Great Big 'Taters | Vi V-40205 |
| 56361-1 | Run, Boy, Run | Vi V-40205 |

Eck Robertson & Family: A.C. (Eck) Robertson, f/poss. v-1; Dr. J.B. Cranfill, f-2; Dueron Robertson, tbj; Nettie Robertson, g; Daphne Robertson, tg.
Dallas, TX   Thursday, October 10, 1929
| 56362-1,-2 | Apple Blossom -2 | Vi unissued |
| 56363-1,-2 | My Frog Ain't Got No Blues -1 | Vi unissued |

A.C. (Eck) Robertson, f; Dueron Robertson, tbj; Nettie Robertson, g; Daphne Robertson, tg.
Dallas, TX   Friday, October 11, 1929
| 56364-1 | Brilliancy Medley | Vi V-40298 |

Eck Robertson, v/sp; poss. Dueron Robertson, sp; acc. Eck Robertson, g.
Dallas, TX   Friday, October 11, 1929
| 56365-1,-2 | My Experience On The Ranch | Vi unissued |

Eck Robertson, f; Dueron Robertson, g.
Dallas, TX   Friday, October 11, 1929
| 56366-1,-2 | The Arkansaw Traveler | Vi unissued |
| 56367-1,-2 | Sally Goodin | Vi unissued |

Eck Robertson & His Family: Eck Robertson, f/v; Nettie Robertson, g/v.
Dallas, TX   Sunday, October 20, 1929

| 56433-1 | The Island Unknown – Part 1 | Vi V-40166 |
| 56434-2 | The Island Unknown – Part 2 | Vi V-40166 |

Eck Robertson recorded after 1942.

DICK ROBERTSON

This extremely prolific artist recorded chiefly popular material, either in his own name (or variants of it such as **Bob Dickson** and **Dan Roberts**) or as incidental vocalist with dancebands. The recordings listed below, however, fall within the scope of this work.

Dick Robertson, v; acc. Frank Novak, f-1/cl-2/ac-3; unknown, g.
New York, NY   Thursday, October 22, 1931

70298-1	Twenty-One Years -1, 2	Vi 23616, MW M-3311
70299-1	Mary And Mother -2, 3	Vi 23616
70300-1	Up In The Mountains -1	Vi 23627, ZoAu EE329
70901-1	That Silver-Haired Daddy Of Mine -1, 2, 3	Vi 23627, MW M-4319, ZoAu EE329

Revs: Montgomery Ward M-3311 by Lewis James (popular), M-4319 by Dick Robertson (popular).

Dan Parker, v; acc. unknown f; unknown, h-1; unknown, g.
New York, NY   c. December 1931

| 1570-3 | They Cut Down The Old Pine Tree -1 | Cr 3248, *Vs 5014*, Summit 177, Lyric 3438 |
| 1571-3 | When The Sunset Turns The Ocean's Blue To Gold | Cr 3248, *Vs 5014*, Summit 177 |

Varsity 5014 as by **Dick Robertson & Band**. Lyric 3438 as by **Frank Luther**.
Rev. Lyric 3438 by Carson Robison.

Dick Robertson, v; acc. Gene Kardos, f; unknown, cl; unknown, ac; unknown, g.
New York, NY   Friday, January 15, 1932

71232-1	The New Twenty-One Years	Vi 23647
71233-1	Fifty Years Repentin'	Vi 23643, MW M-4328, ZoAu EE360, ZoSA 4367
71234-1	Waiting	Vi 23643
71235-1	My Carolina Home	Vi 23647, ZoAu EE360

Matrices 71236/37, recorded at this session but with orchestral accompaniment, are outside the scope of this work.
Revs: Montgomery Ward M-4328 by Bill Elliott; Zonophone 4367 by Jimmie Davis.

Dan Parker, v; acc. prob. Frank Novak, f-1/ac; unknown, c-2; unknown, h-3; unknown, p-4; unknown, g; unknown, sb-5.
New York, NY   Monday, January 18, 1932

1606-1	That Silver-Haired Daddy Of Mine -1, 2, 3	Cr 3265, Htd 22986, *Vs 5001*
1607-3	Up In The Mountains -4, 5	Cr 3265, Htd 22986, *Vs 5001*
1608-1	Fifty Years Repentin' -1, 2	Cr 3266, Htd 22987, *Vs 5072*, CrC/MeC/Stg/Roy 93025
1609-1	New 21 Years	Cr 3266, Htd 22987, *Vs 5072*, CrC/MeC/Stg/Roy 93025

Varsity 5001, 5072 as by **Dick Robertson**.

Dan & Bill Parker: Dick Robertson, poss. Bob Miller, v duet; acc. prob. Frank Novak, f-1/ac-2/x-3; unknown, c-4; unknown, g.
New York, NY   Monday, February 8, 1932

| 1622-2 | When It's Springtime In The Blue Ridge Mountains -2 | Cr 3279, *Vs 5006* |
| 1623-2 | Carry Me Back To The Mountains -1, 3, 4 | Cr 3279, *Vs 5006* |

Varsity 5006 as by **Dick Robertson**.

Bob Dickson-1/**Dan Parker**-2, v; acc. unknown, f; unknown, ac; unknown, g; unknown, sb.
New York, NY   Thursday, February 25, 1932

1639-2	Rhymes – Part 1 -1	Cr 3290, ?Htd 22983, *Vs 5024*
1640-2	Rhymes – Part 2 -1	Cr 3290, ?Htd 22983, *Vs 5024*
1641-2	99 Years – Part 1 -2	Cr 3291, Htd 22984, *Vs 5023*
1642-1	99 Years – Part 2 -2	Cr 3291, Htd 22984, *Vs 5023*

Varsity 5023, 5024 as by **Smith & Band**. Matrices 1641/42 are titled *99 Years – Fox Trot, Pt. 1/Pt. 2* on Varsity 5023.

Dick Robertson, v; acc. Frank Novak, f-1/cl-2/ac-3/v-4; John Cali, g/v-5.
New York, NY   Thursday, April 28, 1932

72518-1	Behind The Big White House -1, 2	Vi 23679
72519-1	I Found A Peanut -3, 4, 5	Vi 23679
72520-1	Let Me Call You Sweetheart -	Vi 23677, MW M-4341
72521-1	If I Ever Meet The Girl Of My Dreams	Vi 23677
72522-1	Medley Of Familiar Tunes – Part 1 -3	Vi 23684, MW M-4311
72523-1	Medley Of Familiar Tunes – Part 2 -3	Vi 23684, MW M-4311

According to the Victor session-sheet, an unidentified pianist arrived at 11.00 a.m. and was dismissed at 12.30 p.m., but it is not known whether he participated in any recordings.
Pressings of Montgomery Ward M-4311 on the red-and-yellow label bear the same titles as Victor 23684, but on later black-label pressings matrices 72522/23 are titled *Medley Of Old Time Waltzes – Part 1/Part 2*.
Rev. Montgomery Ward M-4341 by Frank Luther.

Dan Parker, v; or **Dan & Bill Parker**-1: Dick Robertson, poss. Bob Miller, v duet; acc. poss. Frank Novak, f-2/ac-3; unknown, bj-4; unknown, g-5.
New York, NY   Monday, August 22, 1932

1806-2	Grandmother's Bible -	Cr 3370, Htd 23088, *Vs 5005*
1807-2	I Can't Go To The Poorhouse -1, 3, 4	Cr 3371, Htd 23089, *Vs 5096*
1808-2	The Crime I Didn't Do -1, 2, 5	Cr 3371, Htd 23098, *Vs 5096*
1809-1	My Alabama Home -1, 3, 4	Cr 3369, Htd 23087, *Vs 5005*
1810-2	Missouri Is Calling -2, 5	Cr 3369, Htd 23087, *Vs 5012*

Varsity 5005, 5012 as by **Dick Robertson**, 5096 as by **Harry Dick**.
Matrix 1809 is titled *Alabama Home Of Mine* on Varsity 5005.
Revs: Crown 3370, Homestead 23088 by Johnny Marvin; Varsity 5012 (with same credit) by Clayton McMichen.

Dick Robertson, v; acc. unknown, f; unknown, t; unknown, s; unknown, sg; unknown, p; unknown, g; unknown, sb; unknown, x.
New York, NY   Tuesday, October 3, 1933

14102-1	The Last Round-Up	Me M12813, Pe 12945, Cq 8258, CrC/MeC/Stg/Roy 91631, Min M-920
14103-2	There's A Home In Wyomin'	Me M12813, Pe 12945, Cq 8258, CrC/MeC/Stg/Roy 91631

Other items recorded at this session are beyond the scope of this work.
Rev. Minerva M-920 by Wenatchee Mountaineers (see Elton Britt).

TEXAS JIM ROBERTSON

Texas Jim Robertson, v; acc. prob. own g; Elton Britt, g.
New York, NY   Friday, May 12, 1939

036935-1	What Good Is The Sunshine?	BB B-8207, MW M-8483, RZAu G24745
036936-1	Things That Might Have Been	BB B-8186, MW M-8482, RZAu G24129, Twin FT8810
036937-1	I'm Gonna Throw My Lasso	BB B-8207, MW M-8483, RZAu G24745
036938-1	Bouncin' Along	BB B-8186, MW M-8482, RZAu G24129, Twin FT8810

Acc. prob. Blackie Summers, f; prob. own g.
New York, NY   Wednesday, April 17, 1940

050104-1	'Way Down In Texas (Where The Blue Bonnets Grew)	BB B-8466, RZAu G24421
050105-1	Windy Ben	BB B-8435, RZAu G24776
050106-1	Purple Night On The Prairie	BB B-8466, RZ ME57, RZAu G24421, RZIr IZ1339
050107-1	My Pony's Hair Turned Grey (When My Darling Ran Away)	BB B-8435, RZAu G24776

Revs: Regal-Zonophone ME57, IZ1339 by Texas Jim Robertson (postwar).

Acc. prob. Blackie Summers, f; prob. own g; unknown, sb.
New York, NY   Wednesday, November 27, 1940

057796-1	I'm Gonna Be Long Gone	BB B-8631
057797-1	I'll Be Back In A Year, Little Darling	BB B-8606
057798-1	My Ma, She Told Me So	BB B-8631
057799-1	The Cowboy Isn't Speaking To His Horse	BB B-8606, RZAu G24990

Rev. Regal-Zonophone G24990 by Jake & Carl.

Acc. Bert Hirsch, f; Frank Novak, ac; Carl DeVries, g.
New York, NY   Friday, March 7, 1941

062737-1	There's A Heart In The Heart Of The Rockies	BB B-8706
062738-1	Too Blue To Cry	BB B-8706, Vi 20-2158
062739-1	Birmingham Woman	BB B-8686
062740-1	Brother Henry	BB B-8686

Acc. Frank Novak, f/cl; Chas. Magnante, pac; Jack Shilkret, p; Johnny Cali, bj/g; Ken Binford, g; Gene Traxler, sb; Walter Scanlon, W. Fariss, Earl Waldo, Roy Halle, v quartet.
New York, NY   Friday, June 27, 1941

066151-1	O Bury Me Not On The Lone Prairie (The Dying Cowboy)	Vi 27551

066152-1	Home On The Range	Vi 27550
066153-1	The Cowboy's Dream	Vi 27550
066154-1	Red River Valley	Vi 27552, V-D 84

Acc. Frank Novak, f/cl; Chas. Magnante, ac; Jack Shilkret, p; Johnny Cali, bj/g; Ken Binford, g; Gene Traxler, sb; Walter Scanlon, W. Fariss, Earl Waldo, Roy Halle, v quartet-1.
New York, NY   Monday, June 30, 1941

066160-1	Ridin' Old Paint (And Leadin' Old Dan) -1	Vi 27553
066161-1	In Texas For The Round-Up In The Spring -1	Vi 27551, V-D 84
066162-1	The Texas Song (A Cowboy Lament)	Vi 27553
066163-1	The Border Affair (Mi Amor, Mi Corazon)	Vi 27552

Victor 27550 to 27553 were issued in album P84.

Acc. Bert Hirsch, f; Harry Duncan, f; George Horton, g; Walter Rosnell, g; Lester Braun, sb.
New York, NY   Friday, March 20, 1942

073627-1	(Darling, What I've Been Thru) You'll Never Know	BB B-9017
073628-1	(The Moon And The Water And) Miz O'Reilly's Daughter	BB 33-0503, Vi 20-2158
073629-1	When This War Is Over (The Volunteer's Farewell)	BB B-9017
073630-1	Sweet Baby (Come Back Where You Belong)	BB 33-0503

Texas Jim Robertson recorded after 1942.

THE ROBERTSON FAMILY
See A.C. (Eck) Robertson.

FRANK ROBESON
Pseudonym on Phonycord for Carson Robison.

ROBIN & SOILEAU
See Leo Soileau.

MELVIN ROBINETTE & BYRD MOORE
See Byrd Moore.

CARSON ROBINSON TRIO
The Carson Robison Trio is erroneously credited thus on Lyric 3386 and Taiyo 30005.

PAUL ROBINSON (THE HARMONICA KING)
Paul Robinson, h solo.
Richmond, IN   Wednesday, August 27, 1930
| 16947,-A | Imitations | Ge rejected |

Richmond, IN   Thursday, August 28, 1930
| 16948 | White Mule | Ge rejected |

ROBINSON & EVANS
Pseudonym on Challenge for Melvin Robinette & Byrd Moore (see the latter).

CARSON ROBISON

Carson Robison's first recordings (for Victor, in May 1924) were with the vaudeville artist Wendell Hall. He subsequently acted as house accompanist, for Victor and other labels, to numerous country recording artists, such as the Fiddlin' Powers Family, Kelly Harrell, and Buell Kazee. In 1926-28 he was chiefly engaged in collaborations, both credited and uncredited, with Vernon Dalhart, all of which are listed under the latter. His solo, and some other, recordings from that period, however, are listed below. (But not his accompaniments to popular artists, nor his orchestral recordings in his own name, some of which are detailed in JR.)

In 1928-32 Robison worked chiefly in collaboration with Frank Luther. Their recordings, when issued, might be credited to one or the other, or to both of them, often on no logical principle and sometimes at variance with the musical content. Consequently, for the sake of clarity, *all* their recordings from that period, *both joint and individual*, are listed below, including items by Luther in which Robison's participation is uncertain. Also included are a few recordings involving, and sometimes crediting, Luther's brother Phil Luther Crow. The recordings Frank Luther made after he broke up with Robison are listed separately, under his own name.

Many Robison-Luther collaborations were under pseudonyms (**Bud & Joe Billings**, **Black Brothers**, **Jones Brothers**, etc.). It may be assumed that any pseudonymous item described here as "vocal duet" is sung by Robison and Luther, unless otherwise stated.

In 1932 Robison visited Britain and made numerous recordings, to which he added on visits in 1936 and 1939. None of that material was issued in the U.S. (though a good deal of it was in Australia), but it seems appropriate to document it here, since it hardly differs in repertoire or performance style from his contemporary U.S. recordings.

Carson Robison, v/wh; acc. own g.
New York, NY   Monday, April 5, 1926
   35281-1,-2,-3   Just Whistle   Vi unissued
   35282-1,-2   Strummin' The Blues Away   Vi unissued

Roy Smeck & Carson Robison: Roy Smeck, octachorda; Carson Robison, g.
New York, NY   Monday, April 12, 1926
   35305-1,-2,-3,-4   Twilight Echoes   Vi unissued
   35306-1,-2,-3,-4   Tough Pickin'   Vi unissued

Carson Robison & Roy Smeck: Roy Smeck, octachorda; Carson Robison, g.
New York, NY   Tuesday, April 13, 1926
   141954-2   Tough Pickin'   Co 724-D, CoAu 0627
   141955-3   Twilight Echoes   Co 724-D, CoAu 0627

Columbia 0627 as by **Roy Smeck & Carson Robison**.

Roy Smeck & Carson Robison: Roy Smeck, octachorda; Carson Robison, g.
New York, NY   Saturday, April 24, 1926
   E-2903/04W   Tough Pickin'   Vo 15338, 5135
   E-2905/06W   Twilight Echoes   Vo unissued

Carson Robison, v/wh; acc. unknown.
New York, NY   Thursday, June 17, 1926
   142315-   Just Whistle   Co unissued

Roy Smeck & Carson Robison: Roy Smeck, octachorda; Carson Robison, g.
New York, NY   c. June 1926
   E-3238/40W   Twilight Echoes   Vo 15338, 5135

Carson Robison, v; acc. own g.
New York, NY   Wednesday, July 7, or Thursday, July 8, 1926
   142371-   Strummin' My Blues Away   Co unissued

Roy Smeck & Carson Robison: Roy Smeck, octachorda; Carson Robison, g.
New York, NY   prob. September 11, 1926
   80100-   Twilight Echoes   OK 40705
   80101-   Tough Pickin'   OK 40705

Carson Robison, v/wh; acc. prob. own g.
New York, NY   c. late October 1926
   80207-   Nola   OK 40717
   80208-   Just Whistle   OK 40717

Carson J. Robison, wh; acc. unknown, p.
New York, NY   Wednesday, November 24, 1926
   143148-4   Nola   Co 840-D

New York, NY   Tuesday, November 30, 1926
   143159-5   Whistle-Itis   Co 840-D

Carson Robison, wh; acc. own p-1; Nat Shilkret, p-2.
New York, NY   Wednesday, December 8, 1926
   37111-1   Nola -1   Vi 20382
   37112-1   Whistle-itis -2   Vi 20382

Acc. unknown, p.
New York, NY   January 1927
   11466   Nola   Ed 51939
   11467   Whistle-itis   Ed 51939

Carson Robison (The Kansas Jay Bird), wh; acc. prob. own g.
New York, NY   c. January 31, 1927
   GEX-504-A   Nola   Ge 6070, Ch 15248
   GEX-505-A   Whistle-itis   Ge 6070

Rev. Champion 15248 by Ernest V. Stoneman.

Roy Smeck & Carson Robison: Roy Smeck, octachorda; Carson Robison, g.
New York, NY   Wednesday, March 28, 1928
   35305-   Twilight Echoes   Vi 21277

Rev. Victor 21277 by Roy Smeck & Art Kahn (popular).

Carson Robison & Roy Smeck: Roy Smeck, octachorda; Carson Robison, g.
New York, NY   March 1928

| 18297 | Tough Pickin' | Ed 52260 |
| 18298 | Twilight Echoes | Ed 52260 |

Robison–Luther, prob. v duet; acc. unknown.
New York, NY   Friday, June 8, 1928

| 8022- | Steamboat (Keep Rockin') | Pl unissued |
| 8023- | There's A Whippoorwill A Calling | Pl unissued |

Frank Luther, v; acc. prob. Murray Kellner, f; Carson Robison, h/g.
New York, NY   c. June 15-16, 1928

| GEX-1439-A | The West Plains Explosion | Ge 6530, Ch 15526, Spt 9183 |
| GEX-1440-A | The Hanging Of Charles Birger | Ge 6530, Ch 15526, Spt 9183 |

Champion 15526 as by **Dan Blanchard**.

Frank Luther & Carson Robison & Company, v duet; acc. two unknowns, f; prob. Carson Robison, g/wh-1.
New York, NY   Monday, June 18, 1928

| 18579-B | The Little Green Valley -1 | Ed 52351, 5572 |
| 18580-C | Six Feet Of Earth (Makes Us All Of One Size) | Ed 52351, 5564 |

For duets by Carson Robison & Andrew Jenkins, recorded for OKeh on June 19-20, 1928, see the latter.

Frank Luther, v; acc. unknown, f; unknown, h-1; unknown, cel-2; unknown, bj; unknown, g; poss. Carson Robison, wh-3.
?Chicago, IL   Wednesday, June 20, 1928

| E-7405- | The Song Of The Prune (No Matter How Young A Prune May Be It's Always Full Of Wrinkles) -1, 2 | Vo 5227 |
| E-7406- | Down In De Cane Break -3 | Vo 5227 |

Carson Robison & Frank Luther, v duet; acc. two unknowns, f; Carson Robison, g/wh.
New York, NY   Tuesday, June 26, 1928

E-27778-	In The Hills Of Old Kentucky	Br unissued
E-27779-	The Little Green Valley	Me M12179, Po P9062
E-27780-	Drifting Down The Trail Of Dreams	Me M12179, Po P9062

Melotone M12179, Polk P9062 as by **The Jones Brothers**.

Bud Billings: Frank Luther, v; acc. two unknowns, f; prob. Carson Robison, g.
New York, NY   Friday, June 29, 1928

| 45837-3 | Since Mother's Gone | Vi 21555, Zo 5575, ZoAu EE113 |
| 45838-1 | A Mother's Plea | Vi 21555, Zo 5575, ZoAu EE113 |

Zonophone 5575 possibly as by **Bud & Joe Billings**.

Carson Robison Trio: Frank Luther, v; acc. poss. Murray Kellner, f; Carson Robison, g.
New York, NY   June/July 1928

| 108265- | Since Mother's Gone | Pat 32387, Pe 12466 |
| 108266- | A Mother's Plea | Pat 32387, Pe 12466 |

New York, NY   June/July 1928

| 3255-A | Since Mother's Gone | Ca 8284, Lin 2932, Ro 707 |
| 3256-A | A Mother's Plea | Ca 8288, Lin 2936, Ro 711 |

Rev. all issues by Frank Marvin.

Robison–Luther, prob. v duet; acc. unknown.
New York, NY   Monday, July 2, 1928

| 8022- | Steamboat (Keep Rockin') | Pl unissued |
| 8023- | There's A Whippoorwill A Calling | Pl unissued |

These are additional takes to those of June 8, 1928.

Frank Luther, v; acc. two unknowns, f; prob. Carson Robison, g.
New York, NY   Monday, July 2, 1928

| 8069- | Since Mother's Gone | Ba 7207, Do 0255, Or 1328, Re 8624, Chg 545, Cq 7166 |
| 8070- | A Mother's Plea | Ba 7181, Do 0255, Je 5350, Or 1325, Re 8624, Chg 698, Cq 7166, Pm 3225, Bwy 8166, 8214 |

If matrix 8070 was used, as reported, on Broadway 8214, it replaced the Paramount matrix of this title (21165) by Owen Mills (David Miller) & Frank Welling and presumably adopted the Mills–Welling pseudonymous credit of **Harkins & Owens**. Some issues of matrix 8070 use the control 1678-2.

Bud Billings: Frank Luther, v; or **Bud Billings–Carson Robison**-1, v duet; acc. two unknowns, f; Carson Robison, g/wh-2; Frank Luther, vb.
New York, NY   Tuesday, July 17, 1928

| 46315-3 | I Tore Up Your Picture When You Said Good-bye (But I Put It Together Again) | Vi 21604, Zo 5318, ZoAu EE115 |
| 46316-2 | Do You Still Remember? -1, 2 | Vi 21604, Zo 5318, ZoAu EE115 |

Matrix 46316 on Zonophone 5318 as by **Bud Billings & Carson Robison**.

Carson J. Robison & Frank Luther, v duet; acc. two unknowns, f; prob. Carson Robison, g; prob. Frank Luther, bell-1; unknown, steam-wh-2.
New York, NY   Tuesday, July 17, 1928

| 8022-9 | Steamboat (Keep Rockin') -1, 2 | Ba 7207, Do 0254, Or 1325, Re 8606, Chg 545 |
| 8023-8 | There's A Whippoorwill A Calling | Ba 7181, Do 0254, Je 5350, Or 1328, Re 8606, Chg 698 |

Some issues of matrix 8023 use the control 1677-8.

Bud Billings–Carson Robison, v duet; acc. Murray Kellner, f; Carson Robison, h-1/g; Lew Shilkret, o-2.
New York, NY   Thursday, July 26, 1928

| 46613-2 | Will The Circle Be Unbroken? -2 | Vi 21586, BB B-6406, MW M-8194, Au 212, Twin FT8144 |
| 46614-2 | You'll Never Miss Your Mother Till She's Gone -1 | Vi 21586, BB B-5297, Eld 2168, Sr S-3378, MW M-4479, Au 212, ZoSA 4272 |

Aurora 212 as by **Chester & Rollins**.
Revs: Bluebird B-5297, Electradisk 2168, Sunrise S-3378, Montgomery Ward M-4479 by The Vagabonds; Montgomery Ward M-8194 by the Stamps Quartet; Bluebird B-6406, Twin FT8144 by Vernon Dalhart.

Black Brothers, v duet; acc. unknown, f; unknown, f-1; Carson Robison, g/wh; prob. Frank Luther, x-2/bell-3.
New York, NY   Friday, July 27, 1928

400892-B	The Little Green Valley	OK 45244, Ve 2365-V, Cl 5299-C, PaE R3870
400893-C	Down In The Hills -1, 3	OK 45244, Ve 2354-V, Cl 5288-C, PaE R3870
400894-B	Do You Still Remember? -1, 2, 3	OK 45253, Ve 2411-V, Cl 5347-C, PaE E6143, R3874

Velvet Tone and Clarion issues as by **Carson Robison Trio**. Parlophone E6143 as by **Carson Robison & Frank Luther**.
Velvet Tone and Clarion issues use transfer matrices, as follows: 400892 = 100528; 400893 = 100507; 400894 = 100543.

Frank Luther, v; acc. unknown, f; Carson Robison, h/g.
New York, NY   ? c. July 1928

3016-A,-B	The Wreck Of The Royal Palm	GG/Rad 4200
3017-B	I Wish I Was Single Again	GG/Rad 4141
3017-C	I Wish I Was Single Again	GG/Rad 4299, VD 84299

Van Dyke 84299 as by **Jeff Calhoun**.
The first issues of Grey Gull/Radiex 4141 use a Vernon Dalhart recording of *I Wish I Was Single Again* (matrix 2398). Later issues use the Luther recording above, first as by **Jeff Calhoun**, subsequently as by **Frank Luther**.
Matrices shown on labels are not always correct for the version chosen.
Revs: Grey Gull/Radiex 4141, 4200 by Arthur Fields.

Acc. unknown, f; prob. Carson Robison, h/g.
New York, NY   ? c. July 1928

3031-C	The Butcher Boy	GG/Rad 4133, Mad/VD 5078
3032-A	Jesse James	GG/Rad 4133
3032-B	Jesse James	Mad/VD 5073

Madison/Van Dyke 5073, 5078 as by **Tom Cook**.
The first issues of Grey Gull/Radiex 4133 couple Vernon Dalhart recordings of *Jesse James* (matrix 2344) and *The Butcher Boy* (matrix 2397). Matrices shown on labels are not always correct for the version chosen.
Revs: Madison/Van Dyke 5073 by Vernon Dalhart, 5078 by Arthur Fields.

Carson Robison Trio: Frank Luther, v; or v duet-1; acc. unknown, f; unknown, f-2; Carson Robison, g/wh-3.
New York, NY   July/August 1928

108294-2; 3282	The Prune Song (No Matter How Young A Prune May Be It's Always Full Of Wrinkles)	Ca 8313, Lin 2961, Pat 32386, Pe 12465, Ro 736, Ang 3065, Starr 726, Worth 7051
108295-2; 3283	Down In De Cane Brake -3	Ca 8313, Lin 2961, Pat 32386, Pe 12465, Ro 736
108296-1,-2; 3284	I Tore Your Picture Up When You Said Good-Bye (But I've Put It Together Again) -2, 3	Ca 8307, Lin 2955, Pat 32381, Pe 12460, Ro 730, Ang 3071
108297-1; 3285	Do You Still Remember? -1, 2, 3	Ca 8307, Lin 2955, Pat 32396, Pe 12475, Ro 730

Angelus 3065, Starr 726 as by **Jack Kaufman**. Angelus 3071 as by **Charles Hart**. Worth 7051 as by **Happiness Boys**; matrix 108294 is titled *Prune Song* on that issue. Matrix 108297 is titled *Do You Stil Remember* on Pathé 32396.
Matrices 108296/97 were technically remade as Brunswick matrices B 14212/13 on October 25, 1933 but not issued.
Revs: Pathé 32396, Perfect 12475 by Frank Marvin; Pathé 32381, Perfect 12460 by Irving Kaufman (popular); Angelus 3071 (with same credit) popular.

Black Brothers, v duet; acc. unknown, f; prob. Carson Robison, g/wh; prob. Frank Luther, x.
    New York, NY   Friday, August 3, 1928
    401052-C   I Tore Up Your Picture When You Said Good-bye   OK 45253, PaE E6143, R3874
                          (But I've Put It Together Again)

Parlophone E6143 as by **Frank Luther**; the parenthesized part of the title is omitted on that issue.

Pete Wiggins: Frank Luther, v; acc. prob. Carson Robison, g.
    New York, NY   Monday, August 6, 1928
    401056-A   Hallalujah! I'm A Bum   OK 41092, PaAu A2596
    401057-B   The Bum Song   OK 41092, PaAu A2596

Francis Luther, v; acc. prob. Carson Robison, g; unknown, sp-1.
    New York, NY   Friday, August 10, 1928
    E-28034-   The Bum Song -1   Br 254, 4029, BrE 3858, BrAu 4029, Pan 25221,
                                                           Rex 9819
    E-28035-   Hallelujah, I'm A Bum   Br 254, 4029, BrE 3858, BrAu 4029, Spt S2056,
                                                           Pan 25221, Rex 9819

Supertone S2056, Panachord 25221, Rex 9819 as by **Frank Luther**.
Rev. Supertone S2056 by Buell Kazee.

Francis Luther & Carson Robison, v duet; acc. two unknowns, f; Carson Robison, g/wh; prob. Frank Luther, x.
    New York, NY   Friday, August 10, 1928
    E-28036   Do You Still Remember?   Br 262, 4052, BrAu 262, BrAu 4052
    E-28037-   I Tore Up Your Picture When You Said Goodbye   Br 262, 4052, BrAu 262, BrAu 4052
                          (But I Put It Together Again)

Matrix E-28036 is titled *So You Still Remember* on some Australian Brunswick pressings.

Frank Luther, v; acc. Bert Hirsch, f; Carson Robison, g.
    New York, NY   Wednesday, August 15, 1928
    18653   The Butcher's Boy   Ed 52377, 5594
    N-361   The Butcher's Boy   Ed 11008
    18654   Barbara Allen   Ed 52377, 5596
    N-362   Barbara Allen   Ed 11008

Weary Willie (Pat/Pe)/**Lazy Larry** (Ca/Lin/Ro): Frank Luther, v; acc. prob. Murray Kellner, f-1; Carson Robison, g.
    New York, NY   mid-August 1928
    108317-1; 3319   Who Said I Was A Bum?   Ca 8345, Lin 2993, Pat 32389, Pe 12468,
                                                          Ro 768, HGS 2021
    108318-1,-2;   Jack Of All Trades -1   Ca 8314, Lin 2962, Pat 32389, Pe 12468,
    3320-A   Ro 737, Cq 7846, Ang 3065

Herschel Gold Seal 2021 as by **Happy Jackson**. Angelus 3065 as by **Jack Kaufman**.

John Albin: v/wh-1 duet; or prob. Frank Luther, v-2; acc. unknown, f; prob. Carson Robison, h/g; prob. Frank Luther, jh-3.
    New York, NY   c. August 1928
    31306-2   Blue Ridge Mountain Home -1, 3   Marathon 042
    31307-2   Pappy's Buried On The Hill -2   Marathon 042
                  The Little Green Valley -   Marathon 048
                  Climbin' Up De Golden Stairs -   Marathon 048

It is likely that Marathon 048 uses the matrices 31310 and 31311. These are 7-inch discs.

Weary Willie (Pat/Pe)/**"Lazy" Larry** (Ca/Lin/Ro): Frank Luther, v; acc. Carson Robison, g.
    New York, NY   August/September 1928
    108332-;   Hallelujah! I'm A Bum   Ca 8296, Lin 2944, Pat 32382, Pe 12461,
    3274-A,-C   Ro 719, Ang 3054, Electron 5117,
                                                           MeAu 10072, Regent 1056, StgAu 1133,
                                                           StAu 711, Worth 7014
    108333-; 3275-A   The Bum Song   Ca 8296, Lin 2944, Pat 32382, Pe 12461,
                                                           Ro 719, Ang 3054, Electron 5117,
                                                           MeAu 10072, Regent 1056, StgAu 1133,
                                                           StAu 711, Worth 7014

Different takes of matrix 108332 are reported on Cameo 8296 and Lincoln 2944.
Angelus 3054, Melotone 10072, Sterling 1133, Starr 711 as by **Lazy Larry**. Electron 5117 as by **George Byers**. Regent 1056 as by **Reggie Black**. Worth 7014 as by **Allan Royal**.
Matrix 108332/3274 is titled *Hallelujah I'm A Bum* on Angelus 3054, Electron 5117, Melotone 10072, Regent 1056, Sterling 1133, and *Hallelujah, I'm A Bum* on Starr 711, Worth 7014. On all Australian issues except Sterling 1133, matrix 3275 is subtitled (*The Song Of The Tramp*).

Carson J. Robison & Frank Luther, v duet; acc. two unknowns, f; Carson Robison, g/wh; Frank Luther, x.
    New York, NY   Friday, September 7, 1928

8179-	Do You Still Remember?	Ba 7233, 32058, Ca 8307, Do 0260, 4705, Je 6180, Or 1354, 2180, Re 8643, 10238, Ro 1545, Cq 7735
8180-	Down In The Hills	Ba 7234, Do 0260, Or 1353, Re 8643, Chg 916

Banner 7233, 7234 as by **Carson J. Robison & Francis Luther**. Banner 32058, Conqueror 7735, Jewel 6180, Oriole 2180, Romeo 1545 as by **Carson Robison Trio**. Challenge 916 as by **Francis Evans & Carson Robison**.
Controls appear on various issues instead of, or as well as, the matrices, as follows: 8179 = 1781-2; 8180 = 1783-1.
Revs: Banner 7233, 7234, 32058, Conqueror 7735, Jewel 6180, Oriole 1353, 2180, Regal 10238, Romeo 1545 by Frank Marvin.

Frank Evans: Frank Luther, v; prob. acc. two unknowns, f; Carson Robison, g/wh; own x.
New York, NY   Friday, September 7, 1928

8181-	Never No Mo' Blues	Or 1439

Oriole 1439 uses the control 1959.

Bud & Joe Billings, v duet; acc. two unknowns, f; Carson Robison, g/wh; unknown, vc.
New York, NY   Tuesday, September 11, 1928

47500-2	Down In The Hills	Vi 23534

Bud Billings: Frank Luther, v; acc. unknown, f-1; Carson Robison, h-2/g; unknown, jh-3; unknown, train-wh eff-4.
New York, NY   Tuesday, September 11, 1928

47501-3	The Wreck Of Number Nine -1, 2, 4	Vi V-40021, MW M-8054
47502-1	Jack Of All Trades -1, 2, 3	Vi 21686
47503-1	Who Said I Was A Bum?	Vi 21686

Rev. Montgomery Ward M-8054 by the Georgia Yellow Hammers.

Frank Luther & His Pards: Frank Luther, v; acc. Bert Hirsch, f; Carson Robison, g.
New York, NY   Thursday, September 27, 1928

18765	Jack Of All Trades	Ed 52413, 5616
N-467	Jack Of All Trades	Ed unissued
18766	Who Said I Was A Bum?	Ed 52413, 5614
N-468	Who Said I Was A Bum?	Ed unissued

Frank Luther, v; acc. unknown, f; prob. Carson Robison, h-1/g/wh-2.
New York, NY   Friday, September 28, 1928

8215-	The Porto [sic] Rico Storm -1	Ba 7259, Do 0263, Re 8660, Chg 925, Htd 16390
8216-	An Old Man's Story -1	Ba 6221, Do 4237, Or 1413, Re 8679, Chg 944, Pm 3126, Bwy 8095, 8162
8217-	Where The Silv'ry Colorado Wends Its Way -1, 2	Ba 7259, Chg 925, Htd 16390, Pm 3129, Bwy 8091
8218-	Where The Sunset Turns The Ocean's Blue To Gold -2	Ba S6228, Do 0263, Or 1404, Re 8660, Pm 3129, Bwy 8091

This session was logged as by **Francis Luther** but Banner 7259 and Broadway 8095 are the only issues known to be so credited. Homestead 16390, Oriole 1404, 1413, Challenge 944 as by **Frank Evans**. Challenge 925 as by **Francis Evans**.
Controls appear on various issues instead of, or as well as, the matrices, as follows: 8215 = 1837-3; 8216 = 1895-2, 1127; 8217 = 1838-2, 1122; 8218 = 1859-1, 1123.
Rev. Broadway 8162 by Vernon Dalhart.

Acc. unknown, f; Carson Robison, h/g.
New York, NY   c. September 1928

3128-B	Wreck Of The Titanic	GG/Rad 4131, VD 5112

First issues of Grey Gull/Radiex 4131 use Vernon Dalhart's recording of *Wreck Of The Titanic* (matrix 2396), as by **Jeff Calhoun**. It was replaced by matrix 3128-B, as by both **Jeff Calhoun** and **Frank Luther**.
Matrices shown on labels are not always correct for the version chosen.
Revs: Grey Gull/Radiex 4131 by Arthur Fields; Van Dyke 5112 by Bob Miller.

Carson Robison Trio: Frank Luther, v; acc. poss. Murray Kellner, f; prob. Carson Robison, h/g/wh-1; unknown, jh-2.
New York, NY   September/October 1928

108399-; 3378	Goin' To Have A Big Time Tonight -1, 2	Ca 8345, Lin 2993, Pat 32405, Pe 12484, Ro 768, HGS 2021
108400-1; 3379	The Porto [sic] Rico Storm	Ca 8346, Lin 2994, Pat 32397, Pe 12476, Ro 769
108401-2; 3380	An Old Man's Story	Ca 8346, Lin 2994, Pat 32397, Pe 12476, Ro 769

Romeo 768 as by "**Lazy**" **Larry**. Herschel Gold Seal 2021 as by **Happy Jackson**.
Revs: Pathé 32405, Perfect 12484 by Frank Marvin.

Black Brothers, v duet; acc. unknown, f; Carson Robison, g/wh; Frank Luther, bell/wh-1.
New York, NY   Tuesday, October 9, 1928

401205-A	On A Blue Lagoon	OK 45270

401206-C   Howdy, Old Timer -1   OK 45270, Ve 2391-V, Cl 5325-C

Velvet Tone 2391-V, Clarion 5325-C as by **Carson Robison Trio**. Those issues use the transfer matrix 100535.

Harry Black: Frank Luther, v; acc. unknown, f; unknown, o; poss. Carson Robison, g-1.
New York, NY   Friday, October 26, 1928
410269-A   Christmas Holds No Joy For Me -1   OK 45272
401270-B   Jesus The Light Of The World   OK 45272

Bud Billings: Frank Luther, v; acc. unknown, f; unknown, c; unknown, s; unknown, o.
New York, NY   Wednesday, October 31, 1928
48104-1,-2,-3   Will There Be A Santa Claus In Heaven?   Vi unissued
48105-1,-2,-3   The Baby On The Doorstep   Vi unissued

Frank Luther & Carson J. Robison, v duet; acc. unknown.
New York, NY   Thursday, November 1, 1928
8283-   On A Blue Lagoon   Ba 6219, Je 5449, Or 1409

Jewel 5449, Oriole 1409 as by **Robison & Evans**. Those issues use the control 1854.

Frank Luther, v/y-1; acc. prob. Carson Robison, g.
New York, NY   Thursday, November 1, 1928
8284-   Neapolitan Nights   Ba 6219, Do 4235, Je 5449, Or 1404, Re 8676
8285-2   Goin' To Lay Me Down In The Cold, Cold Ground -1   Do 4239, Or 1412, Re 8681

Jewel 5449, Oriole 1404 as by **Frank Evans**.
Controls appear on various issues instead of, or as well as, the matrices, as follows: 8284 = 1893; 8285 = 1904.
Revs: Domino 4235, Regal 8676 by Roy Smeck's Trio (popular).

Carson Robison, v; acc. two unknowns, f; prob. own g/wh-1; unknown, steamboat-wh-2.
New York, NY   c. November 7, 1928
GEX-2135   The Swanee Kitchen Door -1   Ge 6683, Ch 15626, Spt 9337
GEX-2136   Steamboat (Keep Rockin') -2   Ge 6683, Ch 15626, Spt 9337

Frank Luther, v; acc. unknown, f; Carson Robison, h-1/g-2; unknown, o-3; unknown, bj-4; own jh-5/bell-6.
New York, NY   Thursday, November 8, 1928
8300-   Ohio River Blues -1, 2, 4, 5   Ba 6342, Do 0267, Je 5563, Or 1525, Re 8696, Chg 991
8301-   A Choir Boy Sings All Alone To-Night -3, 6   Ba 6221, Do 4236, Or 1413, Re 8677, Chg 944, Pm 3128, Bwy 8092
8302-   The Baby On The Doorstep -2, 3   Ba S6225, Do 4236, Je 5459, Or 1415, Re 8677, Chg 945, Pm 3128, Bwy 8092

Banner 6342 as by **Carson Robison & Frank Luther**. Challenge 944, 945, Jewel 5459, Oriole 1413, 1415 as by **Frank Evans**.
Matrix 8301 on Broadway 8092 and probably Paramount 3128 as by **Francis Luther**.
Matrix 8301 is titled *A Choir Boy Sings All Alone Tonight*, and matrix 8302 *The Baby On The Door Step*, on Broadway 8092.
Controls appear on various issues instead of, or as well as, the matrices, as follows: 8300 = 2142-2; 8301 = 1894-2, 1124; 8302 = 1860-3, 1125.
Revs: Domino 0267, Regal 8696 by Rodman Lewis (popular).

Acc. unknown, f; Carson Robison, h/g.
New York, NY   Tuesday, November 13, 1928
8309-   Howdy! Old Timer   Pl unissued
8310-   Will The Angels Play Their Harps For Me? (A Beggar's Lament)   Ba S6225, Do 4237, Je 5459, Or 1412, Re 8679, Chg 945, ImpE 2216, 2602, Broadcast 516, Unison 516, Rex 8056

Challenge 945, Jewel 5459, Oriole 1412 as by **Frank Evans**. Broadcast 516, Unison 516 as by **Joe Leigh**. Rex 8056 as by **Frank Ranger**.
The parenthesised subtitle of matrix 8310 does not appear on Imperial 2216, 2602, Broadcast 516, Unison 516, Rex 8056.
Some issues of matrix 8310 use the control 1900-3.
Revs: Imperial 2216, 2602, Rex 8056 by John I. White.

Carson Robison Trio: Frank Luther, v; acc. two unknowns, f; prob. Carson Robison, g.
New York, NY   mid-November 1928
3424-   Will There Be A Santa Claus In Heaven   Ca 8377, Lin 3025, Ro 800
3425-2   The Baby On The Doorstep   Ca 8377, 9219, Lin 3025, 3246, Ro 800, 1021

Revs: Cameo 9219, Lincoln 3246, Romeo 1021 (all as by **Jimmie Price & His Guitar**) by Ed "Jake" West.

Acc. poss. Murray Kellner, f; prob. Carson Robison, h/g.
New York, NY   mid-November 1928
108488-2;   The Sinking Of The Vestris   Ca 8380, Lin 3028, Pat 32411, Pe 12490, Ro 803
3484-B
108489-1;   Will The Angels Play Their Harps For Me?   Ca 8380, Lin 3028, Pat 32411, Pe 12490, Ro 803
3485-B

Frank Luther, v; acc. unknown, f; Carson Robison, h/g.
New York, NY   Friday, November 16, 1928
   8335-2   The Sinking Of The Vestris   Ba S6228, Do 4239, DoC 31004, Je 5462,
                                                          Or 1415, Re 8681, Chg 946, Pm 3126,
                                                          Bwy 8095, Apex 8853, LS 24343, Mc 22343,
                                                          St 8853

Jewel 5462, Oriole 1415 as by **Frank Evans**. Broadway 8095, Paramount 3126 as by **Francis Luther**. Some issues use the controls 1858-1,-3, 1126.
Revs: Challenge 946 by Frank Marvin; Apex 8853, Microphone 22343, Starr 8853 by Vernon Dalhart.

Jimmie Black: Frank Luther, v; acc. unknown, f; Carson Robison, h/g.
New York, NY   Friday, November 16, 1928
   401332-A   The Sinking Of The Vestris   OK 45275
   401333-B   Will The Angels Play Their Harps For Me? OK 45275, PaE E6255, Ariel Z4512

Ariel Z4512 as by **Charles Moore**.
Revs: Parlophone E6255 by Honolulu Strollers; Ariel Z4512 by Singing Serenaders (popular).

Bud Billings: Frank Luther, v; acc. Murray Kellner, f; Carson Robison, h/g; unknown, eff-1.
New York, NY   Monday, November 19, 1928
   49121-3   An Old Man's Story   Vi V-40006
   49122-1   The Sinking Of The Vestris -1   Vi V-40006

New York, NY   Wednesday, November 21, 1928
   48190-2   The Heroes Of The Vestris   Vi V-40021

Frank Luther & His Pards: Frank Luther, v; acc. —— Jaudas, f?; Carson Robison, g.
New York, NY   Thursday, November 22, 1928
   18889   The Sinking Of The Vestris   Ed 52453, 5639
   N-584   The Sinking Of The Vestris   Ed unissued
   18890   An Old Man's Story   Ed 52453, 5687
   N-585   An Old Man's Story   Ed unissued

Frank Luther, v; acc. prob. Murray Kellner, f; Carson Robison, h/g; unknown, eff-1.
New York, NY   Thursday, November 22, 1928
   E28766-   The Sinking Of The Vestris -1   Br 277, Vo 5262
   E28767-   The Heroes Of The Vestris   Br 277, Vo 5262

Vocalion 5262 as by **Tommy Wilson**.

Acc. prob. Carson Robison, g.
New York, NY   Thursday, November 22, 1928
   8343-2   The Bum's Rush   Ba 6229, Do 4240, DoC 31012, 181250,
                                                          Re 8682, Chg 801, 980, Cq 7223, Apex 8858,
                                                          CrC 81250, LS 24347, Mc 22347, St 8858,
                                                          Stg 281250
   8344-   Who Said I Was A Bum?   Do 4240, DoC 31012, Or 1418, Re 8682,
                                                          Cq 7223, 7846, Pm 3147, 20667, Bwy 1226,
                                                          Apex 8858, LS 24347, Mc 22347, St 8858
   8345-2   The Bowery Bums   Ba 6229, Do 0266, DoC 31015, Or 1418,
                                                          Re 8697, Chg 801, 980, Cq 7227, Pm 3147,
                                                          20667, Bwy 1226, 4054, Apex 8859,
                                                          LS 24353, Mc 22353, St 8859

Oriole 1418 as by **Frank Evans**. Conqueror 7846 as by **Weary Willie**. Crown 81250, Domino 181250, Sterling 281250 as by **Buddy Bartlett**. Lucky Strike 24347, and probably 24353, as by **Chic Harris**. Microphone 22353, and probably 22347, as by **Dick Porter**. Matrix 8343 is titled *The Bums Rush* on Banner 6229.
Controls appear on various issues instead of, or as well as, the matrices, as follows: 8343 = 1907-3; 8344 = 1909-1, 1136; 8345 = 1908-2, 1137.
Revs: Crown 81250, Domino 181250, Sterling 281250 (with same credit) by Frank Marvin.

Carson Robison Trio: Frank Luther, v; acc. prob.: Murray Kellner, f; Carson Robison, h-1/g.
New York, NY   c. November 22, 1928
   108509-3; 8944 The Death Of Stonewall Jackson   Pat unissued
   3507-   The Death Of Stonewall Jackson   Ca 9038, Lin 3067, Ro 842
   108510-1   General Robert E. Lee -1   Pat 32449, Pe 12528
   3508-   General Robert E. Lee -1   Ca 9038, Lin 3067, Ro 842

Weary Willie-1/"Lazy" Larry-2: Frank Luther, v; acc. Carson Robison, g/wh-3.
New York, NY   c. November 22, 1928
   108511-1   In The Big Rock Candy Mountains -1, 3   Pat 32415, Pe 12494
   3509-   In The Big Rock Candy Mountains -2   Ca 9014, Lin 3043, Ro 818
   108512-   The Bum Song No. 2 -1   Pat 32415, Pe 12494

A later issue of Perfect 12494 couples matrices 3509 and 3527.

Frank Luther, v; acc. unknown, f-1; Carson Robison, h/g/wh-2; unknown, jh-3.
New York, NY   Wednesday, November 28, 1928

8368-2	Jack Of All Trades -1, 3	Ba 6251, Je 5482, Or 1441, Chg 979, Cq 7846, Htd 16514
8369-3	That Big Rock-Candy Mountain -2	Ba 6251, Do 0266, DoC 31015, 181014, Je 5482, Or 1441, Re 8697, Chg 979, Cq 7227, Htd 16514, Pm 3139, Bwy 8121, Apex 8859, CrC 81014, LS 24353, Mc 22353, St 8859, Stg 281014, ImpE 2243

Jewel 5482, Oriole 1441, Challenge 979, Homestead 16514 as by **Frank Evans**. Conqueror 7846 as by **Weary Willie**. Crown 81014, Domino 181014 as by **Buddy Bartlett**. Sterling 281014 as by **Frank Lewis**. Microphone 22353 as by **Dick Porter**. Matrix 8369 is titled *That Big Rock Candy Mountain* on Paramount 3139, Broadway 8121.
Controls appear on various issues instead of, or as well as, the matrices, as follows: 8368 = 1911-2,-3; 8369 = 1910-2, 1151.
Revs: Paramount 3139, Broadway 8121 by Frank Marvin.

Turney Brothers, v duet; acc. unknown, f; unknown, c; unknown, p.
New York, NY   Wednesday, November 28, 1928

49211-3	Revive Us Again	Vi V-40027
49212-3	At The Cross	Vi V-40027, MW M-8212

Rev. Montgomery Ward M-8212 by Trinity Choir (popular).

Frank Luther & His Pards: Frank Luther, v; acc. Bert Hirsch, f; Carson Robison, g.
New York, NY   Tuesday, December 11, 1928

18932	Mother Was A Lady Or (If Jack Were Only Here)	Ed 52483, 5693
N-623	Mother Was A Lady Or (If Jack Were Only Here)	Ed unissued
18933	Will The Angels Play Their Harps For Me	Ed 52483, 5671
N-624	Will The Angels Play Their Harps For Me	Ed unissued

Frank Luther, v; acc. unknown, f-1; unknown, ac-2; prob. Carson Robison, g; unknown, castanets-3.
New York, NY   Thursday, December 13, 1928

E-28910-	A Gay Caballero -1, 2, 3	Br 4180, BrAu 4180, Spt S2064
E-28911-	The Big Rock Candy Mountains	Vo 5278, Spt S2061, Me M12174

Revs: Vocalion 5278 by Charlie Craver; Melotone M12174 by Bob & Monte.

Weary Willie (Pat/Pe)/**"Lazy" Larry** (Ca/Lin/Ro): Frank Luther, v; acc. unknown, f; Carson Robison, h-1/g; unknown, castanets-2.
New York, NY   c. mid-December 1928

108530-; 3526-A	A Gay Caballero -2	Ca 9019, Lin 3048, Pat 32418, Pe 12497, Ro 823, Ang 3078, Gracelon 4022, MeAu 10084, StAu 726, Worth 7051
108531-; 3527-5	How To Make Love -1	Ca 9014, Lin 3043, Pat 32418, Pe 12494, 12497, Ro 818

Angelus 3078, Gracelon 4022, Melotone 10084, Starr 726 as by **Lazy Larry**; matrix 108530/3526 is titled *The Gay Caballero* on those issues. Worth 7051 as by **Allan Royal**; matrix 108530/3526 is titled *Gay Caballero* on that issue.
Regarding Perfect 12494, see the note on the session of c. November 22, 1928.
Revs: Cameo 9019, probably Lincoln 3048, Romeo 823, Angelus 3078, Gracelon 4022, Melotone 10084, and some issues of Starr 726 by Frank Marvin.

Frank Luther & Carson Robison, v duet; acc. unknown orch.; prob. Carson Robison, wh.
New York, NY   Wednesday, December 26, 1928

E-28928	Old Kentucky Cabin	Br 4222, BrAu 4222, PanAu 12244
E-28929	Blue Lagoon	Br 4222, BrAu 4222, PanAu 12244

Frank Luther, v; acc. unknown, f; unknown, ac; Carson Robison, g.
New York, NY   Wednesday, December 26, 1928

E-28930	Barnacle Bill, The Sailor	Br 4180, BrAu 4180, Spt S2064, PanAu 12293

Matrix E-28930 is titled *Barnacle Bill, The Sailor, Pt. 1* on Panachord 12293.

Bud & Joe Billings, v duet; acc. poss. Sam Freed, f; Carson Robison, h/g; poss. Roy Smeck, sg.
New York, NY   Thursday, December 27, 1928

49299-2	Birmingham Jail	Vi V-40031, Zo 5647
49600-2	Columbus Stockade Blues	Vi V-40031

Intervening matrices are by other artists on other dates.

Acc. Sam Freed, f; Roy Smeck, sg; Carson Robison, g/wh.
Camden, NJ   Friday, December 28, 1928

49419-1	You're As Welcome As The Flowers In May	Vi V-40039, Zo 5376, HMVAu EA1248
49420-2	When The Harvest Moon Is Shining (Mollie Dear)	Vi V-40039, Zo 5376, HMVAu EA1248

Bud Billings: Frank Luther, v; acc. Sam Freed, f; Carson Robison, h-1/g; Roy Smeck, sg-2/bj-3; unknown, jh-4.
   Camden, NJ   Friday, December 28, 1928
     49421-2   How To Make Love -1, 3, 4   Vi V-40043, MW M-4365, Zo 5399
     49422-2   Barnacle Bill, The Sailor -2   Vi V-40043, MW M-1248, M-4310, Zo 5399,
                                                                   ?5725

Montgomery Ward M-4310 possibly as by **Frank Luther**.
Revs: Montgomery Ward M-1248 by Frank Crumit, M-4365 by Cal Stewart.

Frank Luther, v; acc. unknown, f; prob. Carson Robison, h/g.
   New York, NY   ?late 1928/early 1929
     2342-E   May I Sleep In Your Barn Tonight Mister?   GG/Rad 4118, VD 74118

It was Grey Gull's frequent, though not invariable, practice to reuse with a new take letter a matrix that been assigned to an earlier recording of the same title by a different artist; and then to issue that new recording with the same catalogue number as its predecessor, sometimes employing the same pseudonymous artist credit. It is impossible to date those new versions with any accuracy, but this item and the several following may have been recorded about this time.
Grey Gull/Radiex 4118 as by **Jeff Calhoun** or **Frank Luther**. Van Dyke 74118 as by **Martin Dixon**.
Earlier takes of matrix 2342 are by Vernon Dalhart (as **Jeff Calhoun**).
Rev. all issues by Francis Herold (popular).

Acc. unknown, f; prob. Carson Robison, h/g; own jh.
   New York, NY   ?late 1928/early 1929
     2345-C   Rovin' Gambler   GG/Rad 4135, Mad 5027, 50027, VD 5027

Grey Gull/Radiex 4135 as by **Jeff Calhoun**. Madison 5027, 50027, Van Dyke 5027 as by **Tom Cook**.
Some issues use the control 206.
Earlier takes of matrix 2345 are by Vernon Dalhart (as **Jeff Calhoun**).
Revs: Grey Gull/Radiex 4135 by Kenneth Calvert (popular); Madison 5027, 50027, Van Dyke 5027 by Bob Miller.

Tom Cook: Frank Luther, v; acc. unknown, f; prob. Carson Robison, h/g; own jh.
   New York, NY   ?late 1928/early 1929
     2360-E   Hand Me Down My Walking Cane   GG/Rad 4119, Mad 5076, VD 5076, VD 74119

Earlier takes of matrix 2360 are by Johnny Marvin (as **Honey Duke**).
Revs: Grey Gull/Radiex 4119, Van Dyke 74119 by Arthur Fields; Madison 5076, Van Dyke 5076 by Bob Miller.

Acc. unknown, f; prob. Carson Robison, h/g.
   New York, NY   ?late 1928/early 1929
     2419-C   The Letter Edged In Black   GG/Rad 4311, Mad 5045, 50045, VD 5045,
                                                                     84311

Grey Gull/Radiex 4311 as by **Frank Luther**. Van Dyke 84311 as by **Jeff Calhoun**. Madison 5045, 50045, Van Dyke 5045 as by **Tom Cook**.
Some issues use the control 231. Earlier takes of matrix 2419 are by Arthur Fields (but on different issues).
Revs: Grey Gull/Radiex 4311, Van Dyke 84311 by Bob Miller; Madison 5045, 50045, Van Dyke 5045 by Al Bernard (popular).

Frank Luther, v; acc. unknown, f; prob. Carson Robison, h/g; own jh; unknown, train eff.
   New York, NY   ?late 1928/early 1929
     2996-D   Engineer's Dying Child   GG 4208, Mad/VD 5077

Grey Gull 4208 as by **Frank Luther** or **Tom Cook**. Madison/Van Dyke 5077 as by **Tom Cook**.
Earlier takes of matrix 2996 are by Arthur Fields.
Revs: Grey Gull 4208 by Arthur Fields; Madison/Van Dyke 5077 by Walter Bailey (popular).

Tom Cook: Frank Luther, v; acc. unknown, f; prob. Carson Robison, h/g; own jh.
   New York, NY   ?late 1928/early 1929
     212-A   Get Away, Old Man, Get Away   Mad 5028, 50028, VD 5028

The control number 203 shown on the labels of these issues is erroneous.
Revs: Madison 5028, 50028, Van Dyke 5028 by Bob Miller.

Pete Wiggins: Frank Luther, v; acc. unknown, f; unknown, ac; Carson Robison, g; unknown, castanets-1.
   New York, NY   Wednesday, January 9, 1929
     401512-B   A Gay Caballero -1   OK 45295, Pa E6156
     401513-B   Barnacle Bill The Sailor   OK 45295, Pa E6156, PaAu A2779

Parlophone E6156 as by **Pete Wiggin**.
Rev. Parlophone A2779 by Leslie Sarony (English popular).

Black Brothers, v duet; acc. two unknowns, f; Carson Robison, g; prob. Frank Luther, bell-1.
   New York, NY   Wednesday, January 9, 1929
     401514-A   He Left His Religion In The Country   OK 45296
     401515-B   What Has Become Of The Old Church Bells? -1   OK 45296

Francis Luther & Jack Parker: Francis Luther, Jack Parker, v duet; acc. unknown orch.
   New York, NY   Saturday, January 12, 1929
     E-29045-   You Can't Take My Mem'ries From Me   Br 4202, BrAu 4202

| E-29046- | Carolina Moon | Br 4202, BrAu 4202 |

It is not known if Jack Parker is a pseudonym for Carson Robison.

Jimmie Black: Frank Luther, v; acc. two unknowns, f; Carson Robison, g.
New York, NY   Monday, January 14, 1929

| 401526-B | Buffalo Bill | OK 45298 |
| 401527-B | Custer's Last Fight | OK 45298 |

Black Brothers, v duet; acc. two unknowns, f; unknown, p; prob. Carson Robison, g/wh-1.
New York, NY   Monday, January 14, 1929

| 401528-B | Tennessee (I'm Coming Home) | OK 45336 |
| 401529-B | Old Kentucky Cabin -1 | OK 45336, Ve 2354-V, Cl 5288-C |

Velvet Tone 2354-V, Clarion 5288-C as by **Carson Robison Trio**. Those issues use the transfer matrix 100508.

Frank Luther & Carson Robison, v duet; acc. unknown, f; Carson Robison, h/g; unknown, bj; Frank Luther, jh.
New York, NY   Tuesday, January 15, 1929

| 8458- | Sing Hallelujah | Ba S6282, Do 0271, Or 1471, Re 8715, Chg 994 |

Some issues of matrix 8458 use the control 2020-2.

Frank Luther, v; acc. unknown, f-1; unknown, bj-2; Carson Robison, g.
New York, NY   Tuesday, January 15, 1929

| 8459-2 | Barnacle Bill, The Sailor -1, 2 | Ba S6282, 32194, Do 4284, DoC 31059, 181021, Or 1471, 2282, Pe 12717, Re 8733, 10374, Ro 1649, Chg 994, Cq 7312, Pm 20689, Bwy 1248, 4054, Apex 8902, CrC 81021, Roy 81021, St 8902, Stg 281021 |
| 8460-3 | She Waits And Waits | Ba 6342, Do 4306, DoC 31059, 181021, Je 5563, Or 1525, Re 8754, Chg 991, Cq 7327, Apex 8902, CrC 81021, Roy 81021, St 8902, Stg 281021 |

Matrix 8458 on Banner S6282, Regal 8715 as by **Carson J. Robison & Frank Luther**. Canadian issues as by **Buddy Bartlett**, except Apex 8902 as by **Frank Luther**, Domino 31059 as by **"Sailor" Jack**.
Controls appear on various issues instead of, or as well as, the matrices, as follows: 8459 = 2021-2; 8460 = 2141.
Revs: Banner 32194, Oriole 2282, Perfect 12717, Regal 8733, 8754, 10374, Romeo 1649 by Billy Murray (popular);
Paramount 20689 by Irving Kaufman (popular).

Weary Willie (Pat/Pe)/**"Lazy" Larry**(Ca/Lin/Ro): Frank Luther, v; acc. unknown, f-1; prob. Carson Robison, g.
New York, NY   c. January 1929

| 108619-2; 3611 | The Bum's Rush | Ca 9060, Lin 3089, Pat 32431, Pe 12510, Ro 864 |
| 108620- ; 3612 | Barnacle Bill The Sailor -1 | Ca 9060, Lin 3089, Pat 32431, Pe 12510, Ro 864 |

Carson Robison Trio: Frank Luther, v; acc. poss. Murray Kellner, f; Carson Robison, h/g; own jh-1.
New York, NY   January/February 1929

108654-2	His Journey's End	Pat 32438, Pe 12517
3651-	His Journey's End	Ca 9091, Lin 3118, Ro 893
108655-2; 3652-A	The Wanderer's Warning	Ca 9092, Lin 3119, Pat 32449, Pe 12528, Ro 894
108656-2; 3653-1	'Leven Cent Cotton -1	Ca 9092, Lin 3119, Pat 32438, Pe 12517, Ro 894

Matrices 108654-2 and 3651 are different takes.
Revs: Cameo 9091, Lincoln 3118, Romeo 893 by Frank Marvin.

Bud & Joe Billings, v duet; acc. unknown, f; unknown, f-1; unknown, bj-2; Carson Robison, g/wh.
New York, NY   Tuesday, February 5, 1929

| 49922-1 | The Utah Trail -2 | Vi V-40040, MW M-4312, Zo 5402 |
| 49923-2 | Wednesday Night Waltz -1 | Vi V-40040, Zo 5402, HMVAu EA1247 |

Rev. Montgomery Ward M-4312 by Stuart Hamblen.

Frank Luther & Carson Robison, v duet; acc. unknown, f; unknown, f-1; unknown, bj-2; Carson Robison, g/wh; Frank Luther, jh-3.
New York, NY   early February 1929

| E-29290- | My Tennessee Mountain Home -2, 3 | Br 297, Spt S2053 |
| E-29291- | Wednesday Night Waltz -1 | Br 297 |

Frank Luther & His Pards: Frank Luther, v; acc. Murray Kellner, f; Carson Robison, h-1/g; own jh-2.
New York, NY   Tuesday, February 19, 1929

19055-B	How To Make Love -1, 2	Ed 52532
N-746-B	How To Make Love -1, 2	Ed 20006
19056-A	Barnacle Bill The Sailor	Ed 52532, 5678
N-747-B	Barnacle Bill The Sailor	Ed 20006

Matrix 19055 was scheduled for cylinder release but not issued in that form.

Frank Luther, v/y; acc. prob. Carson Robison, g.
New York, NY   Monday, February 25, 1929

8566-3	Lullaby Yodel	Ba 6369, 6466, Do 4304, Je 5585, 5671, Or 1560, Re 8752, Chg 812, Cq 7325, Htd 16055, Pm 3165, Bwy 8102
8567-2	Oklahoma Blues	Ba 6341, Je 5559, Or 1527, Re 8775, Chg 989, Cq 7348, Htd 16056, Bwy 8103, QRS R.9007, Apex 8951, CrC 81066, DoC 181066, Stg 281066
8568-3	My Little Old Home Down In New Orleans	Ba 6341, Do 4304, Je 5559, Or 1527, Re 8752, Chg 989, Cq 7325, Htd 16056, Bwy 8103, QRS R.9007

Crown 81066, Domino 181066, Sterling 281066 as by **Buddy Bartlett**.
Controls appear on various issues instead of, or as well as, the matrices, as follows: 8566 = 2203-3; 8567 = 2140, 1195, 516; 8568 = 2139, 517.
Revs: Jewel 5671, Homestead 16055 by Chezz Chase; Regal 8775, Conqueror 7348, Crown 81066, Domino 181066, Sterling 281066 by Ed (Jake) West.

Bud Billings–Carson Robison, v duet; acc. unknown, f; unknown, f-1; unknown, c-2; Carson Robison, h-3/g-4/wh-5; unknown, p-6; unknown, bj; unknown, sb; Frank Luther, jh-7/wh-8.
New York, NY   Monday, February 25, 1929

48386-2	Dance At Jones's Place -3, 5, 7, 8	Vi V-40073, ZoSA 4232
48387-1	Goin' Back To Texas -2, 4	Vi V-40073
48388-1	Old Kentucky Cabin -1, 2, 4, 5, 6	Vi V-40115, Zo 5491, HMVAu EA730
48389-2	Open Up Dem Pearly Gates For Me -2, 3, 6, 7	Vi V-40115, Zo 5491, HMVAu EA730

Zonophone 5491 as by **Bud Billings & Carson Robison**.
Matrix 48386 is titled *Dance At Jones' Place* on Zonophone 4232.
Rev. Zonophone 4232 by Nelstone's Hawaiians.

Frank Luther & Carson Robison, v duet; acc. unknown, f; Carson Robison, h/g/wh; unknown, bj; Frank Luther, jh.
New York, NY   late February 1929

| E-29379- | The Dance At Jones' Place | Br 4334, BrAu 4334, Spt S2066 |
| E-29380- | Open Up Dem Pearly Gates For Me | Br 4334, BrAu 4334, Spt S2067 |

Revs: Supertone S2066 by Frank Marvin, S2067 by Charlie Craver.

Jimson Brothers, v duet; acc. Murray Kellner, f; Sam Freed, f; Carson Robison, g.
New York, NY   prob. early March 1929

| 19076 | On A Blue Lagoon | Ed 52537 |
| 19077 | Wednesday Night Waltz | Ed 52537 |

Black Brothers, v duet; acc. unknown, f; Carson Robison, h/g; unknown, bj; Frank Luther, jh.
New York, NY   Wednesday, March 6, 1929

| 401692-A | The Dance Down At Jones' Place | OK 45312, Ve 2411-V, Cl 5347-C |
| 401693-A | Open Up Dem Pearly Gates | OK 45312, Ve 2391-V, Cl 5325-C, ReAu G21094 |

Velvet Tone 2391-V, 2411-V, Clarion 5325-C, 5347-C, Regal G21094 as by **Carson Robison Trio**. Those issues use transfer matrices, as follows: 401692 = 100544; 401693 = 100536.
Rev. Regal G21094 by Andrew Jenkins & Carson Robison (see the former).

Bud Billings: Frank Luther, v; acc. Sam Freed, f; Phil Napoleon, c; Carson Robison, g.
Camden, NJ   Friday, March 8, 1929

| 51016-2 | Will The Angels Play Their Harps For Me? | Vi V-40057, MW M-4341, Zo 5422, Zo/RZAu 5422, ZoSA 4225, RZ 5422, RZIr IZ322 |
| 51017-2 | The Wanderer's Warning | Vi V-40057, MW M-4057, Zo 5422, Zo/RZAu 5422, ZoSA 4225, RZ 5422, RZIr IZ322 |

Matrix 51018 is by Luther with Billy Hays & His Orchestra (popular).
Revs: Montgomery Ward M-4057 by Jimmie Rodgers, M-4341 by Dick Robertson.

Carson Robison & Frank Luther, v duet; acc. unknown, f; Carson Robison, h-1/g; unknown, bj; Frank Luther, jh-2.
New York, NY   Monday, March 11, 1929

| 8600- | Open Up Dem Pearly Gates For Me -1, 2 | Ba 6370, Je 5586, Or 1561, Re 8773, Chg 813, Cq 7346, Pm 3225, Bwy 8166, QRS R.9009, ImpE 2642 |
| 8601-3 | Goin' Back To Texas | Ba 6399, Do 4347, Je 5616, Or 1593, Re 8791, Cq 7362, Htd 16143, 23014, QRS R.9009 |

Banner 6399 (and possibly 6370), Regal 8773, Challenge 813, Conqueror 7362 as by **Carson J. Robison & Frank Luther**. QRS R.9009 as by **Robison–Luther**.

Controls appear on various issues instead of, or as well as, the matrices, as follows: 8600 = 2205-2, 520; 8601 = 2247-2, 521.
Revs: Banner 6370, Oriole 1561, Challenge 813 by Ed (Jake) West.

Frank Luther, v; acc. unknown.
New York, NY   Monday, March 11, 1929
   8602-   Coon Dog Yodel   Pl unissued

Frank Luther & Carson Robison, v/wh-1 duet; acc. unknown, f; unknown, bj; Carson Robison, g.
New York, NY   March 1929
   E-29474-   The Utah Trail -1   Br 4296, BrAu 4296, Spt S2062, PanAu 12250
   E-29475-   Goin' Back To Texas   Br 4296, BrAu 4296, Spt S2062, PanAu 12250

Frank Luther, v; acc. unknown.
New York, NY   March 1929
   3378-A   Barnacle Bill The Sailor   GG/Rad 4273, VD 74273
   3397-B   Little Lost Child   GG/Rad 4259, VD 74259
Van Dyke 74259, 74273 as by **Jeff Calhoun**.
Revs: Grey Gull/Radiex 4259 by Arthur Fields (popular), 4273 by Clark & Reese (popular); Van Dyke 74273 by Fay & Sanborn (popular).

Acc. unknown orch; train-eff.
New York, NY   March 1929
   3398-A,-B   The Eastern Train   GG/Rad 4260, Rad 5118, VD 5118, 84260
Van Dyke 84260 as by **Jeff Calhoun**.
Revs: Grey Gull/Radiex 4260, Van Dyke 84260 by Arthur Fields (popular).

Frank Luther, v/y-1; acc. unknown, f-2; Carson Robison, h-3/g.
New York, NY   Tuesday, April 9, 1929
   8629-4   Memphis Yodel -1   Ba 6433, Do 4348, Je 5642, Or 1621, Re 8790,
                                                                  Cq 7361, Htd 16054, Pm 3165, Bwy 8102,
                                                                  ImpE 2124
   8671-   The Alabama Flood -2, 3   Ba 6369, Je 5585, Or 1560, Re 8773, Chg 812,
                                                                  Cq 7346
   8672-   The Death Of Jesse James -2   ARC unissued
   8673-1   The Wanderer's Warning -2, 3   Ba 6464, Do 4379, Je 5667, Or 1649, Re 8825,
                                                                  Cq 7396, Htd 16062, Pm 3178, Bwy 8125,
                                                                  4057
Matrix 8629 is a remake of the March recording of this title by Ed (Jake) West; all listed issues are believed to be derived from this remake rather than from West's original, unissued, version, and are duly credited to Luther.
Matrix 8672 is reported in ARC files as having been remade on April 24 and it is assumed that the common take 5 is from that later session (see below).
Controls appear on various issues instead of, or as well as, the matrices, as follows: 8629 = 2322, 1192; 8671 = 2202-1; 8673 = 2347, 1338.
Revs: Domino 4379, Regal 8825, Conqueror 7396 by Ed (Jake) West; Paramount 3178, Broadway 8125 by Chezz Chase; Imperial 2124 by Frank Marvin (as by **Frank Luther**).

Bud & Joe Billings, v duet; acc. unknown, f; Carson Robison, h-1/g/wh-2; unknown, sg-3; Frank Luther, jh-4/poss. sp-5.
New York, NY   Monday, April 22, 1929
   51650-2   Birmingham Jail No. 2 -2, 3   Vi V-40082, ZoSA 4234
   51651-1   Lonesome Railroad -2, 3   Vi V-40082
   51652-1   Why Did I Get Married? -1, 4, 5   Vi V-40121, 23784
   51653-3   Sailor Jack -1   Vi V-40121
Revs: Victor 23784 by Don Hall Trio (popular); Zonophone 4234 by Vernon Dalhart.

Jimson Brothers, v duet; or Frank Luther, v-1/y-1; acc. unknown, f; unknown, t; unknown, sg; unknown, g; unknown, train-wh eff-2.
New York, NY   c. April 23, 1929
   19169-A   I Wish I Had Died In My Cradle (Before I Grew   Ed 52578, 5709
                       Up To Love You)
   19170-B   Waiting For A Train -1, 2   Ed 52578, 5708

Frank Luther, v/y-1; acc. unknown, f; Carson Robison, h-2/g; unknown, v eff-3.
New York, NY   Wednesday, April 24, 1929
   8672-5   The Death Of Jesse James -2   Ba 6433, Do 4364, DoC 181060, Je 5642,
                                                                  Or 1621, Re 8808, Cq 7377, Bwy 4055,
                                                                  Htd 16054, CrC/MeC 81060, Stg 281060
   8708-3   Blue Yodel No. 4 -1, 3   Ba 6399, Do 4348, Je 5616, Or 1593, Re 8790,
                                                                  Cq 7361, Htd 16143, 23014, Pm 3172,
                                                                  Bwy 8124

Crown/Melotone 81060, Domino 181060, Sterling 281060 as by **Frank Vernon**.
Matrix 8708 is titled *California Blues (Blue Yodel No. 4)* on Banner 6399, Homestead 16143, and may be titled *Blue Yodel No. 4 (California Blues)* on Homestead 23014, Paramount 3172, Broadway 8124.
Controls appear on various issues instead of, or as well as, the matrices, as follows: 8672 = 2323-5; 8708 = 2246-3, 1289.
Revs: Broadway 4055 by Edward L. Crain; Crown/Melotone 81060, Domino 181060, Sterling 281060 by Vernon Dalhart.

Carson Robison Trio: v/wh-1 duet; acc. unknown, f-2; unknown, 2nd f-3; Carson Robison, h-4/g; unknown, bj-5; Frank Luther, jh-6.

New York, NY   April 1929

108739-1; 3761-A	I Wish I Had Died In My Cradle (Before I Grew Up To Love You) -2, 3	Ca 9135, Lin 3162, Pat 32453, Pe 12532, Ro 937
108740-1	Goin' Back To Texas -1, 4	Pat 32461, Pe 12540
3762-B	Goin' Back To Texas	Ca 9135, Lin 3162, Ro 937
108741-1	Open Up Dem Pearly Gates For Me -2, 5, 6	ImpE 2662
108741-2	Open Up Dem Pearly Gates For Me -2, 5, 6	Pat 32461, Pe 12540

Matrices 108740-1 and 3762-B are different takes.
Romeo 937, and possibly matrix 3762 on Cameo 9135, Lincoln 3162, as by **"Lazy" Larry**. Imperial 2662 as by **Carson Robison & Frank Luther**.
Rev. Pathé 32453, Perfect 12532 by Frank Marvin.

Carson Robison, Frank Luther, v duet; or Frank Luther, v-1; acc. unknown, f; Carson Robison, h/g; unknown, bj; Frank Luther, jh-2.

New York, NY   c. April 1929

3845-A; 108883-	The Dance Down At Jones' Place	Ca 9192, Lin 3219, Pat 32464, Pe 12543, Ro 994, Cq 7833
3846- ; 108884-1	Why Did I Get Married? -1, 2	Ba 6532, Ca 9178, Do 4416, Je 5723, Lin 3205, Or 1715, Pat 32474, Pe 12553, Re 8863, Ro 980, Chg 840, Cq 7422, 7725

Pathé 32464, Perfect 12543 as by **"Weary" Willie**. Conqueror 7833 as by **Weary Willie**.
Banner 6532, Domino 4416, Jewel 5723, Oriole 1715, Regal 8863, Conqueror 7422, 7725 as by **Frank Luther**.
Some issues of matrix 3846 use the controls or transfer matrices 8974, 2489-2.
Revs: Cameo 9192, Lincoln 3219, Romeo 994 by Frank Marvin; Banner 6532, Jewel 5723, Oriole 1715, Challenge 840, Conqueror 7725 by John I. White.

Frank Luther, v; acc. Carson Robison, h/g.

New York, NY   c. April 1929

3847-1; 108885-1	Peg Leg Jack	Ca 9178, Lin 3205, Pat 32464, Pe 12543, Ro 980, Cq 7833

Pathé 32464, Perfect 12543 as by **"Weary" Willie**. Conqueror 7833 as by **Weary Willie**.

Carson Robison, v; acc. unknown, f; prob. own h/g; unknown, bj; poss. Frank Luther, jh.

New York, NY   c. May 1, 1929

GEX-2227	Why Did I Get Married	Ge 6854, Ch 15746, Spt 9423
GEX-2228	Jack Of All Trades	Ge 6868, Ch 15766, 45145, Spt 9423
GEX-2229,-A	How To Make Love	Ge rejected

Acc. unknown, f; unknown, bj; prob. own g.

New York, NY   c. May 3, 1929

GEX-2230	Barnacle Bill The Sailor	Ge 6854, Ch 15829, Spt 9422

Acc. unknown, f; prob. own h/g; unknown, bj; poss. Frank Luther, jh-1.

New York, NY   c. early May 1929

GEX-2238-A	'Leven Cent Cotton, Forty Cent Meat -1	Ge 6868, Ch 15746, Spt 9454
GEX-2239	How To Make Love	Ge 6887, Ch 15766, Spt 9422

Matrix GEX-2238 is titled *Eleven Cent Cotton, Forty Cent Meat* on Supertone 9454.
Revs: Gennett 6887, Supertone 9454 by Walter Smith; Champion 15829 by Bill Cox.

Frank Luther, v; or **Frank Luther & Carson Robison**-1, v duet; acc. unknown, f; Carson Robison, h/g/wh-2; unknown, bj.

New York, NY   Wednesday, May 8, 1929

8741-1	Eleven Cent Cotton	Ba 6400, Do 4347, DoC 183006, Je 5618, Or 1595, Re 8791, Cq 7362, Htd 16051, Pm 12784, Bwy 8123, Apex 26143, CrC/MeC 83006, Stg 283006
8742-3	The Utah Trail -1, 2	Ba 6400, De 4364, DoC 183006, Je 5618, Or 1595, ?Pat 32481, Pe 12560, Re 8808, Cq 7377, Htd 16051, Bwy 4056, Apex 8956, CrC/MeC 83006, Stg 283006

Jewel 5618 and possibly Oriole 1598 as by **Carson Robison Trio**. Perfect 12560, ?Pathe 32481 as by **Harry "Rocky" Wilson**. Conqueror 7377 as by **Carson J. Robison & Frank Luther**. Broadway 4056 as by **Jack Walters**. Crown/Melotone 83006, Domino 183006, Sterling 283006 as by **Frank Vernon**.

Controls appear on various issues instead of, or as well as, the matrices, as follows: 8741 = 2269, 1264; 8742 = 2270.
Revs: Broadway 4056 by Edward L Crain; Paramount 12784, Broadway 8123 by The Pickard Family; Apex 8956 untraced.

Carson Robison Trio, v/sp duet; acc. unknown, f; Carson Robison, h/g; unknown, ac.
    New York, NY   Tuesday, May 14, 1929

8752- ; 108928-	Bum Song No. 5 (Happy-Go-Lucky Boy)	Ba 6464, Ca 9245, Je 5667, Lin 3272, Or 1649, Pat 32477, Pe 12556, Ro 1047, Htd 16062

Cameo 9245, Lincoln 3272, Romeo 1047 as by **"Weary" Willie**. Jewel 5667 as by **Carson Robison & Frank Luther**. Some issues use the controls 4022, 2346.
Revs: Pathé 32477, Perfect 12556 by Ed "Jake" West; Cameo 9245, Lincoln 3272, Romeo 1047 by Chezz Chase.

Bud & Joe Billings, v duet; acc. Sam Freed, f; Roy Smeck, sg-1/g; Carson Robison, g/wh-2.
    Camden, NJ   Thursday, May 16, 1929

50887-2	When It's Springtime In The Rockies -2	Vi V-40088, MW M-1412, M-4046, Zo 5465, ZoAu 5465, Twin FT1277
50888-3	Sleepy Rio Grande -1	Vi V-40088, MW M-8130, Zo 5465, ZoAu 5465, Twin FT1277
50891-1	Barnacle Bill The Sailor No. 2	Vi unissued

Matrices 50889/90 are by Fess Williams (see *JR*).
Revs: Montgomery Ward M-1412 by Frank Crumit, M-8130 by Jimmy Long.

Acc. Murray Kellner, f; Earl Oliver, t-1; Roy Smeck, sg; Carson Robison, g/poss. sp-2; unknown, eff-3.
    New York, NY   Tuesday, May 21, 1929

50891-3	Barnacle Bill The Sailor – No. 2 -2, 3	Vi V-40102, Zo 5725, ZoAu EE266, Twin FT1230
53424-2	Left My Gal In The Mountains -1	Vi V-40102, MW M-8124, Zo 5647, ZoSA 4239

Matrix 50891 is titled *Barnacle Bill The Sailor No. 2* on Zonophone 5725.
Revs: Montgomery Ward M-8124 by Jimmie Rodgers; Zonophone 4239 by The Carter Family; Twin FT1230 by Lewis James (popular).

Frank Luther & Carson Robison, v duet; or **Frank Luther**-1, v; acc. poss. Earl Oliver, c; unknown, cl; prob. Roy Smeck, sg; unknown, g.
    New York, NY   Tuesday, May 21, 1929

E-29928	Left My Gal In The Mountains	Br 425, BrC 425, BrE 1170, BrAu 4392, Spt S2061
E-29929	Gonna Lay Me Down In The Cold, Cold Ground -1	Br 4392, BrAu 4392

Rev. Brunswick 425 by Uncle Dave Macon.

Black Brothers, v duet; acc. poss. Earl Oliver, t; poss. Roy Smeck, sg-1/g-2; prob. Carson Robison, g/wh-3.
    New York, NY   Monday, May 27, 1929

401988-A	Left My Gal In The Mountains -1	OK 45345
401989-B	Goin' Back To Texas -2, 3	OK 45345, Ve 2355-V, Cl 5289-C

Velvet Tone 2355-V, Clarion 5289-C as by **Carson Robison Trio**. Those issues use the transfer matrix 100509.
Rev. Velvet Tone 2355-V, Clarion 5289-C by Goebel Reeves.

Frank Luther, v; acc. prob. Murray Kellner, f; Carson Robison, h/g/wh-1; unknown, ac; prob. own bell-2.
    New York, NY   May 1929

E-29952	Barnacle Bill, The Sailor – No. 2 -1, 2	Br 4371, BrAu 4371, PanAu 12293
E-29953	Peg-Leg Jack	Br 4371, BrAu 4371

Matrix E-29952 is titled *Barnacle Bill, The Sailor, Pt. 2* on Panachord 12293.

Acc. unknown orch.
    New York, NY   c. May 1929

3442-B	The Convict And The Bird	GG/Rad 4263, VD 74263
3443-A	When The Works All Done In The Fall	GG/Rad 4264, VD 74264, 5013, Mad 5013, 50013
3444-A	Don't Say I Did It, Jack	GG/Rad 4258, VD 74258
3445-	My Mother Was A Lady	GG/Rad 4267, VD 74267

Van Dyke 74263, 74264 probably as by **Jeff Calhoun**, except some copies of Van Dyke 74264 possibly as by **Tom Cook**. Van Dyke 5013, Madison 5013, 50013 as by **Tom Cook**.
Some issues of matrix 3443 use the control 134.
Rev. all issues popular.

Jimson Brothers, v duet; acc. poss. Earl Oliver, c; poss. Roy Smeck, sg-1/bj-2; prob. Carson Robison, g/wh-3; unknown, train-wh eff-4.
    New York, NY   Monday, June 3, 1929

19230-B	Left My Gal In The Mountains -2, 3	Ed 52608, 5721
N-934	Left My Gal In The Mountains -2, 3	Ed 20007

| 19231-B | Goin' Back To Texas -1, 4 | Ed 52608, 5722 |
| N-935 | Goin' Back To Texas -1, 4 | Ed 20007 |

Edison 5721, 5722, 20007 may never have been issued.

Frank Luther, v; or **Frank Luther & Carson Robison**-1, v duet; acc. poss. Earl Oliver, t; Roy Smeck, sg; Carson Robison, g.

New York, NY   Thursday, June 6, 1929

| 8800-2 | I'm Lonely And Blue | Ba 6463, Ca 9276, Do 4380, Je 5669, Lin 3303, Or 1647, Re 8824, Ro 1078, Cq 7398, Htd 16050, Pm 3170, Bwy 8122, 4057 |
| 8801-1 | Left My Gal In The Mountains -1 | Ba 6465, Do 4380, Je 5668, Or 1648, Pe 12553, Re 8824, Cq 7398, Htd 16061, 23015, Pm 3172, Bwy 8124 |

Cameo 9276, Lincoln 3303, Romeo 1078 as by **"Lazy" Larry**. Matrix 8801 on Regal 8824, Conqueror 7398 as by **Carson J. Robison & Frank Luther**. Perfect 12553 as by **Carson Robison Trio**. Broadway 8124 as by **Robinson Luther**.
Controls appear on various issues instead of, or as well as, the matrices, as follows: 8800 = 4058, 2344-2, 1262; 8801 = 2385, 1290.
Revs: Banner 6463, Cameo 9276, Jewel 5669, Lincoln 3303, Oriole 1647, Romeo 1078, Homestead 16050 by Chezz Chase; Banner 6465, Jewel 5668, Oriole 1648, Homestead 16061, 23015 by Ed (Jake) West.

Frank Luther, v/y; acc. Carson Robison, g.

New York, NY   Thursday, June 6, 1929

| 8802-2 | My Little Lady | Ba 6495, Do 4398, Je 5697, Or 1681, Re 8843, Cq 7410, Htd 16060, Pm 3170, Bwy 8122 |

Some issues use the controls 2444, 1261.
Revs: Banner 6495, Jewel 5697, Oriole 1681, Homestead 16060 by Chezz Chase; Domino 4398, Regal 8843, Conqueror 7410 by Frank Marvin.

Bud & Joe Billings, v duet; acc. two unknowns, f; Earl Oliver, t; Carson Robison, g; Frank Luther, vb.

New York, NY   Monday, June 24, 1929

| 53464-3 | Lonesome Melody | Vi V-40108, Zo 5549, ZoSA 4240, |
| 53465-3 | An Old Fashioned Sweetheart Of Mine | Vi V-40108, Zo 5549, ZoSA 4240, HMVAu EA1247 |

Carson Robison Trio, v/wh-1 duet; acc. unknown, f; poss. Earl Oliver, c-2; unknown, cl-3; prob. Roy Smeck, sg-4/g-5; prob. Carson Robison, g; unknown, train-wh eff-6.

New York, NY   c. June 1929

3930-B; 108891-	Left My Gal In The Mountains -2, 3, 4	Ca 9216, Lin 3243, Pat 32474, Pe 12553, Ro 1018
3931-B; 108909-1	Sleepy Rio Grande Waltz -1, 4	Ca 9217, Do 4565, Lin 3244, Pe 12615, Ro 1019, Cq 7548, Pm 3180, Bwy 8130
3932-B; 108947-	The Railroad Boomer -2, 3, 5, 6	Ca 9216, Do 4442, Lin 3243, Pat 32481, Pe 12560, Re 8885, Ro 1018, Cq 7438, Bwy 4051

Conqueror 7438 as by **Carson Robison's Trio**.
A reported copy of Perfect 12553 uses the different Plaza matrix 8801 rather than matrix 3930/108891. No copy of Pathé 32474 has been reported.
Controls or transfer matrices appear on various issues instead of, or as well as, the matrices, as follows: 3931 = 8945-2, 1371; 3932 = 9076.
Revs: Domino 4442, Regal 8885, Conqueror 7438 by John I. White; Paramount 3180, Broadway 8130, 4051 by Frank Marvin.

Carson Robison, Frank Luther, v/wh duet; acc. unknown, f; unknown, bj; Carson Robison, g.

New York, NY   c. June 1929

| 3946-3; 108946- | The Utah Trail | Ca 9217, Lin 3244, Pat 32481, Pe 12560, Ro 1019 |

Pathé 32481, Perfect 12560 as by **Harry "Rocky" Wilson**.

"Weary" Willie: Frank Luther, v/y; acc. prob. Carson Robison, g.

New York, NY   July/August 1929

| 108926- | My Little Lady | Pat 32485, Pe 12564 |

Rev. Pathé 32485, Perfect 12564 by Frank Marvin.

Frank Luther & His Pards: Frank Luther, v; acc. prob. Murray Kellner, f; Carson Robison, h-1/g/sp-2/eff-2; unknown, ac.

New York, NY   c. August 5, 1929

| 19336-B | Barnacle Bill The Sailor – No. 2 -2 | Ed 52641 |
| N-1061 | Barnacle Bill The Sailor – No. 2 -2 | Ed 20008 |

19337-B	Peg-Leg-Jack -1	Ed 52641
N-1062	Peg-Leg-Jack -1	Ed 20008

Frank Luther, v/y-1; acc. unknown, f; unknown, cl; unknown, sg; poss. unknown, bj; Carson Robison, g; own jh-2.
New York, NY   Tuesday, September 3, 1929

4051-2	My Carolina Sunshine Girl -1	Ba 6533, Ca 9277, Do 4417, Je 5722, Lin 3304, Or 1714, Re 8864, Ro 1079, Cq 7423, Htd 16058, 23006, Bwy 8131
4052-C	Oh That Dumb-bell! -2	Ba 6559, Ca 9291, Do 4416, Je 5746, Lin 3318, Or 1749, Re 8863, Ro 1093, Chg 858, Cq 7422, Bwy 8131

Cameo 9277, 9291, Lincoln 3304, 3318, Romeo 1079, 1093, Broadway 8131 as by **Carson Robison Trio**.
Matrix 4052 is titled *Oh That Dumpbell* on Romeo 1093, *Oh That Dumb-bell* on Cameo 9291, Broadway 8131, and *Oh, That Dumb-bell!* on Banner 6559.
Controls or transfer matrices appear on various issues instead of, or as well as, the matrices, as follows: 4051 = 8956, 2491, 1446; 4052 = 8993, 2576.
Revs: Cameo 9277, Lincoln 3304, Romeo 1079 by Chezz Chase; Banner 6533, Domino 4416, Jewel 5722, Oriole 1714, Regal 8864, Conqueror 7423 by Frank Marvin.

Carson Robison Trio: Frank Luther, v; acc. Carson Robison, h/g.
New York, NY   Tuesday, September 3, 1929

4053-C	John The Drunkard	Ca 9291, Do 4476, Lin 3318, Pat 32504, Pe 12583, Re 8921, Ro 1093, Cq 7466, 7728

Conqueror 7466 as by **Frank Luther**.
Some issues use the transfer matrix 8995.
Revs: Domino 4476, Pathé 32504, Perfect 12583, Regal 8921, Conqueror 7466 by John I. White.

Black Brothers, v duet; acc. unknown, f; unknown, f-1; unknown, sg; unknown, md-2; prob. Carson Robison, g/wh-3.
New York, NY   Thursday, September 5, 1929

402930-A	Sleepy Rio Grande Waltz -2, 3	OK 45374
402931-C	Lonesome Melody -1	OK 45374

Bud Billings–Carson Robison, v duet; acc. unknown, f; unknown, t; unknown, s; poss. Roy Smeck, sg/g-1; Carson Robison, g; unknown, train-wh eff-2.
New York, NY   Monday, September 9, 1929

55679-2	Woman Down In Memphis	Vi V-40139
55680-1	The Railroad Boomer -1, 2	Vo V-40139, ZoSA 4272
55681-2	You Made Me Want To Forget	Vo V-40143
55682-2	Beneath Montana Skies	Vo V-40143

Frank Luther & His Pards: Frank Luther, v; acc. unknown.
New York, NY   c. September 18, 1929

N-1134	Goin' Home	Ed 20009
N-1135	Lay Down Dogies	Ed 20009

Edison 20009 was possibly not issued.

Frank Luther & Ed Faber, v duet; or **Frank Luther**-1, v; acc. unknown, f; unknown, cl-2/s-3; unknown, sg; unknown, g; unknown, train-wh eff-4.
New York, NY   c. September 1929

3626-B	I Left My Gal In The Mountains -2	GG/Rad 4275, VD 74275
3627-B	The Railroad Boomer -3, 4	GG/Rad 4275, VD 74275
3628-A	Polly Wolly Doodle -1	GG/Rad 4274, VD 74274, Gn 185
3629-A	Dixie Way -1	GG/Rad 4274, VD 74274

Van Dyke 74274 as by **Jeff Calhoun**, 74275 as by **Jeff Calhoun & Robert Leavitt**.

Smith & James, v duet; acc. unknown, t; unknown, cl; unknown, g; Carson Robison, g/wh.
New York, NY   ?c. September 1929

135-A,-B	Left My Gal In The Mountains	Mad 5014, 50014, VD 5014, 5119

Rev. Van Dyke 5119 by Gene Autry.

Tom Cook: Frank Luther, v/wh; acc. unknown, f; prob. Carson Robison, g/wh.
New York, NY   ?c. September 1929

136-A,-B	The Girl I Loved In Sunny Tennessee	Mad 5014, 50014, VD 5014

Frank Luther, v; or v duet-1; acc. unknown, f; Carson Robison, h/g; unknown, bj; Frank Luther, jh.
New York, NY   c. September/October 1929

207-A,-B	Oh Dem Golden Slippers	Mad 5029, 50029, VD 5029
208-A,-B	Climbing Up Those Golden Stairs -1	Mad 5029, 50029, VD 5029

Carson Robison Trio, v duet; or **Frank Luther**, v-1/y-1; acc. unknown, f; Carson Robison, g/wh-2.
New York NY   c. October 3, 1929

4158	When It's Springtime In The Rockies -2	Ba 6559, Ca 9314, Do 4441, DoC 181208, Je 5746, Lin 3338, Or 1749, Pat 32492, Pe 12571, Re 8883, Ro 1105, Chg 858, Cq 7437, Bwy 4046, Apex 41064, CrC/MeC/Roy 81208, Stg 281208, Co-Lucky 60408
4159	When The Roses Bloom For The Bootlegger -1	Ba 6560, Ca 9315, Do 4441, DoC 181208, Je 5745, Lin 3339, Or 1750, Pat 32492, Pe 12571, Re 8883, Ro 1106, Cq 7437, Htd 16059, 23007, Apex 41064, CrC/MeC/Roy 81208, Stg 281208

Banner 6559, Jewel 5745, Regal 8883, Conqueror 7437, Homestead 16059, 23007 as by **Carson J. Robison & Frank Luther**. Cameo 9315, Lincoln 3339, Romeo 1106 as by **"Lazy" Larry**. Matrix 4159 on Pathé 32492, Perfect 12571 as by **"Weary" Willie**. Crown/Melotone/Royale 81208, Domino 181208, Sterling 281028 as by **Bob Carson Trio** (matrix 4158)/**Buddy Bartlett** (matrix 4159). Apex 41064 possibly as by **Carson Robison Trio** on both sides.
Controls or transfer matrices appear on various issues instead of, or as well as, the matrices shown, as follows: 4158 = 108999-3, 9064-3, 2575; 4159 = 109014-3, 9056-3, 2545.
It is uncertain which should be taken as the original matrices of these items. The ARC matrices 9056 and 9064, here assumed to be transfer matrices, are dated in the files to October 3; the true recording date may have been slightly earlier.
Revs: Banner 6560, Jewel 5745, Oriole 1750, Homestead 16059, 23007 by Frank Marvin; Cameo 9314, 9315, Lincoln 3338, 3339, Romeo 1105, 1106 by John I. White; Columbia-Lucky 60408 by Louise Massey.

Bud Billings–Carson Robison, v duet; acc. unknown, f; unknown, t; unknown, s; poss. Roy Smeck, sg/g-1; unknown, bj; Carson Robison, g/wh-2.
New York, NY   Monday, October 14, 1929
56778-1	Down On The Old Plantation	Vi V-40191, MW M-8305, ZoSA 4321
56779-1	Sweet Virginia In Old Virginia -2	Vi V-40191, ZoSA 4288
56780-1	Went To See My Gal Last Night -1	Vi V-40153

Rev. Montgomery Ward M-8305 by Ernest V. Stoneman.

Acc. Carson Robison, g; unknown, sp; unknown, eff.
New York, NY   Monday, October 14, 1929
| 56781-2 | Barnacle Bill The Sailor No. 3 | Vi V-40153 |

Frank Luther & Carson Robison, v duet; acc. unknown, c; unknown, cl; unknown, sg; prob. Carson Robison, g; unknown, train-wh-1.
New York, NY   Tuesday, October 22, 1929
| E-31285- | Woman Down In Memphis | Br 4648, BrAu 4648 |
| E-31286- | The Railroad Boomer -1 | Br 4648, BrAu 4648 |

Carson Robison, v; acc. unknown, f; unknown, cl; prob. own h/g; unknown, bj; poss. Frank Novak, bss; Frank Luther, jh.
New York, NY   late October 1929
| GEX-2479 | A Chaw Of Tobacco And A Little Drink | Ge 7051, Ch 15872, Spt 9549 |
| GEX-2480 | Why Ain't I Got No Sweetheart | Ge 7051, Ch 15872, 45145, Spt 9549, Spr 2580 |

Matrix GEX-2479 is titled *A Chew Of Tobacco And A Little Drink* on Supertone 9549.

Robison & Luther, v duet; acc. unknown, cl/s; unknown, sg; prob. Carson Robison, g; poss. Frank Novak, bss.
New York, NY   late October 1929
| GEX-2481-A | Left My Gal In The Mountains | Ge 7019, Ch 15848, 45020, Spt 9567, MW 4990 |
| GEX-2482 | Railroad Boomer | Ge 7019, Ch 15848, 45020, Spt 9567 |

Champion 45020 as by **Carson Robison & Frank Luther**.
Matrix GEX-2481 is titled *I Left My Gal In The Mountains* on Supertone 9567. Rev. Montgomery Ward 4990 by Dick Parman.

Frank Luther & Ed Faber, v/wh duet; acc. Carson Robison, h/g; unknown, bj; poss. Frank Novak, bss.
New York, NY   November 1929
| 3735-B | Goin' Back To Texas | GG/Rad 4288, VD 74288 |

Van Dyke 74288 as by **Jeff Calhoun & Robert Leavitt**.

Frank Luther, v; acc. unknown, f; Carson Robison, h/g; unknown, bj; own jh/sp.
New York, NY   November 1929
| 3736-B | Why Did I Get Married | GG/Rad 4288, VD 74288 |

Van Dyke 74288 as by **Jeff Calhoun**.

Frank Luther & Ed Faber, v duet; acc. unknown.
New York, NY   November 1929
| 3737-B | Woman Down In Memphis | GG/Rad 4287, VD 74287, Gn 185 |

Van Dyke 74287 as by **Jeff Calhoun & Robert Leavitt**.
Revs: Grey Gull/Radiex 4287, Van Dyke 74287 by Mobile Revelers/Alabama Harmonizers (see *B&GR*).

Frank Luther, v; acc. poss. Frank Novak, cl/bscl; unknown, ac; Carson Robison, g; own jh.
    New York, NY   November 1929
    3738-D   Farm Relief Song   GG/Rad/VD 4285, VD 74285

Van Dyke 74285 as by **Jeff Calhoun**.
Matrix 3738 is titled *The Farm Relief Song* on Radiex/Van Dyke 4285.
Revs: Grey Gull/Radiex/Van Dyke 4285, Van Dyke 74285 by Jack Fitts/Bill Black (popular).

Bud Billings–Carson Robison, v duet; acc. Earl Oliver, t; unknown, tb; unknown, as; Carson Robison, h-1/g; unknown, bj; Frank Luther, jh-2/y-3; unknown, d-4.
    New York, NY   Monday, December 23, 1929
    57943-2   His Old Cornet -4   Vi V-40208, ZoSA 4292
    57944-2   Why Ain't I Got No Sweetheart? -1, 2   Vi V-40208, ZoSA 4292
    57945-2   Smoky Mountain Bill -3   Vi V-40217, ZoSA 4363
    57946-1   Cross-Eyed Sue   Vi unissued

Bud Billings: Frank Luther, v/sp; acc. Carson Robison, h/g.
    New York, NY   Monday, December 23, 1929
    57946-2   Cross Eyed Sue   Vi V-40217, ZoSA 4327

Carson Robison Trio: Frank Luther, v/y; or v duet-1; acc. unknown, cl-2; unknown, sg; prob. Carson Robison, g; Frank Luther, y-3.
    New York, NY   Monday, December 30, 1929
    9244-1,-3   Frankie And Johnny   Ba 0581, Ca 0181, Do 4490, Je 5837, Or 1837,
                                                               Pat 32506, Pe 12585, Re 8934, Ro 1200,
                                                               Chg 875, Cq 7480, Htd 16155, Bwy 4052
    9245-2,-3   Woman Down In Memphis -1, 2, 3   Ba 0585, Ca 0185, Do 4490, Je 5841, Or 1841,
                                                                Pat 32506, Pe 12585, Re 8934, Ro 1204,
                                                               Cq 7480

Revs: Banner 0581, 0585, Cameo 0181, 0185, Jewel 5837, 5841, Oriole 1837, 1841, Romeo 1200, 1204, Challenge 875, Homestead 16155 by John I. White; Broadway 4052 by Canova Family.

Frank Luther & Carson Robison, v duet; acc. unknown, cl; Carson Robison, h-1/g; unknown, bj-2; prob. Frank Luther, jh-3.
    New York, NY   Wednesday, January 8, 1930
    E-31764-   Went To See My Gal Last Night -2   Br 405, BrAu 405, Spt S2048
    E-31765-   Why Did I Get Married -1, 3   Br 405, BrAu 405, Spt S2048

Matrix E-31765 is titled *Why Did I Get Married?* on Australian Brunswick 405.

Pete Wiggins: Frank Luther, v/y; acc. Carson Robison, h-1/g.
    New York, NY   Friday, January 10, 1930
    403604-B   I Don't Work For A Living -1   OK 45412, PaE E6357, PaAu A3051, Ariel Z4673
    403605-A   Everybody Does It In Hawaii   OK 45412, PaAu A3051

Rev. Parlophone E6357, Ariel Z4673 by Greene Brothers (see Arthur Fields & Fred Hall).

Bud Billings–Carson Robison, v/sp duet; acc. unknown, f; Carson Robison, h-1/g; unknown, bj.
    New York, NY   Monday, January 20, 1930
    58400-1   Oh Jailer Bring Back That Key -1   Vi V-40221
    59101-1   You'll Get Pie In The Sky When You Die   Vi V-40221

Carson Robison Trio, v duet; acc. unknown, sg; unknown, bj or u; Carson Robison, g/wh.
    New York, NY   Thursday, January 23, 1930
    9306-1,-2   Down On The Old Plantation   Ba 0615, Ca 0215, Do 4511, Je 5871, Or 1871,
                                                                Pe 12595, Re 8956, Ro 1233, Cq 7501,
                                                                CrC/MeC/Roy/Stg 91931
    9307-1,-2   Red River Valley   Ba 0615, Ca 0215, Do 4509, DoC 181365,
                                                                Je 5871, Or 1871, Pe 12591, Re 8954,
                                                                Ro 1233, Cq 7492, Bwy 4058, Apex 41152,
                                                                CrC 81365, Stg 281365, MeC/Min M-919

Canadian issues as by **Frank Luther & Carson Robison**.
Revs: Domino 4511, Perfect 12595, Regal 8956, Conqueror 7501, Broadway 4058 by Frank Marvin; Domino 4509, Perfect 12591, Regal 8954, Conqueror 7492, and all Canadian issues except Melotone/Minerva M-919 by John I. White; Melotone/Minerva M-919 by Patt Patterson & Lois Dexter.

Carson Robison, v; acc. own h/g.
    New York, NY   Wednesday, January 29, 1930
    59130-1   Naw, I Don't Wanta Be Rich   Vi V-40226, MW M-4313
    59131-2   Don't You Believe It   Vi V-40226, MW M-4313

Acc. unknown.
    New York, NY   c. January 1930

| 3795 | I Don't Work For A Living | GG/Rad 2526, VD 82526, Gn 183 |

Grey Gull/Radiex 2526 credit unknown. Van Dyke 82526, Goodson 183 as by **Lew Grant**.
This item has been reported, but not confirmed, as by Frank Luther. The Van Dyke artist credit is elsewhere a pseudonym or alternative credit for Lou Sidney, a popular artist.
Revs: Grey Gull/Radiex 2526, Van Dyke 82526 by Charles Brock (popular); Goodson 183 by The Two Cuckoos (popular).

Acc. unknown, t; unknown, cl; own h/g.
New York, NY   c. January 1930

| 3891-A | Why Ain't I Got No Sweetheart | GG/Rad 4299, Rad 5118, VD 5118, 84299 |
| 3892-B | A Chaw Of Tobacco And A Little Drink | GG/Rad 4303, VD 84303, Empire E5, Phonycord P-99 |

Van Dyke 84299, 84303 as by **Robert Leavitt**. Empire E5 as by **Alec Carson**. Phonycord P-99 as by **Frank Robeson**.
Empire E5, Phonycord P-99 use the control P-133.
Revs: Grey Gull/Radiex 4303, Van Dyke 84303 by Gene Autry; Empire E5, Phonycord P-99 by Al Bernard (on Phonycord with same credit).

Robison & Luther, v duet; acc. unknown, t; poss. Frank Novak, cl; unknown, bj; prob. Carson Robison, g.
New York, NY   c. February 4/5, 1930

| GEX-2584 | Went To See My Gal Last Night | Ge 7141, Ch 15947, Spt 9638 |

This master was damaged and replaced by the remake on matrix GEX-2628-A. Gennett files list the issues shown above, so matrix GEX-2584 may have briefly appeared on them.

Carson Robison, v; acc. unknown, f; unknown, t-1; poss. Frank Novak, cl/bscl; prob. own h/g; unknown, sp-2.
New York, NY   c. February 4/5, 1930

GEX-2585-B	Did You Ever Hear A Gold Fish Sing	Ge 7124, Ch 15941, Spt 9625
GEX-2586-A	I Got A Gal In Kansas -2	Ge 7124, Ch 15947, Spt 9625
GEX-2587-A	I Don't Work For A Living -1, 2	Ge 7141, Ch 15941, Spt 9638

George Thompson: Frank Luther, v; acc. unknown, f; unknown, t; prob. Carson Robison, h-1/g; unknown, ac; unknown, bj.
New York, NY   Wednesday, February 26, 1930

| 150021-2 | Cross Eyed Sue -1 | Co 15532-D |
| 150022-3 | A Chaw Of Tobacco And A Little Drink | Co 15532-D |

Frank Luther & Carson Robison, v duet; acc. unknown, t; unknown, tb; unknown, cl; unknown, md-1/bj-2; Carson Robison, g; unknown, d-3; Frank Luther, y-4.
New York, NY   Wednesday, February 26, 1930

| 150023-2 | His Old Cornet -2, 3 | Co 2134-D, CoJ J1083, ReE MR119, ReAu G20729 |
| 150024-1 | Smoky Mountain Bill -1, 4 | Co 2134-D, CoJ J1083, ReAu G20729 |

Regal MR119 as by **The Regal Rascals**.
Rev. Regal MR119 (with same credit) by Tom Darby & Jimmie Tarlton.

Frank Luther & Carson Robison, v duet; or **Frank Luther**-1, v/y; acc. unknown, cl; unknown, sg; prob. Carson Robison, g.
New York, NY   c. February/March 1930

| | Woman Down In Memphis | QRS Q-1014 |
| | Frankie & Johnnie -1 | QRS Q-1014 |

Carson Robinson–Frank Luther, v duet; acc. unknown orch.; Carson Robison, g/wh-1.
New York, NY   c. February/March 1930

	His Old Cornet	QRS Q-1028
	Smoky Mountain Bill	QRS Q-1028
	Sweet Virginia -1	QRS Q-1029
2034-4	Down On The Old Plantation -1	QRS Q-1029

QRS Q-1029 as by **F. Luther–C. Robinson**.

Frank Luther & Carson Robison, v duet; acc. unknown, t; unknown, tb; unknown, cl; unknown, bj; Carson Robison, g; unknown, d-1; Frank Luther, y-2.
New York, NY   Friday, March 7, 1930

| E-32069- | His Old Cornet -1 | Br 412, BrE 1080 |
| E-32070 | Smoky Mountain Bill -2 | Br 412, BrE 1080 |

Robison & Luther, v duet; acc. unknown, t; poss. unknown, tb; unknown, cl; unknown, bj; prob. Carson Robison, g.
New York, NY   c. March 10, 1930

GEX-2626-A	His Old Cornet	Ge 7152, Ch 15964, Spt 9663
GEX-2627-A	Smoky Mountain Bill	Ge 7152, Ch 15964, Spt 9663
GEX-2628-A	Went To See My Gal Last Night	Ge 7141, Ch 15947, Spt 9638

Carson Robison, v; acc. unknown, t; poss. unknown, tb; own h/g/sp; unknown, bj.
New York, NY   c. March 10, 1930

| GEX-2629-A | Cross Eyed Sue | Ge 7186, Ch 15986, Spt 9662, Spr 2580 |

Acc. unknown, cl-1; own h/g/wh-2.
New York, NY
c. March 10, 1930

GEX-2630-A	Everything Happens For The Best -1	Ge 7186, Ch 16006, Spt 9662
GEX-2631-A	Naw! I Don't Wanta Be Rich -2	Ge 7202, Ch 15986, Spt 9672
GEX-2632-A	Don't You Believe It -2	Ge 7202, Ch 16006, Spt 9672

Frank Luther & Ed Faber, v duet; or **Frank Luther**-1, v; acc. unknown, f; Carson Robison, h/g; unknown, bj; Frank Luther, jh.
New York, NY
c. March 1930

3955	Oh, Dem Golden Slippers -1	Sr 33005, Pic 522, Melba 1047, Simcha 10057
3956	Climbing Up Those Golden Stairs	Pic 522, Melba 1047, Simcha 10057
	His Old Cornet	GG/Rad 4301, VD 84301
3959-A	Smoky Mountain Bill	GG/Rad 4301, Rad 5116, VD 5116, 84301

Radiex/Van Dyke 5116 as by **Carson Robison & Frank Luther**. Van Dyke 84301 as by **Jeff Calhoun & Robert Leavitt**. Sunrise 33005 as by **Bill Moore**. Piccadilly 522 as by **Frank Lucker**. Melba 1047, Simcha 10057 as by **Leslie Gray**. Piccadilly 522, Melba 1047, Simcha 10057 replace matrices 3955 and 3956 with the controls 3680 and 3679 respectively. Revs: Radiex/Van Dyke 5116 by Chezz Chase; Sunrise 33005 untraced.

Carson Robison Trio, v duet; acc. unknown, t; unknown, tb; unknown, cl; unknown, bj; Carson Robison, g; unknown, d.
New York, NY
Friday, April 4, 1930

| 9561-2,-3 | His Old Cornet | Ba 0681, Ca 0281, Do 4549, Je 5933, Or 1933, Pe 12610, Ro 1297, Chg 883, Cq 7538 |

Revs: Banner 0681, Cameo 0281, Jewel 5933, Oriole 1933, Romeo 129, Challenge 883 by Frank Marvin.

Acc. unknown, t; two unknowns, md; Carson Robison, g; Luther, y-1
New York, NY
Friday, April 4, 1930

9570-3	She Was Bred In Old Kentucky	Ba 0705, Ca 0305, Do 4598, DoC 181374, Je 5962, Or 1962, Pe 12630, Re 9015, 10015, Ro 1324, Cq 7584, 7732, CrC/MeC 81374, Stg 281374
9571-1,-3	Just Break The News To Mother	Ba 0704, Ca 0304, Do 4569, Je 5960, Or 1960, Pe 12617, Re 9016, 10016, Ro 1325, Cq 7733, ImpE 2764
9572-1,-2	Smoky Mountain Bill -1	Ba 0680, Ca 0280, Do 4549, Je 5937, Or 1937, Pe 12610, Ro 1296, Cq 7538, Htd 16140

Canadian issues of matrix 9570 as by **Carson Robison & Frank Luther**.
Some issues of matrix 9571 use the controls 2015, 102014.
Revs: Banner 0680, Cameo 0280, Jewel 5937, Oriole 1937, Romeo 1296, Homestead 16140 by Frank Marvin.

Bud Billings–Carson Robison, v duet; acc. John Cali, f/bj; Earl Oliver, c; Frank Novak, s/ac; Roy Smeck, sg; Carson Robison, g.
New York, NY
Tuesday, April 8, 1930

| 59680-1,-2 | Poor Man's Heaven | Vi V-40249, Zo 5695, Twin FT1211 |
| 59681-1 | Leave The Purty Gals Alone | Vi V-40249, Zo 5695, Twin FT1211 |

Travelin' Jim Smith: Carson Robison, v; acc. own h/g.
New York, NY
Monday, April 14, 1930

| 150461-2 | So I Joined The Navy | Co 15547-D |
| 150462-2 | Naw! I Don't Wanta Be Rich | Co 15547-D |

Robison & Luther, v duet; acc. unknown, f; unknown, sg; Carson Robison, wh.
New York, NY
c. April 19, 1930

| GEX-2682 | Sleepy Rio Grande | Ge 7180, Ch 15988, Spt 9697 |
| GEX-2683 | When It's Springtime In The Rockies | Ge 7180, Ch 15988, 33027, 45143, Spt 9697, Spr 2546 |

Champion 45143 as by **Carson Robison & Frank Luther**.
Revs: Champion 33027 untraced; Superior 2546 by Vernon Dalhart & Carson Robison.

Bud Billings: Frank Luther, v; acc. unknown, f; unknown, o; Carson Robison, g.
New York, NY
Thursday, April 24, 1930

| 62207-2 | The Prison Fire | Vi V-40251, MW M-8188, ReE MR910, ZoSA 4363, HMVIn N4227 |
| 62208-3 | The Old Parlor Organ | Vi V-40251 |

Matrix 62207 is titled *The Columbus Prison Fire* on Montgomery Ward M-8188.

Carson Robison, v; acc. unknown, f; unknown, o; own g; prob. Frank Luther, bell-1.
New York, NY
Friday, April 25, 1930

| 150491-2 | Ohio Prison Fire -1 | Co 15548-D |
| 150492-3 | Why Are The Young Folks So Thoughtless | Co 15548-D, RZAu G21835 |

Regal-Zonophone G21835 as by **Carson Robison Trio**. Matrix 150492 is titled *Why Are The Young Folks So Thoughtless?* on that issue.

Frank Tuttle: Frank Luther, v; acc. unknown, f; unknown, o; Carson Robison, g/prob. v-1.
New York, NY   Friday, April 25, 1930

| 150493-1 | The Old Parlor Organ -1 | Ha 1148-H, Ve 2148-V, Di 3148-G, ReE MR208, ReAu G21045 |
| 150494- | The Prison Fire | Ha 1148-H, Ve 2148-V, Di 3148-G |

Revs: Regal MR208 by Frank & James McCravy, G21045 by Jack Miller (popular).

Carson Robison Trio, v duet; acc. unknown, f-1; Carson Robison, h-2/g; unknown, sg; unknown, md-3; unknown, bj-4.
New York, NY   Tuesday, April 29, 1930

| 9655-2 | When The Bloom Is On The Sage -1, 3 | Ba 0704, Ca 0304, Do 4565, DoC 181450, Je 5960, Or 1960, Pe 12615, Re 9016, 10016, Ro 1325, Cq 7548, 7733, Bwy 4060, CrC/MeC/Roy 81450, Stg 281450, Min M-903 |
| 9656-2,-3 | They Cut Down The Old Pine Tree -2, 4 | Ba 0705, Ca 0305, Je 5962, Or 1962, Pe 12616, Re 9015, 10015, Ro 1324, Cq 7549, 7732, Bwy 3297, Apex 26157, CrC/MeC/Roy 93008, Stg 293008, Roy 393008 |

Canadian issues of matrices 9655/56 as by **Carson Robison & Frank Luther**.
Revs: Perfect 12616 by John I. White; Broadway 4060 by Vernon Dalhart; Canadian issues of matrix 9655, except Minerva M-903, by Goebel Reeves; Canadian issues of matrix 9656 by O'Connor Trio (popular).

Frank Luther, v; acc. unknown, f; unknown, o; Carson Robison, g; prob. own bell.
New York, NY   Tuesday, April 29, 1930

| 9657-1 | The Prison Fire | Ba 0707, Ca 0307, Je 5964, Or 1964, Pe 12617, Re 9019, 10019, Ro 1328, Chg 895, Apex 41180, CrC/MeC 81374, DoC 181374, Stg 281374, ImpE 2764 |

Canadian issues of matrix 9657, except possibly Apex 41180, as by **Frank Luther**.
Some issues use the control 2014.
Rev. Banner 0707, Cameo 0307, Jewel 5964, Oriole 1964, Regal 9019, 10019, Romeo 1328, Challenge 895 by John I. White.

Tom Cook: Frank Luther, v; acc. unknown, f; unknown, p; poss. own bell-1.
New York, NY   c. early May 1930

238-A	When They Ring The Golden Bells For You And Me -1	Mad 5053, 50053, VD 5053
239-A	Pictures From Life's Other Side	Mad 5053, 50053, VD 5053
4049	A Picture From Life's Other Side	GG/Rad 4317, VD 84317

Grey Gull/Radiex 4317 as by **Frank Luther**. Van Dyke 84317 as by **Jeff Calhoun**.
Revs: Grey Gull/Radiex 4317, Van Dyke 84317 sacred.

Bud Billings Trio With Carson Robison: Frank Luther, Carson Robison, poss. Phil Luther Crow, v trio; acc. unknown, sg; unknown, bj; Carson Robison, g.
New York, NY   Monday, May 19, 1930

| 62234-3 | Red River Valley | Vi V-40267, MW M-4058, M-4101, RZ MR1311, ZoSA 4288 |

Matrix 62234 is titled *On The Red River Shore* on Montgomery Ward M-4101.
Revs: Montgomery Ward M-4058 by Jimmie Rodgers, M-4101 by Jules Allen.

Bud Billings–Carson Robison, v/wh duet; acc. unknown, s; unknown, ac; unknown, bj; unknown, g; Carson Robison, g; unknown, bbs.
New York, NY   Monday, May 19, 1930

| 62235-2 | Little Cabin In The Cascade Mountains | Vi V-40267, ZoSA 4321, HMVIn N4319 |

Zonophone 4321 as by **Bud Billings**.

Carson Robison, v; acc. unknown.
New York, NY   c. June 2, 1930

| GEX-2707 | So I Joined The Navy | Ge 7219, Ch 16023 |
| GEX-2708-A | Poor Man's Heaven | Ge 7219, Ch 16023 |

Carson Robison Trio, v duet; acc. unknown, f; unknown, t; prob. Frank Novak, cl-1/ac-2/bss-3/x-4; unknown, md-5/bj-6; Carson Robison, g.
New York, NY   Monday, June 9, 1930

| 9790-1 | Poor Man's Heaven -2, 3, 6 | Ba 0743, Ca 0343, Do 4584, Je 5994, Or 1994, Pe 12624, Re 10050, Ro 1358, Cq 7573 |

| 9791-2,-3 | Leave The Purty Gals Alone -1, 4, 5 | Ba 0743, Ca 0343, Do 4583, Je 5994, Or 1994, Pe 12622, Re 10050, Ro 1358, Cq 7572, Broadcast International B-111 |
| 9792-2 | I'm Drifting Back To Dreamland -1, 2, 5 | Ba 0771, Ca 0371, Je 6021, Or 2021, Re 10076, Ro 1387, Chg 897 |

Broadcast International B-111 as by **Robison & Luther**. Matrix 9791 is titled *Leave The Pretty Girls Alone* on that issue.
Revs: Domino 4583, Perfect 12622, 12624, Conqueror 7572, 7573 by Vernon Dalhart; Broadcast International B-111 by McDonald Quartet.

Bud Billings: Frank Luther, v; or **Bud Billings–Carson Robison**-1, v duet; acc. poss. John Cali, f-2/md-3; unknown, c; prob. Frank Novak, cl/ac-4; prob. Carson Robison, g.
New York, NY   Tuesday, June 24, 1930

| 62742-1,-3 | Hello, Young Lindy -2 | Vi 22463, Zo 5725 |
| 62743-1,-2 | It's The Same The Whole World Over -1, 3, 4 | Vi 22463, HMVAu EA1248 |

Carson Robison Trio: Frank Luther, v; or v duet-1; acc. unknown.
New York, NY   Tuesday, June 24, 1930

| 9824- | Hello Young Lindy | Ba 0764, Ca 0364, Je 6015, Or 2015, Pe 12627, Ro 1379, Cq 7582, Htd 16000 |
| 9825- | It's The Same The Whole World Over -1 | Ba 0764, Ca 0364, Je 6015, Or 2015, Ro 1379 |

Revs: Perfect 12627, Conqueror 7582 by Irving Kaufman (popular).

Carson Robison, v; acc. own h/g.
New York, NY   Friday, June 27, 1930

| E33294- | So I Joined The Navy | Br 442, BrE 1065, BrAu 442, PanAu P12174 |
| E33295- | Naw! I Don't Wanta Be Rich | Br 442, BrE 1065, BrAu 442 |

Australian Brunswick 442 as by **Carson–Robison** (matrix E-33294)/**Carson Brothers** (matrix E-33295).
Rev. Panachord P12174 by McFarland & Gardner.

Carson Robison Trio, v duet; acc. unknown, t; unknown, cl-1; unknown, ac; unknown, sg-2; unknown, md-3; unknown, bj-4; Carson Robison, g/wh-5.
New York, NY   Monday, June 30, 1930

| 9834-2,-3 | Moonlight On The Colorado -1, 2, 3, 5 | Ba 0771, Ca 0371, Do 4598, Je 6021, Or 2021, Pe 12630, Re 10076, Ro 1387, Chg 897, Cq 7584, 7734 |
| 9840-1,-2 | My Pretty Quadroon -4 | Ba 0773, Ca 0373, Do 4604, Je 6024, Or 2024, Pe 12633, Re 10079, Ro 1388, Chg 785, Cq 7593 |

Matrices 9835 to 9839 are popular.
Revs: Banner 0773, Cameo 0373, Jewel 6024, Oriole 2024, Romeo 1388, Challenge 785 by Frank Marvin; Perfect 12633, Conqueror 7593 by Vernon Dalhart.

Carson Robison, v; acc. own h/g.
New York, NY   Monday, June 30, 1930

| 9841-1,-2 | Naw, I Don't Wanta Be Rich | Ba 0796, Ca 0396, Do 4601, Je 6046, Or 2046, Pe 12632, Re 10101, Ro 1410, Cq 7592, Bwy 4059, ImpE 2624, Broadcast Twelve 3369 |

Broadcast Twelve 3369 as by **Carson Robison**.
Matrix 9841 is titled *Naw I Don't Wanta Be Rich* on Imperial 2624.
Revs: Perfect 12632, Conqueror 7592 by Frank Marvin; Broadway 4059, Broadcast Twelve 3369 by Vernon Dalhart.

Bud Billings–Carson Robison, v duet; acc. unknown, f; unknown, t; unknown, cl; Frank Luther, cel-1; unknown, md; Carson Robison, g/wh-2.
New York, NY   Tuesday, July 1, 1930

62323-1	When The Bloom Is On The Sage -1, 2	Vi V-40282, MW M-3297, M-4060, ReE MR910, ZoAu EE249, HMVIn N4226
62324-1	Carry Me Back To The Mountains	Vi V-40322, Zo 5900, HMVIn N4217
62325-1	My Pretty Quadroon	Vi V-40282, ZoAu EE249
62326-1	Moonlight On The Colorado	Vi 22478, MW M-1403, Zo 5778, ZoAu EE219, HMVIn N4219

Matrix 62323 is titled *Round-Up Time In Texas* on Montgomery Ward M-3297.
Revs: Montgomery Ward M-1403 by Waring's Pennsylvanians (popular); M-3297 by Gene & Glenn (popular); M-4060 (red-and-yellow label issue) by Carl T. Sprague; M-4060 (black label issue) by Delmore Brothers; HMV N4226 by Frank Luther.

Bud Billings–Carson Robison, v duet; acc. prob. Frank Novak, f-1/cl-2/bss-3; unknown, t; unknown, cl; Frank Luther, cel-4; unknown, bj-5/g-6; Carson Robison, g.
New York, NY   Wednesday, July 9, 1930

| 62331-2 | Never Leave Your Gal Too Long -3, 6 | Vi V-40299, ZoAu EE225 |
| 62332-2 | On The Top Of The Hill -1, 4, 5 | Vi V-40299, ZoAu EE225 |

| 62333-2 | By The Old Oak Tree -2, 3, 5 | Vi 22478, Zo 5778, ZoAu EE219, HMVIn N4219 |
| 62334-1 | Oklahoma Charlie -5 | Vi V-40322, Zo 5900, ZoAu EE266, HMVIn N4217 |

Carson Robison, v; acc. own h/g.
New York, NY   c. early July 1930

| 4103-A | Naw! I Don't Wanta Be Rich | VD 5117, Pic 838, Phonycord P-81 |
| 4104-A | So I Joined The Navy | VD 5120, Pic 838, Phonycord P-81 |

Piccadilly 838 as by **Leyland Franklin**. Phonycord P-81 as by **Frank Robeson**.
A test-pressing of these two matrices exists, made by the Australian World company, presumably anticipating issue on one of its labels.
Some issues use controls, as follows: 4103 = 126; 4014 = 131.
Revs: Van Dyke 5117 by Jack Kaufman (popular), 5120 by Gene Autry.

Frank Luther & Carson Robison, v duet; acc. unknown, f; unknown, t; prob. Frank Novak, cl/bss-1; Frank Luther, cel-2; unknown, g; Carson Robison, g/wh-3.
New York, NY   Wednesday, July 23, 1930

E-33245-	Carry Me Back To The Mountains -3	Br 476
E-33246-	Leave The Purty Gals Alone -1, 2	Br 450
E-33247-	Oklahoma Charlie -1	Br 450

Carson Robison Trio, v duet; acc. unknown, t; prob. Frank Novak, cl/bss-1; unknown, g; Carson Robison, g/wh-2; unknown, train-wh eff-3.
New York, NY   Tuesday, July 29, 1930

9905-1,-2	I'll Never See My Darling Any More -2	Ba 0795, Ca 0395, Je 6047, Or 2047, Pe 12643, Re 10102, Ro 1411, Cq 7631, Htd 16147
9906-1,-2	Carry Me Back To The Mountains -2	Ba 0795, Ca 0395, Je 6047, Or 2047, Pe 12637, Re 10102, Ro 1411, Cq 7603, Htd 16147
9907-1	Never Leave Your Gal Too Long -3	Ba 0796, Ca 0396, Je 6046, Or 2046, Re 10101, Ro 1410
9908-1	Oklahoma Charley -1	Ba 0824, Ca 0424, Do 4642, Je 6075, Or 2075, Re 10131, Ro 1439, Chg 783, Cq 7734

Perfect 12643 as by **Carson Robinson Trio**.
Revs: Perfect 12643, Conqueror 7631, and all issues of matrix 9908 except Conqueror 7734 by Vernon Dalhart; Perfect 12637, Conqueror 7603 by John I. White.

Robison & Luther, v duet; or **Carson Robison**-1, v; acc. unknown, t; prob. Frank Novak, cl/s-2; Frank Luther, cel-3; unknown, g; Carson Robison, g.
New York, NY   c. late July/early August 1930

GEX-2747-A	Carry Me Back To The Mountains	Ge 7261, Ch 16068, 45143, Spt 9735
GEX-2748-A	Oklahoma Charlie	Ge 7261, Ch 16068, Spt 9735
GEX-2749-A	Never Leave Your Gal Too Long -1	Ge 7284, Ch 16090, 45144, Spt 9736
GEX-2750-A	Leave The Purty Gals Alone -1, 2, 3	Ge 7284, Ch 16090, 45144, Spt 9736

In the Gennett files matrices GEX-2747 to 2750 have descriptive comments written in: each is described as "Not hill billy" and then (respectively): "springtime rockies type," "railroad boomer tune," "blues type," and "pop type."

Frank Luther & Carson Robison, v duet; acc. Carson Robison, g/wh-1.
New York, NY   Monday, August 4, 1930

| 150686-1 | Carry Me Back To The Mountains -1 | Co 15588-D, ReAu G21477 |
| 150687-1 | Oklahoma Charley | Co 15588-D |

Harper Brothers, v duet; acc. unknown.
New York, NY   Tuesday, August 19, 1930

| E-33624- | Moonlight On The Colorado | Br 4874 |
| E-34025- | When The Organ Played At Twilight | Br 4874 |

Black Brothers, v duet; acc. unknown, f; unknown, g.
New York, NY   Monday, September 15, 1930

| 404441-B | Moonlight On The Colorado | OK 41453, PaE E6386, PaAu A3089, Ariel Z4660 |
| 404442-B | When The Bloom Is On The Sage | OK 41453, PaE E6386, PaAu A3089 |

Rev. Ariel Z4660 untraced.

Bud Billings–Carson Robison, v duet; acc. two unknowns, f; Carson Robison, h-1/g; Frank Luther, cel-2; unknown, md-3/bj-4.
New York, NY   Tuesday, September 16, 1930

| 63138-2 | Tell Me That You Love Me, Dear -2, 3 | Vi V-40314 |
| 63139-1 | Song Of The Silver Dollar -1, 4 | Vi V-40314, ZoSA 4327 |

Bud & Joe Billings, v duet; acc. three unknowns, f; unknown, g; Carson Robison, g.
New York, NY   Monday, September 29, 1930

| 63676-1,-2 | Somewhere In Old Wyoming | Vi unissued |

| 63677-1,-2,-3 | Drifting And Dreaming | Vi unissued |
| 63678-1,-2 | My Heart Is Where The Mohawk Flows Tonight | Vi unissued |

Bud Billings–Carson Robison, v duet; acc. unknown, f; unknown, t; unknown, tb; prob. Roy Smeck, sg-1/g-2; unknown, md/bj; Carson Robison, g; unknown, sb.
New York, NY   Thursday, October 9, 1930
| 63676-4 | Somewhere In Old Wyoming -2 | Vi 22556, Zo 5809, ZoAu EE231, Twin FT1256 |
| 63677-5 | Drifting And Dreaming -1 | Vi 22556, Zo 5809, ZoAu EE231, Twin FT1256 |

Zonophone 5809, EE231, Twin FT1256 as by **Bud Billings & Carson Robison**.

Harper Brothers, v duet; acc. three unknowns, f; unknown, ac; unknown, p; unknown, g; unknown, sb; poss. Frank Luther, x-1/bell-2.
New York, NY   Monday, October 13, 1930
| E-34852- | Dreamy Rocky Mountain Moon -1 | Br 469 |
| E-34853- | The Church Bells Are Ringing For Mary -2 | Br 469 |

Frank Luther & Carson Robison, v duet; acc. unknown, t; unknown, cl; unknown, ac-1; Frank Luther, cel; unknown, md-2; unknown, g; Carson Robison, g; unknown, x.
New York, NY   Thursday, October 16, 1930
E-34788-	My Heart Is Where The Mohawk Flows To-night	Br 478, BrAu 478
E-34789-	Sleepy Hollow	Br 478, BrAu 478
E-34790-	You're Still My Valentine -1, 2	Br 476

Black Brothers-1/Carson Robison & Frank Luther-2, v duet; acc. unknown, t; prob. Frank Novak, cl-3/bss-4/ac-5; Frank Luther, cel-6; unknown, g; prob. Carson Robison, g; unknown, train-wh eff-7.
New York, NY   Monday, October 20, 1930
404491-B	Oklahoma Charley -1, 3, 4	OK 45487
404492-B	Never Leave Your Gal Too Long -1, 3, 4, 5, 7	OK 45487, Ve 2365-V, Cl 5299-C
404493-B	Carry Me Back To The Mountains -2, 3	Co 15768-D
404494-B	I'll Never See My Darling Anymore -2, 5, 6	Co 15768-D

Velvet Tone 2365-V, Clarion 5299-C as by **Carson Robison Trio**. Those issues use the transfer matrix 100527. The above items are dated as follows in Columbia/OKeh files: 404491, 404494 to October 20; 404492 to October 30; 404493 to October 10. It has been assumed that the latter two dates are misprints.

Carson Robison Trio, v duet; acc. Frank Novak, cl-1/bss-2/ac-3/x-4; Frank Luther, cel-5; unknown, g; Carson Robison, g.
New York, NY   Tuesday, October 21, 1930
150890-1	Oklahoma Charley -1, 2	Ve 7092-V, Di 6066-G, Cl 5109-C
150890-2	Oklahoma Charley -1, 2	ReE MR277, ReAu G21115
150891-2	Leave The Purty Gals Alone -3, 4, 5	Ve 7092-V, 7126-V, Di 6066-G, Cl 5110-C
105891-3	Leave The Purty Gals Alone -3, 4, 5	Cl 5110-C, ReE MR277, ReAu G21115
150892-1	Darling Nellie Gray -1, 3	Ve 7126-V, Cl 5110-C
150893-2	Red River Valley -4, 5	Cl 5109-C, 5243-C

Regal G21115 as by **The Carson Robison Trio**.
Rev. Clarion 5243-C by Gene Autry.

Bud Billings–Carson Robison, v duet; or Frank Luther, v-1; acc. unknown, f; unknown, t-2; Frank Novak, cl/s-3/x; Frank Luther, cel; unknown, g; Carson Robison, g/wh-4.
New York, NY   Monday, October 27, 1930
63174-1	Come Back To-night In My Dreams -2, 3	Vi V-40335, ZoSA 4345
63175-1	Back In The Hills Of Colorado -1, 2, 3	Vi V-40335
63678-3	My Heart Is Where The Mohawk Flows Tonight -4	Vi 23534, Zo 5951, Twin FT1336

Victor 23534, Zonophone 5951, Twin FT1336 as by **Bud & Joe Billings**.
The unknown guitarist may not play on matrix 63678.

Carson Robison Trio, v duet; acc. Frank Novak, cl-1/bscl-2/ac-3; Carson Robison, h-4/g/wh-5; Frank Luther, cel-6/jh-7; unknown, bj-8/g-9.
New York, NY   c. October/November 1930
1017-2	When It's Springtime In The Rockies -1, 5, 9	Cr 3025, Htd 23017, MW M3007, Vs 5045
1018-3	Hand Me Down My Walking Cane -2, 4, 7, 8	Cr 3027, Htd 23018, MW M3006, Vs 5041, Beacon 3001, JDs 3520
1019-5	She'll Be Comin' 'Round The Mountain -2, 4, 8	Cr 3027, Htd 23018, MW M3006, Vs 5041, Beacon 3001, JDs 3521
1020-1	Red River Valley -1, 3, 5, 6, 9	Cr 3025, Htd 23017, MW M3009, Vs 5045, JDs 3521

Varsity 5041 as by **Frank Luther & Carson Robison**, 5045 as by **Carson Robison & Frank Marvin**. Beacon 3001, Joe Davis 3521 as by **Carson Robison & Frank Luther**; Joe Davis 3520 as by **Carson Robinson & Frank Luther**.
Matrix 1018 is titled *Hand Me Down My Walkin' Cane* on Joe Davis 3520.

Frank Luther & Carson Robison, v duet; acc. unknown, cl; unknown, o; prob. Carson Robison, g.

New York, NY   c. October/November 1930
1037-1   When The Organ Played At Twilight   Cr 3020

Acc. unknown orch.
New York, NY   c. October/November 1930
1038-1   Cabin In The Hills   Cr 3020, Bwy 8275

Phil Crow Trio: prob.: Frank Luther, Phil Luther, Carson Robison, v trio; or **Frank & Phil Crow**-1, v duet; or **Bud Billings**-2: Frank Luther, v; acc. unknown, f; unknown, t; two unknowns, cl; unknown, s; unknown, bss; prob. Carson Robison, h-3/g; unknown, bj; prob. Frank Luther, jh-4; unknown, clapping-5.
New York, NY   Thursday, November 6, 1930

63197-2	I'm A-Gittin' Ready To Go -5	Vi 23504, HMV B3886
63198-2	Abraham -1, 4	Vi 23504, HMV B3886
63199-2	He Was Once Some Mother's Boy -2, 3	Vi 23500, MW M-8188
63200-2	The Fate Of The Fleagle Gang -2, 3	Vi 23500, MW M-8188

Matrix 63199 is titled *The Prison* (or *Prisoner's*?) *Child* on Montgomery Ward M-8188.
Several instruments may have been played by Frank Novak.

Carson Robison & Frank Luther, v duet; acc. unknown.
New York, NY   Friday, November 7, 1930

404529-	Come Back Tonight In My Dreams	OK unissued
404530-	Sleepy Hollow	OK unissued

Carson Robison, v; prob. acc. own h/g.
New York NY   Friday, November 7, 1930

404531-	Naw, I Don't Wanna Be Rich	OK 45537
404532-	So I Joined The Navy	OK 45537

Black Brothers, v duet; acc. unknown, t; unknown, ac; unknown, g; poss. Frank Luther, bell.
New York, NY   Friday, November 7, 1930

404539-A	Where Will You Be On Next New Year's Day?	OK 45493, PaE R1096
404540-B	No Christmas Times For Poor Little Nell	OK 45493, PaE R1096

Carson Robison, v/sp; acc. John Cali, bj/sp-1; own g/jh-2/wh-3; unknown, sp.
New York, NY   c. November 19, 1930

GEX-2821-A	Carson Robison's Story – Part 1 -3	Ch 16138
GEX-2822-A	Carson Robison's Story – Part 2 -1, 2	Ch 16138

Bud & Joe Billings, v duet; acc. unknown, f; unknown, c; Frank Novak, cl-1/x-2; poss. Frank Luther, cel-3; unknown, g; Carson Robison, g; Fred Erdman, sp-4.
New York, NY   Wednesday, November 26, 1930

64814-1	When Your Hair Has Turned To Silver (I Will Love You Just The Same) -1, 2	Vi 22588, Zo 5834, ZoAu EE241, HMVIn N4216
64815-1	I'm Alone Because I Love You -3	Vi 22588, Zo 5834, ZoAu EE241, HMVIn N4216
64816-1,-2	The Whistle Boys -4	Vi unissued

Carson Robison & Phil Crow, v/sp duet; acc. unknown, t; Frank Novak, bss; poss. John Cali, bj; prob. Carson Robison, g; poss. Frank Luther, jh.
New York, NY   Wednesday, December 3, 1930

150951-3	Abraham	Co 15627-D, ReE MR405

Carson Robison & Frank Luther, v duet; or **Carson Robison, Frank Luther & Phil Crow**-1, v trio; acc. unknown, t; Frank Novak, cl-2/bss-3/x-4; poss. John Cali, md; prob. Carson Robison, g; unknown, clapping-5/eff-5.
New York, NY   Wednesday, December 3, 1930

150995-2	My Heart Is Where The Mohawk Flows To-night -2, 4	Co 15644-D, ReE MR316, Re/RZAu G21146
150996-2	Sleepy Hollow -2, 4	Co 15644-D, ReE MR316, Re/RZAu G21146
150999-2	I'm Gittin' Ready To Go -1, 3, 5	Co 15627-D, ReE MR433, ReAu G21477

Regal G21477 as by **Carson Robison Trio**.
Matrix 150995 is titled *My Heart Is Where The Mohawk Flows Tonight* on Regal MR316. Matrix 150999 is titled *I'm Gettin' Ready To Go* on Regal G21477.
Matrices 150952 to 150994 are by other artists on other dates; matrices 150997/98 are by Fletcher Henderson (see *JR*).
Rev. Regal MR433 by Frank & James McCravy.

Harper Brothers, v duet; acc. two unknowns, f; unknown, ac; unknown, p; unknown, marimba; unknown, bells.
New York, NY   Thursday, December 11, 1930

E-35736-	Blue Pacific Moonlight	Br 505, Spt S2200
E-35737-	When The Golden Corn Is Waving	Br 505, Spt S2200

Supertone S2200 is marked "cancelled" in company files and may never have been issued.

Cal Carson: Frank Luther or Carson Robison, v; acc. unknown, f; prob. Frank Novak, bscl; prob. Carson Robison, h/g; unknown, oc.

New York, NY   poss. late 1930/early 1931
        Why Did I Get Married   Durium Junior A1
        She Sat In Her Parlor   Durium Junior A3

The instrumentation is confirmed for Durium Junior A3 only.
Durium Juniors were single-sided paper-based discs about 4 inches in diameter. Durium went out of business in March 1931.

Cal & Gid Carson, v duet; acc. prob. Frank Novak, bscl-1; unknown, sg; prob. Carson Robison, g; unknown third man, v eff-2.
   New York, NY   poss. late 1930/early 1931
        Birmingham Jail -1   Durium Junior A2
        Lonesome Railroad -2   Durium Junior A4

Carson Robison Trio, v duet; acc. Frank Novak, cl-1/ac-2; unknown, sg; poss. John Cali, md; Carson Robison, g/wh-3.
   New York, NY   Tuesday, January 20, 1931
   10374-2,-3   Little Sweetheart Of The Prairie -1, 2, 3   Ba 32078, Je 6200, Or 2200, Pe 12683,
                                                             Re 10257, Ro 1568, Cq 7710, Apex 26156,
                                                             CrC/MeC 93005, Stg 293005, Roy 393005
   10375-   Little Sweetheart Of The Mountains   ARC unissued

Revs: Apex 26156, Crown/Melotone 93005, Sterling 293005, Royale 393005 by The O'Connor Trio (Canadian popular).

Acc. unknown, md; Carson Robison, g.
   New York, NY   Friday, January 30, 1931
   10375-6   Little Sweetheart Of The Mountains   Ba 32078, Je 6200, Or 2200, Pe 12683,
                                                             Re 10257, Ro 1568, Cq 7710

Acc. Frank Novak, cl-1/ac-1/x-3; unknown, md; Carson Robison, g/wh-4.
   New York, NY   c. January 1931
   1137-6   Little Sweetheart Of The Prairie -1, 3, 4   Cr 3057, Htd 23019, Bwy 8253, *MW M3003,*
                                                             Vs 5031
   1138-2   Little Sweetheart Of The Mountains -2   Cr 3057, Htd 23019, Bwy 8253, *MW M3003,*
                                                             Vs 5031, Ang 3353, Lyric 3353
   1141-2   I'm Alone Because I Love You -1, 3   Cr 3055, Htd 23055, Bwy 1434, Ang 3309,
                                                             Lyric 3386

Crown 3055, Homestead 23055 as by **Frank Luther & Carson Robinson.** Broadway 1434 as by **Carson Robison & Frank Luther.** Varsity 5031 as by **Frank Luther Duo.** Angelus 3309, Lyric 3386 as by **Robinson Luther.**
Controls appear on various issues instead of, or as well as, the matrices shown, as follows: 1137 = 1963; 1138 = 1964; 1141 = 1965. Matrices 1139/40 are untraced.
Revs: Crown 3055, Homestead 23055 by Harry Shayne (popular); Broadway 1434 by George Stark (popular); Angelus 3309 by Chick Bullock (popular), 3353 by Frankie Saunders (popular).

Frank Luther & Carson Robison, v duet; acc. unknown orch.
   New York, NY   c. January/February 1931
   1181-   When Your Hair Has Turned To Silver   Cr 3070, Htd 23002, Bwy 1450, *Vs 5086,*
                                                             Ang 3342, Lyric 3342, Summit Z101
   1182-   Wabash Moon   Cr 3070, Htd 23002, Bwy 1452, *Vs 5086,*
                                                             Ang 3342

Broadway 1450 as by **Luther Brothers,** 1452 as by **Luther Bros.** Angelus 3342 as by **Jack Turner** (matrix 1181)/**Luther Brothers** (matrix 1182), but some issues have matrix 1181 coupled with an item by Tommie & Willie (popular). Lyric 3342, Summit Z101 as by **Dale & Clyde Russell,** but some issues of the former as by **Jack Turner.**
Crown 3070 may not have been issued.
Some issues use controls, as follows: 1181 = 1999; 1182 = 2005.
Revs: Broadway 1450, 1452 by Fred L. Jeske; Lyric 3342 by Jack Turner or Dale & Clyde Russell (both popular); Summit Z101 by Jack Turner (popular).

Carson Robison Trio, v trio; acc. poss. Frank Novak, f; unknown, p.
   New York, NY   c. February 1931
   1195-3   There's A Rainbow Shining Somewhere   Cr 3079, Htd 23020, Bwy 8256
   1196-1   The Way Of The Cross Leads Home   Cr 3079, Htd 23020, Bwy 8256

Frank Luther, v; or **Carson Robison Trio**-1, v duet; acc. Frank Novak, f-2/cl-3/bscl-4/ac-5/x-6; Carson Robison, h-7/g; unknown, md-8/g-9; Frank Luther, y-10; unknown, train-wh eff-11.
   New York, NY   c. February 1931
   1197-2   The Runaway Boy -3, 6, 7, 8   Cr 3080, Htd 23021, Bwy 8275, *Vs 5079*
   1198-1   Little Green Valley -1, 8   Cr 3080, Htd 23021, *MW M3008, Vs 5047*
   1199-2   Birmingham Jail No. 2 -1, 4, 5, 6, 7, 8   Cr 3081, Htd 23022, Pm 3273, Bwy 8254,
                                                             MW M3007, Vs 5047, JDs 3520, Lyric 3371
   1200-2   Waiting For A Train -9, 10, 11   Cr 3083, Htd 22996, 23062, *Vs 5079*
   1201-   Left My Gal In The Mountains -1, 8   Cr 3081, Htd 23022, Bwy 8257
   1202-1   May I Sleep In Your Barn Tonight Mister? -2, 7, 8   Cr 3082, Htd 22995

1203-1	When The Work's All Done This Fall -2, 7, 8	Cr 3082, Htd 22995
1204-1	Oh Dem Golden Slippers -8	Cr 3083, Htd 22996, 23062
1205-4	Naw I Don't Wanna Be Rich -2, 7, 8	Cr 3084, Htd 22997, Bwy 8274, Vs 5083
1206-1	I Wish I Was Single Again -8	Cr 3084, Htd 22997

All issues of matrix 1205 as by **Carson Robison**. Broadway 8254, Paramount 3273, Lyric 3371 as by **The Luther Brohers**. Varsity 5047 as by **Carson Robison & Frank Luther**.
Matrix 1199 is titled *Birmingham Jail* on Homestead 23022, Montgomery Ward M3007, Varsity 5047, Joe Davis 3520. Matrix 1205 is titled *Naw! I Don't Wanna Be Rich* on Varsity 5083.
Some issues of matrix 1199 use the control 1974.
Revs: Broadway 8254, Paramount 3273, Lyric 3371 by Gunboat Billy & The Sparrow (see Arthur Fields & Fred Hall); Varsity 5083 (as by **Frank Luther Trio**) by Bob Miller.

The Jones Brothers: Frank Luther, Carson Robison, Phil Luther Crow, v trio; or Frank Luther, Carson Robison, v duet-1; acc. prob. Frank Novak, bscl-2/ac-3; unknown, bj-4/g-5.

New York, NY Monday, March 9, 1931

E-36238-A,-B	Jacob's Ladder -2, 4	Me unissued?
E-36239-A,-B	Six Feet Of Earth -1, 3	Me unissued?
E-36240-A,-B	Will The Circle Be Unbroken -3	Me unissued?
E-36241-A	Tell Mother I'll Be There -3, 5	Me M12141, Po P9014, Pan 25079, PanAu P12141

This session was recorded by Brunswick but session-sheets are stamped "SYNDICATE," implying that the products were destined for primary issue on Melotone. Rerecordings of matrices E-36238 to E-36240 (see March 30, 1931 session below) were so issued. Matrix E-36241 was originally logged as by **The Jones Brothers**, but session-sheets note a "correction due to change in artist name from the Jones Bros. to Phil and Frank Luther." All the above issues, however, appear to have been credited as shown.

Eddie Bell: Frank Luther, v; or Frank Luther, Phil Crow, v duet-1; acc. Frank Novak, f-2/cl-3; unknown, h-4; unknown, k-5; unknown, g; poss. Frank Novak, u-6; unknown, octoreen-7.

New York, NY Friday, March 20, 1931

64892-2	Stop Yer Playin' -2, 3, 5	Vi 23547, BB B-5941, Twin FT1941
64893-1	Stop Yer Playin' -	TT C-1558
64894-	Divorce Blues -4, 5, 6, 7	TT C-1558
64895-1	Divorce Blues -2, 4, 5, 6, 7	Vi 23547
68811-	Cornpone In Pot Likker (Whether To Dunk Or Crumble) -1, 2, 3	Vi 23539

Timely Tunes C-1558 as by **Frank Luther**. Victor 23539 as by **Bud Billings**.
Revs: Victor 23539 by Peg Moreland; Bluebird B-5941 by The Three 'Baccer Tags; Twin FT1941 by Delmore Brothers.

Phil & Frank Luther, v duet; acc. Frank Novak, f-1/cl-2/bscl-3/ac-4/bj-5; unknown, g.

New York, NY Monday, March 23, 1931

E-36493-A	You Will Never Miss Your Mother Until She Is Gone -2, 4	Me M12144, Po P9061, Vo 5482, Pan 25041, PanAu P12144
E-36494-A	Can I Sleep In Your Barn Tonight, Mister? -1, 4	Me M12144, Po P9061, Vo 5482, Pan 25065, PanAu P12144
E-36495-A	When The Work's All Done This Fall -1, 3, 5	Me M12143, Po P9075, Vo 5483, Pan 25041
E-36496-A	Oh! Bury Me Not On The Lone Prairie -1	Me M12143, Po P9075, Vo 5483, Pan 25079

At least some issues of Canadian Melotone M12143 use Plaza matrices of these titles by Vernon Dalhart.
Matrix E-36494 is titled *Can I Sleep In Your Barn To-night, Mister?* on Panachord 25065.

Acc. Frank Novak, f-1/cl-2/bscl-3/h-4/ac-5/bj-6; unknown, g; poss. Frank Luther, jh-7/oc-8.

New York, NY Monday, March 30, 1931

E-36428-	Jacob's Ladder -3, 4, 6, 7	Me M12140, Po P9072, Pan 25065, PanAu P12140
E-36429-A	Will The Circle Be Unbroken? -1, 5	Me M12141, Po P9014, PanAu P12141
E-36430-	Six Feet Of Earth -2, 4, 5	Me M12140, Po P9072, PanAu P12140
E-36431-A	Birmingham Jail -1, 3, 4, 8	Me M12280, Po P9089, Vo 5480

Carson Robison Trio: Frank Luther, Carson Robison, v duet; or Frank Luther, Carson Robison, Phil Crow, v trio-1; acc. Frank Novak, bscl-2/x-3; Carson Robison, h-4/g; poss. John Cali, md; unknown, clapping-5.

New York, NY c. March 1931

1235-2	I Want To Dream By The Old Mill Stream -2, 3	Cr 3100, Htd 22998, Bwy 8273, Lyric 3386
1236-1	Sleepy Hollow -	Cr 3100, Htd 22998, Bwy 8274, Lyric 3421
1237-	I'm Gettin' Ready To Go -1, 2, 4, 5	Cr 3124, Htd 22999, Bwy 8273
1238-	Abraham -	Cr 3124, Htd 22999, Bwy 8257

Lyric 3386 as by **Carson Robinson Trio**.
Matrix 1237 is titled *I'm Gittin' Ready To Go* on Broadway 8273.
Some issues of matrix 1235 use the control 2010.
Rev. Lyric 3421 by Frank Marvin.

Frank Luther, Carson Robison, Phil Crow, v trio; acc. unknown, o; prob. Carson Robison, g; prob. Frank Luther, bell.

New York, NY   Wednesday, April 8, 1931
   10550-3   A Tribute To Knute Rockne   Ba 32164, Or 2249, Pe 12705, Re 10341,
                                                     Ro 1623, Cq 7805

Rev. all issues by Roxy Male Quartette (sacred).

Bud Billings: Frank Luther, v; acc. unknown, f; unknown, t; Frank Novak, cl/x; unknown, p; two unknowns, g.

New York, NY   Wednesday, April 22, 1931
   53047-1   Rocky Mountain Lullaby   Vi 22694, Zo 5951, ZoAu EE254, Twin FT1336
   53048-2   My Cradle Sweetheart   Vi 22694, ZoAu EE254

Bud Billings Trio: Frank Luther, Carson Robison, Phil Crow, v trio; or **Carson Robison**-1, v; acc. prob. Murray Kellner, f; unknown, p; Carson Robison, g; unknown, sb.

New York, NY   Wednesday, April 22, 1931
   53050-1   Settin' By The Fire   Vi 23556, Zo 6048, ZoAu EE298
   53051-1   Wolf At The Door -1   Vi 23556, Zo 6048, ZoAu EE298

Carson Robison Trio, v trio; or **Frank Luther**-1, v; acc. Frank Novak, bscl/x-2; poss. Frank Luther, cel-3; poss. Roy Smeck, sg-4/md-5; Carson Robison, g/wh-6.

New York, NY   c. April 1931
   1301-3   My Pretty Quadroon -2, 4   Cr 3140, Htd 23001, Bwy 8280
   1302-3   Bring Your Roses To Her Now -5, 6 Cr 3140, Htd 23001, Bwy 8276
   1303-3   Rocky Mountain Lullaby -1, 3, 4, 5 Cr 3138, Htd 23061, Bwy 8276, *MW M3011*,
                                                         Vs 5060, ImpE 2510

Some issues of matrix 1303 use the control 1933.

Carson Robison Trio, v duet; acc. Frank Novak, ac; poss. Roy Smeck, md; Frank Luther, bell.

New York, NY   c. April 1931
   1316-3   The Little Old Church In The Valley   Cr 3138, Htd 23061, Bwy 8280, *MW M3011*,
                                                     Vs 5060, Ang 3347, Lyric 3347, 3401,
                                                     Summit Z109, ImpE 2510

Montgomery Ward M3011, Varsity 5060 as by **Frank Luther & Carson Robison**. Angelus 3347, Lyric 3347, 3401 as by **Luther & Robison**. Summit Z109 as by **The Luther Brothers**. Imperial 2510 as by **The Radio Imps**.
Matrix 1316 is titled *Little Old Church In The Valley* on Montgomery Ward M3011.
Some issues of matrix 1316 use the controls 1929, 2018.
Revs: Lyric 3401 by Fred L. Jeske; Angelus 3347, Lyric 3347 untraced.

Frank Luther & Carson Robison, v duet; acc. prob. Frank Novak, f-1/ac-2/x-3; prob. Frank Luther, cel-4; unknown, g; Carson Robison, g/wh-5.

New York, NY   Wednesday, May 6, 1931
   151545-1   When It's Night-Time In Nevada -1, 2, 5 Co 2458-D, CoJ J1210, ReE MR405,
                                                            Re/RZAu G21055
   151546-2   Rocky Mountain Lullaby -3, 4   Co 2458-D, CoJ J1210, Re/RZAu G21055

Matrix 151546 on Regal/Regal-Zonophone G21055 as by **Frank Luther**.

Bud Billings–Carson Robison, v/wh-1 duet; acc. unknown, f; Frank Novak, cl-2/sb-3/x-4; unknown, p-5; Carson Robison, g.

New York, NY   Wednesday, May 20, 1931
   69630-1,-2   There Must Be A Bright Tomorrow -2 Vi unissued
   69631-1   Silvery Arizona Moon -1, 3, 5   Vi 22753, Zo 5984, ZoAu EE270, HMVIn N4207,
                                                        Twin FT1357
   69632-1   Southern Moon -3, 5   Vi 22753, Zo 5984, ZoAu EE270, Twin FT1357
   69633-1   Sleepy Hollow -2, 4, 5   Vi 22771, ZoSA 4345

Matrix 69633 is titled *In Sleepy Hollow* on some pressings of Victor 22771.
Rev. HMV N4207 by Jimmie Rodgers.

Frank Luther & Carson Robison, v duet; or **Phil & Frank Luther**-1, v duet; acc. Frank Novak, f-2/cl-3/bscl-4/ac-5/sg-6/g-7; prob. Carson Robison, h-8/g; unknown, bj-9; poss. Frank Luther, jh-10.

New York, NY   Thursday, May 21, 1931
   E-36716-   Abraham -2, 8, 9, 10   Br 536
   E-36717-   I'm Getting Ready To Go -4, 8, 9   Br 536, BrE 1170
   E-36718-   There Must Be A Bright Tomorrow (For Each Me M12187
                  Yesterday Of Tears) -1, 3, 6
   E-36719-   Don't Lay Me On My Back (In My Last Sleep) -1, Me M12187
                  4, 5, 9
   E-36720-A   Lonesome Railroad -1, 4, 7   Me M12280, Po P9089, Vo 5480

Carson Robison Trio, v duet; acc. Frank Novak, f-1/bscl-2/sg-3/x-4; prob. Carson Robison, g.

New York, NY   Wednesday, May 27, 1931

| 10667-3 | There Must Be A Bright Tomorrow (For Each Yesterday Of Tears) -3, 4 | Ba 32210, Or 2289, Pe 12731, Ro 1656, CrC/MeC 91144, Stg 291144, Roy 391144 |
| 10668-2 | The Steer's Lament (Nearin' The End Of The Trail) -1, 2 | Ba 32210, Or 2289, Pe 12731, Ro 1656, CrC/MeC 91144, Stg 291144, Roy 391144 |

Frank Luther, Carson Robison, v duet; or **Frank Luther, Carson Robison, Phil Luther Crow**, v trio-1; acc. unknown, f-2; Frank Novak, cl-3/x-4; Frank Luther, cel-5; unknown, g; Carson Robison, g; prob. Frank Luther, Carson Robison, wh duet-6.

New York, NY   c. May/June 1931

1362-2	When The Moon Comes Over The Mountain -3, 4, 5, 6	Cr 3156, Htd 23060, *MW M3004*, Vs 5033, Lyric 3415, Summit Z135
1363-1	When It's Night-time In Nevada -1, 2, 3, 4, 5, 6	Cr 3156, Htd 23060, *MW M3004*, Vs 5033, Lyric 3438, Summit 109
1364-	The Runaway Train -	Cr 3171, Htd 23057
1365-	Settin' By The Fire -	Cr 3171, Htd 23057

Montgomery Ward M3004 as by **Frank Luther & Carson Robison**. Lyric 3438 as by **The Lewis Trio**. Summit Z135 as by **The Robison Trio**.

Matrix 1363 is titled *When It's Night Time In Nevada* on Montgomery Ward M3004, Varsity 5033.

Revs: Lyric 3415 by Bill Parker, 3438 (as by **Frank Luther**) by Dick Robertson; Summit Z135 by Dick Robertson.

Frank Luther, v; acc. Bill Wirges, p; Carson Robison, g.

New York, NY   Wednesday, June 24, 1931

| 69975-1 | Beautiful Dreamer | Vi unissued |

Bud Billings–Carson Robison, v duet; acc. poss. Frank Novak, cl/x; Frank Luther, cel; unknown, g; prob. Carson Robison, g.

New York, NY   Tuesday, July 21, 1931

| 70201-1 | When The Moon Comes Over The Mountain | Vi 22771 |

Carson Robison Trio, v duet; acc. unknown, ac; unknown, sg; John Cali, md; prob. Carson Robison, g/wh-1.

New York, NY   Tuesday, July 28, 1931

| 10753-2 | When It's Night-Time In Nevada -1 | Ba 32242, Or 8093, Pe 12745, Ro 5093, Cq 7845, Bwy 4069, Mel-O-Dee 302, EBW 5375 |
| 10753-4 | When It's Night-Time In Nevada | Apex 41413, CrC/MeC 91181, Stg 291181, Roy 391181, Min M-903 |

An excerpt from matrix 10753-4 was issued on the Canadian "double-length" discs Domino/Melotone 51023, Sun 251023, Ace 351023.

Edison Bell Winner 5375 uses the transfer matrix 13802-B.

Revs: all issues by Gene Autry, except Broadway 4069 by Martin & Roberts; Minerva M-903 by Robison & Luther; Edison Bell Winner 5375 by Gus Van (popular).

Bud & Joe Billings–Carson Robison: Frank Luther, Carson Robison, prob. Phil Luther Crow, v trio; acc. unknown, p; John Cali, bj/g; Carson Robison, g; Frank Novak, sb; prob. Frank Luther, Carson Robison, wh duet.

New York, NY   Thursday, September 24, 1931

| 70254-1 | In The Cumberland Mountains | Vi 22852, MW M-4046, Zo 6063, Zo/RZAu EE303, HMVIn N4214 |

Bud & Joe Billings, v duet; acc. Frank Novak, cl/ac-1/x; unknown, p; poss. Frank Luther, cel; John Cali, bj/g; Carson Robison, g.

New York, NY   Thursday, September 24, 1931

| 70255-1 | Missouri Valley | Vi 22852, Zo 6063, Zo/RZAu EE303, HMVIn N4214 |
| 70256-1 | Roll On, You Yellow Moon -1 | Vi unissued |

Carson Robison & Frank Luther, v duet; or **Carson Robison Trio**-1: Frank Luther, Carson Robison, Phil Crow, v trio; acc. Frank Novak, cl-2/ac-3/sb-4/x-5; unknown, sg-6; John Cali, g; Carson Robison, g; prob. Frank Luther, Carson Robison, wh duet-7.

New York, NY   Wednesday, September 30, 1931

151819-2	Silvery Arizona Moon -3, 7	Co 2550-D, Re/RZAu G21231
151820-4	When You're Alone (Try To Remember Me) -2, 5, 6	Co 2550-D, Re/RZAu G21231
151821-2	In The Cumberland Mountains -1, 4, 7	Co 2619-D, ReE MR482, Re/RZAu G21356
151822-2	Missouri Valley -	Co 15779-D, ReE MR482, Re/RZ G21372

Matrix 151821 on Regal MR482 as by **Carson Robison, Frank Luther & Phil Crow**.

Regal/Regal-Zonophone G21231 as by **Frank Luther & Carson Robison**.

Carson Robison Trio, v duet/trio-1; acc. unknown, f-2; Carson Robison, h-3/g; poss. Bob Miller, p-4; poss. Roy Smeck, sg-5/md-6; poss. John Cali, g-7.

New York, NY   c. September 1931

1486-3	I'll Be Thinking Of You Little Girl -2, 5, 7	Cr 3221, Htd 23058, *MW M3010, Vs 5051*
1487-1	Give My Love To Nellie, Jack -7	Cr 3221, Htd 23058, *MW M3009, Vs 5050*
1488-2	You're As Pretty As A Picture -4, 6, 7	Cr 3222, Htd 23059, *MW M3010, Vs 5051, Cont C-3014*
1489-2	The Picture On The Wall -1, 3	Cr 3222, Htd 23059, *MW M3008, Vs 5050*

Varsity 5050 as by **Carson Robison & Frank Luther**. Varsity 5051, Continental C-3014 as by **Frank Luther & Carson Robison**.
Matrix 1486 is titled *I'll Be Thinking Of You, Little Gal* on Varsity 5051. Matrix 1487 is titled *Give My Love Too Nelly, Jack*, and matrix 1489 *Picture On The Wall*, on Varsity 5050.
Homestead 23058 was also assigned to a coupling by Vernon Dalhart.
Rev. Continental C-3014 by Bob Miller.

Frank Luther, Carson Robison, prob. Leonard Stokes, v trio; acc. poss. Bob Miller, p; prob. John Cali, md/g; prob. Carson Robison, g; prob. Frank Novak, bbs; prob. Frank Luther, Carson Robison, wh duet.
    New York, NY   Tuesday, October 13, 1931

| 10874-3 | In The Cumberland Mountains | Apex 41440, CrC/MeC 91226, Stg 291226, Roy 391226, Min M-14004 |
| 10874-4 | In The Cumberland Mountains | Ba 32305, Or 8100, Pe 12759, Ro 5100, Cq 7898, Bwy 4046, ImpE 2662, Taiyo 30005 |

Taiyo 30005 (a Japanese issue) as by **Carson Robinson Trio**.

Frank Luther, Carson Robison, v duet; acc. prob. Carson Robison, h/g; prob. John Cali, md.
    New York, NY   Tuesday, October 13, 1931

| 10875-2 | Twenty-One Years | Apex 41440, CrC/MeC 91226, Stg 291226, Roy 391226 |
| 10875-3 | Twenty-One Years | Ba 32305, Or 8100, Pe 12759, Ro 5100, Cq 7898, Bwy 3311, ImpE 2624, Taiyo 30005 |

Taiyo 30005 (a Japanese issue) as by **Carson Robinson Trio**.
Excerpts from matrices 10874-3 and 10875-2 were issued on the Canadian "double-length" discs Domino/Melotone 51023, Sun 251023, Ace 351023.
Revs: Broadway 3311 by Renfro Valley Boys (see Karl & Harty); Domino/Melotone 51023, Sun 251023, Ace 351023 by Gene Autry; Minerva M-14004 by Mus-Kee-Kee Indian Trappers (Canadian).

Frank Luther & Carson Robison, v duet; or **Carson Robison Trio**-1: Frank Luther, Carson Robison, Leonard Stokes, v trio; acc. prob. Frank Novak, cl-2/sb-3/x-4; prob. Carson Robison, h-5/g; poss. Bob Miller, p-6; prob. John Cali, md; prob. Frank Luther, Carson Robison, wh duet-7.
    New York, NY   Friday, October 23, 1931

E-37273-A	Silvery Arizona Moon -2, 4, 6	Me M12278, Po P9087, Vo 5477, Pan 25147
E-37274-A	In The Cumberland Mountains -1, 3, 6, 7	Me M12289, Po P9091, Pan 25162, Mayfair G2078
E-37325-A	Missouri Valley -2, 4, 6	Me M12289, Po P9091, Pan 25162, Mayfair G2078
E-37326-A	Twenty One Years -5	Me M12278, Po P9087, Vo 5477
E-37327-	Twenty-One Years -5	Pan 25147

Mayfair G2078 as by **The Texas Crooners**.
The Brunswick session-sheet for matrices E-37326/27 (which are distinct recordings) specifies that the former was made for "syndicate" use (i.e. on Melotone, etc.) and the latter for issue in England.

Carson Robison Trio, v duet; or Carson Robison, v-1; acc. unknown, f-2; poss. Frank Novak, cl-3/bbs-4; unknown, p-5; poss. John Cali, md-6; unknown, g-7.
    New York, NY   Thursday, January 7, 1932

11092-	I'm Trying The Leaves So They Won't Come Down	ARC unissued
11093-1	What Are You Squawkin' About? -1, 4, 6, 7	Ba 32358, Or 8117, Pe 12785, Ro 5117, Cq 7935, Bwy 4077, CrC/MeC/Stg/Roy 91272
11094-	Missouri Valley	ARC unissued
11095-3	Prosperity Is Just Around Which Corner? -2, 3, 5	Ba 32358, Or 8117, Pe 12785, Ro 5117, Cq 7935, CrC/MeC/Stg/Roy 91272

Matrix 11095 may be titled *Prosperity Is Right* (or *Just*) *Around The Corner* on Crown/Melotone/Sterling/Royale 91272 (or some of those issues).
Rev. Broadway 4077 by John McGhee & Frank Welling.

Carson Robison & Frank Luther, v/wh duet; acc. Frank Novak, cl/x; poss. John Cali, md; prob. Carson Robison, g.
    New York, NY   Wednesday, February 3, 1932

| 152102-1 | When It's Springtime In The Blue Ridge Mountains - | Co 15779-D |
| 152103- | Pals Of The Little Red School | Co 2619-D |

Matrix 152103 was assigned the transfer matrix 130733-1.

Black Brothers, v/wh-1 duet; acc. Frank Novak, cl-2/ac-3/x-4; poss. John Cali, bj/g; prob. Carson Robison, g.

New York, NY   Wednesday, February 3, 1932

365063-1; 405138-	When It's Springtime In The Blue Ridge Mountains -3, 4	OK 41553, Ve 2519-V, Cl 5459-C, RZ MR1311, Re/RZAu G21372
365064-1; 405139-	Pals Of The Little Red School -1, 2, 3	OK 41553, Ve 2519-V, Cl 5459-C, RZ MR2496, Re/RZAu G21356, RZIr IZ683, Twin FT8371

Velvet Tone 2519-V, Clarion 5459-C, Regal/Regal-Zonophone G21372 as by **Carson Robison Trio**.
Regal-Zonophone MR2496, IZ683, Twin FT8371 as by **Carson Robison & His Pioneers**.
Some issues use controls or transfer matrices, as follows: 365063/405138 = 480046-A; 365064/405139 = 480045-A.

Carson Robison & Frank Luther, v/wh-1 duet; acc. Frank Novak, bscl-2/ac-3/x-4; unknown, ac; unknown, g; Carson Robison, g.

New York, NY   Thursday, March 17, 1932

152146-1	Home On The Range -3	Co 2642-D
152147-1	The Tree That Stands By The Road -1, 2, 4	Co 2642-D, Re/RZAu G21448

Carson Robison Trio & The Black Brothers: Carson Robison, v; or **Luther & Robison & The Black Brothers**-1, v duet; acc. Frank Novak, bscl; Carson Robison, h/g; poss. John Cali, md or bj.

New York, NY   Thursday, March 17, 1932

405178-; 365074-	Home On The Range	OK 45572, Ve 2537-V, Cl 5477-C, RZ MR2496, RZAu G21835, RZIr IZ683, Twin FT8371
405179-; 365075-	The Tree That Stands By The Road -1	OK 45572, Ve 2537-V, Cl 5477-C

Velvet Tone 2537-V, Clarion 5477-C as by **Carson Robison Trio**. Regal-Zonophone MR2496, IZ683, Twin 8371 as by **Carson Robison & His Pioneers**. Regal-Zonophone G21835 as by **The Carson Robison Trio**.

Frank Luther With Carson Robison Trio: Frank Luther, v; acc. Frank Novak, f/bscl; unknown, ac; Carson Robison, h/g; poss. John Cali, bj.

New York, NY   Saturday, March 26, 1932

11582-A	99 Years (Still Got 99)	Me M12350, Pan 25230, RZ MR3351, RZIn MR20100, RZIr IZ1087

Matrix 11582 is titled *Ninety Nine (99) Years (Still Got 99)* on Regal-Zonophone MR3351.

Acc. Frank Novak, ac; unknown, ac; poss. John Cali, md; Carson Robison, g; prob. Frank Luther, Carson Robison, Leonard Stokes, v trio.

New York, NY   Saturday, March 26, 1932

11583-A	Strawberry Roan	Me M12350, Pan 25230

Frank Luther & Carson Robison, v duet; acc. Frank Novak, f-1/ac-2; unknown, ac; poss. John Cali, g; Carson Robison, g.

New York, NY   Saturday, March 26, 1932

11584-A	That Silver Haired Daddy Of Mine -2	Me M12371, Pan 25245, RZ MR3351, RZIn MR20100, RZIr IZ1087
11585-	Ma And Pa (Send Their Sweetest Love) -1	Me M12371, Pan 25245

Bud Billings–Carson Robison, v/wh-1 duet; acc. unknown, t-2; Frank Novak, cl-3/ac-4; unknown, p; unknown, sg-5; unknown, g; Carson Robison, g.

New York, NY   Monday, April 4, 1932

72228-2	When The Sun Goes Down On A Little Prairie Town -1, 3	Vi 22997, Zo 6195, Zo/RZAu EE320, HMVIn N4220
72229-1	Ma And Pa (Send Their Sweetest Love) -4, 5	Vi 22997, Zo 6195, Zo/RZAu EE320, HMVIn N4220
72230-1	When We Carved Our Hearts On The Old Oak Tree -2	Vi unissued

HMV N4220 as by **Bud & Joe Billings**.

Carson Robison & His Pioneers: Carson Robison, poss. Frank Luther, unknown, v trio; acc. prob. Carson Robison, h/g; unknown, h; unknown, g.

New York, NY   Monday, April 4, 1932

72231-1	The Cowboy's Prayer	Vi unissued
72232-1	Meet Me Tonight In The Valley	Vi unissued

The session of April 4, 1932 was the last at which Robison and Luther worked together. Luther's subsequent recordings are listed under his own name.

No details.

New York, NY   ?c. April 1932

130891-1	Old Familiar Tunes – Part 1	Co 15773-D
130892-1	Old Familiar Tunes – Part 2	Co 15773-D

Carson J. Robison & His Pioneers: Carson Robison, v; acc. own h/g; John Mitchell, bj/poss. g/v; Bill Mitchell, bj/poss. g/v; Pearl Pickens, v-1; unidentified, jh-2; band, laughing-3.

London, England.   late April 1932

OY-3336-2	I Was Born In Old Wyoming -1, 3	Zo 6136, ZoAu 6136, RZ T6136, RZAu T6136, Twin FT1427
OY-3337-2	Way Out West In Kansas -	Zo 6143, ZoAu 6143, RZ T6143, RZAu T6143, Twin FT1434
OY-3338-2	Going To The Barn Dance Tonight -1, 2	Zo 6136, ZoAu 6136, RZ T6136, RZAu T6136, Twin FT1427
OY-3339-2	Didn't He Ramble -	Zo 6143, ZoAu 6143, RZ T6143, RZAu T6143, Twin FT1434

On some items one of the Mitchell brothers, but it is uncertain which, plays guitar rather than banjo.

Carson J. Robison, wh; acc. orch.; Ray Noble, dir.
London, England. Friday, April 29, 1932

| OY-3346-1 | Nola | Zo 6135, RZ T6135, Twin FT1426 |
| OY-3347-1 | Tree Top Serenade | Zo 6135, RZ T6135, Twin FT1426 |

John & Bill Mitchell Of Carson Robison's Pioneers, bj/v-1 duet.
London, England. Friday, April 29, 1932

| OY-3348-2 | Honeymoon Express -1 | Zo 6144, Twin FT1435 |
| OY-3349-2 | Medley/Intro.: - Whispering, Spain, Strumming Our Troubles Away, Roll On, Mississippi | Zo 6144, Twin FT1435 |

Carson Robison & His Pioneers: Carson Robison, v; acc. unknown, f; Frank Novak, cl-1/bscl-2; own h-3/g; John Mitchell, bj or g/v; Bill Mitchell, bj or g/v; Pearl Pickens, v-4.
London, England. Friday, May 6, 1932

AR-1208-1	The Bum Song -	ReE/RZ MR780, Twin FT1523
AR-1209-1	Hallelujah! I'm A Bum -2, 3	ReE/RZ MR587
AR-1210-2	Polly Wolly Doodle -	ReE/RZ MR780, RZAu G21478, Twin FT1523
AR-1211-2	Cross Eyed Sue -	ReE/RZ MR756, RZAu G21447, Twin FT1545
AR-1212-2	Open Up Dem Pearly Gates -1, 2, 3, 4	ReE/RZ MR600
AR-1213-1	Peg-Leg Jack -2	ReE/RZ MR587, RZAu G21447
AR-1214-1	Meet Me Tonight In The Valley -4	ReE/RZ MR600, RZAu G21478
AR-1215-1	The Engineer's Child -	ReE/RZ MR756, RZAu G21448, Twin FT1545

Regal/Regal-Zonophone MR756, MR780, Twin FT1523, FT1545 as by **Bud & Joe Billings**.

Carson Robison, v/wh-1; acc. unknown orch.; unknown, v trio; unknown, train eff-2.
London, England. early May 1932

GB-4422-2	Everybody's Going But Me -1, 2	DeE F3001, M1219
GB-4423-2	In The Cumberland Mountains	DeE F2972, M1161
GB-4424-2	The Wolf At The Door	DeE F3001, M1219
GB-4425-2	When It's Springtime In The Blue Ridge Mountains	DeE F2972, M1161

Acc. unknown, f-2; own h-3/g; John Mitchell, bj-4/g-5/v; Bill Mitchell, bj-6/g-7/v; Frank Novak, sb; Pearl Pickens, v-8.
London, England. May 1932

A1134	Oh! Susannah -3, 4/6, 5/7, 8	Broadcast Twelve 3203
A1134-X	Oh! Susannah -3	Broadcast Twelve 3203
A1135	Swanee Kitchen Door -1, 2, 5, 7	Broadcast Twelve 3214
A1136	Ain't Ya Coming Out Tonight -3, 4/6, 5/7, 8	Broadcast Twelve 3214, Rex 8297
A1137	Sweet Virginia -1, 2, 5, 7, 8	Broadcast Twelve 3203

Carson J. Robison & His Pioneers: Carson Robison, v; acc. Max Goldberg, t; unknown, cl; unknown, p; own g.
London, England. Thursday, June 2, 1932

| GB-4541-2 | Stack O' Lee Blues – Part 1 | DeE F3026 |
| GB-4542-2 | Stack O' Lee Blues – Part 2 | DeE F3026 |

Carson Robison & His Pioneers: Carson Robison, John Mitchell, Bill Mitchell, v trio; acc. Frank Novak, ac-1; prob. Carson Robison, g.
London, England. Friday, June 24, 1932

AR-1314-1	A Hill Billy Mixture Part 1 Introducing: Casey Jones; Six Feet Of Earth; The Wanderer's Warning -1	ReE MR645
AR-1315-1	A Hill Billy Mixture Part 2 Introducing: Barnacle Bill; Bury Me Not On The Lone Prairie; Will The Angels Play Their Harps For Me	ReE MR645
AX-6451-1	Hill Billy Songs Medley Part 1 Introducing: Open Up Dem Pearly Gates; Will The Angels Play Their Harps; Casey Jones; Bury Me Not On The Lone Prairie; Hallelujah I'm A Bum	CoE DX365

AX-6452-1	Hill Billy Songs Medley Part 2 Introducing: Barnacle Bill; Why Did I Get Married; Naw, I Don't Wanna Be Rich; Cowgirl's Prayer; Hand Me Down My Walking Cane	CoE DX365

Columbia DX365 is a 12-inch record.

Carson J. Robison & His Pioneers: Carson Robison, John Mitchell, Bill Mitchell, v trio; acc. Carson Robison, h; unknown, p; unknown, chimes; unidentified, y.
London, England.   June/July 1932

S-2487	Smoky Mountain Bill	Sterno 1001, Solex SX-139, Plaza P277

Sterno 1001 as by **Carson Robison & His Pioneers**. Plaza P277, an 8-inch English issue, as by **Tony Miller & The Cow-Boys**. Matrix S-2487, assigned the control L-972, is titled *Smokey Mountain Bill* on that issue.

Carson Robison, v; acc. unknown, t-1; own h-2/g/sp-3; John Mitchell, bj or g/v; Bill Mitchell, bj or g/v; unidentified, jh-4.
London, England.   June/July 1932

S-2488	Why Did I Get Married? -2, 3, 4	Sterno 994
S-2489	The Runaway Train -	Sterno 995, Solex SX-139, Plaza P277
S-2490	Goin' Back To Texas -1	Sterno 994
S-2491	Steamboat (Keep Rocking) -	Sterno 995
S-2496	Why Ain't I Got No Sweetheart	Sterno 1001

Sterno 1001 as by **Carson Robison & His Pioneers**. Plaza P277, an 8-inch English issue, as by **Tony Miller & The Cow-Boys**. Matrix S-2489 is assigned the control L-966 on that issue.
Intervening matrices are untraced.

Carson Robison & His Pioneers: Carson Robison, v/sp; acc. Henry ———, f; own h/g; John Mitchell, bj/v/sp; Bill Mitchell, bj/v/sp; unidentified, jh; Pearl Pickens, v/sp; unidentified, wh duet.
London, England.   June/July 1932

X127+7	Goin' To Have A Big Time To-night	4-in-1 1

This item was almost certainly recorded at the preceding Sterno session. Other items on 4-In-1 1 (a "double-play" issue) are by popular artists.

No details.
London, England.   c. June/July 1932

E-1077-A,-B	Hand Me Down My Walking Cane	Durium EN-27

Duriums are single-sided discs containing two recordings; the other item on EN-27 is by the Durium Dance Band (popular).

Carson Robison, v; acc. prob. John Mitchell, Bill Mitchell, Pearl Pickens, v trio; unk. orch. (*Ev'rybody's Going But Me*); or acc. own h/g; unidentified, jh; John Mitchell, Bill Mitchell, v duet (*Get Away Old Man*).
London, England.   c. June/July 1932

E-1078-A,-B	Ev'rybody's Going But Me/Get Away Old Man	Durium EN-25

Acc. prob.: own h/g; John Mitchell, g/v; Bill Mitchell, g/v; poss. Pearl Pickens, v.
London, England.   c. June/July 1932

E-1102-B	Come Along With Me/Coming Round The Mountain	Durium EN-35

According to Robison the group also recorded for Durium *Sleepy Rio Grande* and *Waltz Of The Hills*, but no issues of these items have been traced.

Carson Robison, v/sp; acc. own h-1/g/wh-2; John Mitchell, bj/g/v/sp; Bill Mitchell, bj/g/v/sp; Pearl Pickens, v-3/sp-4; poss. another man, sp; unknown, dog eff/car eff.
London, England.   c. early July 1932

OY-2328-2	The Back Porch – Part 1 -2	Zo 6160, ZoAu 6160, RZ T6160, RZAu T6160, Twin FT1446
OY-2329-2	The Back Porch – Part 2 -1, 3, 4	Zo 6160, ZoAu 6160, RZ T6160, RZAu T6160, Twin FT1446

The Mitchell Brothers, bj duet-1/g duet-2/v duet-3.
London, England.   c. July 1932

JW-773-2	March Medley -1	Eclipse SC50
JW-775-2	Plantation Memories -1	Eclipse 334
JW-777-2	Sittin' By The River -2	Eclipse 334
JW-778-	Hum, Strum Whistle Or Croon -2, 3	Eclipse SC50

These are 7-inch issues.

Carson Robison & His Pioneers: Carson Robison, v/sp; acc. own h/g/wh-1; John Mitchell, bj/g/v/sp; Bill Mitchell, bj/g/v/sp; Pearl Pickens, v/sp; ——— Jackson, unknown others, sp; Bert Firman, sp-2.
London, England.   Thursday, September 15, 1932

OY-3844-2	Making A Record – Part 1	Zo 6224, ZoAu 6224

| OY-3845-3 | Making A Record – Part 2 -1, 2 | Zo 6224, ZoAu 6224 |

Matrix OY-3845 concludes with an excerpt of orchestral playing as on matrix OY-3846.

Carson Robison, v; acc. orch.; Bert Firman, dir.
London, England. Thursday, September 15, 1932

| OY-3846-2 | That's Bound To Be Kentucky | Zo/RZ 6225, ZoAu/RZAu 6225, Twin FT1482 |
| OY-3847-2 | Just Keep Ploddin' Along | Zo/RZ 6225, ZoAu/RZAu 6225, Twin FT1482 |

Acc. own h/g; John Mitchell, bj or g/v; Bill Mitchell, bj or g/v; unidentified, jh.
London, England. Monday, September 26, 1932

| GB-4940-2 | Hot Time In New Orleans | Pan 25328 |

Pearl Pickens, v; acc. unidentified, g.
London, England. Monday, September 26, 1932

| GB-4941-2 | The Song Of The Prairie | Pan 25328 |

Carson Robison, John Mitchell, Bill Mitchell, v trio; acc. unknown, o; prob. Carson Robison, g.
London, England. Monday, September 26, 1932

| GB-4942-1 | The Old Man Of The Mountain | Pan 25290 |

The Mitchel [sic] **Brothers Of Carson J. Robison's Pioneers**: John Mitchell, bj/v/sp; Bill Mitchell, bj/v/sp; Pearl Pickens, sp.
London, England. Monday, September 26, 1932

| GB-4943-2 | We Love To Play For People When They Talk | Pan 25290 |

Carson Robison & His Pioneers: Carson Robison, v; acc. unknown, f-1; own h-2/g/wh-3; John Mitchell, bj or g/v; Bill Mitchell, bj or g/v; prob. Frank Novak, sb; unidentified, jh-4; unknown, chimes-5; Pearl Pickens, v-6.
London, England. c. September 1932

1196	Sing Another Line -4	Broadcast Twelve 3254, Rex 8212
1197	Home On The Range-1, 3, 6 (lead)	Broadcast Twelve 3254, Rex 8130
1198	Climbin' Up The Golden Stairs -2, 5	Broadcast Twelve 3318, Rex 8212
1199	Darling Nellie Gray -1, 3, 6	Broadcast Twelve 3318, Rex 8130

Matrix 1197 on Broadcast Twelve 3254 as by **Pearl Pickens With Carson Robison & His Pioneers**, and on Rex 8130 as by **Carson Robison & His Pioneers (With Pearl Pickens)**.

Carson Robison & His Buckaroos: Carson Robison, v; acc. own h-1/g/wh-2; John Mitchell, bj or g/v; Bill Mitchell, bj or g/v; unidentified, jh-3; Pearl Pickens, v-4; band sp-5; unknown, boat-whistle eff-6.
New York, NY Thursday, October 18, 1934

16135-2	Long Long Ways From Home -2	Cq 8396
16136-2	Ramblin' Cowboy	Cq 8396
16137-1,-2	Goin' To The Barn Dance To-night -1, 3, 4, 5	Ba 33278, Me M13245, Or 8404, Pe 13088, Ro 5404, Cq 8397, CrC/MeC/Stg/Roy 91997, Rex 8415
16138-1	Hot Time In New Orleans To-night -1, 6	Ba 33278, Me M13245, Or 8404, Pe 13088, Ro 5404, Cq 8397, CrC/MeC/Stg/Roy 91997, Rex 8415

Rex 8415 as by **Carson Robison & His Pioneers**.

John Mitchell, bj/v; Bill Mitchell, bj/v; Carson Robison, g/v/wh-1; poss. Pearl Pickens, v.
New York, NY Tuesday, November 27, 1934

16251-1,-2	Heart In The Heart Of Texas	ARC unissued
16252-1	Prairie Town -1	Ba 33327, Me M13294, Or 8424, Pe 13107, Ro 5424, Cq 8487, Cr/Me/Stg/Roy 91972
16253-1	Big Ranch Boss	Ba 33327, Me M13294, Or 8424, Pe 13107, Ro 5424, Cq 8487, Cr/Me/Stg/Roy 91972
16254-1,-2	You'll Never Take My Dreams Away	ARC unissued

Carson Robison, v; acc. own g; prob. John and/or Bill Mitchell, g.
New York, NY Wednesday, February 6, 1935

| 16818- | Happy Go Lucky Carson | ARC unissued |
| 16819-1 | Texas Dan | Cq 8488 |

Acc. own g.
New York, NY Thursday, March 14, 1935

| 17041-1 | Five Thousand Dollars Reward | Cq 8488 |

Carson Robison & His Buckaroos: no details (but prob. as for next session).
New York, NY Monday, April 1, 1935

| 17229-1,-2 | That Old Swiss Chalet In The Rockies | ARC unissued |
| 17230-1,-2 | Little Mother Of The Hills | ARC unissued |

Carson Robison, John Mitchell, Bill Mitchell, v trio; acc. unknown, ac; John or Bill Mitchell, bj-1; Carson Robison, g/wh-2; unknown, sb; unidentified, v-3.

		Wednesday, April 10, 1935
New York, NY
17229-4	That Old Swiss Chalet In The Rockies -2, 3	Vo 02952, RZAu G22592
17230-4	Little Mother Of The Hills -1	Vo 02952, RZAu G22592

Carson Robison, v; acc. Frank Novak, bscl-1/pac-2; own h-3/g/wh-4; John Mitchell, bj or g/v; Bill Mitchell, bj or g/v; unknown, sb; Pearl Pickens, v.

New York, NY   Friday, June 19, 1936
102239-1	So I Joined The Navy -1, 3	MW M-4919, RZ MR2654, Twin FT8486
102240-1	I'm Leavin' On That Blue River Train -1, 2	MW M-4919, RZ MR2339, Twin FT8235, CoSs MZ234
102241-1	The Candle Light In The Window -2, 4	MW M-4917, RZ MR2376, Twin FT8264
102242-1	There's A Bridle Hangin' On The Wall -2	MW M-4917, RZ MR2340, RZIr IZ598, Twin FT8236
102243-1	Ramblin' Cowboy -2	MW M-4915, BB 33-0509, RZ MR2340, RZAu G25012, RZIr IZ598, Twin FT8236
102244-1	I Was Born In Old Wyomin' -1, 3	MW M-4918, RZ MR2654, Twin FT8486

Bluebird 33-0509 as by **Carson Robison**. Regal-Zonophone, Twin issues as by **Carson Robison & His Pioneers**. One of the vocalists does not sing on matrix 102241.

Carson Robison, v; acc. Frank Novak, ac-1; own h-2/g/wh-3; unknown, sb-4.

New York, NY   Friday, June 19, 1936
| 102245-1 | Happy Go Lucky -1, 2, 3, 4 | MW M-4916, HMV BD407, RZIr IZ613 |
| 102246-1 | Texas Dan | MW M-4916, HMV BD407, RZIr IZ613 |

HMV BD407 as by **Carson Robison**. Regal-Zonophone IZ613 as by **Carson Robison & His Pioneers**.

Acc. Frank Novak, ac/bscl-1; John Mitchell, bj/v; Bill Mitchell, bj/v; own g/wh; unknown, sb; Pearl Pickens, v.

New York, NY   Wednesday, July 1, 1936
| 102367-1 | I Left Her Standin' There (With A Doo-Dad In Her Hair) -1 | MW M-4918, RZ MR2376, Twin FT8264 |
| 102368-1 | Home Sweet Home On The Prairie | MW M-4915, RZ MR2339, Twin FT8235, CoSs MZ234 |

Regal-Zonophone MR2339, MR2376, Twin FT8235, FT8264 as by **Carson Robison & His Pioneers**.
Matrix 102367 is titled *I Left Her Standing There (With A Dood-Da In Her Hair)* on Regal-Zonophone MR2376.

Carson Robison & His Pioneers: Carson Robison, v; acc. Frank Novak, bscl-1/sb-2; own h-3/wh-4; unknown, sg-5; John Mitchell, bj/g/v; Bill Mitchell, bj/g/v; unidentified, jh-6; Pearl Pickens Mitchell, v; unidentified, y-7.

London, England.   October 1936
F-2038	Home, Sweet Home On The Prairie -2, 4	Rex 8911, RZAu G40115
F-2039	(a) Darling Nellie Gray, (b) Oh! Susannah, (c) Will The Angels Play Their Harps For Me -3	Rex 8911, RZAu G40115
F-2042	I'm An Old Cow Hand -1, 7	Rex 8922
F-2043	The Cowboy Yodelling Song -1, 3, 4, 5, 6, 7	Rex 8922, RZAu G40123
F-2044	Texas Dan	Rex 9037, RZAu G40118

Matrices F-2040/41 are untraced.

Pearl Pickens Mitchell, v; acc. unknown, sg; John Mitchell, bj/g; Bill Mitchell, bj/g; Carson Robison, g; Frank Novak, sb.

London, England.   October 1936
| F-2045 | My True Love Has Gone | Rex 9100, RZAu G40140 |

Carson Robison, v; acc. Frank Novak, bscl-1/sb-2; own h-3/g/wh-4; John Mitchell, bj/g/v; Bill Mitchell, bj/g/v; Pearl Pickens Mitchell, v; unknown, train eff-5.

London, England.   October 1936
F-2046	Carson Robison Selection No. 2 – Part 1 (Clementine; Camptown Races; Annie Laurie) -3	Rex 9158, RZAu G40161
F-2047	Carson Robison Selection (Continued) (Open Up Dem Pearly Gates; Climbing Up De Golden Stairs; The Old Rugged Cross)	Rex unissued
F-2050	There's A Bridle Hangin' On The Wall	Rex 8951, RZAu G40095
F-2051	Blue River Train -1, 3, 5	Rex 8951, RZAu G40095

Matrices F-2048/49 are untraced.

Carson Robison, v/sp; acc. John Mitchell, bj/v/sp/dancing; Bill Mitchell, bj/v/sp; own g/wh; Pearl Pickens Mitchell, v/sp.

London, England.   November 1936
| F-2074-2 | An Evening On The C R Ranche Part 1 | Rex 8982, RZAu G40109 |
| F-2075 | An Evening On The C R Ranche Part 2 | Rex 8982, RZAu G40109 |

Matrices F-2074/75 are titled *An Evening On The C.R. Ranch Parts 1 & 2* on Regal-Zonophone G40109.

Carson Robison, v/sp-1; acc. own h-2/g/wh-3; John Mitchell, bj/v-4; Bill Mitchell, bj/v-4; prob. Frank Novak, sb; Pearl Pickens Mitchell, v-4/sp.

London, England.   December 1936

F-2090	[unknown title] -4	Rex unissued
F-2091	Rambling Cowboy -3, 4	Rex 9127, RZAu G40157
F-2092	Happy-Go-Lucky -1, 2	Rex 9127, RZAu G40157
F-2093	Selection: Summer Night On The Texas Trail, Roll Along, Little Doggie, Billie Boy	Rex 9100, RZAu G40140

Matrix F-2090 may have been *Long, Long Ways From Home*, which Robison remembered recording for Rex in 1936.
Matrix F-2093 is titled *Carson Robison Selection No. 1* [etc.] on Regal-Zonophone G40140.
One or both of the Mitchells may not play on all titles.

Carson Robison, v/sp; acc. own h/g; unknown, o; unidentified, bj; John Mitchell, v; Bill Mitchell, v; Pearl Pickens Mitchell, v.

London, England.   December 1936

F-2126	Carson Robison Selection No. 2 – Part 2	Rex 9158, RZAu G40161

Carson Robison, v; acc. unknown, sg-1; John or Bill Mitchell, md; John or Bill Mitchell, lg-2; own g; John Mitchell, v; Bill Mitchell, v; Pearl Pickens Mitchell, v; unidentified, y-3.

New York, NY   February 1937

20702	There's A Moon Shinin' Bright On The Prairie Tonight	Rex unissued
20703	Nobody's Darlin' But Mine -1	Rex 9008, RZAu G40123
20704	The Cowboy Romeo -2, 3	Rex 9008, RZAu G40118

These recordings were made by ARC on behalf of the British Rex label.

Acc. Frank Novak, bscl; own h; John or Bill Mitchell, bj/v; John or Bill Mitchell, g/v; Pearl Pickens Mitchell, v.

New York, NY   February 1937

20705	With A Banjo On My Knee	Rex 9037

Carson Robison, John Mitchell, Bill Mitchell, v trio; acc. poss. Frank Novak, bscl-1; unknown, pac; unknown, eo-2; unknown, md-3/g-4; Carson Robison, g/wh; unknown, sb; unidentified, y-5.

London, England.   c. May 3, 1939

R-3531-	There's A Ranch In The Rockies -	Rex 9545, RZAu G40243
R-3532-	Sing Me To Sleep With A Song Of The West -	Rex 9545, RZAu G40243
R-3533-1	Little Swiss Whistling Song -1, 2, 4	Rex 9565, RZAu G40247
R-3534-1	Cowboy's Home In Heaven -3, 5	Rex 9565, RZAu G40258

Carson Robison, John Mitchell, Bill Mitchell, Pearl Pickens Mitchell, v quartet; acc. unknown, pac; Carson Robison, g; poss. unknown, sb.

London, England.   c. June 3, 1939

R-3648-A	South Of The Border	Rex 9574, RZAu G40247
R-3649-B	The West Ain't What It Used To Be	Rex 9574, RZAu G40258
R-3650-	There's A Hole In The Old Oaken Bucket	Rex 9598, RZAu G40250
R-3651-	Cowboy Blues	Rex 9598, RZAu G40250

Carson Robison & His Old Timers: two unknowns, f; John Cali, bj; Carson Robison, g; unknown, sb; Lawrence V. Loy, calls-1.

New York, NY   February 1941

29743-1	The First Two Ladies Cross Over -1	Co 36018, CoC C279
29744-1	Buffalo Boy Go 'Round The Outside -1	Co 36019, CoC C280
29745-1	Darling Nellie Gray -1	Co 36018, CoC C279
29747-1	Oh Susanna -1	Co 36109, CoC C280
29748-1	Dive For The Oyster (Part I) -1	Co 36020, CoC C281
29749-1	Dive For The Oyster (Part II) -1	Co 36020, CoC C281
29750-1	Little Brown Jug	Co 36021, CoC C282
29751-1	'Possum In The 'Simmon Tree	Co 36021, CoC C282

Matrix 29746 is untraced. Columbia 36018 to 36021 were issued in album C-47.

Carson Robison & His Buckaroos: Carson Robison, v; acc. Frank Novak, s/cel; John Gart, ac/Ho; John Cali, bj/g; own g.

New York, NY   Friday, February 28, 1941

062723-1	So I Joined The Navy	BB B-8681
062724-1	Naw, I Don't Wanta Be Rich	BB B-8712
062725-1	Goin' Back To Texas	BB B-8712, RZAu G25012
062726-1	Sleepy Rio Grande	BB B-8681

Carson Robison, v; acc. Del Staigers, t; Frank Novak, pac; Jene Von Hallberg, p; John Cali, g; Ed Brader, tu; Harry Breuer, traps.

New York, NY   Thursday, December 18, 1941

068496-1	Remember Pearl Harbor	BB B-11414
068497-1	Get Your Gun And Come Along (We're Fixin' To Kill A Skunk)	BB B-11415

| 068498-1 | I'm In The Army Now | BB B-11415 |
| 068499-1 | We're Gonna Have To Slap The Dirty Little Jap (And Uncle Sam's The Guy Who Can Do It) | BB B-11414 |

Acc. Frank Pinero, vn; Frank Novak, cl/pac; Jene Von Hallberg, p; John Cali, g; Ed Brader, sb.
New York, NY   Tuesday, January 26, 1942

071718-1	Mussolini's Letter To Hitler	BB B-11459
071719-1	Hitler's Reply To Mussolini	BB B-11459
071720-1	1942 Turkey In The Straw	BB B-11460
071721-1	"Here I Go To Tokio", Said Barnacle Bill, The Sailor	BB B-11460

Acc. Frank Novak, cl/s; Charles Magnante, pac; William Wirges, p; James H. Smith, bj/g; John Cali, g; Melvin Raub, sb.
New York, NY   Friday, April 16, 1942

073836-1	Don't Let My Spurs Get Rusty While I'm Gone	BB B-11546
073837-1	It's Just A Matter Of Time	BB B-11527
073838-1	Plain Talk	BB B-11546
073839-1	The Story Of Jitter-Bug Joe	BB B-11527

Acc. prob.: Frank Novak, f-1/cl-2; own h-3; Charles Magnante, pac; unknown, tin whistle; James H. Smith, bj; John Cali, g; unknown, tu.
New York, NY   Friday, July 17, 1942

075427-1	I'm A Pris'ner Of War	BB unissued
075428-1	Just Wait And See	BB 33-0509
075429-1	The Old Gray Mare Is Back Where She Used To Be -1, 3	BB 33-0808, RZAu G24815, HMVIn NE722
075430-1	I'm Goin' Back To Whur I Come From -2	BB 33-0808, RZAu G24815, HMVIn NE722

Matrix 075429 is titled *The Old Grey Mare Is Back Where She Used To Be* on Regal-Zonophone G24815.
Carson Robison recorded after 1942.

THE ROBISON TRIO

This credit was used on Summit for the Carson Robison Trio.

ROCHFORD & PEGGS

One of them, sg; the other, g; Emry Arthur, v-1.
Chicago, IL   Tuesday, January 17, 1928

C-1527/8	Indiana March	Vo 15654
C-1529/30	Hawaiian Hula	Vo 15654
C-1547/48*	I'm All Alone -1	Vo 5207
C-1549*/50*	Hawaiian Blues -1	Vo 5207

Intervening matrices are by other artists.

ROCKY MOUNTAIN RANGERS

See Frank Luther.

ROCKY MOUNTAINEERS

Pseudonym on Aurora A22022 for the Rex Cole Mountaineers (see Arthur Fields & Fred Hall), and on A22037 for John Wilfahrt's Concertina Orchestra (who are beyond the scope of this work).

HUGH RODEN

Hugh Roden & His Texas Night Hawks: Hugh Roden, f; unknown, sg; unknown, bj-md; unknown, g.
Dallas, TX   Tuesday, June 25, 1929

402720-A	Possum Rag	OK 45363
402721-A	Crazy Rag	OK 45363
402722-A	Deep Sea Waltz	OK 45430
402723-A	Sweetheart Waltz	OK 45430

OKeh 45363 as by **The Texas Night Hawks**.

Hugh Roden & Roy Rodgers: Hugh Roden, f; Roy Rodgers, ac; unidentified, sp-1/v eff-1.
San Antonio, TX   Wednesday, June 4, 1930

404052-	Tulsa Waltz	OK 45465, 16731
404053-	Spanish Waltz	OK 45465, 16731
404060-A	Hogs In The Potato Patch -1	OK 45540
404061-	Chicken In The Garden	OK unissued

OKeh 16731 (a Mexican issue) as by **Duo Robles**. Matrix 404052 is titled *Tulsa* and matrix 404053 is titled *Vals Espanol* on that issue.

Intervening matrices are Mexican.
Rev. OKeh 45540 by Carl Jones.

   San Antonio, TX   Thursday, June 5, 1930
     404062-   Lost Indian   OK unissued

Matrix 404063, blank in OKeh files, may be by these artists.

THE RODEO BOYS

Pseudonym on English Regal Zonophone and Indian Twin for Hinson, Pitts & Coley.

RODEO TRIO

D.A. Champagne, f; Kenneth Deshazo, h/jh-1; Phil Smith, g.
   El Paso, TX   Friday, July 12, 1929
     55243-1,-2   Dreamy Time Gal   Vi unissued
     55244-2   Turkey In The Straw -1   Vi V-40136
     55245-2   Arkansas Traveler   Vi V-40136
   El Paso, TX   Monday, July 15, 1929
     55252-1   1. Bury Me Out On The Prairie 2. Home On The   Vi V-40186
                          Range
     55253-1   1. When The Work's All Done This Fall   Vi V-40186
                          2. Cowboy's Lament

COWBOY RODGERS

This pseudonym was used on Varsity as follows:
on 5034, 5037, 5043, and one side of 5044 (matrix 1551) for Edward L. Crain;
on 5036 for Frankie Marvin;
and on the other side of 5044 (matrix 1828) for Clayton McMichen.

JESSE RODGERS

Jesse Rodgers, v/y; acc. own g.
   San Antonio, TX   Monday, March 26, 1934
     82620-1   Way Down In Mississippi   BB B-5499, MW M-4523, RZAu G22552
     82621-1   The Rambler's Yodel   BB B-5443, MW M-4524, RZAu G22466,
                                                              HMVIn N4316
     82622-1,-2   When The Texas Moon Is Shining   BB unissued
     82623-1   I Wish You Were Here, Dear   BB B-5443, MW M-4524, RZAu G22466,
                                                               HMVIn N4316

Bluebird B-5499, Montgomery Ward M-4523 as by **Jessie Rodgers**.
Matrix 82620 is titled 'Way Down In Mississippi on Regal-Zonophone G22552. Matrix 82621 is titled The Ramblers Yodel on Regal-Zonophone G22466.

Jesse Rodgers, v/y-1; acc. own g.
   San Antonio, TX   Monday, April 2, 1934
     82622-3   When The Texas Moon Is Shining -1   BB B-6256, RZAu G22831, Twin FT8077
     82762-1   My Winding River Home -1   BB B-5632, MW M-4522
     82763-1   All Alone -1   BB B-6256, RZAu G22831, Twin FT8077
     82764-1   Yodelling The Railroad Blues -1   BB B-5689, RZAu G22660
     82765-1   Roughneck Blues -1   BB B-5689, RZAu G22660
     82766-1   My Mary -1   BB B-5632, MW M-4522, M-7043
     82767-1   My Brown-Eyed Texas Rose   BB B-5499, MW M-4523

Jesse Rodgers, v/y-1; acc. Dick Bunyard, sg-2; own g; unknown, train-wh eff-3.
   San Antonio, TX   Tuesday, January 29, 1935
     87738-1   Rattlesnake Daddy -1   BB B-5839, MW M-4785, HMVIn N4373
     87739-1   The Auto Love Song -1   BB B-5839, MW M-4785
     87740-1   Leave Me Alone, Sweet Mama -1   BB B-5942, MW M-5014, RZAu G22552,
                                                              Twin FT1925
     87741-1   Headin' Home -2, 3   BB B-5853, RZAu G22595, HMVIn N4375
     87742-1   The Empty Cot -2   BB B-5910, MW M-4555, RZAu G22588
     87743-1   An Old Rugged Road -2   BB B-5910, MW M-4555, RZAu G22588,
                                                              Twin FT1910
     87744-1   Down In The Hills -2   BB B-5958, MW M-8488, RZAu G22553
     87745-1   Lonely Days In Texas -2   BB B-5958, MW M-8488, RZAu G22553
     87746-1   You Can't Beat Me Talkin' 'Bout You -1   BB unissued
     87747-1   Let Me Call You Mine -2   BB B-5853, RZAu G22595, HMVIn N4375

Revs: Bluebird B-5942, Montgomery Ward M-5014, Twin FT1925 by Jimmie Rodgers; HMV N4373 by Girls Of The Golden West; Twin FT1910 by Judy Rogers (popular).

Acc. own g.
San Antonio, TX
Monday, August 12, 1935

94426-1	Longing For You -1	BB unissued
94427-1	Be Nobody's Darling But Mine	BB B-6066, MW M-4983, HMVIn N4388
94428-1	The Sun Goes Down	BB B-6143, MW M-4788, M-8484, Twin FT8035
94429-1	(In A Little Shanty) Hummin' To My Honey	BB B-6066, MW M-4983, HMVIn N4388
94430-1	Give Me Your Love -1	BB B-6196, MW M-8485, Twin FT8055
94431-1	Jesse's Talking Blues	BB B-6143, MW M-4788
94432-1	Hot Dog Blues -1	BB B-6087, MW M-8486, Twin FT8020
94433-1	When I Was A Boy From The Mountains -1	BB B-6116
94434-1	Old Kentucky Cabin	BB B-6116, MW M-8485, Twin FT8020
94435-1	Window Shopping Mama -1	BB B-6087, MW M-8486

Revs: Bluebird B-6196, Twin FT8055 by Riley Puckett; Twin FT8035 by Dick Hartman's Tennessee Ramblers.

Acc. **Kama's Moana Hawaiians**: Charles Kama, sg; unknown, ti; unknown, g.
San Antonio, TX
Friday, February 28, 1936

99424-1	I'm Writing To You, Little Darling (The Answer To "Nobody's Darling")	BB B-6311, MW M-4787, Twin FT8097
99425-1	Old Pinto, My Pony, My Pal -1	BB B-6364, MW M-4786, Twin FT8115
99426-1	Little Prairie Town -1	BB B-6311, MW M-4787, Twin FT8097
99427-1	San Antonio Blues -1	BB B-6364, MW M-4786, Twin FT8115
99428-1	Lonely Hillbilly -1	BB B-6402, RZAu G23438, HMVIn N4406
99429-1	Tell You About A Gal Named Sal	BB B-6402, MW M-7043, HMVIn N4406

Rev. Regal-Zonophone G23438 by Fred Kirby & Don White.

Acc. **El Patio Trio (Bert, Buddy & Homer)**: unknown, sg; unknown, ti; unknown, g; unknown g-2/y-2; unknown, sp-3.
San Antonio, TX
Saturday, February 27, 1937

07397-1	What You're Doing Is Telling On Me	BB B-6924, MW M-7206, Twin FT8402
07398-1	The Little Girl Dressed In Blue -1	BB B-7018, MW M-7205, RZAu G23267
07399-1	Rounded Up In Glory	BB B-7209, MW M-8484
07400-1	Troubled In Mind And Blue	BB B-6924, MW M-7205, Twin FT8402
07401-1	Back In Jail Again -1, 3	BB B-7042, MW M-7206, RZAu G23272
07402-1	I'm A Roamin' Cowboy	BB B-7209, MW M-7187
07403-1	Just One Little Kiss -1, 2	BB B-7018, MW M-7207, RZAu G23267
07404-1	Second Class Hotel -1	BB B-7042, MW M-7207, RZAu G23272

Rev. Montgomery Ward M-7187 by Sain Family.

Jesse Rodgers recorded after 1942.

JIMMIE RODGERS

Jimmie Rodgers, v/y-1; acc. own g.
Bristol, TN
Thursday, August 4, 1927

39767-4	The Soldier's Sweetheart	Vi 20864, MW M-4452, BB 33-0513, RZAu G23197, HMVAu EA1400
39768-3	Sleep Baby Sleep -1	Vi 20864, 21-0180, ViJ A1466, BB B-6225, MW M-4452, RZ MR2795, RZAu G23197, HMVAu EA1400, Twin FT8585

Matrix 39768 is titled *Sleep, Baby, Sleep* on Bluebird B-6225, Montgomery Ward M-4452, Regal-Zonophone MR2795, G23197, Twin FT8585.

Camden, NJ
Wednesday, November 30, 1927

40751-2	Ben Dewberry's Final Run	Vi 21245, BB B-5482, RZ MR2241, RZAu G23117, RZIr IZ495, HMVAu EA1543, Twin FT8185
40752-1	Mother Was A Lady (If Brother Jack Were Here)	Vi 21433, BB B-5482, MW M-4224, RZ MR2241, RZAu G23193, RZIr IZ495, HMVAu EA1382, Twin FT1808
40753-2	Blue Yodel -1	Vi 21142, 21-0042, BB B-5085, Sr S-3172, MW M-3272, Zo 5158, RZ T5158, RZIr IZ310
40754-2	Away Out On The Mountain -1	Vi 21142, 21-0042, BB B-5085, Sr S-3172, MW M-3272, Zo 5158, Zo/RZAu EE109, RZ T5158, RZIr IZ310, Twin FT1733

Matrix 40753 was first issued as *If Brother Jack Were Here*, then withdrawn for copyright reasons and reissued as *Mother Was A Lady*, then further reissued as shown.

Some early pressings of Victor 21-0042 were made with matrix 41742 (see below) substituted for matrix 40754.

Many LP/CD reissues of matrix 40753 have been edited in the guitar solo after the fourth verse.

Jimmie Rodgers, v/y; acc. **The Three Southerners**: Ellsworth T. Cozzens, sg-1/md-2/u-3; own g-4/u-5; Julian R. Ninde, g-6.

Camden, NJ Tuesday, February 14, 1928

41736-1	Dear Old Sunny South By The Sea -1, 2, 5, 6	Vi 21574, 21-0182, ViJ A1454, BB B-6246, Zo 5341, RZ T5341, RZAu G23188, RZIr IZ317, HMVAu EA1228, HMVIn N4336
41737-2	Treasures Untold -1, 6	Vi 21433, BB B-5838, MW M-4217, Zo/RZAu EE139, HMVIn N4310, Twin FT9115
41738-1	The Brakeman's Blues (Yodeling The Blues Away) -3, 4	Vi 21291, 21-0044, MW M-4214, RZAu G23116, HMVAu EA1542, HMVIn N4364
41739-1	The Sailor's Plea -1, 4, 6	Vi V-40054, BB B-6246, 33-0513, MW M-5036, Zo 5401, ZoAu 5401, RZ T5401, RZAu T5401, RZIr IZ321, HMVIn N4327
41739-2	The Sailor's Plea -1, 4, 6	Vi unissued: *ACM 11 (LP)*

The Three Southerners are credited on only some issues of matrices 41736 and 41739.

Acc. Ellsworth T. Cozzens, sg-1/bj-2; own g.

Camden, NJ Wednesday, February 15, 1928

41740-1	In The Jailhouse Now -2	Vi 21245, BB B-5223, Eld 2109, Sr S-3306, MW M-4721, RZAu G23202, HMVAu EA1406, HMVIn N4309, ZoSA 4342
41741-2	Blue Yodel – No. II (My Lovin' Gal, Lucille) -1	Vi 21291, 21-0181, ViJ A1454, MW M-4214, M-8121, RZ MR3122, RZAu G23116, RZIr IZ1004, HMVAu EA1542, HMVIn N4309, ZoSA 4370, Twin FT8775
41742-2	Memphis Yodel	Vi 21636, 21-0042, MW M-4450, M-4725, Zo 5283, RZ T5283, RZAu G23114, RZIr IZ315, HMVAu EA1540, HMVIn N4291
41743-2	Blue Yodel No. 3	Vi 21531, 21-0177, MW M-4213, Zo 5247, RZ T5247, RZIr IZ314

Matrix 41741 is titled *Blue Yodel – No. 2 (My Lovin Gal Lucille)* on Victor 21-0181, Montgomery Ward M-4214, Regal-Zonophone MR3122. Matrix 41743 is titled *Blue Yodel No. 3 (Evening Sun Yodel)* on Victor 21-0177. Matrix 40142 was pressed in error for matrix 40753 (see above) on some early pressings of Victor 21-0042.

Acc. own g.

Camden, NJ Tuesday, June 12, 1928

45090-1	My Old Pal	Vi 21757, 21-0176, BB B-5609, Zo 5356, Zo/RZAu EE150, RZ T5356, RZIr IZ318, Twin FT1756
45091-1	Mississippi Moon	Vi unissued: *ACM 12 (LP)*; Rdr CD1057, BF BCD15540 (CDs)
45093-1	My Little Old Home Down In New Orleans	Vi 21574, BB B-5609, MW M-4218, Zo 5341, Zo/RZAu EE139, RZ T5341, RZIr IZ317, HMVIn N4336
45094-1	You And My Old Guitar	Vi V-40072, 420-0028, BB B-5083, Eld 2009, Sr S-3170, MW M-4224, Zo 5423, ZoAu 5423, RZ T5423, RZAu T5423, RZIr IZ323, Twin FT1276
45095-1	Daddy And Home	Vi 21757, 21-0043, BB B-5991, MW M-8109, Zo 5356, Zo/RZAu EE150, RZ T5356, RZIr IZ318, Twin FT1756
45096-1	My Little Lady	Vi V-40072, 420-0029, BB B-5838, MW M-4731, Zo 5423, ZoAu 5423, RZ T5423, RZAu T5423, RZIr IZ323, HMV N4371
45097-2	I'm Lonely And Blue	Vi unissued: *ACM 12 (LP)*; Rdr CD1057, BF BCD15540 (CDs)
45098-2	Lullaby Yodel	Vi 21636, BB B-5337, Sr S-3418, MW M-4218, Zo 5283, RZ T5283, RZAu G23114, RZIr IZ315, HMVAu EA1540, HMVIn N4291
45099-1	Never No Mo' Blues	Vi 21531, 21-0043, BB B-6225, Zo 5247, Zo/RZAu EE109, RZ T5247, RZIr IZ314, Twin FT1733

Matrix 45093 is titled *My Little Old Home Town In New Orleans* on Bluebird B-5609, Zonophone 5341.
On some LP/CD reissues of matrix 45096 the first two notes of the guitar introduction have been edited out.
Matrix 45092 is unrelated. Rev. Twin FT1276 by Maurice J. Gunsky (popular).

Acc. C.L. Hutchison, c; James Rikard, cl; John Westbrook, sg; Dean Bryan, g; George MacMillan, sb.

Atlanta, GA Saturday, October 20, 1928

| 47215-3 | My Carolina Sunshine Girl | Vi V-40096, 21-0180, BB B-5556, MW M-4451, Zo 5495, ZoAu 5495, RZ T5495, RZAu T5495, HMVIn N4351 |
| 47216-4 | Blue Yodel No. 4 (California Blues) | Vi V-40014, 21-0175, MW M-4722, M-8124, Zo 5380, ZoAu 5380, RZ T5380, RZAu T5380, RZIr IZ320, HMVPg MH192 |

Acc. C.L. Hutchison, c; James Rikard, cl-1; John Westbrook, sg; Dean Bryan, g; George MacMillan, sb; own v eff-2.
Atlanta, GA   Monday, October 22, 1928

47223-4	Waiting For A Train -1, 2	Vi V-40014, 21-0175, BB B-5163, Eld 2060, Sr S-3244, MW M-8109, Zo 5380, ZoAu 5380, RZ T5380, RZAu T5380, RZIr IZ320, HMVPg MH192
47224-3	I'm Lonely And Blue	Vi V-40054
47224-5	I'm Lonely And Blue	Vi V-40054, MW M-4047, M-4217, Zo 5401, ZoAu 5401, RZ T5401, RZAu T5401, RZIr IZ321, HMVIn N4327

Rev. Montgomery Ward M-4047 by Bud Billings (Frank Luther). Take 5 of matrix 47224 is a technical remastering of take 3.

Acc. unknown, vn; unknown, c; unknown, cl; unknown, p; own g-1; unknown, tu; unknown, traps; Leonard Joy, dir.
New York, NY   Thursday, February 21, 1929

48384-3	Desert Blues	Vi V-40096, 21-0176, MW M-4451, Zo 5495, ZoAu 5495, RZ T5495, RZAu T5495, HMVIn N4351
48385-1	Any Old Time -1	Vi 22488, BB B-5664, MW M-4730, Zo 5780, ZoAu EE221, RZ T5780, HMVIn N4215
48385-2	Any Old Time -1	Vi unissued: *ACM 12* (LP)

Acc. own g.
New York, NY   Saturday, February 23, 1929

49990-2	Blue Yodel No. 5	Vi 22072, MW M-4212, Zo 5548, Zo/RZAu EE185, RZ T5548, Twin FT1824
49991-2	High Powered Mama	Vi 22523, Zo 5808, RZ T5808, RZIr IZ334
49991-	High Powered Mama	Vi unissued: *ACM 12* (LP)
49992-1	I'm Sorry We Met	Vi 22072, 21-0177, ViJ A1466, Zo 5548, Zo/RZAu EE185, RZ T5548, RZIr IZ326, Twin FT1824

It is uncertain whether ACM 12 uses take 1 or 3 of matrix 49991.

Acc. Joe Kaipo, sg; Billy Burkes, g; own g/v eff-1; Weldon Burkes, u; Bob MacGimsey, wh-2.
Dallas, TX   Thursday, August 8, 1929

55307-2	Everybody Does It In Hawaii	Vi 22143, Zo 5577, Zo/RZAu EE189, RZ T5577, RZIr IZ327, HMVIn N4364
55308-1	Tuck Away My Lonesome Blues -2	Vi 22220, 21-0181, BB B-5664, MW M-5036, Zo 5983, Zo/RZAu EE269, RZ T5983, Twin FT1356
55309-2	Train Whistle Blues -1	Vi 22379, MW M-4223, Zo 5697, RZ T5697, RZAu G23113, HMVAu EA1539, HMVIn N4345

Acc. Joe Kaipo, sg; Billy Burkes, g.
Dallas, TX   Saturday, August 10, 1929

| 55332-2 | Jimmie's Texas Blues | Vi 22379, MW M-4212, Zo 5697, RZ T5697, RZAu G23113, HMVAu EA1539, HMVIn N4345 |

Acc. own g.
Dallas, TX   Saturday, August 10, 1929

| 55333-1 | Frankie And Johnny | Vi unissued: *Rdr CD1058, BF BCD15540* (CDs) |
| 55333-2 | Frankie And Johnny | Vi 22143, 21-0044, BB B-5223, Eld 2109, Sr S-3306, MW M-4309, M-4721, Zo 5577, Zo/RZAu EE189, RZ T5577, RZIr IZ327, HMV N4371 |

Rev. Montgomery Ward M-4309 by Leonard Stokes.

Acc. unknown, c; unknown, s; unknown, p; unknown, bj; unknown, sb.
Dallas, TX   Monday, August 12, 1929

| 55344-3 | Frankie And Johnny | Vi unissued |

Acc. Joe Kaipo, sg; own g; L.D. Dyke, saw-1.
Dallas, TX   Monday, August 12, 1929

55345-2	Home Call -1	Vi unissued: *RCA 947-0225 (EP); RCA LPT3073, LPM2213, CPL1-2504(e), RCA(E) RD27241, DPS2021, RCA(J) RA5465 (LPs); Conifer CDRR300, BF BCD15540 (CDs)*
55345-3	Home Call	Vi unissued: *ACM 12 (LP); Rdr CD1058, BF BCD15540 (CDs)*

RCA 947-0025 is included in the EP set RCA EPBT3073.

Acc. Joe Kaipo, sg; Billy Burkes, g; Weldon Burkes, u.
  Dallas, TX   Tuesday, October 22, 1929

56449-	Whisper Your Mother's Name	Vi unissued: *ACM 11 (LP)*
56449-3	Whisper Your Mother's Name	Vi 22319, BB B-5057, Eld 1983, Sr S-3142, MW M-4207, RZ MR2242, RZAu G23193, RZIr IZ496, HMVAu EA1382, HMVIn N4310, Twin FT9115
56449-4	Whisper Your Mother's Name	Vi unissued: *ACM 11 (LP)*

One of the two previously unissued and undesignated takes of matrix 56449 on ACM 11 is take 4; the other is either take 1 or 2.

Acc. Joe Kaipo, sg-1; own g.
  Dallas, TX   Tuesday, October 22, 1929

56450-1	The Land Of My Boyhood Dreams	Vi 23811, BB B-5337, Sr S-3418, MW M-4450, M-4728, RZAu G23190, HMVAu EA1303, HMVIn N4259
56450-2	The Land Of My Boyhood Dreams	Vi unissued: *ACM 12 (LP); BF BCD15540 (CD)*
56450-3	The Land Of My Boyhood Dreams	Vi unissued: *ACM 11 (LP); Rdr CD1058 CD)*
56450-4	The Land Of My Boyhood Dreams	Vi unissued: *RCA LPM2865, RCA(E) RD7644, RCA(J) RA5461 (LPs)*
56453-1	Blue Yodel No. 6	Vi unissued: *ACM 12 (LP)*
56453-2	Blue Yodel No. 6	Vi unissued: *ACM 12 (LP)*
56453-3	Blue Yodel No. 6	Vi 22271, 21-0182, MW M-4211, Zo 5623, ZoAu 5623, RZ T5623, RZAu T5623, RZIr IZ329
56454-	Yodeling Cowboy	Vi unissued: *ACM 12 (LP)*
56454-3	Yodeling Cowboy	Vi 22271, BB B-5991, MW M-4058, M-4213, Zo 5623, ZoAu 5623, RZ T5623, RZAu T5623, RZIr IZ329, HMVIn N4381
56455-1	My Rough And Rowdy Ways -1	Vi 22220, MW M-4215, Zo 6022, Zo/RZAu EE269, RZ T6022, Twin FT1808
56455-2	My Rough And Rowdy Ways -1	Vi unissued: *ACM 12 (LP)*
56455-3	My Rough And Rowdy Ways -1	Vi unissued: *ACM 12 (LP)*
56456-1	I've Ranged, I've Roamed, I've Travelled	Vi unissued: *RCA LPM2865, DPL2-0075, RCA(E) RD7644, RCA(J) RA5461, ACM 12 (LPs); BF BCD15540 (CD)*
56456-2	I've Ranged, I've Roamed, I've Travelled	Vi unissued: *ACM 12 (LP)*
56456-3	I've Ranged, I've Roamed, I've Travelled	BB B-5892, MW M-5013, RZAu G23205, HMVAu E1566, HMVIn N4377

It is uncertain which of the previously unissued takes 1 and 2 of matrix 56454 is used on ACM 12, where it is titled *Yodeling Cowboy [Alt. #1]*. The adjacent item on ACM 12, titled *Yodeing Cowboy [Alt. #2]*, is actually the issued take 3.
Matrix 56454-3 is titled *Yodelling Cowboy* on Regal-Zonophone T5623.
The previously unissued takes 1 and 2 of matrix 56453 and takes 2 and 3 of matrix 56455 are issued on ACM 12, but it is uncertain which is which in each instance.
Matrices 56451/52 are by Burkes Brothers.
Revs: Montgomery Ward M-4058 by Bud Billings (Frank Luther); HMV N4381 by Dick Hartman's Tennessee Ramblers.

Acc. Billy Burkes, g; own v eff.
  New Orleans, LA or Atlanta, GA   Wednesday, November 13, 1929

56528-1	Hobo Bill's Last Ride	Vi 22421, MW M-4210, Zo 5724, Zo/RZAu EE213, RZ T5724, RZIr IZ333, Twin FT1784

Acc. Billy Burkes, g.
  Atlanta, GA   Monday, November 25, 1929

56594-1	Mississippi River Blues	Vi unissued: *ACM 12 (LP); Rdr CD1059, BF BCD15540 (CDs)*
56594-3	Mississippi River Blues	Vi 23535, BB B-5393, MW M-4722, Zo 5983, RZ T5983, RZAu G23199, HMVAu EA1402, HMVIn N4207, Twin FT1356

| 56595-4 | Nobody Knows But Me | Vi 23518, MW M-4724, RZAu G23198, HMVAu EA1401, HMVIn N4322, Twin FT9116 |

Rev. HMV N4207 by Bud Billings (Frank Luther) & Carson Robison (see the latter).

Acc. Billy Burkes, g-1; own g-2.
Atlanta, GA   Tuesday, November 26, 1929

56607-1	Anniversary Blue Yodel (Blue Yodel No. 7) -1, 2	Vi 22488, MW M-4210, Zo 5780, ZoAu EE221, RZ T5780, HMV N4215
56607-	Anniversary Blue Yodel (Blue Yodel No. 7) -1, 2	Vi unissued: *ACM 12 (LP)*; *Rdr CD1059, BF BCD15540 (CDs)*
56608-1	She Was Happy Till She Met You -2	Vi 23681, BB B-5057, Eld 1983, Sr S-3142, MW M-4207, M-4324, RZ MR1335, RZIr IZ388, Zo/RZAu EE352, Twin FT1723
56608-2	She Was Happy Till She Met You -1	Vi unissued: *ACM 12 (LP)*

It is uncertain which of the previously unissued takes 2 and 3 of matrix 56607 is used on ACM 12, Bear Family BCD 15540, and Rounder CD1059.
Matrix 56608 is titled *She's More To Be Pitied Than Censured* on at least some copies of Montgomery Ward M-4324.
Rev. Montgomery Ward M-4324 by Mac (Harry McClintock).

Acc. Billy Burkes, g; own g.
Atlanta, GA   Wednesday, November 27, 1929

| 56617-1 | Blue Yodel Number Eleven | Vi 23796, MW M-4726 |
| 56617-4 | Blue Yodel, #11 | Vi unissued: *BF BCD15540 (CD)* |

Matrix 56617-1 is titled *Blue Yodel No. 11* on Montgomery Ward M-4726.

Acc. Billy Burkes, g.
Atlanta, GA   Thursday, November 28, 1929

56618-1	A Drunkard's Child	Vi 22319, MW M-4221, RZAu G23194, HMVAu EA1385, ZoSA 4343
56619-1	That's Why I'm Blue	Vi 22421, BB B-6198, MW M-4222, Zo 5724, Zo/RZAu EE213, RZ T5724, MR2049, RZIr IZ333, IZ422, Twin FT1784
56620-1	Why Did You Give Me Your Love?	Vi unissued: *ACM 11 (LP)*; *Rdr CD1059, BF BCD15540 (CDs)*
56620-3	Why Did You Give Me Your Love?	BB B-5892, MW M-5013, RZAu G23205, HMVAu EA1566, HMVIn N4377

The issued take of matrix 56620 on 78 rpm has also been reported as -4.

Acc. Bob Sawyer's Jazz Band: unknown, c; unknown, cl; Bob Sawyer, p; unknown, bj; unknown, tu.
Hollywood, CA   Monday, June 30, 1930

| 54849-2 | My Blue Eyed Jane | Vi 23549, BB B-5393, MW M-4222, RZAu G23196, HMVAu EA1339, HMVIn N4302, Twin FT9114 |
| 54849-3 | My Blue Eyed Jane | Vi unissued: *ACM 11 (LP)* |

Matrix 54849-2 is titled *My Blue-Eyed Jane* on Regal-Zonophone G23196.

Jimmie Rodgers, v/y-1; acc. Lani McIntire's Hawaiians: poss. Sam Koki, sg; Lani McIntire, g; unknown, u; unknown, sb.
Hollywood, CA   Monday, June 30, 1930

54850-3	Why Should I Be Lonely -1	Vi 23609, BB B-5082, Sr S-3169, MW M-4204, Zo 6102, Zo/RZAu EE305, RZ T6102, RZIr IZ336, HMV N4221
54851-	Moonlight And Skies	Vi unissued: *ACM 11 (LP)*
54851-3	Moonlight And Skies	Vi 23574, BB B-5000, Eld 1830, 1958, Sr S-3104, MW M-4216, M-4720, RZ MR2200, RZIr IZ469, Zo/RZAu EE369, HMVIn N4322, HMVPg MH187, Twin FT9116, ColR IFB341

It is uncertain which of the previously unissued takes 1 and 2 of matrix 54851 is used on ACM 11.
Zonophone 6102 as by **Jimmy Rodgers**.
Revs: Zonophone 6102, Regal-Zonophone T6102, HMV N4221 by Dick Robertson (popular).

Jimmie Rodgers, v/y; acc. own g.
Hollywood, CA   Tuesday, July 1, 1930

| 54852-2 | Pistol Packin' Papa | Vi 22554, 420-0027, MW M-4316, M-4730, Zo 6011, Zo/RZAu EE232, ZoSA 4342, RZ T6011 |

Revs: Montgomery Ward M-4316 by Jimmy Long; Zonophone 6011, Regal-Zonophone T6011 by Bill Simmons.

Acc. Lani McIntire's Hawaiians: poss. Sam Koki, sg; Lani McIntire, g; unknown, u; unknown, sb.
   Hollywood, CA   Wednesday, July 2, 1930
   54854-2   Take Me Back Again   Vi unissued: *ACM 11 (LP)*
   54854-3   Take Me Back Again   BB B-7600, HMVIn N4422

Acc. Lani McIntire, g.
   Hollywood, CA   Saturday, July 5, 1930
   54855-1   Those Gambler's Blues   Vi 22554, MW M-4211, RZ MR911,
                                                                          Zo/RZAu EE232, ZoSA 4344
   54855-2   Those Gambler's Blues   Vi unissued: *ACM 11 (LP)*

Jimmie Rodgers, v/y-1; acc. Lani McIntire's Hawaiians: poss. Sam Koki, sg; Lani McIntire, g; unknown, u; unknown, sb.
   Hollywood, CA   Monday, July 7, 1930
   54856-1   I'm Lonesome Too   Vi unissued: *ACM 12 (LP)*
   54856-2   I'm Lonesome Too   Vi 23564, BB B5739, MW M-4220, RZ MR1599,
                                                                          RZAu G23189, RZIr IZ401, HMVAu EA1253,
                                                                          Twin FT1822
   54857-1   The One Rose (That's Left In My Heart) -1   BB B-7280

Jimmie Rodgers, v/y; acc. Lani McIntire's Hawaiians: poss. Sam Koki, sg; unknown, p; Lani McIntire, g; unknown, u; unknown, sb.
   Hollywood, CA   Tuesday, July 8, 1930
   54860-1,-2   For The Sake Of Days Gone By   Vi unissued

   Hollywood, CA   Wednesday, July 9, 1930
   54860-3   For The Sake Of Days Gone By   Vi 23651, ViJ A1430, BB B-5784, MW M-4221,
                                                                           Zo/RZAu EE363, HMVIn N4281

Matrix 54860 is titled *For The Sake Of Day's Gone By* on Victor A1430.

Acc. Bob Sawyer's Jazz Band: unknown, c; unknown, cl; Bob Sawyer, p; unknown, bj; own g; unknown, tu.
   Hollywood, CA   Thursday, July 10, 1930
   54861-3   Jimmie's Mean Mama Blues   Vi 23503, 420-0027, MW M-4723, Zo 5859,
                                                                          RZ T5859, RZAu G23115, HMVAu EA1541

Acc. own g/v eff-1.
   Hollywood, CA   Friday, July 11, 1930
   54862-3   The Mystery Of Number Five -1   Vi 23518, BB B-5739, MW M-4223, RZ MR1599,
                                                                        RZAu G23198, RZIr IZ401, HMVAu EA1401,
                                                                      ZoSA 4343, Twin FT1822
   54863-1   Blue Yodel No. 8 (Mule Skinner Blues)   Vi 23503, BB B-6275, MW M-4723, M-8235,
                                                                      Zo 5859, RZ T5859, RZAu G23115,
                                                                      HMVAu EA1541

Matrix 54863 is titled *Blue Yodel No. 8* on Montgomery Ward M-4723, Regal-Zonophone T5859, *Mule Skinner Blues* on Bluebird B-6275, and *Mule Skinner Blues (Blue Yodel No. 8)* on Regal-Zonophone G23115, HMV EA1541.
Rev. Montgomery Ward M-8235 by Gene Autry.

   Hollywood, CA   Saturday, July 12, 1930
   54864-1   In The Jail-House Now – No. 2   Vi 22523, MW M-4315, Zo 5808, RZAu T5808,
                                                                      RZIr IZ334
   54864-   In The Jailhouse Now – No. 2   Vi unissued: *ACM 12 (LP)*

It is uncertain which of the previously unissued takes 2 and 3 of matrix 54864 is used on ACM 12.
Rev. Montgomery Ward M-4315 by Jimmy Long.

Acc. Louis Armstrong, t; Lillian Hardin Armstrong, p.
   Hollywood, CA   Wednesday, July 16, 1930
   54867-2   Blue Yodel No. 9   Vi 23580, MW M-4209, M-4724, RZ MR3208,
                                                                    Zo/RZAu EE300, Twin FT8832,
                                                                    HMVPg MH194, CoSS MZ315

Matrix 54867 is titled *Blue Yodel No. 9 (Standin' On The Corner)* on Regal-Zonophone RZ EE300, HMV MH194, and Twin FT8832.

Jimmie Rodgers, I.N. Bronson, dialog.
   Hollywood, CA   Thursday, July 17, 1930
   1302-1   The Pullman Porters   Vi unissued: *Endangered Species ES1,*
                                                                    ACM 11 (LPs); BF BCD15540(CD)

Matrix 1302-1 is titled *The Pullman Porters With Bronson – (Comedy Skit)* on ACM 11.

Jimmie Rodgers, v/y; acc. Charles Kama, sg; own g.
   San Antonio, TX   Saturday, January 31, 1931
   67133-2   T.B. Blues   Vi unissued: *Franklin Mint 43,*
                                                                    52 (LPs); BF BCD15540 (CD)

| 67133-3 | T.B. Blues | Vi 23535, BB B-6275, MW M-4067, M-4729, RZ MR911, MR2374, RZAu G23199, RZIr IZ616, HMVAu EA1402, ZoSA 4344 |

Rev. Montgomery Ward M-4067 by Gene Autry.
Acc. Shelly Lee Alley, f-1; Alvin Alley, f-1; Charles Kama, sg; M.T. Salazar, g; Mike Cordova, sb.
San Antonio, TX   Saturday, January 31, 1931

67134-1	Travellin' Blues -1	Vi unissued: BF BCD15540 (CD)
67134-2	Travellin' Blues -1	Vi 23564, MW M-4729, RZAu G23112, HMVAu EA1514, HMVIn N4367
67134-3	Travellin' Blues -1	Vi unissued: Rdr CD1060, BF BCD15540 (CDs)
67135-1	Jimmie The Kid (Parts Of The Life Of Rodgers)	Vi 23549, MW M-4731, Zo 6022, RZ T6022, MR3208, RZAu G23196, HMVAu EA1399, HMVIn N4302, HMVPg MH194, Twin FT8832, FT9114
67135-3	Jimmie The Kid	Vi unissued: Rdr CD1060, BF BCD15540 (CDs)

Matrix 67135 is subtitled (*Part Of The Life of Jimmie Rodgers*) on Regal-Zonophone MR3208, HMV MH194; the subtitle is omitted on Zonophone 6022.

Jimmie Rodgers–Sara Carter, v/y duet; acc. Maybelle Carter, g; Sara Carter, g-1.
Louisville, KY   Wednesday, June 10, 1931

69412-1	Why There's A Tear In My Eye	BB B-6698, MW M-7138, RZ ME33, MR2374, MR2429, RZIr IZ616, IZ649, Twin FT8313
69412-3	Why There's A Tear In My Eye	Vi unissued: RCA LPM2865, RCA (E) RD7644, DPM2047, RCA (J) RA5463, RA5501, RA5645 (LPs); BF BCD15865 (CD)
69413-2	The Wonderful City -1	BB B-6810, MW M-7137, RZ MR2455, RZAu G23184, RZIr IZ662, Twin FT8313

Montgomery Ward M-7137, M-7138 as by **Jimmie Rodgers**. Regal-Zonophone ME33 and possibly other issues as by **Jimmie Rodgers & Sara Carter**.
Revs: Bluebird B-6698, Regal-Zonophone ME33, MR2429, IZ649 by Mrs. Jimmie Rodgers.

Jimmie Rodgers, v/y; acc. Clifford Gibson, g-1; own g.
Louisville, KY   Thursday, June 11, 1931

69424-2	Let Me Be Your Side Track -1	Vi unissued: RST BD2057 (LP); Rdr CD1060, RST BDCD6015, BF BCD15540, BMG Heritage 07863 65129 (CDs)
69424-3	Let Me Be Your Side Track	Vi 23621, HMV B-5084, Sr S-3171, MW M-4209, Zo 6056, Zo/RZAu EE363, RZ T6056, HMVIn N4209
69424-4	Let Me Be Your Sidetrack	Vi unissued: BF BCD15540 (CD)

Zonophone 6056 as by **Jimmy Rodgers**. HMV N4209 as by **Jimme Rodgers**.
Matrix 69424-2 is titled *Let Me Be Your Sidetrack* on Bear Family BCD15540.

Jimmie Rodgers (Assisted By The Carter Family): Jimmie Rodgers, v/y/sp; A.P. Carter, v/sp; Sara Carter, v/sp; Maybelle Carter, v/sp; acc. Maybelle Carter, md/g; Sara Carter, g.
Louisville, KY   Thursday, June 11, 1931

69427-1,-2	Jimmie Rodgers Visits The Carter Family	Vi unissued
69427-3	Jimmie Rodgers Visits The Carter Family	Vi unissued: Franklin Mint 34, 52, RCA (J) RA5645 (LPs); BF BCD15865 (CD)
69428-	The Carter Family And Jimmie Rodgers In Texas	Vi unissued: ACM 11 (LP)

Other LP/CD issues of matrix 69427 use take 4, slightly edited and with the spoken coda dubbed in from take 3.
It is uncertain which of the previously unissued takes 1, 2, and 3 of matrix 69428 is used on ACM 11.

Jimmie Rodgers, v/y/sp; Sara Carter, v/y-1/sp; A.P. Carter, v-2/sp; Maybelle Carter, v-2/sp; acc. Maybelle Carter, md-2/g-2; Jimmie Rodgers, g-1; Sara Carter, g.
Louisville, KY   Friday, June 12, 1931

| 69427-4 | Jimmie Rodgers Visits The Carter Family -2 | Vi 23574, MW M-4720, RZ ME34, MR3164, Zo/RZAu EE369, Twin FT8806, HMVPg MH188 |
| 69428-4 | The Carter Family And Jimmie Rodgers In Texas -1 | BB B-6762, MW M-7137, RZ ME34, MR3164, Twin FT8806, HMVPg MH188 |

Matrix 69428 is titled *The Carter Family Visits Jimmie Rodgers* on Montgomery Ward M-7137.
Rev. Bluebird B-6762 by Monroe Brothers.

Jimmie Rodgers, v/y; acc. Cliff Carlisle, sg; Wilbur Ball, g.
Louisville, KY   Saturday, June 13, 1931

| 69432-2 | When The Cactus Is In Bloom | Vi 23636, BB B-5163, Eld 2060, Sr S-3244, MW M-4216, RZ MR2795, Zo/RZAu EE345, Twin FT8585 |

| 69432-3 | When The Cactus Is In Bloom | Vi unissued: *ACM 11 (LP)* |

Matrix 69432 is titled *Round Up Time Out West (When The Cactus Is In Bloom)* on Regal-Zonophone MR2795, Twin FT8585, and possibly Zonophone/Regal-Zonophone EE345.

Acc. Ruth Ann Moore, p.
Louisville, KY Monday, June 15, 1931

69439-2	Gambling Polka Dot Blues	Vi 23636, Zo/RZAu EE345, ZoSA 4365
69439-	Gambling Polka Dot Blues	Vi unissued: *ACM 11, 12 (LPs)*
69439-	Gambling Polka Dot Blues	Vi unissued: *ACM 12 (LP)*

The version of *Gambling Polka Dot Blues* on ACM 11 (side 2, track 5) is duplicated on ACM 12 (side 2, track 7); a different version appears on ACM 12 (side 2, track 6). It is uncertain which of the previously unissued takes 1 and 3 of matrix 69439 any of these items represent.

Acc. Cliff Carlisle, sg; Wilbur Ball, g; own u.
Louisville, KY Monday, June 15, 1931

| 69443-1 | Looking For A New Mama | Vi unissued: *Rdr CD1061, BF BCD15540 (CDs)* |
| 69443-3 | Looking For A New Mama | Vi 23580, BB B-5037, Eld 1966, Sr S-3131, MW M-4203, RZ ME15, MR3002, RZIn MR20215, Zo/RZAu EE300, Twin FT8694 |

Matrices 69440/41 are by Jimmie Strange; matrix 69442 is by Kid Coley (see *B&GR* for both).

Acc. Ruth Ann Moore, p.
Louisville, KY Tuesday, June 16, 1931

| 69448-1 | What's It? | Vi 23609, BB B-5084, Sr S-3171, MW M-4208, Zo/RZAu EE305 |
| 69448- | What's It? | Vi unissued: *ACM 11 (LP)* |

It is uncertain which of the previously unissued takes 2, 3, and 4 of matrix 69448 is used on ACM 11.

Acc. **The Louisville Jug Band**: Clifford Hayes, f; George Allen, cl; Cal Smith, g; Freddie Smith, g; Earl McDonald, j.
Louisville, KY Tuesday, June 16, 1931

| 69449-1 | My Good Gal's Gone Blues | Vi unissued: *ACM 11 (LP); Rdr CD1061, RST JPCD1504-2, BF BCD15540, BMG Heritage 07863 65129 (CDs)* |
| 69449-3 | My Good Gal's Gone – Blues | BB B-5942, MW M-5014, Twin FT1925 |

Acc. own g.
Louisville, KY Wednesday, June 17, 1931

| 69458-1 | Southern Cannon-Ball | Vi 23811, MW M-4728, RZAu G23111, HMVAu EA1503, HMVIn N4259 |
| 69458-4 | Southern Cannonball | Vi unissued: *ACM 11 (LP)* |

Remastering session (Rodgers not present).
Camden, NJ Tuesday, October 27, 1931

| 69032-1 | Jimmie Rodgers' Puzzle Record | Vi unissued |

See note to following session.

Camden, NJ Wednesday, November 11, 1931

| 69032-3 | Rodgers' Puzzle Record | Vi 23621, Zo 6056, ZoSA 4365, RZ T6056, RZAu G23204, HMVAu EA1489, HMVIn N4209 |

For this item extracts from *Train Whistle Blues, Blue Yodel*, and *Everybody Does It In Hawaii* were remastered, to be pressed on a record with three concentric grooves starting at different points on the disc's circumference.
Zonophone 6056 as by **Jimmy Rodgers**. HMV N4209 as by **Jimme Rodgers**.
Take 3 and the unissued take 4 of matrix 69032 were logged as *Jimmie Rodgers' Puzzle Record* but issued as shown, except that take 3 is titled *Rodger's Puzzle Record* on Zonophone 4365.

Jimmie Rodgers, v/y; acc. Dick Bunyard, sg; Red Young, md; Bill Boyd, g; Fred Koone, sb.
Dallas, TX Tuesday, February 2, 1932

| 70645-1 | Roll Along, Kentucky Moon | Vi unissued: *Rdr CD1061, BF BCD15540 (CDs)* |
| 70645-2 | Roll Along Kentucky Moon | Vi 23651, ViJ A1430, BB B-5082, Sr S-3169, MW M-4219, RZ MR3122, RZAu G23188, RZIr IZ1004, HMVAu EA1228, HMVIn N4281, ZoSA 4370, Twin FT8775 |

The previously unissued take 1 of matrix 70645 is used on Rounder CD1061, Bear Family BCD15540 in error for the issued take 2.
Matrix 70645 is titled *Roll Along, Kentucky Moon* on Regal-Zonophone MR3122, G23188, HMV EA1228.

Acc. Dick Bunyard, sg; Red Young, md; Bill Boyd, g; poss. own g; Fred Koone, sb
Dallas, TX Wednesday, February 3, 1932

70646-1	Hobo's Meditation	Vi 23711, MW M-4205, RZ MR3313, RZAu G23192, RZIn MR20064, RZIr IZ1065, HMVAu EA1374, HMVIn N4233, ZoSA 4374, Twin FT8902
70646-2	Hobo's Meditation	Vi unissued: *BF BCD15540* (CD)

Revs: HMV N4233, Zonophone 4374 by Gene Autry.

Acc. Billy Burkes, sg-1/g-2; Weldon Burkes, g; own g-3/v eff-4; Charlie Burkes, u-5; Fred Koone, sb.
   Dallas, TX   Thursday, February 4, 1932

70647-1	My Time Ain't Long -1, 4, 5	Vi unissued: *RCA LPM2865, RCA(E) RD7644, DPM2047, RCA(J) RA5464* (LPs)
70647-2	My Time Ain't Long -1, 4, 5	Vi unissued: *Rdr CD1061, BF BCD15540* (CDs)
70647-3	My Time Ain't Long -1, 4, 5	Vi 23669, BB B-5083, Eld 2009, Sr S-3170, Zo 6159, ZoAu 6159, RZ T6159, RZAu T6159, HMVIn N4210
70648-2	Ninety Nine Years Blues -2, 3	Vi 23669, MW M-4215, Zo 6159, ZoAu 6159, RZ T6159, RZAu T6159, HMV N4210
45091-5	Mississippi Moon -1, 3	Vi 23696, ViJ A1401, JA708, BB B-5136, Eld 2042, Sr S-3217, MW M-4220, RZ MR1853, RZAu G23189, RZIr IZ410, HMVAu EA1253, HMVIn N4252

Rounder CD1061 claims to use take 3 of matrix 70647, and Bear Family BCD 15540 take 1, but take 2 is used in each case. Matrix 70648 is titled *Ninety-Nine Years Blues* on Montgomery Ward M-4215, Regal-Zonophone T6159.

Acc. own g; Fred Koone, g.
   Dallas, TX   Friday, February 5, 1932

45091-3	Mississippi Moon	Vi unissued: *BF BCD15540* (CD)
70649-1	Down The Old Road To Home	Vi 23711, BB B-5081, Sr S-3168, MW M-4202, RZ MR1725, RZAu G23192, RZIr IZ404, HMVAu EA1374

Takes 1 and 2 of matrix 45091 were recorded on June 12, 1928, and takes 4 and 5 on February 4, 1932. There was no take 3 as such, but the sixth take, recorded on February 5, 1932, was designated take 3 (being the third attempt at the item during this February 1932 session).

Acc. own g.
   Dallas, TX   Saturday, February 6, 1932

70650-1	Blue Yodel No. 10 (Ground Hog Rootin' In My Back Yard)	Vi 23696, ViJ A1401, JA708, MW M-4208, M-4725, RZ MR3257, RZIn MR20010, HMVIn N4292, Twin FT8858, CoSs MZ315
55345-4	Home Call	Vi 23681, MW M-4219, Zo/RZAu EE352, HMVIn N4367

Matrix 70650 is titled *Blue Yodel* on Victor A1401.

Acc. Clayton McMichen, f; Dave Kanui, sg; Oddie McWinders, bj; Hoyt "Slim" Bryant, g; George Howell, sb.
   Camden, NJ   Wednesday, August 10, 1932

58960-5	In The Hills Of Tennessee	Vi unissued

Acc. Clayton McMichen, f; Oddie McWinders, bj; Hoyt "Slim" Bryant, g.
   Camden, NJ   Thursday, August 11, 1932

58961-2A	Mother, The Queen Of My Heart	Vi 23721, BB B-5080, Eld 2008, Sr S-3167, MW M-4206, RZ MR1310, RZAu G23195, HMVAu EA1390, HMVIn N4239
58962-1,-2	Prohibition Has Done Me Wrong	Vi unissued
58963-1A	Rock All Our Babies To Sleep	Vi 23721, BB B-5000, Eld 1830, 1958, Sr S-3104, MW M-4201, RZ MR2200, RZAu G23200, RZIr IZ469, HMVAu EA1403, HMVIn N4239, HMVPg MH187, ZoSA 4378, CoIr IFB341
58964-1	Whippin' That Old T.B.	Vi unissued: *Rdr CD1062, BF BCD15540* (CDs)
58964-2	Whippin' That Old T.B.	Vi 23751, BB B-5076, Eld 1999, Sr S-3157, MW M-4204, RZ MR1310, RZAu G23195, HMVAu EA1390

Acc. Clayton McMichen, f-1; Oddie McWinders, bj-2; Hoyt "Slim" Bryant, g-3; own g-4.
   Camden, NJ   Monday, August 15, 1932

58968-2A	No Hard Times -3, 4	Vi 23751, MW M-4205, RZAu G23117, HMVAu EA1534, HMVIn N4251
58968-3	No Hard Times -3, 4	Vi unissued: *ACM 11* (LP); *Rdr CD1062, BF BCD15540* (CDs)
58969-1A	Long Tall Mamma Blues -2, 4	Vi 23766, MW M-4202, HMVIn N4245

| 58970-2A | Peach Pickin' Time Down In Georgia -1, 2, 3 | Vi 23781, BB B-5080, Eld 2008, Sr S-3167, MW M-4200, RZ MR1335, RZAu G23200, RZIr IZ388, HMVAu EA1403, HMVIn N4242, Twin FT1723 |

Matrix 58970 is titled *Peach Picking Time in Georgia* on Montgomery Ward M-4200, Regal-Zonophone G23200, HMV EA1403.

Acc. Clayton McMichen, f; Oddie McWinders, bj; Hoyt "Slim" Bryant, g.
Camden, NJ   Tuesday, August 16, 1932

| 58971-3 | Gambling Barroom Blues | Vi 23766, BB B-5037, Eld 1966, Sr S-3131, MW M-4203, RZ ME15, MR3002, RZAu G23112, RZIn MR20215, HMVAu EA1514, HMVIn N4245, Twin FT8694 |
| 58972-1 | I've Only Loved Three Women | BB B-6810, MW M-7138, RZ MR2455, RZAu G23184, RZIr IZ662, Twin FT8334 |

Matrix 58971 is titled *Gambling Bar Room Blues* on Regal-Zonophone ME15, MR3002, MR20215.
Rev. Twin FT8334 by Cliff Carlisle.

Acc. two unknowns, f; unknown, cl; unknown, p; Hoyt "Slim" Bryant, g.
New York, NY   Monday, August 29, 1932

73324-1	In The Hills Of Tennessee	Vi 23736, BB B-5784, MW M-4200, RZ MR2700, RZAu G23201, HMVAu EA1404, HMVIn N4234, ZoSA 4376, Twin FT8538
73325-1	Prairie Lullaby	Vi 23781, 420-0028, BB B-5076, Eld 1999, Sr S-3157, MW M-4201, RZ MR1725, RZAu G23203, RZIr IZ404, HMVAu EA1405, HMVIn N4242
73326-1	Miss The Mississippi And You	Vi 23736, BB B-5081, Sr S-3168, MW M-4206, RZ MR3257, RZAu G23201, RZIn MR20010, HMVAu EA1404, HMVIn N4234, ZoSA 4376, Twin FT8858
73327-1	Sweet Mama Hurry Home Or I'll Be Gone	Vi 23796, MW M-4726, RZAu G23202, HMVAu EA1406

Matrix 73327 is titled *Sweet Mamma Hurry Home Or I'll Be Gone* on Regal-Zonophone G23202.

Acc. own g.
New York, NY   Wednesday, May 17, 1933

76138-1	Blue Yodel No. 12	Vi 24456, 18-6000, MW M-4727
76139-1	Dreaming With Tears In My Eyes	BB B-7600, MW M-7139, HMVIn N4422
76140-1	The Cow Hand's Last Ride	Vi 24456, 18-6000, MW M-4727, RZAu G23191, HMVAu EA1362
76141-1	I'm Free (From The Chain Gang Now)	Vi 23830, MW M-4453, RZAu G23204, HMVAu EA1489, HMVIn N4263, Twin FT9112

Matrix 76140 is titled *Cowhand's Last Ride* on Victor 18-6000, and mistitled *The Cow Han's Last Ride* on Victor 24456, Regal-Zonophone G23191, HMV EA1462. Victor 18-6000 is a picture disc.

New York, NY   Thursday, May 18, 1933

76139-2	Dreaming With Tears In My Eyes	Vi unissued: RCA LPM2531, RCA(E) RD7505, RCA(J) RA5466, NW NW287 (LPs); Rdr CD1063, BF BCD15540 (CDs)
76151-1	Yodeling My Way Back Home	BB B-7280, MW M-7139, RZ MR2700, Twin FT8538
76160-1	Jimmie Rodgers' Last Blue Yodel	BB B-5281, Eld 2155, Sr S-3362, MW M-4415, RZ MR1702, RZAu G23206, HMVAu EA1567, Twin FT1874

Matrix 76151 is titled *Yodelling My Way Back Home* on Regal-Zonophone MR2700. Matrix 76160 is titled *Jimmie Rogers' Last Blue Yodel* on Bluebird B-5281.
Matrices 76152 to 76156 are by Bert Lown & His Orchestra (popular); matrices 76157 to 76159 are untraced.

New York, NY   Saturday, May 20, 1933

| 76191-1 | The Yodeling Ranger | Vi 23830, BB B-5556, MW M-4453, RZ MR1853, RZAu G23203, RZIr IZ410, HMVAu EA1405, HMVIn N4263, Twin FT9112 |
| 76192-1 | Old Pal Of My Heart | Vi 23816, 420-0029, BB B-5136, Eld 2042, Sr S-3217, RZ MR2242, RZAu G23191, RZIr IZ496, HMVAu EA1362, ZoSA 4378, Twin FT8185 |

Matrix 76191 is titled *The Yodelling Ranger* on Regal-Zonophone G23203.

Acc. John Cali, sg-1/bj-2/g-3; Tony Colicchio, g.
New York, NY   Wednesday, May 24, 1933

76327-1	Old Love Letters (Bring Memories Of You) -1	Vi 23840, BB B-6198, MW M-4454, RZ MR2049, RZAu G23190, RZIr IZ422, HMVAu EA1303, HMVIn N4297, Twin FT9113
76328-1	Mississippi Delta Blues -2	Vi 23816, RZAu G23194, HMVAu EA1385
76331-1	Somewhere Down Below The Dixon Line -3	Vi 23840, MW M-4454, RZAu G23111, HMVAu EA1053, HMVIn N4297, Twin FT9113

Matrix 76327 is titled *Old Love Letters* on Regal-Zonophone MR2049.
Matrices 76329/30 are untraced.

Acc. own g.
New York, NY   Wednesday, May 24, 1933

| 76332-1 | Years Ago | BB BB-5281, Eld 2155, Sr S-3362, MW M-4415, RZ MR1702, MR3313, RZAu G23206, RZIn MR20064, RZIr IZ1065, HMVAu EA1567, Twin FT1874, FT8902 |

Matrix 76332 is titled *Fifteen Years Ago Today* on Regal-Zonophone MR3313, MR20064, IZ1065, Twin FT8902.

Remastering session (Rodgers not present).
London, England.   Monday, October 28, 1935

| WAR3690-1 | Jimmie Rodgers Medley, Part 1 Intro.: My Old Pal; Dear Old Sunny South; Blue Yodel No. 1 | RZ MR1918, RZAu G22792, RZIr IZ414, Twin FT1980 |
| WAR3691-1 | Jimmie Rodgers Medley, Part 2 Intro.: Daddy And Home; Away Out On The Mountain; Blue Yodel No. 4 | RZ MR1918, RZAu G22792, RZIr IZ414, Twin FT1980 |

These items are constructed of edited extracts from the named recordings.

Overdub sessions (Rodgers not present).
Jimmie Rodgers & The Rainbow Ranch Boys: Jimmie Rodgers, v/y; acc. own g; original accompanists-1; plus H.N. "Tommy" Vaden, f; Joseph Hale Talbot III, esg; Chester "Chet" Atkins, g/ldr; Ernest "Ernie" Newton, sb.
Nashville, TN   Friday, March 18, 1955

[54864]; F2-WB-0281	In The Jailhouse Now – No.2	Vi 20/47-6092, HMVPg MH193, HMV HR10092
[54863]; F2-WB-0282	Muleskinner Blues	Vi 20/47-6205, HMV HR10137
[58970]; F2-WB-0283	Peach Picking Time Down In Georgia -1	Vi 20/47-6092, HMVPg MH193, HMV HR10092
[58961]; F2-WB-0284	Mother, The Queen Of My Heart -1	Vi 20/47-6205, HMV HR10137

Matrix F2-WB-0282 is titled *Mule Skinner Blues (Blue Yodel No. 8)* on HMV HR10137. The guitar solo after the fourth verse is edited out on issues of this item.

Nashville, TN   Friday, July 22, 1955

[45099]; F2-WB-3952	Never No Mo' Blues	Vi 20/47-6408, HMV HR10237
[40753]; F2-WB-3953	Blue Yodel, #1 (T For Texas)	Vi unissued: *BF BCD15540 (CD)*
[45095]; F2-WB-3954	Daddy And Home	Vi 20/47-6408, HMV HR10237
[41742]; F2-WB-3955	Memphis Yodel	Vi unissued: *BF BCD15540 (CD)*

Matrix F2-WB-3952 is titled *Never Do Mo' Blues* on HMV HR10237.

MRS. JIMMIE RODGERS

Mrs. Jimmie Rodgers, v; acc. Ernest Tubb, g.
San Antonio, TX   Monday, October 26, 1936
| 02935-1 | We Miss Him When The Evening Shadows Fall | BB B-6698, MW M-7085, RZ ME33, MR2429 |

Revs: Bluebird B-6698, Regal-Zonophone ME33, MR2429 by Jimmie Rodgers; Montgomery Ward M-7085 by Blue Sky Boys.

Acc. Merwyn Buffington, g; Ernest Tubb, g.
San Antonio, TX   Tuesday, March 2, 1937
| 07474-1 | My Rainbow Trail Keeps Winding On | BB B-7339, MW M-7279 |

Revs: Bluebird B-7339 by McClendon Brothers & Georgia Dell; Montgomery Ward M-7279 untraced.

TED RODGERS

Ted Rodgers, v; acc. unknown.
Dallas, TX   Monday, October 28, 1929

| DAL-523 | Sweetheart Of Yesterday | Br/Vo cancelled trial recording |
| DAL-524 | In That Wonderful Garden Of Mine | Br/Vo cancelled trial recording |

See also Hawaiian Songbirds.

RODGERS & NICHOLSON

See the Carolina Ramblers String Band.

RODIK TWINS (VERNA & VERDA)

Verna Rodik, Verda Rodik, v duet; acc. unknown, f; unknown, esg; unknown, g; unknown, sb.
Los Angeles, CA   Monday, August 18, 1941

DLA-2647-A	Did You Ever Go Sailing (Down The River Of Memories)	De 5980
DLA-2648-A	Answer To You Are My Sunshine	De 5980
DLA-2649-A	The Unopened Letter	De 6089
DLA-2650-A	Why Do I Care	De 6089

ROE BROTHERS & MORRELL

Fred Roe, f; Lewis Morrell, bj-1; Henry Roe, g; unidentified, v-2/v duet-3/v trio-4.
Atlanta, GA   Monday, March 28, 1927

143779-1	Goin' Down The Road Feeling Bad -1, 4	Co 15199-D
143780-	Meet Me In St. Louis, Louey	Co unissued
143781-1	The Ship That Never Returned -2	Co 15156-D
143782-2	My Little Mohi -2	Co 15199-D
143783-1	She'll Be Coming Around The Mountain -3	Co 15156-D
143784-	Lillie Sweet Lillie	Co unissued

The Roe brothers also recorded with The Hill Billies and Jack Reedy.

ROEBUCK BROS.

No details.
Atlanta, GA   Tuesday, November 5, 1929

| 149377- | Hold Your Rope | Co unissued |
| 149378- | Who Would Care For You Little Sweetheart | Co unissued |

COWBOY ROGERS

Pseudonym on Continental for Frank Marvin.

ERNEST ROGERS

Ernest Rogers, v; acc. own g.
Atlanta, GA   Friday, January 30, 1925

| 140304-2 | Willie The Weeper | Co 15012-D, Ha 5138-H |
| 140305-2 | My Red-Haired Lady | Co 15012-D, Ha 5138-H |

Acc. own g; Lambdin Kay, prob. sp-1.
Atlanta, GA   Thursday, February 17, 1927

| 37914-1,-2 | Mr. Rogers And Mr. Kay -1 | Vi unissued |
| 37915-2 | Willie, The Chimney Sweeper | Vi 20502, Twin FT1786 |

Revs: Victor 20502, Twin FT1786 by Vernon Dalhart.

Camden, NJ   Monday, May 23, 1927

38920-2	My Red-Haired Lady	Vi 20870
38921-1	Steamboat Bill	Vi 20798
38922-1	Waitin' For The "Robert E. Lee"	Vi 20798
38923-3	The Flight Of "Lucky" Lindbergh	Vi 20671
38924-2	Let Me Be Your Man In The Moon	Vi 20870
38925-2	I've Got The Misery	Vi 21361

Rev. Victor 20671 by Ernest V. Stoneman.

Atlanta, GA   Thursday, February 23, 1928

| 41954-2 | The Mythological Blues | Vi 21361 |
| 41955-1,-2 | We've Gone To The End Of The Rainbow | Vi unissued |

JAMES ROGERS

Pseudonym on one side of Paramount 3088 and Broadway 8076 for Irving Kaufman, a standard popular singer beyond the scope of this work.

ROY ROGERS

Roy Rogers' real name was Leonard Slye.

Roy Rogers, v/y; acc. Hugh Farr, f; Karl Farr, g; Lloyd Perryman, g; Bob Nolan, sb.
   Los Angeles, CA   Thursday, October 28, 1937

Matrix	Title	Issue
LA-1500-A	Cowboy Night Herd Song	ARC unissued: *Co FC37439 (LP)*
LA-1500-B	Cowboy Night Herd Song	ARC unissued: *CSP P4-15542 (LP)*; *ABM ABMMCD1276 (CD)*
LA-1501-A	When The Black Sheep Gets The Blues	ARC 8-04-51
LA-1502-A	That Pioneer Mother Of Mine	ARC 8-04-51
LA-1503-A	Hadie Brown	ARC unissued: *CSP P4-15542, Co FC38907 (LPs)*; *ABM ABMMCD1276 (CD)*

Matrix LA-1503 is titled *My Little Lady (Hadie Brown)* on Columbia FC38907.

Roy Rogers, v/y-1; acc. two unknowns, f; unknown, ac; unknown, o; unknown, sg; unknown, g; unknown, sb; group v-2; unknown, sp-3.
   Los Angeles, CA   Wednesday, March 30, 1938

Matrix	Title	Issue
LA-1616-A	That Pioneer Mother Of Mine -1, 2	Vo/OK 04051, Cq 9007
LA-1617-A	Dust -2, 3	Vo/OK 04050, Cq 9008
LA-1618-A	When A Cowboy Sings A Song	Vo/OK 04050, Cq 9008
LA-1619-A,-B	Listen To The Rhythm Of The Range -1	Vo/OK 04051, Cq 9007

Roy Rogers, v/y-1; acc. two unknowns, f; unknown, pac; unknown, esg; unknown, g; unknown, sb; group v-2; unknown, sp-2; unknown, eff-2.
   New York, NY   Wednesday, June 15, 1938

Matrix	Title	Issue
23091-1	Hi-Yo, Silver! -1, 2	Vo/OK 04190, Cq 9060
23092-1	A Lonely Ranger Am I	Vo 04263
23092-2	A Lonely Ranger Am I	Vo unissued: *Co FC38907 (LP)*
23093-1	Old Pioneer	Vo 04263
23093-2	Old Pioneer	Vo unissued: *Co FC38907 (LP)*
23094-1	Ridin' Ropin'	Vo/OK 04190, Cq 9060
23094-2	Ridin' Ropin'	Vo unissued: *Co FC38907 (LP)*

Acc. Hugh Farr, f; unknown, f; unknown, ac; unknown, sg; prob. Karl Farr, g; prob. Pat Brady, sb.
   Los Angeles, CA   Thursday, September 1, 1938

Matrix	Title	Issue
LA-1706-A	I've Sold My Saddle For An Old Guitar	Vo/OK 05310, Cq 9431
LA-1707-	Side Kick Joe	Vo unissued
LA-1708-A	Colorado Sunset	Vo/OK 04453, RZ MR2931, RZAu G24885
LA-1709-A	There's A Ranch In The Rockies -1	Vo/OK 04453, RZ MR2931
LA-1710-A	When The Sun Is Setting On The Prairie -1	Vo 04389, Cq 9059
LA-1711-A	When I Camped Under The Stars	Vo/OK 04544
LA-1712-A	Born To The Saddle	Vo/OK 04544
LA-1713-A	When Mother Nature Sings Her Lullaby	Vo 04389, Cq 9059

Acc. two unknowns, f; unknown, ac; unknown, sg; unknown, g; unknown, sb.
   Los Angeles, CA   Monday, April 17, 1939

Matrix	Title	Issue
LA-1858-A	Somebody's Smile	Vo/OK 04840
LA-1859-A	I've Learned A Lot About Women	Vo/OK 05094, Cq 9430
LA-1860-A	The Man In The Moon Is A Cowhand -1	Vo/OK 05028, Cq 9333
LA-1861-A	She's All Wet Now -1	Vo/OK 05094, Cq 9430
LA-1862-B	I Hope I'm Not Dreaming Again	Vo/OK 05310, Cq 9431
LA-1863-A	The Mail Must Go Through	Vo unissued: *Co FC38907 (LP)*
LA-1863-B	The Mail Must Go Through	Vo/OK 04840, RZAu G24885

   Los Angeles, CA   Tuesday, April 18, 1939

Matrix	Title	Issue
LA-1868-A	Ridin' Down The Trail	Vo/OK 04923, Cq 9692
LA-1869-A	Here On The Range	Vo/OK 04961, Cq 9334
LA-1870-A	Let Me Build A Cabin	Vo/OK 04961, Cq 9334
LA-1871-A	Headin' For Texas And Home -1	Vo/OK 04923, Cq 9692
LA-1872-A	Rusty Spurs	Vo/OK 05028, Cq 9333

Roy Rogers, v; acc. poss. Carl Cotner, f; poss. Spade Cooley, f; unknown, esg; Dick Reinhart, g; Johnny Bond, sb.
   Los Angeles, CA   Thursday, August 29, 1940

Matrix	Title	Issue
DLA-2102-A	Chapel In The Valley	De 5895, DeAu X1968
DLA-2103-A	You Waited Too Long	De 5876, DeAu X1936
DLA-2104-A	Nobody's Fault But My Own	De 5876, DeAu X1936
DLA-2105-A	No Matter What Happens, My Darling	De 5895, DeAu X1968, DeSA FM5126

Rev. Decca FM5126 by Jimmy Wakely.

Acc. **Jimmy Wakely's Rough Riders**: poss. Carl Cotner, f; poss. Spade Cooley, f; unknown, esg; Jimmy Wakely, g; Dick Reinhart, g; Johnny Bond, sb; v trio (Wakely, Reinhart, Bond) -1.

Los Angeles, CA   Tuesday, September 3, 1940

DLA-2110-A	Silent Night, Holy Night -1	De 5883
DLA-2111-A	O Come All Ye Faithful (Adeste Fideles) -1	De 5883
DLA-2112-A	Wondering Why	De 5916, DeAu X2150, MeC 45415
DLA-2113-A	(Without You Darling) Life Won't Be The Same	De 5916, MeC 45415

The accompaniment credit is omitted on issues of matrices DLA-2112/13. Only one guitar is used on matrices DLA-2110/11.

Roy Rogers, sp/calls; acc. **Cooley's Buckle Busters**: Spade Cooley, f; unknown, g; unknown, sb.

Los Angeles, CA   Wednesday, September 4, 1940

DLA-2114-A	Round The Couple And Swing When You Meet	De 3733, Coral 64016
DLA-2115-A	Round That Couple – Go Through And Swing	De 3734, Coral 64017
DLA-2116-A	Bird In A Cage And Three Rail Pen	De 3734, Coral 64017
DLA-2117-A	Chase That Rabbit – Chase That Squirrel	De 3733
DLA-2117-A,-B	Chase That Rabbit – Chase That Squirrel	Coral 64016
DLA-2118-A	Boy Around A Boy – Girl Around A Girl	De 3735, Coral 64018
DLA-2119-A	Lady 'Round The Lady And The Gent Solo	De 3735, Coral 64018

Roy Rogers, v; acc. Spade Cooley, f; Carl Cotner, f; Homer Rhodes, esg; Gene Haas, eg; Woodrow Wines, g; Rufus Cline, sb.

Los Angeles, CA   Friday, November 29, 1940

DLA-2247-A	New Worried Mind	De 5906
DLA-2248-A	Time Changes Everything	De 5908, DeAu X2150
DLA-2249-A	Yesterday	De 5908
DLA-2250-A	Melody Of The Plains	De 5906

Acc. Spade Cooley, f; Wilmot Hollinger, t; Robert E. Nelson, cl; Gene Haas, g; Rufus Cline, sb.

Los Angeles, CA   Monday, August 25, 1941

DLA-2685-A	Don't Be Blue, Little Pal, Don't Be Blue	De 5986
DLA-2686-A	You Were Right And I Was Wrong	De 6074, MeC 45546
DLA-2687-A	I'm Trusting In You	De 5986
DLA-2688-A	I'll Be Honest With You (Answer To Be Honest With Me)	De 6016

Paul Sells reportedly plays accordion and piano on this session, but neither instrument is audible.

Acc. unknown, f; unknown, t; unknown, ac; unknown, g; unknown, sb.

Los Angeles, CA   Friday, September 4, 1941

DLA-2726-A	Down By The Old Alamo	De 5987, MeC 45467
DLA-2727-A	I Know I Shouldn't Worry (But I Do)	De 6060
DLA-2728-A	A Gay Ranchero (Las Altenitas)	De 5987, MeC 45467
DLA-2729-A	Blue Bonnet Lane	De 6016

Acc. unknown, f; unknown, ac; unknown, g; unknown, sb.

Los Angeles, CA   Saturday, September 12, 1941

DLA-2755-A	Don't Waste Your Love On Me	De 6037
DLA-2756-A	It's Just The Same	De 6074, MeC 45546
DLA-2757-A	A Man And His Song	De 6037
DLA-2758-A	I've Sold My Saddle For An Old Guitar	De 6092

Acc. Spade Cooley, f; unknown, t; Johnny Kiddo, ac; Virgil Dehne, g; Gene Haas, g; Rufus Cline, sb.

Los Angeles, CA   Friday, March 20, 1942

DLA-2955-A	You're The Answer To My Prayer	De 6041
DLA-2956-A	Little Old Church On The Hilltop	De 6060
DLA-2957-A	She Gave Her Heart To A Soldier Boy	De 6041
DLA-2958-A	Think Of Me	De 6092

Roy Rogers also recorded with the Sons Of The Pioneers, and after 1942.

SILAS ROGERS

See Kentucky String Ticklers.

ROGERS & PICKET

Pseudonym on Conqueror for Kirk McGee & Blythe Poteet (see McGee Brothers).

ROGERS BROS. [& BURGHER]

See Kentucky String Ticklers.

ROLAND & YOUNG

Pseudonym on Champion for Andy Patterson & Warren Caplinger (see the latter).

THE ROLLING STONES (JIMMIE ADAMS–BUD JAMISON)

Bud Jamison, h/v/y-1; Jimmie Adams, g/v/y-1.
    Hollywood, CA   Monday, September 15, 1930

61020-3	Down By The Old Rio Grande	Vi V-40316
61021-3	Mountain Angel -1	Vi V-40316

Jimmie Adams was also a member of The Two Cow Hands.

ROPER'S MOUNTAIN SINGERS

Vocal group; unacc.
    Atlanta, GA   Wednesday, November 2, 1927

145078-2	When I Walked The Streets Of Gold	Co 15222-D
145079-2	On The Sea Of Life	Co 15222-D

POSEY RORER & THE NORTH CAROLINA RAMBLERS

Posey Rorer, f; C.M. "Matt" Simmons, g/lv; Frank Miller, tv.
    New York, NY   Monday, September 24, 1928

18749-A,-B	If I Could Hear My Mother Pray Again	Ed unissued
N-452-A,-B	If I Could Hear My Mother Pray Again	Ed unissued
18750-B	Beautiful Beckoning Hands	Ed 5617
N-453	Beautiful Beckoning Hands	Ed unissued
18751-A,-B	He's Coming Back Again	Ed rejected
N-454	He's Coming Back Again	Ed unissued
18752-A,-B,-C	We'll Understand It Better By And By	Ed rejected
N-455-A,-B	We'll Understand It Better By And By	Ed rejected
18753-A,-B,-C	Wild And Reckless Hobo	Ed rejected
N-456-B	Wild And Reckless Hobo	Ed 11009

It is not certain that matrix 18749 was used.
Edison 11009 may not have been released.

    New York, NY   Tuesday, September 25, 1928

18754-A,-B,-C	Blue Eyed Eller	Ed rejected
N-457-A,-B	Blue Eyed Eller	Ed unissued
18755-A,-B,-C	Sweet Sunny South Take Me Home	Ed rejected
N-458-A,-B	Sweet Sunny South Take Me Home	Ed unissued
18756-B	I'll Meet My Mother After All	Ed 52414
N-459-B	I'll Meet My Mother After All	Ed N20005
18757-A,-B,-C	Did You Mean Those Words You Said	Ed rejected
N-460-A,-B	Did You Mean Those Words You Said	Ed unissued

    New York, NY   Wednesday, September 26, 1928

18760-B	As We Sat Beneath The Maple On The Hill	Ed 5615, 52414
N-462-B	As We Sat Beneath The Maple On The Hill	Ed N20005
18761-A,-B,-C	The Drunkard's Dream	Ed rejected
N-463-B	The Drunkard's Dream	Ed 11009
18762-B	Down In A Georgia Jail	Ed 5613
N-464-A,-B	Down In A Georgia Jail	Ed unissued

Edison 11009 may not have been released.

ALBERT ROSE

Albert Rose, v; acc. own or John Hammond, bj.
    Richmond, IN   Wednesday, April 8, 1925

12196-A	Little Birdie	Ge unissued

The plain take of matrix 12196 is by John Hammond, but Gennett ledgers appear to report that the A take is the same title recorded by Rose.

BAYLESS ROSE

This is almost certainly an African-American artist. See *B&GR*.

FREDDIE ROSE

Fred Rose (as he is usually known), in addition to being a prolific composer of songs recorded by country (and other) artists, has occasionally made records, at least one of which has been issued in a country series (Decca 5390). However, his solo prewar recordings are on the whole beyond the scope of this work. For duet recordings with Frank Luther (as by **Frank & Buddy Ross**) and Ray Whitley, see those artists.

JACK ROSE

Jack Rose, v; acc. unknown, p.
    Dallas, TX   Thursday, June 27, 1929

402760-B	Jack And Babe Blues No. 1	OK 45370

    Dallas, TX   Friday, June 28, 1929

402771-A	Jack And Babe Blues No. 2	OK 45370
402772-	I Can't Help Loving You	OK unissued
402773-	Wake Up, Li'l Girl	OK unissued

FRANK & BUDDY ROSS

Pseudonym on Decca for Frank Luther and Fred Rose.

ROSS RHYTHM RASCALS

J.R. Chatwell, f; prob. Warren "Sweet Face" Harrison, f; Speck Bradley, cl/ts; Jack Hinson, p; prob. Aldan "Wimpy" Hutson, tbj; William "Curly" Perrin, g/v-1/y-2; Horace Edmondson, g; Eugene Edmondson, sb/v-3; Pat Perrin, hv-4; band v-5.
    Dallas, TX   Tuesday, February 16, 1937

61799-A	That's Why I'm Jealous Of You -1	De 5384
61800-A	Indiana (Back Home In Indiana) -1	De 5885
61801-A	Business In F	De 5344
61802-A	What's The Use -1	De 5399
61803-A	I Want A Girl (Just Like The Girl That Married Dear Old Dad) -1, 4	De 5399
61804-A	She's Doggin' Me -1, 5	De 5344
61805-A	Tuck Away My Lonesome Blues -1, 2	De 5410
61806-A	Ramona -1	De 5384
61807-A	I Never Knew -3	De 5446
61808-A	Lulu's Back In Town -1	De 5446
61809-A	Over Somebody Else's Shoulder -1	De 5410
61810-A	You Were Meant For Me -1	De rejected

George Uttinger, f; Clarence Clark, t/v-1; Leon Adams, ts; Jack Hinson, p; Eugene Edmondson, tbj/v-2; Horace Edmondson, g/v-3; Lonnie Mitchell, sb; poss. Joe Mendez, d-4; band v-5.
    Dallas, TX   Saturday, December 4, 1937

62900-A	Please Don't Talk About Me When I'm Gone -2	De 5917
62901-B	Rascal Rag	De 5512
62902-A	I'm Happy When You're Happy -2	De 5885
62903-A	Bonnie -2	De 5528
62904-A	Boojie-Woo Blues -3, 4, 5	De 5480
62905-A	There's Gonna Be No Me To Welcome You -1, 4	De 5528

The drummer may also play on other items than those indicated.

George Uttinger, f; Clarence Clark, t/v-1; Leon Adams, ts; Jack Hinson, p; Eugene Edmondson, tbj/v-2; Horace Edmondson, g; Lonnie Mitchell, sb.
    Dallas, TX   Sunday, December 5, 1937

62906-A	Carry Me Back To Ole Virginny -1	De 5512
62907-A	I'm Just A Country Boy At Heart -2	De 5480
62908-A	I'm Sorry	De unissued
62909-A	Congratulate Me	De 5546
62910-A	Lonely Heart Of Mine -2	De 5917
62911-A	Everybody's Swingin' And Truckin'	De rejected
62912-A	Thank You Mr. Moon	De rejected
62913-A	Save It For Me	De 5546

The band took its name from Ross Aldridge, its manager and announcer.

ROSWELL SACRED HARP QUARTET

Vocal quartet; unacc.
    Atlanta, GA   Saturday, October 12, 1940

056538-1	Odem	BB B-8582
056539-1	Jubilee	BB B-8612
056540-1	White	BB B-8612
056541-1	Weeping Mary	BB B-8582

EARL ROUSE & BROTHERS

See Rouse Brothers.

ROUSE BROTHERS

Earl Rouse & Brothers: Earl Rouse, f; Ervin Rouse, f; prob. Gordon Rouse, g; unidentified, v.

New York, NY   Wednesday, June 3, 1936

| 19359-2 | Pedal Your Blues Away | ARC 6-09-54 |
| 19360-1 | I'm So Tired | ARC 6-09-54 |

Only one fiddle is heard on matrix 19360.

Rouse Brothers: Earl Rouse, f; Ervin Rouse, f; prob. Gordon Rouse, g; unidentified, v-1/v duet-2.

New York, NY   Monday, June 8, 1936

19398-	Please Let Me Walk With My Son -2	ARC unissued
19399-	Are You Angry Little Darling -2	ARC unissued
19400-	Some Old Day -2	ARC unissued
19401-	Toll -1	ARC unissued
19402-	Dixieland Echoes	ARC unissued
19403-	Under The Double Eagle	ARC unissued

Ervin Rouse, f/v-1/sp-2; Gordon Rouse, g/v/sp-2; Jack Rouse, v-3/sp-2.

New York, NY   Wednesday, June 14, 1939

037358-1	Orange Blossom Special -1/3, 2	BB B-8218, MW M-8490
037359-1	Craven County Blues -1	BB B-8239, MW M-8491
037360-1	Bum Bum Blues -1	BB B-8239, MW M-8491
037363-1	Some Old Day -1	BB B-8197, MW M-8489
037364-1	Please Let Me Walk With My Son -3	BB B-8197, MW M-8489
037365-1	My Family Circle (Will The Circle Be Unbroken) -1/3	BB B-8218, MW M-8490

Matrices 037361/62 are untraced.

Rouse Brothers groups recorded after 1942.

ALLAN ROYAL

Pseudonym on Worth for Frank Luther (see Carson Robison).

ROYAL HAWAIIANS

Recordings by this group on Paramount (3144-46) and Broadway (8099-101) are beyond the scope of this work.

ROYAL QUARTETTE

Vocal quartet; acc. unknown, p.

New York, NY   Thursday, August 8, 1935

39826-A	Do Your Best Then Wear A Sunny Smile	De 5181
39827-A	On The Jericho Road	De 5181
39828-A	Over In Glory	De 5197
39829-A	Precious Memories	De 5131
39830-A	Keep On The Firing Line	De 5197
39831-A	We'll Soon Be Done With Troubles And Trials	De 5915, 46057
39832-A	Jesus Hold My Hand	De 5130
39833-A	Some Day	De 5131
39834-A	Happy Am I	De 5310
39835-A	Climbing Jacob's Ladder	De 5278
39836-A	The Home-Coming Week	De 5278
39837-A	Look Away To Jesus	De 5915, 46057
39838-A	The Grand Old Story	De 5310
39839-A	Hallelujah	De 5882
39840-A	Lord I Want To Live With Thee	De 5882
39841-A	When I Rest On The Bosom Of My King	De 5130

Decca 46057 as by **Royal Quartet**.

ROYAL SUMNER QUARTET

Vocal quartet; acc. unknown, p.

Atlanta, GA   Saturday, April 2, 1927

| 143877-2 | Fight To Win | Co 15233-D, Ve 7109-V, CL 5143-C |
| 143878-1 | Be A Man | Co 15233-D, Ve 7108-V, CL 5143-C |

Revs: Velvet Tone 7108-C, 7109-C by Benny Borg.

ARCHIE RUFF'S SINGERS

Pseudonym on Aurora A22014 for Buell Kazee (*The Faded Coat Of Blue*) or the Dixieland Four (*Down By The Old Mill Stream*), and on A22026 for the Kanawha Singers.

GEORGE RUNNELS

Pseudonym on Champion for Roy Harvey.

GEORGE RUNNELS & HOWARD HALL
GEORGE RUNNELS & ED SAWYER

Pseudonyms on Champion for Roy Harvey & Bob Hoke (see the former).

DALE & CLYDE RUSSELL

Pseudonym on Lyric and Summit for Frank Luther & Carson Robison (see the latter).

FLOYD RUSSELL

Pseudonym on Silvertone and Supertone for Marion Underwood.

GROVER RUSSELL

See Russell Brothers.

RUSSELL BROTHERS

Russell Brothers: Grady Russell, Grover Russell, v duet; acc. Grady Russell, sg-1/g-2; Grover Russell, g.
    Jackson, MS   Tuesday, October 15, 1935

JAX-155-2	Lost On The Ocean -1	Vo 03142
JAX-156-	The Sailor's Sweetheart -2	ARC unissued
JAX-157-	Boys In Blue -2	ARC unissued

Grover Russell, v/y; acc. Grady Russell, g; own g.
    Jackson, MS   Tuesday, October 15, 1935

| JAX-158- | Yodeling My Way Back Home | ARC unissued |

Russell Brothers: Grady Russell, Grover Russell, v duet; acc. Grady Russell, sg; Grover Russell, g.
    Jackson, MS   Tuesday, October 15, 1935

| JAX-159- | Daisies Won't Tell | ARC unissued |

Grover Russell, v/y; acc. own g.
    Jackson, MS   Tuesday, October 15, 1935

| JAX-160-1 | It's All Comin' Home To You | Vo 03142 |

RUSTIC REVELLERS

Unknown, f; unknown, md; unknown, g; unknown, sb; George Wilson, calls on some items.
    Chicago, IL   Saturday, October 27, 1934

C-9590-A	Soldier's Joy	De 5059
C-9591-B	Knickerbocker Reel	De 5062
C-9592-A	Chicken Reel	De 5062
C-9593-A,-B	Down Yonder	De unissued
C-9594-A,-B	Berry Pickin' Rag	De rejected
C-9595-B	Fiddlin' Away	De 5063
C-9596-C	Sunshine Special	De 5063
C-9597-A,-B	Dixie Get-Together	De 5059

LEONARD RUTHERFORD

Leonard Rutherford, v; acc. own f; Byrd Moore, g.
    Richmond, IN   Monday, October 29, 1928

| 14395 | Build Me A Bungalow Big Enough For Two | Ge rejected |
| 14396 | Lost John | Ge rejected |

Rutherford & Moore: Leonard Rutherford, f; Byrd Moore, g.
    Richmond, IN   Tuesday, October 30, 1928

| 14398 | Good Night Waltz | Ge 6760, Ch 15653, Spt 9377 |

Champion 15653 as by **Norton, Bond & Williams**. Supertone 9377 as by **Green & Russell**.
For other items recorded on October 29-30 in which Rutherford participated see Richard D. Burnett.
Revs: Gennett 6760 by Taylor, Moore & Burnett; Champion 15653 by Moore, Burnett & Rutherford; Supertone 9377 by Asa Martin & Doc Roberts.

Leonard Rutherford, f/v-1; acc. John Foster, g.
    Richmond, IN   Thursday, April 11, 1929

| 15038 | The Girl I Left Behind Me -1? | Ge rejected |
| 15039,-A | Waggoner | Ge unissued |

Leonard Rutherford made most of his recordings in collaboration with Richard D. Burnett or John Foster, under whose names they are listed.

RUTHERFORD & BURNETT
See Richard D. Burnett.

RUTHERFORD & FOSTER
See John D. Foster.

MARSHALL RUTLEDGE
Marshall Rutledge, v; acc. unknown.
    New York, NY   Tuesday, January 20, 1925

    140350-   Out In The Cold World Alone   Co unissued
    140351-   Got Up Soon One Morning   Co unissued

J.P. RYAN
J.P. Ryan, v/y; acc. prob. own g.
    Richmond, IN   Thursday, September 19, 1929

    15634-A   Bed Bug Groan   Ge 7006, Spt 9542
    15635-A   Sad And Lonely Blues   Ge 7006, Ch 15946, Spt 9542

Champion 15946 as by **Frank Clark**. Supertone 9542 as by **John Ryan**.

J.P. Ryan, v/y-1; acc. prob. own h-2/g.
    Richmond, IN   Tuesday, February 18, 1930

    16295   Going To Leave You Darling -1   Ge 7140, Ch 15946, Spt 9690, Spr 2582
    16296-A   Worried Daddy Blues -1   Ge 7140, Spt 9690, Spr 2582
    16297   It Just Suits Me -2   Ch 16342
    16298   Noah And The Lobsters -2   Ge unissued
    16299   The Silver Dagger -2   Ch 16342
    16300   Mother, Sweetheart And Home -2   Cq 7275
    16301   Fair Florella -2   Spr 2527
    16302   Mother's Gone -2   Cq 7275
    16303   Going Gliding Down The Stream -2 Spr 2527

Champion 15946 as by **Frank Clark**; 16342, Supertone 9690 as by **John Ryan**. Superior 2527, 2582 as by **Dan Weber**. Conqueror 7275 as by **Carl Hutchison**.

JOHN RYAN
See J.P. Ryan.

RYE'S RED RIVER BLUE YODELERS
Conrad Brooks, unknown, v duet; acc. Forrest Rye, f-1; unknown, esg; prob. two unknowns, g; unknown, sb.
    Prob. Detroit, MI   prob. 1941

                You Had Time To Think It Over -1   Hot Wax 1616, Mellow 1616
                On Down The Line   Hot Wax 1616, Mellow 1616

Mellow 1616 as by **Rye's Blue Yodelers**.
Forrest Rye recorded after 1942.

S

JOHN SACKETT
Pseudonym on Banner and Challenge for items by the Gentry Brothers featuring solo vocals by Lester McFarland.

SACRED SINGERS
Pseudonym on Ariel Z4725 for Frank & James McCravy (matrix 81155) or Andrew Jenkins & Carson Robison (matrix 400806).

THE SADDLE TRAMPS
J.R. Chatwell, f; unknown, h-1; "Highpockets" Busse, ac; Jimmy Cole, p; unknown, tbj; Bob Fite, g; Julian Akins, sb; unidentified, v duet-2/v trio-3/y duet-4/y trio-5.
    Dallas, TX   Wednesday, June 23, 1937

    DAL-437-1   Away Out There -3, 5   ARC 7-10-53, Vo 03649
    DAL-438-2   There's A Blue Sky Way Out Yonder -3, 5   ARC 7-10-53, Vo 03649
    DAL-439-1   Good-Bye Gal -3, 5   ARC 7-11-65, Vo 03708
    DAL-440-   Rolling Caravan   ARC unissued
    DAL-441-   Rolling Herd   ARC unissued
    DAL-442-1   I'm Thinking Tonight Of My Blue Eyes -2   Vo/OK 04037

DAL-443-	Mama What Makes You That Way	ARC unissued
DAL-444-1	I'm Blue And Lonesome -1, 3, 5	ARC 8-01-56, Vo 03868
DAL-445-	Driftin' On	ARC unissued
DAL-446-	She's Always On My Mind	ARC unissued
DAL-447-2	Hot As I Am	ARC 7-11-65, Vo 03708

Dallas, TX — Thursday, June 24, 1937

DAL-454-2	Givin' Everything Away -3	ARC 7-08-68, Vo/OK 03609, Cq 8942, Co 37709, 20286
DAL-455-2	Just Because No. 3 -2	ARC 7-08-68, Vo/OK 03609, Cq 8942, Co 37709, 20286
DAL-456-2	Mama How Can You Be Mean To Me -1, 2, 4	Vo/OK 04037
DAL-457-	Texas Home	ARC unissued
DAL-458-1	Mama Mama -3, 5	ARC 8-01-56, Vo 03868
DAL-459-	Rocky Mountain Express	ARC unissued
DAL-460-	Hidden Valley	ARC unissued
DAL-467-2	I Don't Care What You Used To Be -2	Vo 03940
DAL-468-1	Hold Them Critters Down -3	Vo 03940
DAL-469-	Cowboy's Call	ARC unissued

Matrices DAL-461 to 466 are by Grace & Curly Gray.

E.J. SAFRIT

E.J. Safrit, v; acc. poss. own g.
Richmond, IN — Saturday, March 7, 1931

| 17581 | [unknown title] | Ge rejected |

"SAILOR" JACK

Pseudonym on Canadian Domino for Frank Luther (see Carson Robison).

SAIN FAMILY

J.C. Cook, poss. g/v; poss. Wesley Jones, g; Mrs. J.L. Sain, v-1.
Charlotte, NC — Friday, February 19, 1937

07184-1	Quitting My Rowdy Ways	BB unissued
07185-1	Singing The Hilo March	BB unissued
07186-1,-2	Two Timing Mama Blues -1	BB unissued
07187-1	Texas Trail	MW M-7187

Rev. Montgomery Ward M-7187 by Jesse Rodgers.

Unknown, f; two unknowns, bj; poss. J.C. Cook, g; poss. Wesley Jones, g.
Charlotte, NC — Friday, February 19, 1937

| 07188-1 | Wabash | BB unissued |
| 07189-1 | Grey Bonnet | BB unissued |

Matrices 07190/91, listed on the Bluebird session-sheet as part of this session, are solos by Wesley Jones, issued as by **Wesley Long** and listed in this book under that name.

SALEM HIGHBALLERS

Henry McCray, f; Robert McCray, bj; Carl McCray, g; Fred McCray, g.
Richmond, VA — Friday, October 18, 1929

403173-	Salem #1	OK unissued
403174-A	Snow Bird On The Ash Bank	OK 45455
403175-	Dinah, Old Lady	OK unissued
403176-B	Going On To Town	OK 45455

Matrices 403171/72 are by Carl McCray.

THEOPHILE SALNAVE

This artist's one release in the Brunswick old-time series (487) is of Creole material (one side a monologue, the other a song with piano accompaniment), and is believed to be beyond the scope of this work.

SAMMY & SMITTY

Sammy Forsmark, esg/v-1; "Smitty" Smith, g/v-2/y-3.
Atlanta, GA — Monday, February 5, 1940

047537-1	Ten Or Eleven Times -1	BB B-8426, MW M-8735
047538-1	Ridin' Down The Sunset Trail -1, 2	BB B-8526, MW M-8737
047539-1	Meet Mother In The Sky -1, 2	BB B-8526, MW M-8737
047540-1	The Song Of Two Roses -1?	BB B-8492, MW M-8736
047541-1	Canoeing With Another Man -2	BB B-8426, MW M-8735
047542-1	I Still Love You, Sweetheart -2, 3	BB B-8492, MW M-8736

JOSEPH SAMUELS

Joseph Samuels was a New York-based studio musician and prolific recording artist in the popular field. A few of his recordings might be judged to fall within the scope of this book.

Joe Samuels & Larry Briers: Joseph Samuels, f; Larry Briers, p.
   New York, NY   c. September 1925

1760-A,-B	Turkey In The Straw	GG 4068, ?Rad 4068
1761-A,-B	Arkansas Traveler	GG 4068, ?Rad 4068

See session of c. February 1928 for later recordings of these items using the same release numbers.

Three Old Cronies: Joseph Samuels, f; Harry Reser, tbj; Steve Porter, calls.
   New York, NY   Monday, March 15, 1926

E-2640/41W	Turkey In The Straw (A "Paul Jones")	Vo 15305, 5134
E-2642/43W	The Arkansas Traveler (A Quadrille)	Vo 15305, 5134

Fiddler Joe & His Boys: Joseph Samuels, f; poss. Harry Reser, tbj; poss. Steve Porter, calls; unknown, wh-1.
   New York, NY   March/April 1926

74094-B	Turkey In The Straw (The Paul Jones) -1	OK 45042, Ha 866-H, Ve 1866-V, Di 2866-G, Cl 5023-C
74095-B	Arkansaw Traveler (A Quadrille)	OK 45042, Ha 866-H, Ve 1866-V, Di 2866-G, Cl 5023-C

Harmony 866-H, Velvet Tone 1866-V, Diva 2866-G, Clarion 5023-C as by **"Pop" Hanks & His Boys**. The subtitles are omitted, and matrix 74095 is titled *Arkansas Traveler*, on those issues.

Joe Samuels, f; acc. unknown.
   New York, NY   unknown date

	Arkansas Traveler And Medley Reels	Sil 5057
	Old Zip Coon And Medley Reels	Sil 5057

Joe Samuels & Larry Briers: Joseph Samuels, f; Larry Briers, p.
   New York, NY   c. February 1928

2716-A	Arkansas Traveler	GG/Rad 4068, Mad 14068
2717-A,-B	Turkey In The Straw	GG/Rad 4068, Mad 14068

A (probably) later pressing of these items on Grey Gull 4068, and all copies of Madison 14068, are as by **Wabash Trio**; those issues use matrix 2717-A rather than -B.

Arkansas Traveler (matrix 218-B) as by **Frisco Players** on Grey Gull 4068, Madison 5041, Van Dyke 5041, and *Turkey In The Straw* (unknown matrix, but not 163-A) as by **White City Jazzers** on Grey Gull/Radiex 4068 are different recordings, possibly not involving Samuels, and beyond the scope of this work.

Joseph Samuels also accompanies Ernest V. Stoneman and Henry Whitter.

THE SANCTIFIED SINGERS

Pseudonym on Parlophone E6400 for Frank & James McCravy (matrix 81155) or Andrew Jenkins & Carson Robison (matrix 400806).

RAY SAND'S HARMONY FOUR

Vocal quartet; acc. "Bill" Lynch, p.
   Richmond, IN   Thursday, October 3, 1929

15732-A	Down On The Levee	Ge 7018, Ch 15874
15733-A	Shine Song	Ge 7018, Ch 15874

Champion 15874 as by **Oak Mountain Four**.

   Richmond, IN   Thursday, November 14, 1929

15885	Back To Alabama In The Spring	Ge rejected
15886	Washington Waddle/Goodbye Big Town	Ge rejected

   Richmond, IN   Thursday, December 26, 1929

16013	Sailin' Away On The Henry Clay	Ge 7078, Ch 15966, Spt 9675
16014,-A,-B	Cross The Mason Dixon Line	Ge rejected
16015-A	Down South Everybody's Happy	Ge 7078, Ch 15966, Spt 9675
16017,-A,-B	I Leave For Dixie Today	Ge rejected

Champion 15966 as by **Oak Mountain Four**. Matrix 16016 is popular.

DILLARD SANDERS

Pseudonym on Supertone for G.B. Grayson & Henry Whitter.

IRENE SANDERS

Irene Sanders, v; acc. Aaron Campbell's Mountaineers: unknown, h-1/v; Aaron Campbell, sg-2/v; prob. Buddy Webber, g/v.

    Richmond, IN   Monday, November 6, 1933

| 19344 | Fond Affection -2 | Ch S-16719, 45056 |
| 19345 | The Widow In The Cottage By The Sea -1 | Ch S-16719, 45056 |

SANDERS TWINS

Pseudonym on Harmony for the Sandlin Brothers.

THE SANDERS TWINS

Pseudonym on Diva for the Sandlin Brothers.

SANDHILLS SIXTEEN

Eight unknown men, tv; three unknown men, bv; three unknown men, bsv; Theo S. Page, v solo-1; E. Ellsworth Giles, v solo-2/dir; acc. Mrs Ellsworth Giles, p.

    Camden, NJ   Thursday, July 21, 1927

38993-2	What Sort O' Robes Do Angels Wear?	Vi 20903
38994-2	Hush! Hush! Somebody's Calling My Name	Vi 20904
38995-1	Shine On Me -1	?Vi 20903
38995-2,-3	Shine On Me -2	?Vi 20903
38996-2	Down By The Riverside	Vi 20904
38997-2	Levee Song/I've Been Working On The Railroad	Vi 20905
38998-2	My Evaline	Vi 20905

It is uncertain which take of matrix 38995 was issued.

SANDLIN BROTHERS

—— Sandlin, —— Sandlin, h duet.

    Atlanta, GA   Saturday, January 31, 1925

| 140315-1 | Traveling Man's Blues (Train Imitations) | Co 315-D, Ha 5108-H, Di 6002-G |
| 140316-2 | Mocking Bird (Bird Calls) | Co 315-D, Ha 5108-H, Di 6002-G |

Harmony 5108-H as by **Sanders Twins**. Diva 6002-G as by **The Sanders Twins**.

SANDY CREEK WOOD CHOPPERS

Pseudonym on Supertone for Walter Coon & His Joy Boys.

TOM SARGENT

Pseudonym on Broadway for Thomas C. Ashley.

BILLY SAWYER

Billy Sawyer, v; poss. acc. own g.

    Atlanta, GA   Sunday, October 25, 1931

| 151930- | Goin' Back To Tenn [sic] Blues | Co unissued |
| 151931- | Swamps Of Old Arkansas | Co unissued |

Billy Sawyer (or Sawyers) also recorded with L.O. Birkhead & R.M. Lane and with A.E. Ward.

SAWYER SISTERS (CELIA & ANN)

Celia Sawyer, Ann Sawyer, v duet; acc. poss. Billy Sawyer, g.

    Atlanta, GA   Monday, October 26, 1931

| 151946- | Don't Leave Me Sally | Co unissued |
| 151947-1 | It's All In The Game | Co 15745-D |

Rev. Columbia 15745-D by the Duncan Sisters.

SAXTON BROS.

Pseudonym on Superior for (David) Fletcher & (Gwen) Foster.

HAZEL SCHERF

Hazel Scherf, v; acc. prob. Archie Porter, h/g.

    Richmond, IN   Wednesday, January 31, 1934

| 19468 | You Can't Blame Me For That | Ch 16728, 45082 |
| 19469 | Married Girls Troubles | Ch 16728, 45082 |

B.E. SCOTT

B.E. Scott, f; acc. Berdina Scott, p.

    prob. New York, NY   c. August 1924

| 1836-3 | The Big Eared Mule | Pm 33156, Pu 9156 |

| 1838-3 | College Horn Pipe | Pm 33156, Pu 9156 |

Matrix 1837 is untraced but probably by this artist.

B.E. Scott, f; unknown, f; unknown, p; unknown, calls-1.
   prob. New York, NY   unknown date

| 919 | The Wagoner -1 | Pm 33167, Pu 9167, Sil 3511 |
| 920 | Devil In The Hay | Pm 33167, Pu 9167, Sil 3511 |

JAMES SCOTT–CLAUDE BOONE

James Scott, Claude Boone, v duet; acc. Cliff Carlisle, sg-1; own g duet.
   Charlotte, NC   Friday, February 19, 1937

| 07174-1 | Memories Of A Shack On The Hill | BB B-6885 |
| 07175-1 | Carolina Trail -1 | BB B-6885 |

Scott & Boone (The Elk Mountain Boys): James Scott, Claude Boone, v duet; acc. Cliff Carlisle, sg-1; own g duet.
   Charlotte, NC   Friday, June 3, 1938

64016-A	Think Of Mother -1	De 5668, MeC 45300
64017-A	Prepare! Prepare! (For The Great Eternity)	De 5644
64018-A	I'm Just A Drunkard's Child	De 5566, Min M-14101
64019-A	Sin Is To Blame	De 5550
64020-A	Gold Holds The Future In His Hand	De 5668, MeC 45300
64021-A	Don't Dig Mother's Grave Before She Is Dead	De 5587, MeC 45270
64022-A	Only A Word (From That Book So Dear)	De 5587, MeC 45270
64023-A	Jesus Hold My Hand	De 5644
64024-A	Father Dear Father Come Home	De 5566, Min M-14101
64025-A	Mary In The Wildwood	De 5550

Claude Boone sings lead and James Scott tenor.

James Scott and Claude Boone probably recorded with Cliff Carlisle at his June 1938 session. Claude Boone recorded after 1942.

SCOTT & BOONE (THE ELK MOUNTAIN BOYS)

See James Scott–Claude Boone.

SCOTT COUNTY TRIO

Pseudonym on Supertone for the Gibson String Trio or Workman, Ramsey & Wolfe (probably the same group; see Gibson String Trio).

SCOTTDALE STRING BAND

Belvie Freeman, bj-md; Barney Pritchard, g; Marvin Head, g.
   Atlanta, GA   Thursday, October 28, 1926

| 9829-A | Aunt Hager's Blues | OK 45074 |
| 9830-A | Southern Blues | OK 45074 |

Prob. Charlie Simmons, bj-md; Barney Pritchard, g; Marvin Head, g; unidentified, v-1/calls-2.
   Atlanta, GA   Monday, March 21, 1927

80599-B	Stone Mountain Wobble	OK 45118
80600-B	Carbolic Rag	OK 45118
80601-B	My Own Iona -1	OK 45142
80602-A	Carolina Glide	OK 45142, Ve 7098-V, Cl 5130-C
80603-B	Chinese Break Down -2	OK 45103, Ve 7097-V, Cl 5130-C
80604-B	In The Shade Of The Parasol -2	OK 45103

Revs: Velvet Tone 7097-V, 7098-V by W.T. Narmour & S.W. Smith.

Prob. Charlie Simmons, bj-md; Barney Pritchard, g; Marvin Head, g; unidentified, calls-1/sp-2.
   Atlanta, GA   Monday, October 10, 1927

81732-A	Down Yonder	OK 45188
81733-A	Hiawatha Breakdown -1	OK 45158
81734-A	Scottdale Stomp -2	OK 45173
81735-A	Old Folks Better Go To Bed -1	OK 45173
81736-A	Hop Light Ladies -1	OK 45158
81737-A	Sea March	OK 45188
81738-A	Goin' Crazy Blues	OK 45201

Rev. OKeh 45201 by Four Virginians.

   Atlanta, GA   Friday, August 10, 1928

| 402126-B | Come Be My Rainbow | OK 45256 |
| 402127-A | Share 'Em -1, 2 | OK 45256 |

| 402128-B | Silver Bell | OK 45279, Ve 2395-V, Cl 5329-C, Re/RZAu G21090 |
| 402129-A | Green Mountain Poker -1, 2 | OK 45279 |

Velvet Tone 2395-V, Clarion 5329-C, Regal/Regal-Zonophone G21090 as by **The Howard Boys**.
Velvet Tone 2395-V, Clarion 5329-C, Regal/Regal-Zonophone G21090 use the transfer matrix 100540-1.
Revs: Velvet Tone 2395-V, Clarion 5329-C, Regal/Regal-Zonophone G21090 by Frank & James McCravy.

Poss. Owen McDearis or Luke Talton, f; Charlie Simmons, bj-md; Barney Pritchard, g; Marvin Head, g; unidentified, sp-1/coughing-1.
    Atlanta, GA   Thursday, March 14, 1929

402315-A	Kohala March	OK 45379
402316-B	Sunset Waltz	OK 45352, 16391
402317-B	Honolulu Moon	OK 45379
402318-B	The Moonshiners' Waltz	OK 45352, 16391
402319-B	Coughdrop Blues -1	OK 45341
402320-B	Waiting For The Robert E. Lee	OK 45341

OKeh 16391 (a Mexican issue) as by **Orquesta De Cuerda Del Sur**. Matrix 402316 is titled *Al Anochecer*, and matrix 402318 *Al Amanacer*, on that issue.

Charlie Simmons, bj-md; Barney Pritchard, g; Marvin Head, g.
    Atlanta, GA   Monday, December 1, 1930

404604-B	Scottdale Highballers	OK 45527
404605-B	Japanese Breakdown	OK 45509
404606-A	Sitting On Top Of The World	OK 45509
404607-B	Charleston Wabble	OK 45527

B.L. Pritchard (Accompanied By The Scottdale String Band): prob. Charlie Simmons, bj-md; Barney Pritchard, g/v-1; Marvin Head, g.
    Grafton, WI   c. April/May 1932

| L-1502-3 | Wang Wang Blues -1 | Pm 3320 |
| L-1503-2 | Stone Mountain Wobble | Pm 3320 |

The Scottdale String Band: prob. Charlie Simmons, bj-md; Barney Pritchard, g; Marvin Head, g.
    Grafton, WI   c. April/May 1932

| L-1513-2 | St. Louis Tickle | Bwy 8336 |
| L-1514-2 | Down Yonder Breakdown | Bwy 8336 |

Matrices L-1504 to L-1512 are untraced.

SCOTTY THE DRIFTER

See Benny Borg.

LISTON SCROGGINS

Liston Scroggins, v/y-1; acc. own g.
    Dallas, TX   Sunday, October 27, 1929

| DAL-495- | Good-Bye To Friends And Home | Br 378, BrAu 378 |
| DAL-496- | I'm Lonely Tonight Sweetheart -1 | Br 378, BrAu 378 |

Matrix DAL-496 is titled *I'm Lonely To-night, Sweetheart* on Australian Brunswick 378.

WALTER B. SEALE
SEALE & VAUGHAN

See Vaughan Quartet & Associated Groups.

JIM SEANEY

Pseudonym on Challenge for Ernest V. Stoneman.

UNCLE JIM SEANEY

Pseudonym on Champion for Ernest V. Stoneman.

JOSEPH SEARS

Pseudonym on Sunrise for Vernon Dalhart.

KELLY & HOWARD SEARS

Kelly Sears, v; or **Kelly Sears & Howard Sears**-1, v duet; acc. The Musical Fools: Kelly Sears, bj; Howard Sears, g.
    Richmond, IN   Wednesday, December 10, 1930

| 17360 | Rambling Blues | Ge rejected |
| 17361 | She Said She Was Going Away | Ge rejected |

```
17362        They Can't Fool Me Anymore              Ge rejected
17363        Do It Some More -1                      Ge rejected
```
Kelly Sears recorded after 1942.

SEBREN & WILSON (HAPPY TWO)
See Vaughan Quartet & Associated Groups.

E. SEGURA & D. HERBERT
SEGURA BROS

Segura Bros: Dewey Segura, ac/v-1; Edier Segura, tri.
New Orleans, LA   Sunday, December 16, 1928

```
147654-1     Bury Me In A Corner Of The Yard -1      Co 40500-F, OK 90000
147655-1     My Sweetheart Run Away -1               Co 40500-F, OK 90000
147656-1     A Mosquito Ate Up My Sweetheart -1      Co 40507-F, OK 90007
147657-1     New Iberia Polka                        Co 40507-F, OK 90007
```

E. Segura & D. Herbert: Dewey Segura, ac/v; Didier Hebert, g.
New Orleans, LA   Tuesday, December 10, 1929

```
111391-2     Far Away From Home Blues                Co 40517-F, OK 90017
111392-2     Rosalia                                 Co 40512-F, OK 90012
111393-2     Your [sic] Small And Sweet              Co 40512-F, OK 90012
```

Revs: Columbia 40517-F, OK 90017 by Didier Hebert.
Dewey and Edier Segura recorded for the Library of Congress in 1934, and Dewey Segura did so again in 1975.

LEON PAPPY SELF & HIS BLUE RIDGE PLAYBOYS
See Leon Selph.

HAROLD SELMAN

Harold Selman, sp; acc. unknown, f; unknown, p; unknown, vc; unknown man, sp-1/laughing-1.
Atlanta, GA   Wednesday, August 8, 1928

```
402094-      Shooting Of Dan McGrew Part 1           OK unissued
402095-      Shooting Of Dan McGrew Part 2           OK unissued
402096-B     The Face On The Bar Room Floor – Part 1 -1   OK 45249
402097-B     The Face On The Bar Room Floor – Part 2      OK 45249
```

LEON SELPH

Blue Ridge Playboys: Leon Selph, f/v-1; Floyd Tillman, eg-2/v-3; Herman Standlee, eg-3/g-2; Moon Mullican, p/v-4; Gus Plant, tbj; Chuck Keeshan, g/v-5; Hezzie Bryant, sb.
San Antonio, TX   Friday, November 20, 1936

```
SA-2538-1    Anything -1, 2                          ARC 7-06-55, Vo 03526
SA-2539-1    Blue Monday -3                          Vo 03589
SA-2540-1    Rhythm In The Air -3                    ARC 7-04-72, Vo 03460
SA-2541-2    Swing Baby Swing -2, 4                  ARC 7-04-72, Vo 03460
SA-2542-1    Gimme My Dime Back -1, 2                ARC 7-06-55, Vo 03526
SA-2543-1    That Old Fashioned Way -2, 5            ARC 7-07-53, Vo 03558
SA-2544-1    Can't Nobody Truck Like Me -1, 2        ARC 7-03-66, Vo 03425
SA-2545-1    Take Me Back To West Texas -3           ARC 7-07-53, Vo 03558
SA-2546-2    You're As Pretty As A Picture -2, 5     Vo 03589
SA-2547-1    Georgia Pines -2, 4                     ARC 7-05-53, Vo 03481
SA-2548-2    Ain't You Kinda Sorry Now -2, 4         ARC 7-05-53, Vo 03481
SA-2549-2    Whose Honey Are You -2, 5               ARC 7-03-66, Vo 03425
```

Leon Selph, f/v-1; Herman Standlee, eg; Eddie Gerard, p; Gus Plant, tbj; Chuck Keeshan, g/v-2; Clarence Standlee, g; Dick Haltom, sb.
Dallas, TX   Monday, June 21, 1937

```
DAL-404-     'Neath The Silvery Moon                 ARC unissued
DAL-405-     Louisiana And You                       ARC unissued
DAL-406-1    Scram -1                                Vo 03685
DAL-407-1    How Can I Help It? -1                   Vo 03685
DAL-408-     Breakin' Up Matches                     ARC unissued
DAL-409-2    The Convict And The Rose -2             Vo/OK 03765
DAL-410-1    I'll Love You In My Dreams -2           Vo/OK 03765
DAL-411-2    Keep Your Nose Out Of Daddy's Business -1   Vo 03620
DAL-412-     Lonesome Trail                          ARC unissued
DAL-413-1    I'm No Good On Earth -1                 Vo 03620
```

Leon Selph's Blue Ridge Playboys: Cliff Bruner, f; Bob Dunn, esg; Mancel Tierney, p; Joe Thames, tbj; Dickie McBride, g; Hezzie Bryant, sb; Leon Selph, v-1; Floyd Tillman, v-2.

Houston, TX   Monday, March 6, 1939

65156-A	What Difference Does It Make -2	De 5663
65157-A	Two More Years (And I'll Be Free) -2	De 5679
65158-A	A Precious Memory -2	De 5696
65159-A	Why Do I Love You -2	De 5696
65160-A	Some Day -1	De 5663
65161-A	If You Should Go Away I'd Cry -1	De 5679

Bob Dunn, esg; Leo Raley, emd; Moon Mullican, p; unknown, g; Hezzie Bryant, sb; Leon Selph, v-1; Gus Plant, v-2.

Houston, TX   Tuesday, September 5, 1939

66417-A	You're My Darling -2	De 5747
66418-A	My Precious Baby Girl -1	De 5747

Leon Pappy Self & His Blue Ridge Playboys: Leon Selph, f/v-1; Ernest "Deacon" Evans, esg; Ralph Smith, p; Howard Oliver, tbj; Gus Plant, g/v-2; Chet Miller, sb.

Saginaw, TX   Sunday, April 28, 1940

DAL-1078-1	Daisy Mae -1	Vo/OK 05559
DAL-1079-2	I'm Sorry I Ever Met You -2	OK 06018
DAL-1080-1,-2	Tell Me If You Love Me	Vo unissued
DAL-1081-2	Sweet Magnolia Blossoms	OK 05709
DAL-1082-1	I'm Just A Country Boy -1	Vo/OK 05559
DAL-1083-2	Nobody Cares About Me -1	OK 06018
DAL-1084-1	Nobody But Me -1	OK 05767
DAL-1085-2	Texas Take Off	OK 05709

Saginaw, TX   Monday, April 29, 1940

DAL-1086-1,-2	When You Smile	Vo unissued
DAL-1087-2	Polecat Stomp	OK 05767

Leon Selph, f/v; Freddie Courtney, ac; Herman Standlee, eg; Gus Plant, g; Dick Haltom, sb.

Fort Worth, TX   Wednesday, March 12, 1941

DAL-1307-1	Natcherly	OK 06174, Cq 9780
DAL-1308-1	Just Forget	OK 06174, Cq 9780
DAL-1309-1	Florene	OK 06276
DAL-1310-1	Lovin' And Leavin'	OK 06276
DAL-1311-1,-2	Teardrops On My Pillow	OK unissued
DAL-1312-1,-2	If You Should Go Away	OK unissued
DAL-1313-1,-2	Some Day	OK unissued
DAL-1314-1,-2	Now That You Have Gone	OK unissued
DAL-1315-1,-2	She's Gone Away	OK unissued
DAL-1316-1,-2	In My Dreams	OK unissued

WALLACE SESTEN & JACK SHOOK

No details.

Chicago, IL   Tuesday, November 13, 1934

TO-1480	Nobody's Sweetheart/Hand Me Down My Walking Cane	ARC unissued trial recording

Jack Shook recorded after 1942.

JILSON SETTERS (J.W. DAY)

See J.W. Day.

SEVEN FOOT DILLY [& OTHERS]

See John Dilleshaw.

BILL SHAFER

Bill Shafer, v/y; acc. own g.

Dallas, TX   Sunday, October 27, 1929

DAL-485-	Broken Engagements	Vo 5413
DAl-486-	Kicking Mule	Vo 5413

ROY SHAFFER

Roy Shaffer (The Lone Star Cowboy), v; acc. own g.

New Orleans, LA   Thursday, March 19, 1936

60826-	Three Thousand Miles From Home	De 5274

60827-	Mother Dear Old Mother	De 5228, MeC 45210, Min M-14063, BrSA SA1101
60828-	The Girl I Left In Kentucky	De 5274
60829-	Don't Forget Me Little Darling	De 5228, MeC 45210, Min M-14076

The subcredit is omitted on Melotone 45210, Minerva M-14063, M-14076, Brunswick SA1101.
Revs: Minerva M-14063 by Fleming & Townsend, M-14076 by Tex Fletcher; Brunswick SA1101 by Rex Griffin.

Roy Shaffer, v; or Roy Shaffer, sp-1; acc. own g.
Chicago, IL   Monday, June 26, 1939

040039-1	The Answer To "Disappointed In Love"	BB B-8303, MW M-8497, RZAu G24329
040040-1	Cowboy Jack	BB B-8303, MW M-8497
040041-1	Shake Hands With Your Mother	BB B-8254, MW M-8494
040042-1	The Great Speckled Bird	BB B-8254, MW M-8494
040043-1	Talking Blues -1	BB B-8234, MW M-8493
040044-1	The Match Box Blues	BB B-8234, MW M-8493
040045-1	Coupon Song	BB B-8213, MW M-8492, Twin FT8875
040046-1	Bury Me Out On The Prairie	BB B-8213, MW M-8492, Twin FT8875
040047-1	Disappointed In Love (I Wish I Had Never Seen Sunshine)	BB B-8267, MW M-8495, RZAu G24329
040048-1	Rockin' Alone In An Old Rocking Chair	BB B-8267, MW M-8495
040049-1	Trouble In Mind	BB B-8289, MW M-8496
040050-1	Jack And Joe	BB B-8289, MW M-8496

SHAMROCK STRING BAND

Unknown, f; unknown, md; unknown, g.
Atlanta, GA   Monday, October 22, 1928

147245-1	Kuhala March	Co 15339-D
147246-2	High-Low March	Co 15339-D
147247-1	Hawaiian Moon Waltz	Co 15534-D
147248-1	Sweetheart Waltz	Co 15534-D

SHANKS BROS. TRIO

Vocal /sp-1 trio; acc. unknown, f; unknown, g; unknown, sb.
Richmond, IN   June-July 1933

19234	We're In The Money	Ch 16631
19235	Charlie's Home -1	Ch 16631
19236	Is That Religion	Ch 16640
19237	She's A Great Great Girl	Ch 16640

Vocal/sp-1 trip; acc. unknown, f; unknown, g; unknown, sb.
Richmond, IN   c. early December 1933

19410	Annie Doesn't Live Here Anymore	Ch 16688
19411	Puddin' Head Jones	Ch 16688
19412	Shanghai Lil	Ch 16704
19413	The Last Round-Up	Ch 16687, 45006
19414	Who's Afraid Of The Big Bad Wolf	Ch 16687
19415	The Night We Met	Ch 16704

Rev. Champion 45006 popular.
Chuck Shanks, named as a royalty payee, is probably a member of the group.

"TED" SHARP, HINMAN & SHARP

Unidentified, f; unidentified, p; unidentified, g.
Richmond, IN   Wednesday, November 8, 1933

19351	The Old Grey Horse Came Out Of The Wilderness	Ch S-16751, 45008
19352	Hell Among The Yearlings	Ch 16712, 45012, MeC 45012
19353	Robinson County	Ge unissued
19354	Pike's Peak	Ch 16712, 45012, MeC 45012
19355	Goin' On Up To Town	Ch S-16766, 45002
19356	Where's My Other Foot	Ch S-16739, 45182
19357	Tuscaloosa Waltz	Ch S-16739, 45182
19358	Aunt Clara's Waltz	Ch S-16766, 45002

Revs: Champion S-16751, 45008 by Aaron Campbell's Mountaineers.

BERT SHAW
BURT SHAW

Pseudonyms on Superior for Jess Hillard.

MIKE SHAW & HIS ALABAMA ENTERTAINERS

Unknown, f; unknown, k-1; unknown, g.
    Atlanta, GA   Wednesday, December 10, 1930

404650-A	Going Crazy	OK 45529
404651-A	May Flower	OK 45529
404652-B	Birmingham Special -1	OK 45518
404653-B	Tennessee River Bottom Blues -1	OK 45518

THEODORE SHAW OF LAWRENCEBURG, TENN.

See Vaughan Quartet & Associated Groups.

SHAW & KERR

Pseudonym on Aurora for
A22018 Richard Brooks & Reuben Puckett (*She's More To Be Pitied Than Censored*) / Vernon Dalhart (*After The Ball*)
A22028 Vernon Dalhart (*The Letter Edged In Black*) / Frank & James McCravy (*The Vacant Chair*).

HUGH SHEARER

Hugh Shearer, v; acc. prob. own bj.
    Richmond, IN   Saturday, August 1, 1931

17909	John Henry	Ge unissued trial recording

SHEFFIELD MALE QUARTET

C.P. Sheffield, tv; J.C. Cronic, tv; C.E. Couch, bv; A.C. Sheffield, bsv; unacc.
    Atlanta, GA   Monday, February 21, 1927

37939-2	What Did He Do	Vi 20554
37940-1	Christ Arose	Vi 20554

J.C. Cronic was probably one of the Cronic Brothers, and possibly the Clarence Cronic who was a member of Smith's Sacred Singers. He and C.P. Sheffield may have been members of Peck's Male Quartette.

THE SHELBY SINGERS

Pseudonym on Columbia for a Bob Miller group.

SHELL CREEK QUARTET

Vocal quartet; unacc.
    Johnson City, TN   Monday, October 15, 1928

147176-1	My Boyhood Days	Co 15355-D
147177-1	Back Where The Old Home Stands	Co 15355-D

SHELOR FAMILY

Shelor Family-1/Dad Blackard's Moonshiners-2: Jesse T. Shelor, f; Pyrhus D. Shelor, f; Clarice Blackard, p/hv-3; Joe B. Blackard, bj/v.
    Bristol, TN   Wednesday, August 3, 1927

39761-3	Big Bend Gal -1, 3	Vi 20865
39762-2	Suzanna Gal -2	Vi 21130
39763-1	Sandy River Belle -2	Vi unissued: *CMF-011-L (LP); 011-D (CD)*
39763-2	Sandy River Belle -2	Vi 21130
39764-2	Billy Grimes, The Rover -1	Vi 20865

B.F. SHELTON

B.F. Shelton, v; acc. own bj.
    Bristol, TN   Friday, July 29, 1927

39734-1	Cold Penitentiary Blues	Vi V-40107
39735-2	Oh Molly Dear	Vi V-40107
39736-2	Pretty Polly	Vi 35838
39737-1	Darling Cora	Vi 35838

Victor 35838 is a 12-inch issue.

FRANK SHELTON

Frank Shelton, v; acc. unknown.
    Johnson City, TN   Thursday, October 18, 1928

147240-	Someone Else May Be There	Co unissued
147241-	Why Have You Left Me Lonely	Co unissued

JOE SHELTON

See the Shelton Brothers.

SHELTON BROTHERS (BOB & JOE)

Bob Shelton, Joe Shelton, v duet; acc. Joe Shelton, md; Bob Shelton, g; or **Joe Shelton**-1, v; acc. own g.

Chicago, IL Friday, February 22, 1935

C-9809-A	Deep Elem Blues	De 5099, 46008
C-9810-A	A Message From Home Sweet Home	De 5135
C-9811-A	The Coupon Song -1	De 5087
C-9812-A	Hang Out The Front Door Key	De 5099

Chicago, IL Saturday, February 23, 1935

C-9813-A	Just Because	De 5100, 46008
C-9814-A	Who Wouldn't Be Lonely	De 5100
C-9815-A	Nothin'	De 5161
C-9816-A	Beautiful Louisiana	De 5079, DeSA FM5106
C-9817-A	Will There Be Any Cowboys In Heaven?	De 5135
C-9818-A	Stay In The Wagon Yard -1	De 5087
C-9819-A	Johnson's Old Grey Mule	De 5161
C-9820-A	'Neath The Maple In The Lane	De 5079

Rev. Decca FM5106 by Margaret West.

Shelton Bros. & Curley Fox: Bob Shelton, Joe Shelton, Curly Fox, v trio; acc. Curley Fox, f; Joe Shelton, md; Bob Shelton, g.

Chicago, IL Monday, August 19, 1935

| C-90251-A | Sal Let Me Chew Your Rosom [sic] Some | De 5137 |
| C-90252-A | Gonna Raid That Chicken Roast [sic] Tonight | De 5137 |

Matrices C-90250 and C-90253 are by Curley Fox.

Shelton Brothers (Bob & Joe), v duet; acc. Joe Shelton, md; Bob Shelton, g.

Chicago, IL Monday, August 19, 1935

| C-90254-A,-AA | Deep Elem Blues No. 2 | De unissued |

Bob Shelton, Joe Shelton, v duet; or Joe Shelton, v-1; acc. Curley Fox, f-2; Joe Shelton, md-3/g-4; Bob Shelton, g-5/j-6.

Chicago, IL Tuesday, August 20, 1935

C-90256-A	When It's Night Time In Nevada -2, 4/5	BrSA SA991, ?DeSA FM5108
C-90257-A,-AA	Bury Me Beneath The Willow -1, 2, 4, 5	De rejected
C-90258-A,-AA	Lover's Farewell -1, 2, 4, 5	De rejected
C-90260-A,-AA	Budded Roses -3, 5	De unissued
C-90261-A,-AA	New John Henry Blues -2, 4/5	De unissued
C-90262-A	Sittin' On Top O' The World -2, 4/5	De 6079, MeC 45551
C-90263-A,-AA	Cheatin' On Your Baby -4, 5	De unissued
C-90264-A,-AA	Match Box Blues -2, 4, 6	De unissued
C-90265-A,-AA	Daddy Don't 'Low No Lowdown Hangin' Around -2, 3, 5	De unissued

Matrix C-90255 is a Ma Perkins radio commercial; matrix C-90259 is by Curley Fox.

Chicago, IL Wednesday, August 21, 1935

| C-90266-A,-AA | Black Sheep -2, 4/5 | De unissued |
| C-90268-A,-AA | Sweet Evalina -3, 5 | De unissued |

Matrix C-90267 is by Curley Fox.

Joe Shelton, v; acc. Curley Fox, f; Bob Shelton, g.

New York, NY Wednesday, December 18, 1935

| 60242-A | Match Box Blues | De 5177 |

Shelton Brothers (Bob & Joe), v duet; or **Joe Shelton**-1, v; acc. Curley Fox, f-2; Joe Shelton, md-3; Bob Shelton, g/j-4.

New York, NY Thursday, December 19, 1935

60243-A	Budded Roses -3	De 5180, DeAu X1117, DeSA FM5496
60243-B	Budded Roses -2, 3	De 5180
60244-A,-AA	I'm Sitting On Top Of The World -2	De 5190, MeC 45218
60245-A	When It's Night Time In Nevada -2	De 5219, ?DeSA FM5108
60246-A	I'm Thinking Tonight Of My Blue Eyes -2	De 5184, DeAu X1118, DeSA FM5109
60247-A	Bury Me Beneath The Willow -2	De 5184, DeAu X1118, MeC 45215
60248-A	The Black Sheep -2	De 5219
60257-A,-C	'Leven Miles From Leavenworth	De 5180, DeAu X1117
60258-B	Daddy Don't 'Low No Low Down Hangin' Around -2, 3	De 5198
60259-B	Deep Elem Blues No.2 -3	De 5198

60261-A	New John Henry Blues -2, 4	De 5173
60262-B	At The Shelby County Fair -1, 2	De 5177
60263-A	Ridin' On A Humpback Mule -2	De 5173

Decca 5173 as by **Shelton Bros. & Curley Fox**, 5184, X1118, Melotone 45215 as by **Joe Shelton & Curly Fox**.
Matrices 60249 to 60252 are by Louis Armstrong (see JR); matrices 60253 to 60256 are popular; matrix 60260 is by Curley Fox.
Revs: Melotone 45215 by Tex Owens; Decca FM5496 by the Carolina Buddys.

Bob Shelton, Joe Shelton, v duet; acc. Curley Fox, f-1; Joe Shelton, md-2; Bob Shelton, g.
New York, NY   Friday, December 20, 1935

60264-	Sweet Evelina -2	De 5261, DeSA FM5111, BrSA SA1201
60265-B	Answer To Just Because -2	De 5170, MeC 45214, Min M-14062
60267-A	Lover's Farewell -1	De 5261, DeSA FM5108, BrSA SA991
60268-B-1	That's A Habit I've Never Had -1	De 5170, DeSA FM5109, MeC 45214
60269-A	Four Or Five Times -1	De 5190, MeC 45218

Matrix 60266 is by Curley Fox.
Revs: Decca FM5111, Brunswick SA1201 by Leo Soileau; Minerva M-14062 by Fleming & Townsend.

Shelton Bros. (Bob & Joe), v duet; or Joe Shelton, v-1; acc. Leon "Lonnie" Hall, f-2; Harry Sorensen, ac; Joe Shelton, md-3; Gene Sullivan, g; Grundy "Slim" Harbert, sb.
Dallas, TX   Wednesday, February 17, 1937

61820-A	Answer To Blue Eyes -2	De 5440
61821-A	I'm Gonna Fix Your Wagon -2	De 5471
61822-A	The Story Of Seven Roses -2	De 5353, DeSA FM5139
61823-A	I'm Here To Get My Baby Out Of Jail -2	De 5409
61824-A	Way Down In Georgia -2, 3	De 5471
61825-A	Aura Lee -3	De 5533
61826-A	Givin' Everything Away -1, 3	De 5367
61827-A	Cinda Lou -3	De 5409
61828-A	New Cinda Lou -3	De 5456

Decca 5353 as by **Shelton Brothers**.
Rev. Decca FM5139 by The Carter Family.

Acc. Lonnie Hall, f-2; Harry Sorensen, ac; Joe Shelton, md-3; Gene Sullivan, g/v-4; Slim Harbert, sb.
Dallas, TX   Thursday, February 18, 1937

61839-A	Deep Elem Blues No. 3 -3	De 5422
61840-A	New Trouble In Mind Blues -2	De 5339
61841-A	That Golden Love (My Mother Gave To Me) -2	De 5468
61842-A	She Was Happy Till She Met You -2	De 5381, DeSA FM5147
61843-A	A Prisoner's Dream -2	De 5381, DeSA FM5147
61844-A	Answer To Prisoner's Dream -2	De 5468
61845-A	Someone To Love You When You're Old -1	De 5440
61846-A	Goodness Gracious Gracie -3	De 5397
61847-A	Nobody But My Baby Is Getting My Love -1, 3	De 5397
61848-A	Uncle Eph's Got The Coon -3, 4	De 5456
61849-A	A Dollar Down And A Dollar A Week -3	De 5339

Decca 5339, 5397 as by **Shelton Brothers**.

Bob Shelton, Joe Shelton, v duet; acc. Harry Sorensen, ac-1; Joe Shelton, md-2; Gene Sullivan, g; Slim Harbert, sb-3.
Dallas, TX   Friday, February 19, 1937

61862-A	Just Because No. 3 -1, 2, 3	De 5367
61863-A	All Night Long	De unissued
61864-A	Alone With My Sorrows	De 5353, DeSA FM5115, BrSA SA1453
61865-A	Go 'Long Mule -1, 2, 3	De 5422

Decca 5353 as by **Shelton Brothers**.
Revs: Decca FM5115, Brunswick SA1453 by Frank Luther.

Bob Shelton, Joe Shelton, v duet; or Joe Shelton, v-1; acc. Lonnie Hall, f; Harry Sorensen, ac; Joe Shelton, md-2; Howard Oliver, tbj; Gene Sullivan, g; Slim Harbert, sb.
Dallas, TX   Sunday, December 12, 1937

63022-A	When You Think A Whole Lot About Someone	De 5508
63023-A	Who Calls You Sweet Mama Now -1	De 5519
63024-A	I Told Them All About You -2	De 5484
63025-A	As Long As I Have You -2	De 5519
63026-A	Blue Kimono Blues	De 5475
63027-A	I'm Gonna Let The Bumble Bee Be -2	De 5545
63028-A	Eight More Years To Go -2	De 5496
63029-A	My Gal Is Mean -1	De 5475
63040-A	Seven Years (With The Wrong Woman) -2	De 5484, 46050

63041-A	Take Me Back To Renfro Valley -2	De 5545
63042-A	You're Standing On The Outside Now	De 5568
63043-A	The Old Mill's Tumbling Down	De 5585
63044-A	The Pig Got Up And Slowly Walked Away	De rejected
63045-A	No Foolin' -2	De 5568
63046-A	Down On The Farm (They All Ask For You)	De 5533
63047-A	If You Want Me You Got To Run Me Down	De rejected
63048-A	By The Stump Of The Old Pine Tree -2	De 5496
63049-A	Far Over The Hill	De 5585
63050-A	Jealous -1	De 5508

Matrices 63030 to 63039 are by Leon's Lone Star Cowboys (see Leon Chappelear).

Acc. Felton "Preacher" Harkness, f; Joe Shelton, emd; Howard Oliver, tbj; Merle Shelton, g; Slim Harbert, sb.
San Antonio, TX   Sunday, September 18, 1938

64534-A	You Can't Put That Monkey On My Back	De 5609
64535-A	Thankful And Thankful Again	De 5609
64536-A	On The Owl-Hoot Trail -1	De 5630
64537-A	She's Somebody's Darling Once More	De 5630
64538-A	Knot Hole Blues -1	De 5653
64539-A	Meet Me Somewhere In Your Dreams	De 5653
64540-A	Those Dusty Roads	De 5717
64541-A-1	Let A Smile Be Your Umbrella On A Rainy Day	De 5606

San Antonio, TX   Monday, September 19, 1938

64542-A	Wednesday Night Waltz	De 5621, 46050
64543-A	Someday Baby -1	De 5645
64544-A	My Own Sweet Darling Wife	De 5723
64545-A	Ace In The Hole	De 5661, 46095
64546-A	Lita -1	De 5621
64547-A	I'm Savin' Saturday Night For You	De 5661
64548-A	My Girl Friend Doesn't Like Me Anymore	De 5645
64549-A	Mandy	De 5669
64550-A	She Gave It All Away -1	De 5678, MeC 45309, Min M-14113
64551-A	Lost Woman	De 5606

Bob Shelton, Joe Shelton, v duet; acc. Cliff Bruner, f-1; Bob Dunn, esg; Leo Raley, emd; prob. Dickie McBride, g; Hezzie Bryant, sb.
Houston, TX   Saturday, March 4, 1939

65130-A	You Can't Put That Monkey On My Back No. 2 -1	De 5665
65131-A	Just Because You're In Deep Elem -1	De 5665
65132-A	That's No Way To Treat The Man You Love -1	De 5678
65133-A	She's My Gal (Right Or Wrong) -1	De 5700
65134-A	I Just Don't Care Anymore	De 5669
65135-A	Bye Bye Baby Bye Bye -1	De 5706
65136-A	(Aye Aye) On Mexico's Beautiful Shore -1	De 5709, MeC 45323, Min M-14113
65137-A	That's Why I'm Jealous Of You -1	De 5706

Bob Shelton, Joe Shelton, v duet; or Joe Shelton, v-1; acc. Cliff Bruner, f-2; Bob Dunn, esg; Leo Raley, emd; prob. Dickie McBride, g; Hezzie Bryant, sb.
Houston, TX   Sunday, March 5, 1939

65146-B	The Pretty Little Girl With A Smile	De 5700
65147-A	Hallelujah I'm Gonna Be Free Again -2	De 5717
65148-A	You Can't Fool A Fool All The Time -2	De 5723
65149-A	You Gotta Quit Cheatin' On Me -1, 2	De 5709
65150-A	How Times Have Changed -2	De 5690
65151-A	You Can't Do That To Me -2	De 5690

Acc. Cliff Bruner, f; Bob Dunn, esg; Leo Raley, emd; prob. Dickie McBride, g; Hezzie Bryant, sb.
Houston, TX   Sunday, September 3, 1939

66380-A,-A-1	Lay Your Hand In Mine	De 5755
66381-A	Old Age Pension Blues -1	De 5811
66382-A	My Grandfather's Clock	De 5739
66383-A	Don't Leave Me All Alone	De 5795

Decca 5795, 5811 as by **Shelton Brothers**.

Houston, TX   Monday, September 4, 1939

66384-A	Dig Me A Grave In Missouri	De 5739
66385-A	Silver Dollar	De unissued
66386-A	Shoutin' In The Amen Corner (A Rhythmic Sermon) -1	De 5760

66387-A	Ain't No Use To Worry Anymore	De 5811
66388-A	I Wish It Wasn't So	De 5795
66389-A	Parking Meter Blues -1	De 5755
66390-B	If You Don't Like My Peaches (Leave My Tree Alone)	De 5787
66391-A	You Can't Get Love (Where There Ain't No Love)	De 5776
66392-A	No Matter What They Say -1	De 5760
66393-B	Don't Take My Darling Away	De 5787
66394-A	I Have My Bed	De 5776

Decca 5795, 5811 as by **Shelton Brothers**.

Shelton Brothers (Bob & Joe), v duet; or Joe Shelton, v-1; acc. Jimmy Thomason, f; Billy McNew, esg; Joe Shelton, emd; Merle Shelton, g; Slim Harbert, sb.

Houston, TX   Saturday, April 6, 1940

92023-A	You Can't Get Me Back When I'm Gone	De 5826
92024-A	Doggone Crazy Blues -1	De 5844
92025-A	Coo See Coo	De 5833, MeC 45356
92026-A	I'll Be Seein' You In Dallas, Alice -1	De 5844
92027-A	Tell Me With Your Blue Eyes	De 5855, DeAu X1926, DeSA FM51??, MeC 45367
92028-A	Somebody Stole My Little Darling -1	De 5855, DeAu X1926, DeSA FM51??, MeC 45367
92029-A	It's Hard To Love And Not Be Loved	De 5865, MeC 45376
92036-A	I'm A Handy Man To Have Around	De 5833, MeC 45356

Matrices 92030 to 92035 are by the Rice Brothers Gang.

Acc. Jimmy Thomason, f; Billy McNew, esg; Joe Shelton, emd; Merle Shelton, g; Slim Harbert, sb; band v-2.

Houston, TX   Sunday, April 7, 1940

92037-A	What's The Matter With Deep Elem -1, 2	De 5898
92038-A	There'll Always Be A Maple On The Hill	De 5826
92039-A	It's A Weary World Without My Blue Eyes -1	De 5865, DeAu X2198, MeC 45376
92040-A	Henpecked Husband Blues	De 5898
92041-A	Beautiful Brown Eyes	De 6079, MeC 45551

Decca 5898 as by **Shelton Bros. (Bob & Joe)**.
Rev. Decca X2198 by Ernest Tubb.

Acc. Jimmy Thomason, f; Billy McNew, esg; Joe Shelton, emd; Bruce Pierce, tbj; Merle Shelton, g; Slim Harbert, sb; band v-2.

Dallas, TX   Friday, April 25, 1941

93659-A	Ida Red -2	De 5946, 46009, MeC 45439
93660-A	Rompin' And Stompin' Around	De 5964
93661-A	Who's Gonna Cut My Baby's Kindling -1, 2	De 5964
93662-A	Love Me Easy (Or Leave Me Alone)	De 5975
93663-A	I'll Never Get Drunk Anymore	De 6021
93664-A	Choo Choo Blues	De 6071, 46095
93665-A	I'm Driftin' And Shiftin' My Gears -1	De 6047
93666-A	I Just Can't Go -1, 2	De 5996, MeC 45475
93667-A	Weary	De 6021

Dallas, TX   Saturday, April 26, 1941

93668-A	I Just Dropped In To Say Goodbye -1	De 6071
93669-A	When It Rains It Really Pours	De 6047
93670-A	South -1	De 5946, 46009, MeC 45439
93671-A	Sittin' On Your Doorstep -1	De 5996, MeC 45475
93672-A	Old Fashioned Locket -1	De 5975

See also the Lone Star Cowboys. The Shelton Brothers' band also recorded as The Sunshine Boys. The Shelton Brothers recorded after 1942.

BILL SHEPARD

See Bill Shepherd.

BILL SHEPHERD

Bill Shepherd, f; Hayes Shepherd, bj; Herb Shepherd, bj; Ed Webb, g; unidentified, v.

Richmond, IN   Friday, January 29, 1932

18343	Bound Steel Blues	Ch S-16383
18344	Aunt Jane Blues	Ch S-16383
18345	Turtle Dove	Ge rejected
18346	Little Red Pink	Ge rejected

18347	Ramblin' Boy	Ge rejected
18348	Coon Jine My Lover	Ge unissued
18349	Queen Sallie	Ge rejected
18350	Going Back On Board Again	Ge unissued
18351	I Wonder Where My Father Is Gone	Ge unissued
18352	I'm Alone In This World	Ge rejected

Champion S-16383 as by **Bill Shepard**.
Hayes Shepherd is believed to have played banjo on one (unidentified) side of Champion S-16383, and Herb Shepherd banjo on the other.
See also Hayes Shepherd.

HAYES SHEPHERD

Hays Shepherd, v; acc. own bj.
Richmond, IN   Saturday, October 5, 1929

| 15749,-A | Mine Own Time Troubles | Ge rejected |

The Appalachia Vagabond, v; acc. own bj.
Knoxville, TN   Friday, March 28, 1930

| K-8035 | Hard For To Love | Vo 5450 |
| K-8036 | Peddler And His Wife | Vo 5450 |

See also Bill Shepherd.

BOB SHERMAN
SHERMAN & LEE

Pseudonyms on Clarion and Velvet Tone for Bob Miller groups.

SHINING LIGHT SACRED DUET

The item thus credited in the Okeh Old Time series (45282) is beyond the scope of this work.

UNCLE JOE SHIPPEE

Uncle Joe Shippee, f; acc. unknown (poss. his daughter), p.
New York, NY   c. January 1926

106559-1	(1) Irish Washerwoman (2) Turkey In The Straw (3) Arkansas Traveler	PA 21163, Pe 11236, Ro 916
106560-1	(1) Miss McCloud's Reel (2) Peel Her Jacket (3) Pig Town Fling	PA 21163, Pe 11236
106561-2	(1) Oh Susanna (2) My Grandmother Lives On Yonder Green (3) Johnny Get Your Gun	PA 21164, Pe 11237, Ro 916
106562-2	(1) Irish Washerwoman (2) White Cockade (3) Marching Thro' Georgia (4) Virginia Reel	PA 21164, Pe 11237

EARL SHIRKEY & ROY HARPER

Roy Harper is a pseudonym for Roy Harvey.

Roy Harvey, v/sp-1; **Earl Shirkey**, y/sp-1; acc. Roy Harvey, g.
Johnson City, TN   Thursday, October 18, 1928

147226-2	Steamboat Man	Co 15326-D
147227-1	When The Roses Bloom For The Bootlegger -1	Co 15326-D
147228-1	Poor Little Joe	Co 15376-D, CoSA DE506
147229-2	We Parted At The Gate	Co 15376-D

Rev. Columbia DE506 by the Red Mountain Trio.

Roy Harper & Earl Shirkey: Roy Harvey, v/sp-1; Earl Shirkey, v-2/y/sp-1; acc. Roy Harvey, g.
New York, NY   Tuesday, March 26, 1929

148130-2	The Yodeling Mule -1, 2	Co 15406-D, Ve 2490-V, Cl 5430-C
148132-	When I'm Gone	Co unissued
148133-	My Mother And My Sweetheart	Co unissued
148134-1	The Cowboy's Lullaby -2	Co 15467-D, RZAu G22059
148135-2	The Bootlegger's Dream Of Home -1	Co 15429-D
148136-1	The Railroad Blues -1	Co 15406-D, Ve 2363-V, 2490-V, Cl 5430-C
148137-2	Keep Bachelor's Hall	Co 15429-D

Velvet Tone 2363-V as by **Rip Hurley & Bob**; 2490-V, Clarion 5430-C as by **Joe Fletcher & Arthur Higgins**.
Matrix 148131 is by Guy Lombardo (popular).
Rev. Velvet Tone 2363-V by Earl & Bell (popular).

Earl Shirkey, y; acc. Roy Harvey, g.
New York, NY   Tuesday, March 26, 1929

| 148138-2 | Kitty Waltz Yodel | Co 15467-D, ReE MR20, RZAu G22059 |

Regal MR20 as by **Alabama Barnstormers**.
Rev. Regal MR20 (with same credit) by Gid Tanner & His Skillet-Lickers.

Earl Shirkey & Roy Harper: Earl Shirkey, v-1/y; Roy Harvey, v-2; acc. prob. Lonnie Austin, f-3; Roy Harvey, g.
    Johnson City, TN   Tuesday, October 22, 1929

149226-1	The Virginian Strike Of '23 -2	Co 15535-D
149227-2	The Policeman's Little Child -2	Co 15642-D
149228-2	My Yodeling Sweetheart -1, 3	Co 15490-D, Ve 2491-V, Cl 5431-C
149229-1	I'm Longing To Belong To Someone -1, 3	Co 15490-D
149230-2	We Have Moonshine In The West Virginia Hills -2	Co 15642-D
149231-2	A Hobo's Pal -2	Co 15535-D

Velvet Tone 2491-V, Clarion 5431-C as by **Joe Fletcher & Arthur Higgins**.
Revs: Velvet Tone 2491-V, Clarion 5431-C by Elzie Floyd & Leo Boswell.

Prob.: Roy Harvey, v; Earl Shirkey, y; acc. Roy Harvey, g.
    Atlanta, GA   Tuesday, April 22, 1930

150341- ; 194936-	Down The Trail To Home Sweet Home	Co unissued
150342- ; 194937-	The Pal That I Love	Co unissued
150344-	Peggy O'Neil	Co unissued
150345-	When I Lost You	Co unissued
150352- ; 194935-	Learning Macfayden To Dance	Co unissued
150353-	Eileen	Co unissued

Matrix 150343 is by Bob Nichols & Hugh Cross (see Clayton McMichen or Hugh Cross); matrices 150346 to 150349 are by the Progressive Four (see *B&GR*); matrices 150350/51 are by Lowe Stokes.

CHESLEY SHIRLEY (THE TEXAS RAMBLER)

Chesley Shirley, v; or Chesley Shirley, h-1; acc. own g.
    Richmond, IN   Wednesday, September 26, 1934

19704	Engine 143	Ge unissued
19705	Only Flirting	Ch 16826, 45075
19706	Make Me A Bed On The Floor -1	Ge unissued
19707	Peek-A-Boo Waltz -1	Ge unissued
19708	Medley: Washington & Lee Swing; My Little Girl; Dixie; Tipperary -1	Ge unissued
19709	My Carolina Girl -1	Ge unissued
19710	The Last Great Round-Up	Ch 16826, 45075

MR. & MRS. W.M. SHIVELY

Vocal duet; acc. unknown, p.
    Richmond, IN   Thursday, September 10, 1931

18006	Nearer My God To Thee	Ch 16604
18007	Sitting At The Feet Of Jesus	Ch 16604
18008	Rock Of Ages	Ge unissued

BILL SHORES & MELVIN DUPREE
SHORES SOUTHERN TRIO

Shores Southern Trio: Bill Shores, f; Frank Locklear, md; Melvin Dupree, g.
    Richmond, IN   Tuesday, April 2, 1929

14994	Wedding Bells Waltz	Ge rejected
14995	Goin' Crazy	Ge 6927, Ch 15768, 45159, MeC 45159
14996	Down Yonder	Ge 6927, Ch 15729
14997	Alabama Jubilee	Ge rejected
14998-A	Back Up And Push	Ge 6842, Ch 15768
14999	Whistling Rufus	Ge 6842, Ch 15729, 45159, MeC 45159
15000	My Blue Ridge Girl	Ge rejected

Champion 15729, 15768, 45159, Melotone 45159 as by **The Augusta Trio**.

Bill Shores & Melvin Dupree: Bill Shores, f; Melvin Dupree, g.
    Atlanta, GA   Wednesday, October 30, 1929

| 149306-2 | Wedding Bells | Co 15506-D |
| 149307-1 | West Texas Breakdown | Co 15506-D |

Bill Shores also recorded with Dupree's Rome Boys and Riley Puckett.

SHORT BROTHERS

Unidentified, v solo/wh duet; acc. prob. own g duet.
   Memphis, TN   Friday, February 24, 1928

400327-	Listen To The Mocking Bird	OK unissued
400328-B	Whistling Coon	OK 45206, PaAu A2553
400329-B	Whistling Rufus	OK 45206, PaAu A2553
400330-	Peek-A-Boo Waltz	OK unissued

SHORT CREEK TRIO

Olen Mayes, f/v; Reuben Burns, bj/v; Charlie Ross, g/v.
   Birmingham, AL   c. July 11-13, 1927

GEX-708-A	Hand Me Down My Walking Cane	Ge 6272, Chg 325, 398
GEX-709,-A	Shoo Fly	Ge rejected

Challenge 325, 398 as by **Logan County Trio**.
Revs: Gennett 6272 by Wyzee Hamilton; Challenge 325 by Welby Toomey, 398 by Ernest V. Stoneman.

Ruben Burns & The Short Creek Trio: Reuben Burns, v; or Reuben Burns, Olen Mayes, Charlie Ross, v trio-1; acc. Olen Mayes, f; Reuben Burns, bj; Charlie Ross, g.
   Birmingham, AL   c. July 30, 1927

GEX-755-A	The Burglar Man	Ge 6222, Ch 15376, Chg 336
GEX-756-A	Nobody's Business	Ge 6222
GEX-757,-A,-B	Only Two More Weeks To Stay Here -1	Ge rejected
GEX-758,-A	Naomi Wise	Ge rejected

Champion 15376 as by **Ruben Burns**. Challenge 336 as by **Henry Decker**.
Revs: Champion 15376, Challenge 336 by Wyzee Hamilton.

Cliff Click & The Short Creek Trio: Cliff Click, f/v/v eff; Olen Mayes, f; Reuben Burns, bj; Charlie Ross, g; unidentified, sp.
   Birmingham, AL   c. August 17, 1927

GEX-815-A	The Buckin' Mule	Ge 6364, Sil 5083, 8177, Spt 9175, Chg 302, Her 75568, Bell 1188
GEX-816,-A	Old Joe Clark	Ge rejected

Silvertone 5083, 8177, Supertone 9175 as by **Cliff Click & Logan County Trio**. Challenge 302 as by **The Logan County Trio**. Bell 1188 as by **Henry County Trio**.
Revs: Silvertone 5083, 8177 by Ben Jarrell (see Da Costa Woltz); Supertone 9175 by Frank Jenkins (see Da Costa Woltz); Challenge 302 by Marion Underwood (see Taylor's Kentucky Boys); Bell 1188 by Doc Roberts.

Ruben Burns & The Short Creek Trio: Reuben Burns, v; acc. Olen Mayes, f; Reuben Burns, bj; Charlie Ross, g.
   Birmingham, AL   c. August 17, 1927

GEX-817-A	Huntin' Me A Home	Her 75575

Rev. Herwin 75575 by The Eva Quartette.

Short Creek Trio: Cliff Click, f/v/v eff; Olen Mayes, f; Reuben Burns, bj; Charlie Ross, g; unidentified, sp.
   Birmingham, AL   c. August 17, 1927

GEX-818-X	The Old Hen Cackled And The Rooster Crowed	Ge 6364, Sil 8178, Spt 9176, Her 75568

Silvertone 8178, Supertone 9176 as by **Logan County Trio**.
Matrix GEX-818 is titled *The Old Hen Cackled, The Rooster Crowed* on Supertone 9176.
Revs: Silvertone 8178, Supertone 9176 by Doc Roberts.

LOREN H. SHORTRIDGE

Loren H. Shortridge, v; acc. poss. own g.
   Richmond, IN   Thursday, October 3, 1929

15730	Old Pals	Ge rejected trial recording

THE SHOW BOAT BOYS

Vocal quartet; unacc.
   Richmond, IN   Saturday, June 28, 1930

16799	Old Time Melodies Part II	Ge 7270, Ch 16077
16800	Old Time Melodies Part I	Ge 7270, Ch 16077
16801	On A Blue And Moonless Night	Ge rejected

FLOYD SHREVE

Floyd Shreve, v; acc. The Three Aces: Leo Soileau, f; own g; Bill (Dewey) Landry, g; Tony Gonzales, d.
   New Orleans, LA   Friday, January 18, 1935

87608-1	Lonesome Blues	BB B-5960

Leo Soileau, f; Floyd Shreve, g; Bill (Dewey) Landry, g; Tony Gonzales, d.
  New Orleans, LA   Friday, January 18, 1935
    87609-1   Darling Of Yesterday   BB B-5960

Floyd Shreve, v; acc. own g.
  Chicago, IL   Saturday, May 4, 1935
    C-9992-A   Louisiana Sweetheart   De 5156
    C-9993-A   Georgia Blues   De 5156
Floyd Shreve recorded with the Hackberry Ramblers and Leo Soileau.

SHRINE MALE QUARTET OF MEMPHIS

Hugh Sandidge, tv; Charles Clark, tv; Walter Moore, bv; William Newton, bsv; acc. Herbert Rohloff, p.
  Memphis, TN   Saturday, September 22, 1928
    47082-1,-2   The Riches Of Love   Vi unissued
    47083-1,-2   The Wayside Cross   Vi unissued

REV. H.L. SHUMWAY

Rev. H.L. Shumway, v; acc. prob. own h/g.
  Richmond, IN   Wednesday, March 12, 1930
    16379   Will The Circle Be Unbroken   Ge rejected
    16380   C&O Freight And Section Crew Wreck   Ge rejected

CONNIE SIDES

Connie Sides, v; acc. Ernest Thompson, h/g.
  New York, NY   Wednesday, September 10, 1924
    81994-2   Underneath The Southern Moon   Co 15009-D, Ha 5135-H
    81995-1   You're As Welcome As The Flowers In May   Co 15008-D, Ha 5134-H
    81996-1   In The Shadow Of The Pine   Co 15009-D, Ha 5135-H
    81997-   Where The River Shannon Flows   Co unissued
Harmony 5134-H, 5135-H as by **Nellie Johnson**.

  New York, NY   Thursday, September 11, 1924
    81998-   Mammy's Little Coal Black Rose   Co unissued
    81999-1   They Made It Twice As Nice As Paradise   Co 15008-D, Ha 5134-H
Harmony 5134-H as by **Nellie Johnson**.
For duets with Ernest Thompson see the latter.

MOSE SIGLER

Mose Sigler, v; acc. unknown, f-1; poss. own g; unknown, u-2.
  Birmingham, AL   c. August 17, 1927
    GEX-831,-A   I Start Going Home At Eleven O'Clock (And Never   Ge rejected
                          Get Home Till One) -1
    GEX-856   I Hope You Don't Feel Hurt -2   Ge 6237, Ch 15350
Intervening matrices are by other artists.
Revs: Gennett 6237, Champion 15350 by Les Backer (popular).
See also Jimmy Yates Groups.

SIMERLY TRIO

George Simerly, two unknowns, v/y-1 trio; acc. prob. own g duet or trio.
  Birmingham, AL   Tuesday, March 30, 1937
    B-53-   Daddy My Pal   ARC unissued
    B-54-3   Going Back To Dixie   ARC 7-06-61
    B-55-   That Little Bit Of Company   ARC unissued
    B-56-5   Ridin' Down The Trail -1   ARC 7-06-61
    B-57-   The Things We Used To Do   ARC unissued
    B-58-   Open Up Them Pearly Gates   ARC unissued

BILL SIMMONS

Bill Simmons, v/y; acc. own g.
  Culver City, CA   Tuesday, March 4, 1930
    54655-1   The Yodeling Cowboy   Vi unissued
Bill Simmons, v/y-1; acc. own g.
  Culver City, CA   Wednesday, March 5, 1930

54655-2	The Yodeling Cowboy -1	Vi unissued
54662-1,-2	The Night Herder	Vi unissued
54663-2	Take Me Back To Old Montana -1	Vi V-40256

Culver City, CA   Thursday, March 6, 1930

| 54674-2 | Wild Roses -1 | Vi V-40256 |

Bill Simmons & His Orchestra: Bill Simmons, v/y-1; acc. unknown, f; Chuck Darling, h; unknown, ac; poss. own g.

Hollywood, CA   Thursday, October 16, 1930

61035-2	The Cowboy's Plea -1	Vi 23533
61036-2	Rocky Mountain Sweetheart	Vi V-40329, MW M-4084, ZoSA 4329
61037-1	My Sweetheart Of Yesterday	Vi V-40329

Victor V-40329 as by **Bill Simmons**. Montgomery Ward M-4084 as by **Tivoli Novelty Orchestra**.
Revs: Montgomery Ward M-4084 by Buster & Jack (see Jack Cawley's Oklahoma Ridge Runners); Zonophone 4329 by Grayson & Whitter.

Bill Simmons & His California Cowboys: Bill Simmons, v; acc. unknown, f; Chuck Darling, h; unknown, ac; poss. own g.

Hollywood, CA   Friday, October 17, 1930

| 61040-2 | My California Home | Vi 23603 |

Bill Simmons, v/y; acc. own g.

Hollywood, CA   Friday, October 17, 1930

| 61041-1 | Rocky Mountain Blues | Vi 23603, Zo 6011, RZ T6011 |
| 61042-1 | The Lonesome Cowboy | Vi 23533 |

Victor 23533 as by **Bill Simmons & His Orchestra**.
Revs: Zonophone 6011, Regal-Zonophone T6011 by Jimmie Rodgers.

Bill Simmons, v; acc. own g.

Los Angeles, CA   Saturday, December 28, 1935

| DLA-289-A | Red Skin Lady | De unissued |
| DLA-290-A | Ozark Mountain Moon | De unissued |

MATT SIMMONS & FRANK MILLER

C.M. "Matt" Simmons, Frank Miller, v duet; acc. Posey Rorer, md; Matt Simmons, g.

Winston-Salem, NC   Thursday, September 22, 1927

81373-	There'll Be No Graveyard There	OK unissued
81374-	That Heavenly Home	OK unissued
81375-	That Old Fashioned Cabin	OK rejected
81376-B	Childhood's Sweet Home	OK 45148
81377-	We'll Never Say Goodbye	OK unissued
81378-A	That Little Old Hut	OK 45148

See also Posey Rorer & The North Carolina Ramblers.

SIMMONS SACRED SINGERS

Vocal quartet; acc. unknown, o.

Winston-Salem, NC   Saturday, September 24, 1927

81397-A	Sleep On Departed Ones	OK 45193
81398-A	Why Don't You?	OK 45238
81399-A	Mother, Oft I Think Of Thee	OK 45238
81600-A	Bloom Brightly, Sweet Roses	OK 45160
81601-A	Death Is Only A Dream	OK 45160
81602-A	Hold To God's Unchanging Hand	OK 45193

Acc. unknown, p.

New York, NY   Tuesday, November 20, 1928

401354-B	Lost	OK 45284
401355-	Precious Memories	OK 45299
401356-B	Swinging 'Neath The Old Oak Trees	OK 45310
401357-A	Work, Sing, Pray	OK 45310
401358-B	The Tree Of Life	OK 45284
401359-	When Jesus Comes	OK 45299

SIMMONS UNIVERSITY BAND

One coupling by this band was issued in the Victor Old Familiar Tunes series (V-40168). The group was originally logged as **Cowboy Band Inc.**, and the same coupling also issued on Bluebird as by **Bluebird Military Band**. It is outside the scope of this work.

JOSH SIMPKINS & HIS RUBE BAND

Pseudonym on Champion for Ezra Buzzington's Rustic Revelers.

OLIVER SIMS

Oliver Sims, h solo.
    Atlanta, GA   Saturday, April 24, 1926

142128-1,-2	Hop About Ladies	Co 15103-D
142129-2	Lost John	Co 15103-D

THE SINGING PREACHERS

Clyde D. King, Gilbert Newland, v duet; acc. unknown, p.
    Chicago, IL   c. March 14, 1928

13546	My Wonderful Dream	Ge 6451

Acc. Reg Peel, p.
    Chicago, IL   c. March 23, 1928

13594	In The Garden	Ge 6451, Ch 15568, 45113, MeC 45113
13595	Memories Of Mother	Ge rejected

Champion 15568, 45113, Melotone 45113 as by **Brandon & Wells**.

Clyde D. King, Gilbert Newland, two unknowns, v quartet; unacc.
    Chicago, IL   c. March 23, 1928

13600	Can The World See Jesus In You	Ge 6432, Ch 15527
13601	The Church In The Wildwood	Ge 6977, Ch 15568, 45113, MeC 45113
13602-A	Since Jesus Came Into My Heart	Ge 6977, Ch 15527
13603	If Your Heart Keeps Right	Ge 6432

Champion 15527, 15568, 45113, Melotone 45113 as by **The Gospel Four**.
Matrix 13596 is by Rev. Clyde D. King; matrices 13597 to 13599 are unrelated.

Rev. Clyde D. King recorded in his own name.

THE SINGING SWEETHEARTS

Records by this group on Champion and Superior (under the pseudonym, on the latter label, of **Blake & Milton**) are believed to be outside the scope of this work.

ALLEN SISSON (CHAMPION FIDDLER OF TENNESSEE)

Allen Sisson, f; acc. John F. Burckhardt, p.
    New York, NY   Wednesday, February 25, 1925

10219-A,-B,-C	Walking Water	Ed 51559, 4981
10220-A	Kentucky Waggoners	Ed 51720, 5166
10221-A,-B	Rocky Road To Dublin	Ed 51559, 5024

    New York, NY   Thursday, February 26, 1925

10224-A,-C	Grey Eagle	Ed 51720
10225-A,-B	Katy Hill	Ed 51690
10226-	Kaiser's Defeat	Ed unissued
10227-	Sally Brown	Ed unissued
10228-A,-B,-C	Cumberland Gap	Ed 51690, 5149
10229-A,-B	Farewell Ducktown	Ed 51522
10230-A	Rymer's Favorite	Ed 51522

ASHER SIZEMORE & LITTLE JIMMIE

Asher Sizemore (The Kentucky Mountaineer), v; acc own g.
    Richmond, IN   Thursday, December 31, 1931

18291	Twenty One Years	Ge unissued
18292	They Say It Is Sinful To Flirt	Ge unissued
18293	Pass The Drunkard By	Ge unissued
18294	The Girl I Loved In Sunny Tennessee	Ge unissued

Asher Sizemore & Little Jimmie, v duet; or **Asher Sizemore**, v-1; or **Little Jimmie Sizemore**, v-2; acc. Asher Sizemore, g/sp-3.
    San Antonio, TX   Monday, April 2, 1934

82750-1	Little Jimmie's Goodbye To Jimmie Rodgers -2	BB B-5445, RZ MR2145, RZAu G22467, Twin FT8106
82751-1	Little Cowboy Jim -2, 3	BB B-5495
82752-1	That Tumbled Down Cabin -1	BB B-5717
82753-1	How Beautiful Heaven Must Be	BB B-5568

82754-1	Free From The Walls Of Grey (Twenty-One Years Is Some Debt To Pay) -1	BB B-5774
82755-1	Memories Of Kentucky -1	BB B-5774, Twin FT1863
82756-1	My West Virginia Home -1	BB B-5717
82757-1	I Miss My Dear Sweet Mother	BB B-5445, RZ MR2145, RZAu G22467, Twin FT8106
82758-1	Shake Hands With Mother Again	BB B-5568
82759-1	1. Chawin' Chewin' Gum. 2. My Little Rooster -2, 3	BB B-5495
82760-1	I Dreamed I Searched Heaven For You -1	BB B-6021, RZAu G22655
82761-1	The Forgotten Soldier Boy -1	BB B-6021, RZAu G22655

Rev. Twin FT1863 by Jimmie Davis.

Asher Sizemore & Little Jimmie recorded after 1942.

THORSTEIN SKARNING & HIS OLD TIME ORCHESTRA

This group, which had one release in the Brunswick old-time series (477), is outside the scope of this work.

BUD SKIDMORE

Pseudonym on Columbia for a Bob Miller group.

BOB SKILES FOUR OLD TUNERS [or TIMERS]

Bob Skiles Four Old Tuners-1/Bob Skiles Four Old Timers-2: Bob Skiles, f; Mrs. Skiles, p; poss. Jack or Dude Skiles, bj; unknown, bbs.
    San Antonio, TX   Tuesday, March 13, 1928

400497-A	Wagner -2	OK 45243
400498-A	Varsovienne -2	OK 45243
400499-B	Uncle Bob's Favorite -1	OK 45225
400500-B	Medley – Scottische [sic] -1	OK 45211, PaE E6038
400501-B	Rye Waltz -1	OK 45211, PaE E6038
400502-B	Casey Jones -1	OK 45225

Parlophone E6038 as by **Bob Style's Old Time Dance Band**. Matrix 400500 is titled *Medley – Schottische* on that issue. Mrs. Skiles was Bob Skiles' mother; Jack and Dude were his sons.

Jack and Dude Skiles later recorded for Variety with Dude Skiles & His Vine Street Boys (see JR).
There is no connection between this family and the artist known as Bob Skyles.

FLOYD SKILLERN "THE MOUNTAIN TROUBADOUR"

Floyd Skillern, v; acc. unknown, sg; unknown, g.
    Hot Springs, AR.   Thursday, March 11, 1937

HS-46-1	I'll Remember You Love In My Prayers	ARC 7-07-60
HS-47-	My Old Fashioned Dad	ARC unissued
HS-48-1	When We Carved Our Hearts On The Old Oak Tree	ARC 7-07-60
HS-49-	What Is A Home Without Love	ARC unissued

SKYLAND SCOTTY

This artist's real name is Scott Wiseman.

Skyland Scotty, v; acc. own h/g.
    Chicago, IL   Wednesday, December 13, 1933

77341-1	Home Coming Time In Happy Valley	BB B-5357, Sr S-3438, MW M-4478
77342-1	Two Little Frogs	BB B-5906, Twin FT1909
77351-1	Great Granddad	BB B-5357, Sr S-3438, MW M-4478
77352-1	Whippoorwill	BB B-5906

Intervening matrices are by Tom & Don.
Rev. Twin FT1909 by the West Brothers Trio.

    Chicago, IL   Friday, March 23, 1934

CP-1035-3	Home Comin' Time	Cq 8308
CP-1036-2	Aunt Jemima's Plaster	Cq 8308
CP-1037-1	Sweet Kitty Clyde	Cq 8307

Acc. own h/g/wh-1.
    Chicago, IL   Saturday, March 24, 1934

CP-1054-1	The Scolding Wife	Cq 8307
CP-1055-1	They Fit And Fit And Fit	Cq 8309
CP-1056-1	Darby's Ram	Cq 8309
CP-1057-1	Gathering Up The Shells From The Seashore	Cq 8306

CP-1058-1	The Whippoorwill Song -1	Cq 8305
CP-1059-1	Great Grand Dad	Cq 8306
CP-1060-1	Keep A Horse Shoe Hung Over The Door -1	Cq 8305

Scott Wiseman also recorded with his wife Myrtle Cooper Wiseman as Lulu Belle & Scotty (and continued to do so after 1942).

BOB SKYLES & HIS SKYROCKETS

Bob Kendrick ("Bob Skyles"), f/cl/ts/v-1; Sanford Kendrick, t/tb/bazooka/sw/v-2; Robert "Curly" Nichols, eg; Doc Kendrick, g; Sparky Stiles, sb; Clifford Kendrick, d-3/wb-4; band v-5. (This instrumentation is collective: all the instruments listed are not heard on every item.)

San Antonio, TX   Thursday, February 25, 1937

07301-1	The Arkansas Bazooka Swing -1, 3	BB B-6876, MW M-7214
07302-1	The Bazooka Stomp -3	BB B-6876, MW M-7214
07303-1	You Gotta Quit Draggin' Around -1, 3	BB B-6882, MW M-7215
07304-1	You Can't Cool A Good Man Down -1, 3	BB B-6882, MW M-7215
07305-1	She's Built Like A Great Big Fiddle -1, 3	BB B-6978, MW M-7216
07306-1	I Got A Crow To Pick With You -1, 3, 5	BB B-6978, MW M-7216
07307-1	We're Not The Hoosier Hot Shots -1, 4	BB B-7092, MW M-7217
07308-1	Sweet As Sugar Blues -1, 3	BB B-7150, MW M-7218
07309-1	The Blue Street Blues -1, 3	BB B-7150, MW M-7218
07310-1	My Love Song Melody -1, 3	BB B-7060, MW M-7219
07311-1	The Drug Store Cowboy -1, 3, 5	BB B-6923, MW M-7220
07312-1	The Lavender Cowboy -1, 2, 3	BB B-7092, MW M-7217, Twin FT8475
07313-1	I Hear Your Music -1, 3	BB B-6923, MW M-7220
07314-1	The Farmer -1, 3, 5	BB B-7017, MW M-7221
07315-1	The Rhythm King -1, 3	BB B-7017, MW M-7221
07316-1	Porter's Love Song -1, 3, 5	BB B-7060, MW M-7219

Take 3 of matrices 07301 and 07307 may also have been issued.
Rev. Twin FT8475 by Jimmie Revard.

Bob Kendrick, f-1/cl/emd/oc-2/v-3; Sanford Kendrick, t/tb/bazooka/sw/v-4; Dave Hughs, ac/p/v-5; Curly Nichols, g; Doc Kendrick, g; Ted Walls, sb; Clifford Kendrick, d; band v-6. (This instrumentation is collective: all the instruments listed are not heard on every item.)

San Antonio, TX   Tuesday, September 14, 1937

014119-1	Blue Accordion Blues -3	BB B-7219, MW M-7351
014120-1	She's Stopped Giving Everything Away -3	BB B-7219, MW M-7353
014121-1	Love Keeps Me Awake -3	BB B-7410
014122-1	My Arkansas Bazooka Gal -3, 4	BB B-7287, MW M-7352, Twin FT8540
014123-1	Napoleon Bonaparte -3	BB B-7447
014124-1	Let's Play Love -3	BB B-7360
014125-1	Turn Loose And Go To Town -2, 3, 4	BB B-7322, MW M-7353
014126-1	What Did I Do? -5	BB B-7322
014127-1	Hot Tamale Pete -3, 4	BB B-7495
014128-1	New Van Buren Blues -3	BB B-7287, MW M-7352
014129-1	The Fox Trot You Saved For Me -1, 3, 4	BB B-7360
014130-1	'Way Out West Of The Pecos -3, 4	BB B-7381, ViJ A1184
014131-1	I Want That Girl -3, 6	BB B-7410
014132-1	What-Cha Gonna Do When Your Wife Comes Home? -3	BB B-7381, ViJ A1184
014133-1	Too Many Times You're Cheatin' On Me -3	BB B-7447
014134-1	Music Of The South -3	BB B-7495, MW M-7351

Rev. Twin FT8540 by Bill Boyd.

Bob Kendrick, f/cl/ts/cowbells-1/v-2; Sanford Kendrick, t/tb/bazooka/sw/v-3; Dave Hughs, t-4/ac/p/v-5; Curly Nichols, g; Doc Kendrick, g/v-6; Ted Walls, sb; Clifford Kendrick, d; band v-7. (This instrumentation is collective: all the instruments listed are not heard on every item.)

San Antonio, TX   Monday, April 4, 1938

022060-1	Swingin' With The Accordion Man -2	BB B-7546
022061-1	Swingin' In Oklahoma -2	BB B-7714
022062-1	No Fault Of Mine -2, 7	BB B-7625, Twin FT8604
022063-1	Laughing Song -6	BB B-7585
022064-1	Ghost Of The Blues -2	BB B-7764
022065-1	Rubber Dolly -4, 5	BB B-7650
022066-1	My Hill Billy Girl -2, 3	BB B-7714
022067-1	The Hill Billy Fiddler -2	BB B-7909
022068-1	Rodeo Ann -2	BB B-7909
022069-1	The Pal That I Loved -2, 3	BB B-7843
022070-1	Blue Bazooka Blues -2	BB B-7546

022071-1	Mr. Bazooka And Miss Clarinet -2	BB B-7815, RZAu G23690
022072-1	Country Cowbells -1, 2, 3	BB B-7585
022073-1	Slow It Down -2, 4	BB B-7650
022074-1	You're Not The Girl For Me -2	BB B-7764
022075-1	Lookin' For The Girl Of My Dreams -2	BB B-7815, RZAu G23690
022076-1	That's All There Is -2	BB B-7625
022077-1	Honky Tonk Gals -2	BB B-7689
022078-1	You're A Cold Hearted Sweetheart -2	BB B-7689
022079-1	I'm Gonna Die With A Broken Heart -2	BB B-7843

Rev. Twin FT8604 by the Three Tobacco Tags.

Bob Kendrick, f/cl/ts/md/saw-1/v-2; Sanford Kendrick, t/tb/bazooka/sb/sw/v-3; Dave Hughs, t/cl-4/ac/sb; Frank Wilhelm, ac/tu/v-5; Max Bennett, p/v-6/scat v-7; Clifford Kendrick, d; band v-8. (This instrumentation is collective: all the instruments listed are not heard on every item.)

San Antonio, TX   Tuesday, October 25, 1938

028553-1	Swat The Love Bug -5	BB B-7998, [MW M-7914]
028554-1	You've Punched Number Four -2	BB B-7963, [MW M-7913]
028555-1	All Night Long -8	BB B-7963, [MW M-7913]
028556-1	Plenty More Fish In The Sea -4, 5	BB B-8029
028557-1	Slap It, Shake It -2	BB B-7932
028558-1	It's Bad To Be A Good Girl -6	BB B-7932
028559-1	Drinking Blues -2	BB B-8080
028560-1	Shake Up Your Gourd Seeds -8	BB B-8029
028561-1	Waltzing With You -1, 2, 3	BB B-8142
028562-1	You're O.K. -2, 3	BB B-8116
028563-1	I Want To Live In Loveland -2, 3	BB B-8102
028564-1	Drifting And Dreaming -2, 3	BB B-8142
028565-1	The Old Grey Goose -2, 3, 7	BB B-8080
028566-1	Jive And Smile -6, 8	BB B-8116
028567-1	My Darling Texas Cowgirl -3	BB B-7983
028568-1	Swing It Drummer Man -2	BB B-8102
028569-1	Moonlight Waltz -3	BB B-7983
028570-1	Honky Tonk Rag -8	BB B-7998, [MW M-7914]

Bob Kendrick, f/cl/sb; Sanford Kendrick, t/sb; Frank Wilhelm, ac/vb/v-1; Max Bennett, p/v-2; Clifford Kendrick, d; Lou Brown (Mrs. Sanford Kendrick), v-3; band v-4. (This instrumentation is collective: all the instruments listed are not heard on every item.)

Houston, TX   Tuesday, April 9, 1940

92058-A	Eskimo Nell -3	De 5841
92059-A	That's Right I Betcha -2, 4	De 5829
92060-A	You've Been Untrue -2	De 5829
92061-A	Maria Elena -2	De 5851, 46087
92062-A	Only In Dreams -2, 4	De 5887, MeC 45396
92063-A,-B	Pokey Joe	De unissued
92064-A,-B	I Like It Here Where I Am -1, 3	De 5841
92065-A	Don't Call Me Boy -2, 4	De 5851
92066-A	I Ain't Got No Girl -2	De 5887, MeC 45396

Bob Kendrick, f/cl/sb/v-1; Sanford Kendrick, t/sb; Max Bennett, p/solovox/v-2; Bob Hemphill, eg; Clifford Kendrick, d. (This instrumentation is collective: all the instruments listed are not heard on every item.)

Los Angeles, CA   Tuesday, October 28, 1941

DLA-2801-A	Goodbye, Adelita, Goodbye -1	De 6017
DLA-2802-A,-B	I Won't Be Back In A Year Little Darling -2	De unissued
DLA-2803-A	By The River Sainte Marie -2	De 6017
DLA-2804-A	Lovely Veil Of White -2	De 6068
DLA-2805-A	I'm Pretending -2	De 46087
DLA-2806-A,-B	One More Drink And I'll Tell It All -2	De unissued
DLA-2807-A	The Love That Used To Be -1	De 6068
DLA-2808-A,-B	Who's Gonna Play In The Band -1	De unissued

SLIM

Pseudonym on Bluebird for Debs Mays (see Jack Pierce).

SLIM DWIGHT

Pseudonym on Bluebird and Electradisk for Dwight Butcher.

SLIM JIM

Pseudonym on Bluebird for Debs Mays (see Jack Pierce).

SLIM TEX
Pseudonym on Varsity and Continental for Dwight Butcher.

SLOANE & THREADGILL

—— Sloane, —— Threadgill, v duet; acc. prob. one of them, g.
    Dallas, TX   c. October 19, 1928

DAL-692-	Clover Blossoms	Br 284
DAL-693-	Down In The Old Cherry Orchard	Br 284
DAL-694-	When The Harvest Moon Is Shining	Br 299, Spt S2053
DAL-695-	When The Cold, Cold Clay Is Laid Around Me	Br 299

Rev. Supertone S2053 by Frank Luther & Carson Robison (see the latter).

SMALL TOWN PLAYERS

Two unknowns, f-1; unknown, sg-2; unknown, bj-3; two unknowns, g; unknown, bird eff-4; unknown, humming eff-5.
    New York, NY   January/February 1930

3868-B	Arkansas Hoedown -1, 3	GG/Rad 4296, VD 4296, 74296, 84296
3869-B	Plantation Mem'ries -2, 4	GG/Rad 4296, VD 4296, 74296, 84296
163-A; 6047-B	Turkey In The Straw -1, 3, 5	VD 5018, Mad 5018, 50018

Van Dyke 4296 as by **Home Folks**, 74296, 84296 as by **Home Folk Fiddlers**. Van Dyke 5018, Madison 5018, 50018 as by **White City Jazzers**.

Recordings of *Turkey In The Straw* on Grey Gull/Radiex 4068 as by **White City Jazzers** are by a different group outside the scope of this work.

Revs: Van Dyke 5018, Madison 5018, 50018 by Melody Hounds (popular).

LESTER SMALLWOOD

Lester Smallwood, v; acc. own h/bj.
    Atlanta, GA   Thursday, October 18, 1928

47197-3	Cotton Mill Girl	Vi V-40181
47198-2	I'm Satisfied	Vi V-40181
47199-1,-2,-3	Sitting In The Parlor	Vi unissued
47200-1,-2	Goin' Down The Road Feelin' Bad	Vi unissued

ROY SMECK

This prolific studio musician accompanied a number of artists included in this book, among them Gene Autry, Elton Britt, Smiley Burnette, Dwight Butcher, Chezz Chase, Virginia Childs, Vernon Dalhart, Kelly Harrell, Frank Luther, Frank & James McCravy, Frank Marvin, Johnny Marvin, Carson Robison, Ed (Jake) West, and John I. White. He was also a member of The Dizzy Trio and recorded duets with Carson Robison, listed under the latter's name. His own recordings in Hawaiian and other idioms, however, are beyond the scope of this book.

Montgomery Ward 1015, credited to **Roy Smeck Hawaiian Orchestra**, and Varsity 8056, credited to **Roy Smeck Trio**, and one side of Varsity 5137, credited to **Roy Smeck's Trio**, are by Frank Marvin.

SMILING SOUTHERNERS

Unknown, v/y-1; acc. two unknowns, g.
    Richmond, IN   Friday, March 10, 1933

19078	For The Sake Of Days Gone By -1	Ge unissued
19079	Roll Along Kentucky Moon	Ge unissued

In the Gennett files, the name (Lunsford) is written after each title. This may refer to Theodore (Ted) Lunsford, but its implication is unknown.

ARTHUR SMITH

Arthur Smith, f; acc. Alton Delmore, g; Rabon Delmore, tg.
    New Orleans, LA   Tuesday, January 22, 1935

87676-1	Lost Train Blues	BB B-5858
87677-1	Fiddlers' Dream	BB B-5843
87678-1	Spring Street Waltz	BB B-5858, RZAu G22597
87679-1	Smith's Waltz	BB B-5896, RZAu G22500
87680-1	Blackberry Blossom	BB B-5896, RZAu G22500
87681-1	Mocking Bird	BB B-5843, B-2434
87682-1	Doin' The Goofus	BB B-5928, MW M-4906
87683-1	Red Apple Rag	BB B-5928, B-2434, MW M-4906

Bluebird B-2434 as by **Arturo Muniz**. Matrix 87681 is titled *El Sinsonte*, and matrix 87683 *Manzana Roja*, on that issue.
Rev. Regal-Zonophone G22597 by the Ray Brothers.

Arthur Smith Trio: Arthur Smith, f/v-1; Alton Delmore, g/v-2; Rabon Delmore, tg/v-3.

Charlotte, NC   Monday, February 17, 1936

99187-1	Cheatham County Breakdown	BB B-6369
99188-1	Dixon County Blues	BB B-6369
99189-1	There's More Pretty Girls Than One -1, 2, 3	BB B-6322, MW M-4822
99190-1	Sugar Tree Stomp	BB B-6927
99191-1	Chittlin' Cookin' Time In Cheatham County -1	BB B-6322, MW M-4822, Vi 27495
99192-1	Fiddlers Blues	BB B-6442
99203-1	Little Darling They Have Taken You From Me -1	BB B-6514, MW M-4859, Twin FT8245
99204-1	Bonaparte's Retreat	BB B-6387
99205-1	Take Me Back To Tennessee -1, 2, 3	BB B-6514, MW M-4859

Bluebird B-6387 as by **Smoky Mt. Fiddler Trio**.
Intervening matrices are by the Monroe Brothers.
Revs: Bluebird B-6387 (with same credit), B-6442 by the Dixie Ramblers [II]; Victor 27495 by the Dixon Brothers; Twin FT8245 by Bill Boyd.

Charlotte, NC   Wednesday, February 17, 1937

07095-1	Straw Breakdown	BB B-6844
07096-1	Cheatham County Breakdown No. 2	BB B-7351
07097-1	Little Darling -1, 2, 3	BB B-6994, MW M-7157
07098-1	The Girl I Love Don't Pay Me No Mind -1, 2, 3	BB B-6913, MW M-7156
07099-1	There's More Pretty Girls Than One – Part 2 -1, 2, 3	BB B-6869, MW M-7155
07118-1	Dickson County Blues No. 2	BB B7351
07119-1	It's Hard To Please Your Mind -1, 2, 3	BB B-6994, MW M-7157
07120-1	Love Letters -1	BB B-6913, MW M-7155
07121-1	Singing Those House Of David Blues -1	BB B-6927, MW M-7156
07122-1	Walking In My Sleep -1, 2, 3	BB B-7043
07123-1	Never Alone -1, 2, 3	BB B-6869
07124-1	Pig At Home In The Pen -1	BB B-7043
07125-1	Florida Blues	BB B-6844
07126-1	Smith's Breakdown	BB B-7511

Montgomery Ward M-7155, M-7156, M-7157 as by **Delmore Brothers**.
Intervening matrices are untraced.
Matrix 07097 is titled *Kilby Jail* on Montgomery Ward M-7157.

Arthur Smith, f/v-1; Alton Delmore, g/v-2; Rabon Delmore, tg/v-3; unidentified, y-4.

Charlotte, NC   Tuesday, August 3, 1937

011898-1	Beautiful Brown Eyes -1, 2, 3	BB B-7221, MW M-7343
011899-1	Beautiful Memories -1, 2, 3	BB B-7203, MW M-7343
011900-1	Beautiful Mabel Clare -1, 2, 3	BB B-7203, MW M-7344
011901-1	Nellie's Blue Eyes -1, 2, 3	BB B-7325, MW M-7344
011902-1	Lonesome For You -1, 2, 3	BB B-7146, MW M-7345
011903-1	Sweet Heaven -1, 2, 3	BB B-7146, MW M-7345
011904-1	Across The Blue Ridge Mountains -1, 2, 3	BB B-7221, MW M-7346
011905-1	Lonesome Ramblers Blues -1, 4	MW M-7346
011906-1	Indian Creek	BB B-7511, MW M-7602
011907-1	Freight Train Moan	BB B-8158, MW M-7602
011908-1	Goin' To Town	BB B-8101, MW M-7603

Arthur Smith, bj/v; Alton Delmore, g; Rabon Delmore, tg.

Charlotte, NC   Tuesday, August 3, 1937

011909-1	I'm Bound To Ride	BB B-7325

Arthur Smith, f/v-1; Alton Delmore, g/v-2; Rabon Delmore, tg/v-3.

Charlotte, NC   Wednesday, January 26, 1938

018745-1	The Answer To "More Pretty Girls Than One" -1, 2, 3	BB B-7437, MW M-7476
018746-1	Henpecked Husband Blues -1, 2, 3	BB B-7498, MW M-7476
018747-1	Stood On The Bridge At Midnight -1	BB B-7437, MW M-7477
018748-1	More Like His Dad Every Day -1	BB B-7498, MW M-7477
018749-1	Lost Love -1, 2, 3	BB B-7651, MW M-7478
018750-1	A Lonesome Day Today -1	BB B-7547, MW M-7478
018751-1	Her Little Brown Hand -1	BB B-7547, MW M-7479
018752-1	Adieu False Heart -1	BB B-7651, MW M-7479
018753-1	The Paris Waltz	BB B-8158, MW M-7603

Montgomery Ward M-7477, M-7478, M-7479 as by **Delmore Brothers**.

Arthur Smith & His Dixieliners: Arthur Smith, v; acc. own f; Howdy Forrester, f-1; Virgil Atkins, bj-2; Billy Byrd, g; Joe Forrester, sb; band v-3.
   Rock Hill, SC   Tuesday, September 27, 1938

Matrix	Title	Issue
027749-1	I've Had A Big Time Today -3	BB B-7982, MW M-7685
027750-1	The Farmer's Daughter	BB B-7893, MW M-7685
027751-1	Gypsy's Warning	BB B-7893, MW M-7686
027752-1	In The Pines -1	BB B-7943, MW M-7686
027753-1	Why Should I Wonder?	BB B-7943, MW M-7687, RZAu G23719
027754-1	When The Roses Grow Around The Cabin Door -3	BB B-8009, MW M-7687
027755-1	I'm Lonesome, I Guess	BB B-8009, MW M-7688
027756-1	Hesitating Blues	BB B-8101, MW M-7688
027757-1	Girl Of My Dreams -1	MW M-7689
027758-1	Give Me Old-Time Music -2, 3	BB B-7982, MW M-7689

Rev. Regal-Zonophone G23719 by Tom Dickey Show Boys.

Arthur Smith, f/v-1; acc. Tommy Magness, f-2; Clyde Moody, g; Bill Westbrook, sb.
   Atlanta, GA   Monday, October 7, 1940

Matrix	Title	Issue
054526-1	K.C. Stomp -2	BB B-8588, MW M-8890
054527-1	Smith's Rag	BB B-8662, MW M-8891
054528-1	It's A Weary World -1	BB B-8588, MW M-8890
054529-1	The Crazy Blues -1	BB B-8662, MW M-8891
054530-1	That's The Love I Have For You -1	BB B-8688, MW M-8892
054531-1	I Wish I'd Never Learned To Love You -1	BB B-8783, MW M-8893
054532-1	Peacock Rag	BB B-8688, MW M-8892
054533-1	Bill Cheatham	BB B-8783, MW M-8893

Arthur Smith recorded after 1942.

BERNARD [SLIM] SMITH

This artist's full name is Charles Bernard Smith.

Bernard Smith, v/y; acc. **His Dixie Combination**: poss. Benny "King" Nawahi, sg; poss. James Ferraro, g; prob. own g.
   New York, NY   Thursday, October 30, 1930

Matrix	Title	Issue
10189-2,-3	Down Where The Taters Grow	Ba 32094, Je 20036 Or 8036, Pe 12668, Re 10294, Ro 5036
10190-1,-2	My Old Home Town	Ba 32094, Je 20036 Or 8036, Pe 12668, Re 10294, Ro 5036

Bernard Smith, v; acc. unknown.
   New York, NY   Tuesday, November 11, 1930

Matrix	Title	Issue
10243-	Jake Itus Blues	ARC unissued
10244-	Toad Frog And The Elephant	ARC unissued

Bernard Smith, v/y; acc. unknown.
   New York, NY   c. November 17, 1930

Matrix	Title	Issue
GEX-2810,-A	Down Where The Taters Grow	Ge rejected
GEX-2811,-A	My Old Home Town	Ge rejected

   New York, NY   c. November 19, 1930

Matrix	Title	Issue
GEX-2823,-A	Toad Frog And The Elephant	Ge rejected
GEX-2824,-A	Jakeitus Blues	Ge rejected

Slim Smith, v; acc. Benny "King" Nawahi, h/sg; prob. own g.
   New York, NY   Thursday, February 5, 1931

Matrix	Title	Issue
67435-1	Bread Line Blues	Vi 23526
67436-1	Otto Wood, The Bandit	Vi 23526

Bernard Smith, v/y; acc. Benny "King" Nawahi, h/sg/md; James Ferraro, g; poss. own g.
   New York, NY   c. March 1931

Matrix	Title	Issue
1254-6	Down Where The 'Taters Grow	Cr 3118, Htd 22990
1255-4	Bread Line Blues	Cr 3118, Htd 22990

Homestead 22990 was also used for a coupling by Edward L. Crain.

Charles B. Smith, v; acc. Benny Goodman, cl; Benny "King" Nawahi, h/sg/md/g; poss. own g.
   New York, NY   Friday, June 26, 1931

Matrix	Title	Issue
151653-	Wish I Had My First Wife Back	Co unissued
151654-1	My Little A-1 Brownie	Co 15755-D

Rev. Columbia 15755-D by Pelican Wildcats.

Bernard Smith & His Hawaiian Hill Billys: no details.
   New York, NY   Friday, June 17, 1932

Matrix	Title	Issue
152215-	Wish I Had My First Wife Back	Co unissued
152216-	Sweetheart Of Long Ago	Co unissued

BLAINE & CAL SMITH

Blaine Smith, Cal Smith, v duet; acc. Blaine Smith, g; one of them, wh-1; both, wh-2; one of them, humming-3.
   Chicago, IL   Thursday, February 9, 1939

C-2478-1	When A Boy From The Mountains Weds A Girl From The Valley -1	Vo 04855
C-2479-1	The Tie That Binds	Vo 04705
C-2480-1	Golden River -2	Vo/OK 04976
C-2481-1	Won't You Waltz "Home Sweet Home" With Me (For Old Times' Sake) -1	Vo 04855
C-2482-1	An Old Sweet Song (For A Sweet Old Lady) -1, 3	Vo/OK 04976
C-2483-1	Whispering Hope	Vo 04705

Blaine Smith recorded after 1942.

BOB SMITH

Bob Smith, banjolin solo.
   Richmond, IN   Monday, July 7, 1930

16813	Three O'Clock In The Morning; Over The Waves	Ge rejected

CHARLES B. SMITH

See Bernard (Slim) Smith.

CHRISTINE SMITH

Christine Smith, v; acc. unknown.
   Chicago, IL   Friday, November 1, 1935

C-1153-1	Chime Bells	ARC unissued trial recording
C-1154-1	Longing To Hear The Train Whistle Blow	ARC unissued

DILLARD SMITH

Dillard Smith, v; acc. prob. own g.
   Richmond, IN   Friday, May 3, 1929

15086,-A	George Collins	Ge rejected

DR. SMITH'S CHAMPION HOSS HAIR PULLERS

Leeman Bone, tv; Graydon Bone, tv; Roosevelt Garner, tv; Odie Goatcher, bsv; Hubert Simmons, bsv; acc. Bryan Lackey, f-1/prob. bj-2; Clark Duncan, f-3; Ray Marshall, md; Leeman Bone, g-4; Dr. H.H. Smith, ldr.
   Memphis, TN   Wednesday, September 12, 1928

47012-2	Save My Mother's Picture From The Sale -1/3, 4	Vi V-40059
47013-2	Up In Glory -1/3	Vi V-40059
47014-2	Just Give Me The Leavings -1, 3, 4	Vi V-40124
47015-1	In The Garden Where The Irish Potatoes Grow -2, 3, 4	Vi 21711
47016-2	Nigger Baby -1, 3, 4	Vi V-40124
47017-1	Going Down The River -1, 3, 4	Vi 21711

GLAD & WOODY SMITH

Glad Smith, Woody Smith, v duet; acc. prob. one of them, g.
   Chicago, IL   Friday, September 28, 1934

C-9532-A	The Old Church Bell In The Steeple	De unissued
C-9533-A,-B	On Our Golden Wedding Day	De unissued

HANK SMITH

Pseudonym on Vocalion for Al Bernard.

HARRY SMITH

These items are hardly within the scope of this work, but are included for the sake of their titles. Harry Smith may be a pseudonym for the popular singer Irving Kaufman.

Harry Smith, v; acc. Emil Velazco, p-o.
   New York, NY   Wednesday, September 5, 1928

401098-C	You Will Never Miss Your Mother Until She Is Gone	OK 45260, PaAu A2675
401099-C	The Death Of Floyd Collins	OK 45260, PaAu A2675

Parlophone A2675 as by **Emil Velazco**.

J. FRANK SMITH

See Smith's Sacred Singers.

TRAVELIN' JIM SMITH

Pseudonym on Columbia for Carson Robison.

JIMMIE SMITH

Pseudonym on Timely Tunes and Aurora for Gene Autry.

JIMMY SMITH

Jimmy Smith, h; acc. Harry Holden, g.
   New York, NY   Wednesday, March 31, 1926

35254-2	Mountain Blues	Vi 20020
35255-3	Southern Melody Soft Shoe Dance "Old Kentucky Home" – "Old Black Joe" – "Swanee River"	Vi 20020

Acc. Frank Banta, p.
   New York, NY   Monday, July 26, 1926

36001-4	Abie's Irish Blues	Vi V-29056
36002-3	Medley Of Reels	Vi V-29056

This issue is in the Irish series.

Acc. Clarence Gaskill, p.
   New York, NY   Friday, August 20, 1926

36055-1,-2,-3,-4	When Down South Morgan Plays The Old Mouth-Organ	Vi unissued

JOE SMITH

Pseudonym on Champion for Harmon Canada.

JOE SMITH (THE COLORADO COWBOY)

Pseudonym on Bluebird & Regal-Zonophone for Dwight Butcher.

JOSEPHUS SMITH

Pseudonym on Grey Gull and Radiex for Vernon Dalhart.

KID SMITH & [HIS] FAMILY

See Walter Smith.

MARSHALL SMITH [& JOHN MARLOR]

Marshall Smith, v; or **Marshall Smith & John Marlor**-1, v duet; acc. unknown, h; unknown, md; unknown, g.
   Atlanta, GA   Wednesday, April 21, 1926

142070-2	Jonah And The Whale -1	Co 15080-D
142071-2	Home In The Rock	Co 15080-D

MERRITT SMITH

Merritt Smith & Keith Pooser (The Two Larks), v duet; acc. unknown, f-1; unknown, g.
   Atlanta, GA   Monday, March 11, 1929

402275-B	The Old Rugged Cross -1	OK 45326
402276-A	Softly And Tenderly -1	OK 45326
402277-	In A Garden	OK unissued
402278-B	Carolina Moon	OK 45318
402279-	Down Among The Sugar Cane	OK unissued
402280-A	Sleepy Head	OK 45318

Acc. unknown, f; unknown, g; unknown, vc.
   New York, NY   Wednesday, July 10, 1929

402518-	Take The Name Of Jesus With You	OK unissued
402519-	Death Is Only A Dream	OK 45474
402520-	The Beautiful Garden Of Prayer	OK 45474
402521-	Somewhere	OK unissued
402522-A,-B	Memories Of Home	OK 45362
402523-	Good Bye Eliza Jane	OK unissued

OKeh 45474 as by **Smith & Pooser**.

Acc. unknown, g.
   New York, NY   Wednesday, July 10, 1929

402524-A	The Lonesome Road	OK 45362

Merritt Smith, v; acc. prob. own g.
  New York, NY   c. August 18, 1930

GEX-2755-A	She Was Bred In Old Kentucky	Ch 33064
GEX-2756,-A	Dear Old Southern Moon	Ge rejected
GEX-2757,-A	I Got A Girl In Tennessee	Ge rejected
GEX-2758,-A	Going Back To Dixie	Ge rejected

Rev. Champion 33064 by **The Arkansas Woodchopper**.

Merritt Smith & Leo Boswell, v duet; acc. prob. Leo Boswell, h-1; prob. own g duet.
  Richmond, IN   Wednesday, September 30, 1931

18064-A	Try Not To Forget	Ch 16358, Spr 2741
18065-A	Sweet Martha Williams	Ch 16358, Spr 2761
18066	On The Banks Of The Brandywine	Ch 16335, Spr 2761
18067	When The Harvest Moon Is Shining	Ch 16335
18068	Daisies Never Tell	Ch 16433
18069	Oh Mary Don't You Weep	Ch 16344, Spr 2825
18070	Jesus Keep Me Near The Fountain	Ch 16344, Spr 2825
18071	The Night Was Dark And Stormy -1	Ch 16433
18072	I Remember When Mother Left Home -1	Spr 2741

Superior 2741 as by **Jim & Jack Burbank**, 2761, 2825 as by **Jack & Jim Burbank**.

  Atlanta, GA   Wednesday, October 28, 1931

151972-1	My Hearts [sic] Turned Back To Dixie	Co 15748-D, ReAu G21556
151973-	Sona My Darling	Co unissued
151974-1	Try Not To Forget	Co 15748-D, ReAu G21556
151975-	When The Harvest Moon Is Shining	Co unissued

Regal G21556 as by **Regal Hill-Billy Singers**.

Merritt Smith (The Voice Of Melodies), v; acc. prob. own g.
  New York, NY   Tuesday, May 1, 1934

15142-	Drifting Down The Blue Ridge Trail	ARC unissued
15143-	My Old New Hampshire Home	ARC unissued
15144-	Down In The Old Cherry Orchard	ARC unissued
15145-	Silver Threads Among The Gold	ARC unissued

OLIVER SMITH & DEWEY CULPEPPER

Oliver Smith, Dewey Culpepper, v duet; acc. prob. one of them, g.
  Birmingham, AL   c. July 8, 1927

GEX-692,-A	For Gambling On The Sabbath Day	Ge rejected

  Birmingham, AL   c. July 9, 1927

GEX-703	Put My Little Shoes Away	Ge rejected

OTHA SMITH

Otha Smith, v; acc. two unknowns, g.
  Richmond, IN   Monday, February 16, 1931

17540	Mannington Blues	Ge rejected

R. SMITH

No details.
  poss. New York, NY   c. late 1925

Medley Of Southern Airs	Pm 33173
Medley Of Old Time Airs	Pm 33173
Harped Rag	Pm 33180
March Medley	Pm 33180

R.B. SMITH–S.J. ALLGOOD

R.B. Smith, S.J. Allgood, bj duet.
  Asheville, NC   prob. Tuesday, August 25, 1925

9278-A	American And Spanish Fandango	OK 45010

Rev. OKeh 45010 by **Ernest Helton**.

SIDNEY SMITH

Sidney Smith, v; acc. prob. own g.
  Dallas, TX   Thursday, October 18, 1928

| DAL-680-A | Just A Little Blue | Br 4266 |
| DAL-681-A | Calling You Sweetheart | Br 4266 |

Acc. own g.
   Dallas, TX   Monday, October 21, 1929

| 56441-1,-2 | Sweet Marie | Vi unissued |
| 56442-1,-2 | Dixieland Blues | Vi unissued |

SLIM SMITH

Slim Smith, v; acc. own g; James Andrews, g-1.
   Memphis, TN   Friday, July 7, 1939

MEM-56-	I Know You've Been Drinking Again	Vo unissued
MEM-57-1	Sad And Alone	Vo 05082, Cq 9335
MEM-58-1	Death Of The Bowery Girl	Vo 05082, Cq 9335
MEM-59-1	Old Muddy Water -1	Vo 05178
MEM-60-	Hello Beautiful Texas	Vo unissued
MEM-61-1	Lonely Little Hobo	Vo 05178
MEM-70-1	Lonesome River Road -1	Vo 05335
MEM-71-1	I Must Be A Good Woman -1	Vo 05335

Intervening matrices are by the Andrews Brothers.

Other recordings with this artist credit are by Bernard Smith.

W.M. SMITH

See Smith & Irvine.

WALTER SMITH

Walter Smith, v; or **Smith & Woodlieff**-1: Walter Smith, Norman Woodlieff, v duet; acc. Posey Rorer, f; Norman Woodlieff, g.
   Richmond, IN   Wednesday, March 20, 1929

14934	I'll Remember You Love In My Prayers -1	Ge 6840, Ch 15812, Spt 9389, Cq 7277
14935-A	I Ain't Gonna Grieve My Lord Anymore -1	Ge 6840, Ch 15812, Spt 9494
14936	It Won't Be Long Till My Grave Is Made -1	Ge 6858, Ch 15730, 45072, Spt 9494
14937	The Old Schoolhouse Play Ground -1	Ge 6809, Ch 15855, Chg 431
14938	I'd Rather Be With Rosy Nell -1	Ge 6858, Chg 431
14939	I Long To Kiss You All The Time -1	Ge unissued
14940	The Bald-Headed End Of A Broom	Ge 6887, Ch 15772, Spt 9454
14941	It's Sad To Leave You, Sweetheart -1	Ge 6809, Ch 15730, 45072, Spt 9389, Cq 7277
14942	Old Johnny Bucker Wouldn't Do	Ge 6825, Spt 9407
14943	The Cat's Got The Measles And The Dog's Got Whoopin' Cough	Ge 6825, Ch 15772, Spt 9407

Champion 15730, 15812, 15855 as by **Jim Taylor & Bill Shelby**, 15772 as by **Jim Taylor**. Supertone 9389 as by **Norris Brothers**, 9407, 9454 as by **Jerry Jordon**, 9494 as by **Jordan & Rupert**. Challenge 431 as by **Conley & Logan**. Conqueror 7277 as by **White & Bryant**.

Matrix 14934 is titled *I'll Remember You Love, In My Prayers* on Supertone 9389. Matrix 14935 is titled *I Ain't Gonna' Grieve My Lord Anymore*, and matrix 14936 is titled *It Won't Be Long 'Till My Grave Is Made*, on Supertone 9494. Matrix 14937 is titled *The Old Schoolhouse Playground*, and matrix 14938 is titled *I'd Rather Be With Rosie-Nell*, on Challenge 431. Matrix 14942 is titled *Old Johnny Bucker Won't Do*, and matrix 14943 is titled *The Cat's Got The Measels, The Dog's Got The Whooping Cough*, on Supertone 9407.

Revs: Gennett 6887, Supertone 9454 by Carson Robison; Champion 15855 by Andy Patterson & Warren Caplinger.

Kid Williams & Bill Morgan: Walter Smith, Buster Carter, v duet; or **Kid Williams**-1: Walter Smith, v; acc. Posey Rorer, f; Buster Carter, bj; Lewis McDaniels, g.
   New York, NY   Thursday, March 27, 1930

9523-1	Please Daddy Come Home	Je 20005, Or 8005, Pe 152, Ro 5005, Htd 16118
9524-1,-2	My Happy Home I Left In Caroline	Je 20005, Or 8005, Pe 145, Ro 5005, Htd 16118
9527-2	I Want To Be Called Pet And Sweetheart	Pe 152
9528-	Don't Be Angry With Me Sweetheart -1	ARC unissued

Matrices 9525/26 are by Lewis McDaniels.

   New York, NY   Friday, March 28, 1930

9531-2	I Know I'll Meet My Mother After All	Ba 32095, Je 20017, Or 8017, Pe 145, Ro 5017, Htd 16106, 23024, Cq 7740
9532-2	Mother Kiss Your Darling	Ba 32095, Je 20017, Or 8017, Ro 5017, Htd 16106, 23024, Cq 7740
9535-2	Aggravating Mother-In-Law -1	Je 20006, Or 8006, Pe 146, Ro 5006
9536-	Love Is A Funny Little Thing -1	Pe 146

At this session Lewis McDaniels also recorded in his own name, and Posey Rorer, Buster Carter, and McDaniels recorded as **Dixie Ramblers [1]**. Matrices 9533/34 are by The Clevelanders (popular).
Revs: Jewel 20006, Oriole 8006, Romeo 5006 by Lewis McDaniels.

Kid Williams/Kid Williams & Bill Morgan-1: Walter Smith, v; or **Kid Williams & Roy Martin**-2: Walter Smith, Lewis McDaniels, v duet; acc. **Texas Mud Splashers**: Pat Patterson, sg; Lois Dexter, tbj; Lewis McDaniels, g.

New York, NY   Monday, May 5, 1930

9705-1	Birmingham Jail -3	Ba 32096, Je 20020, Or 8020, Pe 160, Re 10301, Ro 5020, Htd 16114, 23036, Cq 7739
9706-1,-2	The Prisoner And The Rose -2	Ba 32096, Je 20020, Or 8020, Re 10301, Ro 5020, Htd 16114, 23036
9707-3	When He Died He Got A Home In Hell	Je 20028, Or 8028, Ro 5028, Htd 16094, 23033, Cq 7739
9708-2	I'm Glad I Counted The Cost -1	Je 20028, Or 8028, Ro 5028, Htd 16094, 23033
9709-	Swinging In The Lane With Nel -2	ARC unissued

Matrix 9705 as by **Kid Williams & Bill Morgan** on Conqueror 7739; the accompaniment-credit is omitted on this issue and on Perfect 160, Romeo 5020.

Kid Williams & His Guitar: Walter Smith, v; acc. Lewis McDaniels, g.

New York, NY   Tuesday, May 6, 1930

9714-2	May I Sleep In Your Barn Tonight, Mister?	Pe 160

Kid Smith & His Family: Walter Smith, Thelma Smith, Dorothy Smith, v trio; acc. Odell Smith, f; Thelma Smith, g; Dorothy Smith, u.

Charlotte, NC   Tuesday, May 19, 1931

69313-1	Whisper Softly, Mother's Dying	Vi 23576
69314-2	Little Bessie	Vi 23576

Thelma and Dorothy Smith are Walter Smith's daughters.

Kid Smith & Family: Walter Smith, Thelma Smith, Dorothy Smith, v trio; acc. Thelma Smith, g; Dorothy Smith, u.

New York, NY   Tuesday, December 1, 1936

20346-2	You Give Me Your Love (And I'll Give You Mine)	ARC 7-03-51, Vo 03414
20347-	Whisper Softly Mother's Dying	ARC unissued
20348-	Come Up Here My Little Bessie	ARC unissued
20349-4	Homestead In The Wildwood	ARC 7-04-52, Vo 03443, Cq 8787

Take 4 of matrix 20349 is thought to be a technical rerecording, made on December 8, 1936, of either take 1 or take 2.

Walter Smith, Thelma Smith, Dorothy Smith, v trio; or Walter Smith, Thelma Smith, v duet-1; or Walter Smith, v-2; acc. Thelma Smith, g/y-3; Dorothy Smith, u/y-3.

New York, NY   Wednesday, December 2, 1936

20352-2	Lying Daddy Blues -3	ARC 7-04-76, Vo 03482
20353-2	Mama Cat Blues -2, 3	ARC 7-04-76, Vo 03482
20354-1	Mississippi Freight Train Blues -3	ARC 7-04-52, Vo 03415, Cq 8788
20355-2	Ten I Served And Ten To Serve -1	ARC 7-04-52, Vo 03443, Cq 8787
20356-	It Won't Be Long Till My Grave Is Made	ARC unissued

Walter Smith, Thelma Smith, Dorothy Smith, v trio-1; or Walter Smith, v-2; acc. Thelma Smith, g/y-2; Dorothy Smith, u/y-2.

New York, NY   Saturday, December 5, 1936

20369-2	I'm Not Angry With You Darling -1	ARC 7-03-51, Vo 03414
20370-	Do Not Wait Till I'm Laid 'Neath The Clay	ARC unissued
20371-2	Mama You're A Mess -2	ARC 7-03-52, Vo 03415, Cq 8788

Walter Smith also recorded with the Carolina Buddies, Lewis McDaniels, and the Virginia Dandies.

SMITH & BAND

Pseudonym on Varsity for Dick Robertson.

SMITH & DYAL

No details.

Atlanta, GA   Saturday, November 5, 1927

145130-	Let's Be Sweethearts Again	Co unissued
145131-	I Love You Best Of All	Co unissued

SMITH & IRVINE

W.M. Smith, ——— Irvine, p duet; or **W.M. Smith**-1, p solo.

Richmond, IN   Saturday, October 1, 1932

18814	Sally Gooden -1	Ch 16518

18815	Lonesome Road Blues	Ch 16518
18816	Hand Me Down My Walking Cane	Ch 16508
18817	Don't Let Your Deal Go Down	Ch 16508

Gennett files note that these performances were "with mandolin attachment;" this appears to refer to a device fitted to the piano which modifies its sound to mimic a mandolin.

SMITH & JAMES

This pseudonym was used on Madison and Van Dyke for Bob Miller & Barney Burnett or Frank Luther & Carson Robison, as well as for popular groups.

SMITH & POOSER

See Merritt Smith.

SMITH & WOODLIEFF

See Walter Smith.

SMITH BROTHERS

Roosevelt Smith, William Smith, v duet; acc. Roosevelt Smith, ah; William Smith, g.
    Bristol, TN   Thursday, November 1, 1928

47266-1,-2	There's No-One To Care For Me	Vi unissued

    Bristol, TN   Friday, November 2, 1928

47273-2	My Mother Is Waiting For Me In Heaven Above	Vi V-40201
47274-2	She Has Climbed The Golden Stair	Vi V-40201

SMITH'S CAROLINA CRACKERJACKS

Arthur Smith, f/v; Ralph Smith, bj/v; Sonny Smith, g/v; Luke Tucker, sb/v.
    Rock Hill, SC   Thursday, September 29, 1938

027650-1	I'm Going Back To Old Carolina	BB B-8304, MW M-7735
027651-1	(Old Santa Claus Is Leavin') Just Because	BB B-8304, MW M-7735

Arthur Smith, md/lv; Sonny Smith, g; Ralph Smith, tv.
    Rock Hill, SC   Thursday, September 29, 1938

027652-1	There Are No Disappointments In Heaven	BB B-8376, MW M-7736
027653-1	Your Soul Never Dies	BB B-8376, MW M-7736

Arthur Smith, later better known as Arthur "Guitar Boogie" Smith, recorded after 1942.

SMITH'S GARAGE FIDDLE BAND

Samuel Morgan Peacock, f; John Peacock, g.
    Dallas, TX   Friday, October 26, 1928

DAL-734-	Done Gone	Vo 5287
DAL-735-	Cuban Two Step Rag	Vo 5287
DAL-736-	Beaumont Rag	Vo 5268
DAL-737-	Twinkle Twinkle Little Star	Vo 5268

Samuel Peacock, f; Frank Russell, p-1; John Peacock, g.
    San Antonio, TX   Tuesday, March 12, 1929

SA-211-	Rag Time Annie -1	Vo 5306
SA-212-	Dill Pickle Rag -1	Vo 5306
SA-213-	Miss Iola -1	Vo 5336
SA-214-	Lime Rock	Vo 5336
SA-215-	College Hornpipe	Vo rejected
SA-216-	The Wagoner Hornpipe	Vo rejected

Smith's Garage Band: Samuel Peacock, f; John Peacock, g; poss. Charles Peacock, g.
    Dallas, TX   Tuesday, October 29, 1929

DAL-525-	The Gray Eagle	Vo 5375
DAL-526-	Tom And Jerry	Vo 5375
DAL-527-	Tickle The Strings	Vo rejected
DAL-528-	Schottische	Vo rejected

SMITH'S SACRED SINGERS

J. Frank Smith, lv; Clarence Cronic, tv; Clyde B. Smith, v; Charley Hall, v; Rev. M.L. Thrasher, bsv; acc. Mrs. T.C. Llewellyn, p-1; Clarence Cronic, g-2.
    Atlanta, GA   Friday, April 23, 1926

| 142094-1 | Pictures From Life's Other Side -2 | Co 15090-D |
| 142095-2 | Where We'll Never Grow Old -1 | Co 15090-D |

Atlanta, GA　　　　　　　　　　　　　　　　　　　　　　　　　　　Tuesday, November 2, 1926

143016-3	We Are Going Down The Valley One By One -1	Co 15128-D
143017-	I Want My Father's Own Hand	Co unissued
143018-	Satisfied	Co unissued

Acc. Mrs. T.C. Llewellyn, p; Rev. M.L. Thrasher, scripture reading-1.

Atlanta, GA　　　　　　　　　　　　　　　　　　　　　　　　　　Wednesday, November 3, 1926

| 143033-2 | The Eastern Gate | Co 15110-D |
| 143034-2 | Jesus Prayed -1 | Co 15159-D |

J. Frank Smith, v; acc. Mrs. T.C. Llewellyn, p.

Atlanta, GA　　　　　　　　　　　　　　　　　　　　　　　　　　Wednesday, November 3, 1926

| 143035-1 | The Prodigal's Return | Co 15137-D |

Smith's Sacred Singers: J. Frank Smith, lv; Clarence Cronic, tv; Clyde B. Smith, v; Charley Hall, v; Rev. M.L. Thrasher, bsv; acc. Clyde Smith, f; Clarence Cronic, g.

Atlanta, GA　　　　　　　　　　　　　　　　　　　　　　　　　　Wednesday, November 3, 1926

| 143036-1 | Shouting On The Hills | Co 15110-D |
| 143037-1 | If I'm Faithful To My Lord | Co 15128-D |

J. Frank Smith, v; acc. Clyde Smith, f; Clarence Cronic, g.

Atlanta, GA　　　　　　　　　　　　　　　　　　　　　　　　　　Wednesday, November 3, 1926

| 143038- | Tell My Mother I Will Meet Her | Co unissued |
| 143039-2 | The Drunkard's Child | Co 15137-D |

Smith's Sacred Singers: J. Frank Smith, lv; Joe Day, tv; Willie Fowler, bv; Will Brewer, bsv; acc. Mildred Cowsert, p.

Atlanta, GA　　　　　　　　　　　　　　　　　　　　　　　　　　　　Monday, April 4, 1927

143884-	I'm Only On A Visit Here	Co unissued
143885-2	I Will Sing Of My Redeemer	Co 15144-D
143886-2	He Will Set Your Fields On Fire	Co 15144-D
143887-2	Trace The Footsteps Of Jesus	Co 15173-D
143888-	Jesus Died For Me	Co unissued
143889-2	He Is Coming Back	Co 15173-D
143890-	I'll Go	Co unissued
143891-	In The Happy Long Ago	Co unissued

Acc. unknown, f-1; Mildred Cowsert, p-2; unknown, g-3.

Atlanta, GA　　　　　　　　　　　　　　　　　　　　　　　　　　　　Tuesday, April 5, 1927

143904-2	A Child At Mother's Knee -2	Co 15671-D
143905-2	Beautiful Life -2	Co 15671-D
143906-2	City Of Gold -1, 3	Co 15195-D
143907-	Over In The Glory Land	Co unissued
143908-1	Life's Railway To Heaven -1, 3	Co 15159-D
143909-	The Life Boat	Co unissued
143910-1	Climbing Up The Golden Stairs -1, 3	Co 15195-D

J. Frank Smith, v; acc. unknown.

Atlanta, GA　　　　　　　　　　　　　　　　　　　　　　　　　　　Wednesday, April 6, 1927

143915-	My Mother's Bible	Co unissued
143916-	Was That Somebody You	Co unissued
143917-	Reapers Are Needed	Co unissued

Smith's Sacred Singers: prob.: J. Frank Smith, lv; Joe Day, tv; Willie Fowler, bv; Will Brewer, bsv; acc. poss. Mildred Cowsert, p.

Atlanta, GA　　　　　　　　　　　　　　　　　　　　　　　　　　　Monday, November 7, 1927

145144-2	Keep On Climbing	Co 15351-D
145145-2	Gospel Waves	Co 15208-D
145146-2	He Bore It All	Co 15208-D
145147-	Walking Along With Me	Co unissued
145148-2	I Want To Go To Heaven	Co 15230-D
145149-2	We Shall Rise	Co 15230-D
145150-2	I Am Going That Way	Co 15389-D
145151-	He Lives On High	Co unissued

Atlanta, GA　　　　　　　　　　　　　　　　　　　　　　　　　　　　Tuesday, April 17, 1928

146110-2	Let The Lower Lights Be Burning	Co 15257-D
146111-2	Hold To God's Unchanging Hand	Co 15308-D
146112-2	Waiting On The Golden Shore	Co 15308-D

146113-2	Drifting Down	Co 15257-D
146114-1	Prepare To Meet Thy God	Co 15281-D
146115-2	My Latest Sun Is Sinking Fast	Co 15281-D

Acc. unknown, f; unknown, p.
Atlanta, GA   Tuesday, October 30, 1928

147348-1	The Unclouded Day	Co 15351-D
147349-1	When The Happy Morning Breaks	Co 15389-D
147350-1	Deliverance Will Come	Co 15329-D
147351-2	When Jesus Comes	Co 15371-D
147352-1	The Home Over There	Co 15329-D
147353-2	Lord I'm Coming Home	Co 15371-D

Acc. unknown, f-1; unknown, p-1; unknown, g-2.
Atlanta, GA   Wednesday, April 17, 1929

148338-2	Are You Washed In The Blood Of The Lamb -1	Co 15430-D
148339-2	Jesus Died For Me -1	Co 15430-D
148340-2	Endless Joy Is Waiting Over There -1	Co 15471-D, ReE MR4
148341-2	Working For The Crown -1	Co 15401-D
148344-	Keep The Sunlight In Your Sky -2?	Co 15772-D
148345-2	Meet Me There -2	Co 15401-D
148346-2	What A Gathering That Will Be -2	Co 15471-D, ReE MR4
148347-	When Our Lord Shall Come Again -2?	Co 15772-D

Regal MR4 as by **The Southern Sacred Singers**.
Matrices 148342/43 are by Barbecue Bob (see *B&GR*).

Acc. unknown, p.
Atlanta, GA   Tuesday, November 5, 1929

149379-2	You Can't Do Wrong And Get By	Co 15517-D
149380-2	Labor On	Co 15517-D
149381-2	He Holds Me By The Hand	Co 15579-D
149382-1	My Saviour's Train	Co 15749-D
149383-2	I Have Found The Way	Co 15749-D
149384-2	Echoes From The Glory Shore	Co 15579-D
149385-2	When Our Saviour Comes Again	Co 15494-D
149386-1	His Picture Is In My Heart	Co 15494-D

Atlanta, GA   Friday, April 18, 1930

150283-2	Love Lifted Me	Co 15619-D
150284-2	Is It Well With Your Soul	Co 15706-D
150285-2	The Church In The Wildwood	Co 15551-D
150286-2	Gathering Home	Co 15706-D
150287-1	Jesus Lover Of My Soul	Co 15593-D
150288-1	Work For The Night Is Coming	Co 15593-D
150289-1	There Is A Fountain Filled With Blood	Co 15551-D
150290-2	How Firm A Foundation	Co 15619-D

J. Frank Smith, lv; Ms.——Wheeler, av; Willie Fowler, bv; Bob Coker, bsv; acc.——Cooper, f; Bob Coker, g.
Atlanta, GA   Thursday, December 4, 1930

151029-1	Sing All Your Troubles Away	Co 15659-D
151030-1	In A Little While	Co 15683-D
151031-2	Wayside Wells	Co 15659-D
151032-1	It Won't Be Long	Co 15683-D
151033-1	Old Time Religion For Me	Co 15639-D
151034-2	My Redeemer Lives	Co 15639-D

Smith Sacred Singers: J. Frank Smith, lv; Joe Day, tv; Willie Fowler, bv; Bob Coker, bsv; or unidentified, v duet-1/trio-2; acc. unknown, f-3; Mildred Cowsert, p; prob. Bob Coker, g-4.
Atlanta, GA   Tuesday, July 31, 1934

82838-1	No Stranger Yonder	BB B-5809
82839-1	Let The Lower Lights Be Burning	BB B-5611
82840-1	Hold To God's Unchanging Hand	BB B-5943
82841-1	You Can't Do Wrong And Get By	BB B-5750
82842-1	When They Ring The Golden Bells For You And Me	BB B-5972
82843-1	From The Cross To The Crown	BB B-5943
82844-1	Home On The Banks Of The River	BB B-5671
82845-2	Where We'll Never Grow Old -1	BB B-5721
82846-1	Jesus Is All The World To Me	BB B-5972
82847-1	Stand Up For Jesus	BB B-5809

82854-1	Pictures From Life's Other Side -2, 3, 4	BB B-5606
82855-1	We'll Understand It Better Bye And Bye	BB B-5750
82856-1	God's Children Are Gathering Home	BB B-5606
82857-1	Beyond The Stars Is Home	BB B-5611
82858-1	We'll Work Till Jesus Comes	BB B-5854
82859-1	Jesus Is Calling	BB B-5883
82860-1	Have Thine Own Way, Lord	BB B-5883
82861-1	Saved By Grace	BB B-5854
82862-1	Tell Mother I'll Be There	BB B-5671
82863-1	Since Jesus Came Into My Heart	BB B-5721

Matrices 82848 to 82853 are by Riley Puckett.

Acc. Byron Whitworth, p.
Atlanta, GA   Wednesday, August 7, 1935

94354-1	My Troubles Will Pass Away	BB B-6108
94355-1	We're Living For Jesus	BB B-6137
94356-1	Smile Your Troubles Away	BB B-6092
94357-1	He Is Everything To Me	BB B-6092
94358-1	Won't It Be Wonderful There?	BB unissued
94359-1	He's A Wonderful Saviour	BB B-6165
94360-1	In Our Home Sweet Home	BB B-6121
94361-1	We'll Sing Over Yonder	BB B-6108
94362-1	Wonderful City	BB B-6273
94363-1	Trace The Footsteps Of Jesus	BB B-6183
94364-1	When Our Saviour Comes Again	BB B-6273
94365-1	Good Morning In Glory	BB B-6137

Atlanta, GA   Thursday, August 8, 1935

94366-1	Happy Bye-And-Bye Land	BB B-6121
94367-1	My Redeemer Lives	BB unissued
94378-1	I'll Be Singing 'Round The Throne Someday	BB B-6206
94379-1	Will You Meet Me Up There?	BB B-6206
94380-1	What A Happy Time	BB B-6183
94381-1	Ride On, God's Children	BB B-6222
94382-1	Hallelujah	BB B-6165
94383-1	I'm Going To Live With Jesus	BB unissued

Matrices 94368 to 94377 are by Riley Puckett.
Rev. Bluebird B-6222 by J.E. Mainer's Mountaineers.

SMIZERS DIXIE SERENADERS

Unknown "string band" (thus Vocalion files); unknown, v-1.
Chicago, IL   Wednesday, August 28, 1929

| C-4156-A,-B | Deep River Blues -1 | Vo unissued |
| C-4157-A,-B | Weary Blues | Vo unissued |

SMOKY BLUE HIGHBALLERS

Pseudonym on Velvet Tone and Clarion for the North Carolina Ramblers (see Charlie Poole).

SMOKY MOUNTAIN BOYS

The items below consist of excerpts from Gennett recordings interspersed with dialog, recorded for this purpose, by employees of Gennett Records using the stage names "Slim," "Red," "Ike," and "Joe;" and sound effects also drawn from Gennett recordings. Further details of the source recordings follow each item.

Richmond, IN   Thursday, April 25, 1929

| 15082,-A,-B | Coon Hollow Boys At The Still Part 1 | Ge rejected |

Richmond, IN   Saturday, April 27, 1929

| 15084-C | The Smoky Mountain Boys At The Still Part I | Ge 6871, Ch 15748, Cq 7274 |

Champion 15748 as by **Coon Hollow Boys**. Conqueror 7274 is uncredited.
Matrix 15084-C uses excerpts of matrices 13645, 13639, and 13638, in that order, by The Red Fox Chasers. This item is titled *Coon Hollow Boys At The Still Part I* on Champion 15748, or *The Black Mountain Gang At Their Still Part I* on Conqueror 7274.

Richmond, IN   Monday, May 6, 1929

| 15089-A | The Smoky Mountain Boys At The Still Part II | Ge 6871, Ch 15748, Cq 7274 |

Champion 15748 as by **Coon Hollow Boys**. Conqueror 7274 is uncredited.
Matrix 15089-A uses excerpts of matrices 14727 and 14726 by Pie Plant Pete, and of matrix 14899 (part of *All Out And Down*) by Freeman Stowers (see B&GR).
This item is titled *Coon Hollow Boys At The Still Part II* on Champion 15748, or *The Black Mountain Gang At Their Still Part II* on Conqueror 7274.

SMOKY MOUNTAIN FAMILY

Pseudonym on a late issue of Conqueror 7072 for Peck's Male Quartette (matrix 10081)/Troy Martin & Elvin Bigger (matrix 19272).

SMOKY MOUNTAIN RAMBLERS

Homer "Slim" Miller, f; poss. Lowe Stokes, f-1; Walt McKinney, sg; Raymond Gully, bj-md; "Heavy Martin" (Hugh Cross), g/lv-2; poss. Bill Brown, sp; band v-2/sp.
Knoxville, TN   Friday, March 28, 1930

K-8022-	San Antonio -2	Vo 5422
K-8023-	Back To Old Smoky Mountain -2	Vo 5422
K-8024-	Ain't It Hell, Boys -2	Vo 5451
K-8025-	Down In Tennessee -2	Vo 5451
K-8032/3	No Business Of Mine -2	Vo 5437
K-8034-	Bear Mountain Rag -1	Vo 5437

Matrices K-8026 to 8029 are by the Perry County Music Makers; matrices K-8030/31 are by the Kentucky Holiness Singers. See also the Tennessee Farm Hands.
This artist-credit was also used as a pseudonym on Supertone for H.M. Barnes & His Blue Ridge Ramblers.

SMOKY MOUNTAIN SACRED SINGERS

Vocal group; acc. unknown, g.
Chicago, IL   Wednesday, October 3, 1928

C-2387-	The Old Rugged Cross	Vo 5257
C-2388-	Abide With Me	Vo 5257
C-2389-	We're Marching To Zion	Vo 5311
C-2392-	More Like The Master	Vo 5311

Matrices C-2390/91 are by Sammy Stewart (see JR).
This artist credit was also used as a pseudonym on Vocalion for the Old Southern Sacred Singers.

SMOKY MOUNTAIN TWINS

Pseudonym on Conqueror, Domino, and Regal for the Gentry Brothers.

SMOKY MT. FIDDLER TRIO

Pseudonym on Bluebird B-6387 for the Dixie Ramblers [II] or Arthur Smith Trio (one side each).

SMYTH COUNTY RAMBLERS

Jack Pierce, f/v; Weldon (Jack) Reedy, bj; Malcolm Warley, g/v-1; Carl Cruise, g/v-2.
Bristol, TN   Saturday, October 27, 1928

47229-2	My Name Is Ticklish Reuben -1	Vi V-40144, Au 401
47230-1	Way Down In Alabama -2	Vi V-40144, Au 401

HANK SNOW

Hank, The Yodeling Ranger, v/y; acc. own g.
Montreal, P.Q.   Thursday, October 29, 1936

8132-1	Prisoned Cowboy	BB B-4614, B-4741
8133-1	Lonesome Blue Yodel	BB B-4614, B-4742

Hank Snow, v/y-1/sp-2; acc. Eugene "Johnny" Beaudoin, esg-3; own g.
Montreal, P.Q.   November 6-9, 1937

8278-1	Blue For Old Hawaii -3	BB B-4635, RZAu G23486
8279-1	We Met Down In The Hills Of Old Wyoming -3	BB B-4637, RZAu G25014
8280-1	My San Antonio Mama -1, 3	BB B-4640, B-4741
8281-1	My Little Swiss Maiden -1	BB B-4737, RZAu G25014
8282-1	Was There Ever A Pal Like You	BB B-4640, B-4742
8283-1	The Blue Velvet Band -1, 2	BB B-4635, RZAu G23486
8284-	The Hobo's Last Ride	BB B-4643, RZAu G25040
8285-	The Answer To "That Silver Haired Daddy Of Mine" -1	BB B-4643, RZAu G25040

Hank Snow, v/y/sp-1; acc. Eugene "Johnny" Beaudoin, esg-2; own g.
Montreal, P.Q.   Sunday, February 5-Monday, February 6, 1939

8470-	Someday You'll Care -2	BB B-4657, RZAu G25027
8471-	I'll Ride Back To Lonesome Valley -2	BB B-4661, RZAu G25033
8472-	Bluer Than Blue -2	BB B-4661
8473-	Yodeling Back To You	BB B-4657, RZAu G25027

| 8474- | There's A Picture On Pinto's Bridle -1 | BB B-4655, RZAu G25008 |
| 8475- | The Texas Cowboy | BB B-4655, RZAu G25008 |

Rev. Regal-Zonophone G25033 by Hank Snow (postwar).

Hank Snow, v/y-1/sp-2; acc. Eugene "Johnny" Beaudoin, esg-3; own g; unknown, sb.
Montreal, P.Q.   February 8-10, 1941

8713-	On The Mississippi Shore -1, 3	BB B-4688, RZAu G25098
8714-	Under Hawaiian Skies -3	BB B-4691
8715-	She's A Rose From The Garden Of Prayer -3	BB B-4696, RZAu G25057
8716-	Wandering On -1	BB B-4694, RZAu G25120
8717-	The Broken Wedding Ring -1	BB B-4696
8718-	You Didn't Have To Tell Me -3	BB B-4694, RZAu G25057
8719-	His Message Home	BB B-4691, RZAu G25098
8720-	Answer To "The Blue Velvet Band" -2	BB B-4688

Hank Snow, v/y-1; acc. own g.
Montreal, P.Q.   Friday, January 16, 1942

8864-	When That Someone You Love Doesn't Love You	BB unissued
8865-	I'll Tell The World That I Love You	BB B-4733
8866-	Let's Pretend	BB unissued
8867-	Polka Dot Blues -1	BB B-4729
8868-	I Dream Of The Rainbow's End	BB unissued
8869-	The Alphabet Song	BB B-4729
8870-	The Galveston Rose -1	BB B-4733
8871-	I Traded My Saddle For A Rifle	BB unissued

The date shown is confirmed only for matrix 8865, but the other items were probably recorded on or close to that date.

Acc. Eugene "Johnny" Beaudoin, esg; own g; unknown, sb.
Montreal, P.Q.   Tuesday, April 14, 1942

8946-	Broken Dreams -1	BB B-4737, RZAu G25051
8947-	Let's Pretend -1	BB B-4736
8948-	The Days Are Long And I'm Weary	BB B-4739
8949-	I Traded My Saddle For A Rifle -1	BB B-4736
8950-	When That Someone You Love Doesn't Love You -1	BB B-4739, RZAu G25120
8951-	The Rainbow's End -1	BB B-4737, RZAu G25051

Throughout the above recordings the artist credit takes slightly variant forms such as **Hank**, **"The Yodeling Ranger"**, **Hank** (**"The Yodelling Ranger"**), and **Hank**, **"The Singing Ranger"**.

Hank Snow recorded after 1942.

SNOWBALL & SUNSHINE

Vocal duet; acc. unknown, o; unknown, v group.
Atlanta, GA   Tuesday, November 3, 1931

| 152021-1 | Leave It There | Co 15722-D |
| 152022-1 | When The Saints Go Marchin' In | Co 15722-D |

Rev. Snowball Of Snowball & Sunshine: comic sermon.
Atlanta, GA   Tuesday, November 3, 1931

| 152029-1 | Moses And The Bull Rush – Part 1 | Co 15738-D |
| 152030-1 | Moses And The Bull Rush – Part 2 | Co 15738-D |

Snowball & Sunshine, v duet; acc. unknown; unknown, v group-1.
New York, NY   Friday, January 29, 1932

11180-	Take Your Burden To The Lord	ARC unissued
11181-	When The Saints Go Marching In	ARC unissued
11182-	Paul And Silas	ARC unissued
11183-	I Can't Sit Down -1	ARC unissued
11184-	I Ain't Gonna Study War -1	ARC unissued

LEO SOILEAU

Leo Soileau–Mayuse Lafleur: Leo Soileau, f; Mayuse Lafleur, ac/v.
Atlanta, GA   Friday, October 19, 1928

47201-2	Basile Waltz	Vi 21769
47202-3	Mama, Where You At?	Vi 21769
47203-2	The Criminal Waltz (La Valse Criminale)	Vi 21770
47204-1	Your Father Put Me Out (Ton Pere A Mit D'eor)	Vi 21770

Soileau & Robin: Leo Soileau, f/v-1; Moise Robin, ac/v-2.
Richmond, IN   Saturday, July 13, 1929

15343	Ma Cherie Tite Fille -1	Pm 12808
15344	Easy Rider Blues -1	Pm 12808
15345	Ce Pas La Pienne Tu Pleur -2	Pm 12908
15346-A	Ma Mauvais Fille -2	Pm 12830
15347	La Valse De La Ru Canal -2	Pm 12830
15348	Je Te Recontrais De Le Brulier -2	Pm 12908

Paramount 12830 as by **Robin & Soileau**.
Data are as given in Gennett files. However, Paramount 12830 is reported as bearing the matrices 15347 (*Ma Mauvais Fille*) and 15345-A (*La Valse De La Ru Canal*), and *Je Te Recontrais De Le Brulier* on Paramount 12908 also bears the matrix 15347. See also the note on adjacent recordings by Roy Gonzales.

Leo Soileau–Moise Robin: Leo Soileau, f/v-1; Moise Robin, ac/v-2.
Memphis, TN   Wednesday, September 18, 1929

55534-2	La Valse Penitentiaire (Penitentiary Waltz) -1	Vi 22183, BB B-2184
55535-2	Je Veux Marier (I Want To Get Married) -1	Vi 22183, BB B-2184
55536-2	La Valse De Josephine (Josephine Waltz) -2	Vi 22207
55537-2	Grosse Mama (Big Mama) -2	Vi 22207

Leo Soileau & Moise Robin: Leo Soileau, f/v; Moise Robin, ac/v.
New Orleans, LA   Wednesday, October 2, 1929

NO-261-	La Valse A Moreau	Vo 15845
NO-262-	Demain C'Est Pas Dimanche	Vo 15845
NO-263-	La Valse De Pecaniere	Vo 15852
NO-264-	Le Cleuses De Negre Francaise	Vo 15852

It is uncertain who sings which items.

Soileau Couzens: Leo Soileau, f/v-1; Alius Soileau, f/v-2.
New Orleans, LA   Thursday, November 7, 1929

56502-1	Quand J'Ete Seul Hier Soir (When I Was All Alone Last Night) -1	Vi 22578
56503-1	Allons Boire A Coup (Let's All Take A Drink Together) -1	Vi 22578
56504-1	Trois Jours Apres Ma Mort (Three Days After My Death) -2	Vi 22364
56505-1	Sur Le Chemin Chez Moi (On My Way Home) -2	Vi 22364

Leo Soileau & His Three Aces: Leo Soileau, f/v-1; Floyd Shreve, g; Bill (Dewey) Landry, g; Tony Gonzales, d.
New Orleans, LA   Friday, January 18, 1935

87600-1	Alons A Ville Platte (Let's Go To Ville Platte) -1	BB B-2196
87601-1	Acout Vous Moi Lese (When You Left Me) -1	BB B-2196
87602-1	Le Gran Mamou -1	BB B-2194, MW M-4880
87603-1	Si Vous Moi Voudrez Ame (If You'd Only Love Me) -1	BB B-2194, MW M-4880
87604-1	Petit Ou Gros (Little Or Big) -1	BB B-2197
87605-1	Dites Moi Avant (Tell Me Before)	BB B-2197
87606-1	Hackberry Hop -1	BB B-2171, B-2086
87607-1	Le Valse De Gueydan -1	BB B-2171, B-2086

Matrices 87608/09 are by Floyd Shreve & The Three Aces.

Leo Soileau's Four Aces: Leo Soileau, f/v-1; Floyd Shreve, g/v-2; Bill (Dewey) Landry, g/v-3; band, sp/shouting.
Chicago, IL   Friday, May 3, 1935

C-9970-A	Quand Je Suis Loin De La Maison (When I Am Far Away From Home) -1	De 17013
C-9971-A	Je Ne Tracasse Pas Plus (I Don't Worry Now) -1	De 17013
C-9972-A	La Bonne Valse (Good Time Waltz) -1	De 17008
C-9973-A	Ma Belle Ne M'Aime Pas (My Girl Don't Love Me) -1	De 17012
C-9974-A	L'Ancienne Valse (The Old Time Waltz) -1	De 17012
C-9975-A	Les Blues De La Louisianne (Louisiana Blues)	De 17009, 5116
C-9976-A	Quand Je Suis Bleu (When I Am Blue) -1	De 17010
C-9977-A	Ma Petite Fille (My Little Girl) -1	De 17010
C-9978-A	My Brown Eyed Texas Rose -2	De 5182
C-9979-A	Blue Eyes -2	De 5102
C-9980-A	Green Valley Waltz -2, 3	De 5102
C-9981-A	Corrine Corrina -2, 3	De 5101

Matrix C-9975 is titled *Louisiana Blues* on Decca 5116.
Decca files indicate that O.P. Shreve and Johnny Roberts were also present. O.P. Shreve was the band's manager and probably took no performing part, but Roberts, a singer-guitarist who recorded in his own name, may have participated in either or both roles.

Chicago, IL   Saturday, May 4, 1935

C-9982-A	Let Me Call You Sweetheart (I'm In Love With You) -2	De 5117
C-9983-A	Little Dutch Mill -2	De 5133
C-9984-A	Breeze (Blow My Baby Back To Me) -2	De 5117
C-9985-A	Frankie And Johnnie	De 5133
C-9986-A	Red River Valley -2?	De 5182
C-9987-A	Birmingham Jail -2, 3	De 5157
C-9988-A	Paroi Arcadia Breakdown (Arcadia County Breakdown)	De 17009, 5116
C-9989-A	T'Est Petite Et T'Est Mignonne (You Are Little And You Are Cute) -1	De 17008
C-9990-A	My Wild Irish Rose -2	De 5157
C-9991-A	Nobody's Business If I Do -3	De 5101

Matrix C-9988 is titled *Arcadia County Breakdown* on Decca 5116.
Matrices C-9992/93 are by Floyd Shreve.

Leo Soileau, f/v-1; unidentified, k-2; Floyd Shreve, g/v-3; Bill (Dewey) Landry, g/v-4.
New Orleans, LA   Tuesday, March 17, 1936

NO-60790-A	Valse De Estherwood	De 17016
NO-60791-	Atrape Moi – Je Tombe (Catch Me – I'm Falling) -1	De 17020
NO-60792-	Je M'Ennui Ce Soir (I'm Lonesome Tonight) -1	De 17017
NO-60793-A	Il Ta Prie De Mois (He Took You From Me) -1	De 17016
NO-60794-A	Dans Claire De Lune Avec Toi (In The Moonlight With You) -1	De 17020
NO-60795-	A Ute (Where Are You) -1	De 17017
NO-60796-A	Quand Tu Me Prie De La Maison (When You Took Me From My Home) -1	De 17021
NO-60797-A	Breakdown De Cajin (Cajun Breakdown)	De 17021
NO-60798-	I Only Want A Buddy (Not A Sweetheart) -3	De 5210
NO-60799-	When The Moon Comes Over The Mountain -3	De 5279, DeSA FM5111, BrSA SA1201
NO-60800-	K.C. Railroad -3, 4	De 5262
NO-60801-	Somebody Loves You -2, 3	De 5236, BrSA SA1106
NO-60802-A	Don't Let Your Love Go Wrong -4	De 5210
NO-60803-A	Little Darling Pal Of Mine -3	De 5236, BrSA SA1106
NO-60804-	In The Valley Of The Moon -3	De 5262
NO-60805-	Goodnight Little Girl Of My Dreams -3	De 5299

Revs: Decca FM5111, Brunswick SA1201 by Shelton Brothers.

Leo Soileau, f; Floyd Shreve, g/v; Bill (Dewey) Landry, g.
New Orleans, LA   Wednesday, March 18, 1936

NO-60806-	Chain Store Blues	De rejected
NO-60807-	Every Little Moment	De 5326
NO-60808-	Painting The Clouds With Sunshine	De 5326
NO-60809-	Love Letters In The Sand	De 5215
NO-60810-	Ain't She Sweet	De 5299
NO-60811-	The Unexplained Blues	De 5215
NO-60812-	Wreck Of Old No. 9	De 5279
NO-60813-A,-B	I Get The Blues When It Rains	De rejected

Most 5000-series issues from the March 17-18 session as by **The Four Aces With Leo Soileau**.

Leo Soileau's Rhythm Boys: Leo Soileau, v; acc. own f; poss. Johnny Baker, g; poss. Buel Hoffpauir, g; prob. Tony Gonzales, d; band, sp/shouting.
Dallas, TX   Saturday, February 20, 1937

61892-A	La Bonne Valse	De 17027
61893-A	The Pretty Brunette	De 17049
61894-A	The Old Country	De 17031
61895-A	Valse De Avalon	De 17035
61896-A	La Blues De Port Arthur	De 17058
61897-A	Riche Ou Pauvre (Rich Or Poor)	De 17031
61898-A	La Jeunne Sur La Montagne (The Girl On The Mountain)	De 17035
61899-A	Promise Me	De 17058
61900-A	Ma Jolie Petite Fille	De 17027
61901-A	Crowley Stomp	De 17049

Acc. own f; Julius "Papa Cairo" Lamperez, eg; prob. Harold "Popeye" Broussard, p; Floyd Shreve, g; Tony Gonzales, d; band, sp/shouting.
Dallas, TX   Tuesday, December 14, 1937

63061-A	Partir A La Maison (Going Back Home)	De 17045
63062-A	Avalon	De 17037
63063-A	Chere Liza	De 17047
63064-A	Going Down The Road With You	De 17056
63065-A	In Your Heart You Love Another	De 17056
63066-A	Vous Avez Quelque Chose (You Had Some)	De 17037
63067-A	Valse D'Amour	De 17042
63068-A	Embrace Moi Encore	De 17045
63069-A	Personne N'Aime Pas	De 17042
63070-A	La Valse De La Rosa	De 17047

SOILEAU & ROBIN
SOILEAU COUZENS

See Leo Soileau.

SOLOMON & HUGHES

Ervin Solomon, f; Joe Hughes, f; Joe Solomon, g.
Dallas, TX   Monday, October 14, 1929

| 56380-1 | Ragtime Annie | Vi V-40244, BB B-5142, MW M-4289 |
| 56381- | Sally Johnson | Vi V-40244, BB B-5142, MW M-4289 |

SONS OF ACADIANS

Oran "Doc" Guidry, f; Roscoe Whitlow, sg; Sidney Guidry, g/v; Nathan Guidry, sb.
Dallas, TX   Tuesday, September 5, 1939

66403-A	Aux Balle Chez Te Maurice	De 17054
66404-A	Ca Tait Pas Difference Asteur (It Makes No Difference Now)	De 17052
66405-A	Tu Peu Pas Metre Ce Maquac Sur Mon Dou (You Can't Put That Monkey On My Back)	De 17053
66406-A	Onze Livre De Ciel (Eleven Pounds Of Heaven)	De 17053
66407-A	Rosetta	De 17052
66408-A	Je Me Demande Si Tu Te Cent Comme Mois Je Me Cent (I Wonder If You Feel The Way I Do)	De 17055
66409-A	En Jour A Venir (I'll Get Mine Bye And Bye)	De 17057
66410-A	La Derniere Lettre (The Last Letter)	De 17051
66411-A	Tu Peu Pas L'Omnait Avec Toi (You Cannot Take It With You)	De 17055
66412-A	L'Alle D'Amour (Lover's Lane)	De 17051
66413-A	A Legire Ma Pauvre Idie (Ease My Wearied Mind)	De 17057
66414-A	J'Vas Continue A' T'Aime (I'll Keep On Loving You)	De 17054

THE SONS OF DIXIE

Tony Sepolio, f/v-1; Bob Dunn, esg; Ralph Smith, p; Arthur "Buddy" Duhon, g/v-2; W.E. "Cotton" Plant, sb.
Dallas, TX   Tuesday, October 7, 1941

071102-1	Nobody Cares For Me -2	BB B-8970
071103-1	Bugle Two-Step	BB B-8873
071104-1	The Prisoner's Farewell -1, 2	BB B-8970
071105-1	I'm Always Dreaming Of You -2	BB B-33-0507
071106-1	Don't Ever Go Wrong -2	BB B-33-0507
071107-1	Those Blue Eyes Don't Sparkle Anymore -2	BB B-8873

SONS OF THE OZARKS

"Ozark Red" (poss. Ishmael Loveall), f-1/g-2/v-3; "Freckles" (Farrell "Rusty" Draper), g/v-4; Howard "Froggy" Matson, sb/v-5.
Chicago, IL   Friday, December 8, 1939

044333-1	Drifting Sands -1, 5	BB B-8583, MW M-8743
044334-1	I'm From Missouri -1, 4	BB B-8583, MW M-8743
044335-1	Ozark Kitchen Sweat -1	BB B-8553, MW M-8742
044336-1	Lone Star Pony -1, 3, 4, 5	BB B-8364, MW M-8738, RZAu G24152
044337-1	The Ghost Song -1, 5	BB B-8457, MW M-8740
044338-1	Mountain Mother Of Mine -1, 4	BB B-8553, MW M-8742
044339-1	Plantation Blues -2	BB B-8380, MW M-8739, HMVIn NE635
044340-1	Bluin' In E Minor -2	BB B-8502, MW M-8741
044341-1	The Story Of The Websters And The McGuires -1, 4	BB B-8364, MW M-8738, RZAu G24152

044342-1	My Sweet Irene From Illinois -1, 4	BB B-8502, MW M-8741
044343-1	When Beulah Did The Hula In Missoula -1, 4	BB B-8457, MW M-8740
044344-1	Little Pony, Travel On To Arizona -1, 4	BB B-8380, MW M-8739, HMVIn NE635

[THE] SONS OF THE PIONEERS

Bob Nolan, Tim Spencer, Leonard Slye, v trio; acc. Hugh Farr, f; Leonard Slye, g.
Los Angeles, CA   Wednesday, August 8, 1934

DLA-10-A	'Way Out There	De 5013, DeAu X1299, Pan 25894
DLA-11-A	Tumbling Tumbleweeds	De 5047
DLA-12-A	Moonlight On The Prairie	De 5047
DLA-13-A	Ridin' Home	De 5013, DeAu X1299, Pan 25894

Los Angeles, CA   Thursday, March 7, 1935

DLA-122-A	I Follow The Stream	De 5083
DLA-123-A	There's A Roundup In The Sky	De 5083
DLA-124-A,-B	I Still Do	De rejected
DLA-125-A	Roving Cowboy	De 5218, DeAu X1382, MeC 45235, Min M-14071

Los Angeles, CA   Monday, March 11, 1935

| DLA-139-A | Will You Love Me When My Hair Has Turned To Silver? | De 5082, DeAu X1317 |
| DLA-141-A,-B | Popeyed | De rejected |

Los Angeles, CA   Wednesday, March 13, 1935

| DLA-138-A | When Our Old Age Pension Check Comes To Our Door | De 5082, DeAu X1317, Pan 25874 |
| DLA-140-A | When I Leave This World Behind | De 5218, MeC 45235 |

Matrix DLA-138 is titled *When Our Old Age Pension Cheque Comes To Our Door* on Decca X1317.

Acc. Hugh Farr, f; Karl Farr, g; Leonard Slye, g.
Los Angeles, CA   Wednesday, October 9, 1935

DLA-241-B	Over The Santa Fe Trail	De 5232, DeAu X1205, BrE 04393
DLA-242-A	Song Of The Pioneers	De 5168, BrE 04393
DLA-243-A,-B	The New Frontier	De rejected
DLA-244-A	Echoes From The Hills	De 5168, BrE 04362

Hugh Farr, f; Karl Farr, g.
Los Angeles, CA   Wednesday, October 16, 1935

DLA-245-A	Kilocycle Stomp	De 5178
DLA-246-B	Cajon Stomp	De 5178
DLA-247-A,-B	Kelly Waltz	De rejected

Bob Nolan, Tim Spencer, Leonard Slye, v trio; acc. Hugh Farr, f; Karl Farr, g; Leonard Slye, g.
Los Angeles, CA   Wednesday, October 16, 1935

| DLA-248-A | Westward Ho | De 5275, MeC 45239, Min M-14071, BrE 04362 |

Los Angeles, CA   Friday, May 8, 1936

DLA-358-A,-B	The Hills Of Old Wyomin'	De 5222, DeAu X1179, Pan 25874
DLA-359-A,-B	A Melody From The Sky	De 5222, Pan 25866
DLA-360-A	We'll Rest At The End Of The Trail	De 5248, DeAu X1179, Pan 25866
DLA-361-A	Texas Star	De 5232
DLA-362-A	On A Mountain High	De rejected

Los Angeles, CA   Thursday, June 18, 1936

| DLA-382-A | Blue Bonnet Girl | De 5243, DeAu X1205, Pan 25886 |
| DLA-383-A | Ride, Ranger, Ride | De 5243, Pan 25886 |

Los Angeles, CA   Friday, July 3, 1936

DLA-411-A,-B	Empty Saddles	De 5247, 46160, DE-24, Pan 25873, BrE 04238, Fest DW-039
DLA-412-A	Blue Prairie	De 5248, DeAu X1382, Pan 25889
DLA-413-A	I'm An Old Cowhand (From The Rio Grande)	De 5247, Pan 25873
DLA-414-A	One More Ride	De 5275, MeC 45239, Pan 25889

Dallas, TX   Monday, February 22, 1937

| 61926-A | 'Way Out There | De 5358, Pan 25925 |
| 61927-A | Tumbling Tumbleweeds | De 5358, 46027, 29814, Pan 25925, BrE 04001, Fest DW-02 |

Bob Nolan, Leonard Slye, Lloyd Perryman, v trio; acc. Hugh Farr, f; Karl Farr, g; Leonard Slye, g; Lloyd Perryman, sb.
Los Angeles, CA   Thursday, October 21, 1937

LA-1482-A	My Saddle Pals And I	ARC 8-03-58, Vo/OK 03236, Cq 8941, Ha 1035-H
LA-1483-B	I Love You Nelly	ARC 8-02-62, Vo/OK 03916, Cq 8941, Co 37627, 20226
LA-1484-A	I Wonder If She Waits For Me Tonight	Vo/OK 04136, Cq 8949
LA-1485-A	When The Roses Bloom Again	ARC 8-02-62, Vo/OK 03916, Cq 8949, Co 37627, 20226
LA-1486-A	Heavenly Airplane	OK 05725
LA-1487-B	Billie The Kid	Vo/OK 04136, Ha 1033-H
LA-1488-B	Power In The Blood	ARC 8-04-60, Vo/OK 03399, Co 37757, 20334

Los Angeles, CA   Monday, October 26, 1937

LA-1489-B	Let's Pretend	ARC 8-03-58, Vo/OK 03236
LA-1490-A,-B	Love Song Of The Waterfall	ARC unissued
LA-1491-A	Song Of The Bandit	ARC unissued: *Co FC37439* (LP); *CK37439, Sony J2K-65816, ASV Living Era CD AJA5421* (CDs)
LA-1491-B	Song Of The Bandit	ARC unissued: *CSP P4-15542* (LP)
LA-1492-B	Down Along The Sleepy Rio Grande	ARC 8-01-51, Vo/OK 03880, Ha 1033-H
LA-1493-A	Just A-Wearyin' For You	ARC 8-01-52, Vo/OK 03881, Ha 1070-H
LA-1494-B	Smilin' Through	ARC 8-01-52, Vo/OK 03881, Ha 1070-H

Hugh Farr, f; Karl Farr, g; Lloyd Perryman, g; Bob Nolan, sb.
Los Angeles, CA   Monday, October 26, 1937

LA-1495-A	Kelly Waltz	Vo/OK 04264, Ha 1035-H

Bob Nolan, Leonard Slye, Lloyd Perryman, v trio; acc. Hugh Farr, f; Karl Farr, g; Leonard Slye, g; Lloyd Perryman, sb.
Los Angeles, CA   Monday, October 26, 1937

LA-1496-A	Open Range Ahead	ARC 8-01-51, Vo/OK 03880, Co 20500, CoC C1188

Hugh Farr, f; Karl Farr, g; Lloyd Perryman, g; Bob Nolan, sb.
Los Angeles, CA   Monday, October 26, 1937

LA-1497-A,B	Cajon Stomp	Vo/OK 04264

Bob Nolan, Leonard Slye, Lloyd Perryman, v trio; acc. Hugh Farr, f; Karl Farr, g; Leonard Slye, g; Lloyd Perryman, sb.
Los Angeles, CA   Monday, October 26, 1937

LA-1498-A,-B	Blue Juniata	ARC unissued
LA-1499-A	Send Him Home To Me	Vo/OK 04328
LA-1499-B	Send Him Home To Me	ARC unissued: *Co FC37439* (LP); *CK37439* (CD)

Matrix LA-1499 may have been recorded on October 28. Matrices LA-1500 to 1503 are by Leonard Slye, in his professional name of Roy Rogers, accompanied by the Sons Of The Pioneers.

Acc. Hugh Farr, f-1/bsv-2; Sam Koki, sg; Karl Farr, g; Lloyd Perryman, g; Pat Brady, sb.
Los Angeles, CA   Tuesday, December 14, 1937

LA-1539-A	Hear Dem Bells -1	Vo/OK 04187
LA-1540-A	One More River To Cross -1	OK 05725, Co 20500, CoC C1188
LA-1541-A	You Must Come In At The Door -2	ARC unissued: *Co FC37439* (LP); *CK37439* (CD)
LA-1541-B	You Must Come In At The Door -2	Vo/OK 04187
LA-1542-B	Lead Me Gently Home, Father -1	Vo/OK 03399, Co 37757, 20334
LA-1543-B	The Devil's Great Grand Son -1	Co 20499
LA-1544-B	Dwelling In Beaulah Land -1	Vo/OK 05428, Cq 9447
LA-1545-A	When The Golden Train Comes Down -1	Vo/OK 05347, Cq 9448

Bob Nolan, Leonard Slye, Lloyd Perryman, v trio; or Bob Nolan, v-1; acc. Hugh Farr, f; Sam Koki, sg; Karl Farr, g; Lloyd Perryman, g; Pat Brady, sb.
Los Angeles, CA   Thursday, December 16, 1937

LA-1546-A,-B	The Hangin' Blues	ARC unissued
LA-1547-B	Hold That Critter Down	Co 20499
LA-1548-B	Leaning On The Everlasting Arm	Vo/OK 05428, Cq 9447
LA-1549-A	What You Gonna Say To Peter	Vo/OK 05347, Cq 9448
LA-1550-A	At The Rainbow's End	Vo/OK 04328
LA-1551-B	The Touch Of God's Hand -1	ARC unissued: *Co FC37439* (LP); *CK37439* (CD)
LA-1552-A,-B	Lord, You Made The Cowboy Happy	ARC unissued

Bob Nolan, Tim Spencer, Lloyd Perryman, v trio; acc. Hugh Farr, f; Karl Farr, g; Pat Brady, sb.
Chicago, IL   Thursday, March 27, 1941

93626-A,-B	So Long To The Red River Valley	De 5939, 46160, MeC 45432, BrE 04238, Fest DW-039
93627-A	My Love Went Without Water (Three Days)	De 5977

93628-A	(Goodbye My Darlin') They Drew My Number	De 5941, MeC 45434
93629-A,-B	He's Gone Up The Trail	De 6003
93630-A	A Love That Ended Too Soon	De 5941, MeC 45434
93631-A,-B	Cielito Lindo	De 6003
93632-A	Cool Water	De 5939, 46024, 29814, DE-24, MeC 45432, BrE 04001, Fest DW-02
93633-A	You Don't Love Me But I'll Always Care	De 5977

Matrix 93628 is titled *(Goodbye My Love) They Drew My Number* on Melotone 45434.

Bob Nolan, Tim Spencer, Lloyd Perryman, v trio; acc. Hugh Farr, f; Karl Farr, g; Pat Brady, sb; or Hugh Farr, f-1; Karl Farr, g-1.

Chicago, IL   Tuesday, April 1, 1941

93644-A	There's A Long, Long Trail	De 5963
93645-A	Kelly Waltz -1	De 46059, BrE 04371, Fest DW-038
93646-A	Lonely Rose Of Mexico	De 5963
93647- -	Rye Whiskey	De unissued: MCA MCAD10090 (CD)
93648-A	Wagner Hoedown -1	De 6066
93649-A	Boggy Road To Texas -1	De 6066

Revs: Decca 46059, Brunswick 04371, Festival DW-038 by the Sons Of The Pioneers (postwar).

Los Angeles, CA   Wednesday, September 3, 1941

DLA-2714-A	I Knew It All The Time	De 6035
DLA-2715-B	You Broke My Heart, Little Darlin'	De 5994, MeC 45473
DLA-2716-A	How Was I To Know	De 6046
DLA-2717-A	When The Moon Comes Over Sun Valley	De 5994, MeC 45473

Los Angeles, CA   Tuesday, September 16, 1941

DLA-2763-A	Pay Me No Mind	De 6011
DLA-2764-A	Salt River Valley	De 6035
DLA-2765-A	Tumbleweed Trail	De 6073
DLA-2766-A	Plain Old Plains	De 6011

Los Angeles, CA   Monday, March 23, 1942

DLA-2959-A	Private Buckaroo	De 6042
DLA-2960-A	O-O-Oh, Wonderful World	De 6042
DLA-2961-A	I'll Be Around Somewhere	De 6073
DLA-2962-A	I'm Crying My Heart Out Over You	De 6046

The Sons Of The Pioneers recorded after 1942. See also Tex Ritter, Roy Rogers.

SONS OF THE WEST

Pat Trotter, f; Billy Briggs, esg; Slick Robertson, tbj; Freddy Dean, g; Jimmie Meek, sb/v; band v-1.

Dallas, TX   Friday, September 16, 1938

64524-A	There's Evil In You Chillun -1	De 5641
64525-A	Visions Of The Past -1	De 5657
64526-A	Mama Inez -1	De 5618, MeC 45272, Pan 26017
64527-A	Am I Blue	De 5641
64528-A	Spanish Cavalier	De 5618, MeC 45272, Pan 26017
64529-A	Oh Monah! -1	De 5608
64530-A	I'll Always Be In Love With You	De 5629
64531-A	My Gal Don't Love Me Anymore -1	De 5629
64532-A	Following You Around	De 5657
64533-A	Thinking Of You	De 5608

Pat Trotter, f-1/emd-2; Buck Buchanan, f; Billy Briggs, esg; Loren Mitchell, p; Slick Robertson, tbj; Jess Williams, g; Jimmie Meek, sb/v; unidentified, v duet-3.

Fort Worth, TX   Wednesday, March 19, 1941

DAL-1370-1	I Live In Memory Of You -1	OK 06328
DAL-1371-1	You'll Be Sorry -1	Cq 9861
DAL-1372-1	Our Last Goodbye -2	OK 06196
DAL-1373-1	Sally's Got A Wooden Leg -1	OK 06587
DAL-1374-1	My Prairie Queen -1, 3	OK 06587
DAL-1375-1	Panhandle Shuffle -1	OK 06196
DAL-1376-1	Make A Wreath For Mary -1, 3	OK 06328
DAL-1377-1	I'll Forget I Ever Loved You -1	Cq 9861

The Sons of The West also recorded with Bill Boyd on February 12, 1940.

SOUTH CAROLINA SACRED QUARTETTE

Pseudonym on Supertone for the Carolina Gospel Singers.

SOUTH GEORGIA HIGHBALLERS

Melgie Ward, f/v; Albert Everidge, saw/sp-1; Vander Everidge, g.
Atlanta, GA   Wednesday, October 5, 1927
    81675-   Ida Red   OK unissued
    81676-   Old Sallie Goodwin   OK unissued
    81677-A   Green River Train   OK 45166
    81678-A   Mister Johnson, Turn Me Aloose -1   OK 45166

Vander Everidge, g solo/sp; Melgie Ward, sp; Albert Everidge, sp.
Atlanta, GA   Wednesday, October 5, 1927
    81679-B   Blue Grass Twist   OK 45155
    81680-B   Bibb County Grind   OK 45155

SOUTH SEA SERENADERS

No details.
Atlanta, GA   Tuesday, October 27, 1931
    151954-   My South Sea Rose   Co unissued
    151955-   Palm Breezes   Co unissued
    151958-   Will You Be My Sweetheart   Co unissued
    151959-   In A Cottage On A Hill   Co unissued

Matrices 151956/57 are by the Pelican Wildcats.

THE SOUTHERN BROADCASTERS

Pseudonym on Silvertone 5183 for Da Costa Woltz's Southern Broadcasters.

SOUTHERN HAWAIIANS

The one release with this credit in the Okeh Old Time Tunes series (45395) is beyond the scope of this work.

SOUTHERN KENTUCKY MOUNTAINEERS

Pseudonym on Supertone for Taylor, Moore & Burnett or for Moore, Burnett & Rutherford (see Richard D. Burnett in both instances).

SOUTHERN MELODY BOYS (ODUS & WOODROW)

See Odus & Woodrow.

SOUTHERN MOONLIGHT ENTERTAINERS

George Rainey, f; Luther Luallen, f-1; Willie Rainey, bj; Albert Rainey, g/v-2; Marvin "Dude" Rainey, g.
Knoxville, TN   Tuesday, August 27, 1929
    K-107-   My Carolina Girl -1, 2   Vo 5388
    K-108-   Are You Happy Or Lonesome -2   Vo 5372
    K-109-   Lost John -1, 2   Vo 5460
    K-110-   My Cabin Home -1, 2   Vo 5460
    K-111-   My Blue Ridge Mountain Queen -2 Vo 5372
    K-112-   Dream Waltz -1   Vo 5388
    K-113-   Sister Liz -2   Vo 5407
    K-114-   Buckin' Mule   Vo 5407

George Rainey, f; Willie Rainey, bj; Albert Rainey, g/v; Marvin "Dude" Rainey, g; poss. Bill Brown, sp.
Knoxville, TN   Friday, April 4, 1930
    K-8084-   Then I'll Move To Town   Vo 5440
    K-8085-   How To Make Love   Vo 5440

SOUTHERN MOONSHINERS

Harry Walker, v; acc. **Southern Moonshiners**: unknown, bj; poss. another unknown, bj; unknown g.
Richmond, IN   Tuesday, June 25, 1929
    15271   Yellow Bumblebee   Ge rejected

Southern Moonshiners: unknown, bj; another unknown, bj-1; unknown, g.
Richmond, IN   Tuesday, June 25, 1929
    15273   Mississippi Clog   Ge rejected
    15274   Irish Clog -1   Ge rejected

Matrix 15272 is by Chester Southworth, who may be associated with this group.

SOUTHERN RAILROAD QUARTET

J.M. Drake, tv; H.Q. Sides, tv; C.E. Sides, bv; C.F. Dunn, bsv; acc. Irene Burke, p.
Atlanta, GA   Saturday, October 20, 1928

47213-2	Life's Railway To Heaven	Vi V-40002	
47214-2	God Is Love	Vi V-40002	

SOUTHERN SACRED SINGERS

Vocal quartet; acc. unknown, o; unknown, chimes-1.
New York, NY   Monday, March 11, 1929

401709-B	Work For The Night Is Coming -1	OK 45342	
401710-B	The Wondrous Story	OK 45342	

The Southern Sacred Singers was used as a pseudonym on English Regal for Smith's Sacred Singers.

SOUTHLAND MARIMBA PLAYERS

This pseudonym for the Dixie Marimba Players was used on a coupling issued in the Paramount Old Time Tunes series (3167). The group is outside the scope of this work.

SOUTHLAND'S LADIES QUARTET

Pseudonym on Challenge for the Carolina Ladies Quartette.

THE SOUTHLANDERS

No details.
Birmingham, AL   Thursday, November 15, 1928

BIRM-804	Southern College Medley	Br 4454	
BIRM-805	Sweetheart Of Sigma Chi	Br 4454	

CHESTER SOUTHWORTH

Chester Southworth, v; acc. prob. own g.
Richmond, IN   Tuesday, June 25, 1929

15272	The Jailhouse Blues	Ge rejected	

Matrices 15271, 15273/74 are by the Southern Moonshiners, with whom this artist may be associated.

THE IRENE SPAIN FAMILY

Irene Spain, two unknowns, v trio; acc. unknown, vla; unknown, ah.
Atlanta, GA   Wednesday, March 20, 1929

402388-	He Keeps Me Singing	OK 45340	
402389-A	Leaning On The Everlasting Arms	OK 45322	
402390-B	Since He Came To Stay	OK 45322	
402391-	At The Cross	OK 45340	

Irene Spain was a daughter of Andrew Jenkins and a member of the Jenkins Sacred Singers, with whom this group may be associated.

SPANGLER & PEARSON (OLD VIRGINIA FIDDLERS)

J.W. Spangler, f; Dave Pearson, g.
Richmond, VA   Monday, October 14, 1929

403120-	Climbing Up The Golden Stairs	OK unissued	
403121-	Golden Slippers	OK unissued	
403122-A	Midnight Serenade	OK 45387	
403123-A	Patrick County Blues	OK 45387	

SPARKMAN TRIO

Ruth Sparkman, Rena Sparkman, unknown, v trio; acc. unknown, p.
Birmingham, AL   Monday, November 12, 1928

BIRM-769-	Living For Christ Each Day	Vo 5286	
BIRM-770-	That Beautiful Land	Vo 5286	
BIRM-771-B,-A	Rocking On The Waves	Vo unissued	

Ruth & Rena Sparkman, v duet; acc. unknown, p.
Birmingham, AL   Monday, November 12, 1928

BIRM-772-A,-B	Happy In Him	Vo unissued	

THE SPARROW

See Arthur Fields & Fred Hall.

BUDDY SPENCER TRIO

Pseudonym on ARC labels (and derivatives) for the Frank Luther Trio.

THE SPENCER TRIO
Pseudonym on Supertone for Ted Gossett's Band or Tommy Whitmer's Band.

THE SPINDALE QUARTET
Vocal quartet; unacc.
    Johnson City, TN   Tuesday, October 22, 1929

149220-2	Sweet Peace The Gift Of God's Love	Co 15541-D
149221-1	God Will Take Care Of You	Co 15541-D
149222-2	Face To Face	Co 15488-D
149223-2	Lift Him Up	Co 15488-D

THE SPOONEY FIVE
Prob. Bill Edwards, f; prob. Patt Patterson, md; unknown, bj; prob. Bill Chandler, g; J. Herschel Brown, wb/spoons-1; unknown, sp-2; band v-3.
    Atlanta, GA   Tuesday, November 8, 1927

145172-1	Chinese Rag -1, 2	Co 15234-D
145173-2	My Little Girl -3	Co 15234-D

CARL T. SPRAGUE
Carl T. Sprague, v; acc. own g.
    Camden, NJ   Monday, August 3, 1925

33124-3	Kisses	Vi 19813
33125-1,-2,-3	When The Work's All Done This Fall	Vi unissued

    Camden, NJ   Tuesday, August 4, 1925

33139-2	Bad Companions	Vi 19747
33140-1,-2,-3	Chicken	Vi unissued
33141-1,-2,-3	Sarah Jane	Vi unissued

    Camden, NJ   Wednesday, August 5, 1925

33125-4	When The Work's All Done This Fall	Vi 19747, MW M-8060
33143-2	Following The Cow Trail	Vi 20067, MW M-4468, Au 418, BB B-4957
33144-1,-2,-3	The Kicking Mule	Vi unissued
33145-3	Cowboy Love Song	Vi 20067, Au 418, BB B-4957
33146-1,-2,-3	The Last Great Round-Up	Vi unissued
33147-2	The Club Meeting	Vi 19813

Revs: Montgomery Ward M-4468 by Dwight Butcher, M-8060 by Nat Shilkret (popular).

Acc. C.R. Dockum, f-1; H.J. Kenzie, f-1; own g.
    Camden, NJ   Monday, June 21, 1926

35193-1,-2,-3	Here's To The Texas Ranger -1	Vi unissued
35194-2	If Your Saddle Is Good And Tight	Vi V-40066

Acc. C.R. Dockum, f; H.J. Kenzie, f; own g.
    New York, NY   Monday, June 21, 1926

35539-1,-2,-3	The Boston Burglar	Vi unissued
35540-3	The Gambler	Vi 20534

    New York, NY   Tuesday, June 22, 1926

35541-2	O Bury Me Not On The Lone Prairie (The Dying Cowboy)	Vi 20122, MW M-4060, M-4099, Au 419, BB B-4958
35542-3	The Cowboy's Dream	Vi 20122, MW M-4343, Au 419, BB B-4958
33124-4,-5	Kisses	Vi unissued

Later pressings of Montgomery Ward M-4060 replace matrix 35541 with matrix 77252 by the Delmore Brothers.
Revs: Montgomery Ward M-4099, M-4343 by Jules Allen, M-4060 by Bud Billings (Frank Luther) & Carson Robison (see the latter).

    New York, NY   Wednesday, June 23, 1926

35193-6	Here's To The Texas Ranger	Vi V-40066
35539-4,-5	The Boston Burglar	Vi unissued
35541-4,-5,-6	The Dying Cowboy (O Bury Me Not On The Lone Prairie)	Vi unissued

    New York, NY   Thursday, June 24, 1926

35539-7	The Boston Burglar	Vi 20534

Acc. Olie Olsen, f; Joe Mintz, f; own g.
    Savannah, GA   Wednesday, August 24, 1927

39838-2	Rounded Up In Glory	Vi 20932, MW M-4466

39839-3	Last Great Round-Up	Vi 20932, MW M-4466
39840-2	Cowman's Prayer	Vi 21402
39841-3	The Cowboy	Vi 21402, MW M-4465, M-4783
39842-2	Utah Carroll	Vi 21194
39843-4	The Two Soldiers	Vi 21194

Victor 21402 as by **C.T. Sprague**.
Rev. Montgomery Ward M-4465 by Harry "Mac" McClintock.

Acc. own g.
Dallas, TX — Sunday, October 13, 1929

56374-2	The Wayward Daughter	Vi V-40246, Au 235
56375-	The Prisoner's Meditation	BB B-6258
56376-2	The Cowboy's Meditation	Vi V-40197, MW M-4467, M-4783, Au 233
56377-2	The Last Longhorn	Vi V-40197, MW M-4467, Au 233
56378-	The Cowboy At Church	BB B-6258
56379-2	The Mormon Cowboy	Vi V-40246, Au 235

Carl T. Sprague recorded after 1942.

MAURY SPRAYBERRY

Maury Sprayberry, v; acc. unknown.
Atlanta, GA — Friday, March 18, 1927

| 80567- | Froggy | OK unissued |
| 80568- | Polly Wolly Doodle | OK unissued |

STALSBY FAMILY (SAMMY–DOT–JACKIE)

Sammy Stalsby, Dot Stalsby, Jackie Stalsby, v trio; acc. prob. Harold Whatley, sg; prob. Sammy Stalsby, g.
Dallas, TX — Thursday, April 11, 1940

92076-A	Every Time I Feel The Spirit	De 5866
92077-A	Heaven Bells Ring Out	De 5888
92078-A	Greasy Greens	De 5835
92079-A	My Heart Is Aching	De 5835
92080-A	When We See The Saviour Coming From Above	De 5888
92081-A	I Found The Right Way	De 5866

V.O. STAMPS–M.L. YANDELL

Virgil O. Stamps, M.L. Yandell, v duet; acc. unknown, p.
Memphis, TN — Saturday, September 15, 1928

46171-1,-2	When Jesus Comes	Vi unissued
47032-1	On The Happy Hallelujah Side	Vi V-40084, BB B-5274, Eld 2148, ZoSA 4231
47033-2	Singing While Ages Roll	Vi V-40084, BB B-5274, Eld 2148, ZoSA 4231
47034-1	When The Light Shines Thru	Vi 21722
47035-1,-2	What A Day That Will Be	Vi unissued
47040-1	You Must Come In At The Door	Vi 21722

Intervening matrices are by other artists.

Acc. unknown, f; unknown, p; unknown, vc.
Dallas, TX — Sunday, August 11, 1929

| 55338-2 | Does This Train Go To Heaven | Vi V-40142 |
| 55339-2 | Down On The Farm | Vi V-40142 |

Acc. unknown, p.
Dallas, TX — Sunday, August 11, 1929

| 55340-2 | What A Wonderful Time | Vi V-40183 |
| 55341-2 | No Longer Sad | Vi V-40183 |

STAMPS–BAXTER SCHOOL OF MUSIC

See Stamps Quartet & Associated Groups.

STAMPS QUARTET & ASSOCIATED GROUPS

Stamps Quartet: Palmer Wheeler, tv; Roy Wheeler, tv; Odis Echols, bv; Frank Stamps, bsv; acc. Dwight M. Brock, p.
Atlanta, GA — Thursday, October 20, 1927

40316-2	Give The World A Smile	Vi 21072, 20-2429, BB B-6038, MW M-4250
40317-2	Love Leads The Way	Vi 21072, BB B-6038, MW M-4278
40318-2	Bringing In The Sheaves	Vi 21035, MW M-8107
40319-2	Rescue The Perishing	Vi 21035

Victor 21035 as by **Stamp's Quartet**. Montgomery Ward M-4250, M-4278, M-8107 as by **The Stamps Quartet**.

The Stamps Quartet: Palmer Wheeler, tv; Roy Wheeler, tv; Odis Echols, bv; Frank Stamps, bsv; acc. Dwight M. Brock, p.

    Memphis, TN   Friday, February 10, 1928

41873-1	Wonderful	Vi 21468
41874-1	Let Me Live Close To Thee	Vi 21637, MW M-4278
41875-2	Till He Calls His Reapers	Vi 21468
41876-1	He's With Me All The Way	Vi 21637, MW M-4279

    Memphis, TN   Saturday, February 11, 1928

41878-1	Jesus Is Coming, It May Be Soon	Vi V-40090
41879-1	The Heavenly Chorus	Vi V-40029
41880-1	Walk And Talk With Jesus	Vi 21265, MW M-4250
41881-1	He Bore It All	Vi 21265

Victor 21265 as by **Stamps' Quartet**.

Palmer Wheeler, tv; J.E. Wheeler, tv; Ray Wheeler, bv; Frank Stamps, bsv; Mike O'Byrne, bsv; acc. Dwight M. Brock, p.

    Bristol, TN   Thursday, November 1, 1928

47267-2	I'll Be Happy	Vi V-40029, 20-3314, MW M-4279

    Bristol, TN   Friday, November 2, 1928

47268-2	Like The Rainbow	Vi V-40122
47269-2	Because I Love Him	Vi V-40090, ZoSA 4233
47270-2	Come To The Savior	Vi V-40062
47271-2	Do Your Best, Then Wear A Smile	Vi V-40122
47272-1	We Shall Reach Home	Vi V-40062

Rev. Zonophone 4233 by Frank & James McCravy.

Stamps Quartet: four unknowns, v quartet; acc. unknown, p.

    Dallas, TX   Friday, June 28, 1929

402774-B	The Way To Glory Land	OK 45359, Ve 7096-V
402775-	On The Cross	OK 45385
402776-B	Don't Forget To Pray	OK 45359, Ve 7095-V
402777-	It Will Not Be Long	OK 45385
402778-	Lord Let Me Serve	OK unissued
402779-	Walking With My Lord	OK unissued

Revs: Velvet Tone 7095-V by Frank & James McCravy, 7096-V by the Wisdom Sisters.

Original Stamps Quartet: Virgil O. Stamps, three unknowns, v quartet; acc. unknown, p.

    Dallas, TX   Sunday, October 27, 1929

DAL-503-	He Will Be With Me	Br 375, DeE F3878, RexIr U482
DAL-504-	A Little While Then Glory	Br 375, DeE F3878, RexIr U482
DAL-505-	Cling To The Cross	Br 408
DAL-506-	The Glad Bells	Br 408
DAL-507-	The City Of Gold	Br 418
DAL-508-	Thou Art My Strength	Br 418
DAL-509-	He Keeps My Soul	Br 447
DAL-510-	I'm In The Way	Br 447

This session was logged as by **Original V.O. Stamps Quartette** but issued as shown.

Frank Stamps & His All Star Quartet: —— Hughes, v; —— Long, v; —— Burgess, v; Frank Stamps, bsv; acc. unknown, p.

    Atlanta, GA   Monday, November 25, 1929

56590-1	Living For Jesus	Vi V-40245
56591-1	Reapers Be True	Vi V-40228
56592-1	I'm Only Here On A Visit	Vi V-40228
56593-1	I'm On The Right Road Now	Vi V-40245

    Atlanta, GA   Tuesday, November 26, 1929

56601-1,-2	Oh Declare His Glory	Vi unissued
56602-1,-2	In The Master's Presence	Vi unissued
56603-1	With Joy We Sing	Vi V-40301
56604-2	Working For The Master	Vi V-40320, 20-2429, BB 1853, B-5008, Eld 1965, Sr S-3130, MW M-4285
56605-1	Singing In My Soul	Vi V-40320, 20-3314, BB 1853, B-5008, Eld 1965, Sr S-3130, MW M-4285
56606-1	His Love Leads Home	Vi V-40301

Stamps–Baxter School Of Music: mixed choir; unacc.

    Dallas, TX   Friday, November 29, 1929

| 403386-C | I Am O'ershadowed By Love | OK 45396 |
| 403387-A | I'll Be Singing Forever | OK 45396 |

Frank Stamps & His All Star Quartet: Lester Harley, poss. tv; unknown, tv; unknown, bv; Frank Stamps, bsv; or Lester Harley, v-1; or Frank Stamps, v-2; acc. Dwight M. Brock, p.

Memphis, TN   Thursday, May 22, 1930

59969-	Singing Of Wonderful Love	BB B-5544
59970-	I Will Never Give Up	BB B-5487
59971-	Walking With My Lord	BB B-5487, MW M-8194
59972-	Lord, Let Me Serve -1	BB B-5544
59973-2	It Won't Be Long	Vi 23519
59974-1,-2	What A Day That Will Be	Vi unissued
59975-1	A Song Of Jesus' Love Brings Heaven Down	Vi 23572
59976-2	Endless Joy Is Coming -2	Vi 23572

Matrix 59971 is titled *I Will Walk With My Savior (Walking With My Lord)* on Montgomery Ward M-8194.
Revs: Victor 23519 by Vaughan Quartet; Montgomery Ward M-8194 by Carson Robison.

Memphis, TN   Friday, May 23, 1930

56601-4	Oh Declare His Glory	Vi V-40279
56602-4	In The Master's Presence	Vi V-40279
59977-	Jesus is Precious To Me	MW M-8107
59978-1,-2	Jesus Paid It All	Vi unissued

Matrix 59977 was originally logged as *He's A Wonderful Saviour To Me*.

Original Stamps Quartet: Myrtle Combs, av; Lonnie Combs, v; poss. Virgil O. Stamps, v; one or more unknowns, v; acc. Myrtle Combs, ac-1; unknown, p-2; unknown, g-3.

Dallas, TX   Saturday, November 29, 1930

DAL-6775-	Launch Out On The Sea Of God's Love -3	Br 500, DeE F3745, RexIr U479
DAL-6776-	In Christ, Our Lord -2	Br 500, DeE F3745, RexIr U479
DAL-6777-	Won't We Be Happy -2	Br 508, DeE F3744, RexIr U478
DAL-6778-	Jesus Taught Me How To Smile -1	Br 508, DeE F3744, RexIr U478
DAL-6779-	Walking At My Side -2	Br 555, DeE F3746, RexIr U480
DAL-6780-A	We Will March Alone -2	Br 583
DAL-6785	The Longer I Know Him -1, 2	Br 555, DeE F3746, RexIr U480
DAL-6786-	Old Time Religion For Me -2	Br 569, DeE F3788, RexIr U481
DAL-6787-A	Follow Jesus -2	Br 583
DAL-6788-	My Friend -2	Br 569, DeE F3788, RexIr U481

Matrices DAL-6781 to 6784 are by The Red Headed Fiddlers.

Frank Stamps & His All Star Quartet: J.R. Baxter, Jr., tv; Otis McCoy, tv; Dwight Brock, bv; Frank Stamps, bsv; acc. Mrs. Frank Stamps, p.

Atlanta, GA   Monday, February 15, 1932

70688-1	The Great Redeemer	Vi 23753, MW M-4347
70689-1	Wonderful Love Divine	Vi 23729
70690-1	Homeward Bound	Vi 23854
70691-1	There Is Springtime In My Soul	Vi 23702
70692-1	Skies Will Be Blue	Vi 23702
70693-1	Troubles All Will End	Vi 23660
70694-1	I Want To Hear Him Call My Name	Vi 23753, MW M-4347
70695-1	Dreaming Alone In The Twilight	BB B-5785

J.R. Baxter, Jr., tv; Otis McCoy, tv; Dwight Brock, bv; Frank Stamps, bsv; acc. Mrs. Frank Stamps, p; or Mrs. Frank Stamps, v-1; acc. J.R. Baxter, Jr., p-2; Dwight Brock, p-3.

Atlanta, GA   Tuesday, February 16, 1932

70696-1	I'm Finding Glory -1, 2	Vi 23854
70697-1	Tell Him Now	Vi 23660
70698-1	Dreams Of The Past	BB B-5785
70699-1	I Ain't A-Gonna Let Satan Turn Me 'Roun' -1, 3	Vi 23729

The Stamps Quartet: four unknowns, v quartet; acc. unknown, p.

Dallas, TX   Friday, May 13, 1938

DAL-521-1	Give The World A Smile	Co 37674, 20273
DAL-522-1	There's A Little Pine Log Cabin	Co 37674, 20273
DAL-523-1	Who	Vo/OK 04160, Co 37671, 20270
DAL-524-1	Holy Be Thy Name	Vo/OK 04160, Cq 9105, 9592, Co 37671, 20270
DAL-525-1	Farther Along	Vo/OK 04236, Co 37760, 20337
DAL-526-1	A Beautiful Prayer	Vo/OK 04236, Cq 9105, 9592, Co 37760, 20337
DAL-527-1	Just A Little Talk With Jesus	Vo/OK 04329, Cq 9668, Co 37672, 20271

Dallas, TX Saturday, May 14, 1938
DAL-528-1 The Lord Is With Me Vo/OK 04329, Cq 9668, Co 37672, 20271

See also Owen Brothers & Ellis, some of whose recordings were as, or subcredited, **The** (or **A**) **Stamps Quartet**.

FRED STANLEY

Fred Stanley, v; acc. own g.
Atlanta, GA Tuesday, April 15, 1930
150224-1 The Tie That Binds Co 15559-D
150225-2 The Cottage By The Sea Co 15559-D

JOHN STANLEY'S ORCHESTRA

Pseudonym on Superior for Geo. Pariseau's Orchestra.

LEVI STANLEY

Pseudonym on Challenge for John Hammond.

ROBA STANLEY

The Stanley Trio: R.M. (Rob) Stanley, f/v; Roba Stanley, g/v-1; William Patterson, g.
Atlanta, GA c. August 26, 1924
8696-A Nellie Gray OK 40271
8697-A Whoa! Mule -1 OK 40271

Roba Stanley–William Patterson: William Patterson, h/g; Roba Stanley, g/v.
Atlanta, GA c. August 26, 1924
8698-A Devilish Mary OK 40213
8699-A Mister Chicken OK 40213

Roba Stanley–Bill Patterson: William Patterson, h/g; Roba Stanley, g/v.
Atlanta, GA c. January 9, 1925
8847-A All Night Long OK 40295
8848-A Little Frankie OK 40436

Roba Stanley, Bob Stanley, Bill Patterson: R.M. (Rob) Stanley, f; Roba Stanley, g/v; William Patterson, g.
Atlanta, GA c. January 9, 1925
8852-A Railroad Bill OK 40295

Matrices 8849 to 8851 are untraced but possibly by these artists.

Roba Stanley, v; acc. Henry Whitter, h/g; own g.
Atlanta, GA c. July 4, 1925
9213-A Old Maid Blues OK 45036
9315-A Single Life OK 40436

Matrices 9212, 9214, and 9216 to 9219 are untraced but some at least may be by this artist.
Rev. OKeh 45036 by Ernest V. Stoneman.

RUFUS K. STANLEY

Rufus K. Stanley, v; acc. own bj.
Chicago, IL c. March 1926
2490-1 Only A Tramp Pm 33175
2491-1 Six Feet Of Earth Pm 33175
  Down In Arkansas Pm 33174
  Where The Whippoorwill Is Whispering Pm 33174
  Goodnight

STANLEY & HIGGINS

Prob.: Fred Stanley, Clarence Higgins, v duet; prob. acc. own g duet.
Atlanta, GA Tuesday, April 15, 1930
150230- He's Coming Home To Mother Co unissued
150231- Railroad Love Co unissued

THE STANLEY TRIO

See Roba Stanley.

FRANK STANTON

Pseudonym on Superior for Walter Coon.

STANTON'S JOY BOYS

Pseudonym on Superior for Walter Coon & His Joy Boys.

MASON STAPLETON
STAPLETON BROTHERS

Stapleton Brothers: Mason Stapleton, Mitchell Stapleton, v duet; acc. prob. one of them, h-1; prob. the other, g; one of them, wh-2.

Atlanta, GA   Thursday, April 19, 1928

146140-1	Call Of The Whip-Poor-Will -1	Co 15284-D
146141-1	In A Cool Shady Nook -2	Co 15284-D

Mason Stapleton, v/y-1; acc. own or Mitchell Stapleton, sg; own or Mitchell Stapleton, g; Roy Kingsmore, g-2.

Charlotte, NC   Friday, May 29, 1931

69381-1	The Rafe King Murder Case -2	Vi 23568
69385-1	Strolling Through Life Together -1	Vi 23591
69386-2	Won't You Take Me Back Again -1	Vi 23591

Victor 23568 as by **Mason Stapleton**.
Matrices 69382 to 69384 are by the Three Tobacco Tags.
Rev. Victor 23568 by Johnnie Powell (see Jack & Johnnie Powell).

BOB STAR (THE TEXAS RANGER)

Pseudonym on Montgomery Ward for Edward L. Crain, Frank Marvin, or Johnny Marvin.

STAR SACRED QUARTETTE

Pseudonym on Broadway for the XC Sacred Quartette.

STAR SACRED SINGERS

Pseudonym on Broadway for the Paramount Sacred Four or XC Sacred Quartette.

BLUE STEELE & HIS ORCHESTRA

Several items by this danceband were issued in the Victor Old Familiar Tunes series (V-40140, V-40161, V-40182, and V-40288). For further details of those and other Victor recordings by this group – which is beyond the scope of this work – see *JR*.

GENE STEELE

Gene Steele, v/y-1; acc. Farris "Lefty" Ingram, f; "Jose Cortes" (Alfredo Casares), f-2; David "Pee Wee" Wamble, t-3/p-4; Clifford Z. "Kokomo" Crocker, ac; Elmer "Slim" Hall, g; Calvin "Curly" Noland, sb.

Memphis, TN   Wednesday, July 12, or Thursday, July 13, 1939

MEM-119-1	Ride 'Em, Cowboy, Ride 'Em -1, 2, 4	Vo 05135, Cq 9337
MEM-120-1	Don't Wait 'Till We're Old And Grey -3	Vo 05068, Cq 9336
MEM-124-1	Here's Your Opportunity	Vo 05068, Cq 9336
MEM-125-1	Freight Train Blues -1, 4	Vo/OK 05204

Intervening matrices are by the Swift Jewel Cowboys (who constitute Steele's accompanying group at this session).

Acc. poss. Gene Bagett, lg; own g; unknown, sb.

Memphis, TN   Friday, July 14, 1939

MEM-140-1	Rio Grande Moon	Vo 05135, Cq 9337
MEM-141-1	Just A Little Of The Blues	Vo/OK 05204

Gene Steele recorded after 1942.

STEELMAN SISTERS (SIS & SHANG)

Sis Steelman, Shang Steelman, v/y-1 duet; acc. prob. one of them, g.

Hattiesburg, MS   Thursday, July 23, 1936

HAT-161-2	Those Rambling Blues -1	ARC-6-11-69
HAT-162-3	The Cowgirl's Prayer -1	ARC 7-01-61, Cq 8762
HAT-170-3	Lonesome Valley Sally	ARC 7-01-61, Cq 8762
HAT-171-1	I'm Drifting Back To Dreamland	ARC 6-11-69, Cq 8753

Matrices HAT-170/71 may have been recorded on July 24.
Intervening matrices are by other artists.
Rev. Conqueror 8753 by Jimmie & Eddie Dean.

Birmingham, AL   Saturday, April 10, 1937

B-111-	Going Home To Mother -1	ARC unissued
B-112-	Dear Old Texas Moon	ARC unissued
B-113-	Rusty Rural Mailbox	ARC unissued
B-114-	Carolina Moon	ARC unissued

JOE STEEN

Joe Steen, v/y-1; acc. prob. own g.

Richmond, IN   Tuesday, March 24, 1931

17641,-A	Happy Joe -1	Ge rejected
17642	Ben Dewberry's Final Run	Ch 16258
17643-A	Railroad Jack -1	Ch 16258
17644	I Wonder If They Care To See Me Now -1	Ge rejected

Joe Steen, v; acc. unknown, sg; prob. own g.
Louisville, KY   Tuesday, June 16, 1931

| 69452-1 | The Crazy Engineer | Vi 23634, Au 412, BB B-4953 |
| 69453-1 | I Just Received A Long Letter | Vi 23634, Au 412, BB B-4953 |

Joe Steen, v/y-1; acc. prob. own g.
Chicago, IL   Friday, January 26, 1934

80190-1	I'll Love Ya Till The Cows Come Home -1	BB B-5567
80191-1	Kentucky, My Home -1	BB B-5567
80192-1	Madison Street Rag	BB unissued
80193-1	Soft Baby Feet	BB unissued
80194-1	Nobody Knows About Women	BB unissued
80195-1	Mother, My Sweetheart	BB unissued

"UNCLE BUNT" STEPHENS

"Uncle Bunt" Stephens, f solo.
New York, NY   Monday, March 29, 1926

141874-1	Louisburg Blues	Co 15071-D
141875-3	Left In The Dark Blues	Co 15085-D
141876-2	Sail Away Lady	Co 15071-D
141877-3	Candy Girl	Co 15085-D
141878-	Jenny In The Garden	Co unissued
141879-	Leather Breeches	Co unissued

REV. STEPHENSON & MALE CHOIR

Sermons with singing.
Chicago, IL   c. August 1927

| 4752-2 | Call For Sinners | Pm 3050, Bwy 8181 |
| 4753-1 | The Gospel Train | Pm 3050, Bwy 8181 |

Broadway 8181 as by **Rev. Stone & Male Choir**.
Surrounding matrices are by the Riley Quartette, with whom Rev. Stephenson may be associated.

WILLIAM STEUDEVANT

Wm. Steudevant, v; acc. unknown.
Shreveport, LA   Tuesday, February 18, 1930

| 403812- | Old Pal How I Wonder Where You Are Tonight | OK unissued |
| 403813- | Let's Be Sweethearts Again | OK unissued |

A William Sturdevant, almost certainly the same man as the above, wrote material for, and may have accompanied, Jimmie Davis.

STEVE & HIS HOT SHOTS

Unknown, f; unknown, bj-1; unknown, g; unknown, vc; George P. Stephens, v-2.
Dallas, TX   Tuesday, October 15, 1929

56388-1	The Grape Vine Twist -1	Vi 23699
56389-2	Sour Apple Cider -1	Vi 23699
56390-	My Buddy -2	Vi V-40308

Dallas, TX   Wednesday, October 16, 1929

| 56391- | The Press -1, 2 | Vi V-40308 |

GEORGE STEVENS
STEVENS & DOHLAY

George Stevens, v; or **Stevens & Dohlay**-1, v duet; acc. unknown, sg-2; prob. George Stevens, g.
Grafton, WI   c. April 1932

L-270-2	Lonesome Dreamer Of Love -2	Pm 3252, Bwy 8268
L-273-	Don't Grieve Over Me	Pm 3252, Bwy 8268
	Aunt Betsey's Choice -1	Pm 3246
	The Girl That Wore A Water Fall	Pm 3246

Matrices L-271/72 are untraced but may apply to Paramount 3246.

OTIS STEWART

Pseudonym on Supertone for Owen Gray with Otto Gray's Oklahoma Cowboy Band.

OVIE STEWART & ZELPHA SPARKS

Ovie Stewart, Zelpha Sparks, v duet; acc. poss. one of them, f; poss. the other, g.
Richmond, IN   Monday, December 21, 1931
18265	Rock Me In A Cradle Of Kalua	Ge rejected

Richmond, IN   Tuesday, December 22, 1931
18266	That Good Old Country Town	Ge unissued

STEWART & DILLMAN

Poss. —— Stewart, —— Dillman, v duet; acc. unknown, g.
Richmond, IN   Saturday, June 21, 1930
16780	[unknown title]	Ge rejected trial recording

STEWART'S HARMONY SINGERS

Vocal duet; acc. unknown, md-1; two unknowns, g.
Richmond, IN   Thursday, October 27, 1932
18862-A	Carry Me Back To The Mountains	Ch 16527
18863	I Only Want A Buddy -1	Ch S-16538, MW 4957
18864	My Renfra Valley Home -1	Ch 16527, MW 4957
18865	Do Not Wait Until I'm Under The Clay -1	Ch S-16538

Fred Shepherd is named as a royalty payee in Champion files and may be a member of this group.

CHARLES LEWIS STINE

Chas. L. Stine, v; acc own g.
Camden, NJ   Monday, November 10, 1924
	The Wreck Of The C&O	Vi unissued trial recording

Charles Lewis Stine, v; acc. own g; unknown, train- or boat-wh eff.
New York, NY   Thursday, March 19, 1925
140447-1	The Wreck On The C&O	Co 15027-D, Ha 5145-H
140448-1	The Ship That Never Returned	Co 15027-D, Ha 5145-H

Harmony 5145-H as by **Charles Lewis**.

Acc. own g.
New York, NY   Friday, March 20, 1925
140450-	There's Room In My Album For Your Picture	Co unissued
140455-	Don't Forget My Little Darling	Co unissued

Matrix 140451 is untraced; matrices 140452 to 140454 are popular.

OCIE STOCKARD

Ocie Stockard & The Wanderers: Robert "Buck" Buchanan, f/v-1; Johnny Borowski, f; Harry Palmer, t/v-2; George Bell, p; Ocie Stockard, tbj/v-3; Buster Ferguson, g/v-4; Wanna Coffman, sb.
Dallas, TX   Saturday, September 11, 1937
014022-1	Ain't Nobody Truck Like You -4	BB B-7208
014023-1	Long Ago -3	BB B-7208
014024-1	What's The Matter? -1, 3	BB B-7570
014025-1	There'll Be Some Changes Made -3	BB B-7570
014026-1	Same Thing All The Time -3	BB B-7459
014027-1	One Of Us Was Wrong -3	BB B-7296
014028-1	Black And Blues -2	BB B-7652
014029-1	How Come -3	BB B-7459
014030-1	Please Sing For Me -3	BB B-8021
014031-1	Just Blues -2, 3, 4	BB B-7716
014032-1	Why Shouldn't I -3	BB B-7296
014033-1	To My House -1, 3, 4	BB B-7716
014034-1	Turn Your Lights Down Low -3	BB B-7652
014035-1	Wabash Blues -3	BB B-8021

This session was originally logged as by **The Wanderers**. An undated internal memo from Eli Oberstein determined the change of credit, and all issues were as shown.

Ocie Stockard & His Wanderers: Ocie Stockard, f/v-1; Joe Holley, f/v-2; Cecil Mullins, eg/v-3; Jack Hinson, p; prob. Derwood Brown, g; Wanna Coffman, sb; poss. Curly Hallmark, d.

Fort Worth, TX   Friday, March 7, 1941
    DAL-1238-1,-2   Bass Man Jive   OK 06339
    DAL-1239-1,-2   You Turned Me Down -2   OK unissued
    DAL-1240-1,-2   I Don't Know Nothin' About Lovin' -3   OK unissued
    DAL-1241-1   Jitterbug Katy -3   OK 06339
    DAL-1242-1,-2   Lovin' Baby Blues -1   OK unissued
    DAL-1243-1,-2   I'll Forget You Bye And Bye -1   OK unissued
    DAL-1244-1   Darling Little Memories -1   OK 06151
Ocie Stockard, f/v; Joe Holley, f/hv-1; Cecil Mullins, eg; Jack Hinson, p; Derwood Brown, g; Wanna Coffman, sb; poss. Curly Hallmark, d.
    Fort Worth, TX   Tuesday, March 18, 1941
    DAL-1365-1   Nickel In The Kitty   OK 06228
    DAl-1366-1   You've Got Me There   OK 06228
    DAL-1367-1   You Are My Sunshine -1   OK 06151
    DAL-1368-1,-2   Gee   OK unissued
    DAL-1369-1,-2   Hold Me Daddy   OK unissued

LEONARD STOKES
See Frank Luther.

LEONARD STOKES–GEORGE MORRIS
See J.E. Mainer's Mountaineers.

LOWE STOKES

Lowe Stokes & His North Georgians: Lowe Stokes, f; Clayton McMichen, f; K.D. Malone, cl; Hoke Rice, g/v.
    Atlanta, GA   Monday, October 31, 1927
    145051-3   Home Brew Rag   Co 15241-D
    145052-2   Unexplained Blues   Co 15241-D
Some copies of Columbia 15241-D are as by **Low Stokes & His North Georgians**.

Lowe Stokes, f; unknown, md or bj-md; prob. Perry Bechtel, g; Clayton McMichen, v.
    Atlanta, GA   Friday, October 27, 1928
    147312-2   Wave That Frame   Co 15367-D
    147313-2   Take Me To The Land Of Jazz   Co 15367-D

No details.
    Atlanta, GA   Friday, April 12, 1929
    148256-   San Antonio   Co unissued
    148257-   She's Got Rings On Her Fingers   Co unissued

Lowe Stokes & Mike Whitten: Lowe Stokes, f; Mike Whitten, g.
    Atlanta, GA   Wednesday, October 30, 1929
    149297-2   Katy Did   Co 15486-D
    149298-2   Take Me Back To Georgia   Co 15486-D

Lowe Stokes & His North Georgians: Lowe Stokes, f; Clayton McMichen, f/v-1; Bert Layne, f; Arthur Tanner, bj-md or tbj/v-2; Claude Davis or Hoke Rice, g.
    Atlanta, GA   Friday, November 1, 1929
    149330-2   Sailin' Down The Chesapeake Bay -1 Co 15606-D
    149331-2   Everybody's Doing It -1   Co 15606-D
    149332-2   Left All Alone Again Blues -1   Co 15557-D
    149333-1   Wish I Had Stayed In The Wagon Yard -2   Co 15557-D

Lowe Stokes & "Heavy Martin": Lowe Stokes, f; "Heavy Martin" (Hugh Cross), g.
    Knoxville, TN   Monday, April 7, 1930
    K-8098-   Done Gone   Br/Vo rejected
    K-8099-   Possum Up The Gum Stump   Br/Vo rejected

Lowe Stokes, Homer Miller, Walt McKinney, Heavy Martin, Roger Williams & Bill Brown: Lowe Stokes, f/sp; Homer "Slim" Miller, f/sp; Walt McKinney, sg/poss. sp; unidentified, bj-1; "Heavy Martin" (Hugh Cross), g/prob. sp; Roger Williams, prob. sp; Bill Brown, sp; unidentified, tap-dancing-2.
    Knoxville, TN   Monday, April 7, 1930
    K-8104-   The Drunkard's Tap Dance – Part 1 -1, 2   Br/Vo rejected
    K-8105-   The Drunkard's Tap Dance – Part 2 -1, 2   Br/Vo rejected
    K-8106-   The Great Hatfield-McCoy Feud – Part 1   Br 422
    K-8111-   The Great Hatfield-McCoy Feud – Part 2   Br 422
    K-8112-   The Great Hatfield-McCoy Feud – Part 3   Br 423
    K-8113-   The Great Hatfield-McCoy Feud – Part 4   Br 423
Matrices K-8108/09 are by Alex Hood & His Railroad Boys; matrices K-8107, K-8110 are untraced.

Lowe Stokes & Riley Puckett: Lowe Stokes, f/sp-1; Riley Puckett, g.
    Atlanta, GA   Monday, April 14, 1930

150206-2	Sally Johnson -1	Co 15620-D
150207-2	Billy In The Low Ground	Co 15620-D

Lowe Stokes & His North Georgians: Lowe Stokes, f/hv-1; poss. Hoke Rice or Claude Davis, g; unknown, g; Dan Hornsby, lv; Clayton McMichen, hv-1.
    Atlanta, GA   Tuesday, April 22, 1930

150350-2	Bone Dry Blues	Co 15660-D
150351-2	It Just Suits Me -1	Co 15660-D

Lowe Stokes & Hoke Rice: Lowe Stokes, f; Hoke Rice, g.
    Atlanta, GA   Monday, November 10, 1930

ATL-6603-	Japanese Stomp	Br unissued
ATL-6604-	Liberty Number One	Br unissued

Lowe Stokes & His Pot Lickers: Lowe Stokes, f; Bert Layne, f; poss. Harry Stark, bj; Arthur Tanner, tbj/v; Claude Davis or Hoke Rice, g; band v.
    Atlanta, GA   Tuesday, November 11, 1930

ATL-6607-	Four Cent Cotton	Br 549
ATL-6608-	Rocking My Sugar Lump	Br 549
ATL-6609-	Can I Have Your Daughter	Br unissued
ATL-6610-	Green Mountain Poker	Br unissued
ATL-6611-	Rocking Pony	Br unissued
ATL-6612-	Hey Mister	Br unissued

Harry Stark may not be present on all the above items.

Lowe Stokes, f; Bert Layne, f/v-1; Arthur Tanner, tbj/v-2; Claude Davis or Hoke Rice, g.
    Atlanta, GA   Wednesday, November 12, 1930

ATL-6631-	Kitty And The Baby -2	Br 491
ATL-6632-	Prohibition Is A Failure -1	Br 491

Georgia Pot Lickers: prob.: Lowe Stokes, f; Hoke Rice, g; Dan Tucker, v-1.
    Atlanta, GA   Wednesday, November 12, 1930

ATL-6637-	Chicken Don't Roost Too High -1	Br 595
ATL-6638-	Up Jumped The Rabbit	Br 595

Dan Tucker is doubtless a pseudonym.

Lowe Stokes & R. Puckett: Lowe Stokes, f; Riley Puckett, g.
    Atlanta, GA   Friday, December 5, or Saturday, December 6, 1930

151057-	Julianne Flanagan	Co unissued
151058-	Nigger Eat The Sugar	Co unissued

Lowe Stokes & His North Georgians: Lowe Stokes, f; prob. Clayton McMichen, f/v; prob. Claude Davis or Hoke Rice, g.
    Atlanta, GA   Sunday, December 7, 1930

151077-	You Gotta See Your Mama Every Night	Co unissued
151078-	Pray For The Lights To Go Out	Co unissued
151079-2	Row, Row, Row	Co 15693-D
151080-1	Sailing On The Robert E. Lee	Co 15693-D

Lowe Stokes recorded prolifically as a member of Gid Tanner & His Skillet-Lickers and associated groups, and after 1942. See also Claude (C.W.) Davis, John Dilleshaw, Clayton McMichen, the Smoky Mountain Ramblers, and The Swamp Rooters.

CLYDE STONE & LEM PASCHAL

Prob.: Clyde Stone, Lem Paschal, v duet; acc. unknown.
    New York, NY   Monday, April 27, 1936

19117-	Be No Other Fellow's Sweetheart	ARC unissued
19118-	Ball And Chain Blues	ARC unissued

Lem Paschal was a member of Lem's Down Home Boys.

REV. STONE & MALE CHOIR

Pseudonym on Broadway for Rev. Stephenson & Male Choir.

STONE & BUTLER

Pseudonym on Broadway for the Fruit Jar Guzzlers.

STONE MOUNTAIN BOYS

Pseudonym on Supertone 9456 for The Red Fox Chasers, or on Supertone S2049 for The Beverly Hill Billies.

STONE MOUNTAIN ENTERTAINERS

Pseudonym on Broadway for the Blue Ridge Highballers. (On some copies of Broadway 8158 by the North Carolina Ramblers & Roy Harvey, matrix 20084 is also credited thus.)

STONE MOUNTAIN TRIO

Unknown, f; unknown, bj; unknown, g; unknown, v-1; unknown, wh.
Atlanta, GA   Saturday, March 22, 1930

| ATL-987- | Stone Mountain Waltz -1 | Vo 5457 |
| ATL-988- | Swanee River Waltz | Vo 5457 |

Unknown, f; unknown, bj; unknown, g.
Atlanta, GA   Tuesday, November 11, 1930

| ATL-6613- | Maple Leaf Waltz | Br 543 |
| ATL-6614- | Sundown Waltz | Br 543 |

ERNEST V. STONEMAN

Ernest V. Stoneman, v; acc. own h/ah.
New York, NY   c. September 4, 1924

| 72787-A | The Face That Never Returned | OK unissued |
| 72788-A | The Titanic | OK unissued |

New York, NY   c. January 8, 1925

72787-B	The Face That Never Returned	OK 40288
72788-B	The Titanic	OK 40288
73089-A	Freckle Face Mary Jane	OK 40312
73090-A	My And My Wife	OK 40312

New York, NY   Wednesday, May 27, 1925

73371-A	Uncle Sam And The Kaiser	OK 40430
73372-A	Jack And Joe	OK 40408
73373-A	Sinful To Flirt	OK 40384
73374-A	Dixie Parody	OK 40430
73375-A	The Dying Girl's Farewell	OK 40384
73376-A	The Lightning Express	OK 40408

Ernest V. Stoneman & Emmet Lundy: Emmet Lundy, f; Ernest Stoneman, h/ah.
New York, NY   Wednesday, May 27, 1925

| 73377-A | Piney Woods Girl | OK 40405 |
| 73378-A | The Long Eared Mule | OK 40405 |

Ernest V. Stoneman, v; acc. own h-1/ah.
Asheville, NC   Thursday, August 27, 1925

9284-A	The Sailor's Song	OK 45015
9285-A	Blue Ridge Mountain Blues -1	OK 45009
9286-A	All I've Got's Gone -1	OK 45009
9287-A	The Fancy Ball -1	OK 45015
9288-A	The Kicking Mule -1	OK 45036
9289-A	The Wreck On The C&O -1	OK 7011
9290-A	John Hardy -1	OK 7011

OKeh 7011 is a 12-inch disc.
Rev. OKeh 45036 by Roba Stanley.

Acc. own h-1/ah-2/g-3.
New York, NY   April 1926

74102-B	The Religious Critic -	OK 45051
74103-A	When My Wife Will Return To Me -	OK 45051
74104-A	Asleep At The Switch -1, 2	OK 45044
74105-A	The Orphan Girl -1, 2	OK 45044
74108-A	Kitty Wells -	OK 45048
74109-A	The Texas Ranger -1, 3	OK 45054
74110-A	In The Shadow Of The Pine -	OK 45048
74111-A	Don't Let Your Deal Go Down -3	OK 45054

Matrices 74106/07 are untraced.

Ernest V. Stoneman The Blue Ridge Mountaineer, v; acc. own h/g.
New York, NY   Monday, June 21, 1926

11053-A,-B	Bad Companions	Ed 51788, 5201
11054-A	When The Work's All Done This Fall	Ed 51788, 5188
11055-A,-B,-C	Wreck Of The C&O (Or "George Alley")	Ed 51823, 5198

11056-A	Wild Bill Jones	Ed 51869, 5196	
11057-A	John Henry	Ed 51869, 5194	
New York, NY			Tuesday, June 22, 1926
11058-A	Sinking Of The Titanic	Ed 51823, 5200	
11059-A,-B,-C	Watermelon Hanging On The Vine	Ed 51864, 5191	
11060-B,-C	The Old Hickory Cane	Ed 51864, 5241	
New York, NY			Wednesday, June 23, 1926
11063-B,-C	My Little German Home Across The Sea	Ed 51909	
11064-A,-B	Bury Me Beneath The Weeping Willow Tree	Ed 51909, 5187	

Ernest V. Stoneman & Fiddler Joe: Joe Samuels, f; Ernest V. Stoneman, h/g/v.

New York, NY — between August 16 and 23, 1926

74300-A	Silver Bell	OK 45060
74301-A	May I Sleep In Your Barn Tonight Mister?	OK 45059
74302-A	My Pretty Snow Dear	OK 45060
74303-A	Are You Angry With Me, Darling?	OK 45065

Ernest V. Stoneman, v; acc. own h/g.

New York, NY — between August 16 and 23, 1926

74304-A	The Old Hickory Cane	OK 45059
74305-A	He's Going To Have A Hot Time Bye And Bye	OK 45062
74306-A	The Old Go Hungry Hash House	OK 45062
74307-A	Katie Kline	OK 45065

Ernest Stoneman, v; acc. Hattie Stoneman, f-1; own h/g; poss. Bolen Frost, bj-2.

New York NY — c. August 28, 1926

X-233-A	May I Sleep In Your Barn To-night Mister -1	Ge 3368, Chg 153, 312, Her 75530
X-234	The Girl I Left Behind In Sunny Tennessee -1	Ge 3368, Chg 151, Her 75529
X-235	Silver Bell -1	Ge 3369, 20253, Chg 153, Her 75529
X-236-A	Pretty Snow Dear -1	Ge 3369, Chg 152, Her 75530
X-237-A	Katy Cline -2	Ge 3381, Chg 151, Her 75528
X-238	Barney McCoy -1	Ge 3381, 20253, Chg 152, 309, Her 75528

Revs: Challenge 309, 312 by Vernon Dalhart.

Ernest V. Stoneman & His Dixie Mountaineers: Ernest Stoneman, Kahle Brewer, Walter Mooney, Tom Leonard, Hattie Stoneman, v group; acc. Kahle Brewer, f; prob. Irma Frost, o; Ernest Stoneman, g.

New York, NY — Tuesday, September 21, 1926

36198-2	Going Down The Valley	Vi 20531
36199-2	The Sinless Summerland	Vi 20531
36500-2	In The Golden Bye And Bye	Vi 20223
36501-2	I Will Meet You In The Morning	Vi 20223
36502-1	The Great Reaping Day	Vi 20532
36503-1	I Love To Walk With Jesus	Vi 20224
36504-2	Hallelujah Side	Vi 20224

New York, NY — Friday, September 24, 1926

36507-1	I'll Be Satisfied	Vi 20533

Ernest V. Stoneman–Kahle Brewer: Kahle Brewer, f; Ernest Stoneman, h-1/g.

New York, NY — Friday, September 24, 1926

36508-1	West Virginia Highway	Vi 20237
36509-2	Peek-A-Boo – Waltz -1	Vi 20540

Rev. Victor 20540 by Phil Reeve–Ernest Moody.

Ernest V. Stoneman & His Dixie Mountaineers: Ernest Stoneman, Kahle Brewer, Walter Mooney, Tom Leonard, Hattie Stoneman, v group; acc. Kahle Brewer, f; prob. Irma Frost, o; Ernest Stoneman, g.

New York, NY — Friday, September 24, 1926

36510-2	When The Redeemed Are Gathering In	Vi 20533
36511-1	I Would Not Be Denied	Vi 20532

Kahle Brewer, f; Ernest Stoneman, h-1/ah-2/g-3/v; Bolen Frost, bj; Hattie Stoneman, v; Walter Mooney, v-4; Tom Leonard, v-4.

New York, NY — Friday, September 24, 1926

36512-2	Going Up Cripple Creek -1, 2	Vi 20294
36513-2	Sourwood Mountain -1, 3	Vi 20235
36514-2	The Little Old Log Cabin In The Lane -3, 4	Vi 20235, MW M-8305

Rev. Montgomery Ward M-8305 by Frank Luther & Carson Robison (see the latter).

Kahle Brewer, f; Ernest Stoneman, h-1/g-2/v; Bolen Frost, bj; Hattie Stoneman, v-3.

New York, NY — Saturday, September 25, 1926

36515-2	Ida Red -1, 2	Vi 20302	
36516-2	Sugar In The Gourd	Vi 20294	
36517-2	Old Joe Clark -1, 2, 3	Vi 20302	
36518-2	All Go Hungry Hash House -1, 2	Vi 20237	

Victor 20237 as by **Ernest V. Stoneman**.

Ernest V. Stoneman & The Dixie Mountaineers: Ernest Stoneman, v; acc. Kahle Brewer, f; own h/g; unknown, bj.
New York, NY
Monday, January 24, 1927

11460-A,-C	Bright Sherman Valley	Ed 51951, 5383
11461-A,-C	Once I Had A Fortune	Ed 51935, 5357

The Dixie Mountaineers: Kahle Brewer, f; unknown, bj; Ernest Stoneman, g.
New York, NY
Tuesday, January 25, 1927

11462-A,-B	The Long Eared Mule	Ed 52056
11463-A,-B,-C	Hop Light Ladies	Ed 52056

Ernest V. Stoneman & The Dixie Mountaineers: Ernest Stoneman, v; acc. Kahle Brewer, f; own h/g; unknown, bj.
New York, NY
Tuesday, January 25, 1927

11464-A,-B,-C	Two Little Orphans (Our Mamma's In Heaven)	Ed 51935, 5338
11465-A,-C	Kitty Wells	Ed 51994, 5341

Ernest V. Stoneman Trio: Kahle Brewer, f; Bolen Frost, bj; Ernest Stoneman, g/v.
New York, NY
Thursday, January 27, 1927

80344-A	The Wreck Of The '97	OK unissued: *LC LBC9* (LP)
80345-A	The Little Old Log Cabin In The Lane	OK unissued: *OH OHCS173* (LP)
80346-A	Flop Eared Mule	OK unissued: *Cy 533* (LP); *Co C4K47911* (CD)
80347-A	Lonesome Road Blues	OK 45094
80348-A	Round Town Girl	OK 45094
80349-	Old Joe Clark	OK unissued

Matrix 80346 is titled *Untitled* on Columbia C4K47911.

Ernest V. Stoneman & The Dixie Mountaineers: Ernest Stoneman, v; acc. Kahle Brewer, f; own h/g; Bolen Frost, bj-1.
New York, NY
Friday, January 28, 1927

11481-B,-C	Hand Me Down My Walking Cane -1	Ed 51938, 5297
11482-A,-B	Tell Mother I Will Meet Her	Ed 51938, 5382

Ernest V. Stoneman The Blue Ridge Mountaineer, v; acc. own h/g.
New York, NY
Saturday, January 29, 1927

11483-A	We Courted In The Rain	Ed 51994, 5308

Ernest V. Stoneman & The Dixie Mountaineers: Ernest Stoneman, v; acc. Kahle Brewer, f; own g.
New York, NY
Saturday, January 29, 1927

11484-A,-C	The Bully Of The Town	Ed 51951, 5314

Ernest V. Stoneman, v; acc. Kahle Brewer, f; own h-1/g.
New York NY
Saturday, January 29, 1927

80360-B	The Fatal Wedding	OK 45084
80361-A	The Fate Of Talmadge Osborne -1	OK 45084

Ernest Stoneman, v; acc. Kahle Brewer, f; own h/g.
New York, NY
c. February 5, 1927

GEX-493	The Poor Tramp Has To Live	Ge 6044, Ch 15233, Sil 5001, 8155, 25001, Spt 9255, Chg 244, 324, 398, Her 75535
GEX-494	Sweet Bunch Of Violets	Ge 6065, Ch 15233, Sil 5004, 25004, Her 75541
GEX-495	Kenney Wagner's Surrender	Ge 6044, Ch 15222, Sil 5004, 25004, Her 75535
GEX-496-A	When The Roses Bloom Again	Ge 6065, Ch 15222, Sil 5001, 8155, 25001, Spt 9255, Chg 244, Her 75541

Champion 15222, 15233 as by **Uncle Jim Seaney**. Silvertone 5001, 8155, 25001, 25004, Supertone 9255, Challenge 244 as by **Uncle Ben Hawkins**. Challenge 324, 398 as by **Jim Seaney**.
Revs: Challenge 324 by Welby Toomey, 398 by the Short Creek Trio.

Ernest Stoneman & His Greysen County Boys: Ernest Stoneman, v; acc. Kahle Brewer, f; Bolen Frost, bj; own g.
New York, NY
c. February 5, 1927

GEX-497	Long Eared Mule	Ge 6052, Sil 5003, 25003
GEX-498-A	Round Town Gals	Ge 6052, Ch 15248, Sil 5003, 25003

Champion 15248, Silvertone 5003 as by **Uncle Ben Hawkins & His Boys**. Silvertone 25003 as by **Logan County Trio** (matrix GEX-497)/**Uncle Ben Hawkins & His Gang** (matrix GEX-498).
Rev. Champion 15248 by Carson Robison.

The Dixie Mountaineers-1/Ernest V. Stoneman The Blue Ridge Mountaineer-2: Hattie Stoneman, f; Ernest Stoneman, h/g/v.

New York, NY Tuesday, May 10, 1927

| 11690-C | Fate Of Talmadge Osborne -1 | Ed 52026, 5369 |
| 11691-A | The Orphan Girl -2 | Ed 52077, 5367 |

Rev. Edison 52077 by Vernon Dalhart.

Ernest V. Stoneman & Mrs. Stoneman: Ernest Stoneman, Hattie Stoneman, v duet; acc. Ernest Stoneman, h/g.

New York, NY Tuesday, May 10, 1927

| 11692- | Pass Around The Bottle | Ed unissued |
| 11693-C | The Fatal Wedding | Ed 52026, 5355 |

Ernest Stoneman, v; acc. Hattie Stoneman, f-1/bj-2; own h/g.

New York, NY c. early May 1927

7222-1	Hand Me Down My Walking Cane -1	Ba 1993, Do 3964, Or 916, Re 8324, Htd 16490
7223-1	Pass Around The Bottle -1	Ba 2157, Do 3985, Or 916, Re 8346, Chg 665, Cq 7064, 7755, Htd 16490, Pm 3021, Bwy 8054, Her 75578
7224-1	When The Roses Bloom Again -2	Ba 1993, Do 3964, Or 946, Re 8324, Htd 16498
7225-1	Bully Of The Town	Ba 2157, Ca 8217, Do 3984, Lin 2822, Or 947, Pat 32279, Pe 12358, Re 8347, Ro 597, Chg 665, Cq 7755, Htd 16500, ARC-Bwy 8056

Oriole 916, 946, 947, Homestead 16490, 16498, 16500 as by **Sim Harris**.
Some of the above issues may have been issued incorrectly as by **Vernon Dalhart**. Some, however, such as some issues of Banner 1993, though credited to Ernest Stoneman, use Dalhart masters of the same titles.
Revs: Pathé 32279, Perfect 12358, Paramount 3021, Broadway 8054, ARC-Broadway 8056 by Vernon Dalhart; Herwin 75578 by Arthur Fields.

Mr. & Mrs. Ernest V. Stoneman: Hattie Stoneman, f-1/v-2; Ernest Stoneman, h/g/v.

New York, NY Thursday, May 12, 1927

81075-A,-B	Where The Silvery Colorado Wends Its Way -2	OK unissued
81076-A,-B	Goodbye, Dear Old Step Stone -1	OK unissued
81077-	My Little German Home -2	OK unissued
81078-B	Two Little Orphans -1	OK unissued: OH OHCS173 (LP)
81079-A,-B	The Road To Washington -1	OK 45125
81080-B	The Mountaineer's Courtship -2	OK 45125

Ernest V. Stoneman, v; acc. own h/g.

New York, NY Thursday, May 19, 1927

38763-2	The Poor Tramp	Vi 20672
38764-2	The Fate Of Talmage Osborne	Vi 20672
38765-2	The Old Hickory Cane	Vi 20799
38766-2	'Till The Snow Flakes Fall Again	Vi 20799

New York, NY Saturday, May 21, 1927

| 38918-1 | The Story Of The Mighty Mississippi | Vi 20671 |
| 38919-1,-2 | Joe Hoover's Mississippi Flood Song | Vi unissued |

Matrix 38919 was originally logged as *The Flooded Mississippi River*.
Rev. Victor 20671 by Ernest Rogers.

Acc. own h-1/g.

New York NY late May 1927

7286-	The Old Hickory Cane -1	Do 0187, Pat 32271, Pe 12350, Re 8369
107554-A; 7287-	The Fatal Wedding	Ca 8220, Lin 2825, Ro 600
107554-B; 7287-2	The Fatal Wedding	Ba 2158, Do 3984, Or 946, Pat 32278, Pe 12357, Re 8347, Chg 666, Htd 16498
107555-A,-B	Pass Around The Bottle -1	Ca 8271, Lin 2822, Pat 32278, Pe 12357, Ro 597
107556-A; 7288-3	Sinful To Flirt -1	Ba 2158, Ca 8220, Do 3985, Lin 2825, Or 947, Pat 32271, Pe 12350, Re 8346, Ro 600, Chg 666, Cq 7064, Htd 16500

Oriole 946, 947, Homestead 16498, 16500 as by **Sim Harris**.
Matrix 107554 is titled *Fatal Weddding* on Pathé 32278, Perfect 12357.
Revs: Domino 0187, Regal 8369 by the Gentry Brothers.

E. Stoneman–E.K. Brewer–M. Mooney: Ernest Stoneman, Kahle Brewer, Walter Mooney, v trio; acc. Ernest Stoneman, h-1/g.

Bristol, TN Monday, July 25, 1927

| 39700-1 | Dying Girl's Farewell | Vi 21129 |
| 39701-3 | Tell Mother I Will Meet Her -1 | Vi 21129 |

E. Stoneman–Miss I. Frost–E. Dunford-1/Ernest Stoneman & Miss Irma Frost-2: Ernest Stoneman, Irma Frost, v duet; acc. Ernest Stoneman, h/g; Eck Dunford, sp-1.
    Bristol, TN   Monday, July 25, 1927

39702-1	The Mountaineer's Courtship -1	Vi unissued: *CMF-011-L (LP); 011-D (CD)*
39702-2	Mountaineer's Courtship -1	Vi 20880
39703-3	Midnight On The Stormy Deep -2	Vi unissued: *CMF-011-L (LP); 011-D (CD)*

What is believed to be an excerpt from matrix 39703 is included in *Twisting The Dials – Part 1* by The Happiness Boys on Victor 35953 (a 12-inch issue).
Rev. Victor 20880 by Uncle Eck Dunford.

Ernest V. Stoneman & His Dixie Mountaineers: prob. some or all of: Ernest Stoneman, Kahle Brewer, Walter Mooney, Tom Leonard, Hattie Stoneman, Irma Frost, Edna Brewer, v group; acc. prob. Kahle Brewer, f; Eck Dunford, f; Irma Frost, o; Ernest Stoneman, g.
    Bristol, TN   Monday, July 25, 1927

39704-3	Sweeping Through The Gates	Vi 20844
39705-2	I Know My Name Is There	Vi 21186
39706-2	Are You Washed In The Blood?	Vi 20844, MW M-8136
39707-2	No More Good-byes	Vi 21186
39708-1	The Resurrection	Vi unissued: *CMF-011-L (LP); 011-D (CD)*
39708-2	The Resurrection	Vi 21071
39709-2	I Am Resolved	Vi 21071

Victor 21186 as by **Stoneman's Dixie Mountaineers**.
Rev. Montgomery Ward M-8136 by the Pace Jubilee Singers (see *B&GR*).

Blue Ridge Corn Shuckers: Kahle Brewer, f; Eck Dunford, f/calls; Iver Edwards, h/u; unknown, k; Bolen Frost, bj; George Stoneman, bj; Ernest Stoneman, g/v; unknown, jh.
    Bristol, TN   Wednesday, July 27, 1927

39720-2	Old Time Corn Shuckin', Part 1	Vi 20835
39721-4	Old Time Corn Shuckin', Part 2	Vi 20835

Matrices 39716 to 39719 are by Uncle Eck Dunford.

The Dixie Mountaineers: no details.
    New York, NY   Monday, September 12, 1927

11882	The Little Black Moustache	Ed rejected
11883	Puttin' On The Style	Ed rejected
11884	All Go Hungry Hash House	Ed rejected
11885	Sally Goodwin	Ed rejected

    New York, NY   Tuesday, September 13, 1927

11886	When The Redeemed Are Gathering In	Ed rejected
11887	He Was Nailed To The Cross For Me	Ed rejected

Ernest V. Stoneman, v; acc. own h/g.
    New York, NY   Thursday, September 15, 1927

39182-1,-2	Josephus And Bohunkus	Vi unissued

Ernest Stoneman & The Blue Ridge Corn Shuckers: Ernest Stoneman, v; acc. prob.: Eck Dunford, f; George Stoneman, bj; Bolen Frost, bj; own g; Sam Patton, sp-1; band sp.
    Atlanta, GA   Wednesday, February 22, 1928

41932-2	Possum Trot School Exhibition, Part I -1	Vi 21264
41933-2	Possum Trot School Exhibition, Part II -1	Vi 21264
41934-2	A Serenade In The Mountains, Part 1	Vi 21518
41935-1	A Serenade In The Mountains, Part 2	Vi 21518

Ernest V. Stoneman & Irma Frost, v duet; acc. prob. Eck Dunford, f; Ernest Stoneman, h/g; prob. George Stoneman or Bolen Frost, bj.
    Atlanta, GA   Wednesday, February 22, 1928

41936-1,-2	Claud Allen	Vi unissued

Ernest Stoneman & The Blue Ridge Corn Shuckers: Ernest Stoneman, v; acc. prob.: Eck Dunford, f; own h-1/g; George Stoneman or Bolen Frost, bj; band v-2.
    Atlanta, GA   Wednesday, February 22, 1928

41937-1	The Two Little Orphans	Vi 21648
41938-1,-2	Once I Had A Fortune	Vi unissued
41939-1	The Raging Sea, How It Roars -1, 2	Vi 21648

Matrices 41940 to 41943 are by Uncle Eck Dunford; matrix 41944 is by George Stoneman.

Ernest V. Stoneman & His Dixie Mountaineers: Ernest Stoneman, v; acc. Hattie Stoneman, f/v-1; own h-2/g; Bolen Frost, bj/v-1.
    New York, NY   Tuesday, April 24, 1928

18433-A	He Was Nailed To The Cross For Me -1, 2	Ed 52290, 5536

N-210	He Was Nailed To The Cross For Me -1, 2	Ed unissued: *Cy CD3510* (CD)
18434-B	When The Redeemed Are Gathering In -1, 2	Ed 52290, 5527
N-211	When The Redeemed Are Gathering In -1, 2	Ed unissued: *Cy CD3510* (CD)
18435-A	All Go Hungry Hash House -2	Ed 52350, 5528
N-212	All Go Hungry Hash House -2	Ed unissued: *Cy CD3510* (CD)
18436-B	There'll Come A Time -2	Ed 52350, 5528
N-213	There'll Come A Time -2	Ed unissued: *Cy CD3510* (CD)
18437-A	Sally Goodwin	Ed 52350, 5529
N-214	Sally Goodwin	Ed unissued: *Cy CD3510* (CD)
18438-B	Careless Love -2	Ed 52386, 5530
N-215	Careless Love -2	Ed unissued: *Cy CD3510* (CD)

Matrix N-214 was used for Edison 0000, a developmental disc.

Ernest Stoneman, v; acc. Hattie Stoneman, f; own h/g; Bolen Frost, bj.
New York, NY   Wednesday, April 25, 1928

18440-B	The East Bound Train	Ed 52299, 5548
N-217	The East Bound Train	Ed unissued: *Cy CD3510* (CD)
18441-B	The Unlucky Road To Washington	Ed 52299, 5545
N-218	The Unlucky Road To Washington	Ed unissued: *Cy CD3510* (CD)
18442-B	The Old Maid And The Burglar	Ed 52369, 5531
N-219	The Old Maid And The Burglar	Ed unissued: *Cy CD3510* (CD)
18443-A	Down On The Banks Of The Ohio	Ed 52312
N-220	Down On The Banks Of The Ohio	Ed unissued: *Cy CD3510* (CD)
18444-B	We Parted By The Riverside	Ed 52312, 5635
N-221	We Parted By The Riverside	Ed unissued: *Cy CD3510* (CD)
18445-A	It's Sinful To Flirt	Ed 52386, 5547
N-222	It's Sinful To Flirt	Ed unissued: *Cy CD3510* (CD)

Matrix N-221 is titled *We Parted At The River* on County CD3510.
Matrix 18439 is not by Ernest Stoneman.

Ernest V. Stoneman, v; acc. own h/g.
New York, NY   c. May 1928

| 108203-1 | In The Shadow Of The Pine | Pat 32380, Pe 12459 |

Revs: Pathé 32380, Perfect 12459 by Vernon Dalhart.

Justin Winfield: Ernest Stoneman, v; acc. Herbert Sweet, f; Earl Sweet, bj; own g.
Richmond, IN   Monday, July 9, 1928

14015	New River Train	Ge 6619, Spt 9400
14016-A	John Hardy	Ge 6619
14017-A	Say, Darling, Say	Ge 6733, Spt 9400

Supertone 9400 as by **Uncle Ben Hawkins**.
Stoneman also participated in other recordings made at this session by the Sweet Brothers and Virginia Mountain Boomers.
Rev. Gennett 6733 by G.B. Grayson & Henry Whitter.

Stoneman Family: Eck Dunford, f/v-1; Ernest Stoneman, h/g/v-2; Bolen Frost, bj; Hattie Stoneman, v.
Bristol, TN   Tuesday, October 30, 1928

47248-1,-2	Beautiful Isle O'er The Sea -1, 2	Vi unissued
47249-1,-2,-3	Willie, We Have Missed You	Vi unissued
47252-1,-2	The Fate Of Shelly And Smith -1, 2	Vi unissued
47253-2	The Broken-Hearted Lover -1, 2	Vi V-40030

Matrices 47250/51 are by Clarence Greene; matrices 47254/55 are by Uncle Eck Dunford.

Stoneman Family-1/Ernest Stoneman's Dixie Mountaineers-2: Eck Dunford, f/v-3; unknown, f-4; Ernest Stoneman, h/g/v; Bolen Frost, bj-5; Hattie Stoneman, v-6.
Bristol, TN   Wednesday, October 31, 1928

47256-1,-2	Minnie Brown -1, 3, 5	Vi unissued
47257-1	We Parted By The Riverside -1, 5	Vi V-40030
47258-2	Down To Jordan And Be Saved -2, 3, 4	Vi V-40078
47259-2	There's A Light Lit Up In Galilee -2, 3, 4, 6	Vi V-40078

The Stoneman Family: Ernest Stoneman, Eck Dunford, dialog; acc. Bolen Frost, bj.
Bristol, TN   Wednesday, October 31, 1928

| 47260-2 | Going Up The Mountain After Liquor, Part 1 | Vi V-40016 |
| 47261-2 | Going Up The Mountain After Liquor, Part 2 | Vi V-40016 |

Stoneman Family: Eck Dunford, f/v-1; unknown, f-2; Ernest Stoneman, h/g/v; Bolen Frost, bj; Hattie Stoneman, v.
Bristol, TN   Wednesday, October 31, 1928

| 47262-2 | The Spanish Merchant's Daughter -2 | Vi V-40206 |
| 47263-1,-2 | Twilight Is Stealing O'er The Sea -1 | Vi unissued |

Bristol, TN Tuesday, November 1, 1928
47264-2	Too Late -2	Vi V-40206
47265-1,-2	I Should Like To Marry	Vi unissued

Ernest V. Stoneman & His Dixie Mountaineers: Ernest Stoneman, v; acc. Hattie Stoneman, f; own h/g; Bolen Frost, bj-1/g-2.

New York, NY Wednesday, November 21, 1928
18881-B	Goodbye, Dear Old Stepstone -2	Ed 52489
N-576	Goodbye, Dear Old Stepstone -2	Ed unissued: *Cy CD3510 (CD)*
18882-B	Fallen By The Wayside -2	Ed 52489
N-577	Fallen By The Wayside -2	Ed unissued: *Cy CD3510 (CD)*
18883-B	All I've Got's Gone -1	Ed 52489
N-578	All I've Got's Gone -1	Ed unissued
18884	My Mother And My Sweetheart -1	Ed rejected
N-579	My Mother And My Sweetheart -1	Ed unissued: *Cy CD3510 (CD)*
18885	Remember The Poor Tramp Has To Live -1	Ed rejected
N-580	Remember The Poor Tramp Has To Live -1	Ed unissued: *Cy CD3510 (CD)*
18886-B	The Prisoner's Lament -1	Ed 52461, 5673
N-581	The Prisoner's Lament -1	Ed unissued: *Cy CD3510 (CD)*

Hattie Stoneman, f; Ernest Stoneman, h-1/g/v-2; Bolen Frost, bj-3/g-4/hv-5.

New York, NY Thursday, November 22, 1928
18887	Midnight On The Stormy Deep -1, 2, 4	Ed rejected
N-582	Midnight On The Stormy Deep -1, 2, 4	Ed unissued: *Cy CD3510 (CD)*
18888	The Pretty Mohea (Indian Maid) -1, 2, 3	Ed rejected
N-583	The Pretty Mohea (Indian Maid) -1, 2, 3	Ed unissued: *Cy CD3510 (CD)*
18891-A,-B	I Remember Calvary -1, 2, 3, 5	Ed 52479, 5676
N-586-B	I Remember Calvary -1, 2, 3, 5	Ed N20004
18892-A,-B	He Is Coming After Me -1, 2, 3, 5	Ed 52479, N20004
N-587-A	He Is Coming After Me -1, 2, 3, 5	Ed N20004
18893	West Virginia Highway	Ed rejected
N-588	West Virginia Highway	Ed rejected
18894	Watchman Ring That Bell -3	Ed rejected
N-589	Watchman Ring That Bell -3	Ed unissued: *Cy CD3510 (CD)*

Matrices 18893/94 (N-588/89) were logged as by **The Railsplitters**.
Matrices 18889/90 are by Frank Luther.

Ernest & Eddie Stoneman, v duet; acc. poss.: Ernest Stoneman, h/ah/g; unknown, ah or g; Eddie Stoneman, bj.

New York, NY Monday, January 8, 1934
14545-	Good-bye, Dear Old Stepstone	ARC unissued
14546-	The Railroad Flagman's Sweetheart	ARC unissued
14547-	After The Roses Have Faded Away	ARC unissued
14548-	Meet Me By The Seaside	ARC unissued
14549-	Six Months Is A Long Time	ARC unissued
14550-	My Only Sweetheart	Vo 02901
14551-	I'm Alone, All Alone	ARC unissued
14552-	There's Somebody Waiting For Me	Vo 02632
14553-1	Nine Pound Hammer	Vo 02655

The accompaniment details for this session and those of January 9-10, 1934 are collective and to some extent hypothetical. The instruments are specified in ARC files but it is uncertain who plays what.

Ernest Stoneman, v; acc. own h/g; Eddie Stoneman, bj-1.

New York, NY Tuesday, January 9, 1934
14554-1	Broke Down Section Hand	Vo 02655
14555-	Texas Ranger	Vo 02632
14556-	Prisoner's Advice	ARC unissued
14557-	All I Got's Gone -1	Vo 02901

Ernest & Eddie Stoneman, v duet; acc. prob. Ernest Stoneman, h/ah/g.

New York, NY Wednesday, January 10, 1934
14560-	Golden Bye And Bye	ARC unissued
14561-	Hallelujah Side	ARC unissued
14562-	I'll Live On	ARC unissued
14563-	Reaping Days	ARC unissued

Ernest Stoneman, v; acc. prob. own h/g; Eddie Stoneman, bj.

New York, NY Wednesday, January 10, 1934
14564-	The Sweetest Way Home	ARC unissued

Ernest V. Stoneman also recorded with Uncle Eck Dunford, Frank Jenkins' Pilot Mountaineers, Oscar Jenkins' Mountaineers, Willie Stoneman, Herbert Sweet, the Sweet Brothers, the Virginia Mountain Boomers, and Fields Ward. He continued to record, with the Stoneman Family, after 1942.

GEORGE STONEMAN

George Stoneman, g solo.
    Atlanta, GA   Wednesday, February 22, 1928
    41944-1,-2   Stonewall Jackson   Vi unissued

WILLIE STONEMAN

Willie Stoneman, v; acc. unknown, bj; unknown, g.
    Richmond, IN   Thursday, July 5, 1928
    14005   Katy Lee   Ge 6565, Ch 15565

Champion 15565 as by **Dave Hunt**.
Rev. Champion 15565 by Herbert Sweet.

Willie Stoneman, v/y; acc. unknown, bj; unknown, g.
    Richmond, IN   Friday, July 6, 1928
    14012   Wake Up In The Morning   Ge 6565, Ch 15610, Spt 9083

Champion 15610 as by **Dave Hunt**.
Revs: Champion 15610 by the Virginia Mountain Boomers; Supertone 9083 by Frank Welling (see John McGhee & Frank Welling).

[THE] STONEMAN FAMILY

See Ernest V. Stoneman.

STOVE PIPE NO. 1

This artist, whose real name was Sam Jones, and who appeared once in the Columbia Old Familiar Tunes series, was African-American; see *B&GR*.

HARLEY STRATTON

Pseudonym on Superior for Bradley Kincaid.

KENNETH STRIKER (THE DAKOTA WIZARD)

Kenneth Striker, h; acc. own g.
    Richmond, IN   Saturday, December 7, 1929
    15983   Me Too – Wait For The Wagon   Ge rejected
    15984   The Old Gray Bonnett [sic]   Ge rejected

STRINGFELLOW QUARTET

Vocal quartet; acc. unknown, p.
    Atlanta, GA   Monday, October 26, 1931
    151938-   Just A Little Nearer Home   Co unissued
    151939-1   We'll Reap What We Sow   Co 15726-D
    151940-1   I Want To Hear Him Call My Name   Co 15726-D
    151941-   My Heavenly Homecoming   Co unissued

STRIPLING BROTHERS

Charles Stripling, f; Ira Stripling, g.
    Birmingham, AL   Thursday, November 15, 1928
    BIRM-812-   The Big Footed Nigger In The Sandy Lot   Vo 5321, Me M12181, MeC 93129, Po P9068,
                                                                        Min M-14087
    BIRM-813-   The Lost Child   Vo 5321, Me M12181, MeC 93129, Po P9068,
                                                                        Min M-14086

Charles Stripling, f/v-1; Ira Stripling, g/v-1.
    Chicago, IL   Monday, August 19, 1929
    C-4119-   Dance All Night With A Bottle In My Hand   Vo 5395
    C-4120-   Horse Shoe Bend   Vo 5395
    C-4121-   Get Off Your Money   Vo 5441
    C-4122-   Lost John   Vo 5441
    C-4123-   Big Eyed Rabbit   Vo 5412, 02770, Me M12172, M18027,
                                                                MeC 93131, Min M-14013, M-14086
    C-4124-   Kennedy Rag   Vo 5382, 02761

C-4125-	New Born Blues	Vo 5382, 02761
C-4126-	Coal Mine Blues	Vo 5453, 02739, RZAu G22272
C-4127-A	Red River Waltz	Vo 5366, Me M12173, M18025, Po P9081, Apex 26294, Min M-14011, RZAu G22527
C-4128-A	Moonlight Waltz	Vo 5366, Me M12173, Po P9081, Apex 26294, Min M-14011, RZAu G22527
C-4129-	Midnight Waltz	Vo 5468, 02738, RZAu G22271
C-4130-	June Rose Waltz	Vo 5468, 02738, RZAu G22271
C-4132-	Ranger's Hornpipe	Vo 5453, 02739, RZAu G22272
C-4133-	Railroad Bum -1	Vo 5365
C-4134-	Weeping Willow -1	Vo 5365
C-4135-	Wolves Howling	Vo 5412, 02770, Me M12172, M18027, MeC 93131, Min M-14087

Melotone M18025, M18027 as by **Les Freres Boisvert**.
Matrix C-4123 is titled *Le Reel De La Malbaie*, and matrix C-4135 *Le Reel Du Charretier*, on Melotone M18027. Matrix C-4127 is titled *La Valse De La Riviere Rouge* on Melotone M18025.
Matrix C-4131 is untraced but not by these artists.
Revs: Melotone M18025 by I. Podgorski & J. Pawlak (see *EMOR*); Minerva M-14013 (although as by **Stripling Brothers**) by Gene Clardy & Stan Clements.

New York, NY   Monday, September 10, 1934

38618-A	Silver Lake Waltz	De 5019
38619-A,-B?, -C?,-D?	Down Yonder	De unissued
38620-C	Over The Waves	De 5041
38621-A	Salty Dog	De 5049
38622-A	One Hundred Four	De unissued
38623-A	Sweet Bunch of Daisies	De unissued
38624-A	Birmingham Jail	De 5019
38625-A	Possum Hollow	De 5018
38626-A	Down On The L.N. Railroad	De 5041
38627-C	Whiskers	De 5049
38628-C	Wednesday Night – Waltz	De 5018
38629-A	Bug House	De unissued
38630-C	Sweet Silas	De 5069
38631-A	Chinese Breakdown	De 5069

Matrix 38619 is assigned a single take in one Decca file, but four takes in another.

New Orleans, LA   Thursday, March 12, 1936

60687-A	When Shadows Fade Away	De 5313
60688-	Late In The Evening	De 5246
60689-A	Big Bully	De 5291
60690-A	Coal Valley	De 5547
60691-	You Are Always In My Dreams	De 5267, DeAu X1277, BrSA SA 1074
60692-	Big Four	De 5547
60693-	Pallet On The Floor	De 5267, DeAu X1277
60694-	Mayflower	De 5291
60695-	My Isle Of Golden Dreams	De 5207
60696-A	Boatman's Delight	De 5417
60697-	Forty Drops	De 5313
60698-A	Soft Voices	De 5417
60699-	California Blues	De 5246
60700-	Spanish Flang Dang	De 5207

Rev. Brunswick SA1074 by the Paradise Entertainers.

STROUP QUARTET

Vocal quartet; acc. unknown, p.
Atlanta, GA   Friday, April 20, 1928

146155-2	The Man Behind The Plow	Co 15299-D, Ve 7110-V, Cl 5145-C
146156-2	Dreaming	Co 15299-D, Ve 7111-V, Cl 5145-C

Revs: Velvet Tone 7110-V by the Atco Quartet, 7111-V by Grant Brothers & Their Music.

UNCLE "AM" STUART

Uncle "Am" Stuart, f; acc. unknown, p-1; Gene Austin, bj-2/v-3.
New York, NY   prob. July 7, 1924

13300*/01	Billie In The Low Ground	Vo 14843, 5038, BrC 1003

13302*/03	Old Liza Jane -1, 3	Vo 14846, 5039, BrC 1004
13304/05*	Sally Gooden -1, 3	Vo 14841, 5037, BrC 1002
13306/07*	Dixie	Vo 14888, 5048, BrC 1005
13308*/09	Waggoner	Vo 14840, 5036, BrC 1001
13310*/11	Grey Eagle	Vo 14839, 5035, Sil 3064, BrC 1000
13312/13*	Cumberland Gap -2	Vo 14839, 5035, Sil 3064, BrC 1000
13314*/15	Sourwood Mountain -2	Vo 14840, 5036, BrC 1001
13316/17	Leather Breeches -2	Vo 14841, 5037, BrC 1002
13318/19*	Forki Deer -2	Vo 14846, 5039, BrC 1004
13320/21*	Nigger In The Wood-pile -2	Vo 14919, 5053, Sil 3051, BrC 1006
13322*/23	Old Granny Rattle-Trap -2	Vo 14888, 5048, BrC 1005
13324*/25	George Boker -2	Vo 14919, 5053, Sil 3051, BrC 1006
13328/29*	Rye Straw (Or) The Unfortunate Pup -2	Vo 14843, 5038, BrC 1003

Vocalion 14843 as by "**Am**" Stuart.
Matrices 13326/27 are untraced but possibly by this artist.

UNCLE JOHN STUART

Pseudonym on Challenge for Billy Milton.

BOB STUCKELEY

Pseudonym on Clarion and Velvet Tone for Bob Miller.

BOB STUCKELEY & BEN WEAVER

Pseudonym on Clarion and Velvet Tone for Bob Miller & Barney Burnett.

JUDGE STURDY'S ORCHESTRA

Two unknowns, f; unknown, g; unknown, vc; Judge O. Sturdy, calls.
St. Louis, MO   Thursday, December 3, 1925

34015-2	One Snowy Night – Quadrille	Vi 20530
34016-1	Hiram's Valley – Quadrille	Vi 20102, BB B-5141
34017-2	Moselle – Quadrille	Vi 20530
34018-3	Old Dan Tucker – Country Dance	Vi 20102, BB B-5141

BOB STYLE'S OLD TIME DANCE BAND

Pseudonym (or erroneous credit) on Parlophone for Bob Skiles Four Old Tuners.

SUE & RAWHIDE

See the Crazy Hillbillies Band.

GENE SULLIVAN & WILEY WALKER

See Wiley Walker & Gene Sullivan.

JOE SUMMERS

Pseudonym on Conqueror for Frank Welling.

SUNDY & MUNDY

Pseudonym on Summit for Gunboat Billy & The Sparrow (see Arthur Fields & Fred Hall).

THE SUNSHINE BOYS

Jimmy Thomason, f/v-1; Billy Mack (McNew), esg; Aubrey "Moon" Mullican, p/v-2; Merle Shelton, g; Grundy "Slim" Harbert, sb/v-3; band v-4.
Saginaw, TX   Saturday, May 4, 1940

DAL-1132-1	Pipe Liner Blues -2	OK 05669, Cq 9730
DAL-1133-1	Lay Me Down Beside My Darling -2	OK 05880, Cq 9729
DAL-1134-1	What's The Matter With Deep Elm -3, 4	OK 05810, Cq 9728
DAL-1135-1	Tell Me With Your Blue Eyes -1, 3	Vo/OK 05612
DAL-1136-1	It's A Weary World Without My Blue Eyes -3	OK 05880, Cq 9729
DAL-1137-1	It's Hard To Please Your Mind -1, 3	Vo/OK 05612
DAL-1138-2	Coo-Se-Coo -1, 3	OK 05669, Cq 9730
DAL-1139-2	Forgive And Forget -3	OK 05810, Cq 9728

Jimmy Thomason, f/v-1; Jack Hinson, p; Bruce "Roscoe" Pierce, tbj; Merle Shelton, g; Slim Harbert, sb/v-2.
Fort Worth, TX   Saturday, March 8, 1941

DAL-1251-1	Two And Two Still Make Four -1, 2	OK 06150, Cq 9851
DAL-1252-1	No Good For Nothin' Blues -2	OK 06338
DAL-1253-1,-2	Blue And Lonesome -1?, 2?	OK unissued

DAL-1254-1,-2	I Will Never Leave You	OK unissued	
DAL-1255-2	I'm Checking Out -2	OK 06195, Co 37659	
DAL-1256-1	Sittin' On The Doorstep -2	OK 06240	

Jimmy Thomason, f-1/md-2; Jack Hinson, p; Roscoe Pierce, tbj; Merle Shelton, g; Slim Harbert, sb/v-3; band v-4.
  Fort Worth, TX   Thursday, March 13, 1941

DAL-1317-1	She's A Rounder -1, 2, 3	OK 06540, Co 37426
DAL-1318-1,-2	My Mind Won't Be Worried Anymore!	OK unissued
DAL-1319-2	I'll Dump Your Apple Cart -2, 3	OK 06603
DAL-1320-	Want A Little Home To Go To	OK unissued
DAL-1321-1	Who's Gonna Chop My Baby's Kindlin' -1, 3	OK 06240
DAL-1322-2	Gonna Get Tight -1, 3, 4	OK 06540, Co 37426

Jimmy Thomason, f/v-1; Jack Hinson, p; Roscoe Pierce, tbj/v-2; Merle Shelton, g; Slim Harbert, sb/v-3; band v-4.
  Fort Worth, TX   Tuesday, March 18, 1941

DAL-1359-1	Drinkin' Made A Fool Outa Me -1, 3	OK 06444
DAL-1360-1	That's Bad -2, 4	OK 06603
DAL-1361-1	Who's Been Tendin' To My Business -3	OK 06338
DAL-1362-1	Don't Come Cryin' In My Beer -3	OK 06150, Cq 9851
DAL-1363-1	Monkey Business -3	OK 06195, Co 37659
DAL-1364-1	Women Are My Weakness -3	OK 06444

The OKeh session listed under **Slim Harbert & His OKeh Boys** was originally logged as by The Sunshine Boys. Other groups called The Sunshine Boys recorded after 1942.

SUNSHINE FOUR

Vocal quartet; unacc.
  Atlanta, GA   Thursday, November 4, 1926

143070-1	In My Heart	Co 15119-D
143071-1	Beautiful Land	Co 15119-D
143072-	Broder Jonah	Co unissued
143073-	Hypocrite	Co unissued

SUNSHINE SACRED TRIO

Pseudonym on Champion for Rev. Edward Boone.

R.C. SUTPHIN

R.C. Sutphin, zither solo.
  Richmond, IN   Saturday, August 11, 1928

14136	Medley Of Old Time Songs	Ge rejected

ELLA SUTTON

Ella Sutton, v; acc. Spade Cooley, f; Carl Cotner, f; Paul Sells, pac; Frank Marvin, esg; Jimmy Wakely, g; Dick Reinhart, sb.
  Hollywood, CA   Friday, August 22, 1941

H-475	Blue Mountain Blues	OK unissued
H-476	Nobody's Sorry For Me	OK unissued
H-477-1	Blue Bonnets	OK 06481
H-478-1A	On The Banks Of The Sunny San Juan	OK 06481
H-479	You'll Be Sorry	OK unissued
H-480	I Wish All My Children Were Babies Again	OK unissued

THURSTON SUTTON & RAYMOND SUTTON

Thurston Sutton, Raymond Sutton, v duet; acc. prob. one of them, g.
  Richmond, IN   Friday, October 30, 1931

18137	Brooklyn Theatre Fire	Ge rejected
18138	Two Little Boys	Ge rejected

SUTTON'S SOUTHERN SERENADERS

Pseudonym on Supertone for George R. Pariseau's Orch.

J. DOUGLAS SWAGERTY
MR. & MRS. J. DOUGLAS SWAGERTY

J. Douglas Swagerty, v; or Mr. & Mrs. J. Douglas Swagerty-1, v duet; acc. Mrs. R.L. Forster, p.
  Atlanta, GA   early April 1924

8621-A	My Mother's Prayers Have Followed Me	OK 40151
8622-A	My Mother's Hands	OK 40151

8623-	Life's Railway To Heaven -1	OK 40086
8625-	Sweet Will Of God -1	OK 40086
8626-A	Redeeming Love -1	OK 40366

The pianist's last name may be spelled Foster on the labels of OKeh 40086. Her initials are given as R.M. on OKeh 40366. Matrix 8624, blank in OKeh files, may be by these artists.

Mr. & Mrs. J. Douglas Swagerty, v duet; acc. Mrs. R.M. Forster, p.
Atlanta, GA c. August 26, 1924

8690-A	Throw Out The Life Line	OK 40270
8691-A	Sweeter As The Years Go By	OK 40270
8692-A	Take The Name Of Jesus With You	OK 40216
8693-	Shall We Gather At The River	OK 40216

Acc. Mrs. R.M. Forster, o-1/p-2.
Atlanta, GA c. April 18, 1925

| 9068-A | God Will Take Care Of You -1 | OK 40366 |
| 9069- | My Mother's Bible -2 | OK 40457 |

Acc. Mrs. R.M. Forster, o.
Atlanta, GA c. July 3, 1925

9202-	The Rock That Is Higher Than I	OK 40457
9203-	He'll Never Forget To Keep Me	OK 40485
9204-	Whosoever Meaneth Me	OK 40485

Matrix 9205, blank in OKeh files, may be by these artists.

J. Douglas Swagerty, v; acc. Mrs. R.M. Forster, o.
Atlanta, GA July 1925

| 9206-A | Better Farther On | OK 40435 |
| 9207-A | The Old Fashioned Faith | OK 40435 |

Mr. & Mrs. J. Douglas Swagerty, v duet; acc. unknown, f; unknown, cl; unknown, p; unknown, vc.
Atlanta, GA March 1926

9639-	In The Garden	OK 40636
9640-A	Jesus Will	OK 40596
9641-A	Jesus, Lover Of My Soul	OK 40596
9642-	Land Of Unsetting Sun	OK 40636

J. Douglas Swagerty–Solon Drukenmiller, v duet; acc. unknown.
Atlanta, GA March 1926

| 9643- | 'Til I See My Mother's Face | OK 40620 |
| 9644- | Where He Leads Me, I Will Follow | OK 40620 |

Mr. & Mrs. J. Douglas Swagerty, v duet; acc. unknown, f; unknown, p; unknown, vc.
Atlanta, GA Friday, August 13, 1928

402135-A	There'll Be No Sorrow There	OK 45291
402136-A	I Gave My Life For Thee	OK 45291
402138-	Better Farther On	OK unissued

Matrix 402137, blank in OKeh files, is probably by these artists.

THE SWAMP ROOTERS

Lowe Stokes, f; Bert Layne, f; Hoke Rice, g; unidentified, sp.
Atlanta, GA Wednesday, November 12, 1930

| ATL-6633- | Swamp Cat Rag | Br 556 |
| ATL-6634- | Citaco | Br 556 |

Atlanta, GA Saturday, November 15, 1930

ATL-6678	Gettin' Away	Br unissued
ATL-6679-	Hickory Mountain Breakdown	Br unissued
ATL-6680-	Sally Johnson	Br unissued
ATL-6681-	Shoot The Buffalo	Br unissued

ROY SWEENEY & FAMILY

No details.
Atlanta, GA Thursday, November 10, 1927

| 145200- | She Was Bred In Old Kentucky | Co unissued |
| 145201- | Just One Girl | Co unissued |

HERBERT SWEET

See Sweet Brothers.

SWEET BROTHERS

Herbert Sweet, v; or **Sweet Brothers**-1: Herbert Sweet, Earl Sweet, v duet; acc. Herbert Sweet, f; Earl Sweet, bj-2; Ernest Stoneman, g.
    Richmond, IN   Thursday, July 5, 1928

14006	My Mother And My Sweetheart -1	Ge 6655
14007-A	Prisoner's Lament	Ge 6567, Ch 15565, Spt 9185, 9305
14008	Once I Knew A Little Girl	Ge rejected
14009-B	Somebody's Waiting For Me -1, 2	Ge 6620, Ch 15586, Spt 9323
14010	Falling By The Wayside -2	Ge 6655, Ch 15586, Spt 9185

Matrix 14010 on Gennett 6655 as by **Sweet Brothers**. Champion 15565 as by **John Clark**, 15586 as by **Clark Brothers** (matrix 14009)/**John Clark** (matrix 14010). Supertone 9185 as by **Sam Caldwell**, 9323 as by **Caldwell Brothers**. Revs: Champion 15565 by Willie Stoneman; Supertone 9323 by Miller Wikel.

Virginia Mountain Boomers: Herbert Sweet, f; Earl Sweet, bj; Ernest Stoneman, g; unidentified, v.
    Richmond, IN   Thursday, July 5, 1928

14011	Sugar Hill	Ge 6687

Herbert Sweet, f; Earl Sweet, bj; Ernest Stoneman, g; unidentified, calls.
    Richmond, IN   Monday, July 9, 1928

14018,-A	I Am Gonna Marry That Pretty Little Girl	Ge rejected: Hi BC-2433-1, HLP8001, Cy 535 (LPs)

It is not known which take of matrix 14018 is used on the LP issues.

Herbert Sweet, f; Earl Sweet, bj/v-1; Ernest Stoneman, g/v-2; unknown, g-3.
    Richmond, IN   Tuesday, July 10, 1928

14019	Cousin Sally Brown -1?	Ge 6687
14020,-A	Bluff Hollow Sobs -1?	Ge unissued
14021-A	I Got A Bulldog -1, 2	Ge 6620
14022	East Tennessee Polka -3	Spt 9406
14023-A	Ramblin' Reckless Hobo -2	Ge 6567, Ch 15610, 33043, Spt 9305

Champion 15610 as by **Pine Mountain Ramblers**, 33043 credit unknown.
Matrix 14023 is titled *Rambling, Reckless Hobo* on Supertone 9305.
Revs: Champion 15610 by Willie Stoneman, 33043 by Pie Plant Pete; Supertone 9406 by Leonard Rutherford & John Foster (see the latter).

The Sweet Brothers also accompanied Ernest Stoneman (as Justin Winfield) at this session.

SWEET VIOLET BOYS

See the Prairie Ramblers.

SWIFT JEWEL COWBOYS

Farris "Lefty" Ingram, f-1/cl-2; "Jose Cortes" (Alfredo Casares), f-3; David "Pee Wee" Wamble, c-4/p-5/sb-6; Clifford Z. "Kokomo" Crocker, ac/v-7; Elmer "Slim" Hall, g/v-8; Calvin "Curly" Noland, sb-9/v-10; poss. Jim Sanders, claves-11; band v-12.
    Memphis, TN   Monday, July 10, 1939

MEM-82-2	Chuck Wagon Swing -2, 3, 4, 9	Vo 05133
MEM-83-1	Swingin' At The Circle S -2, 3, 4, 9	OK 05737
MEM-84-1	Little Man -1, 3, 6, 10	Vo 05449
MEM-85-1	Kansas City Blues -2, 4, 7, 8 (lead), 9, 10	Vo/OK 05243, Co 37738, 20315
MEM-86-1	Little Willie Green (From New Orleans) -1, 5, 7, 9	Vo 05188
MEM-87-1	When The Saints Go Marching In -2, 3, 4, 8, 9, 12	Vo/OK 05598
MEM-88-1	Willie The Weeper -2, 4, 8, 9	Vo 05052
MEM-89-1	Bug Scuffle -2, 3, 4, 9, 11	Vo 05499
MEM-90-1	Coney Island Washboard -3, 6, 7 (lead), 8, 10	Vo 05499

Lefty Ingram, f-1/cl-2; "Jose Cortes," f-3/v-4; Pee Wee Wamble, c-5/v-6; Jimmy Riddle, h-7; Kokomo Crocker, ac/p-8/v-9; Slim Hall, g/v-10; Curly Noland, sb/v-11; prob. Jim Sanders, sp-12.
    Memphis, TN   Thursday, July 11, 1939

MEM-91-1	Look Down That Railroad Line -3, 9, 10, 11	Vo/OK 05598
MEM-92-1	Shine On Harvest Moon -2, 3, 5, 6, 8	Vo/OK 05309
MEM-93-1	Memphis Oomph -2, 3, 5	Vo 05052
MEM-94-1	Raggin' The Rails -3, 7, 8	Vo/OK 05369
MEM-95-1	Fan It -2, 5, 7	Vo/OK 05243, Co 37738, 20315
MEM-96-1	Dill Pickle Rag -2, 3, 5, 7	Vo/OK 05309
MEM-97-1	When The White Azaleas Start Blooming -3, 9, 10, 11	OK 05737
MEM-98-1	My Untrue Cowgirl -2, 3, 4, 5, 9	Vo/OK 05369
MEM-99-1	Long White Robe -1, 3, 5, 9, 10, 11	Vo unissued: Ep EG37324 (LP)
MEM-100-	Alexander's Talking Blues -12	Vo unissued

Matrix MEM-99 is titled *When I Put On My Long White Robe* on Epic EG37324.

"Jose Cortes," f-1; Pee Wee Wamble, c; Lefty Ingram, cl/ts-2; Kokomo Crocker, ac/v-3; Slim Hall, g; Curly Noland, sb; band v-4.

    Memphis, TN   Wednesday, July 12, or Thursday, July 13, 1939

MEM-121-1	You Gotta Ho-De-Ho (To Get Along With Me) -3, 4	Vo 05133
MEM-122-1	Memphis Blues -1	Vo 05188
MEM-123-1	Rose Room (In Sunny Roseland) -1, 2	Vo 05449

THE SWING BILLIES

Harvey Ellington, f; Garfield Hammons, bj; Ray Williams, g; Sam Pridgen, g; Charlie Poole (Jr.), v-1; unidentified, 2nd v-2.

    Charlotte, NC   Friday, August 6, 1937

013028-1	Moonshine In The North Carolina Hills -1	BB B-7143
013029-1	St. Louis Blues	BB B-8099
013030-1	Leavin' Home -1	BB B-7121
013031-1	From Buffalo To Washington -1	BB B-7121
013032-1	I Can't Give You Anything But Love, Baby -1, 2	BB B-8099
013033-1	Somebody Loves You Yet -1	BB B-7338, RZ MR2728, Twin FT8546
013034-1	Melancholy Baby -1	BB B-7161
013035-1	If You're Sorry, Say You're Sorry -1	BB B-7143
013036-1	Every Day Away From You -1	BB B-7161
013037-1	Crazy Yodeling Blues -1	BB B-7338, RZ MR2728, Twin FT8546

This group was originally logged as **Blackwoods Swingbillies**.
Matrix 013037 is titled *Crazy Yodelling Blues* on Regal-Zonophone MR2728 and probably Twin FT8546.

SWISS HILLBILLIES

Releases by this group in the Decca Hill Billy series (5862, 5873) are outside the scope of this work. (Other items recorded at the same session were issued in the popular series as by **Frantz & Fritz & Their Swiss Hillbillies** [2559].)

BERT SWOR & DICK MACK

Bert Swor, Dick Mack, dialog; acc. unknown, g; unknown, jh; unknown, v eff-1.

    New York, NY   Tuesday, September 15, 1931

| 151788-1 | Wowdy Dowdy – Part 1 | Co 15707-D |
| 151789-1 | Wowdy Dowdy – Part 2 -1 | Co 15707-D |

Acc. unknown, k-1; unknown, jh-2; unknown, perc-3; unknown, v eff-4; unknown, wh-5.

    New York, NY   Monday, September 28, 1931

151814-1	Wowdy Dowdy – Part 3 -1, 2	Co 15718-D
151815-1	Wowdy Dowdy – Part 4 -1, 2	Co 15718-D
151816-1	Wowdy Dowdy – Part 5 -2, 5	Co 15743-D
151817-1	Wowdy Dowdy – Part 6 -3, 4	Co 15743-D

No details.

    New York, NY   early October 1931

151829-	Wowdy Dowdy – Parts 9-12 inc [sic]	Co unissued
151830-	Wowdy Dowdy – Part 10	Co unissued
151831-	Wowdy Dowdy – Part 11	Co unissued
151832-	Wowdy Dowdy – Part 12	Co unissued

Matrix 151829 should presumably be titled *Wowdy Dowdy – Part 9*.

T

GEORGE TALBOT

Pseudonym on Bell for Otto Gray's Oklahoma Cowboy Band.

ARTHUR TANNER

Arthur Tanner, v; or **Arthur Tanner & Gid Tanner-1**, poss. v duet; acc. Gid Tanner, f; Arthur Tanner, bj.

    Atlanta, GA   Tuesday, January 27, 1925

| 140280- | Floella's Cottage | Co rejected |
| 140281- | Knoxville Girl -1 | Co unissued |

Dixie String Band: Earl Johnson, f; unknown, f-1; Arthur Tanner, bj-2; Lee Henderson, g; poss. Webb Phillips, calls-3.

    prob. New York, NY   c. June 1925

| 2161-1 | Atlanta Special | Pm 33164 |
| 2162-1 | Chickens Don't Roost Too High For Me -1, 2, 3 | Pm 33160, Pu 9160, Sil 3516 |

2163-1	Leather Breeches	Pm 33162, Pu 9162
2167-1	Soldier's Joy -1, 2	Pm 33163, Sil 3516
2170-1	Show Me The Way To Go Home -1, 2	Pm 33166
2171-1	Birmingham Rag	Pm 33164

Matrix 2162 as by **Dixie String Band (Acc. by Webb Phillips)**. Matrix 2162 is mistitled *Leather Breeches* on Silvertone 3516. Matrices 2164 to 2166, 2168/69 are untraced but probably by this group.

Arthur Tanner, v; acc. by Dixie String Band: Earl Johnson, f; own bj; Lee Henderson, g.
   prob. New York, NY   c. June 1925
| 2172-1 | Whoa, Mule, Whoa | Pm 33166 |

Earl Johnson & Lee Henderson: Earl Johnson, f; Lee Henderson, g.
   prob. New York NY   c. June 1925
| 2174-1 | Merry Widow Waltz | Pm 33161 |

Matrix 2173 is untraced but probably by these or related artists.

Arthur Tanner, v; acc. Earl Johnson, f; Lee Henderson, g.
   prob. New York, NY   c. June 1925
2175-1	When I Was Single My Pockets Would Jingle	Pm 33163, Sil 3515, Her 75538
2176-1	The Lightning Express Train	Pm 33160, Pu 9160, Her 75501
2177-1	Little Log Cabin In The Lane	Pm 33161
2179-1	The Knoxville Girl	Pm 33162, Pu 9162, Sil 3515, Her 75538
2180-1	The Burglar Man	Pm 33159, Pu 9159, Sil 3514, Her 75539
2181-1	Devlish Mary	Pm 33159, Pu 9159, Sil 3514, Her 75539

Herwin 75501 as by **Guy Phillips**; matrix 2176 is titled *The Lightning Express* on that issue. Other issues of Herwin 75501 use a recording of *The Lightning Express* by Vernon Dalhart.
Matrix 2179 is titled *That Knoxville Gal* on some issues of Paramount 33162.
Matrix 2178 is untraced but probably by this artist.
Rev. Herwin 75501 by Vernon Dalhart.

Arthur Tanner & His Corn-Shuckers: Arthur Tanner, v; acc. Gid Tanner, f/hv-1; unknown, f; unknown, bj; own g; unidentified, hv-2.
   Atlanta, GA   Friday, April 1, 1927
143850-2	Shack No. 9 -1, 2	Co 15180-D
143851-2	The Jealous Lover	Co 15145-D
143852-2	Knoxville Girl	Co 15145-D

Arthur Tanner, v; acc. prob. own g.
   Atlanta, GA   Friday, April 1, 1927
| 143853-1 | Two Little Children | Co 15180-D |

Acc. Clayton McMichen, f; prob. own g.
   Atlanta, GA   Wednesday, November 2, 1927
145073-	Out In The Pale Moonlight	Co unissued
145074-	My Bonnie's Blue Eyes	Co unissued
145075-	Keep My Grave Clean	Co unissued
145076-	The Sailor Boy	Co unissued

Acc. Clayton McMichen, f; Lowe Stokes, f; Ted Hawkins, md; own g.
   Atlanta, GA   Tuesday, April 17, 1928
| 146108-2 | The Disappointed Lover | Co 15352-D |
| 146109-2 | Sleep On Blue Eyes | Co 15352-D |

Arthur Tanner & Riley Puckett, v duet; or **Arthur Tanner-1**, v; acc. Arthur Tanner, bj; Riley Puckett, g.
   Atlanta, GA   Friday, April 12, 1929
| 148264-1 | Bring Back My Blue-Eyed Boy | Co 15577-D |
| 148265-1 | Gather The Flowers -1 | Co 15577-D |

Arthur Tanner & His Corn-Shuckers: Arthur Tanner, v; acc. Clayton McMichen, f; Lowe Stokes, f; unknown, bj; own g.
   Atlanta, GA   Friday, April 12, 1929
| 148268-1 | Dr. Ginger Blue | Co 15479-D |
| 148269-2 | Lay Me Where Sweet Flowers Blossom | Co 15479-D |

Matrices 148266/67 are by Clayton McMichen.

Arthur Tanner, v; acc. prob. own g.
   Atlanta, GA   Saturday, November 15, 1930
| ATL-6674- | Don't Go Out Tonight, Sweetheart | Br/Vo rejected |
| ATL-6675- | The Sailor Boy | Br/Vo rejected |

GID TANNER

Gid Tanner, v; acc. own f; Riley Puckett, g-1.
New York, NY   Friday, March 7, 1924
    81604-6   Boll Weevil Blues   Co 15016-D
    81627-1   I'm Satisfied   Co 15016-D

Matrices 81605, 81626 are by Riley Puckett; matrices 81606 to 81625 are by other artists.

New York, NY   Saturday, March 8, 1924
    81628-1   [1. Chicken Don't Roost Too High For Me] 2. I   Co 150-D, Ha 5095-H
                  Don't Love Nobody -1

Harmony 5095-H as by **Gibbs & Watson**; matrix 81628 is titled *1. Chicken Roost 2. I Don't Love* on that issue. The first tune (here bracketed) on matrix 81628 is by Riley Puckett alone and so credited.
Revs: Columbia 150-D, Harmony 5095-H by Riley Puckett.

Gid Tanner & George Riley Puckett: Gid Tanner, f/v; Riley Puckett, g.
New York, NY   Saturday, March 8, 1924
    81630-2   Hen Cackle   Co 110-D, Ha 5117-H
    81634-2   Buckin' Mule   Co 110-D, Ha 5117-H
    81635-1   Black Eyed Susie   Co 119-D, Ha 5119-H, ReE G8236
    81638-1   Alabama Gal, Give The Fiddler A Dram   Co 119-D, Ha 5119-H

Harmony 5117-H as by **Tom Carter** (81630)/**Carter & Wilson** (81634), 5119-H as by **Carter & Wilson**.
Matrix 81635 is titled *Black-Eyed Susie* on Regal G8236.
Matrices 81631 to 81633 are by Riley Puckett; matrices 81636/37 are untraced but probably not by Tanner (or Puckett).
Rev. Regal G8236 by Ernest Thompson.

Gid Tanner & Riley Puckett: Gid Tanner, f/v; Riley Puckett, g.
New York, NY   Wednesday, September 10, 1924
    140002-   Prettiest Little Girl In County   Co unissued
    140003-   Whistlin' Rufus (Intro: Big Ball In Town)   Co rejected

Gid Tanner, f/v; Riley Puckett, bj.
New York, NY   Thursday, September 11, 1924
    14004-2   Sourwood Mountain   Co 245-D, Ha 5104-H
    140005-   Cripple Creek   Co rejected
    140019-1   Georgia Railroad   Co 15019-D, Ha 5144-H, Sil 3262

Columbia 15019-D originally as by **Gid Tanner**; later pressings as by **Gid Tanner & Riley Puckett**. Harmony 5104-H, 5144-H, Silvertone 3262 as by **Gibbs & Watson**.
Matrices 140006 to 140018 are by Riley Puckett.

Gid Tanner, f/v-1/sp-2; Riley Puckett, bj-3/g-4/v-5/sp-6.
New York, NY   Friday, September 12, 1924
    140031-1   John Henry -1, 4, 5   Co 15019-D, Ha-5144-H, Sil 3262
    140045-1   The Arkansaw Traveler -2, 4, 6   Co 15017-D, Ha 5143-H
    140046-1   Cumberland Gap -3   Co 245-D, Ha 5104-H
    140047-   Turkey In The Straw -1, 3/4   Co unissued
    140048-2   Be Kind To A Man When He's Down -1   Co 15010-D, Ha 5136-H
    140049-   Sailor Boy -1   Co unissued
    140050-1   Fox Chase -1   Co 15017-D, Ha 5143-H
    140051-1   Don't Grieve Your Mother -1   Co 15010-D, Ha 5136-H

Columbia 15010-D and matrix 140050 on Columbia 15017-D as by **Gid Tanner**. Harmony 5104-H, 5144-H, Silvertone 3262 as by **Gibbs & Watson**. Harmony 5136-H as by **Tom Carter**, 5143-H as by **Carter & Wilson** (140045)/**Tom Carter** (140050).
Intervening matrices are unrelated.

Gid Tanner & His Georgia Boys: Gid Tanner, Fate Norris, v duet; acc. Gid Tanner, f; unknown, bj; Fate Norris, g.
Atlanta, GA   Saturday, October 3, 1925
    141087-2   Old Time Tunes   Co 15059-D
    141088-1   Just Gimme The Leavings   Co 15059-D

Gid Tanner & His Skillet-Lickers With Riley Puckett: Clayton McMichen, f/lv-1; Gid Tanner, f/lv-2/hv-3; Bert Layne, f (on at least some items); unknown (poss. Frank Walker), h-4; Fate Norris, bj/lv-5; Riley Puckett, g/solo v-6/lv-7/hv-8; unidentified, hv-9; unidentified, dog eff-10.
Atlanta, GA   Saturday, April 17, 1926
    142034-2   Hand Me Down My Walking Cane -1, 3, 8, 9   Co 15091-D, CoE 19004
    142035-1   Bully Of The Town -6   Co 15074-D
    142036-1   Pass Around The Bottle And We'll All Take A   Co 15074-D
                  Drink -3, 7, 9
    142037-2   Alabama Jubilee -6   Co 15104-D

142038-1	Watermelon On The Vine -3, 5, 8, 9	Co 15091-D, CoE 19004
142039-1	Don't You Hear Jerusalem Moan -2, 8, 9	Co 15104-D, Ve 2493-V, Cl 5433-C
142040-1	Ya Gotta Quit Kickin' My Dog Aroun' -3, 7, 9, 10	Co 15084-D
142041-3	Turkey In The Straw -3, 4, 7	Co 15084-D

Velvet Tone 2493-V, Clarion 5433-C as by **Jackson Pavey & His Corn Shuckers**.

Gid Tanner & Faith Norris, v duet; acc. Gid Tanner, f; Fate Norris, g.
Atlanta, GA   Tuesday, April 20, 1926

142060-1	S-A-V-E-D	Co 15097-D
142061-2	Where Did You Get That Hat	Co 15097-D
142062-	Frankie Was A Good Woman	Co unissued
142063-1	Goodbye Booze	Co 15105-D
142064-	I'm Tired Of Living On Pork And Beans	Co unissued
142065-	Three Night's [sic] Experience	Co unissued

Rev. Columbia 15105-D by Dock Walsh.

Gid Tanner & His Skillet-Lickers With Riley Puckett: Clayton McMichen, f; Gid Tanner, f/hv-1; Bert Layne, f; Fate Norris, bj; Riley Puckett, g/lv-2; several voices, lv/hv/sp-3.
Atlanta, GA   Tuesday, November 2, 1926

143019-1	Polly Woddle Doo -3	Re/RZAu G20666
143019-2	Polly Woddle Doo -3	Co 15200-D, CoE 19011
143020-	Rock Road To Milledgeville	Co unissued
143021-2	Uncle Bud -1, 2	Co 15134-D

Columbia 15200-D as by **Gid Tanner & His Skillet-Lickers With Riley Puckett & Clayton McMichen**. Regal/Regal-Zonophone G20666 as by **Gid Tanner & His Skillet-Lickers**.

Clayton McMichen, f/poss. hv-1/sp-2; Gid Tanner, f/lv-3/hv-4/v eff-5; Bert Layne, f/sp-6; Fate Norris, bj/poss. hv-7/sp-8; Riley Puckett, g/solo v-9/lv-10/sp-11; unidentified, sp-12.
Atlanta, GA   Wednesday, November 3, 1926

143026-1	Dance All Night With A Bottle In Your Hand -2, 5, 6, 8, 9	Co 15108-D, Ve 2516-V, Cl 5456-C
143027-1	She'll Be Coming 'Round The Mountain -4, 10, 12	Co 15200-D, CoE 19011
143028-1	I Don't Love Nobody -4, 5, 10, 12	Co 15123-D
143029-	Hop Light Ladies	Co unissued
143030-1	I Got Mine -1, 4, 7, 10, 11, 12	Co 15134-D
143031-2	Shortening Bread -4, 10, 12	Co 15123-D, Ve 2493-V, Cl 5456-C
143032-1	Old Joe Clark -3 (chorus), 4, 8?, 10	Co 15108-D

Columbia 15200-D as by **Gid Tanner & His Skillet-Lickers With Riley Puckett & Clayton McMichen**. Velvet Tone 2493-V, 2516-V, Clarion 5433-C, 5456-C as by **Jackson Pavey & His Corn Shuckers**.

Bob Nichols & Gid Tanner: poss. Clayton McMichen, Gid Tanner, v duet; acc. own f duet.
Atlanta, GA   Thursday, November 4, 1926

| 143046- | The Drunkard's Hic-cups | Co unissued |

Gid Tanner, v; acc. own f.
Atlanta, GA   Friday, November 5, 1926

143078-	My Boarding House On The Hill	Co unissued
143079-	The Fate Of William Cheek	Co unissued
143080-	The Drunkard's Courtship	Co unissued
143081-	Don't Forget Me Little Darling	Co rejected

Gid Tanner & His Skillet-Lickers With Riley Puckett & Clayton McMichen: Clayton McMichen, f/sp-1; Gid Tanner, f/hv; Bert Layne, f; Fate Norris, bj; Riley Puckett, g/lv; unidentified, train-wh eff.
Atlanta, GA   Monday, March 28, 1927

| 143785-2 | Casey Jones -1 | Co 15237-D |
| 143786-1 | The Wreck Of The Southern Old '97 | Co 15142-D |

Clayton McMichen, f/solo v-1/sp-2; Gid Tanner, f/hv-3; Bert Layne, f; Fate Norris, bj/lv-4; Riley Puckett, g/solo v-5/lv-6/sp-7; unidentified, sp-8/steel hammering eff-9.
Atlanta, GA   Tuesday, March 29, 1927

143795-2	Dixie -3, 6	Co 15158-D, Ve 2484-V, Cl 5424-C
143796-1,-2	Run Nigger Run -3, 6	Co 15158-D
143797-2	The Girl I Left Behind Me -3, 6	Co 15170-D, Ve 2484-V, Cl 5424-C
143798-2	The Old Gray Mare -3, 6, 8	Co 15170-D, Ve 2516-V, Cl 5456-C
143799-2	John Henry (The Steel Drivin' Man) -3, 6, 8, 9	Co 15142-D
143800-2	Drink 'Er Down -2, 3, 4, 7	Co 15188-D
143801-2	The Darktown Strutters' Ball -1 (verse), 5 (chorus)	Co 15188-D
143802-	Peter Went A Fishing	Co unissued

Velvet Tone 2484-V, Clarion 5424-C as by **Charlie Norris**; Velvet Tone 2516-V, Clarion 5456-C as by **Jackson Pavey & His Corn Shuckers**.

Gid Tanner & Fate Norris, v duet; acc. Gid Tanner, f; Fate Norris, bj.
Atlanta, GA   Thursday, March 31, 1927
   143823-   Grandpapa's Pa Pa   Co unissued
   143824-   Howdy Bill   Co unissued
   143825-2   Football Rag   Co 15165-D
   143826-1   Baby Lou   Co 15165-D

Fate Norris & Gid Tanner: prob. v duet; acc. Gid Tanner, f; Fate Norris, bj or g.
Atlanta, GA   Monday, October 31, 1927
   145046-   Mr. Dooley   Co unissued

Gid Tanner & His Skillet-Lickers With Riley Puckett & Clayton McMichen: Clayton McMichen, f/solo v-1/hv-2/sp-3; Gid Tanner, f/lv-4/hv-5/sp-6; prob. Lowe Stokes, f; Fate Norris, bj/sp-7; Riley Puckett, g/solo v-8/lv-9/hv-10/sp-11; unidentified, dog eff-12.
Atlanta, GA   Monday, October 31, 1927
   145047-2   Old McDonald Had A Farm -1 (verse), 2, 4, 10, 12   Co 15204-D
   145048-3   Bile Them Cabbage Down -5, 9   Co 15249-D
   145049-1   Big Ball In Town -8   Co 15204-D
   145050-3   It's A Long Way To Tipperary -1 (verse), 2, 9   Co 15249-D
              (chorus), 10
   145053-2   Buckin' Mule -3, 6, 7, 11   Co 15237-D
   145054-2   Uncle Bud -5, 9   Co 15221-D
   145005-   Polly Wolly Doodly [sic]   Co unissued

Matrices 145051/52 are by Lowe Stokes.

Gid Tanner & Fate Norris, v duet; acc. Gid Tanner, f; Fate Norris, bj.
Atlanta, GA   Tuesday, November 1, 1927
   145056-2   Please Do Not Get Offended   Co 15217-D
   145057-1   Everyday Will Be Sunday Bye And Bye   Co 15217-D

Gid Tanner & His Skillet-Lickers With Riley Puckett & Clayton McMichen: Clayton McMichen, f; Gid Tanner, f/sp; prob. Lowe Stokes, f; Fate Norris, bj; Riley Puckett, g/v.
Atlanta, GA   Tuesday, November 1, 1927
   145058-2   Johnson's Old Gray Mule   Co 15221-D

Clayton McMichen, f/hv-1/sp-2; Gid Tanner, f/hv-3/v eff -4; Lowe Stokes, f/poss. hv-5; Fate Norris, bj; Riley Puckett, g/solo v-6/lv-7/sp-8; unidentified, chicken eff-9/clogging eff-10.
Atlanta, GA   Tuesday, April 10, 1928
   146000-1   Hen Cackle -2, 9   Co 15303-D
   146001-1   Cumberland Gap -3, 7   Co 15303-D
   146002-2   Cotton-Eyed Joe -3, 7   Co 15283-D
   146003-2   Black-Eyed Susie -3, 7   Co 15283-D
   146004-3   Prettiest Little Girl In The County -1, 2, 3, 7, 8   Co 15315-D, Vo 02917
   146005-3   Slow Buck -2, 4, 8, 10   Co 15267-D, Vo 02985
   146006-1   Settin' In The Chimney Jamb -1, 5, 7   Co 15315-D, Vo 02917
   146007-2   Sal Let Me Chaw Your Rosin -2, 6, 8   Co 15267-D, Vo 02985

The Vocalion issues use dubbing masters, as follows: 146004 = 16943; 146005 = 17133; 146006 = 16944; 146007 = 17132.

Fate Norris & Gid Tanner: prob. v duet; acc. Gid Tanner, f; Fate Norris, bj or g.
Atlanta, GA   Thursday, April 12, 1928
   146040-   Grandpapa's Papa   Co unissued
   146041-   Coon, Coon, Coon   Co unissued

Gid Tanner & His Skillet-Lickers With Riley Puckett & Clayton McMichen: Clayton McMichen, f/sp-1; Gid Tanner, f/hv-2/sp-3; poss. Lowe Stokes, f; Fate Norris, bj/sp-4; Riley Puckett, g/lv-5/sp-6.
Atlanta, GA   Monday, October 22, 1928
   147253-1   Liberty -1, 6   Co 15334-D, Vo 02948
   147254-2   Nancy Rollin -1, 3, 4, 6   Co 15382-D
   147255-1   Old Dan Tucker -2, 5   Co 15382-D
   147256-2   Devilish Mary -2, 5   Co 15709-D

Columbia 15709-D as by **Gid Tanner & His Skillet-Lickers**.
Vocalion 02948 uses the dubbing master 17139.

Clayton McMichen, f/sp-1; Gid Tanner, f/hv; poss. Lowe Stokes, f; Fate Norris, bj/sp-2; Riley Puckett, g/lv/sp-3.
Atlanta, GA   Tuesday, October 23, 1928
   147263-2   Pretty Little Widow -1, 2, 3   Co 15334-D, Vo 02948
   147264-2   Fly Around My Pretty Little Miss   Co 15709-D

Columbia 15709-D as by **Gid Tanner & His Skillet-Lickers**.
Vocalion 02948 uses the dubbing master 17138.

Clayton McMichen, f/lv-1/joint lv-2/poss. hv-3/sp-4; Gid Tanner, f/hv-5/v eff-6/sp-7; Lowe Stokes, f; Fate Norris, bj/hv-8/poss. sp-9; Riley Puckett, g/solo v-10/lv-11/joint lv-12/sp-13; unidentified, wh duet-14.

Atlanta, GA   Monday, April 8, 1929

148200-1	Mississippi Sawyer -4, 7, 9, 13	Co 15420-D
148201-2	It Ain't Gonna Rain No Mo' -2, 5, 12	Co 15447-D
148202-2	Going On Down Town -5, 11	Co 15420-D
148203-2	Flatwoods -1, 4, 5, 13	Co 15472-D, ReE MR20
148208-1	Never Seen The Like Since Gettin' Upstairs -1, 5	Co 15472-D
148209-1	Show Me The Way To Go Home -2, 3, 5, 8, 12, 14	Co 15404-D
148210-2	Cotton Baggin' -4, 6	Co 15404-D
148211-2	The Rovin' Gambler -4, 10	Co 15447-D

Regal MR20 as by **The Alabama Barn Stormers**.
Matrices 148204 to 148207 are by Hugh Cross.
Rev. Regal MR20 (with same credit) by Earl Shirkey & Roy Harper.

Clayton McMichen, f/sp-1; Lowe Stokes, f; Gid Tanner, f (on some items)/hv-2; poss. Bert Layne, f (on some items); Fate Norris, bj; Riley Puckett, g/solo v-3/lv-4/sp-5; unidentified, sp-6.

Atlanta, GA   Tuesday, October 29, 1929

149276-2	Rocky Pallet	Co 15516-D
149277-2	Soldiers Joy -1, 3	Co 15538-D
149278-1	Rock That Cradle Lucy -3	Co 15538-D
149279-1	There'll Be A Hot Time In The Old Town To-Night -2, 4	Co 15695-D
149280-2	Boneparte's Retreat -1, 5	Co 15485-D
149281-2	Hell's Broke Loose In Georgia -1, 5	Co 15516-D
149282-1	Giddap Napoleon -3	Co 15695-D
149283-2	Cripple Creek -3, 6	Co 15485-D

Clayton McMichen, f/sp-1; Lowe Stokes, f; poss. Bert Layne, f; Gid Tanner, poss. f (on some items)/v eff-2; Fate Norris, bj; Riley Puckett, g/solo v-3/sp-4; several unidentified, v eff/sp-5.

Atlanta, GA   Monday, April 14, 1930

150200- ; 194976-2	Leather Breeches -5	Co 15623-D
150201- ; 194977-2	New Arkansaw Traveller -1, 4	Co 15623-D
150202- ; 194978-2	Sugar In The Gourd -3	Co 15612-D
150203-; 194979-2	Georgia Wagner -5	Co 15612-D
150204-2	Sal's Gone To The Cider Mill -2, 3, 5	Co 15562-D
150205-2	Nigger In The Woodpile -2, 3, 5	Co 15562-D

Gid Tanner, Fate Norris & Mel Dupree, v trio; acc. Gid Tanner, f; Fate Norris, bj; Melvin Dupree, g.

Atlanta, GA   Tuesday, April 15, 1930

| 150216-2; 194980-1 | I Don't Bother Work | Co unissued: *Rdr 1035 (LP)* |
| 150217-2; 194981-2 | I Shall Not Be Moved | Co unissued: *Rdr 1035 (LP)* |

Gid Tanner & His Skillet-Lickers With Riley Puckett & Clayton McMichen: Clayton McMichen, f/poss. hv-1; Lowe Stokes, f; poss. Bert Layne, f; Gid Tanner, poss. f/hv; Fate Norris, bj; Riley Puckett, g/lv.

Atlanta, GA   Tuesday, April 15, 1930

| 150222- ; 194875-2 | Devilish Mary -1 | Co 15589-D |
| 150223- ; 194874-2 | Soldier, Will You Marry Me | Co 15589-D |

Clayton McMichen, f; Lowe Stokes, f; poss. Bert Layne, f; prob. Gid Tanner, bj; Riley Puckett, g/solo v-1; several unidentified, v eff/sp-2.

Atlanta, GA   Thursday, December 4, 1930

151024-1,-2	Ride Old Buck To Water -1	Co 15665-D
151025-2	Don't You Cry My Honey -1	Co 15665-D
151026-2	Cacklin' Hen And Rooster Too -2	Co 15682-D
151027-2	Ricketts Hornpipe	Co 15682-D

Clayton McMichen, f; Lowe Stokes, f; poss. Bert Layne, f; prob. Gid Tanner, bj/jh-1/v eff-1; Riley Puckett, g/solo v-2/sp-3.

Atlanta, GA   Friday, December 5, 1930

| 151041- | Hand Me Down My Walking Cane | Co unissued |
| 151042-2 | Bully Of The Town No. 2 -2 | Co 15640-D |

| 151043-2 | Broken Down Gambler -1, 3 | Co 15640-D |
| 151044- | Possum Up The Gum Stump | Co unissued |

Gid Tanner, v; acc. own bj.
Atlanta, GA   Saturday, December 6, 1930

| 151061-2 | If You Want To Go A Courtin' | Co 15716-D |
| 151062-2 | You've Got To Stop Drinking Shine | Co 15716-D |

Gid Tanner & His Skillet-Lickers With Riley Puckett & Clayton McMichen: Clayton McMichen, f/sp-1/poss. wh-2; Lowe Stokes, f/sp-3; Gid Tanner, bj/v eff-4; Riley Puckett, g/solo v-5/sp-6/wh-7; unidentified, sp-8.
Atlanta, GA   Saturday, October 24, 1931

151916-1	Miss McLeods Reel -4, 6, 8	Co 15730-D
151917-1	Four Cent Cotton -5	Co 15746-D
151918-1	Molly Put The Kettle On -1, 3, 5, 6	Co 15746-D
151919-1	Sleeping Lulu -1, 3, 6	Co 15777-D
151920-1	McMichen's Breakdown -3, 4	Co 15777-D
151921-1	Whistlin' Rufus -2, 7	Co 15730-D

Tanner & Puckett: Gid Tanner, f/poss. v-1; Riley Puckett, g/poss.v-1.
Atlanta, GA   Thursday, October 29, 1931

| 151982- | No. 2 Schottiche [sic] | Co unissued |
| 151983- | Parody On Home Sweet Home -1 | Co unissued |

Gid Tanner & His Skillet Lickers: Gid Tanner, f-1/solo v-2/joint lv-3/hv-4/v eff-5/sp-6; Gordon Tanner, f-7/md-8; Ted Hawkins, md; Riley Puckett, g/lv-9/joint lv-10; unidentified, sp on several items.
San Antonio, TX   Thursday, March 29, 1934

82672-1	Georgia Waggoner -1, 5, 7	BB B-5433, MW M-4845
82673-1	Mississippi Sawyer -1, 5, 7	BB B-5433, MW M-4845
82674-1	Back Up And Push -1, 2, 6, 7	BB B-5562, Vi 20-2167
82675-1	Rufus -1, 7	BB B-5434
82676-1	Cumberland Gap On A Buckin' Mule -1, 2, 6, 7	BB B-5434
82677-1	Hawkins' Rag -8	BB B-5435
82678-1	Skillet Licker Breakdown -7	BB B-5435
82679-1	Cotton Patch -1, 2, 6, 7	BB B-5591, HMVIn N4354
82680-1	Ida Red -1, 4, 6, 7, 9	BB B-5488, MW M-4846
82681-1	Down Yonder -1, 7	BB B-5562, Vi 20-2167
82682-1	Git Along -1, 4, 7, 9	BB B-5488, MW M-4846
82683-1	Whoa, Mule, Whoa -1, 3, 4, 7, 10	BB B-5591, HMVIn N4354

RCA 8416-2-R (CD) claims to use matrix 82680-2 but the item is identical to the issued take 1.

Gid Tanner–Riley Puckett: Gid Tanner, v; acc. own f; Ted Hawkins, md-1; Riley Puckett, g/v-2.
San Antonio, TX   Thursday, March 29, 1934

82684-1	Tanner's Boarding House	BB B-5665
82685-1	On Tanner's Farm	BB B-5665
82686-1	I'm Satisfied	BB B-5748
82687-1	Three Nights Drunk -1, 2	BB B-5748

Gid Tanner & His Skillet Lickers: Gid Tanner, f/solo v-1/hv-2; Gordon Tanner, f; Ted Hawkins, md/lv-3; Riley Puckett, g/hv-4; Dan Hornsby, solo v-5/hv-6.
San Antonio, TX   Thursday, March 29, 1934

82692-1	Tra-Le-La-La -2, 3, 4, 6	BB B-5633, MW M-4844
82693-1	Keep Your Gal At Home -1	BB B-5805, MW M-4843
82694-1	Hinkey-Dinkey-Dee -1, 5	BB B-5633, MW M-4844

Matrices 82688 to 82691 are by Ted Hawkins & Riley Puckett.

Gid Tanner, f-1/bj-2/ solo v-3/sp-4; Gordon Tanner, f-5/md-6; Ted Hawkins, md-7; Riley Puckett, g; unidentified, sp-8.
San Antonio, TX   Friday, March 30, 1934

82719-1	I Ain't No Better Now -1, 3	BB B-5805, MW M-4843
82720-1	Tanner's Rag -2, 6, 7, 8	BB B-5657, MW M-4847
82721-1	Tanner's Hornpipe -2, 5, 7, 8	BB B-5657, MW M-4847
82722-1	Soldier's Joy -2, 3, 5, 7	BB B-5658, MW M-4907, Vi 20-2168
82723-1	Flop-Eared Mule -2, 4, 5, 7, 8	BB B-5658, MW M-4907, Vi 20-2168

Gid Tanner, f-1/bj-2/hv-3; Gordon Tanner, f; Ted Hawkins, md/sp; Riley Puckett, g/lv-4/sp; Dan Hornsby, lv-5/sp; unidentified, sp-6; band v-7.
San Antonio, TX   Friday, March 30, 1934

82724-1	Prosperity And Politics – Part 1 -1	BB B-5446
82725-1	Prosperity And Politics – Part 2 -2, 3, 5, 7	BB B-5446
82728-1	Practice Night With The Skillet Lickers – Part 1 -2, 3, 4	BB B-5559

| 82729-1 | Practice Night With The Skillet Lickers – Part 2 | BB B-5559 |
| | -2, 6, 7 | |

Bluebird B-5559 as by **Gid Tanner & His Skillet Lickers With Riley Puckett**.

Matrices 82726/27 are by Ted Hawkins & Riley Puckett.

Gid Tanner participated in many sketch recordings by members of the Skillet-Lickers and associated artists, for which see Clayton McMichen. See also Riley Puckett.

JIMMIE TARLTON

Jimmie Tarlton made numerous recordings with Tom Darby, under whose name they will be found. His solo recordings are listed below. ARC recordings credited to Tarlton are by Darby & Tarlton together and are listed under the former.

Jimmie Tarlton, v; acc. own sg.
    Atlanta, GA   Wednesday, December 3, 1930

151000-2	Careless Love	Co 15651-D
151001-2	By The Old Oaken Bucket Louise	Co 15763-D
151002-2	Lowe Bonnie	Co 15763-D
151003-2	After The Sinking Of The Titanic	Co unissued: *FV FV12504, BF BF15504* (LPs); *Cy CD3503, BF BCD15764* (CDs)
151004-2,-3	New Birmingham Jail	Co 15629-D
151005-2	Roy Dixon	Co unissued: *BF BCD15764* (CD)
151005-3	Roy Dixon	Co 15629-D

    Atlanta, GA   Thursday, December 4, 1930

| 151010-1 | Moonshine Blues | Co 15651-D |
| 151011- | Over The Hills Maggie | Co unissued |

    Atlanta, GA   Monday, February 29, 1932

71629-1	Dixie Mail	Vi 23665, MW M-4329
71630-1	The Weaver's Blues	Vi 23700
71631-2	Sweetheart Of My Dreams	Vi 23665, MW M-4329
71632-1	Ooze Up To Me	Vi 23700

Montgomery Ward M-4329 as by **Jimmy Tarlton**.

Matrices 71627/28 are by Darby & Tarlton.

Jimmie Tarlton recorded after 1942.

TATE BROS. & HICKS

Prob.: ——— Tate, ——— Tate, bj duet; acc. Rhoda Hicks, p.
    Richmond, IN   Saturday, March 1, 1930

| 16342-A | Turkey In The Straw – Soldier's Joy | Ge 7165, Ch 15965 |
| 16343-A | Arkansas Traveler – The Girl I Left Behind Me | Ge 7165, Ch 15965, 33002 |

Rev. Champion 33002 untraced.

Rhoda Hicks also recorded in her own name.

[EX-GOVERNOR] ALF. TAYLOR

Ex-Governor Alf. Taylor's Old Limber Quartet: Nat Taylor, tv; Alfred Taylor, Jr., tv; David Taylor, bv; Bob Wardrep, bsv; unacc.
    New York, NY   Monday, August 11, 1924

30640-1,-2	(1) Heaven Song (2) Standing In The Need Of Prayer	Vi unissued
30641-2	Brother Noah Built An Ark	Vi 19451
30644-1,-2	Nigger Crap Song	Vi unissued

Matrix 30641 was logged as *(1) Brother Noah (2) Chorus Of Beloved*; the latter song does appear in the recording.

Alf. Taylor (Ex-Governor of Tennessee) & His Old Limber Quartet: Nat Taylor, tv; Alfred Taylor, Jr., tv; David Taylor, bv; Bob Wardrep, bsv; Alfred A. Taylor, sp; unacc.
    New York, NY   Monday, August 11, 1924

| 30726-2 | Pharoah's Army Got Drownded | Vi 19451 |

This item was made, on the date shown, as an unnumbered trial recording, and assigned the matrix shown on August 27. It is described on the label of Victor 19451 as "Jubilee Incident to a Fox Chase in the Appalachian Mountains."

The Old Limber Quartet is logged as **Ole Timber Male Quartet**; it is uncertain whether "Limber" or "Timber" is correct.

Ex-Governor Alfred A. Taylor, f; acc. Nat Shilkret, p.
    New York, NY   Monday, August 11, 1924

| | Arkansaw Traveler | Vi unissued trial recording |

Ex-Governor Alfred A. Taylor, poss. f solo.
    New York, NY   Friday, August 15, 1924

| | Nigger's Dream | Vi unissued trial recording |

CAREY TAYLOR & HIS 'GINNY BOYS

Pseudonym on Clarion and Velvet Tone for McMichen's Melody Men.

DAVE & ALICE TAYLOR

Pseudonym on Supertone for Dick Parman & Lowell Smith.

MRS. DENNIS TAYLOR

Mrs. Dennis Taylor, v; acc. unknown, g.
Richmond, IN   c. March 1928

13630	There Was No One To Welcome Me Home	Ge rejected
13631	Does Jennie Remember	Ge rejected

HARTY TAYLOR & KARL DAVIS (OF THE CUMBERLAND RIDGE RUNNERS)

This credit was used on Conqueror 8660 for Karl & Harty.

MR. & MRS. HOMER TAYLOR

See Taylor Trio.

JIM TAYLOR [& BILL SHELBY]

Pseudonym on Champion for Walter Smith [& Norman Woodlieff].

PAUL TAYLOR

Pseudonym on Australian Parlophone for Vernon Dalhart.

T.A. TAYLOR

See C.S. Wagner.

"BIG ROAD" WEBSTER TAYLOR (THE MISSISSIPPI MULE SKINNER)

On the evidence of composer credits, this artist's real name is Ben Webster.

Webster Taylor, v; acc. own g.
Chicago, IL   Friday, March 29, 1929

TC-3204	World In A Jug Blues	Vo unissued trial recording
TC-3205	Sunny Southern Blues	Vo unissued trial recording

Chicago, IL   c. April 17, 1929

C-3302-	World In A Jug Blues	Vo 1271
C-3303-	Sunny Southern Blues	Vo 1271

Though issued in the Vocalion "race" series, these sides were originally intended for the 5000 hillbilly catalogue. Despite his listing in B&GR, this artist seems definitely to have been white.

WILL TAYLOR

Pseudonym on Velvet Tone and Clarion for Riley Puckett.

TAYLOR & BUNCH

Pseudonym on Supertone for Leonard Rutherford & John Foster.

TAYLOR & DAVIS

See Karl & Harty.

TAYLOR & DURBIN

See Taylor Trio.

TAYLOR & WALKER

See Walker's Corbin Ramblers.

TAYLOR–GRIGGS LOUISIANA MELODY MAKERS

Taylor–Griggs Louisiana Melody Makers: F.R. Taylor, f-1; R.C. Grigg, f-2/v-3; Lorene Grigg, md; Ione Grigg, g; Ausie B. Grigg, sb; Clavie Taylor, v-4; Crockett Grigg, bsv-5.
Memphis, TN   Thursday, September 13, 1928

47021-2	Sweet Rose Of Heaven -1, 4	Vi 21768
47022-1,-2	Big Ball Uptown -2, 3, 5	Vi 21768
47023-2	Ione -1, 4	Vi V-40083

Memphis, TN   Friday, September 14, 1928

47028-1,-2	Dreamy Eyes Waltz -1?, 4?	Vi unissued

47029-1	I Wish I Were Single Again -1, 2, 4?	Vi unissued
47030-1	Doris Waltz -1?, 4?	Vi unissued
47031-2	When The Moon Drips Away Into The Blood -2, 3	Vi V-40083

Taylor's Louisiana Melody Makers: F.R. Taylor, f; Bun Hiser, md; Henry Galloway, g; Ausie B. Grigg, sb; Oscar Logan, v.
Memphis, TN   Tuesday, September 24, 1929

55575-	On The Bridge At Midnight	Vi V-40261
55576-2	'Tis All Over Now	Vi V-40261
55577-2	'Mid The Shamrocks Of Shannon	Vi 23613
55578-2	The Garden's Fairest Flower	Vi 23613, ZoSA 4368
55579-2	The Yodler's Serenade	Vi V-40184, Au 227, ZoSA 4295
55580-2	Where The Sweet Magnolias Bloom	Vi V-40184, Au 227, ZoSA 4295

Victor V-40184, Zonophone 4295 as by **Taylor–Griggs Louisiana Melody Makers**.
Rev. Zonophone 4368 by Poplin–Woods Tennessee String Band.

TAYLOR, MOORE & BURNETT

Dick Taylor, f; Richard D. Burnett, bj/sp; Byrd Moore, g/sp.
Richmond, IN   Monday, October 29, 1928

| 14392 | Knoxville Rag | Ge 6760, Ch 15690, Spt 9310 |
| 14393-A | Grandma's Rag | Ge 6706 |

Gennett 6706 as by **Moore, Burnett & Rutherford**. Champion 15690 as by **Norton, Bond & Thomas**. Supertone 9310 as by **Southern Kentucky Mountaineers**.
Surrounding matrices at this session are by various combinations of Richard D. Burnett, Byrd Moore, and Leonard Rutherford. Revs: Gennett 6706 by Moore, Burnett & Rutherford (see Richard D. Burnett), 6760 by Rutherford & Moore; Champion 15690 by Asa Martin & Doc Roberts; Supertone 9310 by Moore, Burnett & Rutherford.

TAYLOR TRIO

Taylor Trio: prob. v trio; acc. unknown, g.
Richmond, IN   Monday, October 6, 1930

17140	The Measly Shame	Ge rejected
17141,-A	Coon Coon Coon	Ge rejected
17142	Lorina	Ge rejected
17143,-A	Bashful Coon	Ge rejected
17144	The Saddest Day Of All	Ge rejected

Mr. & Mrs. Homer Taylor, v duet; acc. unknown, g.
Richmond, IN   Monday, October 6, 1930

| 17145 | Good-Bye Maggie | Ge rejected |
| 17146 | When The Morning Glories Twine | Ge rejected |

Taylor & Durbin, v duet; acc. unknown, g.
Richmond, IN   Monday, October 6, 1930

| 17147 | Jack And May | Ge rejected |
| 17148 | Old Old Love Returns | Ge rejected |

Taylor Trio: prob. v trio; acc. unknown, g.
Richmond, IN   Tuesday, October 7, 1930

| 17149 | I'll Not Kiss You Anymore | Ge rejected |

Mr. & Mrs. Homer Taylor, v duet; acc. unknown, g.
Richmond, IN   Tuesday, October 7, 1930

| 17150 | Faithless Husband | Ge rejected |
| 17133 | In The Valley Of Kentucky | Ge rejected |

Gennett files date matrix 17133 as shown. Matrices 17134 to 17139 are by Madisonville String Band.

TAYLOR'S KENTUCKY BOYS

Jim Booker, f; Marion Underwood, bj; Willie Young, g.
Richmond, IN   Tuesday, April 26, 1927

| 12741-A | Gray Eagle | Ge 6130, Ch 15315, Sil 5082, 8183, Spt 9170 |
| 12742 | Forked Deer | Ge 6130, Ch 15300, Sil 5082, 8183, Spt 9170, Chg 302 |

Champion 15300 as by **The Tennessee Travelers**, 15315 as by **Allen's Creek Players**. Silvertone 5082, 8183, Supertone 9170 as by **Hill's Virginia Mountaineers**. Challenge 302 as by **The Clinch Valley Boys**.
Revs: Champion 15300 by Frank Jenkins (see Da Costa Woltz), 15315 by Price Goodson (see Da Costa Woltz); Challenge 302 by Short Creek Trio.

Marion Underwood & Sam Harris-1/**Aulton Ray**-2: Jim Booker, f-3; unknown, h-4; Marion Underwood, bj/v-5; prob. Willie Young, g; "Sam Harris" (Sam Deatheridge), v-6; Aulton Ray, v-7.

Richmond, IN Tuesday, April 26, 1927

12743-A	Little Red Caboose Behind The Train -1, 4, 5, 6	Ge 6155, Ch 15297, Chg 334, Her 75549
12744-A	The Dixie Cowboy -2, 7	Ge 6177, Ch 15277, Sil 5084, 8150, Spt 9250, Chg 335, Spr 385, Her 75552
12745-A	Just As The Sun Went Down -1, 4, 5, 6	Ge 6177, Ch 15316, Sil 5091, 8148, Spt 9248, Chg 334, Her 75549
12746	Pictures From Life's Other Side -1, 4, 5, 6	Ge 6155, Ch 15316, Sil 5091, 8148, Spt 9248, Chg 393
12747	Soldier Joy -2, 3, 7	Ge 6205
12748-A	Maxwell Girl -2, 3, 7	Ge 6205, Ch 15332, Sil 5084, 8150, Spt 9250, Chg 335, Her 75550

Champion 15297, 15316, Silvertone 5091, 8148, Supertone 9248 as by **The Clinch Valley Boys**. Challenge 334 as by **Borton & Thompson**, 335 as by **Charlie Prescott**, 393 as by **Borton & Lang**.
Matrices 12744 and 12747/48 are logged in Gennett files as by **Aulton Ray Or "Shine"**, but this joke (if joke it is) was not transferred to the label of any issue.
Revs: Champion 15297 by Price Goodson (see Da Costa Woltz); Challenge 393 by Grayson & Whitter.

Aulton Ray, v; acc. prob. own g.

Richmond, IN Wednesday, April 27, 1927

12749-A	True And Trembling Brakeman	Ge 6129, Ch 15277, Chg 269, Spr 385, Her 75552, Bell 1186
12750	Will You Love Me When I'm Old	Ge 6129, Ch 15332, Chg 269, Her 75550

Bell 1186 as by **Carl Bunch**. Rev. Bell 1186 by David Miller.

Marion Underwood, bj; acc. prob. Willie Young, g.

Richmond, IN Wednesday, April 27, 1927

12753	Coal Creek March	Ge 6240, Sil 5080, 8181, Spt 9167

Silvertone 5080, 8181, Supertone 9167 as by **Floyd Russell**.
Matrices 12751/52 are by W.R. Rhinehart (personal recordings).
Rev. all issues by Frank Jenkins (see Da Costa Woltz).

Taylor's Kentucky Boys: Jim Booker, f; Doc Roberts, f; John Booker, g.

Richmond, IN Saturday, August 27, 1927

13044,-A	Turkey In The Straw	Ge rejected
13045,-A	Old Hen Cackled And The Rooster Crowed	Ge rejected
13046-A	Sourwood Mountain	Sil 8179, Spt 9165

Silvertone 8179, Supertone 9165 as by **Hill's Virginia Mountaineers**.
Revs: Silvertone 8179, Supertone 9165 by Doc Roberts.

Marion Underwood, v; acc. Jim Booker, f; Doc Roberts, f; Robert Steele, md; own bj-1; John or Joe Booker, g.

Richmond, IN Saturday, August 27, 1927

13051	Down In The Valley	Ge rejected
13052	Little Old Log Cabin In The Lane	Chg 331
13053	That's What The Old Bachelor's Made Of -1	Chg 331

Challenge 331 as by **Kenneth Borton**.
Only one of the fiddlers may play on matrix 13053.
Matrices 13047/48 are by Booker Orchestra; matrices 13049/50 are by Sam Collins (see *B&GR* for both).

Taylor's Kentucky Boys took their name from their manager Dennis W. Taylor. Jim, John, and Joe Booker were African-American musicians.

TAYLOR'S LOUISIANA MELODY MAKERS

See Taylor–Griggs Louisiana Melody Makers.

SHERMAN TEDDER

Sherman Tedder, sg; acc. unknown, g.

Memphis, TN Saturday, February 25, 1928

400342-	Tulsa Waltz	OK unissued
400343-A	Untitled	OK unissed: Co C4K47911 (CD)

UNCLE FRANK TEMPLETON

Pseudonym on Bell for Walter Peterson.

TENNESSEE FARM HANDS

"Featuring: Ray Gully, Walt McKinney, Henry [sic] Martin, Homer Miller and Slim McCoy" (thus the Brunswick/Vocalion Artist's Card) and therefore poss.: Homer "Slim" Miller, f/sp; Walter McKinney, sg/sp; Raymond Gully, bj-md/sp; "Heavy Martin" (Hugh Cross), g/sp; Slim McCoy (poss. a pseudonym), sp.

Knoxville, TN   Friday, March 28, 1930
  K-8037   A Day On The Farm In Tennessee – Part 1   Br/Vo rejected
  K-8038/39   A Day On The Farm In Tennessee – Part 2   Br/Vo rejected
Slim Miller, Walter McKinney, Ray Gully, and Hugh Cross also recorded at this Knoxville session with the Smoky Mountain Ramblers and Lowe Stokes, and Cross solo. McKinney had previously recorded in Knoxville with (The) Tennessee Ramblers [I].

TENNESSEE FIDDLERS

Pseudonym on Timely Tunes and Aurora for the Happy Hayseeds.

THE TENNESSEE HILL BILLY WITH RUTH & LEO WEST

The Tennessee Hill Billy, v; acc. poss. own bj; poss. Ruth West, g; poss. Leo West, g.
  Charlotte, NC   Friday, February 19, 1937
  07192-1,-2   Back To Oklahoma   BB unissued
  07193-1   I'm Gonna Live Anyhow Until I Die   BB unissued
  07194-1   It's Been A Long Long Time Since I Been Home   BB unissued
  07195-1   Got A Little Home I Call My Home   BB unissued
Ruth West, v; acc. poss. own or Leo West, g.
  Charlotte, NC   Friday, February 19, 1937
  07196-1   Got The Weary Blues   BB unissued
  07197-1,-2   Down In Johnson City   BB unissued
Ruth West, Leo West, v duet; acc. poss. one of them, g.
  Charlotte, NC   Friday, February 19, 1937
  07198-1   Sleep On, Departed One   MW M-7134
  07199-1   Church I Know's You Gwine Miss Me When I'm   BB unissued
                   Gone
Montgomery Ward M-7134 as by **Mainer's Mountaineers**.
Rev. Montgomery Ward M-7134 by Mainer's Mountaineers.

TENNESSEE MOUNTAINEERS

Mixed choir (20 voices, including Roy Hobbs); unacc.
  Bristol, TN   Friday, August 5, 1927
  39775-3   Standing On The Promises   Vi 20860
  39776-1   At The River   Vi 20860
This credit is also used as a pseudonym on Broadway for The Highlanders (see Charlie Poole).

TENNESSEE MUSIC & PRINTING CO. QUARTET

Vocal quartet; acc. unknown, p.
  Atlanta, GA   Tuesday, October 30, 1931
  405076-1   Leave Your Sorrows And Come Along   OK 45558
  405077-1   Joy Bells   OK 45551
  405078-2   Your Best Friend   OK 45558
  405079-1   Hold Up Jesus   OK 45551
  405080-1   Sowing Seed For Heaven's Harvest King   OK 45565
  405081-1   Will The Gates Swing Wide For Me   OK 45565

[THE] TENNESSEE RAMBLERS [I]

The Tennessee Ramblers: Fiddlin' Bill Sievers, f/sp-1; James "Mack" Sievers, bj/v-2/sp-1; Willie Sievers Wiggins, g/sp-1.
  Ashland, KY   late February 1928
  AL-308   A Fiddler's Contest -1   Br 257, Spt S2087
  AL-310   Arkansas Traveller   Br 225, 80096, Spt S2083
  AL-312   Satisfied   Br 257
  AL-314   Cackling Pullet   Br 225, Spt S2083
  AL-316   The Preacher Got Drunk And Laid Down His Bible Br 259, Spt S2063
                   -2
  AL-327   Medley Of Mountain Songs (Hop Out Ladies –   Br 259, Spt S2063
                   Marching Through Georgia – Little Brown Jug)
Matrices AL-318, 321 are by All Star Entertainers; other intervening matrices are untraced, but probably include unissued takes of at least some of the above items.
Revs: Supertone S2087 by Kessinger Brothers; Brunswick 80096 by Bradley Kincaid.

Tennessee Ramblers: Fiddlin' Bill Sievers, f/sp-1; Walter McKinney, sg-2; Mack Sievers, bj/v-3/sp-1; Willie Sievers Wiggins, g/sp-1; unidentified, v-4.

Knoxville, TN   Tuesday, August 27, 1929

K-100-	Garbage Can Blues -3, 4	Vo 5378
K-101-	Tennessee Traveler -1, 3	Vo 5378
K-102-	Ramblers March -2	Vo 5362
K-103-	In My Dear Old Sunny South -2	Vo 5398
K-105-	Hawaiian Medley -2	Vo 5394
K-106-	Give The Fiddlers A Dram -3, 4	Vo 5362

Matrix K-104 is untraced but probably not by this group.

Revs: Vocalion 5394, 5398 by Cal Davenport & His Gang.

The Tennessee Ramblers are believed to have also recorded for Vocalion at the Knoxville session of March–April 1930, but no details have been traced in the files and no releases were made.

TENNESSEE RAMBLERS [II]

Rene O. "Jack" Gillette, f-1/t-2; Cecil "Curley" Campbell, sg/v-3; Tex Martin (Martin Shope), g/v-4; W.J. "Harry" Blair, g or sb/v-5.

Rock Hill, SC   Thursday, February 2, 1939

031983-1	Sugar Blues -2	BB B-8062
031984-1	Trumpet Talking Blues -1, 2	BB B-8081
031985-1	There's A Beautiful Home -1, 3, 4, 5	BB B-8176
031986-1	The Hills Of Home -1, 3, 4/5	BB B-8176, RZAu G24864

Revs: Bluebird B-8062 by Jimmie Revard, B-8081 by Bill Boyd.

Jack Gillette, f/t-1/v-2; Curley Campbell, sg-3/tbj-4/g-5/v-6; Tex Martin, g or sb/v-7; Harry Blair, g or sb/v-8; band v-9; unidentified, y-10.

Atlanta, GA   Thursday, August 24, 1939

041314-1	I'll Keep On Loving You -3, 8	BB B-8253, MW M-8498
041315-1	Don't Put A Tax On The Beautiful Girls -2, 5	BB B-8253, MW M-8498
041316-1	Tonight You Belong To Me -5, 7	BB B-8283, MW M-8500, RZ ME2, Twin FT8908
041317-1	Carry Me Back To Carolina -1, 4, 8	BB B-8283, MW M-8500, RZ ME2, Twin FT8908
041318-1	Four Or Five Times -1, 4, 8, 9	BB B-8298, MW M-8501
041319-1	Hootchie-Kootchie-Koo -1, 4, 7	BB B-8298, MW M-8501
041320-1	The Washboard Man -1, 4, 8	BB B-8334, MW M-8502
041321-1	Doug Ain't Doin' The Jitterbug -1, 4, 8	BB B-8334, MW M-8502
041322-1	There's A Blue Sky 'Way Out Yonder -3, 6, 7, 8, 10	BB B-8268, MW M-8499, RZAu G24417
041323-1	Over The Santa Fe Trail -3, 6, 7, 8	BB B-8268, MW M-8499, RZAu G24417
041324-1	Out On The Lone Prairie -3, 6, 7, 8, 10	BB B-8315, MW M-8503, RZAu G24864
041325-1	Steel Guitar Blues -3	BB B-8315, MW M-8503

Jack Gillette, f/t; Curley Campbell, sg/tbj/tg/v-1; Tex Martin, g or sb/v-2; Harry Blair, g or sb/v-3.

Atlanta, GA   Tuesday, February 6, 1940

047543-1	I'd Love To Be A Cowboy -1, 2, 3	BB B-8481, MW M-8744
047544-1	I Like It That Way -1, 2, 3 (lead)	BB B-8417, MW M-8744
047545-1	I'll Never Let You Cry -1, 2, 3	BB B-8427, MW M-8745
047546-1	Hard-Hearted Love -1, 2, 3 (lead)	BB B-8427, MW M-8745
047547-1	All My Natural Life -3	BB B-8516, MW M-8746
047548-1	'Neath Hawaiian Palms	BB B-8516, MW M-8746
047549-1	Coquette -3	BB B-8417, MW M-8747
047550-1	I Don't Know Why I Should Cry Over You -3	BB B-8481, MW M-8747

Jack Gillette, f-1/t-2/v-3; Curley Campbell, esg-4/tbj-5/v-6; Tex Martin, g or sb/v-7; Harry Blair, g or sb/v-8.

Atlanta, GA   Saturday, October 12, 1940

056530-1	Grab Your Saddle Horn And Blow -1, 4, 6, 7, 8 (lead)	BB B-8571, MW M-8894, RZAu G24943
056531-1	Blue Eyed Baby -1, 2, 5, 8	BB B-8571, MW M-8894
056532-1	Won't You Sometimes Dream Of Me -1, 4, 7, 8	BB B-8678, MW M-8895
056533-1	Sweet Mamma, Tree Top Tall -1, 2, 5, 8	BB B-8678, MW M-8895
056534-1	I'm Through Wishing On Stars -1, 2, 4, 8	BB B-8765, MW M-8896
056535-1	Come Swing With Me -1, 2, 5, 7	BB B-8742, MW M-8896
056536-1	The Beach At Waikiki -3, 4	BB B-8765, MW M-8897
056537-1	Steel Guitar Swing -4	BB B-8742, MW M-8897

Rev. Regal-Zonophone G24943 by Bill Boyd.

Jack Gillette, f-1/t-2; unknown, cl; Curley Campbell, esg-3/tbj-4/v-5; Tex Martin, g or sb/v-6; Harry Blair, g or sb/v-7.

Atlanta, GA   Saturday, October 4, 1941

071090-1	You Certainly Said It -1, 2, 4	BB B-8894
071091-1	You're Always On My Mind -1, 2, 3, 5	BB B-8984
071092-1	Why Should I Be Blue -2, 3, 7	BB B-8984

071093-1	New "Red River Valley" -1, 2, 3, 5, 6 (lead), 7	BB B-8894
071094-1	I Love Hawaii -3	BB B-8941
071095-1	Oh Mary, Don't You Weep -2, 4, 5, 6, 7, (lead)	BB B-8941
071096-1	Don't You Know Or Don't You Care	BB unissued
071097-1	The Unkind Word	BB unissued

For recordings by earlier versions of this group see Dick Hartman's Tennessee Ramblers.
Later lineups of the Tennessee Ramblers recorded after 1942, as Cecil Campbell's Tennessee Ramblers and under other names.

TENNESSEE STRING BAND

This artist credit was used on Aurora and Zonophone for the Poplin-Woods Tennessee String Band.

THE TENNESSEE TRAVELERS

Pseudonym on Champion for Taylor's Kentucky Boys.

TENNESSEE TRIO

The coupling issued with this credit on Vocalion 5472 was also issued on Vocalion 1517 as by the **Tennessee Chocolate Drops**. The group was an African-American stringband; see *B&GR*.

TENNEVA RAMBLERS

See Grant Brothers.

TESS & CASS

Pseudonym on Broadway for Thompson Cates.

JACK TETER

Jack Teter, v; acc. prob. own g.
Grafton, WI c. December 1929

| L-192-2 | When You And I Were Young Maggie | Pm 3235, Bwy 8193 |
| L-193-2 | Silver Threads Among The Gold | Pm 3235, Bwy 8193 |

Acc. unknown.
Grafton, WI c. May 1932

| L-1423- | You Didn't Know The Music (I Didn't Know The Tune) | Bwy 1496 |

Rev. Broadway 1496 popular.
An artist of this name recorded after 1942.

CHAS. TEUSER & HAROLD LAWRENCE

Chas. Teuser, Harold Lawrence, v duet; or Harold Lawrence, v-1; or Chas. Teuser, v-2; acc. unknown.
Richmond, VA Thursday, October 17, 1929

403148-	Jesus, Lover Of My Soul	OK unissued
403149-	The Christian's "Good Night"	OK unissued
403150-	Have Thy Own Way, Lord	OK unissued
403151-	One Sweetly Solemn Thought -1	OK unissued
403152-	The Great Judgment Morning -2	OK unissued

NORWOOD TEW

Norwood Tew, v/y-1; acc. own g.
Charlotte, NC Monday, June 15, 1936

102618-1	Sailor Man Blues -1	BB B-6553
102619-1	Sunny South Is Calling Me	MW M-7235
102620-1	Carolina Yodeling Rambler -1	BB B-6553
102621-1	Harvest Time In Dixie	MW M-7235

Norwood Tew (The Old Lefthander) Assisted By Mrs. Tew: Norwood Tew, Louise Tew, v duet; or Norwood Tew, v-1; acc. Norwood Tew, g.
Charlotte, NC Monday, February 15, 1937

07012-1	If I Could Bring Back My Buddy	BB B-6892, MW M-7232
07013-1	My Old Crippled Daddy	BB B-6892, MW M-7232
07014-1	Little Wooden Doll	BB B-7288, MW M-7233
07015-1	Soon We'll Come To The Old Garden Gate	BB B-7288, MW M-7234
07016-1	Talking To The River -1	BB B-7618
07017-1	Your Mother Still Prays For You	BB B-7791, MW M-7233, RZAu G23689

07018-1   When The Cactus Blooms I'll Be Waiting   BB B-7791, MW M-7234, RZAu G23689

Bluebird B-7618 as by **Norwood Tew "The Old Left Hander"**.
Matrix 07108 is titled *I'll Be Waiting* on Montgomery Ward M-7234.
Rev. Bluebird B-7618 by Wilf Carter.

Norwood & Louise Tew, v duet; or **Norwood Tew**, v-1; acc. Norwood Tew, g.
    Rock Hill, SC   Monday, September 26, 1938

     027709-1   Just A Kerosene Lamp   BB unissued
     027710-1   Louisiana Moon   BB unissued
     027711-1   Lillian Branch -1   BB unissued
     027712-1   Daddy's Gone Where The Good Farmers Go -1   BB unissued
     027713-1   If You Meet A Tramp -1   BB B-7950, RZAu G23751
     027714-1   Two Little Lads -1   BB B-7950, RZAu G23751
     027715-1   At The Bottom Blues -1   BB B-8057
     027716-1   Two Hearts On The Old Willow Tree   BB B-8057
     027717-1   My Old Crippled Daddy Part 2   BB unissued
     027718-1   Your Love Was Like A Rainbow   BB unissued

Norwood Tew also participated in a recording by Wade Mainer & Zeke Morris at the June 1936 session.

TEX SLIM

Pseudonym on Varsity and Continental for Dwight Butcher.

THE TEXANS

Pseudonym on Australian Regal Zonophone for Adolph Hofner & His Texans.

TEXARKANA MELODY BOYS

Pseudonym on Velvet Tone and Clarion for the Leake County Revelers.

TEXAS COWBOY TRIO

See Richmond Melody Boys.

THE TEXAS CROONERS

Pseudonym on Mayfair for Carson Robison.

THE TEXAS DRIFTER

See Goebel Reeves.

THE TEXAS FIDDLIN WAMPUS KAT & HIS KITTENS

See W.B. Chenoweth.

THE TEXAS HIGH FLYERS

See The Hi-Flyers.

THE TEXAS NIGHT HAWKS

See Hugh Roden.

THE TEXAS RANGER

Pseudonym on Superior for Loren H. Abram, on Supertone (S2000 series) for Frank Marvin, and on Varsity for Johnny Marvin.

[THE] TEXAS RANGERS

The Texas Rangers: Gomer "Tenderfoot" Cool, f; Paul "Monty" Sells, ac; Herb "Arizona" Kratoska, bj-1/g; Tex Owens, g-2/v-2/y-2/sp-2; Clarence "Idaho" Hartman, sb/j-3; Bob Crawford, Fran "Irish" Mahaney, Rod "Dave" May, Edward "Tucson" Cronenbold, v quartet; "Alabam," sp; band sp.
    Chicago, IL   Monday, August 27, 1934

     C-9353-   Dude Ranch Party – Part I -2   De 5022, Pan 25694
     C-9354-   Dude Ranch Party – Part II -1, 3   De 5022, Pan 25694

Texas Rangers: Gomer "Tenderfoot" Cool, f; Paul "Monty" Sells, ac; Herb "Arizona" Kratoska, g; Clarence "Idaho" Hartman, sb; Bob Crawford, Fran "Irish" Mahaney, Rod "Dave" May, Edward "Tucson" Cronenbold, v quartet; unidentified, y-1.
    Chicago, IL   Saturday, April 6, 1935

     C-9896-B   Goin' Down To Santa Fe Town   De 5107
     C-9897-B   Prairie Dream-Boat   De 5107
     C-9898-A   Careless Love   De 5139
     C-9899-A   Let The Rest Of The World Go By   De 5217
     C-9900-A   New River Train   De 5139

C-9901-A	Lonesome Valley Sally	De 5217
C-9902-A	The Big Corral	De 5183
C-9903-A	The Trail To Mexico -1	De 5183

Decca 5183 as by **The Texas Rangers**.

Prob. : Gomer "Tenderfoot" Cool, f; Paul "Monty" Sells, ac; Herb "Arizona" Kratoska, bj-1/g; Clarence "Idaho" Hartman, sb/j-2; several unidentified, oc-3; Bob Crawford, Fran "Irish" Mahaney, Rod "Dave" May, Edward "Tucson" Cronenbold, v quartet (Crawford, lv-4; Mahaney, lv-5); unidentified, eff-6.

Hollywood, CA   Thursday, December 4, 1941

H-590-1	The Air Corps Of Uncle Sam -5, 6	OK 06543
H-591-1	I've Changed My Penthouse For A Pup-Tent -4	OK 06543
H-592-1	Pull Out The Stopper -1, 2, 3, 4	OK 06629
H-593-1	I Wonder Why -4	OK 06629

This artist credit is also used as a pseudonym on one side of Minerva M-14027 for Jimmie & Eddie Dean.

TEXAS RUBY [& ZEKE]

Texas Ruby's real name was Ruby Owens; she was a sister of Tex Owens.

Texas Ruby & Zeke: Texas Ruby, Zeke Clements, v/y duet; or **Texas Ruby**-1, v/y; acc. Zeke Clements, g; unknown, sb-2.

Dallas, TX   Monday, February 22, 1937

| 61924-A | Pride Of The Prairie | De 5364, DeAu X1391, Coral 64003, MeC 45202 |
| 61925-A | Blue Yodel No. 1 -1, 2 | De 5364, DeAu X1391, Coral 64003, MeC 45202 |

Texas Ruby recorded after 1942.

TEXAS WANDERERS

Grady Hester, f; Anthony Scanlin, ts-1/p-2; J.D. Standlee, esg; Joe Thames, tbj/v-3; Dickie McBride, g/v-4; W.E. "Cotton" Plant, sb; Jerry Irby, v-5.

Houston, TX   Friday, March 3, 1939

65111-A	I Wonder If You Feel The Way I Do -2, 4	De 5664
65112-A	I'll Never Let You Cry -2, 4	De 5704
65113-A	I'll Always Be Your Buddy -2, 4, 5 (lead)	De 5712
65114-A,-B	Is This A Dream -2, 4	De 5719
65115-A	Meet Me In Loveland -2, 4	De 5691
65116-A	I Still Care For You -2, 4	De 5719
65117-A	Waiting At The End Of The Road -2, 3	De 5712
65118-A	I Wish I'd Never Learned To Love You -2, 4	De 5681
65119-A	In A Little House On The Hill -2, 4	De 5704
65120-A	Rosetta -1, 4	De 5691
65121-A	Wonder Stomp -1	De 5681
65122-A	Jo-Jo -1	De 5664

Grady Hester, f-1/v-2; Anthony Scanlin, ts-3/p-4; J.D. Standlee, esg; Leo Raley, emd/v-5; Johnny Thames, tbj; Aubrey "Red" Greenhaw, g; Dickie McBride, g/v-6; Hezzie Bryant, sb; band v-7.

Houston, TX   Monday, August 28, 1939

66308-A	Those Things I Can't Forget -1, 4, 6	De 5730
66309-A	I Hope I Never Fall In Love Again -1, 4, 6	De 5756
66310-A	Rubber Dolly -1, 4	De 5740
66311-A	Deep Elm Swing -1, 4	De 5775
66312-A	Black Sea Blues -3, 6	De 5740
66313-A	We Couldn't Say Goodbye -1, 4, 6	De 5782
66314-A	Where The Morning Glories Grow -1, 2, 3	De 5800
66315-A	You Gotta Know How To Truck And Swing -1, 3, 6	De 5775
66316-A	How Could You Have Left Me -1, 4, 6	De 5812
66317-A	I Remember -1, 4, 6	De 5818
66318-A	The Night Was Filled With Music -1, 4, 6	De 5884, MeC 45394
66319-A	Give Me Those Old Fashioned Days -1, 4, 6	De 5818
66320-A	Smile And Drive Your Blues Away -1, 3, 6	De 5756
66321-A	When It's Your Time Of Day -1, 4, 6	De 5730
66322-A	Lies -1, 4, 6	De 5782
66323-A	Moonlight On The Prairie -1, 4, 5, 6	De 5800
66324-A	Cry Baby Cry -1, 4, 6, 7	De 5812

Revs: Decca 5884, Melotone 45394 by Burns Brothers.

Buddy Ray, f/v-1; Cameron Hill, eg; Moon Mullican, p/v-2/sp-3; Johnny Thames, tbj; Red Greenhaw, g; Bill Mounce, sb.

Houston, TX			Thursday, April 4, 1940
92010-A	Pipe Liner's Blues -2	De 5831, MeC 45355	
92011-A	Rackin' It Back	De 5831, MeC 45355	
92012-A	When You're Gone -1, 3	De 5843	
92013-A	My Dixieland Girl -2	De 5843	

Buddy Ray, f-1/v-2; Cameron Hill, eg; Moon Mullican, p/v-3; Johnny Thames, tbj; Red Greenhaw, g; Bill Mounce, sb.

Houston, TX			Wednesday, April 10, 1940
92067-A	San Antonio Polka -1	De 5872, MeC 45382, Min M-14126	
92068-A	Dixieland I Hear You Calling Me -1, 3	De 5856	
92069-A	I Wonder If True Love Will Find A Way (Some Day) -2	De 5872, MeC 45382	
92070-A	Sundown Blues -1, 3	De 5856	

Rev. Minerva M-14126 by Jimmie Davis.

This group also recorded as the Modern Mountaineers at their sessions of February 1940 and April 1941.

HERMAN THACKER

Herman Thacker, v; acc. own g.

Dallas, TX			Friday, October 18, 1929
56426-1,-2	Waco Girl	Vi unissued	

THIBODEAUX BOYS

Erby Thibodeaux, f/v-1; Joe Werner, h-2/g/v-3/wh-4; T.C. Thibodeaux, g/v-5.

New Orleans, LA			Friday, April 1, 1938
022008-1	Par De Su Les Lames -4, 5	BB B-2033	
022009-1	La Vieux Valse A Ma Belle -5	BB B-2033	
022010-1	La Manvais Femme -5	BB B-2043	
022011-1	Ma Petite Chere Ami -2, 3	BB B-2043	
022012-1	De Seul Payce -3	BB B-2047	
022013-1	Le Moulin Casay -3	BB B-2047	
022014-1	La Vieux Vals An' Onc Mack -2, 3	BB B-2038	
022015-1	Un Lettre A Ma Belle -2, 3	BB B-2038	
022016-1	Tu Pen Pas Ma Retter De Revere -3	BB B-2051	
022017-1	La Two Step A Erby -1	BB B-2051	
022018-1	La Valse A Rouge -1	BB B-2053	
022019-1	La Breakdown Des Creepers -1	BB B-2053	

ALAN THOMAS

Pseudonym on Australian Capitol for Vernon Dalhart.

BOB THOMAS

Pseudonym on labels of the Grey Gull/Radiex group for Arthur Fields.

GEORGE THOMAS & HIS MUSIC

Pseudonym on Champion for Tommy Dandurand & His Gang.

GREYSEN THOMAS & WILL LOTTY

Pseudonym on Champion for G.B. Grayson & Henry Whitter.

THOMAS & JORDAN

Pseudonym on Conqueror for Cranford & Thompson (see The Red Fox Chasers).

THOMAS TRIO

Vocal duet; acc. unknown, f; unknown, g.

Richmond, IN			Saturday, December 20, 1930
17395,-A	Sadie Ray	Ge unissued	

THOMASSON BROS

Benny Thomasson, f; Jim Thomasson, g.

Dallas, TX			Thursday, June 27, 1929
402756-	Scolding Wife	OK unissued	
402757-	Star Waltz	OK unissued	

BUD THOMPSON

Pseudonym on Crown and Homestead for Bob Miller.

ERNEST [E.] THOMPSON

Ernest Thompson, h/g/v-1.
New York, NY   Friday, April 25, 1924

81724-	War Town Quick Step	Co unissued
81725-2	Mississippi Sawyer	Co 189-D, Ha 5099-H, Ve 7034-V, Di 6004-G
81726-2	Don't Put A Tax On The Beautiful Girls -1	Co 168-D
81727-2	Are You From Dixie? -1	Co 130-D, ReE G8236
81728-1	Little Brown Jug -1	Co 147-D, Ha 5122-H
81729-2	How Are You Goin' To Wet Your Whistle? -1	Co 147-D, Ha 5122-H
81730-2	Red Wing -1	Co 190-D, Ha 5123-H
81731-2	Snow Deer -1	Co 190-D, Ha 5123-H
81732-2	Sparrow Bird Waltz	Co 169-D, Ha 5112-H
81733-2	Kiss Waltz	Co 169-D, Ha 5112-H
81734-1	Yield Not To Temptation -1	Co 158-D, Ha 5096-H, Ve 7032-V, Di 6003-G
81735-2	Life's Railway To Heaven -1	Co 158-D, Ha 5096-H, Ve 7032-V, Di 6003-G
81736-	Yellow Rose In Texas	Co unissued
81737-	Soldier's Joy	Co unissued

Harmony 5122-H, 5123-H as by **Ernest Johnson**. All other Harmony, and all Velvet Tone and Diva, issues as by **Jed Tompkins**.
Matrix 81735 is titled *Life's Railway* on Harmony 5096-H, Velvet Tone 7032-V, Diva 6003-G.
Rev. Regal G8236 by Gid Tanner & Riley Puckett.

Ernest Thompson, h/bj-1/g-2/v-3.
New York, NY   Saturday, April 26, 1924

81742-1	The Wreck Of The Southern Old '97 -2, 3	Co 130-D
81743-2	Lightning Express -2, 3	Co 145-D, Ha 5121-H
81744-1	Chicken Roost Behind The Moon -1, 3	Co 206-D, Ha 5101-H
81745-1	Coon Crap Game -1, 3	Co 206-D, Ha 5101-H
81746-1	Frankie Baker -2, 3	Co 168-D
81747-2	Jessie James -1	Co 145-D, Ha 5121-H
81748-1	Climbing Up The Golden Stairs -1	Co 189-D, Ha 5099-H, Ve 7034-V, Di 6004-G

Harmony 5121-H as by **Ernest Johnson**. All other Harmony issues, and Velvet Tone 7034-V, Diva 6004-G, as by **Jed Tompkins**.
Matrix 81747 is titled *Jesse James* on Harmony 5121-H.

Ernest Thompson, v; acc. own h/g.
New York, NY   Tuesday, September 9, 1924

81961-1	Weeping Willow Tree	Co 15001-D, Ha 5130-H
81983-2	The Little Rosebud Casket	Co 216-D, Ha 5124-H
81984-3	The Old Time Religion	Co 15007-D
81985-2	I'm Going Down To Jordan	Co 15007-D
81986-	John Henry, Steel Driver	Co unissued
81987-2	Sylvester Johnson Lee	Co 15001-D, Ha 5130-H

Harmony 5124-H, 5130-H as by **Ernest Johnson**.
Intervening matrices are by other artists.

Ernest Thompson & Connie Sides: Ernest Thompson, h/prob. bj; Connie Sides, prob. g.
New York, NY   Wednesday, September 10, 1924

| 81992-1 | At A Georgia Camp Meeting | Co 15002-D |
| 81993-1 | Silly Bill | Co 15002-D |

At this session Connie Sides also recorded vocal items accompanied by Ernest Thompson.

Ernest Thompson, h/k-1/bj-2/g-3/v-4.
New York, NY   Thursday, September 11, 1924

140000-1	Whistling Rufus -2, 4	Co 15006-D, Ha 5109-H
140001-1	When You're All In Down And Out -3, 4	Co 15006-D, Ha 5109-H
140032-	Jim Thompson's Old Gray Mule	Co unissued
140033-3	Alexander's Ragtime Band -1	Co 15000-D, Ha 5129-H
140034-2	The Mississippi Dippy Dip -1	Co 15000-D, Ha 5129-H

Harmony 5109-H as by **Jed Tompkins**, 5129-G as by **Ernest Johnson**.
Matrix 140001 is titled *When You're All In, Down, Out* on Harmony 5109-H.
Intervening matrices are by other artists.

New York, NY   Friday, September 12, 1924

| 140035-3 | In The Baggage Coach Ahead -3, 4 | Co 216-D, Ha 5124-H |

Harmony 5124-H as by **Ernest Johnson**.

Ernest E. Thompson, h/g.
Richmond, IN   Tuesday, January 21, 1930

16120	Sparrow Bird Waltz; Good Old Summer Time	Ge 7139
16121,-A	My Little Girl; Goodbye Ma, Goodbye Pa	Ge unissued
16122	Are You From Dixie; Swanee River	Ge 7139

Ernest Thompson, h/g/v-1.
Richmond, IN   Wednesday, January 22, 1930

| 16124 | Bring Me A Leaf From The Sea -1 | Ge rejected |
| 16127 | Snow Dear; Rainbow | Ge unissued |

Matrix 16123 is Mexican; matrix 16125 is by Boyden Carpenter; matrix 16126 is Philippine.

Earnest [sic] **Thompson**, prob. v; acc. own h/g.
Richmond, IN   Saturday, March 29, 1930

16422	Every Little Bit Added To What You Got	Ge rejected
16423	Sweetheart Dance With Me	Ge rejected
16425	I Will Be Dancing With You	Ge rejected
16426	What Is Home Without Babies	Ge rejected
16427	[untitled]	Ge rejected

Matrix 16424 is popular.

FLOYD THOMPSON & HIS HOME TOWNERS

Floyd Thompson & His Home Towners With Jack Tilson: Frank Owens, f; unknown, f; unknown, h; unknown, g; poss. another unknown, g; poss. Floyd Thompson, Jack Tilson, v duet; unknown, 3rd v-1.
Indianapolis, IN   Tuesday, June 19, 1928

IND-628-	Billy Boy	Vo 5258
IND-629-	Little Brown Jug	Vo 5236, Me M12128, Po P9048, Vo 02703, Pan 25028, PanAu P12128
IND-630-	Get Away, Old Man, Get Away -1	Vo 5258
IND-631-	Ida Red	Vo 5236, Me M12128, Po P9048, Vo 02703, Pan 25028, PanAu P12128

Melotone M12128, Polk P9048, Panachord 25028, P12128 as by **Floyd Turner & His Home Towners**.
Matrix IND-628-A,-B was remastered as E-7468W-A,-B, and matrix IND-629-A,-B as E-7469W-A,-B.

Floyd Thompson & His Home Towners With Jack Tilson-1/Floyd Thompson & His Home Towners With Jack Tilson & Frank Owens-2: Frank Owens, f/v-3; unknown, h; unknown, g; poss. another unknown, g; prob. Jack Tilson, v; band v-4.
Indianapolis, IN   Saturday, June 23, 1928

IND-657-	Oh My Darling Clementine -1, 4	Vo 5242
IND-658-	The Old Cabin Home -1, 4	Vo 5242
IND-660-	The Sidewalks Of New York (East Side, West Side) -2, 3, 4	Vo 5233
IND-661-	Rye -2	Vo 5233
IND-662-	'Round Her Neck She Wears A Yeller Ribbon (For Her Lover Who Is Fur, Fur Away) -1	Vo 5266, Me M12251, Pan 25163
IND-663-	I Wonder How She Did It -1	Vo 5266, Me M12251, Pan 25163
IND-664-	The Trail Of The Lonesome Pine -2, 3	Vo 5253
IND-665-	I Hear The Meadows Calling Me -2, 3	Vo 5253

Panachord 25163 as by **Floyd Turner & His Home Towners**; the parenthesized part of the title of matrix IND-662 does not appear on the label of that issue.
Matrix IND-659 is by Emry Arthur.

Floyd Thompson & His Home Towners-1/Floyd Thompson & His Home Towners With Emry Arthur-2: unknown, f; Emry Arthur, h-2/prob. v-2; unknown, g; unknown, v-1.
Chicago, IL   Thursday, July 19, 1928

C-2085-A,-B	I Wonder Do The Old Folks Think Of Me -1	Vo unissued
C-2086-A,-B	Where The Sunset Turns The Ocean Blue To Gold -1	Vo unissued
C-2089-A,-B	Red Wing -2	Vo unissued

Matrices C-2087/88 are by Emry Arthur.

Floyd Thompson & His Home Towners With Emry Arthur: unknown, f; Emry Arthur, h/prob. v; unknown, g.
Chicago, IL   Friday, July 20, 1928

C-2090-A,-B	Snow Deer	Vo unissued
C-2091-A,-B	Mountains Of Virginia	Vo unissued
C-2092-A,-B	Way Down In Georgia	Vo unissued

Unknown, f; Emry Arthur, h/prob. v; two unknowns, g.
Chicago, IL   Friday, August 31, 1928

| C-2286- | Mountains Of Virginia | Vo 5317 |
| C-2287- | Way Down In Georgia | Vo 5317 |

C-2288-	Red Wing	Vo 5331
C-2289-	Snow Deer	Vo 5331

Floyd Thompson & His Home Towners: unknown, f; unknown, g; unknown, v duet.
   Chicago, IL   Friday, August 31, 1928

C-2290-	Where The Sunset Turns The Ocean Blue To Gold	Vo 5300
C-2291-	I Wonder Do The Old Folks Think Of Me	Vo 5300

FRED THOMPSON

Pseudonym on Homestead for Vernon Dalhart.

GEORGE THOMPSON

Pseudonym on Columbia for Frank Luther (see Carson Robison).

UNCLE JIMMY THOMPSON

"Uncle Jimmie" Thompson, f; acc. prob. Eva Thompson Jones, p.
   Atlanta, GA   Monday, November 1, 1926

143002-2	Billy Wilson	Co 15118-D
143003-	High Born Lady	Co unissued
143004-2	Karo	Co 15118-D
143005-	Mississippi Sawyer	Co unissued

Uncle Jimmy Thompson, f/sp; acc. Eva Thompson Jones, p; Bill Brown, sp.
   Knoxville, TN   Saturday, April 5, 1930

K-8092-	High Born Lady	Vo unissued
K-8093-	Lynchburg	Vo 5456
K-8094-	Uncle Jimmy's Favorite Fiddling Pieces (Flying Clouds – Leather Breeches)	Vo 5456
K-8095-	Golden Beauty Waltz	Vo unissued

LOU & NELLIE THOMPSON

Lou Thompson's real name is Lou Pope.

Nellie & Lou Thompson-1/Lou & Nellie Thompson-2, v duet; acc. unknown, p; unknown, g; unknown, wh-3.
   New York, NY   Wednesday, July 6, 1932

12034-	By The Old Swinging Bridge -1, 3	ARC unissued
12035-	When You Were The Queen Of The May -2	ARC unissued

Lew & Nellie Thompson-1/Lou & Nellie Thompson-2, v duet; acc. unknown, p; unknown, g.
   New York, NY   Thursday, July 7, 1932

12036-	Oklahoma Days -1	ARC unissued
12037-	When The Tide Of Happiness Comes Rolling In -2	ARC unissued
12038-	There's A little Faded Flower -1	ARC unissued

Nellie & Lou Thompson-1/Lew & Nellie Thompson-2, v duet; "with novelty acc." (thus Satherley files).
   New York, NY   Monday, July 11, 1932

12047-	I Want To Go Back To The Farm -1	ARC unissued
12048-	Sweet Magnolia Time In Dixie -2	ARC unissued
12049-	In Old New Hampshire -2	ARC unissued

MARVIN THOMPSON

Pseudonym on Velvet Tone and Australian Regal and Regal-Zonophone for Andrew Jenkins & Carson Robison.

THOMPSON & MILES
THOMPSON, CRANFORD & MILES

See The Red Fox Chasers.

REV M.L. THRASHER [& HIS GOSPEL SINGERS]
THE THRASHER FAMILY

Rev. M.L. Thrasher: no details.
   Atlanta, GA   Thursday, April 7, 1927

143937-	Someday, It Won't Be Long	Co unissued
143938-	Yield Not To Temptation	Co unissued
143939-	We Shall Reach It Bye And Bye	Co unissued
143940-	What Shall We Do With Mother	Co unissued

Rev. M.L. Thrasher & His Gospel Singers, v group; acc. unknown, p.
   Atlanta, GA   Wednesday, November 9, 1927

145178-2	Ring Out The Message	Co 15313-D
145179-1	At The Cross	Co 15313-D
145180-2	What Shall We Do With Mother	Co 15207-D
145181-2	Wonderful Grace	Co 15239-D

Acc. unknown, f; unknown, g.
Atlanta, GA   Wednesday, November 9, 1927

| 145182-1 | When The Roll Is Called Up Yonder | Co 15207-D |
| 145183-2 | There's Glory On The Winning Side | Co 15239-D |

Acc. unknown, p.
Atlanta, GA   Wednesday, April 18, 1928

146130-2	When I See The Blood Of The Lamb	Co 15271-D
146131-2	Where The Soul Never Dies	Co 15271-D
146132-2	The Last Mile Of The Way	Co 15294-D
146133-1	You Shall Reap Just What You Sow	Co 15294-D
146134-	Are You Washed In The Blood	Co unissued
146135-	I'm Going Bye And Bye	Co unissued

Atlanta, GA   Thursday, October 25, 1928

147287-2	I'll Keep Singing On	Co 15335-D
147288-2	Walk In The Light Of God	Co 15335-D
147289-2	Just As I Am	Co 15361-D

Acc. unknown, f; unknown, g.
Atlanta, GA   Thursday, October 25, 1928

147290-3	We'll Drop Our Anchor	Co 15361-D
147291-2	Life's Troubled Sea	Co 15626-D
147292-1	Just Over In The Glory Land	Co 15626-D

Acc. unknown, f-1; unknown, p-2; unknown, g-1.
Atlanta, GA   Monday, April 15, 1929

148285-	O Wondrous Love	Co unissued
148286-1	No Room -2	Co 15459-D
148287-2	Jesus Knows How -2	Co 15459-D
148288-2	Just To Be Alone With Jesus -2	Co 15422-D
148289-2	Beautiful Home Awaits -1	Co 15422-D
148290	I'm Going To Live With Jesus	Co unissued

The Thrasher Family, v group; acc. unknown, g.
Atlanta, GA   Monday, April 15, 1929

| 148299-1 | My Savior's Love | Co 15396-D |
| 148300-2 | Reapers, Be True | Co 15396-D |

Rev. M.L. Thrasher & His Gospel Singers, v group; acc. unknown, p.
Atlanta, GA   Monday, October 28, 1929

149266-1	Redeemed	Co 15607-D
149267-2	Don't Forget To Pray	Co 15484-D
149268-2	My Old Cottage Home	Co 15571-D
149269-2	The Answer Comes Back	Co 15571-D

Acc. unknown, f; unknown, g.
Atlanta, GA   Monday, October 28, 1929

| 149270-2 | When We Go To Glory Land | Co 15484-D |
| 149271-1 | Standing On The Promises | Co 15607-D |

The Thrasher Family, v group; acc. unknown, ah; unknown, g.
Atlanta, GA   Monday, October 28, 1929

149272-2	This Is The Reason	Co 15539-D
149273-2	I Have A Friend	Co 15717-D
149274-2	He Will Be With Me	Co 15539-D
149275-1	It Was For Me	Co 15717-D

Rev. M.L. Thrasher also participated in recordings by Smith's Sacred Singers.

THREE 'BACCER TAGS
See (The) Three Tobacco Tags.

THE THREE CRACKERS
See the Canova Family.

THREE DOMINOES

No details.
 San Antonio, TX   Friday, October 18, 1929
  SA-439   Hawaiian Dream Girl   Me M12014, Au A22005
  SA-440   Drifting And Dreaming In Hawaii   Me M12014, Au A22006
Revs: Aurora A22005 by Joe Hall & His Orchestra, A22006 by Charlie Simpson & His Orchestra (both popular).

THE THREE FLORIDIANS

No details.
 New York, NY   Tuesday, May 22, 1934
  15250-   Death Of Young Stribling   ARC unissued
  15251-   My Family Circle   ARC unissued
  15252-   The Duval Count [sic] Blues   ARC unissued
  15253-   The Jacksonville Stomp   ARC unissued
Matrix 15253 is reported in ARC files to be an instrumental.
This group is associated with Luther Higginbotham.

THREE GEORGIA[N] CRACKERS

See the Canova Family.

THREE HOWARD BOYS

Pseudonym on Challenge for Homer Davenport & Young Brothers (see Jess Young), or Homer Davenport solo.

THE THREE KENTUCKY SERENADERS

Pseudonym on Silvertone and Supertone for Roy Harvey groups.

THREE LITTLE MAIDS

Three Little Maids "Overstake Sisters": Eva Overstake, Evelyn Overstake, Lucille Overstake, v trio; acc. Lucille Overstake, g; unidentified, y-1.
 Chicago, IL   Friday, April 14, 1933
  C-554-3   When The Flowers Are Blooming In The Springtime   Cq 8159
  C-555-1   I Hear The Voice Of An Angel   Cq 8159
  C-556-1   Across The Blue Ridge -1   Cq 8158
  C-557-1   It's Just A Tumble Down Shack (But I'd Like To Go Back To My Old Kentucky Home) -1   Cq 8158

Three Little Maids (Eva, Evelyn & Lucille Overstake), v trio; acc. Lucille Overstake, g.
 Chicago, IL   Tuesday, December 12, 1933
  77319-1   Since The Angels Took Mother Away   BB B-5336, Sr S-3417, MW M-4491
  77320-1   In The Harbor Of Home Sweet Home   BB B-5336, Sr S-3417, MW M-4491
  77321-1   I Ain't Gonna Study War No More   BB B-5860
  77322-1   Hear Them Bells   BB B-5860

Overstake Sisters, v trio; acc. unknown.
 Chicago, IL   Friday, May 3, 1935
  TO-1549   When I Grow Too Old To Dream   ARC unissued trial recording

Eva Overstake recorded, as Judy Martin, after 1942. Lucille Overstake recorded, as Lucille Lee, with the Sweet Violet Boys (see The Prairie Ramblers) and, as Jenny Lou Carson, after 1942.

THE THREE MUSKETEERS (TOMMY BOWLES, PAUL ENNIS & JAMES JONES)

Tommy Bowles, Paul Ennis, v/y-1 duet; or Tommy Bowles, v-2/y-2; acc. prob. one of them or James Jones, sg; one of them or James Jones, g.
 Charlotte, NC   Monday, June 22, 1936
  102786-1   Goodbye To The Step Stones   BB B-6525
  102787-1   At Night When The Sun Goes Down   BB B-6525
  102788-1   Bill Green -1   BB B-8129
  102789-1   Chattanooga Mama -2   BB B-8129

THREE OLD CRONIES

See Joseph Samuels.

THE THREE SACKS

Vocal trio; acc. unknown, g.
 New York, NY   Friday, November 18, 1932
  TO-1226   Seven Years With The Wrong Woman   ARC unissued trial recording

THE THREE STRIPPED GEARS

Ralph Durden, md; Marion Brown, g; Cliff Vaughn, g.
    Atlanta, GA   Friday, October 30, 1931

405074-1	Blackberry Rag	OK 45571
405075-1	Alabama Blues	OK 45571

    Atlanta, GA   Monday, November 2, 1931

405092-1	1931 Depression Blues	OK 45553
405093-1	Black Bottom Strut	OK 45553

The mandolinist's name has been reported as B.W. Durden, but Marion Brown remembered his first name as Ralph.

[THE] THREE TOBACCO TAGS

Three 'Baccer Tags: George Wade, md/v; Luther Baucom, md/v; Reid Summey, g/v.
    Charlotte, NC   Friday, May 29, 1931

69382-1,-2	The Sharon School Teacher	Vi unissued
69383-1	Get Your Head In Here	Vi 23571, BB B-5941
69384-1	Ain't Gonna Do It No More	Vi 23571

Rev. Bluebird B-5941 by Frank Luther.

The Three Tobacco Tags: George Wade, md; Luther Baucom, md; Reid Summey, g; unidentified, v.
    Richmond, IN   Tuesday, August 9, 1932

18670	The Teacher's Hair Was Red	Ch 16480
18671	Don't Forget The Sailor Lad	Ch 16480
18672	That's Why We Got Reno Now	Ch unissued
18673	Reno Blues	Ch 16674
18674	Bonus Army Blues	Ch unissued
18675	Back Water Blues	Ch 16674

Three Tobacco Tags: George Wade, md/v; Luther Baucom, md/v; Reid Summey, g/v.
    Charlotte, NC   Tuesday, October 13, 1936

02555-1	I'm Sorry That's All I Can Say	BB B-6790, MW M-7163
02556-1	Why Should It End This Way?	BB B-6790, MW M-7163
02557-1	Mother's Torn And Faded Bible	BB B-6668, MW M-7095, RZAu G23182
02558-1	We'll Know Each Other Up There	BB B-6668, MW M-7095, RZAu G23182
02559-1	V-8 Blues	BB B-6730, MW M-7097, RZ MR2378, Twin FT8293

George Wade, md; Luther Baucom, md/v/sp; Reid Summey, g/v/sp.
    Charlotte, NC   Tuesday, October 13, 1936

02560-1	Courtin' -1	BB B-6730, MW M-7097, RZ MR2378, Twin FT8293

George Wade, md/v-1/y-2/sp-3; Luther Baucom, md/v-4/sp-5; Reid Summey, g/v-6/y-7/sp-8; unidentified, v duet-9.
    Charlotte, NC   Monday, February 15, 1937

07000-1	My Redeemer -1, 4, 6	BB B-7044, MW M-7167
07001-1	Noah's Warning -9	BB B-7044, MW M-7167
07002-1	You Never Trusted Me -9	BB B-6948, MW M-7166
07003-1	Roses -1, 4, 6	BB B-6948, MW M-7166
07004-1	Tall And Handsome Comedy -2, 3, 5, 7, 8, 9	BB B-6853, MW M-7164, Twin FT8336
07007-1	I'm Nobody's Darling But Mine -1, 2, 3, 5, 7	BB B-6853, MW M-7164, Twin FT8336
07008-1	Mother's Old Rockin' Chair -9	BB B-6902, MW M-7165
07009-1	To Bring You Back To Me -1	BB B-6999, MW M-7168
07010-1	My Girl Of The Golden West -1, 4, 6	BB B-6902, MW M-7165
07011-1	Heart Breaking Blues -1, 4, 6	BB B-6999, MW M-7168, Twin FT8400

Matrices 07005/06 are untraced.
Rev. Twin FT8400 by Delmore Brothers.

Prob. Reid Summey, sg-1/g-2/v-3/y-4/sp-5; George Wade, md or g/v-6/y-7/sp-8; Luther Baucom, md or g/v-9/y-10/sp-11; unidentified, v-12.
    Charlotte, NC   Tuesday, August 3, 1937

011859-1	Raindrop Waltz Song -1, 12	BB B-7250, MW M-7328
011860-1	There, Our Love Won't End This Way -1, 6	BB B-7250, MW M-7328
011861-1	You'd Better Lay Off Of Love -2, 6?	BB B-7400, MW M-7329
011862-1	I'm Starving To Death For Love -2, 6?	BB B-7211, MW M-7329
011863-1	Reno Blues -2, 12	BB B-7361, MW M-7330
011864-1	That's Why We've Got Reno Now -2, 3, 6, 9	BB B-7163, MW M-7330
011865-1	Ridin' The Rails -2, 3, 6, 9	BB B-7361, MW M-7331
011866-1	She's Not My Curley Headed Baby -2, 3, 4, 6, 7, 10, 11	BB B-7211, MW M-7331

011867-1	The Hottest Gal In Town -2, 12	BB B-7163, MW M-7332
011868-1	Do You Know What It Means To Be Lonely? -2, 3, 6, 9	BB B-7312, MW M-7332
011869-1	Rainbow Trail -2, 3, 6, 9	BB B-7400, MW M-7333
011870-1	There's An Old Fashioned Lamp (Beside A Window) -2, 3, 6, 9	BB B-7312, MW M-7333
011871-1	Once I Was Young And Pretty -2, 3, 5, 6, 8	BB B-7130, MW M-7334
011872-1	Yes! My Darling Daughter -2, 3, 5, 6, 8	BB B-7130, MW M-7334

George Wade, md/v-1; Luther Baucom, md/v-2; Reid Summey, g/v-3; Bob Hartsell, g; unidentified, v-4/v duet-5.
Charlotte, NC   Tuesday, January 25, 1938

018691-1	Down By The Old Mill Stream -5	BB B-7777, [MW M-7929]
018692-1	I Love You Best Of All -1, 2, 3	BB B-7777, [MW M-7929], RZAu G23658
018693-1	Rock Me To Sleep In An Old Rocking Chair -1, 2, 3	BB B-8572
018694-1	I Have A Little Home -1, 2, 3	BB B-7692, [MW M-7931], RZ MR2845, RZAu G23658, Twin FT8604
018695-1	The Teacher's Hair Was Red -1, 2, 3	BB B-7448
018696-1	My Frazzle Headed Baby -1, 2, 3	BB B-7448
018697-1	Good Gal Remember Me -1, 2, 3	BB B-7482, [MW M-7933]
018698-1	I Was Only Teasing You -4	BB B-7715, [MW M-7930]
018699-1	Never Was A Married Man -1, 2, 3	BB B-7533, [MW M-7932]

Bluebird B-8572 as by **The Tobacco Tags**. Regal-Zonophone MR2845 as by **The Three Yanks**.
Matrix 018694 is titled *No Place Like Home (I Have A Little Home)* on Regal-Zonophone MR2845.
Rev. Twin FT8604 by Bob Skyles.

Unknown, h-1; unknown, bazooka-2; George Wade or Luther Baucom, md; Reid Summey, g; Bob Hartsell, g; unknown, wb-3; unidentified, v; two unidentifieds, sp-4.
Charlotte, NC   Tuesday, January 25, 1938

018700-1	How Can I Keep My Mind On Driving? -2, 4	BB B-7533, [MW M-7932]
018701-1	Be Good, Baby -3	BB B-7482, [MW M-7933]
018702-1	I'm Afraid It's Love -1	BB B-7715, [MW M-7930]

George Wade, sp; acc. prob. Reid Summey, g.
Charlotte, NC   Tuesday, January 25, 1938

| 018703-1 | Lady Twinklepuss | BB B-7692, [MW M-7931], RZ MR2845 |

Poss. George Wade, v; acc. prob. Reid Summey, sg; Bob Hartsell, g.
Charlotte, NC   Tuesday, January 25, 1938

| 018704-1 | With A Pal Like You | BB B-8572 |

The Tobacco Tags: Harvey Ellington, f; Luther Baucom, md/v-1; Reid Summey, g/v-2; Bob Hartsell, g/v-3; unidentified, v-4/v duet-5; two unidentifieds, sp-6.
Rock Hill, SC   Sunday, September 25, 1938

026937-1	Darling, The Answer Is In This Song -1, 2, 3	BB B-7877, MW M-7569, RZAu G23699
026938-1	Honey, Where You Been So Long? -1, 2, 3	BB B-7912, MW M-7699
026939-1	De Way To Spell Chicken -4	BB B-7973, MW M-7699
026940-1	When You Go A-Courtin' -4	BB B-7973, MW M-7571
026941-1	Miss A Miss From Tennessee -3	BB B-8135, MW M-7700
026942-1	Do You Think Of Me? -3	BB B-8135, MW M-7700
026943-1	Midnight On The Stormy Deep -5	BB B-8603, MW M-7569
026944-1	Hawaiian Melody -4	BB B-8603, MW M-7701
026945-1	Just Plain Folks -1, 2, 3	BB B-8647, MW M-7570
026946-1	The Red Patch -4, 6	BB B-7912, MW M-7571
026947-1	Saw Your Face In The Moon -3	BB B-8647, MW M-7701
026948-1	If I Only Had A Home Sweet Home -1, 2, 3	BB B-7877, MW M-7570, RZAu G23699

Regal-Zonophone G23699 as by **Three Tobacco Tags**.

Harvey Ellington, f-1/md-2; Luther Baucom, md/lv/v eff-3; Reid Summey, g/tv-4; Sam Pridgin, sb-5; band sp-6.
Rock Hill, SC   Sunday, February 5, 1939

032659-1	I Love To Ramble In The Roses -2, 4, 5	BB B-8208, RZ G24095
032660-1	Just An Old Lady -2, 4, 5	BB B-8072, [MW M-7928], RZAu G23935
032661-1	Tiny Blue Shoe -2, 4, 5	BB B-8208, RZ G24095
032662-1	Don't Forget The Sailor Lad -2, 4, 5	BB B-8225
032664-1	Yodeling Mule -2, 3	BB B-8225
032666-1	It Can't Be Done -2, 4, 5	BB B-8089, [MW M-7927]
032667-1	I'm Longing For My Carolina Home -2, 4, 5	BB B-8072, [MW M-7928], RZAu G23935
032668-1	Jersey Bull Blues -1, 4, 5, 6	BB B-8089, [MW M-7927]

Regal-Zonophone G23935 as by **The Three Tobacco Tags**.
Luther Baucom may not play mandolin on all items.
Intervening matrices are by Gwen Foster.

Harvey Ellington, f-1/md-2; Luther Baucom, md-3/lv-4; Reid Summey, g/tv-5; Sam Pridgin, sb/prob. v-6; unidentified, v-7.

    Atlanta, GA   Monday, August 21, 1939

041294-1	Would You Care? -2, 4, 5, 6	BB B-8336
041295-1	My Mother's Prayers -2, 4, 5	BB B-8336, RZAu G24952
041296-1	My Love Is Following You -2, 4, 5	BB B-8351, RZAu G24239
041297-1	Who's Sorry Now? -1, 4, 5	BB B-8365
041298-1	Wild Bill Jones -2, 7	BB B-8365
041299-1	Don't Forget Mother -2, 7	BB B-8351, RZAu G24239
041300-1	My Gypsy Dream Girl -1, 7	BB B-8321
041301-1	The Missouri Waltz -2, 3	BB B-8321

Regal-Zonophone G24952 as by **The Wanderers**.

Harvey Ellington, md; Luther Baucom, md/v/sp-1; Reid Summey, g/v-2/sp-3; Sam Pridgin, sb/v-4.

    Atlanta, GA   Thursday, February 8, 1940

047607-1	I'll Get A Pardon In Heaven -2	BB B-8396, MW M-8748, RZAu G24737
047608-1	My Own Iona -2, 4	BB B-8420, MW M-8749
047609-1	Sunset On The Prairie	BB B-8396, MW M-8748, RZAu G24737
047610-1	Sweethearts Forever -2	BB B-8496, MW M-8749
047611-1	I'm Sorry It Ended This Way -2	BB B-8420, MW M-8750, RZAu G24952
047612-1	Pagan Love Song -2	BB B-8496, MW M-8750
047613-1	Let Us All Stay At Home -2	BB B-8538, MW M-8751
047614-1	A Paper Of Pins -1, 2, 3	BB B-8538, MW M-8751

Regal-Zonophone G24737, G24952 as by **The Wanderers**.

Harold Hensley, f; Harvey Ellington, md; Luther Baucom, md; Reid Summey, g; Sam Pridgin, sb; unidentified, v-1/v duet-2.

    Atlanta, GA   Wednesday, October 1, 1941

071056-1	The Best Girl Of All -2	BB B-8855
071057-1	The Little Red Piggy -1	BB B-8995
071058-1	The Gypsy's Warning -1	BB B-8942
071059-1	Anna From Indiana -1	BB B-8942
071060-1	Little Rose Covered Garden -2	BB B-8995
071061-1	You Didn't Mean It Darlin' -1	BB B-8855

For Montgomery Ward M-7169, credited to **Three Tobacco Tags**, see Bob Hartsell.

THE THREE TWEEDY BOYS

See the Tweedy Brothers.

THE THREE VIRGINIANS

Holly Horton, cl; Dick Reinhart, g/v-1; unknown, g.

    Dallas, TX   Wednesday, June 26, 1929

402732-A,-B	Yoo Yoo Blues	OK 45451
402733-A	June Tenth Blues -1	OK 45451
402734-	Hard To Get Papa -1	OK unissued
402735-	Who's Sorry Now	OK unissued

THREE WILLIAMSONS (KITTY, DUCK & AARON)

Kitty Williamson, f/v-1; Duck Williamson, g/v-2; Aaron Williamson, g.

    San Antonio, TX   Saturday, February 27, 1937

07405-1	The Roaster Rag -1	BB B-6937, MW M-7249
07406-1	You Broke My Heart A Million Ways -1	BB B-7819, MW M-7250
07407-1	Ain't Got Nobody -1	BB B-7275, MW M-7251, RZ MR2688
07408-1	Fiddlers' Blues -2	BB B-7819, MW M-7250
07409-1	A Good Man Is Hard To Find -1	BB B-6937, MW M-7249
07410-1	Right Or Wrong -1	BB B-7275, MW M-7251, RZ MR2688

Regal-Zonophone MR2688 as by **Kitty Williams**.

Kitty Williamson later recorded, as Texas Rose, with W. Lee O'Daniel & His Hillbilly Boys.

THE THREE YANKS

Pseudonym on Regal-Zonophone MR2845 for (The) Three Tobacco Tags.

THURSDAY EVENING PRAYER MEETERS

Vocal quartette; acc. unknown, vla.

    Chicago, IL   c. January 1927

4153-2	Don't Let It Be Said Too Late	Her 75543

The control 515 also appears on Herwin 75543. This item is likely to have been released in the Paramount 33000 series, but no such issue has been traced.
Rev. Herwin 75543 by Brown & Bradshaw.

CHARLIE D. TILLMAN & DAUGHTER

Prob. v duet; acc. unknown.
    Atlanta, GA   Wednesday, August 1, 1928

402034-	What Has Become Of The Old Church Bell?	OK unissued
402035-	He Left His Religion In The Country	OK unissued

See also Jewell Tillman Burns & Charlie D. Tillman (who may be the same duet).

FLOYD TILLMAN

Floyd Tillman, v; acc. Cliff Bruner, f; Bob Dunn, esg; Aubrey "Moon" Mullican, p; Leo Raley, emd; own g; Hezzie Bryant, sb.
    Houston, TX   Tuesday, August 29, 1939

66325-A	I Didn't Know	De 5741
66326-A	There Must Be Someone For Me	De 5783
66327-A	I'm Always Dreaming Of You	De 5801
66328-A	Don't Be Blue	De 5741, 46182
66329-A	I Never Felt This Way Before	De 5783
66330-A	Maybe I'll Get By Without You	De 5801
66331-A	I'd Settle Down For You	De 5761
66332-A	It Had To Be That Way	De 5761

Floyd Tillman & His Favorite Playboys: Woodrow M. "Woody" Carter, f-1/eg-2; Ernest "Deacon" Evans, esg; Ralph "Smitty" Smith, p; Howard Oliver, tbj; Floyd Tillman, g/v-3; Chet Miller, sb.
    Dallas, TX   Wednesday, April 30, 1941

93736-A,-B	It's Been A Long Long Time -1, 3	De 5982, 46182
93737-A	All Because Of You -1, 3	De 5982
93738-A	I've Learned My Lesson Now -2, 3	De 5960
93739-B	They Took The Stars Out Of Heaven -2, 3	De 6090
93740-A	Rio Grande -2	De 5960
93741-A	Why Do You Treat Me This Way -2, 3	De 6090, 46102

Rev. Decca 46102 by Floyd Tillman (postwar).
Floyd Tillman also recorded with Leon Selph, the Village Boys, and after 1942.

TIN-CAN JOE

No details.
    New York, NY   Friday, July 31, 1925

140800-	Medley Of Old-Time Waltzes. Part 1: 1. The Sidewalks Of New York. 2. Sweet Rosie O'Grady. 3. After The Ball	Co unissued
140801-	Medley Of Old-Time Waltzes. Part 2: 1. Rock-a-bye Baby On The Tree-top. 2. See-Saw. 3. Peek-a-boo. 4. I Will Be All Smiles To-night, Love	Co unissued
140802-	Medley Of Barn Dances Part 1	Co unissued
140803-	Medley Of Barn Dances Part 2	Co unissued

LEVI TIPTON

Levi Tipton, v; acc. prob. own g.
    Richmond, IN   Wednesday, June 24, 1931

17846	Mountain Railroad	Ge unissued

TIVOLI NOVELTY ORCHESTRA

Pseudonym on Montgomery Ward M-4084 for Bill Simmons.

THE TOBACCO TAGS

See [The] Three Tobacco Tags.

TOM & CHUCK

Tom Murray, Chuck Cook (Charlie Quirk), v duet; acc. own g duet.
    Hollywood, CA   Monday, August 4, 1930

61005-1,-2	White River Road	Vi unissued
61006-1,-2	(By A Window) At The End Of The Lane	Vi unissued

Hollywood, CA			Friday, August 15, 1930
61005-4	White River Road	Vi V-40305	
61006-4	At The End Of The Lane	Vi V-40305	

Tom Murray and Chuck Cook were members of The Beverly Hill Billies and associated groups. Both also recorded with the Hollywood Hillbilly Orchestra, while Murray recorded with Jimmie Adams as The Two Cow Hands.

TOM & DON

Tom Dix, Doyne "Don" Wilson, v duet; or Don Wilson, v-1; acc. Don Wilson, sg; Tom Dix, g; one of them, y-2/wh-2/humming-2.

Chicago, IL			Wednesday, December 13, 1933
77343-1	When It's Prayer-Meetin' Time In The Hollow	BB B-5472, MW M-4482, Victrola Z-353	
77344-1	Peek-A-Boo -2	BB B-6209, Twin FT8057	
77345-1	Arabiana -1	BB unissued	
77346-1	Lonely Nights In Hawaii	BB B-5397, MW M-4482, Twin FT1748	
77347-1	Keep A Light In Your Window Tonight	BB B-5379, Sr S-3460, MW M-4481	
77348-1	A Hill Billy Wedding In June	BB B-5397	
77349-1	Underneath The Blue Hawaiian Sky	BB B-5340, Sr S-3421, MW M-4481	
77350-1	Hawaiian Starlight	BB B-5340, Sr S-3421	

Twin FT1748 as by **Dix & Wilson**.
Victrola Z-353 is a special pressing for the Cole Publishing Co., made in December 1935.
Revs: Bluebird B-5379, Sunrise S-3460 by The Songcopators (popular); B-5472, Victrola Z-353 by The Vagabonds; B-6029, Twin FT8057 by Tom & Roy; Twin FT1748 by Riley Puckett.
Tom Dix also recorded with Roy Weston as Tom & Roy.
Doyne Wilson also recorded with The Hilltoppers.

TOM & ROY

Tom Dix, Roy Weston, v duet; acc. own g duet.

Chicago, IL			Monday, April 24, 1933
75425-1	In The Valley Of The Moon	Vi unissued	
75426-1	Dream Train	Vi 23813	
75427-1	The Chant Of The Jungle	Vi 23813	
75428-1	In My Old Cabin Home In The Mountains	Vi 23804	
75429-1	The Mountain, The Music And You	Vi 23804	
75430-1	Grandfather's Clock – Part 1	Vi 23800	
75431-1	Grandfather's Clock – Part 2	Vi 23800	
75432-1	In My Old Cabin Home In The Mountains	MW M-4241	
75433-1	The Mountain, The Music And You	MW M-4241	
75434-1	Grandfather's Clock – Part 1	BB B-5073, Eld 1996, Sr S-3154, MW M-4242	
75435-1	Grandfather's Clock – Part 2	BB B-5073, Eld 1996, Sr S-3154, MW M-4242	
Chicago, IL			Thursday, July 27, 1933
75953-1	The Convict And The Rose	BB B-5138, Eld 2044, Sr S-3219, MW M-4428	
75954-1	Locked Up In Prison	BB B-5138, Eld 2044, Sr S-3219, MW M-4428	
75955-1	The Mountaineer's Sweetheart	BB B-5198, Eld 2088, Sr S-3279, MW M-4383	
75956-1	That Old Feather Bed On The Farm	BB unissued	
75957-1	Somewhere	BB B-5245, Eld 2128, Sr S-3328, MW M-4402	
75958-1	Dreaming	BB B-5245, Eld 2128, Sr S-3328, MW M-4402	
75959-1	Bells Of Avalon	BB B-5198, Eld 2088, Sr S-3279, MW M-4383	
75960-1	Tomorrow Is Another Day	BB B-6209, Twin FT8057	

Revs: Bluebird B-6209, Twin FT8057 by Tom & Don.
Tom Dix also recorded with Don Wilson as Tom & Don.

PINKY TOMLIN

See Texas Jim Lewis.

TOMMIE & WILLIE

This duo, whose full names are Tommie Reynolds and Willie Robinson, recorded popular material for Gennett, some of which was issued in the Champion 45000 series and on Montgomery Ward. It is beyond the scope of this work.

JED TOMPKINS

Pseudonym on Harmony, Velvet Tone, and Diva for Ernest Thompson.

TONO HOMBRES

Pseudonym on Bluebird, in the Mexican series, for the Tune Wranglers.

THE TOO BAD BOYS

Pseudonym on one side of Paramount 12861 (matrix GEX-2406) for Westbrook Conservatory Entertainers.

WELBY TOOMEY

Welby Toomey, v; acc. Edgar Boaz, g.
   Richmond, IN   Wednesday, September 30, 1925

12355,-A	The Golden Willow Tree	Ge rejected
12356,-A	Meet Me In The Moonlight Alone	Ge rejected
12357,-A	Frankie's Gamblin' Man	Ge rejected

Doc Roberts may play fiddle on some or all of the above items.

Acc. Doc Roberts, f-1; Edgar Boaz, g.
   Richmond, IN   Friday, November 13, 1925

12412	Frankie's Gamblin' Man	Ge 3195, Chg 232, 325
12413	The Golden Willow Tree	Ge 3195, Chg 232
12414-A	Thrills That I Can't Forget	Ge 3228, Chg 159, 504
12415,-A	I'll Take Low And Go Down	Ge rejected
12416,-A	Goodbye Little Girl	Ge unissued
12417-A	Railroad Daddy -1	Ge 3202, Chg 159, 504

Challenge 159, 325 as by **John Ferguson**, 232 as by **Clarence Adams**. Rev. Challenge 325 by Short Creek Trio.

   Richmond, IN   Saturday, November 14, 1925

12420-A	I Wish I Was Single Again -1	Ge 3202, Chg 158
12421,-A	Where Are Your Smiles	Ge rejected
12422-A	Wild Bill Jones	Ge 3228, Chg 158, 324

Challenge 158, 324 as by **John Ferguson**.
Rev. Challenge 324 by Ernest V. Stoneman.

Acc. Doc Roberts, f; Edgar Boaz, g.
   Richmond, IN   c. October 1926

12572	The Death Of John Henry	Ge 6005, Ch 15198, Sil 5002, 8146, Spt 9245, Chg 228, Her 75532
12573	The Drunkard's Dream	Ge rejected
12576	Abraham And Isaac	Ge rejected
12577	Roving Gambler	Ge 6005, Ch 15209, Sil 5006, 8151, Spt 9252, Chg 229, Her 75532
12580	Someday We'll Meet Again	Ge rejected
12581	Little Brown Jug	Ge 6025, Ch 15198, Sil 5002, 8146, Spt 9245, Chg 228, Her 75534
12582	I Had But Fifteen Cents	Ge rejected

Champion 15198, 15209 as by **Herb Jennings**. Challenge 228, 229 as by **Clarence Adams**.
Later pressings of Herwin 75532 replace matrix 12577 with a Vernon Dalhart recording of *The Roving Gambler* (Grey Gull matrix 2345). Another variant issue of Herwin 75532 couples that Dalhart recording with Harkreader & Moore's *Death Of John Henry* (Paramount matrix 4593).
Matrices 12574, 12578/79 are by "Big Boy" George Owens (see *B&GR*); matrix 12575 is by Doc Roberts.
Revs: Champion 15209, Silvertone 5006, 8151, Supertone 9252, Challenge 229, Herwin 75534 by Doc Roberts.

Acc. unknown, h-1; unknown, "jazzbo"-2; unknown, g.
   Richmond, IN   Tuesday, November 22, 1927

GEX-971,-A	You Must Unload -1	Ge rejected
GEX-972,-A	The Faded Coat Of Blue	Ge rejected
GEX-973,-A	Sadie Ray -1	Ge rejected
GEX-974,-A	A Lone Summer Day -2	Ge rejected

At least some, perhaps all, of the instruments were played by the African-American musician Sammy Brown (see *B&GR*).

FRAN TRAPPE

See Charlie Bowman.

THE TRAVELERS

Henry Hartley, f-1/sb-2; Ted "Otto" Morse, t; George (Bill) Thall, cl-3/sb-4; Ted "Buddy" Gilmore, g; unidentified, v-5.
   Chicago, IL   Thursday, April 11, 1935

C-9911-A	Feedin' The Horses -2, 3, 5	De 448, 5453
C-9912-A	The Bottom Of The Lake -2, 3	De 448
C-9913-A,-B	The Little Mouse Parade	De unissued
C-9914-A	When The Pussywillow Whispers To The Catnip -2, 3, 5	De 5453
C-9915-A	Toodle-Oo Rag -2, 3	De 449, 5461
C-9916-A	Raggin' The Fiddle -1, 4	De 449, 5461

The Travelers also accompany Sally Foster on some of her recordings.

THE TRAVELERS QUARTETTE

Vocal quartet; acc. unknown.
   Birmingham, AL   Saturday, July 9, 1927

GEX-697	Give The World A Smile	Ge rejected

ADAM TREHAN

Adam Trehan, ac/v-1; acc. unknown, g.
   New Orleans, LA   Friday, December 14, 1928

147634-2	The Walts [sic] Of Our Little Town -1	Co 40501-F, OK 90001
147635-2	The Pretty Girls Don't Want Me -1	Co 40501-F, OK 90001
147636-1	Do You Think Work Is Hard? -1	Co 40509-F, OK 90009
147637-2	Arcadian Waltz	Co 40509-F, OK 90009

PAUL TREMAINE'S ARISTOCRATS

Two couplings by this danceband were issued in the Victor Old Familiar Tunes series (V-40176, V-40230); they are outside the scope of this work. (The former is listed in *JR*.)

TRENTON MELODY MAKERS

Vocal quartet; unacc.
   Memphis, TN   Wednesday, February 22, 1928

400293-A	Face To Face	OK 45221
400295-	Southern Medley	OK unissued
400296-B	Though Your Sins Be As Scarlet	OK 45221
400298-	Steal Away	OK unissued

Matrices 400294, 400297, blank in OKeh files, are probably by this group.

CARL TRIMBLE

This artist's full name is Carl Eugene Trimble.

Carl Trimble, v; acc. poss. own g.
   Richmond, IN   between December 12 and 26, 1933

19427	Down On The Old Plantation	Ch S-16717, 45050
19428	In A Lonely Little Cottage	Ch S-16717, 45050

Matrix 19428 is titled *Please Take Me Back Again* on Champion 45050.

TRIO GONZALES

Pseudonym on Mexican Decca for the Perry Brothers.

TRIO HERMANOS DE OESTE

Pseudonym on Mexican Bluebird for West Brothers Trio.

ERNEST TUBB

Ernest Tubb, v/y; acc. own g.
   San Antonio, TX   Tuesday, October 27, 1936

02952-1	The Passing Of Jimmie Rodgers	BB B-6693, RZAu G23183, Twin FT8228
02953-1	The Last Thoughts Of Jimmie Rodgers	BB B-6693, RZAu G23183, Twin FT8228
02954-1	Married Man Blues	BB B-8899
02955-1	Mean Old Bed Bug Blues	BB B-8899
02956-1	My Mother Is Lonely	BB B-8966
02957-1	The Right Train To Heaven	BB B-8966

Acc. own g; Merwyn J. Buffington, g-1.
   San Antonio, TX   Tuesday, March 2, 1937

07475-1	The T B Is Whipping Me	BB B-7000
07476-1	Since That Black Cat Crossed My Path -1	BB B-7000

Ernest Tubb, v; acc. Jimmie Short, g; own g.
   Houston, TX   Thursday, April 4, 1940

92006-A	Blue Eyed Elaine	De 5825, 46093, MeC 45350
92007-A	I'll Never Cry Over You	De 5846, 46007, DeSA FM5160
92007-B	I'll Never Cry Over You	De unissued: *BF BCD15853 (CD)*
92008-A	I'll Get Along Somehow	De 5825, 46092, MeC 45350
92008-B	I'll Get Along Somehow	De unissued: *BF BCD15853 (CD)*
92009-A	You Broke A Heart	De 5846

Acc. Dick Ketner, g; own g.
   Los Angeles, CA   Monday, October 28, 1940

DLA-2221-A	I Ain't Gonna Love You Anymore	De 5900
DLA-2222-A	I'm Glad I Met You After All	De 5910
DLA-2223-A	I Cared For You More Than I Knew	De 5938
DLA-2224-A	You'll Love Me Too Late	De 5920

   Los Angeles, CA   Tuesday, October 29, 1940

DLA-2225-A	I've Really Learned A Lot	De 6076, MeC 45548
DLA-2226-A	Swell San Angelo	De 5938
DLA-2226-B	Swell San Angelo	De unissued: *BF BCD15853 (CD)*
DLA-2227-A	I Know What It Means To Be Lonely	De 6054
DLA-2228-A	Please Remember Me	De 5910

   Los Angeles, CA   Wednesday, October 30, 1940

DLA-2231-A	My Rainbow Trail	De 5993
DLA-2232-A	Last Night I Dreamed	De 5920
DLA-2232-B	Last Night I Dreamed	De unissued: *BF BCD15853 (CD)*
DLA-2233-A	I'm Missing You	De 5958, MeC 45450
DLA-2234-A	My Baby And My Wife	De 5900

Ernest Tubb, v/y-1; acc. Fay "Smitty" Smith, esg-2/eg-3; own g; unknown, sb.
   Dallas, TX   Saturday, April 26, 1941

93673-A	Walking The Floor Over You -3	De 5958, 46006, MeC 45450
93674-A	When The World Has Turned You Down -3	De 6023, 46092
93675-A	Our Baby's Book -1, 2	De 6040, 46093
93676-A	I'll Always Be Glad To Take You Back -3	De 5993, 46006
93677-A	Mean Mama Blues -1, 3	De 5976, 46162, MeC 45462
93678-A	I Wonder Why You Said Goodbye -3	De 5976, 46007, DeSA FM 5160, MeC 45462

Ernest Tubb, v; acc. Smitty Smith, esg-1/eg-2; own g; unknown, sb.
   Chicago, IL   Monday, November 17, 1941

93791-A	I Ain't Goin' Honky Tonkin' Anymore -2	De 6007, 46125, MeC 45485
93792-A	I Hate To See You Go -2	De 6084, 46091, MeC 45556
93793-A	Time After Time -2	De 6023, 46091
93794-A	First Year Blues -2	De 6007, MeC 45485
93795-A	Just Rollin' On	De unissued: *BF BCD15853 (CD)*
93796-A	There's Nothing More To Say -2	De 6076, MeC 45548
93797-A	Wasting My Life Away -2	De 6054
93798-A	You May Have Your Picture -1	De 6040

Acc. Oliver E. (Eddie) Tudor, eg; Charles Quirk, g; own g-1; Wesley Tuttle, sb.
   Los Angeles, CA   Friday, July 17, 1942

L-3099-A	That Same Old Story	De 6084, MeC 45556
L-3100-A	Try Me One More Time -1	De 6093, 46047, DeAu X2198
L-3101-A	You Nearly Lose Your Mind -1	De 6067, 46125
L-3102-A	That's When It's Comin' Home To You -1	De 6093
L-3103-A	I Don't Want You After All -1	De unissued: *BF BCD 15853 (CD)*
L-3104-A	I'm Wondering How -1	De 6067

Revs: Decca 46047 by Ernest Tubb (postwar), X2198 by Shelton Brothers.
Ernest Tubb recorded after 1942.

TUBIZE ROYAL HAWAIIAN ORCH.

Recordings by this group on OKeh, including one issue in the Old Time Tunes series (45394), are outside the scope of this work.

THE TUNE WRANGLERS

Tom Dickey, f; Edward (Eddie) Whitley, p; "Red Brown" (Joe Barnes), tbj/v-1; Edwin P. "Buster" Coward, g/v-2; J.Harrell "Curley" Williams, sb/v-3; band v-4; unidentified, y-5.
   San Antonio, TX   Thursday, February 27, 1936

99394-1	Buster's Crawdad Song -2, 4	BB B-6554, MW M-7039
99395-1	Rancho Grande -1, 2, 3	BB B-6554, MW M-7039, Twin FT8224
99396-1	It Was Midnight On The Ocean -2 (lead), 4	BB B-6365, MW M-4764, Twin FT8127
99397-1	They Go Wild Over Me -1	BB B-6310, MW M-4763, Twin FT8096
99398-1	Red's Tight Like That -1 (lead), 4	BB B-6438, MW M-7040, Twin FT8188
99399-1	Ragtime Cowboy Joe -1, 2 (lead), 3	BB B-6438, MW M-7040, Twin FT8188
99400-1	Drivin' The Doggies Along -2 (lead), 4, 5	BB B-6403, MW M-4765
99401-1	Ride On, Old Timer, Ride On -2, 3	BB B-6403, MW M-4765
99402-1	She's Sweet -1	BB B-6326, MW M-4762, Twin FT8114

| 99403-1 | Sarah Jane -1/3, 2 | BB B-6397, MW M-7041 |

Bluebird B-6397 as by **Chicago Rhythm Kings**.
Revs: Bluebird B-6397 (with same credit) by Chicago Rhythm Kings (see JR); Twin FT8096 by Jimmie Davis.

Tom Dickey, f-1/poss. sb-2; Eddie Whitley, p; Red Brown, tbj/v-3; Buster Coward, g/v-4; Curley Williams, sb-1/v-5; band v-6.

San Antonio, TX   Friday, February 28, 1936

99418-1	I'm Wild About That Thing -1, 3 (lead), 6	BB B-6310, MW M-4763
99419-1	Born Too Soon -2, 5 (lead), 6	BB B-6421, MW M-7041, Twin FT8166
99430-1	My Sweet Thing -1, 3 (lead), 6	BB B-6326, MW M-4762, Twin FT8114
99431-1	Texas Sand -1, 3, 4 (lead), 5	BB B-6513, MW M-4766, Vi 20-2070, Twin FT8224
99432-1	Lonesome Blues -1, 4	BB B-6513, MW M-4766
99433-1	I Can't Change It -1	BB B-6365, MW M-4764, Twin FT8127

Matrices 99420 to 99423 are untraced (possibly Mexican); matrices 99424 to 99429 are by Jesse Rodgers.
Revs: Bluebird B-6421 by Dick Robertson (popular); Twin FT8166 by Riley Puckett.

Tom Dickey, f; Eddie Duncan, esg/v-1; George Timberlake, p; Arthur "Eddie" Fielding, tbj; Buster Coward, g/v-2; Eljay "Bill" Dickey, sb/v-3; band v-4.

San Antonio, TX   Saturday, October 24, 1936

02868-1	I Wish You Were Jealous Of Me -1, 2	BB B-6856
02869-1	They Cut Down The Old Pine Tree -2, 3	BB B-6692, MW M-7194
02870-1	Oh, Look At That Baby -1	BB B-6828
02871-1	Sweet Mama Blues -2, 4	BB B-6856, MW M-7199
02872-1	I'll Be Hanged If They're Goin' To Hang Me -2	BB B-6692, MW M-7194, Twin FT8277
02873-1	Hot Peanuts -1	BB B-7867, MW M-7199
02874-1	I Believe In You -2, 4	BB B-6783
02875-1	The One Rose In My Heart -1	BB B-6655, MW M-7195, RZAu G23181
02876-1	Yesterday -2	BB B-6703
02877-1	In The Shadow Of The Pines -1, 2	BB B-6655, MW M-7195, RZAu G23181
02878-1	I've Got No Use For The Women -2	BB B-7089, Twin FT8493
02879-1	The Girl I Left Behind Me -2, 3	BB B-6783, MW M-7200, Twin FT8317
02880-1	Echo Valley -1	BB B-6703
02881-1	Up Jumped The Devil	BB B-6982
02882-1	That Little Texas Town -2, 3	BB B-6828
02883-1	Cielito Lindo -2, 3	BB B-7089, MW M-7200

Revs: Bluebird B-7867, Twin FT8277 by Bill Boyd's Cowboy Ramblers; Twin FT8317 by Jack Pierce's Oklahoma Cowboys.

Tom Dickey, f; Emil Zunker or Cal Callison, ac; Eddie Duncan, esg/v-1; George Timberlake, p; prob. Eddie Fielding, tbj; Buster Coward, g/v-2; Bill Dickey, sb/v-3.

San Antonio, TX   Wednesday, February 24, 1937

07263-1	Let's Go	BB B-6900
07264-1	Get With It	BB B-6900
07265-1	Shine On, New Mexico Moon -2, 3	BB B-7030, MW M-7196
07266-1	Dreams Of Silver And Memories Of Gold -1, 2	BB B-6962, MW M-7197, Twin FT8377
07267-1	When It's Tune Wrangling Time In Texas -1, 2	BB B-6947, MW M-7184, Twin FT8376
07268-1	When The Sun Goes Down In Arizona -2, 3	BB B-6962, MW M-7196
07269-1	Back To Nevada -2, 3	MW M-7197
07270-1	A Little While Ago -1, 2	BB B-7030, MW M-7198
07271-1	Why Do You Knock At My Door? -1	BB B-7076, Twin FT8493
07272-1	That's My Way Of Loving You -1	BB B-7076, MW M-7198
07273-1	Rodeo Rose -2, 3	BB B-6947, MW M-7184
07274-1	Chicken Reel Stomp	BB B-6982, Twin FT8377

Rev. Twin FT8376 by Jimmie Revard's Oklahoma Playboys.

Benjamin (Ben) McKay, f; Eddie Whitley, p/v-1; Red Brown, tbj/v-2; Buster Coward, g/v-3; Charles (Charlie) Gregg, sb/v-4; band v-5/wh-6.

San Antonio, TX   Tuesday, September 14, 1937

014147-1	Who'll Take Your Place When You're Gone -1, 3	BB B-7336
014148-1	When You Think A Whole Lot About Someone -3, 4	BB B-7413
014149-1	Look Out For The Ghost, Red -2, 5	BB B-7830
014150-1	It Don't Mean A Thing -2	BB B-8133
014151-1	Honey, Smile For Me -3	BB B-7336
014152-1	Leave Me With A Smile -2	BB B-7272
014153-1	Black Eyed Susan Brown -3	BB B-7830
014154-1	It Ain't Gonna Rain No Mo' -2, 3, 5	BB B-7272
014155-1	Sweetest Girl In The World -3	BB B-7200
014156-1	Four Leaf Clover -3	BB B-7413, MW M-7367

| 014157-1 | Cowboys And Indians -3, 4 | BB B-7766, MW M-7367, RZAu G23750 |
| 014158-1 | Whistling Waltz -3, 6 | BB B-7200 |

Rev. Bluebird B-8133 by Doug Bine.

Ben McKay, f; Charlie Gregg, f/v-1; Beal Ruff, cl/as; Eddie Whitley, p/v-2; Neal Ruff, tbj; Buster Coward, g/v-3; unknown, sb.
   San Antonio, TX   Tuesday, April 5, 1938

022148-1	Laughter And Tears -1	BB B-7571
022149-1	Old Montana Moon -2, 3	BB B-7612, RZAu G23595
022150-1	Little Love Ship -3	BB B-7703, RZAu G23633
022151-1	Ye Old Rye Waltz	BB B-8032, B-3196
022152-1	Riding For The Rio Grande -1, 3	BB B-8032
022153-1	Sing A Song Of Harvest -1	BB B-7571
022154-1	Shawnee	BB B-7766
022155-1	Blue Bonnet Rhythm	BB B-7673, RZAu G23597
022156-1	Chopo -3	BB B-7612, RZAu G23595
022157-1	Solita -2, 3	BB B-7703, RZAu G23633
022158-1	Rainbow	BB B-7673, B-3196, RZAu G23597

Bluebird B-3196 (a Mexican issue) as by **Tono Hombres**. Matrix 022151 is titled *Centenos Vals*, and matrix 022158 *Arco Iris*, on that issue.

Leonard Seago, f/v-1; Beal Ruff, cl/as; Neal Ruff, cl-2/tbj-3; Olan "Smiley" Whitley, esg; George Timberlake, p; Buster Coward, g/v-4; Curley Williams, sb/v-5.
   San Antonio, TX   Tuesday, October 25, 1938

028593-1	Dixie Moon -1, 3	BB B-7934, MW M-7660
028594-1	Kalua Sweetheart -1, 3, 4, 5	BB B-8014, MW M-7660, RZAu G23789
028595-1	Rio Grande Lullaby -1, 3, 4, 5	BB B-8014, MW M-7661, RZAu G23789
028596-1	Rio Pecos Rose -1, 3, 4, 5	BB B-7992, MW M-7661, RZAu G24043
028597-1	Island Reverie -1, 3	BB B-7966, MW M-7662
028598-1	Hawaiian Honeymoon -1, 3, 4, 5	BB B-7966, MW M-7662, Vi 20-2070
028599-1	Let's Make Believe We're Sweethearts -1, 3, 5	BB B-7972, MW M-7663, RZAu G23750
028600-1	Sweet Fiddle Blues -3, 4	BB B-7992, MW M-7663
028601-1	You Lost A Friend -2	BB B-7947, MW M-7664, RZAu G23749
028602-1	I'll Never Let You Cry -2	BB B-7934, MW M-7664
028603-1	Singing Clarinet Blues -2	BB B-7947, MW M-7665, RZAu G23749
028604-1	I Love Her -2	BB B-7972, MW M-7665

Rev. Regal-Zonophone G24043 by Adolph Hofner.

TURKEY MOUNTAIN SINGERS

Prob.: Bud Landress, tv; C. Ernest Moody, tv; C. Philip Reeve, bv; Clyde Evans, bsv; acc. J.M. Barnette, o.
   Charlotte, NC   Wednesday, August 10, 1927

| 39791-2 | I Am Bound For The Promised Land | Vi 20942 |
| 39792-2 | He Loves Me | Vi 20942 |

Bud Landress, tv; C. Ernest Moody, tv; C. Philip Reeve, bv; Bill Chitwood, bsv; acc. Ira Mashburn, o.
   Atlanta, GA   Sunday, October 21, 1928

47217-2	Does The Pathway Lead Straight	Vi 23602, Au 409
47218-	He Will Never Leave Me	BB B-5542
47219-	Precious Memories	BB B-5542
47220-2	Keep Marching All The Time	Vi 23602, Au 409

The lineups given above are those of the Georgia Yellow Hammers on those dates. For a list of other groups with which members of this circle recorded, see the note at the end of the entry for Georgia Yellow Hammers.

BUCK TURNER

Buck Turner, v/y-1; acc. unknown, sg; prob. own g.
   Fort Worth, TX   Monday, October 5, 1936

FW-1272-1,-3	Sing Sing Blues -1	ARC 7-01-55
FW-1273-	Bootleggers Blues	ARC unissued
FW-1274-	My Baby	ARC unissued
FW-1275-	Hard To Please	ARC unissued
FW-1276-	Death House Blues	ARC unissued
FW-1277-2,-3	Somebody's Darling Not Mine	ARC 7-01-55

CAL TURNER

Pseudonym on Champion for Ted Chestnut.

CAL TURNER & BUD PARKINS

Pseudonym on Superior for Cranford & Thompson (see The Red Fox Chasers).

DAVE TURNER

Pseudonym on Supertone for Dick Parman.

FLOYD TURNER & HIS HOME TOWNERS

Pseudonym on Melotone, Polk, and Australian and British Panachord for Floyd Thompson & His Home Towners.

HAPPY JACK TURNER

See Jack Turner.

"HOBO" JACK TURNER

Pseudonym on Clarion, English Columbia, Diva, Harmony, Puritone, Australian Regal, and Velvet Tone for Ernest Hare.

JACK TURNER

John C. Turner recorded for Gennett as **Jack Turner** and for Decca as **Happy Jack Turner**. A singer of standard and sacred songs, he is beyond the scope of this work.

JAMES TURNER

James Turner, v; acc. poss. own g.
   Atlanta, GA   Friday, March 21, 1930
    ATL-978-   The Lamar Bank Robbery   Br rejected
    ATL-979-   Take This Bunch Of Roses   Br rejected

LEMUEL TURNER

Lemuel Turner, sg solo.
   Memphis, TN   Tuesday, February 7, 1928
    41863-2   'Way Down Yonder Blues   Vi 21292
    41864-1   Tramp Waltz   Vi 21292
   Memphis, TN   Thursday, February 9, 1928
    41869-2   Jake Bottle Blues   Vi V-40052
    41870-2   Beautiful Eyes Of Virginia   Vi V-40052

Victor V-40052 as by **Lemmuel Turner**.

SID TURNER

Pseudonym on Harmograph, Oriole, Pathé, Perfect, and Romeo for Vernon Dalhart.

TURNER & PARKINS

Pseudonym on Superior for Cranford & Thompson (see The Red Fox Chasers).

TURNEY BROTHERS

Pseudonym on Victor V-40027, Montgomery Ward M-8212 for Frank Luther & Carson Robison (see the latter).

BILL TUTTLE

Bill Tuttle, v/y-1; acc. own sg.
   New Orleans, LA   Tuesday, December 10, 1929
    149576-2   The Roamin' Musician -1   Co 15697-D
    149577-2   Gamblin' Bill Driv' On   Co 15697-D

FRANK TUTTLE

Pseudonym on Columbia, Harmony, Velvet Tone, Diva, and English and Australian Regal for Frank Luther (see Carson Robison).

TWEEDY BROTHERS

Harry Tweedy, f; Charles W. Tweedy, p.
   Richmond, IN   Saturday, June 14, 1924
    11922   Ricketts Hornpipe   Ge 5613
    11923   Wild Horse   Ge 5613
    11924   Turkey In The Straw Medley (Turkey In The Straw;   Ge unissued
                      Ain't Gonna Rain No More; Swanee River;
                      Turkey In The Straw; Chicken Reel)
    11925   Chicken Reel   Ge 5488, Sil 4006

Charles W. Tweedy, p solo.
   Richmond, IN   Saturday, June 14, 1924
    11926-A   Repasz Band   Ge 5488, Sil 4006

Harry Tweedy, f; Charles W. Tweedy, p.
    Richmond, IN   Thursday, January 15, 1925
        12124-A   Birdie   Ge 5635, Ch 15148, Sil 4008, Bu 8016
        12125-A   Cripple Creek   Ge 5635, Ch 15148, Sil 4008, Bu 8016
        12126,-A   Sourwood Mountain   Ge rejected
        12127,-A   Oh Aunt Dinah Get Your Nightcap On Ge rejected
Champion 15148 as by **Jennings Bros.**

Harry Tweedy, f; George Tweedy, f; Charles W. Tweedy, p; unidentified, v-1.
    Richmond, IN   c. March 1928
        13653-A   Dance All Night With A Bottle In Your Hand   Ge 6734, Ch 15689, Spt 9174, Vs *5101*
        13654-A   Ida Red -1   Ge 6529, Ch 15689, Spt 9166
        13655-A   Shortenin' Bread   Ge 6529, Ch 15548, Spt 9174, MeC 45004,
                                                             Min M-14061
        13656-A   Birdie   Ge 6483, Ch 15486
        13657   The Bully Of The Town   Ge 6447, Ch 15486
        13658   Liberty   Ge 6447
        13659-A   Sugar In The Gourd   Ge 6483, Ch 15548, MeC 45004, Min M-14061
        13660   My Carolina Home -1   Ge rejected
Champions, Melotone 45004, Minerva M-14061 as by **The Three Tweedy Boys**. Varsity 5101 as by **Buckeye Boys**.
Rev. Varsity 5101 (with same credit) by Archie Porter.

    Richmond, IN   Monday, July 16, 1928
        14050   I Don't Love Nobody -1   Ge rejected

    Richmond, IN   Tuesday, July 17, 1928
        14057   The Mocking Bird   Ge 6604
        14059   My Carolina Home -1   Ge rejected
        14060   Oh Dem Golden Slippers   Ge unissued
        14061   Dixie   Ge 6734
        14062   High School Cadet   Ge rejected
        14063   Lee County Blues   Ge rejected
        14064-A   Buckwheat Batter   Ge 6604, Spt 9166
Matrix 14058 is popular.

Harry Tweedy, f/v-1; Charles W. Tweedy, p/v-1.
    Richmond, IN   Wednesday, May 21, 1930
        16639   Down Yonder   Spr 2784
        16640   Charleston No. 1   Ge unissued
        16641   Home Brew Rag -1   Ge 7240, Ch 16048, 33056, Spt 9748, Spr 2784
        16642   The Alabammy Jubilee   Ge 7240, Ch 16048, 33056, Spt 9748
        16645   Lee County Blues   Ge rejected
        16646   Kanawha Hornpipe   Ge rejected
Matrices 16643/44 are tap-dancing.

TWILIGHT TRAIL BOYS

Vocal trio; acc. unknown, g.
    San Antonio, TX   Sunday, October 30, 1938
        028819-1   Wanderers Of The Wasteland   MW M-7621
        028820-1   Following The Stars   MW M-7621
        028821-1   Moonlight On The Prairie   MW M-7622
        028822-1   Back To The Lone Prairie   MW M-7622
        028823-1   The California Trail   MW M-7623
        028824-1   Over The Santa Fe Trail   MW M-7623
        028825-1   The Rodeo Song   MW M-7624
        028826-1   Press Along To The Big Corral   BB B-8001, MW M-7624, RZAu G23780,
                                                             Twin FT8715
        028827-1   Little Ah Sid   BB B-8001, MW M-7625, RZAu G23780,
                                                             Twin FT8715
        028828-1   Westward-Ho!   MW M-7625
        028829-1   Ridin' The Range   MW M-7626
        028830-1   The Herdin' Song   MW M-7626

THE TWO COW HANDS (JIMMIE ADAMS & TOM MURRAY)

Jimmie Adams, Tom Murray, prob. v duet; acc. own g duet.
    Los Angeles, CA   Monday, February 3, 1930
        LTR-267-A   Red River Valley   Br unissued trial recording

Jimmie Adams also recorded with Bud Jamison as The Rolling Stones, while Tom Murray also recorded with Chuck Cook (Charlie Quirk) as **Tom & Chuck** and with The Beverly Hill Billies.

THE TWO ISLANDERS
See James Brown, Jr. & Ken Landon groups.

U

UNCLE BUD & HIS PLOW BOYS
Pseudonym on Clarion, Velvet Tone, ARC-group labels, and derivatives for Bob Miller.

UNCLE JIM'S OLD TIME FIDDLERS
Pseudonym on Herwin for The Barnstormers.

UNCLE NED & HIS TEXAS WRANGLERS
Prob.: Chick Stripling, f; Sammy Forsmark, esg; Pete Cassell, p/g/poss. v; Slim Hutcheson, bj/prob. v; Gene "Uncle Ned" Stripling, sb; Cicero (Ray) Merneigh, unknown instrument.

Atlanta, GA Monday, August 21, 1939

041216-1	I Found You Among The Roses	BB unissued
041217-1	Sweetheart Of Hawaii	BB unissued
041218-1	Ten Or Eleven Times	BB unissued
041219-1	Canal Street Mama	BB unissued
041220-1	House At The End Of The Lane	BB unissued
041221-1	Canoeing With Another Man	BB unissued

The personnel above is derived from *Rural Radio* (June 1939).
Pete Cassell also recorded in his own name, and Sammy Forsmark as half of Sammy & Smitty and with Hank Penny.

UNCLE PETE & LOUISE
Elmore "Pete" Raines, Louise Collins, v duet; acc. Louise Collins, f; Elmore "Pete" Raines, g.

New York, NY Wednesday, June 14, 1933

13452-1	Only A Tramp	Cq 8342
13453-1	We Ought To Be Thankful For That	Cq 8343
13454-1	The Bible My Mother Gave To Me	Cq 8343
13455-2	A Mother's Plea	Cq 8344
13456-1	Out On A Western Range	Cq 8342
13457-2	Forgive And Forget	Cq 8344

CHARLES UNDERWOOD
See Hack's String Band.

MARION UNDERWOOD
See Taylor's Kentucky Boys.

SOCKO UNDERWOOD
Oliver "Socko" Underwood, v; acc. own g.

Dallas, TX Tuesday, April 8, 1941

063062-1	I'm Only A Convict's Wife	BB B-8752
063063-1	In A Little Village Church Yard	BB B-8722
063064-1	You're Gone And Forget Me	BB B-8722
063065-1	You Got Another Pal	BB B-8752

UNIVERSAL COWBOYS
Darrell Kirkpatrick, f/ac; unknown, f-1; Wilson "Lefty" Perkins, esg; unknown, p-2; James "Doc" Eastwood, tbj; Dick Reinhart, g/v-3; Kermit Whalen, sb.

Dallas, TX Friday, June 23, 1939

DAL-927-2	Hot Mama Stomp -2	Vo/OK 05040
DAL-928-1	I'll Take Her Back (If She Wants To Come Back) -2, 3	Vo/OK 05040
DAL-929-1	Night Spot Blues -2	Vo 05189
DAL-930-1	Oh Marie, Oh Marie -1, 3	Vo 05189
DAL-931-1	Steel Guitar Honky Tonk -2	Vo/OK 04987
DAL-932-1	Don't You Remember Me -1, 3	Vo/OK 04987
DAL-933-1	Cow Town Swing -2	Vo/OK 05107, Cq 9715

DAL-934-1 Aloha Means Goodbye -2, 3   Vo/OK 05107, Cq 9715
Conqueror 9715 as by **Dick Reinhart & His Universal Cowboys**.
Matrix DAL-927 was logged as *Little Rubber Dolly* and so titled in a 1941/42 OKeh catalogue but no copy of OKeh 05040 has been reported with that title.

UNIVERSITY OF TENNESSEE TRIO

Prob. vocal trio; acc. unknown.
Knoxville, TN   Saturday, August 31, 1929
  K-148-   Dixie Medley   Br/Vo rejected trial recording
  K-149-   Down Virginia Way   Br/Vo rejected trial recording

UNKNOWN ARTISTS [I]

Unknown, v; acc. prob. own g.
Atlanta, GA   Tuesday, March 22, 1927
  80617-A   I Cannot Be Your Sweetheart   OK unissued

UNKNOWN ARTISTS [II]

Two unknowns, h.
Atlanta, GA   Wednesday, October 12, 1927
  81767-A   [Medley]   OK unissued: *LC LBC14 (LP)*

UNKNOWN ARTISTS [III]

Female recitation; acc. unknown, vn; unknown, p; unknown, vc; unknown, male v duet.
Atlanta, GA   Wednesday, August 8, 1928
  402099-[A]   [Over The Hills To The Poorhouse]   OK unissued
Matrices 402098, 402100 are also blank in OKeh files and may be by these artists.

UNKNOWN ARTISTS [IV]

Male v duet; or v-1; acc. two unknowns, g.
Atlanta, GA   Friday, March 22, 1929
  402409-   [The Story Of Adam; Show Me The Way To Go   OK unissued
                  Home]
  402410-   [In The Jailhouse Now] -1   OK unissued
These matrices are blank in OKeh files. The lead or solo singer may be Roy Bledsoe, who recorded matrices 402411/12, also unissued. There may also be a connection with John Dilleshaw, who recorded on matrices 402405 to 402408, and may be one of the guitarists, though he is probably not the second vocalist on matrix 402409. The titles are conjectural.

UNKNOWN ARTISTS [V]

Unknown, f; unknown, bj; unknown, g.
Richmond, IN   Saturday, May 24, 1930
  16652   Tennessee Rag   Ge rejected
  16653   The Fun Is All Over   Ge rejected

UNKNOWN ARTISTS [VI]

Unknown woman, v/y; acc. unknown, f; unknown, g.
Fort Worth, TX   c. October 1, 1934
  FW-Test #1   Waltz Of The Hills   Vo rejected
This is not Patsy Montana, who also recorded this song.

UNKNOWN ARTISTS [VII]

Unknown man, v; acc. Audrey "Art" Davis, f; prob. Jim Boyd, g.
Fort Worth, TX   October 1934
  FW-Test #2   When They Baptised Sister Lucy Lee Vo rejected

JACK URBAN (THE ROVIN' MINER)

Jack Urban, v; acc. prob. own h/g.
New York, NY   Thursday, October 18, 1934
  16139-2   I'm A Pennsylvania Bum   Ba 33401, Me M13368, Or 8453, Pe 13131,
                                                      Ro 5453, Cq 8482
  16140-   You'll Never Take Away My Dreams   ARC unissued

New York, NY   Monday, March 18, 1935
17057-1   Innocent Boy   Ba 33401, Me M13368, Or 8453, Pe 13131,
                                                 Ro 5453, Cq 8482

V

THE VAGABOND YODELER

Pseudonym on Superior for Chas. M. DeWitte.

THE VAGABONDS

The Vagabonds (Herald–Dean–Curt): Herald Goodman, Dean Upson, Curt Poulton, v trio; acc. Curt Poulton, g.
Richmond, IN   Friday, January 30, 1933

18987	When It's Harvest Time In Peaceful Valley	Old Cabin unnumbered
18988	Little Mother Of The Hills	Old Cabin unnumbered
18989	Little Shoes	Old Cabin unnumbered?
18990	When It's Lamp Lightin' Time In The Valley	Old Cabin unnumbered
18991	99 Years	Old Cabin unnumbered

These are custom recordings by Gennett. Issues are coupled 18987/18988, 18987/18990, and 18990/18991. No issue has yet been traced bearing matrix 18989. The Old Cabin Co., Inc. was based at 208 Hitchcock Building, Nashville, TN.

The Vagabonds: Herald Goodman, Dean Upson, Curt Poulton, v trio; acc. Curt Poulton, g.
Chicago, IL   Wednesday, April 26, 1933

75460-1	My Pretty Quadroon	Vi 23849
75461-1	Ninety-Nine Years (Is Almost For Life)	Vi 23820, HMVIn N4254
75462-1	Little Shoes	Vi 23801
75463-1	In The Sleepy Hills Of Tennessee	Vi 23801
75464-1	That Little Boy Of Mine	Vi 23820, HMVIn N4254
75465-1	How Beautiful Heaven Must Be	Vi 23809
75466-1	The Old Rugged Cross	Vi 23809
75467-1	My Pretty Quadroon	BB B-5072, Eld 1995, Sr S-3153, MW M-4307, Victrola Z-353, HMVIn N4278
75468-1	Ninety-Nine Years (Is Almost For Life)	BB B-5282, Eld 2156, Sr S-3363, MW M-4307, M-4443, Twin FT1920
75469-1	Little Shoes	BB B-5103, Eld 2019, Sr S-3186, MW M-4239
75470-1	In The Sleepy Hills Of Tennessee	BB B-5103, Eld 2019, Sr S-3186, MW M-4239
75471-1	That Little Boy Of Mine	BB B-5072, Eld 1995, Sr S-3153, MW M-4238
75472-1	How Beautiful Heaven Must Be	BB B-5124, Eld 2034, Sr S-3205, MW M-4240
75473-1	The Old Rugged Cross	BB B-5124, Eld 2034, Sr S-3205, MW M-4240
75474-1	Little Mother Of The Hills	BB unissued

Victrola Z-353 is a special pressing for the Cole Publishing Co., made in December 1935.
Revs: Victor 23849 by the Kelly Brothers; Victrola Z-353 by Tom & Don; HMV N4278 by the Lone Star Cowboys.

Acc. Curt Poulton, g; or unacc.-1.
Chicago, IL   Thursday, July 27, 1933

75474-2	Little Mother Of The Hills	BB B-5197, Eld 2087, Sr S-3278
75944-1	In The Vine-Covered Church 'Way Back Home	BB B-5137, Eld 2043, Sr S-3218, MW M-4382
75945-1	In The Little White Church On The Hill	BB B-6250, Twin FT8058
75946-1	The Death Of Jesse James	BB B-5282, Eld 2156, Sr S-3363, MW M-4443, Twin FT1920
75947-1	When It's Moonlight Down In Lovers' Lane	BB B-5137, Eld 2043, Sr S-3218, MW M-4382
75948-1	I Will Always Call You Sweetheart	BB B-5402, MW M-4455, HMVIn N4323
75949-1	For Ever And Ever More	BB B-5244, Eld 2127, Sr S-3327, MW M-4406
75950-1	The Little Old Brick Church	BB B-5244, Eld 2127, Sr S-3327
75951-1	Livin' On The Mountain	BB B-6184
75952-1	In The Garden -1	BB B-6184

Revs: Bluebird B-6250, Twin FT8058 by the Don Hall Trio (popular).

Chicago, IL   Friday, July 28, 1933
75970-1   Father, Mother, Sister And Brother   BB B-5197, Eld 2087, Sr S-3278, MW M-4406

Chicago, IL   Wednesday, December 6, 1933

77230-1	Leavenworth Jail	BB B-5472
77231-1	At The End Of Sunset Lane	Vi 23855, BB B-5381, Sr S-3462, MW M-4444, HMVAu EA1343, HMVIn N4287
77232-1	When It's Time For The Whippoorwill To Sing	BB B-5402, HMVIn N4323
77233-1	Red River Valley	BB B-5297, Eld 2168, Sr S-3378, MW M-4479

77234-1	Drifting In A Lover's Dream	BB B-5588
77235-1	Give My Love To Mother	BB B-5588, MW M-4455
77236-1	In The Valley Of Yesterday	Vi 23855, BB B-5315, Sr S-3396, MW M-4422, HMVAu EA1343, HMVIn N4287
77237-1	An Old Sweet Song For A Sweet Old Lady	BB B-5381, Sr S-3462, MW M-4444

Revs: all issues of matrix 77233 by Bud Billings (Frank Luther) & Carson Robison (see the latter); Bluebird B-5472 by Tom & Don.

Chicago, IL   Thursday, December 7, 1933

77257-1	Sourwood Mountain	BB B5335, Sr S-3416, MW M-4477
77258-1	When The Work's All Done This Fall	BB B-5300, Eld 2171, Sr S-3381, MW M-4442
77259-1	Four Thousand Years Ago	BB B-5315, Sr S-3396, MW M-4422
77260-1	Barbara Allen	BB B-5300, Eld 2171, Sr S-3381, MW M-4442
77261-1	Sweethearts' Paradise	BB B-5989, Twin FT1943
77262-1	In My Book Of Dreams	BB B-5989, Twin FT1943

Rev. all issues of matrix 77257 by Vernon Dalhart.

VAL & PETE

Pete Martinez, v/y; acc. own sg; Valentin Martinez, g.

San Antonio, TX   Wednesday, March 14, 1928

400510-B	Yodel Blues – (Part 1)	OK 45224, PaE R3871
400511-A	Yodel Blues – (Part 2)	OK 45224, PaE R3871

Valentin Martinez recorded prolifically, in Spanish, for several labels' Mexican series.

VALDESE QUARTETTE

Vocal quartet; acc. unknown, o.

Winston-Salem, NC   Monday, September 19, 1927

81345-A	He Holds Me By The Hand	OK 45199, PaE R3867
81346-	Don't Forget To Pray	OK unissued
81347-A	Waiting The Boatman	OK 45161
81349-B	Walking Along With Me	OK 45199, PaE R3867
81350-B	Just Over The Glory-Land	OK 45161

Matrix 81348, blank in OKeh files, is probably by this group.

VANCE'S TENNESSEE BREAKDOWNERS

Dudley Vance, f; prob. Will McNamara, bj-1; Sam Vance, g; unidentified, v duet-2/calls-3.

Winston-Salem, NC   Thursday, September 22, 1927

81385-A,-B	My Tennessee Mountain Home -2	OK unissued
81386-A,-B	Old Engineer Reuben	OK unissued
81387-A,-B	Wise County Blues	OK unissued
81388-A	Washington County Fox Chase -1	OK unissued: Cy 525 (LP); Co C4K47911, Cy CD3511 (CDs)
81389-B	Tennessee Breakdown -3	OK 45151
81390-B	Ragged Ann -1	OK 45151

Matrix 81388 is titled *Tennessee Mountain Fox Chase* on County 525, CD3511.

THE VASS FAMILY

Frank Vass, poss. Emily Vass, Louisa Vass, Sally Vass, Virginia Vass, v quintet; acc. unidentified, h-1; prob. Virginia Vass, g.

New York, NY   Wednesday, August 4, 1937

62495-A	Paper Of Pins -1	De 5425
62496-A	Soldier Won't You Marry Me? -1	De 5432
62497-A	Deep Blue Sea -1	De 5432
62498-A,-B	Hawg Foot	De rejected
62499-A,-B	Blue Eyed Ellen (The Jealous Lover Of Lone Green Valley) -1	De rejected
62500-A,-B	My Grandmother -1	De rejected
62501-A	Jimmie Randall (The Pizen Song)	De 5425
62502-A,-B	Skip To My Lou -1	De rejected

Frank Vass sings solo parts on matrices 62495/96; one of the women sings solo parts on matrices 62495 to 62497.

G.K. VAUGHAN & W.B. SEALE
G. KIEFER VAUGHAN

See Vaughan Quartet & Associated Groups.

VAUGHAN & SEALE
See Vaughan Quartet & Associated Groups.

VAUGHAN HAPPY TWO
See Vaughan Quartet & Associated Groups.

VAUGHAN QUARTET & ASSOCIATED GROUPS
The James D. Vaughan Music Co. of Lawrenceburg, TN, gospel songbook publishers, sponsored a number of singing groups, some of which recorded for the old-time series of Victor and Paramount. The company also produced records on its own Vaughan label, custom-made usually by Gennett but occasionally by Paramount or other, unidentified, companies. These were issued in a series that began in 1921 at 300; releases were numbered at intervals of 25 (so 300, 325, 350, 375, etc.) and continued at least until 2025; issues above 1850 are believed to have beeen recorded after 1942.

Vaughan Quartet: G. Kiefer Vaughan, tv; unknown, tv; poss. Walter B. Seale, bv; unknown, bsv; or **Vaughan & Loudy**-1: G. Kiefer Vaughan, ——— Loudy, v duet; acc. unknown orch.; or acc. unknown-2.

1921
unknown location

311	Couldn't Hear Nobody Pray -2	Vaughan 300
313	Steal Away -2	Vaughan 300
327	Look For Me	Vaughan 350
332	Waiting At The Gate -1	Vaughan 350
	Someday	Vaughan 325
	Magnify Jesus	Vaughan 325

Vaughan 300 was reissued with later recordings of the titles; see November 6, 1924 session.
There is no information on these recordings in Gennett files, and it is likely that they were made by another company.

Prob. unacc.
Richmond, IN   Saturday, June 17, 1922

11124,-A,-B,-C	Don't Forget To Pray	Vaughan unissued
11125	Vaughan Quartet Medley	Vaughan 400
11126,-A,-B,-C	Drifting Away	Vaughan unissued

Richmond, IN   Monday, June 19, 1922

11127,-A,-B,-C	Is It Well With Your Soul	Vaughan unissued
11128,-A,-B,-C,-D	When Jesus Deems It Best	Vaughan unissued
11129,-A,-B	Echoes From The Glory Shore	Vaughan unissued

Vaughan Quartet: G. Kiefer Vaughan, tv; unknown, tv; Walter B. Seale, bv; unknown, bsv; or **Mr. Vaughn** [sic] & **Mr. Seale**-1, v duet; acc. unknown, p.

Richmond, IN   Tuesday, June 20, 1922

11130,-A,-B,-C	Kentucky Babe	Vaughan unissued
11131,-A,-B	Keep My Hand In Thine -1	Vaughan unissued
11132,-A	Mother Is Waiting For Me -1	Vaughan unissued
11133	Somebody Needs Just You	Vaughan 375

Richmond, IN   Wednesday, June 21, 1922

11134,-A,-B,-C	When The Twilight Shadows Fall	Vaughan unissued
11135,-A,-B,-C	Crossing The Bar	Vaughan unissued
11136,-A,-B,-C	Dreaming Alone In The Twilight	Vaughan unissued
11137	Do You Know Him?	Vaughan 375
11138,-A,-B,-C	My Loved Ones Are Waiting For Me	Vaughan unissued

Vaughan Quartet: G. Kiefer Vaughan, tv; unknown, tv; Walter B. Seale, bv; unknown, bsv; unacc.; or **Mr. Seale & Quartette**-1: Walter B. Seale, lv; acc. v quartet.

Richmond, IN   Thursday, June 22, 1922

11139,-A,-B	I Need The Prayers	Vaughan unissued
11140,-A,-B	Better Than Gold -1	Vaughan unissued
11141	Love-Sick Blues	Vaughan 400

Richmond, IN   Tuesday, April 16, 1923

11404,-A	Crossing The Bar	Vaughan 425
11405	Dreaming Alone In The Twilight	Vaughan 425
11406	Love Sick Blues	Vaughan unissued

Richmond, IN   Sunday, April 21, 1923

11B27	Don't Forget To Pray	Vaughan 500
11B28	Crossing The Bar	Vaughan unissued
11B29	Beautiful Harbor Lights	Vaughan 600
11B30	Love Sick Blues	Vaughan unissued
11B31	Dreaming Alone In The Twilight	Vaughan unissued
11B32	Music In My Soul	Vaughan 625

Vaughan Quartet: G. Kiefer Vaughan, tv; unknown, tv; Walter B. Seale, bv; unknown, bsv; or **Walter B. Seale**-1, v; unacc.; or acc. unknown, p-2.

Richmond, IN   Tuesday, April 23, 1923

11B33-A	Better Than Gold	Vaughan unissued
11B34	Only A Step	Vaughan 650
11B35	When They Ring The Golden Bells For You And Me -1, 2	Vaughan 600
11B36	The Old-Fashioned Cabin	Vaughan 675
11B37	When We Lay Our Burdens Down	Vaughan 750

Richmond, IN   Wednesday, April 24, 1923

11B38	Go To Jesus With It All	Vaughan 700

Richmond, IN   Thursday, April 25, 1923

11B41	I'll Take You Home Again Kathleen -2	Vaughan 725
11B42,-A	Do You Know Him	Vaughan unissued
11B43,-A	Somebody Needs Just You	Vaughan unissued
11B44	Is It Well With Your Soul?	Vaughan 475
11B45	Echoes From The Glory Shore	Vaughan 575
11B46	Vaughan Quartette Medley	Vaughan unissued

Richmond, IN   Friday, April 26, 1923

11B47	My Loved Ones Are Waiting For Me -2	Vaughan 525
11B48	They Left Him Alone	Vaughan 675
11B49	That Little Old Hut	Vaughan unissued

Richmond, IN   Tuesday, April 30, 1923

11429	Drifting Away	Vaughan 475
11430	When Jesus Deems It Best	Vaughan 525
11431	Mother And Home	Vaughan 650

Mr. Seale, v; acc. unknown.

Richmond, IN   Wednesday, May 1, 1923

11432	When They Ring The Golden Bells For You And Me	Vaughan unissued

G. Kiefer Vaughan, v; acc. unknown, p.

Richmond, IN   Wednesday, May 1, 1923

11433	Jesus Is All I Need	Vaughan 625

Vaughan Quartet: G. Kiefer Vaughan, tv; unknown, tv; Walter B. Seale, bv; unknown, bsv; or **Seale & Vaughan**-1, v duet; unacc.; or acc. unknown, p-2.

Richmond, IN   Wednesday, May 1, 1923

11434	Better Than Gold	Vaughan 550
11435	I Need The Prayers	Vaughan 575
11436	Keep My Hand In Thine -1, 2	Vaughan 500
11437	Kentucky Babe	Vaughan 450
11438	Singing A Wonderful Song	Vaughan 700

Richmond, IN   Thursday, May 2, 1923

11442	When Honey Sings An Old Time Song -2	Vaughan 725
11443	That Little Old Hut	Vaughan 750
11444	Mother Is Waiting For Me -1	Vaughan 550
11445	Will The Gates Open For Me?	Vaughan 800
11446	Is It Well With Your Soul	Vaughan unissued
11447	When The Twilight Shadows Fall	Vaughan 450
11448	Jesus Forgives And Forgets	Vaughan 775

Richmond, IN   Friday, May 3, 1923

11449,-A	Somebody Needs Just You	Vaughan unissued
11450	If I Could Hear My Mother Pray Again	Vaughan 775
11451	Dear Old Girl	Vaughan unissued
11452	I'd Like To Go Down South	Vaughan unissued

Richmond, IN   Sunday, May 5, 1923

11457	Bloom Brightly Sweet Roses	Vaughan 800
11458	Massa's In The Cold, Cold Ground	Vaughan unissued
11459	When You And I Were Young Maggie	Vaughan unissued

Walter B. Seale, v; acc. v quartet; Theodore Shaw, p.

Richmond, IN   Friday, April 4, 1924

11823-A	Sin Is To Blame	Vaughan 850

Vaughan Quartet; G. Kiefer Vaughan, tv; prob. Hillman Barnard, tv; Walter B. Seale, bv; prob. Roy Collins, bsv; unacc.; or acc. Theodore Shaw, p-1.
Richmond, IN   Friday, April 4, 1924
| 11824 | Take Him With You -1 | Vaughan 875 |
| 11825 | Don't Forget The Family Prayer | Vaughan 950 |

Vaughan Quartet; G. Kiefer Vaughan, tv; prob. Hillman Barnard, tv; Walter B. Seale, bv; prob. Roy Collins, bsv; or **Seale & Vaughan**-1, v duet; acc. Theodore Shaw, p.
Richmond, IN   Saturday, April 5, 1924
11826	Will You Be There	Vaughan 900
11827-A	Jesus Will Care For Me -1	Vaughan 925
11828-A	O Happy Day	Vaughan unissued

Walter B. Seale v; acc. Theodore Shaw, p.
Richmond, IN   Monday, April 7, 1924
| 11829,-A | What Is He Worth To Your Soul? | Vaughan 950? |

G. Kiefer Vaughan, v; acc. v quartet; Theodore Shaw, p.
Richmond, IN   Monday, April 7, 1924
| 11830,-A | Pal Of My Dreams | Vaughan 975? |

Theodore Shaw Of Lawrenceburg, Tenn., p solo.
Richmond, IN   Monday, April 7, 1924
| 11831-B | Hold 'Er Newt (They're After Us) | Vaughan 825 |

Although logged with the above credit, this item was issued as **Piano Solo by the Author**.

Vaughan Quartet; G. Kiefer Vaughan, tv; prob. Hillman Barnard, tv; Walter B. Seale, bv; prob. Roy Collins, bsv; unacc.
Richmond, IN   Monday, April 7, 1924
| 11832 | Don't You Love Your Daddy Too? | Vaughan 975 |

Roy Collins, bsv; acc. unknown.
Richmond, IN   Monday, April 7, 1924
| K-9 | Asleep In The Deep | Ge unissued |

Hilman [sic] Barnard, v; acc. unknown.
Richmond, IN   Monday, April 7, 1924
| K-10 | Heaven Holds All To Me | Ge unissued |

Vaughan Quartet: unidentified, v; acc. v quartet; Theodore Shaw, p.
Richmond, IN   Tuesday, April 8, 1924
| K-11 | Wake Up, America And Kluck, Kluck Kluck | Vaughan 825 |

This item was logged as by **Solo & Quartette** but issued as shown.

Seale & Vaughan, v duet; acc. v quartet; Theodore Shaw, p.
Richmond, IN   Wednesday, April 9, 1924
| 11833 | Face To Face At Last | Vaughan 875 |

Vaughan Quartet; G. Kiefer Vaughan, tv; prob. Hillman Barnard, tv; Walter B. Seale, bv; prob. Roy Collins, bsv; acc. Theodore Shaw, p.
Richmond, IN   Wednesday, April 9, 1924
| 11834 | We'll Live Again | Vaughan 850 |
| 11835,-A,-B | I'm In His Care | Vaughan 900? |

Walter B. Seale, v; acc. poss. v quartet; Theodore Shaw, p.
Richmond, IN   Friday, April 11, 1924
| 11829-B,-C,-D | What Is He Worth To Your Soul? | Vaughan 950? |

Roy Collins, bsv; acc. unknown.
Richmond, IN   Friday, April 11, 1924
| K-9-A | Asleep In The Deep | Ge unissued |

Vaughan Quartet: G. Kiefer Vaughan, tv; prob. Hillman Barnard, tv; Walter B. Seale, bv; prob. Roy Collins, bsv; unacc.
Richmond, IN   Saturday, April 12, 1924
11835-C,-D	I'm In His Care	Vaughan 900?
11836	I'd Like To Go Down South Once More	Vaughan 1000
11837	Juanita	Vaughan 1000

Walter B. Seale, v; acc. unknown.
Richmond, IN   Saturday, April 12, 1924
| K-12 | Old Folks At Home | Ge unissued |

T. Shaw, poss. p solo.
   Richmond, IN
                                                                                      Saturday, April 12, 1924
    K-13   [untitled]   Vaughan unissued trial recording

G. Kiefer Vaughan, v; acc. v quartet.
   Richmond, IN
                                                                                     Monday, April 14, 1924
    11830-B,-C   Pal Of My Dreams   Vaughan 975?

Vaughan Quartet; G. Kiefer Vaughan, tv; prob. Hillman Barnard, tv; Walter B. Seale, bv; poss. Roy Collins, bsv; acc. Theodore Shaw, p.
   Richmond, IN
                                                                                     Monday, April 14, 1924
    K-14   Sittin' In The Corner   Vaughan 1025

   Richmond, IN
                                                                                    Tuesday, April 15, 1924
    11828-B   O Happy Day   Vaughan 925

Vaughan Quartette; G. Kiefer Vaughan, tv; poss. Hillman Barnard, tv; Walter B. Seale, bv; unknown, bsv; or **Vaughan & Seale**-1, v duet; acc. unknown, p.
   Richmond, IN
                                                                            Tuesday, November 4, 1924
    12065-A   Nearing My Long Sought Home   Vaughan 1050
    12066-B   There's A Bridge O'er The River -1   Vaughan 1050
    12067-B   One At Last   Vaughan 1100

Vaughan Quartette; G. Kiefer Vaughan, tv; poss. Hillman Barnard, tv; Walter B. Seale, bv; unknown, bsv; unacc.; or acc. unknown, p-1.
   Richmond, IN
                                                                       Wednesday, November 5, 1924
    12068-A   Walking With My King -1   Vaughan 1100
    12069-A   Ain't Gwine To Study War No More   Vaughan 1075
    12070-A   Swing Low Sweet Chariot   Vaughan 1075
Matrix 12069 was originally titled *Down By The Riverside*.

Acc. unknown, p.
   Richmond, IN
                                                                       Thursday, November 6, 1924
    12071   Steal Away   Vaughan 300
    12072-B   I Couldn't Hear Nobody Pray   Vaughan 300

Walter B. Seale, v; acc. unknown, p.
   Richmond, IN
                                                                       Thursday, November 6, 1924
    12073XX   The Old Folks At Home   Vaughan 1025
This matrix was made as a trial recording but almost certainly furnished the issue shown.

Vaughan Quartette: poss. G. Kiefer Vaughan, tv; Luther E. Heatwole, bv; Walter B. Seale, prob. bv; poss. F.P. Heatwole, bsv; unacc.; or acc. unknown, p-1.
   Richmond, IN
                                                                    Tuesday, November 3, 1925
    12380-A   Lead Me, Shepherd   Vaughan 1225
    12381-A   Wheel In A Wheel   Vaughan 1150
    12382,-A   When Jesus Comes -1   Vaughan unissued
    12383   Where He Leads Me   Vaughan 1250

Walter B. Seale, v; acc. unknown, p.
   Richmond, IN
                                                            Wednesday, November 4, 1925
    12384-A   The Pearly White City   Vaughan 1325

Vaughan Quartet (or **Quartette**): poss. G. Kiefer Vaughan, tv; Luther E. Heatwole, bv; Walter B. Seale, prob. bv; poss. F.P. Heatwole, bsv; acc. unknown, p; or unacc.-1.
   Richmond, IN
                                                               Wednesday, November 4, 1925
    12385   I Shall Not Pass Again This Way   Vaughan 1275
    12386   Hold To God's Unchanging Hand -1   Vaughan 1250
    12387-A   Over In The Glory Land   Vaughan 1300
    12388   Rocking On The Waves   Vaughan 1125

   Richmond, IN
                                                                  Thursday, November 5, 1925
    12389-A   While The Years Roll On   Vaughan 1125
    12390   Jesus, Lover Of My Soul -1   Vaughan 1350

   Richmond, IN
                                                                    Friday, November 6, 1925
    12391-A   Golden Sunbeams Of Love   Vaughan 1325
    12392   Lord, I Want To Live With Thee   Vaughan 1300
    12393,-A   Tune In On Heaven   Vaughan unissued
    12394-B   The Old Rugged Cross -1   Vaughan 1400

Vaughan Quartette: poss. G. Kiefer Vaughan, tv; Luther E. Heatwole, bv; Walter B. Seale, prob. bv; poss. F.P. Heatwole, bsv; or **Luther E. Heatwole**-1, bv; acc. poss. L.E. Heatwole, p-2; unknown, vc-3.

			Saturday, November 7, 1925
Richmond, IN			
12395	One Sweet Day -2, 3	Vaughan 1200	
12396	God Bless You -1, 2	Vaughan 1425	
12397	A Little Close Harmony	Vaughan 1150	

Vaughan Quartet: poss. G. Kiefer Vaughan, tv; Luther E. Heatwole, bv; Walter B. Seale, prob. bv; poss. F.P. Heatwole, bsv; acc. unknown, p; or unacc.-1.

			Monday, November 9, 1925
Richmond, IN			
12398	The Church In The Wildwood -1	Vaughan 1400	
12399	Mother, Oh My Mother	Vaughan 1200	
12400-A	America	Vaughan 1175	

Walter B. Seale, v; acc. unknown.

			Wednesday, November 11, 1925
Richmond, IN			
12405-A	The Prisoners [sic] Song	Vaughan 1425	
12406	Down Dixie Way	Vaughan unissued trial recording	

Vaughan Quartet: poss. G. Kiefer Vaughan, tv; Luther E. Heatwole, bv; Walter B. Seale, prob. bv; poss. F.P. Heatwole, bsv; acc. unknown, p.

			Wednesday, November 11, 1925
Richmond, IN			
12407-A	Traveling Home	Vaughan 1275	
12408-B	What Wondrous Love	Vaughan 1375	

Prob. unacc.

			Thursday, November 12, 1925
Richmond, IN			
12409-A	Onward Christian Soldiers	Vaughan 1175	
12410	He's My Friend	Vaughan 1350	
12411	When Jesus Comes	Vaughan 1225	

G. Kiefer Vaughan, v; acc. unknown, p; unknown, vc.

			Saturday, November 14, 1925
Richmond, IN			
12423,-A	One Sweet Day	Vaughan rejected	

Seale & Vaughan, v duet; acc. unknown, p.

			Saturday, November 14, 1925
Richmond, IN			
12424	Tune In On Heaven	Vaughan 1375	

Claude A. Sharp, v; acc. unknown, p.

			Saturday, November 14, 1925
Richmond, IN			
12425	West Of The Great Divide	Vaughan unissued	

Gennett files note "wax broken in Eigly's Dept."

F.P. Heatwole, bsv; acc. unknown, p.

			Monday, November 16, 1925
Richmond, IN			
12426	Invictus	Vaughan unissued	

Vaughan Quartet: Hillman Barnard, tv; Otis L. McCoy, tv; W.B. Walbert, bv; A.M. Pace, bsv; unacc.

			c. May 15, 1927
Richmond, IN			
12795-A	O What A Blessing He Is To Me	Vaughan 1450	
12796	When The Home Gates Swing Open	Vaughan 1450	

Some issues of Vaughan 1450 may have been as by **Barnard, McCoy, Walbert & Pace**.

Vaughan Quartet: poss.: Hillman Barnard, tv; Otis L. McCoy, tv; W.B. Walbert, bv; A.M. Pace, bsv; acc. unknown, p-1.

			c. October 23, 1927
Richmond, IN			
13156-A	When You Get It Right	Vaughan 1525	
13157-A	Stilling The Tempest -1	Vaughan 1475	
13158	The Home Coming Week	Vaughan 1500	
13159	O Happy Day	Vaughan 1500	
13160	Love	Vaughan 1525	
13161-A	Where We'll Never Grow Old -1	Vaughan 1475	

Another issue of Vaughan 1475 has the same titles but unaccompanied. These may be from another, undatable, session.

			?late 1927
Unknown location.			
	Happy Jubilee	Vaughan 1550	
	Happy Meeting	Vaughan 1550	
	Love Took It Away	Vaughan 1575	
	I'm Happy Now	Vaughan 1575	

These items have not been traced in Gennett files and may have been custom-recorded by another company, possibly Paramount.

The Vaughan Radio Quartette: poss.: Hillman Barnard, tv; Otis L. McCoy, tv; W.B. Walbert, bv; A.M. Pace, bsv; acc. Johnny Jernigan, p.

Chicago, IL

c. April 1928

| 20507-4 | Take The Name Of Jesus With You | Pm 3096, Bwy 8203 |
| 20509-2 | I Want To Go There | Pm 3096, Bwy 8203 |

Broadway 8203 as by **Wolcott Quartette**. Matrix 20508 is untraced.

Vaughan Happy Two: C.G. Wilson, tv; A.B. Sebren, bv; acc. A.B. Sebren, p.
Richmond, IN

Tuesday, May 22, 1928

13857	Don't Be Knocking	Vaughan 1600
13858-A	Ain't It A Shame	Vaughan 1625
13859	My Didn't It Reign	Vaughan 1625
13860	Come Listen To My Story	Vaughan 1600

Some issues of either or both of Vaughan 1600 and 1625 may have been as by **Sebren & Wilson (Happy Two)**.

Vaughan Quartet-1/Vaughan Quartette-2/The Vaughan Radio Quartette-3: poss.: Hillman Barnard, tv; Otis L. McCoy, tv; W.B. Walbert, bv; A.M. Pace, bsv; acc. unknown, f-4; unknown, p-5; unknown, g-6; unknown, marimba-7.
Chicago, IL

c. June 1928

20684-	He Will Rise And Shine -1	Vaughan 1650
20685-1	Bringing In The Sheaves -2, 4, 5, 6	Pm 3110, Bwy 8107
20686-1	Take The Name Of Jesus With You -3, 4, 7	Pm 3096, Bwy 8203
20687-2	I Want To Go There -3, 5, 6	Pm 3096, Bwy 8203
20688-	Look How This World Has Made A Change -1	Vaughan 1650
20689-2	Jesus Is Precious To Me -2, 5, 6	Pm 3110, Bwy 8107

Broadway 8107 as by **Victory Quartette**, 8203 as by **Wolcott Quartette**. It is not certain whether Broadway 8203 couples matrices 20507/20509 (see session of c. April 1928) or 20686/87; both versions may have been issued.

Vaughan Quartet: Hillman Barnard, tv; Otis L. McCoy, tv; W.B. Walbert, bv-1; G. Kiefer Vaughan, bv-2; A.M. Pace, bsv; acc. Johnny Jernigan, p.
Nashville, TN

Friday, October 5, 1928

47143-1	I Want To Go There, Don't You? -1	Vi V-40045
47144-2	When All Those Millions Sing -1	Vi V-40071, ZoSA 4238
47145-1	The Master Of The Storm -1	Vi 21756, MW M-8116
47146-1	Sunlight And Shadows -1	Vi V-40097
47147-1	My Troubles Will Be Over -1	Vi V-40071
47148-2	His Charming Love -2	Vi V-40045
47149-2	What A Morning That Will Be -1	Vi 21756
47150-2	In Steps Of Light -1	Vi V-40097

Revs: Zonophone 4238 by the McCravy Brothers; Montgomery Ward M-8116 popular.

Vaughan Happy Two: C.G. Wilson, tv; A.B. Sebren, bv; acc. M.B. Stroud, p.
Atlanta, GA

Saturday, October 20, 1928

47209-1,-2	Tell It To The World	Vi unissued
47210-1,-2,-3	Love Waves Of Glory	Vi unissued
47211-3	Chicken	Vi V-40001
47212-3	A Married Man In Trouble	Vi V-40001

Vaughan Quartet: no details.
Richmond, IN

Monday, July 1, 1929

| 15296 | It Will Make Heaven Brighter | Vaughan rejected |

Richmond, IN

Tuesday, July 2, 1929

| 15297 | It's Just Like Heaven | Vaughan rejected |

Sebren & Wilson (Happy Two): C.G. Wilson, tv; A.B. Sebren, bv; acc. unknown, p.
Richmond, IN

Wednesday, July 17, 1929

15363,-A,-B	Dis Train	Vaughan rejected
15364-A	Forever On Thy Hands	Vaughan 1675
15365,-A,-B	Keep On Steppin'	Vaughan rejected
15366-B	Don't Hinder Me	Vaughan 1700

Matrices 15363 to 15366 were logged as by **Vaughan Happy Two** but Vaughan 1700 at least was credited as shown.

Richmond, IN

Thursday, August 8, 1929

| 15416-A | Keep On Steppin' | Vaughan 1700 |
| 15417 | Dis Train | Vaughan 1675 |

Matrices 15416/17 were logged as by **Vaughan Happy Two** but Vaughan 1700 at least was credited as shown.

Acc. L.E. Heatwole, p.
Memphis, TN

Friday, September 20, 1929

55552-	Singing Glory Over There	BB B-6005
55553-2	I Am Looking For The Coming Of The Lord	Vi V-40164
55554-	Living For Christ Each Day	BB B-5541

55555-2	Put My Little Shoes Away	Vi V-40164
55557-	He Knows How	BB B-5541
55558-	I'll Ride On The Clouds With My Lord	BB B-6005

Victor V-40164 as by **Vaughan's Happy Two**. Matrix 55556 is by Blue Steele & His Orchestra (see JR).

Vaughan Quartet: Claude O. Sharpe, tv; G. Kiefer Vaughan, tv; L.E. Heatwole, bv; F.P. Heatwole, bsv; unacc.
Memphis, TN   Friday, September 20, 1929

55559-1	O Such Wondrous Love	Vi 23519
55560-2	Where Is God?	Vi V-40333

Rev. Victor 23519 by Frank Stamps & His All Star Quartet.

Acc. Ms. W.L. Bizzell, p; or unacc.-1.
Memphis, TN   Saturday, September 21, 1929

55561-2	I'll Never Be Lonesome In Heaven	Vi V-40157
55562-2	It's Just Like Heaven	Vi V-40202
55563-2	A Happy Meeting	Vi V-40289
55564-1	Just As Long As Eternity Rolls -1	Vi V-40333

Claude O. Sharpe, tv; G. Kiefer Vaughan, tv; F.P. Heatwole, bv-1; L.E. Heatwole, bv-2; Roy Collins, bsv; unacc.; or acc. L.E. Heatwole, p-3.
Memphis, TN   Saturday, September 21, 1929

55565-2	One At Last -1, 3	Vi V-40157
55566-2	Walking With My King -2	Vi V-40202, BB B-6039, MW M-4277

Montgomery Ward M-4277 as by **Vaughan's Texas Quartet**.

Vaughan's Texas Quartet: Lloyd Gilbert, tv; Eiland Scarborough, tv; Walter B. Seale, bv; Horley Lester, bsv; acc. Lee Myers, p.
Dallas, TX   Wednesday, October 9, 1929

56348-1	I Walk With Jesus	Vi V-40174
56349-1	The Wayfaring Pilgrim	Vi V-40231, MW M-4299
56350-1	We'll Reap What We Sow	Vi V-40257, BB B-6039
56351-2	Heaven All The Way For Me	Vi V-40231, MW M-4277, M-4299
56352-2	That Beautiful Land	Vi V-40257
56353-2	The King Needs Workers	Vi V-40174

Montgomery Ward M-4299 as by **Vaughan Quartet**.

Vaughan Quartet: two unknowns, tv; unknown, bv; unknown, bsv; acc. Mrs. Carl Goble, p.
Richmond, IN   Monday, November 4, 1929

15848	Naturalized For Heaven	Vaughan 1750
15849,-A	A Child At Mother's Knee	Vaughan rejected
15850	When The Holy Ghost Comes Down	Vaughan 1800
15851,-A	His Love Waves Are Rolling On	Vaughan rejected
15852-A	Jesus Is All I Need	Vaughan 1800
15853	Amazing Grace	Vaughan 1750

Hillman Barnard, tv; unknown, tv; unknown, bv; unknown, bsv; or **Hillman Barnard**, tv-1; acc. Mrs. Carl Goble, p.
Richmond, IN   Wednesday, December 4, 1929

15973	It Will Make Heaven Brighter	Vaughan 1725
15974-A	It's Just Like Heaven	Vaughan 1725
15975	My Record Will Be There -1	Vaughan 1775
15976-A	Forever On Thy Hands	Vaughan 1775

Two unknowns, tv; unknown, bv; unknown, bsv; acc. unknown, p.
Memphis, TN   Monday, May 19, 1930

59945-	My Heavenly Home Coming	Vi 23738
59946-2	O Happy Day	Vi 23769
59947-2	Naturalized For Heaven	Vi V-40289
59948-1,-2	My Loved Ones Are Waiting For Me	Vi unissued

Memphis, TN   Tuesday, May 20, 1930

59953-	I Am Happy Now	Vi 23597
59954-	A Beautiful Life	Vi 23597
59955-	When The Holy Ghost Comes Down	BB B-5258, Eld 2138, Sr S-3341
59956-2	I See A Gleam Of Glory	Vi 23769
59957-	It Will Make Heaven Brighter	Vi 23738
59958-	Jesus Leads To Victory	BB B-5258, Eld 2138, Sr S-3341
59959-	His Love Waves Are Rolling On	Vi V-40318
59960-2	When The Home Gates Swing On	Vi V-40318

Vaughan Happy Two: C.G. Wilson, tv; A.B. Sebren, bv; acc. unknown, p.
Richmond, IN   Tuesday, June 10, 1930

16753-B	Set Down	Vaughan 1825
16754	I Will Meet Mother Up There	Vaughan 1825
16755	Fifty Miles Of Elbow Room	Vaughan 1850
16756	But How Did De Goats Git In	Vaughan 1850

Some issues of either or both of Vaughan 1825 and 1850 may have been as by **Sebren & Wilson (Happy Two)**.

Vaughn Trio: three unknowns, v trio; unacc.; or acc. unknown, p-1.
   Richmond, IN   Saturday, March 26, 1932

18474-A	What Are They Doing In Heaven	Chapel 509
18475-A	The Country Where People Don't Die	Chapel 509
18476-A	My Loved Ones Are Waiting For Me	Chapel 510
18477	Death Is Only A Dream	Chapel 510
18478-A	Don't You Love Daddy Too -1	Ge Personal 20393
18479	Shake Hands With Mother Again -1	Ge Personal 20393

It is uncertain how closely associated this group is with the Vaughan Music Co.
Vaughan groups recorded after 1942.

CECIL VAUGHN

Cecil Vaughn, v; acc. own g.
   New York, NY   Wednesday, September 25, 1929

149047-1	Out In The Cold World And Far Away From Home	Co 15465-D
149048-2	The Village Blacksmith	Co 15465-D

   Richmond, IN   Friday, November 22, 1929

15931,-A	Dying Willie	Ge rejected
15932,-A	The Murder Of Jay Legg	Ge rejected
15933	The Banjo Tramp	Ge rejected
15935,-A	The Village Blacksmith	Ge rejected
15937,-A	Out In The Cold World Far Away From Home	Ge rejected

Matrices 15934, 15936 are Mexican.

CHARLEY VAUGHN

Pseudonym on Conqueror for Walter Coon.

CLIFFORD VAUGHN

Clifford Vaughn, v; acc. unknown.
   Atlanta, GA   Saturday, August 11, 1928

402130-	Blue Yodel	OK unissued

Clifford Vaughn is a member of the Three Stripped Gears.

VAUGHN TRIO

See Vaughan Quartet & Associated Groups.

VEL VETERAN

Pseudonym on labels of the Grey Gull/Radiex group for Arthur Fields, and possibly also for Vernon Dalhart.

EMIL VELAZCO

This pipe-organist is given sole artist credit on Australian Parlophone A2675 for sides originally issued on OKeh 45260 as by **Harry Smith**.

ALBERT VERNON

Pseudonym on Lucky Strike for Vernon Dalhart.

BILL VERNON

Pseudonym on Varsity for Vernon Dalhart.

FRANK VERNON

Pseudonym on labels in the Canadian Compo group for Frank Luther (see Carson Robison).

HERBERT VERNON

Pseudonym on English Regal for Vernon Dalhart.

VERNON & HARWELL

No details.
   Memphis, TN   Thursday, February 23, 1928

| 400314- | Drifting | OK unissued |
| 400315- | A Sinner Made Whole | OK unissued |

BILLY VEST

Billy Vest (The Strolling Yodler), v/y; acc. own g.
  Atlanta, GA   Wednesday, April 16, 1930

| 150239-2 | She'll Never Find Another Daddy Like Me | Co 15669-D |
| 150240-2 | I Loved You Better Than You Knew | Co 15669-D |

  New York, NY   Friday, September 19, 1930

| 150827-2 | Yodeling Hobo | Co 15602-D |
| 150828-3 | A Message From Home | Co 15602-D |

  New York, NY   Friday, April 17, 1931

151521-2	Billy's Blue Yodel	Co 15692-D
151522-2	She Died Like A Rose	Co 15692-D
151523-	The Club Held A Meeting	Co unissued
151524-	Little Girl's Plea	Co unissued
151525-	A Crown Of Soft Brown Hair	Co unissued
151526-	Oh! Sir I Was Only Flirting	Co unissued

Billy Vest, v; acc. Aubry Smith, f; Kyle Roop, g; own g.
  Richmond, IN   Wednesday, June 10, 1931

| 17813 | Weeping Willow Tree | Ge unissued trial recording |

Acc. own g.
  New York, NY   Tuesday, April 11, 1933

13224-1	Big City Jail	Ba 32762, Me M12691, Or 8231, Pe 12911, Ro 5231, Vo 5494, Cq 8235
13225-	When It's Honeysuckle Time	ARC unissued
13226-1	The Last Good-Bye	Cq 8236
13227-	Dark Eyes Plea	ARC unissued
13228-2	Frankie And Johnnie No. 2	Ba 32762, Me M12691, Or 8231, Pe 12911, Ro 5231, Cq 8235
13229-1	The Tramp's Last Ride	Vo 5494, Cq 8236

Vocalion 5494 as by **Jack Harper**.

Acc. Bob Vest, g; own g; or **Bob Vest With Billy Vest**-1, v duet; acc. own g duet.
  New York, NY   Monday, August 26, 1935

18007-1	There's Room In My Album For Your Picture -1	ARC 5-12-54, Cq 8574
18008-1	Dear Old Texas	ARC 5-12-54, Cq 8574
18009-	Cowboy Prisoner	ARC unissued
18010-	Electric Chair Blues	ARC unissued

BOB VEST

See Billy Vest.

THE VICTORY FOUR

Vocal quartet; acc. unknown.
  New Orleans, LA   Saturday, December 15, 1928

| 147642- | Don't Forget To Pray | Co unissued |
| 147643- | Look For Me I'll Be There | Co unissued |

VICTORY QUARTETTE

Pseudonym on Broadway for the Vaughan Quartette.

VIKING ACCORDION BAND

Items by this group on Champion and Decca are outside the scope of this work.

[THE] VILLAGE BOYS

Village Boys: Grady Hester, f; J.D. Standlee, esg; Anthony Scanlin, p; Dickie McBride, g/v-1; Floyd Tillman, g/v-2; Hezzie Bryant, sb.
  Houston, TX   Thursday, April 11, 1940

92088-A	I'll Come Back To You -1, 2	De 5845
92089-A	Nothing Matters To Me -1	De 5879
92090-A	Daisy May -2	De 5845

92091-A	Anything That's Part Of You -1	De 5834
92092-A	I'm Gonna Change All My Ways -2	De 5879
92093-A	Gee! But I Feel Blue -1	De 5857
92094-A	The Mountains Will See Her Face No More -2	De 5857
92095-A	Let's Make Believe We're Sweethearts -1	De 5834

The Village Boys: Dickie Jones, f-1/v-2; Buddy Ray, f-3; J.D. Standlee, esg; Mancel Tierney, p; Aubrey "Red" Greenhaw, g; Hezzie Bryant, sb; Edward V. "Babe" Fritsch, v-4/sp-5/wh-6.
Dallas, TX   Wednesday, April 9, 1941

063066-1	A Paul Jones Dance -1, 5, 6	BB B-8717
063067-1	I'm Doin' A Peach Of A Job (With A Little Peach Down In Ga.) -3, 4	BB B-8717
063068-1	Ooh! Mama What Have You Done? -3, 4	BB B-8758
063069-1	I'll Miss You When I'm Gone -2, 3	BB B-8781
063070-1	A Cradle, A Baby And You -1, 4	BB B-8781
063071-1	Heart Shy -3, 4	BB B-8734
063072-1	Boogie Woogie In The Village -1	BB B-8734
063073-1	Sun's Gonna Shine In My Backdoor Someday -1, 4	BB B-8758

The Village Boys: Dickie Jones, f-1; Buddy Ray, f-2; J.D. Standlee, esg; Mancel Tierney, p; Aubrey "Red" Greenhaw, g; Hezzie Bryant, sb; Edward V. "Babe" Fritsch, v-3; band v-4.
Dallas, TX   Friday, October 10, 1941

071154-1	Why? -1, 3	BB B-8886
071155-1	Old Joe Is At It Again -1, 3, 4	BB B-8918
071156-1	The Place For You Is Louisian' -1, 3, 4	BB B-8886
071157-1	Dixieland Girl	BB unissued
071158-1	Baby, I Ain't Satisfied -2, 3	BB B-8918
071159-1	My Dream Heaven	BB unissued

See also Dickie McBride.

VIOLINISTAS

Pseudonym on Mexican Bluebird B-3186 for Jack Pierce & the Oklahoma Cowboys.

VIRGINIA DANDIES

Odell Smith, f; Norman Woodlieff, g/solo v-1/hv-2; Walter Smith, lv-2.
New York, NY   c. late February 1931

1215-2	There's A Mother Old And Gray Who Needs Me Now -1	Cr 3103, Pm 3280, Htd 23025
1218-2	I Wonder If She Cares To See Me Now -1	Pm 3280
1220-1	There's A Beautiful City Called Heaven -2	Cr 3145, Htd 23026
1221-1	God's Getting Worried -2	Cr 3145, Htd 23026
1222-2	'Mid The Green Fields Of Virginia -2	Cr 3103, Pm 3305, Htd 23025
1223-1	I'll Meet Her When The Sun Goes Down	Htd 23027
1224-1,-2	The Cabin With The Roses -2	Pm 3305, Htd 23027

All issues of matrices 1215, 1218 as by **Jake Woodlieff**.
Matrix 1215 is titled *There's A Mother Old And Grey Who Needs Me Now* on Paramount 3280.
Intervening matrices are untraced. According to Woodlieff, other items recorded at this session include *Rosy Nell* (Woodlieff-Smith vocal duet), *Sweet Estelle, What Whiskey Will Do* (Woodlieff vocal solos), and *Shady Grove* (Smith vocal solo). Some or all of these may have been released on untraced Crown and/or Paramount issues. Original Crown issues of matrices 1218 and 1223/24 may also remain to be traced.

This lineup also recorded as the Carolina Buddies. Walter Smith and Norman Woodlieff also recorded in their own names, and Woodlieff with the Four Pickled Peppers and Charlie Poole.

VIRGINIA MALE QUARTET

Vocal quartet; acc. unknown, p.
Richmond, VA   Tuesday, October 15, 1929

403134-B	I Am Wandering Down Life's Shady Path	OK 45388
403135-A	Looking This Way	OK 45453
403136-A	Light Of Life	OK 45388
403137-A	No Night There	OK 45453

VIRGINIA MOUNTAIN BOOMERS

See Sweet Brothers.

VIRGINIA POSSUM TAMERS

Pseudonym on Champion and Montgomery Ward for The Red Fox Chasers. (On Champion 15484 the credit is misspelled **Virginia Possom Tamers**.)

VIRGINIA RAMBLERS

No details.
    Richmond, VA   Friday, October 18, 1929

403183-	Carper Hutchison	OK unissued
403184-	Kitty Wells	OK unissued
403185-	Maple Rag	OK unissued
403186-	Wreck Of Old 97	OK unissued

This artist credit was also used as a pseudonym on Timely Tunes and Aurora for the Floyd County Ramblers.

W

WILD BILL WADE

Wild Bill Wade, v/y; acc. prob. own g.
    Dallas, TX   Monday, June 27, 1929

| 402758-A | Weeping Daddy Blues | OK 45550 |
| 402759-A | Sweetheart | OK 45550 |

GEORGE WADE

George Wade & Francum Braswell, v duet; acc. Francum Braswell, h/g; George Wade, md.
    Johnson City, TN   Monday, October 21, 1929

| 149204-2 | Think A Little | Co 15515-D |
| 149205-2 | When We Go A Courtin' | Co 15515-D |

George Wade & The Caro-Ginians: George Wade, v; acc. unknown, f; unknown, esg-1; own md; three unknowns, g; unknown, v-2.
    Rock Hill, SC   Wednesday, September 28, 1938

027767-1	Down Home	MW M-7702
027768-1	Because You Were Here One Day	MW M-7702
027769-1	Broken-Hearted Cowboy -1	MW M-7659
027770-1	I'm Just A Hitch-Hiker On The Road To Love	MW M-7703
027771-1	Georgia Moon	MW M-7703
027772-1	Old Covered Wagon	MW M-7659
027773-1	Please Give Me Back My Dreams	MW M-7704
027774-1	He Turned Around And Went The Other Way -2	BB B-7904, MW M-7705
027775-1	Long And Bony	BB B-7904, MW M-7705
027776-1	Where The South Begins	MW M-7704

One of the guitarists may be absent on matrix 027769.

George Wade was also a member of the Three Tobacco Tags.

CLIFFORD [C.S.] WAGNER

Clifford Wagner, v; acc. unknown, h; unknown, g.
    Richmond, IN   Thursday, September 25, 1930

| 17082 | Leaving Your Home | Ge rejected |

C.S. Wagner, v; or **C.S. Wagner & T.A. Taylor**-1, v duet; or **T.A. Taylor**-2, v; acc. unknown, h-3; unknown, bj-4; unknown, g; unknown, u-5.
    Richmond, IN   Monday, November 2, 1931

18139	Leaving Your Home -3, 4, 5	Ge rejected
18140	The Factory Girl -1	Ge rejected
18141	Gambling On The Sabbath -2, 4	Ge unissued
18142	Lamp Post On Old Broadway -4, 5	Ge rejected
18143	Longing For You Sweetheart -1	Ge rejected

REV. CHARLES WAKEFIELD & FAMILY
REV. CHARLES WAKEFIELD & MISS MARY WAKEFIELD

Pseudonyms on Superior for Rev. Edward Boone.

JIMMY WAKELY

Jimmy Wakely & His Rough Riders: Jimmy Wakely, Johnny Bond, Dick Reinhart, v trio; acc. Carl Cotner, f-1; Frank Marvin, esg; Jimmy Wakely, g; Johnny Bond, g; Dick Reinhart, sb.
    Los Angeles, CA   Thursday, August 29, 1940

| DLA-2096-A | Too Late -1 | De 5909, DeAu X2069, DeSA FM5126, MeC 45410 |

DLA-2097-A	Maria Elena -1	De 5877, DeAu X1950
DLA-2098-A	Poor Little Rose -1	De 5909, DeAu X2069, MeC 45410
DLA-2099-A	I Wonder Where You Are Tonight	De 5918
DLA-2100-A	Will You Be True To Me -1	De 5918
DLA-2101-A	Cimarron (Roll On) -1	De 5877, DeAu X1950

A contract from Local 47, AFM cites a recording date of August 8.
Rev. Decca FM5126 by Roy Rogers.

Acc. Carl Cotner, f; Frank Marvin, esg; Jimmy Wakely, g; Johnny Bond, g; Dick Reinhart, sb.
Los Angeles, CA   Saturday, September 7, 1940

DLA-2132-A	The Old Ladies' Home	De 5880, DeAu X1959, MeC 45392
DLA-2133-A	The Day You Went Away	De 5899, DeAu X2060, DeSA FM5127, MeC 45402
DLA-2134-A	Cattle Call	De 5880, DeAu X1959, MeC 45392
DLA-2135-A	Rocky Mountain Lullaby	De 5899, DeAu X2060, DeSA FM5127, MeC 45402

Acc. two unknowns, f; prob. Frank Marvin, esg; Dick Reinhart, g; poss. Jimmy Wakely, g; poss. Johnny Bond, sb.
New York, NY   Wednesday, April 9, 1941

68961-A	Be Honest With Me	De 5942, Coral 64037
68962-A	Little Sweetheart (I Miss You)	De 5997

Jimmy Wakely, v; acc. unknown, f; unknown, f/pac; prob. Frank Marvin, esg; Dick Reinhart, g; poss. own g; poss. Johnny Bond, sb.
New York, NY   Wednesday, April 9, 1941

68963-A	There Ain't Gonna Be No Me (To Welcome You)	De 5973, MeC 45460
68964-A	Won't You Remember	De 5942

Jimmy Wakely, Johnny Bond, Dick Reinhart, v trio; acc. two unknowns, f; unknown, pac; prob. Frank Marvin, esg; Dick Reinhart, g; poss. Jimmy Wakely, g; poss. Johnny Bond, sb.
Los Angeles, CA   Tuesday, July 1, 1941

DLA-2491-A	Gone And Left Me Blues	De 5991, Coral 64037, MeC 45471
DLA-2492-A	There Ain't No Use In Crying	De 6055
DLA-2493-A	I'll Never Let You Go	De 5973, DeSA FM5140, MeC 45460
DLA-2494-A	Sailing On A Dream	De 6029

Rev. Decca FM5140 by Christine.

Acc. unknown, t; unknown, h-1; prob. Frank Marvin, esg; unknown, p-2; Dick Reinhart, g; poss. Jimmy Wakely, g; poss. Johnny Bond, sb.
Los Angeles, CA   Thursday, August 14, 1941

DLA-2635-A	Fort Worth Jail -1	De 6029
DLA-2636-A	After Tomorrow -2	De 5991, MeC 45471
DLA-2637-A	That Little Kid Sister Of Mine -2	De 5979
DLA-2638-A	When I Take My Vacation In Heaven	De 5979, Coral 64014

Jimmy Wakely, v; acc. unknown, t; unknown, pac-1/p-2; unknown, esg; poss. Dick Reinhart, g; poss. Johnny Bond, sb.
New York, NY   Monday, October 27, 1941

69867-A	Truck Driver's Coffee Stop -2	De 5995, MeC 45474
69868-A	Don't Bite The Hand That's Feeding You -1	De 5997

Jimmy Wakely, poss. Johnny Bond, poss. Dick Reinhart, v trio; acc. unknown, f; unknown, t; unknown, pac; unknown, esg; poss. Dick Reinhart, g; poss. Johnny Bond, sb.
New York, NY   Monday, October 27, 1941

69869-A	Be My Darlin'	De 6055
69870-A	Froggy Went A Courtin'	De 5995, MeC 45474

Jimmy Wakely & His Rough Riders: Jimmy Wakely, v; or Jimmy Wakely, Johnny Bond, unknown, v trio-1; acc. Spade Cooley, f; Carl Cotner, f; Don Linder, t; unknown, h-2; Frank Marvin, esg; Johnny Bond, g; Fred Whiting, sb.
Los Angeles, CA   Tuesday, June 23, 1942

L-3053-A	There's A Star Spangled Banner Waving Somewhere	De 6059
L-3054-A	Standing Outside Of Heaven -2	De 6059, Coral 64014
L-3055-A	Alone And Lonely	De 6072
L-3056-AA	It's Too Late To Say You're Sorry -1, 2	De 6072

Jimmy Wakely recorded after 1942.

GEORGE WALBURN & EMMETT HETHCOX

George Walburn–Emmett Hethcox-1/Geo. Walburn & Emmett Hethcox-2: George Walburn, f; Emmett Hethcox, g.
Atlanta, GA   c. July 1, 1925

9190-A	K.C. Railroad -1	OK 45004
9191-A	Lee County Blues -2	OK 45024

Revs: OKeh 45004 by The Bouchillon Trio, 45024 by J.D. Harris.

George Walburn & Emmett Hethcox: George Walburn, f; Emmett Hethcox, g.
Atlanta, GA   Tuesday, October 26, 1926

9837-A	Macon Georgia Bound	OK 45066
9838-A	Home Brew	OK 45066

George Walburn, f; unknown, f-1; Emmett Hethcox, g.
Atlanta, GA   Saturday, October 8, 1927

81720-B	Kansas City Railroad Blues -1	OK 45178
81721-B	Lee County Blues	OK unissued: *Cy 544 (LP)*
81722-B	Decatur Street Rag	OK 45305
81723-	Under The Double Eagle	OK unissued
81724-A	Wait For The Lights To Go Out -1	OK 45305
81725-B	Polecat Blues -1	OK 45178

Matrix 81721 is titled *Walburn Stomp* on County 544.

George Walburn's Footscorchers: George Walburn, f; unknown, bj; poss. Emmett Hethcox, g.
Atlanta, GA   Friday, October 30, 1931

151990-1	Halliawika March	Co 15721-D
151991-1	Dixie Flyer	Co 15721-D

CINDY WALKER

Cindy Walker, v; acc. Bruce Hudson, t; Del Porter, cl; Perry Botkin, g; unknown, sb; Lindley "Spike" Jones, d.
Los Angeles, CA   Friday, September 5, 1941

DLA-2730-A	He Knew All The Answers (To A Maiden's Prayer)	De 6022
DLA-2731-A	Waltz Me Around Again Willie	De 5992
DLA-2732-A	I Want Somebody	De 6022
DLA-2733-A	Don't Talk To Me About Men	De 5992

Acc. unknown, t; unknown, esg; unknown, p; unknown, g; unknown, sb.
New York, NY   Tuesday, March 10, 1942

70456-A	It Never Can Be	De 6082, MeC 45554
70457-A	Bye Lo Baby Buntin' (Daddy's Goin' Huntin')	De 6038
70458-A	It's All Your Fault	De 6802, MeC 45554
70459-A	Till The Longest Day I Live	De 6038
70460-A	Now Or Never	De 6057
70461-A	Why I Don't Trust The Men	De 6057

Cindy Walker recorded after 1942.

DAVE WALKER

Pseudonym on Superior for Ernest Branch.

LAWRENCE WALKER

See Walker Brothers.

TEX WALKER

This artist's real name is Thurman J.C. Walker.

Tex Walker, v; acc. unknown.
Chicago, IL   poss. Thursday, February 18, 1937

TI-47	Going Back To Texas	ARC unissued trial recording
TI-48	Back To The Texas Claims & Buckaroo	ARC unissued trial recording

Tex Walker & Sister: Tex Walker, Margie "Toni" Rothel, v duet; or **Tex Walker**-1, v; acc. unknown, f; Tex Walker, g.
New York, NY   Tuesday, March 23, 1937

20861-1	New London Texas School Disaster	ARC 7-05-66
20862-1	If I Could Only Hear My Mother Pray Again -1	ARC 7-05-66

Tex Walker recorded after 1942.

WILEY WALKER & GENE SULLIVAN

Gene Sullivan & Wiley Walker, v duet; or Wiley Walker, v-1; acc. Wiley Walker, f; Gene Sullivan, g.
prob. Saginaw, TX   c. early September 1939

25289-1	All Over Nothing At All -1	Vo/OK 05108
25290-1	Little Rubber Dolly	Vo/OK 05108

Wiley Walker & Gene Sullivan, v duet; or Wiley Walker, v-1; acc. Wiley Walker, f; Gene Sullivan, g; Darrell Kirkpatrick, sb.

Saginaw, TX   Friday, April 19, 1940

DAL-993-2	Don't Be Jealous Of My Yesterdays	OK 06067, Cq 9779
DAL-994-2	Somebody Stole My Little Darlin'	Vo/OK 05524
DAL-995-2	I'm Tired Of Mountain Women	OK 05639
DAL-996-2	Wednesday Night Waltz	OK 05711
DAL-997-2	Texas Duster	Vo/OK 05574
DAL-998-2	And He Looks So Peaceful Now	OK 05639
DAL-999-2	It's All Over Now (I Won't Worry)	Vo/OK 05524
DAL-1000-2	Lola Lee	OK 05711
DAL-1001-2	You Don't Love Me Anymore (Little Darling)	OK 06067, Cq 9779
DAL-1002-1	South Plains Blues -1	Vo/OK 05574

Wiley Walker, Gene Sullivan, v duet; acc. Wiley Walker, f; poss. Foy Willingham, esg-1; Sheldon Bennett, eg-2; Gene Sullivan, g.

Fort Worth, TX   Sunday, March 9, 1941

DAL-1263-1	I Might Have Known -1	OK 6726, Co 37403, 20130
DAL-1264-1	Live And Let Live -1	OK 06374, Co 37665, 20264
DAL-1265-1	When My Blue Moon Turns To Gold Again -1	OK 06374, Co 37665, 20264
DAL-1266-1,-2	Don't Make Me Laugh – I'm Mad -2	OK unissued
DAL-1267-1	There's Always Somebody Else -1	OK 06218
DAL-1268-1,-2	You Married For Money -1	OK unissued
DAL-1269-1,-2	It's Only A Matter Of Time -2	OK unissued
DAL-1270-1	You've Got To Pay The Fiddler -2	OK 06218
DAL-1271-1	So Lonely -1	OK 06600, Co 37419, 20146
DAL-1272-2	A Tiny Baby Bonnet -2	Co 20465
DAL-1273-1	I Want To Live And Love -2	OK 6726, Co 37403, 20130
DAL-1274-1	I Just Don't Want To Be Happy -2	OK 06600, Co 37419, 20146

Columbia 37665, 20264, 20465 as by **Wiley (Walker) & Gene (Sullivan)**.
Rev. Columbia 20465 by Wiley Walker & Gene Sullivan (postwar).
Wiley Walker & Gene Sullivan recorded after 1942.

WALKER BROTHERS

Prob.: Lawrence Walker, f-1/ac-2; unknown, f; unknown, g; unknown (poss. Lawrence Walker), v.

Dallas, TX   Wednesday, October 30, 1929

| DAL-545- | La Breakdown La Louisianne -1 | Br 381, 80084 |
| DAL-546- | La Vie Malheureuse -2 | Br 381, 80084 |

Unknown, f; Lawrence Walker, ac/v-1; two unknowns, g.

New Orleans, LA   Friday, January 18, 1935

87610-1	La Valse Des Pins -1	BB B-2195
87611-1	Jamais Marriez -1	BB B-2195
87612-1	La Valse De Louisiane	BB B-2198
87613-1	Pourquois Vous Etes Si Cannai -1	BB B-2198
87614-1	Alberta -1	BB B-2199, MW M-4882
87615-1	What's The Matter Now? -1	BB B-2199, MW M-4882

Bluebird B-2199, Montgomery Ward M-4882 as by **Lawrence Walker**.
This artist credit was also used on Broadway as a pseudonym for John McGhee & Frank Welling.

WALKER'S CORBIN RAMBLERS

John V. Walker, f-1; Larry Hensley, md/v-2; Mack Taylor, g/v-3; Albert Walker, poss. tg/v-4.

New York, NY   Tuesday, January 23, 1934

14669-1	Stone Mountain Toddle	Vo 02790
14670-1	E Rag	Vo 02790
14671-1	My Baby Keeps Stealin' Sugar On Me -3, 4	Vo 02771
14672-1	Nobody's Business -1	Vo 02648
14673-1	I Had A Dream -2, 3, 4	Vo unissued
14674-1	The Dying Tramp -3, 4	Vo 02678, Pan 25635
14675-	Five Foot Two	Vo unissued

New York, NY   Wednesday, January 24, 1934

14673-2	I Had A Dream -2, 3, 4	Vo 02719
14685-1	I Want A Buddy, Not A Sweetheart -2, 3, 4	Vo 02719, Pan 25635
14686-1	Ned Went A' Fishin' -1	Vo 02667
14687-2	Green Valley Waltz -1	Vo 02648
14688-1	Darktown Strutters Ball -1, 3, 4	Vo 02771

Hensley, Taylor & Walker: Mack Taylor, Larry Hensley, Albert Walker, v trio; acc. Mack Taylor, g.
New York, NY   Thursday, January 25, 1934
    14693-1   It's Hard To Make Gertie   Vo 02639

Larry Hensley, v; acc. own g.
New York, NY   Thursday, January 25, 1934
    14694-2   Match Box Blues   Vo 02678

Walker's Corbin Ramblers: Larry Hensley, md/v; Mack Taylor, g/v; Albert Walker, poss. tg/v.
New York, NY   Thursday, January 25, 1934
    14695-   When You Wore A Tulip   Vo unissued

Hensley & Taylor: Larry Hensley, md; Mack Taylor, g.
New York, NY   Thursday, January 25, 1934
    14696-1   Ruffles and Bustles   Vo 02667
    14697-   Wallin's Creek Blues   Vo unissued
    14698-1   Mandolin King Rag   Vo 02640
    14699-1   Scottdale Stomp   Vo 02640

Hensley, Taylor & Walker: Larry Hensley, Mack Taylor, Albert Walker, v trio; acc. Larry Hensley, md; Mack Taylor, g.
New York, NY   Friday, January 26, 1934
    14702-   Curse Of An Aching Heart   Vo unissued

Taylor & Walker: Mack Taylor, Albert Walker, v duet; acc. Larry Hensley, md; Mack Taylor, g.
New York, NY   Friday, January 26, 1934
    14703-1   Bad Boy   Vo 02639
    14704-   Leave Me With A Smile   Vo unissued

FRANCIS WALLACE

Pseudonym on Gennett for Frank Marvin.

FRANK[IE] WALLACE [& HIS GUITAR]

Pseudonym on various labels for Frank Marvin.

FRED WALLACE

Pseudonym on Canadian Sterling for Frank Marvin.

JERRY WALLACE

Pseudonym on Superior for Pie Plant Pete.

RUTH & WANDA WALLACE

Pseudonym on Challenge for Ruth Donaldson & Helen Jepsen.

"DOCK" [or DOC] WALSH

"Dock" Walsh, v; acc. own bj.
Atlanta, GA   Saturday, October 3, 1925
    141089-1   The East Bound Train   Co 15047-D
    141096-1   The Bull Dog Down In Sunny Tennessee   Co 15057-D
    141097-2   Educated Man   Co 15057-D
    141098-1   I'm Free At Last   Co 15047-D

Intervening matrices are by other artists, recorded in New York, NY.

"Dock" Walsh, v/sp-1; acc. own bj.
Atlanta, GA   Saturday, April 17, 1926
    142028-2   Travelling Man   Co 15105-D
    142029-2   Knocking On The Hen House Door   Co 15075-D, Ve 2486-V, Cl 5426-C
    142030-   Lay Down Baby   Co unissued
    142031-1   In The Pines   Co 15094-D
    142032-2   We Courted In The Rain -1   Co 15075-D, Ve 2486-V, Cl 5426-C
    142033-1   Going Back To Jericho   Co 15094-D

Rev. Columbia 15105-D by Gid Tanner & Faith Norris.

Doc Walsh, v; acc. own bj.
Memphis, TN   Wednesday, September 25, 1929
    55585-1,-2   As I Wandered Over The Hillside   Vi unissued
    55586-1,-2   Aunt Jemimah   Vi unissued
    55587-1   Laura Lou   Vi V-40325
    55588-1   A Precious Sweetheart From Me Is Gone   Vi V-40237

| 55589-2 | Bathe In That Beautiful Pool | Vi V-40237 |
| 55590-2 | We're Just Plain Folks | Vi V-40325 |

Walsh plays slide banjo on matrices 55587 to 55589.

"Dock" Walsh was a member of the Carolina Tar Heels and Pine Mountain Boys. He recorded after 1942.

WALTER FAMILY

Draper Walter, f; Mary Walter, p; Ray Agee, bj-1; Charlie Estes, g; Wilburn Burdette, wb; Charlie Burdette, j.
Richmond, IN   Wednesday, March 29, 1933

19098	Tennessee Wagner	Ch S-16595
19099	Too Young To Get Married -1	Ch S-16595
19100	Flying Cloud Waltz -1	Ch S-16622
19101	Patty On The Turn Pike -1	Ch S-16643
19102	Granny, Will Your Dog Bite -1	Ch S-16643
19103	Walter Family Waltz	Ch S-16622
19104	That's My Rabbit – My Dog Caught It -1	Ch S-16653
19105	Shaker Ben -1	Ch S-16653

The washboard and jug may be absent on matrices 19100, 19103.

JACK WALTERS

Pseudonym on Broadway for Frank Luther (see Carson Robison).

ROBERT WALTON & MCWINDERS

Robert Walton, v; acc. Oddie McWinders, bj; own g.
Memphis, TN   Monday, September 23, 1929

55567-1,-2	Grouch Blues	Vi unissued
55568-1,-2	The Traveling Man	Vi unissued
55569-1,-2	Si's Mule	Vi unissued
55570-1,-2	Six O'Clock Blues	Vi unissued

There may be no vocal on matrix 55570.

THE WANDERERS

Alfredo "Fred" Casares, f/v-1; Holly Horton, cl/v-2; Jack Norwood, p; Marvin Montgomery, tbj; Dick Reinhart, g/v-3; Bert Dodson, sb/v-4.
San Antonio, TX   Monday, January 28, 1935

87728-1	Wanderer's Stomp	BB B-5869, ViJ Jr-28
87729-1	Tiger Rag -1, 3, 4	BB B-5887, HMV JF26, ViJ Jr-26
87730-1	Foot Warmer	BB B-5994
87731-1	No One To Say Goodbye -3	BB B-5887
87732-1	Sweet Uncle Zeke	BB unissued
87733-1	A Good Man Is Hard To Find -4	BB B-5834
87734-1	I Ain't Got Nobody -1, 3, 4	BB B-5869, ViJ Jr-28
87735-1	Nealski	BB B-5994
87736-1	Thousand Miles -2 (lead), 3, 4	BB B-5921, MW M-4559
87737-1	It's You I Adore -4	BB B-5834

Revs: Bluebird B-5921, Montgomery Ward M-4559 by Ray Nichols & His Four Towers Orchestra (popular); HMV JF26, Victor Jr-26 by KXYZ Novelty Band (see JR).

This artist credit was also used as a pseudonym on Australian Regal-Zonophone for (The) Three Tobacco Tags.

ENOS WANNER

Pseudonym on Champion, Superior, and Montgomery Ward for W.C. Childers.

WANNER & JENKINS

Pseudonym on Columbia and Australian Regal for W.C. Childers.

WANNER & WHITE

Pseudonym on Champion, Superior, and Montgomery Ward for W.C. Childers & Clyde G. White.

A.E. WARD & HIS PLOW BOYS

Albert E. Ward, v; acc. own f; Gene Morton, p; Wizener Ward, md or g; Bill Sawyers, g.
Atlanta, GA   Sunday, October 25, 1931

151924-1	The Old Dinner Pail	Co 15734-D
151925-1	Going To Leave Old Arkansas	Co 15734-D
151926-	Down In Texas	Co unissued
151927-	The Blues In The Worsest Way	Co unissued

CROCKETT WARD & HIS BOYS

Crockett Ward, f; Vernon Ward, ah; Sampson Ward, bj; Fields Ward, g/v.
Winston-Salem, NC   Monday, September 26, 1927

81615-	Sad And Lonely	OK unissued
81616-A	Sugar Hill	OK 45179
81617-A	Deadheads And Suckers	OK 45179
81618-B	Love's Affections	OK 45304
81619-B	Ain't That Trouble In Mind?	OK 45304
81620-	Train On The Island	OK unissued

FIELDS WARD

Fields Ward, v; or **Ward & Winfield**-1: Fields Ward, "Justin Winfield" (Ernest V. Stoneman), v duet; acc. **Grayson County Railsplitters**: Eck Dunford, f; Ernest V. Stoneman, h/ah; Sampson Ward, bj; Fields Ward, g; or **Grayson County Railsplitters**-2: Fields Ward, Ernest V. Stoneman, Eck Dunford, v trio; with same acc.

Richmond, IN   Tuesday, March 5, 1929

14861	Way Down In North Carolina	Ge rejected: *Hi BC-2433-1, HLP8001, Cy 534* (LPs)
14862-A	Ain't That Trouble In Mind	Ge rejected: *Hi BC-2433-1, HLP8001* (LPs); *Old Hat CD-1004* (CD)
14863	You Must Be A Lover Of The Lord -2	Ge rejected: *Hi BC-2433-1, HLP8001* (LPs)
14864	Watch And Pray -2	Ge rejected: *Hi BC-2433-1, HLP8001, Cy 534* (LPs)
14865	Good Bye Little Bonnie -1	Ge rejected: *Hi BC-2433-1, HLP8001* (LPs)
14866	Alas My Darling -1	Ge rejected
14867	My Old Sweetheart -1	Ge rejected
14868	The Place Where Ella Sleeps -1	Ge rejected
14869	In Those Cruel Slavery Days -1	Ge rejected: *Hi BC-2433-1, HLP8001* (LPs)
14870	The Sweetest Way Home	Ge rejected: *Hi BC-2433-1, HLP8001* (LPs)

Richmond, IN   Thursday, March 7, 1929

14876	My Only Sweetheart -2	Ge rejected: *Hi BC-2433-1, HLP8001, Cy 534* (LPs)
14877	Tie Up Those Old Broken Cords -1	Ge rejected: *Hi BC-2433-1, HLP8001* (LPs)
14878	The Birds Are Returning -1	Ge rejected: *Hi BC-2433-1, HLP8001* (LPs)
14879	No One Loves You As I Do	Ge rejected: *Hi BC-2433-1, HLP8001* (LPs)
14880	I Don't Know Why I Love Her	Ge rejected

Matrices 14876/77 were logged as by **Ward & Winfield Acc. by Grayson County Railsplitters**.

Fields Ward also recorded with the Buck Mt. Band and Crockett Ward & His Boys, for the Library of Congress, and after 1942.

TOM WARD
TOMMY WARD

Pseudonyms on Superior for Ted Lunsford.

WADE WARD

Wade Ward, v/v eff-1; acc. own bj.
Asheville, NC   Tuesday, September 1, 1925

9316-	Lookout Mountain -1	OK unissued
9317-	A Married Woman's Blues	OK unissued
9318-	Chilly Wind	OK unissued
9319-	Brother Ephram	OK unissued

Matrix 9316 was logged as *Fox Chase* but a test-pressing is titled as shown.

Wade Ward recorded after 1942.

LOUIS WARFIELD

Pseudonym on Paramount and Broadway for Frank Marvin.

PAUL WARMACK & HIS GULLY JUMPERS

Charles Arrington, f; Paul Warmack, md/v; Roy Hardison, bj; Bert Hutcherson, g.
Nashville, TN   Friday, September 28, 1928

47102-1,-2	Tennessee Waltz	Vi unissued

Nashville, TN   Monday, October 1, 1928

47102-4	Tennessee Waltz	Vi V-40067
47103-1,-2,-3	Put My Little Shoes Away	Vi unissued
47104-1,-2	I'm A Little Dutchman	Vi unissued: *RCA CPL2-9507* (LP)
47105-1	The Little Red Caboose Behind The Train	Vi V-40067

It is not known which take of matrix 47104 is used on RCA CPL2-9507.

Charles Arrington, f; Paul Warmack, md; Roy Hardison, bj; Bert Hutcherson, g.
Nashville, TN   Wednesday, October 3, 1928

47128-3	Robertson County	Vi V-40009
47129-2	Stone Rag	Vi V-40009
47130-1,-2	Hell Broke Loose In Georgia	Vi unissued
47131-1,-2	New Five Cents	Vi unissued

HANK WARNER

Hank Warner, v; acc. unknown, f; poss. Bob Miller, p; unknown, g.
New York, NY   Friday, September 13, 1935

18081-1	The Death Of Huey P. Long	ARC 5-11-61, Cq 8544
18082-2	Precious Wife	ARC 5-11-61, Cq 8544

YODELIN' JIMMY WARNER

Pseudonym on Champion for Frank Marvin.

WASHBOARD NOVELTY QUARTETTE

Pseudonym on English Rex for the Maple City Four.

WASHBOARD WONDERS

See Dick Hartman.

VERNON WATERS (THE OZARK RAMBLER)

Vernon Waters, v; acc. prob. unknown, g.
Kansas City, MO   Sunday, November 7, 1929

KC-608	Billy The Kid	Br/Vo rejected
KC-609	Two Gun Joe	Br/Vo rejected

W.L. "RUSTIC" WATERS

W.L. "Rustic" Waters, v; acc. unknown.
New York, NY   between August 10 and 13, 1931

151718-	[unknown title]	Co unissued
151719-	[unknown title]	Co unissued
151720-	Leaning Charming Betsy	Co unissued
151721-	Dixie Flyer	Co unissued
151722-	Habersham Fox Hunt	Co unissued

Acc. prob. own h/k/unknown stringed instrument/poss. another instrument.
New York, NY   Monday, August 24, 1931

151743-	The Nigger Washerwoman	Co unissued
151744-	Step High Lady	Co unissued
151745-	Sleep On Darling Sleep On	Co unissued
151746-2	Lonely As I Can Be	Co 15705-D
151747-2	Sweet Nora Shannon	Co 15705-D

On aural evidence, Waters appears to be a one-man-band. His stringed instrument has some characteristics of a banjo but may be an adapted or specially made instrument, and he may additionally play some kind of (possibly foot-operated) stringed instrument in the bass range.

WATKINS BAND

Unknown, md; unknown, bj; two unknowns, g; unknown, v-1/v eff-2/sp-3/calls-3.
Atlanta, GA   Friday, February 24, 1928

41960-2	Bob Murphy -3	Vi 21405
41961-2	Gideon -3	Vi 21405
41962-1	Little Girl, You Know I Love You -1	Vi V-40041
41963-1	Tom's Rag -2	Vi V-40041

Victor V-40041 as by **Watkins' Band**.
Tom Watkins and Charlie Watkins are members of this band, but it is not known what instruments they played.

DR. CLAUDE WATSON & L.W. McCREIGTON [or McCREIGHT]

Dr. Claude Watson & L.W. McCreigton: one of them, cl; the other, bj.
Dallas, TX   c. October 20, 1925

9383-A	Love My Mamma	OK 45020
9384-A	Chicken Reel	OK 45020

Dr. Claud E. Watson & L.W. McCreight: one of them, bj; the other, bj-u.
   Dallas, TX   c. October 20, 1925
     9386-A   Ballin' The Jack And Nigger Blues   OK 45034

Matrix 9385 is untraced. Rev. OKeh 45034 by McMichen's Home Town Band.

HARVEY WATSON

Pseudonym on Champion, Silvertone, Supertone, and Challenge for Holland Puckett.

LOUIS WATSON

Pseudonym on Supertone for Frank Jenkins (see Da Costa Woltz's Southern Broadcasters).

TOM WATSON

Pseudonym on Silvertone for Riley Puckett or (3263) Vernon Dalhart.

WILMER WATTS

Watts & Wilson: Wilmer Watts, Frank Wilson, v duet; acc. Wilmer Watts, bj; Frank Wilson, g.
   Chicago, IL   January/February 1927
     4168-   The Sporting Cowboy   Pm unissued

Unidentified, v/v duet-1; acc. prob.: Frank Wilson, sg; Wilmer Watts, bj; Charles Freshour, g.
   Chicago, IL   c. April 1927
     4428-3   When The Roses Bloom Again -1   Pm 3006, Bwy 8112
     4431-2   The Empty Cradle -1   Pm 3007, Bwy 8113
     4432-2   Walk Right In Belmont   Pm 3019
     4433-2   The Night Express   Pm 3007, Bwy 8113
     4435-2   The Sporting Cowboy   Pm 3006, Bwy 8112
     4438-   Why Did You Leave Me Poor Bessie   Pm unissued
     4439-1   Chain Gang Special   Pm 3019

Broadway 8112, 8113 as by **Weaver & Wiggins**.
Intervening matrices are untraced but at least some are probably by this group.

Wilmer Watts & The Lonely Eagles: unidentified, v/v duet-1; acc. poss. Palmer Rhyne, sg-2; Wilmer Watts, bj-3; poss. Charles Freshour, g.
   New York, NY   c. October 1929
     GEX-2455   Knocking Down Casey Jones -1, 3   Pm 3210, Bwy 8248
     GEX-2456   Been On The Job Too Long -3   Pm 3210, Bwy 8248
     GEX-2457-A   Charles Guitaw [sic] -1, 3   Pm 3232
     GEX-2458-A   Working For My Sally -3   Pm 3232
     GEX-2459-A   Fightin' In The War With Spain -1, 3   Pm 3254
     GEX-2460-A   Cotton Mill Blues -3   Pm 3254
     GEX-2461-A   She's A Hard Boiled Rose -   Pm 3247, Bwy 8264
     GEX-2462-A   The Fate Of Rhoda Sweetin -   Pm 3247, Bwy 8264
     GEX-2463   Sleepy Desert -1, 2   Pm 3282
     GEX-2464   When The Snow Flakes Fall Again -2   Pm 3282
     GEX-2465   Take This Little Bunch Of Roses -1, 2   Pm 3299
     GEX-2466   Bonnie Bess -1, 2, 3   Pm 3299
     GEX-2467   Ginger Blues   Pm unissued
     GEX-2468   A Soldier Of Honor   Pm unissued
     GEX-2469   Say Darling Won't You Love Me -1, 2, 3   Pm 3242, 3271, Bwy 8289

Matrix GEX-2462 as by **Charles Freshour & The Lonely Eagles**.
The allocation of instruments is uncertain: Rhyne may play guitar and Freshour steel guitar.

Unidentified, v; acc. Wilmer Watts, bj.
   New York, NY   c. October 1929
     GEX-2470-A   Banjo Sam   Pm 3242, 3271, Bwy 8289

WATTS & WILSON

See Wilmer Watts.

"WEARY" WILLIE

Pseudonym on Pathé, Perfect, Conqueror, and various Australian labels for Frank Luther (see Carson Robison), or on Supertone for Jack Golding. The credit sometimes appears as **Weary Willie**.

J.D. WEAVER

This artist's full name is John D. Weaver.

J.D. Weaver, f solo/sp.

Asheville, NC   prob. August 29 or 31, 1925
- 9312-A   Arkansas Traveler   OK 45016
- 9313-A   Hog Drivers   OK 45016

J.D. Weaver also recorded cylinders for Robert W. Gordon in December 1925.

RAYMOND WEAVER & LES APPLEGATE

Raymond Weaver, Les Applegate, v duet; acc. Dick Carmene, p.
Richmond, IN   Tuesday, November 12, 1929
- 15874   [unknown title]   Ge unissued
- 15878,-A   Down Where The Watermelons Grow   Ge rejected

Matrices 15875/76 are unrelated; matrix 15877 is by Jenkins Carmen.

WEAVER & WIGGINS

Pseudonym on Broadway for Watts & Wilson (see Wilmer Watts).

WEAVER BROTHERS

Vance Weaver, Wiley Weaver, v duet; or Wiley Weaver, v-1; acc. Lonnie Austin, f; Vance Weaver, bj-2; Wiley Weaver, g-3; Roy Harvey, g/v-4.
Johnson City, TN   Tuesday, October 22, 1929
- 149236-1   You Came Back To Me -1, 2   Co 15487-D
- 149237-2   Prison Sorrows -3, 4   Co 15487-D

Weaver Brothers String Band: poss.: Lonnie Austin, f; Vance Weaver, bj; Wiley Weaver, g; Roy Harvey, g.
Johnson City, TN   Tuesday, October 22, 1929
- 149238-   Raleigh County Rag   Co unissued
- 149239-   Homesick Boy   Co unissued

JACK WEBB THE 101 RANCH COWBOY

Jack Webb, v; acc. own g.
New York, NY   Tuesday, May 27, 1930
- 62246-1   The Night Guard   Vi V-40285
- 62247-1   The Roving Cowboy   Vi V-40285

DAN WEBER

Pseudonym on Superior for J.P. Ryan.

SAM WEBER

Pseudonym on Superior for Earl Wright & the Arkansas Corndodgers (see George Edgin).

WEBER & BROOKS

Pseudonym on Superior for the Hoosier Hawaiians.

WEE WEE THREE

See The Hilltoppers.

WEEMS STRING BAND

Dick Weems, f; Frank Weems, f; Alvin Conder, bj/v; Jesse Weems, vc.
Memphis, TN   Friday, December 9, 1927
- 145355-2   Davy   Co 15300-D
- 145536-2   Greenback Dollar   Co 15300-D

Alvin Conder also recorded with W.A. Lindsay.

FRANK WELLING [& JOHN McGHEE]
MR. & MRS. FRANK WELLING [& JOHN McGHEE]
WELLING & McGHEE [TRIO]
WELLING & SCHANNEN
WELLING & SHANNON
WELLING–McGHEE–TETER
THE WELLING TRIO
WELLINGS & McGHEE [TRIO]

See John McGhee & Frank Welling.

LEE WELLS & HIS JASPER ALABAMA SACRED HARP SINGERS

Vocal group; acc. (if any) unknown.
New York, NY   Wednesday, April 2, 1930

9549-	Roll Jordan Roll	ARC rejected	
9550-	Jackson	ARC rejected	
9551-	New Hope	ARC unissued	

Acc. unknown, p-1.
New York, NY   Thursday, April 3, 1930

9552-	We'll Soon Be There	ARC rejected	
9553-	Morning Sun	ARC rejected	
9554-	Worlds Unknown	ARC unissued	
9555-	The Morning Trumpet	ARC unissued	
9556-	Sweet Morning	ARC rejected	
(1)9557-2	North Port	Je 20011, Or 8011, Ro 5011	
(1)9558-1,-2	The Christian's Flight	Je 20011, Or 8011, Pe 151, Ro 5011	
9565-1	Religion Is A Fortune	Pe 151	
9566-	All Is Well	ARC unissued	
9567-	Ninety Fifth -1	ARC unissued	
9568-	Ortonville -1	ARC unissued	
9569-	Parting Hands	ARC unissued	

Matrices 9559/60, 9564 are popular; matrix 9561 is by Carson Robison & Frank Luther; matrices 9562/63 are by Frank Marvin.

New York, NY   Friday, April 4, 1930

9573-	Passing Away	ARC unissued	
9574-	Victoria	ARC unissued	
9575-	Anthem On The Savior	ARC unissued	
9576-	Reverential Anthem	ARC unissued	
9577-	Rocky Road	ARC unissued	

WELLS BROTHERS STRING BAND

Unknown, f-1; unknown, p; unknown, bj-2; unknown, g; unknown, 2nd g-3; unknown, v duet.
Charlotte, NC   Friday, January 28, 1938

018797-1	Snow White Stone -1, 2, 3	BB B-7588	
018798-1	Faded Picture -1, 2, 3	BB B-7588	
018799-1	Blue Tail Fly -1, 2, 3	BB unissued	
018800-1	Old Fashioned Man	BB unissued	
018801-1	Montana Anna -3	BB unissued	
018802-1	Away Beyond The Blue -1, 2, 3	BB unissued	

WENATCHEE MOUNTAINEERS

See Elton Britt.

JOE WERNER

Joe Werner recorded with several cajun groups in 1937-1938. The sessions listed below include all those recordings logged or issued under his name, or part of it.

Joe Werner & The Ramblers: Joe Werner, v; acc. Moise Sonnier, f; own h-1/g/wh-2; Roy Romero, sg; Leroy "Happy Fats" LeBlanc, g; unidentified, v-3.
New Orleans, LA   Friday, September 10, 1937

014020-1	The Lonesome Wanderer -2	BB B-7210, MW M-7342	
014021-1	The Answer To "Weeping Willow" -1, 3	BB B-7210, MW M-7342	

Louisiana Rounders: Wayne Perry, f; Joe Werner, h-1/g/v-2/wh-3; Julius "Papa Cairo" Lamperez, g/v-4; unknown, sb or d; Mrs. Joe Werner, v-5; unidentified, v duet-6.
Dallas, TX   Wednesday, December 15, 1937

63071-A	Ayou, Ayou, Mon Petite Chien Pour Edete (Where, Oh Where Has My Little Dog Gone) -1, 2, 3	De 17040	
63072-A	Je Vue Ta Figure Dans La Lune (I Saw Your Face In The Moon) -1, 5	De 17039	
63073-A	Quatre Ou Cinq Fois (Four Or Five Times) -2, 6	De 17041	
63074-A	Bon Whiskey -1, 5	De 17039	
63075-	Le Vieux Arbre De Pin -	De 17046	
63076-A	La Valse A Karo -4, 6	De 17041	
63077-A	Alons Kooche Kooche -4	De 17040	
63078-	Vingt Et Un Ans -	De 17046	

Wayne Perry, f; Joe Werner, h-1/g/v/wh-2.
Dallas, TX   Wednesday, December 15, 1937

63079-A	Wishing -1, 2	De 5495	
63080-A	Answer To Wondering -2	De 5483	

| 63081-A | Valley Rose -2 | De 5495 |
| 63082-A | Me And My Pal From New Orleans -1 | De 5483 |

Matrices 63071 to 63082 were logged as by **Joe Werner & His Wanderers** but issued as shown.

Joe Werner & Ramblers: Joe Werner, v; acc. prob. Oran "Doc" Guidry, f; own h-1/g/wh-2; prob. Leroy "Happy Fats" LeBlanc, g.

New Orleans, LA   Friday, April 1, 1938

022000-1	Just Thinking -2	BB B-7539, RZAu G23662
022001-1	Memory Of Mother -1	BB B-7690
022002-1	Running Around -1	BB B-7539
022003-1	She's A Leatherneck Gal -1	BB B-7639
022004-1	Under The Spell Of Your Love -2	BB B-7575
022005-1	Tommy Cat Blues	BB B-7575
022006-1	Poor Boy -2	BB B-7690
022007-1	She's My Flapper And My Baby -1	BB B-7639

Bluebird B-7539, Regal-Zonophone G23662 as by **Joe Werner & The Ramblers**.
Rev. Regal-Zonophone G23662 by The Old Timers Orchestra (popular).

Acc. unknown, f; own h-1/g/wh-2; unknown, g; unknown, v-3.

New Orleans, LA   Saturday, October 22, 1938

027699-1	She's My Sweetheart Of The Prairie	BB B-2076
027840-1	My Girl Polly -3	BB B-7923
027841-1	Under The Old China Tree -1	BB B-2077
027842-1	My Lover In Dreams -2	BB B-7923
027843-1	Crap Shooters Hop	BB B-2075
027844-1	'Rang 'Tang Bully -1	BB B-2075, MW M-7676
027845-1	Dreaming -1	BB B-2077
027846-1	Story Of The Dying Cowboy -2	BB B-2076, MW M-7676

Joe's Acadians: unknown, f; Joe Werner, h-1/g/v-2; unknown, g; unknown, sp-3.

New Orleans, LA   Saturday, October 22, 1938

027888-1	Les Poules Paus Pas (Chickens Don't Lay) -1, 2	BB B-2064
027889-1	La Valse A'N'Oncle Knute (Uncle Knute's Waltz) -2	BB B-2064
027890-1	Si Tu Voudroit Marriez Avec Moi (Marry Me) -1, 2	BB B-2060
027891-1	La Two-Step A' Chachin (Asa's Two-Step) -2	BB B-2060
027892-1	Il Ya Pas La Claire De Lune (No Moonlight) -2	BB B-2069
027893-1	La Fille De Village (Town Girl) -1, 2	BB B-2069
027894-1	Ammend La Nouville A Mamere (Bring Mother The News) -1, 2, 3	BB B-2054
027895-1	La Valse A Deux Temps (A Two Step Waltz) -2, 3	BB B-2054
027896-1	Joe's Breakdown -1	BB B-2073
027897-1	La Valse De Bayou Granddan -2	BB B-2073
027898-1	La One-Step A Moujeane -2, 3	BB B-2078
027899-1	Je Suis Seul Encore (I'm Alone Again) -1, 2, 3	BB B-2078

Joe Werner also recorded with the Hackberry Ramblers (both under that name and as the Riverside Ramblers) and Thibodeaux Boys.

C.A. WEST

C.A. West, v; acc. own g.

Richmond, IN   Tuesday, December 31, 1929

16043,-A,-B	Pity The Drunkard	Ge rejected
16044	A Mother's Advice	Ge 7098, Spt 9650
16045,-A,-B	Christine Leroy	Ge rejected
16046-A	The Broken Engagement	Chg 429
16047	I Sit Broken Hearted	Spr 2528, Chg 429
16048	Oh! Willie Come Back	Ge 7098, Spt 9650, Spr 2528
16049,-A	I Am So Glad	Ge unissued
16050,-A	The Lot In Canaan's Land	Ge unissued

Superior 2528 as by **Alvin Crawford**. Challenge 429 as by **Clayton Brooks**.

CAL WEST

Cal West, v/y; acc. own g.

Knoxville, TN   Sunday, September 1, 1929

K-165-	Cal West's Yodel Blues – Part 1	Vo 5361
K-166-	Cal West's Yodel Blues – Part 2	Vo 5361
K-167-	At The Party	Vo rejected
K-168-	Preacher Selection	Vo rejected

ED (JAKE) WEST

Ed (Jake) West, v/y; acc. prob. Roy Smeck, sg; poss. own g; unknown, v eff-1/v duet eff-2.
New York, NY   Friday, March 22, 1929

8627-2	Daddy And Home	Ba 6465, Do 4379, Je 5668, Or 1648, Re 8825, Cq 7396, Htd 16061, 16150, 23015, Pm 3154, Bwy 8109, ARC-Bwy 8109
8628-1	Waiting For The Train -2	Ba 6370, Ca 9219, Do 4329, DoC 181066, Je 5586, Lin 3246, Pat 32477, Pe 12556, Re 8775, Ro 1021, Cq 7348, Pm 3154, Bwy 8109, Apex 8951, CrC 81066, Stg 281066
2204-3	Waiting For The Train -1	Or 1561, Chg 813
8629-	Memphis Yodel	Pl unissued

Further takes of matrix 8629, made on April 9, 1929, are by Frank Luther.
Cameo 9219, Lincoln 3246, Romeo 1021 as by **Jimmie Price & His Guitar**. Pathé 32477, Perfect 12556 as by **Harry Wilson**. Apex 8951, Crown 81066, Domino 181066, Sterling 281066 as by **Buddy Bartlett**.
Matrix 8628 may be titled *Waiting For A Train* on some or all of Cameo 9219, Lincoln 3246, Pathé 32477, Perfect 12556, and Romeo 1021.
Controls appear on various issues instead of, or as well as, the matrices, as follows: 8627 = 1210, 2384; 8628 = 1211, 3951.
Revs: ARC-Broadway 8109 by Arkansas Woodchopper; Apex 8951, Crown 81066, Domino 181066, Sterling 281066 (with same credit) by Frank Luther; all others by Frank Luther &/or Carson Robison (see the latter for both).

Eddie "Jake" West, v; acc. unknown.
New York, NY   Saturday, March 23, 1929

401739-	Waiting For A Train	OK unissued

Jake West, v; acc. own g.
New York, NY   Tuesday, June 25, 1929

53868-1,-2	The Wanderer's Warning	Vi unissued
53869-1,-2	Lonesome Daddy Blues	Vi unissued

JACK WEST

Pseudonym on Broadway (4000 series) for Frankie Marvin.

MARGARET WEST

Margaret West, v; acc. unknown.
New York, NY   Tuesday, July 19, 1932

TO-1187	Cowboy's Dream	ARC unissued trial recording

Acc. unknown, g.
New York, NY   Thursday, September 14, 1933

TO-1330	Blue Eyed Ellen	ARC unissued trial recording
TO-1331	The Last Round Up	ARC unissued trial recording

Margret [sic] **West & Her Sagebrush Harmonizers**: Margaret West, v/y-1; acc. unknown, f; unknown, h-2; unknown, bj; unknown, g; unknown, sb.
New York, NY   Monday, December 17, 1934

39165-A,-B	The Yellow Rose Of Texas -1, 2	BrSA SA1076
39166-	Chime Bells -1	DeSA FM5106
39167-A,-B	Silvery Prairie Moon	BrSA SA1076
39168-A,-B	Ridin' Down That Old Texas Trail -2	De unissued

Rev. Decca FM5106 by the Shelton Brothers.

W.W. WEST (RATTLER)

W.W. West, v/laughing-1; acc. prob. own f.
Atlanta, GA   Saturday, January 31, 1925

140311-1	Puttin' On Airs -1	Co 15013-D, Ha 5139-H
140312-2	Sambo	Co 15013-D, Ha 5139-H

WALTON WEST

Walton West, v; acc. prob. own g.
New York, NY   Tuesday, November 12, 1935

60142-A	When A Boy From The Mountain (Weds A Girl From The Valley)	Ch 45161, MeC 45161
60143-A	'Leven Miles From Leavenworth	Ch 45161, MeC 45161, Min M-14041

Rev. Minerva M-14041 by Asa Martin & Roy Hobbs.

New York, NY   Friday, December 13, 1935
   60225-A   In That Vine Covered Chapel (In The Valley)   Ch 45170, MeC 45170
   60226-A   That Golden Love (My Mother Gave To Me)   Ch 45170, MeC 45170

WEST BROTHERS TRIO

Philip West, David West, Billy West, v trio-1; acc. one of them, md; one of them, g; one of them, 2nd g-2.
  New Orleans, LA   Monday, January 21, 1935
   87654-1   Little Shoes -1   BB unissued
   87655-1   I Love You, My Dear -1   BB B-5836
   87656-1   Star Dust -2   BB B-5836, B-2497
   87657-1   Song Of The Islands -1, 2   BB unissued
   87658-1   Mountain Top Rag -2   BB B-5841, B-2497, MW M-4554
   87659-1   Ole Faithful -1, 2   BB B-5841, MW M-4554, Twin FT1909

Bluebird B-2497 (a Mexican issue) as by **Trio Hermanos De Oeste**.
Matrix 87656 is titled *Destello De Estrella*, and matrix 87658 *Cima De La Montana*, on that issue.
Rev. Twin FT1909 by Skyland Scotty.

WEST VIRGINIA COON HUNTERS

W.B. Boyles, f; two unknowns, bj; unknown, g; W.A. Meadows, v.
  Bristol, TN   Friday, August 5, 1927
   39773-2   Greasy String   Vi 20862
   39774-1   Your Blue Eyes Run Me Crazy   Vi 20862

Matrix 39774 is titled *Your Blue Eyes Run* on some copies of Victor 20862.

THE WEST VIRGINIA HILLTOPPERS

Pseudonym on Supertone for Calaway's West Virginia Mountaineers.

WEST VIRGINIA MOUNTAINEERS

No details (but very likely to include John McGhee and Frank Welling, who were present in the studio.)
  Richmond, IN   Wednesday, August 15, 1928
   14148   Ezra's Experience At The Recording Laboratory   Ge rejected

WEST VIRGINIA NIGHT OWLS

Fred Pendleton, f/v; Arville Reed, g/v.
  Camden, NJ   Monday, December 19, 1927
   40764-1,-2   The Fate Of Rose Sarlo   Vi unissued
   40765-1,-2   Give The Flapper A Chew   Vi unissued
   40788-2   Sweet Bird   Vi 21190
   40789-2   I'm Goin' To Walk On The Streets Of Glory   Vi 21533

Victor files erroneously assign the fiddle to Reed and the guitar to Pendleton.
Intervening matrices are by other artists on other dates.
Revs: Victor 21190 by Arville Reed (as **Orville Reed**), 21533 by Blind Alfred Reed.

THE WEST VIRGINIA RAIL SPLITTER

Pseudonym on Champion for The Arkansas Woodchopper.

WEST VIRGINIA RAMBLERS

See Roy Harvey.

WEST VIRGINIA RIDGE RUNNERS

Pseudonym on Superior for the Corn Cob Crushers.

WEST VIRGINIA SNAKE HUNTERS

See John & Emery McClung.

WESTBROOK CONSERVATORY ENTERTAINERS
WESTBROOK CONSERVATORY PLAYERS
WESTBROOK GOSPEL PLAYERS & SOLOIST

Westbrook Conservatory Entertainers: (Walter) John Westbrook, sg/v-1/humming-2; Mrs. John Westbrook, g/v-1/humming-2; unknown man, v-3.
  New York, NY   c. October 1929
   GEX-2397-A   Silent Night -2   Pm 3197, Bwy 8228
   GEX-2398-A   It Came Upon A Midnight Clear   Pm 3197, Bwy 8228
   GEX-2399-A   Will That Circle Be Unbroken -1, 3   Pm 3203, Bwy 8194

GEX-2400-A	Indiana March	Pm 3206, Bwy 8143
GEX-2401-A	Memories Of Hawaii	Pm 3206, Bwy 8143
GEX-2402-A	I Would Walk With My Saviour -1, 3	Pm 3203, Bwy 8194, ARC-Bwy 8194
GEX-2403	Dark Alley Blues	Pm unissued
GEX-2404	Daisies Won't Tell	Pm 3226, Bwy 8263
GEX-2405	If I Only Had A Home Sweet Home	Pm 3226, Bwy 8263
GEX-2406	Corrine Corrina Blues -1	Pm 12861

Paramount 12861 as by **The Too Bad Boys**. Broadway 8143 as by **Hawaiian Trio**.
Matrix GEX-2403 is uncredited in Gennett files but seems likely to be by this group.
Rev. Paramount 12861 (with same credit) by a different, probably African-American group; ARC-Broadway 8194 by Frank & James McCravy.

Westbrook Conservatory Players: (Walter) John Westbrook, sg; poss. Mrs. John Westbrook, g; unknown, u; Bruce Waggoner, v.

Atlanta, GA   Tuesday, November 3, 1931

152023-1	Tell Mother I'll Be There	Re/RZAu G21461
152024-	He Is Our Crucified King	Co unissued
152025-1	The Old Rugged Cross	Co 15741-D, Re/RZAu G21461
152026-	I Would Walk With My Savior	Co 15741-D

Regal/Regal-Zonophone G21461 as by **Westbrook Gospel Players & Soloist**.

AL WESTERLEY

Pseudonym possibly used on labels of the Grey Gull group for Jack Weston.

WESTERN HILLBILLIES

Pseudonym on Canadian Melotone for Glen Rice & His Beverly Hill Billies (see The Beverly Hill Billies).

THE WESTERNERS

See The Massey Family.

ROBERT WESTFALL

Robert Westfall, v; acc. prob. own g.

Richmond, IN   Wednesday, June 10, 1931

17811	My Old Pal	Ge unissued trial recording

DON WESTON

Don Weston, v/y-1; acc. unknown, f-2; prob. own g.

Richmond, IN   Friday, March 16, 1934

19497	That Old Feather Bed On The Farm -2	Ch 16748, 45107
19498	That Mother And Daddy Of Mine	Ch 16825, 45101, MeC 45101
19499	There's An Empty Cot In The Bunkhouse Tonight -2	Ch 16748, 45107, DeAu X1270
19500	Way Out West In Texas -1, 2	Ch S-16779, 45110, MW 4955
19501	When The Hummin' Birds Are Hummin' Low -1	Ch S-16764, 45053, DeAu X1241
19502	The Dying Cowgirl -1	Ch S-16764, 45053, DeAu X1241
19503	When They Changed My Name To A Number -2	Ch S-16779, 45100, MW 4955
19504	Closer To You -2	Ge unissued

Matrix 19499 is titled *There's An Empty Cot In The Bunkhouse Tonite* on Champion 45107. Matrix 19501 is titled *When The Humin' Birds Are Hummin' Low* on Champion 45053.
Revs: Champion 16825, 45101, Melotone 45101 by Buddy DeWitt; Decca X1270 by John McGhee & Frank Welling.

Don Weston, v/y-1; acc. unknown, f; prob. own g.

New York, NY   Friday, July 23, 1937

62440-A	The Maple On The Hill Is Gone -1	De 5421, MeC 45211
62441-A	Old Pal Why Don't You Answer Me	De 5421, MeC 45211

Don Weston recorded after 1942.

JACK WESTON

The recordings listed below sound as if they are the work of a single singer, but is uncertain whether Jack Weston is his true name.

Jack Weston, v; acc. unknown, f-1; unknown, h; unknown, g.

New York, NY   January 1930

3841-A	The Texas Trail -1	GG/Rad 4292, VD 4292, 84292
3842-A	The Little Old Sod Shanty	VD 4293
3842-B	The Little Old Sod Shanty	GG/Rad 4293, VD 84293

Some issues possibly as by **Al Westerley**. Rev. all issues by Bob Miller.

Billy Dalton-1/**George Anthony**-2, v; acc. unknown, h; unknown, g.

New York, NY c. January 1930
111-B	Rock Candy Mountain -1	Mad 5006, 50006, VD 5006
112-A	Hallelujah, I'm A Bum -2	Mad 5006, 50006, VD 5006

JIM WHALEN

Pseudonym on Champion for Miller Wikel.

WHEAT STREET FEMALE QUARTET

This group, which had one release in the Columbia Old Familiar Tunes series (15021-D), was African-American; see B&GR.

BILLY WHEELER

Pseudonym on Broadway for John McGhee.

FRANK WHEELER–MONROE LAMB

Frank Wheeler, Monroe Lamb, v duet; acc. one of them, g.
Dallas, TX Thursday, October 17, 1929
56408-2	Utah Carl's Last Ride	Vi V-40169, MW M-4470
56409-1	Since The Preacher Made Us One	Vi V-40248
56410-	If I Could Only Blot Out The Past	Vi V-40248
56411-1	A Jolly Group Of Cowboys	Vi V-40169, MW M-4470

Victor V-40248 as by **Wheeler & Lamb**.

Wheeler–Lamb, v duet; acc. one of them, h; the other, g.
Memphis, TN Tuesday, May 27, 1930
62513-2	Will You Sometimes Think Of Me	Vi 23755, MW M-4317
62514-2	I'll Ever Be Faithful To You	Vi 23755, MW M-4317
62515-1,-2	The Man Who Follows The Plow	Vi unissued
62516-2	The Farmer Feeds Them All	Vi 23537, MW M-4334, ZoAu EE279

Victor 23755, Montgomery Ward M-4317, Zonophone EE279 as by **Wheeler & Lamb**.

Memphis, TN Wednesday, May 28, 1930
62527-2	Jim Blake, The Engineer	Vi 23537, MW M-4334, ZoAu EE279
62528-1,-2	The Dying Message	Vi unissued
62529-1,-2	When The Roses Come Again	Vi unissued
62530-1,-2	I'll Remember You, Love, In My Prayer	Vi unissued

Zonophone EE279 as by **Wheeler & Lamb**.

WHEELER & LAMB
WHEELER–LAMB

See Frank Wheeler–Monroe Lamb.

WEBB WHIPPLE

Webb Whipple, v; acc. Bill Harper, g.
New York, NY Wednesday, March 30, 1932
405182-A	Don't Hang Me In The Morning	OK 45574
405183-A	The International Bum	OK 45574

These are described in OKeh files as "race vocal."

BOB WHITE

Pseudonym on Domino and Regal for Vernon Dalhart, or on Bell 1188 for Doc Roberts.

FIDDLIN' BOB WHITE

Pseudonym on Bell for Doc Roberts.

CARL WHITE

Carl White, v; acc. The Arkansas Travelers: unknown, f; unknown, md; unknown, bj; unknown, g.
Richmond, IN Thursday, January 12, 1933
18964	Lamp Post On Old Broadway	Ge unissued

CLYDE WHITE

Clyde White, v; acc. unknown, g.
Richmond, IN Monday, July 27, 1931
17895-A	Beside A Lonely River	Ch 16318
17896-A	The Old Man's Story	Ch 16318

Clyde White also recorded with W.C. Childers.

DON WHITE

Don White, v; or **Don White & F. Kirby**-1: Don White, Fred Kirby, v duet; acc. prob. Don White, g.
  Charlotte, NC   Friday, June 19, 1936
  102705-1   Play That Waltz Again (Sleepy Rio Grande) -1   BB B-6459, MW M-5034, Twin FT8189
  102706-1   Mexicali Rose   BB B-6459, MW M-5034, Twin FT8189
  102707-1   Rockin' Chair   BB unissued
  102708-1   What A Friend We Have In Mother   BB unissued

Don White also recorded with Fred Kirby.

GEORGE WHITE [& HIS GUITAR]

Pseudonym on OKeh and Parlophone for Frank Marvin.

GEORGE WASHINGTON WHITE

George Washington White, v; acc. prob. own g.
  Grafton, WI   c. March 1932
  L-1429-1   Idaho Joe   Pm 584
  L-1430-2   Gamblers Blues   Pm 584

JOHN I. WHITE

John I. White, v; acc. unknown.
  New York, NY   Friday, August 9, 1929
  8923-1   The Little Old Sod Shanty   ARC unissued
  8924-1   Great Grandad   ARC unissued

Whitey Johns, v; acc. Roy Smeck, h/g.
  New York, NY   Thursday, September 19, 1929
  8923-2   The Little Old Sod Shanty   Ba 6532, Ca 9321, Do 4440, Je 5723, Or 1715,
                                                                        Pat 32488, Pe 12567, Re 8881, Ro 1118,
                                                                        Chg 840, Cq 7434, 7725, Pm 3190, Bwy 8132,
                                                                        ImpE 2216
  8924-2   Great Grand Dad   Ba 6561, Ca 9314, Do 4440, Je 5749, Or 1751,
                                                                        Pat 32488, Pe 12567, Re 8881, Ro 1105,
                                                                        Chg 852, Cq 7434, Htd 16154

Domino 4440, Pathé 32488, Perfect 12567, Regal 8881, Conqueror 7434, Imperial 2216 as by **(The) Lone Star Ranger**.
Cameo 9314, Romeo 1105 as by **Jimmie Price**. Oriole 1715 and some issues of Jewel 5723 as by **Whitey John**. Some issues of
Romeo 1118 as by **Jimmie Price**; matrix 8923 is titled *Little Old Sod Shanty* on those issues.
Broadway 8132 credits the accompanist as **Alabama Joe**, a pseudonym used elsewhere for Roy Smeck.
Matrix 8923 is titled *My Little Old Sod Shanty* on some issues of Cameo 9321, and *The Little Old Shanty* on Imperial 2216.
Matrix 8924 is titled *Great Grand-Dad* on some issues.
Controls appear on various issues instead of, or as well as, the matrices, as follows: 8923 = 4089, 1694; 8924 = 4090, 2552.
Revs: Banner 6532, Oriole 1715, Challenge 840, Conqueror 7725, Imperial 2216 by Frank Luther (see Carson Robison);
Cameo 9321, Romeo 1118, Paramount 3190, Broadway 8132 by Frank Marvin; Cameo 9314, Romeo 1105 by Carson
Robison.

Acc. unknown, f; unknown, h; unknown, bj; unknown, g; unknown, jh.
  New York, NY   Saturday, October 12, 1929
  9073-A,-C   Farm Relief Song   Ba 6561, Ca 9315, Do 4442, Je 5749, Lin 3339,
                                                                        Or 1751, Pat 32491, Pe 12570, Re 8885,
                                                                        Ro 1106, Chg 852, Cq 7438, Htd 16154,
                                                                        Pm 3208, Bwy 8144

Domino 4442, Pathé 32491, Perfect 12570, Regal 8885, Conqueror 7438, Paramount 3208, Broadway 8144 as by **(The) Lone Star Ranger**. Cameo 9315, Lincoln 3339, Romeo 1106 as by **Jimmie Price**.
Some issues of matrix 9073 use the controls 4140, 2551.
According to John I. White, Roy Smeck accompanied him on many, perhaps all, of his recordings. It may therefore be assumed
that Smeck played one or more of the harmonica, banjo, guitar, and jew's harp heard on the above and subsequent sessions.
Revs: Pathé 32491, Perfect 12570 by Frank Marvin; Cameo 9315, Domino 4442, Romeo 1106 by Frank Luther (see Carson
Robison); Regal 8885, Conqueror 7438 by Carson Robison; Lincoln 3339 untraced.

Acc. unknown, f; unknown, h-1; unknown, bj; unknown, g; unknown, jh-2.
  New York, NY   Wednesday, November 13, 1929
  9136-2,-3   The Crow Song (Caw-Caw-Caw)   Ba 0556, Ca 0156, Je 5810, Or 1810, Pat 32504,
                                                                        Pe 12583, Re 8921, Ro 1176, Chg 878,
                                                                        Cq 7466, 7728, Pm 3208, Bwy 8144
  9137-2,-3   The Deserted Cabin -1   Ba 0556, Ca 0156, Do 4477, Je 5810, Or 1810,
                                                                        Pat 32501, Pe 12580, Re 8922, Ro 1176,
                                                                        Chg 878, Cq 7726

| 9138-2 | When Bill Hilly Plays A Hill Billy Upon His Violin -1, 2 | Ba 0583, Ca 0183, Je 5839, Or 1839, Ro 1205, Htd 16138, 23012 |

Pathé 32501, 32504, Perfect 12580, 12583, Conqueror 7466, 7726, 7728, Homestead 16138, 23012, Paramount 3208, Broadway 8144 as by **(The) Lone Star Ranger**.
Matrix 9138 is titled *When Bill Hilly Plays A Hill Billy* on Homestead 16138.
Revs: Pathé 32504, Perfect 12583, Conqueror 7466, 7728 by Carson Robison; all issues of matrix 9138 by Frank Marvin.

Acc. unknown, f; unknown, o; unknown, g; unknown, bell.
New York, NY   Friday, November 22, 1929

| 9172-3 | At Father Power's Grave | Ba 0560, Ca 0160, Do 4477, Je 5812, Or 1812, Pat 32501, Pe 12580, Re 8922, Cq 7726 |
| 9173- | The Unmarked Grave | Ba 0560, Ca 0160, Je 5812, Or 1812 |

Pathé 32501, Perfect 12580 as by **The Old Sexton**. Conqueror 7726 as by **Lone Star Ranger**.

Acc. unknown, f; unknown, h; unknown, g; unknown, train-wh eff-1.
New York, NY   Wednesday, December 4, 1929

9203-1,-2	The Prison Warden's Secret	Ba 0581, Ca 0181, Je 5837, Or 1837, Pat 32510, Pe 12589, Re 8938, Ro 1200, Chg 875, Cq 7482, 7782, Htd 16155, Pm 3201, Bwy 8141
9204-2	The Train That Never Arrived -1	Ba 0585, Ca 0185, Je 5841, Or 1841, Ro 1204, Pm 3202, Bwy 8142
9205-1,-3	Pappy's Buried On The Hill	Ba 0649, Ca 0249, Je 5904, Or 1904, Pat 32510, Pe 12589, Re 8938, Ro 1268, Cq 7482, 7782, Htd 16065, Pm 3201, Bwy 8141

Cameo 0249, Pathé 32510, Perfect 12589, Regal 8938, Romeo 1268, Challenge 875, Conqueror 7482, 7782, Paramount 3201, 3202, Broadway 8141, 8142, and some issues of Jewel 5904 as by **(The) Lone Star Ranger**. Banner 0649 as by **Lone Star Ranger** or **The Lonesome Cowboy**. Oriole 1904 as by **Whitey Johns**, **Lone Star Ranger**, or **The Lonesome Cowboy**.
Matrix 9205 is titled *My Pappy's Buried On The Hill* on Broadway 8141.
Revs: Banner 0581, 0585, Cameo 0181, 0185, Jewel 5837, 5841, Oriole 1837, 1841, Romeo 1200, 1204, Challenge 875, Homestead 16155 by Carson Robison; Paramount 3202, Broadway 8142 by Frank Marvin.

Acc. unknown, f; unknown, h-1; unknown, g.
New York, NY   Thursday, January 23, 1930

9302-2	I'm Just A Black Sheep	Ba 0618, Ca 0218, Do 4509, Je 5875, Or 1875, Pe 12591, Re 8954, Ro 1237, Cq 7492, Apex 41152, CrC/MeC 81365, Stg 281365, Roy 381365
9302-4	I'm Just A Black Sheep	Cq 7492
9303-3	Hillbilly Courtship -1	Ba 0617, Ca 0217, Je 5873, Or 1873, Ro 1235, Htd 16153, 23016, MeC 91931

Domino 4509, Regal 8954, Conqueror 7492, Apex 41152, Crown/Melotone 81365, Sterling 281365, Royale 381365, Melotone 91931 as by **(The) Lone Star Ranger**. Perfect 12591 as by **The Lone Star Ranger** or **The Lonesome Cowboy**.
Matrix 9303 is titled *Hill Bill Courtship* on Banner 0617 and *Hill Billy Courtship* on Homestead 23016.
Revs: Domino 4509, Perfect 12591, Regal 8954, Conqueror 7492, Apex 41152, Crown/Melotone 81365, Sterling 281365, Royale 381365, Melotone 91931 by Carson Robison; all other issues by Frank Marvin.

Lone Star Ranger, v; acc. poss. Adelyne Hood, f; poss. Ross Gorman, cl; unknown, bj; unknown, g.
New York, NY   Wednesday, February 5, 1930

| 9341-1,-2,-3 | Eleven More Months And Ten More Days | Ba 0649, Ca 0249, Je 5904, Me M12106, Or 1904, Pe 12598, Re 8973, Ro 1268, Chg 877, Cq 7509, 7727, Htd 16065, Pm 3218, Bwy 8150, Apex 41170, CrC 81354, ImpE 2274, 2602, Rex 8056 |

Banner 0649, Perfect 12598, Conqueror 7727 as by **The Lone Star Ranger** or **The Lonesome Cowboy**. Jewel 5904 as by **The Lone Star Ranger** or **Whitey Johns**. Oriole 1904 as by **The Lone Star Ranger**, **Whitey Johns**, or **The Lonesome Cowboy**. Homestead 16065 as by **Whitey Johns**. Rex 8056 as by **Frank Ranger**.
Some issues use the control 1761.
White also participates in matrix 9340 by Adelyne Hood, recorded on this date.
Revs: Perfect 12598, Regal 8973, Challenge 877, Conqueror 7509, 7727, Apex 41170, Crown 81354 by Frank Marvin; Paramount 3218, Broadway 8150 by The Pickard Family; Imperial 2274 by The Radio Imps (popular), 2602, Rex 8056 by Frank Luther (see Carson Robison).

Whitey Johns, v; acc. unknown, f; unknown, h; unknown, bj; unknown, g.
New York, NY   Monday, March 31, 1930

| 9539-3,-4 | Take Care Of The Farmer | Ba 0682, Ca 0282, Je 5935, Or 1935, Pe 12616, Chg 884, Cq 7549 |
| 9540-1 | The Prisoner's Rosary | ARC unissued |

Cameo 0282, Challenge 884, Conqueror 7549 as by **(The) Lone Star Ranger**. Perfect 12616 as by **The Lonesome Cowboy**. Some issues of Banner 0682 as by **The Lone Star Ranger**.
Revs: Perfect 12616, Conqueror 7549 by Carson Robison; all other issues by Adelyne Hood.

Acc. unknown, f; unknown, o; unknown, g.
   New York, NY   Monday, April 14, 1930
   9540-2,-5,-7   The Prisoner's Rosary   Ba 0707, Ca 0307, Je 5964, Or 1964, Pe 12637,
                                                                     Re 9019, Ro 1328, Chg 895, Cq 7603

Banner 0707, Cameo 0307, Conqueror 7603 as by **The Lone Star Ranger**. Perfect 12637 as by **The Lone Star Ranger** or **The Lonesome Cowboy**.
Revs: all issues by Carson Robison.

John White (The Lonesome Cowboy), v; acc. unknown, h; unknown, g.
   New York, NY   Thursday, April 2, 1931
   10541-2   Whoopie-Ti-Yi-Yo (Git Along Little Doggies)   Ba 32179, Or 8066, Pe 12709, 12712, Ro 1629,
                                                                           5066, Cq 7753, MeC/Roy 91249
   10542-2   Strawberry Roan   Pe 12709, 12712, Cq 7753, Roy 91249

Matrix 10541 is titled *Little Doggie* on Perfect 12709, 12712, Romeo 1629, Royale 91249.
   New York, NY   Thursday, April 16, 1931
   10571-1,-2   Strawberry Roan   Ba 32179, Or 8066, Pe 12709, Ro 1629, 5066,
                                                                           MeC 91249

Strawberry Roan on matrix 10571 is the composition of that title by Howard and Vincent, whereas that on matrix 10542 is the composition by Curley Fletcher.
Smith Ballew is erroneously credited as vocalist on Perfect 12709.
John I. White recorded after 1942.

REUBEN WHITE

Pseudonym on Challenge for Wyzee Hamilton.

ZEB WHITE

Zeb White, v; acc. Carson Robison, g/wh-1.
   New York, NY   Saturday, May 21, 1927
   E23286*/87   When You Were Sweet Sixteen   Vo 5189
   E23288/89*   Down The Old Meadow Lane -1   Vo 5189

WHITE & BRYANT

Pseudonym on Conqueror for Walter Smith & Norman Woodlieff.

WHITE & DAWSON

Pseudonym on Supertone for Andy Patterson & Warren Caplinger (see the latter).

WHITE BROTHERS (JOE & BOB)

Joe White, Bob White, v/y-1 duet; acc. one of them, g; the other, tg.
   Columbia, SC   Wednesday, November 2, 1938
   SC-47-   I'm Going Back To Alabama   Vo unissued
   SC-48-1   Southern Moon -1   Vo/OK 04674
   SC-49-   Lover's Warning   Vo unissued
   SC-55-1   When It's Time For The Whippoorwills To Sing   Vo 04530
   SC-56-1   The Fugitive's Lament   Vo 04530
   SC-57-1   Beautiful Brown Eyes   Vo/OK 04674

Matrices SC-50 to SC-54 are by Fisher Hendley & His Aristocratic Pigs.

WHITE CITY JAZZERS

Pseudonym on Madison, Van Dyke, and possibly Grey Gull for Small Town Players. (See also Joseph Samuels.)

WHITE MOUNTAIN ORCHESTRA

E.C. Maxwell, f; Mrs. A.C. Warner, bj; F.L. Maxwell, g; F.M. Maxwell, g.
   El Paso, TX   Tuesday, July 2, 1929
   53290-2   Gooson   Vi V-40185, MW M-4293
   53291-2   Leather Britches   Vi V-40185, MW M-4293
   53292-   Maxwell's Old Rye Waltz   Vi 23619, Au 404
   53293-   Escudilla Waltz   Vi 23619, Au 404

RED WHITEHEAD & DUTCH COLEMAN

See Dutch Coleman.

WHITEY & HOGAN (ROY GRANT & ARVAL HOGAN)

Arval Hogan, md/tv; Roy Grant, g/v.
New York, NY   Wednesday, November 8, 1939

66473-A	Watching You	De 5810
66474-A	You'll Be My Closest Neighbor	De 5758
66475-A	Sunny Side Of Life	De 5758
66476-A	That's The Way With A Broken Heart	De 5810
66477-A	An Old Log Cabin For Sale	De 5817
66478-A	It's Alcatraz For Me	De 5759
66479-A	Gosh! I Miss You All The Time	De 5759
66480-A	Answer To Budded Roses	De 5817
66481-A	Let Me Travel Along	De 5838, MeC 45360
66482-AA	Tell My Mother I'll Meet Her	De 5784
66483-A	I'll Meet You In The Morning	De 5838, MeC 45360
66484-A	Turn Your Radio On	De 5784
66485-A	Ridin' On My Saviour's Train	De 5771
66486-A	Don't Be Knockin'	De 5796
66487-A	I've Changed My Mind	De 5771
66488-A	I Can Tell You The Time	De 5796

Whitey & Hogan recorded after 1942.

WHITFIELD TABERNACLE LONDON CHOIR, ORGAN & H.M. SCOTS GUARDS

Despite appearing in the Paramount and Broadway old-time series, these recordings, which were probably made in London and very likely originally issued on the local Edison Bell Winner label, are outside the scope of this work.

RAY WHITLEY

Ray Whitley, v; or **Ray Whitley & Odis Elder**-1, v duet; acc. unknown, f; prob. Bob Miller, p.
New York, NY   Monday, September 17, 1934

| 15961-2 | Have You Written Mother Lately -1 | Ba 33183, Me M13150, MeC 91865, Or 8379, Pe 13047, Ro 5379, Cq 8383 |
| 15962-1 | The Morro Castle Disaster | Ba 33183, Me M13150, MeC 91865, Or 8379, Pe 13047, Ro 5379, Cq 8383 |

Ray Whitley & Odis Elder, v duet; acc. poss. Frank Novak, bscl; prob. Bob Miller, p; prob. Ray Whitley, g; unknown, sb; unknown, x.
New York, NY   Thursday, September 20, 1934

| 15987-1 | Sittin' On The Old Settee! | Ba 33265, Me M13232, Or 8400, Pe 13085, Ro 5400, Cq 8401 |
| 15988-2 | Old Wishing Well | Ba 33265, Me M13232, Or 8400, Pe 13085, Ro 5400, Cq 8401 |

Ray Whitley, v; acc. unknown.
New York, NY   Monday, September 24, 1934

| 15962-2 | The Morro Castle Disaster | ARC unissued |

Ray Whitley & Otis Elder, v duet; acc. unknown, f; prob. Bob Miller, p; prob. Ray Whitley, g.
New York, NY   Friday, October 5, 1934

| 16039- | Big Ball In Texas | ARC unissued |
| 16040-2 | Singing A Song In Sing Sing | Ba 33252, Me M13219, MeC 91912, Or 8397, Pe 13079, Ro 5397, Cq 8436 |

Matrix 16040 is titled *Singin' A Song In Sing Sing* on Conqueror 8436.

Ray Whitley, v acc. unknown, f; unknown, h; poss. own g.
New York, NY   Saturday, October 27, 1934

| 16279-1 | Pretty Boy Floyd | Ba 33252, Me M13219, MeC 91912, Or 8397, Pe 13079, Ro 5397, Cq 8436 |

Buck Nation & Ray Whitley, v/y duet; acc. prob.: Bill Benner, f; Jake Watts, h-1; Bill Butler, sg; Buck Nation and/or Ray Whitley, g.
New York, NY   Thursday, January 17, 1935

39254-A	End Of Memory Lane	BrSA SA879
39254-B	End Of Memory Lane	De 5065, DeSA FM 5494
39255-A	Ramshackled Shack On The Hill -1	De 5065, DeSA FM 5494, BrSA SA879

Ray Whitley, v/y-1; or **Buck Nation & Ray Whitley**-2, v duet; acc. prob. Bill Benner, f; Jake Watts, h-3; Bill Butler, sg; Ray Whitley and/or Buck Nation, g.
New York, NY   Friday, February 15, 1935

| 39362-A | That Green Back Dollar Bill -3 | De 5078 |
| 39363-A | Big Bad Blues -1, 3 | De 5078 |

39364-	Sweet Little Someone -2	BrSA SA 893
39365-A,-B	My Prairie Pride	De rejected
39366-A	Vine Covered Church -2	De 5114, BrSA SA915
39367-A	Newly Moulded Mound -2, 3	De 5114, BrSA SA917

Brunswick SA915, SA917 possibly as by **Ray Whitley**.
Revs: Brunswick SA893 by Buck Nation, SA915 by Frank Luther, SA917 by Stuart Hamblen.

Ray Whitley, v; acc. prob.: Bill Benner, f; Bill Butler, sg; own g.
New York, NY Thursday, August 22, 1935

| 39873-AA | Will Rogers Your Friend And My Friend | De 5132 |
| 39874-A | The Last Flight Of Wiley Post | De 5132 |

Ray Whitley, v/y-1; acc. prob.: Bill Benner, f; Bill Butler, sg-2; Ken Card, tbj-3; own g; unidentified, v-4.
New York, NY Thursday, February 27, 1936

| 60582-A | Saddle Your Blues To A Wild Mustang -2 | De 5195, DeAu X1142, Pan 25863 |
| 60583-A | Wah-Hoo! -1, 3, 4 | De 5195, DeAu X1142, Pan 25863 |

Ray Whitley, v/y; acc. prob.: Bill Benner, f; Bill Butler, sg; Ken Card, tbj; own g.
New York, NY Monday, March 2, 1936

| 60599-A | My Alabammy Home | De 5205, DeAu X1178 |
| 60851-A | Blue Yodel Blues | De 5205, DeAu X1178 |

Matrix 60599 is titled *My Alabamy Home*, and matrix 60851 *Blue Yodel*, on Decca X1178.

Ray Whitley's Range Ramblers: poss.: Earl Phelps, f; unknown, ac; Ken Card, tbj; Willie Phelps, g; Norman Phelps, sb; Ray Whitley, v/y-1.
New York, NY Tuesday, October 27, 1936

61349-A	Trailin' -1	De 5285
61350-A,-B	I Saw Your Face In The Moon	De 5293
61351-A	You Took My Candy -1	De 5293
61352-A	Just A Little Cough Drop -1	De 5285

Ray Whitley & His 6 Bar Cowboys: Ray Whitley, v; acc. Earl Phelps, f; Ken Card, tbj; Willie Phelps, g; Norman Phelps, sb; unidentified, v duet.
New York, NY Wednesday, October 26, 1938

64700-AA	The Cowboy And The Lady	De 5617, MeC 45273, Min M-14093
64701-A	Back In The Saddle Again	De 5628, Min M-14138
64702-A	Come On Boys We're Ridin' Into Town	De 5617, MeC 45273, Min M-14093
64703-A	On The Painted Desert	De 5628

Rev. Minerva M-14138 by Fred Kirby.

Ray Whitley & His Six Bar Cowboys: Ray Whitley, v; acc. Spade Cooley, f; Ken Card, etg; own, g; Onie Haas, g; Walter Jecker, sb; Fred Rose, v-1.
Hollywood, CA Tuesday, August 19, 1941

HCO-454-1	When You Took Your Love Away	OK 06454, Cq 9863
HCO-455-1	Please Don't Forget Me, Dear	Cq 9864
H-456-1	Darlin' Don't Cry Over Me -1	Cq 9864
H-457-1	How Was I To Know -1	OK 06454, Cq 9863

Ray Whitley also recorded in the Frank Luther Trio, and after 1942.

TOMMY WHITMER'S BAND

Tommy Whitmer, f; Pete Woods, bj; Earl Nossinger, g; Enos Gossett, g.
Richmond, IN Tuesday, September 16, 1930

17044	Fire On The Mountain	Ch 16160, Spt 9776, Spr 2519
17047,-A	Kentucky Limit	Ge rejected
17048	Going To Jail	Spr 2519

Supertone 9776 as by **The Spencer Trio**. Superior 2519 as by **Buddy Young's Kentuckians**.
Intervening and surrounding matrices are by Ted Gossett's Band.
Revs: Champion 16160, Supertone 9776 by Ted Gossett's Band.

J.B. WHITMIRE'S BLUE SKY TRIO

Vocal trio (one man, two women); or v quartet (two men, two women)-1; acc. unknown, p.
Charlotte, NC Thursday, August 5, 1937

011948-1	I'll Meet You In The Morning	BB B-7132, MW M-7718
011949-1	It's An Unfriendly World	BB B-8385, MW M-7718
011950-1	Dream Boat	BB B-7844, MW M-7719
011951-1	A Beautiful Prayer	BB B-8171, MW M-7719
011952-1	Will The Circle Be Unbroken There?	BB B-8512, MW M-7720
011953-1	It Won't Be Very Long	BB B-8171, MW M-7720

011954-1	I'll Be List'ning	BB B-7550, MW M-7721
011955-1	I Dreamed I Met Mother And Daddy	BB B-7550, MW M-7721
011956-1	My Coming Vacation	BB B-7132, MW M-7722
011957-1	Getting Ready To Leave This World -1	BB B-7844, MW M-7722

Atlanta, GA   Tuesday, August 22, 1939

041234-1	Farther Along	BB B-8512, MW M-8508
041235-1	I've Changed My Mind	BB B-8385, MW M-8508
041236-1	Did You Ever Go Sailing	BB B-8310, MW M-8507
041237-1	No Shadows	BB B-8310, MW M-8507
041238-1	An Empty Mansion	BB B-8344, MW M-8506
041239-1	Let Me Go Down To The River	BB B-8344, MW M-8506
041240-1	Turn Your Radio On	BB B-8280, MW M-8504
041241-1	Just Over The Hill	BB B-8366, MW M-8505
041242-1	Just A Little Pine Log Cabin	BB B-8280, MW M-8504
041243-1	I'd Like To Go Back	BB B-8366, MW M-8505

WESLEY WHITSON

Wesley Whitson, sp.
New Orleans, LA   c. October 2, 1929

| TNO-265- | Senator Francois – Part I | Br 391 |
| TNO-266- | Senator Francois – Part II | Br 391 |

HENRY WHITTER

According to the artist himself and other sources, Henry Whitter made his first recordings, for OKeh in New York, NY, on or about March 1, 1923. OKeh files furnish no evidence for this claim.

Henry Whitter, h solo.
New York, NY   c. December 10, 1923

72159-A	Rain Crow Bill Blues	OK 40187
72160-A	Lost Train Blues (Lost John Blues)	OK 40029
72161-A	The Old Time Fox Chase	OK 40029

Matrix 72162 is untraced but probably by Whitter.

Henry Whitter, h-1/g/v-2.
New York, NY   c. December 10, 1923

72163-A	Weeping Willow Tree -1, 2	OK 40187
72164-A	The Stormy Wave Blues -1	OK 40143
72165-A	Broken Engagement Blues -1, 2	OK 40229
72166-A	The Kaiser And Uncle Sam -2	OK 40229
72167-A	Wreck On The Southern Old 97 -1, 2	OK 40015
72168-A	Lonesome Road Blues -1, 2	OK 40015

Henry Whitter, v; acc. own h/g.
New York, NY   c. February 25, 1924

72339-A	Sydney Allen	OK 40109
72340-A	Where Have You Been So Long?	OK 40109
72341-A	The New River Train	OK 40143
72342-A	Chicken, You Better Go Behind The Barn	OK 40077
72344-A	She's Coming Around The Mountain	OK 40063

Matrix 72343 is untraced but probably by Whitter.

Henry Whitter, h solo.
New York, NY   c. February 26, 1924

72347-A	The Weepin' Blues	OK 40120
72348-A	Hop Out Ladies & Shortenin' Bread	OK 40064
72349-A	Double Headed Train	OK 40120

Henry Whitter, h/g/v-1.
New York, NY   c. February 26, 1924

72350-A	Little Brown Jug -1	OK 40063
72351-A	Western Country -1	OK 40077
72352-A	Tippy Two Step Blues	OK 40064

Whitter's Virginia Breakdowners: James Sutphin, f; John Rector, bj; Henry Whitter, g/v-1.
New York, NY   c. July 16, 1924

| 72679-B | 'Round Town Girl -1 | OK 40320 |
| 72680-A | Black-Eyed Susan -1 | OK 40320 |

| 72684-A | Jenny Lind Polka | OK 40211 |
| 72685-A | Nellie Gray | OK 40211 |

Intervening matrices are by other artists.

Henry Whitter, v; acc. own h/g.
New York, NY   c. July 16, 1924

| 72686-A | The Drunkard's Child | OK 40169 |
| 72687-A | Goin' Down The Road Feelin' Bad | OK 40169 |

Whitter's Virginia Breakdowners: James Sutphin, f; John Rector, bj; Henry Whitter, g; unidentified, calls.
New York, NY   c. July 16, 1924

| 72691-A | Sourwood Mountain | OK 7005 |
| 72692-A | Mississippi Sawyer | OK 7005 |

OKeh 7005 is a 12-inch issue.
Matrices 72688 to 72690 are untraced.

Henry Whitter, h-1/g/v-2/v eff-3.
New York, NY   Wednesday, November 19, and Thursday, November 20, 1924

72978-B	Rabbit Race -1, 3	OK 40269
72979-A	Farewell To Thee -1	OK 40269
72982-A	Watermelon Hanging On The Vine -1, 2	OK 40296
72983-A	Ellen Smith -1, 2	OK 40237
72984-A	Keep My Skillet Good And Greasy -1, 2	OK 40296
72985-A	Travelling Man -1, 2	OK 40237
72986-A	The Long Tongued Woman -2	OK 40352
72987-A	The Dollar And The Devil -1, 2	OK 40352

Matrix 72979 was recorded on November 19, matrices 72984 and 72987 on November 20, the rest presumably on one day or the other. Matrices 72980/81 are by other artists.

Henry Whitter, h solo.
New York, NY   Thursday, April 23, 1925

| 73310-A | Lost John | OK 40391 |
| 73311-A | Peek-A-Boo | OK 40391 |

Henry Whitter, v; acc. own h/g.
New York, NY   Thursday, April 23, and Friday, April 24, 1925

73312-A	Love Me While I Am Living	OK 40403
73313-A	My Darling's Black Mustache	OK 40395
73314-	I Wish I Was A Single Girl Again	OK unissued
73315-A	The Clouds Gwine To Roll Away	OK 40395
73316-A	Good-Bye, Old Booze	OK 40403
73317-A	Butcher Boy	OK 40375

Matrix 73312 was recorded on April 23, matrices 73316/17 on April 24, the rest presumably on one day or the other.

Atlanta, GA   Wednesday, July 1, 1925

9210-A	The Story By The Moonlight	OK 45003
9211-A	Liza Jane	OK 45003
9212-A	I Wish I Was A Single Girl Again	OK 40375

New York, NY   Wednesday, April 21, 1926

| 80003-A | Many Times With You I've Wandered | OK 45053 |
| 80004-A | Goin' Down To Jordan To Be Baptized | OK 45053 |

Acc. "Fiddler Joe" (Joe Samuels), f-1; own h-2/g.
New York, NY   Thursday, April 22, 1926

74137-A	I Wish I Was Single Again -2	OK 45045
74138-A	Put My Little Shoes Away -2	OK 45046
74139-	The Old Grey Mare -2	OK unissued
74140-A	The Heart Of Old Galax -2	OK 45045
74141-A	Go Bury Me Beneath The Willow Tree -1, 2	OK 45046
74142-	It's A Rough Road To Georgia -1	OK unissued

Matrix 74141 as by **Henry Whitter With Fiddler Joe**.

Acc. own h/g.
Chicago, IL   c. August 1926

2777-1	There Was An Old Tramp	Bwy 8024, Her 75536
2779-3	Geo. Collins	Bwy 8024, Her 75536
2782-2	The Snow Storm	Pm 33183, Bwy 8023, Her 75537
2783-1	The Explosion At Eccles, West Virginia	Pm 33183, Bwy 8023, Her 75537

Intervening matrices are untraced.

Acc. "Fiddler Joe" (Joe Samuels), f-1; own h-2/g.
  New York, NY   Tuesday, September 7, 1926

80088-A	Hand Me Down My Walking Cane -1	OK 45061
80089-A	Show Me The Way To Go Home -1	OK 45061
80090-	A Woman's Tongue Has No End -2?	OK unissued
80091-	The Burglar Man -2?	OK unissued
80092-	George Collins -2?	OK unissued
80093-	Broken Engagement -2?	OK unissued

OKeh 45061 as by **Henry Whitter & Fiddler Joe**.

Acc. own h/g.
  New York, NY   Monday, October 18, 1926

74396-A	The Broken Engagement	OK 45081
74397-A	George Collins	OK 45081
74398-A	The Burglar Man	OK 45063
74399-A	A Woman's Tongue Has No End	OK 45063
74400-	Overshoes And Leggins	OK unissued

Henry Whitter, h solo.
  Bristol, TN   Tuesday, August 2, 1927

39758-2	Henry Whitter's Fox Chase	Vi 20878, BB B-5259, Eld 2139, Sr S-3342, MW M-4475
39759-2	Rain Crow Bill	Vi 20878, MW M-4475

  Atlanta, GA   Tuesday, October 16, 1928

47183-1	The Lost Girl Of West Virginia	Vi V-40061, Zo 5400
47184-2	Poor Lost Boy	Vi V-40061, MW M-4909, Zo 5400

Henry Whitter, h/sp/v eff-1.
  Memphis, TN   Tuesday, October 1, 1929

56325-2	Fox Chase No. 2 -1	Vi V-40292, BB B-5259, Eld 2139, Sr S-3342, MW M-4909
56326-2	Train Blues	Vi V-40292

Henry Whitter also recorded with G.B. Grayson (some of their records being issued under Whitter's name alone), Kelly Harrell, Fisher Hendley, and Roba Stanley.

WHITTER–HENDLEY–SMALL

See Fisher Hendley.

WHITTER'S VIRGINIA BREAKDOWNERS

See Henry Whitter.

BILLIE WHOOP
BILLY WHOOP

Pseudonyms on Paramount for John McGhee.

CHAS. WIESER

Chas. Wieser, zither solo.
  Chicago, IL   c. March 23, 1928

13604	The Jolly Lumberjack	Ge rejected trial recording

PETE WIGGIN
PETE WIGGINS

Pseudonyms for Frank Luther (see Carson Robison).

SETH WIGGINS
WIGGINS BROTHERS

Pseudonyms on Brunswick 260, for, respectively, Al Bernard, and Al Bernard & James O'Keefe.

WIJSKOWA ORKESTRA

Victor V-21139, a Ukrainian-series issue, with this artist credit is by Jack Pierce & The Oklahoma Cowboys.

MILLER WIKEL

Miller Wikel, v; acc. Bill Charles, f-1; John McGhee, h-2/g.
  Richmond, IN   Monday, June 25, 1928

13918	May I Sleep In Your Barn Tonight, Mister -1	Ch 15545, Cq 7254
13919	Frail Wildwood Flower -2	Ge 6566, Cq 7254

| 13920 | She'll Be Waiting On The Golden Stairs | Ge 6566, Ch 15545, Spt 9323 |

Champion 15545 as by **Jim Whalen**. Supertone 9323 as by **Clem Baker**. Conqueror 7254 as by **Joe Reeves**.
Matrix 13918 is titled *May I Sleep In Your Barn Tonight, Mister?* on Conqueror 7254.
Rev. Supertone 9323 by the Sweet Brothers.

Acc. poss. own g.
New York, NY   c. October 1929

GEX-2421-A	Young Charlotte	Pm 3205
GEX-2422-A	No Home No Home	Pm 3205
GEX-2423	My Old Virginia Home	Pm unissued
GEX-2424	My Trundle Bed	Pm unissued

Matrices GEX-2423/24 are uncredited in Gennett files but seem almost certain to be by this artist.

Acc. two unknowns, g.
Richmond, IN   Tuesday, May 27, 1930

16679,-A	My Old Virginia Home	Ge rejected
16680,-A	Young Charlotte	Ge rejected
16682,-A	My Old Homestead	Ge rejected
16684,-A	A Mother's Goodbye	Ge rejected
16685	No Home No Home	Ge rejected

Intervening matrices are popular.

RILEY WILCOX

Pseudonym on Bell for Holland Puckett.

WILEY, ZEKE, & HOMER (THE SMILIN' RANGERS)

See Morris Brothers (Wiley & Zeke).

JOHN WILFAHRT'S CONCERTINA ORCH.

A few of this prolific artist's recordings appeared, under this credit, in the Brunswick old-time series. They are beyond the scope of this work.

FRANK WILKINS

Pseudonym on Broadway for Frank Welling.

WILKINS & MOORE

Pseudonym on Broadway for John McGhee & Frank Welling or, on Broadway 8327, for Owen Mills (David Miller) & Frank Welling.

WILKINS & SHARON

Pseudonym on Broadway for John McGhee & Frank Welling, or, for Welling & Shannon (see John McGhee & Frank Welling).

WILKINS QUARTET

Vocal quartet; acc. unknown, p.
Atlanta, GA   Friday, April 18, 1930

| 150279-2 | I Am So Glad | Co 15592-D |
| 150280-2 | Glory For The Faithful | Co 15592-D |

WILLARD & FOSTER

See John D. Foster.

CARL WILLIAMS

Carl Williams, v; acc. unknown, f; unknown, g.
Chicago, IL   Tuesday, March 24, 1936

C-1306-1,-2	Smile Your Troubles Away	ARC unissued
C-1307-1,-2	Moonlight Shadows	ARC unissued
C-1308-1,-2	I'm Going To Settle Down	ARC unissued
C-1309-1,-2	Ozark Moon	ARC unissued

"DAD" WILLIAMS

This artist's full name is Frank E. Williams.

"Dad" Williams, f/sp-1; acc. unknown, g-2.
New York, NY   Wednesday, January 30, 1929

| E-29256- | The Dutchman's Serenade -1 | Br 306 |
| E-29257- | Money Musk (Intro: Opera Reel) -2 | Br 306 |

"Dad" Williams also recorded with H.M. Barnes & His Blue Ridge Ramblers.

GEORGE WILLIAMS

George Williams, v; acc. prob. own g.
   Richmond, IN
                                                                                          c. mid-April 1928
    13662   Bonham Bus Line Blues Part I   Bonham 20322

Bonham 20322 is a Gennett personal recording.
Rev. Bonham 20322 by Osborne & Williams (see G.C. Osborne).
George Williams also recorded with G.C. Osborne.

HENRY WILLIAMS

Pseudonym on Marathon for Arthur Fields.

KID WILLIAMS

Pseudonym on ARC labels for Walter Smith.

KID WILLIAMS & ROY MARTIN

Pseudonym on ARC labels for Walter Smith and Lewis McDaniels.

KID WILLIAMS & BILL MORGAN

Pseudonym on ARC labels for Walter Smith and Buster Carter.

KITTY WILLIAMS

Pseudonym on English Regal-Zonophone for the Three Williamsons.

MARC WILLIAMS

Marc Williams "The Cowboy Crooner," v; acc. unknown, f-1; own g-2/u-3.
   Chicago, IL   Thursday, March 22, 1928
    C-1758/59*   Willie The Weeper -3   Br 240
    C-1760/61*   Sam Bass -3   Br 304
    C-1762*/63   The Cowboy's Dream -1, 2   Br 244, Spt S2054

Brunswick 244 as by **Marc Williams** only.

Acc. unknown, f-1; own g.
   Chicago, IL   Friday, March 23, 1928
    C-1764/65*   When The Work's All Done This Fall   Br 244, Spt S2054
    C-1766*/67   Jesse James   Br 269
    C-1768/69   Little Joe, The Wrangler   Br 269
    C-1770/71*   Utah Carroll   Br 304
    C-1772*/73   Bad Companions -1   Br 274
    C-1774*/75   William and Mary (Love In Disguise) -1   Br 274

Brunswick 244, 269 as by **Marc Williams** only.

Acc. own u.
   Chicago, IL   Saturday, March 24, 1928
    C-1782/83*   Sioux Indians   Br 240

Acc. own g.
   Dallas, TX   Thursday, October 31, 1929
    DAL-563-A   The Cowboy's Last Wish   Br 377, Spt S2046, Pan 25623
    DAL-564-A   The Crepe Upon The Little Cabin Door   Br 430, Spt S2051, Pan 25636
    DAL-565-A   Sing, Poor Devil, Sing   Br 377, Pan 25623
    DAL-566-A   Cowboy Jack   Br 430, Pan 25636

Supertone S2046, S2051 as by **Marc Williams** only.
Revs: Supertone S2046 by Buell Kazee, S2051 by John B. Evans.

   Dallas, TX   Wednesday, November 26, 1930
    DAL-6743-A   The Boys In Blue   Br 564, Pan 25247, DeIr W4419
    DAL-6744-A   Curly Joe   Br 544, Pan 25589
    DAL-6745-A   The Night Herding Song   Br 497, Spt S2263, Pan 25510, DeIr W4112
    DAL-6746-A   The Little Old Sod Shanty   Br 564, Pan 25247, DeIr W4419
    DAL-6747-A   The Dying Ranger   Br 497, Pan 25510, DeIr W4412
    DAL-6748-A   Cole Younger   Br 544, Pan 25589

Supertone S2263 and possibly Decca W4112, W4419 as by **Marc Williams** only.
Rev. Supertone S2263 by the Beverly Hill Billies.

Marc Williams, v; acc. own g.
   New York, NY
                                                                        Wednesday, August 15, 1934
    38314-A   William And Mary   De 5327

38315-	The Letter Edged In Black	De 5327	
38316-A	Roy Bean	De 5010, DeE F5265	
38317-A	The Old Chisholm Trail	De 5106, DeE F5265	
38318-A	Give My Love To Nell	De 5106	
38319-A	Twenty-One Years	De 5010	

New York, NY   Friday, August 24, 1934

38420-A	Old Montana	De 5012, Pan 25895
38421-A	When The Work's All Done This Fall	De 5012, Pan 25895
38422-A	Roll Out, Cowboys	Pan 25879
38423-A	Willie The Weeper	De 5011, Pan 25757
38424-A	"Sioux Indians" (A Cowboy Chant)	De 5011, Pan 25757
38425-A	Sunny San Juan	Pan 25879

Acc. unknown, esg.
New York, NY   Tuesday, January 28, 1936

60408-A,-B	My Blue Heaven	De rejected
60409-A,-B	My Melancholy Baby	De rejected
60410-A,-B	I'm Waiting For Ships That Never Come In	De unissued
60411-A	When They Changed My Name To A Number	De 5196, MeC 45219, Min M-14078

Acc. unknown, sg; poss. own g.
New York, NY   Monday, February 24, 1936

60566-A	My Melancholy Baby	De 5216
60567-A	My Blue Heaven	De 5216
60568-A	I'm Waiting For Ships That Never Come In	De 5196, MeC 45219, Min M-14078

MARVIN WILLIAMS (SUNSHINE YODLER)

Marvin Williams, v/y; acc. Hauulea Entertainers: unknown, sg; unknown, g; unknown, u.
San Antonio, TX   Sunday, June 15, 1930

404316-B	Can't Sleep In Your Barn Tonight Mister	OK 45467
404317-B	Lula Whal	OK 45467
404318-A	The Town Of The Lonesome Touch	OK 45483, Ve 2364-V
404319-B	Back Where The Blue Bonnets Grow	OK 45483

Velvet Tone 2364-V as by **Eddie Madden (The Strolling Yodeler)**.
Rev. Velvet Tone 2364-V by Earl & Bell (popular).

ZEKE WILLIAMS & HIS RAMBLING COWBOYS

Zeke Williams, v/y-1; acc. Charlie Gregg, f; Steve Wooden, g/v-2; "Sleepy" Rice, g or sb/v-2; unknown, g or sb.
Dallas, TX   Saturday, June 19, 1937

DAL-380-1	Breeze (Blow My Baby Back To Me) -2	ARC 7-12-64, Vo/OK 03755
DAL-381-1	Don't Forget Me Little Darling -1	ARC 7-09-63, Vo 03635
DAL-382-1	I've Got The Blues For Mammy -1	ARC 7-10-62, Vo 03673, Cq 8950
DAL-383-	Back To Arizona	ARC unissued
DAL-384-	Alley Boogie	ARC unissued

Zeke Williams, v; acc. Charlie Gregg, f; Steve Wooden, g/v-1; "Sleepy" Rice, g or sb/v-2; unknown, g or sb.
Dallas, TX   Tuesday, June 22, 1937

DAL-432-1	The Starlit Trail -1, 2	ARC 7-12-64, Vo/OK 03755
DAL-433-1	Westward Ho -1, 2	ARC 7-09-63, Vo 03635
DAL-434-1	He's Gone, He's Gone Up The Trail -1, 2	Vo 04000
DAL-435-1	I Would If I Could -1/2	ARC 7-10-62, Vo 03673, Cq 8950
DAL-436-	Carolina Moonshiner	ARC unissued

Zeke Williams, v/y-1; acc. prob. Charlie Gregg, f; prob. Steve Wooden, g/v-2/y-3; prob. "Sleepy" Rice, g or sb/v-2/y-3; unknown, g or sb; Hank Holland, sp-4.
San Antonio, TX   Wednesday, November 3, 1937

SA-2881-	Hole In The Wall	ARC unissued
SA-2882-	The Old Chisholm Trail	ARC unissued
SA-2883-1	The Cowboy's Dream -2, 4	ARC 8-01-63, Vo/OK 03892, Co 20553
SA-2884-1	What A Friend We Have In Jesus -2, 4	ARC 8-01-63, Vo/OK 03892, Co 20553
SA-2885-	Missouri Hills	ARC unissued
SA-2886-1	One More Ride -1, 2, 3	Vo 04000

There may be only one guitar on this session.

WILLIAMS & WILLIAMS

Vocal duet; acc. unknown, p.
Atlanta, GA   Tuesday, March 29, 1927

| 143803-2 | In The Garden | Co 15172-D, Ve 7105-V |
| 143804-2 | Though Your Sins Be As Scarlet | Co 15172-D, Ve 7104-V |

Revs: Velvet Tone 7104-V, 7105-V by Chris Bouchillon.

Atlanta, GA   Tuesday, November 8, 1927

| 145164-1,-2 | Will The Circle Be Unbroken | Co unissued |
| 145165-1,-2 | Jesus My Savior | Co unissued |

JIMMIE WILLIAMSON

Jimmie Williamson, v; acc. prob. own bj.
Richmond, IN   Wednesday, February 1, 1928

| 13416,-A | The Dying Texas Ranger | Ge rejected |

WILLIAMSON BROTHERS & CURRY

Arnold Williamson, f; Ervin Williamson, g; Arnold Curry, bj-u; unidentified v solo-1/duet-2/trio-3/calls-4.
St. Louis, MO   Tuesday, April 26, 1927

80751-A	Cumberland Gap -1	OK 45108
80752-B	Warfield -3	OK 45127
80753-B	The Fun's All Over -4	OK 45108
80755-B	Lonesome Road Blues -3	OK 45146
80756-B	The Old Arm-Chair -1	OK 45146
80757-B	Gonna Die With My Hammer In My Hand -2	OK 45127

Matrix 80754 is by Stovepipe No. 1 & David Crockett (see B&GR).

BOB WILLS

Jim Rob Wills & Herman Arnspiger: James Robert "Bob" Wills, f; Herman Arnspiger, g.
Dallas, TX   Friday, November 1, 1929

| TDA-569 | Gulf Coast Blues | Br/Vo cancelled |
| TDA-570 | Wills Breakdown | Br/Vo cancelled |

Bob Wills & His Texas Playboys: Bob Wills, f/v-1/sp; Jesse Thedford Ashlock, f; Arthur D. "Art" Haynes, f/tb; Robert "Zeb" McNally, as; Thomas Elmer "Tommy" Duncan, poss. ts-2/v-3; William Leon McAuliffe, esg-4/eg-5/v-6; Alton Meeks "Al" Stricklin, p; Johnnie Lee Wills, tbj; Clifton G. "Sleepy" Johnson, g; Herman Arnspiger, g; Thomas C. "Son" Lansford, sb; William E. "Smokey" Dacus, d; band v-7.
Dallas, TX   Monday, September 23, 1935

DAL-126-2	Osage Stomp -4	Vo/OK 03096, Co 37701, 20280
DAL-127-1	Get With It -3, 5, 7	Vo/OK 03096, Co 37701, 20280
DAL-128-1,-2	Pray For The Lights To Go Out -1, 4?, 5?, 7?	Vo unissued
DAL-129-2	I Can't Give You Anything But Love -2, 4, 6	Vo/OK 03264, Co 37703, 20282
DAL-130-1	Spanish Two Step -4	Vo/OK 03230, Co 20498
DAL-131-1	Maiden's Prayer -4	Vo/OK 03924, Co 20473, CoC C1157
DAL-132-1	Wang Wang Blues -4	Vo/OK 03173
DAL-133-1	St. Louis Blues -1, 3, 5	Vo unissued: TR TXR-2709 (LP)
DAL-133-2	St. Louis Blues -1, 3, 5	Vo/OK 03076, Co 37605, 20204

Although some attempt has been made to identify individual musicians' contributions, the personnels cited throughout this entry should be regarded as collective.

Bob Wills, f/v-1/sp; Jesse Ashlock, f; Ruth McMaster, f-2; Art Haynes, f/tb; Zeb McNally, as; Leon McAuliffe, esg-3/eg-4/v-5; Al Stricklin, p; Johnnie Lee Wills, tbj; Sleepy Johnson, g/v-6; Herman Arnspiger, g; Son Lansford, sb; Smokey Dacus, d; Tommy Duncan, v-7/y-8; band v-9.
Dallas, TX   Tuesday, September 24, 1935

DAL-134-1	Good Old Oklahoma -3, 7, 9	Vo/OK 03086, Co 37607, 20206
DAL-135-2	Blue River-1, 2, 3, 6 (lead), 7	Vo/OK 03230
DAL-136-1	Mexicali Rose -1, 3	Vo/OK 03086, Cq 9169, Co 37607, 20206
DAL-137-1	I Ain't Got Nobody -3, 7, 8	Vo/OK 03206, *Antone's 102*
DAL-138-2	Never No More Blues -3, 7, 8	Vo/OK 03264, Co 37703, 20282
DAL-139-1	Who Walks In When I Walk Out -4, 5	Vo/OK 03206, *Antone's 102*
DAL-140-2	Old Fashioned Love -1, 3	Vo/OK 03295, Co 37616, 20215
DAL-141-2	Oklahoma Rag -4	Vo/OK 03295, Co 37616, 20215
DAL-142-1	Black And Blue Rag -3	Vo/OK 03139, Co 37612, 20211
DAL-143-2	Sittin' On Top Of The World -1, 4	Vo/OK 03139, Co 37612, 20211
DAL-144-1	Four Or Five Times-1, 3, 9	Vo/OK 03076, Co 37605, 20204
DAL-144-2	Four Or Five Times-1, 3, 9	Vo unissued: *Co C2-40149 (LP)*
DAL-145-2	I Can't Be Satisfied -4, 7, 9	Vo/OK 03173

Rev. Conqueror 9169 by Hoosier Hot Shots.

Bob Wills & Sleepy Johnson: Bob Wills, f; Sleepy Johnson, g.

Dallas, TX   Wednesday, September 25, 1935

DAL-146-1	Smith's Reel	ARC 6-11-58
DAL-147-1	Harmony	ARC 6-11-58
DAL-148-1	Tulsa Waltz	Vo unissued: *CMF 010-L (LP)*; *BF BCD15933 (CD)*
DAL-149-1	Waltz In D	Vo unissued: *CMF 010-L (LP)*; *BF BCD15933 (CD)*

Bob Wills & His Texas Playboys: Bob Wills, f/sp; Jesse Ashlock, f/v-1; Sleepy Johnson, f/g; Everett Stover, t; Ray DeGeer, cl/s; Zeb McNally, s; Leon McAuliffe, esg; Al Stricklin, p; Johnnie Lee Wills, tbj; Herman Arnspiger, g; Joe Frank Ferguson, sb-2/v-3; unidentified (prob. Johnson or Duncan), sb-4; Smokey Dacus, d; Tommy Duncan, v-5; band v-6.

Chicago, IL   Monday, September 28, 1936

C-1475-2	She's Killing Me -2, 5, 6	Vo/OK 03424, Co 37622, 20221
C-1476-1	Weary Of The Same Ol' Stuff -1, 2	Vo/OK 03343, Cq 9041
C-1477-2	No Matter How She Done It -3, 4, 6	Vo/OK 03537, Co 37625, 20224
C-1478-2	Bluin' The Blues -2	Vo/OK 03614

Bob Wills, f/v-1/sp; Jesse Ashlock, f; Sleepy Johnson, f/g/v-2; Everett Stover, t; Ray DeGeer, cl/s; Zeb McNally, s; Leon McAuliffe, esg/v-3; Al Stricklin, p; Johnnie Lee Wills, tbj; Herman Arnspiger, g; Joe Ferguson, sb/v-4; Smokey Dacus, d; Tommy Duncan, v-5; unidentified, y duet-6; band v-7.

Chicago, IL   Tuesday, September 29, 1936

C-1479-1	Steel Guitar Rag	OK 03394
C-1479-2	Steel Guitar Rag	Vo/OK 03394, Co 37620, 20219
C-1480-2	Get Along Home Cindy -5, 7	Vo/OK 03451, Co 37623, 20222
C-1481-2	Trouble In Mind -5	Vo/OK 03343, Cq 9041, Co 37306, 20109, CoC C6366
C-1482-2	What's The Matter With The Mill? -1, 5, 7	Vo/OK 03424, Co 37622, 20221
C-1483-2	Sugar Blues -1	Vo/OK 03361, Co 37619, 20218
C-1484-2	Basin Street Blues -5	Vo/OK 03344, Cq 9040, Co 37618, 20217
C-1485-2	Red Hot Gal Of Mine -5	Vo/OK 03344, Cq 9040, Co 37618, 20217
C-1486-1	Darktown Strutters' Ball -1, 5	Vo unissued: *Encore P14390 (LP)*
C-1486-2	Darktown Strutters' Ball -1, 5	Vo unissued: *BF BCD15933 (CD)*
C-1487-1	Too Busy	Vo/OK 03537, Co 37625, 20224
C-1488-1	Back Home Again In Indiana -5	Vo/OK 03578, CoC C910
C-1489-1,-2	There's A Quaker Down In Quaker Town -2, 3, 4	Vo unissued
C-1490-2	Away Out There -5, 6	Vo unissued: *Co FC-37648 (LP)*; *BF BCD15933 (CD)*

Bob Wills, f; Sleepy Johnson, g; Leon McAuliffe, g.

Chicago, IL   Tuesday, September 29, 1936

C-1492-2	Crippled Turkey	Vo unissued: *CMF 010-L (LP)*; *BF BCD15933 (CD)*

Chicago, IL   Wednesday, September 30, 1936

C-1491-1,-2	Just Friends	Vo unissued

Matrix C-1491 may have been recorded on September 29 despite the Columbia file date of September 30.

Bob Wills, f/v-1/sp; Jesse Ashlock, f; Sleepy Johnson, f/g; Everett Stover, t/v-2; Ray DeGeer, cl/s; Zeb McNally, s; Leon McAuliffe, esg; Al Stricklin, p; Johnnie Lee Wills, tbj/v-3; Herman Arnspiger, g; Joe Ferguson, sb; Smokey Dacus, d; Tommy Duncan, v-4/y-5.

Chicago, IL   Wednesday, September 30, 1936

C-1493-1	Fan It -3	Vo/OK 03361, Co 37619, 20218
C-1494-1	Red Head -2	Vo unissued: *Encore P14390 (LP)*
C-1494-2	Red Head -2	Vo unissued: *BF BCD15933 (CD)*
C-1495-2	Mean Mama Blues -4, 5	Vo/OK 03492, Co 37624, 20223
C-1496-2	There's No Disappointment In Heaven -1(lead), 4	Vo unissued: *Co P15813, Co C2-40149, Time-Life TLCW-07 (LPs)*; *BF BCD15933 (CD)*
C-1497-2	Rockin' Alone In An Old Rockin' Chair -1	Vo unissued: *Co P4-15542 (LP)*; *BF BCD15933 (CD)*
C-1498-1,-2	Bear Cat Mama -1	Vo unissued
C-1499-1	Sleepy Time In Sleepy Hollow -4	Vo unissued: *BF BCD15933 (CD)*
C-1500-1	Bring It On Down To My House -1, 4	Vo/OK 03492, Co 37624, 20223
C-1501-2	I've Got The Wonder Where She Went (Blues) -4	Vo unissued: *Time-Life TLCW-07, Co C2-40149 (LPs)*; *BF BCD15933 (CD)*
C-1502-1,-2	Roll Along Kentucky Moon -4	Vo unissued
C-1503-2	Right Or Wrong -4, 5	Vo/OK 03451, Co 37623, 20222
C-1504-1	Swing Blues #1 -1, 4	Vo/OK 03394, Co 37620, 20219
C-1504-2	Swing Blues #1 -1, 4	Vo unissued: *TR TXR-2709 (LP)*; *BF BCD15933 (CD)*
C-1505-2	Swing Blues #2 -1, 4	Vo/OK 03578

Bob Wills, f/v-1/sp; Jesse Ashlock, f; Cecil Brower, f; Sleepy Johnson, f/g; Everett Stover, t; poss. Robert Lee "Bob" Dunn, tb-2; Ray DeGeer, cl/s; Zeb McNally, s; Leon McAuliffe, esg; Al Stricklin, p; Johnnie Lee Wills, tbj; Herman Arnspiger, g; Joe Ferguson, sb; Smokey Dacus, d; Tommy Duncan, v-3.

Dallas, TX   Monday, June 7, 1937

DAL-212-2	White Heat	Vo/OK 03614
DAL-213-1,-2	I'll Get Mine -3	Vo unissued
DAL-214-1	Dedicated To You -1, 2	Vo/OK 03597
DAL-215-1	Playboy Stomp -2	Vo 03854
DAL-216-2	Steel Guitar Stomp	Vo unissued: Co C2-40149 (LP); BF BCD15933 (CD)
DAL-216-3	Steel Guitar Stomp	Vo/OK 03997, Cq 9039, Co 37628, 20227
DAL-217-1	Rosetta -1	Vo/OK 03659, Antone's 103
DAL-218-2	Bleeding Hearted Blues -2, 3	Vo/OK 03597
DAL-219-1,-2	Down Hearted Blues -1	Vo unissued
DAL-220-1,-2	Ole Jelly Roll Blues -3	Vo unissued

Take 3 of matrix DAL-216 is a technical remastering of take 1.

Bob Wills, f/v-1/sp; Jesse Ashlock, f; Cecil Brower, f; Sleepy Johnson, f/g; Everett Stover, t; Ray DeGeer, cl/s; Zeb McNally, s; Leon McAuliffe, esg/v-2; Al Stricklin, p; Johnnie Lee Wills, tbj; Herman Arnspiger, g; Joe Ferguson, sb; Smokey Dacus, d; Tommy Duncan, v-3/y-4.

Dallas, TX   Tuesday, June 8, 1937

DAL-221-2	Blue Yodel #1 -3, 4	Vo unissued: Co KG32416 (LP); BF BCD15933 (CD)
DAL-222-1	Tulsa Stomp	Vo unissued: Co P15813 (LP); BF BCD15933 (CD)
DAL-222-2	Tulsa Stomp	Vo unissued: TR TXR-2709 (LP); BF BCD15933 (CD)
DAL-223-1,-2	There Are Two Sides To Every Story -1	Vo unissued
DAL-224-1,-2	Thirty-First Street Blues -3, 4	Vo unissued
DAL-225-1,-2	Oh, You Beautiful Doll -1, 3	Vo unissued
DAL-226-1,-2	Mexicali Rose -1	Vo unissued
DAL-227-2	Tie Me To Your Apron Strings Again -1, 3	Vo 03854
DAL-228-1,-2	Keep Knocking But You Can't Come In -2	Vo unissued
DAL-229-1	Never No More Hard Times Blues -3, 4	Co 20473, CoC C1157, RZ ME79, RZIr IZ1365
DAL-229-2	Never No More Hard Times Blues -3, 4	Vo/OK 03924
DAL-230-1	Sunbonnet Sue -1, 3	Vo/OK 03997, Cq 9039, Co 37628, 20227
DAL-230-2	Sunbonnet Sue -1, 3	Vo 03997
DAL-231-1,-2	La Golondrina (The Swallow)	Vo unissued
DAL-232-1,-2,-3	At The Barn Dance (Introducing: The Girl I Left Behind Me)	Vo unissued
DAL-234-1,-2	Dallas Blues	Vo unissued

Matrix DAL-234 may have been recorded on June 9 despite the Columbia file date of June 8.

Bob Wills, f/v-1/sp; Jesse Ashlock, f/v-2; Sleepy Johnson, f/g; Everett Stover, t; Ray DeGeer, cl/s; Zeb McNally, s; Leon McAuliffe, esg/v-3; Al Stricklin, p; Johnnie Lee Wills, tbj; Herman Arnspiger, g; Joe Ferguson, sb; Smokey Dacus, d; Tommy Duncan, v-4.

Dallas, TX   Wednesday, June 9, 1937

DAL-233-1,-2	There Is A Tavern In The Town -3	Vo unissued
DAL-235-2	The New St. Louis Blues -1, 4	Vo/OK 03693, Co 37712, 20289
DAL-236-3	Loveless Love -1, 4	Vo unissued: BF BCD15933 (CD)
DAL-237-2	I'm A Ding Dong Daddy (From Dumas) -1, 4	Vo/OK 03659, Antone's 103
DAL-238-1,-2	I Wish I Could Shimmy Like My Sister Kate -2	Vo unissued
DAL-239-1	Oozlin' Daddy Blues -1, 4	Vo/OK 03693, Co 37712, 20289
DAL-239-3	Oozlin' Daddy Blues -1, 4	Vo unissued: BF BCD15933 (CD)

Matrix DAL-236-3 is a technical remastering of either take 1 or take 2.

Bob Wills, f/v-1/sp; Jesse Ashlock, f; Charles Laughton, t/cl/s; Everett Stover, t; Zeb McNally, s; Leon McAuliffe, esg/v-2; Al Stricklin, p; Sleepy Johnson, tbj; Eldon Shamblin, g; Joe Ferguson, sb-3/v-4; Tommy Duncan, prob. sb-5/v-6/y-7; Smokey Dacus, d; band v-8.

Dallas, TX   Monday, May 16, 1938

DAL-562-1	Black Rider -3, 6	OK 04132
DAL-562-2	Black Rider -3, 6	Vo/OK 04132
DAL-563-1	Everybody Does It In Hawaii -3, 6	Vo/OK 04132
DAL-563-2	Everybody Does It In Hawaii -3, 6	Vo unissued: BF BCD15933 (CD)
DAL-564-1,-2	I'm Free From The Chain Gang Now -3, 6	Vo unissued
DAL-565-1	Alexander's Ragtime Band -2, 3	Vo unissued: BF BCD15933 (CD)
DAL-565-2	Alexander's Ragtime Band -2, 3	Vo/OK 04275, Cq 9156
DAL-566-1	Blue Prelude -4, 5	Vo/OK 05333

DAL-567-1	Down Hearted Blues -1, 3	Vo unissued: *Time-Life TLCW-07*(LP); BF BCD15933 (CD)
DAL-568-1	Little Heaven Of The Seven Seas -3	Vo unissued: *Encore P14390* (LP)
DAL-568-2	Little Heaven Of The Seven Seas -3	Vo unissued: BF BCD15933 (CD)
DAL-569-1	Sophisticated Hula -3	Vo/OK 05333
DAL-570-1	Pray For The Lights To Go Out -1, 3, 8	Vo/OK 05401, Cq 9718, *Antone's 100*
DAL-571-1	Gambling Polka Dot Blues -3, 6, 7	Vo/OK 04275, Cq 9156
DAL-571-2	Gambling Polka Dot Blues -3, 6, 7	Vo unissued: *Co C2-40149* (LP); BF BCD15933 (CD)
DAL-572-1	Keep Knocking (But You Can't Come In) -2, 3	Vo/OK 04184, Cq 9070, Co 37629, 20228
DAL-573-1	Loveless Love -1, 3, 6	Vo/OK 04387

Rev. *Antone's 100* by Bob Wills (postwar).

Jesse Ashlock, f/v-1/sp; Charles Laughton, t/cl/s; Everett Stover, t; Zeb McNally, s; Leon McAuliffe, esg/v-2; Al Stricklin, p; Sleepy Johnson, tbj/v-3; Eldon Shamblin, g; Joe Ferguson, sb-4/v-5; Tommy Duncan, prob. sb-6/v-7/y-8; Smokey Dacus, d; unidentified, v trio-9.

Dallas, TX   Tuesday, May 17, 1938

DAL-574-1	Oh, Lady Be Good -4	Vo unissued: BF BCD15933 (CD)
DAL-574-2	Oh, Lady Be Good -4	Vo/OK 04515, Co 37728, 20305
DAL-575-1	Way Down Upon The Swanee River -4	Vo/OK 04387
DAL-575-2	Way Down Upon The Swanee River -4	Vo unissued: *Co C2-40149* (LP); BF BCD15933 (CD)
DAL-576-1	Don't Stop Loving Me -5, 6	Vo unissued: BF BCD15933 (CD)
DAL-577-1	Oh You Beautiful Doll -4, 7	Vo/OK 04515, Co 37728, 20305
DAL-577-2	Oh You Beautiful Doll -4, 7	Vo unissued: BF BCD15933 (CD)
DAL-578-1	Moonlight And Roses (Bring Mem'ries Of You) -4, 9	Vo/OK 04439, Cq 9155, Co 37727, 20304
DAL-579-1	William Tell -4	Vo unissued: *Encore P14390, Co C2-40149* (LPs); BF BCD15933 (CD)
DAL-580-1	I Wish I Could Shimmy Like My Sister Kate -1, 4	Vo/OK 04439, Cq 9155, Co 37727, 20304
DAL-581-1	Mississippi Delta Blues -4, 7, 8	Vo unissued: *Encore P14390* (LP); BF BCD15933 (CD)
DAL-582-1	Tulsa Stomp -4	Vo/OK 04325, Cq 9400, Co 37725, 20302
DAL-583-1	Empty Bed Blues -4, 7	Vo/OK 04184, Cq 9070, Co 37629, 20228
DAL-584-1,-2	Oh! You Pretty Woman -2, 4	Vo unissued
DAL-585-1	Little Red Head -5, 6	Vo/OK 04325, Co 37725, 20302
DAL-586-1	I'll See You In My Dreams -3, 4	Vo unissued: *Co KG32416* (LP); BF BCD15933 (CD)

Bob Wills, f/sp; Jesse Ashlock, f; Sleepy Johnson, f; Everett Stover, t-1; Charles Laughton, t-2; Leon McAuliffe, esg/v-3; Eldon Shamblin, eg/g; Al Stricklin, p; Johnnie Lee Wills, tbj; Herman Arnspiger, g; Son Lansford, sb; Smokey Dacus, d; Tommy Duncan, v-4; unidentified, v trio-5.

Dallas, TX   Monday, November 28, 1938

DAL-615-1	San Antonio Rose	Vo/OK 04755, Cq 9226, Co 37009, 20035, 52029, V-D 115, RZ ME79, RZIr IZ1365
DAL-616-1	Little Girl, Go Ask Your Mama	Vo/OK 04625, Cq 9210, Co 37731, 20308
DAL-617-1	Carolina In The Morning	Vo/OK 05079, Cq 9354, Co 37735, 20312
DAL-618-1	The Convict And The Rose -1, 4	Vo/OK 04755, Cq 9226, Co 37009, 20035
DAL-619-1	Silver Bells	Vo/OK 04934, Cq 9721, Co 20498
DAL-620-1	Dreamy Eyes Waltz	Vo/OK 05161
DAL-621-1	Beaumont Rag	Vo/OK 04999, Cq 9718, Co 37642, 20241
DAL-622-1	Twinkle Twinkle Little Star	Vo/OK 05401, *Antone's 104*
DAL-625-1	If I Could Bring Back My Buddy -1, 5	Vo/OK 05228
DAL-626-1	Whoa Babe -2, 3	Vo/OK 04625, Cq 9210, Co 37731, 20308

Take 2 of matrix DAL-618, which appears on some issues of Conqueror 9226, is a technical remastering of take 1.

Bob Wills, f/v-1/sp; Jesse Ashlock, f; Sleepy Johnson, f; Everett Stover, t-2; Charles Laughton, t-3/s-4; Zeb McNally, s-5; Joe Ferguson, s-6/v-7; Leon McAuliffe, esg; Al Stricklin, p; Johnnie Lee Wills, tbj; Eldon Shamblin, g; Herman Arnspiger, g; Son Lansford, sb; Smokey Dacus, d; Tommy Duncan, v-8/y-9; band v-10.

Dallas, TX   Tuesday, November 29, 1938

DAL-623-1	Ida Red -8, 10	Vo/OK 05079, Co 37735, 20312
DAL-624-1	Yearning (Just For You) -1, 2, 4, 5?, 6	Vo/OK 04934, Cq 9721
DAL-627-1	I Wonder If You Feel The Way I Do -8	Vo/OK 04566, Cq 9206, Co 37637, 20236, CoC C983, RZAu G23970
DAL-631-1	Prosperity Special	Vo/OK 05228
DAL-633-1	Drunkard's Blues -8, 9	Vo/OK 05282, Cq 9604, Co 37739, 20316
DAL-634-1	You're Okay -2?, 3?, 5?, 7	Vo/OK 04839, Cq 9213, Co 37639, 20238
DAL-635-1	Liza Pull Down The Shades	Vo/OK 04839, Cq 9213, Co 37639, 20238

Rev. Regal-Zonophone G23970 by Light Crust Doughboys.

Bob Wills, f/sp; Jesse Ashlock, f; Sleepy Johnson, f; Everett Stover, t-1; Charles Laughton, t-2/s-3; Zeb McNally, s; Joe Ferguson, s; Leon McAuliffe, esg/v-4; Al Stricklin, p; Johnnie Lee Wills, tbj; Eldon Shamblin, g; Herman Arnspiger, g; Son Lansford, sb; Smokey Dacus, d; Tommy Duncan, v-5.

Dallas, TX   Wednesday, November 30, 1938

DAL-628-1	That's What I Like 'Bout The South -2, 4	Vo/OK 04566, Cq 9206, Co 37637, 20236, CoC C983
DAL-629-1	My Window Faces The South -1, 2, 4	Vo/OK 05161, *Antone's 104, 501*
DAL-630-1	The Waltz You Saved For Me -3, 5	Vo/OK 04999, Cq 9354, Co 37642, 20241

Rev. Antone's 501 by Bob Wills (postwar).

Bob Wills, f; Jesse Ashlock, f; Sleepy Johnson, f; Leon McAuliffe, esg; Al Stricklin, p; Johnnie Lee Wills, tbj; Eldon Shamblin, g; Herman Arnspiger, g; Son Lansford, sb; Smokey Dacus, d.

Dallas, TX   Wednesday, November 30, 1938

DAL-632-1	Don't Let The Deal Go Down	Vo/OK 05282, Co 37739, 20316

Bob Wills, f/v-1/sp; Jesse Ashlock, f; Lewis E. "Louis" Tierney, f; Leon McAuliffe, esg; Al Stricklin, p; Johnnie Lee Wills, tbj/g; Eldon Shamblin, g; poss. Herman Arnspiger, g; Son Lansford, sb; Smokey Dacus, d; Tommy Duncan, v-2; unidentified, v trio-3.

Saginaw, TX   Monday, April 15, 1940

DAL-968-1	You Don't Love Me (But I'll Always Care) -2	Vo unissued: *Co C2-40149 (LP)*
DAL-968-2	You Don't Love Me (But I'll Always Care) -2	Vo/OK 05597, Cq 9720
DAL-969-2	No Wonder -1	Vo/OK 05597, Cq 9720
DAL-970-1	Lone Star Rag	OK 05637, Cq 9604, Co 37749, 20326, CoC C910
DAL-970-2	Lone Star Rag	Vo unissued: *Encore P14390, Co P15813 (LPs); BF BCD15933 (CD)*
DAL-971-1	There's Going To Be A Party (For The Old Folks) -2	Vo unissued: *BF BCD15933 (CD)*
DAL-971-2	There's Going To Be A Party (For The Old Folks) -2	OK 05905, Cq 9386
DAL-972-1	I Don't Lov'a Nobody	OK 05637, Co 37749, 20326
DAL-972-2	I Don't Lov'a Nobody	Vo unissued: *CMF 010-L (LP); BF BCD 15933 (CD)*
DAL-973-1	That Brownskin Gal	Vo unissued: *CMF 010-L (LP); BF BCD15933 (CD)*
DAL-973-2	That Brownskin Gal	OK 05753, Cq 9394
DAL-974-1	Corrine Corrina -1	OK 06530, Co 37428, 20155, CoC C550
DAL-974-2	Corrine Corrina -1	Vo unissued: *BF BCD15933 (CD)*
DAL-975-1	Let Me Call You Sweetheart (I'm In Love With You) -1	Co 20513
DAL-976-1	Blue Bonnet Rag	Vo unissued: *Co C2-40149 (LP)*
DAL-976-2	Blue Bonnet Rag	Vo/OK 05523, Co 37647, 20246
DAL-978-1	Time Changes Everything -2	Vo unissued: *Co CK48958 (CD)*
DAL-978-2	Time Changes Everything -2	OK 05753, Cq 9394, Co 37308, 20111, CoC C6368
DAL-979-2	Medley Of Spanish Waltzes (1) La Golondrina (2) Lady Of Spain (3) Cielito Lindo -3	Vo/OK 05523, Cq 9603, Co 37647, 20246

Matrix DAL-970-1 is titled *Loan Star Rag* on Columbia 37749. Matrix DAL-970-2 is incorrectly identified as take 1 on Encore P14390.

Bob Wills, f/v-1/sp; Jesse Ashlock, f; Louie Tierney, f/s; Walter Earle "Tubby" Lewis, t; Everett Stover, t; Murel Wayne Johnson, cl/s; Zeb McNally, s; Joe Ferguson, s; poss. Lloyd E. "Tiny" Mott, s; Leon McAuliffe, esg; Al Stricklin, p; Johnnie Lee Wills, tbj/g; Eldon Shamblin, g; poss. Herman Arnspiger, g; Son Lansford, sb; Smokey Dacus, d; Tommy Duncan, v-2.

Saginaw, TX   Tuesday, April 16, 1940

DAL-977-1	Bob Wills Special	Vo unissued: *CMF 010-L (LP); BF BCD15933 (CD)*
DAL-977-2	Bob Wills' Special	OK 05694, Cq 9400, Co 37014, 20040, CoC C150, C1026
DAL-980-1/1a	Big Beaver	OK 05905, Cq 9386
DAL-980-1b/1c/2	Big Beaver	Co 37308, 20111, CoC C6368
DAL-980-3	Big Beaver	Vo unissued: *BF BCD15933 (CD)*
DAL-981-1	New San Antonio Rose -2	OK 05694, Cq 9603, Co 37014, 37306, 20040, 20109, 52029, CoC C150, C1026, C6366, V-D 115
DAL-981-2	New San Antonio Rose -2	Vo unissued: *Co B2805 (EP); Co HL9003, Ha HL7036, HS 11358, Ep BG33782, Time-Life STW-119 (LPs)*
DAL-982-1	Wait 'Til You See -1	Vo unissued: *BF BCD15933 (CD)*

| DAL-982-2 | Wait 'Til You See -1 | Vo unissued: *Encore P14390* (LP) |

Some pressings of OKeh 05694 as by **Bob Wills & His Texas Cowboys**.
Matrix DAL-982 is incorrectly identified as take 1 on Encore P14390.
Matrix 977 may have been recorded on April 15 despite the Columbia file date of April 16.

Bob Wills, f/v-1/sp; Louie Tierney, f/s; Tubby Lewis, t; Jamie MacIntosh, t; poss. Everett Stover, t; Don Harlan, cl/s; Wayne Johnson, cl/s; Zeb McNally, s; Leon McAuliffe, esg/v-2; Eldon Shamblin, eg/g; Al Stricklin, p; Son Lansford, sb; Eugene Tomlins, d; Tommy Duncan, v-3.

Fort Worth, TX   Monday, February 24, 1941

DAL-1168-1	Liebestraum	OK unissued: *Co C2-40149* (LP); *BF BCD15933* (CD)
DAL-1168-2	Liebestraum	OK unissued: *Time-Life TLCW-07* (LP); *BF BCD15933* (CD)
DAL-1169-1	Lyla Lou -2	OK 06327, Cq 9819
DAL-1169-2	Lyla Lou -2	OK unissued: *Co FC37468* (LP); *BF BCD15933* (CD)
DAL-1170-1	New Worried Mind -1, 3	OK 06101, Cq 9818, Co 37019, 20045, CoC C331
DAL-1170-3	New Worried Mind -1, 3	OK unissued: *BF BCD15933* (CD)
DAL-1171-2	La Paloma	OK unissued: *Co P15813, FM 75-76, 89-92* (LPs); *BF BCD15933* (CD)
DAL-1172-1	Maiden's Prayer -3	OK 06205, Cq 9824
DAL-1172-2	A Maiden's Prayer -3	OK unissued: *Co CK48958* (CD)
DAL-1173-1	Oh! You Pretty Woman -2	OK 06640, Cq 9821, Co 37022, 20048
DAL-1173-2	Oh! You Pretty Woman -2	OK unissued: *Encore P14390* (LP)
DAL-1174-1	I Found A Dream -3	OK unissued: *Co KG32416* (LP)
DAL-1174-2	I Found A Dream -3	OK unissued: *BF BCD15933* (CD)
DAL-1175-1	The Girl I Left Behind Me	OK unissued: *Co C2-40149* (LP); *BF BCD15933* (CD)
DAL-1175-2	The Girl I Left Behind Me	OK unissued: *Ep EG37324* (LP); *BF BCD15933* (CD)

Matrix DAL-1175-2 is incorrectly identified as take 1 on Epic EG37324.

Bob Wills, f/sp; Louie Tierney, f; Leon McAuliffe, esg; Eldon Shamblin, eg; Al Stricklin, p; Son Lansford, sb; Gene Tomlins, d; Tommy Duncan, v-1.

Fort Worth, TX   Tuesday, February 25, 1941

DAL-1176-1	I Knew The Moment I Lost You -1	OK 06640, Co 37022, 20048
DAL-1176-2	I Knew The Moment I Lost You -1	OK unissued: *BF BCD15933* (CD)
DAL-1177-1	Done And Gone	Cq 9821
DAL-1177-2	Done and Gone	OK unissued: *Encore P14390* (LP)
DAL-1178-1	Twin Guitar Special	OK 06327, Cq 9819
DAL-1178-2	Twin Guitar Special	OK unissued: *Encore P14390* (LP); *Co CK48958, BF BCD15933, ASV Living Era CD AJA5214* (CDs)
DAL-1178-3	Twin Guitar Special	OK unissued: *BF BCD15933* (CD)
DAL-1179-1	Mississippi Delta Blues -1	OK unissued: *Co KG32416* (LP); *BF BCD15933* (CD)

Bob Wills, f/v-1/sp; Louie Tierney, f; Leon McAuliffe, esg; Eldon Shamblin, eg; Al Stricklin, p; Son Lansford, sb; Gene Tomlins, d; Tommy Duncan, v-2.

Fort Worth, TX   Wednesday, February 26, 1941

DAL-1180-1	Take Me Back To Tulsa -1, 2	OK 06101, Cq 9818, Co 37307, 37019, 20045, 20110, CoC C331, C6367
DAL-1180-2	Take Me Back To Tulsa -1, 2	OK unissued: *Co HL9003, Ha HL7036, HS11358, Ep BG33782, Time-Life STW-119* (LPs)
DAL-1181-1	Takin' It Home	OK 06205, Cq 9824
DAL-1181-2	Takin' It Home	OK unissued: *BF BCD15933* (CD)
DAL-1182-1	I'm Sorry We Said Goodbye -2	OK unissued: *BF BCD15933* (CD)
DAL-1183-1	Honey, What You Gonna Do -2	OK unissued: *Co KG32416* (LP)
DAL-1183-2	Honey, What You Gonna Do -2	OK unissued: *BF BCD15933* (CD)

Bob Wills, f/sp; Jesse Ashlock, f; Louie Tierney, f/s; Don Harlan, cl/s; Wayne Johnson, cl/s; Leon McAuliffe, esg/v-1; Al Stricklin, p; Eldon Shamblin, g; Darrell Jones, sb; Gene Tomlins, d; Tommy Duncan, v-2; band v-3.

Hollywood, CA   Wednesday, July 23, 1941

H-372-2	Blue Bonnet Lane -2, 3	Cq 9822
H-372-3	Blue Bonnet Lane -2, 3	OK unissued: *BF BCD15933* (CD)
H-373-1	Bob Wills Stomp	OK 06371, Cq 9820
H-373-2	Bob Wills Stomp	OK unissued: *CMF 010-L* (LP)
H-374-1	Lil Liza Jane -2, 3	OK 06371, Cq 9820, Co 37664, 20263

H-374-2	Lil Liza Jane -2, 3	OK unissued: *BF BCD15933 (CD)*
H-375-1	Please Don't Leave Me -2	OK 6681, Co 36593, 37025, 20051
H-376-1	Don't Count Your Chickens -1	OK unissued: *Time-Life TLCW-07* (LP); *BF BCD15933 (CD)*
H-377-1	Cherokee Maiden -2, 3	OK 06568, Cq 9822, Co 37422, 20149

Bob Wills, f/v-1/sp; Jesse Ashlock, f; Louie Tierney, f/s; Don Harlan, cl/s; Wayne Johnson, cl/s; Leon McAuliffe, esg/v-2; Al Stricklin, p; Eldon Shamblin, g; Darrell Jones, sb; Gene Tomlins, d; Tommy Duncan, v-3.
Hollywood, CA   Thursday, July 24, 1941

	New San Antonio Rose -3	OK unissued: *Time-Life TLCW-07, Co C2-40149* (LPs); *BF BCD 15933 (CD)*
H-378-1	Ride On! (My Prairie Pinto) -3	OK 06568, Co 37422, 20149
H-378-2	Ride On! (My Prairie Pinto) -3	OK unissued: *BF BCD15933 (CD)*
H-379-1	Got A Letter From My Kid Today -3	Cq 9823
H-380-1	It's All Your Fault -2	OK 06598, Co 37420, 20147
H-380-2	It's All Your Fault -2	OK unissued: *BF BCD15933 (CD)*
H-381-1	Goodnight Little Sweetheart -1	OK 06530, Cq 9823, Co 37428, 20155, CoC C550
H-382-1	Dusty Skies -3	OK 06598, Co 37420, 20147
H-383-1	My Life's Been A Pleasure -2	OK 6681, Co 36593, 37025, 20051

Bob Wills, f/sp; Louie Tierney, f; James "Joe" Holley, f; Reuben Daniel "Danny" Alguire or William Alex Brashear or Benny Strickler, t-1; Woodrow "Woodie" Wood, cl-2; Leon McAuliffe, esg/v-3; Doyle Salathiel, eg; Morris "Mo" Billington, p; Darrell Jones, sb; Robert "Bob" Fitzgerald, d; Leon Huff, v-4; Danny Alguire, v-5; band v-6.
Hollywood, CA   Tuesday, July 14, 1942

H-834-1	We Might As Well Forget It -1, 2, 4	OK 6722, Co 37034, 20059
H-835-1	Drop Us Off At Bob's Place -2, 4	OK unissued: *Time-Life TLCW-07* (LP); *BF BCD15933 (CD)*
H-836-1	Home In San Antone -2, 5	OK 6710, V-D 340
H-837-1	That Hot Lick Fiddlin' Man -3, 6	Co 20531
H-838-1	Liberty	Co 37926, 20373, CoC C958

Bob Wills, f/sp; Louie Tierney, f; Joe Holley, f; Cornelius "Neil" Duer, tb-1; Leon McAuliffe, esg/v-2; Doyle Salathiel, eg; Mo Billington, p; Darrell Jones, sb; Bob Fitzgerald, d; Leon Huff, v-3; unidentified, v trio-4.
Hollywood, CA   Wednesday, July 15, 1942

H-839-Inc.	Miss Molly -2, 4	OK unissued: *BF BCD15933 (CD)*
H-839-1	Miss Molly -2, 4	OK 6710, Co 37309, 20122, CoC C6369, V-D 340
H-839-2	Miss Molly -2, 4	OK unissued: *Time-Life TLCW-07* (LP); *Rhino R2-70744, BF BCD 15933 (CDs)*
H-840-1	It Never Can Be -3	OK unissued: *BF BCD15933 (CD)*
H-840-2	It Never Can Be -1, 3	OK unissued: *BF BCD15933 (CD)*
H-841-1	Honeymoon Trail -1, 4	Co 20487, CoC C1175
H-842-1	It Seems Like Yesterday -1, 3	OK unissued: *BF BCD15933 (CD)*
H-843-1	You're From Texas -2	OK 6722, Co 37034, 20059
H-844-1	Goodbye, Liza Jane -2, 4	Co 20555

Matrix H-839-2 is incorrectly identified as take 1 on Time-Life TLCW-07.

Bob Wills, f/v-1/sp; Joe Holley, f; Louie Tierney, f/ts; Danny Alguire, t; Alex Brashear, t; Benny Strickler, t; Neil Duer, tb; Woodie Wood, cl/as; Don Harlan, cl/as/poss. bs-2; George Balay, cl/ts; Leon McAuliffe, esg; Doyle Salathiel, eg; Mo Billington, p; Darrell Jones, sb; Bob Fitzgerald, d; Leon Huff, v-3; Robert Emerson "Bob" Lee, v-4.
Hollywood, CA   Thursday, July 16, 1942

H-845-1	My Confession -1	OK 6703, Co 37030, 20055
H-845-?	My Confession -1	OK unissued: *Ha HL7304, Co P2-12922, P2-13971* (LPs)
H-846-1	Ten Years -3	OK 6692, Co 37405, 20132
H-846-2	Ten Years -2?, 3	OK unissued: *Time-Life TLCW-07* (LP)
H-847-1	This Little Rosary -4	OK unissued: *BF BCD15933 (CD)*
H-848-1	When It's Honey Suckle Time In The Valley -3	OK unissued: *Co C2-40149* (LP); *BF BCD15933 (CD)*
H-849-1	Let's Ride With Bob (Theme Song)	OK 6692, Co 37405, 20132
H-850-1	My Laddie -3	OK unissued: *BF BCD15933 (CD)*
H-851-1	Whose Heart Are You Breaking Now? -3	OK 6703, Co 37030, 20055

Bob Wills also recorded with the Fort Worth Doughboys (see The Light Crust Doughboys) and after 1942.

CHARLIE WILLS

Charlie Wills, v; acc. unknown.
New York, NY   Tuesday, April 20, 1937
| 21010- | In The Baggage Coach Ahead | ARC unissued |

| 21011- | Wreck Of The Old '97 | ARC unissued |

These recordings are also listed in Art Satherley's files, as by **Charlie Wells**, on a sheet otherwise devoted to recordings by Elton Britt. It is uncertain how this should be interpreted.

JOHNNY LEE WILLS & HIS BOYS

Guy "Cotton" Thompson, f/v-1; Lester "Junior" Barnard, eg; Millard Kelso, p; Johnnie Lee Wills, tbj; Harley Huggins, g/v-2; Luther Jay "Luke" Wills, sb; band v-3.

Dallas, TX   Monday, April 28, 1941

93697-A	I Wonder What I'm Goin' To Do -1	De 5957, MeC 45449
93698-A	I'm Sorry That We Said Goodbye -1, 2	De 5948, 46012, MeC 45441
93699-A	Do I Really Deserve It From You? -1	De 5969
93700-A	Memories Of You Dear -2	De 5985
93701-A	Whatcha Know Joe? -1, 3	De 5948, MeC 45441
93702-A	Milk Cow Blues -1	De 5985, 46012
93703-A	Too Long -1	De 5957, MeC 45449
93704-A	Together Forever -1	De 6014, MeC 45483
93705-A	Keep A Light In Your Window Tonight -2	De 6014, MeC 45483
93706-A	Devil's Blues -1	De 5969

Johnnie Lee Wills (as his name is usually spelled) recorded after 1942.

BUCK WILSON & HIS RANGERS

This credit was occasionally used on Diva, Harmony, and Velvet Tone for the group more often called Eddie Younger & His Mountaineers (see Arthur Fields & Fred Hall).

CHARLIE WILSON & HIS HILLBILLIES

Charlie Wilson, f/sp; prob. Roy Hobbs, g; Asa Martin, sp/calls; unknown man, sp.

Richmond, IN   Wednesday, October 19, 1932

| 18850 | Cuttin' At The Point | Ch 16528, MW 8065 |
| 18851 | Shelven Rock | Ch 16528, MW 8065 |

Montgomery Ward 8065 as by **Charlie Wilson & His Hayloft Boys**.

Charlie Wilson, f/sp; Roy Hobbs, md/sp; Asa Martin, g/sp.

Richmond, IN   Wednesday, April 5, 1933

| 19124 | The Beer Party | Ch S-16601, MW 8064 |

Originally logged as by **Charlie Wilson & His Gang** but reportedly issued as shown. Montgomery Ward 8064 as by **Charlie Wilson & His Hayloft Boys**.

Vertner Hatton, f; Jess Hatton, bj; Asa Martin, g/calls; several men, sp.

Richmond, IN   Wednesday, April 5, 1933

| 19125 | Ride The Goat Over The Mountain | Ch S-16601, MW 8064 |

Originally logged as by **Charlie Wilson & His Gang** but reportedly issued either as shown or as by **Martin, Hobbs & Hatton Bros.**. Montgomery Ward 8064 as by **Charlie Wilson & His Hayloft Boys**.
Charlie Wilson is present on matrix 19125 but possibly does not speak.

EDGAR WILSON

Edgar Wilson, v/y-1; acc. poss. own g.

Richmond, IN   c. July 1931

| 17890,-A | Good Bye Old Friends -1 | Ge rejected |
| 17891-A | I Never Will Forget The Night When First We Met | Ch 16348, Spr 2713 |

Revs: Champion 16348, Superior 2713 by W.C. Childers.

FRANK WILSON & HIS BLUE RIDGE MOUNTAIN DUO

Charlie Bowman, f; Frank Wilson, sg; Walter Bowman, bj.

New York, NY   Wednesday, February 20, 1929

| 147971-1 | Polly Ann | Co 15372-D |
| 147975-1 | Katy-Did Waltz | Co 15372-D |

Matrices 147972/73 are by Charlie Bowman & His Brothers; matrix 147974 is popular.
Frank Wilson also recorded with Charlie Bowman, The Hill Billies, and Wilmer Watts.

FRED WILSON

Pseudonym on Harmony for Riley Puckett.

HARRY WILSON

Pseudonym on Pathé 32477 and Perfect 12556 for Ed (Jake) West.

HARRY "ROCKY" WILSON

Pseudonym on Pathé 32476, Perfect 12555 for Dad Pickard (see The Pickard Family), or on Pathé 32481, Perfect 12560 for Carson Robison & Frank Luther.

JIMMIE WILSON'S CATFISH STRING BAND

Poss.: Jack Gillis, f; John Ed Harris, h; Dick Fahrenwald, md; Franklin Ward, bj; Orin Potter, jazz wh/gas pipe; Charlie Potter, bones; poss. unidentified musicians, other instruments; Jimmie Wilson, dir.

Dallas, TX   c. October 21, 1925

9387-A	Over The Waves	OK 45029
9388-A	Let Me Call You Sweetheart	OK 45019
9389-A	Snow Dear	OK 45019
9390-A	Medley Of Old Time Popular Songs	OK 45029

Jack Gillis, f; John Ed Harris, h; Dick Fahrenwald, md; Franklin Ward, bj; Bob Dennis, g/v-1; unknown, u; Speedy Mouleer (or Moulder), sb; Orin Potter, jazz wh/gas pipe; Charlie Potter, bones; unidentified, v trio-2; Jimmie Wilson, dir.

Dallas, TX   Thursday, October 17, 1929

56412-1	She's Comin' 'Round The Mountain -2	Vi V-40163, Au 402, BB B-4950
56413-2	Catfish Medley March	Vi V-40216
56414-1	Polecat Creek	Vi V-40240
56415-1	Argentine Rag	Vi V-40216
56416-1	Catfish Whiskers	Vi V 40163, Au 402, BB B-4950
56417-2	My Two Sweethearts -1	Vi V-40240

On at least some copies of Bluebird B-4950 an unidentified Mexican item was pressed in place of matrix 56412, though the labelling applies to the latter.

TOMMY WILSON

Pseudonym on Vocalion 5262 for Frank Luther (see Carson Robison).

WILSON RAMBLERS

Pseudonym on Broadway for the North Carolina Ramblers & Roy Harvey (see the latter).

JUSTIN WINFIELD

Pseudonym on Gennett for Ernest V. Stoneman.

WING'S ROCKY MOUNTAIN RAMBLERS

Two unknowns, f; unknown, bj; three unknowns, g.

Richmond, IN   Monday, August 27, 1934

19686	Ragged Ann	Ch S-16819, 45019
19687	Whiskers	Ch S-16819, 45019
19688	Jackson County Rag	Ch S-16808
19689	Blue Hills Of Virginia	Ch S-16808

Champion 45019 as by **Wingy's Rocky Mountain Ramblers**.

WINGY'S ROCKY MOUNTAIN RAMBLERS

Champion 45019 by Wing's Rocky Mountain Ramblers was so credited.

CHAS. WINTERS & ELOND AUTRY

Chas. Winters, Elond Autry, v duet; acc. prob. one of them, f; prob. the other, g.

Memphis, TN   Saturday, February 25, 1928

400344-B	Hand Me Down My Silver Trumpet	OK 45207
400345-A,-B	[Flower From My Angel Mother's Grave]	OK unissued
400346-	I'll Be All Smiles Tonight	OK unissued
400347-B	You Tell Me Your Dream And I'll Tell You Mine	OK 45207
400348-	Kelley Waltz	OK unissued

THE WISDOM SISTERS

Vocal trio; prob. unacc.

New Orleans, LA   Wednesday, September 23, 1925

140986-	Amazing Grace	Co unissued
140996-	Sitting At The Feet Of Jesus	Co unissued

Intervening matrices are by other artists.

Unacc.
   Atlanta, GA   Friday, April 23, 1926
   142096-2   Amazing Grace   Co 15093-D
   142097-2   Sitting At The Feet Of Jesus   Co 15093-D
   Atlanta, GA   Thursday, November 4, 1926
   143050-   O For A Closer Walk With God   Co unissued
   143051-   I Saw A Way Worn Traveller   Co unissued
   143052-1   Children Of The Heavenly King   Co 15129-D, Ve 7093-V
   143053-1   A Charge To Keep   Co 15112-D, Ve 7094-V
   143054-2   Jesus Is All The World To Me   Co 15112-D, Ve 7093-V
   143055-2   The Old Time Power   Co 15129-D, Ve 7096-V

Revs: Velvet Tone 7094-V by Frank & James McCravy, 7096-V by the Stamps Quartet.

   Atlanta, GA   Wednesday, March 30, 1927
   143817-2   Hide Thou Me   Co 15153-D
   143818-1   Saviour More Than Life To Me   Co 15153-D
   143819-2   Prayer   Co 15309-D
   143820-2   Why Not Say Yes   Co 15309-D

CECIL WISE

Cecil Wise, v; acc. two or more unknowns, g.
   Richmond, IN   Saturday, April 18, 1931
   17697   Good Bye Dolly Gray   Ge rejected trial recording

WISE STRING ORCHESTRA

Newman Wise, f; C.J. Wise, bj-md; George Wise, g; unidentified, v duet-1.
   Knoxville, TN   Tuesday, August 27, 1929
   K-121   Yellow Dog Blues   Vo 5360
   K-122   How Dry I Am -1   Vo 5360

WLS RADIO ARTISTS

Although these recordings are largely beyond the scope of this work, they are included because of the occasional presence of relevant artists. The participants are listed in the order of their first appearance.

Harold Stafford, sp; Tom Corwin, sp; Ralph Waldo Emerson, calliope/sp; The Four Legionaires, v quartet; Jack & Gene, v duet; acc. unknown, g; unknown, eff.
   Chicago, IL   c. March 15, 1928
   13549-B   The WLS Show Boat, Part No. I   Sil 5199, 8231
   13552   The WLS Show Boat, Part No. II   Sil 5199, 8231

Matrices 13550/51 are popular.

Harold Stafford, sp; Tom Corwin, sp; Ralph Waldo Emerson, calliope; Bradley Kincaid, v; acc. own g; Maple City Four, v quartet; acc. unknown, p.
   Chicago, IL   c. March 19, 1928
   13576-A   The WLS Show Boat, Part No. III   Sil 5200, 8232
   13577-D   The WLS Show Boat, Part No. IV   Sil 5200, 8232
   Chicago, IL   c. March 21, 1928
   13587-A   The WLS Show Boat, Part No. V   Sil 5201, 8233
   13588   The WLS Show Boat, Part No. VI   Sil 5201, 8233

WOLCOTT QUARTETTE

Pseudonym on Broadway for the Vaughan Radio Quartette.

HASKELL WOLFENBARGER

Haskell Wolfenbarger, v; acc. own g.
   Knoxville, TN   Wednesday, August 28, 1929
   K-129-   My Little Girl   Vo 5390
   K-130-   Sailing Out On The Ocean   Vo 5390

DA COSTA WOLTZ'S SOUTHERN BROADCASTERS

Ben Jerrell [sic Ben Jarrell], v; acc. **Da Costa Woltz's Southern Broadcasters**: own f; Frank Jenkins, bj/v-1; Da Costa Woltz, bj/v-1.
   Richmond, IN   early May 1927
   12766   Merry Girl -1   Ge 6143, Her 75565
   12767   Yellow Rose of Texas   Ge 6143

Price Goodson, v; acc. **Da Costa Woltz's Southern Broadcasters**: Ben Jarrell, f; own h; Frank Jenkins, bj; Da Costa Woltz, bj.
Richmond, IN   early May 1927
   12768   Lonesome Road Blues   Ge 6154

Da Costa Woltz's Southern Broadcasters: Ben Jarrell, f; Frank Jenkins, bj; Da Costa Woltz, bj; unidentified, calls.
Richmond, IN   early May 1927
   12769   Richmond Cotillion   Ge 6220, Sil 5183, Chg 407, Her 75554

Silvertone 5183 as by **The Southern Broadcasters**. Challenge 407 as by **Frank Neal & His Boys**. Herwin 75554 credit untraced.
Revs: Challenge 407 by Billy Milton; Herwin 75554 by Holland Puckett.

Ben Jarrell, v; acc. **Da Costa Woltz's Southern Broadcasters**: own f; Frank Jenkins, bj/v; Da Costa Woltz, bj/v.
Richmond, IN   early May 1927
   12770-A   Are You Washed In The Blood Of The Lamb   Ge 6164, Ch 15318, Chg 340, Her 75553

Champion 15318, Challenge 340, possibly Herwin 75553 as by **Jackson Young**.

Frank Jenkins Of Da Costa Woltz's Southern Broadcasters, bj solo.
Richmond, IN   early May 1927
   12773   Home Sweet Home   Ge 6165, Sil 5080, 8181, Spt 9167
   12774   Babtist [sic] Shout   Ge 6187

Supertone 9167 and probably Silvertone 5080, 8181 as by **Louis Watson**. Matrices 12771/72 are by Holland Puckett.
Revs: Silvertone 5080, 8181, Supertone 9167 by Marion Underwood (see Taylor's Kentucky Boys).

Price Goodson, h; acc. own u-1/v-1.
Richmond, IN   early May 1927
   12775   Be Kind To A Man When He Is Down -1   Ge 6154, Ch 15297, Her 75553
   12776-A   Lost Train Blues   Ge 6187, Ch 15315

Champion 15297, 15315, possibly Herwin 75553 as by **Stanley Miller**.
Revs: Champion 15297 by Marion Underwood, 15315 by Taylor's Kentucky Boys.

Da Costa Woltz's Southern Broadcasters: Ben Jarrell, f-1/v; Frank Jenkins, bj/v-2; Da Costa Woltz, bj/v-2.
Richmond, IN   early May 1927
   12777-A   I Know My Name Is There -1, 2   Ge 6164, Ch 15333, Sil 5075, 8167, Spt 9263,
                                                                          Chg 340, Her 75559
   12778   When You Ask A Girl To Leave Her Happy Home -1 Ge 6176
   12779   Take Me Back To The Sweet Sunny South   Ge 6176, Ch 15318, Chg 333, Her 75555

Gennett 6164 as by **Ben Jarrell Acc. Da Costa Woltz's Southern Broadcasters**. Champion 15318, 15333, Silvertone 5075, 8167, Supertone 9263, Challenge 333, 340 as by **Jackson Young**. Herwin 75555 as by **Ben Jarrell**, 75559 credit untraced.
Revs: Champion 15333, Silvertone 5075, 8167, Supertone 9263, Herwin 75559 by Holland Puckett; Herwin 75555 by Vernon Dalhart.

Ben Jarrell, f; Da Costa Woltz, bj; unidentified, calls.
Richmond, IN   early May 1927
   12780   John Brown's Dream   Ge 6220, Sil 5183

Silvertone 5183 as by **The Southern Broadcasters**.

Ben Jarrell, v; acc. **Da Costa Woltz's Southern Broadcasters**: own f; Frank Jenkins, bj; Da Costa Woltz, bj.
Richmond, IN   early May 1927
   12781-A   Old Joe Clark   Ge 6223, Chg 333, Her 75565

Challenge 333 as by **Jackson Young**.

Da Costa Woltz's Southern Broadcasters: Ben Jarrell, f; Frank Jenkins, bj; Da Costa Woltz, bj.
Richmond, IN   early May 1927
   12782   Evening Star Waltz   Ge 6240

Rev. Gennett 6240 by Marion Underwood.

Ben Jarrell, v; acc. **Da Costa Woltz's Southern Broadcasters**: own f; Frank Jenkins, bj.
Richmond, IN   early May 1927
   12783-A   Jack Of Diamonds   Her 75561

Rev. Herwin 75561 by David Miller.

Frank Jenkins Of Da Costa Woltz's Southern Broadcasters, v; acc. own f; or f solo-1.
Richmond, IN   early May 1927
   12787-A   Roving Cowboy   Ge 6223
   12788   Wandering Boy -1   Ge 6165, Ch 15300, Sil 5083, 8177, Spt 9175

Champion 15300 as by **John Burham**. Silvertone 5083, 8177, Supertone 9175 as by **Louis Watson**.
Matrices 12784 to 12786 are by Holland Puckett.
Revs: Champion 15333 by Taylor's Kentucky Boys; Silvertone 5083, 8177, Supertone 9175 by the Short Creek Trio.

WONDER STATE HARMONISTS

Unknown, f; unknown, bj; unknown, g; unknown, vc; unknown, v-1.

Memphis, TN Friday, November 23, 1928

M-840-	El Menio	Vo 5291
M-841-	On The Wing	Vo 5291
M-842-	Turnip Greens -1	Vo 5275
M-843-	Walk Along Al	Vo unissued
M-844-	Petit Jean Gallop	Vo 5346
M-845-	Memory (Means Happiness To Me) -1	Vo 5275
M-846-	Buffalo Rag	Vo unissued
M-847-	My Castle On The Nile -1	Vo 5346

SMOKY WOOD & HIS WOOD CHIPS

Smoky Wood, v; acc. George Uttinger, f; Clarence Clark, t; J.C. Way, esg; own p; Gene Edmondson, tbj; prob. Horace Edmondson, g; Lonnie Mitchell, sb; unidentified, sp-1.

Dallas, TX Sunday, September 12, 1937

014065-1	There's Gonna Be No Me To Welcome You Home	BB unissued
014066-1	Riding To Glory	BB B-7399
014067-1	I'm Sorry	BB B-7660
014068-1	Lonely Heart Of Mine	BB B-7660
014069-1	Woodchip Blues	BB B-7729
014070-1	Keep On Truckin'	BB B-7232
014071-1	Wood's Traveling Blues	BB B-7729
014072-1	Moonlight In Oklahoma -1	BB B-7399
014073-1	Carry Me Back To Virginny	BB B-7232
014074-1	The Doctor	BB unissued

Smoky Wood and J.C. Way played in early lineups of the Modern Mountaineers; the other musicians were members of the Ross Rhythm Rascals.

WOOD & TURNER

Pseudonym on Australian Grand Pree for Vernon Dalhart & Carson Robison.

WOODHULL'S OLD TIME MASTERS

Ransom Terwilliger, f; Floyd Woodhull, ac/o/bells/v; Herb Woodhull, bj; John Woodhull or Tommy Wood, g; John Taggart, sb.

New York, NY Monday, July 14, 1941

066812-1	Oh Susanna	Vi 36400
066813-1	Pop Goes The Weasel	Vi 36400
066814-1	Captain Jinks	Vi 36401
066815-1	Wearing Of The Green	Vi 36401
066816-1	The Girl Behind Me	Vi 36402
066817-1	Triple Right And Left Four	Vi 36402
066818-1	Blackberry Quadrille	Vi 36403
066819-1	Soldier's Joy	Vi 36403

Victor 36400 to 36403, which are 12-inch discs, comprise Victor album C36.

Woodhull's Old Time Masters recorded after 1942.

EPHRAIM WOODIE & THE HENPECKED HUSBANDS
WOODIE BROTHERS

Ephraim Woodie & The Henpecked Husbands: Ephraim Woodie, v; acc. Clay Reed, f; W. Edison Nuckolls, bj; own g.

Johnson City, TN Thursday, October 24, 1929

149260-2	The Last Gold Dollar	Co 15564-D
149261-1	The Fatal Courtship	Co 15564-D

Woodie Brothers: William Lawton Woodie, h/hv; Ephraim Woodie, g/lv.

Charlotte, NC Friday, May 29, 1931

69374-1	Likes Likker Better Than Me	Vi 23579, ZoSA 4348
69375-2	Chased Old Satan Through The Door	Vi 23579, ZoSA 4348

WOODLAWN QUARTETTE

Vocal quartet; acc. unknown, o; or unacc.-1.

Birmingham, AL c. August 1, 1927

GEX-759-A	Let The Lower Lights Be Burning -1	Ge 6238

| GEX-760-A | When The Roll Is Called Up Yonder | Ge 6238, Ch 15330, Sil 5071, 8174, Spt 9270, Chg 337, Her 75567, Bell 1185 |
| GEX-761-A | Rock Of Ages | Ge 6258, Sil 5076, 8171, Spt 9267, Chg 338 |

Champion 15330 and possibly Herwin 75567 as by **The Hamlin Quartette**. Silvertone and Supertone issues as by **Hamlin Male Quartette**. Challenge 337, 338 as by **Hamlin Sacred Quartette**. Bell 1185 as by **The Four Andersons**.
An unnumbered trial recording of *When The Roll Is Called Up Yonder* was made immediately after matrix GEX-760-A.
Revs: Champion 15330 by McDonald Quartette; Silvertone 5076, 8171, Supertone 9267, Herwin 75567 by Eva Quartette; Bell 1185 by McGhee & Welling.

Acc. unknown, o-1/p-2.
   Birmingham, AL   c. August 15, 1927

GEX-805-A	The Vacant Chair -1	Her 75570
GEX-806-A	Tell Mother I'll Be There -1	Ge 6258, Ch 15411, Sil 5071, 8174, Spt 9270, Chg 339, Spr 322, Bell 1184
GEX-807	When You're Gone I Won't Forget -2	Ge 6316, Ch 15433, Sil 5120, 8252, Spt 9152, Chg 417, Her 75570
GEX-812	The Old Oaken Bucket -1	Ge rejected
GEX-813	Darling Nellie Gray -2	Ge rejected
GEX-814	Old Black Joe -2	Ge rejected

Champion 15411, 15433 as by **Hamlin Quartette**. Silvertone and Supertone issues as by **Hamlin Male Quartet** (or **Quartette**). Challenge 339 as by **Hamlin Sacred Quartette**, 417 possibly as by **The Challenge Harmony Four**. Bell 1184 as by **The Four Andersons**. Herwin 75570 possibly as by **The Hamlin Quartette**. Superior 322 credit unknown.
An unnumbered trial recording of *When You're Gone I Won't Forget* was made immediately after matrix GEX-807-A. Intervening matrices are by Wyzee Hamilton.
Revs: Champion 15411, Challenge 339, Superior 322 by Eva Quartette; Silvertone 5120, 8252, Supertone 9152, Challenge 417 by Gold Medal Four; Bell 1184 by McGhee & Welling.

   Birmingham, AL   c. August 17, 1927

GEX-812-A	The Old Oaken Bucket -1	Ge 6347, Ch 15433, Chg 418, Her 75574
GEX-813-A	Darling Nellie Gray -2	Ge 6316, Her 75572
GEX-814-A,-B	Old Black Joe -2	Ge rejected
GEX-825,-A	Onward Christian Soldiers -1	Sil 5073, 8165, Spt 9261, Her 75576
GEX-826	O Come, All Ye Faithful -1	Ge 6290, Ch 15374, Sil 5176, Spt 9140, Chg 337, Her 75576
GEX-827-B	Silent Night – Holy Night -1	Ge 6290, Ch 15374, Her 75557
GEX-828	Juanita -1	Ge 6347, Chg 419, Her 75572

It is uncertain which take of matrix GEX-825 was used for release.
Champion 15374, Herwin 75557, 75572, 75574, 75576 as by **The Hamlin Quartette**. Champion 15433 as by **Hamlin Quartette**. Supertone and probably Silvertone issues as by **Hamlin Male Quartet** (or **Quartette**). Challenge 419, and probably 418, as by **The Challenge Harmony Four**.
Herwin 75557 was also used for an issue by David Miller and Holland Puckett.
An unnumbered trial recording of *Onward Christian Soldiers* was made immediately after matrix GEX-825-A.
Matrices GEX-815 to 818 are by the Short Creek Trio; matrices GEX-819 to 824 are by Geo. L. Hodge (popular).
Revs: Silvertone 5176, Supertone 9140 by McDonald Quartette; Challenge 418 by Luke Minnick's Harmony Four Of WLW (popular), 419 by Harmony Four (see B&GR).

   Birmingham, AL   late August 1927

GEX-846-A	Beautiful Isle Of Somewhere -1	Ge 6420, Sil 5073, 8165, Spt 9261, Chg 338, Her 75573
GEX-847-A	Star Of The East -2	Her 75557
GEX-848-A	My Old Kentucky Home -2	Ge 6285, Ch 15351, Sil 5119, 8245, Spt 9147, Chg 346, Her 75574

Champion 15351, Herwin 75557, 75573, 75574 as by **The Hamlin Quartette**. Silvertone and Supertone issues, Challenge 346 as by **Hamlin Male Quartet** (or **Quartette**). Challenge 338 as by **Hamlin Sacred Quartette**.
Revs: Gennett 6285, Champion 15351, Silvertone 5119, 8245, Supertone 9147, Challenge 346 by Gold Medal Four; Gennett 6420, Herwin 75573 by Eva Quartette.

JAKE WOODLIEFF

Pseudonym on Crown, Homestead, and Paramount for Norman Woodlieff. (See Virginia Dandies.)

NORMAN WOODLIEFF

Norman Woodlieff, v; acc. Posey Rorer, f; own g.
   Richmond, IN   Wednesday, March 20, 1929

14933	Brace Up And Be A Man She Said	Ge rejected trial recording
14944,-A,-B	Why Did You Prove Untrue?	Ge rejected
14946	I Fell In Love With A Married Man	Ge 6824, Chg 428
14947	Brace Up And Be A Man, She Said	Ge 6824, Chg 428

| 14948,-A,-B | What Whiskey Will Do | Ge rejected |

Challenge 428 as by **Jack Logan**.
Matrix 14945 is popular; other intervening matrices are by Walter Smith (mostly with Norman Woodlieff).
Norman Woodlieff also recorded with the Carolina Buddies, Four Pickled Peppers, Charlie Poole, Walter Smith, and the Virginia Dandies.

WOODRUFF BROTHERS (DUCKY & CURLY)

Ducky Woodruff, Curly Woodruff, v duet; acc. unknown, h; prob. one of them, g.
   Atlanta, GA   Wednesday, February 7, 1940

047595-1	Jesse James	BB B-8381, MW M-8752
047596-1	Mountaineer's Home, Sweet Home	BB B-8503, MW M-8754, RZAu G24799
047597-1	Where The Grass Grows Green	BB B-8381, MW M-8752
047598-1	We Buried Her Beneath The Willow	BB B-8503, MW M-8754
047599-1	What Would You Give For Your Soul In The End?	BB B-8477, MW M-8753
047600-1	No Place To Pillow My Head	BB B-8477, MW M-8753, RZAu G24799

LAWRENCE WOODS

Lawrence Woods, v; acc. prob. own g.
   Richmond, IN   Thursday, July 7, 1932

| 18580 | Mississippi Flood | Ge rejected |

   Richmond, IN   Thursday, August 4, 1932

| 18663 | Cowboy Jack | Ch 16517 |
| 18664 | The Cyclone Of Rye Cove | Ch 16517 |

KYLE WOOTEN

Kyle Wooten, h solo.
   Atlanta, GA   Monday, December 1, 1930

404608-A	Red Pig	OK 45539
404609-A	Violet Waltz	OK 45511
404610-A	Choking Blues	OK 45526
404611-B	Fox Chase	OK 45526
404612-B	Lumber Camp Blues	OK 45511
404613-B	Loving Henry	OK 45539

WORKMAN, RAMSEY & WOLF

See Gibson String Trio.

EARL WRIGHT & THE ARKANSAS CORNDODGERS

See George Edgin.

JOE WRIGHT & HIS GUITAR

Pseudonym on Aurora for Frank Marvin.

LE & LEONARD WRIGHT

Le Wright, Leonard Wright, v duet; acc. poss. one of them, g.
   Richmond, IN   Wednesday, August 28, 1929

| 15507 | Every Time I Feel The Spirit | Ge rejected trial recording |

LLOYD WRIGHT

Lloyd Wright, v; acc. prob. own g.
   Richmond, IN   Thursday, October 8, 1931

| 18091 | Fifty Years From Now | Ge unissued |

Acc. Hoosier Hawaiians: several unknowns, sg and/or g.
   Richmond, IN   Thursday, October 8, 1931

| 18093 | Silvery Arizona Moon | Ge unissued |

Matrix 18092 is by Walter Judd.

Lloyd Wright–Monie Chasteen, prob. v duet; poss. acc. own g duet.
   Richmond, IN   Wednesday, January 27, 1932

| 18340 | The Prisoner's Blues | Ge unissued |

Lloyd Wright, v; acc. prob. own g.
   Richmond, IN   Friday, February 26, 1932

| 18430 | 99 Years | Ge unissued |

ROWDY WRIGHT

This artist's given name is Cecil Wright.

"Rowdy" – Cecil Wright, v; acc. **Mac's Haywire Orchestry**: poss. Asa Wright, f; unknown, f; own g.
  poss. San Francisco, CA   c. 1930–31

963-1,-2	The Strawberry Roan Part I	Flexo 8-963-1
964-1,-2	The Strawberry Roan Part II	Flexo 8-964-1

Matrices 963/64 are coupled on an 8-inch flexible disc.

Rowdy Wright (The Jolly Cowboy), v/y-1; acc. poss. own h-2; Ben Jackson, bj; own g.
  Hot Springs, AR   Tuesday, March 9, 1937

HS-37-1	I'm A Wandering Bronco Rider -2	ARC 7-06-52
HS-38-2	I Want To Go Back To My Home On The Range -1	Cq 8841
HS-39-	The Ramblin' Cowboy	ARC unissued
HS-40-1	I'm A Jolly Cowboy	Cq 8841
HS-41-	My Dear Ole Kansas Home	ARC unissued
HS-42-1	Going Down Town	ARC 7-06-52
HS-43	What Makes Your Head So Red	ARC unissued
HS-44-	Pretty Mohee	ARC unissued
HS-45	Red Dog Blues	ARC unissued

  Hot Springs, AR   between March 11 and 14, 1937

HS-50	The Wife That Turned Me Down	ARC unissued

Rowdy Wright, v; or **Rowdy & Vera Wright**-1, v duet; acc. Ben Jackson, bj; Rowdy Wright, g.
  Hot Springs, AR   between March 14 and March 16, 1937

HS-57-	Poor Boy -1	ARC unissued
HS-58-	Cowboy's Sweetheart	ARC unissued
HS-59-	I've Got No Use For The Women	ARC unissued
HS-60-	When The Roses Bloom Again -1	ARC unissued

  Hot Springs, AR   Wednesday, March 17, or Thursday, March 18, 1937

HS-76-	Cowboy's Lament -1	ARC unissued
HS-77-	The Hill Billy Jamboree	ARC unissued
HS-78-2	When I Take My Vacation In Heaven -1	ARC 7-08-56, Cq 8897
HS-79-1	Let The Lower Lights Be Burning -1	ARC 7-08-56, Cq 8897

Matrices HS-78/79 were logged as by **Rowdy & Vera Wright** but issued as by **The Wright Family**.

WRIGHT & McNEW

See The Hoosier Hawaiians.

WRIGHT BROTHERS

Pseudonym on Melotone (US and Canadian), Minerva, Polk, and Vocalion for the Kessinger Brothers.

WRIGHT BROTHERS QUARTET

Vocal quartet; acc. unknown, p; unknown, md; unknown, g.
  Atlanta, GA   Wednesday, April 17, 1929

148326-2	God's Message To Man	Co 15402-D
148327-2	What A Glad Day	Co 15402-D
148328-2	Mother Is With The Angels	Co 15587-D
148329-2	Somebody's Boy	Co 15587-D

The Wright Brothers Gospel Singers on Bluebird, Conqueror, OKeh, and Vocalion are an African-American group; see *B&GR*.

THE WRIGHT FAMILY

See Rowdy Wright.

WYATT & BRANDON

Howard Wyatt, bj-md/v; Luke Brandon, g/v.
  Johnson City, TN   Monday, October 21, 1929

149214-2	Evalina	Co 15523-D
149215-2	Lover's Farewell	Co 15523-D

Wyatt & Brandon were members of the Roane County Ramblers.

THE WYOMING COWBOY

See Charles Baker.

WYZEE, TUCKER & LECROY

See Wyzee Hamilton.

X

XC SACRED QUARTETTE

Vocal quartet, unacc.
   Chicago, IL   c. May 1927

4539-1	One By One	Pm 3051, Bwy 8186
4540-1	Mother Is Gone	Pm 3051, Bwy 8186
4541-1	The Tombs	Pm 3034
4542-2	Going Home Tomorrow	Pm 3034
4543-2	Take Time To Be Holy	Pm 3028
4548-1	Where We'll Never Grow Old	Pm 3031, Bwy 8127
4549-2	There Is No Disappointment In Heaven	Pm 3031, Bwy 8127
4550-2	A Dream Of Home	Pm 3027, Bwy 8187
4551-1	Have Thine Own Way	Pm 3028
4552-1	Bloom Brightly Sweet Rose	Pm 3027, Bwy 8187
4555-2	It Is Well With Your Soul	Pm 3026, Bwy 8126
4556-1	When They Ring Those Golden Bells	Pm 3026, Bwy 8126

Broadways as by **Star Sacred Singers**, except 8186 as by **Star Sacred Quartette**.
Intervening matrices are untraced but may include unissued items by this group.

Y

IRA [& EUGENE] YATES

Ira Yates, v; acc. unknown.
   Johnson City, TN   Tuesday, October 16, 1928

147192-	You'll Never Get To Heaven With Your Powder And Paint	Co unissued
147193-	The Weary Gambler	Co unissued

Ira & Eugene Yates, v duet; acc. prob. one of them, g.
   Johnson City, TN   Wednesday, October 23, 1929

149262-2	Powder And Paint	Co 15581-D, ReE MR56

Regal MR56 as by **The Alabama Barn Stormers**. Matrix 149262 is titled *You'll Never Go To Heaven With Your Powder And Paint* on that issue. Rev. Regal MR56 (with same credit) by Hugh Cross & Riley Puckett.

   Johnson City, TN   Thursday, October 24, 1929

149263-1	Sarah Jane	Co 15581-D

JIMMY YATES GROUPS

Red Mountain Trio: unknown, h-1; Jimmy Yates, sg; two unknowns, g; unknown, v duet-2; unknown, sp; unknown, train eff-3.
   Atlanta, GA   Friday, April 20, 1928

146163-2	The Wang Wang Blues -2	Co 15260-D
146164-1	Home Again Medley -1, 3	Co 15260-D

Jimmy Yates' Boll Weevils: David Lischkoff, f; Jimmy Yates, sg; Alfred McCarty, g; Al Treadway, u/v; unidentified, 2nd v-1.
   Memphis, TN   Tuesday, September 18, 1928

47051-3	Bloody War	Vi V-40065
47052-2	Shoo Fly -1	Vi 21723
47053-1	Smiles	Vi 21723
47054-1,-2	If You'll Be Mine Again	Vi unissued

Rev. Victor V-40065 by Nelstone's Hawaiians.

Red Mountain Trio: Jimmy Yates, sg; unidentified (prob. Yates), musical saw-1; two unknowns, g; unknown, perc eff-2; unknown, v; two unknowns, sp; unknown, shouting-2; unknown, wh.
   Atlanta, GA   Wednesday, October 31, 1928

147362-1	Sailing Down The Chesapeake Bay	Co 15369-D
147363-2	Dixie -2	Co 15369-D, CoSA DE506
147364-1	Carolina Sunshine -1	Co 15462-D
147365-2	Gypsy Love Song (Slumber On, My Little Gypsy Sweetheart) -1	Co 15462-D

Rev. Columbia DE506 by Roy Harper & Earl Shirkey (see the latter).

The Northlanders: unknown, f; Jimmy Yates, sg; unknown, g; poss. Al Treadway, u.
   Birmingham, AL
                                                                                                    Thursday, November 15, 1928
    BIRM-802-   Over The Waves   Vo 5274
    BIRM-803-   Floraine Waltz   Vo 5274

The Four Buzz Saws (Jimmy Yates, Moe Sigler, E.R. Smith & C.D. Linthicum): Jimmy Yates, sg/v-1; E.R. Smith, g/v/sp-2; C.D. Linthicum, g/v-3; Moe Sigler, tg/v-4; unidentified, 2nd v-5.
   Atlanta, GA
                                                                                                         Sunday, March 23, 1930
    ATL-996   Elevator Blues -1, 3 (lead), 4   Vo 1652
    ATL-997   Baptising Sister Lucy Lee -2, 5   Vo 1652

At least one copy exists of Canadian Melotone 12242 on which matrix ATL-996 (shown in wax as ALT-996) is pressed in error for matrix LA-996 by The Texas Drifter (Goebel Reeves).

Jimmy Yates, sg; E.R. Smith, g; C.D. Linthicum, g; Moe Sigler, tg/v-1; unidentified, sp-2.
   Atlanta, GA
                                                                                  Monday, March 24, 1930
    ATL-8008-   Farewell Blues -2   Vo 5471
    ATL-8009-   The Tree Song -1?   Vo 5471

Jimmy Yates, sg; E.R. Smith, g; C.D. Linthicum, g; Moe Sigler, tg; unidentified, v; two or three unidentifieds, humming.
   Atlanta, GA
                                                                              Tuesday, March 25, 1930
    ATL-8010-A   Three O'Clock In The Morning   Me M12105, Po P9055, PanAu P12105
    ATL-8011-A   I'm Forever Blowing Bubbles   Me M12105, Po P9055, PanAu P12105

Any of Sigler, Smith, and Linthicum may be absent from one or more of the recordings made on March 23–25.

THE YELLOW JACKETS [I]

Pine Knob Serenaders: Wilson (Bill) Ingram, h/g; Harley Reynolds, ah; Flanner Terrel, bj.
   Richmond, IN
                                                                                Monday, June 16, 1930
    16768   Apple Cider   Spr 2556

Matrix 16768 was logged as by **Yellow Jacket Trio**.

The Yellow Jackets: Wilson (Bill) Ingram, h/g; Harley Reynolds, ah; Flanner Terrel, bj; unidentified, sw.
   Richmond, IN
                                                                                Monday, June 16, 1930
    16769   Massa's In De Cold, Cold Ground – Little Log   Ge 7262, Ch 16070
                          Cabin, Etc. [sic]

Wilson (Bill) Ingram, h-1/g; Harley Reynolds, ah; unidentified, ah-2; Flanner Terrel, bj/u-3; Bummer Reynolds, bones; two unidentifieds, wh-4.
   Richmond, IN
                                                                                Monday, July 28, 1930
    16849   Over The Waves -2, 4   Ge rejected
    16850   Jay Bird -1   Ge rejected
    16851-A   Heel Toe Polka – Can't Catch A Nigger -1, 3   Ge 7262, Ch 16070

Wilson (Bill) Ingram, h/g; unidentified, h; Harley Reynolds, ah; Flanner Terrel, bj/u; Bummer Reynolds, bones; unidentified, sw-1.
   Richmond, IN
                                                                               Tuesday, July 29, 1930
    16852   Eyes Of Blue -1   Ge rejected
    16853   In The Good Old Summer Time -1   Ge rejected
    16854   Cake Walk And Down In Dixie   Spr 2556

Superior 2556 as by **Pine Knob Serenaders**.

Wilson (Bill) Ingram, h/g; unidentified, h; Harley Reynolds, ah; unidentified, ah-2; Flanner Terrel, bj-1; Bummer Reynolds and/or Flanner Terrel, flexatone-2/sw-2.
   Richmond, IN
                                                                     Wednesday, November 12, 1930
    17237   Believe Me If All Those Endearing Young Charms -2   Ch 16161
    17238   Bill Bailey And Coon, Coon -1   Ch 16161

THE YELLOW JACKETS [II]

Cody Fox & His Yellow Jackets: Willie Boyd, cl; Sonny Fleming, md-1/g-2/v-3; Malcolm "Mack" Bogard, g/v-4; Joe Johnson, sb/v-5; unidentified, v-6; Cody Fox, ldr.
   Chicago, IL
                                                                            Monday, December 14, 1936
    C-1719-1,-2   Put On Your Old Grey Bonnet -1   ARC unissued?
    C-1720-   Tiger Rag -2   ARC 7-04-56, Vo 03452, Cq 8793
    C-1721-   Oh! She's Crazy -2, 4   ARC 7-04-56, Vo 03452, Cq 8793
    C-1722-   Yellow Jacket Blues -2, 4   ARC 7-08-72, Vo 03622
    C-1723-1   I'm Looking Over A Four Leaf Clover -2, 3, 4, 5   ARC 7-05-52, Vo/OK 03493, Cq 8844,
                                                                           Co 38082, 20403
    C-1724-1   Sam The Accordian Man -2, 6   ARC 7-11-55, Vo 03695
    C-1725-   Echo Valley -1, 3   ARC 7-03-59, Vo 03427

			Tuesday, December 15, 1936
Chicago, IL			
C-1726-	Kansas City Kitty -1, 3		ARC 7-08-72, Vo 03622
C-1727-1,-2	China Boy-1		ARC unissued?
C-1728-1,-2	I Can't Give You Anything But Love -1, 4		ARC unissued?
C-1729-2	Wabash Blues -2, 3		ARC 7-11-55, Vo 03427
C-1730-	In A Chapel In The Moonlight -2, 3		ARC 7-03-59, Vo 03427
C-1731-1,-2	Twilight Waltz -2		ARC unissued?
C-1732-2	I Only Want A Buddy – Not A Sweetheart -1, 3		ARC 7-05-52, Vo/OK 03493, Cq 8844, Co 38082, 20403

Matrix C-1732 is titled *I Only Want A Buddy, Not A Sweetheart* on Columbia 38082, 20403.

The Yellow Jackets: Willie Boyd, cl; Sonny Fleming, g; Mack Bogard, g/v-1; Joe Johnson, sb; unidentified, v-2; band sp-3.

			Tuesday, October 26, 1937
Chicago, IL			
C-2034-1	Willie Blow Your Blower -1, 3		Vo 03976
C-2035-1,-2	Mama Don't Allow -2		ARC unissued
C-2036-	My Little Girl -2		ARC 8-02-65, Vo 03914
C-2037-1,-2	I Want A Girl -2		ARC unissued
C-2038-1,-2	Rhythm Maker's Swing -2		ARC unissued
C-2039-1,-2	The Crawdad Song -2		ARC unissued
C-2040-1,-2	I'll Be Thinking Of You Little Girl -2		ARC unissued

Willie Boyd, cl; Sonny Fleming, md-1/g-2/v-3; Mack Bogard, g; Joe Johnson, sb; unidentified, v-4.

			Wednesday, October 27, 1937
Chicago, IL			
C-2041-1,-2	That Little Boy Of Mine -2, 4		ARC unissued
C-2042-	Swinging Rhythm -2, 4		ARC 8-02-65, Vo 03914
C-2043-1	Johnson's Old Gray Mule -1, 3		Vo 03976
C-2044-	Columbus Stockade Blues -2, 4		Vo 04038
C-2045-	Happy Days And Lonely Nights -2, 4		Vo 04038

According to the Satherley files Cody Fox was not present at the October 26–27 session.

THE YODELING RUSTLER

Pseudonym on the Canadian label-group Crown/Domino/Royale/Sterling for Goebel Reeves.

THE YODELING TWINS (GARNER ECKLER & ROLAND GAINES)

See Garner Eckler & Roland Gaines.

YODER'S YOKELS

Pseudonym on Aurora for "Happy" Dixon's Clod Hoppers.

YORK BROTHERS (LESLIE & GEORGE)

Leslie York, George York, v duet; acc. prob. George York, g.

			Wednesday, February 26, 1941
Chicago, IL			
93506-A	My Little Honeysuckle Rose		De 6018
93507-A	You Took My Sunshine With You		De 5933, MeC 45429
93508-A	I'm Saying Goodbye		De 6018
93509-A	Naggin' Young Woman		De 5943
93510-A	Speak To Me Little Darling		De 5933, DeSA FM5137, MeC 45429
93511-A	Got Ramblin' And Gamblin' On My Mind		De 5943

Rev. Decca FM5137 by Pete Cassell.

Leslie York, George York, v duet; or prob. George York, v-1; acc. unknown, esg-2; prob. George York, g; unknown, sb-3.

			prob. 1941
Detroit, MI			
105	Hamtramck Mama -3		Universal 105/106, Mellow 105/405, Hot Wax 105/405, Fortune 120
106	Going Home -3		Universal 105/106, Fortune 180
107	Highland Park Girl -1, 2		Universal 107/108, Fortune 120
108	Detroit Hula Girl -2		Universal 107/108, Fortune 180
405	It Tain't No Good -2		Mellow 105/405, 405/1105, Hot Wax 105/405

Matrix 405 is titled *It Taint No Good* on Mellow 405/1105.
Rev. Mellow 405/1105 by York Brothers (postwar).

Leslie York, George York, v duet; or prob. George York, v-1; acc. Leslie York, eg; George York, g; unknown, sb-2.

			prob. 1941–42
Detroit, MI			
	Blue Skies Turned to Grey		Mellow 1619
	I Don't Want No Part Of You -2		Mellow 1619
	I'll Be Happy Again		Mellow 1620

Goodbye And Good Luck To You	Mellow 1620
Long Gone -2	Mellow 1621
Just Wanting You -2	Mellow 1621
Hail Hail Ol' Glory -2	Mellow 1622
Riding And Singing My Song -2	Mellow 1622
Hillbilly Rose	Mellow 1623
If I Would Never Lose You	Mellow 1623
Life Can Never Be The Same	Mellow 1624
Going Back To The Sunny South	Mellow 1624
Gonna Catch The Train	Mellow 1625
Jealous Hearted Blues	Mellow 1625
Home In Old Tennessee	Mellow 1629
Memories Of You -2	Mellow 1633
New Trail To Mexico -2	Mellow 1633
Rose Of The Rio Grande -2	Mellow 1634
York Brothers Blues -1, 2	Mellow 1634
I Told The Moon About You	Mellow 1636
Maybe Then You'll Care	Mellow 1637
You Stayed Away Too Long	Mellow 1637

Revs: Mellow 1629, 1636 untraced.
Mellow 1630 to 1632 and 1635 are untraced and may be by these artists.

York Brothers-1/York Bros. & Jonnie Lavender-2: Leslie York, George York, v duet; or prob. George York, v-3; or prob. Leslie York, v-4; acc. Leslie York, eg; George York, g; Jonnie Lavender, prob. sb.
   Detroit, MI   prob. 1941–42

Going To The Shindig -1	Mellow 1638
Mother's Sunny Smile -1	Mellow 1638
A Merry Christmas To The Boys Over There -2, 4	Mellow 1640/1641
Not Over Thirty-Five -2	Mellow 1640/1641
I Got My Eyes On You -2, 3	Mellow 1642
You'll Pay For It All -2	Mellow 1642

I Got My Eyes On You on Mellow 1642 possibly as by **George York**.
Mellow 1639 is untraced and may be by these artists.
The York Brothers recorded after 1942.

BUDDY YOUNG'S KENTUCKIANS

Pseudonym on Superior 2519 for Tommy Whitmer's Band, and on 2655, 2731 for Ted Gossett's Band.

CLARENCE YOUNG

Pseudonym on Champion for Frank Welling.

JACKSON YOUNG

Pseudonym on Challenge, Champion, Silvertone, and Supertone for Ben Jarrell (see Da Costa Woltz's Southern Broadcasters).

JESS YOUNG

Homer Davenport & Young Brothers: Jess Young, f; Homer Davenport, bj; prob. Alvin Young, g.
   Richmond, IN   Wednesday, April 22, 1925

12211,-A	Variations – Sweet Bunch Of Daisies	Ge rejected
12212	Hy Patillion	Ge 5719, Sil 4010
12213-A	Maybelle Rag	Ge 3077, Sil 4011
12214-A	The Old Hen Cackled And The Rooster Crowed	Ge 5715, 3021, Sil 4009, Chg 110, 304, Bu 8017
12215	Sequetchic [sic]	Ge unissued
12216	The Fox Chase	Ge 5719, Sil 4010
12217	Going Back To Dixie	Ge rejected
12218	Smoke Behind The Clouds	Ge 3077, Sil 4011

Challenge 110, 304 as by **The Three Howard Boys**.
Revs: Gennett 5715, Silvertone 4009, Challenge 110 by Homer Davenport; Gennett 3021 by John Hammond; Challenge 304 by Murray Kellner; Buddy 8017 by Doc Roberts.

Jess Young, f solo.
   Richmond, IN   Wednesday, April 22, 1925

| 12220 | Young's Hornpipe | Ge unissued |

Gennett files note of matrix 12220: "Don't use in catalog; wrote to sell Personal."
Matrix 12219 is by Homer Davenport.

Young Brothers Tennessee Band: Jess Young, f; unknown, f-1; poss. C.C. Thomas, bj; prob. Alvin Young, g; unidentified, v; unidentified, sp.
    Atlanta, GA   Tuesday, November 8, 1927

    145166-2   Bill Baily [sic] Won't You Please Come Home -1   Co 15219-D, ReAu G20669
    145167-2   Are You From Dixie?   Co 15219-D, ReAu G20669

Matrix 145166 is titled *Bill Bailey, Won't You Please Come Home?* on Regal G20669.

Jess Young's Tennessee Band: Jess Young, f; poss. C.C. Thomas, bj; prob. Alvin Young, g; Dan Hornsby, v.
    Atlanta, GA   Thursday, October 25, 1928

    147293-2   Fiddle Up   Co 15338-D
    147294-2   Oh! My Lawd   Co 15338-D
    147295-   The Fatal Wedding   Co unissued
    147296-   After The Ball   Co unissued

Jess Young, f; prob. Alvin Young, g; Dan Hornsby, v; unidentified, sp-1.
    Atlanta, GA   Friday, April 19, 1929

    148361-2   Sweet Bunch Of Daisies   Co 15400-D
    148362-2   Silver Bell   Co 15400-D
    148363-2   The Old K-C -1   Co 15431-D
    148364-2   Lovin' Henry -1   Co 15431-D

Jess Young, f; unknown, f; prob. Alvin Young, g; Dan Hornsby, v-1; unidentified, v duet-2.
    Atlanta, GA   Monday, November 4, 1929

    149348-2   Take A Look At That Baby -1   Co 15493-D
    149349-2   Old Weary Blues -2   Co 15493-D
    149350-   There's Something Nice About Everyone   Co unissued
    149351-   Wink The Other Eye   Co unissued

EDDIE YOUNGER & HIS MOUNTAINEERS

See Arthur Fields & Fred Hall.

Z

EARL B. ZAAYER

Earl B. Zaayer, h/v-1; acc. Joe ———, g.
    Richmond, IN   Thursday, May 22, 1930

    16647   Ozark Waltz   Ch 16310
    16648   Deep Sea Waltz   Ge unissued
    16649,-A   My Irene -1   Ge unissued

Champion 16310 as by **Earl & Joe**.
Rev. Champion 16310 by Ted Gossett's Band.

ZACK & GLENN

Zack Hurt, Glenn Hewitt, v duet; acc. unknown, f; Glenn Hewitt, g; unknown, vc.
    San Antonio, TX   Monday, March 12, 1928

    400471-B   I'll Take You Home Again, Kathleen   OK 45240, PaAu A2707
    400474-A   Carry Me Back To Old Virginny   OK 45212
    400476-B   Love's Old Sweet Song   OK 45240, PaAu A2707

At least some of matrices 400470, 400472/73, and 400475, blank in OKeh files, are probably by these artists.

Zack Hurt Of Zack & Glenn, v; acc. Glenn Hewitt, g.
    San Antonio, TX   Tuesday, March 13, 1928

    400489-A   Gambler's Lament   OK 45212

Zack Hurt also recorded with The Hi-Flyers.

ZEB & ZEEKE (MEACHAM & CASTEEL)

Roy "Zeb" Meacham or Therould "Zeeke" Casteel, v; acc. prob. one of them, f; prob. the other, g; one of them, wh-1.
    New York, NY   Monday, December 10, 1934

    39159-A,-B   Alabamy Bound   De unissued
    39160-A   I'm A Ding Dong Daddy (From Dumas)   De 5060, MW 8038
    39161-A,-B   How'm I Doin'   De unissued
    39162-A   My Cabin By The Sea -1   De 5060, MW 8038

ZORA & THE HOMETOWNERS

See Zora Layman.

Bibliography

Books

Generic and Label Discographies

Most discographical writing on country music has been published in periodicals rather than books, and the works in this section have been chiefly useful for their approaches to layout and methodology. Obvious exceptions, in that they are more directly relevant, are Rust's *Victor Master Book* and Ginell's *Decca Hillbilly Discography*. I should make it clear that my divergences from Rust are based on my own inspection of the RCA Victor files and of the records concerned, and my disagreements with Ginell's findings, particularly in respect to band personnels, are based upon further research, much of it by Kevin Coffey. Three books listed here—Ginell and Coffey's *Discography of Western Swing*, Meade's *Country Music Sources*, and Sutton and Nauck's *American Record Labels*—were published too late in the production process of this discography to be consulted. They are included as a resource for interested readers.

Dixon, Robert M. W., John Godrich, & Howard Rye. *Blues & Gospel Records 1890–1943*. 4th ed. Oxford: Clarendon, 1997.

Ginell, Cary. *The Decca Hillbilly Discography, 1927–1945*. Westport, CT: Greenwood, 1989.

Ginell, Cary, and Kevin Coffey. *Discography of Western Swing and Hot String Bands, 1928–1942*. Westport, CT: Greenwood, 2001.

Kinkle, Roger D. *The Complete Encyclopedia of Popular Music and Jazz, 1900–1950*. New Rochelle, NY: Arlington, 1974.

Meade, Guthrie T., with Dick Spottswood, and Douglas S. Meade. *Country Music Sources: A Biblio-Discography of Commercially Recorded Traditional Music*. Chapel Hill: Southern Folklife Collection, 2002.

Robertson, Alex. *Canadian Compo Numericals*. Point Claire, P.Q., Canada: author, 1978.

Rust, Brian. *The Victor Master Book*. Volume 2, *1925–1936*. Pinner, Middlesex, England: author, 1969.

———. *Jazz Records 1897–1942*. Rev. ed. London: Storyville, 1970.

———. *The Complete Entertainment Discography*. New Rochelle, NY: Arlington, 1973.

———. *The American Dance Band Discography, 1917–1942*. New Rochelle, NY: Arlington, 1975.

Sears, Richard S. *V-Discs: A History and Discography*. Westport, CT: Greenwood, 1980.

Spottswood, Richard K. *Ethnic Music on Records: A Discography of Ethnic Recordings Produced in the United States, 1893 to 1942*. Urbana: University of Illinois Press, 1990.

Vreede, Max. *Paramount 12000/13000*. London: Storyville, 1971.

Country Music Studies

Most of the works in this section are studies of regions, institutions, or individual artists rather than discographies, but all have been valuable sources of data.

Cauthen, Joyce H. *With Fiddle and Well-Rosined Bow: Old-Time Fiddling in Alabama*. Tuscaloosa: University of Alabama Press, 1989.

Daniel, Wayne W. *Pickin' on Peachtree: A History of Country Music in Atlanta, Georgia*. Urbana: University of Illinois Press, 1990.

Ginell, Cary. *Milton Brown and the Founding of Western Swing*. Urbana: University of Illinois Press, 1994.

Lornell, Kip. *Virginia's Blues, Country, & Gospel Records 1902–1943: An Annotated Discography*. Lexington: University Press of Kentucky, 1989.

Porterfield, Nolan. *Jimmie Rodgers: The Life and Times of America's Blue Yodeler*. Urbana: University of Illinois Press, 1979.

Pugh, Ronnie. *Ernest Tubb: The Texas Troubadour*. Durham, NC: Duke University Press, 1996.

Rorrer, Kinney. *Rambling Blues: The Life & Songs of Charlie Poole*. London: Old Time Music, 1982.

Townsend, Charles. *San Antonio Rose: The Life and Music of Bob Wills*. Urbana: University of Illinois Press, 1976.

Tribe, Ivan M. *Mountaineer Jamboree: Country Music in West Virginia*. Lexington: University Press of Kentucky, 1984.

Wiggins, Gene. *Fiddlin' Georgia Crazy: Fiddlin' John Carson, His Real World, and the World of His Songs*. Urbana: University of Illinois Press, 1987.

Wolfe, Charles K. *The Grand Ole Opry: The Early Years, 1925–35*. London: Old Time Music, 1975.

———. *Tennessee Strings: The Story of Country Music in Tennessee*. Knoxville: University of Tennessee Press, 1977.

———. *The Devil's Box: Masters of Southern Fiddling*. Nashville, TN: Country Music Foundation Press and Vanderbilt University Press, 1997.

———. *A Good-Natured Riot: The Birth of the Grand Ole Opry*. Nashville, TN: Country Music Foundation Press and Vanderbilt University Press, 1999.

Other Studies

Kennedy, Rick. *Jelly Roll, Bix, and Hoagy: Gennett Studios and the Birth of Recorded Jazz*. Bloomington: Indiana University Press, 1994.

Rust, Brian. *The American Record Label Book*. New Rochelle, NY: Arlington, 1978.

Sutton, Allan, and Kurt Nauck. *American Record Labels and Companies: An Encyclopedia (1891–1943)*. Highlands Ranch, CO: Mainspring, 2000.

Periodicals

I have drawn much vital data from articles, interviews, artist discographies, and label numericals, far too numerous to specify, published in the following periodicals:

Bluegrass Unlimited (U.S.)
Country Directory (U.S.)
Country & Western Spotlight (New Zealand)
Country News & Views (Britain)
Cowboy Music World (U.S.)
Devil's Box (U.S.)
Disc Collector (U.S.)
Jamboree (U.S.)
John Edwards Memorial Foundation Quarterly (U.S.)
Journal of Country Music (U.S.)
Matrix (Britain)
Mountain Broadcast & Prairie Recorder (U.S.)

Music Memories (U.S.)
National Hillbilly News (U.S.)
Old-Time Herald (U.S.)
Old Time Music (Britain)
Record Research (U.S.)
Rural Radio (U.S.)
78 Quarterly (U.S.)
Stand By! (U.S.)
Storyville (Britain)
Vintage Jazz Mart (Britain)

Index to Performers

This index contains all performers who appear in the discography in an accompanying role, or as members of a collective entity such as a band or vocal group. An asterisk before the name signifies that the performer also has a main entry in the book, that is, in his/her own name. (An artist whose name appears *only* in a main entry is not included in this index.) Names beginning with "Mc" are indexed as if they began with "Mac."

Following the performer's name is a list of instruments played and/or vocal parts sung, using the abbreviations detailed on pp. 43–44. As in the Index to Titles, references are to artist headings (sometimes, for reasons of space, in shortened form) and page numbers. The latter are cited only for pages where the performer is named. Some performers, for example, in groups with stable line-ups, may participate in sessions on subsequent pages, where their presence is implicit, but those pages are not indexed unless the performer is named on them. Page ranges (e.g., 704–10) are merely shorthand for consecutive page references.

Degrees of uncertainty about a performer's, or an instrument's, presence or role in a performance, such as "prob." or "poss.," have not been taken into account.

A performer's name may appear in slightly different forms in different parts of the discography, perhaps because of variations on record labels or in company files, or for other reasons. In such cases the name has been indexed in its fullest or commonest form. Some names are shared by more than one performer, and, while the index aspires to distinguish between them, it is possible that performers with the same name may sometimes have been conflated in a single entry.

Abbott, Carl, sb Nolan Bush, 147
Abernathy, D[ee], v/bsv Abernathy Quartet, 47; Atco Quartet, 70
Abernathy, Leroy, p Abernathy Quartet, 47; Atco Quartet, 70
Abernathy, Velma, p Atco Quartet, 70
Abernathy, Will, v/sp/ah Blue Ridge Mountain Entertainers, 111; Clarence Greene, 382
Achten, M.J., g J.B. Fuslier, 361
Adams, Harry, v/lg Eldon Baker, 89
Adams, Jimmie, v/y/g Rolling Stones, 813; Two Cow Hands, 918
Adams, Leon, ts Ross Rhythm Rascals, 814
Adkins, Cecil, bj David Miller, 625
Adler, Jerry, h Johnny Bond, 116–17
Agee, Ray, bj Walter Family, 938
Aiken, Oscar, f Emmett & Aiken String Band, 332
Akers, Lundy, v/bj Fred Pendleton, 685
Akins, E.E., f Akins Birmingham Boys, 52; T.H. Phillips, 690
Akins, Julian, v/lg/sb Roy Newman, 657–58; Saddle Tramps, 817
"Alabam," sp Texas Rangers, 899
Albright, Oscar, sb Dr. Humphrey Bate, 97
Alderman, Alonzo Elvis "Tony," v/f Hill Billies, 422–24
Aldridge, Red, f Ralph Hodges, 429
Aldridge, Ross Ross Rhythm Rascals, 814
Aldridge, Talton, v/g Roy Hall, 390
Aleshire, Lennie, f Hugh Cross, 236

Alexander, Bud, md Frank Roberts, Bud Alexander & Fiddlin' Slim Sandford, 755
Alguire, Reuben Daniel "Danny," v/t Bob Wills, 966
Alleman, Toney, v/g Alleman & Walker, 54
Allen, Austin, v/sp/wh/h/tbj/g Allen Brothers, 55–57
Allen, George, cl Jimmie Rodgers, 806
Allen, Lee "Zeke," v/vc Otto Gray, 378–79
Allen, Lee, v/k/g Allen Brothers, 55–57
Allen, Wade "Hy," v/bj Otto Gray, 378–79
Alley, Alvin, f Jimmie Rodgers, 805
*****Alley, Shelly Lee, v/f** Lummie Lewis, 500; Jimmie Rodgers, 805
Allgood, S.J., bj R.B. Smith-S.J. Allgood, 845
Altizer, Billy, v/f Roanoke Jug Band, 751
Altschuler, B., vla Vernon Dalhart, 246
Amendt, Johnny, v/y Johnny Marvin, 606–07
Anderson, Bill, f/bj-g W.B. Chenoweth, 203; Ed Hayes, 414
Anderson, Raymond, v Red Headed Brier Hopper, 732
Andrews, James, v/y/g Andrews Brothers, 60; Slim Smith, 846
Andrews, Tom, g Binkley Brothers Dixie Clodhoppers, 104
Anglin, Jack, v/g Anglin Brothers, 61
Anglin, Jim, v/g Anglin Brothers, 61
Anglin, Red, v/g Anglin Brothers, 61
Anglin, Skinny, h Cherokee Ramblers, 203–04
Applegate, Les, v Raymond Weaver & Les Applegate, 942
Arceneaux, Louis, f/wb Happy Fats, 395
Armstrong, Lillian Hardin, p Jimmie Rodgers, 804

Armstrong, Louis, t Jimmie Rodgers, 804
Arnspiger, Herman, lg/g Light Crust Doughboys, 501; Bob Wills, 960–64
Arrington, Charles, f Paul Warmack, 939–40
*Arthur, Emry, v/sp/h/g Brother James Arnold, 64; Dock Boggs, 116; Jossie Ellers, 331; William Rexroat's Cedar Crest Singers, 744; Rochford & Peggs, 797; Floyd Thompson, 903
Arthur, Henry, v/sg/bj Emry Arthur, 64–65
Arwine, Herman, g Hi-Flyers, 418
Ashabraner, ——, h Nicholson's Players, 659
Ashley, Gerald, h Ashley's Melody Makers, 68
Ashley, Hobart N., v/sg Ashley's Melody Makers, 68
Ashley, Hubert M., v/y/g Ashley's Melody Makers, 68
*Ashley, Thomas C. (Clarence), lv/v/sp/bj/g Blue Ridge Mountain Entertainers, 110–11; Carolina Tar Heels, 173; Byrd Moore, 639
Ashlock, Jesse Thedford, v/sp/f Bill Boyd, 122; John (Dusty) King, 486; Bob Wills, 960–66
Aslakson, Casey, f Casey's Old Time Fiddlers, 197
Atchison, Shelby "Tex," lv/f Gene Autry, 80–81; Bob Miller, 624–25; Patsy Montana, 634–35; Prairie Ramblers, 704–10
Atkins, Jimmy, v/g Hilltoppers, 427
Atkins, Virgil, bj Herald Goodman, 375; Arthur Smith, 842
*Attlesey (Shelton) Bob, v/sp/md/g/u/j Jimmie Davis, 300; Curley Fox, 357; Lone Star Cowboys, 509
*Attlesey (Shelton), Joe, v/sp/md/emd/g Jimmie Davis, 300–301; Curley Fox, 357; Lone Star Cowboys, 509
Austin, Don, v/bj/g Al Clauser, 214
Austin, Gar, f Roy Newman, 658
Austin, Gene, v/bj/calls George Reneau, 740–41; Uncle "Am" Stuart, 880
Austin, Lonnie, sp/f/p H.M. Barnes, 94–95; Four Pickled Peppers, 356; Kelly Harrell, 404; Roy Harvey, 410; Charlie Poole, 699–700; Earl Shirkey & Roy Harper, 832; Weaver Brothers, 942
Autry, Elond, v/f/g Chas. Winters & Elond Autry, 968
*Autry, Gene, v/y/g George Goebel, 372; Frank[ie] Marvin, 602–04
Ayers, Eunice, v Morris Brothers, 643
Ayers, Harry, v/g Grover Rann, 728

Babb, Neal, v/g Freeny Harmonizers, 359
Babineaux, Albert, tri Joe Creduer-Albert Babineaux, 232
"Baby Ray," v/sb Fisher Hendley, 417
Bacon, Ted, vla Gene Autry, 86
Bagett, Gene, lg Gene Steele, 867
Bagwell, James, bv Flat Creek Sacred Singers, 346
Bailey, Alton, tbj Port Arthur Jubileers, 701
Baker, A.G., v Baker's Whitley County Sacred Singers, 90; Ernest Phipps, 690–91
Baker, Arle, g Ashley's Melody Makers, 68
Baker, Bill, v/sp/g Bob Miller, 618
Baker, Ethel, p Ernest Phipps, 691
Baker, Flora, v/ah Mr. & Mrs. J.W. Baker, 90
Baker, Floyd, v/g Eldon Baker, 89
Baker, Jim, g Mr. & Mrs. J.W. Baker, 90
Baker, Johnny, g Leo Soileau, 855
Baker, Vern, v/y/f/g Ashley's Melody Makers, 68; Elton Britt, 127–28
Baker, Wade, v/g Eldon Baker, 89
Balay, George, cl/ts Bob Wills, 966
Ball, A.J., v Elmer Bird, 105–06
*Ball, Wilbur, v/y/g/u Cliff Carlisle, 161–63; Jimmie Rodgers, 806
Ballew, Jess, bv/g Happy Four, 396
Ballew, Smith, v Cruthers Brothers, 239
Bankey, Ray Jack, v/g Jack & Tony, 452
Banks, Lee, sp Fiddlin' John Carson, 177

Banks, Morris "Buddy," v/md Wade Mainer, 584
Banks, Robert "Buck," v/g Wade Mainer, 584
*Bankston, Emmett, v/bj Red Henderson, 415; Earl Johnson, 459–60
Banta, Frank, p Jimmy Smith, 844
Barber, A. Farry, bsv Hendersonville Quartet, 416
Barber, George, md/g Barber & Osborne, 93
*Bare, Ted, v/y/md Carolina Night Hawks, 172
Barfield, "Coot" Cotton & Barfield, 223
*Barfield, Johnny, v/sp/g Bert Layne, 493
Barger, Ray, g Roanoke Jug Band, 751
Barker, Bob, cl Ralph Hodges, 429
*Barnard, Hillman, tv Vaughan Quartet, 925–29
Barnard, Lester "Junior," eg Johnny Lee Wills, 967
Barnes, George, eg Massey Family, 612; Patsy Montana, 636; Prairie Ramblers, 711–12
Barnes, Jack, v/g Jimmie Davis, 300
Barnes, Joe, v/tbj Tune Wranglers, 914–15
Barnett, Ransom, f Shorty McCoy, 531
Barnette, J.M., o Turkey Mountain Singers, 916
Barnum, Herbert, sb Light Crust Doughboys, 502
Barres, Faye, v/y Carrie Mae Moore-Faye Barres, 640
Barret, W.J. (Bill), v/f/calls Dr. Humphrey Bate, 97
Barrett, Amy, v Blue Ridge Mountain Singers, 112
Barrett, Curt, v/y/g Beverly Hill Billies, 102
Barrett, Fred, v/ah Blue Ridge Mountain Singers, 112
Barrett, Patrick. see Uncle Ezra
Barrett, Vella, v Blue Ridge Mountain Singers, 112
Bartley, Moat, tbj Bar-X Cowboys, 92–93
Bassett, Ila, g Green's String Band, 381
Bassett, Jesse, v/g McClendon Brothers, 527–28
Bates, Charles, p George Reneau, 741
Baucom, Luther, lv/sp/md/v eff Three Tobacco Tags, 907–09
Baur, Franklyn, v Vernon Dalhart, 245–46
Baxter, Andrew, f Georgia Yellow Hammers, 367
Baxter, J.R., Jr., tv/p Stamps Quartet, 865
Bean, A.M., tbj Dixie String Band, 320
Beaudoin, Eugene "Johnny," esg Hank Snow, 852–53
Beaver, Landon, v/p Hi-Flyers, 418–20; Dick Reinhart, 739
*Bechtel, Perry, bv/sg/bj/g Taylor Flanagan, 345; Dan Hornsby, 441–42; Clayton McMichen, 568; Lowe Stokes, 870
Belcher, Ed, f Hill Billies, 424
Bell, Burgess, p E.M. Bartlett Groups, 96
Bell, Dwight, bj Thomas C. Ashley, 67
Bell, George, p Roy Newman, 658; Ocie Stockard, 869
Bellow, Ted "Pappy," v/y/g Beverly Hill Billies, 103
Belmard, Bob, f Jimmie Revard, 743
Benner, Bill, f Ken Card, 158; Buck Nation, 650–51; Tex Ritter, 750; Ray Whitley, 952–53
Bennett, Clinton, v Jim[my] Boa, 115
Bennett, Cooper, v/g/sb Doug Bine, 104; Dixie Ramblers [IV], 319; Modern Mountaineers, 630–31
Bennett, Max, scat v/p/vox Bob Skyles, 839
Bennett, Roy C., bv Hendersonville Quartet, 416
Bennett, Sheldon, v/f/eg Hi-Flyers, 419–20; Hank Penny, 685–86; Wiley Walker & Gene Sullivan, 936
Benson, Wayne, sb Hi-Flyers, 419–20
Berry, Mrs. H.S., v/g/u Kentucky Girls, 477
Berry, Hugh, cl Leon Chappelear, 201
Bethel, Melvin "Slats," md E.E. Hack String Band, 386
"Betty Lou," v Dick Hartman's Tennessee Ramblers, 408
Bickford, Charlie, p Doug Bine, 104
Bigger, Elvin, v/g Four Virginians, 357; Troy Martin & Elvin Bigger, 594
Bigger, Richard, f Four Virginians, 357
Billington, Morris "Mo," p Bob Wills, 966
*Bine, Doug, esg Dixie Ramblers [IV], 319

Binford, Ken, g Texas Jim Robertson, 759–60
Bingham, Virgil, v/p Bingham & Wells, 104
Binkley, Amos, bj Binkley Brothers Dixie Clodhoppers, 104
Binkley, Gale, f Binkley Brothers Dixie Clodhoppers, 104
Biondi, Joe, g Vernon Dalhart, 289; Adelyne Hood, 434
Bird, Connie, v/g Elmer Bird, 105–06
Bird, Louis, v Elmer Bird, 105–06
Birkhead, William, v/g George Edgin, 330
Bisbee-Schula, B., p Jasper Bisbee, 107
Bizzell, Ms. W.L., p Vaughan Quartet, 929
Black, Frank, cel/o Frank & James McCravy, 533; Old Southern Sacred Singers, 669
Black, Howard, sb Bob Atcher, 69
Blackard, Clarice, hv/p Shelor Family, 826
Blackard, Joe B., v/bj Shelor Family, 826
Blackburn, Al, v/p/g Frank & James McCravy, 537
Blackweller, Beacham, v/g J.E. Mainer's Mountaineers, 581
Blaeholder, Harry. see Skillet, Hank
Blaikie, Douglas, p Shelly Lee Alley, 58
Blainer, Johnny, tbj Hodgers Brothers, 428
Blair, ——, f/bj/g John McGhee & Frank Welling, 555
Blair, W.J. "Harry," lv/v/sp/sb Campbell Brothers, 154; Dick Hartman's Tennessee Ramblers, 407–09; Tennessee Ramblers [II], 897
Blakeman, Guy, f Garner Eckler & Roland Gaines, 329
Blalock, (Earl?), v/f Blalock & Yates, 108
Blanchard, Clarence, cl Plymouth Vermont Old Time Barn Dance Orch., 698
Blankenship, Daphna, lv/bj/u Blankenship Family, 108
Blankenship, Darius, lv/vc Blankenship Family, 108
Blankenship, William Pool, bsv/f Blankenship Family, 108
Blankenship, William Walter, tv/g Blankenship Family, 108
Blevins, ——, f/bj/g John McGhee & Frank Welling, 555
Blevins, Edd, g Frank Blevins, 108
Blevins, Rubye. see Montana, Patsy
Blind Andy. see Jenkins, Andrew
Bloom, Rube, p Al Bernard, 100
Blue, Bud, sp/p Fiddlin' John Carson, 177; OKeh Medicine Show, 668
Boaz, Edgar, g Doc Roberts, 752; Welby Toomey, 912
Boaz, Gus, f Dixie Crackers, 318; Moody Bible Sacred Harp Singers, 637; North Georgia Four, 663
*Bodine, Loy, v/y/h Charlie Hager, 388; Howard Keesee, 475
Bogan, Henry, vc East Texas Serenaders, 329; Honeyboy & Sassafras[s], 433
Bogard, Malcolm "Mack," v/g Yellow Jackets [II], 976–77
Boggs, Noel, esg Hank Penny, 686
Bolick, Bill, tv/md Blue Sky Boys, 113
Bolick, Earl, lv/g Blue Sky Boys, 113
*Boling, Carl, v/h/tg/tbj Claude Casey, 197
Boling, Ernest, v Carl Boling, 116
Boling, Lawrence, v/g Carl Boling, 116; Claude Casey, 197
*Bond, Johnny, v/g/sb Gene Autry, 85–87; Canova Family, 156; Jimmie Davis, 305; Al Dexter, 315; Dick Reinhart, 739; Tex Ritter, 751; Roy Rogers, 811–12; Jimmy Wakely, 933–34
Bone, Graydon, tv Dr. Smith's Champion Hoss Hair Pullers, 843
Bone, Henry, h Perry County Music Makers, 687
Bone, Leeman, tv/g Dr. Smith's Champion Hoss Hair Pullers, 843
Bonnie Blue Eyes, v Bob Atcher, 69–70
*Booker, Rev. Horace A., v/h/g/u Cliff Carlisle, 161
Booker, Jim, f Taylor's Kentucky Boys, 894–95
Booker, Joe, g Doc Roberts, 753; Taylor's Kentucky Boys, 895
Booker, John, g Doc Roberts, 752; Taylor's Kentucky Boys, 895
Boone, Claude, v/g Cliff Carlisle, 167; Walter Hurdt, 448; James Scott-Claude Boone, 821

Boone, J.W. (Will), lv/g Floyd County Ramblers, 350
Boone, Miss Olive, v Rev. Edward Boone, Mrs. Edward Boone & Miss Olive Boone, 117–18
Boone, Walter, tv/h Floyd County Ramblers, 350
"Boots[ie]," v/bj J.H. Howell, 445–46
Borodkin, Bert, vla Vernon Dalhart, 247–48
Borowski, Johnny, f/oc Milton Brown, 138; Jimmie Davis, 302; Ocie Stockard, 869
Boswell, Catherine, v/p Katherine Baxter & Harry Nelson, 97; Peck's Male Quartette, 683–84
Boswell, Dewey, v Leo Boswell, 119
*Boswell, Leo, v/h/md/g Elzie Floyd & Leo Boswell, 350; Merritt Smith, 845
Botkin, Perry, g Cindy Walker, 935
Bouchillon, Charley, f Chris Bouchillon, 119
Bouchillon, Uris, g Chris Bouchillon, 119
Bowen, Lyall W., cl Johnny Bond, 117
Bowers, W.H., v Avoca Quartette, 87
Bowles, Tommy, v/y/sg/g Three Musketeers, 906
*Bowman, Charlie, v/sp/f/bj/g Bowman Sisters, 121; Hill Billies, 422–24; Frank Wilson, 967
Bowman, Elbert, sp/g/eff Charlie Bowman, 120; Hill Billies, 423–24
Bowman, Jennie, v Bowman Sisters, 121
Bowman, Pauline, v Bowman Sisters, 121
Bowman, Walter, v/sp/bj Charlie Bowman, 120; Frank Wilson, 967
*Boyd, Bill, v/y/g Jimmie Rodgers, 806
*Boyd, Jim, eg/sb/v eff Gene Autry, 81; Bill Boyd, 121–24; Light Crust Doughboys, 504–06; Roy Newman, 656–57; Unknown Artists [VII], 920
*Boyd, John, tv/esg Bill Boyd, 123–24; Light Crust Doughboys, 504–05
Boyd, Willie, cl Yellow Jackets [II], 976–77
Boyett, James Andrew, g Carrie Mae Moore-Faye Barres, 640
Boyles, W.B., f West Virginia Coon Hunters, 946
Brader, Ed, tu/sb Carson Robison, 796–97
Bradley, Hampton. see "Little Boy Blue"
Bradley, Joe "Curley," v Ranch Boys, 725
Bradley, Speck, cl/ts Ross Rhythm Rascals, 814
Bradshaw, Carl, v/y/f/g Renus Rich & Carl Bradshaw, 747
Brady, Pat, sb Patsy Montana, 637; Roy Rogers, 811; Sons Of The Pioneers, 858–59
*Branch, Ernest, v/bj Roy Harvey, 411
Brandon, Luke, v/g Roane County Ramblers, 751; Wyatt & Brandon, 974
Brandt, Larry, ac Al Clauser, 214
Brashear, William Alex, t Bob Wills, 966
Braswell, Francum, h/g George Wade, 933
Bratcher, Bundy, ac W. Lee O'Daniel, 666
Braun, Lester, sb Elton Britt, 130; Zeke Manners, 586; Texas Jim Robertson, 760
Breaux, Cleoma, v/sg/g Amadie Breaux, 126; Clifford Breaux, 127; Joseph Falcon, 334–36
*Breaux, Clifford, v/g Amadie Breaux, 126
*Breaux, Ophy, f Joseph Falcon, 334–35
Breen, May Singhi, u Vernon Dalhart, 245
Brewer, Edna, v Ernest V. Stoneman, 876
Brewer, Kahle, v/f Ernest V. Stoneman, 873–76
Brewer, T.M., v/sp/f/bj/g Fiddlin' John Carson, 176–78
Brewer, Will, bsv Smith's Sacred Singers, 849
Briers, Larry, p Joseph Samuels, 819
Briggs, Billy, esg/sb Hi-Flyers, 418–19; Sons Of The West, 859
Brinkley, J.B., lv/eg Crystal Springs Ramblers, 239; Al Dexter, 315; Light Crust Doughboys, 506–07; Patsy Montana, 636

*Britt, Elton, v/y/g** Beverly Hill Billies, 103; Zeke Manners, 586; Bob Miller, 624; Texas Jim Robertson, 759
Britton, Johnny, g Forrest Copeland & Johnny Britton, 221
*Brock, Allie, v** Louie Donaldson, 323
Brock, D.M., p Palmer Sisters, 673
Brock, Dwight M., bv/p Stamps Quartet, 863–65
Brock, Jessie, v/g Earl McCoy & Jessie Brock, 531
Brokenshire, Norman, sp Johnny Marvin, 606
*Brook, Charles S., v/g** Dixie String Band, 320
Brooks, Conrad, v Rye's Red River Blue Yodelers, 817
Brooks, Guy, v/sp/f Red Fox Chasers, 730–31
Brooks, Ted, v/g Rex Griffin, 384
Broughton, Ted, v/y/sg Hawaiian Songbirds, 412
Broussard, Harold "Popeye," v/p Happy Fats, 396; Leo Soileau, 855
Broussard, Joseph M. "Pee Wee," v/tbj Happy Fats, 396
Brower, Cecil, v/f Bill Boyd, 122–24; Milton Brown, 136–37; Al Dexter, 315; Light Crust Doughboys, 505–06; Patsy Montana, 636; Roy Newman, 657–58; Bob Wills, 962
Brown, Bill, esg Roy Hall, 391
Brown, Bill, g E.E. Hack String Band, 386
Brown, Bill, sp/g Chumbler Family, 212; Cal Davenport, 296; John Dilleshaw, 317; Alex Hood, 435; Clayton McMichen, 566, 568; Ridgel's Fountain Citians, 749; Smoky Mountain Ramblers, 852; Southern Moonlight Entertainers, 860; Lowe Stokes, 870; Uncle Jimmy Thompson, 904
Brown, Boyce, v/g Brown Brothers, 138; Carlisle Brothers, 169
Brown, Clarence, vc Jack Cawley's Oklahoma Ridge Runners, 199
Brown, Derwood, v/g/calls Bill Boyd, 124; Milton Brown, 136–38; Jimmie Davis, 302; Light Crust Doughboys, 500; Ocie Stockard, 869–70
Brown, Earl T., tv Hendersonville Quartet, 416
Brown, Earl, v/g/sb/v eff Roy Newman, 656–58
Brown, Harry, md H.M. Barnes, 94–95
*Brown, J. Herschel, wb/spoons** Spooney Five, 862
Brown, J.C., bsv Alabama Sacred Harp Singers, 53; Denson Quartet, 313
Brown, James, f E.E. Hack String Band, 386
Brown, Joe, f John Dilleshaw, 317
Brown, John, p Little Brown Church Quartet, 508; Prairie Ramblers, 706–07, 712–13
Brown, Lou, v Bob Skyles, 839
Brown, Marion "Peanut," v/y/sp/g Fiddlin' John Carson, 179; Pink Lindsey, 507
Brown, Marion, g Three Stripped Gears, 907
*Brown, Milton, lv/sp/v eff** Light Crust Doughboys, 500
Brown, Mrs Nancy, v Denson Quartet, 313
Brown, Red. *see* Barnes, Joe
Brundage, D.W., p Russell Miller, 627
*Bruner, Cliff, v/f/etg** Shelly Lee Alley, 57–58; Milton Brown, 137; Jimmie Davis, 305; Buddy Jones, 465–66; Charles Mitchell & His Orchestra, 629–30; Rice Brothers' Gang, 747; Leon Selph, 824; Shelton Brothers, 829; Floyd Tillman, 910
Bryan, Byron, bj [E.R.] Nance Family, 648
Bryan, Dean, g Jimmie Rodgers, 800–801
Bryant, Boudleaux, f Hank Penny, 686
Bryant, Hezzie, sb Cliff Bruner, 139–41; Leon Chappelear, 202; Bob Dunn's Vagabonds, 326–27; Buddy Jones, 465; Dickie McBride, 526; Leon Selph, 823–24; Shelton Brothers, 829; Texas Wanderers, 900; Floyd Tillman, 910; Village Boys, 931–32
Bryant, Hoyt "Slim," v/sp/g Bert Layne, 493; Clayton McMichen, 570–73; McMichen's Harmony Boys, 573; Bob Miller, 622; Jimmie Rodgers, 807–08
Bryant, Raymond "Loppy," v/sb Clayton McMichen, 572
Buchanan, Clato, tbj Roy Hall, 390
Buchanan, Robert "Buck," v/f Bill Boyd, 124; Milton Brown, 138; Jimmie Davis, 302; Light Crust Doughboys, 504–05; Sons Of The West, 859; Ocie Stockard, 869
Buckholtz, Buck, d/traps Harry "Mac" McClintock, 529
Bucy, Joshua Floyd, v/y/g Andrews Brothers, 60
Buffington, Merwyn J., g Mrs. Jimmie Rodgers, 809; Ernest Tubb, 913
Buice, Luther, v Buice Brothers, 142
Buice, Marvin, v Buice Brothers, 142
Buice, Paul, v Buice Brothers, 142
Buice, T. Carl, v Buice Brothers, 142
Bullard, Allen, f Crysel Boys, 239
Buller, Sidney "Buddy," lg Ted Daffan's Texans, 240–41
Bumgardner, Howard, v/g J.E. Mainer's Mountaineers, 581
*Bumgarner, Samantha, v/f/bj** Eva Davis, 298
Bunn, Ollie, v/f/bj/g Dixie Reelers, 319; J.E. Mainer's Mountaineers, 581
Bunyard, Dick, sg Jesse Rodgers, 798; Jimmie Rodgers, 806
Burckhardt, John F., p John Baltzell, 90–91; Allen Sisson, 836
Burdette, Charlie, j Walter Family, 938
Burdette, Wilburn, wb Walter Family, 938
Burgess, ——, v Stamps Quartet, 864
Burgess, Bob, v/g Clay Long, 510; Nite Owls, 661
Burgher, Oddis J., bj Kentucky String Ticklers, 478
Burke, Irene, p Southern Railroad Quartet, 860
Burke, Peter, Sr., p Bill Mounce, 645
Burkes, Billy, v/sg/g Burke Brothers, 143; Jimmie Rodgers, 801–03, 807
Burkes, Charlie, u Jimmie Rodgers, 807
Burkes, Weldon, v/g/u Burke Brothers, 143; Jimmie Rodgers, 801–02, 807
Burleson, Curly, v/g/sb Walter Hurdt, 448; Leroy [Slim] Johnson, 461–62
Burnett, Barney, v/y/sp/bj/g/humming Bob McGimsey, 564; Bob Miller, 616–24
Burnett, Hick, g Crook Brothers String Band, 234
*Burnett, Richard D., v/sp/f/bj/g/v eff** Taylor, Moore & Burnett, 894
*Burnette, Smiley, v/v eff** Gene Autry, 78, 80–83
Burns, Reuben, v/bj Short Creek Trio, 833
Burton, Charles, v Light Crust Doughboys, 504–05; Charles Mitchell & His Orchestra, 630
Burton, Mrs. Dora, p Hamp Reynolds' Sacred Harp Singers, 744
Burton, John, v Howard Keesee, 475
Burton, Louis/Lewis, v/h/bj/g Russell & Louis Burton, 146
**Bush, —— ** Pioneer Trio, 698
Bush, ——, bsv Mr. & Mrs. R.N. Grisham, 385
Buskirk, Paul, md Callahan Brothers, 154
Busse, "Highpockets," ac Saddle Tramps, 817
*Butcher, Dwight, v/y/h/g** Prairie Ramblers, 711
Butler, Bill, esg Ken Card, 158; Buck Nation, 650–51; Tex Ritter, 750; Ray Whitley, 952–53
Byles, Ruth, v Range Riders, 727
Byrd, Billy, g Herald Goodman, 375; Arthur Smith, 842
Byrd, Gerry, sg Happy Valley Boys, 397
Byrd, Paul, v/k/g Johnson County Ramblers, 463
Byrley, Nora, v Ernest Phipps, 691

Cady, Cassie, p Plymouth Vermont Old Time Barn Dance Orch., 698
Cady, Linn, d Plymouth Vermont Old Time Barn Dance Orch., 698
Cagle, Bill, v Atco Quartet, 70
Caldwell, George, p Nolan Bush, 147
Calhoun, Bill, hv/g (Charlie) Monroe's Boys, 632
Calhoun, Fred "Papa," p Milton Brown, 136–38; Cliff Bruner, 139; Jimmie Davis, 302
Cali, Johnny, v/sp/f/sg/md/lute/bj/tbj/g Al Bernard, 100;

Vernon Dalhart, 258–59, 289, 292; Graham Brothers, 377; Kanawha Singers, 469; Frank Luther, 518–23; Frank[ie] Marvin, 600; Dick Robertson, 758; Texas Jim Robertson, 759–60; Carson Robison, 780, 782, 785–87, 789–91, 796–97; Jimmie Rodgers, 808

Callahan, Alma, v Callahan Brothers, 152

Callahan, Homer, v/y/h/g/sb Callahan Brothers, 151–54

Callahan, Walter, v/y/g Callahan Brothers, 151–54

Callison, Cal, ac Jimmie Revard, 743; Tune Wranglers, 915

*Campbell, Aaron, v/sg/g Irene Sanders, 819

Campbell, Cecil "Curl[e]y," v/bv/y/sg/esg/bj/tg/tbj/g Dick Hartman's Tennessee Ramblers, 407–08; Tennessee Ramblers [II], 897

Campbell, Grady "Red," v/g Chester Allen & Campbell, 54

Campbell, Lee, tv/h Happy Four, 396

Campbell, Muryel "Zeke," sg/eg/lg Bill Boyd, 123–24; Clifford Gross, 385; Light Crust Doughboys, 503–06

Campbell, William, h Arkansas Barefoot Boys, 63

Cannon, Fonzo, v/g/calls Freeny's Barn Dance Band, 359

Canova, Anne (Anna, Annie), v Canova Family, 155–56

Canova, Julietta [Judy], v/y/sp Canova Family, 155–56

Canova, Leon Canova Family, 155

Canova, Pete, f/g Dwight Butcher, 148–49; Canova Family, 155–56

Canova, Zeke, v/sp/p/g Canova Family, 155–56

Caplinger, Everett, v Warren Caplinger, 157

*Card, Ken, v/bj/etg/tbj Earl & Willie Phelps, 689; Ray Whitley, 953

Carey, Joe, v Parker Quartette, 678

Carlino, William, bj Vernon Dalhart, 266, 274–77, 279–84

*Carlisle, Bill, v/y/sp/h/g Cliff Carlisle, 164–68; Milton & Marion Carlisle, 168; Carlisle Brothers, 168–69

*Carlisle, Cliff, v/y/sg/g/v eff Wilbur Ball, 90; Bill Carlisle, 158–60; Carlisle Brothers, 168–69; Walter Hurdt, 448; Fred Kirby, 486–87; Jimmie Rodgers, 806; James Scott-Claude Boone, 821

Carlisle, Louis, v/sb Bill Carlisle, 160; Cliff Carlisle, 166; Milton & Marion Carlisle, 168

Carlisle, Sonny Boy Tommy, v/y Bill Carlisle, 160; Cliff Carlisle, 166–68; Carlisle Brothers, 169

Carmen, Marcheta, v Jenkins Carmen, 170

Carmene, Dick, p Raymond Weaver & Les Applegate, 942

Carnes, Chet, v/tbj Jimmie Revard, 743

Carpenter, ——, tv Mr. & Mrs. R.N. Grisham, 385

Carpenter, Boyden, v/h/g Boyden Carpenter, 174

Carpenter, Glen, h Asa Martin, 593

Carpenter, Jesse, esg Lunsford Bros., 517

Carpenter, Lewis, f Plymouth Vermont Old Time Barn Dance Orch., 698

Carr, Earl, v/f/sb Jack Pierce, 695–96

*Carson, Fiddlin' John, v/sp/f Rosa Lee Carson, 179; OKeh Medicine Show, 668

Carson, Jenny Lou. see Overstake, Lucille

Carson, Ken "Shorty," v Ranch Boys, 725

Carson, Ken, wh/g Bob Atcher, 70; Ranch Boys, 725–26

*Carson, Rosa Lee, v/y/sp/bj/g Fiddlin' John Carson, 176–79; OKeh Medicine Show, 668

Carter, A.P., v/sp Carter Family, 187–95

Carter, Andrew, f Carter Brothers & Son, 186–87

Carter, Anna, av Chuck Wagon Gang, 209–10

*Carter, Buster, tv/bj Carolina Buddies, 170; Dixie Ramblers [I], 318; Walter Smith, 846

Carter, D.P. "Dad," tv/bsv/md Chuck Wagon Gang, 209–11

Carter, Ernest "Jim," tv/bsv/g Chuck Wagon Gang, 209–11

Carter, George, v/f Carter Brothers & Son, 186–87

Carter, Jimmie, g Carter Brothers & Son, 186–87

Carter, Maybelle, v/y/sp/sg/md/g Carter Family, 187–95

Carter, Sara, v/y/sp/g/ah Carter Family, 187–95

Carter, Woodrow M. "Woody," f/eg Floyd Tillman, 910

Cartwright, Bernard, v/y/f/md Cartwright Brothers, 195–96

Cartwright, Jack, v/y/g Cartwright Brothers, 195–96

Caruthers, Earl, v/f/emd Jimmy Hart, 406; Port Arthur Jubileers, 701

Carver, Noble "Uncle Bozo," tv/g Carver Boys, 196

Carver, Robert, bsv/g Carver Boys, 196

Carver, Warner, lv/f/h/bj Carver Boys, 196

Casares, Alfredo "Fred" ["Jose Cortes"], v/f Gene Steele, 867; Swift Jewel Cowboys, 884–85; Wanderers, 938

Casey, Sara, v Claude Casey, 196

*Cassell, Pete, v/y/p/g Uncle Ned, 919

Cassterers, Horace, v Blue Ridge Sacred Singers, 112

Cassterers, Shaffer, v Blue Ridge Sacred Singers, 112

Casteel, Therould "Zeeke," v/wh/f/g Zeb & Zeeke, 979

Castleman, Homer, bj Blue Ridge Mountaineers, 112

Cates, Toney, v Hart & Cates, 406

Cauley, ——, v/bj Roland Cauley, 198–99

Cavanagh, ——, f Lake & Cavanagh, 489

Cawley, Howard L., f Jack Cawley's Oklahoma Ridge Runners, 199; Leonard C. Fulwider, 361

Ceppos, Mac, f Zeke Manners, 586

Chamblie, Henry, v/g Carroll County Revelers, 174

Chamblie, Jess, f Carroll County Revelers, 174

Champa[i]gne, D.A., f/h Jules Allen, 54; Rodeo Trio, 798

Chandler, Bill, g Spooney Five, 862

Chapman, Chris, wh/traps/bells/v eff/eff Al Bernard, 100; Vernon Dalhart, 246–48; Frank & James McCravy, 533

*Chappelear, Leon, v/y/sp/g Jimmie Davis, 300–302, 304; Lone Star Cowboys, 509

Charles, Bill, f/g Calaway's West Virginia Mountaineers, 150; Miller Wikel, 956

Charles, Harry, v Katherine Baxter & Harry Nelson, 97; Hugh Gibbs String Band, 368; Nelson & Nelson, 653

Chastain, Jeff, lv Happy Four, 396

*Chasteen, Monie, v/g Lloyd Wright, 973

Chatwell, J.R., v/f Bill Boyd, 122–23; Cliff Bruner, 140; Leon Chappelear, 202; Adolph Hofner, 431; Modern Mountaineers, 630–31; Ross Rhythm Rascals, 814; Saddle Tramps, 817

*Chenoweth, W.B., v/f Ed Hayes, 414

Cherry, Clara Belle, lv/md Cherry Sisters, 204

Cherry, Margaret, v/g Cherry Sisters, 204

Cherry, Patsy, v/sg Cherry Sisters, 204

*Chestnut, Ted, v/bj-md Kentucky Thorobreds, 478–79

Childers, Mrs. W.C., v W.C. Childers, 206

Chism, John H., f Pope's Arkansas Mountaineers, 701

Chism, Wallace, tv/g Pope's Arkansas Mountaineers, 701

*Chitwood, Bill, bsv/sp/f Clyde Evans Band, 333; Georgia Yellow Hammers, 367; Gordon County Quartet, 375; Turkey Mountain Singers, 916

Chitwood, Tom, bsv Gordon County Quartet, 375

Choates, Harry, v/f/esg/eg Shelly Lee Alley, 59; Happy Fats, 396

Christian, Ben, f Bar-X Cowboys, 92–93

Christian, Bobby, d/vb Massey Family, 611

Christian, Elwood B. "Elmer," v/f/sb Bar-X Cowboys, 92–93; Ted Daffan's Texans, 240

Christopher, Katherine, g Homer Christopher, 209

Christy, Harold, g J.E. Mainer's Mountaineers, 581

Chumbler, George Elmo "Judge Lee," v/sp/g Chumbler Family, 212; Jim King, 486

Chumbler, Irene, v Chumbler Family, 212

Chumbler, Laura, v Chumbler Family, 212

Chumbler, William "Archie Lee," v/sp/md/ah Chumbler Family, 211–12; John Dilleshaw, 317–18; Jim King, 486; Hoke Rice, 745–46

Cibelli, A., md/vc Casey's Old Time Fiddlers, 197; Frank[ie] Marvin, 604
Clair, Felix St, f Paradise Joy Boys, 674
Clancy, Dolores Jo, v Light Crust Doughboys, 506
Clark, Charles, tv Shrine Male Quartet Of Memphis, 834
Clark, Clarence, v/t Ross Rhythm Rascals, 814; Smoky Wood, 971
*Clark, Duke, v/y/g Kent Bane, 92; Harry Hillard, 425; Jess Hillard, 426
Clark, Gus, g Theo. & Gus Clark, 214
Clark, Kelland "Kid," ac Claude Casey, 197; Hank Penny, 686
Clark, Ray, v/esg Happy Fats, 396
Clark, Theo, f Theo. & Gus Clark, 214
Cleary, William, v Arthur Cornwall & William Cleary, 223
Clem, Harmon, sp/f/g Prince Albert Hunt, 447
Clements(?), Eleanor, v/ac Otis & Eleanor, 670
Clements, Otis, v/y/g Otis & Eleanor, 670
*Clements, Stanley, v/g Gene Clardy & Stan Clements, 212
Clements, Zeke, v/y/g Texas Ruby, 900
Click, Cliff, v/f/v eff Short Creek Trio, 833
Cline, Rufus, sb John (Dusty) King, 486; Roy Rogers, 812
Clint, F., f Tex Ritter, 750
Clotworthy, John, v Paul Crutchfield & John Clotworthy, 239
Coates, Willie, p Claude Casey, 197
Coats, James B., av/p Coats Sacred Quartette, 216
Cobb, Clarence, v/f Madisonville String Band, 580
Cobb, Walter, v/bj E.E. Hack String Band, 386
Cofer, Leon, v/sp/bj/g Cofer Brothers, 216; Georgia Crackers, 365–66
Cofer, Paul, v/sp/f Cofer Brothers, 216; Georgia Crackers, 365–66
Coffey, Charles, v/f Jules Allen, 55
Coffman, Wanna, sb Milton Brown, 136–38; Jimmie Davis, 302; Ocie Stockard, 869–70
Cogar, Thomas, v/y/f John McGhee & Frank Welling, 556
Coggin, A.D., calls Floyd Ming, 629
Coker, Bob, bsv/g Smith's Sacred Singers, 850
Coker, Howard, f Chumbler Family, 211; Hoke Rice, 745
*Cole, Allen D., f Byrd Moore, 639
Cole, Dorothy Ellen, sp Harry "Mac" McClintock, 529
Cole, Faye, v Fay & The Jay Walkers, 337
Cole, Jimmy, p Saddle Tramps, 817
Coleman, Bernice, v/f Ernest Branch & Bernice Coleman, 125–26; Roy Harvey, 411
Coley, David, v/g Hinson, Pitts & Coley, 427
Colicchio, Ralph, eg Elton Britt, 130
Colicchio, Tony, g Jimmie Rodgers, 808
Collier, Alsey, g Collier Trio, 218
Collier, Otto, md Collier Trio, 218
Collier, William, bj Collier Trio, 218
Collins, Clinton, v/f/sb Claude Casey, 197
Collins, Cotton, f Doug Bine, 104
Collins, Jerry, p Dixieland Swingsters, 320
Collins, Louise, v/f Uncle Pete & Louise, 919
Collins, Roy, bsv Vaughan Quartet, 925–26, 929
Collins, Tom, g Nat Bird & Tom Collins, 106
Colucci, Tony, g Al Bernard, 100; Hawkins Brothers, 414
Colvard, Jimmie/Jimmy, esg/sb Claude Casey, 197; Hank Penny, 686
Combs, Lonnie, v Stamps Quartet, 865
Combs, Myrtle, av/ac Stamps Quartet, 865
Compton, Harold, ac Hi Neighbor Boys, 420
Compton, Mack, f Georgia Compton's Reelers, 219
Conder, Alvin, v/bj W.A. Lindsay, 507; Weems String Band, 942
Conger, Tex, g/sb Cliff Bruner, 140–41

Conway, Edward, v Rambling Rangers, 725
Conway, Norwood, v Rambling Rangers, 725
Cook, Chuck, v/g Beverly Hill Billies, 102–03; Hollywood Hillbilly Orchestra, 432; Tom & Chuck, 910; Ernest Tubb, 914
Cook, J.C., v/g Sain Family, 818
Cook, J.H., v North Georgia Four, 663
Cool, Gomer "Tenderfoot," f Happy Hollow Hoodlums, 397; Texas Rangers, 899–900
Cooley, Spade, f Gene Autry, 84, 86; Johnny Bond, 117; Canova Family, 156; Texas Jim Lewis, 499–500; Roy Rogers, 811–12; Ella Sutton, 882; Jimmy Wakely, 934; Ray Whitley, 953
Cooper, ——, f Smith's Sacred Singers, 850
Cooper, Cotton, v/tbj Jimmie Revard, 742
Cooper, Robert Dewey, f North Carolina Cooper Boys, 662–63
Cooper, Thomas Franklin, g North Carolina Cooper Boys, 662–63
Copeland, Leonard, g Roy Harvey, 410
Coppes, Mac, f Elton Britt, 130
*Coquille, Walter, sp/calls Denus McGee, 551
Cordova, Mike, sb Jimmie Rodgers, 805
Cornelison, Ernie, v/g Happy Valley Boys, 397
Cortes, Jose. see Casares, Alfredo "Fred" ["Jose Cortes"]
Corwin, Tom, sp WLS Radio Artists, 969
Costello, Laverne "Slicker," bj Arizona Wranglers, 62
Cotner, Carl, f Gene Autry, 82–87; Al Dexter, 315; Clayton McMichen, 572; Dick Reinhart, 739; Roy Rogers, 811–12; Ella Sutton, 882; Jimmy Wakely, 933–34
Couch, Bonson, bj Walter Couch & Wilks Ramblers, 223
Couch, C.E., bv Sheffield Male Quartet, 826
Couch, Kelly, g Walter Couch & Wilks Ramblers, 223
Courtney, Freddie/Freddy, ac Ted Daffan's Texans, 241; Leon Selph, 824
Courville, Sady D., f Denus McGee, 551
Coward, Edwin P. "Buster," v/g Tune Wranglers, 914–16
Cowsert, Mildred, p Smith's Sacred Singers, 849–50
*Cox, Richard, v/f/g John McGhee & Frank Welling, 562
Cox, Slim, v/f Kenneth Houchins, 444
Cozzens, Ellsworth T., sg/md/bj/u Jimmie Rodgers, 800
Cranfill, Dr. J.B., f A.C. (Eck) Robertson, 757
Cranford, Bob, v/sp/h Blue Ridge Sacred Singers, 112; Red Fox Chasers, 730–31
Crawford, Bob, lv Texas Rangers, 899–900
Credeur, Leon "Crip," v/f Jolly Boys Of Lafayette, 464
Creel, Slomie, p Bill Boyd, 121
Crenshaw, Joseph E. "Elmer," v/sb Lew Preston, 713
Crocker, Clifford Z. "Kokomo," v/ac/p Gene Steele, 867; Swift Jewel Cowboys, 884–85
Crocker, L.F. Palmetto Male Quartette, 674
Crockett, Alan, v/sp/f/bones/jh Crockett [Family] Mountaineers, 233–34; Karl & Harty, 471; Lulu Belle & Scotty, 516; Patsy Montana, 635–36; Prairie Ramblers, 710–13
Crockett, Albert, v/tg/g/calls Crockett [Family] Mountaineers, 233–34
Crockett, Clarence, v/h/g/jh Crockett [Family] Mountaineers, 233–34
Crockett, Elnora, v Crockett [Family] Mountaineers, 234
Crockett, George, f/bj Crockett [Family] Mountaineers, 233–34
Crockett, John, Sr., v/f/bj Crockett [Family] Mountaineers, 233–34
Crockett, Johnny, lv/wh/bj/g Crockett [Family] Mountaineers, 233–34
Cronenbold, Edward "Tucson," v Texas Rangers, 899–900

*Cronic, C.A., **v/tv/g** Smith's Sacred Singers, 848–49
Cronic, J.C. (Clarence), **tv** C.A. Cronic, 234; Peck's Male Quartette, 683; Sheffield Male Quartet, 826
Crook, Herman M., **h** Crook Brothers String Band, 234
Crook, Matthew H., **h** Crook Brothers String Band, 234
*Cross, Hugh, **lv/v/y/sp/wh/g/humming** Clayton McMichen, 568–70; Riley Puckett, 718–19; Ridgel's Fountain Citians, 749; Smoky Mountain Ramblers, 852; Lowe Stokes, 870
Cross, Mary, **v** Hugh Cross, 235–36
Cross, Reggie, **h** Bob Atcher, 69; Prairie Ramblers, 712
Crowder, Clovis, **bsv/f** Crowder Brothers, 237–38
Crowder, Olfa, **lv/y/g** Crowder Brothers, 237–38
Crowder, Ortive, **tv/y/g** Crowder Brothers, 237–38
Crowder, Warren, **md** Crowder Brothers, 237
Crowe, Edward, **md** Pete Pyle, 723
Cruise, Carl, **v/g** Smyth County Ramblers, 852
Crumpler, Denver, **tv** Rangers Quartet, 728
Crysel, Curtis, **md** Crysel Boys, 239
Crysel, Jack, **v/g** Crysel Boys, 239
Culpepper, Dewey, **v/g** Oliver Smith & Dewey Culpepper, 845
Cummings, Hugh, **v** M. Homer Cummings & Son Hugh, 240
Curry, Arnold, **bj-u** Williamson Brothers & Curry, 960
Curtis, Luke, **f** Milner & Curtis, 628
*Cutrell, Dave, **v/g** Otto Gray, 378
Cuttiette, Johnny, **sb** Bar-X Cowboys, 92

Dacus, William E. "Smokey," **d** Bob Wills, 960–64
*Daffan, Ted, **v/esg** Shelly Lee Alley, 57–58; Bar-X Cowboys, 93; Al Dexter, 315; Light Crust Doughboys, 506
Dahl, Ted Stuart Hamblen, 392
Dale, Jimmie, **sg** Jimmy Long, 512
*Dalhart, Vernon, **v/sp/wh/h/jh** Adelyne Hood, 434–35; Kanawha Singers, 469; Murray Kellner, 476; Old Southern Sacred Singers, 668–69
*Dandurand, Tommy, **f** Tom Owens Barn Dance Trio, 672
Dangfield, Wallace, **h/g** Dalton Johnson & Wallace Dangfield, 459
Darbone, Luderin, **v/f** Hackberry Ramblers, 387–88
*Darby, Tom, **v/y/sp/wh/g/humming** Georgia Wildcats, 366
D'Arcy, Philip, **f/h/piccolo/oc** Arthur Fields & Fred Hall, 340–45
*Darling, Chuck, **h** Bill Simmons, 835
*Darling, Denver, **v/g** Zeke Manners, 586
Daulton, Ernest C., **p** Maury Pearson, 683
*Davenport, Homer, **bj** Jess Young, 978
Davenport, Hubert, **h** Cal Davenport, 296
Davenport, Malcolm, **g** Cal Davenport, 296
Davies, Bill, **f** John McGhee & Frank Welling, 555; Red Brush Rowdies, 730
Davis, ——, **g** Clagg & Sliger, 212
Davis, Arnold, **v/h/g** Rambling Kid & The Professor, 724
Davis, Audrey (Art), **v/f/md** Gene Autry, 81–82; Bill Boyd, 121; Jim Boyd & Audrey Davis, 125; Roy Newman, 656–57; Unknown Artists [VII], 920
Davis, Big Bill, **f** Homer Briarhopper, 127
*Davis, Claude [C.W.], **v/sp/md/g** Gibbs Brothers, 368; Bert Layne, 493; Ruth Neal & Wanda Neal, 652; Lowe Stokes, 870–71
Davis, Claude, **md** Hi-Flyers, 418
Davis, Ed, **v/g** Jimmie Davis, 300; Patsy Montana, 634
Davis, Edna, **v** Edna Richards & Edna Davis, 747
*Davis, Eva, **v/bj** Samantha Bumgarner, 142
Davis, Jack, **esg** Jimmie Davis, 300, 302
Davis, Karl, **v/y/sp/md** Cumberland Ridge Runners, 239; Jossie Ellers, 331; Red Foley, 350–51; Doc Hopkins, 441; Karl & Harty, 470–71; Linda Parker, 678

Davis, Link, **v/f** Crystal Springs Ramblers, 239
Davis, Ovie, **v/h/g** Rambling Kid & The Professor, 724
Davis, Slim, **v** Tex Ritter, 750
Davis, Walter, **v/sp/g** Blue Ridge Mountain Entertainers, 110–11
Dawson, Pinkie/Pinky, **sb** Shelly Lee Alley, 58; Lummie Lewis, 500
Day, Joe, **tv** Smith's Sacred Singers, 849–50
Day, Lee, **g/calls** Lonesome Luke, 510
Dean, Freddy, **g** Sons Of The West, 859
Deane, Bill, **v** Bull Mountain Moonshiners, 142
DeArman, Ramon (Ray), **lv/tv/y/sp/sb/v eff** Clifford Gross, 385; Light Crust Doughboys, 501–02, 504–06; Roy Newman, 656
Deason, Morris, **v/tbj/g** Crystal Springs Ramblers, 239
Deatheridge, Sam. *see* Harris, Sam
Decker, Ira, **bj** Lonesome Luke, 510
Decker, Loyal, **v** Deckers, 308
Decker, Luke, **f** Lonesome Luke, 510
Decker, Wayne, **v** Deckers, 308
Dedry, Joe, **f** Asa Martin, 593
Dees, Allen, **g** Jimmie Davis, 298
Dees, Jad, **v/y/g** Beverly Hill Billies, 102–03
DeGeer, Ray, **cl/s** Bob Wills, 961–62
Dehne, Virgil, **g** Roy Rogers, 812
Dell, Georgia, **v/g** McClendon Brothers, 527–28
Delmore, Alton, **v/g** Delmore Brothers, 309–12; Uncle Dave Macon, 578; Arthur Smith, 840–41
Delmore, Rabon, **v/tg/g** Delmore Brothers, 309–12; Uncle Dave Macon, 578; Arthur Smith, 840–41
Dennis, Bob, **v/g** Jimmie Wilson's Catfish String Band, 968
Denson, Delilah, **v** Denson-Parris Sacred Harp Singers, 313
Denson, R.E. (Bob), **tv** Denson-Parris Sacred Harp Singers, 313; Denson Quartet, 313
Denson, S. Whitt (Whit), **av** Alabama Sacred Harp Singers, 53; Denson Quartet, 313; Denson's Sacred Harp Singers Of Arley, Alabama, 313
Denton, Fred, **bj** Morganton Trio, 642
DePaul, Larry "Pedro," **v/ac/vox** Texas Jim Lewis, 499–500
Derry, E.J., Jr, **v/md** Travis B. Hale-E.J. Derry Jr., 389
Deshazo, Kenneth, **h/jh** Rodeo Trio, 798
DeVries, Carl, **sg/g** Wilf Carter (Montana Slim), 184–86; Texas Jim Robertson, 759
Dexter, Lois, **v/tbj** Lewis McDaniels, 539; Patt Patterson, 681–82; Walter Smith, 847
Dezurik, Caroline, **v/y/g** Dezurik Sisters, 316
Dezurik, Mary Jane, **v/y/g** Dezurik Sisters, 316
Dickey, Bill, **v/sb** Tom Dickey Show Boys, 316; Adolph Hofner, 430; Tune Wranglers, 915
Dickey, Eljay "Bill," **v/sb** Tune Wranglers, 915
*Dickey, Tom, **f/sb** Adolph Hofner, 430; Tune Wranglers, 914–15
*Dilleshaw, John, **v/sp/g** A.A. Gray, 378
Dillman, ——, **v** Stewart & Dillman, 869
Dix, Tom, **v/y/wh/g/humming** Tom & Don, 911; Tom & Roy, 911
Dixon, Howard, **v/y/sg** Dorsey & Beatrice Dixon, 321; Frank Gerald & Howard Dixon, 367–68
Dizzy Head. *see* Schaffer, Ed
Dobias, Ameril, **sb** Ralph Hodges, 429
Dockum, C.R., **f** Carl T. Sprague, 862
Dodd, ——, **v** Parker & Dodd, 678
Dodd, Bonnie, **v/sg/g** Bonnie Dodd & Murray Lucas, 322
Dodson, Bert, **lv/sp/sb** Cass County Boys, 198; Light Crust Doughboys, 503; Wanderers, 938
*Dodson, Tiny, **v/f** Fred Kirby, 487; Morris Brothers, 643
*Donaldson, Louie, **v/g** Allie & Pearl Brock, 131

Dooley, Clarence, tv/g [E.R.] Nance Family, 648
Dossey, Len "Dynamite," f Arizona Wranglers, 62; Stuart Hamblen, 393
Douglas, Robert, f Allen Brothers, 55
Dowell, Saxie, v Cruthers Brothers, 239
Downing, Larry, v/g Dixieland Swingsters, 320
Drake, J.M., tv Southern Railroad Quartet, 860
Draper, Farrell "Rusty," v/g Sons Of The Ozarks, 856
Driver, Earl, as Crystal Springs Ramblers, 239
Drukenmiller, Solon, v J. Douglas Swagerty, 883
Duboise, Willie, bj Dixie Ramblers [III], 319
Duer, Cornelius "Neil," tb Bob Wills, 966
Duhon, Arthur "Buddy," v/g Bar-X Cowboys, 93; Modern Mountaineers, 631; Sons Of Dixie, 856
Duhon, Hector, f Dixie Ramblers [II], 319
Duhon, Jesse, g Dixie Ramblers [II], 319
Duhon, Pete, v/sb Hackberry Ramblers, 388
Dumas, Prentis, sg Jimmie Davis, 298–99
Dumont, Louis, v/tbj Hank Penny, 685–86
Duncan, Clark, f Dr. Smith's Champion Hoss Hair Pullers, 843
Duncan, Eddie, v/esg Hank Penny, 686; Tune Wranglers, 915
Duncan, Harry, v/f/cl Zeke Manners, 586; Radio Rubes, 723; Texas Jim Robertson, 760
Duncan, Lula, v Duncan Sisters Trio, 325
Duncan, Slim, f Denver Darling, 295
Duncan, Thomas Elmer "Tommy," v/y/ts/sb Bob Wills, 960–66
*Dunford, Uncle Eck, v/sp/f/g/calls Ernest V. Stoneman, 876–77; Fields Ward, 939
Dunlap, Saloma, p William B. Houchens, 443
Dunlap, Tommy, esg Modern Mountaineers, 630–31
*Dunn, Bob, v/esg/tb Bill Boyd, 124; Milton Brown, 136–37; Cliff Bruner, 140–41; Jimmie Davis, 304; Buddy Jones, 465; Dickie McBride, 526; Modern Mountaineers, 631; Bill Mounce, 645; Roy Newman, 657; Leon Selph, 824; Shelton Brothers, 829; Sons Of Dixie, 856; Floyd Tillman, 910; Bob Wills, 962
Dunn, C.F., bsv Southern Railroad Quartet, 860
Dunn, Julius, v/md/g R.D. Kelly & Julius Dunn, 476
Dunn, Shorty, sb Tex Dunn, 327
*Dupree, Melvin (Mel), v/g Georgia Organ Grinders, 366; Georgia Yellow Hammers, 367; Uncle Bud Landress, 490; Bill Shores & Melvin Dupree, 832; Gid Tanner, 890
Dupuis, Joswell, g Bartmon Montet-Joswell Dupuis, 637
Durden, Ralph, md Three Stripped Gears, 907
Durham, Dave, f/t/k/bj Dixieland Swingsters, 320
Durlacher, Ed, calls Al McLeod's Country Dance Band, 565
Dyke, L.D., saw Jimmie Rodgers, 801
Dykes, Charles, v/g Elmer Bird, 105–06
Dykes, John, v/f Dykes' Magic City Trio, 328

Eanes, Jim, v Roy Hall, 391
Eargle, Mike, sb Rice Brothers' Gang, 746
Earls, Bert, g Alex Hood, 435
Eary, Gladys, p M. Homer Cummings & Son Hugh, 240
Easterday, Jess, v/md/g/sb Roy Acuff, 48–50
Eastwood, James "Doc," tbj Light Crust Doughboys, 502; Universal Cowboys, 919
Echols, Odis, bv Stamps Quartet, 863–64
Eckerd, Everett, v/g Brown Brothers, 138
Edans, ——, h/g Orla Clark, 214
Edmondson, Eugene, v/tbj/sb Ross Rhythm Rascals, 814; Smoky Wood, 971
Edmondson, Horace, v/g Ross Rhythm Rascals, 814; Smoky Wood, 971
Edmonson, Helena Berry, v/g/u Kentucky Girls, 477

Edwards, Bill, f Spooney Five, 862
Edwards, Earl, v/y/g Buck Mt. Band, 141
Edwards, Iver, h/u Uncle Eck Dunford, 325; Ernest V. Stoneman, 876
Edwards, Van, f Buck Mt. Band, 141
*Elder, Odis, v/g Ray Whitley, 952
*Ellers, Jossie, v Brother James Arnold, 64; William Rexroat's Cedar Crest Singers, 744
Ellington, Harvey, f/md Swing Billies, 885; Three Tobacco Tags, 908–09
Elliott, Elmer, v/f North Carolina Ridge Runners, 663
Ellis, Homer, md Milner & Curtis, 628
Ellis, Ira, v/f Freeny Harmonizers, 359
Ellis, Leo, g Milner & Curtis, 628
Ellis, Lonnie, f/md Mississippi 'Possum Hunters, 629
Ellis, Oglesby Lonnie, bsv Owen Brothers & Ellis, 670–71
Elmore, Buster, md/g Jack Cawley's Oklahoma Ridge Runners, 199
Emerson, Ralph Waldo, sp/calliope WLS Radio Artists, 969
Emmett, Dewey, bj Emmett & Aiken String Band, 332
Emmett, R.L., vc Emmett & Aiken String Band, 332
Emmett, Roy, g Emmett & Aiken String Band, 332
Engel, Curly, v/y/tg Texas Jim Lewis, 499
Engel, Vince, ac/p Stuart Hamblen, 393
Enloe, James, p Jimmie Davis, 298
Ennis, Paul, v/y/sg/g Three Musketeers, 906
Erdman, Fred, sp Carson Robison, 785
Erickson, Jack, v Bob Miller, 623
Erwin, Ish, sb Bill Boyd, 124; Roy Newman, 656–58
Eskew, Mary, v Andrew Jenkins, 454
Essig, Abe, f Vernon Dalhart, 261
Estes, Charlie, g Walter Family, 938
Evans, Ben, v/wh/g Cofer Brothers, 216; Georgia Crackers, 365–66
*Evans, Clyde, bsv/g Bill Chitwood, 208; Georgia Yellow Hammers, 367; Moody Quartet, 637; Turkey Mountain Singers, 916
Evans, Ernest "Deacon," esg Shelly Lee Alley, 58–59; Bar-X Cowboys, 93; Cliff Bruner, 139–40; Modern Mountaineers, 631; Leon Selph, 824; Floyd Tillman, 910
Evans, Mutt, v/g Dorsey & Beatrice Dixon, 321
Evans, Neil, v Dixieland Four, 320; Kanawha Singers, 469
Everidge, Albert, sp/saw South Georgia Highballers, 860
Everidge, Vander, sp/g South Georgia Highballers, 860

Fabacher, Francis "Red," g Jolly Boys Of Lafayette, 464
Fabacher, Joseph, ac Jolly Boys Of Lafayette, 464
Fahrenwald, Dick, md Jimmie Wilson's Catfish String Band, 968
Falcon, Cleoma. see Breaux, Cleoma
Fariss, W., v Texas Jim Robertson, 759–60
Farr, Hugh, bsv/f Patsy Montana, 637; Len Nash, 650; Roy Rogers, 811; Sons Of The Pioneers, 857–59
Farr, Karl, lg/g Gene Autry, 86; Patsy Montana, 637; Len Nash, 650; Roy Rogers, 811; Sons Of The Pioneers, 857–59
Farrell, Skip, v Hoosier Hot Shots, 438–39
Featherstone, Phil, v/sp/h/md Golden Melody Boys, 373
Ferera, Frank, sg/g Al Bernard, 100; Vernon Dalhart, 242–43
Ferguson, Buster, v/g Hi-Flyers, 419–20; Dick Reinhart, 739; Ocie Stockard, 869
Ferguson, Gilbert "Bert," wh/p Tom Dickey Show Boys, 316; Adolph Hofner, 430–31; Jimmie Revard, 743
Ferguson, Joe Frank, v/tv/s/sb Al Dexter, 315; Light Crust Doughboys, 506–07; Patsy Montana, 636; Bob Wills, 961–64
Ferraro, James, g Bernard [Slim] Smith, 842
Fielding, Arthur "Eddie," tbj Tune Wranglers, 915

Fields, George, v/sp Honeyboy & Sassafras[s], 433
Fillis, Len, sg/g Vernon Dalhart, 291
Fincher, "Shorty," f Crazy Hillbillies Band, 232
Fincher, Hamilton "Rawhide," v/g Crazy Hillbillies Band, 232
Fincher, Sue, v Crazy Hillbillies Band, 232
Firman, Bert, dir/sp Carson Robison, 793–94
Fisher, Shug, v/sb Beverly Hill Billies, 102; Hugh Cross, 236
Fite, Bob, g Saddle Tramps, 817
Fitzgerald, Robert "Bob," d Bob Wills, 966
*Flanagan, Taylor, tv/p Perry Bechtel, 98; Brunswick Players, 141; Dan Hornsby, 441–42
Fleenor, Gene, g Tex Ritter, 750
Fleming, Reece, v/y/g Fleming & Townsend, 346–48
Fleming, Sonny, v/md/g Yellow Jackets [II], 976–77
Fletcher, David O., v/y/sp/wh/g Fletcher & Foster, 349–50
Floyd, ——, f Nicholson's Players, 659
*Foley, Red, v/y/g/sb Cumberland Ridge Runners, 239; Karl & Harty, 470; Lulu Belle & Scotty, 515; Linda Parker, 678
Ford, Ezra, v/y/f Elton Britt, 129; Bob Miller, 624
*Ford, Oscar, v/y/sp/f/g Clayton McMichen, 569
Forrester, Howard "Howdy," f Herald Goodman, 375; Arthur Smith, 842
Forrester, Joe, sb Herald Goodman, 375; Arthur Smith, 842
Forsmark, Sammy, v/esg Hank Penny, 685; Sammy & Smitty, 818; Uncle Ned, 919
Forster, Mrs. R.M., p/o J. Douglas Swagerty, 882–83
*Foster, Garley, v/wh/h/k/g Carolina Tar Heels, 173; Haywood County Ramblers, 414; Pine Mountain Boys, 697
*Foster, Gwen, v/y/sp/wh/h/g Thomas C. Ashley, 68; Blue Ridge Mountain Entertainers, 110–11; Carolina Tar Heels, 173–74; Fletcher & Foster, 349–50
*Foster, John D., lv/v/g Leonard Rutherford, 816
Foster, Ray, v/t Texas Jim Lewis, 499
Fowler, Willie, bv Smith's Sacred Singers, 849–50
*Fox, Arnum "Curl[e]y," v/sp/f/g Jimmie Davis, 301; Roane County Ramblers, 751; Shelton Brothers, 827–28
Fox, Cody, ldr Yellow Jackets [II], 976
Fralia, Jack, v/p Jack & Bill, 451
Franchini, Anthony, g Vernon Dalhart, 244
Franchini, Frank, g Vernon Dalhart, 255
Francis, Art, p Jimmie Revard, 742
Frankie, Edmond, traps Jimmie Revard, 743
Frazier, Arnold, sp Loren H. Abram, 47
Frazier, Atlee, sb Adolph Hofner, 431
Frazier, Dave, eg Slim Harbert, 398
Freed, Sam, f Kelly Harrell, 404; Carson Robison, 768–69, 771, 774
Freeman, Belvie, bj-md Scottdale String Band, 821
Freeny, Cleveland, md Freeny's Barn Dance Band, 359
Freeny, Hendrix, f Freeny's Barn Dance Band, 359
Freeny, Leslie, f Freeny's Barn Dance Band, 359
Freeny, S. Carlton, tbj Freeny Harmonizers, 359; Freeny's Barn Dance Band, 359
Freshour, Charles, g Wilmer Watts, 941
Frisby, Lew, sb Modern Mountaineers, 630–31
Fritsch, Edward V. "Babe," v/sp/wh Village Boys, 932
Fritz, Eddie, ac Bob Atcher, 70
Frost, Bolen, hv/bj/g Uncle Eck Dunford, 326; Ernest V. Stoneman, 873–74, 876–78
Frost, Irma, v/o Ernest V. Stoneman, 873, 876
Froste, Bert, v/g Jess Johnston, 464
Fruge, Ernest, f Angelas Le Jeunne, 493; Denus McGee, 551
Frye, Cecil, f Moatsville String Ticklers, 630
Frye, Floyd, g Moatsville String Ticklers, 630
Frye, Gordon, f Moatsville String Ticklers, 630
Frye, Zell, tbj Moatsville String Ticklers, 630
Fugate, Willie, bj North Carolina Ridge Runners, 663

Fulkersin, Walter "Shorty," ac Texas Jim Lewis, 499
Fuller, Anson, f Ashley's Melody Makers, 68
*Fulwider, Leonard C., v/g Jack Cawley's Oklahoma Ridge Runners, 199
Fuselier, J.B., v/f Miller's Merrymakers, 627–28
Futrell, Cyrus, f/v eff Arkansas Barefoot Boys, 63

Gabehart, O.S., v Chas. Richardson & O.S. Gabehart, 748
Gaines, Roland, v/y/g Garner Eckler & Roland Gaines, 329; Prairie Ramblers, 705
Galloway, Billy, esg Rice Brothers' Gang, 746
Galloway, Henry, g Taylor-Griggs Louisiana Melody Makers, 894
Galvan, Connie "Pancho," sb W. Lee O'Daniel, 665
Ganus, Cecil, v/md Clarence Ganus, 361–62
Ganus, Clyde, bsv Clarence Ganus, 361–62
Garde, Paul, p Sue Morgan, 642
Gardner, Frank, f Luke Highnight, 422
Gardner, Robert A., v/sp/k/g Lester McFarland & Robert A. Gardner, 542–50; Old Southern Sacred Singers, 668–69
Garner, Clem, v Earl McCoy & Jessie Brock, 531
Garner, Roosevelt, tv Dr. Smith's Champion Hoss Hair Pullers, 843
Garrett, Gene, sb E.E. Hack String Band, 386
Garrett, Virgil "Cricket," f E.E. Hack String Band, 386
Gart, John, ac/Ho Carson Robison, 796
Gaskill, Clarence, p Jimmy Smith, 844
*Gaspard, Blind Uncle, v/f/g Delma Lachney, 488–89
Gass, Aubrey, v/h/traps/wb Al Dexter, 314–15
*Gatin[s], Bill, v/y/sp/j Cherokee Ramblers, 203–04
Gaylor, ——, v/y Elton Britt, 127–28
Gentry, Giles, tv Gentry Family, 365
Gentry, Leonard, tv Gentry Family, 365
Gentry, Paul, bv Gentry Family, 365
Gentry, Wade, bsv Gentry Family, 365
George, ——, v/f/bj/g George & Henson, 365
Gerard, Eddie, p Leon Selph, 823
Gibbs, Bob, md/tbj Hugh Gibbs String Band, 368; Gibbs Brothers, 368
*Gibbs, Hugh, sg/harp-g Gibbs Brothers, 368
Gibbs, Joe, g Hugh Gibbs String Band, 368; Gibbs Brothers, 368
Gibson, "Butch," cl/as Bill Boyd, 123; John Boyd, 125; Hi-Flyers, 418–19
Gibson, B.M., tv Missouri Pacific Lines Booster Quartet, 629
Gibson, John, v Arthur Cornwall, 222
Gibson, L.L., bsv Missouri Pacific Lines Booster Quartet, 629
Gilbert, Lloyd, tv Vaughan Quartet, 929
Giles, E. Ellsworth, dir/v Sandhills Sixteen, 820
Giles, Lem, v/g Beverly Hill Billies, 102–03
Giles, Mrs Ellsworth, p Sandhills Sixteen, 820
Gill, Rusty, v/h/g Bob Atcher, 69; Prairie Ramblers, 712–13
Gillette, Rene O. "Jack," v/f/t Dick Hartman's Tennessee Ramblers, 407; Tennessee Ramblers [II], 897
Gilliland, Henry C., f A.C. (Eck) Robertson, 757
Gillis, Jack, f Jimmie Wilson's Catfish String Band, 968
Gilmer, George, f Madden Community Band, 580
Gilmer, Will, tv/f Leake County Revelers, 494–95
Gilmore, Frank, ac Harry "Mac" McClintock, 529
Gilmore, Ted "Buddy," g Sally Foster, 355; Travelers, 912
Givans, Thomas J., bj Crook Brothers String Band, 234
Glenn, Artice, v/sb Doug Bine, 104
Glenn, Wilfred, v Vernon Dalhart, 245; Old Southern Sacred Singers, 668–69
Glogau, Jack, p Virginia Childs, 208
Goatcher, Odie, bsv Dr. Smith's Champion Hoss Hair Pullers, 843

Goble, Mrs. Carl, p Vaughan Quartet, 929
Goff, Landon, g Loy Bodine, 115
Goldberg, Max, t Carson Robison, 792
*Gonzales, Roy, v/y/g John H. Bertrand, 101
Gonzales, Tony, d Four Aces, 355; Floyd Shreve, 833–34; Leo Soileau, 854–55
Good, Dorothy, v/y/g Girls Of The Golden West, 370–71
Good, Mildred, v Girls Of The Golden West, 370
Goodman, Benny, cl Bernard [Slim] Smith, 842
*Goodman, Herald, v Vagabonds, 921
Goodreau, Ed, calls Tommy Dandurand, 292–93
Goodson, Price, v/h/u Da Costa Woltz's Southern Broadcasters, 970
Gordon, Anna Carter, av Chuck Wagon Gang, 211
Gorman, Johnny, esg/cl/as Rice Brothers' Gang, 746
Gorman, Ross, bscl Vernon Dalhart, 289–91; Adelyne Hood, 434–35; John I. White, 950
Gorodetzer, ——, f Kelly Harrell, 404
Gossett, Enos, g Ted Gossett's Band, 376; Tommy Whitmer's Band, 953
Gottuso, Tony, g Elton Britt, 130; Jimmie Davis, 305
Grader, Julian, v/f/ac Adler Connor & Julian Grader, 219
Graham, J. Warner "Red," bj/g Red Headed Fiddler[s], 732
Graham, William (Bill), t Elton Britt, 130; Jimmie Davis, 304–05
Grant, Claude, v/g Grant Brothers, 377
Grant, Grover, g Grinnell Giggers, 384
Grant, Jack, v/bj-md Grant Brothers, 377
Grant, Roy, v/g Whitey & Hogan, 952
Grantham, Ted, f Milton Brown, 136; Hugh Cross, 236
*Gray, A.A., v/f John Dilleshaw, 317
Gray, Grace, v Curly Gray, 378
Gray, Mrs. Otto, v Otto Gray, 378–79
Gray, Owen, v/sp/g Otto Gray, 378–79
Gray, Paul, f Lone Star Cowboys, 509
Grayson, Shannon, v/md/g Bill Carlisle, 160; Cliff Carlisle, 168; Milton & Marion Carlisle, 168; Carlisle Brothers, 169
Green, A. Judson, f Green's String Band, 381
Green, Herman, f Green's String Band, 381
Green, Howard, g Bull Mountain Moonshiners, 142
Green, J.E., f Mr. & Mrs. J.W. Baker, 90
Green, Jelly, f Range Riders, 727
Green, Joe, traps/vb Vernon Dalhart, 245; Frank & James McCravy, 532
Green, Preston, sb Green's String Band, 381
Green[e], Lem, v Arthur Fields & Fred Hall, 340
*Greene, Clarence, v/tv/sp/f/g Blue Ridge Mountain Entertainers, 110–11; Byrd Moore, 639
Greene, Rosaline, sp Arthur Fields & Fred Hall, 343
Greenhaw, Aubrey "Red," g Bob Dunn's Vagabonds, 326; Dickie McBride, 526; Modern Mountaineers, 631; Texas Wanderers, 900–901; Village Boys, 932
Greenlaw, Vernon "Junior," f Texas Jim Lewis, 499
Greer, Charlie, g Bull Mountain Moonshiners, 142
Greer, Professor I.G., v Professor & Mrs. Greer, 382
Gregg, Charles (Charlie), v/f/sb Tune Wranglers, 915–16; Zeke Williams, 959
*Gregory, Bobby, v/pac Vernon Dalhart, 292
Griffin, Wallace, sb W. Lee O'Daniel, 665–66
Griffith, Lonnie, v/g Blue Ridge Highballers, 109–10; Luther B. Clarke, 214
Grigg, Ausie B., sb Jimmie Davis, 300; Taylor-Griggs Louisiana Melody Makers, 893–94
Grigg, Crockett, bsv Taylor-Griggs Louisiana Melody Makers, 893
Grigg, Ione, g Taylor-Griggs Louisiana Melody Makers, 893
Grigg, Lorene, md Taylor-Griggs Louisiana Melody Makers, 893

Grigg, R.C., v/f Taylor-Griggs Louisiana Melody Makers, 893
Grisham, Miss, p/o Mr. & Mrs. R.N. Grisham, 384–85
Grishaw, Eddy, v/g Hi Neighbor Boys, 420
Grissom, Hovah, p E.B. Holden Quartet, 432
*Gross, Clifford, bsv/f/h Hi-Flyers, 418; Light Crust Doughboys, 501–04
Grosso, Eddie, h/cl Arthur Fields & Fred Hall, 340–44
Groves, Lefty, g Modern Mountaineers, 630
Guidry, Bixy, v/ac Percy Babineaux-Bixy Guidry, 87
Guidry, Murphy, v/g Alley Boys Of Abbeville, 59
Guidry, Nathan, sb Happy Fats, 395–96; Sons Of Acadians, 856
Guidry, Oran "Doc," f Happy Fats, 395–96; Sons Of Acadians, 856; Joe Werner, 944
Guidry, Ray, tbj Happy Fats, 395–96
Guidry, Sidney, v/g Alley Boys Of Abbeville, 59; Sons Of Acadians, 856
Gully, Raymond, bj-md Smoky Mountain Ramblers, 852
Gunkler, Hymie, cl Gene Autry, 83

Haas, Gene, eg Patsy Montana, 637; Roy Rogers, 812
Haas, Onie, g Ray Whitley, 953
Hackworth, Ernest, sb Hi-Flyers, 419
Hadaway, J.B., bv Abernathy Quartet, 47
Hager, Charles, md Loy Bodine, 115
Haines, Hubert, g Arkansas Barefoot Boys, 63
Halbert, Chesley, tbj Doug Bine, 104
Hale, Elizabeth, p Theron Hale, 389
Hale, Mamie Ruth, f/md Theron Hale, 389
Haley, Sonny, sb Ambrose Haley, 389
Hall, Charley, v Smith's Sacred Singers, 848–49
Hall, Clarence, g Big Chief Henry's Indian String Band, 103
Hall, Clayton, v/bj Roy Hall, 391
Hall, Elmer "Slim," v/g Gene Steele, 867; Swift Jewel Cowboys, 884–85
Hall, Fred, v/sp/p Arthur Fields & Fred Hall, 340–45
Hall, Harold, v/bj Big Chief Henry's Indian String Band, 103
Hall, Henry, f Big Chief Henry's Indian String Band, 103
Hall, Herman, bj Mansfield Patrick, 680
Hall, Jay Hugh, hv/g Hall Brothers, 391; Happy-Go-Lucky Boys, 396; Steve Ledford, 495; J.E. Mainer's Mountaineers, 582; Wade Mainer, 584–85
*Hall, Leaford, f Al Dexter, 314
Hall, Leon "Lonnie," v/f Leon Chappelear, 201–02; Jimmie Davis, 303–04; Buddy Jones, 465; Bill Nettles, 654; Shelton Brothers, 828
Hall, Monte, v Bob Palmer & Monte Hall, 673
*Hall, Roy, v/sp/g Hall Brothers, 391
Hall, Ruth, p Carolina Gospel Singers, 171
Hall, Saford, v/g Roy Hall, 391
Hallberg, Jene Von, p Carson Robison, 796–97
Hallbrook, Sam, g [E.R.] Nance Family, 648
Halle, Roy, v Texas Jim Robertson, 759–60
Hallmark, Curly, d Ocie Stockard, 869–70
Haltom, Dick, sb Lummie Lewis, 500; Leon Selph, 823–24
Hamman, Cloet, g East Texas Serenaders, 329
*Hammond, John, v/bj Albert Rose, 813
Hammons, Garfield, bj Swing Billies, 885
Hanks, Josh, v/g Pipers Gap Ramblers, 698
Hanks, Walter, v/tambourine Pipers Gap Ramblers, 698
Hansen, Aleth. see Giles, Lem
*Harbert, Grundy C. "Slim," v/sb Leon Chappelear, 201; Shelton Brothers, 828–30; Sunshine Boys, 881–82
Harbuck, S.M., v McDonald Quartet, 541
Hardin, John, f Hardin & Grinstaff, 398
Hardin, Pete, f Rice Brothers' Gang, 747
Harding, Clarence, v/g Clarence Harding, 398
Harding, Evelyn, v/y Blue Ridge Mountain Girls, 111

Hardison, Roy, bj Paul Warmack, 939–40
Hardy, Lige, bj Blue Ridge Highballers, 110
Harkleroad, Haskell, bj W.C. Childers, 206; Richmond Melody Boys, 748
Harkness, Felton "Preacher," f Shelton Brothers, 829
*Harkreader, Sid, v/sp/wh/f/g Uncle Dave Macon, 574, 576–77
Harlan, Don, cl/as/bs Bob Wills, 965–66
Harley, Lester, tv Stamps Quartet, 865
Harmon, Frank, lv Moody Quartet, 637
*Harold, Richard, v/g Fred Pendleton, 685
Harper, Bill, f/vc Jimmie Davis, 301–03
Harper, Bill, g Webb Whipple, 948
Harper, C.C., v Moody Bible Sacred Harp Singers, 637; North Georgia Four, 663
Harper, Elvin, sv Copperhill Male Quartet, 222
Harper, J.H., v North Georgia Four, 663
Harper, Roy. see Harvey, Roy
Harpold, J.O., v Jackson County Ramblers, 452
Harris, Buddy, v Roy Newman, 656
Harris, Esmond, g Four Pickled Peppers, 356
*Harris, Fern, v Happy Hoosiers, 397
Harris, John Ed, h Jimmie Wilson's Catfish String Band, 968
Harris, Sam, v Taylor's Kentucky Boys, 895
Harrison, Andrew, g Newton County Hill Billies, 658
Harrison, Marcus, md Newton County Hill Billies, 658
Harrison, Spec[k], cl/as/ac Leon Chappelear, 201; Bill Nettles, 654; Range Riders, 727
Harrison, Warren "Sweet Face," f Ross Rhythm Rascals, 814
Hart, ———, v/g Hart & Ogle, 406
*Hart, Jimmy, v/ac/p Port Arthur Jubileers, 701
Hart, Sam, v Hart & Cates, 406
Hartley, Henry, f/sb Travelers, 912
Hartley, Rene "Zeb," f/sb Sally Foster, 355
Hartman, Clarence "Idaho," sb/j Happy Hollow Hoodlums, 397; Texas Rangers, 899–900
*Hartsell, Bob, v/y/g Three Tobacco Tags, 908
Hartsey, Will, v Atco Quartet, 70
Harvey, Johnny, cl Leon Chappelear, 201
*Harvey, Roy, v/sp/g Ernest Branch & Bernice Coleman, 125–26; Charlie Poole, 699–700; Earl Shirkey & Roy Harper, 831–32; Weaver Brothers, 942
Harwell, A.W., tv Friendship Four, 360
Haskell, ———, Pioneer Trio, 698
Hatch, Budd, sb Eddie Dean, 308
Hatcher, Sam "Dynamite," v/h/k Roy Acuff, 48
Hatfield, Della, v Emry Arthur, 66
Hatton, Jess, bj Hatton Brothers, 412; Charlie Wilson, 967
Hatton, Vertner, sp/f Hatton Brothers, 412; Charlie Wilson, 967
Hawkins, Chester, g Oscar [Slim] Doucet, 324
*Hawkins, Ezra (Ted), lv/v/sp/f/md/calls Clayton McMichen, 566, 570; Riley Puckett, 720–21; Arthur Tanner, 886; Gid Tanner, 891
Hawkins, Skipper, sb Leon Chappelear, 201; Stuart Hamblen, 393
Hawkins, Ted. see Hawkins, Ezra (Ted)
Hayes, Buddy, sb Texas Jim Lewis, 499
Hayes, Clifford, f Jimmie Rodgers, 806
Hayes, Edd Kentucky Coon Hunters, 477
Hayes, Selma, v Dewey Hayes, 414
Haynes, Arthur D. "Art," f/tb Bob Wills, 960
Head, Marvin, g Scottdale String Band, 821–22
Heatherington, Charlie "Ezra," v/y/f Beverly Hill Billies, 103
Heatwole, F.P., bv/bsv Vaughan Quartet, 926–27, 929
Heatwole, Luther E., bv/p Vaughan Quartet, 926–29
"Heavy Martin". see Cross, Hugh
*Hebert, Didier, v/g E. Segura & D. Herbert, 823

Hebert, Hal, v/cl/ts Modern Mountaineers, 630
Heck, Chas., calls Reubens, 742
Hedges, Norman, f Stuart Hamblen, 393
Heffernan, George, f Claude Casey, 197
Helleberg, Gus, tu/sb Arthur Fields & Fred Hall, 342–43
Helmick, Mrs. H.E., v Harmon E. Helmick, 415
*Helms, Bill, v/f Home Town Boys, 433; Riley Puckett, 719
*Helton, Ernest, bj/g J.D. Harris, 405
Hemphill, Bob, eg Bob Skyles, 839
Henderson, ———, v/md/g Henderson Brothers, 415
Henderson, C.E., bsv Macedonia Quartet, 542
Henderson, Larry, v/md/g Henderson Brothers, 415
*Henderson, Lee "Red," v/sp/g Emmett Bankston & Red Henderson, 92; Fiddlin' John Carson, 177; Earl Johnson, 459–60
Henderson, Lee, g Arthur Tanner, 885–86
Henderson, Lynn, g Bar-X Cowboys, 92
Henderson, W.K., sp John McGhee & Frank Welling, 557
Henry, ——— Byrd Moore, 640
Hensley, Harold, f Three Tobacco Tags, 909
Hensley, Larry, v/md/g Walker's Corbin Ramblers, 936–37
Henson, Bernard F., v/f/g Richard Cox, 229; John McGhee & Frank Welling, 562
Henson, Bill, v/g Earl Johnson, 460
*Henson, Russell, v/f/bj/g George & Henson, 365
Herbert, Arthur, v Dixieland Four, 320; Kanawha Singers, 469
Hermansen, Howard A., bv/p Moody Bible Institute Trio, 637
*Herring, Pete, v/g Mississippi 'Possum Hunters, 629
Herrington, Criss, f Bill Nettles, 654
Herscher, Lou, v Dwight Butcher, 148
Hester, Grady, v/f Dickie McBride, 526; Modern Mountaineers, 631; Texas Wanderers, 900; Village Boys, 931
Hethcox, Emmett, g George Walburn & Emmett Hethcox, 934–35
Hewitt, Glenn, v/g Zack & Glenn, 979
Hewlett, Jim, t Jimmie Davis, 305; Charles Mitchell & His Orchestra, 629–30
Hicks, Curley, g Grady & Hazel Cole, 217
Hicks, Curly, v/md Leo Boswell, 119
Hicks, Elmer, ac Grady & Hazel Cole, 217
Hicks, Frank, v/sp Andrew Jenkins, 455
Hicks, Jack, v Elmer Bird, 105
*Hicks, Rhoda, v/p/g Tate Bros. & Hicks, 892
Higgins, Clarence, v/g Stanley & Higgins, 866
*Highnight, Luke, v/h/bj Mintons Ozark String Band, 629
Highsmith, Carl, cl/ts Lummie Lewis, 500
Hilbun, Glaston, bsv Coats Sacred Quartette, 216
Hill, Bill, v/f/ah Hill Brothers, 424
Hill, Cameron, eg Texas Wanderers, 900–901
Hill, Dewey, v/h/g Hill Brothers, 424; [E.R.] Nance Family, 648
Hill, Dolphus, md Pelican Wildcats, 684
Hill, Sam[uel], v/ah Hill Brothers, 424; [E.R.] Nance Family, 648
Hill, William H. (Billy), f Texas Jim Lewis, 500
*Hillard, Harry, v/y/g Duke Clark, 213; Hoosier Hawaiians, 435
*Hillard, Jesse, v/y/g/calls Duke Clark, 213
*Hillard, Nelson, v/md Jess Hillard, 425–26
Hilliard, ———, f/g Daddy John Love, 514
Hilliard, Jack, v/g Jack & Leslie, 451
Hinson, Guy, v/g Hinson, Pitts & Coley, 427
Hinson, Jack, p Bill Boyd, 122–23; Ross Rhythm Rascals, 814; Ocie Stockard, 869–70; Sunshine Boys, 881–82
Hirsch, Bert, f Al Bernard, 100; Blue Ridge Gospel Singers, 109; Elton Britt, 130; Vernon Dalhart, 266, 275, 292; Ewen

Hirsch, Bert, f (*continued*)
Hail, 389; Hawkins Brothers, 414; Buell Kazee, 472–73; Texas Jim Robertson, 759–60; Carson Robison, 764–65, 768
Hiser, Bun, md Taylor-Griggs Louisiana Melody Makers, 894
Hitch, W.B., bsv Alcoa Quartet, 53
Hobbs, Cliff, v/y/g Bill Cox, 228–29
Hobbs, Elmer Hobbs Brothers, 428
Hobbs, Jud[d] Hobbs Brothers, 428
Hobbs, Roy "Shorty," v/sp/md/g Callahan Brothers, 153; Asa Martin, 589, 591–92; James Roberts, 756; Tennessee Mountaineers, 896; Charlie Wilson, 967
Hobbs, Sookie. *see* Robison, Carson
Hodges, Almoth, v/sp/h Bob Miller, 618
Hodges, Ernest, f Hodgers Brothers, 428
*****Hodges, Ralph, v/g** Hodgers Brothers, 428
Hoepner, Harry "Tex," v/sb Al Clauser, 214
Hoffpauir, Buel, g Leo Soileau, 855
*****Hofner, Adolph, v/sp/g/calls** Tom Dickey Show Boys, 316; Jimmie Revard, 742–43
Hofner, Emil "Bash," v/esg/eg/etg/tbj Tom Dickey Show Boys, 316; Adolph Hofner, 430–31; Jimmie Revard, 742–43
Hogan, Arval, tv/md Whitey & Hogan, 952
Hogan, Cecil, eg Adolph Hofner, 430
Hogan, John, bj Bill Helms, 415
Hogan, Ty Cobb, g Bill Helms, 415
Hogg, Jack, esg Jimmie Davis, 303; Tex Ritter, 750
Hoke, Bob, v/bj-md Roy Harvey, 410
Holbrook, J.H., bj Mr. & Mrs. J.W. Baker, 90
Holbrook, Roy, tv Abernathy Quartet, 47
Holden, Harry, g Jimmy Smith, 844
Holifield, Algia, v Laurel Firemen's Quartet, 491
Holland, Rev. A.H., sp Flat Creek Sacred Singers, 346
Holland, Hank, sp Zeke Williams, 959
Holley, James "Joe," hv/f Crystal Springs Ramblers, 239; Ocie Stockard, 869–70; Bob Wills, 966
Hollinger, Wilmot "Holly," t Al Dexter, 315; Roy Rogers, 812
Holloway, John M., f/vc Mississippi 'Possum Hunters, 629
Holmes, Floyd "Salty," v/y/sp/h/g/j/bazooka Gene Autry, 80–81; Jo & Alma, 458; Lulu Belle & Scotty, 516; Bob Miller, 624–25; Patsy Montana, 634–36; Prairie Ramblers, 704–13
Holstein, Jim, v/g Jim & Bob, 458
*****Hood, Adelyne, v/sp/f/p** Vernon Dalhart, 271–92; Arthur Fields & Fred Hall, 344; John I. White, 950
*****Hood, Alex, sp/bj** Fay & The Jay Walkers, 337
Hooten, Frances, tbj Leaford Hall, 390
Hopkins, Albert Green (Al), v/y/sp/p/calls Charlie Bowman, 120; Hill Billies, 422–24
*****Hopkins, Doc, v/g** Little Georgie Porgie, 508
Hopkins, Joe, v/g Charlie Bowman, 120; Hill Billies, 422–23
Hopkins, John, v/u Charlie Bowman, 120; Hill Billies, 422–24
Hopkins, Sybil, v Bob Dunn's Vagabonds, 326
Hopson, Bob, sp/g Roy Hall, 390
Horne, George, p Carolina Gospel Singers, 170–71
*****Hornsby, Dan, lv/hv/sp** Perry Bechtel, 98; Taylor Flanagan, 345; Georgia Organ Grinders, 366; Clayton McMichen, 567–70; Wade Mainer, 584–85; Lowe Stokes, 871; Gid Tanner, 891; Jess Young, 979
Horton, George, g Texas Jim Robertson, 760
Horton, Holly, v/sp/cl Roy Newman, 656–58; Three Virginians, 909; Wanderers, 938
Horton, Roy, sb Red River Dave, 732
Horton, Vaughn, esg/eg Elton Britt, 130; Denver Darling, 296; Jimmie Davis, 305; Buddy Jones, 466; Red River Dave, 732
Hoskins, Hervey, g Chuck Darling, 295
Houchens, Karl "Buck," v/cl/ts Dixieland Swingsters, 320
*****Houchins, Kenneth, v/y/g** Patsy Montana, 634–35; Prairie Ramblers, 707–09
Howard, James, v/f Howard-Peak, 445

*****Howard, Lake, v/g** Roland Cauley, 198–99
Howell, George, sb Jimmie Rodgers, 807
Howell, Julius H., v/g J.H. Howell, 445
Hubbard, Carroll, f Bill Boyd, 123–24; Roy Newman, 657–58; W. Lee O'Daniel, 665–66
Hubbard, Dallas, v/bones Four Pickled Peppers, 356
Hubbert, Ernest "Skeeter," t/g Texas Jim Lewis, 499–500
Hudson, Bruce, t Cindy Walker, 935
Huff, Leon, lv/y/g Light Crust Doughboys, 501–02; Charles Mitchell & His Orchestra, 630; W. Lee O'Daniel, 665–66; Bob Wills, 966
Huffstutler, Leonard D., v Huff's Quartette, 446
Huggins, Harley, v/g Dave Edwards, 330; Johnny Lee Wills, 967
Hughes, ——, v Stamps Quartet, 864
Hughes, Joe, f Solomon & Hughes, 856
Hughes, Walter "Sparkplug," sp/g Jack Reedy, 734
Hughes, Walter, g Hill Billies, 424
*****Hughs, Dave, v/t/cl/ac/p/sb** Bob Skyles, 838–39
Humbard, Clement, v/esg/as/md/tbj Humbard Family, 447
Humbard, Leona, v/sb Humbard Family, 447
Humbard, Rex, v/g Humbard Family, 447
Humbard, Ruth, v/ac Humbard Family, 447
Humphries, Cecil, g Humphries Brothers, 447
Humphries, Jess, f Humphries Brothers, 447
Humphries, Ollie, tv/sg Hawaiian Pals, 412
Hundley, R.D., bj Kelly Harrell, 403–04
Hunt, E.L., bv Missouri Pacific Lines Booster Quartet, 629
Hunt, Helen, v Nite Owls, 660
Hunt, K.T., v Avoca Quartette, 87
Hunt, O.M., v Avoca Quartette, 87
Hunter, Chas. "Irontail," v/bj-md Arizona Wranglers, 62
Hurd, Eddie, cl Rice Brothers' Gang, 747
*****Hurdt, Walter, v/y/g** Leroy [Slim] Johnson, 461
Hurt, Charles "Chick," v/sp/md/mandola/tbj/g Gene Autry, 80–81; Happy Valley Family, 397; Jo & Alma, 458; Bob Miller, 624–25; Patsy Montana, 634–36; Prairie Ramblers, 704–13
Hurt, Zack, v/sb Hi-Flyers, 419; Zack & Glenn, 979
Hutcherson, Bert, g Paul Warmack, 939–40
Hutcheson, Slim, v/bj Uncle Ned, 919
Hutchison, C.L., c Jimmie Rodgers, 800–801
*****Hutchison, Frank, v/sp/h/g** OKeh Medicine Show, 668
Hutinger, George, f Lummie Lewis, 500
Hutson, Aldan "Wimpy," tbj/g Leaford Hall, 390; Lummie Lewis, 500; Ross Rhythm Rascals, 814
Hyatt, Leon, v/md/g Julian Johnson & Leon Hyatt, 461
Hyle, D.F., bj W.B. Chenoweth, 203; Ed Hayes, 414
Hyles, Arnold, bsv Rangers Quartet, 728
Hyles, Vernon, lv/g Rangers Quartet, 728

Ingram, Farris "Lefty," f/cl/ts Gene Steele, 867; Swift Jewel Cowboys, 884–85
Ingram, Olive, p Sue Morgan, 642
Ingram, Wilson (Bill), h/g Yellow Jackets [I], 976
Inman, Floyd, tv Macedonia Quartet, 542
Irby, Jerry, v/g Bar-X Cowboys, 93; Modern Mountaineers, 631; Bill Mounce, 645; Texas Wanderers, 900
Irvine, ——, p Smith & Irvine, 847
Isley, Tex, v/g Claude Casey, 196
Ivans, Joe "Hungry," v/md Arizona Wranglers, 62

Jackson, ——, sp Carson Robison, 793
Jackson, Ben, bj Rowdy Wright, 974
Jackson, H.A., bsv Hamp Reynolds' Sacred Harp Singers, 744
*****Jackson, Jack, v/y/g** Binkley Brothers Dixie Clodhoppers, 104
Jackson, James William, f Hugh Gibbs String Band, 368
James, Dewey, bv Carolina Gospel Singers, 170–71

James, Jesse (J.D.), v/md John D. Foster, 353
Jamison, Bud, v/y/h Rolling Stones, 813
Janes, Art, v Maple City Four, 587
Jarrell, Ben, v/f Da Costa Woltz's Southern Broadcasters, 969–70
Jarvis, Reese, f Jarvis & Justice, 453
Jasper, Skeets, f Nolan Bush, 147
Jaudas, ——, f Carson Robison, 767
Jecker, Walter, sb Gene Autry, 84; Ray Whitley, 953
Jefcoats, Buford, tv Coats Sacred Quartette, 216
Jenkins, "Goo[d]by". see Jenkins, Andrew
*Jenkins, Andrew, v/y/sp/wh/f/g W.C. Childers, 206; Jenkins Family, 455–57
Jenkins, DeWitt "Snuffy," bj J.E. Mainer's Mountaineers, 582; Byron Parker, 675
*Jenkins, Frank, v/f/bj Da Costa Woltz's Southern Broadcasters, 969–70
Jenkins, Oscar, bj Frank Jenkins, 455
Jennings, Leonard, ti Four Virginians, 357
Jepsen, Helen, v/g/ti Ruth Donaldson & Helen Jepsen, 323
Jernigan, Johnny, p Vaughan Quartet, 927–28
Johnson, Adous, sb Johnson Brothers' Band, 463
Johnson, C.C. Byrd Moore, 640
Johnson, C.W., g Lonesome Luke, 510
Johnson, Charles, v/sp/g Johnson Brothers, 462–63
Johnson, Clifton G. "Sleepy," bv/f/tg/tbj/g/sb Hi-Flyers, 419; Light Crust Doughboys, 500–502; Dick Reinhart, 739; Bob Wills, 960–64
Johnson, Dan, f Johnson Brothers' Band, 463
*Johnson, Earl, v/sp/f Fiddlin' John Carson, 176–77; Bill Chitwood, 208; Arthur Tanner, 885–86
Johnson, Eula, bj Ernest Phipps, 691
Johnson, J. C., p Frank[ie] Marvin, 596
Johnson, Jess. see Johnston, Jess
Johnson, Joe, v/sb Yellow Jackets [II], 976–77
Johnson, Johnny, sb Ted Daffan's Texans, 241
Johnson, Leo, v/f Johnson Brothers' Band, 463
Johnson, Leroy "Slim," v/g Walter Hurdt, 448; Leroy [Slim] Johnson, 462
Johnson, Lula Bell (Mrs. Earl), v Earl Johnson, 460
Johnson, Paul, v/y/sg/bj Johnson Brothers, 462–63
Johnson, Ras, lv/g Johnson Brothers' Band, 463
Johnson, Roland N., v/f McVay & Johnson, 579; Ernest Phipps, 691
Johnson, W.H., hv/f Johnson Brothers' Band, 463
Johnson, W.V. "Dick," bv Copperhill Male Quartet, 222
Johnson, Wayne, cl/s Bob Wills, 964–66
*Johnston, Jess, v/sp/f/p/g Ernest Branch & Bernice Coleman, 125; Duke Clark, 213; Roy Harvey, 411; Jess Hillard, 425–26; Ted Lunsford, 517; Byrd Moore, 639–40
Jolly, Rita, tv/sp/o [E.R.] Nance Family, 648
Jolly, Valena, sv [E.R.] Nance Family, 648
Jones, Boyce, f Four Aces, 355
*Jones, Buddy, v/y/sp/h/g Jimmie Davis, 299, 301–02
Jones, Buster, esg Jimmie Davis, 302–04; Buddy Jones, 464–66
Jones, Colon, v Riley Puckett, 720
Jones, Dallas, lv/y/g Leake County Revelers, 494–95
Jones, Darrell, sb Dave Edwards, 330; Bob Wills, 965–66
Jones, Dempsey, v/sp/g/ti Golden Melody Boys, 373
Jones, Dick[ie], v/f Cliff Bruner, 139; Dickie McBride, 526; Port Arthur Jubileers, 701; Village Boys, 932
Jones, Eva Thompson, p Uncle Jimmy Thompson, 904
Jones, James, sg/g Three Musketeers, 906
Jones, Judie, v/g Judie & Julie, 468
Jones, Julie, v/g Judie & Julie, 468
Jones, Lindley "Spike," d Ted Daffan's Texans, 241; Dick Reinhart, 739; Cindy Walker, 935

Jones, Louis, v Bill & Louis Jones, 464
Jones, Red, v/y/g/sb Roy Acuff, 48–49; Riley Puckett, 721
Jones, Russell, sg H.M. Barnes, 95
Jones, Sam, etg Bob Dunn's Vagabonds, 327
Jones, Shirley, g Ernest Phipps, 691
Jones, Wesley, v/g Wesley Long, 513; Sain Family, 818
Jordan, Chalmers, v/g Jordan Brothers, 467
Jordan, Hershel, v/g Jordan Brothers, 467
Jordan, Thomas, v/md Jordan Brothers, 467
Joy, Leonard, dir/cel Frank & James McCravy, 534; Johnny Marvin, 606; Jimmie Rodgers, 801
*Justice, Dick, v/sp/g Jarvis & Justice, 453

Kaai, Bob, v/sg/u Jim & Bob, 458
Kainapu, George, u Jimmie Davis, 303
Kaipo, Joe, v/sg Burke Brothers, 143; Jimmie Rodgers, 801–02
Kama, Charles, sg Jesse Rodgers, 799; Jimmie Rodgers, 804–05
Kamplain, Frank, y Arthur Fields & Fred Hall, 342
Kanter, Ben, cl Whitey McPherson, 579
Kanui, Dave, sg Jimmie Rodgers, 807
Kapp, Jack, sp Buell Kazee, 473
Kardos, Gene, f Dick Robertson, 758
*Karnes, Alfred G., v/harp-g/eff Ernest Phipps, 691
Karnes, Rose Carter, sv/y Chuck Wagon Gang, 209–11
Kastner, Roy, g Fiddling Sam Long, 512
Kay, Lambdin, sp [Smilin'] Ed McConnell, 530; Ernest Rogers, 810
*Kazee, Buell, v/sp/bj/g Blue Ridge Gospel Singers, 109
Keenan, ——, f/g Ike Cargill, 158
Keeshan, Charles W. "Chuck," v/g Shelly Lee Alley, 57–58; Bar-X Cowboys, 92–93; Ted Daffan's Texans, 240–41; Bob Dunn's Vagabonds, 326; Leon Selph, 823
Kehm, Frederick "Fritz," d Bob Dunn's Vagabonds, 326
Keiser, Cliff, v Jimmy Long, 511
Keith, Walter, bj Roanoke Jug Band, 751
Kelley, Toby, v/g Port Arthur Jubileers, 701
*Kellner, Murray, f/jh Elton Britt, 130; Vernon Dalhart, 244–70, 278–80, 282, 287–88; Carson Robison, 762–67, 770–71, 774–75, 788
Kelly, Jerry, v/g Kelly Brothers, 476–77
Kelly, John, md Roane County Ramblers, 751
Kelly, Ramon (Raymond), v/sg Kelly Brothers, 476–77
Kelso, Millard, p Johnny Lee Wills, 967
Kendrick, Bob, v/f/cl/ts/md/sb/saw/cowbells Jack Moser, 644; Bob Skyles, 838–39
Kendrick, Clifford, d/wb Dave Hughs, 446; Bob Skyles, 838–39
Kendrick, Doc, v/g Bob Skyles, 838
Kendrick, Sanford, v/t/tb/sb/sw/bazooka Bob Skyles, 838–39
Kendrick, Mrs. Sanford. see Brown, Lou
Kenzie, H.J., f Carl T. Sprague, 862
Kessinger, Clark, f Kessinger Brothers, 479
Kessinger, Luches, g Kessinger Brothers, 479
Ketner, Dick, g Ernest Tubb, 914
Kettering, Frank, v/sb/bb Hoosier Hot Shots, 435–39
Kiddo, Johnny, ac Roy Rogers, 812
Kiker, Harry, sp/f John Dilleshaw, 317
*Kincaid, Bradley, v/y/g WLS Radio Artists, 969
Kincaid, Irma F., p Bradley Kincaid, 485
King, Clyde D., v Singing Preachers, 836
King, Jimmy, esg Bill Nettles, 654
King, John (Dusty), v John (Dusty) King, 486
King, William E., bsv Moody Bible Institute Trio, 637
Kingsmore, Roy, g Mason Stapleton, 867
Kinzele, Grace, g W.C. Childers, 206; Richmond Melody Boys, 748
*Kirby, Fred, v/y/g Cliff Carlisle, 164, 167; Don White, 949

Kirby, Pete "Oswald," v/sg/bj/g Roy Acuff, 49–51
Kirkes, Walker, tbj Bill Boyd, 121–22; Roy Newman, 656–58
Kirkpatrick, Darrell, v/f/ac/emd/lg/sb Hi-Flyers, 418–20; W. Lee O'Daniel, 665; Lew Preston, 713; Dick Reinhart, 739; Universal Cowboys, 919; Wiley Walker & Gene Sullivan, 936
Kiser, Clyde, h/g Claude Davis, 298
Kiser, Rudle, v/y/wh Claude Davis, 298
Kite, Cecil, v Melford Jackson, 452
Kite, Walter, g Cherokee Ramblers, 203–04; Bill Gatin, 363
Kitts, Bill, v Kitts Bros., 487
Kitts, Zeke, v Kitts Bros., 487
Klein, Augie, ac Christine, 209; Red Foley, 351; Patsy Montana, 636; Prairie Ramblers, 711–12
Kleypas, Walter, ac/p Adolph Hofner, 431
Knight, Robert, v/tg/g Carl Boling, 116
Knippers, Cecil Christopher, bv Knippers Bros. & Parker, 488
Knippers, Ottis J., tv Knippers Bros. & Parker, 488
Kob, C. Martin, sb Eddie Dean, 308
Koehler, Esther "Violet," md Coon Creek Girls, 221; A'nt Idy Harper, 402
Koki, Sam, esg Gene Autry, 83–84; Jimmie Rodgers, 803–04; Sons Of The Pioneers, 858
Kolinek, Jake, g Dixie Ramblers [IV], 319
Koone, Fred, g/sb Jimmie Rodgers, 806–07
Kratoska, Herb "Arizona," bj/g Eddie Dean, 308; Happy Hollow Hoodlums, 397; Dick Reinhart, 739; Texas Rangers, 899–900
Krechter, Joe, cl Gene Autry, 86; Johnny Marvin, 607
Kruger, Bill, f Bar-X Cowboys, 93

Laam, Fred, bj Happy Hayseeds, 397
Laam, Ivan, f Happy Hayseeds, 397
*Lachney, Delma, v/f/g Blind Uncle Gaspard, 363
Lackey, Bryan, f/bj Dr. Smith's Champion Hoss Hair Pullers, 843
Lackland, Ray, v Roy Newman, 656–57
Lafleur, Lewis, f Delin T. Guillory-Lewis Lafleur, 385
Lafleur, Mayuse, v/ac Leo Soileau, 853
Lair, John, v/h Cumberland Ridge Runners, 239; Karl & Harty, 470
Lake, Denver, v/g Lake & Cavanagh, 489
Lam, Alva, lv/g Bela Lam, 489
Lam, Rosa, av Bela Lam, 489
LaMagna, Carl, f Texas Jim Lewis, 499
Lamb, Monroe, v/h/g Frank Wheeler-Monroe Lamb, 948
Lamperez, Julius "Papa Cairo," v/esg/eg Happy Fats, 396; Leo Soileau, 855; Joe Werner, 943
Landon, Ken, v/md/g James Brown, Jr. & Ken Landon Groups, 134–35
Landress, Bud, lv/tv/bv/sp/f/bj Bill Chitwood, 208; Georgia Yellow Hammers, 367; Gordon County Quartet, 375; Turkey Mountain Singers, 916
Landress, Mrs. Mary, v Uncle Bud Landress, 490
Landry, Bill (Dewey), v/g Four Aces, 355; Floyd Shreve, 833–34; Leo Soileau, 854–55
*Landry, Sydney, v/y/g Harrington-Landry & Steward, 404
Lane, Bunk, p Kentucky String Ticklers, 478
Lane, Ralph M., f L.O. Birkhead & R.M. Lane, 106
Lange, Evelyn "Daisy," sb Coon Creek Girls, 221; A'nt Idy Harper, 402
Lansford, Thomas C. "Son," sb Bob Wills, 960, 963–65
La Prade, Charley, f Blue Ridge Highballers, 109–10; Luther B. Clarke, 214
Larkin, Forrest "Bob," v/f/p Bob Larkan & Family, 490–91
Lasiter, Mrs. L.T., av Friendship Four, 360
Laughton, Charles, t/cl/s Bob Wills, 962–64

Laurent, Archie, p Leon Chappelear, 202
Lavender, Jonnie, sb York Brothers, 978
Law, Don, wb Shelly Lee Alley, 57
Lawrence, Harold, v Chas. Teuser & Harold Lawrence, 898
Lawson, Sherman, f Frank Hutchison, 450
Lay, Red, v/y/g Vance Knowles-Red Lay, 488
*Layman, Zora, v Frank Luther, 518–25
*Layne, Bert, v/sp/f Virginia Childs, 208; Claude Davis, 296–97; Oscar Ford, 352; Georgia Organ Grinders, 366; Dan Hornsby, 442; Bascom Lamar Lunsford, 517; Clayton McMichen, 566–70; Ruth Neal & Wanda Neal, 652; Riley Puckett, 717, 719; Lowe Stokes, 870–71; Swamp Rooters, 883; Gid Tanner, 887–88, 890
LeBlanc, Leroy "Happy Fats," v/sp/g/sb Nathan Abshire, 47; Happy Fats, 395–96; Joe Werner, 943–44
Lecroy, ——, bj/g Wyzee Hamilton, 393
Ledford, George, v Carolina Ramblers String Band, 172
Ledford, Lily May, v/f/bj Coon Creek Girls, 221; A'nt Idy Harper, 402
Ledford, Rosie, v/g Coon Creek Girls, 221; A'nt Idy Harper, 402
*Ledford, Steve, lv/f/bj/sb Carolina Ramblers String Band, 172; Happy-Go-Lucky Boys, 396; Wade Mainer, 583–84
Ledford, Taft, f/g Carolina Ramblers String Band, 172
Lee, Jack, esg Al Dexter, 314
Lee, Kitty, g Powder River Jack-Kitty Lee, 495
Lee, Lucille. see Overstake, Lucille
Lee, Robert Emerson "Bob," v Bob Wills, 966
Leeper, Jane, v Oklahoma Sweethearts, 668
Leeper, Jean, v Oklahoma Sweethearts, 668
*Leftwich, Woody, v/g Fred Pendleton, 685
Leger, Lourse, sg Alley Boys Of Abbeville, 59
Legg, Ernest, calls Kessinger Brothers, 479
Leonard, Tom, v Ernest V. Stoneman, 873, 876
Lester, Henry, f East Texas Serenaders, 329
Lester, Horley, bsv Vaughan Quartet, 929
Lester, Shorty, tbj East Texas Serenaders, 329
Leverett, Walter, bv Rangers Quartet, 728
Lewis, Dempson, f Lewis Brothers, 500
Lewis, Denmon, g Lewis Brothers, 500
Lewis, Ed, ah Asa Martin, 589
Lewis, Jack Rivers, v/g Texas Jim Lewis, 499–500
Lewis, Walter Earle "Tubby," t Bob Wills, 964–65
Liddel, Frank, f Jimmie Davis, 303; Tex Ritter, 750
Ligget, Walter, v/bj/calls Dr. Humphrey Bate, 97
Lilly, Roy, v/g Fred Pendleton, 685
Linder, Don, t Gene Autry, 85–87; Jimmie Davis, 305; Jimmy Wakely, 934
*Lindsey, Pink, sp/f/md/g/sb Chumbler Family, 212; John Dilleshaw, 316–17
Lindsey, Shorty, sp/tbj John Dilleshaw, 317
Lingo, Rufus, v/f/g Tim Flora & Rufus Lingo, 350
Linthicum, C.D., v/g Jimmy Yates Groups, 976
Linville, Charlie, f Eldon Baker, 89; Tex Ritter, 751
Lischkoff, David, f Jimmy Yates Groups, 975
"Little Boy Blue," v/g Fisher Hendley, 416–17
Little, Morine, g Mumford Bean, 98
Llewellyn, Mrs. T.C., p Smith's Sacred Singers, 848–49
Lockhart, Charlie, v Roy Newman, 657
Locklear, Frank, v/md Melvin Dupree, 327; Uncle Bud Landress, 490; Bill Shores & Melvin Dupree, 832
Logan, Oscar, v Taylor-Griggs Louisiana Melody Makers, 894
Lohman, Dale "Smokey," esg/vib-a-chord Prairie Ramblers, 712
Lombardo, Tony, h/ac/vb Jack Bankey, 92; Jack & Tony, 452
Long, ——, v Stamps Quartet, 864
Long, Andy Iona, esg Gene Autry, 86
Long, Beverly, v/y Jimmy Long, 511–12

Long, Bob, **v/g** Patsy Montana, 635–36; Prairie Ramblers, 709–12
Long, Howard, **v/k** David McCarn, 527
*Long, Jimmie, **v/y/sg/g** Gene Autry, 71, 75–83
Looney, Grady, **v** Atco Quartet, 70
Lormand, Sandy, **v/g** Happy Fats, 396
Loudy, ——, **v** Vaughan Quartet, 923
Love, ——, **v/y** Carolina Buddys, 170
*Love, Daddy John, **v/g** Dixie Reelers, 319; J.E. Mainer's Mountaineers, 581
Loveall, Ishmael, **v/f/g** Sons Of The Ozarks, 856
Loveland, Freddy, **eg** Jack Moser, 644
Loveless, Wendell P., **tv** Moody Bible Institute Trio, 637
Lowe, Hasten, **f** Pipers Gap Ramblers, 698
Lowe, Ike, **bj** Pipers Gap Ramblers, 698
Lowery, Henry C., **v/g** Dixie Ramblers [III], 319
Lowery, Joe, **v/g** Dixie Ramblers [III], 319
Loy, Lawrence V., **calls** Carson Robison, 796
Luallen, Luther, **f** Southern Moonlight Entertainers, 860
*Lulu Belle, **v/y/g** Red Foley, 351
Lunday, Ray, **sg** W. Lee O'Daniel, 665
Lundy, Emmet, **f** Ernest V. Stoneman, 872
Lunsford, Blackwell, **f** Bascom Lamar Lunsford, 516
Lunsford, Leaford, **v/sb** Lunsford Bros., 517; Shorty McCoy, 531
Lunsford, Paul, **v/g** Lunsford Bros., 517; Shorty McCoy, 531
Luse, Harley, **ac** Tex Ritter, 750
*Luther, Frank, **v/y/sp/wh/cel/bells/x/vb/jh/oc** Zora Layman, 492; OKeh Medicine Show, 668; Carson Robison, 762–78, 780–91
*Luther, Phil, **v/sp/sg/bscl/ac/g** Carson Robison, 781, 785, 787–89
Lynch, "Bill," **p** Ray Sand's Harmony Four, 819
Lynch, ——, **y** Keller Sisters & Lynch, 475

Mabie, Milt, **sb** Massey Family, 608–13
McAbee, Jimmy, **sb** Carl Boling, 116
McAdoo, Jimmy, **sb** Crystal Springs Ramblers, 239
Macalester, Johnny, **g** Homer Briarhopper, 127
McAuliffe, Harry C., **v/h/g** Big Slim Aliff, 54
McAuliffe, William Leon, **v/esg/eg/sb** Light Crust Doughboys, 501–02; Bob Wills, 960–66
*McBride, Dickie, **v/g** Cliff Bruner, 139–40; Bob Dunn's Vagabonds, 326; Buddy Jones, 465; Leon Selph, 824; Shelton Brothers, 829; Texas Wanderers, 900; Village Boys, 931
McCarroll, Jimmy, **f** Roane County Ramblers, 751
McCartt, Barney, **y/md** McCartt Brothers & Patterson, 527
McCartt, Luther, **v/y/f/md** Hugh Cross, 235; McCartt Brothers & Patterson, 527
McCarty, Alfred, **g** Jimmy Yates Groups, 975
McClain, E.W., **v** Jackson County Ramblers, 452
McClendon, Buster, **v/h/g** McClendon Brothers, 527–28
McClendon, Ernest ——, **v** McClendon Brothers, 528
McClendon, Rupert, **v/f** McClendon Brothers, 527–28
*McClung, Emery, **v/f** Cleve Chaffin, 200
*McClung, John, **v/wh/g** Cleve Chaffin, 200
McClured, Julius Plato "Nish," **v/bj** Hickory Nuts, 420
McCluskey, Bill, **v** Girls Of The Golden West, 371
McConville, Leo, **t** Arthur Fields & Fred Hall, 340–43
McCord, Don, **v** Arthur Duhon, 325
McCord, J. Fred, **g/sb** Bill Boyd, 121
McCormick, Alice, **p** Blue Ridge Mountaineers, 112
McCormick, Clarence, **h** Blue Ridge Mountaineers, 112
McCoy, Otis L., **tv** Stamps Quartet, 865; Vaughan Quartet, 927–28
*McCray, Carl, **v/g** Salem Highballers, 818
McCray, Fred, **g** Salem Highballers, 818

McCray, Henry, **f** Salem Highballers, 818
McCray, Robert, **bj** Salem Highballers, 818
McCreigton, L.W., **cl/bj/bj-u** Dr. Claude Watson & L.W. McCreigton, 940–41
*McDaniels, Lewis, **lv/y/g** Carolina Buddies, 170; Dixie Ramblers [I], 318; Hawaiian Pals, 412; Patt Patterson, 681; Walter Smith, 846–47
McDearis, Owen, **f** McDearis String Band, 539; Scottdale String Band, 822
McDonald, Alvin, **lv** McDonald Quartet, 539
McDonald, Bud, **v/g** Dave Edwards, 330
McDonald, Earl, **j** Jimmie Rodgers, 806
McDonald, Harold, **tv** McDonald Quartet, 539–40
McDonald, Lovelle, **lv** McDonald Quartet, 540
McDonald, R.F., **v** McDonald Quartet, 541
McDonald, Ralph, **bv** McDonald Quartet, 539–40
MacDowell, Edith, **v/sg** MacDowell Sisters, 542
MacDowell, Grace, **v/sg** MacDowell Sisters, 542
*McFarland, Lester, **v/sp/f/h/k/md/bj/g** Gentry Brothers, 364–65; Old Southern Sacred Singers, 668–69
McFarlane(?), ——, **p** J.D. McFarlane & Daughter, 550
*McGee, Denus, **v/f** Amedie Ardoin, 61–62; Angelas Le Jeunne, 493
McGee, Kirk, **v/f/md/bj/g** McGee Brothers, 552; Uncle Dave Macon, 575–76, 578
McGee, Sam, **v/sp/bj/bj-g** McGee Brothers, 551–52; Uncle Dave Macon, 574–78
McGhee, Alma, **v/humming** John McGhee & Frank Welling, 557–59
*McGhee, John, **v/y/sp/wh/h/o/g/perc/humming** David Miller, 626; Red Brush Rowdies, 730; West Virginia Mountaineers, 946; Miller Wikel, 956
*MacGimsey, Bob, **v/wh** Vernon Dalhart, 288; Frank[ie] Marvin, 604; Jimmie Rodgers, 801
McIntire, Al, **sb** Jimmie Davis, 303
McIntire, Lani, **g** Jimmie Davis, 303; Jimmie Rodgers, 803–04
MacIntosh, Jamie, **b** Bob Wills, 965
Mack, Al, **p** Jimmie Davis, 305
Mack, Billy. *see* McNew, Billy
Mack, Dick, **sp** Bert Swor & Dick Mack, 885
McKay, Benjamin (Ben), **v/f** Jimmie Revard, 742; Tune Wranglers, 915–16
McKinney, —— Byrd Moore, 640
McKinney, J.W. (Joe), **v/bj** Pope's Arkansas Mountaineers, 701
McKinney, Lee F. "Tip," **v/sp** Pope's Arkansas Mountaineers, 701
McKinney, Squeak, **f** Beverly Hill Billies, 102
McKinney, Walt[er], **sp/sg** Smoky Mountain Ramblers, 852; Lowe Stokes, 870; Tennessee Ramblers [I], 896
McLaughlin, Dr. ——, **bj** McLaughlin's Old Time Melody Makers, 564–65
McMadd, Micky, **v** Jim[my] Boa, 115
McMaster, Ruth, **f** Bob Wills, 960
*McMichen, Clayton, **lv/v/hv/y/sp/wh/f/g/v eff/calls** Virginia Childs, 208; Hugh Cross, 235–36; Claude Davis, 297; Oscar Ford, 352; Georgia Organ Grinders, 366; Dan Hornsby, 442; Bob Miller, 622; Fate Norris, 661; Riley Puckett, 717–20; Jimmie Rodgers, 807–08; Lowe Stokes, 870–71; Arthur Tanner, 886; Gid Tanner, 887–91
McMichen, Elmer, **v/f** McMichen's Harmony Boys, 573
MacMillan, George, **sb** Jimmie Rodgers, 800–801
McMillar, Kinman, **v/g** Blue Ridge Hill Billies, 110
McNally, Cy, **v/g** Paradise Joy Boys, 674
McNally, Robert "Zeb," **as** Bob Wills, 960–65
McNamara, Will, **bj** Vance's Tennessee Breakdowners, 922
McNeil, Banks, **f** Floyd County Ramblers, 350
McNeil, Sam, **bj** Floyd County Ramblers, 350

McNew, A.J., v/sg/g Harry Hillard, 425; Hoosier Hawaiians, 435
McNew, Billy, esg Shelton Brothers, 830; Sunshine Boys, 881
Macon, Dorris, g Uncle Dave Macon, 577
*Macon, Uncle Dave, sp/bj/g/v eff/calls McGee Brothers, 552
McPhail, Fred, tv Macedonia Quartet, 542
McReynolds, Charles, f Bull Mountain Moonshiners, 142
McReynolds, William, bj Bull Mountain Moonshiners, 142
McTague, Doug, v/y/g Cowboy Tom's Roundup, 224
McVay, Ancil L., v/md/g McVay & Johnson, 579; Ernest Phipps, 691
McWinders, Oddie, v/bj Clayton McMichen, 571; Bob Miller, 622; Jimmie Rodgers, 807–08; Robert Walton & McWinders, 938
Maggard, Odus, v/bj Odus & Woodrow, 667
Magnante, Charles, ac/pac Vernon Dalhart, 292; Arthur Fields & Fred Hall, 340–45; Texas Jim Robertson, 759–60; Carson Robison, 797
Magness, Tommy, bv/sp/f/md Roy Hall, 390–91; Bill Monroe, 631; Arthur Smith, 842
Mahaffey, G.H. "Hub," v/g/calls Dock Boggs, 115; Dykes' Magic City Trio, 328
Mahaney, Fran "Irish," lv Texas Rangers, 899–900
Mailhes, Frank, v/f Alley Boys Of Abbeville, 59
Mainer, Julia "Princess," v/y/sp Wade Mainer, 584
*Mainer, Wade, lv/sp/h/bj/g Steve Ledford, 495; J.E. Mainer's Mountaineers, 581
Malloy, Joe, v/g/sb Jimmie Revard, 743
Malloy, Martin, sp OKeh Medicine Show, 668
Malone, K.D., cl Clayton McMichen, 566–68; Lowe Stokes, 870
Malone, W.A., cond OKeh Atlanta Sacred Harp Singers, 667
Mang[r]um, Blind Joe, f Blind Joe Mangum-Fred Shriber, 586
*Manners, Zeke, v/ac/pac Beverly Hill Billies, 101–03
Manuel, Preston, g J.B. Fuslier, 361
Mapp, Eddie, h Hoke Rice, 745
Maratti, Arthur, traps Zeke Manners, 586
Marlor, John, v Marshall Smith, 844
Marshall, Ray, md Dr. Smith's Champion Hoss Hair Pullers, 843
Martin, "Heavy". see Cross, Hugh
*Martin, Asa, v/sp/h/g/calls Green Bailey, 88; Ted Chestnut, 204; Hatton Brothers, 412; Dick Parman, 679; Doc Roberts, 753–55; James Roberts, 755–56; Charlie Wilson, 967
Martin, Basil, g Jimmy Johnson's String Band, 461
Martin, Freddie, v/ac Cass County Boys, 198
Martin, Tex, v/y/g/sb Claude Casey, 197; Tennessee Ramblers [II], 897
Martinez, Pete, v/y/sg Val & Pete, 922
Martinez, Valentin, g Val & Pete, 922
*Marvin, Frank[ie], v/y/h/esg/ac/jh/wb/v eff/eff Gene Autry, 71–72, 74–76, 79, 81–87; Canova Family, 156; Eddie Dean, 308; Al Dexter, 315; Johnny Marvin, 606–07; Dick Reinhart, 739; Tex Ritter, 751; Ella Sutton, 882; Jimmy Wakely, 933–34
*Marvin, Johnny, v/y/sg/g/u/v eff Gene Autry, 71; Frank[ie] Marvin, 599
Marvin, Thelma, calls Frank[ie] Marvin, 598
Mashburn, Ira, o Moody Bible Sacred Harp Singers, 637; Turkey Mountain Singers, 916
Mason, Alex, v Dixieland Four, 320; Kanawha Singers, 469
Massengale, Alvis L., f Newton County Hill Billies, 658
Massey, Allen, lv/g Massey Family, 608–13
Massey, Bob, v Vernon Dalhart, 244–45
Massey, Curt, f/t/v eff Massey Family, 608–13
Massey, Doc, f Buddy Jones, 465; Bill Nettles, 653–54
Massey, Dott Curtis, v/f Massey Family, 608
Massey, Henry A. "Dad," sp/f Massey Family, 610–11

Massey, Louise, v/sp/p Massey Family, 608–13
Masters, Kelly, bj/g Kelly Brothers, 476
Masters, Ralph, sg Kelly Brothers, 476
Matson, Howard "Froggy," v/sb Sons Of The Ozarks, 856
Matthews, Ancil, bsv McDonald Quartet, 540
Matthews, Jug, bsv Laurel Firemen's Quartet, 491
Maudlin, Chuck, f Delmore Brothers, 311
*Maus, Harold, g Harold & Hazel, 402
Maxey, Howard, v/sp/f Doctor Lloyd & Howard Maxey, 508
Maxwell, E.C., f White Mountain Orchestra, 951
Maxwell, E.G., f Billie Maxwell, 613
Maxwell, F.L., g White Mountain Orchestra, 951
Maxwell, F.M., g White Mountain Orchestra, 951
May, Rod "Dave," v Texas Rangers, 899–900
Mayes, Kenneth, g Pelican Wildcats, 684
Mayes, Olen, v/f Short Creek Trio, 833
Mayes, Willie Ross, f Pelican Wildcats, 684
Mayhew, Jack, cl Gene Autry, 86–87; Johnny Bond, 117; Dick Reinhart, 739
Mayo, Joseph, gong Arthur Fields & Fred Hall, 340–41
Mays, Debs "Slim," v/sp/g Jack Pierce, 695–96
Meacham, Roy "Zeb," v/wh/f/g Zeb & Zeeke, 979
*Meadows, Clyde, v/h/g Fred Pendleton, 685
Meadows, Elias, tv/g Georgia Yellow Hammers, 367
Meadows, John Paul, bsv Bela Lam, 489
Meadows, W.A., v West Virginia Coon Hunters, 946
Medford, Vaughn, md Haywood County Ramblers, 414
Medley, Jimmie, g Allen Brothers, 55
Meek, Jimmie, v/sb Bill Boyd, 124; Sons Of The West, 859
Meissner, Fritz, tv Maple City Four, 587
Melvin, Sterling "Pops," bsv/sp/sg Perry Bechtel, 98; Brunswick Players, 141; Chumbler Family, 212; John Dilleshaw, 318; Taylor Flanagan, 345; Dan Hornsby, 441–42
Mendez, Joe, d Ross Rhythm Rascals, 814
Meng, Alfred, v Earl McCoy & Jessie Brock, 531
Merneigh, Cicero (Ray) Uncle Ned, 919
Michaels, Shorty, f Bob Atcher, 69–70
Miles, George R., g/calls Crook Brothers String Band, 234
Miles, Paul, v/sp/bj Red Fox Chasers, 730–31
Miller, Bethoven, v/g Miller's Merrymakers, 627–28
*Miller, Bob, v/sp/p/cel/o/g/chimes Gene Autry, 77–80; Elton Britt, 128–29; Smiley Burnette, 145; Dwight Butcher, 148; Cliff Carlisle, 165; Odis Elder, 331; Dan Hornsby, 442; Jake & Carl, 453; Frank Luther, 518–20, 522; Jack Mahoney, 581; Prairie Ramblers, 704–06; Dick Robertson, 758–59; Carson Robison, 789–90; Hank Warner, 940; Ray Whitley, 952
Miller, Charles, g Carolina Night Hawks, 172
Miller, Charlotte, v/sp Bob Miller, 617, 619–20
Miller, Chet, sb Shelly Lee Alley, 58–59; Leon Selph, 824; Floyd Tillman, 876
Miller, Emmett, v/sp OKeh Medicine Show, 668
Miller, Frank, tv/f Blue Ridge Mountaineers, 112; Posey Rorer, 813; Matt Simmons & Frank Miller, 835
Miller, Fred, tbj Frank Blevins, 108
Miller, Gleason "Dock," g North Carolina Ridge Runners, 663
Miller, Homer "Slim," v/sp/f Cumberland Ridge Runners, 239; Red Foley, 350–51; Karl & Harty, 470; Linda Parker, 678; Smoky Mountain Ramblers, 852; Lowe Stokes, 870
Miller, Howard, f Carolina Night Hawks, 172
Miller, Ralph, v/md Carl Boling, 116
Miller, Smoky, cl/as Shelly Lee Alley, 58
Millican, Leroy, eg Light Crust Doughboys, 506
Mills, Emory, f Alex Hood, 435
Milner, Luke, f Milner & Curtis, 628
Milo, Edward, v/y/g Milo Twins, 628

Milo, Edwin, v/y/g Milo Twins, 628
Minevitch, Borrah, p Dizzy Trio, 322
Ming, Rozelle, g Floyd Ming, 629
Ming, Troy, md Floyd Ming, 629
Minter, ——, v/g Melton & Minter, 615
Mintz, Joe, f Carl T. Sprague, 862
Misenheimer, Junior, bj J.E. Mainer's Mountaineers, 581
Mitchell, Bill, v/sp/md/bj/lg/g Frank Luther, 521; Carson Robison, 791–96
Mitchell, Bob, o Bill Elliott, 332
*Mitchell, Charles, esg Cliff Bruner, 141; Jimmie Davis, 301–05
Mitchell, J.M., f Dixie String Band, 320
Mitchell, John, v/sp/wh/md/bj/tbj/lg/g/eff Frank Luther, 521–22; Carson Robison, 791–96
Mitchell, Lonnie, sb Ross Rhythm Rascals, 814; Smoky Wood, 971
Mitchell, Loren, p Bill Boyd, 124; Crystal Springs Ramblers, 239; Sons Of The West, 859
Mitchell, Orville "Rex," v/lg/g Jack Pierce, 695–96
Mitchell, Ova, u Jimmie Davis, 301–03
Mitchell, Pearl Pickens. see Pickens, Pearl
Mitchell, Richard, md Roanoke Jug Band, 751
Moffet[t], Clyde, sb Christine, 209; Red Foley, 351
*Monroe, Bill, lv/tv/v/sp/md/g Monroe Brothers, 632
*Monroe, Charlie, lv/v/y/g Monroe Brothers, 632
*Montana, Patsy, v/y/sp/f Jimmie Davis, 300; Prairie Ramblers, 706
Montgomery, Marvin, lv/sp/k/tg/tbj Bill Boyd, 123–24; Light Crust Doughboys, 503–06; Patsy Montana, 636; Wanderers, 938
Moody, C. Ernest, tv/bv/sp/f/bj-u/g Calhoun Sacred Quartet, 151; Georgia Yellow Hammers, 367; Gordon County Quartet, 375; Moody Bible Sacred Harp Singers, 637; Moody Quartet, 637; North Georgia Four, 663; Phil Reeve & Ernest Moody, 735; Turkey Mountain Singers, 916
Moody, Clyde, lv/md/g Happy-Go-Lucky Boys, 396; Steve Ledford, 495; J.E. Mainer's Mountaineers, 582; Wade Mainer, 584–85; Bill Monroe, 631; Arthur Smith, 842
Mooney, Walter, v Ernest V. Stoneman, 873, 875–76
Moonshine Kate. see Carson, Rosa Lee
*Moore, Byrd, bv/v/sp/g Richard D. Burnett, 144; Clarence Greene, 382; Earl Johnson, 459; Leonard Rutherford, 816; Taylor, Moore & Burnett, 894
Moore, Grady, v/sp/f/sg/g Sid Harkreader, 400
Moore, Herbert L., calls Plymouth Vermont Old Time Barn Dance Orch., 698
Moore, James, h Hoke Rice, 745
Moore, Ruth Ann, p Jimmie Rodgers, 806
Moore, Tiny, v/f/emd Jimmy Hart, 406; Jubileers, 468
Moore, Walter, bv Shrine Male Quartet Of Memphis, 834
Moran, Jack, sb Shelly Lee Alley, 57
More, Frankie, v/sg/md/bj/g Log Cabin Boys, 508
Moresco, Joe, p Buddy Jones, 466
Morgan, Moise, f Joseph Falcon, 335
Morrell, Lewis, bj Roe Brothers & Morrell, 810
Morris, Rev. Frank, v/md Morris Family, 643
Morris, Fred "Happy," v/g/sb Campbell Brothers, 154; Dick Hartman's Tennessee Ramblers, 408–09
*Morris, George, v/g J.E. Mainer's Mountaineers, 582
Morris, Girlie Jean, v/bj Morris Family, 643
Morris, Wiley, v/g Morris Brothers, 643
*Morris, Zeke, hv/v/md/g J.E. Mainer's Mountaineers, 581; Wade Mainer, 582–84; (Charlie) Monroe's Boys, 632; Morris Brothers, 643
Morrison, Abbie, f Morrison Twin Brothers String Band, 644
Morrison, Apsie, f Morrison Twin Brothers String Band, 644

Morrison, Claude, g Morrison Twin Brothers String Band, 644
Morrison, Lawson, g Morrison Twin Brothers String Band, 644
Morse, Al, sb Arthur Fields & Fred Hall, 342–43
Morse, Ted "Otto," t Sally Foster, 355; Travelers, 912
Morton, Gene, p A.E. Ward, 938
Moser, Allan, v/g Jack Moser, 644
Mosley, R.O., bj-md Leake County Revelers, 494–95
Motlow, Johnny, v/bj Akins Birmingham Boys, 52; Rex Griffin, 383
Mott, Lloyd E. "Tiny," s Bob Wills, 964
Moulder, Rankin, tbj Bill Boyd, 121, 123
Mouleer/Moulder, Speedy, sb Jimmie Wilson's Catfish String Band, 968
*Mounce, Bill, sb Buddy Jones, 466; Modern Mountaineers, 631; Texas Wanderers, 900–901
Mullican, Aubrey "Moon," v/sp/p Cliff Bruner, 140–41; Jimmie Davis, 305; Bob Dunn's Vagabonds, 326; Slim Harbert, 398; Buddy Jones, 465–66; Charles Mitchell & His Orchestra, 629–30; Modern Mountaineers, 631; Leon Selph, 823–24; Sunshine Boys, 881; Texas Wanderers, 900–901; Floyd Tillman, 910
Mulligan, Bill, bj Jimmy Johnson's String Band, 461
Mullins, Cecil, v/eg Ocie Stockard, 869–70
Mundy, Shellie Propes, sv Flat Creek Sacred Singers, 346
Munnerlyn, John, tbj East Texas Serenaders, 329
Murray, Bill, ac Tex Ritter, 750
*Murray, Tom "Pappy," v/g Beverly Hill Billies, 101–02; Hollywood Hillbilly Orchestra, 432; Two Cow Hands, 918
Myers, Lee, p Vaughan Quartet, 929

Nance, Earl, bsv [E.R.] Nance Family, 648
Nance, Helen, av/p/o/md Hill Brothers, 424; [E.R.] Nance Family, 648
Nance, Madie, sv [E.R.] Nance Family, 648
Napoleon, Phil, c Carson Robison, 771
*Narmour, W.T., f/g OKeh Medicine Show, 668
*Nation, Buck, v/y/g Airport Boys, 52; Tex Ritter, 750; Ray Whitley, 952
Nations, Marshall, g Nations Brothers, 652
Nations, Shelton, f Nations Brothers, 652
Nawahi, Benny "King," h/sg/md/g Bob Miller, 620; Bernard [Slim] Smith, 842
Neal, ——, md Jess Hillard, 426
Neal, Lawrence D., tv Calhoun Sacred Quartet, 151; Moody Quartet, 637
Neal, Randall "Buddy," g Roy Newman, 656–57
Neal, Thurman, f Roy Newman, 656–57
Neal, Wanda, v Ruth Neal & Wanda Neal, 652
Nelson, Harry Katherine Baxter & Harry Nelson, 97
Nelson, Harry(?), v/g Claude Davis, 297–98
Nelson, Hubert A., v/sp/sg Nelstone's Hawaiians, 653
Nelson, Robert E., cl Roy Rogers, 812
Nettles, Luther, sb Bill Nettles, 653–54
Nettles, Norman, v/g Bill Nettles, 653–54
Newland, Gilbert, v Singing Preachers, 836
Newman, Hamon, tbj Four Pickled Peppers, 356
Newman, Harry, g Loy Bodine, 115
Newman, Syd "Willie (Red)," h/k/perc/flexatone Jack Pierce, 695–96
Newton, Ernie, v/sb Hilltoppers, 427
Newton, Hoyt, f McMichen's Harmony Boys, 573
Newton, Ken, v/wh/f Clayton McMichen, 572
Newton, William, bsv Shrine Male Quartet Of Memphis, 834
Nichols, Bob. see McMichen, Clayton
Nichols, Bob, esg Jimmie Davis, 303
Nichols, Claude, v/f Nichols Brothers, 659

Nichols, Frank, f/g Wyzee Hamilton, 393
Nichols, L.P., v McDonald Quartet, 541
Nichols, Lawrence, v/y/g Nichols Brothers, 659
Nichols, Robert "Curly," eg/g Dave Hughs, 446; Bob Skyles, 838
Nichols, Stanton, v/y/tg Nichols Brothers, 659
Nicholson, Daniel, v/bj/g Carolina Ramblers String Band, 172
Nicholson, Will J., bj Nicholson's Players, 659
Ninde, Julian R., g Jimmie Rodgers, 800
Noble, Cherrie, p Mellie Dunham's Orchestra, 326
Noble, M.A., vc/calls Mellie Dunham's Orchestra, 326
Noble, Ray, dir Carson Robison, 792
Nola, Larry, cl/ts Bill Nettles, 654
Nolan, Bob, v/sb Roy Rogers, 811; Sons Of The Pioneers, 857–58
Noland, Calvin "Curly," v/g/sb Gene Steele, 867; Swift Jewel Cowboys, 884–85
Nolen, Dick, tbj Red Patterson's Piedmont Log Rollers, 682
*Norris, Fate, lv/v/hv/sp/bj/g Georgia Organ Grinders, 366; Clayton McMichen, 566, 568–70; Gid Tanner, 887–90
*Norris, Land, v/bj Fiddlin' John Carson, 175
Norwood, Jack, p Wanderers, 938
Nossinger, Earl, g Ted Gossett's Band, 376; Tommy Whitmer's Band, 953
Novak, Frank, v/f/h/alto cl/bscl/bss/sg/ac/pac/cel/bj/u/sb/x Elton Britt, 129–30; Vernon Dalhart, 290–91; Odis Elder, 331; Graham Brothers, 377; Ernest Hare, 399; Adelyne Hood, 434–35; Frank Luther, 518–23; Frank & James McCravy, 537–38; Frank[ie] Marvin, 604–05; Johnny Marvin, 606–07; Bob Miller, 620, 622; Old Settlers, 668; Dick Robertson, 758–59; Texas Jim Robertson, 759–60; Carson Robison, 777–92, 794–97; Ray Whitley, 952
Nuckolls, W. Edison, bj Ephraim Woodie, 971
Nyland, Einar, v/md/mandola/g Perry Kim & Einar Nyland, 481–82

Oaks, Mrs. (Charlie), v/k/ah Charlie Oaks, 664
Oberstein, Eli, dir Bob McGimsey, 563
O'Brien, Smiley, v/g Delmore Brothers, 311
O'Byrne, Mike, bsv Stamps Quartet, 864
O'Daniel, Mike, f W. Lee O'Daniel, 666
O'Daniel, Pat, tbj W. Lee O'Daniel, 665–66
*O'Daniel, W. Lee, ldr/sp Light Crust Doughboys, 501–02
Odom, Bartie, lv Laurel Firemen's Quartet, 491
Ogden, Jean, v Leaford Hall, 390
Ogden, Mabel, p Al Dexter, 314; Leaford Hall, 390
Ogg, George, v/cl/ts Shelly Lee Alley, 58; Modern Mountaineers, 631
Ogle, ——, v/g Hart & Ogle, 406
Oglesby, Red, v/p Modern Mountaineers, 630–31
O'Keefe, James, v/p Al Bernard, 100; Hill Billies, 423
O'Keefe, Lester, v Blue Ridge Gospel Singers, 109; Old Southern Sacred Singers, 669
Oliver, Earl, t/c Carson Robison, 774–75, 778, 780
Oliver, Howard, tbj Shelly Lee Alley, 59; Leon Chappelear, 201–02; Leon Selph, 824; Shelton Brothers, 828–29; Floyd Tillman, 910
Olsen, Olie, f Carl T. Sprague, 862
O'Neill, H., sp Harry "Mac" McClintock, 528
Orr, Marion, f/g Cherokee Ramblers, 203–04; Bill Gatin, 363
Osborne, Gwyn, md/g Barber & Osborne, 93
O'Shea, Harry, ac Bill Nettles, 654
Overstake, Eva, v Three Little Maids, 906
Overstake, Evelyn, v Three Little Maids, 906
Overstake, Lucille, v/g Prairie Ramblers, 710–11; Three Little Maids, 906
Overstreet, Mahlon B., g Roanoke Jug Band, 751

Owen, Arch, lv Owen Brothers & Ellis, 670–71
Owen, Aubrey, tv/sb Owen Brothers & Ellis, 670–71
Owen, Crawford D. "Babe," lv/g Owen Brothers & Ellis, 670–71
Owen, Freddie, v/sg/md/bj/g Log Cabin Boys, 508
Owen, Herbert "Hub," bv/f Owen Brothers & Ellis, 670–71
Owen, W.A., treble v Hamp Reynolds' Sacred Harp Singers, 744
Owens, Frank, v/f Emry Arthur, 65; Floyd Thompson, 903
Owens, Grady, f Bill Helms, 415
Owens, Luke, v/g Al Dexter, 314; Nite Owls, 659–61
*Owens, Tex, v/y/sp/wh/g Texas Rangers, 899
"Ozark Red," v/f/g Sons Of The Ozarks, 856

Pace, A.M., bsv Vaughan Quartet, 927–28
Padgett, M.B. Zeb Harrelson & M.B. Padgett, 404
Page, Theo S., v Sandhills Sixteen, 820
Painter, Clinton, tv Copperhill Male Quartet, 222
Palmer, Alice, tv Palmer Sisters, 673
Palmer, Andy, v/f Jimmy Johnson's String Band, 461
Palmer, Francis, sb Whitey McPherson, 579
Palmer, Harry, v/t Ocie Stockard, 869
Palmer, Hue Tokah, sv Palmer Sisters, 673
Palmer, Leslie, v/sg Jack & Leslie, 451
Palmer, Sudie Belle, av Palmer Sisters, 673
Parham, A.E., bsv Carolina Gospel Singers, 170–71
Parham, Clyde, tv Carolina Gospel Singers, 170–71
Parker, ——, v Parker & Dodd, 678
Parker, Bill, g Jimmie Davis, 301
Parker, Billy, g Jubileers, 468
*Parker, Chubby (Frederick R.), v/wh/h/bj/tbj Tommy Dandurand, 292–93
Parker, Jack, v Carson Robison, 769
Parker, John Raymond, tv/p Knippers Bros. & Parker, 488
Parker, John W. "Knocky," ac/p Bill Boyd, 123–24; Light Crust Doughboys, 504–06
*Parker, Linda, v Cumberland Ridge Runners, 239
*Parman, Dick, v/y/g Fay & The Jay Walkers, 337; Hodgers Brothers, 428; Kentucky Thorobreds, 478–79
Parsons, Kathryn, v Girl O' Yesterday, 369
Paschal, Lem, v Lem's Down Home Boys, 496; Clyde Stone & Lem Paschal, 871
Pate, Tom, g Fiddlin' Jim Pate, 680
Patent, Harry, sb Buddy Jones, 466
Patrick, Luther, sp/g Wyzee Hamilton, 393
Patterson, Andy, v/y/sp/f/g/calls Warren Caplinger, 156–57; McCartt Brothers & Patterson, 527
Patterson, J.E. "Nubbins," v/g Arizona Wranglers, 62
Patterson, John, bj Carroll County Revelers, 174
Patterson, Patt, md Spooney Five, 862
*Patterson, Patt, v/y/sg/g Lewis McDaniels, 539; Walter Smith, 847
Patterson, William, h/g Roba Stanley, 866
Patton, Sam, sp Ernest V. Stoneman, 876
Paul, Les, v/h/g Rhubarb Red, 744
Paul, Melvin, md/bj Grinnell Giggers, 384
Paulette, Ezra, lv/y/f Beverly Hill Billies, 101–03
Payne, Keith, d Dave Edwards, 330
*Payne, Leon, v/g Bill Boyd, 124
Peacock, Charles, g Smith's Garage Fiddle Band, 848
Peacock, John, g Smith's Garage Fiddle Band, 848
Peacock, Samuel Morgan, f Smith's Garage Fiddle Band, 848
Peak, Charles, v/g Howard-Peak, 445
Pearson, Dave, g Spangler & Pearson, 861
Pearson, Johnnie, v/g Bill Boyd, 124
Peck, Emory, bsv Peck's Male Quartette, 683
Peel, Reg, p Rev. Clyde D. King, 485; Singing Preachers, 836

*Pellerin, Petrick (Dak), v Christine Muszar, 647
*Pendleton, Fred, v/f Richard Harold, 401; West Virginia Night Owls, 946
Pennington, Bill, p Adolph Hofner, 430
Perkins, Wilson "Lefty," esg Bill Boyd, 122–23; Milton Brown, 138; Jimmie Davis, 302; Hi-Flyers, 419; W. Lee O'Daniel, 665; Universal Cowboys, 919
Perrin, Cecil S., v/g Cecil & Vi, 199
Perrin, Pat, hv Ross Rhythm Rascals, 814
Perrin, Vivian, v/g Cecil & Vi, 199
Perrin, William "Curly," v/tv/y/g Bill Boyd, 122–23; Light Crust Doughboys, 502; W. Lee O'Daniel, 665–66; Ross Rhythm Rascals, 814
Perry, Wayne, f Joe Werner, 943
Perryman, Happy, v/g Tex Ritter, 750
Perryman, Lloyd, v/g/sb Jimmie Davis, 303; Tex Ritter, 750; Roy Rogers, 811; Sons Of The Pioneers, 857–58
Petterson, Pat, v Maple City Four, 587
Pettrey, Oliver, v/v/g Joe Gore & Oliver Pettrey, 376
Peveto, A.C., esg Jubileers, 468
*Phelps, Earl, v/y/f/sw Ray Whitley, 953
*Phelps, Norman, sb/d Ray Whitley, 953
*Phelps, Willie, v/g Ray Whitley, 953
Phillips, Albert "Slim," f Al Clauser, 214
Phillips, Bob, v/y Fred Kirby, 486
Phillips, Herman "Zeke," sb Delmore Brothers, 312
Phillips, Jesse, v Dixieland Four, 320; Kanawha Singers, 469
Phillips, T.H. "Red," v/g Akins Birmingham Boys, 52
Phillips, Webb, calls Arthur Tanner, 885
Philyaw, James, v/g Philyaw Brothers, 690
Philyaw, Myrl, v/g Philyaw Brothers, 690
Phipps, Minnie, v Ernest Phipps, 691
Pickard, Bubb, v/g Pickard Family, 691–93
Pickard, George, bsv Calhoun Sacred Quartet, 151
Pickard, Mom, v/p Pickard Family, 691–93
Pickard, Obed "Dad," v/sp/h/jh Pickard Family, 691–93
Pickard, Ruth, v/g Pickard Family, 691–93
Pickens, Pearl, v/sp Carson Robison, 791–96
Pierce, Bruce "Roscoe," v/tbj Cliff Bruner, 141; Slim Harbert, 398; Buddy Jones, 466; Shelton Brothers, 830; Sunshine Boys, 881–82
*Pierce, Jack, v/sp/f Grant Brothers, 377; Smyth County Ramblers, 852
Pilliod, Jody, esg Bill Nettles, 654
Pinero, Frank, vn Carson Robison, 797
Pitman, W.C., Jr., md Gibson String Trio, 368
Pitre, Milton, g John H. Bertrand, 101
Pitts, Jesse D., v/g Hinson, Pitts & Coley, 427
Pitts, Jesse, v/bj Georgia Wildcats, 366
Pitts, Kenneth, lv/bv/sp/f/ac/p/g Bill Boyd, 123–24; Light Crust Doughboys, 502–07; Roy Newman, 658
Pitts, T.T., bsv Avondale Mills Quartet, 87
Plant, Gus, v/tbj/g Shelly Lee Alley, 58–59; Leon Selph, 823–24
Plant, W.E. "Cotton," sb Sons Of Dixie, 856; Texas Wanderers, 900
Pleasant, Ralph, f Johnny Barfield, 93
Pless, Lee, bsv Copperhill Male Quartet, 222
Pollack, Ben, d Whitey McPherson, 579
Pollard, Talmadge, v/k/g Johnson County Ramblers, 463
Poole, Charlie, (Jr.), v Swing Billies, 885
*Poole, Charlie, v/sp/bj Roy Harvey, 409–10
Pooser, Keith, v Merritt Smith, 844
Poplin, Sam, v/f Fisher Hendley, 416–17
Poplin, W.E., v/f Poplin-Woods Tennessee String Band, 701
*Porter, Archer, v/h/g Hazel Scherf, 820
Porter, Del, cl Cindy Walker, 935

Porter, John L. "Steamboat," h Fiddlin' Powers & Family, 704
Porter, Steve, calls Joseph Samuels, 819
Porter, Sylvia, v Archer Porter, 702
Posner, Benny, f Vernon Dalhart, 251
Poteet, Blythe, v/wh/g Sid Harkreader, 401; McGee Brothers, 552
Potter, Charlie, bones Jimmie Wilson's Catfish String Band, 968
Potter, Orin, jazz wh/gas pipe Jimmie Wilson's Catfish String Band, 968
Pottinger, Warren, sg Jimmie Davis, 301
Poulton, Curt, v/g Vagabonds, 921
Powell, Dr. W.M., f Dixie String Band, 320
Power, Bill, bj Cherokee Ramblers, 203–04
Powers, Ada, u Fiddlin' Powers & Family, 703–04
Powers, Carrie, g Fiddlin' Powers & Family, 703–04
Powers, Charlie, v/bj/g Fiddlin' Powers & Family, 703–04
Powers, Eddie, ac Bob Atcher, 69–70
Powers, James Cowan, f Fiddlin' Powers & Family, 703–04
Powers, Orpha, v/md Fiddlin' Powers & Family, 703–04
Presson, Nonnie Smith, v/y/zither Perry County Music Makers, 687
Price, Cecil, u Price-Prosser-Teasley, 714
Priddy, Relder, md Mumford Bean, 98
Pridgen, Millard, v Laurel Firemen's Quartet, 491
Prigden/Pridgin, Sam, v/g/sb Swing Billies, 885; Three Tobacco Tags, 908–09
Pritchard, Barney, v/g Scottdale String Band, 821–22
Propes, Benjamin, tv Flat Creek Sacred Singers, 346
Propes, James Marlowe, bsv Flat Creek Sacred Singers, 346
Propst, Horace, v/g Hickory Nuts, 420
Propst, Perry, f Hickory Nuts, 420
Prosser, Sweeny, sg Honolulu Strollers, 434; Price-Prosser-Teasley, 714
Prow, Aubrey, v/g Madisonville String Band, 580
Puckett, Reuben, v Richard Brooks & Reuben Puckett, 132
*Puckett, Riley, lv/hv/v/sp/wh/bj/g/humming Virginia Childs, 208; Hugh Cross, 235–36; Oscar Ford, 352; Ted Hawkins, 413; Home Town Boys, 433; Dan Hornsby, 442; Clayton McMichen, 565–71; Fate Norris, 661; Lowe Stokes, 871; Arthur Tanner, 886; Gid Tanner, 887–91
Puderer, Johnnie, sb Hackberry Ramblers, 387–88
*Pyle, Pete, lv/tv/y/sp/g Bill Monroe, 631–32

Quinn, Eddie "Snoozer," g Jimmie Davis, 299
Quirk, Charlie. see Cook, Chuck

Raderman, Lou, f/vla Vernon Dalhart, 242, 245–46, 250, 257
Raines, Elmore "Pete," v/g Uncle Pete & Louise, 919
*Raines, Sherman, v/g R.L. Raines, 724
Rainey, Albert, v/g Warren Caplinger, 156; Southern Moonlight Entertainers, 860
Rainey, Allen, calls Gatwood Square Dance Band, 363
Rainey, George, sp/f Warren Caplinger, 156; Southern Moonlight Entertainers, 860
Rainey, Marvin "Dude," g Southern Moonlight Entertainers, 860
Rainey, Willie, bj Warren Caplinger, 156; Southern Moonlight Entertainers, 860
Rainwater, Carl, esg/j Leon Chappelear, 201; Dave Edwards, 330
Rainwater, Floyd, v/y/g Hackberry Ramblers, 387
Rainwater, Lonnie, sg Hackberry Ramblers, 387
Raitz, Samuel, f Vernon Dalhart, 268–70; Kanawha Singers, 469
Raley, ——, g Raley Brothers, 724
Raley, Adrian, sg Raley Brothers, 724

Raley, Leo, v/emd Cliff Bruner, 139–40; Bob Dunn's Vagabonds, 326; Buddy Jones, 465; Leon Selph, 824; Shelton Brothers, 829; Texas Wanderers, 900; Floyd Tillman, 910
Raley, Randall "Red," v/g Cliff Bruner, 139–40
Ramsey, ——, g Clagg & Sliger, 212
Ramsey, Clifton "Rip," sb Bill Boyd, 122; Modern Mountaineers, 630
Ramsey, J.A. Gibson String Trio, 369
Ratraff, Thurman, cl Gene Autry, 86
Raub, Melvin, sb Carson Robison, 797
Ray, Aulton, v Taylor's Kentucky Boys, 895
Ray, Buddy, v/f/g/sb Bar-X Cowboys, 93; Buddy Jones, 466; Dickie McBride, 526; Modern Mountaineers, 630–31; Texas Wanderers, 900–901; Village Boys, 932
Ray, Frankie, f Ralph Hodges, 429
Ray, S. Vardaman, v/g Ray Brothers, 729
Ray, Wade, f Ambrose Haley, 389
Ray, Will E., f Ray Brothers, 729
Reaves, Ira, f/eff Reaves White County Ramblers, 729
Reaves, Isaac "Ike," f Reaves White County Ramblers, 729
Reaves, Lloyd, v/o Reaves White County Ramblers, 729
Rector, John, bj Hill Billies, 422; Henry Whitter, 955
Rector, John, f Rector Trio, 729
Reed, Arville, v/g Blind Alfred Reed, 733; West Virginia Night Owls, 946
Reed, Clay, f Ephraim Woodie, 971
*Reedy, Weldon (Jack), sp/bj/bells H.M. Barnes, 94–95; Hill Billies, 423–24; Smyth County Ramblers, 852
*Reeve, C. Philip, lv/tv/bv/v/sp/g/u Calhoun Sacred Quartet, 151; Clyde Evans Band, 333; Georgia Yellow Hammers, 367; Gordon County Quartet, 375; Moody Bible Sacred Harp Singers, 637; North Georgia Four, 663; Turkey Mountain Singers, 916
Reeve, Jewell, p Calhoun Sacred Quartet, 151
*Reeves, Goebel, v/y/sp/g Canova Family, 155
Register, Mac, p Lummie Lewis, 500
Reid, Sam, v/bj Reid Bros. Band, 738–39
*Reinhart, Dick, lv/tv/esg/md/eg/sb Gene Autry, 85; Johnny Bond, 116–17; Canova Family, 156; Al Dexter, 315; Hi-Flyers, 419; Light Crust Doughboys, 503–04; Johnny Marvin, 607; Roy Rogers, 811–12; Ella Sutton, 882; Three Virginians, 909; Universal Cowboys, 919; Jimmy Wakely, 933–34; Wanderers, 938
Reneau, Frank, p Light Crust Doughboys, 506–07
*Reneau, George, v/h/g Gentry Brothers, 364–65
Reser, Harry, bj/tbj Al Bernard, 100; Joseph Samuels, 819
*Rexroat, William, v/g Brother James Arnold, 64; Emry Arthur, 65; Jossie Ellers, 331
Reynolds, Bronson "Barefoot Brownie," v/h/sb Eldon Baker, 89
Reynolds, Bummer, bones/sw/flexatone Yellow Jackets [I], 976
Reynolds, Harley, ah Yellow Jackets [I], 976
Reynolds, Mahlon, bj Bill Nettles, 654
Rhine, Monte, lg Ambrose Haley, 389
Rhodes, Homer, esg Roy Rogers, 812
Rhodes, Oral, f/sb Roy Acuff, 50
Rhyne, Palmer, sg Wilmer Watts, 941
Rice, "Sleepy," v/y/g/sb Zeke Williams, 959
Rice, Al, v Maple City Four, 587
Rice, Frank, v/bj/g/spoons Mustard & Gravy, 647
Rice, Glen, dir Beverly Hill Billies, 102
*Rice, Hoke, v/y/sp/eg/humming Allie & Pearl Brock, 131; Chumbler Family, 211–12; Claude Davis, 298; John Dilleshaw, 317; Louie Donaldson, 323; Rice Brothers' Gang, 746–47; Lowe Stokes, 870–71; Swamp Rooters, 883
Rice, Paul, v/y/g Rice Brothers' Gang, 746–47

Rich, Brown, vc George Edgin, 330
Richard, Jerry, bj Harry "Mac" McClintock, 529
*Richards, Fred, v/y/g Four Virginians, 357
Richards, John, sp/bells/eff Buell Kazee, 473
Riddle, Jimmy, h Swift Jewel Cowboys, 884
Ridgel, Carthel, g Ridgel's Fountain Citians, 748–49
Ridgel, Charles Ancil, v/md Ridgel's Fountain Citians, 748–49
Ridgel, Leroy, f Ridgel's Fountain Citians, 748–49
Riggins, W.H., v McDonald Quartet, 541
Rikard, James, cl Jimmie Rodgers, 800–801
Riley, Kirby, v/ac Douglas Bellar & Kirby Riley, 99
Ringeisen, Fanny Lou Morris, v/g Morris Family, 643
Ritter, Brooks, bj/bj-md Moatsville String Ticklers, 630
Ritter, Harold, sb Moatsville String Ticklers, 630
Rivera, Rudy, cl Bob Dunn's Vagabonds, 327
Rives, Johnny, f/d Adolph Hofner, 430–31
Roark, George, Jr., v George [Shortbuckle] Roark, 752
Roark, Oda, v George [Shortbuckle] Roark, 752
Roark, Robert, v George [Shortbuckle] Roark, 752
Robbins, Clyde, tv/g Byron Parker, 675
Roberts, Dick, esg Johnny Bond, 117; Jimmie Davis, 305; Al Dexter, 315
*Roberts, Doc, v/f/md/g Green Bailey, 88; Ted Chestnut, 204; Kentucky Thorobreds, 478–79; Asa Martin, 588–93; Dick Parman, 679; James Roberts, 756; Taylor's Kentucky Boys, 895; Welby Toomey, 912
Roberts, Fred, v/f Harmon Canada, 154–55
Roberts, Harold "Little Willie," v/sb Range Riders, 727
*Roberts, James, v/y/md/g Asa Martin, 588–93; Doc Roberts, 754–55
Roberts, Sam, Jr., v eff Johnson Brothers, 463
Roberts, Woodrow, v/g Odus & Woodrow, 667
Robertson, Daphne, tg A.C. (Eck) Robertson, 757
Robertson, Dueron, sp/tbj/g A.C. (Eck) Robertson, 757
Robertson, Jesse "Slick," tbj Bill Boyd, 124; Sons Of The West, 859
Robertson, Nettie, v/g A.C. (Eck) Robertson, 757–58
Robin, Moise, v/ac Leo Soileau, 854
Robinette, Melvin, v/sp/f Byrd Moore, 638
*Robinson, Paul, h Elton Britt, 129
Robinson, Mrs. W.E., p Holman & Robinson, 432
*Robison, Carson, v/sp/wh/h/p/g/calls/eff Al Bernard, 100–101; Blue Ridge Gospel Singers, 109; Vernon Dalhart, 242–82; J.W. Day, 306; Dizzy Trio, 322; Forman Sisters, 352; Ewen Hail, 389; Kelly Harrell, 403; Hill Billies, 424; Adelyne Hood, 434; Andrew Jenkins, 454; Kanawha Singers, 469; Buell Kazee, 472–73; Murray Kellner, 476; John & Emery McClung, 529; Frank & James McCravy, 532, 534; Frank[ie] Marvin, 603; OKeh Medicine Show, 668; Old Southern Sacred Singers, 669; Fiddlin' Powers & Family, 703; Zeb White, 951
Roden, Sonny, p Bill Boyd, 121
Rodgers, Audie "Buffalo," v/g Carolina Ramblers String Band, 172
*Rodgers, Jimmie, v/y/sp/g/u/v eff Carter Family, 189–90
Rodgers, Roy, v/y/ac/g Hawaiian Songbirds, 412; Hugh Roden, 797
Roe, Fred, sp/f H.M. Barnes, 94–95; Hill Billies, 423; Jack Reedy, 734; Roe Brothers & Morrell, 810
Roe, Henry, sp/g H.M. Barnes, 94–95; Hill Billies, 422–23; Jack Reedy, 734; Roe Brothers & Morrell, 810
Rogers, Charlie, v/g Kentucky String Ticklers, 478
Rogers, Eugene "Smokey," bj/g Texas Jim Lewis, 499
Rogers, Joe, v Tex Fletcher, 349
*Rogers, Roy, v/y/sp/g/calls Sons Of The Pioneers, 857–58
Rogers, Silas, v/f Kentucky String Ticklers, 478
Rohloff, Herbert, p Shrine Male Quartet Of Memphis, 834

Romero, Roy, sg Happy Fats, 395; Joe Werner, 943
Roop, Kyle, g Billy Vest, 931
Roper, Ezra, ac Fisher Hendley, 416–17
*Rorer, Posey, f/md Carolina Buddies, 170; Buster Carter & Preston Young, 180; Dixie Ramblers [I], 318; Kelly Harrell, 403; Roy Harvey, 409–10; Charlie Poole, 698–99; Matt Simmons & Frank Miller, 835; Walter Smith, 846; Norman Woodlieff, 972
Rose, Arthur, v Asa Martin, 592; James Roberts, 756
Rose, Fred, v Frank Luther, 524; Ray Whitley, 953
Rosnell, Walter, g Texas Jim Robertson, 760
Ross, Buddy, ac Hugh Cross, 236
Ross, Charlie, v/g Short Creek Trio, 833
Ross, J.S., h/g H.K. Hutchison, 450
Ross, Jack, v Ranch Boys, 725
Rothel, Margie "Toni," v Tex Walker, 935
Rouse, Earl, f Rouse Brothers, 815
Rouse, Ervin, v/sp/f Rouse Brothers, 815
Rouse, Gordon, v/sp/g Rouse Brothers, 815
Rouse, Jack, v/sp Rouse Brothers, 815
Rouse, Jimmy, f Claude Casey, 197
Rowell(?), Chad(?), bj Crazy Hillbillies Band, 232
Rude, Druce, v McLaughlin's Old Time Melody Makers, 564–65
Ruff, Beal, cl/as Adolph Hofner, 430; Tune Wranglers, 916
Ruff, Neal, tbj Tune Wranglers, 916
Rumble, Ed, g/calls Reaves White County Ramblers, 729
Russell, Frank, p Smith's Garage Fiddle Band, 848
Russell, Grady, v/sg/g Madden Community Band, 580; Russell Brothers, 816
Russell, Grover, v/y/g Madden Community Band, 580; Russell Brothers, 816
Russell, Henry, f East Texas Serenaders, 329
Russell, Mischa, f Gene Autry, 85–86; Canova Family, 156
Russell, William B., v/h Harmonica Bill, 401
Russo, Al, bj/g Arthur Fields & Fred Hall, 340–45
*Rutherford, Leonard, v/f Richard D. Burnett, 144; John D. Foster, 353–54
Ruttledge, Oscar, g Richard D. Burnett, 144
Ryan, Gale, v/d/traps Prairie Ramblers, 711–13
Rye, Forrest, f Rye's Red River Blue Yodelers, 817

Sain, Mrs. J.L., v Sain Family, 818
Salathiel, Doyle, eg Johnny Bond, 117; Bob Wills, 966
Salazar, M.T., g Jimmie Rodgers, 805
*Samuels, Joseph, f/g Ernest V. Stoneman, 873; Henry Whitter, 955–56
Sanders, "Chief," v/f Otto Gray, 378–79
Sanders, Jim, sp/claves Swift Jewel Cowboys, 884
Sandford, Fiddlin' Slim, f Frank Roberts, Bud Alexander & Fiddlin' Slim Sandford, 755
Sandidge, Hugh, tv Shrine Male Quartet Of Memphis, 834
Sandor, Olga, p Little Brown Church Quartet, 507
Sannella, Andy, sg/g Vernon Dalhart, 268; Arthur Fields & Fred Hall, 340, 342–43, 345
Sanucci, Frank, ldr Tex Ritter, 750
Sargent, Charles, g Tex Ritter, 750
Savage, George "Little Georgie Porgie," v Little Georgie Porgie, 508
Savoy, Norris, f Nathan Abshire, 47; Happy Fats, 395
Sawyer, Bob, p Jimmie Rodgers, 803–04
*Sawyer[s], Bill[y], v/g L.O. Birkhead & R.M. Lane, 106; Sawyer Sisters, 820; A.E. Ward, 938
Sayre, Harry, p John McGhee & Frank Welling, 563
Scanlin, Anthony, cl/ts/p Shelly Lee Alley, 57–58; Dickie McBride, 526; Texas Wanderers, 900; Village Boys, 931
Scanlon, Walter, v Texas Jim Robertson, 759–60
Scarborough, Eiland, tv Vaughan Quartet, 929

Scarborough, Elmer, tg/tbj Hi-Flyers, 418–20; Dick Reinhart, 739
Schaffer, Ed, v/sg Jimmie Davis, 299–300
Schexnyder, Warnest, g Nathan Abshire, 47; Happy Fats, 395
Schmit, Lucien, vc Vernon Dalhart, 258
Schroeder, Andrew, v/esg/sb Hi-Flyers, 419–20; Lew Preston, 713; Dick Reinhart, 739
Schubert, Adrian, chimes Dwight Butcher, 148
Schultz, Clayton, f Clayton & His Melody Mountaineers, 215
Scoggins, Jerry, v/g Cass County Boys, 198
Scott, Berdina, p B.E. Scott, 820
Scott, Leon, f Cliff Carlisle, 167
Seago, Leon[ard], v/f/emd Ted Daffan's Texans, 241; Adolph Hofner, 430; Jimmie Revard, 743
Seale, Walter B., lv/bv Vaughan Quartet, 923–27, 929
Sebren, A.B., bv/p Vaughan Quartet, 928–29
Segura, Dewey, v/ac E. Segura & D. Herbert, 823
Sells, Paul "Monty," ac/pac/p Gene Autry, 84–87; Johnny Bond, 117; Canova Family, 156; Eddie Dean, 308; Al Dexter, 315; Happy Hollow Hoodlums, 397; Johnny Marvin, 607; Dick Reinhart, 739; Tex Ritter, 751; Roy Rogers, 812; Ella Sutton, 882; Texas Rangers, 899–900
*Selph, Leon, v/f Shelly Lee Alley, 58–59
Selvey, Basil, v/md Fred Pendleton, 685
Sentell, L.K., sp/g Herschel Brown, 133–34
Sepolio, Tony, v/f Bill Mounce, 645; Sons Of Dixie, 856
Setliff, Percy, f Red Patterson's Piedmont Log Rollers, 682
Shaffer, Doyle, g Moatsville String Ticklers, 630
Shahan, Cleo "Doc," g Harry "Mac" McClintock, 529
Shamblin, Eldon, eg Bob Wills, 962–66
Shanks, Arvin Ercil, p Bill Mounce, 645
Shanks, Chuck, v/sp Shanks Bros. Trio, 825
Shannon, William, v/sp John McGhee & Frank Welling, 556
Sharp, Claude A., v Vaughan Quartet, 927
Sharpe, Claude O., tv Vaughan Quartet, 929
Shaw, Elliott, v Vernon Dalhart, 245
Shaw, Theodore, p Vaughan Quartet, 924–26
Sheffield, A.C., bsv Sheffield Male Quartet, 826
Sheffield, C.P., tv Peck's Male Quartette, 683; Sheffield Male Quartet, 826
Shelor, Jesse T., f Shelor Family, 826
Shelor, Pyrhus D., f Shelor Family, 826
Shelton, Bob. see Attlesey (Shelton), Bob
Shelton, Curley/Curly, v/tv/md/g Tiny Dodson's Circle-B Boys, 322; Wade Mainer, 585
Shelton, Jack, lv/g Tiny Dodson's Circle-B Boys, 322; Wade Mainer, 585
Shelton, Joe. see Attlesey (Shelton), Joe
Shelton, Merle, g Shelton Brothers, 829–30; Sunshine Boys, 881–82
Shepherd, Fred Stewart's Harmony Singers, 869
*Shepherd, Hayes, v/bj Bill Shepherd, 830
Shepherd, Herb, bj Bill Shepherd, 830
Sherbs, Alice, g Bob Larkan & Family, 490–91
Sherbs, William Holden, g Bob Larkan & Family, 490–91
Sherman, ——, bsv Friendship Four, 360
Sherrill, Herb, g Hiter Colvin, 219
Sherrill, Homer, bv/f Blue Ridge Hill Billies, 110; Wade Mainer, 583; Morris Brothers, 643; Byron Parker, 675
Shield, Roy, p John Baltzell, 90; Ted Markle, 587
Shilkret, Jack, p Vernon Dalhart, 242, 245; Texas Jim Robertson, 759–60
Shilkret, Lew, o Carson Robison, 763
Shilkret, Nat, dir/p/o Vernon Dalhart, 242, 268; Frank & James McCravy, 531; A.C. (Eck) Robertson, 757; Carson Robison, 761; Alf. Taylor, 892
*Shores, Bill, f Melvin Dupree, 327; Riley Puckett, 717
Short, Cal "Sleepy," h Arizona Wranglers, 62

Short, Jimmie, g Ernest Tubb, 913
Showalter, E.F., v/f W.C. Childers, 206; Richmond Melody Boys, 748
Shreve, Danny, v/g Hackberry Ramblers, 388
*Shreve, Floyd, v/g Four Aces, 355; Hackberry Ramblers, 387–88; Leo Soileau, 854–55
Shriver, Fred, pac Blind Joe Mangum-Fred Shriber, 586
Shucks, Jake, bj Jimmy Johnson's String Band, 461
Shults, Samuel C., f/calls John Baltzell, 91
Shunatona, Chief, v/sp/tomtom Cowboy Tom's Roundup, 224
Sides, C.E., bv Southern Railroad Quartet, 860
*Sides, Connie, v/g Ernest Thompson, 902
Sides, H.Q., tv Southern Railroad Quartet, 860
Sievers, Fiddlin' Bill, sp/f Tennessee Ramblers [I], 896
Sievers, James "Mack," v/sp/bj Tennessee Ramblers [I], 896
Sigler, Moe, v/tg Jimmy Yates Groups, 976
Signorelli, Frank, p Jimmie Davis, 305
Simerly, George Simerly Trio, 834
*Simmons, Bill, v/y/g Happy Hayseeds, 397
Simmons, Charlie, bj-md Scottdale String Band, 821–22
Simmons, Hubert, bsv Dr. Smith's Champion Hoss Hair Pullers, 843
*Simmons, Matt, lv/g Posey Rorer, 813
Simmons, Willie, v Hill Brothers, 424
Sims, Harry, f Christine, 209; Red Foley, 351
Sims, James Leroy "Roy," h Arkansas Barefoot Boys, 63
Singer, Lou, vb Bob Atcher, 70
Sirillo, A., v/bj/g Bob Miller, 623
Sirinski, Koby, f Bob Atcher, 70
Sizemore, Little Jimmie, v Asher Sizemore & Little Jimmie, 836
Skeen, A.J. Buffalo Ragged Five, 142
Skiles, Dude, bj Bob Skiles Four Old Tuners, 837
Skiles, Jack, bj Bob Skiles Four Old Tuners, 837
Skiles, Mrs., p Bob Skiles Four Old Tuners, 837
Skillet, Hank, f Beverly Hill Billies, 101–03
Skookum, v/sp Cowboy Tom's Roundup, 224
Slagle, Claude, bj Grant Brothers, 377
Sloane, ——, v/g Sloane & Threadgill, 840
Slye, Leonard. see Rogers, Roy
Small, Marshall, bj Fisher Hendley, 416
Smalle, Ed, humming Vernon Dalhart, 244
Smeck, Roy, h/sg/octachorda/md/bj/g/u/jh Gene Autry, 75–77, 80; Elton Britt, 128; Smiley Burnette, 145; Dwight Butcher, 148; Chezz Chase, 202–03; Virginia Childs, 208; Vernon Dalhart, 260–61, 263, 289, 292; Dizzy Trio, 322; Kelly Harrell, 404; Adelyne Hood, 434–35; Frank Luther, 521–22; Frank & James McCravy, 534; Frank[ie] Marvin, 600, 603–05; Johnny Marvin, 607; Carson Robison, 761, 768–69, 774–77, 780, 784, 788–89; Ed (Jake) West, 945; John I. White, 949
*Smith, Arthur, f Delmore Brothers, 310; Herald Goodman, 375
*Smith, Arthur, lv/v/f/md Smith's Carolina Crackerjacks, 848
Smith, Arthur, v/f Smith's Carolina Crackerjacks, 848
Smith, Aubry, f Billy Vest, 931
Smith, Bulow, v/y/g Perry County Music Makers, 687
Smith, Byron, v Carlisle Brothers, 169; Bo Norris, 661
*Smith, Cal, v/wh/g/humming Jimmie Rodgers, 806
Smith, Charles, f Riley Puckett, 721
Smith, Clyde B., v/f Smith's Sacred Singers, 848–49
Smith, Dorothy, v/y/u Walter Smith, 847
Smith, Dr. H.H., ldr Dr. Smith's Champion Hoss Hair Pullers, 843
Smith, E.R., v/sp/g Jimmy Yates Groups, 976
Smith, Eddie, v/h/sb Denver Darling, 295–96; Lunsford Bros., 517; Hank Penny, 686; Radio Rubes, 723

Smith, Evelyn, v Carolina Gospel Singers, 171
Smith, Fay "Smitty," esg/eg Ernest Tubb, 914
Smith, Freddie, g Jimmie Rodgers, 806
Smith, Gid. see Smith, Walter "Gid"
Smith, J. Frank, lv Smith's Sacred Singers, 848–50
Smith, James H., bj/g Carson Robison, 797
Smith, Jim E., f H.M. Barnes, 94–95
Smith, Kenneth, v/g Plantation Boys, 698
Smith, Lowell E., v/p/u Dick Parman, 679
Smith, Odell, sp/f Carolina Buddies, 170; Roy Harvey, 410–11; Charlie Poole, 700; Walter Smith, 847; Virginia Dandies, 932
Smith, Olan, v/g Plantation Boys, 698
Smith, Phil, g Rodeo Trio, 798
Smith, Ralph, v/bj Smith's Carolina Crackerjacks, 848
Smith, Ralph C. "Smitty," p Shelly Lee Alley, 58–59; Ted Daffan's Texans, 240–41; Modern Mountaineers, 631; Leon Selph, 824; Sons Of Dixie, 856; Floyd Tillman, 910
Smith, Roosevelt, v/g/ah Carson Brothers-Smith, 180; Smith Brothers, 848
Smith, Shell W., f/g W.T. Narmour & S.W. Smith, 649–50; OKeh Medicine Show, 668
*Smith, Slim, v/f/g Andrews Brothers, 60
Smith, Smitty, v/sb Rex Griffin, 384
Smith, Smitty, v/y/g Sammy & Smitty, 818
Smith, Sonny, v/g Smith's Carolina Crackerjacks, 848
Smith, Spencer, bv Macedonia Quartet, 542
Smith, Thelma, v/y/g Walter Smith, 847
Smith, W.J., v Eva Quartette, 333
Smith, W.M., p Smith & Irvine, 847
*Smith, Walter "Gid," lv/v/h/v eff Carolina Buddies, 170; Lewis McDaniels, 539; Virginia Dandies, 932
Smith, William, v/g Smith Brothers, 848
Smitha, Les, f Jimmy Johnson's String Band, 461
Smithmire, W.E., bsv McDonald Quartet, 539–40
Snodgrass, Logan. see Conger, Tex
Snow, Gus, g Eddie Dean, 308
Snyder, Elmer, v Fay & The Jay Walkers, 337; Dick Parman, 679
Snyder, "Herman the Hermit," bj Stuart Hamblen, 393
Soileau, Alius, v/f Oscar [Slim] Doucet, 324; Leo Soileau, 854
*Soileau, Leo, v/f Wilfred Fruge-Leo Soileau, 360; Floyd Shreve, 834
Soldi, Andrew "Cactus," f Texas Jim Lewis, 499
Solomon, Ervin, f Solomon & Hughes, 856
Solomon, Joe, g Solomon & Hughes, 856
Sonnier, Lennis, v/g Hackberry Ramblers, 387–88
Sonnier, Moise, f Happy Fats, 395; Joe Werner, 943
Sooter, Rudy, g Jimmie Davis, 303; John (Dusty) King, 486; Tex Ritter, 750
Sorensen, Art, tb Ezra Buzzington's Rustic Revelers, 149
Sorensen, Harry, ac Ted Daffan's Texans, 240; Roy Newman, 658; Shelton Brothers, 828
Sosson, Marshall, f Bob Atcher, 70
*Spain, Irene, v/p/o Jenkins Family, 455–57
Spain, Mary Lee, v Jenkins Family, 455–56
Spanier, Muggsy, c Whitey McPherson, 579
Spann, L.S., tv Missouri Pacific Lines Booster Quartet, 629
Sparkman, Rena, v Sparkman Trio, 861
Sparkman, Ruth, v Sparkman Trio, 861
Sparks, Zelpha, v/f/g Ovie Stewart & Zelpha Sparks, 869
Sparrow, John, tv/g Pope's Arkansas Mountaineers, 701
Spencer, Samuel, v Hugh Gibbs String Band, 368
Spencer, Tim, v Sons Of The Pioneers, 857
Spivey, Douglas, v/y/g Pine Ridge Boys, 697
Spivey, Ina Mae, v Jimmy Long, 511
Spriggins, Ace, g Stuart Hamblen, 393
Spurgeon, Glen, v/y/g Nicholson's Players, 659

Stafford, Harold, sp WLS Radio Artists, 969
Stagner, "Smoky Mountain" Glenn, v/g Uncle Dave Macon, 578
Staigers, Del, t/c Vernon Dalhart, 251–55; Carson Robison, 796
Stalsby, Dot, v Stalsby Family, 863
Stalsby, Jackie, v Stalsby Family, 863
Stalsby, Sammy, v/g Rambling Rangers, 725; Stalsby Family, 863
Stamps, Frank, bsv Stamps Quartet, 863–65
Stamps, Mrs. Frank, v/p Stamps Quartet, 865
*Stamps, V.O., v Stamps Quartet, 864–65
Standlee, Clarence, g Leon Selph, 823
Standlee, Herman, eg Leon Selph, 823–24
Standlee, J.D., esg Dickie McBride, 526; Modern Mountaineers, 631; Texas Wanderers, 900; Village Boys, 931–32
*Stanley, Fred, v/g Bascom Lamar Lunsford, 517; Stanley & Higgins, 866
Stanley, R.M. (Rob), v/f Roba Stanley, 866
Stanton, Floyd, p John A. McDermott, 539
Stapleton, Mitchell, v/h/sg/g Mason Stapleton, 867
Stark, Harry, v/bj/humming Hoke Rice, 746; Lowe Stokes, 871
Statham, Jack, ac Eddie Dean, 308
Staton, Bill, ac Roy Newman, 657–58
Steagall, Alfred, g Kelly Harrell, 403–04
Steele, Robert, md Taylor's Kentucky Boys, 895
Steeley, A.L. "Red," f Red Headed Fiddler[s], 732
Steeley, Mildred, g Red Headed Fiddler[s], 732
Stephens, George P., v Steve & His Hot Shots, 868
Stephens, Haig, sb Jimmie Davis, 305
Stephens, J.D., bj/g Duel Frady, 358
Stephens, Robert, bj Clayton McMichen, 565
Stephens, Robert, Jr., cl Clayton McMichen, 565
Stern, Hank, tu/sb Johnny Bond, 117; Vernon Dalhart, 292
Stewart, ——, v Stewart & Dillman, 869
Stewart, Carl, v/f/sb Lunsford Bros., 517; Hank Penny, 685–86
Stewart, Danny, sg Whitey McPherson, 579
Stewart, Dixon. see "Baby Ray"
Stewart, Ed, v/tg/g Carl Boling, 116
Stewart, Lanier, v Lonesome Singer, 510
Stidman, W.R., v Avoca Quartette, 87
Stier, Cliff, sb Dixieland Swingsters, 320
Stiles, Sparky, sb Bob Skyles, 838
*Stockard, Ocie, v/f/tg/bj Milton Brown, 136–38; Jimmie Davis, 302; Hi-Flyers, 418
Stockton, Oscar, f Dixie Ramblers [III], 319
Stokes, Ernest, v/bj/g/spoons Mustard & Gravy, 647
Stokes, Leonard, v/md/g/oc Frank Luther, 518–25; J.E. Mainer's Mountaineers, 582; Byron Parker, 675; Carson Robison, 790–91
*Stokes, Lowe, hv/sp/f/o/g Claude Davis, 297; John Dilleshaw, 317–18; Oscar Ford, 352; Georgia Organ Grinders, 366; Ted Hawkins, 413; Bert Layne, 493; Clayton McMichen, 565–70; Smoky Mountain Ramblers, 852; Swamp Rooters, 883; Arthur Tanner, 886; Gid Tanner, 889–91
Stone, Cliffie, v/sb Tex Ritter, 751
Stone, M.L. "Rocky," f Tex Ritter, 750
Stone, Oscar, f/calls Dr. Humphrey Bate, 97
Stoneman, Eddie, v/bj Ernest V. Stoneman, 878
*Stoneman, Ernest V., v/sp/bj/g/ah Uncle Eck Dunford, 325–26; Frank Jenkins, 455; Sweet Brothers, 884; Fields Ward, 939
*Stoneman, George, v/bj/g Uncle Eck Dunford, 326; Ernest V. Stoneman, 876

Stoneman, Hattie, v/f/md/bj Uncle Eck Dunford, 325–26; Ernest V. Stoneman, 873, 875–78
Stout, Joe, v/g Lone Star Cowboys, 509
Stover, Everett, v/t Bob Wills, 961–65
Streets, Curtis, v Rambling Rangers, 725
Strickland, William A. "Flip," v/md Warren Caplinger, 157
Strickler, Benny, t Bob Wills, 966
Stricklin, Alton Meeks "Al," p Bob Wills, 960–66
Stripling, Charles, v/f Stripling Brothers, 879
Stripling, Chick, f Uncle Ned, 919
Stripling, Gene "Uncle Ned," sb Uncle Ned, 919
Stripling, Ira, v/g Stripling Brothers, 879
Stroud, M.B., p Vaughan Quartet, 928
Stubb, Lloyd "Stubby," sb Earl & Willie Phelps, 689
Stubbs, Mina, p Patrick (Dak) Pellerin, 684
Stutes, Bradley "Sleepy," v/g Happy Fats, 396
Stutes, Hector, f Dixie Ramblers [II], 319
Sullivan, Don, v/y/wh/g Ozark Boys, 672
Sullivan, Gene, v/lg/g Leon Chappelear, 201; Roy Newman, 657–58; Shelton Brothers, 828; Wiley Walker & Gene Sullivan, 935–36
Summerall, Vol, tv/g Laurel Firemen's Quartet, 491
Summers, Blackie, f Texas Jim Robertson, 759
Summers, Marshall, g Moatsville String Ticklers, 630
Summey, Clell, v/sg Roy Acuff, 48–49
Summey, Reid, tv/y/sp/sg/g Three Tobacco Tags, 907–09
Sumrall, Chealous, bv Coats Sacred Quartette, 216
Sutton, Raymond, v/g Thurston Sutton & Raymond Sutton, 882
Swaim, Loyce (Bud) "Tex," h/g Jimmie Davis, 301–05; Charles Mitchell & His Orchestra, 629–30
Swanson, Carl, tv/y/md Jake & Carl, 453
Sweet, Earl, v/bj Ernest V. Stoneman, 877; Sweet Brothers, 884
Sweet, Herbert, v/f Ernest V. Stoneman, 877; Sweet Brothers, 884
Sykes, Warren, h/spoons Rice Brothers' Gang, 746
Symons, Bob[by], v/esg/eg Al Dexter, 314; Clay Long, 510; Nite Owls, 659–61

Taggart, John, sb Woodhull's Old Time Masters, 971
Tallent, Johnnie, v Ted Hawkins, 413
Talton, Luke, f Scottdale String Band, 822
*Tanner, Arthur, v/bj/bj-md/tbj/g Fate Norris, 661; Riley Puckett, 719; Lowe Stokes, 870–71
Tanner, Elmo, v Charlie Craver, 231; Buell Kazee, 473
*Tanner, Gid, lv/hv/sp/f/bj/jh/v eff Ted Hawkins, 413; Home Town Boys, 433; Clayton McMichen, 566, 568–70; Fate Norris, 661; Riley Puckett, 715–16, 720; Arthur Tanner, 885–86
Tanner, Gordon, f/md Ted Hawkins, 413; Riley Puckett, 720; Gid Tanner, 891
Tanner, Tom, v/g Hilltoppers, 427
Tanton, F.M., tv Avondale Mills Quartet, 87
Tapley, F.G., tv Avondale Mills Quartet, 87
*Tarlton, Jimmie, v/y/sp/wh/sg/humming Tom Darby & Jimmie Tarlton, 293–95
Taylor, Alma, v Happy Valley Family, 397; Jo & Alma, 458
Taylor, Clavie, v Taylor-Griggs Louisiana Melody Makers, 893
Taylor, David, bv Alf. Taylor, 892
Taylor, Dick, f Taylor, Moore & Burnett, 894
Taylor, Earl, g Four Pickled Peppers, 356
Taylor, F.R., f Taylor-Griggs Louisiana Melody Makers, 893–94
Taylor, Harty, v/y/g Cumberland Ridge Runners, 239; Jossie Ellers, 331; Red Foley, 350–51; Doc Hopkins, 441; Karl & Harty, 470–71; Linda Parker, 678
Taylor, Homer, v Taylor Trio, 894

Taylor, Mrs. Homer, v Taylor Trio, 894
Taylor, Jack, v/sp/g/sb Gene Autry, 80–81; Happy Valley Family, 397; Jo & Alma, 458; Lulu Belle & Scotty, 516; Bo Miller, 624–25; Patsy Montana, 634–36; Prairie Ramblers, 704–13
Taylor, Jo, v Happy Valley Family, 397; Jo & Alma, 458
Taylor, Kenny, g Jimmy Hart, 406
Taylor, Mack, v/g Walker's Corbin Ramblers, 936–37
Taylor, Marvin, v/y/g Pine Ridge Boys, 697
Taylor, Nat, tv Alf. Taylor, 892
Taylor, T.A., v Clifford (C.S.) Wagner, 933
Teasley, Harold M., sg Price-Prosser-Teasley, 714
Terhune, Max, sp/v eff Ezra Buzzington's Rustic Revelers, 149–50
Terrel, Flanner, bj/u/sw/flexatone Yellow Jackets [I], 976
Terry, Lucy, p Roy Harvey, 410; Charlie Poole, 699–700
Terwilliger, Ransom, f Woodhull's Old Time Masters, 971
*Teter, Jack, v/g John McGhee & Frank Welling, 557
Tew, Louise, v Norwood Tew, 898–99
*Tew, Norwood, v/y/g Wade Mainer, 583
Thall, George "Bill/Willie," v/cl/s/as/sb Sally Foster, 355; Massey Family, 611; Prairie Ramblers, 705–12; Travelers, 912
Thames, Joe, v/tbj Cliff Bruner, 139–40; Buddy Jones, 465; Leon Selph, 824; Texas Wanderers, 900
Thames, Johnny, v/bj/tbj Bill Boyd, 122; Cliff Bruner, 140; Modern Mountaineers, 630–31; Texas Wanderers, 900–901
Thibodeaux, Ambrose, f Happy Fats, 396
Thibodeaux, Bobby, p Four Aces, 355
Thibodeaux, Erby, v/f Thibodeaux Boys, 901
Thibodeaux, Robert, p Happy Fats, 395
Thibodeaux, T.C., v/g Thibodeaux Boys, 901
Thiele, Ed/Ted, f Vernon Dalhart, 247–48, 250
Thomas, C.C., bj Jess Young, 979
Thomas, Dick, g Dwight Butcher, 148
Thomas, Etha K., p R.C. Garner, 363
Thomas, Gilbert, v/g John Busby & Gilbert Thomas, 147
Thomas, Henry, f Claude Davis, 298; Jim King, 486
Thomas, J.E., tv Alcoa Quartet, 53
Thomas, J.H., tv Alcoa Quartet, 53
Thomas, Joe Grady, sb Bill Nettles, 654
Thomas, Ralph, p Johnny Bond, 117
Thomason, Jimmy, v/f/md/g Doug Bine, 104; Dixie Ramblers [IV], 319; Slim Harbert, 398; Modern Mountaineers, 630–31; Shelton Brothers, 830; Sunshine Boys, 881–82
Thomasson, John, f Blue Ridge Highballers, 110
Thompson, ——, bsv Happy Four, 396
Thompson, ——, v Chumbler Family, 212
Thompson, A.P., v/sp/g Blue Ridge Sacred Singers, 112; Red Fox Chasers, 730–31
Thompson, Donald, bj Carolina Night Hawks, 172
*Thompson, Ernest [E.], v/h/k/bj/g Boyden Carpenter, 174; Connie Sides, 834
Thompson, Guy "Cotton," v/f Dave Edwards, 330; Johnny Lee Wills, 967
Thornhill, Jack, v/sb Tex Ritter, 750
*Thrasher, Rev. M.L., bsv Smith's Sacred Singers, 848–49
Threadgill, ——, v/g Sloane & Threadgill, 840
Tierney, Lewis E. "Louis," f/s/ts Dave Edwards, 330; Bob Wills, 964–66
Tierney, Mancel, v/p Bob Dunn's Vagabonds, 326–27; Dave Edwards, 330; Dickie McBride, 526; Leon Selph, 824; Village Boys, 932
*Tillman, Charlie D., v Jewell Tillman Burns & Charlie D. Tillman, 145
Tillman, Elizabeth, p Jewell Tillman Burns & Charlie D. Tillman, 145
*Tillman, Floyd, v/eg Leon Selph, 823–24; Village Boys, 931

Tilson, Jack, v Floyd Thompson, 903
Timberlake, George, p Jimmie Revard, 743; Tune Wranglers, 915
Tinnon, Ben, f Grinnell Giggers, 384
Todd, Clarence, v/f/bj/g Dixie Reelers, 319; J.E. Mainer's Mountaineers, 581
Todd, Mazy, f McGee Brothers, 552; Uncle Dave Macon, 575–76
Tomlin, Pinky, v Texas Jim Lewis, 499
Tomlins, Eugene, d Bob Wills, 965–66
Touchet, Maxie, d Alley Boys Of Abbeville, 59
Touchstone, James D., v/sp/h/g Nelstone's Hawaiians, 653
Townsend, Respers, v/y/h/sg/k/md/g Fleming & Townsend, 346–48
Trappe, Fran, ac Charlie Bowman, 121; Bowman Sisters, 121
Travers, Fred Tony, pac John (Dusty) King, 486
Traxler, Gene, sb Elton Britt, 130; Texas Jim Robertson, 759–60
Traylor, Forest, p Jack Pickell, 694
Treadway, Al, v/u Jimmy Yates Groups, 975–76
Treat, Homer, bj Ashley's Melody Makers, 68
Treme, John L. "Tommy," esg Nolan Bush, 147
Trietsch, Ken, lv/g/bb Ezra Buzzington's Rustic Revelers, 149–50; Hoosier Hot Shots, 435–39
Trietsch, Paul "Hezzie," v/motor horn/k/perc/jh/wb/sw/j Ezra Buzzington's Rustic Revelers, 149; Hoosier Hot Shots, 435–39
Tronson, Rube, f Tommy Dandurand, 292–93
Trotter, Pat, f/emd Bill Boyd, 124; Sons Of The West, 859
True, Jack, v/sb Al Dexter, 314; Clay Long, 510; Nite Owls, 659–61
*Tubb, Ernest, v/y/g Mrs. Jimmie Rodgers, 809
Tucker, ——, bj/g Wyzee Hamilton, 393
Tucker, Dan, v Lowe Stokes, 871
Tucker, Houston, md Madisonville String Band, 580
Tucker, Hubert, g Luke Highnight, 422
Tucker, Luke, v/sb Smith's Carolina Crackerjacks, 848
Tucker, Noah, sb Madisonville String Band, 580
Tudor, Oliver E. (Eddie), eg/g Gene Autry, 84–86; Ernest Tubb, 914
Turner, Charlie, v/sp Charles S. Brook & Charlie Turner, 131
Turner, Forrest A., md Jack Cawley's Oklahoma Ridge Runners, 199; Leonard C. Fulwider, 361
Tuttle, Wesley, sb Ernest Tubb, 914
Tweedy, Charles W., p Tweedy Brothers, 917–18
Tweedy, Harry, f Tweedy Brothers, 917–18
Tyler, Don, v/g Nolan Bush, 147; Jubileers, 468
Tyler, Jesse, p Jubileers, 468

Uncle Ezra, v Hoosier Hot Shots, 436
Underwood, Charles, v/y/g E.E. Hack String Band, 386
Underwood, Loyal "Sheriff," sp Arizona Wranglers, 62
Underwood, Marion, v/bj Byrd Moore, 638; Taylor's Kentucky Boys, 894–95
Underwood, Oliver "Sock," v/g Cliff Bruner, 141; Buddy Jones, 466; Bill Mounce, 645
Upson, Dean, v Vagabonds, 921
Uttinger, George, f Ross Rhythm Rascals, 814; Smoky Wood, 971

Vaden, H.N. "Tommy," ldr/f Jimmie Rodgers, 809
Valentine, Buddy, sb New Dixie Demons, 655
Vance, Bill, sb Bob Atcher, 69–70
Vance, Dudley, f Vance's Tennessee Breakdowners, 922
Vance, Sam, g Vance's Tennessee Breakdowners, 922
Vanvink, Raney, g Homer Christopher, 209
Vass, Emily, v Vass Family, 922
Vass, Frank, v Vass Family, 922

Vass, Louisa, v Vass Family, 922
Vass, Sally, v Vass Family, 922
Vass, Virginia, v/g Vass Family, 922
Vaughan, Cooney, p Madden Community Band, 580
Vaughan, G. Kiefer, tv/bv Vaughan Quartet, 923–29
*Vaughn, Cliff[ord], v/g Three Stripped Gears, 907
Veach, Rachel, v/bj Roy Acuff, 50
Velazco, Emil, p-o Harry Smith, 843
Venuti, Joe, f Johnny Marvin, 606
Vermillion, Myrtle, v/ah Dykes' Magic City Trio, 328
Vest, Bob, v/g Billy Vest, 931
Vest, L. Vernal, v/u Robert Hoke & Vernal West, 431; Fred Pendleton, 685
Vincent, Willie, v/sg/g/sb Dixie Ramblers [II], 319; Happy Fats, 396
Vitovsky, Bill, esg Leaford Hall, 390; Buddy Jones, 466
Vodola, Tom, f Arthur Fields & Fred Hall, 340–44
Vogt, ——— Pioneer Trio, 698
Voss, Lester J., sb Shelly Lee Alley, 58

*Wade, George, v/y/sp/md Three Tobacco Tags, 907–08
Waggoner, Bruce, v Melton & Waggoner, 615; Westbrook Conservatory Entertainers, 947
Waggoner, Paul, g Light Crust Doughboys, 506
Wakefield, Bill, v/g Lake Howard, 445
*Wakely, Jimmy, v/g/sb Johnny Bond, 116–17; Jimmie Davis, 305; Johnny Marvin, 607; Dick Reinhart, 739; Roy Rogers, 812; Ella Sutton, 882
Walbert, W.B., bv Vaughan Quartet, 927–28
Waldo, Earl, v Texas Jim Robertson, 759–60
Walker, A.L., g Buell Kazee, 473
Walker, Albert, v/tg Walker's Corbin Ramblers, 936–37
*Walker, Cindy, v Texas Jim Lewis, 499
Walker, Frank, v/sp/h Clayton McMichen, 569; Wade Mainer, 584; Gid Tanner, 887
Walker, Harry, v Southern Moonshiners, 860
Walker, Jimmy, v/g Lone Star Cowboys, 509
Walker, John V., f/md Alex Hood, 435; Walker's Corbin Ramblers, 936
Walker, Lawrence, v/f/ac Alleman & Walker, 54; Walker Brothers, 936
*Walker, Wiley, v/f Lew Childre, 207
Wallace, Dave, tbj Buddy Jones, 466
Wallace, H.D., bv Peck's Male Quartette, 683
Wallace, Jerry, md/bj/g Clayton McMichen, 572–73; Asa Martin, 589
Walls, Ted, sb Dave Hughs, 446; Bob Skyles, 838
Walsh, Dock, v/sp/bj Carolina Tar Heels, 173–74; Haywood County Ramblers, 414; Pine Mountain Boys, 697
Walsh, Eugene Dan, v/g Texas Jim Lewis, 499–500
Walter, Draper, f Walter Family, 938
Walter, Mary, p Walter Family, 938
Walton, Staley, g Dr. Humphrey Bate, 97
Wamble, David "Pee Wee," v/t/c/p/sb Gene Steele, 867; Swift Jewel Cowboys, 884–85
*Ward, Albert E., v/f L.O. Birkhead & R.M. Lane, 106
*Ward, Fields, v/g Crockett Ward, 939
Ward, Franklin, bj Jimmie Wilson's Catfish String Band, 968
Ward, Madeline Carlyle Brooks & Madeline Ward, 132
Ward, Melgie, v/sp/f South Georgia Highballers, 860
Ward, Otto "Gabe," lv/v/cl/bscl Ezra Buzzington's Rustic Revelers, 149; Hoosier Hot Shots, 435–39
Ward, Reginald "Reggie," sb Bill Nettles, 654; Rice Brothers' Gang, 747
Ward, Sampson, bj Crockett Ward, 939; Fields Ward, 939
Ward, Vernon, ah Crockett Ward, 939
Ward, Virgi, f Harry "Mac" McClintock, 528
*Ward, Wade, v/bj/v eff Buck Mt. Band, 141

Ward, Wizener, md/g A.E. Ward, 938
Wardrep, Bob, bsv Alf. Taylor, 892
Ware, Thurman, f Madden Community Band, 580
Warley, Malcolm, v/g Smyth County Ramblers, 852
Warner, Mrs. A.C., bj White Mountain Orchestra, 951
Warren, Doc, p Cliff Bruner, 139–40
Warren, Elmer, f/k Dick Hartman's Tennessee Ramblers, 408–09
Warren, Oliver, lv/g Rambling Rangers, 725
Watkins, Charlie Watkins Band, 940
Watkins, Everett "Shorty," v/g Blue Ridge Hill Billies, 110
Watkins, Tom Watkins Band, 940
Watson, El, h/bones Johnson Brothers, 463
Watson, Wayne, sb Roy Hall, 391
Watts, Clyde, g Phil Reeve & Ernest Moody, 735
Watts, Jake, lv/y/h/g Jake & Carl, 453; Buck Nation, 650–51; Ozark Boys, 672; Tex Ritter, 750; Ray Whitley, 952
Way, J.C., esg Bill Boyd, 122; Modern Mountaineers, 630; Smoky Wood, 971
Weaver, Liston, sb Leaford Hall, 390
Weaver, Vance, v/bj Weaver Brothers, 942
Weaver, Wiley, v/g Weaver Brothers, 942
Webb, Ed, g Bill Shepherd, 830
Webber, Buddy, v/g/sb Aaron Campbell's Mountaineers, 154; Irene Sanders, 819
Weems, Dick, f Weems String Band, 942
Weems, Frank, f Weems String Band, 942
Weems, Harold, g W.A. Lindsay, 507
Weems, Jesse, vc Weems String Band, 942
Weiner, N., t Frank[ie] Marvin, 600
Welling, Frank, lv/v/sp/wh/sg/g/u Richard Cox, 229; John McGhee & Frank Welling, 553–63; David Miller, 626; Red Brush Rowdies, 730; West Virginia Mountaineers, 946
Welling, Thelma, v John McGhee & Frank Welling, 555, 561
Wellington, Larry, ac/p Massey Family, 608–13
Wellman, Jack, sp/g Red Gay & Jack Wellman, 364
Wells, ———, v Bingham & Wells, 104
Wells, Arthur, bj Blue Ridge Highballers, 109; Luther B. Clarke, 214
Wells, Charlie. see Robison, Carson
Wells, Clifford, tbj W. Lee O'Daniel, 665
Wells, J.L., bv Alcoa Quartet, 53
Wells, Willie, v/g/sb Hi-Flyers, 418–19
Welsh, ———, v/sp Honeyboy & Sassafras[s], 433
Wenzel, Art, ac Johnny Bond, 117; Sally Foster, 355
Werner, Mrs. Joe, v Joe Werner, 943
*Werner, Joe, v/wh/h/g Hackberry Ramblers, 387; Thibodeaux Boys, 901
Wesbrooks, Willie "Cousin Wilbur," bsv/sp/sb Bill Monroe, 631–32
West, Billy, v West Brothers Trio, 946
West, David, v West Brothers Trio, 946
West, Ed, v/g Airport Boys, 52
West, Leo, v/g Tennessee Hill Billy, 896
West, Lloyd, v/sb Airport Boys, 52
West, Philip, v West Brothers Trio, 946
West, Ruth, v/g Tennessee Hill Billy, 896
Westbrook, Bill, sb Arthur Smith, 842
Westbrook, (Walter) John, v/sg/humming Jimmie Rodgers, 800–801; Westbrook Conservatory Entertainers, 946–47
Westbrook, Mrs. John, v/g/humming Westbrook Conservatory Entertainers, 946–47
Westley, Ozzie, g Christine, 209; Red Foley, 351
*Weston, Don, v/y/sg/g Asa Martin, 593
Weston, Roy, v/g Tom & Roy, 911
Whalin, June, hv/g W. Lee O'Daniel, 665
Whalin, Kermit, esg/sb W. Lee O'Daniel, 666; Universal Cowboys, 919

Whatley, Harold, v/sg Rambling Rangers, 725; Stalsby Family, 863
Wheeler, Gordon K. "Buck," sb Adolph Hofner, 430–31; Jimmie Revard, 743
Wheeler, J.E., tv Stamps Quartet, 864
Wheeler, Ms. ——, av Smith's Sacred Singers, 850
Wheeler, Palmer, tv Stamps Quartet, 863–64
Wheeler, Ray, bv Stamps Quartet, 864
Wheeler, Roy, tv Stamps Quartet, 863–64
*White, Clyde G., v/k W.C. Childers, 205–06
*White, Don, v/f/esg Fred Kirby, 486–87
White, Jimmy, v/g Bob Palmer & Jimmy White, 673
*White, John I., v/sp Adelyne Hood, 434
White, Ruth, v/sb Jimmie Davis, 300
Whitehead, Millard, v/g Ridgel's Fountain Citians, 748–49
Whitehead, Red, h Dutch Coleman, 217
Whiting, W. Fred, sb Gene Autry, 85–87; Al Dexter, 315; Dick Reinhart, 739; Jimmy Wakely, 934
Whitley, Edward (Eddie), v/p Jimmie Revard, 742; Tune Wranglers, 914–16
Whitley, Olan "Smiley," esg Adolph Hofner, 430
*Whitley, Ray, v/y/g Ken Card, 158; Odis Elder, 331; Frank Luther, 521–22; Buck Nation, 650–51
Whitlow, Roscoe, sg Sons Of Acadians, 856
Whitney, Gail, v Bill Boyd, 123
Whittaker, Clyde, g Alex Hood, 435
Whitten, Mike, g Lowe Stokes, 870
*Whitter, Henry, v/sp/h/g/v eff G.B. Grayson & Henry Whitter, 380–81; Kelly Harrell, 403; Fisher Hendley, 416; Roba Stanley, 866
Whitworth, ——, v Andrew Jenkins, 455
Whitworth, Byron, p Smith's Sacred Singers, 851
Wiggins, Willie Sievers, sp/g Tennessee Ramblers [I], 896
*Wikel, Miller, v/f/g John McGhee & Frank Welling, 555; Red Brush Rowdies, 730
Wilder, Uncle John, f Plymouth Vermont Old Time Barn Dance Orch., 698
Wilhelm, Frank, v/tu/ac/vb Bob Skyles, 839
Wilkerson, Holland, v Bertha Hewlett, 418
Wilkins, John T., tv Hendersonville Quartet, 416
Willard, ——, v John D. Foster, 355
Willard, Bill, bj Fiddlin' John Carson, 179
Williams, Arthur, tv Abernathy Quartet, 47
Williams, Daniel H., f East Texas Serenaders, 329; Honeyboy & Sassafras[s], 433
Williams, Frank E. "Dad," f H.M. Barnes, 94–95
*Williams, George, v/g G.C. Osborne, 670
Williams, J. Harrell "Curl[e]y," v/g/sb Jimmie Revard, 742–43; Tune Wranglers, 914–15
Williams, J. S. (Jess), g Bill Boyd, 124; Sons Of The West, 859
Williams, Johnny, f Adolph Hofner, 430
Williams, Ray, g Swing Billies, 885
Williams, Roger, sp Lowe Stokes, 870
Williams, Spencer, p Phil Pavey, 682
Williams, Velma, sb Roy Acuff, 50–51
Williamson, Aaron, g Three Williamsons, 909
Williamson, Arnold, f Williamson Brothers & Curry, 960
Williamson, Duck, v/g Three Williamsons, 909
Williamson, Ervin, g Williamson Brothers & Curry, 960
Williamson, Kitty "Texas Rose," v/y/f W. Lee O'Daniel, 666; Three Williamsons, 909
Willingham, Foy, esg Lew Preston, 713; Wiley Walker & Gene Sullivan, 936
Wills, Charlie, v Bob Wills, 966
*Wills, James Robert "Bob," v/sp/f/v eff Light Crust Doughboys, 500

*Wills, Johnny Lee, v/tbj/g Bob Wills, 960–64
Wills, Luther Jay "Luke," sb Johnny Lee Wills, 967
Willson, Parker, bv/bsv/sp/v eff Light Crust Doughboys, 504–07
Wilson, C.G., tv Vaughan Quartet, 928–29
Wilson, Cecil "Tex," f Hi Neighbor Boys, 420
Wilson, Clyde, sb Tex Ritter, 750
Wilson, Doyne "Don," v/y/wh/sg/esg/humming Hilltoppers, 427; Tom & Don, 911
*Wilson, Frank, v/sp/sg/g H.M. Barnes, 94–95; Charlie Bowman, 120; Hill Billies, 424; Jack Reedy, 734; Wilmer Watts, 941
Wilson, Fred, v Otto Gray, 378–79
Wilson, Happy, g Tex Dunn, 327
Wilson, Lonnie, g/sb Roy Acuff, 49–51
Wimberly, Wallace K., tbj Dixie Ramblers [III], 319
Wines, Woodrow, g Roy Rogers, 812
Wirges, William F. "Bill," dir/p/o Blue Ridge Gospel Singers, 109; Vernon Dalhart, 266, 270; Dixieland Four, 320; Kanawha Singers, 469; Frank Luther, 518; Jack Major, 586; Old Southern Sacred Singers, 669; Carson Robison, 789, 797
Wise, Bee, bj Clarence Greene, 382
Wise, C.J., bj-md Wise String Orchestra, 969
Wise, George, g Wise String Orchestra, 969
Wise, Newman, f Wise String Orchestra, 969
Wise, Omer, Sr., g Clarence Greene, 382
Wiseman, Chuck, f/g Walter Hurdt, 448; Leroy [Slim] Johnson, 461–62
Wiseman, Lulu Belle. see Lulu Belle
*Wiseman, Scott, v/y/wh/h/bj/g Lulu Belle & Scotty, 515–16; Prairie Ramblers, 708
Wiseman, Smoky, v/f/g Walter Hurdt, 448; Leroy [Slim] Johnson, 461–62
Wisrock, ——, md Red Headed Fiddler[s], 732
Wisrock, Albert, g Red Headed Fiddler[s], 732
Wofford, Ms., p Copperhill Male Quartet, 222
Wofford, Woodrow Wilson "Slim," v Hi Neighbor Boys, 420
Wolf[e], Louis Gibson String Trio, 369
Wolfe, Kenneth "Pappy," tv/traps/wb/sw/eff Dick Hartman's Tennessee Ramblers, 407–09
Wolverton, Jim, bsv/bj Leake County Revelers, 494–95
Womble, ——, v/y Carolina Buddys, 170
Wong, Prince, f/sg Dwight Butcher, 148
*Wood, John B. "Smoky," v/p/g Bill Boyd, 122; Modern Mountaineers, 630
Wood, Tommy, g Woodhull's Old Time Masters, 971
Wood, Woodrow "Woodie," cl/as Bob Wills, 966
Woodal, Hershel, sb Cliff Bruner, 141; Jimmie Davis, 301–05; Buddy Jones, 464, 466; Charles Mitchell & His Orchestra, 629–30
Woodall, Dennis, sg Shorty McCoy, 531
Woodall, Waite "Chief," f Harry "Mac" McClintock, 529
Woodard, Lynn, g Richard D. Burnett, 144
Wooden, Steve, v/y/g Hi-Flyers, 419; Zeke Williams, 959
Woodhull, Floyd, v/ac/o/bells Woodhull's Old Time Masters, 971
Woodhull, Herb, bj Woodhull's Old Time Masters, 971
Woodhull, John, g Woodhull's Old Time Masters, 971
Woodie, William Lawton, hv/h Ephraim Woodie, 971
*Woodlieff, Norman, hv/g Carolina Buddies, 170; Four Pickled Peppers, 356; Charlie Poole, 698; Walter Smith, 846; Virginia Dandies, 932
Woods, ——, bj McMichen's Harmony Boys, 573
Woods, Francis, v/g Poplin-Woods Tennessee String Band, 701

Woods, Jack, md/v eff Poplin-Woods Tennessee String Band, 701
Woods, Louise, p Poplin-Woods Tennessee String Band, 701
Woods, Oscar, v/sp/g Jimmie Davis, 299–300
Woods, Pete, bj Ted Gossett's Band, 376; Tommy Whitmer's Band, 953
Woods, Vera, v Dick Reinhart, 739
Woody, Buddy, ac Dixie Ramblers [IV], 319
Woolbright, Mack, v/g Charlie Parker, 676
Wooten, Art, bv/sp/f Bill Monroe, 631–32
Workman, Dan Gibson String Trio, 369
Worsham, R.E., v Moody Bible Sacred Harp Singers, 637; North Georgia Four, 663
Wray, Pete, v/g Texas Jim Lewis, 499–500
Wright, Asa "Ace," f/g Harry "Mac" McClintock, 528–29; Rowdy Wright, 974
Wright, Babe, p Light Crust Doughboys, 506
*Wright, Cecil "Rowdy," g Harry "Mac" McClintock, 529
Wright, Earl, v/g George Edgin, 330
Wright, Jasper "Jake," v/g Lew Preston, 713
*Wright, Lloyd, v/sg/g Harry Hillard, 425; Hoosier Hawaiians, 435
Wright, Vera, v Rowdy Wright, 974

Wyatt, Howard, v/bj/bj-md Roane County Ramblers, 751; Wyatt & Brandon, 974
Wyble, Jimmy, eg Bill Mounce, 645
Wynn, Wm. F., h/g Harry Reed & Wm. F. Wynn, 733
Wyrick, Arthur, g Blind Alfred Reed, 733

Yandell, M.L., v V.O. Stamps-M.L. Yandell, 863
*Yates, Eugene, v/g Blalock & Yates, 108
*Yates, Ira, v/g Blalock & Yates, 108
York, George, v/g York Brothers, 977–78
York, Leslie, v/eg York Brothers, 977–78
York, Mrs. N.R., sv Friendship Four, 360
Young, Alvin, g Jess Young, 978–79
Young, Gilbert, sg Claude Casey, 197
Young, Preston, v/g Buster Carter & Preston Young, 180
Young, Red, md Jimmie Rodgers, 806
Young, T.S., tv/md John D. Foster, 355
Young, Willie, g Taylor's Kentucky Boys, 894–95
Youngblood, Byron "Barney," sb Jimmy Hart, 406; Port Arthur Jubileers, 701

Zinkan, Joe, sb Delmore Brothers, 311
Zunker, Emil, ac Tune Wranglers, 915

Index to Titles

This index includes all titles listed in the discography, except title variants that appear only in session notes. References are to artist headings (sometimes, for reasons of space, in shortened form) and page numbers.

Alphabetization is "word by word" ("nothing before something") so that *I Would If I Could* comes before *Ice Man Blues* and *Ain't I Right?* before *Ain't It A Shame*. Hyphens and apostrophes are ignored, so that *I'd Settle Down For You* comes before *Ida Red* and *Katy On Time* before *Katy-Did Waltz*.

Medleys of songs have been broken up and the individual titles indexed. Thus the medley (a) *Darling Nellie Gray*, (b) *Oh! Susannah*, (c) *Will The Angels Play Their Harps For Me* creates three entries. If the medley has its own title, that too is indexed: thus *Carson Robison Selection (Continued) (Open Up Dem Pearly Gates; Climbing Up De Golden Stairs; The Old Rugged Cross)* creates entries for the three titles in the medley and a further entry for *Carson Robison Selection (Continued)*.

Variant forms of a title are, in general, indexed separately, but minor variations in punctuation and spelling have been merged into single entries, usually for the most common form of the title. It must be emphasized that this is an index of titles, not of tunes. A tune that was given different titles by different artists or record labels will be indexed under all those titles. Conversely, different tunes that share a single title will be indexed together under that title.

$10,000 Reward For The Chicken (That Roosts Too High For me) R.L. Raines, 724
11 More Months And 10 More Days Part 2 Frank Dudgeon, 324
11:99 Blues Duke Clark, 213
1199 Blues Duke Clark, 213
12th Street Blues Melvin Dupree, 327
12th Street Rag Texas Jim Lewis, 499; Pink Lindsey, 507; Roy Newman, 657
13 More Steps Frank[ie] Marvin, 604
13 Years In Kilbie Prison Tom Darby & Jimmie Tarlton, 295
15 Miles From Birmingham Delmore Brothers, 311
18 Months, Little Darlin' Bill Mounce, 645
1930 Drought Bob Miller, 620
1931 Depression Blues Three Stripped Gears, 907
1936 Floods [The] Red Foley, 351
1936 Tornado Elton Britt, 129
1942 Turkey In The Straw Johnny Bond, 117; Denver Darling, 296; Carson Robison, 797
1982 Blues Jimmie Davis, 300
30 Minutes Behind The Time Duke Clark, 213
31st Street Blues Leon Chappelear, 201
4, 6, 7 Hill Billies, 424
4000 Years Ago Otto Gray, 380
41 Days In Jail William H. Powell, 703
99 Years George Edgin, 330; Harry Hillard, 425; Vagabonds, 921; Lloyd Wright, 973
99 Years—Part 1, 2 Dick Robertson, 758
99 Years (Still Got 99) Carson Robison, 791
99 Years Blues Jess Hillard, 426

Abandoned Waltz [The] Bartmon Montet-Joswell Dupuis, 637
Abbeville Jolly Boys Of Lafayette, 464
Abbeville Breakdown Alley Boys Of Abbeville, 59
ABC Of Religion Fern Harris, 404
Abdul Abubul Amir Duke Clark, 213
Abe's Waltz Amedie Ardoin, 61
Abide With Me Buice Brothers, 142; Friendship Four, 360; Little Brown Church Quartet, 507; Jimmy Long, 512; Smoky Mountain Sacred Singers, 852
Abie's Irish Blues Jimmy Smith, 844
Abounding Sin And Abounding Grace Rev. J.O. Hanes & Male Choir, 394
Abraham Carson Robison, 785, 787–88
Abraham And Isaac Welby Toomey, 912
Absent Arthur Cornwall & William Cleary, 223
Accordion Joe Dave Hughs, 446
Ace [An] Bill Boyd, 123
Ace In The Hole New Dixie Demons, 655; Bud Rainey, 724; Shelton Brothers, 829
Aces Breakdown Four Aces, 356
Acorn Stomp East Texas Serenaders, 329
Acout Vous Moi Lese (When You Left Me) Leo Soileau, 854
Across The Blue Ridge Three Little Maids, 906
Across The Blue Ridge Mountains Arthur Smith, 841
Across The Great Divide Stuart Hamblen, 393
Action Speaks Louder Than Words Buddy Jones, 465
Adam And Eve Otto Gray, 378–79; Nelstone's Hawaiians, 653; Charlie Oaks, 664
Adam And Eve—Part 1–4 Chris Bouchillon, 120

Ada's Quadrille John Baltzell, 91
Adieu False Heart Arthur Smith, 841
Adieu Rosa Denus McGee, 551
Adios Bill Mounce, 645
Advice To Husband Seekers Warren Caplinger, 157
Advice To Wife Seekers Warren Caplinger, 157
Afraid Range Riders, 727
After Hours Blues Jimmie Revard, 742
After I'm Gone Johnny Bond, 117
After My Laughter Came Tears Leaford Hall, 390
After The Ball Fiddlin' John Carson, 178; Homer Christopher, 209; Collier Trio, 218; Crockett [Family] Mountaineers, 233; Vernon Dalhart, 246–48; Tom Darby & Jimmie Tarlton, 293; Dorsey & Beatrice Dixon, 322; Humphries Brothers, 447; Bradley Kincaid, 483–84; W.W. Macbeth, 526; Walter C. Peterson, 688; Tin-Can Joe, 910; Jess Young, 979
After The Ball Game Is Over Carson Bros., 180
After The Ball Is Over Vernon Dalhart, 248
After The Old Barn Dance Arthur Fields & Fred Hall, 342, 344
After The Rain Parker Quartette, 679
After The Roses Have Faded Away Ernest V. Stoneman, 878
After The Round-Up Hank Keene, 474
After The Sinking Of The Titanic Jimmie Tarlton, 892
After The Sunrise Chuck Wagon Gang, 210
After The War Is Over Charles Nabell, 647
After Thinking It Over Jimmy Hart, 406
After Tomorrow Gene Autry, 85–86; Jimmy Wakely, 934
After Twenty-One Years Gene Autry, 79
After You Left Me Alone Ted Daffan's Texans, 241
After You Said You Were Leaving Light Crust Doughboys, 506
After You've Gone Dixie Demons, 318; Hoosier Hot Shots, 438; Kelly Brothers, 477
After You've Said Goodbye Bill Nettles, 654
Aged Mother Cleve Chaffin, 200; Crowder Brothers, 237–38; John McGhee & Frank Welling, 553; Asa Martin, 590
Aggravating Lula Love Asa Martin, 590
Aggravating Mother-In-Law Walter Smith, 846
Ah Woo! Ah Woo! To You Hoosier Hot Shots, 437
Ah! Suzette Chere Patrick (Dak) Pellerin, 684
Aimer Et Perdre (To Love And Lose) Joseph Falcon, 335
Aimez-Moi Ce Soir (Love Me Tonight) Amedie Ardoin, 62
Ain't Goin' To Be Treated This Way Mustard & Gravy, 647
Ain't Goin' To Grieve My Lord No More Kentucky Coon Hunters, 477
Ain't Goin' To Lay My Armour Down Kentucky Coon Hunters, 477
Ain't Going To Lay My Armor Down McVay & Johnson, 580
Ain't Gonna Do It No More Arthur Cornwall, 222; Three Tobacco Tags, 907
Ain't Gonna Give You None Hackberry Ramblers, 388
Ain't Gonna Grieve My Lord Anymore Canova Family, 156
Ain't Gonna Grieve My Mind Vernon Dalhart, 286–87
Ain't Gonna Grieve My Mind Any More Vernon Dalhart, 286
Ain't Gonna Marry No More Tom Darby & Jimmie Tarlton, 294
Ain't Gonna Rain No More Tweedy Brothers, 917
Ain't Gonna Sin No More Elmer Bird, 106
Ain't Got No Money Babe Thomas C. Ashley, 67
Ain't Got Nobody Three Williamsons, 909
Ain't Gwine To Study War No More Vaughan Quartet, 926
Ain't I Right? Johnny Barfield, 94
Ain't It A Shame Vaughan Quartet, 928
Ain't It A Shame To Keep Your Honey Out In The Rain Uncle Dave Macon, 575
Ain't It Hard (To Love One That Don't Love You) Milo Twins, 628

Ain't It Hard To Love Delmore Brothers, 310
Ain't It Hell, Boys Smoky Mountain Ramblers, 852
Ain't Misbehavin' Patrick (Dak) Pellerin, 685
Ain't Never Comin' Back Philyaw Brothers, 690
Ain't No Bugs On Me Fiddlin' John Carson, 177, 179
Ain't No Tellin' Dwight Butcher, 149
Ain't No Use To High Hat Me Thomas C. Ashley, 68
Ain't No Use To Worry Anymore Shelton Brothers, 830
Ain't Nobody Truck Like You Ocie Stockard, 869
Ain't Nobody's Business Earl Johnson, 459
Ain't Satisfied Hackberry Ramblers, 388
Ain't She Coming Out Tonight Bill Boyd, 122
Ain't She Sweet Dixie Demons, 318; Tex Fletcher, 349; Freeny Harmonizers, 359; Hoosier Hot Shots, 437; Bob Larkan & Family, 490; Clayton McMichen, 566; McMichen's Harmony Boys, 573; Leo Soileau, 855
Ain't That A Shame Allen Brothers, 55
Ain't That Kind Of A Cat Yodel Hoke Rice, 745
Ain't That Skippin' And Flyin' Allen Brothers, 55
Ain't That Too Bad Nite Owls, 660; Rice Brothers' Gang, 746
Ain't That Trouble In Mind? Crockett Ward, 939; Fields Ward, 939
Ain't We Crazy? Bradley Kincaid, 485; Harry "Mac" McClintock, 529
Ain't Ya Comin' Out Tonight Vernon Dalhart, 242–43, 256; Carson Robison, 792
Ain't You Kinda Sorry Now Leon Selph, 823
Ain't You Sorry Now Jubileers, 468
Aint'cha Comin' Out Tonight Bill Cox, 225
Air Corps Of Uncle Sam [The] Texas Rangers, 900
Airship That Never Returned [The] Vernon Dalhart, 269
Akron Disaster [The] Frank Luther, 520
Alabama Blues Bill Cox, 225; Three Stripped Gears, 907
Alabama Breakdown Herschel Brown, 134
Alabama Dream Frank Roberts, Bud Alexander & Fiddlin' Slim Sandford, 755
Alabama Flood Vernon Dalhart, 286; Andrew Jenkins, 455; Carson Robison, 772
Alabama Flood Song Vernon Dalhart, 286
Alabama Gal Riley Puckett, 718
Alabama Gal (Won't You Come Out Tonight?) Fiddlin' John Carson, 175
Alabama Gal, Give The Fiddler A Dram Gid Tanner, 887
Alabama Girl, Ain't You Comin' Out Tonight? Frank Hutchison, 450; Earl Johnson, 460
Alabama Hills McClendon Brothers, 528
Alabama Jubilee Cleve Chaffin, 200; Cherokee Ramblers, 203; Homer Christopher, 209; Bill Helms, 415; Clayton McMichen, 565; W. Lee O'Daniel, 666; Rice Brothers' Gang, 746; Bill Shores & Melvin Dupree, 832; Gid Tanner, 887
Alabama Lullaby Delmore Brothers, 309–10; Lester McFarland & Robert A. Gardner, 548
Alabama Moon Clay Long, 510
Alabama Rag Freeman & Ashcraft, 358
Alabama Square Dance—Part 1, 2 Chumbler Family, 211
Alabama Trot Roane County Ramblers, 751
Alabammy Jubilee [The] Tweedy Brothers, 918
Alabamy Bound 'Lasses & Honey, 491; Zeb & Zeeke, 979
Alamo March Paradise Entertainers, 674
Alamo Polka Hi-Flyers, 420
Alamo Rag Adolph Hofner, 431
Alamo Steel Serenade Adolph Hofner, 431
Alamo Waltz Light Crust Doughboys, 501
Alarm Clock Blues Dwight Butcher, 148
Alas My Darling Fields Ward, 939
Alberta Walker Brothers, 936
Alcatraz Island Blues Delmore Brothers, 311
Alcatraz Prisoner Hall Brothers, 391

Alcatraz Prisoner Part 2 Hall Brothers, 392
Alcoholic Blues Deford Bailey, 88; Clayton McMichen, 566; Riley Puckett, 718
Aldeline Waltz East Texas Serenaders, 329
Aldora Waltz Dixie String Band, 320
Alecazander Johnson Brothers, 463
Alexander's Ragtime Band Hoosier Hot Shots, 437; Clayton McMichen, 572; Ernest Thompson, 902; Bob Wills, 962
Alexander's Talking Blues Swift Jewel Cowboys, 884
Alice Blue Gown Bill Boyd, 123; Milton Brown, 137; Light Crust Doughboys, 506
Alice From Dallas Buddy Jones, 465
Alimony Blues Buddy Baker, 89; Jimmie Davis, 300; Al Dexter, 315
Alimony Woman Bill Cox, 225–26
All Aboard For Blanket Bay Loren H. Abram, 47
All Alone Dan Hornsby, 442; Jesse Rodgers, 798
All Alone By The Sea Side Fiddlin' John Carson, 176
All Alone In This World Jimmie Davis, 303
All Ashore Ranch Boys, 727
All Because Of Lovin' You Light Crust Doughboys, 505
All Because Of You Floyd Tillman, 910
All Because You Said Goodbye Jimmie Davis, 305
All Bound Down Haywood County Ramblers, 414
All Bound Down In Prison Riley Puckett, 720
All Bound Down In Texas Tom Darby & Jimmie Tarlton, 294
All Bound 'Round With The Mason Dixon Line Riley Puckett, 718
All Day Long Warren Caplinger, 157
All Dolled Up Jimmie Revard, 743
All For The Sake Of Her Mitchell Brothers, 630
All Go Hungry Hash House Binkley Brothers Dixie Clodhoppers, 104; Cofer Brothers, 216; Uncle Dave Macon, 574; Ernest V. Stoneman, 874, 876–77
All Gone Now Clyde Evans Band, 333
All I Do Is Dream Claude Casey, 197
All I Do Is Dream Of You W. Lee O'Daniel, 666
All I Ever Do Is Wait Prairie Ramblers, 712
All I Got's Done Gone Doc Roberts, 755
All I Got's Gone Ernest V. Stoneman, 878
All I Want Is You Al Dexter, 315
All In Down And Out Blues Uncle Dave Macon, 578
All In Vain Nolan Bush, 147
All In, Down And Out Richard Brooks & Reuben Puckett, 132
All Is Quiet On The Old Front Porch Tonight Dick Hartman's Tennessee Ramblers, 408
All Is Well Lee Wells, 943
All I've Got Is Done Gone Doc Roberts, 752
All I've Got Is Gone Clayton McMichen, 571
All I've Got's Gone Uncle Dave Macon, 573; Asa Martin, 591; Ernest V. Stoneman, 872, 878
All My Friends Wade Mainer, 584
All My Life Light Crust Doughboys, 503
All My Natural Life Tennessee Ramblers [II], 897
All My Sins Are Taken Away Kelly Harrell, 404
All My Sins Been Taken Away Crowder Brothers, 237
All Night And All Day Long Hank Penny, 686
All Night Long Roy Acuff, 48; Clarence Ganus, 362; Frank Hutchison, 449; Earl Johnson, 460; Zora Layman, 492; Byrd Moore, 638; Shelton Brothers, 828; Bob Skyles, 839; Roba Stanley, 866
All Night Long Blues Richard D. Burnett, 144; John D. Foster, 354
All Of My Sins Are Taken Away Buffalo Ragged Five, 142
All Old Bachelors Are Hard To Please Georgia Yellow Hammers, 367
All Over A Smile Pete Pyle, 723

All Over Nothing At All Wiley Walker & Gene Sullivan, 935
All Praise Our King Freeman Quartette, 359
All Praise The Lord Clarence Ganus, 362
All That I'm Asking Is Sympathy Nite Owls, 660
All That I've Got's Done Gone Doc Roberts, 754
All The Glory Is Gone Frank Luther, 521; Bob Miller, 624
All The Good Times Are Passed And Gone Fred & Gertrude Gossett, 376; Monroe Brothers, 633
All The Good Times Are Past And Gone Carolina Ramblers String Band, 172; Ozark Boys, 672
All Through The Night Clayton McMichen, 572
All Will Be Well When The Night Is Past [E.R.] Nance Family, 649
Allen Brothers' Rag Allen Brothers, 57
Allen Vane Clayton McMichen, 569
Allen's Lying Blues Allen Brothers, 57
Alley Boogie Zeke Williams, 959
Alley Cat Stomp Shelly Lee Alley, 58
Alligator Song Adelyne Hood, 434
Allon A Tassone (Let's Go To Tassone) Denus McGee, 551
Allons Boire A Coup (Let's All Take A Drink Together) Leo Soileau, 854
Almost Persuaded Hugh Gibbs String Band, 368; John McGhee & Frank Welling, 561
Aloha Means Goodbye Universal Cowboys, 920
Aloha Oe (Farewell To Thee) Clayton McMichen, 567
Aloha Sunset Land James Brown, Jr. & Ken Landon Groups, 134
Aloma James Brown, Jr. & Ken Landon Groups, 135; Jim & Bob, 458
Alone Shelly Lee Alley, 58
Alone And Lonely Jimmy Wakely, 934
Alone And Lonesome Cliff Carlisle, 162–63
Alone At Home Delin T. Guillory-Lewis Lafleur, 385
Alone Because I Love You Oliver & Allen, 670
Alone In Lonesome Valley Beverly Hill Billies, 102
Alone With My Sorrow Jimmy Long, 511
Alone With My Sorrows Gene Autry, 77; Jimmy Long, 512; Shelton Brothers, 828
Along Life's Journey Jordan Brothers, 467
Alons A Ville Platte (Let's Go To Ville Platte) Leo Soileau, 854
Alons Kooche Kooche Joe Werner, 943
Alon's Rendezvous (Let's Go To The Rendezvous) Happy Fats, 396
Alphabet Song [The] Hank Snow, 853
Alpine Milk Man Beverly Hill Billies, 103
Alpine Milkman Yodel Elton Britt, 128
Alto Waltz Tom Darby & Jimmie Tarlton, 294
Altoona Freight Wreck [The] Vernon Dalhart, 254–55; Riley Puckett, 721
Altoona Wreck [The] Vernon Dalhart, 255
Always Alone Bob Atcher, 70; Ted Daffan's Texans, 241; Massey Family, 612
Always Been A Rambler Wade Mainer, 583
Always Blue, Lonesome Too Maynard Britton, 131
Always In Dreams You're A Pal Gene King, 485
Always In The Way Cromwell Brothers, 234; Lester McFarland & Robert A. Gardner, 546; Asa Martin, 588
Always Lift Him Up And Never Knock Him Down Blind Alfred Reed, 733
Always Marry Your Lover Dick Reinhart, 739
Always Remember Kelly Brothers, 477
Always Think Of Mother Richard Brooks & Reuben Puckett, 132
Always Waiting For You Dorsey & Beatrice Dixon, 321
Always Wrong Golden Rod & Red Hat Of Wsai, 373

Always Wrong, Part 1, 2 Golden Rod & Red Hat Of Wsai, 373
Am I Blue? Milton Brown, 137; Whitey McPherson, 579; Jimmie Revard, 743; Sons Of The West, 859
Am I Happy? Adolph Hofner, 430
Amadie Two Step Amedie Ardoin, 62
Amapola (Pretty Little Poppy) Gene Autry, 86
Amarillo Waltz A.C. (Eck) Robertson, 757
Amazing Grace Dye's Sacred Harp Singers, 328; Friendship Four, 360; North Georgia Four, 663; Vaughan Quartet, 929; Wisdom Sisters, 968–69
Amber Tresses Carter Family, 190
Amber Tresses Tied In Blue W.C. Childers, 205; Oscar L. Coffey, 216
Ambitious Father Chris Bouchillon, 120
America Vaughan Quartet, 927
American And Spanish Fandango R.B. Smith-S.J. Allgood, 845
American Eagle Georgia Compton's Reelers, 219
Ammend La Nouville A Mamere (Bring Mother The News) Joe Werner, 944
Among My Souvenirs Vernon Dalhart, 276
Anchored In Love Carter Family, 187
And A Little Child Shall Lead Them Lester McFarland & Robert A. Gardner, 547
And He Looks So Peaceful Now Wiley Walker & Gene Sullivan, 936
And Now You Farmers Louis Adler, 51
And So You Have Come Back To Me Bradley Kincaid, 483
And Still No Luck With You Dick Hartman's Tennessee Ramblers, 408
And That Was Irish Too Chubby Parker, 677
And The Cat Came Back Doc Roberts, 753
And The Cat Came Back The Very Next Day Doc Roberts, 752
And The Very God Of Peace E. Arthur Lewis, 498
And The Very God Of Peace Sanctify You Wholly E. Arthur Lewis, 497
And The Wise Old Owl Said Hoo Vernon Dalhart, 290
Angel Boy Gene Autry, 80
Angel Of East Tennessee Karl & Harty, 471
Angel Of The Shore [The] Bill Cox, 229
Angeline, The Baker Uncle Eck Dunford, 326
Angels In Heaven Know I Love You Bradley Kincaid, 483
Angels Tell My Mother I'll Be There Mr. & Mrs. R.N. Grisham, 384
Angels, Please Tell Mother Central Mississippi Quartet, 200
Angry Leon Chappelear, 201; Maple City Four, 587
Animal Fair Walter C. Peterson, 688
Animation Dye's Sacred Harp Singers, 328
Anna From Indiana Clayton McMichen, 572; Three Tobacco Tags, 909
Anna Lou Light Crust Doughboys, 504
Anna Mae Miller's Merrymakers, 628
Annabelle Hoosier Hot Shots, 438
Anna-May Bob Miller, 620
Annie Dear, I'm Called Away [Blind] Jack Mathis, 613
Annie Doesn't Live Here Anymore Shanks Bros. Trio, 825
Annie Laurie Billy Bishop, 107; Cliff Bruner, 140; Carson Robison, 795
Annie Laurie Swing Bill Boyd, 123
Anniversary Blue Yodel (Blue Yodel No. 7) Jimmie Rodgers, 803
Anniversary Blue Yodel No. 7 Gene Autry, 73; Lonesome Cowboy [II], 509
Another Alabama Camp Meetin' Wade Mainer, 584
Another Man's Wife Fisher Hendley, 416
Answer Comes Back [The] Rev. M.L. Thrasher, 905

Answer To "Disappointed In Love" [The] Roy Shaffer, 825
Answer To "Greenback Dollar" J.E. Mainer's Mountaineers, 582
Answer To "Honky Tonk Blues" Al Dexter, 314
Answer To "More Pretty Girls Than One" [The] Arthur Smith, 841
Answer To "My Precious Darling" Shelly Lee Alley, 59; Arthur Duhon, 325
Answer To "That Silver Haired Daddy Of Mine" [The] Hank Snow, 852
Answer To "The Blue Velvet Band" Hank Snow, 853
Answer To "Two Little Rosebuds" Wade Mainer, 583
Answer To 21 Years [The] Gene Autry, 78; Zora Layman, 492; Jimmy Long, 512; Frank[ie] Marvin, 605
Answer To 99 Years Red Headed Brier Hopper, 732
Answer To Big Rock Candy Mountain Fisher Hendley, 416
Answer To Birmingham Jail [An] Jordan Brothers, 467
Answer To Blonde Headed Baby Crowder Brothers, 238
Answer To Blue Eyes Morris Brothers, 643; Bill Nettles, 654; Shelton Brothers, 828
Answer To Broken Engagement Frank Gerald & Howard Dixon, 368
Answer To Budded Roses Whitey & Hogan, 952
Answer To Disappointed Love Clay Long, 510
Answer To Great Speckled Bird Roy Hall, 390
Answer To I'll Be Back In A Year, Little Darlin' (I'll Be Waiting For You, Darlin') Massey Family, 612
Answer To It Makes No Difference Now Wilf Carter (Montana Slim), 185; Hi-Flyers, 419
Answer To Just Because Rhubarb Red, 744; Shelton Brothers, 828
Answer To Maple On The Hill—Part 1, 2, 4 Dorsey & Beatrice Dixon, 321
Answer To Maple On The Hill—Part 2 Dixie Reelers, 319
Answer To Ninety-Nine Years [The] Elton Britt, 129
Answer To Nobody's Darling [The] Gene Autry, 82; Lew Childre, 207
Answer To Nobody's Darling But Mine Jimmie Davis, 301; Tex Ritter, 750
Answer To Prisoner's Dream Shelton Brothers, 828
Answer To Red River Valley Gene Autry, 81
Answer To Sparkling Blue Eyes Roy Acuff, 49
Answer To Swiss Moonlight Lullaby Wilf Carter (Montana Slim), 184
Answer To The Gypsy's Warning Harmonica Bill, 401
Answer To The Last Letter Rex Griffin, 384
Answer To The Prisoner's Dream Blue Sky Boys, 113; Karl & Harty, 471
Answer To Twenty-One Years Log Cabin Boys, 508
Answer To Weeping Willow Carter Family, 194; Joe Werner, 943
Answer To What Would You Give In Exchange For Your Soul Bill Cox, 228
Answer To Wondering Bill Nettles, 654; Joe Werner, 943
Answer To You Are My Sunshine Bob Atcher, 70; Pine Ridge Boys, 697; Rodik Twins, 810
Anthem On The Savior Lee Wells, 943
Antioch [J.T.] Allison's Sacred Harp Singers, 60; Original Sacred Harp Choir, 670
Anuiant Et Bleue Roy Gonzales, 375
Any Old Time Gene Autry, 73; Buddy Jones, 466; Jimmie Rodgers, 801
Any Time Ambrose Haley, 390; Dave Hughs, 446
Anything Leon Selph, 823
Anything That's Part Of You Village Boys, 932
Anywhere Is Home Dorsey & Beatrice Dixon, 321; Wade Mainer, 585
Apple Blossom A.C. (Eck) Robertson, 757

Apple Blossom Time Charlie Mitchell & His Kentucky Ridge Runners, 630
Apple Blossoms Charles Baker, 89
Apple Cider Yellow Jackets [I], 976
Apple Song [The] Arthur Fields & Fred Hall, 340
Apple Tree—Part 1, 2 Dick Hartman's Tennessee Ramblers, 409
Applejack Reid Bros. Band, 739
Apres Jengler A Toi Alley Boys Of Abbeville, 59
Apron String Blues [The] Pine Mountain Boys, 697
Arabella Blues Jimmie Davis, 299; Ted Lunsford, 517
Arabiana Tom & Don, 911
Arcade Blues Uncle Dave Macon, 575
Arcadia County Breakdown Leo Soileau, 855
Arcadian One Step Joseph Falcon, 335
Arcadian Waltz Adam Trehan, 913
Are You A Christian John McGhee & Frank Welling, 556
Are You Angry Little Darling Rouse Brothers, 815
Are You Angry With Me, Darling? Blue Ridge Highballers, 110; Ernest V. Stoneman, 873
Are You From Dixie ('Cause I'm From Dixie Too) Prairie Ramblers, 707
Are You From Dixie? Blue Sky Boys, 114; Hugh Cross, 237; John McGhee & Frank Welling, 555; Dick Parman, 679; Poplin-Woods Tennessee String Band, 701; Ernest Thompson, 902–03; Jess Young, 979
Are You Goin' To Leave Me Lil Bill Carlisle, 160
Are You Going To Leave The Old Home Rosa Lee Carson, 180
Are You Going To Leave Your Old Home Today? Kelly Harrell, 404
Are You Happy Or Lonesome Richard D. Burnett, 144; Hugh Cross, 236; John D. Foster, 354; Southern Moonlight Entertainers, 860
Are You Havin' Any Fun Hoosier Hot Shots, 439
Are You Lonesome For Me (Tonight Old Pal) Hi Neighbor Boys, 420
Are You Lonesome Tonight? James Brown, Jr. & Ken Landon Groups, 134; Carter Family, 193
Are You Marching With The Savior? Delmore Brothers, 310
Are You Ready My Friend Philyaw Brothers, 690
Are You Sorry, Are You Blue Bonnie Dodd & Murray Lucas, 322
Are You Sure? Bob Atcher, 69; Dorsey & Beatrice Dixon, 321
Are You Thinking Of Me Darling? Roy Acuff, 50
Are You Tired Of Me, Darling? Bill Cox, 225; Jimmie Davis, 301; Dick Hartman's Tennessee Ramblers, 408; Earl McCoy & Jessie Brock, 531; Lester McFarland & Robert A. Gardner, 543; [Blind] Jack Mathis, 613; Raymond Render, 740
Are You Tired Of Me, My Darling? Carter Family, 192
Are You Washed In The Blood Of The Lamb Uncle Dave Macon, 576; Smith's Sacred Singers, 850; Da Costa Woltz's Southern Broadcasters, 970
Are You Washed In The Blood? John McGhee & Frank Welling, 553, 560; Ernest V. Stoneman, 876; Rev. M.L. Thrasher, 905
Argentine Rag Jimmie Wilson's Catfish String Band, 968
Arizona Blues Phil Pavey, 682
Arizona Days Tex Ritter, 750
Arizona Girl I Left Behind Me [The] Billie Maxwell, 614
Arizona Lullaby Leon Payne, 683
Arizona Moon Tex Dunn, 327
Arizona Stomp East Texas Serenaders, 329
Arizona Trail Tex Dunn, 327
Arizona Yodeler [The] Dezurik Sisters, 316
Arkansas Bazooka Swing [The] Bob Skyles, 838
Arkansas Bill Green Barnyard Steve, 95
Arkansas Hard Luck Blues Lonnie Glosson, 372

Arkansas Hoedown Small Town Players, 840
Arkansas Hotel [The] George Edgin, 330
Arkansas Pullet Reaves White County Ramblers, 729
Arkansas Sheik [The] Clayton McMichen, 568; Riley Puckett, 719
Arkansas Stump Speech (Bring Me A Load Of Corn In The Fall) Pope's Arkansas Mountaineers, 701
Arkansas Stump Speech (Marry A Widow) Pope's Arkansas Mountaineers, 701
Arkansas Traveler—The Girl I Left Behind Me Tate Bros. & Hicks, 892
Arkansas Traveler (A Quadrille) [The] Joseph Samuels, 819
Arkansas Traveler (Step Right Back And Watch Her Smile) Shorty McCoy, 531
Arkansas Traveler [The] Arkansas Woodchopper, 64; John Baltzell, 91; Fiddlin' John Carson, 175; Crockett [Family] Mountaineers, 233; Jess Hillard, 425; Frank Luther, 525; Alphus McFayden, 550; Clayton McMichen, 571, 573; Red Fox Chasers, 730; George Reneau, 740–41; Doc Roberts, 752; Rodeo Trio, 798; Joseph Samuels, 819; Uncle Joe Shippee, 831; J.D. Weaver, 942
Arkansas Traveler And Medley Reels Joseph Samuels, 819
Arkansas Travelers Uncle Dave Macon, 574
Arkansas Traveller Emry Arthur, 66; Kessinger Brothers, 479; Tennessee Ramblers [I], 896
Arkansas Wagner Reaves White County Ramblers, 729
Arkansas Waltz Bob Larkan & Family, 491
Arkansas Wanderer Edward L. Crain, 230
Arkansaw Sweetheart Herb Cook, 220; Hawaiian Songbirds, 413
Arkansaw Traveler J.W. Day, 306; William B. Houchens, 443; A.C. (Eck) Robertson, 757; Gid Tanner, 887; Alf. Taylor, 892
Arkansaw Traveler (A Quadrille) Joseph Samuels, 819
Arkansaw Traveller Robert Cook's Old Time Fiddlers, 220
Arkansaw Wampus Cat W.B. Chenoweth, 203
Army Blues Hank Penny, 687
Army Rookie Polka Massey Family, 612
Around The Corner At Smokey Joe's Slim Harbert, 398
Arthur And Freddie (Part I, II) (Thank You For Your Information) Arthur Fields & Fred Hall, 344
As Far As The Gate Doctor Lloyd & Howard Maxey, 508
As Free A Little Bird As Can Be John Hammond, 394
As I Wandered Over The Hillside "Dock" Walsh, 937
As Long As I Have You Shelton Brothers, 828
As Long As I Live Johnny Marvin, 607
As Long As I've Got My Horse Gene Autry, 83
As Long As You're With Me Jolly Boys Of Lafayette, 464
As The Train Rattled On Professor & Mrs. Greer, 383
As We Parted At The Gate Roy Harvey, 410
As We Ride Down The Old Prairie Trail Al Clauser, 214
As We Sat Beneath The Maple On The Hill Posey Rorer, 813
As Willie And Mary Strolled By The Seashore McGee Brothers, 552
Asa's Two-Step Joe Werner, 944
Ash Can Blues Cliff Carlisle, 164
Asheville Osey Helton, 415
Asheville Blues Callahan Brothers, 151
Asleep At The Switch Lester McFarland & Robert A. Gardner, 547; Pie Plant Pete, 694; Ernest V. Stoneman, 872
Asleep In Jesus Giddens Sisters, 369
Asleep In The Briny Deep Blue Sky Boys, 114; Doc Hopkins, 441
Asleep In The Deep Vaughan Quartet, 925
Assassination Of J.B. Marcum Richard D. Burnett, 144
Assi Dans La Fenetre De Ma Chambre (Sitting In The Window Of My Room) Blind Uncle Gaspard, 363
At A Georgia Camp Meeting Ernest Thompson, 902

At Dawning (I Love You) Jack Major, 585
At Father Power's Grave Charlie Craver, 231; Vernon Dalhart, 289; John I. White, 950
At Last My Dreams Have Come True Burke Brothers, 143
At Night When The Sun Goes Down Three Musketeers, 906
At Sunset I'm Going Home Praetorian Quartet, 704
At The Barn Dance (Introducing: The Girl I Left Behind Me) Bob Wills, 962
At The Battle Front John McGhee & Frank Welling, 556
At The Bottom Blues Norwood Tew, 899
At The Close Of A Long Long Day James Brown, Jr. & Ken Landon Groups, 135; Frank Luther, 519; Rice Brothers' Gang, 747
At The Cross Fiddlin' John Carson, 178; Hartford City Trio, 407; John McGhee & Frank Welling, 553; Carson Robison, 768; Irene Spain Family, 861; Rev. M.L. Thrasher, 905
At The Darktown Strutters' Ball Hoosier Hot Shots, 436
At The End Of Memory Lane Cherry Sisters, 204
At The End Of Sunset Lane Vagabonds, 921
At The End Of The Hobo's Trail Goebel Reeves, 736
At The End Of The Lane Jimmie Revard, 743; Tom & Chuck, 911
At The End Of The Sunset Trail Hoke Rice, 745
At The Old Barn Dance Gene Autry, 83
At The Old Church Door David Miller, 626
At The Old Maids Ball Hoosier Hot Shots, 436
At The Party Cal West, 944
At The Rainbow's End Chuck Wagon Gang, 210; Sons Of The Pioneers, 858
At The River Tennessee Mountaineers, 896
At The Shelby County Fair Shelton Brothers, 828
At The Spring Adolph Hofner, 431
At Twilight Old Pal Of Yesterday Frank Gerald & Howard Dixon, 367
Atlanta Blues Earl & Willie Phelps, 689
Atlanta Bound Frank Dudgeon, 324; Johnny Marvin, 606
Atlanta Special Arthur Tanner, 885
Atrape Moi—Je Tombe (Catch Me—I'm Falling) Leo Soileau, 855
Attendre Pour Un Train John H. Bertrand, 101; Roy Gonzales, 375
Au Clair De La Lune (By The Light Of The Moon) Christine Muszar, 647
Au Revoir Cherie (Bye Bye Sweetheart) Joseph Falcon, 335
August Waltz Amadie Breaux, 126
Augusta Georgia Blues Crowder Brothers, 237
Augusta Rag Melvin Dupree, 327
Aunt Aline Amedie Ardoin, 61
Aunt Betsey's Choice George Stevens, 868
Aunt Clara's Waltz "Ted" Sharp, Hinman & Sharp, 825
Aunt Dinah's Quilting Party Floyd County Ramblers, 350
Aunt Hager's Blues Scottdale String Band, 821
Aunt Jane Blues Bill Shepherd, 830
Aunt Jemimah "Dock" Walsh, 937
Aunt Jemima's Plaster Skyland Scotty, 837
Aunt Mandy's Barn Dance—Part 1, 2 John Dilleshaw, 317
Aura Lee Shelton Brothers, 828
Austin Breakdown Jess Hillard, 426
Auto Club March R.D. Kelly & Julius Dunn, 476
Auto Love Song [The] Jesse Rodgers, 798
Automobile Of Life [The] Roy Acuff, 49
Automobile Ride Through Alabama—Part 1, 2 Red Henderson, 415
Aux Bal Se Te Maurice Happy Fats, 396
Aux Balle Chez Te Maurice Sons Of Acadians, 856
Aux Long Du Bois Happy Fats, 396
Avalon Milton Brown, 137; Hoosier Hot Shots, 438; Light Crust Doughboys, 504; Leo Soileau, 856

Avalon Blues W.T. Narmour & S.W. Smith, 649–50
Avalon Quick Step W.T. Narmour & S.W. Smith, 650
Avoyelles (Parish Name) Delma Lachney, 489
Awaiting The Chair Wilf Carter (Montana Slim), 181–82
Away Beyond The Blue Wells Brothers String Band, 943
Away Out On The Mountain Frank[ie] Marvin, 595–96; Riley Puckett, 719; Jimmie Rodgers, 799, 809
Away Out On The Old Saint Sabbeth Carter Family, 191
Away Out There Callahan Brothers, 153; Tex Dunn, 327; Saddle Tramps, 817; Bob Wills, 961
(Aye Aye) On Mexico's Beautiful Shore Shelton Brothers, 829
Ayou, Ayou, Mon Petite Chien Pour Edete (Where, Oh Where Has My Little Dog Gone) Joe Werner, 943

B Flat Rag Madisonville String Band, 580
Babe East Texas Serenaders, 329
Babtist [sic] Shout Da Costa Woltz's Southern Broadcasters, 970
Baby Charles Brooks, 132
Baby (You're As Sweet As Honey To Me) Dave Edwards, 331
Baby All Night Long Blue Ridge Mountain Entertainers, 111
Baby And The Gambler [The] Delma Lachney, 488
Baby Be On Your Way Dick Reinhart, 739
Baby Call Your Dog Off Ridgel's Fountain Citians, 749
Baby Chile Four Pickled Peppers, 356
Baby Girl Delmore Brothers, 312
Baby I Can't Use You Tom Darby & Jimmie Tarlton, 295
Baby Keep Stealin' Milton Brown, 138
Baby Lou Gid Tanner, 889
Baby On The Doorstep [The] Carson Robison, 766
Baby When You Coming Back Home Allen Brothers, 57
Baby Won't You Come Along Leon Chappelear, 201
Baby Won't You Please Come Home Cliff Bruner, 139; W. Lee O'Daniel, 666
Baby Your Mother Jimmie Revard, 743
Baby Your Mother (Like She Babied You) Jimmie Davis, 304
Baby Your Time Ain't Long Hill Billies, 424
Baby You're Throwing Me Down Delmore Brothers, 311
Baby You're Thru Foolin' Me Johnny Bond, 116
Baby You've Let Me Down Modern Mountaineers, 631
Baby, Come Kiss Your Honey Johnson Brothers, 463
Baby, Give Me Some Of That Light Crust Doughboys, 505
Baby, I Ain't Satisfied Village Boys, 932
Baby, Please Come Back Bob Miller, 622
Babylon Is Fallen Down Cleve Chaffin, 200
Baby's Lullaby Blue Ridge Mountain Girls, 112; Jimmie Davis, 298; Girls Of The Golden West, 370
Bachelor Blues Steve Ledford, 495
Bachelor's Blues Bill Carlisle, 159
Back Biting Blues Duke Clark, 213
Back Home Again In Indiana Bob Wills, 961
Back Home In Tennessee Bill Cox, 224; Hugh Cross, 235
Back Home In The Blue Ridge Mountains Gene Autry, 77
Back In '67 Prairie Ramblers, 711
Back In California Odus & Woodrow, 667
Back In Indiana Hoosier Hot Shots, 436
Back In Jail Again Jesse Rodgers, 799
Back In My Home Town Lester "Pete" Bivins, 107; Frank Hutchison, 450
Back In Tennessee Clayton McMichen, 568, 571
Back In The Hills Of Colorado Beverly Hill Billies, 102; Carson Robison, 784
Back In The Old Green Hills Arthur Fields & Fred Hall, 342
Back In The Old Sunday School Beverly Hill Billies, 102; John McGhee & Frank Welling, 563; Bess & Tee Prewitt, 713

Back In The Saddle Again Gene Autry, 84; Eddie Dean, 308; Ray Whitley, 953
Back In The Years Etowah Quartet, 333
Back In Your Own Back Yard Roy Newman, 657
Back On Montana Plains Patsy Montana, 636
Back On The Texas Plains Riley Puckett, 722
Back Porch—Part 1, 2 [The] Carson Robison, 793
Back Ridin' Old Trails Again Wilf Carter (Montana Slim), 186
Back To Alabama In The Spring Ray Sand's Harmony Four, 819
Back To Arizona Zeke Williams, 959
Back To Birmingham Delmore Brothers, 311
Back To Carolin' Carl Boling, 116
Back To Hawaii And You Bob Palmer & Monte Hall, 673
Back To Johnson City J.E. Mainer's Mountaineers, 582
Back To Mexico Carolina Tar Heels, 173
Back To My Georgia Home Bert Layne, 493; Clayton McMichen, 570
Back To My Home In Smokey Mountain Riley Puckett, 721
Back To My Mountain Home Prairie Ramblers, 705
Back To My Wyoming Home Frank Gerald & Howard Dixon, 368
Back To Nevada Tune Wranglers, 915
Back To Oklahoma Tennessee Hill Billy, 896
Back To Old Kentucky Hugh Cross, 236
Back To Old Smokey Mountain Gene Autry, 77
Back To Old Smoky Mountain Gene Autry, 77; Hugh Cross, 237; Dick Hartman's Tennessee Ramblers, 407; Kenneth Houchins, 444; W. Lee O'Daniel, 666; Smoky Mountain Ramblers, 852
Back To That Dear Old Farm Ezra Buzzington's Rustic Revelers, 149–50
Back To The Blue Ridge Roy Harvey, 411
Back To The Farm Emmett Bankston & Red Henderson, 92
Back To The Harbor Of Home Sweet Home John McGhee & Frank Welling, 557; David Miller, 626; Parker & Dodd, 678
Back To The Hills Of Carolina Red Fox Chasers, 731
Back To The Lone Prairie Twilight Trail Boys, 918
Back To The Texas Claims & Buckaroo Tex Walker, 935
Back Up A Little Bit Hank Penny, 686
Back Up And Push Cherokee Ramblers, 204; Georgia Organ Grinders, 366; Bill Monroe, 632; Bill Shores & Melvin Dupree, 832; Gid Tanner, 891
Back Water Blues Dewey & Gassie Bassett, 96; Uncle Dave Macon, 576; Byrd Moore, 638; Three Tobacco Tags, 907
Back Where The Blue Bonnets Grow Marvin Williams, 959
Back Where The Old Home Stands Shell Creek Quartet, 826
Back Yard Stomp Nite Owls, 660; Prairie Ramblers, 710
Bacon And Cabbage Blind Joe Mangum-Fred Shriber, 586
Bacon Rind Prairie Ramblers, 708
Bad Blues Modern Mountaineers, 631
Bad Boy Walker's Corbin Ramblers, 937
Bad Companions Vernon Dalhart, 271; Doc Hopkins, 441; Asa Martin, 588; Happy Massey, 608; George Reneau, 741; Carl T. Sprague, 862; Ernest V. Stoneman, 872; Marc Williams, 958
Bad Girl Airport Boys, 52
[Bad Lee Brown] John Dilleshaw, 316
Bad Mule Georgia Crackers, 366
Bad Reputation Fleming & Townsend, 347
Bagatelle Massey Family, 612
Baggage Coach Ahead [The] Fiddlin' John Carson, 176; Vernon Dalhart, 245; Girl O' Yesterday, 369; Lester McFarland & Robert A. Gardner, 544; George Reneau, 740
Bailey Waltz Luke Highnight, 422
Bake That Chicken Pie Jackson County Ramblers, 453; Uncle Dave Macon, 575

Baker Boy [The] Patrick (Dak) Pellerin, 685
Balance Six Quadrille National Barn Dance Orchestra, 651
Bald Faced Steer [The] Bill Bender, 99
Bald Top Mountain Harry "Mac" McClintock, 528
Bald-Headed End Of A Broom [The] Blevins & Blair, 109; Walter Smith, 846
Bald-Headed End Of The Broom [The] George Reneau, 740; Ridgel's Fountain Citians, 749
Balking Mule [The] Frank & James McCravy, 533
Ball And Chain Lem's Down Home Boys, 496
Ball And Chain Blues Happy Bud Harrison, 406; Clyde Stone & Lem Paschal, 871
Ballin' The Jack And Nigger Blues Dr. Claude Watson & L.W. McCreigton, 941
Balsam Gap Jubilee Breakdowners From Balsam Gap, 126
Baltimore Fire Charlie Poole, 700
Baltimore Waltz Delma Lachney, 488
Banana Peeling Mama Fleming & Townsend, 348
Band Played On [The] Hoosier Hot Shots, 440; Massey Family, 612
Band Rehearsal For Old Settler's Reunion -Part 1, 2 Paul Crutchfield & John Clotworthy, 238
Bandit Cole Younger Edward L. Crain, 229–30
Banjo Joe Bill Cox, 228
Banjo Marmolo E.E. Hack String Band, 386
Banjo Pickin' Girl Coon Creek Girls, 221
Banjo Rag Gibson String Trio, 369; Herald Goodman, 375
Banjo Sam Wilmer Watts, 941
Banjo Tramp [The] Cecil Vaughn, 930
Bank Bustin' Blues John McGhee & Frank Welling, 562
Bank Failures Bob Miller, 620
Bankhead Blues Nations Brothers, 652
Banquet In Misery Hall [The] Dan Hornsby, 442
Baoille Delma Lachney, 488
Baptising Sister Lucy Lee Jimmy Yates Groups, 976
Bar Hotel Al Dexter, 315
Bar None Ranch [The] Goebel Reeves, 738
Barbara Allen Vernon Dalhart, 264–67, 271, 291; Arthur Fields & Fred Hall, 339; Newton Gaines, 361; Doc Hopkins, 441; Bradley Kincaid, 482, 484; Frank Luther, 524; Carson Robison, 764; Vagabonds, 922
Barbara Polka Adolph Hofner, 431
Barbecue Down In Georgia—Part 1, 2 Herschel Brown, 134
Barber's Blues Frank[ie] Marvin, 597
Barefoot Boy With Boots Asa Martin, 591
Barefoot Boy With Boots On Bill Cox, 226; Otto Gray, 379; Asa Martin, 589
Barefoot Days Eddie Dean, 307–08
Barn Dance—Part 1, 2 National Barn Dance Orchestra, 651
Barn Dance Of Long Ago Girls Of The Golden West, 371
Barn Dance On The Mountain Part I, II Claude Davis, 297
Barn Dance Rag Bill Boyd, 122; Roy Newman, 656
Barn Yard Romp Hi-Flyers, 419
Barnacle Bill Carson Robison, 792–93
Barnacle Bill The Sailor Arthur Fields & Fred Hall, 339; Frank Luther, 523; Carson Robison, 768–70, 772–73
Barnacle Bill The Sailor—No. 2 Carson Robison, 774–75
Barnacle Bill The Sailor No. 2 Vernon Dalhart, 288; Carson Robison, 774
Barnacle Bill The Sailor No. 3 Carson Robison, 777
Barney McCoy Arkansas Woodchopper, 63; Uncle Eck Dunford, 325; Bradley Kincaid, 482; Walter Morris, 642; Ernest V. Stoneman, 873
Barnyard Conference [The] [E.R.] Nance Family, 648
Barnyard Frolic Carolina Ramblers String Band, 172
Barnyard Hymn Midkiff, Spencer & Blake, 616
Barnyard Imitations Ezra Buzzington's Rustic Revelers, 150
Barnyard Serenade G.B. Grayson & Henry Whitter, 381

Barnyard Stomp Jimmie Davis, 300; Jess Hillard, 426
Barnyard Tumble Bill Carlisle, 159
Barrel House Blues Jap Magee, 580
Barroom Blues Dixie Ramblers [II], 319
Barroom Message [The] Jimmie Davis, 298
Barrow County Stomp Theo. & Gus Clark, 214
Bartender's Daughter [The] Light Crust Doughboys, 506
Bashful Bachelor [The] David McCarn, 527
Bashful Beau Murphy Brothers, 646
Bashful Coon Taylor Trio, 894
Basile Waltz Leo Soileau, 853
Basin Street Blues Bob Dunn's Vagabonds, 326; Bob Wills, 961
Bass Blues Ezra Buzzington's Rustic Revelers, 149
Bass Man Jive Ocie Stockard, 870
Batchelors' Hall [The] Fiddlin' John Carson, 176
Bath House Blues Ashley's Melody Makers, 68
Bathe In That Beautiful Pool "Dock" Walsh, 938
Battle Axe And The Devil [The] Bill Cox, 228
Battleship Maine Professor & Mrs. Greer, 383; Richard Harold, 402
Battleship Of Maine [The] Red Patterson's Piedmont Log Rollers, 682
Bay Rum Blues Thomas C. Ashley, 68; Kenneth Houchins, 443; David McCarn, 527
Bayou Courtebleau Oscar [Slim] Doucet, 324
Bayou Pom Pom One Step Angelas Le Jeunne, 493
Bayou Teche Columbus Fruge, 360
Bazooka Stomp [The] Bob Skyles, 838
Be A Daniel Deal Family, 307
Be A Man Royal Sumner Quartet, 815
Be At Home Soon Tonight, My Dear Boy Kelly Harrell, 403
Be Careful Boys, Don't Go Too Far Carter Family, 192
Be Careful Girls Lulu Belle & Scotty, 516
Be Careful What You Say Vernon Dalhart, 289
Be Careful With Those Eyes Rice Brothers' Gang, 746
Be Good, Baby Three Tobacco Tags, 908
Be Home Early Tonight Leon McGuire, 564
Be Home Early Tonight My Dear Boy Otto Gray, 379
Be Honest With Me Roy Acuff, 50; Gene Autry, 84; Red Foley, 351; Light Crust Doughboys, 506; Prairie Ramblers, 712; Jimmy Wakely, 934
Be Just Like Your Daddy Stuart Hamblen, 393
Be Kind To A Man When He Is Down Da Costa Woltz's Southern Broadcasters, 970
Be Kind To A Man When He's Down Fiddlin' John Carson, 175, 177, 179; North Carolina Ridge Runners, 663; Pie Plant Pete, 695; Gid Tanner, 887
Be My Darlin' Dick Reinhart, 739; Jimmy Wakely, 934
Be No Other Fellow's Sweetheart Clyde Stone & Lem Paschal, 871
Be Nobody's Darling But Mine Jesse Rodgers, 799
Be Of Good Cheer Jenkins Family, 457
Be Ready Ridgel's Fountain Citians, 748
Beach At Waikiki [The] Tennessee Ramblers [II], 897
Beale Street Blues Bill Boyd, 122; Nite Owls, 660
Beale Street Mama Milton Brown, 137; Hoosier Hot Shots, 438
Bear Cat Mama W. Lee O'Daniel, 666; Bob Wills, 961
Bear Cat Mama From Horner's Corner[s] Gene Autry, 74; Jimmie Davis, 299; Ted Lunsford, 517
Bear Cat Papa Frank[ie] Marvin, 604
Bear Cat Papa Blues Gene Autry, 74–75
Bear Creek Blues Carter Family, 195
Bear Creek Hop Clifford Gross, 385; Light Crust Doughboys, 506
Bear Me Away On Your Snowy White Wings Fiddlin' John Carson, 179

Bear Mountain Rag Smoky Mountain Ramblers, 852
Bear's Gap Earl & Willie Phelps, 689
Beatrice Fairfax, Tell Me What To Do Hoosier Hot Shots, 440
Beatrice Snipes Frank Luther, 519; Bob Miller, 623
Beau Of Oak Hill [The] Tommy Dandurand, 293
Beaumont Bill Boyd, 123
Beaumont Rag Cliff Bruner, 140; East Texas Serenaders, 329; Oscar & Doc Harper, 402; Light Crust Doughboys, 504; Prairie Ramblers, 711; Smith's Garage Fiddle Band, 848; Bob Wills, 963
Beautiful Garland Brothers & Grinstead, 362
Beautiful Bearded Lady [The] Zora Layman, 492
Beautiful Beckoning Hands Posey Rorer, 813
Beautiful Belle Bob Larkan & Family, 490
Beautiful Bells Leake County Revelers, 495
Beautiful Brown Eyes Roy Acuff, 49; Shelton Brothers, 830; Arthur Smith, 841; White Brothers (Joe & Bob), 951
Beautiful City Of God Frank & James McCravy, 533
Beautiful City Of Zion Clarence Ganus, 362
Beautiful Dream [A] Grady & Hazel Cole, 217
Beautiful Dreamer Carson Robison, 789
Beautiful Eyes Of Virginia Lemuel Turner, 917
Beautiful Garden Of Prayer [The] Jenkins Family, 456; Frank & James McCravy, 534; John McGhee & Frank Welling, 557, 562; Merritt Smith, 844
Beautiful Girl Of The Prairie Wilf Carter (Montana Slim), 185
Beautiful Harbor Lights Vaughan Quartet, 923
Beautiful Hawaiian Shores Bill Nettles, 654
Beautiful Heaven Milton Brown, 137; Nite Owls, 660
Beautiful Heaven Must Be Dick Hartman's Tennessee Ramblers, 407
Beautiful Home Carter Family, 195
Beautiful Home Awaits Rev. M.L. Thrasher, 905
Beautiful Home Somewhere Ashford Quartette, 67; Deal Family, 307
Beautiful Home Sweet Home Homer Briarhopper, 127
Beautiful Isle Arthur Cornwall & William Cleary, 223; Mrs. Leon Hinkle, 427; Melody Boys, 615
Beautiful Isle O'er The Sea Carter Family, 195; Ernest V. Stoneman, 877
Beautiful Isle Of Somewhere Lester McFarland & Robert A. Gardner, 544; Maple City Four, 587; Woodlawn Quartette, 972
Beautiful Isle Of Sorrow Jimmy Long, 511
Beautiful Lady In Blue [A] Dixie Ramblers [II], 319; Earl & Willie Phelps, 689
Beautiful Land Monroe Quartette, 633; Paramount Sacred Four, 674; Sunshine Four, 882
Beautiful Land Of Glory Clarence Ganus, 362
Beautiful Life [A] Chuck Wagon Gang, 210; Monroe Brothers, 633; Byron Parker, 675; Smith's Sacred Singers, 849; Vaughan Quartet, 929
Beautiful Louisiana Johnson County Ramblers, 464; Shelton Brothers, 827
Beautiful Love Uncle Dave Macon, 578
Beautiful Mabel Clare Arthur Smith, 841
Beautiful Mary Jimmie Davis, 301; Four Aces, 356
Beautiful Memories Arthur Smith, 841
Beautiful Northwest Country Bob Palmer & Jimmy White, 673
Beautiful Ohio Light Crust Doughboys, 504; Ranch Boys, 726
Beautiful Prayer [A] Stamps Quartet, 865; J.B. Whitmire's Blue Sky Trio, 953
Beautiful River Allen Quartette, 57
Beautiful Stars Dorsey & Beatrice Dixon, 321
Beautiful Texas Gene Autry, 79–80; Milton Brown, 136;

Jimmie Davis, 300; Farmer Sisters, 336; Dick Hartman's Tennessee Ramblers, 407; Light Crust Doughboys, 501; Massey Family, 609; W. Lee O'Daniel, 666
Beautiful Valley Theron Hale, 389
Beautiful, Beautiful Brown Eyes Blue Sky Boys, 113
Beaver Cap Allen Brothers, 55; Riley Puckett, 720
Beaver Creek Texas Jim Lewis, 499; Prairie Ramblers, 712
Beaver Valley Breakdown Lonesome Luke, 510
Because Cliff Bruner, 140; Ted Daffan's Texans, 241; Patrick (Dak) Pellerin, 684
Because He Loved Her So Cofer Brothers, 216
Because He Was Only A Tramp Wyzee Hamilton, 393
Because I Have Lost You Adolph Hofner, 430
Because I Love Him Laurel Firemen's Quartet, 491; Peck's Male Quartette, 683; Stamps Quartet, 864
Because You Were Here One Day George Wade, 933
Beckley Rag Roy Harvey, 410
Bed Bug Blues Jimmie Davis, 301
Bed Bug Groan J.P. Ryan, 817
Bed Bugs Makin' Their Last Go Round Byrd Moore, 638
Bee Hunt On Hill For Sartin Creek Part 1, 2 [A] Clayton McMichen, 569
Beech Fork Blues Richard Cox, 229
Beech Fork Special John McGhee & Frank Welling, 561
Been Foolin' Me, Baby Wade Mainer, 583
Been Married Three Times Ernest Mull, 646
Been On The Job Too Long Wilmer Watts, 941
Been To The East—Been To The West Leake County Revelers, 494
Beer And Skittles Massey Family, 612
Beer Barrel Polka (Roll Out The Barrel) Hoosier Hot Shots, 439
Beer Drinkin' Blues Pete Pyle, 723
Beer Drinkin' Mama Light Crust Doughboys, 505
Beer Joint Blues Shelly Lee Alley, 59
Beer Parlor Jive Hi-Flyers, 420
Beer Party [The] Charlie Wilson, 967
Beer Song [The] Frank Luther, 519
Bees Are Humming Around The Flowers Phil Reeve & Ernest Moody, 735
Bees Are In The Hive [The] Jimmie Revard, 743
Before I Grew Up To Love You East Texas Serenaders, 329
Before You Say Farewell Jimmie Davis, 299
Beggar Joe Tom Darby & Jimmie Tarlton, 294
Beggar's Daughter [The] Hoke Rice, 746
Behind The Big White House Bob Miller, 621, 623; Dick Robertson, 758
Behind The Clouds Burl Ives, 451
Behind The Clouds (Are Crowds And Crowds Of Sunbeams) Vernon Dalhart, 255
Behind The Hen House Lewis McDaniels, 538
Behind The Parlor Door J.E. Mainer's Mountaineers, 581; Pickard Family, 692–93
Behind These Gray Walls Vernon Dalhart, 253–55; Kenneth Houchins, 444
Behind Those Gray Walls Vernon Dalhart, 254
Behind Those Stone Walls Carter Family, 192
Believe Me If All Those Endearing Young Charms Yellow Jackets [I], 976
Bell Clapper Mama Bill Carlisle, 159
Bell Clappin' Mama Bill Carlisle, 160
Belle Of Point Claire Artelus Mistric, 629
Belle Of The Ball Duke Clark, 213
Bells Of Avalon Tom & Roy, 911
Bells Of Hawaii Dixie Girls, 318
Below The Rio Grande Rice Brothers' Gang, 747
Ben Dewberry's Final Run Frank[ie] Marvin, 595–97; Jimmie Rodgers, 799; Joe Steen, 868

Ben Hur Perry Brothers, 687
Ben Hur March Collier Trio, 218
Ben Tucker Reel Pie Plant Pete, 694
Ben Wheeler Stomp Leon Chappelear, 201
Bend Down, Sister Johnny Marvin, 606
Beneath A Bed Of Daisies Johnny Marvin, 607
Beneath A Sheltering Pine Patt Patterson, 682
Beneath An Old Maple Dorsey & Beatrice Dixon, 322
Beneath Montana Skies Carson Robison, 776
Beneath That Lonely Mound Of Clay Roy Acuff, 50
Beneath The Old Pine Tree Carlisle Brothers, 169
Beneath The Stars Pleaman S. Neal's Harmony Three, 652
Beneath The Weeping Willow Tree Bill Carlisle, 159; Kelly Harrell, 403
Bennie, The Bumble Bee, Feels Bum Dixieland Swingsters, 320
Benton County Hog Thief Arkansas Barefoot Boys, 63
Berry Pickin' Rag Rustic Revellers, 816
Berry Picking Time Johnny Barfield, 94; George Goebel, 372; Buck Nation, 650
Beside A Lonely River Clyde White, 948
Beside The Ocean Blue Howard Keesee, 475
Bessie's Monkey Arthur Cornwall, 223
Best Friend I Ever Had [The] Bill Cox, 226
Best Girl Of All [The] Three Tobacco Tags, 909
Best Of Friends Must Part [The] Roy Hall, 391
Best Pal I Had Is Gone [The] Callahan Brothers, 154
Bethel Dye's Sacred Harp Singers, 328
Betsey Brown Walter Morris, 642
Betsy Brown Hill Billies, 423
Betsy From Pike Bill Bender, 99
Better Farther On J. Douglas Swagerty, 883
Better Get Off Your High Horse Baby Roy Newman, 657
Better Get Out Of My Way Vernon Dalhart, 255–57
Better Home [The] Ruth Donaldson & Helen Jepsen, 323; Frank & James McCravy, 535
Better Quit It Now Adolph Hofner, 430
Better Quit Your Rowdy Ways Henderson Brothers, 416
Better Range Is Home [A] Delmore Brothers, 311
Better Than Gold Vaughan Quartet, 923–24
Betty Brown Sally Foster, 355
Beulah Land Jenkins Family, 456
Beware Blind Alfred Reed, 733
Beyond Black Smoke Dorsey & Beatrice Dixon, 322
Beyond Prison Walls Bob Miller, 621
Beyond The Clouds Light Crust Doughboys, 507; Rangers Quartet, 728
Beyond The Clouds Is Light Gordon County Quartet, 376
Beyond The Last Mile Rex Griffin, 384
Beyond The River Carolina Gospel Singers, 170
Beyond The Starry Plane Red Brush Singers, 730
Beyond The Stars Is Home Smith's Sacred Singers, 851
Biarritz Massey Family, 612
Bib-A-Lollie-Boo Chubby Parker, 676–77
Bibb County Grind South Georgia Highballers, 860
Bibb County Hoe Down John Dilleshaw, 317
Bible Is Good Enough For Me [The] John McGhee & Frank Welling, 555
Bible My Mother Gave To Me [The] Uncle Pete & Louise, 919
Bible's True [The] Uncle Dave Macon, 574
Big At The Little, Bottom At The Top Bill Carlisle, 160
Big Bad Bill (From The Badlands) Texas Jim Lewis, 500
Big Bad Blues Ray Whitley, 952
Big Ball In Memphis Georgia Yellow Hammers, 367
Big Ball In Texas Delmore Brothers, 311; Prairie Ramblers, 704; Ray Whitley, 952
Big Ball In Town Warren Caplinger, 156; Gid Tanner, 889

Big Ball Uptown Taylor-Griggs Louisiana Melody Makers, 893
Big Beaver Bob Wills, 964
Big Bend Gal Shelor Family, 826
Big Bully Stripling Brothers, 880
Big City Jail Billy Vest, 931
Big Corral [The] Beverly Hill Billies, 102; Light Crust Doughboys, 503; Massey Family, 608; Ranch Boys, 726; Texas Rangers, 900
Big Daddy Blues Jimmie Revard, 742
Big Dallas Blues Curly Gray, 378
Big Eared Mule William B. Houchens, 443; Nicholson's Players, 659; Doc Roberts, 753; B.E. Scott, 820
Big Eared Mule (The Two Bit Whirl) [The] Shorty McCoy, 531
Big Fat Gal Lester "Pete" Bivins, 107
Big Fat Gal Of Mine Carl Boling, 116
Big Footed Nigger Roane County Ramblers, 751
Big Footed Nigger In The Sandy Lot [The] Stripling Brothers, 879
Big Four Stripling Brothers, 880
Big House Blues Shelly Lee Alley, 58–59; Light Crust Doughboys, 507
Big Little Family Of The Hills [The] Radio Rubes, 723
Big Mama Leo Soileau, 854
Big Mama Blues Buddy Jones, 465
Big Moon Patsy Montana, 635
Big Night Tonight Walter C. Peterson, 688
Big Noise From Kokomo Hoosier Hot Shots, 439
Big Ranch Boss Carson Robison, 794
Big River Blues Carolina Buddys, 170
Big Rock Candy Mountain [The] Stuart Hamblen, 392; Goebel Reeves, 738
Big Rock Candy Mountains—No. 2 [The] Stuart Hamblen, 392
Big Rock Candy Mountains [The] Vernon Dalhart, 284; Ernest Hare, 399; Harry "Mac" McClintock, 529; Frank[ie] Marvin, 598; Carson Robison, 768
Big Sandy Valley Dewey Golden, 372
Big Shot Daddy Blues Bill Nettles, 654
Big String Band Jimmie Revard, 742
Big Town Fling Tommy Dandurand, 292
Big White Rooster And The Little Brown Hen [The] Ed Hayes, 414
Big-Eyed Rabbit Samantha Bumgarner, 142; Stripling Brothers, 879
Big-Mouthed Elephant And The Long-Eared Mule [The] Bob Miller, 622
Bile Dem Cabbage Down Carolina Ramblers String Band, 173; Crockett [Family] Mountaineers, 233; Clayton McMichen, 571; Parker & Dodd, 678; Riley Puckett, 716
Bile Them Cabbage Down Dixie Crackers, 318; Uncle Dave Macon, 574; Gid Tanner, 889
Bill Bailey Perry Bechtel, 98; Homer Briarhopper, 127
Bill Bailey And Coon, Coon Yellow Jackets [I], 976
Bill Bailey, Ain't That A Shame John McGhee & Frank Welling, 555
Bill Bailey, Won't You Please Come Home Al Bernard, 101; John McGhee & Frank Welling, 555
Bill Baily [sic] Won't You Please Come Home Jess Young, 979
Bill Cheatam Blind Joe Mangum-Fred Shriber, 586
Bill Cheatham Arthur Smith, 842
Bill Cheatum Light Crust Doughboys, 501
Bill Green Three Musketeers, 906
Bill Johnson Bill & Louis Jones, 464; Clayton McMichen, 568; Riley Puckett, 719
Bill Mason Roy Harvey, 410; Charlie Poole, 700
Bill Morgan And His Gal Buster Carter & Preston Young, 181

Bill The Bar Fly Tex Ritter, 750
Bill Was A Texas Lad J.D. Farley, 336
Bill Wishes He Was Single Again Bill Chitwood, 208
Billboard Frank Roberts, Bud Alexander & Fiddlin' Slim Sandford, 755
Billie Boy Massey Family, 611
Billie Gray Hartford City Trio, 407
Billie In The Low Ground Uncle "Am" Stuart, 880
Billie The Kid Sons Of The Pioneers, 858
Billy Massey Family, 611
Billy Boy Boyden Carpenter, 174; Ray Covert, 224; Bradley Kincaid, 483; Frank Luther, 524; Floyd Thompson, 903
Billy Boy, Billy Boy Al McLeod's Country Dance Band, 565
Billy Grimes, The Rover Shelor Family, 826
Billy In The Low Ground Dr. Humphrey Bate, 97; Richard D. Burnett, 144; Fiddlin' John Carson, 175; Robert Cook's Old Time Fiddlers, 220; Fiddlin' Powers & Family, 703; Doc Roberts, 753; Lowe Stokes, 871
Billy In The Low Grounds [sic] Doc Roberts, 752
Billy In The Lowland J.W. Day, 306
Billy On The Low Ground Oscar & Doc Harper, 402
Billy Richardson's Last Ride Vernon Dalhart, 261–64, 281; George Goebel, 372
Billy The Kid Bill Bender, 99; Vernon Dalhart, 265–66, 268; Vernon Waters, 940
Billy Venero Harry "Mac" McClintock, 528–29
Billy Venero Part 1, 2 Billie Maxwell, 613
Billy Wilson Uncle Jimmy Thompson, 904
Billy's Blue Yodel Billy Vest, 931
Bingo Was His Name Chubby Parker, 677
Bird Dog Waltz Roane County Ramblers, 751
Bird In A Cage And Three Rail Pen Roy Rogers, 812
Bird In A Gilded Cage [A] Frank & James McCravy, 534
Bird With The Broken Pinion [The] Frank & James McCravy, 533
Birdie Roy Harvey, 411; Kessinger Brothers, 480; John & Emery McClung, 530; John McGhee & Frank Welling, 561; Fiddlin' Powers & Family, 703; Tweedy Brothers, 918
Birdie Darling Elzie Floyd & Leo Boswell, 350
Birds Are Returning [The] Fields Ward, 939
Birds In The Brook Leake County Revelers, 494
Birds Were Singing Of You [The] Carter Family, 189
Birmingham McDonald Quartet, 541; Pope's Arkansas Mountaineers, 701; George Reneau, 740
Birmingham Daddy Gene Autry, 76
Birmingham Jail Cliff Carlisle, 162; Tom Darby & Jimmie Tarlton, 293; Dezurik Sisters, 316; Dick Hartman's Tennessee Ramblers, 407; Fred Kirby, 487; Lester McFarland & Robert A. Gardner, 545; Byrd Moore, 638; Roy Newman, 657; Pickard Family, 692; Carson Robison, 768, 786–87; Walter Smith, 847; Leo Soileau, 855; Stripling Brothers, 880
Birmingham Jail No. 2 Cliff Carlisle, 163; Tom Darby & Jimmie Tarlton, 294; Frank Dudgeon, 324; Carson Robison, 772, 786
Birmingham Prisoner [The] Clay Long, 510
Birmingham Rag Tom Darby & Jimmie Tarlton, 294; Arthur Tanner, 886
Birmingham Special Mike Shaw, 826
Birmingham Town Tom Darby & Jimmie Tarlton, 293
Birmingham Woman Texas Jim Robertson, 759
Birth Of The Blues [The] Light Crust Doughboys, 504
Biscuit Jim "Sunshine" Pritchard, 714
Biscuit Shootin' Susie Bill Bender, 99
Bits Of Blues Sid Harkreader, 400
Bitter Creek Oscar & Doc Harper, 402
Bitter Pill Blues Thomas C. Ashley, 67
Black And Blue Blues Blind Alfred Reed, 733
Black And Blue Rag Bob Wills, 960

Black And Blues Ocie Stockard, 869
Black And Tan Rag Bill Boyd, 122
Black And White Rag Milton Brown, 137; Humphries Brothers, 447
Black Annie Georgia Yellow Hammers, 367
Black Bayou One Step Anatole Credure, 232
Black Bottle Blues George E. Harris, 404–05
Black Bottom Blues Gene Autry, 77
Black Bottom Strut Three Stripped Gears, 907
Black Eyed Susan Brown Hoosier Hot Shots, 436; W. Lee O'Daniel, 665; Earl & Willie Phelps, 689; Tune Wranglers, 915
Black Eyed Susie J.W. Day, 306; Hill Billies, 423; J.P. Nester, 653; Hank Penny, 686; Doc Roberts, 752; Gid Tanner, 887, 889
Black Hawk Waltz Kessinger Brothers, 480
Black Jack David Cliff Carlisle, 168; Carter Family, 195
Black Jack Davy Part I, II Professor & Mrs. Greer, 382
Black Jack Moonshine Tom Darby & Jimmie Tarlton, 294
Black Lake Waltz E.E. Hack String Band, 386
Black Mustache Gene Clardy & Stan Clements, 212
Black Outlaw Steer Bill Bender, 99
Black Pine Waltz Gwen Foster, 353
Black Rider Bob Wills, 962
Black Sea Blues Texas Wanderers, 900
Black Sheep Richard Brooks & Reuben Puckett, 133; Warren Caplinger, 157; Tom Darby & Jimmie Tarlton, 294–95; Doc Hopkins, 441; (Charlie) Monroe's Boys, 632; Shelton Brothers, 827
Black Sheep Blues E.E. Hack String Band, 386; Charlie Hager, 388
Black Sheep Of The Family [The] Fruit Jar Guzzlers, 360
Black Snake John Henry Howard, 444
Black Snake Moan E.E. Hack String Band, 386
Blackberry Blossom Richard D. Burnett, 144; Arthur Smith, 840
Blackberry Quadrille Woodhull's Old Time Masters, 971
Blackberry Rag J.D. Harris, 405; Three Stripped Gears, 907
Black-Eyed Susan Henry Whitter, 954
Blackie's Gunman Carter Family, 195
Blanket Me With Western Skies Patsy Montana, 636
Blazin' The Trail Patsy Montana, 634
Bleeding Hearted Blues Bob Wills, 962
Blessed Jesus, Hold My Hand Morris Brothers, 643
Blessed Redeemer Maury Pearson, 683
Blind Boy [The] Emry Arthur, 66
Blind Boy's Lament Pickard Family, 693
Blind Child Delmore Brothers, 310; Otto Gray, 379; Harvey Irwin, 451
Blind Child's Prayer [The] Cliff Carlisle, 166; Fisher Hendley, 417; Lester McFarland & Robert A. Gardner, 543
Blind Child's Prayer Part 1, 2 [The] Clayton McMichen, 568
Blind Girl [The] Bradley Kincaid, 483–85
Blind Man [The] Buell Kazee, 473
Blind Man And His Child [The] Red Fox Chasers, 730
Blind Man's Lament [The] Crockett [Family] Mountaineers, 233
Blonde Headed Baby Crowder Brothers, 237
Blonde Headed Girl Red Foley, 351
Blonde Headed Mama Blues Shelly Lee Alley, 58
Blonde-Headed Woman Hi-Flyers, 420
Blood Of Jesus Saved Me [The] Dorsey & Beatrice Dixon, 322
Bloodstained Dress [The] Emry Arthur, 66
Bloody War John D. Foster, 354; Jimmy Yates Groups, 975
Bloom Brightly Sweet Rose XC Sacred Quartette, 975
Bloom Brightly Sweet Roses Peck's Male Quartette, 684; Simmons Sacred Singers, 835; Vaughan Quartet, 924

Blooming Youth Denson-Parris Sacred Harp Singers, 313; Huggins & Philips Sacred Harp Singers, 446
Blow That Lonesome Whistle Anglin Brothers, 61
Blow The Whistle Zeke Manners, 586
Blow Yo' Whistle, Freight Train Delmore Brothers, 310
Blow Your Whistle Freight Train Milo Twins, 628
Blow, Whistle, Blow Bob Atcher, 69
Blowin' Down The Road Woody Guthrie, 386
Blowin' The Blues Chuck Darling, 295; Fleming & Townsend, 346
Blue Accordion Blues Bob Skyles, 838
Blue And Lonesome Fleming & Townsend, 348; Sunshine Boys, 881
Blue And The Gray [The] Tom Darby & Jimmie Tarlton, 294
Blue Arizona Moon Bill Carlisle, 160
Blue Bazooka Blues Bob Skyles, 838
Blue Bell Hill Billies, 424; Dick Parman, 679
Blue Bonnet Girl Sons Of The Pioneers, 857
Blue Bonnet Governor Bar-X Cowboys, 93
Blue Bonnet Lane Roy Rogers, 812; Bob Wills, 965
Blue Bonnet Rag Bob Wills, 964
Blue Bonnet Rhythm Tune Wranglers, 916
Blue Bonnet Waltz Hi-Flyers, 418; Light Crust Doughboys, 501
Blue Bonnet Yodelling Blues Arthur Duhon, 325
Blue Bonnets Ella Sutton, 882
Blue Days Gene Autry, 73; Allie & Pearl Brock, 131; Hinson, Pitts & Coley, 427; Daddy John Love, 514
Blue Devil Rag Jack Cawley's Oklahoma Ridge Runners, 199
Blue Dreams Cliff Carlisle, 167
Blue Eyed Baby Al Dexter, 314; Tennessee Ramblers [II], 897
Blue Eyed Blonde Bill Cox, 228
Blue Eyed Boy Morris Family, 644
Blue Eyed Darling Roy Acuff, 50
Blue Eyed Ellen Elton Britt, 128; Frank Luther, 525; Margaret West, 945
Blue Eyed Ellen (The Jealous Lover Of Lone Green Valley) Vass Family, 922
Blue Eyed Eller Posey Rorer, 813
Blue Eyed Girl Hill Billies, 423; Patt Patterson, 682
Blue Eyed Jane Parker & Dodd, 678
Blue Eyed Sailor Bill Cox, 228
Blue Eyed Sally Bill Cox, 227; Sam & Fred Friend, 359; Light Crust Doughboys, 504
Blue Eyes Blue Ridge Hill Billies, 110; Bill Carlisle, 159; Cliff Carlisle, 165; Dixieland Swingsters, 320; Hackberry Ramblers, 387; Roy Harvey, 409–11; Fisher Hendley, 417; Leo Soileau, 854
Blue Eyes Lullaby Rex Griffin, 383
Blue Eyes Waltz Amadie Breaux, 126
Blue For A Red Headed Daddy Dick Hartman's Tennessee Ramblers, 408
Blue For My Blue Eyes Bill Cox, 228
Blue For Old Hawaii Hank Snow, 852
Blue Galilee Hendersonville Quartet, 416
Blue Grass Hayseed Harmonica Bill, 401
Blue Grass Rag Doc Roberts, 755
Blue Grass Twist South Georgia Highballers, 860
Blue Guitar Light Crust Doughboys, 503
Blue Guitars Light Crust Doughboys, 504
Blue Hawaii Gene Autry, 82; Lester McFarland & Robert A. Gardner, 546; Oliver & Allen, 669
Blue Hawaiian Moonlight Nite Owls, 661
Blue Hills Of Virginia [The] McDonald Quartet, 541; Clayton McMichen, 571; Wing's Rocky Mountain Ramblers, 968
Blue Hours Light Crust Doughboys, 504
Blue Juniata Sons Of The Pioneers, 858
Blue Kimono Blues Shelton Brothers, 828

Blue Lagoon Carson Robison, 768
Blue Man Leaford Hall, 390
Blue Man's Blues Dave Edwards, 331
Blue Melody Hank Penny, 686
Blue Monday Leon Selph, 823
Blue Monday Morning Blues Albert Cain, 150
Blue Montana Skies Gene Autry, 83
Blue Moon Dewey & Gassie Bassett, 97
Blue Mountain Blues Ella Sutton, 882
Blue Mountain Home In The West Bob Palmer & Jimmy White, 673
Blue Mountain Sally Goodin George Edgin, 330
Blue Mountain Shack Beverly Hill Billies, 102; Bill Cox, 229
Blue Pacific Moonlight Fred L. Jeske, 458; Carson Robison, 785
Blue Pining For You Jimmy Long, 511
Blue Prairie Sons Of The Pioneers, 857
Blue Prelude Bob Wills, 962
Blue Railroad Train Delmore Brothers, 309
Blue Ridge Blues Hank Penny, 686; George Reneau, 740–41
Blue Ridge Home I Love [The] Jack Pierce, 696
Blue Ridge Lullaby Kenneth Houchins, 444
Blue Ridge Mountain Blues Bill Cox, 225–26; Vernon Dalhart, 249; Cal Davenport, 296; John D. Foster, 354; Sid Harkreader, 400; Hill Billies, 423; Whitey McPherson, 579; Charlie [& Bud] Newman, 655; Riley Puckett, 716, 721; James Roberts, 756; Ernest V. Stoneman, 872
Blue Ridge Mountain Home Carson Robison, 764
Blue Ridge Mountain Queen Lew Childre, 207
Blue Ridge Mountain Sweetheart Buck Nation, 651
Blue Ridge Ramblers' Rag H.M. Barnes, 95
Blue Ridge Sweetheart Roy Acuff, 49; Vernon Dalhart, 288
Blue River Prairie Ramblers, 704; Bob Wills, 960
Blue River Train Carson Robison, 795
Blue Skies Dixieland Swingsters, 320; Bob Dunn's Vagabonds, 326
Blue Skies Above Leroy [Slim] Johnson, 462
Blue Skies Are Gray Skies Carl Boling, 116
Blue Skies Turned to Grey York Brothers, 977
Blue Sparks Kelly Brothers, 476
Blue Steel Blues Ted Daffan's Texans, 240
Blue Steele Blues Bar-X Cowboys, 93
Blue Street Blues [The] Bob Skyles, 838
Blue Tail Fly Wells Brothers String Band, 943
Blue Undertaker's Blues—Part 1–4 Goebel Reeves, 735
Blue Velvet Band [The] Hank Snow, 852
Blue Waltz Dixie Ramblers [II], 319
Blue Weary And Lonesome Panhandle Pete, 674
Blue Yodel Frank[ie] Marvin, 595; Riley Puckett, 718; Jimmie Rodgers, 799; Clifford Vaughn, 930
Blue Yodel—No. 4 Frank[ie] Marvin, 599
Blue Yodel—No. 9 Frank[ie] Marvin, 605
Blue Yodel—No. II (My Lovin' Gal, Lucille) Jimmie Rodgers, 800
Blue Yodel Blues Ray Whitley, 953
Blue Yodel No. 1 Whitey McPherson, 579; Frank[ie] Marvin, 594; Jimmie Rodgers, 809; Texas Ruby, 900; Bob Wills, 962
Blue Yodel No. 10 Jess Hillard, 426
Blue Yodel No. 10 (Ground Hog Rootin' In My Back Yard) Jimmie Rodgers, 807
Blue Yodel No. 12 Jimmie Rodgers, 808
Blue Yodel No. 2 Frank[ie] Marvin, 595–97
Blue Yodel No. 2 (My Lovin' Gal Lucille) Whitey McPherson, 579
Blue Yodel No. 3 Whitey McPherson, 579; Frank[ie] Marvin, 597; Hoke Rice, 745; Jimmie Rodgers, 800
Blue Yodel No. 4 Frank[ie] Marvin, 598; Hoke Rice, 745; Carson Robison, 772; Jimmie Rodgers, 809

Blue Yodel No. 4 (California Blues) Jimmie Rodgers, 801
Blue Yodel No. 5 Gene Autry, 71; W.C. Childers, 206; Howard Keesee, 474; Whitey McPherson, 579; Frank[ie] Marvin, 601; Jimmie Rodgers, 801
Blue Yodel No. 6 Gene Autry, 71; Cliff Carlisle, 161; W.C. Childers, 206; Frank[ie] Marvin, 602; Jimmie Rodgers, 802
Blue Yodel No. 7 Frank[ie] Marvin, 603; Bill Monroe, 632
Blue Yodel No. 8 Gene Autry, 73; Frank[ie] Marvin, 604
Blue Yodel No. 8 (Mule Skinner Blues) Jimmie Rodgers, 804
Blue Yodel No. 9 Harry Hillard, 425; Ted Lunsford, 517; Jimmie Rodgers, 804
Blue Yodel Number Eleven Jimmie Rodgers, 803
Blue Yodel, #1 (T For Texas) Jimmie Rodgers, 809
Blue Yodel, #11 Jimmie Rodgers, 803
Blueberry Hill Gene Autry, 84
Bluebird Waltz Big Chief Henry's Indian String Band, 103; Collier Trio, 218
Blue-Eyed Elaine Gene Autry, 86; Ernest Tubb, 913
Blue-Eyed Ella Kelly Harrell, 403; Roy Harvey, 409
Bluefield Murder [The] Emry Arthur, 66; Roy Harvey, 410
Bluer Than Blue Hank Snow, 852
Blues (My Naughty Sweetie Gives To Me) Hoosier Hot Shots, 440
Blues [The] Gace Haynes & Eugene Ballenger, 414
Blues De Basille Amedie Ardoin, 62
Blues De Leebou Joseph Falcon, 336
Blues Have Gone [The] Fleming & Townsend, 347
Blues In A Bottle Prince Albert Hunt, 447
Blues In Jail Bob Atcher, 70
Blues In The Bottle Jimmie Revard, 742
Blues In The Worsest Way [The] A.E. Ward, 938
Blues Is Nothing Bill Boyd, 123
Blues Negres (Niggar Blues) Joseph Falcon, 335
Blues On My Mind Ted Daffan's Texans, 241
Blues When It Rains Bill Boyd, 124
Blues, Why Don't You Let Me Alone? Roy Newman, 658
Bluest Blues Ted Daffan's Texans, 241
Bluff Hollow Sobs Sweet Brothers, 884
Bluin' In E Minor Sons Of The Ozarks, 856
Bluin' The Blues Bob Wills, 961
Blushing Bride Golden Melody Boys, 373
Boarding House Bells Are Ringing [The] Fletcher & Foster, 349
Boarding House Bells Are Ringing Waltz Kessinger Brothers, 480
Boarding House Blues [The] Lloyd Burdette, 143
Boat Song March Murphy Brothers, 646
Boatin' Up Sandy Hill Billies, 423
Boatman's Dance Byrd Moore, 639
Boatman's Delight Stripling Brothers, 880
Bob Christmas Carter Brothers & Son, 187
Bob Murphy Cherokee Ramblers, 203; Watkins Band, 940
Bob Walker William B. Houchens, 443
Bob Wills Special Bob Wills, 964
Bob Wills Stomp Bob Wills, 965
Bobby Boy—Part 1, 2 Graham Brothers, 377
Bobby Boy, Oh Boy, Oh Boy Maple City Four, 587
Bob's Medley Bob McGimsey, 564
Body In The Bag [The] Stan Davis, 306
Bogey Alley Louie Donaldson, 323
Boggy Road To Texas Sons Of The Pioneers, 859
Boil Dem Cabbage Down Earl Johnson, 459
Boil The Cabbage Down W.E. Bowden, 120
Boil Them Cabbage Down Fiddlin' John Carson, 176
Bold Knights Of Labor [The] Oscar L. Coffey, 216
Boling Rag Carl Boling, 116
Boll Weevil W.A. Lindsay, 507; Charlie Oaks, 664
Bollweevil Blues Cherokee Ramblers, 203; Gid Tanner, 887

Bon Whiskey Joe Werner, 943
Bonaparte's Retreat Crockett [Family] Mountaineers, 233; A.A. Gray, 378; Arthur Smith, 841
Bone Dry Blues Lowe Stokes, 871
Boneparte's Retreat Gid Tanner, 890
Bonham Bus Line Blues Part I George Williams, 958
Bonnie Ross Rhythm Rascals, 814
Bonnie Bess Wilmer Watts, 941
Bonnie Blue Eyes Roy Acuff, 49; Carter Family, 194; Hackberry Ramblers, 387; Leake County Revelers, 495
Bonnie Blue Eyes—Part 2 Dorsey & Beatrice Dixon, 321
Bonnie Blue Waltz Richard D. Burnett, 144
Bonnie Blues Eyes Joseph Falcon, 336
Bonnie Little Girl Blind Alfred Reed, 733
Bonus Army Blues Three Tobacco Tags, 907
Boo Hoo Blues Lunsford Bros., 517
Boog-A-Boo Baby Buddy Jones, 465; Roy Newman, 658
Boogie Woogie Cowboy Patsy Montana, 637
Boogie Woogie In The Village Village Boys, 932
Boogie Woogie Johnson Jubileers, 468
Boogie-Woogie Johnny Barfield, 93
Boojie-Woo Blues Ross Rhythm Rascals, 814
Book Of Etiquette [The] Capt. Appleblossom, 158
Book Of Life [The] J.H. Howell, 445
Book That Mother Gave Me [The] Rev. Edward Boone, Mrs. Edward Boone & Miss Olive Boone, 118
Booley Wooger Prairie Ramblers, 712
Booneville Stomp Dutch Coleman, 217
Bootlegger Song [The] Georgia Wildcats, 366
Bootleggers Blues Buck Turner, 916
Bootlegger's Dream James Brown, Jr. & Ken Landon Groups, 135
Bootlegger's Dream Of Home [The] Earl Shirkey & Roy Harper, 831
Bootlegger's Joint In Atlanta Part 3,4 [A] John Dilleshaw, 318
Bootlegger's Joint In Atlanta Pt. 1, 2 [A] Chumbler Family, 212
Bootlegger's Lullaby [The] Emry Arthur, 67
Bootlegger's Plea [The] Bill Cox, 225
Bootlegger's Song [The] Emry Arthur, 66
Bootlegger's Story Frank Gerald & Howard Dixon, 368
Boots And Saddle Riley Puckett, 722
Booze Drinkin' Daddy Chester Allen & Campbell, 54
Border Affair (Mi Amor, Mi Corazon) [The] Tex Fletcher, 348; Texas Jim Robertson, 760
Born In Hard Luck Chris Bouchillon, 119; Harmon Canada, 154
Born To Be Blue Jimmie Davis, 304
Born To Lose Ted Daffan's Texans, 241
Born To The Saddle Roy Rogers, 811
Born Too Soon Tune Wranglers, 915
Boston Burglar [The] Fiddlin' John Carson, 176; Vernon Dalhart, 246–49; Frank Hutchison, 450; Frank Luther, 525; Pie Plant Pete, 694–95; Riley Puckett, 717; Carl T. Sprague, 862
Boston Fancy Mellie Dunham's Orchestra, 326
Boston Waltz [The] Richmond Melody Boys, 748
Bottom Of The Lake [The] Travelers, 912
Bouncin' Along Texas Jim Robertson, 759
Bound For Canaan [J.T.] Allison's Sacred Harp Singers, 60; OKeh Atlanta Sacred Harp Singers, 667
Bound For The Promised Land Harmon E. Helmick, 415
Bound Steel Blues Bill Shepherd, 830
Bound To Look Like A Monkey Jimmie Revard, 743
Bouquet Waltz Oscar & Doc Harper, 402
Bouquets Of June Waltz W.T. Narmour & S.W. Smith, 650
Bow Legged Irishman Ted Gossett's Band, 376

Bow Wow Blues Allen Brothers, 55; Hoosier Hot Shots, 436
Bower Of Prayer [The] Charles Butts Sacred Harp Singers, 149
Bowery Bums [The] Ernest Hare, 399; Carson Robison, 767
Box Car Blues Buddy Baker, 89; Cliff Carlisle, 161
Box Car Yodel Cliff Carlisle, 163
Boy Around A Boy—Girl Around A Girl Roy Rogers, 812
Boy From North Carolina [A] Claude Casey, 197
Boy In Blue [The] Stuart Hamblen, 392
Boy The Ladies Saved From Jail [The] Rambling Kid & The Professor, 725
Boy Who Stuttered And The Girl Who Lisped [The] Stan Davis, 306
Boy, Take Your Time Prairie Ramblers, 711
Boyd's Blues Bill Boyd, 122
Boyd's Kelly Waltz Bill Boyd, 124
Boyd's Tin Roof Blues Bill Boyd, 124
Boyhood Days Down On The Farm Little Georgie Porgie, 508
Boys [sic] Best Friend [The] Walter Coon, 220
Boy's Best Friend Is His Mother [A] Vernon Dalhart, 244–46, 281; Charlie Oaks, 664
Boys In Blue Edward L. Crain, 230; Russell Brothers, 816; Marc Williams, 958
Boys Keep Away From The Girls Bill Chitwood, 208
Brace Up And Be A Man, She Said Norman Woodlieff, 972
Brakeman Blues Whitey McPherson, 579
Brakeman's Blues (Yodeling The Blues Away) [The] Jimmie Rodgers, 800
Brakeman's Blues [The] Cliff Carlisle, 161; Frank[ie] Marvin, 595–96
Brakeman's Reply [The] Cliff Carlisle, 161, 164
Branded Wherever I Go Roy Acuff, 50; Denver Darling, 296
Brave Engineer [The] Carver Boys, 196; Roy Harvey, 409
Brave Soldier [The] Rosa Lee Carson, 179
Braying Mule Uncle Dave Macon, 575
Bread Line Blues Bernard [Slim] Smith, 842
Break The News To Mother Arthur Fields & Fred Hall, 338; Andrew Jenkins, 453
Breakdown De Cajin (Cajun Breakdown) Leo Soileau, 855
Breakin' My Heart Over You Ted Daffan's Texans, 240
Breakin' Up Matches Leon Selph, 823
Breaking Of The St. Francis Dam John McGhee & Frank Welling, 554; Edd Rice, 744
Breeze Riley Puckett, 718–19
Breeze (Blow My Baby Back To Me) Dick Hartman's Tennessee Ramblers, 409; Leo Soileau, 855; Zeke Williams, 959
Breezin' Along With The Breeze Hoosier Hot Shots, 437
Brick Yard Joe Doc Roberts, 753
Bright And Golden Lights Reed Family, 734
Bright Fiery Cross [The] R.C. Garner, 363
Bright Lights In The Graveyard Georgia Crackers, 366
Bright Little Valley [The] Chubby Parker, 677
Bright Mohawk Valley [The] David Gauthier, 364; Knight Sisters, 487
Bright Sherman Valley Luther B. Clarke, 214; Kelly Harrell, 403; Doctor Lloyd & Howard Maxey, 508; Frank Luther, 523; Lester McFarland & Robert A. Gardner, 543; Holland Puckett, 715; Goebel Reeves, 737; Ernest V. Stoneman, 874
Bright Tomorrow Ernest Phipps, 691
Brighten The Corner Hartford City Trio, 407
Brighten The Corner Where You Are Kanawha Singers, 469; John McGhee & Frank Welling, 556, 561
Brilliancy Forrest Copeland & Johnny Britton, 221
Brilliancy And Cheatum A.C. (Eck) Robertson, 757
Brilliancy Medley A.C. (Eck) Robertson, 757
Bring Back My Blue Eyed Sweetheart Philyaw Brothers, 690

Bring Back My Blue-Eyed Boy Boyden Carpenter, 174; Riley Puckett, 719; Red Headed Brier Hopper, 731; Arthur Tanner, 886
Bring Back My Blue-Eyed Boy To Me Carter Family, 188
Bring Back My Boy Carter Family, 194; Ted Chestnut, 204
Bring Back My Buddie George Edgin, 330
Bring Back My Darling Jack & Jean, 451
Bring Back My Wandering Boy Blue Sky Boys, 114; W.C. Childers, 206
Bring Back The Greenback Dollar Dixieland Swingsters, 320
Bring Back The Old Time Music John McGhee & Frank Welling, 555
Bring Back The One I Love Dewey Hayes, 414
Bring Back The Sunshine And Roses Bill Cox, 225–26
Bring Back To Me My Wandering Boy Emry Arthur, 65
Bring It Down To The Jailhouse, Honey Hackberry Ramblers, 387
Bring It On Down To My House Charlie Mitchell & His Kentucky Ridge Runners, 630; Bob Wills, 961
Bring It On Down To My House Honey Milton Brown, 138
Bring It On Home To Grandma Shelly Lee Alley, 58; Cliff Bruner, 140
Bring It On Home To Me Al Dexter, 314
Bring Me A Bottle Leake County Revelers, 494
Bring Me A Leaf From The Sea Blue Ridge Mountain Entertainers, 111; Carolina Tar Heels, 173; Vernon Dalhart, 277, 279; Red Fox Chasers, 731; Ernest Thompson, 903
Bring Me Back My Darling Allie & Pearl Brock, 131
Bring Mother The News Joe Werner, 944
Bring Them In Clagg & Sliger, 212
Bring Your Roses To Her Now Beverly Hill Billies, 102; Carson Robison, 788
Bring Your Roses To Your Mother Elton Britt, 128
Bringin' Home The Bacon Cliff Bruner, 139
Bringing In The Sheaves Eva Quartette, 333; Earl Johnson, 460; Mountain Singers Male Quartet, 645; Parker & Dodd, 678; Stamps Quartet, 863; Vaughan Quartet, 928
Bristol Tennessee Blues Hill Billies, 423
Britt's Reel Elton Britt, 127
Broadway Blues Allie & Pearl Brock, 131
Broadway Mama Bill Boyd, 124
Broadway Moon Lester McFarland & Robert A. Gardner, 549
Broder Jonah Sunshine Four, 882
Broke Down Section Hand Ernest V. Stoneman, 878
Broke Man Blues Georgia Wildcats, 366
Broken Down Gambler Gid Tanner, 891
Broken Down Tramp [The] Carter Family, 194
Broken Dreams Hank Snow, 853
Broken Engagement [The] Kelly Harrell, 403; Jo & Alma, 459; Lester McFarland & Robert A. Gardner, 545; Massey Family, 611; Charlie Oaks, 664; Holland Puckett, 715; Riley Puckett, 721; C.A. West, 944; Henry Whitter, 956
Broken Engagement Blues Henry Whitter, 954
Broken Engagements Bill Shafer, 824
Broken Heart Roy Acuff, 50; Carlisle Brothers, 169; Dewey Hayes, 414
Broken Hearted Blues Al Dexter, 314; Daddy John Love, 514
Broken Hearted Family [The] Anglin Brothers, 61
Broken Hearted Girl Dorsey & Beatrice Dixon, 322
Broken Hearted Lover Carolina Buddies, 170; Carter Family, 190, 193; Cal Davenport, 296; Delmore Brothers, 311; Ernest V. Stoneman, 877
Broken Hearted Mother [A] Buddy Dewitt, 313
Broken Hearted Vow [The] George Edgin, 330
Broken Man [The] Bill Boyd, 121
Broken Promises John D. Foster, 354
Broken Tambourine [The] Harry "Mac" McClintock, 529
Broken Vows Bob Atcher, 69

Broken Wedding [The] Emry Arthur, 66
Broken Wedding Ring [The] Hank Snow, 853
Broken-Down Cowboy Wilf Carter (Montana Slim), 183
Broken-Hearted Charles Mitchell & His Orchestra, 629; George [Shortbuckle] Roark, 752
Broken-Hearted Cowboy George Wade, 933
Broken-Hearted Wife Johnson Brothers, 463
Bronc That Wouldn't Bust [The] Arkansas Woodchopper, 64
Broncho Bustin' Blues Phil Pavey, 682
Bronco Bill Asa Martin, 591–92
Bronco Mustang Buck Nation, 650
Brooklyn Theatre Fire Thurston Sutton & Raymond Sutton, 882
Broomstick Buckaroo Gene Autry, 85
Brother Ephram Wade Ward, 939
Brother Henry Texas Jim Robertson, 759
Brother Noah Built An Ark Alf. Taylor, 892
Brother Of Missouri Joe [The] Bob Miller, 625
Brother Of Old Missouri Joe Prairie Ramblers, 709
Brother Take Warning Roy Acuff, 50; Delmore Brothers, 310
Brother, Be Ready For That Day Grady & Hazel Cole, 217
Brotherhood [The] John McGhee & Frank Welling, 561
Brown Bottle Blues Slim Harbert, 398
Brown Eyed Sweet Adolph Hofner, 430
Brown Eyes Blue Sky Boys, 114; Edith & Sherman Collins, 218; Bill Cox, 226; Fisher Hendley, 416; Wade Mainer, 582
Brown Jug Blues Ezra Buzzington's Rustic Revelers, 149
Brown Kelly Waltz—Part 1, 2 A.C. (Eck) Robertson, 757
Brown Mule Slide Chumbler Family, 211; Jim King, 486; Hoke Rice, 746
Brown Skin Blues Dick Justice, 468
Brown Skin Gal (Down The Lane) Massey Family, 609
Brownie Special Milton Brown, 136
Brownie's Stomp Milton Brown, 136
Brown's Dream Fiddlin' Powers & Family, 703
Brown's Ferry Blues Bill Cox, 226; Delmore Brothers, 309; McGee Brothers, 552
Brown's Ferry Blues—Part 2, 3 Delmore Brothers, 310–11
Brown's Ferry Blues No. 2 Callahan Brothers, 153
Brown's Ferry Blues, No. 4 Philyaw Brothers, 690
Brownstown Girl Kessinger Brothers, 480
Bruddah Brown Monroe Quartette, 634
Bruno Hauptmann's Fate Buck Nation, 651
Bryan's Last Fight Vernon Dalhart, 250
Buck Creek Gal Doc Roberts, 752
Buck Creek Girls Fiddlin' Powers & Family, 703
Buck Dancer's Choice McGee Brothers, 551
Buck Jones Rangers' Song Frank Luther, 518
Buckaroo Stomp Massey Family, 609
Buckeye Medley Quadrille John Baltzell, 90
Buck-Eyed Rabbits Hill Billies, 423
Buckin' Mule Carolina Ramblers String Band, 172; J.D. Harris, 405; Short Creek Trio, 833; Southern Moonlight Entertainers, 860; Gid Tanner, 887, 889
Bucking Broncho Girls Of The Golden West, 370
Buckwheat Batter Tom Owens Barn Dance Trio, 672; Tweedy Brothers, 918
Budded Rose [The] Delmore Brothers, 310; Light Crust Doughboys, 504; Charlie Poole, 699
Budded Roses Roy Harvey, 410; Daddy John Love, 514; Asa Martin, 593; Red Fox Chasers, 731; Shelton Brothers, 827
Buddies In The Saddle Carter Family, 195
Buddy Jimmy Long, 512
Buddy Boy Elton Britt, 130
Buddy Won't You Roll Down The Line Uncle Dave Macon, 576
Buffalo Bill Vernon Dalhart, 286; Carson Robison, 770
Buffalo Boy Go 'Round The Outside Carson Robison, 796

Buffalo Gals Frank Luther, 524; Shorty McCoy, 531; Pickard Family, 692–93; Ranch Boys, 726–27
Buffalo Gal's Medley Crockett [Family] Mountaineers, 234
Buffalo Girl Alexander & Miller, 53; Tommy Dandurand, 293
Buffalo Girls Tom Owens Barn Dance Trio, 672
Buffalo Rag Wonder State Harmonists, 971
Buffalo Range Frank Luther, 522
Buffalo Skinner [The] Bill Bender, 99
Bug House Stripling Brothers, 880
Bug In The Taters Hill Billies, 424
Bug Scuffle Swift Jewel Cowboys, 884
Bugle Call Rag Leon Chappelear, 201
Bugle Two-Step Sons Of Dixie, 856
Build Me A Bungalow William Rexroat's Cedar Crest Singers, 744
Build Me A Bungalow Big Enough For Two Leonard Rutherford, 816
Bull At The Wagon Lewis Brothers, 500
Bull Dog Down In Tennessee Ted Bare, 93; Fred Pendleton, 685
Bull Dog In Tennessee Lester "Pete" Bivins, 107
Bull Dog Sal Thomas C. Ashley, 68
Bull Fight In Mexico [A] Chris Bouchillon, 119
Bull Frog Serenade Hoosier Hot Shots, 440
Bulldog Greenville Trio, 382; Monroe Quartette, 634
Bulldog Down In Sunny Tennessee [The] Carolina Tar Heels, 173; "Dock" Walsh, 937
Bully Of The Town [The] Fiddlin' John Carson, 176; Cherokee Ramblers, 203; Sid Harkreader, 400; Earl Johnson, 459; Kessinger Brothers, 480; Frank Luther, 524; Lester McFarland & Robert A. Gardner, 542; Clayton McMichen, 565; Frank[ie] Marvin, 594; Byrd Moore, 638; North Carolina Hawaiians, 663; Ernest V. Stoneman, 874–75; Gid Tanner, 887; Tweedy Brothers, 918
Bully Of The Town No. 2 Gid Tanner, 890
Bully Song—Part 1, 2 [The] Vernon Dalhart, 283
Bum Bum Blues Rouse Brothers, 815
Bum Hotel [The] Uncle Dave Macon, 578
Bum On The Bum Ramblin' Red Lowery, 515
Bum Song [The] Vernon Dalhart, 283; Arthur Fields & Fred Hall, 339; Ernest Hare, 399; Harry "Mac" McClintock, 528–29; Carson Robison, 764, 792
Bum Song No. 2 [The] Vernon Dalhart, 284; Jack Golding, 374; Harry "Mac" McClintock, 529; Carson Robison, 767
Bum Song No. 5 (Happy-Go-Lucky Boy) Carson Robison, 774
Bumble Bee [The] E.M. Bartlett Groups, 96
Bum-Dalay Land Norris, 662
Bummelpetuss [sic] Walter C. Peterson, 688
Bummin' On The I.C. Line Clayton McMichen, 571; Bob Miller, 622
Bum's Rush [The] Charlie Craver, 231; Ernest Hare, 399; Carson Robison, 767, 770
Bunch Of Cactus On The Wall [The] Cliff Carlisle, 166
Buncombe Chain Gang Haywood County Ramblers, 414
Buncombe County Blues Crowder Brothers, 237–38
Bundle Of Old Southern Sunshine [A] Jimmie Revard, 743
Bungalow Big Enough For Two Four Pickled Peppers, 356
Bunkhouse Jamboree Massey Family, 611
Burglar And The Old Maid [The] Fiddlin' John Carson, 177
Burglar Man [The] Frank Hutchison, 450; Pine Ridge Ramblers, 698; Riley Puckett, 716; Short Creek Trio, 833; Arthur Tanner, 886; Henry Whitter, 956
Burglar Man And Old Man No. 2 Benny Borg, 118
Burial Of The Miner's Child Jack & Tony, 452; John McGhee & Frank Welling, 556
Burial Of Wild Bill Frank Jenkins, 455

Burning Kisses John McGhee & Frank Welling, 558
Burning Of Cleveland School J.H. Howell, 446
Burning Of The Kimball House [The] Macon String Trio, 579
Bury Me Beneath The Roses Fred Kirby, 487
Bury Me Beneath The Weeping Willow Tree Ernest V. Stoneman, 873
Bury Me Beneath The Willow Claude Davis, 297; Shelton Brothers, 827
Bury Me In A Corner Of The Yard E. Segura & D. Herbert, 823
Bury Me In Old Kentucky Jimmie Davis, 299–300
Bury Me In The Hill Billy Way Bill Cox, 228
Bury Me In The Tennessee Mountains Bill Cox, 225; Arthur Fields & Fred Hall, 341
Bury Me 'Neath The Weeping Willow Light Crust Doughboys, 502; Asa Martin, 590
Bury Me 'Neath The Willow Tree Riley Puckett, 721
Bury Me Not On A Lone Prairie Vernon Dalhart, 271
Bury Me Not On The Lone Prairie W.C. Childers, 205; Vernon Dalhart, 264, 271; Pickard Family, 691; Carson Robison, 792
Bury Me On The Lone Prairie Otto Gray, 379
Bury Me On The Prairie Jimmy Johnson's String Band, 461; Bradley Kincaid, 482
Bury Me Out On The Prairie Edward L. Crain, 230; Delmore Brothers, 309; Farm Hands, 336; Bradley Kincaid, 484; Ranch Boys, 726–27; Rodeo Trio, 798; Roy Shaffer, 825
Bury Me Out On The Prairie (I Got No Use For The Women) Ranch Boys, 726
Bury Me Under The Weeping Willow Carter Family, 187; Delmore Brothers, 310
Business In "F" Light Crust Doughboys, 502; Ross Rhythm Rascals, 814
Bust Down Stomp John Dilleshaw, 317
Busted Bank Blues John McGhee & Frank Welling, 561
Buster's Crawdad Song Tune Wranglers, 914
But How Did De Goats Git In Vaughan Quartet, 930
But I Do You Know I Do David Miller, 626
But Now It's Only A Dream Anglin Brothers, 61
But The World Treats Real Salvation In Such A Funny Way E. Arthur Lewis, 497
Butcher Boy Vernon Dalhart, 270; Bradley Kincaid, 483; Frank Luther, 524; James Roberts, 756; Carson Robison, 763; Henry Whitter, 955
Butcher Man Blues Buddy Jones, 465
Butcher's Boy (The Railroad Boy) [The] Buell Kazee, 472
Butcher's Boy [The] Blue Sky Boys, 114; Carolina Night Hawks, 172; Vernon Dalhart, 265; Kelly Harrell, 403; Carson Robison, 764
Buttercup Grady Family, 376
Butterscotch Rag Gibson String Trio, 369
Buvez Plus Jamais (Never Drink No More) Joseph Falcon, 335
Buy A Half Pint And Stay In The Wagon Yard Earl Johnson, 460
By A Cottage In The Twilight Roy Harvey, 411
By A Little Bayou Dwight Butcher, 148; McDonald Quartet, 541
By A Window Bill Boyd, 122
By A Window At The End Of The Lane Beverly Hill Billies, 102; Cliff Bruner, 139; Tom & Chuck, 910
By And By You Will Forget Me Fred Pendleton, 685
By Himself Dorsey & Beatrice Dixon, 322
By The Banks Of The Rio Grande Delmore Brothers, 309
By The Cottage Door Perry County Music Makers, 687
By The Grave Of Nobody's Darling Wilf Carter (Montana Slim), 184

By The Grave Of Nobody's Darling (My Darling's Promise) Jimmie Davis, 303; Girls Of The Golden West, 371; Prairie Ramblers, 709
By The Honeysuckle Vine Lester McFarland & Robert A. Gardner, 548
By The Light Of The Moon Christine Muszar, 647
By The Old Garden Gate Jack & Johnnie Powell, 703
By The Old Oak Tree Carson Robison, 783
By The Old Oaken Bucket, Louise Tom Darby & Jimmie Tarlton, 295; Frank Gerald & Howard Dixon, 368; Buck Nation, 651; Jimmie Tarlton, 892
By The Old Swinging Bridge Lou & Nellie Thompson, 904
By The Old Swinging Bridge Across The Rim Frank & James McCravy, 538
By The Ozark Trail George E. Logan, 508; Jimmy Long, 511
By The River Sainte Marie Bob Skyles, 839
By The Sea Hal O'Halloran's Hooligans, 667
By The Silvery Rio Grande Ted Chestnut, 204; Girls Of The Golden West, 370
By The Silv'ry Moonlight Trail Wilf Carter (Montana Slim), 182
By The Sleepy Rio Grande Elton Britt, 128; Stuart Hamblen, 392
By The Stump Of The Old Pine Tree Arty Hall, 390; Shelton Brothers, 829
By The Touch Of Her Hand Carter Family, 192
By The Waters Of Minnetonka Jim & Bob, 458
Bye And Bye [Smilin'] Ed McConnell, 530; Frank & James McCravy, 531–32, 536
Bye And Bye You Will Forget Me Kelly Harrell, 403; Robert Hoke & Vernal West, 432; Lewis McDaniels, 538
Bye And Bye You'll Soon Forget Me Anglin Brothers, 61
Bye Bye Baby New Dixie Demons, 655
Bye Bye Blues Benny Borg, 118; Hoosier Hot Shots, 437; Earl & Willie Phelps, 689
Bye Bye Mama North Georgia Four, 663
Bye Bye Sweetheart Joseph Falcon, 335
Bye Bye, Baby, Bye Bye Roy Hall, 391; Shelton Brothers, 829
Bye Lo Baby Buntin' (Daddy's Goin' Huntin') Cindy Walker, 935
Bye, Bye, My Love Bill Carlisle, 160

C & N.W. Railroad Blues Byron Parker, 675
C & O Wreck [The] George Reneau, 740
C&O Excursion Frank Hutchison, 449
C&O Freight And Section Crew Wreck Rev. H.L. Shumway, 834
C. & N.W. Blues Bert Bilbro, 103
C. & O. Whistle Fruit Jar Guzzlers, 360
C.C. & O. No. 558 Hill Billies, 423
C.C.C. Lament Bobbie & Ruby Ricker, 748
Ca Tait Pas Difference Asteur (It Makes No Difference Now) Sons Of Acadians, 856
Cabin Home Golden Melody Boys, 373
Cabin In The Hills Carson Robison, 785
Cabin Just Over The Hill Doc Hopkins, 441
Cabin With Roses At The Door John D. Foster, 355
Cabin With The Roses [The] Virginia Dandies, 932
Cabin With The Roses At The Door [The] John D. Foster, 354
Cacklin' Hen And Rooster Too Gid Tanner, 890
Cackling Hen Fruit Jar Guzzlers, 360; J.D. Harris, 405; Hill Billies, 422; Jess Hillard, 425
Cackling Pullet Fiddlin' John Carson, 176; Tennessee Ramblers [1], 896
Cactus Bill Joe Harvey, 409
Cactus Blossoms Prairie Ramblers, 707

Cafe Song [The] Honeyboy & Sassafras[s], 433
Cajon Stomp Sons Of The Pioneers, 857–58
Cajun Breakdown Miller's Merrymakers, 628; Leo Soileau, 855
Cajun Crawl Hackberry Ramblers, 387
Cake Eatin' Man Jimmie Revard, 742
Cake Walk And Down In Dixie Yellow Jackets [1], 976
Cal West's Yodel Blues—Part 1, 2 Cal West, 944
Calamity Jane Vernon Dalhart, 289; Arthur Fields & Fred Hall, 344; Adelyne Hood, 434–35
Calamity Jane (From The West) Vernon Dalhart, 289; Adelyne Hood, 434
Calcasieu Wilfred Fruge-Leo Soileau, 360
Calgary Roundup [The] Wilf Carter (Montana Slim), 182–83
Calico Rag [The] Al Dexter, 314
California Blues Bill Cox, 224; Stripling Brothers, 880
California Blues (Blue Yodel No. 4) Gene Autry, 72
California Murderer Roy Harvey, 411
California Trail [The] Twilight Trail Boys, 918
Caliope Lewis Brothers, 500
Call For Me And I'll Be There Gene Autry, 86
Call For Sinners Rev. Stephenson, 868
Call Me Back Again Lester McFarland & Robert A. Gardner, 545
Call Me Back Pal O' Mine Hugh Cross, 235; Jimmie Davis, 303; Lester McFarland & Robert A. Gardner, 545; Riley Puckett, 719
Call Me Back Pal Of Mine Gene Autry, 73
Call Me Pal Of Mine Frank Gerald & Howard Dixon, 367
Call Of Mother Love [The] Vernon Dalhart, 290
Call Of The Canyon [The] Gene Autry, 85; Ranch Boys, 727
Call Of The Cumberlands Cumberland Mountain Fret Pickers, 239
Call Of The Range Wilf Carter (Montana Slim), 186
Call Of The Whip-Poor-Will Mason Stapleton, 867
Callahan Doc Roberts, 754
Callahan Rag Roane County Ramblers, 751
Callahan's Reel Dykes' Magic City Trio, 328; Fiddlin' Powers & Family, 703
Called Home Bush Brothers, 147
Called To Foreign Fields Roy Harvey, 412
Called To The Foreign Field Alfred G. Karnes, 471
Calling Aloha To Me Jim & Bob, 458
Calling Ole Faithful Fred Kirby, 487
Calling The Prodigal Highleys, 421; John McGhee & Frank Welling, 556
Calling You Sweetheart Sidney Smith, 846
Calvary Denson-Parris Sacred Harp Singers, 313; Dye's Sacred Harp Singers, 328; Golden Echo Boys, 372
Campbells Are Coming Tommy Dandurand, 293
Camptown Races Carson Robison, 795
Can A Boy Forget His Mother Frank & James McCravy, 533–37
Can I Forget? Mr. & Mrs. R.N. Grisham, 385
Can I Get You Now Allen Brothers, 57
Can I Have Your Daughter Lowe Stokes, 871
Can I Sleep In Your Barn Tonight, Mister? Vernon Dalhart, 263, 265, 285; Kelly Brothers, 477; Frank Luther, 524; Charlie Poole, 699; Carson Robison, 787
Can I Sleep In Your Barn? Harry "Mac" McClintock, 529
Can The Circle Be Unbroken (Bye And Bye) Carter Family, 192
Can The World See Jesus In You Singing Preachers, 836
Can You Forgive Roy Hall, 391
Can You, Sweetheart, Keep A Secret? Lester McFarland & Robert A. Gardner, 543–44
Canaan's Land Original Sacred Harp Choir, 670

Canada Waltz Prince Albert Hunt, 447
Canal Street Mama Uncle Ned, 919
Candle Light In The Window [The] Carson Robison, 795
Candy Girl "Uncle Bunt" Stephens, 868
Cannon Ball Blues Carter Family, 193; Frank Hutchison, 450
Cannon Ball Rag David Miller, 627
Cannon-Ball [The] Carter Family, 189; Delmore Brothers, 311
Canoeing With Another Man Sammy & Smitty, 818; Uncle Ned, 919
Can't Blame Me For That Troy Martin & Elvin Bigger, 594
Can't Ease My Evil Mind Light Crust Doughboys, 506
Can't Feel At Home Carter Family, 189
Can't Nobody Truck Like Me Shelly Lee Alley, 58; Cliff Bruner, 139; Leon Selph, 823
Can't Put That Monkey On My Back Riley Puckett, 722
Can't Sleep In Your Barn Tonight Mister Marvin Williams, 959
Can't Tell About These Women Wade Mainer, 584
Can't Use Each Other Bill Boyd, 123
Can't We Make Up Again Bill Cox, 229
Can't We Start All Over Slim Harbert, 398
Can't Yo' Heah Me Callin' Caroline Vernon Dalhart, 267; Dan Hornsby, 442
Can't You Hear Me Calling, Caroline? Vernon Dalhart, 281; Melford Jackson, 452
Can't You Hear Me Say I Love You Travis B. Hale-E.J. Derry Jr., 389
Can't You Hear That Night Bird Crying Blue Sky Boys, 113
Can't You Remember When Your Heart Was Mine? Carolina Tar Heels, 173
Canyon Song [The] George Edgin, 330
Captain Dan's Last Trip Bob Miller, 619
Captain George, Has Your Money Come? W.T. Narmour & S.W. Smith, 649
Captain Jinks Woodhull's Old Time Masters, 971
Captain Tell Me True Clay Long, 510
Captain With His Whiskers [The] Aaron Campbell's Mountaineers, 154
Captain Won't You Let Me Go Home Tom Darby & Jimmie Tarlton, 294
Capture Of Albert Johnson [The] Wilf Carter (Montana Slim), 181
Car Hoppin' Mama Al Dexter, 314
Car Hop's Blues Ted Daffan's Texans, 240
Carbolic Rag Barber & Osborne, 93; Scottdale String Band, 821
Care Of Uncle Sam Denver Darling, 296
Careless Hoosier Hot Shots, 439; Light Crust Doughboys, 506
Careless Love Emry Arthur, 66; Theo. & Gus Clark, 214; C.A. Cronic, 234; Joseph Falcon, 335; Johnson Brothers, 462; Howard Keesee, 475; Lester McFarland & Robert A. Gardner, 542; Asa Martin, 593; Byrd Moore, 639; Riley Puckett, 720; Hoke Rice, 745; Ernest V. Stoneman, 877; Jimmie Tarlton, 892; Texas Rangers, 899
Careless Love (Bring My Baby Back) Delmore Brothers, 311
Careless Lover Byrd Moore, 638
Careless Soul McClendon Brothers, 528
Carmelita Jerry Behrens, 99
Carnal Mennagerie [sic] [The] E. Arthur Lewis, 497–98
Carolina Girl Jackson County Ramblers, 452
Carolina Glide Scottdale String Band, 821
Carolina Home Hackberry Ramblers, 387
Carolina In The Morning Bob Wills, 963
Carolina Moon Cruthers Brothers, 239; Frank Luther, 522; Lester McFarland & Robert A. Gardner, 546; Riley Puckett, 719; Carson Robison, 770; Merritt Smith, 844; Steelman Sisters, 867

Carolina Moonshiner Hill Billies, 424; Zeke Williams, 959
Carolina Rolling Stone Bob Calen, 151
Carolina Stompdown Aiken County String Band, 51
Carolina Sunshine Fred Richards, 747; Jimmy Yates Groups, 975
Carolina Sweetheart Callahan Brothers, 153
Carolina Trail James Scott-Claude Boone, 821
Carolina Train Clayton McMichen, 570
Carolina Yodeling Rambler Norwood Tew, 898
Carolina's Best Grady Family, 376
Carolina's Callin' Hugh Cross, 236
Caroline Moonshine Charlie Bowman, 121
Caroline Sunshine Girl Riley Puckett, 721
Caroline Train Bert Layne, 493
Carper Hutchison Virginia Ramblers, 933
Carrie, Sarrie And Me Kelly Brothers, 477
Carroll County Blues W.T. Narmour & S.W. Smith, 649; Byron Parker, 675; Doc Roberts, 754
Carroll County Blues No. 2 W.T. Narmour & S.W. Smith, 649
Carroll County No. 3 W.T. Narmour & S.W. Smith, 649
Carry Me Back To Alabama Delmore Brothers, 310
Carry Me Back To Carolina Tennessee Ramblers [II], 897
Carry Me Back To Dixie Thomas Brown, 138
Carry Me Back To Old Virginny Chief Pontiac, 205; W.W. Macbeth, 526; Lester McFarland & Robert A. Gardner, 547; Zack & Glenn, 979
Carry Me Back To Ole Virginny Ross Rhythm Rascals, 814
Carry Me Back To The Blue Ridge Walter Hurdt, 448
Carry Me Back To The Lone Prairie Milton Brown, 138; Light Crust Doughboys, 502; Massey Family, 609; Ranch Boys, 725
Carry Me Back To The Mountains Chuck Wagon Gang, 210; Flannery Sisters, 346; Girls Of The Golden West, 371; Dick Robertson, 758; Carson Robison, 782–84; Stewart's Harmony Singers, 869
Carry Me Back To Virginny Smoky Wood, 971
Carry Me Over The Tide Odus & Woodrow, 667
Carry Me Over The Warm Desert Sands Massey Family, 611
Carry The Good Work On Buddy Jones, 465
Carry Your Cross With A Smile J.E. Mainer's Mountaineers, 582
Carson Robison Selection (Continued) Carson Robison, 795
Carson Robison Selection No. 2- Part 1, 2 Carson Robison, 795–96
Carson Robison's Story—Part 1, 2 Carson Robison, 785
Carter Family And Jimmie Rodgers In Texas [The] Carter Family, 190; Jimmie Rodgers, 805
Carter's Blues Carter Family, 188
Carve That Possum Uncle Dave Macon, 575
Casey County Jail Cliff Carlisle, 166
Casey Jones Deford Bailey, 88; Al Bernard, 100; Fiddlin' John Carson, 175; Vernon Dalhart, 247–49, 281; Dixie Demons, 318; Hart & Ogle, 406; Riley Puckett, 715; George Reneau, 740; Carson Robison, 792; Bob Skiles Four Old Tuners, 837; Gid Tanner, 888
Casey's Old-Time Waltz Casey's Old Time Fiddlers, 197
Casey's Whistle Lester McFarland & Robert A. Gardner, 542–43
Cash River Waltz L.O. Birkhead & R.M. Lane, 106
Cast Thy Bread Upon The Water Clarence Ganus, 362
Cast Thy Bread Upon The Waters Frank & James McCravy, 537
Cat Came Back [The] Fiddlin' John Carson, 175; Otto Gray, 380; Riley Puckett, 720–21
Cat Rag Melvin Dupree, 327
Cata Houla Breakdown Jolly Boys Of Lafayette, 464

Catahoula Stomp Joseph Falcon, 335
Catch Me—I'm Falling Leo Soileau, 855
Catch On And Let's Go Roy Newman, 657
Catfish Medley March Jimmie Wilson's Catfish String Band, 968
Catfish Whiskers Jimmie Wilson's Catfish String Band, 968
Cathedral In The Pines Charles Hogg, 431; Fred Kirby, 487
Cats Are Bad Luck Jimmie Revard, 743
Cat's Got The Measles And The Dog's Got Whoopin' Cough [The] Walter Smith, 846
Cat's Whiskers [The] Patt Patterson, 681
Cattle Call Light Crust Doughboys, 505; Tex Owens, 671; Jimmy Wakely, 934
Cattlesburg James Brown, Jr. & Ken Landon Groups, 135
Cause All My Good Times Are Taken Away Bill Cox, 225
Cause I Don't Mean To Cry When You're Gone Delmore Brothers, 311
Cause My Baby's Gone Walter Hurdt, 448
Cave Love Has Gained The Day Kelly Harrell, 404
Ce Pas La Pienne Tu Pleur Leo Soileau, 854
Cemetary Sal Paradise Joy Boys, 674
Cemetery Sal Bill Boyd, 123; Roy Newman, 657–58
Central, Hello Hinson, Pitts & Coley, 427
C'Est Mauvais De Dire Un Mensonge (It's A Sin To Tell A Lie) Joseph Falcon, 336
C'Est Si Triste Sans Lui (It Is So Blue Without Him) Joseph Falcon, 334
C'Est Tard Et Le Temps Partir (It's Late And Time To Go) Joseph Falcon, 336
Chain Gang Blues Riley Puckett, 720
Chain Gang Song [The] Vernon Dalhart, 244–46, 248
Chain Gang Special Wilmer Watts, 941
Chain Store Blues Leo Soileau, 855
Chain Store Blues—Part 1, 2 Bob Miller, 620
Chamberlin And Lindy (Our Hats Are Off To You) Vernon Dalhart, 271
Chan Se Tige Happy Fats, 396
Change All Around [A] Wade Mainer, 583
Change In Business Claude Casey, 196; Fletcher & Foster, 349; Fred Kirby, 487
Change In Business All Around [A] Fletcher & Foster, 349
Chant Of The Jungle [The] Tom & Roy, 911
Chapel In The Valley Roy Rogers, 811
Charge To Keep [A] Wisdom Sisters, 969
Charge To Keep I Have [A] John McGhee & Frank Welling, 563
Charles A. Lindbergh, Jr. Bob Miller, 621
Charles Giteau [sic] Kelly Harrell, 404
Charles Guitaw [sic] Wilmer Watts, 941
Charleston Hornpipe [The] John W. Daniel, 293
Charleston No. 1 W.T. Narmour & S.W. Smith, 649; Doc Roberts, 755; Tweedy Brothers, 918
Charleston No. 2 W.T. Narmour & S.W. Smith, 649
Charleston No. 3 W.T. Narmour & S.W. Smith, 649
Charleston Rag Aiken County String Band, 52
Charleston Wabble Scottdale String Band, 822
Charley Boy (We Love You) Vernon Dalhart, 271
Charley, He's A Good Old Man Kelly Harrell, 404
Charley's Low-Down Weary Blues—Part 1, 2 Elmer Bird, 106
Charlie And Nellie Carter Family, 194
Charlie Boy Vernon Dalhart, 271
Charlie Boy (We Love You) Vernon Dalhart, 271
Charlie Brooks Bradley Kincaid, 483
Charlie Karo Fiddlin' Powers & Family, 704
Charlie's Home Shanks Bros. Trio, 825
Charlotte Hot Step Fletcher & Foster, 349
Charlotte Rag J.H. Howell, 446

Charming Bessie Lee [Blind] Jack Mathis, 613
Charming Betsy Roy Acuff, 48; Fiddlin' John Carson, 176; Claude Davis, 297; Georgia Organ Grinders, 366; Land Norris, 662; Dick Parman, 680
Charming Bill McGee Brothers, 552
Charming Billy (Billy Boy) Andrew Jenkins, 454
Chas. A Brooks Holland Puckett, 715
Chase That Rabbit—Chase That Squirrel Roy Rogers, 812
Chased Old Satan Through The Door Ephraim Woodie, 971
Chasing Squirrels Four Virginians, 357
Chattanooga Blues Allen Brothers, 55; Lester McFarland & Robert A. Gardner, 543
Chattanooga Mama Allen Brothers, 56–57; Three Musketeers, 906
Chaw Of Tobacco And A Little Drink [A] Carson Robison, 777, 779
Chawin' Chewin' Gum Asher Sizemore & Little Jimmie, 837
Cheat 'Em Allen Brothers, 55; Red Headed Fiddler[s], 732
Cheatham County Breakdown Arthur Smith, 841
Cheatham County Breakdown No. 2 Arthur Smith, 841
Cheatin' Jimmie Revard, 743
Cheatin' On Me Jimmy Hart, 406; Dick Hartman's Tennessee Ramblers, 408
Cheatin' On You Baby Hank Penny, 686
Cheatin' On Your Baby Bill Boyd, 122; Rice Brothers' Gang, 746; Shelton Brothers, 827
Cheer Along The Way Peck's Male Quartette, 684
Cheesy Breeze Milton Brown, 136
Cher Ami Ma Vie Est Ruini (Dear Friend My Life Is Ruined) Delma Lachney, 488
Chere Liza Leo Soileau, 856
Chere Te Mon Miller's Merrymakers, 628
Chere Te Te (Honey Child) J.B. Fuslier, 361
Chere Tite Fille Hackberry Ramblers, 388; Happy Fats, 395
Chere Tu Tu Miller's Merrymakers, 628
Chere Yeux Noirs Oscar [Slim] Doucet, 324
Cherie A You Toi Te? Hackberry Ramblers, 388
Cherokee Maiden Denver Darling, 296; Charlie Wills, 966
Cherokee Rag Big Chief Henry's Indian String Band, 103
Cherokee Rose Dick Reinhart, 739
Chesapeake Bay Walter Couch & Wilks Ramblers, 224
Chester Blues Bert Bilbro, 104
Chevrolet Car McGee Brothers, 552
Chevrolet Six [The] Frank Hutchison, 450
Chew Of Tobacco And A Little Drink [A] Frank Luther, 518
Chewing Chawin' Gum Richard Cox, 229
Chewing Chewing Gum Lake Howard, 445
Chewing Gum Carter Family, 187
Cheyenne E.F. Morgan, 641; Everett Morgan, 642
Chicago Blues Harry Hillard, 425
Chicago Bound Blues Leroy Roberson, 752
Chicken John & Emery McClung, 530; Carl T. Sprague, 862; Vaughan Quartet, 928
Chicken Don't Roost Too High Clayton McMichen, 571; Lowe Stokes, 871
Chicken Don't Roost Too High For Me—2 Riley Puckett, 715
Chicken Don't Roost Too High For Me Gid Tanner, 887
Chicken In The Barn Lot Lane's Old Time Fiddlers, 490
Chicken In The Barnyard Kessinger Brothers, 479
Chicken In The Garden Hugh Roden, 797
Chicken Pie Dusty Rhodes, 744
Chicken Reel E.F. "Poss" Acree, 48; Warren Caplinger, 156; Farm Hands, 336; Hugh Gibbs String Band, 368; Kessinger Brothers, 481; Roy Newman, 656; Harry Reed & Wm. F. Wynn, 733; Doc Roberts, 754; Rustic Revellers, 816; Tweedy Brothers, 917; Dr. Claude Watson & L.W. McCreigton, 940

Chicken Reel Stomp Tune Wranglers, 915
Chicken Roost Behind The Moon Ernest Thompson, 902
Chicken Roost Blues Cliff Carlisle, 164, 166; Raley Brothers, 724
Chicken Sermon [The] Honeyboy & Sassafras[s], 433
Chicken Sneeze Kentucky String Ticklers, 478
C-h-i-c-k-e-n Spells Chicken McGee Brothers, 552
Chicken, You Better Go Behind The Barn Henry Whitter, 954
Chicken, You Can't Roost Too High For Me Uncle Tom Collins, 219
Chickens Don't Lay Joe Werner, 944
Chickens Don't Roost Too High For Me Arthur Tanner, 885
Child At Mother's Knee [A] Allen Quartette, 57; Smith's Sacred Singers, 849; Vaughan Quartet, 929
Childhood Days Georgia Yellow Hammers, 367
Childhood Dreams Cliff Carlisle, 162–63
Childhood's Sweet Home Matt Simmons & Frank Miller, 835
Children I Must Go Uncle Dave Macon, 577
Children Of The Heavenly King Wisdom Sisters, 969
Chill Tonic Hank Penny, 686
Chilly Wind Wade Ward, 939
Chime Bells Elton Britt, 129; Ozark Boys, 672; Christine Smith, 843; Margaret West, 945
Chimes Jim & Bob, 458
Chimes Of Arcady Frank Luther, 525
Chimes Of Hawaii Kelly Brothers, 476
Chin Music Sid Harkreader, 401
China Boy Carl Boling, 116; Leon Chappelear, 201; Kelly Brothers, 477; Rice Brothers' Gang, 746; Yellow Jackets [II], 977
Chinaman's Song Dusty Rhodes, 744
Chinatown, My Chinatown Milton Brown, 136; Nite Owls, 660; W. Lee O'Daniel, 665
Chinese Blues Pickard Family, 691
Chinese Breakdown Carolina Ramblers String Band, 172; North Carolina Hawaiians, 663; Jack Reedy, 734; Hoke Rice, 745; Scottdale String Band, 821; Stripling Brothers, 880
Chinese Honeymoon Doug Bine, 104; Milton Brown, 137
Chinese Rag Spooney Five, 862
Ching Chow Jimmy Johnson's String Band, 461
Chinky Pin Kessinger Brothers, 480
Chiquita Red Foley, 352
Chiselin' Daddy Prairie Ramblers, 710–11
Chiselin' Mama Prairie Ramblers, 711
Chisholm Trail Jules Allen, 55; Ranch Boys, 726–27
Chittlin' Cookin' Time In Cheatham County Bill Cox, 228; Arthur Smith, 841
Choctaw Beer Blues Roy Gonzales, 375
Choctaw County Rag Ray Brothers, 729
Choctaw Waltz Big Chief Henry's Indian String Band, 103
Choir Boy Sings All Alone Tonight [The] Vernon Dalhart, 282–83; Carson Robison, 766
Choking Blues Kyle Wooten, 973
Choking The Reeds Eldon Baker, 89
Choo Choo Blues Shelton Brothers, 830
Chopo Tune Wranglers, 916
Chorus Jig Mellie Dunham's Orchestra, 326
Chris Visits The Barber Shop Chris Bouchillon, 119
Christ Arose Sheffield Male Quartet, 826
Christ Arose! Buice Brothers, 142
Christ Is Keeping My Soul Humbard Family, 447
Christ Is Mine, Forever Mine McDonald Quartet, 541
Christian Soldier Denson Quartet, 313
Christian Warfare [The] Original Sacred Harp Choir, 670
Christian's "Good Night" [The] Chas. Teuser & Harold Lawrence, 898
Christian's Flight [The] Lee Wells, 943

Christians Hope [The] Alabama Sacred Harp Singers, 53; Denson-Parris Sacred Harp Singers, 313; Denson's Sacred Harp Singers Of Arley, Alabama, 313
Christine Leroy Blue Ridge Mountain Singers, 112; C.A. West, 944
Christmas Holds No Joy For Me Carson Robison, 766
Christmas Time Will Soon Be Over Fiddlin' John Carson, 177
Christofo Colombo Vernon Dalhart, 245
Chuck Wagon Blues Diamond D Boys, 316; Patsy Montana, 635
Chuck Wagon Swing Swift Jewel Cowboys, 884
Chums For Fifty Years Asa Martin, 593
Church At The Foot Of The Hill [A] Dorsey & Beatrice Dixon, 322
Church Bells Are Ringing For Mary [The] Frank & James McCravy, 533; Carson Robison, 784
Church Bells Told [The] Buck Nation, 651
Church By The Side Of The Road [The] Hoosier Duo, 435
Church I Know's You Gwine Miss Me When I'm Gone Tennessee Hill Billy, 896
Church In The Wildwood [The] Calhoun Sacred Quartet, 151; Carter Family, 191; Chuck Wagon Gang, 210; Gentry Family, 365; Jenkins Family, 456–57; Little Brown Church Quartet, 508; Pickard Family, 693; Riley Quartette, 749; Singing Preachers, 836; Smith's Sacred Singers, 850; Vaughan Quartet, 927
Church Of God Is Right Otis & Tom Mote, 644
Church Of Long Ago [The] Doc Hopkins, 441; [Smilin'] Ed McConnell, 530–31
Church Point Breakdown Hackberry Ramblers, 388
Church Point Waltz Amedie Ardoin, 62
Cielito Lindo Otis & Eleanor, 670; Sons Of The Pioneers, 859; Tune Wranglers, 915; Bob Wills, 964
Cielito Lindo (Beautiful Heaven) Milton Brown, 137; Nite Owls, 660
Cimarron (Roll On) Jimmy Wakely, 934
Cincinnati Breakdown Blue Ridge Mountain Entertainers, 111
Cincinnati Hornpipe Lake & Cavanagh, 489
Cincinnati Hornpipe And Devine's Hornpipe William B. Houchens, 443
Cincinnati Rag Clarence Greene, 382; Byrd Moore, 639
Cinda Hill Billies, 423
Cinda Lou Shelton Brothers, 828
Cindy Vernon Dalhart, 272–73; Fisher Hendley, 416; Bradley Kincaid, 483–84; Shorty McCoy, 531; Clayton McMichen, 566; Riley Puckett, 718; George Reneau, 740
Cindy In The Meadows Samantha Bumgarner, 142
Cinque Pieds Deux Patrick (Dak) Pellerin, 684
Circle Has Been Broken [The] Frank Luther, 518–19; Parker & Dodd, 678
Circus Day Rag Claude Davis, 298
Circus Days [The] Harry "Mac" McClintock, 529
Circus Parade Mustard & Gravy, 647
Ciribiribin Massey Family, 612
C'Ist Je Pourez Et Avec Toi Ce Soir (If I Could Be With You) Patrick (Dak) Pellerin, 685
Citaco Swamp Rooters, 883
City Of Gold Golden Echo Boys, 372; Alfred G. Karnes, 472; Smith's Sacred Singers, 849; Stamps Quartet, 864
City Of Rest McDonald Quartet, 540
City Of Sighs And Tears [The] Lester McFarland & Robert A. Gardner, 545
City On The Hill J.E. Mainer's Mountaineers, 581
Clarinet Marmalade Light Crust Doughboys, 504
Classic Medley Robert Barringer, 96
Claud Allen Ernest V. Stoneman, 876
Clayton Case [The] Dutch Coleman, 217

Clementine Ranch Boys, 727; Carson Robison, 795
Clementine (The Bargain Queen) Adelyne Hood, 435
Clementine: Little Ah Sid Ranch Boys, 726
Cleveland Hospital Disaster Warren Caplinger, 157
Cliffside Rag Grady Family, 376
Climb Up, Ye Chillun, Climb Kanawha Singers, 469
Climbing Jacob's Ladder Armstrong & Highley, 64; Royal Quartette, 815
Climbing The Stairs Jack Major, 586
Climbing Up De Golden Stairs Vernon Dalhart, 279–82; Kanawha Singers, 469; Carson Robison, 764, 795
Climbing Up Dem Golden Stairs John McGhee & Frank Welling, 557
Climbing Up The Golden Stairs Carson Bros., 180; Georgia Crackers, 366; Happy Four, 396; John McGhee & Frank Welling, 554; Carson Robison, 794; Smith's Sacred Singers, 849; Spangler & Pearson, 861; Ernest Thompson, 902
Climbing Up Those Golden Stairs Vernon Dalhart, 281; Carson Robison, 776, 780
Clinch Mountain Clinch Mountain Singers, 215
Cling To The Cross Stamps Quartet, 864
Clinton Quadrille John Baltzell, 91
Close Your Bright Eyes Earl Johnson, 460
Closer To You Don Weston, 947
Cloud And Fire Ernest Phipps, 691
Clouds Gonna Roll Away Fern Harris, 404
Clouds Gwine Roll Away Bill Cox, 225–26
Clouds Gwine To Roll Away [The] Henry Whitter, 955
Clouds Of Glory Alfred G. Karnes, 472
Clouds Will Soon Roll By [The] Pine Ridge Boys, 697
Clover Blossom Lester McFarland & Robert A. Gardner, 542
Clover Blossoms Hugh Cross, 235; Bob McGimsey, 564; Bob Miller, 620; "Peg" Moreland, 641; Riley Puckett, 719; Sloane & Threadgill, 840
Club Had A Meeting [The] Walter Coon, 221
Club Held A Meeting [The] Billy Vest, 931
Club Meeting [The] Carl T. Sprague, 862
Cluck Old Hen G.B. Grayson & Henry Whitter, 380; Hill Billies, 423; Frank Hutchison, 450; Fiddlin' Powers & Family, 703
Clyde Barrow And Bonnie Parker Dwight Butcher, 148; Frank Luther, 522
Coal Creek March Taylor's Kentucky Boys, 895
Coal Creek Mines [The] G.B. Grayson & Henry Whitter, 381
Coal Mine Blues Allen Brothers, 55; Stripling Brothers, 880
Coal Miner's Blues Carter Family, 195; Prairie Ramblers, 705
Coal Miner's Dream [A] Miner Hawkins, 413
Coal Tipple Blues Doc Roberts, 755
Coal Valley Stripling Brothers, 880
Coat And Pants Do All The Work (And The Vest Gets All The Gravy) [The] Hoosier Hot Shots, 437
Coat And Pants Do All The Work [The] Hoosier Hot Shots, 437
Cocaine Dick Justice, 468
Coffee In The Morning, Kisses In The Night Jim & Bob, 458
Cold And Hungry Goebel Reeves, 737–38
Cold Icy Floor Pipers Gap Ramblers, 698
Cold Penitentiary Blues George Edgin, 330; B.F. Shelton, 826
Cole Younger Marc Williams, 958
College Hornpipe Jasper Bisbee, 107; William B. Houchens, 443; Maddux Family, 580; B.E. Scott, 821; Smith's Garage Fiddle Band, 848
College Quadrille Jasper Bisbee, 107
Collin's Reel William B. Houchens, 443
Colorado Blues Girls Of The Golden West, 370
Colorado Memories Cherry Sisters, 204; Ranch Boys, 727
Colorado Sunset Frank Luther, 525; Roy Rogers, 811

Colorado Trail Bob Miller, 624
Columbus Prison Fire John McGhee & Frank Welling, 559
Columbus Stockade Cliff Carlisle, 162
Columbus Stockade (Go And Leave Me If You Wish To) Flannery Sisters, 346
Columbus Stockade Blues Anglin Brothers, 61; Cliff Carlisle, 162; Tom Darby & Jimmie Tarlton, 293; Jimmie Davis, 305; Fred Kirby, 487; Carson Robison, 768; Yellow Jackets [II], 977
Columbus Waltz J.B. Fuslier, 361
Combination Rag East Texas Serenaders, 329
Come A Little Closer Nite Owls, 661
Come Along Children, Come Along Four Pickled Peppers, 356
Come Along Down To The Old Plantation Eldon Baker, 89
Come Along Little Children J.H. Howell, 445
Come Along With Me Carson Robison, 793
Come And Be Saved L.V. Jones, 467
Come And Dine Happy Four, 396
Come And Drift With Me Fleming & Townsend, 347
Come And Kiss Me, Baby Darling Holland Puckett, 715
Come And Meet Me J.B. Fuslier, 361
Come Back Little Darling Roy Acuff, 51
Come Back Little Pal Roy Acuff, 50; Roy Hall, 390
Come Back Sweetheart Cliff Carlisle, 164; Happy-Go-Lucky Boys, 397
Come Back To Me My Darling Al Dexter, 315
Come Back To The Hills Flannery Sisters, 346; Fisher Hendley, 417; Frank[ie] Marvin, 604
Come Back To Your Dobie Shack Wade Mainer, 582
Come Back Tonight In My Dreams Lester McFarland & Robert A. Gardner, 548; Carson Robison, 784–85
Come Back, Lottie Ashley's Melody Makers, 68
Come Be My Rainbow Clover Leaf Old Time Fiddlin' Team, 215; Riley Puckett, 718; Scottdale String Band, 821
Come Easy, Go Easy Bill Boyd, 123
Come Home Father Walter Coon, 220
Come Listen To My Story Vaughan Quartet, 928
Come On McDonald Quartet, 540
Come On And Swing Me Adolph Hofner, 430
Come On Board The Ship Of Glory P.H. Ashworth, 69
Come On Boys We're Ridin' Into Town Ray Whitley, 953
Come On Buddie, Don't You Want To Go Uncle Dave Macon, 577
Come On Over To My House (Ain't Nobody Home But Me) Jimmie Davis, 301–02
Come Over And See Me Sometime Georgia Yellow Hammers, 367
Come Swing With Me Tennessee Ramblers [II], 897
Come Take A Trip In My Airship Fred Pendleton, 685
Come Thou Fount John McGhee & Frank Welling, 557
Come To The Savior Stamps Quartet, 864
Come Up And See Me Some Day Jimmie Revard, 743
Come Up Here My Little Bessie Walter Smith, 847
Come Ye Disconsolate Mrs. Leon Hinkle, 427
Comical Ditty [A] Lester McFarland & Robert A. Gardner, 547
Comin' Down The River Curly Gray, 378
Comin' 'Round The Mountain—No. 1 Frank Luther, 524
Comin' 'Round The Mountain—No. 2 Frank Luther, 524
Comin' 'Round The Mountain—Part 4 Frank Luther, 524
Coming Chuck Wagon Gang, 211; McDonald Quartet, 540; Majestic [Male] Quartet, 585; Owen Brothers & Ellis, 671
Coming From The Ball Roy Acuff, 50
Coming Of The King [The] Bill Nettles, 654
Coming Round The Mountain Uncle Dave Macon, 576; Carson Robison, 793
Coming Soon I Know You'll Take Me E. Arthur Lewis, 498

[Commercial—Old Sams Soda] Wade Mainer, 583
Common Bill Arthur Fields & Fred Hall, 339
Companions Draw Nigh Wade Mainer, 584
Complete For All The World Bush Brothers, 147
Concert Hall On The Bowery [A] Benny Borg, 118
Concertina Waltz Karl & Harty, 471
Concord Denson-Parris Sacred Harp Singers, 313
Concord Rag J.E. Mainer's Mountaineers, 582
Coney Island Lloyd Burdette, 143
Coney Island Baby Roy Acuff, 48; McKinney Brothers, 564
Coney Island Washboard Swift Jewel Cowboys, 884
Coney Isle Frank Hutchison, 449
Confessin' (That I Love You) Milton Brown, 138; W. Lee O'Daniel, 666
Confession D'Amour (Confession Of Love) Sydney Landry, 490
Confession Of Love Sydney Landry, 490
Confidence Dye's Sacred Harp Singers, 328
Congratulate Me W. Lee O'Daniel, 666; Ross Rhythm Rascals, 814
Connie's Got Connections In Connecticut Hoosier Hot Shots, 439
Constant Sorrow Hall Brothers, 391
Constantly Abiding John McGhee & Frank Welling, 554, 560
Contented Hobo [The] Asa Martin, 589–90
Continuer De Sonner (Keep A' Knockin' (But You Can't Come In)) Clifford Breaux, 127
Conversation With A Mule Arty Hall, 390
Conversation With Death (By A Blind Girl) Vernon Dalhart, 283
Conversion Denson-Parris Sacred Harp Singers, 313
Convict And The Bird [The] Jack Mahoney, 581; Carson Robison, 774
Convict And The Rose [The] Blue Sky Boys, 114; Edith & Sherman Collins, 218; Vernon Dalhart, 249, 251–52, 255, 281; Pine Ridge Boys, 697; Leon Selph, 823; Tom & Roy, 911; Bob Wills, 963
Convict's Dream [The] Gene Autry, 82
Convict's Lament Crockett [Family] Mountaineers, 234
Convict's Prayer Lew Preston, 713
Convict's Return [The] Jack Mahoney, 581
Convict's Song [The] Bobby Gregory, 383
Convict's Soul [The] Goebel Reeves, 738
Coo See Coo Shelton Brothers, 830
Coo-Coo Bird [The] Thomas C. Ashley, 67
Cool Penitentiary Fruit Jar Guzzlers, 360
Cool Water Bob Atcher, 69; Sons Of The Pioneers, 859
Coon Crap Game Ernest Thompson, 902
Coon Dog Cartwright Brothers, 195
Coon Dog Yodel Carson Robison, 772
Coon From Tennessee Georgia Crackers, 365; Charlie Poole, 699
Coon Hollow Boys At The Still Part 1 Smoky Mountain Boys, 851
Coon Hunt Otto Gray, 379
Coon Hunting Blues Jones County Boys, 467
Coon Jine My Lover Bill Shepherd, 831
Coon That Had The Razor [The] Uncle Dave Macon, 576
Coon, Coon, Coon Leake County Revelers, 494; Gid Tanner, 889; Taylor Trio, 894
Coon-Hunting In Moonshine Hollow Uncle Bud Landress, 490
Coo-Se-Coo Sunshine Boys, 881
Copenhagen Milton Brown, 136; Light Crust Doughboys, 502
Copper And The Gunman [The] Arthur Fields & Fred Hall, 339
Copper Head Mama Bill Carlisle, 159

Coquette New Dixie Demons, 655; Nite Owls, 660; W. Lee O'Daniel, 666; Tennessee Ramblers [II], 897
Corbin Slide Alex Hood, 435
Corinth OKeh Atlanta Sacred Harp Singers, 667
Corn Dodger No. 1 Special George Edgin, 330
Corn Fed Mama Jimmie Davis, 301
Corn Licker & Barbecue—Part 1, 2 Fiddlin' John Carson, 178
Corn Licker Blues (A Delirious Yodel) Chezz Chase, 202
Corn Licker Rag Callahan Brothers, 152
Corn Licker Still In Georgia [A]—Part 1–14 Clayton McMichen, 566–70
Corn Pone And Pot Licker Crumbled Or Dunked Bob Miller, 620
Corn Pone And Pot Likker (Crumbled Or Dunked)—Part 1, 2 Bob Miller, 620
Corn Shuckers Frolic [The] Calaway's West Virginia Mountaineers, 150
Corn Shucking Party In Georgia Herschel Brown, 133
Cornbread Wyzee Hamilton, 393
Cornpone In Pot Likker (Whether To Dunk Or Crumble) Carson Robison, 787
Corns On My Feet McClendon Brothers, 527
Coronation Daniels-Deason Sacred Harp Singers, 293
Corpse At The Express Office [The] Mr. & Mrs. Ed Lindsey, 507
Corrina, Corrina Blue Ridge Mountain Entertainers, 111
Corrine Corrina Cliff Bruner, 139; Hugh Cross, 236; Clayton McMichen, 569; Roy Newman, 656; Hal O'Halloran's Hooligans, 667; Leo Soileau, 854; Bob Wills, 964
Corrine Corrina Blues Westbrook Conservatory Entertainers, 947
Cotillion—Part 1, 2 National Barn Dance Orchestra, 651
Cottage By The Sea [The] Fred Stanley, 866
Cottage By The Wayside Fred Kirby, 486
Cottage Hornpipe John W. Daniel, 293
Cottage On The Hill Dixie Ramblers [II], 319
Cottle Waltz Cottle Brothers, 223
Cotton Baggin' Gid Tanner, 890
Cotton Mill Blues Lester "Pete" Bivins, 107; Chumbler Family, 212; Daddy John Love, 514; Wilmer Watts, 941
Cotton Mill Colic David McCarn, 527
Cotton Mill Girl Earl McCoy & Jessie Brock, 531; Lester Smallwood, 840
Cotton Patch Gid Tanner, 891
Cotton Patch Rag John Dilleshaw, 316
Cotton Patch Serenade W.B. Chenoweth, 203
Cotton Pickers' Drag Grinnell Giggers, 384
Cotton-Eyed Joe Fiddlin' John Carson, 177; Carter Brothers & Son, 187; Dykes' Magic City Trio, 328; Adolph Hofner, 431; Pope's Arkansas Mountaineers, 701; Gid Tanner, 889
Cottonfield Blues Fleming & Townsend, 347
Cottonwood Reel Happy Hayseeds, 397
Coughdrop Blues Scottdale String Band, 822
Couldn't Hear Nobody Pray Vaughan Quartet, 923
Countin' Cross Ties Clayton McMichen, 571; Bob Miller, 622
Counting The Fords Pass By Honeyboy & Sassafras[s], 433
Country Blues Dock Boggs, 115; J.E. Mainer's Mountaineers, 582
Country Church Yard [The] Andrew Jenkins, 453
Country Cowbells Bob Skyles, 839
Country Doctor (Doc. Brown Has Moved Upstairs)—Part 1, 2 Jack Major, 586
Country Girl J.B. Fuslier, 361
Country Girl Valley Tom Darby & Jimmie Tarlton, 294
Country Ham And Red Gravy Uncle Dave Macon, 578
Country Where People Don't Die [The] Vaughan Quartet, 930

County Boy Blues Roy Marsh, 587
County Fair—Part 1, 2 Herschel Brown, 134
Coupon Song [The] Bill Monroe, 632; Roy Shaffer, 825; Shelton Brothers, 827
Courtin' Three Tobacco Tags, 907
Courtin' Cowboy Frank Luther, 522
Courtin' Days Waltz Leake County Revelers, 495
Courtin' In The West Virginia Hills Leroy [Slim] Johnson, 462
Courtin' The Widow Willard Hodgin[s], 429
Courville And McGee Waltz Denus McGee, 551
Cousin Cindy's Wedding Arthur Fields & Fred Hall, 343, 345
Cousin Sally Brown Sweet Brothers, 884
Cousinne Lilly John H. Bertrand, 101
Covered Wagon Headin' West Wilf Carter (Montana Slim), 183
Covered Wagon Rolled Right Along [The] Hoosier Hot Shots, 440; Texas Jim Lewis, 499
Cow Hand's Last Ride [The] Jimmie Rodgers, 808
Cow Town Swing Universal Cowboys, 919
Cow Trail To Mexico [The] Jules Allen, 55
Cowards Over Pearl Harbor Denver Darling, 295
Cowboy [The] Carl T. Sprague, 863
Cowboy And The Lady [The] Ray Whitley, 953
Cowboy At Church [The] Carl T. Sprague, 863
Cowboy Blues Wilf Carter (Montana Slim), 182; Carson Robison, 796
Cowboy Dance Ranch Boys, 726–27
Cowboy Don't Forget Your Mother Wilf Carter (Montana Slim), 182
Cowboy Honeymoon [A] Patsy Montana, 635
Cowboy Isn't Speaking To His Horse [The] Texas Jim Robertson, 759
Cowboy Jack Arkansas Woodchopper, 63; Callahan Brothers, 153; Bill Carlisle, 159; Carter Family, 191; Leon Chappelear, 200; Girls Of The Golden West, 370; "Peg" Moreland, 641; Ranch Boys, 726–27; Roy Shaffer, 825; Marc Williams, 958; Lawrence Woods, 973
Cowboy Joe Beverly Hill Billies, 102
Cowboy Johnnie's Last Ride Cliff Carlisle, 166
Cowboy Love Call Girls Of The Golden West, 371
Cowboy Love Song Carl T. Sprague, 862
Cowboy Lullaby Wilf Carter (Montana Slim), 182
Cowboy Medley Bill Bender, 99
Cowboy Night Herd Song Roy Rogers, 811
Cowboy Prisoner Billy Vest, 931
Cowboy Rhythm Patsy Montana, 635
Cowboy Rider [A] Joseph Falcon, 334
Cowboy Romeo [The] Carson Robison, 796
Cowboy Song Cliff Carlisle, 162–63
Cowboy Tom's Roundup Part 1 Cowboy Tom's Roundup, 224
Cowboy Tom's Roundup Part 2 Red River Valley Cowboy Tom's Roundup, 224
Cowboy Trail [The] Buell Kazee, 473
Cowboy Wedding In May [The] Wilf Carter (Montana Slim), 183
Cowboy Who Never Returned [A] Wilf Carter (Montana Slim), 185
Cowboy Yodel Gene Autry, 71–72; Chuck Wagon Gang, 210; Romaine Lowdermilk, 515; Frank[ie] Marvin, 605
Cowboy Yodelling Song [The] Carson Robison, 795
Cowboys Ain't Stupid Like Cupid Zora Layman, 492
Cowboy's Airplane Ride Wilf Carter (Montana Slim), 185
Cowboys And Indians Tune Wranglers, 916
Cowboy's Best Friend Zora Layman, 492–93
Cowboy's Best Friend Is His Horse [A] George Goebel, 372
Cowboy's Best Friend Is His Pony [A] Wilf Carter (Montana Slim), 181
Cowboy's Call Saddle Tramps, 818
Cowboys Christmas Ball Tex Ritter, 749
Cowboy's Dizzy Sweetheart [The] Goebel Reeves, 738
Cowboy's Dream Jules Allen, 55; Arkansas Woodchopper, 63; Charlie Craver, 231; Vernon Dalhart, 271; Otto Gray, 378; Bradley Kincaid, 485; Light Crust Doughboys, 502; Al McLeod's Country Dance Band, 565; Massey Family, 608–09; Ranch Boys, 726–27; Goebel Reeves, 736–37; Texas Jim Robertson, 760; Carl T. Sprague, 862; Margaret West, 945; Marc Williams, 958; Zeke Williams, 959
Cowboy's Dying Dream Cliff Carlisle, 167
Cowboy's Evening Song (Goin' Home) Vernon Dalhart, 267
Cowboy's Farewell [The] Buell Kazee, 472; Powder River Jack-Kitty Lee, 496
Cowboy's Heaven Gene Autry, 77–78; Dwight Butcher, 148; Girls Of The Golden West, 371; Jimmy Long, 512; Frank[ie] Marvin, 605
Cowboy's Heavenly Dream [The] Wilf Carter (Montana Slim), 183
Cowboy's Herding Song (Lay Down, Dogies) Vernon Dalhart, 267
Cowboy's High-Toned Dance [The] Wilf Carter (Montana Slim), 182
Cowboy's Home In Heaven Carson Robison, 796
Cowboy's Home Sweet Home Edward L. Crain, 230; Jimmie Davis, 299
Cowboy's Honeymoon [A] Patsy Montana, 635
Cowboy's Lament (The Dying Cowboy) Al Bernard, 100
Cowboy's Lament [The] Jules Allen, 55; Capt. Appleblossom, 158; Vernon Dalhart, 271, 285; Ewen Hail, 389; Harry "Mac" McClintock, 528; Ken Maynard, 614; Buck Nation, 650; Ranch Boys, 725–27; Rodeo Trio, 798; Rowdy Wright, 974
Cowboy's Last Wish [The] Marc Williams, 958
Cowboy's Letter From Home W.C. Childers, 206
Cowboy's Love Song Jules Allen, 55; Patt Patterson, 681
Cowboy's Lullaby [The] Tex Dunn, 327; Goebel Reeves, 737; Earl Shirkey & Roy Harper, 831
Cowboy's Lullabye Goebel Reeves, 737
Cowboy's Meditation Leo Boswell, 119; David Gauthier, 364; Kenneth Houchins, 444; Carl T. Sprague, 863
Cowboy's Mother Wilf Carter (Montana Slim), 183
Cowboy's Plea [The] Bill Simmons, 835
Cowboy's Pony In Heaven Wade Mainer, 583
Cowboy's Prayer [The] Dewey Hayes, 414; Goebel Reeves, 737; Carson Robison, 791
Cowboy's Quickstep Robert Cook's Old Time Fiddlers, 220
Cowboy's Secret [The] Goebel Reeves, 737
Cowboy's Sweetheart Frank[ie] Marvin, 605; Rowdy Wright, 974
Cowboy's Swing Hank Penny, 686
Cowboy's Trademarks Gene Autry, 85; Cowboy Tom's Roundup, 224
Cowboy's Wife [The] Billie Maxwell, 614
Cowboy's Wild Song To His Herd Carter Family, 192
Cowboy's Yodel Gene Autry, 73
Cowgirl Jean Bill Carlisle, 160
Cowgirl's Dream [The] Girls Of The Golden West, 370
Cowgirl's Prayer Carson Robison, 793; Steelman Sisters, 867
Cowhand's Guiding Star [The] Wilf Carter (Montana Slim), 182
Cowman's Lament Tex Fletcher, 348
Cowman's Prayer Carl T. Sprague, 863
Cradle And The Music Box [The] Sally Foster, 355

Cradle Days Wade Mainer, 583
Cradle Song L.C. Fulenwider, 360; Blind Joe Mangum-Fred Shriber, 586
Cradle, A Baby And You [A] Village Boys, 932
Cradle's Empty (Baby's Gone) Frank & James McCravy, 534
Crafton Blues Milton Brown, 137; Hi-Flyers, 418; Jimmie Revard, 742
Crap Shooter Bob Kerby & George Barton, 479
Crap Shooters Hop Joe Werner, 944
Crash Of The Akron [The] Bob Miller, 624
Craven County Blues Rouse Brothers, 815
Crawdad Song E.E. Hack String Band, 386; Texas Jim Lewis, 499; Lone Star Cowboys, 509; Asa Martin, 593; Yellow Jackets [II], 977
Crawford March Rainey Old Time Band, 724
Crawling And Creeping Asa Martin, 593
Crazy About Women Len Nash, 650
Crazy Blues Cliff Carlisle, 161; Crysel Boys, 239; Arthur Smith, 842
Crazy Coon Walter Morris, 642
Crazy Cracker Walter Morris, 642
Crazy Engineer [The] Joe Steen, 868
Crazy Joe Mansfield Patrick, 681
Crazy Rag Hugh Roden, 797
Crazy Yodeling Blues Swing Billies, 885
Creole Belle Tim Flora & Rufus Lingo, 350
Creole Girl Rev. Horace A. Booker, 117; Walter Coon, 221
Creole Waltz [The] Dudley & James Fawvor, 337
Crepe On The Cabin Door James Roberts, 756
Crepe On The Door Bill Cox, 228
Crepe On The Little Cabin Door [The] W.C. Childers, 206; Vernon Dalhart, 262
Crepe On The Old Cabin Door [The] Vernon Dalhart, 261–62, 268, 272
Crepe Upon The Little Cabin Door [The] Marc Williams, 958
Cricket On The Hearth Elmer Bird, 105; Billy Bishop, 107; Edd Rice, 744
Crime At Quiet Dell [The] John McGhee & Frank Welling, 562
Crime Does Not Pay Frank Luther, 522
Crime I Didn't Do [The] Gene Autry, 77; Frank Dudgeon, 324; Dick Robertson, 759
Crime Of Harry Powers Bob Miller, 621
Crime Of The D'Autremont Brothers Johnson Brothers, 463
Criminal Waltz (La Valse Criminale) [The] Leo Soileau, 853
Criminal's Fate [The] Fleming & Townsend, 348
Cripple Creek Crockett [Family] Mountaineers, 233; Fruit Jar Guzzlers, 360; Hill Billies, 422; Light Crust Doughboys, 506; Fiddlin' Powers & Family, 703; Doc Roberts, 752; Gid Tanner, 887, 890; Tweedy Brothers, 918
Crippled Turkey Bob Wills, 961
Crockett's Reel Prairie Ramblers, 710
Crooked Creek Blues Blue Ridge Mountain Entertainers, 110
Crooked John Kentucky String Ticklers, 478
Crooning Bachelor Pine Ridge Boys, 697
Croquet Habits Freeny's Barn Dance Band, 359
Cross Eyed Boy And School Days [The] Little Georgie Porgie, 508
Cross Eyed Butcher [The] Golden Melody Boys, 373; Kelly Brothers, 477
Cross Eyed Butcher And The Cackling Hen [The] Uncle Dave Macon, 575
Cross Eyed Sue Ramblin' Red Lowery, 515; Carson Robison, 778–80, 792
Cross My Heart Dick Reinhart, 739
Cross On The Hill [The] Jones Brothers Trio, 467
Cross On The Prison Floor [The] Lester McFarland & Robert A. Gardner, 546
Cross Patch Milton Brown, 138; W. Lee O'Daniel, 666
Cross The Mason Dixon Line Ray Sand's Harmony Four, 819
Crossed Old Jordan's Stream Elmer Bird, 106
Cross-Eyed Cowboy From Abilene Light Crust Doughboys, 503
Cross-Eyed Gal On The Hill Bill Boyd, 123
Cross-Eyed Gal That Lived Upon The Hill Gene Autry, 76
Crossfiring Blues Allen Brothers, 56
Crossing The Bar Carolina Quartette, 172; Copperhill Male Quartet, 222; Vaughan Quartet, 923
Crossing The Tide Jenkins Family, 457
Crow [sic] Dad Song Honeyboy & Sassafras[s], 433
Crow Black Chicken Leake County Revelers, 494
Crow Song Caw-Caw-Caw [The] Vernon Dalhart, 288; John I. White, 949
Crowley Blues Amedie Ardoin, 62
Crowley Breakdown Amadie Breaux, 126
Crowley Stomp Leo Soileau, 855
Crowley Waltz Hackberry Ramblers, 387
Crown Him Bela Lam, 489
Crown Him Lord Of All Peck's Male Quartette, 684
Crown Of Soft Brown Hair [A] Billy Vest, 931
Cry Baby Cry Texas Wanderers, 900
Cryin' Holy Unto My Lord Bill Monroe, 631
Crying Holy Roy Hall, 390; Wade Mainer, 585
Crying Myself To Sleep Bob Atcher, 69
Crying The Blues Again Ted Daffan's Texans, 240
Cuba Alabama Sacred Harp Singers, 53
Cuban Appetizer Dick Hartman's Tennessee Ramblers, 408
Cuban Soldier Carter Family, 191, 194
Cuban Two Step Rag Smith's Garage Fiddle Band, 848
Cubanola Glide Dan Hornsby, 442
Cuckoo Is A Pretty Bird Bradley Kincaid, 483
Cuckoo She's A Fine Bird [The] Kelly Harrell, 403
Cuckoo Song Louis Adler, 51
Cuddle Up A Little Closer, Lovey Mine Hoosier Hot Shots, 440
Cuddled In My Mammy's Arms Frank[ie] Marvin, 605
Cumberland Blues Kentucky Thorobreds, 479; Doc Roberts, 755
Cumberland Gap Richard D. Burnett, 144; Carolina Ramblers String Band, 172; Carson Bros., 180; Hill Billies, 423; Frank Hutchison, 450; Land Norris, 662; Fiddlin' Powers & Family, 703; Doc Roberts, 755; Allen Sisson, 836; Uncle "Am" Stuart, 881; Gid Tanner, 887, 889; Williamson Brothers & Curry, 960
Cumberland Gap On A Buckin' Mule Gid Tanner, 891
Cumberland Mountain Deer Race Uncle Dave Macon, 577–78
Cumberland Mountains Flannery Sisters, 346
Cumberland Valley 'Lasses & Honey, 491
Cumberland Valley Waltz Clayton McMichen, 570
Cumbling [sic] Gap Osey Helton, 415
Curley Headed Baby No. 3 Edith & Sherman Collins, 218
Curley-Headed Woman Richard D. Burnett, 144
Curley's New Talkin' Blues Curley Fox, 357
Curly Joe Charles Baker, 89; Marc Williams, 958
Curly-Headed Baby Riley Puckett, 721
Curly-Headed Baby—Part 2 Leatherman Sisters, 495
Curse Of An Aching Heart Thompson Cates, 198; Vernon Dalhart, 251; Jimmie Davis, 303; Walker's Corbin Ramblers, 937
Curtain Of Night Cleve Chaffin, 200
Curtains Of Night Cleve Chaffin, 200; Grant Brothers, 377; Ramblin' Red Lowery, 515

Custer's Last Fight Vernon Dalhart, 286; Carson Robison, 770
Cuttin' At The Point Charlie Wilson, 967
Cyclone Of Ryecove [The] Carter Family, 188; Lawrence Woods, 973
Cynda Bill Chitwood, 208

D Waltz [The] E.E. Hack String Band, 386
Dad In The Hills Gene Autry, 73
Daddy Hugh Cross, 236; Frank & James McCravy, 534
Daddy And Home Arkansas Woodchopper, 63; Gene Autry, 72; Bill Cox, 224; Nicholson's Players, 659; Red River Dave, 733; Jimmie Rodgers, 800, 809; Ed (Jake) West, 945
Daddy And Son John McGhee & Frank Welling, 563
Daddy Blues Rosa Lee Carson, 180; John McGhee & Frank Welling, 554
Daddy Dear I Can't Forget You Callahan Brothers, 153
Daddy Don't 'Low No Lowdown Hangin' Around Shelton Brothers, 827
Daddy In The Hills Joe Cook, 220
Daddy Is Gone Crowder Brothers, 238
Daddy My Pal Simerly Trio, 834
Daddy Park Your Car Allen Brothers, 57
Daddy Song—Part 1, 2 [The] Uncle Bud Landress, 490
Daddy Won't Have No Easy Rider Here Tom Darby & Jimmie Tarlton, 294
Daddy, You Are Too Late Philyaw Brothers, 690
Daddy's Gone Where The Good Farmers Go Norwood Tew, 899
Daddy's Got The Deep Elm Blues Jimmie Revard, 742
Daddy's In The Dog House Now Al Dexter, 314
Daddy's Lullaby John McGhee & Frank Welling, 563
Daddy's Wonderful Pal Raymond Render, 740
Dad's Favorite Waltz Dick Hartman's Tennessee Ramblers, 407
Dad's Getting Fuzzy Dutch Coleman, 218
Dad's Little Boy Herald Goodman, 375
Dad's Little Texas Lad Wilf Carter (Montana Slim), 186
Dad's Vacant Chair Cousin Levi, 224
Daffy Over Taffy Lulu Belle & Scotty, 515
Daisies Never Tell Merritt Smith, 845
Daisies Won't Tell Aaron Campbell's Mountaineers, 154; Jack Golding, 374; Roy Harvey, 409; Hill Billies, 423–24; Johnson Brothers' Band, 463; Clayton McMichen, 568; Moore Sisters, 640; Russell Brothers, 816; Westbrook Conservatory Entertainers, 947
Daisy Mae Leon Selph, 824
Daisy May Village Boys, 931
Dallas Blues Bob Wills, 962
Dallas Bound Oscar & Doc Harper, 402
Dallas County Jail Blues Gene Autry, 75
Dalton Round-Up Leonard C. Fulwider, 361
Damaged Goods Walter Coon, 221
Dan O'Brien's Raffle Fred Lehman, 496
Dan, The Banana Man Bill Nettles, 654
Dance All Night With A Bottle In My Hand Stripling Brothers, 879
Dance All Night With A Bottle In Your Hand Georgia Crackers, 365; Gid Tanner, 888; Tweedy Brothers, 918
Dance At Jones' Place [The] Carson Robison, 771
Dance At Jones's Place Carson Robison, 771
Dance Away Polka Dixie Ramblers [IV], 319
Dance Down At Jones' Place [The] Carson Robison, 771
Dance In The Light Of The Moon Emmett & Aiken String Band, 332
Dance To Those Sobbin' Blues Bill Boyd, 123
Dance Wid A Gal, Hole In Her Stocking William B. Houchens, 443

Dance With A Gal With Hole In Her Stocking Doc Roberts, 753
Dance With A Girl With A Hole In Her Stocking, Leather Breeches, Big-Eared Mule Doc Roberts, 753
Danced All Night With A Bottle In My Hand Crazy Hillbillies Band, 232
Dancer [The] Delma Lachney, 488
Dancing 'Round The Apple Tree Arthur Fields & Fred Hall, 342–43, 345
Dancing To The Rhythm Of My Heart James Brown, Jr. & Ken Landon Groups, 134
Dancing With My Shadow Louisiana Strollers, 514
Dancing With Tears In My Eyes Lester McFarland & Robert A. Gardner, 548
Dandy Dan Ashley's Melody Makers, 68
Dang My Pop-Eyed Soul Bill Cox, 228
Dang My Rowdy Soul Cliff Carlisle, 165
Dangerous Nan McGrew Bob Miller, 619
Daniel In The Den Of Lions North Carolina Cooper Boys, 662
Dans Claire De Lune Avec Toi (In The Moonlight With You) Leo Soileau, 855
Dans Le Chere De La Lune Happy Fats, 395
Dans Le Grand Bois (In The Forest) Hackberry Ramblers, 388
Danville Blues Fred Richards, 747
Danville Girl Dock Boggs, 116
Darbone's Breakdown Hackberry Ramblers, 387
Darbone's Creole Stomp Hackberry Ramblers, 387
Darby Ram Uncle Dave Macon, 577
Darby's Ram Bascom Lamar Lunsford, 517; Skyland Scotty, 837
Dark Alley Blues Westbrook Conservatory Entertainers, 947
Dark And Stormy Weather Carter Family, 195
Dark Bedroom Blues Hi-Flyers, 419
Dark Eyes Dorsey & Beatrice Dixon, 321; Sid Harkreader, 400; Roy Harvey, 409; Morris Family, 643; Dick Parman, 679; Riley Puckett, 720
Dark Eyes Plea Billy Vest, 931
Dark Haired True Lover Carter Family, 194
Dark Holler Blues Thomas C. Ashley, 67
Dark Road Is A Hard Road To Travel [A] G.B. Grayson & Henry Whitter, 381
Darkey's Wail [The] Riley Puckett, 718
Darkness All Around Me Dick Hartman's Tennessee Ramblers, 408
Darktown Strutter's [sic] Ball [The] John McGhee & Frank Welling, 560
Darktown Strutters Ball Milton Brown, 137; Fiddlin' John Carson, 178; Leon Chappelear, 201; Walter C. Peterson, 688; Riley Puckett, 720; Gid Tanner, 888; Walker's Corbin Ramblers, 936; Bob Wills, 961
Darlin' Clementine Bradley Kincaid, 485
Darlin' Don't Cry Over Me Ray Whitley, 953
Darlin', I've Loved Way Too Much Elton Britt, 130
Darling Child Blue Ridge Highballers, 110
Darling Chloe Harmonica Bill, 401
Darling Cora Buell Kazee, 472; B.F. Shelton, 826
Darling Corey Monroe Brothers, 633
Darling Daisies Carter Family, 191
Darling Do You Miss Me Dorsey & Beatrice Dixon, 321
Darling Ease My Worried Mind Dick Reinhart, 739
Darling How Can You Forget So Soon Gene Autry, 84
Darling Little Girl Lew Preston, 713
Darling Little Joe Carter Family, 191
Darling Little Memories Ocie Stockard, 870
Darling Little Sweetheart Crowder Brothers, 237
Darling Mustache [The] Professor & Mrs. Greer, 383

Darling Nell Fred Kirby, 486
Darling Nellie Across the Sea Carter Family, 189
Darling Nellie Gray Alexander & Miller, 53; Carver Boys, 196; Hill Billies, 423; W.W. Macbeth, 526; Clayton McMichen, 567; Asa Martin, 589; Chubby Parker, 676–77; Riley Puckett, 716; Carson Robison, 784, 794–96; Woodlawn Quartette, 972
Darling Nellie Grey Charlie Oaks, 664
Darling Nelly Gray Roland Cauley, 199
Darling Of Yesterday Floyd Shreve, 834
Darling Rose Marie Bill Cox, 229
Darling The Sunshine Grows Brighter Oliver & Allen, 670
Darling Think Of What You've Done Jack & Leslie, 452; Karl & Harty, 471
Darling Think What You Have Done Morris Brothers, 643
Darling What Do You Care Elton Britt, 130
Darling You Know Dick Reinhart, 739
Darling Zelma Lee Uncle Dave Macon, 576
Darling, Do You Know Who Loves You? Bill Cox, 229; Fisher Hendley, 416; Oklahoma Sweethearts, 668
Darling, Do You Love Another Prairie Ramblers, 712
Darling, I'm Still In Love With You Happy-Go-Lucky Boys, 397
Darling, It's All Over Now Al Dexter, 315
Darling, The Answer Is In This Song Three Tobacco Tags, 908
(Darling, What I've Been Thru) You'll Never Know Texas Jim Robertson, 760
Darling, Where Have You Been So Long? Grant Brothers, 377
Darling's Black Mustache Doctor Lloyd & Howard Maxey, 508
Darned Old Mule From Georgia [The] Benny Borg, 118
Darneo Blue Ridge Highballers, 109
Daughter Of Calamity Jane [The] Adelyne Hood, 435
Daughter Of Moonshine Bill [The] Kelly Brothers, 477
Daughter Of San [The] Hoosier Hot Shots, 436
Davey Crockett Chubby Parker, 677
David Blues Bill Boyd, 122
Davidson County Blues Deford Bailey, 88
Davis Limited [The] Jimmie Davis, 299
Davis Rag Cowboy Pioneers, 224
Davis' Salty Dog Jimmie Davis, 300
Davy Weems String Band, 942
Dawn [The] Cowboy Tom's Roundup, 224
Dawn On The Prairie Wilf Carter (Montana Slim), 185
Dawn Waltz [The] Jack Cawley's Oklahoma Ridge Runners, 199
Day At The County Fair- Part 1, 2 [A] Clayton McMichen, 568
Day Has Come [The] Adelyne Hood, 434
Day I Left Home [The] Emry Arthur, 66
Day On The Farm In Tennessee—Part 1, 2 [A] Tennessee Farm Hands, 896
Day You Came Along [The] Al Dexter, 314
Day You Left Me [The] Hi-Flyers, 420
Day You Went Away [The] Jimmy Wakely, 934
Days Are Blue Callahan Brothers, 153; Asa Martin, 593
Days Are Long And I'm Weary [The] Hank Snow, 853
Days Of Forty-Nine [The] Jules Allen, 54
Days Of My Childhood Plays [The] Alfred G. Karnes, 472
De Blues Prairie Ramblers, 704
De Camptown Races Kanawha Singers, 469
De Clouds Are Gwine To Roll Away Vernon Dalhart, 242–43
De Ladies Man Bradley Kincaid, 483
De Sad Moment Carolina Gospel Singers, 171
De Seul Payce Thibodeaux Boys, 901

De Way To Spell Chicken Three Tobacco Tags, 908
Deacon Jones East Texas Serenaders, 329
Deacon's Calf [The] Georgia Yellow Hammers, 367
Deacon's Prayer [The] Vernon Dalhart, 291
Deadheads And Suckers Crockett Ward, 939
Deal [The] Kenneth Houchins, 444; Frank Hutchison, 450
Dear Daddy, You're Gone Wade Mainer, 583
Dear Evalina, Sweet Evalina W. Lee O'Daniel, 666
Dear Friend My Life Is Ruined Delma Lachney, 488
Dear Little Darling Jake & Carl, 453
Dear Little Dream Girl Of Mine Gene Autry, 86
Dear Little Girl Leon Chappelear, 202
Dear Loving Mother And Dad Wade Mainer, 584
Dear Mother Has Taught Me The Way Bill Cox, 228
Dear Mother I'll Think Of You Maynard Britton, 131
Dear Old Dad Of Mine Gene Autry, 86
Dear Old Daddy Elton Britt, 129; Cliff Carlisle, 163
Dear Old Daddy Of Mine Wilf Carter (Montana Slim), 181, 183
Dear Old Dixie Jordan Brothers, 467
Dear Old Dixieland Eldon Baker, 89; Clayton McMichen, 567; Riley Puckett, 718
Dear Old Girl Dan Hornsby, 442; Vaughan Quartet, 924
Dear Old Mother Hank & Slim Newman, 656; Red Headed Brier Hopper, 732
Dear Old Southern Moon Elton Britt, 127; Merritt Smith, 845
Dear Old Sunny South Jimmie Rodgers, 809
Dear Old Sunny South By The Sea George Edgin, 330; Buddy Jones, 466; Jimmie Rodgers, 800
Dear Old Tennessee Nichols Brothers, 659
Dear Old Texas Billy Vest, 931
Dear Old Texas Blues George E. Harris, 404–05
Dear Old Texas Moon Steelman Sisters, 867
Dear Old Western Skies Gene Autry, 79, 81
Dear To The Heart Of The Shepherd Clagg & Sliger, 212
Dear, I Love You Thomas C. Ashley, 67
Dear, Oh[!] Dear Vernon Dalhart, 245, 247, 249
Dearest Pal Is My Mother [The] Jack Bankey, 92
Dearest Sweetest Mother Hugh Cross, 235
Death Has Caused Me To Ramble Julian Johnson & Leon Hyatt, 461
Death House Blues Buck Turner, 916
Death Is No More Than A Dream Claude Davis, 298; Paramount Sacred Four, 675
Death Is Only A Dream Allen Quartette, 57; Jenkins Family, 457; Simmons Sacred Singers, 835; Merritt Smith, 844; Vaughan Quartet, 930
Death Of Clark, The Bandit [The] Hoke Rice, 746
Death Of Dr. Snook [The] Roy Pick, 691
Death of Floella Ruth Neal & Wanda Neal, 652
Death Of Floyd Bennett [The] Vernon Dalhart, 280–81
Death Of Floyd Collins [Waltz] [The] Fiddlin' John Carson, 176; Vernon Dalhart, 247, 250–51, 253, 255, 257, 281; Charlie Oaks, 664; Harry Smith, 843
Death Of Frank Bowen [The] Bill Cox, 224
Death Of Huey P. Long [The] Hank Warner, 940
Death Of J.B. Marcum [The] Ted Chestnut, 204
Death Of Jack "Legs" Diamond [The] Bob Miller, 621
Death Of Jesse James [The] Al Clauser, 214; Carson Robison, 772; Vagabonds, 921
Death Of Jimmie Rodgers [The] Gene Autry, 78; Bradley Kincaid, 485
Death Of John Henry (Steel Driving Man) Uncle Dave Macon, 574
Death Of John Henry [The] Welby Toomey, 912
Death Of Laura Parson [sic] [The] H.K. Hutchison, 450
Death Of Little Joe [The] W.C. Childers, 206
Death Of Lura Parsons [The] Vernon Dalhart, 269–70

Death Of Mother Jones [The] Gene Autry, 74
Death Of My Mother-In-Law [The] Lester McFarland & Robert A. Gardner, 546, 548
Death Of Oswald [The] Dixie Ramblers [II], 319
Death Of Stonewall Jackson [The] Carson Robison, 767
Death Of The Bowery Girl Slim Smith, 846
Death Of Williams Jennings Bryan [The] Charlie Oaks, 664
Death Of Young Stribling Three Floridians, 906
Death's River Paul Crutchfield & John Clotworthy, 239
Death's Shadow Song Vernon Dalhart, 266
Decatur Street Rag George Walburn & Emmett Hethcox, 935
Dedicated To You Bob Wills, 962
Dedication To Mother [A] John McGhee & Frank Welling, 557
Deed I Do Bill Boyd, 122
'Deed We Do Prairie Ramblers, 709
Deep Blue Sea Vass Family, 922
Deep Congress Avenue Shelly Lee Alley, 58
Deep Elem Blues Prairie Ramblers, 706; Rhubarb Red, 744; Shelton Brothers, 827
Deep Elem Blues No. 3 Shelton Brothers, 828
Deep Elem Blues No.2 Rhubarb Red, 744; Shelton Brothers, 827
Deep Elm Blues Lone Star Cowboys, 509
Deep Elm Swing Texas Wanderers, 900
Deep In The Heart Of Texas Gene Autry, 86; John (Dusty) King, 486; Patsy Montana, 637
Deep Mississippi Blues Jimmie Davis, 301
Deep River Blues Dewey Hayes, 414; Smizers Dixie Serenaders, 851
Deep Sea Blues Fred Kirby, 487
Deep Sea Waltz Hugh Roden, 797; Earl B. Zaayer, 979
Deer Walk Doc Roberts, 753
Del Rio Waltz East Texas Serenaders, 329
Delighting In The Love Of God Owen Brothers & Ellis, 671
Deliverance Will Come Uncle Dave Macon, 575; Smith's Sacred Singers, 850
Dellaide Happy Fats, 396
Demain C'Est Pas Dimanche Leo Soileau, 854
Democratic Donkey (Is In His Stall Again) [The] Bill Cox, 228
Depot Blues Crowder Brothers, 237
Depression Medley Blue Ridge Mountain Girls, 112
Der Fuehrer's Face Johnny Bond, 117; Arthur Fields & Fred Hall, 345
De's Bones Gwine Rise Again Frank & James McCravy, 533
Dese Bones Gonna Rise Again Dick Hartman's Tennessee Ramblers, 407
Dese Bones Gwine Rise Again Frank & James McCravy, 536; Prairie Ramblers, 712
Desert Blues Cliff Carlisle, 161, 163; Lewis McDaniels, 538; Whitey McPherson, 579; Jimmie Rodgers, 801
Desert Lullaby Johnny Barfield, 94
Deserted Cabin [The] John I. White, 949
Deserted Lover Four Aces, 356
Detroit Hula Girl York Brothers, 977
Devil And Mr. Hitler [The] Denver Darling, 296
Devil In Georgia [The] Doc Roberts, 753
Devil In The Hay B.E. Scott, 821
Devil In The Woodpile J.D. McFarlane & Daughter, 550
Devil Of The Sierras [The] Bill Bender, 99
Devil Song [The] [Smilin'] Ed McConnell, 530
Devil With The Devil [The] Roy Newman, 658
Devilish Mary Bill Boyd, 123; T.H. Phillips, 690; Riley Puckett, 715; Red Fox Chasers, 731; Roba Stanley, 866; Gid Tanner, 889–90
Devilism [sic] Mary W. Lee O'Daniel, 666
Devil's Blues Johnny Lee Wills, 967

Devil's Dream E.F. "Pat" Alexander, 53; Jasper Bisbee, 107; Tommy Dandurand, 293; Clifford Gross, 385; Hobbs Brothers, 428; William B. Houchens, 443; Kessinger Brothers, 479; Clayton McMichen, 570, 573; Uncle Dave Macon, 576
Devil's Great Grand Son [The] Sons Of The Pioneers, 858
Devil's No Relation [The] Ruth Donaldson & Helen Jepsen, 323
Devil's Serenade Richmond Melody Boys, 748
Devlish Mary Arthur Tanner, 886
Dex Yeux De Goo Goo Patrick (Dak) Pellerin, 684
Diamond In The Rough Uncle Dave Macon, 575
Diamond Joe Georgia Crackers, 365
Diamonds And Roses Lester McFarland & Robert A. Gardner, 547
Diamonds In The Rough Carter Family, 188
Dick And I Dick Hartman's Tennessee Ramblers, 408
Dick's Hoedown Dick Hartman's Tennessee Ramblers, 408
Dickson County Blues No. 2 Arthur Smith, 841
Did He Ever Return? Fiddlin' John Carson, 177
Did You Ever Go Sailing (Down The River Of Memories) Rodik Twins, 810
Did You Ever Go Sailing? Lulu Belle & Scotty, 516; J.B. Whitmire's Blue Sky Trio, 954
Did You Ever Hear A Goldfish Sing? Pie Plant Pete, 695; Carson Robison, 779
Did You Ever Hear A String Band Swing Light Crust Doughboys, 503
Did You Ever See The Devil, Uncle Joe? Fiddlin' Powers & Family, 704; Red Fox Chasers, 730; Doc Roberts, 754
Did You Mean Those Words You Said Posey Rorer, 813
Did You See My Lovin' Henry Warren Caplinger, 157
Diddy, Wah, Diddy With A Blah! Blah! Al Dexter, 314
Didi Wa Didi Bill Cox, 228
Didn't He Ramble Fiddlin' John Carson, 178; Carson Robison, 792
Didn't They Crucify My Lord Blue Sky Boys, 113; Philyaw Brothers, 690
Dig Me A Grave In Missouri Shelton Brothers, 829
Diga Diga Do Hoosier Hot Shots, 439
Dill Pickle Jim Couch, 223
Dill Pickle Rag Dr. Humphrey Bate, 97; Corn Cob Crushers, 222; Four Pickled Peppers, 356; Midkiff, Spencer & Blake, 616; Smith's Garage Fiddle Band, 848; Swift Jewel Cowboys, 884
Dill Pickles Billy Milton, 628
Dill Pickles Rag Kessinger Brothers, 480; McLaughlin's Old Time Melody Makers, 565
Dillinger's Warning Lone Star Cowboys, 509
Dinah Leon Chappelear, 201; Roy Newman, 656; Land Norris, 662
Dinah, Old Lady Salem Highballers, 818
Dingy Miner's Cabin [The] Ted Chestnut, 204
Dip And Dive Al McLeod's Country Dance Band, 565
Dip Me In The Golden Sea Frank & James McCravy, 533–34, 536–37
Dipping In The Golden Sea Rev. Horace A. Booker, 117
Dirty Dish Rag Blues Light Crust Doughboys, 505
Dirty Dog Jimmie Revard, 742
Dirty Dog Blues Modern Mountaineers, 630
Dirty Hangout Where I Stayed—Part 1, 2 [The] Hoke Rice, 745
Dirty Hangover Blues W. Lee O'Daniel, 666
Dis Ja Liebe Spim Adolph Hofner, 431
Dis Train Dick Hartman's Tennessee Ramblers, 407; S.E. Mullis, 646; Vaughan Quartet, 928
Disappointed In Love (I Wish I Had Never Seen Sunshine) Roy Shaffer, 825

Disappointed Lover [The] Arthur Tanner, 886
Disez Goodbye A Votre Mere (Tell Your Mother Goodbye) Denus McGee, 551
Dissatisfied Loy Bodine, 115; Hackberry Ramblers, 387; Riley Puckett, 720
Distant Land To Roam [A] Carter Family, 188
Dites Moi Avant (Tell Me Before) Leo Soileau, 854
Ditty Wah Ditty Bill Carlisle, 160
Dive For The Oyster (Part I, II) Carson Robison, 796
Dividing Line Odus & Woodrow, 667
Divorce Blues Carson Robison, 787
Dixie Earl Johnson, 459; Kessinger Brothers, 481; Chesley Shirley, 832; Uncle "Am" Stuart, 881; Gid Tanner, 888; Tweedy Brothers, 918; Jimmy Yates Groups, 975
Dixie ('Way Down South In Dixie) Doc Roberts, 752
Dixie And Yankee Doodle Dr. D.D. Hollis, 432
Dixie Boll Weevil Fiddlin' John Carson, 175
Dixie Cowboy Fiddlin' John Carson, 175; Taylor's Kentucky Boys, 895
Dixie Darling Poole Family, 701
Dixie Division Fiddlin' John Carson, 175
Dixie Flyer George Walburn & Emmett Hethcox, 935; W.L. "Rustic" Waters, 940
Dixie Flyer Blues Deford Bailey, 88
Dixie Get-Together Rustic Revellers, 816
Dixie Mail Jimmie Tarlton, 892
Dixie Medley W.W. Macbeth, 526; Massey Family, 610; University Of Tennessee Trio, 920
Dixie Moon Tune Wranglers, 916
Dixie Moonbeam Gibson String Trio, 369
Dixie Parody Ernest V. Stoneman, 872
Dixie Rag Jess Hillard, 426
Dixie Ramblers Waltz Dixie Ramblers [II], 319
Dixie Schottische Green's String Band, 381
Dixie Shadows Frank[ie] Marvin, 596
Dixie Waltz Hiter Colvin, 219; Dixie String Band, 320
Dixie Way Vernon Dalhart, 287; Carson Robison, 776
Dixieland Modern Mountaineers, 631
Dixieland Blues Sidney Smith, 846
Dixieland Echoes Rouse Brothers, 815
Dixieland Girl Village Boys, 932
Dixieland I Hear You Calling Me Texas Wanderers, 901
Dixieland Sweetheart Rex Griffin, 383
Dixie's Hottest Dixie Ramblers [II], 319
Dixon County Blues Arthur Smith, 841
Do I Really Deserve It From You? Johnny Lee Wills, 967
Do It Some More Kelly & Howard Sears, 823
Do Lord Do Remember Me Elmer Bird, 106; R.C. Garner, 363; John Henry Howard, 444
Do Lord Remember Me Ernest Phipps, 690; Prairie Ramblers, 705
Do Not Ask Me Why I'm Weeping John D. Foster, 354
Do Not Wait Till I'm Laid Beneath The Clay Elmer Bird, 106
Do Not Wait 'Till I'm Laid 'Neath The Clay Amory Male Quartette, 60; Alfred G. Karnes, 472; Walter Smith, 847
Do Not Wait Until I'm Under The Clay Stewart's Harmony Singers, 869
Do Re Mi Woody Guthrie, 386
Do Right Daddy Blues Gene Autry, 74–75; Kenneth Houchins, 443
Do Round My Lindy Fiddlin' John Carson, 176
Do Something Rice Brothers' Gang, 746
Do The Hula Lou Milton Brown, 136
Do We Have To Be Apart Bill Mounce, 645
Do You Rice Brothers' Gang, 747
Do You Call That Religion? Monroe Brothers, 632
Do You Ever Miss Me Light Crust Doughboys, 506

Do You Ever Think Of Me? Alley Boys Of Abbeville, 59; Fiddlin' John Carson, 179; Jimmie Davis, 302; Nite Owls, 660
Do You Know Him? Lyric Quartette, 525; Vaughan Quartet, 923–24
Do You Know What It Means To Be Lonely? Three Tobacco Tags, 908
Do You Love Me, Mother Darling? Dewey & Gassie Bassett, 97
Do You Still Remember? Carson Robison, 763–65
Do You Think I'll Make A Soldier [E.R.] Nance Family, 649
Do You Think Of Me? Three Tobacco Tags, 908
Do You Think That You Could Love Me Gibbs Brothers, 368
Do You Think Work Is Hard? Adam Trehan, 913
Do You Want To See Mother Again? Dixie Reelers, 320
Do You Wonder Why Roy Acuff, 51
Do Your Best—Then Wear A Sunny Smile McDonald Quartet, 540
Do Your Best And Wear A Smile Peck's Male Quartette, 683
Do Your Best Then Wear A Sunny Smile Royal Quartette, 815
Do Your Best, Then Wear A Smile Stamps Quartet, 864
Dobie Shack Hackberry Ramblers, 387
Doctor [The] Smoky Wood, 971
Do-Do-Daddling Thing Fleming & Townsend, 347
Does He Ever Think Of Me Raymond Render, 740
Does Jennie Remember Mrs. Dennis Taylor, 893
Does Jesus Care? Morris Brothers, 643; Prairie Ramblers, 709
Does My Baby Love Me, Yes Sir! Jimmie Revard, 743
Does She Ever Think Of Me? Raymond Render, 740
Does The Pathway Lead Straight Turkey Mountain Singers, 916
Does This Train Go To Heaven? Frank & James McCravy, 537; V.O. Stamps-M.L. Yandell, 863
Does True Love Live Today? Lester McFarland & Robert A. Gardner, 547
Does Your Path Seem Long Bush Brothers, 147
Doesn't Matter Anymore Bob Atcher, 70
Dog And Gun (An Old English Ballad) Bradley Kincaid, 485
Dog Gone Them Blues Jess Hillard, 425
Dog House Blues Bill Monroe, 631
Doggone Blues Jimmy Long, 511–12
Doggone Crazy Blues Shelton Brothers, 830
Dog-Gone Mule Hodgers Brothers, 428
Doggone That Train Jimmie Davis, 299
Dogs In The Ash Can Lonesome Luke, 510
Dogwood Mountain Land Norris, 662
Doin' It Right Lew Preston, 713
Doin' It The Old Fashioned Way Roy Acuff, 48
Doin' The Best I Can Vernon Dalhart, 244–45
Doin' The Goofus Arthur Smith, 840
Doin' The Raccoon John Boyd, 125
Doin' Things On The Farm Lew Preston, 713
Dollar A Week Furniture Man Emmett Bankston & Red Henderson, 92
Dollar And The Devil [The] Bill Cox, 225; Frank & James McCravy, 534–36; Lester McFarland & Robert A. Gardner, 545; Henry Whitter, 955
Dollar Down And A Dollar A Week [A] Shelton Brothers, 828
Dollar Down And A Dollar A Week With Chicken Pie Arkansas Woodchopper, 64
Dollar Is All I Crave Cliff Carlisle, 166
Dollar's All I Crave [A] Carlisle Brothers, 169
Dominicker Duck [The] Fiddlin' John Carson, 178
Dominion Hornpipe A.C. (Eck) Robertson, 757
Donald Rag [The] Martin Melody Boys, 594
Done And Gone Bob Wills, 965

Done Gone Kessinger Brothers, 480; Clayton McMichen, 570; Massey Family, 610; A.C. (Eck) Robertson, 757; Smith's Garage Fiddle Band, 848; Lowe Stokes, 870
Done Gone Crazy Herschel Brown, 134
Done Sold My Soul To The Devil Dave Edwards, 331
Donkey On The Railroad Track Hill Billies, 423
Don't Accuse Your Lover Claude Casey, 196
Don't Ask Me Why I'm Weeping John D. Foster, 353
Don't Be Angry With Me Darling Red Headed Brier Hopper, 731
Don't Be Angry With Me Sweetheart Walter Smith, 846
Don't Be Ashamed Of Mother Bill Carlisle, 160
Don't Be Blue Floyd Tillman, 910
Don't Be Blue For Me Ted Daffan's Texans, 241; Massey Family, 612
Don't Be Blue, Little Pal, Don't Be Blue Karl & Harty, 471; Roy Rogers, 812
Don't Be Jealous Of My Yesterdays Wiley Walker & Gene Sullivan, 936
Don't Be Knocking Atco Quartet, 70; Parker Quartette, 679; Peck's Male Quartette, 684; Rainbow Quartette, 724; Vaughan Quartet, 928; Whitey & Hogan, 952
Don't Bite The Hand That's Feeding You Gene Autry, 85; Jimmy Wakely, 934
Don't Break Her Heart Boy Jimmie Davis, 303
Don't Break My Heart Dick Reinhart, 739
Don't Bring Lulu New Dixie Demons, 655
Don't Call Me Boy Bob Skyles, 839
Don't Cause Mother's Hair To Turn Grey J.E. Mainer's Mountaineers, 581
Don't Check Out On Me Slim Harbert, 398
Don't Come Cryin' In My Beer Sunshine Boys, 882
Don't Count Your Chickens Charlie Wills, 966
Don't Cry For Me When I'm Gone Al Dexter, 314
Don't Cry My Darlin' Johnny Barfield, 93
Don't Cry, Little Sweetheart, Don't Cry Vernon Dalhart, 292
Don't Dig Mother's Grave Before She Is Dead James Scott-Claude Boone, 821
Don't Do Me That Way Gene Autry, 74
Don't Drop A Slug In The Slot Bill Boyd, 123
Don't Ever Go Wrong Sons Of Dixie, 856
Don't Ever Leave Me Alone Buddy Jones, 466
Don't Ever Marry A Widow Bill Cox, 225
Don't Ever Say Adieu Dick Reinhart, 739
Don't Ever Trust A Friend Hackberry Ramblers, 387
Don't Fall Too Deep In Love Lester McFarland & Robert A. Gardner, 546, 548
Don't Forget Me Monroe Brothers, 633
Don't Forget Me Darling Delmore Brothers, 310; David Miller, 626
Don't Forget Me Little Darling Carter Family, 192; Jess Hillard, 426; Buell Kazee, 473; Wade Mainer, 584; Bob Miller, 623; David Miller, 626; Parker & Dodd, 678; Red Patterson's Piedmont Log Rollers, 682; Roy Shaffer, 825; Gid Tanner, 888; Zeke Williams, 959
(Don't Forget Me) Dear Little Darling Vernon Dalhart, 292
Don't Forget Mother Three Tobacco Tags, 909
Don't Forget My Little Darling Charles Lewis Stine, 869
Don't Forget That Jesus Loves You Eddie Dean, 308
Don't Forget The Family Prayer Vaughan Quartet, 925
Don't Forget The Old Folks Jewell Tillman Burns & Charlie D. Tillman, 145; [Smilin'] Ed McConnell, 530–31
Don't Forget The Sailor Lad Three Tobacco Tags, 907–08
Don't Forget This Song Carter Family, 188, 193
Don't Forget To Drop A Line To Mother Frank & James McCravy, 535–36
Don't Forget To Pray Abernathy Quartet, 47; Stamps Quartet, 864; Rev. M.L. Thrasher, 905; Valdese Quartette, 922; Vaughan Quartet, 923; Victory Four, 931
Don't Get Married Emry Arthur, 67
Don't Get One Woman On Your Mind Willard Hodgin[s], 430
Don't Get Too Deep In Love Wade Mainer, 584
Don't Get Trouble In Your Mind Frank Blevins, 108; J.E. Mainer's Mountaineers, 582
Don't Get Weary Children Uncle Dave Macon, 578
Don't Go Away Unsaved Hall Brothers, 392
Don't Go In The Lion's Cage Tonight Zora Layman, 492
Don't Go Out J.E. Mainer's Mountaineers, 582
Don't Go Out Tonight, My Darling G.B. Grayson & Henry Whitter, 380
Don't Go Out Tonight, Sweetheart Arthur Tanner, 886
Don't Go 'Way, Doggone Ya Dick Hartman's Tennessee Ramblers, 407
Don't Grieve After Me Ernest Phipps, 691
Don't Grieve Over Me Carson Brothers-Smith, 180; George Stevens, 868
Don't Grieve Your Mother W.C. Childers, 205; Lester McFarland & Robert A. Gardner, 544; John McGhee & Frank Welling, 558, 560; Gid Tanner, 887
Don't Hang Me In The Morning Graham Brothers, 377; Webb Whipple, 948
Don't Hinder Me Vaughan Quartet, 928
Don't Lay Me On My Back Eldon Baker, 89
Don't Lay Me On My Back (In My Last Sleep) Lester McFarland & Robert A. Gardner, 549; Carson Robison, 788
Don't Leave Me (With A Broken Heart) Shelly Lee Alley, 59
Don't Leave Me All Alone Shelton Brothers, 829
Don't Leave Me Alone Wade Mainer, 584
Don't Leave Me Now Airport Boys, 52; Modern Mountaineers, 631
Don't Leave Me Sally Sawyer Sisters, 820
Don't Leave Mother Alone Johnnie Gates, 363
Don't Let It Be Said Too Late Thursday Evening Prayer Meeters, 909
Don't Let Me Be In The Way Delmore Brothers, 309
Don't Let Me Down Old Pal Wilf Carter (Montana Slim), 183
Don't Let Me Stand In Your Way Roy Newman, 658
Don't Let Me Worry Your Little Mind Carlisle Brothers, 169
Don't Let My Mother Know Canova Family, 156
Don't Let My Ramblin' Bother Your Mind Delmore Brothers, 311
Don't Let My Spurs Get Rusty While I'm Gone Carson Robison, 797
Don't Let The Barrel Go Dry Bill Boyd, 125
Don't Let The Blues Get You Down Buck Mt. Band, 141
Don't Let The Deal Go Down Vernon Dalhart, 263; Kessinger Brothers, 480; W. Lee O'Daniel, 665; Bob Wills, 964
Don't Let Your Deal Go Down Fiddlin' John Carson, 177; Vernon Dalhart, 262; Jess Hillard, 425; Nelson Hillard, 426; Lake Howard, 445; Riley Puckett, 719, 721; Smith & Irvine, 848; Ernest V. Stoneman, 872
Don't Let Your Deal Go Down Blues Charlie Poole, 699
Don't Let Your Deal Go Down Medley Charlie Poole, 699
Don't Let Your Love Go Wrong Leo Soileau, 855
Don't Let Your Mother Know (The Way I Am To Go) Dwight Butcher, 149
Don't Let Your Sweet Love Die Bob Atcher, 70; Roy Hall, 391
Don't Let Your Sweet Love Die (Like Flowers In The Fall) Denver Darling, 295
Don't Lie To An Innocent Maiden Light Crust Doughboys, 506
Don't Lie To Me Roy Marsh, 587
Don't Love A Smiling Sweetheart Willard Hodgin[s], 429

Don't Love Nobody Uncle Dave Macon, 576
Don't Make Me Go To Bed (I'll Be Good) Bill Cox, 228
Don't Make Me Go To Bed And I'll Be Good Roy Acuff, 51
Don't Make Me Laugh—I'm Mad Wiley Walker & Gene Sullivan, 936
Don't Make Me Wait Too Long Dick Reinhart, 739
Don't Marry A Man If He Drinks John McGhee & Frank Welling, 557
Don't Marry A Widow Vernon Dalhart, 291
Don't Marry The Wrong Woman Bill Carlisle, 159; Cliff Carlisle, 165
Don't Mention Me Carlisle Brothers, 169
Don't Monkey 'Round My Widder Karl & Harty, 471
Don't Put A Tax On The Beautiful Girls Tennessee Ramblers [II], 897; Ernest Thompson, 902
Don't Put Me Off The Train Bradley Kincaid, 482–83
Don't Put Off Salvation Too Long Carolina Ladies Quartet, 171
Don't Reckon It'll Happen Again Sid Harkreader, 400
Don't Say Goodbye Hi-Flyers, 419
Don't Say Goodbye If You Love Me Blue Sky Boys, 114; Claude Casey, 197; Jimmie Davis, 301; Buddy Jones, 466; Morris Brothers, 643
Don't Say Goodbye Little Darling Bob Atcher, 70; Prairie Ramblers, 712
Don't Say Good-Bye When You Go Anglin Brothers, 61
Don't Say I Did It, Jack Carson Robison, 774
Don't Say No Honolulu Strollers, 434
Don't Sell Pa Any More Rum Giddens Sisters, 369
Don't Send My Boy To Prison Duke Clark, 213
Don't Sing Aloha When I Go John McGhee & Frank Welling, 557
Don't Stay After Ten Grover Rann, 729
Don't Stop Loving Me Bob Wills, 963
Don't Stop Praying Andrew Jenkins, 455
Don't Take Me Back To The Chain Gang Gene Autry, 78
Don't Take My Darling Away Shelton Brothers, 830
Don't Take My Darling Boy Away David Miller, 626
Don't Take My Memories Johnny Barfield, 94
Don't Take The Sweet Out Of Sweetheart Sally Foster, 355
Don't Talk To Me About Men Cindy Walker, 935
Don't Tell Me Goodbye (If You Love Me) Bill Cox, 229
Don't Think Anymore About Me Prairie Ramblers, 713
Don't Think It Ain't Been Charmin' Dick Reinhart, 739
Don't Trouble Me Clayton McMichen, 572
Don't Try It For It Can't Be Done Riley Puckett, 719
Don't Try It, It Can't Be Done Pie Plant Pete, 695
Don't Try To Cry Your Way Back To Me Dixieland Swingsters, 320
Don't Wait 'Till We're Old And Grey Gene Steele, 867
Don't Waste Your Love On Me Roy Rogers, 812
Don't Waste Your Tears On Me Gene Autry, 82
Don't Waste Your Tears Over Me, Little Girl Jimmie Revard, 743
Don't You Believe It Carson Robison, 778, 780
Don't You Care Shelly Lee Alley, 58
Don't You Cry My Honey Gid Tanner, 890
Don't You Cry Over Me Jimmie Davis, 305
Don't You Grieve Your Mother John McGhee & Frank Welling, 561
Don't You Hear Jerusalem Moan Gid Tanner, 888
Don't You Hear Jerusalem Mourn Edward Carson, 174
Don't You Know Or Don't You Care Tennessee Ramblers [II], 898
Don't You Love Daddy Too Vaughan Quartet, 930
Don't You Love Your Daddy Dick Parman, 679
Don't You Love Your Daddy Too? Johnson County Ramblers, 464; McClendon Brothers, 528; Jack Pickell, 694; Vaughan Quartet, 925
Don't You Remember Me Universal Cowboys, 919
Don't You Remember The Time Callahan Brothers, 152; Freeny's Barn Dance Band, 359; Lester McFarland & Robert A. Gardner, 543; Clayton McMichen, 566; Riley Puckett, 717
Don't You See That Train? Delmore Brothers, 310
Don't You Think Of Sister And Brother Willard Hodgin[s], 429
Don't You Want To Go John McGhee & Frank Welling, 557
Don't You Want To Go (To That Happy Home On High) Eldon Baker, 89
Don't You Weep Anymore Darlin' Johnny Bond, 116
Don't You Worry 'Bout Me When I'm Gone Pete Pyle, 723
Doodle Doo Doo Vernon Dalhart, 242
Dor Mon Enfant Dor Roy Gonzales, 375
Dor, Baby, Dor Happy Fats, 395
Doris Waltz Taylor-Griggs Louisiana Melody Makers, 894
Double Crossin' Daddy Prairie Ramblers, 713
Double Eagle March Cal Davenport, 296; Hugh Gibbs String Band, 368
Double Headed Train Henry Whitter, 954
Double Trouble Blues Walter Hurdt, 447
Double-Crossing Mama Prairie Ramblers, 712
Doug Ain't Doin' The Jitterbug Tennessee Ramblers [II], 897
Doughboy Hop Light Crust Doughboys, 502
Doughboy Rag Light Crust Doughboys, 501
Doughboys Theme Song #1, 2 Light Crust Doughboys, 501
Dovie Darling Callahan Brothers, 153
Down A Mountain Trail Gene Autry, 82
Down Along The Sleepy Rio Grande Sons Of The Pioneers, 858
Down Among The Budded Roses J.E. Mainer's Mountaineers, 582
Down Among The Budding Roses Happy Valley Family, 398; Lewis McDaniels, 538
Down Among The Faded Roses Hi Neighbor Boys, 420
Down Among The Hills Of Tennessee Morgan Denmon, 312
Down Among The Shady Woodland North Carolina Cooper Boys, 663
Down Among The Sugar Cane Tom Darby & Jimmie Tarlton, 294; Merritt Smith, 844
Down And Out Blues Jimmy Long, 511–12; James Roberts, 756
Down At Polka Joe's Bill Boyd, 124
Down At The Bottom Of The Mountain Arthur Fields & Fred Hall, 340, 342, 344
Down At The End Of Memory Lane Jimmie Davis, 304
Down At The Old Country Church Jimmie Davis, 299
Down At The Old Man's House Thomas C. Ashley, 68
Down At The Roadside Inn Al Dexter, 315
Down By The Cane Brake Smiley Burnette, 145
Down By The Hawthorn Tree Fred Pendleton, 685
Down By The Mississippi Shore Richard Brooks & Reuben Puckett, 132
Down By The Moss Covered Spring Fisher Hendley, 417
Down By The Old Alamo Roy Rogers, 812
Down By The Old Cabin Door Arthur Fields & Fred Hall, 341
Down By The Old Mill Stream Cliff Carlisle, 162; Dixieland Four, 320; John McGhee & Frank Welling, 559; Uncle Dave Macon, 574; Prairie Ramblers, 706; Riley Puckett, 716–17; Three Tobacco Tags, 908
Down By The Old Rio Grande Rolling Stones, 813
Down By The Old Rustic Well Frank Luther, 520; Bob Miller, 623

Down By The Railroad Track Bradley Kincaid, 485; Buck Nation, 650
Down By The River Uncle Dave Macon, 574
Down By The Riverside Lester McFarland & Robert A. Gardner, 542; Sandhills Sixteen, 820
Down By The Weeping Willow Tree H.K. Hutchison, 450
Down By The Window Where My Mother Used To Pray Frank & James McCravy, 536–37
(Down By The) O-H-I-O Milton Brown, 136; Hoosier Hot Shots, 439
Down Del Rio Way Red River Dave, 732
Down Dixie Way Vaughan Quartet, 927
Down Hearted Blues Virginia Childs, 208; Clayton McMichen, 566, 572; Roy Newman, 657; Riley Puckett, 718; Bob Wills, 962–63
Down Hilo Way Ted Daffan's Texans, 240
Down Home McClendon Brothers, 528; George Wade, 933
Down Home Rag Happy Hollow Hoodlums, 397; Hoosier Hot Shots, 438; Doc Roberts, 755
Down In A Georgia Jail Posey Rorer, 813
Down In A Southern Town Claude Davis, 297
Down In A Southern Town Yodel Hoke Rice, 745
Down In Arkansas Cofer Brothers, 216; Bill Cox, 225; Crystal Springs Ramblers, 239; Dave Edwards, 331; Pickard Family, 691–92; Riley Puckett, 717; Reaves White County Ramblers, 729; Rufus K. Stanley, 866
Down In Arkansaw Uncle Dave Macon, 574
Down In Atlanta Claude Davis, 297
Down In Baltimore Odus & Woodrow, 667
Down In Caroline Cliff Carlisle, 167
Down In De Cane Brake/Break Carson Robison, 762–63
Down In Dixie Land Bill Cox, 227
Down In Florida On A Hog Tom Darby & Jimmie Tarlton, 293
Down In Georgia Charlie Poole, 699
Down In Happy Valley Johnson Brothers, 462
Down In Indiana Clarence Ganus, 362
Down In Johnson City Tennessee Hill Billy, 896
Down In Jungle Town Dave Edwards, 331; Hoosier Hot Shots, 438; Walter C. Peterson, 688
Down In Lone Green Valley Frank Hutchison, 450
Down In Louisiana Ezra Buzzington's Rustic Revelers, 150
Down In New Orleans Dewey & Gassie Bassett, 97
Down In Old Alabama Rex Griffin, 383
Down In Old Kentucky Clayton McMichen, 571; Asa Martin, 592
Down In Tennessee Russell & Louis Burton, 146; Smoky Mountain Ramblers, 852
Down In Tennessee Blues Homer Davenport, 296
Down In Tennessee Valley Emry Arthur, 64
Down In Texas A.E. Ward, 938
Down In The Cane Break Hartford City Trio, 407; Pickard Family, 693
Down In The Diving Bell Lulu Belle & Scotty, 516
Down In The Dumps Johnny Bond, 116
Down In The Hills Carson Robison, 763, 765; Jesse Rodgers, 798
Down In The Jail House On My Knees Cliff Carlisle, 161
Down In The Lone Star State Dwight Butcher, 149
Down In The Old Cherry Orchard Tom Darby & Jimmie Tarlton, 294; Sloane & Threadgill, 840; Merritt Smith, 845
Down In The Old Home Town Oscar Ford, 352; Arty Hall, 390; Bob Miller, 625
Down In The Valley Arthur Fields & Fred Hall, 343; Ted Hawkins, 413; Hoosier Hot Shots, 436; Frank Luther, 524; Taylor's Kentucky Boys, 895
Down In The Willow Wade Mainer, 583
Down In Union County Roy Acuff, 49

Down On Penny's Farm Bentley Boys, 100
Down On The Banks Of The Ohio Blue Sky Boys, 113; Red Patterson's Piedmont Log Rollers, 682; Ernest V. Stoneman, 877
Down On The Banks Of The Yazoo Bob Calen, 151
Down On The Farm Uncle Tom Collins, 219; Vernon Dalhart, 255, 268; Wesley Long, 513; Asa Martin, 588, 593; Ruth Neal & Wanda Neal, 652; Chubby Parker, 676; Prairie Ramblers, 707; V.O. Stamps-M.L. Yandell, 863
Down On The Farm (They All Ask For You) Shelton Brothers, 829
Down On The L.N. Railroad Stripling Brothers, 880
Down On The Levee Ray Sand's Harmony Four, 819
Down On The Old Plantation Tex Fletcher, 349; Doc Hopkins, 441; Carson Robison, 777–79; Carl Trimble, 913
Down On The Ozark Trail Clayton McMichen, 568
Down South Delmore Brothers, 310
Down South Blues Dock Boggs, 115
Down South Everybody's Happy Ray Sand's Harmony Four, 819
Down South Where The Sugar Cane Grows Fiddlin' John Carson, 177
Down Sunshine Lane Ambrose Haley, 389
Down The Arizona Trail Walter Hurdt, 448
Down The Colorado Trail Tex Ritter, 750
Down The Hobo Trail To Home Asa Martin, 591
Down The Lane Of Memory Lester McFarland & Robert A. Gardner, 550; Prairie Ramblers, 711
Down The Lane To Home Sweet Home John McGhee & Frank Welling, 558; Clayton McMichen, 568
Down The Old Cattle Trail Wilf Carter (Montana Slim), 182
Down The Old Meadow Lane Hill Billies, 424; Zeb White, 951
Down The Old Ohio River Valley Kenneth Houchins, 444
Down The Old Road To Home Jimmie Rodgers, 807
Down The Ozark Trail Clayton McMichen, 571
Down The River Of Golden Dreams R.D. Kelly & Julius Dunn, 476; Lester McFarland & Robert A. Gardner, 548
Down The River We Go John Dilleshaw, 317
Down The Road Samantha Bumgarner, 142; W.A. Lindsay, 507
Down The Trail Hi-Flyers, 419
Down The Trail To Home Sweet Home Deckers, 308; Earl Shirkey & Roy Harper, 832
Down The Yodeling Trail At Twilight Wilf Carter (Montana Slim), 184
Down To Jordan And Be Saved Ernest V. Stoneman, 877
Down To The Club Hill Billies, 423
Down Virginia Way University Of Tennessee Trio, 920
Down Where The Coosa River Flows Vernon Dalhart, 274
Down Where The Cotton Blossoms Grow Hugh Cross, 235; Frank & James McCravy, 534
Down Where The Roses Go To Sleep Lester McFarland & Robert A. Gardner, 550; Bob Miller, 625
Down Where The Swanee River Flows Hugh Cross, 235–36; Otto Gray, 379; Melford Jackson, 452; David Miller, 626
Down Where The Taters Grow Bernard [Slim] Smith, 842
Down Where The Violets Grow Leon Payne, 683
Down Where The Watermelon Grows Phil Reeve & Ernest Moody, 735
Down Where The Watermelons Grow Avoca Quartette, 87; Raymond Weaver & Les Applegate, 942
Down With Gin Claude Casey, 197
Down With The Old Canoe Dorsey & Beatrice Dixon, 322
Down Yonder Herschel Brown, 133; Clayton McMichen, 566; Hoke Rice, 745; Rice Brothers' Gang, 746; Doc Roberts, 755; Rustic Revellers, 816; Scottdale String Band, 821; Bill Shores

& Melvin Dupree, 832; Stripling Brothers, 880; Gid Tanner, 891; Tweedy Brothers, 918
Down Yonder (In The Valley) Dick Hartman's Tennessee Ramblers, 408
Down Yonder Breakdown Scottdale String Band, 822
Downfall Of Adam Richard Cox, 229
Downfall Of Paris Mumford Bean, 98; Hickory Nuts, 420; W.A. Hinton, 427; Murphy Brothers, 646
Dr. Ginger Blue Arthur Tanner, 886
Draft Board Blues Cliff Bruner, 141
Draftee Blues Johnny Bond, 117
Drag Along Blues Roy Newman, 656
Draggin' It Around Bill Boyd, 122
Dragging The Bow Cliff Bruner, 140; Hi-Flyers, 419; Massey Family, 610
Dratenik The Tinker Polka Adolph Hofner, 431
Dream A Little Dream Of Me Cliff Carlisle, 164
Dream Boat J.B. Whitmire's Blue Sky Trio, 953
Dream Book Of Memories Stuart Hamblen, 392
Dream Of A Miner's Child Vernon Dalhart, 252
Dream Of Home [A] Andrew Jenkins, 454; Morris Family, 643; XC Sacred Quartette, 975
Dream Of Love Jimmie Davis, 304
Dream Of The Miner's Child [The] Vernon Dalhart, 251–53, 255; Johnson Brothers, 463; Morris Brothers, 643
Dream Shadows East Texas Serenaders, 329
Dream Trail Clayton McMichen, 572
Dream Train Cliff Bruner, 139; Riley Puckett, 722; Tom & Roy, 911
Dream Valley Massey Family, 612
Dream Waltz Southern Moonlight Entertainers, 860
Dreamed I Searched Heaven For You Monroe Brothers, 633
Dreaming Adolph Hofner, 430; Stroup Quartet, 880; Tom & Roy, 911; Joe Werner, 944
Dreaming Alone In The Twilight Stamps Quartet, 865; Vaughan Quartet, 923
Dreaming Of Mother Claude Davis, 297
Dreaming Of The Old Homestead Sam & Fred Friend, 359
Dreaming Of You Al Dexter, 314
Dreaming With Tears In My Eyes Jimmie Rodgers, 808
Dreams Of Days Gone By Plantation Boys, 698
Dreams Of Love McDearis String Band, 539
Dreams Of Silver And Memories Of Gold Tune Wranglers, 915
Dreams Of The Ozarks Mintons Ozark String Band, 629
Dreams Of The Past Stamps Quartet, 865
Dreams Of The Southland Vernon Dalhart, 251–52, 254
Dreamy Autumn Waltz Poplin-Woods Tennessee String Band, 701
Dreamy Eyes Bill Carlisle, 160
Dreamy Eyes Waltz Taylor-Griggs Louisiana Melody Makers, 893; Bob Wills, 963
Dreamy Land Bay Elton Britt, 130
Dreamy Moon Of Tennessee Fleming & Townsend, 347
Dreamy Prairie Moon Wilf Carter (Montana Slim), 184
Dreamy Rocky Mountain Moon Carson Robison, 784
Dreamy Time Gal Rodeo Trio, 798
Dreary Black Hills Bill Bender, 99
Drift Along Pretty Moon Bill Cox, 228
Drifter—Part 1, 2 [The] Goebel Reeves, 735–36
Drifter's Buddy (A True Story) [The] Goebel Reeves, 737
Drifting Bill Carlisle, 160; Frank & James McCravy, 531; Moore Sisters, 641; Vernon & Harwell, 931
Drifting Along Jerry Behrens, 98; Hackberry Ramblers, 387; Modern Mountaineers, 630
Drifting And Dreaming Carson Robison, 784; Bob Skyles, 839

Drifting And Dreaming (Sweet Paradise) Bar-X Cowboys, 92; Roy Newman, 657
Drifting And Dreaming In Hawaii Three Dominoes, 906
Drifting Away Vaughan Quartet, 923–24
Drifting Back To Dixie Stuart Hamblen, 392
Drifting Back To Dreamland Homer Christopher, 209; John D. Foster, 354
Drifting Down John McGhee & Frank Welling, 556; Peck's Male Quartette, 684; Smith's Sacred Singers, 850
Drifting Down The Blue Ridge Trail Merritt Smith, 845
Drifting Down The Trail Of Dreams Vernon Dalhart, 278–79; Carson Robison, 762
Drifting In A Lover's Dream Four Novelty Aces, 356; Vagabonds, 922
Drifting On Fleming & Townsend, 346; Saddle Tramps, 818
Drifting Sands Sons Of The Ozarks, 856
Drifting Through An Unfriendly World Wade Mainer, 585
Drifting Together Bill Carlisle, 160
Drifting Too Far From The Shore Roy Acuff, 49; Carolina Gospel Singers, 171; Arty Hall, 390; Judie & Julie, 468; Monroe Brothers, 632
Driftwood Humbard Family, 447; Jack Pierce, 696
Driftwood On The River Elton Britt, 130
Drill, Ye Tarriers, Drill Chubby Parker, 677
Drink 'Er Down Gid Tanner, 888
Drink Her Down Sid Harkreader, 401
Drink More Cider Jimmy Johnson's String Band, 461
Drink The Barrel Dry Bill Boyd, 124
Drinker's Child [The] Rosa Lee Carson, 179
Drinkin' Made A Fool Outa Me Sunshine Boys, 882
Drinking Blues Chester Allen & Campbell, 54; Bob Skyles, 839
Drive Away Your Troubles With A Song Jenkins Family, 457
Drive My Blues Away Callahan Brothers, 153
Drivin' The Doggies Along Tune Wranglers, 914
Driving Saw-Logs On The Plover Pierre La Dieu, 488
Droan Waltz [The] Grapevine Coon Hunters, 377
Drop Us Off At Bob's Place Charlie Wills, 966
Drowsy Moonlight Frank[ie] Marvin, 595–96
Drug Store Cowboy [The] Bob Skyles, 838
Drunk And Nutty Blues Allen Brothers, 57
Drunk Man Blues Blue Ridge Mountain Entertainers, 110
Drunk Man's Blues Kentucky Thorobreds, 478
Drunkard [The] E.F. Morgan, 641
Drunkard's Blues Buddy Jones, 464; Bob Wills, 963
Drunkard's Child [The] Lewis McDaniels, 538; Jimmie Rodgers, 803; Smith's Sacred Singers, 849; Henry Whitter, 955
Drunkard's Child's Plea [The] Lester McFarland & Robert A. Gardner, 545
Drunkard's Courtship [The] Gid Tanner, 888
Drunkard's Doom [The] Frank Blevins, 108; Ted Chestnut, 204
Drunkard's Dream [The] Thomas C. Ashley, 67; Morgan Denmon, 312; Lester McFarland & Robert A. Gardner, 544; Charlie Oaks, 664; Riley Puckett, 716; Posey Rorer, 813; Welby Toomey, 912
Drunkard's Hell [The] Maynard Britton, 131; Vernon Dalhart, 254
Drunkard's Hiccoughs J.E. Mainer's Mountaineers, 582; Reaves White County Ramblers, 729
Drunkard's Hic-cups [The] Fiddlin' John Carson, 176; Clayton McMichen, 566; Gid Tanner, 888
Drunkard's Lone Child [The] Vernon Dalhart, 254, 258; Arthur Fields & Fred Hall, 338; Otto Gray, 379
Drunkard's Own Child [The] Lester McFarland & Robert A. Gardner, 545
Drunkard's Resolution [A] Fleming & Townsend, 347

Drunkard's Tap Dance—Part 1, 2 [The] Lowe Stokes, 870
Drunkard's Waltz J.B. Fuslier, 361
Drunkards Warning Benny Borg, 118; Hinson, Pitts & Coley, 427
Drunken Hiccoughs Ray Gaddis, 361; Holland Puckett, 715
Drunken Man's Dream [The] Doc Roberts, 754
Drunken Sailor Medley John Baltzell, 90
Dry And Dusty Morrison Twin Brothers String Band, 644
Dry Bones Bascom Lamar Lunsford, 517
Dry Gin Rag W.T. Narmour & S.W. Smith, 649–50
Dry Landers [The] Patt Patterson, 681
Dry Those Tears Little Darlin' Modern Mountaineers, 631
Dry Town Blues Leake County Revelers, 495
Dry Voters And Wet Drinkers Bob Miller, 618
Dry Votin' Wet Drinkers Bob Miller, 617
Dry Votin', Wet Drinkin' Better-Than-Thou Hypocritical Blues [The] Bob Miller, 617
Dry Your Eyes, Little Girl Rice Brothers' Gang, 747
Dry, Dry, Dry John D. Foster, 354
Duane Street Dye's Sacred Harp Singers, 328
Dublin Bay Lester McFarland & Robert A. Gardner, 543
Duchess Had The Duke For Dinner Bob Miller, 625
Duck Foot Sue Buckeye Boys, 141; Bob Miller, 616–17, 623
Duck Shoes Rag Grinnell Giggers, 384
Ducky Daddy Doc Hopkins, 441
Dude Cowboy Hoosier Hot Shots, 440; Massey Family, 611
Dude Ranch Cowhands [The] Gene Autry, 83
Dude Ranch Party—Part I, II Texas Rangers, 899
Dunbar-Midkiff Jig Midkiff, Spencer & Blake, 616
Duplin County Blues Roland Cauley, 198
Durang Hornpipe Kessinger Brothers, 480
Durang Hornpipe Medley John Baltzell, 90
Durang's Hornpipe William B. Houchens, 443; Kessinger Brothers, 479; Massey Family, 610
Durna [sic] Hornpipe Clayton McMichen, 570
Dusky Stevedore Light Crust Doughboys, 504
Dust Gene Autry, 82; Roy Rogers, 811
Dust Bowl Blues Woody Guthrie, 386
Dust Bowl Refugee Woody Guthrie, 386
Dust Can't Kill Me Woody Guthrie, 386
Dust Off That Old Piano Roy Newman, 657
Dust Pan Blues Gene Autry, 71–72; Frank[ie] Marvin, 600; Jack Pierce, 696
Dust Pneumonia Blues Woody Guthrie, 386
Dusty Miller Capt. M.J. Bonner, 117
Dusty Old Dust Woody Guthrie, 386
Dusty Road Al Dexter, 314
Dusty Roads Duncan Sisters, 325
Dusty Skies Texas Jim Lewis, 500; Charlie Wills, 966
Dusty Trails Wilf Carter (Montana Slim), 184
Dutchman's Daughter [The] Johnson Brothers, 463
Dutchman's Serenade [The] "Dad" Williams, 957
Duval Count [sic] Blues [The] Three Floridians, 906
Duval[l] County Blues Bill Carlisle, 159; Luther Higginbotham, 421; James Roberts, 756
Dwelling In [The] Be[a]ulah Land Katherine Baxter & Harry Nelson, 97; John McGhee & Frank Welling, 554; Sons Of The Pioneers, 858
Dying Boy's Message [The] Howard Haney, 395
Dying Boy's Prayer [The] Charles Baker, 89; Blue Sky Boys, 113; Wade Mainer, 583
Dying Brake[s]man [The] Roy Harvey, 411; Pine Ridge Ramblers, 698
Dying Cowboy ([O] Bury Me Not On The Lone Prairie) [The] Vernon Dalhart, 267; Carl T. Sprague, 862
Dying Cowboy [The] Jules Allen, 55; Arkansas Woodchopper, 63; Asa Martin, 590; Holland Puckett, 715

Dying Cowboy On The Prairie [The] Girls Of The Golden West, 370
Dying Cowgirl [The] Gene Autry, 78; Don Weston, 947
Dying For Someone To Love Me Jossie Ellers, 331; B.F. Kincaid, 482
Dying From Home, And Lost Jenkins Family, 457
Dying Girl [The] Bob Miller, 624
Dying Girl's Farewell [The] Callahan Brothers, 153; Lester McFarland & Robert A. Gardner, 546; Ernest V. Stoneman, 872, 875
Dying Girl's Message [The] Vernon Dalhart, 248, 252, 263; Sid Harkreader, 400; Lester McFarland & Robert A. Gardner, 545; Asa Martin, 588
Dying Hobo [The] Russell & Louis Burton, 146; Rosa Lee Carson, 179; Arthur Fields & Fred Hall, 339; Travis B. Hale-E.J. Derry Jr., 389; Kelly Harrell, 403; Clayton McMichen, 567
Dying Hobo's Prayer [The] Chas. M. Dewitte, 314
Dying In Ashville [sic] Jail Crowder Brothers, 238
Dying Message [The] Frank Wheeler-Monroe Lamb, 948
Dying Mother [The] Carter Family, 195
Dying Mother's Prayer [The] Wilf Carter (Montana Slim), 182
Dying Mountaineer [The] Ranch Boys, 725
Dying Nun [The] Foreman Family, 352
Dying On Calvary Rev. Edward Boone, Mrs. Edward Boone & Miss Olive Boone, 118
Dying Ranger [The] Arkansas Woodchopper, 63; Cartwright Brothers, 196; Marc Williams, 958
Dying Rustler [The] Red Foley, 351
Dying Soldier (Brother Green) [The] Buell Kazee, 473
Dying Soldier [The] Carter Family, 189; Clarence Ganus, 362
Dying Texas Ranger [The] Jimmie Williamson, 960
Dying Thief [The] Uncle Dave Macon, 576
Dying Tramp [The] Walker's Corbin Ramblers, 936
Dying Truckdriver [The] Delmore Brothers, 311
Dying Willie Cecil Vaughn, 930

E Rag Walker's Corbin Ramblers, 936
Each Day I'll Do A Golden Deed North Georgia Four, 663
Eagle Rock Blues Byrd Moore, 639
Earl Johnson's Arkansaw Traveler Earl Johnson, 460
Early In The Mornin' Kanawha Singers, 469
Early Morning Blues Bill Nettles, 654
Early, Early In The Morning Leroy Roberson, 752
Ease My Troubled Mind Buddy Jones, 465
Ease My Wearied Mind Sons Of Acadians, 856
Ease My Worried Mind Cliff Bruner, 140
East Bound Train Blue Sky Boys, 114; Carolina Buddys, 170; George Edgin, 330; Frank Luther, 524; Lester McFarland & Robert A. Gardner, 544; Asa Martin, 588, 590; Riley Puckett, 720; Ernest V. Stoneman, 877; "Dock" Walsh, 937
East Cairo Street Blues Bill Cox, 226
East Carolina Waltz Roland Cauley, 198
East Tennessee Blues Elmer Bird, 105; Richard Cox, 229; Hill Billies, 422; Johnson Sisters Trio, 464
East Tennessee Polka Sweet Brothers, 884
East Tennessee Quiver Dixieland Swingsters, 320
East Texas Drag East Texas Serenaders, 329
East Virginia Buell Kazee, 472
East Virginia Blues Thomas C. Ashley, 68; Carter Family, 191
East Virginia Blues No. 2 Carter Family, 192
Easter Anthem Original Sacred Harp Choir, 670
Easter Day Dorsey & Beatrice Dixon, 321
Eastern Gate [The] Delmore Brothers, 311; John McGhee & Frank Welling, 554; Morris Brothers, 643; Smith's Sacred Singers, 849

Eastern Train [The] Carson Robison, 772
Easy Rider McGee Brothers, 552
Easy Rider—Easy Rider Buddy Jones, 465
Easy Rider Blues Jimmie Davis, 301; Leo Soileau, 854
Easy Ridin' Papa Milton Brown, 137
Easy Rollin' Sue Buddy Jones, 465
Eat At The Welcome Table Jenkins Family, 457
Ebenezer Fred Pendleton, 685
Eblution Carolina Gospel Singers, 171
Echo Valley Tune Wranglers, 915; Yellow Jackets [II], 976
Echoes From Around The Old Cabin Door Willard Hodgin[s], 429
Echoes From The Glory Shore Paramount Sacred Four, 674; Smith's Sacred Singers, 850; Vaughan Quartet, 923–24
Echoes From The Hills Chuck Wagon Gang, 210; Patsy Montana, 635; Sons Of The Pioneers, 857
Echoes Of My Plantation Home Red Foley, 351
Echoes Of Shenandoah Valley H.M. Barnes, 95
Echoes Of The Chimes Hill Billies, 423
Echoes Of The Ozarks Fiddling Sam Long, 512
Echoing Hills Yodel Back To Me Wilf Carter (Montana Slim), 186
Edom OKeh Atlanta Sacred Harp Singers, 667
Educated Man "Dock" Walsh, 937
Egan One Step Amadie Breaux, 126
Egyptian Ella Nite Owls, 660; Pat-Halley-Jardine, 680
Eight Ball Blues Nite Owls, 660
Eight More Years To Go Shelton Brothers, 828
Eight of January Ted Gossett's Band, 376
Eighth Of January Arkansas Barefoot Boys, 63; Dr. Humphrey Bate, 97; Fox Chasers, 357; Richmond Melody Boys, 748
Eileen Earl Shirkey & Roy Harper, 832
El Capitan Massey Family, 611
El Menio Wonder State Harmonists, 971
El Rancho Grande Light Crust Doughboys, 502; Otis & Eleanor, 670
El Rancho Grande (My Ranch) Gene Autry, 84
Elder Bigby's Discourse Part 1, 2 [Smilin'] Ed McConnell, 530
Elder Jackson's Sermon Part 1, 2 [Smilin'] Ed McConnell, 530
Election Day In Kentucky—Part 1/I, 2/II Buell Kazee, 473–74
Electric Chair Blues Bill Cox, 229; Billy Vest, 931
Electric Light Schotische John Baltzell, 91
Elevated Railroad In The City [The] Hall Brothers, 392
Elevator Blues Jimmy Yates Groups, 976
Eleven Cent Cotton Vernon Dalhart, 284–85; Carson Robison, 773
Eleven Cent Cotton—Forty Cent Meat Loren H. Abram, 47
Eleven Cent Cotton And Forty Cent Meat Al Bernard, 101
Eleven Cent Cotton Forty Cent Meat—Part 1, 2 Bob Miller, 616
Eleven Months And Ten Days More Vernon Dalhart, 289
Eleven Months And Ten More Days Arthur Fields & Fred Hall, 340
Eleven Months In Leavenworth Gene Autry, 79
Eleven More Months And Ten More Days Vernon Dalhart, 289–90; Arthur Fields & Fred Hall, 343; Hi-Flyers, 419; John I. White, 950
Eleven More Months And Ten More Days—Part 1, 2 Bill Elliott, 332
Eleven More Months And Ten More Days Pt 1–4 Arthur Fields & Fred Hall, 343–44
Eleven Pounds Of Heaven Roy Newman, 658; Sons Of Acadians, 856
Eli Green's Cake Walk Uncle Dave Macon, 577–78

Ella Ree Kanawha Singers, 469
Ella Ree (Carry Me Back To Tennessee) Kanawha Singers, 469
Elle A Plurer Pour Revenir (She Cried To Come Back But She Couldn't) Percy Babineaux-Bixy Guidry, 87
Elle M'A Oublie (She Has Forgotten Me) Joseph Falcon, 334
Ellen Smith Henry Whitter, 955
Ellis March Hauulea Entertainers, 412
Elton Two Step Miller's Merrymakers, 628
Embers Graham Brothers, 377
Embrace Moi Encore Leo Soileau, 856
Emmaline Light Crust Doughboys, 504
Emmett Quadrille John Baltzell, 91
Empty Barrels Arthur Fields & Fred Hall, 343
Empty Bed Blues Bob Wills, 963
Empty Cell [The] Buell Kazee, 473
Empty Cot [The] Jesse Rodgers, 798
Empty Cradle [The] Leon Chappelear, 201; Vernon Dalhart, 280–81; Hart Brothers, 407; Doc Hopkins, 441; Wilmer Watts, 941
Empty Mansion [An] Chuck Wagon Gang, 211; J.B. Whitmire's Blue Sky Trio, 954
Empty Pocket Blues Emry Arthur, 65; Frank Luther, 523
Empty Saddles Ranch Boys, 727; Sons Of The Pioneers, 857
Empty Stall [An] Prairie Ramblers, 710
Empty Stocking [The] Lulu Belle & Scotty, 516
En Jour A Venir (I'll Get Mine Bye And Bye) Sons Of Acadians, 856
End Of A Bandit's Trail Eddie Dean, 307
End Of Memory Lane Callahan Brothers, 153; Carlisle Brothers, 168; Kenneth Houchins, 444; Buck Nation, 651; Ray Whitley, 952
End Of My Round-Up Days Gene Autry, 82–83
End Of Public Enemy Number One [The] Buck Nation, 651
End Of The Lane Modern Mountaineers, 631
End Of The Road Dave Hughs, 446
End Of The Shenandoah [The] Arthur Fields & Fred Hall, 338
End Of The Trail [The] Gene Autry, 81
End Of The World [The] Jimmie Davis, 305
End Of Twenty One Years Red Headed Brier Hopper, 732
Endless Glory Buice Brothers, 142
Endless Glory To The Lamb Bush Brothers, 147
Endless Joy Is Coming Stamps Quartet, 865
Endless Joy Is Waiting Over There Smith's Sacred Singers, 850
Enforcement Blues [The] Allen Brothers, 55
Engine 143 Chesley Shirley, 832
Engine One-Forty-Three Carter Family, 188
Engineer Blues Walter Hurdt, 447
Engineer Frank Hawk Rainey Old Time Band, 724
Engineer Joe Willard Hodgin[s], 429
Engineer On The Mogull Fiddlin' John Carson, 177
Engineer's Child [The] Chuck Wagon Gang, 210; Vernon Dalhart, 255–56, 281; Carson Robison, 792
Engineer's Dream [The] Vernon Dalhart, 268–69
Engineer's Dying Child [The] Vernon Dalhart, 255; Arthur Fields & Fred Hall, 338; Carson Robison, 769
Engineer's Hand Was On The Throttle [The] Willard Hodgin[s], 429
Engineer's Last Run [The] Blue Ridge Mountain Singers, 112
'Er Somethin' Vernon Dalhart, 282
Ersula I Love You Jap Magee, 580
Es Ce Que Tu Pense Jamais A Moi? (Do You Ever Think Of Me?) Alley Boys Of Abbeville, 59
Escudilla Waltz White Mountain Orchestra, 951
Eskimo Nell Bob Skyles, 839

Est-ce Que Tu M'Aimes Happy Fats, 396
Esther [J.T.] Allison's Sacred Harp Singers, 60
Et La Bas Hackberry Ramblers, 388
Eternity Peck's Male Quartette, 684
Ethan Lang Emry Arthur, 65
Etiquette Johnny Marvin, 606
Etiquette Blues Hoosier Hot Shots, 438
Evalina Wyatt & Brandon, 974
Evangeline's Song Christine Muszar, 647
Evening Bells Are Ringing [The] Carter Family, 192
Evening On The C R Ranche Part 1,2 [An] Carson Robison, 795
Evening Prayer [An] John McGhee & Frank Welling, 563
Evening Prayer Blues Deford Bailey, 88
Evening Shade Waltz Milner & Curtis, 628
Evening Star Capt. McKinney & E.L. Graham, 564
Evening Star Waltz Da Costa Woltz's Southern Broadcasters, 970
Ever So Quiet Hoosier Hot Shots, 438–39
Everglades Beverly Hill Billies, 102
Everglades Blues [The] Carrie Mae Moore-Faye Barres, 640
Evergreen Tree By The River [The] Rambling Kid & The Professor, 725
Every Day Away From You Swing Billies, 885
Every Day Blues Samantha Bumgarner, 142; Buddy Jones, 466
Every Day Is Mother's Day To Me Fred Kirby, 487
Every Jack Must Have A Jill Arthur Fields & Fred Hall, 345
Every Little Bit Added To What You Got Claude Davis, 297; Ernest Thompson, 903
Every Little Moment Leo Soileau, 855
Every Man A King Louisiana Boys, 513
Every Race Has A Flag But The Coons Uncle Tom Collins, 219
Every Sunday Night Back Home Frank Luther, 521; Bob Miller, 624
Every Time I Feel (Charlie) Monroe's Boys, 632
Every Time I Feel The Spirit Golden Echo Boys, 372; Stalsby Family, 863; Le & Leonard Wright, 973
Everybody Does It In Hawaii Jack Foy, 358; Ernest Hare, 399; Frank[ie] Marvin, 602; Carson Robison, 778; Jimmie Rodgers, 801; Bob Wills, 962
Everybody Gets A Letter But Me Ozark Boys, 672
Everybody Has The Right To Be Screwy (In His Own Way) Elton Britt, 130
Everybody Kiss Your Partner New Dixie Demons, 655
Everybody Kiss Your Partner (The Whistle Song) Massey Family, 610; W. Lee O'Daniel, 665
Everybody Knows It! Milner & Curtis, 628
Everybody Loves My Baby (But My Baby Don't Love Nobody But Me) Hoosier Hot Shots, 440
Everybody Loves My Marguerite Milton Brown, 138
Everybody Stomp Hoosier Hot Shots, 436
Everybody To The Punchin' Kessinger Brothers, 481
Everybody Two Step Roane County Ramblers, 751
Everybody Will Be Happy Over There Deal Family, 306; Peck's Male Quartette, 683
Everybody Works But Father Elmer Bird, 106; Loy Bodine, 115; Fiddlin' John Carson, 176; Johnson Brothers' Band, 463; Riley Puckett, 717
Everybody's Been Some Mother's Darling Wilf Carter (Montana Slim), 184
Everybody's Blues John D. Foster, 354; Roy Newman, 657
Everybody's Doing It Lowe Stokes, 870
Everybody's Going But Me Carson Robison, 792
Everybody's Happy There [E.R.] Nance Family, 648
Everybody's Knocking At My Door Earl Powell, 702

Everybody's Swingin' And Truckin' Ross Rhythm Rascals, 814
Everybody's Truckin' Modern Mountaineers, 630
Everybody's Tryin' To Be My Baby Johnny Barfield, 93; Rex Griffin, 383; Roy Newman, 658
Everyday Dirt David McCarn, 527
Everyday In The Saddle Tex Ritter, 749–50
Everyday Will Be Sunday Bye And Bye Uncle Tom Collins, 219; Gid Tanner, 889
Everything Happens For The Best Carson Robison, 780
Everything I Do, I Sure Do Good Hoosier Hot Shots, 439
Everything Is Lovely Down In Dixie Land W. Lee O'Daniel, 666
Everything Is Peaches 'Neath The Old Apple Tree Roy Newman, 658
Everything's Gonna Be All Right Jimmie Revard, 743
Everywhere You Go Roy Newman, 657
Evil In You Children Bill Boyd, 122
Evil Stingaree Buddy Jones, 465
Evoline Chief Pontiac, 205
Ev'rybody's Going But Me Carson Robison, 793
Ev'ryone's Out—So Let's Stay In To-Night W. Lee O'Daniel, 666
Exhilaration [J.T.] Allison's Sacred Harp Singers, 60
Exhortation Denson-Parris Sacred Singers, 313
Explosion At Eccles, West Virginia [The] Henry Whitter, 955
Explosion In The Fairmount Mines Blind Alfred Reed, 733
Export Gal [The] Louisiana Lou, 513
Eyes Are Watching You Roy Acuff, 49
Eyes Of Blue Yellow Jackets [I], 976
Eyes Of Texas [The] Bill Boyd, 122; Milton Brown, 137; Light Crust Doughboys, 504
Eyes To The Sky Gene Autry, 82
Ezra's Experience At The Recording Laboratory West Virginia Mountaineers, 946

F Waltz Bob Kerby & George Barton, 479
Face I See At Evening [A] Bob Atcher, 70; Gene Autry, 84
Face On The Bar Room Floor—Part 1,2 [The] Harold Selman, 823
Face That Never Returned [The] Ernest V. Stoneman, 872
Face To Face Dempsey Quartette, 312; Mrs. Leon Hinkle, 427; John McGhee & Frank Welling, 563; Spindale Quartet, 862; Trenton Melody Makers, 913
Face To Face At Last Vaughan Quartet, 925
Factory Girl [The] Clifford (C.S.) Wagner, 933
Faded Bunch Of Roses Holland Puckett, 715
Faded Coat Of Blue [The] Carter Family, 192; Buell Kazee, 473; David Miller, 626; Welby Toomey, 912
Faded Flowers Carter Family, 191
Faded Knot Of Blue [The] Vernon Dalhart, 282
Faded Letter [The] Vernon Dalhart, 253
Faded Love Letters Of Mine Girls Of The Golden West, 371
Faded Picture Wells Brothers String Band, 943
Faded Rose [The] Lew Preston, 713
Faded Roses Thomas C. Ashley, 68
Fading Away William Rexroat's Cedar Crest Singers, 744
Fair Ellen Bradley Kincaid, 482–83
Fair Eyed Ellen Blue Sky Boys, 113
Fair Florella J.P. Ryan, 817
Fair Young Lover Zora Layman, 492
Fairy Dance Lake & Cavanagh, 489
Fais Do-Do Negre (Go To Sleep Nigger) Amadie Breaux, 126
Fais Pas Ca Hackberry Ramblers, 388
Faithful Little Cowboy Charles Mitchell & His Orchestra, 630
Faithful Lovers [The] John D. Foster, 354
Faithless Husband Tom Darby & Jimmie Tarlton, 295;

Foreman Family, 352; Frank Gerald & Howard Dixon, 368; Taylor Trio, 894
Fall In Behind John McGhee & Frank Welling, 559
Fallen By The Wayside Barber & Osborne, 93; Ernest V. Stoneman, 878
Fallen Leaf Paul Hamblin, 393
Falling By The Wayside Charlie Poole, 699; Sweet Brothers, 884
Falling Leaf Crazy Hillbillies Band, 232; George R. Pariseau's Orchestra, 675; L.K. Reeder, 734
Falling Leaves Massey Family, 610
False Hearted Girl Delmore Brothers, 310
False Hearted Lover's Blues Dock Boggs, 116
Falsefying [sic] **Mamma** Jimmy Long, 511
Fame Apart From God's Approval Uncle Dave Macon, 578
Family Circle [The] Byron Parker, 675
Family Prayers Bob Atcher, 69
Fan It Bill Boyd, 122; Milton Brown, 137; Swift Jewel Cowboys, 884; Bob Wills, 961
Fancy Ball [The] Ernest V. Stoneman, 872
Fancy Nancy Kenneth Houchins, 443
Fancy Nancy (Every Day Dirt No. 2) David McCarn, 527
Fannie Moore Ken Maynard, 614
Fannin' [sic] **Street Blues** Bill Nettles, 654
Far Across The Deep Blue Sea Blue Ridge Mountain Entertainers, 111
Far Away From Home Blues E. Segura & D. Herbert, 823
Far Away From My Old Virginia Home Andrews Brothers, 60
Far Away In Hawaii Vernon Dalhart, 263
Far Away In The South Central Mississippi Quartet, 199
Far Away On The Sleepy Rio Grande Chas. M. Dewitte, 314
Far Back In My Childhood Oscar L. Coffey, 217
Far Beyond The Blue Sky Dykes' Magic City Trio, 328
Far Beyond The Starry Sky Cliff Carlisle, 168
Far In The Mountain Red Headed Fiddler[s], 732
Far Over The Hill Shelton Brothers, 829
Fare You Well Old Joe Clark Fiddlin' John Carson, 175
Farewell Jenkins Family, 456
Farewell Blues Virginia Childs, 208; Hoosier Hot Shots, 438; Clayton McMichen, 571; Jimmy Yates Groups, 976
Farewell Ducktown Allen Sisson, 836
Farewell Kentucky Morris Brothers, 643
Farewell My Loved One Crowder Brothers, 238
Farewell My Loved Ones Crowder Brothers, 238
Farewell Nellie Carter Family, 194
Farewell To Prague Adolph Hofner, 431
Farewell To The Range Jimmie Davis, 303
Farewell To Thee Homer Christopher, 209; Clayton McMichen, 567; Henry Whitter, 955
Farewell Waltz Doc Roberts, 753–54
Farm Girl Blues Carolina Tar Heels, 173
Farm Relief Uncle Dave Macon, 577
Farm Relief Blues Bob Miller, 617–18
Farm Relief Song Vernon Dalhart, 288; Carson Robison, 778; John I. White, 949
Farmer [The] Bob Skyles, 838
Farmer Feeds Them All [The] Frank Wheeler-Monroe Lamb, 948
Farmer Gray Loy Bodine, 115; Hoosier Hot Shots, 436
Farmer Grey Hinson, Pitts & Coley, 427
Farmer In The Dell Walter C. Peterson, 688
Farmer Is The Man That Feeds Them All [The] Fiddlin' John Carson, 175
Farmer Song [The] Pie Plant Pete, 694
Farmer Took Another Load Away [The] Lake & Cavanagh, 489
Farmer's Blues John Dilleshaw, 317

Farmer's Daughter Lulu Belle & Scotty, 516; Clayton McMichen, 568; Riley Puckett, 719; Arthur Smith, 842
Farmer's Dream [The] Oscar Ford, 352
Farmer's Girl [The] Delmore Brothers, 310
Farmer's Holiday Hank Keene, 474
Farmer's Letter To The President [The] Bob Miller, 617–18
Farmer's Medley Quadrille John Baltzell, 90
Farmer's Not In The Dell [The] Light Crust Doughboys, 505
Farming By The Fire Pie Plant Pete, 695
Farrell O'Gar's Favorite William B. Houchens, 443
Farther Along Roy Acuff, 50; Wade Mainer, 584; (Charlie) Monroe's Boys, 632; Pine Ridge Boys, 697; Stamps Quartet, 865; J.B. Whitmire's Blue Sky Trio, 954
Farwell [sic] **Father I Am Dying** E. Arthur Lewis, 498
Fast Train Blues Lonnie Glosson, 372
Fatal Courtship [The] Ephraim Woodie, 971
Fatal Derby Day [The] Bradley Kincaid, 484; Red Headed Brier Hopper, 731
Fatal Flower Garden Nelstone's Hawaiians, 653
Fatal Rose Of Red [The] Leo Boswell, 119; W.C. Childers, 206
Fatal Run [The] Cliff Carlisle, 162–63
Fatal Shot [The] Canova Family, 155
Fatal Wedding [The] Vernon Dalhart, 252; Arthur Fields & Fred Hall, 338; Bradley Kincaid, 482, 484; Charlie Oaks, 664; Red Headed Fiddler[s], 732; George Reneau, 741; Ernest V. Stoneman, 874–75; Jess Young, 979
Fatal Wedding Night [The] Richard D. Burnett, 144
Fatal Wreck Of The Bus J.E. Mainer's Mountaineers, 581
Fate Of Chris Liveley And Wife Blind Alfred Reed, 733
Fate Of Dewey Lee [The] Carter Family, 193
Fate Of Edward Hickman [The] Andrew Jenkins, 454; Edd Rice, 744
Fate Of Elba, Alabama [The] Andrew Jenkins, 455
Fate Of Ellen Smith [The] Green Bailey, 88
Fate Of Gladys Kincaid [The] Morganton Trio, 642
Fate Of Kinnie Wagner [The] Vernon Dalhart, 262
Fate Of Mildred Doran [The] Vernon Dalhart, 273
Fate Of Old Strawberry Roan [The] Wilf Carter (Montana Slim), 183
Fate Of Rhoda Sweetin [The] Wilmer Watts, 941
Fate Of Rose Sarlo [The] West Virginia Night Owls, 946
Fate Of Santa Barbara Bascom Lamar Lunsford, 516
Fate Of Shelly And Smith [The] Ernest V. Stoneman, 877
Fate Of Talma[d]ge Osborne Ernest V. Stoneman, 874–75
Fate Of Talt Hall Green Bailey, 88
Fate Of The Battleship Maine Doc Hopkins, 441
Fate Of The Fleagle Gang [The] Carson Robison, 785
Fate Of The Lindbergh Baby [The] Kenneth Houchins, 443
Fate Of The Shenandoah [The] Vernon Dalhart, 250
Fate Of The Sunset Trail [The] Wilf Carter (Montana Slim), 183
Fate Of Walter Harris [The] Ted (Straw) Henley, 417
Fate Of Will Rogers And Wiley Post [The] Bill Cox, 227
Fate Of William Cheek [The] Gid Tanner, 888
Father Alone J.H. Howell, 446
Father Put The Cow Away Prairie Ramblers, 712
Father, Dear Father Dixie Reelers, 319
Father, Dear Father, Come Home Blue Sky Boys, 114; James Scott-Claude Boone, 821
Father, Mother, Sister And Brother Vagabonds, 921
Father's A Drunkard And Mother Is Dead Walter Coon, 221
Faux Pas Tu Bray Cherie Hackberry Ramblers, 388
Favorite Two Step Byrd Moore, 638
Fe Fe Ponchaux Joseph Falcon, 334
Feather Your Nest Dick Hartman's Tennessee Ramblers, 408
Feed Your Soul Milton & Marion Carlisle, 168
Feedin' The Horses Travelers, 912

Feels Good Dick Hartman's Tennessee Ramblers, 408
Feet, Don't Fail Me Bill Carlisle, 160
Feller That Looked Like Me [The] Hill Billies, 423
Fellow That Looks Like Me [The] Professor & Mrs. Greer, 383; Asa Martin, 588
Fellow That's Just Like Me [The] Charlie [& Bud] Newman, 655
Ferdinand The Bull Dixieland Swingsters, 320; Hoosier Hot Shots, 438
Fetch It On Down To My House Dick Hartman's Tennessee Ramblers, 408
Fetch Me Down My Trusty 45 Prairie Ramblers, 709
Few More Years [A] Reed Family, 734
Fiddle And Guitar Runnin' Wild Walter Hurdt, 448
Fiddle Up Jess Young, 979
Fiddleobia Dixieland Swingsters, 320
Fiddler Joe Vernon Dalhart, 285
Fiddler's [sic] Convention In Georgia Part 2 [A] Clayton McMichen, 566
Fiddlers Blues Arthur Smith, 841; Three Williamsons, 909
Fiddler's Contest [The] Blue Ridge Mountain Entertainers, 111; Tennessee Ramblers [I], 896
Fiddlers' Convention In Georgia—Part 1 [A] Clayton McMichen, 566
Fiddlers' Convention Part 3, 4 Clayton McMichen, 570
Fiddler's Dram Clayton McMichen, 573
Fiddlers' Dream Arthur Smith, 840
Fiddler's Tryout In Georgia—Part 1, 2 [A] John Dilleshaw, 317
Fiddlin' Away Rustic Revellers, 816
Fiddlin' Bill Andrew Jenkins, 454
Fiddlin' Bootleggers—Part I, II [The] Claude Davis, 297
Fiddlin' Medley (Old Time Fiddlers' Medley) Clayton McMichen, 566
Fiddlin' Rufus Earl Johnson, 460
Fiddlin' The Fiddle James Brown, Jr. & Ken Landon Groups, 135; East Texas Serenaders, 329
Fiddling Soldier Bill Cox, 228
Fields On Fire Dorsey & Beatrice Dixon, 322
Fifteen Dollars A Week Tom Dickey Show Boys, 316
Fifteen Years Ago Buell Kazee, 473
Fifteen Years Ago Today Pine Ridge Ramblers, 697
Fifty Cents Harry "Mac" McClintock, 529
Fifty Miles Of Elbow Room Carter Family, 195; Vaughan Quartet, 930
Fifty Years Ago Wyzee Hamilton, 393; Clayton McMichen, 567
Fifty Years Ago Waltz Curley Fox, 357
Fifty Years From Now Frank Luther, 519–20; Harry "Mac" McClintock, 529; Lloyd Wright, 973
Fifty Years Repentin' Ernest Hare, 399; Bob Miller, 621; Dick Robertson, 758
Fifty-One Beers Karl & Harty, 471
Fight To Win Royal Sumner Quartet, 815
Fightin' In The War With Spain Wilmer Watts, 941
Fightin' Son-Of-A-Gun [The] Zeke Manners, 586
Filipino Baby Bill Cox, 228
Fill My Way Every Day With Love Kentucky Mountain Choristers, 478
Filling Station Blues Andrews Brothers, 60
Fillmore Denson-Parris Sacred Harp Singers, 312; Hamp Reynolds' Sacred Harp Singers, 744
Final Farewell [The] Bill Carlisle, 159
Final Ride Of Jimmie Bryan Lowell Moore, 640
Find My Precious Home Fred Kirby, 487
Finger Ring Zeb Harrelson & M.B. Padgett, 404
Finger-Prints (Upon The Window Pane) Lester McFarland & Robert A. Gardner, 550; Bob Miller, 624

Fire Ball Mail Roy Acuff, 50
Fire In The Mountain Fiddlin' John Carson, 176; Clayton McMichen, 573
Fire On The Mountain Riley Puckett, 718; Tommy Whitmer's Band, 953
Fireman Save My Child Harry "Mac" McClintock, 529
Firing Line [The] Ernest Phipps, 691
First Time In Jail Fleming & Townsend, 347
First Two Ladies Cross Over [The] Carson Robison, 796
First Whippoorwill Song [The] Blue Ridge Mountain Girls, 111; Bradley Kincaid, 484
First Year Blues Ernest Tubb, 914
Fisherman's Daughter Leroy [Slim] Johnson, 462
Fisherman's Luck Dorsey & Beatrice Dixon, 321
Fisher's Hornpipe Hill Billies, 422; Clayton McMichen, 573; George R. Pariseau's Orchestra, 675
Fisher's Hornpipe And Opera Reel William B. Houchens, 443
Fisher's Maid [The] Richard Harold, 402
Fishing Blues [The] Lew Childre, 207
"Fishing Time" Square Dance National Barn Dance Orchestra, 651
Five Cent Cotton Bob Miller, 622
Five Cent Glass Of Beer Bob Miller, 620
Five Foot Two Walker's Corbin Ramblers, 936
Five Foot Two, Eyes Of Blue Range Riders, 728
Five Foot Two, Eyes Of Blue (Has Anybody Seen My Girl?) Hugh Cross, 237
Five Long Years Light Crust Doughboys, 506
Five Man Blues Dixieland Swingsters, 320
Five Miles/Intro Emry Arthur, 66
Five Nights' Experience Mustard & Gravy, 647
Five Piece Band [The] Hi-Flyers, 418
Five Thousand Dollars Reward Carson Robison, 794
Five Up Henry L. Bandy, 92
Flag That Train Carlisle Brothers, 169
Flamin' Mamie Hilltoppers, 427; Hank Penny, 686
Flat Foot Floogee [The] Hoosier Hot Shots, 438
Flat Tire Blues Jack Jackson, 452
Flat Wheel Train Blues—Nos. 1, 2 Red Gay & Jack Wellman, 364
Flat-Footed Nigger Fiddlin' John Carson, 176; Dixie Ramblers [III], 319
Flatwood Crazy Hillbillies Band, 232
Flatwoods Gid Tanner, 890
Flee As A Bird Edward Morgan, 641
Flemington Kidnapping Trial [The] Bob Miller, 624–25
Flight Of "Lucky" Lindbergh [The] Ernest Rogers, 810
Flitting Away Oscar L. Coffey, 216; Uncle Dave Macon, 577
Floatin' Down Bill Boyd, 122
Floating Down A River Kelly Brothers, 477
Floating Down The Stream Of Time J.E. Mainer's Mountaineers, 582
Floating Down To Cotton Town Hoke Rice, 746
Floella's Cottage Arthur Tanner, 885
Flood Song Vernon Dalhart, 286
Flop Eared Mule H.M. Barnes, 95; Blue Ridge Highballers, 109; Byrd Moore, 638; Charlie Poole, 700; Poplin-Woods Tennessee String Band, 701; Ernest V. Stoneman, 874; Gid Tanner, 891
Floraine Waltz Jimmy Yates Groups, 976
Floral Wreaths Vernon Dalhart, 282
Floreene Waltz Madisonville String Band, 580
Florence Dye's Sacred Harp Singers, 328
Florene Leon Selph, 824
Florida Dye's Sacred Harp Singers, 328
Florida Blues Arthur Smith, 841
Flow Rain Waltz Mumford Bean, 98

Index to Titles

Flower From My Angel Mother's Grave [A] McGee Brothers, 552; John McGhee & Frank Welling, 558, 560; Charles Nabell, 647; Chas. Winters & Elond Autry, 968
Flower Of My Dreams Cliff Carlisle, 167
Flower Of Texas Bill Boyd, 124
Flower Of The Valley [The] Cliff Carlisle, 166
Flowers At Edinburgh John Baltzell, 91
Flowers Blooming In The Wildwood Coon Creek Girls, 221
Flowers From Mother's Grave W.C. Childers, 205
Flowers Now Roy Harvey, 412
Flowers Of Edinburgh And Sandy Bottom George R. Pariseau's Orchestra, 675
Flowers On The Open Grave Rev. Edward Boone, Mrs. Edward Boone & Miss Olive Boone, 118
Floyd Collins' Dream Vernon Dalhart, 258
Floyd Collins' Fate Arthur Fields & Fred Hall, 340
Floyd Collin's [sic] Fate Arthur Fields & Fred Hall, 338
Floyd Collins In Sand Cave Andrew Jenkins, 453
Floyd Collins Waltz Vernon Dalhart, 256–57
Fly Around My Pretty Little Miss Frank Blevins, 108; Samantha Bumgarner, 143; Gid Tanner, 889
Fly Away And Sing Freeman Quartette, 359
Fly Away Birdie To Heaven Walter Coon, 221
Fly, Birdie, Fly Roy Acuff, 49
Fly, Butterfly! Prairie Ramblers, 711
Fly, Butterfly! #2 Prairie Ramblers, 712
Flyin' Clouds Charlie Poole, 699
Flying Cloud Blue Ridge Highballers, 110
Flying Cloud Waltz Walter Family, 938
Flying Clouds Uncle Jimmy Thompson, 904
Flying Engine Reaves White County Ramblers, 729
Foggy Dew [The] Bradley Kincaid, 485
Foggy Mountain Top [The] Carter Family, 188
Folks Back Home [The] Ray Brothers, 729
Follow Jesus Bela Lam, 489; Stamps Quartet, 865
Follow Long (The Louisiana Song) Louisiana Boys, 513
Follow The Bugle Dick Hartman's Tennessee Ramblers, 409
Follow The Golden Rule Charles Nabell, 647
Following The Cow Trail Carl T. Sprague, 862
Following The Stars Hilltoppers, 427; Twilight Trail Boys, 918
Following You Around Sons Of The West, 859
Fond Affection Carter Family, 188; Walter Coon, 221; Clarence Greene, 382; Irene Sanders, 820
Foot Warmer Light Crust Doughboys, 505; Wanderers, 938
Football Rag Gid Tanner, 889
Footprints In The Snow Big Slim Aliff, 54; Cliff Carlisle, 168
For Ever And Ever More Vagabonds, 921
For Gambling On The Sabbath Day Oliver Smith & Dewey Culpepper, 845
For Goodness Sakes Don't Say I Told You Uncle Dave Macon, 577
For Me Etowah Quartet, 333
For Me And My Gal Dick Parman, 680
For Old Times Sake Pink Lindsey, 507
For Sale, A Baby Bradley Kincaid, 484
For Seven Long Years I've Been Married Kelly Harrell, 404
For The First Time In Twenty-Four Years Vernon Dalhart, 290
For The One I Love Is You Adolph Hofner, 431
For The Sake Of Days Gone By Bill Cox, 226; Jimmie Rodgers, 804; Smiling Southerners, 840
For The Soul That's Redeemed Lyric Quartette, 525
For Work I'm Too Lazy Newton Gaines, 361
Forbidden Love Grady & Hazel Cole, 217
Forever On Thy Hands Vaughan Quartet, 928–29
Forget Me And Be Happy Carl Boling, 116

Forget Me Not James Brown, Jr. & Ken Landon Groups, 135
Forgive And Forget Sunshine Boys, 881; Uncle Pete & Louise, 919
Forgotten Soldier Boy [The] Monroe Brothers, 633; Asher Sizemore & Little Jimmie, 837
Forked Deer J.W. Day, 306; Fox Chasers, 357; Kessinger Brothers, 479; A.C. (Eck) Robertson, 757; Taylor's Kentucky Boys, 894
Forki Deer Uncle "Am" Stuart, 881
Forkied [sic] Deer John W. Daniel, 293
Forks Of Sandy Charlie Poole, 699
Forky Dear Charlie Bowman, 120
Forsaken Claude Casey, 196
Forsaken Girl [The] Frank Luther, 520
Forsaken Love Carter Family, 187; Lake Howard, 445; Roy Lyons, 525
Fort Smith Breakdown Luke Highnight, 422
Fort Worth Jail Dick Reinhart, 739; Jimmy Wakely, 934
Fort Worth Rag Jack Cawley's Oklahoma Ridge Runners, 199; Light Crust Doughboys, 502
Fort Worth Stomp Crystal Springs Ramblers, 239
Fortunes Galore Goebel Reeves, 735, 737
Forty Drops Stripling Brothers, 880
Forty Per Cent Earl McCoy & Jessie Brock, 531
Four Cent Cotton Lowe Stokes, 871; Gid Tanner, 891
Four Cent Tobacco And Forty Cent Meat Bob Miller, 620
Four Day Blues Riley Puckett, 721
Four Leaf Clover Four Pickled Peppers, 356; Tune Wranglers, 915
Four Night's Experience Thomas C. Ashley, 67
Four O'Clock Blues McKinney Brothers, 564
Four Or Five Times Cliff Bruner, 139; Leon Chappelear, 201; Shelton Brothers, 828; Tennessee Ramblers [II], 897; Joe Werner, 943; Bob Wills, 960
Four Sons-Of-A-Gun [The] Uncle Tom Collins, 219
Four Stone Walls And A Ceiling Arthur Fields & Fred Hall, 344–45
Four Thousand Years Ago Georgia Organ Grinders, 366; Hoosier Hot Shots, 436; Bradley Kincaid, 483; Vagabonds, 922
Four, Five Or Six Times Milton Brown, 136
Fourteen Days In Georgia Blue Ridge Highballers, 110; Walter Couch & Wilks Ramblers, 223
Fourteen Little Puppies Doc Hopkins, 441
Fourth Avenue Blues Hoke Rice, 745
Fourth Of July Bill Chitwood, 208
Fourth Of July At A Country Fair Georgia Yellow Hammers, 367
Fourth Of July At The Country Fair Bill Chitwood, 208
Fox And The Hounds Jimmie Revard, 742
Fox Chase Deford Bailey, 88; Lonnie Glosson, 372; Ted Gossett's Band, 376; Uncle Dave Macon, 573; Gid Tanner, 887; Kyle Wooten, 973; Jess Young, 978
Fox Chase In Georgia Land Norris, 662
Fox Chase No. 2 Loy Bodine, 115; Henry Whitter, 956
Fox Chase Stomp Jack Reedy, 734
Fox Hunter's Luck Walter Hurdt, 448
Fox In The Mountain Fruit Jar Guzzlers, 360
Fox Trot You Saved For Me [The] Bob Skyles, 838
Frail Wildwood Flower Miller Wikel, 956
Frank Du Pree [sic] Andrew Jenkins, 453
Frank Dupre[e] Vernon Dalhart, 250, 255
Frankie Dykes' Magic City Trio, 328
Frankie And Albert Arkansas Woodchopper, 64
Frankie And Johnn[ie/y] Arkansas Woodchopper, 63; Gene Autry, 71; Clayton McMichen, 572; Frank[ie] Marvin, 604; Riley Puckett, 722; Carson Robison, 778–79; Jimmie Rodgers, 801; Leo Soileau, 855

Frankie And Johnn[ie/y] (You'll Miss Me In The Days To Come) Frank[ie] Marvin, 601; Nite Owls, 660; Riley Puckett, 720
Frankie And Johnnie No. 2 Billy Vest, 931
Frankie Baker Ernest Thompson, 902
Frankie Baker—Part I, II Emry Arthur, 66
Frankie Dean Tom Darby & Jimmie Tarlton, 294
Frankie Silvers Thomas C. Ashley, 68; Byrd Moore, 639
Frankie Silver's Confession Clarence Greene, 382; Byrd Moore, 639
Frankie Was A Good Woman Gid Tanner, 888
Frankie's Gamblin' Man Welby Toomey, 912
Franklin Blues [The] McGee Brothers, 551
Franklin County Blues Dixie Ramblers [III], 319
Franklin Roosevelt's Back Again Bill Cox, 228
Freak Medley Golden Melody Boys, 373
Freckle Face Mary Jane Ernest V. Stoneman, 872
Free A Little Bird—1930 Model Roane County Ramblers, 751
Free A Little Bird Allen Brothers, 55
Free A Little Bird As I Can Be, No. 2 Clayton McMichen, 572
Free Again Wade Mainer, 583
Free As I Can Be McClendon Brothers, 527
Free From The Walls Of Grey (Twenty-One Years Is Some Debt To Pay) Asher Sizemore & Little Jimmie, 837
Free Little Bird Carolina Ramblers String Band, 172; Dykes' Magic City Trio, 328; Ridgel's Fountain Citians, 749
Free Wheelin' Hobo Elton Britt, 129; Bob Miller, 622–23
Free-Wheeling Blues Allen Brothers, 56
Freight Train Blues Roy Acuff, 48; Miss Jimmie Allen, 54; Billy Brooks, 132; Callahan Brothers, 153; Pete Cassell, 198; Gene Steele, 867
Freight Train Moan Arthur Smith, 841
Freight Train Ramble Tom Darby & Jimmie Tarlton, 294
Freight Train Whistle Blues No. 2 Callahan Brothers, 153
Freight Wreck At Altoona [The] Vernon Dalhart, 255–56, 279
Freight Wreck of No. 52 Fred Richards, 747
French Blues Nathan Abshire, 48; Sydney Landry, 490
French Town Blind Uncle Gaspard, 363
French Two-Step Hackberry Ramblers, 388
Fresh Eggs Fred L. Jeske, 458
Fresno Blues Crockett [Family] Mountaineers, 233
Friday Night Waltz Ray Brothers, 729
Friendless And Sad Karl & Harty, 470
Friends Of Long Ago Asa Martin, 588
Friends Of Yesterday Buddy Baker, 89
Frisco Blues Allen Brothers, 55
Frisco One-Step Joseph Falcon, 335
Frivolous Frisco Fan Dwight Butcher, 148
Frog Song [The] Vernon Dalhart, 283
Frog Tuplets Smiley Burnette, 145
Frog Went A-Courtin' [The] Canova Family, 155; Buell Kazee, 472
Froggie Went A-Courting Eldon Baker, 89; Bradley Kincaid, 482
Froggy Maury Sprayberry, 863
Froggy Went A Courtin' Jimmy Wakely, 934
Frolic Of The Wampus Cat W.B. Chenoweth, 203
From A Cabin In Kentucky Karl & Harty, 471
From Broadway To Heaven Four Pickled Peppers, 356
From Buffalo To Washington Swing Billies, 885
From Cradle Bars To Prison Bars Frank Luther, 519; Bob Miller, 623
From Earth To Heaven Uncle Dave Macon, 576
From Hell To Arkansas Otto Gray, 379

From Jerusalem To Jericho R.C. Garner, 363; Lulu Belle & Scotty, 516; Uncle Dave Macon, 574, 578
From Monday On Dixie Demons, 318
From Now On Make Your Whoopee At Home Jess Hillard, 426
From Shore To Shore (Charlie) Monroe's Boys, 632
From The Cross To The Crown Smith's Sacred Singers, 850
From The Heart Of The West Bob Palmer & Monte Hall, 673
From The Heart Of The West (Came You) Bob Palmer & Monte Hall, 673
From The Indies To The Andes In His Undies Hoosier Hot Shots, 439
From The Palms Of Hawaii Dick Hartman's Tennessee Ramblers, 407
From The Start (And To The End) Bill Mounce, 645
Frontier Breakdown Jack Pierce, 696
Frosty Mornin' Bill Boyd, 123
Frozen Girl [The] Delmore Brothers, 309
Fruit Jar Blues Allen Brothers, 56
Fruit Wagon Gal Slim Harbert, 398
Fry St. Blues Frank Roberts, Bud Alexander & Fiddlin' Slim Sandford, 755
Fugitive From A Chain Gang [A] Bob Miller, 623
Fugitive's Lament [The] Delmore Brothers, 310; Milo Twins, 628; White Brothers (Joe & Bob), 951
Full House Blues Range Riders, 727
Fulton County Moonshiners, 638
Fun Is All Over [The] John & Emery McClung, 530; Unknown Artists [V], 920
Funny Old Hills [The] Prairie Ramblers, 710
Funny Old World Rolls Along [The] Bill Elliott, 332
Funny When You Feel That Way Carter Family, 194
Fun's All Over [The] Kenneth Houchins, 444; Midkiff, Spencer & Blake, 616; Williamson Brothers & Curry, 960
Furniture Man Bill Chitwood, 208
Fussin' Mama Cliff Carlisle, 165
Fuzzy Rag Riley Puckett, 718

G Rag Georgia Yellow Hammers, 367; Earl Johnson, 460
Gabe Kentucky String Ticklers, 478
Gabriel's Trumpet Morris Brothers, 643
Gal I Left Behind [The] Cliff Carlisle, 167
Gal I Left Behind Me [The] Jules Allen, 55
Gal Like Me [A] Patt Patterson, 682
Gal Like You [A] Bill Bruner, 139
Gal Of Mine Took My Licker From Me Fletcher & Foster, 349
Gal On The Log [The] Capt. M.J. Bonner, 117
Gal That Got Stuck On Everything She Said [The] Uncle Dave Macon, 576
Gallop To Georgia W.T. Narmour & S.W. Smith, 649–50
Gallopin' To Gallup (On The Santa Fe Trail) Patsy Montana, 636
Galloping Dominoes 'Lasses & Honey, 491
Gals Don't Mean A Thing (In My Young Life) Massey Family, 613
Galveston Rose [The] Hank Snow, 853
Gambler [The] Carl T. Sprague, 862
Gambler's Advice [The] Fleming & Townsend, 347
Gamblers Blues Ted Lunsford, 517; George Washington White, 949
Gambler's Confession [The] Fleming & Townsend, 348
Gambler's Dying Words [The] Sid Harkreader, 400; Panhandle Pete, 674
Gambler's Lament Zack & Glenn, 979
Gambler's Return Jimmie Davis, 299–300
Gamblers Yodel Delmore Brothers, 311
Gamblin' Bill Driv' On Bill Tuttle, 917

Gamblin' Cowboy Asa Martin, 592
Gamblin' Dan Cliff Carlisle, 165
Gamblin' Jim Tom Darby & Jimmie Tarlton, 293
Gamblin' Yodel Delmore Brothers, 310
Gambling Barroom Blues Jimmie Rodgers, 808
Gambling Blues Roy Harvey, 411; Buell Kazee, 472
Gambling Man Samantha Bumgarner, 143; Land Norris, 662
Gambling On The Sabbath McClendon Brothers, 527; Red Headed Brier Hopper, 732; Clifford (C.S.) Wagner, 933
Gambling On The Sabbath Day William Hanson, 395; George Reneau, 741
Gambling Polka Dot Blues Harry Hillard, 425; Jimmie Rodgers, 806; Bob Wills, 963
Gang's All Here [The] Louie Donaldson, 323
Gangster's Brother [The] Kenneth Houchins, 444
Gangster's Moll [The] Light Crust Doughboys, 501
Gangster's Warning [A] Gene Autry, 73–74, 77; Loy Bodine, 115; Deckers, 309; Frank[ie] Marvin, 604
Gangster's Yodel [The] Bill Cox, 226
Garbage Can Blues Tennessee Ramblers [1], 897
Garbage Man Buddy Jones, 465
Garbage Man Blues Milton Brown, 136; Roy Newman, 656
Garden Of My Heart Rev. Calbert Holstein & Sister Billie Holstein, 433
Garden Of Prayer Wade Mainer, 584
Garden's Fairest Flower [The] Taylor-Griggs Louisiana Melody Makers, 894
Garfield March Kessinger Brothers, 479
Gas Run Out [The] Pine Mountain Boys, 697
Gasport One Step Anatole Credure, 232
Gastonia Gallop David McCarn, 527
Gate To Go Through Jimmy Johnson's String Band, 461
Gates Of Gold Avoca Quartette, 87
Gather The Flowers Arthur Tanner, 886
Gather The Golden Sheaves Jenkins Family, 457
Gathering Buds Judie & Julie, 468
Gathering Flowers From The Hills Wade Mainer, 583
Gathering Flowers From The Hillside Carter Family, 193; Delmore Brothers, 311
Gathering Home Smith's Sacred Singers, 850
Gathering Up The Shells From The Seashore Otto Gray, 379; Skyland Scotty, 837
Gay Caballero [A] Vernon Dalhart, 284; Jack Golding, 374; Carson Robison, 768–69
Gay Ranchero (Las Altenitas) [A] Massey Family, 611; Roy Rogers, 812
Gayest Old Dude That's Out [The] Uncle Dave Macon, 578
Gee Ocie Stockard, 870
Gee But I Hate To Go Home Alone Leaford Hall, 390
Gee! But I Feel Blue Village Boys, 932
Gee! But It's Great Walking Back Home Jimmie Revard, 743
Gee, But I'm Lonesome Tonight Lester McFarland & Robert A. Gardner, 548
Gee, But It's Great To Meet A Friend (From Your Home Town) Arthur Fields & Fred Hall, 345; Prairie Ramblers, 708
Gene The Fighting Marine Graham Brothers, 377; Ernest Hare, 399–400
General Logan A.C. (Eck) Robertson, 757
General Robert E. Lee Carson Robison, 767
Gentle Anna Lester McFarland & Robert A. Gardner, 543
Gentle Annie Asa Martin, 589
Gentle Presence Mrs. Leon Hinkle, 427
George Boker Uncle "Am" Stuart, 881
George Collins Emry Arthur, 66; Elmer Bird, 105; Roy Harvey, 410; Jess Johnston, 464; Riley Puckett, 720; Dillard Smith, 843; Henry Whitter, 956
Geo. Collins Henry Whitter, 955

George Washington Pope's Arkansas Mountaineers, 701
Georgia J.P. Nester, 653
Georgia Barbecue At Stone Mountain—Part 1, 2 [A] John Dilleshaw, 317
Georgia Black Bottom [The] Georgia Crackers, 365
Georgia Blues Samantha Bumgarner, 143; Bill Helms, 415; Floyd Shreve, 834
Georgia Brown Blues Bill Cox, 226
Georgia Bust Down John Dilleshaw, 317; Kentucky String Ticklers, 478
Georgia Camp Meeting Carolina Mandolin Orchestra, 171; Jenkins Family, 456; Leake County Revelers, 495; McLaughlin's Old Time Melody Makers, 565
Georgia Gal Hoke Rice, 746
Georgia Girl Andrew Jenkins, 454
Georgia Hobo [The] Cofer Brothers, 216
Georgia Home Arthur Fields & Fred Hall, 340
Georgia Is My Home Oscar Ford, 352
Georgia Jubilee Hoke Rice, 746
Georgia Man Georgia Organ Grinders, 366
Georgia Moon Cliff Carlisle, 165; George Wade, 933
Georgia Mountain Home Jordan Brothers, 467
Georgia Pines Leon Selph, 823
Georgia Railroad Gid Tanner, 887
Georgia The Dear Old State I Love Harmonica Bill, 401
Georgia Waggoner Gid Tanner, 891
Georgia Wagner Fiddlin' John Carson, 176; Gid Tanner, 890
Georgia Wildcat Breakdown Clayton McMichen, 571
Georgia Wobble Blues Carroll County Revelers, 174
Georgiana Moon Clayton McMichen, 571
Georgia's Three-Dollar Tag Fiddlin' John Carson, 179
Georgie Buck Hill Billies, 423
German Waltz East Texas Serenaders, 329
Get A Move On, Cowboy Jerry Abbott, 47
Get A Transfer John McGhee & Frank Welling, 554–55
Get Aboard That Southbound Train Bill Boyd, 122; Jim Boyd & Audrey Davis, 125
Get Along Home Cindy Lulu Belle & Scotty, 516; Bascom Lamar Lunsford, 516; Bob Wills, 961
Get Along Home, Miss Cindy Pope's Arkansas Mountaineers, 701
Get Along Little Doggies Cowboy Tom's Roundup, 224; Kenneth Houchins, 443; Harry "Mac" McClintock, 528
Get Along Little Dogie Tex Ritter, 750
Get Along Little Dogies Cartwright Brothers, 196; Eddie Dean, 308
Get Along, Cindy Milton Brown, 136
Get Along, Little Pony, Get Along Nite Owls, 660
Get Along, Old Paint Fred Kirby, 487
Get Away From That Window Pickard Family, 691, 693
Get Away Jordan Four Novelty Aces, 356; Paramount Sacred Four, 675
Get Away Old Man Carson Robison, 793
Get Away Old Man Get Away Vernon Dalhart, 266–67, 269, 291; Frank & James McCravy, 538; Johnny Marvin, 606; Charlie [& Bud] Newman, 655; Carson Robison, 769; Floyd Thompson, 903
Get Away, Old Maids Get Away Chubby Parker, 677
Get Her By The Tail On A Down Hill Drag Cliff Carlisle, 166
Get Hot W. Lee O'Daniel, 665
Get Hot (For Your Loving Daddy) Nite Owls, 660
Get Hot Or Go Home Hi-Flyers, 419; Prairie Ramblers, 712
Get It Ready Nite Owls, 660–61
Get Me Out Of This Birmingham Jail Pickard Family, 693
Get Off Your Money Stripling Brothers, 879
Get On Board, Aunt Susan Jimmie Davis, 299
Get Out And Get Under The Moon Riley Puckett, 722

Get Understanding Brother James Arnold, 64
Get With It Tune Wranglers, 915; Bob Wills, 960
Get Your Gun And Come Along (We're Fixin' To Kill A Skunk) Denver Darling, 296; Carson Robison, 796
Get Your Head In Here Arthur Cornwall, 223; Lake Howard, 445; Three Tobacco Tags, 907
Gettin' Away Swamp Rooters, 883
Gettin' That Low Down Swing Modern Mountaineers, 630
Getting Into Trouble Land Norris, 662
Getting Ready To Leave This World Chuck Wagon Gang, 210–11; J.B. Whitmire's Blue Sky Trio, 954
Getting Tired Of Railroading Jimmy Johnson's String Band, 461
Ghost [The] Adolph Hofner, 431
Ghost And The Graveyard [The] Prairie Ramblers, 705
Ghost In The Graveyard Prairie Ramblers, 710
Ghost Of Robert E. Lee [The] Massey Family, 613
Ghost Of The Blues Bob Skyles, 838
Ghost Song [The] Sons Of The Ozarks, 856
Giddap Napoleon Gid Tanner, 890
Gideon Watkins Band, 940
Gideon's Band Hill Billies, 424
Gig-A-Wig Blues Light Crust Doughboys, 504
Gigger Waltz No. 2 Grinnell Giggers, 384
Giggers Waltz [The] Grinnell Giggers, 384
Gilderoy's Reel John Baltzell, 91
Gilmar [sic] Waltz Leake County Revelers, 495
Gimme Good Old Sorghum Any Old Time Vernon Dalhart, 287
Gimme My Dime Back Leon Selph, 823
Gin Mill Blues Light Crust Doughboys, 505
Ginger Blue Charlie Oaks, 664
Ginger Blues Wilmer Watts, 941
Ginger Ridge Quadrille John Baltzell, 91
Ginsang [sic] Blues Elmer Bird, 105
Ginseng Blues Elmer Bird, 106
Gippy Get Your Hair Cut Kessinger Brothers, 481
Gipsy's Warning [The] Vernon Dalhart, 266
Girl Behind Me [The] Woodhull's Old Time Masters, 971
Girl By The Rio Grande [The] Asa Martin, 592
Girl Friend Of The Whirling Dervish [The] Hoosier Hot Shots, 438
Girl From Natchez [The] Hoke Rice, 746
Girl I Left Behind [The] Gene Autry, 72; John Baltzell, 91; Frank[ie] Marvin, 601–02
Girl I Left Behind In Sunny Tennessee [The] Ernest V. Stoneman, 873
Girl I Left Behind Me Alexander & Miller, 53; Jasper Bisbee, 107; Carolina Ramblers String Band, 172; Vernon Dalhart, 249; Arthur Fields & Fred Hall, 338; John D. Foster, 354; Dalton Johnson & Wallace Dangfield, 459; Kessinger Brothers, 479; Doctor Lloyd & Howard Maxey, 508; John A. McDermott, 539; Uncle Dave Macon, 574; Doc Roberts, 753–54; Leonard Rutherford, 816; Gid Tanner, 888; Tune Wranglers, 915; Bob Wills, 965
Girl I Left Behind Me—Medley Jasper Bisbee, 107
Girl I Left In Danville [The] Dorsey & Beatrice Dixon, 321
Girl I Left In Kentucky [The] Green Bailey, 88; Roy Shaffer, 825
Girl I Left In Sunny Tennessee [The] Charlie Poole, 699
Girl I Left So Blue [The] Bill Carlisle, 160
Girl I Love [The] Joe Creduer-Albert Babineaux, 232
Girl I Love Don't Pay Me No Mind Tiny Dodson's Circle-B Boys, 322; Arthur Smith, 841
Girl I Love In Tennessee [The] Oscar Ford, 352
Girl I Loved In Sunny Tennessee [The] Frank & James McCravy, 538
Girl I Loved In Sunny Tennessee [The] Morgan Denmon, 312; Red Fox Chasers, 731; Carson Robison, 776; Asher Sizemore & Little Jimmie, 836
Girl I Met In Bluefield [The] Chas. M. Dewitte, 314
Girl In The Blue Velvet Band [The] Cliff Carlisle, 165; Tex Fletcher, 349
Girl Of My Dreams Milton Brown, 136; Cliff Bruner, 139; Rice Brothers' Gang, 747; Arthur Smith, 842
Girl Of The Prairie Beverly Hill Billies, 103
Girl On The Greenbrier Shore [The] Carter Family, 195
Girl On The Mountain [The] Leo Soileau, 855
Girl Slipped Down [The] Dr. D.D. Hollis, 432
Girl That Lived On Polecat Creek [The] Willard Hodgin[s], 429–30
Girl That Wore A Water Fall [The] George Stevens, 868
Girl That Worries My Mind J.H. Howell, 446
Girl That You Betrayed [The] Bob Miller, 616
Girl That You Loved Long Ago [The] Cliff Bruner, 140
Girls Don't Worry My Mind [The] Delmore Brothers, 309
Girls Of To-day Chris Bouchillon, 120
Girls, Don't Refuse To Kiss A Soldier Karl & Harty, 471
Girls . . . Girls . . . Girls Bar-X Cowboys, 93
Git Along Delmore Brothers, 311; Gid Tanner, 891
Git Along Home Cindy Roy Newman, 656
Git Along Little Doggies Tex Ritter, 749
Git Along Little Dogies Ranch Boys, 726–27
Gittin' Tired Rambling Rangers, 725
Gittin' Upstairs Ridgel's Fountain Citians, 749
Give Him One More As He Goes Carter Family, 195
Give It To Me, Daddy Dick Hartman's Tennessee Ramblers, 408
Give Me A Bottle Of I Don't Care What Newton County Hill Billies, 659
Give Me A Chaw Tobacco Carter Brothers & Son, 187
Give Me A Home In Montana Patsy Montana, 634
Give Me A Straight Shooting Cowboy Girls Of The Golden West, 371; Patsy Montana, 636
Give Me Back My Fifteen Cents Binkley Brothers Dixie Clodhoppers, 104
Give Me Back My Five Dollars Uncle Dave Macon, 578
Give Me Back My Heart Ted Lunsford, 517
Give Me Back My Texas Home Dick Hartman's Tennessee Ramblers, 407
Give Me Back The Fifteen Cents Capt. McKinney & E.L. Graham, 564
Give Me Flowers While I'm Living Troy Martin & Elvin Bigger, 594
Give Me My Roses Now Blue Sky Boys, 114
Give Me Old-Time Music Arthur Smith, 842
Give Me Roses While I Live Carter Family, 191
Give Me That Old Time Religion Elmer Bird, 106
Give Me The Roses While I Live Coon Creek Girls, 221
Give Me Those Old Fashioned Days Texas Wanderers, 900
Give Me Your Hand Buffalo Ragged Five, 142; Deal Family, 307
Give Me Your Heart Claude Davis, 297–98; Bert Layne, 493
Give Me Your Love Jesse Rodgers, 799
Give Me Your Love And I'll Give You Mine Carter Family, 193
Give My Baby My Old Guitar Happy Fats, 396
Give My Love To Mother Vagabonds, 922
Give My Love To Nell Blue Ridge Mountain Singers, 112; Dick Hartman's Tennessee Ramblers, 408; Roy Harvey, 410; Bradley Kincaid, 483–84; North Carolina Cooper Boys, 662; Marc Williams, 959
Give My Love To Nell, O! Jack Lester McFarland & Robert A. Gardner, 545
Give My Love To Nellie David Miller, 627
Give My Love To Nellie, Jack Asa Martin, 590; David Miller, 626; Carson Robison, 790

Give That Nigger Ham Charlie Parker, 676
Give The Fiddler[s] A Dram Carter Brothers & Son, 186; Clayton McMichen, 571; Tennessee Ramblers [I], 897
Give The Flapper A Chew West Virginia Night Owls, 946
Give The World A Smile Corley Family, 222; Laurel Firemen's Quartet, 491; McDonald Quartet, 540–41; Stamps Quartet, 863, 865; Travelers Quartette, 913
Give Us Another Lincoln Alexander & Apple, 53
Givin' Everything Away Saddle Tramps, 818; Shelton Brothers, 828
Glad Bells [The] McDonald Quartet, 541; Stamps Quartet, 864
Gladiola Time Elton Britt, 129
Glee Club March Jimmy Johnson's String Band, 461
Glide Waltz Green's String Band, 381
Gloom And Darkness Precede The Dawn M. Homer Cummings & Son Hugh, 240
Gloomy Sunday Light Crust Doughboys, 503
Glorious Gospel Train [The] Frank & James McCravy, 537
Glorious Light Is Dawning Dorsey & Beatrice Dixon, 322
Glorious Night Blues Allen Brothers, 56
Glory Bye And Bye Bela Lam, 489
Glory For The Faithful McMillan Quartet, 573; Wilkins Quartet, 957
Glory Glory Glory Glory To The Lamb Elmer Bird, 106
Glory Is Coming McMillan Quartet, 573
Glory Is Now Rising In My Soul Blue Ridge Singers, 112
Glory Land Way [The] Carson Family Sacred Quartette, 180; Jenkins Family, 457; McDonald Quartet, 540
Glory Now Is Rising In My Soul McDonald Quartet, 540
Glory On The Big String Dr. D.D. Hollis, 432
Glory Special [The] Rangers Quartet, 728
Glory To God He's Come Home Ruth Donaldson & Helen Jepsen, 323
Glory To The Lamb Carter Family, 192
Glory Train [The] Deal Family, 307
Glory Way [The] Carolina Gospel Singers, 171
Go Along Bum And Keep On Bumming Along Johnny Marvin, 607
Go Along Mule Uncle Dave Macon, 575
Go And Leave If You Wish To Carlisle Brothers, 169
Go And Leave Me If You Wish Buck Mt. Band, 141; Pie Plant Pete, 695
Go And Leave Me If You Wish To Lester McFarland & Robert A. Gardner, 545
Go Bury Me Fred & Gertrude Gossett, 376
Go Bury Me Beneath The Willow Tree Henry Whitter, 955
Go By The Way Of The Cross John McGhee & Frank Welling, 554, 563
Go Easy Blues Prairie Ramblers, 704
Go Easy Mabel Delmore Brothers, 311
Go Feather Your Nest Hugh Cross, 236; Riley Puckett, 719
Go In And Out The Window Massey Family, 611
Go Long Mule (Parody) Bill Cox, 224
Go 'Long, Mule Vernon Dalhart, 242; Louisiana Lou, 513; Shelton Brothers, 828
Go On, Nora Lee Uncle Dave Macon, 577
Go On, We'll Soon Be There Owen Brothers & Ellis, 671
Go Tell Aunt Tabby Perry Bechtel, 98
Go To Jesus With It All Vaughan Quartet, 924
Go To Sleep My Darling Baby Dezurik Sisters, 316
Go To Sleep Nigger Amadie Breaux, 126
Go 'Way And Let Me Sleep Thomas C. Ashley, 68
Go Your Way Dick Reinhart, 739
God Be With You Kanawha Singers, 469
God Be With You 'Till We Meet Again Uncle Dave Macon, 576
God Bless You Vaughan Quartet, 927

God Gave Noah The Rainbow Sign Carter Family, 188, 193
God Holds The Future In His Hands Monroe Brothers, 632; Riley Quartette, 749
God Is Love MacDowell Sisters, 542; Southern Railroad Quartet, 861
God Is Still On The Throne Rev. Joseph Callender, 154; Highleys, 421; Chas. Richardson & O.S. Gabehart, 748
God Leads His Dear Children Along Rev. Joseph Callender, 154
God Must Have Loved America Gene Autry, 86
God Pity The Life Of A Cowboy Edward L. Crain, 230
God Put A Rainbow In The Clouds Delmore Brothers, 311
God Sent My Little Girl Blue Sky Boys, 114
God Shall Wipe All Tears Away S.E. Mullis, 646
God Shall Wipe Our Tears Away Deal Family, 307
God Will Take Care Of You Katherine Baxter & Harry Nelson, 97; Eddie Dean, 307; Jenkins Family, 457; Jimmy Long, 512; Parker & Dodd, 678; Spindale Quartet, 862; J. Douglas Swagerty, 883
God's Children Are Gathering Home Allen Quartette, 57; Central Mississippi Quartet, 200; Smith's Sacred Singers, 851
God's Getting Worried Virginia Dandies, 932
God's Indictment Rev. C.M. Grayson, 380
God's Love John McGhee & Frank Welling, 554; Palmetto Male Quartette, 674
God's Love Will Shine Fred Kirby, 487
God's Message To Man Wright Brothers Quartet, 974
Goin' Back Home Jordan Brothers, 467
Goin' Back To Georgia Delmore Brothers, 311
Goin' Back To Old Montana Patsy Montana, 635
Goin' Back To Tenn [sic] Blues Billy Sawyer, 820
Goin' Back West In The Fall J.E. Mainer's Mountaineers, 581
Goin' Crazy Blues Scottdale String Band, 821
Goin' Down That Lonesome 'Frisco Line Georgia Wildcats, 366
Goin' Down The River Of Jordan J.E. Mainer's Mountaineers, 581
Goin' Down The Road Dick Hartman's Tennessee Ramblers, 408; Hill Billies, 422; Pie Plant Pete, 695
Goin' Down The Road Feelin' Bad H.M. Barnes, 95; Cliff Carlisle, 165; Carolina Ramblers String Band, 172; Cherokee Ramblers, 204; Crazy Hillbillies Band, 232; Hill Billies, 423; McKinney Brothers, 564; Roe Brothers & Morrell, 810; Lester Smallwood, 840; Henry Whitter, 955
Goin' Down To Jordan To Be Baptized Henry Whitter, 955
Goin' Down To Santa Fe Town Massey Family, 609; Texas Rangers, 899
Goin' Down To Town Charlie Craver, 231; Len Nash, 650
Goin' On Up To Town "Ted" Sharp, Hinman & Sharp, 825
Goin' 'Round And 'Round This World Jack Moser, 644
Goin' South Bob Atcher, 70
Goin' To Have A Big Time To-night Vernon Dalhart, 257–58; McClendon Brothers, 527; Land Norris, 662; Carson Robison, 765, 793
Goin' To Lay Me Down In The Cold, Cold Ground Carson Robison, 766
Goin' To The West Next Fall Green Bailey, 88
Goin' To Town Arthur Smith, 841
Goin' Up The Country Clifford Gross, 385
Goin' Up To Dallas Leon Chappelear, 202
Goin' Up-Town Dr. Humphrey Bate, 97
Goin' Where The Climate Suits My Clothes Fiddlin' John Carson, 178
Going A Courtin' Fletcher & Foster, 350
Going Across The Sea Henry L. Bandy, 92; Richard D. Burnett, 144; Crook Brothers String Band, 234; Uncle Dave Macon, 574

Going Along Downtown Riley Puckett, 716
Going Around The World Emry Arthur, 65; Richard D. Burnett, 144
Going Back Home Leo Soileau, 856
Going Back On Board Again Bill Shepherd, 831
Going Back To Alabama Cliff Carlisle, 163; Asa Martin, 593
Going Back To Arizona Arizona Wranglers, 62
Going Back To Dixie "Peg" Moreland, 641; Simerly Trio, 834; Merritt Smith, 845; Jess Young, 978
Going Back To Jericho "Dock" Walsh, 937
Going Back To Louisiana Lou Buddy Jones, 466
Going Back To Mississippi Girls Of The Golden West, 370
Going Back To My Texas Home Bill Boyd, 121; Tom Darby & Jimmie Tarlton, 294
Going Back To Texas Cowboy Tom's Roundup, 224; Farmer Sisters, 336; Carson Robison, 771-75, 777, 793, 796; Tex Walker, 935
Going Back To The One I Love Frank Luther, 518
Going Back To The Sunny South York Brothers, 978
Going Crazy Johnson County Ramblers, 464; Mike Shaw, 826; Bill Shores & Melvin Dupree, 832
Going Down In Georgia Howard Keesee, 475
Going Down The Lee Highway G.B. Grayson & Henry Whitter, 381
Going Down The River Dr. Smith's Champion Hoss Hair Pullers, 843
Going Down The Road Delma Lachney, 489
Going Down The Road With You Leo Soileau, 856
Going Down The Valley Happy Valley Family, 397; John McGhee & Frank Welling, 559; Peck's Male Quartette, 684; Ernest V. Stoneman, 873
Going Down The Valley One By One Carlisle Brothers, 169; Old Southern Sacred Singers, 669
Going Down To Carbin [sic] Town Dewey Golden, 372
Going Down To Cripple Creek Fiddlin' John Carson, 177
Going Down To Lynchburg Town—Intro: Don't Let Your Deal Go Down Blue Ridge Highballers, 110
Going Down To New Orleans Vernon Dalhart, 287
Going Down Town Fisher Hendley, 416; Madden Community Band, 580; Rowdy Wright, 974
Going Gliding Down The Stream J.P. Ryan, 817
Going Home Vernon Dalhart, 268; McDonald Quartet, 540; Carson Robison, 776; York Brothers, 977
Going Home To Mother Bob Atcher, 69; Happy Fats, 396; Steelman Sisters, 867
Going Home Tomorrow XC Sacred Quartette, 975
Going On Down Town Gid Tanner, 890
Going On To Town Salem Highballers, 818
Going Out West This Fall Red Foley, 351
Going Slow Homer Christopher, 209
Going To Georgia Wade Mainer, 583
Going To Heaven On My Own Expense Callahan Brothers, 152
Going To Jail Tommy Whitmer's Band, 953
Going To Leave Old Arkansas A.E. Ward, 938
Going To Leave You Darling J.P. Ryan, 817
Going To Raise A Rucus Tonight Georgia Yellow Hammers, 367
Going To Ride That Midnight Train Georgia Yellow Hammers, 367
Going To The Ball 'Lasses & Honey, 491
Going To The Barn Dance Tonight Carson Robison, 792, 794
Going To The County Fair Fiddlin' John Carson, 177
Going To The Mill Uncle Dave Macon, 577
Going To The Shindig York Brothers, 978
Going To The Wedding Sally Ann Hill Billies, 422

Going To The Wedding To Get Some Cake Newton County Hill Billies, 659
Going Up Brushy Fork Milton Brown, 137; Kessinger Brothers, 480
Going Up Cripple Creek Ernest V. Stoneman, 873
Going Up The Mountain After Liquor, Part 1, 2 Ernest V. Stoneman, 877
Going Where The Sugar Cane Grows Fiddlin' John Carson, 179
Gold Coast Express Patsy Montana, 634
Gold Diggers Grady Family, 376
Gold Holds The Future In His Hand James Scott-Claude Boone, 821
Gold Mine In The Sky Charles Hogg, 431
Gold Mine In Your Heart [A] Gene Autry, 84
Gold Star Mothers Vernon Dalhart, 256
Gold Watch And Chain Carter Family, 191
Gol-Darn Wheel Massey Family, 610
Golden Barefoot Days Eddie Dean, 308
Golden Beauty Waltz Uncle Jimmy Thompson, 904
Golden Bye And Bye Ernest V. Stoneman, 878
Golden Harp [The] [J.T.] Allison's Sacred Harp Singers, 60
Golden Lariat Wilf Carter (Montana Slim), 185
Golden Memories Of Mother And Dad Wilf Carter (Montana Slim), 184
Golden Memories Waltz Owen Brothers & Ellis, 671
Golden River Stuart Hamblen, 392; Blaine & Cal Smith, 843
Golden Slippers H.M. Barnes, 94; Vernon Dalhart, 266, 272–73, 291; Dykes' Magic City Trio, 328; Edgewater Sabbath Singers, 329; Tony Hammes, 394; Frank Luther, 524; Spangler & Pearson, 861
Golden State Limited [The] Bill Cox, 226
Golden Sunbeams Of Love Vaughan Quartet, 926
Golden Sunset Jack & Jean, 451
Golden Sunset Trail [The] Lone Star Cowboys, 509
Golden Tomorrow Ahead [A] Massey Family, 611
Golden Train [The] Bill Cox, 227
Golden Tresses Clog Russell Miller, 627
Golden Waltz Red Gay & Jack Wellman, 364
Golden Wedding Anniversary Waltz Paradise Entertainers, 674
Golden Wedding Ring [The] Clayton McMichen, 570
Golden West [The] Vernon Dalhart, 288
Golden Willow Tree [The] Welby Toomey, 912
Golden Wings Bob Miller, 617
Goldstine And Lavinskie Walter Coon, 221
Gone And Left Me Blues Jimmy Wakely, 934
Gone But Not Forgotten Emry Arthur, 66
Gonna Buy Me A Brand New Suit Arthur Fields & Fred Hall, 342, 345
Gonna Catch The Train York Brothers, 978
Gonna Change My Business All Around Buddy Jones, 466
Gonna Die With My Hammer In My Hand Williamson Brothers & Curry, 960
Gonna Get Tight Sunshine Boys, 882
Gonna Get Tight Tonight Ted Daffan's Texans, 241
Gonna Have A Big Time Tonight Roy Acuff, 48
Gonna Have A Feast Here Tonight Prairie Ramblers, 704–05
Gonna Have A Good Time Tonight Arthur Cornwall, 223
Gonna Have 'Lasses In De Mornin' Golden Melody Boys, 373
Gonna Keep My Skillet Good & Greasy John Henry Howard, 444
Gonna Kill Myself (Good Gracious Me) Bill Carlisle, 159
Gonna Lay Down My Old Guitar Delmore Brothers, 309
Gonna Lay Down My Old Guitar—Part 2 Delmore Brothers, 311
Gonna Lay Me Down In The Cold, Cold Ground Carson Robison, 774

Gonna Make Whoopee Tonight Bill Cox, 227
Gonna Quit Drinkin' When I Die Callahan Brothers, 153; Arthur Cornwall, 222; Fleming & Townsend, 346, 348
(Gonna Quit My Ramblin') Some Of These Days Panhandle Pete, 674
Gonna Quit My Rowdy Ways Carl Boling, 116; Callahan Brothers, 151
Gonna Raid That Chicken Roast [sic] Tonight Shelton Brothers, 827
Gonna Raise A Ruckus Fiddlin' John Carson, 179
Gonna Raise A Ruckus Tonight Warren Caplinger, 157; Carlisle Brothers, 169
Gonna Raise A Rukus Tonight Roy Acuff, 48
Gonna Raise Ruckus Tonight Hugh Cross, 235; Riley Puckett, 718
Gonna Raise Some Bacon At Home Dutch Coleman, 217
Gonna Raise The Ruckus Tonight Charlie Bowman, 120
Gonna Ride Till The Sun Goes Down Johnny Barfield, 93
Gonna Swing On The Golden Gate Fiddlin' John Carson, 177
Good Bye Blues James Brown, Jr. & Ken Landon Groups, 134
Good Bye Dolly Gray Cecil Wise, 969
Good Bye Eliza Jane Merritt Smith, 844
Good Bye Little Bonnie Red Fox Chasers, 731; Fields Ward, 939
Good Bye Mama Jimmie Mattox, 613
Good Bye My Charming Bessie Kent Bane, 92
Good Bye Old Friends Edgar Wilson, 967
Good Bye Step Stone Walter Coon, 221
Good Bye To My Stepstone [E.R.] Nance Family, 649
Good Bye Waltz Doc Roberts, 753
Good Bye, My Blue Bell Richard Brooks & Reuben Puckett, 132
Good Bye, My Darlin' John D. Foster, 353
Good Cocaine (Mama Don't Allow It) Elmer Bird, 106
Good Evening, Mama Dewey & Gassie Bassett, 97
Good Fellow Leake County Revelers, 495
Good For Nothing Gal Roy Hall, 390
Good Gal Remember Me Three Tobacco Tags, 908
Good Gracious Gracie! Light Crust Doughboys, 506
Good Lord Takin' Care Of The Poor Folks Frank & James McCravy, 536
Good Luck Old Pal Kenneth Houchins, 444
Good Luck Old Pal ('Till We Meet Bye And Bye) Gene Autry, 79
Good Man Is Hard To Find [A] Milton Brown, 136; Roy Newman, 657; Three Williamsons, 909; Wanderers, 938
Good Man Is Waiting For You [A] James Roberts, 756
Good Morning In Glory Smith's Sacred Singers, 851
Good Morning Mr. Zip, Zip, Zip Walter C. Peterson, 688
Good Morning Waltz Red Gay & Jack Wellman, 364
Good News From Home Arthur Fields & Fred Hall, 341
Good Night Jack Major, 586
Good Night Run Chris Bouchillon, 120
Good Night Waltz Blue Ridge Mountain Entertainers, 111; George Edgin, 330; Kessinger Brothers, 479; Leake County Revelers, 494; Leonard Rutherford, 816
Good Night, Little Girl Of My Dreams Elton Britt, 128–29; Frank Luther, 522; Leo Soileau, 855
Good Old Beer Frank Luther, 520; Bob Miller, 623
Good Old Bible Line [The] Uncle Dave Macon, 578
Good Old Country Town Hank & Slim Newman, 656
Good Old Fashioned Hoedown Gene Autry, 85; Prairie Ramblers, 712
Good Old Oklahoma Bob Wills, 960
Good Old Summer Time Humphries Brothers, 447; Ernest Thompson, 903

Good Old Time Religion Is A Million Miles Ahead E. Arthur Lewis, 498
Good Old Times (Are Coming Back Again) Bill Elliott, 332
Good Old Turnip Greens H.K. Hutchison, 450; W.A. Lindsay, 507; Massey Family, 610; Pie Plant Pete, 694
Good Old Way [The] Denson-Parris Sacred Harp Singers, 313
Good Time Papa Blues Jimmie Davis, 301
Good Time Waltz Leo Soileau, 854
Goodbye Alexander Dan Hornsby, 442
Goodbye And Good Luck To You York Brothers, 978
Good-Bye Betty Asa Martin, 589, 591
Goodbye Big Town Ray Sand's Harmony Four, 819
Goodbye Booze Delmore Brothers, 311; Jim & Charlie, 458; Fred Pendleton, 685; Charlie Poole, 699; Gid Tanner, 888
Good-bye Brownie Roy Acuff, 49
Goodbye Dixie Dear Gibbs Brothers, 368
Goodbye Forever Shelly Lee Alley, 59
Goodbye Forever, Darling E.B. Owens, 671
Good-Bye Gal Saddle Tramps, 817
Goodbye Little Darling Johnson & Lee, 462; Light Crust Doughboys, 506
Goodbye Little Girl Welby Toomey, 912
Goodbye Little Pal Of My Dreams Wilf Carter (Montana Slim), 181, 183
Good-bye Little Sweetheart Forever Madisonville String Band, 580
Goodbye Ma, Goodbye Pa Ernest Thompson, 903
Good-Bye Maggie Monroe Brothers, 633; Taylor Trio, 894
Goodbye Maggie, Goodbye Darling Roy Harvey, 411
Goodbye Mama Blues Walter Hurdt, 447
Good-Bye Mary Dear Charlie Poole, 700
Good-Bye Mr. Greenback Pickard Family, 693
Good-bye My Bonnie, Good-bye Carolina Tar Heels, 173
(Goodbye My Darlin') They Drew My Number Sons Of The Pioneers, 859
Goodbye My Honey—I'm Gone Grant Brothers, 377
Good-Bye My Honey I'm Gone Panhandle Pete, 674; Pickard Family, 692
Goodbye My Little Cherokee Tex Ritter, 751
Goodbye Old Pal Cliff Carlisle, 166
Good-Bye Pinto Gene Autry, 83
Goodbye Sin Rangers Quartet, 728
Goodbye Summer, Hello Winter Walter Coon, 221
Good-Bye Sweet Liza Jane Charlie Poole, 700
Good-Bye Sweetheart Joe Gore & Oliver Pettrey, 376; Byrd Moore, 638; Renus Rich & Carl Bradshaw, 747
Goodbye Sweetheart Goodbye Richard D. Burnett, 145; Callahan Brothers, 153; Roy Harvey, 411
Good-Bye To Friends And Home Liston Scroggins, 822
Goodbye To My Stepstones Daphne Burns, 145
Goodbye To Old Mexico Prairie Ramblers, 711
Goodbye To The Plains Carter Family, 194
Goodbye To The Step Stones Three Musketeers, 906
Goodbye, Adelita, Goodbye Bob Skyles, 839
Goodbye, Baby, Goodbye McClendon Brothers, 528
Goodbye, Dear Old Stepstone Ernest V. Stoneman, 875, 878
Goodbye, Little Blue Eyes, Don't Cry Lew Preston, 713
Goodbye, Little Darlin', Goodbye Gene Autry, 84; Elton Britt, 130; Red River Dave, 733
Good-bye, Little Girl, Good-bye Frank & James McCravy, 532
Goodbye, Liza Jane Fiddlin' John Carson, 176; Pickard Family, 693; Charlie Wills, 966
Goodbye, My Lover, Goodbye Emry Arthur, 65; Kanawha Singers, 469; Frank Luther, 525; Moatsville String Ticklers, 630; Pie Plant Pete, 695
Good-Bye, Old Booze Jimmie Davis, 303; Rambling Rangers, 725; Henry Whitter, 955

Goodbye, Old Paint Charlie Craver, 230; Harry "Mac" McClintock, 528; Ranch Boys, 726–27; Tex Ritter, 749
Goodness Gracious Gracie Jimmie Revard, 743; Shelton Brothers, 828
Goodness Me! Holy Gee! Vernon Dalhart, 251
Good-Night Darling Clarence Greene, 382
Goodnight Little Sweetheart Charlie Wills, 966
Goodnight Mother Massey Family, 612
Goodnight Taps Jim & Bob, 458
Goofus Bill Boyd, 122; Milton Brown, 137; Cumberland Ridge Runners, 239; Hoosier Hot Shots, 437
Goo-Goo Eyes B.F. Kincaid, 482
Gooseberry Pie Beverly Hill Billies, 102; Benny Borg, 118; Doc Hopkins, 441; Bradley Kincaid, 484; Red Headed Brier Hopper, 731
Gooson White Mountain Orchestra, 951
Gosh[!] I Miss You All The Time Gene Autry, 78; Jimmy Long, 512; Whitey & Hogan, 952
Gospel Cannon Ball Delmore Brothers, 312; Karl & Harty, 471; Wade Mainer, 585
Gospel Ship Carter Family, 193; Frank Hutchison, 449
Gospel Tide Is Rolling On [The] McDonald Quartet, 540
Gospel Train [The] Perry Bechtel, 98; Kanawha Singers, 469; Rev. Stephenson, 868
Gospel Waves Smith's Sacred Singers, 849
Got A Buddy I Must See Perry County Music Makers, 687
Got A Freight Train On My Mind Dwight Butcher, 148
Got A Home In That Rock J.E. Mainer's Mountaineers, 581
Got A Letter From My Kid Today Charlie Wills, 966
Got A Little Home I Call My Home Tennessee Hill Billy, 896
Got Drunk And Got Married Emry Arthur, 66
Got No Silver Nor Gold Blues Uncle Dave Macon, 576
Got No Time Virginia Childs, 208
Got No Use For [The] Women Crowder Brothers, 237–38
Got Ramblin' And Gamblin' On My Mind York Brothers, 977
Got The Farm Land Blues Carolina Tar Heels, 173
Got The Fever In My Bones Canova Family, 155
Got The Guitar Blues Byrd Moore, 639
Got The Jake Leg Too Ray Brothers, 729
Got The Kansas City Blues Delmore Brothers, 309
Got The Weary Blues Tennessee Hill Billy, 896
Got Them Drunken Blues Bill Cox, 225
Got Up Soon One Morning Marshall Rutledge, 817
Gotta Hit That Texas Trail Tonight Prairie Ramblers, 711
Governor Al Smith Uncle Dave Macon, 576
Governor Al Smith For President Carolina Night Hawks, 172
Governor Alf Taylor's Fox Chase Hill Billies, 422
Governor's Ball [The] Light Crust Doughboys, 502
Governor's Pardon (The Clock Song) [The] Vernon Dalhart, 257
Governor's Pardon [The] Vernon Dalhart, 256–58
Grab Your Saddle Horn And Blow Tennessee Ramblers [II], 897
Grace Greater Than Our Sins Moody Bible Institute Trio, 637
Grady's Daughter Charlie [& Bud] Newman, 656
Gram-pa Snazzy Fryin' Eggs Prairie Ramblers, 711
Gran Prairie Happy Fats, 396
Grand Galle Li Fils A Moncre Pierre Patrick (Dak) Pellerin, 684
Grand Horn Pipe J.W. Day, 306
Grand Old Chariot Ashford Quartette, 67
Grand Old Story [The] Knippers Bros. & Parker, 488; Royal Quartette, 815
Grand Roundup [The] W.C. Childers, 205
Granddad's Cuspidor Buck Nation, 651

Grandfather's Clock Carolina Buddys, 170; Fred L. Jeske, 458; Chubby Parker, 677
Grandfather's Clock—Part 1, 2 Tom & Roy, 911
Grandfather's Liver (Ain't Whut It Used To Wuz) Wyzee Hamilton, 393
Grandma And Grandpa Dick Hartman's Tennessee Ramblers, 408
Grandma's Rag Taylor, Moore & Burnett, 894
Grandma's Rockin' Chair Johnny Marvin, 607
Grandmother's Bible Frank Luther, 518; McDonald Quartet, 541; Dick Robertson, 759
Grandpapa's Frolic Calaway's West Virginia Mountaineers, 150
Grandpapa's Papa Gid Tanner, 889
Granny Get Your Hair Cut Dutch Coleman, 218
Granny, Will Your Dog Bite Floyd County Ramblers, 350; Walter Family, 938
Granny's Old Arm-Chair Crockett [Family] Mountaineers, 233; Clarence Harding, 398; Zora Layman, 492
Grapevine Twist [The] Al McLeod's Country Dance Band, 565; Steve & His Hot Shots, 868
Grapevine Waltz [The] Grapevine Coon Hunters, 377
Grass Is Just As Green [The] Frank Luther, 525
Grave Beneath The Pines [The] Henderson Brothers, 416
Grave By The Whispering Pine [The] Goebel Reeves, 736
Grave In The Pines [The] Clayton McMichen, 569
Grave Of Little Mary Phagan [The] Fiddlin' John Carson, 176
Grave Of Rosa Lee George E. Logan, 508
Grave On The Green Hillside [The] Carter Family, 188
Graveyard Blues Jimmie Davis, 301; Bob Dunn's Vagabonds, 326; Roy Newman, 657; Paradise Joy Boys, 674
Gray Cat On The Tennessee Farm [The] Uncle Dave Macon, 575
Gray Eagle Green's String Band, 381; Smith's Garage Fiddle Band, 848; Taylor's Kentucky Boys, 894
Greasy Greens Stalsby Family, 863
Greasy Possum Fisher Hendley, 416
Greasy String Jackson County Ramblers, 452; West Virginia Coon Hunters, 946
Greasy Wagon Roy Harvey, 411
Great Airplane Crash [The] John McGhee & Frank Welling, 558
Great And Final Judgment [The] Wade Mainer, 585
Great Big 'Taters A.C. (Eck) Robertson, 757
Great Change Since I've Been Born Golden Echo Boys, 372
Great Dust Storm [The] Woody Guthrie, 386
Great Final Judgment [The] Dewey & Gassie Bassett, 97
Great Grand Dad Skyland Scotty, 837–38; John I. White, 949
Great Grandad Cass County Boys, 198; Clarence Harding, 398; John I. White, 949
Great Grandad And Grandma Harmonica Bill, 401
Great Grandma Zora Layman, 492
Great Hatfield-McCoy Feud—Part 1, 2 [The] Lowe Stokes, 870
Great Judg[e]ment Morning [The] Roy Acuff, 50; Friendship Four, 360; Doc Hopkins, 441; Frank & James McCravy, 535, 537; Chas. Teuser & Harold Lawrence, 898
Great Reaping Day [The] Carson Family Sacred Quartette, 180; Roy Harvey, 411; Kentucky Mountain Choristers, 478; J.E. Mainer's Mountaineers, 582; Ernest V. Stoneman, 873
Great Redeemer [The] Laurel Firemen's Quartet, 491; Stamps Quartet, 865
Great Reunion [The] Bill Cox, 228
Great Round Up [The] Charles Nabell, 647
Great Shining Light [The] Roy Acuff, 49; Herald Goodman, 375

Great Ship Went Down [The] Cofer Brothers, 216
Great Speckle Bird Roy Acuff, 48
Great Speckle Bird No. 2 Roy Acuff, 49
Great Speckled Bird (New Version) [The] Morris Brothers, 643
Great Speckled Bird [The] Hall Brothers, 391; Jack & Leslie, 451; (Charlie) Monroe's Boys, 632; Roy Shaffer, 825
Great Titanic [The] Vernon Dalhart, 258
Great Transactions Done [The] Rev. J.O. Hanes & Male Choir, 394
Greatest Mistake In My Life [The] Jimmie Davis, 303
Green Backed Dollar Bill Dr. Humphrey Bate, 97
Green Mountain Earl Johnson, 460
Green Mountain Poker Scottdale String Band, 822; Lowe Stokes, 871
Green Mountain Polka Blue Ridge Highballers, 109; Dixie Ramblers [I], 318
Green River Osey Helton, 415
Green River March Roane County Ramblers, 751
Green River Train South Georgia Highballers, 860
Green River Waltz Clifford Gross, 385
Green Valley John D. Foster, 353
Green Valley Trot Light Crust Doughboys, 506
Green Valley Waltz Richard D. Burnett, 144; Warren Caplinger, 157; George Edgin, 330; Hackberry Ramblers, 387; McCartt Brothers & Patterson, 527; Roane County Ramblers, 751; Leo Soileau, 854; Walker's Corbin Ramblers, 936
Greenback Dollar Thomas C. Ashley, 68; Callahan Brothers, 153; Daddy John Love, 514; Weems String Band, 942
Greenback Dollar—Part 1, 3 Dorsey & Beatrice Dixon, 321; Morris Brothers, 643
Greenville Blow Oliver & Allen, 669
Grey Bonnet Sain Family, 818
Grey Cat [The] Uncle Dave Macon, 578
Grey Eagle Roland Cauley, 198; J.D. Harris, 405; Allen Sisson, 836; Uncle "Am" Stuart, 881
Grey Eyed Darling Ted Daffan's Texans, 240
Grey Skies Light Crust Doughboys, 505
Grosse Mama (Big Mama) Leo Soileau, 854
Grouch Blues Robert Walton & McWinders, 938
Ground Hog Land Norris, 661; Jack Reedy, 734
Ground Hog Blues Ernest Mull, 646
Gruver Meadows Andrew Jenkins, 454
Guess Who's In Town Bill Boyd, 122
Gueydan Breakdown Nathan Abshire, 48
Gueydon Two-Step J.B. Fuslier, 361
Guian Valley Waltz Jarvis & Justice, 453
Guide Me Oh My Saviour Guide Asa Martin, 588
Guide Me, O Thou Great Jehovah Loveless Twins Quartet, 514
Guided By Love (Charlie) Monroe's Boys, 632
Guitar Blues Carl Boling, 116; Cliff Carlisle, 163; Bill Cox, 225; Dezurik Sisters, 316
Guitar Duet Blues Jack Cawley's Oklahoma Ridge Runners, 199
Guitar Fantasy Hi Neighbor Boys, 420
Guitar Lullaby Bob Osborne, 670
Guitar March Harold Maus, 613
Guitar Medley Harold Maus, 613
Guitar Polka Al Dexter, 315
Guitar Rag Golden Melody Boys, 373; Roy Harvey, 411; Leroy [Slim] Johnson, 461
Guitar Runaway Crowder Brothers, 238
Gulf Breeze Waltz East Texas Serenaders, 329
Gulf Coast Blues Light Crust Doughboys, 504; Riley Puckett, 721; Bob Wills, 960

Gulf Coast Special Adolph Hofner, 431
Guns And Guitars Gene Autry, 82
Guy Massey's Farewell Vernon Dalhart, 256–58
Guy Who Stole My Wife [The] Hoosier Hot Shots, 440
Gwine Down To Town Asa Martin, 588
G'wine To Raise A Rucas Tonight Warren Caplinger, 156
Gwine Up Imperial Quartet, 451
Gypsies Warning [The] David Miller, 627
Gypsy Lady Jenkins Carmen, 170; Modern Mountaineers, 631
Gypsy Love Song (Slumber On, My Little Gypsy Sweetheart) Jimmy Yates Groups, 975
Gypsy Love Song (Slumber On, My Little Gypsy Sweetheart) (Gypsy Yodel) McDonald Quartet, 541
Gypsy Swing Al Dexter, 314
Gypsy's Warning [The] Arkansas Woodchopper, 63; Vernon Dalhart, 265, 268; Andrew Jenkins, 454; Arthur Smith, 842; Three Tobacco Tags, 909

Habersham Fox Hunt W.L. "Rustic" Waters, 940
Habit [The] Arkansas Woodchopper, 63
Habit I Never Have Had [The] Stanley Clements, 215
Ha-Cha-Nan (The Daughter Of San) Hoosier Hot Shots, 436
Hackberry Hop Leo Soileau, 854
Hackberry Trot Hackberry Ramblers, 387
Had Nothing Else To Do W.A. Lindsay, 507
Hadie Brown Roy Rogers, 811
Hail Hail Ol' Glory York Brothers, 978
Hail Hail The Gang's All Here Walter C. Peterson, 688
Hail To The King Huff's Quartette, 446
Hail West Virginia Kanawha Singers, 469
Hale's Rag Theron Hale, 389
Half Has Never Yet Been Told [The] John McGhee & Frank Welling, 558
Half Way To Arkansas Lonesome Luke, 510
Hall[e/a]elujah! [J.T.] Allison's Sacred Harp Singers, 60; Daniels-Deason Sacred Harp Singers, 293; Perry Kim & Einar Nyland, 481; Hamp Reynolds' Sacred Harp Singers, 744; Royal Quartette, 815; Smith's Sacred Singers, 851
Hall[e/a]lujah[!] I'm A Bum Vernon Dalhart, 283; Arthur Fields & Fred Hall, 339; Ernest Hare, 399; Harry "Mac" McClintock, 529; Carson Robison, 764, 792; Jack Weston, 948
Hallelujah All The Way John McGhee & Frank Welling, 560
Hallelujah I'm Gonna Be Free Again Shelton Brothers, 829
Hallelujah In My Soul Laurel Firemen's Quartet, 491
Hallelujah Side [The] Chumbler Family, 212; John McGhee & Frank Welling, 554, 563; Ernest V. Stoneman, 873, 878
Hallelujah To The Lamb Hill Brothers, 424; Ridgel's Fountain Citians, 748
Hallelujah We Shall Rise Red Fox Chasers, 730
Hallelujah[!] He Is Mine Bush Brothers, 147; McDonald Quartet, 540; Riley Quartette, 749
Hallelujah[!] There's A Rainbow In The Sky Vernon Dalhart, 289–90; Adelyne Hood, 434
Halliawika March George Walburn & Emmett Hethcox, 935
Halls-Mills Case [The] Vernon Dalhart, 264
Ham And Bone Part No. 1, 2 Loren H. Abram, 47
Ham And Eggs Blue Ridge Mountain Entertainers, 111
Ham Beats All Meat Dr. Humphrey Bate, 97
Hamilton's Special Breakdown Wyzee Hamilton, 393
Hamtramck Mama York Brothers, 977
Hand Car Yodel [The] Bill Cox, 225
Hand In Hand We Have Walked Along Together Carolina Tar Heels, 173
Hand In Hand With Jesus Fortner Family Mixed Quartette, 353

Hand Me Down My Silver Trumpet Chas. Winters & Elond Autry, 968
Hand Me Down My Walking Cane Vernon Dalhart, 265, 273, 291; Joseph Falcon, 336; Sid Harkreader, 400; Kelly Harrell, 403; Earl Johnson, 459; Frank Luther, 524; Lester McFarland & Robert A. Gardner, 542; McMichen's Harmony Boys, 573; Johnny Marvin, 606; North Carolina Hawaiians, 663; Pie Plant Pete, 694; Carson Robison, 769, 784, 793; Wallace Sesten & Jack Shook, 824; Short Creek Trio, 833; Smith & Irvine, 848; Ernest V. Stoneman, 874–75; Gid Tanner, 887, 890; Henry Whitter, 956
Hand Of Fate [The] George Reneau, 741
Hand That Rocks The Cradle [The] John McGhee & Frank Welling, 556
Handful Of Earth From Mother's Grave [A] Vernon Dalhart, 261
Handsome Blues Cliff Carlisle, 166
Handsome Molly G.B. Grayson & Henry Whitter, 380
Handsome Texas Buckaroo Zora Layman, 492
Handy Man Blues McClendon Brothers, 528
Hang Down Your Head And Cry Asa Martin, 591
Hang It In The Hen House Arthur Fields & Fred Hall, 343–44; Jimmy Long, 512
Hang On, Brother Frank Luther, 518
Hang Out The Front Door Key Blue Sky Boys, 114; Lone Star Cowboys, 509; Shelton Brothers, 827
Hang Out Your Front Door Key Lew Childre, 207; Riverside String Band, 751
Hang Over Blues Bar-X Cowboys, 93
Hang Your Pretty Things By My Bed Shelly Lee Alley, 59
Hangin' Blues [The] Sons Of The Pioneers, 858
Hanging Of Charles Birger [The] Vernon Dalhart, 280, 282; Carson Robison, 762
Hanging Of Edward Hawkins [The] Green Bailey, 88
Hanging Of Eva Dugan [The] Vernon Dalhart, 290
Hanging Of The Fox (Edward Hickman—Slayer Of Little Marion Parker) [The] Vernon Dalhart, 279
Hangman Hold Your Rope Oscar Chandler, 200
Hangman, Hangman, Slack The Rope Charlie Poole, 699
Hank Keene's Song Of The Crow Hank Keene, 474
Hannah Chris Bouchillon, 119
Hannah My Love Canova Family, 155–56
Hannah Won't You Open The Door? McGee Brothers, 552
Han'some Joe (From The Land Of The Navaho) Patsy Montana, 636
Happiest Days Of All Carter Family, 190
Happy Denus McGee, 551
Happy All The Time Peck's Male Quartette, 683
Happy Am I Knippers Bros. & Parker, 488; [E.R.] Nance Family, 648; Royal Quartette, 815
Happy And Gay Fleming & Townsend, 347
Happy Band [A] McDonald Quartet, 540
Happy Bill Daniel's Quadrille (Part I, II) John A. McDermott, 539
Happy Bye-And-Bye Land Smith's Sacred Singers, 851
Happy Cowboy Eldon Baker, 89; Bill Bender, 99; Claude Casey, 197; Light Crust Doughboys, 503; Prairie Ramblers, 710
Happy Days (I'll Never Leave Old Dixieland Again) Goebel Reeves, 737
Happy Days And Lonely Nights Yellow Jackets [II], 977
Happy Days Long Ago Bradley Kincaid, 483
Happy Days Of Yore Jim & Charlie, 458
Happy Go Lucky Boy [A] Frank[ie] Marvin, 599–600
Happy Go Lucky Carson Carson Robison, 794
Happy Hawaiian Blues Hawaiian Songbirds, 412
Happy Hickey—The Hobo Delmore Brothers, 310
Happy Home Waltz Collier Trio, 218

Happy Hour Breakdown Newton County Hill Billies, 658
Happy In Him Eddie Dean, 307; Sparkman Trio, 861
Happy In Prison Ernest Phipps, 691
Happy In The Prison Carter Family, 194
Happy Joe Joe Steen, 868
Happy Jubilee Vaughan Quartet, 927
Happy Land [J.T.] Allison's Sacred Harp Singers, 60
Happy Meeting Vaughan Quartet, 927, 929
Happy On The Mississippi Shore Delmore Brothers, 311
Happy Or Lonesome Carter Family, 191; Steve Ledford, 495
Happy Pilgrims Bush Brothers, 147
Happy Sailor [The] Denson's Sacred Harp Singers Of Arley, Alabama, 313
Happy Song Of Praise [A] Freeman Quartette, 359
Happy Spirit (Charlie) Monroe's Boys, 632
Happy Warrior [The] Bob Miller, 622
Happy With Him McDonald Quartet, 541
Happy-Go-Lucky Carson Robison, 795–96
Happy-Go-Lucky Breakdown Happy-Go-Lucky Boys, 397
Harbor Of Home Sweet Home Red Brush Rowdies, 730
Hard Cider Song Crockett [Family] Mountaineers, 233
Hard For To Love Hayes Shepherd, 831
Hard Hearted Mama Jimmie Davis, 302–03
Hard Luck Blues Dock Boggs, 116; Bill Cox, 226; Curly Gray, 378
Hard Luck Boy [The] Honeyboy & Sassafras[s], 433
Hard Luck Guy [A] Arkansas Woodchopper, 63
Hard Luck Jim John McGhee & Frank Welling, 555
Hard Luck Mamma Duncan Sisters, 325
Hard Luck Soldier [The] Lewis McDaniels, 538
Hard Time Blues Tom Darby & Jimmie Tarlton, 295
Hard Times Breakdown Aiken County String Band, 51
Hard Times In Arkansas Bob Miller, 618
Hard To Get Papa Three Virginians, 909
Hard To Please Buck Turner, 916
Hard-Hearted Love Tennessee Ramblers [II], 897
Harem Scarem R.D. Kelly & Julius Dunn, 476
Harlan Town Tragedy Asa Martin, 593
Harmonica Rag Chuck Darling, 295
Harmonies Of Heaven Majestic [Male] Quartet, 585
Harmony Bob Wills, 961
Harped Rag R. Smith, 845
Harrisburg Itch Aiken County String Band, 51
Harvest Field [The] Owen Brothers & Ellis, 671
Harvest Home Waltz Gene Clardy & Stan Clements, 212
Harvest Time Bill Boyd, 121
Harvest Time In Dixie Norwood Tew, 898
Harvey Logan Byrd Moore, 638
Has Anybody Here Seen Kelly? Dan Hornsby, 442
Has Anybody Seen My Gal Jack Pierce, 696
Hash House Hattie Dick Reinhart, 739
Haste To The Wedding Tommy Dandurand, 292
Hatfield-McCoy Feud John McGhee & Frank Welling, 555; Red Brush Rowdies, 730
Haunted Hunter Billie Maxwell, 614
Haunted Road Blues Blue Ridge Mountain Entertainers, 111
Hauthan Waltz E.E. Hack String Band, 386
Havana River Glide Asa Martin, 591
Have A Feast Here Tonight Monroe Brothers, 633
Have A Little Talk With Jesus Jones Brothers Trio, 467
Have A Sunny Smile Clarence Ganus, 362
Have Courage To Only Say No Dorsey & Beatrice Dixon, 322
Have I Lost Your Love Forever (Little Darling) Light Crust Doughboys, 507
Have No Desire To Roam Blue Sky Boys, 113
Have Thine Own Way XC Sacred Quartette, 975
Have Thine Own Way, Lord Paul Crutchfield & John

Clotworthy, 238; John McGhee & Frank Welling, 554; Smith's Sacred Singers, 851
Have Thy Own Way, Lord Chas. Teuser & Harold Lawrence, 898
Have You Ever Been In Heaven? Jimmie Davis, 303
Have You Ever Been Lonely? (Have You Ever Been Blue) W. Lee O'Daniel, 666
Have You Found Someone Else To Love You Jimmy Long, 511
Have You Found Someone Else? Gene Autry, 77; Jimmy Long, 512
Have You Written Mother Lately Ray Whitley, 952
Haven Of Dreams Roy Acuff, 49
Haven Of Rest [The] Rev. Joseph Callender, 154; Jenkins Family, 456–57; Frank & James McCravy, 533; John McGhee & Frank Welling, 553, 561
Hawaii Stuart Hamblen, 392
Hawaii Land James Brown, Jr. & Ken Landon Groups, 134
Hawaiian Blues Rochford & Peggs, 797
Hawaiian Chimes Are Calling James Brown, Jr. & Ken Landon Groups, 135
Hawaiian Dream Girl Three Dominoes, 906
Hawaiian Honeymoon Hank Penny, 686; Tune Wranglers, 916
Hawaiian Hula Rochford & Peggs, 797
Hawaiian Hurricane Kelly Brothers, 477
Hawaiian Medley Tennessee Ramblers [I], 897
Hawaiian Melody Three Tobacco Tags, 908
Hawaiian Moon Waltz Shamrock String Band, 825
Hawaiian Skies Lew Preston, 713
Hawaiian Star Dust Kelly Brothers, 476
Hawaiian Starlight Tom & Don, 911
Hawg Foot Vass Family, 922
Hawk And [The] Buzzard Fiddlin' John Carson, 176–77
Hawkin Sisters Kelly Brothers, 477
Hawkins Rag Ted Hawkins, 413; Gid Tanner, 891
Hawk's Got A Chicken Doc Roberts, 754
Hay Tank Toodle All Day Professor & Mrs. Greer, 383
Hayseed Rag Dizzy Trio, 322
He Abides John McGhee & Frank Welling, 554, 561, 563
He Answers Prayers Today Rev. Edward Boone, Mrs. Edward Boone & Miss Olive Boone, 118
He Bore It All Carolina Gospel Singers, 170–71; Rangers Quartet, 728; Smith's Sacred Singers, 849; Stamps Quartet, 864
He Cares For Our Souls, Not Our Sighs Frank & James McCravy, 535
He Carved His Mother's Name Upon The Tree Lester McFarland & Robert A. Gardner, 543
He Cometh Kentucky Thorobreds, 479
He Died In The Little Shirt His Mother Made Dewey & Gassie Bassett, 97
He Gave His Life Wade Mainer, 585
He Hideth My Soul John McGhee & Frank Welling, 555
He Holds Me By The Hand Smith's Sacred Singers, 850; Valdese Quartette, 922
He Included Me John McGhee & Frank Welling, 556
He Is Coming After Me Ernest V. Stoneman, 878
He Is Coming Back Smith's Sacred Singers, 849
He Is Coming To Us Dead G.B. Grayson & Henry Whitter, 380
He Is Everything To Me Smith's Sacred Singers, 851
He Is King E.M. Bartlett Groups, 96
He Is My Friend And Guide Byron Parker, 675
He Is Our Crucified King Westbrook Conservatory Entertainers, 947
He Just Makes Us Willing Ruth Donaldson & Helen Jepsen, 323

He Keeps Me Singing Perry Kim & Einar Nyland, 481; John McGhee & Frank Welling, 553, 560; Irene Spain Family, 861
He Keeps My Soul Corley Family, 222; E.B. Holden Quartet, 432; McDonald Quartet, 541; Stamps Quartet, 864
He Knew All The Answers (To A Maiden's Prayer) Cindy Walker, 935
He Knows How Hall County Sacred Singers, 392; Happy Four, 396; McDonald Quartet, 540; Vaughan Quartet, 929
He Leads Me Home Jenkins Family, 456
He Left His Religion In The Country Carson Robison, 769; Charlie D. Tillman & Daughter, 910
He Left The One Who Loved Him For Another Wilf Carter (Montana Slim), 185; Lester McFarland & Robert A. Gardner, 550
He Lives On High Avoca Quartette, 87; Dalton Johnson & Wallace Dangfield, 459; Holland Puckett, 715; Smith's Sacred Singers, 849
He Loved Me So Flat Creek Sacred Singers, 346
He Loves Me Turkey Mountain Singers, 916
He Loves Me So Roland Cauley, 199
He Never Came Back Carter Family, 194; Oscar L. Coffey, 216; "Peg" Moreland, 641; Pickard Family, 693
He Pardoned Me Bush Brothers, 147; Price Family Sacred Singers, 714
He Rambled Barber & Osborne, 93; Charlie Poole, 700
He Rescued Me Parker Quartette, 679
He Rode The Strawberry Roan Wilf Carter (Montana Slim), 181
He Rose Unknown Morris Family, 644
He Said If I Be Lifted Up Majestic [Male] Quartet, 585
He Set Me Free Chuck Wagon Gang, 211
He Sure Can Play A Harmonica (It's The Second Best Thing That He Does) Vernon Dalhart, 244
He Sure Can Play A Harmoniky Harry "Mac" McClintock, 529
He Sure Can Play The Harmonica Vernon Dalhart, 245
He Took A White Rose From Her Hair Carter Family, 192
He Took You From Me Leo Soileau, 855
He Touched Me And Made Me Whole Perry Kim & Einar Nyland, 481
He Turned Around And Went The Other Way George Wade, 933
He Was A Good Man (But He's Dead And Gone) Bob Miller, 622
He Was A Traveling Man Smiley Burnette, 145; Prairie Ramblers, 709
He Was A Travellin' Man Charlie Craver, 231
He Was Nailed To The Cross For Me Ernest V. Stoneman, 876–77
He Was Once Some Mother's Boy Carson Robison, 785
He Went In Like A Lion (But Came Out Like A Lamb) Carolina Buddies, 170
He Will Be With Me Stamps Quartet, 864; Rev. M.L. Thrasher, 905
He Will Be Your Savior Too Bill Carlisle, 160
He Will Lead Me Home Vernon Dalhart, 255
He Will Never Cast You Out Moody Bible Institute Trio, 637
He Will Never Leave Me Turkey Mountain Singers, 916
He Will Rise And Shine Vaughan Quartet, 928
He Will Set Your Fields On Fire Johnson County Ramblers, 463; Monroe Brothers, 633; Smith's Sacred Singers, 849
He Won The Heart Of [My] Sarah Jane Uncle Dave Macon, 574, 578
He Would Hum A Little Tune All Day Long Arthur Fields & Fred Hall, 342
Heaben Paramount Sacred Four, 675
Headin' Back To Texas Red Foley, 351

Headin' For Texas And Home Roy Rogers, 811
Headin' For That Land Of Gold Wilf Carter (Montana Slim), 185
Headin' For The Rio Grande Prairie Ramblers, 709; Tex Ritter, 750
Headin' For The Texas Plains Nite Owls, 660
Headin' Home Jimmie Davis, 303; Jesse Rodgers, 798
Heah Dem Bells Vernon Dalhart, 275
Hear Dem Bells Vernon Dalhart, 274, 276; Hill Billies, 423; Sons Of The Pioneers, 858
Hear Them Bells Three Little Maids, 906
Heart Breaking Blues Three Tobacco Tags, 907
Heart Broken Blues Bill Carlisle, 159
Heart Broken Prisoner Bill Cox, 228
Heart Broken Vow [The] George Edgin, 330
Heart In The Heart Of Texas Elton Britt, 129; Carson Robison, 794
Heart Of Old Galax [The] Henry Whitter, 955
Heart Of Sorrow Delmore Brothers, 311
Heart Shy Village Boys, 932
Heart That Is Broken For You [A] Bill Nettles, 654
Heart That Was Broken For Me [The] Roy Acuff, 51; Carter Family, 194; Mr. & Mrs. R.N. Grisham, 385; Jimmy Long, 511; Chas. Richardson & O.S. Gabehart, 748
Heartaches And Tears Johnny Barfield, 94
Heartaching Blues Uncle Dave Macon, 576
Heartbroken Girl Troy Martin & Elvin Bigger, 594
Hearts Aglow Rev. Walt Holcomb, 432
Heave Ho—The Anchor Emry Arthur, 64
Heaven All The Way For Me Vaughan Quartet, 929
Heaven Bells Are Ringing Wade Mainer, 585
Heaven Bells Ring Out Stalsby Family, 863
Heaven Bound Gold McClendon Brothers, 527
Heaven For Me Coats Sacred Quartette, 216
Heaven Holds All For Me Blue Sky Boys, 113
Heaven Holds All To Me Vaughan Quartet, 925
Heaven In My Soul Perry Kim & Einar Nyland, 481
Heaven Is My Home Chuck Wagon Gang, 211; Paramount Quartet, 674
Heaven Song Alf. Taylor, 892
Heavenly Airplane Sons Of The Pioneers, 858
Heavenly Armor Dye's Sacred Harp Singers, 328
Heavenly Chorus [The] Stamps Quartet, 864
Heavenly Light Is Shining On Me Delmore Brothers, 310
Heavenly Port [The] [J.T.] Allison's Sacred Harp Singers, 60; Denson-Parris Sacred Harp Singers, 312
Heavenly Sunshine Edgewater Sabbath Singers, 329; Humbard Family, 447
Heavenly Train [The] Bill Carlisle, 160
Heaven's My Home [J.T.] Allison's Sacred Harp Singers, 60
Heaven's Radio Carter Family, 195
Heavy Hearted Blues Tom Darby & Jimmie Tarlton, 294
Hebrew And Home Brew Chris Bouchillon, 120
He'd Have To Get Under, Get Out And Get Under Hoosier Hot Shots, 439
Heel And Toe W.T. Narmour & S.W. Smith, 649
Heel And Toe—Polka Light Crust Doughboys, 501
Heel Toe Polka—Can't Catch A Nigger Yellow Jackets [I], 976
Helena Jack Pierce, 696
Hell Among[st] The Yearlings John Dilleshaw, 317; Hobbs Brothers, 428; Kessinger Brothers, 479; "Ted" Sharp, Hinman & Sharp, 825
He'll Be With Me Palmer Sisters, 673
Hell Bound For Alabama Fiddlin' John Carson, 177
Hell Broke Loose In Georgia Fiddlin' John Carson, 176; Murray Kellner, 476; Paul Warmack, 940
He'll Find No Girl Like Me Sid Harkreader, 401

Hell In Texas Daca, 240
He'll Never Forget To Keep Me J. Douglas Swagerty, 883
Hell On The Wabash Tom Owens Barn Dance Trio, 672
He'll Set Your Fields On Fire Morris Brothers, 643
He'll Tell Us All About It McDonald Quartet, 540
He'll Understand John McGhee & Frank Welling, 559
Hell Up Flat Rock Jess Hillard, 426
Hell-Bound Train [The] Bill Cox, 225; Frank Hutchison, 450; [Smilin'] Ed McConnell, 530–31
Hello Beautiful Texas Slim Smith, 846
Hello Bill Brown Vernon Dalhart, 288
Hello Central, Give Me Heaven Richard Brooks & Reuben Puckett, 132; Frank & James McCravy, 532, 536; Riley Puckett, 716–17
Hello My Baby Fred Kirby, 487
Hello Stranger Carter Family, 194
Hello World Doggone John McGhee & Frank Welling, 557, 559
Hello World Doggone You John McGhee & Frank Welling, 558
Hello World Song (Don't You Go 'Way) Andrew Jenkins, 455
Hello, Central! Give Me Heaven Carter Family, 192; Lester McFarland & Robert A. Gardner, 547
Hello, Young Lindy Carson Robison, 782
Hell's Broke Loose In Georgia Gid Tanner, 890
Hell's Poppin' In The Barnyard Lake & Cavanagh, 489
Hel'n Georgia William B. Houchens, 443
Help Me Lose The Blues Johnny Bond, 117
Help Me To Find The Way Palmer Sisters, 673
Hen And The Rooster Fiddlin' John Carson, 178
Hen Cackle Bill Chitwood, 208; Earl Johnson, 459; Gid Tanner, 887, 889
Hen Cacklin' Piece Whit Gaydon, 364
Hen House Door Is Locked [The] Carolina Tar Heels, 173
Hen Pecked Man Cliff Carlisle, 166; Kelly Harrell, 404; Raley Brothers, 724
Henhouse Blues Bentley Boys, 100
Henpecked Husband Blues Shelton Brothers, 830; Arthur Smith, 841
Henpecked Papa E.E. Hack String Band, 386
Henry Clay Beattie Kelly Harrell, 403; Red Fox Chasers, 731
Henry Ford's Model A Oscar Ford, 352
Henry Judd Gray Johnson Brothers, 462
Henry Lee Dick Justice, 468
Henry Whitter's Fox Chase Henry Whitter, 956
Henry, Did You Weed The Cabbage Patch ("Yes, Pappy, Yes") Arthur Fields & Fred Hall, 343
Henry's Made A Lady Out Of Lizzie Vernon Dalhart, 277
Her Black Sheep Is In The Fold Louisiana Lou, 513
Her Little Brown Hand Arthur Smith, 841
Her Name Was Hula Lou Carolina Tar Heels, 173
Her Name Was Rosita Red River Dave, 733
Herdin' Song [The] Twilight Trail Boys, 918
Here Comes Pappy Bill Boyd, 124
Here Comes Your Pappy (With The Wrong Kind Of Load) Nite Owls, 660
Here I Am Allen Brothers, 57
"Here I Go To Tokio," Said Barnacle Bill, The Sailor Carson Robison, 797
Here On The Range Roy Rogers, 811
Here, Rattler, Here (Calling The Dog) George Reneau, 740
Here's To The Texas Ranger Carl T. Sprague, 862
Here's Your Opportunity Lew Childre, 207; Gene Steele, 867
Heroes' Last Flight [The] Vernon Dalhart, 269–70
Heroes Of The Vestris [The] Carson Robison, 767
He's A Beaut Earl Johnson, 460

He's A Curbstone Cutie (They Call Him Jelly Bean) Hi-Flyers, 418–19
He's A Hillbilly Gaucho Hoosier Hot Shots, 440
He's A Ramblin' Man Ramblin' Red Lowery, 515
He's A Ring Tail Tornado Karl & Harty, 471
He's A Wonderful Savior To Me Harmony Four, 401
He's A Wonderful Saviour Smith's Sacred Singers, 851
He's An Army Man Dixie Ramblers [IV], 319
He's Calling All Laurel Firemen's Quartet, 491; Owen Brothers & Ellis, 671
He's Calling You Owen Brothers & Ellis, 671
He's Coming Again Chuck Wagon Gang, 211; Deal Family, 307
He's Coming Back Again Posey Rorer, 813
He's Coming Home To Mother Stanley & Higgins, 866
He's Coming To Us Dead G.B. Grayson & Henry Whitter, 380
He's Going To Have A Hot Time Bye And Bye Ernest V. Stoneman, 873
He's Gone Up The Trail Sons Of The Pioneers, 859
He's Gone, He's Gone Up The Trail Zeke Williams, 959
He's In The Jail House No. 2 Gene Autry, 73
He's In The Jail House Now Bill Bruner, 139
He's My Friend Vaughan Quartet, 927
He's On The Chain Gang Now Adelyne Hood, 434
He's Only A Miner Killed In The Ground Ted Chestnut, 204
He's The Best Friend I Can Find Rev. Edward Boone, Mrs. Edward Boone & Miss Olive Boone, 118
He's Too Far Gone Frank Luther, 518
He's Up With The Angels Now Uncle Dave Macon, 578
He's Waiting For Me Jack & Jean, 451
He's With Me All The Way McDonald Quartet, 540; Stamps Quartet, 864
Hesitating Blues Arthur Smith, 842
Hesitation Blues Milton Brown, 137; Hank Penny, 686
Hesitation Blues (Oh! Baby Must I Hesitate) Reaves White County Ramblers, 729
Hesitation Mama Deford Bailey, 87
Hey Buddy, Won't You Roll Down The Line Allen Brothers, 57
Hey Hey Pretty Mama Fleming & Townsend, 347
Hey Hey, I'm Memphis Bound Delmore Brothers, 309
Hey Mister Lowe Stokes, 871
Hey Toots Dick Reinhart, 739
Hi De Ho Baby Mine Delmore Brothers, 310
Hi Hattin' Blues Roy Acuff, 49
Hi Lee Hi Lo Fredricksburg Future Farmers, 358
Hi O, Hi O (Night Herding Song) Girls Of The Golden West, 370
Hi Rinkum Inktum Doodle Red Foley, 351
Hiawatha Breakdown Scottdale String Band, 821
Hickman Rag Charlie Bowman, 120; Hill Billies, 422
Hickory Mountain Breakdown Swamp Rooters, 883
Hidden Valley Ranch Boys, 726; Saddle Tramps, 818
Hide Away Oscar Ford, 352; Frank & James McCravy, 533–34
Hide Me John McGhee & Frank Welling, 554, 561
Hide Thou Me Wisdom Sisters, 969
Hi-De-Hi Doug Bine, 104
Hiding In The Shadow Of The Rock Maury Pearson, 683
Hi-Flyer Stomp Hi-Flyers, 419
High And Dry Blues Nite Owls, 661
High Behind Blues Jimmie Davis, 300
High Born Lady Uncle Jimmy Thompson, 904
High Falutin' Newton Patsy Montana, 636; W. Lee O'Daniel, 666
High Geared Daddy Jimmie Davis, 302
High Geared Mama Jimmie Davis, 301

High Mountain Blues Hackberry Ramblers, 387
High Powered Mama Gene Autry, 73; Jimmie Rodgers, 801
High School Cadet Tweedy Brothers, 918
High Sheriff Aiken County String Band, 51
High Sheriff From Georgia Georgia Wildcats, 366
High Silk Hat And A Walking Cane [A] Ernest Hare, 399; Kanawha Singers, 469; Frank[ie] Marvin, 598–99
High Silk Hat And Gold Top Walking Cane Bill Cox, 225
High Society Jolly Boys Of Lafayette, 464
High Steppin' Mama Gene Autry, 74; Cliff Carlisle, 162; Bill Nettles, 654
High Steppin' Mama Blues Gene Autry, 74–75
High Toned Dance [The] Lowell Cheetham, 203
High Water Waltz Bartmon Montet-Joswell Dupuis, 637
High, Wide And Handsome Prairie Ramblers, 709; Tex Ritter, 750
Higher Chuck Wagon Gang, 210
Higher Up The Monkey Climbs [The] Bob Larkan & Family, 491
Highland Fling John Baltzell, 91
Highland Park Girl York Brothers, 977
High-Low March Shamrock String Band, 825
Highway Blues Merle McGinnis, 564
Highway Hobo Johnny Barfield, 94; Bert Layne, 493
Highway Man Lester "Pete" Bivins, 107; Carson Bros., 180; Bill Cox, 228; Charlie Poole, 699; Harvey Powell, 702
Highways Are Happy Ways Walter C. Peterson, 688
Highways Are Happy Ways (When They Lead The Way To Home) Tex Fletcher, 349
Hilarious Zeb McLaughlin's Old Time Melody Makers, 565
Hill Billie Blues Uncle Dave Macon, 573
Hill Billy Bill Texas Jim Lewis, 499
Hill Billy Boy From The Mountains Jake & Carl, 453
Hill Billy Fiddler [The] Bob Skyles, 838
Hill Billy Jamboree [The] Rowdy Wright, 974
Hill Billy Mixture Part 1, 2 [A] Carson Robison, 792
Hill Billy Shack In The Valley Jack Pierce, 696
Hill Billy Songs Medley Part 1, 2 Carson Robison, 792–93
Hill Billy Swing Jimmie Revard, 743
Hill Billy Wedding In June [A] Gene Autry, 79; Frank Luther, 522; Bob Miller, 624; Tom & Don, 911
Hill-Billy Bride [The] Benny Borg, 119
Hillbilly Courtship John I. White, 950
Hill-Billy Love Song Vernon Dalhart, 284
Hillbilly Rose York Brothers, 978
Hillbilly Stomp W. Lee O'Daniel, 665
Hillbilly Valley Wilf Carter (Montana Slim), 182
Hills Of Carolin' Carl Boling, 116
Hills Of Carolina [The] Lester McFarland & Robert A. Gardner, 547
Hills Of Home [The] Tennessee Ramblers [II], 897
Hills Of Idaho Bill Elliott, 332
Hills Of Old Kentucky [The] Charles Nabell, 647
Hills Of Old Wyomin' [The] Light Crust Doughboys, 504; Tex Ritter, 750; Sons Of The Pioneers, 857
Hills Of Tennessee [The] Sid Hampton, 394; Byrd Moore, 639
Hills Quadrille John Baltzell, 91
Hilo March Homer Christopher, 209
Hindenburg Disaster [The] Wilf Carter (Montana Slim), 184
Hinkey-Dinkey-Dee Gid Tanner, 891
Hinky Dinky Dee Dan Hornsby, 442
Hinky Dinky Parley Voo No. 2 Prairie Ramblers, 707
Hinky Dinky Parley Voo Part 1 Prairie Ramblers, 707
Hiram's Valley—Quadrille Judge Sturdy's Orchestra, 881
His Charming Love Vaughan Quartet, 928
His Coming Draweth Nigh Parker Quartette, 679
His Death Was Not In Vain [E.R.] Nance Family, 648

His Journey's End Carson Robison, 770
His Last Words (Tell Me Sweetheart That You Love Me) Ralph Hodges, 429
His Love Leads Home Stamps Quartet, 864
His Love Waves Are Rolling On Vaughan Quartet, 929
His Message Home Hank Snow, 853
His Name Is Jesus Carolina Quartette, 172
His Old Cornet Carson Robison, 778–80
His Parents Haven't Seen Him Since Harry "Mac" McClintock, 529; Chubby Parker, 676–77
His Picture Is In My Heart Smith's Sacred Singers, 850
His Promise To Me John McGhee & Frank Welling, 563
His Trade Marks Bill Bender, 99
His Way Is Best Deal Family, 307
His Way With Thee Jenkins Family, 457
History In A Few Words Dan Hornsby, 442
Hitch Hike Blues Hall Brothers, 391
Hitch Hike Bums Tom Darby & Jimmie Tarlton, 295
Hitch Hiking Blues Bill Cox, 229
Hitch Old Dobbin To The Shay Again Texas Jim Lewis, 500
Hitch Up The Horse And Buggy Prairie Ramblers, 710
Hiter's Favorite Waltz Hiter Colvin, 219
Hitler's Reply To Mussolini Johnny Bond, 117; Denver Darling, 296; Carson Robison, 797
Hittin' The Trail Wilf Carter (Montana Slim), 182; Pine Ridge Ramblers, 697; Tex Ritter, 750
Hi-Yo, Silver! Roy Rogers, 811
Hobo And The Cop [The] Goebel Reeves, 737
Hobo And The Pie [The] Jack Mahoney, 581
Hobo Bill's Last Ride Gene Autry, 72; Cliff Carlisle, 161; Frank[ie] Marvin, 603; Jimmie Rodgers, 802
Hobo Blues Cliff Carlisle, 161, 164; Walter Hurdt, 448
Hobo From The T & P Line—Part I, II [The] Bob Miller, 618
Hobo Jack The Rambler Frank Gerald & Howard Dixon, 368
Hobo Jack's Last Ride Cliff Carlisle, 161, 164
Hobo Life George E. Logan, 508; David McCarn, 527
Hobo Tramp [The] Tom Darby & Jimmie Tarlton, 294
Hobo Yodel Gene Autry, 71–72; Jimmy Long, 510–11
Hobo Yodel No. 2 Jimmy Long, 511
Hobo's Blues [The] Wilf Carter (Montana Slim), 181
Hobo's Convention [The] Boyden Carpenter, 174
Hobo's Dream [The] Loy Bodine, 115
Hobo's Dream Of Heaven Wilf Carter (Montana Slim), 182
Hobo's Fate Cliff Carlisle, 167
Hobo's Grave [The] Goebel Reeves, 736
Hobo's Last Letter [The] Goebel Reeves, 736–37
Hobo's Last Ride [The] Buell Kazee, 473; Hank Snow, 852
Hobo's Life Is A Happy Life [A] Ernest Hare, 399
Hobo's Life Is Lonely [A] Andrews Brothers, 60
Hobo's Lullaby Bill Cox, 228; Goebel Reeves, 737
Hobo's Meditation Jimmie Rodgers, 807
Hobo's Pal Roy Harvey, 411; Earl Shirkey & Roy Harper, 832
Hobo's Paradise Byrd Moore, 638
Hobo's Paradise (Big Rock Candy Mountain) Bill Boyd, 122
Hobo's Prayer [The] Goebel Reeves, 738
Hobo's Return [The] Ted Lunsford, 517
Hobo's Song To The Mounties [The] Wilf Carter (Montana Slim), 182
Hobo's Spring Song [The] Charlie Craver, 231; Harry "Mac" McClintock, 529
Hobo's Sweetheart [The] Goebel Reeves, 738
Hobo's Warning Jimmie Davis, 299
Hobo's Yodel Wilf Carter (Montana Slim), 183; Fred Richards, 748
(Ho-dle-ay) Start The Day Right Hoosier Hot Shots, 439
Hoe Down Vernon Dalhart, 287
Hog Calling Blues Lew Childre, 207

Hog Drivers J.D. Weaver, 942
Hog Eye Pope's Arkansas Mountaineers, 701
Hog Face Blues Clayton McMichen, 571
Hog Horse Canova Family, 155
Hog Killing Day—Part 1, 2 Clayton McMichen, 567
Hogs In The Potato Patch Hugh Roden, 797
Hog-Trough Reel Clayton McMichen, 571
Hokey Pokey Frankie Barnes, 94
Hokey, Pokey, Diddle, Run Ted Bare, 93
Hold 'Er Eb'ner Hoosier Hot Shots, 437
Hold 'Er Newt (They're After Us) Vaughan Quartet, 925
Hold 'Er, Newt Jimmie Davis, 300
Hold Fast To The Right Carter Family, 194; Dick Hartman's Tennessee Ramblers, 408; Lester McFarland & Robert A. Gardner, 545
Hold Him Down Cowboy Walter Hurdt, 448
Hold It A Little Longer Buddy Jones, 465
Hold Me Rice Brothers' Gang, 746
Hold Me Daddy Ocie Stockard, 870
Hold On Little Doggies Bill Boyd, 122
Hold On To That Thing Bill Boyd, 125
Hold On To The Sleigh Uncle Dave Macon, 575
Hold On, Little Dogies, Hold On Gene Autry, 81
Hold That Critter Down Sons Of The Pioneers, 858
Hold That Wood-Pile Down Uncle Dave Macon, 575
Hold Them Critters Down Saddle Tramps, 818
Hold Thou To Me Classic City Quartet, 214
Hold To God's Unchanging Hand Amory Male Quartette, 60; Simmons Sacred Singers, 835; Smith's Sacred Singers, 849–50; Vaughan Quartet, 926
Hold Up Jesus Tennessee Music & Printing Co. Quartet, 896
Hold Your Rope Roebuck Bros., 810
Holding The Sack Jimmie Revard, 742
Holding To His Hand Of Love Chuck Wagon Gang, 211
Hole In The Wall Adolph Hofner, 430; Zeke Williams, 959
Holiness Mother Karl & Harty, 470–71
Hollywood Mama Billy Casteel, 198
Holy Be Thy Great Name Chuck Wagon Gang, 211; Rangers Quartet, 728
Holy Be Thy Name Majestic [Male] Quartet, 585; Stamps Quartet, 865
Holy City [The] Maury Pearson, 683
Holy Manna Johnson Brothers' Band, 463
Holy Trinity [The] McDonald Quartet, 540
Home (Answer To "Home On The Range") Fred Kirby, 487
Home Again Medley Jimmy Yates Groups, 975
Home Ain't Nothin' Like This McGee Brothers, 552
Home Beyond The Sunset Buffalo Ragged Five, 142
Home Brew George Walburn & Emmett Hethcox, 935
Home Brew Party Herschel Brown, 133
Home Brew Rag Cherokee Ramblers, 204; Roanoke Jug Band, 751; Lowe Stokes, 870; Tweedy Brothers, 918
Home By The Sea Carter Family, 191
Home Call Jimmie Rodgers, 802, 807
Home Comin' Time Skyland Scotty, 837
Home Coming Time In Happy Valley Happy Valley Boys, 397; Clarence Harding, 398; Skyland Scotty, 837
Home Coming Waltz Bill Boyd, 125
Home Coming Week [The] Buice Brothers, 142; Deal Family, 307; Leatherman Sisters, 495; McDonald Quartet, 540; Royal Quartette, 815; Vaughan Quartet, 927
Home Corral Patsy Montana, 634
Home In Caroline Jimmie Davis, 300
Home In Indiana Bill Boyd, 124
Home In Old Tennessee York Brothers, 978
Home In San Antone Charlie Wills, 966
Home In Sunlit Valley Bill Cox, 226
Home In Tennessee Carter Family, 192

Home In The Mountains Vernon Dalhart, 288
Home In The Rock Otis & Tom Mote, 644; Marshall Smith, 844
Home In The Sky Wade Mainer, 584
Home Of The Soul Cliff Carlisle, 168; Charlie Oaks, 664
Home On The Banks Of The River Flat Creek Sacred Singers, 346; Smith's Sacred Singers, 850
Home On The Plains Carl Boling, 116
Home On The Range—Part 1–6 Frank Luther, 524
Home On The Range [A] Jules Allen, 54; Arkansas Woodchopper, 63; James Brown, Jr. & Ken Landon Groups, 135; Lowell Cheetham, 203; Cherokee Ramblers, 204; Vernon Dalhart, 267; Hi-Flyers, 419; Hank Keene, 474; Frank Luther, 521; Johnny Marvin, 607; Ken Maynard, 614; Patt Patterson, 681; Ranch Boys, 725–26; Texas Jim Robertson, 760; Carson Robison, 791, 794; Rodeo Trio, 798
Home On The River Delmore Brothers, 311
Home Over There [The] Old Southern Sacred Singers, 669; Peck's Male Quartette, 684; Smith's Sacred Singers, 850
Home Sweet Home Amadie Breaux, 126; Happy Hayseeds, 397; Lester McFarland & Robert A. Gardner, 547; Clayton McMichen, 567; Da Costa Woltz's Southern Broadcasters, 970
Home Sweet Home In Tennessee Lester McFarland & Robert A. Gardner, 546
Home Sweet Home In Texas Girls Of The Golden West, 370
Home Sweet Home In The Rockies Pete Pyle, 723
Home Town Blues Jimmie Davis, 298; Roane County Ramblers, 751
Home Town Rag Homer Christopher, 209; Home Town Boys, 433
Home Town Waltz Ray Brothers, 729
Home With Mother And Dad In The West Lester "Pete" Bivins, 107
Home, Sweet Home On The Prairie Carson Robison, 795
Homeland Mrs. Leon Hinkle, 427
Homeless Child Daddy John Love, 514
Homesick And Blue Cousin Levi, 224
Homesick Boy Dewey & Gassie Bassett, 97; Weaver Brothers, 942
Homesick Daddy Happy Bud Harrison, 406
Homesick For Heaven Kenneth Houchins, 444
Homesick For My Old Cabin Patsy Montana, 634
Homespun Gal Harry "Mac" McClintock, 529
Homestead In The Wildwood Walter Smith, 847
Homestead On The Farm [The] Carter Family, 188, 193
Homeward Bound Stamps Quartet, 865
Homme Abondonne Guidry Brothers, 385
Hona Hona Hawaii James Brown, Jr. & Ken Landon Groups, 134
Honest Confesson Is Good For The Soul Uncle Dave Macon, 578
Honest Farmer [The] Fiddlin' John Carson, 176, 179
Honest I Do Bob Atcher, 70
Honey Four Novelty Aces, 356
Honey Baby Mine Frank Gerald & Howard Dixon, 368; Lew Preston, 713
Honey Child J.B. Fuslier, 361
Honey Does You Love Your Man Four Aces, 355
Honey I'm Ramblin [sic] Away Delmore Brothers, 312
Honey In The Rock Carter Family, 194
Honey It's Just Because Frank Gerald & Howard Dixon, 368
(Honey I've Got) Everything But You Tom Emerson's Mountaineers, 332
Honey Song (Honey, I'm In Love With You) [The] Massey Family, 613
Honey This Time I'm Gone Slim Harbert, 398
Honey, Don't Turn Me Down Buddy Jones, 466

Honey, Honey, Honey Poplin-Woods Tennessee String Band, 701
Honey, Smile For Me Tune Wranglers, 915
Honey, What You Gonna Do Bob Wills, 965
Honey, What's The Matter Now? Walter Hurdt, 448
Honey, Where You Been So Long? Three Tobacco Tags, 908
Honeymoon Express Carson Robison, 792
Honeymoon Stomp Doc Roberts, 755
Honeymoon Stream Hugh Cross, 236
Honeymoon Trail Charlie Wills, 966
Honeymoon Waltz Cartwright Brothers, 195; Nations Brothers, 652; Doc Roberts, 753
Honeysuckle Charlie Poole, 700
Honeysuckle Blues Richard Cox, 229; Leroy [Slim] Johnson, 462
Honeysuckle Rag Blue Ridge Mountain Entertainers, 111
Honeysuckle Rose Earl & Willie Phelps, 689
Honeysuckle Schottische Massey Family, 609
Honeysuckle Time John McGhee & Frank Welling, 562; Red Fox Chasers, 730
Honeysuckle Waltz Ray Brothers, 729
Honky Tonk Baby Al Dexter, 314
Honky Tonk Blues Jimmie Davis, 302; Al Dexter, 314
Honky Tonk Chinese Dime Al Dexter, 315
Honky Tonk Gals Bob Skyles, 839
Honky Tonk Mama Hi-Flyers, 419
Honky Tonk Mamma Hi Neighbor Boys, 420
Honky Tonk Mammas Roy Acuff, 49
Honky Tonk Rag Bob Skyles, 839
Honky Tonk Shuffle Light Crust Doughboys, 506
Honky Tonk Swing Bill Monroe, 632
Honky Tonky Jump [The] Hi-Flyers, 419
Honky-Tonk Gal Modern Mountaineers, 631
Honolulu Flapper Gal Hi-Flyers, 419
Honolulu Moon Clayton McMichen, 568; Scottdale String Band, 822
Honolulu Rag James Brown, Jr. & Ken Landon Groups, 135
Honolulu Stomp H.M. Barnes, 95; James Brown, Jr. & Ken Landon Groups, 134
Honolulu Sweetheart Of Mine James Brown, Jr. & Ken Landon Groups, 134
Hook And Line Dykes' Magic City Trio, 328; Hatton Brothers, 412; Fisher Hendley, 416; George [Shortbuckle] Roark, 752
Hoopee Scoopee Bobby Gregory, 383
Hoopy Scoopy Vernon Dalhart, 292
Hooray For St. Nick Vernon Dalhart, 283–84
Hoosier Rag [The] Four Horsemen, 356
Hoosier Stomp Hoosier Hot Shots, 435
Hootchie-Kootchie-Koo Tennessee Ramblers [II], 897
Hootin' Nannie Annie Texas Jim Lewis, 499
Hop About Ladies Oliver Sims, 836
Hop Along Peter Happy Valley Boys, 397; Fisher Hendley, 417; Wade Mainer, 583
Hop Along, Sister Mary Gentry Family, 365
Hop High Ladies, The Cake's All Dough Uncle Dave Macon, 575
Hop Light Ladies Blue Ridge Highballers, 110; Robert Cook's Old Time Fiddlers, 220; Ted Hawkins, 413; Scottdale String Band, 821; Ernest V. Stoneman, 874; Gid Tanner, 888
Hop Light, Lady Fiddlin' John Carson, 176; J.C. Glasscock, 371
Hop Out Ladies Tennessee Ramblers [I], 896
Hop Out Ladies & Shortenin' Bread Henry Whitter, 954
Hop Pickin' Time In Happy Valley Prairie Ramblers, 706
Hopefull [sic] Walter Booth Andrew Jenkins, 454
Hop-Head Joe Nite Owls, 660
Hornpipe Medley Nat Bird & Tom Collins, 106
Horse Neck Daddy Bill Cox, 228

Horse Shoe Bend Stripling Brothers, 879
Horses Work, Not Me! Hobo Jim, 428
Horsie Keep Your Tail Up Lew Childre, 207
Horsie! Keep Your Tail Up! (Keep The Sun Out Of My Eyes) Light Crust Doughboys, 506
Hot As I Am Saddle Tramps, 818
Hot Corn Asa Martin, 591, 593
Hot Corn—Cold Corn Kentucky String Ticklers, 478
Hot Dog Blues Jesse Rodgers, 799
Hot Dog Stomp Roy Newman, 656
Hot Dog, A Blanket And You [A] Hoosier Hot Shots, 438
Hot Foot Kessinger Brothers, 479–80
Hot Foot Step And Fetch It W.B. Chenoweth, 203
Hot Hula Lips Kelly Brothers, 477
Hot Lip Baby Bill Cox, 228
Hot Lips Hoosier Hot Shots, 437
Hot Mama Stomp Universal Cowboys, 919
Hot Peanuts Tune Wranglers, 915
Hot Pepper Bob Osborne, 670
Hot Potato Stomp Roy Newman, 657
Hot Romance Massey Family, 609
Hot Sausage Mama Asa Martin, 593
Hot Tamale Pete Bob Skyles, 838
Hot Time Dick Hartman's Tennessee Ramblers, 407
Hot Time In New Orleans Carson Robison, 794
Hot Time In New Orleans To-night Carson Robison, 794
Hot Time In The Old Town Tonight Wilfred Brancheau, 126
Hot Time Mama Hank Penny, 686
Hottest Gal In Town [The] Three Tobacco Tags, 908
Hottest Little Baby In Town Claude Casey, 197
Hottest Mama In Town [The] Bill Nettles, 654
Houchins Waltz Clifford Gross, 385
Hound Dog Blues [The] Doc Hopkins, 441; Karl & Harty, 471
House At The End Of The Lane [The] Milton Brown, 136; W.C. Childers, 206; Vernon Dalhart, 266; McGee Brothers, 552; W. Lee O'Daniel, 666; Uncle Ned, 919
House By The Side Of The Road [The] Macedonia Quartet, 542
House Carpenter—Part 1, 2 [The] Professor & Mrs. Greer, 383
House Carpenter (An Old English Ballad) [The] Bradley Kincaid, 485
House Carpenter [The] Thomas C. Ashley, 67
House Cat Mama Bill Carlisle, 159
House Of David Blues Cherokee Ramblers, 203; Ted Gossett's Band, 376; Clayton McMichen, 566
House of Prayer Rev. Walt Holcomb, 432
House Upon A Rock [The] [E.R.] Nance Family, 648
House Where Love Had Died [The] Bob Miller, 623
House Where Love Has Died [The] Bob Miller, 624
House Where We Were Wed [The] Blue Sky Boys, 114; Karl & Harty, 470
Houston Blues Shelly Lee Alley, 58
Houston Shuffle Bar-X Cowboys, 93
Houston Slide Prince Albert Hunt, 447
How Are You Goin' To Wet Your Whistle? Ernest Thompson, 902
How Beautiful Heaven Must Be Knippers Bros. & Parker, 488; Light Crust Doughboys, 501; Hank & Slim Newman, 656; North Georgia Four, 663; Peck's Male Quartette, 683; Ruth Pippin & Thelma Davenport, 698; Prairie Ramblers, 707; Bess & Tee Prewitt, 713; Riley Quartette, 749; Asher Sizemore & Little Jimmie, 836; Vagabonds, 921
How Can A Broke Man Be Happy Dorsey & Beatrice Dixon, 321
How Can A Poor Man Stand Such Times And Live Blind Alfred Reed, 733

How Can I Go On Without You James Brown, Jr. & Ken Landon Groups, 134
How Can I Help It? Leon Selph, 823
How Can I Keep My Mind On Driving? Three Tobacco Tags, 908
How Can I Leave Thee Moore Sisters, 641
How Can You Be Mean To Me Fleming & Townsend, 347
How Can You Say You Love Me? Eddie Dean, 308
How Can You Treat Me This Way Shelly Lee Alley, 59
How Come Ocie Stockard, 869
How Come You Do Me Like You Do Milton Brown, 138; Freeny Harmonizers, 359; Hoosier Hot Shots, 440; Riley Puckett, 722; Range Riders, 728
How Could You Have Left Me Texas Wanderers, 900
How Dry I Am Wise String Orchestra, 969
How Firm A Foundation Dye's Sacred Harp Singers, 328; Moody Bible Institute Trio, 637; Smith's Sacred Singers, 850
How Foolish Of Me Massey Family, 613
How I Got My Gal Clyde Evans Band, 333
How I Got My Wife Bill Chitwood, 208; Byrd Moore, 638
How I Love My Mabel Red Fox Chasers, 731
How I Love Pretty Little Liza Carolina Buddies, 170
How I Miss You Tonight Adolph Hofner, 430
How Long? Cofer Brothers, 216
How Low Do The Blues Want To Go Johnny Bond, 117; Denver Darling, 296
How Many Biscuits Can I Eat? Gwen Foster, 353
How Many Biscuits Can You Eat Dr. Humphrey Bate, 97
How Many Times Doug Bine, 104; Roy Newman, 657
How My Yodel[l]ing Days Began Wilf Carter (Montana Slim), 182, 184
How Tedious And Tasteless The Hours E. Arthur Lewis, 498
How Times Have Changed Shelton Brothers, 829
How To Make Love Carson Robison, 768–70, 773; Southern Moonlight Entertainers, 860
How Was I To Know Sons Of The Pioneers, 859; Ray Whitley, 953
How Well I Remember Carl Jones, 466
How Will It Be With Your Soul? Jenkins Family, 457
How Wonderful Heaven Must Be Eva Quartette, 333; Paramount Sacred Four, 674
Howdy Do Blues Bill Nettles, 654
Howdy, Bill Bill Chitwood, 208; Gid Tanner, 889
Howdy[!/,] Old Timer Carson Robison, 766
Howell's Railroad J.H. Howell, 445
How'm I Doin' Zeb & Zeeke, 979
How's Your Folks And My Folks (Down In Norfolk Town) Ambrose Haley, 389
How'Ya Gonna Keep 'Em Down On The Farm Hoosier Hot Shots, 438
Huckleberry Blues Dykes' Magic City Trio, 328
Huckleberry Picnic Massey Family, 612
Hula Blues [The] Jim & Bob, 458
Hula Lou Dave Edwards, 331
Hula Nights Honolulu Strollers, 434
Hull's Victory Mellie Dunham's Orchestra, 326
Hum, Strum Whistle Or Croon Carson Robison, 793
Hungry Hash House Fate Norris, 661; Charlie Poole, 699
Hungry Hash House Blues Bill Cox, 224
Huntin' Blues Buddy Jones, 465
Huntin' Me A Home Short Creek Trio, 833
Huntsville Blues Curly Gray, 378
Huntsville Jail [The] Chester Allen & Campbell, 54
Hurrah For Arkansas (In The Hills Of Arkansas) McDonald Quartet, 541
Hurray Johnnie Hurray Bob Miller, 624
Hurray, I'm Single Again Zora Layman, 492
Hurry Johnnie Hurry Bob Miller, 616

Hurry, Johnny, Hurry Jim[my] Boa, 114; Tom Emerson's Mountaineers, 332; Bob Miller, 616, 623; Prairie Ramblers, 704; Rice Brothers' Gang, 747
Husband And Wife Were Angry One Night Charlie Poole, 699
Hush Little Baby Don't You Cry Uncle Dave Macon, 577
Hush My Baby Hush My Honey Gal Jack Major, 586
Hush! Hush! Somebody's Calling My Name Sandhills Sixteen, 820
Hush! Somebody's Calling My Name Mississippi Juvenile Quartette, 629
Hush-A-Bye Baby Blues Happy Bud Harrison, 405
Husking Bee Walter Coon, 220; Crockett [Family] Mountaineers, 233
Husks With The Swine Brother James Arnold, 64
Hut In The Cotton Fields [The] Plantation Boys, 698
Hut On The Back Of The Lot [The] Lester McFarland & Robert A. Gardner, 546, 548
Hutchison's Rag Frank Hutchison, 450
Hut-Sut Song (A Swedish Serenade) [The] Hoosier Hot Shots, 440
Hy Patillion Jess Young, 978
Hymns My Mother Sang Blue Sky Boys, 113; Karl & Harty, 470
Hymns They Sang (At Mother's Grave) Karl & Harty, 471
Hypocrite Sunshine Four, 882

I Ain't A Bit Drunk George [Shortbuckle] Roark, 751–52
I Ain't A-Gonna Let Satan Turn Me 'Roun' Stamps Quartet, 865
I Ain't Goin' Honky Tonkin' Anymore Ernest Tubb, 914
I Ain't Goin' To Study War No More Golden Echo Boys, 372
I Ain't Goin' To Work Tomorrow Carter Family, 187
I Ain't Goin' Your Way Buddy Jones, 465
I Ain't Gonna Give Nobody None O' This Jelly Roll Cliff Bruner, 139
I Ain't Gonna Grieve My Lord Anymore Walter Smith, 846
I Ain't Gonna Let Ol' Satan Turn Me 'Round Jimmie Davis, 302
I Ain't Gonna Let Satan Turn Me 'Round Jimmie Davis, 301
I Ain't Gonna Love You Anymore Ernest Tubb, 914
I Ain't Gonna Stay Here Long Delmore Brothers, 309
I Ain't Gonna Study War Snowball & Sunshine, 853
I Ain't Gonna Study War No More Three Little Maids, 906
I Ain't Got Long To Stay Uncle Dave Macon, 575
I Ain't Got No Gal Dave Hughs, 446
I Ain't Got No Girl Bob Skyles, 839
I Ain't Got No Home In This World Anymore Woody Guthrie, 386
I Ain't Got No Sweetheart Claude Davis, 297; Bert Layne, 493
I Ain't Got Nobody Canova Family, 155; Wanderers, 938; Bob Wills, 960
I Ain't Got Nobody (And Nobody Cares For Me) Hoosier Hot Shots, 437
I Ain't Got Nowhere To Travel Delmore Brothers, 309
I Ain't Lazy I'm Just Dreamin' Red Foley, 351
I Ain't No Better Now Gid Tanner, 891
I Ain't Nobody's Darling Pipers Gap Ramblers, 698
I Always Told You Not To Do That Percy Babineaux-Bixy Guidry, 87
I Am A Fugitive From A Chain Gang Dwight Butcher, 148
I Am A Man Of Constant Sorrow Emry Arthur, 64
I Am Bound For Home Hall County Sacred Singers, 392
I Am Bound For That City Farmer Sisters, 337
I Am Bound For The Promised Land Alfred G. Karnes, 471; Old Southern Sacred Singers, 669; Turkey Mountain Singers, 916

I Am Coming Home John McGhee & Frank Welling, 554, 560
I Am Dreaming Of Mother Daddy John Love, 514
I Am Feeling Love Waves Coats Sacred Quartette, 216
I Am Going Down The Road Feeling Bad Riley Puckett, 716
I Am Going Home E.M. Bartlett Groups, 96; Happy Fats, 396
I Am Going Over There Owen Brothers & Ellis, 671
I Am Going That Way Monroe Brothers, 633; Smith's Sacred Singers, 849
I Am Gonna Marry That Pretty Little Girl Sweet Brothers, 884
I Am Happy Now Percy Babineaux-Bixy Guidry, 87; Vaughan Quartet, 929
I Am Happy With My Saviour Riley Cole Quartet, 217
I Am Just A Gambler Frank[ie] Marvin, 603
I Am Just What I Am Homer Briarhopper, 127; Karl & Harty, 471
I Am Lonely Buell Kazee, 473
I Am Looking Daily For My Saviour E. Arthur Lewis, 497
I Am Looking For The Coming Of The Lord Vaughan Quartet, 928
I Am My Mamma's Darling Child Samantha Bumgarner, 142
I Am O'ershadowed By Love Owen Brothers & Ellis, 671; Stamps Quartet, 865
I Am On My Way To Heaven Hill Brothers, 424; [E.R.] Nance Family, 649
I Am Praying For You Maury Pearson, 683
I Am Ready To Go Monroe Brothers, 633
I Am Redeemed At Last McDonald Quartet, 540
I Am Resolved John McGhee & Frank Welling, 554, 560; Ernest V. Stoneman, 876
I Am So Glad C.A. West, 944; Wilkins Quartet, 957
I Am So Lonely Joseph Falcon, 336
I Am Sure He Won't Drink It Again Elmer Bird, 105
I Am Thine O Lord John McGhee & Frank Welling, 563
I Am Thinking Tonight Of The Old Folks Monroe Brothers, 633
I Am Waiting With Jesus E.M. Bartlett Groups, 96
I Am Walking In The Light J.E. Mainer's Mountaineers, 581
I Am Wandering Down Life's Shady Path Virginia Male Quartet, 932
I Been Here A Long, Long Time Odus & Woodrow, 667
I Believe I'm Entitled To You Carlisle Brothers, 169
I Believe In God Moody Quartet, 637
I Believe In You Tune Wranglers, 915
I Believe It Blue Sky Boys, 113
I Believe It For My Mother Told Me So Delmore Brothers, 310
I Believe The Good Old Bible Ruth Donaldson & Helen Jepsen, 323
I Belong To This Band [J.T.] Allison's Sacred Harp Singers, 59
I Betcha My Heart I Love You Zeke Manners, 586
I Bought A Rock For A Rocky Mountain Gal Wilf Carter (Montana Slim), 186
I Called And Nobody Answered Roy Acuff, 50
I Can Do Without You In The Daytime Smiley Burnette, 145
I Can Never Forget Emry Arthur, 64
I Can Remember The Kind Things Mother Did Willard Hodgin[s], 429
I Can Tell You The Time Lyric Quartette, 525; Wade Mainer, 585; Whitey & Hogan, 952
I Can Whip Any Man But Popeye Smiley Burnette, 145
I Can, I Do, I Will North Georgia Four, 663
I Cannot Be Your Sweetheart Carter Family, 192; Howard-Peak, 445; Unknown Artists [I], 920
I Cannot Call Her Mother Roy Harvey, 410; Charlie Poole, 699

I Cannot Get Beyond His Love Moody Bible Institute Trio, 637
I Cannot Tell A Lie Clayton McMichen, 572
I Can't Be Bothered Buddy Jones, 465
I Can't Be Satisfied Bob Wills, 960
I Can't Change It Otto Gray, 379; Tune Wranglers, 915
I Can't Dance (Got Ants In My Pants) Roy Newman, 656
I Can't Do Without You Joseph Falcon, 335
I Can't Feel At Home In This World Anymore Pete Cassell, 198; Edith & Sherman Collins, 218
I Can't Forget (No Matter How I Try) Bill Boyd, 124
I Can't Get Her Started Otis & Tom Mote, 644
I Can't Give You Anything But Love Milton Brown, 138; Hoosier Hot Shots, 436; W. Lee O'Daniel, 666; Bob Wills, 960; Yellow Jackets [II], 977
I Can't Give You Anything But Love, Baby Swing Billies, 885
I Can't Go To The Poorhouse Bob Miller, 622; Dick Robertson, 759
I Can't Help It, I Still Love You Johnny Barfield, 94
I Can't Help Loving You Jack Rose, 814
I Can't Lose That Longing For You Ambrose Haley, 389
I Can't Sit Down Snowball & Sunshine, 853
I Can't Tame Wild Women Bill Boyd, 122
I Can't Tell Why I Love You Tom Darby & Jimmie Tarlton, 293; Frank Gerald & Howard Dixon, 368
I Can't Think Of Everything John McGhee & Frank Welling, 563
I Can't Use You Anymore Buddy Jones, 465
I Cared For You More Than I Knew Ernest Tubb, 914
I Choose Jesus Jenkins Family, 456
I Could Not Call Her Mother Bradley Kincaid, 483
I Could Tell By The Look On His Face Clayton McMichen, 572
I Couldn't Hear Nobody Pray Vaughan Quartet, 926
I Cried For You Roy Newman, 658; Rice Brothers' Gang, 746
I Cried For You (Now It's Your Turn To Cry Over Me) Nite Owls, 660
I Did It And I'm Glad Texas Jim Lewis, 499
I Didn't Hear Anybody Pray Dorsey & Beatrice Dixon, 322
I Didn't Hear Anyone Pray Karl & Harty, 471
I Didn't Know Floyd Tillman, 910
I Didn't Think I'd Care Bar-X Cowboys, 93
I Didn't Want You To Know Roy Acuff, 51
I Done It Wrong Bill Carlisle, 160
I Don't Belong In Your World (And You Don't Belong In Mine) Gene Autry, 83
I Don't Bother Work Claude Davis, 297; Gid Tanner, 890
I Don't Care Pete Pyle, 723; Dick Reinhart, 739
I Don't Care (Life's A Jamboree) Hoosier Hot Shots, 439
I Don't Care Anymore Red Foley, 351
I Don't Care If I Never Wake Up Uncle Dave Macon, 575
I Don't Care If You Never Come Round Earl Powell, 702
I Don't Care What You Used To Be Clayton McMichen, 568; Saddle Tramps, 818
I Don't Get It Bill Mounce, 645
I Don't Know Nothin' About Lovin' Ocie Stockard, 870
I Don't Know Why I Love Her Delmore Brothers, 310; Fields Ward, 939
I Don't Know Why I Should Cry Over You Tennessee Ramblers [II], 897
I Don't Let The Girls Worry My Mind Crowder Brothers, 237
I Don't Like The Blues No-How Carolina Tar Heels, 173
I Don't Lov'a Nobody Bob Wills, 964
I Don't Love Anybody But You Rex Griffin, 383; Hank Penny, 686
I Don't Love Anyone But You Roy Newman, 658
I Don't Love Nobody Russell & Louis Burton, 146; Cherokee Ramblers, 204; Earl Johnson, 459; Clayton McMichen, 571; Riley Puckett, 715; Hoke Rice, 746; Doc Roberts, 754; Gid Tanner, 887–88; Tweedy Brothers, 918
I Don't Mind Cliff Carlisle, 163; W. Lee O'Daniel, 666
I Don't Need No 'Lasses To Sweeten Liza Jane Arthur Fields & Fred Hall, 344
I Don't Reckon It'll Happen Again Uncle Dave Macon, 574
I Don't Reckon That'll Happen Again Fate Norris, 661
I Don't Wanna Go To School Light Crust Doughboys, 502
I Don't Want Anyone But You Dickie McBride, 526
I Don't Want No Part Of You York Brothers, 977
I Don't Want No Woman Maynard Britton, 131
I Don't Want To Get Married Arthur Fields & Fred Hall, 344; Ernest Hare, 399
I Don't Want To Hear Your Name Callahan Brothers, 152
I Don't Want To Hear Your Name No. 2 Callahan Brothers, 153
I Don't Want To Set The World On Fire Gene Autry, 86
I Don't Want You After All Ernest Tubb, 914
I Don't Want You Mama Howard Keesee, 475
I Don't Want Your Gold Or Silver Claude Davis, 298
I Don't Want Your Greenback Dollar Claude Davis, 298
I Don't Work For A Living Bill Gatin, 363; Ernest Hare, 399; Frank[ie] Marvin, 601; Carson Robison, 778–79
I Don't Worry Bar-X Cowboys, 93
I Don't Worry Now Leo Soileau, 854
I Dream Of The Rainbow's End Hank Snow, 853
I Dream Of Your Bonnie Blue Eyes Bob Atcher, 69
I Dreamed I Met Mother And Daddy Rangers Quartet, 728; J.B. Whitmire's Blue Sky Trio, 954
I Dreamed I Searched Heaven For You Bill Carlisle, 160; Karl & Harty, 470; Knippers Bros. & Parker, 488; Asher Sizemore & Little Jimmie, 837
I Dreamed Of An Old Love Affair Jimmie Davis, 305; Charles Mitchell & His Orchestra, 630
I Feel Like Going On Frank & James McCravy, 535
I Feel Like Traveling On John McGhee & Frank Welling, 554–56, 560
I Feel So Blue Fleming & Townsend, 347
I Feel The Draft Coming On Bill Nettles, 654
I Feel The Same As You Jimmie Davis, 304
I Fell In Love With A Married Man Norman Woodlieff, 972
I Find A Pretty Girl Delma Lachney, 489
I Follow The Stream Sons Of The Pioneers, 857
I Found A Dream Bob Wills, 965
I Found A Peach In Orange, New Jersey Arthur Fields & Fred Hall, 345
I Found A Peanut Dick Robertson, 758
I Found My Cowgirl Sweetheart Bob Atcher, 69
I Found The Right Way Stalsby Family, 863
I Found The Way Cousin Levi, 224
I Found This Love On Calvary Huff's Quartette, 446
I Found You Among The Roses Carter Family, 195; Bill Cox, 225; Uncle Ned, 919
I Found You Out (When I Found You In Somebody Else's Arms) Bob Dunn's Vagabonds, 327; Jack Golding, 374
I Gave My Life For Thee Ruth Neal & Wanda Neal, 652; J. Douglas Swagerty, 883
I Get My Whiskey From Rockingham Earl Johnson, 459
I Get The Blues When It Rains Tex Fletcher, 349; Riley Puckett, 722; Leo Soileau, 855
I Get The Same Old Story Karl & Harty, 471
I Give In So Easy Prairie Ramblers, 711
I Got A Bulldog Sweet Brothers, 884
I Got A Crow To Pick With You Bob Skyles, 838
I Got A Gal In Kansas Carson Robison, 779
I Got A Girl In Mexico Otis & Tom Mote, 644
I Got A Girl In Tennessee Merritt Smith, 845

I Got A Home In That Rock Carolina Ladies Quartet, 171
I Got A Home In The Beulah Land Carolina Ramblers String Band, 172
I Got A Papa Down In New Orleans Virginia Childs, 208
I Got A Red Hot Mama Fred Kirby, 486
I Got Drunk And I Got Married Emry Arthur, 66
I Got Her Boozy Callahan Brothers, 153
I Got Mine C.L. Ballen & Amos Ballen, 90; Kent Bane, 92; Chris Bouchillon, 120; Fiddlin' John Carson, 175; Bill Chitwood, 208; Four Aces, 355; Jenkins Family, 456; John McGhee & Frank Welling, 553; "Peg" Moreland, 641; Gid Tanner, 888
I Got My Eyes On You York Brothers, 978
I Got Some Of That John McGhee & Frank Welling, 562
I Got The Blues Shelly Lee Alley, 58
I Got The Blues For Mammy Bill Boyd, 124
I Got The Carolina Blues Dick Hartman's Tennessee Ramblers, 407
I Got The Freight Train Blues Red Foley, 351
I Got The Kansas City Blues Delmore Brothers, 310
I Got The Spring Fever Blues W. Lee O'Daniel, 666
I Got Those Drunken Blues Bill Cox, 226
I Got Worry On My Mind Nite Owls, 661
I Gotta Feelin' Stuart Hamblen, 392
I Gotta Ketch Up With My Settin' Clayton McMichen, 572
I Guess I've Got To Be Goin' Delmore Brothers, 309
I Guess You Don't Care Anymore Bill Boyd, 124
I Guess You Forgot Adolph Hofner, 431
I Guess You'll Soon Forget Pete Pyle, 723
I Guess You're Laughing Now Adolph Hofner, 430
I Had A Darling Little Girl Bela Lam, 489
I Had A Dream Walker's Corbin Ramblers, 936
I Had A Girl Duke Clark, 213; Harry Hillard, 425
I Had But Fifteen Cents Bill Chitwood, 208; Welby Toomey, 912
I Had But Fifty Cents Arthur Cornwall, 222; Jack Golding, 374; Otto Gray, 379
I Had Someone Before I Had You Milton Brown, 137
I Had Someone Else Before I Had You (And I'll Have Someone After You're Gone) Light Crust Doughboys, 505; Nite Owls, 660
I Hang My Head And Cry Gene Autry, 86
I Hate To Be Called A Hobo Frank Dudgeon, 324; Arthur Fields & Fred Hall, 343–44
I Hate To Lose You Cliff Bruner, 140; Hank Penny, 686
I Hate To Say Goodbye To The Prairie Gene Autry, 82
I Hate To See You Go Ernest Tubb, 914
I Have A Friend Rev. M.L. Thrasher, 905
I Have A Little Home Three Tobacco Tags, 908
I Have An Aged Mother Carter Family, 189
I Have Been Redeemed Macedonia Quartet, 542
I Have Entered The Land Of Corn And Wine E. Arthur Lewis, 498
I Have Found A Honey Light Crust Doughboys, 503
I Have Found The Way Monroe Brothers, 633; Smith's Sacred Singers, 850
I Have Hung My Old Guitar On The Wall Bonnie Dodd & Murray Lucas, 322
I Have Kept My Promise, Darling Bonnie Dodd & Murray Lucas, 322
I Have Lost You Darling, True Love G.B. Grayson & Henry Whitter, 381
I Have My Bed Shelton Brothers, 830
I Have My Dog Goebel Reeves, 738
I Have No Loving Mother Now Blue Ridge Mountain Entertainers, 111; Kelly Harrell, 404
I Have No Mother In This World Charlie Allen, 54
I Have No Mother Now Harvey Irwin, 451; Charlie Oaks, 664

I Have No One To Love Me (But The Sailor On The Deep Blue Sea) Carter Family, 187; Lake Howard, 445
I Have Read Of A Beautiful City Frank & James McCravy, 537
I Have To Raise My Voice In Song Harmony Four, 401
I Haven't Got A Pot To Cook [In] Prairie Ramblers, 707
I Hear A Voice Mr. & Mrs. R.N. Grisham, 385
I Hear An Old Train A'Comin' Jim Boyd & Audrey Davis, 125
I Hear Dem Bells Andrew Jenkins, 454
I Hear The Meadows Calling Me Floyd Thompson, 903
I Hear The Ozark Mountains Calling Me Ozark Boys, 672
I Hear The Voice Of An Angel Graham Brothers, 377; Three Little Maids, 906
I Hear Your Music Bob Skyles, 838
I Heard His Voice McDonald Quartet, 540
I Heard My Mother Call My Name In Prayer Lester McFarland & Robert A. Gardner, 550; John McGhee & Frank Welling, 563
I Heard Somebody Call My Name Kelly Harrell, 404
I Heard The Wicked Pray Karl & Harty, 471
I Hide My Face And Cry Karl & Harty, 471
I Hold His Hand Albertville Quartet, 53; Harmony Four, 401
I Hope I Never Fall In Love Again Texas Wanderers, 900
I Hope I'm Not Dreaming Again Roy Rogers, 811
I Hope She's Satisfied Happy-Go-Lucky Boys, 397
I Hope You Don't Feel Hurt Mose Sigler, 834
I Hope You Have Been True Prairie Ramblers, 709
I Hope You're Happy Now Dixie Ramblers [IV], 319
I Hung My Head And Cried Elton Britt, 130; Jimmie Davis, 305; John (Dusty) King, 486
I Intend To Make Heaven My Home Fiddlin' John Carson, 179
I Just Can't Forget The Past Shelly Lee Alley, 59
I Just Can't Forget You Old Pal Wilf Carter (Montana Slim), 183
I Just Can't Go Shelton Brothers, 830
I Just Can't Say Goodbye Pete Pyle, 723
I Just Don't Care Anymore Prairie Ramblers, 711; Shelton Brothers, 829
I Just Don't Want To Be Happy Wiley Walker & Gene Sullivan, 936
I Just Dropped In To Say Goodbye Shelton Brothers, 830
I Just Had Fifteen Cents Prairie Ramblers, 705
I Just Received A Long Letter Joe Steen, 868
I Just Wanna Play With You Hoosier Hot Shots, 440
I Just Want You Gene Autry, 83
I Just Want Your Stingaree Milton Brown, 138
(I Keep Lying, Lying) Little White Lies Lonesome Singer, 510
I Killed My Daddy Ike Cargill, 158
I Knew It All The Time Sons Of The Pioneers, 859
I Knew The Moment I Lost You Bob Wills, 965
I Know Everything Frank Luther, 523
I Know His Voice Charlie Oaks, 665
I Know I Love You, But I Don't Know Why Leon Chappelear, 201
I Know I Shouldn't Worry (But I Do) Roy Rogers, 812
I Know I'll Be Happy In Heaven Delmore Brothers, 310
I Know I'll Meet My Mother After All Walter Smith, 846
I Know I'll See My Mother Again Light Crust Doughboys, 507
I Know I've Got The Meanest Mama Ike Cargill, 158
I Know My Lord Will Keep Me E.M. Bartlett Groups, 96
I Know My Name Is There Ernest V. Stoneman, 876; Da Costa Woltz's Southern Broadcasters, 970
I Know That Jesus Set Me Free Ernest Phipps, 691
I Know That My Redeemer Lives Maury Pearson, 683

I Know That My Redeemer Liveth Earl Johnson, 460
I Know The Reason Why Hi-Flyers, 420
I Know There Is Somebody Waiting Eldon Baker, 89; Vernon Dalhart, 271, 273; Farmer Sisters, 336; Flannery Sisters, 346; Grover Rann, 729; Bobbie & Ruby Ricker, 748
I Know There Is Somebody Waiting (In The House At The End Of The Lane) Vernon Dalhart, 264, 266
I Know There'll Be Music In Heaven Lem's Down Home Boys, 496
I Know There's Somebody Waiting Vernon Dalhart, 266
I Know We're Saying Goodbye Roy Acuff, 50
I Know What It Means To Be Lonely Richard Cox, 229; Ernest Tubb, 914
I Know What It Means To Be Lonesome Bill Carlisle, 160; Pete Cassell, 198
I Know What You're Thinkin' Dick Reinhart, 739
I Know You Feel The Way I Do Happy Fats, 396
I Know You've Been Drinking Again Slim Smith, 846
I Knowed I'd Settle Down Crockett [Family] Mountaineers, 234
I Laughed So Hard I Nearly Died Arthur Fields & Fred Hall, 342, 344
I Learned About Women From Her Lew Childre, 207; Jack Golding, 375; Goebel Reeves, 735–36
I Leave For Dixie Today Ray Sand's Harmony Four, 819
I Left Because I Loved You Kentucky Thorobreds, 479
I Left Her At The River Tom Darby & Jimmie Tarlton, 294
I Left Her Standin' There (With A Doo-Dad In Her Hair) Dezurik Sisters, 316; Carson Robison, 795
I Left Ireland And Mother Lester McFarland & Robert A. Gardner, 547
I Left My Gal In The Mountains Hugh Cross, 236; Kelly Brothers, 477; Clayton McMichen, 569; Carson Robison, 776
I Left My German Home Charlie Poole, 700
I Left My Heart In Old Kentucky Dwight Butcher, 149
I Left My Heart In Texas Massey Family, 612
I Left My Home In The Mountains Wade Mainer, 584
I Left The Highway Very Dissatisfied Joseph Falcon, 336
I Like Bananas (Because They Have No Bones) Hoosier Hot Shots, 436; Light Crust Doughboys, 503; W. Lee O'Daniel, 665; Earl & Willie Phelps, 689
I Like It Here Where I Am Bob Skyles, 839
I Like It That Way Tennessee Ramblers [II], 897
I Like Molasses Hank Penny, 686
I Like Mountain Music Elton Britt, 128; James Brown, Jr. & Ken Landon Groups, 135; Hoosier Hot Shots, 436; Kelly Brothers, 477; Earl & Willie Phelps, 689
I Like To Go To Back In The Evening (To That Old Sweetheart Of Mine) Jim[my] Boa, 115
I Live In Memory Of You Sons Of The West, 859
I Long For Old Wyoming Wilf Carter (Montana Slim), 182
I Long For The Pines Tom Darby & Jimmie Tarlton, 295
I Long For Your Love Each Day Bill Cox, 227
I Long To Kiss You All The Time Walter Smith, 846
I Long To See My Mother Delmore Brothers, 310
I Long To See The One I Left Behind Vernon Dalhart, 287
I Lost A Wonderful Pal (When I Lost You) Vernon Dalhart, 260
I Lost My Gal Again Nite Owls, 660
I Lost My Girl Earl Johnson, 460
I Lost My Love In The Ohio Flood Tex Fletcher, 349
I Lost My Sunshine Ted Daffan's Texans, 241
I Love Coal Miners Aunt Molly Jackson, 452
I Love Everything That You Do Jimmie Davis, 303
I Love Hawaii Tennessee Ramblers [II], 898
I Love Her Tune Wranglers, 916
I Love Her Just The Same Girls Of The Golden West, 371

I Love My Baby Thomas C. Ashley, 68; Bill Boyd, 124
I Love My Baby (My Baby Loves Me) Roy Newman, 657–58
I Love My Daddy Too Patsy Montana, 634
I Love My Fruit Prairie Ramblers, 711
I Love My Mountain Home Carolina Tar Heels, 173
I Love My Savior, Too Chuck Wagon Gang, 211; Humbard Family, 447
I Love My Saviour Byron Parker, 675; Rice Brothers' Gang, 746
I Love My Sweetheart The Best Kelly Harrell, 403
I Love My Toodlum-Doo Gibbs Brothers, 368
I Love My Woman Maynard Britton, 131
I Love No One But You Lunsford Bros., 517
I Love Nobody But You Clarence Ganus, 362
I Love Only You Julian Johnson & Leon Hyatt, 461
I Love Somebody Arkansas Barefoot Boys, 63; Land Norris, 662
I Love The Hills Of Tennessee Sid Harkreader, 400
I Love The Jailer's Daughter Bill Cox, 225
I Love The Life Of A Cowboy Lem's Down Home Boys, 496
I Love The Silver In Your Hair Morris Brothers, 643
I Love To Raise My Voice Majestic [Male] Quartet, 585
I Love To Raise My Voice In Song Palmetto Male Quartette, 674
I Love To Ramble In The Roses Three Tobacco Tags, 908
I Love To Tell His Love McDonald Quartet, 540; McMillan Quartet, 573
I Love To Tell Of His Love Chuck Wagon Gang, 210
I Love To Tell The Story Foundation Quartette, 355; John McGhee & Frank Welling, 556; Peck's Male Quartette, 684
I Love To Walk With Jesus John McGhee & Frank Welling, 556, 560; Ernest V. Stoneman, 873
I Love Virginia Arthur Fields & Fred Hall, 340
I Love You Milton Brown, 136; Hackberry Ramblers, 388
I Love You As Before Rex Griffin, 384
I Love You Best Of All Blue Ridge Hill Billies, 110; Hugh Cross, 235; Louie Donaldson, 323; Farmer Sisters, 336; Kentucky Thorobreds, 478; Clay Long, 510; Dick Parman, 679; Smith & Dyal, 847; Three Tobacco Tags, 908
I Love You But I Don't Know Why Leon Chappelear, 200
I Love You I Do Julian Johnson & Leon Hyatt, 461
I Love You In The Same Old Way (Darling Sue) Frank & James McCravy, 535
I Love You Nellie Leo Boswell, 119; Elzie Floyd & Leo Boswell, 350; Rex Griffin, 383
I Love You Nelly Sons Of The Pioneers, 858
I Love You Sweetheart, I Love You Fleming & Townsend, 347
I Love You The Best Of All Lester McFarland & Robert A. Gardner, 545
I Love You Too Much Canova Family, 156
I Love You, My Dear West Brothers Trio, 946
I Loved Her In The Moonlight Thos. A. Burton, 146
I Loved Her Till She Done Me Wrong Wilf Carter (Montana Slim), 183
I Loved You Better Than You Knew Anglin Brothers, 61; Carter Family, 191; Delmore Brothers, 311; Bradley Kincaid, 483; Billy Vest, 931
I Loved You Once Jimmie Davis, 305
I Made A Mistake Pete Pyle, 723
I Married A Mouse Of A Man Prairie Ramblers, 710–11
I Married The Wrong Woman Cliff Carlisle, 165
I May Be Wrong Wilf Carter (Montana Slim), 186
I Mean Corrina Jack Moser, 644
I Mean To Live For Jesus Blind Alfred Reed, 733
I Met Her At A Ball One Night Wade Mainer, 584
I Might Have Known Wiley Walker & Gene Sullivan, 936

I Miss My Dear Sweet Mother Asher Sizemore & Little Jimmie, 837
I Miss My Mother And Dad Zeke & George Morris, 643
I Miss My Swiss Wilf Carter (Montana Slim), 182
I Miss The Girl (That Misses Me) Bill Nettles, 653
I Must Be A Good Woman Slim Smith, 846
I Must See My Mother Asa Martin, 591
I Must Tell Jesus Old Southern Sacred Singers, 669
I Need A Sweetheart Carl Boling, 116
I Need One Sweet Letter From You Bill Boyd, 122
I Need The Prayers Blue Sky Boys, 113; Vaughan Quartet, 923–24
I Need The Prayers Of Those I Love Delmore Brothers, 310; Karl & Harty, 470
I Need Thee All The Time Carson Family Sacred Quartette, 180
I Need Thee Every Hour Katherine Baxter & Harry Nelson, 97; M. Homer Cummings & Son Hugh, 240; Little Brown Church Quartet, 508
I Never Felt So Blue Ashley's Melody Makers, 68; Adolph Hofner, 430
I Never Felt This Way Before Floyd Tillman, 910
I Never Knew Leon Chappelear, 201; W. Lee O'Daniel, 665; Ross Rhythm Rascals, 814
I Never Loved But One Carter Family, 190
I Never Will Forget The Night When First We Met Edgar Wilson, 967
I Never Will Marry Carter Family, 191
I Now Have A Bugle To Play Delmore Brothers, 312
I Once Did Have A Sweetheart Reed Children, 734
I Once Knew A Little Girl Thomas C. Ashley, 67
I Once Loved A Girl Knight Sisters, 487
I Once Loved A Sailor Charlie Poole, 699
I Once Loved A Young Man J.E. Mainer's Mountaineers, 582
I Only Want A Buddy [Not A Sweetheart] Sally Foster, 355; Massey Family, 611; Patsy Montana, 635; Riley Puckett, 721; Ranchers, 727; Leo Soileau, 855; Stewart's Harmony Singers, 869; Yellow Jackets [II], 977
I Ought To Break Your Neck [For Breakin' My Heart] Ambrose Haley, 389; Roy Newman, 658
I Played My Heart And Lost Roy Hall, 391
I Played On My Spanish Guitar Johnson Brothers, 463
I Remember Texas Wanderers, 900
I Remember Calvary Ernest V. Stoneman, 878
I Remember When Mother Left Home Merritt Smith, 845
(I Said Goodbye To Everything) When I Said Goodbye To You Lester McFarland & Robert A. Gardner, 547
I Sat Upon The River Bank Fletcher & Foster, 349
I Saw A Man At The Close Of Day G.B. Grayson & Henry Whitter, 381
I Saw A Way Worn Traveller Wisdom Sisters, 969
I Saw My Mother Kneeling Ruth Donaldson & Helen Jepsen, 323
I Saw Your Face Bill Boyd, 123
I Saw Your Face In The Moon Cliff Bruner, 139; Jimmie Davis, 303; Nite Owls, 660; Joe Werner, 943; Ray Whitley, 953
I See A Gleam Of Glory Vaughan Quartet, 929
I See That Certain Something (In Your Eyes) Shelly Lee Alley, 58
I Settled It All Ashley's Melody Makers, 68
I Shall Go Home In The Morning Rangers Quartet, 728
I Shall Know By The Print Of The Nails On His Hand Emry Arthur, 65
I Shall Not Be Moved Roland Cauley, 199; Claude Davis, 298; Dixie Reelers, 319; Bertha Hewlett, 418; Frank & James McCravy, 532, 536–37; Gid Tanner, 890
I Shall Not Pass Again This Way Vaughan Quartet, 926

I Shall See Him Bye And Bye Light Crust Doughboys, 507
I Should Like To Marry Ernest V. Stoneman, 878
I Sit Broken Hearted C.A. West, 944
I Smell Your Hoecake Burning Rosa Lee Carson, 180
I Start Going Home At Eleven O'Clock (And Never Get Home Till One) Mose Sigler, 834
I Still Believe In You Charles Mitchell & His Orchestra, 630
I Still Care For You Texas Wanderers, 900
I Still Do Sons Of The Pioneers, 857
I Still Got Ninety-Nine Howard Keesee, 475
I Still Have A Place In My Heart For You Jack & Tony, 452
I Still Love You Prairie Ramblers, 710
I Still Love You, Sweetheart Sammy & Smitty, 818
I Still Think Of You Modern Mountaineers, 631
I Still Think Of You Sweet Nellie Dean Wilf Carter (Montana Slim), 185
I Still Write Your Name In The Sand Bill Cox, 228; Parker & Dodd, 678
I Surely Am Living A Ragtime Life W.A. Lindsay, 507
I Surrender All Friendship Four, 360; John McGhee & Frank Welling, 554, 559; D.T. Mayfield, 614
I Take To You Dick Hartman's Tennessee Ramblers, 408
I Thank You, Mister Moon Tom Dickey Show Boys, 316
I Think I'll Give Up (It's All Over Now) Rex Griffin, 384
I Think I'll Turn Your Damper Down Jimmie Davis, 303; Buddy Jones, 465
I Think That I've Been Fair Ted Daffan's Texans, 241
I Thought About You Bill Mounce, 645
I Thought I Was Dreaming Edith & Sherman Collins, 218
I Thought I'd Forgotten You Carrie Mae Moore-Faye Barres, 640
I Thought You Meant It Hi-Flyers, 420
I Tickled Her Under The Chin Emry Arthur, 65–66; Asa Martin, 589, 591
I Tickled Nancy Uncle Dave Macon, 574
I Told The Moon About You York Brothers, 978
I Told The Stars About You Frank Gerald & Howard Dixon, 368; Lester McFarland & Robert A. Gardner, 549; Odus & Woodrow, 667
I Told Them All About You Walter Hurdt, 448; Hank Penny, 686; Riley Puckett, 722; Shelton Brothers, 828
I Told You So Ted Daffan's Texans, 240; Jimmie Davis, 305
I Told You That I Would Never Forget You John McGhee & Frank Welling, 560
I Took It Claude Casey, 197; Dixie Ramblers [II], 319; Lester McFarland & Robert A. Gardner, 546
I Took My Time Agoin' (But, Oh! How I Hurried Back) Bob Miller, 620
I Tore Up Your Picture When You Said Good-bye (But I['ve] Put It Together Again) Jack Major, 586; Carson Robison, 763–64
I Tore Your Picture Up When You Said Good-bye (But I've Put It Together Again) Carson Robison, 763
I Traced Her Little Footsteps In The Snow Red Foley, 351
I Traded My Saddle For A Rifle Hank Snow, 853
I Truly Love But One Charlie Allen, 54
I Truly Understand, You Love Another Man George [Shortbuckle] Roark, 752
I Trusted You Once Too Often Dick Reinhart, 739
I Used To Love Somebody Uncle Dave Macon, 577
I Used To Love You (But It's All Over Now) Massey Family, 612; Roy Newman, 658
I Used To Wear A White Hat North Carolina Cooper Boys, 662
I Walk Backwards To Keep From Goin' Straight Willard Hodgin[s], 430
I Walk With Jesus Vaughan Quartet, 929
I Walked And Walked Akins Birmingham Boys, 52

I Wandered Away From Home Gibbs Brothers, 368
I Wanna Be A Cowboy's Sweetheart Patsy Montana, 634; W. Lee O'Daniel, 666
I Wanna Be A Cowboy's Sweetheart No. 2 (I've Found My Cowboy Sweetheart) Patsy Montana, 635
I Wanna Be A Western Cowgirl Patsy Montana, 636
I Wanna Be Loved Edith & Sherman Collins, 218; Bill Cox, 228
(I Wanna Go Where You Go, Do What You Do) Then I'll Be Happy Nite Owls, 660
I Want A Buddy, Not A Sweetheart Walker's Corbin Ramblers, 936
I Want A Feller Bill Boyd, 124; Light Crust Doughboys, 506
I Want A Gal Bill Carlisle, 160
I Want A Girl Walter C. Peterson, 688; Jimmie Revard, 742; Yellow Jackets [II], 977
I Want A Girl (Just Like The Girl That Married Dear Old Dad) Hoosier Hot Shots, 437; Dan Hornsby, 442; Light Crust Doughboys, 503; Ross Rhythm Rascals, 814
I Want A Good Woman Cliff Carlisle, 163
I Want A Nice Little Fellow Kelly Harrell, 403
I Want A Pardon For Daddy Gene Autry, 83; Benny Borg, 118; Vernon Dalhart, 261
I Want A Sweetheart Jim King, 486
I Want A Waitress Light Crust Doughboys, 506
I Want A Woman Raley Brothers, 724
I Want Her Tailor-Made Jimmie Davis, 300
I Want It Dick Hartman's Tennessee Ramblers, 408
I Want My Black Baby Back Fletcher & Foster, 349
I Want My Boots On When I Die Johnny Marvin, 607
I Want My Father's Own Hand Smith's Sacred Singers, 849
I Want My Life To Count For Jesus Chas. Richardson & O.S. Gabehart, 748
I Want My Life To Tell For Jesus Methodist Ministers Quartet, 615
I Want My Life To Testify Freeman Quartette, 359; Hendersonville Double Quartet, 416
I Want My Mama Blues Prairie Ramblers, 704
I Want My Mammy Buddy Baker, 89
I Want My Rib E.E. Hack String Band, 386; Clayton McMichen, 571; Hank Penny, 686
I Want Some Home Brew Orla Clark, 214
I Want Somebody Cindy Walker, 935
I Want Somebody Like You Bar-X Cowboys, 93
I Want Somebody To Cry Over Me Light Crust Doughboys, 501
I Want That Girl Bob Skyles, 838
I Want The Whole World To Know I Love You Bob Dunn's Vagabonds, 326
I Want To Ask The Stars Callahan Brothers, 154
I Want To Be A Cowboy's Sweetheart Patsy Montana, 634, 636
I Want To Be A Real Cowboy Girl Chuck Wagon Gang, 210; Girls Of The Golden West, 371
I Want To Be A Worker For The Lord John McGhee & Frank Welling, 556
I Want To Be Called Pet And Sweetheart Walter Smith, 846
I Want To Be Like Jesus [Smilin'] Ed McConnell, 530
I Want To Be Loved Wade Mainer, 584
I Want To Be There Frank & James McCravy, 532
I Want To Be Where You Are Callahan Brothers, 153
I Want To Do My Best Owen Brothers & Ellis, 671
I Want To Dream By The Old Mill Stream Frank & James McCravy, 538; Carson Robison, 787
I Want To Get Married Leo Soileau, 854
I Want To Go—I Want To Go [E.R.] Nance Family, 649
I Want To Go Back Bill Boyd, 124

I Want To Go Back To My Home On The Range Rowdy Wright, 974
I Want To Go Back To My Old Mountain Shack John McGhee & Frank Welling, 555
I Want To Go Back To The Farm Lou & Nellie Thompson, 904
I Want To Go There Ruth Donaldson & Helen Jepsen, 323; Frank & James McCravy, 532, 536; Vaughan Quartet, 928
I Want To Go There, Don't You? Blue Ridge Singers, 112; Frank & James McCravy, 537; John McGhee & Frank Welling, 554; Vaughan Quartet, 928
I Want To Go To Heaven Smith's Sacred Singers, 849
I Want To Go Where Jesus Is Ernest Phipps, 690
I Want To Hear Him Call My Name Stamps Quartet, 865; Stringfellow Quartet, 879
I Want To Live And Love Wiley Walker & Gene Sullivan, 936
I Want To Live Beyond The Grave North Canton Quartet, 662
I Want To Live In Loveland Bob Skyles, 839
I Want To Live Like Daddy Grady & Hazel Cole, 217
I Want To Love Him More Blue Ridge Sacred Singers, 112
I Want To Make Heaven My Home Fiddlin' John Carson, 179
I Want To See My Mother (Ten Thousand Miles Away) Johnson Brothers, 463
I Want To Walk In The Heavenly Way Dick Hartman's Tennessee Ramblers, 408
I Want To Waltz With You Honey E.E. Hack String Band, 386
I Want To Wander In The Cumberland Mountains Riley Puckett, 721
I Want You By My Side Edith & Sherman Collins, 218
I Want You Every Day Phil Reeve & Ernest Moody, 735
I Wanta Be A Cowboy's Dreamgirl Patsy Montana, 636
I Wanta Be Where You Are Fleming & Townsend, 346
I Wants My Lulu John McGhee & Frank Welling, 555
I Was A Pal To Daddy Chas. M. Dewitte, 314
I Was Born 4000 Years Ago Frank Luther, 524
I Was Born About 10,000 Years Ago Crockett [Family] Mountaineers, 233; Kelly Harrell, 403
I Was Born Four Thousand Years Ago Fiddlin' John Carson, 179; Gentry Brothers, 364; Lester McFarland & Robert A. Gardner, 542
I Was Born In Old Wyoming Carson Robison, 792, 795
I Was Born In Pennsylvania Kelly Harrell, 403
I Was Born In The Mountains Elton Britt, 128
I Was Only Teasing You Three Tobacco Tags, 908
I Was So Happy Adolph Hofner, 431
I Was There When It Happened Perry Kim & Einar Nyland, 481
I Went Down Into The Garden Price Family Sacred Singers, 714
I Went To Honolulu Just To Get Myself A Lei Prairie Ramblers, 707
I Went To Honolulu To Get A Lei Prairie Ramblers, 707
I Went To See My Sweetheart Daddy John Love, 514; Lewis McDaniels, 539
I Will Always Call You Sweetheart Vagabonds, 921
I Will Be All Smiles Tonight Frank Jenkins, 455; Bradley Kincaid, 483
I Will Be All Smiles To-night, Love Tin-Can Joe, 910
I Will Be Dancing With You Ernest Thompson, 903
I Will Live For My Savio[u]r E. Arthur Lewis, 497–98
I Will Meet Mother Up There Vaughan Quartet, 930
I Will Meet My Precious Mother Dorsey & Beatrice Dixon, 321; Morris Brothers, 643

Index to Titles 1071

I Will Meet You Eldon Baker, 89
I Will Meet You In The Morning Carson Family Sacred Quartette, 180; Ernest V. Stoneman, 873
I Will Ne'er Forget My Mother And My Home Vernon Dalhart, 244
I Will Never Give Up Stamps Quartet, 865
I Will Never Leave You Sunshine Boys, 882
I Will Never Move Again Duncan Sisters Trio, 325
I Will Never Turn Back Morris Brothers, 643
I Will Not Be Removed Kentucky Holiness Singers, 478
I Will Praise Him Hallelujah John McGhee & Frank Welling, 559–60
I Will See You Tonight In My Dreams Joe Cook, 220
I Will Shout His Praise In Glory Perry Kim & Einar Nyland, 481
I Will Sing Of My Redeemer Jenkins Family, 457; Perry Kim & Einar Nyland, 481; Log Cabin Boys, 508; Lester McFarland & Robert A. Gardner, 542; Smith's Sacred Singers, 849
I Will Sing Of My Saviour E. Arthur Lewis, 497
I Will Slip Away Home Rangers Quartet, 728
I Will Tell A Wondrous Story Joe Reed Family, 734
I Wish All My Children Were Babies Again Gene Autry, 86; Ella Sutton, 882
I Wish I Could Shimmy Like My Sister Kate Cliff Bruner, 140; Hoosier Hot Shots, 437; Bob Wills, 962–63
I Wish I Had A Sweetheart (Like That Old Sweetheart Of Mine) Jimmie Davis, 305
I Wish I Had Died In My Cradle (Before I Grew Up To Love You) Max Friedman, 359; Arty Hall, 390; Lester McFarland & Robert A. Gardner, 546; Carson Robison, 772–73
I Wish I Had My First Wife Back Old Settlers, 668
I Wish I Had My Whiskey Back Uncle Dave Macon, 577
I Wish I Had Never Seen Sunshine Wilf Carter (Montana Slim), 184; Jimmie Davis, 301; Philyaw Brothers, 690; Prairie Ramblers, 709; Johnny Roberts, 756
I Wish I Had Someone To Love Me Bradley Kincaid, 484
I Wish I Stayed In The Wagonyard Wyoming Jack O'Brien, 665
I Wish I Was A Mole In The Ground Bascom Lamar Lunsford, 516–17
I Wish I Was A Single Gal Again Canova Family, 155
I Wish I Was A Single Girl Again Vernon Dalhart, 249, 285; Sid Harkreader, 400; Kelly Harrell, 403; Riley Puckett, 722; Henry Whitter, 955
I Wish I Was In Tennessee Fred Pendleton, 685
I Wish I Was Single Again Vernon Dalhart, 259, 270; Riley Puckett, 716, 722; Carson Robison, 763, 787; Welby Toomey, 912; Henry Whitter, 955
I Wish I Were A Mole In The Ground Green Bailey, 88
I Wish I Were A Single Girl Again Riley Puckett, 720
I Wish I Were Single Again Taylor-Griggs Louisiana Melody Makers, 894
I Wish I'd Never Been Born Prairie Ramblers, 710
I Wish I'd Never Learned To Love You Shelly Lee Alley, 59; Arthur Smith, 842; Texas Wanderers, 900
I Wish I'd Never Met You Blue Ridge Mountain Singers, 112; Buddy Jones, 465
I Wish It Wasn't So Bob Atcher, 69; Shelton Brothers, 830
I Wish That Gal Was Mine Herschel Brown, 133
I Wish The Train Would Wreck Maynard Britton, 131
I Wish They'd Do It Now John McGhee & Frank Welling, 558
I Wish You Knew The Way I Feel Bill Boyd, 124
I Wish You Well Tom Dickey Show Boys, 316
I Wish You Were Here, Dear Jesse Rodgers, 798

I Wish You Were Jealous Of Me Nite Owls, 660; Rice Brothers' Gang, 746; Tune Wranglers, 915
I Wish You Were With Me Tonight Johnny Roberts, 757
I Wished I Was A Single Girl Again Vernon Dalhart, 259
I Woke Up One Morning In May Didier Herbert, 418
I Wonder (If She Is Blue) Jimmie Davis, 300
I Wonder Do The Old Folks Think Of Me Floyd Thompson, 903–04
I Wonder How She Did It Floyd Thompson, 903
I Wonder How The Folks Are At Home Karl & Harty, 470
I Wonder How The Old Folks Are At Home Jackson County Ramblers, 453
I Wonder How They Live At Home Rev. Edward Boone, Mrs. Edward Boone & Miss Olive Boone, 118
I Wonder If He's Singing To The Angels To-night Frank Luther, 518
I Wonder If She Cares To See Me Now Virginia Dandies, 932
I Wonder If She Waits For Me Tonight Sons Of The Pioneers, 858
I Wonder If She's Blue Jimmie Davis, 300; Massey Family, 609
I Wonder If The Moon Is Shining? Roy Hall, 391
I Wonder If They Care To See Me Now Joe Steen, 868
I Wonder If True Love Will Find A Way (Some Day) Texas Wanderers, 901
I Wonder If 'Twas Very Wrong Red Fox Chasers, 731
I Wonder If You Feel The Way I Do Gene Autry, 84; Bill Monroe, 631; Prairie Ramblers, 710; Sons Of Acadians, 856; Texas Wanderers, 900; Bob Wills, 963
I Wonder If You Love Me George & Henson, 365
I Wonder If You Miss Me Tonight Jack Golding, 374
I Wonder If You Still Remember Vernon Dalhart, 270, 272
I Wonder What I'm Goin' To Do Johnny Lee Wills, 967
I Wonder What's The Matter Dixie Ramblers [IV], 319
I Wonder Where My Darling Is Tonight Delmore Brothers, 312
I Wonder Where My Father Is Gone Bill Shepherd, 831
I Wonder Where You Are Jimmie Davis, 302
I Wonder Where You Are Tonight Bob Atcher, 70; Roy Hall, 391; Jimmy Wakely, 934
I Wonder Who's Kissing Her Now Jimmie Davis, 302; Clayton McMichen, 572; Dick Parman, 679–80
I Wonder Who's Sorry Now Carlisle Brothers, 169
I Wonder Why Thos. A. Burton, 146; Herb Cook, 220; Texas Rangers, 900
I Wonder Why Nobody Cares For Me Golden Melody Boys, 373
I Wonder Why You Said Goodbye Ernest Tubb, 914
I Wonder Will My Mother Be On That Train? Frank Luther, 523
I Won't Accept Anything For My Soul Dorsey & Beatrice Dixon, 321
I Won't Be Back In A Year Little Darling Bob Skyles, 839
I Won't Be Blue No More Earl Powell, 702
I Won't Be Worried Wade Mainer, 584
I Won't Care Pine Ridge Boys, 697
I Won't Care (A Hundred Years From Now) Bob Atcher, 69
I Won't Have Any Troubles Anymore Rice Brothers' Gang, 747
I Won't Have To Cross Jordan Alone Laurel Firemen's Quartet, 491
I Won't Mind Prairie Ramblers, 712
I Won't Miss You When You Go Away Buddy Jones, 466
I Won't Never Get Drunk Anymore Pipers Gap Ramblers, 698
I Won't Stand In Your Way Johnny Bond, 116

I Worship The Lord Owen Brothers & Ellis, 671
I Would If I Could Zeke Williams, 959
I Would If I Could But I Can't Callahan Brothers, 151; New Dixie Demons, 655
I Would Not Be Denied Elmer Bird, 105; John McGhee & Frank Welling, 554, 563; Ernest V. Stoneman, 873
I Would See Jesus [J.T.] Allison's Sacred Harp Singers, 60; Charles Butts Sacred Harp Singers, 149
I Would Walk With My Savio[u]r Westbrook Conservatory Entertainers, 947
I Wouldn't Mind Dying Carter Family, 191
I Wouldn't Take Nothing For My Journey Dick Parman, 680
I Wouldn't Trade The Silver In My Mother's Hair Frank Luther, 518; John McGhee & Frank Welling, 563
I Wouldn't Trade The Silver In My Mother's Hair (For All The Gold In The World) Ambrose Haley, 389
Ice Man Blues Johnny Barfield, 94; Lee Frazier, 358
Ice Water Blues Deford Bailey, 88
I'd Die Before I'd Cry Over You Roy Hall, 391
I'd Like To Be In Texas Bradley Kincaid, 485
I'd Like To Be In Texas (When They Round Up In The Spring) Vernon Dalhart, 262–63
I'd Like To Be In Texas For The Round Up In The Spring Leon Chappelear, 200
I'd Like To Be Your Shadow In The Moonlight Carlisle Brothers, 169
I'd Like To Go Back Lulu Belle & Scotty, 516; J.B. Whitmire's Blue Sky Trio, 954
I'd Like To Go Down South Vaughan Quartet, 924
I'd Like To Go Down South Once More Vaughan Quartet, 925
I'd Like To Hear Elijah Pray Again Ruth Donaldson & Helen Jepsen, 323
I'd Like To Live There With You [E.R.] Nance Family, 648
I'd Like To Send A Message Up To Heaven Arthur Fields & Fred Hall, 339
I'd Like To Take An Aeroplane To Heaven Arthur Fields & Fred Hall, 340
I'd Love A Home In The Mountains Gene Autry, 81
I'd Love To Be A Cowboy Tennessee Ramblers [II], 897
I'd Love To Be A Cowboy (But I'm Afraid Of Cows) Patsy Montana, 636
I'd Love To Call You Sweetheart Jimmie Davis, 304
I'd Love To Fall Asleep Hugh Cross, 236
I'd Love To Live In Loveland Martin Melody Boys, 594
I'd Love To Live In Loveland (With A Girl Like You) Bar-X Cowboys, 92; Light Crust Doughboys, 503
I'd Rather Be An Old-Time Christian Mount Vernon Quartet, 645
I'd Rather Be With Rosy Nell Walter Smith, 846
I'd Rather Have Jesus Chuck Wagon Gang, 210; Coats Sacred Quartette, 216; Tiny Dodson's Circle-B Boys, 322
I'd Rather Stay Out In The Rain Meridian Hustlers, 615
I'd Settle Down For You Floyd Tillman, 910
Ida Red Roy Acuff, 49; Carson Bros., 180; Roland Cauley, 199; Dykes' Magic City Trio, 328; Frank Luther, 524; Clayton McMichen, 573; Land Norris, 662; Fiddlin' Powers & Family, 703; Riley Puckett, 717; Shelton Brothers, 830; South Georgia Highballers, 860; Ernest V. Stoneman, 874; Gid Tanner, 891; Floyd Thompson, 903; Tweedy Brothers, 918; Bob Wills, 963
Ida! (Sweet As Apple Cider) Hoosier Hot Shots, 436
Ida, Sweet As Apple Cider Milton Brown, 138; W. Lee O'Daniel, 665
Idaho Joe George Washington White, 949
Ider Red Clayton McMichen, 571
Ie Mes Beaux Yieux Guidry Brothers, 385

If Brother Jack Were Here Arkansas Woodchopper, 63; Frank[ie] Marvin, 596
If Father And Mother Would Forgive Ashley's Melody Makers, 68
If He Should Come Again Chumbler Family, 212
If Heaven's Any Better Rangers Quartet, 728
If I Came From A Monkey E. Arthur Lewis, 498
If I Can Count On You Bill Boyd, 123
If I Could Be With You Patrick (Dak) Pellerin, 685
If I Could Bring Back My Buddy Gene Autry, 78; Jimmy Long, 512; Norwood Tew, 898; Bob Wills, 963
If I Could Drift Back There Again Sam & Fred Friend, 359
If I Could Hear My Mother Wade Mainer, 583
If I Could Hear My Mother Pray Again Vernon Dalhart, 263; Gentry Brothers, 364; Jenkins Family, 456–57; Earl McCoy & Jessie Brock, 531; Lester McFarland & Robert A. Gardner, 542; McGee Brothers, 552; [E.R.] Nance Family, 648; Jack Pickell, 694; Posey Rorer, 813; Vaughan Quartet, 924
If I Could Only Blot Out The Past Arkansas Woodchopper, 63; McGee Brothers, 551–52; Frank Wheeler-Monroe Lamb, 948
If I Could Only Hear My Mother Pray Again Callahan Brothers, 152; Tex Walker, 935
If I Could See Mother Tonight Vernon Dalhart, 287
If I Cry You'll Never Know Jimmie Davis, 302
If I Didn't Care Light Crust Doughboys, 505
If I Die A Railroad Man Green Bailey, 88; Grant Brothers, 377
If I Don't Love You (There Ain't A Cow In Texas) Light Crust Doughboys, 504
If I Ever Get To Heaven Roy Newman, 658
If I Ever Leave The South Happy Fats, 396
If I Ever Meet The Girl Of My Dreams Dick Robertson, 758
If I Had Listened To Mother Wade Mainer, 584
If I Had Listened To My Mother Tom Darby & Jimmie Tarlton, 294
If I Had My Druthers Charlie Craver, 231; Harry "Mac" McClintock, 529
If I Had My Way Light Crust Doughboys, 505; Nite Owls, 661; Jack Pierce, 696; Bud Rainey, 724
If I Had Only Had A Home Sweet Home Hugh Cross, 235
If I Had Somebody Fleming & Townsend, 348
If I Had You Jimmy Long, 512
If I Knew Where I Was Going To Die Old Settlers, 668
If I Lose, I Don't Care Charlie Poole, 699
If I Lose, Let Me Lose J.E. Mainer's Mountaineers, 582
If I Only Could Blot Out The Past Lester McFarland & Robert A. Gardner, 547; Jimmie Revard, 743
If I Only Had A Home McGee Brothers, 552
If I Only Had A Home Sweet Home Kentucky Thorobreds, 479; Dick Parman, 679; Pie Plant Pete, 695; Three Tobacco Tags, 908; Westbrook Conservatory Entertainers, 947
If I Was Rich By Gum Ike Cargill, 158
If I Would Never Lose You York Brothers, 978
If I'm Faithful To My Lord Smith's Sacred Singers, 849
If I'm Wrong, I'm Sorry Buddy Jones, 466
If It Hadn't Been For You Texas Jim Lewis, 499
If It Wasn't For Mother And Dad Fisher Hendley, 417; Jack & Leslie, 451
If It Wasn't For The Rain Gene Autry, 84
If It's Wrong To Love You Charles Mitchell & His Orchestra, 630
If Jesse James Rode Again Massey Family, 609
If Jesus Goes With Me Emry Arthur, 65
If Jesus Leads This Army Howard Haney, 395
If Jesus Should Come Bill Carlisle, 160
If Mothers Could Live On Forever Ed McBride, 527
If One Won't Another One Will Carter Family, 190

Index to Titles

If The Light Has Gone Out In Your Soul Ernest Phipps, 691
If The River Was Whisky Charlie Poole, 700
If The Stork Comes To Our House Prairie Ramblers, 706
If There Wasn't Any Women In The World Fiddlin' John Carson, 176
If They String Me Up Jimmie Revard, 743
If Today Were The End Of The World Gene Autry, 83
If Tomorrow Never Comes Jimmie Davis, 304
If To-night Should End The World Bela Lam, 489
If We Can't Be Sweethearts Why Can't We Be Pals Al Dexter, 314
If You Call That Gone, Good Bye Rex Griffin, 383
If You Can't Get Five Take Two Milton Brown, 137
If You Can't Get The Stopper Out Break Off The Neck Fiddlin' John Carson, 177
If You Can't Hold The Man You Love Virginia Childs, 208
If You Can't Tell The World She's A Good Little Girl (Just Say Nothing At All) Vernon Dalhart, 263
If You Cared (You'd Have Spared Me This Trouble) Dickie McBride, 526
If You Don't Believe I'm Leavin' Jack Pierce, 696
If You Don't Like My Ford Coupe, Don't You Cadillac Me Owen Brothers & Ellis, 671
If You Don't Like My Peaches (Leave My Tree Alone) Shelton Brothers, 830
If You Don't Really Care Wilf Carter (Montana Slim), 186
If You Ever Had The Blues Homer Briarhopper, 127
If You Ever Learn To Love Me Tom Darby & Jimmie Tarlton, 294
If You Have The Blues Dick Hartman's Tennessee Ramblers, 408
If You Love Your Mother Morris Brothers, 643
If You Love Your Mother (Meet Her In The Skies) Buell Kazee, 472; Lester McFarland & Robert A. Gardner, 545
If You Meet A Tramp Norwood Tew, 899
If You Only Believed In Me Gene Autry, 86
If You See My Little Mountain Gal (Tell Her I'm Coming Back) Arthur Fields & Fred Hall, 344
If You See My Little Mountain Girl Arthur Fields & Fred Hall, 342
If You See My Saviour (Charlie) Monroe's Boys, 632; Odus & Woodrow, 667
If You Should Go Away Leon Selph, 824
If You Should Go Away I'd Cry Leon Selph, 824
If You Think I'm Not Worthy Bess Pennington, 685
If You Want Me You Got To Run Me Down Shelton Brothers, 829
If You Want To Go A Courtin' Gid Tanner, 891
If You Want To See A Girl That's [sic] Bobbie & Ruby Ricker, 748
If You Won't Be Mean To Me Nite Owls, 660
If You'd Only Love Me Leo Soileau, 854
If You'll Be Mine Hawaiian Pals, 412
If You'll Be Mine Again Jimmy Yates Groups, 975
If You'll Come Back Bill Boyd, 124; Light Crust Doughboys, 506
If You'll Let Me Be Your Little Sweetheart Gene Autry, 79
If You'll Let Me Be Your Sweetheart Rambling Rangers, 725
If You'll Take Me Back Bill Nettles, 654
If Your Heart Keeps Right Kanawha Singers, 469; Singing Preachers, 836
If Your Love Like The Rose Should Die Vernon Dalhart, 271, 273
If Your Saddle Is Good And Tight Carl T. Sprague, 862
If You're Sorry, Say You're Sorry Swing Billies, 885
Il Ta Prie De Mois (He Took You From Me) Leo Soileau, 855
Il Ya Pas La Claire De Lune (No Moonlight) Joe Werner, 944
I'll Always Be A Rambler Gene Autry, 74–75
I'll Always Be Glad To Take You Back Ernest Tubb, 914
I'll Always Be In Love With You Sons Of The West, 859
I'll Always Be True To You Bill Nettles, 654
I'll Always Be Your Buddy Texas Wanderers, 900
I'll Always Be Your Little Darling Bill Carlisle, 160
I'll Always Keep Smiling For You Wilf Carter (Montana Slim), 186
I'll Always Love You Claude Casey, 197; Karl & Harty, 471
I'll Always Love You (Should I Live A Thousand Years) Rice Brothers' Gang, 747
I'll Always Love You Darlin' Cecil & Vi, 199
I'll Be A Friend Of Jesus Wade Mainer, 583
I'll Be A Friend To Jesus Mr. & Mrs. R.N. Grisham, 384–85
I'll Be All Smiles Tonight Allen Brothers, 55; Carter Family, 191; Chuck Wagon Gang, 210; Oscar L. Coffey, 216; Andrew Jenkins, 455; Lester McFarland & Robert A. Gardner, 543; Linda Parker, 678; Reed Children, 734; Chas. Winters & Elond Autry, 968
I'll Be All Smiles To-night Love Luther B. Clarke, 214
I'll Be All Smiles, Love Bill Carlisle, 160
I'll Be Around Somewhere Sons Of The Pioneers, 859
I'll Be Back Home Georgia Peaches, 366
I'll Be Back In A Year (Little Darlin') Bill Boyd, 124; Red Foley, 351; Prairie Ramblers, 712; Texas Jim Robertson, 759
I'll Be Down Dick Hartman's Tennessee Ramblers, 408
I'll Be Faithful Cliff Bruner, 141
I'll Be Glad When You're Dead You Rascal You Milton Brown, 136
I'll Be Gone For Awhile Pete Pyle, 723
I'll Be Hanged (If They're Gonna Hang Me) Zora Layman, 492; Prairie Ramblers, 709
I'll Be Hanged If They're Goin' To Hang Me Tune Wranglers, 915
I'll Be Happy Stamps Quartet, 864
I'll Be Happy Again York Brothers, 977
I'll Be Happy Today Jimmie Davis, 299
I'll Be Here A Long, Long Time Allen Brothers, 56; Asa Martin, 593
I'll Be Home Some Day Carter Family, 192
I'll Be Honest With You (Answer To Be Honest With Me) Roy Rogers, 812
I'll Be In The Army For A Stretch Elton Britt, 130
I'll Be Listening Warren Caplinger, 157
I'll Be List'ning J.B. Whitmire's Blue Sky Trio, 954
I'll Be No Stranger There Chuck Wagon Gang, 211
I'll Be Ready Murphy Sacred Singers, 646
I'll Be Ready When The Bridegroom Comes McVay & Johnson, 580
I'll Be Satisfied Ernest V. Stoneman, 873
I'll Be Seein' You In Dallas, Alice Shelton Brothers, 830
I'll Be Singing Forever Stamps Quartet, 865
I'll Be Singing 'Round The Throne Someday Classic City Quartet, 214; Smith's Sacred Singers, 851
I'll Be There Frank & James McCravy, 535
I'll Be There, Mary Dear Roy Harvey, 410
I'll Be Thinking Of The Days Gone By Callahan Brothers, 152
I'll Be Thinking Of You Little Gal Gene Autry, 71–73; Frank[ie] Marvin, 603
I'll Be Thinking Of You Little Girl Gene Autry, 72, 75; Cecil Brown, 133; Texas Jim Lewis, 499; Carson Robison, 790; Yellow Jackets [II], 977
I'll Be True To The One I Love Jimmie Davis, 305; Joseph Falcon, 336; Frank Luther, 524; Prairie Ramblers, 708

I'll Be True While You're Gone Gene Autry, 85; Patsy Montana, 637
I'll Be Waiting For You Darling Patsy Montana, 636; Prairie Ramblers, 713
I'll Be Washed Carolina Tar Heels, 173
I'll Be With You Mother Sid Hampton, 394
I'll Be With You When The Roses Bloom Again Richard D. Burnett, 144; Carver Boys, 196; Vernon Dalhart, 254, 268–69; Frank Luther, 523
I'll Carry On Hi-Flyers, 420
I'll Climb The Blue Ridge Mountains Back To You Hugh Cross, 235
I'll Come Back Dear (If You're Still In Love With Me) Buddy Jones, 466
I'll Come Back To You Prairie Ramblers, 712; Village Boys, 931
I'll Die Before I Tell You Elton Britt, 130
I'll Dump Your Apple Cart Sunshine Boys, 882
I'll Ever Be Faithful To You Frank Wheeler-Monroe Lamb, 948
I'll Find A Sweet Rest Parker Quartette, 679
I'll Find You Bill Boyd, 123
I'll Fly Away Humbard Family, 447
I'll Forget Dear (That I Ever Loved You) Bob Dunn's Vagabonds, 327
I'll Forget I Ever Loved You Sons Of The West, 859
I'll Forget You Bye And Bye Ocie Stockard, 870
I'll Forgive You (But I Can't Forget) Roy Acuff, 51; Cliff Bruner, 140
I'll Get A Pardon In Heaven Three Tobacco Tags, 909
I'll Get Along Fleming & Townsend, 347
I'll Get Along Somehow Vernon Dalhart, 288–89; Arthur Fields & Fred Hall, 341, 345; Ernest Tubb, 913
I'll Get By Hi-Flyers, 419
I'll Get By (As Long As I Have You) Bob Dunn's Vagabonds, 327
I'll Get By Somehow Massey Family, 611
I'll Get It Shelly Lee Alley, 58
I'll Get Mine Light Crust Doughboys, 504; Bob Wills, 962
I'll Get Mine Bye And Bye Wilf Carter (Montana Slim), 186; Duke Clark, 213; Jimmie Davis, 300; Jess Hillard, 426; Buddy Jones, 465; Sons Of Acadians, 856
I'll Get Mine Bye And Bye No. 2, 3 Buddy Jones, 465
I'll Go Smith's Sacred Singers, 849
I'll Go Flipping Through The Pearly Gates Hodgers Brothers, 428
I'll Go On Loving You Lester McFarland & Robert A. Gardner, 549
I'll Go Riding Down That Texas Trail Gene Autry, 82
I'll Go Where You Want Me To Go Jenkins Family, 456; Old Southern Sacred Singers, 669
I'll Journey On Crowder Brothers, 237
I'll Keep My Old Guitar Adolph Hofner, 430
I'll Keep My Skillet Good And Greasy Uncle Dave Macon, 578
I'll Keep On Loving You Cliff Bruner, 140; Light Crust Doughboys, 505; Sons Of Acadians, 856; Tennessee Ramblers [II], 897
I'll Keep On Smiling Cliff Bruner, 140; Ted Daffan's Texans, 241
I'll Keep On Wishing For You Patsy Montana, 636
I'll Keep Singing On Rev. M.L. Thrasher, 905
I'll Keep Thinking Of You Shelly Lee Alley, 59; Cliff Bruner, 141
I'll Know Him Harmony Four, 401
I'll Lead A Christian Life Elder Golden P. Harris, 405
I'll Live On Carson Family Sacred Quartette, 180; Monroe Brothers, 633; Old Southern Sacred Singers, 669; Ernest V. Stoneman, 878
I'll Love Ya Till The Cows Come Home Joe Steen, 868
I'll Love You In My Dreams Leon Selph, 823
I'll Love You Till I Die Prairie Ramblers, 712
I'll Make A Ring Around Rosie Hoosier Hot Shots, 438
I'll Make It My Home Bush Brothers, 147
I'll Marry May In June Arthur Fields & Fred Hall, 343
I'll Meet Her When The Sun Goes Down Vernon Dalhart, 275–76; Pickard Family, 693; Virginia Dandies, 932
I'll Meet My Mother After All Posey Rorer, 813
I'll Meet My Precious Mother Fisher Hendley, 417
I'll Meet You At The Roundup In The Spring Wilf Carter (Montana Slim), 185
I'll Meet You In Loveland Frank Luther, 518
I'll Meet You In The Morning Majestic [Male] Quartet, 585; Whitey & Hogan, 952; J.B. Whitmire's Blue Sky Trio, 953
I'll Miss You When I'm Gone Dickie McBride, 526; Village Boys, 932
I'll Ne'er Forget My Mother And My Home Vernon Dalhart, 248
I'll Never Be Lonesome In Heaven Vaughan Quartet, 929
I'll Never Be Yours G.B. Grayson & Henry Whitter, 380
I'll Never Cry Over You Nite Owls, 660; Ernest Tubb, 913
I'll Never Fall In Love Again Delmore Brothers, 312
I'll Never Forsake You Carter Family, 195
I'll Never Get Drunk Anymore Lymon Norris, 662; Red Patterson's Piedmont Log Rollers, 682; Riley Puckett, 717; Shelton Brothers, 830
I'll Never Go There Any More (The Bowery) Uncle Dave Macon, 576
I'll Never Leave Old Dixie Again Walter Morris, 642
I'll Never Leave Old Dixieland Again Happy Valley Boys, 397
I'll Never Let The Devil Win [Smilin'] Ed McConnell, 530–31
I'll Never Let You Cry Alley Boys Of Abbeville, 59; Hi-Flyers, 419; Tennessee Ramblers [II], 897; Texas Wanderers, 900; Tune Wranglers, 916
I'll Never Let You Go Jimmy Wakely, 934
I'll Never Let You Go (Little Darlin') Gene Autry, 85
I'll Never Love You Ezra Buzzington's Rustic Revelers, 150
I'll Never Say "Never Again" Again Leon Chappelear, 201; Prairie Ramblers, 706
I'll Never Say Goodbye Light Crust Doughboys, 507
I'll Never Say Goodbye (Just So Long) Jimmie Davis, 306
I'll Never See Her Again Fleming & Townsend, 347
I'll Never See My Darling Anymore Carson Robison, 783–84
I'll Never Smile Again Gene Autry, 85; Elton Britt, 130
I'll Never Tell You That I Love You Rex Griffin, 384
I'll Never Worry Over You Bill Nettles, 654
I'll Not Be Your Sweetheart Joe Gore & Oliver Pettrey, 376
I'll Not Forget You Daddy John McGhee & Frank Welling, 558
I'll Not Kiss You Anymore Taylor Trio, 894
I'll Not Marry At All Kentucky Thorobreds, 479
I'll Play This For You Percy Babineaux-Bixy Guidry, 87
I'll Pray For You Denver Darling, 295
I'll Reap My Harvest In Heaven Roy Acuff, 50
I'll Remember You Love Brock & Dudley, 131
I'll Remember You Love In My Prayers Loren H. Abram, 47; Emry Arthur, 65; Blue Ridge Mountain Singers, 112; Four Pickled Peppers, 356; Hall Brothers, 391; Lester McFarland & Robert A. Gardner, 544; Pie Plant Pete, 695; Holland Puckett, 715; Floyd Skillern "The Mountain Troubadour," 837; Walter Smith, 846
I'll Remember You, Love, In My Prayer Odus & Woodrow, 667; Frank Wheeler-Monroe Lamb, 948

I'll Remember Your Love (In My Prayers) Lake Howard, 445
I'll Ride Back To Lonesome Valley Hank Snow, 852
I'll Ride On The Clouds With My Lord Freeman Quartette, 359; Vaughan Quartet, 929
I'll Rise, When The Rooster Crows Binkley Brothers Dixie Clodhoppers, 104
I'll Roll In My Sweet Baby's Arms Buster Carter & Preston Young, 181
I'll See You Again Hinkey Myers, 647
I'll See You In My Dreams Bob Wills, 963
I'll Serve The King Of Glory Carolina Gospel Singers, 171
I'll Smoke My Long Stemmed Pipe W.C. Childers, 205
I'll Soon Be Rolling Home Hoosier Hot Shots, 437
I'll Still Write Your Name In The Sand Freeman & Ashcraft, 358
I'll String Along With You Milton Brown, 137
I'll Take Care Of Your Cares Prairie Ramblers, 709
I'll Take Her Back Jimmie Revard, 743
I'll Take Her Back (If She Wants To Come Back) Universal Cowboys, 919
I'll Take Low And Go Down Welby Toomey, 912
I'll Take You Back Again Shelly Lee Alley, 58; Bill Boyd, 124
I'll Take You Home Again, Kathleen Bradley Kincaid, 485; Riley Puckett, 717; Vaughan Quartet, 924; Zack & Glenn, 979
I'll Tell The World (She's A Good Little Girl) Bob Dunn's Vagabonds, 327
I'll Tell The World That I Love You Hank Snow, 853
I'll Tell You About The Women Fleming & Townsend, 346
I'll Tell You What I Saw Last Night Hickory Nuts, 420
I'll Think Of You Mitchell Brothers, 630
I'll Think Of You Sweetheart Arthur Fields & Fred Hall, 340
I'll Tickle Nancy Uncle Dave Macon, 578
I'll Travel Alone Ted Daffan's Texans, 240
I'll Wait For You Gene Autry, 85; Patsy Montana, 637
I'll Wait For You Dear Al Dexter, 315
I'll Wear A White Robe Central Mississippi Quartet, 199–200
Ill-Fated Akron [The] John McGhee & Frank Welling, 563
Ill-Fated Morro Castle [The] Buck Nation, 651
Ils La Volet Mon Trancas Joseph Falcon, 335
I'm A Broken Hearted Cowboy Dwight Butcher, 149
I'm A Child Of The King John McGhee & Frank Welling, 556
I'm A Cow Poke Pokin' Along Gene Autry, 87
I'm A Diamond From The Rough Allen Brothers, 55
I'm A Ding Dong Daddy (From Dumas) Light Crust Doughboys, 503; Bob Wills, 962; Zeb & Zeeke, 979
I'm A Do Right Cowboy Tex Ritter, 750
I'm A Do Right Papa Leon Chappelear, 201
I'm A Dog House Daddy Dixie Ramblers [IV], 319
I'm A Fool To Care Ted Daffan's Texans, 240
I'm A Free Little Bird Elmer Bird, 106
I'm A Fugitive From A Chain Gang Frank Luther, 519; Bob Miller, 623
I'm A Gold Diggin' Papa Fred Kirby, 486
I'm A Gonna Be In That Glad Band Jones Brothers Trio, 467
I'm A Handsome Man Bob Hartsell, 409
I'm A Handy Man To Have Around Shelton Brothers, 830
I'm A Heart-Broken Mama Virginia Childs, 208
I'm A High Steppin' Daddy Bill Boyd, 123
I'm A Jolly Cowboy Rowdy Wright, 974
I'm A Little Dutchman Paul Warmack, 939
I'm A Lone Star Cowboy J.D. Farley, 336
I'm A Lonely Hobo Brown Brothers, 138
I'm A Lonesome Cowboy Jim[my] Boa, 114; Goebel Reeves, 737
I'm A Long Time Traveling Away From Home [J.T.] Allison's Sacred Harp Singers, 59

I'm A Man Of Constant Sorrow Emry Arthur, 66
I'm A Natural Born Cowboy Tex Ritter, 750
I'm A Pennsylvania Bum Jack Urban, 920
I'm A Poor Pilgrim J.E. Mainer's Mountaineers, 582
I'm A Pris'ner Of War Carson Robison, 797
I'm A Pris'ner Of War (On A Foreign Shore) Johnny Bond, 117; Denver Darling, 296
I'm A Railroad Man (Waiting On A Weary Train) Gene Autry, 76
I'm A Rambler Dewey Hayes, 414
I'm A Roamin' Cowboy Jesse Rodgers, 799
I'm A Rolling Deal Family, 307
I'm A Rootin' Shootin' Tootin' Man From Texas New Dixie Demons, 655
I'm A Stern Old Bachelor Chubby Parker, 676–77
I'm A Straight Shooting Cowboy Walter Hurdt, 448
I'm A Swingin' Hill Billie Singer Modern Mountaineers, 630
I'm A Texas Cowboy Arkansas Woodchopper, 63
I'm A Tough Shooting Hombre From Texas Carl Boling, 116
I'm A Truthful Fellow Frank[ie] Marvin, 604
I'm A Truthful Fellow (True Blue Bill) Frank[ie] Marvin, 604
I'm A Twelve O'Clock Feller (In A Nine O'Clock Town) Al Bernard, 100
I'm A Wandering Bronco Rider Rowdy Wright, 974
I'm A Wandering Ranger Tex Fletcher, 348
I'm A Wild And Reckless Cowboy (From The West Side Of Town) Patsy Montana, 635
(I'm A) Hillbilly Boy From The Mountains Jake & Carl, 453
I'm Afraid It's Love Three Tobacco Tags, 908
I'm Afraid Of Bees New Dixie Demons, 655
I'm A-Gittin' Ready To Go Carson Robison, 785
I'm A-Goin' Away In The Morn Uncle Dave Macon, 575
I'm Alabama Bound Delmore Brothers, 311
I'm All Alone Rochford & Peggs, 797
I'm Alone Again Joe Werner, 944
I'm Alone Because I Love You Callahan Brothers, 152; Lester McFarland & Robert A. Gardner, 548; Carson Robison, 785–86
I'm Alone In This World Blue Ridge Gospel Singers, 109; Bill Shepherd, 831
I'm Alone, All Alone Ernest V. Stoneman, 878
I'm Always Dreaming Of You Bob Atcher, 69; Gene Autry, 76–77; Jimmy Long, 511; Sons Of Dixie, 856; Floyd Tillman, 910
I'm Always Out Of Luck E.M. Bartlett Groups, 96
I'm Always Thinking Of You Emry Arthur, 66–67
I'm Always Whistling The Blues Allen Brothers, 56
I'm An Old Cow Hand Carson Robison, 795
I'm An Old Cowhand (From The Rio Grande) Patsy Montana, 634; Sons Of The Pioneers, 857
I'm A-Ridin' Up The Old Kentucky Mountain Patsy Montana, 636
I'm As Free A Little Birdie As Can Be John D. Foster, 354
I'm As Pretty Little Bird As I Can Be John Hammond, 394
I'm Atlanta Bound Gene Autry, 75–76
I'm Beginning To Care Gene Autry, 83–84
I'm Blue Rosa Lee Carson, 180
I'm Blue And Lonesome Gene Autry, 75; Fleming & Townsend, 346; Frank[ie] Marvin, 604; Saddle Tramps, 818
I'm Bound For Home Buffalo Ragged Five, 142; North Canton Quartet, 662
I'm Bound For The Promised Land John McGhee & Frank Welling, 562
I'm Bound To Ride Arthur Smith, 841
I'm Building A Home Roy Acuff, 49
I'm Building Me A Home, Sweet Home Grady & Hazel Cole, 217

I'm Checking Out Sunshine Boys, 882
I'm Comin' Home Darlin' Gene Autry, 86; Eddie Dean, 308
I'm Coming Back To Dixie And You Richard Brooks & Reuben Puckett, 132
I'm Counting On The Mountain Moon Dickie McBride, 526
(I'm Crying 'Cause I Know I'm) Losing You Nite Owls, 660
I'm Crying My Heart Out Over You Sons Of The Pioneers, 859
I'm Doin' A Peach Of A Job (With A Little Peach Down In Ga.) Village Boys, 932
I'm Doin' That Thing Fred L. Jeske, 458
I'm Doin' The Best I Can Vernon Dalhart, 244
I'm Doing It Too Hi-Flyers, 420
I'm Doomed To Follow The Bugle Smiley Burnette, 145
I'm Dreaming Of Someone I Love Bonnie Dodd & Murray Lucas, 322
I'm Dreaming Tonight Of The Old Folks Dickie McBride, 526
I'm Driftin' And Shiftin' My Gears Shelton Brothers, 830
I'm Drifting Back To Dreamland Vernon Dalhart, 278; Jimmie Davis, 303; Flannery Sisters, 346; John D. Foster, 354; Kelly Brothers, 476–77; John McGhee & Frank Welling, 558; W. Lee O'Daniel, 666; Riley Puckett, 717, 721; Carson Robison, 782; Steelman Sisters, 867
I'm Drinking My Troubles Down Walter Hurdt, 448
I'm Finding Glory Stamps Quartet, 865
I'm Forever Blowing Bubbles Lester McFarland & Robert A. Gardner, 545; John McGhee & Frank Welling, 559; Clayton McMichen, 566; Riley Puckett, 717; Jimmy Yates Groups, 976
I'm Free Hall County Sacred Singers, 392
I'm Free (From The Chain Gang Now) Jimmie Rodgers, 808; Bob Wills, 962
I'm Free A Little Bird As I Can Be Clayton McMichen, 572
I'm Free Again Lester McFarland & Robert A. Gardner, 543; John McGhee & Frank Welling, 554, 560
I'm Free At Last "Dock" Walsh, 937
I'm From Missouri Sons Of The Ozarks, 856
I'm Gettin' Nowhere Jimmie Revard, 743
I'm Getting Absent Minded Over You Nite Owls, 661
I'm Getting Ready To Go Arty Hall, 390; Riley Puckett, 720; Carson Robison, 787–88
I'm Gittin' Ready To Go Carson Robison, 785
I'm Glad For Your Sake Melody Boys, 615
I'm Glad I Counted The Cost Hill Brothers, 424; Walter Smith, 847
I'm Glad I Met You After All Ernest Tubb, 914
I'm Glad I'm A Bum Arthur Fields & Fred Hall, 341, 344; Jack Hagwood, 388; Ernest Hare, 399
I'm Glad I'm A Hobo Cliff Carlisle, 165
I'm Glad I'm Free Happy Bud Harrison, 406
I'm Glad I'm Married Roy Harvey, 410
I'm Glad I'm One Of Them Carson Family Sacred Quartette, 180
I'm Glad It's Over Now Radio Rubes, 723
I'm Glad My Wife's In Europe Fiddlin' John Carson, 175, 177, 179; George Reneau, 741
I'm Glad That Jesus Won Rev. Joseph Callender, 154
I'm Glad We Didn't Say Goodbye Roy Hall, 391
I'm Glory Bound L.V. Jones, 467
I'm Goin [sic] Crazy Hugh Gibbs String Band, 368
I'm Goin' Back To Coney Isle Lester "Pete" Bivins, 107
I'm Goin' Back To My Little Mountain Shack Al Clauser, 214
I'm Goin' Back To Red River Valley Tex Fletcher, 348
I'm Goin' Back To Whur I Come From Carson Robison, 797
I'm Goin' To Walk On The Streets Of Glory West Virginia Night Owls, 946

I'm Goin' West Hank Keene, 474
I'm Goin' West To Texas Patsy Montana, 636
I'm Going Monroe Brothers, 633
I'm Going Away Delmore Brothers, 310; Bartmon Montet-Joswell Dupuis, 637
I'm Going Away (Cause You Don't Treat Me Right) Clarence Ganus, 362
I'm Going Away And You Can't Bring Me Back Hickory Nuts, 420
I'm Going Away From The Cotton Fields Hugh Cross, 235
I'm Going Away To Leave You Hickory Nuts, 420
I'm Going Away To Leave You, Love Uncle Dave Macon, 574
I'm Going Back Jack & Jean, 451
I'm Going Back To Alabama Delmore Brothers, 309; White Brothers (Joe & Bob), 951
I'm Going Back To Caroline Lester "Pete" Bivins, 107
I'm Going Back To North Carolina Kelly Harrell, 403
I'm Going Back To Old Carolina Smith's Carolina Crackerjacks, 848
I'm Going Back To Old Texas Tex Owens, 671
I'm Going Back To Sadie Buddy Jones, 466
[I'm Going Back To The Farm] Paul Crutchfield & John Clotworthy, 238
I'm Going Back To The Girl I Love Emry Arthur, 66
I'm Going Back To The Mountains Fisher Hendley, 417
I'm Going Back To 'Tucky Pie Plant Pete, 695
I'm Going Bye And Bye Rev. M.L. Thrasher, 905
I'm Going Down To Jordan Ernest Thompson, 902
I'm Going Higher Someday Ruth Donaldson & Helen Jepsen, 323
I'm Going Home Ruth Donaldson & Helen Jepsen, 323; Troy Martin & Elvin Bigger, 594
I'm Going Home This Evening Karl & Harty, 470
I'm Going Home To Die No More Blue Ridge Gospel Singers, 109; Giddens Sisters, 369; George Long, 510
I'm Going Home To My Wife Chumbler Family, 212
I'm Going Through Frank & James McCravy, 537
I'm Going To Georgia Carolina Tar Heels, 173; Grant Brothers, 377; Riley Puckett, 719
I'm Going To Get Me A Honky Tonky Baby Buddy Jones, 466
I'm Going To Leave The Old Home Edgewater Sabbath Singers, 329
I'm Going To Live With Jesus Smith's Sacred Singers, 851; Rev. M.L. Thrasher, 905
I'm Going To Settle Down Hugh Cross, 236; Riley Puckett, 719; Carl Williams, 957
I'm Going To Take The Train To Charlotte Fiddlin' John Carson, 177
I'm Going Where The Blues Ain't Never Known Ike Cargill, 158
I'm Going Where The Chilly Winds Don't Blow Riley Puckett, 718
I'm Gonna Be Long Gone Texas Jim Robertson, 759
I'm Gonna Be Long Gone (When I Go Away) Johnny Bond, 117
I'm Gonna Change All My Ways Village Boys, 932
I'm Gonna Change My Way Delmore Brothers, 310
I'm Gonna Cook Your Goose Slim Harbert, 398
I'm Gonna Die With A Broken Heart Bob Skyles, 839
I'm Gonna Fix Your Wagon Prairie Ramblers, 711; Shelton Brothers, 828
(I'm Gonna Get High And Say) Goodbye To The Blues Dickie McBride, 526
I'm Gonna Have A Cowboy Weddin' Patsy Montana, 636
I'm Gonna Hop Off The Train Bill Boyd, 121
I'm Gonna Learn To Swing Clayton McMichen, 572
I'm Gonna Let The Bumble Bee Be Shelton Brothers, 828

I'm Gonna Live Anyhow Until I Die Tennessee Hill Billy, 896
I'm Gonna Live On High Hoke Rice, 746
I'm Gonna Move Further Down The Road Robert N. Page, 672
I'm Gonna Ride Clay Long, 510
I'm Gonna Ride In Elijah's Chariot John McGhee & Frank Welling, 553
I'm Gonna Ride To Heaven On A Streamline Train Wilf Carter (Montana Slim), 182
I'm Gonna Rise Up Clarence Ganus, 362
I'm Gonna Round Up My Blues Gene Autry, 84
I'm Gonna Sail Away Jones Brothers Trio, 467
I'm Gonna Say Goodbye To The Blues Modern Mountaineers, 631
I'm Gonna Sit Right Down And Write Myself A Letter Earl & Willie Phelps, 689
I'm Gonna Throw My Lasso Texas Jim Robertson, 759
I'm Gonna Yodel My Way To Heaven Frank[ie] Marvin, 604–05; Johnny Marvin, 607
I'm Grievin' For Believin' In A Lie Dickie McBride, 526
I'm Gwine Back To Dixie Leake County Revelers, 495
I'm Gwine To Heaven When I Die Jenkins Family, 457
I'm Happy In Prison Crowder Brothers, 238
I'm Happy Now Vaughan Quartet, 927
I'm Happy When You're Happy Al Dexter, 314; Ross Rhythm Rascals, 814
I'm Happy With My Savior McDonald Quartet, 540
I'm Headin' For Home Sweet Home Bill Carlisle, 160
I'm Headin' For That Ranch In The Sky Cliff Bruner, 140
I'm Here To Get My Baby Out Of Jail Tex Fletcher, 348; Karl & Harty, 470; Shelton Brothers, 828
I'm His At Last Buice Brothers, 142; McDonald Quartet, 540
I'm Hittin' The Trail Wilf Carter (Montana Slim), 184
I'm Homesick For Heaven Warren Caplinger, 157; Frank & James McCravy, 535
I'm Homesick For Heaven Tonight Frank & James McCravy, 536
I'm Hot Like That Hoke Rice, 745
I'm Human Too Massey Family, 613
I'm In Heaven Arthur Fields & Fred Hall, 341, 345
I'm In Here A Long Long Time Allen Brothers, 57
I'm In His Care Vaughan Quartet, 925
I'm In Love With You Honey Bill Boyd, 124
I'm In The Army Now Carson Robison, 797
I'm In The Doghouse Again Dick Reinhart, 739
I'm In The Doghouse Now Buddy Jones, 465
I'm In The Doghouse Now No. 2 Buddy Jones, 465
I'm In The Glory Land Way Jack & Leslie, 451; J.E. Mainer's Mountaineers, 582
I'm In The Jail House Now—No. 2 Frank[ie] Marvin, 603
I'm In The King's Highway Rangers Quartet, 728
I'm In The Way Stamps Quartet, 864
I'm Jealous Of The Twinkle In Your Eye Bill Boyd, 123
I'm Just A Black Sheep Jack Jackson, 452; John I. White, 950
I'm Just A Country Boy Leon Selph, 824
I'm Just A Country Boy At Heart Ross Rhythm Rascals, 814
I'm Just A Drunkard's Child James Scott-Claude Boone, 821
I'm Just A Gambler Frank[ie] Marvin, 603
I'm Just A Hitch-Hiker On The Road To Love George Wade, 933
I'm Just A Lonesome Cowboy Goebel Reeves, 737
I'm Just A Poor Hillbilly Looking Fer A Hill Prairie Ramblers, 711
I'm Just A Ramblin' Gambler Willard Hodgin[s], 429
I'm Just A Ramblin' Man Cliff Carlisle, 168
I'm Just A Yodeling Rambler Kenneth Houchins, 444
I'm Just An Outcast Bar-X Cowboys, 93
I'm Just As Happy (As I've Ever Been) Nite Owls, 660

I'm Just Going Down To The Gate Dear Ma Vernon Dalhart, 287
I'm Just Here To Get My Baby Out Of Jail Blue Sky Boys, 113
I'm Just Here To Get My Baby Out Of Jail—Part 2 Dorsey & Beatrice Dixon, 321
I'm Just Passin' Through Rex Griffin, 383
I'm Just Wild About Harry Hoosier Hot Shots, 439
I'm Knocking At Your Door Again Jimmie Davis, 305
I'm Leavin' On That Blue River Train Carson Robison, 795
I'm Leavin' This Town Fleming & Townsend, 346
I'm Leavin' You Delmore Brothers, 309, 312
I'm Leaving My Troubles Behind Al Dexter, 314
I'm Led By Love Huff's Quartette, 446
I'm Left All Alone Joseph Falcon, 336
I'm Lending You To Uncle Sammy Bob Atcher, 70
I'm Livin' On The Mountain Log Cabin Boys, 508
I'm Living The Right Life Now J.E. Mainer's Mountaineers, 582
I'm Lonely And Blue Gene Autry, 72; Cliff Carlisle, 161; Hoke Rice, 745; Carson Robison, 775; Jimmie Rodgers, 800–801
I'm Lonely Since Mother's Gone Nichols Brothers, 659
I'm Lonely Tonight Sweetheart Liston Scroggins, 822
I'm Lonely Too Ashley's Melody Makers, 68
I'm Lonesome For The Lone Range Dwight Butcher, 149
I'm Lonesome For You Caroline Odis Elder, 331; Girls Of The Golden West, 370
I'm Lonesome Tonight Leo Soileau, 855
I'm Lonesome Too Monie Chasteen, 203; Bill Cox, 225; Ted Lunsford, 517; Jimmie Rodgers, 804
I'm Lonesome, I Guess Arthur Smith, 842
I'm Lonesome, Sad And Blue Fred Kirby, 486
I'm Longing For My Carolina Home Three Tobacco Tags, 908
I'm Longing For My Old Kentucky Home B.F. Kincaid, 482
I'm Longing To Belong To Someone Earl Shirkey & Roy Harper, 832
I'm Looking Ahead Arthur Fields & Fred Hall, 341
I'm Looking For A Brand New Mama Harry Hillard, 425
I'm Looking For A Gal Frank[ie] Marvin, 603
I'm Looking For A Girl Hoosier Hot Shots, 436
I'm Looking For A Sweetheart (Not A Friend) Red Foley, 352
I'm Looking For The Bully Of The Town Prairie Ramblers, 707
I'm Looking Over A Four Leaf Clover Louisiana Strollers, 514; Yellow Jackets [II], 976
I'm Losing My Mind Over You Ted Daffan's Texans, 240; Al Dexter, 315
I'm Mighty Blue Jack & Jean, 451
I'm Missing You Ernest Tubb, 914
I'm Mississippi Bound Delmore Brothers, 309
I'm Nine Hundred Miles From Home Fiddlin' John Carson, 175
I'm No Good On Earth Leon Selph, 823
I'm No Stranger To Jesus Bush Brothers, 147; McDonald Quartet, 541
I'm Nobody's Darling But Mine Three Tobacco Tags, 907
I'm Nobody's Darling On Earth Kelly Harrell, 404
I'm Not Angry With You, Darling Four Pickled Peppers, 356; Walter Smith, 847
I'm Not As Good As I Appear W.C. Childers, 205
I'm Not Coming Home Tonight Bob Atcher, 69
I'm Not Satisfied Here Palmetto Male Quartette, 674
I'm Not Sorry Now Happy Fats, 396
I'm Not Turning Back Cousin Levi, 224
I'm Not Turning Backward Wade Mainer, 583

I'm Old And Feeble Fiddlin' John Carson, 179
I'm On My Journey Home Denson Quartet, 313; Dye's Sacred Harp Singers, 328
I'm On My Way Kentucky Holiness Singers, 478
I'm On My Way Back Asa Martin, 592
I'm On My Way To A Holy Land Grady & Hazel Cole, 217
I'm On My Way To Canaan's Land Panhandle Pete, 674
I'm On My Way To Glory Deal Family, 307; Lyric Quartette, 525
I'm On My Way To Heaven R.C. Garner, 363; Jenkins Family, 457; [E.R.] Nance Family, 648
I'm On My Way To The Promised Land Bill Carlisle, 160
I'm On The Chain Gang Now Arthur Fields & Fred Hall, 340
I'm On The Right Road Now Stamps Quartet, 864
I'm On The Right Side Now Freeman Quartette, 359
I'm On The Sunny Side Jenkins Family, 457; John McGhee & Frank Welling, 554, 560–61
I'm Only A Convict's Wife Socko Underwood, 919
I'm Only A Dude In Cowboy Clothes Wilf Carter (Montana Slim), 184
I'm Only Here On A Visit Stamps Quartet, 864
I'm Only On A Visit Here Freeman Quartette, 358; E.B. Holden Quartet, 432; Smith's Sacred Singers, 849
I'm Only Suggesting This Happy Jack, 397
I'm Over The Jordan Tide R.C. Garner, 363
I'm Paying The Price Wilbur Ball, 90
I'm Pining For The Pines And Caroline Arthur Fields & Fred Hall, 342–43
I'm Popeye The Sailor Man Frank Luther, 523
I'm Poundin' The Rails Again Johnny Bond, 116
I'm Pretending Bob Skyles, 839
I'm Putting You Out Of My Mind Dixie Ramblers [IV], 319
I'm Reading Your Letter Again, Dear Bob Atcher, 70
I'm Ready To Reform Rex Griffin, 383
I'm Redeemed Alcoa Quartet, 53
I'm Returning To My Log Cabin Home Thos. A. Burton, 146
I'm Ridin' Down The Trail To Albuquerque Al Clauser, 214
I'm Ridin' Now Walter Hurdt, 448
I'm Ridin' The Trail Back Home Clayton McMichen, 572
I'm Riding Around Them Cattle Woody Leftwich, 496
I'm Riding The Blinds On A Train Headed West Frank[ie] Marvin, 601
I'm Riding The Blinds On A West Bound Train Frank[ie] Marvin, 601
I'm Rollin' On Prairie Ramblers, 705
I'm Rolling Along Buell Kazee, 473
I'm Sad And Blue Perry County Music Makers, 687
I'm Sailing On Harmony Four, 401
I'm Satisfied Earl Johnson, 459; Lester Smallwood, 840; Gid Tanner, 887, 891
I'm Satisfied In Loving You Dick Reinhart, 739
I'm Satisfied With You Vernon Dalhart, 251, 257–58
I'm S-A-V-E-D Blue Sky Boys, 114; Georgia Yellow Hammers, 367; Karl & Harty, 470
I'm Savin' Saturday Night For You Cliff Carlisle, 166; Roy Newman, 657; Shelton Brothers, 829
I'm Savin' Up Coupons (To Get One Of Those) Lew Childre, 207
I'm Saving Up Coupons "Peg" Moreland, 641
I'm Saying Goodbye York Brothers, 977
I'm Serving Days Leon Chappelear, 201
I'm Sitting On Top Of The World Leon Chappelear, 201; Shelton Brothers, 827
I'm Sitting Sad And Lonely Red Headed Brier Hopper, 731
I'm Smiling (Just To Hide A Broken Heart) Shelly Lee Alley, 59
I'm So Alone With The Crowd Ambrose Haley, 389
I'm So Glad That Jesus Found Me Jenkins Family, 456

I'm So Glad Trouble Don't Last Always Jimmy Long, 511
(I'm So Lonely) Since My Darling Went Away Ernest Branch & Bernice Coleman, 126
I'm So Lonesome Tonight Claude Casey, 197
I'm So Sorry Bar-X Cowboys, 93
I'm So Tired Rouse Brothers, 815
I'm So Used To You Now Shelly Lee Alley, 58
I'm Sorry Ross Rhythm Rascals, 814; Smoky Wood, 971
I'm Sorry I Ever Met You Leon Selph, 824
I'm Sorry I Made You Cry Dan Hornsby, 442; Jack Major, 586; Nite Owls, 661
I'm Sorry I Said Goodbye Ted Daffan's Texans, 240
I'm Sorry It Ended This Way Three Tobacco Tags, 909
I'm Sorry Now Carlisle Brothers, 169; Jimmie Davis, 305; Hi-Flyers, 419
I'm Sorry That We Said Goodbye Johnny Lee Wills, 967
I'm Sorry That You've Gone Bill Mounce, 645
I'm Sorry That's All I Can Say Carlisle Brothers, 169; Byron Parker, 675; Three Tobacco Tags, 907
I'm Sorry We Met Gene Autry, 72–73; Howard Keesee, 474–75; Jimmie Rodgers, 801
I'm Sorry We Said Goodbye Bob Wills, 965
I'm Starving To Death For Love Three Tobacco Tags, 907
I'm Still A Fool Over You Jimmie Davis, 304
I'm Still In Love With You Shelly Lee Alley, 58; Cliff Bruner, 140
I'm Still Waiting For You Wilf Carter (Montana Slim), 183
I'm Taking My Audition To Sing Up In The Sky Warren Caplinger, 157
I'm The Child To Fight Uncle Dave Macon, 576
I'm The Lady That's Known As Lou Adelyne Hood, 434–35
I'm The Man That Rode The Mule Around The World Vernon Dalhart, 263
I'm The Man That Rode The Mule 'Round The World Charlie Poole, 699
I'm The Man That's Been Forgotten No. 1, 2 Johnny Marvin, 607
I'm The One Jimmie Davis, 305
I'm The Roughest And Toughest Fred Kirby, 487
I'm Thinking Tonight Of Mother Julian Johnson & Leon Hyatt, 461
I'm Thinking Tonight Of My Blue Eyes Bob Atcher, 69; Gene Autry, 86; Carroll Black, 107; Wilf Carter (Montana Slim), 186; Carter Family, 188, 193; Denver Darling, 295; Jimmie Davis, 305; Karl & Harty, 470; Massey Family, 613; Saddle Tramps, 817; Shelton Brothers, 827
I'm Thinking Tonight Of You Dear Fisher Hendley, 416
I'm Through Wishing On Stars Tennessee Ramblers [II], 897
I'm Through With Women Walter Hurdt, 448
I'm Through With Women Blues Ike Cargill, 158
I'm Through With You Little Girl Hi Neighbor Boys, 420
I'm Tired Of Everything But You Roy Newman, 658
I'm Tired Of Living Here Alone Blue Ridge Highballers, 110
I'm Tired Of Living On Pork And Beans Gid Tanner, 888
I'm Tired Of Mountain Women Wiley Walker & Gene Sullivan, 936
I'm Tired Of You Cliff Bruner, 140
I'm Troubled, I'm Troubled Blue Sky Boys, 113
I'm Trusting In You Roy Rogers, 812
I'm Trying The Leaves So They Won't Come Down Carson Robison, 790
I'm Tying The Leaves Hinkey Myers, 647
I'm Tying The Leaves So They Won't Come Down Warren Caplinger, 157; Log Cabin Boys, 508; Lester McFarland & Robert A. Gardner, 547
I'm Up In The Air About Mary Riley Puckett, 719
I'm Waitin' Mabel Jimmie Revard, 743
I'm Waiting For Ships That Never Come In Jimmie Davis,

303; Jack Dawson, 306; Jack & Bill, 451; Marc Williams, 959
I'm Walking In The Light Owen Brothers & Ellis, 671
I'm Wastin' My Time Prairie Ramblers, 712
I'm Wearin' The Britches Now Bill Carlisle, 159
I'm Wild About That Thing Tune Wranglers, 915
I'm Wondering How Ernest Tubb, 914
I'm Wondering Now Shelly Lee Alley, 58; Jimmie Davis, 304
I'm Working On A Building Carter Family, 192
I'm Worried Now Delmore Brothers, 310; Milo Twins, 628
I'm Writing A Letter To Heaven Vernon Dalhart, 292
I'm Writing To You, Little Darling (The Answer To "Nobody's Darling") Jesse Rodgers, 799
I'm Your Real And True Friend Buddy Jones, 465
Imitating The Birds On The Mountain—Part 1, 2 Garley Foster, 353
Imitations Paul Robinson, 760
In 1960 You'll Find Dixie Looking Just The Same Hugh Cross, 235
In 1992 Bill Cox, 225; Vernon Dalhart, 290; Arthur Fields & Fred Hall, 342
In A Box Car Around The World Cliff Carlisle, 166
In A Chapel In The Moonlight Yellow Jackets [II], 977
In A City Far Away Chris Bouchillon, 119
In A Cool Shady Nook McGee Brothers, 551; Mason Stapleton, 867
In A Cottage By The Sea Carolina Buddies, 170
In A Cottage On A Hill South Sea Serenaders, 860
In A Friendly Sort Of Way [Smilin'] Ed McConnell, 530–31
In A Garden Chumbler Family, 212; Merritt Smith, 844
In A Graveyard On The Hill Ernest Hare, 399
In A Home Far Away Ruth Neal & Wanda Neal, 652
In A Land Where The Sun Goes Down Hi-Flyers, 419
In A Little Garden Riley Puckett, 722
In A Little Green Valley Al Dexter, 314
In A Little Gypsy Tea Room Beverly Hill Billies, 103; Light Crust Doughboys, 503; Riley Puckett, 721
In A Little House On The Hill Texas Wanderers, 900
In A Little Inn Way Out In Indiana Elton Britt, 129
In A Little Red Barn Leon Chappelear, 201; Light Crust Doughboys, 504
In A Little Red Barn On A Farm Down In Indiana Frank Luther, 522
(In A Little Shanty) Hummin' To My Honey Jesse Rodgers, 799
In A Little Town In Old Kentucky Elmer Bird, 106
In A Little Village Churchyard Carter Family, 194; J.E. Mainer's Mountaineers, 582; Socko Underwood, 919
In A Little While Bush Brothers, 147; Smith's Sacred Singers, 850
In A Lonely Jail Lymon Norris, 662
In A Lonely Little Cottage Carl Trimble, 913
In A Lonely Village Churchyard John McGhee & Frank Welling, 560
In A Mansion Of Aching Hearts Vernon Dalhart, 247
In A Shanty Down In Shanty Town Johnny Marvin, 607
In A Shanty In Old Shantytown Bar-X Cowboys, 92; Ambrose Haley, 389; Rhoda Hicks, 421; Rice Brothers' Gang, 747
In A Sleepy Country Town Johnny Barfield, 93
In All My Dreams Bill Cox, 225
In An Old Dutch Garden (By An Old Dutch Mill) Hoosier Hot Shots, 439
In An Old Log Cabin Ranch Boys, 726
In An Old Log Cabin (By An Old Log Fire) W. Lee O'Daniel, 665
In An Old Southern Home Plantation Boys, 698
In Arkansas Jimmie Davis, 299

In Berry Picking Time Sally Foster, 355; "Peg" Moreland, 641
In Christ, Our Lord Stamps Quartet, 865
In Days Of Yesterday Al Dexter, 314
In Dear Old Tennessee Arthur Fields & Fred Hall, 342
In Dear Old Tennessee (Where Someone Waits For Me) Arthur Fields & Fred Hall, 341
In El Rancho Grande Milton Brown, 136
In Gethsemane, Alone Carolina Gospel Singers, 170
In Heaven [E.R.] Nance Family, 648
In Kansas Lester McFarland & Robert A. Gardner, 545; Chubby Parker, 677
In Kentucky Lester McFarland & Robert A. Gardner, 548
In Lover's Lane Farmer Sisters, 336
In My Book Of Dreams Vagabonds, 922
In My Cabin Tonight Jimmie Davis, 301
In My Childhood Days Red Foley, 351
In My Dear Old Southern Home Monroe Brothers, 632
In My Dear Old Sunny South Tennessee Ramblers [I], 897
In My Dreams Leon Selph, 824
In My Heart Sunshine Four, 882
In My Heart There Rings A Melody Moody Bible Institute Trio, 637
In My Heart You'll Always Be Mine Jimmie Davis, 304
In My Little Home In Tennessee Blue Sky Boys, 113; Rambling Kid & The Professor, 725
In My Old Cabin Home Fiddlin' John Carson, 177
In My Old Cabin Home In The Mountains Tom & Roy, 911
In My Old Kentucky Home Len & Joe Higgins, 421
In Nineteen Ninety-Two Arthur Fields & Fred Hall, 344
In Old New Hampshire Lou & Nellie Thompson, 904
In Old Wyoming Hinson, Pitts & Coley, 427
In Ole' Oklahoma Light Crust Doughboys, 505; Patsy Montana, 636
In Our Hearts The Bells Of Heaven Sweetly Chime E. Arthur Lewis, 498
In Our Home Sweet Home Smith's Sacred Singers, 851
In Our Little Home Sweet Home Jack Jackson, 452
In Steps Of Light Vaughan Quartet, 928
In Texas For The Round-Up In The Spring Texas Jim Robertson, 760
In That City That The Bible Calls Four Square Rev. Edward Boone, Mrs. Edward Boone & Miss Olive Boone, 117
In That Crowning Day L.V. Jones, 466
In That Happy Home Over Yonder George Long, 510
In That Home Beyond The Sky Dutch Coleman, 218
In That Morning Moody Bible Sacred Harp Singers, 637
In That Old Fashioned Buggy Johnny Roberts, 756
In That Vine Covered Chapel (In The Valley) Delmore Brothers, 311; W. Lee O'Daniel, 665; Walton West, 946
In That War W.A. Lindsay, 507
In That Wonderful Garden Of Mine Ted Rodgers, 810
In The Baggage Coach Ahead Vernon Dalhart, 244–46, 248, 281, 285, 291; Arthur Fields & Fred Hall, 338; Otto Gray, 379; Andrew Jenkins, 454; Frank Luther, 523–24; Ernest Thompson, 902; Charlie Wills, 966
In The Beautiful Land Rev. Joseph Callender, 154
In The Big Rock Candy Mountain No. 2 Bill Cox, 224
In The Big Rock Candy Mountains Jack Golding, 374; Carson Robison, 767
In The Blue Hills Of Virginia Delmore Brothers, 311; Frank Luther, 518
In The Blue Of The Night Cliff Bruner, 139
In The Chapel In The Moonlight Ranch Boys, 727
In The City Where There Is No Night Owen Brothers & Ellis, 671
In The Cradle Of My Dreams Gene Autry, 77; Jimmy Long, 512

In The Cumberland Mountains Carson Robison, 789–90, 792
In The Days Of Yesterday Al Dexter, 314
In The Dog House Now Prairie Ramblers, 708
In The Echo Of My Heart Bob Atcher, 70
In The Evening Hugh Cross, 235; Jack & Jean, 451
In The Evening Take Me Home Gentry Family, 365
In The Fall Of '29 Light Crust Doughboys, 501
In The Forest Hackberry Ramblers, 388
In The Garden Arthur Cornwall & William Cleary, 223; Highleys, 421; Dalton Johnson & Wallace Dangfield, 459; Light Crust Doughboys, 502; MacDowell Sisters, 542; Lester McFarland & Robert A. Gardner, 544; John McGhee & Frank Welling, 553, 560–61; Montgomery Quartet, 637; Ruth Pippin & Thelma Davenport, 698; Singing Preachers, 836; J. Douglas Swagerty, 883; Vagabonds, 921; Williams & Williams, 960
In The Garden Of My Heart Rev. Joseph Callender, 154
In The Garden Where The Irish Potatoes Grow Dr. Smith's Champion Hoss Hair Pullers, 843
In The Gloaming Frank & James McCravy, 532; Dixie Mason, 608
In The Golden Bye And Bye Ashford Quartette, 67; Ernest V. Stoneman, 873
In The Golden West With You Jack Pierce, 695
In The Good Old Days (Part 1, 2) Len Nash, 650
In The Good Old Days Of Long Ago Uncle Dave Macon, 575
In The Good Old Summer Time Richard Brooks & Reuben Puckett, 132; Gentry Brothers, 365; Hugh Gibbs String Band, 368; Leake County Revelers, 494; Uncle Dave Macon, 575; Walter C. Peterson, 688; Riley Puckett, 717; Yellow Jackets [I], 976
In The Happy Long Ago Smith's Sacred Singers, 849
In The Happy Over Yonder Mount Vernon Quartet, 645
In The Harbor Of Home Sweet Home Edd Rice, 744; Three Little Maids, 906
In The Heart Of Kentucky Max Friedman, 359
In The Heart Of The Beverly Hills Beverly Hill Billies, 102
In The Heart Of The City Johnny Barfield, 94
In The Heart Of The City That Has No Heart Emry Arthur, 65
In The Hills Of Arkansas Bob Miller, 618, 622–23
In The Hills Of Carolina Gene Autry, 77
In The Hills Of Caroline Joe Cook, 220
In The Hills Of Old Kentucky Cliff Carlisle, 162; Vernon Dalhart, 278–79; Bradley Kincaid, 485; Oliver & Allen, 670; Dick Parman, 679–80; Carson Robison, 762
In The Hills Of Old Kentucky (My Mountain Rose) Melton & Waggoner, 615
In The Hills Of Old Virginia Hugh Cross, 236; Hill Brothers, 424; Clayton McMichen, 569
In The Hills Of Pennsylvania Elton Britt, 129
In The Hills Of Roane County Blue Sky Boys, 114
In The Hills Of Tennessee Hugh Cross, 235; Vernon Dalhart, 288; Clarence Greene, 382; Jess Johnston, 464; Byrd Moore, 639; Jack Moore, 640; Jimmie Rodgers, 807–08
In The Hills Over There Eldon Baker, 89
In The Hour Of Trial Frank & James McCravy, 531
In The House At The End Of The Road Happy Fats, 396
In The Jailhouse Now Arkansas Woodchopper, 63; Ernest Hare, 399; Frank[ie] Marvin, 595–97; Jimmie Rodgers, 800; Unknown Artists [IV], 920
In The Jail-House Now—No. 2 Jimmie Rodgers, 804, 809
In The Jailhouse Now No. 2 Gene Autry, 73
In The Land Beyond The Blue Wade Mainer, 583
In The Land Of Beginning Again John D. Foster, 354
In The Land Of The Never Was Goebel Reeves, 735
In The Land Of The Sky Cliff Carlisle, 164

In The Land Of Zulu Gene Autry, 83
In The Land Where The Roses Never Fade Ralph E. Johnson, 462
In The Land Where's She's At Rest Anglin Brothers, 61
In The Little Shirt That Mother Made For Me Bradley Kincaid, 484–85
In The Little White Church On The Hill Bob Miller, 624; Vagabonds, 921
In The Master's Presence Stamps Quartet, 864–65
In The Mission By The Sea Zora Layman, 492
In The Moonlight Hinson, Pitts & Coley, 427
In The Moonlight With You Leo Soileau, 855
In The Morning Light Crust Doughboys, 507
In The Old Carolina State (Where The Sweet Magnolias Bloom) Uncle Dave Macon, 575
In The Pines Tex Dunn, 327; Clayton McMichen, 571; Bill Monroe, 632; Arthur Smith, 842; "Dock" Walsh, 937
In The Royal Hawaiian Hotel Nite Owls, 661
In The Shade Of The Old Apple Tree Richard Brooks & Reuben Puckett, 132; Milton Brown, 137; Crockett [Family] Mountaineers, 233; Jack Golding, 374; Kentucky Thorobreds, 479; B.F. Kincaid, 482; Frank & James McCravy, 532; Clayton McMichen, 567; McMichen's Harmony Boys, 573; Uncle Dave Macon, 576; Dick Parman, 680; Pickard Family, 692; Riley Puckett, 718
In The Shade Of The Old Pine Tree Fred Kirby, 486
In The Shade Of The Parasol Barber & Osborne, 93; Scottdale String Band, 821
In The Shadow Of Clinch Mountain Carter Family, 194
In The Shadow Of The Cross Majestic [Male] Quartet, 585; Rangers Quartet, 728
In The Shadow Of The Pine Gene Autry, 72; Kelly Harrell, 404; Earl Johnson, 460; M.O. Keller, 475; Doc Roberts, 752; Connie Sides, 834; Ernest V. Stoneman, 872, 877
In The Shadow Of The Pines Carter Family, 194; Robert Hoke & Vernal West, 431; Buell Kazee, 473; Leake County Revelers, 495; Lester McFarland & Robert A. Gardner, 545; Asa Martin, 592; Tune Wranglers, 915
In The Sleepy Hills Of Tennessee Vagabonds, 921
In The Streets Of Laredo Bradley Kincaid, 483
In The Sweet Bye And Bye Sid Harkreader, 400; Frank Luther, 524; Uncle Dave Macon, 576
In The Time Of Long Ago Walter Morris, 642
In The Town Where I Was Born Vernon Dalhart, 288; "Peg" Moreland, 641
In The Valley Of Broken Hearts Hart & Cates, 406
In The Valley Of Kentucky Lester McFarland & Robert A. Gardner, 546; Taylor Trio, 894
In The Valley Of The Moon Gene Autry, 78–79; Frank Luther, 522; Leo Soileau, 855; Tom & Roy, 911
In The Valley Of The Shenandoah Carter Family, 195
In The Valley Of Yesterday Vernon Dalhart, 292; Frank Luther, 521; Vagabonds, 922
In The Valley Where The Bluebonnets Grow Andrew Jenkins, 455
In The Village By The Sea James Johnson, 461
In The Vine-Covered Church 'Way Back Home Vagabonds, 921
In The West Where Life Is Free Jimmie Davis, 302
In The Year Of Jubilo Frank Jenkins, 455
In Those Cruel Slavery Days Fields Ward, 939
In Your Heart You Love Another Leo Soileau, 856
Indian Creek Arthur Smith, 841
Indian Dance Ted Markle, 587
Indian Dawn Jack Major, 585
Indian Tom Tom [The] Big Chief Henry's Indian String Band, 103
Indian War Whoop Hiter Colvin, 219; Floyd Ming, 629

Indiana Hoosier Hot Shots, 437; Kanawha Singers, 469
Indiana (Back Home In Indiana) Ross Rhythm Rascals, 814
Indiana March Rochford & Peggs, 797; Westbrook Conservatory Entertainers, 947
Indiana Pal Of Mine Howard Keesee, 475
Indian's Dream [The] Big Chief Henry's Indian String Band, 103
Innocent Boy Jack Urban, 921
Innocent Convict [The] Kenneth Houchins, 444
Innocent Of Murder Brown Brothers, 138
Innocent Prisoner Cliff Carlisle, 164; Bradley Kincaid, 484; Frank Luther, 520
Inside The Gate Laurel Firemen's Quartet, 491
Inspiration Allen Brothers, 56
Instalment [sic] Song [The] Claude Casey, 197
International Bum [The] Webb Whipple, 948
Intoxicated Rat Dorsey & Beatrice Dixon, 321
Intro. They're Wearing 'Em Higher In Hawaii Johnny Marvin, 606
Intro: W.W. Macbeth, 526
Invictus Vaughan Quartet, 927
Ione Taylor-Griggs Louisiana Melody Makers, 893
Irene Waltz Collier Trio, 218
Irish Christening [The] Chubby Parker, 677
Irish Clog Southern Moonshiners, 860
Irish Frolic [The] Mintons Ozark String Band, 629
Irish Police [The] Tom Darby & Jimmie Tarlton, 293
Irish Wash Woman Kessinger Brothers, 481
Irish Washerwoman Tommy Dandurand, 293; William B. Houchens, 443; Nicholson's Players, 659; Tom Owens Barn Dance Trio, 672; Doc Roberts, 753; Uncle Joe Shippee, 831
Irish Washerwoman, Kitty Clyde [The] Doc Roberts, 753
Irishman And The Barber [The] Cromwell Brothers, 234
Is It Far? Flat Creek Sacred Singers, 346; Murphy Sacred Singers, 646
Is It True Canova Family, 156; Red Foley, 352
Is It True What They Say About Dixie Hoosier Hot Shots, 437; Massey Family, 610; Rice Brothers' Gang, 746
Is It Well With Your Soul? Carolina Quartette, 172; [E.R.] Nance Family, 648; Jack Pickell, 694; Praetorian Quartet, 704; Smith's Sacred Singers, 850; Vaughan Quartet, 923–24
Is My Name Written There Frank & James McCravy, 537
Is She Praying There? (Charlie) Monroe's Boys, 632
Is That Religion Shanks Bros. Trio, 825
Is There No Chance For Me Tonight Love Red Headed Brier Hopper, 732
Is There No Kiss For Me Tonight Love? Benny Borg, 118
Is There Still Room For Me Jimmie Revard, 743
Is There Still Room For Me ('Neath The Old Apple Tree) Clayton McMichen, 572
Is This A Dream Texas Wanderers, 900
Is Your Name Written There Herald Goodman, 375
I'se Born In A Texas Town Patt Patterson, 682
I'se Goin' From The Cotton Fields John McGhee & Frank Welling, 554
I'se Gwine Back To Dixie Uncle Dave Macon, 575; Grover Rann, 729
Island Reverie Tune Wranglers, 916
Island Unknown—Part 1, 2 [The] A.C. (Eck) Robertson, 758
Isle Of Capri Beverly Hill Billies, 103; Fredricksburg Future Farmers, 358; Prairie Ramblers, 705; Riley Puckett, 721
Isles Across The Sea Lew Preston, 713
It Ain't Gonna Rain No Mo' Airport Boys, 52; Fiddlin' John Carson, 175; Hank Penny, 686; Gid Tanner, 890; Tune Wranglers, 915
It Ain't Gonna Rain No More Vernon Dalhart, 242
It Ain't No Fault Of Mine Cliff Carlisle, 166; Graham Brothers, 377

It Ain't No Good Johnny Barfield, 94; Jimmie Revard, 742
It Ain't No Place For Me Clarence Gill, 369
It Ain't Nobody's Bizness Lulu Belle & Scotty, 516
It Ain't Nobody's Biz'ness What I Do Hoosier Hot Shots, 437
It Ain't Right Dick Hartman's Tennessee Ramblers, 408; New Dixie Demons, 655
It Ain't So Good Richard Cox, 229
It Came Upon A Midnight Clear Westbrook Conservatory Entertainers, 946
It Came Upon The Midnight Clear Frank & James McCravy, 536
It Can't Be Done Allen Brothers, 56; Cotton Butterfield, 149; Lew Childre, 207; Otto Gray, 378–79; Three Tobacco Tags, 908
It Cleanseth Me Perry Kim & Einar Nyland, 481
It Didn't Do Nothing But Rain Lew Childre, 207
It Doesn't Matter Claude Casey, 197
It Doesn't Matter Now Shelly Lee Alley, 59
It Don't Do Nothing But Rain Lew Childre, 207
It Don't Mean A Thing Range Riders, 727; Tune Wranglers, 915
It Had To Be That Way Floyd Tillman, 910
It Is Better Farther On Carter Family, 194
It Is Love Morris Brothers, 643
It Is So Blue Without Him Joseph Falcon, 334
It Is Well Gospel Sanctified Singers, 376
It Is Well With Your Soul XC Sacred Quartette, 975
It Is You, Just You, Jesus Needs Maury Pearson, 683
It Just Suits Me J.P. Ryan, 817; Lowe Stokes, 871
It Keeps On Raining Paradise Joy Boys, 674
It Looks Like Lucy Arthur Fields & Fred Hall, 345
It Looks Like Rain In Cherry Blossom Lane Ambrose Haley, 389
It Looks To Me Like A Big Time Tonight Sid Harkreader, 400
It Made You Happy When You Made Me Cry Rice Brothers' Gang, 747
It Makes A Lot Of Difference Now Shelly Lee Alley, 59
It Makes No Difference Now Gene Autry, 85; Cliff Bruner, 140; Wilf Carter (Montana Slim), 185; Jimmie Davis, 303; Tom Dickey Show Boys, 316; Fisher Hendley, 417; Light Crust Doughboys, 504; Sons Of Acadians, 856
It Makes No Never Mind Red Foley, 351; Prairie Ramblers, 713
It Might Have Been Worse Byrd Moore, 640
It Must Be Love Bob Dunn's Vagabonds, 326
It Must Have Been Something I Et Arthur Fields & Fred Hall, 344
It Never Can Be Cindy Walker, 935; Charlie Wills, 966
It Pays To Serve Jesus Carlyle Brooks & Madeline Ward, 132; Lester McFarland & Robert A. Gardner, 548
It Seems I've Always Held Your Hand Frank Luther, 520
It Seems Like Yesterday Charlie Wills, 966
It Tain't No Good York Brothers, 977
It Takes A Little Rain With The Sunshine Fiddlin' John Carson, 176
It Takes A Long Tall Brownskin Gal Dick Parman, 679–80
It Takes An Old Hen To Deliver The Goods Cliff Carlisle, 167
It Took My Breath Away Shelly Lee Alley, 59
It Was For Me Perry Kim & Einar Nyland, 481–82; Rev. M.L. Thrasher, 905
It Was Midnight On The Ocean Tune Wranglers, 914
It Was Only A Dream Hall Brothers, 391
It Was Wonderful Then (And It's Wonderful Now) Massey Family, 612
It Will Always Be Wonderful There Peck's Male Quartette, 684

It Will Have To Do Until The Real Thing Comes Along Elton Britt, 129
It Will Make Heaven Brighter Vaughan Quartet, 928–29
It Will Matter But Little At Last M. Homer Cummings & Son Hugh, 240
It Will Not Be Long Carolina Gospel Singers, 171; Stamps Quartet, 864
It Won't Be Long Shelly Lee Alley, 59; Carolina Ladies Quartet, 171; Parker Quartette, 679; Smith's Sacred Singers, 850; Stamps Quartet, 865
It Won't Be Long (Till I'll Be Leaving) Roy Acuff, 50; Anglin Brothers, 61
It Won't Be Long Now Sid Harkreader, 401
It Won't Be Long Till My Grave Is Made Walter Smith, 846–47
It Won't Be Long, It May Be Soon Rev. Joseph Callender, 154
It Won't Be Very Long E.M. Bartlett Groups, 96; J.B. Whitmire's Blue Sky Trio, 953
It Won't Do You No Good Dick Reinhart, 739
It Won't Happen Again Bill Cox, 225
It Won't Happen Again For A Hundred Years Or More Fiddlin' John Carson, 177
It Won't Happen Again For Months Bill Chitwood, 208
It Won't Hurt No More Buster Carter & Preston Young, 181
It Worries Me Lummie Lewis, 500
Italian Dream Waltz Madisonville String Band, 580
Italy Bascom Lamar Lunsford, 517
It'll Aggravate Your Soul Carter Family, 192
It'll Never Happen Again Binkley Brothers Dixie Clodhoppers, 104
It's A Cowboy's Night To Howl Wilf Carter (Montana Slim), 186
It's A Lonely Trail Dixieland Swingsters, 320; Hoosier Hot Shots, 439
It's A Lonely Trail (When You're Travelin' All Alone) Hoosier Hot Shots, 438
It's A Lonesome Old Town (When You're Not Around) Nite Owls, 661
It's A Long Lane That Doesn't Have A Turning Johnny Barfield, 94
It's A Long Long Road To Travel Alone Carter Family, 195
It's A Long Way To Tipperary John & Emery McClung, 530; Gid Tanner, 889
It's A Long, Long Way To Tipperary Jimmie Revard, 743
It's A Lovely Day Tomorrow Massey Family, 612
It's A Rough Road To Georgia Henry Whitter, 955
It's A Shame To Whip Your Wife On Sunday Fiddlin' John Carson, 177
It's A Sin To Tell A Lie Elton Britt, 129; Joseph Falcon, 336; Riley Puckett, 722
It's A Weary World Arthur Smith, 842
It's A Weary World Without My Blue Eyes Shelton Brothers, 830; Sunshine Boys, 881
It's Alcatraz For Me Whitey & Hogan, 952
It's All Because That I Love You Ike Cargill, 158
It's All Coming Home To You Jimmie Davis, 300; Russell Brothers, 816
It's All Gone Now Arthur Cornwall, 223
It's All In The Game Sawyer Sisters, 820
It's All My Fault Adolph Hofner, 430
It's All Over Now Modern Mountaineers, 631
It's All Over Now (I Won't Worry) Cliff Bruner, 140; Wilf Carter (Montana Slim), 185; Wiley Walker & Gene Sullivan, 936
It's All Over Now I'm Glad We're Through Johnny Barfield, 94
It's All So Sweet Jimmie Revard, 743

It's All Your Fault Cindy Walker, 935; Charlie Wills, 966
It's An Unfriendly World Anglin Brothers, 61; J.B. Whitmire's Blue Sky Trio, 953
It's Awful What Whiskey Will Do Hawaiian Pals, 412
It's Bad To Be A Good Girl Bob Skyles, 839
It's Been A Long Long Time Floyd Tillman, 910
It's Been A Long Long Time Since I Been Home Tennessee Hill Billy, 896
It's Been So Long Light Crust Doughboys, 503
It's Been Years (Since I've Seen My Mother) Jimmie Davis, 301
It's Best To Behave Adolph Hofner, 430
It's Blues Morris Brothers, 643
It's Funny What Love Will Make You Do Light Crust Doughboys, 506
It's Funny What Whiskey Will Do Elmer Bird, 106
It's Funny When You Feel That Way Woody Leftwich, 496; Asa Martin, 589; Frank[ie] Marvin, 598–99
It's Great To Be Back In The Saddle Again Wilf Carter (Montana Slim), 186
It's Hard Eldon Baker, 89
It's Hard But It's True Jimmie Davis, 304
It's Hard To Be Bound Down In Prison Asa Martin, 592; Riley Puckett, 716
It's Hard To Be Shut Up In Prison David Miller, 626
It's Hard To Kiss Your Sweetheart Richard Brooks & Reuben Puckett, 132
It's Hard To Leave You, Sweet Love Lewis McDaniels, 539
It's Hard To Love And Can't Be Loved Buster Carter & Preston Young, 180; Harvey Powell, 702
It's Hard To Love And Not Be Loved Shelton Brothers, 830
It's Hard To Make Gertie Walker's Corbin Ramblers, 937
It's Hard To Please Your Mind Philyaw Brothers, 690; Arthur Smith, 841; Sunshine Boys, 881
It's Just A Matter Of Time Carson Robison, 797
It's Just A Tumble Down Shack (But I'd Like To Go Back To My Old Kentucky Home) Three Little Maids, 906
It's Just Like Heaven Freeman Quartette, 359; Parker Quartette, 679; Vaughan Quartet, 928–29
It's Just Like Heaven To Me Palmetto Male Quartette, 674
It's Just My Imagination Bill Mounce, 645
It's Just The Same Roy Rogers, 812
It's Killing Me Bill Cox, 227
It's Kinda Late To Be Sorry Jimmy Hart, 406
It's Late And Time To Go Joseph Falcon, 336
(It's Mighty Cold) When The Sun Goes Down Buddy Jones, 465
It's More Than I Can Bear Dutch Coleman, 218
It's Movin' Day Charlie Poole, 700
It's My Time Now Jimmie Revard, 742
It's Nobody's Business But My Own John McGhee & Frank Welling, 560
It's None Of Your Business Lake Howard, 445
It's Only A Matter Of Time Wiley Walker & Gene Sullivan, 936
It's Only An Old Fashioned Cottage Riley Puckett, 720
It's Roundup Time In Reno Gene Autry, 83
It's Sad To Leave You, Sweetheart Walter Smith, 846
It's Simple To Flirt Riley Puckett, 716
It's Sinful To Flirt Vernon Dalhart, 259; Milo Twins, 628; Ernest V. Stoneman, 877
It's So Hard To Be Just A Pal To You Pete Pyle, 723
It's Spring In The Rockies Again Peaceful Valley Folk, 683
It's Takin' Me Down Delmore Brothers, 310
It's The Same The Whole World Over Carson Robison, 782
It's The Top Of Everything Miller's Merrymakers, 628
It's Tight Like That Freeny Harmonizers, 359; Earl & Willie Phelps, 689; Hoke Rice, 745

It's Time To Say Aloha Frank Luther, 522
It's Time To Say Aloha To You Vernon Dalhart, 292
It's Too Bad For You Allen Brothers, 56
It's Too Late To Say You're Sorry Jimmy Wakely, 934
It's Too Late To Say You're Sorry Now Al Dexter, 315
It's Tough On Everybody Buddy Baker, 89
It's True I'm Just A Convict Goebel Reeves, 737
It's Up To You Al Dexter, 315
It's You I Adore Wanderers, 938
It's Your Worry Now Denver Darling, 295; Light Crust Doughboys, 506
I've Always Been A Rambler G.B. Grayson & Henry Whitter, 380–81
I've Always Loved My Old Guitar Walter Hurdt, 448
I've Anchored in Love Divine Carver Boys, 196
I've Been Drafted Bill Mounce, 645
I've Been Hoodooed Canova Family, 155–56
I've Been Listening In On Heaven Rangers Quartet, 728
I've Been Looking For A Sweetheart Ike Cargill, 158
I've Been Married Three Times Chris Bouchillon, 120
I've Been Redeemed John McGhee & Frank Welling, 553; Norris Quartet, 662
I've Been To The Pen And I'm Goin' Again (Gosh Darn My Rowdy Soul) Charlie Craver, 232
I've Been Working On The Railroad Sandhills Sixteen, 820
I've Changed My Mind Jones Brothers Trio, 467; Rangers Quartet, 728; Whitey & Hogan, 952; J.B. Whitmire's Blue Sky Trio, 954
I've Changed My Penthouse For A Pup-Tent Texas Rangers, 900
I've Cried My Last Tear Over You Canova Family, 156
I've Done The Best I Could Tex Ritter, 751
I've Found A Friend Blue Sky Boys, 114; Bush Brothers, 147
I've Found A Hiding Place Chuck Wagon Gang, 211; Rangers Quartet, 728
I've Found A New Baby Bill Mounce, 645
I've Found My Love Bill Cox, 229
I've Found Somebody New Texas Jim Lewis, 500
I've Got A Bimbo Down On The Bamboo Isle Hoosier Hot Shots, 437
I've Got A Gal Dixie Ramblers [II], 319
I've Got A Gal In Baltimore Georgia Crackers, 366
I've Got A Gal In Ev'ry State Prairie Ramblers, 712
I've Got A Gal In The Mountains Hank Keene, 474
I've Got A Girl Named Susie Doc Roberts, 753
I've Got A House In Chicago Pete Herring, 418
I've Got A Pocketful Of Dreams Prairie Ramblers, 710
I've Got A Silver Haired Sweetheart In The Golden West Patsy Montana, 636
I've Got A White Man Working For Me Fiddlin' John Carson, 178
I've Got A Woman On Sourwood Mountain Earl Johnson, 460
I've Got Enough Of Your Foolin' Slim Harbert, 398
I've Got It Roy Newman, 658
I've Got Man Trouble Zora Layman, 492
I've Got My Heart On My Sleeve Jimmie Davis, 305
I've Got No Honey Babe Now Frank Blevins, 108
I've Got No Use For The Women Tune Wranglers, 915; Rowdy Wright, 974
I've Got The Big River Blues Delmore Brothers, 309
I've Got The Blues W. Lee O'Daniel, 666
I've Got The Blues #2 Shelly Lee Alley, 58
I've Got The Blues For Mammy Milton Brown, 137; Zeke Williams, 959
I've Got The Blues In My Heart Lew Preston, 713
I've Got The Chain Store Blues Allen Brothers, 55
I've Got The Jail House Blues Gene Autry, 75

I've Got The Misery Ernest Rogers, 810
I've Got The Mourning Blues Uncle Dave Macon, 574
I've Got The Railroad Blues Delmore Brothers, 310; George Reneau, 741
I've Got The Right Key Baby Hank Penny, 686
I've Got The Walkin' Blues Roy Newman, 658
I've Got The Wonder Where She Went (Blues) Bob Wills, 961
I've Got These Oklahoma Blues Kenneth Houchins, 444
I've Got Those Oklahoma Blues Bill Boyd, 124
I've Got To Be Gittin' Away Anglin Brothers, 61
I've Got Trouble In Mind Jimmie Revard, 742
I've Grown So Lonely For You Happy Fats, 396
I've Grown So Used To You Frank & James McCravy, 538; Lester McFarland & Robert A. Gardner, 547
I've Had A Big Time Today Arthur Smith, 842
I've Had The Blues Before Johnny Bond, 117
I've Just Been A Brakeman Callahan Brothers, 152
I've Learned A Lot About Women Roy Rogers, 811
I've Learned My Lesson Now Floyd Tillman, 910
I've Lost My Love Lake Howard, 445
I've Lost You So Why Should I Care Nite Owls, 660
I've Loved You So True Lewis McDaniels, 539
I've Nothing To Live For Now Dickie McBride, 526; Lester McFarland & Robert A. Gardner, 550
I've Only Loved Three Women Jimmie Rodgers, 808
I've Ranged, I've Roamed, I've Travelled Jimmie Rodgers, 802
I've Really Learned A Lot Ernest Tubb, 914
I've Rode The Southern And The L. & N. Callahan Brothers, 153
I've Sold My Saddle For An Old Guitar Roy Rogers, 811–12
I've Started For The Kingdom John Henry Howard, 444
I've Still Got A Place In My Heart For You Jack Bankey, 92
I've Still Got Ninety Nine Morgan Denmon, 312
I've Still Got Niney-Nine Monroe Brothers, 633
I've Tried So Hard To Forget You Jimmie Davis, 304
I've Waited Honey, Waited Long For You Dick Parman, 680
I've Waited Long For You Kentucky Thorobreds, 479; Dick Parman, 679
I've Waited Too Long To Prepare Paramount Sacred Four, 675
I've Wandered To The Village Tom Land Norris, 662
Ivy Bob Palmer & Monte Hall, 673
Ivy Covered Cabin Parker & Dodd, 678
Ivy Covered Cabin Home Frank Luther, 519

Jack And Babe Blues No. 1, 2 Jack Rose, 814
Jack And Jill Johnny Marvin, 607
Jack And Joe Hill Brothers, 424; McDonald Brothers, 539; Riley Puckett, 717; George Reneau, 741; Roy Shaffer, 825; Ernest V. Stoneman, 872
Jack And Mae Blankenship Family, 108
Jack And Mary Russell & Louis Burton, 146
Jack And May Russell & Louis Burton, 146; Tom Darby & Jimmie Tarlton, 294; Golden Melody Boys, 373; Roy Harvey, 409; Bess Pennington, 685; Taylor Trio, 894
Jack Lafiance At The Telephone Jos. P. Landry, 490
Jack Lafiance On De Crawfish Jos. P. Landry, 490
Jack O' Diamonds Jules Allen, 54; Bill Bender, 99; Lew Childre, 207; Patt Patterson, 681
Jack Of All Trades Prairie Ramblers, 705; Carson Robison, 764–65, 768, 773
Jack Of Diamonds Lew Childre, 207; Da Costa Woltz's Southern Broadcasters, 970
Jack The Yodeling Mule Earl Powell, 702
Jacks Creek Watlz Doc Roberts, 753
Jack's Polka Jack Pierce, 696

Jackson Lee Wells, 943
Jackson County Bill Cox, 224
Jackson County Rag Wing's Rocky Mountain Ramblers, 968
Jacksonville Stomp [The] Three Floridians, 906
Jacobs [sic] Ladder Chumbler Family, 212
Jacob's Ladder Frank & James McCravy, 531–32, 536; Carson Robison, 787
Ja-Da Jimmie Revard, 743
Ja-Da (Ja-da, Ja-da, Jing-Jing-Jing) Prairie Ramblers, 711
Jai Maitritte Pas Sa Hackberry Ramblers, 388
Jai Pas Bien Fey Hackberry Ramblers, 387
Jai Passe Devonde Ta Parte Hackberry Ramblers, 387
Jai Pres Parley Hackberry Ramblers, 387
Jail Bird [The] Holland Puckett, 715
Jail House Blues Amedie Ardoin, 62; Gene Autry, 75–76; Johnny Marvin, 606; Chester Southworth, 861
Jail House Now George Edgin, 330
Jailer's Daughter [The] Bill Cox, 226
Jailhouse Lament Tex Ritter, 750
Jailhouse Rag David Miller, 627
Jake Bottle Blues Lemuel Turner, 917
Jake Leg Blues Byrd Moore, 639
Jake Leg Rag W.T. Narmour & S.W. Smith, 649
Jake Leg Wobble Ray Brothers, 729
Jake Walk Blues Allen Brothers, 55
Jake Walk Papa Asa Martin, 592
Jakeitus Blues Bernard [Slim] Smith, 842
Jam Making Time Hoosier Hot Shots, 436
Jamais Marriez Walker Brothers, 936
Jammin' On The Steel Guitar Bar-X Cowboys, 93
Japanese Breakdown Scottdale String Band, 822
Japanese Sandman Rice Brothers' Gang, 746
Japanese Stomp Lowe Stokes, 871
Jaw Bone Pope's Arkansas Mountaineers, 701
Jay Bird Dalton Johnson & Wallace Dangfield, 459; Yellow Jackets [I], 976
Jazz Baby Bill Cox, 228
Jazz Mad Man Dick Hartman's Tennessee Ramblers, 408
Jazzbo Joe Light Crust Doughboys, 505
Je Jais Pos C Cannye (Ain't Misbehavin') Patrick (Dak) Pellerin, 685
Je Marche Nuit Et Jour Douglas Bellar & Kirby Riley, 99
Je Me Demande Si Tu Te Cent Comme Mois Je Me Cent (I Wonder If You Feel The Way I Do) Sons Of Acadians, 856
Je Me Trouve Une Dolie Fille (I Find A Pretty Girl) Delma Lachney, 489
Je M'En Suis Alle (I'm Going Away) Bartmon Montet-Joswell Dupuis, 637
Je M'En Vas Dans Le Chemin (Going Down The Road) Delma Lachney, 489
Je M'Ennui Ce Soir (I'm Lonesome Tonight) Leo Soileau, 855
Je Ne Tracasse Pas Plus (I Don't Worry Now) Leo Soileau, 854
Je Serais Vrai A Quelqu'un J'Aime (I'll Be True To The One I Love) Joseph Falcon, 336
Je Suis Laissee Seule (I'm Left All Alone) Joseph Falcon, 336
Je Suis Parti Sous Le Grand Chemin Tres Dissatisfe (I Left The Highway Very Dissatisfied) Joseph Falcon, 336
Je Suis Se Seul (I Am So Lonely) Joseph Falcon, 336
Je Suis Seul Encore (I'm Alone Again) Joe Werner, 944
Je Tai Toujors Dis Dene Pas Fair Sa (I Always Told You Not To Do That) Percy Babineaux-Bixy Guidry, 87
Je Te Recontrais De Le Brulier Leo Soileau, 854
Je Vas Jamais Lessair Pleurer (I'll Never Let You Cry) Alley Boys Of Abbeville, 59

Je Veux M'Achete Un Fuse Qui Brille John H. Bertrand, 101
Je Veux Marier (I Want To Get Married) Leo Soileau, 854
Je Vous Jamise Kete Braie Four Aces, 356
Je Vue Ta Figure Dans La Lune (I Saw Your Face In The Moon) Joe Werner, 943
Jealous Hi-Flyers, 419; Nite Owls, 660; Shelton Brothers, 829
Jealous Hearted Blues York Brothers, 978
Jealous Hearted Me Carter Family, 194
Jealous Hearted Me No. 2 Edith & Sherman Collins, 218
Jealous Lover Jimmie Davis, 300; Hinson, Pitts & Coley, 427; Arthur Tanner, 886
Jealous Lover Of Lone Green Valley [The] Vernon Dalhart, 254, 258, 268
Jealous Mary Charlie Poole, 700
Jealous Sweetheart [The] Johnson Brothers, 463
Jealous Woman Won't Do [A] Callahan Brothers, 154
Jeep's Blues Port Arthur Jubileers, 701
Jeff Davis J.D. Harris, 405
Jefferson County Blues Dixie Ramblers [III], 319
Jefferson Street Rag Roy Harvey, 411
Jelly Roll Special Al Dexter, 314
Jellyroll Blues Jimmie Davis, 301
Jenn[ie/y]'s Strawberry Festival—Part 1, 2 Bob Miller, 617
Jennie Baker Jimmy Johnson's String Band, 461
Jennie Barn Bound Asa Martin, 593
Jennie Lee Bill Boyd, 123
Jennie Lou Bill Boyd, 125
Jennie My Own True Love Emry Arthur, 66
Jenny In The Garden "Uncle Bunt" Stephens, 868
Jenny Lind Polka Roy R. Harper, 402; Hill Billies, 424; Henry Whitter, 955
Jenny On The Railroad Carter Brothers & Son, 187
Jeremiah Hopkins' Store At Sand Mountain—Part 1, 2 Clayton McMichen, 569
Jericho Road Majestic [Male] Quartet, 585
Jerry, Go Ile That Car Harry "Mac" McClintock, 528
Jersey Bull Blues Three Tobacco Tags, 908
Jersey Side Jive Charles Mitchell & His Orchestra, 629
Jerusalem Morn Mountain Singers Male Quartet, 645
Jerusalem, Mourn Warren Caplinger, 156; Bill Chitwood, 208
Jess & Duke's Salty Gob [sic] Duke Clark, 213
Jesse And Duke's Salty Gob [sic] Jess Hillard, 426
Jesse Blues Bill Boyd, 122
Jesse James Bill Bender, 99; Fiddlin' John Carson, 177; Bill Chitwood, 208; Vernon Dalhart, 250–51, 265, 268, 281; Bascom Lamar Lunsford, 516; Harry "Mac" McClintock, 528; Clayton McMichen, 572; Riley Puckett, 716; George Reneau, 740; Carson Robison, 763; Marc Williams, 958; Woodruff Brothers, 973
Jesse's Talking Blues Jesse Rodgers, 799
Jessie Cliff Bruner, 140
Jessie James Ken Maynard, 614; Ernest Thompson, 902
Jessie Polka Adolph Hofner, 431
Jessie's Sister Cliff Bruner, 141
Jesus Died For Me Huggins & Philips Sacred Harp Singers, 446; Smith's Sacred Singers, 849–50
Jesus Filled My Life With Sunshine Ruth Donaldson & Helen Jepsen, 323
Jesus Forgives And Forgets Vaughan Quartet, 924
Jesus Getting Us Ready For That Great Day Ernest Phipps, 690
Jesus Gives Me Peace Canova Family, 155
Jesus Has Lifted Me Ruth Donaldson & Helen Jepsen, 323
Jesus Has Pardoned Me Paramount Sacred Four, 674
Jesus Hold My Hand Chuck Wagon Gang, 211; Denson-Parris Sacred Harp Singers, 313; Majestic [Male] Quartet, 585; Prairie Ramblers, 706; Royal Quartette, 815; James Scott-Claude Boone, 821

Jesus Is All I Need Vaughan Quartet, 924, 929
Jesus Is All The World To Me Jenkins Family, 457; Smith's Sacred Singers, 850; Wisdom Sisters, 969
Jesus Is All To Me W.C. Childers, 205
Jesus Is Calling Giddens Sisters, 369; Jenkins Family, 456; Smith's Sacred Singers, 851
Jesus Is Coming Leslie Hughes, 446
Jesus Is Coming Back Again Jenkins Family, 456
Jesus Is Coming, It May Be Soon Stamps Quartet, 864
Jesus Is Getting Us Ready Joe Reed Family, 734
Jesus Is Getting Us Ready For That Great Day Baker's Whitley County Sacred Singers, 90
Jesus Is Mine Blue Ridge Sacred Singers, 112
Jesus Is My Headlight Hartwic Brothers, 409
Jesus Is Over All Eva Quartette, 333
Jesus Is Precious To Me Stamps Quartet, 865; Vaughan Quartet, 928
Jesus Is Tenderly Calling Parker & Dodd, 678
Jesus Is The Light Laurel Firemen's Quartet, 491
Jesus Is True Fortner Family Mixed Quartette, 353
Jesus Keep Me Near The Fountain Merritt Smith, 845
Jesus Knows How Freeman Quartette, 358; Rev. M.L. Thrasher, 905
Jesus Knows The Way Clarence Ganus, 362
Jesus Lead Me There McDonald Quartet, 540
Jesus Leads To Victory Vaughan Quartet, 929
Jesus Leads, I'll Follow On Buffalo Ragged Five, 142
Jesus My All Carlisle Brothers, 169
Jesus My Savior Williams & Williams, 960
Jesus Paid It All Carolina Gospel Singers, 170–71; Deal Family, 307; Euclid Quartette, 333; Gentry Family, 365; Golden Echo Boys, 372; Stamps Quartet, 865
Jesus Paved The Way Dewey & Gassie Bassett, 97
Jesus Prayed Smith's Sacred Singers, 849
Jesus Savio[u]r Pilot Me Friendship Four, 360; Jimmy Long, 512
Jesus Taught Me How To Smile Stamps Quartet, 865
Jesus The Light Of The World Carson Robison, 766
Jesus Will J. Douglas Swagerty, 883
Jesus Will Care For Me Vaughan Quartet, 925
Jesus You Taught Me How To Smile Duncan Sisters Trio, 325
Jesus, I Come Jenkins Family, 457
Jesus, Lover Of My Soul Little Brown Church Quartet, 508; Uncle Dave Macon, 576; Rambling Rangers, 725; Smith's Sacred Singers, 850; J. Douglas Swagerty, 883; Chas. Teuser & Harold Lawrence, 898; Vaughan Quartet, 926
Jesus, The Holy Child Edith & Sherman Collins, 218
Jeunes Gens Campagnard Denus McGee, 551
Jeuste Parcque (Just Because) Joseph Falcon, 335
Jewett [J.T.] Allison's Sacred Harp Singers, 60
Jew's Harp Bill Arthur Fields & Fred Hall, 340
Jig Bill Boyd, 124
Jig In G Light Crust Doughboys, 503
Jig Time Dave Edwards, 330
Jill's Polka Jack Pierce, 696
Jim And Me R.C. Garner, 363; Red Fox Chasers, 731
Jim Blake Vernon Dalhart, 269, 272–73, 281; Lonesome Cowboy [II], 509
Jim Blake, The Engineer Frank Wheeler-Monroe Lamb, 948
Jim Blake's Message Carter Family, 194
Jim Thompson's Old Gray Mule Ernest Thompson, 902
Jimbo Jambo Land Shorty Godwin, 372
Jimmie And Sallie Dorsey & Beatrice Dixon, 322
Jimmie Brown The Newsboy Carter Family, 188
Jimmie Bryan's Final Ride Lowell Moore, 640
Jimmie On The Railroad Fiddlin' John Carson, 175
Jimmie Randall (The Pizen Song) Vass Family, 922

Jimmie Rodgers' Last Blue Yodel Jimmie Rodgers, 808
Jimmie Rodgers' Life Bradley Kincaid, 485
Jimmie Rodgers' Medley, Part 1, 2 Jimmie Rodgers, 809
Jimmie Rodgers' Puzzle Record Jimmie Rodgers, 806
Jimmie Rodgers Visits The Carter Family Carter Family, 190; Jimmie Rodgers, 805
Jimmie The Kid Gene Autry, 74; Ted Lunsford, 517; Jimmie Rodgers, 805
Jimmie The Kid (Parts Of The Life Of Rodgers) Jimmie Rodgers, 805
Jimmie's Mean Mama Blues Jimmie Rodgers, 804
Jimmie's Texas Blues Jimmie Rodgers, 801
Jimmie's Travelin' Blues Jimmie Davis, 302
Jimmy Bone 'Lasses & Honey, 491
Jim's Windy Mule Prairie Ramblers, 705
Jingle Bells Hoosier Hot Shots, 437
Jingle Jangle Jingle Gene Autry, 87; Tex Ritter, 751
Jitterbug Jive Bill Boyd, 124
Jitterbug Katy Ocie Stockard, 870
Jive And Smile Bob Skyles, 839
Jobbin Gettin' There [sic] Crook Brothers String Band, 234
Joe Bowers Bill Bender, 99
Joe Hoover's Mississippi Flood Song Ernest V. Stoneman, 875
Joe Turner Blues Milton Brown, 136; Orla Clark, 214; Hi-Flyers, 419; Adolph Hofner, 431
Joe Turner's Blues Lester McFarland & Robert A. Gardner, 543
Joe's Breakdown Joe Werner, 944
Jog Along, Boys Gentry Family, 365
John Baltzell's Reel John Baltzell, 91
John Brown Reid Bros. Band, 738
John Brown's Dream Da Costa Woltz's Southern Broadcasters, 970
John Dillinger Dwight Butcher, 148
John Hardy Eva Davis, 298; Buell Kazee, 472; Ernest V. Stoneman, 872, 877
John Hardy Blues Roy Harvey, 411
John Hardy Was A Desperate Little Man Carter Family, 187
John Henry Deford Bailey, 88; Callahan Brothers, 154; Sid Harkreader, 400; Hugh Shearer, 826; Ernest V. Stoneman, 873; Gid Tanner, 887
John Henry Blues Fiddlin' John Carson, 175; Gentry Brothers, 365; Earl Johnson, 459
John Henry The Steel Driving Man G.B. Grayson & Henry Whitter, 380; Earl McCoy & Jessie Brock, 531; Gid Tanner, 888
John Henry Was A Little Boy J.E. Mainer's Mountaineers, 581
John Henry, Steel Driver Ernest Thompson, 902
John In The Army Fiddlin' John Carson, 178
John Law And The Hobo Goebel Reeves, 737
John Makes Good Licker Fiddlin' John Carson, 177
John Makes Good Liquor—Part 3, 4 Fiddlin' John Carson, 177–78
John My Lover J.P. Nester, 653
John T. Scopes Case [The] Vernon Dalhart, 250
John T. Scopes Trial (The Old Religion's Better After All) [The] Vernon Dalhart, 250
John T. Scopes Trial [The] Vernon Dalhart, 248, 250; Charlie Oaks, 664
John The Baptist Vernon Dalhart, 259
John The Drunkard Carson Robison, 776
Johnnie Land Norris, 662
Johnnie Darlin' Vernon Dalhart, 292
Johnnie, Get Your Gun Earl Johnson, 460; Fate Norris, 661
Johnny And Jane—Part 1, 2 Frank Hutchison, 450

Johnny Bring The Jug 'Round The Hill Kessinger Brothers, 480
Johnny Goodwin Bull Mountain Moonshiners, 142
Johnny Grey Uncle Dave Macon, 578
Johnny Inchin' Along Doc Roberts, 753
Johnny Long, The Engineer Vernon Dalhart, 288
Johnny Lover Roanoke Jug Band, 751
Johnny Private Happy Jim Parsons, 680
Johnny The Drunkard Asa Martin, 589
Johnny, Get Your Gun Bill Chitwood, 208; Archer Porter, 702; Uncle Joe Shippee, 831
Johnny's Gone To Cuba John Hammond, 394
John's Trip To Boston Fiddlin' John Carson, 177
Johnson Boy Grant Brothers, 377
Johnson Boys Hill Billies, 423
Johnson City Blues Clarence Greene, 382
Johnson City Hop Carolina Ramblers String Band, 172
Johnson City Rag Roane County Ramblers, 751
Johnson Gal Leake County Revelers, 494
Johnson's Grass Rag Red Headed Fiddler[s], 732
Johnson's Old Gray Mule Gid Tanner, 889; Yellow Jackets [II], 977
Johnson's Old Grey Mule Georgia Yellow Hammers, 367; Earl Johnson, 459; J.E. Mainer's Mountaineers, 581; Riley Puckett, 715; Shelton Brothers, 827
Joilie Schvr Rouge (Pretty Red Hair) Happy Fats, 396
Jo-Jo Texas Wanderers, 900
Joke Song [The] Bailey Briscoe, 127
Joking Henry G.B. Grayson & Henry Whitter, 381
Jolie (Brunette) Jolly Boys Of Lafayette, 464
Jolie Blonde Hackberry Ramblers, 387
Jolie Fille (Pretty Girl) Hackberry Ramblers, 388
Jolie Fille Qui Ta Fa Avec Moi Douglas Bellar & Kirby Riley, 99
Jolie Petite Blonde Alley Boys Of Abbeville, 59
Jolie Petite Fille Alley Boys Of Abbeville, 59; Hackberry Ramblers, 387
Jolly Blacksmith Theron Hale, 389
Jolly Boys' Breakdown Jolly Boys Of Lafayette, 464
Jolly Group Of Cowboys Four Pickled Peppers, 356; Frank Wheeler-Monroe Lamb, 948
Jolly Lumberjack [The] Chas. Wieser, 956
Jonah E. Arthur Lewis, 497
Jonah And The Whale Uncle Dave Macon, 574; Marshall Smith, 844
Jonah's Scriptural Submarine John D. Foster, 354
Jones And Bloodworth Case Carl Conner, 219
Jones And Bloodworth Execution [The] Vernon Dalhart, 258–59
Jones County Blues Jones County Boys, 467
Jones Stomp Port Arthur Jubileers, 701
Jordan Is A Hard Road To Travel Doctor Lloyd & Howard Maxey, 508; Uncle Dave Macon, 575
Josephine Dave Edwards, 330
Josephine Waltz Leo Soileau, 854
Josephus And Bohunkus Ernest V. Stoneman, 876
Josh And I Kessinger Brothers, 480
Journey Home [J.T.] Allison's Sacred Harp Singers, 60
Joy Among The Angels Deal Family, 307
Joy Bells Tennessee Music & Printing Co. Quartet, 896
Joy Bells In My Soul (Charlie) Monroe's Boys, 632
Joy For The Redeemed Murphy Sacred Singers, 646
Joy To The World! Golden Hour Mixed Quartette, 373
Juanita Carlisle Brothers, 169; Vaughan Quartet, 925; Woodlawn Quartette, 972
Jubilee Roswell Sacred Harp Quartet, 814
Judas Sold Christ Rev. C.M. Grayson, 380
Judge Done Me Wrong [The] Willard Hodgin[s], 430

Judgement Morning Pipers Gap Ramblers, 698
Jug Of Wine And You [A] W. Lee O'Daniel, 665
Jug Rag Prairie Ramblers, 704
Juke Box Jump Hi-Flyers, 420
Juke Box Rag Bob Dunn's Vagabonds, 327
Jule Girl Blue Ridge Highballers, 110
Julia Waltz Leake County Revelers, 494
Julianne Flanagan Lowe Stokes, 871
Jumpin' And Jerkin' Blues Bill Carlisle, 159
June Bug [The] Queen Trio, 723
June Rose Waltz Stripling Brothers, 880
June Tenth Blues Three Virginians, 909
June Wedding Waltz Clayton & His Melody Mountaineers, 215
Jungle Town Bill Boyd, 123
Jungle Waltz Leake County Revelers, 495
Jus Pasque Happy Fats, 396
Just A Baby's Prayer At Twilight Dan Hornsby, 442
Just A Blue Eyed Blonde Leon Chappelear, 201
Just A Cottage Walter Hurdt, 448
Just A Dream Milton Brown, 136
Just A Few More Days Carter Family, 194
Just A Girl That Men Forget Jimmie Davis, 303
Just A Good Time Gal Jimmie Revard, 743
Just A Honky Tonk Gal Dick Reinhart, 739
Just A Kerosene Lamp Lester McFarland & Robert A. Gardner, 550; Prairie Ramblers, 705; Norwood Tew, 899
Just A Little Blue Sidney Smith, 846
Just A Little Cough Drop Ray Whitley, 953
Just A Little Dream Bill Bruner, 139
Just A Little Happiness Herb Cook, 220
Just A Little Home For The Old Folks James Brown, Jr. & Ken Landon Groups, 134
Just A Little Lovin' Bill Nettles, 653
Just A Little Nearer Home Stringfellow Quartet, 879
Just A Little Of The Blues Gene Steele, 867
Just A Little Pine Log Cabin J.B. Whitmire's Blue Sky Trio, 954
Just A Little Talk With Jesus Rangers Quartet, 728; Stamps Quartet, 865
Just A Little While Deal Family, 307; Edgewater Sabbath Singers, 329; Leatherman Sisters, 495
Just A Lonely Cowboy W.C. Childers, 206
Just A Lonely Hobo Cliff Carlisle, 161, 163
Just A Melody Vernon Dalhart, 258–59, 262–63, 266
Just A Message Hank Penny, 686
Just A Message From Carolina Johnson Brothers, 463
Just A Rollin' Stone Jimmie Davis, 305
Just A Song At Childhood Cliff Carlisle, 166
Just A Song Of Old Kentucky Monroe Brothers, 633
Just A Stranger Chas. M. Dewitte, 314
Just A Wayward Boy Cliff Carlisle, 167
Just A While Texas Jim Lewis, 499
Just An Evening At Home Ranch Boys, 726
Just An Old Birthday Present (From An Old Sweetheart Of Mine) Grace & Scotty MacLean, 565
Just An Old Chimney Stack Clayton McMichen, 572
Just An Old Fashioned Gospel Is Needed Today Rev. & Mrs C.A. Dougherty, 324
Just An Old Fashioned Locket Elton Britt, 128; Dick Parman, 680
Just An Old Lady Three Tobacco Tags, 908
Just An Old Spanish Custom Vernon Dalhart, 290
Just Another Broken Heart Carter Family, 193
Just Around The Bend Frank Luther, 518
Just Around The Bend (From The Rainbow's End) Frank & James McCravy, 538
Just As I Am Rev. M.L. Thrasher, 905

Just As Long As Eternity Rolls Vaughan Quartet, 929
Just As Rich As You Rev. Horace A. Booker, 117
Just As The Sun Went Down Bill Cox, 226, 228; Andrew Jenkins, 453; B.F. Kincaid, 482; Frank & James McCravy, 532, 534; Wade Mainer, 582; Riley Puckett, 716; Taylor's Kentucky Boys, 895
Just As We Used To Do Riley Puckett, 721
Just As Your Mother Was John McGhee & Frank Welling, 560
Just At Twilight Fleming & Townsend, 348
Just A-Wearyin' For You Sons Of The Pioneers, 858
Just Because Joseph Falcon, 335; Hackberry Ramblers, 387; Lone Star Cowboys, 509; Nelstone's Hawaiians, 653; Prairie Ramblers, 705; Rhubarb Red, 744; Shelton Brothers, 827
Just Because (Of You Little Girl) Jimmie Davis, 305
Just Because No. 3 Saddle Tramps, 818; Shelton Brothers, 828
Just Because She Made Them Goo Goo Eyes B.F. Kincaid, 482
Just Because You're In Deep Elem Elton Britt, 130; Prairie Ramblers, 711; Shelton Brothers, 829
Just Before The Battle Mother Benny Borg, 118; Arthur Fields & Fred Hall, 338; Monroe Quartette, 633; Charlie Oaks, 664; Old Southern Sacred Singers, 669
Just Before The Last Fierce Charge Green Bailey, 88
Just Beyond The Gates Mr. & Mrs. R.N. Grisham, 384
Just Blues Ocie Stockard, 869
Just Break The News To Mother Vernon Dalhart, 248; Old Southern Sacred Singers, 669; Riley Puckett, 716; Carson Robison, 780
Just Bumming A Railroad Train Riley Puckett, 716
Just Come On In Gene Autry, 81; Prairie Ramblers, 706
Just Drifting Ted Daffan's Texans, 241
Just Fooling Around Ted Daffan's Texans, 241
Just For A Girl Jack Dunigan, 326
Just For Old Time's Sake Rex Griffin, 383; Hank Penny, 686
Just For Tonight Bar-X Cowboys, 93
Just Forget Leon Chappelear, 201; Morgan Denmon, 312; Hank Penny, 686; Leon Selph, 824
Just Forgive And Forget Jimmie Davis, 302; Philyaw Brothers, 690
Just Friends Bob Wills, 961
Just From College Billy Brooks, 132
Just From Tennessee Uncle Dave Macon, 574
Just Gimme The Leavings Gid Tanner, 887
Just Give Me The Leavings Dr. Smith's Champion Hoss Hair Pullers, 843
Just Good-Bye I Am Going Home Roy Harvey, 411
Just How Pretty You Smile Morris Brothers, 643
Just Inside The Eastern Gate John McGhee & Frank Welling, 560
Just Inside The Pearly Gates Roy Acuff, 50; Anglin Brothers, 61
Just Keep Ploddin' Along Carson Robison, 794
Just Keep Waiting Till The Good Time Comes Charlie Poole, 700
Just Kiss Yourself Goodbye John McGhee & Frank Welling, 557
Just Like You Arthur Duhon, 325
Just Lonesome Nelstone's Hawaiians, 653
Just Make My People Think You Care Dewey & Gassie Bassett, 96
Just Married Riverside String Band, 751
Just Once More Hackberry Ramblers, 387
Just Once Too Often Light Crust Doughboys, 504
Just One Girl Walter C. Peterson, 688; Roy Sweeney & Family, 883

Just One Little Kiss Callahan Brothers, 153; Fleming & Townsend, 346; Red Foley, 351; Jesse Rodgers, 799
Just One More Ride Wilf Carter (Montana Slim), 186
Just One Time Philyaw Brothers, 690
Just One Way To The Pearly Gates Uncle Dave Macon, 578; Wade Mainer, 583
Just One Year Callahan Brothers, 153; (Charlie) Monroe's Boys, 632
Just Outside The Door Calhoun Sacred Quartet, 151
Just Over In The Glory Land Carson Family Sacred Quartette, 180; Hill Brothers, 424; John McGhee & Frank Welling, 563; J.E. Mainer's Mountaineers, 582; Rev. M.L. Thrasher, 905
Just Over Jordan Warren Caplinger, 156
Just Over The Glory-Land Valdese Quartette, 922
Just Over The Hill J.B. Whitmire's Blue Sky Trio, 954
Just Over The River Carson Family Sacred Quartette, 180; Garland Brothers & Grinstead, 362
Just Over The Smiling Sea Ruth Neal & Wanda Neal, 652
Just Partners Rex Griffin, 384
Just Pickin' Roy Harvey, 410
Just Plain Folks Arkansas Woodchopper, 63; Charles Baker, 89; Clagg & Sliger, 212; Bradley Kincaid, 485; Lester McFarland & Robert A. Gardner, 546; John McGhee & Frank Welling, 555–56; Sue Morgan, 642; Three Tobacco Tags, 908
Just Refined Jimmie Revard, 742
Just Remember Lunsford Bros., 517
Just Rollin' On Ernest Tubb, 914
Just Sitting On Top Of The World Milton Brown, 136
Just Tell Me That You Love Me Yet Pine Ridge Boys, 697
Just Tell Them That You Saw Me Vernon Dalhart, 250, 281; Andrew Jenkins, 454; Buell Kazee, 472; Frank & James McCravy, 538; Clayton McMichen, 572; Uncle Dave Macon, 574
Just The Same Sweet Thing To Me Delmore Brothers, 311
Just The Thought Of Mother Clarence Ganus, 362
Just Thinking Joe Werner, 944
Just Thinking Of You Ted Daffan's Texans, 241
Just To Be Alone With Jesus Rev. M.L. Thrasher, 905
Just To Break My Heart Allie & Pearl Brock, 131
Just To Ease My Worried Mind Roy Acuff, 50
Just Try To Picture Me Down In Tennessee Bill Cox, 227
Just Wait And See Texas Jim Lewis, 500; Carson Robison, 797
Just Wanting You York Brothers, 978
Just Wear A Smile Coats Sacred Quartette, 216
Just Whistle Carson Robison, 761
J'Vai Jouer Celea Pour Toi (I'll Play This For You) Percy Babineaux-Bixy Guidry, 87
J'Vas Continue A' T'Aime (I'll Keep On Loving You) Sons Of Acadians, 856
J'Vas Tamey Camaime (I Love You) Hackberry Ramblers, 388

K. C. Whistle Gentry Brothers, 365
K.C. Blues Frank Hutchison, 450
K.C. Brown Dick Justice, 468
K.C. Railroad Leo Soileau, 855; George Walburn & Emmett Hethcox, 935
K.C. Railroad (Going Down The Road Feeling Bad) Riley Puckett, 721
K.C. Stomp Arthur Smith, 842
K.C. Whistle Blues Duke Clark, 213
Kaiser And Uncle Sam [The] Charlie Oaks, 664; Henry Whitter, 954
Kaiser's Defeat Allen Sisson, 836
Kalua Loha Light Crust Doughboys, 504

Kalua Sweetheart Tune Wranglers, 916
Kamona March Corn Cob Crushers, 222
Kanawha County Rag Kessinger Brothers, 480
Kanawha Hornpipe Tweedy Brothers, 918
Kanawha March Kessinger Brothers, 479
Kangaroo Blues Cliff Bruner, 140
Kansas City Blues Deford Bailey, 88; Leon Chappelear, 201; Bill Cox, 228; Roy Newman, 658; Swift Jewel Cowboys, 884
Kansas City Kitty Ezra Buzzington's Rustic Revelers, 150; Ambrose Haley, 389; Louisiana Strollers, 514; Yellow Jackets [II], 977
Kansas City Rag Prairie Ramblers, 708
Kansas City Railroad Blues George Walburn & Emmett Hethcox, 935
Kansas City Reel Bob Larkan & Family, 491
Karo Uncle Jimmy Thompson, 904
Kasoos Hornpipe Massey Family, 611
Kate's Snuff Box Fiddlin' John Carson, 178
Katie Cline Fisher Hendley, 416
Katie Dear Blue Sky Boys, 113
Katie Dear (Silver Dagger) Callahan Brothers, 152
Katie Kline Pipers Gap Ramblers, 698; Ernest V. Stoneman, 873
Katinka Dan Hornsby, 442
Katy Cline Monroe Brothers, 633; Red Fox Chasers, 731; Ernest V. Stoneman, 873
Katy Dear Tiny Dodson's Circle-B Boys, 322
Katy Did Lowe Stokes, 870
Katy Hill Bill Monroe, 631; Allen Sisson, 836
Katy Lee Willie Stoneman, 879
Katy On Time Prince Albert Hunt, 447
Katy-Did Waltz Frank Wilson, 967
Kawanha [sic] Waltz Frank Roberts, Bud Alexander & Fiddlin' Slim Sandford, 755
Keep A Happy Heart Rangers Quartet, 728
Keep A Horse Shoe Hung Over The Door Skyland Scotty, 838
Keep A Knockin' Milton Brown, 138
Keep A' Knockin' (But You Can't Come In) Clifford Breaux, 127
Keep A Light In Your Window Tonight James Brown, Jr. & Ken Landon Groups, 135; Frank Luther, 522; Lester McFarland & Robert A. Gardner, 550; Bob Miller, 624; W. Lee O'Daniel, 665; Tom & Don, 911; Johnny Lee Wills, 967
Keep An Eye On Your Heart Hoosier Hot Shots, 440
Keep Bachelor's Hall Earl Shirkey & Roy Harper, 831
Keep Holding On McDonald Quartet, 540
Keep In De Middle Of De Road Kanawha Singers, 469
Keep In The Middle Of The Road Frank & James McCravy, 534
Keep Knocking (But You Can't Come In) Bob Wills, 962–63
Keep Marching All The Time Turkey Mountain Singers, 916
Keep Me On The Firing Line Perry Kim & Einar Nyland, 481
Keep Me On The Firing Line Jesus Perry Kim & Einar Nyland, 482; E. Arthur Lewis, 498
Keep My Grave Clean Arthur Tanner, 886
Keep My Hand In Thine Vaughan Quartet, 923–24
Keep My Skillet Good And Greasy Uncle Dave Macon, 573; Henry Whitter, 955
Keep On Climbing L.V. Jones, 467; Smith's Sacred Singers, 849
Keep On Keeping On Ruth Donaldson & Helen Jepsen, 323; Bob Miller, 617–18, 622–23
Keep On Shining, Colorado Moon Jack Pierce, 696
Keep On Steppin' Vaughan Quartet, 928
Keep On The Firing Line Carter Family, 195; Howard Haney, 395; Humbard Family, 447; Royal Quartette, 815

Keep On The Sunny Side Carter Family, 187, 193; Asa Martin, 590
Keep On The Sunny Side Of Life Harmon E. Helmick, 415
Keep On Truckin' Smoky Wood, 971
Keep Praying Claude Casey, 197
Keep Rollin' Lazy Longhorns Gene Autry, 86
Keep Smiling Old Pal Wilf Carter (Montana Slim), 183
Keep Smiling Thru' Ralph E. Johnson, 462
Keep Straight Ahead Forman Sisters, 352
Keep The Camp Fires Burning Delmore Brothers, 310
Keep The Sunlight In Your Sky McDonald Quartet, 540; Smith's Sacred Singers, 850
Keep Truckin' Hi Neighbor Boys, 420
Keep Your Eyes On Jesus Amory Male Quartette, 60
Keep Your Gal At Home Gid Tanner, 891
Keep Your Light Shining Bush Brothers, 147
Keep Your Love Letters, I'll Keep Mine McClendon Brothers, 528
Keep Your Nose Out Of Daddy's Business Leon Selph, 823
Kelley Waltz Cartwright Brothers, 195; Len Nash, 650; Chas. Winters & Elond Autry, 968
Kelly Swing Cliff Bruner, 140
Kelly Waltz Oscar & Doc Harper, 402; Light Crust Doughboys, 501; Richmond Melody Boys, 748; Sons Of The Pioneers, 857–59
Kenesaw Mountain Rag John Dilleshaw, 317
Kenion Clog John Baltzell, 91
Kennedy Rag Stripling Brothers, 879
Kennesaw Mountain Blues [The] Andrew Jenkins, 454
Kenney Wagner's Surrender Ernest V. Stoneman, 874
Kennie Wagner's Surrender Vernon Dalhart, 264
Keno, The Rent Man Cofer Brothers, 216
Kentucky Karl & Harty, 471
Kentucky Babe Vaughan Quartet, 923–24
Kentucky Bean With His Double Barreled Shot Gun [The] Walter C. Peterson, 688
Kentucky Blues Elmer Bird, 105; Prairie Ramblers, 704
Kentucky Bootlegger Fruit Jar Guzzlers, 360
Kentucky Bride's Fate [The] Lester McFarland & Robert A. Gardner, 545
Kentucky Days Duke Clark, 213; Harry Hillard, 425
Kentucky Is Calling Me McKinney Brothers, 564
Kentucky Jig Dick Hartman's Tennessee Ramblers, 407
Kentucky Limit Tommy Whitmer's Band, 953
Kentucky Lullaby Gene Autry, 77
Kentucky Miner's Wife—Part 1, 2 (Ragged Hungry Blues) Aunt Molly Jackson, 452
Kentucky Moonshiner John D. Foster, 354
Kentucky Plow Boy's March E.E. Hack String Band, 386
Kentucky Stomp Elmer Bird, 105
Kentucky Sweetheart Milton & Marion Carlisle, 168
Kentucky Waggoners Allen Sisson, 836
Kentucky Wedding Chimes Len & Joe Higgins, 421
Kentucky, My Home Joe Steen, 868
Kentucky, Sure As You're Born Roy Newman, 658
Kept For Jesus Canova Family, 155
Kept On The Firing Line E. Arthur Lewis, 498
Kethcup Arthur Fields & Fred Hall, 345
Key Hole Blues Frank Roberts, Bud Alexander & Fiddlin' Slim Sandford, 755
Keyhole In The Door [The] Jimmie Davis, 300; Holland Puckett, 715
Kickapoo Medicine Show—Part 1, 2 Clayton McMichen, 569
Kickin' It Off Bill Mounce, 645
Kicking Mule [The] Fiddlin' John Carson, 175; John B. Evans, 333; Sid Hampton, 394; McGee Brothers, 552; Bill Shafer, 824; Carl T. Sprague, 862; Ernest V. Stoneman, 872

Kid In The Three Cornered Pants [The] Hoosier Hot Shots, 437
Kidder Cole Bascom Lamar Lunsford, 517
Kidnapped Baby [The] Goebel Reeves, 738
Kidnapper's Story [The] Buck Nation, 651
Kidnapping Is A Terrible Crime Dwight Butcher, 148
Kileau March Melvin Dupree, 327
Killem Light Crust Doughboys, 501
Killie-Cranky Forrest Copeland & Johnny Britton, 221
Killin' Blues Byrd Moore, 639
Killing Of Tom Slaughter [The] Clayton McMichen, 569
Kilocycle Stomp Sons Of The Pioneers, 857
Kimball House Ted Hawkins, 413
King Cotton Stomp Rice Brothers' Gang, 746
King I Love [The] Freeman Quartette, 359
King Kong Kitchie Kitchie Ki-Me-O Chubby Parker, 676–77
King Needs Workers [The] [E.R.] Nance Family, 648; Vaughan Quartet, 929
King Of Borneo Vernon Dalhart, 286
King Of The Hobos Hobo Jim, 428
Kingdom Comin' [The] Willard Hodgin[s], 429
Kingdom Land Hall Brothers, 391
Kings Head E.M. Lewis, 498; Tom Owens Barn Dance Trio, 672
Kinnie Wagner Vernon Dalhart, 255, 257
Kinnie Wagner's Surrender Vernon Dalhart, 261
Kinston Blues Claude Casey, 197
Kiss Me W.T. Narmour & S.W. Smith, 650
Kiss Me Quick Georgia Yellow Hammers, 367
Kiss Me Waltz Murphy Brothers, 646; W.T. Narmour & S.W. Smith, 649
Kiss Me, Cindy Oscar Ford, 352; J.E. Mainer's Mountaineers, 582
Kiss Waltz Theron Hale, 389; Capt. McKinney & E.L. Graham, 564; Charlie Poole, 699; Ernest Thompson, 902
Kisses Carl T. Sprague, 862
Kissin' On The Sly Uncle Dave Macon, 575
Kissing Is A Crime Carter Family, 192
Kissing Song [The] Chubby Parker, 677
Kitten With The Big Green Eyes [The] Hoosier Hot Shots, 439
Kittie Wells North Carolina Cooper Boys, 662
Kitty And The Baby Lowe Stokes, 871
Kitty Blye Roy Harvey, 410
Kitty Clyde Adolph Hofner, 430; William B. Houchens, 443
Kitty Hill Bill Chitwood, 209
Kitty Ki Crockett [Family] Mountaineers, 233
Kitty Puss Land Norris, 662
Kitty Waltz Carter Family, 188; Clarence Greene, 382; Hill Billies, 423
Kitty Waltz Yodel Earl Shirkey & Roy Harper, 832
Kitty Wells Vernon Dalhart, 254; Sid Harkreader, 400; Hill Billies, 423; Doc Hopkins, 441; Pickard Family, 691, 693; Ernest V. Stoneman, 872, 874; Virginia Ramblers, 933
Klucker Blues [The] [Smilin'] Ed McConnell, 530
Knee Deep In Cotton Blackberry Dudes, 108
Kneel At The Cross Blue Sky Boys, 114; Chuck Wagon Gang, 210; Euclid Quartette, 333; Fortner Family Mixed Quartette, 353; Moody Quartet, 637
Knickerbocker Reel Rustic Revellers, 816
Knock Around The Kitchen Jess Hillard, 426
Knocking At The Door John McGhee & Frank Welling, 553
Knocking Down Casey Jones Wilmer Watts, 941
Knocking On The Hen House Door Lester "Pete" Bivins, 107; "Dock" Walsh, 937
Knock-Kneed Susie Jane Asa Martin, 593
Knocky-Knocky Light Crust Doughboys, 504

Knot Hole Blues Shelton Brothers, 829
Knotty Head Jake Fiddlin' John Carson, 178
Knoxville Blues McGee Brothers, 552
Knoxville Girl Ted Chestnut, 204; Lester McFarland & Robert A. Gardner, 543; Asa Martin, 590; Riley Puckett, 715; Arthur Tanner, 885–86
Knoxville Rag Taylor, Moore & Burnett, 894
Kohala March Scottdale String Band, 822
Kohalo Rag Herschel Brown, 133
Koots Town E.M. Lewis, 498
Krawdad [sic] Song Honeyboy & Sassafras[s], 433
Kuhala March Shamrock String Band, 825

L&N Brakeman [The] Clarence Gill, 369
L. And N. Rag Alex Hood, 435
La Blouse Francaise (French Blues) Sydney Landry, 490
La Blues De Port Arthur Leo Soileau, 855
La Bonne Valse Leo Soileau, 855
La Bonne Valse (Good Time Waltz) Leo Soileau, 854
La Breakdown A Pete Hackberry Ramblers, 388
La Breakdown Des Creepers Thibodeaux Boys, 901
La Breakdown La Louisianne Walker Brothers, 936
La Chanson D'Evangeline (Evangeline's Song) Christine Muszar, 647
La Danse Carre Denus McGee, 551
La Danseuse (The Dancer) Delma Lachney, 488
La Delaisser John H. Bertrand, 101
La Derniere Lettre (The Last Letter) Sons Of Acadians, 856
La Femme Qui Jovait Les Cartes Alleman & Walker, 54
La Fiesta Massey Family, 612
La Fille A Oncle Elair (Uncle Elair's Daughter) Joseph Falcon, 335
La Fille De La Compaigne (Country Girl) J.B. Fuslier, 361
La Fille De Village (Town Girl) Joe Werner, 944
La Fille Du Jolier John H. Bertrand, 101
La Fille Que J'Aime (The Girl I Love) Joe Creduer-Albert Babineaux, 232
La Golondrina Bill Boyd, 124; Milton Brown, 137; Bob Wills, 964
La Golondrina (The Swallow) Bob Wills, 962
La Jeunne Sur La Montagne (The Girl On The Mountain) Leo Soileau, 855
La Jolie Fille N'En Veut Plus De Moi (The Nice Girl Don't Want Me Any More) Joseph Falcon, 335
La Louisiana (Louisiana) Delma Lachney, 488
La Manvais Femme Thibodeaux Boys, 901
La Marche De La Noce (Wedding March) Joseph Falcon, 334
La Musique Encore, Encore Dixie Ramblers [II], 319
La Nouvelle Marche De Marris Happy Fats, 396
La Nuit De Samedi (Saturday Night Waltz) Joseph Falcon, 336
La One-Step A Moujeane Joe Werner, 944
La Paloma Bob Wills, 965
La Place Mon Couer Desire Happy Fats, 395
La Polka A Gilbent Happy Fats, 396
La Rille Cajen Denus McGee, 551
La Robe Barre (Striped Dress) J.B. Fuslier, 361
La Stompe Creole [sic] Harrington-Landry & Steward, 404
La Turtape De Saroied (The Turtape Of Saroied) Amedie Ardoin, 62
La Two Step A Erby Thibodeaux Boys, 901
La Two-Step A' Chachin (Asa's Two-Step) Joe Werner, 944
La Valse A Aristil Creduer Angelas Le Jeunne, 494
La Valse A Austin Ardoin Amedie Ardoin, 62
La Valse A Columbus (Columbus Waltz) J.B. Fuslier, 361

La Valse A Deux Temps (A Two Step Waltz) Joe Werner, 944
La Valse A Karo Joe Werner, 943
La Valse A Moreau Leo Soileau, 854
La Valse A Papa Jolly Boys Of Lafayette, 464
La Valse A Rouge Thibodeaux Boys, 901
La Valse A Thomas Ardoin Amedie Ardoin, 62
La Valse A Tidom Hanks Angelas Le Jeunne, 493
La Valse Ah Abe (Abe's Waltz) Amedie Ardoin, 61
La Valse A'N'Oncle Knute (Uncle Knute's Waltz) Joe Werner, 944
La Valse Crowley (The Waltz Crowley) Joseph Falcon, 335
La Valse D'Auguste (August Waltz) Amadie Breaux, 126
La Valse De Amities (Love Waltz) Amedie Ardoin, 62
La Valse De Baldwin Joseph Falcon, 335
La Valse De Bayou Granddan Joe Werner, 944
La Valse De Boutte Dechuminen Nathan Abshire, 48
La Valse De Church Point Angelas Le Jeunne, 493
La Valse De Creole (The Creole Waltz) Dudley & James Fawvor, 337
La Valse De Gueydan Amedie Ardoin, 62
La Valse De Josephine (Josephine Waltz) Leo Soileau, 854
La Valse De La Lafayette Jolly Boys Of Lafayette, 464
La Valse De La Prison (Waltz Of The Prison) Hackberry Ramblers, 388
La Valse De La Rosa Leo Soileau, 856
La Valse De La Ru Canal Leo Soileau, 854
La Valse De La Veuve Angelas Le Jeunne, 493
La Valse De L'Amour Happy Fats, 395
La Valse De Lange Au Paille Denus McGee, 551
La Valse De Louisiane Walker Brothers, 936
La Valse De Madame Sosten (Mrs. Sosten Waltz) Joseph Falcon, 335
La Valse De Pecaniere Leo Soileau, 854
La Valse De Rebot (Drunkard's Waltz) J.B. Fuslier, 361
La Valse De Riceville Nathan Abshire, 48
La Valse De Rosalie (Rosalie Waltz) Denus McGee, 551
La Valse Des Chantiers Petroliferes (Waltz Of The Oil Field) Amedie Ardoin, 62
La Valse Des Pins Walker Brothers, 936
La Valse Des Pins (Pinewood Waltz) Amadie Breaux, 126
La Valse Des Reid Denus McGee, 551
La Valse Des Yeux Bleus (Blue Eyes Waltz) Amadie Breaux, 126
La Valse Du Ballard Amedie Ardoin, 62
La Valse Du Bayou (The Waltz Of The Bayou) Percy Babineaux-Bixy Guidry, 87
La Valse Du Bayou Plaquemine (Plaquemine Bayou Waltz) Amadie Breaux, 127
La Valse Du Bayou Sauvage Angelas Le Jeunne, 493
La Valse Du La Compaign J.B. Fuslier, 361
La Valse Du Mariage Guidry Brothers, 385
La Valse Du Texas Angelas Le Jeunne, 494
La Valse Du Vieux Temp (Old-Time Waltz) Hackberry Ramblers, 388
La Valse Du Vieux Temps (The Old Time Waltz) Amadie Breaux, 126
La Valse La Prison Douglas Bellar & Kirby Riley, 99
La Valse Penitentiaire (Penitentiary Waltz) Leo Soileau, 854
La Veuve De La Coulee Happy Fats, 396
La Vie Malheureuse Walker Brothers, 936
La Vieux Two Step Francais Happy Fats, 396
La Vieux Vals An' Onc Mack Thibodeaux Boys, 901
La Vieux Valse A Ma Belle Thibodeaux Boys, 901
L'Abandonner (The Abandoned Waltz) Bartmon Montet-Joswell Dupuis, 637
Labor On Smith's Sacred Singers, 850
Lacassine Waltz Anatole Credure, 232

Lad From Old Virginia [A] Carter Family, 192
Ladies' Man (Or A Devil With The Women) [The] Frank Luther, 523
Ladies On The Steamboat Richard D. Burnett, 144
Ladies' Quadrille Happy Hayseeds, 397
Lady Gay Buell Kazee, 472
Lady In Red [The] Beverly Hill Billies, 103; Prairie Ramblers, 706
Lady Killin' Cowboy Tex Ritter, 750
Lady Of Spain Bob Wills, 964
Lady Of The Lake Mellie Dunham's Orchestra, 326
Lady 'Round The Lady And The Gent Solo Roy Rogers, 812
Lady That's Known As Lou [The] Arthur Fields & Fred Hall, 344
Lady Twinklepuss Three Tobacco Tags, 908
Lady Washington Reel Plymouth Vermont Old Time Barn Dance Orch., 698
Lady, Be Good Hi-Flyers, 418
Lafayette (Allon A Luafette) Joseph Falcon, 334
Lake Arthur Stomp Miller's Merrymakers, 628
Lake Arthur Two-Step Adler Connor & Julian Grader, 219
Lake Arthur Waltz Miller's Merrymakers, 628
Lake Charles Shuffle Happy Fats, 396
Lake Charles Waltz Anatole Credure, 232; Four Aces, 356
Lake Of Ponchatrain [The] Pie Plant Pete, 695
Lakes Of Pontchartrain Pie Plant Pete, 694
Lalita Dixie Ramblers [II], 319
L'Alle D'Amour (Lover's Lane) Sons Of Acadians, 856
Lamar Bank Robbery [The] James Turner, 917
L'Amour Indifferent (Careless Love) Joseph Falcon, 335
Lamp Lighting Time In Heaven J.E. Mainer's Mountaineers, 582
Lamp Lighting Time In The Valley Gilbert Betz, 101; Hart Brothers, 407; Roy Harvey, 411
Lamp Post On Old Broadway Clifford (C.S.) Wagner, 933; Carl White, 948
Lamplighter's Dream [The] Herald Goodman, 375
L'Ancienne Valse (The Old Time Waltz) Leo Soileau, 854
Land Of Beulah Dye's Sacred Harp Singers, 328
Land Of Liberty And Love Crowder Brothers, 238
Land Of My Boyhood Dreams [The] Jimmie Rodgers, 802
Land Of The Never Was Goebel Reeves, 736–37
Land Of The Sweet Bye And Bye [The] Bill Cox, 227
Land Of Unsetting Sun J. Douglas Swagerty, 883
Land Where The Roses Never Fade [The] Eddie Dean, 308
Land Where We Never Grow Old [The] Sid Harkreader, 400
Land Where We'll Never Grow Old Jenkins Family, 456
Lane County Bachelor Bill Bender, 99; B.F. Kincaid, 482
Lanse Des Belaire Denus McGee, 551
Larry O'Gaff Tommy Dandurand, 293
Las Gaviotas (Seagulls) Massey Family, 612
Last Days In Georgia Byrd Moore, 639
Last Farewell [The] Fred Pendleton, 685
Last Flight [The] Vernon Dalhart, 269
Last Flight Of Wiley Post [The] Ken Card, 158; Ray Whitley, 953
Last Gold Dollar Samantha Bumgarner, 142; Ephraim Woodie, 971
Last Goodbye [The] Dewey & Gassie Bassett, 97; Oklahoma Sweethearts, 668; Hank Penny, 686; Billy Vest, 931
Last Great Round-Up [The] Arkansas Woodchopper, 64; Chesley Shirley, 832; Carl T. Sprague, 862–63
Last Letter [The] Bob Atcher, 69; Gene Autry, 85; Wilf Carter (Montana Slim), 186; Bill Cox, 229; Jimmie Davis, 304; Rex Griffin, 384; Morris Brothers, 643; Goebel Reeves, 736; Sons Of Acadians, 856
Last Longhorn [The] Carl T. Sprague, 863
Last Love Call Yodel [The] Rex Griffin, 384

Last Mile [The] John McGhee & Frank Welling, 555; Johnny Marvin, 607; Red Brush Rowdies, 730
Last Mile Of The Way [The] Blue Sky Boys, 114; Drum Quartet, 324; Duncan Sisters Trio, 325; John B. Evans, 334; Jack & Leslie, 451; Lester McFarland & Robert A. Gardner, 545; John McGhee & Frank Welling, 560; Jack Pickell, 694; Rev. M.L. Thrasher, 905
Last Move For Me [The] Carter Family, 193
Last Moving For Me [The] Leo Boswell, 119
Last Night Broken Hearted Clayton McMichen, 568
Last Night I Dreamed Ernest Tubb, 914
Last Night I Had A Dream Of Home Campbell Brothers, 154
Last Night I Was Your Only Darling Delmore Brothers, 312
Last Night Was The End Of The World Hugh Cross, 235
Last Night When My Willie Came Home Uncle Dave Macon, 574
Last Night While Standing By My Window Blue Sky Boys, 114
Last Of The 21 Year Prisoner [The] Frank Luther, 521
Last Old Dollar is Gone [The] Rosa Lee Carson, 179
Last Ride Down Lariat Trail [The] Wilf Carter (Montana Slim), 183
Last Round-Up [The] Gene Autry, 79; Beverly Hill Billies, 103; Hank Keene, 474; Ranch Boys, 725, 727; Dick Robertson, 759; Shanks Bros. Trio, 825; Margaret West, 945
Last Scene Of The Titanic [The] Frank Hutchison, 449
Last Shot Got Him [The] W.B. Chenoweth, 203; Mississippi 'Possum Hunters, 629
Last Thoughts Of Jimmie Rodgers [The] Ernest Tubb, 913
Last Trip Of The Old Ship Jimmie Davis, 304
Last Wednesday Night Blind Uncle Gaspard, 363
Late In The Evening Stripling Brothers, 880
Late Last Night When Willie Frank Blevins, 108
Laughin' And Cryin' Allen Brothers, 56
Laughin' And Cryin' Blues Allen Brothers, 55
Laughin' Rufus Earl Johnson, 460
Laughing Song H.P. Houser, 444; Bob Skyles, 838
Laughter And Tears Tune Wranglers, 916
Launch Out On The Sea Of God's Love Stamps Quartet, 865
Laura Lou Ted Daffan's Texans, 241; "Dock" Walsh, 937
L'Aurevoir D'Une Mere (Mother's Farewell) Delma Lachney, 489
Lauterbach Archer Porter, 702
Lauterbach Waltz Kessinger Brothers, 481
Lavender Cowboy Vernon Dalhart, 292; Ewen Hail, 389; Bob Skyles, 838
LaVerne, My Brown Eyed Rose Wilf Carter (Montana Slim), 186
Lawd, I Want To Be Right Imperial Quartet, 451
Lawson Murder [The] [E.R.] Nance Family, 648
Lawyer Skinner Smiley Burnette, 145
Lay Down Baby "Dock" Walsh, 937
Lay Down Baby Blues Clarence Greene, 382; Byrd Moore, 639
Lay Down Doggies (Cowboy's Night Song) Vernon Dalhart, 268
Lay Down Dogies Carson Robison, 776
Lay Down My Sword And Shield Mustard & Gravy, 647
Lay Down, Baby, Take Your Rest Carolina Tar Heels, 173
Lay Down, Doggies Vernon Dalhart, 268
Lay Me Down Beside My Darling Sunshine Boys, 881
Lay Me Where My Mother Is Sleeping Roy Hall, 390
Lay Me Where My Mother's Sleeping Clarence Ganus, 362
Lay Me Where Sweet Flowers Blossom Arthur Tanner, 886
Lay My Head Beneath A Rose Vernon Dalhart, 258–59
Lay My Head Beneath The Rose Carter Family, 194; Bill Cox, 226; Lester McFarland & Robert A. Gardner, 544
Lay Your Hand In Mine Shelton Brothers, 829

Lazy Acres Massey Family, 612
Lazy Farmer Boy [A] Buster Carter & Preston Young, 181
Lazy Kate Leake County Revelers, 495
Lazy Lou'siana Moon Lester McFarland & Robert A. Gardner, 548
Lazy Old Mary Will You Get Up Walter C. Peterson, 688
Lazy River Hoosier Hot Shots, 440; Buck Nation, 651
Lazy River Moon Bill Nettles, 653
Lazy Tennessee Sid Harkreader, 400
Lazy Texas Longhorns Johnny Marvin, 607
Le Bebe Et Le Gambleur (The Baby And The Gambler) Delma Lachney, 488
Le Blues De Petit Chien (Little Dog Blues) Amadie Breaux, 126
Le Cleuses De Negre Francaise Leo Soileau, 854
Le Fille De St. Martin Happy Fats, 395
Le Garcon Boulanger (The Baker Boy) Patrick (Dak) Pellerin, 685
Le Garcon Chez Son Pere Guidry Brothers, 385
Le Garcon Negligent Guidry Brothers, 385
Le Gran Mamou Leo Soileau, 854
Le Mellaige Happy Fats, 396
Le Midland Two-Step Amedie Ardoin, 62
Le Moulin Casay Thibodeaux Boys, 901
Le Nouveau Lafayette (New Lafayette) Joseph Falcon, 335
Le One Step A Martin (Martin's One Step) Amadie Breaux, 127
Le Petit One Step Angelas Le Jeunne, 493
Le Pond De Nante John H. Bertrand, 101
Le Recommendation Du Soulard Guidry Brothers, 385
Le Reponse De Blues De Bosco Happy Fats, 396
Le Soldat Fatigue John H. Bertrand, 101
Le Valse De Gueydan Leo Soileau, 854
Le Valse De Mon Reve (Waltz Of My Dream) Joseph Falcon, 335
Le Valse D'Utah (Utah Waltz) Amadie Breaux, 126
Le Vieux Arbre De Pin Joe Werner, 943
Le Vieux Breakdown (The Old Breakdown) Joseph Falcon, 335
Le Vieux Soulard Et Sa Femme (The Old Drunkard And His Wife) Joseph Falcon, 334
Lead Kindly Light Loveless Twins Quartet, 514
Lead Me Delmore Brothers, 310
Lead Me Gently Home, Father Drum Quartet, 324; Friendship Four, 360; Sons Of The Pioneers, 858
Lead Me Higher Up The Mountain John McGhee & Frank Welling, 555; Red Brush Rowdies, 730
Lead Me Saviour Friendship Four, 360
Lead Me, Shepherd Vaughan Quartet, 926
Leaf By Leaf The Roses Fall Holland Puckett, 715
Leaf From The Sea [A] Wade Mainer, 582
Leake County Blues Leake County Revelers, 495
Leake County Breakdown Leake County Revelers, 495
Leake County Two Step [The] Freeny's Barn Dance Band, 359
Leanin' On The Hitchin' Rail Charlie Marshall, 587
Leanin' On The Old Top Rail Jimmie Davis, 304
Leanin' On The Ole Top Rail Patsy Montana, 636
Leaning Charming Betsy W.L. "Rustic" Waters, 940
Leaning On The Everlasting Arm Sons Of The Pioneers, 858
Leaning On The Everlasting Arms John McGhee & Frank Welling, 556, 563; Irene Spain Family, 861
Learning Macfayden To Dance Earl Shirkey & Roy Harper, 832
Learning McFadden To Waltz Roy Harvey, 409
Leather Breeches Carter Brothers & Son, 187; Robert Cook's Old Time Fiddlers, 220; Tommy Dandurand, 293; Clifford Gross, 385; William B. Houchens, 443; Earl Johnson, 460;

Leather Breeches (*continued*)
  Leake County Revelers, 494; Doc Roberts, 753; "Uncle Bunt" Stephens, 868; Uncle "Am" Stuart, 881; Arthur Tanner, 886; Gid Tanner, 890; Uncle Jimmy Thompson, 904
Leather Briches [*sic*] Tim Flora & Rufus Lingo, 350
Leather Britches W.A. Hinton, 428; White Mountain Orchestra, 951
L'Eau Haute (High Water Waltz) Bartmon Montet-Joswell Dupuis, 637
Leave It There Ruth Donaldson & Helen Jepsen, 323; [Smilin'] Ed McConnell, 530–31; Frank & James McCravy, 532, 535–36; Snowball & Sunshine, 853
Leave It Up To Uncle Jake Zeke Manners, 586
Leave Me Alone, Sweet Mama Jesse Rodgers, 798
Leave Me Darling I Don't Mind Crowder Brothers, 237
Leave Me If You Wish Hackberry Ramblers, 387
Leave Me With A Smile Tune Wranglers, 915; Walker's Corbin Ramblers, 937
Leave The Old Sheep Alone Uncle Dave Macon, 577
Leave The Purty Gals Alone Carson Robison, 780, 782–84
Leave Your Sorrows And Come Along Tennessee Music & Printing Co. Quartet, 896
Leavenworth Duel Frady, 358
Leavenworth Jail Vagabonds, 921
Leaves Of Shamrock [The] Riley Puckett, 718
Leaving Dear Old Ireland Charlie Poole, 700
Leaving Here Blues Kentucky String Ticklers, 478
Leaving Home Charlie Poole, 699; Swing Billies, 885
Leaving North Carolina Carolina Ramblers String Band, 172
Leaving On That Train Anglin Brothers, 61; Delmore Brothers, 311
Leaving On The New River Train Crazy Hillbillies Band, 232
Leaving Smiles [Smilin'] Ed McConnell, 530
Leaving The Farm Roland Cauley, 198
Leaving Town Blues Bill Cox, 225
Leaving You Blues Jap Magee, 580
Leaving Your Home Clifford (C.S.) Wagner, 933
Led By The Lord Of All E.B. Holden Quartet, 432
Lee County Blues Tweedy Brothers, 918; George Walburn & Emmett Hethcox, 935
Lee County Rag Asa Martin, 589
Leechburg Polka Dick Hartman's Tennessee Ramblers, 408
Left All Alone Cliff Carlisle, 163
Left All Alone Again Blues Lowe Stokes, 870
Left In The Dark Blues "Uncle Bunt" Stephens, 868
Left My Gal In The Mountains Gene Autry, 71; Lonesome Cowboy [II], 509; Carson Robison, 774–77, 786
Lefty's Breakdown Prairie Ramblers, 704
Legire Ma Pauvre Idie (Ease My Wearied Mind) [A] Sons Of Acadians, 856
Lei Ilima James Brown, Jr. & Ken Landon Groups, 135
Leleaux Breakdown Four Aces, 356
Lend Your Aid [E.R.] Nance Family, 648
Lenoir County Blues Roland Cauley, 198
Lenox Charles Butts Sacred Harp Singers, 149
Les Blues De Bosco Happy Fats, 395
Les Blues De Crowley (Crowley Blues) Amedie Ardoin, 62
Les Blues De La Louisianne (Louisiana Blues) Leo Soileau, 854
Les Blues De La Prison (The Jail House Blues) Amedie Ardoin, 62
Les Blues De Voyage (Travel Blues) Amedie Ardoin, 62
Les Blues Du Texas Denus McGee, 551
Les Crepes A'Nasta Happy Fats, 395
Les Ecrivis Dan Platin Happy Fats, 395
Les Poules Paus Pas (Chickens Don't Lay) Joe Werner, 944
Les Tete Fille Lafayette Happy Fats, 396

Les Tracas Du Hobo Blues Amadie Breaux, 126
Let A Smile Be Your Umbrella On A Rainy Day Shelton Brothers, 829
Let Her Go Ted Daffan's Texans, 240
Let Her Go God Bless Her J.E. Mainer's Mountaineers, 581
Let Her Go I'll Meet Her Richard D. Burnett, 145; John D. Foster, 354
Let Him Go God Bless Him Thomas C. Ashley, 68
Let Him Lead You Jack & Jean, 451
Let It Alone Chris Bouchillon, 119
Let It End This Way Leon Payne, 683
Let Jesus Convoy You Home Rangers Quartet, 728
Let Me Be Your Man In The Moon Ernest Rogers, 810
Let Me Be Your Salty Dog Morris Brothers, 643
Let Me Be Your Side Track Jess Hillard, 426; Howard Keesee, 475; Jimmie Rodgers, 805
Let Me Bring It To Your Door Shelly Lee Alley, 58
Let Me Build A Cabin Roy Rogers, 811
Let Me Call You Mine Jesse Rodgers, 798
Let Me Call You Sweetheart Clayton McMichen, 566; Melton & Minter, 615; Nicholson's Players, 659; Walter C. Peterson, 688; Riley Puckett, 717; Dick Robertson, 758; Jimmie Wilson's Catfish String Band, 968
Let Me Call You Sweetheart (I'm In Love With You) Vernon Dalhart, 266; Leo Soileau, 855; Bob Wills, 964
Let Me Call You Sweetheart Again Rex Griffin, 383
Let Me Down Easy John McGhee & Frank Welling, 558
Let Me Go Down To The River J.B. Whitmire's Blue Sky Trio, 954
Let Me Go Home Mount Vernon Mixed Quartet, 645
Let Me Hear The Songs My Mother Used To Sing Frank & James McCravy, 534
Let Me Hear You Say "I Love You" Claude Casey, 197
Let Me Join The C.C.C. Al Dexter, 315
Let Me Live And Love You Jimmie Revard, 743
Let Me Live Close To Thee Stamps Quartet, 864
Let Me Play With It Dick Hartman's Tennessee Ramblers, 408
Let Me Rest Forman Sisters, 352
Let Me Ride By Your Side In The Saddle Light Crust Doughboys, 504
Let Me Sleep On The Edge Of The Prairie Girls Of The Golden West, 371
Let Me Smile My Last Smile At You Cliff Bruner, 141
Let Me Travel Along Whitey & Hogan, 952
Let My Peaches Be Riley Puckett, 722
Let That Liar Alone Emry Arthur, 65
Let That Mule Go Aunk! Aunk! Bradley Kincaid, 483
Let The Church Roll On Carter Family, 189; S.E. Mullis, 646
Let The Lower Lights Be Burning Katherine Baxter & Harry Nelson, 97; Jenkins Family, 457; Smith's Sacred Singers, 849–50; Woodlawn Quartette, 971; Rowdy Wright, 974
Let The Rest Of The World Go By Lester McFarland & Robert A. Gardner, 545; John McGhee & Frank Welling, 560; Clayton McMichen, 566; Melton & Minter, 615; Riley Puckett, 717; Ranch Boys, 727; Texas Rangers, 899
Let The Song Ring Out John McGhee & Frank Welling, 556
Let Us All Stay At Home Three Tobacco Tags, 909
Let Us Be Lovers Again Monroe Brothers, 633
Let Us Try My Dream Dixie Ramblers [III], 319
Let Your Shack Burn Down Fisher Hendley, 416
Letart Isle Jackson County Ramblers, 452
Let's All Get Good And Drunk Prairie Ramblers, 712
Let's All Go Down To Grandpa's Bar-X Cowboys, 93
Let's All Go Home Uncle Dave Macon, 577
Let's All Have Another Beer Karl & Harty, 471
Let's All Take A Drink Together Leo Soileau, 854
Let's Be Friends Again Tom Darby & Jimmie Tarlton, 295

Let's Be Lovers Again Carter Family, 192
Let's Be Sweethearts Again Oliver & Allen, 669; Smith & Dyal, 847; William Steudevant, 868
Let's Count The Stars Together Adolph Hofner, 431
Let's Do It Honey Shelly Lee Alley, 59
Let's Dream Of Each Other Bill Carlisle, 159
Let's Get Together Jimmy Long, 511
Let's Go Johnson & Lee, 462; Tune Wranglers, 915
Let's Go Back To The Bible Wilf Carter (Montana Slim), 186
Let's Go Down To The Old State Fair Hank Keene, 474
Let's Go Dreaming Charles Mitchell & His Orchestra, 630
Let's Go Fishing Hackberry Ramblers, 388
Let's Go Honky-Tonkin' Tonight Bar-X Cowboys, 93
Let's Go To Tassone Denus McGee, 551
Let's Go To The Rendezvous Happy Fats, 396
Let's Go To Ville Platte Leo Soileau, 854
Let's Have The Old Time Ring E. Arthur Lewis, 497–98
Let's Incorporate Dick Hartman's Tennessee Ramblers, 409
Let's Make Believe We're Sweethearts Light Crust Doughboys, 505; Tune Wranglers, 916; Village Boys, 932
Let's Not And Say We Did Hoosier Hot Shots, 440
Let's Play Love Bob Skyles, 838
Let's Pretend Hank Snow, 853; Sons Of The Pioneers, 858
Let's Ride With Bob (Theme Song) Charlie Wills, 966
Let's Spend The Night In Hawaii Hi-Flyers, 419
Let's Start All Over Again Jimmy Hart, 406
Let's Start Life All Over Bob Atcher, 70
Let's Tell Our Dream To The Moon Bob Atcher, 70
Let's Tie The Knot Cliff Carlisle, 165
Letter Edged In Black Cotton Butterfield, 149; Fiddlin' John Carson, 176; Vernon Dalhart, 246, 251–54, 281, 285, 291–92; Bradley Kincaid, 485; Frank Luther, 523, 525; George Reneau, 741; Carson Robison, 769; Marc Williams, 959
Letter From Home [The] Ted Chestnut, 204
Letter From Home Sweet Home [The] Asa Martin, 591; Charles Nabell, 647
Letter I Never Did Mail [The] Bill Boyd, 125
Letter That Came Too Late [The] Lester McFarland & Robert A. Gardner, 543
Letter That Never Came [The] Blue Ridge Mountain Singers, 112; Pie Plant Pete, 694; Charlie Poole, 699
Letter That Went To God [The] Bob Atcher, 69; Byron Parker, 675
Letter To A Soldier [A] Ted Daffan's Texans, 241
Letter To Dad In The Skies [A] Bill Carlisle, 159
Letter To Mother [A] Judie & Julie, 468
Letting Jesus Lead Blue Ridge Sacred Singers, 112
Lettres D'Amour Dans Le Sable (Love Letters In The Sand) Joseph Falcon, 336
Levee Breaking Blues—Part I, II Happy Bud Harrison, 406
Levee Song Sandhills Sixteen, 820
'Leven Cent Cotton Vernon Dalhart, 284; Bob Miller, 617; Carson Robison, 770
'Leven Cent Cotton And Forty Cent Meat Bob Miller, 618
'Leven Cent Cotton, Forty Cent Meat Carson Robison, 773
'Leven Miles From Leavenworth Shelton Brothers, 827; Walton West, 945
Levison Reel John Baltzell, 91
Lexington Blues Porter Phillips, 690
Liberty Herschel Brown, 133–34; Fiddlin' John Carson, 176; Moody Bible Sacred Harp Singers, 637; Gid Tanner, 889; Tweedy Brothers, 918; Charlie Wills, 966
Liberty Number One Lowe Stokes, 871
Lie He Wrote Home [The] Frank Luther, 520; Bob Miller, 624; Radio Rubes, 723
Liebestraum Bob Wills, 965
Lies Bar-X Cowboys, 92; Texas Wanderers, 900

Life Ain't Worth Living When You're Broke John McGhee & Frank Welling, 555
Life And Death Of Jesse James Uncle Dave Macon, 577
Life And Death Of John Dillinger [The] Wilf Carter (Montana Slim), 181–82
Life Boat [The] Carolina Ladies Quartet, 171; Jo & Alma, 459; Frank & James McCravy, 537; Smith's Sacred Singers, 849
Life Can Never Be The Same York Brothers, 978
Life In The City Leroy Roberson, 752
Life Is A Mighty Long Time Prairie Ramblers, 707
Life Is But A Dream Johnnie & Jack, 459
Life Is Like A Mountain Railroad Bradley Kincaid, 485
Life Line Blue Sky Boys, 113
Life Of A Tramp [The] Red Fox Chasers, 731
Life Of Jimmie Rodgers [The] Gene Autry, 79; Bradley Kincaid, 485
Life Of Tom Watson Vernon Dalhart, 253, 255
Life On An Ocean Wave Malcolm Legette, 496
Life On The Ocean Wave Frank[ie] Marvin, 599
Life Time Man [The] Duke Clark, 213
Life's Evening Sun Is Sinking Low Massey Family, 610
Life's Ev'nin' Sun Wade Mainer, 584
Life's Ocean Waves Are Rolling On Owen Brothers & Ellis, 671
Life's Railway To Heaven Allen Quartette, 57; Rev. Horace A. Booker, 117; Buice Brothers, 142; Calhoun Sacred Quartet, 151; Crowder Brothers, 238; Sid Harkreader, 401; Fred Kirby, 487; [Smilin'] Ed McConnell, 530–31; John McGhee & Frank Welling, 558–59; Montgomery Quartet, 637; Pickard Family, 693; George Reneau, 740–41; Smith's Sacred Singers, 849; Southern Railroad Quartet, 861; J. Douglas Swagerty, 883; Ernest Thompson, 902
Life's Troubled Pathway Bill Carlisle, 160
Life's Troubled Sea Rev. M.L. Thrasher, 905
Lifetime Prisoner Duke Clark, 213
Lift Him Up Spindale Quartet, 862
Lift Up The Standard Ruth Donaldson & Helen Jepsen, 323
Light Foot Bill Arkansas Woodchopper, 64
Light Of Homer Rogers [The] Dorsey & Beatrice Dixon, 322
Light Of Life Virginia Male Quartet, 932
Lighthouse Song [The] Honeyboy & Sassafras[s], 433
Lightning Bug Blues Allen Brothers, 56
Lightning Express (Please, Mr. Conductor) Vernon Dalhart, 257
Lightning Express [The] Blue Sky Boys, 114; Fiddlin' John Carson, 175; Crockett [Family] Mountaineers, 233; Vernon Dalhart, 249, 253; Frank Hutchison, 449; Bradley Kincaid, 484; Lester McFarland & Robert A. Gardner, 544; Pie Plant Pete, 695; Riley Puckett, 715; George Reneau, 741; Ernest V. Stoneman, 872; Ernest Thompson, 902
Lightning Express Train [The] Arthur Tanner, 886
Lights Along The Shore Palmetto Male Quartette, 674
Lights In The Valley J.E. Mainer's Mountaineers, 581
Lights In The Valley Outshine The Sun Homer Briarhopper, 127
Lights Out Ranch Boys, 727
Like A Monkey Likes Cocoanuts Hoosier Hot Shots, 438
Like An Angel You Flew Into Everyone's Heart (Lindbergh) Vernon Dalhart, 270
Like The Doctor Said Buddy Jones, 465
Like The Rainbow Stamps Quartet, 864
Like You Bill Boyd, 123
Likes Likker Better Than Me Ephraim Woodie, 971
Lil Liza Jane Taylor Flanagan, 345; Massey Family, 611; Bob Wills, 965; Charlie Wills, 966
Lillian Branch Norwood Tew, 899
Lillie Dale Asa Martin, 593

Lillie Sweet Lillie Roe Brothers & Morrell, 810
Lilly Dale Asa Martin, 589
Lilly Of The Valley [The] Elmer Bird, 105
Lilly Reunion [The] Roy Harvey, 411
Lily Of The Valley [The] Happy Valley Family, 398; John McGhee & Frank Welling, 554, 561; Jack Pickell, 694
Lily That Bloomed For Me [The] Clayton McMichen, 572
Limber Neck Blues W.T. Narmour & S.W. Smith, 649
Lime Rock Smith's Garage Fiddle Band, 848
Limehouse Blues Hoosier Hot Shots, 436
Lincoln County Blues Nations Brothers, 652
Linda May Polka Rice Brothers' Gang, 747
Lindbergh (The Eagle Of The U.S.A.) Vernon Dalhart, 269–71
Lindy Proximity String Quartet, 714
Line That Used To Be In Front [The] E. Arthur Lewis, 498
Lineman's Serenade H.M. Barnes, 94
Lion Rag Kelly Brothers, 476
Lips That Touch Liquor Shall Never Touch Mine John D. Foster, 354
Liquor Bowl Blues Bill Cox, 229
Listen To The Mocking Bird Billy Bishop, 107; Elton Britt, 127; Curley Fox, 357; Theron Hale, 389; Bela Lam, 489; Leake County Revelers, 494; Light Crust Doughboys, 506; Fiddling Sam Long, 512; W.W. Macbeth, 526; Massey Family, 611; William Rexroat's Cedar Crest Singers, 744; Short Brothers, 833
Listen To The Rhythm Of The Range Roy Rogers, 811
Listen To The Story Of Sleepy Hollow Bill Girls Of The Golden West, 370
Listen To The Voice Jimmy Long, 511
Lita Shelton Brothers, 829
Little Acadian Girl Hackberry Ramblers, 388
Little Ah Sid Arkansas Woodchopper, 63; Ranch Boys, 726–27; Twilight Trail Boys, 918
Little Alice Summers Charlie Craver, 231
Little Annie Lake Howard, 445
Little Annie Rooney Walter C. Peterson, 688
Little Bar Fly [The] Light Crust Doughboys, 506
Little Bessie Blue Sky Boys, 113; Tom Darby & Jimmie Tarlton, 294; Dorsey & Beatrice Dixon, 321; Buell Kazee, 472; Holland Puckett, 715; Red Headed Brier Hopper, 732; Walter Smith, 847
Little Betty Brown Milton Brown, 137; Kessinger Brothers, 481
Little Birdie Coon Creek Girls, 221; Vernon Dalhart, 251; John Hammond, 394; Wade Mainer, 583; Land Norris, 662; Holland Puckett, 715; Albert Rose, 813
Little Bit Of Lovin' From You [A] Cliff Carlisle, 167
Little Black Bronc Al Clauser, 214
Little Black Moustache [The] Vernon Dalhart, 254, 258; Lulu Belle & Scotty, 515; Asa Martin, 589; Ernest V. Stoneman, 876
Little Black Mustache [The] Vernon Dalhart, 257, 273; Arthur Fields & Fred Hall, 338; Nations Brothers, 652
Little Black Train [The] Carter Family, 193; Harmon E. Helmick, 415
Little Black Train Is Coming [The] Emry Arthur, 64
Little Blossom Arkansas Woodchopper, 63; Bill Cox, 229
Little Blossom—Part 1, 2 Edward L. Crain, 229–30
Little Blue Eyed Blonde, Goodbye Pete Pyle, 723
Little Blue Haird [sic] Boy Cumberland Mountain Fret Pickers, 239
Little Blue Ridge Girl Clayton McMichen, 567
Little Bonnie Eldon Baker, 90; Ridgel's Fountain Citians, 749
Little Boy Working On The Road J.W. Day, 306
Little Brown Church [The] Montgomery Quartet, 637
Little Brown Eyed Girl Dick Reinhart, 739

Little Brown Head Orla Clark, 214
Little Brown Jug Roland Cauley, 199
Little Brown Jug [The] Uncle Tom Collins, 219; Vernon Dalhart, 277, 282; G.W. Fields, 345; Taylor Flanagan, 345; W.A. Hinton, 427; John Henry Howard, 444; Kessinger Brothers, 480–81; Frank Luther, 524; Clayton McMichen, 566; Clyde Martin, 593; Massey Family, 611; Chubby Parker, 676–77; Pie Plant Pete, 695; Riley Puckett, 718; George Reneau, 740–41; Carson Robison, 796; Tennessee Ramblers [I], 896; Ernest Thompson, 902; Floyd Thompson, 903; Welby Toomey, 912; Henry Whitter, 954
Little Brown Jug Goes Modern [The] Denver Darling, 296
Little Brown-Eyed Lady Adolph Hofner, 430
Little Bunch Of Roses Frank Blevins, 108; Clarence Greene, 382; Judie & Julie, 468; Howard Keesee, 475; Murphy Brothers, 646
Little Cabin In The Cascade Mountains Carson Robison, 781
Little Child Shall Lead Them [A] David Miller, 626–27
Little Close Harmony [A] Vaughan Quartet, 927
Little Cory Clarence Gill, 369
Little Cotton Mill Girl Bob Miller, 620
Little Cowboy Jim Asher Sizemore & Little Jimmie, 836
Little Darling Lew Preston, 713; Johnny Roberts, 756; Arthur Smith, 841
Little Darling Pal Of Mine Lysle Byrd, 150; Carter Family, 187, 193; Hill Brothers, 424; Leo Soileau, 855
Little Darling They Have Taken You From Me Arthur Smith, 841
Little Darling, I'll Be Yours Clayton McMichen, 572; Pine Ridge Boys, 697
Little David Play On Your Harp Joe Reed Family, 734
Little Dobe Shack [The] Carter Family, 192
Little Dobie Shack [The] Bill Carlisle, 159; Carlisle Brothers, 168
Little Doctor Fell In The Well Charlie Poole, 700
Little Dog Blues Amadie Breaux, 126
Little Dog Waltz Charlie Poole, 699
Little Dog Yodel Ralph Richardson, 748
Little Dolly Driftwood Grover Rann, 728
Little Dutch Mill Leo Soileau, 855
Little Empty Cradle Chezz Chase, 202–03
Little Empty Crib [The] Hank Keene, 474
Little Fairy George R. Pariseau's Orchestra, 675
Little Farm Home Gene Autry, 79
Little Farm House Upon The Hill Kenneth Houchins, 443
Little Flower Girl [The] Andrew Jenkins, 454
Little Foot Prints Ernest Branch & Bernice Coleman, 125
Little Frankie Roba Stanley, 866
Little Girl Dressed In Blue [The] Hugh Cross, 237; Light Crust Doughboys, 504; Frank Luther, 522; Jesse Rodgers, 799
Little Girl In Carolina Lester McFarland & Robert A. Gardner, 549
Little Girl Of My Dreams Dick Reinhart, 739
Little Girl That Played On My Knee [The] Carter Family, 194
Little Girl You've Done Me Wrong Hall Brothers, 391
Little Girl, Go Ask Your Mama Bob Wills, 963
Little Girl, Go Ask Your Mother Claude Casey, 197
Little Girl, I'm So Blue Without You Rice Brothers' Gang, 747
Little Girl, You Know I Love You Watkins Band, 940
Little Girl's Plea Billy Vest, 931
Little Grave In Georgia [The] Earl Johnson, 460
Little Green Mound On The Hill [The] Chuck Wagon Gang, 210
Little Green Mound On The Hillside Hank Keene, 474
Little Green Valley [The] Arkansas Woodchopper, 63;

Vernon Dalhart, 279–80; Farmer Sisters, 336; Dick Hartman's Tennessee Ramblers, 407; Carson Robison, 762–64, 786
Little Grey Church In The Valley [The] Frank Luther, 522
Little Grey Home In The West Eddie Dean, 308
Little Heaven Of The Seven Seas Bob Wills, 963
Little High Chair [A] Happy Fats, 396
Little Hill-Billy Heart Throb Odis Elder, 331; Light Crust Doughboys, 503
Little Home Down In The Valley [The] Otis & Eleanor, 670
Little Home in Tennessee Farmer Sisters, 337
Little Home Of Long Ago Lester McFarland & Robert A. Gardner, 549–50
Little Home On The Hill Fleming & Townsend, 348
Little Home Upon The Hill Fleming & Townsend, 346
Little Honey Bee Bill Carlisle, 159
Little Honky Tonk Headache Light Crust Doughboys, 506
Little Honky Tonk Heart-throb Light Crust Doughboys, 506
Little Hula Girl Jimmy Hart, 406
Little Indian Napanee Duke Clark, 213; David Miller, 626
Little Janie Green Cofer Brothers, 216
Little Jimmie's Goodbye To Jimmie Rodgers Asher Sizemore & Little Jimmie, 836
Little Joe Carter Family, 194; Doc Hopkins, 441; Bradley Kincaid, 485; Monroe Brothers, 633; Charles Nabell, 647; Prairie Ramblers, 707–08
Little Joe The Hobo Curly Gray, 378
Little Joe The Wrangler Jules Allen, 54; Arizona Wranglers, 62; Leon Chappelear, 200; Everett Cheetham, 203; Lew Childre, 207; Edward L. Crain, 230; Ranch Boys, 726–27; Goebel Reeves, 737; Marc Williams, 958
Little Kaplan Happy Fats, 396
Little Lady Whitey McPherson, 579
Little Log Cabin By The Sea Carter Family, 187
Little Log Cabin By The Stream [The] Fiddlin' John Carson, 177
Little Log Cabin In The Lane John D. Foster, 353; Lester McFarland & Robert A. Gardner, 546; Riley Puckett, 718; Arthur Tanner, 886
Little Log Hut In The Lane [The] Carter Family, 189
Little Log Shack I Can Always Call My Home [A] Wilf Carter (Montana Slim), 181, 183
Little Lost Child Frank Luther, 523; Carson Robison, 772
Little Love [A] Wade Mainer, 584
Little Love Ship Tune Wranglers, 916
Little Lulie Homer Briarhopper, 127; Dick Justice, 468
Little Maggie Wade Mainer, 583
Little Maggie With A Dram Glass In Her Hand G.B. Grayson & Henry Whitter, 381
Little Maiden Of The Mountain Chas. M. Dewitte, 313
Little Mamie Elmer Bird, 105–06
Little Man Swift Jewel Cowboys, 884
Little Marian McLean Bob Miller, 621
Little Marian Parker Vernon Dalhart, 278–79; Andrew Jenkins, 454
Little Marion Parker Vernon Dalhart, 276, 279
Little Mary Jane Charlie Craver, 231
Little Mary Phagan Rosa Lee Carson, 179; Vernon Dalhart, 247, 251, 255
Little Maud Bela Lam, 489
Little Maumee Riley Puckett, 719
Little Mohee Hall Brothers, 391; Kelly Harrell, 403; Buell Kazee, 472; Bradley Kincaid, 483; Flora Noles, 661; Pie Plant Pete, 695
Little More Sugar In The Coffee Fiddlin' John Carson, 178
Little Moses Carter Family, 188; Harmon E. Helmick, 415; Jo & Alma, 458
Little Mother Of Mine Deckers, 309

Little Mother Of The Hills Edith & Sherman Collins, 218; Farmer Sisters, 336; Bob Miller, 624; James Roberts, 756; Carson Robison, 794–95; Vagabonds, 921
Little Mouse Parade [The] Travelers, 912
Little Nan Oscar Ford, 352
Little Nell Lester McFarland & Robert A. Gardner, 545
Little Nellie Morris Brothers, 643
Little Nellie's Waltz Bob Larkan & Family, 491
Little Newsboy [The] Andrew Jenkins, 454
Little Nigger Baby George Reneau, 740
Little Ola Tom Darby & Jimmie Tarlton, 294
Little Old Band Of Gold Gene Autry, 84
Little Old Brick Church [The] Vagabonds, 921
Little Old Cabin In The Lane Girls Of The Golden West, 370; Fiddlin' Powers & Family, 703
Little Old Cabin In The Mountain [The] Andrew Jenkins, 455
Little Old Church In The Valley [The] W.C. Childers, 206; Jimmy Long, 511; Lester McFarland & Robert A. Gardner, 548; Dixie Mason, 608; Carson Robison, 788
Little Old Church On The Hilltop Roy Rogers, 812
Little Old Cross Road Store John McGhee & Frank Welling, 563
Little Old Farm House Upon The Hill Kenneth Houchins, 444
Little Old Hut [The] Beard's Quartette, 98
Little Old Jail House [The] Asa Martin, 589–91
Little Old Locket Of Gold Patsy Montana, 636
Little Old Log Cabin By The Stream Ted Chestnut, 204
Little Old Log Cabin In The Lane Binkley Brothers Dixie Clodhoppers, 104; Fiddlin' John Carson, 175; Roland Cauley, 199; Vernon Dalhart, 269; Doc Hopkins, 441; Bradley Kincaid, 483; Uncle Dave Macon, 574; David Miller, 626; Fiddlin' Powers & Family, 703; Riley Puckett, 715; Ernest V. Stoneman, 873–74; Taylor's Kentucky Boys, 895
Little Old Sod Shanty [The] Jules Allen, 55; Charlie Craver, 231; Jack Weston, 947; John I. White, 949; Marc Williams, 958
Little Old Sod Shanty On My Claim Bill Bender, 99
Little Old Sod Shanty On The Claim Ranch Boys, 726–27
Little Old Sweet Lady Jim[my] Boa, 115; Bob Miller, 624
Little Or Big Leo Soileau, 854
Little Or Big, Give It To Me Joe Creduer-Albert Babineaux, 232
Little Pal Bill Carlisle, 160; John McGhee & Frank Welling, 557–58; Wade Mainer, 583; Byron Parker, 675
Little Pal Of Mine Bobby Gregory, 383
Little Pale Face Girl [The] Johnnie Gates, 363
Little Paper Boy Julian Johnson & Leon Hyatt, 461
Little Pardner Gene Autry, 84
Little Picture Playhouse Jimmie Revard, 743
Little Pony, Travel On To Arizona Sons Of The Ozarks, 857
Little Poplar Log House On The Hill Callahan Brothers, 152; Carter Family, 195
Little Prairie Town Jesse Rodgers, 799
Little Prayer For Me [A] Jimmie Revard, 742
Little Princess Footsteps [The] Newton County Hill Billies, 658
Little Rabbit And Rabbit Where's Your Mammy Crockett [Family] Mountaineers, 234
Little Rag Doll Big Slim Aliff, 54; Stuart Hamblen, 393
Little Ragamuffin [The] Hank Keene, 474
Little Ranch House On Circle B Blue Ridge Mountain Girls, 112
Little Ranch House On The Old Circle B [The] Gene Autry, 77–78
Little Red Caboose Vernon Dalhart, 286; Bob Miller, 618–19

Little Red Caboose Behind The Train [The] Bob Miller, 616, 618, 622; Pickard Family, 692; Taylor's Kentucky Boys, 895; Paul Warmack, 939
Little Red Head Bob Wills, 963
Little Red Lantern Bob Miller, 619
Little Red Patch On The Seat Of My Trousers [The] Wilf Carter (Montana Slim), 184
Little Red Piggy [The] Three Tobacco Tags, 909
Little Red Pink Bill Shepherd, 830
Little Red Shawl That Mother Wore [The] Alexander & Apple, 53
Little Red Shoes Bill Cox, 228; Monroe Brothers, 632
Little Rendezvous In Honolulu [A] Hackberry Ramblers, 387
Little Rock Getaway Light Crust Doughboys, 505
Little Rose Covered Garden Three Tobacco Tags, 909
Little Rose Covered Shack [The] Elton Britt, 127
Little Rose Of The Prairie Patsy Montana, 635
Little Rosebud Casket [The] Ernest Thompson, 902
Little Rosebuds Wade Mainer, 583
Little Rosewood Casket Vernon Dalhart, 248–49, 251–52, 281; Cal Davenport, 296; Bradley Kincaid, 482–83, 485; Frank Luther, 525; George Reneau, 741
Little Rubber Dolly Light Crust Doughboys, 505; Wiley Walker & Gene Sullivan, 935
Little Sadie Thomas C. Ashley, 67
Little Sally Waters Uncle Dave Macon, 577
Little Seaside Village Roy Harvey, 411
Little Shack Around The Corner Asa Martin, 593
Little Shack By The Maple Fleming & Townsend, 347
Little Shirt My Mother Made For Me [The] Charlie Craver, 231
Little Shoes Vagabonds, 921; West Brothers Trio, 946
Little Silver Haired Sweetheart Of Mine Wilf Carter (Montana Slim), 181
Little Sir Echo Gene Autry, 84; Riley Puckett, 722
Little Sod Shanty Al Dexter, 314
Little Star W.T. Narmour & S.W. Smith, 649
Little Star Of Heaven Charles Mitchell & His Orchestra, 630
Little Story [A] Callahan Brothers, 153
Little Stranger Hall Family, 392
Little Stream Of Whiskey Richard D. Burnett, 144
Little Streams Of Whiskey John D. Foster, 354
Little Street Where Old Friends Meet [A] Frank Luther, 518, 522
Little Sweetheart Sid Harkreader, 400
Little Sweetheart (I Miss You) Dick Reinhart, 739; Jimmy Wakely, 934
Little Sweetheart Come And Kiss Me Roy Hall, 391
Little Sweetheart Of The Mountain Dick Hartman's Tennessee Ramblers, 407
Little Sweetheart Of The Mountains Lester McFarland & Robert A. Gardner, 548; Johnny Marvin, 606; Carson Robison, 786
Little Sweetheart Of The Ozarks Tex Fletcher, 349; Patsy Montana, 635
Little Sweetheart Of The Prairie Hank Keene, 474; Johnny Marvin, 606; Bob Miller, 620; Carson Robison, 786
Little Sweetheart Pal Of Mine Red Fox Chasers, 731
Little Sweetheart, I'm In Prison Karl & Harty, 471
Little Sweetheart, Little Pal Of Mine Kenneth Houchins, 443
Little Swiss Whistling Song Carson Robison, 796
Little Talk With Jesus [A] Majestic [Male] Quartet, 585; Ernest Phipps, 691
Little Texas Cowgirl Tex Dunn, 327
Little Turtle Dove Bascom Lamar Lunsford, 517; Prairie Ramblers, 712
Little While Ago [A] Tune Wranglers, 915
Little While Then Glory [A] Stamps Quartet, 864

Little White House [The] Rambling Kid & The Professor, 725
Little White Lies Cliff Bruner, 140
Little White Rose Cliff Carlisle, 164, 166; Murphy Brothers, 646
Little White Washed Cabin [The] William Hanson, 395
Little Whitewashed Chimney At The End Jess Hillard, 426
Little Wild Rose Bill Carlisle, 159
Little Willie Green (From New Orleans) Swift Jewel Cowboys, 884
Little Wooden Doll Norwood Tew, 898
Little Wooden Whistle Bill Boyd, 123
Little Wooden Whistle Wouldn't Whistle [The] Massey Family, 610
Little Yeller Dog [A] Fred L. Jeske, 458
Live And Let Live Roy Acuff, 51; Denver Darling, 296; Jimmie Davis, 305; Wiley Walker & Gene Sullivan, 936
Live Anyhow Till I Die B.F. Kincaid, 482
Liverpool Hornpipe William B. Houchens, 443
Livin' In The Mountains Gene Autry, 71; Lonesome Cowboy [I], 509; Frank[ie] Marvin, 602
Livin' On The Mountain Vagabonds, 921
Living And Loving In Style Bill Nettles, 654
Living For Christ Each Day McDonald Quartet, 540; Sparkman Trio, 861; Vaughan Quartet, 928
Living For Jesus Freeman Quartette, 359; McDonald Quartet, 541; Stamps Quartet, 864
Living In Glory Divine Johnson Brothers Quartette, 463
Living On Easy Street Prairie Ramblers, 710
Living On The Glory Side Lyric Quartette, 525
Living On The Love Of God McDonald Quartet, 540
Living On The Mountain, Baby Mine Roy Acuff, 49
Living On The Sunny Side Majestic [Male] Quartet, 585
Liza Jane Perry Bechtel, 98; Carter Brothers & Son, 186; Kessinger Brothers, 480; John & Emery McClung, 530; McQueen Quartet, 579; Riley Puckett, 716; Henry Whitter, 955
Liza Pull Down The Shades Bob Wills, 963
Liza Up In The 'Simmon Tree Bradley Kincaid, 483
Liza, Curl Your Hair Breakdowners From Balsam Gap, 126
Locked Up In Prison Tom & Roy, 911
Locket Of Gold Bar-X Cowboys, 93; Ted Daffan's Texans, 241
Locomotive Blues Bert Bilbro, 104
Log Cabin Blues [The] Chezz Chase, 202
Log Cabin Call Archer Porter, 702
Log Cabin Home Rosa Lee Carson, 180
Log Cabin In The Lane Clayton McMichen, 571
Log Cabin On The Hill Johnson & Lee, 462
Logan County Blues Frank Hutchison, 449
Lola Lee Stuart Hamblen, 393; Wiley Walker & Gene Sullivan, 936
London Bridge Walter C. Peterson, 688
London Polka John Baltzell, 91
Lone And Sad J.D. Harris, 405
Lone Child [The] Rosa Lee Carson, 179
Lone Cowboy [The] Smiley Burnette, 145; Red Foley, 350
Lone Driftin' Riders [The] Patt Patterson, 682
Lone Eagle (Lindy To Mexico) Vernon Dalhart, 276
Lone Indian Dr. D.D. Hollis, 432
Lone Prairie Otto Gray, 378
Lone Star Bill Boyd, 122; Patsy Montana, 634; Ranch Boys, 726
Lone Star Lullaby Patsy Montana, 636
Lone Star Pony Sons Of The Ozarks, 856
Lone Star Rag Bob Wills, 964
Lone Star Trail [The] Ken Maynard, 614
Lone Summer Day [A] Welby Toomey, 912
Lonely Brock & Dudley, 131; Cliff Carlisle, 167

Lonely And Blue, Pining For You Jimmy Long, 511–12
Lonely And Sad Odus & Woodrow, 667
Lonely As I Can Be W.L. "Rustic" Waters, 940
Lonely Blues [The] Roy Hall, 390
Lonely Child [The] Ashley's Melody Makers, 68
Lonely Cowboy—Part 1, 2 Arthur Miles, 616
Lonely Cowgirl Girls Of The Golden West, 370
Lonely Days In Texas Jesse Rodgers, 798
Lonely Drifter [The] Asa Martin, 591
Lonely Grave [The] Grant Brothers, 377
Lonely Graveyard Cliff Carlisle, 164
Lonely Heart Of Mine Ross Rhythm Rascals, 814; Smoky Wood, 971
Lonely Hillbilly Jesse Rodgers, 799
Lonely Hobo Jimmie Davis, 299
Lonely Little Hobo Slim Smith, 846
Lonely Little Orphan Child Cliff Carlisle, 167
Lonely Memories Joe Cook, 220
Lonely Nights In Hawaii Tom & Don, 911
Lonely Prisoner [The] Dorsey & Beatrice Dixon, 321
Lonely Ranger Am I [A] Roy Rogers, 811
Lonely River Gene Autry, 86
Lonely Rose Massey Family, 611
Lonely Rose Of Mexico Sons Of The Pioneers, 859
Lonely Since Norma's Gone Clarence Bowlin, 120
Lonely Sweetheart Philyaw Brothers, 690
Lonely Tomb Wade Mainer, 584
Lonely Tramp [A] Tim Flora & Rufus Lingo, 350
Lonely Valley Cliff Carlisle, 163
Lonely Village Churchyard John McGhee & Frank Welling, 554, 556
Lonesome Blue Ridge Hill Billies, 110
Lonesome (I Need You) Fleming & Townsend, 347
Lonesome And Blue Lester McFarland & Robert A. Gardner, 549
Lonesome And Lonely Burke Brothers, 143
Lonesome And Weary Blues Callahan Brothers, 153
Lonesome As Can Be Claude Casey, 197
Lonesome Blue Yodel Hank Snow, 852
Lonesome Blues Bowman Sisters, 121; Dutch Coleman, 217; Leake County Revelers, 495; Floyd Shreve, 833; Tune Wranglers, 915
Lonesome Boy's Letter Back Home [A] Vernon Dalhart, 263
Lonesome Cowboy Dwight Butcher, 148; Lonesome Cowboy [II], 509; Bob McGimsey, 564; Bill Simmons, 835
Lonesome Daddy Blues Ed (Jake) West, 945
Lonesome Day Today [A] Arthur Smith, 841
Lonesome Dove [The] Roy Hall, 391
Lonesome Downhearted And Blue Kenneth Houchins, 443
Lonesome Dreamer Of Love George Stevens, 868
Lonesome For Caroline Cliff Carlisle, 164
Lonesome For Mother And Home Jerry Behrens, 98
Lonesome For My Baby Tonight Wilf Carter (Montana Slim), 182
Lonesome For You Carter Family, 189; Bill Cox, 227; Arthur Smith, 841
Lonesome For You Annabelle Pine Ridge Boys, 697; Prairie Ramblers, 712
Lonesome For You, Darling Carter Family, 195; Leatherman Sisters, 495
Lonesome Freight Train Blues Callahan Brothers, 154
Lonesome Frisco Line Tom Darby & Jimmie Tarlton, 294
Lonesome Homesick Blues Carter Family, 195
Lonesome In Dreams Bill Carlisle, 159
Lonesome In The Pines Tom Darby & Jimmie Tarlton, 293
Lonesome Jailhouse Blues Delmore Brothers, 309
Lonesome Life Of Worry J.H. Howell, 446
Lonesome Lost Gal Blues Crowder Brothers, 237

Lonesome Lovesick Prisoner Philyaw Brothers, 690
Lonesome Lullaby Fred Kirby, 486
Lonesome Mama Blues Hi-Flyers, 419; Clayton McMichen, 568
Lonesome Melody Carson Robison, 775–76
Lonesome Mountain [The] Bob Atcher, 69
Lonesome Old River Blues Roy Acuff, 50
Lonesome Pine Joseph Falcon, 335
Lonesome Pine Special Carter Family, 189
Lonesome Railroad Tom Darby & Jimmie Tarlton, 294; Carson Robison, 772, 786, 788
Lonesome Railroad Blues Fred Pendleton, 685
Lonesome Ramblers Blues Arthur Smith, 841
Lonesome River Road Slim Smith, 846
Lonesome Road [The] Beverly Hill Billies, 103; Delta Twins, 312; Arthur Fields & Fred Hall, 343; Jack & Bill, 451; Leland Johnson, 461; Roy Newman, 656; Merritt Smith, 844
Lonesome Road Blues Dwight Butcher, 148; Duke Clark, 213; Corn Cob Crushers, 222; John Henry Howard, 444; Kessinger Brothers, 481; W. Lee O'Daniel, 666; Fred Pendleton, 685; George Reneau, 740–41; Smith & Irvine, 848; Ernest V. Stoneman, 874; Henry Whitter, 954; Williamson Brothers & Curry, 960; Da Costa Woltz's Southern Broadcasters, 970
Lonesome Scenes Of Winter Odus & Woodrow, 667
Lonesome Steel Guitar Ted Daffan's Texans, 241
Lonesome Trail Al Clauser, 214; Walter Couch & Wilks Ramblers, 224; Arthur Fields & Fred Hall, 341; Leon Selph, 823
Lonesome Trail Ain't Lonesome Anymore [The] Prairie Ramblers, 710
Lonesome Train Blues Hank Penny, 687
Lonesome Train Whistling Blues Tex Owens, 671
Lonesome Valley—Part 2 Dixie Reelers, 319
Lonesome Valley [The] Roy Acuff, 49; Carter Family, 189, 193; Morgan Denmon, 312; Bill Elliott, 332; Elzie Floyd & Leo Boswell, 350; Clarence Greene, 382; Frank Hutchison, 449; Lester McFarland & Robert A. Gardner, 543; David Miller, 625–27; Byrd Moore, 639
Lonesome Valley Sally Girls Of The Golden West, 370; Linda Parker, 678; Steelman Sisters, 867; Texas Rangers, 900
Lonesome Wanderer [The] Joe Werner, 943
Lonesome Weary Blues Roy Harvey, 410; Ramblin' Red Lowery, 515
Lonesome Without My Baby Kelly Brothers, 476
Lonesome Yodel Blues Delmore Brothers, 309
Lonesome Yodel Blues No. 2 Delmore Brothers, 310
Lonesome, Broke And Weary Asa Martin, 593
Lonesome, That's All Massey Family, 611
Long Ago Vernon Dalhart, 262–64; Ocie Stockard, 869
Long And Bony George Wade, 933
Long Chain Charlie Blues Bill Cox, 226
Long Eared Mule Dixie Ramblers [I], 319; Hill Billies, 422; Kessinger Brothers, 480; Ernest V. Stoneman, 872, 874
Long Gone Richard Brooks & Reuben Puckett, 132; Travis B. Hale-E.J. Derry Jr., 389; York Brothers, 978
Long Gone From Bowling Green Allen Brothers, 57
Long Horn Pipes [And] Reels Ted Markle, 587
Long John Ted Daffan's Texans, 241
Long Legged Daddy Blues Bill Carlisle, 159
Long Lonesome Road Johnny Bond, 116; Howard Keesee, 474
Long Long Ways From Home Carson Robison, 794
Long Lost Sweetheart Four Pickled Peppers, 356
'Long Side The Santa Fe' Trail Jules Allen, 55
Long Sought Home [J.T.] Allison's Sacred Harp Singers, 60
Long Tall Mama Blues Happy Bud Harrison, 405
Long Tall Mamma Blues Jimmie Rodgers, 807

'Long The Rio Grande Massey Family, 613
Long Time Ago Otis McDonnell, 541
Long Tongue Women Johnny Barfield, 94; Warren Caplinger, 157; Riley Puckett, 716–17
Long Tongued Woman [The] Warren Caplinger, 157; Henry Whitter, 955
Long Way To Tipperary Fiddlin' John Carson, 177; Frank Hutchison, 449
Long White Robe Bob Miller, 619, 625; Swift Jewel Cowboys, 884
Long, Lean, Lanky Lew Arthur Fields & Fred Hall, 341
Long, Long Ago Milton Brown, 138; Dick Hartman's Tennessee Ramblers, 407; Bradley Kincaid, 484; Roy Newman, 657; W. Lee O'Daniel, 666; Chubby Parker, 677; James Roberts, 755
Longer I Know Him [The] Stamps Quartet, 865
Longest Train [The] Roy Acuff, 49; J.E. Mainer's Mountaineers, 581; Riley Puckett, 721
Longest Train I Ever Saw [The] Grant Brothers, 377; Howard Keesee, 475; Riley Puckett, 720, 722
Longest Train I Ever Seen Clayton McMichen, 570
Longest Way Home [The] Richard Brooks & Reuben Puckett, 133
Longing For Hawaii Fleming & Townsend, 347
Longing For Home Fay & The Jay Walkers, 337; Jack Golding, 374
Longing For Mother Fleming & Townsend, 347
Longing For My Mississippi Home Wilf Carter (Montana Slim), 183
Longing For Old Virginia Carter Family, 192
Longing For You Cliff Carlisle, 165; Fleming & Townsend, 348; Hackberry Ramblers, 388; Jesse Rodgers, 799
Longing For You Sweetheart Clifford (C.S.) Wagner, 933
Longing To Hear The Train Whistle Blow Christine Smith, 843
Lonnie's Fox Chase Lonnie Glosson, 372
Lonnie's Hard Luck Lonnie Glosson, 372
Look Away From The Cross Carter Family, 195
Look Away To Calvary Flat Creek Sacred Singers, 346
Look Away To Jesus Royal Quartette, 815
Look Before You Leap Charlie Poole, 700
Look Down That Railroad Line Swift Jewel Cowboys, 884
Look For Me Frank & James McCravy, 533, 536; Vaughan Quartet, 923
Look For Me I'll Be There Victory Four, 931
Look For The Rainbow Parker Quartette, 678
Look How This World Has Made A Change Carter Family, 194; Vaughan Quartet, 928
Look Inside The Glory Gate [A] Bush Brothers, 147
Look On And Cry Roy Hall, 390; Wade Mainer, 584
Look On The Bright, Beautiful Side Owen Brothers & Ellis, 671
Look On The Right Side Hoosier Hot Shots, 439
Look Out For The Ghost, Red Tune Wranglers, 915
Look Out For The Window Emry Arthur, 67
Look Out, I'm Shifting Gears Cliff Carlisle, 166
Look Up, Look Down The Lonesome Road Delmore Brothers, 310
Look What Those Blue Eyes Did To Me Karl & Harty, 471
Look What You Done Fleming & Townsend, 347
Look Who's Squawkin' Slim Harbert, 398
Look Who's Talkin' Ted Daffan's Texans, 241
Lookin' For A Hill Billy Bride Jack Pierce, 695
Lookin' For A Mama Fleming & Townsend, 346
Lookin' For The Girl Of My Dreams Bob Skyles, 839
Looking At The World Thru Rose Colored Glasses New Dixie Demons, 655
Looking For A Gal Woody Leftwich, 496

Looking For A New Mama Jimmie Rodgers, 806
Looking For Somebody To Love Hank Penny, 686
Looking For Tomorrow Carlisle Brothers, 168
Looking This Way Frank & James McCravy, 533; Phil Reeve & Ernest Moody, 735; Virginia Male Quartet, 932
Looking To My Prayer Hill Brothers, 424; [E.R.] Nance Family, 648; Red Fox Chasers, 730
Lookout Mountain Wade Ward, 939
Lookout Valley Waltz Clayton & His Melody Mountaineers, 215
Lopez The Bandit Stuart Hamblen, 393
Lord I'm Coming Home Callahan Brothers, 152; Hugh Gibbs String Band, 368; Smith's Sacred Singers, 850
Lord I'm In Your Care Carter Family, 194
Lord Is My Shepherd [The] Frank Luther, 523
Lord Is Watching Over Me [The] Prairie Ramblers, 711
Lord Is With Me [The] Stamps Quartet, 866
Lord, I Want To Live With Thee Royal Quartette, 815; Vaughan Quartet, 926
Lord, I'm Coming Hom Old Southern Sacred Singers, 669
Lord, Lead Me On Chuck Wagon Gang, 211
Lord, Let Me Serve Stamps Quartet, 864–65
Lord, You Made The Cowboy Happy Sons Of The Pioneers, 858
Lord's Prayer [The] Frank Luther, 523
Loreena Karl & Harty, 470
Loreina Lester McFarland & Robert A. Gardner, 546, 548
Lorena Blue Ridge Mountain Singers, 112; Hugh Cross, 235; Jo & Alma, 458; Red Headed Brier Hopper, 731
Lorena, The Slave Delmore Brothers, 310
Lorina Taylor Trio, 894
Lorrainna Hugh Cross, 236
Lose Your Blues And Laugh At Life Jimmie Revard, 742
Lost Ashford Quartette, 67; Light Crust Doughboys, 503; Simmons Sacred Singers, 835
Lost Boy Blues Palmer McAbee, 526
Lost Child [The] Stripling Brothers, 879
Lost Dog Walter Hurdt, 448
Lost French Flyers (Captains Nungesser & Coli) [The] Vernon Dalhart, 269–70
Lost Girl Of West Virginia [The] Henry Whitter, 956
Lost Indian Hugh Roden, 798
Lost John Deford Bailey, 88; Eldon Baker, 89; Blevins & Blair, 109; Richard D. Burnett, 144; Lonnie Glosson, 372; J.H. Howell, 445; Leonard Rutherford, 816; Oliver Sims, 836; Southern Moonlight Entertainers, 860; Stripling Brothers, 879; Henry Whitter, 955
Lost John Dean Bascom Lamar Lunsford, 516
Lost Love Asa Martin, 588; Riley Puckett, 719, 721; Arthur Smith, 841
Lost Love Blues Dock Boggs, 116
Lost Mamma Blues Homer Christopher, 209
Lost On Life's Sea Bill Carlisle, 159
Lost On The Ocean Anglin Brothers, 61; Russell Brothers, 816
Lost Train Blues Arthur Smith, 840; Da Costa Woltz's Southern Broadcasters, 970
Lost Train Blues (Lost John Blues) Henry Whitter, 954
Lost Wagon [The] Bill Boyd, 121
Lost Waltz Moatsville String Ticklers, 630
Lost Woman Shelton Brothers, 829
Lot In Canaan Land Laurel Firemen's Quartet, 491
Lot In Canaan's Land [The] [E.R.] Nance Family, 648–49; C.A. West, 944
Loud Mouth Modern Mountaineers, 630; Nite Owls, 660
Louisa Waltz East Texas Serenaders, 329
Louisburg Blues "Uncle Bunt" Stephens, 868
Louise Proximity String Quartet, 714
Louise Louise Blues Milton Brown, 138

Louisiana Delma Lachney, 488
Louisiana And You Leon Selph, 823
Louisiana Blues Cliff Carlisle, 164; Carlisle Brothers, 168; Leo Soileau, 854
Louisiana Breakdown Hackberry Ramblers, 387
Louisiana Hop Walter Coon, 220
Louisiana Mazurka Amadie Breaux, 126
Louisiana Moon Gene Autry, 77–78; Farmer Sisters, 336; Hackberry Ramblers, 387; Kenneth Houchins, 444; Bill Nettles, 654; Norwood Tew, 899
Louisiana Special Joseph Falcon, 336
Louisiana Susie Al Bernard, 101
Louisiana Sweetheart Hackberry Ramblers, 388; Floyd Shreve, 834
Louisville Burglar [The] Hickory Nuts, 420
Lou'siana Herb Cook, 220
Love McDonald Quartet, 540; Vaughan Quartet, 927
Love Always Has Its Way Gentry Brothers, 364; Lester McFarland & Robert A. Gardner, 543; McGee Brothers, 552; George Reneau, 741
Love Bug Will Bite You (If You Don't Watch Out) [The] Texas Jim Lewis, 499
Love Burning Love Roy Newman, 658
Love Call Yodel Rex Griffin, 383
Love Enough For Me McDonald Quartet, 539, 541
Love Flower Waltz Pelican Wildcats, 684
Love Gone Cold Johnny Bond, 117
Love Has Been The Ruin Of A Many Young Maid Texas Jim Lewis, 499
Love Has Been The Ruin Of A Many Young Man Texas Jim Lewis, 499
Love Hunting Blues McClendon Brothers, 528
Love I Have For You [The] Jimmie Davis, 305
Love In Bloom Milton Brown, 136
Love Is A Funny Little Thing Walter Smith, 846
Love Is A Ticklish Thing Willard Hodgin[s], 430
Love Is No Pleasure Ramblin' Red Lowery, 515
Love Is The Key Chuck Wagon Gang, 211
Love Keeps Me Awake Bob Skyles, 838
Love Keeps Me Singing Flat Creek Sacred Singers, 346
Love Land And You Milton Brown, 136
Love Leads The Way Stamps Quartet, 863
Love Letters Arthur Smith, 841
Love Letters In The Sand Joseph Falcon, 336; Leo Soileau, 855
Love Lifted Me Emry Arthur, 64; Clagg & Sliger, 212; McDonald Quartet, 541; Smith's Sacred Singers, 850
Love Me Easy (Or Leave Me Alone) Shelton Brothers, 830
Love Me Only Johnny Barfield, 94
Love Me Or Leave Me Dixieland Swingsters, 320
Love Me Tonight Amedie Ardoin, 62
Love Me While I Am Living Henry Whitter, 955
Love Me, Darling, Love Me Lake Howard, 445
Love My Mamma Dr. Claude Watson & L.W. McCreigton, 940
Love Of Jesus Covers The World [The] Peck's Male Quartette, 684
Love Ship Pink Lindsey, 507
Love Sick Blues Beard's Quartette, 98; Rex Griffin, 384; McQueen Quartet, 579; Vaughan Quartet, 923
Love Somebody Crook Brothers String Band, 234; Luke Highnight, 422; Uncle Dave Macon, 574
Love Song Of The Waterfall Sons Of The Pioneers, 858
Love That Ended Too Soon [A] Sons Of The Pioneers, 859
Love That Lies Johnson County Ramblers, 464
Love That Used To Be [The] Bob Skyles, 839
Love Took It Away Vaughan Quartet, 927
Love Waltz Amedie Ardoin, 62

Love Waves Of Glory Vaughan Quartet, 928
Loved Ones [The] [J.T.] Allison's Sacred Harp Singers, 60
Loveless Love Milton Brown, 136; Dixie Ramblers [II], 319; Curley Fox, 357; Dick Hartman's Tennessee Ramblers, 407; Bob Wills, 962–63
Lovelight In The Starlight Rice Brothers' Gang, 746
Lovely Veil Of White Bob Skyles, 839
Lover Of The Lord Huggins & Philips Sacred Harp Singers, 446
Lover Who Loved Me Last Spring [The] Louisiana Lou, 513
Lovers' Call Waltz Poplin-Woods Tennessee String Band, 701
Lovers Dream George R. Pariseau's Orchestra, 675
Lover's Farewell Carter Family, 189; Bill Cox, 229; Lake Howard, 445; Shelton Brothers, 827–28; Wyatt & Brandon, 974
Lovers Goodbye Hall Brothers, 392
Lover's Lane Carter Family, 194; Sons Of Acadians, 856
Lovers' Leap Bill Cox, 228
Lover's Lullaby Yodel Wilf Carter (Montana Slim), 182
Lover's Message Warren Caplinger, 157
Lovers Return Carter Family, 192
Lover's Waltz Clayton McMichen, 570
Lover's Warning Delmore Brothers, 310; White Brothers (Joe & Bob), 951
Love's A Game That Two Can Play Pete Pyle, 723
Love's Affections Crockett Ward, 939
Love's Old Sweet Song Frank & James McCravy, 532; Ralph Richardson, 748; Zack & Glenn, 979
Love's Ship Lester McFarland & Robert A. Gardner, 548
Lovin' And Leavin' Leon Selph, 824
Lovin' Baby Blues Ocie Stockard, 870
Lovin' Blues Byrd Moore, 639
Loving Henry Kyle Wooten, 973; Jess Young, 979
Loving You Too Well Roy Hall, 391
Low And Blue Asa Martin, 593
Low And Lonely Roy Acuff, 51
Low Blues Hi-Flyers, 420
Low Bridge!—Everybody Down (Fifteen Years On The Erie Canal) Vernon Dalhart, 285
Low Down Hanging Around Asa Martin, 591
Low Down Jail House Blues Earl Powell, 702
Low Down Woman Blues Kenneth Houchins, 443
Lowe Bonnie Jimmie Tarlton, 892
Lu Lu Gal Asa Martin, 592
Luckiest Man In Love [The] Goebel Reeves, 738
Lucky Lindy Vernon Dalhart, 269–71
Lucy Long Prairie Ramblers, 710
Lucy Wants Insurance Green B. Adair, 51
Lula From Honolulu Prairie Ramblers, 711
Lula Wall Bill Chitwood, 209; Red Fox Chasers, 731
Lula Whal Marvin Williams, 959
Lullaby Baby Flannery Sisters, 345
Lullaby Lady (From Lullaby Lane) Bingham & Wells, 104
Lullaby Land John McGhee & Frank Welling, 556
Lullaby Song Louis Adler, 51
Lullaby Yodel Gene Autry, 72; Cotton Butterfield, 149; Morgan Denmon, 312; Hoke Rice, 745; Carson Robison, 771; Jimmie Rodgers, 800
Lulu Lee Coon Creek Girls, 221
Lulu Lou Slim Harbert, 398
Lulu Love Ernest Branch & Bernice Coleman, 125
Lulu Wall Carter Family, 188; A'nt Idy Harper, 402; Bascom Lamar Lunsford, 517
Lulu Walls Carter Family, 193
Lulu Walsh Walter Morris, 642
Lulu's Back In Town Joseph Falcon, 336; Earl & Willie Phelps, 689; Ross Rhythm Rascals, 814
Lumber Camp Blues Kyle Wooten, 973

Lumberton Wreck Roland Cauley, 198
Lunatic's Lullaby [The] Dan Hornsby, 442
Lura Parsons Vernon Dalhart, 272
Lye Soap John Dilleshaw, 317
Lying Daddy Blues Walter Smith, 847
Lying Woman Blues Roy Acuff, 50
Lyla Lou Bob Wills, 965
Lynchburg Uncle Jimmy Thompson, 904
Lynchburg Town Hill Billies, 424; Charlie Poole, 700

Ma And Pa (Send Their Sweetest Love) Johnny Marvin, 607; Carson Robison, 791
Ma And Pa And Me Arthur Fields & Fred Hall, 342
Ma Belle Mellina Happy Fats, 396
Ma Belle Ne M'Aime Pas (My Girl Don't Love Me) Leo Soileau, 854
Ma Blonde Est Partie (My Blonde Went Away And Left Me) Amadie Breaux, 126
Ma Chere Basett J.B. Fuslier, 361
Ma Chere Belle Hackberry Ramblers, 387
Ma Chere Bouclett (My Curly Headed Girl) J.B. Fuslier, 361
Ma Chere Catain J.B. Fuslier, 361
Ma Chere Jolite J.B. Fuslier, 361
Ma Chere Joui Rouge J.B. Fuslier, 361
Ma Chere Vieux Maison Dan Swet J.B. Fuslier, 361
Ma Cherie (My Cherie) Joe Creduer-Albert Babineaux, 232
Ma Cherie Tite Fille Leo Soileau, 854
Ma Ferguson Capt. M.J. Bonner, 117
Ma Jolie Petite Fille Leo Soileau, 855
Ma Julie Noir So (My Pretty Black Eyes) Miller's Merrymakers, 628
Ma Maison Aupres De L'Eau Roy Gonzales, 375
Ma Mauvais Fille Leo Soileau, 854
Ma Petite Blonde (My Little Blonde) Delin T. Guillory-Lewis Lafleur, 385
Ma Petite Chere Ami Thibodeaux Boys, 901
Ma Petite Fille (My Little Girl) Leo Soileau, 854
Ma Valse Preferee (My Favorite Waltz) Joseph Falcon, 335
Ma! (He's Making Eyes At Me) Sally Foster, 355; Riley Puckett, 722
Ma! (She's Making Eyes At Me) Nite Owls, 660
Ma, She's Making Eyes At Me Hoosier Hot Shots, 439
Mabelle Tete Catin Happy Fats, 396
Mable Ain't Able Hi-Flyers, 420
Macon Georgia Bound George Walburn & Emmett Hethcox, 935
Macon, Georgia Breakdown Hoke Rice, 745
Madam Atchen (Mrs. Atchen) Amedie Ardoin, 61
Madam Donnez Moi Les Angelas Le Jeunne, 494
Madam I've Come To Marry You Lulu Belle & Scotty, 516
Madam Queen Adelyne Hood, 434
Madame Young Donnez Moi Votre Plus Jole Blonde (Madam Young, Give Me Your Sweetest) Denus McGee, 550
Madeira Bill Boyd, 123
Mademoiselle From Armentieres Al McLeod's Country Dance Band, 565
Madison Street Rag Joe Steen, 868
Maggie Dear, I'm Called Away Roy Harvey, 410; Asa Martin, 589
Magnify Jesus Vaughan Quartet, 923
Magnolia One Step Nations Brothers, 652
Magnolia Waltz Cherokee Ramblers, 204; Leake County Revelers, 494
Mah Yaller Gal Fisher Hendley, 416
Maid Of Mexico Lew Preston, 713
Maiden's Plea [The] Bert Peck, 683
Maiden's Prayer Bob Wills, 960, 965

Mail Man Blues—Part I, II Happy Bud Harrison, 406
Mail Must Go Through [The] Roy Rogers, 811
Mailman's Warning [The] Red Foley, 351
Make A Change In Business Duke Clark, 213
Make A Wreath For Mary Sons Of The West, 859
Make Down The Bed And We'll All Sleep Together Jess Hillard, 426
Make His Praises Ring E.M. Bartlett Groups, 96
Make Jesus Your Choice Jenkins Family, 456
Make Me A Bed On The Floor Leake County Revelers, 494; Chesley Shirley, 832
Make Me A Cowboy Again "Peg" Moreland, 641
Make Me A Cowboy Again For A Day Patt Patterson, 682
Make Me A Pallet George Edgin, 330
Make Me A Pallet On The Floor George Edgin, 330
Make Room In The Lifeboat For Me Delmore Brothers, 311
Makes No Difference What Life May Bring Cliff Carlisle, 168
Making A Baby From Georgia Hi-Flyers, 419
Making A Record—Part 1, 2 Carson Robison, 793–94
Making Little Ones Out Of Big Ones Frank[ie] Marvin, 603
Malinda Gets Married Green B. Adair, 51
Mama Cat Blues Walter Smith, 847
Mama Don't Allow Yellow Jackets [II], 977
Mama Don't Allow It Milton Brown, 137; Leon Chappelear, 201
Mama Don't Allow No Easy Riders Here Happy Bud Harrison, 406
Mama Don't Allow No Hanging Around Hackberry Ramblers, 387
Mama Don't Allow No Low Down Hangin' Around Byrd Moore, 638
Mama Don't Be So Mean To Me Callahan Brothers, 153
Mama Don't Like Music Smiley Burnette, 145
Mama Don't Like No Music Bill Boyd, 121
Mama Gets What She Wants Light Crust Doughboys, 505
Mama Grows Hot, Papa Grows Cold Johnson Sisters Trio, 464
Mama How Can You Be Mean To Me Saddle Tramps, 818
Mama I Wish't I'd Listened To You Charles S. Brook & Charlie Turner, 132
Mama Inez Sons Of The West, 859
Mama Inez (Oh! Mom-E-Nez) Massey Family, 612
Mama Mama Saddle Tramps, 818
Mama Take Your Time Philyaw Brothers, 690
Mama Why Treat Me That Way Callahan Brothers, 152
Mama Won't Allow No Low Down Hanging Around Riley Puckett, 718
Mama Won't Let Me Light Crust Doughboys, 505
Mama You're A Mess Walter Smith, 847
(Mama) What Makes You That Way? Fleming & Townsend, 346; Saddle Tramps, 818
Mama, Don't Make Me Go To Bed Wade Mainer, 584
Mama, Where You At? Leo Soileau, 853
Mama's Crying For Me Wilfred Fruge-Leo Soileau, 360
Mama's Getting Hot And Papa's Getting Cold Bill Boyd, 122; Jimmie Davis, 302
Mama's Getting Young Hank Penny, 686
Mama's Gone, Goodbye Bob Dunn's Vagabonds, 326
Mama's Nanny Goat Fiddlin' John Carson, 179
Mame E.F. "Pat" Alexander, 53
Mamie Que J'Aime Tant (Mamie I Love So Much) Patrick (Dak) Pellerin, 685
Mamma Toot Your Whistle Byrd Moore, 638
Mammoth Cave Waltz Blind Joe Mangum-Fred Shriber, 586
Mammy's Little Black-Eyed Boy Cartwright Brothers, 196
Mammy's Little Coal Black Rose Otto Gray, 380; Connie Sides, 834
Mammy's Lullaby Ollie Hess, 418

Mammy's Pickaninny Hoke Rice, 746
Mammy's Precious Baby Bradley Kincaid, 484; Lester McFarland & Robert A. Gardner, 549
Man And His Song [A] Roy Rogers, 812
Man Behind The Plow [The] Jackson County Ramblers, 453; Stroup Quartet, 880
Man From Memphis [The] Clay Long, 510
Man In The Moon Is A Cowhand [The] Roy Rogers, 811
Man Man What A Band! New Dixie Demons, 655
Man Of Galilee [The] Parham Bros. Quartette, 675
Man On The Flying Trapeze [The] Aaron Campbell's Mountaineers, 154; Harry "Mac" McClintock, 528
Man That Rode A Mule Around The World [The] Dwight Butcher, 148
Man That Rode The Mule Around The World Uncle Dave Macon, 577
Man Who Follows The Plow [The] Frank Wheeler-Monroe Lamb, 948
Man Who Wrote Home Sweet Home Never Was A Married Man [The] Charlie Parker, 676
Man With The Big Black Mustache [The] Johnny Marvin, 607
Man With The Whiskers [The] Hoosier Hot Shots, 438
Man, Poor Man Lester McFarland & Robert A. Gardner, 546
Mandolin King Rag Walker's Corbin Ramblers, 937
Mandolin Rag H.M. Barnes, 95; Ted Hawkins, 413; Doc Roberts, 753
Mandy Shelton Brothers, 829
Mandy Lee Buell Kazee, 472; Frank & James McCravy, 532
Mandylyn Quadrille Medley John Baltzell, 91
Maneater Doc Roberts, 754
Mannington Blues Otha Smith, 845
Mansion Of Aching Hearts [The] Blue Ridge Mountain Singers, 112; Bill Cox, 227; Hugh Cross, 235; Andrew Jenkins, 454; Lester McFarland & Robert A. Gardner, 547
Mansion There For Me [A] Rev. Edward Boone, Mrs. Edward Boone & Miss Olive Boone, 118
Mansions In The Sky Wade Mainer, 585
Many Happy Returns Of The Day Lester McFarland & Robert A. Gardner, 549
Many Many Years Ago Vernon Dalhart, 246–49; Lester McFarland & Robert A. Gardner, 542
Many Times I've Wandered Vernon Dalhart, 248
Many Times With You I Wandered Sid Harkreader, 400
Many Times With You I've Wandered David Miller, 626; Parker & Dodd, 678; Henry Whitter, 955
Many Troubles Blues Dick Parman, 679
Many Years Ago Vernon Dalhart, 287; Asa Martin, 593
Maple In The Lane [The] "Peg" Moreland, 641
Maple Leaf Waltz Stone Mountain Trio, 872
Maple On The Hill—Part 2 (Drifting To That Happy Home) Wade Mainer, 583; Prairie Ramblers, 707
Maple On The Hill [The] Buckeye Boys, 141; Callahan Brothers, 153; Tom Darby & Jimmie Tarlton, 294; Farmer Sisters, 336; Frank Luther, 525; John McGhee & Frank Welling, 562; Uncle Dave Macon, 576; J.E. Mainer's Mountaineers, 581; Peaceful Valley Folk, 683; Holland Puckett, 715
Maple On The Hill Is Gone [The] Don Weston, 947
Maple On The Hill No. 4 Arty Hall, 390; Prairie Ramblers, 708
Maple Rag Virginia Ramblers, 933
March Along With The Christ E.M. Bartlett Groups, 96
March In "D" Homer Christopher, 209
March Medley Carson Robison, 793; R. Smith, 845
March Of The Roses Dick Hartman's Tennessee Ramblers, 407

March Winds Goin' To Blow My Blues All Away Carter Family, 192
Marcheta Bob Dunn's Vagabonds, 327
Marching Thro' Georgia Uncle Joe Shippee, 831
Marching Through Flanders Charlie Oaks, 664
Marching Through Georgia Kessinger Brothers, 481; Walter C. Peterson, 688; Tennessee Ramblers [I], 896
Margie Dick Hartman's Tennessee Ramblers, 409; Hoosier Hot Shots, 437; Earl & Willie Phelps, 689; Riley Puckett, 722
Maria Elena Gene Autry, 86; Bob Skyles, 839; Jimmy Wakely, 934
Maria Elina Adolph Hofner, 431
Marian Parker Murder [The] John McGhee & Frank Welling, 553
Marie Rice Brothers' Gang, 746
Marie Buller Joseph Falcon, 334
Mariechen Walzer Walter C. Peterson, 688
Marinita Light Crust Doughboys, 506
Marion Massacre [The] John McGhee & Frank Welling, 557
Market House Blues Jimmie Davis, 299
Marksville Blues Blind Uncle Gaspard, 363
Married Girls Troubles Buell Kazee, 472; Hazel Scherf, 820
Married Life Blues Lester "Pete" Bivins, 107; Bill Cox, 225, 227; Oscar Ford, 352; Byron Parker, 675
Married Man [The] Emry Arthur, 66
Married Man Blues Nite Owls, 660; Ernest Tubb, 913
Married Man In Trouble [A] Vaughan Quartet, 928
Married Woman Blues Morris Brothers, 643
Married Woman's Blues Louisiana Strollers, 514; Wade Ward, 939
Marry Me Joe Werner, 944
Marsha Run Away Walter Morris, 642
Marsovia Waltz Hill Billies, 424; Louisiana Strollers, 514
Martha Campbell Doc Roberts, 752–53
Marthis Campbell J.W. Day, 306
Martins And The Coys [The] Hoosier Hot Shots, 439
Martin's One Step Amadie Breaux, 127
Mary And Mother Dick Robertson, 758
Mary Anna Brown Barr Brothers, 95
Mary Dear Gene Autry, 84; Richard Harold, 402
Mary Don't Go Emry Arthur, 66
Mary Dow Arkansas Woodchopper, 64
Mary Had A Little Lamb Massey Family, 611; Walter C. Peterson, 688
Mary In The Wildwood James Scott-Claude Boone, 821
Mary Jane Modern Mountaineers, 631
Mary Jane Waltz Kessinger Brothers, 481
Mary Lou Light Crust Doughboys, 505; Clayton McMichen, 572; Roy Newman, 657; Rice Brothers' Gang, 747
Mary Of The Wild Moor Blue Sky Boys, 114; Lester McFarland & Robert A. Gardner, 546; Charlie Oaks, 664
Mary Phagan Charlie Oaks, 664
Mary Wore Three Links Of Chain Bradley Kincaid, 483
Mary, Don't You Weep Georgia Yellow Hammers, 367
Mary, The Prairie And I Texas Jim Lewis, 499
Mary's Breakdown Allen Brothers, 57
Mary's One Step Amadie Breaux, 126
Massa's In De Cold, Cold Ground Len & Joe Higgins, 421
Massa's In De Cold, Cold Ground—Little Log Cabin, Etc. [sic] Yellow Jackets [I], 976
Massa's In The Cold, Cold Ground Alexander & Miller, 53; Chuck Wagon Gang, 210; Mississippi Juvenile Quartette, 629; Archer Porter, 702; Vaughan Quartet, 924
Master Needs You [The] E.B. Holden Quartet, 432
Master Of The Storm [The] Freeman Quartette, 359; Riley Quartette, 749; Vaughan Quartet, 928

Match Box Blues Roy Newman, 657–58; Paradise Joy Boys, 674; Roy Shaffer, 825; Shelton Brothers, 827; Walker's Corbin Ramblers, 937
Matilda Higgins Smiley Burnette, 145
Matrimonial Intentions Buddy Baker, 89
Matrimony Bill Vernon Dalhart, 291
Maudaline Perry County Music Makers, 687
Maw And Paw And Me Arthur Fields & Fred Hall, 340
Maxwell Girl Taylor's Kentucky Boys, 895
Maxwell's Old Rye Waltz White Mountain Orchestra, 951
May Days And Grey Days Bob Miller, 625
May Dearest May Bela Lam, 489
May Flower Mike Shaw, 826; Stripling Brothers, 880
May I Sleep In Your Barn Tonight Mister? Vernon Dalhart, 265; Lester McFarland & Robert A. Gardner, 544; Charlie Poole, 700; Red Fox Chasers, 730; George Reneau, 741; James Roberts, 756; Carson Robison, 769, 786; Walter Smith, 847; Ernest V. Stoneman, 873; Miller Wikel, 956
Maybe New Dixie Demons, 655
Maybe I'll Get By Without You Floyd Tillman, 910
Maybe Next Week Sometime Allen Brothers, 56; Lester "Pete" Bivins, 107; John McGhee & Frank Welling, 561–62
Maybe Next Week Sometime—No. 2 Allen Brothers, 56
Maybe Some Lucky Day Golden Melody Boys, 373
Maybe Then You'll Care York Brothers, 978
Maybe You'll Think About Me Rex Griffin, 384
Maybe, Baby It's Me Al Dexter, 315
Maybelle Rag Jess Young, 978
Mayflowers Steve Homesley, 433
Mayor Of Bayou Pom Pom Part I, II Walter Coquille, 222
Mayor Of Bayou Pom Pom—Part III (On Traffic) [The] Walter Coquille, 222
Mayor Of Bayou Pom Pom—Part IV (On Hunting & Fishing In The Bayou) [The] Walter Coquille, 222
Mayor Of Bayou Pom Pom—Pt. 5, 6 [The] Walter Coquille, 222
Mazurka De La Louisiane (Louisiana Mazurka) Amadie Breaux, 126
McAbee's Railroad Piece Palmer McAbee, 526
McBeth Mine Explosion Warren Caplinger, 157
McCarroll's Breakdown Roane County Ramblers, 751
McCloud's Reel Kessinger Brothers, 480
McDonald's Farm Warren Caplinger, 156; McDonald Quartet, 541
McDonald's Reel Jasper Bisbee, 107
McDowell Blues Hall Brothers, 391
McGee's One Step Denus McGee, 551
McKinley Riley Puckett, 719
McKinney Waltz East Texas Serenaders, 329
McLeod's Reel Tommy Dandurand, 293; Bob Larkan & Family, 491; Tom Owens Barn Dance Trio, 672
McMichen's Breakdown Gid Tanner, 891
McMichen's Reel Clayton McMichen, 568
Me And My Brother Joe Arthur Fields & Fred Hall, 342
Me And My Burro Beverly Hill Billies, 103; Hilltoppers, 427; Ranch Boys, 726
Me And My Gal Oscar Ford, 352
Me And My Pal From New Orleans Joe Werner, 944
Me And My Shadow Dixie Demons, 318; Johnny Marvin, 607
Me And My Still Canova Family, 156
Me And My Wife's Wedding Ernest Mull, 646
Me And The Man In The Moon Jack Golding, 374
Me Too—Wait For The Wagon Kenneth Striker, 879
Me, The Moon And My Gal Fleming & Townsend, 346
Meadlowlark Canova Family, 155
Meadow Brook Waltz East Texas Serenaders, 329
Mean OKeh Atlanta Sacred Harp Singers, 667

Mean Hangover Blues Buddy Jones, 466
Mean Mama Callahan Brothers, 151
Mean Mama Blues Gene Autry, 73; Charles Mitchell & His Orchestra, 630; Ernest Tubb, 914; Bob Wills, 961
Mean Mean Mama (From Meana) Light Crust Doughboys, 506
Mean Mistreater Blues Bob Dunn's Vagabonds, 326
Mean Old Ball And Chain Blues Kenneth Houchins, 443
Mean Old Bed Bug Blues Ernest Tubb, 913
Mean Old Jailhouse Blues Daddy John Love, 514
Mean Old Lonesome Blues Buddy Jones, 464
Mean Old Sixty Five Blues Buddy Jones, 466
Mean Papa Blues Roy Marsh, 587
Mean Woman Blues Rex Griffin, 383
Meanest Thing Blues Whitey McPherson, 579
Meant For Me Bill Boyd, 123
Measly Shame [The] Taylor Trio, 894
Meat House Blues—Brumfield, 139
Medicine Show—Act I-VI [The] OKeh Medicine Show, 668
Medicine Show [The] Chris Bouchillon, 119
Medley Roland Cauley, 199; Jim Couch, 223; Fisher Hendley, 416; Unknown Artists [II], 920
Medley—Part 1, 2 Johnny Marvin, 606
Medley—Scottische [sic] Bob Skiles Four Old Tuners, 837
Medley Of Barn Dances Part 1, 2 Tin-Can Joe, 910
Medley Of Bar-Room Songs Prairie Ramblers, 707
Medley Of Breakdowns Asa Martin, 592
Medley Of Familiar Tunes—Part 1, 2 Dick Robertson, 758
Medley Of Kiddie Rhymes Little Georgie Porgie, 508
Medley Of Mountain Songs Tennessee Ramblers [I], 896
Medley Of Old Familiar Tunes, Part I, II Pie Plant Pete, 694
Medley Of Old Favorites—Part 1, 2 Billy Bishop, 107
Medley Of Old Fiddlers Favorites Nat Bird & Tom Collins, 106
Medley Of Old Songs Alexander & Miller, 53
Medley Of Old Southern Melodies Len & Joe Higgins, 421
Medley Of Old Time Airs R. Smith, 845
Medley Of Old Time Dance Tunes/Intro Hill Billies, 424
Medley Of Old Time Fiddlers' Favorites—No. 1, II Robert Cook's Old Time Fiddlers, 220
Medley Of Old Time Jigs Chief Pontiac, 205
Medley Of Old Time Jigs And Reels Part 1, 2 Billy Milton, 628
Medley Of Old Time Melodies Asa Martin, 589
Medley Of Old Time Popular Songs Jimmie Wilson's Catfish String Band, 968
Medley Of Old Time Songs R.C. Sutphin, 882
Medley Of Old Time Tunes Archer Porter, 702
Medley Of Old Time Waltzes Tommy Dandurand, 293; Bobby Gregory, 383; Asa Martin, 589; Archer Porter, 702
Medley Of Old Timers Archer Porter, 702
Medley Of Old-Time Dance Tunes—Part I, II Crockett [Family] Mountaineers, 233
Medley Of Old-Time Waltzes. Part 1, 2 Tin-Can Joe, 910
Medley Of Reels Mellie Dunham's Orchestra, 326; Jimmy Smith, 844
Medley Of Southern Airs R. Smith, 845
Medley Of Southern Songs Barr Brothers, 95
Medley Of Spanish Waltzes Bob Wills, 964
Medley Of Two-Steps Chief Pontiac, 205
Medley Old Time Favorites (Part 1, II) Walter C. Peterson, 688
Medley/Intro. Carson Robison, 792
Medley: Washington & Lee Swing Chesley Shirley, 832
Meet Her When The Sun Goes Down Fiddlin' John Carson, 177
Meet Me At The Crossroads, Pal Goebel Reeves, 738

Meet Me At The Ice-House Dick Hartman's Tennessee Ramblers, 408
Meet Me At Twilight Vernon Dalhart, 260
Meet Me By Moonlight, Alone Carter Family, 187
Meet Me By The Ice House Lizzie Hoosier Hot Shots, 436
Meet Me By The Moonlight Alone Carter Family, 193
Meet Me By The Seaside Ernest V. Stoneman, 878
Meet Me Down In Honky Tonk Town Al Dexter, 315
Meet Me In Dreamland Richard Brooks & Reuben Puckett, 133
Meet Me In Hawaii Price-Prosser-Teasley, 714
Meet Me In Honeysuckle Time Cromwell Brothers, 234
Meet Me In Loveland Texas Wanderers, 900
Meet Me In St. Louis, Louey Roe Brothers & Morrell, 810
Meet Me In The Moonlight John D. Foster, 354; Troy Martin & Elvin Bigger, 594
Meet Me In The Moonlight Alone Welby Toomey, 912
Meet Me Somewhere In Your Dreams Shelton Brothers, 829
Meet Me There John McGhee & Frank Welling, 554; Smith's Sacred Singers, 850
Meet Me Tonight In Dreamland Vernon Dalhart, 248, 267; Claude Davis, 297–98; Jimmie Davis, 303; Jack Major, 586; Melton & Minter, 615; Riley Puckett, 718
Meet Me Tonight In Dreams Bob Dunn's Vagabonds, 326
Meet Me Tonight In The Cowshed Tex Fletcher, 349; Hoosier Hot Shots, 438
Meet Me Tonight In The Valley Carson Robison, 791–92
Meet Mother In The Skies Emry Arthur, 65
Meet Mother In The Sky Sammy & Smitty, 818
Meet Your Mother In The Skies Allen Brothers, 55
Meetin' Time In The Hollow Oliver & Allen, 670
Meeting In The Air Carter Family, 195; Humbard Family, 447
Melancholy Baby Swing Billies, 885
Melancholy Moon Lester McFarland & Robert A. Gardner, 548
Melancholy Yodel Blues Jack Major, 586
Mellow Mountain Moon Beverly Hill Billies, 102; Hollywood Hillbilly Orchestra, 432; Frank Luther, 522; W. Lee O'Daniel, 666
Melody From The Sky [A] Tex Ritter, 750; Sons Of The Pioneers, 857
Melody Of Hawaii Dick Hartman's Tennessee Ramblers, 407
Melody Of The Plains Roy Rogers, 812
Melon Time In Dixieland Jack & Bill, 451
Memoire De Mom Happy Fats, 396
Memories Roy Bledsoe, 108; Richard Brooks & Reuben Puckett, 133; Jimmie Davis, 303; Leake County Revelers, 494; Light Crust Doughboys, 503; Moore Sisters, 641
Memories (Mothers' Song) Jack Pickell, 694
Memories In The Moonlight Fisher Hendley, 416
Memories Of A Shack On The Hill James Scott-Claude Boone, 821
Memories Of Charley Poole Claude Casey, 196
Memories Of Floyd Collins Clarence Ganus, 362; Ozark Warblers, 672
Memories Of Galilee Mississippi Juvenile Quartette, 629
Memories Of Hawaii Westbrook Conservatory Entertainers, 947
Memories Of Home Merritt Smith, 844
Memories Of Huey Long Johnny Roberts, 756
Memories Of Jimmy [sic] Rodgers Light Crust Doughboys, 501
Memories Of Kentucky Asher Sizemore & Little Jimmie, 837
Memories Of Long Ago McKinney Brothers, 564
Memories Of Mother Ted Hawkins, 413; Singing Preachers, 836

Memories Of My Carolina Girl Delmore Brothers, 310
Memories Of My Father Callahan Brothers, 153
Memories Of My Grey Haired Mother In The West Wilf Carter (Montana Slim), 183
Memories Of My Little Old Log Shack Wilf Carter (Montana Slim), 185
Memories Of My Silver Haired Daddy Gene Autry, 80
Memories of Old Dick Hartman's Tennessee Ramblers, 408
Memories Of Sam P. Jones Jenkins Family, 456
Memories Of That Silver Haired Daddy Blue Ridge Mountain Girls, 112
Memories Of That Silver Haired Daddy Of Mine Gene Autry, 79
Memories Of The South Before The War Charles Nabell, 647
Memories Of You York Brothers, 978
Memories Of You Dear Johnny Lee Wills, 967
Memories That Haunt Me Cliff Carlisle, 163–64
Memories That Make Me Cry Cliff Carlisle, 162
Memories That Never Die Wilf Carter (Montana Slim), 186
Memories Waltz Leake County Revelers, 495
Memory (Means Happiness To Me) Wonder State Harmonists, 971
Memory Lane Wade Mainer, 584; Rambling Rangers, 725
Memory Of Mother Joe Werner, 944
Memory That Lingers [The] Fleming & Townsend, 347
Memory That Time Cannot Erase [A] Leo Boswell, 119; Vernon Dalhart, 270–71, 273, 276–78
Memory Waltz Kelly Brothers, 476
Memphis Blues Milton Brown, 137; Nite Owls, 660; Swift Jewel Cowboys, 885
Memphis Gal Lonesome Cowboy [II], 509
Memphis Mama Blues Bill Cox, 227
Memphis Oomph Swift Jewel Cowboys, 884
Memphis Special Blues Howard Keesee, 474
Memphis Yodel Cliff Carlisle, 161; Carson Robison, 772; Jimmie Rodgers, 800, 809; Ed (Jake) West, 945
Memphis Yodel No. 4 Ramblin' Red Lowery, 515
Men Will Wear Kimonos Bye And Bye [The] E.M. Bartlett Groups, 96
Mercredi Soir Passe' (Last Wednesday Night) Blind Uncle Gaspard, 363
Mercy Mercy Blues Allen Brothers, 57
Mermentan Stomp Hackberry Ramblers, 387
Merry Christmas To The Boys Over There [A] York Brothers, 978
Merry Girl Da Costa Woltz's Southern Broadcasters, 969
Merry Widow Waltz A.A. Gray, 378; Leake County Revelers, 494; Arthur Tanner, 886
Merry-Go-Roundup [The] Gene Autry, 84; Hoosier Hot Shots, 439
Merrymakers' Hop Miller's Merrymakers, 628
Merrymakers Stomp Lummie Lewis, 500
Mes Yeux Bleus (My Blue Eyes) Joseph Falcon, 335
Message From Home [A] Leon Chappelear, 200; Christine, 209; Billy Vest, 931
Message From Home Sweet Home [A] Frank Jenkins, 455; Shelton Brothers, 827
Message Of A Broken Heart Asa Martin, 591
Message Of Faith [A] Rev. J.O. Hanes & Male Choir, 395
Messin' Around Roy Newman, 656
Methodist Pie Ashley's Melody Makers, 68; Gene Autry, 75; Doc Hopkins, 441; Bradley Kincaid, 482, 484
Mexicali Rose Gene Autry, 82; Milton Brown, 137; Don White, 949; Bob Wills, 960, 962
Mexican Beans M.S. Dillehay, 316
Mexican Medley Ranch Boys, 726

Mexican Rag Tom Darby & Jimmie Tarlton, 294; David McCarn, 527
Mexican Waltz Kessinger Brothers, 481
Miami Storm [The] Vernon Dalhart, 261
'Mid The Green Fields Of Virginia Carter Family, 190; Virginia Dandies, 932
'Mid The Shamrocks Of Shannon Taylor-Griggs Louisiana Melody Makers, 894
Midnight Blues Jimmie Davis, 299; Hank Penny, 686
Midnight Flyer Texas Jim Lewis, 500
Midnight Mama Allen Brothers, 57
Midnight On The Stormy Deep Carolina Buddys, 170; Gentry Brothers, 364; Lester McFarland & Robert A. Gardner, 542; B.L. Reeves, 735; Ernest V. Stoneman, 876, 878; Three Tobacco Tags, 908
Midnight On The Stormy Sea Blue Sky Boys, 113
Midnight Patrol Dick Reinhart, 739
Midnight Serenade Red Brush Rowdies, 730; Spangler & Pearson, 861
Midnight Serenade Waltz Kessinger Brothers, 481
Midnight Special Bill Cox, 225; Otto Gray, 379
Midnight Waltz Moonshiners, 638; W.T. Narmour & S.W. Smith, 649–50; Stripling Brothers, 880
Midnight, The Unconquered Outlaw Wilf Carter (Montana Slim), 183
Midwest Dust Storm [The] Bill Carlisle, 159
Mighty Close To Heaven Chuck Wagon Gang, 211
Mighty Lak A Rose Vernon Dalhart, 267; Honolulu Strollers, 433
Mighty The Lord Rangers Quartet, 728
Mike The Turk Dusty Rhodes, 744
Mildred Doran's Last Flight Vernon Dalhart, 273
Milenberg Joys Hoosier Hot Shots, 438; Light Crust Doughboys, 502
Milenburg Joys Leon Chappelear, 201
Military March Medley Kelly Brothers, 476
Milk And Honey Jenkins Family, 456
Milk Cow Blues Cliff Bruner, 139; Johnny Lee Wills, 967
Mill Blues Bill Boyd, 124
Miller's Reel William B. Houchens, 443
Million Dollar Smile W. Lee O'Daniel, 666
Mills' Waltz Happy Hayseeds, 397
Milwaukee Blues Roy Harvey, 411; Charlie Poole, 700
Mind Your Own Business Johnson County Ramblers, 464; Asa Martin, 589
Mine Is For Mary G.B. Grayson & Henry Whitter, 380
Mine Own Time Troubles Hayes Shepherd, 831
Mineola Rag East Texas Serenaders, 329
Miner's Blues [The] Frank Hutchison, 450
Miner's Doom [The] Vernon Dalhart, 267
Miner's Life [A] Bill Cox, 227
Miner's Prayer [The] Vernon Dalhart, 278–79; Hart Brothers, 406
Minnie Brown Ernest V. Stoneman, 877
Minnie The Mermaid Earl & Willie Phelps, 689
Minnie The Moocher Dave Edwards, 331
Minnie The Moocher At The Morgue Smiley Burnette, 145
Minor Blues Lester "Pete" Bivins, 107
Minstrel Hall Roy Harvey, 409
Misbehavin' Mama Allen Brothers, 56–57
Miserable John H. Bertrand, 101
Misery On My Mind Clayton McMichen, 572
Miss A Miss From Tennessee Three Tobacco Tags, 908
Miss Brown Carter Brothers & Son, 187
Miss Iola Smith's Garage Fiddle Band, 848
Miss Jackson Tennessee Goebel Reeves, 737
Miss 'Liza, Poor Gal Grant Brothers, 377
Miss Lucy Long Phil Reeve & Ernest Moody, 735

Miss McCloud's Reel Uncle Joe Shippee, 831
Miss McLeod's Reel John A. McDermott, 539; Gid Tanner, 891
Miss Me When I'm Gone J.E. Mainer's Mountaineers, 582
Miss Molly Charlie Wills, 966
Miss Moonshine Frank[ie] Marvin, 600
Miss The Mississippi And You Jimmie Rodgers, 808
Mississippi Blues Cliff Carlisle, 163
Mississippi Bound Johnson & Lee, 462
Mississippi Breakdown Leake County Revelers, 495; Mississippi 'Possum Hunters, 629; W.T. Narmour & S.W. Smith, 650
Mississippi Clog Southern Moonshiners, 860
Mississippi Delta Blues Jimmie Rodgers, 809; Bob Wills, 963, 965
Mississippi Dippy Dip [The] Ernest Thompson, 902
Mississippi Echoes Ray Brothers, 729
Mississippi Flood [The] Vernon Dalhart, 268–69, 271; Lawrence Woods, 973
Mississippi Flood Song (On The Old Mississippi Shore) [The] Vernon Dalhart, 269
Mississippi Freight Train Blues Walter Smith, 847
Mississippi Home Walter Hurdt, 448
Mississippi Jubilee Earl Johnson, 460
Mississippi Moon Jess Hillard, 426; Jimmie Rodgers, 800, 807
Mississippi Moon Waltz Leake County Revelers, 495
Mississippi Mud Bill Boyd, 123; Roy Newman, 657
Mississippi Muddle Hank Penny, 686
Mississippi River Blues Jack & Leslie, 451; Ted Lunsford, 517; Hank & Slim Newman, 656; Pine Ridge Boys, 697; Jimmie Rodgers, 802
Mississippi Sandman Modern Mountaineers, 630
Mississippi Sawyer Arkansas Woodchopper, 64; Roland Cauley, 199; Robert Cook's Old Time Fiddlers, 220; Fisher Hendley, 416; Hill Billies, 422; Earl Johnson, 460; Kessinger Brothers, 480; Clayton McMichen, 573; Red Fox Chasers, 730; Gid Tanner, 890–91; Ernest Thompson, 902; Uncle Jimmy Thompson, 904; Henry Whitter, 955
Mississippi Shadows McLaughlin's Old Time Melody Makers, 565
Mississippi Square Dance—Part 1, 2 Freeny's Barn Dance Band, 359
Mississippi Valley Gene Autry, 76
Mississippi Valley Blues Gene Autry, 76; Carolina Buddys, 170; Chuck Wagon Gang, 210; Farmer Sisters, 336; Jimmy Long, 511; Johnny Marvin, 607
Mississippi Waters Canova Family, 156
Mississippi Wave Waltz W.T. Narmour & S.W. Smith, 650
Mississippi Waves Waltz W.T. Narmour & S.W. Smith, 649
Missouri Hills Zeke Williams, 959
Missouri I'm Calling Gene Autry, 76
Missouri Is Calling Gene Autry, 76; Jimmy Long, 510–11; Dick Robertson, 759
Missouri Joe Elton Britt, 130; Bob Miller, 616–19
Missouri Mule Bob Miller, 616–17
Missouri Stuff Russell Miller, 627
Missouri Valley Carson Robison, 789–90
Missouri Waltz E.F. "Poss" Acree, 48; Dave Edwards, 331; John D. Foster, 354; W.W. Macbeth, 526; Clayton McMichen, 567; Ranch Boys, 726; Three Tobacco Tags, 909
Mistakes Massey Family, 612; Nite Owls, 660; Jimmie Revard, 743
Mister Chicken Imperial Quartet, 451; Roba Stanley, 866
Mister Johnson Uncle Dave Macon, 577
Mister Johnson, Turn Me Aloose South Georgia Highballers, 860
Mister Moon Clayton McMichen, 566
Mistook In The Woman I Found Bob Miller, 625

Mistook In The Woman I Love Bob Miller, 625; Prairie Ramblers, 708–09
Mistook In The Woman I Loved Elton Britt, 130; Tex Fletcher, 349
Mistreated Blues Carolina Buddies, 170; Leon Chappelear, 201
Mitchell Blues Wade Mainer, 584
Moatsville Blues Moatsville String Ticklers, 630
Mobile—Alabam Vernon Dalhart, 288, 291
Mobile Bay Vernon Dalhart, 275
Mobile County Blues Nelstone's Hawaiians, 653
Mocking Bird John Baltzell, 91; Bert Bilbro, 104; Canova Family, 155; Happy Hayseeds, 397; Homer Lovell, 514; Arthur Smith, 840; Tweedy Brothers, 918
Mocking Bird (Bird Calls) Sandlin Brothers, 820
Mocking Bird Breakdown Sid Harkreader, 400
Mockingbird Song Medley [The] Uncle Dave Macon, 576
Model Church—Part I, II [The] John McGhee & Frank Welling, 557
Model Church [The] Bill Cox, 227; Asa Martin, 588
Modern Modern Mountaineers, 631
Modern Cannon Ball Denver Darling, 296
Modern Mama Cliff Carlisle, 162
Mohana Blues Bert Bilbro, 103
Moi Et Ma Belle Alley Boys Of Abbeville, 59
Mollie Darling Vernon Dalhart, 254
Mollie Married A Travelin' Man J.H. Howell, 446
Mollie Rinktum Bill Cox, 228
Molly Bland Hall Family, 392
Molly Darling Vernon Dalhart, 267; Texas Jim Lewis, 499; Ramblin' Red Lowery, 515
Molly Married A Travelling Man Uncle Dave Macon, 576
Molly Put The Kettle On Leake County Revelers, 494; Gid Tanner, 891
Mon Camon Le Case Que Je Sui Cordane Douglas Bellar & Kirby Riley, 99
Mon Chere Bebe Creole (My Creole Sweet Mama) Denus McGee, 551
Mon Couer T'Appelle (My Heart Aches For You) Joseph Falcon, 335
Mon Cour Me Fais Ci Mal Hackberry Ramblers, 388
Mon Cuore Et Pour Toit Happy Fats, 395
Mon Dernier Bon Soir Alleman & Walker, 54
Monday Morning Blues Jack Pierce, 695
Money Ain't No Use Anyhow Gene Autry, 75
Money Ain't No Use Anyway Gene Autry, 73–74
Money Cannot Buy Your Soul Anglin Brothers, 61
Money Can't Make Everybody Happy John McGhee & Frank Welling, 562
Money Cravin' Folks Blind Alfred Reed, 733
Money Musk Jasper Bisbee, 107; Chief Pontiac, 205; Clifford Gross, 385; William B. Houchens, 443
Money Musk (Intro: Opera Reel) "Dad" Williams, 957
Money Musk And Little Reel George R. Pariseau's Orchestra, 675
Money Musk Medley John Baltzell, 90
Money Won't Make Everybody Happy John McGhee & Frank Welling, 560–62
Money You Spent Was Mine [The] Al Dexter, 315
Monita Charles Mitchell & His Orchestra, 630
Monkey Blues Allen Brothers, 55–56
Monkey Business Sunshine Boys, 882
Monkey In The Dog Cart Leake County Revelers, 494
Monkey On A String Charlie Poole, 699
Monkey Show Henry L. Bandy, 92
Monkey Song Georgia Wildcats, 366; Harry Hickox, 420
Monkeys Is The Cwaziest People! Prairie Ramblers, 710
Monroe County Blues Roy Harvey, 411

Monroe Stamp Hiter Colvin, 219
Montana Patsy Montana, 634
Montana Anna Wells Brothers String Band, 943
Montana Moon Red Foley, 351
Montana Plains Patsy Montana, 634
Mood Indigo Rice Brothers' Gang, 746
(The Moon And The Water And) Miz O'Reilly's Daughter Texas Jim Robertson, 760
Moon Hangs Low (On The Ohio) [The] Patsy Montana, 636
Moonlight And Roses Hugh Cross, 237
Moonlight And Roses (Bring Mem'ries Of You) Frank Luther, 523; Bob Wills, 963
Moonlight And Skies Gene Autry, 77; Leon Chappelear, 200; Garner Eckler & Roland Gaines, 329; Hank & Slim Newman, 656; Jimmie Rodgers, 803
Moonlight And Skies (No. 2) Jimmie Davis, 301
Moonlight Blues Bill Carlisle, 160
Moonlight Clog Gene Clardy & Stan Clements, 212
Moonlight Down In Lovers' Lane Gene Autry, 79
Moonlight In Oklahoma Smoky Wood, 971
Moonlight On Biscayne Bay Magnolia Trio, 580
Moonlight On The Colorado R.D. Kelly & Julius Dunn, 476; Riley Puckett, 720–21; Carson Robison, 782–83
Moonlight On The Mountain Ralph Hodges, 429
Moonlight On The Prairie Sons Of The Pioneers, 857; Texas Wanderers, 900; Twilight Trail Boys, 918
Moonlight On The River James Brown, Jr. & Ken Landon Groups, 134
Moonlight Prison Blues Wilf Carter (Montana Slim), 182
Moonlight Shadows Carl Williams, 957
Moonlight Waltz Bob Skyles, 839; Stripling Brothers, 880
Moonlight Waters Modern Mountaineers, 631
Moonlight, Shadows And You Riley Puckett, 722
Moonshine Charlie Oaks, 664
Moonshine Bill Allen Brothers, 56
Moonshine Blues Lew Childre, 207; Pine Ridge Ramblers, 697; Jimmie Tarlton, 892
Moonshine Hollow Band [The] Georgia Yellow Hammers, 367
Moonshine In The Hills [The] Bill Cox, 224
Moonshine In The Kentucky Hills E.F. "Pat" Alexander, 53
Moonshine In The North Carolina Hall [sic] Claude Casey, 196
Moonshine In The North Carolina Hills Swing Billies, 885
Moonshine In The West Virginia Hills George A. Norman, 661
Moonshine Kate Fiddlin' John Carson, 177
Moonshiner And His Money Charlie Bowman, 120
Moonshiner's Ball Breakdowners From Balsam Gap, 126
Moonshiner's Daughter [A] Sid Hampton, 394
Moonshiner's Daughter And I [The] Bill Cox, 227
Moonshiner's Dream [The] Riley Puckett, 719
Moonshiner's Dream Of Home [The] Ted Bare, 93
Moonshiner's Serenade George R. Pariseau's Orchestra, 675
Moonshiners' Waltz [The] Scottdale String Band, 822
Moose River Mine Song (The Glitter Of Gold) [The] Earl & Willie Phelps, 689
More About Jesus Clyde & Chester Cassity, 198
More Good Women Gone Wrong Wade Mainer, 584
More Like His Dad Every Day Arthur Smith, 841
More Like The Master Smoky Mountain Sacred Singers, 852
More Like Your Dad Every Day Uncle Dave Macon, 576
More Pretty Girls Than One—Part 3 Frank Gerald & Howard Dixon, 368
More To Pity Four Aces, 356
Mormon Cowboy [The] Carl T. Sprague, 863
Morning Blues Lester "Pete" Bivins, 107
Morning Star (Waltz) Blalock & Yates, 108; Reubens, 742

Morning Sun Lee Wells, 943
Morning Trumpet [The] [J.T.] Allison's Sacred Harp Singers, 60; Lee Wells, 943
Morris Dance William B. Houchens, 443
Morro Castle Disaster [The] Light Crust Doughboys, 501; Ray Whitley, 952
Moselle—Quadrille Judge Sturdy's Orchestra, 881
Moses And The Bull Rush—Part 1, 2 Snowball & Sunshine, 853
Mosquito Ate Up My Sweetheart [A] E. Segura & D. Herbert, 823
Mosquito Song [The] Arthur Fields & Fred Hall, 341
M-O-T-H-E-R Riley Puckett, 718
Mother And Dad Jenkins Family, 457; Fred Kirby, 486; Earl & Willie Phelps, 689
Mother And Home Vernon Dalhart, 244, 246; Hinson, Pitts & Coley, 427; Vaughan Quartet, 924
Mother And Son John McGhee & Frank Welling, 563
Mother Came To Get Her Boy From Jail Wade Mainer, 583
Mother Dear Has Gone Away Holiness Singers, 432
Mother Dear Is Waiting Bush Brothers, 147
Mother Dear Old Mother Roy Shaffer, 825
Mother Here's A Bouquet For You Gene Autry, 82
Mother I'm Coming Back Someday Philyaw Brothers, 690
Mother Is Gone Holiness Singers, 432; XC Sacred Quartette, 975
Mother Is Waiting For Me Vaughan Quartet, 923–24
Mother Is With The Angels Wright Brothers Quartet, 974
Mother Kiss Your Darling Walter Smith, 846
Mother Mine Al Dexter, 314
Mother Now Your Saviour Is My Saviour Too E. Arthur Lewis, 497
Mother Of The Valley Chuck Wagon Gang, 210
Mother Still Prays For You Ruth Donaldson & Helen Jepsen, 323
Mother Still Prays For You Jack Ruth Donaldson & Helen Jepsen, 323; Wade Mainer, 584
Mother Tell Me Of The Angels Flat Creek Sacred Singers, 346
Mother Wants To See You Lester McFarland & Robert A. Gardner, 550
Mother Was A Lady Vernon Dalhart, 283
Mother Was A Lady (If Brother Jack Were Here) Jimmie Rodgers, 799
Mother Was A Lady Or (If Jack Were Only Here) Vernon Dalhart, 283; Carson Robison, 768
Mother Watch O'er And Guide Me Andrews Brothers, 60
Mother Went Her Holiness Way Blue Sky Boys, 114
Mother, A Father, A Baby [A] Dorsey & Beatrice Dixon, 322
Mother, Look Down And Guide Me Burns Brothers, 146
Mother, My Sweetheart Joe Steen, 868
Mother, Oft I Think Of Thee Simmons Sacred Singers, 835
Mother, Oh My Mother Vaughan Quartet, 927
Mother, Pal And Sweetheart Callahan Brothers, 152; Ramblin' Red Lowery, 515
Mother, Queen Of My Heart James Roberts, 756
Mother, Sweetheart And Home J.P. Ryan, 817
Mother, The Queen Of My Heart Dwight Butcher, 148; Carolina Buddys, 170; Jess Hillard, 426; Ralph Hodges, 429; Doc Hopkins, 441; Jimmie Rodgers, 807, 809
Mother-In-Law M.S. Dillehay, 316
Mother-In-Law Blues Allen Brothers, 56; Goebel Reeves, 736–37
Motherless Children Carter Family, 188
Mother's Advice [A] Kentucky Thorobreds, 479; [E.R.] Nance Family, 648–49; Holland Puckett, 715; C.A. West, 944
Mother's Always Waiting Ernest Branch & Bernice Coleman, 126

Mother's Answer (To All Going Home But One) [A] Anglin Brothers, 61
Mother's Beautiful Hands Red Headed Brier Hopper, 732
Mother's Crazy Quilt Benny Borg, 119; W. Lee O'Daniel, 665
Mother's Dream Maynard Britton, 131; Mustard & Gravy, 647
Mother's Dying Wish [A] Arthur Fields & Fred Hall, 338–40
Mother's Face I Long To See Walter Morris, 642
Mother's Farewell Loy Bodine, 115; Delma Lachney, 489
Mother's Gone R.N. Johnson, 462; J.P. Ryan, 817
Mother's Gone From The Cabin Andrews Brothers, 60
Mother's Goodbye [A] Miller Wikel, 957
Mother's Grave Vernon Dalhart, 250–53, 255; John B. Evans, 334
Mother's In Heaven Tonight Emry Arthur, 66
Mother's Knee Aaron Campbell's Mountaineers, 154
Mother's Last Farewell Kiss Charlie Poole, 700
Mother's Last Prayer [A] Bill Nettles, 653
Mother's Lullaby Buddy Baker, 89
Mother's Missing Now Rev. Edward Boone, Mrs. Edward Boone & Miss Olive Boone, 118
Mother's Old Red Shawl Arthur Fields & Fred Hall, 338
Mother's Old Rockin' Chair Three Tobacco Tags, 907
Mother's Picture On The Old Cabin Wall Mustard & Gravy, 647
Mother's Plea [A] W.C. Childers, 206; Hugh Cross, 235; David Miller, 626; Carson Robison, 762; Uncle Pete & Louise, 919
Mother's Plea For Her Son [The] Charlie Poole, 700
Mother's Prayers For Jack Howard Haney, 395
Mother's Prayers Guide Me Roy Acuff, 49
Mother's Song Of Love Frank[ie] Marvin, 601–02
Mother's Sunny Smile York Brothers, 978
Mother's Torn And Faded Bible Three Tobacco Tags, 907
Mother's Waltz Roy Harvey, 411
Mother's Wayward Son [A] Red Headed Brier Hopper, 732
Moundsville Prisoner John McGhee & Frank Welling, 558
Mount Pisgah Blues Rector Trio, 729
Mount Zion Denson-Parris Sacred Harp Singers, 313
Mountain Ain't No Place For A Bad Man [The] Robert Barringer, 95
Mountain Angel Rolling Stones, 813
Mountain Blues Jimmy Smith, 844
Mountain Boy Hilltoppers, 427; Frank[ie] Marvin, 605
Mountain Boy Makes His First Record—Part I, II [A] Buell Kazee, 473
Mountain Daddy Blues Emry Arthur, 66
Mountain Dew Lulu Belle & Scotty, 516; Bascom Lamar Lunsford, 516
Mountain Dew Blues Dick Hartman's Tennessee Ramblers, 407
Mountain Goat Jack Pierce, 696
Mountain Home Prairie Ramblers, 710
Mountain Man [The] E.M. Lewis, 498
Mountain Mother Of Mine Sons Of The Ozarks, 856
Mountain Railroad Levi Tipton, 910
Mountain Rangers Mellie Dunham's Orchestra, 326
Mountain Ranger's Lullaby Garner Eckler & Roland Gaines, 329
Mountain Reel Charlie Poole, 699
Mountain Rhythm Jack Pierce, 695
Mountain Sweetheart Wade Mainer, 584; Red Fox Chasers, 730
Mountain Top Rag West Brothers Trio, 946
Mountain, The Music And You [The] Tom & Roy, 911
Mountaineer's Courtship [The] Ernest V. Stoneman, 875–76
Mountaineer's Home, Sweet Home Woodruff Brothers, 973
Mountaineer's Love Song Hill Billies, 422
Mountaineers Song Louis Adler, 51

Mountaineer's Sweetheart [The] Tom & Roy, 911
Mountains Ain't No Place For Bad Men Vernon Dalhart, 292; Arthur Fields & Fred Hall, 339; Kanawha Singers, 469; Frank[ie] Marvin, 598
Mountains Of Tennessee [The] Carter Family, 192
Mountains Of Virginia Floyd Thompson, 903
Mountains Will See Her Face No More [The] Prairie Ramblers, 712; Village Boys, 932
Mountain-Top Samantha Bumgarner, 142
Mourn, Jerusalem, Mourn Warren Caplinger, 157
Mouse Been Messin' Around [A] Bill Carlisle, 160
Mouses' Ear Blues Cliff Carlisle, 165
Mouth Harp Blues Emry Arthur, 66
Moving Day In Jungletown Hoosier Hot Shots, 438
Mowin' Machine [The] Charlie Marshall, 588
Mr. And Mrs. Is The Name Leon Chappelear, 201
Mr. Bazooka And Miss Clarinet Bob Skyles, 839
Mr. Brown, Here I Come Fletcher & Foster, 349
Mr. Deep Blue Sea Crystal Springs Ramblers, 239
Mr. Dooley Gid Tanner, 889
Mr. Frog Went A-Courtin' Len Nash, 650
Mr. Ghost Goes To Town Zeke Manners, 586
Mr. McKinley Homer Briarhopper, 127
Mr. Rhythm Massey Family, 609
Mr. Rogers And Mr. Kay Ernest Rogers, 810
Mr. W. Lee O'Daniel And His Hillbilly Boys (Theme Song) W. Lee O'Daniel, 666
Mrs. Atchen Amedie Ardoin, 61
Mrs. Jimmie Rodgers' Lament Bradley Kincaid, 485
Mrs. Murphy's Chowder Arkansas Woodchopper, 63; Jack Golding, 374
Mrs. Sosten Waltz Joseph Falcon, 335
Muddy Moon Blues Range Riders, 727
Muddy Water (A Mississippi Moan) Vernon Dalhart, 264
Mug Of Ale [A] Light Crust Doughboys, 503
Mule Skinner Blues (Blue Yodel #8) Roy Acuff, 50
Mule Song (Missouri Mule) [The] Bob Miller, 622
Mule Song [The] Vernon Dalhart, 284–85
Muleskinner Blues Bill Monroe, 631; Jimmie Rodgers, 809
Murder Of J. B. Markham [sic] [The] Lester McFarland & Robert A. Gardner, 545
Murder Of Jay Legg [The] Cecil Vaughn, 930
Murder Of Little Marion Parker [The] Arthur Fields & Fred Hall, 339
Murder Of Nellie Brown [The] Frank Jenkins, 455
Murder Of The Lawson Family [The] Carolina Buddies, 170; Red Fox Chasers, 731
Murillas [sic] Lesson Huggins & Philips Sacred Harp Singers, 446
Murilla's Lesson—Intro. What A Friend We Have In Jesus Johnson Brothers' Band, 463
Murillo's Lesson [J.T.] Allison's Sacred Harp Singers, 60; Charles Butts Sacred Harp Singers, 149; George Long, 510
Muscle Shoal Blues Deford Bailey, 88
Muscle Shoals Blues Elmer Bird, 105
Music Goes 'Round And Around [The] Hal O'Halloran's Hooligans, 667; Prairie Ramblers, 706
Music In My Soul Bush Brothers, 147; Vaughan Quartet, 923
Music Maestro Please Charles Hogg, 431
Music Man [The] Warren Caplinger, 157
Music Of The Old Cow Bell [The] Pickard Family, 691
Music Of The South Bob Skyles, 838
Muskakatuck Waltz Nicholson's Players, 659
Muskrat Land Norris, 662
Muskrat Medley Uncle Dave Macon, 574
Muskrat Rag Jarvis & Justice, 453
Mussolini's Letter To Hitler Johnny Bond, 117; Denver Darling, 296; Carson Robison, 797

Must I Hesitate? Bill Boyd, 122
Must Jesus Bear The Cross Alone John McGhee & Frank Welling, 556, 561
Mustang Gray Bill Bender, 99
My Adobe Hacienda Massey Family, 612
My Alabama Home Gene Autry, 71, 76; Bill Cox, 225; Jack Jackson, 452; Jimmy Long, 511; Dick Robertson, 759
My Alabama Rose Bill Cox, 227
My Alabammy Home Ray Whitley, 953
My Alpine Yodelling Sweetheart Morris Nelson, 653
My And My Wife Ernest V. Stoneman, 872
My Angel Sweetheart Fisher Hendley, 416
My Arkansas Bazooka Gal Bob Skyles, 838
My Arkansas Sweetheart Jimmie Davis, 299
My Ashville [sic] Home In Caroline Johnson Brothers, 463
My Baby Buck Turner, 916
My Baby And My Wife Ernest Tubb, 914
My Baby Can't Be Found Fleming & Townsend, 347
My Baby Don't Love Me Fay & The Jay Walkers, 337; Doc Roberts, 754
My Baby Just Cares For Me Frank[ie] Marvin, 603
My Baby Keeps Stealin' Sugar On Me Walker's Corbin Ramblers, 936
My Baby Loves Me Al Dexter, 314
My Baby Loves Me, I Know Bill Boyd, 124
My Baby Loves Shortenin' Bread Doc Roberts, 752
My Baby Rocks Me (With One Steady Roll) Roy Newman, 658
My Baby's Back In town Buddy Baker, 89
My Baby's Hot Earl & Willie Phelps, 689
My Baby's Lullaby Patsy Montana, 634
My Ball And Chain Bill Boyd, 122
My Bear Cat Mountain Gal Texas Jim Lewis, 499
My Beaumont Mama Blues Leroy Roberson, 752
My Beautiful Home L.V. Jones, 467
My Best Friend Elton Britt, 129
My Big Swiss Cheese Johnny Marvin, 607
My Birmingham Rose Bill Boyd, 125
My Blonde Went Away And Left Me Amadie Breaux, 126
My Blue Bonnet Girl Jimmie Davis, 302
My Blue Eyed Boy Karl & Harty, 470; Asa Martin, 590
My Blue Eyed Jane Callahan Brothers, 154; Ted Lunsford, 517; Jimmie Rodgers, 803
My Blue Eyes Al Dexter, 315; Joseph Falcon, 335
My Blue Eyes Are Not My Blue Eyes Now Al Dexter, 315
My Blue Heaven Georgia Compton's Reelers, 219; Jimmie Davis, 304; Light Crust Doughboys, 502; Marc Williams, 959
My Blue Ridge Girl Bill Shores & Melvin Dupree, 832
My Blue Ridge Mountain Bride Old Hank Penny, 687
My Blue Ridge Mountain Damsel Ted Bare, 93
My Blue Ridge Mountain Home Vernon Dalhart, 266–67, 272–73, 279, 282; Walter C. Peterson, 688
My Blue Ridge Mountain Queen Clayton McMichen, 566; Charlie [& Bud] Newman, 656; Riley Puckett, 718; Southern Moonlight Entertainers, 860
My Blue Ridge Sweetheart Bill Cox, 226
My Blue-Eyed Girl And I Crockett [Family] Mountaineers, 233
My Blues Have Turned To Sunshine Wilf Carter (Montana Slim), 183
My Boarding House On The Hill Gid Tanner, 888
My Boat Is Sailing James Brown, Jr. & Ken Landon Groups, 134
My Bone's Gonna Rise Again David McCarn, 527
My Bones Is Gonna Rise Again Arthur Cornwall, 223
My Bonnie Hoosier Hot Shots, 440; Nicholson's Players, 659

My Bonnie Lies Over The Ocean Cliff Bruner, 140; Hi-Flyers, 419; Leake County Revelers, 494
My Bonnie's Blue Eyes Arthur Tanner, 886
My Boyhood Days Shell Creek Quartet, 826
My Boyhood Happy Days John D. Foster, 354–55
My Boy's Voice Vernon Dalhart, 271, 273–75
My Brave Buckaroo Walter Hurdt, 448
My Brown Eyed Prairie Rose Wilf Carter (Montana Slim), 185
My Brown Eyed Texas Girl Nite Owls, 660
My Brown Eyed Texas Rose Jimmie Davis, 301; Stuart Hamblen, 392; Light Crust Doughboys, 501; Tex Ritter, 750; Jesse Rodgers, 798; Leo Soileau, 854
My Buddy Roy Bledsoe, 108; Happy Bud Harrison, 405; Light Crust Doughboys, 502–03; Riley Puckett, 721; Steve & His Hot Shots, 868
My Buddy, My Daddy, My Pal Bob Atcher, 69
My Burdens Rolled Away John McGhee & Frank Welling, 563
My Cabin By The Sea Zeb & Zeeke, 979
My Cabin Home Southern Moonlight Entertainers, 860
My Cabin Home Among The Hills Asa Martin, 589
My California Home Bill Simmons, 835
My Cannibal Maiden Jimmy Long, 511
My Carolina Girl Georgia Yellow Hammers, 367; Chesley Shirley, 832; Southern Moonlight Entertainers, 860
My Carolina Home Vernon Dalhart, 264, 269, 273, 275; Farmer Sisters, 337; Arthur Fields & Fred Hall, 339; John D. Foster, 354; Fred Kirby, 487; Lester McFarland & Robert A. Gardner, 543; Clayton McMichen, 565, 567; Riley Puckett, 717, 721; Dick Robertson, 758; Tweedy Brothers, 918
My Carolina Mountain Rose Gene Autry, 77; Light Crust Doughboys, 502
My Carolina Sunshine Girl Gene Autry, 72; Wilbur Ball, 90; Rice Brothers' Gang, 747; Carson Robison, 776; Jimmie Rodgers, 801
My Carolina Sweetheart Fred Kirby, 486; Magnolia Trio, 580
My Castle On The Nile Wonder State Harmonists, 971
My Catalina Mountain Rose Jimmy Long, 512
My Cherie Joe Creduer-Albert Babineaux, 232
My Christian Friends In Bonds Of Love Elder Golden P. Harris, 405
My City Girl Fleming & Townsend, 347
My Clinch Mountain Home Carter Family, 188, 193; Happy Valley Family, 398
My Coming Vacation J.B. Whitmire's Blue Sky Trio, 954
My Confession Charlie Wills, 966
My Cotton Pickin' Darling W. Lee O'Daniel, 665
My Courting Days Are Gone Crowder Brothers, 238
My Courting Days Are Over Crowder Brothers, 237
My Cradle Sweetheart Carson Robison, 788
My Creole Sweet Mama Denus McGee, 551
My Cross-Eyed Beau Girls Of The Golden West, 371
My Cross-Eyed Girl Gene Autry, 76
My Cross-Eyed Nancy Jane Bill Nettles, 653
My Curly Headed Girl J.B. Fuslier, 361
My Cute Gal Sal Jack Cawley's Oklahoma Ridge Runners, 199
My Dad Jack Pierce, 696
My Daddy, My Mother And Me -?3, 6 Cliff Bruner, 139
My Dad's Dinner Pail Harry "Mac" McClintock, 528
My Dark Eyed Sweetheart Bar-X Cowboys, 93
My Darling Little Girl Callahan Brothers, 154
My Darling Nell Fred Kirby, 486
My Darling Nellie Gray Vernon Dalhart, 248
My Darling Of The Valley Prairie Ramblers, 712
My Darling Texas Cowgirl Bob Skyles, 839

My Darling Wife Cecil & Vi, 199
My Darling's Black Mustache Henry Whitter, 955
My Daughter Wished To Marry Uncle Dave Macon, 578
My Dear Baby Girl Warren Caplinger, 158
My Dear Little Mother Johnny Roberts, 756
My Dear Old Arizona Home Girls Of The Golden West, 371; Patsy Montana, 635
My Dear Old Daddy Cliff Carlisle, 164
My Dear Old Happy Valley Home Cliff Carlisle, 161
My Dear Old Mountain Home Oscar L. Coffey, 217
My Dear Old Southern Home Jack & Johnnie Powell, 702
My Dear Old Sunny South By The Sea Howard Keesee, 474
My Dear Ole Kansas Home Rowdy Wright, 974
My Didn't It Reign Vaughan Quartet, 928
My Dixie Darling Carter Family, 193
My Dixie Home Andrew Jenkins, 454; Howard Keesee, 475; Asa Martin, 591
My Dixie Sweetheart Jimmie Davis, 299
My Dixieland Girl Texas Wanderers, 901
My Dream Hill Brothers, 424
My Dream Heaven Village Boys, 932
My Dreaming Of You Gene Autry, 71; Jimmy Long, 511; Frank[ie] Marvin, 597
My Dreams Come True Wilf Carter (Montana Slim), 185
My Evaline Sandhills Sixteen, 820
My Evolution Girl Carolina Buddies, 170
My Experience On The Ranch A.C. (Eck) Robertson, 757
My Eyes Are Growing Dimmer Every Day Georgia Yellow Hammers, 367
My Faith Is Clinging To Thee McDonald Quartet, 541; Riley Quartette, 749
My Faithful Old Pinto Pal Wilf Carter (Montana Slim), 184
My Family Circle Fisher Hendley, 416; Three Floridians, 906
My Family Circle (Will The Circle Be Unbroken) Rouse Brothers, 815
My Family Has Been A Crooked Set McGee Brothers, 552
My Far Away Home Allen Quartette, 57
My Fat Gal Sherman Raines, 724
My Fat Girl Chris Bouchillon, 119
My Father Died A Drunkard Tom Darby & Jimmie Tarlton, 294
My Father Doesn't Love Me Lewis McDaniels, 538–39
My Father Is Rich In House And Lands (The Child Of A King) Frank & James McCravy, 537
My Favorite (Mon Favori) Joseph Falcon, 335
My Favorite Blues John D. Foster, 354
My Favorite Waltz Joseph Falcon, 335
My Fickle Sweetheart Ernest Branch & Bernice Coleman, 126
My First Bicycle Ride Uncle Eck Dunford, 325
My Ford Sedan Fiddlin' John Carson, 177
My Frazzle Headed Baby Three Tobacco Tags, 908
My Free Wheelin' Baby Ernest Branch & Bernice Coleman, 126
My Friend McDonald Quartet, 541; Stamps Quartet, 865
My Friend Divine Harmony Four, 401; Laurel Firemen's Quartet, 491
My Frog Ain't Got No Blues A.C. (Eck) Robertson, 757
My Gal Don't Love Me Anymore Sons Of The West, 859
My Gal Is Mean Shelton Brothers, 828
My Gal Kate Crysel Boys, 239
My Gal On The Rio Grande Massey Family, 609
My Gal Sal Roy Acuff, 49; John Boyd, 125; Leon Chappelear, 201
My Gal's A Lulu Clayton McMichen, 572
My Gal's With My Pal Tonight Light Crust Doughboys, 505
My Galveston Gal Milton Brown, 137

My Gamblin' Days Bill Cox, 227
My Girl—She's A Lulu Emry Arthur, 66
My Girl Don't Love Me Leo Soileau, 854
My Girl Friend Doesn't Like Me Anymore Shelton Brothers, 829
My Girl Has Gone And Left Me Hall Brothers, 391
My Girl In Sunny Tennessee Dorsey & Beatrice Dixon, 321
My Girl Is A High Born Lady McGee Brothers, 552
My Girl Of The Golden West Three Tobacco Tags, 907
My Girl Polly Joe Werner, 944
My Girl With Auburn Hair Clarence Ganus, 362
My Girl's A High Born Lady Uncle Dave Macon, 575
My Glorious Saviour Freeman Quartette, 359
My God The Spring Of All My Joys Elder Golden P. Harris, 405
My Good Gal Has Thrown Me Down Callahan Brothers, 152
My Good Gal's Gone—Blues Jimmie Rodgers, 806
My Good Gal's Gone Blues Jimmie Rodgers, 806
My Grandfather's Clock Shelton Brothers, 829
My Grandmother Vass Family, 922
My Grandmother Lives On Yonder Green Uncle Joe Shippee, 831
My Grandpappy's Gun Al Bernard, 100
My Gypsy Dream Girl Three Tobacco Tags, 909
My Gypsy Girl Charlie Poole, 700
My Happiest Day Bush Brothers, 147
My Happy Home I Left In Caroline Walter Smith, 846
My Happy Song McDonald Quartet, 540
My Head Went Round And Round Prairie Ramblers, 713
My Heart Aches For You Joseph Falcon, 335
My Heart Belongs To An Angel Dick Reinhart, 739
My Heart Belongs To The Girl Who Belongs To Somebody Else Lester McFarland & Robert A. Gardner, 548
My Heart Is Aching Stalsby Family, 863
My Heart Is Broken Uncle Bud Landress, 490
My Heart Is Broken For You Dixie Reelers, 319
My Heart Is In The Hills Of Carolina Lew Childre, 207
My Heart Is Stamped With Your Name Claude Casey, 197
My Heart Is Where The Mohawk Flows Tonight Blue Ridge Mountain Girls, 111; Carson Robison, 784–85
My Heart Makes A Monkey Out Of Me Jubileers, 468
My Hearts [sic] Turned Back To Dixie Merritt Smith, 845
My Heart's In Mississippi Central Mississippi Quartet, 199
My Heart's In The Heart Of The Blue Ridge Claude Casey, 197
My Heart's Tonight In Texas Carter Family, 192
My Heavenly Homecoming Stringfellow Quartet, 879; Vaughan Quartet, 929
My Heavenly Sweetheart Fred Kirby, 486
My Herdin' Song Eddie Dean, 308; Massey Family, 610
My Hero Perry Brothers, 687
My High Silk Hat And Gold Top Walking Cane Bill Cox, 225
My Hill Billy Baby Rex Griffin, 384
My Hill Billy Girl Bob Skyles, 838
My Hillside Kentucky Home Plantation Boys, 698
My Home Carolina Buddys, 170
My Home Among The Hills Carter Family, 195
My Home In Arkansas Plantation Boys, 698
My Home In Dixie-Land Fiddlin' John Carson, 178
My Home In The Hills Of Caroline Buddy Jones, 464
My Home On The Prairie Otis & Eleanor, 670
My Home On The Western Plains Jack Pierce, 696
My Home Sweet Home Parker Quartette, 679
My Home, My Baby And Me Buddy Jones, 465
My Home's Across The Blue Ridge Mountains Carolina Tar Heels, 173; Carter Family, 194; Delmore Brothers, 311

My Homestead On The Farm Asa Martin, 592
My Honey Nicholson's Players, 659
My Honey Lou Carter Family, 194
My Honeymoon Bridge Broke Down Wilf Carter (Montana Slim), 184
My Horses Ain't Hungry Vernon Dalhart, 268; Tim Flora & Rufus Lingo, 350; Kelly Harrell, 403; Frank Luther, 524
My Hula Love James Brown, Jr. & Ken Landon Groups, 134
My Hulu Girl Frank[ie] Marvin, 598
My Idea Of Heaven Rice Brothers' Gang, 746
My Irene Earl B. Zaayer, 979
My Irish Molly O Walter C. Peterson, 688
My Island Reverie Charles Mitchell & His Orchestra, 629
My Isle Of Golden Dreams Honolulu Strollers, 433; Clayton McMichen, 566; Riley Puckett, 717; Stripling Brothers, 880
My Ivy Covered Cabin Home Frank Luther, 518
My Jesus I Love Thee Carolina Ladies Quartet, 171
My Katie Fred Richards, 747
My Kentucky Cabin Buddy Dewitt, 313
My Kentucky Mountain Girl Vernon Dalhart, 287
My Kentucky Mountain Sweetheart Jack Major, 585
My Ladder Of Dreams Arthur Duhon, 325
My Laddie Charlie Wills, 966
My Lady Nicholson's Players, 659
My Last Letter Blue Sky Boys, 114
My Last Moving Day Eddie Dean, 307; Monroe Brothers, 633
My Last Old Dollar Harry "Mac" McClintock, 528
My Last Old Yodel Song Wilf Carter (Montana Slim), 185
My Latest Sun Is Sinking Fast Smith's Sacred Singers, 850
My Life's Been A Pleasure Charlie Wills, 966
My Lindy Dear H.K. Hutchison, 450
My Little A-1 Brownie Bernard [Slim] Smith, 842
My Little Blonde Delin T. Guillory-Lewis Lafleur, 385
My Little Blue Heaven Tom Darby & Jimmie Tarlton, 295
My Little Buckaroo Massey Family, 610; Oliver & Allen, 669; Ranch Boys, 726
My Little Cajun Girl Happy Fats, 396
My Little Cow Pony And I Beverly Hill Billies, 103
My Little Darling Brown Brothers, 138; Julian Johnson & Leon Hyatt, 461
My Little Dream Girl Shelly Lee Alley, 59
My Little Georgia Rose Doc Hopkins, 441; Lester McFarland & Robert A. Gardner, 546
My Little German Home Ernest V. Stoneman, 875
My Little German Home Across The Sea Ernest V. Stoneman, 873
My Little Girl Carolina Buddys, 170; Leon Chappelear, 201; Cherokee Ramblers, 204; Hugh Gibbs String Band, 368; Hackberry Ramblers, 387; Hoosier Hot Shots, 440; David Miller, 626–27; Walter C. Peterson, 688; Chesley Shirley, 832; Leo Soileau, 854; Spooney Five, 862; Ernest Thompson, 903; Haskell Wolfenbarger, 969; Yellow Jackets [II], 977
My Little Girl I Love You Jimmie Revard, 742
My Little Grass Shack In Kealakekua, Hawaii Happy Valley Boys, 397
My Little Grass Shack In Kealukekua James Brown, Jr. & Ken Landon Groups, 135
My Little Grey Haired Mother In The West Wilf Carter (Montana Slim), 181, 183
My Little Home Down In New Orleans Howard Keesee, 474
My Little Home In Alabama Thos. A. Burton, 146
My Little Home In Tennessee Harmon Canada, 154; Carter Family, 190; Hugh Cross, 235; Vernon Dalhart, 253–55; Buggs Emerick, 332; Sid Harkreader, 400; Bradley Kincaid, 483
My Little Honeysuckle Rose York Brothers, 977

My Little Hut In Carolina Dick Hartman's Tennessee Ramblers, 407
My Little Indian Napanee David Miller, 626
My Little Lady Jack Foy, 358; Howard Keesee, 474; Carson Robison, 775; Jimmie Rodgers, 800
My Little Mohee Daca, 240
My Little Mohi Roe Brothers & Morrell, 810
My Little Mountain Home John McGhee & Frank Welling, 562
My Little Mountain Lady, Queen Of Alabam' McClendon Brothers, 527
My Little Nappanee Four Pickled Peppers, 356
My Little Old Home Down In New Orleans Carson Robison, 771; Jimmie Rodgers, 800
My Little Old Nevada Home Girls Of The Golden West, 370
My Little Old Sod Shanty On The Claim Chubby Parker, 677
My Little Old Southern Home By The Sea George Edgin, 330
My Little Ozark Mountain Home Kenneth Houchins, 444
My Little Pal Cliff Carlisle, 164
My Little Prairie Flower Texas Jim Lewis, 500
My Little Precious Sonny Boy Claude Casey, 197
My Little Rambling Rose Morgan Denmon, 312
My Little Ranch Home Arthur Duhon, 325
My Little Red Ford Daddy John Love, 514
My Little Rooster Asher Sizemore & Little Jimmie, 837
My Little Sadie Cliff Carlisle, 168
My Little Sod Shanty On The Claim Chubby Parker, 676
My Little Swiss And Me Wilf Carter (Montana Slim), 182
My Little Swiss Maiden Hank Snow, 852
My Little Texas Town Fred Kirby, 486
My Little Yoho Lady Wilf Carter (Montana Slim), 183–84
My Lonely Boyhood Days Cliff Carlisle, 163–64
My Long Journey Home Monroe Brothers, 632
My Long Lost Pal Bill Cox, 227
My Long Stem Pipe W.C. Childers, 206
My Lord Will Come For Me Morris Brothers, 643
My Lord's Gonna Move This Wicked Race Frank Luther, 523
My Lost Lover On The Sea Asa Martin, 589
My Louisiana Girl Jimmie Davis, 299
My Louisiana Sweetheart Bill Nettles, 654
My Love Shelly Lee Alley, 59
My Love Divine Bill Cox, 229
My Love Is A Cowboy (Old Cowboy Song) Powder River Jack-Kitty Lee, 496
My Love Is But A Lassie 'O Arkansas Woodchopper, 64
My Love Is Following You Three Tobacco Tags, 909
My Love Shall Never Fail Miller's Merrymakers, 628
My Love Song Melody Bob Skyles, 838
My Love Went Without Water (Three Days) Sons Of The Pioneers, 858
My Loved Ones Are Waiting For Me Blue Ridge Gospel Singers, 109; Carolina Ladies Quartet, 171; Vaughan Quartet, 923–24, 929–30
My Lover In Dreams Joe Werner, 944
My Lover On The Deep Blue Sea Asa Martin, 590
My Lovin' Kathleen Cliff Carlisle, 166
My Loving Brother (Rock Of Ages) [Smilin'] Ed McConnell, 530
My Lulu Wilf Carter (Montana Slim), 184; Frank[ie] Marvin, 598
My Lulu Gal Charlie Craver, 232
My Ma, She Told Me So Texas Jim Robertson, 759
My Mama Always Talked To Me John Hammond, 394
My Mama Told Me Jimmie Davis, 303
My Mamma Scolds Me For Flirting Carolina Tar Heels, 173

My Mammy Lew Childre, 207
My Mammy's Cabin Charles Brooks, 132
My Mammy's Yodel Song Woody Leftwich, 496; Frank[ie] Marvin, 597–99
My Man Fred Kirby, 486
My Man's A Jolly Railroad Man Rosa Lee Carson, 180
My Mary Milton Brown, 136; Lew Childre, 207; Jimmie Davis, 305; Stuart Hamblen, 392; Light Crust Doughboys, 502; Jesse Rodgers, 798
My Mary Jane Vernon Dalhart, 290–92
My Melancholy Baby Light Crust Doughboys, 503; Marc Williams, 959
My Memory Lane Claude Casey, 197
My Midnight Man Allen Brothers, 56
My Million Dollar Smile Light Crust Doughboys, 502; Patsy Montana, 636
My Mind Won't Be Worried Anymore! Sunshine Boys, 882
My Mississippi Home Goebel Reeves, 736
My Missoula Valley Moon Wilf Carter (Montana Slim), 186
My Missouri Home James Brown, Jr. & Ken Landon Groups, 134
My Montana Sweetheart Wilf Carter (Montana Slim), 181
My Mother Buell Kazee, 472; Earl & Willie Phelps, 689
My Mother And Dear Old Dad Brown Brothers, 138
My Mother And My Sweetheart Roy Harvey, 410, 412; Earl Shirkey & Roy Harper, 831; Ernest V. Stoneman, 878; Sweet Brothers, 884
My Mother Is Lonely Ernest Tubb, 913
My Mother Is Waiting Edward Carson, 174; Wade Mainer, 583
My Mother Is Waiting For Me In Heaven Above Smith Brothers, 848
My Mother Scolds Me For Flirting Thomas C. Ashley, 68
My Mother Was A Lady Ted Chestnut, 204; Lonesome Cowboy [II], 509; Carson Robison, 774
My Mother-In-Law Emry Arthur, 66; John McGhee & Frank Welling, 562
My Mothers [sic] Call Tex Owens, 672
My Mother's Beautiful Hands Bradley Kincaid, 485
My Mother's Bible Allen Quartette, 57; Jewell Tillman Burns & Charlie D. Tillman, 145; Jimmie Davis, 304; Frank & James McCravy, 533; John McGhee & Frank Welling, 553; Smith's Sacred Singers, 849; J. Douglas Swagerty, 883
My Mother's Evening Prayer Frank & James McCravy, 538
My Mother's Grave Elmer Bird, 105
My Mother's Hands McGee Brothers, 552; George [Shortbuckle] Roark, 752; J. Douglas Swagerty, 882
My Mother's Humming Lullaby Vernon Dalhart, 246
My Mother's Old Bible Is True Frank & James McCravy, 535
My Mother's Old Red Shawl Vernon Dalhart, 255, 268; Zora Layman, 492
My Mother's Prayer Melody Boys, 614
My Mother's Prayers Three Tobacco Tags, 909
My Mother's Prayers Have Followed Me Old Southern Sacred Singers, 669; J. Douglas Swagerty, 882
My Mother's Rosary (Ten Baby Fingers And Ten Baby Toes) Leon Chappelear, 202
My Mother's Tears Elton Britt, 128
My Mother's Two Step Amedie Ardoin, 61
My Mountain Gal Goebel Reeves, 735
My Mountain Girl Goebel Reeves, 737
My Mountain Home Sweet Home Roy Acuff, 48
My Name Is John Johannah Kelly Harrell, 404
My Name Is Johnny Brown Joe Gore & Oliver Pettrey, 376
My Name Is Ticklish Reuben Smyth County Ramblers, 852
My Native Home Carter Family, 194
My North Carolina Home Thomas C. Ashley, 68
My North Georgia Home Fiddlin' John Carson, 176

My Nose E.M. Bartlett Groups, 96
My Ohio Shore Jerry Behrens, 98
My Oklahoma Home Gene Autry, 71; Vernon Dalhart, 291
My Old Blackie Joe Cook, 220
My Old Boarding House Pickard Family, 692
My Old Cabin Home Hugh Cross, 236
My Old Canadian Home Wilf Carter (Montana Slim), 186
My Old Carolina Home Bill Cox, 225
My Old Coon Dog George [Shortbuckle] Roark, 751; Doc Roberts, 753
My Old Cottage Home Allen Quartette, 57; Carter Family, 189; Ed Helton Singers, 415; Jimmy Long, 511; John McGhee & Frank Welling, 556; Rev. M.L. Thrasher, 905
My Old Crippled Daddy (& Part 2) Norwood Tew, 898–99
My Old Dog And Me Tex Owens, 671
My Old Dog Tray Light Crust Doughboys, 502
My Old Fashioned Dad Floyd Skillern "The Mountain Troubadour," 837
My Old Fashioned Sweetheart Fred Kirby, 486
My Old Flame Zora Layman, 492
My Old Home Town Bernard [Slim] Smith, 842
My Old Home Town Girl Bill Bruner, 139
My Old Home Town Waltz Amedie Ardoin, 62
My Old Homestead Miller Wikel, 957
My Old Homestead By The Sea Asa Martin, 591
My Old Iowa Home Beverly Hill Billies, 102
My Old Kentucky Home Alexander & Miller, 53; Bowman Sisters, 121; Chief Pontiac, 205; Clayton McMichen, 566; Russell Miller, 627; Riley Puckett, 717; Woodlawn Quartette, 972
My Old Lasso Is Headed Straight For You Wilf Carter (Montana Slim), 186
My Old Log Cabin Home Bill Cox, 225
My Old Maid (In The Shade Of The Old Apple Tree) Hilltoppers, 427
My Old Model T Canova Family, 156
My Old Montana Home Wilf Carter (Montana Slim), 183
My Old Mountain Home Raymond Render, 740
My Old Mule Riley Puckett, 721
My Old New Hampshire Home Elry Cash, 197; Lester McFarland & Robert A. Gardner, 546; Merritt Smith, 845
My Old Pal Bill Cox, 224; Red River Dave, 733; Jimmie Rodgers, 800, 809; Robert Westfall, 947
My Old Pal Of Yesterday Gene Autry, 76; Farmer Sisters, 336; Judie & Julie, 468; Jimmy Long, 511
My Old Plantation And You Loy Bodine, 115
My Old Plantation Home Plantation Boys, 698
My Old Rose Frank & James McCravy, 534
My Old Saddle Horse Is Missing Fred Kirby, 486
My Old Saddle Pal Gene Autry, 81
My Old Sweetheart B.F. Kincaid, 482; Fields Ward, 939
My Old Used To Be (Mon Vieux D'Autrefois) Joseph Falcon, 335
My Old Virginia Home Carter Family, 192; Johnson Brothers, 463; Miller Wikel, 957
My Ole Dog And Me Tex Fletcher, 349; W. Lee O'Daniel, 666
My Only Romance Is Memories Of You Wilf Carter (Montana Slim), 185
My Only Sweetheart Ernest V. Stoneman, 878; Fields Ward, 939
My Own Blues Woody Leftwich, 496
My Own Iona Cotton Mill Weavers, 223; Scottdale String Band, 821; Three Tobacco Tags, 909
My Own Sweet Darling Wife Shelton Brothers, 829
My Own True Lover Emry Arthur, 67
My Ozark Mountain Home George Edgin, 330; Linda Parker, 678; Jimmie Revard, 743

My Pal—Jimmie Davis Buddy Jones, 464
My Pal Of Yesterday Bill Bruner, 139
My Pipe, My Slippers And You Elton Britt, 129
My Poncho Pony Patsy Montana, 636
My Pony's Hair Turned Grey (When My Darling Ran Away) Texas Jim Robertson, 759
My Poodle Dog Hugh Cross, 236; Riley Puckett, 717
My Poodle Doodle Dog Johnny Barfield, 93
My Prairie Pride Ray Whitley, 953
My Prairie Queen Sons Of The West, 859
My Prayer Carolina Gospel Singers, 170; Mr. & Mrs. R.N. Grisham, 385
My Precious Baby Girl Leon Selph, 824
My Precious Bible Copeland Chorus, 221
My Precious Darling Shelly Lee Alley, 58
My Precious Mother Avoca Quartette, 87
My Precious Saviour Allen Quartette, 57
My Precious Sonny Boy Milton Brown, 136
My Pretty Black Eyes Miller's Merrymakers, 628
My Pretty Little Indian Napanee David Miller, 627
My Pretty Quadroon Beverly Hill Billies, 102; Dixieland Swingsters, 320; Keller Sisters & Lynch, 475; Light Crust Doughboys, 502; Carson Robison, 782, 788; Vagabonds, 921
My Pretty Snow Dear Madisonville String Band, 580; Ernest V. Stoneman, 873
My Puppy Bud Riley Puckett, 717
My Rainbow Trail Ernest Tubb, 914
My Rainbow Trail Keeps Winding On Mrs. Jimmie Rodgers, 809
My Ramblin' Days Are Through Wilf Carter (Montana Slim), 185
My Rambling Days Are Over Dwight Butcher, 148
My Ranch Gene Autry, 84; Nite Owls, 660
My Record Will Be There Vaughan Quartet, 929
My Red River Valley Home Red River Dave, 732
My Redeemer Bertha Hewlett, 418; John McGhee & Frank Welling, 556; George Reneau, 740; Chas. Richardson & O.S. Gabehart, 748; Three Tobacco Tags, 907
My Redeemer Lives Carolina Gospel Singers, 170; McDonald Quartet, 541; Smith's Sacred Singers, 850–51
My Red-Haired Lady Lew Childre, 207; Ernest Rogers, 810
My Renfra Valley Home Stewart's Harmony Singers, 869
My Renfro Valley Home Red Foley, 351; Karl & Harty, 470
My Rockin' Mama Cliff Carlisle, 167
My Rocky Mountain Queen Asa Martin, 591
My Rocky Mountain Sweetheart Cliff Carlisle, 163
My Rose Of Tennessee Hoosier Hawaiians, 435
My Rose Of The Prairie Gene Autry, 82
My Rough And Rowdy Ways Gene Autry, 72; Bill Cox, 225; Jimmie Rodgers, 802
My Saddle Pals And I Sons Of The Pioneers, 858
My San Antonio Mama Hank Snow, 852
My Sarah Jane John D. Foster, 354
My Savior First Of All John McGhee & Frank Welling, 556
My Savior's Love Rev. M.L. Thrasher, 905
My Saviour Understands Milton & Marion Carlisle, 168
My Saviour's Train Monroe Brothers, 633; Smith's Sacred Singers, 850
My Shack By The Track Bill Cox, 227
My Sheep Know My Voice Highleys, 421
My Shy Little Bluebonnet Girl Gene Autry, 80
My Silent Love Rhoda Hicks, 421
My Silver Haired Mom Kenneth Houchins, 444
My Sister And I Massey Family, 612
My Skinny Sarah Jane Walter Hurdt, 448
My Smokey Mountain Gal Delmore Brothers, 310
My Smoky Mountain Home Roy Harvey, 411

My Son Joshua Bob Osborne, 670
My Song Of The West Patsy Montana, 636
My Soul Is Lost Crowder Brothers, 238
My Soul Will Shout Hallelujah Jones Brothers Trio, 467
My South Sea Rose South Sea Serenaders, 860
My South Sea Sweetheart Kelly Brothers, 476
My Southern Movements Dick Hartman's Tennessee Ramblers, 408
My Southland Elton Britt, 128
My Star Of The Sky Gene Autry, 82–83; Arthur Duhon, 325
My Steppin' Gal Shelly Lee Alley, 58
My Sunny Alabama Home Clarence Ganus, 362
My Sweet Chiquita Tex Ritter, 750
My Sweet Farm Girl Blue Ridge Mountain Entertainers, 111
My Sweet Floetta David Miller, 626; Parker & Dodd, 678
My Sweet Irene From Illinois Sons Of The Ozarks, 857
My Sweet Little Clover Ernest Branch & Bernice Coleman, 126
My Sweet Little Mother Of The Range Fred Kirby, 487
My Sweet Mountain Rose Roy Hall, 391
My Sweet Thing Tune Wranglers, 915
My Sweetheart Across The Sea Richard D. Burnett, 144
My Sweetheart Darling Rice Brothers' Gang, 747
My Sweetheart Has Gone And Left Me Crowder Brothers, 238; J.H. Howell, 446
My Sweetheart In Tennessee Richard D. Burnett, 144
My Sweetheart In The Moon Jimmy Long, 511
My Sweetheart Is A Shy Little Fairy Red Patterson's Piedmont Log Rollers, 682
My Sweetheart Is A Sly Little Miss Carolina Buddies, 170
My Sweetheart Of Yesterday Bill Simmons, 835
My Sweetheart Run Away E. Segura & D. Herbert, 823
My Sweetheart Was Discouraged Wilfred Fruge-Leo Soileau, 360
My Sweetheart, My Mother And Home Vernon Dalhart, 264
My Sweetheart's Gone And Left Me Crowder Brothers, 238
My Sweetheart's Letter Carl Boling, 116
My Task Jack Pickell, 694
My Tennessee Girl Carl Jones, 466
My Tennessee Mountain Home Vernon Dalhart, 284; Carson Robison, 770; Vance's Tennessee Breakdowners, 922
My Tennessee Sweetheart George & Henson, 365
My Texas Girl Carter Family, 193
My Texas Home Crystal Springs Ramblers, 239
My Texas Sweetheart Shelly Lee Alley, 59; Wilf Carter (Montana Slim), 186
My Time Ain't Long Jess Hillard, 426; Jimmie Rodgers, 807
My Time Will Come Someday Cliff Bruner, 141
My Tootsie Wootsie Gal Bill Cox, 229
My Traveling Night Cliff Carlisle, 166
My Trouble Blues Byrd Moore, 639
My Troubled Mind Rice Brothers' Gang, 747
My Troubles Don't Trouble Me No More Al Dexter, 315
My Troubles Will Be Over Freeman Quartette, 358; McDonald Quartet, 540; Vaughan Quartet, 928
My Troubles Will Pass Away Smith's Sacred Singers, 851
My True And Earnest Prayer Wilf Carter (Montana Slim), 185
My True Love Has Gone Carson Robison, 795
My Trundle Bed Frank Gerald & Howard Dixon, 368; Miller Wikel, 957
My Two Sweethearts Jimmie Wilson's Catfish String Band, 968
My Two-Time Mama Cliff Carlisle, 163
My Untrue Cowgirl Swift Jewel Cowboys, 884
My Valley Of Memories Bob Miller, 624
My Vine Covered Home In The Blue Ridge Blue Ridge Mountain Girls, 112

My Virginia Rose Carter Family, 192
My Virginia Rose Is Blooming Carter Family, 193
My West Virginia Home Asher Sizemore & Little Jimmie, 837
My Wife And Sweetheart Bill Cox, 228
My Wife Died On Friday Night Crook Brothers String Band, 234
My Wife Died Saturday Night Dr. Humphrey Bate, 97
My Wife Has Gone And Left Me Lloyd Burdette, 143
My Wife Is On A Diet Hoosier Hot Shots, 439
My Wife Left Me McGee Brothers, 552
My Wife Went Away And Left Me Daddy John Love, 514; Charlie Poole, 699
My Wife, She Has Gone And Left Me Kelly Harrell, 404
My Wife's Done Gone And Left Me Jack Hagwood, 388
My Wife's Gone To The Country Warren Caplinger, 157
My Wife's Wedding Chris Bouchillon, 120
My Wild Irish Rose Chuck Wagon Gang, 210; Hugh Cross, 235; Honolulu Strollers, 433; Leake County Revelers, 494; W.W. Macbeth, 526; Lester McFarland & Robert A. Gardner, 544; Melody Boys, 614; Walter C. Peterson, 688; Riley Puckett, 719; Leo Soileau, 855
My Winding River Home Jesse Rodgers, 798
My Window Faces The South Bob Wills, 964
My Wishing Song W. Lee O'Daniel, 665
My Wonderful Dream Singing Preachers, 836
My Wonderful One Bill Boyd, 123
My Yodeling Days Are Through Wilf Carter (Montana Slim), 185
My Yodeling Sweetheart Wilf Carter (Montana Slim), 185; Earl Shirkey & Roy Harper, 832
Myself Denus McGee, 551
Myster [sic] Of No. 5 [The] Harry Hillard, 425
Mysteries Of The World Uncle Dave Macon, 577
Mystery Of No. 5 [The] Howard Keesee, 475
Mystery Of Number Five [The] Jimmie Rodgers, 804
Mystery Of Old Number Five Dwight Butcher, 148
Mythological Blues [The] Ernest Rogers, 810

N.R.A. Blues Bill Cox, 226
Na Marjanse Jimmie Revard, 742
Na Pas Des Mouche Sur Moi (There Ain't No Flies On Me) Patrick (Dak) Pellerin, 685
Nagasaki Dixieland Swingsters, 320; Roy Newman, 658; Rice Brothers' Gang, 746
Naggin' Young Woman York Brothers, 977
Nailed To The Cross Holman & Robinson, 432; Frank & James McCravy, 531; John McGhee & Frank Welling, 559
Nancy Jane Light Crust Doughboys, 500
Nancy Rollin Gid Tanner, 889
Nancy Rowland Fiddlin' John Carson, 175; Carter Brothers & Son, 187
Naomi Wise Thomas C. Ashley, 67; Vernon Dalhart, 253–55; Morgan Denmon, 312; Red Fox Chasers, 731; Short Creek Trio, 833
Napoleon Bonaparte Bob Skyles, 838
Napoleon March Collier Trio, 218
Napoleon's March Perry Brothers, 687
Nashville Blues Deford Bailey, 88; Delmore Brothers, 310
Natcherly Leon Selph, 824
Natchitocheo (French Town) Blind Uncle Gaspard, 363
National Blues Richard Cox, 229
Natural Bridge Blues Roy Hall, 391
Naturalized For Heaven Parker Quartette, 679; Vaughan Quartet, 929
Naughty, Naughty Jimmie Revard, 742
Naw! I Don't Wanta Be Rich Carson Robison, 780, 782–83
Naw, I Don't Wanna Be Rich Carson Robison, 785, 787, 793
Naw, I Don't Wanta Be Rich Carson Robison, 778, 782, 796

Nealski Wanderers, 938
Neapolitan Nights Carson Robison, 766
Neapolitan Two Step Kessinger Brothers, 481
Near The Cross Paramount Sacred Four, 674; Parker & Dodd, 678
Nearer My God To Thee Eva Quartette, 333; Jimmy Long, 512; Frank Luther, 524; Uncle Dave Macon, 576; Mr. & Mrs. W.M. Shively, 832
Nearer The Sweeter [The] John McGhee & Frank Welling, 554, 561
Nearing My Long Sought Home McDonald Quartet, 540; Vaughan Quartet, 926
'Neath An Indian Summer Moon Leon Payne, 683
'Neath Hawaiian Palms Tennessee Ramblers [II], 897
'Neath The Bridge At The Foot Of The Hill Roy Hall, 391
'Neath The Maple In The Lane Shelton Brothers, 827
'Neath The Old Apple Tree Clayton McMichen, 567; Riley Puckett, 718–19
'Neath The Old Pine Tree Leon Payne, 683
'Neath The Old Pine Tree At Twilight Magnolia Trio, 580
'Neath The Purple On The Hills Cliff Bruner, 141
'Neath The Silvery Moon Leon Selph, 823
'Neath The Weeping Willow Tree Hackberry Ramblers, 387
Nebuchadneez[a/e]r Bob Miller, 620
Ned Went A' Fishin' Walker's Corbin Ramblers, 936
Negro Supper Time Nations Brothers, 652
Nellie Bly Massey Family, 612
Nellie Dare Elzie Floyd & Leo Boswell, 350
Nellie Dare And Charl[ey/ie] Brooks Vernon Dalhart, 254, 268
Nellie Gray Roba Stanley, 866; Henry Whitter, 955
Nellie's Blue Eyes Arthur Smith, 841
Nellie's Not The Same Nell Now Prairie Ramblers, 713
Nervy Bum [A] Frankie Barnes, 94
Nevada Johnnie Cliff Carlisle, 167
Never Alone Hall Brothers, 391; D.T. Mayfield, 614; Ruth Neal & Wanda Neal, 652; Phil Reeve & Ernest Moody, 735; Arthur Smith, 841
Never Alone Waltz Red Headed Fiddler[s], 732
Never Be As Fast As I Have Been G.B. Grayson & Henry Whitter, 381
Never Break A Promise Jimmie Davis, 304
Never Drink No More Joseph Falcon, 335
Never Grow Old Tex Owens, 672
Never Had Such A Time In My Life Johnson County Ramblers, 464
Never Leave Your Gal Too Long Carson Robison, 782–84
Never Let The Devil Get The Upper Hand Of You Carter Family, 194
Never Let You Cry Over Me Bill Boyd, 124
Never Make Love No More Uncle Dave Macon, 575
Never No Mo' Blues Cliff Carlisle, 161; Whitey McPherson, 579; Carson Robison, 765; Jimmie Rodgers, 800, 809
Never No More Blues Hugh Cross, 235; Bob Wills, 960
Never No More Hard Times Blues Bob Wills, 962
Never Seen The Like Since Gettin' Upstairs Gid Tanner, 890
Never Slept Last Night Modern Mountaineers, 630
Never Take No For An Answer Lulu Belle & Scotty, 516
Never To Be Sweethearts Again Dorsey & Beatrice Dixon, 321
Never Was A Married Man Three Tobacco Tags, 908
New "Boogie Woogie" [The] Johnny Barfield, 94
New "Comin' 'Round The Mountain" [The] Fiddlin' John Carson, 179
New "Givin' Everything Away" Riley Puckett, 722
New "Red River Valley" Dick Hartman's Tennessee Ramblers, 407; Tennessee Ramblers [II], 898
New 21 Years Dick Robertson, 758

New Answer To Twenty-One Years Blue Ridge Mountain Girls, 112
New Arkansaw Traveller Gid Tanner, 890
New Birmingham Jail Big Slim Aliff, 54; Jimmie Tarlton, 892
New Birmingham Jail No. 3 Callahan Brothers, 152
New Born Blues Stripling Brothers, 880
New Britain Denson-Parris Sacred Harp Singers, 312; Original Sacred Harp Choir, 670
New Broom Fox Chasers, 357
New Brown's Ferry Blues Log Cabin Boys, 508
New Carroll County Blues—No. 1-3 [The] W.T. Narmour & S.W. Smith, 650
New Century Hornpipe John Baltzell, 91
New Charleston—No. 1–3 [The] W.T. Narmour & S.W. Smith, 650
New Chattanooga Blues Allen Brothers, 56
New Chattanooga Mama Lake Howard, 445
New Cinda Lou Shelton Brothers, 828
New Coon In Town Mumford Bean, 98; Four Virginians, 357; Uncle Dave Macon, 577
New Crawdad Song Log Cabin Boys, 508
New Curly Headed Baby J.E. Mainer's Mountaineers, 581
New Day Is Comin' Mighty Soon [A] Dwight Butcher, 148
New Deal Blues Allen Brothers, 57
New Dixie Fate Norris, 661
New Do Right Dady Leon Chappelear, 202
New Dress For Ida Red [A] Dixieland Swingsters, 320
New Falling Rain Blues Cliff Bruner, 141
New False Hearted Girl Delmore Brothers, 312
New Five Cents Paul Warmack, 940
New Ford Car [The] Uncle Dave Macon, 576
New Frontier [The] Chuck Wagon Gang, 210; Sons Of The Pioneers, 857
New Greenback Dollar Roy Acuff, 48
New Ground Blues Dutch Coleman, 217
New Harmony Waltz Richmond Melody Boys, 748
New Hope Lee Wells, 943
New Hosanna Dye's Sacred Harp Singers, 328
New How-Do-You-Do Dick Hartman's Tennessee Ramblers, 407
New Iberia Polka E. Segura & D. Herbert, 823
New It Makes No Difference Now Dickie McBride, 526
New Jail [The] Buell Kazee, 473
New Jelly Roll Blues Al Dexter, 314
New Jerusalem Way [The] Mount Vernon Quartet, 645
New John Henry Blues Shelton Brothers, 827–28
New Lafayette Joseph Falcon, 335
New Lamp Lighting Time In The Valley Herald Goodman, 375
New Liberty Cherokee Ramblers, 203
New London School Tragedy (In Eastern Texas) Elton Britt, 129
New London Texas School Disaster Tex Walker, 935
New Lost Train Blues J.E. Mainer's Mountaineers, 581
New Mama Bill Cox, 226
New Maple On The Hill Crowder Brothers, 237
New Mean Mama Blues Shelly Lee Alley, 58
New Memories Of You That Haunt Me Cliff Carlisle, 167
New Money Doc Roberts, 753
New Orleans Patrick (Dak) Pellerin, 685
New Orleans Is The Town I Like Best Fletcher & Foster, 349
New Orleans Mama Blues Happy Bud Harrison, 405
New Prisoner's Song Dock Boggs, 116
New River Train [The] Al Bernard, 100; Roland Cauley, 198; Vernon Dalhart, 247–49; Sid Harkreader, 400; Kelly Harrell, 403; Dick Hartman's Tennessee Ramblers, 407; Jess Hillard, 425; Frank Luther, 525; Massey Family, 608; Monroe

New River Train [The] (continued)
    Brothers, 632; Ernest V. Stoneman, 877; Texas Rangers, 899;
    Henry Whitter, 954
New Roswell Schottische Massey Family, 611
New Salty Dog [A] Allen Brothers, 56
New San Antonio Rose Roy Hall, 391; Texas Jim Lewis, 499;
    Bob Wills, 964; Charlie Wills, 966
New Sensation [The] E.M. Bartlett Groups, 96
New Six Or Seven Times Bill Boyd, 123
New Soldier's Farewell Al Dexter, 315
New Spanish Two-Step Bill Boyd, 124
New St. Louis Blues [The] Bob Wills, 962
New Steel Guitar Rag Bill Boyd, 123
New Talking Blues Chris Bouchillon, 120; Herschel Brown, 133
New Talking Blues No. 2 Herschel Brown, 134
New Trail To Mexico York Brothers, 978
New Trouble Frank Gerald & Howard Dixon, 368
New Trouble In Mind Blues Shelton Brothers, 828
New Twenty One Years Ernest Hare, 399; Frank Luther, 519;
    Bob Miller, 621–22; Dick Robertson, 758
New Van Buren Blues Bob Skyles, 838
New Worried Mind Elton Britt, 130; Roy Rogers, 812; Bob
    Wills, 965
New York Hobo [The] Tom Darby & Jimmie Tarlton, 294
(New) Jeep's Blues Light Crust Doughboys, 505
Newly Moulded Mound Buck Nation, 651; Ray Whitley, 953
Newmarket Wreck [The] Mr. & Mrs. J.W. Baker, 90; George
    Reneau, 740
Next To Your Mother Who Do You Love Madisonville String
    Band, 580
Next Year Prairie Ramblers, 704
Nice Girl Don't Want Me Any More [The] Joseph Falcon, 335
Nick Nack Song [The] Ridgel's Fountain Citians, 749
Nickel In The Kitty Ocie Stockard, 870
Nickety Nackety Now Now Now Chubby Parker, 676–77
Nigger Baby John Dilleshaw, 317; A.A. Gray, 378; Dr. Smith's
    Champion Hoss Hair Pullers, 843
Nigg[a/e]r Blues Joseph Falcon, 335; 'Lasses & Honey, 491
Nigger Crap Song Alf. Taylor, 892
Nigger Eat The Sugar Lowe Stokes, 871
Nigger In The Cotton Patch Earl Johnson, 460
Nigger In The Woodpile Happy Hoosiers, 397; Uncle "Am"
    Stuart, 881; Gid Tanner, 890
Nigger Loves A Watermellon [sic] Bill Cox, 224
Nigger Loves A Watermelon [A] Bill Cox, 226
Nigger On The Wood Pile Earl Johnson, 460
Nigger Stays At Home E.M. Lewis, 498
Nigger Talking Blues No. 2 Herschel Brown, 134
Nigger Washerwoman [The] W.L. "Rustic" Waters, 940
Nigger, Will You Work? Fisher Hendley, 416
Nigger's Dream Alf. Taylor, 892
Night Express [The] Wilmer Watts, 941
Night Guard [The] Jack Webb, 942
Night Herder [The] Bill Simmons, 835
Night Herdin' Lullabye Tex Owens, 671
Night Herding Song George Goebel, 372; Marc Williams, 958
Night I Fell In Love [The] Bill Cox, 229
Night In A Blind Tiger—Part 1, 2 [A] Clayton McMichen, 569
Night In Carolina [A] Dick Hartman's Tennessee Ramblers, 408
Night In June [A] Walter C. Peterson, 688
Night My Mother Died [The] Cleve Chaffin, 200
Night Spot Blues Universal Cowboys, 919
Night That You Nestled In My Arms [The] Roy Newman, 657

Night Time Down South Adolph Hofner, 430
Night Time Is The Right Time Crowder Brothers, 238
Night Time On The Prairie Fred Kirby, 487
Night Train To Memphis Roy Acuff, 50
Night Was Dark And Stormy [The] Merritt Smith, 845
Night Was Filled With Music [The] Texas Wanderers, 900
Night We Met [The] Shanks Bros. Trio, 825
Night We Said Goodbye [The] Hi-Flyers, 420
Night Wind [The] Hi-Flyers, 419
Nights Of Gladness Bert Layne, 493
Nina One-Step Bartmon Montet-Joswell Dupuis, 637
Nine Hundred Miles From Home Riley Puckett, 720
Nine Miles Out O' Town Nite Owls, 660
Nine O'Clock Breakdown Newton County Hill Billies, 658
Nine Or Ten Times Shelly Lee Alley, 58
Nine Pound Hammer Frank Blevins, 108; Blue Ridge
    Mountain Entertainers, 111; G.B. Grayson & Henry Whitter,
    381; Hill Billies, 423; Ernest V. Stoneman, 878
Nine Pound Hammer Is Too Heavy Monroe Brothers, 632
Ninety And Nine [The] Vernon Dalhart, 285; Rev. Clyde D.
    King, 485; Maury Pearson, 683; Chas. Richardson & O.S.
    Gabehart, 748
Ninety Fifth Denson's Sacred Harp Singers Of Arley, Alabama,
    313; OKeh Atlanta Sacred Harp Singers, 667; Lee Wells, 943
Ninety Nine Years Blues Jimmie Rodgers, 807
Ninety-Nine Years Carolina Ramblers String Band, 172; Jess
    Hillard, 426; Asa Martin, 591
Ninety-Nine Years—Part 1, 2 [I,II] Graham Brothers, 377;
    Lester McFarland & Robert A. Gardner, 549
Ninety-Nine Years (Is Almost For Life) Asa Martin, 590;
    Vagabonds, 921
Ninety-Nine Years In Jail Clarence Greene, 382
Ninety-Nine's My Name Callahan Brothers, 153
No Business Of Mine Smoky Mountain Ramblers, 852
No Christmas Times For Poor Little Nell Carson Robison, 785
No Daddy Blues Cliff Carlisle, 161; Bill Nettles, 653
No Deep True Love Dewey & Gassie Bassett, 97
No Depression Carter Family, 194
No Dice Bill Boyd, 125
No Disappointment In Heaven Blue Sky Boys, 113; Rev. &
    Mrs C.A. Dougherty, 324; Perry Kim & Einar Nyland, 481
No Disappointments In Heaven Ruth Donaldson & Helen
    Jepsen, 323
No Drunkard Can Enter That Beautiful Home Bill Carlisle, 160
No Drunkard Can Enter There Delmore Brothers, 310
No Drunkards Can Enter There Anglin Brothers, 61
No Fault Of Mine Bob Skyles, 838
No Foolin' Walter Hurdt, 448; Range Riders, 727; Shelton
    Brothers, 829
No Good For Nothin' Blues Sunshine Boys, 881
No Hard Times Dwight Butcher, 148; Jimmie Rodgers, 807
No Hiding Place Down There (Sister Lucy) Frank & James
    McCravy, 533
No Home Blue Sky Boys, 113; Plantation Boys, 698
No Home No Home Miller Wikel, 957
No Home, No Place To Pillow My Head (Charlie) Monroe's
    Boys, 632
No Huggin' Or Kissin' Dick Hartman's Tennessee Ramblers, 408
No Letter In The Mail Roy Acuff, 50; Bill Monroe, 631
No Letter In The Mail Today Bill Carlisle, 160; Happy-Go-
    Lucky Boys, 397
No Letter Today Ted Daffan's Texans, 241
No Longer Lonely R.L. Barksdale, 94; Humbard Family, 447
No Longer Sad V.O. Stamps-M.L. Yandell, 863

No Low Down Hanging Around Allen Brothers, 56; John McGhee & Frank Welling, 562
No Mama Blues Leon Chappelear, 201
No Matter How He Done It Walter Hurdt, 448
No Matter How She Done It Bob Wills, 961
No Matter What Happens Lunsford Bros., 517; Pine Ridge Boys, 697
No Matter What Happens, My Darling Rice Brothers' Gang, 747; Roy Rogers, 811
No Matter What They Say Shelton Brothers, 830
No Moonlight Joe Werner, 944
No More Hoosier Hot Shots, 437
No More Dying Armstrong & Highley, 64; Frank & James McCravy, 533, 535–37
No More Good-byes Ernest V. Stoneman, 876
No More The Moon Shines On Lorena Carter Family, 189
No More To Ride The Rails Chas. M. Dewitte, 314
No Name Blues Clayton McMichen, 571
No Nance Georgia Compton's Reelers, 219
No Never Alone Roy Hall, 391; John McGhee & Frank Welling, 557; Ruth Neal & Wanda Neal, 652
No Night There Virginia Male Quartet, 932
No No Positively No Carolina Buddies, 170
No One Delmore Brothers, 310; Rambling Rangers, 725
No One Else Can Take Your Place McGee Brothers, 552
No One Knows Foundation Quartette, 355
No One Left To Love Me Mitchell Brothers, 630
No One Loves You As I Do Fields Ward, 939
No One To Call Me Darling Gene Autry, 71
No One To Kiss Me Goodnight Bob Atcher, 70; Ramblin' Red Lowery, 515; Johnny Marvin, 607; Dick Reinhart, 739
No One To Say Goodbye Wanderers, 938
No One To Welcome Me Home Blue Sky Boys, 113; Carver Boys, 196; Georgia Yellow Hammers, 367
No One's Going To Miss Me When I'm Gone Golden Melody Boys, 373
No One's Hard Up But Me Red Brush Rowdies, 730
No Other Fellow's Sweetheart Lem's Down Home Boys, 496
No Other's Bride I'll Be Carter Family, 193
No Path Of Sunshine Arthur Duhon, 325
No Place Like Home Daddy John Love, 514
No Place To Lay His Head Rev. Edward Boone, Mrs. Edward Boone & Miss Olive Boone, 118
No Place To Pillow My Head Anglin Brothers, 61; Karl & Harty, 470; Woodruff Brothers, 973
No Romance In Your Soul Hoosier Hot Shots, 440
No Room Rev. M.L. Thrasher, 905
No Room For A Tramp Roy Harvey, 411
No Shadows J.B. Whitmire's Blue Sky Trio, 954
No Sorrow There Elder Golden P. Harris, 405
No Stranger Yonder McMillan Quartet, 573; Parker Quartette, 679; Peck's Male Quartette, 684; Smith's Sacred Singers, 850
No Tears In Heaven Drum Quartet, 324
No Telephone In Heaven Carroll Black, 107; Carter Family, 188
No Wedding Bells Carlisle Brothers, 169
No Wonder Bob Wills, 964
No, No, Nora Hoosier Hot Shots, 439; New Dixie Demons, 655
No, Not One Emry Arthur, 65; Canova Family, 155
No. 2 Schottiche [sic] Riley Puckett, 720; Gid Tanner, 891
Noah And The Lobsters J.P. Ryan, 817
Noah's Ark Harmonica Bill, 401
Noah's Warning Three Tobacco Tags, 907
Noah's Wife (Lived A Wonderful Life) Hoosier Hot Shots, 440
Nobody Red Foley, 351
Nobody Answered Me Warren Caplinger, 157

Nobody But Me Leon Selph, 824
Nobody But My Baby Is Getting My Love Shelton Brothers, 828
Nobody Cares Carlisle Brothers, 169; Jenkins Family, 456
Nobody Cares About Me Leon Selph, 824
Nobody Cares For Me Ralph Hodges, 429; Sons Of Dixie, 856
Nobody Cares If I'm Blue Canova Family, 155; Carolina Tar Heels, 174
Nobody Knows About Women Joe Steen, 868
Nobody Knows But Me Dwight Butcher, 148; Harry Hillard, 425; Howard Keesee, 475; Jimmie Rodgers, 803
Nobody Knows But Me And You Bob Atcher, 70
Nobody Knows My Name Joe Cook, 220
Nobody Knows My Troubles But Me Fiddlin' John Carson, 178
Nobody Knows The Trouble I've Seen Anglin Brothers, 61
Nobody Knows What's On My Mind Blues Buddy Baker, 89
Nobody Like You Hackberry Ramblers, 387
Nobody Loves Me Herschel Brown, 133
Nobody Loves My Soul Prairie Ramblers, 709
Nobody To Love Carolina Night Hawks, 172; Frank Luther, 518; McDonald Quartet, 541; Massey Family, 609–10; Bob Miller, 621
Nobody Wants Me Cliff Carlisle, 162
Nobody Wants To Be My Baby Rex Griffin, 384
Nobody's Business Emry Arthur, 65; Jerry Behrens, 99; Warren Caplinger, 156; Carolina Ramblers String Band, 173; Jimmie Davis, 298; Clyde Martin, 593; Bob Miller, 625; Ernest Mull, 646; Charles Nabell, 647; Riley Puckett, 721–22; Short Creek Trio, 833; Walker's Corbin Ramblers, 936
Nobody's Business But My Own Earl & Willie Phelps, 689
Nobody's Business If I Do Riley Puckett, 716; Leo Soileau, 855
Nobody's Darlin' But Mine Joseph Falcon, 335
Nobody's Darling Cumberland Ridge Runners, 240; G.B. Grayson & Henry Whitter, 380; Lester McFarland & Robert A. Gardner, 545; North Carolina Ridge Runners, 663; Grover Rann, 729
Nobody's Darling But Mine Gene Autry, 81; Jimmie Davis, 301, 303; Doc Hopkins, 441; Light Crust Doughboys, 502; Wade Mainer, 583; Earl & Willie Phelps, 689; Prairie Ramblers, 705; Tex Ritter, 750; Carson Robison, 796
Nobody's Darling On Earth Uncle Dave Macon, 577; Wade Mainer, 583; North Carolina Cooper Boys, 663; Raymond Render, 740
Nobody's Fault But My Own Roy Rogers, 811
Nobody's Little Girl Frank & James McCravy, 538
Nobody's Lonesome For Me Jimmie Davis, 303
Nobody's Sorry For Me Ella Sutton, 882
Nobody's Sweetheart Hugh Cross, 237; Hoosier Hot Shots, 436; Wallace Sesten & Jack Shook, 824
Nobody's Sweetheart Now Wesley Long, 513
Noko-No March James Brown, Jr. & Ken Landon Groups, 135
"Nol Pros" Nellie Bascom Lamar Lunsford, 516
Nola Carson Robison, 761, 792
None Greater Than Lincoln Dr. D.D. Hollis, 432
Nonie Shelly Lee Alley, 58
Nora Darling Roland Cauley, 199
Norfolk Flip Melvin Dupree, 327
North Asheville Blues Crowder Brothers, 237
North Carolina Blues Crowder Brothers, 237–38; Lewis McDaniels, 538
North Carolina Moon Callahan Brothers, 152; Wade Mainer, 584
North Carolina Textile Strike [The] John McGhee & Frank Welling, 557
North Port Lee Wells, 943

North-Bound Train Nelstone's Hawaiians, 653
Northeast Texas Milner & Curtis, 628
Norwegian Waltz And Chicken Reel Harry Reed & Wm. F. Wynn, 734
Not A Word From Home Roy Acuff, 51
Not A Word Of That Be Said Wade Mainer, 585
Not Made With Hand Huggins & Philips Sacred Harp Singers, 446
Not Made With Hands [J.T.] Allison's Sacred Harp Singers, 60
Not Over Thirty-Five York Brothers, 978
Not Turning Back Dorsey & Beatrice Dixon, 321
Nothin' Shelton Brothers, 827
Nothing Between Paul Crutchfield & John Clotworthy, 238; Old Southern Sacred Singers, 669
Nothing But The Blood John McGhee & Frank Welling, 563
Nothing But The Blood Of Jesus Canova Family, 156; Old Southern Sacred Singers, 669
Nothing But The Blues Delmore Brothers, 311
Nothing From Nothing Leaves You Cofer Brothers, 216
Nothing Goes Hard With Me Elmer Bird, 106
Nothing Like Old Time Religion Bateman Sacred Quartet, 97
Nothing Matters Anymore Massey Family, 612
Nothing Matters To Me Village Boys, 931
Nothing To Do, But John McGhee & Frank Welling, 556
Noveau Grand Gueyan Happy Fats, 395
Now And Forever Dixieland Swingsters, 320
Now He's In Heaven Callahan Brothers, 154
Now I Am All Alone Joe Gore & Oliver Pettrey, 376
Now I Am Lonesome And Blue Cecil & Vi, 199
Now I Feel The Way You Do Bill Boyd, 125
Now I Know Somebody Doesn't Care Bob Atcher, 69
Now Or Never Cindy Walker, 935
Now She's Gone (I'm Sittin' On Top Of The World) Morris Brothers, 643
Now That You Have Gone Leon Selph, 824
Now That You're Gone (Oh My Darling!) Bob Atcher, 70
Now You Care No More For Me Johnny Bond, 117
Now You're Gone I Can't Forget You Jack & Leslie, 451
Number 111 J.E. Mainer's Mountaineers, 581
Numbers Blues [The] Johnny Barfield, 94
Nutty Song Pie Plant Pete, 694

O Bear Me Away On Your Snowy Wings Uncle Dave Macon, 576
O Beautiful Land Kitts Bros., 487
O Blessed Day Freeman Quartette, 359
O Bury Me Not On The Lone Prairie Arthur Fields & Fred Hall, 339
O Bury Me Not On The Lone Prairie (The Dying Cowboy) Texas Jim Robertson, 759; Carl T. Sprague, 862
O Come All Ye Faithful (Adeste Fideles) Roy Rogers, 812
O Come, All Ye Faithful Woodlawn Quartette, 972
O Dem Golden Slippers Roy Harvey, 411
O For A Closer Walk With God Wisdom Sisters, 969
O Glorified City Hall County Sacred Singers, 392
O Happy Day Canova Family, 155; Vaughan Quartet, 925–27, 929
O How I Miss You Tonight John McGhee & Frank Welling, 560
O How She Lied Rhoda Hicks, 421
O Jailer Bring Back That Key Pie Plant Pete, 694
O Lights Of Home Freeman Quartette, 359
O Mother How We Miss You Lubbock Texas Quartet, 515
O Rock Of Ages Hide Thou Me Chuck Wagon Gang, 211
O Such Wondrous Love Vaughan Quartet, 929
O Take Me Back Byrd Moore, 640
O Think Of The Home Over There Frank & James McCravy, 534

O Wand'rer On Life's Troubled Sea E. Arthur Lewis, 497
O What A Blessing He Is To Me Vaughan Quartet, 927
O Why Not Tonight Blue Ridge Gospel Singers, 109; Giddens Sisters, 369
O Wondrous Love Rev. M.L. Thrasher, 905
O! Dem Golden Slippers Vernon Dalhart, 275
O! Little Town Of Bethlehem Golden Hour Mixed Quartette, 373
O! Molly Dear Go Ask Your Mother Kelly Harrell, 403
O! Susanna Riley Puckett, 716
O&C Railroad Wreck John McGhee & Frank Welling, 558
O, Susanna! Dan Hornsby, 442
O.S.T. Gal Happy Fats, 396
Oakville Twister Hoosier Hot Shots, 436
Oberlin Amedie Ardoin, 62
Object Of My Affection [The] Milton Brown, 136; Texas Jim Lewis, 499
Ocean Of Life Dorsey & Beatrice Dixon, 321
Ocean Waves Casey's Old Time Fiddlers, 197; Tom Owens Barn Dance Trio, 672; Pie Plant Pete, 694
Ocean Waves Call Archer Porter, 702
Oceana Roll Dan Hornsby, 442
Odem Roswell Sacred Harp Quartet, 814
O'ershadowed By God's Love Palmetto Male Quartette, 674
Off To Honolulu Hank Penny, 687
Off To The War I'm Going Fletcher & Foster, 349
Off To War Earl McCoy & Jessie Brock, 531
Oh Aunt Dinah Get Your Nightcap On Tweedy Brothers, 918
Oh Baby Blues (You Won't Have No Mama At All) Light Crust Doughboys, 505
Oh Baby! Oscar [Slim] Doucet, 324
Oh Baby, You Done Me Wrong Uncle Dave Macon, 577
Oh Bury Me Beneath The Willow Arthur Fields & Fred Hall, 343
Oh Bury Me Not On The Lone Prairie (The Dying Cowboy) Vernon Dalhart, 266
Oh Bury Me Out On The Prairie Vernon Dalhart, 291
Oh Bury Me Out On The Prairie (The Cowboy's Lament) Travis B. Hale-E.J. Derry Jr., 389
Oh By Jingo Light Crust Doughboys, 502
Oh By Jingo! Hoosier Hot Shots, 438
Oh By Jingo! (Oh By Gee, You're The Only Girl For Me) Dave Edwards, 330
Oh Captain, Captain Tell Me True Vernon Dalhart, 254; Elzie Floyd & Leo Boswell, 350
Oh Christofo Columbo Charlie Craver, 232
Oh Darling Bob Atcher, 69
Oh Darling Come Back Byron Parker, 675
Oh Darling You're Breakin' My Heart Girls Of The Golden West, 371
Oh Death (Charlie) Monroe's Boys, 632
Oh Declare His Glory Buice Brothers, 142; Johnson Brothers Quartette, 463; McDonald Quartet, 540; Stamps Quartet, 864–65
Oh Dem Golden Slippers Al Bernard, 100; Vernon Dalhart, 281; Frank Luther, 524; Chubby Parker, 676–77; Carson Robison, 776, 780, 787; Tweedy Brothers, 918
Oh Didn't He Ramble Hill Billies, 424
Oh For The Life Of A Hobo Arthur Fields & Fred Hall, 343–44
Oh For The Wild And Wooley West Gene Autry, 71
Oh Gee, There Ain't No Justice Arthur Fields & Fred Hall, 340
Oh How I Love Jesus Phil Reeve & Ernest Moody, 735
Oh How I Miss You Tonight Cliff Bruner, 139
Oh How I Need My Mother Frank Luther, 524
Oh How It Hurt E.M. Bartlett Groups, 96

Oh Jailer Bring Back That Key Charlie Craver, 231; Pie Plant Pete, 695; Carson Robison, 778
Oh Josephine, My Josephine Hackberry Ramblers, 388
Oh Little Children Crowder Brothers, 238
Oh Lord Rambling Rangers, 725
Oh Lord Show Me The Light Callahan Brothers, 153
Oh Lovin' Babe Uncle Dave Macon, 577
Oh Mama, Why Didn't I Listen To You? Dwight Butcher, 148
Oh Marie, Oh Marie Universal Cowboys, 919
Oh Mary, Don't You Weep Edward Carson, 174; Morris Family, 643; Reid Bros. Band, 738; Merritt Smith, 845; Tennessee Ramblers [II], 898
Oh Miss Lizzie Chris Bouchillon, 120
Oh Molly Dear B.F. Shelton, 826
Oh Mo-nah Maple City Four, 587
Oh Monah! Sons Of The West, 859
Oh My Darling Clementine Floyd Thompson, 903
Oh Susanna Vernon Dalhart, 274–75; Nicholson's Players, 659; Chubby Parker, 676–77; Pie Plant Pete, 695; Carson Robison, 796; Uncle Joe Shippee, 831; Woodhull's Old Time Masters, 971
Oh Susannah Rice Brothers' Gang, 747
Oh Suzanna, Ring The Banjo Bill Bender, 99
Oh Suzzana Chubby Parker, 676
Oh Sweet Daddy, Oh Pshaw Dick Hartman's Tennessee Ramblers, 408
Oh Sweet Mama Bill Cox, 229
Oh Sweet Mama Blues Hoke Rice, 745
Oh That Cow Fleming & Townsend, 347
Oh That Dumb-bell! Carson Robison, 776
Oh That Nasty Raid Bill Cox, 229
Oh Those Tombs Roy Hall, 391
Oh Wanderer On Life's Troubled Sea E. Arthur Lewis, 498
Oh Wasn't I Getting Away Claude Davis, 297
Oh What A Fool I've Been Shelly Lee Alley, 59
Oh What A Joy To Sing Coats Sacred Quartette, 216
Oh Where Is My Little Dog Gone? Hill Billies, 424
Oh Why Did I Ever Get Married J.E. Mainer's Mountaineers, 582
Oh Wonderful Day Bush Brothers, 147
Oh Yes? Take Another Guess Hank Penny, 686
Oh You Beautiful Doll Bob Wills, 962–63
Oh You Can't Fool An Old Hoss Fly Vernon Dalhart, 242
Oh You Pretty Woman Cliff Bruner, 139
Oh You Pretty Woman! Milton Brown, 136
Oh! Adam Had 'Em Vernon Dalhart, 290
Oh! Beautiful City Amory Male Quartette, 60
Oh! Bright Home Forman Sisters, 352
Oh! Bury Me Not On The Lone Prairie Carson Robison, 787
Oh! By Jingo Dan Hornsby, 442
Oh! Come Deal Family, 307
Oh! For The Life Of A Hobo Arthur Fields & Fred Hall, 343
Oh! For The Wild And Woolly West Frank[ie] Marvin, 602
Oh! For The Wild And Wooly West Frank[ie] Marvin, 602
Oh! How She Lied Joe Foss, 353
Oh! Mom-E-Nez Massey Family, 612
Oh! My Lawd Jess Young, 979
Oh! She's Crazy Yellow Jackets [II], 976
Oh! Sir I Was Only Flirting Billy Vest, 931
Oh! Susanna Vernon Dalhart, 275; Light Crust Doughboys, 503
Oh! Susannah Carson Robison, 792, 795
Oh! Swing It Jimmie Revard, 743
Oh! We Miss You Carson Brothers-Smith, 180
Oh! What I Know About Roscoe New Dixie Demons, 655
Oh! Willie Come Back C.A. West, 944
Oh! You Beautiful Doll Hoosier Hot Shots, 439

Oh! You Pretty Woman Bob Wills, 963, 965
Oh! You Rogue (You Stole My Heart) New Dixie Demons, 655
Oh, For The Wild And Woolly West Frank[ie] Marvin, 602
Oh, Happy Day Majestic [Male] Quartet, 585
Oh, Hide You In The Blood Monroe Brothers, 633
Oh, How I Hate It Carolina Tar Heels, 173
Oh, I Want To See Him Forman Sisters, 352; Peck's Male Quartette, 684
Oh, It's Great To Be A Doctor Vernon Dalhart, 292
Oh, Johnny, Oh Riley Puckett, 722
Oh, Lady Be Good Bob Wills, 963
Oh, Little Town Of Bethlehem Frank & James McCravy, 536
Oh, Look At That Baby Tune Wranglers, 915
Oh, My Goodness Dick Hartman's Tennessee Ramblers, 408
Oh, My Pretty Monkey Kelly Harrell, 403
Oh, No She Don't Bill Boyd, 122
Oh, Take Me Back Carter Family, 195
(Oh, The Whippoorwill Sings In The Sycamore) Just The Same Jack Major, 585
Oh, Where Is My Wandering Boy Tonight Nelson & Nelson, 653
Ohio Lovers Thomas C. Ashley, 67
Ohio Prison Fire [The] Bob Miller, 619–20; Carson Robison, 781
Ohio River Blues Vernon Dalhart, 282, 284; Carson Robison, 766
Ohio River Flood [The] Roscoe & Samuel Dellinger, 309
Ohio Sweetheart Gene King, 485
Okay Baby Hoosier Hot Shots, 439
OKeh Washboard Breakdown Herschel Brown, 134
Oklahoma Jack Moser, 644
Oklahoma Blues Chuck Wagon Gang, 210; Ernest Hare, 399; Frank[ie] Marvin, 596–98; Jack Pierce, 695; Carson Robison, 771
Oklahoma Blues No. 2 Frank[ie] Marvin, 598
Oklahoma Charley Carson Robison, 783–84
Oklahoma Charlie Carson Robison, 783
Oklahoma City Blues Buddy Jones, 465
Oklahoma Days Lou & Nellie Thompson, 904
Oklahoma Kid [The] Goebel Reeves, 736
Oklahoma Medley Jack Pierce, 696
Oklahoma Rag Prince Albert Hunt, 447; Bob Wills, 960
Oklahoma Rounder Jimmie Revard, 742
Oklahoma Sunshine Patt Patterson, 682
Oklahoma Waltz Jack Cawley's Oklahoma Ridge Runners, 199
Oklahoma, Land Of The Sunny West Frank[ie] Marvin, 599–601
Old Account Settled [An] Perry Kim & Einar Nyland, 481
Old Account Settled Long Ago [The] Perry Kim & Einar Nyland, 482
Old Account Was Settled [An] Blue Sky Boys, 113
Old Account Was Settled Long Ago [The] Deal Family, 307; Andrew Jenkins, 455; John McGhee & Frank Welling, 554, 561
Old Age Pension Blues Shelton Brothers, 829
Old Age Pension Check Roy Acuff, 49
Old Alberta Plains Wilf Carter (Montana Slim), 183
Old And Faded Picture [The] J.E. Mainer's Mountaineers, 581
Old And In The Way Fiddlin' John Carson, 175, 177, 179
Old And Only In The Way Arkansas Woodchopper, 63; Ted Chestnut, 204; Kentucky Girls, 478; Lester McFarland & Robert A. Gardner, 546, 548; Charlie Poole, 700
Old Apple Tree [The] Frank Gerald & Howard Dixon, 368; A'nt Idy Harper, 402; Riley Puckett, 722
Old Arapahoe Trail [The] Beverly Hill Billies, 103

Old Ark's A'Moving [The] John Dilleshaw, 317; A.A. Gray, 378
Old Arm Chair [The] Thomas C. Ashley, 68; Charlie Parker, 676; R.L. Raines, 724; Williamson Brothers & Curry, 960
Old Aunt Betsy Frank Blevins, 108
Old Aunt Peggy, Won't You Set 'Em Up Again? Fiddlin' John Carson, 175
Old Axe Shop [The] Bill Cox, 225
Old Barn Dance [The] Wilf Carter (Montana Slim), 184
Old Bay Mule Of Mine Melton & Minter, 615
Old Bell Cow [The] Dixie Crackers, 318
Old Bill Moser's Ford Vernon Dalhart, 257–58
Old Bill Mosher's Ford Archer Porter, 702
Old Black Crow In The Hickory-Nut Tree Allen Brothers, 56; Hugh Cross, 236
Old Black Dog Dick Justice, 468
Old Black Joe Len & Joe Higgins, 421; Clayton McMichen, 566; Riley Puckett, 716; Jimmy Smith, 844; Woodlawn Quartette, 972
Old Black Mountain Trail Patsy Montana, 634
Old Black Sheep Elzie Floyd & Leo Boswell, 350; Lester McFarland & Robert A. Gardner, 543
Old Black Steer (Old Cowboy Song) [The] Powder River Jack-Kitty Lee, 496
Old Black Steer [The] Patt Patterson, 681
Old Blind Dog Jimmy Johnson's String Band, 461
Old Blind Heck Chris Bouchillon, 120
Old Breakdown [The] Joseph Falcon, 335
Old Brown Pants [The] Frank Morris, 642
Old Buckaroo Goodbye Gene Autry, 83
Old Buddies Wilf Carter (Montana Slim), 186
Old Bureau Drawer [The] Vernon Dalhart, 283
Old Buzzard Doc Roberts, 752
Old Cabin Home [The] Floyd Thompson, 903
Old California Prairie Ramblers, 710
Old Chain Gang [The] Crowder Brothers, 238; Doc Hopkins, 441; Karl & Harty, 471
Old Cherry Tree, Sweet Marie [The] Bert Bilbro, 104
Old Chisholm Trail [The] Edward L. Crain, 230; Girls Of The Golden West, 370; Tex Hardin, 398; Harry "Mac" McClintock, 528; Patt Patterson, 681; Marc Williams, 959; Zeke Williams, 959
Old Chisolm [sic] Trail Patt Patterson, 681
Old Chuck Wagon Days Wilf Carter (Montana Slim), 186
Old Church Bell In The Steeple [The] Glad & Woody Smith, 843
Old Church Choir [The] Jimmy Long, 512
Old Clay Pipe [The] Roy Harvey, 410
Old Concert Hall In The Bowery [The] Hoke Rice, 745
Old Coon Steve Homesley, 433
Old Coon Dog Bradley Kincaid, 484
Old Coon Dog Blue Fleming & Townsend, 348
Old Corn Liquor Frank Hutchison, 450
Old Corn Mill Russell & Louis Burton, 146
Old Corral [The] Ranch Boys, 726
Old Cottage Home [The] Lester McFarland & Robert A. Gardner, 545; Charlie Oaks, 664; Holland Puckett, 715
Old Country [The] Leo Soileau, 855
Old Covered Bridge [The] Vernon Dalhart, 292; Asa Martin, 592; Morris Brothers, 643; Dick Parman, 679
Old Covered Wagon Gene Autry, 81; George Wade, 933
Old Cowboy Zora Layman, 492; Prairie Ramblers, 709
Old Cross Roads [The] Doc Hopkins, 441
Old Crossroad [The] Monroe Brothers, 633
Old Dad Frank Jenkins, 455
Old Daddy Dear Hugh Cross, 236
Old Dan Tucker Fiddlin' John Carson, 176; Hill Billies, 424; Frank Luther, 524; Uncle Dave Macon, 574; Gid Tanner, 889
Old Dan Tucker—Country Dance Judge Sturdy's Orchestra, 881
Old Days Medley McLaughlin's Old Time Melody Makers, 565
Old Deacon Johnson Duke Clark, 213
Old Deacon Jones Wesley Long, 513
Old Dinner Pail [The] A.E. Ward, 938
Old Dog Tray—Hard Times Len & Joe Higgins, 421
Old Drunkard And His Wife [The] Joseph Falcon, 334
Old Eliza Jane Doc Roberts, 753
Old Elm Tree [The] John McGhee & Frank Welling, 562
Old Engineer Reuben Vance's Tennessee Breakdowners, 922
Old Faded Photograph [An] Rex Griffin, 383
Old Familiar Tunes—Part 1, 2 Carson Robison, 791
Old Family Album Arthur Fields & Fred Hall, 343; Frank[ie] Marvin, 601
Old Family Doctor [The] Frank Luther, 522
Old Fashioned Dipper (That Hangs On A Nail) Elton Britt, 128
Old Fashioned Faith [The] John McGhee & Frank Welling, 562; J. Douglas Swagerty, 883
Old Fashioned Hoedown Texas Jim Lewis, 499
Old Fashioned Home In New Hampshire [An] Lester McFarland & Robert A. Gardner, 549
Old Fashioned Locket Burns Brothers, 146; Frank & James McCravy, 533; Clayton McMichen, 572; Dick Parman, 679–80; Riley Puckett, 722; Shelton Brothers, 830
Old Fashioned Love Roy Acuff, 49; Bill Boyd, 122; Cliff Bruner, 139; Dixie Demons, 318; Whitey McPherson, 579; Bob Wills, 960
Old Fashioned Man Wells Brothers String Band, 943
Old Fashioned Meeting Blue Sky Boys, 113
Old Fashioned Mother Ike Cargill, 158
Old Fashioned Picture [An] Vernon Dalhart, 260–61
Old Fashioned Picture Of Mother Asa Martin, 588–89; Doc Roberts, 754
Old Fashioned Shack [An] Red Foley, 351
Old Fashioned Square Dance [The] Billy Milton, 628
Old Fashioned Sweetheart Buddy Jones, 465; Fred Kirby, 486
Old Fashioned Sweetheart Of Mine [An] Carson Robison, 775
Old Fashioned Waltz Homer Christopher, 209
Old Fiddle Blues [The] Hackberry Ramblers, 388
Old Fiddler Joe Johnny Barfield, 94; Doc Hopkins, 441
Old Fiddler's Song [The] Vernon Dalhart, 258–59
Old Flannigan Blue Ridge Mountaineers, 112
Old Folks At Home Monroe Quartette, 634; Nicholson's Players, 659; Vaughan Quartet, 925–26
Old Folks Back Home [The] Gene Autry, 78; Jimmy Long, 512
Old Folks Better Go To Bed Scottdale String Band, 821
Old Folks Dance Medley—Part 1, 2 Arthur Fields & Fred Hall, 343
Old Folks Get In Bed Oscar Ford, 352
Old Frying Pan And The Old Camp Kettle [The] Fiddlin' John Carson, 176
Old Gal Of Mine Walter C. Peterson, 688
Old Gatville Quadrille Colonel John A. Pattee, 681
Old Go Hungry Hash House [The] Ernest V. Stoneman, 873
Old Granny Rattle-Trap Uncle "Am" Stuart, 881
Old Gray Bonnet [The] Walter C. Peterson, 688
Old Gray Bonnett [sic] [The] Kenneth Striker, 879
Old Gray Goose Is Dead [The] Pickard Family, 693
Old Gray Haired Man [The] Edward L. Crain, 229–30

Old Gray Horse [The] Pickard Family, 691
Old Gray Mare [The] Gene Autry, 82; Milton Brown, 138; Lew Childre, 207; Vernon Dalhart, 277, 282; Gid Tanner, 888
Old Gray Mare Is Back Where She Used To Be [The] Carson Robison, 797
Old Grey Goose [The] Carolina Tar Heels, 173; John Henry Howard, 444; Bob Skyles, 839
Old Grey Goose Is Dead [The] Boyden Carpenter, 174; Karl & Harty, 470; Pickard Family, 693
Old Grey Horse Ain't What He Used To Be [The] Fiddlin' John Carson, 178
Old Grey Horse Came Out Of The Wilderness [The] "Ted" Sharp, Hinman & Sharp, 825
Old Grey Mare [The] Carolina Ramblers String Band, 172; Lew Childre, 207; Vernon Dalhart, 275, 277; Johnny Marvin, 606; Land Norris, 662; Henry Whitter, 955
Old Grey Mare Kicking Out Of The Wilderness Earl Johnson, 460
Old Gulf Coast [The] Leroy [Slim] Johnson, 462
Old Hat [The] Leake County Revelers, 494
Old Hayloft Waltz [The] Farm Hands, 336
Old Hen Cackle Deford Bailey, 88; Clayton McMichen, 573
Old Hen Cackled Chief Pontiac, 205; Clayton McMichen, 571
Old Hen Cackled And The Rooster Crowed [The] Short Creek Trio, 833; Taylor's Kentucky Boys, 895; Jess Young, 978
Old Hen Cackled And The Rooster's Going To Crow [The] Fiddlin' John Carson, 175
Old Hickory Cane [The] Ernest V. Stoneman, 873, 875
Old Hitchin' Rail [The] Charlie Marshall, 588
Old Home Brew [The] Dorsey & Beatrice Dixon, 321
Old Home Nest Hart & Cates, 406
Old Home Place [The] Cliff Carlisle, 167; Chapman Quartet, 200
Old Hymns Are Best [E.R.] Nance Family, 648
Old Ice Man [The] Happy Fats, 396
Old Jake Gillie Kessinger Brothers, 479
Old Jim Crow [The] Land Norris, 662
Old Jimmy Sutton G.B. Grayson & Henry Whitter, 380
Old Joe Dr. Humphrey Bate, 97; Sid Harkreader, 400
Old Joe Bone Carter Brothers & Son, 187
Old Joe Clark H.M. Barnes, 94; Fiddlin' John Carson, 177; Fruit Jar Guzzlers, 360; Hill Billies, 422; Doc Hopkins, 441; Bradley Kincaid, 484; Light Crust Doughboys, 502; Clayton McMichen, 573; Fiddlin' Powers & Family, 703; Riley Puckett, 715; Short Creek Trio, 833; Ernest V. Stoneman, 874; Gid Tanner, 888; Da Costa Woltz's Southern Broadcasters, 970
Old Joe Clarke Clayton McMichen, 571
Old Joe Is At It Again Village Boys, 932
Old Joe Turner Blues Cliff Bruner, 140
Old John Hardy Thomas C. Ashley, 67
Old Johnny Bucker Wouldn't Do Walter Smith, 846
Old K-C [The] Jess Young, 979
Old Kentucky Cabin Carson Robison, 768, 770–71; Jesse Rodgers, 799
Old Kentucky Dew Ralph Hodges, 429; John McGhee & Frank Welling, 559, 562
Old Kentucky Home William B. Houchens, 443; Jimmy Smith, 844
Old Kitty Kate (On The Mississippi Line) [The] Vernon Dalhart, 287
Old Ladies' Home [The] Frank Luther, 519; Ed McBride, 527; Jimmy Wakely, 934
Old Lady And The Devil Bill & Belle Reed, 733
Old Lady Blues Hiter Colvin, 219

Old Liza Jane Uncle "Am" Stuart, 881
Old Log Cabin For Sale [An] Rangers Quartet, 728; Whitey & Hogan, 952
Old Lonesome Blues Bowman Sisters, 121
Old Love Letters (Bring Memories Of You) Jimmie Rodgers, 809
Old Maid [The] Jossie Ellers, 331; Buell Kazee, 472
Old Maid And The Burglar [The] Ernest V. Stoneman, 877
Old Maid Blues Roba Stanley, 866
Old Maids' Brown [sic]Ferry Blues Riley Puckett, 721
Old Maid's Last Hope (A Burglar Song) Uncle Dave Macon, 573
Old Maid's Song [The] Jossie Ellers, 331
Old Man Crip Jolly Boys Of Lafayette, 464
Old Man Duff Frank[ie] Marvin, 604–05
Old Man Of The Mountain [The] Texas Jim Lewis, 500; Carson Robison, 794
Old Man On The Hill George Reneau, 741
Old Man's Drunk Again [The] Uncle Dave Macon, 575
Old Man's Story [An] Arkansas Woodchopper, 63; Hall Brothers, 391; John McGhee & Frank Welling, 563; Monroe Brothers, 633; Carson Robison, 765, 767; Clyde White, 948
Old Master's Runaway McGee Brothers, 552
Old McDonald Had A Farm Gid Tanner, 889
Old Mill Wheel [The] Eddie Dean, 307; Buck Nation, 651
Old Miller's Will [The] Edward Carson, 175; Carson Bros., 180
Old Mill's Tumbling Down [The] Shelton Brothers, 829
Old Mississippi Moon Prairie Ramblers, 712
Old Missouri Moon Gene Autry, 81; Claude Casey, 197; Kenneth Houchins, 443
Old Molly Hair Fiddlin' Powers & Family, 704
Old Molly Hare Carter Brothers & Son, 187; Crockett [Family] Mountaineers, 233; Clayton McMichen, 567; Riley Puckett, 719
Old Money Musk Quadrille Colonel John A. Pattee, 681
Old Montana Marc Williams, 959
Old Montana Moon Tune Wranglers, 916
Old Mountain Dew Delmore Brothers, 311
Old Mountain Man [The] Herald Goodman, 375
Old Muddy Water Slim Smith, 846
Old Mule [The] Edward Carson, 175
Old Musician And His Harp [The] Charlie Oaks, 664
Old Musicians Harp [The] Everett Morgan, 642
Old Nevada Moon Patsy Montana, 636
Old New Hampshire Village [The] Asa Martin, 588
Old November Moon Gene Autry, 83; Light Crust Doughboys, 505
Old Number Three Bradley Kincaid, 483
Old Oak Tree [The] Ranch Boys, 726
Old Oaken Bucket [The] Honolulu Strollers, 433; Woodlawn Quartette, 972
Old Old Love Returns Taylor Trio, 894
Old Pal Arkansas Woodchopper, 63; Fred Richards, 747
Old Pal How I Wonder Where You Are Tonight William Steudevant, 868
Old Pal Of My Heart Jimmie Rodgers, 808
Old Pal of Yesterday Girls Of The Golden West, 370
Old Pal Why Don't You Answer Me Don Weston, 947
Old Pals Loren H. Shortridge, 833
Old Parlor Organ [The] Carson Robison, 780–81
Old Pinto Massey Family, 609
Old Pinto And Me Bill Cox, 229
Old Pinto, My Pony, My Pal Jesse Rodgers, 799
Old Pioneer Massey Family, 612; Roy Rogers, 811
Old Plantation Melodies Vernon Dalhart, 274; Adelyne Hood, 434

Old Plantation Melody Vernon Dalhart, 275–78
Old Polka Alexander & Miller, 53
Old Rabbit W.A. Lindsay, 507
Old Race Horse [The] Theron Hale, 389
Old Rachel Frank Hutchison, 449
Old Rattler Ernest Mull, 646
Old Red Floyd Ming, 629
Old Red Barn Medley Quadrille John Baltzell, 90
Old Red Cradle [The] Lulu Belle & Scotty, 516
Old Revival Meetin' [An] Prairie Ramblers, 712
Old River Valley Frank Luther, 518
Old Rock Jail Behind The Old Iron Gate [The] Georgia Yellow Hammers, 367
Old Rocket Prairie Ramblers, 706
Old Rockin' Chair [An] Dixieland Swingsters, 320
Old Rose And A Curl [An] Rex Griffin, 384
Old Rose Waltz Massey Family, 609
Old Rub Alcohol Blues Dock Boggs, 116
Old Ruben Wade Mainer, 585
Old Rugged Cross [The] California Aeolians, 151; Carter Family, 191; Arthur Cornwall & William Cleary, 223; Sid Harkreader, 400; Jenkins Family, 456; Light Crust Doughboys, 502; [Smilin'] Ed McConnell, 530–31; Frank & James McCravy, 533, 536; Lester McFarland & Robert A. Gardner, 544; John McGhee & Frank Welling, 561; Montgomery Quartet, 637; [E.R.] Nance Family, 648; Jack Pickell, 694; George Reneau, 741; Carson Robison, 795; Merritt Smith, 844; Smoky Mountain Sacred Singers, 852; Vagabonds, 921; Vaughan Quartet, 926; Westbrook Conservatory Entertainers, 947
Old Rugged Road [An] Jesse Rodgers, 798
Old Saddle For Sale [An] Patsy Montana, 636
Old Sallie Goodman Fiddlin' John Carson, 175
Old Sallie Goodwin South Georgia Highballers, 860
(Old Santa Claus Is Leavin') Just Because Smith's Carolina Crackerjacks, 848
Old Schoolhouse Play Ground [The] Walter Smith, 846
Old Sefus Brown Wyzee Hamilton, 393
Old Shep Red Foley, 351; Jack & Leslie, 452; Pine Ridge Boys, 697
Old Ship Is Sailing For The Promised Land [The] Fiddlin' John Carson, 178
Old Ship Of Zion [J.T.] Allison's Sacred Harp Singers, 60; Uncle Dave Macon, 574; Ernest Phipps, 690
Old Shoes A-Draggin' Bob Miller, 623
Old Shoes And Leggin's Uncle Eck Dunford, 326
Old Southern Home Carolina Ramblers String Band, 172
Old Spinning Wheel [The] Frank Luther, 521; Riley Puckett, 721; Ranch Boys, 725, 727
Old Sport Reel William B. Houchens, 443
Old Spring Of Love [The] W. Lee O'Daniel, 665
Old Step Stone [The] "Peg" Moreland, 641
Old Sweet Song (For A Sweet Old Lady) [An] Lester McFarland & Robert A. Gardner, 550; Blaine & Cal Smith, 843; Vagabonds, 922
Old Sweetheart Of Mine [An] Martin Melody Boys, 594
Old Sweethearts Of Mine George Edgin, 329
Old Swinnie Fiddlin' Powers & Family, 703
Old Three Room Shack [An] Roy Acuff, 49
Old Ties Uncle Dave Macon, 575
Old Time Breakdown Miller's Merrymakers, 628
Old Time Cinda Hill Billies, 422
Old Time Corn Shuckin', Part 1, 2 Ernest V. Stoneman, 876
Old Time Favorites Medley Walter C. Peterson, 688
Old Time Fox Chase [The] Henry Whitter, 954
Old Time Melodies Everett Morgan, 642
Old Time Melodies Part I, II Walter C. Peterson, 688; Show Boat Boys, 833

Old Time Power Jewell Tillman Burns & Charlie D. Tillman, 145; John McGhee & Frank Welling, 560; Wisdom Sisters, 969
Old Time Religion For Me Smith's Sacred Singers, 850; Stamps Quartet, 865
Old Time Southern Revival Jenkins Family, 456
Old Time Tune Medley Herschel Brown, 133
Old Time Tunes Gid Tanner, 887
Old Time Waltz [The] Amadie Breaux, 126; Leo Soileau, 854
Old Timer Jimmie Davis, 304; Massey Family, 612
Old Timer From Caroliner Johnson Brothers, 463
Old Tobacco Mill [The] Leo Boswell, 119; Golden Melody Boys, 373; Hi-Flyers, 419
Old Trail [The] Gene Autry, 83
Old Traveling Man [The] Charlie [& Bud] Newman, 656
Old Tunes Joseph Falcon, 334
Old Uncle Bill Al Bernard, 100
Old Uncle Dudy (Keep Fiddling On) Coon Creek Girls, 221
Old Uncle Jessie Uncle Eck Dunford, 326
Old Uncle Joe McKinney Brothers, 564
Old Uncle Ned Fiddlin' John Carson, 176; Hill Billies, 424
Old Village Church [The] Lester McFarland & Robert A. Gardner, 545
Old Virginia Breakdown Dixie Ramblers [I], 319
Old Virginia Moon Carl Boling, 116
Old Virginia Rambler Earl Powell, 702; Holland Puckett, 715
Old Virginia Reel—Part 1, 2 Fiddlin' Powers & Family, 704
Old Virginny Lullaby Bob Palmer & Monte Hall, 673
Old Voile Blue Ridge Mountaineers, 112
Old Waggoner Crazy Hillbillies Band, 232
Old Water Mill By A Waterfall [An] Bill Boyd, 122; Milton Brown, 137; W. Lee O'Daniel, 665
Old Waterfall Jimmie Revard, 743
Old Weary Blues Jess Young, 979
Old Whisker Bill, The Moonshiner Buell Kazee, 472
Old White Mule [The] Len & Joe Higgins, 421
Old Wishing Well Jake & Carl, 453; Ray Whitley, 952
Old Woman And The Cow [The] Gene Autry, 74
Old Wooden Leg Blevins & Blair, 109
Old Wooden Rocker [The] Bradley Kincaid, 485; Maple City Four, 587; Chubby Parker, 677
Old Yazoo W. Lee O'Daniel, 666
Old Zip Coon Charlie Craver, 231
Old Zip Coon And Medley Reels Doc Roberts, 753; Joseph Samuels, 819
Old Zip Coon Medley Colonel John A. Pattee, 681
Old-Fashioned Cabin [The] Vaughan Quartet, 924
Old-Fashioned Cottage [An] Hugh Cross, 236; Blind Alfred Reed, 733
Old-Fashioned Hill Flat Creek Sacred Singers, 346
Old-Fashioned Photograph Of Mother Frank & James McCravy, 534
Oldtime Medley Girl O' Yesterday, 369; Imperial Quartet, 451
Old-Time Religion [The] Old Southern Sacred Singers, 669; Reid Bros. Band, 738; Ernest Thompson, 902
Old-Time Waltz Hackberry Ramblers, 388
Old-Time Westerner [An] Jimmie Revard, 743
Ole Bill Jackson Brown Log Cabin Boys, 508
Ole Dan Tucker Frank Luther, 524
Ole Faithful Gene Autry, 81; Prairie Ramblers, 704; Riley Puckett, 721; Ranch Boys, 725; West Brothers Trio, 946
Ole Jelly Roll Blues Bob Wills, 962
Ole Joe Clark Carolina Ramblers String Band, 173
Ole Pardner Ranch Boys, 726
Ole Rattler Cumberland Ridge Runners, 239
Olney Dye's Sacred Harp Singers, 328
Ommie Wise G.B. Grayson & Henry Whitter, 380
On A Blue And Moonless Night Show Boat Boys, 833

On A Blue Lagoon Carson Robison, 765–66, 771
On A Chinese Honeymoon W. Lee O'Daniel, 666
On A Cold Winter Night J.E. Mainer's Mountaineers, 581
On A Good Time Straw-Ride Al Bernard, 100
On A Green Mountainside In Virginia Hugh Cross, 237
On A Hill Lone And Gray Carter Family, 190–91
On A Mountain High Sons Of The Pioneers, 857
On A Road That Winds Down To The Sea Earl & Willie Phelps, 689
On A Slow Train Through Arkansaw Al Bernard, 100
On A Slow Train Thru Arkansaw Al Bernard, 100
On A Summer's Day Pleaman S. Neal's Harmony Three, 652
On A Sunday Afternoon Walter C. Peterson, 688
On A Tennessee Trail Charlie Craver, 232
On A Tom Thumb Golf Course Walter Coon, 221
On Christ The Solid Rock I Stand Jenkins Family, 456
On Desert Sands Gibson String Trio, 369
On Down The Line Rye's Red River Blue Yodelers, 817
On Her Wedding Morn Harwood Entertainers, 412
On Jordan's Stormy Bank John McGhee & Frank Welling, 556
On Mexico's Beautiful Shore Prairie Ramblers, 711
On Mobile Bay Vernon Dalhart, 276; Dan Hornsby, 442
On My Way Back Home Monroe Brothers, 633
On My Way Back Home (En Route Chez Moi) Joseph Falcon, 335
On My Way Home Leo Soileau, 854
On My Way To Canaan Land Philyaw Brothers, 690
On My Way To Canaan's Land Carter Family, 189
On My Way To Glory Monroe Brothers, 633
On My Way To Jesus Bush Brothers, 147
On My Way To Lonesome Valley Cliff Carlisle, 161
On My Way With Jesus McDonald Quartet, 540
On Our Golden Wedding Day Glad & Woody Smith, 843
On Some Foggy Mountain Top Monroe Brothers, 632
On Tanner's Farm Gid Tanner, 891
On That Dixie Bee Line Vernon Dalhart, 259
On That Old Gospel Ship Monroe Brothers, 633
On The 14th Of November Porter Phillips, 689
On The Banks Of A Lonely River Tom Darby & Jimmie Tarlton, 295
On The Banks Of Old Tennessee Fiddlin' John Carson, 178; G.B. Grayson & Henry Whitter, 381
On The Banks Of That Silvery Stream Warren Caplinger, 157
On The Banks Of The Brandywine Merritt Smith, 845
On The Banks Of The Kaney Big Chief Henry's Indian String Band, 103
On The Banks Of The Ohio Callahan Brothers, 152; Walter Coon, 221; Clarence Greene, 382; Clayton McMichen, 570; Monroe Brothers, 632; Philyaw Brothers, 690
On The Banks Of The Old Ohio Bert Layne, 493
On The Banks Of The Old Omaha Andrew Jenkins, 454
On The Banks Of The Old Tennessee Byrd Moore, 638
On The Banks Of The Rio Grande Cliff Carlisle, 165
On The Banks Of The Silvery Stream Warren Caplinger, 157
On The Banks Of The Sunny San Juan Eddie Dean, 308; Ella Sutton, 882
On The Banks Of The Sunny Tennessee Mr. & Mrs. J.W. Baker, 90
On The Banks Of The Wabash B.F. Kincaid, 482; Lester McFarland & Robert A. Gardner, 547
On The Banks Of The Wabash Far Away Kanawha Singers, 469
On The Battle Fields Of Belgium Charlie Poole, 699
On The Bowery Sid Harkreader, 401
On The Bridge At Midnight Taylor-Griggs Louisiana Melody Makers, 894

On The Colorado Trail Frank Luther, 520
On The Cross Stamps Quartet, 864
On The Dixie Bee Line Vernon Dalhart, 263
On The Dixie Bee Line (In That Henry Ford Of Mine) Uncle Dave Macon, 574
On The Dummy Line Pickard Family, 693
On The Glory Road Bush Brothers, 147; Mountain View Quartet, 645
On The Good Old Santa Fe Frank & James McCravy, 538
On The Happy Hallelujah Side V.O. Stamps-M.L. Yandell, 863
On The Hill Over There Blue Ridge Gospel Singers, 109
On The Hills Over There Blue Ridge Gospel Singers, 109; Doc Hopkins, 441
On The Jericho Road Chuck Wagon Gang, 211; Propes Quartet, 714; Rice Brothers' Gang, 746; Royal Quartette, 815
On The Lone Prairie Carlisle Brothers, 169
On The Mississippi Shore Hank Snow, 853
On The Old Chisholm Trail Cartwright Brothers, 195
On The Old Hay Ride In The Morning Arthur Fields & Fred Hall, 342
On The Old Plantation Blue Sky Boys, 113
On The Other Side Of Jordan Riley Puckett, 719
On The Owl-Hoot Trail Shelton Brothers, 829
On The Ozark Mountain Trail Frank[ie] Marvin, 604
On The Painted Desert Ray Whitley, 953
On The Plains Of Texas Thomas Brown, 138
On The Prairie Dixieland Swingsters, 320
On The Red River Shore Patt Patterson, 681
On The Resurrection Morning We Shall Rise Bela Lam, 489
On The Riverside Blind Uncle Gaspard, 363
On The Road To California Len Nash, 650
On The Road To Happiness Lester McFarland & Robert A. Gardner, 546
On The Road To Tennessee Crockett [Family] Mountaineers, 233
On The Rock Where Moses Stood Carter Family, 189, 193
On The Royal Glory Road Coats Sacred Quartette, 216
On The Sea Of Galilee Carter Family, 191
On The Sea Of Life [E.R.] Nance Family, 648; Roper's Mountain Singers, 813
On The Sunny Side Of The Rockies Jimmie Davis, 305; Girls Of The Golden West, 371; Prairie Ramblers, 709
On The Sunny Side Of The Street Rice Brothers' Gang, 746
On The Texas Plains Bill Boyd, 121
On The Texas Prairie Beverly Hill Billies, 103
On The Top Of The Hill Carson Robison, 782
On The Wing Wonder State Harmonists, 971
On To Victory Mr. Roosevelt Light Crust Doughboys, 501
On Top Of Old Smokey Gentry Brothers, 364
On Top Of Old Smoky Bradley Kincaid, 483; George Reneau, 741; Bobbie & Ruby Ricker, 748
On Top Of The Hill Bill Boyd, 122
On Top Of The World Hackberry Ramblers, 387
On Treasure Island Girls Of The Golden West, 371; Peaceful Valley Folk, 683; Prairie Ramblers, 706
On Wisconsin Walter C. Peterson, 688
On Your Way Hi Neighbor Boys, 420
Once A Bum, Always A Bum Hobo Jim, 428
Once I Had A Darling Mother Callahan Brothers, 151; (Charlie) Monroe's Boys, 632
Once I Had A Fortune Tom Darby & Jimmie Tarlton, 295; Ernest V. Stoneman, 874, 876
Once I Had A Sweetheart Tom Darby & Jimmie Tarlton, 294
Once I Knew A Little Girl Sweet Brothers, 884
Once I Was Young And Pretty Three Tobacco Tags, 908
Once You Were My Little Darling Jack & Jean, 451

One At Last McDonald Quartet, 540; Missouri Pacific Lines Booster Quartet, 629; Vaughan Quartet, 926, 929
One By One XC Sacred Quartette, 975
One Cold December Day Dick Justice, 468
One Dark And Rainy Night Fletcher & Foster, 349
One Dark And Stormy Night Thomas C. Ashley, 68
One Eleven Special Curley Fox, 357
One Horse Shay Bo Norris, 661
One Hundred Four Stripling Brothers, 880
One Is My Mother Four Virginians, 357
One Kiss Dick Reinhart, 739
One Little Kiss Garner Eckler & Roland Gaines, 329; Wade Mainer, 584; Melody Boys, 614
One Little Word Carter Family, 191; Morris Brothers, 643
One Moonlight Night Charlie Poole, 700
One More Day In Prison Al Dexter, 314
One More Drink And I'll Tell It All Bob Skyles, 839
One More Kiss Before I Go Lewis McDaniels, 539
One More Ride Sons Of The Pioneers, 857; Zeke Williams, 959
One More River To Cross Light Crust Doughboys, 501; Uncle Dave Macon, 578; Sons Of The Pioneers, 858
One More Tear Johnny Bond, 117
One Night As I Lay Dreaming R.L. Barksdale, 94; Golden Echo Boys, 372; Frank & James McCravy, 532, 536–37
One Night Of Heaven With You Bill Cox, 226
One Of God's Days Frank & James McCravy, 531, 533
One Of These Days Peck's Male Quartette, 684
One Of Us Was Wrong Milton Brown, 136; Hank Penny, 686; Ocie Stockard, 869
One Old Shirt Roy Acuff, 49
One Rose (That's Left In My Heart) [The] Gene Autry, 82–83; Leon Chappelear, 201; Jimmie Rodgers, 804
One Rose [The] Milton Brown, 138
One Rose In My Heart [The] Tune Wranglers, 915
One Snowy Night—Quadrille Judge Sturdy's Orchestra, 881
One Step A Cain Angelas Le Jeunne, 494
One Step A Marie (Mary's One Step) Amadie Breaux, 126
One Step De Chataignier Angelas Le Jeunne, 493
One Step De Chupic Denus McGee, 551
One Step De Laccissine Nathan Abshire, 48
One Step De L'Amour Hackberry Ramblers, 388
One Step De Mamou Denus McGee, 551
One Step De Morse Nathan Abshire, 48
One Step Des Chameaux Amedie Ardoin, 62
One Step Des McGee (McGee's One Step) Denus McGee, 551
One Step D'Oberlin Amedie Ardoin, 62
One Step Du Maraist Bouler Angelas Le Jeunne, 493
One Step More Pete Cassell, 198
One Sweet Day Vaughan Quartet, 927
One Sweet Letter Hackberry Ramblers, 388
One Sweet Letter From You Cliff Bruner, 139; Light Crust Doughboys, 504; W. Lee O'Daniel, 667; Hank Penny, 686
One Sweetly Solemn Thought Chas. Teuser & Harold Lawrence, 898
One Thing At A Time Bill Boyd, 124
One Thousand Miles Away From Home Frank[ie] Marvin, 605
One To Love Me J.E. Mainer's Mountaineers, 581
One Who Set You Free [The] Crowder Brothers, 237
One Year Ago Today Dewey & Gassie Bassett, 97
One Year Ain't Long Crowder Brothers, 238
One, Two, Three, Four Jimmie Davis, 303; Walter C. Peterson, 688
One-Eyed Sam Eldon Baker, 89; Hoosier Hot Shots, 440; 'Lasses & Honey, 491
Onion Eating Mama Cliff Carlisle, 166

Only A Broken Heart Steve Ledford, 495
Only A Bum Ernest Hare, 399
Only A Faded Rose Clayton McMichen, 572
Only A Miner Kentucky Thorobreds, 479
Only A Prayer Jenkins Family, 457
Only A Rosebud Frank & James McCravy, 531, 538
Only A Step Vaughan Quartet, 924
Only A Step To The Grave McGee Brothers, 552
Only A Tear Andrew Jenkins, 454
Only A Tramp Ted Chestnut, 204; Rufus K. Stanley, 866; Uncle Pete & Louise, 919
Only A Word (From That Book So Dear) James Scott-Claude Boone, 821
Only As Far As The Gate Sid Harkreader, 400
Only As Far As The Gate, Dear Ma Uncle Dave Macon, 574
Only Childhood Sweethearts Lester McFarland & Robert A. Gardner, 549
Only Flirting Lester McFarland & Robert A. Gardner, 547–48; Chesley Shirley, 832
Only Girl (I Ever Cared About) [The] Carter Family, 194
Only Girl I Ever Loved [The] Ernest Branch & Bernice Coleman, 125; Charlie Poole, 700
Only In Dreams Bob Skyles, 839
Only Let Me Walk With Thee Blue Sky Boys, 113
Only One Step More Blue Sky Boys, 114; Girls Of The Golden West, 371; Prairie Ramblers, 711
Only Star [The] Delmore Brothers, 311
Only The Best M. Homer Cummings & Son Hugh, 240
Only Time Can Tell Bar-X Cowboys, 93
Only Trust Him Old Southern Sacred Singers, 669
Only Two More Weeks To Stay Here Short Creek Trio, 833
Only Waiting Loveless Twins Quartet, 514
Only Way [The] Claude Davis, 298
Only You Ted Daffan's Texans, 241
Onward Christian Soldiers Old Southern Sacred Singers, 669; Vaughan Quartet, 927; Woodlawn Quartette, 972
Onward Ye Soldiers Hendersonville Double Quartet, 416
Onze Livre De Ciel (Eleven Pounds Of Heaven) Sons Of Acadians, 856
Ooh! Mama What Have You Done? Village Boys, 932
O-O-Oh, Wonderful World Sons Of The Pioneers, 859
Ooze Up To Me Jimmie Tarlton, 892
Oozlin' Daddy Blues Bill Cox, 228; Bob Wills, 962
Open Range Ahead Sons Of The Pioneers, 858
Open Up Dem Pearly Gates Carson Robison, 771, 792, 795
Open Up Dem Pearly Gates For Me Carson Robison, 771, 773
Open Up Them Pearly Gates Beverly Hill Billies, 103; Simerly Trio, 834
Opera Reel Jasper Bisbee, 107; Lake & Cavanagh, 489
Orange Blossom Special Roy Hall, 390; Bill Monroe, 632; Rouse Brothers, 815
Oregon Trail [The] Eddie Dean, 308; Girls Of The Golden West, 371; Peaceful Valley Folk, 683; Prairie Ramblers, 706; Tex Ritter, 750
Organ Grinder's Swing Hilltoppers, 427; Zeke Manners, 586
Organ-Grinder Blues Jimmie Davis, 300
Original Arkansas Traveler Part 1, 2 [The] Clayton McMichen, 567
Orlando [Smilin'] Ed McConnell, 530
Orphan Boy [The] Lester McFarland & Robert A. Gardner, 546
Orphan Child [The] Fiddlin' John Carson, 176; Fleming & Townsend, 347; Lake Howard, 445
Orphan Girl [The] David Gauthier, 364; Buell Kazee, 472; Bradley Kincaid, 483; Lester McFarland & Robert A. Gardner, 545; Len Nash, 650; Riley Puckett, 717; Ernest V. Stoneman, 872, 875

Ortonville Dye's Sacred Harp Singers, 328; OKeh Atlanta Sacred Harp Singers, 667; Lee Wells, 943
Osage Indian Girl Hi-Flyers, 419
Osage Stomp Bob Wills, 960
Osson Joseph Falcon, 334
Other Way [The] Cliff Bruner, 140
Otto Wood Red Fox Chasers, 731
Otto Wood, The Bandit Carolina Buddies, 170; Bernard [Slim] Smith, 842
Oublies Mois Jamais Petite Happy Fats, 395
Our American Girl Vernon Dalhart, 274
Our Baby Boy Milton Brown, 137
Our Baby's Book Ernest Tubb, 914
Our Blue Haired Boy Jack Mahoney, 581
Our Director March H.M. Barnes, 95
Our Dreams Come Drifting Back Four Aces, 356
Our Friend Crowder Brothers, 238
Our Friend Is Gone Crowder Brothers, 238
Our Happy Little Cabin Home Arthur Fields & Fred Hall, 344
Our Home Town Mountain Band (& Pt 1, 2) Arthur Fields & Fred Hall, 344
Our Last Good-Bye Buddy Dewitt, 313; Sons Of The West, 859
Our Last Goodnight Hi-Flyers, 420
Our Little Blue Haired Boy "Sunshine" Pritchard, 714
Our Little Dream House In Lullaby Lane W. Lee O'Daniel, 665
Our Little Romance Is Through Adolph Hofner, 430
Our Mansion Is Ready Crowder Brothers, 237
Our Old Family Album Kenneth Houchins, 443; Frank[ie] Marvin, 601
Our Old Grey Mare (She's Old And Bent) Johnny Marvin, 606
Our Partner's Phonograph Record (Song Our Partner Sang) Karl & Harty, 470
Our President And The Farmers Fleming & Townsend, 347
Our Schoolboy Days Buffalo Ragged Five, 142
Our Senator Huey Long Benny Borg, 119
Our Watchword McMillan Quartet, 573
Out In The Cold World Lester McFarland & Robert A. Gardner, 547–48
Out In The Cold World Alone Marshall Rutledge, 817
Out In The Cold World And Far Away From Home Cecil Vaughn, 930
Out In The Cold World Far Away From Home Cecil Vaughn, 930
Out In The Great North West Vernon Dalhart, 288–89
Out In The Pale Moonlight Arthur Tanner, 886
Out Near The Rainbow's End Hi-Flyers, 419
Out Of Place Roy Newman, 658
Out Of Town Blues Jimmie Davis, 298; Jess Hillard, 426
Out Of Town Blues (Dallas) Jimmie Davis, 298
Out On A Western Range Uncle Pete & Louise, 919
Out On An Island Frank[ie] Marvin, 603
Out On Loco Range Massey Family, 609
Out On The Desert Kelly Brothers, 477
Out On The Farm Barnyard Steve, 95
Out On The Lone Prairie Patsy Montana, 635; Tex Ritter, 750; Tennessee Ramblers [II], 897
Out On The Lone Star Cow Trail Dick Devall, 313
Out On The Ocean Ashford Quartette, 67
Out On The Western Plains Johnson Brothers, 463
Out Where West Winds Blow Dickie McBride, 526
Outcast [The] William Rexroat's Cedar Crest Singers, 744
Outlaw John Dillinger Frank Luther, 522
Ouvrez Grand Ma Fenetre (Raise My Window High) Joseph Falcon, 335

Over At The Old Barn Dance Frank[ie] Marvin, 602–03
Over At Tom's House Blue Ridge Mountain Entertainers, 111
Over By The Crystal Sea Cliff Carlisle, 167
Over In Glory Royal Quartette, 815
Over In The Glory Land McDonald Quartet, 540; Smith's Sacred Singers, 849; Vaughan Quartet, 926
Over Moonlit Waters Cliff Bruner, 140
Over On The Other Side Of Glory Perry Bechtel, 98
Over Sixty Doug Bine, 104
Over Somebody Else's Shoulder Ross Rhythm Rascals, 814
Over The Garden Wall Carter Family, 191
Over The Hill Cliff Bruner, 140
Over The Hills Delmore Brothers, 311
Over The Hills In Carolina Daddy John Love, 514
Over The Hills In Caroline Claude Davis, 298
Over The Hills Maggie Jimmie Tarlton, 892
Over The Hills To The Poorhouse W.C. Childers, 205; "Peg" Moreland, 641; Bert Peck, 683; Edd Rice, 744; Unknown Artists [III], 920
Over The Mountain Uncle Dave Macon, 577–78
Over The Ocean Waves Tommy Dandurand, 293
Over The River Rex Griffin, 384
Over The Road I'm Bound To Go Uncle Dave Macon, 576
Over The Santa Fe Trail Sons Of The Pioneers, 857; Tennessee Ramblers [II], 897; Twilight Trail Boys, 918
Over The Sea Bill Chitwood, 208
Over The Sea Waltz McCartt Brothers & Patterson, 527
Over The Teacups Hackberry Ramblers, 387
Over The Tide Buice Brothers, 142
Over The Trail Elton Britt, 130; Cliff Bruner, 140
Over The Waves Breakdowners From Balsam Gap, 126; Cartwright Brothers, 196; Collier Trio, 218; Green's String Band, 381; Humphries Brothers, 447; Frank Hutchison, 449; W.W. Macbeth, 526; Miller's Merrymakers, 628; Charlie Oaks, 664; Perry Brothers, 687; Walter C. Peterson, 688; Doc Roberts, 754; Bob Smith, 843; Stripling Brothers, 880; Jimmie Wilson's Catfish String Band, 968; Jimmy Yates Groups, 976; Yellow Jackets [I], 976
Over The Waves Waltz Bill Boyd, 125; Kessinger Brothers, 480
Over There Wilfred Brancheau, 126
Over Yonder Frank & James McCravy, 537
Overshadowed By His Love Propes Quartet, 714
Overshoes And Leggins Henry Whitter, 956
Oxford (Miss.) Blues Bill Nettles, 653
Oyster Stew Chris Bouchillon, 120
Ozark Kitchen Sweat Sons Of The Ozarks, 856
Ozark Moon Carl Williams, 957
Ozark Mountain Moon Bill Simmons, 835
Ozark Mountain Queen Sam & Fred Friend, 359
Ozark Mountain Rose Bonnie Dodd & Murray Lucas, 322
Ozark Mystery [The] Roy Pick, 691
Ozark Rag East Texas Serenaders, 329
Ozark Stomp Ambrose Haley, 389
Ozark Trail Roy Marsh, 587; Len Nash, 650
Ozark Waltz Morrison Twin Brothers String Band, 644; Earl B. Zaayer, 979

Pa, Ma And Me Bill Chitwood, 208
Pack My Things Harold & Hazel, 402
Package Of Love Letters [A] Louisiana Lou, 513
Paddy On The Hand Car Red Headed Fiddler[s], 732
Paddy Ryan's Favorite Irish Jig John Baltzell, 91
Paddy Won't You Drink Some Cider Clayton McMichen, 568; Riley Puckett, 719
Paddy, Won't You Drink Some Good Old Cider? Bob Larkan & Family, 491
Paddy's Irish Pup Melton & Minter, 615

Padlock Key Blues Allen Brothers, 57
Pagan Love Song Lester McFarland & Robert A. Gardner, 546; Three Tobacco Tags, 909
Page Mister Volstead Bob Miller, 620
Page Mr. Volstead Bob Miller, 620
Paint A Rose On The Garden Wall Lester McFarland & Robert A. Gardner, 550; Prairie Ramblers, 705
Painting The Clouds With Sunshine Leo Soileau, 855
Pal Of Long Ago Jimmie Davis, 302
Pal Of Mine, Please Come Home Woody Leftwich, 496
Pal Of My Dreams Vaughan Quartet, 925–26
Pal Of My Sunny Days Howard Keesee, 475
Pal Of Pals Jerry Behrens, 98
Pal That I Love [The] Earl Shirkey & Roy Harper, 832
Pal That I Loved [The] Bob Skyles, 838
Pal That Is Always True [The] Doc Hopkins, 441; Lester McFarland & Robert A. Gardner, 549
Pale Moonlight Wade Mainer, 584
Pallet On The Floor Madden Community Band, 580; Stripling Brothers, 880
Palm Breezes South Sea Serenaders, 860
Pals Bob Palmer & Monte Hall, 673
Pals Of The Little Red School Bill Elliott, 332; Carson Robison, 790–91
Pals Of The Prairie Tex Owens, 671
Pals Of The Saddle Red Foley, 352
Pan American Blues Deford Bailey, 88
Pan American Express Deford Bailey, 87
Panama Happy Hollow Hoodlums, 397
Pan-American Man Cliff Carlisle, 167
Pandora Waltz John Baltzell, 92
Panhandle Blues Otis & Eleanor, 670
Panhandle Jack Ernest Hare, 399
Panhandle Pete Gene Autry, 83
Panhandle Shuffle Sons Of The West, 859
Panting For Heaven Bowman Family, 121
Pants That My Pappy Gave To Me [The] Hoosier Hot Shots, 439
Papa Please Buy Me An Airship James Johnson, 461
Papal Anthem A 100% Song [The] R.C. Garner, 363
Papa's Billie Goat Uncle Dave Macon, 573
Papa's Billy Goat Fiddlin' John Carson, 175, 177, 179; Vernon Dalhart, 259; Riley Puckett, 716
Papa's Gettin' Mad Jimmie Revard, 743
Papa's Going Crazy—Mama's Going Mad Bob Atcher, 69
Papa's Gone Nite Owls, 660
Papa's Got A Home Andrew Jenkins, 454
Paper Of Pins Bradley Kincaid, 482–83; Three Tobacco Tags, 909; Vass Family, 922
Pappy Is Buried On The Hill Arthur Fields & Fred Hall, 340
Pappy's Breakdown Dick Hartman's Tennessee Ramblers, 407
Pappy's Buried On The Hill Vernon Dalhart, 290; Arthur Fields & Fred Hall, 339; Carson Robison, 764; John I. White, 950
Par De Su Les Lames Thibodeaux Boys, 901
Paradise Alley Elmer Bird, 105
Paradise In The Moonlight Gene Autry, 83
Pardon Came Too Late [The] Arthur Fields & Fred Hall, 339
Pardon Of Sidna [sic] Allen Vernon Dalhart, 259
Pardon Of Tom Mooney [The] Bob Miller, 621
Parents I Left Alone Pine Ridge Ramblers, 697
Paris Waltz [The] Arthur Smith, 841
Parish Name Delma Lachney, 489
Parking Meter Blues Shelton Brothers, 830
Parlor Is A Pleasant Place To Sit In Sunday Night [The] Hugh Cross, 235
Parody On Home Sweet Home Uncle Nick Decker, 308; Riley Puckett, 720; Gid Tanner, 891

Paroi Arcadia Breakdown (Arcadia County Breakdown) Leo Soileau, 855
Parting Hand OKeh Atlanta Sacred Harp Singers, 667
Parting Hands Lee Wells, 943
Partir A La Maison (Going Back Home) Leo Soileau, 856
Partner, It's The Parting Of The Way Massey Family, 610
Pas Aller Vita Hackberry Ramblers, 388
Pa's Birthday Fiddlin' John Carson, 178
Pas La Belle De Personne Que Moi (Nobody's Darlin' But Mine) Joseph Falcon, 335
Pass Around The Bottle Al Bernard, 101; Georgia Yellow Hammers, 367; Frank Luther, 525; North Carolina Hawaiians, 663; Ernest V. Stoneman, 875
Pass Around The Bottle And We'll All Take A Drink Gid Tanner, 887
Pass It On Arthur Cornwall & William Cleary, 223
Pass Me Not O/Oh Gentle Savior John McGhee & Frank Welling, 556, 561
Pass The Drunkard By Asher Sizemore & Little Jimmie, 836
Passing Away Denson-Parris Sacred Harp Singers, 313; Lee Wells, 943
Passing Of Jimmie Rodgers [The] Ernest Tubb, 913
Passing Of Little Joe [The] Peaceful Valley Folk, 683
Passing Policeman Lysle Byrd, 150; Johnson Brothers, 463
Pat That Butter Down Land Norris, 662
Patent Leather Boots Elton Britt, 130
Pathway [The] Bush Brothers, 147
Patrick County Blues Spangler & Pearson, 861
Patty On The Turnpike Hobbs Brothers, 428; Kessinger Brothers, 479; Fiddlin' Powers & Family, 703; Walter Family, 938
Paul And Silas Snowball & Sunshine, 853
Paul Jones (Arkansas Traveler) Adolph Hofner, 431
Paul Jones Dance [A] Village Boys, 932
Pauvre Garcon Joseph Falcon, 335
Paw's Old Mule Riley Puckett, 720
Pay Day Fight Cliff Carlisle, 167
Pay Me Back My Fifteen Cents Carter Brothers & Son, 187
Pay Me No Mind Airport Boys, 52; Jimmie Davis, 305; Sons Of The Pioneers, 859
Pea Picking Papa Jimmie Davis, 300; Jess Hillard, 425
Peace Rev. Joseph Callender, 154
Peaceful Sleep Ruth Neal & Wanda Neal, 652
Peaceful Valley Christine, 209; Frank Luther, 519; Parker & Dodd, 678
Peach Picking Time Down In Georgia Jimmie Rodgers, 808–09
Peach Picking Time In Georgia Bert Layne, 493; W. Lee O'Daniel, 665
Peach Tree Shuffle Hank Penny, 686
Peaches Down In Georgia Georgia Yellow Hammers, 367
Peacock Rag Arthur Smith, 842
Peacock Strut Gibson String Trio, 369
Peanut Special Byron Parker, 675
Pearl Bryan Richard D. Burnett, 144; Vernon Dalhart, 261–62, 264; Bradley Kincaid, 483
Pearl Bryant Roy Harvey, 410
Pearl Quadrille John Baltzell, 90
Pearly Gates Monroe Brothers, 633
Pearly White City [The] Friendship Four, 360; Frank & James McCravy, 533; Vaughan Quartet, 926
Pedal Your Blues Away Rouse Brothers, 815
Peddler And His Wife Hayes Shepherd, 831
Pedestal Clog Dance Bill Boyd, 124
Peek-A-Boo Beverly Hill Billies, 102; J.C. Glasscock, 371; Fisher Hendley, 416; Uncle Dave Macon, 578; Walter C. Peterson, 688; Archer Porter, 702; Tin-Can Joe, 910; Tom & Don, 911; Henry Whitter, 955

Peek-A-Boo Waltz Chesley Shirley, 832; Short Brothers, 833; Ernest V. Stoneman, 873
Peel Her Jacket Uncle Joe Shippee, 831
Peg And Awl Carolina Tar Heels, 173; Kelly Harrell, 403
Peggy Lou Cliff Bruner, 140
Peggy O'Neil Johnnie & Jack, 459; Earl Shirkey & Roy Harper, 832
Peg-Leg Jack Smiley Burnette, 145; Frank Luther, 522; Carson Robison, 773–74, 776, 792
Penick [J.T.] Allison's Sacred Harp Singers, 60; OKeh Atlanta Sacred Harp Singers, 667; Original Sacred Harp Choir, 670
Penitentiary Blues Buddy Baker, 89; Bill Carlisle, 159; Cliff Carlisle, 166; Jess Hillard, 425; Reid Bros. Band, 738
Penitentiary Bound Blue Ridge Mountain Entertainers, 110
Penitentiary Waltz Leo Soileau, 854
Penitientiary Blues Jimmie Davis, 299
Pennsylvania Hop Dick Hartman's Tennessee Ramblers, 407
Pennsylvania Pal Bob Atcher, 69
Perhaps Jack Major, 586
Perished In The Snow Lester McFarland & Robert A. Gardner, 547–48
Perrodin Two Step Angelas Le Jeunne, 493
Persian Lamb Gibson String Trio, 369
Personne N'Aime Pas Leo Soileau, 856
Pete Knight, The King Of The Cowboys Wilf Carter (Montana Slim), 182–83
Pete Knight's Last Ride Wilf Carter (Montana Slim), 184
Peter Went A Fishing Clayton McMichen, 573; Gid Tanner, 888
Peter Went Fishing Fiddlin' John Carson, 176
Petit Jean Gallop Wonder State Harmonists, 971
Petit Ou Gros (Little Or Big) Leo Soileau, 854
Petit Ou Gros, Donne Moi Le (Little Or Big, Give It To Me) Joe Creduer-Albert Babineaux, 232
Petit Tes Canaigh Angelas Le Jeunne, 493
Pharoah's Army Got Drownded Alf. Taylor, 892
Phil The Fluter's Ball Hoosier Hot Shots, 439
Pick That Bass Hoosier Hot Shots, 437; New Dixie Demons, 655
Pickaninny Lullaby Song Uncle Dave Macon, 575
Pickanninny [sic] Lullaby Cartwright Brothers, 196
Pickaway Green's String Band, 381
Pickin' And Playin' Doc Roberts, 755
Pickin' Cotton Blues Jimmie Revard, 742
Pickin' Off Peanuts John Dilleshaw, 317
Pickin' On The Old Guitar Albert Cain, 150
Pickwick Club Tragedy [The] Arthur Fields & Fred Hall, 338
Picnic In The Wildwood [The] Vernon Dalhart, 259
Picture From Life's Other Side [A] Benny Borg, 118; W.C. Childers, 206; Vernon Dalhart, 272; Gentry Brothers, 364; Sid Harkreader, 400; Kelly Brothers, 477; Frank Luther, 523; John McGhee & Frank Welling, 558; Carson Robison, 781
Picture No Artist Can Paint Leake County Revelers, 495; Lester McFarland & Robert A. Gardner, 546
Picture Of Life's Other Side [A] Bradley Kincaid, 484
Picture Of Mother's Love [The] Uncle Bud Landress, 490
Picture Of My Home [The] Charlie Oaks, 665
Picture On My Dresser [The] Fleming & Townsend, 347
Picture On The Mantle [The] Bob Atcher, 69
Picture On The Wall Blue Sky Boys, 114; Carter Family, 190; W.C. Childers, 206; Cotton Mill Weavers, 223; Farmer Sisters, 337; Georgia Yellow Hammers, 367; John McGhee & Frank Welling, 558, 560–61; Carson Robison, 790
Picture That Is Turned To The Wall [The] Vernon Dalhart, 260
Picture That Is Turned Toward The Wall [The] Vernon Dalhart, 246, 248; Sue Morgan, 642

Picture That's Turned To The Wall [The] Arthur Fields & Fred Hall, 338
Picture Turned To The Wall [The] Vernon Dalhart, 250
Pictures From Life's Other Side Blue Sky Boys, 114; Vernon Dalhart, 260; Jenkins Family, 457; Carson Robison, 781; Smith's Sacred Singers, 849, 851; Taylor's Kentucky Boys, 895
Pictures Of My Mother Gene Autry, 73
Pictures Tonight North Carolina Cooper Boys, 662
Pig Angle Clarence Greene, 382; Byrd Moore, 639
Pig At Home In The Pen Arthur Smith, 841
Pig Got Up And Slowly Walked Away [The] Shelton Brothers, 829
Pig Town Fling Uncle Joe Shippee, 831
Pike's Peak "Ted" Sharp, Hinman & Sharp, 825
Pile Drivin' Papa Allen Brothers, 56
Piles Of It New Dixie Demons, 655
Pilgrim's Song [A] Land Norris, 662
(Pin A Bluebonnet On Your New Bonnet) Bluebonnet Hi-Flyers, 419
Pin Solitaire (Lonesome Pine) Joseph Falcon, 335
Pine Island Miller's Merrymakers, 628
Pine Prairie Joseph Falcon, 336
Pine State Honky Tonk Claude Casey, 197
Pine Tree Richmond Melody Boys, 748
Pine Tree On The Hill [The] Ralph Hodges, 429; Asa Martin, 589; Red Headed Brier Hopper, 732
Pinewood Waltz Amadie Breaux, 126
Piney Woods Girl Ernest V. Stoneman, 872
Pining For The Pines In Carolin' Dwight Butcher, 148
Pins And Needles (In My Heart) Bob Atcher, 70
Pipe Liner Blues Sunshine Boys, 881
Pipe Liner's Blues Modern Mountaineers, 631; Texas Wanderers, 901
Pi-Rootin' Around Jimmie Davis, 302
Pisgah [J.T.] Allison's Sacred Harp Singers, 60; Charles Butts Sacred Harp Singers, 149
Pistol Packin' Mama Al Dexter, 315
Pistol Packin' Papa Gene Autry, 73, 75; Jimmie Rodgers, 803
Pistol Pete Dwight Butcher, 148
Pistol Pete's Midnight Special Dave Cutrell, 240
Pity The Drunkard C.A. West, 944
Pity The Tramp Fruit Jar Guzzlers, 360
Place For You Is Louisian' [The] Village Boys, 932
Place Prepared For Me [The] [E.R.] Nance Family, 648
Place Where Ella Sleeps [The] Fields Ward, 939
Plain Old Me Ambrose Haley, 389
Plain Old Plains Sons Of The Pioneers, 859
Plain Talk Carson Robison, 797
Plant A Watermelon On My Grave Otto Gray, 379
Plant A Weeping Willow On My Grave (When I Go) Frank Luther, 524
Plant Some Flowers By My Grave Jimmie Davis, 305; McClendon Brothers, 528
Plant Sweet Flowers On My Grave John Dilleshaw, 318; Jo & Alma, 458
Plantation Blues Sons Of The Ozarks, 856
Plantation Memories Carson Robison, 793
Plantation Mem'ries Small Town Players, 840
Plaquemine Bayou Waltz Amadie Breaux, 127
Play Me That Single Time Jazz Massey Family, 610
Play On, Little David Parker Quartette, 679
Play That Waltz Again (Sleepy Rio Grande) Don White, 949
Play To Me Gypsy James Brown, Jr. & Ken Landon Groups, 135
Playboy Stomp Bob Wills, 962
Playboy's Breakdown Jimmie Revard, 742
Playing Around Walter Hurdt, 448

Playmates Riley Puckett, 722
Plea Of A Mother [The] Cliff Carlisle, 162
Plea To Young Wives [A] John McGhee & Frank Welling, 557
Please Come Back Lunsford Bros., 517
Please Come Back To Me Light Crust Doughboys, 501
Please Come Home Prairie Ramblers, 710
Please Daddy Come Home Walter Smith, 846
Please Do Not Get Offended Gid Tanner, 889
Please Don't Do That Nite Owls, 661
Please Don't Fool Me Pete Pyle, 723
Please Don't Forget Me, Dear Ray Whitley, 953
Please Don't Leave Me Charlie Wills, 966
Please Don't Love Nobody When I'm Gone Jake & Carl, 453
Please Don't Say We're Through Carl Boling, 116
Please Don't Sell My Pappy No More Rum Clayton McMichen, 572
Please Don't Stay Away Rice Brothers' Gang, 747
Please Don't Talk About Me When I'm Gone Roy Acuff, 48; Ross Rhythm Rascals, 814
Please Give Me Back My Dreams George Wade, 933
Please Let Me Broadcast To Heaven Lester McFarland & Robert A. Gardner, 550
Please Let Me Walk With My Son Rouse Brothers, 815
Please Papa Come Home Roy Harvey, 410; Log Cabin Boys, 508
Please Pass The Biscuits, Pappy (I Like Mountain Music) W. Lee O'Daniel, 666
Please Pay In Advance Allen Brothers, 57
Please Pull Down Your Curtain Johnny Barfield, 94
Please Remember Me Ernest Tubb, 914
Please Send Me To Jail, Judge! Prairie Ramblers, 711
Please Sing For Me Ocie Stockard, 869
Please Stay Home Tonight Bill Cox, 225
Please Take Me Back To My Darling Earl & Willie Phelps, 689
Please, Mr. Moon, Don't Tell On Me Dick Hartman's Tennessee Ramblers, 408
Plenty More Fish In The Sea Bob Skyles, 839
Pleur Plus' Columbus Fruge, 360
Pleyel's Hymn Dye's Sacred Harp Singers, 328; Original Sacred Harp Choir, 670
Plodding Along Eldon Baker, 89
Plow Boy Hop Grinnell Giggers, 384
Plucky Lindy's Lucky Day Vernon Dalhart, 286
Plush Covered Album [The] Doc Hopkins, 441
Po' Mourner Jules Allen, 54
Poca River Blues Jarvis & Justice, 453
Poche Town Joseph Falcon, 334
Podunk Toddle Freeny Harmonizers, 359
Point Clear Blues Columbus Fruge, 360
Poker Alice Bob Miller, 619
Pokey Joe Bob Skyles, 839
Polecat Blues Fiddlin' John Carson, 179; Roy Hall, 391; George Walburn & Emmett Hethcox, 935
Polecat Creek Jimmie Wilson's Catfish String Band, 968
Polecat Stomp Leon Selph, 824
Policeman's Little Child [The] Earl Shirkey & Roy Harper, 832
Polka Dot Blues Hank Snow, 853
Polka Four Kessinger Brothers, 481
Polka Medley/Intro Hill Billies, 424
Polka Quadrille National Barn Dance Orchestra, 651
Pollo James Brown, Jr. & Ken Landon Groups, 135
Polly Ann Frank Wilson, 967
Polly Woddle Doo Gid Tanner, 888
Polly Woddle Doodle Vernon Dalhart, 282
Polly Wolly Doodle Walter Coon, 221; Vernon Dalhart, 284; Massey Family, 611; Carson Robison, 776, 792; Maury Sprayberry, 863
Polly Wolly Doodly [sic] Gid Tanner, 889
[Polly Wolly Woodle] Dick Parman, 679
Ponce A Moi (Think Of Me) J.B. Fuslier, 361
Pony Boy Walter C. Peterson, 688
Pony Express [The] Vernon Dalhart, 290
Pool Playin' Papa Prairie Ramblers, 713
Poor Blind Child [The] Tex Fletcher, 349
Poor Boy Edward L. Crain, 230; Duel Frady, 358; Stuart Hamblen, 393; Riley Puckett, 721; Joe Werner, 944; Rowdy Wright, 974
Poor Boy (Pauvre Garcon) Joseph Falcon, 335
Poor Boy Long Ways From Home Buell Kazee, 472
Poor But A Gentleman Still Oscar L. Coffey, 216
Poor Convict Blues Hoke Rice, 745
Poor Drunkard's Dream [The] Wade Mainer, 585
Poor Ellen Smith Dykes' Magic City Trio, 328
Poor Fish [The] Charlie Craver, 231
Poor Forgotten Man Bob Miller, 622
Poor Girl Story [The] Rosa Lee Carson, 180
Poor Girl's Waltz Jarvis & Justice, 453
Poor Little Bennie Bela Lam, 489
Poor Little Country Maid [The] Hoosier Hot Shots, 440
Poor Little Doggie Bonnie Dodd & Murray Lucas, 322
Poor Little Honky Tonk Girl Al Dexter, 315
Poor Little Joe Roy Harvey, 410; Earl Johnson, 460; McDonald Brothers, 539; Charlie Oaks, 664; Red Patterson's Piedmont Log Rollers, 682; Earl Shirkey & Roy Harper, 831
Poor Little Orphan Boy Buell Kazee, 472
Poor Little Orphaned Boy Carter Family, 191
Poor Little Rose Bob Atcher, 70; Jimmy Wakely, 934
Poor Little Thing Cried Mammy Canova Family, 155
Poor Lone Girl Zora Layman, 492
Poor Lonesome Boy (The Unfaithful Lover) Ralph Hodges, 429
Poor Lost Boy Henry Whitter, 956
Poor Man, Rich Man (Cotton Mill Colic No. 2) David McCarn, 527
Poor Man's Blues Frank[ie] Marvin, 597
Poor Man's Friend No. 1, 2 Johnny Roberts, 756
Poor Man's Heaven Carson Robison, 780–81
Poor Miners Farewell Aunt Molly Jackson, 452
Poor Mistreated Me Ted Daffan's Texans, 241
Poor Naomi Wise A'nt Idy Harper, 402
Poor Old Dad Walter Coon, 221; Uncle Dave Macon, 576
Poor Old Jane Four Pickled Peppers, 356
Poor Old Mare Vernon Dalhart, 287
Poor Old Slave [The] Foreman Family, 352
Poor Ole Davy Prairie Ramblers, 710
Poor Orphan Boy Jack & Leslie, 451
Poor Orphan Child [The] Carter Family, 187
Poor Papa (He's Got Nothing At All) Hoosier Hot Shots, 439
Poor Sinners, Fare You Well Uncle Dave Macon, 574
Poor Tramp [The] Ernest V. Stoneman, 875
Poor Tramp Has To Live [The] Ernest V. Stoneman, 874
Poor Unlucky Cowboy Stuart Hamblen, 393
Poor Wayfaring Stranger [A] John McGhee & Frank Welling, 563
Poor Widow [The] Cliff Carlisle, 167
Pop Goes The Weasel Carver Boys, 196; Kessinger Brothers, 481; Woodhull's Old Time Masters, 971
Pop Goes The Weazel Massey Family, 611
Pope Waltz Reaves White County Ramblers, 729
Popeyed Sons Of The Pioneers, 857
Poppa's Gettin' Old Dewey & Gassie Bassett, 97
Pore Little Thing Cried Mammy Canova Family, 156
Pork Chops Tom Darby & Jimmie Tarlton, 295

Porquoi Es-Tu Triste? (Why Are You Sad) Four Aces, 356
Porter's Love Song Bob Skyles, 838
Portland Belle Tim Flora & Rufus Lingo, 350
Portland Fancy Plymouth Vermont Old Time Barn Dance Orch., 698
Portland Maine Orla Clark, 214
Porto [sic] Rico Storm [The] Carson Robison, 765
Portsmouth Kessinger Brothers, 480
Possum Hollow Stripling Brothers, 880
Possum Hunt [The] Fisher Hendley, 416
Possum Hunt On Stump House Mountain—Part 1, 2 Clayton McMichen, 567
'Possum In The 'Simmon Tree Carson Robison, 796
'Possum On The Rail Mississippi 'Possum Hunters, 629
Possum Pie Uncle Dave Macon, 577
Possum Rag Hugh Roden, 797
Possum Trot School Exhibition, Part I, II Ernest V. Stoneman, 876
Possum Up A Gum Stump, Cooney In The Hollow Charlie Bowman, 120; Hill Billies, 422
Possum Up The Gum Stump Lowe Stokes, 870; Gid Tanner, 891
Potato Song Pie Plant Pete, 695
Pourquoi Que Tu Laise Moi (Why Are You Leaving Me) Clifford Breaux, 127
Pourquoi Tu M'Aime Pas Alley Boys Of Abbeville, 59
Pourquois Te En Pen Alley Boys Of Abbeville, 59
Pourquois Vous Etes Si Cannai Walker Brothers, 936
Powder And Paint Ira Yates, 975
Powder River, Let 'Er Buck Powder River Jack-Kitty Lee, 496
Power In The Blood Sons Of The Pioneers, 858
Power's Crimes Hart & Ogle, 406
Practice Night At Chicken Bristle—Part I, II Bob Miller, 618
Practice Night With The Skillet Lickers—Part 1, 2 Gid Tanner, 891–92
Prairie Blues Wilf Carter (Montana Slim), 182; Phil Pavey, 682
Prairie County Waltz Bob Larkan & Family, 491
Prairie Darling Tex Dunn, 327
Prairie De Pin (Pine Prairie) Joseph Falcon, 336
Prairie Dream-Boat Texas Rangers, 899
Prairie Lullaby Dwight Butcher, 148; Light Crust Doughboys, 502; Jimmie Rodgers, 808
Prairie Maiden Paul Hamblin, 393
Prairie Moon Hi Neighbor Boys, 420; Pie Plant Pete, 695
Prairie Moonlight And You Ranch Boys, 726
Prairie Of Love Jimmie Davis, 302
Prairie Rose Leon Chappelear, 201
Prairie Skies Beverly Hill Billies, 102
Prairie Soileau Two Step Amedie Ardoin, 61
Prairie Sunset Wilf Carter (Montana Slim), 183
Prairie Town Carson Robison, 794
Praise The Lord It's So John McGhee & Frank Welling, 554, 560
Pray For Me Mother Frank Luther, 524
Pray For The Lights To Go Out Milton Brown, 136; Bill Cox, 225; Poplin-Woods Tennessee String Band, 701; Lowe Stokes, 871; Bob Wills, 960, 963
Prayer Wisdom Sisters, 969
Prayer Meetin' Time In The Mountain Fred Kirby, 487
Prayer Of The Drunkard's Little Girl [The] Blind Alfred Reed, 733
Preacher And The Bear [The] Al Bernard, 101; Honeyboy & Sassafras[s], 433; Kentucky Thorobreds, 479; John McGhee & Frank Welling, 553; New Dixie Demons, 655; Prairie Ramblers, 707; Riley Puckett, 716–17
Preacher And The Cowboy [The] Wilf Carter (Montana Slim), 184

Preacher Blues Allen Brothers, 56; Bill Chitwood, 208
Preacher Got Drunk And Laid Down His Bible [The] Tennessee Ramblers [I], 896
Preacher Made Us One [The] Charles Nabell, 647
Preacher Selection Cal West, 944
Precious Hiding Place Moody Bible Institute Trio, 637
Precious Jesus I'll Be There Fred Kirby, 487
Precious Jewel [The] Roy Acuff, 50; Elton Britt, 130; Delmore Brothers, 312; Wade Mainer, 585
Precious Love, Please Come Home McClendon Brothers, 528
Precious Memories McDonald Quartet, 541; Wade Mainer, 585; Norris Quartet, 662; Royal Quartette, 815; Simmons Sacred Singers, 835; Turkey Mountain Singers, 916
Precious Memory [A] Leon Selph, 824
Precious Name (Take The Name Of Jesus With You) Old Southern Sacred Singers, 669
Precious One Kelly Brothers, 477
Precious Sonny Boy Prairie Ramblers, 706
Precious Sweetheart From Me Is Gone [A] "Dock" Walsh, 937
Precious Thoughts Of Mother Grady & Hazel Cole, 217
Precious Wife Hank Warner, 940
Prenez Courage (Take Courage) Joseph Falcon, 334
Prepare Me Oh Lord Cliff Carlisle, 168
Prepare To Meet Thy God Flat Creek Sacred Singers, 346; Smith's Sacred Singers, 850
Prepare To Meet Your Mother Frank & James McCravy, 534
Prepare! Prepare! (For The Great Eternity) James Scott-Claude Boone, 821
Prescription For The Blues Virginia Childs, 208
Present Joys Alabama Sacred Harp Singers, 53
Press [The] Steve & His Hot Shots, 868
Press Along To Glory Land Riley Puckett, 716
Press Along To The Big Corral Twilight Trail Boys, 918
Pressing Along Peck's Male Quartette, 684
Prettiest Little Girl In County Gid Tanner, 887
Prettiest Little Girl In The County Gid Tanner, 889
Pretty Blue Eyes Arthur Duhon, 325
Pretty Boy Floyd Woody Guthrie, 386; Massey Family, 609; Bob Miller, 624; Ray Whitley, 952
Pretty Brunette [The] Leo Soileau, 855
Pretty Fair Miss Fiddlin' Powers & Family, 703
Pretty Gal's Love [A] Fisher Hendley, 416
Pretty Girl Hackberry Ramblers, 388
Pretty Girls Don't Want Me [The] Adam Trehan, 913
Pretty Little Blue-Eyed Sally Hugh Cross, 235
Pretty Little Dear Vernon Dalhart, 266–67; Light Crust Doughboys, 504; Charlie [& Bud] Newman, 655
Pretty Little Doggies Cartwright Brothers, 196
Pretty Little Dream Girl Bill Boyd, 123
Pretty Little Girl Curly Gray, 378; E.E. Hack String Band, 386; Fisher Hendley, 416
Pretty Little Girl With A Smile [The] Frank Luther, 524; Shelton Brothers, 829
Pretty Little Girls Are Made To Marry Philyaw Brothers, 690
Pretty Little Indian Napanee Rector Trio, 729
Pretty Little Naponee Johnny Barfield, 94
Pretty Little Pink Bradley Kincaid, 483–84
Pretty Little Poppy Gene Autry, 86
Pretty Little Widder Clayton McMichen, 573
Pretty Little Widow Gid Tanner, 889
Pretty Mama, You're Doin' Wrong Fleming & Townsend, 346
Pretty Mohea (Indian Maid) [The] Ernest V. Stoneman, 878
Pretty Mohee Rowdy Wright, 974
Pretty Polly Dock Boggs, 116; Coon Creek Girls, 221; Frank Luther, 525; Lester McFarland & Robert A. Gardner, 542; Red Fox Chasers, 731; B.F. Shelton, 826

Pretty Pond Lillies George R. Pariseau's Orchestra, 675
Pretty Quadroon [The] James Brown, Jr. & Ken Landon Groups, 135; W.C. Childers, 206; Texas Jim Lewis, 499
Pretty Red Hair Happy Fats, 396
Pretty Snow Dear Ernest V. Stoneman, 873
Pretty White Rose [A] Elmer Bird, 106
Pretzels Bob Miller, 620
Price I Had To Pay [The] Callahan Brothers, 153
Price Of Cotton Blues Allen Brothers, 56
Prickly Heat Bill Boyd, 122
Pride Of The Ball Blalock & Yates, 108; Clarence Greene, 382; Lexington Red Peppers, 500; Byrd Moore, 639
Pride Of The Prairie Patsy Montana, 635; Tex Owens, 671; Texas Ruby, 900
Pride Of The Prairie Blues Jess Hillard, 425
Pride Of The Prairie, Mary Aaron Campbell's Mountaineers, 154
Primrose Hill [J.T.] Allison's Sacred Harp Singers, 60; Daniels-Deason Sacred Harp Singers, 293
Princess Poo-poo-ly Has Plenty Papaya Prairie Ramblers, 711
Prison Bound Blues Emry Arthur, 66
Prison Clock (The Governor's Pardon) [The] Vernon Dalhart, 256
Prison Fire [The] Carson Robison, 780–81
Prison Sorrows Weaver Brothers, 942
Prison Warden's Secret [The] W.C. Childers, 206; John I. White, 950
Prisoned Cowboy Hank Snow, 852
Prisoner And The Rose [The] Walter Smith, 847
Prisoner At 23 [A] Ted Chestnut, 204
Prisoner At The Bar [The] Arkansas Barefoot Boys, 63; Arkansas Woodchopper, 63; Cotton Butterfield, 149; Lulu Belle & Scotty, 516; "Peg" Moreland, 641
Prisoner Boy Fiddlin' Jim Pate, 680
Prisoner For Life [A] Jules Allen, 54; Ken Maynard, 614
Prisoner Is My Son [The] Lester McFarland & Robert A. Gardner, 547
Prisoner No. 999 Asa Martin, 590–91; Bob Miller, 623
Prisoners [sic] Love Letters [The] Jack Mahoney, 581
Prisoners [sic] Song [The] Vaughan Quartet, 927
Prisoners [sic] Sweetheart [The] Elmer Bird, 106
Prisoner's Adieu [A] Modern Mountaineers, 631
Prisoner's Advice Ernest V. Stoneman, 878
Prisoner's Blues [The] Lloyd Wright, 973
Prisoner's Child [The] Kenneth Houchins, 443; John McGhee & Frank Welling, 559
Prisoner's Dream [The] Allen Brothers, 55, 57; Blue Sky Boys, 113; Andrew Jenkins, 454; Karl & Harty, 470; Lulu Belle & Scotty, 516; Shelton Brothers, 828
Prisoner's Farewell Andrews Brothers, 60; Cecil & Vi, 199; Bill Nettles, 653; Sons Of Dixie, 856
Prisoner's Lament [The] Ernest V. Stoneman, 878; Sweet Brothers, 884
Prisoner's Last Song [The] Philyaw Brothers, 690
Prisoner's Letter [The] Dale Hunter, 447
Prisoner's Letter To The Governor [The] Bob Miller, 619, 623
Prisoner's Meditation [The] Carl T. Sprague, 863
Prisoner's Plea Frank Gerald & Howard Dixon, 368
Prisoner's Radio [The] Harmonica Bill, 401
Prisoner's Rosary [The] John I. White, 950–51
Prisoner's Song [The] Alley Boys Of Abbeville, 59; Beverly Hill Billies, 103; Wilf Carter (Montana Slim), 186; Vernon Dalhart, 242–46, 256–57, 281, 291–92; Jimmie Davis, 305; Ranch Boys, 727; Goebel Reeves, 737; George Reneau, 741
Private Buckaroo Gene Autry, 86; Sons Of The Pioneers, 859
Prize Fighter [The] 'Lasses & Honey, 491
Prize Winner Joseph Falcon, 335

Prodigal Son—Part 1, 2 [The] Perry Kim & Einar Nyland, 481
Prodigal Son [The] Roy Acuff, 50; Hart & Cates, 406; Hart Brothers, 407
Prodigal's Return [The] Smith's Sacred Singers, 849
Prohibition—Yes Or No—Part 1, 2 Clayton McMichen, 570
Prohibition Blues Maynard Britton, 131; Clayton McMichen, 569
Prohibition Has Done Me Wrong Jimmie Rodgers, 807
Prohibition Is A Failure Lowe Stokes, 871
Promenade All Four Virginians, 357
Promise In Store Dorsey & Beatrice Dixon, 321
Promise In The Book Of Life Dorsey & Beatrice Dixon, 322
Promise Me Leo Soileau, 855
Promise Me You'll Always Be Faithful Delmore Brothers, 310
Promise To Be True While I'm Away John (Dusty) King, 486
Promise To The Faithful [The] Carolina Gospel Singers, 171
Promised Land [The] Charles Butts Sacred Harp Singers, 149; Jenkins Family, 456; Frank & James McCravy, 531
Prosperity And Politics—Part 1, 2 Gid Tanner, 891
Prosperity Is Just Around Which Corner? Carson Robison, 790
Prosperity Special Bob Wills, 963
Protection Denson's Sacred Harp Singers Of Arley, Alabama, 313
Proving My Love Howard Keesee, 475
Prune Song (No Matter How Young A Prune May Be It's Always Full Of Wrinkles) [The] Carson Robison, 763
Prune Song [The] Adolph Hofner, 431
Pryel's Hymn Daniels-Deason Sacred Harp Singers, 293
Puckett Blues Riley Puckett, 721
Puddin' Head Jones Shanks Bros. Trio, 825
Pull Out The Stopper Texas Rangers, 900
Pullman Porters [The] Jimmie Rodgers, 804
Pumpkin Pies That Mother Used To Make Warren Caplinger, 157
Punchin' The Dough Jules Allen, 55
Purer in Heart Calhoun Sacred Quartet, 151
Purple Night On The Prairie Texas Jim Robertson, 759
Purple Sage In The Twilight Gene Autry, 86
Purty Polly John Hammond, 394
Push Them Clouds Away Fisher Hendley, 417
Pussy, Pussy, Pussy Bill Boyd, 124; Light Crust Doughboys, 505
Pussycat Rag Claude Davis, 297
Pussywillow Port Arthur Jubileers, 701
Put Away My Little Shoes Girls Of The Golden West, 370
Put It Down Range Riders, 727
Put Me In My Little Bed Leake County Revelers, 494; Uncle Dave Macon, 576
Put Me In Your Pocket Bill Boyd, 123; Light Crust Doughboys, 501; W. Lee O'Daniel, 666
Put Me Off At Buffalo W.C. Childers, 205
Put Me On The Trail To Carolina Delmore Brothers, 310
Put My Little Shoes Away Big Slim Aliff, 54; Wilf Carter (Montana Slim), 183; Chuck Wagon Gang, 210; Vernon Dalhart, 259, 271; Gentry Brothers, 365; Frank Luther, 525; Lester McFarland & Robert A. Gardner, 546; Asa Martin, 592; Ruth Neal & Wanda Neal, 652; Riley Puckett, 717; Red Fox Chasers, 731; Oliver Smith & Dewey Culpepper, 845; Vaughan Quartet, 929; Paul Warmack, 939; Henry Whitter, 955
Put On An Old Pair Of Boots (And Saddle Up Your Horse) Prairie Ramblers, 707
Put On An Old Pair Of Shoes Prairie Ramblers, 705; Riley Puckett, 721
Put On Your Old Blue Dress Johnny Roberts, 756–57

Put On Your Old Gray Bonnet Asa Martin, 589; Holland Puckett, 714
Put On Your Old Grey Bonnet Milton Brown, 136; Dixie Ramblers [II], 319; Dixieland Four, 320; James Johnson, 461; Clayton McMichen, 572; Prairie Ramblers, 706; Hoke Rice, 746; Yellow Jackets [II], 976
Put On Your Old Red Flannels Hoosier Hot Shots, 439
Put Your Arms Around Me, Honey Pine Ridge Boys, 697
Put Your Arms Around Me, Honey (I Never Knew Any Girl Like You) Clayton McMichen, 572
Put Your Little Arms Around Me Ted Daffan's Texans, 240
Put Your Little Foot Right Out Massey Family, 611
Put Your Troubles Down The Hatch Bill Boyd, 125
Puttin' On Airs W.W. West, 945
Puttin' On Style Vernon Dalhart, 257, 259
Puttin' On The Style Vernon Dalhart, 254, 257–58, 273; Kenneth Houchins, 443; Massey Family, 610; Ernest V. Stoneman, 876

Quaker Waltz [The] Newton County Hill Billies, 659
Quand Je Quite Ta Maison (When I Leave Your Home) Joseph Falcon, 335
Quand Je Suis Bleu (When I Am Blue) Leo Soileau, 854
Quand Je Suis Loin De La Maison (When I Am Far Away From Home) Leo Soileau, 854
Quand Je Suis Partis Pour Le Texas (When I Left Home For Texas) Joseph Falcon, 334
Quand J'Ete Seul Hier Soir (When I Was All Alone Last Night) Leo Soileau, 854
Quand Tu Me Prie De La Maison (When You Took Me From My Home) Leo Soileau, 855
Quatre Ou Cinq Fois (Four Or Five Times) Joe Werner, 943
Que Ces Que Ma Chere Four Aces, 356
Queen City Square Dance Meridian Hustlers, 615
Queen Sallie Bill Shepherd, 831
Queen's Waltz E.E. Hack String Band, 386
Quel Espoire (What's The Use) Alley Boys Of Abbeville, 59
Quelqun Est Jalous (Somebody Is Jealous) Delin T. Guillory-Lewis Lafleur, 385
Qu'Est Que J'Ai Fait Pour Etre Peuni Si Longtemps? (What Did I Do To Be Punished So Long?) Percy Babineaux-Bixy Guidry, 87
Quiera Mi Jesusita Massey Family, 612
Quit Hanging Around, Baby Asa Martin, 593
Quit Knockin' On The Jail House Door Willard Hodgin[s], 429–30
Quit That Ticklin' Me Fiddlin' John Carson, 177
Quit Treatin' Me Mean Delmore Brothers, 311; Milo Twins, 628
Quitter La Maison Hackberry Ramblers, 387
Quitting My Rowdy Ways Sain Family, 818

Rabbit Blues Jack Pierce, 696
Rabbit Chase Charlie Parker, 676
Rabbit Hunt—Part 1, 2 [The] Bert Layne, 493
Rabbit In The Pea Patch Vernon Dalhart, 292; Uncle Dave Macon, 575; Pickard Family, 691–92
Rabbit Race Henry Whitter, 955
Rabbit Stole The Pumpkin [The] John H. Bertrand, 101
Rabbit Up The Gum Stump Hiter Colvin, 219
Rabbs Creek Elton Britt, 127
Raccoon And The Possum [The] Fiddlin' John Carson, 178
Raccoon On A Rail Home Town Boys, 433
Race Between A Ford And Chevrolet Oscar Ford, 352
Rackin' It Back Modern Mountaineers, 631; Texas Wanderers, 901
Radio Mama 'Lasses & Honey, 491
Rafe King Murder Case [The] Mason Stapleton, 867

Rag Time Annie Corn Cob Crushers, 222; Floyd County Ramblers, 350; Oscar & Doc Harper, 402; Prince Albert Hunt, 447; Kessinger Brothers, 481; Light Crust Doughboys, 502; Massey Family, 610; Midkiff, Spencer & Blake, 616; Charlie Poole, 699; Red Headed Fiddler[s], 732; A.C. (Eck) Robertson, 757; Smith's Garage Fiddle Band, 848; Solomon & Hughes, 856
Ragan Denson-Parris Sacred Harp Singers, 312; OKeh Atlanta Sacred Harp Singers, 667
Ragged Ann Vance's Tennessee Breakdowners, 922; Wing's Rocky Mountain Ramblers, 968
Ragged Ann Rag Humphries Brothers, 447
Ragged Annie Hill Billies, 423
Ragged But Right Buddy Jones, 465; Mitchell Brothers, 630; Riley Puckett, 720
Ragged Jim McGee Brothers, 552
Ragged Pat Cecil & Vi, 199
Raggedy Riley Rosa Lee Carson, 179
Raggin' The Blues (At The Old Piano) Massey Family, 611
Raggin' The Fiddle Travelers, 912
Raggin' The Rails Swift Jewel Cowboys, 884
Raging Sea, How It Roars [The] Ernest V. Stoneman, 876
Rags Vernon Dalhart, 263
Ragtime Chicken Joe Asa Martin, 592
Ragtime Cowboy Joe Girls Of The Golden West, 371; Massey Family, 611; Ranch Boys, 725; Tune Wranglers, 914
Ragtime Man W.A. Lindsay, 507
Railroad Bill Cleve Chaffin, 200; Cotton & Barfield, 223; Georgia Crackers, 365; Frank Hutchison, 450; Otis & Tom Mote, 644; Riley Puckett, 716; Roba Stanley, 866
Railroad Blues Chester Allen & Campbell, 54; Richard Brooks & Reuben Puckett, 132; Roy Harvey, 411; Hauulea Entertainers, 412; Kentucky String Ticklers, 478; Daddy John Love, 514; McGee Brothers, 552; Nations Brothers, 652; Roy Newman, 657; Earl Shirkey & Roy Harper, 831
Railroad Boomer [The] Roy Acuff, 49; Gene Autry, 71; Bowman Sisters, 121; Jenkins Carmen, 170; Pine Ridge Boys, 697; Riley Puckett, 722; Goebel Reeves, 737; Rice Brothers' Gang, 747; Carson Robison, 776–77
Railroad Bum Goebel Reeves, 736; Stripling Brothers, 880
Railroad Corral [The] Bill Bender, 99
Railroad Daddy Welby Toomey, 912
Railroad Flagman's Sweetheart [The] Frank Jenkins, 455; Ernest V. Stoneman, 878
Railroad Jack Joe Steen, 868
Railroad Love Stanley & Higgins, 866
Railroad Lover George Reneau, 741
Railroad Lover For Me [A] Emry Arthur, 66
Railroad Of Life [The] Jenkins Family, 456
Railroad Take Me Back Bowman Sisters, 121
Railroad Tramp [The] Walter Morris, 642
Railroad Under The Sea Bill Cox, 226
Railroader [The] Blind Alfred Reed, 733
Railroadin' And Gamblin' Uncle Dave Macon, 577–78
Railway Flagman's Sweetheart [The] Frank Jenkins, 455
Rain Odis Elder, 331
Rain Crow Bill Henry Whitter, 956
Rain Crow Bill Blues Henry Whitter, 954
Rain On The Roof Elton Britt, 129
Rainbow Light Crust Doughboys, 506; Ernest Thompson, 903; Tune Wranglers, 916
Rainbow Division [The] Tom Darby & Jimmie Tarlton, 294
Rainbow Island Charles Mitchell & His Orchestra, 629
Rainbow Lady Ike Cargill, 158
Rainbow On The Rio Colorado Gene Autry, 86
Rainbow Trail Al Dexter, 315; Three Tobacco Tags, 908
Rainbow Valley Gene Autry, 81
Rainbow Waltz Ted Hawkins, 413

Rainbow's End Tex Dunn, 327; Hank Snow, 853
Raincrow Canova Family, 155
Raindrop Waltz Ted Hawkins, 413; Fisher Hendley, 417
Raindrop Waltz Song Three Tobacco Tags, 907
Rainin' On The Mountain Delmore Brothers, 311
Rainy Day Blues Ted Daffan's Texans, 240
Raise My Window High Joseph Falcon, 335
Raise Rough House Tonight Bill Chitwood, 208
Raise The Roof In Georgia Prairie Ramblers, 708
Raise Your Window Joseph Falcon, 335
Raising 'Ell McLaughlin's Old Time Melody Makers, 565; Raggedy Ann's Melody Makers, 724
Raleigh County Rag Weaver Brothers, 942
Rambler's Blues Cliff Carlisle, 162; Jess Hillard, 425; Buddy Jones, 464
Ramblers March Tennessee Ramblers [I], 897
Ramblers' Rag Bill Boyd, 121; Dick Hartman's Tennessee Ramblers, 408
Ramblers Stomp Doug Bine, 104
Rambler's Yodel [The] Jesse Rodgers, 798
Ramblin' Hackberry Ramblers, 387
Ramblin' Boy Eldon Baker, 89; Carter Family, 195; Fleming & Townsend, 346; Clayton McMichen, 568; Wade Mainer, 585; Riley Puckett, 720; Bill Shepherd, 831
Ramblin' Cowboy Buddy Baker, 89; Frank[ie] Marvin, 605; Carson Robison, 794–96; Rowdy Wright, 974
Ramblin' Hobo Bill Cox, 226
Ramblin' Hobo Blues Emry Arthur, 67
Ramblin' Jack Cliff Carlisle, 165
Ramblin' John Four Pickled Peppers, 356
Ramblin' Minded Blues Delmore Brothers, 309
Ramblin' Railroad Boy [The] Bill Cox, 225
Ramblin' Reckless Hobo Richard D. Burnett, 144; Sweet Brothers, 884
Ramblin' Red Head [The] Ramblin' Red Lowery, 515
Ramblin' Red's Memphis Yodel No. 1–3 Ramblin' Red Lowery, 515
Rambling Blues Charlie Poole, 700; Kelly & Howard Sears, 822
Rambling Freight Train Yodel Bob Hartsell, 409
Rambling Gambler Dorsey & Beatrice Dixon, 321
Rambling Gambling Rounder [A] Fleming & Townsend, 348
Rambling Lover Dick Reinhart, 739
Rambling Woman [The] Ashley's Melody Makers, 68
Rambling Yodel Sam Andrew Jenkins, 455
Rambling Yodler Cliff Carlisle, 166
Ramona Jimmie Davis, 298; Ross Rhythm Rascals, 814
Ramshackle Shack Wade Mainer, 584
Ramshackled Shack On The Hill Carlisle Brothers, 169; Kenneth Houchins, 444; Buck Nation, 651; Ray Whitley, 952
Ranchman's Daughter [The] Floy England, 332
Rancho Grande Massey Family, 609; Tune Wranglers, 914
Rancho Grande (My Ranch) Nite Owls, 660
Rancho Pillow Massey Family, 613
'Rang 'Tang Bully Joe Werner, 944
Range In The Sky [The] Doc Hopkins, 441
Range Riders' Stomp [The] Range Riders, 727
Ranger's Hornpipe Stripling Brothers, 880
Rascal Rag Ross Rhythm Rascals, 814
Rat Cheese Under The Hill Kessinger Brothers, 480
Rattler Frank Dudgeon, 324
Rattler Tree'd A 'Possum Reaves White County Ramblers, 729
Rattlesnake Happy Hayseeds, 397
Rattlesnake Daddy Callahan Brothers, 152; Bill Carlisle, 158; Jesse Rodgers, 798

Rattlesnake Rag G.C. Osborne, 670
Rattlin' Cannonball Wilf Carter (Montana Slim), 185
Rattlin' Daddy Bill Carlisle, 159
Raymond Denson-Parris Sacred Harp Singers, 312
Rayne Breakdown Happy Fats, 395
Rayne Special Joseph Falcon, 335
Razor Jim Buddy Baker, 89
Razors In De Air Vernon Dalhart, 287
Razz Ma Tazz Stomp Hi-Flyers, 418–19
Reaching To You Mr. & Mrs. R.N. Grisham, 384; Chas. Richardson & O.S. Gabehart, 748
Read The Bible Karl & Harty, 471
Ready To Go, I'll Be Ashford Quartette, 67
Reapers Buffalo Ragged Five, 142
Reapers Are Needed Smith's Sacred Singers, 849
Reapers Be True McDonald Quartet, 540; Stamps Quartet, 864; Rev. M.L. Thrasher, 905
Reaping Days Ernest V. Stoneman, 878
Reaves Waltz Reaves White County Ramblers, 729
Reckless Hobo George & Henson, 365; Lymon Norris, 662
Reckless Love Canova Family, 155
Reckless Motorman Carter Family, 195
Reckless Night Blues Allen Brothers, 56
Reckless Rambler Buck Mt. Band, 141
Reckless Tex Goebel Reeves, 737
Reckless Tex From Texas Goebel Reeves, 738
Red And Green Signal Lights [The] G.B. Grayson & Henry Whitter, 381
Red Apple Rag Arthur Smith, 840
Red Creek Land Norris, 662
Red Dog Blues Rowdy Wright, 974
Red Fox Chasers Makin' Licker Part I, II, 3, 4 [The] Red Fox Chasers, 731
Red Handkerchief Adolph Hofner, 431
Red Head Bob Wills, 961
Red Hot Breakdown Earl Johnson, 459
Red Hot Fannie Hoosier Hot Shots, 438
Red Hot Gal Of Mine Bob Wills, 961
Red Hot Mama Bill Nettles, 654
Red Hot Mama From Way Out West Leon Chappelear, 202
Red Hot Papa Hank Penny, 686
Red Hot Rambling Dan Allen Brothers, 56
Red Hot Town Kelly Brothers, 477
Red Lips Bill Boyd, 123
Red Lips—Kiss My Blues Away Roy Acuff, 49; Cliff Bruner, 139
Red Nightgown Blues Jimmie Davis, 300; Jess Hillard, 426
Red Or Green G.B. Grayson & Henry Whitter, 380
Red Pajama Sal Allen Brothers, 57
Red Patch [The] Three Tobacco Tags, 908
Red Pig Kyle Wooten, 973
Red River Delma Lachney, 488
Red River Blues Jimmie Davis, 301
Red River Lullaby Gene Autry, 80
Red River Rose Cliff Bruner, 141
Red River Valley [The] Arizona Wranglers, 62; Beverly Hill Billies, 101; W.C. Childers, 205; Hugh Cross, 235; Arthur Fields & Fred Hall, 339; Sid Harkreader, 401; Bradley Kincaid, 483–85; Harry "Mac" McClintock, 529; McGee Brothers, 552; Bob McGimsey, 564; Riley Puckett, 718, 722; Ranch Boys, 725–27; Texas Jim Robertson, 760; Carson Robison, 778, 781, 784; Leo Soileau, 855; Two Cow Hands, 918; Vagabonds, 921
Red River Valley Blues Wilf Carter (Montana Slim), 185
Red River Valley Rose Asa Martin, 592–93
Red River Waltz Stripling Brothers, 880
Red Rose Christine, 209

Red Rose Of Texas North Carolina Cooper Boys, 662
Red Rose Rag Fletcher & Foster, 349
Red Roses, Sweet Violets So Blue McClendon Brothers, 528
Red Sails In The Sunset Beverly Hill Billies, 103; Eddie Dean, 308; Girls Of The Golden West, 371; Prairie Ramblers, 706; Riley Puckett, 722
Red Skin Lady Bill Simmons, 835
Red Steer Dykes' Magic City Trio, 328
Red Wagon Buddy Jones, 466
Red White And Blue Holland Puckett, 715
Red Wing Blue Ridge Highballers, 110; Cliff Carlisle, 163; Carolina Mandolin Orchestra, 171; Homer Christopher, 209; Fox Chasers, 357; Tony Hammes, 394; Honolulu Strollers, 433; Buell Kazee, 473; W.W. Macbeth, 526; John McGhee & Frank Welling, 561; Clayton McMichen, 571; Roy Newman, 656; Walter C. Peterson, 688; Riley Puckett, 718; George Reneau, 740; Ernest Thompson, 902; Floyd Thompson, 903–04
Redeemed Abernathy Quartet, 47; Allen Quartette, 57; Buffalo Ragged Five, 142; Golden Echo Boys, 372; North Georgia Four, 663; Rev. M.L. Thrasher, 905
Redeeming Love Bush Brothers, 147; J. Douglas Swagerty, 883
Redeeming Star Mr. & Mrs. R.N. Grisham, 385
Redell Breakdown J.B. Fuslier, 361
Red-Headed Music Maker Whitey McPherson, 579
Red-Headed Widow Was The Cause Of It All [A] Willard Hodgin[s], 429–30
Red's Tight Like That Tune Wranglers, 914
Reel Of Old Tunes Ted Markle, 587
Re-election Of The Mayor Of Bayou Pom Pom—Part 1, 2 [The] Walter Coquille, 222
Reformatory Blues Frank Luther, 518
Regal March Kessinger Brothers, 481
Reilly's Reel William B. Houchens, 443
Rejoice In God Clarence Ganus, 362
Rejoicing On The Way Avondale Mills Quartet, 87
Religion Ain't Nothing To Play With Bob McGimsey, 563
Religion Is A Fortune Alabama Sacred Harp Singers, 53; Lee Wells, 943
Religious—Swanee River Song E. Arthur Lewis, 497–98
Religious Critic [The] Ernest V. Stoneman, 872
Remember Cliff Bruner, 140; Modern Mountaineers, 631
Remember Me Warren Caplinger, 158; Lulu Belle & Scotty, 516
Remember Me, O Mighty One Alcoa Quartet, 53
Remember Pearl Harbor Carson Robison, 796
Remember The Old Folks Back Home Emry Arthur, 66
Remember The Poor Tramp Has To Live Ernest V. Stoneman, 878
Remember Your Mother Frank & James McCravy, 537
Remember You're Mine Al Dexter, 315
Renfro Valley Miss Jimmie Allen, 54
Renfro Valley Home Happy Valley Boys, 397; Riley Puckett, 721
Reno Blues Three Tobacco Tags, 907
Reno Street Blues Hi-Flyers, 420
Reno Valley Walter Judd, 468
Repasz Band Tweedy Brothers, 917
Repasz Band March H.M. Barnes, 94; Green's String Band, 381
Reply To Nobody's Darling Bobbie & Ruby Ricker, 748
Reply To The Weeping Willow [The] Lester McFarland & Robert A. Gardner, 545
Rescue From Moose River Gold Mine [The] Wilf Carter (Montana Slim), 183
Rescue Of The PN-9 [The] Vernon Dalhart, 250

Rescue The Perishing Kanawha Singers, 469; Stamps Quartet, 863
Resting In The Current Of His Love Knippers Bros. & Parker, 488
Resurrected Denson-Parris Sacred Harp Singers, 313; Dye's Sacred Harp Singers, 328
Resurrection [The] Ernest V. Stoneman, 876
Resurrection Morning [The] Frank & James McCravy, 535
Return Again Dye's Sacred Harp Singers, 328; OKeh Atlanta Sacred Harp Singers, 667; Hamp Reynolds' Sacred Harp Singers, 744
Return Of A Wandering Boy [The] Lowell Moore, 640
Return Of Barnacle Bill [The] Frank Luther, 523
Return Of Country Boy [The] Cartwright Brothers, 196
Return Of Mary Vickery [The] Vernon Dalhart, 267
Return Of The Gay Caballero [The] Vernon Dalhart, 289
Return To Red River Valley [The] Bill Nettles, 654
Return To The Prairie Frank Luther, 523
Returning Home Wilfred Fruge-Leo Soileau, 360
Returning To My Cabin Home Gene Autry, 77
Returning To My Old Prairie Home Wilf Carter (Montana Slim), 182–83
Reuben Oh Reuben Emry Arthur, 66
Reubens Special [The] Reubens, 742
Reverential Anthem Denson-Parris Sacred Harp Singers, 313; Lee Wells, 943
Revival Meeting In Dixie Jenkins Family, 456
Revive Us Again Carson Robison, 768
Rheumatism Blues Gene Autry, 75–76
Rhode Island Red Mintons Ozark String Band, 629
Rhyme Your Sweetheart Hoosier Hot Shots, 440
Rhymes—Part 1, 2 Dick Robertson, 758
Rhythm And Romance W. Lee O'Daniel, 665
Rhythm In E Leroy [Slim] Johnson, 461
Rhythm In The Air Leon Selph, 823
Rhythm In The Hills Tom Emerson's Mountaineers, 332
Rhythm Is Our Business Roy Newman, 656
Rhythm King Jack Golding, 374; Bob Skyles, 838
Rhythm Maker's Swing Yellow Jackets [II], 977
Rhythm Of The Hoof Beats Gene Autry, 84
Rhythm Of The Range Gene Autry, 82
Rhythmatism Frank Luther, 523
Rice City Stomp Hackberry Ramblers, 387
Rich Man And Joe Smith [The] Emry Arthur, 65
Rich Man And The Poor Man [The] Bob Miller, 622
Rich Or Poor Leo Soileau, 855
Rich Young Ruler [The] Atco Quartet, 70
Riche Ou Pauvre (Rich Or Poor) Leo Soileau, 855
Riches Of Love [The] Copeland Chorus, 221; Shrine Male Quartet Of Memphis, 834
Richmond Blues John D. Foster, 354
Richmond Cotillion Da Costa Woltz's Southern Broadcasters, 970
Richmond Polka Kentucky String Ticklers, 478; Kessinger Brothers, 480
Richmond Square Charlie Poole, 700
Rickett's Hornpipe Green's String Band, 381; Lake & Cavanagh, 489; Clayton McMichen, 573; Poole Family, 701; Gid Tanner, 890; Tweedy Brothers, 917
Ride Along Adolph Hofner, 430
Ride Along Little Gal Fleming & Townsend, 348
Ride And Shine On The Dummy Line Robert N. Page, 672
Ride Beneath The Texas Moon Tex Owens, 671
Ride 'Em Cowboy Clyde Martin, 593; Jimmie Revard, 742
Ride 'Em, Cowboy, Ride 'Em Gene Steele, 867
Ride For The Open Range Wilf Carter (Montana Slim), 186
Ride Old Buck To Water Gid Tanner, 890

Ride On! (My Prairie Pinto) Charlie Wills, 966
Ride On, God's Children Smith's Sacred Singers, 851
Ride On, Old Timer, Ride On Tune Wranglers, 914
Ride Tenderfoot Ride Gene Autry, 83; Charles Hogg, 431
Ride That Mule Hill Billies, 424
Ride The Goat Over The Mountain Charlie Wilson, 967
Ride, Ranger, Ride Sons Of The Pioneers, 857
Ride, Ride, Ride Tex Ritter, 750
Ride-Ride-Ride Girls Of The Golden West, 370
Ridge Of Sighs [The] Sue Morgan, 642
Ridge Runnin' Roan Beverly Hill Billies, 102; Tex Fletcher, 348
Ridin' A Maverick Wilf Carter (Montana Slim), 183
Ridin' Down That Old Texas Trail Frank Luther, 521; Massey Family, 608; Margaret West, 945
Ridin' Down The Arizona Trail Jimmie Davis, 302
Ridin' Down The Canyon Gene Autry, 81; Cass County Boys, 198; Prairie Ramblers, 704; Jimmie Revard, 742; Rice Brothers' Gang, 747
Ridin' Down The Canyon When The Desert Sun Goes Down Prairie Ramblers, 706
Ridin' Down The Sunset Trail Sammy & Smitty, 818
Ridin' Down The Trail Roy Rogers, 811; Simerly Trio, 834
Ridin' Down The Trail To Albuquerque Tex Ritter, 750
Ridin' High Massey Family, 612
Ridin' Home Red Foley, 351; Sons Of The Pioneers, 857
Ridin' In An Old Model "T" Dixie Ramblers [III], 319
Ridin' My Jenny Crowder Brothers, 238
Ridin' Old Paint (And Leadin' Old Dan) Texas Jim Robertson, 760
Ridin' Old Paint [A] Patsy Montana, 634; Tex Ritter, 749
Ridin' Old Paint And Leadin' Old Ball Bill Boyd, 121
Ridin' Ole Paint And Leadin' Old Bald Light Crust Doughboys, 501
Ridin' On A Humpback Mule Bill Boyd, 121; Shelton Brothers, 828
Ridin' On A Humped Backed Mule Cumberland Ridge Runners, 239
Ridin' On A Rainbow Red Foley, 351
Ridin' On Down That Road Jack & Johnnie Powell, 703
Ridin' On My Saviour's Train Whitey & Hogan, 952
Ridin' Ropin' Roy Rogers, 811
Ridin' That Lonesome Train Cliff Carlisle, 167
Ridin' The Blinds To The Call Of The Pines Cliff Carlisle, 167
Ridin' The Rails Three Tobacco Tags, 907
Ridin' The Range Gene Autry, 81; Ranch Boys, 726; Twilight Trail Boys, 918
Ridin' The Sunset Trail Patsy Montana, 635
Ridin' The Trail Back Home Ambrose Haley, 389
Riding & Roping Jordan Brothers, 467
Riding All Day Gene Autry, 82
Riding And Singing My Song York Brothers, 978
Riding By The Rio Grande Walter Hurdt, 448
Riding For The Rio Grande Tune Wranglers, 916
Riding In A Chevrolet Six Oscar Ford, 352
Riding Old Paint Leading Old Bald Stuart Hamblen, 393
Riding On That Train Forty-Five Wade Mainer, 583
Riding On The Elevated Railroad Frank[ie] Marvin, 597–98
Riding On The Glory Waves McDonald Quartet, 540
Riding On The Old Ferris Wheel Bill Boyd, 124; Hank Penny, 686
Riding The Billows For Home Paramount Sacred Four, 675
Riding To Eternity E.M. Bartlett Groups, 96
Riding To Glory Smoky Wood, 971
Riding To See The Sun Go Down Morris Brothers, 643
Right Always Wins Fleming & Townsend, 347

Right Key (But The Wrong Keyhole) [The] Cliff Bruner, 139
Right Or Wrong Bill Boyd, 122; Milton Brown, 137; Hackberry Ramblers, 388; Hauulea Entertainers, 412; Jap Magee, 580; Three Williamsons, 909; Bob Wills, 961
Right String But The Wrong Yo-Yo [The] Jubileers, 468
Right Train To Heaven [The] Ernest Tubb, 913
Right Upon The Firing Line Owen Brothers & Ellis, 671
Right Will Always Win McDonald Quartet, 540; Paramount Sacred Four, 674
Right Will Win Freeman Quartette, 359
Rights Of Man [The] Fiddling Sam Long, 512
Riley The Furniture Man Georgia Crackers, 365
Riley's Hen-House Door Riley Puckett, 721
Ring Around The Rosy Walter C. Peterson, 688
Ring Dem Heavenly Bells Rev. Horace A. Booker, 117; Frank & James McCravy, 533
Ring My Mother Wore [The] Ernest Branch & Bernice Coleman, 125
Ring Out The Message Rev. M.L. Thrasher, 905
Ring Song [The] Little Georgie Porgie, 508
Ring The Bell, Watchman Charlie Oaks, 664
Ring The Bells Of Freedom Rev. Calbert Holstein & Sister Billie Holstein, 433
Ring The Bells Of Heaven John McGhee & Frank Welling, 563
Ring Them Heavenly Bells Frank & James McCravy, 534
Ring Waltz Clayton McMichen, 566; Riley Puckett, 716–17
Ringtail Tom Cliff Carlisle, 165
Rio Grande Floyd Tillman, 910
Rio Grande Lullaby Tune Wranglers, 916
Rio Grande Moon Gene Steele, 867
Rio Grande Waltz Bill Boyd, 122
Rio Pecos Rose Tune Wranglers, 916
Rip Rip Snortin' Two Gun Gal [A] Patsy Montana, 636
Rip Van Winkle Bradley Kincaid, 483
Rip Van Winkle Blues Uncle Bud Landress, 490
Rippling Waves Waltz Mellie Dunham's Orchestra, 326
Rise When The Rooster Crows Uncle Dave Macon, 574
Rising Sun [The] Roy Acuff, 49
Rising Sun Blues Thomas C. Ashley, 68; Tom Darby & Jimmie Tarlton, 295
River Blues Bill Boyd, 122
River Of Jordan Carter Family, 187, 193
River Shannon Second Blessing E. Arthur Lewis, 498
River Stay Away From My Door Vernon Dalhart, 291
River, Stay 'Way From My Door Cliff Bruner, 139
Riviere Rouge (Red River) Delma Lachney, 488
Road Is Way Too Long [The] Johnny Bond, 116
Road To Washington [The] Ernest V. Stoneman, 875
Road Weary Hobo Claude Casey, 197
Roadside Drifter Asa Martin, 593
Roadside Rag Hi-Flyers, 419
Roamer's Memories [The] Girls Of The Golden West, 370
Roamin' Harry "Mac" McClintock, 529
Roamin' In The Gloamin' Girls Of The Golden West, 371
Roamin' In Wyomin' Bill Cox, 227
Roamin' Jack Ted Hawkins, 413
Roamin' Musician [The] Bill Tuttle, 917
Roamin' My Whole Life Away Wilf Carter (Montana Slim), 183
Roane County Rag Roane County Ramblers, 751
Roaster Rag [The] Three Williamsons, 909
Robert E. Lee Poplin-Woods Tennessee String Band, 701
Robertson County Paul Warmack, 940
Robin Hood James Brown, Jr. & Ken Landon Groups, 135
Robinson County L.O. Birkhead & R.M. Lane, 106; "Ted" Sharp, Hinman & Sharp, 825

Rochester Schottische Light Crust Doughboys, 501; Massey Family, 611
Rock About My Sara Jane Uncle Dave Macon, 575
Rock All Of Our Babies To Sleep Charlie [& Bud] Newman, 656
Rock All Our Babies To Sleep Binkley Brothers Dixie Clodhoppers, 104; Fay & The Jay Walkers, 337; Charlie [& Bud] Newman, 655; Dick Parman, 679; Riley Puckett, 715; Phil Reeve & Ernest Moody, 735; George Reneau, 741; Jimmie Rodgers, 807
Rock Amid The Waves [The] Murphy Sacred Singers, 646
Rock And Rye Polka Texas Jim Lewis, 499; Massey Family, 611
Rock Candy Mountain Arthur Fields & Fred Hall, 339; Jack Weston, 948
Rock City Blues J.H. Howell, 446
Rock House Gamblers Cleve Chaffin, 200
Rock Island Buell Kazee, 472
Rock Me In A Cradle Of Kalua Ovie Stewart & Zelpha Sparks, 869
Rock Me In The Cradle Of Kalua Blue Ridge Mountain Girls, 111
Rock Me To Sleep In An Old Rocking Chair Three Tobacco Tags, 908
Rock Me To Sleep In My Rocky Mountain Home Vernon Dalhart, 292; Bob Hartsell, 409; Frank Luther, 522
Rock Of Ages Buice Brothers, 142; Arthur Cornwall & William Cleary, 223; Eva Quartette, 333; Golden Echo Boys, 373; Jimmy Long, 512; Lester McFarland & Robert A. Gardner, 545; Moultrie Georgia Quartet, 644; Mr. & Mrs. W.M. Shively, 832; Woodlawn Quartette, 972
Rock Of Ages Keep My Soul Jones Brothers Trio, 467
Rock Road To Milledgeville Gid Tanner, 888
Rock That Cradle Lucy Cofer Brothers, 216; Gid Tanner, 890
Rock That Is Higher Than I [The] J. Douglas Swagerty, 883
Rock That's Higher Than I [The] John McGhee & Frank Welling, 563
Rock-A-Bye Baby Walter C. Peterson, 688; Riley Puckett, 717
Rock-abye Baby On The Tree-top Tin-Can Joe, 910
Rock-A-Bye Moon James Brown, Jr. & Ken Landon Groups, 134; Roy Newman, 657
Rockdale Rag Bar-X Cowboys, 92
Rockin' Alone (In An Old Rockin' Chair) Blue Ridge Mountain Girls, 111; Judie & Julie, 468; Light Crust Doughboys, 504; Frank Luther, 519; Maple City Four, 587; Bob Miller, 623–24; Tex Owens, 671; Roy Shaffer, 825; Bob Wills, 961
Rockin' Blues Jimmie Davis, 300
Rockin' Chair Don White, 949
Rockin' Rollin' Mama Buddy Jones, 465
Rockin' Yodel Leake County Revelers, 494
Rocking Chair Lullaby Buck Nation, 651
Rocking My Sugar Lump Lowe Stokes, 871
Rocking On The Waves Deal Family, 307; Fortner Family Mixed Quartette, 353; McDonald Quartet, 540–41; Propes Quartet, 714; Sparkman Trio, 861; Vaughan Quartet, 926
Rocking Pony Lowe Stokes, 871
Rockingham Herschel Brown, 133; Roy R. Harper, 402; Kessinger Brothers, 481
Rocky Mountain Blues Bill Simmons, 835
Rocky Mountain Express Al Clauser, 214; Saddle Tramps, 818
Rocky Mountain Goat Ted Gossett's Band, 376; Clifford Gross, 385; Kentucky Thorobreds, 479; Light Crust Doughboys, 502; Doc Roberts, 753
Rocky Mountain Lullaby Albee Sisters, 53; Elton Britt, 130; Carson Robison, 788; Jimmy Wakely, 934

Rocky Mountain Rose Lester McFarland & Robert A. Gardner, 548; Johnny Marvin, 606
Rocky Mountain Sal Arthur Fields & Fred Hall, 341–43
Rocky Mountain Sweetheart Bill Simmons, 835
Rocky Palace Earl Johnson, 460
Rocky Pallet Gid Tanner, 890
Rocky Road Alabama Sacred Harp Singers, 53; Cliff Carlisle, 167; Lee Wells, 943
Rocky Road To Dinah's House Fiddlin' Powers & Family, 703
Rocky Road To Dublin Osey Helton, 415; Hill Billies, 424; Allen Sisson, 836
Rodeo Ann Bob Skyles, 838
Rodeo Queen Patsy Montana, 636
Rodeo Rose Tune Wranglers, 915
Rodeo Song [The] Twilight Trail Boys, 918
Rodeo Sweetheart Patsy Montana, 635
Rodgers' Puzzle Record Jimmie Rodgers, 806
Roe Rire Poor Gal Uncle Dave Macon, 576
Roll Along Covered Wagon Ranch Boys, 726
Roll Along Jordan Light Crust Doughboys, 504
Roll Along Kentucky Moon Gene Autry, 78; Dwight Butcher, 148; Wilf Carter (Montana Slim), 185; Jimmie Davis, 304; Ralph Hodges, 429; Jimmie Rodgers, 806; Smiling Southerners, 840; Bob Wills, 961
Roll Along Moonlight Yodel Wilf Carter (Montana Slim), 184
Roll Along Prairie Moon Dwight Butcher, 149; Eddie Dean, 308; Girls Of The Golden West, 371; Earl & Willie Phelps, 689; Prairie Ramblers, 706
Roll Along, Jordon Eldon Baker, 89
Roll Back The Carpet Riley Puckett, 721
Roll Dem Cotton Bales Vernon Dalhart, 288, 291
Roll Down The Line Allen Brothers, 56
Roll 'Em Girls, Roll 'Em Warren Caplinger, 157
Roll 'Em On The Ground Fate Norris, 661
Roll In My Sweet Baby's Arms Monroe Brothers, 633
Roll It Down Allen Brothers, 56; John McGhee & Frank Welling, 562
Roll It Down Baby John McGhee & Frank Welling, 562
Roll Jordan Roll Lee Wells, 943
Roll On Blue Moon Cliff Carlisle, 164–65; McDonald Quartet, 541
Roll On Buddy Roy Acuff, 51; Charlie Bowman, 120; Monroe Brothers, 633
Roll On Dreamy Texas Moon Wilf Carter (Montana Slim), 184
Roll On Freight Train Henderson Brothers, 415
Roll On Old Troubles Roll On Bill Carlisle, 160
Roll On River Vernon Dalhart, 286
Roll On The Ground Hill Billies, 424
Roll On, Boys Carolina Tar Heels, 173
Roll On, Daddy, Roll On Pine Mountain Boys, 697
Roll On, John Buell Kazee, 472
Roll On, Mississippi Carson Robison, 792
Roll On, Mississippi, Roll On Freeny Harmonizers, 359; W. Lee O'Daniel, 666
Roll On, Roll On Fred Kirby, 486
Roll On, You Yellow Moon Carson Robison, 789
Roll Out, Cowboys Marc Williams, 959
Roll Them Clouds Away Vernon Dalhart, 290
Roll Up The Carpet Light Crust Doughboys, 501
Roll Your Own Dick Hartman's Tennessee Ramblers, 409
Rollin' Along Prairie Ramblers, 712
Rollin' Down The Great Divide Bill Boyd, 125
Rollin' Home Ezra Buzzington's Rustic Revelers, 150
Rollin' On Monroe Brothers, 633; Prairie Ramblers, 704
Rollin' Pin Woman Bill Cox, 226

Rollin' River Jess Hillard, 426
Rolling Caravan Saddle Tramps, 817
Rolling Herd Saddle Tramps, 817
Romance Ended [The] Lester McFarland & Robert A. Gardner, 546
Rome Georgia Bound Carroll County Revelers, 174
Rome Wasn't Built In A Day Jim & Bob, 458
Rompin' And Stompin' Around Shelton Brothers, 830
Rooky Toody Dick Reinhart, 739
Room For Jesus Kentucky Thorobreds, 479
Room In Heaven For Me Carter Family, 189
Rooster Blues Cliff Carlisle, 167
Rooster Crow Medley Uncle Dave Macon, 574
Rooster On The Limb Mustard & Gravy, 647
Roosters Comb Fisher Hendley, 416
Root Hog Or Die Jack Foy, 358; Byrd Moore, 639
Rootin' Tootin' Cowboy Wilf Carter (Montana Slim), 184
Rootin' Tootin' Shootin' Cowboy Dewey & Gassie Bassett, 97
Rope Around My Picture [A] Vernon Dalhart, 292
Rosalee Crockett [Family] Mountaineers, 233; Pie Plant Pete, 695
Rosalia E. Segura & D. Herbert, 823
Rosalie Beverly Hill Billies, 103
Rosalie Waltz Denus McGee, 551
Rosalita Al Dexter, 315
Rosco Trillion Bill Helms, 415
Rose And A Prayer [A] Red Foley, 351
Rose Conley G.B. Grayson & Henry Whitter, 380
Rose In Her Hair [The] Earl & Willie Phelps, 689
Rose Of Heaven Johnson Brothers, 463
Rose Of Mexico Lew Preston, 713
Rose Of Mother's Day Buddy Dewitt, 313
Rose Of My Heart Wilf Carter (Montana Slim), 183
Rose Of Santa Fe Ted Daffan's Texans, 241; Lew Preston, 713
Rose Of Sante Fe Patt Patterson, 682
Rose Of Sharon [The] California Aeolians, 151
Rose Of Shenandoah Valley Clayton McMichen, 572
Rose Of The Alamo Adolph Hofner, 431
Rose Of The Border Texas Jim Lewis, 500
Rose Of The Rio Grande York Brothers, 978
Rose Room Milton Brown, 138
Rose Room (In Sunny Roseland) Swift Jewel Cowboys, 885
Rose Waltz [The] Blind Joe Mangum-Fred Shriber, 586; W.T. Narmour & S.W. Smith, 649–50
Rose With A Broken Stem [The] Jess Johnston, 464; North Carolina Cooper Boys, 663
Rosedale, Everyone's Home Town Hoosier Hot Shots, 438
Roseland Melody [The] Milton Brown, 137
Roseland Waltz Doug Bine, 104
Rosenthal's Goat Lester McFarland & Robert A. Gardner, 545
Roses Three Tobacco Tags, 907
Roses Bloom Again Homer Briarhopper, 127
Roses In The Sunset Port Arthur Jubileers, 701
Rose's Sister Hank Penny, 686
Rosetta Sons Of Acadians, 856; Texas Wanderers, 900; Bob Wills, 962
Rosey Lee Slim Harbert, 398
Rosie Nite Owls, 660
Roughest Gal In Town [The] Buddy Jones, 465
Roughneck Blues Allen Brothers, 57; Jesse Rodgers, 798
Round And Round (Yas, Yas, Yas) Prairie Ramblers, 708
Round Dice Reel Uncle Dave Macon, 577
'Round Her Neck She Wears A Yeller Ribbon (For Her Love Who Is Fur, Fur, Away) Bob Dunn's Vagabonds, 327
'Round Her Neck She Wears A Yeller Ribbon (For Her Lover Who Is Fur, Fur Away) Floyd Thompson, 903
Round That Couple—Go Through And Swing Roy Rogers, 812

Round The Couple And Swing When You Meet Roy Rogers, 812
Round The World On A Dime Roy Newman, 658
Round Town Blues John Henry Howard, 444
Round Town Gals Ernest V. Stoneman, 874
Round Town Girl Ernest V. Stoneman, 874; Henry Whitter, 954
Round Town Girls Blue Ridge Highballers, 110; Hill Billies, 423; Ruth Neal & Wanda Neal, 652
Rounded Up In Glory Massey Family, 609; Jesse Rodgers, 799; Carl T. Sprague, 862
Rounder's Luck Callahan Brothers, 153
Roundin' Up The Yearlings Cumberland Ridge Runners, 240
Round'n-Around'n-Around Pie Plant Pete, 694
Round-Up Hop Miller's Merrymakers, 628
Round-Up In Cheyenne Gene Autry, 79; Girls Of The Golden West, 370–71
Roundup In The Fall [The] Wilf Carter (Montana Slim), 181
Roundup In The Spring [The] Asa Martin, 591; Patt Patterson, 681
Roundup Lullaby [A] Massey Family, 609
Round-Up Time In Dreamland Bob Hartsell, 409
Round-Up Time In Heaven Wilf Carter (Montana Slim), 183; Fred Kirby, 486; Massey Family, 609–10
Roundup Time In Sunny Old Alberta Wilf Carter (Montana Slim), 184
Round-Up Time In Texas Girls Of The Golden West, 370; Hart & Ogle, 406
Rovin' Little Dark[e]y [A] Chubby Parker, 676–77
Rovin' Moonshiner [The] Asa Martin, 590–91
Roving Cowboy Buell Kazee, 472; Sons Of The Pioneers, 857; Jack Webb, 942; Da Costa Woltz's Southern Broadcasters, 970
Roving Gambler Crockett [Family] Mountaineers, 234; Vernon Dalhart, 247, 249–50, 252, 265, 291; Kelly Harrell, 403; Frank Luther, 524; Pie Plant Pete, 694; George Reneau, 741; Carson Robison, 769; Gid Tanner, 890; Welby Toomey, 912
Row Us Over The Tide Blue Sky Boys, 113; Clarence Ganus, 362; Kelly Harrell, 404; Bela Lam, 489; Lulu Belle & Scotty, 516; Mr. & Mrs. E.C. Mills, 628
Row, Row, Row Lowe Stokes, 871
Rowan County Feud [The] Ted Chestnut, 204
Roy Bean Marc Williams, 959
Roy Dixon Jimmie Tarlton, 892
Royal Clog Ernest Helton, 415
Royal Diadem [The] John McGhee & Frank Welling, 557
Royal Telephone [The] Blue Sky Boys, 114; Happy Valley Family, 397; [Smilin'] Ed McConnell, 530–31; Lester McFarland & Robert A. Gardner, 547–48
Rub Alcohol Blues Ernest Mull, 646
Rubber Doll Rag Uncle Bud Landress, 490
Rubber Dolly Perry Bechtel, 98; Roy Hall, 391; Bob Skyles, 838; Texas Wanderers, 900
Rube Band Rehearsal, Part 1, 2 Ezra Buzzington's Rustic Revelers, 149
Rubens Train Carolina Ramblers String Band, 172
Rubin Jess Johnston, 464
Ruck Tuckin' Baby Dick Reinhart, 739
Rude And Rambling Man Carolina Tar Heels, 173
Ruffles and Bustles Walker's Corbin Ramblers, 937
Rufus Gid Tanner, 891
Rufus Blossom McGee Brothers, 552
Rufus Rastus Mississippi 'Possum Hunters, 629
Rummy Kentucky Bay Rum Bottlers, 477
Run Along Home With Lindy Fiddlin' John Carson, 176
Run Along Home, Sandy Fiddlin' John Carson, 177
Run Smoke Run Doc Roberts, 753

Run Them Coons In The Ground Clifford Gross, 385
Run, Boy, Run A.C. (Eck) Robertson, 757
Run, Johnny, Run Luke Highnight, 422
Run, Nigger, Run Dr. Humphrey Bate, 97; Fiddlin' John Carson, 175; Sid Harkreader, 400; Uncle Dave Macon, 574; Gid Tanner, 888
Runaway Boy [The] Bobby Gregory, 383; Hank Keene, 474; Carson Robison, 786
Runaway Train [The] Vernon Dalhart, 245–47, 250, 252, 291; Carson Robison, 789, 793
Runaway Train Blues Bill Cox, 228
Runnin' Wild Albert Cain, 150; Dixie Demons, 318; Hoosier Hot Shots, 438; John McGhee & Frank Welling, 558; W. Lee O'Daniel, 665
Running Around Joe Werner, 944
Running Blues [The] Georgia Yellow Hammers, 367
Rural Rhythm Hoosier Hot Shots, 439; Light Crust Doughboys, 503
Rustic Clog Russell Miller, 627
Rustic Schottische Clifford Gross, 385
Rustler's Fate [The] Carlisle Brothers, 168
Rusty Rural Mailbox Steelman Sisters, 867
Rusty Spurs Roy Rogers, 811
Ruth's Rag Grinnell Giggers, 384
Rycove Cyclone Asa Martin, 590
Rye Floyd Thompson, 903
Rye Straw Clayton McMichen, 568; Riley Puckett, 720; Doc Roberts, 754
Rye Straw (Or) The Unfortunate Pup Uncle "Am" Stuart, 881
Rye Strawfields Uncle Dave Macon, 574
Rye Waltz Bob Skiles Four Old Tuners, 837
Rye Whiskey Tex Ritter, 749; Sons Of The Pioneers, 859
Rye Whiskey, Rye Whiskey Tex Ritter, 749
Rymer's Favorite Allen Sisson, 836

S.J. Rafferty Reel John Baltzell, 91
S.O.S. Vestris John McGhee & Frank Welling, 556
Sabula Blues Golden Melody Boys, 373
Sad And Alone Slim Smith, 846
Sad And Lonely Lew Preston, 713; Rambling Rangers, 725; Crockett Ward, 939
Sad And Lonely Blues J.P. Ryan, 817
Sad And Lonely Mountain Boy Parker & Dodd, 678
Sad And Lonesome Day Carter Family, 192
Sad Lover [The] Vernon Dalhart, 263–64, 269
Sad Memories Roy Acuff, 49; Callahan Brothers, 154
Sad Song [The] Keller Sisters & Lynch, 476; Bob Miller, 621
Sad, Sad Story [The] Buddy Dewitt, 313
Saddest Day Of All [The] Taylor Trio, 894
Saddle Up The Grey Carter Brothers & Son, 187
Saddle Your Blues To A Wild Mustang Light Crust Doughboys, 503; Ray Whitley, 953
Sadie Green (The Vamp Of New Orleans) Milton Brown, 137; Roy Newman, 657
Sadie Ray Charlie Allen, 54; Thomas C. Ashley, 68; Lester McFarland & Robert A. Gardner, 547; Holland Puckett, 715; Thomas Trio, 901; Welby Toomey, 912
Safe In The Arms Of Jesus Jenkins Family, 456; Old Southern Sacred Singers, 669
Safe In the Homeland Central Mississippi Quartet, 199
Safety First Rev. Walt Holcomb, 432
Saga Of Susie Brown (Ril-A-Ral-A-Ree) [The] Happy Jim Parsons, 680
Sage Brush Shuffle Adolph Hofner, 431
Sagebrush Dance Patt Patterson, 681
Sail Along, Silv'ry Moon Gene Autry, 83
Sail Away Home [E.R.] Nance Family, 648

Sail Away Ladies Henry L. Bandy, 92; Uncle Dave Macon, 575
Sail Away Lady Parker & Dodd, 678; "Uncle Bunt" Stephens, 868
Sail On Jenkins Family, 456
Sailin' Away On The Henry Clay Ray Sand's Harmony Four, 819
Sailing Along Roy Acuff, 49
Sailing Along To Hawaii James Brown, Jr. & Ken Landon Groups, 134
Sailing Blues Buddy Jones, 466
Sailing Down The Chesapeake Bay Lowe Stokes, 870; Jimmy Yates Groups, 975
Sailing On Hartwic Brothers, 409
Sailing On A Dream Jimmy Wakely, 934
Sailing On The Bay Of Tripoli Clayton McMichen, 568
Sailing On The Ocean Luke Highnight, 422
Sailing On The Robert E. Lee Dave Edwards, 330; Bert Layne, 493; Clayton McMichen, 567; Lowe Stokes, 871
Sailing Out On The Ocean Haskell Wolfenbarger, 969
Sailing Ship [The] Crowder Brothers, 237
Sailing To Glory Chumbler Family, 212
Sailor Boy Carter Family, 192; Massey Family, 612; Arthur Tanner, 886; Gid Tanner, 887
Sailor Boy's Farewell Vernon Dalhart, 251; Flora Noles, 661
Sailor Jack Carson Robison, 772
Sailor Man Blues Norwood Tew, 898
Sailor On The Deep Blue Sea Doc Roberts, 754
Sailor's Dream Richmond Melody Boys, 748
Sailor's Farewell Stuart Hamblen, 392
Sailor's Hornpipe John Baltzell, 91; Chief Pontiac, 205; Massey Family, 610; Doc Roberts, 753
Sailor's Plea [A] Sid Hampton, 394; Howard Keesee, 474–75; Pie Plant Pete, 695; Jimmie Rodgers, 800
Sailor's Song [The] Ernest V. Stoneman, 872
Sailor's Sweetheart Dick Hartman's Tennessee Ramblers, 409; Dan Hornsby, 442; Patsy Montana, 634; Russell Brothers, 816
Saints Go Marching In [The] Monroe Brothers, 633
Sal Got A Meatskin Carlisle Brothers, 168
Sal Let Me Chaw Your Rosin Gid Tanner, 889
Sal Let Me Chew Your Rosom [sic] Some Shelton Brothers, 827
Sale Of Simon Slick—Part 1, 2 Georgia Yellow Hammers, 367
Salem #1 Salem Highballers, 818
Sales Tax Blues Crowder Brothers, 237–38
Sales Tax On The Women Dorsey & Beatrice Dixon, 321
Sales Tax Toddle Nations Brothers, 652
Sallie Gooden A.C. (Eck) Robertson, 757
Sallie Goodwin Arkansas Woodchopper, 64
Sallie Johnson Robert Cook's Old Time Fiddlers, 220
Sallie Johnson And Billy In The Low Ground A.C. (Eck) Robertson, 757
Sally Aim [sic] Frank Blevins, 108
Sally Ann Fiddlin' John Carson, 176; Hill Billies, 422–23; Doc Roberts, 754
Sally Brown Allen Sisson, 836
Sally Do You Love Me Rice Brothers' Gang, 747
Sally Gooden G.B. Grayson & Henry Whitter, 380; Frank Hutchison, 450; Doc Roberts, 754; Smith & Irvine, 847; Uncle "Am" Stuart, 881
Sally Goodin Crockett [Family] Mountaineers, 233; Clifford Gross, 385; Kessinger Brothers, 480; Clayton McMichen, 573; Pickard Family, 692; Fiddlin' Powers & Family, 703; A.C. (Eck) Robertson, 757
Sally Goodwin Riley Puckett, 717; Ernest V. Stoneman, 876–77

Sally In The Garden Crockett [Family] Mountaineers, 233
Sally Johnson Cartwright Brothers, 195; John D. Foster, 354; Oscar & Doc Harper, 402; Kessinger Brothers, 479; Lewis Brothers, 500; Solomon & Hughes, 856; Lowe Stokes, 871; Swamp Rooters, 883
Sally Let Your Bangs Hang Down Bill Carlisle, 160; Bill Cox, 228; Prairie Ramblers, 711
Sally, Let Me Chaw Your Rosin Some Poplin-Woods Tennessee String Band, 701
Sally's Got A Wooden Leg Sons Of The West, 859
Sally's Not The Same Old Sally Cumberland Ridge Runners, 239; Ambrose Haley, 390
Sal's Gone To The Cider Mill Gid Tanner, 890
Sal's Got A Meatskin Laid Away Bob Atcher, 69; Doc Roberts, 753
Salt Lake City Blues McGee Brothers, 552
Salt River Kessinger Brothers, 480
Salt River Valley Sons Of The Pioneers, 859
Salty Dog Stripling Brothers, 880
Salty Dog Blues Allen Brothers, 55; McGee Brothers, 552
Salty Dog, Hey Hey Hey Allen Brothers, 57
Salvation Has Been Brought Down Light Crust Doughboys, 507
Salvation Is For All Rev. Edward Boone, Mrs. Edward Boone & Miss Olive Boone, 118
Sam Bass Harry "Mac" McClintock, 528; Marc Williams, 958
Sam Hall Tex Ritter, 750
Sam Stover And The Clergyman Chris Bouchillon, 120
Sam The Accordian Man Yellow Jackets [II], 976
Sam, The College Leader Man Hoosier Hot Shots, 439
Sam, The Old Accordian Man Adolph Hofner, 431
Sambo W.W. West, 945
Same Old Moon James Brown, Jr. & Ken Landon Groups, 135
Same Old Moon Is Shining [The] Jimmie Davis, 304
Same Old You To Me [The] Wade Mainer, 584
Same Thing All The Time Ocie Stockard, 869
Sammie, Where Have You Been So Long Dock Boggs, 115
Samuel Hall Bill Bender, 99
San Hoosier Hot Shots, 436
San Antonio Cartwright Brothers, 196; Roy Harvey, 409–10; Asa Martin, 589, 591; W. Lee O'Daniel, 665; Smoky Mountain Ramblers, 852; Lowe Stokes, 870
San Antonio Blues Jesse Rodgers, 799
San Antonio Moonlight Jubileers, 468
San Antonio Polka Texas Wanderers, 901
San Antonio Rose Cliff Bruner, 140; Bob Wills, 963
Sand Cave George Ake, 52
Sand Class Reel John Baltzell, 90
Sand Mountain Drag John Dilleshaw, 317
Sand Reel John Baltzell, 91
Sand Will Do It Pie Plant Pete, 694
Sandy Land Fiddling Sam Long, 512
Sandy River Belle Blue Ridge Highballers, 110; Shelor Family, 826
Sandy River Bells Dixie Ramblers [I], 319
Sanford Barnes Ted Hawkins, 413
Santa Barbara Earthquake [The] Green Bailey, 88; Vernon Dalhart, 248, 250
Santa Claus, That's Me! Vernon Dalhart, 283–84
Santa Fe Trail [The] Bill Bender, 99; Powder River Jack-Kitty Lee, 496; Charlie Marshall, 588; Massey Family, 609
Santa Fe' Folks Fiesta Riley Puckett, 721
Sara Jane Gentry Brothers, 365; Arty Hall, 390
Sarah Jane Lester McFarland & Robert A. Gardner, 542; Carl T. Sprague, 862; Tune Wranglers, 915; Ira Yates, 975
Sardis Bowman Family, 121
Saro Warren Caplinger, 156–57
Sassafras Blues Hawkins Brothers, 414

Sassafras Rag Gibson String Trio, 369
Sassy Sam Uncle Dave Macon, 575
Satisfied J.E. Mainer's Mountaineers, 581; Smith's Sacred Singers, 849; Tennessee Ramblers [I], 896
Satisfied At Last Dorsey & Beatrice Dixon, 321
Saturday Night Breakdown Leake County Revelers, 495
Saturday Night Rag Bill Boyd, 122; Light Crust Doughboys, 501
Saturday Night Stroll Jimmie Davis, 300
Saturday Night Waltz Joseph Falcon, 336; Bob Larkan & Family, 491
Sauerkraut Riley Puckett, 717
Sauerkraut Is Bully Ralph Richardson, 748
Savannah River Stride Aiken County String Band, 52
Save It For Me Lummie Lewis, 500; Ross Rhythm Rascals, 814
Save My Mother's Picture From The Fire B.F. Kincaid, 482
Save My Mother's Picture From The Sale Uncle Dave Macon, 574; R.L. Raines, 724; Dr. Smith's Champion Hoss Hair Pullers, 843
S-A-V-E-D Gid Tanner, 888
Saved By Grace Mrs. Leon Hinkle, 427; Jimmy Long, 511; Smith's Sacred Singers, 851
Saved By His Sweet Grace Bush Brothers, 147; Carolina Quartette, 172
Saved! Moody Bible Institute Trio, 637
Savingest Man On Earth [The] Uncle Eck Dunford, 325
Saviour Lead Me Lest I Stray Riley Quartette, 749
Saviour Lead Them (Orphans) Jimmy Long, 511
Saviour More Than Life To Me Wisdom Sisters, 969
Saviour Said [The] Carolina Gospel Singers, 171
Saw Mill Blues Jordan Brothers, 467
Saw Mill Blues No. 1 Johnnie Gates, 363
Saw Your Face In The Moon Three Tobacco Tags, 908
Saw-Mill Blues No. 2 Johnnie Gates, 363
Saxophone Waltz Riley Puckett, 721
Say A Little Prayer For Me East Texas Serenaders, 329
Say A Prayer For Mother's Baby Graham Brothers, 377
Say Darling Won't You Love Me Wilmer Watts, 941
Say, Darling, Say Ernest V. Stoneman, 877
Scarecrow Song [The] Prairie Ramblers, 712
Scatter Seeds Of Kindness E. Arthur Lewis, 497–98
Scatter The Seeds Of Kindness E. Arthur Lewis, 498
Scatterbrain Mama Delmore Brothers, 311
School Day Dreams Bill Bruner, 139
School Day Sweetheart Asa Martin, 593
School Days Richard Brooks & Reuben Puckett, 133; Johnnie & Jack, 459; John McGhee & Frank Welling, 559; Walter C. Peterson, 688
School House Fire [The] Dorsey & Beatrice Dixon, 321
School House On The Hill Carter Family, 191
Schoolhouse Dreams Thos. A. Burton, 146; Lester McFarland & Robert A. Gardner, 549
Schotische [sic] Dance Poole Family, 701
Schottische Tom Dickey Show Boys, 316; Smith's Garage Fiddle Band, 848
Schwartz Gingerale Commercial Harry "Mac" McClintock, 529
Schwartz Gingerale Song Harry "Mac" McClintock, 529
Scolding Wife [The] Holland Puckett, 715; Skyland Scotty, 837; Thomasson Bros, 901
Scope's [sic] Trial Charles Nabell, 647
Scotch Reel John Baltzell, 91
Scottdale Highballers Scottdale String Band, 822
Scottdale Stomp Asa Martin, 589; Scottdale String Band, 821; Walker's Corbin Ramblers, 937
Scottische [sic] Edward Carson, 175
Scottish Bag Pipe Happy Hoosiers, 397
Scram Leon Selph, 823

Screech Owl Canova Family, 155
Se Mallereux Happy Fats, 396
Se Pas La Pan Hackberry Ramblers, 387
Se Toute Sain Comme Moi Ma Saine Alley Boys Of Abbeville, 59
Sea March Scottdale String Band, 821
Sea Of Galilee Carter Family, 193
Seaboard Waltz Roland Cauley, 199
Seagulls Massey Family, 612
Searching For A Pair Of Blue Eyes Daddy John Love, 514
Searcy County Rag Ashley's Melody Makers, 68
Seaside Polka Kessinger Brothers, 481
Seaside Schottische Clifford Gross, 385
Second Class Hotel H.P. Houser, 444; Jesse Rodgers, 799
Second Love Asa Martin, 588
Second Street Blues Four Aces, 356
See Mama Ev'ry Night Bill Boyd, 123
See See Ryder Frank Roberts, Bud Alexander & Fiddlin' Slim Sandford, 755
See That Coon In A Hickory Tree Delmore Brothers, 311
See That My Grave Is Kept Green Carter Family, 191; Bela Lam, 489
See The Black Clouds A Breakin' Over Yonder Chubby Parker, 677
See Them Pine Trees Waving Anglin Brothers, 61
Seeing My Gal Bill Carlisle, 160
Seeing Nellie Home Hart & Ogle, 406
Seeing Nellie Home (Quilting Party) Lester McFarland & Robert A. Gardner, 544
See-Saw Tin-Can Joe, 910
Select Banjo Waltz Uncle Dave Macon, 577
Selection: Summer Night On The Texas Trail, Roll Along, Little Doggie, Billie Boy Carson Robison, 796
Senator Francois—Part I, II Wesley Whitson, 954
Send Back My Wedding Ring Riley Puckett, 716–17
Send Him Home To Me Sons Of The Pioneers, 858
Send The Light Lester McFarland & Robert A. Gardner, 547
Send This Letter To My Mother John D. Foster, 354
Seneca Square Dance Fiddling Sam Long, 512
Sentenced To Life Behind These Gray Walls Vernon Dalhart, 253
Sentimental Gentleman From Georgia Leon Chappelear, 202; Hoosier Hot Shots, 435
Separation Blues Jess Johnston, 464
Sequetchic [sic] Jess Young, 978
Serenade In The Mountains, Part 1, 2 [A] Ernest V. Stoneman, 876
Serenaders' Waltz East Texas Serenaders, 329
Sergeant! Can You Spare A Girl Prairie Ramblers, 712
Sermon To Men [A] Rev. J.O. Hanes & Male Choir, 395
Serves 'Em Fine David McCarn, 527
Serving The Master Blue Ridge Sacred Singers, 112
Set Down Vaughan Quartet, 930
Settin' By The Fire Carson Robison, 788–89
Settin' In The Chimney Jamb Gid Tanner, 889
Settle Down Blues Buddy Jones, 465
Settling Down For Life Jimmie Davis, 298
Seven And A Half J.E. Mainer's Mountaineers, 581
Seven Beers With The Wrong Man Bob Atcher, 69; Texas Jim Lewis, 499
Seven Beers With The Wrong Woman Karl & Harty, 471; Texas Jim Lewis, 499
Seven Come Eleven Johnny Marvin, 606–07
Seven Days From Now Ernest Hare, 399
Seven Long Years Red Foley, 351
Seven Long Years In Prison Grant Brothers, 377
Seven Long Years Of Trouble Dick Parman, 679
Seven Mile Ford Rag Jack Reedy, 734

Seven More Days Gene Autry, 80; Eddie Dean, 308; Tex Fletcher, 349; Jimmy Long, 512
Seven Years Hardin & Grinstaff, 398
Seven Years With The Wrong Man Hibbard Sisters, 420; Zora Layman, 492; Frank Luther, 521
Seven Years With The Wrong Woman Cliff Carlisle, 164; Jess Hillard, 426; Frank Luther, 519, 521; Lester McFarland & Robert A. Gardner, 550; Bob Miller, 623; Parker & Dodd, 678; Shelton Brothers, 828; Three Sacks, 906
Seventeen Years Ago Callahan Brothers, 152
Sewing Machine Blues Jimmie Davis, 300
Shack By The Side Of The Road [A] Bill Carlisle, 160
Shack No. 9 Arthur Tanner, 886
Shackles And Chains Jimmie Davis, 303
Shade Of The Pines Billy Bishop, 107
Shadow Song [The] Vernon Dalhart, 265
Shadows Frank & James McCravy, 537
Shadows And Dreams Asa Martin, 591–92
Shadrach Bob McGimsey, 563
Shady Grove Kentucky Thorobreds, 479
Shady Grove My Darling Prairie Ramblers, 704
Shady Tree Fiddlin' Powers & Family, 704
Shake Hands With Mother Carolina Buddys, 170; Central Mississippi Quartet, 200; Wade Mainer, 583
Shake Hands With Mother Again Bill Cox, 227; Happy Valley Family, 398; John McGhee & Frank Welling, 563; Reeves Family, 738; Asher Sizemore & Little Jimmie, 837; Vaughan Quartet, 930
Shake Hands With Your Mother Roy Shaffer, 825
Shake It And Take It Bill Nettles, 653
Shake It, Ida, Shake It Allen Brothers, 56
Shake Little Lula Reid Bros. Band, 739
Shake My Mothers [sic] Hand For Me Warren Caplinger, 158
Shake My Mother's Hand For Me Wade Mainer, 585; Bill Monroe, 632
Shake Up Your Gourd Seeds Bob Skyles, 839
Shake Your Dogs Hoosier Hot Shots, 437
Shake Your Feet Hoosier Hot Shots, 436
Shaker Ben Walter Family, 938
Shall It Be You John McGhee & Frank Welling, 557
Shall Not Be Moved Homer Briarhopper, 127
Shall We Gather At The River Alcoa Quartet, 53; Kanawha Singers, 469; Uncle Dave Macon, 576; Peck's Male Quartette, 684; J. Douglas Swagerty, 883
Shall We Meet Golden Echo Boys, 373
Shamrock Schottische Doc Roberts, 754
Shanghai In China Carolina Tar Heels, 173
Shanghai Lil Shanks Bros. Trio, 825
Shanghai Rag Herschel Brown, 133
Shanghai Rooster Dusty Rhodes, 744
Shanghai Rooster Blues Allen Brothers, 56
Shanghai Rooster Yodel Cliff Carlisle, 162
Shanghai Rooster Yodel No. 2 Cliff Carlisle, 164
Shannon Waltz East Texas Serenaders, 329
Shanty-Man's Life [The] Pierre La Dieu, 488
Share 'Em Scottdale String Band, 821
Sharon School Teacher [The] Three Tobacco Tags, 907
Sharpsburg [J.T.] Allison's Sacred Harp Singers, 60
Shattered Love Grady & Hazel Cole, 217
Shawnee Tune Wranglers, 916
She Ain't Built That Way Asa Martin, 588, 590
She Buckaroo [The] Patsy Montana, 634
She Came Rollin' Down The Mountain Blue Ridge Mountain Girls, 111; Callahan Brothers, 153
She Can't Be Satisfied Al Dexter, 314; Walter Hurdt, 448
She Come Rolling Down The Mountain Prairie Ramblers, 706

She Cost Two Dollars And Seventy Cents Arthur Fields & Fred Hall, 342
She Cried To Come Back But She Couldn't Percy Babineaux-Bixy Guidry, 87
She Did Not Get Her Baby Out Of Jail Karl & Harty, 471
She Died Like A Rose Billy Vest, 931
She Doodle Dooed Chris Bouchillon, 119
She Fell For The Villian's [sic] Moustache Hank Keene, 474
She Gave Her Heart To A Soldier Boy Roy Rogers, 812
She Gave It All Away Shelton Brothers, 829
She Gave Me The Bird Light Crust Doughboys, 505
She Gave Up Oscar & Doc Harper, 402
She Goes The Other Way Ted Daffan's Texans, 240
She Had A Little Pig John Dilleshaw, 317
She Has Climbed The Golden Stair Smith Brothers, 848
She Has Forgotten Me Joseph Falcon, 334
She Is A Flower From The Fields Of Alabama Richard D. Burnett, 144
She Is My Gal Jimmie Revard, 742
She Is Only A Bird In A Gilded Cage Roy Harvey, 410
She Is Spreading Her Wings For A Journey Wade Mainer, 584
She Is Waiting For You In That Happy Home Campbell Brothers, 154
She Just Kept Kissing On Kelly Harrell, 404
She Just Wiggled Around Shelly Lee Alley, 58
She Left A Runnin' Like A Sewing Machine Jimmie Davis, 299
She Lied To Me Emry Arthur, 66
She Lived Down By The Firehouse Pie Plant Pete, 695
She Lives 'Round The Bend A Ways Arthur Fields & Fred Hall, 343
She Loves It So Shelly Lee Alley, 58
She Might Have Seen Better Days Breakdowners From Balsam Gap, 126
She Never Came Back Uncle Nick Decker, 308; Pickard Family, 693
She No Longer Belongs To Me Roy Acuff, 48
She Rests By The Swanee River John McGhee & Frank Welling, 558
She Said She Was Going Away Kelly & Howard Sears, 822
She Sat In Her Parlor Carson Robison, 786
She Shook It On The Corner Carolina Tar Heels, 174
She Sleeps Beneath The Daisies Beverly Hill Billies, 102
She Takes Her Time Dick Hartman's Tennessee Ramblers, 409
She Taught Me To Yodel Elton Britt, 130
She Tells Me That I Am Sweet Fletcher & Foster, 349
She Thinks First Of You Judie & Julie, 468
She Tickles Me Dorsey & Beatrice Dixon, 321
She Waits And Waits Ernest Hare, 399; Carson Robison, 770
She Waits For Me There Carlisle Brothers, 169
She Was A Lulu North Georgia Four, 663
She Was A Moonshiner's Daughter Chezz Chase, 202
She Was A Pip Cliff Carlisle, 164
She Was A Washout In The Blackout Hoosier Hot Shots, 440
(She Was Always) Chewing Gum Uncle Dave Macon, 574
She Was Bred In Old Kentucky Clagg & Sliger, 212; Dan Hornsby, 442; B.F. Kincaid, 482; Frank & James McCravy, 534; Carson Robison, 780; Merritt Smith, 845; Roy Sweeney & Family, 883
She Was Happy Till She Met You Jimmie Rodgers, 803; Shelton Brothers, 828
She Was Only Flirting Roy Hall, 391
She Was The Daughter Of A Butterfly And He Was The Son Of A Bee Prairie Ramblers, 712
She Waves As His Train Passes Willard Hodgin[s], 429

She Won't Be My Little Darling Delmore Brothers, 311
She Won't Pay Me No Mind Walter Hurdt, 448
She Wouldn't Shelly Lee Alley, 58
She Wouldn't Be Still Pine Mountain Boys, 697
She Wouldn't Do It Gene Autry, 74–75
Shear The Sheep Bobbie Gatwood Square Dance Band, 364
Shed Your Tears Upon Me Roy Hall, 391
Sheep And The Hog Walking Through The Pasture Robert Cook's Old Time Fiddlers, 220
Sheik Of Araby [The] Milton Brown, 137; Hoosier Hot Shots, 438
Shelby County Moonshiners, 638
Shelby Disaster [The] Dan Hornsby, 442
She'll Be Comin' 'Round The Mountain Hill Billies, 423; Frank Luther, 524; Dick Parman, 679; Pickard Family, 691; Carson Robison, 784; Gid Tanner, 888
She'll Be Comin' 'Round The Mountain No. 2 Bill Cox, 224
She'll Be Comin' Round The Mountain When She Comes H.M. Barnes, 95; Al McLeod's Country Dance Band, 565
She'll Be Coming Around The Mountain Dick Parman, 679; Roe Brothers & Morrell, 810
She'll Be There Blue Sky Boys, 114; Fisher Hendley, 417; Ralph Hodges, 429
She'll Be Waiting On The Golden Stairs Miller Wikel, 957
She'll Never Find Another Daddy Like Me Billy Vest, 931
Shelven Rock Charlie Wilson, 967
Shepherd Of Love [The] Jimmy Long, 511
Shepherd Of The Air Frank Luther, 521; Bob Miller, 624
Shepherd Show Me How To Go Mrs. Leon Hinkle, 427
Sherburne Huggins & Philips Sacred Harp Singers, 446
Sheriff And The Robber [The] Charlie Craver, 231
Sheriff Sale [The] Charles Nabell, 647
Sheriff's Sale Harwood Entertainers, 412; Frank[ie] Marvin, 605
Sherman Valley Bascom Lamar Lunsford, 516
She's A Cousin Of Mine Four Pickled Peppers, 356
She's A Darn Good Gal Buster Carter & Preston Young, 181
She's A Flower From The Fields Of Alabama Emry Arthur, 64; Crazy Hillbillies Band, 232; John D. Foster, 353
She's A Great Great Girl Shanks Bros. Trio, 825
She's A Hard Boiled Rose Wilmer Watts, 941
She's A High Geared Mama Charlie Mitchell & His Kentucky Ridge Runners, 630
She's A Hot Shot Baby Johnson & Lee, 462
She's A Hum Ding Mama Jack & Leslie, 451
She's A Hum Dum Dinger Gene Autry, 74; Jess Hillard, 425; Buddy Jones, 466
She's A Hum Dum Dinger (From Dingersville) Jimmie Davis, 299
She's A Hum-Dum Dinger—Part 2 (From Dingersville) Jimmie Davis, 299
She's A Leatherneck Gal Joe Werner, 944
She's A Low Down Mama Gene Autry, 74, 76
She's A Low Down Mamma Gene Autry, 74
She's A Rose From The Garden Of Prayer Hank Snow, 853
She's A Rounder Sunshine Boys, 882
She's A Wants Everything Takes Anything Gal Prairie Ramblers, 712
She's All Mine Jimmie Revard, 742
She's All Wet Now Roy Rogers, 811
She's Always On My Mind Gene Autry, 75; Callahan Brothers, 153; Fleming & Townsend, 346; Frank[ie] Marvin, 604; Saddle Tramps, 818
She's Anybody's Gal Walter Hurdt, 448
She's Built Like A Great Big Fiddle Bob Skyles, 838
She's Comin' 'Round The Mountain Vernon Dalhart, 249; Jimmie Wilson's Catfish String Band, 968
She's Coming Around The Mountain Henry Whitter, 954

She's Coming Now John Busby & Gilbert Thomas, 147
She's Doggin' Me Bill Boyd, 123; Roy Newman, 657; Ross Rhythm Rascals, 814
She's Gone Away Leon Selph, 824
She's Gone But I'll Meet Her In Heaven Bill Carlisle, 159
She's Got A Great Big Army Of Friends Jack Golding, 374; Hoosier Hot Shots, 440
She's Got Everything At Her Command Tom Dickey Show Boys, 316
She's Got Her Jinx On Me Buddy Jones, 465
She's Got Me Worried Leon Chappelear, 202
She's Got Rhythm Now Walter Hurdt, 448
She's Got Rings On Her Fingers Lowe Stokes, 870
She's Got The Best In Town Buddy Jones, 465
She's Got The Habit Walter Hurdt, 448
She's Got The Money Too Uncle Dave Macon, 577–78
She's Just That Kind Fleming & Townsend, 346, 348; Frank[ie] Marvin, 604; Hank Penny, 686
She's Just That Kind—No. 2 Fleming & Townsend, 347
She's Just That Kind No. 2 Callahan Brothers, 153
She's Killing Me Bill Boyd, 123; Callahan Brothers, 152; Jack & Leslie, 451; Nichols Brothers, 659; Bob Wills, 961
She's Long She's Tall Dick Hartman's Tennessee Ramblers, 407
She's Mine, All Mine G.B. Grayson & Henry Whitter, 380
She's More Like Her Mother Every Day Fiddlin' John Carson, 178
She's More To Be Pitied Than Censured Richard Brooks & Reuben Puckett, 132; Charlie Hager, 388; Wyzee Hamilton, 393; Lester McFarland & Robert A. Gardner, 547–48
She's My Curly Headed Baby Callahan Brothers, 151; Dick Hartman's Tennessee Ramblers, 407
She's My Curly Headed Baby No. 2, 3 Callahan Brothers, 152–53
She's My Flapper And My Baby Joe Werner, 944
She's My Gal (Right Or Wrong) Shelton Brothers, 829
She's My Honey Bee Honeyboy & Sassafras[s], 433
She's My Mama And I'm Her Daddy John McGhee & Frank Welling, 555
She's My Red Hot Gal Shelly Lee Alley, 58
She's My Red Hot Gal (From New Orleans) Shelly Lee Alley, 58
She's My Sweetheart Of The Prairie Joe Werner, 944
She's Not My Curley Headed Baby Three Tobacco Tags, 907
She's Not My Curly Headed Baby Bob Atcher, 69
She's Old And Bent Frank[ie] Marvin, 600
She's Old And Bent (But She Just Keeps Hoofin' Along) Frank[ie] Marvin, 599
She's Old And Bent But She Gets There Just The Same Frank[ie] Marvin, 599
She's One Of Those Hackberry Ramblers, 388
She's Only A Bird In A Gilded Cage Elzie Floyd & Leo Boswell, 350; John D. Foster, 354
She's Runnin' Around Leon Chappelear, 202
She's Runnin' Wild Bill Nettles, 654
She's Selling What She Used To Give Away Buddy Jones, 465; Bill Nettles, 654
She's Selling What She Used To Give Away No. 2 Buddy Jones, 465
She's Sleeping 'Neath The Maple Fred Pendleton, 685
She's So Different Shelly Lee Alley, 58
She's Somebody's Darling Once More Blue Sky Boys, 114; Shelton Brothers, 829
She's Still That Old Sweetheart Of Mine Light Crust Doughboys, 501
She's Stopped Giving Everything Away Bob Skyles, 838
She's Sweet Tune Wranglers, 914

She's The Only Girl I Love Uncle Dave Macon, 576
She's The Sunshine Of Moonshine Valley Al Dexter, 314
She's The Tie That Binds Lester McFarland & Robert A. Gardner, 546
She's The Treasure Of Them All Bill Nettles, 654
She's Too Good For Me Arthur Fields & Fred Hall, 342
She's Too Young (To Play With The Boys) Light Crust Doughboys, 506
She's Waiting For Me Cliff Carlisle, 162
She's Waiting For Me (Fort Benning Blues) Georgia Wildcats, 366
She's 'Way Up Thar Hal O'Halloran's Hooligans, 667
She's Winkin' At Me Roy Hall, 391
Shian, Crenbells, Tony Boy Melford Jackson, 452
Shift Gears Truck And Go Bill Nettles, 654
Shine Cliff Bruner, 139; Dixie Demons, 318
Shine On Harvest Moon Milton Brown, 137; Cliff Carlisle, 162; Vernon Dalhart, 274–76; Lester McFarland & Robert A. Gardner, 549; Roy Newman, 656; Jack Pierce, 696; Swift Jewel Cowboys, 884
Shine On Me Cliff Carlisle, 166; Gospel Sanctified Singers, 376; Ernest Phipps, 691; Sandhills Sixteen, 820
Shine On, New Mexico Moon Tune Wranglers, 915
Shine On, Pale Moon Gene Autry, 80
Shine On, Rocky Mountain Moonlight Tex Fletcher, 349; Grace & Scotty MacLean, 565; Patsy Montana, 635
Shine Song Ray Sand's Harmony Four, 819
Shine Your Light For Others Cliff Carlisle, 168
Shining City Over The River Dorsey & Beatrice Dixon, 321
Shining For The Master Emry Arthur, 64
Ship Of Glory Price Family Sacred Singers, 714
Ship Sailing Now J.E. Mainer's Mountaineers, 581
Ship That Never Returned [The] Kent Bane, 92; Vernon Dalhart, 251, 255, 258, 281; Roscoe & Samuel Dellinger, 309; Bradley Kincaid, 482, 485; Asa Martin, 590; Roe Brothers & Morrell, 810; Charles Lewis Stine, 869
Ship That's Sailing High [The] Elmer Bird, 106; Buell Kazee, 472
Ship Without A Sail [The] McGee Brothers, 552
Shippin' Sport Doc Roberts, 753
Shipping Port Jimmy Johnson's String Band, 461
Shirkin' Mama Blues Bill Carlisle, 159
Shirley Hoosier Hot Shots, 439
Shirt Tail Blues Jimmie Davis, 301
Shivering in The Cold Lester McFarland & Robert A. Gardner, 545
Sho' Fly, Don't Bother Me Uncle Dave Macon, 575
Shoes We Have Left Are All Right [The] Arthur Fields & Fred Hall, 340
Shoesole Rag Mintons Ozark String Band, 629
Shoo Fly Crockett [Family] Mountaineers, 234; Short Creek Trio, 833; Jimmy Yates Groups, 975
Shoo Fly Don't Bother Me McGee Brothers, 552
Shoo! Fly Kessinger Brothers, 481
Shoot That Turkey Buzzard Breakdowners From Balsam Gap, 126; Doc Roberts, 753
Shoot The Buffalo Swamp Rooters, 883
Shootin' Creek Charlie Poole, 700
Shooting Of Dan McGrew—Part 1, 2 Brunswick Players, 141; Harold Selman, 823
Short Dresses And Bobbed Hair Andrew Jenkins, 454
Short Life And It's Trouble Wade Mainer, 583
Short Life In Trouble Haywood County Ramblers, 414
Short Life Of Trouble Anglin Brothers, 61; Emry Arthur, 66; Blue Ridge Mountain Entertainers, 110; Blue Sky Boys, 113–14; Richard D. Burnett, 144; John D. Foster, 354; G.B. Grayson & Henry Whitter, 381; Buell Kazee, 472; Riley Puckett, 721

Shortenin' Bread Dykes' Magic City Trio, 328; W.A. Hinton, 428; Earl Johnson, 459; Clayton McMichen, 573; Reaves White County Ramblers, 729; Doc Roberts, 754; Gid Tanner, 888; Tweedy Brothers, 918
Shortenin' The Bread Kessinger Brothers, 480
Short'nin' Bread Cherokee Ramblers, 204
Shorty's Nightmare Massey Family, 609
Shot The Innocent Man Cliff Carlisle, 167
Shotgun Wedding [The] Jimmie Davis, 300
Shout And Shine For Jesus Jenkins Family, 456
Shout Lou Samantha Bumgarner, 142
Shout Lula G.B. Grayson & Henry Whitter, 380
Shout, Mourner, You Shall Be Free Uncle Dave Macon, 575
Shout, Oh Lulu Roy Acuff, 49
Shoutin' In The Amen Corner (A Rhythmic Sermon) Shelton Brothers, 829
Shouting Hallelujah All The Way John McGhee & Frank Welling, 554
Shouting In The Air Deal Family, 307
Shouting On The Hills Johnson County Ramblers, 463; Smith's Sacred Singers, 849
Show Boat Blues Chezz Chase, 202
Show Me A Man That Won't Prairie Ramblers, 711
Show Me The Way To Go Home Bill Boyd, 122; Milton Brown, 137; Frank[ie] Marvin, 594; Arthur Tanner, 886; Gid Tanner, 890; Unknown Artists [IV], 920; Henry Whitter, 956
Shreve Breakdown Hackberry Ramblers, 387
Shreveport County Jail Blues Buddy Jones, 465
Shrine At The Miracle Grave [The] Charlie Craver, 231
Shuber's Hoe Down Clyde Martin, 593
Shuffle, Feet, Shuffle Fisher Hendley, 416
Shufflin' Gal Cliff Carlisle, 167
Shut The Door Dixieland Swingsters, 320
Shut Up In Coal Creek Mine Green Bailey, 88
Shy Anne From Old Cheyenne Patsy Montana, 636
Shy Little Ann From Cheyenne Patsy Montana, 636
Si Dur D'Etre Seul (So Hard To Be Alone) Amedie Ardoin, 62
Si Tu Voudroit Marriez Avec Moi (Marry Me) Joe Werner, 944
Si Vous Moi Voudrez Ame (If You'd Only Love Me) Leo Soileau, 854
Side Kick Joe Roy Rogers, 811
Side-Line Blues Thomas C. Ashley, 68; Gwen Foster, 353
Sidewalk Waltz [The] Jimmie Revard, 743
Sidewalks Of New York Walter C. Peterson, 688; Tin-Can Joe, 910
Sidewalks Of New York (East Side, West Side) [The] Vernon Dalhart, 249; Andrew Jenkins, 454; Floyd Thompson, 903
Sidney Allen Vernon Dalhart, 252
Sierra Sue Gene Autry, 85; Elton Britt, 130; Red River Dave, 733
Sigh And Cry Blues Dave Edwards, 331
Sighing Winds [The] Ramblin' Red Lowery, 515
Silent Church On The Hill Dewey & Gassie Bassett, 96
Silent Night Ruth Neal & Wanda Neal, 652; Westbrook Conservatory Entertainers, 946
Silent Night, Holy Night Roy Rogers, 812; Woodlawn Quartette, 972
Silly Bill Hill Billies, 422; Ernest Thompson, 902
Silver Bell Clayton McMichen, 565; Scottdale String Band, 822; Ernest V. Stoneman, 873; Jess Young, 979
Silver Bells Bob Wills, 963
Silver Dagger [The] J.P. Ryan, 817
Silver Dollar Denver Darling, 295; Delmore Brothers, 311; Shelton Brothers, 829

Silver Haired Daddy Of Mine Gene Autry, 76; Maze & Jones, 614
Silver Haired Mother Of Mine Gene Autry, 81
Silver Lake Waltz Stripling Brothers, 880
Silver Lining [The] Jenkins Family, 456
Silver Moon Johnson Brothers' Band, 463; Jack Major, 585
Silver Nail Bob Larkan & Family, 491
Silver Threads Dick Hartman's Tennessee Ramblers, 407
Silver Threads Among The Gold Alexander & Miller, 53; Fiddlin' John Carson, 178; Chief Pontiac, 205; Andrew Jenkins, 454; Frank & James McCravy, 532; Clayton McMichen, 566; Riley Puckett, 716; Merritt Smith, 845; Jack Teter, 898
Silver Valley Blue Ridge Mountain Girls, 111
Silver-Haired Mother Frank Luther, 518
Silvery Arizona Moon Carson Robison, 788–90; Lloyd Wright, 973
Silvery Bell Gibson String Trio, 369
Silvery Prairie Moon Odis Elder, 331; Margaret West, 945
Simple To Flirt Lester McFarland & Robert A. Gardner, 547
Simpson County Carver Boys, 196
Sin And The Remedy Rev. J.O. Hanes & Male Choir, 394
Sin Has Caused So Many Tears Bill Carlisle, 159
Sin Is To Blame James Scott-Claude Boone, 821; Vaughan Quartet, 924
Since Baby's Learned To Talk Uncle Dave Macon, 577
Since Dear Old Mother's Gone David Miller, 626
Since He Came To Stay Irene Spain Family, 861
Since I Gave My Heart To You Jack & Tony, 452
Since I Have Been Redeemed John McGhee & Frank Welling, 561
Since I Left The City Joe Cook, 220
Since I Lost My Darling Prairie Ramblers, 712
Since I Married That Actor Man John McGhee & Frank Welling, 559
Since I Met My Mother-In-Law Steve Ledford, 495; Wade Mainer, 584
Since I Put A Radio Out In The Henhouse Cass County Boys, 198
Since I've Grown So Used To You George E. Harris, 404–05
Since Jesus Came Into My Heart Peck's Male Quartette, 684; Singing Preachers, 836; Smith's Sacred Singers, 851
Since Mother's Gone Vernon Dalhart, 282; David Miller, 626; Carson Robison, 762
Since Mother's Gone From The Old Home Vernon Dalhart, 290
Since My Baby's Gone Away Fletcher & Foster, 349
Since My Dear Old Mother's Gone Charlie Oaks, 665
Since My Mother's Dead And Gone Eddie Dean, 307
Since She Took My Licker From Me Fiddlin' John Carson, 179
Since That Black Cat Crossed My Path Ernest Tubb, 913
Since The Angels Carried My Mother Home To Glory Ted (Straw) Henley, 417
Since The Angels Took Mother Away Three Little Maids, 906
Since The Angels Took My Mother Far Away Blue Sky Boys, 114
Since The Preacher Made Us One Frank Wheeler-Monroe Lamb, 948
Since We Landed Over Here Bill Cox, 225
Since We Put A Radio Out In The Hen House Hoosier Hot Shots, 440
Since You Called Me Sweetheart Elkins Stringed Steppers, 331
Since You Left Me All Alone Earl & Willie Phelps, 689
Since You Left Me, Hon Jimmie Revard, 742
Since You Said Goodbye To Me Massey Family, 612

Sinful To Flirt Blue Ridge Mountain Singers, 112; Louisiana Lou, 513; Ernest V. Stoneman, 872, 875
Sing A Little Swing Song Dixieland Swingsters, 320
Sing A Song For The Blind Blue Sky Boys, 113
Sing A Song Of Harvest Tune Wranglers, 916
Sing All Your Troubles Away Smith's Sacred Singers, 850
Sing Another Line Carson Robison, 794
Sing Cowboy Sing W. Lee O'Daniel, 666; Tex Ritter, 750
Sing Fa-Da Riddle, Sing Dey (Or Poor Old Mare) Vernon Dalhart, 287
Sing Fa-Da-Riddle, Sing Dey Vernon Dalhart, 287
Sing Hallelujah Vernon Dalhart, 283–85; Carson Robison, 770
Sing Hallelujah And Hozanna Freeman Quartette, 359
Sing It And Tell It Jenkins Family, 456
Sing It Fast And Hot Prairie Ramblers, 712
Sing Me A Hill-Billy Ballad Red Foley, 351
Sing Me A Melody Of The Mountains Dwight Butcher, 149
Sing Me A Song Of The Mountains Girls Of The Golden West, 370
Sing Me A Song Of The Saddle Gene Autry, 82
Sing Me A Song Of The South John McGhee & Frank Welling, 562
Sing Me A Song Of The Sunny South Greensboro Boys Quartet, 382
Sing Me To Sleep With A Song Of The West Carson Robison, 796
Sing Nightingale Jack Pierce, 696
Sing Of His Goodness Forever E.M. Bartlett Groups, 96
Sing Of His Word Peck's Male Quartette, 684
Sing Old Hymns To Me Copeland Chorus, 221
Sing On Brother, Sing! Vernon Dalhart, 274
Sing On, Brother, Sing Vernon Dalhart, 274–76
Sing Sing Blues Buck Turner, 916
Sing The Old Hymns To Me Frank & James McCravy, 533
Sing To Me Of Heaven Denson-Parris Sacred Harp Singers, 313
Sing, Poor Devil, Sing Marc Williams, 958
Sing, Sing, Sing (With A Swing) Hilltoppers, 427
Singin' In The Saddle Patsy Montana, 636; Tex Ritter, 750
Singin' Steel Blues (The Waco Wail) Dickie McBride, 526
Singin' The Low Down Blues Down Low Cliff Bruner, 140
Singing A Song In Sing Sing Ray Whitley, 952
Singing A Wonderful Song Vaughan Quartet, 924
Singing Along The Way Bush Brothers, 147
Singing An Old Hymn McDonald Quartet, 541; Clayton McMichen, 571; Bob Miller, 622
Singing And Swinging For Me Bill Boyd, 124
Singing Clarinet Blues Tune Wranglers, 916
Singing Glory Over There Vaughan Quartet, 928
Singing Hills [The] Gene Autry, 84
Singing In My Soul Stamps Quartet, 864
Singing My Hill Billy Song Beverly Hill Billies, 103
Singing My Troubles Away Delmore Brothers, 310; Milo Twins, 628
Singing My Way To Glory Roy Acuff, 48
Singing Of Wonderful Love Stamps Quartet, 865
Singing On The Journey Home McDonald Quartet, 540; McMillan Quartet, 573
Singing The Blues With My Old Guitar Bill Bruner, 139
Singing The Hilo March Sain Family, 818
Singing The Story Of Grace Palmer Sisters, 673
Singing Those House Of David Blues Arthur Smith, 841
Singing To Victory McDonald Quartet, 541
Singing While Ages Roll V.O. Stamps-M.L. Yandell, 863
Single Girl, Married Girl Carter Family, 187, 193; Hardin & Grinstaff, 398
Single Life Roba Stanley, 866

Single Life Is Good Enough For Me Red Foley, 351
Single Life Is Good Enough For Me (Crooning Bachelor) Garner Eckler & Roland Gaines, 329
Sinking In The Lonesome Sea Carter Family, 192
Sinking Of The Great Titanic Vernon Dalhart, 281
Sinking Of The Submarine S-4 [The] John McGhee & Frank Welling, 553
Sinking Of The Submarine S-51 Vernon Dalhart, 251
Sinking Of The Titanic [The] Vernon Dalhart, 247; George Reneau, 741; Ernest V. Stoneman, 873
Sinking Of The Vestris [The] Golden Melody Boys, 373; Carson Robison, 766–67
Sinless Summerland [The] Deal Family, 307; Ernest V. Stoneman, 873
Sinner And The Song [The] Frank & James McCravy, 538
Sinner Made Whole [A] Vernon & Harwell, 931
Sinner Sinks In Sad Despair [The] Alfred G. Karnes, 472
Sinner You Better Get Ready Monroe Brothers, 633
Sinner's Prayer [A] Jimmie Davis, 305
Sioux Indians Marc Williams, 958
"Sioux Indians" (A Cowboy Chant) Marc Williams, 959
Sippin' Cider Vernon Dalhart, 284–85
Siree Peaks [The] Everett Cheetham, 203
Si's Mule Robert Walton & McWinders, 938
Sisco Harmonica Blues Carver Boys, 196
Sister Jackson Mustard & Gravy, 647
Sister Liz Southern Moonlight Entertainers, 860
Sister Lucy Frank & James McCravy, 534
Sister Lucy Lee Bill Boyd, 123
Sittin' By The Old Corral Wilf Carter (Montana Slim), 186
Sittin' By The River Carson Robison, 793
Sittin' In The Corner Vaughan Quartet, 926
Sittin' On The Doorstep Sunshine Boys, 882
Sittin' On The Moon Cliff Bruner, 140
Sittin' On The Old Settee Rex Griffin, 383; Judie & Julie, 468
Sittin' On The Old Settee! Ray Whitley, 952
Sittin' On Top O' The World Shelton Brothers, 827
Sittin' On Your Doorstep Shelton Brothers, 830
Sittin' Round The Fireside Eldon Baker, 90
Sitting At The Feet Of Jesus Carolina Ladies Quartet, 171; Mr. & Mrs. W.M. Shively, 832; Wisdom Sisters, 968–69
Sitting In The Parlor Lester Smallwood, 840
Sitting In The Window Of My Room Blind Uncle Gaspard, 363
Sitting On Top Of The World William Hanson, 395; Light Crust Doughboys, 504; Scottdale String Band, 822; Bob Wills, 960
Six Feet Of Earth Vernon Dalhart, 278–79, 281; Highleys, 421; Frank & James McCravy, 531–32; Carson Robison, 787, 792; Rufus K. Stanley, 866
Six Feet Of Earth (Makes Us All Of One Size) Carson Robison, 762
Six Feet Of Earth Makes Us All One Size Oscar L. Coffey, 217
Six Feet Of Papa Virginia Childs, 208
Six Months Ain't Long John D. Foster, 354; Monroe Brothers, 633
Six Months In Jail Ain't Long Emry Arthur, 66
Six Months Is A Long Time Ernest V. Stoneman, 878
Six Nights Drunk—Part 1, 2 Emmett Bankston & Red Henderson, 92
Six O'Clock Blues Robert Walton & McWinders, 938
Six White Horses Bill Monroe, 631
Six Women Done Me Wrong Bill Cox, 227
Sixteen Days In Georgia Kessinger Brothers, 479
Sixty Six Frank Roberts, Bud Alexander & Fiddlin' Slim Sandford, 755
Sixty-Seven Gals In Savannah Prairie Ramblers, 709

Skater's Waltz Perry Brothers, 687
Skeedee-Waddle-Dee-Waddle-Do Hoosier Hot Shots, 438–39
Skeeter And Bumble-Bee Bob Miller, 616
Skidd More Blue Ridge Highballers, 109
Skies Will Be Blue Stamps Quartet, 865
Skillet Licker Breakdown Gid Tanner, 891
Skip To Ma Lou, My Darling Uncle Eck Dunford, 325
Skip To My Lou Crockett [Family] Mountaineers, 234; Frank Luther, 525; Vass Family, 922
Skip To My Lou My Darling Georgia Organ Grinders, 366
Skipping And Flying Allen Brothers, 55, 57
Skunk In The Collard Patch Earl & Willie Phelps, 689
Skyland Rag Rector Trio, 729
Slap It, Shake It Bob Skyles, 839
Sleep Baby Sleep Homer Christopher, 209; Ollie Hess, 418; Hill Billies, 423; Frank[ie] Marvin, 595; Charlie [& Bud] Newman, 655; Walter C. Peterson, 688; Riley Puckett, 716, 718; Renus Rich & Carl Bradshaw, 747; Jimmie Rodgers, 799
Sleep Darlin' Sleep On Johnny Barfield, 94
Sleep On John Busby & Gilbert Thomas, 147
Sleep On Blue Eyes Arthur Tanner, 886
Sleep On Darling Sleep On W.L. "Rustic" Waters, 940
Sleep On Departed Ones Simmons Sacred Singers, 835
Sleep On, Brown Eyes Claude Davis, 297
Sleep On, Departed One Tennessee Hill Billy, 896
Sleeping At The Foot Of The Bed Clarence Ganus, 362
Sleeping In The Manger Tom Darby & Jimmie Tarlton, 294
Sleeping Late Uncle Eck Dunford, 325
Sleeping Lula Richard D. Burnett, 144; Carver Boys, 196; Clifford Gross, 385
Sleeping Lulu Richard D. Burnett, 144; Richard Cox, 229; Gid Tanner, 891
Sleeping Time Waltz Gene Clardy & Stan Clements, 212
Sleepy Creek Wail Elmer Bird, 105
Sleepy Desert Wilmer Watts, 941
Sleepy Head Merritt Smith, 844
Sleepy Hollow Claude Davis, 298; Howard Keesee, 475; Carson Robison, 784–85, 787–88
Sleepy Lou Uncle Dave Macon, 575
Sleepy Rio Grande Louisiana Strollers, 514; Carson Robison, 774, 780, 796
Sleepy Rio Grande Waltz Carson Robison, 776
Sleepy Time Gal Hal O'Halloran's Hooligans, 667
Sleepy Time In Sleepy Hollow Bob Wills, 961
Sleepy Waltz Hi-Flyers, 419
Sleepy-Time In Caroline Eddie Dean, 308
Slide Daddy, Slide Allen Brothers, 56; John McGhee & Frank Welling, 562
Slighted Sweetheart Roy Lyons, 525
Slim Gal Bill & Louis Jones, 464; Clayton McMichen, 567; Riley Puckett, 719
Slim's Blues Oscar [Slim] Doucet, 324
Slim's Talkin' Blues Part 1, 2 Jack Pierce, 696
Slippery Elm Tree Len & Joe Higgins, 421
Slipping Clutch Blues Allen Brothers, 57
Slow And Easy Roy Newman, 656
Slow Buck Gid Tanner, 889
Slow Buck Reel Lane's Old Time Fiddlers, 490
Slow Down Mr. Brown Light Crust Doughboys, 504
Slow Guitar Blues Jack Cawley's Oklahoma Ridge Runners, 199
Slow It Down Bob Skyles, 839
Slow Time Waltz Mumford Bean, 98
Slow Wicked Blues Tom Darby & Jimmie Tarlton, 294
Slue-Foot Lou Frank[ie] Marvin, 601

Slue-Foot Lue Gene Autry, 71
Slu-Foot Lou Frank[ie] Marvin, 600
Slufoot On The Levee Light Crust Doughboys, 506
Small Town Blues Bill Nettles, 654
Small Town Mama Buddy Jones, 465
Small Town Mama No. 2 Buddy Jones, 465
Smile And Drive Your Blues Away Texas Wanderers, 900
Smile For Me W. Lee O'Daniel, 665
Smile Your Troubles Away Smith's Sacred Singers, 851; Carl Williams, 957
Smile, Darn Ya, Smile Bar-X Cowboys, 92
Smiles Hugh Cross, 235; Dave Edwards, 330; John McGhee & Frank Welling, 561; Riley Puckett, 719; Jimmie Revard, 743; Jimmy Yates Groups, 975
Smiles Thru Tear Drops Prairie Ramblers, 712
Smilin' Through Sons Of The Pioneers, 858
Smiling Sea Ruth Neal & Wanda Neal, 652
Smiling Through Tears Bill Cox, 229
Smiling Watermelon Bill Chitwood, 208
Smith's Breakdown Arthur Smith, 841
Smith's March (New Orleans) Leake County Revelers, 495
Smith's Rag Arthur Smith, 842
Smith's Reel Bob Wills, 961
Smith's Waltz Arthur Smith, 840
Smoke Behind The Clouds Georgia Organ Grinders, 366; Jess Young, 978
Smoke Goes Out The Chimney Just The Same [The] Fiddlin' John Carson, 177
Smoke Went Up The Chimney Just The Same [The] Wilf Carter (Montana Slim), 182–83
Smokey Mokes Raggedy Ann's Melody Makers, 724
Smoking Habit [The] Arthur Fields & Fred Hall, 345
Smoky Mountain Poole Family, 701
Smoky Mountain Bill Carson Robison, 778–80, 793
Smoky Mountain Bill And His Song Delmore Brothers, 309
Smoky Mountain Blues George Reneau, 740
Smoky Mountain Boys At The Still Part I, II [The] Smoky Mountain Boys, 851
Smoky Mountain Far Away Johnson Brothers, 463
Smoky Mountain Home Hugh Cross, 236; Clayton McMichen, 570–71
Smoky Mountain Moon Roy Acuff, 49
Smoky Mountain Rag Roy Acuff, 49
Smoky Mountain Schottische Prairie Ramblers, 708
Smoky Mountain Waltz Roane County Ramblers, 751
Smoky Mt Blues Jack & Jean, 451
Smoky Row Doc Roberts, 753
Snake Eyed Killing Dude Canova Family, 155
Snap Bean Blues Roland Cauley, 198
Snatch 'Em Back Blues Byrd Moore, 638
Sneeze Song—If You'll Ker-Ker-Chooey Me (Then I'll Ker-Chooey You) [The] Vernon Dalhart, 247
Sneeze Song (If You'll Ker-Ker-Chooey Me) [The] Vernon Dalhart, 249
Sneeze Song [The] Vernon Dalhart, 247
Sneezing Song [The] Vernon Dalhart, 249
Snow Bird On The Ash Bank Salem Highballers, 818
Snow Covered Face Patt Patterson, 681–82
Snow Dear Ernest Thompson, 903; Jimmie Wilson's Catfish String Band, 968
Snow Deer Buell Kazee, 473; Light Crust Doughboys, 506; Ernest Thompson, 902; Floyd Thompson, 903–04
Snow Storm [The] Henry Whitter, 955
Snow White Roses Ted Daffan's Texans, 241
Snow White Stone Wells Brothers String Band, 943
Snowflakes Roscoe & Samuel Dellinger, 309; Prairie Ramblers, 705

So Blue Cliff Carlisle, 166
So Hard To Be Alone Amedie Ardoin, 62
So I Joined The Navy Carson Robison, 780–83, 785, 795–96
So I'll Have Part Of You Bonnie Dodd & Murray Lucas, 322
So Lonely Wiley Walker & Gene Sullivan, 936
So Lonely So Blue Bill Carlisle, 159
So Long Frank Roberts, Bud Alexander & Fiddlin' Slim Sandford, 755
So Long Pal Al Dexter, 315
So Long To The Red River Valley Sons Of The Pioneers, 858
So Long, Baby Bill Carlisle, 160
So May You Frank & James McCravy, 533
So Now You Come Back To Me Joe Cook, 220
So Straight, My Lad Allen Brothers, 57
So This Is Venice Dan Hornsby, 442
So Tired Cliff Bruner, 139
So Tired Of Dreaming W. Lee O'Daniel, 666
So Tired Of Waiting Adolph Hofner, 430
So Tired Of Waiting Alone Bill Boyd, 123
Soap Box Blues Jack Pierce, 696
Soap In The Wash Pan Jimmy Johnson's String Band, 461
Soap Suds Over The Fence Capt. McKinney & E.L. Graham, 564
Socker On The Kisser [A] Asa Martin, 589
Sod Buster With The Jug Handle Ears [The] Elton Britt, 129
Soft Baby Feet Joe Steen, 868
Soft Music [J.T.] Allison's Sacred Harp Singers, 60; Original Sacred Harp Choir, 670; Hamp Reynolds' Sacred Harp Singers, 744
Soft Voices Stripling Brothers, 880
Softly And Tenderly Frank & James McCravy, 537; Old Southern Sacred Singers, 669; George Reneau, 741; Merritt Smith, 844
Softly And Tenderly Jesus Is Calling Foundation Quartette, 355
Soldier And The Lady [The] Coon Creek Girls, 221
Soldier Boy In Blue Lester McFarland & Robert A. Gardner, 545
Soldier Boy Stomp Lew Preston, 713
Soldier Joy Taylor's Kentucky Boys, 895
Soldier Of Honor [A] Wilmer Watts, 941
Soldier Won't You Marry Me? Vass Family, 922
Soldier, Soldier, Will You Marry Me Bradley Kincaid, 483
Soldier, Will You Marry Me Gid Tanner, 890
Soldiers Bonus [The] Benny Borg, 119
Soldier's Dream Charlie Oaks, 664
Soldiers Joy Arkansas Woodchopper, 64; Blue Ridge Highballers, 110; Herschel Brown, 133; Fiddlin' John Carson, 176; Roland Cauley, 199; Robert Cook's Old Time Fiddlers, 220; Tommy Dandurand, 293; Zeb Harrelson & M.B. Padgett, 404; Fisher Hendley, 416; Kessinger Brothers, 480; Clayton McMichen, 573; Uncle Dave Macon, 574; North Carolina Hawaiians, 663; Archer Porter, 702; Rustic Revellers, 816; Arthur Tanner, 886; Gid Tanner, 890–91; Ernest Thompson, 902; Woodhull's Old Time Masters, 971
Soldier's Joy Hill Billies, 424
Soldier's Joy Hornpipe John Baltzell, 91
Soldier's Poor Little Boy [The] Johnson Brothers, 463
Soldier's Return [The] Goebel Reeves, 737–38
Soldier's Story [The] Eddie Dean, 307
Soldier's Sweetheart [The] Green Bailey, 88; Jimmy Long, 512; Frank[ie] Marvin, 595; Jimmie Rodgers, 799
Solita Tune Wranglers, 916
Some Day Bateman Sacred Quartet, 97; Modern Mountaineers, 631; Royal Quartette, 815; Leon Selph, 824; Vaughan Quartet, 923

Some Day I'll Wander Back Again John D. Foster, 355
Some Day In Wyomin' Gene Autry, 80
Some Day We'll Meet Our Mother Mr. & Mrs. R.N. Grisham, 385
Some Day You Are Gonna Be Sorry Philyaw Brothers, 690
Some Family Honeyboy & Sassafras[s], 433
Some Girls Do And Some Girls Don't Karl & Harty, 471
Some Glad Day Monroe Brothers, 633; Lew Preston, 713
Some Little Bug Is Goin' To Get You Some Day Bradley Kincaid, 484
Some Mother's Boy Elmer Bird, 106
Some Must Win—Some Lose Jimmie Davis, 304
Some Of These Days Milton Brown, 136; Vernon Dalhart, 267; Hoosier Hot Shots, 437; Light Crust Doughboys, 502; Roy Newman, 657
Some Of These Days You're Gonna Be Sad Delmore Brothers, 311
Some Old Day Rouse Brothers, 815
Some One Ernest Branch & Bernice Coleman, 126; Canova Family, 156; Tex Ritter, 751
Some One Is Praying For You Maury Pearson, 683
Some Other Man Jimmie Davis, 305
Some Sweet Day Bye And Bye Land Norris, 662
Somebody Hank Penny, 687
Somebody But You Don't Mean Me Jules Allen, 54
Somebody Cares J.E. Mainer's Mountaineers, 582
Somebody Is Jealous Delin T. Guillory-Lewis Lafleur, 385
Somebody Knows Lester McFarland & Robert A. Gardner, 543; Prairie Ramblers, 710–11; Rangers Quartet, 728
Somebody Loves Me Hoosier Hot Shots, 437; Lyric Quartette, 525; Roy Newman, 656
Somebody Loves You Frank Luther, 522; Leo Soileau, 855
Somebody Loves You Yet Swing Billies, 885
Somebody Makes Me Think Of You Blue Sky Boys, 113
Somebody Needs Just You Vaughan Quartet, 923–24
Somebody Stole My Gal John Boyd, 125; Milton Brown, 137
Somebody Stole My Little Darling Shelton Brothers, 830; Wiley Walker & Gene Sullivan, 936
Somebody Waiting For You Happy Massey, 608
Somebody's Been Using It Bill Boyd, 122
Somebody's Been Using That Thing Milton Brown, 137; Callahan Brothers, 153
Somebody's Boy Wright Brothers Quartet, 974
Somebody's Darling Astray John McGhee & Frank Welling, 558
Somebody's Darling Not Mine Four Pickled Peppers, 356; Prairie Ramblers, 707; Buck Turner, 916
Somebody's Knocking At Your Door [E.R.] Nance Family, 649
Somebody's Smile Prairie Ramblers, 710; Roy Rogers, 811
Somebody's Tall And Handsome Carolina Tar Heels, 173
Somebody's Waiting Cousin Levi, 224
Somebody's Waiting For Me Duke Clark, 213; Jack & Leslie, 451; Riley Puckett, 721; Sweet Brothers, 884
Somebody's Waiting For You Bradley Kincaid, 485; Riley Puckett, 717
Somebody's Wrong About The Bible Philyaw Brothers, 690
Someday Baby Shelton Brothers, 829
Someday Somewhere Sweetheart Red Foley, 352
Someday Soon Adolph Hofner, 430
Someday Sweetheart Vernon Dalhart, 267; Melody Boys, 615; W. Lee O'Daniel, 666
Someday We'll Meet Again Welby Toomey, 912
Someday You'll Care Hank Snow, 852
Someday You'll Know You Did Wrong John (Dusty) King, 486
Someday You're Gonna Be Blue Johnny Bond, 117

Someday, It Won't Be Long Jewell Tillman Burns & Charlie D. Tillman, 145; Rev. M.L. Thrasher, 904
Someone Else May Be There Frank Shelton, 826
Someone Else May Be There While I'm Gone McGee Brothers, 552
Someone Else You Care For Jimmie Revard, 743
Someone I Love W.T. Narmour & S.W. Smith, 649–50
Someone In Heaven Is Thinking Of You Bill Boyd, 123; W. Lee O'Daniel, 665
Someone Is Alone Adolph Hofner, 430
Someone Owns A Cottage Ernest Branch & Bernice Coleman, 125
Someone Thinks Of Someone Adolph Hofner, 430
Someone To Go Home To Patsy Montana, 635
Someone To Love You When You're Old Morris Brothers, 643; Shelton Brothers, 828
Someone Will Welcome You M. Homer Cummings & Son Hugh, 240
Someone's Last Day Blue Sky Boys, 114
Something Eatin' On Me Blues Ike Cargill, 158
Something Got A Hold Of Me Carter Family, 195
Something Wrong With My Gal Red Fox Chasers, 730
Something's Always Sure To Tickle Me Uncle Dave Macon, 575
Something's Going To Happen, Honey Richard Brooks & Reuben Puckett, 132
Something's Got To Change Somewhere Fleming & Townsend, 346
Sometime Hawaiian Songbirds, 413; Frank & James McCravy, 537
Sometime We'll Say Goodbye Clarence Ganus, 362
Sometime We'll Understand Mrs. Leon Hinkle, 427; Frank & James McCravy, 537
Sometime You Will Pray Fortner Family Mixed Quartette, 353
Sometime You'll Pray Clarence Ganus, 362
Sometime, Somewhere Jewell Tillman Burns & Charlie D. Tillman, 146; Peck's Male Quartette, 684
Sometimes Adolph Hofner, 431
Somewhere Merritt Smith, 844; Tom & Roy, 911
Somewhere Down Below The Dixon Line Jimmie Rodgers, 809
Somewhere In Arkansas Ashley's Melody Makers, 68
Somewhere In Old Wyoming Frank Luther, 522; Lester McFarland & Robert A. Gardner, 548; Riley Puckett, 720; Carson Robison, 783–84
Somewhere Somebody's Waiting W.C. Childers, 205
Somewhere Somebody's Waiting For You Carlisle Brothers, 169; Bradley Kincaid, 484; Pie Plant Pete, 695
Somewhere West Of Heaven Massey Family, 613
Somewhere, Someone Is Waiting Clover Leaf Old Time Fiddlin' Team, 215
Son Hath Made Me Free [The] Chuck Wagon Gang, 210
Son Of A Gun "Sunshine" Pritchard, 714
Son, Please Come Home Brown Brothers, 138
Sona My Darling Merritt Smith, 845
Song For Mother [A] Tex Fletcher, 349
Song Of Hawaii W. Lee O'Daniel, 667
Song Of Jesus' Love Brings Heaven Down [A] Stamps Quartet, 865
Song Of Sorrow [The] Frank[ie] Marvin, 597
Song Of The Bandit Sons Of The Pioneers, 858
Song Of The Bandits Bill Cox, 225
Song Of The Blind Karl & Harty, 470
Song Of The Blind Man [The] Arthur Fields & Fred Hall, 340
Song Of The Brown Family Bob Miller, 622

Song Of The Condemned Vernon Dalhart, 289; Arthur Fields & Fred Hall, 340
Song Of The Doodle Bug Georgia Yellow Hammers, 367
Song Of The Failure Vernon Dalhart, 278–79
Song Of The Golden West Fred Kirby, 487
Song Of The Harvest Grover Rann, 729
Song Of The Islands West Brothers Trio, 946
Song Of The Lariat Massey Family, 610
Song Of The Old Ding Dong Adelyne Hood, 435
Song Of The Orphan Girl Richard D. Burnett, 144
Song Of The Pioneers Sons Of The Pioneers, 857
Song Of The Prairie [The] Carson Robison, 794
Song Of The Prune (No Matter How Young A Prune May Be It's Always Full Of Wrinkles) [The] Carson Robison, 762
Song Of The Range [The] Jim & Bob, 458
Song Of The Saddle Light Crust Doughboys, 504; Pine Ridge Ramblers, 697
Song Of The Sea [The] Miner Hawkins, 413; Goebel Reeves, 735
Song Of The Shut-In [The] Vernon Dalhart, 282
Song Of The Silver Dollar Carson Robison, 783
Song Of The Tramp Malcolm Legette, 496
Song Of The Wanderer Milton Brown, 137
Song Of The Wanderer (Where Shall I Go?) Vernon Dalhart, 264–65
Song Of The Waterfall Bill Boyd, 123
Song Of Two Roses [The] Sammy & Smitty, 818
Song Of Wonderful Love [The] John McGhee & Frank Welling, 556
Song To Hawaii [A] James Brown, Jr. & Ken Landon Groups, 135
Songbird Yodel Bill Boyd, 121; Hawaiian Songbirds, 412
Songs My Mother Used To Sing [The] Lester McFarland & Robert A. Gardner, 546, 548
Songs Of Adoration Copeland Chorus, 221
Sonny Boy Hackberry Ramblers, 387
Sons Of Sorrow Dye's Sacred Harp Singers, 328
Soon We'll Be Going Home Knippers Bros. & Parker, 488
Soon We'll Come To The Old Garden Gate Norwood Tew, 898
Soon We'll Pass Away Denson-Parris Sacred Harp Singers, 313
Sophisticated Hula Happy Valley Boys, 397; Bob Wills, 963
Sopping The Gravy Kessinger Brothers, 480
Sorrow On My Mind Bob Atcher, 70
Sorry (I'll Say I'm Sorry) Cliff Bruner, 141
So's Your Old Lady Johnny Marvin, 606
Soucis Quand J'Etais Gamin (Troubles When I Was A Boy) Joseph Falcon, 335
Soul Winner For Jesus Old Southern Sacred Singers, 669
Sour Apple Cider Steve & His Hot Shots, 868
Sour Dough Dan Prairie Ramblers, 711
Sour Wood Mountains Fiddlin' Powers & Family, 703
Sourwood Mountain Crockett [Family] Mountaineers, 233; Fruit Jar Guzzlers, 360; Hill Billies, 423; Kessinger Brothers, 480; Bradley Kincaid, 482, 484; Frank Luther, 524; Clayton McMichen, 573; Doc Roberts, 755; Ernest V. Stoneman, 873; Uncle "Am" Stuart, 881; Gid Tanner, 887; Taylor's Kentucky Boys, 895; Tweedy Brothers, 918; Vagabonds, 922; Henry Whitter, 955
Sourwood Mountain Medley Uncle Dave Macon, 575
Sourwood Mt Frank Luther, 524
South Airport Boys, 52; Bar-X Cowboys, 93; Texas Jim Lewis, 499; Light Crust Doughboys, 506; Shelton Brothers, 830
South Bound Train Dick Hartman's Tennessee Ramblers, 407
South Carolina Blues Chris Bouchillon, 119
South Of The Border Riley Puckett, 722; Carson Robison, 796

Index to Titles

South Of The Border (Down Mexico Way) Gene Autry, 84; Massey Family, 611
South Of The Mason Dixon Line Jack Pierce, 695
South Plains Blues Wiley Walker & Gene Sullivan, 936
South Sea Serenade Kelly Brothers, 477
South Solon Quadrille [The] Gibson String Trio, 369
South Texas Swing Adolph Hofner, 431
Southern Blues Scottdale String Band, 821
Southern Cannon-Ball Jimmie Rodgers, 806
Southern College Medley Southlanders, 861
Southern Flower Waltz Clifford Gross, 385
Southern Jack Fletcher & Foster, 349
Southern Jane Fleming & Townsend, 348
Southern Medley Beard's Quartette, 98; Charlie Poole, 700; Trenton Melody Makers, 913
Southern Melodies W.W. Macbeth, 526
Southern Melodies—Part 1, 2 Bob McGimsey, 564
Southern Melody Soft Shoe Dance Jimmy Smith, 844
Southern Moon Delmore Brothers, 310; Carson Robison, 788; White Brothers (Joe & Bob), 951
Southern Moon Waltz George Edgin, 330
Southern No. 111 Roane County Ramblers, 751
Southern Railroad Homer Christopher, 209
Southern Seas McDearis String Band, 539
Southern Whistling Coon Sid Harkreader, 400; McGee Brothers, 552
Southern Whoopee Song Anglin Brothers, 61
Southwest Mine Disaster John McGhee & Frank Welling, 558
Sow 'Em On The Mountain (Reap 'Em In The Valley) Carter Family, 189
Sowing And Reaping Rev. J.O. Hanes & Male Choir, 394
Sowing On The Mountain Coon Creek Girls, 221
Sowing Seed For Heaven's Harvest King Tennessee Music & Printing Co. Quartet, 896
Spain Carson Robison, 792
Spanish Cavalier David Miller, 626–27; Riley Puckett, 716; Sons Of The West, 859
Spanish Fandango Bill Boyd, 124; John Dilleshaw, 316
Spanish Flang Dang Stripling Brothers, 880
Spanish Medley Of Waltzes Jimmie Revard, 742
Spanish Merchant's Daughter [The] Ernest V. Stoneman, 877
Spanish Rag Herschel Brown, 133
Spanish Rose Al Dexter, 315
Spanish Two Step Adolph Hofner, 431; Bob Wills, 960
Spanish Waltz Jack Pierce, 696; Hugh Roden, 797
Sparkin' My Gal Bill Carlisle, 159
Sparklets Waltz Bert Layne, 493
Sparkling Blue Eyes Cliff Bruner, 141; Bill Carlisle, 160; Wade Mainer, 584
Sparkling Blue Eyes No. 2 Wade Mainer, 585
Sparkling Brown Eyes Bill Cox, 228
Sparrow Bird Waltz Ernest Thompson, 902–03
Spartanburg Blues Homer Christopher, 209
Spartanburg Jail Hall Brothers, 391
Speak Evil Of No Man Dorsey & Beatrice Dixon, 322
Speak My Lord Perry Kim & Einar Nyland, 481
Speak To Me Little Darling York Brothers, 977
Speaking The Truth Bascom Lamar Lunsford, 517
Speckled Peas [The] [E.R.] Nance Family, 648
Speed Elkins Stringed Steppers, 331
Speed Maniac Chris Bouchillon, 120
Speed The Plow Farm Hands, 336
Spell O' The Moon [The] Jack Major, 586
Spend A Night In Argentina Gene Autry, 85
Spider And The Fly [The] Lester McFarland & Robert A. Gardner, 547

Spinning Room Blues Dorsey & Beatrice Dixon, 321; Hinson, Pitts & Coley, 427
Spirit Of Love Watches Over Me [The] Carter Family, 191
Spit Devil Rag Doc Roberts, 755
Spooning 'Neath A Western Sky Jack Pierce, 696
Sporting Bachelors [The] Buell Kazee, 472
Sporting Cowboy [The] Wilmer Watts, 941
Spreading Maple [The] Bill Cox, 229
Spring Heel Hornpipe Jess Hillard, 426
Spring Place Reel C.L. Ballen & Amos Ballen, 90
Spring Roses Richard D. Burnett, 144; Byrd Moore, 640
Spring Street Waltz Arthur Smith, 840
Springing Up Within My Soul Rev. Edward Boone, Mrs. Edward Boone & Miss Olive Boone, 118
Spring's Tornado Graham Brothers, 377
Springtime And Flowers Asa Martin, 592
Springtime In Glory Propes Quartet, 714
Springtime In The Blue Ridge Mountains Flannery Sisters, 345
Springtime In The Mountains Fleming & Townsend, 347
Springtime In The Rockies John McGhee & Frank Welling, 559
Springtown Shuffle Crystal Springs Ramblers, 239
Square Dance—Part 1, 2 National Barn Dance Orchestra, 651
Square Dance Fight On Ball Top Mountain—Part 1, 2 [The] John Dilleshaw, 317
Squeeze Box Polka Massey Family, 613
Squint Eyed Cactus Jones Vernon Dalhart, 289–90
Squire And The Deacon [The] Ernest Hare, 399
St. James Gibson String Trio, 369
St. Jobe's Waltz Red Headed Fiddler[s], 732
St. Louis Blues [The] Bill Boyd, 121; Milton Brown, 136; Callahan Brothers, 151; Pete Cassell, 198; Virginia Childs, 208; Four Horsemen, 356; Hoosier Hot Shots, 440; Jim & Bob, 458; Lester McFarland & Robert A. Gardner, 543; Clayton McMichen, 566; Whitey McPherson, 579; Johnny O'Brien, 665; Jack Pierce, 696; Swing Billies, 885; Bob Wills, 960
St. Louis Tickle Jim Couch, 223; Humphries Brothers, 447; Scottdale String Band, 822
St. Louis Woman (Got Her Diamond In The Hock Shop Now) Clayton McMichen, 572
St. Regious Girl Carter Family, 194
St. Regis Valley Tex Fletcher, 348
Stack O' Lee Blues—Part 1, 2 Carson Robison, 792
Stackalee Frank Hutchison, 449
Stack-O-Lee Fruit Jar Guzzlers, 360
Stamp Collector [The] Prairie Ramblers, 711
Stand By Me Frank & James McCravy, 533, 535–36
Stand Up And Sing For Your Father Frank Morris, 642
Stand Up For Jesus Giddens Sisters, 369; Mountain Singers Male Quartet, 645; Smith's Sacred Singers, 850
Standin' In Need Of Prayer Four Novelty Aces, 356
Standin' Neath The Old Pine Tree Hank Penny, 687
Standin' On The Pier In The Rain Stuart Hamblen, 392
Standing By A Window North Carolina Cooper Boys, 663
Standing By The Highway Claude Davis, 298
Standing In The Need Of Prayer John & Emery McClung, 530; Alf. Taylor, 892
Standing On The Promises John McGhee & Frank Welling, 563; Tennessee Mountaineers, 896; Rev. M.L. Thrasher, 905
Standing On The Promises Of God Giddens Sisters, 369
Standing Outside Chuck Wagon Gang, 210
Standing Outside Of Heaven Jimmy Wakely, 934
Star Boarder Blues Bill Cox, 227
Star Dust Cliff Bruner, 140; West Brothers Trio, 946
Star Kovarna Jimmie Revard, 742
Star Of The East Woodlawn Quartette, 972

Star Waltz Thomasson Bros, 901
Starlight Schottische Massey Family, 613
Starlight Waltz John Baltzell, 92
Star-Lit Heaven Warren Caplinger, 157–58
Starlit Trail [The] Zeke Williams, 959
Stars & Guitars In Sunny Mexico Cliff Carlisle, 162
Stars (Are The Windows Of Heaven) Vernon Dalhart, 260–61
Stars Over Laredo Red River Dave, 732
Stars With Stripes Goebel Reeves, 738
Start A Little Rainbow In My Heart Jubileers, 468
Started Out From Texas Girls Of The Golden West, 370
Starting Life Anew With You Wade Mainer, 583
Starving To Death On A Government Claim Edward L. Crain, 230
Static Stomp Hi-Flyers, 419
Station H.O.B.O. Goebel Reeves, 736–37
Station Will Be Changed After A While Uncle Dave Macon, 574
Stay All Night And Don't Go Home Oscar L. Coffey, 216
Stay Away From My Chicken House Gene Autry, 71; Frank[ie] Marvin, 600–601
Stay In The Wagon Yard "Peg" Moreland, 641; Shelton Brothers, 827
Stay In Your Own Back Yard Hackberry Ramblers, 387
Stay On The Farm Pie Plant Pete, 695
Stay On The Right Side Doug Bine, 104
Stay On The Right Side Sister Milton Brown, 137; Light Crust Doughboys, 504
Stay Out Of The South Hoosier Hot Shots, 436
Stay Out Of The South (If You Want To Miss Heaven On Earth) Light Crust Doughboys, 504
Steal Away Trenton Melody Makers, 913; Vaughan Quartet, 923, 926
Stealing Through The Shadows Al Dexter, 314
Steamboat Vernon Dalhart, 280
Steamboat (Keep Rockin') Vernon Dalhart, 280, 282; Carson Robison, 762–63, 766, 793
Steamboat Bill Al Bernard, 101; Smiley Burnette, 145; Fiddlin' John Carson, 176; Kessinger Brothers, 481; Riley Puckett, 715; Ernest Rogers, 810
Steamboat Man Earl Shirkey & Roy Harper, 831
Steamboat Whistle Blues Roy Acuff, 48
Steel A Goin' Down Buell Kazee, 473
Steel Driving Man Fruit Jar Guzzlers, 360
Steel Guitar Blues Roy Acuff, 49; Tennessee Ramblers [II], 897
Steel Guitar Chimes Roy Acuff, 49
Steel Guitar Honky Tonk Universal Cowboys, 919
Steel Guitar Hula Hank Penny, 686
Steel Guitar Rag Bob Wills, 961
Steel Guitar Stomp Bob Wills, 962
Steel Guitar Swing Tennessee Ramblers [II], 897
Steel Guitar Wobble Lunsford Bros., 517
Steeley Rag [The] Red Headed Fiddler[s], 732
Steer's Lament (Nearin' The End Of The Trail) [The] Carson Robison, 789
Step High Lady W.L. "Rustic" Waters, 940
Step High Waltz Roane County Ramblers, 751
Step It Fast Amadie Breaux, 126
Step Light Ladies Dick Hartman's Tennessee Ramblers, 407
Step Lively Jimmy Johnson's String Band, 461
Step On It Joseph Falcon, 336
Step Stone Floyd County Ramblers, 350; Bascom Lamar Lunsford, 517
Stephensville Blues Johnson & Lee, 462
Stepping In The Light John McGhee & Frank Welling, 554–55

Stepping Stones To Heaven Karl & Harty, 471
Stern Old Bachelor Carolina Night Hawks, 172; Carter Family, 194
Steward Long Bow Green's String Band, 381
Still Got 99 Home Town Boys, 433
Still Still With Thee Loveless Twins Quartet, 514
Still Talkin' Dick Hartman's Tennessee Ramblers, 407
Still There's A Spark Of Love Bill Carlisle, 160; Tex Fletcher, 348
Still There's A Spark Of Love—Part 2 Bill Carlisle, 160
Still Write Your Name In The Sand Home Town Boys, 433
Stilling The Tempest Avondale Mills Quartet, 87; Vaughan Quartet, 927
Stockade Blues Fiddlin' John Carson, 179; Georgia Crackers, 366; "Sunshine" Pritchard, 714
Stolen Love Red Fox Chasers, 730
Stompin' At The Honky Tonk Bob Dunn's Vagabonds, 326
Stone Mountain Memorial Vernon Dalhart, 250–53
Stone Mountain Rag Roanoke Jug Band, 751
Stone Mountain Tank Explosion Andrew Jenkins, 454
Stone Mountain Toddle Walker's Corbin Ramblers, 936
Stone Mountain Waltz Stone Mountain Trio, 872
Stone Mountain Wobble Scottdale String Band, 821–22
Stone Rag Maddux Family, 580; Paul Warmack, 940
Stonewall Jackson Alexander & Miller, 53; George Stoneman, 879
Stoney Creek Rag Allen D. Cole, 217
Stoney Point Tom Owens Barn Dance Trio, 672
Stoney Point And Mule Skinner's Delight Fiddling Sam Long, 512
Stony Point Alexander & Miller, 53; Clifford Gross, 385
Stood On The Bridge At Midnight Arthur Smith, 841
Stop And Fix It Dick Reinhart, 739
Stop And Listen Blues William Hanson, 395
Stop And Look For The Train Andrew Jenkins, 455
Stop That Delin T. Guillory-Lewis Lafleur, 385
Stop That Knocking At My Door Uncle Dave Macon, 575
Stop Yer Playin' Carson Robison, 787
Storm On The Sea (The Sinking Of The Steamship Vestris) [A] Ed Helton Singers, 415
Storm That Struck Miami [The] Fiddlin' John Carson, 179
Storms Are On The Ocean [The] Carter Family, 187, 193; Delmore Brothers, 311
Storms May Rule The Ocean John D. Foster, 354
Stormy Hawaiian Weather Kelly Brothers, 477
Stormy Wave Blues [The] Henry Whitter, 954
Story Book Call [The] Walter C. Peterson, 688
Story By The Moonlight [The] Henry Whitter, 955
Story Of A Dear Old Lady [A] Bob Miller, 625
Story Of Adam [The] Pink Lindsey, 507; Unknown Artists [IV], 920
Story Of C.S. Carnes [The] Dan Hornsby, 442
Story Of Charlie Lawson [The] Morris Brothers, 643
Story Of Frieda Bolt [The] Floyd County Ramblers, 350
Story Of George Collins [The] Dorsey & Beatrice Dixon, 322
Story Of Gerald Chapman Carl Conner, 219
Story Of Jitter-Bug Joe [The] Carson Robison, 797
Story Of John Hardy Dixieland Swingsters, 320
Story Of Love Divine [The] McClendon Brothers, 527
Story Of Seven Roses [The] Arty Hall, 390; Shelton Brothers, 828
Story Of The Dying Cowboy Joe Werner, 944
Story Of The Gambler Arthur Fields & Fred Hall, 340–41
Story Of The Knoxville Girl Blue Sky Boys, 113
Story Of The Mighty Mississippi [The] Ernest V. Stoneman, 875
Story Of The Preacher And The Bear Riley Puckett, 722
Story Of The Seven Roses Prairie Ramblers, 708

Story Of The Websters And The McGuires [The] Sons Of The Ozarks, 856
Story That The Crow Told Me [The] Carolina Buddies, 170
Stove Pipe Blues Kentucky String Ticklers, 478
Stranger Blues Roy Hall, 390
Strashidlo (The Ghost) Adolph Hofner, 431
Straw Breakdown Arthur Smith, 841
Strawberries Riley Puckett, 715
Strawberry Blues Reaves White County Ramblers, 729
Strawberry Roan Arizona Wranglers, 62; Beverly Hill Billies, 102; Bill Boyd, 121; Crowder Brothers, 238; Paul Hamblin, 393; Light Crust Doughboys, 503; Frank[ie] Marvin, 605; Bob Miller, 620; Patsy Montana, 636; Buck Nation, 650; Ranch Boys, 725–27; Carson Robison, 791; John I. White, 951
Strawberry Roan—Part I, II [The] W.C. Childers, 206; Rowdy Wright, 974
Streak O'Lean—Streak O' Fat John Dilleshaw, 317; A.A. Gray, 378
Streamlined Cannon Ball [The] Roy Acuff, 50
Streamlined Mama Lake Howard, 445; Buddy Jones, 465
Streamlined Yodel Song Wilf Carter (Montana Slim), 186
Streets Of Laredo Bradley Kincaid, 484
Streets Of New York [The] Hoosier Hot Shots, 440
Streets Of That City [The] Rev. Horace A. Booker, 117; Cliff Carlisle, 161
Stretch Of 28 Years [A] Cliff Carlisle, 166
String Bean Mama Bill Carlisle, 159; James Roberts, 756
Strip Tease Swing Ted Daffan's Texans, 241
Striped Dress J.B. Fuslier, 361
Strollers Waltz Louisiana Strollers, 514
Strolling Home With Jenny Gibbs Brothers, 368
Strolling Through Life Together Mason Stapleton, 867
Strummin' My Blues Away Vernon Dalhart, 248; Carson Robison, 761
Strummin' The Blues Away Carson Robison, 761
Strumming Our Troubles Away Carson Robison, 792
Strut Your Material Prairie Ramblers, 704
Struttin' Around Bar-X Cowboys, 93
Struttin' 'Round Sid Harkreader, 400
Struttin' The Neck Carl Boling, 116
Stuck Up Blues Roy Acuff, 50
Study War No More Arty Hall, 390
Stumbling Light Crust Doughboys, 504
Stump Of The Old Pine Tree [The] Gene Autry, 80
Stump Speech In The 10th District [A] Bascom Lamar Lunsford, 517
Stuttering Billy Tim Flora & Rufus Lingo, 350
Su Charin Hackberry Ramblers, 387
Su Parti A La Maison (I Am Going Home) Happy Fats, 396
Suckin' Cider Otto Gray, 380
Suffering Child Made Happy [A] John McGhee & Frank Welling, 555
Suffering Redeemer [The] Perry Kim & Einar Nyland, 482
Sugar Cliff Bruner, 139; Monie Chasteen, 203
Sugar Babe Hugh Cross, 237; Doc Hopkins, 441; Lulu Belle & Scotty, 516
Sugar Baby Dock Boggs, 115; Benny Borg, 118
Sugar Baby Blues Bill Nettles, 654
Sugar Blues Rice Brothers' Gang, 746; Tennessee Ramblers [II], 897; Bob Wills, 961
Sugar Cane Mama Bill Carlisle, 159; Cliff Carlisle, 165; Carlisle Brothers, 169
Sugar Daddy Blues Bill Cox, 226
Sugar Hill Crockett [Family] Mountaineers, 233; Prairie Ramblers, 712; Sweet Brothers, 884; Crockett Ward, 939
Sugar In My Coffee Crockett [Family] Mountaineers, 234
Sugar In The Gourd Fiddlin' John Carson, 175; Clayton McMichen, 573; Fiddlin' Powers & Family, 703; Ernest V. Stoneman, 874; Gid Tanner, 890; Tweedy Brothers, 918
Sugar Plum Blues Warren Caplinger, 157
Sugar Tree Stomp Arthur Smith, 841
Suicide Blues John Busby & Gilbert Thomas, 147
Sullivan's Hollow Freeny's Barn Dance Band, 359
Summer's County Rag E.F. "Pat" Alexander, 53
Summertime In Old Kentucky Vernon Dalhart, 284–86
Summertime On The Beeno Line Uncle Dave Macon, 578
Sun Goes Down [The] Jesse Rodgers, 799
Sun Has Gone Down On Our Love [The] Cliff Bruner, 141; Charles Mitchell & His Orchestra, 630
Sun Of My Soul Frank Luther, 523
Sun Of The Soul [The] Carter Family, 190
Sunbonnet Gal [Smilin'] Ed McConnell, 530
Sunbonnet Sue Cliff Bruner, 139; Light Crust Doughboys, 500; Bob Wills, 962
Sunday Morning Blues Queen Trio, 723
Sunday On The Farm Grace & Scotty MacLean, 565
Sundown Blues Wilf Carter (Montana Slim), 182; Texas Wanderers, 901
Sundown On The Prairie Tex Ritter, 751
Sundown Polka Al Dexter, 315
Sundown Waltz Stone Mountain Trio, 872
Sunlight And Shadows Vaughan Quartet, 928
Sunlight And Starlight Nolan Bush, 147
Sunny Home In Dixie Frank Jenkins, 455
Sunny Land Jack Golding, 374
Sunny San Antone Patsy Montana, 636
Sunny San Juan Marc Williams, 959
Sunny Side Of Life Blue Sky Boys, 113; Whitey & Hogan, 952
Sunny South By The Sea Cliff Carlisle, 163; Chuck Wagon Gang, 210
Sunny South Is Calling Me Norwood Tew, 898
Sunny Southern Blues "Big Road" Webster Taylor, 893
Sunny Tennessee Fiddlin' John Carson, 178; Floyd County Ramblers, 350; Roy Hall, 390; Harvey Irwin, 451; Lester McFarland & Robert A. Gardner, 546; Asa Martin, 589; Riley Puckett, 720
Sunny Waltz W.T. Narmour & S.W. Smith, 649; Nations Brothers, 652
Sunrise Frank & James McCravy, 537; John McGhee & Frank Welling, 563
Sunrise On The Guinea Farm Al Clauser, 214
Sun's Gonna Shine In My Backdoor Someday Village Boys, 932
Sunset (Sunset) Amedie Ardoin, 62
Sunset Gates Of Gold Howard Haney, 395
Sunset Is Coming (But The Sunrise We'll See) Chuck Wagon Gang, 211
Sunset March Charlie Poole, 699
Sunset On The Prairie Three Tobacco Tags, 909
Sunset Trail Buck Nation, 651
Sunset Trail To Texas [The] Bill Boyd, 124
Sunset Valley Bar-X Cowboys, 93
Sunset Waltz Grinnell Giggers, 384; Scottdale String Band, 822
Sunshine Al Dexter, 315
Sunshine Alley Stuart Hamblen, 393
Sunshine And Daisies Cliff Carlisle, 165
Sunshine And Paradise Milner & Curtis, 628
Sunshine And Shadows Emry Arthur, 66
Sunshine In Dixie Modern Mountaineers, 631
Sunshine In My Soul Arthur Cornwall & William Cleary, 223
Sunshine In The Shadows Carter Family, 189
Sunshine Special Rustic Revellers, 816
Sunshine Train [The] Knippers Bros. & Parker, 488

Sur Le Borde De L'Eau (On The Riverside) Blind Uncle Gaspard, 363
Sur Le Chemin Chez Moi (On My Way Home) Leo Soileau, 854
Surprise Party Of The Mayor Of Bayou Pom Pom—Part 1, 2 [The] Walter Coquille, 222
Susan Brown Dick Hartman's Tennessee Ramblers, 408
Susan Jane Frank & James McCravy, 534
Susan Van Duzan Buck Nation, 650
Susie Ann Charlie [& Bud] Newman, 655; George Reneau, 740–41
Susie Brown Jake & Carl, 453
Susie Lee Uncle Dave Macon, 577
Suzanna Gal Shelor Family, 826
Svestkova Alej (The Prune Song) Adolph Hofner, 431
Swaller-Tail Coat Frank Luther, 521
Swallow [The] Bob Wills, 962
Swallows [The] John H. Bertrand, 101
Swamp Cat Rag Swamp Rooters, 883
Swamps Of Old Arkansas Billy Sawyer, 820
Swanee Hoosier Hot Shots, 439
Swanee Blue Jay Frank[ie] Marvin, 595–96
Swanee Kitchen Door Carson Robison, 766, 792
Swanee River Bowman Sisters, 121; Fiddlin' John Carson, 177; Jim Couch, 223; Len & Joe Higgins, 421; E. Arthur Lewis, 498; Riley Puckett, 716; Jimmy Smith, 844; Ernest Thompson, 903; Tweedy Brothers, 917
Swanee River Waltz Stone Mountain Trio, 872
Swanee Sweetheart Sid Hampton, 394
Swapping Song [The] Bradley Kincaid, 482
Swat The Love Bug Bob Skyles, 839
Sway Back Pinto Pete Wilf Carter (Montana Slim), 182
Sweeping Through The Gates John McGhee & Frank Welling, 559, 561; Ernest V. Stoneman, 876
Sweet Adeline (You're The Flower Of My Heart) Frank & James McCravy, 534
Sweet Adeline At The Still John McGhee & Frank Welling, 558–59, 562
Sweet Allalee Blue Sky Boys, 113; Lester McFarland & Robert A. Gardner, 544
Sweet And Low Foundation Quartette, 355
Sweet As Sugar Blues Bob Skyles, 838
Sweet As The Flowers In May Time Carter Family, 190
Sweet As The Roses Of Spring Cliff Carlisle, 167
Sweet Baby (Come Back Where You Belong) Texas Jim Robertson, 760
Sweet Betsie From Pike Doc Hopkins, 441
Sweet Betsy From Pike Crockett [Family] Mountaineers, 233; Frank Dudgeon, 324; Doc Hopkins, 441; Bradley Kincaid, 485; Harry "Mac" McClintock, 528; Ken Maynard, 614; Ranch Boys, 726
Sweet Beulah Bill Elton Britt, 128
Sweet Bird Sid Harkreader, 401; Richard Harold, 402; West Virginia Night Owls, 946
Sweet Birds Prairie Ramblers, 706
Sweet Bunch Of Daisies Cleve Chaffin, 200; Cherry Sisters, 204; Claude Davis, 297; Bob Dunn's Vagabonds, 327; Hill Billies, 423; Humphries Brothers, 447; Fred Lehman, 496; John McGhee & Frank Welling, 561; Clayton McMichen, 565–66, 572; Ruth Neal & Wanda Neal, 652; Charlie [& Bud] Newman, 655–56; Nicholson's Players, 659; Stripling Brothers, 880; Jess Young, 979
Sweet Bunch Of Violets Ernest V. Stoneman, 874
Sweet Bye And Bye Bela Lam, 489; Uncle Dave Macon, 576; Mount Vernon Quartet, 645; George Reneau, 740
Sweet Canaan [J.T.] Allison's Sacred Harp Singers, 60
Sweet Carlyle E.B. Owens, 671

Sweet Cider Time Cliff Carlisle, 164
Sweet Daddy From Tennessee Fleming & Townsend, 347
Sweet Elaine Vernon Dalhart, 277
Sweet Evalina Blue Sky Boys, 113; Shelton Brothers, 827
Sweet Evalina My Gal Perry Bechtel, 98
Sweet Evalina, Dear Evalina Asa Martin, 589
Sweet Evelina Arkansas Woodchopper, 63; Johnnie & Jack, 459; Phil Reeve & Ernest Moody, 735; Shelton Brothers, 828
Sweet Fern Carter Family, 188; A'nt Idy Harper, 402; Red Fox Chasers, 731
Sweet Fiddle Blues Tune Wranglers, 916
Sweet Floetta David Miller, 626
Sweet Floreine Clayton McMichen, 570
Sweet Florine Bert Layne, 493; Asa Martin, 593
Sweet Freedom [E.R.] Nance Family, 648–49
Sweet Genevieve Frank & James McCravy, 534
Sweet Georgia Brown Milton Brown, 137; Leon Chappelear, 201; Jim & Bob, 458; Kelly Brothers, 477; Light Crust Doughboys, 503; Jack Pierce, 695
Sweet Golden Daisies Kentucky Girls, 478
Sweet Happy Home John McGhee & Frank Welling, 557
Sweet Hawaiian Chimes Dezurik Sisters, 316
Sweet Heaven Arthur Smith, 841
Sweet Heaven In My View Carter Family, 194
Sweet Heaven When I Die Grant Brothers, 377
Sweet Hour Of Prayer Lester McFarland & Robert A. Gardner, 544; John McGhee & Frank Welling, 562; Uncle Dave Macon, 576
Sweet Inniscarra Bradley Kincaid, 485
Sweet Jennie Lee Milton Brown, 136
Sweet Kentucky Lou Bill Cox, 226
Sweet Kitty Clyde Skyland Scotty, 837
Sweet Kitty Wells Bradley Kincaid, 482–84
Sweet Lips (Kiss My Blues Away) Al Dexter, 314
Sweet Little Girl In Blue [A] Joe Cook, 220
Sweet Little Girl Of Mine Crowder Brothers, 238; Greensboro Boys Quartet, 382; Macedonia Quartet, 542; Modern Mountaineers, 630
Sweet Little Old Lady Vernon Dalhart, 284; Bob Miller, 616
Sweet Little Someone Ray Whitley, 953
Sweet Locust Blossoms Odus & Woodrow, 667
Sweet Lorene Jimmie Davis, 302
Sweet Magnolia Blossoms Leon Selph, 824
Sweet Magnolia Time In Dixie Lou & Nellie Thompson, 904
Sweet Mama Blues Tune Wranglers, 915
Sweet Mama Hurry Home Rex Griffin, 383
Sweet Mama Hurry Home Or I'll Be Gone Jimmie Rodgers, 808
Sweet Mama Put Him In Low Karl & Harty, 471
Sweet Mama Tree Top Tall Massey Family, 610
Sweet Mamma, Tree Top Tall Tennessee Ramblers [II], 897
Sweet Marie Elmer Bird, 105; Bull Mountain Moonshiners, 142; Frank & James McCravy, 534; Walter Morris, 642; Sidney Smith, 846
Sweet Martha Williams Merritt Smith, 845
Sweet Milk And Peaches W.T. Narmour & S.W. Smith, 649–50
Sweet Morning [J.T.] Allison's Sacred Harp Singers, 60; Lee Wells, 943
Sweet Nannie Lisle Cliff Carlisle, 166
Sweet Nellie Brown Johnson Brothers, 463
Sweet Nora Shannon W.L. "Rustic" Waters, 940
Sweet Old Lady Dwight Butcher, 148
Sweet Pal Bob Miller, 621
Sweet Peace, Gift Of God's Love John McGhee & Frank Welling, 560–61

Sweet Peace, The Gift Of God's Love Frank & James McCravy, 537; Spindale Quartet, 862
Sweet Potato Bill New Dixie Demons, 655
Sweet Prospect [J.T.] Allison's Sacred Harp Singers, 60; OKeh Atlanta Sacred Harp Singers, 667
Sweet Refrain Roy Harvey, 410
Sweet River OKeh Atlanta Sacred Harp Singers, 667
Sweet Rivers [J.T.] Allison's Sacred Harp Singers, 60
Sweet Rose Of Heaven Leake County Revelers, 495; Taylor-Griggs Louisiana Melody Makers, 893
Sweet Rosie O'Grady Hugh Cross, 235; G.B. Grayson & Henry Whitter, 380; Walter C. Peterson, 688; Tin-Can Joe, 910
Sweet Sally Light Crust Doughboys, 506
Sweet Sarah Blues Tom Darby & Jimmie Tarlton, 294
Sweet Silas Stripling Brothers, 880
Sweet Sixteen Charlie Poole, 700
Sweet Sixteen Next Sunday Georgia Organ Grinders, 366
Sweet Someone Rice Brothers' Gang, 746
Sweet Story Of Old [The] Bela Lam, 489
Sweet Sue—Just You Leon Chappelear, 201; Dixie Demons, 318; Hoosier Hot Shots, 437
Sweet Summer Has Gone Away Uncle Eck Dunford, 326
Sweet Sunny South Arkansas Woodchopper, 63; Roy Harvey, 409–10; Red Patterson's Piedmont Log Rollers, 682; Charlie Poole, 700
Sweet Sunny South Take Me Home Posey Rorer, 813
Sweet Talkin' Mama Al Dexter, 315; Hank Penny, 686
Sweet Thing Callahan Brothers, 154; Nite Owls, 660
Sweet Uncle Zeke Wanderers, 938
Sweet Violets Callahan Brothers, 153; Uncle Dave Macon, 576; Earl & Willie Phelps, 689; Prairie Ramblers, 706
Sweet Violets #2 Prairie Ramblers, 706
Sweet Violets No. 3 Prairie Ramblers, 708
Sweet Virginia Carson Robison, 779, 792
Sweet Virginia In Old Virginia Carson Robison, 777
Sweet Will Of God J. Douglas Swagerty, 883
Sweet William Claude Davis, 297; George & Henson, 365; Russell Henson, 418
Sweet William And Fair Ellen—Part 1, 2 Professor & Mrs. Greer, 382–83
Sweet Wimmin' Jimmie Mattox, 613
Sweet, The Memory Of My Mother Paul Crutchfield & John Clotworthy, 239
Sweeter As The Years Go By Carlyle Brooks & Madeline Ward, 132; J. Douglas Swagerty, 883
Sweeter Than All Frank & James McCravy, 537
Sweeter Than An Angel Light Crust Doughboys, 504
Sweetest Flower Elton Britt, 128; East Texas Serenaders, 329
Sweetest Flower Waltz Ashley's Melody Makers, 68; East Texas Serenaders, 329
Sweetest Girl [The] Bill Boyd, 122
Sweetest Girl In All The World Maynard Britton, 131
Sweetest Girl In The World Tune Wranglers, 915
Sweetest Girl In Town Oscar Ford, 352
Sweetest Mother Central Mississippi Quartet, 199; Humbard Family, 447
Sweetest Of All My Dreams Frank Luther, 518
Sweetest Story Ever Told [The] Hoosier Duo, 435; Frank & James McCravy, 533
Sweetest Way Home [The] Ernest V. Stoneman, 878; Fields Ward, 939
Sweetheart Wild Bill Wade, 933
Sweetheart Dance With Me Ernest Thompson, 903
Sweetheart Days McMichen's Harmony Boys, 573
Sweetheart Lane Frank Luther, 521
Sweetheart Of Hawaii Uncle Ned, 919

Sweetheart Of Long Ago Bernard [Slim] Smith, 842
Sweetheart Of Mine Shelly Lee Alley, 59; Lummie Lewis, 500
Sweetheart Of My Childhood Days Wilf Carter (Montana Slim), 181, 183
Sweetheart Of My Dreams Jimmie Tarlton, 892
Sweetheart Of Sigma Chi Milton Brown, 137; Southlanders, 861
Sweetheart Of The Saddle Patsy Montana, 634
Sweetheart Of The Smokies Carl Boling, 116
Sweetheart Of The Valley Jerry Behrens, 98; Jimmie Davis, 305
Sweetheart Of West Texas Jimmie Davis, 302
Sweetheart Of Yesterday John Busby & Gilbert Thomas, 147; Ted Rodgers, 810
Sweetheart Rose Ted Daffan's Texans, 241
Sweetheart This Is Goodbye Adolph Hofner, 431
Sweetheart Wait For Me Rice Brothers' Gang, 746–47
Sweetheart Waltz Moonshiners, 638; Hugh Roden, 797; Shamrock String Band, 825
(Sweetheart) Please Be True To Me Jimmie Davis, 303
Sweetheart, I Have Grown So Lonely Hill Brothers, 424
Sweetheart, Let's Grow Old Together Elton Britt, 129; Jack Pierce, 696
Sweetheart, You're In My Dream Frank[ie] Marvin, 599
Sweethearts And Kisses Bill Cox, 227
Sweetheart's Farewell Wilf Carter (Montana Slim), 186
Sweethearts Forever James Brown, Jr. & Ken Landon Groups, 134; Three Tobacco Tags, 909
Sweethearts Or Strangers Bob Atcher, 70; Gene Autry, 86; Bill Boyd, 125; Jimmie Davis, 305
Sweethearts' Paradise Vagabonds, 922
Sweetheart's Promise [A] W.C. Childers, 206
Sweetie Dear Jules Allen, 55
Swell San Angelo Ernest Tubb, 914
Swing Baby Swing Leon Selph, 823
Swing Blues #1 Bob Wills, 961
Swing Blues #2 Bob Wills, 961
Swing It Drummer Man Bob Skyles, 839
Swing Little Indians Swing Hoosier Hot Shots, 440
Swing Low Sweet Chariot Jenkins Family, 457; Kanawha Singers, 469; Earl & Willie Phelps, 689; Vaughan Quartet, 926
Swing Me Jimmie Revard, 742
Swing Out On The Premises E.M. Bartlett Groups, 96
Swing Steel Swing Bill Boyd, 125
Swing The Door Of Your Heart Open Wide J.E. Mainer's Mountaineers, 582
Swing Time Cowgirl Patsy Montana, 636
Swing Wide Yo' Golden Gate Parker Quartette, 679
Swing With The Music Adolph Hofner, 430–31
Swing Your Partner Four Virginians, 357
Swingin' And Truckin' Crystal Springs Ramblers, 239
Swingin' At The Circle S Swift Jewel Cowboys, 884
Swingin' In Oklahoma Bob Skyles, 838
Swingin' On That New River Train Bill Nettles, 654
Swingin' To Glory Crystal Springs Ramblers, 239
Swingin' With The Accordion Man Bob Skyles, 838
Swinging Down The Lane (I'd Rather Be Rosy Nell) Buster Carter & Preston Young, 180
Swinging Down The Old Orchard Lane Lester McFarland & Robert A. Gardner, 550; Prairie Ramblers, 706
Swinging In The Lane Vernon Dalhart, 288; Roscoe & Samuel Dellinger, 309; Hugh Gibbs String Band, 368; William Rexroat's Cedar Crest Singers, 744
Swinging In The Lane With Nel Walter Smith, 847
Swinging 'Neath The Old Oak Trees Avoca Quartette, 87; Simmons Sacred Singers, 835
Swinging On The Garden Gate Milton Brown, 136

Swinging On The Golden Gate Jimmy Long, 511; Frank & James McCravy, 535–36
Swinging Rhythm Yellow Jackets [II], 977
Swinging With Dora Hoosier Hot Shots, 438
Swinging With Gilbert Claude Casey, 197
Swingsters Lullaby Dixieland Swingsters, 320
Swiss Moonlight Lullaby Wilf Carter (Montana Slim), 181
Swiss Yodel Beverly Hill Billies, 102; Elton Britt, 128
Sycamore Lane Gene Autry, 85
Sydney Allen Vernon Dalhart, 251, 253, 255–56; Henry Whitter, 954
Sylvester Johnson Lee Ernest Thompson, 902
Sympathy Dewey & Gassie Bassett, 97
Symphony Of Calls [A] Rev. J.O. Hanes & Male Choir, 394
Syncopated Swing Leroy [Slim] Johnson, 461

T B Is Whipping Me [The] Ernest Tubb, 913
T For Texas Cliff Carlisle, 161
T.B. Blues Gene Autry, 74–75; Frank[ie] Marvin, 605; Jimmie Rodgers, 804–05
T.B. Blues No. 2 Callahan Brothers, 152
Ta Oblis De Vernier Happy Fats, 396
Tableau Clog Clifford Gross, 385
Tableau Clog Dance Bill Boyd, 124
Taffy-Pulling Party [The] Uncle Eck Dunford, 325
Tail Of Halley's Comet Happy Hayseeds, 397
'Tain't A Fit Night Out For Man Or Beast New Dixie Demons, 655
'Tain't No Lie Uncle Tom Collins, 219
'Tain't No Use Otis & Eleanor, 670
Take A Circle Around The Moon Byrd Moore, 640
Take A Drink On Me Charlie Poole, 699
Take A Look At That Baby Jess Young, 979
Take A 'Tater And Wait E.M. Bartlett Groups, 96; Clarence Ganus, 362; Pete Herring, 418
Take Away This Lonesome Day Delmore Brothers, 310
Take Back The Ring Roy Harvey, 410
Take Back Your Gold Walter Morris, 642
Take Care Of The Farmer John I. White, 950
Take Courage Joseph Falcon, 334
Take Him With You Vaughan Quartet, 925
Take It Slow And Easy Milton Brown, 136; Johnny Marvin, 606; Hank Penny, 686
Take Me As I Am W.T. Narmour & S.W. Smith, 649
Take Me Back Anglin Brothers, 61
Take Me Back Again Bob Atcher, 70; Cliff Bruner, 140; Ted Daffan's Texans, 240; Jimmie Rodgers, 804
Take Me Back Into Your Heart Gene Autry, 86
Take Me Back Little Darling Philyaw Brothers, 690
Take Me Back To Alabama Anglin Brothers, 61
Take Me Back To Col-ler-rad-da Fer To Stay Chuck Wagon Gang, 210; Charlie Craver, 231; Maple City Four, 587; Charlie Marshall, 588
Take Me Back To Colorado Arkansas Woodchopper, 63
Take Me Back To Georgia Lowe Stokes, 870
Take Me Back To Home And Mother Roy Harvey, 410
Take Me Back To My Boots And Saddle Gene Autry, 83; Girls Of The Golden West, 371; Peaceful Valley Folk, 683; Prairie Ramblers, 706; Riley Puckett, 722; Tex Ritter, 750
Take Me Back To My Carolina Home Sid Harkreader, 401; Riley Puckett, 721
Take Me Back To My Dear Old Georgia Home Harmon Canada, 155
Take Me Back To My Home In The Mountains Roy Newman, 658
Take Me Back To My Home On The Plains Buck Nation, 651
Take Me Back To My Old Carolina Home Riley Puckett, 717

Take Me Back To My Old Mountain Home Earl Johnson, 460
Take Me Back To Old Montana Wilf Carter (Montana Slim), 181; Bill Simmons, 835
Take Me Back To Renfro Valley Chuck Wagon Gang, 210; Girls Of The Golden West, 371; Linda Parker, 678; Shelton Brothers, 829
Take Me Back To Tennessee Ramblin' Red Lowery, 515; Arthur Smith, 841
Take Me Back To Texas Leaford Hall, 390
Take Me Back To The Range Delmore Brothers, 310
Take Me Back To The Sweet Sunny South Da Costa Woltz's Southern Broadcasters, 970
Take Me Back To The Valley (Charlie) Monroe's Boys, 632
Take Me Back To Tulsa Bob Wills, 965
Take Me Back To West Texas Leon Selph, 823
Take Me Back To Your Heart Nite Owls, 660
(Take Me Back To) The Wide Open Places Frank Luther, 525
Take Me Home Elton Britt, 129; Lloyd Burdette, 143; Old Settlers, 668
Take Me Home Boys Bob Miller, 624
Take Me Home Boys Tonight Hilltoppers, 427
Take Me Home Boys Tonight (Take Me Home) Crowder Brothers, 237
Take Me Home Little Birdie Bascom Lamar Lunsford, 517
Take Me Home To My Grandma Asa Martin, 592
Take Me Home To My Mother George Edgin, 330
Take Me Home To My Wife Theo. & Gus Clark, 214
Take Me Home To The Sweet Sunny South J.E. Mainer's Mountaineers, 581
Take Me Home, Poor Julia Uncle Dave Macon, 575
Take Me In The Lifeboat J.E. Mainer's Mountaineers, 581
Take Me Out To The Ball Game Hoosier Hot Shots, 437; Dan Hornsby, 442
Take Me To The Land Of Jazz Lowe Stokes, 870
Take The Name Of Jesus With You Peck's Male Quartette, 684; Merritt Smith, 844; J. Douglas Swagerty, 883; Vaughan Quartet, 928
Take The Name Of Jesus With You (The Precious Name) Old Southern Sacred Singers, 669
Take The News To Mother Callahan Brothers, 153
Take The Train To Charlotte Fiddlin' John Carson, 178
Take Them For A Ride David McCarn, 527
Take This Bunch Of Roses James Turner, 917
Take This Letter To My Mother C.A. Cronic, 234; Clyde Meadows, 614; C.W. Parker, 675
Take This Little Bunch Of Roses Wilmer Watts, 941
Take This Message To Mother Dick Hartman's Tennessee Ramblers, 407
Take This Message To My Mother R.C. Garner, 363
Take Those Lips Away Doc Roberts, 753
Take Those Mountains Out Of My Way Peaceful Valley Folk, 683
Take Time To Be Holy Hendersonville Quartet, 416; Holman & Robinson, 432; XC Sacred Quartette, 975
Take Up Thy Cross Blue Sky Boys, 113; Leo Boswell, 119; Lester McFarland & Robert A. Gardner, 550; Chas. Richardson & O.S. Gabehart, 748
Take Your Burden To The Lord Snowball & Sunshine, 853
Take Your Burdens To The Lord Fiddlin' John Carson, 179
Take Your Foot Out Of The Mud McLaughlin's Old Time Melody Makers, 565
Take Your Foot Out Of The Mud And Put It In The Sand Dr. Humphrey Bate, 97
Take Your Girlie To The Movies Johnny Marvin, 606
Take Your Hand Off My Can Prairie Ramblers, 711

Index to Titles 1151

Take Your Pack On Your Back And Go Back To Your Shack (In The Carolinas) Old Settlers, 668
Take Your Time Papa John McGhee & Frank Welling, 562
Takin' It Home Bob Wills, 965
Takin' Off Milton Brown, 137; Modern Mountaineers, 631; Roy Newman, 657
Taking The Census—Part 1, 2 Clayton McMichen, 569
Taking Those Last Steps Bob Miller, 623
Tale Of A Ticker [A] Vernon Dalhart, 289
Talkin' About My Gal Green B. Adair, 51
Talkin' 'Bout You Earl & Willie Phelps, 689
Talkin' Dust Bowl Blues Woody Guthrie, 386
Talking About You Milton Brown, 136
Talking Blues Chris Bouchillon, 119; Harmon Canada, 154; Curley Fox, 357; Bill Gatin, 363; Roy Shaffer, 825
Talking Nigger Blues Herschel Brown, 133
Talking To The River Norwood Tew, 898
Tall And Handsome Comedy Three Tobacco Tags, 907
Tall Mamma Blues Jess Hillard, 426
Tallapoosa Bound John Dilleshaw, 317; A.A. Gray, 378
Tamiami Trail Roy Newman, 657; Pat-Halley-Jardine, 680
Tanner's Boarding House Gid Tanner, 891
Tanner's Hornpipe Gid Tanner, 891
Tanner's Rag Gid Tanner, 891
Tant Que Tu Est Avec Moi (As Long As You're With Me) Jolly Boys Of Lafayette, 464
Tar And Feathers Fisher Hendley, 416
Tariff Bill Song [The] Vernon Dalhart, 289, 291
T'As Vole Mon Chapeau (You Have Stolen My Hat) Amadie Breaux, 126
Taunt Aline (Aunt Aline) Amedie Ardoin, 61
Taxes On The Farmer Feeds Them All Fiddlin' John Carson, 179
Taxi Jim 'Lasses & Honey, 491
Taxicab Driver's Blues Buddy Jones, 466
Taylor's Quickstep John D. Foster, 354
TB Killed My Daddy Julian Johnson & Leon Hyatt, 461
T-Bone Steak John McGhee & Frank Welling, 562
Te A Pas Raison Alley Boys Of Abbeville, 59
Te Bonne Pour Moir Estere Alley Boys Of Abbeville, 59
Te Jolie Te Petite Happy Fats, 396
Te Kaplan (Little Kaplan) Happy Fats, 396
Te Ma Faite Kite Hackberry Ramblers, 387
Te Ma Lessa Jolie Blonde Miller's Merrymakers, 628
Te Ma Pris De La Maison Hackberry Ramblers, 387
Te Petite Et Te Meon Hackberry Ramblers, 387
Tea For Two Light Crust Doughboys, 505
Teach Me To Forget Leon Payne, 683
Teacher's Hair Was Red [The] Three Tobacco Tags, 907–08
Teardrops On My Pillow Leon Selph, 824
Tears Lester McFarland & Robert A. Gardner, 548; Bob Miller, 625
Tears In My Beer Karl & Harty, 471
Tears I've Shed Over You Kelly Brothers, 476–77
Tears On My Pillow Gene Autry, 85; Jimmie Davis, 305; Massey Family, 612
Teasin' Fritz Charlie Poole, 699
Teeny Weeny Jimmy Hart, 406
Telegraph Shack Ernest Branch & Bernice Coleman, 126
Telephone Girl [The] Orville Reed, 734
Telephone To Glory Morris Brothers, 643
Television In The Sky Warren Caplinger, 157
Tell Her Not To Wait For Me Byron Parker, 675
Tell Her To Come Back Home Uncle Dave Macon, 575
Tell Him Now Stamps Quartet, 865
Tell Him To Come Back Sweet Fern (Charlie) Monroe's Boys, 632

Tell It Again Jewell Tillman Burns & Charlie D. Tillman, 146; Bela Lam, 489; Frank & James McCravy, 534
Tell It Everywhere You Go Flat Creek Sacred Singers, 346
Tell It To Me Grant Brothers, 377
Tell It To The World Vaughan Quartet, 928
Tell It With Joy [E.R.] Nance Family, 648
Tell Me Hugh Cross, 235; Herald Goodman, 375; Riley Puckett, 719
Tell Me Before Leo Soileau, 854
Tell Me Dear (Don't You Care) Dickie McBride, 526
Tell Me If You Love Me Leon Selph, 824
Tell Me Little Gal, Ain't I Your Feller? Prairie Ramblers, 713
Tell Me Pretty Mama Crystal Springs Ramblers, 239
Tell Me That You Love Me Carter Family, 190
Tell Me That You Love Me, Dear Carson Robison, 783
Tell Me What's The Matter Now Albert Cain, 150
Tell Me Where My Eva's Gone Uncle Eck Dunford, 326
Tell Me Why Dave Hughs, 446
Tell Me Why Little Girl Tell Me Why Cliff Bruner, 140
Tell Me Why My Daddy Don't Come Home Bill Boyd, 125
Tell Me With Your Blue Eyes Leroy [Slim] Johnson, 462; Shelton Brothers, 830; Sunshine Boys, 881
Tell Me You'll Always Remember Log Cabin Boys, 508
Tell Me, Little Coquette Jimmie Revard, 743
Tell Mother I Will Meet Her Ernest V. Stoneman, 874–75
Tell Mother I'll Be There Roy Acuff, 49; Brown & Bradshaw, 138; Eddie Dean, 307; Carson Robison, 787; Smith's Sacred Singers, 851; Westbrook Conservatory Entertainers, 947; Woodlawn Quartette, 972
Tell Mother I'll Meet Her J.E. Mainer's Mountaineers, 582; Red Fox Chasers, 730
Tell My Baby I'm Gone Fleming & Townsend, 348
Tell My Mother I Will Meet Her Smith's Sacred Singers, 849
Tell My Mother I'll Meet Her Whitey & Hogan, 952
Tell My Mother I'm In Heaven Maple City Four, 587; Bob Miller, 624
Tell You About A Gal Named Sal Jesse Rodgers, 799
Tell Your Mother Goodbye Denus McGee, 551
Telling The Stars About You Roscoe & Samuel Dellinger, 309
Temperance Is Coming Arthur Fields & Fred Hall, 341
Temperance Is Coming (Part I, II) Arthur Fields & Fred Hall, 344
Temperance Reel William B. Houchens, 443
Tempted And Tried Dorsey & Beatrice Dixon, 322
Ten Cent Piece Reaves White County Ramblers, 729
Ten Hours A Day—Six Days A Week Frank Luther, 520
Ten I Served And Ten To Serve Walter Smith, 847
Ten Little Miles Prairie Ramblers, 709
Ten Or Eleven Times Sammy & Smitty, 818; Uncle Ned, 919
Ten Or Twelve Times, Maybe More Bill Carlisle, 160
Ten Pretty Girls Cliff Bruner, 141
Ten Thousand Tomorrows Leon Payne, 683
Ten Tiny Toes Jimmie Davis, 302
Ten Years Charlie Wills, 966
Tend To Your Business Buddy Jones, 465
Tend To Your Knitting Jerry Abbott, 47
Tender Recollections Charles Baker, 89
Tenderfoot [The] Bill Bender, 99; Tex Fletcher, 348
Tennessee (I'm Coming Home) Carson Robison, 770
Tennessee Blues Kenneth Houchins, 443; Bill Monroe, 631; Charlie Poole, 700
Tennessee Breakdown Vance's Tennessee Breakdowners, 922
Tennessee Coon Bachelor Buddies, 87; Georgia Yellow Hammers, 367
Tennessee Coon Hunt Whit Gaydon, 364
Tennessee Fish Fry Massey Family, 612
Tennessee Girls Dykes' Magic City Trio, 328

Tennessee Go-By Gace Haynes & Eugene Ballenger, 414
Tennessee Jail Bird Lester McFarland & Robert A. Gardner, 543, 545
Tennessee Jubilee Uncle Dave Macon, 577
Tennessee Mountain Gal Jack Major, 586
Tennessee Rag Unknown Artists [V], 920
Tennessee Red Fox Chase Uncle Dave Macon, 577
Tennessee River Bottom Blues Mike Shaw, 826
Tennessee Roll Curley Fox, 357
Tennessee Swing Herald Goodman, 375
Tennessee Tess Among The Hills Chezz Chase, 203
Tennessee Tornado Uncle Dave Macon, 578
Tennessee Traveler Tennessee Ramblers [I], 897
Tennessee Wagner Walter Family, 938
Tennessee Wagoner Fiddlin' John Carson, 179
Tennessee Waltz Roane County Ramblers, 751; Paul Warmack, 939
Tennessee Yodel G.E. Lancaster, 490
Tennessee Yodel Man Blues Andrew Jenkins, 455
Tenting Tonight On The Old Camp Ground Mount Vernon Quartet, 645
Tequila Hop Blues W.T. Narmour & S.W. Smith, 650
Tequilla Rag Cliff Bruner, 141
Terrell Texas Blues Oscar & Doc Harper, 402
Terrible Day George [Shortbuckle] Roark, 752
Terrible Marriage [The] Stanley Clements, 215; Otto Gray, 379
Terrible Mississippi Flood [The] Arthur Fields & Fred Hall, 338
Terrible Tupelo Storm [The] Earl & Willie Phelps, 689
T'Est Petite A Ete T'Est Meon (You Are Little And You Are Cute) Dudley & James Fawvor, 337
T'Est Petite Et T'Est Mignonne (You Are Little And You Are Cute) Leo Soileau, 855
Texas Harold & Hazel, 402
Texas Blues Gene Autry, 72–73; Lester "Pete" Bivins, 107; Cliff Carlisle, 161; Rosa Lee Carson, 179; Howard Keesee, 475
Texas Bound Rosa Lee Carson, 180
Texas Breakdown Light Crust Doughboys, 501; W.T. Narmour & S.W. Smith, 649
Texas Centennial March Light Crust Doughboys, 502
Texas Centennial Waltz Light Crust Doughboys, 501
Texas Cowboy [The] Jules Allen, 54; David Gauthier, 364; Hank Snow, 853
Texas Dan Carson Robison, 794–95
Texas Drifter's Warning [The] Goebel Reeves, 735–36
Texas Duster Wiley Walker & Gene Sullivan, 936
Texas Fair Leake County Revelers, 495
Texas Farewell Fiddlin' Jim Pate, 680
Texas Gals Hill Billies, 423
Texas Girl Carter Family, 192
Texas Hambone Blues Milton Brown, 137
Texas Home Everett Morgan, 642; Saddle Tramps, 818
Texas Hop Ted Hawkins, 413
Texas Kickin' Maud Leake County Revelers, 494
Texas Moon Girls Of The Golden West, 371
Texas Plains Gene Autry, 80; Leon Chappelear, 201; Stuart Hamblen, 393; Light Crust Doughboys, 502; Prairie Ramblers, 704
Texas Possum Trot W.B. Chenoweth, 203
Texas Quickstep Red Headed Fiddler[s], 732
Texas Rag Elton Britt, 127
Texas Ranger [The] Cartwright Brothers, 196; Lester McFarland & Robert A. Gardner, 543; Macon String Trio, 579; Bobbie & Ruby Ricker, 748; Ernest V. Stoneman, 872, 878
Texas Rangers [The] Harry "Mac" McClintock, 528

Texas Sand Leroy [Slim] Johnson, 461; Tune Wranglers, 915
Texas Shuffle W.T. Narmour & S.W. Smith, 650
Texas Song (A Cowboy Lament) [The] Texas Jim Robertson, 760
Texas Song Of Pride Light Crust Doughboys, 505
Texas Star Chuck Wagon Gang, 210; Port Arthur Jubileers, 701; Sons Of The Pioneers, 857
Texas Star (Dedicated To The Texas Centennial) Massey Family, 610
Texas Stomp Roy Newman, 658
Texas Take Off Leon Selph, 824
Texas Trail [The] Charlie Craver, 230; Sain Family, 818; Jack Weston, 947
Texas Wagoner A.C. (Eck) Robertson, 757
Texas Waltz Cottle Brothers, 223; Red Headed Fiddler[s], 732
Tex's Dance Prairie Ramblers, 704
Thank God For Everything Uncle Dave Macon, 578
Thank You Mr. Moon W. Lee O'Daniel, 666; Ross Rhythm Rascals, 814
Thankful And Thankful Again Shelton Brothers, 829
That Bad Man Stacklee David Miller, 626
That Beautiful Home Murphy Sacred Singers, 646
That Beautiful Land Hendersonville Quartet, 416; Frank & James McCravy, 537; McDonald Quartet, 540; Sparkman Trio, 861; Vaughan Quartet, 929
That Beautiful Picture Roy Acuff, 49
That Big Rock-Candy Mountain Carson Robison, 768
That Brownskin Gal Bob Wills, 964
That City For Shut-Ins Light Crust Doughboys, 501
That City Of Rest Riley Cole Quartet, 217
That Crazy War Lulu Belle & Scotty, 516
That First Love Of Mine Wilf Carter (Montana Slim), 186
That Funny Old World Goes Rolling Along Arthur Fields & Fred Hall, 344
That Goes On For Days And Days Arthur Fields & Fred Hall, 342, 344
That Goes On For Days And Days Pt 1, 2 Arthur Fields & Fred Hall, 344
That Golden Love (My Mother Gave To Me) Shelton Brothers, 828; Walton West, 946
That Good Old Country Town Vernon Dalhart, 277; Ovie Stewart & Zelpha Sparks, 869
That Good Old Country Town (Where I Was Born) Kanawha Singers, 469
That Good Old Time Religion Is A Million Miles Ahead E. Arthur Lewis, 498
That Good Old Utah Trail Fred Kirby, 486
That Great Judgment Day (Is Coming To All) Cliff Carlisle, 167
That Green Back Dollar Bill Ray Whitley, 952
That Heavenly Home Matt Simmons & Frank Miller, 835
That High Born Gal Of Mine Uncle Dave Macon, 574
That Honky-Tonky Rhythm Adolph Hofner, 430
That Hot Lick Fiddlin' Man Charlie Wills, 966
That Is All I Need To Know Carolina Ladies Quartet, 171
That Kind Wade Mainer, 584
That Little Bit Of Company Simerly Trio, 834
That Little Black Mustache Oscar L. Coffey, 217; Jack Golding, 375
That Little Boy Of Mine Bar-X Cowboys, 92; W.C. Childers, 206; Eddie Dean, 308; Deckers, 309; Fred L. Jeske, 458; [Smilin'] Ed McConnell, 530–31; Lester McFarland & Robert A. Gardner, 549; Asa Martin, 591; Vagabonds, 921; Yellow Jackets [II], 977
That Little Girl Of Mine Julian Johnson & Leon Hyatt, 461
That Little Kid Sister Of Mine Gene Autry, 85; Jimmy Wakely, 934
That Little Old Hut Jenkins Family, 457; Knippers Bros. &

Parker, 488; Matt Simmons & Frank Miller, 835; Vaughan Quartet, 924
That Little Old Hut Was A Mansion To Me W.C. Childers, 205
That Little Old Shirt That Mother Made For Me Red Headed Brier Hopper, 732
That Little Shack I Call My Home Sweet Home Dixie Ramblers [III], 319
That Little Shirt My Mother Made For Me Johnny Barfield, 94
That Little Texas Town Tune Wranglers, 915
That Little Town Adolph Hofner, 430
That Lonesome Train Fleming & Townsend, 347
That Lonesome Valley Carolina Ramblers String Band, 173; Jenkins Family, 456
That Makes Me Give In Bill Boyd, 122
That Mother And Daddy Of Mine Gene Autry, 78; Don Weston, 947
That Nasty Swing Cliff Carlisle, 166
That Old Brown Derby Charlie Craver, 231
That Old Covered Bridge Dick Parman, 679
That Old Faded Rose Vernon Dalhart, 292
That Old Fashioned Cabin Matt Simmons & Frank Miller, 835
That Old Fashioned Photograph Buckeye Boys, 141
That Old Fashioned Way W. Lee O'Daniel, 666; Leon Selph, 823
That Old Feather Bed On The Farm Gene Autry, 79; Tom & Roy, 911; Don Weston, 947
That Old Go Hungry Hash House Where We Board Charlie Craver, 231
That Old Home Town Of Mine (Is Still Alive) Prairie Ramblers, 705
That Old Irish Mother Of Mine Riley Puckett, 718, 722
That Old Rockin' Chair Carl Boling, 116
That Old Sweetheart Of Mine Leon Chappelear, 201; Frank Gerald & Howard Dixon, 368; Jack Golding, 374
That Old Swiss Chalet In The Rockies Carson Robison, 794–95
That Old Tiger Rag Byrd Moore, 638
That Old True Love Dorsey & Beatrice Dixon, 321
That Old Vacant Chair Dorsey & Beatrice Dixon, 321
That Old Wooden Rocker Vernon Dalhart, 276; Zora Layman, 492
That Old, Old Story Jenkins Family, 456
That Pioneer Mother Of Mine Roy Rogers, 811
That Ramshackle Shack Gene Autry, 77; Bill Boyd, 122
That Same Old Story Ernest Tubb, 914
That Saxophone Waltz Riley Puckett, 720
That Silver Haired Daddy Of Mine Girls Of The Golden West, 370; Log Cabin Boys, 508; Jimmy Long, 511; Frank Luther, 521; Frank & James McCravy, 538; Lester McFarland & Robert A. Gardner, 549; Dick Robertson, 758; Carson Robison, 791
That Silver-Haired Mother Dwight Butcher, 148; Light Crust Doughboys, 501
That Sweetie Of Mine Red Fox Chasers, 731
That Three Point Two Blue Ridge Hill Billies, 110
That Tumbled Down Cabin Asher Sizemore & Little Jimmie, 836
That Tumbledown Shack By The Trail Wilf Carter (Montana Slim), 183
That Tumble-Down Shack In Athlone Bradley Kincaid, 485
That Wabash Rag Four Pickled Peppers, 356
That Will Be A Happy Moment [E.R.] Nance Family, 648
That Woman Don't Treat John Right Fiddlin' John Carson, 178
That Wonderful Day Carolina Quartette, 172

That Yodelin' Gal—Miss Julie Delmore Brothers, 310
That Yodeling Gal Of Mine Kenneth Houchins, 443–44
That'll Do Now, That'll Do Herald Goodman, 375
That'll Make A Change In Business Jess Hillard, 426
That's A Habit I Never Had "Peg" Moreland, 641
That's A Habit I've Never Had Shelton Brothers, 828
That's A Plenty John McGhee & Frank Welling, 558
That's All I Want To Know Tom Dickey Show Boys, 316
That's All There Is Bob Skyles, 839
That's Bad Sunshine Boys, 882
That's Bound To Be Kentucky Carson Robison, 794
That's Home Sweet Home To Me Asa Martin, 589
That's How Donkey's [sic] Were Born Smiley Burnette, 145
That's How I Feel, So Goodbye Delmore Brothers, 311
That's How I Got My Start Gene Autry, 73–75
That's How I Need You John McGhee & Frank Welling, 561
That's My Blue Heaven George E. Harris, 404
That's My Gal Jimmie Revard, 742
That's My Paradise Hugh Cross, 237
That's My Rabbit—My Dog Caught It Walter Family, 938
That's My Way Of Loving You Tune Wranglers, 915
That's No Business Of Mine Clayton McMichen, 570; Riley Puckett, 720
That's No Way To Treat The Man You Love Shelton Brothers, 829
That's Right I Betcha Bob Skyles, 839
That's The Blue Heaven For Me George E. Harris, 405
That's The Good Old Sunny South Ezra Buzzington's Rustic Revelers, 150
That's The Love I Have For You Arthur Smith, 842
That's The Way With A Broken Heart Whitey & Hogan, 952
That's What I Learned In College Hoosier Hot Shots, 437
That's What I Like 'Bout The South Bob Wills, 964
That's What Ruined Me E.M. Bartlett Groups, 96
That's What The Old Bachelor's Made Of Taylor's Kentucky Boys, 895
That's When It's Comin' Home To You Ernest Tubb, 914
That's When You Broke My Heart Burns Brothers, 146
That's When You Take The Blues Fleming & Townsend, 348
That's Where I Met My Girl Hoosier Hot Shots, 440
That's Where My Money Goes Uncle Dave Macon, 577
That's Where The West Begins Patsy Montana, 636
That's Why I Left The Mountain Gene Autry, 71
That's Why I Left The Mountains Gene Autry, 72; Arthur Fields & Fred Hall, 345; Jimmy Long, 511
That's Why I Love Him So Jack Pickell, 694
That's Why I Sigh And Cry Hi-Flyers, 419
That's Why I Waited So Long Zeke Manners, 586
That's Why I'm All Alone Bill Bruner, 139
That's Why I'm Blue Gene Autry, 72–73; Cliff Carlisle, 161; Byron Parker, 675; Jimmie Rodgers, 803
That's Why I'm Jealous Of You Bill Boyd, 123; Ross Rhythm Rascals, 814; Shelton Brothers, 829
That's Why I'm Nobody's Darling Gene Autry, 82; Jimmie Davis, 302
That's Why The Boys Leave The Farm Alfred G. Karnes, 472
That's Why We Got Reno Now Three Tobacco Tags, 907
That's Why We've Got Reno Now Three Tobacco Tags, 907
Them Golden Slippers Vernon Dalhart, 282
Them Good Old Times Bob Miller, 622
Them Good Old Times (Are Comin' Back Again) Ernest Hare, 399–400
Them Hill-Billies Are Mountain-Williams Now Hoosier Hot Shots, 436
Them Old Hitch Hiking Blues Kenneth Houchins, 443
Them Thirty Nines Of Mine Rector Trio, 729
Them Two Gals Of Mine Uncle Dave Macon, 575

Theme Song, etc. *[sic]* Light Crust Doughboys, 504
Then Honey I Will Come Back To You Edward Carson, 175
Then I Got Drunk Again John McGhee & Frank Welling, 558
Then I'll Move To Town Southern Moonlight Entertainers, 860
Then My Love Began To Wane Elry Cash, 197
Then The World Began Charlie Craver, 232
There Ain't Gonna Be No Afterwhile Jimmie Davis, 300
There Ain't Gonna Be No Me (To Welcome You) Lew Preston, 713; Jimmy Wakely, 934
There Ain't No Flies On Auntie Akins Birmingham Boys, 52
There Ain't No Flies On Me Patrick (Dak) Pellerin, 685
There Ain't No Use In Crying Modern Mountaineers, 631; Jimmy Wakely, 934
There Ain't No Use In Crying Now Gene Autry, 85
There Ain't No Use Workin' So Hard Carolina Tar Heels, 173
There Are Just Two 'I's In Dixie Bob Miller, 625
There Are Just Two I's In Dixie Hoosier Hot Shots, 439
There Are Just Two I's In Dixie (Two Blue Eyes That Mean The World To Me) Jake & Carl, 453
There Are No Disappointments In Heaven Smith's Carolina Crackerjacks, 848
There Are Two Sides To Every Story Bob Wills, 962
There Is A Fountain Old Southern Sacred Singers, 669
There Is A Fountain Filled With Blood Copperhill Male Quartet, 222; Giddens Sisters, 369; John McGhee & Frank Welling, 553, 562; Smith's Sacred Singers, 850
There Is A Name Riley Quartette, 749
There Is A New Name Written Down In Glory Leslie Hughes, 446
There Is A Tavern In The Town Bar-X Cowboys, 92; Bob Wills, 962
There Is A Vacant Chair At Home For You John McGhee & Frank Welling, 558
There Is Glory in My Soul Highleys, 421
There Is Joy E.F. "Pat" Alexander, 53
There Is No Disappointment In Heaven XC Sacred Quartette, 975
There Is No More That I Can Say Carlisle Brothers, 169
There Is No Place Like Home For A Married Man Asa Martin, 588
There Is Power In The Blood Tiny Dodson's Circle-B Boys, 322; John McGhee & Frank Welling, 554, 561; Peck's Male Quartette, 684
There Is Somebody Waiting For Me Duke Clark, 213
There Is Springtime In My Soul Stamps Quartet, 865
There Is Sunshine In My Soul John McGhee & Frank Welling, 553, 560
There Is Sunshine In My Soul Today John McGhee & Frank Welling, 561; Peck's Male Quartette, 684
There Must Be A Bright Tomorrow Carson Robison, 788
There Must Be A Bright Tomorrow (For Each Yesterday Of Tears) Lester McFarland & Robert A. Gardner, 550; Carson Robison, 788–89
There Must Be Someone For Me Floyd Tillman, 910
There Shall Be Showers Of Blessing Eddie Dean, 307; Jenkins Family, 456
There Was A Time Blue Sky Boys, 114; Denver Darling, 296
There Was An Old Tramp Henry Whitter, 955
There Was No One To Welcome Me Home Mrs. Dennis Taylor, 893
There We'll Spend Eternity Clarence Ganus, 362
There Will Be A Bright Tomorrow Carson Brothers-Smith, 180
There Will Come A Time Blue Ridge Mountain Entertainers, 110

There, Our Love Won't End This Way Philyaw Brothers, 690; Three Tobacco Tags, 907
There'll Always Be A Maple On The Hill Shelton Brothers, 830
There'll Be A Change In Business Roy Harvey, 411
There'll Be A Day Bob Atcher, 70
There'll Be A Hot Time In The Old Town To-Night Gid Tanner, 890
There'll Be Joy, Joy, Joy Carter Family, 192
There'll Be No Blues Up Yonder Wilf Carter (Montana Slim), 183
There'll Be No Distinction There Carter Family, 195; Blind Alfred Reed, 733
There'll Be No Graveyard There Matt Simmons & Frank Miller, 835
There'll Be No Kisses To-night Ashley's Melody Makers, 68
There'll Be No Liars There Hickory Nuts, 420
There'll Be No Sorrow There J. Douglas Swagerty, 883
There'll Be One More Fool In Paradise Vernon Dalhart, 289
There'll Be One More Fool In Paradise Tonight Vernon Dalhart, 289
There'll Be Some Changes Made Milton Brown, 138; Hoosier Hot Shots, 440; Roy Newman, 657; Nite Owls, 660; W. Lee O'Daniel, 666; Ocie Stockard, 869
There'll Come A Day Massey Family, 613
There'll Come A Time Blue Sky Boys, 113; Carlisle Brothers, 169; Al Dexter, 315; Hackberry Ramblers, 388; Roy Harvey, 410; Jolly Boys Of Lafayette, 464; Karl & Harty, 470; David Miller, 626; Charlie Poole, 699; Ernest V. Stoneman, 877
There'll Never Be Another Pal Like You Gene Autry, 85
There's A Beautiful City Called Heaven Virginia Dandies, 932
There's A Beautiful Home Karl & Harty, 470; Tennessee Ramblers [II], 897
There's A Blue Sky Out Yonder Arthur Fields & Fred Hall, 342
There's A Blue Sky Over Yonder Hugh Cross, 237
There's A Blue Sky Way Out Yonder Saddle Tramps, 817; Tennessee Ramblers [II], 897
There's A Bridge O'er The River Vaughan Quartet, 926
There's A Bridge Over The River Beard's Quartette, 98
There's A Bridle Hangin' On The Wall Judie & Julie, 468; Prairie Ramblers, 709; Carson Robison, 795
There's A Brown Skin Girl Down The Road Somewhere A.C. (Eck) Robertson, 757
There's A Cabin In The Pines Cliff Carlisle, 165
There's A Chill On The Hill Tonight Jimmie Davis, 304
There's A Girl In The Heart Of Maryland John McGhee & Frank Welling, 561
There's A Gold Mine In The Sky Gene Autry, 83; Jimmie Davis, 303
There's A Good Gal In The Mountains Gene Autry, 74; Kenneth Houchins, 443
There's A Good Girl In The Mountains Gene Autry, 76
There's A Grave In The Wilderness Dewey & Gassie Bassett, 97
There's A Great Day Coming John McGhee & Frank Welling, 563
There's A Green Hill Far Away J.E. Mainer's Mountaineers, 582
There's A Guiding Star John McGhee & Frank Welling, 557
There's A Hard Time Coming Fiddlin' John Carson, 176; Riley Puckett, 720
There's A Heart In The Heart Of The Rockies Texas Jim Robertson, 759
There's A Hole In The Old Oaken Bucket Carson Robison, 796
There's A Home In Wyomin' Elton Britt, 128; James Brown,

Jr. & Ken Landon Groups, 135; Ranch Boys, 727; Dick Robertson, 759
There's A Joy In Righteous Living Emry Arthur, 65
There's A Lamp In The Window Tonight Cliff Carlisle, 167
[There's A Land Beyond The Starlight] Paul Crutchfield & John Clotworthy, 239
There's A Light Lit Up In Galilee Ernest V. Stoneman, 877
There's A Light Shining Bright Bill Boyd, 124
There's A Little Box Of Pine On The 7:29 Bingham & Wells, 104; Asa Martin, 592
There's A little Faded Flower Lou & Nellie Thompson, 904
There's A Little Gray Mother Dreaming Light Crust Doughboys, 502
There's A Little Green Mill (By A Little Green Hill) Hi-Flyers, 419
There's A Little Grey Mother Dreaming Jim & Bob, 458
There's A Little Old Lady Waiting Gene Autry, 79–80
There's A Little Pine Log Cabin Lulu Belle & Scotty, 516; Stamps Quartet, 865
There's A Little Rosewood Casket Sid Harkreader, 400
There's A Lonesome Road Delmore Brothers, 311
There's A Long, Long Trail Sons Of The Pioneers, 859
There's A Love-Knot In My Lariat Wilf Carter (Montana Slim), 184; Texas Jim Lewis, 499
There's A Man Goin' Around Takin' Names Carolina Tar Heels, 173
There's A Man Goin' 'Round Takin' Names G.B. Grayson & Henry Whitter, 381
There's A Man That Comes To Our House (Every Single Day) Prairie Ramblers, 708–09
There's A Moon Shinin' Bright On The Prairie Tonight Carson Robison, 796
There's A Mother Always Waiting Blue Ridge Mountain Girls, 112; W.C. Childers, 205
There's A Mother Always Waiting You At Home Pine Ridge Boys, 697
There's A Mother Always Waiting You At Home Sweet Home Charles Nabell, 647
There's A Mother Old And Gray Hugh Cross, 236; Roy Harvey, 411
There's A Mother Old And Gray Who Needs Me Now Roy Harvey, 410; Jack & Leslie, 451; Edd Rice, 744; Virginia Dandies, 932
There's A Mouse Been Messin' Around Bill Carlisle, 159
There's A New Star In Heaven Tonight—Rudolph Valentino Vernon Dalhart, 260
There's A New Star In Heaven Tonight (Rudolph Valentino) Vernon Dalhart, 260
There's A New Star In Heaven To-night Rudolph Valentino Vernon Dalhart, 259
There's A New Star Up In Heaven (Baby Lindy Is Up There) Bob Miller, 621
There's A Palace Down In Dallas Adolph Hofner, 431
There's A Picture In My Heart Jimmie Revard, 743
There's A Picture On Pinto's Bridle Hank Snow, 853
There's A Picture On The Easel In The Parlor Frank Luther, 524
There's A Place In My Home For Mother Frank Gerald & Howard Dixon, 368
There's A Quaker Down In Quaker Town Bob Wills, 961
There's A Rainbow Shining Somewhere Carson Robison, 786
There's A Ranch In The Rockies Jimmie Davis, 303; Carson Robison, 796; Roy Rogers, 811
There's A Ranch In The Sky Patsy Montana, 635
There's A Reason Why I Love You More Carrie Mae Moore-Faye Barres, 640
There's A Roundup In The Sky Sons Of The Pioneers, 857

There's A Silver Moon On The Golden Gate Girls Of The Golden West, 371; Roy Newman, 657
There's A Spark Of Love Still Burning John McGhee & Frank Welling, 553
There's A Spark Of Love Still Burning (In The Embers Of My Heart) Vernon Dalhart, 264
There's A Star In The Heavens Adolph Hofner, 431
There's A Star Spangled Banner Waving Somewhere Elton Britt, 130; Arthur Fields & Fred Hall, 345; Jimmy Wakely, 934
There's A Tavern In The Town Hoosier Hot Shots, 440
There's A Trail That's Winding Morris Brothers, 643
There's A Treasure Up In Heaven Emry Arthur, 66
There's A Vacant Chair At Home Sweet Home John McGhee & Frank Welling, 559
There's A Warm Spot In My Heart For Tennessee Moore Sisters, 641
There's A Whippoorwill A Calling Vernon Dalhart, 280; Carson Robison, 762–63
There's Always A Welcome At Home Four Aces, 356
There's Always Somebody Else Wiley Walker & Gene Sullivan, 936
There's An Empty Cot In The Bunkhouse Tonight Gene Autry, 79; Girls Of The Golden West, 371; Light Crust Doughboys, 502; Massey Family, 608; Don Weston, 947
There's An Old Easy Chair By The Fireplace Frank Luther, 524
There's An Old Family Album In The Parlor Eddie Dean, 308
There's An Old Fashioned House On A Hillside Jimmie Davis, 305
There's An Old Fashioned Lamp (Beside A Window) Three Tobacco Tags, 908
There's Another One Waiting Hi-Flyers, 419
There's Evil In Ye Children W. Lee O'Daniel, 666
There's Evil In Ye Children, Gather 'Round Jimmie Davis, 300
There's Evil In You Chillun Sons Of The West, 859
There's Evil In Your Children Jess Hillard, 425
There's Glory In My Soul John McGhee & Frank Welling, 556
There's Glory On The Winning Side Rev. M.L. Thrasher, 905
There's Going To Be A Party (For The Old Folks) Bob Wills, 964
There's Gold In Them Thar Hills Frank[ie] Marvin, 605
There's Gonna Be No Me To Welcome You Ross Rhythm Rascals, 814
There's Gonna Be No Me To Welcome You Home Smoky Wood, 971
There's Just One Way To The Pearly Gates Uncle Dave Macon, 578
There's More Good Woman [sic.] Gone Wrong Bill Cox, 227
There's More Pretty Girls Than One George Edgin, 330; John D. Foster, 354; Prairie Ramblers, 707
There's More Pretty Girls Than One—Part 1, 2 Riley Puckett, 721; Arthur Smith, 841
There's More Purty Gals Than One John D. Foster, 353
There's No Disappointment In Heaven Eddie Dean, 307; Gentry Brothers, 365; Light Crust Doughboys, 502; Lester McFarland & Robert A. Gardner, 542; Peck's Male Quartette, 684; Prairie Ramblers, 707; Bob Wills, 961
There's No Friend Like Jesus Eddie Dean, 307
There's No Hell In Georgia Luke Highnight, 422
There's No Hiding Place Down Here Carter Family, 192
There's No Hiding Place Down There Lulu Belle & Scotty, 516

There's No Light In The Window (Of The House On The Hill) Lester McFarland & Robert A. Gardner, 549
There's No One Like Mother To Me Carter Family, 194; Lester McFarland & Robert A. Gardner, 545
There's No One Like The Old Folks John D. Foster, 354
There's No Other Friend Like Mother Philyaw Brothers, 690
There's No Other Love For Me Blue Sky Boys, 114
There's No Place For The Devil In My Home Prairie Ramblers, 712
There's No Place Like Home Earl Johnson, 460; Asa Martin, 591
There's No Use Denying (A Woman's As Good As A Man) Dutch Coleman, 218
There's No Use In Loving You Al Dexter, 315
There's No Use To Worry Now Bill Nettles, 654
(There's No Use) Knocking On The Blinds Merle McGinnis, 564
There's No-One To Care For Me Smith Brothers, 848
There's Not A Friend Canova Family, 155
There's Nothing More To Say Ernest Tubb, 914
There's One Born Every Minute Vernon Dalhart, 245
There's Only One Love In A Lifetime Gene Autry, 84
There's Room In My Album For Your Picture Charles Lewis Stine, 869; Billy Vest, 931
There's So Much That I Forgot Elton Britt, 130
There's Somebody Waiting For Me Lester McFarland & Robert A. Gardner, 547; Ernest V. Stoneman, 878
There's Someone Awaiting For Me Carter Family, 189
There's Someone Waiting For You Asa Martin, 591
There's Something Nice About Everyone Jess Young, 979
There's Sunshine In My Soul Clagg & Sliger, 212
There's Sunshine In My Soul Today Kanawha Singers, 469
There's Trouble On My Mind Today Delmore Brothers, 311
These Bones Gonna Rise Again John McGhee & Frank Welling, 555
These Bones G'wina Rise Again Frank & James McCravy, 531
These Bones Gwine Rise Again John D. Foster, 354
They All Got A Wife But Me Ernest Branch & Bernice Coleman, 126
They Always Pick On Me Harvey Irwin, 451
They Are All Going Home But One Anglin Brothers, 61; Karl & Harty, 470
They Are Calling Me Over The Tide Highleys, 421
They Are Wild Over Me Wesley Long, 513
They Call Her Hula Lou Duke Clark, 213
They Call Her Mother Carter Family, 195
They Can Only Fill One Grave Roy Acuff, 51
They Can't Fool Me Anymore Kelly & Howard Sears, 823
They Can't Shoot Me In The Morning Prairie Ramblers, 711
They Crucified My Savior Eva Quartette, 333
They Cut Down The Old Pine Tree Gene Autry, 72; Arthur Fields & Fred Hall, 341; Hart & Ogle, 406; Frank Luther, 522; Frank[ie] Marvin, 604; Paul Mason, 608; Ranch Boys, 726; Rice Brothers' Gang, 746; Dick Robertson, 758; Carson Robison, 781; Tune Wranglers, 915
They Don't Roost Too High For Me Earl Johnson, 460
They Drew My Number (Goodbye My Darling) Lunsford Bros., 517
They Fit And Fit And Fit Skyland Scotty, 837
They Go Googoo, Gaga, Goofy Over Gobs Bill Boyd, 124; Hoosier Hot Shots, 440
They Go Wild Over Me Tune Wranglers, 914
They Go Wild Simply Wild Over Me Hoosier Hot Shots, 436; Leake County Revelers, 494; New Dixie Demons, 655
They Left Him Alone Vaughan Quartet, 924
They Made It Twice As Nice As Paradise Connie Sides, 834
They Said My Lord Was A Devil Wade Mainer, 583

They Said My Lord's The Devil Zeke & George Morris, 643
They Say It Is Sinful To Flirt Delmore Brothers, 310; Asher Sizemore & Little Jimmie, 836
They Say It's The End Of The Trail Old Paint Cliff Carlisle, 166
They Tell Me Love's A Pleasure Grover Rann, 728
They Took The Stars Out Of Heaven Floyd Tillman, 910
They're After Me Uncle Dave Macon, 578
They're All Home But One Blue Sky Boys, 113
They're All Just The Same To Me Hank Penny, 686
They're At Rest Together Callahan Brothers, 154
They're Burning Down The House I Was Brung Up In Elton Britt, 130; Prairie Ramblers, 708, 710
They're Hanging Old Jonesy Tomorrow Bob Miller, 619–20, 623
They're Off New Dixie Demons, 655
They're Positively Wrong Elton Britt, 130
They've All Got A Wife But Me John D. Foster, 354
Things I Don't Like To See Uncle Dave Macon, 578
Things That Might Have Been Roy Acuff, 50; Al Dexter, 315; Bob Miller, 622; Red River Dave, 732; Texas Jim Robertson, 759
Things We Used To Do [The] Simerly Trio, 834
Think A Little George Wade, 933
Think It Over Nite Owls, 660
Think Of Me J.B. Fuslier, 361; Walter Hurdt, 448; Roy Rogers, 812
Think Of Me Thinking Of You Blue Ridge Hill Billies, 110; Jimmie Davis, 298
Think Of Mother James Scott-Claude Boone, 821
Think Of Mother All The Time Pie Plant Pete, 695
Thinking Wilf Carter (Montana Slim), 186; Jimmie Revard, 742
Thinking Of The Days I Did Wrong Claude Davis, 297
Thinking Of The Days I've Done Wrong Claude Davis, 296
Thinking Of You Light Crust Doughboys, 505; Sons Of The West, 859
Thinking Only Of You Lunsford Bros., 517
Thinking Tonight Of My Sweetheart Otis & Tom Mote, 644
Third Of July [The] Red Brush Rowdies, 730
Third Party Gatwood Square Dance Band, 364
Thirteen More Steps Deckers, 309; Patt Patterson, 682
Thirteen Steps Four Pickled Peppers, 356
Thirty Three Years In Prison Tex Ritter, 750
Thirty Years Luther Higginbotham, 421
Thirty-First Street Blues Leake County Revelers, 495; Light Crust Doughboys, 502; Bob Wills, 962
This Crazy Thing Tom Dickey Show Boys, 316
This Evening Light Blue Sky Boys, 114
This Is God's Will E. Arthur Lewis, 498
This Is Like Heaven To Me Blue Sky Boys, 114; Carter Family, 191
This Is The Chorus Hoosier Hot Shots, 436
This Is The Reason Rev. M.L. Thrasher, 905
This Life Is Hard To Understand Light Crust Doughboys, 507
This Little Rosary Charlie Wills, 966
This Means Our Last Goodbye Pine Ridge Boys, 697
This Morning—This Evening So Soon Clarence Ganus, 362
This Morning, This Evening, So Soon Milton Brown, 136
This Night Is Mine Dickie McBride, 526
This Old Dirty Jail Edith & Sherman Collins, 218
This Train Lulu Belle & Scotty, 516
This World Is Not My Home Kentucky Thorobreds, 479; John McGhee & Frank Welling, 563; J.E. Mainer's Mountaineers, 581; Monroe Brothers, 632; Prairie Ramblers, 705
This World Of Sorrow Panhandle Pete, 674

Thomas E. Watson Vernon Dalhart, 253–55
Thomastown [sic] Breakdown Bill Helms, 415
Thompson's Old Gray Mule Buckeye Boys, 141; Pickard Family, 692–93
Those Blue Eyes Don't Sparkle Anymore Ted Daffan's Texans, 241; Sons Of Dixie, 856
Those Campaign Lyin' Sugar Coated Ballot-Coaxin' Farm Relief Blues Bob Miller, 617
Those Dark Eyes [Blind] Jack Mathis, 613
Those Dark Eyes I Love So Well Fay & The Jay Walkers, 337
Those Dusty Roads Shelton Brothers, 829
Those Eyes Of Grey Bob Atcher, 69
Those Gambler's Blues Frank[ie] Marvin, 604; Jimmie Rodgers, 804
Those Gone And Left Me Blues Johnny Bond, 116
Those Loving Lies Shelly Lee Alley, 58
Those Mean Mama Blues Lummie Lewis, 500
Those Memories Break My Heart Philyaw Brothers, 690
Those Old Time Days Georgia Peaches, 366
Those Out Of Town Girls George Edgin, 330
Those Rambling Blues Steelman Sisters, 867
Those Things I Can't Forget Texas Wanderers, 900
Those Were The Very Last Words He Said Arthur Fields & Fred Hall, 342, 345
Thou Art Gone Murphy Sacred Singers, 646
Thou Art My Strength Stamps Quartet, 864
Though We Never Meet Again Massey Family, 612
Though Your Sins Be As Scarlet Maury Pearson, 683; Trenton Melody Makers, 913; Williams & Williams, 960
Though You're Not Satisfied With Me Riley Puckett, 722
Thousand Good Nights [A] Milton Brown, 138
Thousand Mile Blues Bill Boyd, 121; Light Crust Doughboys, 505
Thousand Miles Wanderers, 938
Thousand Miles From Texas [A] Vance Knowles-Red Lay, 488
Three Babes [The] Professor & Mrs. Greer, 383
Three Black Sheep Howard-Peak, 445
Three Blind Mice Dan Hornsby, 442
Three Days After My Death Leo Soileau, 854
Three Drowned Sisters [The] Vernon Dalhart, 264–65, 271
Three Forks Of Kentucky River Fiddlin' Powers & Family, 703
Three Forks Of Sandy Kessinger Brothers, 480
Three In One Two-Step East Texas Serenaders, 329
Three Leaves Of Shamrock Roy Harvey, 410; Lester McFarland & Robert A. Gardner, 543
Three Little Fishes Hoosier Hot Shots, 439
Three Men Went A Hunting Byrd Moore, 639
Three Naughty Kittens Light Crust Doughboys, 505
Three Night's [sic] Experience Gid Tanner, 888
Three Nights Drunk Gid Tanner, 891
Three Nights Experience John B. Evans, 333; Earl Johnson, 459
Three O'Clock In The Morning H.M. Barnes, 95; Wilfred Brancheau, 126; Clayton McMichen, 566; Riley Puckett, 718; Bob Smith, 843; Jimmy Yates Groups, 976
Three Perished In The Snow Harvey Powell, 702
Three Pictures Of Life's Other Side Hank & Slim Newman, 656
Three Shif-less Skonks Light Crust Doughboys, 504
Three Thousand Miles From Home Roy Shaffer, 824
Three Wishes Bradley Kincaid, 484; Red Headed Brier Hopper, 731
Three Women To Every Man Carlisle Brothers, 169
Thrills That I Can't Forget Welby Toomey, 912
Through This World I Sadly Roam Rangers Quartet, 728

Throw Open Your Door Chapman Quartet, 200
Throw Out The Life Line Alcoa Quartet, 53; Mountain Singers Male Quartet, 645; Riley Puckett, 716; J. Douglas Swagerty, 883
Throw The Old Cow Over The Fence Dr. Humphrey Bate, 97
Tickle Her Hackberry Ramblers, 387
Tickle The Strings Smith's Garage Fiddle Band, 848
Tickle Toe Adolph Hofner, 431
Ticklish Reuben Charlie Parker, 676
Tidy Up And Down The Old Brass Wagon Patt Patterson, 681
Tie Me To Your Apron Strings Riley Puckett, 722
Tie Me To Your Apron Strings Again Johnson County Ramblers, 464; Frank Luther, 519; John McGhee & Frank Welling, 560; Hal O'Halloran's Hooligans, 667; Bob Wills, 962
Tie That Binds [The] Gene Autry, 72; James Johnson, 461; Blaine & Cal Smith, 843; Fred Stanley, 866
Tie Up Those Old Broken Cords Fields Ward, 939
Tiger Rag Leon Chappelear, 201; Hoosier Hot Shots, 440; Kelly Brothers, 477; Maple City Four, 587; Roy Newman, 656; Wanderers, 938; Yellow Jackets [II], 976
Tiger Rag Blues Amadie Breaux, 126
Tight Like That Otis & Tom Mote, 644
'Til I See My Mother's Face J. Douglas Swagerty, 883
Tildy Johnson Lulu Belle & Scotty, 516
Till He Calls His Reapers Stamps Quartet, 864
Till The Longest Day I Live Cindy Walker, 935
Till The Roses Bloom Again Delmore Brothers, 310
'Till The Snow Flakes Fall Again Ernest V. Stoneman, 875
Till We Meet Again Vernon Dalhart, 267; Kentucky Thorobreds, 479; John McGhee & Frank Welling, 559; Clayton McMichen, 566; Melton & Minter, 615; Riley Puckett, 717
Till We Meet Again (God Be With You) Frank & James McCravy, 534
Till Your Returning Clay Long, 510
Tim Brook Carver Boys, 196
Time After Time Ernest Tubb, 914
Time Alone Bob Atcher, 70
Time Changes Everything Roy Rogers, 812; Bob Wills, 964
Time For Me To Go Dorsey & Beatrice Dixon, 322
Time Is Now [The] [E.R.] Nance Family, 648–49
Time Rhythm Leroy [Slim] Johnson, 461
Time Table Blues Capt. Appleblossom, 158
Time That Used To Be In Front [The] E. Arthur Lewis, 497
Time Will Come [The] Vernon Dalhart, 244–45
Time Will Tell Bob Atcher, 70
Time Won't Heal My Broken Heart Ted Daffan's Texans, 241
Times Ain't Like They Used To Be Thomas C. Ashley, 68; Carolina Tar Heels, 174
Times Am Gittin' Hard Al Bernard, 100–101
Times Are Getting Hard Bailey Briscoe, 127
Times Are Not Like They Used To Be Fiddlin' John Carson, 178
Tin Roof Blues Roy Newman, 656
Tiny Baby Bonnet [A] Wiley Walker & Gene Sullivan, 936
Tiny Blue Shoe Three Tobacco Tags, 908
Tiny Shoe [The] Arthur Cornwall, 223
Tiny Toys [Smilin'] Ed McConnell, 530
Tiple Blues Allen Brothers, 55
Tipperary Walter C. Peterson, 688; Chesley Shirley, 832
Tipperary Moonlight Greenville Trio, 382
Tipple Blues Allen Brothers, 57; Kentucky String Ticklers, 478
Tippy Two Step Blues Henry Whitter, 954
Tired Of Me Crystal Springs Ramblers, 239
Tired Of Mother—Part 1, 2 Vernon Dalhart, 279

Tired Of Ramblin' Rambling Rangers, 725
Tired Of The Same Thing All The Time Milton Brown, 137
Tired Of You Shelly Lee Alley, 59
'Tis A Picture From Life's Other Side Old Southern Sacred Singers, 668
'Tis All Over Now Taylor-Griggs Louisiana Melody Makers, 894
'Tis Home Because Mother Is There Lester McFarland & Robert A. Gardner, 543
'Tis Jesus Maury Pearson, 683
'Tis So Sweet To Trust In Jesus Old Southern Sacred Singers, 669
'Tis Sweet To Be Remembered Loy Bodine, 115; Hilltoppers, 427; Lester McFarland & Robert A. Gardner, 546, 548
'Tis The Old Time Religion Moultrie Georgia Quartet, 644
'Tis Wonderful Mr. & Mrs. R.N. Grisham, 384
Tit Willow Hoosier Hot Shots, 438
Titanic [The] Ernest V. Stoneman, 872
To Be Named Clinch Mountain Singers, 215
To Bring You Back To Me Three Tobacco Tags, 907
To Leave You Would Break My Heart Fisher Hendley, 417
To Love And Be Loved Milton & Marion Carlisle, 168; Carlisle Brothers, 169
To Love And Lose Joseph Falcon, 335
To My House Ocie Stockard, 869
To Tell The Truth (I Told A Lie) Dickie McBride, 526
To The End Of The Trail Walter Hurdt, 448
To The Work Alfred G. Karnes, 472
To Wed You In The Golden Summertime Riley Puckett, 716–17
To Welcome The Travelers Home Fiddlin' John Carson, 176
To Welcome The Travellers Home Fiddlin' John Carson, 176
Toad (Saut' Crapaud) [The] Columbus Fruge, 360
Toad Frog And The Elephant Bernard [Slim] Smith, 842
Tobacco State Swing Hank Penny, 686
Together Forever Johnny Lee Wills, 967
Token In Blues G.C. Osborne, 670
Tokio Rag Ted Hawkins, 413
Toll Rouse Brothers, 815
Toll The Bells Buell Kazee, 473
Tom And Jerry Uncle Dave Macon, 575; Smith's Garage Fiddle Band, 848
Tom Bigbee River Charlie Marshall, 588
Tom Cat And Pussy Blues Jimmie Davis, 300
Tom Cat Blues Cliff Carlisle, 164; Otto Gray, 379
Tom Cat Rag Bill Boyd, 124; Light Crust Doughboys, 504
Tom Dooley G.B. Grayson & Henry Whitter, 381
Tom Joad—Part 1, 2 Woody Guthrie, 386
Tom Noonan (Bishop Of Chinatown) Arthur Fields & Fred Hall, 341
Tom Sherman's Barroom Dick Devall, 313
Tom Tom Dance Cowboy Tom's Roundup, 224
Tom Watson Special Fiddlin' John Carson, 175
Tombigbee River Farewell Karl & Harty, 470
Tombs [The] XC Sacred Quartette, 975
Tomcattin' Around Buddy Jones, 465
Tommy Cat Blues Joe Werner, 944
Tomorrow Is Another Day Tom & Roy, 911
Tom's Rag Watkins Band, 940
Tonight I Have A Date Light Crust Doughboys, 503
Tonight I'm Blue And Lonely Adolph Hofner, 430
Tonight You Belong To Me Cliff Bruner, 139; Hank Penny, 686; Tennessee Ramblers [II], 897
Too Blue To Cry Texas Jim Robertson, 759
Too Busy Bob Wills, 961
Too Busy! Roy Newman, 657
Too Good To Be True Leon Chappelear, 200–201

Too Late Gene Autry, 85; W.C. Childers, 206; Jimmie Davis, 305; Foreman Family, 352; Light Crust Doughboys, 506; Ernest V. Stoneman, 878; Jimmy Wakely, 933
Too Late To Start All Over Charles Mitchell & His Orchestra, 630
Too Late To Worry Al Dexter, 315
Too Late You Have Come Back To Me W.C. Childers, 206
Too Late, Little Girl, Too Late Ted Daffan's Texans, 241
Too Late, Too Late Holland Puckett, 715
Too Long Bob Dunn's Vagabonds, 326; Johnny Lee Wills, 967
Too Many Parties And Too Many Pals Jack Dawson, 306; Leland Johnson, 461; John McGhee & Frank Welling, 555, 557, 560
Too Many Tears Elton Britt, 130
Too Many Times You're Cheatin' On Me Bob Skyles, 838
Too Tight Rag E.E. Hack String Band, 386
Too Young To Get Married Crazy Hillbillies Band, 232; Walter Family, 938
Too Young To Marry Charlie Poole, 699
Toodle Lolly Day Bob Miller, 617
Toodle-Oo Rag Travelers, 912
Toodle-Oo Sweet Mama Leon Chappelear, 202
Toodle-Oo, So Long, Goodbye James Brown, Jr. & Ken Landon Groups, 134
Toodle-Oodle-Oo Bob Dunn's Vagabonds, 326
Took My Gal A-Walkin' Charlie Poole, 700
Toot Toot Tootsie Goodbye New Dixie Demons, 655
Toot, Toot, Tootsie, Goo'bye Hoosier Hot Shots, 437
Topsy Turvy Mert's Hometown Serenaders, 615
Torch Dance William B. Houchens, 443
Tortope D'Osrun Amedie Ardoin, 62
Tossing The Baby So High Uncle Dave Macon, 575
Tostape De Jennings (Tostape Of Jennings) Amedie Ardoin, 62
Tote Your Load [Smilin'] Ed McConnell, 530
Totten' The Poke Jimmie Revard, 743
Touch Of God's Hand [The] Sons Of The Pioneers, 858
Touched In The Head Dixieland Swingsters, 320
Tough Pickin' Carson Robison, 761–62
Touring Yodel Blues Tom Darby & Jimmie Tarlton, 294
Tout Que Reste C'Est Mon Linge Amedie Ardoin, 62
Town Girl Joe Werner, 944
Town Of The Lonesome Touch [The] Marvin Williams, 959
Toy-Town Jamboree Hoosier Hot Shots, 438
Trace The Footsteps Of Jesus Smith's Sacred Singers, 849, 851
Trade With Your Home Man Uncle Dave Macon, 577
Tragedy Of Will Rogers And Wiley Post Bob Miller, 625
Tragedy On Daytona Beach Andrew Jenkins, 454
Trail Blazer's Favorite Cleve Chaffin, 200
Trail Of The Lonesome Pine (In The Blue Ridge Mountains Of Virginia) [The] Clayton McMichen, 572
Trail Of The Lonesome Pine [The] Frank & James McCravy, 533; Clayton McMichen, 567; Dick Parman, 679–80; Riley Puckett, 718; Floyd Thompson, 903
Trail Of The Mountain Rose Al Clauser, 214
Trail To California [The] Tex Hardin, 398
Trail To Home Sweet Home Wilf Carter (Montana Slim), 181, 183; Rex Griffin, 383
Trail To Mexico [The] Bill Bender, 99; Cass County Boys, 198; Harry "Mac" McClintock, 528; Massey Family, 608; Len Nash, 650; Texas Rangers, 900
Trailin' Ray Whitley, 953
Trailing Arbutus Christine, 209
Trailrider's Lullaby Wilf Carter (Montana Slim), 181
Trail's End [The] Buck Nation, 651
Train 45 G.B. Grayson & Henry Whitter, 380

Train Blues Henry Whitter, 956
Train Carry My Girl Back Home Wade Mainer, 583
Train Done Left Me And Gone [The] Uncle Dave Macon, 578
Train No. 45 G.B. Grayson & Henry Whitter, 380
Train No. 52 Rambling Rangers, 725
Train On The Island J.P. Nester, 653; Crockett Ward, 939
Train Song [The] Bill Boyd, 121
Train Special Walter Hurdt, 448
Train That Carried The Girl From Town Frank Hutchison, 449
Train That Never Arrived [The] Arthur Fields & Fred Hall, 338–40; John I. White, 950
Train Whistle Blues Shelly Lee Alley, 58; Emry Arthur, 65; Gene Autry, 72; Cliff Carlisle, 161; Bill Cox, 227; Jimmie Rodgers, 801
Training Camp Blues Karl & Harty, 471
Training Camp Shuffle Adolph Hofner, 431
Train's Done Left Me [The] Carolina Tar Heels, 173
Trakas En Ede Happy Fats, 396
Tra-Le-La-La Gid Tanner, 891
Tramp [The] Vernon Dalhart, 259; Jack Golding, 374; Lester McFarland & Robert A. Gardner, 546; McGee Brothers, 552
Tramp On The Street [The] Grady & Hazel Cole, 217
Tramp Song [The] Blue Ridge Mountain Singers, 112; Ernest Hare, 399
Tramp Waltz John Baltzell, 91; Lemuel Turner, 917
Tramp, Tramp, Tramp, The Boys Are Marching John A. McDermott, 539
Tramp's Dream [The] E.M. Lewis, 498
Tramp's Last Ride [The] Billy Vest, 931
Tramp's Mother [The] Girls Of The Golden West, 370; Goebel Reeves, 735–37
Travel Blues Amedie Ardoin, 62
Traveler's Rest Kentucky String Ticklers, 478
Travelin' Blues Leon Chappelear, 201; Bill Cox, 225; Lummie Lewis, 500
Travelin' North Fletcher & Foster, 350
Traveling Along Blues Walter Hurdt, 448
Traveling Coon Sid Harkreader, 401
Traveling Down The Road Uncle Dave Macon, 577–78
Traveling Home Carlisle Brothers, 169; Vaughan Quartet, 927
Traveling Life Alone Carlisle Brothers, 168
Traveling Man Prince Albert Hunt, 447; Robert Walton & McWinders, 938
Traveling Man Blues Cliff Carlisle, 165
Traveling Man's Blues Dick Reinhart, 739
Traveling Man's Blues (Train Imitations) Sandlin Brothers, 820
Traveling Pilgrim [J.T.] Allison's Sacred Harp Singers, 60
Traveling Preacher Frank Roberts, Bud Alexander & Fiddlin' Slim Sandford, 755
Traveling Train Frank Roberts, Bud Alexander & Fiddlin' Slim Sandford, 755
Traveling Yodel Blues Tom Darby & Jimmie Tarlton, 294
Travellin' Blues Gene Autry, 74; Freeny Harmonizers, 359; Frank[ie] Marvin, 605; Jimmie Rodgers, 805
Travelling Coon Claude Davis, 297
Travelling Man "Dock" Walsh, 937; Henry Whitter, 955
Trav'ling On The Glory Road Jo & Alma, 458
Treasure Untold Vernon Dalhart, 283; Frank[ie] Marvin, 596
Treasures Untold Loy Bodine, 115; Howard Keesee, 475; Asa Martin, 592; Jimmie Rodgers, 800
Tree Of Life [The] Simmons Sacred Singers, 835
Tree Song [The] Elm City Quartet, 332; Jimmy Yates Groups, 976
Tree That Father Planted For Me [The] Frank Luther, 521

Tree That Stands By The Road [The] Carson Robison, 791
Tree Top Serenade Carson Robison, 792
Trial Of Bruno Richard Hauptmann—Part I, II [The] Bill Cox, 227
Trial Testing Time Frank Gerald & Howard Dixon, 368
Triangle Blues Roanoke Jug Band, 751
Tribulation Days Odus & Woodrow, 667
Tribute To Knute Rockne [A] Carson Robison, 788
Triflin' Gal Jimmie Revard, 742
Triflin' Mama From Dixie Fleming & Townsend, 348
Triflin' Woman Blues Daddy John Love, 514
Trifling Mama Blues Leon Chappelear, 200; Jimmie Davis, 300
Trinity Waltz Milton Brown, 136
Trip To New York (Part I-IV) [A] Charlie Poole, 700
Trip To The City [A] Green B. Adair, 51
Trip To Town [A] Sid Harkreader, 400
Triple Right And Left Four Woodhull's Old Time Masters, 971
Trois Jours Apres Ma Mort (Three Days After My Death) Leo Soileau, 854
Tropical Isle Of Somewhere Kelly Brothers, 477
Trotting Along The Road Bob Miller, 625
Trottting Along The Road Bob Miller, 625
(Trouble Ends) Out Where The Blue Begins Jack Pierce, 696
Trouble In Mind Leon Chappelear, 201; Whitey McPherson, 579; Roy Shaffer, 825; Bob Wills, 961
Trouble In Mind No. 3 Jack & Leslie, 451
Trouble On My Mind Cliff Carlisle, 167
Trouble Trouble Roy Acuff, 49
Trouble Worries Me Andrews Brothers, 60
Troubled Heart Of Mine Ted Daffan's Texans, 241
Troubled In Mind And Blue Jesse Rodgers, 799
Troubled Mind Lew Preston, 713
Troubled Minded Blues Cliff Carlisle, 167
Troubled Waters Zora Layman, 492
Troubles Bill Boyd, 124; Light Crust Doughboys, 505
Troubles All Will End Majestic [Male] Quartet, 585; Stamps Quartet, 865
Troubles When I Was A Boy Joseph Falcon, 335
Troublesome Blues Roland Cauley, 199
Truck Driver's Blues Cliff Bruner, 140; Leroy [Slim] Johnson, 462; Light Crust Doughboys, 506
Truck Drivers' Coffee Stop Dick Reinhart, 739; Jimmy Wakely, 934
Truck Drivers' Sweetheart Karl & Harty, 471
Truckin' (Truck-Truck-Truckin' Along) Prairie Ramblers, 706
Truckin' On Down Cliff Bruner, 139
True And Trembling Brakeman Cliff Carlisle, 162; Bradley Kincaid, 484; Paul Mason, 608; Taylor's Kentucky Boys, 895
True Blue Bill Gene Autry, 73–75; Frank[ie] Marvin, 604
True Love Divine Emry Arthur, 66
True Love Is A Blessing Bobbie & Ruby Ricker, 748
True Lover Callahan Brothers, 152
True Sweetheart [A] Philyaw Brothers, 690
True To The One I Love Johnny Barfield, 94
Truly I Promise To Love You Leon Chappelear, 201
Trumpet Talking Blues Tennessee Ramblers [II], 897
Trundle Bed Frank & James McCravy, 533–34
Trusting My Redeemer Jenkins Family, 456
Trusting My Sweetheart Crowder Brothers, 237–38
Trusty Lariat [The] Harry "Mac" McClintock, 529
Try And Play It Mansfield Patrick, 680
Try It Once Again Shelly Lee Alley, 58
Try Me One More Time Ernest Tubb, 914
Try Not To Forget Merritt Smith, 845

Try To Win Some Soul To Him Allen Quartette, 57
Trying To Be Happy McDonald Quartet, 541
Trying To Be True Modern Mountaineers, 631
Tu Aura Regret Harrington-Landry & Steward, 404
Tu M'a Quite Dans La Misere Happy Fats, 395
Tu Ma Quite Seul (The Prisoner's Song) Alley Boys Of Abbeville, 59
Tu Pen Pas Ma Retter De Revere Thibodeaux Boys, 901
Tu Peu Depend Si Moi (You Can Depend On Me) Alley Boys Of Abbeville, 59
Tu Peu Pas L'Omnait Avec Toi (You Cannot Take It With You) Sons Of Acadians, 856
Tu Peu Pas Metre Ce Maquac Sur Mon Dou (You Can't Put That Monkey On My Back) Sons Of Acadians, 856
Tu Peus Pas Me Faire Ca (You Can't Put That Monkey On My Back) Alley Boys Of Abbeville, 59
Tu Va Partir Seul (When You Are Gone Alone) Joe Creduer-Albert Babineaux, 232
Tuck Away My Lonesome Blues W. Lee O'Daniel, 666; Jimmie Rodgers, 801; Ross Rhythm Rascals, 814
Tuck Me In Red Brush Rowdies, 730
Tuck Me To Sleep Dixie Girls, 318
Tuck Me To Sleep (In My Old Kentucky Home) Hugh Cross, 235; Riley Puckett, 718, 722
Tug Boat Kessinger Brothers, 480; Light Crust Doughboys, 502
Tugboat And Pineywoods Massey Family, 610
Tulsa Stomp Bob Wills, 962–63
Tulsa Twist Dickie McBride, 526
Tulsa Waltz Jack Cawley's Oklahoma Ridge Runners, 199; Jimmie Revard, 742; Hugh Roden, 797; Sherman Tedder, 895; Bob Wills, 961
Tumble Down Shack In My Dreams Girls Of The Golden West, 370
Tumbled Down Shack In Dixie Land [The] Bob Palmer & Monte Hall, 673
Tumble-Down Shack In Dixieland [The] Bob Palmer & Monte Hall, 673
Tumbleweed Tenor Smiley Burnette, 145
Tumbleweed Trail Bill Boyd, 125; Sons Of The Pioneers, 859
Tumbling Tumbleweeds Gene Autry, 80; Bill Boyd, 122; Ranch Boys, 725; Sons Of The Pioneers, 857
Tu-N'As Laisser Seul (You Left Me Alone) Four Aces, 356
Tune In On Heaven McGee Brothers, 552; Vaughan Quartet, 926–27
Tupelo Blues Floyd Ming, 629
Turkey Buzzard Hill Billies, 424
Turkey Gobbler Theron Hale, 389
Turkey Hash Arty Hall, 390
Turkey In De Straw Dr. D.D. Hollis, 432
Turkey In The Hay Fiddlin' John Carson, 177
Turkey In The Straw Emry Arthur, 66; John Baltzell, 91; Fiddlin' John Carson, 175; Chief Pontiac, 205; Robert Cook's Old Time Fiddlers, 220; Jim Couch, 223; John W. Daniel, 293; Hobbs Brothers, 428; William B. Houchens, 443; Kessinger Brothers, 479; Frank Luther, 524; W.W. Macbeth, 526; Alphus McFayden, 550; Clayton McMichen, 573; Nicholson's Players, 659; Walter C. Peterson, 688; Archer Porter, 702; Red Fox Chasers, 730; George Reneau, 740–41; Doc Roberts, 754; A.C. (Eck) Robertson, 757; Rodeo Trio, 798; Joseph Samuels, 819; Uncle Joe Shippee, 831; Small Town Players, 840; Gid Tanner, 887–88; Taylor's Kentucky Boys, 895; Tweedy Brothers, 917
Turkey In The Straw—Soldier's Joy Tate Bros. & Hicks, 892
Turkey In The Straw (A "Paul Jones") Joseph Samuels, 819
Turkey In The Straw (The Paul Jones) Joseph Samuels, 819
Turkey In The Straw Medley Tweedy Brothers, 917
Turkish Lady [The] Bradley Kincaid, 482

Turn About Swing Bill Nettles, 654
Turn Away Carolina Gospel Singers, 171; Lubbock Texas Quartet, 515
Turn Loose And Go To Town Bob Skyles, 838
Turn Your Lights Down Low Ocie Stockard, 869
Turn Your Radio On Blue Sky Boys, 114; Lulu Belle & Scotty, 516; Whitey & Hogan, 952; J.B. Whitmire's Blue Sky Trio, 954
Turned Around Blues Lee Frazier, 358
Turnip Greens Shorty Godwin, 372; W.A. Lindsay, 507; Wonder State Harmonists, 971
Turnpike Reel William B. Houchens, 443
Turpentine Arthur Fields & Fred Hall, 345
Turtape Of Saroied [The] Amedie Ardoin, 62
Turtle Dove Bill Shepherd, 830
Tuscaloosa Waltz Ray Brothers, 729; "Ted" Sharp, Hinman & Sharp, 825
'Twas Love Devine [sic] Rainbow Quartette, 724
'Twas Only A Dream Frank Gerald & Howard Dixon, 368
Tweedle-O-Twill Gene Autry, 86; Texas Jim Lewis, 500
Twelfth Street Rag Arizona Wranglers, 62; Hauulea Entertainers, 412
Twelve Cent Cotton Rollin' In Wealth Buck Nation, 651
Twenty One Years Edward L. Crain, 230; Doc Hopkins, 441; Karl & Harty, 470; Lester McFarland & Robert A. Gardner, 548; Bob Miller, 618–19, 621; Riley Puckett, 720; Dick Robertson, 758; Carson Robison, 790; Asher Sizemore & Little Jimmie, 836; Marc Williams, 959
Twenty One Years Is A Long Time Lester McFarland & Robert A. Gardner, 547
Twenty Years In Prison Green Bailey, 88
Twenty-Five Years From Now Al Bernard, 101; Elm City Quartet, 332
Twenty-One Years—Part 2 Lester McFarland & Robert A. Gardner, 549; Bob Miller, 622
Twilight Echoes Carson Robison, 761–62
Twilight Is Stealing Carolina Quartette, 172; Dykes' Magic City Trio, 328
Twilight Is Stealing O'er The Sea Ernest V. Stoneman, 877
Twilight On The Prairie Carl Boling, 116; Wilf Carter (Montana Slim), 181
Twilight On The Trail Elton Britt, 129; Ranch Boys, 726
Twilight Waltz Yellow Jackets [II], 977
'Twill All Be Glory Over There Mr. & Mrs. R.N. Grisham, 384
'Twill Be All Glory Over There Deal Family, 307
'Twill Be Glory Bye And Bye Blue Ridge Gospel Singers, 109
'Twill Be Sweet When We Meet Jimmie Davis, 301–02
'Twill Not Be Long Kitts Bros., 487
Twin Guitar Special Bob Wills, 965
Twinkle Little Star Oscar & Doc Harper, 402; Earl Johnson, 460; Martin Melody Boys, 594; Red Fox Chasers, 730
Twinkle Twinkle Little Star Massey Family, 609; Smith's Garage Fiddle Band, 848; Bob Wills, 963
Two And Two Still Make Four Sunshine Boys, 881
Two Babes Karl & Harty, 470
Two Babes In The Woods Red Fox Chasers, 731
Two Brothers Are We Johnson Brothers, 463
Two Chairs On The Porch For You And Me Vance Knowles-Red Lay, 488
Two Cowgirls On The Lone Prairie Girls Of The Golden West, 370
Two Drummers [The] Morgan Denmon, 312
Two Eyes In Tennessee Cliff Carlisle, 167
Two Eyes Of Blue Bill Carlisle, 159
Two Faithful Lovers John D. Foster, 354
Two False Lovers Red Fox Chasers, 730
Two Fragments Jules Allen, 55

Two Gun Cowboy [The] Wilf Carter (Montana Slim), 182; Frank[ie] Marvin, 598
Two Gun Joe Vernon Waters, 940
Two Hearts On The Old Willow Tree Norwood Tew, 899
Two Little Boys Dorsey & Beatrice Dixon, 321; Thurston Sutton & Raymond Sutton, 882
Two Little Children Bill Cox, 228; Joe Reed Family, 734; Arthur Tanner, 886
Two Little Frogs Skyland Scotty, 837
Two Little Girls In Blue Leo Boswell, 119; W.C. Childers, 206; Uncle Tom Collins, 219; M.O. Keller, 475; Bradley Kincaid, 484; Bela Lam, 489; Morganton Trio, 642; Walter C. Peterson, 688
Two Little Girls Loved One Little Boy Lester McFarland & Robert A. Gardner, 547
Two Little Lads Four Virginians, 357; Norwood Tew, 899
Two Little Orphans Carolina Buddys, 170; Bradley Kincaid, 483–84; Jimmy Long, 512; David Miller, 626; Ernest V. Stoneman, 875–76
Two Little Orphans (Our Mamma's In Heaven) Ernest V. Stoneman, 874
Two Little Pretty Birds Jack Major, 586; Maple City Four, 587
Two Little Rosebuds Dorsey & Beatrice Dixon, 321; Tiny Dodson's Circle-B Boys, 322
Two Little Sweethearts Cliff Carlisle, 166
Two Lives [The] Frank & James McCravy, 533, 535–37
Two Locks Of Hair Hart & Ogle, 406
Two Log Cabin Orphans Jenkins Family, 457
Two More Years (And I'll Be Free) Shelly Lee Alley, 59; Elton Britt, 130; Jimmie Davis, 304; Light Crust Doughboys, 505; Leon Selph, 824
Two Old Soldiers [The] Charlie Craver, 231
Two Orphans [The] Elzie Floyd & Leo Boswell, 350; Lester McFarland & Robert A. Gardner, 544; Ruth Neal & Wanda Neal, 652; George Reneau, 741
Two Robes R.C. Garner, 363
Two Sisters Bradley Kincaid, 482–83
Two Soldiers [The] Carl T. Sprague, 863
Two Step De Eunice Amedie Ardoin, 61
Two Step De La Prairie Soileau (Prairie Soileau Two Step) Amedie Ardoin, 61
Two Step De La Tell J.B. Fuslier, 361
Two Step De La Ville Platte Denus McGee, 551
Two Step De Mama (My Mother's Two Step) Amedie Ardoin, 61
Two Step D'Elton Amedie Ardoin, 62
Two Step Du Grand Maraist Denus McGee, 551
Two Step Quadrille Tommy Dandurand, 293
Two Step Waltz [A] Joe Werner, 944
Two Sweethearts Carter Family, 191; Tex Owens, 671
Two Timing Mama Blues Walter Hurdt, 448; Sain Family, 818
Two-Faced Preacher Karl & Harty, 471
Two-In-One Chewing Gum Uncle Dave Macon, 578
Two-Step De Le Momou J.B. Fuslier, 361
Two-Time Mama Blues Dale Hunter, 447
Tying A Knot In The Devil's Tail Powder River Jack-Kitty Lee, 496
Tying Knot's [sic] In The Devil's Tail Arizona Wranglers, 62

Ugly Gal's Got Something Hard To Beat [An] Willard Hodgin[s], 430
Un Fussi Qui Brille Roy Gonzales, 375
Un Lettre A Ma Belle Thibodeaux Boys, 901
Uncle Abner And Elmer At The Rehearsal, Part I, II Golden Melody Boys, 373
Uncle Bob's Favorite Bob Skiles Four Old Tuners, 837

Uncle Booker's Hoedown (Buffalo Gal) Crockett [Family] Mountaineers, 233
Uncle Bud Gid Tanner, 888–89
Uncle Dave And Sid On A Cut-Up Uncle Dave Macon, 577
Uncle Dave's Banjo Medley Uncle Dave Macon, 576
Uncle Dave's Beloved Solo Uncle Dave Macon, 575
Uncle Dave's Favorite Religious Melodies Uncle Dave Macon, 576
Uncle Dave's Travels—Part 1 (Misery In Arkansas) Uncle Dave Macon, 577
Uncle Dave's Travels—Part 2 (Around Louisville, Ky.) Uncle Dave Macon, 577
Uncle Dave's Travels—Part III (In And Around Nashville) Uncle Dave Macon, 577
Uncle Dave's Travels—Part IV (Visit At The Old Maid's) Uncle Dave Macon, 577
Uncle Elair's Daughter Joseph Falcon, 335
Uncle Eph's Got The Coon Anglin Brothers, 61; Prairie Ramblers, 708–09; Shelton Brothers, 828
Uncle Fraley's Formula Smiley Burnette, 145
Uncle Hiram's Trip To The City—Part 1, 2 Paul Crutchfield & John Clotworthy, 239
Uncle Jimmy's Favorite Fiddling Pieces Uncle Jimmy Thompson, 904
Uncle Joe Uncle Eck Dunford, 326; Macon Quartet, 579
Uncle Knute's Waltz Joe Werner, 944
Uncle Ned Willard Hodgin[s], 429; Leake County Revelers, 495; Uncle Dave Macon, 575; Chubby Parker, 676–77
Uncle Ned's Waltz Grinnell Giggers, 384
Uncle Noah's Ark Gene Autry, 80; Blue Ridge Hill Billies, 110; Prairie Ramblers, 704
Uncle Sam And The Kaiser Ernest V. Stoneman, 872
Uncle Sammy David Miller, 626
Uncle Zeke Light Crust Doughboys, 503
Unclouded Day [The] Cliff Carlisle, 168; R.N. Johnson, 462; Old Southern Sacred Singers, 669; Paramount Sacred Four, 674; Peck's Male Quartette, 684; Chas. Richardson & O.S. Gabehart, 748; Smith's Sacred Singers, 850
Uncloudy Day [The] Peck's Male Quartette, 683
Under A Southern Moon Lew Childre, 207
Under Dakota's Cross Paul Hamblin, 393
Under Fiesta Stars Gene Autry, 85
Under Hawaiian Skies Hank Snow, 853
Under His Wings Carolina Ladies Quartet, 171; Hendersonville Quartet, 416
Under The Blood Jenkins Family, 457
Under The Blood Of Jesus Jenkins Family, 457
Under The Double Eagle Blue Ridge Highballers, 110; Bill Boyd, 121; Milton Brown, 137; Fisher Hendley, 416; Hi-Flyers, 419; Bob Larkan & Family, 490; Perry Brothers, 687; Charlie Poole, 700; Red Fox Chasers, 730; Rouse Brothers, 815; George Walburn & Emmett Hethcox, 935
Under The Double Eagle March Kessinger Brothers, 481
Under The Light Of The Texas Moon Wilf Carter (Montana Slim), 183
Under The Moon Jimmie Revard, 743
Under The Moon With You Dixie Ramblers [II], 319
Under The Old Apple Tree Gene Autry, 76
Under The Old Cherry Tree Frank Gerald & Howard Dixon, 368
Under The Old China Tree Joe Werner, 944
Under The Old Kentucky Moon Clayton McMichen, 572; Morris Brothers, 643
Under The Old Sierra Moon Lester McFarland & Robert A. Gardner, 550
Under The Old Umbrella Graham Brothers, 377; Lester McFarland & Robert A. Gardner, 550; Bob Miller, 625
Under The Pale Moonlight Richard D. Burnett, 144

Under The Silvery Moon Cliff Bruner, 139
Under The Spell Of Your Love Joe Werner, 944
Underneath The Blue Hawaiian Sky Tom & Don, 911
Underneath The Cotton Moon Melton & Waggoner, 615
Underneath The Mellow Moon Melvin Dupree, 327; Clayton McMichen, 566; Riley Puckett, 717
Underneath The Southern Moon Claude Davis, 297; Connie Sides, 834
Underneath The Sugar Moon Roy Harvey, 410
Underneath The Sun Bar-X Cowboys, 92
Underneath The Texas Moonlight Fred Kirby, 487
Understand It Better Bye-And-Bye Morris Brothers, 643
Une Pias Ici Et Une Pias La Bas Hackberry Ramblers, 388
Unexplained Blues Louisiana Strollers, 514; Hoke Rice, 745; Leo Soileau, 855; Lowe Stokes, 870
Unfortunate Brakeman [The] Elmer Bird, 106
Unfriendly World Tiny Dodson's Circle-B Boys, 322
Union County Hugh Cross, 236
Unkind Word [The] Tennessee Ramblers [II], 898
Unknown Soldier [The] George Edgin, 330
Unknown Soldier's Grave [The] Vernon Dalhart, 253–55
Unloaded Gun Cliff Carlisle, 166
Unlock This Doghouse Door Hi-Flyers, 419
Unlucky Man Allen Brothers, 56
Unlucky Me Fleming & Townsend, 347
Unlucky Road To Washington [The] Ernest V. Stoneman, 877
Unmarked Grave [The] Howard Keesee, 475; Lester McFarland & Robert A. Gardner, 547; Bob Miller, 621; John I. White, 950
Unopened Letter [The] Rodik Twins, 810
Until I Return To You Roy Hall, 391
Until We Meet Again Adolph Hofner, 431
Until You Went Away Nolan Bush, 147
Untrue Lover [The] Fleming & Townsend, 347
Unwanted Children Frank Luther, 520
Unwanted Dream McClendon Brothers, 528
Unwanted Sweetheart Lonesome Singer, 510
Up Country Blues Deford Bailey, 88
Up In Glory Dr. Smith's Champion Hoss Hair Pullers, 843
Up In The Mountains Dick Robertson, 758
Up Jumped The Devil Byron Parker, 675; Tune Wranglers, 915
Up Jumped The Rabbit Lowe Stokes, 871
Up North Blues [The] Byrd Moore, 639
Upstairs John H. Bertrand, 101
Using That Thing Doug Bine, 104
Utah Carl Charles Nabell, 647
Utah Carl's Last Ride Frank Wheeler-Monroe Lamb, 948
Utah Carrol Cartwright Brothers, 196
Utah Carroll Charles Baker, 89; Bill Bender, 99; Carl T. Sprague, 863; Marc Williams, 958
Utah Mormon Blues Phil Pavey, 682
Utah Trail [The] Arthur Fields & Fred Hall, 339; Hoosier Hawaiians, 435; Bob Palmer & Monte Hall, 673; Ranch Boys, 725; Carson Robison, 770, 772–73
Utah Waltz Amadie Breaux, 126
Ute (Where Are You) [A] Leo Soileau, 855

V-8 Blues Three Tobacco Tags, 907
Vacant Cabin Door [The] Cliff Carlisle, 165
Vacant Chair [The] Arthur Fields & Fred Hall, 338; Frank & James McCravy, 533; Woodlawn Quartette, 972
Vagabond Yodel Chas. M. Dewitte, 314
Vagabond Yodel No. 2 Chas. M. Dewitte, 314
Vagabond's Dream [A] Roy Acuff, 49
Vain Ton Don A Ma Mort Happy Fats, 395
Vain World, Adieu Denson-Parris Sacred Harp Singers, 313
Valley In The Hills Gene Autry, 74; Frank[ie] Marvin, 604
Valley Of Memories Frank Luther, 520
Valley Of Peace Carlisle Brothers, 169
Valley Rose Joe Werner, 944
Valse A Alcee Poulard Amedie Ardoin, 62
Valse A Pap Denus McGee, 551
Valse Brunette Amedie Ardoin, 62
Valse D'Amour Leo Soileau, 856
Valse De Avalon Leo Soileau, 855
Valse De Boscoville Adler Connor & Julian Grader, 219
Valse De Estherwood Leo Soileau, 855
Valse De Gueydan John H. Bertrand, 101
Valse De La Louisianne Angelas Le Jeunne, 493
Valse De La Pointe D'Eglise (Church Point Waltz) Amedie Ardoin, 62
Valse De Maria Bueller Happy Fats, 395
Valse De Mon Vieux Village (My Old Home Town Waltz) Amedie Ardoin, 62
Valse De Pointe Noire Angelas Le Jeunne, 493
Valse Des Opelousas Amedie Ardoin, 62
Valse Des Vachers Denus McGee, 551
Valse Du La Penitencier Denus McGee, 551
Valse Du Puit D'Huile Denus McGee, 551
Vamp [The] Dan Hornsby, 442
Van Buren Bill Boyd, 123
Variations—Sweet Bunch Of Daisies Jess Young, 978
Varsovienna Massey Family, 609
Varsovienne Bob Skiles Four Old Tuners, 837
Vas Y Carrement (Step It Fast) Amadie Breaux, 126
Vaughan Quartet Medley Vaughan Quartet, 923
Vaughan Quartette Medley Vaughan Quartet, 924
Vestris Disaster [The] John McGhee & Frank Welling, 556
Victoria Alabama Sacred Harp Singers, 53; Dye's Sacred Harp Singers, 328; Lee Wells, 943
Victory Ahead Emry Arthur, 65
Victory In Jesus Jones Brothers Trio, 467
Victory Is Coming Parker Quartette, 679
Vie Vals Hackberry Ramblers, 388
Vien A La Maison Avec Moi (You'll Come Home With Me) Percy Babineaux-Bixy Guidry, 87
Vien Don Ma Reguin (Come And Meet Me) J.B. Fuslier, 361
Vieux Airs (Old Tunes) Joseph Falcon, 334
Vigilante Man Woody Guthrie, 386
Village Blacksmith [The] Cecil Vaughn, 930
Village By The Sea Lake Howard, 445
Village Grave Blue Ridge Sunshine Boys, 113
Village School Nelstone's Hawaiians, 653
Vine Covered Cabin In The Valley Gene Autry, 81
Vine Covered Church Buck Nation, 651; Ray Whitley, 953
Vine Covered Cottage [The] Jack Cawley's Oklahoma Ridge Runners, 199
Vingt Et Un Ans Joe Werner, 943
Vinton High Society Hackberry Ramblers, 387
Violet Waltz Kyle Wooten, 973
Virginia Blues Bill Carlisle, 158; Cliff Carlisle, 161; Hoosier Hot Shots, 436, 438
Virginia Bootleggers Red Fox Chasers, 731
Virginia Mann Schottische Polka Kessinger Brothers, 481
Virginia Moonshiner [The] Asa Martin, 588
Virginia Reel John A. McDermott, 539; National Barn Dance Orchestra, 651; Colonel John A. Pattee, 681; Uncle Joe Shippee, 831
Virginia Reel Medley—Part I, II John A. McDermott, 539
Virginian Strike Of '23 [The] Earl Shirkey & Roy Harper, 832
Vision Of Deams Hi-Flyers, 418

Visions Of The Past Sons Of The West, 859
Visiting Sal's House In Moonshine Hollow Uncle Bud Landress, 490
Viva Tequila Tex Ritter, 751
Voice In The Old Village Choir [The] Johnny Marvin, 607; Bob Miller, 621
Voice In The Valley [A] Christine, 209
Voice In The Village Choir [The] John McGhee & Frank Welling, 562
Volunteer Organist [The] Harmonica Bill, 401; John McGhee & Frank Welling, 555
Vous Avez Quelque Chose (You Had Some) Leo Soileau, 856
Vous Avez Quitte Avec Que Unde Dotre Four Aces, 356
Vous Etes Gentille (You're Sweet) Joseph Falcon, 335
Vous Etes Si Doux (You Are So Sweet) Joseph Falcon, 335
Vous M'Avez Donne Votre Parole (You Gave Me Your Word) Denus McGee, 551
Vous Me Fois Espere Four Aces, 356

Wabash Sain Family, 818
Wabash Blues Roy Acuff, 49; Milton Brown, 136; Delmore Brothers, 311; Adolph Hofner, 431; Hoosier Hot Shots, 438; Clayton McMichen, 568; Johnny O'Brien, 665; Jack Pierce, 696; Price-Prosser-Teasley, 714; Hoke Rice, 746; Ocie Stockard, 869; Yellow Jackets [II], 977
Wabash Cannon Ball Roy Acuff, 48; Loy Bodine, 115; Bill Carlisle, 160; Carter Family, 188, 195; Orla Clark, 214; Hugh Cross, 235–36; Roy Hall, 391
Wabash Cannon Ball No. 2 Morris Brothers, 643
Wabash Cannon-Ball Blues [The] Delmore Brothers, 311
Wabash Moon Carson Robison, 786
Waco Girl Herman Thacker, 901
Wages Of Sin Is Death [The] Jenkins Family, 457
Waggoner John D. Foster, 354; Clifford Gross, 385; Light Crust Doughboys, 502; Doc Roberts, 754; Leonard Rutherford, 816; Uncle "Am" Stuart, 881
Waggoner's Hornpipe George R. Pariseau's Orchestra, 675
Wagner William B. Houchens, 443; Bob Skiles Four Old Tuners, 837
Wagner Hoedown Sons Of The Pioneers, 859
Wagon Train Gene Autry, 81
Wagon Train Keep Rollin' Along Fred Kirby, 487
Wagon Wheels Albert E. Dell, 309; Frank Luther, 521; Ranch Boys, 727
Wagon Yard Lew Childre, 207
Wagoner Arkansas Woodchopper, 64; Kentucky Thorobreds, 479; B.E. Scott, 821
Wagoner Hornpipe [The] Smith's Garage Fiddle Band, 848
Wagoner's Hornpipe Red Headed Fiddler[s], 732
Wagoner's Lad (Loving Nancy) [The] Buell Kazee, 473
Wah Hoo Bill Boyd, 122
Wah-Hoo! Hoosier Hot Shots, 436; Ray Whitley, 953
Waikiki Blues James Brown, Jr. & Ken Landon Groups, 134
Wait For Me Harold & Hazel, 402
Wait For The Lights To Go Out George Walburn & Emmett Hethcox, 935
Wait For The Wagon Elton Britt, 128
Wait 'Til You See Bob Wills, 964–65
Wait Till The Clouds Roll By Emry Arthur, 66; Uncle Dave Macon, 578
Wait Till The Sun Shines Nellie John McGhee & Frank Welling, 559, 562; Melody Boys, 614; Riley Puckett, 716
Waitin' For The Evenin' Mail Riley Puckett, 720
Waiting Dick Robertson, 758
Waiting At The End Of The Road Texas Wanderers, 900
Waiting At The Gate Vaughan Quartet, 923

Waiting Dear, For You Adolph Hofner, 431
Waiting For A Ride Cliff Carlisle, 166
Waiting For A Train Gene Autry, 72; Wilf Carter (Montana Slim), 186; Sid Hampton, 394; Buddy Jones, 466; Riley Puckett, 719; Hoke Rice, 745; Carson Robison, 772, 786; Jimmie Rodgers, 801; Ed (Jake) West, 945
Waiting For The Boatman (To Guide Us O'er) Odus & Woodrow, 667
Waiting For The Railroad Train Pie Plant Pete, 694
Waiting For The Robert E. Lee Perry Bechtel, 98; Homer Christopher, 209; Light Crust Doughboys, 504; Ernest Rogers, 810; Scottdale String Band, 822
Waiting For The Train Ed (Jake) West, 945
Waiting Old Pal For You Al Dexter, 314
Waiting On The Golden Shore Smith's Sacred Singers, 849
Waiting The Boatman Ashford Quartette, 67; Hall Brothers, 391; Valdese Quartette, 922
Wake Up In The Morning Willie Stoneman, 879
Wake Up Jacob Prince Albert Hunt, 447
Wake Up, America And Kluck, Kluck Kluck Vaughan Quartet, 925
Wake Up, Li'l Girl Jack Rose, 814
Wake Up, You Drowsy Sleeper Charlie Oaks, 665
Wal I Swan Riley Puckett, 717
Walk Along Al Wonder State Harmonists, 971
Walk Along John Luke Highnight, 422
Walk And Talk With Jesus Stamps Quartet, 864
Walk In The Light Of God Rev. M.L. Thrasher, 905
Walk Right In Belmont Wilmer Watts, 941
Walk That Lonesome Valley J.E. Mainer's Mountaineers, 581
Walk The Streets Of Glory John & Emery McClung, 530
Walk, Tom Wilson, Walk Uncle Dave Macon, 575
Walkin' Blues John Dilleshaw, 317; Rex Griffin, 383
Walkin' Georgia Rose Pelican Wildcats, 684
Walkin' My Blues Away Jimmie Davis, 306
Walkin' The Streets Of Laredo [A] Newton Gaines, 361
Walkin' Up Town Arkansas Woodchopper, 64
Walking Along With Me Smith's Sacred Singers, 849; Valdese Quartette, 922
Walking At My Side Stamps Quartet, 865
Walking Down The Railroad Track Frank[ie] Marvin, 597
Walking Home From An Old Country School Hank Penny, 686
Walking Home With Jesus P.H. Ashworth, 69
Walking In My Sleep Roy Acuff, 49; Al Dexter, 315; Dixie Reelers, 319; Prairie Ramblers, 709; Arthur Smith, 841
Walking In The King's Highway Carter Family, 194; Gordon County Quartet, 376
Walking In The Light [Smilin'] Ed McConnell, 530
Walking In The Light (Of The Lord) Lake Howard, 445
Walking In The Parlor Hill Billies, 423; Dr. D.D. Hollis, 432; Pickard Family, 691
Walking In The Shoes Of John Fisher Hendley, 417
Walking In The Sunlight Uncle Dave Macon, 576
Walking In The Way With Jesus Blind Alfred Reed, 733
Walking My Baby Back Home Riley Puckett, 722
Walking On The Streets Of Glory Roy Harvey, 409–10
Walking The Floor Over You Bob Atcher, 70; Ernest Tubb, 914
Walking The Highway Arthur Cornwall, 222
Walking The Last Mile Jess Hillard, 426; Bob Miller, 623; Parker & Dodd, 678
Walking Water Allen Sisson, 836
Walking With Jesus Avoca Quartette, 87
Walking With My King Vaughan Quartet, 926, 929
Walking With My Lord Etowah Quartet, 333; Stamps Quartet, 864–65

Walking With My Savior Freeman Quartette, 358
Wallin's Creek Blues Walker's Corbin Ramblers, 937
Walls of White Jimmie Davis, 304
Walter Family Waltz Walter Family, 938
Walts [sic] Of Our Little Town [The] Adam Trehan, 913
Waltz Crowley [The] Joseph Falcon, 335
Waltz I Love (La Valse J'Aime) [The] Joseph Falcon, 335
Waltz In D Bob Wills, 961
Waltz Me Around Again Willie Chris Bouchillon, 119; Cindy Walker, 935
Waltz Medley Raggedy Ann's Melody Makers, 724
Waltz Of Dreams E.E. Hack String Band, 386
Waltz Of My Dream Joseph Falcon, 335
Waltz Of Roses Prince Albert Hunt, 447
Waltz Of The Bayou [The] Percy Babineaux-Bixy Guidry, 87
Waltz Of The Hills [The] Arthur Fields & Fred Hall, 340, 342–43; Ernest Hare, 399; Patsy Montana, 634–35; Unknown Artists [VI], 920
Waltz Of The Long Wood Percy Babineaux-Bixy Guidry, 87
Waltz Of The Oil Field Amedie Ardoin, 62
Waltz Of The Prison Hackberry Ramblers, 388
Waltz Quadrille—Part 1, 2 National Barn Dance Orchestra, 651
Waltz That Carried Me To My Grave (La Valce Qui Ma Portin D Ma Fose) [The] Joseph Falcon, 334
Waltz That Carried Me To My Grave [The] Joseph Falcon, 336
Waltz The Hall Doc Roberts, 753
Waltz Time Melody (Varso-Vienna) Massey Family, 612
Waltz You Saved For Me [The] Milton Brown, 137; Dixie Ramblers [II], 319; Fred L. Jeske, 458; Light Crust Doughboys, 503; Bob Wills, 964
Waltzes Of The South Plains Cartwright Brothers, 196
Waltzing With You Bob Skyles, 839
Wampus Cat [The] Lulu Belle & Scotty, 516
Wampus Kitty Mama Jimmie Davis, 300
Wander Down The Valley Dixieland Swingsters, 320
Wanderer [The] Emry Arthur, 65
Wanderers (My Lop Eared Mule, My Broken Down Horse And Me) Ranch Boys, 726
Wanderers (My Lop-Eared Mule, My Broken-Down Horse 'N' Me) Massey Family, 610
Wanderers Of The Wasteland Twilight Trail Boys, 918
Wanderer's Stomp Wanderers, 938
Wanderer's Warning [The] Kenneth Houchins, 443; Carson Robison, 770–72, 792; Ed (Jake) West, 945
Wanderin' Vernon Dalhart, 283–84
Wandering Boy [The] Carter Family, 187; Howard Haney, 395; Lulu Belle & Scotty, 516; Goebel Reeves, 737; Da Costa Woltz's Southern Broadcasters, 970
Wandering Child Come Home North Georgia Four, 663
Wandering Child, Oh, Come Home Mississippi Juvenile Quartette, 629; Peck's Male Quartette, 684
Wandering Cowboy [The] Cartwright Brothers, 196; Patt Patterson, 681
Wandering Gypsy Girl Emry Arthur, 65
Wandering Hobo [The] Asa Martin, 590
Wandering Hobo's Song [The] Kenneth Houchins, 444
Wandering Lamb Bob McGimsey, 563
Wandering Man [The] Hackberry Ramblers, 387
Wandering On Hank Snow, 853
Wang Wang Blues Sid Harkreader, 401; Clayton McMichen, 572; Jack Pierce, 696; Scottdale String Band, 822; Bob Wills, 960; Jimmy Yates Groups, 975
Wang Wang Harmonica Blues Carver Boys, 196
Wanna Be A Man Like Dad Fleming & Townsend, 346
Want A Little Home To Go To Sunshine Boys, 882
Want My Black Baby Back Walter Couch & Wilks Ramblers, 224

War Baby's Prayer [The] Bob Atcher, 69
War Town Quick Step Ernest Thompson, 902
Warden's Secret [The] Arthur Fields & Fred Hall, 340–41
Warfield Williamson Brothers & Curry, 960
Warhorse Game Georgia Yellow Hammers, 367
Warm Knees Blues Allen Brothers, 56
Warning Dream [The] John Dilleshaw, 318
Warning To Boys [A] Vernon Dalhart, 283
Warning To Girls [A] Vernon Dalhart, 283
Was I Drunk? New Dixie Demons, 655
Was It Tears Hackberry Ramblers, 388
Was That All I Meant To You Bob Dunn's Vagabonds, 326
Was That Somebody You Smith's Sacred Singers, 849
Was There Ever A Pal Like You Hank Snow, 852
Was Willst Du Haben (What Will You Have) Cartwright Brothers, 196
Was You There When They Took My Lord Away Uncle Dave Macon, 577
Washboard Man [The] Tennessee Ramblers [II], 897
Washing Mama's Dishes Carolina Tar Heels, 173
Washington And Lee Swing Blue Ridge Mountain Entertainers, 111; James Brown, Jr. & Ken Landon Groups, 134; Milton Brown, 137; Light Crust Doughboys, 504
Washington County Fox Chase Vance's Tennessee Breakdowners, 922
Washington Quadrille Jimmy Johnson's String Band, 461
Washington Waddle Ray Sand's Harmony Four, 819
Wasn't She A Dandy Hill Billies, 424
Wasted Tears Pete Pyle, 723
Wasting My Life Away Ernest Tubb, 914
Watch And Pray Fields Ward, 939
Watcha Gonna Do Hi-Flyers, 420
Watching The Clouds Roll By Gene Autry, 78; Jimmy Long, 511
Watching The Moon Fred Richards, 748
Watching The Trains Come In Vernon Dalhart, 284
Watching The World Go By Bill Boyd, 121
Watching You [E.R.] Nance Family, 648; Whitey & Hogan, 952
Watchman Ring That Bell Ernest V. Stoneman, 878
Water Under The Bridge Bradley Kincaid, 485
Watermelon Hangin' On That Vine Monroe Brothers, 632
Watermelon Hanging On De Vine Binkley Brothers Dixie Clodhoppers, 104
Watermelon Hanging On The Vine Ernest V. Stoneman, 873; Henry Whitter, 955
Watermelon On The Vine J.E. Mainer's Mountaineers, 582; Gid Tanner, 888
Watermelon Smilin' On The Vine Bela Lam, 489; Uncle Dave Macon, 574; Frank[ie] Marvin, 596; Johnny Marvin, 606; Prairie Ramblers, 710
Wave On The Sea [The] Carter Family, 195
Wave That Frame Lowe Stokes, 870
Waxia Special Oscar [Slim] Doucet, 324
Way Beyond The Blue Cleve Chaffin, 200
Way Dow [sic] In Arkansas Golden Melody Boys, 373
Way Down In Alabam' Claude Davis, 297
Way Down In Alabama Smyth County Ramblers, 852
Way Down In Arkansas McGee Brothers, 552
Way Down In Arkansaw Hoosier Hot Shots, 440
'Way Down In Caroline Clayton McMichen, 571
Way Down In Florida On A Bum Byrd Moore, 638
Way Down In Georgia Earl Johnson, 460; McDonald Quartet, 541; Fiddlin' Powers & Family, 703; Shelton Brothers, 828; Floyd Thompson, 903
Way Down In Jail On My Knees Sid Harkreader, 400; David Miller, 627
Way Down In Mississippi Jesse Rodgers, 798

Index to Titles

'Way Down In Missouri Bill Boyd, 121
Way Down In North Carolina Fields Ward, 939
'Way Down In Texas (Where The Blue Bonnets Grew) Texas Jim Robertson, 759
Way Down On The Farm Asa Martin, 593
Way Down South Ruth Neal & Wanda Neal, 652; Doc Roberts, 755
Way Down South By The Sea Hoke Rice, 745
Way Down The Old Plank Road Uncle Dave Macon, 574
Way Down Upon The Swanee River Chief Pontiac, 205; Texas Jim Lewis, 499; Bob Wills, 963
'Way Down Yonder Blues Lemuel Turner, 917
'Way Down Yonder In Carolina Roy Newman, 656
'Way Fer Down In The Holler Otis & Eleanor, 670
Way Of The Cross Leads Home [The] Joseph & Peter Higgins, 421; Carson Robison, 786
Way Out On The Mountain Jimmie Davis, 298; Frank[ie] Marvin, 595
'Way Out There Bill Boyd, 122; Hall Brothers, 391; Riley Puckett, 722; Sons Of The Pioneers, 857
Way Out West Henderson Brothers, 416
Way Out West In Kansas Vernon Dalhart, 242–43; Carson Robison, 792
Way Out West In Texas Gene Autry, 78; Don Weston, 947
'Way Out West Of The Pecos Bob Skyles, 838
Way Over In The Promised Land John McGhee & Frank Welling, 557
Way To Glory Land [The] Corley Family, 222; Peck's Male Quartette, 684; Stamps Quartet, 864
Way Up On Clinch Mountain (Drunken Hiccough Song) J.W. Day, 306
Way Up There Frank Luther, 521; Massey Family, 611; Bob Miller, 624
Wayfaring Pilgrim [The] Vaughan Quartet, 929
Wayne County Blues Billy Casteel, 198; Roland Cauley, 199
Waynesburgh Doc Roberts, 752
Wayside Cross [The] Shrine Male Quartet Of Memphis, 834
Wayside Wells Smith's Sacred Singers, 850
Wayward Boy [The] Charlie Poole, 700
Wayward Daughter [The] Carl T. Sprague, 863
Wayward Son [The] Goebel Reeves, 737
Wayward Traveller Grover Rann, 729
Wayworn Traveler [The] Carter Family, 193
We All Grow Old In Time Charlie Craver, 231
We All Love Mother Crowder Brothers, 237–38
We Are Boys From North Carolina Claude Casey, 196
We Are Climbing Chuck Wagon Gang, 211
We Are Drifting Down The Rugged Stream Of Time Karl & Harty, 471
We Are Going Down The Valley Allen Quartette, 57; Jenkins Family, 457
We Are Going Down The Valley One By One Smith's Sacred Singers, 849
We Are Journeying On Price Family Sacred Singers, 714
We Are Marching Home John McGhee & Frank Welling, 557
We Are Up Against It Now Uncle Dave Macon, 575
We Both Were Wrong Hi-Flyers, 419
We Buried Her Blue Sky Boys, 113
We Buried Her Beneath The Willow Sally Foster, 355; Woodruff Brothers, 973
We Buried Her Beneath The Willow (Ridge Runners' Tribute To Linda Parker) Karl & Harty, 470
We Can Only Have One Mother John D. Foster, 355
We Can't Be Darlings Anymore J.E. Mainer's Mountaineers, 582
We Couldn't Say Goodbye Texas Wanderers, 900
We Courted In The Rain Thomas C. Ashley, 68; Ernest V. Stoneman, 874; "Dock" Walsh, 937

We Found Her Little Pussy Cat Light Crust Doughboys, 505
We Got A Home In The Heavenly Sky Reeves Family, 738
We Gotta Look Into This Mert's Hometown Serenaders, 615
We Have Met And We Have Parted Frank Blevins, 108; Cromwell Brothers, 234
We Have Moonshine In The West Virginia Hills Earl Shirkey & Roy Harper, 832
We Just Can't Get Along Light Crust Doughboys, 507
We Like It Johnny Marvin, 607
We Love To Play For People When They Talk Carson Robison, 794
We Met Down In The Hills Of Old Wyoming Hank Snow, 852
We Might As Well Forget It Charlie Wills, 966
We Miss Him When The Evening Shadows Fall Mrs. Jimmie Rodgers, 809
We Miss You Mother Chuck Wagon Gang, 210
We Miss You Precious Darling Edward Carson, 174
We Must Have Beer Light Crust Doughboys, 505
We Need A Change In Business All Around Uncle Dave Macon, 577
We Never Dream The Same Dream Twice Bob Atcher, 70; Gene Autry, 85; Massey Family, 612
We Never Speak As We Pass By Vernon Dalhart, 286
We Ought To Be Thankful For That Uncle Pete & Louise, 919
We Parted At The Gate Homer Briarhopper, 127; Earl Shirkey & Roy Harper, 831
We Parted By The Riverside Blue Sky Boys, 114; B.F. Kincaid, 482; Prairie Ramblers, 705; Ernest V. Stoneman, 877
We Played A Game Jimmie Revard, 743
We Read Of A Place That's Called Heaven Monroe Brothers, 633
We Sat Beneath The Maple On The Hill Vernon Dalhart, 258, 262–63
We Shall All Be Reunited Lloyd Burdette, 143; Alfred G. Karnes, 472
We Shall Have Glory Afterwhile Chuck Wagon Gang, 211
We Shall Meet Bye And Bye Frank & James McCravy, 537
We Shall Meet On That Beautiful Shore Red Fox Chasers, 730
We Shall Reach Home Freeman Quartette, 359; Stamps Quartet, 864
We Shall Reach It Bye And Bye Rev. M.L. Thrasher, 904
We Shall Rise Carter Family, 195; Byron Parker, 675; Smith's Sacred Singers, 849
We Shall See The King Someday John McGhee & Frank Welling, 559
We Shall Wear A Crown William Rexroat's Cedar Crest Singers, 744
We Were Pals Together Claude Davis, 297
We Will March Alone Stamps Quartet, 865
We Will March Through The Streets Of The City Carter Family, 190
We Will Meet At The End Of The Trail Vernon Dalhart, 262
We Will Meet At The End Of The Trail (A Tribute To Rudolph Valentino) Vernon Dalhart, 262
We Will Miss Him Wade Mainer, 584
We Will Not Forget Brown Brothers, 138
We Will Outshine The Sun Cofer Brothers, 216; Roy Harvey, 410
We Will Rise And Shine Carolina Gospel Singers, 171
We Will Understand It Better Bye And Bye Frank & James McCravy, 537
Weak And Sinful Soul Andrews Brothers, 60
Wearing Of The Green Woodhull's Old Time Masters, 971
Weary Shelton Brothers, 830

Weary Blues Leon Chappelear, 201; Light Crust Doughboys, 504; Roy Newman, 656; Smizers Dixie Serenaders, 851
Weary Gambler [The] Ira Yates, 975
Weary Little Pony Prairie Ramblers, 706
Weary Lonesome Blues Roy Acuff, 51; Delmore Brothers, 310; Milo Twins, 628
Weary Mind Blues Fleming & Townsend, 348
Weary Of The Same Ol' Stuff Bob Wills, 961
Weary Prodigal Son Carter Family, 189
Weary River Roy Acuff, 50
Weary Steel Blues Ted Daffan's Texans, 241
Weary Traveller Cliff Carlisle, 168
Weary Troubled Me Prairie Ramblers, 710
Weary, Worried And Blue Bob Atcher, 70; Ted Daffan's Texans, 241
Weave Room Blues Dorsey & Beatrice Dixon, 321; Fisher Hendley, 417
Weaver's Blues [The] Jimmie Tarlton, 892
Weaver's Life Dorsey & Beatrice Dixon, 321
Weddin' In The Wildwood Otis & Eleanor, 670
Wedding Bells Allen Brothers, 55; Bill Shores & Melvin Dupree, 832
Wedding Bells Waltz Elton Britt, 128; Melvin Dupree, 327; Bill Shores & Melvin Dupree, 832
Wedding March Joseph Falcon, 334
Wedding Of The Winds Green's String Band, 381
Wednesday Night Leaford Hall, 390
Wednesday Night Waltz Cruthers Brothers, 239; Kessinger Brothers, 479; Leake County Revelers, 494; North Carolina Hawaiians, 663; Riley Puckett, 721; Doc Roberts, 754; Carson Robison, 770–71; Shelton Brothers, 829; Stripling Brothers, 880; Wiley Walker & Gene Sullivan, 936
Wednesday Rag Bob Dunn's Vagabonds, 327
Wee Dog Waltz Joe Foss, 353
Week End At Sam Stover's [A] Chris Bouchillon, 120
Weeping Blues Bill Boyd, 124; Henry Whitter, 954
Weeping Daddy Blues Wild Bill Wade, 933
Weeping Mary [J.T.] Allison's Sacred Harp Singers, 60; Roswell Sacred Harp Quartet, 814
Weeping Pilgrim [J.T.] Allison's Sacred Harp Singers, 60
Weeping Willow Earl Johnson, 460; Stripling Brothers, 880
Weeping Willow Lane Hugh Cross, 237
Weeping Willow Tree Richard D. Burnett, 144; Daphne Burns, 145; Lester McFarland & Robert A. Gardner, 544; Monroe Brothers, 633; Holland Puckett, 714; Red Fox Chasers, 730; George Reneau, 741; Ernest Thompson, 902; Billy Vest, 931; Henry Whitter, 954
Weeping Willow Valley Happy Valley Boys, 397
Weighed And Found Wanting Rev. J.O. Hanes & Male Choir, 395
Welcome The Traveler Home Fiddlin' John Carson, 177
Welcome The Travelers Home No. 2 Fiddlin' John Carson, 177
We'll Be At Home Again Mr. & Mrs. R.N. Grisham, 384
We'll Be Married When The Sun Goes Down Buster Carter & Preston Young, 181
We'll Bust Them Trucks John McGhee & Frank Welling, 561
We'll Drop Our Anchor Rev. M.L. Thrasher, 905
We'll Have Weather Loren H. Abram, 47
We'll Know Each Other Up There Three Tobacco Tags, 907
We'll Live Again Vaughan Quartet, 925
We'll Love Each Other Over There Parham Bros. Quartette, 675
We'll Meet Again In Peaceful Valley Wilf Carter (Montana Slim), 184
We'll Meet At The End Of The Trail Girls Of The Golden West, 370
We'll Meet At The Foot Of The Hill Jack & Jean, 451

We'll Meet By The Bend In The River Roy Newman, 657
We'll Never Be Sweethearts Again John Boyd, 125
We'll Never Say Goodbye Frank & James McCravy, 533; McDonald Quartet, 541; Matt Simmons & Frank Miller, 835
We'll Reap What We Sow McDonald Quartet, 541; Stringfellow Quartet, 879; Vaughan Quartet, 929
We'll Rest At The End Of The Trail Ambrose Haley, 390; W. Lee O'Daniel, 665; Ranch Boys, 726; Tex Ritter, 750; Sons Of The Pioneers, 857
We'll Ride The Tide Together Jimmie Revard, 743
We'll Sing On That Shore Palmer Sisters, 673
We'll Sing Over Yonder Smith's Sacred Singers, 851
We'll Soon Be Done With Troubles And Trials Coats Sacred Quartette, 216; Royal Quartette, 815
We'll Soon Be There Lee Wells, 943
We'll Sow Righteous Seed Bill Cox, 226
We'll Sow Righteous Seed For The Reaper Riley Puckett, 716
We'll Talk About One Another Lewis McDaniels, 539
We'll Understand It Better Parker Quartette, 679
We'll Understand It Better By And By Posey Rorer, 813
We'll Understand It Better Bye And Bye Kentucky Mountain Choristers, 478; Frank & James McCravy, 531; Smith's Sacred Singers, 851
We'll Work Till Jesus Comes Smith's Sacred Singers, 851
Went To See My Gal Last Night Carson Robison, 777–79
Went Up In The Clouds Of Heaven Ernest Phipps, 691
We're Drifting On Amory Male Quartette, 60; Mr. & Mrs. R.N. Grisham, 384
We're Floating Down The Stream Of Time George Reneau, 741
We're Gonna Have A Good Time Tonight Bert Bilbro, 104
We're Gonna Have To Slap The Dirty Little Jap Johnny Bond, 117
We're Gonna Have To Slap The Dirty Little Jap (And Uncle Sam's The Guy Who Can Do It) Denver Darling, 295; Carson Robison, 797
We're Happy In The U.S.A. Modern Mountaineers, 631
We're In The Money Shanks Bros. Trio, 825
We're Just Plain Folks "Dock" Walsh, 938
We're Living For Jesus Parker Quartette, 679; Smith's Sacred Singers, 851
We're Marching To Zion Smoky Mountain Sacred Singers, 852
We're Not The Hoosier Hot Shots Bob Skyles, 838
We're Riding On The Dummy Dummy Line Bill Cox, 225
We're Saying Goodbye Eddie Dean, 308
We're The Sweet Violet Boys Prairie Ramblers, 710
Were You Sincere Gene Autry, 83
Were You There? Wade Mainer, 585; Bill Monroe, 632; S.E. Mullis, 646
West Ain't What It Used To Be [The] Carson Robison, 796
West Coast Special Arizona Wranglers, 62
West Kentucky Limited E.E. Hack String Band, 386
West Of Rainbow Trail Wilf Carter (Montana Slim), 186
West Of The Great Divide Vaughan Quartet, 927
West Plains Explosion [The] Vernon Dalhart, 280, 282; Carson Robison, 762
West Texas Breakdown Bill Shores & Melvin Dupree, 832
West Texas Stomp Light Crust Doughboys, 502
West Virginia Blues [The] Fred Pendleton, 685
West Virginia Gals Hill Billies, 424
West Virginia Girl Dick Justice, 468
West Virginia Highway Ernest V. Stoneman, 873, 878
West Virginia Hills Kanawha Singers, 469; Moatsville String Ticklers, 630
West Virginia Rag [The] Frank Hutchison, 449
West Virginia Railroad Blues Andrews Brothers, 60

Index to Titles

West Virginia Sally Ann Byrd Moore, 639
West Virginia Special Kessinger Brothers, 480
West Wind Blues Ted Daffan's Texans, 241
West, A Nest And You [The] Al Clauser, 214; Ranch Boys, 726
Western Country Henry Whitter, 954
Western Hobo Carter Family, 188
Western Union Doctor Lloyd & Howard Maxey, 508
Westward Ho Sons Of The Pioneers, 857; Zeke Williams, 959
Westward Ho For Reno Adelyne Hood, 435
Westward-Ho! Twilight Trail Boys, 918
We've Been Chums For Fifty Years Dick Parman, 679
We've Come A Long Way Together Gene Autry, 84
We've Gone To The End Of The Rainbow Ernest Rogers, 810
We've Got To Have 'Em, That's All Blind Alfred Reed, 733
We've Said Our Last Goodbye Lew Preston, 713
Whale Did, I Know He Did [The] Mustard & Gravy, 647
What A Change Laurel Firemen's Quartet, 491
What A Change One Day Can Make Grady & Hazel Cole, 217
What A Day That Will Be McDonald Quartet, 540; Mount Vernon Mixed Quartet, 645; V.O. Stamps-M.L. Yandell, 863; Stamps Quartet, 865
What A Friend Peck's Male Quartette, 684
What A Friend We Have In Jesus Arthur Cornwall & William Cleary, 223; John McGhee & Frank Welling, 553; [E.R.] Nance Family, 648; Old Southern Sacred Singers, 669; Zeke Williams, 959
What A Friend We Have In Mother Wilf Carter (Montana Slim), 184; Dixie Reelers, 319; Lester McFarland & Robert A. Gardner, 550; Charlie Mitchell & His Kentucky Ridge Runners, 630; Don White, 949
What A Gathering That Will Be John McGhee & Frank Welling, 557, 561; Smith's Sacred Singers, 850
What A Glad Day Wright Brothers Quartet, 974
What A Happy Time Parker Quartette, 679; Smith's Sacred Singers, 851
What A Morning That Will Be Vaughan Quartet, 928
What A Wonderful Feeling Humbard Family, 447
What A Wonderful Mother Of Mine Wilf Carter (Montana Slim), 186
What A Wonderful Mother You'd Be Jack & Bill, 451
What A Wonderful Saviour Is He Wade Mainer, 585
What A Wonderful Time V.O. Stamps-M.L. Yandell, 863
What A Wonderful Time That Will Be Knippers Bros. & Parker, 488
What A Wondrous Love Golden Echo Boys, 372
What About You? Jenkins Family, 457
What Are They Doing In Heaven Carolina Gospel Singers, 171; Frank & James McCravy, 534; Vaughan Quartet, 930
What Are They Doing In Heaven Today Frank & James McCravy, 533, 536
What Are You Going To Do Brother? Wade Mainer, 584
What Are You Going To Do With Baby Hodgers Brothers, 428
What Are You Squawkin' About? Carson Robison, 790
What Can I Give In Exchange Dorsey & Beatrice Dixon, 321
What Caused Me To Roam Arthur Duhon, 325
What Did He Do? Paramount Quartet, 674; Sheffield Male Quartet, 826
What Did I Do To Be Punished So Long? Percy Babineaux-Bixy Guidry, 87
(What Did I Do To Be So) Black And Blue Roy Newman, 657
What Did I Do? Bob Skyles, 838
What Difference Does It Make? Wilf Carter (Montana Slim), 185; Leon Selph, 824

What Do I Do Now Hi-Flyers, 420
What Does It Matter As Long As I Have You Jimmy Long, 511
What Does The Deep Sea Say Anglin Brothers, 61; Carter Family, 191; Vernon Dalhart, 287; Clarence Harding, 398; Lester McFarland & Robert A. Gardner, 547; Bob Miller, 621, 623
What Else Can I Do Jimmie Davis, 304
What Good Is The Sunshine? Texas Jim Robertson, 759
What Good Will It Do Roy Acuff, 50; Jimmie Davis, 304; Clayton McMichen, 572
What Happened Jimmie Davis, 306
What Has Become Of The Old Church Bell? Charlie D. Tillman & Daughter, 910
What Has Become Of The Old Church Bells? Carson Robison, 769
What Have You Done Blue Sky Boys, 113
What I Saw In Havana Dick Parman, 680
What If My Dreams Don't Come True? Leroy [Slim] Johnson, 462
What Is A Home Without Babies Roy Harvey, 410
What Is A Home Without Love Arkansas Woodchopper, 64; Floyd Skillern "The Mountain Troubadour," 837
What Is He Worth To The Soul Blue Ridge Sacred Singers, 112
What Is He Worth To Your Soul? Vaughan Quartet, 925
What Is Home Without Babies Charlie Poole, 700; Red Fox Chasers, 731; Ernest Thompson, 903
What Is Home Without Baby Dick Hartman's Tennessee Ramblers, 408
What Is Home Without Love Edith & Sherman Collins, 218; Tom Darby & Jimmie Tarlton, 294; Roy Harvey, 409–10; Monroe Brothers, 632; Philyaw Brothers, 690
What Is Life Lived Alone Al Dexter, 315; Buddy Jones, 466
What Is So Rare Hoosier Hot Shots, 439
What Kind Of Shoes You Gwine To Wear William Rexroat's Cedar Crest Singers, 744
What Love Bush Brothers, 147
What Love! Bush Brothers, 147
What Made The Wild Cat Wild Humphries Brothers, 447
What Makes Him Do It? Daddy John Love, 514
What Makes Your Head So Red? Charlie Marshall, 587–88; Rowdy Wright, 974
What More Can I Say Jimmie Davis, 305
What Shall Our Answer Be George Long, 510
What Shall We Do With Mother Carolina Ladies Quartet, 171; Rev. M.L. Thrasher, 904–05
What Size Do You Need Shelly Lee Alley, 58
What Sort O' Robes Do Angels Wear? Sandhills Sixteen, 820
What Sugar Head Licker Will Do Buster Carter & Preston Young, 181
What The Engine Done Al Bernard, 101
What Whiskey Will Do Norman Woodlieff, 973
What Will I Do, For My Money's All Gone Uncle Eck Dunford, 325
What Will You Do With Jesus? Maury Pearson, 683
What Will You Take In Exchange (For Your Soul) Edith & Sherman Collins, 218
What Wondrous Love Vaughan Quartet, 927
What Would The Profit Be? Monroe Brothers, 633
What Would You Do With Gabriel's Trumpet Roy Acuff, 49
What Would You Give Rangers Quartet, 728
What Would You Give (In Exchange For Your Mother-In-Law) Jake & Carl, 453; Prairie Ramblers, 709
What Would You Give For Your Soul In The End? Woodruff Brothers, 973
What Would You Give In Exchange For Your Soul No. 2 Massey Family, 611

What Would You Give In Exchange For Your Soul No. 5 Philyaw Brothers, 690
What Would You Give In Exchange For Your Soul? Prairie Ramblers, 707
What Would You Give In Exchange[?] Wade Mainer, 582; Monroe Brothers, 632
What Would You Give In Exchange[?] No. 5 Edith & Sherman Collins, 218
What Would You Give In Exchange[?]—Part 2–4 Monroe Brothers, 633
What Would You Give In Exchange[?]—Part 5 Dorsey & Beatrice Dixon, 321
What You Gonna Do—What You Gonna Say Girls Of The Golden West, 371
What You Gonna Do (This Year My Friend) Fleming & Townsend, 347
What You Gonna Do When The Rent Comes 'Round (Rufus Rastus Johnson Brown) Massey Family, 612
What You Gonna Do With The Baby G.B. Grayson & Henry Whitter, 381
What You Gonna Say To Peter Sons Of The Pioneers, 858
What You Mean To Me Melody Boys, 614
What You Need Now Is Sanctification E. Arthur Lewis, 497
What You're Doing Is Telling On Me Jesse Rodgers, 799
Whatcha Gonna Do Four Aces, 356
Whatcha Gonna Do When Your Licker Gives Out? Fiddlin' John Carson, 178
What-Cha Gonna Do When Your Wife Comes Home? Bob Skyles, 838
What-Cha Gonna Do With The Baby? Happy-Go-Lucky Boys, 397
Whatcha Know Joe? Johnny Lee Wills, 967
What's Bob Done Bill Mounce, 645
What's Gonna Happen To Me Gene Autry, 85
What's It? Jimmie Rodgers, 806
What's The Matter Now? Shelly Lee Alley, 58; Walker Brothers, 936
What's The Matter With Deep Elem Shelton Brothers, 830
What's The Matter With Deep Elm Sunshine Boys, 881
What's The Matter With The Mill? Bob Wills, 961
What's The Matter With You, Darling Jimmie Davis, 305
What's The Matter? Ocie Stockard, 869
What's The Reason (I'm Not Pleasin' You) Hugh Cross, 237; Texas Jim Lewis, 499; Riley Puckett, 721
What's The Use Alley Boys Of Abbeville, 59; Bill Boyd, 123; Jimmie Revard, 742; Ross Rhythm Rascals, 814
What's Wrong With Me Now? Claude Casey, 197
What's Yo' Name Nite Owls, 660
Wheel In A Wheel Vaughan Quartet, 926
Wheel Of The Wagon Is Broken [The] Milton Brown, 137; Light Crust Doughboys, 503; Patsy Montana, 634; Peaceful Valley Folk, 683
Wheezie Anna Milton Brown, 137
When W. Lee O'Daniel, 665
When A Boy From The Mountain (Weds A Girl From The Valley) Walton West, 945
When A Boy From The Mountains (Weds A Girl From The Valley) Jimmie Davis, 301; Blaine & Cal Smith, 843
When A Cowboy Sings A Song Roy Rogers, 811
When A Lady Meets A Gentleman Down South Ambrose Haley, 389
When A Man Get's [sic] Over Sixty Bob Miller, 625
When A Man Is Married Grant Brothers, 377
When A Man's Got A Woman Allen Brothers, 57
When A Man's Lonesome Callahan Brothers, 153
When Abraham And Isaac Rushed The Can Fiddlin' John Carson, 175
When All The Singers Get Home Buice Brothers, 142

When All Those Millions Sing Vaughan Quartet, 928
When Beulah Did The Hula In Missoula Sons Of The Ozarks, 857
When Bill Hilly Plays A Hill Billy Upon His Violin John I. White, 950
When Clouds Have Vanished Clayton McMichen, 568
When Daddy Played The Old Banjo Johnny Barfield, 93
When Down South Morgan Plays The Old Mouth-Organ Jimmy Smith, 844
When Dreams Come True Moore Sisters, 641
When Father Is Gone Crowder Brothers, 238
When Father Put The Paper On The Wall Capt. Appleblossom, 158
When Father Was A Boy Jimmy Long, 511
When First I Fell In Love Uncle Dave Macon, 577
When Gabriel Blows His Trumpet For Me Dorsey & Beatrice Dixon, 322
When God's Singers Reach Glory [E.R.] Nance Family, 648
When Grape Juice Turns To Wine Carl McCray, 538
When He Calls Me I Will Answer Gospel Sanctified Singers, 376
When He Died He Got A Home In Hell Walter Smith, 847
When Honey Sings An Old Time Song Vaughan Quartet, 924
When I Am Blue Leo Soileau, 854
When I Am Far Away From Home Leo Soileau, 854
When I Bid The Prairie Good-Bye Wilf Carter (Montana Slim), 185
When I Bought That Wedding Ring Vernon Dalhart, 290
When I Camped Under The Stars Roy Rogers, 811
When I Can Read My Title Clear Maury Pearson, 683
When I Come To The End Of The Trail Joe Cook, 220
When I Dream Of My Red River Home Bob Miller, 625
When I Feel Froggie, I'm Gonna Hop Cliff Carlisle, 167
When I Find My Dear Daddy Is Waiting Bill Boyd, 121
When I First Laid Eyes On You Gene Autry, 84
When I First Met You Claude Casey, 197
When I Get To The End Of The Way Frank & James McCravy, 533
When I Get You Alone Tonight Dick Parman, 680
When I Go A Courtin' My Best Gal Bill Nettles, 654
When I Grow Too Old To Dream Bill Carlisle, 159; Prairie Ramblers, 705; Riley Puckett, 721–22; Three Little Maids, 906
When I Had But Fifty Cents Thomas C. Ashley, 68; Binkley Brothers Dixie Clodhoppers, 104; Warren Caplinger, 157; Charlie Craver, 231; "Peg" Moreland, 641; Archer Porter, 702; Riley Puckett, 716
(When I Had) My Pony On The Range Bill Boyd, 125
When I Hear You Call O-Le-O-La-E Johnny Marvin, 607
When I Kissed That Girl Good-Bye Johnny Marvin, 607
When I Laid My Bible Down Karl & Harty, 471
When I Lay My Burden Down Roy Acuff, 50
When I Leave This World Behind Sons Of The Pioneers, 857
When I Leave Your Home Joseph Falcon, 335
When I Left Home For Texas Joseph Falcon, 334
When I Left My Good Old Home Charlie Poole, 699
When I Lived In Arkansas Hugh Cross, 236; Clayton McMichen, 569
When I Look To The West (I Think Of You) Arthur Fields & Fred Hall, 341
When I Lost You Earl Shirkey & Roy Harper, 832
When I Met You At The Gate Oscar [Slim] Doucet, 324
When I Move To That New Range Eddie Dean, 307
When I Need Lovin' Prairie Ramblers, 709
When I Put On My Long White Robe Bob Miller, 617
When I Reach Home Laurel Firemen's Quartet, 491

Index to Titles   **1169**

When I Reach My Home Eternal J.E. Mainer's Mountaineers, 581
When I Rest On The Bosom Of My King Royal Quartette, 815
When I Say Hello To The Rockies Wilf Carter (Montana Slim), 185
When I See The Blood Jenkins Family, 457; Alfred G. Karnes, 471
When I See The Blood Of The Lamb Rev. M.L. Thrasher, 905
When I Shall Cross Over The Dark Rolling Tide George Reneau, 741
When I Take My Sugar To Tea Milton Brown, 137; Hank Penny, 686
When I Take My Vacation In Heaven Baker's Whitley County Sacred Singers, 90; Deckers, 308; Ruth Donaldson & Helen Jepsen, 323; Dick Hartman's Tennessee Ramblers, 407; Frank Luther, 520; Frank & James McCravy, 538; Lester McFarland & Robert A. Gardner, 547; Bob Miller, 624; Hank & Slim Newman, 656; Jimmy Wakely, 934; Rowdy Wright, 974
When I Take My Vacation On Heaven's Bright Shore Mount Vernon Quartet, 645
When I Walk Into Your Parlor Byrd Moore, 640
When I Walked The Streets Of Gold Roper's Mountain Singers, 813
When I Was A Baby Four Pickled Peppers, 356
When I Was A Boy From The Mountains Blue Ridge Hill Billies, 110; Jesse Rodgers, 799
When I Was A Boy From The Mountains (And You Were A Girl From The Hills) Beverly Hill Billies, 102; Frank Luther, 522; Lester McFarland & Robert A. Gardner, 549
When I Was All Alone Last Night Leo Soileau, 854
When I Was Born Fisher Hendley, 416
When I Was Single Frank Luther, 525; Lester McFarland & Robert A. Gardner, 542
When I Was Single My Pockets Would Jingle John D. Foster, 353; Arthur Tanner, 886
When I Won You Nolan Bush, 147
When I Wore My Daddy's Brown Derby Frank & James McCravy, 538; Earl & Willie Phelps, 689
When I Yoo Hoo In The Valley Lulu Belle & Scotty, 516
When I'm Back In Tennessee Riley Puckett, 722
When I'm Dead And Gone Cliff Carlisle, 167
When I'm Far Away Charlie Poole, 700
When I'm Four Times Twenty Elton Britt, 129
When I'm Gone Carter Family, 189; Earl Shirkey & Roy Harper, 831
When I'm Gone You'll Be Blue Fleming & Townsend, 347
When I'm Gone You'll Soon Forget Gene Autry, 84; Lloyd Burdette, 143; Lester McFarland & Robert A. Gardner, 544; Riley Puckett, 716–17
When I'm Gone, Don't You Grieve Milton Brown, 136–37
When I'm Gone, You'll Soon Forget Me Riley Puckett, 722
When I'm In A Far Away Land Johnson & Lee, 462
When I'm Travelling Little Darling Andrews Brothers, 60
When I'm Walking With My Sweetness Rice Brothers' Gang, 746
When I'm With You Vernon Dalhart, 251
When Irish Eyes Are Smiling Bradley Kincaid, 485; Riley Puckett, 722
When It Gets Dark Hall Brothers, 391
When It Rains It Really Pours Shelton Brothers, 830
When It's Apple Blossom Time Up In The Berkshires Old Hank Penny, 687
When It's Blossom Time In Old Caroline Rice Brothers' Gang, 747
When It's Harvest Time Elton Britt, 128

When It's Harvest Time In Old New England Elton Britt, 128
When It's Harvest Time In Peaceful Valley Eddie Dean, 308; Dick Hartman's Tennessee Ramblers, 407; Pioneer Trio, 698; Vagabonds, 921
When It's Harvest Time My Sweet Angeline Arkansas Woodchopper, 63
When It's Harvest Time, Sweet Angeline Beverly Hill Billies, 102; Milton Brown, 138; Howard Keesee, 475
When It's Honey Suckle Time In The Valley Charlie Wills, 966
When It's Honeysuckle Time Billy Vest, 931
When It's Hottest Time Down South Fleming & Townsend, 347
When It's Lamp Lightin' Time In The Valley Gene Autry, 78; Edith & Sherman Collins, 218; Frank Dudgeon, 324; Roy Harvey, 411; Frank Luther, 520; Lester McFarland & Robert A. Gardner, 549; Asa Martin, 591–92; Tex Ritter, 750; Vagabonds, 921
When It's Lamplighting Time Up In Heaven Callahan Brothers, 153
When It's Moonlight Down In Lovers' Lane Vagabonds, 921
When It's Moonlight On The Meadow Plantation Boys, 698
When It's Moonlight On The Prairie "Peg" Moreland, 641
When It's Nightime In Nevada Lester McFarland & Robert A. Gardner, 549
When It's Night-Time In Nevada Deckers, 308; Frank[ie] Marvin, 604; Carson Robison, 788–89; Shelton Brothers, 827
When It's Peach Pickin' Time In Georgia Dwight Butcher, 148; Hugh Cross, 236; Jimmie Davis, 302; Clayton McMichen, 569; Riley Puckett, 722
When It's Prayer Meetin' Time In The Hollow Blue Ridge Mountain Girls, 112; Log Cabin Boys, 508; Massey Family, 609; Tom & Don, 911
When It's Prayer-Time On The Prairie Jake & Carl, 453; Bob Miller, 625
When It's Roll-Call In The Bunk House Wilf Carter (Montana Slim), 185
When It's Round-Up Time In Heaven Jimmie Davis, 300–301; Light Crust Doughboys, 501
When It's Roundup Time In Texas Cliff Carlisle, 164
When It's Springtime In The Blue Ridge Mountain Al Clauser, 214
When It's Springtime In The Blue Ridge Mountains Bill Elliott, 332; Lester McFarland & Robert A. Gardner, 549; Dick Robertson, 758; Carson Robison, 790–92
When It's Springtime In The Rockies Gene Autry, 83; Arthur Fields & Fred Hall, 341; Ernest Hare, 399; Leake County Revelers, 495; Lester McFarland & Robert A. Gardner, 547; Bob Palmer & Monte Hall, 673; Ranch Boys, 725; Red River Dave, 732; Carson Robison, 774, 777, 780, 784
When It's Summertime In A Southern Clime Delmore Brothers, 309
When It's Sunset Time In Sunny Tennessee Dwight Butcher, 148
When It's Time For The Whippoorwill To Sing Anglin Brothers, 61; Delmore Brothers, 311; Vagabonds, 921
When It's Time For The Whippoorwills To Sing White Brothers (Joe & Bob), 951
When It's Time To Shear The Sheep I'm Coming Back Harry "Mac" McClintock, 529
When It's Tooth Pickin' Time In False Teeth Valley Pine Ridge Boys, 697
When It's Tune Wrangling Time In Texas Tune Wranglers, 915
When It's Twilight In Sweetheart Lane Bill Boyd, 122

When It's Twilight Over Texas Wilf Carter (Montana Slim), 185
When It's Winter In The Ozarks Arthur Fields & Fred Hall, 341
When It's Your Time Of Day Texas Wanderers, 900
When Jesus Appears Dorsey & Beatrice Dixon, 321
When Jesus Beckons Me Home Frank Luther, 520; [Smilin'] Ed McConnell, 530–31
When Jesus Came My Way Hall County Sacred Singers, 392
When Jesus Comes Corley Family, 222; Drum Quartet, 324; Peck's Male Quartette, 684; Rainbow Quartette, 724; Simmons Sacred Singers, 835; Smith's Sacred Singers, 850; V.O. Stamps-M.L. Yandell, 863; Vaughan Quartet, 926–27
When Jesus Deems It Best Vaughan Quartet, 924
When Jimmie Rodgers Said Good-bye Gene Autry, 79; Kenneth Houchins, 444
When Jimmy Rodgers Said Goodbye Dwight Butcher, 148
When Katie Comes Down To The Gate Murphy Brothers, 646
When Lulu's Gone Roy Acuff, 48
When Mama Goes Out The Maid Comes In Bar-X Cowboys, 93
When Maple Leaves Are Falling Claude Davis, 296
When Married Folks Are Out Of Cash Bill Chitwood, 208
When Mother Nature Sings Her Lullaby Roy Rogers, 811
When Mother Prayed For Me Pine Ridge Boys, 697
When My Baby Comes To Town Modern Mountaineers, 631
When My Blue Moon Turns To Gold Again Zeke Manners, 586; Wiley Walker & Gene Sullivan, 936
When My Dream Boat Comes Home Massey Family, 610
When My Dreams Come True Bill Boyd, 123
When My Life Work Is Ended Frank & James McCravy, 533
When My Louie Sings His Yodel-Laddy-Hoo Lew Childre, 207
When My Saviour Calls Me Home Rambling Kid & The Professor, 725
When My Wife Will Return To Me Ernest V. Stoneman, 872
When Night Comes On Bill Cox, 229
When Night Falls Bob Dunn's Vagabonds, 326
When Old Age Pension Check Comes To Our Door Diamond D Boys, 316
When Once Again We'll Go Home Bill Cox, 227
When Our Lord Shall Come Again Lester McFarland & Robert A. Gardner, 542; Monroe Brothers, 633; Smith's Sacred Singers, 850
When Our Old Age Pension Check Comes To Our Door Sons Of The Pioneers, 857
When Our Saviour Comes Again Smith's Sacred Singers, 850–51
When Our Wonderful Savior Comes Down Bill Cox, 228
When Paw Was Courtin' Maw Hoosier Hot Shots, 438
When Polly Walk Thru The Hollyhock [sic] Jack Golding, 374
When Reubin Comes To Town Uncle Dave Macon, 576
When Rhododendrons Bloom Again Grace & Scotty MacLean, 565
When Shadows Fade Away Stripling Brothers, 880
When Silver Threads Are Gold Again Carter Family, 193
When Somebody Thinks You're Wonderful Crystal Springs Ramblers, 239
When Summer Comes Again Lewis Brothers, 500
When That Some Body Else Was You Wilf Carter (Montana Slim), 186
When That Someone You Love Doesn't Love You Hank Snow, 853
When The Angels Carry Me Home Cliff Carlisle, 167
When The Autumn Leaves Are Turning To Gold Walter Coon, 221

When The Autumn Leaves Fall Odus & Woodrow, 667
When The Bees Are In The Hive Hugh Cross, 236; Girls Of The Golden West, 370; Roy Harvey, 409, 411; Jo & Alma, 458; Judie & Julie, 468
When The Birds Begin Their Singing In The Trees Georgia Yellow Hammers, 367
When The Black Sheep Gets The Blues Roy Rogers, 811
When The Bloom Is On The Sage Beverly Hill Billies, 101; Vernon Dalhart, 292; Hollywood Hillbilly Orchestra, 432; Hoosier Hawaiians, 435; Frank Luther, 522; Clayton McMichen, 570; Carson Robison, 781–83
When The Bloom Is On The Sage (Round-Up Time In Texas) Clayton McMichen, 571
When The Blue Bells Bloom Carlisle Brothers, 169
When The Blue Eyes Met The Brown Leon McGuire, 564
When The Book Of Life Is Opened Bill Nettles, 654
When The Bright Prairie Moon Is Rolling By Wilf Carter (Montana Slim), 183
When The Cactus Blooms I'll Be Waiting Norwood Tew, 899
When The Cactus Is In Bloom Cliff Carlisle, 162; Buddy Jones, 465; Jimmie Rodgers, 805–06
When The Candle Lights Are Gleaming Lester McFarland & Robert A. Gardner, 550
When The Circus Came To Town Dave Hughs, 446
When The Clock Struck Seventeen Goebel Reeves, 735
When The Cold, Cold Clay Is Laid Around Me Sloane & Threadgill, 840
When The Curtains Of Night Are Pinned Back By The Stars Zora Layman, 492
When The Dew Is On The Rose W.C. Childers, 206; Duke Clark, 213; Harry Hillard, 425
When The Evening Sun Goes Down Cliff Carlisle, 166
When The Flowers Are Blooming In The Springtime Three Little Maids, 906
When The Flowers Bloom Again In The Ozarks Hugh Cross, 236
When The Flowers Bloom In Springtime Richard Brooks & Reuben Puckett, 132; Claude Davis, 297
When The Flowers Bloom In The Spring Claude Davis, 297
When The Flowers Bloom In The Springtime Claude Davis, 297–98
When The Flowers Of Montana Were Blooming Patsy Montana, 634
When The Gates Of Glory Open Bush Brothers, 147
When The Golden Corn Is Waving Carson Robison, 785
When The Golden Leaves Are Falling Gene Autry, 82
When The Golden Moon Is Shining Four Pickled Peppers, 356
When The Golden Rod Is Blooming Hugh Cross, 236
When The Golden Rod Is Blooming Once Again Golden Melody Boys, 373
When The Golden Train Comes Down Sons Of The Pioneers, 858
When The Goldenrods Are Waving Kenneth Houchins, 443; Frank Luther, 520
When The Good Lord Sets You Free Carolina Tar Heels, 173
When The Happy Morning Breaks Smith's Sacred Singers, 850
When The Harvest Days Are Over Lester McFarland & Robert A. Gardner, 546; Uncle Dave Macon, 578
When The Harvest Days Are Over, Jessie Dear Buell Kazee, 472; John McGhee & Frank Welling, 558
When The Harvest Moon Is Shining Sloane & Threadgill, 840; Merritt Smith, 845
When The Harvest Moon Is Shining (Mollie Dear) Carson Robison, 768
When The Holy Ghost Comes Down Vaughan Quartet, 929

When The Home Gates Swing On Vaughan Quartet, 929
When The Home Gates Swing Open Missouri Pacific Lines Booster Quartet, 629; Vaughan Quartet, 927
When The Hummin' Birds Are Hummin' Low Don Weston, 947
When The Humming Birds Are Humming Gene Autry, 78
When The Leaves Begin To Fall Lester McFarland & Robert A. Gardner, 546, 548
When The Leaves Turn Green Bowman Sisters, 121
When The Leaves Turn Red And Fall Frank Luther, 518–19
When The Light Shines Thru V.O. Stamps-M.L. Yandell, 863
When The Lightning Struck The Coon Creek Party Line Hoosier Hot Shots, 440
When The Light's Gone Out In Your Soul J.E. Mainer's Mountaineers, 582
When The Lilac Blooms Golden Melody Boys, 373
When The Lillies Bloom Again (In Old Kentucky) Ted Hawkins, 413
When The Liquor Flows Again Elmer Bird, 105
When The Locust Is In Bloom Bob Atcher, 69
When The Mailman Says No Mail Today Gene Autry, 78
When The Maple Leaves Are Falling Claude Davis, 297; Clayton McMichen, 567; Riley Puckett, 718
When The Mellow Moon Is Shining Frank Luther, 519; Bob Miller, 623
When The Mighty Trumpet Sounds Mr. & Mrs. R.N. Grisham, 385
When The Moon Comes Over Sun Valley Sons Of The Pioneers, 859
When The Moon Comes Over The Mountain Cliff Carlisle, 163; Deckers, 308; Lester McFarland & Robert A. Gardner, 549; Frank[ie] Marvin, 604; Carson Robison, 789; Leo Soileau, 855
When The Moon Drips Away Into The Blood Taylor-Griggs Louisiana Melody Makers, 894
When The Moon Shines Down Upon The Mountain Vernon Dalhart, 272–73, 275; Stuart Hamblen, 392
When The Moon Shines Down Upon The Mountains Louisiana Lou, 513
When The Moon Shines On The Mississippi Valley Gene Autry, 80; Light Crust Doughboys, 503
When The Morning Glories Grow Louie Donaldson, 323
When The Morning Glories Twine Taylor Trio, 894
When The Old Cow Went Dry Carlisle Brothers, 169; Bo Norris, 661
When The Organ Played At Twilight Carson Robison, 783, 785
When The Organ Played O' Promise Me Zora Layman, 492
When The Oriole Sings Again Bill Elliott, 332
When The Poppies Bloom Again Massey Family, 610
When The Pussywillow Whispers To The Catnip Travelers, 912
When The Raindrops Pattered On Our Old Tin Hats Bob Palmer & Jimmy White, 673
When The Ransomed Get Home Blue Sky Boys, 113
When The Redeemed Are Gathering In Warren Caplinger, 156; Carson Brothers-Smith, 180; Red Fox Chasers, 730; Ernest V. Stoneman, 873, 876–77
When The Rent Man Comes Around Walter Hurdt, 448
When The Rest Of The Crowd Goes Home (I Always Go Home Alone) Frank & James McCravy, 538
When The Roll Is Called Up Yonder Bela Lam, 489; John McGhee & Frank Welling, 553, 560; Uncle Dave Macon, 576; Rev. M.L. Thrasher, 905; Woodlawn Quartette, 972
When The Roses Bloom Again Elton Britt, 130; Hugh Cross, 235; Vernon Dalhart, 268; Frank Luther, 524; Lester McFarland & Robert A. Gardner, 542; Sons Of The Pioneers, 858; Ernest V. Stoneman, 874–75; Wilmer Watts, 941; Rowdy Wright, 974
When The Roses Bloom Again For The Bootlegger Earl Johnson, 460; Asa Martin, 588
When The Roses Bloom For The Bootlegger Carson Robison, 777; Earl Shirkey & Roy Harper, 831
When The Roses Bloom In Dixie Bill Cox, 225, 227; Asa Martin, 590
When The Roses Bloom In Dixieland Eldon Baker, 89; Blue Sky Boys, 114; Carter Family, 188
When The Roses Come Again Carter Family, 191; [Blind] Jack Mathis, 613; Frank Wheeler-Monroe Lamb, 948
When The Roses Grow Around The Cabin Door Arthur Smith, 842
When The Roses Wave In Dixie Farmer Sisters, 336
When The Round Up's Done This Fall Ken Maynard, 614
When The Saints Go Marching Home Frank Luther, 523; Frank & James McCravy, 533, 535
When The Saints Go Marching In Fiddlin' John Carson, 179; Kentucky Mountain Choristers, 478; Philyaw Brothers, 690; Snowball & Sunshine, 853; Swift Jewel Cowboys, 884
When The Shadows Flee Away Frank & James McCravy, 537
When The Shanghai Takes His Ride Raley Brothers, 724
When The Snowflakes Fall Again Bill Cox, 227; Frank Jenkins, 455; Byrd Moore, 638; Wilmer Watts, 941
When The Spring Roses Are Blooming Odus & Woodrow, 667
When The Springtime Comes Again Carter Family, 189
When The Stars Begin To Fall Blue Sky Boys, 113; Rambling Kid & The Professor, 725
When The Sun Goes Down Delta Twins, 312; Bob Palmer & Monte Hall, 673; Rambling Rangers, 725
When The Sun Goes Down Again Leo Boswell, 119; Bill Boyd, 122; Vernon Dalhart, 274–76, 281; Hank & Slim Newman, 656
When The Sun Goes Down Behind The Hill (And The Moon Begins To Rise) Canova Family, 156
When The Sun Goes Down In Arizona Tune Wranglers, 915
When The Sun Goes Down On A Little Prairie Town Carson Robison, 791
When The Sun Hides Away For The Day Dwight Butcher, 148
When The Sun Is Setting On The Prairie Roy Rogers, 811
When The Sun Says Good-Night To The Prairie Wilf Carter (Montana Slim), 184
When The Sun Sets On My Swiss Chalet Bill Boyd, 122
When The Sun Sets On The Sierra Leon Payne, 683
When The Sun Sets Someday Roy Hall, 390
When The Sunset Turns The Ocean Blue To Gold Foundation Quartette, 355
When The Sunset Turns The Ocean's Blue To Gold Dick Robertson, 758
When The Swallows Come Back To Capistrano Gene Autry, 85
When The Sweet Bye And Bye Is Ended Allen Quartette, 57; Rainbow Quartette, 724
When The Texas Moon Is Shining Jesse Rodgers, 798
When The Tide Of Happiness Comes Rolling In Lou & Nellie Thompson, 904
When The Train Comes Along Uncle Dave Macon, 578
When The Tumbleweeds Come Tumbling Down Again Gene Autry, 82–83
When The Twilight Shadows Fall Vaughan Quartet, 923–24
When The Valley Moon Was Low Blue Sky Boys, 114
When The Violets Bloom Again In The Springtime Magnolia Trio, 580
When The Wandering Boy Comes Home Frank Luther, 519

When The Weeping Willow Smiles Happy Fats, 396
When The White Azaleas Start Blooming Wilf Carter (Montana Slim), 185; Sally Foster, 355; Jake & Carl, 453; Frank Luther, 518–19; Massey Family, 609; Bob Miller, 624; Swift Jewel Cowboys, 884
When The Whole World Turns You Down Charles Nabell, 647
When The Whole World Turns You Down (Go Back To Your Mother And Home) Vernon Dalhart, 251
When The Wild Flowers Are In Bloom Beverly Hill Billies, 103
When The Wild, Wild Roses Bloom Frank Luther, 520; Bob Miller, 624
When The Women Get In Power Bill Cox, 226
When The Works All Done In The Fall Carson Robison, 774
When The Work's All Done Next Fall Vernon Dalhart, 285
When The Work's All Done This Fall Jules Allen, 55; Cartwright Brothers, 195; W.C. Childers, 205; Vernon Dalhart, 271–72; Bradley Kincaid, 483–84; Pie Plant Pete, 694; George Reneau, 741; Carson Robison, 787; Rodeo Trio, 798; Carl T. Sprague, 862; Ernest V. Stoneman, 872; Vagabonds, 922; Marc Williams, 958–59
When The Work's Done This Fall Gentry Brothers, 365
When The World Forgets [Smilin'] Ed McConnell, 530–31
When The World Has Turned You Down Ernest Tubb, 914
When The World's On Fire Carter Family, 189
When The World's On Fire—Part 2 (Charlie) Monroe's Boys, 632
When There's Tears In The Eyes Of A Potato Hoosier Hot Shots, 440; Roy Newman, 657
When They Bapti[s/z]ed Sister Lucy Lee Light Crust Doughboys, 502; Unknown Artists [VII], 920
When They Changed My Name To A Number Vernon Dalhart, 291; Red River Dave, 732; Don Weston, 947; Marc Williams, 959
When They Play Rural Rhythm Bill Boyd, 122
When They Ring The Golden Bells Alfred G. Karnes, 472; Frank & James McCravy, 532, 537; Jack Pickell, 694
When They Ring The Golden Bells For You And Me Carson Robison, 781; Smith's Sacred Singers, 850; Vaughan Quartet, 924
When They Ring Those Golden Bells Cherry Sisters, 204; Arthur Cornwall & William Cleary, 223; [E.R.] Nance Family, 648; XC Sacred Quartette, 975
When They Ring Those Golden Bells For You And Me Foundation Quartette, 355
When This Evening Sun Goes Down Carter Family, 194
When This War Is Over (The Volunteer's Farewell) Texas Jim Robertson, 760
When We All Get To Heaven Jenkins Family, 457; John McGhee & Frank Welling, 553, 557, 560
When We Carved Our Hearts On The Old Oak Tree Lester McFarland & Robert A. Gardner, 549; Carson Robison, 791; Floyd Skillern "The Mountain Troubadour," 837
When We Cross That Great Divide Johnny Roberts, 756
When We Go A Courtin' George Wade, 933
When We Go A Honky Tonkin' Al Dexter, 315
When We Go To Glory-Land Flat Creek Sacred Singers, 346; Rev. M.L. Thrasher, 905
When We Held Our Hymn Books Together Delmore Brothers, 310
When We Kissed And Said Good-bye Bill Nettles, 654
When We Lay Our Burdens Down Vaughan Quartet, 924
When We Meet Again Cliff Carlisle, 168
When We Meet On That Beautiful Shore Fiddlin' John Carson, 176
When We Meet On The Beautiful Shore Bill Cox, 224

When We Put On An Old Pair Of Shoes Jordan Brothers, 467
When We Reach Our Happy Home Light Crust Doughboys, 501
When We Rise To Meet Our Friend Duncan Sisters Trio, 325
When We See The Saviour Coming From Above Stalsby Family, 863
When We Sing Of Home Bill Cox, 224
When We Turn Out The Old Town Band Bob Palmer & Monte Hall, 673
When We're Traveling Thru The Air Ruth Donaldson & Helen Jepsen, 323
When Winter Weaves Its Silver In Our Hair Pine Ridge Ramblers, 697
When You And I Were Young Maggie Fiddlin' John Carson, 175; Chief Pontiac, 205; Collier Trio, 218; William B. Houchens, 443; Frank & James McCravy, 532; Clayton McMichen, 566; Roy Newman, 657; Riley Puckett, 716; George Reneau, 740; Jack Teter, 898; Vaughan Quartet, 924
When You Are Gone Alone Joe Creduer-Albert Babineaux, 232
When You Ask A Girl To Leave Her Happy Home Da Costa Woltz's Southern Broadcasters, 970
When You Come To The End Of The Day Otto Gray, 380
When You Come To The Rainbow's End Cherry Sisters, 204
When You Don't, Others Do Anglin Brothers, 61
When You Get It Right Vaughan Quartet, 927
When You Go A-Courtin' Hill Billies, 424
When You Go A-Courtin' Fletcher & Foster, 349; Three Tobacco Tags, 908
When You Have No One To Love You Pine Ridge Boys, 697
When You Hear Me Call Light Crust Doughboys, 502; Johnny Marvin, 607; W. Lee O'Daniel, 666
When You Know You're Not Forgotten By The Girl You Can't Forget Richard Brooks & Reuben Puckett, 132; Jimmie Davis, 304; Lester McFarland & Robert A. Gardner, 547
When You Leave, You'll Leave Me Sad Allen Brothers, 56
When You Left Me Leo Soileau, 854
When You Played The Old Church Organ Elton Britt, 129
When You Played The Organ Bob Miller, 624
When You Smile Leon Selph, 824
When You Think A Whole Lot About Someone Shelton Brothers, 828; Tune Wranglers, 915
When You Took Me From My Home Leo Soileau, 855
When You Took Your Love Away Ray Whitley, 953
When You Were A Boy On My Knee Johnny Roberts, 756
When You Were Sweet Sixteen Hill Billies, 424; Zeb White, 951
When You Were The Queen Of The May Lou & Nellie Thompson, 904
When You Wore A Tulip Cliff Carlisle, 162; Hugh Cross, 235, 237; Walter C. Peterson, 688; Pickard Family, 693; Riley Puckett, 718; Walker's Corbin Ramblers, 937
When You Wore A Tulip (And I Wore A Big Red Rose) Hoosier Hot Shots, 437; Light Crust Doughboys, 503; John & Emery McClung, 530
When Your Hair Has Turned To Silver Carson Robison, 786
When Your Hair Has Turned To Silver (I Will Love You Just The Same) Bar-X Cowboys, 92; Frank Luther, 522; Lester McFarland & Robert A. Gardner, 548; Carson Robison, 785
When Your Old Wedding Ring Was New Grace & Scotty MacLean, 565
When You're A Long Long Way From Home Richard Brooks & Reuben Puckett, 133; Red River Dave, 732
When You're All In Down And Out Ernest Thompson, 902

When You're Alone (Try To Remember Me) Carson Robison, 789
When You're Far Away Vernon Dalhart, 258–59, 262–63
When You're Far Away From Home Tom Darby & Jimmie Tarlton, 294
When You're Far From The Ones Who Love You Clayton McMichen, 568
When You're Gone Modern Mountaineers, 631; Texas Wanderers, 901
When You're Gone I Won't Forget Lester McFarland & Robert A. Gardner, 544; John McGhee & Frank Welling, 561; Riley Puckett, 716–17; Woodlawn Quartette, 972
When You're In The Graveyard And I'm Away Downtown In Jail Elry Cash, 197
When You're Nobody's Boy But Your Mothers [sic] Jack Golding, 374
When You're Smiling Hoosier Hot Shots, 438
When You're Smiling (The Whole World Smiles With You) Cliff Bruner, 140
When You're Thinking Of The One That You Forgot Port Arthur Jubileers, 701
Where An Angel Waits For Me Charles Mitchell & His Orchestra, 630
Where Are The Pals Of Long Ago Cliff Carlisle, 167
Where Are You Leo Soileau, 855
Where Are You Going, Alice? G.B. Grayson & Henry Whitter, 381
Where Are You Now? Elton Britt, 130
Where Are Your Smiles Welby Toomey, 912
Where Did You Get That Hat Gid Tanner, 888
Where Has My Little Dog Gone? Hoosier Hot Shots, 438
Where Have You Been My Pretty Little Girl John Henry Howard, 444
Where Have You Been So Long? Henry Whitter, 954
Where He Leads Me Joseph & Peter Higgins, 421; Rangers Quartet, 728; Vaughan Quartet, 926
Where He Leads Me I'll Follow Johnson County Ramblers, 463
Where He Leads Me, I Will Follow J. Douglas Swagerty, 883
Where Is God? Drum Quartet, 324; Palmetto Male Quartette, 674; Vaughan Quartet, 929
Where Is My Boy Tonight Wilf Carter (Montana Slim), 184; Jimmie Davis, 305; Sid Harkreader, 400; [Smilin'] Ed McConnell, 530–31; Lester McFarland & Robert A. Gardner, 544; John McGhee & Frank Welling, 561
Where Is My Mama? Vernon Dalhart, 275–76, 279; Sid Harkreader, 401; Daddy John Love, 514; McGee Brothers, 552; John McGhee & Frank Welling, 558, 560–61; Rambling Rangers, 725; Red River Dave, 732
Where Is My Mamma Fletcher & Foster, 349; Lester McFarland & Robert A. Gardner, 544; John McGhee & Frank Welling, 558
Where Is My Mother? Carl McCray, 538
Where Is My Sailor Boy? Delmore Brothers, 311; Monroe Brothers, 633
Where Is My Wandering Boy Canova Family, 155
Where Is My Wandering Boy Tonight Vernon Dalhart, 255, 285; Giddens Sisters, 369; Log Cabin Boys, 508; Riley Puckett, 716
Where Is Your Boy Tonight? Ashford Quartette, 67
Where My Memory Lies Cliff Carlisle, 167
Where My Saviour Leads Me I'll Follow All The Way E. Arthur Lewis, 498
Where Romance Calls Cliff Carlisle, 165; Wade Mainer, 584
Where Shall I Be Carolina Gospel Singers, 171; Carter Family, 189; Deal Family, 307; Dorsey & Beatrice Dixon, 322; Charlie Parker, 676; Philyaw Brothers, 690
Where Southern Roses Climb Cliff Carlisle, 163

Where The Beautiful Red River Flows Flannery Sisters, 346
Where The Bloom Is On The Sage Clayton McMichen, 570
Where The Blue Grass Grows Stuart Hamblen, 393
Where The Bluebirds Nest Again Tom Darby & Jimmie Tarlton, 294
Where The Colorado's Flowing Arthur Fields & Fred Hall, 341
Where The Coosa River Flows Vernon Dalhart, 271–72, 274–75
Where The Deep Water Flows Ted Daffan's Texans, 240
Where The Gates Swing Outward Never Emry Arthur, 65; John McGhee & Frank Welling, 554, 556; Old Southern Sacred Singers, 669
Where The Golden Poppies Grow Hugh Cross, 237; Bob Palmer & Jimmy White, 673
Where The Grass Grows Green Woodruff Brothers, 973
Where The Longhorn Cattle Roam Fred Kirby, 487
Where The Love Light Never Dies McClendon Brothers, 528
Where The Mississippi Washes Goebel Reeves, 737
Where The Morning Glories Grow Clover Leaf Old Time Fiddlin' Team, 215; Cofer Brothers, 216; Hugh Cross, 235; Massey Family, 610; Roy Newman, 658; Riley Puckett, 719; Texas Wanderers, 900
Where The Morning Glories Twine Around The Door Hugh Cross, 235; Ralph Hodges, 429
Where The Mountains Kiss The Sky Ranch Boys, 725
Where The Mountains Meet The Moon Red Foley, 351; Massey Family, 612
Where The Mountains Tiptoe To The Sea Elton Britt, 128
Where The Old Red River Flows Loy Bodine, 115; Jimmie Davis, 299; Pine Ridge Boys, 697
Where The Ozarks Kiss The Sky Jim[my] Boa, 115; Lester McFarland & Robert A. Gardner, 548; Bob Miller, 624
Where The Red Red Roses Grow Richard Brooks & Reuben Puckett, 132; Bill Cox, 225–26; Wade Mainer, 583
Where The Rhododendron Grows Beverly Hill Billies, 103
Where The River Shannon Flows Lew Childre, 207; Chuck Wagon Gang, 210; Tom Darby & Jimmie Tarlton, 294; John Dilleshaw, 316; Sid Harkreader, 400; Lester McFarland & Robert A. Gardner, 544; Clayton McMichen, 567; Walter C. Peterson, 688; Connie Sides, 834
Where The Roses Never Fade Roy Hall, 390; Ralph E. Johnson, 462
Where The Sage Brush Billows Roll Patsy Montana, 634; Prairie Ramblers, 706
Where The Shy Little Violets Grow Riley Puckett, 722
Where The Silvery Colorado Wends Its Way Emry Arthur, 65; Carter Family, 194; Ernest V. Stoneman, 875
Where The Silvery Sea (Meets The Golden Shore) Bob Miller, 624
Where The Silv'ry Colorado Wends Its Way Eddie Dean, 308; Leake County Revelers, 495; Carson Robison, 765
Where The Skies Are Always Blue Clayton McMichen, 571
Where The Soul Never Dies Blue Ridge Sacred Singers, 112; Blue Sky Boys, 113; Rev. M.L. Thrasher, 905
Where The Soul Of Man Never Dies Anglin Brothers, 61; Jack & Leslie, 451
Where The South Begins George Wade, 933
Where The Southern Crosses The Dog W.T. Narmour & S.W. Smith, 650
Where The Sunset Turns The Ocean Blue To Gold Floyd Thompson, 903–04
Where The Sunset Turns The Ocean's Blue To Gold Carson Robison, 765
Where The Sweet Magnolias Bloom Lester McFarland & Robert A. Gardner, 546; Bill Nettles, 654; Taylor-Griggs Louisiana Melody Makers, 894
Where The Sweet Magnolias Grow Buell Kazee, 472

Where The Western Horizon Begins Jack Pierce, 695
Where The Whippoorwill Is Whispering GoodNight Roy Harvey, 411; Charlie Poole, 700; Rufus K. Stanley, 866
Where We Never Grow Old Arthur Cornwall & William Cleary, 223; Vernon Dalhart, 272; Gentry Brothers, 364; Arty Hall, 390; Old Southern Sacred Singers, 668
Where We'll Never Grow Old Carter Family, 190; Giddens Sisters, 369; Alfred G. Karnes, 471; Frank Luther, 523; Frank & James McCravy, 537; McDonald Quartet, 540; Smith's Sacred Singers, 849–50; Vaughan Quartet, 927; XC Sacred Quartette, 975
Where Will You Be On Next New Year's Day? Carson Robison, 785
Where You Been So Long, Corrine? Milton Brown, 136
Where You Going Honey Hoosier Hot Shots, 436
Where Your Sweetheart Waits For You, Jack Billie Maxwell, 614
Where, Oh Where Has My Little Dog Gone Joe Werner, 943
Where's My Other Foot "Ted" Sharp, Hinman & Sharp, 825
Where's My Sweetie Now Asa Martin, 592
While Ages Roll Away Laurel Firemen's Quartet, 491
While Eternal Ages Roll Charlie Parker, 676
While I Was In Arkansas Lester McFarland & Robert A. Gardner, 545
While The Band Is Playing Dixie Russell & Louis Burton, 146
While The Days Are Going By Frank & James McCravy, 537
While The Leaves Came Drifting Down Charles Nabell, 647
While The Years Roll On Eva Quartette, 333; McDonald Quartet, 540; Vaughan Quartet, 926
While You Are Out Cheatin' On Me Oklahoma Sweethearts, 668
Whip The Devil Around The Stump J.D. Harris, 405
Whippin' That Old T.B. Jimmie Rodgers, 807
Whippoorwill Canova Family, 155; Vernon Dalhart, 288; Skyland Scotty, 837
Whippoorwill Song [The] Skyland Scotty, 838
Whippoorwill Waltz Madisonville String Band, 580
Whip-Poor-Will's Song [The] Uncle Eck Dunford, 325
Whiskers Stripling Brothers, 880; Wing's Rocky Mountain Ramblers, 968
Whisper Again That You Love Me Al Dexter, 314
Whisper Goodbye Bob Atcher, 69
Whisper Softly, Mother's Dying Walter Smith, 847
Whisper Your Mother's Name Gene Autry, 72–73; Light Crust Doughboys, 502; Lewis McDaniels, 538; Jimmie Rodgers, 802
Whispering Clayton McMichen, 572; Carson Robison, 792
Whispering Friends Christine, 209
Whispering Hope Blue Sky Boys, 114; Lester McFarland & Robert A. Gardner, 544; Monroe Quartette, 633; Blaine & Cal Smith, 843
Whistle And Blow Your Blues Away Riley Puckett, 722
Whistle Boys [The] Carson Robison, 785
Whistle Song [The] Vernon Dalhart, 288; Arthur Fields & Fred Hall, 340–42
Whistle, Honey, Whistle Hall Brothers, 391
Whistlebee Dr. D.D. Hollis, 432
Whistle-itis Carson Robison, 761
Whistlin' Joe From Ko Ko Mo Hoosier Hot Shots, 436
Whistlin' Rufus (Intro: Big Ball In Town) Gid Tanner, 887
Whistling Bob Bob McGimsey, 564
Whistling Coon W.T. Narmour & S.W. Smith, 649; Nations Brothers, 652; Short Brothers, 833
Whistling Rufus Cotton & Barfield, 223; Kessinger Brothers, 480; J.D. McFarlane & Daughter, 550; John McGhee & Frank Welling, 557; McLaughlin's Old Time Melody Makers, 565; Bill Shores & Melvin Dupree, 832; Short Brothers, 833; Gid Tanner, 891; Ernest Thompson, 902
Whistling Songbird [The] Tom Darby & Jimmie Tarlton, 294
Whistling Waltz Tune Wranglers, 916
White Roswell Sacred Harp Quartet, 814
White Cockade Uncle Joe Shippee, 831
White Flower For You Dorsey & Beatrice Dixon, 321
White Heat Bob Wills, 962
White House Of Our Own [A] Lester McFarland & Robert A. Gardner, 550
White House On The Hill [The] Dick Hartman's Tennessee Ramblers, 408
White Lightning Georgia Yellow Hammers, 367
White Mule Floyd Ming, 629; Paul Robinson, 760
White River Bottom Clyde Martin, 593
White River Road Tom & Chuck, 910–11
White River Stomp Jack Cawley's Oklahoma Ridge Runners, 199; Leon Chappelear, 201
White Rose [The] Emry Arthur, 65; Cliff Carlisle, 163; Red Patterson's Piedmont Log Rollers, 682
White Wings Billy Bishop, 107
Whitehouse Blues Pine Ridge Boys, 697; Charlie Poole, 699
Whiter Than Snow Jenkins Family, 456
Whitter's Rabbit Hunt Fisher Hendley, 416
Who Bit The Wart Off Grandma's Nose Fiddlin' John Carson, 178
Who Broke The Lock On The Hen-House Door? H.M. Barnes, 95; Texas Jim Lewis, 499
Who Broke The Lock? Dick Hartman's Tennessee Ramblers, 408
Who Calls You Sweet Daddy Now? W. Lee O'Daniel, 666
Who Calls You Sweet Mama Now? Roy Newman, 657; Range Riders, 727; Shelton Brothers, 828
Who Comes In At My Back Door Slim Harbert, 398
Who Could Tell A Mother's Thoughts Bowlin & Van Winkle, 120
Who Is That A-Comin' Down The Mountain Vernon Dalhart, 287
Who Is That? Etowah Quartet, 333
Who Said I Was A Bum? Vernon Dalhart, 283; Carson Robison, 764–65, 767
Who Stole The Cherries Off Aunt Minnie's Bonnet Hank Keene, 474
Who Stole The Lock Otto Gray, 379
Who Stole The Lock Off The Henhouse Door? Frank Luther, 523
Who Threw Mush In Grandpa's Whiskers? Bobby Gregory, 383
Who Walks In When I Walk Out Leon Chappelear, 201; Bob Wills, 960
Who Will Be My Friend Ramblin' Red Lowery, 515
Who Will Care For Mother Now Charlie Oaks, 664
Who Will Love You When I'm Gone? Prairie Ramblers, 711
Who Would Care For You Little Sweetheart Roebuck Bros., 810
Who Wouldn't Be Lonely Blue Sky Boys, 113; Lone Star Cowboys, 509; Shelton Brothers, 827
Who? Majestic [Male] Quartet, 585; Stamps Quartet, 865
Whoa Babe Bob Wills, 963
Whoa Back Buck Canova Family, 155; Lulu Belle & Scotty, 516
Whoa Mule Elmer Bird, 106; Bill Chitwood, 208; Hill Billies, 423; Riley Puckett, 716
Whoa! Mule Hill Billies, 422; Roba Stanley, 866
Whoa, Buck, Whoa Canova Family, 156
Whoa, Mule, Whoa Al Clauser, 214; Leonard C. Fulwider, 361; Hinson, Pitts & Coley, 427; Chubby Parker, 676–77; Dick Parman, 679; Arthur Tanner, 886; Gid Tanner, 891

Whoah Mule W.A. Lindsay, 507
Whole Dam Family [The] Bill Cox, 228
Whole World Is Waiting (For Dreams To Come True) [The] Vernon Dalhart, 274–75
Who'll Be To Blame? Macedonia Quartet, 542
Who'll Take Your Place When You're Gone Tune Wranglers, 915
Whoop 'Em Up, Cindy Uncle Dave Macon, 574
Whoopee Ti Yi Yo Bill Bender, 99
Whoopee Ti-Yi-Yo Git Along Little Doggies Girls Of The Golden West, 370
Whoopee Ti-Yi-Yo, Git Along Little Dogies Edward L. Crain, 230
Whoopie Ti Yi Yo, Git Along Little Dogies Beverly Hill Billies, 102
Whoopie-Ti-Yi-Yo (Git Along Little Doggies) John I. White, 951
Who's Afraid Of The Big Bad Wolf Shanks Bros. Trio, 825
Who's Been Giving You Corn? W.T. Narmour & S.W. Smith, 649
Who's Been Here Since I've Been Gone? Doc Roberts, 753
Who's Been Here? Al Dexter, 315
Who's Been Tendin' To My Business Sunshine Boys, 882
Who's Cryin' Sweet Papa Now Modern Mountaineers, 630
Who's Goin' To Shoe Your Pretty Little Feet McClendon Brothers, 527
Who's Going To Love Me Fletcher & Foster, 349
Who's Gonna Bite Your Ruby Lips Bob Miller, 625
Who's Gonna Chop My Baby's Kindlin' Sunshine Boys, 882
Who's Gonna Cut My Baby's Kindling Shelton Brothers, 830
Who's Gonna Kiss Your Lips, Dear Darling Carolina Tar Heels, 173
Who's Gonna Play In The Band Bob Skyles, 839
Who's Gonna Shoe Your Pretty Little Feet Karl & Harty, 470
(Who's It Who Loves You) Who's It, Huh? Vernon Dalhart, 247
Who's It, Who Loves You—Who's It, Huh? Vernon Dalhart, 248
Who's Sorry Now? Milton Brown, 136; Hoosier Hot Shots, 439; Nite Owls, 661; W. Lee O'Daniel, 665–66; Three Tobacco Tags, 909; Three Virginians, 909
Who's That Calling? Eddie Dean, 308
Who's That Knockin' On My Window Carter Family, 195
Who's The Best Fiddler? Fiddlin' John Carson, 178
Whose Heart Are You Breaking Now? Charlie Wills, 966
Whose Honey Are You Leon Selph, 823
Whosoever Meaneth Me John McGhee & Frank Welling, 554; Mountain Singers Male Quartet, 645; J. Douglas Swagerty, 883
Whosoever Surely Meaneth Me John McGhee & Frank Welling, 557, 560
Why Ain't I Got No Sweetheart Carson Robison, 777–79, 793
Why Ain't I Happy At All Vernon Dalhart, 271
Why Are The Young Folks So Thoughtless Carson Robison, 781
Why Are You Blue Shelly Lee Alley, 58–59
Why Are You Leaving Me Clifford Breaux, 127
Why Are You Sad Four Aces, 356
Why Can't We Be Sweethearts (Once Again?) Frank & James McCravy, 538
Why Did I Leaford Hall, 390
Why Did I Cry? Hank Penny, 687
Why Did I Get Married Carson Robison, 772–73, 777–78, 786, 793
Why Did It Have To Be Al Dexter, 315
Why Did The Blue Skies Turn Grey? Bill Carlisle, 160

Why Did They Dig Ma's Grave So Deep? Canova Family, 156
Why Did Things Happen This Way? Claude Casey, 197
Why Did We Ever Part Wilf Carter (Montana Slim), 186
Why Did You Give Me Your Love? Jimmie Rodgers, 803
Why Did You Leave Me Carl Boling, 116
Why Did You Leave Me Alone? Elton Britt, 130; Carrie Mae Moore-Faye Barres, 640
Why Did You Leave Me Poor Bessie Wilmer Watts, 941
Why Did You Lie To Me Light Crust Doughboys, 507
Why Did You Prove Untrue? Norman Woodlieff, 972
Why Did You Teach Me To Love You Hi-Flyers, 419
Why Do I Care Rodik Twins, 810
Why Do I Dream Such Dreams? Bar-X Cowboys, 93
Why Do I Love You Leon Selph, 824
Why Do I Think Of Someone Al Dexter, 315
Why Do The Men Love The Women? Bill Nettles, 654
Why Do You Bob Your Hair, Girls? J.E. Mainer's Mountaineers, 582; Blind Alfred Reed, 733
Why Do You Cry, Little Darling? Carter Family, 195
Why Do You Knock At My Door? Tune Wranglers, 915
Why Do you Treat Me Like Dirt Under Your Feet Jimmie Davis, 304
Why Do You Treat Me This Way Floyd Tillman, 910
Why Don't We Do This More Often Dick Reinhart, 739
Why Don't You Bob Your Hair Girls—No. 2 Blind Alfred Reed, 733
Why Don't You Come Back To Me Gene Autry, 71–72, 76; Blue Ridge Hill Billies, 110; Claude Casey, 197; Pete Cassell, 198
Why Don't You Give Me My Memories? Johnny Barfield, 93
Why Don't You Go John McGhee & Frank Welling, 557
Why Don't You Leave Me Alone Pete Pyle, 723
Why Don't You? Simmons Sacred Singers, 835
Why Have You Left Me Lonely B.L. Reeves, 735; Frank Shelton, 826
Why I Don't Trust The Men Cindy Walker, 935
Why Must You Leave Me My Darling Sally Foster, 355
Why Not Confess Blue Sky Boys, 114; Bill Cox, 229
Why Not Make Heaven Your Home Wade Mainer, 585
Why Not Say Yes Wisdom Sisters, 969
Why Not Tonight Emry Arthur, 65; John McGhee & Frank Welling, 556
Why Should I Be Blue Tennessee Ramblers [II], 897
Why Should I Be Lonely Jimmie Rodgers, 803
Why Should I Be To Blame Jimmie Davis, 304
Why Should I Care Carolina Tar Heels, 174; Jimmie Davis, 304
Why Should I Care If You're Blue Rex Griffin, 383
Why Should I Cry Over You? Bob Atcher, 70; Adolph Hofner, 430
Why Should I Feel So Lonely? Kenneth Houchins, 443
Why Should I Feel Sorry For You Now? Wilf Carter (Montana Slim), 186
Why Should I Wonder? Arthur Smith, 842
Why Should I Worry Now Shelly Lee Alley, 58
Why Should It End This Way? Melody Boys, 614; Three Tobacco Tags, 907
Why Shouldn't I Jack Moser, 644; Ocie Stockard, 869
Why Stay Outside Clarence Ganus, 362
Why There's A Tear In My Eye Carter Family, 189–90; Jimmie Rodgers, 805
Why? Village Boys, 932
Wicked Treatin' Blues Hoke Rice, 745
Wid Hog In The Woods Lonesome Luke, 510
Widow Hayse [The] Green's String Band, 381
Widow In The Cottage By The Sea [The] Irene Sanders, 820
Widow's Daughter [The] Dixieland Swingsters, 320

Widow's Lament [The] Prairie Ramblers, 711
Widow's Son [The] Cliff Carlisle, 162
Wife That Turned Me Down [The] Rowdy Wright, 974
Wigglin' Mama Cliff Carlisle, 167
Wild Doug Bine, 104
Wild And Reckless Hobo Vernon Dalhart, 248, 270; Jimmie Davis, 299; Morgan Denmon, 312; Hill Brothers, 424; Bob Miller, 618–19; Fiddlin' Powers & Family, 703; Posey Rorer, 813
Wild And Reckless Hoboes George Reneau, 741
Wild And Woolly West [The] Frank[ie] Marvin, 601
Wild And Woolly Willie Bob Miller, 625
Wild Bill Jones Eva Davis, 298; Kelly Harrell, 403; Wade Mainer, 584; George Reneau, 741; Ernest V. Stoneman, 873; Three Tobacco Tags, 909; Welby Toomey, 912
Wild Cat Hollow Johnson Brothers, 463
Wild Cat Mama (The Answer to Do Right Papa) Leon Chappelear, 201
Wild Cat Mama Blues Gene Autry, 76
Wild Cat Rag Clayton McMichen, 570; Asa Martin, 591
Wild Cat Woman And A Tom Cat Man [A] Cliff Carlisle, 166
Wild Flowers Richmond Melody Boys, 748
Wild Geese Ted Gossett's Band, 376
Wild Goose Chase Kessinger Brothers, 480
Wild Goose Waltz Jess Hillard, 426
Wild Hogs In The Red Brush Frank Hutchison, 450
Wild Horse Charlie Bowman, 121; Fruit Jar Guzzlers, 360; Frank Hutchison, 449; Kessinger Brothers, 479; Charlie Poole, 699; Tweedy Brothers, 917
Wild Horse On Stoney Point [The] J.W. Day, 306
Wild Horse-Soldier's Joy Crockett [Family] Mountaineers, 233
Wild Hoss Hill Billies, 424
Wild Indian Leroy [Slim] Johnson, 461
Wild Man Of Borneo [The] Carl Jones, 466
Wild Roses Bill Simmons, 835
Wild Wagoner [The] J.W. Day, 306
Wild West Rambler Crowder Brothers, 238
Wild Western Moonlight Flannery Sisters, 346
Wild Women Blues Pine Mountain Boys, 697
Wildcat Mama Gene Autry, 76
Wilderness Arthur Fields & Fred Hall, 342
Wildflower Indian Maid Massey Family, 611
Wildflower Waltz Kessinger Brothers, 481; Jack Pierce, 696
Wildwood Flower Carter Family, 187, 193
Wiley Wills [sic] Last Flight Bob Miller, 625
Wilf Carter Blues Wilf Carter (Montana Slim), 185
Wilkes County Blues Gwen Foster, 353
Will And Wiley's Last Flight Bill Cox, 227
Will David Play His Harp For Me? Rev. Edward Boone, Mrs. Edward Boone & Miss Olive Boone, 117
Will I Ever Find My True Love Frank Luther, 524
Will I Ride The Range In Heaven Prairie Ramblers, 707–08
Will I See You Again Dick Reinhart, 739
Will It Be You Morris Family, 643
Will It Pay? Lester McFarland & Robert A. Gardner, 547; Charlie Oaks, 665
Will My Mother Know Me There? Blue Ridge Sunshine Boys, 113; Carter Family, 191; L.V. Jones, 467; Old Southern Sacred Singers, 669
Will Rogers Your Friend And My Friend Ken Card, 158; Ray Whitley, 953
Will Sweethearts Know Each Other There Dock Boggs, 116
Will That Circle Be Unbroken Westbrook Conservatory Entertainers, 946
Will The Angels Play Their Harps Carson Robison, 792
Will The Angels Play Their Harps For Me Blue Sky Boys, 114; Thompson Cates, 198; Bradley Kincaid, 483; Maple City Four, 587; Carson Robison, 766–68, 771, 792, 795
Will The Angels Play Their Harps For Me? (A Beggar's Lament) Carson Robison, 766
Will The Circle Be Unbroken Bye And Bye Morris Brothers, 643
Will The Circle Be Unbroken There? J.B. Whitmire's Blue Sky Trio, 953
Will The Circle Be Unbroken? Roy Acuff, 50; Carter Family, 191; Edith & Sherman Collins, 218; Golden Echo Boys, 373; Frank & James McCravy, 532, 535–36; John McGhee & Frank Welling, 560; Monroe Brothers, 633; Tex Owens, 671; Carson Robison, 763, 787; Rev. H.L. Shumway, 834; Williams & Williams, 960
Will The Gates Open For Me? Vaughan Quartet, 924
Will The Gates Swing Wide For Me Tennessee Music & Printing Co. Quartet, 896
Will The Lighthouse Shine On Me Crowder Brothers, 238
Will The Roses Bloom In Heaven Carter Family, 190; George E. Logan, 508; Lester McFarland & Robert A. Gardner, 547
Will There Be A Great Judgment Morning Plantation Boys, 698
Will There Be A Santa Claus In Heaven? Carson Robison, 766
Will There Be Any Cowboys In Heaven? Lone Star Cowboys, 509; Shelton Brothers, 827
Will There Be Any Fiddlers Up There? McClendon Brothers, 528
Will There Be Any Flowers Bill Cox, 229
Will There Be Any Stars In My Crown Sid Harkreader, 400; Jenkins Family, 456; John McGhee & Frank Welling, 556; Old Southern Sacred Singers, 669
Will There Be Any Yodelers In Heaven? Girls Of The Golden West, 370
Will There Be Any Yodeling In Heaven? Girls Of The Golden West, 371
Will They Deny Me When They're Men John McGhee & Frank Welling, 557
Will You Always Love Me Darling Carlisle Brothers, 169
Will You Be Lonesome Too? Delmore Brothers, 311
Will You Be My Sweetheart South Sea Serenaders, 860
Will You Be There Vaughan Quartet, 925
Will You Be True Bob Atcher, 70
Will You Be True To Me Jimmy Wakely, 934
Will You Ever Think Of Me Riley Puckett, 719
Will You Love Me When I'm Old Charles S. Brook & Charlie Turner, 132; Jimmie Davis, 301; Lester McFarland & Robert A. Gardner, 546, 548; L.K. Reeder, 734; Taylor's Kentucky Boys, 895
Will You Love Me When My Carburetor Is Busted Otis & Tom Mote, 644
Will You Love Me When My Hair Has Turned To Silver? Chuck Wagon Gang, 210; Sons Of The Pioneers, 857
Will You Meet Me Just Inside Carlisle Brothers, 169
Will You Meet Me Over Yonder? Chuck Wagon Gang, 210
Will You Meet Me Up There? Carolina Gospel Singers, 171; Smith's Sacred Singers, 851
Will You Miss Me When I'm Gone? Carter Family, 187, 193
Will You Miss Me, Darling, Miss Me? Dewey & Gassie Bassett, 97
Will You Miss Your Lover Bill Carlisle, 160
Will You Sometimes Think Of Me Frank Wheeler-Monroe Lamb, 948
Will You Think Of Me? Grady & Hazel Cole, 217; Adolph Hofner, 431
Will You Wait For Me, Little Darlin'? (Sequel To "I'll Be Back In A Year") Elton Britt, 130; Red Foley, 352
Will Your Heart Ache When I'm Gone Jack & Leslie, 451

Will, The Weaver Charlie Parker, 676
William And Mary Marc Williams, 958
William and Mary (Love In Disguise) Marc Williams, 958
William Jennings Bryan's Last Fight Vernon Dalhart, 249
William Tell Bob Wills, 963
Willie After The Ball John McGhee & Frank Welling, 562
Willie And Kate Fred Pendleton, 685
Willie Blow Your Blower Yellow Jackets [II], 977
Willie Mabery Warren Caplinger, 157
Willie Moore Richard D. Burnett, 144
Willie My Darling Roy Harvey, 410
Willie The Weeper Ernest Rogers, 810; Swift Jewel Cowboys, 884; Marc Williams, 958–59
Willie, Poor Boy Roy Harvey, 409
Willie, The Chimney Sweeper Ernest Rogers, 810
Willie, We Have Missed You Ernest V. Stoneman, 877
Willie, Willie, Will You? Hoosier Hot Shots, 439
Willing Workers Mountain View Quartet, 645
Willing? Loyal? Ready? Central Mississippi Quartet, 199
Willis Mabry (In The Hills Of Rowan County) Warren Caplinger, 157
Wills Breakdown Bob Wills, 960
Wilson Clog Russell Miller, 627
Wimbush Rag Theo. & Gus Clark, 214
Wind Pine Ridge Boys, 697
Wind Swept Desert (Desert Blues) [The] Bill Boyd, 121
Wind The Little Ball Of Yarn Odus & Woodrow, 667
Windham Georgia Sacred Harp Quartet, 366
Winding Stream [The] Carter Family, 191
Windmill Tillie Hoosier Hot Shots, 440
Window Shopping Mama Jesse Rodgers, 799
Windowshade Blues Allen Brothers, 56
Windy Ben Texas Jim Robertson, 759
Windy Bill Tex Fletcher, 348
Wine, Women And Song Al Dexter, 315; Texas Jim Lewis, 499; Prairie Ramblers, 712
Winging My Way To Wyoming Beverly Hill Billies, 103
Wings Of An Eagle Johnson Brothers, 462
Wink The Other Eye E.E. Hack String Band, 386; Theron Hale, 389; Jess Young, 979
Winona Echoes W.T. Narmour & S.W. Smith, 649–50
Winona Rag Ray Brothers, 729
Wire Grass Drag Earl Johnson, 460
Wise County Blues Vance's Tennessee Breakdowners, 922
Wise Old Owl [The] Hi-Flyers, 420
Wish I Had My First Wife Back Bernard [Slim] Smith, 842
Wish I Had My Time Again Hatton Brothers, 412
Wish I Had Never Met You Plantation Boys, 698
Wish I Had Stayed In The Wagon Yard Lowe Stokes, 870
Wish I Was A Single Girl Again Vernon Dalhart, 273; Lulu Belle & Scotty, 516
Wish Me Good Luck On My Journey Claude Davis, 298
Wish That Gal Were Mine Buster Carter & Preston Young, 180
Wish To The Lord I Had Never Been Born Luther B. Clarke, 214
Wishing Joe Werner, 943
With A Banjo On My Knee Patsy Montana, 635; Carson Robison, 796
With A Pal Like You Three Tobacco Tags, 908
With A Song In My Heart Gene Autry, 82
With A Twist Of The Wrist Hoosier Hot Shots, 440
With Joy We Sing Carolina Gospel Singers, 171; Dempsey Quartette, 312; Freeman Quartette, 358; Stamps Quartet, 864
With My Banjo On My Knee Louisiana Lou, 513
With My Guitar Harold & Hazel, 402
With My Mother Dead And Gone Elmer Bird, 106

With So Many Reasons Massey Family, 612
With You Still In My Heart Adolph Hofner, 431
Within My Father's House Lake Howard, 445
Within The Circle Blue Sky Boys, 113
(Without You Darling) Life Won't Be The Same Roy Rogers, 812
WLS Show Boat, Part No. I-VI [The] WLS Radio Artists, 969
Wolf At The Door Carson Robison, 788, 792
Wolf County Blues Asa Martin, 592
Wolfe's Trail Dick Hartman's Tennessee Ramblers, 407
Wolves Howling Stripling Brothers, 880
Woman Blues [A] Jess Hillard, 425
Woman Down In Memphis Carson Robison, 776–79
Woman I Love [The] Four Pickled Peppers, 356
Woman Suffrage Bill Cox, 225; Lester McFarland & Robert A. Gardner, 545
Woman Who Done Me Wrong [The] Bob Miller, 625
Woman's Answer To "What Is Home Without Love" Frank Gerald & Howard Dixon, 368
Woman's Answer To 21 Years Blue Ridge Mountain Girls, 111
Woman's Answer To Nobody's Darling Sally Foster, 355; Patsy Montana, 634; Prairie Ramblers, 707
Woman's Been After Man Ever Since Blind Alfred Reed, 733
Woman's Blues [A] Jimmie Davis, 299
Woman's Suffrage George Reneau, 741
Woman's Tongue Has No End [A] Henry Whitter, 956
Woman's Tongue Will Never Rest [A] Lester McFarland & Robert A. Gardner, 546
Women ('Bout To Make A Wreck Out Of Me) [The] Buddy Jones, 464
Women Are My Weakness Sunshine Boys, 882
Women Of Today Carl Boling, 116
Women Please Quit Knocking (At My Door) Bill Carlisle, 159
Women Rule The World Fred Richards, 747
Women Wear No Clothes At All [The] Bob Larkan & Family, 491
Women Will Talk Bobbie & Ruby Ricker, 748
Women, Women, Women Shelly Lee Alley, 58
Wonder Is All I Do Roy Acuff, 49
Wonder Stomp Texas Wanderers, 900
Wonder Valley Beverly Hill Billies, 102; Chuck Wagon Gang, 210; Frank Luther, 522; Plantation Boys, 698; Ranch Boys, 725
Wonder Who's Kissing Her—Part 2 Frank Gerald & Howard Dixon, 368
Wonderful Chuck Wagon Gang, 211; Drum Quartet, 324; McDonald Quartet, 540; Stamps Quartet, 864
Wonderful Child Lone Star Cowboys, 509
Wonderful City Beard's Quartette, 98; Carter Family, 190; Jimmie Rodgers, 805; Smith's Sacred Singers, 851
Wonderful Day [A] Dorsey & Beatrice Dixon, 321
Wonderful Grace Rev. M.L. Thrasher, 905
Wonderful King Huff's Quartette, 446
Wonderful Love Riley Quartette, 749
Wonderful Love Divine Stamps Quartet, 865
Wonderful One Roy Newman, 657
Wonderful Peace Frank & James McCravy, 537
Wonderful Story Of Love Moody Bible Institute Trio, 637; Riley Quartette, 749
Wonderful There Delmore Brothers, 310
Wonderful Time [A] Deal Family, 307; Peck's Male Quartette, 684
Wonderful Voice Of Jesus Owen Brothers & Ellis, 671
Wondering Tex Fletcher, 349; Jack Golding, 374; Hackberry Ramblers, 387
Wondering Why Roy Rogers, 812

Wondrous Love Clarence Ganus, 362; Georgia Sacred Harp Quartet, 366
Wondrous Story [The] E. Arthur Lewis, 497; Southern Sacred Singers, 861
Won't Be Worried Long J.E. Mainer's Mountaineers, 581
Won't It Be Wonderful There? Knippers Bros. & Parker, 488; Smith's Sacred Singers, 851
Won't Somebody Pal With Me? Carlisle Brothers, 169; Wade Mainer, 583
Won't Somebody Tell My Darling Fisher Hendley, 416
Won't The Angels Let Mama Come Home Clarence Ganus, 362
Won't We Be Happy Coats Sacred Quartette, 216; Stamps Quartet, 865
Won't You Be Mine Thos. A. Burton, 146
Won't You Be The Same Old Pal Wilf Carter (Montana Slim), 183
Won't You Come Back To Me Elry Cash, 197; Rice Brothers' Gang, 747
Won't You Come Back To Me My Precious Darling Johnny Barfield, 94
Won't You Come Home? Allen Brothers, 56
Won't You Come Over To My House Riley Puckett, 716–17
Won't You Come Over To My House (Intro. "Daddy") Frank & James McCravy, 533
Won't You Forgive Me? Jimmie Davis, 305
Won't You Please Come Home Bill Boyd, 123
Won't You Remember Dick Reinhart, 739; Jimmy Wakely, 934
Won't You Ride In My Little Red Wagon Hank Penny, 686
Won't You Sometimes Dream Of Me Tennessee Ramblers [II], 897
Won't You Take Me Back Again Mason Stapleton, 867
Won't You Wait Another Year Light Crust Doughboys, 506
Won't You Waltz "Home Sweet Home" With Me (For Old Times' Sake) Blaine & Cal Smith, 843
Won't You Waltz Home Sweet Home With Me Hugh Cross, 236
Won't-Cha Cecil & Vi, 199
Wood Street Blues Deford Bailey, 88
Woodchip Blues Smoky Wood, 971
Woodchuck On The Hill [The] E.M. Lewis, 498
Wooden Wedding [The] Happy Jack, 397
Woodman Spare That Tree Jack Mahoney, 581
Wood's Traveling Blues Smoky Wood, 971
Wooly Booger Dick Reinhart, 739
Wooten Quadrille John Baltzell, 91
Work—Watch—Pray Ashford Quartette, 67
Work Don't Bother Me Carolina Buddies, 170; Chumbler Family, 212
Work For The Night Is Coming Jenkins Family, 456; Nelson & Nelson, 653; Smith's Sacred Singers, 850; Southern Sacred Singers, 861
Work In 1930 Fisher Hendley, 416
Work In The Harvest Field E.M. Bartlett Groups, 96
Work, Sing, Pray Simmons Sacred Singers, 835
Workers For Jesus Albertville Quartet, 53
Workin' Habits W.C. Childers, 205
Working And Singing Deal Family, 307
Working At The Wrong Keyhole Modern Mountaineers, 631
Working For My Lord Uncle Dave Macon, 578
Working For My Sally Wilmer Watts, 941
Working For The Crown Smith's Sacred Singers, 850
Working For The King Of Kings Owen Brothers & Ellis, 671; Peck's Male Quartette, 684
Working For The Master McDonald Quartet, 539, 541; Stamps Quartet, 864

Working On The Railroad Blankenship Family, 108; Melody Boys, 614
Working So Hard Fletcher & Foster, 350
World In A Jug Blues "Big Road" Webster Taylor, 893
World Treats Real Salvation [The] E. Arthur Lewis, 498
Worlds Unknown Lee Wells, 943
Worried Blues Samantha Bumgarner, 143; Crowder Brothers, 237; Frank Hutchison, 449
Worried Daddy Blues J.P. Ryan, 817
Worried Man Blues Carolina Ramblers String Band, 172; Carter Family, 189, 193
Worried Mind Roy Acuff, 50; Airport Boys, 52; Ted Daffan's Texans, 240; Texas Jim Lewis, 499
Worst Old Blues Crowder Brothers, 237
Worst Old Blues (I Ever Had) Crowder Brothers, 238
Worthy Odis Elder, 331
Worthy Of Estimation Uncle Dave Macon, 576
Would If I Could (But I Can't) Callahan Brothers, 152
Would You Jimmie Davis, 300
Would You Care Roy Acuff, 50; Bonnie Dodd & Murray Lucas, 322; Charles Nabell, 647; Red River Dave, 733; Three Tobacco Tags, 909
Would You Ever Think Of Me Golden Melody Boys, 373
Would You Leave Me Alone Little Darling Rex Griffin, 384
Would You Take Me Back Again? Johnny Marvin, 606
Wouldn't Give Me Sugar In My Coffee Uncle Dave Macon, 575
Wowdy Dowdy—Part 1–6, 9–12 Bert Swor & Dick Mack, 885
Wreck Between New Hope And Gethsemane Doc Hopkins, 441
Wreck of "1256" [The] Vernon Dalhart, 251
Wreck Of C. & O. Number 5 [The] Vernon Dalhart, 266
Wreck Of Happy Valley [The] Cliff Carlisle, 167
Wreck Of No. 52 Cliff Carlisle, 165
Wreck Of Number 4 [The] Green Bailey, 88
Wreck Of Number Nine [The] Vernon Dalhart, 263, 267, 271; Carson Robison, 765
Wreck Of Old 97 Virginia Ramblers, 933
Wreck Of Old No. 9 Leo Soileau, 855
Wreck Of The 12:56 Vernon Dalhart, 281
Wreck Of The 12:56 On The C. And O. Vernon Dalhart, 251
Wreck Of The 1256 Vernon Dalhart, 250, 254, 279
Wreck Of The 1256 (On The Main Line Of The C. & O.) [The] Vernon Dalhart, 247
Wreck Of The '97 [The] Arizona Wranglers, 62; Vernon Dalhart, 242; Arthur Fields & Fred Hall, 338; Ernest V. Stoneman, 874
Wreck Of The C&O Cleve Chaffin, 200; Charles Lewis Stine, 869
Wreck Of The C&O (Or "George Alley") Ernest V. Stoneman, 872
Wreck Of The C&O Sportsman Roy Harvey, 411–12
Wreck Of The C. & O. No. 5 Vernon Dalhart, 266, 269, 273, 281
Wreck Of The Circus Train Vernon Dalhart, 292
Wreck Of The F.F.V. [The] Duke Clark, 213
Wreck Of The G. & S.I. [The] Happy Bud Harrison, 406
Wreck Of The N & W Cannon Ball Vernon Dalhart, 285
Wreck Of The No. 9 Vernon Dalhart, 264, 273; Pie Plant Pete, 694
Wreck Of The Number Nine [The] Vernon Dalhart, 265, 279
Wreck Of The Old 97 Vernon Dalhart, 242, 257, 265; Arthur Fields & Fred Hall, 338; Clayton McMichen, 571; Charlie Wills, 967
Wreck Of The Old Southern 97 Vernon Dalhart, 281
Wreck Of The Old Thirty-One Doc Hopkins, 441

Wreck Of The Royal Palm [The] Vernon Dalhart, 264–65; Carson Robison, 763
Wreck Of The Royal Palm Express [The] Vernon Dalhart, 263
Wreck Of The Shenandoah [The] Vernon Dalhart, 250–52, 281
Wreck Of The Six Wheeler [The] Newton Gaines, 361
Wreck Of The Southern No. 97 Vernon Dalhart, 242
Wreck Of The Southern Old '97 [The] Vernon Dalhart, 243, 248; Gid Tanner, 888; Ernest Thompson, 902
Wreck Of The Tennessee Gravy Train [The] Uncle Dave Macon, 577
Wreck Of The Titanic Vernon Dalhart, 270; Carson Robison, 765
Wreck Of The Virginian [The] Blind Alfred Reed, 733
Wreck Of The Westbound Air Liner [The] Fred Pendleton, 685
Wreck Of Virginian No. 3 [The] Roy Harvey, 410
Wreck Of Virginian Train No. 3 [The] John McGhee & Frank Welling, 553
Wreck On The C&O [The] Charles Lewis Stine, 869; Ernest V. Stoneman, 872
Wreck On The C. & O. Road Bradley Kincaid, 483
Wreck On The Highway Roy Acuff, 50
Wreck On The Mountain Road Red Fox Chasers, 730
Wreck On The Southern 97 [The] George Reneau, 740
Wreck On The Southern Old 97 [The] Vernon Dalhart, 242; Kelly Harrell, 403; Henry Whitter, 954
Write A Letter To Mother J.E. Mainer's Mountaineers, 581
Write A Letter To My Mother Roy Harvey, 410; Charles Nabell, 647; Charlie Poole, 700
Write A Letter To Your Mother Jimmie Davis, 304
Write Me A Song About Father Arkansas Woodchopper, 63
Write Me Sweetheart Roy Acuff, 51
Written Letter [The] Cliff Carlisle, 161, 163
Wrong Keyhole Stuart Hamblen, 392
Wrong Man And The Wrong Woman (Went Back Together Again) [The] Elton Britt, 129
Wrong Man And The Wrong Woman [The] Zora Layman, 492; Red Headed Brier Hopper, 732
Wrong Road [The] Hall Brothers, 391
Wyoming For Me Rambling Rangers, 725
Wyoming Trail [The] Dwight Butcher, 148

Y. Z. Special Cherokee Ramblers, 203
Ya Gotta Quit Kickin' My Dog Aroun' Gid Tanner, 888
Yadkin River Johnson Brothers, 463
Yancey Special Light Crust Doughboys, 505
Yankee Doodle Hank Penny, 686; Walter C. Peterson, 688; Pipers Gap Ramblers, 698
Yazoo Red Bob Miller, 622
Yazoo Train On The Arkansas Line [The] Vernon Dalhart, 286
Yazoo, Mississippi Arthur Fields & Fred Hall, 342
Ye Must Be Born Again Rev. Edward Boone, Mrs. Edward Boone & Miss Olive Boone, 118
Ye Old[e] Rye Waltz Massey Family, 611; Tune Wranglers, 916
Year Ago Tonight [A] Gene Autry, 85
Year Of Jubilo Georgia Crackers, 366; Chubby Parker, 677
Yearling's In The Canebrake Capt. M.J. Bonner, 117
Yearning (Just For You) Cliff Bruner, 140; Bob Wills, 963
Years Ago Jimmie Rodgers, 809
Years Ago I Had A Lover Fleming & Townsend, 348
Yellow Bumblebee Southern Moonshiners, 860
Yellow Cat Came Back [The] Oscar Chandler, 200
Yellow Dog Blues Wise String Orchestra, 969
Yellow Gal Land Norris, 661

Yellow Jacket Blues Yellow Jackets [II], 976
Yellow Rose In Texas Ernest Thompson, 902
Yellow Rose Of Texas [The] Gene Autry, 77–78; Leo Boswell, 119; Bill Boyd, 123; Ernest Branch & Bernice Coleman, 125; Milton Brown, 137; Karl & Harty, 470; Ranch Boys, 726–27; Margaret West, 945; Da Costa Woltz's Southern Broadcasters, 969
Yes Good Lord Bill Cox, 229
Yes I Know Rev. Calbert Holstein & Sister Billie Holstein, 433
Yes I'm Free Fruit Jar Guzzlers, 360
Yes She Do—No She Don't Hoosier Hot Shots, 436
Yes Sir, That's My Baby Roy Acuff, 48; Georgia Compton's Reelers, 219; Dixie Demons, 318
Yes Sir[!] Doug Bine, 104; Milton Brown, 137
Yes We Have A Friend In Daddy Warren Caplinger, 158
Yes! My Darling Daughter Three Tobacco Tags, 908
Yes! We Have No Bananas Rice Brothers' Gang, 747
Yes, I Got Mine Fleming & Townsend, 347
Yes, Indeed I Do Bert Bilbro, 104; Arthur Cornwall, 222
Yes, My Mother Comes From Ireland Fred Kirby, 487
Yes, Pappy, Yes Arthur Fields & Fred Hall, 345
Yes-Suh W. Lee O'Daniel, 666
Yesterday Roy Rogers, 812; Tune Wranglers, 915
Yesterday's Roses Gene Autry, 86
Yield Not To Temptation Clyde & Chester Cassity, 198; Ernest Thompson, 902; Rev. M.L. Thrasher, 904
Yip, Yip Yowie, I'm An Eagle Prairie Ramblers, 705
Yo Yo Mama Jimmie Davis, 300
Yodel Macon Quartet, 579
Yodel Blues—(Part 1, 2) Val & Pete, 922
Yodel Lady Tex Fletcher, 349
Yodel Your Troubles Away Jimmy Long, 511–12
Yodelin' Daddy Blues John McGhee & Frank Welling, 555
Yodelin' Gene Gene Autry, 71
Yodelin' Teacher [The] Goebel Reeves, 738
Yodeling Back To You Hank Snow, 852
Yodeling Bill Bobby Gregory, 383
Yodeling Blues Buck Mt. Band, 141
Yodeling Cowboy Bill Cox, 225; Lonesome Cowboy [II], 509; Frank[ie] Marvin, 602, 605; Jimmie Rodgers, 802; Bill Simmons, 834–35
Yodeling Cowboy's Last Song [The] Rex Griffin, 383
Yodeling Cow-Girl Wilf Carter (Montana Slim), 183
Yodeling Drifter [The] Kenneth Houchins, 443
Yodeling Hillbilly Wilf Carter (Montana Slim), 182
Yodeling Hobo Gene Autry, 73; Frank[ie] Marvin, 603; Johnny Marvin, 607; Billy Vest, 931
Yodeling Joe Joe Harvey, 409
Yodeling Love Call Wilf Carter (Montana Slim), 185
Yodeling Memories Wilf Carter (Montana Slim), 185
Yodeling Mule Earl Shirkey & Roy Harper, 831; Three Tobacco Tags, 908
Yodeling My Babies To Sleep Wilf Carter (Montana Slim), 186
Yodeling My Way Back Home Jimmie Rodgers, 808; Russell Brothers, 816
Yodeling Radio Joe Red Foley, 351
Yodeling Ranger W. Lee O'Daniel, 666; Jimmie Rodgers, 808
Yodeling The Blues Away Frank[ie] Marvin, 600
Yodeling Them Blues Away Gene Autry, 71; Cliff Carlisle, 161; Frank[ie] Marvin, 599–600
Yodeling Trailrider [The] Wilf Carter (Montana Slim), 182
Yodelling Blues Hank Keene, 474
Yodelling Cowboy Frank[ie] Marvin, 603
Yodelling The Railroad Blues Jesse Rodgers, 798
Yodler's Serenade [The] Taylor-Griggs Louisiana Melody Makers, 894
Yoo Yoo Blues Three Virginians, 909

York Brothers Blues York Brothers, 978
You Ain't Been Living Right Vernon Dalhart, 290
You Ain't Got Nothin' I Can't Do Without Delmore Brothers, 312
You Ain't Talking To Me Charlie Poole, 699; Jack & Johnnie Powell, 702
You And My Old Guitar Howard Keesee, 474; Jimmie Rodgers, 800
You Are A Little Too Small Carolina Tar Heels, 173
You Are Always In My Dreams Stripling Brothers, 880
You Are As Welcome As Flowers In May John McGhee & Frank Welling, 562
You Are False But I'll Forgive You Buell Kazee, 472
You Are Hard To Please Joseph Falcon, 335
You Are Little And You Are Cute Dudley & James Fawvor, 337; Leo Soileau, 855
(You Are Mine) 'Til The End Of The Waltz Frank & James McCravy, 538
You Are My Flower Carter Family, 195
You Are My Love Roy Acuff, 50
You Are My Sunshine Airport Boys, 52; Bob Atcher, 69; Gene Autry, 85; Wilf Carter (Montana Slim), 186; Jimmie Davis, 304; Pine Ridge Boys, 697; Rice Brothers' Gang, 746; Ocie Stockard, 870
You Are So Sweet Joseph Falcon, 335
You Are The Light Of My Life Gene Autry, 86
You Belong To Me Airport Boys, 52; Artelus Mistric, 629
You Better Let That Liar Alone Carter Family, 194; Frank Luther, 523
You Better Stop That Cattin' 'Round Bill Boyd, 124
You Blotted My Happy School Days Edith & Sherman Collins, 218
You Broke A Heart Ernest Tubb, 913
You Broke My Heart A Million Ways Three Williamsons, 909
You Broke My Heart, Little Darlin' Sons Of The Pioneers, 859
You Brought A New Kind Of Love To Me Clayton McMichen, 570
You Brought Sorrow To My Heart Johnny Bond, 117; Denver Darling, 296; Slim Harbert, 398
You Came Back To Me Weaver Brothers, 942
You Came My Way Happy Bud Harrison, 406
You Can Be A Millionaire With Me Grady & Hazel Cole, 217
You Can Depend On Me Airport Boys, 52; Alley Boys Of Abbeville, 59; Cliff Bruner, 139; Hi-Flyers, 419
You Can Make Me Happy Shelly Lee Alley, 58
You Can Tell She Comes From Dixie New Dixie Demons, 655
You Cannot Take It With You Buddy Jones, 465; Sons Of Acadians, 856
You Can't Beat Me Talkin' 'Bout You Jesse Rodgers, 798
You Can't Blame Me For That Vernon Dalhart, 277; Hazel Scherf, 820
You Can't Break The Heart Of A Farmer Prairie Ramblers, 711
You Can't Come In Bill Boyd, 122
You Can't Cool A Good Man Down Bob Skyles, 838
You Can't Do That To Me Hi-Flyers, 420; Shelton Brothers, 829
You Can't Do Wrong And Get By Eldon Baker, 89; Hall County Sacred Singers, 392; Smith's Sacred Singers, 850
You Can't Fool A Fool All The Time Shelton Brothers, 829
You Can't Forget The Day You Was Born Fiddlin' John Carson, 178
You Can't Get Love (Where There Ain't No Love) Shelton Brothers, 830

You Can't Get Me Back When I'm Gone Shelton Brothers, 830
You Can't Get Milk From A Cow Named Ben Fiddlin' John Carson, 177
You Can't Give Your Kisses To Somebody Else Bill Cox, 225
You Can't Keep A Good Man Down E.M. Bartlett Groups, 96
You Can't Make A Monkey Out Of Me Ashford Quartette, 67; Eva Quartette, 333; Gentry Family, 365; Hodgers Brothers, 428
You Can't Make Me Worry Anymore Ted Daffan's Texans, 241
You Can't Put That Monkey On My Back Alley Boys Of Abbeville, 59; Shelton Brothers, 829; Sons Of Acadians, 856
You Can't Put That Monkey On My Back No. 2 Shelton Brothers, 829
You Can't Ride My Mule Chumbler Family, 212
You Can't Stop Me From Dreaming Philyaw Brothers, 690
You Can't Take My Mem'ries From Me Carson Robison, 769
You Can't Tame Wild Women Carl Boling, 116
You Can't Tell About The Women Nowadays Jimmie Davis, 300
You Can't Win Arthur Fields & Fred Hall, 341
You Certainly Said It Tennessee Ramblers [II], 897
You Denied Your Love Carter Family, 195
You Didn't Have To Tell Me Hank Snow, 853
You Didn't Know The Music (I Didn't Know The Tune) Jack Teter, 898
You Didn't Mean It Darlin' Three Tobacco Tags, 909
You Didn't Mind Saying Goodbye Ted Daffan's Texans, 241
You Didn't Want A Sweetheart Karl & Harty, 471
You Don't Care Johnny Bond, 117
You Don't Know My Mind Bob Dunn's Vagabonds, 326
You Don't Love Me Happy Valley Boys, 397
You Don't Love Me (But I'll Always Care) Cliff Bruner, 140; Massey Family, 612; Sons Of The Pioneers, 859; Bob Wills, 964
You Don't Love Me Anymore Adolph Hofner, 431
You Don't Love Me Anymore (Little Darlin') Charles Mitchell & His Orchestra, 630; Rice Brothers' Gang, 747; Wiley Walker & Gene Sullivan, 936
You Fooled Around And Waited Too Long Nite Owls, 660
You Gave Me Your Word Denus McGee, 551
You Get A Line And I'll Get A Pole Girls Of The Golden West, 370
You Give Me Your Love Blue Sky Boys, 113
You Give Me Your Love (And I'll Give You Mine) Anglin Brothers, 61; Lester McFarland & Robert A. Gardner, 543; Walter Smith, 847
You Go To Your Church I'll Go To Mine Highleys, 421
You Go Your Way, I'll Go Mine Bill Nettles, 654
You Gonna Get Something You Don't Expect Fiddlin' John Carson, 178
You Gonna Pray Dewey & Gassie Bassett, 97
You Got Another Pal Socko Underwood, 919
You Got That Thing Rice Brothers' Gang, 746
You Got To Be Holy Rangers Quartet, 728
You Got To Go To Work Rex Griffin, 384
You Got To Hi De Hi Cliff Bruner, 139
You Got To Live Your Religion Every Day Parker Quartette, 678
You Got What I Want Light Crust Doughboys, 505
You Gotta Go Texas Jim Lewis, 500
You Gotta Ho-De-Ho (To Get Along With Me) Swift Jewel Cowboys, 885
You Gotta Know How To Truck & Swing Modern Mountaineers, 631; Texas Wanderers, 900
You Gotta Let My Dog Alone Fiddlin' John Carson, 178

Index to Titles

You Gotta Live Your Religion Every Day Laurel Firemen's Quartet, 491
You Gotta Quit Cheatin' On Me Shelton Brothers, 829
You Gotta Quit Draggin' Around Bob Skyles, 838
You Gotta See Mama Every Night Earl & Willie Phelps, 689
You Gotta See Your Mama Every Night Lowe Stokes, 871
You Gotta Take Off Your Shoes (To Sing A Hillbilly Song) Tom Emerson's Mountaineers, 332
You Had Some Leo Soileau, 856
You Had Time To Think It Over Rye's Red River Blue Yodelers, 817
You Have Learned To Love Another Jo & Alma, 458
You Have Stolen My Hat Amadie Breaux, 126
You Know What I Mean Shelly Lee Alley, 58
You Left Me Alone Four Aces, 356
You Left Me Last Night Broken Hearted Gibbs Brothers, 368
You Left Your Brand On My Heart Wilf Carter (Montana Slim), 185
You Let Me Down Johnny Bond, 117; Karl & Harty, 471
You Lied About That Woman—Part 1, 2 Allie & Pearl Brock, 131
You Look Awful Good To Me Chris Bouchillon, 119
You Look Pretty In An Evening Gown Prairie Ramblers, 706
You Lost A Friend Tune Wranglers, 916
You Love Me Or You Don't (Make Up Your Mind) Bob Atcher, 69
You Made Me Want To Forget Carson Robison, 776
You Make My Heart Go Boom Fisher Hendley, 417
You Married For Money Wiley Walker & Gene Sullivan, 936
You May Be Sorry Al Dexter, 315
You May Belong To Somebody Else, But I Love You Just The Same Hoosier Hot Shots, 436
You May Forsake Me Wade Mainer, 584
You May Have Your Picture Ernest Tubb, 914
You Met A Gal Dick Hartman's Tennessee Ramblers, 408
You Must Be A Lover Of The Lord Fields Ward, 939
You Must Come In At The Door Sons Of The Pioneers, 858; V.O. Stamps-M.L. Yandell, 863
You Must Unload Deal Family, 307; Ruth Donaldson & Helen Jepsen, 323; Blind Alfred Reed, 733; Welby Toomey, 912
You Nearly Lose Your Mind Ernest Tubb, 914
You Never Can Tell Dick Reinhart, 739
You Never Cared For Me Jerry Abbott, 47
You Never Mentioned Him To Me Carolina Gospel Singers, 171
You Never Miss Your Mother Until She's Gone G.B. Grayson & Henry Whitter, 380
You Never Trusted Me Three Tobacco Tags, 907
You Ought To Be Arrested And Put In Jail Land Norris, 662
You Oughta See My Fann[ie/y] Dance Nite Owls, 660; Prairie Ramblers, 710
You Remind Me Of The Girl That Used To Go To School With Me Vernon Dalhart, 291
You Said Something When You Said Dixie Hoosier Hot Shots, 438
You Said We'd Always Drift Together Bill Carlisle, 160
You Shall Be Free Bill & Belle Reed, 733
You Shall Be Free Monah Bill Boyd, 122
You Shall Reap Just What You Sow Rev. M.L. Thrasher, 905
You Shall Reap What You Sow Owen Brothers & Ellis, 671
You Stayed Away Too Long York Brothers, 978
You Take It Bill Boyd, 124
You Taught Me How To Love You Now Teach Me To Forget Buell Kazee, 473
You Tell Her Cause I Stutter Rice Brothers' Gang, 746
You Tell Her I Stutter Benny Borg, 118
You Tell Me Your Dream (I'll Tell You Mine) Cherry Sisters, 204; Jimmie Davis, 303

You Tell Me Your Dream And I'll Tell You Mine Chas. Winters & Elond Autry, 968
You Tied A Love Knot In My Heart Carter Family, 195
You Told Me A Lie Jimmie Davis, 305
You Took My Candy Ray Whitley, 953
You Took My Sunshine Hi Neighbor Boys, 420
You Took My Sunshine With You York Brothers, 977
You Turned Me Down Ocie Stockard, 870
You Waited Too Long Bob Atcher, 70; Gene Autry, 85; Roy Rogers, 811
You Were Glad You Had Broken My Heart Jerry Behrens, 98
You Were Meant For Me Ross Rhythm Rascals, 814
You Were Right And I Was Wrong Prairie Ramblers, 712; Roy Rogers, 812
You Were With Me In The Waltz Of My Dreams Wilf Carter (Montana Slim), 186
You Will Always Be My Darling Al Dexter, 315
You Will Never Miss Your Mother Until She Is Gone Fiddlin' John Carson, 175; George Reneau, 740; Carson Robison, 787; Harry Smith, 843
You'd Be Surprised Hoosier Hot Shots, 440; Riley Puckett, 717
You'd Better Lay Off Of Love Three Tobacco Tags, 907
You'd Rather Forget Than Forgive Jimmie Davis, 298
You'll Always Be Mine In My Dreams Wilf Carter (Montana Slim), 184
You'll Always Have My Heart Bob Atcher, 70
You'll Be Comin' Back Some Day Jimmie Davis, 302
You'll Be Mine In Apple Blossom Time Lester McFarland & Robert A. Gardner, 548
You'll Be My Closest Neighbor Whitey & Hogan, 952
You'll Be Sorry Gene Autry, 86; Jimmie Davis, 305; Sons Of The West, 859; Ella Sutton, 882
You'll Be Sorry Bye And Bye Dickie McBride, 526
You'll Be Sorry, Dear, You'll Pay Pine Ridge Boys, 697
You'll Come Home With Me Percy Babineaux-Bixy Guidry, 87
You'll Find Her With The Angels David Miller, 626; Pie Plant Pete, 694
You'll Find Your Mother There W.B. Chenoweth, 203
You'll Get "Pie" In The Sky When You Die Charlie Craver, 231; Carson Robison, 778
You'll Have To Wait Till My Ship Comes In Patsy Montana, 636
You'll Hear The Bells In The Morning Chubby Parker, 677
You'll Love Me Too Late Ernest Tubb, 914
You'll Miss Me Blind Alfred Reed, 733
You'll Miss Me Some Sweet Day Buddy Jones, 465
You'll Miss Me When I'm Gone Cliff Carlisle, 166; Charlie Oaks, 665
You'll Never Admit You're Sorry Hi-Flyers, 419
You'll Never Find A Daddy Like Me Nelstone's Hawaiians, 653
You'll Never Get To Heaven With Your Powder And Paint Ira Yates, 975
You'll Never Know Carlisle Brothers, 169
You'll Never Make No Lovin' Wife Bill Cox, 227
You'll Never Miss Your Mother Till She's Gone Fiddlin' John Carson, 179; Gentry Brothers, 364; Lester McFarland & Robert A. Gardner, 544; Troy Martin & Elvin Bigger, 594; Riley Puckett, 716; Carson Robison, 763
You'll Never Miss Your Mother Until She's Gone Fiddlin' John Carson, 177
You'll Never Miss Your Mother Until She's Gone No. 2 Fiddlin' John Carson, 177
You'll Never Miss Your Mother Untill [sic] She Has Gone George Reneau, 741

You'll Never Take Away My Dreams Vernon Dalhart, 292; Jack Urban, 920
You'll Never Take My Dreams Away Carson Robison, 794
You'll Only Have One Mother Rice Brothers' Gang, 747
You'll Pay For It All York Brothers, 978
You'll Pay Some Day Bob Dunn's Vagabonds, 326
You'll Want Me To Want You Someday Johnny Barfield, 94
You'll Want Someone To Love You When You're Old "Peg" Moreland, 641
Young Boy Left His Home One Day [A] Charlie Poole, 699
Young Brothers Buddy Dewitt, 313
Young Charlotte Miller Wikel, 957
Young Freda Bolt Carter Family, 195
Young Man Zora Layman, 492
Young Man, You'd Better Take Care Dwight Butcher, 148
Young McDonald Had A Horse Jerry Abbott, 47
Young Rambler [The] Joe Gore & Oliver Pettrey, 376; Fred Pendleton, 685
Young's Hornpipe Jess Young, 978
Your [sic] Small And Sweet E. Segura & D. Herbert, 823
Your Best Friend Tennessee Music & Printing Co. Quartet, 896
Your Best Friend Is Always Near J.E. Mainer's Mountaineers, 582
Your Blue Eyes Run Me Crazy West Virginia Coon Hunters, 946
Your Chestnut Hair Is Dimmed With Snow Dewey Hayes, 414
Your Enemy Cannot Harm You Frank Luther, 523
Your Father Put Me Out (Ton Pere A Mit D'eor) Leo Soileau, 853
Your Heart Has Turned To Stone Arthur Duhon, 325
Your Heart Should Belong To Me Roy Hall, 391
Your Last Chance Joseph Falcon, 336
Your Lonesome Daddy Loved You All The Time Prairie Ramblers, 712
Your Love And Mine [Blind] Jack Mathis, 613
Your Love Was Like A Rainbow Norwood Tew, 899
Your Love Was Not True Hall Brothers, 391
Your Low-Down Dirty Ways Carolina Tar Heels, 173
Your Mother Always Cares For You W.C. Childers, 205
Your Mother Still Prays For You [Blind] Jack Mathis, 613; Norwood Tew, 898
Your Mother Still Prays For You, Jack Carter Family, 192; Otto Gray, 378–79
Your Mother Wonders Where You Are Tonight Perry Kim & Einar Nyland, 481
Your Mother's Always Waiting W.C. Childers, 205
Your Mother's Going To Leave You Bye And Bye Emry Arthur, 65
Your Own Sweet Darling Wife Light Crust Doughboys, 501; Patsy Montana, 634
Your Promise Was Broken Jimmie Davis, 304
Your Saddle Is Empty Tonight Cliff Carlisle, 167
Your Soul Never Dies Smith's Carolina Crackerjacks, 848
Your Voice Is Ringing Gene Autry, 77
Your Wagon Needs Greasing Fletcher & Foster, 349
You're A Cold Hearted Sweetheart Bob Skyles, 839
You're A Dog Prairie Ramblers, 711
You're A Flower Blooming In The Wildwood Edith & Sherman Collins, 218
You're A Heavenly Thing Roy Acuff, 48
You're A Horse's Neck Hoosier Hot Shots, 438
You're A Little Too Small Thomas C. Ashley, 67
You're A Million Miles From Nowhere Leon Chappelear, 202
You're All The World To Me Slim Harbert, 398
You're Always A Baby To Mother Vernon Dalhart, 255

You're Always On My Mind Adolph Hofner, 430; Tennessee Ramblers [II], 897
You're As Pretty As A Picture Jimmie Revard, 743; Carson Robison, 790; Leon Selph, 823
You're As Welcome As The Flowers In May Allie & Pearl Brock, 131; Hugh Cross, 235; Jimmie Davis, 303; Farmer Sisters, 336; Lester McFarland & Robert A. Gardner, 543; John McGhee & Frank Welling, 558; Carson Robison, 768; Connie Sides, 834
You're Awfully Mean To Me Wade Mainer, 584
You're Bound To Look Like A Monkey Roy Harvey, 411
You're Bound To Look Like A Monkey When You Grow Old Milton Brown, 137
You're Breaking My Heart Ted Daffan's Texans, 241
You're Breaking My Heart ('Cause You Don't Care) Jimmie Davis, 305
You're Burnin' Me Up (Turnin' Me Down) Virginia Childs, 208
You're Driving Me Crazy (What Did I Do) Hoosier Hot Shots, 437
You're Everything Sweet Dick Hartman's Tennessee Ramblers, 409
You're From Texas Charlie Wills, 966
You're Going To Be Sorry Oklahoma Sweethearts, 668
You're Going To Leave The Old Home Jim (There's A Mother Waiting You At Home Sweet Home) Lester McFarland & Robert A. Gardner, 546
You're Going To Leave The Old Home Jim Tonight Benny Borg, 118
You're Going To Leave The Old Home Tonight Benny Borg, 119
You're Going To Leave The Old Home, Jim Thomas C. Ashley, 68; R.C. Garner, 363
You're Gone And Forget Me Socko Underwood, 919
You're Gonna Be Sorry Claude Casey, 197
You're Gonna Be Sorry You Let Me Down Carter Family, 195
You're Gonna Miss Me Mama Ike Cargill, 158
You're Gonna Miss Me When I'm Gone (Charlie) Monroe's Boys, 632
You're Gonna Miss Me, Hon! "Peg" Moreland, 641
You're In My Heart To Stay Leon Chappelear, 201
You're Just A Flower From An Old Bouquet Ranch Boys, 725
You're Just About Right Bill Boyd, 124
You're Just Like A Dollar Bill Bill Carlisle, 160
You're Mean To Me Jimmie Revard, 742
You're My Darling Roy Acuff, 50; Bob Atcher, 69; Jimmie Davis, 304; Leon Selph, 824
You're My Inspiration Airport Boys, 52
You're My Old Fashioned Sweetheart Jack & Tony, 452
You're No Good Anymore Dave Edwards, 330
You're Not The Girl For Me Bob Skyles, 839
You're Nothing More To Me Carter Family, 194
You're O.K. Bob Skyles, 839
You're Okay Bob Wills, 963
You're On My Mind Ted Daffan's Texans, 240
You're On The Right Side Of The Ocean Radio Rubes, 723
You're Simply Delish Frank[ie] Marvin, 603
You're So Different Hank Penny, 686
You're Standing On The Outside Now Shelton Brothers, 829
You're Still My Darling Bar-X Cowboys, 93
You're Still My Valentine Carson Robison, 784
You're Sweet Joseph Falcon, 335
You're The Answer To My Prayer Roy Rogers, 812
You're The One I Care For Hi-Flyers, 419
You're The Only Star (In My Blue Heaven) Roy Acuff, 48;

Gene Autry, 82–83; Claude Casey, 197; Fred Kirby, 487; Light Crust Doughboys, 505; Patsy Montana, 636
You're The Only Star In Heaven Plantation Boys, 698
You're The Picture Of Your Mother Jimmie Davis, 299
You're The Red Red Rose Of My Heart Dick Reinhart, 739
You're The World's Sweetest Girl Frank Luther, 518
You're Tired Of Me Bill Boyd, 122; Milton Brown, 136
Yours And Mine W. Lee O'Daniel, 665
You've Been A Friend To Me Carter Family, 194; Uncle Dave Macon, 576, 578
You've Been Fooling Me, Baby Carter Family, 192
You've Been Tom Cattin' Around Jimmie Davis, 300
You've Been Untrue Bob Skyles, 839
You've Broken My Heart Dear Hi-Flyers, 420
You've Broken Your Promise Pete Pyle, 723
You've Got It Shelly Lee Alley, 58
You've Got Just What It Takes Buddy Jones, 466
You've Got Love In Your Heart Al Dexter, 314
You've Got Me There Ocie Stockard, 870
You've Got Me Worried Now Shelly Lee Alley, 58
You've Got To Hi-De-Hi Hackberry Ramblers, 387
You've Got To Pay The Fiddler Wiley Walker & Gene Sullivan, 936
You've Got To Righten That Wrong Carter Family, 195
You've Got To See Daddy Ev'ry Night Rice Brothers' Gang, 747
You've Got To See Mama Every Night (Or You Can't See Mama At All) Roy Acuff, 48
You've Got To See Mamma Ev'ry Night (Or You Can't See Mamma At All) Prairie Ramblers, 711

You've Got To Stop Drinking Shine Gid Tanner, 891
You've Got To Stop Fussin' At Me Bar-X Cowboys, 93
You've Got To Walk That Lonesome Valley Monroe Brothers, 633
You've Gotta Eat Your Spinach, Baby Dick Hartman's Tennessee Ramblers, 408
You've Made A Dream Come True Shelly Lee Alley, 58
You've Punched Number Four Bob Skyles, 839
Yukon Steve And Alaska Ann Vernon Dalhart, 290
Yum Yum Blues Curley Fox, 357; Bert Layne, 493; Clayton McMichen, 570–72; Nite Owls, 660

Z' Amours Marianne Christine Muszar, 647
Zacatecas Cartwright Brothers, 196
Za-Zoo-Za New Dixie Demons, 655
Zeb Terney's Stomp Hi Neighbor Boys, 420
Zeb Tourney's Gal (Feud Song) Bradley Kincaid, 485
Zeb Turney's Gal Arkansas Woodchopper, 63; Vernon Dalhart, 253, 255–56
Zebra Dun Jules Allen, 55; Tex Fletcher, 348
Zebra Dunn (Cowboy Song) Floy England, 332
Zeb's Gal Susanna Bob McGimsey, 564
Zelma Ted Hawkins, 413
Zenda Waltz Bill Boyd, 124; Green's String Band, 381
Zenda Waltz Song Light Crust Doughboys, 505
Zends [sic] Waltz Raggedy Ann's Melody Makers, 724
Zettie Zum Zum On The Zither Maple City Four, 587
Zions Hill Rev. Calbert Holstein & Sister Billie Holstein, 433
Zip Zip Zipper Light Crust Doughboys, 506